W9-BQW-323

The Old Rose Adventurer

Each Morn a thousand Roses
brings, you say;
Yes, but where leaves the
Rose of Yesterday?

The Rubaiyát of Omar Khayyám
FitzGerald translation

Jean-Pierre Vibert, 1777–1866

The Old Rose Adventurer

The Once-Blooming Old European Roses, and More

BRENT C. DICKERSON

Timber Press
Portland, Oregon

Are roses an end in themselves
or a beginning?

American Rose Annual
30: 215

ISBN 0-88192-466-0

Printed in Hong Kong

Published in 1999 by
Timber Press, Inc.
The Haseltine Building
133 S.W. Second Avenue, Suite 450
Portland, Oregon 97204, U.S.A.

Library of Congress Cataloging-in-Publication Data

Dickerson, Brent C.
    The old rose adventurer : the once-blooming old European roses, and more / Brent C.
Dickerson.
        p.   cm.
    Includes bibliographical references (p.   ) and index.
    ISBN 0-88192-466-0
    1. Old roses. 2. Old roses—Varieties. I. Title.
SB411.65.O55D53   1999
635.9'33734—dc21
                                                                                    98-19092
                                                                                    CIP

Contents

Authorial Testimony

"I request, in advance, the indulgence of the Public for this work, which nothing but the interest which I have in this wonderful genus makes me undertake; the proceeds from this work will never compensate me for the time, research, and effort I put into it." [V1]

"When a traveller gives an account of the country he has been wandering over, he frequently delays writing his description until he has been somewhat accustomed to the place, its manners, customs, and inhabitants; and thus, instead of mentioning what struck him at first sight, and is, in reality, the most amusing and instructive, he publishes his work as a hard outline, deficient in those light shades and fine touches, without which his picture is unequal and incomplete. Thus it is with writers upon experimental subjects: they frequently suppose that a certain quantity of technical knowledge is previously in possession of the reader, and omitting some necessary part of their descriptions upon this assumption, the theory to the reader is incomplete, and baffles his endeavours to act upon it. With a desire to avoid these errors, the memorandums in the following pages have been noted down from time to time; they are the result of an examination of all the works upon the subject accessible to the author, during a practice commenced in perfect ignorance, and ended by almost certain success." [AHB]

These lucubrations are due to a fortuitous confluence of chance, generous assistance, unintended preparation, and bent of personality. We are sincerely convinced that there is not one reader who could not have done as well as or indeed better than the present author given a similar confluence; and indeed there must be many readers and *non*-readers whose talents would have turned this farrago into something much more worthy of its noble subject than is the collection of shreds and patches with which this author presents the charitable reader. But we find, as so often, that those who could have done the task better have turned their high talents to other endeavors in which opportunity to shine is more challenging, and obtention of the goal more remote; at any rate, they have not yet made themselves conspicuous. We have mean-while been left to concentrate our own slender abilities upon the matter at hand, and hope that the outcome will serve until those more able savants find time to divert themselves with it.

No one can have been more fortunate in the assistance and cooperation obtained in the preparation of both the previous book, *The Old Rose Advisor,* and the present one, *The Old Rose Adventurer.* Those who take a dim view of human nature will find their opinion scorned by the facts themselves in this case; help of diverse sorts has been provided by many, each in his or her own particular way or ways, most of the time indeed in a way which could not have been undertaken or accomplished by anyone else. It is always the profound fear of anyone expressing appreciation that some significant, kind, labored, wise, or friendly act will be forgotten, and that the benevolent will be neglected, particularly when a project has extended over many years, traveling many paths and by-ways in the course of its desultory accomplishment. And so it is here! Those not mentioned here, whose names and deeds, bright in the esteem of the author but temporarily obscured by the ever-thickening mists of the passage of time—do not believe that your kindness is regarded as nothing, or that your effort was wasted; indeed, your gracious assistance, while modestly stepping away from our mental spotlight, lies by that very fact rather at the heart of these endeavors. We renew our thanks to those cited in the previous volume; to be working with such stalwarts at the ready has supported these efforts not only in the obtention or clarification of data, but also in providing strength to the often flagging spirit of an author who, like Cowper in his poem "The Castaway," found himself "whelmed in deeper gulfs than he." But we cannot deny ourselves the honor of again remembering the continuing support of Georges Massiot, Cathrine Lewis-Ida, the American Rose Society, and the British Royal National Rose Society. Of new, or previously unmentioned, stalwarts, let us list, in no particular order: Erich Unmuth, Ivan Louette, Ed Wilkinson, Pascal Dupuis, Alice Flores, Karl King, Hedi and Wernt Grimm (whose many efforts toward a complete publication of Pinhas's important watercolors merit much more support than they have obtained), Henry Kuska, Linda Dixon, Garry Williams,

Debbie Andelin, Henry Rankin, Mel Hulse, Judy Pineda, Bill Grant, Sally Festing, Trevor Nottle, the many supportive and enlightened reviewers whose attentions the previous volume had the good fortune to arrest, Daniel Lemonnier, Marianne Ahrne, Allan Hansson, Philippe Gautreau, Marie-Hélène Dupuis, E. Charles Nelson, Colette Tremblay, Osama Kasbari, and Stephen Pascal.

"Reader, I have put into thy hands what has been the diversion of some of my idle and heavy hours. If it has the good luck to prove so of any of thine, and thou hast but half so much pleasure in reading as I had in writing it, thou wilt as little think thy money, as I do my pains, ill bestowed. Mistake not this for a commendation of my work; nor conclude, because I was pleased with the doing of it, that therefore I am fondly taken with it now it is done. He that hawks at larks and sparrows has no less sport, though a much less considerable quarry, than he who flies at nobler game … Thus he who has raised himself above the alms-basket, and, not content to live lazily on scraps of begged opinions, sets his own thoughts on work, to find and follow truth, will (whatever he lights on) not miss the hunter's satisfaction; every moment of his pursuit will reward his pains with some delight; and he will have reason to think his time not ill spent, even when he cannot much boast of any great acquisition. This, Reader, is the entertainment of those who let loose their own thoughts, and follow them in writing; which thou oughtest not to envy them, since they afford thee an opportunity of the like diversion, if thou wilt make use of thy own thoughts in reading. It is to them, if they are thy own, that I refer myself; but if they are taken on trust from others, it is no great matter what they are; they are not following truth, but some meaner consideration; and it is not worth while to be concerned what he says or thinks, who says or thinks only as he is directed by another. If thou judgest for thyself I know thou wilt judge candidly, and then I shall not be harmed or offended, whatever be thy censure." [HUM]

"Too often do reviewers remind us of the mob of Astrologers, Chaldeans, and Soothsayers gathered before the 'writing on the wall,' and unable to read the characters or make known the interpretation. We have a right to rejoice when a true seer comes at last, some man in whom is an excellent spirit, to whom have been given light, wisdom, and understanding; who can accurately read the 'Mene, Mene, Tekel, Upharsin' of an original mind (however unripe, however inefficiently cultured and partially expanded that mind may be); and who can say with confidence, 'This is the interpretation thereof'." [CBë] "My poor Book … will, if the Fates permit, get itself disengaged from the Abysses by and by. It is very torpid, after all I can do for it; but it is authentic, indisputable; and earnest men may by patience spell out for themselves the lineaments … What else is the use of Writing? To explain and encourage grand dumb [i.e., mute] Acting, that is the whole use of speaking, and Singing, and Literaturing! That or nearly so." [Letter from Thomas Carlyle to Karl August Varnhagen von Ense, June 8, 1845]

"I am also glad that I have been able to look into the faces of men who love so much, and who have done so much towards the cultivation of the Queen of all Flora—the Rose. (Loud applause.)" [NRS13/29]

But I'm going to be immoral, now
I mean to show things really as they are,
Not as they ought to be, for I avow,
That till we see what's what in fact, we're far
From much improvement with that virtuous plough
Which skims the surface, leaving scarce a scar
Upon the black loam long manured by vice,
Only to keep its corn at the old price.

Byron
Don Juan XII:40

Abbreviations

These should not be confused with the quotation references, which are translated in our Bibliography.

A	Alba	Macro	Macrophylla
Ag	Agathe	Maj	Majalis
Arv	Arvensis	Mk	Musk
B	Bourbon	MR	Mossy Remontant
Bks	Banksia	Mult	Multiflora
Br.	breeder	N	Noisette
Brac	Bracteata	Nut	Nutkana
Bslt	Boursault	p(p).	page(s)
C	Centifolia	Pern	Pernetiana
ca.	approximately	Pim	Pimpinellifolia or Spinosissima
Can	Canina	Pol	Polyantha
cf.	compare	poss.	possibly
Ch	China	*q(q).v.*	which see
Cin	Cinnamomea	Rbg	Rubiginosa
Cl	Climbing, Climber	Rg	Rugosa
CP	Centifolia Pompon	Rox	Roxburghii
D	Damask	Rubr	Rubrifolia or Glauca
DP	Damask Perpetual	Semp	Sempervirens
F	Foetida	Set	Setigera
fl.	flourished	*sic*	as in original
G	Gallica	Soul	Soulieana
HB	Hybrid Bourbon	syn(s).	synonym(s), synonym(s) of, synonymous, synonymous with, synonymy
HCh	Hybrid China		
Hem	Hemisphaerica	T	Tea
HMk	Hybrid Musk	trans.	translation, translator
HN	Hybrid Noisette	Turb	Turbinata
HP	Hybrid Perpetual	unc.	uncertain
HT	Hybrid Tea	unk.	unknown
Hug	Hugonis	*v.*	see
Hult	Hulthemia	var.	variety, variety of
i.e.	that is	Vil	Villosa
Law	Lawrenciana	Vir	Virginiana
Lv	Laevigata	*viz.*	namely
M	Moss	W	Wichuraiana
Macra	Macrantha	Xan	Xanthina
		?	questionable
		???	otherwise unknown or reference lost

The Rose
is the
Queen of Flowers,
Messieurs;
it is enough to
remember
this old adage.

*Annales du Comice Horticole
de Maine-et-Loire*
59: 207

CHAPTER ONE

Preliminary

Circumspective

The course of any endeavor follows that of human life. It has an infancy, a childhood, a youth, and the various stages of maturity ending with that kind senescence which allows a growing acquaintanceship with oblivion before one quite goes to reside with it. In our previous book, *The Old Rose Advisor,* which dealt with the major repeat-blooming old roses and their closest relatives, we surveyed together what could be called the carefree youth of rose progress, a period in which breeders and rosarians exulted in the new richness of their world, most often without method or understanding, but yet with a bright and indomitable spirit of questing and trial. Now we turn both backwards and forwards, first to see the infancy and childhood of rose breeding, in which wide and wondering eyes blinked in surprise at what Nature had provided and what Nature would allow; and then to see a wiser and more serious middle age begin, an age in which the confidence of increasing understanding was buttressed by the counsel of experience.

Our first dozen or so chapters examine what are considered by many to be at the heart of "Old Roses," the classic once-blooming European shrub roses. It has become a standard posture by many to look at supposed confusion in the characteristics of these groups and then to throw up one's hands, as one cries, in frustration, "Let's just call them all 'Old Garden Roses'!" Close study of original sources, however, reveals that, once the full array of categories, and their characteristics, is understood, there are very few roses that do not fit rather clearly into one category or another. Certainly, there are some cultivars that are simply anomalies, but no more than we find today in our well-understood groups of Modern Hybrid Teas, Floribundas, and Grandifloras. Very amusing it is to find modernity blandly applying higher standards to the Past than it does to itself!

After these initial dozen or so, and then a chapter of dibs and dabs—some of them very important dibs or dabs—we proceed through chapters on what might be termed "old Oriental shrub roses," then climbers both Oriental and European, bringing us at length to the immediate precursors of the present rose era. We will have traveled together from the days of the French Revolution and Napoléon (with a few memories from earlier) to the end of World War I; from the days of Gainsborough to early Picasso; from Mozart to Hot Jazz. And though Reader and Author may begin with a chaconne or minuet, and end with the Charleston, the dances that Old Roses lead us through are, like Mozart, Picasso, Jazz, Gainsborough, and even that grim dance of War itself, never anything less than compelling testimony to the vitality of the human spirit.

Historical

"The history of the Rose reaches back to furthest antiquity and is lost in the mists of time. It is quite difficult to know what its origin was, and who the people were who first practiced its culture." [l'H51] "The state of rose-growing with the ancients was doubtless dependent upon the differing degrees of civilization. All things considered, if we dart a glance into those far-off times, we see Man, hardly emerged from ignorance and barbarism, surrounding the temples of his gods with trees and gardens, decorating their altars with flowers and fruits, adorning their idols, and proving to us, by example of all people and all ages, that Man always tends to look to Nature for his sweetest pleasures. The origin of the culture of the Rose is lost in the mists of time, and the darkness which covers the birth of civilization covers it as well." [V2] "However, it will do to believe that the rose originated in Persia, as, today, one finds several species which grow naturally in that part of Asia; and in the time of Solomon, king of the Jews, 10 centuries before Jesus Christ, people grew it in the area of Jericho. But—how are we to be sure that the rose grown by the Jews was the flower which we know by that name today? Different commentators on the Hebrew texts differ. Gesenius, in his *Lexicon Manuale Hebraicum et Chaldaicum,* made the observation that the word *khavaltselech,* applied to the rose by certain authors, was understood variously by ancient interpreters, sometimes as being the Lily, sometimes as the Narcissus—and, as for him, he thought it was the Colchicum. All things considered, it is fairly difficult to see today's rose in these two passages from *Ecclesiasticus,* written 700 years after Solomon, or 300 years before Jesus Christ: 'I grow my branches *on high,* like the Palms of Cadiz and the roses of Jericho.—Listen to me, O sacred seeds! and bear fruit like the roses planted at the water's edge.' Our roses don't have branches *on high,* unless we graft them that way; it would thus be necessary to suppose that the Jews grafted their on high stocks, and that the varieties which they would have cultivated would have been particularly fond of damp areas, being used to decorate along the waterside. Thus, one is not able to do more than conjecture about the culture of the rose with the Hebrew peoples. As to the ancient Egyptians, what has been handed down is no more certain." [l'H51]

"Egypt, the first civilized country about which we have somewhat clear ideas, shows us that, under several of its pharaohs, culture was brought to a fairly high degree of perfection. Everyone is inclined to believe that these people had some success in growing flowers. In the history of the Jewish people, there are several mentions of roses; the book of *Ecclesiastes* speaks of that of Jericho. One sees it figuring in the religion and ornaments of the high priest. Thus, the Rose took a distinguished place among Flowers; and if it couldn't be called their *Queen,* one can at least that it had prerogatives." [V2] "According to Monsieur Bonastre, who is much occupied with the study of Egyptian antiquities, the rose is indeed mentioned in the Coptic manuscripts—but he never saw it on any of the Egyptian monuments, despite his many researches." [l'H51]

"Greece, which received from Egypt one part of its culture and laws, didn't shut its eyes to the knowledge which, since, has been considered necessary to the happiness of people. Quickly perfecting the lessons of their tutors, the Greeks achieved, in the Sciences and the Arts, that supremacy that no contemporary society of today can dispute; it is easy to believe, then, that those who—in those Arts which depend upon design—left us some models which are still justly admired, would have had the taste and particular genius which was characteristic of their nation in decorating their gardens and all that pertains to the culture of Pleasure." [V2] "With the Greeks, the history of the Rose seems less obscure; and everyone believes that it was grown quite a long time before Homer, who lived 800 years before the Christian era began, because the great Greek poet writes in his *Iliad* of the brilliant coloration of the rose to convey the rising of the sun—the saffron which perfumes the air of his roses. Herodotus, three centuries later, notes as well a province of Macedonia where roses with sixty petals and a perfume more agreeable than that of other roses grew wild—this seems equivocal." [l'H51] "It is only at this stage that we can find some at least slightly certain evidences of the rose-culture passed on to them from Egypt. The frequent use which they made of flowers in sacrifices, in public ceremonies, and even in their meals, doesn't allow us to doubt that this culture [of rose growing] was wide-spread and attended to, though we

are in the dark about their flower-beds and greenhouses. Several places in Greece took their names from the flowers they chose to grow. The city of Rhodes, according to the testimony of several authors, was so called because of the quantity of roses grown in the neighborhood. Pausanias, who left us very precious details on these lands, confirms this. With these people, inclined to voluptuousness as much by the influence of the climate as by that of their religion, the rose was considered to be the aristocrat of all flowers; it was called by the ancients the 'Splendor of Plants' and, since the time of Pliny, it has been regarded as the Queen of Flowers, as well as a universal panacea. Sappho and Anacreon composed odes in its glory, and several peoples agree in giving it a supernatural origin. Protected by the beautiful Grecian sky, it was placed on the top rung of Flowers, and occupied in the empire of Flora a place which it never ought to lose." [V2]

"The Romans also grew the Rose from very early times. It was, as with the Greeks, the Queen of Flowers and the indispensable ornament for all the public and private festivals. The use of them would be particularly lavish at the festivals of Venus and of Flora. These ancient peoples put such an emphasis on the luxury of roses that they would top off their event by covering the chairs and tables of the party-goers at festivals with a pretty thick layer of roses. Some emperors would indeed strew them in the halls of their palaces. But the person who outdid all of this was Nero, in a fête given in the Gulf of Baies, where had been put some skiffs, and beds for sporting, in which women of distinction would play hostess. According to Suetonius, the expense for the roses alone amounted to more than four million sesterces, or five hundred thousand *francs* of our money. To undertake such prodigality during the seasons when Italy didn't produce any roses, the gardeners were obliged to get the flowers from Egypt. But later, in the reign of Nero, they established some forcing-houses which were heated by the means of running hot water through pipes; this is where they put lilies and roses, which produced, in the month of December, some flowers fairly abundantly, to satisfy the needs of their masters. Thus it was, according to Seneca, that the Roman gardeners undertook, in that time, to force roses in hot-houses heated by pipes of warm water; and here it is, the 19th Century, some 1800 years later, and we look on the *thermosiphon* as a new discovery! It can thus be assumed that, at the beginning of the Christian era, the Art of Gardening was pretty well as advanced with the Greeks and Romans as it is today [1851] in France, and that our 'new procedures' of growing are most often simply 'old Athens at its best'." [l'H51]

"According to Pliny, Roman gardeners propagated the rose by seed; however, usually, it was by separating suckers, which gave flowers more quickly; he makes no mention of grafting. Now, if, at that time, someone would propagate by seed, it would not be astonishing that the Romans would have some remontant roses which, however, due to revolutions and the invasions of barbarians, have not come down to us. We have it from Pliny and Virgil that several sorts of roses were grown in Rome: Carthaginian Roses, which bloomed in Winter those of Campania and Miletus, which bloomed later; those of Preneste, or *Paestum,* which bloomed a first time in Spring and a second time in the Fall. Which of these do we have? In vain do we search for them throughout Italy. Messrs. de Jussieu and Landresse have, in these latter days, sought the twice-bearing Rose of Preneste at Paestum and its neighborhood—it's not to be found!" [l'H51]

"In general, the ancients brought roses to a high degree of perfection. Suspended in swags or arranged in crowns, roses are always to be found ornamenting temples, altars, and statues of the gods, or on the tables and brows of the joyous disciples of Epicurus. The ancients, like the moderns, made the rose the subject of some of the most happy allusions. An image of fugitive Beauty, an attribute of Modesty, a symbol of Decency—it is especially found in the guise of ingenious symbols, helping the imagination of poets, adorning the brow with innocence and the bosom with beauty. But which roses were grown in these various eras? Which rose served to adorn the crowns of Anacreon, immortal bard of this flower; which gave the sparkle of its freshness to the charms of the voluptuous Aspasie? Muses, at least tell us which those were that inspired the too-tender Sappho!

"Without a doubt, some of these roses were double, as the artistic monuments seem to testify. Everything that the ancient authors have left us on this subject can only serve to give rise to conjectures yet more cloudy. It is at least certain that, if perhaps rose-growing was very widespread, the species or varieties concerned in it were few. Pliny, among the ancients, is the one who says the most about them—and the few roses he mentions are unrecognizable to us because he doesn't describe them sufficiently. Many diverse opinions have been set forth concerning this, none of which is satisfying; it is probable that this point of Natural History can never be clarified. This author tells us, in one of his books—while talking about the labors which take place at various times of the year—'In this month, one dresses the grapevines and roses,' implying large-scale growing. We furthermore have incontestable proofs that, in those times, the Romans made use of them prodigiously, and that they grew them themselves. Virgil, in his *Georgics,* mentions some roses in the environs of *Paestum* that would bloom two times [a year]; from this, it can be inferred that the Quatre-Saisons [*i.e., Damask Perpetual*] was known to the ancients. But a person does not reflect that this author made free use of poetic license; and that, several lines further on, he speaks of double-bearing grape-vines and sheep that bear twice a year. Virgil was a good farmer as well as a good poet, and doubtless did not really believe that the Beech could be grafted on the Chestnut, nor the Pear on the Ash—but he writes from a society which, aspiring to rule the world, and proud of its success, needed to be touched deeply, and which had an exalted imag-

ination that was not content with simple, obvious truths. The wars which preceded and followed the decay of the Roman Empire brought about neglect of Roses; their palmy days disappeared with those of Athens and Rome, and it seems as if they fell into disuse for several centuries." [V2]

"Still, there is a people who, after the Romans and Egyptians, were much occupied with growing roses—the Moorish people of Spain. According to several Arab authors, the Moors would propagate roses by seed which they sowed in August, September, and October; by offsets and separating the runners, which they did in January by budding on branches and roots and finally by suckers and by grafting on the Briar. There is no doubt that the culture of the Rose made great progress in the hands of the conquerors of Spain; keep in mind, however, that we find today in their works some assertions which seem to be taken from the *Thousand and One Nights,* such as the *Blue Rose* which they grew, and which came from the coast of Alexandria; and grafting on almond trees, apple trees, jujube trees, and others. All in all, aside from these little tales made to divert us, the *Book of Agriculture,* by Ebn-el-Awam, Arab author who lived in the Twelfth Century, includes, on the culture of the rose (according to Monsieur de la Neuville's translation), some precepts which are certainly better than those promulgated by the ancient authors—and indeed than those put out by the authors who wrote at the beginning of this present century [the 1800s] . . .

"In France, growing the Rose seems to go back to the first years of the establishment of the Franks in the [three] Gauls. Under Chilperic I, grandchild of Clovis [Clovis lived 466–511]—the first Christian king—it was positively established, such that Gregory of Tours, in his *History of the Franks,* reports that in 584 the roses bloomed in January [*stated just so; see Gregory of Tours VI:44*], and that in 589, they gave a rebloom in November [*or, at least, "bloomed in November," though indeed "the fruit-trees flowered a second time in the Fall, giving a second crop as heavy as the first"; see Gregory of Tours IX:44*]. However, at that time, the sorts grown were not very many; and it is indeed possible that the only one they knew was the Rose of France, that is, the Provins [*Rosa gallica*]. Some authors, however, doubtless basing their thoughts on that second bloom in the years 584 and 589, mentioned by the Frankish author, have advanced that they grew the Bifera rose, also called the Quatre-Saisons and the Damask. We believe that they have fallen into an error. The appearance of the roses in January 584 was an exceptional fact which was regarded as a prodigy . . . The bloom in November 589 was not any more natural, because the fruit trees also had a Fall bloom [*as had the apple trees in 584*] . . . This particularity, that it was regarded as a prodigy, doesn't prove that the rose of the Franks was biferous, because it would then be necessary to say that they also had remontant fruit trees. It was a simple growth phenomenon which can easily be explained today [*by the series of disasters which Gregory of Tours mentions as preceding these second blooms, including, in 584, a plague of locusts, late frosts, a hailstorm, and then a drought; in 589, more hailstorms, and floods*] . . . Whatever the case, we aren't saying that the Franks grew only the Provins Rose—that would be asserting too much . . .

"Up until Charlemagne, the culture of the Rose seems not to have made much progress [in France]; and indeed, in some areas, the rose was so precious that a person couldn't grow it without permission. But that great emperor of the west, who revived Letters, Science, and Art, recognized the merit of the Queen of Flowers, recommended growing it, and so growing roses probably began to increase. In the Middle Ages, roses became the subject of a very important trade in several provinces of France, particularly in some areas of Provins and Rouen. It was then that the Rose obtained, with us [the French], the homage which had been rendered it by the Greeks and Romans. It was the symbol of Innocence; the prize of Virtue in the fête of the *Rosière de Salency,* the origin of which goes back to St. Médard, bishop of Noyon, who lived under Clovis I. It was also the symbol of Beauty, of Pleasure, or Gentleness, and of Voluptuousness. In assemblies, in all families, companies, corporations, etc., there would be bouquets of roses. At table, during fêtes, people would be crowned with these blossoms, and they would be strewn on the table linen and the floor. It was much the same as with the Romans, only roses never presided over those scandalous scenes so characteristic of the reigns of Caligula and Nero.

"Marchangy tells us that, in the Fourteenth Century, they grew, in the neighborhood of Rouen, fields of roses of several *arpens* for the uses of various festivals; and that they sold some 50,000 *francs*'-worth of roses every year. This sum, which seems enormous, is not surprising if one considers the great use of rose-water then, and the role that these flowers played in certain ceremonies. Thus it is, then, that, in the *droits seigneuriaux,* many of the dues were in bushels of roses, for the *seigneur* to make rose-water. The dukes and peers of France, be they princes or indeed merely children of France, were obliged to bring some roses to the parliament at Paris in April, May, and June. There was a sort of dues called *la baillée des roses,* and no one who had a peerage in the realm of the *département,* except for our kings and queens, was exempt from it. The kings of Navarre were subjected to this, and Henri IV explained to the procurer-general [*of Navarre?*] that neither he nor his predecessors had ever failed to meet this obligation. The day the *seigneur* would pay his dues was a holiday. The lessor was made to strew some roses, flowers, and scented herbs throughout the parliamentary chambers. It all culminated, before the audience [with the *seigneur*], in a splendid dinner with the presidents, counselors, and indeed clerks and ushers. He would pass through each room, and offer to all the officers a bouquet of roses; there was no one down to the assistants to the clerk who did *not* have his own right to some roses. The parliament had its

own rose officer [*faiseur de roses*], called the Court Rose-er [*Rosier de la Cour*], at whose place the dukes and peers were to buy the makings of their presents. However, with the Seventeenth Century, these customs and usages disappeared, and, of all the old fêtes and ceremonies of the Rose, only that of the court Rose-er remains.

"During this long period of glory for the Rose, a few new varieties appeared. The Comte de Brie, coming back from the last crusade in 1270, brought from Syria the Damask or Bifera Rose. In 1563, Claude Mollet, in his *Théâtre des Plans et du Jardinage,* enumerated eight: The Provins Roses, the Incarnate Roses [*possibly the Damasks*], the Centifolias, the Double Musk, the Double Velvety Roses [*presumably Gallicas of the 'Mahaeca' sort*], the Double White Roses [*Albas*], the Double Yellow Roses [*Hemisphaericas*], and the Dutch Roses [*possibly the Agathes, the so-called 'Belgicas'*]. Sweet, in his *Florilegium,* illustrates, in 1612, ten crudely-designed roses, without giving any names. Seventeen years later, Parkinson shows twenty-four species or varieties." [l'H51]

In Haudebourg (Marie-Thérèse Haudebourg, *Roses et Jardins,* Hachette, Paris, 1995), one reads (source not specified) of the rich horticultural ferment of Germany (Augsburg, Nuremberg, Cologne, Ulm), flourishing since the Middle Ages; and one goes on to find there information from the well-known Belgian horticulturalist of the first half of the nineteenth century—connected in particular with the subject of tree-fruit—Van Mons, indicating that the Seventeenth-Century Dutch would plant beds of roses to be open-pollinated, thereafter sowing successive generations of seed from the most double flowers. What roses were they using in these operations? Let us review what *Le Jardinier Hollandois* (by Jan van der Groen, Amsterdam, 1669) has to say—not entirely comprehensibly, and with some variation between the Dutch and French texts of the bi-lingual book—on the subject of roses:

"To have roses, one plants them from buds [*The Dutch text has* oculiren—*eyes; the French text of the book has* bourgeons—*shoots*]; one may also shield-graft them, one on the other, at the end of July when the moon wanes. They can also be supplied from the runners [*grosses racines*], which should be planted four inches deep [ca. 1 dm] and left uncovered. But ground-roses [*see below*] and those from the dunes multiply [themselves] profusely. Here are the names of the roses you find in the Netherlands: Firstly, the Musk Rose, [*the Dutch text has 'Muscus', the French 'Muscate'*]; then the Morlyne Roses [*French text: 'Morlines'; could this be a reference to roses from the royal estates in Malines or Mechlin in Belgium?*], the pale and the red; the Month Roses [*presumably the Damask Perpetuals usually called, in French, 'Tous-les-Mois' ('All-the-Months'), of which this would then be the earliest mention*]; the single Musk Rose [*presumably, then, the Musk Rose previously mentioned was the double one*]; the roses with 300 petals [*presumably the Centifolias*]; the fruit-bearing roses [*presumably the Villosas*]; the Provins roses [*Gallicas*]; the double yellow Provins roses [*presumably Rosa hemisphaerica 'Multiplex'*]; the Camelot roses [*these romantic-sounding roses, so redolent of King Arthur, Guinevere, and the knights of the Round Table, are otherwise unknown, and we have no clue as to what they might be*]; double ground-roses [*'Erdrosen' or 'roses de terre'; from what follows, this would seem to refer to the Briar, Rosa rubiginosa*]—there are three sorts of ground-roses, the double and the single [*'Negelantier duppelt und einfach' or 'esglantier double, simple'*], and the yellow; some Turkish roses [*the term 'Turkish Rose' has been used for Rosa foetida 'Bicolor'*]; some Cinnamon roses [*probably Rosa majalis, of which there were single and double forms*]; and some velvet roses [*'rauche' or 'velues', undoubtedly referring to the 'Mahaeca' or 'Holoserica' or 'Tuscany' group of Gallicas*]. All these sorts can be planted to make hedges or shrubs, aside from the double Musk roses, which a person puts in pots, because it is necessary to protect them in the Winter, or to cover the bark with bran or black millet."

Hmm! Other than the existence of Camelot Roses, the question of what the "Morlyne Roses" might be, and the possible early appearance of the 'Tous-les-Mois', there are no particular surprises here; as neither Albas nor regular Damasks are mentioned, presumably the Camelot Roses and Morlyne Roses are one or the other of these (Agathes and Turbinatas would be other, weaker, possibilities).

"Up to 1680, a person found exactly nothing on how to grow roses; one sees that they were given no attention by fanciers, who preferred auriculas, tulips, and carnations; and, in the works which consider the culture of plants, not a word on the Rose. *La Maison Rustique,* of Maister Charles Estienne and Jean Liébaut, printed in 1680, is the first work which talks about propagation by graft and by seeds; but it observes that this latter method doesn't give any great advantages, because it is necessary to wait several years to see any bloom. Finally, we arrive at the last years of the Seventeenth Century, though without finding any movement in the taste of the fanciers in the direction of Roses. La Quintynie treats it as a very ordinary plant; however, he sees the advantage of grafting it, which gives some specimens which bloom in the Fall when one uses a shield-graft with a growing eye. The varieties which he mentions as being grown at the time (1690) number fourteen [*or fifteen, and the date is 1695*], among which we find the *Rose de Hollande à Cent feuilles, la Rose de Virginie, de Provins, de Damas,* a *Tous-Mois* rose—which has its red flowers in a cluster—a rose *with single flowers the color of red velvet with the underside of its petals a sallow yellow*—it's easy to see this is the Poppy Rose [*Rosa foetida 'Bicolor'*], the striped rose which is a sort of dwarf Dutch Rose easily grown in pots, etc. [*the rest are 'the fragrant Rose, and the Rose without a scent,' 'the milk-white Rose,' 'the tinted white rose, the pale Reds, the flesh-colored Roses,' Rosa hemisphaerica and the white Musk Rose*]." [l'H51]

"The following era would see in France, and particularly in Italy, England, and Holland, the creation of numerous varieties coming from the types Canina, Gallica, Centifolia, and sometimes Damascena. This is a period certainly very rich in the improvement of the Rose but the materials recording the work of the horticulturists are very skimpy." [Cx]

Whatever their methods, then, whatever species they used, whoever the breeders might have been, the Dutch, particularly in the period approximately 1790 to 1820, overshadowed the rest of Europe in the production of new roses. "It is probable that, in the beginning, the first sowing of rose seed was done off-the-cuff. It was perhaps in Holland that these first attempts were made; certainly, they were growing roses from seed before we [French] were, but it would be difficult to determine when they began. The Provins Rose, long since distributed throughout a large part of Europe, was doubtless one of the first they sowed; and this explains why, for a great many years, the varieties of this rose were pretty nearly the only ones grown. These roses, continually inbred, have long maintained nearly unchanged their distinctive characteristics. In Holland, they attracted great interest, and the larger part of the collections there are still [in 1826] comprised of only Provins Roses and the Belgiques [Agathes], with hardly any exceptions. Surrounded as we are by legions of these roses, we are forced to be very circumspect in accepting them because it has become pretty difficult to find any foliage or flowers distinctly different from those we already have in this group." [V2]

"When, nowadays, you consider that growing roses goes back to the most remote antiquity, and that it was known by all civilized peoples, how can it fail to astonish us that it is only in our own days that anyone [in France] has occupied himself with multiplying them from seed? Our astonishment redoubles further when we note that, well before this era, the patient Dutch would sow Tulips and wait for a space of six or eight years for Nature to put the final touches on the brilliant colors of that flower; and when, in our country, Monsieur Duhamel and other celebrated agriculturists had already found out how Nature gave variations by means of sowing seed, how is it that, with such hints, we [French] didn't sooner get to the results we subsequently obtained? It is indeed only in the last twenty-five or thirty years that anyone has occupied himself to advantage with propagating roses by grafting or seed." [V2] "During the whole Eighteenth Century, the culture of the Rose stood still [in France]. Grafting on the Briar, mentioned by Charles Estienne and Jean Liébaut in 1680, was but rarely employed for propagation. One still couldn't find, in the greater number of gardens, more than a few specimens of two or three varieties which were multiplied by suckers or by dividing the bushes." [l'H51]

"With the Nineteenth Century begins a new era for the Rose. The Dutch who had had good results sowing Hyacinths, Tulips, Carnations, etc., thought of submitting the Rose to this mode of propagation; and, from this moment, the culture of the genus made rapid progress. Within a few years, there appeared numerous varieties of Gallicas, bred in the Dutch nurseries. In France, people were also more serious about Roses. While the Generalissimo of the Armies of Louis XVIII—as père Loriquet put it—that is, the Emperor Napoléon—ranged his battalions on the plains of Austerlitz, Jena, Eylau, and Friedland, Empress Joséphine arranged in battle-formation a less bellicose army . . . In short, from 1805 up to the moment when she lost the imperial throne, Empress Joséphine, a passionate lover of flowers, busied herself with collecting all the varieties of Roses produced in Holland, Belgium, and England. She encouraged and protected Dupont, the first grower and collector of roses in France. At length, she would give a great and fortunate impulse to rose-growing." [l'H51] "If anyone wants a . . . striking proof of the influence that can affect our tastes, our pleasures, and I could say our morals—those which, by the stature of their position, show the way to those who surround them—I would mention Joséphine de Beauharnais, that virtuous woman, who, worthy to begin with because of her status at that lofty level at which circumstances placed her, rendered such great services to ornamental horticulture. Who doesn't know that she brought together at Malmaison one of the richest collections of plants and shrubs; and that she took great pains, here and in other countries, to seek out whatever was rare. Roses were especially favored by her; she honored Monsieur Dupont with particular good will, and didn't think it beneath her to join him in their undertakings. The impetus that she gave to Horticulture was sooner felt where she lived; and it is really from that time that the importance of the discoveries in this genus dates, as well as the improvement of the methodology and the increase in the number of fanciers. Her virtues and good will would command love and respect; her example would enliven everyone around her—a friendly rivalry born in the hearts of those who weren't strangers to flower-growing. And when, at the same time, I [Vibert] would, with difficulty, pry some secrets from Nature, didn't the hope I had of such august protection guide my first tries? Didn't it keep my courage up?" [V2]

"Several successfully overcame the initial difficulties. Messrs. Vilmorin, Dupont, and Descemet attached their names to this beautiful genus; and, since, several intellectuals have devoted themselves to classifying them and describing their characteristics. Vilmorin père and Dupont are the ones who, in our country [France], began to collect the varieties this beautiful genus offers. At a time I am unable to specify, but which goes back more than twenty years [to ca. 1800 or before], a pretty large number—for the time—of roses was received from [Schwarzkopf in] Hesse, says a note I have in hand, several of which, under other names, remain in our collections. I think, with some reason, that the number of roses which were cultivated in France didn't exceed a hundred species or varieties, even counting many sorts of little interest which have subsequently been dropped." [V2]

"Dupont sowed few roses; but he had a beautiful collection which was composed of one hundred and ten species or varieties, among which could be found a variety of Centifolia which was

single. At the same time, Vilmorin père was also busying himself with rose-culture; then, later, came Hardy of the Luxembourg, Descemet at St.-Denis, Godefroy at Ville d'Avray, Vibert at Chennevières-sur-Marne, etc. In 1814, these horticulturists were still the only ones particularly concerned with growing roses, and the number of varieties climbed no higher than 182." [l'H51] "In 1810, Monsieur Descemet, who had a particular interest in this flower, was the one who had brought together the greatest number it is from this time that seedlings of some importance began to appear; and my [Vibert's] first were only in 1812." [V2] "The nurseries of Descemet, at St.-Denis, were threatened with destruction by the barbaric armies which surrounded Paris in July 1815. Monsieur Vibert zealously bought the collection of roses." [l'H51] "I bought, in 1814 and 1815, all the roses in the collection of this grower, who had brought the number of species or varieties to two hundred and fifty. But he had about ten thousand seedlings, of which half were three or four years old. Nearly all these roses bloomed in 1816, 1817, and 1818. The success surpassed my expectations; a great number of roses of premier merit came from these seedlings, the results having some important consequences in the rose world. Up until then, Holland had maintained its supremacy, though the Provins roses were pretty nearly the only ones they grew. The few they had of other sorts came for the most part from our country [France]. Little favored by Nature for the ripening of hips, England delivered into commerce some roses from its own soil, but also a rather large number of exotic species, interesting, for the most part, from their foliage and the diversity of their characteristics. Since then, some good Pimpinellifolias and nearly all our Mosses have come from there. However, though British pride may suffer by this admission, today it is to us [the French] that they owe their most beautiful varieties, of which the greater number come from here . . . Some Chinas are about the only roses we have gotten from Italy. Such, pretty nearly, were the components of our collections in 1818." [V2]

"The major part of the roses grown at the time Louis XVIII gained—for the second time—the throne of his fathers was composed of only Gallica roses. But the Chinas soon began to be sown more frequently, producing, after several years, some varieties which bloom nearly the whole year—those called [Hybrid] Perpetuals. The Teas followed close on the heels of the Chinas. Monsieur Bréon gave this country, in 1819, the Bourbon Rose, some seeds of which he sent to Monsieur Jacques, at that time gardener in chief at the estate of Neuilly. At pretty nearly the same time, Monsieur Louis Noisette received from one of his brothers, living in the U.S., another new sort, which has been called the Noisette Rose. All of these new reblooming roses, to which we must add the 'Rose du Roi' [DP] . . . , brought about the abandonment of most of the old Gallica varieties. "Once France had returned its sword to its scabbard, the young horticulturists devoted themselves peacefully to the sweet work of gardening. Messrs.

Desprez, Vibert, Verdier, Hardy, Laffay, Prévost of Rouen, etc., followed the trail blazed by Dupont and Descemet. New fanciers appeared on all sides. Sowings increased, making such a quantity of marvelous roses that, in 1828, Desportes, in his *Rosetum Gallicum,* enumerated 2,562. Today [1851], one can count up to *five thousand,* which take their turn in being admired by rose fanciers. Each year sees a further considerable surge of new varieties." [l'H51] "France need not envy foreign lands at all; and if rose-growing has not yet completely attained the degree of perfection possible, at least it can be said that the chest full of secrets pried from Nature is kept with care by those who have made a special study of this wonderful subject. My [commercial] relations show me that we aren't the only ones interested: England, Holland, Italy, Poland, indeed Russia have knowledgeable fanciers and some enlightened growers who pursue their work with zeal and indeed with success …

"Roses no longer need envy other genera. All alone, they bring together all the pleasures that Nature has distributed to the flower kingdom." [V2]

Descriptive

"We should let [the Reader] know the technical language that the naturalists have created to make themselves comprehensible with precision and concision, and to not burden their style with circumlocutions so often repeated that they bog their writing down in such a manner as to make it unintelligible …

"1°. **About the Corolla.** Roses are always *polypetalous,* which is to say that they are composed of more than one petal, never less than five, unless they are abortive; *regular,* which is to say that they are composed of parts which are similar in form and size. In the corolla, one looks at the number of petals. When they are quite lacking, one says that the flower is *apetalous;* should there be five, the flower is *single;* if there are two or three rows of them, it is *semi-double;* if there are many, but you can still find some stamens in the center, it is *double;* if there are only a very few stamens, it is *very double;* finally, if all the pistils and stamens have been metamorphosed into petals, the blossom is *full.* Collectors of roses complain that these words *double, semi-double, very double,* etc., do not state with mathematical precision the number of petals in a flower; but as that precision means little to botanists, because they regard double flowers as monstrosities without interest for research, these epithets have been consecrated by usage time out of mind, and have been those used up through the present. Still to be noted in the rose is the size of its corolla; its form, hemispherical or simply plump, or flat—which is to say forming a straight, horizontal plane; or, finally, is it *cupuliform,* hollowed in the center, in a way resembling a cup.

"2°. **About the Petals.** A person studies the petals from the standpoint of their outer tip, their limb, their nub, and their general form. The *tip* … is the free extremity of the petal, as opposed to that which is connected at its bottom to the flower. It can be *truncate,* which is to say as if abruptly cut; *rounded; notched,* with a greater or lesser cut-out; *cordiform,* notched and forming two rounded lobes [like a heart]; *pointed; acuminate,* terminating in a sharp, elongated point; *fringed,* cut into several small, fine strips; *sinuate,* having several not very projective lobes; *dentate,* etc.

"The *limb* is the whole body of the petal [between the tip and the nub]. It can be *bristly,* or *villose,* on the *upper surface* ['*above*'] or on the *lower surface* ['*beneath*']; *striped,* marked with regular lines; *furrowed,* having large, dark lines like furrows; *navicular,* bulging lengthwise like a turnip; *concave,* hollowed both in length and width; *convex,* hollowed beneath and bulging above; *rolled; convoluted,* rolled several times; *ragged; flat;* etc.

"It could be *thin, thick, transparent, opaque, white, pink, red,* etc.; *panaché* ['*plumed*' or '*flamed*'], with longitudinal rays which are fairly large and having two or three tints; *lined,* the same, except with narrower rays, like lines; *maculate,* with large touches of another tint; *touched,* with some smaller touches; *punctuate* ['*spotted*'], with small, rounded touches; *pointillé,* covered with small points of another tint.

"As far as the edges go, they say: *entire,* with neither lobes nor divisions; *dentate,* the edge having little teeth; *lobed,* divided into two or several pretty large parts; *oval; ovoid,* approaching the oval form; *rounded,* nearly round; *obronde,* slightly rounded; *cordiform,* heart-shaped; *lanceolate,* elongated oval, pointed at the two extremities; *elongate,* three times longer than wide; *linear,* very narrow, and five or six times longer than wide; *spatulate,* in the form of a spatula.

"The *nub* of the petal … can differ from the limb by color and by consistency. It is *long; very long; large; very large;* etc.

"3°. **About the Stamens.** A stamen is composed of the *filament* …, attached to the receptacle, and the *anther* …, a small yellow sac full of *pollen* or fecund powder. When the stamen lacks the anther, it is called *sterile* or *abortive.* One looks for their number and their arrangement.

"4°. **About the Pistils.** A pistil is composed of the *ovary,* or embryo of the seed, the *style,* a filament of greater or lesser length, and the *stigmas,* a small bulge at the tip pierced with a hole which is imperceptible to the naked eye, and which serves to give passage to the fecundating liquid found in the pollen. One looks for the number of styles; they are on the fruit, or they project from it. They can be *free,* not fused; *fused,* united into a cylindrical column; *glabrous,* without hairs and absolutely smooth; *villose,* having some hairs; *cottony, tomentose,* covered with interlaced, very fine, hairs; *silky,* covered with long, fine, glossy hairs. One may further note that they are *persistent* after bloom, or *caducous,* which is to say falling with the petals or slightly after.

"5°. **About the Ovary.** Several botanists consider the embryo of the fruit as constituting the *ovary,* and give this name to that which we call the *calyx tube,* though this title is not exactly correct. Others call the *ovaries* the embryonic seeds found in the fruit before fertilization. We have adopted this latter terminology. One observes the number of ovaries, their form, and their *pubescence,* which is to say, if they are villose, or glabrous.

"6°. **About the Calyx.** For us, as for Lindley and other authors, the calyx is composed of the *tube,* a part which is fleshy, oval, or rounded, placed immediately under the flower and constituted of the *fruit* before the petals fall; the *receptacle,* or *disk,* a part to which are attached the petals and the stamens; some *sepals* or *calycinate divisions,* consisting of five foliaceous divisions subtending the petals.

"The tube of the calyx may be *round* or *spherical*; *oval*; *cylindrical*; *fusiform,* in the form of a spindle; *turbinate,* in the form of a top; *pyriform,* in the form of a pear; *pisiform,* small and rounded, in the form of a pea; *constricted,* narrowed in one part, then inflated above and below; *compressed,* flattened on both sides; *depressed,* flattened at the summit or the base so as to be wider than long.

"One looks for its pubescence, and calls it: *glabrous,* without hairs; *smooth,* without roughness; *pubescent,* having some hairs; *hairy,* having fewer but longer hairs; *villose,* having hairs both thick and long; *lanate,* overspread with large, interlaced hairs; *cottony* or *tomentose,* covered with small, intercrossing hairs, as with cotton; *silky,* covered with fine, smooth, glossy hairs; *setigerous* (which should not be confused with *silky*), bearing some large hairs or bristles which are long and thick; *bristly,* or *hispid,* covered with bristles and prickles; *prickly,* bearing small prickles; *viscous,* covered with a sticky, moist material, which is ordinarily scented; *glandulose,* bearing some small glands; *hispid-glandulose* [or *glandular-stipitate*], having bristles terminating in a gland; *glossy*; *rugose,* covered with small roughnesses; *nude,* with neither hairs nor glands.

"One notices the color: *red, black, yellow,* etc.; its consistency: *slender* or *fleshy.* Its position: *hanging, nodding, upright,* or *erect.*

"The receptacle or disk can be: *large, narrow, thin, thick, very evident, not very evident* or *obscure, flattened, plump* or *inflated, conical, convex.* It could be *very open,* which is to say, having a large *throat* for the passage of the styles; *hardly open*; *closed at the throat,* or shutting the throat of the calyx.

"The sepals one studies in respect of their duration: they are *deciduous,* or *caducous,* when they fall at the same time as the petals, or shortly thereafter; *persistent,* when they only fall a little before maturity of the fruit; *permanent,* when they don't fall at all. One calls them *entire,* without teeth; *nearly entire,* almost without teeth; *simple,* without deep divisions; *compound,* deeply divided; *appendiculate,* bearing one or several appendages; *foliaceous,* not thick, and having a fairly large limb, giving it the appearance of a leaf; *narrow, wide, thick,* etc. Their form has the same description as that of a petal or a leaflet, which see. Their pubescence can be the same as that of the calyx tube . . . One calls them *connivent*

when they are united from the base; *divergent* when their extremities are well parted; *convergent* when their extremities are quite close together.

"The fruit is studied in the same manner as we have given for the tube of the calyx. One further observes if it is *crowned* by the sepals, and if these latter fall before maturity, or if they are permanent; if the pubescence is persistent or if it is lost before maturity.

"7°. **About the Peduncle.** It can be *simple,* which is to say without any division, and then the flower which it bears is *solitary*; simply *bifurcate,* it is divided into two pedicels, and then the flowers are *geminate*; *trifurcate,* or divided into three pedicels; *ramose,* divided into more than three pedicels; *dichotomous,* divided and subdivided two by two; *trichotomous,* divided and subdivided three by three; *corymbiferous,* when all the pedicels are about the same length, in the manner of umbels. In this case, one says that the flowers are in a *corymb*; in any other circumstance with a ramose peduncle, the flowers are in a *cluster.*

"One looks to see if the peduncle is *thick* or *inflated* at the summit; if it is *pubescent,* or *nude,* all its length or only in one part; if it is *long* and surpassing the foliage; if it is *short,* or within the foliage; if it is *erect,* or vertical; *nodding*; or *hanging.* As to the pubescence, one calls it *glabrous,* with neither hairs nor glands nor prickles; *unarmed* with neither prickles nor bristles; *scabrous,* if bestrewn with elevated points or tubercles which make it rough to the touch. Finally, to express its pubescence, one employs the same terminology as used for the calyx tube, which see. The pedicels are studied in quite the same manner as are the peduncles.

"8°. **About the Bracts.** One calls bracts, or *floral leaves,* some small leaves which are often of another form and another color than the others, and which accompany the flower and are placed on the peduncles and pedicels. One looks for their presence, and in that case one says that the peduncle is *bracteate*; in their absence, one says that they are *lacking.* Sometimes they are *caducous* and fall right after bloom; other times, they are *persistent.* One calls them *subulate* when they are long, narrow, and pointed like an awl; *acuminate,* terminating in a point; *linear,* long, very narrow, of the same width all their length; *lanceolate,* oval-elongate, like a lance; *cordiform,* heart-shaped; *pectinate,* having deep, narrow, parallel divisions along the sides, like the teeth in a comb; *wide, narrow, elliptical,* etc. One observes their pubescence: *glabrous, villose, glandulose,* etc.; their color: *tinted with pink, ringed with red.* They can be *entire*; *divided*; *lobed*; etc.

"9°. **About the Stipules.** These are some small leaves of variable form placed at the base of the petiole of the large leaves, and sometimes adherent to them. One observes their *presence* or *absence*; if they are more or less *distinct*; *free,* which is to say nonadherent to the petiole; *adnate,* attached to the petiole to a determined length; *caducous,* falling before the leaf; *persistent.* Considering them from the aspect of their form, one calls them *pectinate,* and indicates if the segments are *capillary,* which is to say thin and rounded like hair; *crenelate*; *dentate*; *lacinate*, divided into narrow strips; *linear*; *dilated* or enlarged at the base or at the tip; *flattened*; *concave*; *convex*; *notched*; *bifurcate*, parted into two long divisions; *subulate*, formed like an awl; *narrow*; *wide*; etc. Their edges can be: *fringed with glands* or *with hairs*; *ciliate*, bearing hairs in rows, like eyelashes; *glandulose*; *villose*; *dentate*; *lacinate*; *pectinate*; etc. One observes their pubescence above and beneath, and says of it: *nude*, or without pubescence; *silky*; *villose*; *glandulose*. Their coloration is also of importance, particularly when it is necessary to determine the characteristics of a variety.

"10°. **About the Petiole.** Supporting the leaf, connecting it to the plant. When the petiole is lacking, the leaf is *sessile*. Never is the *common petiole*—which is to say, the one attaching to the stem—lacking in the Rose, and so the leaf cannot be sessile; but the *particular petiole*, which is to say that which attaches the leaflets to the common petiole, sometimes is lacking, and so the *leaflet is* sessile. One examines to see if the petiole is *feeble*; *strong*; *long*; *short*; *nude*, which is to say without hair, nor glands, nor prickles; *glabrous*; *unarmed*; *villose*; *tomentose* or *cottony*; *glandulose* and in this case, one looks for whether the glands are *sessile* or *pedicellate*; *armed* with prickles above or beneath, and one sees if the prickles are *large, short, slender, fine, straight, curved,* or *hooked*. One looks further to see if the petiole is *edged* with a membrane; if it is *compressed* or *flattened*; *cylindrical*; *caniculate* or creased with a deeper or shallower channel along its length.

"11°. **About the Leaf.** The leaf of the Rose, one sole species excepted, is *compound*, which is to say that it is formed by a group of several small leaves called *leaflets* on a common petiole. *Rosa simplicifolia* [*Hulthemia persica*] is the only exception. Its single leaflet borne on a simple petiole constitutes a *simple leaf*. The leaf of the rose is *pinnate*, because the leaflets are in paired opposites; it is *pinnate with an odd one*, because it always terminates in an odd leaflet. One counts the number of leaflets, and as this number varies more or less on the same individual, one notes the smallest number and the largest, and one says that the leaf is composed of from three to nine leaflets, or from three to five, or from five to thirteen, etc., etc.

"Considered from the aspect of its form, a leaflet can be: *lanceolate*, elongated in such a manner that its length is at least triple its width, and that it be like a lance in the way it diminishes from its middle to each tip; *oval,* if the transverse diameter at the middle is the largest, and if the distance from the center of the diameters be the same between them, with the edges more or less rounded at the base and at the summit; *oval-enlarged,* if the base or the summit be larger than the middle; *ovoid,* oval like an egg, which is to say larger at the summit than at the base; *obovate,* a reversed oval; *rounded* or *orbicular,* if the diameters all around are nearly equal; *elliptical,* if the diameters of the center and those of two points taken at a certain distance from the center are equal; *spatulate,* if one oval or rounded leaflet is contracted before the base, which preserves a certain width; *linear,* several times longer than wide, with parallel edges.

"The base of a leaflet can be: *rounded*; *attenuate,* if it diminishes little by little such that it could be confused with the petiole; *notched,* if the edges of the leaflet attach at a point the petiole in such a way as to make an oblique angle. If the notched leaflets are oval at the base, one calls them *cordiform*. The tip of a leaflet can be: *obtuse,* or rounded; *acute,* when it is formed by a non-blunt angle; *pointed* if this angle is very sharp; *acuminate,* if it is prolonged into a point.

"From the standpoint of its edges, a leaflet can be: *entire,* if the exterior line of its circumference is continuous without interruption; *dentate,* if this line is interrupted at set distances by small sharp in-cut and out-cut angles; *simply dentate,* if the two sides of the teeth are equal; *toothed like a saw,* or *serrate,* if one of the sides is larger than the other, making oblique teeth rather like those of a saw; *doubly dentate,* if the large teeth of it have smaller ones beside them; *regularly dentate,* if the dentations are all pretty much equal; *irregularly dentate,* if the teeth are unequal; *crenelate,* if the two sides of the tooth are equal and unite in the manner of a semi-circle. The teeth are *sharp* is their edges come together in a not very open angle; *obtuse* if that angle is open and blunt at the tip. If the teeth are long, one says that the leaflet is *profoundly dentate*; if they are wide, one calls them *largely dentate*; if they are very small, one calls it *denticulate* or finely dentate. One further observes if the edges are *ciliate*; *villose*; *glandulose*; etc.

"Considering its two surfaces, a leaflet can be: *flat,* if neither elevation nor depression is observed; *concave,* forming somewhat of a spoon; *convex,* forming something of a cowl; *undulate,* having elongate and rounded elevations on the surface coming from either above or beneath; *pleated,* if one sees some long, sharp elevations; *crisped,* having short, numerous or rounded elevations; *wrinkled,* if the elevations are numerous, short, and with a slender ridge; *channeled,* if the two sides are creased along the face of the leaflet for the whole length of it. The two surfaces of a leaflet, scrutinized from the standpoint of their vestiture, can be: *nude,* without any other process arising from their surface; *glabrous,* without hairs; *glossy*; *glaucous,* with a bluish or sea-green effect produced by the presence of a very fine bluish white powder, such as the bloom one sees on plums; *veined,* if the vessels which go along the surface are very visible; *nerved,* marked with protrusive nerves; *hispid,* covered with thick hairs; *bristly,* covered with blunt bristles; *silky,* covered with small soft hairs which are slanting, elongate, and glossy; *downy,* covered with small silky hairs which are very short, in which case one also calls it pubescent; *cottony* or *tomentose,* covered with blunt, numerous hairs which are interlaced; *lanate,* covered with numerous blunt branched hairs, which are interlaced and pretty thick. They can further be *viscous,* endowed with a mucilaginous matter; *glandulose,* or charged with glands; *prickly,* or armed with prickles. Finally, they are *rugose, irregular, rough,* etc.

"The coloration of the leaflets is important to observe; they are: *pale,* or a green tending towards a light shade; *yellowish*; a green which is *dark,* or gay; *glaucous*; *reddish*; *purple*; *striped*; *marbled*; *spotted*; *splotched* with various tints.

"The leaflets can be: *thin*; *thick*; *transparent*; *opaque*; *soft*; *hard*; *stiff*; *coriaceous*; *crisp*; *tenacious.*

"Considering their duration, one calls the leaves *deciduous* or *falling* if they fall each year at the beginning of Winter; *caducous* if they fall before then; *persistent* if they stay all Winter without falling, or are replaced by others [then] *permanent* if they dry on the bush without falling, as with some species of Oak.

"Under the name of leaf, one understands the ensemble of leaflets, petiole, and stipules.

"12°. **About the Stems.** Under this name, we include—as do the rose fanciers—the stem proper, the canes, the branches, the secondary branches, and the flowering branches. The *stem* [or *trunk*] is that part which arises directly from the roots. It its youth it takes the name *shoot.* The stem is *upright* or *erect,* when it grows vertically; *inclined* when it departs from the vertical line; *sprawling,* extending over the ground, and in this case it is called *rampant* when it grows roots at the nodes. However, the botanists who have written on Roses frequently employ that word for *sprawling,* and we have followed their example. The stem is *flexuose* when it has several rounded bends; *sarmentose* when it is slender, much elongated, and appropriate for palisading.

"It is called *nude* when it is lacking hairs and prickles; *unarmed* when it has neither bristles nor prickles; *glabrous* when it is nude and smooth; *hispid* when it bears some bristles; *armed* or prickly when it has some prickles; *glandulose* when it bears some glands; *pubescent* when it has hairs. To express its coloration and its pubescence, one uses the same terminology as for the leaflets and other organs. With the *shoots,* one notes if they be *straight* or *arching,* or *flexuose*; if they are *glabrous* and *unarmed,* or *hispid* and *prickly,* etc.

"All the characteristics of the stems are found also on the canes and branches, and are described in the same manner. However, one observes if these latter are *clustered,* bearing several from the same point; *divergent,* separating from the stem at nearly right angles; *upright,* growing vertically; *fastigiate,* clustered in *fasces* and close to the stem; *nodding*; *hanging,* as with the Weeping Willow; *stiff,* upright with a manner of stiffness; *flagelliform,* rod-shaped; *geniculate* forming an angular flexuosity at each node. Several writers improperly call *geniculate* canes as *articulated*; myself, to bend to the will of the language of fanciers and growers [as opposed to that of botanists], several times I have used that expression in their sense.

"13°. **About the Armature.** Under this title, we encompass the prickles, the bristles, and indeed the glands. With the prickles, one studies their duration. One says that they are *caducous* when they fall with or after the leaves and don't stay on the wood

longer than two years; *persistent* when they become entirely woody, very hard, and stay several years on the old wood. Relative to their position, they are *sparse,* placed without order here and there; *grouped,* several close together at certain places, while lacking in other places; *geminate,* placed in pairs; *stipulary,* placed under the stipules—sometimes they'll be found there in twos or threes. *Close-set*; *dispersed*; *intermingled with bristles.* One examines their relative proportions and calls them *equal* or *unequal.* They are ordinarily *simple,* sometimes *compound* as in *Rosa simplicifolia* [*Hulthemia persica*]; *alike,* all straight or all hooked; *dissimilar,* some straight, others hooked. "One calls them *straight, in an arc, curved, hooked, very hooked* to specify the four degrees of curvature which it is necessary to observe. As to their forms, they are *thin, long, short, thick*; their base is *enlarged, thick, compressed, decurrent* (which is to say prolonged stemwards). They are *setiform,* which is to say that they have degenerated into bristles. One studies their coloration, and calls them *pale, yellowish, red,* etc.

"The bristles seem to be abortive prickles. They are *numerous, rare, close-set, stiff, soft, equal, unequal, green,* colored with various tints that a person determines; *grouped, sparse, glandulose* (surmounted by a gland). The glands are *sessile, pedicellate, spherical, oval, disformed* (which is to say, of irregular form), *fragrant, scentless, viscous,* etc. One determines their coloration as one did for the bristles.

"14°. **About the Roots.** The roots of the Rose are not of much importance to study as far as Botany goes; however, one observes that in some species they are *tap-rooted* and have few runners, while with others they *run,* which is to say they have many runners which travel from one piece of ground to the next. We note that these two properties of the roots—particularly the latter— change in different circumstances. For example, all the roses which have been propagated by bud, and principally those which have been propagated several times by runners, run prodigiously. Roses grown from seed are the only ones which develop their roots in a manner native to the sort, the only ones, consequently, which should be studied from this aspect.

"15°. **About the Bush.** All herbaceous with a woody stem, persisting for one or several years, as a *tree,* a *shrub,* or a *bush.* The difference between these three sorts of woody vegetation has not been rigorously observed by most botanists, and never by those who are only concerned with Roses. The *bush* is from several inches up to four feet high [ca. 1 dm to 1.3 m]; the *shrub* is from four feet to fifteen [ca. 1.3–5 m]; and the *tree,* from fifteen to a hundred and more [ca. 5 m upwards]. There are roses three or four inches [ca. to 1 dm] in height—the Lawrencianas; there are some from twenty to twenty-five feet high [ca. 6.6–8.3 m], and nevertheless all are bushes for certain authors, and shrubs for others.

"Be that as it may, one calls a rose which is a bush *high* when it is more than six or seven feet high [ca. 2–2.3 m]; *medium-sized,* when it is from four to six [ca. 1.3–2 m]; *low,* when from two to four [ca. 6 dm to 1.3 m]; *dwarf,* when it does not surpass two feet [ca. 6 dm]. It is *bushy* when its branches are numerous and its foliage thick; *diffuse,* when its numerous canes crisscross and jut out irregularly; *erect,* when its branches tend to grow vertically; with a *dense look,* when its canes and foliage seem to form a close-set mass; *rampant,* or *trailing,* when its stems sprawl; *climbing* or *sarmentose* when its stems are long, thin, and appropriate for training against a wall; *arborescent,* tall, and having a thick stem, forming a trunk; *thin,* not very leafy and with slender canes; *forming a bush,* bushy and rounded; *pyramidal,* growing vertically, and diminishing gradually from the base to the summit; etc., etc.

"One studies as well the general coloration of the foliage, and calls the bush a green which is *gay, pale, somber, sad, dark, light, glaucous, reddish,* etc.

"We end here the glossology of the Rose by challenging fanciers to describe several specimens by consulting this chapter, the easiest and quickest way to familiarize one's self with the technical terms consecrated by usage." [MaCo]

Rhapsodic

"Roses—one of the brightest works of the Plant Kingdom, sung by poets of all nations and ages, gathered by the hands of Beauty, of which it is the emblem." [Lam] "More than ever, Roses inspire the admiration of those who grow them. It could be said that this superb genus rewards better than any other the tedious efforts of the grower by the numerous and beautiful varieties people raise nowadays." [No28] "No shrub carries it off like the Rose; and its blossoms, pleasing in their form and perfume, and by their profusion, win out over all the others." [AbR]

"The Rose has its thousands of admirers, and with that generous ardour which particularly distinguishes those who engage in floricultural pursuits, many have laboured to point out the method of culture they have successfully practiced, and by so doing have led others to seek amusement from the same source, and to realise the same pleasure experienced by themselves. Perhaps no flower of modern times has been more universally patronised than the Rose, and the results of this extended patronage have been indeed remarkable. What vast improvements may even our modern florists and amateurs record in this flower. We have not only new features and improved forms in almost every group of Summer Roses, which it is more particularly my purpose now to speak of, but we have a new tribe, a numerous Autumnal race, sprung chiefly from the monthly and four seasons Roses, which a few years since the most sanguine or far-sighted cultivator could not have anticipated beholding. These are indeed valuable, and it is not in the least my wish to depreciate them. I am quite ready to acknowledge that we find a rich treasure in the Autumnal gems, often gladdening the garden with their lively and varied tints, when even the Dahlia, Autumn's own flower, has shrunk blighted

from the chilling frosts. In pleading for the Rose of Summer, I only seek for it a fair share of honour, and in so doing I cannot help protesting against the unpardonable neglect with which some Rose cultivators seem inclined to treat it. I am my own gardener, so far as relates to Roses, attending personally to many of their wants, whether real or fancied, and, like many lovers of flowers, find pleasure in anticipating the period of flowering. To speak more plainly, I sometimes build castles in the air. A sultry sun has driven me into a cool shady bower, where I have for some time been revelling amidst the glories of a June Rose garden, calling up to view one individual specimen after another, until I have raised a host of half-forgotten favourites each in full dress, a gorgeous spectacle, and to which, notwithstanding every effort of the imagination, I could find no parallel among the Autumnal kinds. Where, indeed, among the latter shall we find such a huge mass of beauty as is presented to our view in a finely bloomed specimen of 'Mme. Plantier' [HN], in a 'Brennus' [HB], a 'Fulgens' [*i.e.,* 'Malton', HCh], or a 'Beauty of Billard' [*i.e.,* 'Beauté de Billard', HCh]? Where among the latter, shall we find the brilliancy of a 'Feu Brillant' [G], or 'L'Éblouissante de La Queue' [G], or the sweetness and beauty of many of those old globular-shaped Provence Roses? Where in autumn can we find anything approaching in delicacy of beauty to 'La Séduisante' [A], 'Félicité' [A], and in dry weather to 'Sophie de Marsilly' [A]? Those compact-growing, full-petalled, regular-shaped garden Roses, too, are indispensable to all collections where exhibiting is an object in view, or where perfection in a Rose is desiderated. Among these, '[Comte] Boula de Nanteuil' [G] as a dark Rose reigns supreme; 'Kean' [G] as a scarlet is almost unequalled; and 'Grandissima' [G], 'D'Aguesseau' [G], and 'Columelle' [G], of various shades of crimson, are perfect; and these are Summer Roses.

"The Moss tribe is replete with beauty, and the varieties which compose it must from their distinctness ever form an interesting feature in the Rose garden. But have we any Autumnal Moss? Certainly none worthy of the name. With June these lovely Roses fade, and the glory of the Rose garden is departed. If we turn again to the Hybrid Chinese, and view the perfect symmetry of form so strikingly displayed in 'Coupe d'Hébé' [HB], we shall find that although this Rose 'has but a summer's reign,' it will live in our remembrance when numbers of the longer blooming ones are faded and forgotten. We cannot surely dispense with the 'Persian Yellow' [F], the double Yellow Briar, or 'Harrisonii' [*i.e.,* 'Harison's Yellow', F]. Yet these are Summer Roses. The only objection urged against them is the transitoriness of their flowers. But they are so perfect of their kind, and till we have the like or superior, blooming for a more extended period, they must find place in every Rose garden. It is then, I think, but just and fair for Rose cultivators to consider whether the disregard with which they treat this one great compartment—Summer Roses—is merited, whether by excluding or neglecting such they will not materially lessen the beauty of their gardens. If it be so, then their presence and beauty will be secured." [P2/43–45]

"*Almanach des Roses,* dedicated to the Ladies, by T. Guerrapain . . . Born and raised out in the country, forced by habit and led by taste and circumstances to different sorts of useful and agreeable growing, I have seen myself—with astonishment—in the decline of my career become the passionate friend of the Rose. Struck by the variety of forms and colors that Nature has given prodigiously to this part of the Plant Kingdom, I have been charmed into comparing them with your sex. As they are the Queen of Flowers, so are you also my queens and the ornament of Society. If sometimes, in cultivating them, one is pricked by their light thorns, it is always necessary to take precaution and proper address, the same homage which is due you; you know to punish the guilty who do not give you enough respect and consideration without harming them.

"A man of the world accustomed to tell you sweet things he doesn't really think has indeed a vast field of action in which to sow his imaginings; but a man of the fields always consults Nature, finds it ever true, and makes its truthfulness his own habit. Forced, by solitude, to reflect and compare, and surrounded by Roses, each of which is prettier than the next, he finds no other object to compare them with than you, *Mesdames.*" [C-T, with an elegant bow, no doubt]

Practical

"Cultivate yourself as well as your roses." [ARA28/230]

"ROSES. *Rosa*; Lin. (Icosandrie—polygynie.) Calyx monophyllous, persistent, tubular and expanded beneath, constricted at the orifice, limb divided into 5 pieces; corolla divided into five petals in the form of a reversed heart inserted on the calyx and at its orifice; stamens numerous, having the same insertion; seeds numerous, hispid, arranged in the calyx tube, which becomes a globular or ovoid berry. This genus comprises about seventy species which have supplied more than two hundred varieties, and which, without a doubt, will further bring us a yet greater number." [No26] "Having given this detailed description of Roses, I will seize this opportunity to offer a few thoughts . . . Their habit, branches, and foliage are quite as varied as their colors. Some of them grow with an astonishing vigor, and can be grown ownroot, as well as on [tree-rose] stems—such as the Albas, the Sans-Pareilles [*a kind of Gallica*], 'Ornement de Parade' [G], and the 'Sans Épine de la Chine' [Bslt], etc. Others grow some strong canes which in turn give rise to more slender ones which bear the flowers and bend downwards in garlands—such as 'Bicolor' [F] and the Lucidas. And, finally, others make well-rounded bushes: the Provins and the various sorts of 'Brun' [dark Gallicas]. Some are notable for the size and unusual form of their foliage. Such, among others, is the Centifolia 'Bullata'; others, by their unique

and original form, such as 'Bipenné' [C], 'À Feuille de Chanvre' [C], and 'Subrotundi folia crenata' [C]; and others, last of all, by the color of this same foliage, such as the Glaucas, the Lucidas, etc. Some blossoms are nicer half-open than they are entirely open, such as the Chinas. Others are just as beautiful in bud as they are fully open, such as the Centifolias, Mosses, Damasks, and the Carnées [Agathes?]; others, to be striking, make us wait until they are fully open—'Jaune Double' [*Rosa hemisphaerica*], the Uniques [C], 'Mahaeca' [G], as well as the sorts of *Brun, Veloutée, Pourpre,* and *Cramoisi* [all G]. At first glance, some people can't see any difference between a number of varieties, and imagine that they are all the same under different names, particularly with the dark-colored sorts; before making a definite judgment, however, I would like to say to them that they can be told apart by the thickness of the bush, the leaves, and the blossoms; at that point, their comparison will allow them to perceive the striking and distinctive characteristics that a person wouldn't see just at a glance. Also, to judge the merit and beauty of a rose, it is necessary to wait until the second or third year after planting the bush. It is but rarely that the growth of the first year will bring enough development to a blossom to allow it to be appreciated.

"The strength and vigor of a specimen, concerning those which are grafted, also has a great influence on the character of the blossom; this is—it can't be gainsaid—a family which is the most perfect and the most varied that Nature has given us; and I repeat, it is truly astonishing that this superb production does not have more enthusiasts than it has at present, particularly considering how easy they are to grow. Doubtless, it is this ease which has made people disdain giving them the attention they deserve nevertheless, an enlightened fancier whose taste is such can show his talent with these more than he could with any other flower because of the variety of forms in the genus, in the arrangement of the rosarium, and by the mix of colors. Can anything more magnificent be seen in Flowers than a bed of roses in which the colors are placed and combined with taste and discernment, whatever be the form of the bed—regular or irregular, circular or in a half-moon, oval or square, or planted in an 'amphitheater'? A person can make it in several ways, be it to make the eye go from low to high, from delicate colors to darker colors, or perhaps with darker placed next to lighter, making by this mix of striking contrasts a blend which accentuates the different shades of the flowers. With roses on tall stocks, a person can make covered walks, *berceaux,* pergolas, and little paths, gradually mixing with them lower specimens, giving them the form of garlands or festoons; the shade from the high-stems makes a person able to contemplate the riches of the colors and the delicious perfumes of the low-stems. Indeed, it is proper to mention that the sorts which are the most precious due to the elegance and beauty of their forms, the freshness of their colors, and the suavity of their perfume do better grafted on the Briar on stems two or three feet high [ca. 6–10 dm] than on stems four, five, or six feet high [to ca. 2 m]. It would seem that they want to be close to us so we can flatter them! On the other hand, the large and vigorous sorts which charm and seduce us at first sight, but which don't merit further attention, do well on high stems. Nature tells us the place that each should occupy in our gardens and shrubberies. You can't do better than to listen to her!" [C-T]

"*Culture of Roses. About the Terrain.* Roses grow more or less well in all sorts of ground; however, they generally prefer light, free earth, slightly cool, amended from time to time with good soil. They do perfectly in light limestone soil, and the delicate varieties, such as the Lawrencianas, Chinas, etc., do well in dark, fertile soil and heath-soil. The Briar, on which they graft all the varieties, is not picky about its soil; nevertheless, it grows with great vigor in ground which is substantial and easily cultivated.

"*About the Exposure.* One should give the rose neither too much nor too little sun. Full exposure out in the open, however, does it no harm when it can take advantage of the open air. In gardens enclosed between walls of a certain height, they do better when exposed to the rising and setting sun than with a northern or mid-day exposure. Finally, to use the expression of gardeners, it likes a semi-sunny exposure.

"*About Propagation of the Rose.* A person propagates roses, 1°, by seed; 2°, by runners; 3°, from suckers and cuttings; 4°, by grafting. From seed, one obtains new varieties, but one is never certain to reproduce and multiply those from which one got the seeds . . . As to the other modes of propagation, a person reproduces what he already has, but doesn't obtain anything new. However, if a notable sport occurs on some branch or cane of the rose, one can fix this sport by graft and thus form a new variety that can be propagated by the same method, as well as by that of layering and cuttings, should one want some own-root specimens . . .

"*By Seed.* The seed is collected in the Fall, as soon as mature, leaving it in the fruit up to the moment of sowing. If one wants to obtain double or full blossoms, it is necessary to favor seed collected from double varieties so they give you that or at least semi-doubles. The single ones only produce a few semi-doubles, and indeed only a few of those. When gardeners want to raise hybrid varieties, they take the precaution, when bloom is in full swing, of cutting some blooming stems of one sort, and shaking the pollen from it upon the stamens of another species [*Boitard of course means—we hope—that one should shake the pollen upon the stigmas of another species*]. It does not do to mix the seed of species and varieties all together, because it is always very useful to know for certain what type the varieties obtained came from. It is best to sow the seeds as soon as they are mature. In that case, they all germinate the following Spring; otherwise, if a person waits for the next growing season, they don't sprout for two or three years. However, if one doesn't have any beds prepared for them, a person can still wait until Spring; but then it is necessary to stratify them . . .

"*About the Sowing.* One may put them in pots or in beds. If in pots, what you do is to make use of heath-soil, sometimes pure (for the delicate sorts), sometimes mixed with some well-ripened manure, or indeed with some pure but lighter soil. If one sows in a bed, it is necessary to choose, if possible, an exposure to the rising sun, at the foot of a wall. One lightens and digs the soil, and amends it with well-rotted manure; the lighter it is, the better chance of success. One removes the seed from the fruit; and if this operation takes place as soon as it is mature, one sows them without further ado; if it is necessary to wait until the Spring, it is a good idea to let them soak in water at least twenty-four hours before sowing. Be it in pot or bed, it is not necessary to cover the seeds with more than five or six *lignes* of soil [to ca. ³/₄ in or 1.4 cm] at most; otherwise, the little plant will etiolate and die before being able to get to the surface. One then the whole crop with some chopped moss if the soil is prone to become crusty.

"When Winter commences to make itself felt, one puts the pots into the orangery to protect them from the frost, and one covers the beds with [garden] litter or dry leaves. In Spring, the greater part of the seeds will sprout, with the rest doing so the following year. We will not enter into great detail about the care to give the seedlings; it will suffice to say that the methods are the same as are undertaken for all the other sorts of shrub seedlings . . .

"So that the roses don't become spindly, it is necessary to sow them thinly. If they be sown too thickly, it is absolutely necessary to thin them out, and prick out those that sprout. The younger they are for this operation, the less the pricked-out specimens suffer; nevertheless, ordinarily their bloom will be retarded a year . . .

"*From Runners.* One calls runners those rooted shoots which spring from the foot of the plant or the roots of older roses. One lifts them in the Fall in ordinary soil, in Spring in swampy or very wet soil . . . When the rose is stingy with its runners, one can sometimes force it to give them by cutting off the plant at ground level. Other times, to be sure of their having rooted, one heaps up soil around the foot of the plant, cuts the blooming stem off at the mound, and the shoots which come from the foot of the plant root in this soil.

"*From Suckers.* The Rose suckers like all other shrubs, and can be taken from them pretty easily.

"*From Cuttings.* All roses do not take equally well to cuttings; though, with much effort, a frame, and some *cloches,* one can force even the most recalcitrant ones to send out roots . . . Cuttings are made in the Spring from the wood of the previous year. One cuts them five or six inches long [ca. 1.25–1.5 dm]; then, after having cut off the leaves, if there are any, one puts them into heath-soil, and then puts them into a *cloche* with clouded glass. One plants them pretty close together because they will become sufficiently apart as one removes the dead ones . . .

"*On Pruning.* Several fanciers go to the length of preparing roses for springtime pruning by an autumnal shearing—altogether useless, unless it be simply for neatness. They do this pre-pruning in October. Pruning of the Rose is ordinarily done in the Spring during the first days of March. It consists of cutting out all the dead or sick branches, as well as those which are poorly placed and which will be replaced, be it by an already-formed branch, be it by a bud capable of forming such. One shortens the shoots of the preceding year, cutting them back to one, two, or more eyes, if one wants to have some very beautiful roses. Some sorts, however, demand that one cut them long; and others like to be only lightly trimmed of their twigs to give a great quantity of flowers. One can only learn all of this by experience, because pruning varies not only by species and variety, but also by climate and terrain. Should one want some flowers in the Fall from a rose that only blooms once a year, it is necessary to put off the pruning until June. Last of all, the biferous roses, and the Quatre-Saisons [*referring to Damask Perpetuals*], are only pruned after they have given their first bloom [of the season]. Should a person want to retard the bloom of a rose only some fifteen days or three weeks, one only submits the bush to its pruning after the growth has begun and the shoots have already grown six to eight *lignes* long [ca. ³/₄–1 in or ca. 1.75–2.25 cm]." [MaCo]

"A pillar rose is one in which the canes have been trained about a central support in a definite form and to any desired height within the reach of the variety in use. The side shoots are rigorously pruned short—not cut off completely, please note—to follow the post or pillar form. From these shortened shoots arise the bloom-growths of the next season, and the blooms being thus produced close to the central stem, there is a pleasing formality or regularity in their appearance. The training must be carefully renewed and continued after the blooming season, and it is best regularly to select new shoots from the roots, cutting away those two or more years old." [ARA18/87]

"I am an advocate of own-root roses, particularly for the locality in which I reside [Washington, D.C.] and localities of similar climatic conditions. However, I am not so short-sighted as to overlook facts derived from actual experience often accompanied by much sadness and disappointment. Certain roses *will not* produce on their own roots. This admission does not weaken my stand for own-root roses, because other roses do not produce for me when budded, and some not either way." [ARA26/56]

"Roses are not only good to see and to smell, but their hips are good for food. A fine old lady of eighty-two years [in 1923] told me recently of her trip seventy years ago [in 1853] with her parents over the Oregon Trail. In Montana their oxen were poisoned by eating laurel. Delayed and without supplies, they lived three days on wild rose hips, then joining themselves to a passing emigrant train." [ARA23/186] "It is time for rose-growers and persons in other sections of the country than California to recognize that roadsides filled with roses for miles give a distinction and attraction to a section that can hardly be secured any other way [*as well as providing food for stranded motorists*]." [ARA18/21–22] "Mar-

shall N. Dana, of [Portland, Oregon], tells me that he uses the thorns of 'Mme. Caroline Testout' [HT] rose by inserting in them the usual phonograph needle so as to give him something he can fasten in the needle-holder. When this mounted thorn is put on the disc, there results, he declares, soft sweet tones." [ARA20/159]

"To study plants not at all from the scientific or botanical point of view, but considering their ornamental value—that is the subject which we propose to consider with the help of our able professionals. We begin with Roses. A choice rose should have the following qualities: Canes as upright as possible, of great or moderate vigor. This range of vigor or growth is necessary to meet the requirements of varying sites. Foliage abundant and ample. Flowers well 'clothed,' as the good expression of gardeners has it, producing a better effect than other roses. Some pretty-flowered varieties . . . are 'naked,' and thus incomplete. It doesn't matter how many thorns are on the stems; the less there are, the easier it is to put the blossoms together in a bouquet. But the varieties with stickers so numerous and clinging that they seem to be mossy are very distinct and should have their own category. The more floriferous or remontant the rose, the more ornamental it is in the garden.—However, some varieties which have little or no rebloom should be grown. As to the form of the flower, it is necessary to consider as the Type . . . the most beautiful—that of the Centifolia . . . However, the ones having peony- or poppy-shaped blossoms are not to be spurned. They indeed are more effective in big beds than Anemones . . . A rose should be firmly held on its stem; those that nod, though they be of beautiful form and coloration . . . are not irreproachable. A rose should be full or nearly full—which is to say that the stamens and pistils should disappear beneath or amongst the petals. The more the petals are rounded and well-disposed—that is, imbricated—the more perfect the blossom is. Small and medium-sized roses have their merit just like the big ones do . . . A rose should be fragrant; a pretty rose without perfume is like a pretty woman without spirit. The brighter a coloration a rose has, the more distinct it is from the common color—the pale pink of 'Hermosa' [B], for example—the more effective it is. A rose with flowers having all these characteristics is a plant of great merit. Of all shades, red is the most abundant; white and yellow are still rare. Violet blue or imperial blue we have already—sky blue has yet to be found. Who will find it? Probably someone who isn't looking for it." [RJC62/106–107] "The Rose, because of its perfection of form, color, and perfume, should be viewed close-up. Don't think of growing it in beds or as a specimen at a great distance from the walk in parks and gardens. It should always be close to the stroller—to catch his eye, and to surround him with fragrance." [RJC62/161]

"A fancier's rose would be distinguished by beautiful foliage; the flowers—be they solitary or in a cluster—should be well-rounded, with nicely-shaped petals arranged elegantly and symmetrically one on another, always decreasing in size up to the center near the ovary, as with the Centifolia, which will always be a model the noted painters will choose. All the roses which, like the choice Gallicas, the beautiful flesh-colored ones, the little pompons and cluster-flowered ones, etc., and, notably, Noisette's China from Florence, are pretty closely modeled—aside from size—on the beautiful regularity of the double Centifolia, and are the only ones worthy of the efforts of distinguished fanciers." [BJ24]

"The Rose, the Queen of Flowers, is in all its glory! The plenteous collection at the Luxembourg is notable from the strength of the specimens and the innumerable quantity of blossoms with which each bush is crowned. After having admired this beautiful field of Roses—because that is what it is—a person should undertake his flori-maniacal or roso-maniacal investigations at the locations of various fanciers and horticultural merchants. This is often painful, as I know, because then it is necessary to scour all the precincts of Paris." [dH46/156] "It is quite astonishing to see in what numbers seedlings are produced by the Paris rose fanciers." [MH45/8–9] "How many roses owe their ephemeral reputation to nothing but blundering observations? How often have time and experience popped these beautiful dreams of the imagination, born of nothing but impression? But why is it that Nature does not bring such sweet illusions into reality? Or why is it that our vagabond imagination or our insatiable desires make us seek new pleasures among the improbable?" [V2] "Last year, in California, the writer planted over a thousand varieties of roses, and during the past summer and early fall threw away, as absolutely useless, over 90 per cent of the new varieties, all of which had been highly recommended in various catalogues. It will readily be seen that while private experimenters with unlimited means may still try to keep track of the annual variety flood, the average amateur cannot." [ARA26/53] "There is no doubt at all that a standard list of dependable roses would be desirable for beginners; but, after a man has grown the three Radiances [all HT], 'Gruss an Teplitz' [B], and 'Frau Karl Druschki' [HP], he is pretty well capable of choosing for himself, and he loses half the fun of rose-growing if someone else picks out his varieties for him." [ARA28/212] "The catalogues convinced me that I was ordering 68 yellow roses, or at least roses in which yellow predominated. Experience has taught that 33 of them have so little yellow that they must be discarded as unfit. Is this shocking or a fair average?" [ARA26/97] "It is obvious to any thoughtful rose-lover that catalogue descriptions of roses do not always describe." [ARA17/43] "My advice to those who are about to grow the latest novelties in Roses is—don't; but if you do, obtain them from the raiser." [NRS24/163] "All roses are good, and some are better than others." [ARA29/103] "To a beginner trying to become acquainted with rose varieties, this [variation in the description of rose coloration] is quite confusing. Perhaps the disagreement regarding colors is unavoidable; differences of climate and soil may cause color changes. Some varieties seem to have a natural tendency to vary in color." [ARA25/100] "When one reads five or six opinions of a rose, one has a better idea what it is." [ARA30/165]

Explanatory

"Botanists are not in accord concerning the number of species … because some regard as a mere variety what others regard as a species, and vice-versa. I am going to keep well away from embroiling myself in these difficulties, which I leave to the savants for resolution. It will suffice for me to point out among the many sorts of roses those which, by their foliage, sparkle, and perfume, might merit a fancier's attention." [BJ09] "Messieurs Dumont de Courset, Bosc, de Pronville, and Féburier have discussed [roses] in the course of dealing with the general science of Botany; it is, however, to be regretted that these adepts have not entered into greater detail on each individual among the respective types—they never mention more than a few in this rich family. All the quick and often varying descriptions do nothing for the fancier except leave him in a continual state of indecision or error. I will try to discharge the arduous task that these gentlemen have had too much to talk about to undertake, leaving aside individual details no matter how useful to everyone desiring to know something about this Queen of the Shrubbery. In the final analysis, what is the fancier to do if he wants to choose between several beauties in the same family? What sort of guide is it if it only has a few names, or scant descriptions? How indeed can the merchant respond to questions, each stranger than the foregoing one? How to understand many of these barbarous names which we find in several catalogs?—names inane to the extreme, which, at bloom time, leave us with nothing but disgust and regret at having been tricked? A lover of the Rose, I write their history to satisfy myself; as well as to put each fancier on guard against finding what he thinks is special in the names listed in several catalogs, only to receive—as has happened to me—four or six plants of the same thing under different names. You can refer to me for the description of each Rose!" [LeR]

"The great varietie of Roses is much to bee admired, beeing more than is to be seen in any other shrubby plant that I know, both for colour, forme and smell. I haue to furnish this garden thirty sorts at the least, euery one notably differing from the other, and all fit to be here entertained: for there are some other, that being wilde and of no beautie or smell, we forebeare, and leaue to their wilde habitations. To distinguish them by their colours, as white, Red, incarnate, and yellow, were a way that many might take, but I hold it not so conuenient for divers respects: for so I should confound those of divers sorts one among another, and I should not keepe that method which to me seemeth most conuenient, which is, to place and ranke euery kind, whether single or double, one next unto the other, that so you may the better understand their varieties and differences." [PaSo]

"Cultivars are listed by the names under which they were origi-nally introduced—when determinable—or, where there is any doubt [in the author's mind] as to synonymy, under the name with which they enjoyed the widest distribution [when first re-leased]. The ritual of 'release to commerce' being the deciding fac-tor, the names introducers provided are preferred to those be-stowed by the breeder . . . The date for the cultivar is that of the year in which it was released to commerce, with, for instance, a rose originally announced in late 1885 as being for the '1885–1886 season' being listed here an 1885 rose. Main entries in [square brackets] [*sic*] refer to those roses which are, or seem to be, extinct, but which are nevertheless important or interesting enough that to leave them out of this account would be a disser-vice. Names in (round brackets or parentheses) [*sic*] are syno-nyms or translations. It is worth remembering that a 'synonym,' in this connection, is not a word or name of equal merit to be used interchangeably with the 'original' name; it is an appellation which is 'incorrect' for some reason, which has however been used at some point, and which should be kept in mind should it pop up in research material or on a label in some rosarium. The next element in an entry is the name of the breeder and/or intro-ducer, followed by the date of introduction. In the item 'Laxton/G. Paul, 1876', Laxton is the breeder and G. Paul the introducer, which will be the order followed throughout. A solitary name in-dicates the introducer" [from *The Old Rose Advisor*], who may or may not be the breeder as well. We report the parentages as the breeders or their contemporaries recorded them. "The parentages . . . are always open to question, and yet are never to be regarded as intentional or sinister mis-statements by those from whom I have culled the information. The *fact* in many cases being un-ascertainable, the *conjecture* of an expert—usually the breeder—surely weighs in as important evidence. Following the parentages are the quotations, arranged in whatever order their content sug-gested, but generally beginning with remarks on color and other characteristics of the blossom, continuing with characteristics of the leaves and plant in general, and ending with such cultural and/or historical data as is available and relevant. Each quotation is followed by a code designation indicating the work from which it came, which designation is 'translated' for would-be researchers in the reference key located in the Bibliography . . . My guiding principle in choosing the format and arrangement of this book has been primarily to serve the needs of the 'rank and file' gar-dener, who is the backbone of all horticulture, and then, secon-darily, to provide for the special needs of the enthusiast and the researcher. Because of this, I have avoided some of the more ab-struse flights of botanical fancy in favor of the conventions of horticulture, which are clearer and more familiar to the majority of those using this book." [from *The Old Rose Advisor*]

A note on the illustrations: Aside from the frontispiece, which is a reproduction of Jehan Georges Vibert's portrait of his grand-father Jean-Pierre Vibert, all of the illustrations in this book are from either the *Journal des Roses* of Lyon, edited by Cherpin, or the better-known *Journal des Roses* of Melun, edited by the Cochets and Bernardin. Alas, the copies of the journals from which the il-lustrations are reproduced have suffered from the binder's knife, and sometimes parts of the images or their lettering have been lopped off. Nevertheless, these illustrations convey, to our way of thinking, a much more accurate idea of the feeling their contem-poraries had about the roses than could any photographs of the present day of the same roses. Any relic of the past is to be cher-ished not only for itself, but also for the message it relays to us about its origins and the society in which it appeared; these illus-trations help us to clear away the interfering mind-set of the pre-sent to focus more sharply on the cultivars in their true milieu, an act of justice we owe them—and, indeed, one that we owe our-selves to validate our appreciation of these precious survivors.

Regrettably, we are unable to furnish notes on the artists themselves; in this, we imitate the faults of the periodicals that originally published the illustrations. Those interested in the artistic and historical aspects of horticultural illustration who can find out information on these talented but nearly anonymous art-ists will be doing a valuable piece of work in following up on their interests and providing the world with biographical and aesthet-ic notes on them. Several of the plates are group shots in which one or more of the illustrated cultivars are, for one reason or an-other, not included in this book. In a number of cases, the artist has used within the illustration a shortened form or misspelled version of the name of the cultivar, or has indeed illustrated the cultivar under a completely different and invalid synonym. We refer the Reader to the correct version of the name as we have it in the text of this book. Within each section (*Gallica*, etc.) we illus-trate the cultivars chronologically. Plates of several of the cultivars in this volume will be found in *The Old Rose Advisor*.

"What a pity it is that these fine, fragrant old Roses are dropping out of commerce!" [NRS28/34] "After all, one comes back to these old-fashioned roses as one does to old music and old poetry. A garden needs old associations, old fragrances, as a home needs things that have been lived with." [ARA28/63] "As in collecting old furniture, it is much nicer to make a discovery in a farmyard than to buy from a catalogue; and I clutch at the driver's arm more ex-citedly for a strange rose than for an old ladder-back chair. But identifying periods and styles in antiques is child's play com-pared to identifying old roses!" [ARA28/64] "I wish some rose his-torian would write an article on these old lost roses—an article that should have more periods than question marks!" [ARA28/66]

CHAPTER TWO

Gallicas

"The French Rose (Rosa Gallica, of botanists) is a native inhabitant of the continent of Europe, growing abundantly in the hedges of France and Italy." [WRP] "In the *Florae Romanae* of Sebastiani, published at Rome in 1818, this rose, Rosa Sempervirens, and Rosa canina, are said to be the only roses growing naturally in the Papal States." [WRP] "Its stems, moderately be-thorned, grow to a height of 2 or 3 feet [ca. 6—10 dm]; its blossom, formed of large petals colored purple red or very dark red, while scentless, is valuable because of the sparkle it produces. The abundance and duration of its bloom only enhances its ornament." [Fr] "This rose is widely known and cultivated, not only in France, but also in all the countries of central Europe." [JF] "This was one of the roses introduced at the earliest period to our gardens. The year 1596 is given by botanists as the date of its introduction into England ... The semi-double Red Rose, or *Officinal Rose,* grown in Surrey for the druggists, is of this family, and a very slight remove from the original species, which is of the same color, with but one range of petals, or single. All the roses of this group are remarkable for their compact and upright growth, and many for the multiplicity of their petals, and tendency to produce variegated flowers. Many of the spotted, variegated, and striped varieties are very singular and beautiful. The formation of the flower, in most of the superior modern varieties of Rosa gallica, is very regular ... Some of the new varieties lately introduced, and much prized in France, do not bloom well in England, the change of climate being very unfavorable, but in our [American] dry and warm climate they attain a perfect development." [WRP]

"This rose takes its name from its great abundance in hedges and other uncultivated grounds in France ... It is a very great seed-bearer, and has consequently been much used by florists in crossing with other varieties to produce new sorts; the results have been hundreds, in many instances more astonishing for their exalted names than for any other merits; yet there are many of the most perfect character, composed of numerous and regularly formed petals, with colours of almost every imaginable shade" [Bu], "from violet purple and dark red to the most delicate pink." [JF] "They are particularly noted for the size and brilliant color of their blossoms. The single or semi-double specimens are, in the eyes of several fanciers, preferable to those with perfectly double flowers. These lattermost, however, while indeed more delicate and sparser, ought equally to be sought out." [CM]

"Their blossoms are double and a deep, velvety crimson. This color, darker in several individuals, has perhaps given rise to the fable of black roses, which have no merit other than rarity." [BJ09] "The 'Arab Blue' rose ... mentioned in the Twelfth Century ... is no doubt violet like that of the Germans [*i.e.,* 'Veilchenblau', Mult]. It is Alphonse Karr's 'Gardener's Blue'. Ibn-el-Façel, to name one of many, specifies better than his contemporaries that this rose is more a deep violet." [ExRé] "They use the name 'Veloutée' [*i.e.,* 'velvety'] for those Provins roses with which the petals, when exposed to strong light, give a reflection." [CM] "It is among the Provins roses that one finds the darkest-colored roses. These bushes are also generally the stockiest; they have wood which is thick and short; they fill out freely, and make more regular bushes than the others." [BJ40]

"Seedlings of *R. gallica* not infrequently show marbling of the petals with spots of different shapes and colors." [T&R] "In this group are to be found many interesting striped, marbled, and spotted Roses, singularly beautiful, and which, although highly popular in France, do not seem to suit the taste of English Rose cultivators. To see them in perfection, they should be viewed early in the morning before a summer's sun has dimmed their beauty; the colours of these Roses, in particular, fly at the Fire King's approach, when the contrast often becomes too feeble to please." [P] "Nearly all the striped, mottled, and variegated roses have originated in this group; the recent varieties and improvements of character have gone beyond all calculation, and we may safely arrive at the conclusion that roses of every imaginable colour, except blue and black, will be in cultivation at no distant period; and then it will be nothing remarkable to see white roses edged with crimson, and crimson edged with white." [Bu]

"All hues are here, and the flowers are remarkable for their brilliancy, fulness, perfect outline, and regularity in the disposition of the petals. Hence it will be inferred, that they are well adapted for growing for exhibition; and such is the case. But is there no other quality desirable? Yes, one—sweetness—and it is added to the rest." [P] "They are generally not very fragrant." [JF]

"The *Provins Proper* are very vigorous plants, the wood is big, upright, and clothed with slender thorns. The foliage is very lush, somewhat flat, and a beautiful dark green." [JR9/75] "The French Roses approach nearer to the Provence [*i.e.,* Centifolia] than to any other group: they are distinguished from them by a more upright and compact growth; the prickles are also smaller and less numerous, and the flowers are more flat." [P] "The distinguishing features of this family are strong upright flower-stalks, want of large prickles, rigid leaves, and compact growth." [Bu] "It is distinguished by leaflets more or less hairy or pubescent, especially along the edge, and in which the crenelatures are ordinarily glandulose; by its stems clothed with prickles; by its bristly peduncles, which are a little glandular and covered over more or less with fine prickles, as are the petioles." [Lam]

"The Provins Rose is grown profusely in gardens. All soils are good for it; it nevertheless makes the bushiest plants and gives more numerous and better-colored blossoms in a light, warm soil. This sort cannot be overused in gardens, say landscape gardeners. They can be sited in any exposure, at the back of beds, under lone trees, in the middle of lawns, along waterways." [CM] "They all do best grown on their own roots; their growth is such as will require to be kept under with the knife, and they bear pruning much better than the [Centifolia] or Moss Rose. The best period for the operation is from November to early in the spring; thin out the wood where it is thick, and cut back the young shoots to three or four eyes of the wood of the preceding year's growth. When the pruning of a plant is finished, there should be no shoots crossing any others, and every shoot or branch should stand free and straight. The plants require manure or rich compost dug in among their roots once a year, unless the ground is of a very rich nature; in that case, once in two years will be sufficient. If some of the plants are pruned in November, and others in March, or after the foliage begins to appear, it will make about eight or ten days difference in their time of blooming. This practice is often resorted to in Europe, which greatly retards their bloom in cool or moist climates; but with us the results are not so decisive, yet they are quite perceptible. Many of the sorts sucker freely; in such cases the superfluous ones should be removed in the spring, and planted where wanted, or destroyed." [Bu] "Most of the varieties of Rosa gallica are robust and all are hardy, and flourish equally as bushes on their own roots, grafted or budded on short stems, or as standards; but they cannot be recommended for tall standards, as their growth is too compact to be graceful. To grow them fine for exhibition as single blooms, or 'show-roses,' the clusters of buds should be thinned early in June, taking at least two-thirds from each; manure should also be laid round their stems on the surface, and manured water given to them plentifully in dry

weather. With this description of culture, these roses will much surpass any thing we have heretofore seen in this country . . . In winter pruning, shorten the strong shoots to within six or eight buds of the bottom; those that are weak cut down to two or three buds." [WRP]

"The Provins Rose was one of the first to be introduced into horticultural gardens. Some authors also call it *Rosa Milesiana,* so called because it grows abundantly around Miletus in Asia Minor. It was also grown in great quantity at Provins (Seine-et-Marne) and environs, as well as at Surrey (England) for the needs of the druggists and parfumiers of these two countries. It has as well its political history, as the semi-double scarlet red variety, which served druggists and parfumiers, was adopted as a distinct symbol or, more properly, a device of the prince royal of England, Count Egmont, who took the title Comte de Champagne around 1277. This rose was brought from Syria some years previously to Provins by Thibaut, Comte de Brie, returning from a crusade." [JR9/73] "It was in 1238, upon the return from the 4th Crusade, that Thibault VI, called *le Chansonnier,* brought back from the Holy Land the famous red rose, of which the sort is maintained at Provins. It came from the valley of Damascus . . .

"An historian of Provins, Monsieur Opoix, has traced its origin to the most distant times. According to him, the rose of Provins is the same as the Rose of Sharon mentioned by the bard in the Canticles, as the Milesian Rose mentioned in Pliny, and as the rose the spines of which tore at the feet of Venus as she flew to the aid of Adonis. Be that as it may, it is certain that, shortly after its debut in Provins, this rose figured in religious ceremonies, and that they were made into crowns carried at the procession of the Fête-Dieu, and were, as well, an item in the accounts of the church of St. Quiriace, of Provins, where is seen the expense: *'Pro capellis roseis in festo sancti sacramenti.'*

"Soon after, our rose gained entry into the apothecary's shop. These pharmacists would make conserves and candies from the petals which, for centuries, the city of Provins would bestow—often with enthusiasm, often with quite the opposite—upon kings, queens, dukes, marquises, and archbishops who made their solemn entry there, or who laid siege under its solid walls." [JR1/7/9] ("Provins roses are regarded as being tonic, astringent, stimulating, strengthening, and laxative. One may make from it a syrup, a conserve, or a powder that can be used successfully in cases of indigestion, vomiting, hemorrhages, and diarrhea. These flowers are more effective when infused in vinegar or wine. They are commonly pressed into astringent and resolutive fomentations, particularly for contusions of the head, sprains of the parts with tendons, blood loss, and violent migraines. Unguent or pomade of roses is applied to the lips to take care of chapping." [Lam]) "We have dug up the names of some of these worthies of other centuries to whom these presents were made. These confections were, to our ancestors, quite a tax, and quite bitter for all their sweetness . . . [*We omit the notes on the visiting dignitaries, from the visit paid in 1310 by Philippe de Marigny, Archbishop of Sens, to that of Charles X, which occurred on September 18, 1828.*]

"It was in the 17th century that rose-growing in Provins reached its greatest development. The vogue was such that everyone had a hand in it: Provins households and pharmacists would give themselves over to vying to improve the production of this useful and royal product to such a degree that, as a historian of 1600 tells it, the shops of the latter encroached on the main street . . ." [JR1/7/9]

"Always known in France, [the Gallicas] alone accounted for more than half of the roses known [around 1800]. Their colors went from delicate pink to deep violet, and the 'purples' and 'velvets' were especially in fashion." [Gx] "60 years ago [ca. 1825], the collection of Messrs. Loddiges, at Hackney (England), was composed of 2,000 varieties of Provins roses. But the greater number of these had nothing remarkable about them other than their sonorous names, and only a few remain in collections known to me." [JR9/74] "Until the introduction of the perpetual blooming varieties [the Gallica] was the favorite Rose of our English gardens. Upwards of one thousand varieties of this family alone have been cultivated; such, however, has been the increase of Perpetual Roses, during the last twenty years [*i.e.,* 1857–1877], that the Gallica and other summer blooming roses (excepting the very choicest kinds) have long been thrown out of cultivation." [JC] "In 1860, a pharmacist of Provins, successor to the old apothecaries, sent to England 150 boxes of dried conserves and 115 of liquid [*presumably rose water*], and the previous year had received an order from America for 36 thousand kilograms of rose-petals!—going to show that no one, not even the rose, is a prophet in his own land." [JR1/7/9]

"With full hands, Nature has lavished diversity on this class—diversity capable of trying the patience of the most indefatigable fancier who grows them from seed. The immense quantity of varieties, the imperceptible shadings [of difference] between them, the likeness of their characteristics, their ambiguous connection with the others that exist, the marks of doubtful hybridity—all conspire to throw a person into a labyrinth from which theory and the greatest experience are always insufficient to extricate him." [V1] "No rose, not even the Centifolia, offers the interested fancier such a great number of varieties. In the Centifolia, the varieties can be distinguished by the forms of the foliage—resembling that of other plants—or by marked differences in the blossom and its external parts. In the Provins rose, all you can go by are the color, shadings, and size of the flower. It is rare to find two specimens which are exactly alike in all their parts. Thus, we have a multitude of varieties uniquely distinct one from the other in the number and disposition of the flowers, by the size of the corolla, and by their color; but the nuances which these colors are capable of taking, from the lightest red to purple and the darkest violet, are so

numerous that a certain Belgian rose fancier [*most probably Parmentier*] has four hundred varieties of the Provins Rose all by himself." [CM] "Cross-pollination so perverts them in certain cases that I have, in the Gallica class, some varieties which do not retain one single characteristic of the sort from which came the seed." [V1]

"The varieties and sub-varieties of the Provins are nearly innumerable; disciplined fanciers, however, need concern themselves only with those which offer forms and colorations both distinct and striking; a well-chosen few is sufficient for an enlightened collection." [J-A/571] "They come in such numbers that it is quite difficult to classify them well, due to the different names growers have given them; however, everybody should have one." [LeR]

"The *Gallica* . . . and its hybrids, after having for a long time stood at the head of a brilliant cohort of Roses has perhaps fallen the farthest [in estimation] in the eyes of the moderns because of its real or imaginary faults. It nevertheless has not lost its intrinsic value as a summer rose, as it is one of the hardiest, least demanding, most abundant, and most elegantly perfumed." [R-H63/184] "The varieties I am going to describe should never be allowed to disappear from collections." [JR9/75]

Rosa gallica

"Bush 2–3 feet high [to ca. 1 m]; canes bristling with small caducous prickles; petioles, stipules, nerves, and peduncles bearing glandular bristles; leaves rounded, pretty stiff, glabrous and brownish green above, pubescent and glaucous beneath; blossoms single, fragrant, and very deep purple-red, with sepals totally 'beardless' or non-pinnate." [J-A/567] "The Provins rose, in truth, originates in the southern part of Europe . . . Its stems are in general not very robust, dividing into numerous canes which are glabrous, and armed with thorns which are unequal and nearly straight. Its ovaries are globular, but sometimes oval, especially before the petals fall. Its peduncles are covered with blackish glands; its leaves are most commonly composed of five or seven leaflets which are oval, acute, dark green, very glaucous beneath, and borne on a common petiole which is glandulose and prickly. Its flowers, solitary—or, more like it, two or three together—are a more or less dark red, not very fragrant, two to three inches big [to ca. 8 cm]; they appear in June and July. Its fruits are round, reddish brown, and about five to six *lignes* in size [ca. $^1/_2$–$^3/_4$ in]." [CM]

Horticultural Varieties

À Fleurs de Rose Tremière de la Chine
trans. "With Flowers Like Those of the Rose of Sharon"
Pelletier, pre-1828

"Flowers rosy crimson, petals edged and mottled with blush, large and double; form, cupped. Habit, branching; growth moderate. A pretty Rose." [P] "Flowers medium-sized, full, well-formed, red with nuances." [JR1/7/11] "Canes upright, with light green bark; prickles rare, gray, intermingled with several small bristles strewn over the

À Fleurs de Rose Tremière de la Chine *continued*

branches; leaves of five or seven leaflets which are oblong, pointed, and finely dentate; flowers very double, medium in size, cupped while opening, and at that point looking like the Rose of Sharon, but then succeeding to a plumper form; otherwise, they are well formed and in clusters. Petals a delicate pink mixed with white at the edge, close-together, crisped, irregularly notched at the summit." [No28]

À Fleurs Marbrées   Listed as 'Marmorea' (G).

[À Grand Cramoisi]
syn. 'Grand Cramoisi de Trianon'; trans. "With Big Crimson Ones
     [*i.e.,* Blossoms]"
Trianon, pre-1818

"The most remarkable and darkest of the Purples; the blossom is not very double, but makes up for it by being quite regular." [CM] Not to be confused with 'Grand Cramoisi de Vibert' (G).

Abailard
syns. 'Abaillard', 'Abeilard', 'Abelard'
Sommesson, pre-1826

"Delicate pink, very rich form." [J-As/55] "Blossoms medium-sized, very double, flesh, superb, looking like 'Pompon Bazard', but of a paler color." [No26] "Very beautiful." [Go] Not to be confused with Robert's two-L'd offering of 1845, below.

Abaillard
syns. 'Abailard', 'Abeilard', 'Abelard'
Robert, 1845

"Roseate, marbled, tall." [WRP] "Not very vigorous; thorns close-set, blossom plumed light pink and dark pink; the rose is medium-sized and very double." [S] Not to be confused with Sommesson's one-L'd cultivar, above.

Abeilard   See 'Abailard' (G) and 'Abaillard' (G).

Abelard   See 'Abailard' (G) and 'Abaillard' (G).

[Achille]
syns. 'Belle Italienne', 'Louis XVI', 'Superbe Brune'
Breeder unknown, pre-1810

"Deep violet red." [LS] "Wood strong and vigorous, armed with numerous fairly hooked thorns; leaves the somber ones of the Gallicas, stiff to the touch; numerous buds, not covered [*i.e.,* by the sepals]. The blossoms are double and of the greatest beauty. They are four inches across [ca. 1 dm], and deep velvety purple; its form is that of an oval saucer. Some petals are large and thick, and offer a great brilliancy to the eye, grafted high. Opening June 5–10." [LeR] "Wood, leaves, calyxes, and buds have nothing remarkable, but the blossom is of great beauty; while not very double, it is three inches across [ca. 7.5 cm], and superbly colored velvety deep purple without any shading. The petals are well formed and quite big. It's as perfect a rose as this group could give us! It also enjoys the feature of exhaling a delicious perfume." [C-T] "Guerrapain described this variety; it was in the collection of the Soucelle château." [Gx] Achilles, moody Greek warrior of the Trojan War; he would want us to recall with him his friend Patroclus.

Adèle
Descemet, pre-1814

"Rose." [Cal] "Pink, medium size, full, medium height." [Sn] "Desportes saw this rose in Descemet's nurseries." [Gx]

Adèle Courtoise
Breeder unknown, pre-1842

"Blossom medium-sized, full; color, delicate pink." [S] "Medium height." [Sn]

Adèle Heu
Vibert, 1816

"Deep pink." [V9] "Dark red." [GJB] "*Flower* large, quite double, light red or intense purple pink." [Pf] "Purple violet, medium to large, full, moderate fragrance, tall." [Sn] "Flowers fine rosy purple, covered with white dots, of medium size, double; form, expanded. Habit, erect; growth, moderate. A showy Rose." [P] "Blossom medium-sized, full, very well formed, slightly flat; the buds are good for bouquets because they keep a long time without opening fully. Color, beautiful purple pink touched silvery white." [S] The name of this cultivar, from Vibert's first commercial season, commemorates his recently deceased wife. We do not consider 'Duc d'Orléans' or 'Henri IV' to be synonyms of this cultivar.

Adèle Prévost
Breeder unknown, pre-1836

"Flesh." [V4] "[A] silvery blush." [FP] "Flowers beautiful blush, their centre pink, the lower petals slightly reflexing soon after expansion, leaving the centre petals erect in the form of a cup, large and full; form, fine. Habit, erect; growth, vigorous. A very superior Rose." [P] "Flower large, strong, quite full, well formed; color, pink and salmony pink; this variety is much to be recommended for its rich bloom." [S] "The name commemorates a celebrated rosarian, [and] stands out because of the abundance of its bloom, the exquisite form of its blossoms, and its delicate pink color." [R-H63/184]

[Admirable]
syns. 'Carmosina', 'Chremesina Scintillans', 'Couleur de Sang',
     'L'Admirable', 'Mirabilis', 'Multiplex', 'Superbissima'
Holland, pre-1787

"Red." [Cal] "Flower full, scarlet red. Calyx nearly globular, turbinate; peduncle hispid; stem prickly; thorns sparse, caducous; petioles glandulose, prickly; leaflets ovate-lanceolate, doubly serrate, glandulose at their edges. Description. The bush rarely grows over three feet [ca. 1 m]. The stem and canes are green, and bear numerous short prickles which readily come off at the touch, as do the glands distributed there. The villose petals come with reddish brown glands, feebly pediculate, and bearing short prickles. The leaflets, in 3's or 5's, are ovate-lanceolate, acuminate, double serrate, and glandulose along the edge. The blossom is ordinarily solitary on the peduncle, globular, and fat; the calyx is round-pyriform, without narrowing at the neck, and bestrewn with glands of a red tending towards brown. Of the 5 sepals, three are pinnatifid. The corolla is very strong and full. It is only in the late blossoms that one sees some yellow stamens in the middle. At expansion, the petals are very bright carmine, but they lose their sparkle as soon as the mid-day sun, or rain, hits them, and take on a dull color coming close to violet. Observations. This one is seemingly due to breeding, and should be regarded as a cross between the French Rose and the Velvety Rose. Some [sub]varieties can be found in several gardens under various names, only distinguishable by the flowers being more double or less double. The 'Sanguineo-Purpurea Simplex' shown in our eighth cahier would seem to be the original of this one. Reproduction is easily done, more by its numerous suckers than by layers, which root easily." [Rsg] "According to Desportes, it came from Holland." [Gx] See also 'Cramoisie' (G).

Admirable de Lille See 'Orphise' (G).

Adonis
Descemet, pre-1814

"Bright red." [Cal] "Bright pink, flat." [BJ40] "Light red, flat." [GJB] Adonis, handsome Greek youth much disputed by Aphrodite and Persephone.

Adonis
Breeder unknown, pre-1829

"*Buds* marbled with red. *Flower* medium-sized, regular, light even pink." [Pf] "Medium-sized, full; color, flesh pink." [S] "As a pretty pale blush or rosy white variety, is quite worth cultivation." [WRP]

Adriadne Listed as 'Ariane' (G).

Agar
Vibert, 1843

"Deep rose color, spotted, with a rosette centre." [WRP] "Medium-sized, double, deep pink, spotted, rosette." [V8] "Pink, medium size, full, moderate scent, average height." [Sn] Not to be confused with Laffay's pre-1836 Gallica of the same name.

Agathe Majestueuse
Possibly a synonym for 'Aimable Rouge' (G), *q.v.* See also 'Majestueuse' (Ag).

Agénor
Vibert, 1832

"Flower medium-sized, full, purple shaded scarlet red; cupped; well-formed and much to be recommended; foliage bright and abundant." [S] "Red, medium size, full, medium scent, average height." [Sn] Agenor, son of Poseidon, ruler of Tyre, father of Europa and Cadmus, *inter alia*.

[Aglaé Adanson]
Vibert, 1823

"Pink, spotted." [BJ40] "Flowers large, semi-double, purplish, plumed with light pink." [No26] "Lilac." [God] "Flowers rose, spotted with white, very large and double; form, cupped." [P] "A fine mottled rose, something like ['Agar'] in color, but much larger, and finely formed." [WRP] "*Peduncle* long. *Ovary* ovoid, often glabrous at the tip. *Flower* medium-sized, full, light pink, paler at the edges." [Pf] "To Mme. Aglaé Adanson, daughter of the celebrated botanist of that name, and author of *Maison de Campagne*, a work in 3 vol." [BJ24] A letter by Aglaé Adanson on *Pinus palustris* appears in AnFrII/377. See also 'Charlotte de Lacharme' (G).

[Aigle Brun]
syns. 'Altissima', 'La Très Haute'; trans. "Brown Eagle"
Breeder unknown, pre-1811

"Dark velvet." [Cal] "Beautiful semi-double blossoms, blackish velvety bright crimson." [J-A/567] "Medium-sized, double or a little more, purple, very velvety." [Pf, adding that it is the typical form of the Provins Rose] "Semi-double, a less deep purple [than that of 'Aigle Noir']." [No26] "In the same season [as that when 'Rosa Mundi' (G)

blooms], you can also enjoy a variety much esteemed for the beauty and sparkle of its colors, though it is nothing more than semi-double. It is called 'Aigle Brun'. The wood, foliage, and calyx are like those of the Provins. At least, the flower is as large, but it is to be preferred due to its velvety brown, so dark that it seems black, which its many golden yellow stamens heighten in effect. There are twelve petals. Rose fanciers count it as one of the most beautiful sorts on which to lavish their attentions." [C-T] "This is the original of the most beautiful 'Velvets' and 'Purples'. Its wood is slender though strong; prickles fine and rare; leaves the somber ones of the sort; buds pointed and covered over by the extensions of the calyx. The blossom is medium-sized, semi-double, and a velvety brown, so dark that it seems marked with touches of black on many petals; the golden stamens—which are profuse—give it a look both rich and ravishing. This charming rose is only two and a half inches across [ca. 6.5 cm]. Opens from the 5th to the 10th of June." [LeR]

[Aigle Noir]
syn. 'Maheca Nova'; trans. "Black Eagle"
Godefroy, 1818

"Velvety purple." [LS] "Flowers the same [as those of 'Aigle Brun'], but quite double." [J-A/567] "Blossoms semi-double, medium-sized, velvety purple." [AC] "A very deep purple." [No26] "Pink, nuanced." [V9]

Aigle Rouge Listed as 'Mahaeca' (G).

Aimable Amie
trans. "Likable [Female] Friend"
Trianon, pre-1818

"Blossom medium-sized, full, deep pink." [S] "Described by De Pronville, it grew in the Trianon nurseries." [Gx] We have been unable to substantiate a suggested date of 1813.

Aimable Emma Listed as 'Belle Hélène' (G).

[Aimable Pourpre]
trans. "Likable Purple"
Holland, pre-1811

"Purple." [V9] "Dark." [Cal] "The wood of this rose is remarkable by its yearly growth, its color, and its brown prickles. The elongate, delicate, finely dentate, bright green foliage is very pretty. The calyx as well as the bud are rounded and flattened. The blossom, three inches across [ca. 7.5 cm], is not very double; but it compensates for this through the richness of its color, which is a purple black. It is passably fragrant. Its petals are big, wide, and thick. It blooms at the beginning of June." [C-T] "This is a variety of the Provence [*sic*], wood, thorns, leaves, and buds reveal its classification . . . Its color, which is a well-pronounced purple tending towards black-brown . . . You should graft it high because of its sparkle. Opens from June 1–7." [LeR]

Aimable Rouge
syns. 'Centfeuilles d'Angleterre', 'Hortensia', 'Le Triomphe', 'Rose Hortensia', 'Royal Virgin Rose'; poss. syns., 'Agathe Majestuese', 'Great Royal'; trans. "Likable Red"
Godefroy, pre-1811

"Pale rose." [Cal] "Distinctive form, red blotched white and hydrangea pink." [J-As/59] "Interesting by way of the beautiful Hydrangea pink of its flowers, which are white along the edge of the petals and slightly globose in the center. At the Trianon, several specimens

Aimable Rouge *continued*

of this variety take on a great intensity of color. This is the English Centifolia of Monsieur Noisette, and the 'Rose-Hortensia' of Monsieur Godefroy." [CM] "Pink, medium size, full, moderate scent, tall." [Sn] "This one is distinguished by its green wood armed with numerous hooked thorns. Its leaves are oval and deeply toothed. The calyx is constricted at the top, and is covered over with brown points. The buds are round, and crowned with the calyx-membranes; half-open, they are beautifully formed. The blossoms are large and very double; the petals are wavy, and a lighter pink than those of the [common] Centifolia, mixed with white, particularly just at anthesis. They have a sweet, pleasant scent, blooming at the end of June." [C-T] "This variety was in the nurseries of Cels and Dupont; it was also, says Redouté, in the Dutch catalogs; De Pronville believes it the 'Royal Virgin Rose' of Miss Lawrance; Desportes gives as synonyms 'Le Triomphe', and 'Agathe Majestueuse'." [Gx]

Aimable Sophie   Listed as 'Belle Hélène' (G).

Alaine

This rose-pink cultivar, attributed to "Robert & Moreau, 1849," is not attested in the old literature; the firm Robert & Moreau did not exist in 1849. Possibly it is Vibert's 'Aline' of 1816, *q.v.*

Alba   Listed as 'Gallica Alba' (G).

Alcime
Vibert, 1845

"Purple flesh." [Ÿ] "Medium size, double, very dark violet." [R&M62] See also 'Alcine' (G).

Alcine
Vibert, 1834

"Crimson pink, spotted." [V4] See also 'Alcime' (G).

Aldégonde   Listed as 'Rouge Formidable' (G).

Alector Cramoisi
syn. 'Major'
Dupont, pre-1811

"Velvety crimson." [LS] "Crimson red." [Ÿ] "This variety has nothing to note in its wood, leaves, calyxes, or buds. Its blossom is large, double, beautiful crimson red, producing a grand effect. Its petals are quite big, its perfume is sweet and pleasant." [C-T]

Alexandre Laquement
syn. 'Alexandre Laquemont'
Breeder unknown, pre-1885

"Violet, spotted red." [LS] "Flower medium-sized, full; color, violet-ish pink, marbled and spotted bright pink." [S] "Tall." [Sn]

Alfieri
Vibert, 1833

"Crimson." [V4] "Blossom medium-sized, full; lilac-y pink." [S] "Violet pink . . . average height." [Sn] Vittorio Alfieri, 1749–1803, Italian dramatist and tragic poet.

Alika
syn. 'Grandiflora'?
Hansen, 1906

"'Alika' is a Gallica or Hybrid Gallica rose. Unlike most Gallicas, it

grows to six foot [ca. 2 m]. It suckers and forms arching thickets. It has fragrant, single or semi-double reddish flowers with a central yellowish eye. And it is very hardy. There is a specimen in our local arboretum that puts on quite a show each June. Oh, I forgot—it's musical! If you stand near it on a warm sunny afternoon, it hums (okay, it's really the bumblebees swarming in and out, but with your eyes closed, it's hard not to imagine the bush itself if buzzing)." [Contributor, requesting anonymity, from the Internet] "*R. gallica* 'Grandiflora' is mentioned in a Regel & Kesselring catalog from 1881. That was a big nursery which sold to Finland, too. We had several sanitariums here [Finland] where the Russian elite from St. Petersburg spent their summers . . . In this catalog, 'Grandiflora' is not marked as being double . . ." [Another contributor, also requesting anonymity, from the Internet] 'Alika', brought to the United States from Russia by Professor N. E. Hansen of North Dakota, in commerce by 1930.

[Aline]
Vibert, 1816

"Medium-sized, full, flesh." [V8] "Delicate and very seductive pink." [J-A/569] "Medium-sized, full; color, white nuanced flesh." [S]

Altissima   Listed as 'Aigle Brun' (G).

Ambroise Paré
syn. 'Ambrose Paré'
Vibert, 1846

"Deep purple, striped and spotted white." [JR9/75] "Bright purple touched deep purple." [S] "Medium-sized, full, deep purple, spotted, in a rosette." [R&M62] "Deep purple red, medium size, full, tall." [Sn] Not to be confused with Moreau-Robert's 1865 Tea of the same name. Ambroise Paré, 1517–1590, French surgeon.

Amélie de Mansfield
Breeder unknown, pre-1842

"Violet pink." [Ÿ] "Blossom medium-sized, full; color, bright pink." [S]

Amitié   Listed as 'L'Amitié' in Chapter 3 on Damasks.

Anacréon
Vibert, 1828

"Light purple, marbled." [V4] "Lilac pink." [V9] "*Flower* medium-sized or large, plump, nearly full, light purple, a little wine-lee or deep pink, with pale edges." [Pf] "*Flowers,* large or middle-sized, very double, convex; of a light purple, inclining to claret, or deep red with pale edges." [Go] "Light purple red, medium size, very full, moderate to tall." [Sn] "Violet purple, spotted with blush, large and double; form, expanded. Habit, branching; growth, vigorous. A distinct Rose." [P] Anacreon, convivial ancient Greek poet. It appears that Vibert released no fewer than three Gallicas under this name, in 1819, 1828, and 1836, with his successor Robert releasing yet another in 1854 for good measure. It is exceedingly difficult to separate out these different cultivars, as the Anacreontic interest in wine colored the choice of which rose was to bear this name such that all are similarly vinous in hue.

Ancienne Pivoine   Listed as 'Bourbon' (G).

André du Pont   Listed as 'Rouge Formidable' (G).

Anémone Listed as 'Renoncule' (G). See also 'Ornement de la Nature' (G).

Anémone Ancienne Listed as 'Ornement de la Nature' (G).

Antonia d'Ormois Listed as 'Antonine d'Ormois' (G).

Antonine d'Ormois
syn. 'Antonia d'Ormois'
Vibert, 1835
"Flesh." [V4] "Pale flesh, full, medium-sized, globular, beautiful." [LF] "Blush, their centre rosy flesh, large and very double, beautiful; form, expanded. Growth, vigorous." [P] "Of most splendid form." [WRP] "Tall." [Sn]

Aramis
Vibert, 1845
"White and deep rose, variegated." [WRP] "Medium-sized, full, cupped, well formed; color, white striped with pink." [S] "Flowers French white, striped with rose, of medium size, double; form, cupped. Habit, erect; growth, moderate. A very pretty Rose." [P] Aramis, one of the Three Musketeers.

Archévêque Listed as 'Pourpre Charmant' (G). See also 'L'Évêque' (G).

Archiduc Charles Listed as 'Belle Hélène' (G). Not to be confused with the China 'Archiduc Charles'.

Ardoisée Listed as 'Busard Triomphant' (G).

Ariadne Listed as 'Ariane' (G).

Ariane
syns. 'Adriadne', 'Ariadne'
Vibert, 1818
"Light purple." [V9] "Rose." [Cal] "Light purple." [GJB] "Flowers full, reflexing, deep pink." [AC] *Canes* vertical, very thorny. *Flower* medium-sized, full, plump, regular, deep pink or light purple." [Pf] Not to be confused with Vibert's Alba of the same name of the same year! Ariane, alias Ariadne, assisted Theseus in escaping from the Minotaur, with scant thanks from T.; Dionysus, however, saw to a personal reward for her on Naxos.

Arlequin
Vibert, pre-1821
"Crimson." [Cal] "Red mixed with pink." [Ÿ] "Pale red, prettily marbled, and very double." [WRP] "Medium-sized, full, light red, marbled." [V8] "Feeble growth; flower medium-sized, full; color, red marbled with crimson. While not remontant, this flower nevertheless has its good points. In winter, this rose should be protected from the cold." [S] Arlequin, alias Harlequin, restless inamorato of Columbine in the *Commedia del'Arte*. See also 'Pourpre Marbrée' (G).

Assemblage des Beautés
syn. 'Rouge Éblouissante'; trans. "Gathering of Beauties"
Delaâge, 1823
"Purple." [Ÿ] "Blossoms medium-sized, a very sparkling crimson, the richest of all in color." [No26] "Blossom big, well doubled, bright velvety purple." [S] *Flowers*, middle-sized, of a brilliant crimson." [Go] "Not quite full enough of petals, but deserves its name, for its varied and finely colored crimson and scarlet flowers on one stem are always admired." [WRP] "Purple-red, medium size, full, moderate to tall." [Sn] "Flowers crimson scarlet, shaded with purplish crimson, of medium size, double; form, expanded. Habit, erect; growth, moderate. A most abundant bloomer, a showy and beautiful Rose. A good seed-bearer." [P] "Was a part of the collections at the Soucelle château; mentioned by Desportes." [Gx] The attribution "Fr. Annuaire" which one sees refers to a French almanac, not to a breeder. Not to be confused with an obscure pre-1810 Gallica of the same name.

Athalie Listed as 'Fanny Bias' (G).

Atropurpurea Listed as 'Subnigra' (G).

Austriaca Listed as 'Rosier d'Amour' (G).

Avenant Listed as 'Belle Biblis' (G).

Bacchante
Breeder unknown, pre-1811
"Wine red." [LS] "Wood strong and vigorous. Leaves oval, yellow green, quite dentate. Calyx and bud round, not covered at all [by the sepals]. Blossom of the size of [that of] 'Bordeaux' or 'Rosier des Dames', extremely double, vinous violet, no doubt accounting for the name 'Bacchante'. It has a sweet scent, and blooms around June 10." [C-T] A bacchante was a (usually frenzied) female devotee of Bacchus; today's equivalent may perhaps be found in singles bars Friday nights.

[Baraguay]
syn. 'Baraguey'
Hardy, 1819
"Cindery." [LS] "Very precious variety with very well-formed ashy blossoms, often indeed without thorns." [J-A/570] Louis Baraguay d'Hilliers, 1764–1813, French general who died perhaps of sheer dismay during the Napoleonic retreat from Moscow.

Beau Narcisse
Miellez, pre-1828
"Purple." [RG] "Blossom medium-sized, full; color, deep purple, often striped light purple." [S] "Purple-violet, medium size, full, tall." [Sn] Narcisse, alias Narcissus, the self-absorbed male beauty of mythology.

Beauté de la Malmaison
Breeder unknown, pre-1885
"Medium-sized, full; color, deep red, marbled with violet." [S] Malmaison, the palace of the Empress Joséphine, patroness of botany in general and roses in particular.

[Beauté Insurmontable]
syn. 'Lyre de Flore'; poss. syns., 'Panachée Superbe', 'Phoenix'; trans. "Unsurpassable Beauty"
Holland, pre-1811
"Dark." [Cal] "Red." [LS] *Flowers*, full, small, very regular; of a deep pink; very early, being the first-blowing of the Provins roses." [Go] "To the eyes of certain fanciers, this rose might well merit the grandiose name it has been given. The quite double blossom, larger than that of the Pompon, shows three colors. The ground is purple, mixed or plumed with deep pink and delicate pink; the petals are crinkled and arch back onto the calyx; it has a sweet and pleasant scent, and blooms from the beginning of June to the 10th. It can be counted as one of the pretty ones." [C-T]

Beauté Renommée
trans. "Renowned Beauty"
Holland, pre-1811 (*not* Vibert, 1845)

"Red" [Cal] "Pink, small to medium size, full, very fragrant, tall." [Sn] "Wood and leaves a yellow green, ashy and glaucous. Calyx and bud round, not covered at all [by the sepals]. Blossom two inches across [ca. 5 cm], quite double, of beautiful form, a pretty bright purple red, with a pleasant scent. This rose can be classified among the prettiest of the sort." [C-T] "Originated in Holland, described by Guerrapain." [Gx]

[Beauté Surprenante]
trans. "Amazing Beauty"
Descemet/Vibert, pre-1820

"Flesh white." [V9] "Pale rose." [Cal] "Blossoms white, with a pink heart, medium-sized, leaves glaucous." [No26] *Thorns* feeble. *Leaves* glaucous. *Ovary* globular, glabrous, except at the base which is covered with red glands, as is the peduncle. *Sepals* slightly foliaceous; three are edged on two sides with numerous appendages. *Flower* medium-sized, full, flesh, nearly white." [Pf] "Desportes gives it as an obtention by Descemet; Prévost got it from Vibert." [Gx] Sometimes cataloged as an Alba.

[Beauté Tendre]
syn. 'Rouge Rayé'; trans. "Delicate Beauty"
Dupont, pre-1810

"Pale rose." [Cal] "Superb blossom, well formed, very double, large, beautiful bright red." [S] "The name under which it is sold would seem to announce a variety of delicate coloration; but, on the contrary, the very double large blossom is deep pink; its petals are large, notched in the middle, vinous white beneath, veined darker red above; between these colors there is a mix of white which is the distinctive characteristic of this rose." [C-T] "Here is a hybrid between the Centifolia and the Provins, of which latter it has all the characteristics—its wood, its thorns, and its leaves; of the former, it has the flower, the elegance, and the beauty. It's as rounded and double as the Centifolia, having the same form . . . Its perfume is delicious. Its petals are lighter along the edges, on which one can see some marks of purple. This is a perfect rose, a precious plant to grow. The blossoms open from the 10th to the 15th of June, just as the Agathes are finishing." [LeR] Not to be confused with the pre-1813 Alba of the same name.

[Beauté Touchante]
trans. "Touching Beauty"
Miellez, pre-1813

"Red." [LS] "Grown by Dupont; Desportes says it was bred by Miellez." [Gx]

Bellard
syn. 'Bellart'; probable syn., 'Bellotte', *q.v.*
Breeder unknown, pre-1842

"Nuanced pink." [Ÿ] "Blossom very large, very full; color, bright pink, with a light pink exterior." [S] "Light pink, large, very full, moderate height." [Sn]

Bellart Listed as 'Bellard' (G).

Belle Aimable
syn. 'Pale Rouge Panaché'; trans. "Amiable Beauty"
Holland, pre-1811

"Wood delicate and slender. Leaves a fairly gay yellowish green, pleasantly toothed. Calyx well rounded, as is the bud. Blossom the size of the Pompons, a pretty pale red plumed white, sweet and pleasant scent. This could be considered as a fanciful beauty; it is cute, delicate, fresh, and elegant. It blooms around the end of May." [C-T] "Came from Holland, says Desportes." [Gx]

Belle Alliance Listed as 'Tricolore' (Holland, G).

Belle Biblis
syn. 'Avenant'
Descemet, pre-1820

"Violet pink, medium size, full, moderate scent, medium height." [Sn] "Blossom large, full, plump, beautiful pink." [S] "Flowers deep flesh pink when newly opened, changing paler after expansion, large and very double; form, expanded. Habit, erect; growth, moderate. An abundant bloomer, a pretty and desirable Rose." [P]

Belle Bourbon Listed as 'Rouge Formidable' (G).

[Belle Brun]
syn. 'Belle en Brun'; trans. "Brown Beauty"
Breeder unknown, pre-1811

"Violet purple." [LS] "Has the same characteristics as 'Mahoeca' [*sic*], but differing in that it is velvety as soon as the bud starts opening instead of like the other, which needs to be fully open and touched by the sun. The blossom's petals, large and thick, seem to have been cut from a piece of crimson velvet. This one can be counted among the beauties; it has a sweet, pleasant scent." [C-T] "This one is a masterpiece of delicacy, and comes from seed of 'Aigle Brun', the characteristics it has borrowed down to a T. The flower, however, by being very double, is perfect, as well as large, velvety, and purple violet . . . Some stamens remain, which work to enhance its rich coloration, and should make it regarded as one of the perfect ones in this big family. They open starting June 9–10." [LeR]

Belle de Crécy Listed as a Hybrid China in Appendix 1.

Belle de Hesse Listed as 'Illustre' (G).

Belle de Yébles
syn. 'Belle de Zelbes'; trans. "Yèbles Beauty"
Desprez, pre-1835

"Flowers blush, their circumference rose." [P] "Blossom medium-sized, full, plump, bright red." [S] Yèbles was the location of Desprez' nursery.

Belle de Zelbes Listed as 'Belle de Yèbles' (G).

Belle des Jardins
trans. "Beauty of the Gardens"
Guillot fils, 1872
Seedling of 'Perle des Panachées' (G).

"Purple-violet, striped white, large, full, tall." [Sn] "Medium-sized, full." [S] "Sown by Monsieur Guillot fils, 1865, released to commerce by him in 1872. Very vigorous bush, springing from 'Perle des Panachées'; blossom large, full, well formed; in color, red, purple, violet, bright carmine, plumed and striped pure white. Hard to freeze, it resisted the cold of the winter of 1879–1880 admirably. Prune it little and very long. Does well as a bedder." [JR10/35–36]

Belle Doria
Parmentier, pre-1847

"Ashen lilac." [Y] "Blossom medium-sized, full; color, dirty lilac touched with white, carmine center." [S]

Belle en Brun Listed as 'Belle Brun' (G).

Belle Évêque Listed as 'L'Évêque' (G).

Belle Flore
trans. "Flora the Beautiful"
Descemet, pre-1813

"Pale rose." [Cal] "Red, shaded." [Y] "Wood and leaves those of the Gallica in medium proportions; a few fine thorns; its buds and numerous blossoms are a beautiful velvety violet crimson color; very double; petals notched and crinkled, pale beneath; slightly larger than those of the Bordeaux [i.e., 'Rosier des Dames'], each having a green leaf replacing the central stamens, which gives them an infinite grace; the color in the middle is darker than that of the outer portion. This rose, grafted at four feet [ca. 1.3 m], makes a very rounded bush; its perfume is delicious. Opens June 1–9." [LeR] "Grown by Du Pont, mentioned by Redouté; Desportes gives it as an obtention of Descemet's." [Gx] The breeder Vétillart has also been mentioned in connection with this cultivar, with a date of 1826; another cultivar of the same name? At any rate, Flore, alias Flora, our deity-patroness-lobbyist on site at Olympus.

Belle Galathée
trans. "Beautiful Galatea"
Descemet, pre-1813

"Pink." [V9] "Flesh." [LS] "Desportes says Descemet raised it." [Gx] Galathée, alias Galatea, either the unfortunate inamorata of Acis, or the fortunate *objet d'art* of Pygmalion.

Belle Hébé Listed as an Agathe.

Belle Hélène
syns. 'Aimable Emma', 'Aimable Sophie', 'Archiduc Charles', 'Clémence Isaure'; trans. "Beautiful Helen"
Descemet, pre-1818

"Blush." [Cal] "Pink, large." [BJ40] "Blossoms delicate pink; beautifully formed; charming plant." [J-A/570] "Flowers rosy crimson, of medium size, very double; form, cupped." [P] "Blossom large, full, very well formed; color, crimson; outer petals light pink." [S] "*Epidermis* green. *Thorns* brown. *Ovary* short, nearly finger-like, glabrous at the tip. *Sepals*, sometimes 6, foliaceous, 3 pinnatifid. *Flower* large, full or very double; light pink, edges ordinarily pale." [Pf] "Desportes says that this rose was bred by Descemet, who also called it 'Clémence Isaure'. Prévost gives as synonyms L. Noisette's 'Archiduc Charles' and Calvert of Rouen's 'Aimable Emma'." [Gx] I cannot confirm the suggested date of pre-1813 for this; Vibert's first commercial season was in 1816. Not to be confused with Vibert's Gallica of the same name. Helen the Beautiful, alias Helen of Troy, whose story perhaps demonstrates that beauty can be the beast.

Belle Hélène
Vibert, pre-1829

"*Flower* medium-sized, very full, intense purple, nuanced with violet." [Pf] Not to be confused with Descemet's Gallica of the same name. Again, the ornamental but troublesome Helen the Beautiful, alias Helen of Troy.

Belle Herminie
syns. 'Ponctuée', 'Punctata'; trans. "Beautiful Herminie"
Coquerel, 1819

"Purple spotted, of medium size, semi-double." [P] "Light lilac, pale edge." [LS] "Flowers semi-double, bright purple, spotted white." [dP] "Pink, medium size, very full, very fragrant, tall." [Sn] "*Flowers*, semi-double, small or middle-sized; of a bright pink, spotted." [Go] "*Canes* brown purple, glandulose, thornless. *Flower* medium-sized, full, light lilac-flesh with pale edges." [Pf] "In 1816, I sowed the seed of 'Belle Herminie' (single rose, Descemet), the only [spotted rose] we had in the Provins group at that time; and over twenty-five years, I have constantly sown the seeds of improvements of this rose. Today [1844], there are at my place more than four thousand seedlings of these sorts [spotted and striped] of roses." [V8] Vibert had acquired Descemet's nursery stock in 1815; it could be that he held 'Belle Herminie' for breeding purposes without releasing it commercially, subsequently selling propagation rights to Coquerel, who released it in 1819. This, however, is speculation.

Belle Isis Listed in Chapter 4 on Agathes.

Belle Italienne Listed as 'Achille' (G).

Belle Mignon Listed as 'Belle Mignonne' (G).

Belle Mignonne
syns. 'Belle Mignon', 'Petite Louise'; trans. "Beautiful Cutie"
Prévost, pre-1819

"*Flower* small, nearly full, symmetrical, light pink. The inner petals are often rayed white." [Pf]

[Belle Olympe]
trans. "Beautiful Olympia"
Descemet, pre-1820

"Red flowers, very beautiful in effect." [J-As/56] "Grown by Descemet, says Desportes." [Gx]

Belle Parade
trans. "Beautiful Parade" [as in "succession of flowers"]
Holland, pre-1811

"Delicate lilac." [Y] "Wood strong and vigorous, not very thorny, growing luxuriantly profusely. Leaves oval, dentate. Calyx, elongate. Bud, same, well covered by the membranes of the first [i.e., "calyx membranes," alias "sepals"]. Blossom large, quite double; color, incarnate or light cerise, very fragrant, coming up to six to eight on the same stem, around June 5. For form, number of flowers, and perfume, it can be placed among the pleasant sorts." [C-T]

Belle Pourpre
trans. "Beautiful Purple"
Holland, pre-1813

"Violet purple." [Y] "Dark." [Cal] "According to Desportes, it came from Holland; this rose was grown at Du Pont's." [Gx]

Belle Rubine Listed as 'Belle Villageoise' (G).

Belle sans Flatterie

trans. "Beautiful, and Not Euphemistically So"

Holland, pre-1806

"Rose." [Cal] "Lilac pink." [LS] "Red." [Ÿ] "Superb flesh blossoms." [JAs/56] "Violet pink, medium sized, full, tall." [Sn] "Blossoms medium-sized, very double, a light pink, regularly waved." [No26] "*Leaflets* bullate, undulate. *Flower* medium-sized, full, pale lilac pink." [Pf] "Grown at Du Pont's and at Godefroy's as well, as Prévost received it from this latter." [Gx]

Belle Sultane

syns. 'Cumberland', 'de Cumberland', 'Grande Sultane'; trans. "Beautiful Sultana"

Holland, 1795

"Light pink, in numerous bouquets." [No26] "*Leaves,* having one or two very small leaflets at the base of the terminal leaflet. *Tube of calyx,* smooth at the summit. *Flowers,* semi-double, large, of a light brilliant pink." [Go] "*Ovary* glabrous at the tip. *Flower* large, double, of a light, bright, intense pink all its own. The leaves of this rose often bear one or two very small leaflets at the base of the odd one." [Pf] "Came from Holland. Redouté says it was Du Pont who distributed it into our collection. Prévost also calls it 'Cumberland'." [Gx] There is the greatest amount of confusion between this cultivar, 'Grand Sultan', and 'Le Grand Sultan' (G), all of which see. The name 'Belle Sultane' has also been used as a synonym for the redoubtable 'Mahaeca' (G), which *also* see.

Belle Villageoise

syns. 'Belle Rubine', 'La Rubanée' [there was also an earlier 'La Rubanée'], 'Panaché Double', 'Village Maid'; trans. "Beautiful Village Maid"

Vibert, 1839

"Pink rayed with white and violet." [LF] "White, striped with rose and purple, variable, large and full. Growth vigorous." [GeH] "Flower medium sized, nearly full; color, violet, marbled white." [S] "Large, full, cupped, white plumed pink and purple, or purple plumed white and pink." [JR9/75] "Violet, striped white, medium size, full, tall." [Sn] "A well known rose, varying much in color, and in some situations, has red or carnation colored, in others slate colored or purple stripes." [WRP] "The first of the fine double striped roses, and has been cultivated under these three names [*viz., 'Belle Rubine', 'Panaché Double', 'Village Maid'*]; the flowers are perfectly double, and very like a fine Bizarre Carnation, having stripes of deep rose, pink, and white, regularly over the petals, from the base to the apex." [Bu] "Flowers white, striped with rose and purple, the stripes varying in breadth, sometimes the one and sometimes the other colour preponderating, large and full; form, cupped. Habit, pendulous; growth, small. A beautiful Rose when displayed in true character, which is rather rare." [P]

Belle Virginie

trans. 'Beautiful Virginia'

Breeder unknown, pre-1828

"Blossom medium-sized, full; color, lilac." [S] "Violet pink, medium size, full, tall." [Sn] *Cf.* 'Virginie' (G) and the pre-1827 Hybrid China 'Belle de Vernier'.

[Bellotte]

Vibert, pre-1826

"Pink." [V9] "Flower medium-sized, crimson." [God]

Bérénice

Vibert, 1818

"Rose-red, large, full, tall." [Sn] "Large, full, light purple." [V8] "Flowers rose and crimson, shaded with slate, very rich and beautiful, very large and full; form, globular. Habit, pendulous; growth, vigorous." [P] Not to be confused with Racine's Gallica of the same name.

[Bérénice]

Racine, pre-1829

"*Ovary* glabrous at the tip. *Flowers* medium-sized, full, regular, beautiful light bright pink, together in elegant, upright, multifloral corymbs." [Pf]

Bishop Listed as 'L'Évêque' (G).

Bishop's Listed as 'L'Évêque' (G).

Bizarre Changeant Listed as 'Pourpre Marbrée' (G).

Bizarre Triomphant

Thought-provoking as this name is, we list it under 'Busard Triomphant' (G).

Blanchefleur Listed as a Centifolia.

Bleu Listed as 'Busard Triomphant' (G), and about as "blue" as today's "blue" roses.

Blood Listed as 'Hector' (G).

Blood d'Angleterre Listed as 'Hector' (G).

Blutpurpurne Rose Listed as 'Sanguineo-Purpurea Simplex' (G).

Bossuet

Breeder unknown, pre-1846

"Flower medium-sized, full; color, crimson edged carmine." [S] Not to be confused with Vibert's ca. 1836 Hybrid Perpetual of the same name. Jacques Bénigne Bossuet, 1627–1704, influential French bishop and critic.

Boula de Nanteuil Listed as 'Comte Boula de Nanteuil' (G).

Boule de Neige Listed as 'Globe White Hip' (G).

Bouquet Charmante

syns. 'Bouquet Superbe', 'Pâle Rouge Superbe', 'Vénus Mère'; trans. "Charming Bouquet"

Holland, pre-1811

"Very bright pink." [LS] "Incarnate." [V9] "Rosy purple, brilliant, large, and full." [P] "Large, full, light purple." [V8] "*Flower* medium-sized or large, full, regular, very intense and brilliant pink. The first blossom of each corymb normally nods somewhat on its stalk, which is vertical, and on the highest side is surrounded by buds or secondary flowers which project beyond it." [Pf] "The wood, leaves, calyxes, and buds are nothing out of the ordinary. The blossom, two inches across [ca. 5 cm], is quite double, beautifully formed, with wavy petals, and a bright red, across which whitish nuances play. It has an elegant scent, and can be counted among the number of beauties. It opens around June 10." [C-T] "According to Desportes, it came from Holland." [Gx]

Bouquet Rose de Vénus Listed as an Agathe.

Bouquet Superbe Listed as 'Bouquet Charmante' (G).

[Bourbon]

syns. 'Ancienne Pivoine', 'Des Alpes sans Épines', 'Formosa', 'Inermis Sub Albo Violacea', 'Jéricho', 'Malvina', 'Mauve', 'Pivoine',
'Pivoine de Jéricho', 'Pivoine Mauve', 'Rose Mauve', 'Visqueuse'
Breeder unknown, pre-1811

"Flesh, striped pink." [BJ30] "Sparkling pink." [God] "Semi-double, medium-sized, pink striped with purple." [No26] "Blossoms pretty large, semi-double; form, regular; petals striped, bright pink on a pale ground." [BJ24] "The petals are striped and mottled with pink on a pale ground, and the semi-double flowers, regular in form, keep coming up until August." [CM] "*Canes* glandulose, unarmed. *Flower* medium-sized, multiplex, lilac flesh nuanced purple pink." [Pf] "It differs from ['L'Évêque' (G)] in its wood, which is tinted with pink on the sunny side. The leaves are a somber green, oval, edged with pink, very finely dentate. The buds of the flower are a pretty delicate pink, terminate in a point, and have little covering. The blossom is large, and of a red which is bright and gay. Its petals are large, thick, and notched in the middle; when open, it rather looks like a half-open Peony; it has a very nice scent. This rose, while not very double, can be admitted into the number of beautiful ones because of its sparkle." [C-T] Bourbon, name of the on-again off-again ruling house of France; political realities being what they were no doubt inspired the wide synonymy.

Burgundiaca Listed as 'Pompon de Bourgogne' (G).

Burgundica Listed as 'Pompon de Bourgogne' (G).

Busard Triomphant

syns. 'Ardoisée', 'Bizarre Triomphant', 'Bleu', 'Mahaeca de Dupont',
'Pourpre Ardoisée', 'Rose Bleu', 'Violette Bronzée'
Busard?, pre-1811

"Dark violet." [Cal] "Velvety crimson." [LS] "Blossoms double, medium-sized, slaty purple, and marbled with lilac." [AC] "Bluish crimson, tigered brown; blossoms well formed." [J-As/63] "*Canes* purple. *Flower* medium-sized, nearly full, slaty bluish purple, usually marbled with deep violet." [Pf] "Wood and leaves yellow-green. Calyx and bud round, barely covered. Flower very large, to four inches across [ca. 1 dm], pretty double, a beautiful velvety crimson, sweet scent, blooming [around June 10]. This rose is very effective." [C-T] "Mentioned by Redouté, grown by Du Pont." [Gx] See also 'Mahaeca' (G).

Button Listed as 'Pompon de Bourgogne' (G).

Calvert Listed as 'Globe White Hip' (G).

Camayeux

syns. 'Camaien', 'Camaieu', 'Camaïeux', 'Camailleux', etc., etc.
Gendron/Vibert, 1830

"Lilac pink, striped." [V9] "Violet red, striped white." [BJ53] "Lilac pink lined white and pink." [JR9/75] "Violet pink, striped white, medium size, full, very fragrant, medium to tall." [Sn] "A pretty rosy lilac, distinctly striped with blush white, perfectly double, always opening well." [Bu] "Pink rayed with lilac, full, flat, medium-sized." [LF] "Rather small . . . often has bud in centre." [WRP] "Flowers rose, striped with lilac, of medium size, full. Sometimes pretty, but a small, bad grower." [P] "Very beautiful." [S] As Joyaux has discovered, this rose evidently was grown from seed by one Gendron of Angers, France, and first bloomed in 1826. Vibert himself varied in his spelling of this

cultivar's name; we assign the name under which it was originally introduced by him.

Capricorn

syns. 'Capricorne', 'Capricornus'
Miellez, 1819

"Bright red." [Cal] "Blossoms beautiful, very regular, very double, an intense velvety purple." [No26] *Flower* small or mid-sized, very full, plump, regular, bright pink." [Pf] "Medium-sized, imbricated, red." [God] "Pink, medium size, full, moderate height." [Sn] "Double, petals crowded, small, terminal." [BJ24] "Very pretty flowers, very numerous quite wide petals separated at an angle as with Camellia 'Hexangularis'." [J-As/56] Probably synonymous with the Centifolia 'Capricornus', *q.v.*

Carmosina Listed as 'Admirable' (G).

Captain Williams

Breeder unknown, pre-1843

"Deep carmine." [Ÿ] "Light red, medium size, moderate scent, average height." [Sn]

Cardinal de Richelieu Listed as a Hybrid China.

Carmin Brillant

trans. "Brilliant Carmine"
Holland, pre-1813

"Fine carmine." [WRP] "Crimson." [Cal] "Red." [Ÿ] "Blossoms medium-sized, light purple, carmine in the center." [BJ30] "Medium-sized, very double, nuanced." [No26] "Well and expressively named; it would facilitate the love of flowers to a great degree if their names were always expressive of colour or character; but the title is often all the quality the article can boast of." [Bu] "Came from Holland, grown at Du Pont's, mentioned by Redouté." [Gx] *Cf.* the Centifolia 'Carmin Brillant'.

Carmin Liseré Listed as 'Perle de l'Orient' (G).

Carmosina Listed as 'Cramoisie' (G).

Catinat

Vibert, 1838

"Violet, spotted." [BJ40] "Medium-sized, full, violet spotted with purple." [V8] "Violet-purple, medium size, very full, medium to tall." [Sn] "Flowers purple and crimson, shaded and spotted, their centre filled with numerous small petals, of medium size, very double; form, cupped. Habit, erect; growth, vigorous." [P] Nicolas de Catinat, 1637–1712; very calm Marshal of France.

Céleste Listed as 'Grand Sultan' (G).

Centfeuilles d'Angleterre Listed as 'Aimable Rouge' (G).

Cérisette la Jolie

syns. 'Junon', 'Surpasse Tout'; trans. "Pretty Cherry-ling"
Breeder unknown, pre-1811

"Large, nearly full, cherry color." [BJ53] "Light red, large, full, tall." [Sn] "Flowers rich rosy crimson, sometimes shaded with purple, even, beautiful, large, and full; form, cupped. Habit, erect; growth, moderate. A fine Rose; very handsome on the tree." [P] "Wood green, nearly thornless. Leaves long, pointed, much dentate, folding back on themselves and recurved on their petiole. Bud round, barely covered

Cérisette la Jolie *continued*

by the calyx membranes. This last [*i.e., the calyx*] is long and very slightly constricted at the tip. The blossom, of medium size, is double, prettily formed, and of a beautiful cherry red color, nearly carmine. This doubtless is why it was called 'Cerisette'; its perfume is sweet and pleasant. It blooms June 15." [C-T] "Charming hybrid of the Agathes, Centifolias, and Gallicas. Its wood is … [*one word indecipherable*] …green, slightly feeble, and nearly thornless; its leaves are oval and terminate in a point, and are gay green; the bud is barely covered, and fairly elongate; the blossom is two and a half inches across [ca. 6.5 cm], double, dainty, a beautiful cerise red—nearly carmine, which gives foundation to the name given it by the Dutch. Its perfume is very elegant while sweet. Some of its petals stay white, which demonstrates the polygamy between two Gallicas, Centifolias, and Agathes, and some Alba. This rose comes well caparisoned with leaves and buds, all close-set and bushy. Ravishing! Opens June 1." [LeR]

César Beccaria

Robert, 1855

"White, spotted lilac." [S] "Large, full, white plumed lilac and pink." [JR9/126] "White and violet, large, full, average height." [Sn] "8–10 cm [ca. 3–4 in], white ground, striped and spotted with lilac and violet, flat, in a rosette, green pip at the center, admirable form." [R&M62] Possibly by Vibert, pre-1851 (*v.* JR17/78). Possibly a hybrid between Gallica and Centifolia. Cesare Bonesana, Marchese di Beccaria; 1738–1794; penal philosopher and rhetorician.

Chapelain d'Arenberg

Breeder unknown, pre-1885

"Blossom medium-sized, full, well-formed; color, bright pink." [S] Joyaux supposes a possible attribution of Parmentier, pre-1847. Arenberg, German duchy.

Charlemagne

Said to be a synonym for 'Président Dutailly', listed as a Damask Perpetual (and illustrated) in *The Old Rose Advisor*.

Charles de Mills

Breeder unknown, pre-1885

"Deep purple red, large, full, tall." [Sn] "Blossom large, full; color, orange [!], edged pinkish lilac." [S] We are as of yet unable to crack the shell of mystery surrounding the origins of this cultivar. It is implicative that there are two other obscure Gallicas that appeared at the same time with similar coloration and names, 'Charles Lemayeux' and 'Charles Lemoine', *qq.v.* That Lemoine was a name known in French horticulture is perhaps worth mentioning.

[Charles Lemayeux]

Breeder unknown, pre-1885

"Blossom large, full, well-formed; color, deep carmine." [S] *Cf.* 'Charles de Mills' (G) and 'Charles Lemoine' (G).

[Charles Lemoine]

Breeder unknown, pre-1885

"Blossom medium-sized, full; color, velvety purple lilac." [S] *Cf.* 'Charles de Mills' (G) and 'Charles Lemayeux' (G).

[Charlotte de Lacharme]

Vibert, 1822 (but see below concerning this date)

"The most magnificent blossoms, pink, spotted white." [J-As/61]

"Medium-sized, double, a purple-pink plumed pale pink." [BJ24] "Blossom medium-sized, blackish, spotted with white." [God] "*Flower* medium-sized, very multiplex, light pink, spotted. *Fruit* oval-pyriform, red, smooth, very small." [Pf] "Monsieur Boitard has forgotten certain things [*in his editorship of the 1824* Bon Jardinier]. It was in June 1823 that I [Vibert] saw him for the first time. He returned the visit, accompanied by Monsieur Godefroy, nurseryman at Ville d'Avray, who justly enjoys a merited reputation … It was he [Boitard] who, that same day, evincing a desire to do so, named 'Charlotte de Lacharme' and 'Aglaé Adanson' … Couldn't it have been stated that these roses came from me?" [V2] "Very pretty." [No26]

Château de Namur

trans. "Castle of Namur"

Quétier, pre-1842

"Vigorous bush; canes irregular, bumpy; thorns of varying size; leaves small, regularly dentate; flower medium-sized, full; color, very dark violet striped bishop's violet; crimson center." [S] Namur, Belgian city, notably besieged in 1695; for particulars of a sort, see *Tristram Shandy*, by Laurence Sterne, Vol. I, Ch. 21, *et seq.*

Chremesina Scintillans Listed as 'Admirable' (G).

Claire d'Olban

Vibert, 1825

"Deep pink." [V9] "*Shrub* much armed. *Ovary* large, very short. *Flower* medium-sized, full, regular, bright deep pink with pale edges." [Pf] Often classed as a Damask, and perhaps a Gallica/Damask hybrid; but the "very short" ovary tips it into the Gallica camp.

Clémence Isaure Listed as 'Belle Hélène' (G).

[Clio]

Descemet, pre-1820

"Deep red." [Cal] "Incarnate." [V9] "Flesh." [LS] "Seedling of Descemet's, mentioned by Desportes." [Gx] Clio, the increasingly busy Greek muse of History.

Cocarde Pâle

trans. "Pale Cockade"

Breeder unknown, pre-1813

"Pink, white, and red." [Ÿ] "This variety was in the nurseries of Du Pont." [Gx]

Cocarde Royale Listed as 'Grand Monarque' (G).

Columelle

syn. 'Columella'

Vibert, 1841

"Large, full, crimson purple." [V8] "A deep, bright pink, shaded with flush on the margin of its petals; sometimes it produces self-colored flowers, but is always first rate and remarkably distinct." [WRP] "Flowers rich rosy crimson, often shaded with violet, the outer petals exquisitely disposed, slightly reflexing before the flower falls, of medium size, full; form, cupped, perfect. Habit, branching; growth, moderate … A fine Rose." [P] Not to be confused with Moreau-Robert's 1860 Damask of the same name. Columelle, alias Lucius Junius Moderatus Columella, Roman gardening and agricultural writer of the 1st century A.D.

Complicata

Breeder unknown, date uncertain

"Pink, large, single, light scent, moderate height." [Sn] "Perhaps a *Rosa canina* or *R. macrantha* hybrid, with strong arching branches reaching to 5 feet in height [ca. 1.75 m] and as much across, well clothed in large, pointed, clear green leaves. The large blooms, as much as 5 inches wide [ca. 1.25 dm], are single, of pure brilliant pink, paling to white around the circle of yellow stamens. This is without doubt one of the most strikingly beautiful of single pink roses, and is a good hearty plant." [T4]

Comte Boula de Nanteuil

syns. 'Boula de Nanteuil', 'Comte de Nanteuil'
Roeser/Noisette, 1834

"Deep crimson blossoms . . . One of the best of this shade." [R-H63/185] "Rich crimson and purple, very large and full; a well formed and excellent flower, and a first-rate show rose." [JC] "Crimson-purple, fades easily; worthless." [EL] "[A] most splendid flower of perfect form, crimson purple, very large, and none more admired." [WRP] "Large, full, light purple." [V8] "Large, full, velvety purple." [Gp&f52] "Large, full, violet purple." [JR9/74] "Pink." [BJ40] "[A] rose of the richest crimson-purple, with a centre, at times, of a vivid red. It varies, however, very much in different seasons, and, while sometimes splendid in coloring, is occasionally dull and cloudy." [FP] "One of the best varieties of this sort. Very vigorous growth; canes hardy, proudly showing off the beautiful blossoms; blackish carmine, mixed with flesh pink; the very large, very full flower is ball-shaped." [S] "Flowers crimson purple, their centre sometimes fiery crimson, the largest shaded dark rose, very large and full; form, compact. Habit, branching; growth, moderate. A splendid Rose, which should be in every collection." [P]

Comte de Nanteuil Listed as 'Comte Boula de Nanteuil' (G).

Comte Foy de Rouen

Lecomte, pre-1827

"Pale pink." [LS] "Delicate pink." [V9] "Flowers bright rose, very large and double; form, cupped." [P] "Blossom large, very full, well formed; delicate pink." [S] "*Flowers*, more double, more regular, more variegated. Bearing much resemblance to the *Gallica versicolor.*" [Go] "This should not be mixed up with the one called 'Général Foy' [*q.v.*]. Flowers four to five inches across [ca. 10–12 cm], very full, delicate pink, having the form of the ordinary Centifolia." [No28] "*Canes* glandulose, nearly thornless. *Leaflets* oblong-lanceolate. *Peduncle* large, glandulose. *Ovary* short, turbinate-pyriform, sometimes glabrous at the tip. *Flower* very large, full, light or pale pink, slightly fragrant." [Pf] The name should possibly simply be 'Comte Foy'; the "de Rouen" was added to distinguish it from another 'Comte Foy', a Noisette, which was *not* "from Rouen." One sees Savoureux listed as the breeder; Lecomte's roses were evidently taken over by Savoureux about 1828.

Conditorum

trans. "Of or associated with savory things"
Dieck, 1900

"Brown pink." [LS] "The rose used in Hungary for attar and preserving. Recorded in 1900, but it is undoubtedly a very old form . . . It forms a bushy plant with loose tousled flowers, semi-double, of rich, magenta-crimson tone, slightly flushed and veined with purple in hot weather, and showing yellow stamens. 3 to 4 feet [ca. 1–1.33 m]." [T4]

Cora

Lecomte, pre-1828

"Purple violet." [V9] "Brown violet." [LS] "Blossoms double, small, profuse, in a corymb, velvety deep red." [AC] "*Flower* small, full, regular, velvety, purple violet." [Pf] "Purple violet red, small, full, average height." [Sn] "Flowers medium-sized, very double, a velvety purple, slightly globose at the center, and tending somewhat towards the form of a Ranunculus." [No28] "Flowers rich dark crimson purple, of medium size, full; form, expanded. Habit, erect; growth, moderate." [P] "*Shrub*, small, with straight branches. *Thorns*, scattered, fine, rather bent, interspersed with small bristles. *Leafstalks*, glandulous. *Leaflets*, three to five in number; oval or lanceolated; irregularly toothed, green, whitish underneath. *Flowers*, small, double, numerous, very well formed; of a dark velvety violet, united in clusters of three or four; and having the appearance of a ranunuculus. *Petals*, symmetrically distributed, rolled in a ring towards the centre, with white bases." [Go] Not to be confused with the pre-1819 'Cora à Pétales Variés', which, according to LeRouge, had large, yellowish pink blossoms, and extremely large, brown-margined leaves. One sees Savoureux listed as the breeder; Lecomte's roses were evidently taken over by Savoureux about 1828.

Cosimo Ridolfi

Vibert, 1842

"Flowers lilac rose, spotted, of medium size, very double; form, compact." [P] "Of the usual size, full double, purplish crimson, spotted." [WRP] "Medium-sized, full, crimson purple, spotted." [V8] "Flower medium size, full, [petals] much crowded; color, lilac touched crimson." [S] "Violet purple, medium size, full, medium to tall." [Sn]

Couleur de Sang Listed as 'Admirable' (G).

[Couronne de Salomon]

trans. "Solomon's Crown"
Breeder unknown, pre-1819

"The wood of this hybrid of the Reds [*i.e., regular Gallicas*] and the Browns [*i.e., such as 'Aigle Brun'*] is very vigorous, upright, and bestrewn with little touches of black. The shoots or growths of the year look a lot like those of the 'Sans Pareille Rose' [*q.v.*]. Its flowers are very double and quite large, flat, and are a beautiful, very intense pink or indeed red which, once open, are always surrounded by eight to ten buds, forming a crown, which justifies the wonderful name deserving everyone's attention. It is spring-blooming, opening from June 1 to 5." [LeR]

[Couronnée]

trans. "Crowned"
Breeder unknown, circa 1811

"Blush." [Cal] "Two sorts or new varieties, grown from seed, and which haven't been distributed in the trade at all, can figure with ['Aigle Brun' and 'Rosa Mundi'] for decorating rose-beds and the shrubberies of cottage gardeners. The first, called 'Couronnée', a light and delicate violet, has nothing unusual in its wood more than being strong and vigorous. Its leaves are beautiful, numerous, irregularly dentate, and a gay green, sorting well with the blossoms—a good thing in roses. The calyx is oval and constricted at the tip. The bud, of the same form, is completely covered and crowned with the membranes of the former. The flower is large—three and a half inches

[**Couronnée**] *continued*
[ca. 8.5 cm] across—delicate light violet in color. This very fragrant rose blooms around June 10. Grafted on the Briar, this shrub will give blossoms that, by their sparkle and number, may proudly take a place beside their companions of the same sort. [*The second sort "grown from seed" is* 'Grande Violette Claire']." [C-T]

Cramoisi Listed as 'Pompon de Bourgogne' (G). See also 'Cramoisie' (G).

Cramoisi des Alpes Listed as 'Grand Corneille' (G).

Cramoisi Incomparable Listed as 'Velours Pourpre' (G).

Cramoisi Majeur Listed as 'Hector' (G).

Cramoisi Picoté
trans. "Picotee Crimson"
Vibert, 1834
"Lilac, finely mottled with purple." [WRP] "Medium-sized, full, crimson violet, minutely punctuated." [V8] "Blossom crimson red, spotted violet." [S] "A distinct and curious slate-colored rose; delicately spotted, but not so pretty and brilliant as the old Picotee [?], its spots having a reddish brown appearance." [WRP] "Red violet, small, full, medium height." [Sn]

[**Cramoisie**]
syns. 'Carmosina', 'Crimson-Coloured Provins Rose', 'Kermosina';
trans. "Crimson"
Breeder unknown, pre-1791
"*Flowers*, full, middle-sized; of a crimson-red, turning to purple." [Go] "Dark purple." [Cal] "*Flower* medium-sized, red, nearly full." [Pf] "Very double flowers, and a light red, which grows rapidly and forms beautiful heads when grafted." [CM] "Its quite double blossom is colored deep crimson which goes to purple. It has two varieties, one of which having blossoms colored blackish purple mixed with light red, and the other with flowers washed red and purple on a red ground. These quite bright and distinct nuances makes these Roses very pleasing; but they have only a feeble scent." [Fr] Probably synonymous with 'Admirable', which also see. See also 'Cramoisi' (G).

Cramoisie Éblouissante
syn. 'L'Infante d'Espagne'; trans. "Sparkling Crimson"
Holland, pre-1811
"Sparkling crimson." [Ÿ] "Crimson purple." [Cal] "Wood brown-green, nearly completely covered with small flexible thorns. Leaves long, much dentate and doubly so. Calyx and bud round, barely covered. Blossoms extremely double, well formed, the size of 'Bordeaux' [*i.e.*, 'Rosier des Dames'], sparkling crimson, just like the name says. It blooms around the fifth of June, and can be counted among the beauties, as much for its form as for its color." [C-T] "Probably synonymous with De Pronville's and Redouté's 'Cramoisi Brillant'." [Gx] See also 'Subnigra' (G).

[**Cramoisie Triomphante**]
syns. 'La Plus Élégante', 'Superbe'; trans. "Triumphant Crimson"
Holland, pre-1811
"Crimson, plumed pink." [LS] "Wood and leaves typical Provins, but in larger proportions. Calyx round; bud covered, pointed; flower the size of the Pompon; color, crimson, sparkling, mixed or plumed with a lighter color, pleasant scent." [C-T]

Crignon de Montigny
syn. 'Montigny'
Breeder unknown, pre-1842
"Violet red." [Ÿ] "Flowers medium-sized, full, beautiful bright pink." [JR1/8/9]

Crimson-coloured Provins Rose Listed as 'Cramoisie' (G).

Cumberland Listed as 'Belle Sultane' (G).

Cynthie
Descemet, pre-1820
"Rose." [Cal] "Flowers very large, full, well formed, delicate pink." [JR1/8/9] "Pale pink flowers, delicately margined light purple, recommendable because of its abundant bloom; it is inferior, however, to ... 'Louis-Philippe'." [R-H63/184] "Flowers pale rose, their circumference almost blush, large and full; form cupped, perfect. Habit, erect; growth, moderate. An abundant bloomer, and a beautiful Rose." [P] I cannot confirm the suggested date of pre-1815. Cynthie, alias perhaps Cynthia, beloved of the Roman poet Propertius, but, methinks, somewhat of a pill; still, if he loved her ...

D'Aguesseau
Vibert, 1836
"Brilliant crimson shaded and slightly mottled; perfectly formed, and a beautiful rose." [JC] "Large, full, crimson." [V8] "Large, full, bright red." [BJ53] "Large, full, crimson shaded black." [JR9/74] "Well-formed, slightly plump, bright red." [JR1/8/9] "Purple-red, medium-sized, full, average height." [Sn] "Blossom medium-sized, of beautiful plump form, really 'built'; one of the most beautiful roses of this sort; color, purple, shaded with deep crimson." [S] "Fiery crimson, occasionally shaded with dark purple, glowing, large, and full; form, compact, perfect. Habit, erect; growth, moderate. A superb Rose. A good show Rose." [P] The date 1823 sometimes seen for this cultivar is incorrect. Henri François d'Aguesseau, 1668–1751; French jurist.

Daphné
Vibert, 1819
"Rose." [Cal] "Blossom full, medium-sized, globular; color, light pink." [S] "Light pink, medium size, full, tall." [Sn] Daphné, alias Daphne, sensible nymph who preferred a life in Botany to one with Apollo.

De Cumberland Listed as 'Belle Sultane' (G).

De la Reine Listed as 'Regina Dicta' (G).

De Schelfhont
syn. 'De Schelfhout'
Parmentier, ca. 1840
"Whitish pink, medium size, full, tall." [Sn] "Blossom medium-sized, full; color, white, nuanced flesh pink." [S]

[**De Van Eeden**]
syn. 'Purpurea Velutina Parva'; probable syn., 'L'Obscurité'
Van Eeden, 1810
"*Shrub* with basal non-rooting suckers 0.3–0.6 m long [ca. 1–2 ft]; *prickles* unequal, fairly numerous and almost straight, sparse on the blooming shoots. *Leaflets* ovate-oblong, rounded at the base, acute, green above, slightly tomentose beneath; doubly dentate; petiole villose, with very small straight prickles; stipules slightly dentic-

ulate, gland-edged; pedicels villose; *receptacles* rounded; *sepals* short, pointed, quite entire, villose within, a little hispid without, like the receptacle. *Flowers* 3–4 at the tips of the laterals, medium-sized; *petals* 3-seriate, brilliant purple on opening with an admirable violet-velvety look from the play of light, enhanced by golden stamens at the center; *styles* villose, almost tufted. This magnificent Gallica was grown from seed by Van Eeden, a nurseryman of Haarlem, who enriched the garden at Malmaison with it in 1810 . . . After the death of Joséphine [*in 1814*], this lovely rose disappeared from Malmaison, and is still unknown on its own roots. It survives grafted in a few private gardens, but loses its prostrate habit. Grafting, however, if anything *increases* the bulk of the flowers as well as their brilliance. As with all Gallicas, the petals finally blacken before falling—the explanation of the so-called 'black rose.' It strikes easily on its own roots by mounding up the prostrate stems, and is undemanding; one should, however, resist the urge to straighten up these naturally creeping suckers." [T&R] We alas know few of the names of the Dutch nurserymen who were responsible for so many of the early roses; Van Eeden must represent both himself and his colleagues for us.

Des Alpes sans Épines   Listed as 'Bourbon' (G).

Desiré Parmentier
Parmentier, pre-1841

"Bright pink." [Ÿ] "Large, full, well-formed, flesh." [BJ53] "Deep vivid pink, large and full; form, compact, perfect. Habit, branching; growth, moderate. A showy and beautiful Rose." [P]

Die Berühmte   Listed as 'Illustre' (G).

Dométil Bécar   Listed as a Centifolia.

[Don de Guérin]
trans. "Guérin's Gift"
Breeder unknown (but probably Guérin), pre-1846

"Bright rose, full shell, superb, perfect." [WRP] "Flowers vivid even rose, sometimes shaded with light purple, large and full; form, compact, perfect. Habit, branching; growth, vigorous. A beautiful Rose." [P] Modeste Guérin, important pioneering rose breeder.

Dona Sol
Vibert, 1842

"Currant red, touched white." [Ÿ] "Medium-sized, full, rosette in the middle, purple red spotted purple, perfect form." [dH44/156] "Blossom medium-sized, full, [petals] very crowded; Centifolia form; color, bright grenadine, touched with white." [S] "Large, purplish crimson." [WRP] "Large, very double red flowers, shaded with crimson, and spotted with rose, of strong growth, and will be very liable to run into one colour in rich heavy soils." [Bu] "Flowers purplish rose, spotted with white, of medium size, very double; form, compact. Habit, pendulous; growth, robust; partakes slightly of the Provence." [P]

Double Brique
trans. "Double Brick," the latter presumably referring to the perhaps brick-red color
Breeder unknown, pre-1842

"Purple-red, medium size, full, tall." [Sn] "Light pink, darker center." [Ÿ] "Blossom medium-sized, full; color, bright crimson." [S] There was "also" a 'Grande Brique' in 1811 . . . but we can find no evidence that 'Double Brique' dates to a suggested 1830.

Double Velvet Rose   Listed as 'Holoserica Multiplex' (G).

Du Maître d'École
trans. "From the School-Master," but see below
Coquereau, 1831

"Lilac pink." [Ÿ] "Delicate rose, large and full." [P] "Flowers large, very full, delicate pink changing to lilac." [JR1/8/9] "Violet pink, medium size, very full, very fragrant, tall." [Sn] "Maître-École" is the name of an area in the city of Angers, in France, where several breeders had property: Coquereau had land there in the 1830s–1840s; Moreau-Robert had a *clos* ("enclosure") there by 1866, perhaps handed down from his predecessors Vibert, Robert, and/or Robert & Moreau; later, ca. 1900, Chédane-Guinoisseau also owned property at Maître-École.

Du Mortier   Listed as 'Dumortier' (G)

Du Pont   Listed as 'Rouge Formidable' (G).

Duc d'Arenberg
syn. 'Prince d'Arenberg'
Breeder unknown, pre-1836

"Purple." [V4] "Amaranthine deep violet." [LS] "Flowers medium-sized, full, red fading to pink." [JR1/8/9] "Medium-sized, full, light purple." [V8] "Flowers lively rose, their circumference inclining to lilac, large and full; form, compact. Habit, erect; growth, vigorous. Flowers produced in clusters, the surrounding buds projecting far beyond the centre flower." [P] Arenberg, German duchy.

Duc d'Orléans
Vibert, 1831

"Pink, spotted." [V9] "Purple, nuanced." [LS] "Blossom medium-sized, full; color, light crimson sprinkled with deep crimson." [S] "Pink, spotted, double, medium-sized." [LF] "Purple-red, medium size, full, tall." [Sn] "[A] fine and brilliant flower, large, beautifully cupped, and distinctly spotted with white, and also of robust and vigorous habits." [WRP] "Flowers rich cherry rose, covered with small white spots, large and double; form, cupped, perfect; petals, smooth and fine. Habit, branching; growth, vigorous. An excellent variety, but not double enough for a show Rose. There is a standard of this variety in the Nurseries here, whose stem, at three feet [ca. 1 m] from the ground, measures ten inches in circumference [ca. 2.55 dm]. A good seed-bearer." [P] This particular Duc d'Orléans was probably the well-liked eldest son of Louis-Philippe I, Ferdinand, who died in a coach accident.

Duc de Bordeaux
Vibert, 1820

"Violet." [Cal] "Lilac pink." [V9] "Crimson purple." [LS] "Crimson red." [Ÿ] "Charming rose of a light violet tint." [J-A/569] "Rosy lilac, large and full." [P] "Blossoms full, large, light lilac pink." [AC] "Medium-sized, of a uniform, very sparkling, crimson purple." [No26] "*Thorns* hooked. *Flower* large, full, regular, light even lilac pink." [Pf] "Violet pink, large, full, average height." [Sn]

Duc de Fitzjames
Breeder unknown, pre-1837

"Light purple, medium size, full, tall." [Sn] "Blossom slaty blue, of a beautiful globular form; foliage abundant, of a glossy deep green." [S]

Duc de Guiche

syn. 'Sénat Romain'
Breeder unknown, pre-1810

"Lilac-pink of a very distinct color." [J-A/569] "Rose." [Cal] "Flowers crimson, large and full." [P] "Flowers large, full, violet red." [JR1/8/10] "Large very double flowers, purplish pink." [dP] "Striking in its vigor and the size of its flower." [BJ30] "*Canes* large and thick. *Leaflets* oblong, very acute. *Flower* very large, full, lilac pink. Sometimes it takes on a slaty lilac tint when the temperature is very high." [Pf] "This variety was at the Soucelle château; Prévost, who describes it, gives 'Sénat Romain' as a synonym." [Gx] "We would have been menaced by the Roman Senate but for the good fortune of having discovered that this rose was the same as 'Duc de Guiche'." [V2] Contrary to some listings, Prévost does not claim it as his obtention; he appears to have first gotten involved with roses ca. 1811.

Duchesse d'Angoulême

syn. "Wax Rose"
Miellez(?), 1818(?)

"Blush." [Cal] "Flowers full, medium-sized, in clusters, flesh at the center and white along the edge." [AC] "Blossoms very numerous, white, then flesh when well open. The plant makes a thick bush." [No26] "Flowers blush, their centre pink, wax-like, of medium size, full; form, cupped. Habit, erect; growth, moderate. This variety is often called the Wax Rose, and is very beautiful, though not adapted for exhibition." [P] "*Tube of calyx,* smooth at the summit. *Flowers,* in clusters; full, very regular, middle-sized; white at the circumference, flesh-coloured in the centre. *Petals,* very thin and transparent." [Go] "An old but deservedly a favorite variety: its color is so delicate and its form so perfect that it must always be admired; the habit of the plant is most luxuriant, and rather more erect than most other members of this family [Gallica × Centifolia hybrids]." [WRP] "It is said that this is the *white rose provence* of the English. It distinguishes itself by its medium-sized flowers, which are very double, a white lightly washed with pink, and fairly numerous. The canes are quite close-set and are effective when grafted on a stem [*i.e., as a "tree rose" or "standard"*]." [CM] Considered a Gallica × Centifolia or possibly a Gallica × Damask hybrid. The Duchesse d'Angoulême, daughter of Louis XVI and Marie-Antoinette.

Duchesse de Berry

syn. 'Duchesse de Berri'
Vibert, 1818

"Pale rose." [Cal] "Large, double, pink." [V8] "Blossom large, full; color, pink, shaded carmine." [S] "Flowers light pink, and brilliant in form and in color." [J-A/569] "*Flower* very large, regular, full and plump, semi-double or double, bright light pink." [Pf] "Light pink, very large, lightly double, very fragrant, tall." [Sn] "The same [as 'Duchesse d'Angoulême'], only larger." [BJ30] Grouping with the Centifolias or the Agathes has also been suggested.

Duchesse de Buccleuch

Vibert, 1837

"Bright pink, large, splendid." [WRP] "Light red." [JR1/8/10] "Very large, deep rose colored, and full double." [WRP] "Large, full, deep pink." [V8] "Bright crimson, tinted lavender." [Ỹ] "Deep pink, very large, full, tall." [Sn] "Flowers lively crimson, their circumference inclining to lavender blush, very large and full; form, cupped, perfect.

Habit, erect; growth, vigorous. A beautiful Rose." [P] Misspellers have exercised their fertile imaginations on "Buccleuch," a noble Scots family of long standing.

Duchesse de Montebello
Listed as a Hybrid Noisette in Appendix 1.

Duchesse de Reggio
Listed as 'Fanny Bias' (G).

Dumortier

syn. 'Du Mortier'
Parmentier, pre-1843

"Blossom medium-sized, full; color, bright pink." [S] Probably equivalent to the Hybrid China 'Deuil du Maréchal Mortier', which see in our Appendix 1.

Dupont
Listed as 'Rouge Formidable' (G).

[Dupuytren]

Cartier, 1823

"Very bright crimson, giving over to very intense black velvet from the center to the limb of the petals to reappear with more sparkle along the edges; corolla very full, exterior petals very gracefully arranged in very numerous cups one atop the other; central petals imbricated—making a wonderful combination. It is one of the richest Provins roses." [J-As/57] Guillaume Dupuytren, French royal surgeon, 1777–1835.

Dwarf Austrian Rose
Listed as 'Rosier d'Amour' (G).

Dwarf Burgundy
Listed as 'Pompon de Bourgogne' (G).

Dwarf Red Rose
Listed as 'Pompon de Bourgogne' (G).

Edmond Duval

Parmentier, ca. 1835

"Blossom medium-sized, full; color, bright pink." [S] "Tall." [Sn]

Elise Novella
Listed as 'Elise Rovella' (G).

Elise Rovella

syn. 'Elise Novella'
Breeder unknown, pre-1842

"Blossom medium-sized, full; color, flesh pink." [S] "[*Size of plant*] average to tall." [Sn]

Emilie Verachter

Parmentier, 1840

"Medium-sized, full; color, bright pink." [S] "A small upright bush with small leaves, large stipules, and few prickles. Smooth rounded heps. Clear bright pink, full of quartered petals with green pointel. Little scent." [T4]

[Empereur]

Breeder unknown, pre-1810

"Dark red." [Cal] "Lilac pink." [BJ40] "Existed in 1810 in the collections of the Soucelle château." [Gx] Listed as "rejected and superseded" by Prince in 1846. The eponymous emperor would of course be Napoléon.

Enchantress
Listed as 'L'Enchanteresse' (G).

Estelle

Breeder unknown, pre-1810

"Flesh pink." [Ỹ] "Blossom small, full; color, pink, shaded flesh white." [S] "Pink, medium size, very full, very fragrant, average to tall." [Sn] "Was at the Soucelle château; mentioned by Prévost." [Gx]

Esther
Vibert, 1845

"Purple pink." [Ÿ] "Rose, variegated with claret." [WRP] "6–7 cm [ca. 2½ in], double, pink plumed with wine-lee." [VPt48/app] "Flowers rose, striped with dark red, of medium size, double." [P] "Light pink, striped purple, medium size, full, tall." [Sn] " Not to be confused with Vibert's 1819 Gallica of the same name.

Eucharis
Descemet/Vibert, pre-1820

"Large, full, deep pink." [V8] "Light pink." [LS] "Flowers bright rose, their circumference pale rose, large and full." [P] "Blossoms semi-double, large, numerous, bright purple." [No26] "Full, large, light pink." [AC] "*Canes* glandulose, thornless. *Ovary* short, turbinate, often lacking. *Glands* of the *peduncles, ovaries,* and *sepals* brown, viscous, fragrant. *Flower* large, full, regular, light pink with pale edges." [Pf] We cannot substantiate the date of 1815 suggested for this rose.

[Eudoxie]
Descemet, pre-1820

"Dark rose." [Cal] *Cf.* the Damask of the same name.

Eulalie le Brun Listed as a Centifolia.

Fanny Bias
syns. 'Athalie', 'Duchesse de Reggio'
Vibert, 1819

"Large, full, delicate pink." [V8] "Large, full, flesh, pink center." [JR9/74] "*Flower* large, full, regular, flesh or light pink with pale edges." [Pf] "Flowers very large, very double, incarnate." [No26] "A great favorite, and has few compeers. Every one admires it; the colour is also scarce in the family, being pale blush shading to bright pink towards the centre; it is extremely double, and is greatly to be admired for its symmetry; it is a free bloomer." [Bu] "Flowers blush, their centre rosy, large and full; form, compact, perfect, the texture of the petals delicate. Habit, erect; growth, moderate. A beautiful Rose." [P] "Moderate scent." [Sn] "This magnificent rose has been growing as a bush on its own roots for 15 years [*i.e., since 1812*] at Monsieur Sommesson's, who calls it 'Duchesse de Reggio'. Many fanciers who bought it at St. Denis when Monsieur Descemet's stock was sold by appearance and without names, call it whatever they feel like; but the merchant [*Vibert*] who collected whatever remained unsold [*when Descemet fled in 1815*], after having found it there—or, the same year, among his seedlings—gave it the name 'Fanny Bias'." [J-As/65] "Whatever the veracious Monsieur Pirolle might say, I [*Vibert*] found 'Fanny Bias' in 1817." [JPV]

Fanny Elssler
Vibert, 1835

"Purplish pink spotted with white, full, beautiful." [LF] "Poppy pink." [LS] "Blossom medium-sized, full; color, light pink, spotted with deep pink." [S] "Pink, medium size, full, average height." [Sn] "[A] new and pretty spotted rose." [WRP] The suggested date of 1820 for this cultivar is incorrect; the honoree was only 10 at the time: Fanny Elssler, celebrated ballerina, lived 1810–1884; daughter of the composer Haydn's factotum.

Fanny Parissot
syn. 'Fanny Pavetot'
Breeder unknown, 1819

"Deep pink, large, very full, medium scent, tall." [Sn]

Fanny Pavetot Listed as 'Fanny Parissot' (G).

Ferdinand de Buck
syn. 'Feu de Buck'
Breeder unknown, pre-1842

"Flowers medium-sized, full, bright red." [JR1/8/10] "Blossoms medium-sized, full, colored bright pink." [S]

Feu Amoureux
trans. "Fire of Love"
Breeder unknown, pre-1811

"Deep purple." [Ÿ] "Its wood is … green, and armed with numerous thorns which are broad-based and red. The leaves are long, finely dentate, and unequal [in size]. The bud is round and barely covered [by the sepals]. The calyx is small, elongated, and constricted at the tip. The blossoms, perhaps the largest of the sort, are quite double; the petals are large, and a lightish wine-lee color. They open around the end of June, and are scentless. Right at anthesis, it has the form of a flat head of cabbage—a look all its own." [C-T] The Fire of Love, a striking phenomenon still frequently discernible in members of species *Homo sapiens* at times, though it is not always clear whether the effect is malign or benign; the subject remains under close study by several workers, who have hopes of producing a report soon. See also 'Des Peintres' (C).

Feu de Buck Listed as 'Ferdinand de Buck' (G).

[Feu de Vesta]
syn. 'Vesta'; trans. "Vesta's Fire"
Coquerel, pre-1829

"*Flower* large, double, velvety, light bright crimson. This rose, said to be the same as that called 'Temple d'Apollon', differs from it by its [growth] buds, which are not red; by its longer and more pointed [flower] buds; and finally by its flower, which is a lighter crimson, and has fewer petals." [Pf] Vesta, goddess of the hearth.

Fleurs de Pelletier
trans. "Pelletier's Flowers"
Pelletier, pre-1842

"Blossom medium-sized, full; color, cherry edged slatey red." [S] "Light red, medium size, very full, medium height." [Sn] *Cf.* 'Pelletier' (G).

Formosa Listed as 'Bourbon' (G).

Fornarina
Vétillart, 1826

"Blackish purple." [RG] "Purple, nuanced." [LS] La Fornarina, tempestuous Italian inamorata of Lord Byron; in a letter (not to the present author), he mentions "her great black eyes flashing through her tears, and the long black hair, which was streaming drenched with rain over her brows and breasts." See also under Vibert's 'Fornarina', below.

Fornarina
Vibert, 1841

"Roseate spotted with white." [WRP] "A cupped flower, deep rose

Fornarina *continued*

color, marbled with white." [WRP] "Medium-sized, full, pink, spotted with white." [V8] "Medium-sized, full; color, light pink spotted with deep pink." [S] To be confused with neither Vétillart's Gallica of 1826, above, nor with Robert & Moreau's Mossy Remontant, both of the same name.

Foucheaux
Breeder unknown, pre-1846

"Light red." [Ÿ] "Blossom medium-sized, full; color, velvety carmine." [S] *Not* 'Foucher' (Vibert, 1828), which was "large, full, light pink." [Pf] There was an Abbé Faucheur who was an active horticulturist ca. 1830 . . .

François Foucquier
Breeder unknown, pre-1885

"Very large, full; color, bright crimson." [S]

Fulgens
Vibert, ca. 1830 (?)

"Delicate bright pink." [LS] "Pink, medium size, semi-double, average to tall." [Sn] It is perhaps worth remarking that the name is not typically Vibertian . . . 'Fulgens' is also a synonym of the Hybrid China 'Malton' (Guérin, 1829), which is "cherry carmine red."

Gaillarde Marbrée Listed as 'Noire Couronnée' (G).

Galatée
Dubourg, pre-1828

"Blossoms very double, flesh, with petals which are very thin and nearly transparent." [BJ30] See also 'Belle Galathée' (G).

[Gallica Alba]
syn. 'Rosea'
Breeder unknown, pre-1811

"Blush white." [LS] "A sort called 'Gallica Alba' or, indeed, 'Rosea', because its blossom isn't white at all, but pinkish. It is quite double, and has a sweet, agreeable scent. The wood is also green, armed with numerous slender straight prickles. The leaves are pointed, and of medium size, finely dentate. The calyx is oval, and narrowed at the top. The bud is elongate, and overtopped with the calyx membrane [*i.e., sepals*]. This kind isn't without merit." [C-T]

[Gallica Alba Flore Plena]
Breeder unknown, pre-1811

"This rose resembles the 'Tous-Mois' [Damask Perpetual] in its wood, its leaves, and its thorns. It differs from it by the form of its calyx, which is less elongate and more inflated, and by that of the bud, which is less pointed. The blossoms do not come in as great a number on the same petiole; they are very double, and often have in their middle the beginnings of other flowers. They are white, with some tints of pink. This is a hybrid variety which can be classed among the originals of the species; it looks a little like the Frankfort Agathe." [C-T]

Garnet Striped Rose Listed as 'Rosa Mundi' (G).

[Gazella]
Breeder unknown, pre-1906

"Deep pink." [LS] See also 'Grazella' (G).

Gazelle
Breeder unknown, pre-1843

"Flowers delicate rose, very large." [P] Possibly a Hybrid Bourbon. See also 'Grazella' (G). One would be inclined to state that a gazelle is a mighty peculiar animal to name a rose after, until one reflects that most roses are named after representatives of an even more questionable species . . . But probably from, or in honor of, nurseryman Gazelle, of Ghent, Belgium.

Général Donadière Listed as 'Général Donadieu' (G).

Général Donadieu
syn. 'Général Donadière'
Breeder unknown, pre-1842

"Bright crimson, superb, compact." [WRP] "Flowers purplish red, very double; form, compact." [P] "Flower large, full; color, flesh pink." [S]

[Général Foy]
Pelletier, 1827

"Ruby, full, flat, very large, beautiful." [LF] "This shouldn't get mixed up with the variety which has borne this name for several years [*'Général Foy' (Boutigny, 1825), Damask*], nor with the rose called 'Comte Foy' [*'Comte Foy de Rouen' (Lecomte, pre-1827), Gallica; nor should it indeed be confused with Vibert's spotted Gallica of 1844 of the same name*]. Bush with vigorous growth, erect stems nearly without prickles, with rough blackish bristles; leaves ordinarily composed of seven leaflets, rarely five, in which some are oval and others oblong, simply dentate; flowers very large in size, full, well formed, flat in form, in corymbs; central petals wine-lee red, outer petals lighter, irregularly incised at the tip, very crowded and regularly-arranged on the inside." [No28] Maximilien Sébastien Foy, 1775–1825; French general and war historian; fought at Waterloo.

Général Moreau
F. Moreau, pre-1885 (poss. 1870)

"Medium-sized, full; color, purple pink." [S]

Gentil Listed as 'Les Trois Mages' (G).

Georges Vibert
Robert, 1853

"Purple, spotted with white." [Ÿ] "Rosy purple, striped with white, medium size." [EL] "Violet purple, plumed white." [BJ70] "Medium-sized, full, violet purple plumed white and pink." [JR9/75] "Medium-sized bush; blossom violet purple red, plumed white; large, flat, full. One of the best Provins roses." [S] "Large, full, tall." [Sn] "Purple-red suffused with violet, striped with white, large and full. Growth moderate." [GeH] "Seven to eight cm [ca. 3 in], full, purple red with some violet, very well plumed with white, flat, rosette at the center, beautiful form, vigorous, one of the most interesting of this series." [M-LIV/324] Georges Vibert, grandson of the master rose breeder Jean-Pierre Vibert—the successful artist Jehan Georges Vibert.

Gil Blas
Breeder unknown, pre-1843

"Flowers deep reddish rose." [P] "Flower large, full, flat; color, light pink, touched with bright pink." [S] Gil Blas, hero of the semi-picaresque French novel of the same name by Lesage, the three parts of which were successively published in 1715, 1724, and 1735.

Gilloflower Rose Listed as 'Pompon de Bourgogne' (G).

[Giselle]
Vibert, 1843

"Flowers rose, spotted, of medium size, full." [P] "Medium-sized, full, pink, spotted." [V8] See 'Grazella' (G).

Globe Blanc Listed as 'Globe White Hip' (G).

Globe Hip Listed as 'Globe White Hip' (G).

[Globe White Hip]
syns. 'Boule de Neige', 'Calvert', 'Globe Blanc', 'Globe Hip'
Lee, pre-1826

"Blossoms nearly double, large, an extremely pure white, superb." [No26] "Received from England 3 years ago [*making 1827*]. A very pure white, the only one so far we have in this species." [BJ30] "Medium-sized, full, globular, creamy white in the middle, one of the oldest of the [Hybrid Gallica × Centifolia] group, raised by Mr. Lee the elder of Hammersmith, England." [JR9/126] "Flowers creamy white, of medium size, full; form, globular. Habit, erect; growth, small. An abundant and early bloomer." [P] "*Peduncles* long, glandulose. *Ovary* glabrous, ovoid, with a long, narrow neck. *Flower* large, double, semi-globular, white." [Pf] "Raised from seed in England, many years since. This is now much surpassed by some of our new white roses, but still is a favorite variety. Its habit is most luxuriant; and if grafted on the same stem with 'George the Fourth' [*sic; 'George IV' (Rivers, 1820), Hybrid China*], or some other vigorous-growing dark variety, the union will have a fine effect." [WRP]

Gloire de France
trans. "Glory of France"
Hardy, pre-1836

"Pale pink." [V4] "Lilac pink, full, flat, very large, superb." [LF] "Deep shaded rose, superb." [WRP] "Purple pink to lilac white, large, very full, average height." [Sn] "Very vigorous bush; flower very large, full, flat; color, bright pink, exterior of petals pinkish lilac." [S] "An immense rose, of the most luxuriant habit, having a fine effect grown as a standard, but, like some other very large roses, its flowers are irregularly shaped." [WRP] "Flowers deep rose, their circumference of a lilac blush, very large and full; form, expanded. Habit, erect; growth, robust." [P] We cannot verify the "1819" or the "1828" sometimes given for this cultivar. Joyaux gives an attribution of "Bizard, 1828."

Gloire des Jardins
trans. "Glory of the Gardens"
Descemet, pre-1815

"Cerise pink." [V9] "Cherry red." [GJB] "A large bright red, fully imbricated, and always perfectly double." [Bu] "A deep red, now cast aside." [WRP]

Gloriette
Breeder unknown, pre-1885

"Vigorous; flower large, full, very well formed; color, salmon." [S] *Cf.* the Centifolia and the Hybrid Noisette, both of the same name.

Gonsalve Listed as 'Gonzalve' (G).

Gonzalve
syn. 'Gonsalve'
Vibert, 1835

"Crimson pink." [V4] "Flowers violet red, of medium size, full; form, globular." [P]

[Gracilis]
Vibert, pre-1836

"7–9 cm [ca. 3 in], full, flat, white, flesh center, very floriferous." [R7M62] Not to be confused with the Boursault hybrid. See also 'Grazella' (G).

Grand Condé Listed as 'Rouge Formidable' (G).

Grand Corneille
syn. 'Cramoisi des Alpes'; trans. "Great Corneille"
Trébucien, pre-1829

"Flowers medium-sized, full, bright pink." [JR1/8/9] "*Peduncle* long. *Flower* medium-sized, full, bright purple red." [Pf] Pierre Corneille, French dramatist, lived 1606–1684. Corneille, like this rose's breeder Trébucien, was a Rouennais.

Grand Cramoisi de Trianon
Listed as 'À Grand Cramoisi' (G).
See also 'Grand Cramoisi de Vibert' (G).

Grand Cramoisi de Vibert
trans. "Vibert's Big Crimson"
?Vibert, 1818?

"Crimson." [LS] "Light crimson." [Y̆] "Red, medium size, full, medium height." [Sn] Curious that we find no early mention of this cultivar … Not to be confused with 'À Grand Cramoisi' (G), which was not very full, and was deep purple.

[Grand Monarche]
syns. 'Cocarde Royale', 'Grand Monarchie'; trans. "Great Monarch"
Holland, pre-1818

"Flowers very large, bright pink, beautiful." [No26] "Flowers large, full, pale pink." [Pf] "Well-shaded carmine-cerise, most regular form, beautiful." [J-As/62] "Still a very precious rose. I can't stop admiring its beautiful forms, a bright cerise circle in the middle of the blossom surrounded by an outer counter-circle ornamented pink and enamel white." [J-A/569] "Preferable to ['Ornement de Parade']; brighter color." [dP] "Rejected and superseded." [WRP] "Coming from Holland, this rose in mentioned by Redouté, de Pronville, and Desportes. Prévost gives, as synonymous, Hardy's 'Cocarde Royale'." [Gx]

Grand Monarchie Listed as 'Grand Monarche' (G).

[Grand Napoléon]
Sevale & Haghen, 1809

"Large violet blossoms; very double." [BJ30] "Double, large, intense violet, not very numerous." [No26] "Sub-variety of ['L'Évêque'], blossoms prettier." [BJ24] "Grown from seed at Brussels by Messrs. Sevale and Haghen, who dedicated it to the emperor." [Gx]

Grand Palais de Laeken
syn. 'Palais de Laeken'; trans. "Great Palace of Laeken"
Laeken, 1824

"Pink, shaded." [LS] "Flowers medium-sized, very full, bright pink." [JR1/8/10] "Pink; among the largest and most beautiful of the tribe." [Go] "Light pink, medium size, full, tall." [Sn] The palace of Laeken, refurbished by Napoléon for Joséphine; later of use to the Belgian royals.

[Grand Sultan]
syns. 'Céleste', 'Grand Turban'
Descemet, pre-1820

"Very large, pink." [V8] "Large, very full, delicate flesh." [BJ53] "*Leaves* light green. *Flower* very large, full, pale pink or flesh." [Pf] "Rejected and superseded." [WRP] "Bred by Descemet, according to Desportes. This is probably Miss Lawrance's 'Sultan Rose'. Prévost says that, at Rouen, it was called 'Grand Turban', and 'Céleste' at Le Havre." [Gx] See also 'Belle Sultane' and 'Le Grand Sultan'; all of these Sultans and Sultanas are much confused.

Grand Turban Listed as 'Grand Sultan' (G).

[Grande Brique]
trans. "Large Brick"
Breeder unknown, pre-1811

"Light wine-lee." [LS] "Flowers double, very large, superb, Peony-form, a beautiful bright pink." [No26] Possibly a hybrid between Gallica and Centifolia. *Cf.* 'Double Brique' (G).

Grande Brune Listed as 'Nouveau Monde' (G).

Grande et Belle
trans. "Big and Beautiful"
Holland, pre-1811

"Deep crimson." [RG] "Purple pink." [LS] "Light wine-lee." [LS] "This rose looks like ['Ornement de Parade'], but it grows even more vigorously; indeed, a person can raise it on a stem [*i.e., grow it as a tree rose or "standard"*] own-root, which is a precious characteristic. Its leaves are more deeply toothed. The calyx and bud are a little rounder. The blossom is of the same size and form, but the color is a little darker; as for the rest, check what was said under 'Ornement de Parade'." [C-T]

Grande Henriette Listed as 'L'Enchanteresse' (G).

Grande Pompadour Listed as 'Pourpre Charmant' (G). Note also reference under 'Passe-Velours' (G).

Grande Sultane Listed as 'Belle Sultane' (G). See also 'Le Grand Sultan' (G).

[Grande Violette Claire]
trans. "Large Light Violet"
Breeder unknown, ca. 1811

"Pale violet." [LS] "The second [variety, of which 'Couronnée' was the first] resembles ['Couronnée'] in wood and foliage. Its flower is only semi-double, with ten petals; but it is very large, growing four inches [ca. 1 dm] and more across. This rose, grafted on the Briar raised from a cutting, will nevertheless shine in beds. It can also make a splash there grown on its own roots, due to its vigor and the beauty of its foliage." [C-T]

Grande, Violette, et Belle Listed as 'Roxelane' (G).

Grandesse Royale Listed as 'Great Royal' (G).

Grandeur Royale Listed as 'Great Royal' (G).

Grandiflora Listed as 'Alika' (G).

Grandissima Listed as 'Louis-Philippe' (G).

Grazella
Choose a Gallica: 'Gazella' (deep pink), 'Gazelle' (delicate rose), 'Giselle' (spotted), 'Gracilis' (white, flesh center). *Qq.v.*

Great Royal
syns. 'Grandesse Royale', 'Grandeur Royale', 'Hortensia', 'Pivoine', 'Pivoine des Hollandais', 'Rose Pivoine', 'Regalis'
England, pre-1813

'Rose.' [Cal] "*Flower* very large, full, light lilac pink." [Pf] "The blossoms are a pink tending towards Hydrangea pink, and globular, even when mature." [CM] "Blossoms globular, even when they have developed, red tending towards Hydrangea-pink." [AC] "Rather tufted *bush* 0.5–0.8 m high [ca. 1.5–2 ft high]; *prickles* of differing lengths, more or less close-set. *Leaflets* 5, ovate, thick, rugose, green above, tomentose beneath and at margins; petioles villose, mostly prickly; stipules large, denticulate. *Flowers* with little scent, 3–4 at the tips of the canes; pedicels and *receptacles* glandular hairy; *sepals* 3 pinnatifid, 2 entire, pointed or spatulate, similarly covered in hairs on the outside, whitish woolly within; *corolla* semi-double; *petals* 4–5-seriate, darker pink than those on the common Centifolia; stamens few, some petalloid and crumpled; styles long, subfasciculate." [T&R] Possibly a hybrid between Gallica and Centifolia. 'Aimable Rouge' (G), 'Bourbon' (G), 'Holoserica Regalis' (G), and 'Passe-Princesse' (G), all of which see, are very possibly synonymous.

Gros Provins Panaché Plate 4
trans. "Big Plumed Gallica"
Fontaine, pre-1852

"Large, full, deep violet, large white rays." [Gp&f52] "Blossom large, well formed; color, violet red, striped white." [S] "Among the best [Gallicas] with corollas striped with various shades of carmine, the *Journal des Roses* has chosen the variety called 'Gros Provins Panaché' [*sic*] as the one to offer its subscribers a picture of, so that notice can be taken of the floral splendor that fashion, in abandoning these roses, has deprived our gardens of. The rose shown is one of the most recommendable in the Provins category of those with blossoms of various shades. Monsieur S. Cochet got it from our late regretted colleague Monsieur Denis Hélye of the *Musée d'Histoire Naturelle* in Paris with no other dignity than the name 'Gros Provins Panaché'; all research undertaken to discover some trace of its history and the name of its breeder has been fruitless. The *Journal des Roses* would receive with pleasure any information which anyone would be so kind as to impart concerning this charming Provins." [JR10/72] No response forthcame.

Grosse Cerise
trans. "Big Cerise"
Dupont, pre-1810

"Red." [Y] One also sees the attribution "Van Houtte, 1843."

Haddington
Breeder unknown, date uncertain

"Dark purple-red, yellow center, small to medium size, semi-double, average height." [Sn] Haddington, possibly Thomas Hamilton, Earl of Haddington, favorite of James VI of Scotland; or Haddington, county town of East Lothian, Scotland.

Hector

syns. 'Blood', 'Blood d'Angleterre', 'Cramoisi Majeur', 'Noire', 'Sang', 'Sanguine d'Angleterre'
Holland, pre-1819

"Purple." [Cal] "Violet." [LS] "Flowers large, double, of a less deep velvety carmine." [No26] "Blossoms medium-sized, full; color, violet, with a slatey pink center." [S] "Violet pink, medium size, full, tall." [Sn] "The most besought Provence rose in our gardens has extremely double blossoms; it is given the various names 'Noire', 'Cramoisi', 'Sang' because of the scarlet color of its petals." [CM] "Wood, thorns, leaves, and buds those of the Gallica, but enlarged; perhaps it is a variety of the Provence. Its numerous flowers are large and vie with those of the 'Sans Pareille Pourpre', which it much resembles. Its color is sparkling, velvety crimson red; very double. It should be grafted high. Opens 10–19 of June." [LeR] "This rose, coming from Holland, was in Parmentier's nurseries. According to Desportes, its synonym in England was 'Blood'." [Gx] Hector, supreme Trojan hero, Achilles' foe and antagonist.

Héloïse

Vibert, 1834

"Flesh." [V4] "Blush white." [Y] "Bush with nearly thornless canes; calyx-tube oval-pyriform, bearing—as do the peduncles—several black fragrant glands; sepals viscous, long, three or four of them pinnatifid; flower large or medium, full, pale pink or flesh, nuanced with purplish pink." [S]

Helvetius

Desprez, ca. 1830

"A rosy-violet colour, very large, and double to the centre." [Bu] "Blossom large, full, red with lilac edges." [JR1/8/10] "Flowers rosy lilac, large and double; form, compact. A hybrid, probably between the Damask and French." [P] Claude Adrien Helvetius, 1715–1771, French philosopher.

Henri Foucquier

Breeder unknown, pre-1842

"Flowers large, very full, delicate pink." [JR1/8/10]

Henri Quatre

Calvert, 1821

"Bright red." [Cal] "Flowers large, semi-double, light purple tending towards incarnadine." [MonLdeP] "Very double; very dark, very brilliant pink." [J-A/570] "Blossom double, large; color, bright purple pink or light red." [S] Cf. 'Henri IV', the Damask. Henri Quatre, alias Henri IV "of Navarre," King of France, lived 1553–1610.

Hippolyte

Breeder unknown, pre-1842

"Bright carmine nuanced violet." [JR1/8/10] "Light violet, medium size, full, tall." [Sn] Hippolyte, alias Hippolytus, good boy who preferred chastity to his stepmother Phaedra, alas with fatal results.

[Holoserica]

syns. 'Holosericea', 'Maheck à Fleurs Simples', 'Velvet Rose'; trans. "Thoroughly Silky"
Breeder unknown, pre-1629

"Ovary globular. Calyx with many appendages. Peduncle hispid and glandulose. Petioles prickly beneath. Leaves ovoid, hispid beneath, and saw-toothed with large teeth . . . The blossom, of a deep purple, has two rows of petals speckled with violet, and some filaments and anthers of a golden yellow. The much-appendaged calyx segments have reddish-brown glands on the outside. The globular ovary narrows in the upper portion. The leaves are a thoroughgoing green above, matte green beneath, and are composed of five to seven ovoid lobes which are serrated with large teeth, terminate in one single tooth, and have distinct veins, as well as glands along the edges. The petioles are armed with prickles, and also bear glands. This rose is not very spiny, and blooms in June." [Rsg] "The old stemme or stock of the veluet Rose is couered with a dark coloured bark, and the young shootes of a sad greene with very few or no thornes at all upon them: the leaues are of a sadder greene colour then in most sorts of Roses, and very often seuen on a stalke, many of the rest hauing but fiue: . . . the single is a broad spread flower, consisting of fiue or sixe broad leaues [petals] with many yellow threads in the middle . . . all of them [i.e., all the Holosericas of whatever doubleness] of a smaller s[c]ent then the ordinary red Rose [i.e., the ordinary Gallica]." [PaSo] "Rose with nearly round seed-buds, and peduncles hispid: stem and petioles hispid and prickly, leaves winged: leaflets ovate, and villose beneath: flowers of a deep purple colour; blossom single, semi-double, or full of petals [i.e., in the various forms] . . . [Andrews'] drawing represents the single, semi-double, and completely double-flowered velvet Roses, easily distinguished when in flower, but when out of bloom not the slightest difference is discernible." [A] See also under 'Holoserica Regalis' (G).

[Holoserica Duplex]

syn. 'Semi-Double Velvet Rose'
Breeder unknown, pre-1629

"The double hath two rowes of leaues [i.e., petals], the one large, which are outermost, the other smaller within, of a very deepe red crimson colour like vnto crimson velvet, with many yellow threads [stamens] in the middle; and yet for all the double rowe of leaues, these Roses stand but like single flowers." [PaSo]

[Holoserica Multiplex]

syns. 'Double Velvet Rose', 'Holosericea Plena', 'Rosier Noir', 'Violaceo Purpurea Nigricans Holosericea Plena'
Breeder unknown, pre-1629

"There is another double kinde that is more double than ['Holoserica Duplex'], consisting oftentimes of sixteene leaues [petals] or more in a flower, and most of them of equal bignesse, of the colour of the first single rose of this kinde, or somewhat fresher." [PaSo] "Corolla full. Calyx segments winged. Ovary globular. Peduncles glandular. Leaves ovoid, saw-toothed . . . The petals of this very full rose—which reflex on themselves around the center—are a very deep red, changing to blackish velvet. The sepals are glandular, and have numerous appendages. The nearly globular ovary has glands as does the peduncle. Its leaves, which have large irregular teeth along the edges, and which ordinarily consist of five ovoid lobes, are fresh green above and paler beneath, and terminate in a point. The stipules are long and edged with small glands. This rose is also called the black rose—however, it is, in fact, only a variety of the single velvety rose with violet reflections—and this is only the case when it is favorably sited as to the sun such that the flowers—which usually are only a very deep red—develop these blackish-violet tints. There are

[Holoserica Multiplex] *continued*
two further black roses." [Rsg] It remains to be determined how the various Holosericas, Mahaecas, and Tuscanies relate to each other.

Holoserica Plena Listed as 'Holoserica Multiplex' (G).

Holoserica Regalis
syn. 'Royale Veloutée'
Schwarzkopf, pre-1815
    "Flower double; color purple tending towards black; calyx nearly globular, glabrous; segments with a double appendage; peduncles and petioles bristly and thin; stem spiny; leaflets oval, doubly serrate … The bush grows 2–3 ells high [ca. 7.5–11.25 ft; 2.3–4 m], growing a quantity of canes which are long and slender, and which bear short prickles which are easy to rub off, and rough to the touch. The petioles are bristly, and ordinarily bear oval acuminate leaflets bearing teeth which are glandulose along the edge, and which waft an agreeable scent like that of the French Rose (Rosa gallica). The calyx is nearly globular, and glabrous; its segments have a double appendage, and are covered with very close-set red glands. The double flowers aren't very muddled; the petals are a deep purple and become so dark— particularly when the blossoms open late, when pretty much kept from the burning rays of the sun—that it would nearly be reasonable to call it the Black Rose. The inwards of the blossom holds a few golden yellow stamens and several small deep carmine petals, enhancing further the charms of this superb kind of rose. The glabrous and globular fruits are quite red at maturity, and stay on the rose all Winter. *Native to*: Germany; this rose was, to the best of my knowledge, first grown from seed at Napoleonshöhe by Herr Schwarzkopf, director of the gardens. *Bloom-Time*: June. *Observations*: This variety of rose probably takes its origin from the Velvet Rose (*Rosa holosericea*), of which it is still uncertain whether it is a species all its own, or a variety of the French Rose. Propagation is effected by layering or suckers, which lattermost are not as common as they are with the other velvet roses. This rose often blooms light purple, not showing the beautiful transitory blue of its petals, such that a person could take it to be quite another sort. The exposure and season in particular seem to be the causes of this change in color; it is perhaps also possible that its age contributes, because I have noticed that this deterioration of the blossoms seems more frequent among aged roses than young ones." [Rsg]

Horatius Coclès
Miellez, pre-1828
    "Bright red." [RG] "Rose-red, large, full, good form." [Jg]

Hortense de Beauharnais
Vibert, 1834
    "Deep pink, spotted, beautiful." [LF] "Blossom medium-sized, full; color, delicate pink, spotted bright pink." [S] "Though described as *Rose vif Ponctuée* [*i.e.*, "Spotted bright Pink"], is not worthy of that distinction; these faint spots seen in it after close inspection, are too faint to be deserving of notice." [Bu] "Flowers rose, their circumference rosy lilac, large and full; form, compact. Habit, erect; growth, vigorous." [P] Hortense de Beauharnais, the Empress Joséphine's daughter by her first marriage; wife of Louis Bonaparte, and Queen of Holland; lived 1783–1837.

Hortensia
Synonym shared by 'Aimable Rouge' (G) and 'Great Royal' (G).

[Illustre]
syns. 'Belle de Hesse', 'Die Berühmte', 'La Glorieuse', 'La Prédestinée', 'La Triomphante', 'Surpasse Singleton'; trans. "Illustrious"
Descemet, pre-1820
    "Dark rose." [Cal] "Light pink clouded lilac, very agreeable coloration and form." [J-As/67] "*Flowers*, full, middle-sized; lilac-pink, sometimes shaded with light purple." [Go] "Raised by Descemet, says Desportes." [Gx] Possibly, even probably, by Schwarzkopf of Hesse.

Impératrice Joséphine Listed as 'Francofurtana' (Turb).

Impériale Listed as 'Regina Dicta' (G).

Incomparable
Holland, pre-1813
    "Purple, nuanced." [V9] "Deep pink." [Ÿ] "Dark." [Cal] "Came from Holland, says Desportes; Du Pont grew it in his nurseries." [Gx]

Inermis Sub albo Violacea Listed as 'Bourbon' (G).

Ingénue
trans. "Ingenuous"
Vibert, 1833
    "White, buff centre, compact." [WRP] "Flowers creamy white, of medium size, double; form, cupped. Habit, branching; growth, moderate; foliage of a pale green." [P] "Most undoubtedly a descendant of the Globe Hip, with flowers of the purest white, the centre of the flower inclining to yellow; this is one of the finest white roses known, and, like the Globe Hip, it is of the most luxuriant habit." [WRP] Vibert released a similarly colored 'L'Ingénue' Gallica in 1849, listed below.

Ipsilanté Listed as 'Ypsilanti' (G).

[Isabelle]
Descemet, pre-1820
    "Maroon purple." [LS] "*Flower* small or medium-sized, very full, plump, regular, velvety, purple red marbled violet purple." [Pf] "Flowers crimson, mottled and shaded with purple, of medium size, full; form, compact, neat; the petals small, closely and regularly disposed (Ranunculus-like). Habit, erect; growth, moderate." [P] "One of Descemet's seedlings, mentioned by Desportes." [Gx] Not to be confused with the flesh-colored 'Isabelle' of Prévost fils, given as a synonym of 'Grande Agathe Nouvelle'.

Jeanne Hachette
Vibert, 1842
    "Reddish crimson, spotted, large and double." [P] "Large, double, crimson red, spotted." [V8] "Flower large, full; color, carmine, spotted with grenadine." [S] "Very large, double, red spotted very profusely with crimson." [WRP] "The flowers are almost as large as our old [Damask] Perpetual 'Jeanne Hachette', but much darker in colour, being a red suffused with crimson spots." [Bu] Jeanne Hachette, real name Jeanne Laisné, spirited defendress of Beauvais, France; fl. 1472.

Jeannette
Descemet, pre-1815
    "Red." [RG] "Beautiful red, and very prettily formed." [J-As/62]

Jenny Duval See 'Jenny' (Hybrid China) in Appendix 1.

Jéricho Listed as 'Bourbon' (G).

[Jeune Henry]

trans. "Young Henry"
Descemet, pre-1815

"Bush with purple canes; blossom full, of a dark bright pink." [S] "An obtention of Descemet's mentioned by Desportes." [Gx] Possibly a Centifolia. The distinctions between this 'Jeune Henry' and the Descemet Damask Perpetual of the same name and date are difficult to draw and indeed perhaps illusory: "The boundary between Gallica and Portland is not as easy to draw as one might think." [JR12/170]

Joséphina

Savoureux?, pre-1813

"Pale pink." [Ÿ] "Flowers semi-double, medium-sized, bright pink, spotted." [AC] "Double." [Pf] "Was in the nurseries of Dupont; it is mentioned by Prévost." [Gx] To be confused with neither the "velvety brown violet" 'Joséphine' in LeRouge nor perhaps Prévost's pale-edged deep pink 'Joséphine'.

Joséphine Parmentier

Parmentier, ca. 1840

"Blossom medium-sized, full; color, bright pink." [S]

Juanita

Vibert, 1836

"Medium-sized, full, pink, pale at the edge." [V8] "Flowers lively rose, paler in colour towards their circumference, plentifully sprinkled with white dots, of medium size, full; form, expanded. Habit, branching; growth, moderate." [P] The suggested date of 1834 seen elsewhere appears incorrect.

Julie d'Étanges

Vibert, 1834

"Medium-sized, full, delicate pink." [V8] "Flowers rosy lilac, their circumference inclining to blush, large and full; form, cupped, perfect. Habit, erect; growth, vigorous. Varies much as to quality; sometimes very beautiful. A hybrid, partaking a little of *R. alba*. A good Rose for a pot." [P]

Juliette

Miellez, pre-1828

"Carmine." [RG] "Carmine, medium size, not very full, flat, growth 7 [on a scale of 10], upright." [Jg] 'Juliette' is also a synonym for 'Mahaeca' (G), *q.v.*

Junon

syns. 'Belle Junon', 'Juno', 'Junonis', 'Rouge Agréable'; trans. "Juno"
Dupont, pre-1811

"Bright red." [Cal] "Beautiful crimson with wide ashy edges, blossoms very double." [J-As/62] "Whitish pink, large, full, tall." [Sn] "*Flowers* numerous, small or medium-sized, regular, very double, bright pink." [Pf] "Blossoms very double, a light even red. This rose grows rapidly, and forms beautiful heads when grafted." [AC] "There is nothing out of the ordinary in its wood or its foliage, but the blossom is a beautiful deep pink, often plumed white; its form is very nice; grafted on the Briar, this rose makes a nicely rounded head, giving many flowers and pleasant to see." [C-T] "Hybrid between the Centifolia and the Provins. Wood and leaves, those of the one and the other; flower, pleasant in shape; color, a very intense carminey pink —dark, indeed—and often plumed white. It bears many blossoms

quite surrounded by leaves and buds. It has little scent. Grafted, it makes a pretty, rounded, head. It blooms from the 10th to the 15th of June. Several petals are split between white and pink." [LeR] "Described by Guerrapain and in the *Nouveau Duhamel*, was in the nurseries of Dupont and Godefroy." [Gx] Juno, Roman goddess, protector of women. See also 'Cerisette la Jolie', 'Minerve', and 'Roi des Pourpres'.

Kean

syn. 'Shakespeare'
Laffay, pre-1843

"Bright crimson, shaded shell, large, very splendid." [WRP] "Always a beautiful rose, in size first rate, and in shape quite perfection; color bright reddish crimson, sometimes approaching to scarlet." [WRP] "Flower large, full, beautiful carmine, perfect form." [Gp&f52] "Rich velvety-crimson, flowers large and full, and perfectly formed; one of the most perfect and constant show roses." [JC] "Large, full, velvety purple, scarlet crimson center." [JR9/74] "Blossoms medium-sized or large, full, light red." [JR1/8/11] "Large, full, opening widely; color, velvety grenadine with a scarlet center." [S] "Purple-red, salmon center, medium size, full, tall." [Sn] "Flowers rich velvety purple, their centre crimson scarlet, large and full; form, compact, perfect. Habit, branching; growth, vigorous. A beautiful Rose, worthy of a place in the most limited collection." [P] Edmund Kean, 1787–1833; English actor particularly noted for Shakespearean roles.

Kermosina   Listed as 'Cramoisie' (G).

König von Sachsen

trans. "King of Saxony"
Ruschpler, 1878

"Vigorous bush; canes strong, short, very thorny; leaves light green, deeply serrated; color, bright pink." [S] *Cf.* the Centifolia 'Reine de Saxe'.

Koniginrosa   Listed as 'Regina Dicta' (G).

L'Admirable   Listed as 'Admirable' (G).

L'Amitié   Listed as a Damask.

L'Archvêque   Listed as 'La Provence' (G). See also 'Pourpre Charmant' (G).

L'Enchanteresse

syns. 'Enchantress', 'Grande Henriette'
François, 1826

"Intense pink nuanced purple, full, regular." [BJ30] "Bright flesh pink." [Ÿ] "*Flower* large, full, light intense bright pink, becoming pale." [Pf] "Flowers very large, full, red with paler edges." [JR1/8/11] "Light pink, large, full, tall." [Sn] "Flowers light even rose, of medium size, full; form, cupped, perfect. Habit, erect; growth, moderate. An abundant bloomer, and a fine Rose." [P] "An old and most beautiful variety, so double and finely shaped that it may be considered a prize-rose of the first character." [WRP]

L'Évêque

syns. 'Belle Évêque', 'Bishop', 'Bishop's', 'La Cocarde', 'Provins Double', 'Purpureo-Violaceo Magna', 'The Bishop'; trans. "The Bishop"
Breeder unknown, pre-1790

"Deep violet." [LS] "Purple." [Cal] "Violet petals, spotted with white." [dP] "Blossoms large, double, violet color, picked-out with little white

L'Évêque *continued*

spots." [BJ24] "Flowers large, double, violet in color, slightly striped, ticked with small white spots." [CM] "Very beautiful blossoms of large dimensions, beautiful crimson violet." [J-A/568] "Shaded pink." [Bu] "Light red or pink." [WRP] "Light violet red, medium size, very full, medium to tall." [Sn] "Violet pink, much favored, illustrated by Miss Lawrance and Redouté. It had numerous sub-varieties, such as 'Manteau Pourpre', 'Rose Marron', 'Rose Noire de Hollande', and 'Grande Violette'." [Gx] "Very beautiful variety; flowers large, double; in color, violet, slightly striped, sometimes picked out with little white points. It has some sub-varieties which are only sports of this one. It is, however, necessary to point out the one that low flattery caused to be named 'Napoléon', and which is known, in Godefroy's nursery, under the name 'Grand Alexandre'." [dP] "Has the wood and foliage of the Provins—but this rose is later blooming; the blossom is very double, and less than two inches across [ca. 5 cm]. The petals, a beautiful velvety purple, are beautifully formed. It has a sweet scent." [C-T] "Its leaves are nearly oval, from three to five on the same [petiole], close together, tipped by a point, deeply toothed. The bud is round, and nearly nude. The calyx is oval, and covered with small brown bristles, as is its stalk. The thorns are brown, hooked, and massed at the place where the leaf attaches to the branch. The blossoms, one or two per stem, are very double, and deep violet; the petals are fluted. This faintly-scented rose looks like a flat cockade." [C-T] "Notable by way of the singularity of its leaves being fairly distant on the upright shoots, which are sparsely armed with fine prickles; buds inflated, poorly covered [by the sepals], coming singly or in ones or twos on each peduncle. When the flower opens, it is large and flat as a cockade; the petals are wavy, deep violet, and muddled. They resemble the Agathes a little, of which this is the Type. Being grafted does a lot for it. Blooms June 9–10." [LeR] "*Stems* somewhat reddish, with recurved prickles; *branches* diffuse, with fairly numerous, small, unequal, almost straight, ephemeral *prickles*, densely distributed, especially at the extremities of the plant. *Leaflets* 5, stiff, rounded ovate, dark green, glabrous above, tomentose beneath; petioles villose, glandular, with many small, inclined prickles. *Flowers* faintly scented, 1–3 at the tips of the canes; pedicels long, hispid; *receptacles* rounded, almost glabrous, sometimes glandular; *sepals* pinnatifid, glabrous or glandular hairy; *corolla* large; petals 2–3-seriate, a fine purple-violet, broad, cordately notched or subcrenate; styles fasciculate. This beautiful and long-known cultivar of the Provins Rose is grown in almost all gardens. It is the parent of many violet colored derivatives, all notable for their brilliant colors, they themselves having given rise to seedlings of different shades, more or less double, some striped or spotted with white, others white towards the base, and all very fine. Flower-growers have preferred the single or semi-double to the double cultivars. Botanists, however, disdain them, considering them degenerate and a sign of impermanence of species in *Rosa*." [T&R] "Ancient variety [*already in 1824*]." [MonLdeP] "One of the oldest." [BJ30]

L'Infante d'Espagne Listed as 'Cramoisie Éblouissante' (G).

L'Ingénue
trans. "The Ingenuous One"
Vibert, 1849

"Flowers full, from 8–9 cm across [to ca. 3½ in], pure white, with a rosette and [green] pip at the center." [M-V49/235] Not to be confused with Vibert's similarly colored Gallica of 1833, 'Ingénue'.

[L'Obscurité]
trans. "The Darkness"; probable syn., 'De Van Eeden', *q.v.*
Van Eeden/Prévost, pre-1820

"Dark brown." [V9] "Very beautiful purple passing to velvet brown." [J-A] "Blossoms semi-double, of a brown tending towards puce." [No26] "Tending towards violet." [BJ30] "Medium-sized, velvety." [God] "*Flower* medium-sized, double, velvety, intense even deep violet purple." [Pf] "*Flowers,* semi-double, middle-sized, regular; of a shaded violet-purple." [Go] "Why, when talking about 'L'Obscurité', the name of which is known generally, [do Redouté and Thory] give it under the name of Monsieur Van Eeden?" [V2]

La Cocarde Listed as 'L'Évêque' (G).

La Glorieuse Listed as 'Illustre' (G).

La Grande Junon Listed as 'Minerve' (G).

La Grande Obscurité Listed as 'Passe-Velours' (G).

La Grande Violette Listed as 'Roxelane' (G).

La Maculée
syns. 'Maculata', 'Pulmonaire'; trans. "The Blotched One"
Dupont, pre-1810

"Blossoms medium-sized, semi-double, purple, with lighter touches at the petals' nubs." [dP] "Bright pink, marbled." [LS] "Pink, striped purple-red, medium size, lightly full, tall." [Sn] "*Canes* slender, out-thrust, often arching at the tip; armed with strong thorns, the longest of which are falcate. *Flower* medium-sized or large, double or semi-double, bright purple pink, spotted. As the first spotted variety, and mother of several other much-esteemed varieties, I believe this rose merits a small place in big collections." [Pf] "This variety, though not beautiful, should be cultivated by those who propagate roses from seed, as its seeds are apt to produce spotted or streaked sub-varieties." [Go]

La Magnifique Listed as 'Pourpre Charmant' (G).

La Nationale
syn. 'Nationale Tricolore'
Breeder unknown, pre-1836

"Deep pink, striped and marbled." [V4] "Flowers medium-sized, full, red, shaded and blotched." [JR1/8/11] "A bright rosy colour, striped or mottled with purplish crimson, but with a shower of rain and an hour of sun its variegation is lost." [Bu] "Rose-red, medium size, full, tall." [Sn] "Flowers bright rosy crimson, paler at their circumference, the ground colour growing paler and becoming mottled shortly after expansion, large and full; form, expanded. Habit, erect; growth, moderate." [P] "One of the prettiest of its class." [WRP] We cannot confirm the suggested date of pre-1834 seen elsewhere.

La Négresse Listed as 'Superbe en Brun' (G).

La Neige
trans. "The Snow"
Robert, 1853

"Seven to eight cm [ca. 3 in], full, white, imbricated, form flat, with a rosette and green pips at the center; wood and foliage dark green, vigorous." [M-LIV/325] "6–8 cm [ca. 2½–3 in] ... Superb." [R&M62]

La Panachée Listed as 'Rosa Mundi' (G).

La Plus Belle des Ponctuées
trans. "The Most Beautiful of the Spotted Ones"
Breeder unknown, pre-1929

"Deep pink, medium size, full, tall." [Sn] "A spotting of pale pink on a rich pink ground …A very vigorous constitution, and makes a fine shrub of luxuriant greenery, amid which the pink flowers shine in contrast. They are loose-petalled with muddled centres. Essentially a plant for garden effect. 6 feet [ca. 2 m]." [T4] We cannot confirm the attribution and date of "Hébert, 1829" seen for this rose; nor, if accepted, could we explain why it had not been mentioned in the subsequent hundred years.

La Plus Élégante Listed as 'Cramoisie Triomphante' (G).

La Prédestinée Listed as 'Illustre' (G).

[La Provence]
syn. 'L'Archévêque', shared with 'Pourpre Charmant'
Breeder unknown, pre-1819

"Wood, thorns, leaves, and naked buds those of the group. Its blossom is velvety crimson, four inches across [ca. 1 dm], late to bloom. It is grafted high, where it cuts a majestic figure. I have no doubt that the Gallica and [this cultivar] have produced, through crops of their seed, all the beauties which I am going to describe [*i.e., the Purples (such as 'Pourpre Charmant') and the Browns (such as 'Belle Brune')*]. Opens June 25–30." [LeR]

La Pucelle
trans. "The Maiden"; especially refers to Joan of Arc
Dubourg, pre-1811

"Pink." [Ÿ] "*Flower* small or medium-sized, full, red, with pale edges." [Pf] "Large, full, bright purple pink." [JR1/8/11] "It is very small in all its proportions, and can't be mistaken for anything else. Its wood is slender, delicate, and clothed rather with bristles than with prickles. The very small leaves are well formed, finely dentate, and of a gay green. The bud is pointed, and covered over with the membranes [sepals] of the calyx, which is elongate and constricted from one end to the other. The blossom grows no larger than that of the common Pompon [*Pompon de Bourgogne*], but has a color which is gayer and more delicate. Furthermore, this sort has the benefit of being very fragrant; though it isn't very double, it is worth growing." [C-T] "This pretty Pompon, of which the origin is unknown, finds no place in any catalog except for that of Monsieur Guerrapain, who gave it to me. All the details are in miniature. Its growth is low and slender and light green, as are the leaves which are small and disc-shaped, the whole rather covered with bristles than with thorns. The buds are pointed and covered over by the extensions of the calyx, and come in up to nines on each peduncle. The blossom is a little larger than that of the 'Pompon de Bourgogne'; its color is a bright pink in the center, and lighter along the petal edges. It can be compared to one of the nine sisters [*the Muses?*], insofar as it is fresh and pretty. Opens June 10–15." [LeR] "Described by Guerrapain, mentioned by Redouté." [Gx] "From Monsieur Dubourg, according to the younger Monsieur Margat." [Pf] See also 'Pucelle de Lille' (G).

La Revenante Listed as 'Revenante' (G).

La Rubanée Listed as 'Belle Villageoise' (G).

La Tendresse
trans. "Tenderness"
Dupont, pre-1820

"Pale rose." [Cal] "Light pink." [Ÿ] "Violet pink, charming blossoms." [J-As/58] "Mentioned by De Pronville as being an old variety of Du Pont's, this rose finds a place in Godefroy's catalog." [Gx]

La Très Haute Listed as 'Aigle Brun' (G).

La Triomphante Listed as 'Illustre' (G).

La Villageoise Listed as 'Rosa Mundi' (G). See also 'Belle Villageoise' (G).

La Ville de Londres
trans. "The Town of London"
Vibert, pre-1844

"Shaded rose, very large and good." [FP] "Very large, bright pink." [V8] "Blossom very large, full; color, deep pink." [S] "A new variety, possessing in its bright vivid rose color, and perfect shape, all that can be wished for in a rose." [WRP] "Flowers deep rose, their circumference blush, very large and full; form, cupped, perfect. Habit, branching; growth, moderate. Very fine." [P] Vibert visited England and doubtless London about the time of this cultivar.

[Le Grand Sultan]
syns. 'Grand Sultan', 'Grande Sultane'
Breeder unknown, pre-1819

"Blossom large, red." [God] "Flowers purple and crimson, shaded, large and very double; form, expanded. Habit, branching; growth, robust." [P] "Wood and leaves of the Gallica, enlarged. Buds wide-spreading, not overtopped [by the sepal appendages]. Blossom large, centifolia [form], purplish crimson, petals large, rather like those of 'Pourpre Charmant' [G]. This beautiful rose merits all the efforts of fanciers. Opens June 9–10. Some stamens remain." [LeR] See also 'Belle Sultane' (G) and 'Grand Sultan' (G).

Le Grand Triomphe Listed as 'Nouvelle Pivoine' (G).

Le Pérou
syns. 'Baron de Gossard', 'Pérou de Gossard'; trans. "Peru"
Gossard/Parmentier, pre-1826

"Cerise, nuanced violet flame." [Ÿ] "*Flower* medium-sized, full, purple." [Pf] "Blossom medium-sized, full; color, velvety cerise, with very deep grenadine reflections." [S] "Peru" was used as an expression referring to great wealth, much as "El Dorado" is.

Le Triomphe Listed as 'Aimable Rouge' (G).

Léa
syns. 'Lée', 'Rose Lée'
Vétillart, ca. 1825

"Bright rose-red." [GJB] "Large, full, beautiful bright pink." [R&M62] "Bright red." [Ÿ] "Beautiful bright pink, full, cupped, large, superb." [LF]

Ledonneau-Leblanc
Breeder unknown, pre-1834?

"White and pink." [LS] "White, large, full, tall." [Sn] We cannot verify this date.

Lée Listed as 'Léa' (G).

Les Saisons d'Italie

trans. "The Seasons of Italy"
Breeder unknown, date uncertain

"Light purple red, medium size, very full, very fragrant, tall." [Sn]

Les Trois Mages

syn. 'Gentil'; trans. "The Three Magi"
Gentil, 1823

"Flowers similar [*to those of 'Princesse Éléonore' (G)*], but not as big and of a more delicate pink." [No26] "The blossoms nearly always come in threes. *Canes* very long, vertical. *Leaves* distant. *Leaflets* 5 or 7, undulate; the low pair is distant from the base of the petiole. *Flower* medium sized, very full and very plump, bright pink." [Pf] Has also been called a Damask.

Louis XVI   Listed as 'Achille' (G).

Louis-Philippe

syn. 'Grandissima'
?Hardy, 1824?

"Velvety red, full, globular, large, beautiful." [LF] "Large, full, bright pink." [V8] "Crimson, nuanced." [Ÿ] "Pinkish-blush, light margin." [FP] "Large, full, crimson pink, occasionally purple." [JR9/74] "Sizable blooms, deep crimson in color." [R-H63/183] "Flowers large, full, crimson red nuanced carmine." [JR1/8/11] "Light violet pink, large, full, average height." [Sn] "Flowers rosy crimson, sometimes purplish, very large and full; form, compact, perfect. Habit, branching; growth, moderate. A fine show Rose." [P] I am unable to verify the "Hardy, 1824," though it certainly dates from pre-1844. See also Miellez' Hybrid Bourbon 'Louis-Philippe', from pre-1835. Not to be confused with Guérin's China 'Louis-Philippe' of 1834, nor with Duval's 1832 Damask Perpetual 'Louis-Philippe I'. At any rate, they all commemorate King Louis-Philippe of France, lived 1773–1850, reigned 1830–1848, the "Citizen-King."

Louis van Tyll

Breeder unknown, pre-1846

"Crimson, nuanced." [Ÿ]

Lucile Duplessis

syn. 'Lucille'
Vibert, 1836

"Red-pink, spotted." [V4] "Medium-sized, full, deep pink, spotted." [V8] "Very pretty pink, spotted with white." [WRP] "Flower medium-sized, full; color, crimson spotted with pink." [S]

Lucille   Listed as 'Lucile Duplessis' (G).

Lustre de l'Église

syns. 'Duchesse d'Orléans', 'Grandesse Royale', 'Pivoine', 'Pourpre
    Double'; trans. "Lustre of the Church"
Holland, pre-1819

"Bright red." [Cal] "Blossoms purple, not very numerous, medium sized. Bush tall." [No26] "Pink, small, full, very fragrant, average height." [Sn] "This charming sub-variety of the Gallica and of some pink flowers [*sic*] comes to us as a seedling from the Dutch. Its Centifolia wood betrays its origin; but all these indicia are manifested in medium-sized proportions. The buds are overtopped [by the sepal appendages]. The flower is larger than that of the 'Bordeaux' [*i.e.*, 'Rosier des Dames'], a deep pink like the Hydrangea—nearly crim-

son. This rose is very double and bright. It is grafted at four feet [ca. 1.3 m]. Opens June 10–19." [LeR] "Included by Redouté among the roses called Grand Saint François." [Gx] We cannot substantiate the pre-1813 date suggested elsewhere. This cultivar shares color and some synonyms with 'Great Royal' (G).

Lycoris

Vibert, 1835

"Deep pink, spotted white." [WRP] "Carmine." [Ÿ] "Deep pink, spotted, with marbled foliage." [V4] "A new variety, of a fine vivid rose color, marbled and spotted in a very distinct and beautiful manner." [WRP]

Lyre de Flore   Listed as 'Beauté Insurmontable' (G).

Macrantha Rubicunda

Breeder unknown, pre-1877

"Flowers large, very double, light red." [JR1/8/11]

Maculata   Listed as 'La Maculée' (G).

Madelon Friquet

Vibert, 1842

"Roseate, spotted, expanded, perfect." [WRP] "Medium-sized, full, pink, spotted, flat, well-formed." [V8] "Blossoms large, very full, beautiful form, bright pink." [JR1/8/11] "Of perfect shape, rose spotted with blush, and remarkably full of petals." [WRP] "Flowers rosy lilac, plentifully sprinkled with small white spots, small and full; form, compact. Habit, branching; growth, small. A very neat and pretty Rose." [P] The date of 1830 suggested elsewhere for this cultivar appears incorrect.

Mahaeca

syns. 'Aigle Rouge', 'Belle Sultane', 'Juliette', 'Maheck', 'Maheka',
    'Mahoeca', 'Mutabilis', 'Rose du Sérail', 'Rose Sultane'
Holland/Dupont, ca. 1795

"Fiery cerise crimson nicely shaded brown, beautiful flowers a little more than semi-double." [J-A/568] "Scarlet." [Cal] "'Mahaeca', or 'Belle Sultane', naturally finds a place beside ['Superbe en Brun' and 'Velours Pourpre'], differing in its small prickles which are abundant and brown with a slightly recurved green tip. The blossoms' petals, the same size as the preceding [*i.e.*, ca. 1½–2 in or ca. 4–5 cm across], are wavy and ragged, and are a beautiful purple color which looks velvety in the sunlight. This rose can easily be mistaken for another sort coming from the garden at the Natural History Museum, given to me under the name 'Manteau Pourpre'." [C-T] "Superb variety of Provins or Provence. Wood short, thorns profuse and small, slightly hooked; flowers large, nearly double, of a sparkling lustrous bronze, only becoming purplish with the action of the sun, making it velvety; its petals are crumpled and cut. This pretty rose is limpid, and makes itself seen—even in the middle of those like it—by the sparkle of its color and the profusion of flowers borne by the plant; it makes a well-rounded head, and looks charming grafted on a five-foot stem; the stamens it still has are golden, and serve it well. Opens beginning June 9–10." [LeR] "Too well known to require a description, this is one of the most magnificent of all the gallicas. It demands no special care, needing only exposure to full sun to bring out the full brilliance of the colors. Rather rarely, completely single blossoms can be found on it. It came to us from Dutch nurseries almost thirty years ago, and was distributed by Dupont. Several gardeners refer to it as 'la Belle Sultane'." [T&R]

"They call 'Mahéca' several Provins roses having petals which have the look of the most beautiful velvet. They vary from single flowers to the most double. You can distinguish them by their darker or lighter nuances." [BJ30] "We owe to 'Mahoeca' first of all, and then to those roses which come from it—all of which set seed—a quantity of superb varieties which are basically purple and violet, in which the color, generally, becomes somber a little after the flower opens; and among which are many which are, or become, plumed, striped, or marbled." [V2]

If only we knew what the name 'Mahaeca' signifies! There is a notion I have been unable to run down that there was a Sultana by the name of "Mahika" at some point . . . Whatever the case, the relationships and identities involved in the Holoserica—Mahaeca—Tuscany complex can be depended upon to beguile the hours of rose researchers both patient and impatient.

Mahaeca de Dupont Listed as 'Busard Triomphant' (G), but see also 'Mahaeca' (G) itself.

Maheck Listed as 'Mahaeca' (G).

Maheck à Fleurs Simples Listed as 'Holoserica' (G).

Maheka Listed as 'Mahaeca' (G).

Mahoeca Listed as 'Mahaeca' (G).

Major Listed as 'Alector Cramoisi' (G).

Malesherbes
Vibert, 1834

"Red pink, spotted." [BJ40] "Red, nuanced purple." [Ý] "Medium-sized, full, purple, spotted." [V8] "Flowers very large, very full, and shaded red." [JR1/8/11] "Soon fades unless sheltered from the sun, as is the case with all roses that are purple and slate color." [WRP] "Purple-red, large, very full, average height." [Sn] "It is more of a Chinese hybrid than a Gallica, and is the more desirable, as its growth is thereby improved; the flowers are very double, rosy purple, spotted with white." [Bu] "Flowers clear purple, their centre bright red, very large and full. Habit, branching; growth, moderate." [P] Chrétien Guillaume de Lamoignon de Malesherbes, French statesman loyal to King Louis XVI; guillotined; lived 1721–1794.

Malvina Listed as 'Bourbon' (G).

[Manette]
Écoffay, 1820

"Pink." [Cal] "*Flower* medium-sized, full, plump, regular, deep pink or red, often with pale edges." [Pf] "Beautiful violet, slatey edges, flowers very double and of a very rich form in the manner of the rose 'Duputren' [*sic*; 'Dupuytren']." [J-As/58] *Cf.* 'Nanette' (G).

[Manteau d'Évêque] Plate 1
trans. 'Bishop's Mantle'
Breeder unknown, pre-1819 (probably pre-1814)

"Violet, spotted white." [LS] "Flowers large, double, violet in color, slightly striped, sometimes punctuated with small white points." [AC]

Manteau Pourpre
syn. 'Manteau Rouge'; trans. 'Purple Mantle'
Breeder unknown, pre-1811

"Purple." [Cal] "Red." [Ý] "Very bright carmine, most effective flowers." [J-As/62] "Blossoms large, petals very large, a shining violet purple." [BJ24] "Less double than 'Évêque', but as strong-growing; the flowers are large, the petals very large, and a sparkling purple." [CM] "The blossom [of 1.5–2 in or 4–5 cm across] has a very elegant form; its color is very fresh, a bright deep pink. It is not very double, but it has a very agreeable perfume. The outer petals are edged with a red darker than that found in 'Mahaeca'; the underside is silvery, doubtless the reason it was called 'Manteau Pourpre'—which however doesn't really fit, because in no way is it purple. Its petals are wavy, cut, and elegantly arranged on the calyx. As for the rest, this rose has nothing remarkable in either its wood or its foliage. This latter is nevertheless pretty elegant; the leaves are long, deeply toothed, and a bright green. The calyx of the flower is round and well formed. The buds are graceful, though poorly covered by the calyx membranes [*i.e., sepals*]. All in all, this rose is one of the most perfect sorts we have; it blooms around May 30." [C-T] "Beautiful variety of the Gallica. Flower elegant in form. Its color is a deep, brilliant pink. It has an elegant scent. The outer part of the petals is darker than at the center, which validates the name 'Manteau' [*"Mantle" or "Robe"*]. This rose is crinkled and cut; it should be regarded as one of the perfect ones in the group. Opens June 10–19." [LeR] "Described by Guerrapain and De Pronville, mentioned by Redouté; Desportes says its synonym is 'Manteau Rouge'." [Gx] 'Manteau Pourpre' is also a synonym of 'Rouge Formidable' (G), *q.v.*

Manteau Rouge
Synonym shared by 'Manteau Pourpre' and 'Rouge Formidable', *qq.v.*

Manteau Royal
trans. "Royal Mantle"
Descemet, pre-1820

"Very brilliant, shining with Roman purple; several florists call it the grenadine rose." [J-A/567] "Flowers double, medium-sized, and flame-colored." [AC] "*Flower* medium-sized, very multiplex, bright red, velvety and fiery crimson at the center, or bright carmine and not velvety." [Pf] We cannot confirm the date of 1810 suggested elsewhere for this cultivar.

Marbled Listed as 'Marmorea' (G).

Marbrée Listed as 'Marmorea' (G).

Marcel Bourgoin
Corboeuf-Marsault, 1898

"Red with violet reflections." [LS] "Deep violet red, large, full, medium scent, tall." [Sn]

Marie-Antoinette
Vibert, 1829

"Lilac pink." [LS] "Large, full, crimson lilac." [V8] "Flowers lilac-rose, large and full." [P] "Violet pink, large, full, tall." [Sn] The date of 1825 suggested for this cultivar appears incorrect. Queen Marie-Antoinette of France, lived 1755–1793, Austrian-born wife of Louis XVI of France; has a reputation for being a silly, but met her execution with dignity.

Marie Stuart

Dubourg, 1820

"Crimson pink." [V9] "Large blossoms of a bright pink, very full and tinted." [BJ30] "Flower large, imbricated, bright red." [God] "Flowers very double, very large, a delicate light pink, superb, but sometimes a little irregular." [No26] "Crop of 1818, first bloom in 1820. *Peduncles* in erect corymbs. *Flowers* numerous, overtopping the foliage, medium-sized, full, regular, light purple, with brown touches along the edges. Ordinarily, the last flowers are deep pink." [Pf] Marie Stuart, alias Mary Stuart, alias Mary Queen of Scots, lived 1542–1587.

Marie Tudor

Breeder unknown, pre-1846

"Cerise." [LS] "Slaty violet red." [Ÿ] Marie Tudor, alias Mary Tudor, alias Bloody Mary; queen of England, lived 1516–1558.

Marjolin

Hardy/Roeser, 1829

"Flowers purplish slate, very large and full; form, cupped. Habit, branching; growth, robust. A bold Rose." [P] "*Shrub,* armed with only a few short bristles. *Leaflets,* regularly toothed; of a light vivid green. *Flowers,* numerous, very large and very full, well made, attaining sometimes five inches in diameter [ca. 1.3 dm]; of a crimson-red, very dark, and inclining to violet." [Go] "Fairly vigorous; stems straight and bearing only small bristles; foliage very handsome, a slightly glossy light green; leaflets oblong, lanceolate, regularly dentate; blossoms two or three together on the same cane, numerous, full, very large in size, sometimes up to five inches across [ca. 1.3 dm], very well formed; petals a very deep crimson violet, rolled into a ring in the center, large, often cordiform at the edge. This superb variety belongs to the Provins group." [SAP29/265–266] Dr. Marjolin, one of Hardy's colleagues at the Luxembourg Palace gardens.

Marmorea

syns. 'À Fleurs Marbrées', 'Marbled', 'Marbrée', 'Marmoreo', 'Semi-Double Marbled Rose
Breeder unknown, pre-1754

"Pale rose." [Cal] "Very elegant blossoms, though semi-full; beautiful pink tints." [J-As/54] "This Marbled Variety of the 'Officinalis', or French Red Rose, is, like the Striped, a variety of colour only: for although all the three Roses appear distinct from each other when in flower; yet, when out of bloom, it is scarcely possible to distinguish the one from the other. We have sometimes observed the foliage of this variety more undulated or waved than the others; a trifling difference, it if is even a constant character;—but most likely a mere casualty of growth. It is exactly of the same bushy habit as the other two; and, like them, equally subject to mildew in the autumn." [A] "Corolla marbled. Calyx winged and hairy. Ovary ovoid. Leaves oval ... This rose is moderately large, double, and slightly flat. The greater part of the petals are a pale red, and have a bluish tint and light touches, making the marbling. The sepals are edged with hairs, and have glands along the outside, especially in the middle. The ovary is ovoid. The peduncle is moderately glandulose. The leaves, composed usually of five oval lobes of a dark green above, always slightly curved, extend to a point, and are bestrewn with glossy patches which however are a little dull. This rose is seemingly a variety of the Provins or Province." [Rsg] "*Bush,* 0.9–1.2 m high [ca. 3 ft]; *prickles* small, short, unequal, almost straight, very dense, mainly on the blooming branches. *Leaf-*

lets 5 or 7, mostly rounded ovate, green above, paler beneath; petioles slightly tomentose, with many small recurved prickles; stipules fairly broad, acute. *Flowers* almost scentless, 7.5 cm [ca. 3 in] or more in diameter, clustered at the branch tips; *receptacles* ovoid, glabrous or glandular hispid; pedicels wholly covered in short acicles and sessile glands; *sepals* pinnatifid; *petals* 2–3-seriate, pale pink spotted darker pink to give a marbled effect; *stamens* numerous; *stigmas* short, in a sessile hemispherical head ... Our rose makes a fine display grafted on the Briar. It is in demand, not only because of its variegation, but also because it is only semi-double, which fanciers prefer, in general, to single or full blossoms." [T&R] "Described and illustrated by Redouté, this is the 'Marbled Rose' of Miss Lawrance." [Gx]

Marmoreo   Listed as 'Marmorea' (G).

Mauve   Listed as 'Bourbon' (G).

Mazeppa

Breeder unknown, pre-1841

"Bright red, edged and marbled with white, and superb." [WRP] "Medium or large, plump, shaded pink, petal edges paler." [BJ53] "Pink, medium size, full, tall." [Sn] Ivan Stepanovich Mazeppa, lived ca. 1645–1710; courageous Cossack known to the kings of Poland, Russia, and Sweden.

Mécène

Vibert, 1844

"White and lilac." [LS] "Medium-sized, double, white, plumed pink." [Gp&f52] "A very beautiful expanded flower, white variegated with rose color." [WRP] "7 cm [ca. 2³⁄₄ in], double, ground-color white, striped with pink, flat." [VPt48/app] "White, striped violet pink, medium size, full, tall." [Sn] "Flowers white, striped with rose, of medium size, double; form, compact. Habit, erect; growth, moderate, shoots very smooth." [P] Mécène, alias Gaius Clinius Mecaenas, died 8 B.C., enlightened Roman patron of the Arts, friend of Augustus.

Meleagris   Listed as 'Pintade' (G).

Mercédès

Vibert, 1847

"8 cm [ca. 3 in], double, ground-color white, plumed with lilac pink, globular." [VPt48/app] "Medium-sized bush; flower large, full, white, plumed with lilac pink." [S] Possibly a Gallica × Centifolia hybrid.

Mexica Aurantia   Listed as 'Tricolore' (Holland, G).

Minerve

syn. 'La Grande Junon'
Miellez, pre-1811

"Rose." [Cal] "Deep red." [LS] "Very deep pink." [Ÿ] "This one resembles ['Junon'] in form, color, and bloom-time; it nevertheless differs in its wood, which is more slender, greener, and less clothed with stickers; smaller leaves; rounder calyx; bud better covered and set off by the calyx membranes [*sepals*], which are longer and lacier; and by the weaker perfume. Nevertheless, they can be seen as two sisters who are difficult to distinguish at first sight—though the color of 'Minerve' is a little darker than that of 'Junon'." [C-T] "Desportes says this is Descemet's 'La Grande Junon'." [Gx] Minerve, alias Minerva, the Roman goddess of wisdom, too seldom invoked these days.

Mirabilis   Listed as 'Admirable' (G).

Mme. de Tressan

syn. 'Mme. Tressant'

Sommesson, 1822

"Blossoms of a beautiful, very finished, pure pink color, brilliant from the smile of the Graces." [J-As/62] ("In truth, as the author said, 'All he doesn't do is—write in [*plain*] French'." [V2]) "*Canes* well armed. *Flower* large, full, pale pink or flesh." [Pf] Often considered a Damask.

Mme. Hébert   Listed as 'Président de Sèze' (G).

Mme. Tressant   Listed as 'Mme. de Tressan' (G).

Mme. Ville

Breeder unknown, pre-1885

"Medium-sized, full; color, bright carmine." [S]

Moïse

syn. 'Moyse'

"Bright pink." [LS] "Large, full, light purple." [V8] "Flowers large, full, a superb fiery cherry red." [No35] "*Flowers*, full, large; of a superb flame-coloured red." [Go] "Flowers medium-sized, full, very bright red." [JR1/8/11] "Rose-red, medium size, full, tall." [Sn] "Flowers rosy carmine, shaded with purplish slate, large and very double; form, expanded. Habit, erect; growth, moderate." [P] Moïse, alias Moses, leader of the Israelites.

Montalembert

Robert, 1852

"Deep lilac." [Ÿ] "Medium bush; flower dark violet plumed and often spotted with white and crimson, large, full, globular." [S] Charles Forbes de Tryon, Comte de Montalembert; French historian; lived 1810–1870.

Montézuma

Coquerel, pre-1830

"Lilac pink edged pale." [LS] "*Canes* nearly thornless, bestrewn with glands. *Petiole* glandulose above, glabrous beneath, armed or unarmed. *Leaflets* close-set, ordinarily arching. *Peduncle* glandulose at the tip, often glabrous at the base. *Ovary* short, digitate or hemispherical, glabrous at the tip. *Flower* large, full, semi-globular, bright lilac pink, sometimes with some lead color, paler along the edge." [Pfs] One sees the date "1806" connected with this cultivar; this is an unlikely date. The fact that it first shows up in Prévost's supplemental listing implies introduction in or about 1829. Montezuma, sometimes called Moctezuma, lived ca. 1480–1520, gracious and unfortunate last emperor of the Aztecs.

Montigny   Listed as 'Crignon de Montigny' (G).

Moyse   Listed as 'Moïse' (G).

Multiplex   Listed as 'Admirable' (G).

Mutabilis   Listed as 'Mahaeca'(G).

Nain   Listed as 'Rosier d'Amour' (G); but see also the equally *nain* 'Pompon de Bourgogne' (G).

Nanette

Breeder unknown, pre-1848

"Flowers rosy crimson, marbled with purple, of medium size, very double; form, cupped. Habit, erect; growth, moderate. A very pretty Rose, blooming later than others of the [Gallica] group." [P] *Cf.* the Gallica 'Manette'.

Napoléon

Hardy, 1846

"Large, full, bright crimson red, very beautiful." [Gp&f52] "Very large, very double, bright pink shaded purple." [JR9/74] "[A] most abundant bloomer, and a very handsome erect-growing rose." [JC] "Flowers bright rose, shaded with purple, very large and double; the petals large and thick. Habit, erect; growth, robust; foliage, bold and fine. A decided acquisition." [P] One sees the breeder's name "Hardy" varied to "Hervez" in one reference, not significantly, methinks (probably from misreading of a handwritten manuscript). Not to be confused with the 1814 Gallica of the same name, which was possibly by Dupont. Napoléon Bonaparte, dynamic figure in French history, lived 1769–1821; to us, perhaps most significant as the divorcer of his Empress Joséphine, who then turned her attentions to other interests—roses, for one …

Narcisse de Salvandy

Parmentier/Van Houtte, 1843

"Medium-sized, double wine-lee red, petal edges yellowish white." [R&M62] "Violet red, medium size, full, average height." [Sn] "Again, one of Louis Parmentier's obtentions—that indefatigable breeder whose happy efforts we have noted in our article on the Pimpinellifolia rose 'Marbrée d'Enghien' [*q.v.*]. Here again is one of the many joys which he kept to himself, and which only his death enabled to be brought to the attention of the horticultural public. This time, we have a new Provins rose, a variety with a striping of a sort all its own, and which I have had the good luck to pick up in one of the lots from the celebrated collection from Enghien … Description. Bush of vigorous growth, with upright canes clothed with numerous small, straight, brown thorns; leaves with five leaflets of a beautiful intense green, blossoms pretty big, with six or eight rows of petals of a bright red, bordered all the way round with a cream white band; this band goes to the middle of the petal, and often cuts it in two down to the nub; stamens of a beautiful yellow, visible in the center of the blossom; ovary? … [*sic*]" [V-H50–51]

Nationale Tricolore   Listed as 'La Nationale' (G).

Néala

Vibert, 1822

"Crimson lilac." [V9] "Lilac crimson." [BJ40] "*Flower* medium sized, full, very regular, semi-globular, violet-purple or wine-lee with pale edges." [Pf] "Flowers deep rose, paler at their circumference, of medium size, full." [P]

Négretienne   Listed as 'Subnigra' (G).

Negrette   Listed as 'Subnigra' (G).

Nero   Listed as 'Néron' (G).

Néron

syn. 'Nero'

Laffay, 1841

"Violet crimson, prettily shaped, and very double." [WRP] "Blossom crimson red marbled violet blue, medium-sized, full." [S] "Me-

Néron *continued*

dium-sized, full, violet crimson, spotted." [V8] "Medium size, crimson, violet blue, marbled." [R&M62] "Violet red, medium size, full, tall." [Sn] "Flowers chocolate, marbled with slate, their centre red sprinkled with chocolate spots, of medium size, full; form, cupped, the lower petals often turning back the flowers before falling, becoming inversely cupped. Habit, branching; growth, vigorous. A singular and beautiful variety." [P] Néron, alias Nero, Roman emperor, lived A.D. 37–68; made music to an enflamed crowd.

Nestor
Vibert, 1834

"Large, full, crimson." [V8] "Flowers large, full, crimson red." [JR1/8/11] In the inventory of the rosarium at L'Haÿ, we see reference made to an otherwise unknown "Flesh, tinted" Gallica of this name, attributed to "Cochet, 1896." Nestor, king of Pylos, aged advisor to the Greeks at Troy.

Nigrette Listed as 'Subnigra' (G).

Nigritiana Listed as 'Superbe en Brun' (G).

Noire Listed as 'Hector' (G). See also 'Rosier Noir' (G).

[Noire Couronnée]
syn. 'Gaillarde Marbrée'; trans. 'Crowned Black'
Dupont, pre-1810

"Narrow wavy *leaflets* often touched yellow; *ovary* globular, often glabrous at the tip; *sepals* short, pointed, three with appendages; *flower* large or medium-sized, very double, velvety, purple violet marbled crimson red." [Pf] "Grown at Du Pont's, mentioned by Redouté." [Gx]

Noire de Hollande Listed as 'Subnigra' (G).

Noire Pourpre Panachée Listed as 'Ombre Panachée' (G).

Nouveau Intelligible
trans. "New Intelligible"
Breeder unknown, pre-1811

"Wood slender, leaves small, oval, very bullate. Calyx and bud round and inflated. Blossom three inches across [ca. 7.5 cm], a beautiful deep violet, quite double and fragrant, blooming [around June 10]." [C-T]

Nouveau Monde
syn. 'Grande Brune'; trans. "New World"
Breeder unknown, pre-1811

"Wood strong and vigorous, nearly thornless. Leaves oval, dark green, glaucous beneath, largely dentate; they bend back onto their stem. Calyx and bud large and round. Flower quite double, purple violet, dark and velvety; petals thick. It has a sweet, pleasant scent, and opens around June 10." [C-T] Possibly by Descemet.

Nouveau Rouge
trans. "New Red"
Breeder unknown, pre-1811

"Cerise." [Ÿ] "Wood delicate; leaves nearly round, finely dentate, a nice green. Calyx and bud round, nearly glabrous. Blossom the same size as [*that of 'De Meaux'*] . . . , having a sweet fragrance; very double, having a pretty form; beautiful sparkling purple red. It could be

regarded as perfect in its group." [C-T] The name of this cultivar is possibly 'Nouveau Rouge, Pourpre, et Noir', which we will suppress, pending verification.

Nouveau Vulcain
trans. "New 'Vulcain'"
Breeder unknown, pre-1885

"Blossom medium-sized, full; color, deep violet." [S] "Violet red, medium size, full, medium height." [Sn] The name is very typical of those of the Napoleonic era; it seems there was an old 'Vulcain' that this superseded. We cannot, however, substantiate a date of 1820, which has been suggested. Whatever the case, Vulcain, alias Vulcan, Roman god of fire and the forge.

[Nouvelle Gagnée]
trans. "New Obtention"
Miellez, pre-1813

"Pink." [RG] "Was in Du Pont's nurseries; Desportes got it from Miellez." [Gx] Alas that we have run across no further description of this, which was possibly a Gallica × Centifolia cross.

Nouvelle Pivoine
syns. 'Le Grand Triomphe', 'Pivoine de Lille'; trans. "New 'Pivoine'"
Lille, pre-1818

"Bright and slatey red." [LS] "Slatey violet red." [Ÿ] "Blossoms large, full, violet with a red center." [JR1/8/12] "Beautiful variety with big, globular blossoms of a very bright pink in the center and delicate along the edges." [BJ24] "Perhaps the most beautiful of the Provins roses. The flower is large, double, and a delicate pink which is, however, more intense in the center." [CM] "Blossoms very large and a beautiful red, preferable to those of the old one [*old 'Pivoine'*]— beautiful as they can be." [J-A/570] Pivoine, alias Peony, whether old or new, referring to a certain less rose-like flower form.

Nouvelle Transparente
trans. "New 'Transparente'"
Miellez, 1835

"Large, full, crimson pink." [V8] "Large, full, double, or a rosy crimson hue." [WRP] "Flowers brilliant rosy crimson, large and full." [P] "Transparent" to be understood in the sense of "limpid" or "clear." We have been unable to confirm the suggested date of 1833.

Octavie
Coquerel, pre-1829

"Luminous pink." [Ÿ] "Blossoms full, medium-sized, light pink with pale edges." [AC] "*Flower* medium-sized or large, full, light pink, with pale edges." [Pf] "Flowers light pink, their circumference blush, of medium size, full; form, expanded[.] Habit, branching; growth, robust. A very good Rose." [P] The suggested date of 1800 appears incorrect. Not to be confused with Vibert's *deep* pink Gallica of the same name.

Oeillet Double
trans. "Double Carnation"
Prévost, ca. 1835

"Striped lilac pink." [LS] "Blushing lilac." [Ÿ] We have been unable to verify the introducer and date, as well as a suggested date of 1829. Had Prévost introduced it in that year (or before), it would have been listed in his catalog of that year, or his supplement dating to the next.

Oeillet Flamand

trans. "Flemish Carnation"
Vibert, 1845

"White, striped with red, like a variegated carnation; double." [CA96] "White, striped with rose, like a variegated carnation, double flowers, of medium size; the foliage is very dark." [EL] "Medium-sized, double, flat, striped pink, red, and white." [Gp&f52] "An expanded flower, richly variegated with white and deep rose colored stripes." [WRP] "Pink, striped white, medium size, full, tall." [Sn] "Vigorous bush; blossom pink, plumed with white and light red; medium size, flat, double." [S] "Flowers white, distinctly striped with rose and rosy lilac, large and very double; form, expanded. Habit, erect; growth, moderate . . . A very desirable variety, producing its flowers more frequently true in character than the general run of striped Roses." [P]

Oeillet Parfait   Plate 2

trans. "Perfect Carnation"
Foulard, 1841

"Rose, striped with white and crimson, superb." [MH45/Aug.Ad.3] "Pure white, with petals which are streaked with large crimson-pink bands; the blossoms aren't the largest, but they are perfect in form and color, and—to be sure—count among the finest striped Roses." [R-H63/184] "Medium-sized, full, globular, red plumed lilac white and purple." [JR9/75] "Pink plumed with pure white and crimson, superb." [LF] "Reddish violet, striped purple, medium size, full, medium scent, dwarf." [Sn] "Blush, striped with violet-rose; inferior to ['Oeillet Flamand']." [EL] "Red, striped lilac and purple, of medium size, full, of flat form. Growth dwarf." [GeH] "Medium-sized, full, well-formed, white, plumed with red." [BJ53] "Medium-sized, full, pink, plumed lilac or purple, globular." [V8] "The most constant of the striped ones, never with a unicolored blossom . . . flower medium-sized, lilac and purple." [S] "Flowers pure white, distinctly striped with rosy crimson, the latter colour shaded with purple, of medium size, double; form, cupped. Habit, erect; growth, small. Beautiful when true, like a scarlet bizarre Carnation. Somewhat hybridized, partaking slightly of the Damask." [P]

"[A] hybrid between the Gallica and the Damask and greatly esteemed." [WRP] "Has created quite a sensation in England, and is now advertised at the round price of one guinea. It is beautifully striped, like a Bizarre Carnation, with rose, red and white, is of a fine globular form, and considered one of the best of the group." [Bu] "Very distinct and beautiful." [JC] "Gave most enchanting violet-shaded, tight little flowers like expensive French roses in the days of picture hats, but the bush is erratic and shy." [ARA28/64] "The rose 'Oeillet Parfait' . . . has always been considered as belonging to the Damasks. This classification constitutes an error, because our pretty variety has more of an affinity with the Provins than with any other form of the family. Its ovary is relatively short in comparison with that of the Damask Rose, which is much elongated. The multi-floral inflorescence of this latter differs completely from that of 'Oeillet Parfait', which should be considered unifloral, because rarely is it pluri-floral, except on the very vigorous canes; its leaflets, more rounded than those of the rose from Syria [i.e., Rosa ×damascena], its growth, its form—in a word, its look, all resemble those of the Gallica type. 'Oeillet Parfait' is certainly the non-remontant rose having the most constant striping, and never have I seen or heard of it producing uni-colored blossoms." [JR3/168] "Would seem to be a development of Rosa gallica rather than of Rosa damascena; at least, the short description given of it comes closer to the former. Monsieur Verdier says that it can be had of Monsieur Foulard, a fancier in Le Mans. This variety is considered to be the most beautiful among the striped ones. We are given the following particulars: bush not very vigorous, with numerous fine thorns; bark often tinted purple at the tip of the growth (this is much more characteristic of R. gallica than of R. damascena, which has large, unequal thorns); sepal tube rounded (elongate in the Damask); sepals short (very long and curved in the Damask). This flower would seem to be one of the best of the sort." [SRh50/55] "Superb." [Gp&f52]

Officinalis

syns. 'Pourpre', 'Pourpre Semi-Double'; trans. "Performing an office" [in other words, it's useful!]
Breeder unknown, ca. 1200?

"Purple red." [Y̆] "Semi-double . . . large, a pretty intense light red." [CM] "Medium-sized, double, scarlet red." [JR9/74] "The pale red one, R. officinalis, is grown abundantly around Paris and Provins for the uses of perfumery and medicine." [BJ17] "Bush about 0.9 m high [nearly 3 ft]; prickles weak, sparse, unequal, almost straight. Leaflets acute ovate, denticulate; petioles hispid, glandular, with small hooked prickles; stipules acute, denticulate, glandular. Flowers semi-double, notable for their size and fine purplish red petals; pedicels 1–2 together at the branch tips, hispid; receptacles ovoid, glandular hairy at the base; sepals 3 pinnatifid and 2 entire. Although a native of southern France, this rose seems to dislike too warm a site in our gardens. The soil in which it is grown affects the size of the blooms. This is the rose grown principally for use in pharmaceuticals—from it is made syrup and conserves." [T&R] "Rose, with globular seed-buds; the flowers are large, red, and astringent; peduncles hispid; the stem and petioles hispidly prickly; the leaflets are nearly egg-shaped, and villous beneath. This large grand Rose is both useful as well as ornamental. The flowers are used in medicine (whence its term officinal) in preference to many other restoratives. By the Arabian physicians, they were in great estimation for their mild astringent and corroborant virtues, most particularly in phthisical cases. The flowers cannot be too quickly dried, as slowly drying of them impairs both their colour and quality. They are prepared as a conserve, by an infusion of honey. The bloom is but of short duration, but the succession is rapid. It is of a semi-double character, and of a fine red colour; from three to four feet high [ca. 1–1.33 m], and very bushy. It is in great perfection during the months of June, July, and August, and is extremely beautiful. Its foliage is rather rough and coarse, and when out of bloom in the autumn it is very subject to mildew." [A] Cf. 'Purpurine de France' (G).

Ohl

Hardy, 1838?

"Shaded lake." [MH50/421] "Large blossom, with large petals, a beautiful deep crimson." [An42/328] "Violet, red center." [Y̆] "Flower large, full, violet-y bright carmine red, superb." [Gp&f] "Flowers large, very full, well formed, violet purple with a bright red center." [JR1/8/12] "Velvety-crimson, colour very rich and beautiful, flowers large and finely shaped." [JC] "Violet pink, medium size, very full, tall." [Sn] "Flowers violet purple, their centre brilliant red, large and full. Habit,

Ohl *continued*

branching; growth, robust. A fine show Rose." [P] We cannot verify the dates 1830 or 1838 sometimes given; at any rate, it is pre-1842.

Oleifolia

Dieck, 1900

"Deep pink, large, very full, tall." [Sn]

Ombre Panachée

syn. 'Noire Pourpre Panachée'; trans. "Plumed [*i.e., 'Multicolored'*] Darkness"

Breeder unknown, pre-1811

"Dark purple." [Cal] "Velvety purple." [Ÿ] "Wood vigorous and strong, tending towards brown. Leaves long, well formed, and regularly dentate. Calyx and round buds barely covered. Flower four inches or more across [ca. 1 dm +], acceptably double, very fragrant, beautifully colored velvety purple, tending towards black; petals thick, some of them folding back, as with ['Panachée Superbe'], which, by mixing with those in a natural position, make this rose multicolored. This is one of the most beautiful sorts you can grow, particularly due to its size." [C-T] Note that 4 in or 1 dm was considered attractively large in 1811.

Ombre Superbe

syns. 'Pourpre Noir', 'Sanguineo-Purpurea Atra'; trans. "Superb Darkness"

Holland, pre-1811

"Dark purple." [Cal] "Black purple." [LS] "Red." [Ÿ] "An old black rose (so called), but not so dark colored as many of its class, being only a deep shaded purple." [WRP] "Flowers flat, sparkling purple changing to black. Calyx much winged and glandulose on the back. Ovary globulose. Leaves nearly ovoid, dark green … This rose is double, and its petals are a sparkling purple changing to black. The pistils and the filaments of the stamens are sulphur-colored, and the anthers are golden. The calyx is pinnatifid. The globular ovary, fat and bestrewn with glands, narrows gradually towards the peduncle, which is also glandulose, and which it joins without any constriction. The leaves are composed of three to five lobes of a dark green, nearly ovoid and terminating in a sharp point. The stem is armed with medium spines. After a careful comparison, I suspect that this rose, also commonly called the black rose—and which shouldn't be confused with ['Holoserica Multiplex']—is a double variety of the single velvety rose [*presumably 'Holoserica'*]." [Rsg] "Variety of the Provins or Provence; wood, thorns, and leaves those of its class; the flowers are no more than three and a half inches across [ca. 9 cm], double; they are well seconded by their leaves and buds, which come in sevens or eights on each peduncle, well crowned by the extended part of the calyx, which is fairly unusual in this group. The blossom is double, a beautiful purple black in which several petals have white nuances on one side of the blossom, a characteristic peculiar to this variety; the central petals cover the few remaining stamens. This is a true fancier's flower. They open the 5–10 of June." [LeR] "Came from Holland, says Desportes; described by Guerrapain." [Gx]

Ombrée Parfaite

trans. "Perfect Shaded-One"

Vibert, 1823

"Medium-sized, full, violet, nuanced." [V8] "*Flowers*, streaked in

regular stripes of pure white on the sides of the petals." [Go] "Full double, of medium size, and violet shaded." [WRP] "Flowers medium-sized, full, variable violet." [JR1/8/12] "*Flower* medium-sized, full, regular, umbrageous violet purple." [Pf]

Omphale

Vibert, 1839

"Roseate, spotted." [WRP] "Pink, spotted." [Ÿ] "Medium-sized, full, spotted pink." [R&M62] "Flowers rosy pink, sometimes spotted with white, large and very double; form, cupped. Habit, erect; growth, moderate. The ground colour of this Rose is sweetly pretty and distinct." [P] Not to be confused with Vibert's "pale rose" [Cal] Gallica of the same name of 1820. Omphale, queen of Lydia, much involved with Hercules; the depth and breadth of Vibert's knowledge of classical mythology is remarkable.

Ornement de Carafe   Listed as 'Ornement de Parade' (G).

Ornement de la Nature

syns. 'Anémone Ancienne', 'Rose Anémone'; trans. "Nature's Ornament"

Holland, pre-1813

"Deep rose." [Cal] "Lilac pink." [LS] "Violet pink, large, full, tall." [Sn] "*Flower* small, regular, quite double, hypocrateriform, light lilac pink. The stolons of this rose are usually flat and palmate before appearing above ground." [Pf] "Grown by Du Pont, who received it from Holland under this name; mentioned by Redouté; according to Prévost, called 'Rose Anémone' at Rouen." [Gx]

[Ornement de Parade]

syn. 'Ornement de Carafe'; trans. "Parade Ornament," which one might guess implies that, in the succession or "parade" of roses, this constitutes an ornament

Holland, pre-1811

"Deep pink." [BJ40] "Bright red." [Cal] "Blossoms purple, very double." [BJ30] "Beautiful and numerous blush white blossoms in a cluster." [J-A/570] "Blossoms numerous, purple, very double, in corymbs." [No26, on 'Ornement de Carafe'] "Large, semi-double, violet purple." [No26, on 'Ornement de Parade'] "*Flower* medium-sized, full, regular, light or deep pink." [Pf] "Gives blossoms which are at least three inches across [ca. 7.5 cm] when fully open." [CM] "Its wood is nearly thornless, particularly on those branches bearing flowers. The leaves are oval and deeply toothed. The calyx is large, green, inflated, and slightly constricted at the tip. The bud is round and barely covered [*i.e., by the sepals*]. The growth bud is very protrusive. The blossom is the color of that of 'Junon' [*i.e., 'beautiful deep pink'*]; in form, it resembles that of the *Agathes* [*i.e., flat and compact, like a cockade*], but it is larger. This rose, with a scent both sweet and pleasant, can be counted among the beautiful sorts, and well merits its name. Grafted on the Briar, this bush grows vigorously and forms a nicely rounded head." [C-T] "Came from Holland, says Desportes; described by Guerrapain, it was in the nurseries of Du Pont and Godefroy; Prévost also called it 'Ornement de Carafe'." [Gx] Sometimes equated with 'Couronne de Salomon' [*q.v.*].

Orpheline de Juillet

trans. "July [Female] Orphan"

Breeder unknown, pre-1836

"Violet purple." [V4] "Purple red, medium size, very full, tall." [Sn]

"Flowers crimson purple, sombre, the base of the petals fiery red, the latter colour occasionally running out in streaks towards the circumference, large and very double; form, expanded. Habit, erect; growth, moderate. The effect produced by the contrast of colour in this variety is admirable." [P]

Orphèse Listed as 'Orphise' (G).

Orphise
syns. 'Admirable de Lille', 'Orphèse', 'Rouge Admirable'
Vibert, pre-1826

"Purple crimson." [GJB] "Purple, nuanced." [BJ40] "*Flower* large, full, symmetrical, light purple, sometimes deep pink." [Pf] See also 'Pourpre Charmant' (G).

Palais de Laeken Listed as 'Grand Palais de Laeken' (G).

Pale Rouge Panaché Listed as 'Belle Aimable' (G).

Pâle Rouge Superbe Listed as 'Bouquet Charmante' (G).

Pallas
syn. 'Reine des Pourpres'
Miellez, pre-1811

"Blossom large, full, purple." [S] "This rose well merits the name it has been given because of its size, form, and rich color. Its wood is armed with numerous brown prickles which are flexible and not very sharp. Its long leaves are dark green. The calyx is oval, and constricted from top to bottom. The bud is round, and barely covered. The very double, stamenless blossom is at least as large as that of 'Pourpre Charmant', but not quite as dark. It blooms later; it has a sweet, pleasant scent. It is one of the beauties, and one of the big ones!" [C-T] "When it is opening, its petals are charged with purple. Its perfume is delicious, which is rare in this sort. Wood, thorns, leaves, and nearly naked buds [are all] those of the Gallica. Opens June 19–20." [LeR] Pallas, an epithet for the redoubtable goddess Athena.

Panaché Listed as 'Rosa Mundi' (G).

Panaché Double Listed as 'Belle Villageoise' (G).

Panachée Superbe
trans. 'Superb Plumed One'
Holland, pre-1811

"Dark red." [Cal] "Velvety purple." [Ÿ] "*Flowers,* full, small, very regular; of a deep pink; very early, being the first-blowing of the Provins roses." [Go] "The wood and leaves of this rose have nothing of the unusual, nor do its calyxes or buds; but the double flower, some three inches across [ca. 7.5 cm], has a beautiful form. The top surface of the petals is a very dark velvety purple; beneath, they tend towards a beautiful red; some of them fold back naturally, making a beautiful contrast in the mix of the two colors, a distinctive characteristic of this rose. It's a true fancier's flower, because of its color; what is more, it has a very nice perfume. It blooms around June 10." [C-T] The name 'Panachée Superbe' is also a synonym of 'Beauté Insurmontable' (G), *q.v.*

Paquita
Breeder unknown, pre-1841

"Flowers violet, large and full." [P] "Flowers medium-sized or

large, full, well-formed, violet-ish." [JR1/8/12] "Bright pink." [Ÿ] We cannot confirm the suggested date of pre-1838.

Parvifolia Listed as 'Pompon de Bourgogne' (G).

Passe-Princesse
Prévost, pre-1813

"Rose." [Cal] "*Flowers*, full, very large; of a light lilac-pink." [Go] "Grown by Du Pont, mentioned by Desportes." [Gx] Possibly synonymous with 'Great Royal' (G).

Passe-Velours
syn. 'La Grande Obscurité'
Descemet, pre-1820

"Dark purple." [Cal] "Deep violet." [V9] "Brown crimson." [LS] "Flowers of the fullest, very beautiful—and hardly different from 'Grande Pompadour' [*see 'Pourpre Charmant'*]—if indeed there is any difference at all." [J-As/63] "*Flower* medium-sized, double, very velvety, brown-purple or deep purple. *Petals* very thick, darker at the tip than at the base." [Pf] "Raised by Descemet, mentioned by Desportes; called 'Grande Obscurité' at Rouen, according to Prévost." [Gx] We have been unable to substantiate the pre-1813 date sometimes suggested for this cultivar.

[Pelletier]
Pelletier, ca. 1825

"*Shrub* very floriferous. *Flowers* early, medium-sized, full, symmetrical, pale pink." [Pf] See also 'Fleurs de Pelletier' (G).

Pepita
F. Moreau, ca. 1850?

"Delicate pink." [LS] We have been unable to verify the attribution or date of this cultivar.

[Perle de l'Orient]
syn. 'Carmin Liseré'; trans. "Pearl of the Orient"
Schwarzkopf/Godefroy, pre-1811

"Dark purple." [Cal] "Orangey bluish red." [BJ30] "Flowers a slightly orange-ish red." [No26] "*Flower* medium-sized, full (often only double in own-root specimens), symmetrical, purple red with edges nuanced violet." [Pf] "The second [*Perle*] was given me under the name 'Perle de l'Orient'. Its wood and leaves have the same characteristics as those of ['Perle de Weissenstein']. The flower's calyx is longer. The bud is round, and covered over [*by the sepals*]. The very fragrant blossom is well formed and delicate pink in color. The petals are veined darker pink. They [*i.e., the "Perles"*] can be counted as among those which merit cultivation." [C-T] "Wood, thorns, and leaves those of its sister ['Perle de Weissenstein']. Calyx longer, buds much overtopped by the calyx appendages. Blossom double, well formed, delicate pink. Petals veined with more intense pink. Well scented, a marked characteristic of these two pretty hybrids. Opens June 5–10." [LeR]

Perle de Vaseingtein Listed as 'Perle de Weissenstein' (G).

Perle de Weissenstein
trans. "Pearl of Weissenstein"
Schwarzkopf, 1773

"Dark rose." [Cal] "Brown, purple center." [LS] "Deep purple veined brown." [Ÿ] "I'll describe some varieties which come close to the Centifolias in form and color, such as the *Perles*, of which there are two

Perle de Weissenstein *continued*

sorts. The first is called 'Perle de Vaseingtein' [*sic*]. Its wood is be-strewn with very small, straight, brown stickers. Its leaves are long, dark green, finely dentate, and borne on a green petiole. The calyx is round, and covered over [*i.e., by the sepals*]. The blossom is medium-sized and well-formed; the petals are wavy and light brown veined darker brown." [C-T] "The leaves are elongate, dark green, and borne on a light green petiole ... of medium size, well formed, double, light brown veined darker brown; the petals are crinkled. This sub-vari-ety of the Gallicas is new and charming. Opens June 5–10." [LeR, mixing up the two Schwarzkopf Perles in his listings] Weissenstein, Germany, home base for Schwarzkopf.

Perle des Panachées
trans. "Pearl of the Plumed Ones"
Vibert, 1845

"Very double, white, variegated with lilac and pale violet, exceed-ingly beautiful. The present [1846] price at Paris is $4, it being quite new." [WRP] "7 cm [ca. 2¾ in], plumed with lilac or pale violet, very beautiful." [VPt48/app] "Medium-sized, full, globular, ground of white plumed lilac and pale violet." [JR9/75] "Growth vigorous." [GeH] "Flowers white, striped with rose-colour, the marking very clear and distinct, of medium size, full; form, expanded. Habit, erect; growth, moderate ... One of the best of the striped Roses." [P]

Petite Chalons   Listed as 'Pompon de Bourgogne' (G).

Petite Louise   Listed as 'Belle Mignonne' (G).

Petite Orléanaise
trans. "Small One from Orléans"
Breeder unknown, pre-1843

"Flowers small or medium-sized, very full, beautiful pink." [JR1/8/12] "Pink, medium size, very full, average height." [Sn]

Petite Provins   Listed as 'Rosier d'Amour' (G).

Petite St. François   Listed as 'Pompon de Bourgogne' (G).

Phénice
syn. 'Phénix'
Vibert, 1843

"Cherry spotted, roseate centre." [WRP] "Pink, plumed carmine." [LS] "Flowers reddish rose, spotted, of medium size, full." [P] "Blossom medium-sized, full; color, delicate pink, spotted carmine." [S] "Medi-um-sized, full, red-pink, spotted, in a rosette." [V8] Phénice, alias the Phoenix, mythical bird whose interesting habits give us the phrase "to rise from the ashes."

Phénix   Listed as 'Phénice' (G), but see also 'Beauté Insurmontable' (G).

Phoebus
Breeder unknown, 1818

"Red." [Cal] "Bright pink." [Ÿ] *Cf.* the "lilac-blush" Damask of the same name. Phoebus, alias Apollo, Olympian in charge of (among other matters) the Arts.

Phoenix   Listed as 'Beauté Insurmontable' (G).

Pintade
syn. 'Meleagris'; trans. "Guinea-Fowl"
Loiseleur-Deslongchamps, pre-1817

"Pink, spotted white." [RG] "Mentioned by Redouté, it's the *Gallica Meleagris* of the Nouveau Duhamel." [Gx]

Pivoine
Synonym shared by 'Bourbon' (G) and 'Great Royal' (G), *qq.v.* See also 'Nouvelle Pivoine' (G).

Pivoine de Jéricho   Listed as 'Bourbon' (G).

Pivoine de Lille   Listed as 'Nouvelle Pivoine' (G).

Pivoine des Hollandais   Listed as 'Great Royal' (G).

Pivoine Mauve   Listed as 'Bourbon' (G).

Pluton
syns. 'Pulton', 'Rose Pluton', 'Rose Pulton'
Breeder unknown, pre-1799

"Blackish purple." [LS] "Very deep purple." [Ÿ] "Medium-sized, full, very deep violet, the darkest." [R&M62] "Illustrated by Miss Lawrance." [Gx] Pluton, alias Pluto, alias Hades, alias God of the Dead; his realm is no doubt "very deep violet, the darkest."

Pompon
syns. 'Pompon Panachée', 'Pompon Robert'
Robert & Moreau, 1857

"Pink plumed with white." [JDR57/37] "4–5 cm [ca. 1¾ in], full, bright pink plumed with white and lilac, green pip at the center, vig-orous." [R&M62] Not to be confused with 'Pompon-Marbré', a Moss of the same year.

Pompon Cramoisi   Listed as 'Pompon de Bourgogne' (G).

Pompon de Bourgogne
syns. 'Burgundiaca', 'Burgundica', 'Button', 'Cramoisi', 'Dwarf Burgundy', 'Dwarf Red Rose', 'Gilloflower Rose', 'Parvifolia', 'Petite Chalons', 'Petite St. François', 'Pompon Cramoisi', 'Pompon St. François', 'Pompone', 'Remensis', 'Shell'; trans. "Pompon from Burgundy"
Breeder unknown, pre-1629

"[A] bright rosy pink of very neat form." [Bu] "Very small and pretty, rose colored, and full double." [WRP] "Light purple." [V9] "Flow-ers deep red, very small and double; form, cupped. Growth, small." [P] "A beautiful miniature shrub, adorns the fertile valleys in the neighbourhood of Dijon with its very-double but small, solitary, crimson blossoms." [Go] "The Burgundy Rose has very double blos-soms, charming in form and beauty; it should be chosen over oth-ers." [C'H] "At its greatest height, it's no more than a foot tall [ca. 3 dm]; but it makes a pretty bush on which the flowers, quite full though pe-tite and charming in form, resemble glowing pompons. By their number, they give the whole bush the grace and sparkle of an elegant bouquet. It has a stable variety, with blossoms which are deep pur-ple at the center, and lighter at the edges of the corolla, which is called *Rosier Pompon Pourpre* or 'Rosier Nain de Champagne' and which looks good with it, remaining its rival without either harming it or losing anything itself." [Fr] "The crimson one [*i.e., pompon rose*], also called Saint-François, can't be confused with any other—there's no mistaking it! It is good to mention in regard to this rose that if you want a display of flowers, it's necessary to refrain from pruning it in the spring, because it always bears them [*blossoms*] at the tips of the canes; you'd lose them that year. If this operation is necessary, to rejuvenate the bush, it should be done as soon as the bloom is past. This rose makes very pretty borders because it keeps its leaves nearly all year and takes well to the clippers." [C-T] "This rose is found at the Trianon and in several nurseries, and looks exactly like the Gallica in all characteristics. It is the smallest of pompons; it is only known as a double; its blossom is violet purple. Grafted on the Briar, it makes an attractive head which covers itself with blossoms in July." [AC] "On its own roots, the 'Pompon de Bourgogne' looks very pretty in pots, though it only lasts there for two years. After this length of time, it is necessary to put it out in the open ground. It is pruned after bloom to make new wood. This is the reason it is only effective for two years when it is grafted on a stem—because you can't make it produce a nice 'head' there." [BJ24] "A small bush of a thing; thorns rare, short, and nearly equal; leaflets rough, oval-acute, finely dentate; sepals oval; in June, a large number of small light purple blossoms, very double; some terminal, others overtopped by the young canes. It is found in Portugal, and this is probably why it's called the *Rose from Portugal*, though this name more especially pertains to a Centifolia variety which the English call 'Lisbon Rose'." [BJ30] "This Rose groweth always low and small, otherwise in most respects like vnto the ordinary redde Rose, and with few or no thornes vpon it: the Flowers or Roses are double, thicke, small and close, not so much spread open as the ordinary red ... yet in some places I haue seene them more layde open then these, as they grew in my garden, being so euen at the toppes of the leaues [*petals*], as if they had been clipt off with a pair of sheeres, and are not so fully of so red a colour as the red Prouince Rose, and of small or weak s[c]ent as the ordinary red Rose, or not so much." [PaSo] "Known around 1620. In the Middle Ages [*which we might note preceded 1620*], the people of Italy and eastern France believed it had sprung from the earth on the spot where St. Francis of Assisi [*lived 1182–1226*] underwent self-mortification in the dead of winter." [ExRé]

"This beautiful Dwarf Rose is certainly a very distinct species, and generally known by the appellation of Burgundy Rose. It is an early-blooming Rose, and makes a brilliant appearance. The flowers are very double, of a rich red purple when in perfection, but of a paler or bluer colour when retiring. It is very easily distinguished from any other dwarf Rose, by the striking resemblance which it bears to the Ranunculus, and from which a good specific name might have been derived, had not the leaves (ever the most important characteristic) furnished an unexceptional title [*Parvifolia*], recently adopted by professor Willdenow in his *Specie[s]-Plantarum*." [A] "Stems nearly glabrous, thin, short, branched, and upright; leaves with 5–7 leaflets, small, villose beneath and along the edges; blossoms double, small, but charming and the prettiest pink. There's as double a variety with purple red flowers—the *pourpre de Bourgogne* of gardeners. You can see another variety, white, at Monsieur Noisette's." [BJ17] "Varieties. Flower growers distinguish three: one with double flowers, called 'Pompon de Paris'; another, with white blossoms, can be found in the collection of Monsieur Noisette; and, finally, the third, with large purple flowers." [CM]

"Flowers double, small, dark crimson. Ovary half-ovoid. Calyx segments divided. Peduncles smooth. Petioles lanate above, bristly beneath. Stem and canes with few prickles ... The blossoms of this rose, which are small, double, and deep crimson, have a little of the form of a Ranunculus, and come out at the end of May and beginning of June. The calyx segments have, along their edges, inside, and on their backs, a light tomentum; three of them have two or three filiform appendages along the edge, and foliaceous appendages at the tip. The ovary, which is half-oval, smooth, and light green, joins the same-colored peduncle without constriction—sometimes it's a little reddish and bears glandular hairs; it is solitary. The leaves are composed of three, five, and sometimes seven sessile lobes, slightly rough to the touch, finely dentate at an angle, dark green, without any gloss above; a light matte green beneath, veins evident. The petioles, having short bristles, are bristly here and there on the underside, and have medium-sized, lacy stipules terminating in a point which is short and straight; edged with small glands. There are only a few solitary prickles on the stem and branches. It seems that there are two varieties of this rose—one is bigger, with larger, more expanded leaves and flowers; the other is smaller, and has some flowers in which the petals press on each other in a confused way. Its name tells the land of its birth." [Rsg] "*Shrub* dwarf, forming a thick bush. *Canes* thin, straight, fastigiate, armed at their base with small sparse thorns which are straight or slightly curved and intermingled with several bristles; at their tip, they are smooth or bestrewn with several small prickles. *Leaves* very small, grayish-green. *Petiole* villose, glandulose, armed beneath with several small prickles. *Stipules* narrow, long, with a short, erect point; edged with glands. *Leaflets* 5–7, rarely 3, stiff, flat, oblong-lanceolate, acute, rarely oval, glabrous above, pale beneath, and pubescent along the mid-vein, which forms a ridge and is glandulose. *Serration* fine, even, very acute, lanate, and usually glandulose. *Peduncles* erect, bestrewn with several glands; often coming in 3's. *Bracts* nearly always in the form of the stipule, and terminating in 1 or 3 leaflets. *Ovary* oval or slightly digitate, usually glabrous and glaucous, often purplish. *Sepals* short, sub-pubescent; 3 are appendiculate. *Bud* rounded. *Flower* very small, full, light purple, ordinarily lacking scent. *Styles* 25–40, free. I readily join in the opinion of the people who think that there are nearly as many reasons to put this among the *Gallicas* as there are to put it among the *Centifolia Pompons*." [Pf]

[Pompon de Bourgogne à Fleurs Blanches]

trans. "'Pompon de Bourgogne' with White Flowers"
Mauget, 1827

"Very small rose with pure white petals, flesh at the center, with a pretty look." [An42/328] "Flowers white, their centre pink, very glossy, very small and very double; form, cupped. A pretty Rose." [P] As we see in our entry on 'Pompon de Bourgogne', there was, at least as early as 1817, another (?) white 'Pompon de Bourgogne'.

Pompon Panachée Listed as 'Pompon' (G).

Pompon Robert Listed as 'Pompon' (G).

Pompon St. François Listed as 'Pompon de Bourgogne' (G).

Pompone Listed as 'Pompon de Bourgogne' (G).

Ponctuée Listed as 'Belle Herminie' (G).

Pontiana Listed as 'Rouge Formidable' (G).

Porcia Listed as 'Rouge Formidable' (G).

Pourpre Listed as 'Officinalis' (G).

Pourpre Ardoisée Listed as 'Busard Triomphant' (G).

Pourpre Charmant
syns. 'Grande Pompadour', 'L'Archévêque', 'La Magnifique', 'Rouge
    Admirable'; trans. "Charming Purple"
Breeder unknown, pre-1811
"Purple." [Cal] "Deep purple." [LS] "Deep pink or purple." [Ÿ] "Blossoms medium-sized, very double, sparkling purple, color even and
velvety." [BJ24] "*Flower* large, double, velvety, bright purple." [Pf]
"Looks a lot like 'Manteau Pourpre', but the flowers are very double,
medium-sized, numerous, sparkling purple of an even and very velvety color." [CM] "Blooms a lot." [dP] "Very numerous blossoms; old
variety which maintains its primitive character." [BJ30] "Deep purple
red, large, lightly double, average height." [Sn] "This plant, by the
beauty of its coloration and the rich velvetiness of its petals, etc., still
produces 'mirages' and, particular, a rich synonymy." [J-As/63] "The
wood, leaves, calyx, and bud aren't remarkable at all; but the flowers,
largest of the sort, grow three to four inches across [ca. 7.5 cm to 1
dm]; its petals are large, thick, bright, and a beautiful velvety purple;
they have a sweet scent. This variety, grafted on the Briar, makes a
very nice 'head' which gives many blossoms. It is also known under
the name 'Archévêque'." [C-T] "Very characteristic wood and leaves of
the Provins; thorns short; buds large, inflated, nude, seven to eight
per peduncle, which divides into long pediculate pedicels which are
pretty strong but which however have difficulty bearing the weight
of these blossoms, which are the fullest and largest of this copious
group. They resemble some Peony; the petals are large, thick, and not
raggedy; a beautiful deep purple—but when the sun animates them,
they become velvety violet. Their perfume is sweet and pleasant. You
should bud them high. By its profusion, this rose should be considered as one of the ravishing works of God. It blooms from June 5–10."
[LeR] "This variety, described by De Pronville and mentioned by Redouté, was grown by Du Pont." [Gx]

Pourpre Cramoisi Listed as 'Rouge Formidable' (G).

Pourpre Marbrée
syns. 'Arlequin', 'Bizarre Changeant'; trans. "Marbled Purple"
Paillard?, pre-1821
"Violet purple." [LS] *Flower* small or medium-sized, very full,
bluish violet purple, marbled." [Pf] See also 'Arlequin' (G).

Pourpre Noir Listed as 'Ombre Superbe' (G).

Pourpre Rouge Listed as 'Temple d'Apollon' (G).

Pourpre Semi-Double Listed as 'Officinalis' (G).

Président de Sèze
syn. 'Mme. Hébert'
Hébert, 1828
"Violet pink." [LS] "Flowers pretty numerous, large, very double,
well formed, cupped when just opening, then rather plumpish, in a corymb. Petals a violet pink in the middle, lilac-y at the edge, much folded in the center, slightly notched." [No35] "*Shrub*, vigorous. *Branches*,
straight. *Thorns*, not much curved, numerous. *Leaflets*, five in number; lanceolated or oblong, regularly toothed, pale green. *Flowers*, of
a lilac-pink in the centre, paler at the circumference; very double, nu-

merous, well formed; first cup-shaped, afterwards convex, growing in
clusters. *Petals*, well arranged at the edges, rumpled in the centre." [Go]

Prince d'Arenberg Listed as 'Duc d'Arenberg' (G).

Prince Frédéric
Parmentier, ca. 1840
"Flowers large, very full, beautiful form, bright red." [JR1/8/12]
"Tall." [Sn]

Princesse de Nassau
Miellez, 1840?
"Deep pink." [LS]

Princesse de Portugal
Pelletier, pre-1828
"*Flower* very large, full, bright cerise pink. In the shade, or in
damp and cold seasons, some of the blossoms abort." [Pf] Sometimes
classed as a Damask.

[Princesse Éléonore]
Miellez, pre-1826
"Flowers large, double, well formed, a crimson red. Wood nearly
thornless." [No26]

Provins Ancien
trans. "Old Gallica"
P. Cochet, pre-1906
"Light pink." [LS]

Provins Double Listed as 'L'Évêque' (G).

Provins Marbré Listed as 'Marmorea' (G).

Provins Oeillet Listed as 'Rosa Mundi' (G).

Pucelle de Lille
syns. 'La Pucelle', 'Théagène'; trans. "'Pucelle' from Lille" [differenti-
    ating it from Dubourg's 'La Pucelle', *q.v.*]
Miellez, pre-1828
"Dark red." [RG] "Deep pink, nuanced." [Ÿ] "Blossoms deep purple,
very full and regular." [BJ30] "*Flower* medium-sized or large, full, regular, very bright purple-pink." [Pf] "Deep pink, medium size, full, average height." [Sn]

Pulmonaire Listed as 'La Maculée' (G).

Pulton Listed as 'Pluton' (G).

Pumila Listed as 'Rosier d'Amour' (G).

Punctata Listed as 'Belle Herminie' (G).

Purpurea Listed as 'Purpurine de France' (G).

Purpurea Velutina Parva Listed as 'De Van Eeden' (G).

Purpureo-Violaceo Magna Listed as 'L'Évêque' (G).

[Purpurine de France]
syn. 'Purpurea'
Breeder unknown, pre-1770
"Its stems, nearly thornless, grow straight upright to three or four
feet high [ca. 1–1.33 m]. Its leaves are comprised of 3 or 5 large oval
leaflets, pubescent beneath. The small sepals are completely undi-

vided, while the flowers are quite fragrant, rather more semi-double than completely double, [and] are of a very brilliant purple-red. But this passes quickly, and it can be said that their perfect beauty lasts no longer than a day. It has two stable varieties: (1), in which the blossom is doubler, tinted bluish red, and lasts longer; and another, called 'Rosa Mundi', in which the very double flower is a dark red washed with pale red." [Fr] "It likes the vicinity of the town of Provins, where it was born." [C'H] Possibly synonymous with 'Officinalis' (G).

Regalis Listed as 'Great Royal' (G).

[Regina Dicta]
syns. 'De la Reine', 'Impériale', 'Koniginrosa'; trans. "Called 'The Queen'"
Breeder unknown, pre-1791
    "Pink." [V9] "The blossoms, of medium size, are a beautiful light violet; the petals are edged white." [CM] "*Flower* medium-sized, full, symmetrical, varying from pink to light purple, often mottled." [Pf] "This rose is so called because its double blossom is often surmounted by another sort of flower which grows from its center, the petals of which seem to form a crown. It is colored a beautiful purple red." [Fr]

Reine de Perse
trans. "Queen of Persia"
Breeder unknown, pre-1825
    "Flowers medium-sized, double, a sparkling red." [No26] "Flowers medium-sized, full, a lightly-blushing white." [JR1/8/12] "Light pink, small to medium size, very full, very fragrant, tall." [Sn]

Reine des Amateurs
trans. "Queen of the Fanciers"
Hébert, pre-1829
    "Lilac-y flesh." [V4] "Delicate pink, double." [BJ40] "Lilac, bordered pale." [LS] "Lilac pink, full, globular, large." [LF] "Flowers large, very full, light lilac pink, graceful form." [JR1/8/12] "Light violet pink, medium size, very full, medium scent, tall." [Sn] "*Canes* armed with thorns which are brown, uneven, slender (the largest, falcate), intermingled with brown bristles. *Leaflets* 5 or 7, deep green, narrow, lanceolate, undulate, glabrous except under the main veins, which are ordinarily pubescent. *Peduncle* glandulose. *Ovary* glabrous, very small, turbinate. *Flower* large, full, regular, globular, lilac pink with pale edges. *Petals* thin, having need of being protected from the intensity of the rays of the sun." [Pfs]

Reine des Nègres Listed as 'Superbe en Brun' (G).

Reine des Pourpres Listed as 'Pallas' (G).

Reine Marguerite Listed as 'Tricolore' (Holland, G).

Remensis Listed as 'Pompon de Bourgogne' (G).

Renoncule
syns. 'Anémone', 'Rose Renoncule'; trans. "Ranunculus"
Cartier/Dupont, pre-1810
    "Deep red." [Cal] "Purple; pretty, small pompon, nearly black." [J-A/568] "Blossoms medium-sized, very double, petals short, close-set, folding back when open, nuanced from violet to bright purple red." [CM, BJ24] "Sometimes these flowers are proliferous, under

which conditions they lose their sparkle." [AC] "Takes its name from being like that flower; it is a great and persistent bloomer, of very double form, showing a profusion of mottled rosy purple flowers all over the plant." [Bu] "Its wood is delicate; its thorns are small, straight, numerous, and brown. The leaves are oval, terminating in an obtuse point, edged pink, and finely dentate. The blossoms are a beautiful light purple, of the size and form of a medium-sized Ranunculus, so double that it seems as if someone has been pleased to attach two flowers to the same stalk, and to press the petals of one upon those of the other. There runs along the edges of these last [*i.e., the petals*] a light white tint which is not disagreeable. Some blossoms also have the makings of new flowers; doubtless, attentive culture would make it proliferous." [C-T] "Placed in our 'Rejected' list of roses three years ago [*making 1843*]." [WRP] "Illustrated in Rössig, described by De Pronville, grown at Du Pont's." [Gx]

Renoncule Noirâtre Listed as 'Roi des Pourpres' (G).

Renoncule Ponctué
trans. "Spotted Ranunculus"
Vibert, 1833
    "Pink, spotted." [V4] "Poppy." [LS] "Red, spotted, compact." [WRP] "Very double, beautifully spotted and marbled with rose, crimson, and white; nothing in the division like it." [Bu] "Medium-sized, full, bright red, spotted and marbled." [BJ53] "Light red, small, full, medium height." [Sn] "Flowers rose, mottled with blush, and often edged with cherry, small and full; form, compact, becoming reflexed before the flowers fall, the petals regularly and closely disposed, Ranunculus-like. Habit, erect; growth, vigorous. A neat and beautiful *little* Rose." [P] "Happily named; for it is much like a ranunculus, both in its form and in the disposition of its colors, and is a peculiar and beautiful variety." [WRP]

Revenante
syn. 'La Revenante'; trans. "Prepossessing"
Miellez, pre-1826
    "Pink." [LS] "Cerise or light pink." [Ÿ]

Roi des Pourpres
syn. 'Renoncule Noirâtre'; trans. "King of the Purples"
Descemet, pre-1817
    "Dark purple." [Cal] "Purple, nuanced." [V9] "Crimson, nuanced." [LS] "Very double, even light red-purple; becomes very intense." [BJ24] "Blossom medium-sized, very full; color, crimson shaded grenadine." [S] "Flowers...very lively in coloring, and very distinct in form." [J-A/568] "Blossoms medium-sized, very double, blooming one after the other for a long time." [dP] "Like 'Gallica' [*i.e., 'Cramoisie'*] in color, and only differing in having larger, doubler blossoms." [CM] "Has some similarity to ['Junon']. Flowers more double and larger, with the same intensity of color." [AC] "Very pretty small pompon, which is a real Gallica in miniature. The buds are round and small, overtopped by the appendages of the calyx, which is unusual in this sort. Its flower, which is only an inch in diameter [ca. 2.5 cm], is very double, well-formed, and a purplish violet brown. This pretty variety is new, and should have some charm for the fancier. It should be grafted at three feet [ca. 1 m]. Opens June 10." [LeR] We cannot substantiate the suggested date of 1800.

Rosa Mundi Plate 1

syns. 'Garnet Striped Rose', 'La Panachée', 'La Villageoise', 'Panaché', 'Provins Oeillet', 'Rosemonde', 'Versicolor'

Breeder unknown, pre-1581

"White lined with red, semi-double, very numerous, but not lasting very long." [BJ24] "*Flower* large, double, plumed-rayed white and deep pink or cerise." [Pf] "Flower rose-red, striped and variegated with white, fragrant. Growth vigorous." [GeH] "Flowers white, striped with carnation, large and semi-double; form, expanded. Habit, branching; growth, moderate. An abundant seed-bearer, and the parent of most of the striped French Roses." [P] "Quite remarkable due to its flowers which are large but not very long-lasting, nearly scentless, of a very light pink with little touches and large plumes of a more or less dark red which cover the bushes entirely in July." [CM] "Has an old-fashioned air reminiscent of the old, candy-striped tulips." [ARA28/64] "It is so well known that it is useless to describe it. I'll only say that it seems to me to be the most fragrant sort." [C-T] "Illustrated by Miss Lawrance and Redouté." [Gx]

"Rose, with globular seed-buds; flowers large, and elegantly striped; peduncles hispid; the stem and petioles are hispid and prickly; the leaflets are nearly egg-shaped, and villose beneath. This elegant Striped variety of the Rosa Gallica is certainly more attractive than its original, the 'Officinalis'. Its fine red striped acquire a comparatively superior brilliance, by their contrast with the white; from which analogous circumstance we believe the name of *Rosa Mundi* has been originally derived from a collateral reference to that celebrated lady in the reign of Henry the Second, commonly called Fair Rosamund (signifying Rose-mouth). Thus, like the Rose, the colour of her lips was heightened by the comparative delicacy of her fair complexion; and which the Author has no doubt will be considered as a fair excuse, however remote or questionable the etymology. Like all other variegated Roses, an exactitude of character is never to be expected; we having sometimes seen it more divided than our figure represents, and at others so much less so as to be nearly one half white, and the other red." [A] "*Bush* 0.6–0.9 m high [ca. 2–3 ft]; *canes* bristling with unequal *prickles*, the longer ones hooked and the shorter ones almost straight. *Leaflets* 7, oblong, acute, rounded at the base, glabrous above, tomentose beneath; glandular on the margins; *petioles* villose, sometimes a little prickly; *stipules* simple, acute, edged with sessile glands. Flowers faintly scented, mostly in threes at the branch tips.; *receptacles* subglobose, hispid; *pedicels* hispid; *bracts* 2, oval, most often leafy and glandular like the stipules; *sepals* short, 3 pinnatifid and 2 simple, acute, downy within, downy mixed with sessile glands on the outside; *corolla* always semi-double, never full; *petals* delicate pink striped with a more or less bright red. *Hips* globose, reddish. The variegations which distinguish this variety often disappear, and it is not rare to see in the same year variegated blossoms followed by those of just one color. This tendency to revert requires that the plant be renewed frequently by grafting. It is known … in England as 'Rosamunde' after the beautiful and intelligent mistress of Henry II … *Rosa gallica versicolor* blooms better in shade than in full sun. It does very well grafted, but own-root shrubs give larger and more brilliant flowers." [T&R]

"The most ancient of this [*striped Gallica*] division, and is a striped sportive variety of the old semi-double red Rosa Gallica, or Official Rose. The flowers are large, boldly striped with bright red and white, and it has been frequently confounded with the 'York and Lancaster', which is a pure Damask, very different in the appearance of its flowers, and entirely distinct in its habit, [*the Damask variety*] being a strong growing plant, and attaining to thrice the height of the present variety. The 'Rosa Mundi' often loses its stripes entirely, and returns to its parent … and where a bed of them is allowed to remain and expand themselves, perhaps four out of five will change to the red variety." [WRP] "This one's a variety of the 'Pivoine de Jéricho' [*i.e.*, 'Bourbon'] (so it isn't the same), which often shows a crimson variegation. These two, along with 'Aigle Brun', could be regarded as the Type of the whole group. It has short wood, like 'Pivoine de Jéricho', but the leaves aren't as dark. Its pointed buds can often be found solitary, producing some pretty large roses much variegated, like Carnations, a white ground with bands … [*one word indecipherable; possibly 'liseré', i.e., 'edged'*] … a more or less deep crimson, semi-double with beautiful stamens which enhance the flower. Its petals are large and thick, and not ragged. It has no scent. This is why you should graft it high as its sister 'Pivoine de Jéricho', with which it blooms at the same time. It is most effective." [LeR]

Rose Anémone Listed as 'Ornement de la Nature' (G). See also 'Renoncule' (G).

Rose Bleu Listed as 'Busard Triomphant' (G).

Rose du Maître d'École Listed as 'Du Maître d'École' (G).

Rose du Sérail Listed as 'Mahaeca' (G).

Rose Hortensia Listed as 'Aimable Rouge' (G). See also 'Great Royal' (G), which has the synonym 'Hortensia'.

Rose Lée Listed as 'Léa' (G).

Rose Marguerite Listed as 'Tricolore' (Holland, G).

Rose Mauve Listed as 'Bourbon' (G).

Rose Pivoine Listed as 'Great Royal' (G).

Rose Pluton Listed as 'Pluton' (G).

Rose Pulton Listed as 'Pluton' (G).

Rose Renoncule Listed as 'Renoncule' (G).

Rose Sultane Listed as 'Mahaeca' (G).

Rosea Listed as 'Gallica Alba' (G).

[Rosemary]

Vibert, 1842

Seedling of 'Boule de Neige' (G).

"Large, full, lilac-y pink, spotted white." [Gp&f52] "Large, full, pink, spotted, rosette, with marbled leaves." [V8] "Large, roseate, spotted, rosette form, with marbled foliage." [WRP] "Flowers rose, spotted, large and full." [P] "Shrub vigorous, leaves large for the sort, marbled with yellowish splotches, a characteristic which so far is unique in the Provence roses. Flower medium-sized, full, with a rosette in the center, pink, spotted with deep pink. Seedling of 'Boule de Neige' [G]." [M-L42/351]

Rosemonde Listed as 'Rosa Mundi' (G).

Rosier d'Amour

syns. 'Austriaca', 'Dwarf Austrian Rose', 'Nain', 'Petit Provins', 'Pumila', 'Rosier d'Autriche'; trans. "Rose-Bush of Love"
Breeder unknown, pre-1806

"Deep pink." [Ÿ] "*Subshrub* 0.5–0.6 m high [ca. 1.5–2 ft]; *canes* simple or more often branched, glandular hispid; *prickles* straight or curved, those at the branch tips persistent, but soon falling from the base of the canes, leaving numerous scars. *Leaflets* (3–) 5, obtuse ovate, rarely acute ovate, firm, doubly dentate, gland-edged, glabrous and green above, glaucous and pubescent beneath; petioles villose, glandular, with recurved prickles. *Flowers* 1–3 at the tips of the canes, fragrant; pedicels and ovoid *receptacles* glandular hirsute; *sepals* lanceolate, appendiculate, almost as long as the petals, glandular outside, tomentose within; *petals* 5, large for a small plant, whitish outside, light purple within. *Hips* pyriform, somewhat bristly, reddish or orange, long-persistent in winter. This rose grows spontaneously all over Germany, where it is known as the Rose of Austria. It is the type of the *Gallica* group of our gardens—yet is scarcely known in France. Du Pont's specimen passed, with [*the rest of*] his collection, to the Luxembourg [*palace, in Paris*]; but this year, we have found it in Le Dru's collection, and it is from there that our model [*for Redouté's plate*] comes. Cultivation in France seems to have increased its overall size, compared with wild specimens received direct from Germany … The roots … rapidly extend far and wide, especially in arable land, where the resulting suckers impede the harvest of crops, and defy efforts at eradication." [T&R]

Rosier d'Autriche Listed as 'Rosier d'Amour' (G).

Rosier des Parfumeurs

trans. "Rose-Bush of the Perfumers"
P. Cochet?, date unknown
"Light pink." [Ÿ]

Rosier Noir Listed as 'Holoserica Multiplex' (G).

Rouge Admirable

Synonym shared by 'Orphise' (G) and 'Pourpre Charmant' (G), *qq.v.*

Rouge Admirable Strié

trans. "Striped 'Rouge Admirable'"
Vibert, pre-1836
"Striped purple." [V4]

Rouge Éblouissante Listed as 'Assemblage des Beautés' (G).

[Rouge Formidable]

syns. 'Aldégonde', 'André Du Pont', 'Belle Bourbon', 'Du Pont', 'Dupont', 'Grand Condé', 'Manteau Pourpre', 'Manteau Rouge', 'Pontiana', 'Porcia', 'Pourpre Cramoisi', 'Violet Brillant'; trans. "Formidable Red"
Breeder unknown, pre-1811

"Crimson." [Cal] "Violet purple." [LS] "Fiery red; superb blossoms." [J-As/64] "*Canes* much armed. *Leaflets* oblong, arched, pendant. *Flower* medium-sized, very double, intense purple-red. From 1819 to 1824, I received this rose under the six following names: 'Manteau Pourpre', 'Porcia', 'Manteau Rouge', 'Aldégonde', 'Belle Bourbon', 'Pourpre Cramoisi'. With five others much less known—which I don't mention—this completes a synonymy of 14 names." [Pf] "*Bush*

0.9–1.2 m high [ca. 3–3.5 ft]; *stems* dark green; *branches* diffuse, numerous; *prickles* short, unequal, dense. *Leaflets* 5 or 7, ovate or round, firm and brittle, bidenticulate, gland-edged, glabrous above, villose beneath, with a few small prickles; stipules enlarged, denticulate. *Flowers* clustered at the tips of the canes; pedicels long, more or less hispid; *receptacles* globose or elongate ovoid, glandular hispid as are the pinnatifid *sepals*; *corolla* large; petals 7–8-seriate, brilliant red, with a pleasant though not penetrating perfume." [T&R] "This variety is…not so large [*as 3–4 in across (ca. 0.75–1 dm)*]; its color is a deep brown; the petals are crinkled; it is equally effective [*as 'Pourpre Charmant'*] grafted on the Briar." [C-T] "Its shoots are vigorous; its wood is armed with strong thorns; leaves, the somber ones of the Provins, of which this is a direct descendant. Buds inflated, flat, found in tens or twelves on each peduncle, which is divided into pedicules and pedicels, each one bearing a rose which is very large and very double, and of a deep brown red. When open, some petals are crinkled, though they are quite thick. In size, it nearly equals that of 'Pourpre Charmant'. One must graft this beautiful variety, and it should be done on a high stem [*i.e., making a standard or tree-rose out of it*]. Opens starting June 10–19. No fragrance." [LeR] "Rejected and superseded [*in 1846*]." [WRP]

Rouge Rayé Listed as 'Beauté Tendre' (G).

[Rouge Superbe Actif]

trans. "Potent Superb Red"
Breeder unknown, pre-1811

"Wood and leaves a yellow green; calyx and bud round. Blossom of the same size as [that of 'Bella Victoria', Gallica, breeder unknown, pre-1811; flower velvety crimson, the size of that of 'Pompon de Bourgogne'], well formed, very double, beautiful bright red, nice scent, blooming [around June 10–20]." [C-T]

Roxelane

syns. 'Grande, Violette, et Belle', 'La Grande Violette'
Breeder unknown, 1811

"Deep pink; flowers semi-double, but very beautiful." [J-As/64] "New sort or variety which bloomed for the first time in 1811, and which is still not in commerce [*still writing in 1811*]. This rose has the habit, wood, leaves, buds, and calyxes of 'Mahaeca' or 'Belle Sultane', but in larger, stronger proportions. It is announced as being able to be grown on its own roots. Its blossom is much larger, and its color not quite so dark; but its perfume is stronger and more elegant. This rose will merit the attentions of the fancier; it will make a beautiful head grafted on the Briar, and will give a great quantity of bloom; they come five to six on the same stem. Well set off by the foliage—a single branch makes a perfect bouquet." [C-T]

Royal Marbré

trans. "Marbled Royal"
Breeder unknown, pre-1837

"Lilac and purple, marbled." [WRP] "Flesh, marbled pink." [Ÿ] "Flowers red and purple, marbled, of medium size, full." [P] "Blossom medium-sized, very full; color, carmine, marbled pink." [S] "Red and pink, medium size, very full, tall." [Sn] An attribution and date of "Moreau-Robert, 1850" has been given for this cultivar; but, as we see above, Prince had it in 1846; and the firm of Moreau-Robert was not in existence yet in either 1846 or 1850.

Royal Virgin Rose Listed as 'Aimable Rouge' (G).

Royale Veloutée Listed as 'Holoserica Regalis' (G).

Ruban Doré Listed as 'Tricolore' (Holland, G).

Sanchette
syn. 'Sanchetti'
Vibert, 1837
    "Crimson." [LS] "Medium-sized, full, crimson pink." [V8] "Flowers even rose, very large and full; form, cupped, exquisite. Habit, erect; growth, robust. A noble Rose." [P]

Sanchetti Listed as 'Sanchette' (G).

Sang Listed as 'Hector' (G).

Sang de Boeuf Listed as 'Sanguineo-Purpurea Simplex' (G).

Sanguine d'Angleterre Listed as 'Hector' (G).

Sanguineo-Purpurea Atra Listed as 'Ombre Superbe' (G).

[Sanguineo-Purpurea Simplex]
syns. 'Blutpurpurne Rose', 'Sang de Boeuf'
Breeder unknown, pre-1820
    "This flower is single, medium-sized, and oxblood color. Its calyx is moderately pinnate. The ovary is thick, oval, nearly cup-shaped, and—like the peduncles—villose. The rose's leaves are oval, acuminate towards the tip, singly dentate; their upper side is light green, dull green and hirsute beneath. The petioles are armed with sparse prickles; and the shoots have a moderate amount [of prickles]. Going by its look, this rose comes from the Holoserica called the double one [*i.e., 'Holoserica Multiplex'; see also 'Admirable'*]." [Rsg] If indeed a parent of 'Admirable', obviously pre-1787 in date.

[Sans Pareille Pourpre]
trans. "Unparalleled Purple"
Breeder unknown, pre-1811
    "Violet." [Cal] "Velvety crimson, very rich in form and color." [J-A] "'Sans Pareille Pourpre', which blooms at . . . the end of June, well merits the beautiful name given it. Few can rival it in beauty of form and richness of color. The wood is strong and vigorous, and armed with straight, red, pointed thorns of differing sizes. The leaves are long, pointed, and regularly dentate, nearly always to the number of five on the same stalk. The calyx and the flower bud are oval. This is a superb velvety violet; the outer petals reflex onto the calyx, the others stretch upwards contrarily, making it look like a sort of pompon, characteristics which are all its own. It has an elegant scent. This rose is one of the most perfect in the family. Grafted on the Briar, it does well, and makes a wonder effect budded on the same stock with 'Unique Blanche' and 'Unique Carnée'; they bloom at the same time, and make a charming contrast." [C-T] "Comes from 'La Provence' [*q.v.*], having all its characteristics in the wood, thorns, and leaves. There are few which could rival ['Pourpre Charmant']; this one does in its size, beauty, form, vigor, wood, and the brilliance of its colors. The prickles of the 'Sans Pareille Pourpre' are strong and straight or indeed often hooked; the buds are inflated and somewhat covered [by the sepals]—unusual in this group—are as numerous on each peduncle; the blossom is large, full, a beautiful velvety purple crimson; the petals are crowded . . . it is very late, opening from the 20th to the 29th of June." [LeR]

[Sans Pareille Rose]
trans. "Unparalleled Pink"
Breeder unknown, pre-1811
    "Rose." [Cal] "The wood, leaves, calyxes, and buds are just like those of ['Sans Pareille Pourpre']; however, it has fewer thorns. The blossom is large, quite double, and delicate pink in the middle, which grades insensibly to the outer petals, which are nearly white; it is very fragrant. About the end of June, this rose gives a quantity of astonishing blossoms. I don't know any sort that grows as vigorously as this one; often the season's shoots are five or six feet long or more [ca. 1.66–2 m +]. Grafted on the Briar (on which it does perfectly well), it can make *berceaux* and pergolas." [C-T] "This one is a hybrid from mixing pollen of the Browns, the Pinks, and the Whites. Its wood is the strongest, the most out-shooting, and the most vigorous of all. The rose grows to perhaps ten to twelve feet [ca. 3.33–4 m], has few thorns, and is bestrewn throughout with brown prickles. It could make a charming pergola—only 'Couronne de Salomon' and 'Victorine la Couronnée' can rival it in vigor. The buds are numerous, its blossoms are large, quite double, of a delicate pink, intense at the center, which diminishes gradually out to the exterior petals which are nearly white. It is very fragrant, and resembles no other. In opening, it flattens out like the Rose of Sharon. All in all, it can be regarded as a perfect flower. Blooms June 9–10." [LeR]

Scharlachglut
trans. "Scarlet Glow"
Kordes, 1952
From 'Alika' (G) × 'Poinsettia' (HT).
    "Deep red, large, single, tall." [Sn]

Semi-Double Marbled Rose Listed as 'Marmorea' (G).

Semi-Double Velvet Rose Listed as 'Holoserica Duplex' (G).

Sénat Romain Listed as 'Duc de Guiche' (G).

Séguier
Vibert, 1836?
    "Purple violet, spotted." [V4] "Flowers violet purple, spotted with red, of medium size, full." [P] "Flowers full, from 6 to 7 cm [ca. 2¹⁄₂ in], amaranthine slatey purple, brighter at the center, spotted red and violet." [l'H55/53] "Violet purple and white, medium size, full, average height." [Sn] Possibly Chancellor Pierre Séguier, patron of the Académie Française, also invoked in connection with the Centifolia Pompon 'De Meaux'.

Shakespeare Listed as 'Kean' (G).

Shell Listed as 'Pompon de Bourgogne' (G).

Sterckmanns Listed as 'Triomphe de Sterckmanns' (G).

[Subnigra]
syns. 'Atropurpurea', 'Négretienne', 'Negrette', 'Nigrette', 'Noire de
    Hollande', 'Subnigra Marron'; trans. "Nearly Black"
Breeder unknown, pre-1811
    "Blossoms double, medium-sized, violet purple tending towards black, which however lightens when the flower opens." [CM] "This rose is regarded by fanciers as one of the most beautiful of this large group—the most majestic of the Gallicas; buds round and slightly pointed, not covered [by the sepals]. The blossom has a light scent,

and is not very double—these would seem to be disadvantages, but the whole makes up for the failings of its parts by its most beautiful form. It is a velvety deep brown, nearly black, a little bigger than the Bordeaux [*i.e., 'Rosier des Dames'*]—making it a perfect flower. Opens June 5–10." [LeR] Possibly synonymous with 'Cramoisie Éblouissante'; possibly synonymous with 'Superbe en Brun'.

Subnigra Marron Listed as 'Subnigra' (G).

Superb Tuscan
syn. 'Tuscany Superb'
England?, pre-1838?
"[A] seedling from the Old Tuscany, with larger and more double flowers, very dark, perhaps more so than its parent, but less brilliant." [WRP] "Deep purple red, medium size, full, medium scent, tall." [Sn] "Flowers dark purple, mottled with crimson, of a rich velvety appearance, very large and double; form, expanded. Habit, branching; growth, moderate." [P]

Superbe Listed as 'Cramoisie Triomphante' (G).

Superbe Brune Listed as 'Achille' (G). See also 'Superbe en Brun' (G).

[Superbe en Brun]
syns. 'La Négresse', 'Nigritiana', 'Reine des Nègres'
Dupont, pre-1810
"Brown touches on deep crimson petals." [dP] "Deep velvet." [Cal] "Blossoms very double, beautiful velvety purple." [J-A/568] "Blossom small, full, velvety; a very dark violet purple." [S] "The very beautiful blossoms are like those of 'Velours Pourpre', except that their color is darker and they have petals splotched with very striking touches of brown." [CM] "Blossoms a very deep crimson, petals maculated with brown touches which are very obvious, especially before the blossom is fully open." [AC] "*Thorns* very hooked. *Flower* medium-sized, double, velvety, deep purple, shaded with brown." [Pf] "This rose differs from ['Velours Pourpre'] in having thorns which are larger at the base, and nearly always paired. The blossom is two inches across [ca. 5 cm], pretty double, and flat; the petals are a deep velvety purple, covering over the few stamens it has." [C-T] "This beautiful variety of Gallica is the largest, freshest, and prettiest—indeed, the most elegant." [LeR] "Described by De Pronville and mentioned by Redouté and Desportes. Dupont grew it; some would call it 'La Négresse'." [Gx] See also 'Subnigra' (G).

Superbissima Listed as 'Admirable' (G).

Surpasse Singleton Listed as 'Illustre' (G).

Surpasse Tout Listed as 'Cérisette la Jolie' (G).

Temple d'Apollon
syns. 'Cramoisi Brillant', 'Cramoisissimo Amplo', 'Pourpre Rouge', 'Vesta'; trans. "Temple of Apollo"
Breeder unknown, 1816
"Crimson." [Cal] "Deep violet" [LS] "Large double flowers, sparkling, velvety, very beautiful." [dP] "Blossoms large, very double, nuanced at the center with the most sparkling crimson." [AC] "Flowers of a very sparkling crimson, well shaded brown velvet; beautiful form." [J-A/567] "Superb, large, semi-double." [BJ24] "Blossoms very large, semi-double, purple, superb." [No26] "Buds, long and pointed;

flowers large, semi-double, without very many petals; velvety, bright, light crimson." [S] "[*Growth*] *Buds* red. *Sepals* short. *Flower* large, double, velvety crimson. See '[Feu de] Vesta' for the difference." [Pf] "Flowers light vivid crimson, shaded with purple, large and double; form, expanded. Habit, erect; growth, moderate. A very showy Rose." [P] Calvert tells us that it first *bloomed* in 1816.

The Bishop Listed as 'L'Évêque' (G).

Théagène Listed as 'Pucelle de Lille' (G).

[Tour Malakoff]
Robert, 1856
"Blossom globular, pink." [JDR56/41] "10–12 cm [ca. 4–4³/₄ in], full, lilac-y flesh pink, globular, vigorous." [R&M62] Malakoff's Tower, a feature of the temporary defenses of Sebastopol in the Crimean War. Not to be confused with the well-known violet Centifolia from Soupert & Notting, 'Tour de Malakoff', released the following year.

Tricolore
syns. 'Belle Alliance', 'Mexica Aurantia', 'Reine Marguerite', 'Rose Marguerite', 'Ruban Doré'; trans. "Tricolor"
Stegerhoek, pre-1821
"Variegated red, white, and purple." [WRP] "Velvety crimson rayed with yellowish white." [LF] "Purple plumed with white." [V4] "Very double, deep violet purple, petals striped with white and yellow lines." [BJ30] "Flowers medium-sized, very abundant, purplish rayed white." [JR1/8/13] "From Holland, showing a combination of the colors purple, white, and yellowish, often quite distinct. The central petals are always much smaller." [BJ30] "Is now a very old variety; its flowers prettily striped with yellowish white, on a purple ground." [WRP] "*Ovary* globular, big, and bulging, much constricted at the neck. Its diameter equals or surpasses that of the bud. *Flower* small, quite double, velvety, purple, with a white line down the middle of each petal." [Pf] "Flowers brilliant crimson and purple, shaded and mottled, with a streak of cream tracing the centre of each petal, of medium size, double; form, expanded. Habit, erect; growth, moderate. A distinct and pretty Rose." [P] Evidently came to Vibert ca. 1821 via the nurseryman Lee in England. See also the 'Tricolore' (G) by Lahaye.

Tricolore
Lahaye père, 1827
"*Canes* unarmed. *Flower* large, full or double, symmetrical, bright purple-pink, becoming lilac-pink." [Pf]

Tricolore de Flandre Plate 3
trans. "'Tricolore' from Flanders"
Van Houtte, 1846
"6–7 cm [ca. 2¹/₂ in], full, ground-color white, striped and plumed with purple red and violet." [VPt48/app] "Pink-white, striped violet, medium size, very full, medium scent, average height." [Sn] "Medium-sized, full, white ground, plumed red, purple, and white." [Gp&f52, BJ53] "Medium bush; blossom with a white background, striped and plumed purple red and violet, medium sized … The flowers are well borne, numerous, very full, somewhat plump, and formed of nearly even petals which are rounded, recurved, and tightly packed." [S] "Flowers white, striped with crimson, lilac, and amaranth, of medium size, full. Raised at Gand [*i.e., Ghent*] in 1844. Introduced in 1846. This variety is spoken very highly of on the Continent, but has not,

Tricolore de Flandre *continued*

as far as we know, bloomed in England." [P] "Has been called a hybrid Gallica, [and] is another meritorious striped form, but it is far from the Gallica proper because of its slightly climbing manner, making it better for adorning walks than growing as a bush." [R-H63/184] "Growth moderate." [GeH]

"Monsieur Louis Van Houtte, of Ghent, published a cut of a remarkable Provins rose, the rights to which he has bought. This rose, which—to the eyes of certain people—has but one fault, that it doesn't rebloom—if the blossom is as beautiful, as regular, as striped as the illustration would have us believe—this rose will re-awaken the interest of fanciers in growing roses which, though they bloom but once, give us charming, graceful, ravishing blossoms. The rose in question has—according to the cut—the coloration of a very beautiful slatey carnation. The ground-color is white, but full of irregular stripes varying from delicate pink to carmine red to poppy, then to violet. Everybody should know a few of our roses called *Provins-Panachés* [*i.e., 'Striped Gallicas'*]. A person still sees them, with pleasure, in church-gardens, to which Fashion relegates them because they *don't rebloom*. This one will be one of the most beautiful." [dH47/327]

"I saw it at a fancier's in 1847. I marveled at it, flabbergasted. The rose, studded with at least ten flowers, made a beautiful bush; its wood, not very thorny, its little leaves of a beautiful green and firmly held—but with grace—its flowers of medium size, very double, slightly globular and formed of rounded petals which were close-set and regularly imbricated. As to color, the ground was a pure white enhanced with pink and deep carmine stripes fading to red, then to violet purple. Alas! It disappeared. No longer was it seen in gardens; one searched in vain through the sellers' lists. One must tell the whole story: 'Tricolore de Flandre' belonged to the Gallicas and was not re-montant." [RJC60/167] "A treasure." [ARA28/64]

Triomphe de Flore

trans. "Flora's Triumph"

Descemet, pre-1821

"Delicate pink." [V4] "Blush." [Cal] "Tender red." [Ÿ] "Deep pink; charming flowers." [J-As/64] "Delicate rose, of medium size, full." [P] "Delicate pink, full, medium-sized, beautiful." [LF] "Blossoms full, medium-sized, pink with pale edges." [AC] "Full and very double." [BJ30] "Light pink, medium size, very full, light scent, tall." [Sn] "*Canes* fat, glandulose, unarmed, usually purple at the tip. *Flower* medium-sized, very full, symmetrical, pink with pale edges." [Pf] "Given by Desportes as an obtention of Descemet's." [Gx] We cannot confirm the suggested date of pre-1813.

Triomphe de Sterckmanns

syn. 'Sterckmanns'; trans. "Sterckmanns' Triumph"

Vibert, 1847

"Bright pink." [LS] "Delicate pink." [Ÿ] "Blossom medium-sized, full; color, bright red." [S] "Light red, large, full, average height." [Sn] Vibert probably purchased the propagation rights to this rose from the triumphant breeder Sterckmanns.

Turenne

Vibert, 1846

"Bright red." [LS] "Flowers rose, large and full." [P] "Large, full,

pink." [Gp&f52] Henri de la Tour d'Auvergne, Vicomte de Turenne, lived 1611–1675; successful Marshal-General for Louis XIV.

Tuscany

Breeder unknown, pre-1820

"Flowers blackish crimson, velvety, large and semi-double. Habit, erect; growth, vigorous." [P] "Deep violet purple, small, lightly full, very fragrant, tall." [Sn] "Very dark and very fragrant. Growth vigorous." [GeH] "Is not black, but of a very dark rich crimson; in richness of colour it has very few equals, and to behold it in its beauty it must be seen before the sun affects it. Its deficiency is want of petals, but it forms an excellent parent from which to procure seed; for being profuse in pollen, you can always readily obtain it to impart to other sorts richness of colour." [Bu] "Not so dark as several other varieties; the color is a very dark blackish crimson, very brilliant; it is not full double, and having its parts perfect, it produces abundance of seeds." [WRP] "In a Scotch garden I have seen a hedge of the old velvety crimson 'Tuscany' flowering profusely as late as September." [NRS24/33]

"Rose with nearly round seed-buds and hispid peduncles: stem and petioles hispid and prickly: leaves winged: leaflets ovate, pointed, and sawed, villose and glaucous beneath: flowers of a deep purple colour, rolled back, with a few marks of white: blossoms semi-double. [There is also a] variety with marbled flowers. The first of these elegant varieties is well known in the gardens by the appellation of the Tuscan Rose, and is the most esteemed of all the dark roses for its rich and deep colour: it may well compare with the finest velvet. The small particle of white on the edge of some of the petals, instead of blemishes may be regarded as an enlivening contrast. —The marbled variety, although it bears a very different aspect, can only be regarded as an irregular variation; never to be relied on, as it depends so much on its cultivation and the casualty of a wet or dry season." [A] See also the various Holosericas and 'Mahaeca' (G), which are obvious close congeners, and one of which may well be synonymous (with a name thus having nomenclatural precedence to the name "Tuscany"). Tuscany, area of Italy with Florence as its capital.

Tuscany Superb   Listed as 'Superb Tuscan' (G).

Valence Dubois

Fontaine, 1880

"Pink, medium size, full, average height." [Sn] We have been unable to validate this attribution and date.

Van Artevelde

Parmentier, pre-1847

"Deep pink, large, very full, tall." [Sn] We cannot confirm the attribution or date; it is curious that this cultivar is unmentioned in the old literature.

Van Huyssum

Parmentier, ca. 1845

"Blossom large, semi-double; color, bright red with violet." [S] Possibly a Hybrid China. See also 'Vandhuisson' (HB).

Velvet Rose   Listed as 'Holoserica' (G).

Velours Pourpre

syn. 'Cramoisi Incomparable'; trans. "Purple Velvet"

Holland, pre-1811

"Bright red." [Cal] "The very double, medium-sized flowers—

crimson, tending towards violet—are nuanced a lighter purple around the center." [CM] "The name given this rose is quite appropriate. Its wood is green, clothed with small brown prickles. The leaves are elongated and contracted at the base. The calyx is elongate, and covered over with brown bristles. The bud is nearly naked. The blossom is no more than an inch and a half across [ca. 4 cm]; it is very double, and a beautiful deep velvety purple; its petals are wavy, and fold back onto the calyx." [C-T] "The bud . . . resembles the most beautiful bizarre ranunculus . . . this is truly a pompon of the greatest beauty, meriting all the efforts of the fancier. Graft it at three feet [ca. 1 m]. They open June 1–9." [LeR] "Desportes says this rose came from Holland; it was described by de Pronville and mentioned by Redouté; it was grown in Du Pont's nurseries." [Gx] Not to be confused with Prévost's 'Velours Pourpre Nouveau', the blossoms of which were 2–2½ in across (ca. 5–6.5 cm).

Vénus Mère   Listed as 'Bouquet Charmante' (G).

Versicolor   Listed as 'Rosa Mundi' (G). See also 'York and Lancaster' (D).

Vesta
Synonym shared by 'Feu de Vesta' (G) and 'Temple d'Apollon' (G).

Victor Parmentier
Parmentier, pre-1847
   "Light red, medium size, full, moderate scent, tall." [Sn]

Village Maid   Listed as 'Belle Villageoise' (G).

Ville de Toulouse
trans. "City of Toulouse"
Brassac, 1876
   "Carmine." [LS] "Carmine pink." [Ÿ] "Pink, medium size, full, average height." [Sn]

Violaceo Purpurea Nigricans Holosericea Plena   Listed as 'Holoserica Multiplex' (G).

Violet Brillant   Listed as 'Rouge Formidable' (G).

Violette Bronzée   Listed as 'Busard Triomphant' (G).

[Virginie]
Vibert, 1825
   "Large, full, pink." [V8] "Flowers rose, large and full; form, cupped." [P] There was evidently also an obscure pre-1820 Gallica of the same name by Descemet.

Visqueuse   Listed as 'Bourbon' (G).

Wax Rose   Listed as 'Duchesse d'Angoulême' (G).

Ypsilanti
syn. 'Ipsilanté'
Vibert, 1821
   "Deep pink." [V9] "Dark rose red." [GJB] "Blossoms full, large, bright pink." [AC] *Flower* large, full, plump, symmetrical, light bright pink." [Pf] "Flowers soft even rose, the summits of the petals slightly reflexed, and growing paler soon after expansion, large and full; form, compact, perfect. Habit, erect; growth, robust. A superb show Rose." [P] Alexander Ypsilanti (1792–1828) and Demetrius Ypsilanti (1793–1832), brothers, fighters for Greek independence.

Zoé
Miellez, pre-1826
   "Blossoms beautiful, very double, large, a bright pink at the center, and pale at the edges." [No26] "Purple." [LS] "Pink, large, very full, medium scent, tall." [Sn] We cannot confirm the suggested 1810 for this cultivar. Not to be confused with the Moss of the same name. Zoé, possibly Empress Zoë of the Byzantine Empire, lived 978–1050; competent Empress who also had a good eye for marriageable men.

CHAPTER THREE

Damasks

"This is a Rose which was first introduced into Europe by the Phoenicians . . . , the culture of which was perfected by the Syrians, says Avicenne, who saw them in the Tenth Century. Brought to Europe by Thibault IV, Comte de Champagne, following the 7th Crusade (1254), illustrated in 1508 in the book of hours of Anne de Bretagne." [ExRé] "Some believe this species originated in Spain, but it is much more likely that they come from Syria." [JF] The reader will recall that the Phoenicians had colonies in Spain. "Damas, or, in the Syriac tongue, Demeschk, was the name of the founder of that city [Damascus, Syria] which also gave its name to this group of roses. This name is familiar to all those involved with the Rose be it as writer or grower, and it is certain that the Damask rose was the favorite rose sung by the ancient poets of all countries because of its considerable perfume. The primitive Type of the Damask with single flowers originated in Syria from which it was introduced into Europe around 1573; but Johnson, in his *Histoire du Jardinage*—says the learned Linacre [Physician Royal to the English kings Henry VII and Henry VIII], who died in 1524 —has the first introduction of the Damask from Italy [*we read in Testu that Matthioli, in 1554, said that it had been in Italy for several years already, adding that Monardes, in 1551, stated that it had been grown in Spain for thirty years, and much longer in Italy, France, and Germany*]. Which of these two dates is correct? That's all I know, but it's obvious that this rose has been grown in gardens for many centuries, and that it has given us all the best sorts we have—nearly all of which have disappeared from collections. While we're on dates, let me also tell you what Sanut, on the subject of Damask Roses, tells us in 1187. When Saladin took Jerusalem from the Crusaders, he wanted to purify the walls of the Mosque of Omar, which the Christians had used as a church; he commanded that the aforementioned walls be washed with rosewater brought from Damascus, and it took at least 500 camels to bring all this [rose] water they used. The variety used is still [1885] grown in the gardens of Damascus. [JR9/179–180]

"Its very spiny stems grow to 7 or 8 feet in height [ca. 2.3–2.6 m], and are clothed with a greenish bark. Its leaves are composed of two pairs of oval lobes [*i.e.,* leaflets], tipped by an odd one, all of them shadowed green above, taking on a brown tint along the edges, which are slightly serrate; and pale green beneath. Borne on a bristly peduncle, and contained in a calyx both winged and hirsute, the blossoms are more or less double, depending on the ground and the culture, and are colored a very delicate pale red, wafting a very agreeable scent." [Fr]

"The Damask Rose, is so called from its having been brought originally to Europe from Damascus, in Syria. The variety thus introduced, was the old semi-double light red variety, which, as well as some others, are still grown in the gardens of that city, and the original type of the species with single flowers is said to be a native of Syria. The name of the Damask Rose has long been familiar to every reader of English poetry, as it has been eulogized more than any other species, and its beauties portrayed with a poet's license. In these glowing descriptions, the truth, as is frequently the case in poetry, has been entirely lost sight of, for, in plain unvarnished prose, it must be conceded that the original Damask Rose, and the earlier varieties, such as have been the roses of our poets, though peculiarly fragrant, are most uninteresting flowers. However, we must not ungratefully deprecate them, since they are the types of our present new, beautiful and fragrant varieties." [WRP]

"All the Damask Roses, to the number of 133 varieties, are very vigorous, perfect in form and color, and possess an exquisite perfume, which made it much besought by the ancients." [JR9/179–180] "The Rosa Pesti of Virgil could be regarded as a variety of the Damask. According to him, it bloomed twice a year." [AC] "The Damask Rose may be considered as the 'author' of all the typical sorts known under the names *Bifera, Portland,* and *Perpetual.* The Bifera or Quatre-Saisons was the first offspring, the Portland the second, and the Perpetuals of recent origin . . . The Damask Rose [proper] makes a bushy plant three or four feet high [ca. 1–1.3 m]. Its slightly arching, delicate green stems are armed with numerous slender, reddish, unequal thorns, the longest of them recurving; its leaves are composed of seven pointed, oval leaflets, heavily toothed, and 'waffly' or pleated, pale green above and pubescent beneath. The petiole is hirsutulous and has at its base some three or four small recurved prickles; the blossoms are borne on upright stems which do not jut out much, but which form in panicles; the sepal-tube is clothed with reddish bristles; it is elongate, not very large, and—in some of them—is nothing more than an inflated extension of the pedicel; the sepals are elongate, spatulate, and indeed foliaceous at the tip; they reflex even in the bud stage; the corolla is composed of three or four rows of outstretched, notched petals; they are more or less double; their color is pink, and their scent is pretty nearly that of the Centifolia, but more elegant. The Damask sometimes blooms in the Fall with old specimens … It serves as a stock on which to graft. In budding and especially with shield-grafts, it easily 'takes.' The rose propagators making use of 'forced grafts' at first made use of the Damask, because it is common and easily put in pots, and because it could be kept growing continuously; but as it throws up many suckers from its roots, changing the run of the sap of the stock and necessitating an overplus of work, they for the most part abandoned it in favor of the Briar, on which the graft at least 'takes' more easily." [JDR54/30]

"This rose from the 'Tous-Mois' [Damask Perpetual] originated in the southern part of Europe and Asia. Is it a variety of the 'Tous-Mois'? —or is the 'Tous-Mois' one of the Damask? I have nothing to say as far as that goes. It's enough to know that it has everything from red up to white … It grows own-root or grafted, making large, thick bushes, covered with medium-sized roses which are more than semi-double, having some stamens which enhance it. Sometimes they come all together on one common peduncle, other times in small clusters borne on long peduncles. They are two inches across [ca. 5 cm]; they vary from red to white." [LeR] "Its characteristics approach those of the Centifolia closely; it can be distinguished by: more numerous canes, having stronger or longer thorns; smaller blossoms, but they come in upright and often thick clusters. Another notable difference, which separates it from the Gallica as well, is the ease with which it can be propagated by budding." [JR17/94] "The Damask Rose is frequently confounded with the [Centifolia] and Gallicas, which is not to be wondered at when the mixture of the various species by impregnation is indiscriminately practised every year, often producing plants and flowers, about whose family scarcely two judges could agree … They all have that delicious and agreeable odor so peculiar to the 'old fashioned Damask Rose,' and also produce their flowers in clusters; they have a long succession of bloom … They are all distinguished by long spreading branches thickly set with prickles; the foliage is strong, of a pale green, and deeply nerved." [Bu] "The fairly numerous varieties of which this sort is comprised, though much resembling [the Agathes and the Damask Perpetuals], also for the most part have something of the look of the *Provins* roses. Nevertheless, they can be distinguished easily from them by the following characteristics: *Thorns* stronger and composed of prickles which are normally more numerous,

larger, hooked or falcate, and large-based. *Leaflets* more villose beneath, often larger and more rounded. *Peduncles* more bristly and arranged in multifloral corymbs. *Ovary* narrow at the base, widened at the tip, not much inflated, looking like a top or upside-down cone. *Flowers* more fragrant." [Pf]

"The Damaske Rose bush is more usually noursed up to a competent height to stand alone (which we call Standards) than any other Rose: the bark both of the stock and branches is not fully so green as the red or white Rose [*i.e.*, the Gallica or Alba]: the leaues are greene with an eye of white vpon them, so like vnto the red Rose, that there is no great difference between them, but that the leaues of the red Rose seem to bee of a darker greene. The flowers are of a fine deepe blush colour, as all know, with some pale yellow threads in the middle, and are not so thicke and double as the white, nor being blowne, with so large and great leaues [*i.e.*, petals] as the red, but of the most excellent sweet pleasant scent, far surpassing all other Roses or Flowers, being neither heady nor too strong, nor stuffing or vnpleasant scent, as many other flowers." [PaSo]

"The Damask Rose is one of the most common in our parterres; it wafts a pleasant scent, but its flowers fade and it loses its leaves easily." [AC] "The Damask Roses are very hardy, thriving well either as standards or dwarfs. They do not form compact-headed trees, but their growth is graceful; rather more rambling than that of the French Roses [*i.e.*, Gallicas]. They flower abundantly: in some instances the flowers rest among the leaves and branches which surround them; in others they are elevated above. It is chiefly from the petals of this species, in common with those of the Provence (R. Centifolia), that Rose-water is distilled." [P] "The roses of this neat and elegant family have a pretty effect arranged in a mass, and like the varieties of Rosa alba, they are so beautiful in contrast with the dark roses … The pruning recommended for Rosa gallica will also do for these roses." [WRP] "They are the first to bloom, come again in the Fall, and often last until frost, especially if a person goes to the effort in July of pruning and stripping the plant of leaves, and to water during dry periods." [AC] "Grafted on dwarf stocks or stems, and left to itself in some corner of the garden, it produces there the same effect as the *Alba* roses." [JR9/179–180]

"The Damask held the top place in our gardens for a long time; there were more than 100 varieties, represented today almost solely by 'Mme. Hardy' [*i.e.*, 'Félicité Hardy'] … Another beautiful white, 'Mme. Zoutmann', is still to be found in some collections. To add to these, one can still find, but only with difficulty, 'Leda' or 'Damas Peint', carminy lilac, and '[La] Ville de Bruxelles', salmony red." [JR17/94] "To sum up, the Damask Rose is a very interesting sort in that it blooms all Summer, or at least two times a year, in Spring and in Fall. This is what, in the final analysis, makes it to be preferred in the garden—that we can have roses in Winter." [CM]

Rosa ×damascena

Possibly a cross between *Rosa phoenicia* and *R. gallica* where these
species' ranges overlap in Asia Minor.

"Grows to a height of eight to ten feet [ca. 2.6–3.1 m], has a thorny
stem covered with a greenish bark; its thorns are short; and its leaves
an umbrageous green above, and a pale green beneath; the edges are
often brown; peduncles armed with bristly hairs; calyx winged and
hispid; blossoms, a pale delicate red, barely double; their scent is very
agreeable; the fruits are long and smooth." [AbR] "*Canes* straight or
flexuose, vertical or diffuse, armed with prickles intermingling with
bristles. *Leaves* composed of five or seven *leaflets* which are glabrous
above, villose or pubescent beneath. *Serration* ordinarily simple or
villose, sometimes glandulose. *Peduncles* hispid-glandulose or simply glandulose, ordinarily together in open multifloral corymbs, projecting from the surrounding foliage. *Sepals* ordinarily villose or
glandulose, shorter than the petals. *Ovary* glandulose or glabrous,
rarely hispid, short, turbinate or obconical, always widened at the
neck, and without any noticeable constriction. *Flowers* ordinarily
fragrant." [Pf] "The Damask Rose makes a compact bush growing five
to six feet tall [ca. 1.6–2 m]. Its very numerous branches bear sparse
red hooked thorns. Its leaves have seven leaflets which are oval acute,
pale green above, lightly villose beneath, on a common peduncle
which is villose and armed with several prickles. Its flowers, which
sparkle in May and June, and September and October, are upright,
sometimes in a smaller cluster, sometimes in a bouquet of ten to
twelve medium-sized blossoms, borne on long peduncles, separated
from each other; they are more than two inches in size [ca. 5 cm];
their scent is nearly the same as that of the Centifolia Rose; their col-
or varies from red to white. Last of all, they are more or less double.
Such are the distinguishing characteristics of the species." [CM]

Rosa ×damascena 'Subalba'

syn. 'À Pétale Teinté de Rose'

"Bushy *shrub* 0.9–1.2 m tall [ca. 3 ft]; *prickles* unequal, some
straight, some recurved, reddish. *Leaflets* 5, simply dentate, glabrous
above, pubescent and sometimes purplish beneath; petiole villose,
glandular, with some recurved prickles. *Flowers* 2–3, subpaniculate at
the branch tips; *pedicels* glandular-hispid; bracts recurved, acute; receptacles inflated midway and *sepals* elongate, pointed, pinnatifid,
both of them hirsute; *petals* 5, notched, white flushed with pink; bud
darkish red … This elegant bush produces a large quantity of charming blossoms successively for more than a month. It grows in Southern Europe and is thought to be a native of Spain. For a long time rare
in gardens and confined to a few nurseries, today fanciers hasten to
obtain it now that single-flowered roses are no longer disdained." [T&R]

Rosa ×richardii   Listed as 'Sancta' (D).

Horticultural Varieties

À Bouquets   Listed as 'Argentée' (D).

À Fleurs Rouges Doubles   Listed as 'Red Damask' (D).

À Pétale Teinté de Rose   Listed above as *Rosa ×damascena*
'Subalba'.

À Pétales Variés   Listed as 'York and Lancaster' (D).

Abondante   Listed as 'Belle Couronnée' (D).

Abyssinian Rose   Listed as 'Sancta' (D).

Agathe   For the various Agathes, see Chapter 4.

Alba   Listed as 'Fausse Unique' (D).

Angèle

Breeder unknown, pre-1846

"Flowers light carmine, very large and very double; of compact
form." [P] "A pretty bright-colored rose, very double and distinct."
[WRP] "Very well formed." [S]

[Argentée]

syns. 'À Bouquets', 'Elongata'; trans., "Silvery"

Breeder unknown, pre-1811

"Superb flesh-colored satiny blossoms, very numerous, sometimes in bouquets, sometimes in clusters at the tip of the canes."
[J-As/57] "Very effective because of its corymbs composed of 5–20
flowers which are double, medium-sized, and pink, and which cover
the bush." [BJ24] "Numerous clusters. In bloom pretty long due to the
succession [of flowers blooming in each cluster]." [dP] "Much more
common [than its typical form, 'Red Damask']; its blossoms are medium-sized, white, and washed with pink in the middle." [CM] "*Shrub,*
armed with strong crooked thorns. *Flowers,* small, double, flesh-
coloured." [Go] "Commonly called the Silvery Damask because of its
leaflets which are white and cottony beneath, but more notable because of its numerous very full clusters of medium-sized, double,
flesh-colored blossoms." [BJ30] "This rose grows vigorously … and
gives an enormous quantity of flowers, nearly as pretty and as large
as those of the Centifolia. It would seem to be a hybrid variety produced by mixing the 'Tous-les-Mois' [Damask Perpetual] with some
sort of fruiting Centifolia, such as the Agathes or the Sans Pareilles.
The wood is nearly as thorny as that of the 'Tous-les-Mois'. Its leaves
are oval and pointed. The buds are crowned by the 'leaflets' or sections of the calyx, which latter is round and nearly glabrous. The
leaves and blossoms are slightly glabrous." [C-T] "Sub-variety of the
Damask and Alba, it has canes which are close-set and stubby, forming a well-rounded … [*word indecipherable*] … head. Each of its
branches produces a corymb of more than thirty to forty flowers,
which are medium-sized, very double, and delicate pink—it seems
as if there were a light, thin gauze of a delicate white over their color,
giving it a silvery look. As far as I am concerned, there is nothing so
fresh-looking as this gauzy transparence, nor as original as this pretty variety. Blooms June 19. Leaves downy." [LeR]

Babet

syn. 'Babette'

Breeder unknown, pre-1838

"Large, full; color, flesh." [S] "Flowers full, medium-sized, and
flesh." [AC] "*Flowers,* middle-sized, flesh-colour, very pretty." [Go]

Babette   Listed as 'Babet' (D).

Beauté Virginale   Listed as 'Virginale' (D).

Bélisaire

syn. 'Belisarius'
Breeder unknown, pre-1829

"Charming and vigorous bush; blossoms numerous, mid-sized, very double, in a corymb, at first a delicate pink, then pale or flesh. The peduncles and ovaries bear glandular bristles." [R-H29/21] "*Shrub*, vigorous, with straight branches, armed with numerous, uneven thorns, enlarged at the base, mixed with glandulous bristles. *Leaves*, of a pale green, composed of five or seven leaflets, regularly toothed; some oval, some oblong. *Flowers*, numerous, in clusters, very double; middle-sized. *Petals*, pale pink, when they expand; becoming paler, or flesh-coloured. *Tube of calyx*, and *Peduncle*, covered with glandulous bristles." [Go] Bélisaire, alias Belisarius, ca. 505–565, gloried general for Byzantium under Justinian I.

Belisarius Listed as 'Bélisaire' (D).

Bella Donna

trans. "Beautiful Lady"
Breeder unknown, pre-1844

"[A] delicate pink and a profuse bloomer." [Bu] "Of distinct habit." [WRP] "Soft lilac pink, large and double; form, expanded. Habit, branching; growth, moderate." [P]

Belle Auguste

syn. 'La Belle Augusta'
Vibert, pre-1824

"Flesh." [V9] "A blush, changing to nearly white, fully double, a strong grower, and flowers profusely." [Bu] "From seed; very double, regular, flesh." [MonLdeP] "*Bush*, diffuse. *Canes*, slender. *Flower*, nodding, large, full, flesh at the center, edges nearly white." [Pf]

Belle Couronnée

syns. 'Abondante', 'Bifera Coronata', 'Cels', 'Celsiana', 'De Cels',
'Incarnata Maxima', 'La Coquette', 'Mutabilis', 'Nutabilis', 'Van Huysum'; trans., "Crowned Beauty," the "crowned" referring to either the circlet of stamens or the sepal appendages that overtop the flower bud
Cels, pre-1817

"Flowers numerous, flesh, then white." [dP] "Blossoms very large, semi-double, a light pink or flesh, then white." [No26] "Flowers semidouble, light pink, continuing a long time, largest of the sort." [BJ30] "Blossoms semi-full, but very beautiful. This old plant, though widely grown, will always be held in esteem by fanciers because it has the merit of covering itself in bloom, and of presenting, often on the same canes, some corollas entirely flesh-colored, or white, or pink, and indeed others will be composed of equal portions of two or three of these colors." [J-As/65]

"This rose owes its name to Monsieur Cels, who discovered it [*possibly in Holland*]. This charming shrub is notable because of its canes which bear white and pink blossoms in the same corymb all at the same time." [AC] "This rose is, without contradiction, one of the most beautiful varieties of the Quatre-Saisons rose. Because of its beauty, I owe it specific mention. What is notable about this rose is that its canes bear, at one time, both white and pink blossoms in the same corymb; it is more elegant and lighter in color than the sort which serves as its Type [*'Bifera'? Possibly 'Red Damask'?*]. We are indebted to Monsieur Cels, whose celebrated name it bears, for the

knowledge of this charming rose; and it spread from his nursery into other gardens. It is an excellent acquisition for fanciers." [CM]

"This very beautiful variety of Damask is due to the efforts of Monsieur Cels. Its wood, however, takes after that of the Centifolia, as do its thorns; its leaves are those of the 'Tous-Mois' [Damask Perpetual]. Its beautiful blossoms are elegant, and of a light pink mixed with white—large as the Type [*?*], but infinitely more beautiful. It is a precious obtention for fanciers. Blooms June 19. Its petals are limpid and notched." [LeR] "*Bush* 0.8–0.9 m tall [ca. 2¹/₂ ft]; *prickles* short, unequal, the longest almost straight, with very numerous, scattered, stiff glandular bristles which readily detach leaving small blackish scars. *Leaflets* 5 or 7, ovate. Simply dentate, light green above, paler beneath; petioles glandular, with many small reddish nearly straight prickles; stipules acute, denticulate, gland-edged. *Flowers* very numerous, often 7.5 cm [ca. 3¹/₂ in] in diameter, perfumed, erect, subcorymbose at the branch tips; peduncles and pedicels covered in stiff, unequal, viscous stipitate glands; *receptacles* fusiform, subglabrous in the upper part, glandular below; *sepals* pinnatifid, slightly downy within, glandular without; *petals* 5–6-seriate, cordately notched, those at the center curled and crumpled, soft pink at anthesis, but quickly fading to white such that the bush seems covered in pink and white blossoms at the same time. *Hips* rarely setting. This is dedicated to Jacques-Martin Cels, author of learned discourses on agriculture and other subjects, who first distributed the rose to French gardens, although it had been known much earlier in Haarlem and is shown in the paintings of Van Huysum. Only ordinary culture is needed, and it thrives grafted on the Briar; but to prolong bloom, it should be shaded from full sun." [T&R] "So called ['Van Huysum'] because of the well known painter who often included it in his work … Propagated by Cels." [Gx]

One often sees a date of "pre-1750" given for this cultivar, evidently based upon supposed representations of it in aesthetic paintings (rather than botanical renderings). Did any gardener know it "much earlier in Haarlem"? It is an iffy thing to adduce facts from the Arts! Imagination often runs far ahead of fact; that is why we have recourse to the Arts—they supply what Science is too effete to produce. Be that as it may, however, it is curious that such a distinct cultivar received no notice from such dedicated and wide-ranging early rosarians as Rössig, Andrews, or—most particularly—Guerrapain, who loved Damasks and Damask Perpetuals; the first mention of it we find in the literature is indeed as an Alba in the *Bon Jardinier* almanac of 1817. A couple of years later, LeRouge groups it as a Damask, in which classification it has since remained. Most curious of all, perhaps, is the fact that *never* does Vibert list it for sale by his nursery; hints as to the reason for this may be drawn perhaps from our remarks on the name of the cultivar, below.

Long beloved by rosarians under the name 'Celsiana', it is painful to discover that this familiar name is not correct! The name 'Celsiana' is first found in Redouté and Thory; and they were well known for their habit of rebaptizing cultivars. Listen to the lament of Vibert (who later was to suffer for such affronts to the insiders in court circles): "Why is it that, for a large portion of these cultivars [in Redouté and Thory's work *Les Roses*], we have been forced to exhaust ourselves in conjectures to divine what it was the artist meant to depict? Very few are described under their horticultural name … This system of reform also harms those very varieties which this useless innova-

Belle Couronnée *continued*

tion means to protect. To what will we be reduced if all those who would like to venture to reform nomenclature, having no less right than Messieurs Redouté and Thory, decide to do it? . . . Why is it that the authors haven't deigned to let us in on the motives which led them to make these changes?" [V2] Those familiar with *Les Roses* will recall the format of the book: text on cultivar, plate on cultivar, text on cultivar, plate on cultivar, etc. The text is inevitably headed by a fine-sounding Latinate name, which is perhaps reasonable with the "botanicals"—the wild forms of roses—but much less so with well-known cultivars. For instance, the long-cultivated (even in Redouté's time) Gallica 'L'Évêque' is headed, in the text, *Rosa gallica purpureo-violacea magna,* a name probably not used before *Les Roses* was published, and certainly not after. It was a fanciful, high-sounding name to enhance the tone of the text—a practice not confined to Redouté and Thory, one might mention; this was followed by a name in the vernacular. In the same tradition, the rose introduced as 'Belle Couronnée' has, as its textual heading in Redouté and Thory, *Rosa damascena celsiana,* with "Rosier de Cels" as its vernacular name there. In the accompanying plate of Redouté's, the supposed name 'Celsiana' is entirely forgotten; the cultivar is inscribed "Rosa damascena" on the one side of the plate, and "Rosier de Cels" on the other. We turn to the text, and find Redouté and Thory consciously dedicating it with this magniloquent name to Jacques-Martin Cels, their old colleague in the court botanical circles at Malmaison in the days of the Empress Joséphine. But it is first mentioned in the literature, in the 1817 *Bon Jardinier* almanach as "the Belle Couronnée from Cels," without description, perhaps mute testimony to its immediate newness; Le-Rouge makes the connection for us two years later by describing as his "No. 104" the Rose from Cels (*Rose de Cels*) and repeating its name 'Belle Couronnée'; and Noisette revalidates LeRouge's information in his own book published a few years later. We must accede to the intentions of the introducer of the rose, Monsieur Cels, and know it by the name he gave it; the nonce-name bestowed by the back-slapping Redouté and Thory has no validity other than long erroneous usage.

And what of the Cels family?: "French horticulture suffered a heavy loss with the death of Monsieur François Cels, who died at Montrouge no older than 61 years old. The vast works he directed for thirty years [*i.e., since approximately 1802*] with so much ability—and, we might add, with so much devotion to honor and the prosperity of his country—was founded around the end of the last century by his father, who, from being a mere fancier, became the most notable grower of his time . . . The horticultural work which Cels père set himself to, starting with nothing more than merit, opened a new career in which he was able to bring to reality what his imagination put before him . . . The business of Cels père, continued by his son . . . exercised the very best influence upon the developments which soon were taking place here in the study and culture of exotic plants in three ways: botanical studies, artistic reproduction, and garden ornamentation. Indeed, while Monsieur François Cels marched so worthily in the footsteps of his father, Malmaison found itself being created by the pencil of Berthaut—Malmaison which shone among our gardens with such sparkle, but with the brevity of a beautiful flower. The treasures from [Cels at] Montrouge would find elegant sanctuary where the wife [*Joséphine*] of the First Consul [*Napoléon*] made a home for plants from everywhere in the world. This illustri-

ous woman . . . was pleased to herself go to Cels' and choose some plants, many of which reminded her of the colony [*Martinique*] where she was born and where she spent her youth. But the greatest advantage . . . was that of daily exercising at Malmaison the talent of artists and the genius of savants . . . Monsieur François Cels, whose commercial relations were immense, was a member of the Council of Administration of the horticultural society of Paris, which, a few months before he was taken away from us, gave this useful citizen a token of its sincere and deep esteem in choosing him, in a public meeting, to receive its great Gold Medal. It could be said that, on this high occasion, the master retired to his Tower with his students' award in his hands." [AnFr32/359–360]

Belle d'Auteuil
trans. "Auteuil Beauty"
Prévost?, pre-1826

"A large and perfect show-rose of great beauty; the color bright roseate, with fine foliage." [WRP] "Flowers rosy lilac, large and full; form, globular. Habit, branching; growth, robust. The leaflets are very short and round, forming a fine foliage." [P] "*Prickles* short. *Leaflets* very close-set, oval, large, slender, slightly pubescent beneath. The lateral ones are sessile and overlap at the base. Ovary turbinate-pyriform. *Flower* medium or large, very full, regular, very pale lilac-pink or flesh." [Pf] Auteuil has associations with Ternaux and Laffay.

Belle Fleur   Listed as 'Damas Violacé' (D).

Belle Superbe   Listed as 'Don Pedro' (D).

Bifera Coronata   Listed as 'Belle Couronnée' (D).

Blush Damask
Breeder unknown, pre-1806

"Pale pink." [LS] "Pink, medium size, full, tall." [Sn] "I have a suspicion it may be a hybrid with a Scots Brier; it is certainly not a typical Damask. It forms a large, very twiggy bush . . . bearing neat dark leaves, and is well covered in June with multitudes of nodding blooms. They are lilac-pink when half open, reflexing into a ball, lilac-white at the edges." [T4] One sees the attribution "England, 1759", which we have been unable to verify.

Botzaris
Robert, 1856

"White, yellowish." [JDR56/41] "7–9 cm [ca. 3–3³/4 in], full, pure white, yellowish when opening, flat, perfect form." [R&M62] "White, small, full, medium to tall." [Sn] "The hep is not of true Damask shape." [T4] Markos Botzaris, 1788–1823; fighter for Greek independence.

Bouquet Tout Fait   Listed as 'Red Damask' (D).

Bride of Lille   Listed as 'Triomphe de Lille' (D).

Carnea Virginalis   Listed as 'Virginale' (D).

Cels   Listed as 'Belle Couronnée' (D).

Celsiana   Listed as 'Belle Couronnée' (D).

Coralie
Breeder unknown, pre-1836

"White with a pink heart." [V4] "*Flowers,* middle-sized, very double, well formed, flesh-coloured; very pretty." [Go] "[A] beautifully formed rose, of a pale flesh-color, with rosy centre, to which several of this [Damask] family are inclined." [WRP] "Soft blush, bright flesh in their centre; of medium size, full; form, cupped. Habit, pendulous; growth, moderate. Closely resembles 'Deeseflore' [*sic*]." [P]

Corimbosa Listed as 'Red Damask' (D).

Damas Violacé
syns. 'Belle Fleur', 'La Divinité'; trans., "Violet-y Damask"
Godefroy, 1820

"White, and purple-violet interiorly; very double." [MonLdeP] "*Ovary* turbinate, obconical, glabrous at the tip. *Flower* medium-sized, very full, very pale pink or flesh. *Petals* numerous, very slender, the interior ones folded and finely undulate." [Pf] "*Shrub,* armed with a few thin scattered thorns, mixed with glanduous bristles." [Go]

Damascena Petala Variegata Listed as 'York and Lancaster' (D).

Dame Blanche
trans. "White Lady"
Miellez, pre-1830

"Flesh white." [V9] "Pure white; buds red." [AC] "Flowers double, large, white with some flesh." [BJ30] "Double, large, of a pure white when expanded; the buds as red as those of the Hundred-leaved rose [*i.e., the Centifolia 'Unica'*]" [Go] "Large, double, full; color of the blossom, pure white; color of the bud, pink." [S]

De Cels Listed as 'Belle Couronnée' (D).

Déesse Flore
trans. "Goddess Flower"
Vibert, 1827

"Pearly blush, full double, beautiful." [WRP] "Blush white, cerise at the heart." [S-V] "Flowers medium-sized, full, nearly white, very pretty." [No28] "A first-rate variety, with flowers rather larger than [those of] 'Coralie', and much like it in color: when about half expanded they are most beautiful." [WRP] "Flowers almost white, their centre rosy pink; of medium or small size, full; form, expanded. Habit, branching; growth, moderate. An abundant bloomer; the tree very beautiful when in full bloom." [P] Not to be confused with the pre-1826 'Déesse Flore de Florence', an Alba concerning which we have no description. Or could they be the same? Vibert ranged widely to bring his customers new roses . . .

Don Pedro
syn. 'Belle Superbe'
Breeder unknown, pre-1811

"Delicate pink." [LS] "Blush white." [Ÿ] "This one blooms [at the beginning of June]. Its wood is delicate and brownish. The leaves are elongate, pale green, and glaucous. The calyx and bud are also elongate. The blossom, three inches across [ca. 7.5 cm], is quite double, beautifully shaped, delicate pink, and fragrant. It has several attractive characteristics; often in the middle of the blossom you'll find some little green leaves—not disagreeable." [C-T] Not to be confused with the Alba 'Dom Pedro'.

Duc de Cambridge
Laffay, pre-1841

"Light ruby, full, flat, very large, superb." [LF] "Large, full, purple." [V8] "Blossom large, full, very well formed; color, deep grenadine; ex-

terior petals edged with crimson." [S] "Large, full, purple red." [JR9/180] "Red, medium size, full, medium scent, tall." [Sn] "At first thought to be a Hybrid China, will perhaps be better grouped with the Damask Roses, of which it largely partakes. It is a very fine rose, quite distinct, of a vivid rose color, and robust luxuriant growth." [WRP] "Deep purplish rose, large and full; form, compact, perfect. Foliage of a dark green, the young leaves edged with reddish-brown. Habit, branching; growth, robust." [P] The Duke of Cambridge referred to would be the seventh son of George III of England, Adolphus Frederick (1774–1850), quondam viceroy of Hanover.

Duc de Chartres
syn. 'Nouveau Triomphe'
Godefroy, 1820

"Blush." [Cal] "*Flowers* numerous, medium-sized, full, light pink." [Pf] The Duke of Chartres, one of the titles which the eventual king Louis-Philippe I (lived 1773–1850) held; not king yet in 1820.

Elongata Listed as 'Argentée' (D).

Eudoxie
Breeder unknown, pre-1848

"Flowers vivid rose, of a rosy lilac tint towards their circumference, large and double; form, cupped. Habit, branching; growth, vigorous; the shoots densely covered with spines. A very showy Rose." [P] *Cf.* the Gallica of the same name.

[Fausse Unique]
syns. 'Alba', 'Provins Blanc'; trans., "False 'Unique'"
Breeder unknown, pre-1818

"*Flower* large, full, white, bright flesh center; very beautiful when it opens, which unfortunately does not happen very often." [Pf] "Medium-sized, white, hybridized with the Alba." [No26] "Has white blossoms and has long been confused with varieties of the Alba. It is also widely found in gardens." [dP] "Common in the nurseries, but quite remarkable." [MonLdeP] "Has similarities with the Centifolia 'Unique' [*i.e., 'Unica'*]." [BJ24] "All this is a variety of the red [*either the red 'Tous-les-Mois' (Damask Perpetual) or 'Red Damask' (D)*], all the characteristics of which it has. Several naturalists have called it 'Fausse Unique'—inappropriately. It is a sister of the white 'Tous-Mois', and is worth the efforts of the fancier. Opens [June] 10–19." [LeR]

Félicité Hardy Plates 5 & 15
syn. 'Mme. Hardy'
Hardy, 1832

"Large, full, white, cupped." [V8] "White, flat." [BJ40] "Flat, white." [GJB] "Pure white, full, cupped, large, superb." [LF] "Blush white." [Ÿ] "White, large, very full, flat form, very fragrant; sometimes comes with green centre, but very beautiful when in perfection. A difficult sort to grow from cuttings." [EL] "Larger [than the Gallica 'Globe White Hip'], fully as pure, more double, and an abundant bloomer; the foliage and wood are also stronger. The French describe it '*grande pleine, blanche, creusée*': or in other words, large very double pure white, and of a cup or bowl form." [Bu] "[A] large and very full rose of the purest white. It has but one fault,—that of sometimes showing a green bud in the centre. But for this, it would be almost unrivalled among white roses." [FP] "Occasionally delicately tinged with flesh, large and full; form, cupped. Habit, erect; growth, vigorous, frequent-

Félicité Hardy *continued*

ly producing the flowers in large clusters." [P] "It is not a pure Damask rose, as its leaves have scarcely any pubescence; but a more magnificent rose does not exist for its luxuriant habit and large and finely shaped flowers place it quite first among the white roses." [WRP] "Of all the white roses in this [Damask] group, [this] is the best. In form, purity of color, and abundant bloom, as in vigor and hardiness, it is absolutely without rival; no other is better for beds in the sward or lawn; for the best bloom, however, it must not be pruned too close." [R-H63/127] "This charming and precious variety has its blossoms in corymbs; those in the middle open first, thus being crowded by the other buds, giving it a most graceful look; though its foliage be light green, the rose never appears anything but white and more than pretty; the plant producing it is extra hardy, doing well both grafted and own-root; also, it takes well to being forced." [S]

"Hybrid of Portland and Damask . . . dedicated to Mme. Hardy. A very vigorous bush with long, erect canes which are light green and armed with numerous un-equal thorns, long and straight for the most part; the leaves are large, smooth, nearly all with 7 leaflets which are regularly dentate, a handsome green above and slightly pubescent beneath. One notes that here, as with many other roses, the lower leaves have oval-rounded leaflets, while the higher leaves are oval-elliptical. The leafstalk is hispid and slightly prickly. The blossoms are a very pure white, full, flat above, 3.75 inches across [ca. 8 cm], centifolia perfume, in corymbs on long and strong thorny stems; bud, large, round, pink outside; ovary oval, hispid; some sepals become foliaceous at the top and pinnatifid on the sides. This rose is one of the best introductions in a long time." [R-H32]

Long beloved under the name 'Mme. Hardy', it was nevertheless originally introduced as 'Félicité Hardy', and was distributed as such, at least for a time; Billberg, in far-off Stockholm, Sweden, indeed cited it as 'Félicité Hardy' in 1836.

Folio Variegata   Listed as 'York and Lancaster' (D).

Général Foy
Boutigny, 1825
"Blossoms very double, medium-sized, deep brilliant pink." [No26] "*Flower* small, full, regular, bright pink with flesh edges." [Pf] "Very well formed." [Go] Maximilien Sébastien Foy, 1775–1825; French general and war historian; fought at Waterloo. See also the Gallica 'Général Foy'.

Gloire de Guilan
Hilling, 1949
"Pink, medium size, very full, very fragrant, tall." [Sn] "A most attractive sprawling shrub up to 3 or 4 feet [ca. 1–1.3 m], with fresh green leaves and small curved prickles. The cupped blooms soon open flat, being quartered, and with some petals remaining folded, in a particularly clear and beautiful pink. In the Caspian provinces of Iran, whence it was brought and named by Nancy Lindsay, this rose is used for making attar of roses." [T4]

Impératrice de Hollande   Listed as 'Roi des Pays-Bas' (D).

Incarnata Maxima   Listed as 'Belle Couronnée' (D).

Hebe's Lip   Listed as a Rubiginosa.

Henri IV
Trébucien, pre-1829
"Very large flower, bright pink." [BJ30] "Lively rose-red, rather large." [GJB] "*Bush* vigorous. *Shoots* large, purple at the tip in their youth. *Prickles* sparse, short, thick, unequal, in an arc, intermixed with glandular bristles. *Leaves* composed of five or more usually seven leaflets, purple before fully developed. *Petiole* large, cylindrical, gland-covered, armed beneath with several very short prickles. *Stipules* narrow, entire, glandular-ciliate, covering half the length between the base of the petiole and the first pair of leaflets. Leaflets ovoid-oblong, pointed, serrate, glabrous above, villose beneath. *Peduncles* long, glandulose, disposed in a corymb. *Ovary* turbinate, glandulose. *Sepals* glandulose, reflexed, terminating in a linear point; 3 bear several appendages. *Flower* large (sometimes to five inches across [ca. 1.25 dm]), full, regular, bright pink." [Pf] Henri IV, king of France; lived 1553–1610; assassinated. *Cf.* 'Henri Quatre', the Gallica.

Ismène
Vibert, 1845
"Large, delicate incarnate." [WRP] "Flowers delicate flesh-colour, large and full." [P] Not to be confused with the 1852 Moss. Ismène, alias Ismene, a daughter of Oedipus, beloved of Theoclymenus, with fatal results.

Ispahan
syn. 'Pompon des Princes'
Breeder unknown, pre-1832
"Pink, medium-sized, lightly double, very fragrant, tall." [Sn] "A fine bushy, upright shrub, up to five feet or so [ca. 1.6 m +], and extremely free-flowering in clusters, although its small rather shiny leaves suggest other parentage than pure Damask." [T4] Ispahan or Isfahan, much-sung ancient capital of Persia.

Kazanlyk
syn. 'Trigintipetala'
Keller?, 1689?
"Pink, medium size, lightly double, very fragrant, tall." [Sn] "The variety from which the celebrated Bulgarian Attar of Roses is made." [GeH] "It is a similar type to York and Lancaster, *R. damascena* 'Versicolor', with spindly growth up to 6 feet or so [ca. 2 m], soft light green leaves, and rather small flowers, loosely double, of soft pink." [T4] Kazanlyk or Kazanlik, centrally located rose-loving city in Bulgaria.

King of Holland   Listed as 'Roi des Pays-Bas' (D).

L'Amitié
trans. 'Friendship'
Stegerhoek/Dupont, pre-1813
"Flesh." [Ÿ] "Fairly large semi-double flowers, pink, spotted white; a very precious variety." [J-A/562–563] "Grown by Du Pont, says Redouté." [Gx] At any rate, Amity or Friendship, beautiful as a flower, and often as fleeting.

La Belle Augusta   Listed as 'Belle Auguste' (D).

La Coquette   Listed as 'Belle Couronnée' (D).

La Divinité   Listed as 'Damas Violacé' (D).

[La Félicité]

syn. 'Unique Panachée'; trans., "Bliss"
Dupont, pre-1810

"Flowers a light pink, speckled with white." [No26] "Blush." [Cal] "Flowers pink with some flesh nuances; should be grafted." [dP] "Large flowers ... a little more than semi-double, very numerous, entirely or partially flesh pink on the same cane." [J-A/562] "Blossom medium-sized, semi-double, spotted and with much pluming and raying; deep pink." [S] "No different from ['York and Lancaster'] except in its often maculate blossoms, in which the blotches, coming in longitudinal streaks, are usually more frequent and a darker pink." [Pf] "Sister of ['York and Lancaster']. This much-discussed hybrid is also the result of pollen of the 'Tous-Mois' and some Albas. It has the wood and foliage of ['York and Lancaster'], as well as its thorns. Its very numerous buds expand into medium-sized white blossoms which are ruffled, semi-double, most fresh and ... [one word illegible] ... Sometimes they are playful, and tend to return to the pink Type. Nothing is so like it as ['York and Lancaster'] in wood, thorns, leaves, and the form of the blossoms, which, like those of the [common] Damask ['Red Damask'?], come in two ways [i.e., in big corymbs or in small clusters]." [LeR]. The mottled character of Bliss is worth pondering.

La Négresse

trans. "The Negress"
Vibert, 1842

"Medium-sized, double, deep purple; the darkest of the sort." [V8] "Not so black as its name implies, only a very superb double crimson, very large, expanded, and fully double." [Bu] "By far the darkest Damask rose known; its flowers are of a deep crimson purple." [WRP] "Medium-sized, full, flat; color, deep grenadine." [S] "Flowers dark clouded purple; of medium size, full; form, expanded. Habit, branching; growth, small. A neat dark Rose, and the darkest of the Damask." [P]

La Ville de Bruxelles

trans. "The City of Brussels"
Vibert, 1836

"Rose-colored flowers, very large and double: this is a distinct and fine new variety." [WRP] "Pink, singular foliage." [V4] "Large, full, bright pink." [JR9/180] "Blossom large, full, flat; color, pale pink, veined pink." [S] "Medium or large, full, light red." [BJ53] "Salmon pink, large, full, tall." [Sn] "Vivid rose edged blush, large, full. Growth vigorous." [GeH] "A very large rose with salmony flowers, vigorous, floriferous, and easy of culture." [R-H63/127] "Rose color, large, full, flat; branching habit." [EL] "Very double, of a bright rose colour, with strong foliage [but we wonder if Buist's manuscript read "strange" foliage rather than "strong"; note Vibert's comment in the quotation above from V4]." [Bu] "Bright glossy rose, full and very handsome, a robust growing rose; makes a good pillar or standard." [JC] "Light vivid rose, the color gradually receding from their centre leaving the edges of a rosy blush; large and full; form, expanded. Habit, branching; growth, vigorous. A beautiful Rose." [P] "A very beautiful rose, of delicate waxy tint and vigorous growth." [FP] It is perhaps an adequate gauge of the amount of original research done previous to this present work to note that, though it is superabundantly clear that this very well known and much grown cultivar was introduced prior to 1849—aside from Vibert's mention of it in his catalog of 1836 (and those

succeeding), there are, for instance, Buist in 1844, Prince in 1846, and W. Paul in 1848, reprints of all of these authors' books having been generally available for quite some time—nevertheless, writer after writer (be it of books, articles, or catalogs) has disserved his or her readers by blandly copying a date of "1849" for 'La Ville de Bruxelles'. Old rose literature is replete with such examples of mere copywork, with not only wrong information on dates but also on breeders and rose names being lazily relayed from generation to generation. Fie, brother and sister writers! For shame! We are here to perform a service for our faithful readers, not simply to splash ink on pages!

La Virginale Listed as 'Virginale' (D).

Lady Curzon Listed as a Rugosa.

Lady White

Turner, 1901
From Rosa ×macrantha × R. ×damascena.

"White, touched red." [LS] "White, striped red, large, lightly double, tall." [Sn] "White tinted with pink, petals large and smooth, very free flowering, semi-double. Growth vigorous." [GeH] 'Lady White', not to be confused with 'Dame Blanche' ("White Lady").

Lavalette

syn. 'Valette'
Vibert, 1823

"Rose-red." [GJB] "Flowers rose; of medium size, full." [P] "Prickles red, short, unequal, sparse; the strongest with a large base; intermixed with red bristles. Leaves composed of 5 large, wide, elliptical leaflets, slightly arching, notched at the base, rounded at the summit, glabrous above, pubescent beneath. Flower medium-sized, full, regular, light lilac pink. This rose has so particular a look that it could perhaps just as well be assigned to the Undetermined Hybrids as here." [Pf] Antoine Marie Chamans, Comte de Lavalette, lived 1769–1830; French statesman and memoirist.

Leda

syns. 'Leila', 'Painted Damask'
England?, pre-1831

"White, margined lilac, full, flat, beautiful." [LF] "White." [GJB] "Medium-sized, full, flat, edged pink." [V8] "White, tigered with lilac." [BJ40] "Blush, edged with lake." [EL] "White." [V9] "Perhaps not a true Damask, but a very distinct and pretty variety, with white flowers edged with pink, 'blanche bordée de rose'." [Bu] "Yellowish white, red along the edge, medium size, full, medium height." [Sn] "Moderate growth." [JC] "Its large and thick foliage and painted flowers are quite unique, but like most of the variegated roses, it is inconstant, as its flowers are sometimes pure white; in general, however, the outer edge of each petal is tinged with fine purple." [WRP] "Blush, tinged with flesh, the petals often margined with lake; of medium size, full; form, expanded. Habit, branching; growth, robust; leaves broad, short, and handsome. A beautiful Rose when the lake margin is perfect." [P] We cannot find any reference antedating 1831 referring to the distinctive red margin in this cultivar; the 1827 reference, seemingly the source of the dating quoted by other writers for this cultivar, is to a flower that is "beautiful pink" (see under 'Pink Leda', below); thus, it pains us to point out that the name 'Leda' should therefore belong evidently to what we call 'Pink Leda', while the "blanche bordée de rose" variety—much better known today—should perhaps be called not

Leda *continued*

'Leda' but, well, what? 'Painted Damask', we suppose, or 'White Leda'. At any rate, until the situation clarifies, let us refer comments about the pink, unbordered form to the entry on 'Pink Leda'. Leda, mother of Castor and Pollux, Helen of Troy, and Clytemnestra, etc., to a greater or lesser degree aided in this by Zeus in the form of a swan. One might like to have a discussion with Leda about things.

Leila See 'Leda' (D).

Léon Lecomte

Breeder unknown, 1854?

"Rose-red and yellow, large, full, tall." [Sn] "A big strong bush with good, smooth leaden-green foliage … The flowers are of a rich warm pink fading paler and showing darker veins. Sweet scent. 5 to 6 feet [ca. 1.6–2 m]" [T4] We cannot verify the date.

Louis Cazas

Breeder unknown, pre-1850?

"Light pink, medium size, very full, medium fragrance, tall." [Sn] We cannot verify the date.

Marguerite de Flandre

Breeder unknown, pre-1885

"Flower large, full; color, flesh pink." [S] Presumably, Margaret, Countess of Flanders and wife of Philip of Burgundy; lived 1350–1405. *Cf.* the Centifolia of the same name.

Marie-Louise Listed in Chapter 4 as an Agathe.

Merveille du Monde Listed as 'Roi des Pays-Bas' (D).

Mme. Carré

Breeder unknown, pre-1885

"Medium-sized, full; color, flesh white." [S]

Mme. Hardy Listed as 'Félicité Hardy' (D).

Mme. Lambert

Breeder unknown, pre-1848

"Flowers bright red, very large and full." [P]

Mme. Soëtmans Listed as 'Mme. Zoutmann' (D).

Mme. Stolz

England?, pre-1848

"[A] pale straw or lemon color." [FP] "Blossom medium-sized, full, cupped; color, straw yellow." [S] "Large, full, cupped, straw color." [JR9/180] "Nicely formed, distinct and pretty." [JC] "Pale straw, cupped, sweetly scented, foliage light green. Growth vigorous." [GeH]

Mme. Tressant Listed as 'Mme. de Tressan' among the Gallicas.

Mme. Zoëtmans Listed as 'Mme. Zoutmann' (D).

Mme. Zoutmann

syns. 'Mme. Soëtmans', 'Mme. Zoëtmans'

Marest, 1830

"Delicate cream-color, tinged with buff." [FP] "Medium-sized, full, white." [BJ53] "Medium-sized, full, white with some flesh." [Gp&f52] "Large, full, cupped, delicate flesh fading to pure white." [JR9/180] "The palest flesh, often white, shape perfect, the most beautiful of all light roses; moderate growth." [JC] "Yellowish white, large, very full, tall." [Sn] "Delicate flesh, changing to white, glossy, large, very full, flat form, fragrant, five to seven leaflets; a splendid white rose." [EL] "Large very full blossom of creamy white, and quite showy … [I]t should be pruned only moderately." [R-H63/127] "Creamy white shaded with buff, large, full, very light green foliage. Growth vigorous." [GeH] "Delicate flesh, changing to white, glossy, large and full; form, cupped. Habit, branching; growth, vigorous. A beautiful Rose, well worthy of a place in the most limited collection." [P]

Monstrueux

trans. "Monstrous"

Breeder unknown, pre-1830

"Pink." [BJ40] "Large, full, globular; color, pale pink." [S] Not to be confused with Vibert's Damask Perpetual 'Arielle' of 1845, sometimes called 'Damas Monstrueux'.

Multiflora Listed as 'Red Damask' (D).

Mutabilis Listed as 'Belle Couronnée' (D). See also 'Marie-Louise' (Ag) and 'Unica' (C). Not to be confused with the well-known single China.

Noémie

Vibert, 1845

"Flowers of a dark rose colour, spotted in a slight degree, large and full." [P] "Large, full; color, deep pink, touched with cerise pink." [S]

Nouveau Triomphe Listed as 'Duc de Chartres' (D).

Nutabilis Listed as 'Belle Couronnée' (D).

Oeillet Parfait Listed as a Gallica.

Olympe

Vibert, 1843

"Medium-sized, full, crimson purple." [V8] "A fine French variety, of the usual size, the color crimson purple." [WRP] "Flowers purplish crimson; of medium size, full." [P]

Omar Khayyám

Simpson/Kew/Knight/Notcutts, 1947

"Light pink, small, very full, medium scent, average height." [Sn] "Light green wood and dark prickles and thorns; leaves small, downy, pale green." [T4] Raised at Kew (first bloom, 1894) from seed of a rose found growing at Nashipur, Persia, on the grave of Omar Khayyám (died A.D. 1123), savant and author of the *Rubáiyát*, notably translated into English by Edward FitzGerald. The story goes that a specimen from the Royal Botanic Gardens, Kew, was planted on FitzGerald's grave, where one Frank Knight found it and turned it over to Notcutts for propagation.

We may wish to recall here three quatrains from Omar's work (we use the enumeration of FitzGerald's fifth version). Some readers, students of verisimilitude, may wish to have at hand jugs of wine and loaves of bread:

(5) Iram indeed is gone with all his Rose,
     And Jamshyd's Sev'n-ring'd Cup where no one knows;
          But still a Ruby kindles in the Vine,
     And many a Garden by the Water blows.

(9) Each Morn a Thousand Roses brings, you say;
　　 Yes, but where leaves the Rose of Yesterday?
　　　　 And this first Summer month that brings the Rose
　　 Shall take Jamshyd and Kaikobad away.

(19) I sometimes think that never blows so red
　　 The Rose as where some buried Caesar bled;
　　　　 That every Hyacinth the Garden wears
　　 Dropt in her lap from some once lovely head.

We are assured that Reviewers already have, by heart, Omar's lines about the Moving Finger (71).

Oratam
Jacobus, 1939

From *Rosa ×damascena* × 'Souvenir de Claudius Pernet' (Pern).

"Pink center, yellow base and reverse." [Y̆] "Coppery pink, yellow nubs, large, full, very fragrant, tall." [Sn] "Dark, broad, glossy leaves." [T4] "A modern Hybrid Damask of rich glowing color. The large, double, copper-orange-pink flowers with yellow petal reverses, are lovely but in a color to be used with care. June-blooming and with rugose, leathery, yellow-green foliage, it grows 6 to 8 feet tall [ca. 2–2.6 m] and makes a handsome pillar. The rich damask fragrance is a lovely attribute." [W]

Painted Damask   Listed as 'Leda' (D).

Panachée
syn. 'Variegated Damask'; trans., 'Plumed'
Godefroy, ca. 1820

"*Leaves,* pubescent. *Flowers,* middle-sized, double, white variegated with pink." [Go] Also attributed to Girardon.

Parure des Vierges
trans. "Ornament of the Virgins"
Breeder unknown, pre-1810

"Pure white." [Y̆] "*Ovary* glabrous at the neck. *Flower* medium-sized, multiplex, white. Aside from these characteristics, this rose is further distinguished from ['York and Lancaster' and 'La Félicité'] by its leaflets, which are more rounded, and paler." [Pf] "Was in the collection of the Soucelle Château, and mentioned by Desportes and Prévost." Certainly pre-1810; I cannot verify the 1801 in Y̆, which also mistakenly lists it as a Moss.

Pénélope
Vibert, 1818

"Deep rose." [Cal] "Large, very full; color, bright grenadine." [S] "Flowers purplish red, large and very double. Growth, robust." [P] "Remarkable for its fine foliage; the edges of its leaves tinged with red; the flowers of a very deep rose, globular, large and distinct." [WRP] Penelope, the patient and wily wife of Odysseus.

Péricles
Vibert, pre-1826

"Purple." [LS] "Medium-sized, double, pink, marbled." [R&M62] "Purple, medium size, very full, growth 8 [*on a scale of 10*]." [Jg] Not to be confused with Laffay's flesh pink Hybrid China of the same name and era. Péricles, alias Pericles, 495–429 B.C., Athenian statesman.

Petite Agathe   See 'Sommesson' (Ag).

Phoebus
Breeder unknown, pre-1848

"Flowers lilac blush, their centre rosy crimson, large and full; form, compact. Habit, erect; growth, moderate, producing short thick shoots. Foliage fine." [P] *Cf.* the Gallica of the same name. Phoebus, alias Apollo, who, as overseer of the Muses, presides over our authorial efforts—to good effect, one hopes.

Pink Leda
Breeder unknown, pre-1827

"Medium-sized, full, flesh pink." [JR9/180] "Worthy of appearing in all gardens. Its blossoms are the most beautiful carmine lilac when it is in good sun, but their tint fades easily and turns to pale pink or white when it is not taken care of or in bad soil, and then it loses nearly all its value." [R-H63/127] "Beautiful pink color, very agreeable form; wood thornless." [J-As/58] See our pained discussion under 'Leda' (D).

Pompon des Princes   Listed as 'Ispahan' (D).

Pope
Laffay, pre-1844

"Large and distinct, crimson purple, and inclines to bloom in autumn." [WRP] "Medium-sized, double, crimson purple." [V8] "Globular." [JR9/180] "Very vigorous bush; blossom very large, full, much compacted; very floriferous; color, carmine, shaded purple." [S] "Crimson and purple shaded, their centre sometimes fiery, very large and full; form, compact. Habit, branching; growth, moderate. A free bloomer, very dark in colour, and altogether a superb Rose." [P] The Hybrid Bourbon 'Dembrowski' (Vibert, 1840) sported from this; presumably the introduction of 'Pope' thus predates 1840 (unless for one reason or another Vibert had pre-release specimens of 'Pope'; Laffay is known to have bought propagation rights to Vibert's unreleased seedlings upon occasion). At any rate, considering Laffay's Anglophile tendencies, the name probably commemorates great but diminutive English poet Alexander Pope (1688–1744), author of such as *The Dunciad* and *The Rape of the Lock,* and friend of Jonathan Swift. We have above given a few lines from Omar; perhaps the patient Reader will enjoy as well the closing lines from Pope's *The New Dunciad,* non-rosy though they be, by way of complement, and by way of sop to the present Author, to whom these lines have often occurred in the course of his work:

In vain, in vain,—the all-composing Hour
Resistless falls: The Muse obeys the Pow'r.
She comes! she comes! the sable Throne behold
Of *Night* Primeval, and of *Chaos* old!
Before her, *Fancy's* gilded clouds decay,
And all its varying Rainbows die away.
Wit shoots in vain its momentary fires,
The meteor drops, and in a flash expires.
[. . .]
Thus at her felt approach, and secret might,
Art after *Art* goes out, and all is Night.
See skulking *Truth* to the old Cavern fled,
Mountains of Casuistry heap'd o'er her head!
Philosophy, that lean'd on Heav'n before,
Shrinks to her second cause, and is no more.
Physic of *Metaphysic* begs defence,

Pope *continued*

> And *Metaphysic* calls for aid on *Sense!*
> See *Mystery* to *Mathematics* fly!
> In vain! they gaze, turn giddy, and die.
> *Religion* blushing veils her sacred fires,
> And unawares *Morality* expires.
> Nor *public* Flame, nor *private,* dares to shine;
> Nor *human* Spark is left, nor Glimpse *divine!*
> Lo! thy dread Empire, CHAOS! is restor'd;
> Light dies before thy uncreating word:
> Thy hand, great Anarch! lets the curtain fall;
> And Universal Darkness buries All.

Pride of Lille Listed as 'Triomphe de Lille' (D).

Princesse de Portugal Listed as a Gallica.

Professeur Émile Perrot

Perrot/Turbat, 1931

"Light pink, medium size, lightly double, very fragrant, tall." [Sn] If we construe correctly, Graham Thomas equates this cultivar with 'Trigintipetala', our 'Ispahan'. Sangerhausen offers a date of 1930 for 'Professeur Émile Perrot'.

Provins Blanc Listed as 'Fausse Unique' (D).

Red Damask

syns. 'À Fleurs Rouges Doubles', 'Bouquet Tout Fait', 'Corimbosa', 'Multiflora', 'Rouge', 'Rubro-Purpurea'

England?, pre-1789

"Bright red." [Ŷ] "Rose color, very fragrant." [WRP] "Light red, medium size, full, very fragrant, tall." [Sn] "The Red Damask rose which one finds at the Trianon and in several nurseries, is marvelously effective because of its corymbs composed of six to twelve blossoms which are medium-sized, pink, borne on peduncles which are long and which jut out, covering the bush with numerous bouquets. [Its subvarieties:] 'Argentée' . . . 'Fausse Unique', and 'À Bouquets Couleur de Chair'; but these sub-varieties are of moderate interest." [CM] "The one which seems to me to be the most beautiful is the Damask with very double red flowers, also called 'Corimbosa' and 'Bouquet Tout Fait', doubtless because the blossoms are very numerous on the same stem, one branch making a pretty full bouquet of beautiful form. Its canes are nearly entirely covered with big, long, brown, slightly recurved thorns. The 'eye' or growth bud is large and protrusive. The leaves are oval-obtuse, terminating in a point, and are edged light pink. Its buds are pointed, and in quasi-umbels, very close to each other, sometimes up to thirty on the same petiole; they are completely covered and crowned with the calyx-leaflets [*sepals*], which are long and deeply cut. The calyx, as with that of the 'Tous-Mois', is long, and covered over with brown points or bristles. The flowers are large, beautiful, sparkling pink, and fragrant. This rose grows vigorously and strongly; on its own roots, it can be raised on a nice stem. It is as resistant to great frosts as it is to great heat, which often damage the ordinary 'Quatre-Saisons'. It gives a prodigious quantity of flowers which continue until frost if you take the precaution of cutting back the branches it puts out. It looks good grafted on the Briar." [C-T] "Corolla double, purple-red. Ovary ovoid, large, and covered with white bristles. Peduncles bristly and stiff. Leaves a slightly dark green, oval, and terminating in a point . . . This rose is

double, and a purple-pink at the center. The petals closest to the center have some yellow rays, and the outermost ones are of a fainter color. Three of its calyx segments bristle with spines, and most often have a double appendage. The large, slightly heavy, ovoid, bristly ovary is a matte green, and extends into a peduncle which is also charged with hairs. The leaves are composed of five or seven oval leaflets which terminate in a point, and are slightly dark green above, and paler beneath. The stem, branches, and young growths bristle with hairs and spines. This rose blooms in June." [Rsg]

Roi des Pays-Bas

syns. 'Impératrice de Hollande', 'King of Holland', 'Merveille du Monde'; trans., "King of The Netherlands"

Breeder unknown, pre-1826

"Rose-red." [GJB] "Pink." [BJ40] "Bright red." [Ŷ] "Blossom large, full, well-formed, light red." [S] "[A] very old variety, with immense globular flowers, and curious sepals; so that the flower-bud seems surrounded with leaves." [WRP] "Flowers deep pink, large and full; form, cupped. A beautiful Rose." [P] "*Leaflets* very large. *Ovary* very fat, oval-digitate, elongate, slightly constricted at the neck. *Flower* large, nearly full, an even, bright, intense light pink." [Pf] William I, King of The Netherlands 1813–1840; abdicated.

Rose à Parfum de Bulgarie

trans. "Bulgaria's Perfume Rose"

Breeder unknown, date uncertain

Rose-colored cultivar that we only know from the listing in Trevor Griffith's *The Book of Old Roses*; it should be compared with 'Kazanlyk'.

Rose à Parfum de Grasse

trans. "Perfume Rose from Grasse"

Breeder unknown, date uncertain

"Pink, medium size, full, very fragrant, tall." [Sn] Sangerhausen attributes its origin to the "Orient." Grasse, Alpes-Maritimes, France, a city much concerned with the perfume industry.

Rose d'Hivers

trans. "Winters Rose"

Breeder unknown, date uncertain

Small, pink-to-white roses.

Rose de Puteau

Breeder unknown, pre-1826

"Pink." [Ŷ] Possibly synonymous with 'Bifera' (Damask Perpetual); spelling of name possibly "Rose de Puteaux." One Monsieur Puteaux was, about this time, gardener-in-chief at the palace of St.-Cloud, Sèvres, France.

Rose of St. John Listed as 'Sancta' (D).

Rose Verreux

syn. 'Verhaux'

Breeder unknown, pre-1848

"Flowers red, tinged with lilac, paler towards their circumference; of medium size, full form, globular." [P]

Rosemonde

Toutain, 1825

"Pink, plumed white." [LS] "Striped red and white." [Ŷ] Could 'Rosemonde' actually be the Gallica 'Rosa Mundi'?

Rosier de Damas

trans. 'Damask Rose' [!]

France, 1840?

"Pink, medium size, full, medium scent, average height." [Sn]

Rouge Listed as 'Red Damask' (D).

Rubro-Purpurea Listed as 'Red Damask' (D).

Sancta

horticultural syns. 'Abyssinian Rose', 'Rose of St. John'; botanical
  syn., *Rosa ×richardii*

Dammann, 1895?

"Pale pink." [Ÿ] Plant dwarf and spreading, *or* low and erect, with single blush-white blossoms of five or six petals in few-flowered corymbs. "Evidence of this rose was found in the Egyptian tombs of the Second to Fifth Centuries A.D. (discovered by Monsieur Flinders Petrie and Dr. Schweinfurth in the region of Fayoum). Rediscovered between 1839 and 1843 living in the gardens around the churches and cemeteries of Tigré, Abyssinia, by Messieurs Lefebvre, A. Petit, and Quartin-Dillon. Seemingly introduced from Asia Minor to Tigré (then in the Axoum empire) in the time of St. Frumentius [*4th century A.D.*]." [ExRé] Other authors have supplied their readers with information from sources outside our normal sphere of activity; we knit together, with appreciation, the following facts from Charlotte Testu, in *Les Roses Anciennes,* Dr. Hurst's writings in Graham Thomas' *The Graham Stuart Thomas Rose Book,* and *Roses* by Roger Phillips and Martyn Rix, drawing also on the preceding quote from ExRé. The cultivar is supposed to be a hybrid between *Rosa gallica* and *R. phoenicia* originating in Asia Minor, where the ranges of the two species overlap. (Phillips and Rix, basing their opinion on technical characteristics of the flower, feel that one parent was a member of the *synstylae* group of roses [as *Rosa arvensis*], the other perhaps *R. gallica.*) It was perhaps used by the Egyptians for funereal purposes in the second to fifth centuries A.D. (see below). Meanwhile, in the fourth century A.D., St. Frumentius—born in Phoenicia—was about converting Abyssinians to Christianity, and perhaps introduced a rose familiar from his homeland into the country. Achille Richard described it, as *Rosa sancta,* in his *Flore d'Abyssinie* of 1848, giving it the name of "sancta" or "holy" because of its use around churches in the Christian province of Tigré, Ethiopia—this usage perhaps a relic of St. Frumentius' efforts. In 1888, Sir Flinders Petrie found dried remains of a rose in a tomb in Lower Egypt. These he sent to the Royal Botanic Gardens, Kew, whence Dr. Oliver forwarded them to Professor Crépin, director of the Brussels Botanical Garden, who *compared* them with 'Sancta', but who did not *identify* them with 'Sancta' (see Testu, p. 61). At any rate, the botanist Terraciano collected 'Sancta' in Abyssinia, whence came its introduction about 1895 into European horticulture by the Neapolitan nursery firm Dammann. The firm of George Paul or that of William Paul introduced it into England about 1902. Because Andrews had earlier used the name *Rosa sancta* for another rose, this name was dropped in 1922 by Rehder, who rebaptized it *R. richardii*. See also Ivan Louette's important related researches on *R. abyssinica* in the publication *Rosa Belgica*. We maintain 'Sancta' as a cultivar name until the plant's botanical status is substantiated.

Sémiramis

Vibert, 1841

"Salmon-rose, centre fawn." [JC] "Large, double, coppery pink." [V8] "Quite novel in color, and a most perfect and beautiful rose: the center of the flower is of a bright fawn-color, and its marginal petals of a delicate roseate. This fine variety ought to be in every collection." [WRP] "Very vigorous plant; flower large, full, growing in a cluster; color, bright pink shaded pale pink, center fawn-color, exterior of the petals flesh pink." [S] "Flowers fawn in their centre, shaded with glossy pink; their circumference of a pinky flesh, to which colour the centres change soon after expansion; large and very double; form, expanded. Habit, pendulous; growth, moderate. A distinct and beautiful Rose." [P] The "pendulous" growth perhaps suggested to Vibert the Hanging Gardens of Babylon, which in turn suggest Semiramis, dynamic Babylonian queen who, among other efforts, built the tomb of Ninus which proved of interest to Pyramus and Thisbe. Brought up by doves, she indeed ultimately changed into a dove and flew to heaven, a sort of behavior which is not often seen at present.

Silvia

syn. 'Sylvia'

Vibert, 1819

"Light purple." [V3, V4, V9] "Pale rose." [Cal] "Cerise pink." [BJ40] "Large, full, purple red." [V8] "*Shrub* very vigorous. *Leaflets* oval, large, very villose beneath, slightly so above. *Peduncles* very long, together in very open corymbs. *Ovary* oblong-digitate. *Flower* medium-sized or large, nearly full, beautiful intense cerise pink, even and lasting." [Pf]

St. Nicholas

James/Hilling, 1950

"Pink, medium size, lightly double, tall." [Sn] Said on the one hand to possibly be a Damask × Gallica cross, on the other to be a sport of 'Hebe's Lip'; if the latter, then owed to the Rubiginosa chapter. But, more authoritatively, "this very beautiful rose appeared spontaneously in the garden whose name it bears, owned by The Hon. Robert James at Richmond, Yorkshire." [T4]

Subalba Listed as *Rosa ×damascena* 'Subalba'.

Sylvia Listed as 'Silvia' (D).

Trigintipetala Listed as 'Kazanlyk' (D).

Triomphe de Lille

syns. 'Bride of Lille', 'Pride of Lille'; trans., "Triumph of Lille"

Vibert, pre-1826

"Flesh." [V9] "Bush with prickles which are rare, slender, sparse, mixed with numerous glandular bristles." [S] "*Petiole* rising at the end, around the last pair of leaflets. *Leaflets* with the lateral edges ordinarily up-bent. *Serration* very deep, very sharp, glandulose. *Ovary* obconical, very glandulose. *Flower* nodding, medium-sized, full, white, with a pink center." [Pf] The name is not characteristically Vibertian, and perhaps implies that he bought exclusive proprietary rights to it from a Lillois; breeders Cardon, Miellez, and Rameau are all associated with Lille in the era of the cultivar's introduction.

Triomphe de Rouen

Lecomte, 1826

"Blossoms very large, very double, a beautiful lilac pink." [No26] "*Flower* large, full, light pink." [Pf] "Large, full, shaded pink." [JR9/180]

Triomphe de Rouen *continued*

"Flowers soft even pink, the tops of the petals slightly turning over soon after expansion, large and full; form, expanded. Habit, branching; growth, robust. A beautiful Rose, possessing some of the characters of the Hybrid Chinese." [P] Lecomte was a Rouennais.

Trois Mages Listed as 'Les Trois Mages' (G).

Turner's Crimson Damask
Turner, 1901
"Bright crimson. —Vigorous. —Bush. —Semi-single." [Cat12]

Valette Listed as 'Lavalette' (D).

Van Huysum Listed as 'Belle Couronnée' (D), though we see occasional modern references to another, fully pink, mysterious, 'Van Huysum'.

Variegated Damask Listed as 'Panachée' (D), but see also 'York and Lancaster' (D).

Verhaux Listed as 'Rose Verreux' (D).

Versicolor Listed as 'York and Lancaster' (D).

Véturie
syn. 'Véturine'
Vibert, 1842
"Roseate, peculiar shoots and foliage." [WRP] "Medium-sized, full, pink, wood and foliage singular." [V8] "Flowers rose-colour, of medium size, full; the wood and foliage presenting a very singular appearance." [P]

Véturine Listed as 'Véturie' (D).

Virginale
syns. 'Beauté Virginale', 'Carnea Virginalis', 'La Virginale'
Descemet, pre-1811
"Blush." [Cal] "White." [Y̆] "White, medium-sized, full, tall." [Sn] "The wood resembles that of the 'Tous-Mois' [Damask Perpetual], but has fewer prickles. The leaves are oval, deeply toothed, and ashy green. The calyx is long, and contracted at the tip. The flower bud is pointed and delicate pink. The blossom is medium-sized, well-formed, delicate flesh color, and grows three to four to a stalk. The name 'Virginale' fits pretty well due to its color." [C-T] "A variety indirectly from the pink 'Tous-Mois'…three or four [blossoms] come on the same petiole, nicely seconded by its leaves." [LeR] "Bred by Descemet, described by Guerrapain, was in the Du Pont nurseries." [Gx]

Volumineuse See 'Volumineuse' (Ag) and 'La Volumineuse' (DP).

York and Lancaster
syns. 'À Pétales Variés', 'Damascena Petala Variegata', 'Folio Variegata', 'Versicolor'
Monardes, pre-1551
"White, striped with pale red, large and full." [P] "Blossom medium-sized, semi-double; white, plumed and rayed with light pink." [S] "Blossoms white, plumed with red." [No26] "White and pink striped, large, full; form globular, growth vigorous." [CA93] "Often striped, and frequently one half pink and the other half white." [Bu] "Beautiful flowers little more than semi-double, white, pretty large and plumed delicate pink." [J-A/562] "Pale rose or white, sometimes

striped, fragrant, summer flowering … Growth … is vigorous and free." [GeH] "An historical favorite, named in 1551 in memory of the end of the bloody English 'War of the Roses.' Buds and flowers are wonderfully marked with irregular blotches or stripes of pale red and white, and sometimes of solid color. Do not cut off faded blooms and you will have, in late fall, a beautiful display of red 'marbles'." [C-Ps29] "The rose 'York and Lancaster' has some similarity to 'Versicolor' ['Rosa Mundi' (G)], though its colors aren't as lively. This variety has been known for quite a long time; but it is not much thought of except as a collector's item; its sub-variety, 'La Félicité', is preferred." [CM] "Illustrated in Miss Lawrance, Andrews, Rössig, Redouté." [Gx]

"Adult *stems* with few, sparse, recurved *prickles* little widened at the base; flowering *canes* bristling with unequal, reddish prickles, some very weak, others stronger. *Leaflets* 5 or 7, acute, ovate, bright green above, paler and pubescent beneath and on the margins, simply and not deeply dentate, entire at the base; petioles villose, covered with small sessile reddish glands; stipules slightly tomentose. *Flowers* sweetly scented, many together in a lax terminal panicle; *receptacles* narrowed at both ends, a little swollen in the middle, together with the elongated pedicel, which bristles from many viscous, scented glands; bracts 2, acute, ovate, pubescent on the margins; *sepals* 3 pinnatifid, 2 entire, longly spatulate, downy within, glandular without; *petals* 4–5-seriate, those at the center cupped and crumpled, most often white, spotted or striped with pink, the same bush often giving all pink and all white blossoms. This beautiful cultivar … was propagated by Dupont, who had it from England under the name *R. damascena bicolor*. It should not be confused with …'La Félicité' or with *R. gallica* 'Versicolor', as Rössig incorrectly calls it. It is still rather rare in gardens, and needs a sheltered site. It can be grown on its own roots, but does better grafted on canina." [T&R] "Corolla moderately full, touched and plumed with red and white. Ovary ovoid, pointed. Peduncle glabrous. Leaves slightly rough, oval, terminating in a point … The blossoms of this rose are moderately double, the petals fully wide-spreading, wavy, plumed and touched with white and red; most of the rays, however, lose themselves in the background [*milieu*], and the pink color is a little lighter than in the striped rose proper. This rose, which was found in a garden in that city [*York? or Lancaster?*], was sent from England under the name York and Lancaster Rose … It blooms in June. The calyx segments are short and moderately winged. The oval ovary narrows towards the peduncle, which it grades into without constriction. The glabrous petioles are a light green, like the young shoots. The leaves are, for the most part, composed of five oval oblong lobes terminating in a point; close-set; dark grass-green above, pale green beneath; shallowly, and frequently doubly, dentate. The large stipules extend for much of the length of the petiole." [Rsg] "Blossom a dull white nuanced pale red. Ovary turnip-shaped. Calyx with several rows of leaflets. Leaves oval-acuminate and denticulate …This flower has a ground of white, which however is nuanced red, which merges into the white in the upper part of the petal. The calyx is open and slight; the sepals come in several rows—the front ones are long and pointed. The ovary has the form of a turnip, and bears like the peduncle glands and small fine red prickles. The leaves are oval-acuminate, and come with deep and often double dentation; above, they are a beautiful deep green; beneath, a shaded green, as if felt. The shoots have sparse large thorns, and many small ones. Going by its look, this flower takes its origin from the white 'Tous-Mois' [Damask Perpetual] on which some pollen from a red rose [Gallica] had fallen." [Rsg]

"Rose with oblong seed-buds: peduncles and petioles hispid and glandular; prickles of the branches scattered and straight: leaflets oblong, and villose beneath: petals sweet-scented, red, white, and striped. These varieties of Damask species are known in the gardens by the title of the York and Lancaster Roses. They are seldom longer in bloom than July and August, and, like all striped flowers, are subject to vary; for although the red, white, and striped are all cultivated as distinct plants, they are found with stripes more or less on the white; and sometimes the red rose may be seen, like our specimen [in Andrews' plate], with one half the petals nearly white. They possess an agreeable fragrance, and are used in medicine as a gentle laxative." [A]

"Wood strong and vigorous, pretty much covered all over with reddish brown stickers. Leaves large, nearly round, beautiful dark green. Calyx also covered with much elongated prickles, like those on the wood, but weaker. Buds pointed, well covered by the calyx-membranes [sepals], to the number of twenty-five to thirty on the common stalk, which divides first into four or five, then subdivides further. This is the variety which is the most profuse. Flower medium-sized, double, beautiful white plumed delicate pink, very fragrant. This one of the Damasks could be awarded the palm as much for its foliage as for the colors of the blossom and the quantity produced. They open from June 10th to the 15th." [C-T] "This rose is one of the most beautiful of the hybrids between the Damasks and the Albas. This is the one that should be called 'Bicolore Yorck et lancastre' [sic]—it leaves no doubt about the unification of the two families. This rose is historical, and the other [?] is only a 'Tous-Mois'. Its wood is strong and branching, and is armed with brown thorns; leaves large, dark green; buds pointed, very numerous, twenty to thirty on the same peduncle, which is subdivided into pedicules and pedicels; much overtopped by the extensions of the calyx. Flower, semi-double, ground-color white, plumed with delicate pink, very fragrant; some of the same [peduncle] are completely pink, like the Type—others are all white. It will also rebloom when treated like the preceding [i.e., Damask Perpetuals]. No variety has flowers which are fresher or prettier." [LeR]

"This Rose in the forme and order of the growing, is neerest vnto the ordinary damaske rose, both for stemme, branch, leafe and flower: the difference consisting in this, that the flower (being of the same largenesse and doublenesse as the damaske rose) hath the one halfe of it, sometimes of a pale whitish colour, and the other halfe, of a paler damaske colour then the ordinary; this happeneth so many times, and sometimes also the flower hath diuers stripes, and markes in it, as one leaf [petal] white, or striped with white, and the other half blush, or striped with blush, sometimes also all striped or spotted ouer, and other times little or no stripes or markes at all, as nature listeth to play with varieties, in this as in other flowers: yet this I haue observed, that the longer it abideth blowen open in the sun, the paler and the fewer stripes, markes or spots will be seene in it: the smell whereof is of a weake damaske rose s[c]ent." [PaSo]

"The most fascinating thing in ownership of this quaint Rose is its unique and historical background, which we here briefly recite. One of the great romances, immortalized by Shakespeare in 'Henry VI', was connected with a conflict lasting thirty years and in history as the 'War of the Roses'. Two branches of the royal family of England, the House of York and the House of Lancaster, both descended from a common ancestor, Edward III, claimed the right to the throne. A bloody war between the partisans of the two houses started in 1455. The House of York had for a rallying sign a white Rose while the Lancastrians selected a rose Rose. Success ebbed and flowed until 1485 when Richard III of York was defeated and killed at the battle of Bosworth. But peace was not completely restored for a year, when in 1486, both houses were united by the marriage of Henry VII of Lancaster with Elizabeth of York. The legend says that this marriage was brought about by the discovery on the same bush of a Rose partly white and red. The war-weary people were quick to attribute the phenomenon to some supernatural interference; the legend was still current in 1551, when a Rose-collector actually found a bush bearing strangely variegated roses, red and white, no two alike, some striped, some blotched, some half and half while others were either all red or all white. This curiosity was instantly called 'York and Lancaster', and became in great demand among the descendants of the belligerents; for three centuries it could be found in many gardens of England. However, in the nineteenth century, Rose progress was so rapid that this charming Rose fell into oblivion. While the name remained a cherished memory, the true stock became very scarce and somewhat mixed. In 1925 we were fortunate to discover in an old English collection a few plants of the genuine strain, from which were propagated the plants we are now offering … While there have been several variegated Roses of different types, 'York and Lancaster' is the only variegated Rose known of the Damask species from which high grade attar of Roses is distilled." [C-P30]

CHAPTER FOUR

Agathes

"Some varieties have been classed by Rose fanciers in a separate division, as 'Agathe Roses'. These have curled foliage, and pale colored, compact flowers, remarkable for their crowded petals." [WRP] "The Agathe group, having very double blossoms with densely packed petals, curled and crumpled at the center." [T&R] "Regarded by some as a species [*Rosa belgica*], others construe it as a variety [*of Centifolia*]. The leaflets of the leaves rarely reach the number of five. The blossoms are red or white, and have a rather agreeable sweet scent." [BJ17] "Several hybrids of the Provence Rose are close to the Gallica; nurserymen call them Agathes." [CM]

"The roses known in commerce under the name Agathes are still kinds of Gallicas." [J-A/571] "The Agathe-leafed ones only differ from [*the Gallicas proper*] by their remarkable waved [*ondulé*] foliage; the blossoms are large and generally pale, and the petals are positioned one against the other with the greatest neatness." [JR9/75] "The Agathe group can be distinguished within this group [*i.e., Gallicas*]—very double [blossoms], tight, flat, usually pale pink." [Gx] "The Agathe group should be considered as so many hybrids from the cockade Gallicas, some red Centifolias, and several Albas." [LeR] "Would indeed seem to be the same [*as the Damask Perpetual 'Tous-les-Mois'*], or simply a variety." [BJ09] "This rose, regarded by most fanciers as a variety of the Damask Rose, differs enough from it to merit the title of species. Its ovaries are more covered, and aren't constricted at all; they are hardly glandulose; the calyx leaflets [*i.e., sepals*] are nearly always simple. The leaflets of the leaves rarely exceed the number five; its blossoms are red or white, and exhale an elegant scent." [CM]

"This sort . . . has much similarity to the Gallica rose [*and, we might add because of the description following, to the Damask Perpetual we know as 'Rose de Rescht'*]. Branches fairly upright, to five or six feet [ca. 1.6–2 m], thorns rare and reddish. Canes covered with black, viscous, pedicellate glands, as are the peduncles and ovaries; leaves with 5 nearly round leaflets terminating in a point, whitish and lanate beneath; flowers of a violet red, two inches across [ca. 5 cm], nearly scentless; calyx with leaflets [*sepals*], of which 3 are always pinnate." [BJ17, associating the Agathes with the Turbinatas and Provence Roses] "Their wood is slender and

armed with fine prickles, and of a yellowish green color. Its leaves are light green, oval, and terminate in a point; the close-set branches make a nice rounded bush. The bud is naked and fat. The blossom is very double, and flat when open." [LeR] "The leaves are pubescent beneath, lightly saw-toothed along the edges; the peduncles and calyxes are pubescent, and without prickles; the ovaries are large and oval; the blossoms have very little scent, and are pale flesh, or a slightly darker red." [Lam] "*Shrub* vigorous, forming a thick bush. *Canes* long, diffuse, geniculate, armed with prickled intermingled with bristles; *prickles* long, unequal, the strongest of them hooked. *Leaves* of 5–7 leaflets. *Petiole* villose, glandulose, armed beneath with hooked prickles. *Leaflets* large, oval, obtuse, slightly villose beneath. *Serration* simple. *Peduncles* very long, trichotomous, armed with prickles below the bracts, glandulose above; gathered into elegant multifloral corymbs which are very open, and which project from the foliage. *Ovary* narrow, very long, fusiform, glandulose, constricted at the neck, shorter than the petals, 3 of them bearing several long divergent appendages. *Flowers* ordinarily double, and very fragrant. *Fruit* red, elongate, inflated in the middle, narrow at the two ends." [Pf]

Some used the term "Provence Roses" for the Agathes, meantime distinguishing them from the Centifolias, the Damasks, and the Gallicas: "This rose originates in the southern part of Europe. It has some close resemblance to the Provins or Gallica, and indeed some with the Centifolia. Several authors have considered it a variety of these two species; however, its oval (sometimes rounded) leaves, very glabrous above but indeed a little villose beneath, quite dentate, the pinched and elongate calyx leaflets [*i.e., sepals*], and finally its corymbs, require that it be distinguished form other roses. The Provence rose grows from five to six feet tall [ca. 1.6–2 m]. Its main-stems are fairly straight and are armed with several reddish prickles. Its ovaries are often oval during bloom, but nearly always globular when the fruit is mature. Its canes as well as its peduncles are covered with pedicellate, black, viscous glands. Its leaves, composed of five leaflets which are nearly round and which terminate in a point, and which are dark green above and very glaucous beneath, are borne on a common glandulose peduncle. Its flowers, which appear during the months of June and July, are two inches in size [ca. 5 cm], a more or less dark red, nearly scentless, and single, semi-double, or double. Light warm soils are the ones which are best for the Provence Rose; nevertheless, it grows in all, as long as it is not too wet." [CM] "[The Provence Rose is a] sort of Provins rose in which several differ only by their sparser thorns, some black pedicellate glands (more numerous [*than in the Provins proper*]), some slightly longer leaves which are denticulate and tomentose beneath; blossoms in corymbs, not very fragrant; sepals pinnate and non-pinnate as in many other varieties." [J-A/570] "The varieties brought together under this name distinguish themselves from the second section of Damask roses ... by their much longer *ovary* which is always *constricted* at the tip, and having its greatest diameter not at the tip but rather at the middle; finally, by their *sepals,* three or more of which are completely edged with distichous, spatulate, or lanceolate (never subulate) appendages." [Pf]

It thus is unwise to assume—as many have—that the term "Provence Roses" inevitably refers to what we know as Centifolias; it obviously signified the Agathes to at least some very distinguished rosarians. As we realize from the group's history, related in the following, the Agathes have every right to have been called "Provence" roses, perhaps indeed more right than have the Centifolias:

"Known around 1435. Bearing the name of a Christian martyr of the Provence region, to which the rose was brought in the Middle Ages. Victor Boreau found it growing wild in the middle of France, and described it under the name given by Miller [*Rosa incarnata*]. Introduced into Anjou from Provence by King René [*who lived 1409–1480*]. Grown by Claude Mollet in 1563. This is the *gallica pallidior* of Bauhin (1671). Illustrated on parchments in [*the then-holdings of the Roseraie de l'Haÿ*] museum." [ExRé]

"The Agathe roses have produced many derivatives which are much sought after for their great floriferousness . . . The differences between them are very slight—notably, the habit and petal color, and such characteristics equally trivial in the eyes of botanists. However, we think that a massed display of Agathe roses, grafted on the Briar 0.6–0.9 m tall [ca. 2–3 ft], closely planted and arranged in tiers, would give a fine effect, the more so since these shrubs, which almost all bloom at the same time, would offer an immense quantity of very double blossoms of varying shades lasting for over a month." [T&R]

We resurrect the Agathe grouping as one which, though partaking of characteristics of the Gallicas, Centifolias, Damasks, Damask Perpetuals, Turbinatas, "and several Albas," displayed them in a fairly set way such that the Agathes have their own identity, recognized in their era by those who grew and knew these and all the old European roses.

À Fleur d'un Rouge Pâle Listed as 'Blush Belgic' (Ag).

À Petites Fleurs Listed as the 'Enfant de France' (Ag) from Holland. See also 'Sommesson' (Ag), the 'Petite Agathe'.

Agathe Couronnée Listed as 'Marie-Louise' (Ag). See also 'Victorine la Couronnée' (Ag).

Agathe Incarnata Listed as 'Blush Belgic' (Ag).

Agathe Nouvelle Listed as 'Héloïse' (Ag).

Agathe Rose Listed as 'Marie-Louise' (Ag).

Augustine Pourprée Listed as 'Marie-Louise' (Ag).

Beauté Rare Listed as 'Sapho' (Ag).

[Beauté Superbe Agathée]
syn. 'Pétronille'; trans., "Agathed Superb Beauty"
Breeder unknown, pre-1811

"Wood and leaves yellowish green. Calyx very small; pointed bud enveloped by the sepals. Flower Agathe-form, two inches across [ca. 5 cm], quite double, beautiful light pink, bright, sweetly scented; one of the prettiest of the group." [C-T] "This one's a sub-variety of the Centifolia, of which it has the slender wood, thorns, and leaves, all of them a yellowish green. Its buds are very numerous on the same peduncle, and are overtopped by the calyx appendages. The large blossoms—which their thin stems bear with some difficulty—are quite double, 'agathed', lilac red at the center, pure lilac at the petal edges; once open, the blossoms round out and become like snowballs; its Type would seem to be the Agathe 'Royale'. Opens June 10–15." [LeR]

Belgic Blush Listed as 'Blush Belgic' (Ag).

Belgic Provence Listed as 'Blush Belgic' (Ag).

Belgica
Specific epithet for the Agathes when construed as a separate species. The Latin "Belgica" refers to The Netherlands (Horticulture's "Holland") as well as to Belgium.

Belgic Rose Listed as 'Blush Belgic' (Ag).

Belgica Flore Rubicante Listed as 'Blush Belgic' (Ag).

Belgica Rubra Listed as 'Rouge Belgique' (Ag).

[Belle Hébé]
trans. "Beautiful Hebe"
LeRouge, pre-1820

"Bright red." [Cal] "Bright pink, flesh center." [LS] "Very rich; large, and beautiful form; very bright and sparkling cerise." [J-A/565] "This variety, mentioned by Redouté, was in LeRouge's nurseries." [Gx] Listed (as no. 238) by LeRouge as "new in 1820." Hebe, daughter of Zeus and Hera, quondam cup-bearer to the gods, personification of youth, wife of deified Hercules.

Belle Isis
trans. "Beautiful Isis"
Parmentier, ca. 1845

"Flower large, full; color, bright flesh pink." [S] "Whitish pink, medium size, full, tall." [Sn] "Neat little light-green leaves, coarsely toothed; this character and the prickly stems denote possible Centifolia parentage, together with the winged and elegant calyx, but the flowers and flower stalks are pure Gallica." [T4] Testu also conjectures

Belle Isis *continued*

some hybridity between *Rosa gallica* and *R. centifolia* here; see as well our quote from Charles Malo (CM) about the Agathes or Provences in the head-note to this chapter . . . Anyhow, Isis, the ancient Egyptian nature goddess, *belle* now as then.

Bijarre   Listed as 'Francfort Agathé' (Ag).

Blanda   Listed as 'Blush Belgic' (Ag).

Blässe Niederlandische Rose   Listed as 'Blush Belgic' (Ag).

Blush Belgic
syns. 'À Fleur d'un Rouge-Pâle', 'Belgic Blush', 'Belgic Provence', 'Belgic Rose', 'Belgica Flore Rubicante', 'Blanda', 'Blässe Niederlandische Rose', 'Carné', 'De Bruxelles', 'De Flandre', 'Duchesse d'Angoulême', 'Flamande', 'Incarnata', 'La Grande Belgique', 'Marie-Louise', 'Pallidior', 'Rubicans'
Breeder unknown, pre-1754

"Medium-sized, imbricated, flesh." [God] "Of a delicate silvery blush color, very double, and blooms in profuse clusters." [WRP] "Foliage dark green; charming small quite double flowers." [J-A/571]

"Flower pale, moderately double; calyx pinnate; ovary oval; shoots and petioles prickly; leaves oval and acuminate . . . This blossom is of medium size, pale pink, and very nearly scentless; it is also called the little Flemish Rose. It is very floriferous. Its calyx is pinnate. Its ovary is oval, and its peduncle is somewhat short; both bear fine prickles. The leaves are a *pré* green towards the top, and light towards the base; they have simple serration, and come in 5–7. The shoots bear numerous unequal prickles." [Rsg] "Its thorny stems grow to a height of three feet [ca. 1 m], and are clothed with leaves composed of 5 to 7 oval lobes [*i.e.,* leaflets], pubescent beneath, lightly serrated along the edges. Borne on velvety peduncles, and composed of a great number of pale flesh-colored petals in a very large calyx, the blossoms have more beauty than perfume; they appear towards the end of Spring. They make superb terminal clusters in which the successive blossomings last more than six weeks. This sort has two [sub]varieties which bloom about the same time, and which are no less estimable . . . ['Rouge Belgique' and 'Petite de Flandre']." [Fr]

"This rose has all the characteristics in wood, foliage, calyx, and bud of ['Royale' (Ag) and 'Prolifère' (Ag)—which is to say the branches are slender and close-set, with rather pretty but usual leaves, calyx unmentioned, buds not distinguished], but the blossom differs in that it is larger, not at all proliferous, and a more delicate pink." [C-T] "Densely branched; *prickles* numerous, especially towards the tips of the canes, unequal, reddish, almost straight. *Leaflets* stiff, denticulate, each tooth gland-tipped, dark green and glabrous above, paler and tomentose beneath. *Flowers* clustered at the branch tips; *petals* very numerous and densely packed . . . *Hips* very rarely set . . . It has produced numerous derivatives differing only in the degree of pinkness of the corolla. It blooms at the end of June, and is very common in gardens, where it was formerly known under the name of M[arie]-Louise'." [T&R] (See also our remarks under 'Marie-Louise'.)

"Rose, with globose seed-buds, slightly glandular; peduncles hispidly glandular; flowers crowded, and of a pale flesh-colour; leaflets are ovate, and pointed, the stem and petioles prickly. This fine pale variety of the Belgic Rose is much esteemed. Its flowers are in succession abundant, but rarely more than two are in perfection at

one time. A considerable degree of sameness certainly pervades the Dutch species, to which a judicious curtailment will be very serviceable, by excluding those very trivial florescent varieties from a figurative description; by which abbreviation, a much greater degree of interest will be attached to those that actually possess a character sufficiently distinct, to require a separate figure, and at the same time it will get rid of an heterogeneous mass of superlative phrases made use of occasionally by way of discrimination. The Author will nevertheless give as satisfactory a reason as possible for the apparent expulsion of any of this attractive genus. [Andrews'] figure was made from a fine plant in the nursery of Messrs. Colville, King's Road [in Chelsea, England], in the month of July, from which period till September it is in constant bloom." [A]

Boule Hortensia   Listed as 'Majestueuse' (Ag).

Bouquet Parfait   Listed as 'Royale' (Ag).

Bouquet Rose de Vénus
trans. "Venus' Pink Bouquet"
Breeder unknown, pre-1819

"Very pretty pompon, hybrid between an Agathe and some Alba. Its wood is slender, yellowish, and dotted [with prickles]; leaves light green and round; wood and leaves like a smaller version of those of 'Victorine [la Couronnée]'. The buds are elongate. The blossom is very double, flesh pink, and mixed with touches of white; smaller than the Bordeaux [*i.e.,* 'Rosier des Dames' (CP)]; in a perfect bouquet. This charming miniature is still pretty rare, only being known in the garden of Malmaison. Everyone who sees it wants to own it to grow in pots, in which it grows wonderfully well. It needs to be grafted at three or four feet [ca. 1–1.33 m] to make it easy to enjoy. It is very double. It opens June 9–10; it has some scent." [LeR] "Grown in the nurseries of Monsieur LeRouge, businessman and organist at Dôle—says Redouté." [Gx] LeRouge's remarks, quoted above, do not seem consistent with his having been its breeder, which was formerly the attribution.

Caprice du Zéphyre   Listed as 'Marie-Louise' (Ag).

Carné   Listed as 'Blush Belgic' (Ag).

Cocarde   Listed as 'Majestueuse' (Ag).

De Bruxelles   Listed as 'Blush Belgic' (Ag).

De Flandre   Listed as 'Blush Belgic' (Ag).

De Hollande   Listed as 'Majestueuse' (Ag).

[De la Malmaison]
trans. 'From Malmaison'
Pelletier, pre-1826

"*Flower* medium-sized or large, full, pale pink." [Pf] "Pelletier's seedling mentioned by Desportes and Prévost." [Gx] Malmaison, the palace of the rose-loving Empress Joséphine.

Delphiniana   Listed as the 'Enfant de France' (Ag) from Holland; this synonym is one of Redouté's and Thory's Latinate noncenames.

Duchesse d'Angoulême

For the Agathe, listed as 'Blush Belgic' in Chapter 4; for the Gallica known also as the 'Wax Rose', see 'Duchesse d'Angoulême' in Chapter 2.

Éloïse Listed as 'Héloïse' (Ag).

Elouise Listed as 'Héloïse' (Ag).

Enfant de France

syns. 'À Petites Fleurs', 'Delphiniana', 'Grand-Dauphin', 'Le Grand-Dauphin', 'Le Jeune Roi Dauphin', 'Roi de Rome', 'Roi de Rome de Holland'; trans., "Child of France"
Holland/Dupont, ca. 1802

"Light purple." [BJ40] "Bright red." [Cal] "Flowers full, medium sized, deep pink." [AC] "Regular, medium-sized, very double, violet purple, beautiful." [No26] "Medium-sized, full, regular, a shaded violet purple." [BJ30] "Very bright carminy crimson; pretty ranunculus form." [J-A/570] "Medium-sized, full, light purple." [Pf] "Sub-variety of the Gallica, of which it has, in miniature, all the characteristics up to the round, uncovered buds. Its flower is no larger than that of the 'Pompon de Bourgogne', a beautiful crimson; some green leaves replace the central stamens. This pretty pompon flattens out like a cockade when it is open. Its perfume is delicious. Opens June 12 to 15." [LeR] "Formerly bore the name 'Roi de Rome'; today it is 'Le Grand Dauphin'. It has the same characteristics [as 'Duchesse d'Angoulême' (Ag)—that is, our 'Marie-Louise'], but its color is darker, a beautiful Hydrangea pink. It originally came to us from Brussels under the name 'Enfant de France'." [CM, his last sentence mixing up the Holland 'Enfant de France' with the Brussels 'Enfant de France]

"*Bush* about 0.9 m high [nearly 3 ft]; *canes* with many small, unequal, almost straight prickles, especially in the upper portion, mixed with pedicellate glands. *Leaflets* 5, rather dark green, small, oblong ovate, rounded at the base, acute at the tip, glabrous above, slightly tomentose beneath and on the margins; petioles glandular, with small, very short prickles; stipules decurrent, acute, gland-edged. *Flowers* 2 (−3) at the tips of the canes; *receptacles* and *pedicels* reddish, glandular hispid; *sepals* 3 pinnatifid, 2 simple, glandular without, whitish woolly within; *petals* very numerous and quite crowded, rather dark pink, overlapping in the fashion of a military pompon, entirely hiding the sepals. *Hips* pyriform, red. Remarkable both for the beauty and the singularity of its blossoms, this was introduced about 1802 by Dupont, who claims that it was known during the reign of Louis XV [*reigned 1715–1774*], and that the Dutch dedicated it to the Dauphin, whence the name 'Child of France'. It is rare on its own roots, but commonly found grafted on the Briar." [T&R] "According to Du Pont, who distributed it, this variety was known in the reign of Louis XV, and the Dutch had dedicated it to the Grand Dauphin. Lelieur, in 1811, baptized it 'Roi de Rome'; De Pronville, in 1818, called in the 'Grand Dauphin'." [Gx] This is possibly Fillassier's 'Petite de Flandre', the second sub-variety of 'Blush Belgic' along with 'Rouge Belgique', in which case its date would move back to pre-1791 (and its name would change to 'Petite de Flandre')—*but* we have been unable to substantiate this. See also the 'Enfant de France' from Brussels, below, with which names, synonyms, and facts were freely mixed in the 1820s.

[Enfant de France]

syns. 'Enfant de France de Bruxelles', 'Grand-Dauphin', 'Le Grand Dauphin', 'Roi de Rome'; trans., "Child of France"
Brussels, pre-1824

"Flesh-color . . . nothing but a sub-variety of ['Marie-Louise'], which has a darker color." [BJ24] "*Flower* small or medium-sized, full, plump, very symmetrical, light bright even pink." [Pf] See also the 'Enfant de France' from Holland, above, its Siamese twin in confusion.

Enfant de France de Bruxelles Listed as 'Enfant de France' (Ag), the one from Brussels.

Fatime

Descemet/Vibert, 1820

"Blossoms very full, very graceful, and beautiful pink." [J-As/55] "Of the usual size, rose color, spotted." [WRP] "Flower medium-sized, double or very double, pink, spotted." [S] "Given by Desportes as an obtention of Descemet's." [Gx] Fatime, alias Fatima, lived A.D. 606–632; daughter of Mohammed.

Feu Non Rouge Listed as 'Feunon Rouge' (Ag).

[Feunon Rouge]

trans. "Red *Feunon*"
Breeder unknown, pre-1811

"Wood delicate and slender, leaves oval, much dentate, pointed. Calyx and bud elongate. Blossom the size and color of the 'Bordeaux' rose [*i.e.,* 'Rosier des Dames' (CP)], but flatter; very double; sweet scent; blooms on June 15; worth growing." [C-T]

Flamande Listed as 'Blush Belgic' (Ag).

[Francfort Agathé]

syn. 'Bijarre'; trans., "Agathed Francofurtana"
Breeder unknown, pre-1811

"This rose is quite an original, and I presume that it is the same as a variety which was given to me under the name 'Bijarre', which I alas cannot compare it with because the specimen of this latter perished last Winter. Neither the wood nor the leaves are remarkable at all. The calyx membranes, which are round and glabrous, crown and accompany the bud, which is flat and big. The very double blossom, three inches across [ca. 7.5 cm], is pale pink mixed with white; petals crinkled and ragged; it is fragrant, and is a long time in opening fully." [C-T]

Grand-Dauphin Listed as 'Enfant de France' (Ag), both forms.

Grande Agathe Listed as 'Henriette' (Ag).

Grande Agathe Nouvelle Listed as 'Héloïse' (Ag).

Grande Agathée Listed as 'Henriette' (Ag).

[Héloïse]

syns. 'Agathe Nouvelle', 'Éloïse', 'Elouise', 'Grande Agathe Nouvelle', 'Nouvelle Héloïse'
Descemet, 1816

"Blossoms full, large, flesh pink." [AC] "*Canes* nearly thornless. *Ovary* oval-pyriform, bestrewn (like the *peduncle*) with several fragrant black glands. *Sepals* long, viscous, 3–4 of them pinnatifid. *Flower* medium-sized or large, full, flesh or pale pink, nuanced pur-

[Héloïse] *continued*

ple pink." [Pf] "Bred by Descemet, mentioned by Desportes; Prévost says that it was also called 'Agathe Nouvelle'." [Gx]

Henriette
syns. 'Grande Agathe', 'Grande Agathée'
Dupont, pre-1810

"The wood, calyx, and bud all have the *Agathe* characteristics—that is, they [*i.e.,* the blossoms] come seven or eight on the same petiole, making a corymb- or umbel-bouquet. But the flower differs from those of the [typical] Agathes in that it is at least as large as that of a Centifolia, slightly flat, and beautiful cherry red. This rose has some merit, first by the form and look of its buds and flowers, and then because it blooms late, not opening until the end of June or beginning of July. The bush, grafted on the Briar, makes a good head—strong and well-rounded—making a sight both striking and pleasant. It can't be denied that this rose is due the efforts of the rose fancier, and can be classed among the most beautiful sorts or varieties." [C-T] "Close-set Agathe wood; leaves longer, nearly like those of the Centifolia. The blossoms are large, and flatten out when they open, which doubles their size. These beautiful roses come in eights or tens on the same stalk in the form of a corymb or perfect bouquet. Its color is a full, bright red, a little lighter along the edges of the petals. It is very double, and has the benefit of blooming late. It should be considered one of the beauties. Opens June 20–25." [LeR]

Incarnata   Listed as 'Blush Belgic' (Ag).

Incomparable   Listed as 'Soleil Brillant' (Ag).

Invincible   Listed as 'Soleil Brillant' (Ag).

La Cocarde   Listed as 'Majestueuse' (Ag).

La Grande Belgique   Listed as 'Blush Belgic' (Ag).

Le Grand-Dauphin   Listed as 'Enfant de France' (Ag), both forms.

Le Jeune Roi Dauphin   Listed as 'Enfant de France' (Ag), the one from Holland.

Le Majestueuse   Listed as 'Majestueuse' (Ag).

Le Triomphe   Listed as 'Majestueuse' (Ag).

Lucrèce   Listed as 'Majestueuse' (Ag).

Majestueuse
syns. 'Boule Hortensia', 'Cocarde', 'De Hollande', 'La Cocarde', 'Le Majestueuse', 'Le Triomphe', 'Lucrèce', 'Maxima'; trans., "Majestic"
Holland, pre-1790

"Pale rose." [Cal] "Bright crimson." [WRP] "Light pink." [Ÿ] "*Bud* red. *Flower* medium-sized, full, plump, light pink." [Pf] "Wood, leaves, calyxes, and buds not unusual at all. The blossom, three inches across [ca. 7.5 cm], is well formed, and a beautiful crimson color; its petals are large, thick, and velvety. It has a sweet scent, and also blooms around June 10." [C-T] "Bush with erect canes, glabrous and smooth in some parts; blossom double, medium-sized, regular, plump, bright pink, edges often pale." [S] "Desportes says it came from Holland; it was described by Guerrapain. Descemet's 'La Cocarde' and 'Lucrèce' are synonyms, says Prévost." [Gx]

Marie-Louise
syns. 'Agathe Couronnée', 'Agathe Rose', 'Augustine Pourprée', 'Belle Flamande', 'Caprice du Zéphyre', 'Mutabilis', 'Orphée de Lille', 'Tendresse Admirable'
Malmaison, 1811?

"Pale rose." [Cal] "Flesh." [V9] "Flesh, white when fully open, very abundant." [BJ30] "Blossoms medium-sized, double, white lightly washed with pink, fairly abundant, very thickly set." [BJ24] "Light pink, medium size, full, very fragrant, moderate height." [Sn] "*Bush* diffuse. *Canes* flexuose. *Leaves* ordinarily pendant. *Flower* medium-sized, quite multiplex, light pink or pale." [Pf] Graham Stuart Thomas gives a date of 1811 for this cultivar; Prévost tells of having received it from Malmaison in 1813. Owing to one of the synonyms of 'Blush Belgic' (Ag) being 'Marie-Louise', there is confusion between the two cultivars. Worse, the mauve-pink cultivar distributed in modern times as 'Marie-Louise' does not conform to the descriptions in the old literature. Hmm! Could this modern *parvenu* be something else? Could the original 'Marie-Louise' indeed be only a synonym of 'Blush Belgic'? Marie-Louise, daughter of Francis I of Austria, second wife of Napoléon; Empress of the French and Grand Duchess of Parma; lived 1791–1847.

Maxima   Listed as 'Majestueuse' (Ag).

Multiflora   Listed as 'Royale' (Ag).

Mutabilis   Listed as 'Marie-Louise' (Ag).

Nouvelle Héloïse   Listed as 'Héloïse' (Ag).

Orphée de Lille   Listed as 'Marie-Louise' (Ag).

Pallidior   Listed as 'Blush Belgic' (Ag).

Petite Agathe   Listed as 'Sommesson' (Ag).

Petite de Flandre   See 'Blush Belgic' (Ag) and 'Enfant de France' (Ag; the one from Holland); see also 'Sommesson', the 'Petite Agathe'.

[Petite Renoncule Violette]
trans. "Small Violet Ranunculus"
Vibert, pre-1820

"*Bush* up to 45 cm tall [ca. 18 in]; *canes* diffuse, covered in the upper part with very numerous needles and in the lower part with a few sparse unequal prickles mixed with glands. *Leaves* drooping in a noticeable way; *leaflets* 5(–7), elliptic, bidenticulate, green and glabrous above, paler beneath; petioles glandular hispid, with small straight prickles. *Flowers* 1(–2), lateral and terminal, small; *sepals* pinnatifid, short, scarcely overtopping the petals in bud; petals 8–10-seriate, purple to dark violet, paler towards the base, densely packed like those of a double *Ranunculus*. *Hips* pyriform, red or dark orange, persisting throughout much of the Winter. This is a variant of the Provins Rose, in the Agathe group, having very double blooms with densely packed petals curled and crumpled at the center. We found it last Summer in the rich collection of Ledru, and fanciers can obtain it from Vibert's nursery. It seems related to Descemet's seedling 'Petite Violette', but the rose under discussion is a little larger. It requires shade and only ordinary culture. Ledru prunes it very hard." [T&R]

Pétronille   Listed as 'Beauté Superbe Agathée' (Ag).

Précieuse Listed as 'Prolifère' (Ag).

[Prolifère]

syn. 'Précieuse'; trans., "Proliferative"
Dupont?, pre-1804

"Flowers fairly large, pink, bearing a second abortive bud at the center of the petals." [No26] "Medium-sized, imbricated, pink." [God] "This is a monstrosity . . . from their center come one or two buds which rarely open." [dP] "Hybrid with Centifolia." [R-H29/21] "Plant moderately vigorous; canes slender and out-spreading; thorns light brown; leaves ordinarily in 5 leaflets, the odd one spatulate, the others oval; blossoms not very numerous, very double, well-formed, medium size, two or three together, petals of a pink which is sometimes a bit pale, slightly notched at the tip; outer petals lightly ruffled, central petals rolled into a ring." [S] "This bush has the form and appearance of ['Royale']. The blossom is of medium size, well-formed, pretty, a very delicate pink; the petals are shell-shaped. In the middle, there ordinarily comes another flower, and from this second, a third. I have seen them open successively; they are borne on a petiole which is generally flat and often bearing some slender leaflets which are long and arranged in stages. Some other times, there come up to four or five buds from the middle of the principal flower; this monstrosity depends upon the strength and vigor of the stock on which the plant is grafted. This rose is successfully grown on the Briar, on which it takes a good form and maintains itself. I have seen one which has existed for seven to eight years, getting stronger every year." [C-T] "Grown by Du Pont, mentioned by Redouté and Desportes." [Gx]

Regalis Listed as 'Royale' (Ag).

Roi de Rome Listed as 'Enfant de France' (Ag), both forms.

Roi de Rome de Holland Listed as 'Enfant de France' (Ag), the Dutch one.

[Rouge Belgique]

syns. 'Belgica Rubra', 'Vitex Spinosa'; trans., "Red Belgic"
Breeder unknown, pre-1791

According to Fillassier, a subvariety of 'De Flandre', *i.e.*, 'Blush Belgic': "[It] has blossoms colored a darker red [than 'De Flandre']." [Fr] "*Leaflets* dark green, often marbled yellow, wavy edges. *Flower* large, double, very intense and bright pink." [Pf]

Royale

syns. 'Bouquet Parfait', 'Multiflora', 'Regalis'; trans., "Royal"
Godefroy, pre-1811

"Pale rose." [Cal] "Medium-sized, imbricated, pink." [God] "*Flower* small, full, regular, light pink or cerise mottled with red." [Pf] "Large quite double blossoms, and a beautiful deep pink." [J-A/571] "Very distinct flowers, because of the form and mix of white and pink showing over the surface of the petal." [J-As/55] "Very common; blossoms numerous; pink touched with red." [dP] "Its color is a light cerise red; along the petal edges there are some white shadings which enhance it. The compactness of all its parts should make it considered as one of the beauties for the garden. Opens June 9–10." [LeR] "One of the first to bloom." [CM] "Its branches are close-set and slender, making a good head when grafted on the Briar. There is nothing striking in the leaves, which are pretty enough, nor in the thorns. The blossom could be included among the beautiful because of its form and color; it is quite double, and of a beautiful light cerise red. There runs along the petal edges some white shadings—which makes a good effect." [C-T] "*Bush* about 75 cm high [ca. 30 in]; canes dense, slender, especially in the upper part, armed with short, unequal prickles, the larger ones wider at the base. *Leaflets* 5(–7), stiff, subrotund, bidentate, the teeth sometimes tipped with small glands, glabrous above, tomentose beneath; petioles somewhat villose, with small prickles; stipules decurrent, acute. *Flowers* medium-sized, often in a cluster at the tips of the canes; receptacles subovoid, subglabrous; pedicels glandular hispid; *corolla* very double; *petals* rather bright pink, those at the center curled and crumpled; *stamens* absent; *styles* partly free, partly fasciculate. Agathe 'Royale' blooms in early Spring, and continues for a long time. The outer petals are often flushed whitish or darker red, giving an attractive look to the blossom." [T&R] "Described by De Pronville and Guerrapain, described and illustrated by Redouté; Prévost says that he saw it at Godefroy's under the name 'Bouquet Parfait'." [Gx] "Rejected and superseded." [WRP] Not to be confused with the Alba 'La Royale', a synonym for 'Great Maiden's Blush' (A).

Rubicans Listed as 'Blush Belgic' (Ag).

Sapho

syn. 'Beauté Rare'
Vibert, 1818

"In the eyes of all the fanciers, this rose is one of the prettiest of the Provins group. The very double blossom, the size of the 'Bordeaux' [*i.e.,* 'Rosier des Dames' (CP)], is flat once open. It shows three colors: the middle is purple, and the edges, in expanding, show a mixture of deep pink and delicate pink. The petals are creped and reverse onto the calyx. Its canes are a little weak and divergent, the one going high, the next low, giving a pleasing originality to the plant. Blooms June 1–6." [LeR] Sapho, alias Sappho, 6th century B.C. poetess of Lesbos, evidently the first to bestow on the Rose the lasting office of Queen of Flowers.

Soleil Brillant

syns. 'Incomparable', 'Invincible'; trans., "Bright Sun"
Holland, pre-1790

"Bright red." [Cal] "Deep pink." [LS] "'Soleil Brillant' should find a place in that class [*i.e.,* the class of roses which merit cultivation]. This variety has no very striking characteristic in wood, leaves, or thorns. The flower buds are ordinarily yellow-green; the calyx is oval. This flower has the size of the Centifolia, and is as double; no stamens; deep unshaded pink; petals ragged and wavy. It's a pretty variety with a nice perfume." [C-T] No doubt the "ragged and wavy" "bright red" petals suggested a blazing sun.

Sommesson

syn. 'Petite Agathe'
Pelletier, pre-1820

"*Canes* flexuose, much armed. *Flower* small, full, lilac pink." [Pf] "*Shrub,* armed with numerous thorns, mostly strong and crooked." [Go] Monsieur Sommesson, Parisian rose breeder, fl. in the 1820s.

Tendresse Admirable Listed as 'Marie-Louise' (Ag).

Victorine la Couronnée
trans. "Victorine the Crowned"
Breeder unknown, pre-1811

"Light pink, striped red, medium size, full, light scent, moderate height."[Sn] "A charming kind, with slender, delicate, and nearly thornless wood. The leaves are nearly round, deeply serrated, and beautiful green, coming very close to the blossom, which is very fetching. Calyx round, constricted at the tip. Bud the same form, nicely crowned by the calyx membranes [*sepals*], which are incised feather-style, growing more than an inch long [ca. 2.5 cm]. Flower Centifolia-form, two and a half inches across [ca. 6–7 cm], of a slightly lighter pink [*than that of the common Centifolia*], very fragrant, and blooming about the same time [*as the common Centifolia*]." [C-T] "Several botanists derive this one from the Centifolias—but it doesn't have any of their characteristics. Rather, its jutting-out growth, upright and vigorous, yellowish green and punctuated with touches of brown, as well as its disk-shaped leaves and its few thorns—all these signs proclaim its Agathe origin, of which it is a hybrid with one of the darker Gallicas. These same leaves are set in close to the buds, which are profuse and nicely crowned by the calyx appendages, which extend nearly an inch further [ca. 2.5 cm] in the form of little feathers. The blossom is not very double; its size is more than medium; its pink color is so delicate that it is hard to stop looking at it—one feels softened by the sweetness of its colors; several petals are marked to a greater or lesser degree with a more intense or ore delicate pink. There are hardly any other roses so delicate and so pretty! They bloom June 5–10." [LeR]

Vitex Spinosa Listed as 'Rouge Belgique' (Ag).

Volumineuse
trans. "Massy"
Breeder unknown, pre-1828

"Pink, large, full." [Jg] *Cf.* 'La Volumineuse', the pre-1835 Damask Perpetual.

CHAPTER FIVE

Centifolias

"The north-west of Asia, which has been signalized as the fa- ther-land of the rose-tree, introduces to our admiration the *Rosa centifolia,* the most esteemed of all, and celebrated by po- ets of every age and country, with which the fair Georgians and Circassians adorn their persons." [Go] "Originated in the Cau- casus." [JF] "The *Cent feuilles* ["*Hundred-leaves*"] Rose, which it would be better to call the *Cent pétales* ["*Hundred-petals*"] Rose." [AC] "It is the Centifolia which gives us those beautiful ros- es which are notable in their rounded form and by the delicious perfume they waft; this is what they're talking about in common parlance when they talk generally about roses. Up until these latter days, only the semi-double or doubles were known; but Monsieur Dupont grew from seed the single Type, which has ba- sic differences from all the [other] known varieties; its leaves are a more delicate green; furthermore, it is quite rare. The Centifo- lia grows from six to eight feet [ca. 2–2.6 m]; it blooms in the middle of Spring. By chance, it will give a second crop of flowers in the Fall. We call it the Centifolia; this is not correct—we should call it Centi-Petala. But such is the usage; and we know that usage is a tyrant. The Dutch gardeners count the varieties of Centifolia in the hundreds! It's a fact that this rose has pro- duced nearly as many by cultivation as the Provins rose." [CM]

"This very celebrated and justly popular rose has been an in- habitant of English Gardens for nearly three hundred years [*writing in 1844*]; its native country is rather obscure, though vague tradition says it comes from the east, a term of great breadth and length; however, Bieberstein asserts having seen it grow on the Caucasus. Some suppose that this is the rose men- tioned by Pliny as being a great favorite among the Romans. In this taste the modern world still agree, for it disputes the palm of beauty with its sisters of the present day; although it has been crossed and amalgamated with many others, none of the proge- ny outvies the parent in size, beauty, perfection, and fragrance. In the humid air of Britain, it blooms for two months in the sum- mer, around almost every cottage; but with us [*in the United States*], two or three weeks in June display every flower, and if the weather is very hot, they flower and fade in a day. I confess that

there is great difficulty in deciding on the varieties that do be- long to this species." [Bu] "*Rosa centifolia* differs from *R. gallica* by: 1. *Leaflets* soft to the touch, more or less pendant, always gland-edged, rather deeply dentate (those of *gallica* being firm, as if brittle, finely dentate, more or less whitish beneath, and rarely gland-edged). 2. *Petioles* hispid but always lacking prick- les (those of *gallica* being more or less armed). A fancier with a little experience can distinguish the two species at a glance." [T&R]

"*Bush* with divergent canes, forming a low, diffuse shrub armed with unequal thorns (the largest curved into a scythe), intermingled with bristles and glands. *Leaves* distant and not very numerous, composed of 5 (rarely 7) leaflets. *Petiole* glan- dulose. *Leaflets* glabrous above, villose or pubescent beneath. *Serration* simple or double, normally glandulose. *Peduncles* long, bestrewn or covered with pediculate glands, sometimes solitary, more normally in 2's to 5's or in paucifloral corymbs. *Ovary* glandulose; oval, oblong, or fusiform, rarely turbinate, al- ways longer than wide and more or less constricted at the tip. *Sepals* glandulose (these glands, and all those on the bush— which has an abundance of them—are viscous and fragrant), terminating in a point or very long leaflet, exceeding the tip of the bud; 3 of them have very long, divergent appendages along the sides. They are wide-spreading or erect after bloom, but do not reflex. *Bud* conical. *Flower* nodding in many varieties, up- right in others, wafting a very elegant scent, and nearly always having a regular and very agreeable form due to the arrange- ment of the petals. *Fruit* red, oval, sometimes oblong, rarely round. The Centifolias lose their leaves early in the Fall. Their growth ceases rather earlier than that of the greater part of oth- er species. Their [growth] buds are protrusive and quick to de- velop, in general. Grafted, the majority of the varieties . . . rarely have a career both shining and long-lived. It is thus prudent to also keep them own-root." [Pf] "Of moderate vigor, and barely growing to perhaps four feet in height [ca. 1.3 m]. Its canes, though firm, are somewhat slender, irregular, with the young growths being reddish; the blossoms, solitary or in groups of two or three on the most vigorous branches, are large, very full, and globular, with large petals of a beautiful pink; they diffuse an elegant perfume." [JF] "Canes to 5 to 6 feet [ca. 1.6–2 m] with thorns unequal and hooked; branches and canes divergent; leaves composed of 7 oval leaflets, lightly villose and glaucous beneath; petioles villose, glandular, and prickly; flowers often more than 2 inches across [ca. 5 cm], bright pink, elegant scent." [BJ17] "There are three varieties of the [common] Centifolia, and three of the *Hollande* [*evidently 'Grande Centfeuille de Holland'*] which are distinguished by the greater or lesser size of the blossoms, or the lighter or darker color. To begin with, the branches of the *Hollande* are very divergent; its flowers come all along the canes in great quantities like garlands, much seconded by the leaves. Its petals reflex back on the calyx. Their color is lively and bright; they are veined pretty strongly with a pink which is darker than the ground-color. The [common] Centifolia, on the other hand, is lower, the wood is subject to decay, flowers produced only at the branch-tips, often solitary, smaller, paler—it should give way to the *Hollande*, which should always be preferred." [LeR]

"I won't stop to work out the characteristics of the ordinary Centifolia, so well known all over; but it nevertheless has varieties either more or less beautiful—but, still, I am unable to catch at all of them or to classify them in their proper places. If I would dare to do so, I would bring certain reproaches to this rose to which everyone nevertheless seems to accord the palm —everyone, that is, except for certain fanciers. To begin with, this plant doesn't make bushes either as beautiful or as compact as other sorts—particularly the 'Tous-Mois' [*Damask Perpetual*]. Its blossoms aren't accompanied by enough leaves; having these would set them off, and make them more valuable. The wood often becomes scurfy and dies after two years, or nearly, and needs to be renewed. Its buds don't have the lightness and elegance of those of the 'Tous-Mois', nor do they make as pretty bouquets. Nor does their perfume seem as delicate to me." [C-T]

"The Provence Roses [*meaning the Centifolia Roses*] are deliciously fragrant; their habit is for the most part branching, or pendulous; and among them are some of the finest globular-shaped Roses grown. The foliage is bold and handsome; the leaflets broad and wrinkled, in many instances obtuse, the edges deeply serrated. The prickles on the branches are very unequal; some are fine and straight, others large at their base, and falcate. These points, with the drooping habit, and usually globular flowers, serve as marks by which we distinguish them. They thrive well either as dwarfs or standards; but some varieties require the fostering care of the cultivator to tempt them to produce their flowers in full beauty. To ensure complete success, plant them in a soil made rich, and water them occasionally in spring with liquid manure. All, except the vigorous growers, which are in many instances hybrids, should be subjected to close pruning." [P]

"Monsieur de Pronville asserts, with good reason, that one would do better to call it *Rosa centipetalae* . . . Specific characters. Irregular branches forming a diffuse bush; numerous thorns, unequal, nearly straight; distant leaves composed of five dusky green leaflets, doubly dentate, nodding, much subject to rust, falling very early; leafstalk glandulose, usually unarmed; peduncle long, covered with bristles; stipules channeled; sepals foliaceous; flowers solitary or clustered in groups of 2–5, very full, globular, nodding, very fragrant. Culture. The Centifolia Rose is not of difficult culture; however, it likes sun much better than shade, and prefers a good loam to all other soils. It is absolutely necessary to grow it on its own roots. I know that very often one is obliged to graft it to 'fix' a variety which tends to disappear or to propagate it from others which, on their own roots, give bad results; but, whenever one can, one had best avoid grafting, as the plants end up dying at the end of only a few years. It's no better to bud; make a habit of propagating them by offset or sucker. This rose doesn't rebloom—what a crime! — and that's why a rose so beautiful and fragrant is today somewhat neglected. But there's a way to make it rebloom. It is explained by a fine Langrois named Douette-Richardot, in a little brochure published by him in 1827, and dedicated by him to Posterity (*Procédés pour Obtenir des Roses de toutes Éspèces deux Fois par An*, by Nicolas Douette-Richardot). I'd like very much to make his procedure known, but with due caution, and with no guarantee of success: 'If the fancier is anxious for a double crop, if he wants to gather in September roses yet more beautiful than those which embellished his garden in June, he must: 1°. Immediately after first bloom, completely defoliate the bush, and the branches which bore the blossoms must be pruned back such that no more than two or three eyes, depending on the vigor of the branch, are left. 2°. Then use a brush [*vergette*] to clean the rose and get rid of the moss trying to cover it. 3°. Next, turn your hand to the ground surrounding the rose to a distance of one foot [ca. 3 dm] from the trunk, so that the next step will be easier. 4°. Place around the rose to a distance of 4 inches from the trunk [ca. 1 dm], in earth that has been well-raked, 25 cow dew-claws (those of the young ones are the tenderest and best, giving roses a brighter color and nicer scent). Place these dew-claws point down, such that the cup [*godet*] is nearly at ground level [*à fleur de terre*] and the bush is completely surrounded. Re-do this the following November. The rains which come in Summer and Fall, or which are replaced by frequent waterings, fill the cups; they soften and dissolve at last. The fatty part spreads onto the root-hairs [*chevelu*] of the bush, making an excellent fertilizer, speeding growth, and ensuring the reproduction of flowers. It is by taking such precautions that you can, in September, display the beauty of these charming flowers which, from the ancients of Théos to today, have always been the symbol of joy and pleasure.' As everyone knows, new varieties of roses come sometimes from seed, sometimes from sports. Well! It is perhaps among the Centifolias that one most frequently finds sports, and, oddly enough, nearly all the varieties which so originate have a tendency to metamorphose back to the original; in such cases, it is necessary to resort to grafting to retain the sport. Pruning. Some say, prune long; others, prune short; prune right after bloom; prune in February. As for me, I prune my Centifolias right after the end of severe cold. The plants of moderate vigor, I cut short; the more vigorous, a little longer—and I always get a very good bloom. When the plant gets too old and seems to be decaying, you rejuvenate it by cutting it back to ground level. Loiseleur-Deslongchamps advises that this be done right after bloom. He says that, this way, one gets canes that are vigorous enough to give blossoms the following year. Finally, to bring in La Bretonnerie, one can retard the bloom of Centifolias by picking off their buds as soon as they start appearing, indeed doing the same with their leaves. Buc'hoz says (*Monographie de la Rose et de la Violette*, Paris, 1804, page 102), 'regrow for us to marvel at, bringing their beauty back and giving autumnal blossoms. However, you shouldn't repeat this procedure every year on the same plant, as that would wear it out. Perhaps it was a donkey that taught us this method, having come into to garden and munched on some roses!'. Hardiness. The Centifolias are very hardy and can withstand 25 or indeed 30 degrees of cold." [JR10/93–95]

"Nature, always wise in dispensing the favors she heaps on us, compensates and consoles the poor cottager in his misery by seeing to it that this beautiful flower grows as well in his patch of land as it does on the grounds of the golden palaces of the great. This rose is robust; all terrains suit it, as does any exposure. Always active and alert, it burrows into the deepest recesses of the bosom of its mother to draw out the sugar necessary for the subsistence of its roots, the vigor of its wood, the excellence of its perfume, and the beauty of its colors." [LeR] "The Dutch Centifolia, be it the scented or unscented—all require the same culture: a cool spot, a little sun, and strong soil. They are pruned in March, cutting off only the dry tips. They can bloom in the Fall if you prune them in Spring back to a foot or a foot and a half [ca. 3–4.25 dm]. These Dutch roses—if you can get them going as tree-roses, displaying their beautiful and delicate stock-in-trade in season—are indeed beautiful." [LaQ] "Standards of some of the varieties, if grown on a strong, clayey soil, form fine objects of ornament, as their large globular flowers are so gracefully pendant. In this description of soil, also, if grown as dwarfs, they will not flourish, unless they are worked on the Dog Rose, or Sweet Briar; but in light sandy soils it will be advisable to cultivate them on their own roots. The freedom with which they grow in light sandy soils points out this method of culture on such soils as the most eligible. In pruning, they require a free use of the knife: every shoot should be shortened to three or four buds in February. If not pruned in this severe man-

ner, the plants soon become straggling and unsightly. In poor soils, they should have annually, in November, a dressing of rotten manure on the surface of the bed, to be washed in by the rains of winter." [WRP] "They require a free rich loamy soil; close pruning, that is shortening the shoots of the preceding year to three or four eyes, keeps them in the best order; choosing the month of February for this operation." [Bu] "The Cabbage Rose [Centifolia] is a somewhat weak grower in heavy soil, though in a light soil it grows vigorously. As a general rule, it needs close pruning." [FP] "All the Centifolias love a rich soil, well-fertilized; they should also be closely pruned." [R-H63/183] "The greater part of the Centifolias don't live long grafted. There are, however, some exceptions, because I have seen, a few years ago, an ordinary centifolia grafted on the Briar at the five-foot mark [ca. 1.6 m] in which the stem was six inches around [ca. 1.5 dm], and the head more than 18 feet around [ca. 6 m]. It was no older than ten or twelve years, and hadn't been pruned for five or six; its roses were superb. This is, at any rate, a pretty rare exception to the rule; it is more prudent to have all the beautiful varieties own-root." [An32/373] "They thrive best upon their own roots, and a bed of the Old Cabbage Rose should be in every rosarium." [JC]

"The Cabbage rose, or *Rosa centifolia,* is a persistent plant about old house-sites. I knew of one place in the Middlesex Fells Park, of Boston, when the land was first acquired, where this species had persisted for probably a hundred years. It was on the site of an old house in which tradition stated that children lost their lives over a hundred years ago [*i.e.,* ca. 1800] in a fire. If this could be secured in large quantities, it would make a low cover-shrub that would be very charming in the color of its flowers." [ARA18/21] "*Rosa Centifolia* (*Ouard Beledy* of the Arabs). I only saw it grown in quantity in the fields of Fayoum [Egypt]. It is multiplied by suckers which are planted in February in some trenches prepared beforehand by a workman. They subsequently water them copiously for abundant bloom, and fertilize them well, to be purchased by the government to make rose water … The roses are pruned every year, and they come into full production in the second year. The number of flowers begins to decline about the sixth year. They are then moved into other soil." [AnFrVI/101]

"This superb species has given us numerous varieties." [JF] "The Centifolia varieties have always been small in number in our gardens. Monsieur Vibert, one of the rosarians who most cultivated this type, certainly never found any Centifolia or its sport ever to produce fertile seeds, excepting only the single variety; few plants, however, are so apt to sport as this. Monsieur Vibert would collect these variations, and some of the more notable are still grown; many fanciers believe, wrongly, that these were developed from seed. We might name, among others, the Moss Rose, or—more mossy—'Cristata', the rose 'Des Peintres', Dutch in origin … 'Unique Panachée', and finally 'Pompon', a charming miniature of the Type, found growing wild, in 1735, on a mountain in the vicinity of Dijon by a gardener who took cuttings from it. Other varieties present unusual foliar variations: the 'Lettuce-Leafed Rose' ['Bullata'], for example." [JF] "The varieties in commerce [in 1893] are down to 'Des Peintres', 'Crétée' ['Cristata'], 'À Feuilles Bullées' ['Bullata'], 'À Feuilles Bipennées' ['À Feuilles de Céleri'], 'Unique Blanche' ['Unique'], 'Unique Panachée'." [JR17/78]

We must add a note on use of the term "Provence Roses." This term has never had a consistent meaning in the rose world, with contemporaries in the same country varying the meaning. As we shall see in a moment, the term has been used not only (1) to designate Centifolias but also (2) to refer to hybrids between Centifolias and Gallicas. As we saw in Chapter 4, the Agathes were (3) called "Provence Roses," not consciously as possible hybrids between Centifolias and Gallicas, but in their own right. Finally, as is frequently a subject of discussion or note among rosarians, (4) there is confusion with the term "Provins Roses"—meaning *Gallicas*—not only rendering ambiguous what is meant by "Provence Roses," but also producing its own hybrid term of nebulous significance, "Province Roses." No assumptions should be made when the term is run across in the literature; no definition is "correct." "A very old rose amateur in France informed Mr. Rivers that the species with single flowers is found in a wild state in the southern provinces; and it is therefore very probable that it was called the Provence Rose, from growing more abundantly in that locality. It has, however, an additional name in France, it being also called the 'Rose à Cent Feuilles,' from the botanical name, Rosa centifolia, or Hundred-Leaved Rose. Hybrid roses, between this and Rosa gallica, are denominated Provence Roses by the French amateurs of the present day. Mr. Rivers remarks that, when he was a young rose-fancier, this name often misled him, as he was very apt to think that it referred to the Scotch and other small and thickly-leaved roses, and did not for a moment suppose that the term was applied to the petals or flower-leaves." [WRP]

"This rose is one of the best known and most generally cultivated; it's the one that gives us those beautiful roses remarkable for their rounded, globular form, the great number of their petals, the exquisite perfume which they waft, and the light tint of red which rejoices the eye without fatiguing it. The Type of this rose, of which the varieties are innumerable, is little known. As the flowers are always sterile because of the transformation of the sexual organs into petals, it is not known in its natural state. I have, however, seen one with single flowers at Monsieur Dupont's place, which that wise and able rose-grower had grown from seed coming from a semi-double rose; it isn't different in any way from the double except in the petals, reduced to the number of five. Otherwise, it had the same form, the same color, and the same characteristics in the other parts. What is astonishing is that this rose hasn't yet been found wild, at least to my knowledge, despite the research of all the botanists. It seems very probable to me that it owes its existence to one of the wild species we know; and though the single rose I spoke of isn't like any of these, it is to be believed that, despite its singleness, it retains touches of our cultivated rose. The species to which it comes closest is Rosa gallica, which is perhaps the primitive Type." [Lam]

"In 1816, Rau stated that it is native to northern Persia. Rössig claims that the Dog Rose (*R. canina*) is the prototype of *R. centifolia* perfected by cultivation over many centuries. If this were so, the specimen with single flowers raised from seed in Dupont's nursery would be its predecessor." [T&R]

"We mentioned that the Centifolia came from the region of the Caucasus mountains. The botanical explorer Bieberstein certainly found wild specimens, far from any habitation, giving the same double blossoms found in cultivated sorts. The Type, with single flowers, is unknown in the wild, but can be obtained in some gardens from seeds from the double varieties." [JF] "The year 1596 is cited as the date it was introduced into cultivation." [JR9/20]

Few subjects in rose history are murkier than the origins and progress of the Centifolia roses. It is exceedingly doubtful that any of the ancient roses mentioned by Theophrastus or Pliny the Elder correspond to our Centifolia (*v.* Testu [pp. 13–14], and Hurst in G. S. Thomas [p. 306]); Hurst's research indicated to him that it was neither "a wild species as many have supposed, nor is it a simple primary hybrid like the Damask Roses. It is a complex hybrid of four distinct wild species" [T4]—the Gallica, *Rosa phoenicea, R. moschata,* and *R. canina.* How this combination may have been effected is open to speculation. One of the great lacunae in rose knowledge concerns how the Dutch rose breeders went about their business in the 16th, 17th, and 18th centuries. If only we knew what conditions they worked under, what cultivars or species they bred with, indeed their names and affiliations! We at least know that all of these species mentioned by Hurst were available to the Dutch, if not on the primary level, at least through roses descended from these species. As Hurst points out by way of example, a simple cross of the Damask Perpetual 'Bifera' with an Alba would bring all of these species into play. References to occasional autumnal rebloom in the Centifolia perhaps support relation to 'Bifera' or some congener. We cannot, or at least do not, know how the 'Common Centifolia' came into being; it was associated with the Dutch at least by 1601, when Clusius described it as *Rosa centifolia batavica* (we rely on Testu and Gravereaux for these background facts). It quickly produced a rival, evidently the first of many sports, as, by 1616, Franeau was describing its variety 'Grande Centfeuille de Hollande'. By 1629, Parkinson listed 'Rubra', and had heard rumors of a white variant. It evidently sported the Moss Rose by 1696, a cultivar we will consider in due course in Chapter 7.

"In the [18th] Century, they were distinguished in our gardens—where they were abundantly cultivated—under the name 'Rose de Hollande à cent feuilles', which would seem to indicate they entered France from that country." [JR5/44] The pace of sports and variants began to pick up. A 'Single' is recorded by 1754, though it was evidently little known and quickly forgotten, being at length replaced by Dupont's circa 1804 'À Fleurs Simples'. The white 'Unique' showed up by 1777. With the beginning of the careers of Dupont and Descemet around 1800, collection of sports and development of new cultivars began to magnify the group such that, though the *Bon Jardinier* of 1806 could only muster six cultivars—and that even with including the Moss Rose and the two pompons, by 1820 Vibert was listing nearly two dozen, not counting the new hybrids which were coming into being:

"This group of non-remontant roses, which are called by the name *Hybrid Centifolias,* is comprised of roses intermediate between the Provins and the Centifolia. They share nearly equally the characteristics of both parents; thus it is that they have the wood and thorns of the Centifolia, and foliage pretty much like that of the Provins. You've got to be very sharp to be able to make out the telling characteristics . . ." [JR9/39] "All of these [hybrids] are of an extraordinary purity of color." [JR9/126] "This beautiful group has only 70 varieties, and in its habit much resembles the Provins roses; or, to say it better, it is intermediate between the Provins and the Centifolia. Less vigorous than the Provins, its branches are more nodular, less upright, and clothed with slender and numerous pale green thorns; the foliage is much like that of the Centifolia, but the leaves are also more flexible and closer together than the Centifolia's. The blossoms are nearly all light-colored, which makes a great contrast with the dark colors of their parent the Provins. The origin of the group is unknown to me, but it was formed in 1826 by Messieurs Vibert and Hardy." [JR9/125]

"Nature, with the Centifolia, seems inclined to exhibit the full extent of means at her disposal, and offers the man who knows how to look at things vast scope for his meditations." [V2] "The Centifolia Rose is truly the rose par excellence." [CM]

Rosa ×*centifolia*
—is defined by 'Common Centifolia' (C), *q.v.*

ℋorticultural 𝒱arieties

[À Feuille de Chêne]
syns. 'À Feuilles de Chêne', 'À Feuilles de Chêne Vert', 'Grandidentata', 'Ilicifolia', 'Quercifolia'; trans., "Oak-Leafed"
Trianon, pre-1811
"Rose." [Cal] "Flowers medium-sized, double, pink in color; leaves like those of the Live Oak." [AC] "The wood resembles that of the common Centifolia. The leaves—which in no way look like those of the Oak—are beautiful, oval, close-set on the petiole, bordered and whipped with brown, deeply toothed, and *surdentelées.* The buds are round, and come in umbels of five to seven on the same petiole. They are crowned by the calyx divisions, which are much cut. This last [*i.e.,* the calyx] is small and round, glutinose, releasing to the touch a perfume like that of the Moss. The blossom is medium-sized, and of the form and color of the [common] Centifolia." [C-T] "*Bush* not very vigorous, armed with feeble, sparse thorns. *Canes* purplish. *Leaves* remote. *Stipules* entire, fringed with glands, very close-set on the non-blooming canes. *Leaflets* ovoid, undulate, arching, pointed, usually grooved, often bullate. *Serration* unequal, very large. *Ovary* short, oval-globular or turbinate. *Flower* medium-sized, very full, flesh or pale pink; has difficulty opening." [Pf]

À Feuilles Bipinnées Listed as 'À Feuilles de Céleri' (C).

À Feuilles Crénelées
syns. 'À Feuilles Rondes Crénelées', 'À Folioles Crénelées', 'Crenata'; trans., "With Scalloped Leaves"
Dupont, pre-1804
"*Leaflets* rounded, edged with deep, very large dentations. This rose is very stingy with its flowers, which are small, full, and pink." [Pf] "This rose rarely blooms, and is not yet well known." [dP] "Remarkable by way of its smaller leaflets [in comparison with 'Common Centifolia'], which are strongly crenelate." [Lam]

"There's nothing to be noted in the wood. Its leaves are nearly round, very pretty, and much dentate. The blossom is the size of the Bordeaux [*i.e.,* 'Rosier des Dames' (CP)], quite double, prettily shaped, a delicate pink, fragrant, blooming ten or twelve days later [than June 10–20]. This rose, with its charming foliage, makes a beautiful head grafted on the Briar. It is one of the most beautiful sorts a person could grow! Ordinarily, the flowers are solitary or alone at the tips of the branches. Five or six buds, half open, accompanied by its pretty foliage, makes one of the most beautiful bouquets that Roses can give." [C-T] "The wood, while firm, is delicate and slender; its leaves are small and round, and are deeply scalloped, the teeth edged light brown; its blossoms—with which it is fairly stingy—are very double, bright pink, a little larger than the Bordeaux, Centifolia-form. Grafted, it makes a well-rounded, very neat bush. The blossoms open from June 20 to 25." [LeR]

"Moderately bushy *shrub* about 0.6 m tall [ca. 2 ft]; *canes* numerous, glandular-hispid, with small, almost straight prickles which drop readily so that mature branches are unarmed. *Leaflets* 3–5, round or subrotund, cordate at the base, deeply crenate, each lobe tipped with a glandular point, and denticulate on the margins; dark green above, paler beneath; petioles tomentose, unarmed. *Flowers* 1–3 at the tips of the canes, like those of the 'Common Centifolia', but smaller and less fragrant; pedicels covered in sticky scented glandular hairs; receptacles ovoid, rather short, bristly like the *sepals*; *petals* many, those at the center rather curled and crumpled. Said to have been raised from seed by Du Pont, who distributed it, 'À Feuilles Crénelées' is sought out for its odd foliage, and blooms but rarely on its own roots. Grafted plants bloom freely, if unpruned. It is rather scarce in collections." [T&R] "Takes all its merit from its leaves." [CM] "A too-indulgent regimen will return [it] to being the 'Common Centifolia'." [V2]

À Feuilles Crépues Listed as 'Bullata' (C).

À Feuilles Crispées Listed as 'À Feuilles de Céleri' (C).

[À Feuilles de Céleri]

syns. 'À Feuilles Bipinnées', 'À Feuilles Crispées', 'À Feuilles de
   Groseillier', 'À Feuilles de Groseillier de Maquereau', 'À Feuilles
   de Persil', 'Bipenné', 'Bipinnata', 'Crépue', 'Crispa', 'Gooseberry-
   Leaved', 'Grossularifolia'; trans., "Celery-Leafed"

Dupont, pre-1802

Sport of 'À Feuilles Crénelées' (C).

   "['À Feuilles Crénelées'] has fairly evidently produced another
variety yet more remarkable, in which the leaves are doubly pinnate,
composed of leaflets which are also rounded and obtuse. I have seen
these two . . . in the garden of Monsieur Dupont." [Lam] *Flower* medium-sized, full, globular, light pink." [Pf] "Its flowers rarely reach any
notable size." [dP] "The blossoms are perfectly double, a beautiful
pink; the leaves, toothed at their edges and as if crimped. This variety is worth growing because of its bizarre foliage." [CM] "Vigorous
bush; canes short, clothed with many thorns; foliage dark green;
flower medium-sized, full, exterior petals cordate; color, light pink."
[S] "Flowers rose, of medium size, full; form, globular. Foliage very
curious." [P] "Leaves remarkable due to the way the leaflets are
waved." [AC] "Another subvariety of the Centifolia, from which it differs only by the foliage, which resembles that of the Gooseberry or
Celery. Its blossom is a beautiful Centifolia of perfect scent and a
pleasant coloration. They open from the 9th to the 10th of June." [LeR]
"Leaflets smaller, rounded, creped, giving it a more compact look; often some revert to the primitive form." [BJ09] "The leaves have some
resemblance to those of celery. Its blossoms are medium-sized, full,
globular, light pink." [JR5/44] "Its leaves are, perhaps, as much like
imperfectly curled parsley as celery." [WRP]

   "Neither its wood nor its thorns are notable at all. Its leaves are divided into two or three segments, deeply cut, dentate, even doubly so,
edged and plumed during growth with light brown; these little nice-
ties alone make it sought out. Also, sometimes several leaves of this
rose take on—more or less—the form of those of the [common]
Centifolia, telling us the original Type of this variety, and making it
even more singular. The buds are pretty as is the blossom, which resembles a small Centifolia in shape, color, and scent." [C-T] "Subvariety of ['Rosier des Dames' (CP)], from which it differs only in its cut
foliage; sometimes, however, these cuts disappear, and then this Rose
is just like the other one." [BJ17] "['À Feuilles de Céleri'] and ['À
Feuilles Crénelées'], which a too-indulgent regimen will return to
being the 'Common Centifolia' . . . I [Vibert] have seen ['À Feuilles de
Céleri'] degenerate into ['À Feuilles Crénelées'], and this latter produce canes of the 'Common Centifolia' the same year." [V2] "Once
common, it has now become very rare, perhaps because of extreme
susceptibility to aphids, which make the blossoms unsightly. It can
be obtained on its own roots only by layering, in which state it grows
slowly unless in a moist soil and a very favorable position. Grafted on
the Briar it grows vigorously, and is best left alone—we have seen
fine plants perish as a result of over-attention." [T&R]

À Feuilles de Chanvre

syn. 'Cannabina'; trans., "Hemp-Leaved"

Breeder unknown, pre-1811

   "Light pink." [LS] "Pinkish white." [Y̆] "It is as singular as ['Bullata'],

but doesn't produce the same effect. Its wood is very slender and delicate, and the leaves are exactly the same as those of Hemp—long,
slender, pointed, and serrate. I can't say anything about the flower, as
I've only had the rose for two months; but I am assured that it is a
[true] Centifolia." [C-T]

À Feuilles de Chêne Listed as 'À Feuille de Chêne' (C).

À Feuilles de Chêne Vert Listed as 'À Feuille de Chêne' (C).

À Feuilles de Chou Listed as 'Bullata' (C).

À Feuilles de Groseillier Listed as 'À Feuilles de Céleri' (C).

À Feuilles de Groseillier de Maquereau Listed as 'À Feuilles
   de Céleri' (C).

À Feuilles de Laitue Listed as 'Bullata' (C).

À Feuilles de Persil Listed as 'À Feuilles de Céleri' (C).

À Feuilles Gaufrées Listed as 'Bullata' (C).

À Feuilles Rondes Crénelées Listed as 'À Feuilles Crénelées' (C).

À Fleurs Doubles Violettes

France, date uncertain

   "Violet purple, medium size, full, medium scent, tall." [Sn] Not to
be confused with the pre-1818 China of the same name.

À Fleurs Panachées Listed as 'Variegata' (C).

[À Fleurs Simples]

trans. "With Single Flowers"

Dupont, pre-1804

   "Rose." [Cal] "Flowers large, bright pink; leaves a more delicate
green than those of the common. This rose is, however, rarely completely single." [AC] "*Ovary* ovoid-fusiform. *Flower* medium-sized,
bright pink, single, semi-double, or double (5–12 petals). [Pf] "Similar
to the [common] Centifolia . . . except for having only 5 petals, *stems*
less prickly and pedicels and *sepals* with fewer glands. The plate [in
Les Roses by Thory and Redouté] is made from the plant in Noisette's
nursery, probably the only one now in France, having come to him after the dispersal of Dupont's collection, where it was raised from
seed." [T&R] "A very scarce rose; and as the incipient ground of so
many beautiful varieties, we regard it as peculiarly valuable. It is a
singular circumstance, that from Spain and Italy, where the Province
[*sic*] is supposed to be indigenous, and thence imported to us [the
British], we should never have heard of the 'Single Province', much
less received the plant; which we can in no way account for, unless
the superior beauty of the 'Common Province', joined to its great
abundance, may have rendered the idea of importing those with single flowers superfluous. Our figure [in Andrews' book] was taken
from the only plant we have ever seen, at the nursery of Mr. Shailer,
of Little Chelsea." [A] Not to be confused with another 'Single' (C),
recorded in 1754.

À Folioles Crénelées Listed as 'À Feuilles Crénelées' (C).

À Odeur de Punaise Listed as 'Le Rire Niais' (C).

À Odeur Ingrate Listed as 'Le Rire Niais' (C).

Adéline
Vibert, 1830

"Medium-sized, full, pink, plump." [V8] "Vivid rose, paler towards their circumference; of medium size, full; form, compact. Habit, branching, fine; growth, moderate; fine dark foliage. A showy Rose." [P] Possibly a Centifolia × Gallica hybrid.

Adrienne de Cardoville
V. Verdier?, 1845

"Large, full, cupped, crimson pink." [JR9/20] "Rosy crimson, large and full; form, cupped, fine. Habit, branching; growth, moderate. A good and distinct Rose. Raised in the neighborhood of Paris [*which, in* P, *almost always—if not indeed always—refers to Victor Verdier*]. Introduced in 1845." [P] Possibly a Centifolia × Gallica hybrid.

[Aglaia]
Descemet?, pre-1811

"Wood and foliage slender and delicate. Calyx long, constricted at the tip. Bud pink, terminating in a point, not well covered by the calyx membranes. Flower well formed, two and a half inches across [ca. 6.25 cm], petals fluted, a pretty pink shading to lilac mixed with white, as fragrant as its two companions ['Euphrosine l'Élégante' and 'Thalie la Gentille'], blooming at the same time." [C-T] Probably, like "its two companions," a hybrid between a Centifolia and the Damask 'Argentée'. Aglaia, one of the three Graces, her name meaning "brightness." Going by the names of her "two companions," perhaps the full name of this cultivar was originally "Aglaia la Brillante" or the like—but such is not recorded anywhere. Not to be confused with 'Aglaia', the Lambertiana.

Alain Blanchard
Vibert, 1839

"Large, semi-double, crimson violet, and spotted." [WRP] "Pink, striped." [Ÿ] "Dark violet, spotted, large and double." [P] "Flower medium-sized, full, well formed; color, pink spotted with bright red." [S] "Large, semi-double, deep violet spotted bright red; rich coloration." [R&M62] "Blossoms large, not very many petals, deep violet, spotted." [SRh54/59] "Dark violet-red; large; growth vigorous." [GeH] "Red violet, medium size, full, tall." [Sn] "Mid-green, rather unattractive foliage." [T4]

Alba
syn. 'Blanche Double'; trans., "White"
Breeder unknown, pre-1775

"Blossom large, full, well formed, pure white." [S] Parkinson had heard rumors of a white Centifolia by 1629: "It is said of diuers, that there is a white Prouince Rose, whereof I am not *oculatus testis,* and therefore I dare not giue it to you for a certainty, and indeed I haue some doubt, that it is the greater and more double white rose [*i.e., of the Alba group*] . . . : when I am my selfe better satisfied, I shall bee ready to satisfie others." [PaSo, with admirable ethics] *Cf.* 'Unique' (C).

Anaïs Ségales
Vibert, 1837

"Medium-sized, full, crimson pink." [V8] "Medium or large, full, lilac-y pink." [BJ53] "Rose-red, medium size, full, medium scent, medium to tall." [Sn] "Not very vigorous; foliage small; blossom medium-sized, full, flat form; color, crimson pink." [S] "Rosy crimson . . . cir-

cumference rosy lilac, large and full; form, expanded, perfect. Habit, branching; growth, moderate." [P] A Centifolia × Gallica hybrid.

Anna Listed as 'My Lady Kensington' (C).

Ballady
Perrot, 1934?

"Pink, large, full, medium height." [Sn]

Batavica Listed as 'Grande Centfeuille de Hollande' (C).

Belle de Vilmorin Listed as 'Unique Carnée' (C).

Belle Junon Listed as 'Junon' (G).

Bipenné Listed as 'À Feuilles de Céleri' (C).

Bipinnata Listed as 'À Feuilles de Céleri' (C).

Black Boy
Kordes, 1958

Modern contribution to the group with medium-sized crimson flowers. Not to be confused with the Climber of the same name by A. Clark.

Blanche Double Listed as 'Alba' (C). See also 'Unica' (C).

Blanche Unique Listed as 'Unica' (C).

Blanchefleur
trans. "Whiteflower"
Vibert, 1835

"Of the most delicate flesh color, or nearly white very distinct, and even now one of the finest roses." [WRP] "Its flowers are the most delightful flesh white, and it blooms with such profusion that no other Rose of the same tint can compare." [R-H63/184] "Medium-sized, full, flesh white." [V8] "Blossom large, full, globular; color, flesh pink." [S] "Pure white, . . . is a very free grower, flowers perfectly double and abundant." [Bu] "Flowers white, slightly tinged with flesh, large and full; form, compact, perfect. Habit, erect; growth, moderate. An abundant and early bloomer very beautiful on the tree. A good Pot Rose." [P] "White, tinged with blush, medium size, flat, very full, highly scented. One of the earliest to blossom; the flowers produced in great profusion. A valuable garden rose." [EL] A Centifolia × Gallica hybrid.

Blue Boy
Kordes, 1958

"Violet-red, large, full, very fragrant, medium to tall." [Sn] Close comparison with Gainsborough's similarly (nick)named production indicates negligible duplication.

Bullata
syns. 'À Feuilles Crépues', 'À Feuilles de Chou', 'À Feuilles de Laitue', 'À Feuilles Gaufrées', 'Knobby-Leaved', 'Monstrueuse'; trans., "Embossed"
Dupont, 1809

"Rose." [Cal] "Deep pink." [BJ40] "Pink, full, cupped, very large, superb." [LF] "Deep rose, large, and very double form, globular. Foliage very singular." [P] "Flowers very double, very regular, not very numerous; leaves large, undulate, crisped." [No26] "Flowers large and double; leaves undulate, contorted, and striking because of their size." [AC] *Leaflets* very large, extraordinarily bullate, undulate, and arching. *Flower* large, full, globular, light even pink, intense and brilliant.

Bullata *continued*

The foliage is as singular as the bush is vigorous." [Pf] "Has that large and curious inflated foliage, which we have no expressive name for, but which the French call 'bullé'; it is a vigorous-growing plant, with flowers like the ['Common Centifolia']." [WRP] "Foliage very bullate, having a certain resemblance to the leaf of cultivated lettuce. Flowers large, full, globular, beautiful pink. Beautiful variety." [JR5/44] "Foliage waffly like the leaves of the Milan cabbage." [JR9/20] "This variety is to the Centifolia 'Des Peintres' what ['À Feuilles de Céleri'] and ['Rosier des Dames' (CP)] are—not coming from seed at all, but from a trick of nature in the leaves of a branch, the trick being fixed by grafting." [BJ17] "Rapidly returns to being 'Des Peintres' if neglected." [V2]

"This rose is classed with the Centifolias, having all of the characteristics; it differs in its foliage, which is of rare beauty, being large and billowing like that of lettuce or cabbage. The blossom, which opens at the same time as those of the [*common*] Centifolia, is also the same in size, form, and color, with an equally elegant scent. 'Bullata' brings together virtues not found in the [*common*] Centifolia—branches closer-set and less divergent (making a more beautiful head grafted on the Briar), and more beautiful foliage closer to the blossom. This variety will always show up well, and will make quite a splash in beds of ornamental shrubs because of its leaves, which are unique in its group. They are so massive that their stalk can't hold them up; those at the bottom of the cane droop gracefully onto the stem; often they are ten to eleven inches long [ca. 2.5–2.6 dm], and six, seven, or eight inches wide [ca. 1.5–2 dm]." [C-T] "The flowers … which are often hidden beneath [the leaves]. This is a novel pleasure, due to the close proximity of all parts." [LeR]

"*Leaflets* rugose and bullate, often very gross and concave beneath; petioles pubescent, sometimes with a few fine recurved prickles. Otherwise exactly as for *R. centifolia* … This beautiful modification of *R. centifolia,* known in gardens as the rose with embossed or blistered foliage, or better as the lettuce-leafed rose, has been propagated by Dupont, whose name, *Rosa Bullata,* we have retained. It has many virtues over and above those of the common Centifolia; the closer-set, less divergent branches which form a beautiful head when grafted on the Briar; the singular leaves, so voluminous that the petiole seems to have difficulty supporting them; the beauty, size, rounded shape, and sweet perfume of the flowers. It can only be perpetuated as a graft, and as such it is delicate and short-lived. In our rose garden at Belleville near Paris, we have tried to get it on its own roots by layering, but obtained only sparse bushes with inferior blossoms." [T&R] "Rose with roundish seed-buds: peduncles and petioles hispid and glandular: the prickles of the branches scattered and straight: leaves large, of an oblong-ovate form, knobby, and of a pale green colour: flowers double. This monstrous-leaved variation of the Province Rose is an importation from Holland in the summer of 1815, when we made a drawing of it at the nursery of Messrs. Colville, but deferred figuring it at that time, that we might be certain of its character being a permanent one, and now have no doubt about it, having seen it in bloom for two successive summers in more than one collection, retaining unaltered its large and knobby foliage. It is at present a new and rare plant." [A] "Described in the *Nouveau Duhamel,* illustrated by Redouté, this beautiful rose was propagated by Dupont." [Gx]

Bunte Provinrose   Listed as 'Variegata' (C).

Cabbage

Sometimes intending Centifolias generally; but, when specific, 'Common Centifolia' (C), *q.v.*

Cannabina   Listed as 'À Feuilles de Chanvre' (C).

[Capricornus]
syn. 'Rouge Vif'
Breeder unknown, pre-1811

"Bright red." [Cal] "Beautiful variety; flowers very double, intense velvety purple, very regular." [BJ30] "The wood and leaves have nothing remarkable about them; they are a glaucous green. The calyx is round, the bud is pointed and covered by the sepals. The quite double blossom is beautifully shaped, two inches across [ca. 5 cm], bright sparkling red, and pleasantly scented. This rose could be considered among the pretty ones of this race." [C-T] "Grown by Du Pont, described by Guerrapain." [Gx] Capricornus, alias Capricorn, zodiacal sign and another name of the irrepressible Pan.

Carnea   Listed as 'Unique Carnée' (C).

Caroline de Berri   Listed as 'Foliacée' (C).

Caryophyllata   Listed as 'Oeillet' (C).

Caryophyllea   Listed as 'Oeillet' (C).

Changeante   Listed as 'Unique' (C).

Charles-Quint
Robert, 1856

"Blossom white, ribboned pink." [JDR56/41] "6–8 cm [ca. 2$^1\!/_2$–3 in], full, white ribboned with lilac-y pink, globular, well held, vigorous." [R&M62] "Blossom white, edged lilac pink." [S] "White and violet pink, medium size, full, tall." [Sn]

Childling
syns. 'Grand Cels', 'La Digittaire', 'La Variable', 'Mère Gigogne', 'Prolifera', 'Prolifère'
Breeder unknown, pre-1759

"Rose." [Cal] "Quite singular variety in which one finds, in place of the pistil, a small bud which develops and often gives a new flower; each of its canes bears but one blossom at its tip. The look of the proliferous rose is pleasant." [CM] "0.6 m high [ca. 2 ft] on its own roots; *stems* and *foliage* similar to those of *R. centifolia* with the exception of the long *sepals* and proliferating flowers. This combines two varieties on one plant: 'Foliacée' and 'Prolifére'. It is considered to be a sport of *R. centifolia gigantea* or *pictorum* [*i.e.,* 'Grand Centfeuille de Hollande' or 'Des Peintres'], much esteemed for the largest flowers of the group and for their fragrance. The monstrous growth of this rose is a product of the soil quality, fertilizer, atmospheric conditions, frequent watering, and other circumstances. Nevertheless, growers cannot rely on success for their pains—often only ordinary blossoms are the outcome. Dupont grows it but does not list it because of the continual vagaries." [T&R] "There are Roses which, at the center of the flower, produce another Rose—and sometimes foliage. Monsieur Marchand displayed this sort to the Royal Academy of Sciences of Paris in 1703 and 1707. It's a monstrosity which gives these roses the name *Prolifères.*" [C'H, unclear whether intending this particular cultivar] *Cf.* 'Foliacée' (C).

Chou

Sometimes intending Centifolias generally; but, when specific, 'Common Centifolia' (C), *q.v.*; see also 'Bullata' (C).

Ciudad de Oviedo

trans. "City of Oviedo"
Spain, date uncertain

"Deep pink." [Y] Oviedo, proud city, capital of its province in Spain.

Common Centifolia

syns. 'Cabbage', 'Chou', 'Communis'
Breeder unknown (probably Dutch), pre-1596

"Rose color, large, full, globular, fragrant. A very desirable garden variety." [EL] "[The flowers] only differ from those of 'Des Peintres' in size, which is less." [S] "Flowers rose colour, the outer petals changing to paler rose; form globular, very large and full, and highly fragrant; habit of growth moderate." [JC] "Rosy pink … circumference changing paler soon after expansion; the tops of the petals sometimes slightly reflexing, large and full; form, globular. Habit, branching; growth, vigorous." [P] "The colour is a clear delicate pink, the wood strong, distantly studded with thorns." [Bu] "Of a round cupped form, very compact before expansion, and never becoming flat … It flourishes most in a half shady position, the direct rays of our [American] sun being too powerful and often killing the shoots." [WRP] "This rose grows 6 or 8 feet tall [ca. 2–2.6 m]; it blooms in Spring, and sometimes gives some blossoms in the Fall." [AC] "Rose with nearly round seed-buds, and peduncles hispid and glandular: flowers of a deep flesh-colour, and very sweet-scented; leaflets egg-shaped, pointed, sawed, and villose beneath. This rose is one of the most abundant; and, from being extremely common, is perhaps best known, but the least valued. Yet, if fragrance and beauty were instead of scarcity to fix a price, very few would be deserving of a higher sum. We have sometimes seen this fine Rose, in well cultivated luxuriant plants, acquire the height of nearly fifteen feet [ca. 5 m], adorning the front of a house in a most elegant manner during the summer months." [A] "This old and beautiful queen of gardens is too well known for it to be of any use to describe it." [Pf]

"*Shrub,* vigorous. *Thorns,* uneven; the largest scythe-shaped. *Leaflets,* edged with glands. *Flowers,* drooping, large, of a beautiful pink; fragrant, full. *Calyx,* viscous. *Fruit,* oblong." [Go] "Ovary ovoid and peduncles bestrewn with pediculate glands. Calyx segments with medium-sized appendages and glandular bristles. Petioles bearing glands and several prickles beneath. Leaves pinnate, with the odd one, oval, doubly dentate, tomentose beneath, lightly purpled along the edges. Stem bearing many prickles … This rose—its name coming from the large number of petals in the blossom—is seemingly a variety of the Dog Rose [*Rosa canina*] which arose from cultivation, a variety with reddish wood and canes, resembling the Dog Rose in habit and prickles. Its corolla, always slightly spherical, twists in on itself at the center, as with the Dog Rose, and its large cordiform petals are of an increasingly bright color the nearer they are to the center. The calyx segments bear, on the outside, pediculate glands, and have a white down within and along the edges; there is an appendage at the tip, and several more along the edges. The ovoid ovary grades into the peduncle without narrowing at the base, growing toward a bulge at the ovary. The leaves are bestrewn with glandular red bristles, and are usually composed of five to seven ovoid lobes, doubly dentate, purple along the edges, dull green without brightness on the upper side, paler and bearing white bristles on the lower. The dark brown stem is a clear green here and there. Its shoots are green and much covered with prickles which are shield shaped at the base, slightly hooked, and brown and light brown. Bloom-time is around June 15." [Rsg]

"Growth vigorous, canes of medium size, branching; bark somber green, with numerous brown, nearly straight, unequal, very large thorns. Leaves somber green, slightly rugose, of 5–7 oval and dentate leaflets; leafstalk pretty strong, also somber green. Flowers nearly four inches across [ca. 1 dm], very full, globular, flattened, solitary on the branchlets, in clusters of 3–5 on the more vigorous branches; color, beautiful bright pink; long stem, slender and strong; petals large, concave, those of the center smaller and crumpled. Calyx pear-shaped … very hardy … Its origin is lost in the misty past." [JF] "Shrub 1.8–2.1 m high [ca. 5–6 ft]; *branches* with numerous almost straight unequal *prickles*. Leaflets 5 (–7), deeply bidentate, dark green, underside pubescent; margins and petiole glandular hairy, the latter unarmed. *Receptacles* thick, ovoid, strongly bristly like the pedicels; *sepals* concave, 3 pinnatifid and leaflike, 2 simple, glandular on the outside, downy within; *corolla* rounded, of numerous pink *petals* becoming darker towards the center of the flower. Up to the present, no native home was known for this rose, but in 1816 Rau stated that it is native to Northern Persia … To obtain the maximum number of fine blooms, prune the bush in February to keep it dwarf." [T&R]

"Will always ornament the gardens of both rich and poor." [J-A/565]

Communis Listed as 'Common Centifolia' (C).

Comtesse de Ségur

V. Verdier, 1848

"Medium-sized, full, delicate flesh." [BJ53] "Pale flesh, clear and beautiful, full, fine." [FP] "Vigorous bush; flower medium-sized, full; color, delicate pink." [S] Possibly a hybrid between Centifolia and Gallica.

Constance Listed as 'My Lady Kensington' (C).

Constance des Hollandaises Listed as 'My Lady Kensington' (C).

Cramoisi Listed as 'Rubra' (C).

Crenata Listed as 'À Feuilles Crénelées' (C).

Crépue Listed as 'À Feuilles de Céleri' (C); see also 'Bullata' (C).

Cricks' Listed as 'Yorkshire Provence' (C).

Crispa Listed as 'À Feuilles de Céleri' (C).

D'Hollande Listed as 'Grande Centfeuille de Hollande' (C).

De Descemet Listed as 'Descemet' (C).

De Hollande Listed as 'Grande Centfeuille de Hollande' (C).

Decora Listed in Chapter 6 on Centifolia Pompons.

Des Peintres Plate 6

syns. 'Major Multiplex', 'Maxima Multiplex', 'Souchet', 'Vierge'; trans., "[The One] of the Painters"
Breeder unknown, pre-1806

"Pink, very large, full, cupped, superb." [LF] "Very large, semi-dou-

Des Peintres *continued*

ble, of a lively color tending towards scarlet." [No26] "Bright red." [Cal] "Sport of the common Centifolia. Flower large, full, nodding, admirably formed, pink becoming darker at the center." [JR10/95] "Very double blossom of a bright pink, three inches across [ca. 8 cm]. One can't grow enough of this rose, which for a long time has been admired by fanciers." [An32/313] "Beautiful pink, very large, very double, and held so gracefully that, up till the present, [the blossoms of this variety] have been preferred as the models for our most well-known painters." [J-A/563] "Resembles the Common or Cabbage Rose." [P] "Flower large, very full, semi-globular, nodding, light bright pink. No essential difference from the common Centifolia except in its larger volume." [Pf] "*Flowers,* larger and more vivid than in [the common Centifolia]." [Go] "This is a big 'Hollande' of four and a half inches across [ca. 1.2 dm], with the petals folding back onto the calyx, conversely to those which stay erect, doubling the volume. This is the one used by the painters, and which seems exaggerated in their pictures; it is not very double, which makes it lighter and more elegant. It should be cut short." [LeR] "Flowers full, central petals a very bright incarnate; three to four per corymb; leaves not reddish at the base, large, stiff, pale beneath." [AC] "Its leaves are very large; its flowers, extremely full, are quite big. Horticultural fanciers grow it under the name 'Rosier des Peintres' because it really is the flower chosen to serve as a model. These are the beautiful roses seen in still-lifes, the dimensions of which seem to be exaggerated, though they in truth are nothing other than what Nature gives us." [BJ09]

"They call 'Des Peintres' a variety with large double flowers, the color of which is extremely intense, and which was grown at the Trianon under the name 'Souchet'." [BJ30] "On to the rose which the nurserymen call 'De Peintre' [*sic*]: its blossoms are a beautiful pink, with an elegant scent; their size is about three and a half inches [ca. 9 cm]; they are composed of twelve to fifteen rows of well-colored petals. Let us add that it is less double than the rose 'de Hollande' [*presumably 'Grande Centfeuilles de Hollande'*]." [CM] "It differs little from the rose 'de Hollande', which is nearly 4 inches in diameter [ca. 1 dm], but it doesn't always open as well; both these two are a beautiful bright pink, and have an elegant scent." [BJ17]

"Bush attaining the height of 70 cm to 1.20 m [ca. 2⅓–4 ft]; numerous canes covered with nearly straight unequal thorns; leaves composed of 5–7 deeply toothed leaflets, dull green, and having some glandular bristles along the edges, as have the petioles; flower rounded, very large and very double, of excellent form and of a pink tint becoming darker in the middle of the blossom." [S] "Rose, with many folds, and nearly round seed-buds: the peduncles and petioles are hispid and glandular: the prickles of the branches are scattered, straight, and slightly reflexed: leaflets egg-shaped, villous beneath, with glandular margins. This variety of the Common Province [*sic*] is the most fragrant of all the Roses, and therefore particularly desirable; for, although it cannot be ranked among the rare, it is nevertheless one of the most beautiful. Its sweetness, joined to the abundance of its blossoms, has rendered it an object of culture, for the purpose of distillation, as it yields a much greater quantity of scented water than any other rose. It is generally denominated the Cabbage Province, from the extreme complexity of its petals, which sometimes adhere so closely together as to prevent entirely their expansion without bursting:—a circumstance that frequently occurs

in the vegetable from which its specific distinction is derived, and which we regard to be unequivocally good, as we should every similitude of equally easy reference. By the closeness and superabundance of its petals only, is it distinguished from the Common Province, of which it is certainly an interesting variety." [A]

"All things considered, I am not quite comfortable in classing this beautiful variety of rose as a Centifolia (it's also often called 'Grosse Hollande'). This rose has indeed the habit and wood of the Centifolia; however, its leaves are more rounded, and toothed more shallowly. The buds are longer, as are the petioles which bear them. The blossom, less substantial, and more elegant, appears about the same time—around mid-June—taking the form of a vase; the petals are wavier; those along the edge, instead of growing upright, reverse onto the calyx, making this rose seem larger. It truly does look like those one sees in paintings. Some fanciers also give out as 'Des Peintres' the one called 'Feu Amoureux' [G] … particularly because of its size and volume. Whatever name people finally settle on, it is a constant that these are two beautiful and very effective varieties." [C-T]

There is a certain amount of confusion between 'Des Peintres' and 'Grande Centfeuille de Hollande'; the distinctions seem to be that 'Des Peintres' has a better form than 'Grande Centfeuille de Hollande', and is less double, but has more difficulty in opening its blossoms; the leaves of 'Grande Centfeuille de Hollande' have reddish tints along the base or perhaps edges, tints which 'Des Peintres' lacks.

Descemet

syn. 'De Descemet'
Descemet, pre-1820

"Blossoms also [like those of 'Des Peintres'] very strong, very double, and simultaneously bright and beautifully colored, and elegantly shaped." [J-A/563] "*Shrub,* throwing up numerous suckers. *Flowers,* very large, semi-double; of a bright light pink, fragrant." [Go] "Flowers rich even rose, changing to pale rose, large and double; form, cupped. Habit, branching; growth, vigorous. A beautiful Rose: a good seed-bearer." [P] "Dark red." [Cal] "[The collection] of one of the first growers who attained much distinction—Descemet, of St. Denis [*suburb of Paris, France*]—was cut up by the English troops in 1814 [*Descemet was also mayor of St. Denis*]; when the horticulturist, unable to obtain indemnification from [the] government, proceeded to Russia, and re-established himself [in Odessa] with honour and success." [Go] Descemet was one of the first to practice controlled cross-breeding, keeping written records of his crosses and the behavior of his breeding material. The government failing to bail out Descemet, the remnants of these records were purchased, along with Descemet's nursery-stock and breeding material, by Vibert, who introduced many or most of Descemet's subsequent productions. Vibert was deeply influenced by Descemet's work.

Dianthaeflora Listed as 'Oeillet' (C).

Dominic Boccardo Listed as 'Dométile Bécar' (C).

Dométile Bécar Plate 7

syn. 'Dominic Boccardo', 'Dometille Beccard', and all permutations too numerous to list
Breeder unknown, pre-1853

"Large, full, light pink, striped with white." [BJ53] "Blossom large, full, cupped,; color, bright pink striped white." [S] "Flesh colour, striped with rose. Growth moderate." [GeH] "Light pink, striped white, medium size, full, medium scent, average to tall." [Sn] "To talk about a rose on which one has no information is not an easy thing. This, however, is the case at hand with the Provins rose 'Dometil Beccard' [*sic*] …All in all, despite such research, after having consulted a heap of books—perhaps not the good ones—and catalogs, after having written to several rosarians from whom I thought to receive some morsel on this pretty variety, I have gotten nothing. Who was the fortunate breeder of 'Dometil Beccard'? When was this rose first sold? …'Dometil Beccard' belongs to that series of Provins roses which are plumed, often striped, and have the quality of a bloom which is abundant and of long duration—just the thing for a non-remontant rose. It has some similarity to the variety 'César Beccaria', such that the two have been confused several times. The rose with which we are concerned makes a very vigorous bush, giving blossoms which are large, full, well-formed, and white with some flesh, striped with bright pink and lilac. It is one of the best Provins roses." [JR17/120] Listed in BJ53 as a Centifolia.

Dometille Beccard Listed as 'Dométile Bécar' (C).

Duc d'Angoulême
Holland, 1821

"Deep pink." [BJ40] "Red." [Cal] "Bright pink." [LS] "Dark red, medium size, full, medium scent, tall." [Sn] "Large, full, deep pink." [V8] "Slightly departs from the habits of the true Provence Rose; it is finely shaped, and of a vivid rose-color." [WRP] Not to be confused with anything called 'Duchesse d'Angoulême'. Possibly a hybrid between Centifolia and Gallica. The Duc d'Angoulême—of the various holders of that title, the most likely intended is Louis Antoine de Bourbon (1775–1844), dauphin, son of King Charles X of France; renounced his claim to the throne in 1830.

Duc de Brabant
Breeder unknown, pre-1854

"Blossoms bright pink, very large, and very beautiful." [SRh54/59] "Red, medium size, full, tall." [Sn] "Vigorous bush; strong canes, clothed with hooked thorns which are wood-colored; leaves elongate, dark green; flower large, full, very well formed; color, bright pink." [S] "Duc de Brabant" is the title traditionally held by the eldest son of the king of Belgium.

Duchesse de Coutard
Breeder unknown, pre-1885

"Blossom medium-sized, full; color, delicate pink." [S] *Cf.* the Hybrid China 'Comtesse de Coutard'.

Dutch Provence Listed as 'Grande Centfeuille de Hollande' (C).

Eugénie Chamusseau
Breeder unknown, date uncertain

"Deep pink." [Ÿ] *Cf.* the Hybrid Perpetual 'Eugénie Guinoisseau', also a deep pink.

Eulalie Lebrun
Vibert, 1845

"Flowers white, striped with rose and lilac, of medium size, full." [P] "Medium-sized, full, plumed with pink and lilac, often with three colors, the only one of the sort [*i.e.*, the only striped Centifolia/Gallica hybrid]." [V8] "Medium bush; flower white, striped with lilac pink, medium-sized, flat, full." [S] "White, striped violet-pink, medium size, full, average height." [Sn] Hybrid between Centifolia and Gallica.

Euphrosine l'Élégante
Descemet, pre-1811

"Dark rose." [Cal] "Delicate red-pink or cherry red." [Ÿ] "Very vigorous bush; flower medium-sized; color, deep crimson." [S] "Wood and leaves a delicate and gay green. Calyx round; long bud. Flowers three inches across [ca. 7.5 cm], well formed, elegant, a red which is delicate, bright, and gay; very fragrant. This rose, well complemented by its foliage and numerous buds, is most gratifying, giving a perfect bouquet—doubtless the origin of its name 'Euphrosine', one of the three *Graces*; it blooms from June 10th to the 20th." [C-T] "Buds numerous, overtopped by the calyx appendages. Flower two inches across [ca. 5 cm], very fragrant, delicate bright gay pink, very double, forming perfect bouquets well surrounded by leaves, this very elegant flower would seem to be a hybrid between the Centifolia and the Damask 'Argentée'. Blooms around [June] 9–10." [LeR]

Fantin-Latour
Breeder unknown, date uncertain

"Pink, large, full, tall." The origin of this now-popular rose is evidently unattested. Phillips and Rix state that it is a China or Hybrid Tea hybrid, with possible Gallica infusion, dating to about 1900. Henri Fantin-Latour, French painter, 1836–1904.

Feu Amoreux Listed as a Gallica.

Flore Magno
Synonym shared by 'Foliacée' (C) and 'Grande Centfeuille de Hollande' (C), *qq.v.*

Foliacée
syns. 'Caroline de Berri', 'Flore Magno'; trans., "Leafy"
Holland, pre-1808

"Luminous pink." [Ÿ] "Rose." [Cal] "Very large, full, pink." [V8] "Flesh, large, full, rose delicate." [R&M62] "Large, full double, of a delicate rosy incarnate hue." [WRP] "Flowers light rose, very large and full; form, globular." [P] "Blossoms pink, notable for their long calycinate divisions [sepals], which are foliaceous and lanceolate." [No26] "Sepals transformed into pinnatifid leaflets. Large flowers, opening poorly." [JR5/44] "*Ovary* pretty nearly lacking. *Sepals* transformed into incised, pinnatifid leaflets. *Flowers* large, full, semi-globular, light pink, not always opening perfectly." [Pf] "Canes sometimes trifoliate or unifoliate at the tip; flowers solitary at the tip of the cane, usually bearing, at the center, the rudiments of another blossom, which in turn opening sometimes gives another rose which is also proliferous; thus, a person can see three or four all lined up; sepals drawn out into deeply incised leaves." [AC] "Light pink, large, full tall." [Sn] "Vigorous bush." [S] "These names come from the way that the tips of the leaflets and calyx develop long leaves, which are profoundly dentate and glandulose, and which grow up around the blossom, from the center of which comes a smaller rose." [BJ17] "Another variety, straight from the [common] Centifolia, making a pretty head grafted; its wood, thorns, and leaves indicate its origin. In the middle of each blossom—which is very big—there is another bud instead of stamens; this, when it opens, often produces another—and sometimes two, the one in the other." [LeR, on 'Foliacée'] "*Shrub* 0.3–0.6 m high [ca. 1–2 ft]; *stems* and *foliage* similar to *the* [common] *Centifolia*, from

Foliacée *continued*

which it differs only by the long leafy *sepals* formed at the expense of the receptacle, which is almost absent…The Foliaceous Rose was introduced by Descemet, Professor of Agriculture and Director of the botanical garden and nurseries of the Czar of Russia at Odessa. It is propagated only by grafting or layering. As grown on its own roots by Pelletier, it produces many very fine blooms, but we have seen magnificent grafted specimens in Descemet's former nursery ["now" owned by Vibert] at St.-Denis, near Paris. Sometimes the flowers are proliferous and leafy at the same time. Culture is the same as for the [common] Centifolia, pruning hard to encourage good, typical blooms." [T&R]

A Horticultural Drama. Act I, 1819. "Here, without a doubt, is the most beautiful and newest of the varieties coming from the Agathe, not looking at all like anything in that group, except for the blossom, which leaves no doubt as to its origin. It was chosen by the Princess of this name ['Caroline de Berri'] from among more than four hundred given her in a bouquet as the most beautiful; and she gave it her name. It is said that it was brought to us by the English, who took it from the southern part of America. Its wood is strong, and armed with numerous thorns. The color of its wood is green; and its red thorns—big or small—are hooked; some are straight, and some are a nice green. Its leaves are oval, long like those of the Cherry or *Charmille,* each one three and a half inches long [ca. 8 cm], and two wide across the middle [ca. 5 cm]; they terminate in a sharp point, are light green, and doubly dentate; its buds are wide and flat, like those of the Agathes, round, inflated, overtopped by the appendages of the calyx which are cut feather-style. And surrounding the bud and the flower, which is only two inches across [ca. 5 cm], very double, and a pretty pink with white touches when they open … [*Le-Rouge lost his way in the sentence; we never learn what surrounds the bud and flower!*]. Its petals reverse onto the calyx, making it look like a little ball. The stamens in the center are replaced by a pretty bouquet of small green leaves, which often exceed the flower by two inches [ca. 5 cm]. All in all, this pretty rose is a masterpiece. Opens June 5–10." [LeR, on 'Caroline de Berri']

Act II, 1824. "The *Journal de Paris* announced, about six years ago, around the end of the bloom season, the discovery of a rose supposedly grown from seed by a grower who enjoyed, for his part, a merited reputation, but who—at that time, at least—had never sown any rose seed. Much as the editing of this article was not very intelligible, it was nevertheless possible for several persons to see that the author had intended to talk about one of the two varieties of foliaceous Centifolias. It was known that these roses are sometimes very pretty: One of these was presented to HER HIGHNESS MADAME LA DUCHESSE DE BERRI, who, believing it new on the word of the author, very much wanted to allow her name to be given to it. This favor was a distinguished one—we had not at that time seen any other such example of good will. The name of the grower was unknown as far as this nursery was concerned; and if Her Highness couldn't recompense the long-term effort [to develop the variety], she at least gave strong encouragement by her favor. Dupont, whom Mme. Joséphine Beauharnais honored with her high protection, never dared to give *her* name to a rose. I [Vibert] well know that, before these times, several beautiful Dutch roses, abandoning the names they had borne up till then along with the place of their birth, awoke

to a beautiful new day here [in France], astonished by their new luck; it was, without a doubt, the tribute of knowledge—or homage to self-love—but at least their birth had been a mystery; they weren't officially known by the persons whose names they bore; and the journals didn't sound off about their renaming. But in *this* case, the error is a grave one, and the intention doesn't excuse the fact. The rose concerned in this has characteristics so particular that I cannot begin to conceive how it could have given rise to such a mistake. With names so distinguished, a person can't just seize on them without shouldering the greatest responsibilities. In such cases, zeal does not always suffice—a deep understanding of *what's what* becomes indispensable; and for us to accurately depict the virtues and graces which stand out so distinctly in Her Highness, we have the right to demand one of those perfect flowers that Nature in stingy about giving us, and that is consistent with sustained spirit and perseverance in the face of whatever might happen [*Vibert is alluding to the personal qualities of the Duchesse de Berri*]. Be that as it may, everyone wanted to know about this new marvel; from all over France, and even further, I received many letters asking me for details about this rose. Fanciers are impatient—I know the feeling—they are not always satisfied with fine reasoning: I had indeed spoken the truth—this rose was expensive, and people would want something *novel* for their money. I had obtained irrefutable proof that this was a Dutch variety which had been grown in France for more than eighteen years, and by me for twelve; but such was the impression that the public announcement had made that many people, though they had it already, bought it for themselves. The reasons they expressed to me were plausible enough: How could we believe (they would say to me) that a grower, so outstanding in his own affairs, who had his own interests to look out for and his own reputation to sustain—how could such a person make such a mistake? When a person doesn't raise roses from seed, how could anyone dare to give out as a result of his own sowings a rose known for so long and which nearly every fancier has? To lie to the Public is still the way of the world—it's far from uncommon! But to mislead people, though undoubtedly unintentionally, with 'Son Altesse Mme. la Duchesse de Berri'—all a person can think is that ignorance abounds, if he doesn't try not to think about it at all! As for me, I am quite convinced that it was nothing but an overplus of zeal which lead this particular rosarian into such error, a rosarian whose reputation is otherwise beyond reproach." [V2] But who was this rosarian who had such an overplus of zeal? On to Act III:

Act III, 1849. "Let's not forget to mention the rose 'Caroline de Berry' [*sic*]. In the obituary on Monsieur Tamponnet, published in the *Journal d'Horticulture Pratique* in 1844, we paid that estimable grower a just tribute, and cited a fact which is not absolutely true concerning the rose 'Caroline de Berry'. It *is* quite true that Monsieur Tamponnet offered, around 1820, to Mme. la Duchesse de Berry, a rose *as having been grown from seed,* which was sold at 20 francs, and which, due to its having been so named furnished cut flowers to the [Berri?] château. But here stops the truth. All the horticulturists knew that Monsieur Tamponnet had never sown any rose seed, and when Monsieur Vibert looked into the origin of this rose, he found out that it was quite precisely the *Centifolia flore magno* of the Dutch, offered under that name, since 1808, in the catalogs of Messieurs Descemet and Dupont. This rose did *not* come from seed—it is one of the numerous sports of the Centifolia, and gives, though indeed rarely, perfect flowers. The name *Cent-feuilles foliacée* has prevailed in France; no more is it known under this [earlier] name. Monsieur Godefroy, of Ville d'Avray, assisted at Monsieur Vibert's at that time in the verification which was made from two specimens which had been obtained at Tamponnet's. Monsieur Vibert believed it necessary to bring up, in print, this unfortunate error made by one of our most honorable growers—and Monsieur Tamponnet himself admitted to it by his silence." [M-V49/102–103] Curtain.

[Gaspard Monge]
Robert, 1854

"Flower large, globular, light pink." [JDR55/18] "Double, globular when opening, from 9–10 cm [to ca. 4 in], light pink with a little lilac." [I'H55/51] "From 9–11 cm [to ca. 4 in], double, light pink with some lilac, globular, vigorous." [R&M62] Possibly a hybrid between Centifolia and Gallica. Not to be confused with the 1874 crimson Hybrid Perpetual of the same name.

Gloriette
Robert, 1854

"Flowers large, flesh." [JDR55/18] "Flower full, opening wide, 6–8 cm [ca. 2½–3 in], salmony flesh white." [I'H55/53] "Beautiful coloration, very vigorous." [R&M62] *Cf.* the Gallica and the Hybrid Noisette of the same name.

[Goliath]
syn. 'Maxima'
Girardon, 1829

"Bright pink." [S] "Light roseate, large." [WRP] "Blossoms very big." [JR5/44] "Bouquets of two or three blossoms, to four inches [ca. 1 dm] and more, elegant, of a deep pink with some violet. From seed of the 'Grosse de Hollande' [*i.e.,* 'Grand Centfeuille de Hollande' or possibly (mistakenly) 'Des Peintres']." [R-H29/77] "*Canes* strong, purplish. *Sepals* non-foliaceous. *Flower* large, very full; globular, light pink. Doesn't always open well, better than ['Foliacée']." [Pf] "*Shrub,* vigorous. *Thorns,* very fine, and numerous. *Leaflets,* oblong, large, of a fine green. *Flowers,* two or three together, very pretty, nearly five inches broad [ca. 1.8 dm]; of a violet pink. *Sepals,* resembling the Hundred-leaved rose. *Buds,* oblong, and very large. *Fruit,* conical." [Go] "Arose from the 'Hollande': Centifolia *Goliath,* raised by Monsieur Girardon at Bar-sur-Aube in 1826–1829. *Journal de la Société d'Agronomie Pratique* May 1829, p. 198." [Marginalia added by Pierre-Philémon Cochet in his copy of Prévost] Goliath, the Gittite, whose size was *not* ca. 1 dm but rather six cubits and a span [ca. 10 ft 9 in; ca. 3.28 m].

Gooseberry-Leaved Listed as 'À Feuilles de Céleri' (C).

[Grand Bercam]
syn. 'Grand Berkam'
Prévost?, pre-1826

"Among the darkest, being a deep rose colour; flowers quite large, though not so perfect as some others." [Bu] "*Flower* medium or large, double, hypocrateriform, light bright pink." [Pf] "Semi-double." [S] Prévost does not claim it as his own in his book.

Grand Berkam Listed as 'Grand Bercam' (C).

Grand Cels Listed as 'Childling' (C).

Grand Rosier de Hollande Listed as 'Grande Centfeuille de Hollande' (C).

Grande Centfeuille de Hollande
syns. 'Batavica', 'De Hollande', 'Dutch Provence', 'Grand Rosier de Hollande', 'Great Double Damask Province', 'Great Royal', 'Grosse Centfeuilles de Hollande', 'Grosse de Hollande', 'La Rose de Batavie', 'Maxima'; trans., "Big Centifolia from Holland"
Holland, pre-1616

"Flowers rose, very large and full; form, globular. Closely resembles the Common Provence." [P] "Very large, bright red, equally fragrant, but less double than ['Common Centifolia']. It is much esteemed for forcing, and unlike the Cabbage Rose, it expands fully. This variety appears to have existed longer, and to be more widely disseminated in our [American] Atlantic Gardens than any other." [WRP] "Even larger than ['Common Centifolia'], being four to five inches in diameter [ca. 1–1.25 dm]; colour red; buds large and very splendid, and is the most common rose in the country—called the *Cabbage Rose* [*a frequent name of* 'Common Centifolia'], from which it differs very materially in the wood not having such strong prickles, though of more free growth, the flower also expands fully, which the cabbage never does." [Bu] "Light pink, large, very full, medium scent, tall." [Sn] "Very large flowers, which however don't keep the rounded form when they open; leaves usually reddish along the edge." [AC] "Also [like 'Des Peintres'] very large, but more double." [BJ09] "Nearly 4 inches in diameter [ca. 1 dm]." [BJ17] "The blossoms are at least as voluminous as those of 'Des Peintres', but much more poorly formed." [J-A/564] "Vigorous bush, with canes tinted purple; sepals not foliaceous; flower large, very full, globular, light pink." [S] "The leaflets aren't as big [as those of 'Common Centifolia'], and are rather saw-toothed than crenelate, with shallower dentation; ovaries fat and conical; blossoms of a darker red. The other characteristics are the same with these two plants." [Lam] "The stems of this rose are branching, diffuse, bristling with prickles; its leaves are composed of five leaflets which are fairly large and ordinarily reddish along the edge; its blossoms, in clusters of three to five, are very double and quite fragrant, beautiful red, and of an extraordinary size—some have been seen up to four inches across [ca. 1 dm]." [CM]

"Its thorny stems grow to 2 or 3 feet high [ca. 6 dm to 1 m], and are clothed with leaves composed sometimes of 5 but more often of 3 large, oval, separate lobes [*i.e.,* leaflets] of a dark green lightly washed purple along the edges. Colored a very bright red or incarnate, the blossoms are large, well-rounded, and furnished with a great number of petals which, when the flower is fully open, fold back gracefully. They are borne on peduncles bristling with brown whiskers, and usually come in terminal clusters, in which the buds, opening successively, extend over nearly two months the bloom of this Rose, which commences in the middle of Spring." [Fr] "This Rose . . . hath his barke of a reddish or browne colour, whereby it is soone discerned from other Roses. The leaues are likewise more reddish then in others, and somewhat larger, it usually groweth very like the Damask rose, and much to the same height: the flowers or roses are of the same deepe blush colour that the damaske roses are, or rather somewhat deeper, but much thicker, broader, and more double, or fuller of leaues [*i.e.,* petals] by three parts almost, the outer leaues turning themselues back, when then flower hath stood long blowne, the middle part it selfe (which in all other roses almost haue some yellow

Grande Centfeuille de Hollande *continued*

threds in them to be seene) being folded hard with small leaues, without any yellow almost at all to be seene, the s[c]ent whereof commeth neerest vnto the damaske rose, but yet is short of it by much, howsoeuer many doe thinke it as good as the damask, and to that end I haue known some Gentlewomen haue caused all their damask stockes to bee grafted with prouince Roses, hoping to haue as good water, and more store of them then of damask Roses; but in my opinion it is not halfe so good a s[c]ent as the water of damaske Roses: let euery one follow their own fancie." [PaSo]

"Improvement of the Centifolia by the Dutch. Described by Franeau in *Le Jardin d'Hyver* in 1616. Grown by Claude Mollet in 1563 [*this is we suspect a typographical error for 1663*] and by La Quintynie in 1680. *Zebendena* of the pharmacists, in the *Rhodologia* of Rosemberg (1631). Later became the 'Rose des Peintres'." [ExRé, incorrect in the final sentence; see our notes distinguishing the two cultivars at the end of the entry on 'Des Peintres']

Grande Renoncule Violâtre Listed as 'Grande Renoncule Violette' (C).

Grande Renoncule Violette

syn. 'Grande Renoncule Violâtre'; trans., "Big Violet Ranunculus"
Breeder unknown, pre-1885
"Pink." [LS] "Medium-sized, full, very well formed; color, pink." [S]

Grandidentata Listed as 'À Feuille de Chêne' (C).

Great Double Damask Province Listed as 'Grande Centfeuille de Hollande' (C).

Great Royal

Synonym of 'Grande Centfeuille de Hollande' (C), *q.v.*; see also the Gallica 'Great Royal'.

Gros Chou d'Hollande

syn. 'Grosse Hollande'; trans., "Big Cabbage from Holland"
Vibert?, pre-1820
"*Leaflets,* usually doubly toothed. *Tube of calyx,* very long, often humped in the centre, smooth, not much tightened in the throat. *Flowers,* full, middle-sized, irregular, of a light pink." [Go] Possibly synonymous with 'Grosse de Hollande', *i.e.,* 'Grande Centfeuille de Hollande' (C). The name is obviously not one Vibert would give to one of his own seedlings.

Grosse de Hollande Listed as 'Grande Centfeuille de Hollande' (C); name sometimes used in error for 'Des Peintres' (C).

Grosse Centfeuilles de Hollande Listed as 'Grande Centfeuille de Hollande' (C); name sometimes used in error for 'Des Peintres' (C).

Grosse Hollande Listed as 'Gros Chou d'Hollande' (C).

Grossularifolia Listed as 'À Feuilles de Céleri' (C).

Guenille Listed as 'Oeillet' (C).

[Héloïse]

syns. 'Maiden's Blush', 'Rougeau Virginale'
Breeder unknown, 1818
"Pale rose." [Cal] "The English call this 'Maiden's Blush'. All in all,

it's a Centifolia smaller than the 'Hollande' [*presumably 'Grande Centfeuille de Hollande'*], but which has a prettier coloration; it makes a well-rounded head because it has a compact habit—rare among the Centifolias." [LeR] Possibly a Centifolia × Gallica hybrid. *Cf.* the Agathe of the same name.

Hollande See 'Hollandica' (C) and 'Grande Cenfeuille de Hollande' (C).

[Hollandica]

Breeder unknown, pre-1695
"The 'Hollande' roses would seem, due to their precocity as compared with [Agathes, Mosses, the various Uniques, etc., etc.], to be owed pride of place in this charming scene [*i.e.,* the charming literary tableau of Roses which Guerrapain is about to present to the Reader]. You may count three varieties which are distinguished by the greater or lesser size of the blossoms. The wood, leaves, prickles, and calyx are the same size and sort as with the Centifolias, and it's pointless to describe them. The branches are more divergent; the flowers, more numerous than with the Centifolias, come all along the canes, making a sort of garland; they waft a nice perfume. They are very double, sometimes breaking [the bud] in opening, particularly when the season is a rainy one. Their color is a deeper pink than the Centifolias have. Their petals are in *coquilles* [shell- or scoop-shaped form], sprinkled with veins which are darker than the main color. These sorts have a tendency to put out a lot of runners, and thus could be considered inconvenient in small gardens." [C-T] The name encompasses a series of cultivars.

Horatius Coclès Listed as a Gallica.

Hulda

Vibert, 1845
"Velvety grenadine." [S] "Flowers dark velvety purple, of medium size, double." [P] "Medium-sized, semi-double, velvety flame purple." [R&M62] A Centifolia × Gallica hybrid.

Hypacia

syn. 'Hypathia'
Hardy, pre-1844
"Medium-sized, full, red, often spotted, globular." [V8] "Medium-sized, full, red-pink, rayed and striped white." [JR9/39] "Bright pink." [Ÿ] "A new variety of much beauty; flowers perfectly cupped, and of the most regular shape; color deep pink, occasionally mottled: this is a distinct and charming rose." [WRP] "Flowers rosy red, veined and spotted with white, of medium size, full; form, cupped, perfect. Habit, branching; growth, vigorous. A beautiful Rose." [P] "Vigorous bush; canes very strong, clothed with flat, recurved thorns; leaves pointed, strongly dentate; flower large, full, globular; color red, spotted grenadine." A Centifolia × Gallica hybrid.

Hypathia Listed as 'Hypacia' (C).

Ilicifolia Listed as 'À Feuille de Chêne' (C).

Incarnata Listed as 'My Lady Kensington' (C).

Ingrata Listed as 'Le Rire Niais' (C).

Jacquinot

Breeder unknown, pre-1848

"Flowers deep rose, with a streak of white tracing the centre of each petal, of medium size, double; form, expanded. Habit, branching; growth, moderate. A pretty and distinct Rose." [P] "Vigorous bush; blossom medium-sized, full, flat; color, bright pink, striped with white." [S]

Juanita

Robert, 1855

"5–7 cm [ca. 2$\frac{1}{2}$ in], full, beautiful light pink, well spotted and sabled with white." [R&M62] "Medium-size, full, pink, paler edge." [S]

Junon Listed as a Gallica.

Justine Ramet

Vibert, 1845

"Flowers purplish rose, of medium size, full." [P] "Medium-sized, full, purple pink." [R&M62] "Blossom medium-sized, full; light lilac." [S] "Average height." [Sn]

Knobby-Leaved Listed as 'Bullata' (C).

La Digittaire Listed as 'Childling' (C).

La Louise

syn. 'Louise Simplex'
Dupont, pre-1810

"Flesh." [LS] "Purple red, yellow center, medium size, lightly full, tall." [Sn] "Monsieur Dupont grew this from seed. It has the look of being the Type of the Centifolias—same wood, same leaves (but paler); flowers large, with five petals of the most beautiful pink, as if transparent; having golden stamens, which give a ravishing charm to this very pretty and very delicate rose. Grafted, it gains in beauty. Opens June 10–19." [LeR] "This single rose, mentioned in the *Nouveau Duhamel* and the *Bon Jardinier* of De Launay, was grown from seed by Du Pont." [Gx]

La Noblesse

trans. "Nobility"
Pastoret/Soupert & Notting, 1857

"Pink with tintings." [Ÿ] "Light pink, large, full tall." [Sn] "Light rose with bright carmine centre, large and full. Growth vigorous." [GeH] "Vigorous, hardy bush." [C]

La Reine de Provence Listed as 'Reine des Centfeuilles' (C).

La Rose de Batavie Listed as 'Grande Centfeuille de Hollande' (C).

La Transparente Listed as 'Unique Carnée' (C).

La Variable Listed as 'Childling' (C).

Lacteola Listed as 'Unique' (C).

Laura Listed as 'Laure' (C).

Laure

syn. 'Laura'
Breeder unknown, pre-1836

"Lilac-pink." [BJ40] "Hydrangea pink." [V4] "Flowers deep rosy pink, large and full; form, cupped, perfect. Habit, pendulous; growth,

moderate or vigorous. The flowers are produced in graceful clusters, containing ten or twelve flowers each, when the plant is in a vigorous state." [P] A Centifolia × Gallica hybrid.

Le Rire Niais

syns. 'À Odeur de Punaise', 'À Odeur Ingrate', 'Ingrata', 'Putidula'; trans., "Foolish Laughter"
Dupont, pre-1810

"Pink, medium size, full, average height." [Sn] "The scent approaches that of excrement." [CM] "Du Pont gave this charming name to the rose commonly called 'Cent Feuilles à Odeur de Punaise'; it's the 'Centifolia Ingrata' of the *Nouveau Duhamel*." [Gx]

Leea Rubra

Breeder unknown, pre-1906

"Pink." [LS] "Pink, center deep pink, medium size, full, medium scent, tall." [Sn]

Louise Simplex Listed as 'La Louise' (C).

Maid of the Valley Listed as 'Unique Panachée' (C).

Maiden's Blush For the Centifolia, listed as 'Héloïse' (C).

Marguerite de Flandre

Breeder unknown, pre-1862

"6–8 cm [ca. 2$\frac{1}{2}$–3 in], full, slatey deep red, vigorous." [R&M62] *Cf.* the Damask of the same name.

Maxima

Synonym shared by 'Goliath' (C), 'Grande Centfeuille de Hollande' (C), and 'Regina' (C), *qq.v.*

Mère Gigogne Listed as 'Childling' (C).

Minette

Vibert, 1819

"Blossom small, full; color, pink edged blush white." [S] "Rose." [Cal] "Light pink, medium size, full, average height." [Sn] "*Canes* diffuse, jutting-out, glabrous, and smooth; unarmed at the tip; ordinarily bestrewn at their base with several *prickles* which are feeble, hooked, and intermingled with some bristles. *Leaves* of 5 or 7 leaflets, aside from one or two small ones which are usually found at the base of the odd one. *Petiole* cylindrical, villose, glandulose, often armed beneath with very small hooked prickles. *Leaflets* elliptical, obtuse, light green and glabrous above, pale and villose beneath, crenelate along the edges. *Crenelature* silky, non-glandulose. *Peduncle* glabrous below the bracts, glandulose above. *Ovary* oval or ovoid, glabrous. *Sepals* villose, non-glandulose, terminating in a foliaceous linear point; three bear at their base several long incised appendages, which are serrate and glandulose. *Flower* small or medium-sized, full, very light pink with pale edges. The look of this rose, its various characteristics, and (above all) its peduncles which are glabrous above the bracts make me depart from the usual opinion which places it among the *Provins* or *Provences*." [Pf] Guessing, Prévost therefore places it among the Albas; we retain "the usual opinion" and leave it among the Centifolias and Hybrid Centifolias (as which lattermost Calvert classes it).

Mme. d'Hébray
Pradel, 1857

"White, striped pink, large, full, average height." [Sn] "Moderate growth flower bright pink, much striped and blotched with white; large, full." [S] It has been suggested that this is synonymous with 'Unique Panachée'(C); those in a position to do so may wish to make trial of this conjecture.

Mme. l'Abbey
Breeder unknown, pre-1846

"Bright rose, large and full." [FP] "Large, bright roseate." [WRP] "Flowers brilliant rose, large and full; form, cupped. Draws closely towards the Hybrid French." [P] Evidently a Centifolia × Gallica hybrid. *Cf.* the supposed Hybrid Perpetual 'Mme. A. l'Abbley' or 'Mme. A. l'Abbey'.

Monstrueuse Listed as 'Bullata' (C).

Multiflora Listed as 'Oeillet' (C).

Mutabilis

For the Centifolia, listed as 'Unique' (C).

Mutabilis Variegata Listed as 'Unique Panachée' (C).

[My Lady Kensington]
syns. 'Anna', 'Constance', 'Constance des Hollandaises', Incarnata';
    also, "Kensington" has provided rich fodder for misspellers
Breeder unknown, pre-1819

"Flowers very large, a nuanced flesh pink. A hybrid with the Gallica." [No26] "There is absolutely nothing else in this populous family which can rival this one. Its wood is very vigorous, its leaves very large, its buds (much overtopped by the appendages of the calyx) are round and inflated, close-set as they develop; flower four and a half inches across [ca. 1.2 dm], bright pink (more beautiful than carmine) in the center, which mixes onto the large exterior petals, which are washed purest white. They open between June 10 and 15." [LeR] "Wood and leaves of the Gallica, of which it is a hybrid with the Centifolia. Blossom that of this latter, large, bright pink within and white along the edge. This is the 'Constance' from Holland." [LeR]

Neige Listed as 'Unique' (C).

Nivea Listed as 'Unique' (C).

Oeillet
syns. 'Caryophyllata', 'Caryophyllea', 'Dianthaeflora', 'Guenille',
    'Onguiculata Cariophillata', 'Unguiculata', 'Unguiculata
    Caryophyllata', 'Multiflora'; trans., "Carnation"
Poilpré, 1789

"Light pink, small." [BJ40] "Bright rose-red." [GJB] "Variegated." [Cal] "Flowers light rose, small, and very double; of a singular appearance." [P] "Semi-double." [Go] "Very small, full, with fringed petals." [JR4/21] "A curious variety, with imperfect lacinated petals, unlike any other rose, and something like a pink." [WRP] *Flower* small, double, light or pale pink. *Petals* very small, clawed and as if pediculate with a limb which is nearly triangular and normally tricuspid." [Pf] "Very small, pink, slashed." [V8] "Very small, pink, bizarre." [R&M62] "Blossoms have very small petals which are clawed, crenelate, and jagged at the summit. [There is] a sub-variety with white flowers."

[No26] "Its petals narrow into a claw, as do the petals of a Carnation, the scent of which it indeed shares." [BJ09] "'Oeillet', a name which arises from its petals, in part abortive, with a ragged and dentate limb, the base of which narrows into a long white nub, giving it the look of a Carnation." [BJ17] "Vigorous bush; blossom very small, full; a pink 'Bizarre'." [S] "Very singular, and should be taken note of. It doesn't grow very high; its flowers are small—smaller by at least half than those of the [common] Centifolia. The petals are very much like those of the Carnation; they are small, very lacy, longly clawed at their base, enlarged in the upper part, incised, crenate at their summit, and altogether *sui generis*. What is more, these blossoms share even the scent of the Carnation. Monsieur Dupont grows this pretty variety." [Lam] "True fanciers think absolutely nothing of 'Oeillet'." [BJ30]

"This sort, or variety, though quite different from ['Renoncule'], could be placed alongside that one, just like Carnations succeed Ranunculuses in order of bloom-time. This is a miniature which Monsieur Dupont released to commerce under the name 'Onguiculata Cariophillata'. Few varieties there are that have foliage as beautiful as this. As it can't be confused with any other, let's only talk about the flower. It is small, and a pretty pink whipped with white. The petals are cut or toothed along the edge; the base terminates in a nub, just like Carnations. If the truth be known, it looks more like this last than it does like a rose. This singularity alone makes it worth looking for, its nice form, beautiful foliage, and sufficient perfume being by way of *lagniappe*." [C-T] "A degeneration of the Centifolia, from which it retains the wood, the thorns, and the leaves, as well as the vigor. Its blossom is a monstrosity representing a double Carnation. Its petals are ragged and toothed, their bases narrowing into a long white nub. The pink color is sprinkled with white. Sometimes it is playful and returns to the Type." [LeR]

"Rose with ovate, glandular seed-buds: the empalement glandular, and extending beyond the blossoms: flowers small, flesh-coloured, and very sweet-scented, with numerous halbert-shaped petals: footstalks and petioles hispid and glandular: leaflets ovate, sawed, villose beneath. This curious little Rose is one of the novelties recently imported from Holland, and known there by the French title of Rose Oeillet, or Pink Rose [*i.e.*, 'Pinks' as in *Dianthus*]. It certainly very much resembles the genus *Dianthus* in the size, form, and colour of the flowers: even their odour is like [that of] the carnation: in every other particular it is quite a provincialis. Whether this singular alteration has been produced by grafting, or is only an accidental transformation, we cannot learn. It is evidently an expulsion of petals from the common Province Rose; and Nature, true to its first position, is still struggling (though ineffectually) to pass the barrier of its confinement, which may be seen by two of the petals, that obtrude in spite of all restraint. [Andrews'] figure was delineated from a plant at the Nursery of Mr. Knight, of the King's Road, Chelsea, this summer, 1816." [A]

"Slightly tufted *bush* about 0.6 m high [ca. 2 ft]; *stems* divergent, green, with fairly numerous *prickles,* some very small, others long, reddish, slightly recurved, especially those near the stipules. *Leaflets* 3–5, acute ovate, bright green above, paler and tomentose beneath, margins lightly hirsute, with glandular hairs; petioles villose, often more or less viscous glandular; stipules elongate, acute, incised, villose, glandular. Flowers 3(–6), terminal; peduncle with small unequal acicles; pedicels with minute prickles mixed with stiff glandular hairs, the lateral ones bearing acute, oval bracts; *receptacles* ovoid, a little constricted at the tip, partially covered in sessile, viscous glands; *sepals* 3, pinnatifid, 2 simple, tomentose within, and similarly glandular without and on the margins; *corolla* rather small, cup-shaped; petals 5–6-seriate, irregularly notched, those at the center crumpled, a delicate pink streaked with yellowish white spots; claw elongate, white; styles long, villose. *Hips* identical to those of the *Centifolia*. This rose, the flowers of which resemble a carnation, had a chance origin from a plant of Centifolia which had degenerated in a garden at Mantes-sur-Seine in 1800. It can be propagated only by budding or layering, and Dupont preserved and multiplied it under the name of *R. caryophyllata*. It reverts readily to the parent variety; so, to keep it, one must renew it by budding on the hedge rose or vigorous shoots of the Alba, which produces magnificent heads and many blossoms. It is rarely found on its own roots, and favors a situation facing East." [T&R]

"We have, for many years, seen the rose 'Oeillet' proclaimed as having been found at Mantes, coming from a degenerated Centifolia. The fact of the matter is that this rose, which originated more than thirty-five years ago [*writing in 1824, making it 'earlier than 1789', this latter being, incidentally, the year in which the French Revolution commenced*], was grown at Le Mans from a crop of Centifolia seed (it is Monsieur Poilpré, grower at Le Mans, to whom we owe the release to commerce of several good roses, who was the first to propagate this rose, from which he obtained the Centifolias 'Anémone' [*1814*] and 'Sans Pétales' [*1809*])." [V2]

"A veritable monstrosity, but it shows the form and color of a double carnation in such a way as to put one in the mind of the other. Here's what they say about this rose. Around the year 1800, a Centifolia rose degenerated in a garden in Mantes; it kept the foliage of its kind; it gave full, pink flowers, which were however smaller. One could suppose to have found the scent of a carnation, because they [*the blossoms, presumably*] have some resemblance to that flower, the middle of the petals having a ragged, toothed limb, the base of which narrows into a long white claw. Such a singularity makes people refer to it as 'Guenille' [*i.e.,* "The Rag"]." [CM]

Onguiculata Cariophillata Listed as 'Oeillet' (C).

Prolifera Listed as 'Childling' (C).

Prolifère Listed as 'Childling' (C).

Putidula Listed as 'Le Rire Niais' (C).

Quercifolia Listed as 'À Feuille de Chêne' (C).

Red Provence Listed as 'Rubra' (C).

Regina
syns. 'Maxima', 'Sultana'; trans., 'Queen'
Breeder unknown, pre-1885
"Pink, medium size, very full, very fragrant, tall." [Sn] "Very vigorous bush; canes strong, much clothed with short thorns, which are hooked and blackish green; blossom large, full, opening with difficulty; color, bright pink." [S] See under 'Maxima' (C) for Centifolias sharing that synonym. See also 'Belle Sultane' (G), 'Grand Sultan' (G), and 'Regina Dicta' (G)

Reine de Saxe
trans. "Queen of Saxony"
Roseraie de l'Haÿ, date uncertain
"Light pink, medium size, full, medium scent, tall." [Sn] *Cf.* the Gallica 'König von Sachsen'.

Reine des Centfeuilles
syn. 'La Reine de Provence'; trans., "Queen of the Centifolias"
Belgium, 1824
"Flesh, full, cupped, medium size, beautiful." [LF] "Really deserves to be the queen of this division. Its large and finely shaped globular flowers have a good effect when suspended from a standard: these are of a pale lilac rose-color, distinct and beautiful." [WRP] "Light pink, large, very full, medium scent, tall." [Sn] "Blossoms double, very large, quite beautiful, light pink. The bush has very vigorous growth." [No26] "*Shrub,* very vigorous. *Flowers,* double, very large, very beautiful; of a light pink." [Go] "Flowers glossy lilac blush, large and very double; form, globular. Habit, branching; growth, vigorous; shoots very spinous. A beautiful Rose, with fine even petals." [P] "Raised in Belgium in 1824." [S]

Robert le Diable
Breeder unknown, pre-1885
"Blossom medium-sized, full; color, purple, shaded with bluish crimson." [S] "Violet purple red, medium size, very full, average height." [Sn] "Scarlet pink." [Ÿ] We cannot verify the date "1850" sometimes given for this cultivar; Verrier finds unquestioned hybridity, mentioning Gallica and China alongside Centifolia. Robert, Duke of Normandy, called "le Diable" ("the Devil"); died in Nicaea in 1035, returning from a pilgrimage to Jerusalem; father of William the Conqueror (his only—and illegitimate—son).

Rosalie Listed as 'Unique Carnée' (C).

Röte Centifolie
trans. "Red Centifolia"
Krause, 1938
"Deep red, medium size, very full, very fragrant, tall." [Sn]

Rouge Listed as 'Rubra' (C).

Rouge Vif Listed as 'Capricornus' (C).

Rougeau Virginale Listed as 'Héloïse' (C).

Rubiginosa Listed as 'Rubra' (C).

Rubra
syns. 'Cramoisi', 'Red Provence', 'Rouge', 'Rubiginosa'; trans., "Red"
Breeder unknown, pre-1629
"The blossoms are, in effect, a crimson red, three inches in size [ca. 7.5 cm], and nearly scentless." [CM] "Large, of a deep red, but the fragrance is not very pronounced." [AC] "Pink." [LS] "As the former [*i.e.,* 'Grande Centfeuille de Hollande'] was called *incarnata,* so this is called *Batavica centifolia rubra,* the difference being not very great: the stemme or stocke, and the branches also in this, seeming not to be so great but greener, the barke being not so red; the leaues of the same largenesse with ['Grande Centfeuille de Hollande']. The flowers are not altogether so large, thicke and double, and of a little deeper damaske or blush colour, turning to a red Rose, but not comming

Rubra *continued*

neere the full colour of the best red Rose, of a s[c]ent not so sweete as ['Grande Centfeuille de Hollande'], but comming somewhat neere the s[c]ent of the ordinary red rose [*i.e.*, the Gallica], yet exceeding it. This rose is not so plentifull in bearing as ['Grande Centfeuille de Hollande']." [PaSo]

Stratosféra
trans. "Stratosphere"
Böhm, 1934
   "Purple-red, large, very full, medium scent, tall." [Sn]

Sultana   Listed as 'Regina' (C).

Superb Striped Unique   Listed as 'Unique Panachée' (C).

Thalia   Listed as 'Thalie la Gentille' (C).

Thalie la Gentille
syn. 'Thalia'; trans., "Thalia the Pleasant"
Descemet?, pre-1811
   "Rose." [Cal] "Red." [Y] "Flowers deep rose; form, cupped." [P] "Deep pink, small, very full, moderate scent, tall." [Sn] "This rose resembles in form and shape its sister or companion 'Euphrosine [l'Élégant]'; but it is smaller, and of a more delicate red; it is as fragrant, blooming at the same time. You can find the same resemblance between their wood and their foliage. They are two pretty varieties, as is . . . 'Aglaia' [C]." [C-T] "This one has the wood, thorns, and leaves of its sister 'Euphrosine [l'Élégant]', also producing perfect bouquets of the greatest freshness in the tenderest pink color, but smaller; also, it is similarly bedecked all the way around with buds and foliage. These two sisters are hybrids between the Centifolia and the Damask 'Argentée'; they however haven't got one bit of resemblance to either. Bloom-time around June 9–10." [LeR] Thalie, alias Thalia, the third of the three Graces commemorated by roses in this chapter; the Graces are in particular charge of spreading the joy of Nature, and no doubt find Roses to aid them much in their task.

Théone
Noisette, pre-1820
   "Small bush, to three to four feet [ca. 1–1.33 m]; stem armed with large and small prickles, the large ones flattened and forming a hook towards the base; leaves composed of five flat leaflets which are oval and lightly dentate; flowers beautiful, medium-sized, very full, bright pink, with long peduncles. This variety is a hybrid of Centifolia and Damask. From my seedlings." [No28] "A very beautiful variety." [Go] Théone, Theone, or Theonoe; depending upon which Theone interested Monsieur Noisette, either sister of the Egyptian king Theoclymenus, thwarting her brother's designs on Helen of Troy; or abducted sister of Calchas (the soothsayer of Trojan times who suggested the wooden Trojan Horse).

Tour de Malakoff
trans. "Tower of Malakoff"
Pastoret/Soupert & Notting, 1857
   "Purple-violet, large, full, tall." [Sn] "Vigorous growth, very hardy; flower large, full, purple passing to deep violet." [S] See G. S. Thomas' appreciative description in his work. Not to be confused with Robert's 1856 Gallica of similar name, which was pink. 'Tour de Malakoff', *not* referring to an inquisitive saunter about the town just outside the walls of Paris; rather, Malakoff's Tower in the temporary defenses of Sebastopol, Crimea, during the Crimean War.

Tulipe Paltot   Listed as 'Unique Panachée' (C).

Unguiculata   Listed as 'Oeillet' (C).

Unguiculata Caryophyllata   Listed as 'Oeillet' (C).

Unica   Listed as 'Unique' (C).

Unica Spectabilis   Listed as 'Unique Admirable' (C).

Unique   Plate 6
syns. 'Changeante', 'Lacteola', 'Mutabilis', 'Neige', 'Nivea', 'Unica', 'Unique Blanche', 'White Provence'; trans., "Singular"
Richmond/Grimwood, 1777
   "Pure white, full, cupped, medium-sized, beautiful." [LF] "Flowers medium-sized or small, full, white." [JR5/45] "Large, full, cupped, very pure porcelain white." [JR9/20] "The buds proclaim a deep pink blossom, which however is thoroughly white within. Could it be a variety of the White Rose [*i.e.*, the Alba] . . . ?" [BJ09] "The petals splotched pink on the outside, and alabaster white within, make us pardon the lack of grace in its form." [J-A/564] "Has its buds tinted bright red on the outside, but . . . the blossom is the purest white. [There is] another variety of the same name [*'Unique Carnée'*?], exterior of the petals white, and the center of the flower a beautiful pink." [BJ17] "Flowers paper white, perhaps the purest white rose grown, form cupped, moderate size and full, though the petals are not very evenly disposed, habit moderate; a most beautiful rose." [JC] "A sported branch from the old variety [*'Common Centifolia'*?], differing in colour, and also in the shape of the flower, being weaker, having the petals more crumpled, and not so cupped; the colour is pure white, though it is liable to sport, for I have seen in a pretty blush, and is some instances striped and margined." [Bu] "Exterior of buds tinted the most intense pink, making a person believe that the open flower will have an inside of the same color—though it turns out to be the purest white. This rose, published by Dupont, was found on a farm, where it had been grown a long time." [AC] "[A] genuine English rose, which was found by Mr. Grimwood, then of the Kensington Nursery (England), in some cottage-garden, growing among plants of the common Cabbage Rose. It is a very double flower, the buds edged with pink, and is very beautiful both before and after expansion. This variety was from the first much esteemed, and plants of it were sold at very high prices. Most probably this was not a seedling from the Old Cabbage Rose, as that is too double to bear seed in the English climate, but was what is called by florists a sporting branch or sucker." [WRP] "Pure white, medium size, full, fragrant. Growth vigorous." [GeH] "Flowers paper white, large and full; form, deeply cupped. Habit, erect; growth, vigorous. A good white Rose, well suited for clumping." [P] "*Leaflets* with the serration double and very glandulose. *Ovary* ovoid, hispid-glandulose. *Bud* red. *Flower* medium-sized, full, white." [Pf] "Still finds itself in some fanciers' collection; now [1827], however, that we begin to have higher expectations, we don't have the patience to bear its notchings and the difficulty it has in opening, faults that formerly were overshadowed by the great beauty of its sparkling white and the pink splashes on its outside." [J-As/59] "A good rose, similar but inferior to 'Mme. Hardy'." [EL]
   "Rose, with seed-buds nearly round; peduncles and petioles

hispid and glandular: the stem and branches are prickly, scattered, straight, and slightly bent back: the leaflets are villous beneath, with slightly glandular margins. Among the recent additions to this genus, the 'White Province', or 'Rose Unique', is indisputably the most valuable. Its introduction in 1777 was entirely accidental, through the medium of the later Mr. Grimwood, nurseryman, a great admirer and collector of roses, who, in an excursion [*in 1775* (T4)] which he usually made every summer, in passing the front garden of Mr. Richmond, a baker near Needham in Suffolk, there perceived the present charming plant, where it had been placed by a carpenter who found it near a hedge on the contiguous premises of a Dutch merchant, whose old mansion he was repairing. Mr. Grimwood, requesting a little cutting of it, received from Mr. Richmond the whole plant; when Mr. G., in return for a plant so valuable, presented him with an elegant silver cup with the Rose engraved upon it; and which is commemoration has furnished food for many a convivial hour. It is of a dwarf growth, and remains in flower near six weeks longer than the other Province Roses; which renders it still the more estimable. We wish it had been in our power to have accounted for its having been till so lately a stranger to us, and whence indigenous; but at present [*1805?*] our information is entirely confined to the knowledge of its casual introduction; and until some further light is thrown on the subject, to elucidate its genealogy, we shall regard it as a native." [A]

"Flower double and white. Outer petals pale green beneath, with blood-color along their edges. Calyx oblong, pear-shaped, bristly; peduncles umbeliferous, nearly prickly, bristly; canes and petioles glandulose and bristly. Leaflets oval, doubly serrate, glandulose along the edges . . . Bush always low, rarely rising above three feet [ca. 1 m]. The stem and canes—green touched with brown—are armed with many thorns which are more or less large and scattered at unequal distances. The young shoots are green, and bear reddish prickles as well as glandular bristles. The spine-covered petioles bear two false leaves, one of which is always a little higher than the other on the stem. The fragrant leaflets, to the number of five or rarely seven, are obtuse around the tip, doubly dentate, and glandulose along the edge. The peduncles are ordinarily tripartite, and covered with glandulose red bristles. The calyx is oblong, nearly pear-shaped, quite open at the top, and covered (like the winged sepals) with red pediculate glands. The very full flower, of a sparkling whiteness, very dense, and very cupped, is much like that of the [common] Centifolia. The exterior petals are a pale green on the back, and have a blood-colored tint towards the tip, particularly before the flower is fully open. Before opening, the buds are quite red at the tip—so much so that it can't be believed that they will produce white roses. When the flower nears its end, it happens that several petals take on a pale purple color approaching the color of peach blossoms. *Native Land.* This kind of rose has been known in England for more than a century. From there, gardeners have spread it to the rest of Europe. *Bloom-Time.* The beginning of July. *Observations.* The origin of this sort of rose is not known. Some trace it to the Province Rose, others to the Centifolia; yet others class it with the Albas. But though in its habit it resembles the first two more, it is nevertheless very distinct such that it can't be regarded as a Province Rose. Thus it is that I believe it to be its own species. As this sort of Rose rarely makes suckers from its roots, it is usually propagated by shield-graft or bud on the [*common*] Centifolia." [Rsg]

"The first [of the "Uniques"], called 'Nivea' by Monsieur Dupont, and more usually 'Unique Blanche', has wood armed with numerous thorns which are large at the base, red [*at first?*], very sharp, whitish green [*at maturity?*], and slightly hooked. The leaves are oval—nearly round—deeply dentate, and edged brownish red. The calyx, also oval, is covered over, as is the petiole, with similarly-colored bristles. The buds are nearly round, barely covered [by the sepals], and red on the outside; looking at it, you'd think a red blossom was about to open—but a person is pleasantly surprised by its matte white color; it is large, and the petals are thick and velvety. Though this rose is not as double as the [common] Centifolia, it compensates by its other virtues." [C-T] "All in all, this rose is unique in beauty. It's called 'Neige' ["Snow"] because its petals are a very pure white. Its wood is armed with strong, fairly numerous thorns; the leaves are those of the *Hollandes*, of which this is a hybrid with the Albas, the scent of which is similar. It has the rounded form of the [common] Centifolia. Its numerous buds, sharing the same peduncle, are close to the foliage; their bright pink tint promise a red flower before they open—but a person is pleasantly surprised when, opening, they show such a beautiful white, with a light green on the outer base of the petals, which are large, firm, and quite thick. The blossoms are borne wonderfully on the peduncles and pedicels—which are strong, and make perfect, ravishing, bouquets. Sometimes they vary, taking on a hint of red at the tip of the petals (which are very white within). Who could want it to return to its Type? It's really something grafted on the same stock with its sisters the 'Unique Carnée' from Vilmorin, and the rose called 'Pourpre Charmant' [G]." [LeR] "The rose 'Unique', which is to say 'Unique in Beauty.' The long and short of it is that this rose is the most beautiful of all those we grow in our gardens today [1821]. Some nurserymen entitle this rose 'Blanc de Neige', doubtless because its petals are a pure white; others, 'Changeante', because these same petals are bright red on the exterior and a perfect white within; but, as Monsieur Noisette has a sub-variety with entirely pink blossoms [*presumably 'Unique Rose'*], this name 'Changeante' only really fits the white variety. Monsieur Bosc regards this rose as a hybrid between the Centifolia and the Alba; indeed, it approaches the latter in its scent and form and the former in its leaves and thorns. Most botanists, however, are in accord in putting it among the Centifolias. 'Unique' is commonly propagated by grafting on the Briar. It is usually planted in beds close by the house, the better to enjoy the sparkle of the blossoms when they begin to open." [CM]

"*Shrub* 0.6 m high. *Flowers* 1–4 at the branch tips, rounded, moderately large, a little less double than in the 'Common Centifolia'; *petals* cordately notched, dull velvety white; otherwise, like the remainder of the Centifolias. This rose, known as 'Rose Unique' or 'Snow-White Rose', was named *R. mutabilis* by Persoon because the bud, bright red at first, opens dulls white, retaining a reddish hue only in the 5 outermost petals, although the center petals also retain a pink flush—a throwback to the 'Common Centifolia', from which it is derived . . . It blooms a little later than the other Centifolias. In the absence of seeds, it can be propagated from cuttings or layers; but is normally grafted on the Briar. However, it succeeds better, and has finer blossoms, if worked on vigorous stocks of the 'Quatre-Saisons' rose. It should be pruned hard in February." [T&R]

"Has remained the only one [sport] up till the present [1826]—at least, as far as I [Vibert] know—which has kept its white color

Unique *continued*

without change; but it will at length betray its origin. This rose is one of those which merit the close scrutiny of enlightened observers. It is perhaps the earliest authentic sport that we have; it is still the only one that has kept so long without showing any inclination to return to the Type, despite being grown all over. Last of all, it is the only one in which sporting has changed the color so noticeably." [V2]

"It would be better to call this 'Centifolia Alba', because the particularity of having the main petals red on the outside is common in other sorts, such as the Belgica [Agathe], the Alba, and many of the Chinas; but the very double blossoms, of the purest white, will always make it a sought-out variety." [BJ30]

[Unique Admirable]

syn. 'Unica Spectabilis'
Descemet, pre-1820

"Rose." [Cal] "Blossom medium-sized, full; yellowish-pink." [S] "*Leaves* distant. *Serration* simple. *Ovary* oval-turbinate. *Flower* medium-sized, full, regular, light bright red." [Pf] "A variety which, says Prévost, was raised by Descemet." [Gx]

Unique Anglaise   Listed as 'Unique Rose' (C).

Unique Blanche   Listed as 'Unique' (C).

[Unique Carnée]

syns. 'Belle de Vilmorin', 'Carnea', 'La Transparente', 'Rosalie',
      'Vilmorin'; trans., "Fleshy 'Unica'"
Vilmorin, pre-1811
Sport or seedling of 'Common Centifolia' (C).

"Blush." [Cal] "Large, full, flesh-colored." [V8] "Flowers bright flesh-colour, large and full. A very pleasing Rose." [P] "Blossoms very double and regular, not very abundant." [BJ30] "Less full than the Centifolia 'Des Peintres', but of a very tender flesh color, and having a sort of very agreeable transparence, which makes it easily distinguished and much besought." [BJ17] "Sometimes resumes that original pink color of the common Centifolia, of which it is a sport; while rare, it is nevertheless worth seeking out." [J-A/564] "Very delicate flesh color; leaves, lighter green [than those of 'Common Centifolia'], tomentose beneath, not very leafy." [BJ17] "Stems bristly; blossoms medium-sized, flesh-pink color; leaves light green and slightly lanate beneath." [AC] "*Ovary* ovoid, barely attaining in length double its width. *Flower* medium-sized, flesh, nearly full." [Pf] "There's a darker sub-variety." [No26] "Due to the great-grandmother of Monsieur Vilmorin." [Vibert in SNH65/345] "Everybody knows that 'Vilmorin', in particular, grafted, produces flesh-colored, pink, and indeed variegated roses on the same specimen, a certain indication that it will soon return to being the [common] Centifolia." [V2]

"The second [of the 'Uniques'] differs from ['Unique'] by its longer foliage, larger blossoms, and beautiful flesh color. There is nothing fresher-looking than this rose! Its petals are transparent as porcelain. It would seem that it was Monsieur Vilmorin-Andrieux who released it to commerce; thus it is that it can be found under the name 'Belle de Vilmorin'. What a pretty gift he has given the fanciers! This rose can be playful and sometimes has flowers with petals half pink and half flesh." [C-T] "This beautiful rose, the masterpiece of all the flesh-colored ones, comes from Monsieur Vilmorin, who grew it from seed of the Centifolia, of which it has the form and grace . . . In

the final analysis, a person couldn't see anything more perfect that this flower; its wood, thorns, and leaves are those of the Hollande. It is flesh-colored, and often the roses return to the Type; I have seen some half flesh and half pink, others all pink. They are large and very double, and should be considered the best of all similar." [LeR]

"*Bush* on its own roots about 0.6 m tall [ca. 2 ft]; stems more or less bristling with prickles and stiff glandular hairs according to age and the climate in which it grows. Leaflets light green, tomentose beneath; petiole glandulose, rough to the touch. *Flowers* medium-sized, almost fully double, (1–) 2–3 at the tips of the canes, fragrant, at length a very pleasant flesh color distinct from that of the common Centifolia, but similar to that of 'Bifera' [Damask Perpetual], which is distinguished by the shape of the receptacle and the almost round, simply dentate leaflets. This fine rose commemorates Vilmorin, who had a complete collection of roses before Dupont did, and who introduced and propagated it some 15 or 16 years ago. It is very prone to color mutation, especially when vigorous, so that on a single stock one finds flesh-colored, pink, and motley blossoms. It can also transform wholly into a plant with flowers like those of the common Centifolia, but slightly smaller, in which state some nurserymen offer it as the 'Pink Vilmorin Rose'. It needs to be renewed by grafting, since it inevitably becomes lost if left to itself, and layers take with difficulty." [T&R] "Propagated around 1800 by Monsieur de Vilmorin . . . this variety is mentioned by Dumont de Courset, described in the *Nouveau Duhamel,* and described and illustrated in Redouté. Prévost gives as synonyms 'La Transparente' and 'Rosalie'." [Gx]

Unique Panachée   Plate 6

syns. 'Maid of the Valley', 'Mutabilis Variegata', 'Superb Striped
      Unique', 'Tulipe Paltot'; trans., "Plumed 'Unique'"
Chaussée/Cardon, 1821
Sport of 'Unique' (C).

"Pure white, rayed with carmine, full, cupped, large." [LF] "Large, very full, white, plumed bright pink." [BJ53] "White, striped with lake; though they are very capricious in their coloring, sometimes opening pure white, and occasionally light rose." [FP] "Much marbled with pink in the center of the flower. It doesn't maintain its characteristic in all locales." [BJ30] "A most inconstant rose, in some soils producing flowers beautifully striped, in others entirely red, and in the soil of Mr. Rivers' nursery, most frequently pure white. In Sussex, where it has bloomed finely in its variegated character, it has been honored with a new name, and is there known as 'the Maid of the Valley'." [WRP] "We now [1826] have that beautiful rose with plumed blossoms—or, to put it better, blossoms which have petals showing two colors. In 1825, I [*Vibert*] saw several beautiful specimens, all the blossoms of which were like that." [V2] "*Leaflets,* doubly toothed, with very glandulous teeth. *Flowers,* full, middle-sized, white. *Petals,* white, striped and veined inside with bright pink." [Go] "Flowers white striped with lake, but sporting much, sometimes coming altogether white, and sometimes wholly red; large and full; form, cupped. Habit, erect; growth, vigorous, shoots very spinous. This is one of the most beautiful Striped Roses known; but there is some difficulty in keeping it in true character. To assist in this, avoid a rich soil; let it be planted in a mixture of good turfy loam, burnt earth, and old mortar or brick rubbish, two parts of the former and one of each of the latter." [P]

"*Flower* completely like that of ['Unique'], from which it is nothing other than a sport, with this difference: the inner petals are plumed-rayed with very bright pink. This striping is very pronounced in light, sandy soils; however, in strong ground—clayey and compact—it often disappears completely. This rose was distributed in Rouen around 1821 by one Car[d]on, then caretaker of the city hall garden. For a long time, the discovery of this sub-variety was attributed to him. However, dependable people now assure us that this Car[d]on had received this rose from the late Mme. Chaussée, at that time a distinguished fancier in Le Havre; but they are unable to tell us if the fixing of this sport was the work of Mme. Chaussée, or if she only got it from another." [Pf] "Often beautiful." [JC] See also 'Mme. d'Hébray' (C).

Unique Rose
syn. 'Unique Anglaise'; trans., "Pink 'Unica'"
Cels, pre-1810

"Double, large, a beautiful pink, with a very elegant scent." [No26] "*Flower* medium-sized or large, nearly full, light bright pink. This rose is distinct from the common Centifolia in its shorter *ovary*, often by the form and color of its flowers, but especially by its stronger thorns similar to those of 'Unique Blanche'." [Pf] "'Unique Rose', or 'Unique Anglaise', without having all the rare merits of [the other Uniques, 'Unique' and 'Unique Carnée'], is nevertheless nothing to look down upon. Its leaves are also edged pink, having as well little ashen bristles. The fragrant blossom, of a pretty shade of pink, is not very large; it looks like the [common] Centifolia, all the virtues of which it shares." [C-T] "The wood of this one is brown. [It has the] thorns and leaves of its kin. Buds protrusive; blossom very double, not as large as that of the [common] Centifolia; a pretty pink; petals raggedy; elegant scent; comes into bloom the 10th to the 15th of June." [LeR] "Grew in the collection of the château Soucelle." [Gx]

[Unique Rouge]
trans. "Red 'Unique'"
Breeder unknown, pre-1824

"Lively rose-red." [GJB] "Fairly large, red." [BJ24] "Ovary shorter than that of the 'Common Centifolia'. Blossom medium-sized, nearly full; bright pink." [S]

Variegata
syns. 'À Fleurs Panachées', 'Bunte Provinrose'
Breeder unknown, pre-1775

"[There are] the Panachées, the red and the white, in which the pink-colored petals are, with the one, veined with red, and, in the other, pale pink or deep pink." [CM] "Blossoms superb, plumed like a Gallica, but more double." [No26] "Rose with seed-buds nearly round: peduncles, stem, and footstalks hispid and prickly: flowers striped or blotched: leaflets ovate, pointed, sawed, villose and glaucous beneath. Of this elegant variety of the Province Rose we have seen several plants in bloom, all varying from each other; more or less marked, stronger or paler in colour according to the strength of the plant, or the favourable state of weather during their inflorescence. [Andrews'] figure was delineated from plants in the Nursery of Mr. Lee in the autumn of 1826, although from its being the first time of its flowering it is probable it may eventually flower in the spring season." [A]

Vierge de Cléry
trans. "Virgin of Cléry"
Baron-Veillard, 1888

"White, large and full. Growth vigorous, floriferous." [GeH] "White, medium size, full, tall." [Sn]

Vilmorin   Listed as 'Unique Carnée' (C).

Wellington
Calvert, 1832

"Flower medium-sized, full, outspread; color, bright pink." [S] "Retains its fine globular character to the very last; its rich crimson colour and dwarf habit makes it very desirable." [Bu] "Pink, large, full, medium height." [Sn] "One of the largest of this division, something like 'Grand Bercam' in the color of its flowers, which are of a beautiful deep rose, very double, nearly as much so as those of the ['Common Centifolia']. This forms a splendid standard." [WRP] "Flowers vivid even rose, of medium size, and double; form, cupped. Habit, branching; growth, vigorous." [P] Possibly a Centifolia × Gallica hybrid. Arthur Wellesley, 1st Duke of Wellington, lived 1769–1852; not a favorite with fans of Napoléon.

White Provence   Listed as 'Unique' (C).

Yorkshire Provence
syn. 'Cricks'
Breeder unknown, pre-1821

"Bright rose." [Cal] "Has very much the appearance of the old Cabbage [*i.e.*, 'Common Centifolia'] ...though a shade darker, and opens its flowers more freely." [Bu] Perhaps from nurseryman James Cricks of Rochford, England—not, however, in Yorkshire.

CHAPTER SIX

Centifolia Pompons and Pompon Mosses

"The Pompon roses, which succeed the Chinas [in bloom-time], are too well known to need minute description. There are two pink sorts, the big [*i.e.,* 'Rosier des Dames' (CP)] and the small [*i.e.,* 'De Meaux' (CP)]; the former is infinitely more beautiful than the latter." [C-T] "The Roses in this group are remarkable for their diminuativeness. They are well adapted for edgings to the Rosarium, or Rose-clumps generally. They are sometimes planted in masses, in which manner they look well, as they are of neat growth, and bloom profusely; but they do not last long in flower: and for this reason we should hesitate to recommend them, except under particular circumstances." [P] "Because of their numerous and magnificent little blossoms, which expand in May, these varieties are very good to border rose beds. They can be propagated very easily by offsets, and can be shorn the same as boxwood." [JR9/20, referring to the Gallicas 'Pompon de Bourgogne' and 'Pompon de Bourgogne à Fleurs Blanches' as well as the CP 'De Meaux']

"Some people will find it curious that I [Vibert] have placed the Pompons among the Uncertain Hybrids, as several consider them to be Centifolias. I would tell them that the Pompon Roses have none of the special characteristics of that class. The disposition of the blossoms—very close to the leaves—and their manner of growth would be sufficient to keep me from putting them there. Monsieur Descemet assured me that he had occasionally found them among Gallica seedlings, but never among those from the Centifolias. In my case, let me tell you what happened: In 1816, a Pompon grafted on a vigorous Briar, after having bloomed produced a very strong cane. The cane was only an outgrowth of a shoot from the original; but, in fifteen days, it became so strong in its upper portion that, as a precaution, I staked it. The leaves which would develop on it were large, very thick, and resembled—as did the wood—that from the variety known under the name 'Mère Gigogne' [*i.e.,* 'Childling' (C)]." [V1]

À Balais Listed as 'Comtesse de Chamoïs' (CP).

À Bordures Listed as 'Comtesse de Chamoïs' (CP).

À Douze Pétales Listed as 'À Fleurs Presque Simples' (CP).

[À Fleurs Presque Simples]
syns. 'À Douze Pétales', 'À Sept Pétales'; trans., "With Nearly Single Blossoms"
Charpentier/Lemeunier, 1807

"Bush from 15–20 inches high [ca. 4–5 dm]; canes upright; thorns slightly hooked; leaflets small, pubescent, light green; in *May,* small single pink flowers." [J-A/574] "Weak *shrub* scarcely 0.5 m high [ca. 1½ ft], like ['De Meaux'] …but a little less prickly and with only (5–) 6–7 petals, some distinctly pointed. *Hips* small, elongate, red, commonly abortive. We have grown this rose since 1815 and it constantly gives blossoms with 6 or 7 petals, although 5 have been seen. It was raised in 1807 by Auvé-Charpentier, a surgeon of Sablé near La Flèche. The Pompon Rose is a fertile hybrid of *R. centifolia* and *R. gallica,* regarded as a species by DeCandolle but grouped among the Centifolias by many authors. It differs from these by the simply dentate leaflets, prickly petioles, paired flowers, and very dis-similar stature." [T&R] "This variety has much in common in flower and foliage with 'Pompon Varin' [CP], and is itself perhaps nothing more than a Pompon degenerating or returning to its Type." [V1]

À Sept Pétales Listed as 'À Fleurs Presque Simples' (CP).

Bordeaux des Dames Listed as 'Rosier des Dames' (CP).

Burgundiaca Listed as 'Rosier des Dames' (CP). See also 'Pompon de Bourgogne' (G).

Burgundy Listed as 'Pompon de Bourgogne' (G). See also 'Rosier des Dames' (CP).

[Calypso Petite]
trans. "Little Calypso"
Descemet, pre-1820

"Rose." [Cal] "Rosy blush, very large." [WRP] "Bright crimson, and very beautifully formed." [J-As/56] "Variety straight from the 'Hollande' [C], of which it has all the characteristics, except that all its parts are very close-set. With its plenteous flowers, it makes ravishing corymbs; they are very double, two-thirds smaller than the Type; color, violet pink. They make pretty bushes—well rounded. They bloom from the 1st to the 9th of June." [LeR] Calypso, the captivating admirer of Odysseus; but perhaps referring to 'Calypso', the Boursault.

Chamoïs Listed as 'Comtesse de Chamoïs' (CP).

Common Pompon Listed as 'De Meaux' (CP).

[Comtesse de Chamoïs]

syns. 'À Balais', 'À Bordures', 'Chamoïs', 'Fasciculée', 'Fastigiata', 'Rose Bordée de Blanc'

Descemet, ca. 1810

"*Canes* and *stems* slender, vertical. Leaflets large, oval-rounded. *Flower* small or medium-sized, full, semi-globular, pink." [Pf] See also 'Pompon Varin' (CP).

De Bordeaux Listed as 'Rosier des Dames' (CP).

De Champagne Listed as 'De Meaux' (CP).

De Meaux

syns. 'Common Pompon', 'De Champagne', 'Dijonensis', 'Miniature', 'Pompon Commun', 'Pompon Rose'; engagingly, sometimes the synonymy of 'Rosier des Dames' [CP] and 'Pompon de Bourgogne' [G], qq.v., make incursions on 'De Meaux'; trans., 'From [the city of] Meaux'

Séguier, 1637 (but see below)

"Pale roseate." [WRP] "*Flower* very small, light or pale pink." [Pf] "Light rose, very small and full. Habit, erect; growth, small." [P] "Small, very full, globular, bright pink nuanced lilac." [JR9/20] "Flowers rosy-pink and lilac; very small and compact, habit quite dwarf; a most beautiful little rose." [JC] "Very double, very strong blossoms, center pretty widely cupped, bright pink with delicate pink edges." [J-A/574] "Its blossoms are a little larger than those of the Burgundy Rose [*i.e.,* 'Pompon de Bourgogne' (G)]; their scent can hardly be detected." [BJ09] "Even better than the 'Pompon de Bourgogne', it displays a head covered with flowers; it is better branched and makes a tighter bush." [CM] "Thoroughly dwarf in habit and flower, but endowed with the characteristics of [the larger Centifolias]." [R-H63/183] "Was a great favorite with my grandmother. She would walk about the garden with a bunch of it in her hand, gathered with very short stems. I imagine she liked it because of its perfume; it was not much to look at. This Rose was a pompon, or miniature Provence Rose, habit dwarf and compact, flower small, rosette, colour mauve or washed-out red." [NRS22/98] Testu relays to us that it would seem to have appeared in the garden of Dominique Séguier, Bishop of Meaux, in 1637—and that it was also said to have been introduced into horticulture in 1789. Yet others were convinced that "it was found in 1735 by a Dijonnais gardener, who saw it while cutting brush in the nearby mountains . . . The roots grow many stems which, considering their height, are strong. The stems become branched, and are covered in Spring with a multitude of blossoms of very agreeable form, bright incarnate at the heart, grading to flesh color at the edge. Their size is like that of a 25-sou coin, or sometimes like a little *écu*—they're not as pretty then. They have an elegant scent. The sun destroys the beauty of its colors, making them fade too quickly." [AbR] "Found, according to an author whom I copy, in 1735, wild, by a Dijonnais gardener. The fact would seem to be true—the name supports it, and I [Vibert] well remember that, in my youth [ca. 1780–1790], Pompon roses were not rare." [SNH65/344] Alas for that!—for, had they been rarer, descriptions of them and tales of their origins would not have become so terribly confused. Along with the usual Pompons, which we call 'De Meaux' (CP), 'Pompon de Bourgogne' (G), and 'Rosier des Dames' (CP), with their various color-sports, I suspect that there is some confusion with *R. majalis* 'Flore-Pleno'.

"Corolla double, pale red. Ovary oval. Sepals adorned with several appendages. Leaves oval-lanceolate, terminating in a point. Peduncles bristling with hairs . . . As elegant in form as it is petite, this rose is double, pale red around the edges, always brighter towards the center, flat, and the petals are slightly recurved. The calyx segments, bestrewn with red glands, bear numerous appendages along their edges, and a long foliaceous appendage at the tip. The oval glandulose ovary is mossy in the upper portion. The peduncles are charged with hairs and several glands. The greater part of the leaves are composed of five slender oval-lanceolate leaflets bordered with sharp teeth, grass green above, paler beneath, with hairs bordering the serration. The petioles have some thin prickles, and some lacy stipules which are pointed and back-curving. The thorns arming the young branches are small and not very numerous." [Rsg]

"Low, branched bush; *prickles* sparse, slender, almost straight. Leaflets (3–) 5, ovate, rugose, light green, tomentose beneath; simply dentate, a little ciliate, margins glandular; petioles villose. *Flowers* fully double, sweetly scented, mostly in pairs at the tips of the branches; pedicels, *receptacles,* and the pinnatifid *sepals* hispid from black, stalked, slightly sticky glands; *petals* numerous, pink deepening towards the center of the blossom. This is probably a variety derived from either *R. centifolia* or the Provence Rose, with which it has much in common. Many further derivatives are known with white, striped, or almost single flowers . . . To encourage new growth in the Spring, one should prune hard after bloom, as the stems and principal branches die back. Propagation is by division of the old rootstocks in the Fall." [T&R]

"Bush growing no higher than 50–60 cm [ca. 20–24 in], making a small, rounded plant; stems with light green bark, upright, cylindrical, fairly robust, thorny; thorns narrow, subulate, nearly straight; canes floriferous, branching, more or less vigorous depending upon whether they come from the base or the tip of the stem, thorny, thorns like those of the stems, intermixed with gland-bearing hairs; bark slightly colored brown, becoming more intense toward the upper part of the cane; leaflets, 3– (nearly always) 5—rarely 7—tender matte green; stipules entire, small or medium-sized, edges glandular-ciliate; narrow axils, with auricles adhering to the petiole; stipules of the peduncular leaf with large axil, terminating in a point like an auricle; petioles slightly glandulose and tomentose, rarely prickly; leaflets small, oval, rounded at the base, abruptly pointed at the tip, slightly tomentose beneath, with simple dentation, ciliate-glandulose; blossom often solitary, sometimes geminate, rarely in paucifloral corymbs (rare if not on very vigorous canes); bracts rare, lanceolate, ciliate-glandulose along the edges, tomentose beneath; peduncles fairly long, very straight, very glandulose; receptacles floriferous, glandulose or very glandulose, small, ovoid-ellipsoid at the base, a little constricted at the tip before anthesis; sepals more or less narrow, the tips overtopping the open corolla, spinulate, edges ciliate-glandulose, as are those of the spinules, tomentose within, velvety and slightly glandulose in the internal portion, reflexing after the petals fall; corollas small, very full, cupped; nearly flat after anthesis, deep flesh pink when opening, paler at the edge, fading to pale pink; exterior petals large, emarginate at the tip, shorter than the sepals; central ones more muddled, as if imbricated, allowing the style to appear; styles glabrous, free, slightly divergent. Blooms in May, whence its common name May Pompon." [S]

Decora

Roseraie de l'Haÿ, date uncertain

"Pink, small, very full, light scent, tall." [Sn] "Midway between 'Spong' and 'De Meaux'." [T4]

Dijonensis Listed as 'De Meaux' (CP).

Fasciculée Listed as 'Comtesse de Chamoïs' (CP).

Fastigiata Listed as 'Comtesse de Chamoïs' (CP).

Gros Pompon Listed as 'Rosier des Dames' (CP).

Juno Rose Listed as 'Petite Junon de Hollande' (CP).

Junon Argentée Listed as 'Petite Junon de Hollande' (CP).

Little Gem

W. Paul, 1880

"Crimson, very small, full; a miniature sort." [EL] "Rosy crimson, small, double, well-mossed; a miniature moss Rose, valuable for decorations." [GeH] "Light red, small, full, very fragrant, moderate height." [Sn] "Dwarf growth; miniature rose, charming for gardens, vases, and bouquets; blossom small, full, well mossed; color, crimson. The open blossoms are no larger than a *franc*; the petals are small, proportionately well formed, and magnificently arranged during the whole course through which the flower goes." [S]

Miniature Listed as 'De Meaux' (CP).

Minor Listed as 'Rosier des Dames' (CP).

Mossy de Meaux

syns. 'Pompon Mousseux', 'Pomponia Muscosa'

England, pre-1813

"Blush, peach centre, pretty, small and full." [FP] "Very small, full, pink." [V8] "Very small, cupped, pretty." [LF] "Flowers blush, their centre pale pink, small and full; form, cupped. Habit, dwarf. A very pretty and interesting Rose, but of rather delicate growth in most situations. Prune closely. Decidedly not adapted for a Standard Rose." [P] "Very small, and is the earliest of roses, blooms in clusters, of a delicate pink colour; the plant is very dwarf, and difficult of cultivation, unless in a sandy rich soil, where it grows and holds permanently." [Bu] "*Shrub* distinctly smaller in all its parts. *Flower* very small, full, pale pink." [Pf]

"Discovered five-and-twenty years ago [*making 1813*] in the garden of an old lady in the west of England, of whom it was purchased by a nurseryman for five guineas,—certainly a sport, as the Rose de Meaux is known never to bear seed in England." [Go] "Found by Mr. Sweet in a garden at Taunton, England, in 1814. He obtained possession of the plant for five pounds; and afterwards distributed the young plants at one guinea each … This is one of the prettiest of roses, and one of the first to make its appearance in June, gladdening us with its early clusters of small and finely-shaped flowers. It is not well adapted for a standard; for when grafted or budded, it is but a short-lived plant, at least in the generality of soils; on its own roots, in light rich soils, it may be grown in great perfection." [WRP] "The price is still [1824] too high for everyone to have it." [MonLdeP] "Very precious and still [in 1826] not very widely distributed . . . it's a miniature 'Common Moss'." [J-A/574] "It comes from England, and begins [in 1830] to be propagated." [BJ30]

"Rose with nearly round seed-buds: empalements and peduncles mossy, small-flowered and flesh-coloured: the leaflets are ovate, pointed, small, with finely sawed glandular margins: a dwarf shrub, stem and petioles with red straight prickles. This beautiful little Rose is called the Mossy Pompone. It is a most elegant variety of the Rosa nana, or Rose de Meaux; and although a mere variation, its mossy appendage gives it an appearance so distinct that it may be instantly recognized as a novelty, which is more than can be truly said for nineteen out of twenty of those generally called New Roses. Our figure [in Andrews' book] was made from plants at the Hammersmith Nursery, where it was first raised in the summer of 1815." [A] "At most 0.3 m tall [ca. 1 ft]; *prickles* small, very numerous and dense, unequal, almost straight, mixed with glandular hairs. *Leaflets* 3 or 5, glabrous above, glandular beneath and on the margins and petioles. *Flowers* 2–3 at the tips of the branches; whole inflorescence up to the sepals covered with viscous, branched, moss-like glands; bracts much elongated, spatulate and leafy at the tip; *petals* around 8–10-seriate, the same color as the regular ['De Meaux']. This derivative of ['De Meaux'] came to us from England, where a white variant is also grown in Kennedy's Nursery. Devotees of rose culture have over the years noted an increase in the number of moss roses, often arising from seed of non-mossy ancestors." [T&R]

Normandica Listed as 'Rosier des Dames' (CP).

[Nouveau Petite Serment]

trans. "New Little Oath" or perhaps "New 'Little Oath'"

Breeder unknown, pre-1811

"Wood much armed with hooked red thorns. Leaves oval, deeply and finely dentate, of a gay green. Calyx and buds round, like those of the Agathes, nicely crowned by the sepals, which develop, surrounding the blossom and exceeding it by about three *lignes* [ca. ³⁄₈ in], a very distinctive characteristic of this rose. Flowers about the size of the small 'St. François' or crimson pompon [*i.e.*, 'Pompon de Bourgogne' (G)], but exceedingly double, a beautiful deep purple, which lightens very gradually from the middle of the blossom to the edge. It has a sweet and agreeable scent. This rose is a pretty miniature, and is worth seeking out." [C-T]

Petite de Hollande Listed as 'Rosier des Dames' (CP).

Petite Ernestre Listed as 'Petite Junon de Hollande' (CP).

Petite Hollande Listed as 'Rosier des Dames' (CP).

Petite Junon de Hollande

syns. 'Juno Rose', 'Junon Argentée', 'Petite Ernestre', 'Roi de Perse'; trans., "Little 'Junon' from Holland" [for the big 'Junon', see Chapter 2 on Gallicas]

Holland, pre-1820

"*Flower* small, full, light or pale pink." [Pf] "Blush, very neat and pretty." [WRP]

Pompon Blanc

trans. "White Pompon"

Breeder unknown, pre-1811

"Wood green, nearly thornless; leaves oval, toothed and retoothed, about an inch long [ca. 2.5 cm], often striped with white and yellow. Calyx long, overspread with green bristles. Bud round, crowned with the calyx membranes which are nicely cut. Flowers of the size and form of the Pompon [*presumably 'De Meaux'*], very double, beautiful white, same scent, later to bloom." [C-T] Possibly synonymous with 'White De Meaux' (CP).

Pompon Commun Listed as 'De Meaux' (CP).

Pompon de Kingston

trans. "Pompon from Kingston"; but as to *which* Kingston—that of
   Jamaica, that English one "on Hull," or that other English one
   "upon the Thames"—we are left to guess. We perhaps vote for
   the Thamesish one, due to its proximity to botanical Kew

Breeder unknown, pre-1817

"Flower flesh-colored, small." [BJ40] "Blossoms very small, full, pink." [SRh54/59] "Only can be distinguished from the [common] Centifolia by its flowers, which are the same size as those of ['Rosier des Dames' (CP)], but a pale pink; it has a sub-variety with smaller blossoms." [BJ17] "Flowers like those of the Pompon [*presumably 'De Meaux'*], but leaves like those of the common Centifolia." [No26] "The sub-variety called 'Kingston' differs from ['Rosier des Dames'] in the smallness of its flowers, which much resemble those of the little 'Pompon de Bourgogne'." [dP] In other words, it resembles (1) 'Common Centifolia', (2) 'Rosier des Dames', (3) 'De Meaux', and (4) 'Pompon de Bourgogne'. "An ancient variety, very small, rose colored, full double and pretty." [WRP] "Pretty vigorous bush; flower very small, full; flesh." [JR4/21] "*Shrub,* of moderate height . . . *Flowers,* very small, flesh-coloured, very double." [Go]

Pompon des Dames Listed as 'Rosier des Dames' (CP).

Pompon Mousseux Listed as 'Mossy De Meaux' (CP).

Pompon Rose Listed as 'De Meaux' (CP).

Pompon Spong Listed as 'Spong's' (CP).

[Pompon Varin]

syns. 'Centfeuilles Nain', 'Sara'
Breeder unknown, pre-1819

"Blossoms semi-double, small, pink along the circumference and more intense in the center." [AC] "Flowers irregular, nuanced with bright red and delicate pink." [BJ24] "Leaflets oval-rounded. *Ovary* oval-pyriform. *Flower* small, double, light pink, center more intense. Own-root, this rose sometimes sports suckers of the common Pompon [*probably referring to 'Rosier des Dames'*]." [Pf] "I [Vibert] frequently saw, at Monsieur Descemet's—and several people have been able to see it at my place—'Pompon Varin' springing from the same base as canes of the ordinary Pompon. The characteristics of each variety were quite pronounced on their respective canes; these same bases would produce evidences of the two varieties indiscriminately." [V1] "A person often sees 'Pompon Varin' on its own roots giving rise to the common Pompon and, at the same time, to a small kind of Centifolia which is the 'Chamoïs' rose of several people (the same, I [Vibert] believe, as 'Fasciculée') [referring to 'Comtesse de Chamoïs' (Descemet, pre-1810)]." [V2] "In 1826, a 'Pompon Varin' at my [*i.e.,* Prévost's] place gave me a shoot larger than the others, covered with leaves obviously larger than those of that variety . . . *Name:* in memory of the able grower who, for 40 years, directed Rouen's botanical garden." [Pf]

Pomponia Muscosa Listed as 'Mossy De Meaux' (CP).

Provincialis Hybrida Listed as 'Spong's' (CP).

Roi de Perse Listed as 'Petite Junon de Hollande' (CP).

Rose Bordée de Blanc Listed as 'Comtesse de Chamoïs' (CP).

Rosier de Bourgogne à Grandes Fleurs Listed as 'Rosier des Dames' (CP).

Rosier des Dames

syns. 'Bordeaux des Dames', 'Burgundiaca', 'De Bordeaux', 'Gros
   Pompon', 'Minor', 'Normandica', 'Petite de Hollande', 'Petite
   Hollande', 'Pompon des Dames', 'Rosier de Bourgogne à
   Grandes Fleurs'; trans., 'The Ladies' Rose-Bush'
Breeder unknown, pre-1791

"*Flower* small, full, pale pink or flesh." [Pf] "Bright pink." [Ÿ] "Its blossoms, smaller than those of ['Grande Centfeuille de Hollande' (C)], are larger than those of ['Pompon de Bourgogne' (G)]." [BJ09] "Its blossoms, the color of those of Centifolia 'Des Peintres', and of the same form, are smaller by half." [BJ17] "It's a 'Des Peintres' shrunk to half-size; it is charming." [J-A/564] "Pink, small, full, medium scent, average height." [Sn] "Flowers an agreeable pale pink color. Ovaries glandulose, ovoid. Peduncles villose. Leaves ovoid, pointed . . . This double rose is smaller than the common Centifolia, but it has the same form when open; the tint is always brighter at the center. The calyx segments terminate in a foliaceous point, and bear glands and several appendages. Its ovoid ovary is equipped with bristles and glands, as is the long peduncle which bears it. The ovoid, pointed leaves, serrated with large sharp teeth, are a grass green above, paler beneath, and purplish along the edges when young. The stipules are medium-sized and glandulose. The petioles have little prickles beneath, and the young shoots and branches are armed with light brown thorns." [Rsg]

"Long leaves edged pink, much serrated, five leaflets per stalk. Calyx small, long, covered—as is the petiole—with brown bristles. Thorns small, sharp, enlarged at the base, slightly hooked; blossoms well-formed, a pretty pink, like that of the flesh-colored pompon [*perhaps 'De Meaux'?*]. They come after this last, and before those of the [common] Centifolia, and continue to ornament the garden alongside a crowd of other sorts which try to rival it. This variety, grafted on the Briar, is effective, giving many blossoms over a long period, always with renewed elegance, no doubt the source of its surname 'Rosier des Dames'." [C-T] "Small Centifolia, variety of the large one, of which it has all the characteristics—wood, leaves, and thorns as well as coloration, but on a smaller scale. It is full of grace in this small format. This rose is delicate own-root; grafted, it is more robust, loving a southern exposure, which evidences the locale it came from. Further north, its blossoms have difficulty opening, and its buds abort. It makes a pretty, well-rounded head. It is also grafted in a pyramid on [*Briar*] shoots from the bottom to the top. You must go to the effort of pruning it after bloom to help the new shoots grow . . . This is one of the best to grow." [LeR] "Grown in the greater part of our gardens." [CM]

"*Shrublet* about 45 cm tall [ca. 18 in]; *prickles* unequal, sharp, a little recurved, slightly dilated at the base, mixed with pedicellate glands, mainly concentrated towards the tips of the canes. *Leaflets* 5 or 7, medium-sized, subrotund, crenate with ciliate and glandular margins, bright green above, paler and tomentose beneath; petioles

Rosier des Dames *continued*

villose, unarmed; *stipules* decurrent, acute, gland-edged. *Flowers* 4–6 at the branch tips; peduncle and pedicels glandular hispid up to one third of the way up the *receptacles*; *sepals* 2 entire, 3 pinnatifid, glandular outside, villose within; petals 7–8-seriate as in the 'Common Centifolia', but blossoms smaller. *Hips* as in the [common] Centifolia. This dwarf rose suckers freely to form thickets, and should be kept in check annually. The flower is in no way different from that of *R. centifolia,* and in a good soil the first blooms may be as large. Parisian nurserymen grow it in frames, and thus kept it is one of the first to appear in Spring in the flower market. Seed raised from it has produced many very lovely novelties." [T&R]

Spong's

syns. 'Pompon Spong', 'Provincialis Hybrida'
Spong, 1805

"Bright rose." [Cal] "Light rose, early, cupped." [WRP] "Flowers pale rose, small, and very double; form, cupped." [P] "Pale rose, flowers small; a pretty free flowering rose, and useful for edging or for a small bed." [JC] "Blush-pink, fine small and double. Growth dwarf." [GeH] "Violet pink, small, very full, medium scent, average height." [Sn] "Rose with nearly round seed-buds: peduncles hispid and glandular: leaves both large and small: the leaflets are ovate-pointed and serrate: flowers grow mostly in bunches: stem low and branching, with prickles towards the base. This dwarf rose is an elegant variety between the Province species and Rosa nana or Rose de Meaux, so much partaking of the characters of both, that in the gardens of the Hon. W. Irby there were two plants of it that had forsaken their station; or, as it is termed, run away, and returned to their first original character; the one becoming a Rose de Meaux, and the other a Province Rose, after having flowered one year . . . This, however, does not frequently occur; and when it does, it is owing to a change of soil before it has been well established. It is commonly known by the appellation of the Spong Rose, from having been first raised in quantities by a gardener of that name." [A]

White De Meaux

Breeder unknown, pre-1824

"White, with tintings." [LS] Listed without description by J-A. See also 'Pompon Blanc' (CP).

CHAPTER SEVEN

Mosses

"One of the most curious variations of the Centifolia, and certainly one of the most beautiful, is the Moss Rose, which always holds a special place in the collections of true Rose fanciers. Where did it come from? No one can say with any certainty; all we know is that the honor is disputed between Holland and England, and that the first Moss rose seen in France was brought there from England at the end of the last [*i.e.,* 18th] century by Mme. de Genlis. Whatever the case, the place of origin of the first Moss Rose is of little importance now that its seedlings have given rise to a great number of new ones which themselves comprise a large division of Roses." [R-H63/183] "This much admired rose is unquestionably a mere variety of the [Centifolia]; although its origin remains in obscurity, it has repeatedly been proven to produce flowers, without any moss, on either buds, leaves, or branches. In 1836 a plant in my nursery had a large shoot on it that sported back to the [Centifolia], and entirely destitute of its mossy coat. I believe that Sir James Smith mentions, in *Rees's Cyclopaedia,* that in Italy it loses its mossiness almost immediately through the influence of climate. It was first noticed about the years 1720 to 1724, and is mentioned by Miller in 1727. There is no rose that has been, and is still so highly esteemed as the Moss." [Bu]

"The old Moss Rose is identical with the old Cabbage Rose, except that its glands are compound, and not simple as in the Cabbage Rose; and it is this multiple branching of the gland-bearing organs that gives its flower-buds and stalks the mossy appearance that is so much admired. The exquisite and unique double fragrance peculiar to the old Moss Rose is due to the rich aromatic odour of the mossy glands mingling with the refined old Rose scent of the petals that charms us so much in the old Cabbage Rose." [NRS22/38] "The Moss Rose is notable as much by the size, bright color, and excellent scent of its flowers as by the abundance of the long, branching, herbaceous bristles, charged with reddish glands and looking like certain mosses, with which the peduncles, ovaries, and canes are covered. Its blossoms are a beautiful pink, perfectly double, and three or more inches in size [7.5 cm +]; its petals and stamens are like those of 'Des Peintres' [C]." [CM] "There is no one who does not admire the green and delicate bristles which cover over so gracefully the peduncles and buds. These roses, already very interesting at this stage, become yet better when their sepals open. Through the vegetal fleece which begins to part one can perceive with nothing but a sweet emotion the blush of the flower soon to open. It is then that this rose seduces every eye, and that Innocence itself can't help admiring in these roses the charms of a laughing and voluptuous Flora who seems to call for the caresses of Zephyrus." [J-A/564–565] "It is the Centifolia Moss which, by its green fringe and the silky divisions of its calyx, offers the most interesting characteristics for the horticulturalist. It is certain that this curious modification happens, but rarely, on branches of the common Centifolia; we have seen the opposite at the home of our collaborator Monsieur Jamain, a moss rose with one branch reverting to the Centifolia. It was Mme. de Genlis, or so it is said, who first saw the Moss in England and introduced it into France; but the *Jardinier Fleuriste* of 1746 notes it as being cultivated at that time in le Contentin, around Metz, and along the English Channel. It was brought to this country [France] by Fréard Ducastel, who found it at Carcassonne, where it had been known for half a century. Another curious modification is presented by 'Cristata', distinguished by its crested calyx set in leaves like frilled parsley. Vibert received it from a botanist in Fribourg, who himself found it on an old degenerated Centifolia plant in the garden of a ruined castle." [JF] "Some few years since a traveller in Portugal mentioned that the Moss Rose grew wild in the neighborhood of Cintra; but most likely, the plants were stragglers from some garden, as I have never seen this assertion properly authenticated. The origin of the Double Moss Rose, like that of the Old Double Yellow Rose (Rosa sulphurea) is therefore left to conjecture . . . That it is merely an accidental sport of the common Provence Rose is strengthened by the fact, that plants produced by the seed of the Moss Rose do not always show moss: perhaps not more than two plants out of three will be mossy, as has been often proved . . . What can be more elegant than the bud of the Moss Rose, with its pure rose-colour, peeping through that beautiful and unique envelope? The assertion advanced by some writers that this Rose when cultivated in

Italy 'loses its mossiness almost immediately, through the influence of climate,' is puerile, when the fact is so well known to us that it retains this distinctive character at New-Orleans, and at other localities far exceeding Italy in an approach to a tropical climate." [WRP]

"The Moss Roses are mostly of delicate growth, though some are vigorous and robust in habit, and form good standards, but as a rule they all succeed best when grown upon low stocks, or otherwise upon their own roots … They require rather high cultivation and close pruning, and generally speaking rather better treatment than ordinary kinds. In wet or cold soils they do not thrive, a warm dry soil being required, and this well supplied annually with manure. If at any time they appear to decline in health, they should be taken up and replanted into fresh loamy soil, and cut hard back." [JC] "With few exceptions they require close pruning, rich soil, and high culture. On account of their beautiful buds they are great favorites." [CA96]

"The Moss Rose in this country [U.S.A.] is a plant of very difficult culture if not in a rich sandy soil; but if it is once fairly established in a rich deep loam, it will make shoots six feet long [ca. 2 m]; when such can be obtained its permanency is sure. To encourage their growth, fresh soil, well incorporated with manure, should be dug in about their roots every winter. The pruning must be done sparingly; if the plants are kept low they never do well, often dying off as soon as they have done blooming. I have lost three or four hundred in a single season by overdoing the operation; but if they are kept in bushes four or five feet above ground [to ca. 1.6 m] they will grow admirably; they also delight in an airy exposed situation. Moss Roses in variety are very scarce, even in Europe; no establishment can supply them in any quantity. The new sorts are all budded on the French Eglantine." [Bu] "Moss Roses, when grown on their own roots, require a light and rich soil: in such soils, they form fine masses of beauty in beds on lawns. In cold and clayey soils they in general succeed much better worked on the Dog Rose, forming beautiful standards. I have ascertained that they establish themselves much better on short stems, from two to three feet in height [ca. to 1 m], than on taller stems. If short, the stem increases in bulk progressively with the head, and the plants will then live and flourish a great many years. A very erroneous impression exists in regard to the hardihood of the Moss Rose. It will withstand almost any degree of cold much better than excessive heat. In fact, the old Moss Province Rose, and the white and striped sportive varieties, and others of delicate growth, flourish most in a northern exposure, or at least one that is sheltered from the extreme heat of noonday, such as may be termed a half-shaded position. The new seedling varieties which are mostly of vigorous growth, do not exact any such precaution, but appear to flourish with as little attention as the commonest garden varieties. To insure a succession of bloom, the plants intended to flower early should be pruned in October, and those for the second series the beginning of May—shortening their shoots, as recommended for the Provence Roses. Give them also an abundant annual dressing of manure on the surface, in November." [WRP] "They all require high enrichment. All excepting the strongest growers should be closely pruned; and, in the Northern States, it is well to give them protection in winter by means of pine-boughs, or by laying them down like raspberries." [FP]

"Every day, people say, write, or print *rosier mousseux, rose mousseuse*; however, those who write about roses shouldn't ignore the fact that the epithet *muscosa* doesn't translate that way at all. The botanists who imposed the Latin name on the rose it characterizes were consistent; those who translated it into French didn't bother to be. *Muscosa, muscosus* means *mossy* [*moussue, moussu*], or *covered with moss. Mousseux* serves to designate a liquid which produces froth, and is much more appropriate to characterize the wine of Champagne and beer than a rose." [Pfs]

"The Moss Rose … has a history which is very interesting, if slightly murky. Its long glandular bristles function as question marks to plant physiologists and teratologists both of the present and the future, as well as to all lovers of sports or Nature's pranks —Nature's little joke, it would seem—and to all those who seek to know "why" for this or that. What is more, it has been the object of scholarly controversies between the most knowledgeable grammarians. Had Vaugelas still been with us when people were debating whether the adjective should be '*mousseux*' or '*moussu*', he no doubt would have joined his voice with those of Bescherelle, Lhomond, and Jobelin, henchmen of the Latin scholars, and shown that it should be *rose moussue* and not *rose mousseuse*. As usage is the better guide in the creation of words, however, we will continue to say *Rose mousseuse* despite the jeers of *Ithos* and *Pathos*—such is the vogue! say the gentlemen of the *Académie*.

"One writes the history of nations, for better or worse, by consulting old archives, excavating tumuli, collecting old coins, deciphering ancient monuments, and in studying the mentality of people and the illnesses of kings and great men who leave a trace of their passage here below. But alas! —to write the history of plants, the *cartulaires* are rare or very recent, the medals are lacking, the old monuments—meaning the plants—fall prey to insects, or are buried in the coal pits or calcareous bedrock of some *Meximieu*. And so, what do we fix on to clarify the origin of plant varieties? Some short and abbreviated lines in Reviews, some suspect notes, some hypotheses which are more in the way of guesswork. There are, however, other things allowing us to put things in an order approaching Truth—precise facts, and studious recent experiences which give weight to certain old conjectures.

"The first trace of the Moss Rose is found, we believe, in Philip Miller's *Gardener's Dictionary* [*a note adds:* Ph. Miller, born in 1681, dying in 1771. Superintendent of the English apothecary's garden at Chelsea; his botanical knowledge and his taste for gardening allowed him to make the garden which he directed the most magnificent botanical establishment in Europe in his life-time. Some highly regarded works are due to him.], a celebrated work which was translated into all languages. Here is … the note which he devotes to this … 'Rose rubra, plena, spinosissima, pedoncula muscosa. Boerh. Ind. Alt. 2, p. 252. Red rose with double flowers, and the thorniest, in which the peduncles are completely covered with moss, commonly called the *Provence Moss Rose. R. Muscosa*—The twenty-second sort is called *Mossy Provins Rose* because of the similarity this plant has with the Common Provins Rose; however, it is certainly a distinct sort, because, though the stems and shoots [*rejetons*] of this plant look a lot like those of the 'Common', it nevertheless is difficult to propagate, which is not the case with the regular sort. This one rarely puts out runners, and the branches that a person cuts only take root after a considerable length of time, and most often one is obliged to graft them on a stock of other roses—but these last plants aren't as long-lived as cuttings. The stems and branches of this rose are heavily armed with brown spines; the peduncles and calyxes are covered with long bristles like moss; its blossoms are a crimson red and have a pleasant scent.'

"It should be noted well that Ph. Miller, or at least his translator, wrote, for the same rose 'Rosier de Provence' on the one hand, and, on the other 'Rosier de Provins'. Is there, in this designation of one plant under two different names, merely an error in translation due to the similarity of 'Provins' and 'Provence,' or has the author indeed confused the two roses in question? Either one of these two hypotheses is equally acceptable, because the Rose of Provence is not without affinity to the Rose of Provins …

"From the historical point of view, the reference which Ph. Miller makes to his Moss Rose is more than suggestive. He cites Boerhaave, the celebrated intellectual to whom is due *Index plantarum Lugduno-Batavorum,* published in 1720, which is to say 'List of Plants from the Garden of the Academy of Leyden.' Without this citation, one would be able to suppose that the Moss Rose originated in England, as the greater part of authors have written, while it would seem probable that it was first grown in Leyden, in Holland, if (at any rate) one can base anything on the date of publications. If I am not mistaken, the first edition of Ph. Miller's book (*loc. cit.*) is from 1724, while that of Boerhaave's in 1720.

"N. Desporte[s], who usually is quite knowledgeable, has however written, concerning the Moss Rose, 'Grown in England, in 1724, by Robert Furber; at Leyden, in 1727, by Boerhaave. Introduced into France, around 1777, by Mme. de Genlis' (*Roses Cultivées en France au Nombre de 2,562 Espèces ou Variétés* …, Paris, Le Mans, 1829, p. 34). It is probable that Desporte[s] copied his citations from some ill-informed work, or that it got in due to the error of a facetious correspondent—because it is clear as day that Boerhaave was the first author to speak of the rose in question. As to Mme. de Genlis, it is necessary to use a little prudence in accepting her version.

"Whence came this Moss Rose? — *That is the question!* No other document anterior to the citation of Boerhaave or the note of Miller seems to exist. The singularity of its physiology makes it taken as its own species by several well-versed authors. Today, we can't hesitate any longer [in believing that] this was the exact moment of its appearance in Horticulture. It took on itself the burden of revealing its teratological origin—that of being a sport—by fairly frequently showing on the same specimen canes bearing mossy blossoms mixed with canes of the pure Centifolia.

"Besler (1612) didn't grow it in his garden at Eichstad (*Hortus Eystettensis*), because, had he known of it, he undoubtedly would have drawn it, as he did for all the other roses known in his time.

"If you don't mind, let us pass by the whole constellation of old authors who have mentioned the Moss Rose in their works, because to cite them will make us range far and wide without much benefit (at least, such is our supposition, not having consulted them all) …

"If Loiseleur-Deslongchamps [*La Rose, son Histoire* …, Audot, Paris, 1844] doesn't tell us anything new himself on Moss Roses, he *does* insert in his work some interesting observations concerning them which were told to him by Vibert. Here are some extracts of these observations:

"'In 1810, we still had only the Common Moss; in 1844, there were about thirty varieties, including those grown particularly for seed [*in other words, unreleased breeding varieties*], the number of Mosses surpasses seventy; within four years, there will be more than a hundred, and I can indeed promise that this number, too, will be surpassed. If you want the basis for my option—here it is: It is not so much Time as Means which controls the obtention of a certain number of roses of several sorts. These elements of production exist today, and, speaking for myself, more than sixty specimens of various Mosses are grown at my place alone for their seeds, and in two years I could double that number. It is quite important to note that this is due to accidents—which is to say, "accidents" springing from the Mosses which chance has rendered single, semi-double, or loosely double, making fertile these roses which, naturally, can't reproduce themselves because they are too double. These fertile ones have given us a great quantity of Mosses. Rose history presents nothing else analogous …

"'If this degeneration of the Centifolias into Mosses had not affected doubleness at all, we would very probably have had to content ourselves with the [few] varieties due to sporting. But, fortunately for us, such was not the case. Prompted merely by the number of petals, two births have taken place which have given us a single Moss and a double [*i.e., not full*] Moss. This fact, which, thirty years ago, would no doubt not have been noticed, cannot fail to make us turn our eyes towards an era in which growing roses from seed can fill a person with zeal …

"'Most Moss sports have been "caught" in France and England, only 'Cristata' falling to Switzerland's share. Here are the names of Mosses which came accidentally—that is, from sporting:

In France
>   Single Moss
>   Semi-Double Moss
>   Dwarf Moss
>   Deep Pink Moss
>   Flesh-Colored Moss
>   Semi-Double Striped Moss
>   Proliferous Moss
>   'Zoé'
>   'Sans Sépales'
>   'Unique de Provence'
In England
>   'Common Moss'
>   White Moss, of which there are two sorts, only one still being grown
>   'À Feuilles de Sauge'
>   Pompon Moss

"'As much as possible, I have followed in these lists the order in which these Moss sports occurred …

"'The first Moss from seeds was 'De La Flèche', grown by a fancier from that town about twenty years ago [*i.e., 1824*]. It was followed after an interval of ten years by the red Moss from the Luxembourg; shortly afterwards appeared 'Lancel', which I believe originated in Belgium or the north of France. Over a period of twelve to fifteen years, I only obtained three or four Mosses from seed. As we see, we don't always move along quickly—but it mustn't be forgotten that only the single and semi-double Mosses gave us the seed which we [otherwise] would have lacked. It's different nowadays. The semi-double or loosely double varieties have since become numerous, and the number grows every day. When we sow the seeds we are given, we don't get more than a certain number of plants which will provide mossy roses; three to four months after they come up, a person can recognize which ones are and aren't Mosses. These last provide some roses which are more or less distinct, varying to some degree from the Centifolia—constituting our "hybrids." Lately, it has been possible for me to succeed with some cross-fertilization between the Mosses and some spotted Gallicas; right now, I have several marbled and spotted semi-double varieties which give me hopes that we will have some [completely] double ones before long. These Mosses are so altered from the characteristic physiology that they give runners like the parent Gallicas …

"'It is necessary to place among the Hybrid Mosses that pretty variety, still unique in its color and stripes, latterly entered into commerce under the name 'Lansezeur' or 'Panaget'. Among the seed-grown Mosses—semi-double, double, and full—we now

have pretty nearly all shades or colors besides those tinged violet; the more or less dark purples leave something to be desired in the way of size, being ordinarily no more than a large medium size …
>   'Vibert
>   'Angers, March 16, 1844'

"These remarks by Vibert are those of a practitioner very much 'in the know' on all that concerns roses …

"Duval, horticulturalist at Chaville, published the following remarks on two Moss Roses, which aren't lacking in interest from the point of view of raising [new] varieties. Here are his remarks:

"'In 1830, I grafted several specimens of ['À Feuilles de Sauge'], which grew perfectly well. At the end of 1831, I only had one left unsold. I cut it back to two eyes, from which came two growths which bore the exact characteristics which distinguish this variety, and which bore flowers exactly conforming to what one would expect. But the plant also developed—on the heel of the graft—two other growths which also bloomed, but in which the wood, the leaves, and the blossoms were, in a word, quite the same as those of the 'Common Moss'. In 1833, I again cut these growths quite short, and they developed in the same way—that is, the same individual bore leaves and flowers of two varieties, even while coming from one and the same eye. Might one not induct from this fact that the Moss 'À Feuilles de Sauge', interesting as it is, is nothing more than a sport fixed by Art and maintained by Cultivation? One knows that, in parallel cases, plants have a tendency to revert to their Type. I therefore think that it is also probable that the Moss 'À Feuilles de Sauge' comes from the 'Common Moss', and that this latter will predominate over the former … In 1832, I noted among my 'Prolifère' Mosses an individual in which the blossoms opened out wonderfully. But my attention was drawn more particularly to a branch in which the very beautiful flowers were completely lacking moss on their ovary. The wood was less thorny—glabrous and lacking the viscous matter which, in 'Prolifère', comes off on the fingers, wafting a most elegant scent. The very voluminous blossoms were paler. This branch had two eyes, which I cut and grafted. They 'took' nicely, and grew beautifully in 1833, but didn't bloom. I'll watch them in 1834. Though these grafts be vigorous, the wood is always weak and a little contorted; the leaves, though very ample, are of a thin texture like the Centifolias. Despite the tendency such have to revert to the Centifolia, these are certainly not like any [previously] known or described. It gives promise of a new variety with blossoms of a very large size.'

"The same grower tells us, in the same book, about another anomaly seen upon a Moss Rose: 'Two years ago, I noted in the *Annales de Flore* [*et de Pomone*] a sport produced on the Moss Rose 'Prolifère' which gave me a new variety of Centifolia. The same thing happened again on the 'Common Moss'. I had planted two of these roses at the foot of a wall in the middle. In the month of September, 1835, two shoots grew from the ground to the height of about six inches [ca. 1.5 dm]. Winter stopped their growth, but didn't make them lose their leaves, which stayed on all during the harsh season. In Spring, their growth continued to the point at which one of the two—indeed a Moss—was three feet high [ca. 1 m]. The other, which grew into a bouquet of five flowers, is a true 'Common Centifolia', entirely lacking in moss. This fact confirms me in the notion that the 'Common Moss' is nothing other than a sport coming from the Centifolia, and which always has a propensity to return to the Type.'" [JR32/173–187]

"Shailer (1852) states that the Moss Rose was not much cultivated in England until 1755, but that his father was an extensive grower of it at Little Chelsea in 1788, and it was in that year and in that place that the first white Moss Rose appeared as a bud-variation on the old Moss Rose." [NRS22/42] "On June 15th, 1819, Henry Shailer, of Little Chelsea, exhibited at the Horticultural Society, London, nine kinds of Moss Roses, including his White Moss Rose." [NRS23/198]

"Last year [1842], by crossing a Moss and a Hybrid China ('Athalin', one of the best pod-parents), I developed some varieties of premier merit, one of them with numerous large, full, well-formed, flat, delicate pink blossoms, just as good as the 'Common Moss', or better because of its good growth. A second one, with a carminey blossom, with only 15–18 petals, will be one of my best pod-parents, I think, for that new class of hybrid mosses, whence should come, after several years, a new series of mossy perpetuals, just as hybrid." [R-H44/478] "Of late years the greatest attention has been devoted to the production of seminal varieties." [WRP] "A remarkable illustration of the effects of hybridizing is met with here. There have been introduced lately some Moss Roses of the most vigorous growth, with shining foliage; and others bearing flowers in the autumn. The former have been produced by crossing the Moss with the Hybrid China Roses, or *vice-versâ*: the latter by bringing together the Moss and Perpetual … Besides these, there are some varieties possessing some of the characteristics of the French Rose. Such are 'Célina' and 'Luxembourg'." [P] "Nobody concerned himself with Moss Roses more than Monsieur Vibert. What he had previously done for roses which were striped, marbled, spotted, and plumed, he spent 12 years in doing for Mosses. Since that time, more than 12,000 plants of these roses have been brought to bloom, and more than 1,000 specimens have been grown with the sole end of producing seed. All that long experience could add to a rare perseverance, all combinations possible with the purpose of obtaining hybrids good for modifying the characteristics of Mosses—all has been tried and trialled by him; furthermore, he predicted the results. When the perpetual Moss '[Perpétuelle] Mauget' was raised, he positively declared that soon

the number would increase—it was only a question of time and intelligent attempts. Towards the goal of obtaining some reblooming Mosses and striped Mosses, much time has been expended; it was often necessary to modify or change the mode of proceeding; and nobody knows better than myself—who, over twelve years, directed under Monsieur Vibert these long and interesting experiments—all the zeal and patience that he put to the service of his idea. In 1846, the firm already had, from its seeds, three varieties of semi-double perpetual Mosses, from repeated sowings of which grew the predictions of their author. These last years have seen more than fifty new varieties of full and semi-double Mosses born—among them can be found the deepest colors. What is more, he has raised three striped Mosses, two of which are full, one semi-double. Among the non-reblooming Mosses, aside from those entering our catalog this year [1862], more than 200 full and double varieties are under study; their characteristics are in general very distinct; but they need to be studied to better judge of the differences between themselves and those already out." [R&M62] "The entirety of *Centifolia Mosses* and *Hybrid Centifolia Mosses* comprises [in 1885] 261 varieties." [JR9/58]

"At the present day, when the annual progeny of new Perpetual roses from the nurseries of France, with a humble re-enforcement from those of England, has eclipsed by numbers the old garden favorites, the well-remembered roses of our infancy, the Moss alone stands in tranquil defiance of this gay tide of innovation. Nothing can eclipse and nothing can rival her. She is, and ever will be, the favorite of poetry and art; and the eloquence of her opening buds, half wrapped in their mossy envelope, will remain through all generations a chosen interpreter of the languages of youth and beauty." [FP]

À Fleur d'Anémone Listed as 'De La Flèche' (M). See also 'Anémone' (M).

À Fleurs d'Anémone Listed as 'Anémone' (M). See also 'De La Flèche' (M).

À Fleurs Pâles See 'Gracilis' (M).

À Long Pédoncle
syn. 'À Longs Pédoncules'; trans., "With a Long Flower-Stalk"]
Robert, 1851

"Light pink." [Ÿ] "Six centimeters [ca. 2¼ in], double, globular, flesh pink." [M-LIV/162] "Medium-sized, flesh pink, globular, in groups of 20–25 blossoms." [Gp&f52] "Rose-red, medium size, full, tall." [Sn] "Very curious." [R&M62]

À Longs Pédoncules Listed as 'À Long Pédoncle' (M).

Adèle Pavié
Vibert/Robert, 1851

"Blush." [FP] "Flesh." [FP] "8 centimeters [ca. 3 in], double, flesh white, in a rosette, beautiful form." [R&M62] "Pink-white, medium size, full, medium scent, moderate height." [Sn]

Alcime

Robert & Moreau, 1861

"8–10 centimeters [ca. 3–4 in], cupped, purple red, corymbiferous." [R&M62]

Alice Leroi

syn. 'Alice Leroy'

Vibert, 1843

"Lilac pink." [VPt45/160] "Large, double, lilac-y pink." [V8] "Very beautiful blossom, to be recommended to collectors; flower large, full, mossed regularly and abundantly; color, light lilac pink, shaded bright pink around the center." [S] "Pale purple, well mossed; good foliage." [GeH] "Light violet pink, medium size, full, tall." [Sn] "Rosy-pink with handsome mossy buds, moderate size and full, free-flowering and good habit; a good and useful rose, forming a good standard." [JC] "Lilac blush, shaded with rose, their centre deep rose, very large and double, well mossed; form, cupped, perfect. Growth, vigorous. A distinct and beautiful Rose; thrives well as a standard; should be pruned moderately close." [P] "Blossoms large, double, lilac pink; leaves large, having kept well the characteristics of the Type. This Moss, as with ['Comtesse de Murinais'], is vigorous and hardier, on the Briar, than were our old sorts." [M-L43/49] "Another of the very new sorts; in growth it forms a great contrast to ['Mauget'], being a very strong and free grower, and appears to suit our climate well; the flowers are large and very double, of a rosy lilac colour, and frequently rose edged with lilac." [Bu] "Very good." [WRP] See also 'Mlle. Alice Leroy', the Mossy Remontant from 1856.

Alice Leroy　Listed as 'Alice Leroi' (M).

[Anémone]

syns. 'À Fleurs d'Anémone', 'Mousseux Anémone'

Mauget, 1844

"Flowers even light crimson, their centre petals curling among the stamens, of medium size, double; form, cupped. Growth, vigorous. Requires but little pruning." [P] "Medium-sized, double, bright pink." [V8] "Blossom more than 6 cm across [ca. 2 1/2 in], the outer petals are large and outspread; the center petals are turbinate and make a sort of cockade under which hide some stamens—which will probably disappear after several bloom seasons; this will then be a superb bright carmine Moss Rose—far indeed, however, from having the form of an anemone, which is what the name would lead one to believe." [dH44/205] "A very distinct variety, with shoots very slender and graceful; flowers bright pink, petals incurved, much like those of some double Anemones." [WRP] Not to be confused with Lemeunier's 1824 Moss 'De La Flèche', which has the synonym 'Anémone'.

Angélique Quétier

Quétier, 1839

"The flowers medium size . . . of a delicate rose color." [WRP] "Pale lilac-rose. Growth free and well mossed." [GeH] "Medium-sized, double, delicate pink, singular foliage." [V8] "Violet pink, large, very full, light scent, tall." [Sn] "[A] strong growing plant, with rather singular foliage; the flowers are very double, of a cherry red colour." [Bu] "Flower large, very well formed, cupped, much to be recommended for a buttonhole, which, due to the moss-cover, gives it the form of a crown; color, lilac pink." [S] "Flowers rosy lilac, petals even, large and very double; well mossed; form, cupped; exquisite in the bud state.

Growth, vigorous, forming a head densely clothed with foliage. A free blooming and good variety, thriving well as a Standard." [P]

Anni Welter

Welter, 1906

From 'Cristata' (M) × 'La France' (HT or B).

"Deep pink, large, full, medium scent, tall." [Sn] "Flower pure deep pink, very large, quite full, fragrant. Bush vigorous, quite mossy, floriferous, hardy." [JR31/22]

Aristide　Listed as 'Mlle. Aristide' (M).

Aristobule

Foulard/Moulins, 1849

"Delicate red." [Ÿ] "Blossom medium-sized, full; color, deep pink, shaded or touched with light pink." [S] "Large, full flower of a light red, lightly nuanced with violet blue, and marked with large whitish points." [M-V49/230] "Pink, medium size, full, moderate scent, tall." [Sn] Aristobule, alias Aristobulus, either (1) Aristobulus of Alexandria, fl. 180 B.C., Biblical commentator and supposed teacher of Ptolemy VII; (2) Aristobulus of Cassandria, fl. 4th century B.C., historian for Alexander the Great; (3) Aristobulus I, Prince of Judaea, known for brutality, husband of Salome, fl. 104 B.C.; or (4) Aristobulus II, quondam ruler of Judaea, son of Salome, loser in power struggle involving Caesar, Pompey, and himself, dying of poison in 49 B.C. Or it could be named after somebody's horse.

Asepala

syn. 'Sans Sépales'; trans., "Without Sepals"

Foulard/V. Verdier, 1840

"White and flesh." [Ÿ] "Flesh coloured, the edges of the petals pale rose, affording a very distinct variety." [Bu] "A distinct variety, with incarnate flowers of medium size, tinged with pale rose on the edges." [WRP] "Small, full, flesh, pink edges, with very short sepals." [R&M62] "Whitish pink, medium size, full, tall." [Sn] "Blossom small, full, tightly packed, very remarkable due to the moss which surrounds the branches and leaves; also sometimes called Mossy Carnation Rose; color, white, shaded flesh, sometimes edged pink." [S] "Flowers white shaded with flesh, and sometimes edged with rose colour, the edges of the petals curled, small and full; form, compact. Habit, erect; growth, moderate. More curious than beautiful." [P] "This charming rose . . . has been in the propagation-beds of Monsieur [V.] Verdier since 1837; he received it from Monsieur Foulard, a fancier at Le Mans. The canes are red, thorny, and mossy; the leaves have five or seven leaflets, large, beautiful dark green margined purple, and finely dentate; the petiole is reddish and mossy; the young leaves are a yellow green, with purple edges and serrations. The blossom is 5 cm across [ca. 2 in], with short, slightly crinkled petals, purplish pink at the tip, grading to the near-white of the nub, showing a few stamens at the center. It is very well held by a strong stalk, which is red and mossy; the bud is nearly round, with extremely short calycinate sepals—whence doubtless comes the name—which are reddish and covered with moss. Ordinarily, there is on a common peduncle one open blossom accompanied by two buds and three large green and purplish bracts placed where the three pedicels join. This rose, which has an elegant perfume, is truly seductive, as much because of its pretty flower in which the petals seem edged with purple as because of its vari-colored foliage, the nuances of which receive a particular sparkle when the light passes over it. It really merits a much wider distribution than it at present enjoys." [An40/279–280]

Barillet
V. Verdier, 1850

"Blossom large, full, cupped; color, deep carmine." [S]

Bérangère
Vibert, 1849

"Blossom medium-sized, full, cupped; color, light pink mashed with deep pink." [S] "Carmine, marbled." [Ÿ] "Pink, large, full, medium height." [Sn] "Flowers full, from 7–8 cm across [ca. 3 in], delicate pink; brown foliage; vigorous growth." [M-V49/234] Evidently *not* commemorating Pierre Jean de Béranger, 1780–1857, amiable French poet, obnoxious to the Bourbons.

Blanche Anglaise Listed as 'White Bath' (M).

Blanche de Bath Listed as 'White Bath' (M).

Blanche Mousseuse Listed as 'White Bath' (M).

Blanche Nouvelle Listed as 'White Bath' (M).

Blanche Simon
Moreau-Robert, 1862

"White, large, full, tall." [Sn] "7–9 cm [ca. 3 in], full, flat, green pip at the center, pure white, beautiful form, vigorous." [R&M62]

Blush
Hooker, pre-1838

"Blossom medium-sized, full; color, lilac pink." [S] "Flowers lilac blush, of medium size, double; form, compact. Habit, erect; growth, robust. Foliage curious, thickly clothing the stems, forming a dense bush or tree. Raised at Brenchley, in Kent [England]. A good seed-bearer." [P]

Capitaine Basroger
Moreau-Robert, 1890

"Large full flowers, bright carmine, shaded with rich purple; very fine." [C&Js98] "Produces a few late blooms." [T4] "Bright velvety crimson. Growth vigorous." [GeH] "Light red and purple, large, full, tall." [Sn]

Capitaine John Ingram
Laffay, 1854

"Velvety moiré purple." [BJ70] "Flower full, mid-sized, velvety black purple." [l'H55/52] "Flower medium-sized, deep purple." [JDR55/18] "Beautiful form, of a nearly-black, velvet-like purple." [R-H63/183] "Dark velvety purple, large size, double and full; very handsome." [C&Js98] "Purple-crimson, color non-permanent; dark, small foliage, in five leaflets." [EL] "Vigorous growth." [S] "Dedicated to a captain of the Horse Guard of Her Majesty the Queen of England." [JR9/127] The year 1856 often given for this cultivar appears incorrect.

Carné Listed as 'Vilmorin' (M).

Catherine de Wurtemburg
Vibert, 1843

"Flower medium-sized, full, delicate pink, showing at the center of the blossom some more or less long filaments clustered in a fascicle, as with some of the Provins roses. This singularity had not previously been noted in this sort. This interesting variety, raised this year [*i.e.*, 1842–1843 season], will be released to commerce next year [*i.e.*, 1843–1844 season]." [M-L43/49] "Flower large, very full, beautiful form; color, delicate pink." [S] "Deep pink; well mossed. Growth vigorous." [GeH] "Greatly esteemed. Its growth is very vigorous, the flowers of a rosy blush color, and double, with stamens." [WRP] "Flowers delicate rose, large and very double; form, compact, fine. Prune very little." [P] Princess Catherine of Wurtemburg, wife of Jérôme Bonaparte who was the youngest brother of Napoléon Bonaparte.

Célina
syns. 'Céline', 'Coelina', 'La Gracieuse'
Hardy/Portemer, pre-1843

"Crimson-purple." [EL] "[A] deep, rosy crimson, sometimes verging to purple." [FP] "Large, double, deep crimson shaded black." [JR9/59] "Medium-sized, full, bright red, passing to violet." [BJ58] "Rich crimson shaded purple, double, well mossed." [GeH] "Deep red, large, full, tall." [Sn] "Velvety purple and crimson, buds well mossed, and very beautiful; flowers moderate size, full, and when newly opened very beautiful; habit of growth rather too dwarf; requires rich soil and close pruning." [JC] "Flowers deep rosy crimson, shaded with dark purple, a streak of white occasionally tracing the centre of a petal; colour brilliant when newly opened; large and double; form, expanded. Growth, vigorous. A beautiful Rose; thrives well as a standard. A good seed-bearer." [P] "One of the very best dark crimson varieties we yet possess: its foliage has a peculiarly dark glossy-green tint, quite distinct; its flowers are large and double, but not quite full at the centre, color very brilliant but deep crimson, in some seasons slightly tinged with purple; this will probably supersede the Luxembourg Moss [*i.e.*, 'Ferrugineux du Luxembourg'], which only a few years since was our only deep-colored moss rose. ['Céline's] habit is not quite so robust." [WRP] "An old favorite in our gardens which no new Rose has yet surpassed in its class; it is a vigorous, compact bush, admirably floriferous, of which the flowers, perfectly shaped and the most beautiful crimson red, have an abundance of Moss; few Roses are better for planting in beds, but they need close pruning." [R-H63/183]

Céline Listed as 'Célina' (M).

Chapeau de Napoléon Listed as 'Cristata' (M).

Christata Listed as 'Cristata' (M).

Clémence Beaugrand Listed as 'Mme. Clémence Beauregard' (M).

Clifton Moss Listed as 'White Bath' (M).

Coelina Listed as 'Célina' (M).

Common Moss
syns. 'Communis', 'Ordinaire'
Breeder unknown, pre-1720

"Pale rose, very beautiful in the bud. Difficult to propagate from cuttings. None others in the class except 'Crested' ['*Cristata*'] and 'Gracilis' can rank with this in quality." [EL] "Among them all it is questionable if there is one so very beautiful in bud as the common Moss Rose, generally known under the name of *Red Moss*, in contradistinction, I suppose, to white, for it is not red; it is purely rose-colour, and in bud is truly lovely, but when full blown it has no peculiar attraction." [Bu] "*Flowers*, full, middle-sized or large; light pure pink."

Common Moss *continued*

[Go] "Vigorous bush; canes vigorous, clothed with very small thorns and with moss; foliage dark green, rough to the touch; small leaves [*a mistake for 'stipules,' perhaps?*], reddish green; blossom very large, full, strongly mossed; color, pale pink." [S] "Still one of the most beautiful of the whole family. Its flowers are large and full, and of a pale rose-color and globular form. It is more abundantly mossed than most of its progeny; and none of them surpass it, indeed very few equal it, in the beauty of its half-opened bud. Its growth is tolerably vigorous, and foliage fine." [FP] "Light pink, large, full, tall." [Sn] "In Germany and near Berlin, this rose grows as high as several trees do." [AC] "Its very thorny stems don't grow more than two or three feet high [ca. 6 dm to 1 m]. Its leaves, composed of 3 or 5 leaflets, are a beautiful matte green, and highly scented. Its blossom, as double as that of the [common] Centifolia, is much more fragrant and a bright crimson in color. Both the peduncle which supports it and the calyx where the petals repose are covered with a light silky greenish moss, which brings attention to the sparkle of this beautiful rose, one of the most charming of the family." [Fr] "Thrives well as a Standard." [P] "Should be grown upon its own roots in rich soil." [JC] "The blossoms—so large and so double—exhale so elegant a scent…the tips of the canes and the calyxes of the flowers are covered with soft, branching spines, of a brownish green, which are long, fragrant, and look like moss. It's difficult to find it own-root; most commonly it is on a stem grafted on the Briar." [BJ09] "Can be forgiven its slight faults because of the beauty of its foliage and buds; Nature seems to have wanted to bestow a light covering on it which we call Moss, whence comes its name. It makes itself noticed by the vivacity of its colors, the elegance of its form, the freshness of its coloration, and the balmy perfume wafting from all parts. This rose could be regarded as the Phoenix of its sort, but it doesn't always do well grafted on the Briar, not forming a good head; thus it is that fanciers prefer to grow this kind own-root; but it gives few suckers or runners, and the wood takes two years to root when a person wants to propagate it. It is said that there is a white-blossomed variety, but I haven't been able to get it." [C-T]

"The origin of this beautiful Rose, has ever been considered as enveloped in obscurity; but we have no hesitation in assigning it to the Province [*sic*], to which it assimilates in every particular,–with the addition of a rich luxuriant moss, that gives it a decided superiority, and at the same time a specific distinction. In proof of our opinion, we have recently seen both the Moss and Province Rose at one time, in high perfection, on the same plant; and to remove all doubt, the plant was dug up, to show that it was but one individual root. We have since seen three more plants of the same description. Two of them had been propagated by layers from the mossy shoots. The major part of them returned to their origin, the Province." [A]

"Ovary ovoid. Calyx partially winged. Calyx, ovary, and peduncle charged with green and brownish red viscous glands. Stem and petioles prickly…Considering the habit of this rose, which was found in the Alps, it will be taken as a variety of the Centifolia or the Provins rose; but if its habit is closer to the first, the paler color of its flowers, which open after mid-June, bring it closer to the second. Its calyx, of which three lobes are winged with numerous appendages, is, like the appendages, peduncles, and petioles, covered with balsam-scented, viscous, glandular bristles, making a sort of red-brown and green moss. The ovary is oval and charged with mossy glands and green

bristles. The leaves, usually composed of two or three pairs of lobes with an odd one, are a dull grass-green on their surface, paler beneath; they are bestrewn with bristles and red glands like those found along the double serration, the veins, and the straight, long, lacy stipules. The stem is covered with glands and small prickles, which are straight and sharp. They are denser yet on the [basal] shoots, but less so on the branches. The stem and branches are a slightly brown color. This rose needs protection planted on the north or east side." [Rsg]

"Differs from the single moss rose…only by the fully double *flowers,* which are up to 8 cm in diameter [ca. 3 in], or more, with many series of *petals,* those at the center crumpled, inrolled and concealing the projecting, divergent *styles.* Roessig claims that this rose grows naturally in the Alps, but no naturalist before him ventured to give a habitat. Andrews maintains it as a native of England—but English artists consider many plants as native in the absence of a known habitat. However that may be, the double moss rose is widespread and one of the loveliest decorations of our gardens today by virtue of its flower and its perfume. Culture is the same as for the [common Centifolia], from which it differs only by the 'mossy' calyx." [T&R]

"Not very vigorous; branches of medium size, divergent; bark somber green, reddish where the sun strikes, bristling with very numerous brown prickles which are straight, very fine, and unequal. Leaves somber green, rugose, composed of 5–7 oval, dentate leaflets, the two at the base much smaller than the others; leafstalk slender, hirsute, slightly reddish. Flowers about three inches across [ca. 7.5 cm], very full, globular, well formed, solitary on the smaller branches, in 3's or 5's on the larger; color, a beautiful bright pink; outer petals large and concave, inner petals more muddled. Calyx pyriform . . . One of the most beautiful roses; its stem as well as its calyx are covered with a well-developed silky down, rather like the fine moss found in the woods, giving the rose and particularly the bud a uniquely seductive look; it is very fragrant, very hardy." [JF] "Still a model of perfection." [R-H63/183]

Communis Listed as 'Common Moss' (M).

Comtesse de Murinais
Vibert, 1843

"White, tinged with some flesh." [CA88] "Large, double, pure white." [JR9/59] "[A] big and beautiful nearly white rose, but inferior to 'White Bath' in form and nuance; however, it is much hardier and more useful." [R-H63/183] "One of the best of the White Mosses. Its flowers, though not so double as the Old Moss, are large, and of the purest white; and the growth is very vigorous." [FP] "White, tinged with flesh; not inclined to mildew." [EL] "Large and double though not very full, robust habit; one of the hardiest of the white Moss Roses." [JC] "Very vigorous plant, making a shrub; flower large, very full, cupped; light pink, lightly shaded white." [S] "White, large, full, medium scent, tall." [Sn] "Large, double, white, the first [Moss] of this color raised from seed." [V8] "Flowers pale flesh when newly opened, soon changing to white, large and very double; form, cupped. Growth, vigorous. Raised from seed by Monsieur Vibert in 1843, and is, according to his authority, the only White Moss Rose ever raised from seed. Forms a fine Standard." [P] "A fine hybrid damask variety, with large double white, or pale incarnate flowers. This was obtained from seed . . . This new and highly prized Rose is of the most vigorous growth, and will flourish in soils and locations where the other White Moss varieties will not succeed. It has bloomed but one season in this country [U.S.A.], but we may anticipate a rich display during the summer of the present year." [WRP] "Flower large, double, white, very light tint of flesh at the center; leaves large, having like the wood some resemblance to the white 'Quatre-Saisons' [*probably meaning Laffay's Damask-derived Mossy Remontant of 1835, 'Quatre Saisons Blanc Mousseux'*]. This moss is still the only one of its color coming from seed; it can set some hips." [M-L43/48–49]

Comtesse Doria
Portemer, 1854

"Sparkling crimson." [BJ70] "Medium-sized, crimson red." [JDR55/10] "Non-remontant, flower medium-sized (six to seven cm [ca. 2½ in]), full, sparkling crimson." [I'H55/34] "Red, medium size, full, medium scent, tall." [Sn]

Coralie
Miellez, ca. 1860

"Blossom medium-sized, very double, well-formed, flesh, very pretty." [S]

Couleur de Chair Listed as 'Vilmorin' (M).

Cramoisi Listed as 'Crimson' (M).

Crested Moss Listed as 'Cristata' (M).

Crested Provence Listed as 'Cristata' (M).

Crimson
syns. 'Cramoisi', 'Crimson Moos', 'Damas Mousseux', 'Damask', 'Tinwell Moss'
Tinwell/Lee, pre-1827

"Very dark pink, flowers *semi-double,* but very beautiful." [J-As/62] "Light crimson, very mossy." [WRP] "Somewhat belies its name; for its flowers are rather of a deep rose than crimson. It is, however, a beautiful variety." [FP] "Crimson, semi-double; poor." [EL] "When opening, a shade deeper in colour than the 'Common Moss', the foliage larger, wood stronger and more mossy, and if the old Moss Rose has a competitor, it is this." [Bu] "Flowers rose, large and double; form expanded, well mossed. Growth vigorous; foliage large and fine." [P] "Deep red, medium size, very full, tall." [Sn] "Medium-sized, double, deep crimson. Was found in the garden of a clergyman at Tinwell in Rutlandshire (England), then sent to Mr. Lee, horticulturalist of Hammersmith, who entered it into commerce. This rose was most valuable at the time of its release as being, at that time, the darkest." [JR9/58] "Originated in the garden of a clergyman at Tinwell in Rutlandshire. This is a more luxuriant grower than the Old Moss ... It is an excellent rose for beds; for, if its shoots are pegged to the ground with small hooks, the surface is soon covered with its luxuriant foliage and flowers. For this purpose it is better on its own roots, as worked plants so treated would throw up too many suckers." [WRP]

Crimson Globe
W. Paul, 1890

"Deep crimson cherry red." [Ÿ] "Fine large globular flowers, deep rich crimson, richly mossed." [C&Js98] "Deep crimson, large and full crested, beautifully mossed." [GeH] "Often remaining 'balled'." [T4] "Deep red, large, full, tall." [Sn]

Crimson Moos Listed as 'Crimson' (M).

Crispée Listed as 'Cristata' (M).

Cristata Plates 8 & 9
syns. 'Chapeau de Napoléon', 'Christata', 'Crested Moss', 'Crested Provence', 'Crispée', 'Rose Crépue'; trans., "Crested"
Kitzer/Roblin/Portemer père, Vibert, 1827
Sport of 'Common Centifolia' (C).

"Pink, petals foliated with moss, large, superb." [LF] "Large, full, pink, mossy sepals." [V8] "Pink, medium size, very full, very fragrant, medium to tall." [Sn] "Pale rosy-pink, changing to pale rose; globular, very large and full, the buds beautifully crested; an interesting and beautiful rose; habit moderate." [JC] "*Flowers* full, large, fragrant, of a bright light pink. *Sepals,* three of them bordered with appendages, divided into numerous short linear leaflets, in a striking and elegant form, but having no analogy with Moss roses; very beautiful." [Go] "Its peculiarity consists in a curious and very beautiful mossy growth about the calyx. This growth is developed in proportion to the vigor of the plant: therefore it should be strongly manured and closely pruned, as should the whole race of Provence roses." [FP] "It should here be mentioned, that, if grown in a poor soil, its buds often lose their crest, and become plain, like the Provence Rose." [WRP] "This shrub has all the characteristics of the Centifolia Rose. Of the five *sepals* which surround the corolla, two are edged on each side—and one on one side only—with multipartite, or 4–5 times divided, appendages, subdivided into short linear strips bestrewn with very small fragrant glands. Each of these appendages, looked at from where it arises, looks like a little fairly regular bush, much thickened at the tip. Some similar foliaceous processes are often found on the common petiole. *Flower* large, full, light bright pink, fragrant. This superb rose would be wronged if you were to suppose that this out-of-the-ordinary calyx looked like the mossy calyx of the roses going by that name [*i.e.,* "Moss Roses"]. According to what I have been told, it originated in Switzerland, and had been found by a botanist at the top of an old tower which was part of a former fort." [Pf] "These appendages make them very frilly. Sometimes these same appendages recurve to the base of the pedicels of the leaflets closest to the blossoms, which are medium-sized, bright pink, and very fragrant." [No35] "The nickname of this Rose was naturally suggested by the resemblance of the unopened bud to the three-cornered hat of Napoleon. Its sepals have a peculiar cockscomb-like growth not to be found in any other variety. Flowers are medium size, semi-double, pale rosy pink, and somewhat fragrant." [C-Ps30]

"The very best of the group; its striking peculiarity consists in the green silken mossy fringe surrounding the sepals of the calyx, as it were, half enveloping the bud—a regular moustache, far more elegant and beautiful in the estimation of refined taste than any of those worn by the exquisites of the day. Its bright rosy pink buds are large, the bloom opening very perfect and pendant. If grown on a standard, about two to four feet high [ca. 6.6–13 dm], the beauty is improved. This very curious rose is said to be a sport from the ['Common Centifolia'], and when fully expanded it might be taken for a fine variety of such, though the foliage is stronger, and of a better colour than the original." [Bu] "No rose can be more singular and beautiful than this. The buds, before expansion, are so clasped by its fringed sepals, that they present a most unique and elegant appearance, totally unlike

Cristata *continued*

any other rose. When the flower is fully expanded, this peculiar beauty vanishes, and it has merely the appearance of a superior variety of the Provence Rose." [WRP]

"It was found growing in a crevice in a wall in Fribourg (Switzerland)." [JR9/20] "The rose 'Cristata' was found in Switzerland, around 1826–1827, by a botanist high on an old tower at an old castle from the Middle Ages which was the location of a command center at or near Fribourg; and, according to our friend and collaborator Monsieur Pétrus Rosina, it was Monsieur Kitzer, citizen of the Fribourg canton, who sent this beautiful Centifolia, in 1827, to Monsieur Roblin, chief gardener at the Palais Bourbon in Paris. He, in turn, gave it to Messieurs Vibert and Portemer père, rosarians well-known for their great merit." [JR9/57] "Due to some one in Fribourg, Switzerland, whose name, to my [Vibert's] great regret, I am unable to find in my papers. [*A note adds:*] ... Around 1826, a botanist from Fribourg wrote to me that, in the garden of an old castle, an aged specimen of the Centifolia had partially degenerated, and showed a singular variation from the Moss Rose. Due to the kindness of this person, I received two grafts of the two parts of this specimen. Housed at my place, these grafts reproduced the Centifolia and 'Cristata'." [SNH65/345] "It is probable that it has only been grown since about 1827 or 1828. It was Monsieur Vibert, grower and zealous fancier at St.-Denis, near Paris, who was the first to sell it. You graft it onto a vigorous Briar; it is, however, good to also have some own-root specimens, because the greater part of the Centifolias don't live long grafted. There are, however, some exceptions." [An32/372–373] "Monsieur Vibert presented to the *Société d'Horticulture* a Centifolia rose which he has grown for three years, and of which the calyx shows a singularity yet more astonishing than that of the Moss Rose. Of the five sepals of the calyx, two are bordered on each side, and one on one side only, with multifid appendages—divided and subdivided to the fourth or fifth degree into short linear strips bestrewn with very small linear glands. These appendages replace leaflets—or are nothing indeed more than the leaflets, though extraordinarily developed, that one sees along the edges of three of the calycinate sepals in several roses. This extraordinary development, however, is curious, and gives an added value to the rose, which otherwise already has the merit of being a beautiful Centifolia." [R-H29/78–79]

"We believe that we should place among the Mosses the Centifolia 'Cristata', introduced into France and propagated by Monsieur Vibert. This rose, by the singularity of its calycinate divisions—which are infinitely mossy and fringed—could be considered one of the most interesting sports which art could grasp at." [BJ30]

Cumberland Belle

Dreer/Dingee & Conard, 1900

Sport of 'Princesse Adélaïde' (M).

"A pretty silvery rose in colour, and ... not inclined to mildew." [NRS28/33] "Light pink, large, very full, medium scent, tall." [Sn] "Rare sort, often high-climbing, delightful rose-red bud." [Ck] "Growth very vigorous." [GeH] "This is a grand novelty and a real good thing; a true Climbing Moss Rose. It is of American origin, having been found growing in a private garden in the historic Cumberland Valley [U.S.A.]. The original plant is said to have had 118 buds and flowers on it at one time. The flowers are full and double; color, fine soft silver rose; the buds are nicely mossed and deliciously fragrant." [C&Js07] "It is a wonderfully fine climber. The original plant is said to have grown fifteen feet [ca. 5 m] the first season ... Our stock is the Genuine Variety received direct from the introducer, a noted florist in the Cumberland Valley." [C&Js03]

D'Arcet

Robert, 1851

"Eight cm [ca. 3 in], full, a beautiful scarlet red." [M-L4/162] "Medium-sized, full, scarlet red, beautiful form." [Gp&f52] "Flower much to be recommended to Horticulture because of its mossy buds, which in certain locales are much besought for bouquets. This moss differs much from the usual covering on Centifolia Mosses—it looks like a velvety pile; blossom large, full, flat; color, crimson red." [S] "Deep red, large, full, tall." [Sn] Probably Jean Pierre Joseph Darcet, French chemist, 1777–1844; or his father, Jean Darcet, physician and chemist, 1725–1801.

Damas Mousseux Listed as 'Crimson' (M).

Damask Listed as 'Crimson' (M).

De Candolle

Portemer, 1857

"Flower large, delicate pink." [JDR57/37, as a Damask] "Pink, large, full, medium scent, tall." [Sn] "Vigorous bush, clothed with large and numerous thorns; leaves of five to seven rounded, dark green leaflets; flower large, very full, well formed, delicate pink, center bright pink, petals edges shielded with carmine; in a corymb of 12–15." [l'H57/195] Augustin Pyramus De Candolle, influential Swiss botanist, 1778–1841.

[De La Flèche]

syns. 'À Fleur d'Anémone', 'Anémone', 'Sanguinea', 'Scarlet Moss'; trans., "From [the town of] La Flèche"

Lemeunier, 1824

Seedling from 'Single Moss' (M) or 'Semi-Double' (M).

"Purple pink." [V9] "Medium-sized, double, purple red." [V8] "Deep pink, small." [BJ40] "A pretty brilliant rose, with flowers nearly as small as the Pompone Moss [*i.e.*, *'Mossy De Meaux'*], but not so double." [WRP] "Flowers purplish red, of medium size, double, well mossed; form, cupped." [P] "Blossoms cupped into a beautiful Anemone, deep pink, not very double, but quite interesting; young wood, leaves, ovaries, and sepals covered with moss." [J-As/58] "Blossom an inch and a half across [ca. 4 cm], having, along the circumference, three rows of petals of a very bright pink; at the center is a beautiful cluster of stamens of a beautiful yellow; fragrant; leaves small, and edged with purple. Vigorous growth; very thorny." [An32/313] "Branches and foliage very odd." [JR9/58] "Very singular. The petioles and leaves, like the flowers, are covered with mossy glands. This pretty variety was raised by Monsieur Lemeunier, employed by the local tax collector's office in La Flèche. It is not yet well known in collections; it came from the single Moss." [BJ30] "Came from seed grown by Monsieur Le Meunier [*sic*] ... This rose—singularly notable due to the dark brown tint in all its parts—is much mossier than any other; the moss which covers it goes under the leaf veins, along their serration and indeed their epidermis; the blossom, the petals of which—elongate in form—are no more than forty or forty-five in number, gives hope of ability to set seed." [V2] "*Canes* purple, bristling with numerous long prickles, covered with glands. *Leaflets* purple in their youth, mossy beneath and along their edges. *Flower* small, double, hypocrateriform, bright deep pink." [Pf] "*Bush* 45–50 cm high [ca. 18–20 in], perhaps more; young *branches* reddish brown, later grayish; prickles very numerous and dense, unequal, straight, extending up to the pedicels. *Leaves* at first strikingly reddish, later green; *leaflets* 5 or 7, dark green, rather small, elongate, acute, base rounded, glabrous above, densely covered in often branched glands beneath and along the margins. *Flowers* always erect, never nodding as with the common moss rose, (1-) several at the tips of the canes; *receptacles*, peduncles, and pedicels longly aciculate; *petals* 4–5-seriate, converging on the center as with the Centifolia 'Anémone'; dark pink, some striped paler pink or whitish; stamens very long. *Hips* not seen. Lemeunier grew this from seed and sent it to us requesting that it be named after his home town, La Flèche. At a glance it can be distinguished from the common moss rose; and it seems to prefer shade, the blossoms promptly withering on our two-year-old plant when exposed to full sun." [T&R] See also 'Anémone' (M).

Delphine Listed as 'Delphinie' (M).

[Delphinie]

syn. 'Delphine', 'La Delphinie'
Breeder unknown, pre-1846
   "Flowers of a small size and brilliant rose color." [WRP] "Blossom small, cup-shaped; color, bright flesh." [S] "Flowers bright rose, small; form, cupped. Growth, vigorous." [P] Possibly a Hybrid Bourbon/Moss hybrid; see 'Princesse Adélaïde' (M). Possibly, along with the latter, by Laffay, ca. 1845.

Des Peintres For the Moss, listed as 'Rubra' (M).

Don Pedro

Roseraie de l'Haÿ, date uncertain
   "Light pink, medium size, full, moderate height." [Sn] Possibly synonymous with the Damask 'Don Pedro', *q.v.* Not to be confused with the Alba 'Dom Pedro'.

Double White Striped Moss Listed as 'Panachée Pleine' (M).

Dr. Marjolin

Robert & Moreau, 1860
   "7–9 cm [ca. 3–3½ in], full, very globular, bright red, brighter at the center." [R&M62] "Vigorous growth; blossom medium-sized, full, globular, glossy bright red." [S] Dr. Marjolin, horticulturist primarily associated with the Luxembourg Palace gardens in Paris.

Duchesse d'Abrantès

Robert, 1851
   "Incarnate." [Ÿ] "Deep rose, well mossed. Growth vigorous." [GeH] "Blossom large, very full, shaded pink." [S] "8–9 cm [ca. 3¼ in], full, flesh pink, in a rosette, very beautiful." [R&M62] "Pink-white, large, full, tall." [Sn] Abrantès, Portuguese town and stronghold dating to 300 B.C.

Duchesse d'Istrie

Portemer, 1855
   "Changeable crimson." [Ÿ] "Rose color, not valuable." [EL] "Deep pink, medium size, full, tall." [Sn] Possibly by Laffay; but introduced by Portemer. Istrie, alias Istria, peninsula at the top of the Adriatic Sea.

Duchesse de Verneuil

Portemer, 1856
   "Delicate flesh pink." [BJ70] "Pink-white, medium size, full, tall." [Sn] "A delightful, bright, and healthy rose." [T4]

Ducis

Robert & Moreau, 1857
   "7–8 cm [ca. 3 in], full, flat, light pink shaded with lilac, corymbiferous." [R&M62] "Vigorous." [S]

Elisabeth Brow Listed as 'Elizabeth Rowe' (M).

Elizabeth Rowe

syn. 'Elisabeth Brow'
Breeder unknown, pre-1888
   "Pale pink." [Ÿ] "Bright satiny pink; very large and double; fragrant and finely mossed." [CA88] "Light pink, medium size, full, tall." [Sn] Possibly 'Elisabeth Grow'? *Cf.* Laffay's 'John Grow', etc.

Emilie

Breeder unknown, pre-1885
   "Blossom small, full, folded center; color, pure white." [S] "White, small, full, medium height." [Sn] Probably 'Emmeline' (M), *q.v.*

Emmeline

Robert & Moreau, 1859
   "6–7 cm [ca. 2½ in], full, flat, in a rosette, pure white, corymbiferous." [R&M62] "Flower small, full; central petals curly; blooms in corymbs; color, pure white." [S] *Cf.* 'Emilie' (M).

Etna

Vibert, 1845
   "Brilliant crimson with a purplish tinge, of large size, and very double. A beautiful Rose." [P] "7–8 cm [ca. 3 in], fiery purple." [VPt48/app] "Blossoms full, a flame purple." [SRh54/60] "Crimson tinged with purple. Not of first rank." [EL] "One of the finest, very large and full, delightfully fragrant; color bright crimson, shaded with purple; very mossy." [CA88] "Very beautiful large, full, very well-formed blossom; color, bright carmine, misted with grenadine." [S] "A new French variety of the usual size, cupped form, double, of a purplish flame color, and very beautiful." [WRP] "Red, medium size, very full, tall." [Sn] Mt. Etna, the Sicilian volcano, host to Empedocles and one slipper.

Eugène Verdier

E. Verdier, 1872
   "Very large, very full, beautiful form, crimson red, darker in the middle." [JR9/59] "Vermilion colour, medium size, very double, sweet-scented. Growth vigorous." [GeH] "Red, medium size, very full, medium scent, average to tall growth." [Sn] The breeder/introducer proudly named the cultivar after himself; our notes on Monsieur E. Verdier and his life will be found in the entry on the HP 'Mme. Eugène Verdier' in *The Old Rose Advisor*.

Félicité Bohain

syn. 'Félicité Bohan'
Breeder unknown, pre-1866
   "Bright rose, large and full." [FP] "Intense pink and bright pink." [Ÿ] "Flower large, full; color, bright pink." [S]

Félicité Bohan Listed as 'Félicité Bohain' (M).

[Ferrugineux du Luxembourg]
syn. 'Luxembourg'; trans., "The Luxembourg's Rusty One"
Hardy, pre-1834

"Bright crimson red." [BJ40] "Bright red, full, flat, medium-sized, beautiful." [LF] "Bright crimson scarlet; large and very mossy." [CA88]

Flore Pallido Listed as 'Vilmorin' (M).

François de Salignac
Robert, 1854

"Flower very full, flat, in a rosette, from 7–9 cm [ca. 3 in], amaranth in color." [I'H55/51] "7–8 cm, very full, amaranth, flat, in a rosette, vigorous." [R&M62]

Frédéric Soullier
Laffay, 1854

"Large, full, deep crimson." [JR9/59] "Flower very large, full, cupped, purplish crimson, very fragrant." [I'H55/52] "Deep red, large, full, average to tall growth." [Sn] "Crimson shaded with purple, large and full, a well formed and excellent rose; habit moderate." [JC] "Frédéric Soullier, young painter who died in Italy around 1839." [JR9/127]

Général Clerc
syn. 'Général Clerq'
Laffay/Portemer, 1845

"Medium-sized, full, purple red, slaty." [R&M62] "Well imbricated." [I'H59/110] "Non-remontant; vigorous; medium-sized flower, very full, deep purple red." [JDR59/43] "Deep purple red, medium size, full, tall." [Sn] "Introduced into commerce by Portemer fils." [S]

Général Clerq Listed as 'Général Clerc' (M).

Général Kléber
Robert, 1856

"9–10 cm [ca. 3¾ in], full, beautiful tender pink nuanced with light lilac, imbricated, perfect." [R&M62] "Pink, large, full, tall." [Sn] Jean Baptiste Kléber, 1753–1800, distinguished French general under Napoléon; assassinated in Egypt.

Gewohnliche Moss Rose Listed as 'Common Moss' (M).

Gloire des Mousseuses Listed as 'Gloire des Mousseux' (M)

Gloire des Mousseux
syns. 'Gloire des Mousseuses', 'Glorie de Mezel', etc.; trans., "Glory of the Mosses"
Laffay, 1852

"Carminy pink." [Ÿ] "Flesh pink, center pink." [BJ70] "Very large and double, and of a blush-color." [FP] "One of the best of this sort; its well-mossed flowers are large, full, and beautifully nuanced carmine, but less globular than ['Common Moss']." [R-H63/183] "Pale rose, very large, full, flat form; not attractive in the bud; the foliage is very large." [EL] "Pale rose, the outer petals whitish, one of the largest and best of the Moss Roses, buds large and handsome; habit very vigorous, forming a good standard." [JC] "Nine to ten centimeters [ca. 3¾ in], full, flesh pink, petals folded into a channel. Very beautiful and very vigorous." [M-L4/287] "Vigorous growth; flower large, full, imbricated; carmine pink with a darker center, in rosettes." [S] "Flesh-pink with deeper centre, large and full; of globular, imbricated form. Growth vigorous; well mossed." [GeH]

Glorie de Mezel Listed as 'Gloire des Mousseux' (M).

Goethe
Lambert, 1911
From *Rosa multiflora* × a Moss Rose.

"Red, small, lightly full, tall." [Sn] Johann Wolfgang von Goethe, lived 1749–1832; influential German poet, dramatist, and critic.

Golden Moss
Dot, 1932

"Gold-yellow, medium size, full, medium scent, moderate height." [Sn] "Here is one of the rarest rose-treats of all time—a yellow Moss Rose, the first one ever produced. Moss Roses have been grown in gardens since the sixteenth century [*au contraire!*], but they have been confined to pink, red, and white. Pedro Dot, of Spain, who has produced so many sensational roses during the past few years, scrambled 'Blanche Moreau' [MR] . . . , 'Souv[enir] de Claudius Pernet' [Pern], and 'Frau Karl Druschki' [HP], and the result was Druschki's strong growth, Pernet's color, and Moreau's moss. Fat pinkish buds open a rich golden buff with a pinkish tint. The flowers are about 3 inches in diameter [ca. 7.5 cm], fully double, and twice fragrant—the corolla has a delicious Rose perfume which is almost hidden under the pungent scent of the mossy calyx. The plant is symmetrical in growth with attractive foliage." [C-Pf32] "Can be used as a pillar (mature plants will make 8-foot canes [ca. 2.6 m]), or if trimmed will make a shapely bush, 4 feet high [ca. 1.3 m] and as much through." [C-Pf34]

Gracieuse Listed as 'Gracilis' (M). See also 'Célina' (M).

Gracilis
syns. 'À Fleurs Pâles'? [see below], 'Gracieuse', 'Minor', 'Prolific'; trans., "Graceful"
Prévost, pre-1829

"Medium-sized, full, pink." [V8] "Dwarf, roseate, distinct, globose." [WRP] "Deep pink buds, surrounded with delicate, fringe-like moss. The most beautiful of all the moss roses." [EL] "Deep pink, buds handsomely mossed, flowers large, globular, full and of good shape, an excellent Rose; habit moderate." [JC] "Flowers deep pink, large, and full, well mossed; form, globular. An abundant blooming variety, with fine large foliage; excellent for clumping. Growth, vigorous; forming a good Standard." [P] "Full and imbricated, produced in clusters. Growth very vigorous." [GeH] "Vigorous growth, richly shaded by thick foliage of a glossy green; blossom small, full, globular; color, bright pink." [S] *The Prolific Moss* is not the 'Prolifère' of the French, but a dwarf variety of the common Moss, and a most abundant bloomer. This is known by the French florists as the Minor Moss: it is a most excellent variety to keep in pots for forcing." [WRP] "Sub-variety of ['Common Moss'], from which it only differs in its more slender canes, its larger *leaflets*, and its more consistently nodding *flowers*, which are often paler." [Pf] Not claimed by Prévost, who lists 'À Fleurs Pâles' as a synonym of 'Gracilis'; if the consistently described as deep-pink 'Gracilis' is indeed, perversely, 'À Fleurs Pâles', which one is hesitant to accept, then the correct name and attribution for this cultivar is 'À Fleurs Pâles' (Vibert, pre-1826). Claims via the synonym 'Minor' for "Laffay, pre-1834," as the correct attribution seem incorrect.

Henri Martin
Laffay/Portemer, 1863

"Shaded velvety carmine, good." [FP] "Medium-sized, full, purple red." [JR9/59] "Red, not valuable." [EL] "Medium size flowers, bright rosy red; free bloomer." [C&Js98] "The flowers are rather small, bright crimson, and not so double as most. It is lightly mossed … June-flowering only." [C-Ps25] "Deep red, well mossed, free blooming. Growth vigorous." [GeH] "Vigorous growth; blossom large, globular, full, shining red." [S] "Red, medium size, lightly full, tall." [Sn] "A few unkempt bristles on the calyx and pedicel. It is very floriferous and the semi-double blooms are cerise-red. In the fall it is especially attractive with a great profusion of red 'marbles' (*i.e.*, seed hips), quite showy after a snowfall." [C-Ps29]

Incarnate Listed as 'Vilmorin' (M).

Indiana
Vibert, 1845

"Of cupped form, rose color, and very double." [WRP] "Flowers rose, of medium size, very double." [P] Not to be confused with Vibert's 1834 Gallica of the same name. *Indiana*, 1831 novel by George Sand.

Ismène
Robert, 1852

"Six centimeters (ca. 2.25 inches), full, flesh pink nuanced with lilac, in a rosette at the center. Vigorous." [M-L4/287] "Vigorous growth with large blossom which is full; interior in a rosette; color, flesh pink, shaded lilac." [S] "Whitish pink, medium size, full, tall." [Sn] Ismène, alias Ismene, whom we met among the Damasks.

James Mitchell
E. Verdier, 1861

"Flower medium-sized, full, very well formed, deep pink nuanced lilac, slaty." [I'H61/265] "Dark blossom, with slaty lilac." [S] "Rose-shaded, full." [FP] "Deep violet pink, medium size, full, tall." [Sn] "Vigorous plant of bushy yet wide-spraying habit, with neat, bronzy leaves." [T4]

Jean Bodin
Vibert, 1848

"Pink, globular." [BJ70] "Beautiful form." [R&M62] "6 cm [ca. 2¼ in], full, pink, globular, perfect form." [M-L48/427] "Pink, medium size, full, tall." [Sn] "Very vigorous growth; canes much clothed with short, straight thorns which are compressed at the base; leaf dark green, hard to the touch; blossom large, full, globular, surrounded profusely with moss, making the flower seem flat; color, bright pink; recommended for forcing in March." [S] The year 1846 often given for this cultivar appears incorrect. Jean Bodin, 1530–1596, French economic and political scholar.

Jean Monford Listed as 'Jeanne de Montfort' (M).

Jeanne de Montfort
syn. 'Jean Monford'
Robert, 1853

"Ten to twelve centimeters [ca. 4–4½ in], full, flesh pink flecked with light violet at the end of the petals, flat, blooming in corymbs of twelve to fifteen blossoms; beautiful form and of premier merit." [M-L4/322] "Rose color, quite pretty in bud, subject to mildew, not free." [EL] "Growth vigorous, clusters of 12–15 blossoms, sparse, very large, flat, full; flesh pink flecked with light violet." [S] "Whitish pink, medium size, full, tall." [Sn] The year 1851 often given for this cultivar appears incorrect.

Jenny Lind
Laffay, 1845

"Very beautiful blossom with its own particular look, the moss enveloping the buds very tastefully; blossom medium-sized, nearly full; color, bright pink; very graceful; its pink coloration shows through the light and abundant moss which overspreads the buds." [S] "Small, full, pink, blooms on canes covered over with a thick moss." [R&M62] Jenny Lind, the "Swedish Nightingale"; 1820–1887; Swedish-born singer.

John Crou Listed as 'John Grow' (M).

John Grou Listed as 'John Grow' (M).

John Grow
syns. 'John Crou', 'John Grou'
Laffay/Portemer, 1859

"Large, full, violet crimson red." [JR9/59] "Blossom large, red, shaded deep purple." [S] "Non-remontant, vigorous; flower large, full, violet crimson." [JDR59/43] "Very vigorous shrub, large flower, very full, imbricated, violet crimson." [I'H59/110] "Violet red, large, very full, tall." [Sn]

Joséphine
Breeder unknown, pre-1846

"Lake, beautiful." [WRP] "Flowers deep rose, of medium size, double; form, globular." [P]

Julie de Marsan Listed as 'Julie de Mersan' (M).

Julie de Mersan
syns. 'Julie de Marsan', 'Julie de Mersent'
Thomas, 1854

"Non-remontant, flower medium-sized, full, well-formed, deep pink, striped with white." [I'H55/34] "Rose, shaded with blush." [FP] "Blossom medium-sized, full, flat; color, deep pink, striped white." [S] "Rosy-pink, moderate size, blooming in clusters, buds small and very pretty." [JC]

Julie de Mersent Listed as 'Julie de Mersan' (M).

L'Obscurité
trans. "Darkness"
Lacharme, 1848

"Medium size, full, very deep crimson." [BJ53] "Blossom large, full, opening wide; color, deep velvety grenadine." [S] Darkness, what we grope through in studying Old Roses.

La Caille
trans. "The Quail," (but see below)
Robert & Moreau, 1857

"Velvety bright pink." [Ÿ] "5–6 cm [ca. 2–2¼ in], full, flat, bright pink nuanced with violet, very floriferous." [R&M62] Probably Nicolas Louis de la Caille, French mathematician and astronomer.

La Delphinie Listed as 'Delphinie' (M).

La Diaphane
trans. "The Translucent One"
Laffay, 1848

"7–8 cm [ca. 3 in], full, pink, in a rosette, anemone-form." [R&M62] "Flowers blush rose, large and very double; form, globular. Habit, pendulous; growth, moderate. A free bloomer. This Rose is very pretty in bud; the colour of the flowers is remarkably clear, and the form superb. It was raised by M. Laffay of Bellevue, from whom we expect to receive it this autumn. It is a hybrid between the Moss and French." [P] "Bush not very vigorous; canes weak; blossom large, full, globular, well-held; color, light pink." [S]

La Gracieuse   Listed as 'Célina' (M). See also 'Gracilis' (M).

La Neige
trans. "Snow"
Moranville, 1905
Seedling of 'Blanche Moreau' (MR)

"Pure white of medium size, full. Growth vigorous, floriferous." [GeH] "White, medium size, full, tall." [Sn]

Lafontaine
Robert, 1852

"5–7 cm [ca. 2–2$^1/_5$ in], delicate pink, nuanced. Superb." [M-L52/287] "Blossom large, full, flat; color, delicate pink, shaded with deep pink." [S] Probably intended for Jean de La Fontaine, French *littérateur,* lived 1621–1695.

Lane
syn. 'Latone'
Robert, 1860

"Blush, large and full." [FP] "Very large, full, delicate pink lightly shaded with carmine." [JR9/59] Not to be confused with 'Laneii' (M). Lane, British nurseryman.

Laneii   Plate 10
syns. 'Lane', 'Lanes'
Laffay/Lane, 1846

"Large, red-violet, nuanced with lilac." [R&M62] "Large, very full, lilac-y pink." [Gp&f52] "Large, full, well formed, bright red." [BJ58] "Deep brilliant rose, a beautiful round handsome bud and well mossed, flowers very large, full, and excellent; one of the best Moss Roses grown." [JC] "Large, bold flowers, very double, full, and fragrant; color rich crimson, delicately shaded with rosy purple; very mossy." [CA88] "Blossom large, full, flat; color, bright crimson … The canes of this variety are so 'climbing' that, especially in England, it is often used on rocks or for pyramids." [S] "Flowers rosy crimson, occasionally tinged with purple, large and full; form, globular. Buds broad and bold, fine in form when first expanding, foliage very large." [P] "Red, good foliage, with five leaflets; not subject to mildew. Propagates with great difficulty from cuttings." [EL] "A vigorous and beautiful rose; flowers large, full, and globular; color, a light rosy-crimson. The buds are large, full, and well mossed; its growth is vigorous; and, under good cultivation, the whole plant, with its large and bright-green foliage, bears a striking appearance of thrift and health." [FP] "Very vigorous plant; flowers large, full, well formed, bright red. Magnificent variety, the most beautiful of the mosses." [I'H53/204] The year 1845 often given for this cultivar appears incorrect. Not to be confused with 'Lane' (M).

Lanes   Listed as 'Laneii' (M).

[Lansezeur]
Panaget, pre-1846

"Deep crimson, veined with lilac." [WRP] "Purplish crimson, streaked with rosy lilac, of medium size, double; form, cupped." [P] Possibly synonymous with 'Panaget' (M), *q.v.*

Latone   Listed as 'Lane' (M).

Le Lobèrde
Breeder unknown, date uncertain

"Pink, medium size, very full, tall." [Sn] The name is no doubt a mistake for—something else.

Little Gem   Though mossy, listed as a Centifolia Pompon due to its use in the garden.

Louis Gimard
Pernet père, 1877

"Very vigorous growth; blossom large, full; color, bright pink." [S] "Beautiful bright red, said to be very good for growing in pots." [JR1/12/13] "Pink, large, full, tall." [Sn]

Louise Verger
Robert & Moreau, 1860

"8–9 cm [ca. 3$^1/_2$ in], cupped, beautiful bright pink, more delicate along the edges, vigorous." [R&M62] "Vigorous growth; flower medium-sized, cupped, full, beautiful shining pink." [S]

Lucie Duplessis
syn. 'Lucile Duplessis'
Robert, 1854

"6–7 cm [ca. 2$^1/_2$ in], flesh white, in a rosette, very floriferous." [R&M62] "Flower medium-sized, flat, flesh-colored." [JDR55/18] "Flowers flat, rosette-form, 6–7 cm, flesh white, in clusters." [I'H55/51] "Pink-white, medium size, full, tall." [Sn] "Blossom medium-sized, full; color, crimson, spotted with pink." [S, evidently confused]

Lucile Duplessis   Listed as 'Lucie Duplessis' (M).

Luxembourg
Synonym shared by 'Ferrugineux du Luxembourg' (M) and 'Pourpre du Luxembourg' (M).

Mal Davoust
Erroneous and disturbing synonym derived from the abbreviation of *Maréchal,* "Mal." Listed as 'Maréchal Davoust' (M).

Malvina
Vibert/V. Verdier, 1841

"Medium-sized, double, pink." [V8] "A good rose, with clusters of pink flowers." [FP] "Also [like 'Rubra'] a free seeder; the flowers are pink, very compact, but it will never gratify the nasal organ." [Bu] "Really a good double rose; the whole plant is distinct in character; flowers full sized, and very double, of a bright rose-color slightly tinged with lilac." [WRP] "Pink, large, full, tall." [Sn] "Flowers rosy pink, produced in clusters, large and full, well mossed; form, cupped. Habit, branching; growth, vigorous. A fine Rose, well adapted for a Standard." [P] Said to be a hybrid—no doubt with a Gallica, considering the woes to which it puts the nasal organ. A rare, documented instance of something which was undoubtedly common, Vibert selling propagation rights in his own cultivar to another nurseryman; how many cultivars which we attribute to others were actually bred by the prolific, enterprising, and successful Vibert?

Maréchal Davoust
syn. 'Mal Davoust'
Robert, 1853

"7–9 cm, full, globular, bright red." [R&M62] "Blossom full, globular, red." [JDR56/40] "Flower large, full, glossy red." [S] "Rose red, large, full, tall." [Sn] There are dubieties about the actual year (as opposed to the intended year) of introduction of this. Robert seems to have experienced a set-back in its production, possibly delaying its debut until 1856. The rose seems to have possibly been intended to commemorate Luis Nicholas Davout (note spelling), Duke of Auerstädt, Prince of Eckmühl, and Marshal of France; lived 1770–1823; French military man serving under Napoléon.

Marie de Blois
Robert, 1852

"Rosy-lilac, large and full." [FP] "Nine to ten centimeters [ca. 3¾–4 in], very full, light pink, satined with lilac, globular, stands out." [M-L4/287–288] "Rose color, double, not mossy, poor." [EL] "Bright rose, large and full, an excellent rose, with well mossed handsome buds; habit robust and good." [JC] "Light pink, large, full, tall." [Sn] "Rose-cerise, large, full. Growth vigorous." [GeH] "Without being as good as ['Baron de Wassenaër', 'Capitaine John Ingram', 'Célina', 'Common Moss', 'Comtesse de Murinais', 'Gloire des Mousseux', 'Prolifère', or 'White Bath'], is nevertheless still above the generality of Moss Roses." [R-H63/183]

[Marie-Victoria Benoît]
Puyravaud, 1905
Seedling of 'Eugénie Guinoisseau' (MR).

"Blossom beautiful satiny pink, very large, cupped, fragrant; bush very vigorous with long rigid canes; flower solitary; foliage beautiful dark green, ample; small short thorns, which are reddish and close together. This kind will be much in demand for forcing, to which it takes very well . . . [D]edicated to the daughter of a distinguished horticulturalist of Périgeux." [JR29/151]

[Mauget]
Prévost, 1840

"Medium-sized, full, deep purple." [V8] "Full flowers, bright pink, bush very generous with bloom, raised in 1840." [dH44/204] Not to be confused with 'Perpétuelle Mauget', the 1844 Mossy Remontant by Mauget, which see for notes on Monsieur Mauget.

Ménage
Robert & Moreau, 1858

"Bright pink." [LS] "7–9 cm [ca. 3¼ in], full, flat, beautiful bright carminy pink, very well formed." [R&M62] Possibly commemorating Gilles Menage (note spelling), French philologist and satirist, lived 1613–1692.

[Miniature Moss]
Rivers, pre-1838
Seedling of 'Rivers' Single Crimson Moss' (M).

"Light crimson." [WRP] "One which Mr. Rivers originated from seed in his endeavors to raise a superior dark variety from the Single

Moss Rose. Its flowers are small, of a bright pink, and pretty, though only semi-double." [WRP]

Minor Listed as 'Gracilis' (M).

Mlle. Aristide
syn. 'Aristide'
Laffay, 1858

"Blossom medium-sized, full; color, velvety carmine with very dark crimson." [S] "Large, full, globular, shaded purple." [JR9/58]

Mme. Clémence Beauregard
syn. 'Clémence Beaugrand'
Laffay, 1851

"Blossom very large, full, outspread; color, bright crimson, shaded lilac." [S] "Soft pink, a handsome and well mossed bud, flower large, having a fine broad petal, not very full; a good rose, of free habit." [JC] "Pink, medium size, full, tall." [Sn]

Mme. de la Roche-Lambert
Robert, 1851

"Seven to eight centimeters [ca. 3 in], full, globular, a beautiful amaranth red." [M-L4/163] "8–10 cm [ca. 3¼–4 in], full, amaranth red, globular." [R&M62] "Flower large, full, globular, very well formed; color, amaranth." [S] "Deep red, large, full, medium to tall." [Sn]

Mme. Rose Chéri
Laffay, 1850

"Vigorous growth; branches velvety; leaves blackish green; flower medium-sized, full; color, delicate pink." [S] "Pink, medium size, full, tall." [Sn]

Mme. Soupert
Robert, 1851

"Vigorous bush; corymbiferous; flower medium-sized, full, in a rosette; color, bright cerise red. Very mossy and very floriferous." [S] If meant to honor the wife of the rosarian Jean Soupert of Luxembourg, it is of interest that the Souperts were already known to Robert in 1851; Soupert was, at the time, working for another nurseryman (one Wilhelm), and didn't open his own rose business (with Notting) until 1855.

Monsieur Pélisson Listed as 'Pélisson' (M).

Moscosa Japonica Listed as 'Moussue du Japon' (M).

Mossy de Meaux Though mossy, listed, due to its garden use, in Chapter 6 on Centifolia Pompons and Mossy Pompons.

Mottled Moss Listed as 'Prolifère' (M).

Mousseux du Japon Listed as 'Moussue du Japon' (M).

Moussue du Japon
syns. 'Moscosa Japonica', 'Mousseux de Japon'
Breeder unknown, pre-1906

"A fine crimson." [NRS28/33] "Flower deep rose, large, semi-double. Growth vigorous; well mossed. Distinct." [GeH] "Flower crimson, very deeply mossed, the stems appear to be covered with apple-green moss. Growth vigorous, distinct." [GeH] "Deep pink, medium size, lightly full, tall." [Sn] Appears to have originated in the Cochet circle of rose breeders and rosarians in France about the time there was

Moussue du Japon *continued*
much experimentation in that group utilizing the Japanese rose *Rosa rugosa* . . .

Moussue de Meaux Listed as 'Mossy De Meaux' (CP).

Moussue Partout Listed as 'Zoé' (M).

Mousseuse Blanche Nouvelle Listed as 'White Bath' (M).

Mousseux Ancien Listed as 'Common Moss' (M).

Mousseux Anémone Listed as 'Anémone' (M).

New White Moss Listed as 'White Bath' (M).

Ninette
Robert & Moreau, 1857
"4–5 cm [ca. 1½–2 in], full, bright cherry red, very well formed, very floriferous." [R&M62]

Nuits d'Young
syn. 'Old Black'; trans., 'Young's Nights'
Laffay, 1845
"Purplish-red, a sullied shade." [EL] "Deep purple and very double." [R-H63/183] "Medium-sized, full, velvety deep maroon purple." [BJ58] "Rich velvety purple, large broad petals and full deep flowers, very fragrant." [C&Js02] "Flower blackish crimson, double and well mossed, fragrant. Growth vigorous." [GeH] "Of a very dwarfed growth, and small deep-purple flowers." [FP] "Vigorous growth; wiry upright canes; flower very double, much imbricated, outspread; color, very dark and velvety maroon purple." [M-V50/215] "Deep purple red, medium size, very full, tall." [Sn] The English poet Edward Young (1683–1765) and his poem "Night Thoughts" are commemorated by the Anglophile Laffay.

Oeillet Panaché
trans. "Plumed Carnation"
C. Verdier, 1888
"Pink, striped red." [LS] "White, striped red, medium size, full, medium scent, moderate height." [Sn]

Olavus
Nielsen, 1932
From either 'Cristata' (M) or 'Blanche Moreau' (MR) × 'Mme. Édouard Herriot' (Pern).
"Salmon pink, medium size, lightly full, tall." [Sn]

Old Black Listed as 'Nuits d'Young' (M).

Old White Moss Listed as 'White Moss Rose' (M).

Ordinaire Listed as 'Common Moss' (M).

Pale-Flowered Listed as 'Vilmorin' (M).

Panachée
syns. 'Semi-Double Striped Moss', 'Variegata'; trans., "Plumed"
Shailer, 1818? (But see below)
Sport of either 'White Moss Rose' (M) or 'White Bath' (M).
"Variegated." [Cal] "Medium-sized, striped." [V8] "Pure white plumed pink in the fashion of Flemish carnations; ovary mossy on one side, smooth on the other." [J-As/58] "*Canes* ordinarily unarmed, covered with glands. *Leaves* glaucous in color. *Ovary* ovoid-fusiform,

on which the short and not-very-abundant moss is arranged in longitudinal bands alternating with glabrous bands. *Flower* medium-sized, double, nearly white, plumed and rayed with light pink." [Pf] "The striped Moss, coming from a cane of the white Moss, was found in the environs of Rouen. We owe to this sporting one of the most curious roses in this class—one of the most striking changes that the Mosses have seen. This barely double rose—more frequently semi-double—but much striped—shows a pretty constant singularity. The ovary, the bottom of which is glabrous, is only partially mossy; and the moss, less pronounced than in other varieties, is arranged in longitudinal bands on the upper part." [V2] "This charming Striped Variety is another acquisition to the Mossy tribe, and, we think, of equal value with the White; and though very distinct in its character from that plant, it yet betrays a powerful affinity in many particulars, so as to leave but little doubt of its origin being nearly the same. In flower it approaches nearest to the 'York and Lancaster' Rose, which in size and colour it much resembles. This is likewise the production of Mr. Shailer, who propagated it at the same time as the White variety, and is equally scarce, principally owing to its being treated with too little care before it was sufficiently established. We have no doubt, however, that in time it will be equally as hardy as any other." [A]

Panachée Pleine
syn. 'Double White Striped Moss'; trans., "[The] Full Plumed [One]"
Breeder unknown, pre-1844
"Medium-sized, full, white or flesh-colored, often striped." [V8] "Small, full, white, sometimes plumed pink." [BJ53] "Medium-sized, full, white or carmine, often plumed." [R&M62] "Has as yet produced flowers of pure white striped with pink, but it may be expected (like many other striped roses) to produce flowers pure white or pink." [Bu] "Was received two years since from France [*making 1844; considering that Buist could already comment about it in that year, likely it was introduced in 1843*], and has proved a very pretty rose; its flowers are pale flesh-color striped with pink, and generally constant." [WRP] "Flowers white or flesh-colour, occasionally beautifully streaked with rose, of medium size, very double; form, cupped. Growth, vigorous. Probably a sport from the White Bath Moss, which it resembles closely in some points. A beautiful Rose at all times, especially when the stripes are regularly developed. To assist in this, plant it in a rather poor, but fresh soil (turfy loam, for instance), giving only sufficient manure to keep the plant moderately vigorous." [P] Vibert also offered a pre-1836 Moss 'Panachée Double', *double* having of course fewer petals than *pleine*.

[Panaget]
Breeder unknown, pre-1844
"Medium-sized, not very double, purple striped with red, the only one so far." [V8] "Medium-sized, double, purple, spotted with red." [R&M62] "A very distinct flower." [WRP] Possibly synonymous with 'Lansezeur' (M), *q.v.* Monsieur Panaget, rosarian of Rennes, France; fl. 1840s–1850s.

Parkjuwel
trans. "Park Jewel"
Kordes, 1956
From 'Independence' (HT) × a red Moss Rose
"Red, large, full, medium scent, tall." [Sn]

Parkzauber

trans. "Park Magic"

Kordes, 1956

"Deep red, large, full, medium scent, tall." [Sn]

Parmentier

Robert/Vibert, 1847

"9–10 cm [ca. 1 dm], double, deep pink, cupped." [M-L47/361] "9–10 cm, double, light pink." [R&M62] "Deep pink, large, full, tall." [Sn] "Blossom large, full; delicate pink." [S] Louis-Joseph-Ghislain Parmentier, rosarian, lived 1782–1847; had a very distinguished collection of roses—including many bred by himself over 30 years and kept to himself—in Enghien, Belgium; after his death, at least some of these roses were sold off and distributed by others.

Pélisson

syn. 'Monsieur Pélisson'

Vibert, 1849

"Flowers full, 6 cm across [ca. 2¼ in], deep pink, in a rosette, petals folded." [M-V49/235] "Blossom large, full, made up of folded petals, giving the rose a rosette form; color, bright crimson." [S] "Red, large, full, medium height." [Sn] Monsieur Pélisson, rose breeder, possibly of Marseilles, France.

Pompon   Listed as 'Mossy De Meaux' in Chapter 6 on Centifolia Pompons and Mossy Pompons.

[Ponctuée]

trans. "Spotted"

Laffay, 1846

"Pink, spotted." [LS] "Flowers rose, spotted with white, large and very double." [P] A parent of 'Princesse Royale' (M). To be confused with neither Hébert's similarly named Moss of 1829 nor the Mossy Remontant 'Ma Ponctuée', the 1857 release of Guillot père and Clément.

Pourpre   Listed as 'Rubra' (M).

Pourpre du Luxembourg

syn. 'Luxembourg'; trans., "[The] Purple [One] from the Luxembourg [Palace]"

Hardy, 1848

"Purple." [Ÿ] "A deep crimson, moderately double, and of growth nearly as vigorous as [that of 'Laneii' (M)], with which the deep hue of its buds forms a striking contrast." [FP] "Purple red, medium size, lightly full, tall." [Sn] "Flowers deep crimson, often shaded with purple, of medium size, and double; form, expanded. Growth, vigorous. A beautiful Rose, not unsuitable for a short pillar, or a standard; requires but little pruning. A good seed-bearer." [P] "Grown from seed by Monsieur Hardy, medium-sized, very double, deep purplish red." [JR9/58]

[Pourpre Violet]

Breeder unknown, pre-1862

"Medium-sized, full, violet purple." [R&M62] Cf. 'Purpurea Rubra' (M).

Précoce

trans. "Early"

Vibert, 1843

"Light red." [BJ70] "Medium-sized, full, red-pink, sometimes spotted at the edge, early." [V8] "An early variety, the flower deep pink, sometimes mottled near the border." [WRP] "Flowers rosy red, sometimes spotted at their circumference, of medium size, full. A very early blooming variety." [P] "Rose-red, medium size, full, tall." [Sn]

Presque Simple   Listed as 'Semi-Double' (M).

Prince de Vaudémont   Listed as 'Princesse de Vaudémont' (M).

Princess Alice

A. Paul, 1853

Seedling of 'Pourpre du Luxembourg' (M).

"Raised from '[Pourpre du] Luxembourg'. Violet-rose, not well mossed." [EL] "Blush, pink centre." [FP] "Delicate flesh." [BJ70] "Deep pink, large, full, tall." [Sn] "Blossom large, full; color, deep pink, with a crimson center, petal edges delicate pink." [S] Princess Alice, daughter of Queen Victoria of England and Prince Albert, lived 1843–1878; married the Grand Duke of Hesse.

Princesse Adélaïde

Laffay, 1845

"Carmine." [Ÿ] "Large, full, flesh." [BJ53] "Pale rose, of medium size and good form." [CA90] "Flat." [R&M62] "Medium-sized, full, delicate pink, in a corymb." [Gf56] "Large, full, carminy red." [JR9/59] "Delicate rose." [WRP] "Extra large flowers, very double and sweet; color bright rosy pink; lovely green moss." [C&Js98] "Rose-red, medium size, full, tall." [Sn] "Pale rose, medium size, not very mossy, but good in bud and flower; dark foliage, which is often variegated." [EL] "Flowers pale glossy rose, blooming in large clusters, large and full; form, compact. Habit, erect; growth, vigorous. A fine Rose for a sunny wall or pillar. Does not flower well in a rich soil, nor when closely pruned. Evidently a hybrid, probably between the Moss and some Hybrid Bourbon Rose." [P] "A big, strong-growing bush with fine, crinkly leaves of great size, and enormous flowers of bright, shining pink, not too double, and very sweet. The large buds are heavily mossed, somewhat bronzy, and sometimes apt to split before opening properly." [C-Ps25] "Remarkable for the extreme vigor of its growth." [FP] "Used as a climbing rose to ornament pillars and to make much elevated beds." [S] "Flowers large, numerous, appearing in clusters of from 3 to 15. Color, fine satiny rose. The growth of this variety is extraordinary. It is one of a new tribe raised between the Bourbons and the Moss, and sufficiently mossy to be classed among the latter. It is probably one of the first of a class of perpetual Mosses which ere long will take a rank among the perpetual bloomers." [MH45/28] "The first variety produced of what will hereafter constitute a new class … *Mossy Bourbon Roses* … The present variety is of the same vigorous habit as the Bourbon family; the flowers are produced in immense clusters, and are large, full double, and of magnificent appearance. This Rose is one to which [the French] attach the title of 'une Fleur parfaite,' a perfect flower. The second and only additional ["mossy Bourbon"] hybrid yet obtained is 'La Delphinie' [*i.e.,* 'Delphinie'], with flowers of a small size and brilliant rose color." [WRP] See also 'Delphinie' (M).

Princesse Amélie

Robert, 1851

"Lilac-y blush." [Ÿ] "7–8 cm [ca. 3 in], full, lilac-y carmine." [R&M62] "Bush covered over with light green bark clothed in very brown thorns; calyx tube ovoid, constricted at the neck; flower pink, large, nearly full." [S]

Princesse Bacciochi

Moreau-Robert, 1866

"Flower full, shining pink." [S] "Pink, medium size, full, tall." [Sn]

Princesse de Vaudémont

syn. 'Prince de Vaudémont'

Robert, 1854

"Pink, good." [FP] "Flower full, globular, form and scent of the Centifolia, from 5–6 cm [ca. 2¼ in], light pink." [l'H55/52] "Light pink, medium size, full, average height." [Sn] Not to be confused with Vibert's ca. 1825 Moss of the same name.

Princesse Royale   Plate 6

trans. 'Royal Princess'

Portemer, 1846

From 'Ponctuée' (M) × 'Tuscany' (G).

"Salmon-flesh, full, fine form." [FP] "7 cm [ca. 2¾ in], full, pink." [VPt48/app] "Flowers rosy flesh, large and full; form, globular, beautiful, well mossed; flower stalks very erect." [P] "Medium-sized, full, flesh pink." [BJ58] "Brilliant carmine." [Y̆] "Flowers fairly large, full, well-formed, pink." [SRh54/60] "Medium-sized, very full, imbricated, delicate flesh." [JR9/59] "Pale flesh, very compact and full, flowers rather small, though quite distinct and very beautiful; habit moderate." [JC] "Vigorous bush; blooms in clusters; flower medium-sized, full, globular, delicate flesh pink." [S] "Grown from seed by Monsieur Laffay; its flowers are salmony, and of medium size, but perfect in form, particularly when the bush is pruned closely." [R-H63/183] "The Rose with which we are concerned is a result of my [i.e., Portemer's] sowings, and worthy I believe of being favorably included in all the choice collections. The canes are vigorous, light green, and having short thorns of a saffron color. The leaves are composed of five to seven large, dark green, oval, pointed, much serrated, lightly ciliate leaves. The stalk is upright and very mossy, as are the ovary and calyx, which are nearly lacking any 'pinch'. The blossoms are 5 or 6 cm across [ca. 2¼ in]; they are very full, plump, beautifully colored flesh pink, and perfectly formed. They open well, and always come in pretty full panicles." [An46/42–43] As Portemer's claims to having raised this cultivar are first-hand, and those for Laffay are second-hand, courtesy William Paul, we feel constrained to accept Portemer. However, at the same time it should be pointed out that the cultivar is entirely characteristic of Laffay, that Laffay was releasing similar Mosses at the same time, that several of Laffay's other Mosses were released through Portemer, and that William Paul kept abreast of the French rose situation quite closely; nevertheless, it could well be true that (a) Portemer drew inspiration from Laffay, and made similar crosses; and (b) that W. Paul made an incorrect assumption or simply misunderstood something.

"This would indeed be the most splendid of moss roses if its flowers were quite double; they are not so, but still more than semi-double, and the number of its petals seems to increase annually, as in the '[Rivers'] Single Crimson' Moss, which, from being quite single, is now semi-double. 'Princesse Royale' is, if possible, still more robust in its habit than ['Ferrugineux du Luxembourg']; it makes shoots five to seven feet [ca. 1.8–2.5 m] in one season; its leaves and shoots in spring are of a deep red; it gives a profusion of flowers, which are of a very deep crimson purple, mottled with bright red; when in bud, or half expanded, they are very beautiful. As this rose bears seed freely, it will most probably be the parent of some unique varieties." [WRP, having seemingly received a wrongly identified rose as 'Princesse Royale']

Prolifère

syn. 'Mottled Moss'

Philippe, pre-1826

"Flowers deep rose, large and full, too full to open well at all times; form, cupped. Growth, vigorous. A good forcing Rose." [P] "Flowers, large, very full, the colour of the common Moss rose; expanding with difficulty, but extremely beautiful." [Go] "Large, very full, light red." [R&M62] "A very free bloomer, though the mottled part of its character is not easily detected. It grows freely, and forms a fine variety of a deep rose colour." [Bu] "Large, full, lilac-y pink—the variety still grown by certain firms for the flower-growers of Paris and environs—not the common Moss, though that's what they call it." [JR9/58] "A very beautiful variety, resembling the Old Moss." [FP] "A variety not far from the Type, but it is lower, bushier, and possibly more floriferous, as it blooms profusely, all these qualities making it precious for bedding." [R-H63/183] "Red, medium size, full, tall." [Sn] "Shrub vigorous. Calyx very mossy. Bud large, rounded. Flower large, very full, light pink becoming pale. Petals arranged disorderly. A characteristic which one knows from roses which have difficulty opening is the case here; it is the complete reversal of the sepals on the ovary long before the bud opens. It is thus probable that, in wet, cold spells, a portion of the buds of this variety will abort." [Pf] "An old French variety of vigorous habit, producing very large globular flowers, with petals that are crisp or curled before the expansion of the flower, whence it derived its name of 'Mottled Moss'. The flowers do not open well in the humid climate of England, but beneath our powerful sun they develope themselves with great beauty." [WRP] Not to be confused with 'Prolific' (M), i.e., 'Gracilis' (M).

Prolific   Listed as 'Gracilis' (M). See also 'Prolifère' (M).

Provence Moss   Listed as 'Unique de Provence' (M).

Purpura Rubra   Listed as 'Purpurea Rubra' (M).

Purpurea Rubra

syn. 'Purpura Rubra'; trans., "Purple Red"

Breeder unknown, pre-1870

"Red purple." [BJ70] "Purple, large and full." [FP] "Purplish-red, a bad color." [EL] "Violet purple, large full flowers, very double and fragrant; nicely mossed; one of the best." [C&Js98] Possibly from "Paul, 1866," but we can neither verify the date nor determine which Paul is intended.

Reine-Blanche

trans. "White Queen"

Robert & Moreau, 1857

"Pure white, flowers of good size and tolerably double." [JC] "Flowers large, full, perfectly white, very regular in form, but a little flat." [R-H63/183] "Pure white, of the 'Mme. Hardy' sort." [JDR57/37] "Large, full, well formed, pure white." [JR9/59] "White, large, full, medium scent, tall." [Sn] "White, a shy blooming sort." [EL] "Has difficulty blooming." [S] "7–9 cm [3–3½ in], full, flat, in a rosette, pure white, often with a green pip in the center, corymbiferous, vigorous." [R&M62]

Reine des Mousseuses Listed as 'Reine des Moussues' (M).

Reine des Moussues
syn. 'Reine des Mousseuses'; trans., "Queen of the Mosses"
Robert & Moreau, ca. 1860
"Medium-sized, full, flesh pink." [R&M62] "Light pink, medium size, full, tall." [Sn] Not claimed as one of their own by Robert & Moreau in their 1862 catalog; possibly an error for 'Gloire des Mousseux' (M)?

[Rivers' Single Crimson Moss]
syn. 'Single Crimson'
Rivers, pre-1838
"Flowers brilliant crimson, changing to purplish crimson, large and single, sometimes semi-double; form, expanded. Growth, vigorous; foliage, of a fine dark green." [P] "The number of its petals seems to increase annually, as in the '[Rivers'] Single Crimson Moss', which, from being quite single, is now semi-double." [WRP] See also 'Single' (M).

Robert Fortune
Robert, 1853
"Five to seven cm [2–2½ in], double, striped lilac and pale violet, globular, vigorous—a characteristic still unique in the Mosses." [M-L53/322] Robert Fortune, important horticultural adventurer, lived 1812–1880.

Robert Léopold
Buatois, 1941
"Bright pink." [Y] Color reportedly tends towards the apricot or peach range in this modern Moss.

Rose Crépue Listed as 'Cristata' (M).

Rose Foncé Listed as 'Rubra' (M).

Rotrou Listed as 'Routrou' (M).

Rouge Listed as 'Rubra' (M).

Routrou
syn. 'Rotrou'
Vibert, 1849
"Blossom full, red nuanced pinkish lilac." [S] "Flowers full, 6 cm across, bright lilac pink, darker at the center; flat form." [M-V49/235–236] "Reddish violet, medium size, full, tall." [Sn] Jean de Routrou, French dramatist, lived 1609–1650.

Rubra
syns. 'Des Peintres', 'Pourpre', 'Rose Foncé', 'Rouge'; trans., "Red"
England, pre-1777
"The flowers are bright red, imbricated, and perfectly double." [Bu] "Medium-sized, full, purple." [V8] "*Leaflets* edged with a purple border before mature. *Flower* medium-sized, double, light red or intense deep pink." [Pf] "The whole plant is very mossy, and has a brown appearance; it is a free grower, and appears to do better in this climate than any of the others; it seeds profusely without artificial means. I have several plants from it without any mossy appearance, and others distinctly mossy." [Bu] "Introduced—so it is said—from England into France in 1777 by Mme. de Genlis, this rose is described by Desportes." [Gx]

Sanguinea Listed as 'De La Flèche' (M).

Sans Sépales Listed as 'Asepala' (M).

Scarlet Moss Listed as 'De La Flèche' (M).

[Semi-Double]
syn. 'Presque Simple'
Vibert, pre-1826
"Deep pink." [V9] "Large, half-double, bright pink." [Go] Not to be confused with a purple 'Semi-Double' Moss of 1844.

Semi-Double Striped Moss Listed as 'Panachée' (M).

Shailer's White Moss Listed as 'White Moss Rose' (M).

Simple Listed as 'Single (M).

Single
syn. 'Simple'
Wandes, 1807
"Pink." [V9] "Red." [Cal] "Rose-red, single." [GJB] "*Flower* medium-sized, single or semi-double, light bright pink." [Pf] "Pink, medium size, single, medium fragrance, tall." [Sn] "Rose with egg-shaped seed-buds; empalements and peduncles mossy; petioles and younger branches hispid and glandulously viscous; flowers single; spines of the branches numerous and straight. The Single Moss Rose, like the Single Province, has till lately been unknown to us. It was raised from seed promiscuously amongst other Moss Roses, by some gardener in the country, and sold indiscriminately with the rest, not being considered of greater value; but having been made known to some more intelligent cultivators, it has increased in estimation, and is certainly an interesting plant, as it indicates a distinct species from the provincialis, of which it has hitherto been regarded as only a variety. It will sometimes be found with semi-double flowers on the same plant, as our specimen exhibits an attempt in one of the blossoms to exceed the limits prescribed to single Roses. [Andrews'] drawing was made from the collection of the Countess de Vandes, at Bayswater, last summer, 1810." [A] "*Bush* 0.6–0.9 m high [ca. 2–3 ft], covered in numerous, straight, unequal, very sharp *prickles. Leaflets* 5, ovate, pubescent beneath; unequally dentate and glandular towards the margins; petiole villose, unarmed. *Pedicels, receptacles* and pinnatifid *sepals* covered with long, greenish-brown, glandular, viscous, moss-like outgrowths giving off a sweet and penetrating fragrance. *Petals* 5, light pink. *Hips* not seen. The single-flowered moss rose, still very rare in France, came to us from England where it bloomed for the first time in the gardens of the Countess of Wandes at Bayswater in 1807. Some consider it a variety of *R. centifolia* or *provincialis,* but it seems to us a distinct species. It needs a good soil and resents exposure to wet. One specimen on Briar stock on Boursault's garden produces roses with 6–7 petals; from an examination of the stamens we infer that, stimulated by grafting, the moss rose tends towards doubling." [T&R] "Distinct and compact plant." [WRP] "The Centifolia Moss with single flowers that one can see growing wild in Italy is probably only a sport, its congenitor being the double moss introduced into France from Holland in 1596." [JR9/58] See also 'Rivers' Single Crimson Moss' (M).

Single Crimson Listed as 'Rivers' Single Crimson Moss' (M).

Soeur Marthe

Vibert, 1848

"Full flowers, from 7 to 8 cm across [ca. 3 in], light pink, darker at the center." [M-V49/236] "Pink, large, full, tall." [Sn]

Striped Moss

Synonym shared by 'Oeillet Panaché' (M), 'Panachée' (M), and 'Panachée Pleine' (M).

Tinwell Moss   Listed as 'Crimson' (M).

Transparente   Listed as 'Vilmorin' (M).

Unique de Provence

syn. 'Provence Moss'; trans., "'Unique' from Provence"

Robert/Vibert, 1844

Sport of 'Unica' (C).

"Medium-sized, full, pure white, narrow petals." [V8] "Pure white, full, cupped, medium size, beautiful." [LF] "Pure white, large and full." [FP] "Medium-sized, full, white, sometimes rayed with pink." [Gp&f52] "Flower medium-sized, quite full, pure white. It's one of the mossy Centifolias; charming." [An42/328] "Globose." [WRP] "Medium-sized, full, pure white, sport of the Centifolia 'Unique' more than probably, because its foliage, wood, and flowers are exactly the same, except that the blossoms of the one are entirely clothed with a beautiful moss." [JR9/58] "Pure white, in dry weather slightly tinted . . . ; habit dwarf and delicate." [JC] "Flowers pure white, occasionally tinted with lake after expansion, large and full, well mossed; form, cupped. Habit, erect; growth, moderate; shoots, very spinous. Rather a poor grower. Said to be a sport from the 'Unique' or White Provence." [P] "Is a fac simile of the old 'Unique,' or 'White [Provence] Rose,' only mossed; its habit is similar, and equally robust, with large white flowers, blooming in the same magnificent clusters; it is yet quite rare, but with the present facilities of propagating, it cannot long remain so." [Bu] "This beautiful white rose offers a fine contrast to 'Célina', and equally deserves a place in every garden." [WRP] Existed by 1841, exhibited in 1842 by Vibert, evidently not introduced until 1844. Robert was Vibert's nursery foreman at the time.

Variegata   Listed as 'Panachée' (M).

Vilmorin

syns. 'Carné', 'Couleur de Chair', 'Flore Pallido', 'Incarnate', 'Pale-Flowered', 'Transparente'

Vilmorin, ca. 1805

"Pale pink, full, cupped, very large, beautiful." [LF] "Delicate blush, large, very fine, globose." [WRP] "Large, full, flesh." [Gp&f52] "Medium or large, full." [BJ53] "The blossoms are very double, a perfect flesh color, and fragrant; it is the 'false Cuisse de Nymphe' of Dupont. Monsieur Vilmorin raised this variety about fifteen years ago [*making about 1805*]." [CM] "A most beautiful variety of the color of that well known rose, the Celestial [A],—so exactly intermediate between the white moss and the common, that it is quite necessary in a collection." [WRP] "[Andrews'] figure represents a delicate Pale Variety, of the common, old (but ever favorite) species, taken from the nursery of Mr. Shailer of Little Chelsea, and at present considered as a rare plant: but which we regard as only a variety of colour, considering the latitude of growth to which Roses in general are subject." [A] "Growth somewhat more moderate; the flower is large and full, the foliage fine, and stems

and buds well mossed; color, clear pale pink." [FP] "Flowers blush, their centre inclining to pink when newly expanded, well mossed, large and full; form, cupped. Habit, branching; growth, moderate; foliage, fine. A beautiful Rose." [P] "Very spiny and covered with moss. Flower two inches across [ca. 5 cm], delicate pink; very ample foliage." [An32/313] "*Shrub* vigorous. *Flower* medium-sized, full, flesh." [Pf]

Violacea   Listed as 'Violacée' (M).

Violacée

syn. 'Violacea'; trans., "Violetted"

Soupert & Notting, 1876

"Large, full, steel blue, shaded violet." [JR9/59] "Blossom large, full, peony-form, steel blue shaded bishop's violet, passing to incarnate gray; very mossy." [S] "Steel-blue shaded with violet, changing to greyish pink, large and full. Growth vigorous." [GeH] "Purple-violet, large, full, medium scent, tall." [Sn]

Virginal   Listed as 'White Bath' (M).

Waltraud Nielsen

Nielsen, 1932

From 'Cristata' (M) × 'Arabella' (HT).

"Rose-red, large, full, light scent, tall." [Sn]

White Bath

syns. 'Blanche Anglaise', 'Blanche de Bath', 'Blanche Nouvelle', 'Clifton Moss', 'New White Moss', 'Virginal'

Salter, 1817

Sport of 'Common Moss' (M).

"Pure white, sometimes striped, very mossy, globose." [WRP] "Large, full, globular, pure white striped carmine, sport of 'Common Moss'. Found at Clifton, near Bristol (England) in 1817." [JR9/58] "The best of white Mosses when 'done well by,' but unfortunately very capricious and subject to be ugly if the ground or weather don't suit it." [R-H63/183] "An admirable White Moss, large and full in flower, and exquisite in bud. As it is of moderate growth, it will bear close pruning." [FP] "White, sometimes tinged with flesh, attractive in bud and open flower; generally five leaflets, of straggling habit. Much the best white moss." [EL] "White, large, full, very fragrant, average height." [Sn] "Flowers paper-white, occasionally producing striped or pink petals, well mossed, exquisite in bud, large and full; form, globular. Habit, erect; growth, moderate. A beautiful Rose, and still the best White Moss." [P] "This rose differs from [Shailer's older 'White Moss Rose'] in the following characteristics: *Shrub* more vigorous, having more thorns. *Leaflets* larger and greener. *Moss* longer and more abundant. *Flower* more consistently white, larger, and fuller." [Pf] "A pure white, of rather delicate growth, and rather deficient in the 'mossy coat' so much admired in this tribe. If it had the beauty, while in bud, of the old moss, it would be an invaluable acquisition; it is said to have originated from a sportive branch of the common Moss Rose. In England, about thirty-five years ago, when it first 'came out,' it brought in the guineas at a great rate." [Bu] "Rose with ovate seed-buds: empalement and peduncles mossy: footstalks and younger branches viscose and glandular: leaflets ovate, sawed, and glandular: spines of the branches scattered. This Rose is called the Bath Moss, to distinguish it from one denominated Shailer's White Moss. Both of them, we believe, were casual variations at first, afterwards improved by culture, and although nearly twenty years have elapsed since their first introduction as novelties, they are still considered rare plants, not being so easily increased or preserved as the generality of this fine genus." [A] "Very beautiful and distinct." [JC]

White Moss Rose
syns. 'Ancienne', 'Blanc Carné', 'Blanche', 'Double White Moss
    Provins Rose', 'Old White Moss', 'Shailer's White Moss'
Shailer, 1788
Sport of 'Rubra' (M).

"Flesh white, full, cupped, medium." [LF] "Large, full, with some flesh, center darker." [JR9/58] "I have often seen the old White Moss have one half the flower white and the other half pink." [Bu] "Flowers French white, of medium size, full; form, cupped. Growth, delicate. Inferior to the 'White Bath' Moss." [P] "This has not so much moss as ['White Bath'], and is not pure white, but inclining to a pale flesh-color; it is also much more delicate in habit." [WRP] "Glaucous foliage, globose." [WRP] "Shrub not very vigorous. Leaflets glaucous in color, oval, obtuse, or rounded. Flower medium-sized, full, white; often flesh at the center before fully open." [Pf] "Rose, with egg-shaped seed-buds; empalement, peduncles, and petioles, glandulously viscous; leaflets of an oval shape, villose beneath, with small viscous glands on their edges; spines of the branches numerous, and straight. To the industry of Mr. Shailer, Nurseryman, of Little Chelsea [England], we are indebted for this delicate new Moss Rose, an acknowledged production between the [Common] Moss and White Province, or Rose Unique [i.e., 'Unique'], and which is certainly a valuable addition to this lovely tribe. It evidently bears the compound characters of both plants, with a foliage very distinct from either of them; yet it cannot be deemed perfectly a white flower, since a delicate pale blush pervades the centre of the blossom; this, however, we regard as no diminution of its beauty, and probably not a permanent character, but owing to a tender habit, which time and culture may remove, when it becomes more abundant. At present it is a very scarce Rose, and requires a sheltered situation. The soil in which most Roses thrive best is a light, sandy soil. Some grow very luxuriant in a stony or gravelly situation. This succeeds better with a considerable portion of rich bog earth." [A]

"Similar to the ['Common Moss'] except that the blooms are white with a very slight pink flush—never perfectly white. Shailer, the English nurseryman, first distributed this beautiful rose four to five years ago. It is presumed to be a hybrid between Rosa centifolia nivea and the 'Common Moss'; it certainly offers some of the characters of both. Boursault introduced it to France, where it is much propagated, though as yet it is not widespread. Andrews lists five varieties of Moss Rose. The white Moss Rose needs a sheltered situation and flourishes only in a gritty and somewhat moist soil." [T&R] "In Gard. Chron., 1852, p. 759 (November 27), the following account by H. Shailer, Chapel Nursery, Battersea Fields, appears:— 'In speaking of the first production of the White Moss Rose, which took place in the year 1788, the first birth was from a sucker or underground shoot. My father, Henry Shailer, Nurseryman, of Little Chelsea, an extensive grower of Moss Roses, perceiving it to be a lusus naturae from a stool of the Red Moss ['Rubra'], cut it off and budded it on the White Provins [sic] or Rose La Blanche Unique [sic]. The buds flowered the following season a pale blush. He budded it again the following season; it became much whiter. It figured in Andrews' Rosery under the name of 'Shailer's White Moss'. He then sold it out, the first plants to

Lord Kimbolton'." [NRS23/195–196] "Introduced into France by Boursault, grown by Vilmorin, Cels, and Noisette; it's described and illustrated by Andrews and Redouté." [Gx]

White Provence Listed as 'Unique de Provence' (M).

William Grow
Laffay/Portemer, 1858
"Medium-sized, full, very deep violet velvety crimson." [JR9/59] "Medium-sized, full, velvety violet." [R&M62] "Deep violet red, medium size, full, average height." [Sn] "Vigorous growth, clothed with numerous thorns; leaves of 5–7 leaflets, dark green; blossoms medium-sized, very full, imbricated, very dark velvety crimson violet, in a corymb of 6–8." [JDR58/37]

William Lobb
syn. 'William Loff'
Laffay/Portemer, 1855
"Violet ash, or slate." [BCD] "Carmine." [Ÿ] "Velvety-lake, very distinct." [FP] "Violet-red, not an attractive sort." [EL] "Deep bright pink, large and handsome flowers; very free bloomer." [C&Js98] "Medium-sized, full or nearly full, violet with azure shadings, blooms in a cluster." [JR9/59] "Medium-sized, full, carmine nuanced with azure violet, corymbs of 10–15 flowers." [R&M62] "Medium-sized, very floriferous, in large corymbs, violet carmine." [BJ77] "Very vigorous bush; leaves of five large, dark green leaflets; blossoms medium-sized, very abundant, grouped in corymbs of 20–25 per panicle, carmine shaded with azure-bluish violet." [I'H55/246]

William Loff Listed as 'William Lobb' (M).

Yellow Moss
Walter, 1932
From "Old Moss Rose" (? 'Common Moss'?) × 'Mme. Édouard Herriot' (Pern).
"Yellow, medium size, lightly full, medium scent, average height." [Sn]

Zaïre
Vibert, 1849
"Flowers full, from 7 to 8 cm across [ca. 3 in], deep pink, with long flower-stalks." [M-V49/236] "Deep pink, medium size, full, tall." [Sn] Probably named after the play by Voltaire.

Zenobia
W. Paul, 1892
"Flower soft satin-rose, large, full, buds well mossed. Growth vigorous." [GeH] "Pink, large, full, very fragrant, tall." [Sn] Zenobia, interesting, learned, militant, multilingual Queen of Palmyra; fl. 3rd century A.D.

Zoé
syns. 'Moussue Partout', 'Zoé Barbet'
Forest, 1829
"Light pink, bright." [BJ40] "Medium-sized, very double, pink." [BJ53] "Medium-sized, full, pink, very mossy throughout." [V8] "The flowers of this singular variety are much like the common Moss Rose." [WRP] "Large, full, cupped, light pink, very odd plants bearing moss on all its parts—leaves, branches, and buds are entirely covered." [JR9/58] "Rose, mossy leaves and flowers, globose." [WRP] "A new Moss,

Zoé *continued*

again coming from a sport, notable due to its leaflets which are folded back and often covered with a very fine rust-colored moss." [BJ30] "Named after one of the girls of Monsieur H. Barbet, fancier located in Rouen, to whose kindness I owe this singular variety. *Canes* vigorous, bristling with numerous and long thorns, covered with viscous glands. *Petiole* covered with moss. *Stipules* glabrous above. *Leaflets* 5, rarely 7, ovoid, entire at the base, dentate at the tip; covered above with brown viscous moss; beneath, pale and bestrewn with little puffs of moss. Their lateral edges roll downwards, making each one look like a pipe. *Peduncle* covered with viscous moss, as is the ovary, which is oval or ovoid. *Sepals* mossy; 3 are foliaceous, pinnatifid, and longer than the two others. *Flower* medium-sized, quite double, fragrant, a light and very bright pink. The futility of my research into finding out the origin of this rose makes me desire all the more warmly that mystery and lies would finally cease to preside over the birth of interesting varieties." [Pf]

Zoé Barbet Listed as 'Zoé' (M).

CHAPTER EIGHT

Mossy Remontants

"This new genre is ... an important development Nature has given us; but true rosarians can't yet [in 1856] consider it to be in anything more than the early stages. All things considered, with the exception of two or three varieties, all the others leave much to be desired in bloom, color, growth, and moss." [JDR56/7] "It is only within the last few years [*i.e.,* just prior to 1877] that any really fine Perpetual Moss Roses have been raised; we have, however, now a few first-rate varieties in this class, possessing the properties of the Moss Rose, with the desirable addition of blooming in the Autumn. Many of the varieties are somewhat difficult to propagate, and only the more vigorous growers do well upon the Dog Rose. I find, however, that all of them grow freely upon the Manetti stock, especially the dwarf growers. They require rich soil and close pruning." [JC] "The Perpetual Mosses have their uses, because they extend the season of the Mosses proper; aside from that, however, there isn't a lot to recommend them, as their vigor is limited, and they aren't very mossy." [R-H63/294] "They rebloom more or less freely, and the moss, less developed, less reddish, is less graceful in effect than is the case with its progenitor." [JR17/94] "The flowers are not oppressed with moss, although they have sufficient to denote their origin ... [T]here is no doubt of this becoming eventually one of the most interesting groups. They require the same treatment as the Moss." [P]

"They are very difficult to propagate; their skinny branches only give us flat 'eyes' during the whole season—or, close to the blossom, an herbaceous eye which, budded, rarely takes. No more can they be multiplied, like other roses, by runners or cuttings, because they only rarely root. We think that the most auspicious time to propagate them is in the Spring by shield grafts *sur corps.* To graft this way, in January or February you cut some canes from the rose you want to propagate; these canes are quite ripe, and the eyes are in a good state of development—two essential qualities rarely found in the growth of Moss Roses in Summer and Fall. You bury the branches in the ground so the sap isn't allowed to run; and—when the moment comes—you dig them up to choose the desirable eyes, and graft them. Perhaps before long we will get some varieties which are easier to propagate." [JDR56/7]

"The first remontant moss rose was, without a doubt, the 'Quatre-Saisons [Blanc Mousseux]' with semi-double white flowers. We don't think that craft played a part in its origin, because its wood and particular manner of growth indicates a spontaneous creation, be it by sport or seed. The first product of horticultural art was, if we don't err, 'Perpétuelle Mauget'." [JDR56/7] "Then a fairly good number of others appeared around 1850 and the following years, which is to say the time when could be found all those beautiful Hybrid Perpetuals. It seems probable that the moss roses of this [remontant] series are mongrels, or from hybrids." [JR32/188] Hence, not "Remontant Mosses" (as these cultivars are, genetically, not simply Mosses that rebloom), but rather "Mossy Remontants."

Alfred de Dalmas
Laffay/Portemer, 1855

"Pink." [JDR55/49] "Pink, edged white." [Mz55–56/38] "Rose, edges rosy-white, blooming in clusters, full." [FP] "Very full, in a corymb, pink at the center, edged blush white." [Gf56] "Medium-sized, full, center pink, corymbiferous." [R&M62] "Centre of flower rose coloured, outer petals rosy white, medium, full, fragrant, floriferous." [GeH] "Pink, small flowers, of poor quality; the wood is very thorny; straggling habit." [EL] "Very vigorous growth, branches with nearly imperceptible thorns; bloom quite remontant, medium in size; in corymbs; color, pink. One of the best mosses." [S] "Light pink, small, very full, tall." [Sn] "Vigorous bush clothed with strong and numerous prickles of maroon and yellowish; leaves of 7 apple green leaflets; flower medium-sized, very full, in a cluster of 8–12, pink center, petal edges blush white." [l'H55/246] See also 'Mousseline' (MR), which is not a synonym but rather a sibling in confusion; we cite the differences in our entry on 'Mousseline'.

Baron de Wassenaër
syn. 'Baronne de Wassenaër'
V. & C. Verdier, 1854

"Bright lilac-y red, globular." [BJ77] "Deep rose; buds pretty, and quite well mossed." [EL] "Very large, nearly full, globular, beautiful bright icy pink." [JR9/58] "A very vigorous rose, of a bright red, and flowering in clusters." [FP] "Deep rose and well mossed, cupped, in clusters." [GeH] "Vigorous growth; flower medium-sized, plump,

Baron de Wassenaër *continued*

nearly full, very mossy, blooming in clusters; color, violet pink on up-per surface, blush white beneath." [S] "A vigorous bush with large flowers which are full, globular, the most beautiful carmine red, and grouped in fours or fives." [R-H63/183] "Deep rose, very large and double, buds moderately well mossed, habit vigorous, a very showy and useful rose; forms a good standard." [JC] "Violet pink, medium size, full, tall." [Sn] "Canes of medium size, loose, light green, bristling with occasional thorns and numerous glandular bristles of a brown-red color. Thorns straight, widened at the base, much pointed to-wards the tip, brown red, variable in size; those of less than medium size as well as the very small ones are mixed with the simple glan-dular bristles which clothe the canes. Leaves composed of five or sev-en leaflets of medium size of a beautiful green, covering the bush lightly. The leaflets are fairly thin, soft, oval, sessile, and slightly cor-date at the base, pointed at the tip, finely toothed with simple denta-tion along the two edges of the upper part, entire and only ciliate along the edges of the lower part. The upper face of the leaflets is a beautiful light green inclining a bit to olive, and sometimes showing a slight 'bloom' which gives them a light glaucous tint. The underside is made a very pale green with numerous short, fine, white, non-glandular bristles. The rachis, to which the leaflets are attached, is only angled at the point where the two leaflets nearest the tip arise from the rachis; it is creased into channels above, and armed with several very small prickles beneath; on all parts, bristling with glan-dular hairs—excepting beneath the portion attached to the stipule, which is glabrous. The stipules or 'earlings' are large, glabrous on both sides, edged with glandular cilia, attached to the rachis for three-quarters of their length; the free portion makes an elongated triangle parallel to the petiole. The blossoms are of medium size, beautiful light pink, full without being muddled, perfect in form, and having a fragrance of the most elegant sort. They come up to ten in a cluster at the tips of certain canes; they never come one at a time. The outer petals are largely obovate, often slightly notched at the tip, of a beautiful and fresh pink color within, flesh white with some vi-olet on the outer face; they are erect, well imbricated, and form a cup, the more muddled inner petals folding back lightly to the center of the flower." [l'H54/254–255]

Baronne de Wassenaër Listed as 'Baron de Wassenaër' (MR).

Bicolor

syn. 'Bicolore'
Lacharme, 1855

"Pink, spotted." [JDR55/49] "Vigorous bush; flower medium-sized, nearly full, bright pink, spotted with violet." [l'H56/2] "Vigorous bush; blossom medium sized, quite full, opening well; color, pink, marbled or spotted with violet." [S]

Bicolore Listed as 'Bicolor' (MR).

Blanche Moreau Plate 14

syn. 'Blanche Roberts'
Moreau-Robert, 1880
From a parent-group including 'Comtesse de Murinais' (M), 'Quatre Saisons Blanc Mousseux' (MR), and two unintroduced seedlings (see below).

"White, claimed to be a true remontant." [EL] "Large full flowers, fine creamy white, elegantly tinged with rosy blush, nicely mossed;

very fragrant and beautiful." [C&Js98] "Pure white, large, full, perfect form, produced in corymbs. Growth vigorous, well mossed, hardy. The finest white Moss Rose." [GeH] "White, medium size, full, moder-ate fragrance, tall." [Sn] "Very vigorous growth with upright canes; opening well; corymbiferous; flower large, full; color, pure white." [S] "Extremely vigorous bush with upright, robust canes covered with very fine thorns which are nearly mossy and somber green; very beautiful dark green foliage composed of 5–7 leaflets; ovary and ca-lyx with the most beautiful green moss, and having 6–8 sepals which are equally mossy and which project 2–3 cm [ca. 1 in] beyond the bud; flower large, full, opening well, perfect in form, and the most beautiful pure white; in clusters. This magnificent variety was raised from several Mossy Remontant pod-parents of delicate pink and pure white which are not in commerce; you can also rest assured that this beautiful plant will not be the last remontant white Moss; it doesn't look like any of the other white Mosses developed up till now, the earlier ones always having in wood and moss a yellowish or sul-phurous tint. This beautiful obtention will be, for forcing, bouquets, and sales in bulk, the most wonderful success till now in white ros-es, and will be grown by the thousands to these ends. This extra vig-orous plant should be pruned long, and only reblooms on stems sev-eral years old." [JR4/164–165]

"It is to Monsieur Moreau-Robert, the honorable *rosiériste* from Angers, that we owe the beautiful Moss Rose 'Blanche Moreau', which sprang from a natural cross of the Moss Roses 'Comtesse de Muri-nais' and 'Quatre Saisons Blanc [Mousseux]'. This cross, which dates from 1858–1860, only produced a few hips at first, which themselves only produced three plants: two with single blossoms and the third with nearly full flowers having the color and form of [those of] 'Mère de St.-Louis' [HP]. Having found in this specimen a seed-bearer able to produce good results, Monsieur Moreau-Robert grew it for a pret-ty long time to the end of making it remontant—which was achieved around 1869 or 1870. The first try having partially succeeded, it was necessary to try again—but with certain changes. The able rose-grower planted a hundred specimens of the four following varieties: 'Comtesse de Murinais', the above seedling, 'Quatre Saisons Blanc Mousseux', and another seedling not in commerce with semi-double very delicate pink blossoms, and freely remontant. These roses were planted as close as possible so that natural pollination would have the best chance to take place. The first two years, only a few hips formed, but none of them ripened fully. Tired of waiting, Monsieur Moreau-Robert was going to pull up these roses when the idea came to him to leave the roses to themselves, as is. The following year, the roses—which hadn't been pruned—grew very vigorously and showed a certain number of fruits which ripened perfectly. Having collected and down these seeds with care, Monsieur Moreau-Robert got thirty specimens which bloomed for the first time in Spring 1876; and among these he found 'Mousseline' and 'Blanche Moreau', which were entered into commerce in Fall 1880 [*actually, 'Mousseline' was held back until Fall, 1881*] ...A stem of this rose, presented to the Société d'Horticulture d'Angers in June, 1881, bore 41 blossoms or buds; also, the members present unanimously voted a silver medal as appropriate to the fortunate raiser of this beautiful obtention ... [This rose] has the advantage of being an excellent pod-parent. In the last number of the *Journal des Roses*, mention was made of the presentation to the Société d'Horticulture d'Angers of a tree-rose 'Blanche Moreau' covered with seed. Monsieur Moreau-Robert has let us in on the fact that, for some time, he gathered several hundred of these fruits on two-year-old specimens, grafted *en repassage*, preferably on the '[Général] Jacqueminot' [HP] types. In the year 1883, this able raiser had four to five hundred specimens of unusual vigor, from which he chose the most beautiful 175, which he put to graft the same year. Most curiously, in these seedlings, all the sorts of the genus could be found, excepting the *Teas*, the *Noisettes*, and the *Bourbons*. *Mosses* showed up to the degree of 50%; *Gallicas*, 10%; the same for non-mossy *Centifolias*, *Damasks*, and *Albas*; the rest were *Hybrid Perpetuals* and indeed some *Climbers*. Some specimens were so mossy that it was difficult to see the cane beneath. Others are impossible to classify, at least for the moment. Their colors are equally various: some bright sparkling red, some pink, delicate pink, flesh, and pure white, this last particularly among the 'Mosses' and 'Albas'. Many of these seedlings have already bloomed this year, observations being made carefully and often; but the best bloom will most certainly be next year in June, and Monsieur Moreau-Robert calls upon [professional] rosarians and [amateur] fanciers who are interested to come to his place and study this strange situation. Monsieur Moreau-Robert is still sowing seed of this same variety, and we don't doubt that the future holds several surprises for us; we look forward to seeing soon some beautiful and excellent new varieties of Mossy Remontants." [JR9/136–137] See also 'Mlle. Marie-Louise Bourgeoise' (MR).

Blanche Roberts   Listed as 'Blanche Moreau' (MR).

Céline Briant
Robert, 1853

"5–6 cm [ca. 2¼ in], full, light pink, petals narrow, folded; in a rosette; very floriferous, in corymbs of 8 to a dozen blossoms; freely remontant." [M-L53/320] Not to be confused with Robert's Damask Perpetual of the same name of 1852!

Césonie
Robert & Moreau, 1859

"Carmine." [Ÿ] "Blossom medium-sized, full, crimson." [S] "6–7 cm [ca. 2½ in], full, globular, carminy pink, very corymbiferous, wood very much of a hybrid nature." [R&M62] "Deep pink, medium size, full, tall." [Sn]

Circé
Robert, 1855

"4–6 cm [ca. 2 in], full, delicate pink spotted with white, flat." [R&M62] Not to be confused with W. Paul's similarly named HT of 1916. Circé, alias Circe, bewitching Odyssean temptress who, in the best tradition of bewitching temptresses, turned men into animals.

Clémence Robert
Robert & Moreau, 1863

"9–11 cm [ca. 4 in], full, outspread, very bright pink, very mossy, corymbiferous, very fragrant." [M-R65] "Vigorous growth; corymbiferous; blossom large, opening wide, full, very fragrant; color, bright pink." [S]

Delille
Robert, 1852

"Flesh." [Ÿ] "Five centimeters [ca. 2 in], full, light red passing to flesh pink satined with lilac; in a rosette." [M-L4/288] "Blossom light red, fading to flesh pink." [S] "Appeared at the same time as ['René

d'Anjou' (MR)], which it is much like. It is, however, less remontant." [JDR56/48] Jacques Delille, French poet, lived 1738–1813.

Deuil de Paul Fontaine   Plate 13
trans. "Mourning for Paul Fontaine"
Fontaine, 1873

"Flowers very large and fine; colour purplish-red, shaded, opens freely." [JC] "Red, shaded crimson, large, full; not mossy; worthless." [EL] "Dark purple red, large, full, medium scent, moderately tall." [Sn] "Purple, shaded crimson-red, large, full. Growth vigorous." [GeH] "It was in a sowing of rose seeds made in 1867 by Monsieur Fontaine, horticulturist-rosarian of Clamart, near Paris, that was found the beautiful remontant Moss Rose ...'Deuil de Paul Fontaine'. The original bloomed the first year from seed, so Monsieur Fontaine tells us, who was able to bud this beautiful variety. After having studied it for several years to ascertain whether it rebloomed well, he entered it into commerce in Fall of 1873. This rose is vigorous, with wood which is sturdy without being 'big', clothed with numerous thorns; its foliage is light green and very mossy; its flower, cupped, opening very well, is a very handsome purple red illumined flame within and shaded mahogany without. The provenance of this variety is difficult to establish, the breeder tells us; he thinks that the seeds he sowed were from a collection of non-remontant Mosses which he grew at that time. Granting this, he entered into commerce three [remontant] Mosses from these same seeds: 'Mme. Legrand', 'Mme. Charles Salleron', a pretty plant which received the gold medal at the Soissons exhibition, and finally 'Deuil de Paul Fontaine'." [JR6/127]

Eugène de Savoie
Robert & Moreau, 1860

"Bright red, large and full." [FP] "10–12 cm [ca. 4–4½ in], full, flat, bright red, very floriferous, admirable, very effective, the most fragrant of the sort." [R&M62] "Medium growth, very floriferous; flower large, full, flat, very fragrant; color, bright red." [S] "A very unusual Rose of bright pink; good grower." [C&Js11] Eugène de Savoie, alias Prince Eugene, alias François Eugène de Savoie-Carignan, impressive Austrian general, lived 1663–1736.

Eugénie Guinoisseau   Plate 12
Guinoisseau-Flon, 1864

"Cerise." [Ÿ] "Large, full, well formed, cherry red passing to purple." [M-R65] "Bright cherry, changing to violet, large, full, and well mossed." [FP] "Crimson red, changing to lilac purple, large, full. Growth vigorous." [GeH] "Purple-red, large, full, tall." [Sn] "Of all the moss roses now in commerce [in 1884, 'Eugénie Guinoisseau'] is certainly one of the best and most freely remontant. This beautiful rose was grown from seed by Monsieur Bertrand Guinoisseau, rosarian-horticulturalist, 14 St.-Barthélemy Road, in Angers [France], who dedicated it to his daughter and entered it into commerce in Fall 1864 at the same time as the Hybrid Perpetual 'Héliogabale'. The vigorous shrub makes a rounded bush bearing canes covered with very numerous red prickles. The leaves are a beautiful dark green with five or seven oval, pointed, finely dentate leaflets; the peduncle is very mossy. The blossoms ... are upright, full, well formed, and measure 8–10 cm [ca. 3½–4 in]; the petals are cucullate ['*cuculés*': hood-shaped, scoop-shaped, shell-shaped], cherry red changing to violet red. The rose 'Eugénie Guinoisseau', being very floriferous, merits a worthy place in all rose collections." [JR8/169]

Fornarina

Robert & Moreau, 1861

"Shining carmine." [Ÿ] "6–8 cm [ca. 2½–3 in], full, flat, in a rosette, bright carmine red, very floriferous." [R&M62] "Vigorous growth, very floriferous; blossom medium-sized, full, flat, center a rosette, carminy bright red." [S] Not to be confused with the several Gallicas of the same name. La Fornarina, tempestuous inamorata of Byron's.

Gabrielle Noyelle

Buatois, 1933

"Salmony orange." [Ÿ] "Orange-salmon, large, full, medium scent, tall." [Sn]

Général Dinot   Listed as 'Général Drouot' (MR).

Général Drouet   Listed as 'Général Drouot' (MR).

Général Drouot

syns. 'Général Dinot', 'Général Drouet'

Vibert, 1847

"Double purple." [Mz52–53/32] "Medium-sized, nearly full, purple." [BJ53] "6–8 cm [ca. 2½–3 in], double, purple, very vigorous." [R&M62] "6–7 cm [ca. 2½–2¾ in], double, purple, very vigorous . . . Bears hips." [M-L47/362] "Purple red, medium size, lightly double, tall." [Sn] "Flowers purplish crimson, of medium size, double. Growth, vigorous." [P] "It grows pretty vigorously, but its flowers, of a crimson purple, are no more than semi-double." [R-H63/294] "Easy of culture; the color is deeper [than that of 'Perpétuelle Mauget'], approaching to crimson purple, but the flower is semi-double." [MH50/514] "Purplish crimson, the best dark variety; grows freely upon the Manetti [*sic*; '*Manettii*'] stock, but will not succeed upon the Briar." [JC] "Vigorous growth; canes yellowish green, clothed with thorns which are flat at the base and straight; leaves brown nuanced dark brown; young growths clothed with reddish brown moss; flower medium-sized, semi-full, not very remontant; color, bright grenadine." [S] "The flower . . . has a particular grace, an attraction which makes it distinct among the most beautiful productions of horticulture: a calyx overspread with a light, scented moss composed of bristles which are hispid, glandulose, and viscose . . . Raised in 1845 [but not released until 1847] by one of our subscribers, Monsieur Vibert, enlightened horticulturalist, at Angers. Little known by fanciers, and not wide-spread in commerce, it will be highly regarded, particularly if one considers that its purple red coloration places it among the most distinct varieties. And what a fortunate triumph! —a Moss Rose which reblooms in the Fall! The dedication was made to Count Antoine Drouot, general of the Empire, making it doubly deserving of favor from lovers of Moss Roses: As a novelty notable for its distinctive character, it is a step forward; as a dedication, it is homage to one of the greatest glories of Lorraine . . . This rose is being propagated by many horticulturalists in Paris and the outlying areas." [M-V50/209–211] Robert, Vibert's foreman at the time, possibly had a hand in developing this rose—sometimes it is attributed to him. On the basis of the quote above, however, the writer of which seeming to have superior knowledge about the circumstances of the cultivar (as, when it was *raised*, rather than simply its release date), we opt for attribution to Vibert.

Gloire d'Orient

trans. "Glory of the Orient"

Beluze, 1855

"Deep pink, spotted." [Mz55–56/38] "Blossom medium-sized, full, deep pink." [S] "Deep pink, medium size, full, tall." [Sn]

Hermann Kegel

Portemer, 1849

"Violet crimson plumed white." [Mz52–53/32] "Violet carmine." [Ÿ] "Blossoms medium-sized, violet crimson, sometimes nuanced or striped with lilac." [M-V49/233] "Pretty vigorous plant; flowers medium-sized, nearly full, violet red, sometimes lightly spotted white." [I'H53/173] "Vigorous growth; flower medium-sized, full; color, violet red, sometimes striped crimson." [S] "Deep violet red, medium size, full, tall." [Sn] "[In 1850] the most recent, and perhaps the best, of this group. It is a free grower, similar in color to ['Général Drouot'], but more double." [MH50/514] "This is a very vigorous, freely remontant bush; its habit is spreading; its canes, stalks, and calyx tubes are clothed in numerous unequal, closely-set, nearly filiform prickles of a reddish brown, and glandulose; leaves lightly tinted reddish as they appear, glandulose, composed of 5–7 leaflets which are oblong, rounded at the tip, and dentate; corollas large, from .05 to .06 m [*sic*; ca. 2–2½ in], full; outer petals outspreading, rounded; central petals spatulate, nearly upright, a magnificent deep red nuanced violet, solitary at the tip of a very short stalk widening gradually into a calyx divided into five long, lacy sections, of which two are acuminate and entire, and three have foliaceous appendages. Because of its coloration, this rose is certainly the most beautiful of the Mosses." [V-H49/534]

Hortense Vernet

Robert & Moreau, 1861

"White, tinged with light rose, fine, large, and full." [FP] "Fine rosy carmine; large, full, and sweet; buds beautifully mossed." [CA88] "Whitish pink, medium size, full, moderate scent, tall." [Sn] "Vigorous growth; flower large, full, flat, in a rosette; color, white washed delicate pink." [S] "9–11 cm [ca. 3¾–4¼ in], full, flat, rosette at center, white washed with delicate pink, quite overspread with a very thick moss in the form of prickles, rich foliage, corymbiferous, the most mossy of the sort." [R&M62]

Impératrice Eugénie   Plate 11

Guillot père, 1855

"Bright pink." [Mz55–56/38] "Well-formed." [R&M62] "We saw, in the Fall of 1853, some quite double blossoms of beautiful coloration and elegant form on this variety–rather like those of 'Perpétuelle de Neuilly' [*HP, V. Verdier, 1834; one of the first Hybrid Perpetuals*]." [JDR56/7] "Growth vigorous, floriferous; flower medium-sized, full, glossy bright pink." [S] "Empress Eugénie; lived 1826–1920; wife of Louis Napoléon." [from *The Old Rose Advisor*, p. 117] Not to be confused with the pink Hybrid Bourbon of 1855 from Beluze nor with the slate-colored Hybrid Perpetual of 1854 by Delhommeau.

James Veitch

syn. 'James Weltch'

E. Verdier, 1864

"Deep violet, shaded with crimson, large and double." [FP] "Very large, full, deep slaty violet, nuanced flame." [M-R65] "Violet-crimson, a sullied color, medium or large size, poor shape; blooms freely, very subject to mildew." [EL] "Deep violet shaded with rosy-crimson, flowers large and double, free blooming, one of the best perpetual moss." [JC] "Deep violet red, medium size, full, tall." [Sn] "Medium growth; blossom medium-sized, full; color, deep slaty violet, shaded flame. Blooms in clusters." [S] "Very vigorous, remontant, and floriferous; flowers full, 9 cm across [ca. 3½ in], grouped in 3–8 blossoms per corymb, deep slaty violet, nuanced flame." [l'H64/327] James Veitch, British nurseryman.

James Weltch   Listed as 'James Veitch' (MR).

John Cranston
E. Verdier, 1861

"Violet-red, medium size." [EL] "Crimson-shaded, full." [FP] "Flower medium-sized or large, full, violet crimson shaded with bright red." [l'H61/265] "Vigorous growth; violet-red." [S] "Shaded violet-crimson, colour rich and good, flowers of moderate size, expanded, full, and well formed; habit free." [JC] John Cranston, our JC, British rosarian and author.

John Fraser
Granger/Lévêque, 1861

"10–12 cm [ca. 4–4¾ in], full, beautiful bright red nuanced with carmine." [R&M62] "Remontant Moss, vigorous bush, beautiful glaucous green foliage, wood covered with reddish prickles, calyx covered with a beautiful thick green moss, flowers very large (10–12 cm), well formed, beautiful bright red nuanced carmine, very remontant." [l'H61/167]

Ma Ponctuée
trans. "My Spotted [One]"
Guillot père & Clément, 1857

"Spotted cherry red." [JDR57/37] "Light red, medium size, full, medium height." [Sn] "Vigorous growth; flower medium-sized, full; color, cherry red, sometimes striped with white." [S] "Medium sized, full, cherry red, spotted, vigorous." [R&M62] "Strong canes; flower medium red, cherry, spotted." [l'H57/195]

Marie de Bourgogne
Robert, 1853

"Bright rose, medium size." [EL] "Blossom full, light red, very mossy." [S] "6–7 cm [ca. 2½ in], full, light red, narrow petals, cupped, very well formed, very floriferous." [R&M62] "Pink flower, in a cluster, medium-sized; much praised variety when it first came out; only passable these days [a mere 3 years later!]." [JDR56/48] "Flowers large, very full, light red-pink; petals very thick-set, muddled; globular while opening, then cupped, very well formed; canes vigorous, tipped with 5 or 6 blossoms." [l'H54/12] "Rose red, medium size, full, tall." [Sn] "Six to seven centimeters [ca. 2½ in], very full, light red-pink, petals narrow and very close-set; globular while opening, then cupped, very well formed, canes upright and vigorous, terminating in five or six blossoms. A rose of the first merit in this series." [M-L4/322] "Pretty good variety." [l'H56/251]

Marie Leczinska
Moreau-Robert, 1865

"Deep pink." [Ÿ] "6–8 cm [ca. 2½–3 in], full, globular, a nuanced light red, very floriferous and vigorous, reblooms freely." [M-R65] "Blossom medium-sized, globular; very floriferous, much covered with moss; color, bright red." [S] Queen Marie Leczinska, wife of Louis XV, daughter of the King of Poland.

Maupertuis
Moreau-Robert, 1868

"Deep red, medium size, full, tall." [Sn] "Vigorous growth; flower medium-sized, full, very mossy; color, deep velvety red, fading to crimson." [S] Pierre Louis Moreau de Maupertuis, French mathematician, lived 1698–1759.

Mélanie Waldor
Moreau-Robert, 1865

"Blossom medium-sized, flat; color, lilac pink, white center." [S] Not to be confused with Vibert's 1836 Gallica of the same name.

Melchior Salet   Listed as 'Salet' (MR).

Mlle. Alice Leroy
Trouillard, 1856

"Medium growth; blossom medium-sized, full; color, delicate pink." [S] Not to be confused with the Moss 'Alice Leroi' (Vibert, 1843, rosy lilac pink).

Mlle. Marie-Louise Bourgeoise
Corboeuf-Marsault, 1890

"White." [LS, calling it a synonym of 'Blanche Moreau' (MR)] "White, yellow center, large, full, very fragrant, moderately tall." [Sn]

Mme. Charles Salleron
Fontaine/E. Verdier, 1867

"Blossom large, full, carmine shaded fiery red." [S] "Flowers large, full, sparkling crimson red illumined with flame, having some analogy, in its coloration, with the H.P. 'Monte-Christo' [Fontaine, 1861]." [l'H68/50] Sibling of 'Deuil de Paul Fontaine' (MR).

Mme. de Staël
Robert & Moreau, 1857

"Delicate flesh." [JDR57/37] "5–7 cm [ca. 2–2½ in], full, cupped, flesh pink, very delicate, superb." [R&M62] Mme. Anne Louise Germaine, Baronne de Staël Holstein (née Necker), lived 1766–1817; French authoress.

Mme. de Villars
Beluze, 1847

"Delicate pink, spotted." [Mz55–56/38] "Beautiful pink." [Ÿ]

Mme. Édouard Ory
syn. 'Monsieur Édouard Ory'
Robert, 1854

"Flowers quite full, globular, from 6 to 8 cm [ca. 2½–3 in], bright carmine pink, in 1's to 5's at the tips of the canes." [l'H55/52] "Medium-sized, full, bright carminy pink, very remontant." [Gf56] "Carmine-red, of medium size, full; one of the best in the class, which is not saying much for the class." [EL] "'Mme. Édouard Ory', with its pink-shaded white flowers, is one of the best of this sort; the bush is pretty vigorous, and its blossoms, of a beautiful carmine pink, are large, full, and beautifully shaped." [R-H63/294] "Reddish-crimson, globular, very large, and full, habit free and good; one of the best and most constant in the autumn." [JC] "This magnificent rose is of the first order because of its scent as well as for its abundant manner of blooming, and should be grown especially for the splendid bud, just the thing for bouquets. The blossom is of exemplary form." [S] "Vigorous bush; canes big and upright; bark glandulose, with numerous unequal, fine, sharp thorns. Foliage plentiful, somber green, slightly

Mme. Édouard Ory *continued*

puffy, composed of 5–7 oval leaflets, rounded at each end; petiole slender, the same color as the leaves. Blossoms 7–8 cm [ca. 3 in], quite full, globular, solitary or sometimes in 2's or 3's; color, a beautiful pink, more intense at the center; outer petals large, concave; central petals more interfolded and muddled; flower-stalk short, thick, covered with small, fine, very numerous bristles, rather like those of the 'Common Moss'. Ovary elongate, grading insensibly into the stalk, wide in the upper portion; sepals foliaceous. The blossoms of this variety are notable and very elegant in their fragrance; they bloom somewhat in the midst of the leaves; very beautiful bud. This fairly hardy rose can stand up to Parisian Winters." [JF] "Plant of premier merit." [R&M62]

Mme. Landeau

Moreau-Robert, 1873

"Light red, striped, medium size, full, tall." [Sn] "Very vigorous growth, open; blossom medium-sized, full; color, light red, spotted white." [S] "Red, medium size, full; not valuable." [EL]

Mme. Legrand

Fontaine, 1863

"Large, very full, bright carminy pink." [M-R65] "Rose-red, large, full, tall." [Sn] Sibling rose to 'Deuil de Paul Fontaine' (MR).

Mme. Louis Lévêque

Lévêque, 1898

"Delicate flesh." [Ÿ] "Flower flesh colour, deeper centre, well mossed, good foliage, free. Growth vigorous." [GeH] "Salmon pink, large, full, moderate height." [Sn] Not to be confused with the 1873 HP of the same name.

Mme. Moreau

Moreau-Robert, 1872

"Fine vermilion red, veined with white; very large." [CA88] "Red, large, full." [EL] "Bright rose, veined and shaded with red, flowers large, full, and expanded, scent of the Old Moss, distinct and good." [JC] "Carmine-purple, striped white, large, full. Growth vigorous." [GeH] "Light orange red, striped white, large, full, very fragrant, tall." [Sn] "Very vigorous growth; flower very large, very full; color, vermilion red, lined with white; good variety." [S]

Mme. Platz

Moreau-Robert, 1864

"7–9 cm [ca. 3–3½ in], full, flat, imbricated, very bright pink passing to delicate pink, reblooms very freely." [M-R65] "Vigorous growth; blossom medium-sized, full, flat; very fragrant; bright pink passing to delicate pink." [S]

Mme. William Paul

syn. 'Mrs. William Paul'

Moreau-Robert, 1869

"Bright rose, large and full, finely formed and cupped; a good free blooming rose." [JC] "Vigorous growth, opening well; floriferous; blossom large, full, globular; color, light red or bright pink." [S] "Light red, medium size, full, tall." [Sn] Commemorating the wife of the well-known British rosarian and author, our P.

Monsieur Édouard Ory Listed as 'Mme. Édouard Ory' (MR).

Mousseline

trans. 'Muslin'

Moreau-Robert, 1881

From a parent-group including 'Comtesse de Murinais' (M), 'Quatre Saisons Blanc Mousseux' (MR), and two unintroduced seedlings (see 'Blanche Moreau', above).

"Blush white." [Ÿ] "Flower white, tinted when first opened. Growth vigorous." [GeH] "Whitish pink, medium size, full, tall." [Sn] "Extra fine; large, very full and delightfully fragrant; color pure white, sometimes delicately shaded with rosy blush, elegantly mossed and very beautiful. A continuous bloomer." [CA90] "Very vigorous growth; canes upright and robust, clothed with very fine thorns—nearly moss; flower large, full, opening well; color white, lightly blushing when opening, fading to pure white; this beautiful variety is a veritable *Quatre Saisons*, always in bloom." [S] 'Mousseline' and 'Alfred de Dalmas', though frequently listed as synonyms by many modern authors and catalog-writers, were two distinct cultivars. The clearest distinguishing differences would seem to be: (1) *Color.* 'Mousseline' is blush-white fading to white; 'Alfred de Dalmas' is consistently cited as having a pink center with blush-white edges; (2) *Blossom Quality.* The blossom of 'Mousseline' was considered "beautiful" in whatever degree; that of 'Alfred de Dalmas' was not called "beautiful" or anything of the sort, and indeed was called "of poor quality" by one observer; (3) *Clusters.* For 'Mousseline', no habit of blooming in clusters is ever mentioned; for 'Alfred de Dalmas', cluster-blooming is frequently mentioned; (4) *Thorns.* The thorns of 'Mousseline' are "fine"; those of 'Alfred de Dalmas' are "strong and numerous," and the plant is "very thorny" (aside from one perhaps ambiguous comment from another observer about "nearly imperceptible thorns"); (5) *Size of Blossom.* The flower of 'Mousseline' is described as "large" in the old days, then appearing "medium" to modern eyes; that of 'Alfred de Dalmas' is described as "small" or "medium" both in the old days and in more modern times. All things considered, then, it should not be overly difficult to sort out the two cultivars when all these indicia are present.

Mrs. William Paul Listed as 'Mme. William Paul' (MR).

Oscar Leclerc

Robert, 1853

"Red tinged with violet." [EL] "Blossom medium-sized, full; deep red, spotted white; foliage deep green, touched with hints of yellow." [S] "Five to six centimeters [ca. 2–2¼ in], full, deep pink with some lilac, spotted and splotched with white, canes strong and upright, foliage well spotted with yellowish-white flecks." [M-L4/323]

Perpetual Red Moss Listed as 'Perpétuelle Mauget' (MR).

Perpetual White Moss Listed as 'Quatre Saisons Blanc Mousseux' (MR).

[Perpétuelle Mauget]

syn. 'Perpetual Red Moss'

Mauget, 1844

"Medium-sized, full, bright pink." [BJ53] "Flowers bright rose, of medium size, full; form, cupped; growth, moderate. A beautiful Rose." [P] "Vigorous growth; blossom medium-sized, full, flat; blooms without interruption until Winter begins; color, bright pink, center crimson." [S] "Foliage very strong, calycinate sepals as developed as those of the Centifolia; flower large, full, very fragrant, delicate pink. Raised in 1841." [dH44/204] "I think it likely that ['Perpétuelle Mauget'], which is the handsomest of all, was raised from the Crimson Perpetual [*probably meaning 'Rose du Roi' (DP)*]." [P] "One of the loveliest roses in existence, but one of the most difficult to cultivate. It is of the softest rose-color, large, full, and finely shaped. The portrait of it in the *Rose Garden* [*by William Paul*] is true in every respect." [MH50/514]

"This long dreamed of, and wished for rose, has at last made its appearance; the wood appears of a very delicate growth, and quite short; how far it is to meet our expectations, remains yet to be ascertained; the French extol it very highly. My correspondent has sent me a few plants, one only of which appears to be alive." [Bu] "Of large size, expanded form, deep rose color, and full double. This desideratum of its class, which is said to bloom the whole summer, was originated in France by Mr. Mauget. The price there is still about $3, which may serve to indicate its estimation. The plants imported for the first [time] in 1844, being very small, I have not yet been able to decide on its merits from my own observations; and we must rely for the present on the great favor with which it has been greeted in France. There is one happy circumstance in our favor as regards Roses of the perpetual character, which is, that our powerful [American] sun is fully adequate to develope any such characteristic, and even to a greater degree than in France." [WRP]

"This pretty triumph, raised in 1841 by Monsieur Mauget, Orléans horticulturist, is to be recommended by the perfect form of the blossom, the bright color of the petals, and the happy arrangement of these lattermost in the calyx; foliage a delicate green, leaflets of medium size, wood vigorous, canes very floriferous . . . This Rose is as hardy as the old Moss; it is a mistake to suppose the contrary." [dH44/227] "Recently, we have had the opportunity to see at the homes of several fanciers in the north and west of France some strong specimens of the Perpetual Moss Rose . . . It must be stated that this rose grows little; we could indeed say that it nearly spoils a collection when, grown as it has been up till now, one would see on the Briar some thick canes, stocky, crowned with numerous buds— of which only one or two open more or less well. It doesn't have the elegance of our Common Moss, being without such a graceful habit—that sort of attitude that I could call *insouciant,* a carefree elegance, a majestic 'who cares?' which is as pleasing in a rose as it is in a beautiful woman. I think I see embarrassment in this Mossy Perpetual—I would nearly say 'boredom.' It doesn't grow, it doesn't die, it's as if it had the rickets; you've got to bud ten specimens to get one out of it. We have made every effort to find a way to grow this Rose which comports with its nature, and a mode of propagation which will finally allow us to enjoy Moss Roses in the Fall. We believe we have found it out, and are at least a *little* sure that we have a solution to the problem. Instead of budding the growing 'eye' on the young canes of the Briar . . . in a frame or greenhouse in the Spring, it is necessary to graft a *dormant* eye around the beginning of the Fall—and not on one of the young growths of the Briar, but *rather on its* [mature] *stem.*" [dH46/181–182]

"This rose is the first example of a natural cross between the Mosses and the [Damask] Perpetuals. The announcement of a reblooming Moss Rose made a sensation in the horticultural world. The Moss Rose is so beautiful that just the idea of enjoying it all Summer long made everybody want one. Soon, however, it lost its charm.

Instead of vigorous growth, abundant bloom, thick foliage, and mossy-looking canes, it had weakly shoots, a few puny blossoms, feeble and yellowish foliage, with rickety canes having pretty sparse moss—characteristics you'll still find in this rose when it is planted in poor, hot soil, and when nobody makes the effort to cut back the growths and eliminate the Spring bloom, essential to do it you want to enjoy a good Fall bloom. Whatever the case, however much this Rose has to offer in the perfect form of its flowers, the brilliant coloration of its petals and their attractive arrangement in the calyx, whatever the merit of its beautiful delicate green foliage, the size of its leaflets, the number of buds which develop on each cane—be all this as it may, this Rose is less beautiful than the 'Common Moss' of the springtime. The blossom is flatter, the growth more spindly, the moss less pronounced; the shoots, generally stunted, don't have the grace of out ordinary Moss Roses when they spread before our eyes their floral magnificence in May or June . . . Its bright pink color, nuanced with purple, so beautiful here [*in an accompanying illustration*], disappears sometimes, making the rose a delicate pink . . . The diameter of the blossom, which here is 10 centimeters [ca. 4 in], is sometimes not so large as that. The buds, which seem enormous, aren't exaggerated at all; but through perspective, the moss which envelops them stands out more on paper than indeed on the plant. It is usually in the Fall that the rose is the most vigorous. Its culture, it must be admitted, has till now been fairly difficult—you've got to bud ten stocks to get just one success. We have finally found the solution to the problem. Instead of budding a growing eye on young canes of the Briar . . . it is necessary to bud a *dormant eye* around the beginning of the Fall, and not on the young canes of the Briar, but indeed on the trunk. Own-root, this Rose is never any good." [PIB] Monsieur Mauget of Orléans, France, humble and successful breeder of roses from circa 1825–1849.

Pompon Perpétuel
trans. "Perpetual Pompon"
Vibert, 1849

"Small, full, delicate pink." [BJ58] "4–5 cm [ca. 1½–2 in], full, crimson pink, in a rosette, spotted." [R&M62] Has been called a Centifolia and a Damask Perpetual, but was introduced as a Mossy Remontant.

Quatre Saisons Blanc Mousseux
syn. 'Perpetual White Moss'; trans., "Mossy White *Quatre-Saisons*"
["Quatre Saisons" being another name for Damask Perpetuals]
Laffay, 1835
Said to be a sport from 'Bifera' (DP).

"Full, white." [BJ40] "White, sometimes striped with crimson, blooming in clusters and very mossy." [War] "White, buds handsome and well mossed, flowers good size and tolerably double, blooming in clusters." [JC] "Flowers white, of medium size, double; form, expanded, blooming in large trusses, very mossy, but produced sparingly in the autumn." [P] "A sport from White Damask [*guesses Ellwanger*]. White, tinged with flesh, flowers in clusters, medium size, semi-double or double, coarse form; but little mossed, unattractive either in bud or flower; the name is a deception, as it very rarely blooms in the autumn. Greatly inferior to 'White Bath' (M), and also 'Comtesse de Murinais' (M)." [EL] "*Shrub,* vigorous, armed with thorns. *Thorns,* fine, of a violet-purple. *Leaves,* composed of five sessile leaflets. *Leaflets,* oval, of a bright green on the upper surface, rather glaucous on the under. *Calyx,* entirely covered with branching bristles, long and

Quatre Saisons Blanc Mousseux *continued*

very close, producing a more agreeable effect than any other Moss rose. *Flowers,* very full, white; the petals elegantly disposed." [Go] "Still an excellent variety; its white flowers, in orderly clusters, make it perhaps the most interesting of the group." [R-H63/294]

Raphael

Robert, 1856

"Flesh-color, flowering in corymbs, large, full." [FP] "7–9 cm [ca. 3–3½ in], full, delicate flesh pink, globular, corymbs of 12–20 flowers." [R&M62] "Blossom full, flesh pink; very mossy." [S] Raphael, alias Raffaello Santi, Italian artist, lived 1483–1520, died of "overindulgence."

René d'Anjou

Robert, 1853

"Delicate pink." [Ÿ] "Deep pink, small, full, average height." [Sn] "Flower pink, medium-sized, a pretty good variety." [JDR56/48] "Flower soft pink, well mossed. Growth vigorous." [GeH] "Six to seven centimeters [ca. 2⅕ in], double, deep pink passing to delicate pink, globular, canes straight and vigorous, usually bearing only one blossom, ovary covered with numerous small stickers terminating in a light moss. Very curious rose, freely remontant." [M-L4/323] "Bush moderately vigorous; flowers medium-sized, full, bright pink. Good variety, freely re-blooming." [I'H56/252] *Singer* seems to have mixed up his notes: "Vigorous growth; very beautiful blossom, large, full, of irreproachable form; color, carmine shaded with scarlet." [S] René I of Anjou, King of Naples, enlightened patron of the Arts, lived 1409–1480.

Salet

syn. 'Melchior Salet'

Lacharme, 1854

"Beautiful pink." [Mz55–56/38] "Large, full, bright pink, passing to light pink." [Gf56] "Remontant; flower large, full, bright pink fading to light pink along the edge." [I'H55/34] "Medium-sized, full, globular, bright pink, lighter at the edge, corymbiferous." [R&M62] "Long canes, medium-sized flesh-pink blossom." [JDR55/10] "Light rose, large and full; also pretty in bud. A free blooming, excellent rose." [CA88] "Vigorous and hardy … the full and large blossoms are an irreproachable carmine pink." [R-H63/294] "Light rose, medium size, flat form, fairly good buds, very free. The best in the class, after 'Soupert & Notting'." [EL] "A recurrent bloomer. Blooms are bright rose, edged with blush-pink. Vigorous grower." [C-Ps26] "Plant with long canes; blossom medium-sized, full, very well formed; color, bright pink above, paler beneath; very remontant variety, scent of musk, floriferous, especially in the Fall." [S]

Sophie de Marsilly

Robert & Moreau, 1863

"5–7 cm [ca. 2–2½ in], full, flat, bright pink spotted with white." [M-R65] "Pink, striped white, medium size, full, medium scent, tall." [Sn] "Vigorous growth." [S] Though often met with as a regular Moss, introduced as a Mossy Remontant.

Soupert et Notting

syn. 'Soupert & Notting'

Pernet père, 1874

"Very large, full, beautiful plump form, bright pink, very fragrant, reblooming, one of the most interesting of the series." [BJ77] "Fine bright rose, of perfect form, very large and full, remarkably sweet; the finest of all the *Perpetual Moss.*" [JC] "Rose-red, large, very full, medium scent, medium height." [Sn] "Bright rose, large, very full, globular, fragrant. Growth dwarf, floriferous." [GeH] "Dwarf growth, floriferous; blossom large, very full, globular, Centifolia scent; color, bright pink, shaded crimson." [S] "Rose color, very large, very full, globular form, highly scented, not very mossy, a true ever-blooming rose, five leaflets only. The flowers are sometimes malformed, but they are infinitely superior to all others of the same class." [EL] Jean Soupert (1834–1910) and Pierre Notting (1825–1896) of Luxembourg, important rose breeders and nurserymen; see our notes on them in *The Old Rose Advisor,* pp. 136 and 145.

Souvenir de Pierre Vibert

trans. "In Memory of [Jean-]Pierre Vibert"

Moreau-Robert, 1867

"Red, nuanced." [Ÿ] "Blossom very large, full; color, very deep red, shaded with crimson and bishop's violet." [S] "Deep red, large, full, tall." [Sn] Jean-Pierre Vibert, 1777–1866, a great rosarian, a great man; see our notes on him in *The Old Rose Advisor,* pp. 18–21, to which further research can add (1) that he served in Napoléon's Italian campaign as a sergeant in the elite corps of *les Voltigeurs,* and was severely wounded in the battle for Naples; and (2) that at some point in the mid or late 1820s, he attempted to *donate* to the French *Jardin des Plantes* in Paris a large collection of rose cultivars for study purposes—which generous offer was refused because the *Jardin* declared itself only interested in pure species. This of *les Voltigeurs* tells us something about Vibert's physical appearance, and perhaps gives us some insights into his brave and forward personality as well. As found by our matchless colleague Georges Massiot in *Les Soldats du 1er Empire* (by Liliane & Fred Funcken), *les Voltigeurs* were chosen from those soldiers who were short (less than 1.6 m or ca. 5 feet) and of great agility. They were deployed at the center of the companies of fusiliers, and were charged with the responsibility of harrying the enemy by spreading out before the oncoming masses and firing at will to break their ranks. Vibert maintained these tactics throughout his life in the several controversies in which he participated. We still have not found Vibert's place of burial! Future reader, you who find his tomb, tenderly lay a rose upon it on behalf of the present author, for, indeed, "we should wreathe his tomb with our homage and our respect." [V6] For a unique and previously unknown portrait of Jean-Pierre Vibert, which we were fortunate enough to discover in the last moments of our researches, see the frontispiece.

Validé

Robert & Moreau, 1857

"Light pink." [JDR57/37] "Flower bright pink, shaded carmine." [S] "6–8 cm [ca. 2½–3 in], full, flat, in a rosette, bright carminy pink, very well formed." [R&M62] Validé, possibly meaning "Valideh," title of the mother of the Sultan-to-be.

Venus

Welter, 1904

From 'Mme. Moreau' (MR) × 'Deuil de Paul Fontaine' (MR).

"Red, large, very full, average height." [Sn] "Very large, very full blossom, beautiful fiery red, meritorious plant which adds to the group and is expected to come to something." [JR31/177] Venus, goddess of Love or something like.

CHAPTER NINE

Albas

"The most beautiful of European roses, while being at the same time the most vigorous and the largest. Under cultivation, it has produced a number of varieties—non-remontant, yes, but admirable in form and color." [JF] "The white rose of the gardens has been cultivated from time immemorial. Although the original single white or blush has seldom been seen in cultivation, yet the double is very frequent, keeping ward at the door of the cottage, or towering by the window casements of our oldest homesteads. It is often called the white climbing rose." [Bu] "Introduced to the English gardens in 1597. In some of the old farm and cottage gardens of Hertfordshire and Essex ... a semi-double variety is frequent; this is but a slight remove from the single flowering original species, and grows luxuriantly without culture in any neglected corner ... The roses of this division may be easily distinguished by their green shoots, leaves of a glaucous green, looking as if they were covered with a grayish impalpable powder, and flowers generally of the most delicate colors, graduating from pure white to a bright but delicate pink." [WRP] "All of these [Albas] are so pure in color that some might think them porcelain." [JR9/126] "Probably the most fragrant of all." [NRS28/33] "It makes a very vigorous shrub of impressive stature. Its flowers are pretty large, semi-double or indeed sometimes double on the same specimen. They may be used to advantage to make hedges." [JF] "Its heavily thorned stems, growing to 3 or 4 feet high [ca. 1–1.3 m], and the epidermis which covers them, show all the way to the tips of the canes a whitish tint, a pale green, which hints at the color of the blossoms to be produced. This vigorous Rose comes in two varieties [in 1791]: one gives flowers which only have two or three rows of petals; the blossoms of the other are very double, well spread out, to good effect. Both of these two waft a sweet, slightly musky, scent." [Fr]

"Rose with smooth egg-shaped seed-buds and hispid peduncles: flowers white: leaflets ovate and pointed, with serrated margins, slightly downy on the under side: stem between erect and spreading, nearly smooth on the upper part, but furnished with strong spines towards the base. This Rose is a native of Britain, and considered as the first on the list of Garden Roses removed from the common hedge or Dog Rose [*Rosa canina*], its charm-

ing wild original. The flowers are very fugitive, so soon falling off that a specimen in fine bloom is not easily procured. It is the source of several fine varieties, and flowers during the summer months, but is in very few collections." [A] "*Shrub* vigorous, forming a tall bush. *Shoots* and *canes* smooth, ordinarily green and glaucous, sometimes yellowish, often reddish on the sunny side; armed with prickles which are sparse, uneven, hooked or straight, usually strong, with or without bristles, sometimes unarmed. *Leaves* glaucous, composed of 5 to 7 leaflets. *Petiole* usually villose or glandulose, armed beneath with prickles which are nearly always hooked. *Stipules* ordinarily narrow, flat, and fringed with glands. *Leaflets* rounded, oval or ovoid, obtuse or acute, glabrous above, pale and usually villose or pubescent beneath. *Serration* usually simple, sometimes double, hirsutulose or lanate, rarely glandulose. *Bracts* lanceolate, straight, nearly always concave, glaucous, lanate or glabrous. *Peduncle* hispid-glandulose above the bracts, glabrous beneath. In several varieties, it is glabrous top to bottom, in several others it is quite hispid. *Ovary* glaucous, globular, digitate, turbinate, oval, oblong, or fusiform; hispid, glandulose, or glabrous. *Sepals* long, reflexed, glabrous or bristling with glandular hairs; all, or more often 2 or 3, are pinnatifid and caducous. *Flower* white, flesh, or pink, usually fragrant. *Disk* thick. *Petals* concave. *Styles* free. *Fruit* red, globular, oval, oblong, or fusiform. I [Prévost] have thought it necessary to divide the varieties of this species into two divisions [(1) those like the typical form of the species and (2) those seemingly of hybrid origin], each division itself being subdivided into three sections by color of the flower [white, flesh, pink]. It would doubtless be better to characterize these sections by the form of the ovary, its smoothness or glandulation, the armor of its peduncles, etc. However, over and above the fact that these characteristics are very variable, it would be unhelpful to separate some varieties which the same look renders inseparable." [Pf] "The original stock is spineless; but many of its progeny, in consequence, probably, of hybridization, have spines in greater or less number. The upper surface of the leaves has a glaucous or whitish tinge, and the shoots are of a clear green." [FP]

"One needs to be careful about confusing this sort with the varieties of the Centifolia or others which are white. The White Rose, which one commonly sees in the mountains of Europe, produces a shrub which grows from six to fifteen or eighteen feet high [ca. 2–6 m]; canes upright, strong, numerous, armed with thorns; leaves composed of seven or more often five glabrous, oval leaflets of a dark green above and pale beneath. Blossoms often come in threes at the ends of the small canes; they bloom in June, are slightly flesh-colored when they begin to open, then they become quite white; they have a pleasant scent." [AC] "The principal characters distinguishing the White Roses from other series are the ovate, simply dentate leaflets, pubescent below, and the abruptly rounded bases of the receptacles." [T&R] "I [Vibert] would like to remark at this point that the roses of this group have developed some plusses which we don't always find to such a pronounced degree in the other sorts. Their wood, their habit, their foliage, and the form and arrangement of their thorns makes them easy to distinguish, even in the absence of their flowers. This ease with which they are distinguished adds much to the merit of their blossoms, which further have the advantage of a great variety of forms; their colors, which today extend from white to light purple, don't show the maddening variations of the Provins group. I have found only Albas in crops deriving from individuals belonging to the Alba group; I don't think they can be pollinated by the Provinses except after several successive crosses." [V2] "This type of rose is distinguished from the others principally by the following characteristics: stem smooth and greenish, armed with occasional thin, slightly recurved, thorns; leaflets oval, to the number of five or seven, simply dentate, blackish green and purpled above and whitish beneath; petioles hirsutulous and with prickles; flowers in a corymb at the tips of the canes, borne on peduncles covered with glandular bristles; sepal-tube ovoid, rounded at the base, resembling a reversed thimble; corolla large, composed of several rows of petals of a matte white or pink, depending upon the variety. Opening, they have some flesh color, and become white. The Type of this species is evidently the White Hedge Rose (*alba flore simplici*). It is said that a German doctor named George Heller discovered it in the Hessian Rhineland. Rössig describes it under the name 'alba humilis'. Be that as it may, today it is very common in our countryside. [JDR54/30]

"Desvaux asserts that the single white *R. alba* has never been seen in the wild. However, Poiret says that it is found in Southern Europe, and Bastard records it from hilly places in the high Poitou [France], near Angers and Saumur, and finally we have already said that it is to be found in the Rhineland region of Hesse." [T&R] "Not indigenous to France, but pretty common in southern Germany, and above all in Austria and around Würtzburg." [JF] "The rose *Alba flore simplici* or White Hedge Rose ... in which the blossoms are pure white, originated in central Europe, principally in Germany, from which it was brought into cultivation in 1597.

There also exists another variety, which grows wild in Bavaria and Saxony which was introduced at the same time under the name *Alba humilis* or *Rosier Blanc Rampant,* but it was forgotten because of its tendency to spread through the ground." [JR9/126] "Its fruit is smooth, its peduncle hispid, stems and petioles armed with thorns; its blossom is never perfectly double. It has given us several pretty varieties. Some are simply semi-double; others flesh-colored; some have a slightly pink heart; and, last of all, one has low canes." [AbR]

"The story of the Alba is lost in the mists of time ... The Alba is perhaps in the *Hortus sanit[at]us*—I don't have this incunabulum, so I can't give you its date—but I find a picture of it in old Besler (1612) and a bunch of other *Hortus*. Le Bouc says Tragus mentions it, as do Ma[t]thiole and Gesner—and I wonder who indeed *doesn't* have it, as Perès the botanist lets fall a word on its behalf. Gaspard Bauhin indeed, in his *Pinax*, says that Pliny talks about it. As to the Moderns, recent though they be, they're no clearer. Linné keeps from compromising himself by assuring us that it grows in Europe (*in Europa*). Pretty vague! —say Déséglise, Gemelin [*sic; Gmelin meant, perhaps?*], DeCandolle, Gilibert, Cariot, Fourreau, Willdenow, Lindley, Trattinck, etc., etc., who don't agree with each other very well when it comes to saying where the Alba *does* come from. All in all, it seems that this old sort is naturalized particularly in hedges and enclosures, and planted in all the cottage gardens. I have forgotten who contributed the thought that the Alba was a hybrid of *Rosa canina* (*églantier*) and one of the Gallicas. It is certain that the Hill Rose (*R. collina* Jacquin), on which modern rose-writers spill a lot of ink, has very numerous things in common with this old rose." [JR26/35] "Recognizable [under the name 'Campanian Rose'] ... from its light green and bluish foliage. Had a reputation with the Romans for its perfume. Probably resulted from a cross between the common Briar [*Rosa canina*] and the *Rose of Paestum* [*Rosa ×damascena* or Damask Perpetual variety]." [ExRé] "We have in the Alba class several varieties hybridized with the Briar." [V2]

"At the time of Dupont [ca. 1790–1815], only about ten Albas were known. Monsieur Descemet didn't add more than four." [V2] "[Around 1800], the Alba roses, with so delicate a coloration, accounted for about twelve varieties." [Gx] "Around 1820, they enthusiastically grew [about fourteen] varieties of Alba. In 1824, Monsieur Vibert had more than seventy varieties of Alba." [JDR54/30] "Today [1826], I [Vibert] know and grow more than sixty varieties, all of them interesting." [V2] "But since that era [ca. 1824], the remontants have prevailed, and the Albas, like the Centifolias, Gallicas, and Damasks, have been neglected. Today [1854], a person can only find a few sorts of Albas, preserved by chance, due to their hardiness, in some old town-houses." [JDR54/30]

"The culture of the Alba is just like that of the Centifolia, Gallica, and Damask. These sorts cross easily, and nearly effortlessly; it is, however, necessary to say that their flowers are only large and beautiful in proportion to the treatment they are given. All of them are very hardy, and multiply by runners, so one isn't put to the trouble of having to graft them. They are precious for ornamenting large gardens; grouped or singly in beds, they produce a marvelous effect all Spring." [JDR54/31] "This very vigorous shrub is appropriate for grafting." [BJ30] "Grafts don't take very easily on its branches; but, once one does, it does very well and lives a long time." [JDR54/31] "In pruning, they require to be treated in the same method as Gallic Roses; but budded plants, about two or three feet high [ca. 6 dm to 1 m], are great beauties; their beautiful soft white flowers are brought nearer the eye, contrasting agreeably on the foliage of the plant; they are all free growers, and require the knife to keep them thin and in proper bounds; they may in all other respects be treated as hardy roses." [Bu] "They always bloom abundantly and bear close pruning; in this respect they may be treated as recommended for the French [Gallica] Roses." [WRP]

"The old-fashioned White Rose should not certainly be forgotten, as it is associated with childhood. It is one of the three first Roses that opened their buds to the writer. Who can forget the old White Rose, as it was trained up the side of the house? We have seen a rose-bush, of this variety, trained fifteen feet high [ca. 5 m]." [BBF] "The full variety is much cultivated, and as it grows some meters high, it is frequently used to cover walls and frameworks. I must say that, used in this way, it leaves nothing to be desired, particularly because of its longevity and duration." [JR8/60–61]

Rosa ×alba

"Everybody knows and [*word omitted in original; probably to the effect of "loves"*] this European shrub and its milk-white blossoms." [BJ09] "From the mountains of Europe." [BJ24] "From the mid-lands of France. 8–10 feet tall [ca. 2.6–3.3 m], not very nicely shaped; thorns rare; leaflets a green both glaucous and somber, simply and deeply dentate; sepals reflexed; calyx-tube nude, obovate; peduncles often hispid." [BJ30] "Shrub of 6 to 7 feet [ca. 2–2.3 m]; stems upright, strong, with strong thorns having broad bases, as have the petioles; peduncles with pedicellate glands; leaves of 5 oval leaflets of a dark green, or glaucous-looking; flowers slightly flesh-colored when they're just opening, then very white, but with a scent that is not very pleasant." [BJ17]

"This species is distinguished by its peduncles bristling with small, fine prickles, as do the calyxes, and indeed very often the ovaries; by its pubescent petioles ... Its stems are three to four feet high [ca. 1–1.3 m], bearing numerous canes, which branch, and are clothed with thorns, stipulate alternate leaves composed of five to seven oval leaflets, sometimes a little rounded, glabrous on both sides, green and dark above, slightly whitish beneath, borne on pubescent petioles; rachis also pubescent, bearing several very skimpy small prickles. The flowers are solitary or nearly fasciculate, lateral and terminal, borne on simple peduncles which are long, cylindrical, and bestrewn with prickles which are fine, straight, unequal, and very numerous, much more rare and indeed almost lacking on the ovaries; finer and more numerous on the calyxes, where they are only rough, glandulose bristles. The ovary is oval, and more or less elongate; the

calyx divisions are hispid and a little pinnatifid. The corolla is white, large, and has a not-very-agreeable scent; the petals are notched into a heart at their tip. These blossoms double easily." [Lam]

"This rose, commonly found on the elevated mountains of Europe, is a shrub of vigorous growth, reaching from six and seven feet [ca. 2 and 2.3 m] up to twelve and indeed sometimes fifteen feet [ca. 4 and indeed sometimes 5 m]. Its leaves are composed of seven or more often five leaflets which are oval, glabrous, a green rather darker above, pale beneath, and borne on pubescent petioles and bearing prickles. Its flowers, which arise in June, are placed at the tip of small branches often in threes, on nearly hispid peduncles; they are slightly flesh-colored when they begin to open, then they become very white; their diameter is in excess of two inches [ca. 5 cm]; their scent is disagreeable; they hardly last at all. Be that as it may, from time out of mind the White Rose has been grown in our gardens. Here's why: All terrain suits it; it is effective in beds; furthermore, it is—by way of the vigor of its growth—very appropriate to serve as a stock on which to graft other sorts; last of all, it offers a great number of varieties with semi-double and double blossoms—pretty interesting, as we shall see." [CM]

Horticultural Varieties

À Feuilles de Chanvre Listed as 'Cymbaefolia' (A).

À Feuilles de Pêcher
syn. 'Persicifolia'; trans., "Having Leaves Like Those of the Peach-Tree"
Pelletier, pre-1817
"Vigorous bush; [leaf] pointed, regularly dentate; blossom medium-sized, full; color, white." [S] Possibly synonymous with 'Cymbaefolia' (A).

À Fleurs Doubles Listed as 'Plena' (A).

À Fleurs Roses Listed as 'Elisa' (A).

[Alba Bifera]
trans. "Double-Bearing Alba"
Augeul, 1843
"Blossom from 5 to 6 cm across [ca. 2–2¼ in], very full, well formed, beautiful lilac white. This variety may be found at Monsieur Augeul's on the Boulevard des Lices; it is all the more precious because we have nearly no other remontant Roses in this group." [dH44/429–430]

Alba Rosea Listed as 'Beauté Tendre' (A).

Alba Rubigens Listed as 'Lesser Maiden's Blush' (A).

Alice
Parmentier, ca. 1830
"Blossom medium-sized, full; color, white, shaded flesh color." [S]

Amélia
syn. 'Amélie'
Vibert, 1823
"Blossom large, semi-double, pink, odd due to its color." [BJ24]

Amélia *continued*

"Blossoms full, medium sized, pale pink." [AC] "Flower medium-sized, full; color, bright pink." [S] "Pink, medium size, full, moderate fragrance, tall." [Sn] "*Thorns* sparse, uneven, needle-like, falcate, intermixed with bristles. *Leaflets* arching, not pendant. *Serration* simple, pubescent, not glandulose. *Peduncle* hispid-glandulose above the bracts. *Ovary* ovoid, constricted at the neck, hispid-glandulose. *Sepals* foliaceous, can be considered *persistent* because nearly all of them can still be found on most of the fruits in December and January. *Flower* large, multiplex, light pink. *Fruit* large, oval." [Pf]

Amélie   Listed as 'Amélia' (A).

Anglaise   Listed as 'Lesser Maiden's Blush' (A).

Armide
Vibert, 1818

"Flesh white." [Y] "Blossoms very double, medium-sized, flesh with pale edges." [AC] "Light pink, medium size, full, medium scent, tall." [Sn] "*Leaflets* with very obvious veining. *Serration* acute. *Peduncle* hispid-glandulose above the bracts. *Ovary* digitate-turbinate, longer than broad, hispid-glandulose. *Flower* medium-sized, nearly full, bright flesh with pale edges." [Pf] Armide, alias Armida, sorceress and seductress of the crusader Rinaldo in Tasso's epic *Jerusalem Delivered*.

[Arva Leany]
Geschwind/Lambert, 1911

"Cream with red." [EU] "Vigorous bush, upright, semi-climbing; big flower, full, fragrant; cream yellow with a delicate carmine pink tint. Very floriferous." [JR36/42]

Astrée
trans. "Starry"
Breeder unknown, pre-1842

"Very large, double, pink." [V8] "Very large, bright pink." [WRP] "A new [*in 1846*], large, and fine French variety, of a roseate hue." [WRP] "Flowers pink, changing to delicate lilac blush after opening, very large and very double; form, globular. Habit, branching; growth, moderate." [P] Astrée, either "starry" or Astraea, goddess of Equity and Innocence who left Earth, no doubt for lack of partisans.

Aureata   Listed as 'Lesser Maiden's Blush' (A).

Aurora   Listed as 'Belle Aurore' (A).

Aurore   Listed as 'Belle Aurore' (A).

Beauté Tendre
syns. 'Alba Rosea', 'Enfant de France', 'Regia'; trans., "Delicate
   Beauty"
Breeder unknown, pre-1813

"Pale rose." [Cal] "Delicate pink." [V9] "Blossoms . . . very large and very beautiful, beautiful white with a whisper of pink." [J-A/566] "*Flower* medium-sized, full, regular, flesh, with nearly white edges. This rose differs from ['Great Maiden's Blush'] in its more glaucous leaflets, which are rounder and more obtuse, and in its shorter ovary (its diameter is to its height as 5 is to 4)." [Pf]

Bella Donna   Listed as 'Great Maiden's Blush' (A).

Bella Donna Flore Minore   Listed as 'Lesser Maiden's Blush' (A).

Belle Amour
trans. "Beautiful Love"
Breeder unknown, date uncertain

"Light orange-pink, medium size, full, very fragrant, tall." [Sn, adding that it was found in a cloister]

Belle Aurore
syns. 'Aurora', 'Aurore', 'Belle Aurore Poniatowska', 'Ex Albo Rosea',
   'Purpurascens', 'Royale Aurore'; trans., "Beautiful Aurora"
Holland, pre-1799

"Flowers medium-sized, regular, blushing white suffused yellow." [BJ17] "Light lilac-pink." [Y] "Tinted purplish, touched with yellow." [JDR54/31] "Always liked due to its well-formed medium-sized flowers, washed orange-pink within." [J-A/566] "The blossoms are two and a half inches across [ca. 6.5 cm], are nearly double, regular, in which the petals are tinted that purplish color which one sees at sunrise, and which has something of yellow in it. This nuance is so perfect, says Monsieur de Pronville, that it justifies the name 'Aurore' given the rose." [CM] "Blossoms medium-sized, semi-double, not very numerous, regular, of a white tending towards yellow; leaves glaucous." [No26] "Flowers not very numerous, semi-double, lightly purplish; leaves glaucous." [dP] "Flesh white, superb form, but the flowers are very rare, which is why nearly no one grows it. Its flowers are the most abundant when it is only pruned after bloom." [J-As/66] "Bush with branches which are angular at the base; blossom medium-sized, very full, pale pink, edged very pale lilac flesh." [S]

"This sort can't fail to please lovers of delicate colors who also admire the scent of roses. The nearly glabrous wood resembles that of 'Sans Épine de la Chine' [Bslt]. The small, oval, finely-cut or dentate leaves, quite remote from their petiole, fold back on themselves; they are a glaucous green. The very elongated calyx is overspread with brown prickles, as is its stalk. The bud is pointed. The blossom, three inches across [ca. 8 cm], is not very double; but its great freshness is well worthy of the beautiful name given it. It could be set alongside 'Unique Carnée' [C] because of the similarity of their virtues; but, in my opinion, this one gets the nod due to the elegance of its perfume." [C-T] "This one is a hybrid between the Albas and the *Nymphes* [*i.e.,* either 'Great Maiden's Blush' or 'Lesser Maiden's Blush', or 'Belle Thérèse']. Its wood is that of the 'Tous-Mois' [DP], its leaves are those of the Albas; its buds—overtopped by the prolongations of the calyx, are tinted golden yellow before opening, like those of ['Great Maiden's Blush'], with which it has much in common. Once open, it is medium-sized; its petals are muddled, though thick and rounded. Their color is a white blended into pink, lighter along the edges, and more flesh at the center. The golden tint beneath is near the ovary. It merits the name *Regias varietas aureata*. Opens along with the *Nymphes*." [LeR]

"*Canes* thick, straight, tinted violet purple on the side exposed to the sun. *Leaflets* glaucous, slightly purplish beneath, when young. *Peduncle* usually glabrous beneath the bracts, hispid-glandulose above. *Ovary* oval-fusiform, hispid-glandulose. *Flower* large, multiplex, light delicate purple flesh. *Petals* large, thick." [Pf]

"Shrubby *bush* 0.6–0.9 m high [ca. 2–3 ft]; *branches* glabrous; *prickles* slightly recurved, closely set at the base of the canes, sparse towards the tips. *Leaflets* 5, suborbicular, green above, tomentose beneath; petioles curiously curved upwards, villose, prickly. *Flowers* many, subumbellate at the branch tips; peduncles and *receptacles* densely aciculate; *receptacles* fusiform, as is characteristic of *R. damascena*; *sepals* much longer than the bud, pinnatifid and much dilated at the tip, glandular outside, whitish-woolly within; *corolla* fairly large; *petals* 6–7-seriate, pink tending towards yellow; *styles* in many groups. One of the finest of all shrub roses, this is much sought out both for the fine form of the blossom and for its delicate color, which suggests a sunrise—whence the names 'Rose Aurore' and 'Rose Belle Aurore'. To these, we link the name of Aurore Poniatowska, an aspiring student of Redouté's. The plant demands a sheltered site, and gives fine blossoms when grafted on the wild Briar. Although listed for a long time in nursery catalogs, it is in comparatively few gardens. It was introduced into France from Holland at the end of the Eighteenth Century, and propagated by Dupont." [T&R] "It was also in the Descemet nurseries. It was described in the *Nouveau Duhamel*." [Gx]

"'Belle Aurore', which is my [*i.e.,* Vibert's] 'Ex Albo Rosea', is well known under these two names, and is Dutch in origin. What end is served to dedicate it—after it has been around for twenty-five years—to one Miss Poniatowski, especially when, in the Albas, we already have one by that name? The author [Redouté] lets us know that this Mademoiselle was his student, and that she showed good talent for drawing flowers. I am quite sure that she is likable and even pretty—moreover, that she was foreign—this was more than enough to motivate an act of gallantry or good-will. But why borrow from Holland to dedicate to a young person a rose probably older than she? Is it not, in some ways, paying debts with the money of others? Are we [in France] so impoverished these days that French growers are unable to supply one *new* rose to Monsieur Redouté for this gesture?" [V2]

Belle Aurore Poniatowska Listed as 'Belle Aurore' (A).

Belle de Ségur
trans. "Beauty from Ségur"
Lelieur/Vibert, pre-1826
"Flesh." [V9] "Flesh pink." [Y̆] "Medium-sized, full, flesh." [V8] "Flowers double, medium-sized, a pale flesh." [AC] "Nearly thornless; one of the best, with quite double flesh blossoms." [BJ30] "Light pink, medium size, full, tall." [Sn] "Blossom medium-sized, full, plump. Very vigorous variety, noticeable by way of its handsome foliage; color, flesh pink edged pale pink." [S] "*Shrub* nearly thornless. *Ovary* digitate, glabrous. *Flower* medium-sized, nearly full, symmetrical, pale flesh." [Pf] "Flowers soft rosy flesh, edges blush, beautiful, of medium size, full; form, cupped. Habit, erect; growth, vigorous; foliage, fine dark green." [P] We do not regard this as synonymous with 'Joséphine Beauharnais' (A).

Belle Elisa Listed as 'Elisa' (A).

Belle Fille Listed as 'Great Maiden's Blush' (A).

Belle Thérèse
syns. 'Cuisse de Nymphe à Ovaire Lisse', 'Cuisse de Nymphe Emué';
  trans., "Beautiful Theresa"
Dumont de Courset, 1802
"Bright pink." [God] "Bright flesh." [Y̆] "Medium-sized, double, pink." [V8] "Double, large, delicate pink." [BJ24] "Flowers double, medium-sized, flesh white." [AC] "Whitish pink, medium size, full, medium scent, tall." [Sn] "*Ovary* ovoid or digitate, oblong, glabrous. *Flower* medium-sized, bright even flesh." [Pf] "Flowers deep pink,

large and double; form, cupped. Habit, erect; growth, moderate. A free bloomer, and showy." [P] "Very beautiful blossom, very well formed; one of the best varieties of this sort; very vigorous plant; flower large, full, cupped; color, bright pink." [S] "Found in Descemet's nurseries, mentioned by Redouté . . . Prévost received it from Vibert under the name 'Belle Thérèse'." [Gx]

Blanc Ordinaire Listed as 'Plena' (A).

Blanche de Belgique
trans. "[The] White [One] from Belgium," or perhaps "Belgian Alba"
Breeder unknown, pre-1846
"Very large and double flowers of the purest white." [WRP] "Blossom medium-sized, nearly full, very floriferous; color, pure white." [S] "Flower white, very floriferous. Growth moderate." [GeH] "White, large, full, medium scent, tall." [Sn] "Flowers white, their centre tinted with sulphur, of medium size, full; form, compact. Habit, branching; growth, moderate; foliage, dark green." [P] Though WRP finds it an old variety ("with all the characters of this division"), we still find no substantiation for a frequently seen attribution of "Vibert, 1817."

Bleu Céleste Listed as 'Céleste' (A).

Blush Hip
syn. 'New Blush Hip', "new" not to be understood as implying that
  there was also an "Old Blush Hip," but rather something along
  the lines of: "Here's 'Blush Hip', and it's *new*."
Breeder unknown, pre-1846
"Blossom large, full; color, flesh pink." [S] "Flowers delicate blush, their centre flesh, of medium size, full; form, compact. Habit, branching; growth, vigorous. Forms a splendid Pole Rose. An abundant and early bloomer; the flowers exquisite when about half blown." [P]

Camille Bouland
syn. 'Camille Boulan'
Prévost, pre-1826
"Delicate pink." [V9] "Bright pink, globular." [WRP] "Flowers delicate rose, of medium size, very double; form, globular." [P] "Flower large." [S] "*Ovary* short, digitate, glabrous. *Flower* medium-sized, semi-globular, very multiplex, light even pink." [Pf]

Candide
Vibert, 1831
"Flesh." [V4] "Flowers white, tinged with fawn; form, compact." [P] "Blossom medium-sized, full, quite tightly-packed; color, white, shaded a deep dull orange." [S] The name is something of a pun, primarily being taken from the protagonist of Voltaire's novel, no doubt, but also meaning *candida*, that is, "shining white," singularly appropriate for an *Alba*.

Cannabina Listed as 'Cymbaefolia' (A).

Carné Listed as 'Great Maiden's Blush' (A).

Caroline d'Angleterre
syn. 'Sara'; trans., "Caroline of England"
Calvert, 1822
"Flowers full, small, and a pale pink." [AC] "*Canes* slender, diffuse, armed with *prickles* which are sparse, red, and aciculate. *Peduncles* hispid-glandulose above the bracts, glabrous beneath. *Ovary* oval, glabrous. *Flower* small, full, globular, regular, pale pink, becoming

Caroline d'Angleterre *continued*

nearly white." [Pf] Queen Caroline of England, lived 1768–1821; much-tried spouse of her cousin George IV, who barred her from his coronation.

Céleste

syns. 'Bleu Céleste', 'Céleste Blanche', 'Celestial', 'Celestis', 'Erubescens', 'Nova Coelestis', 'Nuancée de Bleu'; trans., "Celestial"
Dupont, pre-1810

"White." [Cal] "Flesh." [Ÿ] "Incarnate white." [WRP] "Medium-sized, double, white." [V8] "Transparent, large, white." [God] "Blossoms pretty large, very beautiful form, superb white with a light yellowish tint." [J-A/566] "Light pink, large, full, very fragrant, tall." [Sn] "Medium-sized, full." [JR9/126] "*Ovary* ovoid. *Flower* medium-sized, full, white." [Pf] "Flesh colour, beautifully tinted with the most delicate pink, of medium size, double; form, cupped. Habit, erect; growth, moderate." [P] "Blush, glaucous foliage. Growth very vigorous, summer flowering." [GeH] "Glaucous leaves." [No26] "Tube of calyx oval." [S] "Still adorns many an old garden, and when it is in flower it is one of the loveliest of all flowering shrubs. It will attain a height of seven feet [ca. 2.3 m] or more." [NRS28/33]

"Rose with egg-shaped seed-buds and hispid peduncles: flowers of a pale flesh colour, and semi-double: leaves spreading: leaflets nearly glaucous, ovate, pointed, and sawed: stem and petioles prickly, and nearly glaucous. This delicate Rose is called celestial: it is very nearly allied to the 'Belladonna', or 'Maiden's Blush' [*i.e.*, in both cases, 'Great Maiden's Blush']. The superior delicacy of the 'Erubescens' is not confined to the flowers, but pervades even the leaves and stems, which are covered with a glaucous bloom, like that on fruit, conveying an idea of freshness that even the texture of its branches seems to indicate, easily breaking short off, whilst the stems of most other roses are of a tougher character. Flowers during the months of June and July." [A]

"Monsieur Dupont, already cited as a great rose fancier, has released to commerce a new sort which can rival [the three *Uniques*], and is placed in the same group. It is called Alba Nova Coelestis, in French *Nouvelle Rose Blanche Céleste*. The wood and foliage have nothing out of the ordinary to them. Its blossoms are an extremely delicate and light white; one can see on the petals, under certain conditions of sunlight, azure blue reflections, giving it the surname 'Céleste'. In truth, it is a pretty variety with much finesse; nevertheless, it doesn't please every fancier, some of whom want nothing of this blue reflection—which is, if the truth be known, its greatest merit. But I believe that I have noted that this virtue depends principally on exposure and culture. This rose likes to be out in the open and in the sun, in a site more dry than damp." [C-T] "Doesn't differ from the first 'Unique' rose [*i.e.*, 'Unica', (C)] except that the outer petals, pure white, take on a celestial blue tint." [BJ17] "The wood and leaves indicate its origin. This beautiful rose was given us by Monsieur Dupont. Its blossoms are very double, and a very pure white, like those of 'Unique Blanche' [*i.e.*, 'Unica' (C)]. They are two and a half inches [ca. 6.5 cm] in circumference [*sic; "diameter," perhaps?*], with small ragged interior petals. They turn in on themselves; their translucence makes them take on a bluish tint, which gives a basis for the name 'Céleste'. They open June 1–9." [LeR] "Already distributed into gardens . . . the very double blossoms, as pure a white as those of the

rose 'Unique', are more than thirty *lignes* large [ca. 3³⁄₄ in], with interior petals small, ragged, back-rolled, and of a sort of transparence giving them a blue tint." [CM] "Where . . . have you seen that 'Céleste Blanche' had bluish shadings? Dupont, whose imagination was not always closely reined in [*the writer, Vibert, knew Dupont well*], was the first who said he saw them; a father's love no doubt affected his vision, as, less fortunate than he, we today see in this rose a beautiful white, but nothing more." [V2] "Thory and Vibert state that this blue nuance is only an illusion produced by the effect of shadows or by the imagination of Dupont, who grew it from seed." [JDR54/31]

Céleste Blanche   Listed as 'Céleste' (A).

Celestial   Listed as 'Céleste' (A).

Celestis   Listed as 'Céleste' (A).

Chloris

syn. 'Cloris'
Descemet, pre-1820

"Blush." [Cal] "Flesh." [V9] "Flowers delicate flesh, small and full; form, compact. Habit, erect; growth, small. Very pretty." [P] "Light pink, medium size, full, moderate fragrance, tall." [Sn] "*Ovary* ovoid-oblong, hispid-glandulose. *Flower* small or medium-sized, much doubled, symmetrical, flesh-colored becoming nearly white." [Pf] "Desportes says that this was one of Descemet's obtentions." [Gx] Sometimes thought to be synonymous with 'Elisa' (A), *q.v.*; we are dubious. "Chloris, better known under the name Flora." [MaCo] "Chloris: they say that she was [Amphion and] Niobe's daughter, originally called Meliboia; but, when the children of Amphion were shot down by Artemis and Apollo, she and Amyklas were the only two to survive, because they prayed to Leto. But Meliboia turned so green from fear—and stayed green the rest of her life—that instead of Meliboia her name became Chloris." [Pausanias II:21:10] "'Tis said that Hippodameia first gathered the sixteen women to give thanks to Hera for her marriage to Pelops, and first celebrated Hera's games with them; and they also record that the winner was Chloris, the only surviving daughter of Amphion." [Pausanias V:16:4] "Neleus, king of Pylos, married Chloris, the daughter of Amphion." [Pausanias IX:36:4] "Chloris, spouse of Zephyrus." [JR14/147]

Claudine

Vibert, 1823

"Flowers semi-double, medium-sized, and white." [AC] "*Ovary* ovoid, bristling with green bristles, glandulose. *Sepals* foliaceous, pinnatifid. *Flower* small, white, multiplex." [Pf]

Cloris   Listed as 'Chloris' (A).

Couleur de Chair   Listed as 'Lesser Maiden's Blush' (A).

Cuisse de Nymphe   Listed as 'Great Maiden's Blush' (A).

Cuisse de Nymphe à Ovaire Lisse   Listed as 'Belle Thérèse' (A).

Cuisse de Nymphe Emué   Listed as 'Belle Thérèse' (A).

Cuisse de Nymphe Grande   Listed as 'Great Maiden's Blush' (A).

Cuisse de Nymphe Naine   Listed as 'Lesser Maiden's Blush' (A).

Cymbaefolia

syns. 'À Feuilles de Chanvre', 'Cannabina'; trans., "Hemp-Leafed"
Flobert/Pelletier, 1807

"Monstrosity. Flowers small, double, a matte white." [MonLdeP] "Stems glabrous and thornless, with leaflets which are whitish and cottony beneath; blossoms clustered or axillary, white and double, with calycinate leaflets simple and elongate." [BJ30] "Leaflets lanceolate and much toothed like a saw along their edges." [CM] "The leaves look a little like those of hemp." [No26] "*Canes* nearly thornless. *Peduncles* glabrous. *Ovary* glabrous, ovoid, with a narrow neck. *Sepals* entire, glabrous. *Flower* small, multiplex, white." [Pf] "Mention of this plant is made for the first time in the *Bon Jardinier* of 1812. One reads on p. 685, about *Rosa alba*, '... It has several varieties. —One, among others, very new and given this year of 1810 to the *Jardin des Plantes* and to several nurseries, under the name *Rosa cymbaefolia*, is notable by the singularity of its leaves which are fairly distant, composed almost always of five leaflets of a pale and nearly glaucous green, narrow, elongate, pointed, saw-toothed, looking much like the leaves of a Peach or Hemp. The blossoms, of medium size and white, are fairly double, and of a beautiful white. We owe this [rose] to Monsieur Amédée Le Pelletier...' The only new information concerning the origin of *Rosa cymbaefolia*, which was only *propagated* by Le Pelletier, nurseryman at Mesnil-le-Montant ... near Paris, while it had been *observed* for the first time by Flobert, nurseryman at Pinon, near Laon." [JR11/169] Possibly—even probably—synonymous with 'À Feuilles de Pêcher', in which case 'Cymbaefolia' is the older name.

Double Listed as 'Plena' (A).

Duc d'York

syns. 'Rose d'York', 'White Rose of York'
Miellez, pre-1818

"Flowers large, double, well-formed, flesh color." [No26] "Flowers very large, very double, with some flesh-color; admirably effective; wood reddish and thornless." [J-A/566] "Has larger blossoms [than has 'Great Maiden's Blush'], with a more decided flesh color." [dP] "De Pronville calls it 'Le Duc d'York'." [Gx] Possibly commemorating Frederick Augustus, Duke of York and Albany, lived 1763–1827.

Duplex Listed as 'Semi-Plena' (A).

Elisa

syns. 'À Fleurs Roses', 'Belle Elisa', 'Elisa Blanche', 'Elise', 'Elize',
   'Nova Incarnata', 'Rosée du Matin'
Charpentier, pre-1810

"Delicate pink." [V9] "Large, incarnate, beautiful." [WRP] "The blossoms, coming in sixes to eights, are semi-double; the petals are tinted delicate pink around the nub, which fades insensibly towards the limb." [CM] "Flowers medium-sized, double, with petals pink at the nub, white on the limb." [No26] "Has similarities to 'Belle Aurore', of which it seems to be a sub-variety." [BJ24] "*Thorns* straight, very long. *Peduncle* hispid both beneath and above the bracts. *Ovary* ovoid, obconical, hispid-glandulose. *Flower* large, full, flesh with nearly white edges." [Pf] "Wood strong and vigorous, gay green, short prickles which are brown and flexuose. Leaves oval, deeply toothed, beautiful green. Calyx long, covered over with slender stickers. Bud oval, covered by its sepals. Flower well formed, double, no stamens, two or three inches across [ca. 5–8 cm]; an attractive delicate pink; petals

dainty, small, much crumpled; scent sweet and pleasant; blooms at the beginning of June." [C-T] "This is a superb hybrid between the Alba and the 'Red Damask', of which it has the wood and the hooked thorns; large light green leaves. Buds inflated, much overtopped by the extensions of the calyx. Flower well formed, like the 'Hollande' [C], of which it has the form and the plumpness. Very double, no stamens, three inches across [ca. 8 cm], delicate flesh color, lighter along the petal edges, darker within; petals large and thick; pleasant perfume. Nowhere will you find a sweeter color than that of this beautiful rose. Opens 1–9 of June." [LeR]

Elisa Blanche Listed as 'Elisa' (A).

Elise Listed as 'Elisa' (A).

Elize Listed as 'Elisa' (A).

Enfant de France For the Alba, listed as 'Beauté Tendre' (A).

Erubescens Listed as 'Céleste' (A).

Esmeralda

V. Verdier, 1847

"Flowers delicate flesh, their margin white, of medium size, full." [P] Esmeralda, gypsy girl of interest to certain priests and hunchbacks in Victor Hugo's novel *Notre-Dame de Paris* (1831).

Étoile de la Malmaison

trans. "Star of Malmaison"
Breeder unknown, pre-1844

"Incarnate, white border, perfect." [WRP] "Medium-sized, full, flesh." [V8] "Quite new, incarnate and much esteemed in France, but rare here [U.S.A.]." [WRP] "Flowers flesh, fading to French white, large and full; form, cupped. Habit, erect; growth, vigorous. A showy Rose, with fine dull green leaves." [P] "Foliage thick, of a very dark green; color, flesh white, becoming white after several days." [S] Malmaison, palace of the Empress Joséphine.

Évratin Listed as 'Evratina' (A).

[Evratina]

syns. 'Évratin', 'Muscade Rouge'
Bosc, 1809

"Pale red." [BJ40] "Indigenous [to France], and very vigorous; grows to 6 to 8 feet [ca. 2–2.6 m]; branches and canes have few thorns; leaves slightly coriaceous and a somber green; at the tips of the canes, numerous panicles of medium-sized flowers, which are double and flesh-colored, but which never open fully; peduncles and oval [calyx] tubes very hispid." [BJ30] "Very strong bush, of an umbrageous green, with nearly straight thorns which are short and nearly nude on the canes; leaves slightly coriaceous, a somber green, of five to seven leaflets which are oblong-obtuse, simply dentate; flowers medium-sized, numerous, a pale red, with very hispid peduncles; fruit oval. 'Muscade Rouge' from the Dutch, the flowers are red, double, and in very numerous corymbs." [No26] "This rose, of which the native land is unknown, came to us from Holland under the name *rose muscade rouge*. We owe the possession of it to the fancier Évrat; and, by way of recognition, Monsieur Bosc gave this rose the name of his friend. The 'Évratin' rose is very vigorous; its stems have few prickles; its leaves are composed of five to six leaflets which are often oval. obtuse, and a dark green, glossy above and pale beneath;

[Evratina] *continued*

its blossoms, which shine in June and July, are a pale red, lightly fragrant, two inches big [ca. 5 cm], and come in a pendant panicle at the cane-tip; the calyx-leaflets are very long and glandulose. These characteristics make it easily distinguishable from the White Rose [*i.e., the Alba proper*]. The 'Évratin' rose is an excellent acquisition, not only by the profusion and beauty of its panicles of flowers, but further by the beautiful color of its leaves and the vigor of its growth … One finds, in several nurseries, a double-flowered variety of the 'Évratin', which was originally received from Holland under the name *muscade rouge double*. This variety also exists at Lille in the collection of Monsieur Cardon; it should be better known than it is at present." [CM] "The Type [specimen] of this rose was lost in the destruction of the demonstration garden [*école*]." [MonLdeP]

Ex Albo Rosea Listed as 'Belle Aurore' (A).

Fanny
Breeder unknown, pre-1848
  "Flowers salmon blush, large; form, expanded." [P] "Flower large, full, flat; color, bright crimson." [S]

[Fanny Rousseau]
Vibert, 1817
  "*Bush* delicate. *Canes* splotched with brown at their base. *Flower* medium-sized, nearly full, regular, flesh." [Pf]

Fanny Sommerson Listed as 'Fanny-Sommesson' (A).

Fanny-Sommesson
syn. 'Fanny Sommerson'
Vibert, pre-1826
  "Flower large, flesh white." [God] "Blossoms very double, large, and flesh; wood thornless, beautiful foliage." [J-A/566] "Rosy lilac blush, of medium size, full; form, compact. Habit, erect; growth, moderate." [P] "*Bush* vigorous, nearly thornless. *Ovary* oval-digitate. *Flower* medium-sized, full, plump, regular, light pink becoming flesh." [Pf] "A new [*!*] and very fine variety, is a most robust grower, producing rose-colored flowers, extremely double, and finely shaped, a little imbricated, but so perfect that this variety may be considered a good show-rose." [WRP] From the hyphenated name of this cultivar, one might to good effect suppose that Vibert had obtained proprietary rights to it from Sommesson; but this is speculation.

Félicité
syn. 'Félicité Parmentier'; trans., "Happiness"
Parmentier, pre-1836
  "Flesh." [V4] "Rosy flesh, margin blush, large, full." [GeH] "Flesh, full, flat, medium-sized, superb." [LF] "Flesh color, convex, very pretty." [WRP] "Medium-sized, full, flesh, plump." [V8] "Medium-sized, full, deep flesh." [JR9/126] "Most beautiful, very double curled, splendid light pink blush." [FICaVI/229] "A new, distinct, and beautiful rose; its flowers are exactly like a fine double ranunculus, of a most delicate flesh-colour." [WRP] "A large double rose, of a delicate flesh-color, and a most symmetrical shape." [FP] "Pink-white, medium size, very full, very fragrant, tall." [Sn] "Good habit." [JC] "Very vigorous bush making a strong plant; flower large, full, petals crowded; color, flesh, edged flesh pink." [S] "Flowers rosy flesh, their margin white, exquisite in bud, of medium size, full; form, compact. Habit, erect; growth, robust.

A very abundant bloomer, and indispensable even in a small collection." [P] Possibly dates to 1834. Though the rose has become known most often as 'Félicité Parmentier', the "Parmentier" appears to be a later addition prompted by the existence of other roses with the name "Félicité"; in other words, to differentiate, it was called "'Félicité (Parmentier)'," just as with the cultivar immediately preceding in which the "-Sommesson" was added to differentiate from other roses named 'Fanny'. The original name must still take precedence.

Félicité Parmentier Listed as 'Félicité' (A).

Ferox
trans. "Ferocious"
Breeder unknown, pre-1844
  "Incarnate, very spiny." [WRP] "Medium-sized, full, flesh, very thorny." [V8] "Flowers white. Habit, curious." [P] "A very anomalous variety of this family, as most of its members are thornless, but this is completely covered with those fierce defenders; its flowers are of a pretty tinted white, very double and perfect." [WRP] "Vigorous bush; canes much clothed in thorns; leaves pointed, of a yellowish green; color, pure white." [S]

Flore Pleno Listed as 'Plena' (A).

Gabrielle d'Estrées
Vibert, 1819
Seedling of 'Elisa' (A).
  "Pink." [V9] "Blush." [Cal] "Flower large, with a flesh heart." [God] "*Leaflets* slightly bullate, glaucous above, villose beneath. *Ovary* turbinate-pyriform. *Flower* medium-sized, full or very multiplex, pale flesh, becoming white." [Pf] Gabrielle d'Estrées, much beloved mistress of Henri IV, lived 1573?–1599.

Grande Cuisse de Nymphe Listed as 'Great Maiden's Blush' (A).

Great Maiden's Blush Plate 15
syns. 'Bella Donna', 'Belle Fille', 'Carné', 'Cuisse de Nymphe', 'Cuisse de Nymphe Grande', 'Grande Cuisse de Nymphe', 'Incarnata Major', 'La Royale', 'La Virginale', 'Maiden's Blush', 'Regalis'
Breeder unknown, pre-1754
  "Pure incarnate, large, beautiful." [WRP] "Medium-sized, full, pink." [V8] "Blossom medium-sized, full, globular; color, whitish pink." [S] "Very double flowers are a pale flesh pink of an extremely delicate shade; it is unfortunate that we do not see it in more gardens." [JF] "The blossoms, pinkish flesh in color, are smaller [than those of 'Nova Coelestis'], but very pretty." [BJ17] "The flowers, larger than three inches [ca. 7.5 cm], come one after the other for a long time, and are lightly washed with pink at the heart before being fully open." [CM] "Flowers soft blush, colour of the buds exquisite, of medium size, double; form, globular. Habit, branching; growth, moderate." [P] "*Peduncle* hispid above the bracts. *Ovary* hispid, digitate, longer than wide. *Flower* medium-sized, nearly full, flesh with pale edges." [Pf] "Pink-white, large, very full, very fragrant, tall." [Sn] "Rose with egg-shaped seed-buds, and hispid peduncles. Flowers crowded, of a pale flesh colour. Leaves spreading. Leaflets broadly egg-shaped and sharp-pointed. Stem and petioles prickly." [A]
  "Flower full, blush, tending towards red. Calyx winged. Ovary ovoid, bestrewn with red hairs. Peduncles hispid. Branches and young growths glabrous … This double rose, light flesh in color, nearly

white on the outside, blush inclining to red on the inside, is medium in size, and, ordinarily, its petals remain slightly recurved on themselves. Its color being analogous to the tint of virgins [*!*], it has acquired the name 'Belle Fille' [*i.e., "daughter-in-law"; one might note a bit of a* lapsus *in reasoning here*]. Its calyx, equipped with several appendages, is bestrewn with pediculate glands. The ovoid, slender, light green ovary—slightly pointed towards the peduncle—is charged with greenish bristles slightly tinted red. The peduncle, bearing two and often three bracts, has the same characteristics as the ovary. The leaves, dark green above, paler green and veined beneath, are oval, serrated with large teeth, and borne on petioles armed beneath with small, slightly recurved prickles. The stipules are long, edged with sharp teeth, and charged with red glands. The stems of this rose are weak, and it rarely puts out shoots from the base. This rose should not be confused with a Damask rose, which it much resembles." [Rsg] "Its wood is like that of ['Hispida Villosa']. The leaves are nearly round, and deeply toothed. The thorns are long, slightly hooked, wide, and red at the base. The calyx is large, long, and covered with bristles. The buds are round and numerous, sometimes with ten to twelve on the same stem, giving what is more well-formed blossoms, nearly as large and double as those of ['Hispida Villosa']. It is one of the most beautiful roses we have. I should note that this rose loves full sun, that the flowers degenerate on the Briar, and that it is necessary to grow it 'own-root'." [C-T] "Sub-variety of the Alba and some Red [*i.e.,* Gallica], this is one of this group's perfections. Its wood is that of the Alba, as are its thorns and leaves. Buds round and numerous on the same stalk, subdivided into fairly strong pedicules and pedicels, each one bearing one blossom as double as the Centifolia, well formed, a little more of a pretty flesh pink—intense at the center of the petals, and lighter along the edges. The petals are quite thick. This beautiful rose is three inches across [ca. 7.5 cm]. Opens starting June 1." [LeR]

"*Shrub* 0.6–0.9 m high [ca. 2–3 ft], with smooth, greenish *canes*; *prickles* sparse, a little curved. *Leaflets* ovate, pubescent, pale beneath; *petiole* villose, prickly. *Flowers* many together at the tips of the branches; pedicels glandular-hispid; *receptacles* ovoid, abruptly rounded at the base, with a few even bristles; *petals* very large, white flushed pink, in many series. Similar to ['(Petite) Cuisse de Nymphe' ('Lesser Maiden's Blush')], and, because of the larger blossoms (7.5 cm upwards), commonly called 'Grande Cuisse de Nymphe'. The English call it 'Great Maiden's Blush'. To ensure a succession of fine blooms, some of the buds should be sacrificed." [T&R]

"There cannot be a Rose better known than this delicate species, under the title of The Maiden's Blush. It is considered, among the Garden Roses, as the second in progressive routine from the wild species, but must certainly be ranked among the first in beauty. [Andrews'] figure represents what is called the Clustered variety, an appellation we have not adopted, as it would have compelled us to have given two other nominal varieties; the one, whose flowers are rather smaller; the other, with flowers less crowded. But when the latitude of growth that appertains to this luxuriant tribe is considered, they may with propriety be regarded as the variations of culture only. During the months of July and August this Rose is in the greatest perfection. We have frequently remarked the foliage of this Rose, upon most old plants, to be of a very dark or blackish green; but, on the younger ones, to be nearly the same in colour as the minor variety [*i.e.,*

'Lesser Maiden's Blush']." [A] "[Given the name 'Cuisse de Nymphe'] in 1802 by Dumont de Courset; it's the Alba Incarnata or the *R. carnea* of the *Nouveau Duhamel*. Prévost received it from Vibert under the name 'La Royale'." [Gx]

Henriette Campan
Breeder unknown, pre-1830

"Medium-size, double, light purple." [V8] "Medium-size, full, flat; color, grenadine." [S] "Flowers dark purplish rose, of medium size, full; form, expanded. Habit, branching; growth, moderate. A beautiful and distinct Rose." [P] "*Shrub* vigorous. *Canes* ordinarily green, smooth, slightly glaucous. *Prickles* very rare, slender, irregularly sparse. *Leaves* distant. *Petiole* villose, glandulose, armed beneath with strong prickles. *Stipules* long, glabrous, with ciliate-glandulose edges. *Leaflets* 5, very large, oval or ovoid, pointed, glabrous and dark green above, pale, very nerve-reticulate and glabrous beneath, except along the main veins, which are sub-pubescent. *Serration* simple, sharp, bristly or glabrous. *Peduncles* very long, glabrous at their base, bestrewn above the bracts with glandular bristles, ordinarily coming in 2's to 5's. Bracts linear-lanceolate. Ovary glabrous, very smooth, slightly glaucous, ovoid, narrowed at the tip. *Sepals* bestrewn with fine glands, terminating in a linear leaflet; 3 are edged with very long appendages. *Flower* medium-sized or large (2.5–3.5 inches across [ca. 6.5–9 cm]), nearly full, regular, bright very brilliant purplish pink. *Petals* 70–80, crowded, pale beneath. *Styles* 40–60, villose, free, not projecting. I don't know the origin of this beautiful and singular rose, which probably received another name from its raiser. I have never seen it except at a fancier's place, who received it from a correspondent. It is to the kindness of that fancier that I owe its possession." [Pfs] Jeanne Louise Henriette Campan, reader to French royal children, superintendent of girls' schools under Napoléon; authoress; lived 1752–1822.

Incarnata Major   Listed as 'Great Maiden's Blush' (A).

Jeanne d'Arc
Vibert, 1818
Seedling of 'Elisa' (A).

"White." [V9] "Flowers very full, medium-sized, pure white." [AC] "Flowers regular, bowl-shaped, medium-sized." [dP] "Pink-white, medium size, very full, very fragrant, tall." [Sn] "Flowers delicate flesh, their margin blush, of medium size, full: form, cupped. Habit, branching; growth, robust." [P] "*Canes* geniculate, armed with strong thorns, having a well-hooked tip, intermixed with several bristles only at the base of the cane. *Peduncles* hispid both above and below the bracts. *Ovary* oval-pyriform, hispid-glandulose. *Flower* medium-sized, very full, globular, sometimes slightly flesh-colored at the center when opening, but always white after fully open." [Pf] "From 'Belle Elisa' [*i.e.,* 'Elisa' (A)]." [V2] Jeanne d'Arc, alias Joan of Arc, alias St. Joan, inspired French heroine, lived 1412–1431.

Joséphine Beauharnais
Vibert, 1823

"Pink." [V9] "Flesh white." [BJ40] "Large globular flowers, very double, white, tinted with rosy buff." [WRP] "*Ovary* glabrous, digitate, very short. *Flower* medium-sized, very full, symmetrical, bright flesh with pale edges." [Pf] Joséphine [de] Beauharnais, alias Empress Joséphine, quondam and much-loved wife of Napoléon, superlatively

Joséphine Beauharnais *continued*
important patroness of the Rose and rose progress, lived 1763–1814. Vibert, very much a partisan of Napoléon, was much inspired by Joséphine (from afar) to pursue his own work in roses; he would have had to have felt immense pride in this rose to have named it after her.

Königin von Dannemark
syns. 'Naissance de Vénus', 'Queen of Denmark', 'Reine de Danemark'; trans., "Queen of Denmark"
Booth/Flottbeck, 1826
Seedling of 'Great [?] Maiden's Blush' (A).

"Light pink, center darker." [Ÿ] "Clear rosy pink." [FP] "Large blush, superb, compact." [WRP] "Blossom medium-sized, full, flat; color, pink shaded with crimson." [S] "Medium-sized, full, white, pink center." [BJ53] "Medium-sized, full, cupped, salmony pink, paler margin. One of the oldest of the group, which came to us [in France] from Germany, passing through England." [JR9/126] "Delicate flesh-rose with darker centre, medium size, full. Growth vigorous." [GeH] "Flowers rosy pink, their margin paler, of medium size, full; form, cupped. Habit, erect; growth, moderate. A beautiful Rose; a hybrid." [P] "Pretty vigorous bush with upright canes armed with a good number of unequal, red, very hooked thorns; leaves of five to seven leaflets, some cordiform, the others elliptical, somber green, heavily dentate; flowers numerous, large, perfect, in corymbs; the petals are an attractive delicate pink within, and white and cordiform along the edge; peduncle and tube bearing small bristles; a superb flower of very distinct merit." [An37/373] "An old but estimable variety, produces flowers of first rate excellence as prize-flowers: so much was this esteemed when first raised from seed, that plants were sent from Germany to England at five guineas each." [WRP] Interesting information obtained by Graham S. Thomas from O. Sonderhausen of Denmark (and related in full in *The Graham Stuart Thomas Rose Book*, p. 51) indicates that this cultivar, a seedling from 'Maiden's Blush', presumably 'Great Maiden's Blush', first bloomed in 1816, and, at first called 'New Maidenblush', received limited distribution (perhaps not commercially) ca. 1820–1821. After propagation, it was released as 'Königin von Dannemark' (note spelling) in 1826. There is some supposition of Damask (or perhaps Damask Perpetual) complicity in this Alba hybrid.

La Remarquable
trans. "The Noticeable [One]"
Breeder unknown, pre-1833

"White." [V4] "Beautiful white." [WRP] "Medium-sized, full; color, virginal white." [S] "Flowers white; form, cupped, sometimes do not open. Growth, robust." [P]

La Royale
Synonym shared by 'Great Maiden's Blush' (A) and 'Plena' (A), *qq.v.*

La Surprise
trans. "The Surprise"
Poilpré, 1823

"Medium-sized, white." [God] "Very beautiful medium-sized very double flowers; wood thornless and slightly brown." [J-A/566] "Blossoms small, very double, pure white; wood thornless, mahogany-colored." [No26] "*Canes* brown, thornless. *Ovary* oval-fusiform, hispid-glandulose. *Flower* small, nearly full, white." [Pf] The "surprise" would be the brown color of the canes.

La Virginale   Listed as 'Great Maiden's Blush' (A).

Le Gras St.-Germain   Listed as 'Mme. Legras de St. Germain' (A).

Lesser Maiden's Blush
syns. 'Alba Rubigens', 'Anglaise', 'Aureata', 'Bella Donna Flore Minore', 'Couleur de Chair', 'Cuisse de Nymphe Naine', 'Petite Cuisse de Nymphe', 'Regia Carnea', 'Rubigens', 'Small Maiden's Blush'
Royal Botanic Gardens, Kew, 1797

"Flesh." [V9] "Flowers flesh colour, small and full." [P] "Small size, full double and incarnate hue." [WRP] "Medium, flesh, regular in form." [BJ30] "The buds, before they open, have a yellow tint, a characteristic peculiar to this variety. This is doubtless what gives this rose its surname 'Aureata'." [C-T] "The flowers, in size twenty-seven to twenty-eight *lignes* [ca. 3.38 in], regular, a very pale pink at first, then passing to the flesh color which they keep when open." [CM] "Blossoms a very pale pink at first, soon passing to the flesh color which it keeps when open." [AC] "*Peduncle* glabrous below the bracts. *Ovary* ovoid-oblong, glaucous, glabrous, or bestrewn with some glandular hairs. *Flower* medium-sized, much doubled, flesh, sometimes light pink before fully open." [Pf] "Same origin as ['Great Maiden's Blush', *i.e.,* says LeRouge, a cross between Alba and Gallica]. Its wood is greener and thinner, though strong, and bears more thorns; the veins of the Centifolia are more pronounced, and are like those of the Albas [*sic*; LeRouge probably intended 'the veins are more pronounced than those of the Centifolia']. The blossoms are half the size of those of ['Great Maiden's Blush'], and are a more uniform, more delicate flesh pink; very profuse on their peduncles, one lone branch makes a perfect bouquet. Opens June 1." [LeR] "Very vigorous plant, forming a bush; branches often growing 2 m high [ca. 6 ft]." [S]

"Rose with egg-shaped seed-buds, and hispid peduncles. Flowers numerous, smallish, and of a pale flesh colour. Leaves spreading. Leaflets egg-shaped and pointed. Stem and petioles prickly. This minor Variety of the '[Great] Maiden's Blush', like the larger one, is said to possess two equally trivial variations. The only observable distinction in this variety is the very small size of its flowers, compared with the preceding figure. Yet, as it delineates the latitude of growth annexed to this species, it stands in no great need of an apology. But how could we have apologized, in a satisfactory manner, for the introduction of four more intermediate varieties, we know not; but rather think we must have borrowed the specific character of the present species, and blushed for their intrusion. The specific we have adopted [to wit, 'Bella Donna, var. flore minore'] is only retained among cultivators for this minor Variety, doubtless with the intention of preserving an appearance of greater distinction." [A]

Lucrèce
Vibert, 1847

"Flowers pale rose, their centre deep rose, very large and double; form, globular." [P] "8–9 cm [ca. 3¼ in], double, pink, darker at the center, globular, nearly unarmed." [M-L47/360]

Maiden's Blush   Listed as either 'Great Maiden's Blush' (A) or 'Lesser Maiden's Blush' (A).

Marie de Bourgogne
Vibert, pre-1844

"Roseate spotted, incarnate." [WRP] "Flowers rose, spotted with white, of medium size, very double." [P]

Maxima Multiplex
trans. "Largest Double"
Prévost?, pre-1829

"*Shrub* vigorous, making a very tall bush. *Peduncle* glabrous beneath the bracts, hispid-glandulose above. *Ovary* ovoid-fusiform, hispid-glandulose on the central peduncle in each corymb, glabrous on the laterals. *Sepals* glandulose, foliaceous; 3 are pinnatifid. *Flower* large, multiplex, white, slightly nankeen in the center before being fully open. *Petals* large." [Pf, who does not claim it as his own]

Ménage
Vibert, 1847

"6 cm [ca. 2¼–2½ in], full, flesh, plump; filet at the center." [M-L47/360] "Flowers flesh colour, of medium size, full; form, cupped." [P] "Medium-sized, full, wide-spreading; color, flesh pink." [S] Not to be confused with Robert & Moreau's similarly named Moss of 1858, *q.v.*

Mme. Audot
V. Verdier, 1844

"A pale flesh-color." [FP] "Medium-sized, full, delicate flesh." [Gp&f52] "Large, full, wide-spreading; color, flesh pink." [S] "Large, full, cupped; bright flesh, edged creamy flesh." [JR9/126] "Glossy flesh, edges creamy blush, large and full; form, cupped. Habit, branching; growth, moderate. A beautiful Hybrid Rose." [P]

Mme. Hardy
"'Mme. Hardy' is a Damask rose." [WRP] See under 'Félicité Hardy' (D).

Mme. Legras de St. Germain
syn. 'Le Gras St.-Germain'
Breeder unknown, pre-1846

"7–8 cm [ca. 3 in], full, white." [VPt48/app] "Large, full, pure white, yellowish center." [JR9/126] "Blossom very large, full; color, virginal white, cream at the center." [S] "A white rose of peculiar delicacy, and very graceful in its habit of growth." [FP] "Creamy white, large, full. Growth moderate." [GeH] "White, very large, very full, tall." [Sn] "Flowers pure white, their centre sometimes creamy, very large and full; form, expanded. Habit, branching; growth, moderate. A free bloomer, and superb White Rose." [P]

Monica
Breeder unknown, pre-1838

"Medium size, full; color, delicate pink." [S] *Cf.* 'Monique' (A).

Monique
Prévost, 1828

"Flowers double, medium-sized, and a light pink." [AC] "Sown in February, 1826; first bloom in 1828. *Canes* geniculate, smooth, nearly thornless. *Prickles* lacking or very rare, and only found at the base and tip of vigorous canes. *Leaves* of 5 ovoid leaflets, acuminate, glabrous above, pale and sub-pubescent beneath. *Serration* large and simple. *Peduncles* glabrous below the bracts, bestrewn above with several glandular bristles. *Bracts* lanceolate, acuminate, entire. *Ovary* oval-pyriform, nearly glabrous. *Sepals* glandulose, terminating in a

leaflet. *Flower* medium-sized, globular, regular, very multiplex, light even pink, bright and brilliant. *Petals* 60 to 80, orbiculate, concave." [Pf] *Cf.* 'Monica' (A).

Multiple
Listed as 'Semi-Plena' (A).

Muscade Rouge
Listed as 'Evratina' (A).

Naissance de Vénus
Listed as 'Königin von Dannemark' (A).

New Blush Hip
Listed as 'Blush Hip' (A).

Nouvelle Semonville
Listed as 'Semonville à Fleurs Doubles' (A).

Nova Coelestis
Listed as 'Céleste' (A).

Nova Incarnata
Listed as 'Elisa' (A).

Nuancée de Bleu
Listed as 'Céleste' (A).

Persicifolia
Listed as 'À Feuilles de Pêcher' (A).

Petite Cuisse de Nymphe
Listed as 'Lesser Maiden's Blush' (A).

Petite Lisette
syn. 'Hybrida cum Bifera', 'Hybride Bumbifera'; trans., "Wee Lisette"
Vibert, 1817

"Blossoms double, medium-sized, flesh." [AC] "Rose." [Cal] "Whitish pink, small, full, average height." [Sn] "*Leaflets* pointed. *Ovary* glabrous and glaucous at the tip. *Flower* medium-sized, quite double, flesh, becoming nearly white." [Pf] This very delightful rose has been apportioned to the following groups by various writers: Alba, Agathe, Centifolia, Damask, Gallica. As one synonym tells us, it is a hybrid with the 'Bifera', a Damask Perpetual.

Placidie
Prévost/Vibert, 1820
Sport of 'Great Maiden's Blush' (A).

"Flowers semi-double, medium-sized, and a bright pink." [AC] "This rose saw the light of day as a sport from ['Great Maiden's Blush'] that I noted and enfixed in 1820. The name is Monsieur Vibert's, whom I authorized to that effect. *Flower* small or medium-sized, multiplex, bright even pink. *Petals* bullate and undulate. This rose differs from ['Great Maiden's Blush'], from which it came, by the following characteristics: *Canes* slender, vertical, smooth, nearly always unarmed. *Leaflets* small, narrow, deep green, non-glaucous. *Peduncle* more slender, slightly glandulose, but non-hispid. *Ovary* very long, much more narrow, slightly glandulose, non-hispid; often gibbose. *Sepals* less divided. *Flower* much smaller, of a beautiful bright even pink. *Petals* undulate and bullate. [Pf]

Plena
syns. 'À Fleurs Doubles', 'Blanc Ordinaire', 'Double', 'Flore Pleno', 'La Royale', 'Rose de l'Hymen'; trans., "Full"
Breeder unknown, pre-1770

"This one is surely a variety of ['Semi-Plena']; its wood is feebler than that of the semi-double; thorns sparse; each branchlet usually bears three buds, which have a slight pink tint before opening; once open, they are a pretty white slightly washed nankeen-color in the center of the petals, which are plump and short. The whole is en-

Plena *continued*

hanced by a little green leaf at the heart. Its frail branches have trouble holding up under the mass of bloom. It has the benefit of blooming earlier than the others—it blooms in May. Grafted, it forms a well-rounded head." [LeR] "Has become quite common . . . is quite a marvel in the foreground of boskets." [CM]

"Calyx segments winged, terminating in a foliaceous appendage or leaf, and entirely covered with red hairs. Ovary oval, bristly, glandulose. Peduncles prickly. Petioles with prickles beneath. Leaflets ovoid pointed . . . This rose, which blooms in June, is only moderately double, and has slightly upturned petals. Its anthers, like arrowheads, are deep yellow. The segments of its calyx are pinnatifid and bestrewn with red hairs on their backs. The oval ovary is similarly hispid. The peduncles are armed with prickles and bristles. The leaves, composed of five to seven ovoid lobes—which are ovoid, pointed, dentate, dark green above, pubescent and whitish beneath—are attached to a common petiole armed beneath with backhooked prickles. The growths of the current season have reddish shield-shaped thorns." [Rsg]

"Diffusely branched *shrub* up to 3–3.6 m high [ca. 9–11 ft]; *branches* smooth, fresh green in youth, with sparse, slightly recurved *prickles*; current shoots almost always glabrous and unarmed. *Leaflets* 5 or 7, rounded, dark green above, paler and pubescent beneath; petiole villose, with small hooked prickles. *Flowers* 1–4, lateral and terminal; peduncles and pedicels glandular hispid, *receptacles* less so or almost glabrous; *sepals* alternately entire and pinnatifid; *corolla* rarely full, very often semi-double, with the characteristic fragrance of *Rosa alba*; *petals* white, cordately notched. Left to itself, this rose always tends to throw single blossoms, and others with only 7–8 petals. The bud is often lightly flushed with pink. It has been illustrated in many works, but the early plates by Dodonaeus and J. Bauhin are poor. The Double or Semi-Double White Rose flourishes in wild places as in vineyard and garden hedgerows, tolerating shade and demanding little care. By virtue of its height it can make good hedges." [T&R]

"[Andrews'] figure of the White Rose exhibits an appearance of novelty, as one of the flowers represents a tie or knot in the middle, and which we have never before seen in the double white rose, the petals of which are numerous, but loose, with a few straggling stamens in the centre. Of these variations in the flowers there were many instances in the plant from which our drawing was made in the nursery of Messrs. Whitley and Brames in 1810." [A]

Pompon Blanc Parfait

trans. "Perfect White Pompom"
E. Verdier, 1876

"Palest flesh, changing to Pompon Blanc damask." [JC] "Flower small, full, well-formed; very delicate flesh." [JR4/21] "Blossom small, very delicate, fading to pure white." [S] "Whitish pink, small, full, medium scent, tall." [Sn]

Princesse de Lamballé

Miellez, pre-1830

"White." [V4] "Pure white, full, medium-sized, superb." [LF] "Medium-sized, full, pure white, sometimes tinted flesh." [JR9/126] "White, medium size, full, very fragrant, tall." [Sn] "One of the finest in this division, possessing all the characters of the species in its foliage,

branches and flowers: these are of the purest white, and of the most perfect and beautiful shape." [WRP] "Very vigorous bush; beautiful medium pink, full, petals crowded; color, pure white, sometimes shaded very light flesh pink." [S] "Flowers pure white, sometimes delicately tinted with flesh, of medium size, full; form, compact. Habit, branching; growth, vigorous in some places, in others shy and delicate. A lovely Rose." [P] Marie Thérèse Louise de Savoie-Carignano, Princesse de Lamballé; French-Italian princess whose loyalty to her friend Marie-Antoinette and the king resulted in her death at the hands of a Paris mob more interested in politics than virtue; lived 1749–1792.

Purpurascens Listed as 'Belle Aurore' (A).

Queen of Denmark Listed as 'Königin von Dannemark' (A).

Regalis Listed as 'Great Maiden's Blush' (A).

Regia Listed as 'Beauté Tendre' (A).

Regia Carnea Listed as 'Lesser Maiden's Blush' (A).

Reine de Danemark Listed as 'Königin von Dannemark' (A).

Rose d'York Listed as 'Duc d'York' (A).

Rose de l'Hymen Listed as 'Plena' (A).

Rosée du Matin Listed as 'Elisa' (A).

Royale Aurore Listed as 'Belle Aurore' (A).

Rubigens Listed as 'Lesser Maiden's Blush' (A).

Sappho

The "England, 1817," attribution one sees for this belongs rather to a Pimpinellifolia 'Sappho', not an Alba. The 'Sappho' that Sangerhausen records in its collection is perhaps Vibert's white 1847 Damask Perpetual of nearly the same name, 'Sapho'.

Sara Listed as 'Caroline d'Angleterre' (A).

Semi-Duplex Listed as 'Semi-Plena' (A).

Semi-Plena

syns. 'Duplex', 'Multiple', 'Semi-Duplex', 'Suaveolens', 'Vierge';
    trans., "Partially Full"
Breeder unknown, pre-1754

"Medium-sized, white, multiplex, fragrant." [Pf] "Handsome, large." [WRP] "Rose with smooth, egg-shaped seed-buds, and hispid peduncles. Flowers white, and semi-double. Leaves nearly of a glaucous green. Leaflets broadly egg-shaped, sharp-pointed, with serrated margins. Stem between erect and spreading, nearly smooth on the upper part, but furnished with strong thorns towards the base. This semi-double Rose so nearly resembles the single in its habit and foliage, that it can only be regarded as a florescent variety; for, when the plant is not in bloom, it is scarcely possible to distinguish the one from the other: but when in flower it certainly forms a very distinct appearance from its original, and is by far the more desirable plant: not that its beauty is by any means considerable; but as it preserves a regular progressive approach to completely double flowers (generally regarded as the perfection of the plant), it is on that account particularly estimable. Like its original, it is only retained by those who wish to have every distinct rose, to form a complete collection. Its flowers are of a fine white, but not of long continuance. The foliage is of a bluish or glaucous green. In habit, its native origin (the wild species) is very discernible. It is at present rather a scarce plant, from not possessing attraction sufficient to recommend it as an object of general culture." [A] "This rose—very common in our gardens—would seem to be the Type of many sweet and charming varieties; only the semi-double and the double are grown. The semi-double has strong wood, shooting out upright canes; its shoots grow twelve to fifteen feet high [ca. 4–5 m], straight up; the thorns are strong but not very profuse; its epidermis is smooth. Seed sown from this rose still provides the best stock for grafts, which do marvelously well on it. The blossoms are semi-double. The petals are large, quite thick, and a very pure white, with numerous stamens which enhance it. It looks just right between the Browns [*i.e.,* the dull-colored roses] and the bright ones. Grafting helps it quite a bit." [LeR] "Probably arising from the wild rose [*i.e.,* the single Alba]." [OB]

[Semonville]
Charpentier, pre-1815

"Flowers semi-double with a coppery yellow tint." [J-A/570] "*Thorns* long, intermixed with glandular bristles. *Leaflets* with very evident veins. *Peduncle* hispid-glandulose above the bracts. *Ovary* globular, hispid. *Flower* medium-sized, double or multiplex, light coppery pink." [Pf] "Peduncles stiff, short, very hispid; blossoms semi-double, of a yellowish flesh. Hybrid from 'Evratina'." [No26] "Comes from the Alba and ['Evratina']; blossoms a yellowish flesh, semi-double." [dP] "Grown from seed at the Luxembourg flower-garden; a hybrid with 'Evratina', and notable in its peduncles, which are short, straight, and very hispid, as is the oval calyx tube; its blossoms are flesh tending towards yellow." [BJ30] "This variety is very precious as a seed-bearer. Monsieur Hardy calls its progeny the most brilliant." [J-As/64] "These two roses ['Semonville' and 'Semonville à Fleurs Doubles'], pollinated by the Capucine [*i.e.,* 'Austrian Copper' (F)]—should it happen that specimens in bloom be found (one could leave the Capucine in a pot in the cold-house up till May)—

would very probably give, more than any others, the beautiful yellow roses and double Capucines we've been looking for." [J-A/570–571]

[Semonville à Fleurs Doubles]
syn. 'Nouvelle Semonville'
Hardy, 1823

"Beautiful double flowers, more pronounced yellow-copper tint [than has 'Semonville']." [J-A/570] "Blossoms superb, large, a coppery pink; same wood and character as the regular 'Semonville'." [No26]

Small Maiden's Blush Listed as 'Lesser Maiden's Blush' (A).

Suaveolens Listed as 'Semi-Plena' (A).

Superbe
Breeder unknown, pre-1846

"White." [LS] "White, full." [Jg]

Vaucresson
Breeder unknown, pre-1885

"Medium size, full; color, flesh pink." [S]

Vénus
Breeder unknown, pre-1846

"Pure white." [WRP] "Pure white; form, cupped." [P] "Medium-sized, full, outspread; color, virginal white." [S] Not to be confused with the Moss of the same name. Vénus, alias Venus, Roman goddess overseeing much human pleasure, with perhaps its due proportion of resultant human pain a necessarily secondary consideration to meeting Nature's propagative goals.

Vierge Listed as 'Semi-Plena' (A).

White Rose of York Listed as 'Duc d'York' (A).

Zénobie
Vibert, pre-1844

"Pale rose." [WRP] "Rose, of medium size, full." [P] Zénobie, alias Zenobia, dynamic Palmyran queen whom we have already met among the Mosses; fl. A.D. 267–272.

CHAPTER TEN

Hemisphaericas

"This rose, commonly called the Yellow Rose, originated in the Levant. Ovaries very large and fairly spiny; canes long and diffuse, needing to be supported and trained against fences; flowers light yellow, scentless, appearing in June; leaves glaucous, simply dentate, scentless, of delicate consistence. This rose has a variety with double flowers called the Big Yellow Rose, in which, however, the blossoms open poorly, nearly always aborting if the precaution of protecting it against rain isn't taken. The sub-variety, the Dwarf Yellow Rose, is afflicted with the same difficulty in opening, and demands (what is more) a dry terrain and a warm exposure. The sulphur yellow rose is often confused with the Capucine Rose [*Rosa foetida*], from which it has obvious differences in its leaves and thorns." [AC] "A native probably of Armenia and Persia, and was first introduced into Europe early in the Seventeenth Century by Clusius. It was first brought to his notice when seeing a paper model of a yellow Rose which had been brought from Constantinople, and he very soon succeeded in obtaining plants of the variety from friends living there. Lindley, 1820, describes it as a species, and calls it *R. sulphurea,* giving Persia and Constantinople as its origin. Linnaeus evidently had not seen it, or he would never have thought the Double Yellow Rose the same as the Sweet Briar. Parkinson [1629] knew it as *R. hemisphaerica* ... There is a specimen growing at Burghley House, the Marquis of Exeter's seat at Stamford, in Lincolnshire, that was brought from France by a French cook, and the late Mr. Mackintosh and Mr. Gilbert, the gardeners, used to refer to it as the Burghley Rose, or the Yellow Provence Rose; but Mr. Rivers, who had seen it, said it was nothing else than the genuine Double Yellow Rose. *The Botanical Register,* 1815, gives an excellent account of this interesting Rose ... I have it growing in my garden, and with me the blooms are very double and rather difficult to open. The colour is a pure sulphur yellow. The reason why it is not extensively grown in this country is the difficulty in propagation and cultivation. It requires a fairly warm position, as the smallest amount of moisture damages the blooms." [NRS30/235–236] "An old inhabitant of some gardens, but a very shy bloomer, showing its flowers very sparingly, and, some years, none. We have seen the bushes bending with their load of flowers. They are large, very double, of a pale-yellow. On account of its peculiar habits, it is not worth its room in the garden." [BBF66]

"There is nothing in common between the yellow Briar [*Rosa foetida*] and this, though indeed many people take it as a variety of this lattermost." [BJ30] "There is such a similarity between this species and *Rosa lutea* [*i.e., R. foetida*] that one would seem to owe its origin to the other; they however differ in that the one in question has no smelly leaves, its leaflets are glaucous and slender, and the flowers, which double easily, are a sulphur yellow." [Lam]

"The origins of this old and good rose are lost in the mists of time. It is reported by some authors that it was introduced into England around the end of the 16th century by Nicholas Lete, London businessman, who had brought it from Constantinople, to which it had in turn been brought from Syria. But these first specimens introduced soon died, and another London businessman by the name of Jean de Franqueville reintroduced it into the main gardens of England, where it was propagated in large quantities. In botanical writings, this rose is cited as a species originating in the Levant, and as never having been seen bearing single flowers in the wild ... I had always supposed that the single yellow *Capucine* was the Type of the Sulphur Yellow Rose as well as of 'Persian Yellow', and I believe I was and still am right ... As for the rest, here is what Dr. Hooker says: 'The single variety of *Rosa Sulphurea* was found in the wild by Dr. Thomson, in the west of Himalaya, Kishtevar Province, 7,500 feet [ca. 2500 m] above sea level, and by Griffith as well in Afghanistan. Though known in the garden for more than a century, the fatherland of this beautiful plant was only recently discovered. Both of these—the single and the double—are grown en masse in the gardens of Persia and other such countries. The single variety has since also been found growing wild on Mount Sypilus ...' (Dr. Hooker, *Gardener's Chronicle,* January 7, 1857 [*the preceding is a retranslation back into English from French*]). The Sulphurea group has but two varieties, which, in their habit, exactly resemble the Capucine [*Rosa foetida*]." [JR11/14] "Described for the first time in 1762 [*though it must be said here that Parkinson knew both the single and double forms in*

1629], this rose received latterly the names *R. glaucophylla* Ehrh. and *R. sulfurea* Ait. For a long time, it was only known in its double-flowered horticultural form. Its wild Type, discovered in Persia and Asia Minor, was described for the first time in 1859 by MM. Boissier and Balansa under the name *R. Rapini*. In 1860, the same Type received the name *R. Bungeana* Boissier et Buhse." [V-H80/104]

"In many gardens, ['Multiplex' and 'Pompon Jaune'] are ignored because, all in all, their peccadillos are rather discouraging. They nevertheless give now and then some blossoms free from the problems which, depending upon atmospheric conditions, dry out or kill their too-delicate petals. But the flowers which escape these problems sparkle with beauty and freshness. This regrettably rare circumstance is only dependent upon soil, exposure, and especially the proximity of a wall or tree which gives them fortunate protection." [J-A/559] "That these two beautiful varieties are so difficult to grow is a pity, because they are different from all the others in their color." [LeR] "This rose, one of the most beautiful of the genus, has the serious handicap of opening its flowers poorly—that is, frequently splitting the sepals and letting the petals out, which, at this stage, deforms the blossoms and makes the flower disagreeable to look at. Because of this handicap, many fanciers drop it from their collections. I think that there is a very easy way to give the plant the place it should occupy in our gardens. It consists of shading the rose when its buds have grown to a size which indicates they will open within fifteen days. A gauze or other such may be used, as long as the direct rays of the sun are intercepted, because, after the morning dew, they bring on the bloom so vigorously that it sparkles! This fact is validated by the roses which open well and which, as everyone can confirm, have nothing more than the advantage of being located in the center of the bush, or under foliage sufficiently thick to allow them the slow development they need to expand their numerous petals perfectly. This very inconsiderable effort, one which is taken with many other plants, can even so be avoided if one takes the precaution of always planting this rose in a northern exposure, or at least in a sufficiently shaded place. This theory was confirmed to me by Monsieur Mathieu of Neuilly, who told me of having noted, in Switzerland, in the fossées of an old fortress, a double yellow rose which had a northern exposure, its blossoms always opening perfectly. This was due not only to the plant's exposure, but also to the fact that this specimen had been left to itself and not had the pruning which many growers make the mistake of practicing indiscriminately on all their roses. It is necessary, with the rose in question, to be very careful in such checks to the plant's growth, as, in pruning out the shoots of the previous year, one eliminates the roses which should bloom over the next three or four years—because, in this race, the flowers are terminal. Another reason which should be considered in *not* pruning this rose is that, aside from the elimination of the blossoms, all the cut-back branches would have taken on themselves a large amount of sap on behalf of the roses which would otherwise have appeared; not finding an adequate outlet, the sap becomes too much for what remains; it would thus be more reasonable not to cut back the branches which had bloomed the previous year . . . As it is more than probable that the run of the sap is the only cause of the irregularity in the bloom of this rose, one might suppose that girdling the blooming canes would give a good result; it's something which I propose to try, and which I ask fanciers to attempt." [An36/117–119]

"Came from the East, where in all likelihood it is found with single blossoms; I can only speak here to the double-flowered variety. There isn't anyone who can't pick out its branches and foliage from those of other Roses. Its flowers rarely open well. It is said that, to bring this about, it is necessary to bend the bud and hold it against the soil. As for the rest, if this rose is given the high treatment with watering, etc., its flowers crack; if a person forgets and it's given too much sun, the flower's peduncle desiccates right next to the calyx, and the blossom perishes before opening. Perhaps it is picky about the soil, maybe about the exposure. I have seen it do very well in several gardens, and indeed in a window (when some plants are grown in a window, it is necessary to water them more often, sometimes putting them into the shade, and in particular to turn the pots every day; otherwise, the light would bring about flowers on only one side, and the sun would dry out the roots which would be exposed to its intensity too much). Its blossoms are absolutely scentless." [BJ09] "I've only had the enjoyment of it once, on a plant grafted on the Briar." [BJ17] "The double yellow Rose is of great account, both for the rarity, and doublenesse of the flower, and had it s[c]ent to the rest, would of all other be of highest esteeme." [PaSo]

Rosa hemisphaerica

horticultural syns., 'Jaune Simple', 'Simplex'
Introducer unknown, pre-1629

"Leaves glaucous green; blossoms sulphur yellow and single." [J-A/558] "From the Levant. Stems, branches, and petioles armed with prickles both numerous and geminate. The stem grows to 4 to 6 feet [ca. 1.3–2 m]; leaves of 5–7 leaflets which are oval, glabrous, pale green, and nearly glaucous beneath; flowers a sulphur yellow, scentless, and an inch and a half across [ca. 4 cm]; ovaries very large, light, spiny." [BJ17] "This rose, which is grown in our gardens under the name 'Rosier Jaune' ['Yellow Rose'], passes as originating in the Levant. It has long been regarded, in France, as a variety of the Capucine Rose [*Rosa foetida*]; but it presents some differences which can no longer be misunderstood—for example, its leaves are glaucous, simply dentate, scentless, and of a delicate consistency; the prickles with which the canes are armed are more obviously curved; as for the rest, the habit and other characteristics are the same. The sulphur-yellow rose grows vigorously; its ovaries are very large and fairly spiny. Its long, diffuse canes need to be secured and staked; its blossoms are light yellow and scentless; they are an inch and a half in diameter [ca.

Rosa hemisphaerica continued
4 cm], and appear in June. This rose loses its leaves very late." [CM]
"Nobody knows the single flowered type." [No26]

"This single yellow Rose is planted rather for variety then any other good vse. It often groweth to a good height, his stemme being great and wooddy, with few or no prickles upon the old wood, but with a number of small prickles like haires, thicke set, upon the younger branches, of a dark colour somewhat reddish, the barke of the young shootes being of a sad greene reddish colour: the leaues of this Rose bush are smaller, rounder pointed, of a paler greene colour, yet finely snipt about the edges, and more in number, that is, seuen or nine on a stalke or ribbe, then in any other Garden kinde, except the double of the same kind that followeth next: the flower is a small single Rose, consisting of five leaues [petals], not so large as the single Spanish Muske Rose, but somewhat bigger then the Eglantine or sweete Briar Rose, of a fine pale yellow colour, without any great s[c]ent at all when it is fresh, but a little more, yet small and weake when it is dried." [PaSo]

Previous commentators have evidently assumed that Parkinson's words, just quoted, refer to *Rosa foetida*; the description, however, is more consonant with *R. hemisphaerica,* particularly noting plant coloration and spination; and, of course, Parkinson refers to what is certainly the Hemisphaerica cultivar 'Multiplex' as being "the double *of the same kind*" (emphasis mine). Parkinson—always a close observer—reinforces this by writing in the entry on "the double yellow Rose" that this latter is "in all parts like vnto the former single kinde," which would not be the case were one *R. foetida* and one *R. hemisphaerica.*

Horticultural Varieties

Double Jaune Listed as 'Multiplex' (Hem).

Jaune Ancien Listed as 'Multiplex' (Hem).

Jaune Double Listed as 'Multiplex' (Hem).

Jaune Simple Listed as *Rosa hemisphaerica.*

Minor Listed as 'Pompon Jaune' (Hem).

Multiplex Plate 6
syns. 'Double Jaune', 'Jaune Ancien', 'Jaune Double', 'Sulphurea';
    trans., "Double"
Breeder unknown, pre-1629

"One of our honorable subscribers, President Carré, writes us from Tours: 'In my childhood—and it has alas been quite a long time since then—I saw, and I will always remember it, some beautiful roses of a magnificent yellow, which I have never since seen. Having the greatest desire to get myself this rose, I requested it from many people here, but in vain. At last, a gardener obtained for me, two or three years ago, some slips of this famous yellow rose. However, due probably to my unenlightened efforts, of the four slips, all of which had given me some leaves in the Spring, three are already dead; the fourth is still with me, and I'm quite afraid that it will be going the way of its three brothers if I can't prevail on you to come to my aid.'

The rose in question is our beautiful, ravishing Yellow Rose (*Rosa sulfurea*), so common at Alexandria, according to Bellon, who says this is the only sort he saw. The Yellow Rose has fallen out of cultivation, as have many others, because fanciers busy themselves chasing after such insignificant and ephemeral novelties as 'Fidouline' [*forgotten, extinct pre-1844 HP*], 'Mlle. Rachel' [*forgotten, extinct 1841 Bourbon from Monsieur Beluze*], etc., which are unworthy of even an ordinary collection. The Yellow Rose, if the truth be known, is a little difficult to grow. Its blossoms open poorly if exposed to the rain, the same if a too-bright sun desiccates them. Trained against a wall, and under the care of someone who will protect it against these dangers, it will give us some superb blossoms, and everybody will at that point like it better than they do the most sumptuous so-called *remontant* roses." [dH47/76]

"At the extremity of Asia, towards Constantinople, the *Rosa sulphurea* displays its very-double flowers of a brilliant yellow." [Go] "Very large, very full, deep yellow, opens with difficulty." [JR11/14] "In June and July, double flowers, almost always aborting when the bush isn't near enough to a wall protecting it from rain." [BJ24] "They are also very liable to the attacks of insects." [FP] "Blooms a bit after the single one. Its wood is green as it grows, later taking on a gray tinge. Its thorns are numerous, some of them with a wide base, strong, much hooked; others are smaller and flexible. Its calyx is big, short, wide, and flattened; these last two characteristics are unique to this species. The leaves, with seven to nine leaflets on the same leafstalk, are oval, dentate, and a pale green. The flower buds are large, round, and covered and crowned with the calyx-membranes, which are longer and larger than in [*the rest of*] the whole genus. The blossoms are very big, and so double that they frequently break. This rose is one of the most difficult to grow; if it gets too much sun, the flowers desiccate before fully opening; if, on the other hand, it's in too much shade, they rot and break without fully developing. Grafting it onto the Briar takes care of some of these problems. It is also necessary to plant it in a position where it will not be hit by the sun's rays from sunrise to ten or eleven." [C-T] "Put it into a sunrise to noon exposure; don't forget to water it when it dries out; plant it where its buds are protected from the rain. This rose has no scent. It has the habit of the Centifolia. Its thorns are very numerous and flexible. Its wood is green, and its leaves small. Opens June 1–9." [LeR] "Its very thorny stems are feeble and hold themselves up poorly. They manage 5 or 6 feet in length [ca. 1.6–2 m], and bear several slender branches, similarly armed with spines which are short as well as reddish. Its leaves are a light green, and are composed of 2 or 3 pairs of finely dentate leaflets, with an odd one at the tip. There are two sorts, one with single flowers [*see above*] . . . The other has double flowers subject to aborting and to rotting without fully opening, particularly in rainy years, or when the site is too warm." [Fr]

"The *double yellow Rose* only likes a moderate amount of sun; it likes to be cool and left alone—that's why it is neither necessary to tie them up nor to wrap them [in the Winter]. When you prune it, you shouldn't cut off anything more than the dry tips of the branches. It needs to be protected from heavy rains; otherwise the blossoms deteriorate and don't open well. This is why they make them a shelter when the year is too rainy. To improve the bloom and keep the buds from aborting, it's a good idea to pinch them out a good deal before letting them open. To carry them from year to year, before the bloom is past you should cut the plant back pretty short; and if they make much growth in the Fall, cut it back again the following March or April." [LaQ] "On young stems, the blossoms generally open badly, especially if pruned too hard; only old stems sheltered from both rain and sun can bear this beautiful rose to perfection. Not all soils and climates suit it: it blooms in France and Germany, but according to Andrews has not yet bloomed in gardens in or around London." [T&R] "In very damp and indeed swampy earth, it is said that the blossoms open more easily." [S] "It grows better in damp areas than in dry. It needs little pruning." [JF]

"It is a very old inhabitant of the gardens of Europe, though comparatively rare here [U.S.A.]. In Scotland, twenty-five years ago [*making ca. 1819*], I saw a plant of it, which was then considered a great curiosity, though it appeared to have been there a quarter of a century; it always showed a profusion of buds, but rarely a well blown flower; it never felt the pruning knife, being left to nature. History first notices it as being cultivated in Turkey … It is said that the gardens of Florence, Leghorn, and other parts of Tuscany, produce this rose in perfection, which proves that it requires a dry rich soil and an even temperature to bring it to perfection." [Bu] "One of the most ancient and beautiful varieties known to European gardens, introduced there in 1629. The flower is large, bright yellow, very double, and of globular form: its foliage is particularly delicate, with a glaucous pubescence; and its shoots have a greenish yellow tinge, very unlike the single yellow [presumably *Rosa foetida*], yet Mr. Rivers has ventured a supposition that it was produced from that variety fertilized by the Damask, which is also of Oriental origin." [WRP]

"This well-known rose needs no description." [LeR] "Sulphur-colored rose; glaucous. Flower full, yellow. Calyx hemispherical, glandulose; peduncles glabrous; stem and petioles prickly; thorns sparse; leaflets obovate, serrate, glaucous; stipules serrate. *Description.* The stem attains 4–6 feet in height [ca. 1.3–2 m]. It is a gray brown and covered with fine, yellowish prickles, as are the delicate shoots, which are long and brownish yellow. The petioles have mossy prickles. The leaves have no scent and are distinct from all other sorts of roses by their green-tending-to-gray color. There are seven ovate, cupped leaflets, which are obtuse, nearly wedge-shaped near the stem, and serrate. The short and glabrous peduncle ordinarily comes singly at the tip of the young shoots. The calyx is perfectly hemispherical, without obvious narrowing beneath the blossom; often it seems quite glabrous, and it is only after careful scrutiny that a person discovers several glands on the surface and on the semipinnatifid segments of the calyx. The sulphur-colored flowers are so full that it is unusual to see them develop perfectly. Indeed, they often die without opening during damp, cold periods. The blossom being extremely full, none of the sexual organs can be seen, and no fruit is ever produced. *Native to:* Persia (?). *Bloom Time:* July. *Observations.* A thousand ways to get perfect flowers from this rose have been proposed; but this end is rarely attained if the exposure and conditions are not at all favorable. As a rule, it is only very old and strong plants which bear flowers, especially when they are found in heavy, clayey soil and are never exposed to the burning mid-day sun. In very light or very fertile soil, they bourgeon too much, growing many delicate shoots and buds which only rarely develop. Propagation is normally by suckers, which however hardly ever produce blossoms before the sixth year." [Rsg]

"Rose with smooth seed-buds flatly rounded: leaves oval, sawed at the edges, and nearly glaucous: petioles prickly: flowers terminate the smaller branches: blossom yellow: petals numerous and crowded together: stem branching, and armed with crooked spines. Native of the Levant. This fine yellow Rose is a native of the Levant, and not to be met with in flower in any of the nursery-grounds near London. We have not seen it even in a budding state nearer than Brentford, in the collection of the Duke of Northumberland at Sion House, whence our drawing was begun last year from a fine plant with numerous buds, not one of which expanded sufficiently perfect for us to represent. To complete our figure, we this year received some fine specimens communicated by the Hon. W. Irby, collected from a gentleman's garden in the neighbourhood of Farnham, a distance of between twenty and thirty miles, and we believe the nearest approximation to the metropolis in which it can be found in perfect bloom. Even in the most congenial situations it is subject to an irregularity of inflorescence form the extreme complexity of its petals, occasionally bursting at the sides, and destroying the symmetry of its appearance. We have never seen it lighter in colour than we have represented, certainly much too deep a yellow to exemplify the pallid hue of sulphur. It flowers in the month of June, and was introduced to this country [Great Britain] in the year 1629." [A]

"Extremely vigorous growth; branches slender, long, and much-nodding; bark light green, armed with numerous upright thorns which are close together, unequal, fine, and very sharp. Leaves pale green, glaucous beneath, composed of 5–7 or sometimes 9 rounded and dentate leaflets; leafstalk slim, with fine, pointed prickles. Flowers about 2.5 inches across [ca. 6 cm], very full, quite globular, opening with difficulty, no scent, solitary or rarely more than one color, pale yellow, darker within; outer petals large and in a cup, central petals smaller and very numerous, completely hiding the center of the blossom; stem short, glabrous, nodding under the weight of the flower. Calyx globular, slightly flattened at the top, and generally glabrous; sepals leaf-like. This variety is not well known, despite having been for many years the only double yellow rose available … Suffers in the worst Winters." [JF]

"Very tall *bush.* Thorns strong, hooked, sparse, rare at the tip of the canes, lacking and replaced by numerous and long bristles at their base. *Leaves* glabrous and very glaucous. *Petiole* armed with straight, needle-like thorns. *Stipules* much constricted at their base, dilated at the summit, terminating in a free linear-lanceolate point, subulate, incised, and serrate. *Leaflets* 5, 7, or 9; elliptical, oblong, or obovate, obtuse. *Serration* acute, profound, convergent, normally simple. *Peduncles* ordinarily solitary and glabrous. *Ovary* large, hemispherical, glabrous, or more usually bestrewn with glandular points. *Sepals* simple, or bearing several appendages. *Flower* medium-sized, very full, globular and regular, beautiful yellow. Has difficulty opening. The epithet *Sulphurea* seems to me to be little in harmony with the bright golden yellow coloration of this Rose, which, when it opens well (something which, alas, is fairly rare), cedes nothing in perfection of form to the Centifolia." [Pf]

"Grown, from time out of mind, in our gardens; but … you don't meet up with many of them." [CM] "This rose was grown in Parmentier's collection at Enghien (Belgium); Guerrapain mentions it, and it's the 'Lutea Flore Pleno' of De Pronville." [Gx]

[Pompon Jaune]
syns. 'Minor', 'Sulphurea Nana'; trans., "Yellow Pompom"
Breeder unknown, pre-1806

"There is further a variety with very small, very double blossoms called 'Pompon Jaune'. I've got a bush, but I've never seen a blossom." [BJ09] "Small, double, globular, brilliant yellow." [JR11/14] "Flower very small, full; sulphur yellow, opening with difficulty." [JR4/21] "The small very double blossoms are quite as rare [as those of 'Multiplex'], and open with even more difficulty." [J-A/558–559] "The blossom, fuller and more beautiful [than that of 'Multiplex'], has yet even more difficulty opening." [BJ24] "Its blossom is certainly more beautiful [than that of 'Multiplex'], but its development sustains difficulties just as great; it is necessary to give it a warm exposure, just like with the large yellow rose; just the same, it needs to be planted in a dry site." [CM] "Flowers bright yellow, small, and double; form, globular. Habit, dwarf." [P] "*Shrub* dwarf. *Canes* very spindly. *Thorns* lacking, replaced by long bristles all the length of the canes. *Leaves* small, close-set. *Flower* very small, full, sulphur yellow. This rose is very stingy with its flowers, which rarely open well." [Pf]

"Now it is time to talk about 'Pompon Jaune', *Rosa sulphurea nana*. Its wood is green, delicate, and nearly entirely covered with fine, long, flexible stickers of the same color as the wood, though a lighter shade. The leaves are oval, deeply toothed, yellow-green, and come five to a petiole. This rose is even touchier to grow than ['Multiplex']. I have grown it for four years, and haven't seen one blossom you could call pretty. Going by the delicacy of its growth, which gets no more than six or ten inches high [ca. 1.5–2.5 dm], it should be called a miniature. Its rarity should make it much besought by fanciers." [C-T] "Another variety of the Briar of this color [*R. foetida*]; same wood, thorns, and leaves as ['Multiplex' (Hem)], in miniature. Buds inflated and overtopped, like the other, by the calyx appendages. It is very stingy with its flowers, which are less than half the size of those of the other, very double, and subject to the same problems. It should be grafted at three feet [ca. 1 m], if you want it to do well, on the Briar. Quite vigorous, one lone branch gave me, in 1816, more than twenty buds—not one of which opened due to the continual rain that year." [LeR, ruefully]

Simplex Listed as *Rosa hemisphaerica*.

Sulphurea Listed as 'Multiplex' (Hem).

Sulphurea Nana Listed as 'Pompon Jaune' (Hem).

CHAPTER ELEVEN

Foetidas

"These are simply wild Roses native in some parts of Europe, nearly single, and lovely in colour. The '[Austrian] Copper', as it is called, is the form best known; it is quite single, the petals being a most beautiful shade of coppery red, with orange yellow inclined to buff on the under sides. The others, 'Single Yellow' [*i.e., Rosa foetida,* the typical form], 'Persian Yellow', and 'Harrisonii' [*sic*; 'Harison's Yellow'], are also noted for their colour, being hardly surpassed in this point by any [other] known Roses. The two last named are double though by no means full, and are no doubt hybrid forms, but 'Harrisonii' is the best grower. They like a dry soil, will not succeed in suburban or smoky atmosphere, and all do best on their own roots, the suckers being encouraged and taken off when rooted if required to form fresh plants. It is best not to prune them at all, beyond cutting out dead wood; the shoots might be thinned, but there is no advantage in this with single Roses, where quantity of bloom is the thing desired; and they should not be shortened, as flower-bearing shoots often issue from the buds near the tips." [F-M] "This is easily recognized by the foetid scent of the flowers, but has pleasantly fragrant leaves which smell like apples when bruised. It is undemanding in culture; and, left to itself, attains a great height and could cover an arbor, but it resents pruning. It should not be confused with the Dog Rose nor the Sweetbriar, which are also referred to as *'Eglantier'* by many authors. It grows in England, Germany, and in southern France; several authors consider it native to the Paris area. We have never seen the double-flowered cultivar; but it is claimed to occur in gardens in the valley of Montmorency. Perhaps it has been confused with *Rosa sulfurea* [*i.e., R. hemisphaerica*], which is very different. Vilmorin has grown an attractive dwarf sort from seed." [T&R] "I have found ... the varieties of *Rosa lutea* Mill., particularly 'Bicolor' and 'Persian Yellow', trained on walls, which is very beautiful during bloom, but—alas! —too fleeting to recommend." [JR8/61] "Sarmentose canes covered with yellow or scarlet-orange blossoms. The bush does better, is less sarmentose, and lasts longer in mountainous country." [JR26/181]

"To bloom Austrian Briars in perfection, the soil should be moist, and the air dry as well as pure. But little manure is necessary, as they grow freely in any tolerably good and moist soil; neither do they require severe pruning, but merely the strong shoots shortened, most of the twigs being left on the plant, as they, generally, produce flowers in great abundance." [WRP] "It should not be pruned too closely; but the shoots may with great advantage be pinched back in midsummer, thus causing them to throw out a great number of lateral shoots, and correcting the loose and straggling habit of the bush. The bloom, with this treatment, is very profuse." [FP]

"This species was described for the first time by Dalechamps in 1587. It successively received the names *R. foetida* Herrm., *R. Eglanteria* L., *R. chlorophylla* Ehrh., *R. vulpina* Wallr., and *R. bicolor* Jacq. It is found wild in Asia Minor, Persia, Afghanistan, and eastern Tibet. Here and there in Europe it is found subspontaneously." [V-H80/104] "The roses in this category originated in the south of Europe. They can be found wild in the mountains of Italy, in Spain, especially in Persia, and other places. They were introduced into cultivation in 1596. All are very vigorous. The canes are a glossy chocolate color; the thorns are slender and pointed; the leaves are composed of 9–15 leaflets, which are quite rounded and toothed, and which have a very strong odor, as have the blossoms, nearly all of which are yellow." [JR11/13] "This is a small family of roses, very distinct in all its characteristics; a native of Southern Europe and of some parts of the east ... Its stems are spiny, and of a reddish or brownish color. Its leaves are small, and its growth somewhat straggling. The colors of its flowers are copper and yellow in various shades." [FP] "The two groups *Capucine* roses [*i.e.,* the Foetidas] and the *Sulphur Yellow* roses [*i.e.,* the Hemisphaericas]—which, for me, should be but one group, because there is no difference between them: wood, thorns, foliage, growth, flowers, nearly all the same color; the foliage in both groups having the same scent, approaching that of the Pimpinellifolias, but stronger; finally, the characteristics evident from their birth being exactly the same, I don't know why they are classed separately." [JR11/13]

"To tell the truth, the Capucine [*Rosa foetida* 'Bicolor'] and Sulphur Yellow Roses [*Rosa hemisphaerica*] bloom in April–May, which works against crossing them with those that bloom later. This problem, however, can be handled by transplanting the one set, and in protecting the others during Winter. What is more, the roses called Chinas, with semi-double and double blossoms, since they're always blooming, can always be used to pollinate the yellow roses, and vice-versa, giving two procedures which it is very important to try." [J-A/559] "I [Vibert] have found Pimpinellifolias in crops from the single yellow rose [*Rosa foetida*] which had inherited only a part of its color." [V2] "Simply through sowing seed —particularly that of the Capucine—people are trying to obtain a semidouble variety, from which will be found more easily, from seed, the true desideratum, a double variety. But these roses rarely give perfect seed, though indeed the ovaries seem ready to harvest—which doesn't happen very often. This year, at the Luxembourg, several specimens of this rose are covered with quite red hips, looking very good. Though many, as is usual, will be sterile, we have hopes that Monsieur Hardy, the able and zealous director of that garden, will have in such a large crop a good number of perfect seeds—which couldn't be in better hands." [J-A/560] "Strange to say, though the flowers are invariably single, they never produce seed. In this country [U.S.A.] it is also with extreme difficulty, and only by fertilizing its flowers, that seed can be perfected: if the flowers are examined they will all be found deficient in pollen, which accounts for this universal barrenness." [WRP] "It is seldom that any seedlings have been obtained from it, as its flowers, even in the single varieties, are usually barren. They may, however, be made productive by fertilizing them with the pollen of other varieties." [FP]

"Everyone knows *Rosa Lutea* (Mill.) / *Rosa Eglanteria* (Linnaeus), grown for centuries for the beauty of its large blossoms of the most beautiful yellow. Everybody also knows its variety with bicolored flowers, *Rosa Lutea punicea* or *Capucine Rose,* which has a richness of coloration unequalled in any other rose. These two differ only in the color of their petals, and indeed a person often sees *R. punicea* bearing, on certain branches, some sulphur-yellow blossoms, or some half-yellow and half-nasturtium-orange. Authors mention this odd happening in many a place, and this latter form has indeed received the name from Dupont *R. Tulipa* [*v.* 'Rose Tulipe']. The fructification of *Rosa Lutea* has, we believe, been much less studied than the plant proper—probably for the very good reason that this rose rarely bears fruit. Under the skies of Brie, fructification of Miller's Type is indeed so rare that, for our part, we had last year, for the first time in our life, the chance to gather 12 hips. Though there had already been some incidences of this rose seeding, it has been even less so with its bicolored form. Sometime before 1824, Souchet raised from seed of *R. Lutea punicea* a rose with very thorny canes and a pale yellow flower, which he called *R. L. Var. Flore Pallido* [*v.* 'Pallida'], and which he grew at that time in the large kitchen garden of the king, at the Trianon. Does this form still exist? We have no idea . . . We

have already tried a number of times to artificially pollinate *R. lutea*—without success! Last year [1894, or, more probably, 1893], as in preceding years, we tried to artificially pollinate all the flowers of a [would-be] pod-parent. Pollens of the most varied sorts were pressed into service; we used viscous liquid from the stigmas, nectary fluid, Lecoq's honeyed water, Koelreuter's oils, and weak acids recommended by Dr. Aldrige to the end of instigating, if possible, the dehiscence of the pollen grains, formation of the fertilizing tube, and—thusly—introduction of the cells from the stigmas. Of 200 flowers thus treated, two hips developed to attain their normal size. Our joy was uncontained! We had forced an ordinarily sterile plant to produce fruits. Alas! —this joy didn't last long. Shortly afterward, we stood before another *R. Lutea* of which the flowers had been left alone, and of the approximately 250 blossoms produced, *10* had borne fruit! In a word, the blossoms left to themselves had 'taken' in the proportion 4%; and those artificially pollinated gave only 1%. Instead of helping Mother Nature, we had paralyzed her work. The reader may think that we want to 'kill the thing we love'—far from it; never more than now have we been a militant proponent of artificial pollination, which, as a general rule, gives excellent results. To every rule, however, there is an exception, and such is the case here. We have taken some notes on the 12 hips we had the chance to collect, under good conditions, from the rest. At the moment of anthesis, the stigmas become covered with a viscous coating, which however is slight (it is very abundant and red in variety *punicea*). In the Type, this covering only manifests itself the day after the flower opens. *Anthers* elongate, dehiscing with difficulty, containing pollen fairly irregular in form, and which, studied under the microscope, would not seem abortive. On this point, we are pretty much ready to affirm that it is in the female organ of the blossom where we will find the causes of the habitual sterility of *Rosa Lutea. Mouth of the Receptacle* surmounted by a crown of bristles which surround the cluster of stigmas. *Styles* about 30, velvety, distinct, tipped by stigmas which are nearly purple (purple in *punicea*), united into a globose or subglobose head. *Sepals* sometimes entire, sometimes pinnatifid. *Hips* glabrous, globular and orange yellow in maturity. *Ovary* containing about 30 ovules; however, *mirabile dictu,* only one developed in each of the twelve fruits we collected. Each pericarp contained only *one seed* which had developed very much, and it didn't resemble a rose seed in the least. This nearly spherical seed was attached to the trophosperm by an umbilical cord which adhered to the seed. This cord was persistent, cylindrical, about half the width of the seed, and about 3 mm long [ca. $^1/_8$ in]. This strangely formed seed looked exactly like an animal's heart in which the pulmonary artery was represented by the podosperm or umbilical cord. It would be interesting to know if this single fertilized ovule in each of our gathered fruits is exceptional, or if all the Rosa Lutea hips contain but one enormous, strangely-formed seed, and if, consequently, never more than one ovule out of the 30 is fertilized. This latter scenario would not be unique in the Plant Kingdom. In effect, the *gland*, in the acorn or filbert, etc., which forms the young part of the fused or dry syncarp has an ovary of 3 chambers, each containing two ovules. Through unexplained phenomena, *all these ovules except one abort,* and the *mature* fruit has only *one chamber* and *one seed.* The causes of the ovular abortion, leaving but one—are they the same in both scenarios? Of this abortion, normal in certain dry indehiscent syncarpic fruits—was it a mere coincidence in the twelve fruits we collected? *'That is the question'!* We know very well that the monoid fecundation of unisexual flowers of the Oak has little to do with the primarily direct fertilization of the hermaphroditic blossoms of the Rose. Also, we make no conclusions; we only pose the question, and will receive with gratitude all communications on the subject." [JR18/4–6]

Rosa cerea Listed as *Rosa foetida.*

Rosa foetida Plate 16
botanical syns. R. cerea, R. lutea; horticultural syns., 'À Fleurs
Simples Couleur de Cire', 'Eglanteria Lutea', 'Jaune Simple'
Herrmann, 1542

"Large, single, cupped, pale yellow." [JR11/13] "Reddish very thorny wood; leaves fragrant, glabrous, glossy throughout; flowers numerous, solitary, single, and bright yellow." [J-A/558] "Blossoms single and yellow, but making a fairly beautiful appearance because of their number; its foliage is also very pretty and a beautiful green; crumpled between the fingers, it gives a Pippin apple [pomme-de-reinette] scent. This bush grows numerous branching canes which, above all else, are very thorny. It comes from Germany." [BJ09] "The single yellow rose, or 'Eglantine' rose of Linnaeus, springs up in poor terrain. Its blossoms develop there a color which is more vivid than when it is in a fertile soil. This rose grows in the mountains of Germany and Italy, in Switzerland, in England, and we grow it in our [French] gardens. It blooms around the end of May; it forms branched shrubs which grow five to six feet tall [ca. 1.6–2 m], covered with an immense quantity of blossoms which are scentless, but very sparkling, particularly in the sunshine. It's usually seen in country gardens in the second row in beds, against rocks, and indeed alone in the middle of lawns. It's just as good in parterres and against the walls of ornamental gardens. The leaves of the yellow rose have seven leaflets which are oval, deeply toothed, 8–10 *lignes* long [ca. 1–1¼ in], glabrous on both sides, and scented. The name 'Eglantine', which was given to it by Linnaeus, brings about frequent confusion with our hedge rose [*Rosa rubiginosa*], commonly called the 'Eglantine'… The yellow Eglantine, which is found in the middle of France, particularly around Aix, bears blossoms of a more or less light yellow, or of a deep poppy. Something worthy of note is that the leaves of this rose, lightly bruised, waft a balsamic scent, while a fetid odor, rather like that of *punaise*, exhales from the corolla." [CM] "This rose blooms in mid-May, just like [*Rosa foetida* 'Bicolor']. The wood is a glossy red when growing, afterwards developing a yellow tint; its thorns are long, very sharp, and nearly straight. The leaves are rounded, very serrate, and tipped with a point, and has five to nine leaflets per peti-

ole, which is green. The calyx of the flower is round, smooth, and shiny. The bud is pointed; the blossom is composed of five large, wide petals of a beautiful sulphur yellow. They come, as with ['Bicolor'], all along the branches, and keep on for nearly a month." [C-T] "It is not so frequently found in bloom near London as most other Roses, the atmosphere not being congenial to it. In France it is altogether as abundant; for in the summer of 1817 we found most luxuriant plants in all the flower-markets and most of the public streets in Paris." [A]

"Flowers yellow, the color of wax. Calyx half-winged. Ovary globulose, smooth. Leaves with lobes ovoid and nodding; serrated with deep, pointed serrations. Peduncles smooth, light green. Stem prickly … This rose, which blooms at the same time as the May Rose [*Rosa majalis*], gives five-petaled blossoms of a yellow the color of wax. The sexual parts are the same color. The calyxes are half-winged, are partially appendiculate at the tip, lanate along the edge, and on the outside are bestrewn with soft glandular bristles. The globular, smooth, glossy ovaries are, like the peduncles, light green. The leaves are composed of five to seven ovoid, nodding leaves, which come to a long point; they are usually doubly dentate; the petioles have short, isolated bristles along the edge beneath; the flower-bearing shoots are thornless; but at the point at which they join the bush, small shield-shaped prickles may be found, a dark brown in color, growing in pairs; the stem in clearly spiny, and of a brown green like that of the branches and young growths. I have not given this rose the name 'Eglantine' because its foliage has very little scent, as opposed to that of the true Eglantine, with red blossoms, having a very obvious wine scent." [Rsg] "*Stem* often over 3.6 m tall [ca. 11 ft]; *branches* and branchlets numerous, spreading, slender, greenish-brown; *prickles* straight, distant. *Leaflets* 5 or 7, ovate, obtuse, deeply bidentate, glandular, somewhat shiny and sticky, dark green above, paler beneath; *petioles* rough to the touch, more or less armed with small prickles. *Flowers* 1–3 at the branch tips on glabrous pedicels; *receptacles* globose, glabrous; *sepals* subulate, entire or pinnatifid; corolla to 7 cm across [ca. 2½ in]; *petals* 5, of a beautiful pale yellow; *styles* in a globose head, with more or less dark purple stigmas." [T&R] "*Shrub* tall, diffuse. *Canes* with a glossy brown epidermis. *Thorns* long, straight, uneven, sparse. *Bristles* lacking, except at the base of the shoots and the vigorous canes. *Petiole* glandulose, usually unarmed. *Stipules* entire, glabrous, fringed with glands, narrow and rolled under to the base; dilated, flat, and subulate at the tip. *Leaflets* 7 or 9, oval or ovoid, concave, glabrous and smooth above, glandulose, fragrant, and often slightly villose beneath. *Serration* double, glandulose. *Peduncle* glabrous. *Ovary* glossy, glabrous, globular. *Sepals* slightly hispid-glandulose; 3 nearly always bear 3–5 small subulate appendages. *Corolla* single, yellow, having an unpleasant odor. *Fruit* flattened, crowned by the reflexing sepals; usually, it aborts." [Pf]

"All the Arab authors who talk about Roses mention this one, which Crépin, among others, believes to have been grown for a very long time in Western Asia. Ibn-el-Façel, in the Twelfth Century, notes that its color is Jonquil yellow." [ExRé] "The name *Rosa foetida* was given to the wild yellow rose of Persia by Herrmann in 1762, under the impression that the blooms had an unpleasant odor, and this offensive designation has been revived by the later botanists under the rule of priority, but it is safe to say that rose-lovers will continue to use *R. lutea* when referring to the botanical status of the yellow Brier group." [ARA19/14]

Rosa foetida 'Bicolor' Plate 17

syns. 'Austrian Copper', 'Capucine', 'Comtesse', 'Cuivré', 'Eglanteria
    Punicea', 'Punicea', 'Rosier d'Austriche', 'Rosier-Ponceau'
Gerard, 1596

"Copper-red and golden yellow. The delight of landscape architects for flashing color in a shrub border. The single blooms, coppery red on the inside and vivid yellow on the outside of the petals, give the effect of a bush covered with brilliant butterflies." [C-Pf34] "A most singular rose; the inside of each petal is of a bright copper red, the outside inclining to sulphur." [WRP] "Coppery-red, very striking shade, semi-double." [EL] "Always single, with admirable tints of velvety poppy-red and golden yellow, often blended together." [JF] "Medium-sized, single, cupped, center ochraceous coppery red, exterior yellow." [JR11/13] "The red is a thin film laid over the yellow." [NRS21/100] "Hardy, mildew and black-spot resistant, and, unlike 'American Beauty' [HP], grows without much attention . . . 'Austrian Copper' is bright coppery red, the reverse of the petals being a golden yellow. My ten-year-old bush is 6 feet in height [ca. 2 m], 20 feet in circumference [ca. 6.6 m], the pendulous branches spreading in all directions and in June literally covered with thousands of blooms—a ravishing riot of color, it is then absolute queen of my garden." [ARA25/103] "Its stems, armed with short, brown thorns, are somewhat feeble, and put out several slender branches. Its very numerous flowers are single and remarkable by the color of their petals—light yellow on the face, and coppery purple beneath. They have neither scent nor duration, but their reign is a very brilliant one, though momentary. This rose has a variety in which, interiorly, the blossom is tinted bright crimson, while the exterior is yellowish. It, too, is single, and has less sparkle while being quite as fleeting." [Fr] "Its flowers are single, pale yellow within, velvety poppy-red without. This rose is always sterile and, considering that as well as the mixed color of the blossom, many botanists have come to the conclusion that it is a hybrid between *R. foetida* and another, red-flowered, species." [JF] "Differs from [the typical form] only in: 1. *Petals* of a fine ochraceous color within, yellow-orange without, sometimes striped yellow or purplish (Dupont's Rose Tulipe); 2. *Stems* and *branches* flushed red, whereas the yellow briar has them greenish-gray; 3. *Flowers* less foetid, and *leaves* less fragrant. In spite of these differences, most naturalists consider both roses to be one and the same species, for the simple reason that both may occur on one stem . . . [*Rosa foetida* 'Bicolor'] suckers freely and is adaptable to all soils." [T&R] "Differs from its type in bearing flowers of a pale yellow without, and deep orange within. Sub-varieties are cultivated at Lyons bearing yellow and red flowers on the same tree." [Go]

"Its wood is lightly touched brownish red. Its thorns are long, brown at the base, green at the tip, and nearly straight. The leaves are oval, small, and deeply toothed, with seven to eight leaflets on the same petiole, which last is green and armed with prickles of the same color which are slender and flexile. The calyx is round, smooth, and of a beautiful glossy green on a light brown petiole. The bud is long, and covered over with the calyx membranes. The blossoms are composed of five petals, nasturtium [orange] on the upper surface, pale yellow on the lower. Sometimes it gives solely yellow or solely orange flowers, and sometimes the two colors are mixed on the upper surface. They come all along the branch, young and old blossoms all mixed, and make very sparkling garlands." [C-T] "As to the Capucine

Rose, it is called Bicolor is allusion to its two colors yellow and red it's also called 'd'Autriche' [*i.e.,* "From Austria"]—nobody really knows why. The main stems and leaves of the Capucine Rose much resemble those of the Yellow Rose but its blossoms are larger, and its petals more deeply cut at the tips. The flowers . . . are single, a light yellow within, and a copper tending towards purple without; their smell is not agreeable; they fade easily. The Capucine Rose requires a northern exposure." [CM]

"Flowers single, an intensifying orange on the backs, ochre yellow within. Calyx segments having filiform appendages, but not very many. Ovary shiny, globular. Oval leaves drooping, terminating in a point, dentate, glossy. Peduncle and petiole glabrous . . . The orange or flame-colored rose bears single flowers composed of five petals ochre in color within and intense orange or flame on the outside; the styles and stigmas are deep brown red; the filaments and anthers are wax-color. The flower, which appears at the end of the month of May and the beginning of June, always stays a little twisted. The calyx segments, edged with a light white tomentum, have simple appendages, are filiform along the edges, and have a medium-sized appendage at their tip as well as some greenish bristles on their outer surface. Its glossy, light green ovary narrows at the short peduncle with the same gloss and tint. Both of them are glabrous. The leaves are composed of five to seven lobes, which are sessile, oval, nodding, sharply toothed, often doubly so, teeth angled towards the tip, dark green, shiny on the upper surface, light green and not shiny beneath; the petioles are accompanied on the underside by short bristles; and the tip of the straight, slightly serrate, stipule inclines backwards. The stem and branches are armed with light brown prickles. This rose likes good open exposure at noon and sundown. Reproducing from seed, it is very likely that this rose is a species all its own." [Rsg]

"It's a fact that this rose presents some great difficulties in research because, the Capucine Briar being very early, it gives fewer opportunities than others [*i.e.,* for breeding experiments] . . . It gives little seed, and rarely. It is said that, planted in a vase, and put out into the open ground in Spring, it is less parsimonious with its seed—an experiment easy to test." [BJ24] "A singular anomaly presented itself this year in the Capucine Rose or Ponceau Rose, Rosa eglanteria Var.: punicea [*sic*]. This early rose began to bloom at the end of April, and the warmth which obtains then made the blossoms open so quickly that, by the middle of May, they were nearly all gone. This hurried bloom initially worked against the flowers and gave the blossoms smaller size and a lighter color; later, however, the bloom began to go as usual, and lasted up until the first days of this month [*?*]. It was then that I noticed on a strong rose bush of this sort that the greater number of blossoms had two or three rows of petals, and that several of the others had more or less enlarged filaments. I report this fact which I thought interesting because a while ago they were talking about a double Capucine Rose raised in Belgium, which, so far as I know, has not yet appeared in either commerce or in French collections [*see* 'Jaune Double']. I have taken measures to pollinate a few of these semi-double flowers, and marked the branches to try grafting to perpetuate this duplicature." [An40/282–283]

"Was grown in Syria, Tripolitania, and Tunisia under the sway of the Saracens, who no doubt brought it to Europe. It was particularly distributed in Austro-Hungary, under the name 'Austrian Briar' . . . Described by the botanist Cornuti in 1635." [ExRé] "If you look for the date the Capucine was first known, you won't find it mentioned prior to the 17th century. It was only in 1635 that Cornuti (*Canadensium plantarum historia*) described a rose to which he gave the name *punicea*. According to the old botanist, [']this rose is much besought for the elegance of its coloration; on the exterior, its petals are saffrony, and, on the interior, poppy-red. Indeed, sometimes yellow lines at the base of the blossom add yet more to its elegance.['] Cornuti thought that Lobel mentioned this plant, and that it was known to the poets and ancient agronomes Virgil, Horace, and Columella. But nothing more is certain, and it is with only the greatest reservations, after studying the texts, that one can put any faith in Cornuti's words. The important thing is that Cornuti was the first to give the Capucine Rose a specific botanic name in good standing. Taking it further, Cornuti's priority would seem to be absolutely unrecognized or at least ignored. Usually, *Rosa punicea* is attributed to Miller. In 1640, Parkinson (*Theatricum Botanicum*, p. 1018) illustrates and describes the same plant under the name *Rosa sylvestris austriaca flore phoeniceo,* to which he gives the synonym *The Vermilion Rose of Austria.* This rose differs from the yellow rose [*Rosa foetida* proper] in particular due to its coloring. We see appearing for the first time the name 'Austrian Rose' that, later, is used by all the authors. In 1710 and 1720, the Leyden garden catalogs (*Index Plantarum,* etc.; *Index alter,* etc.) mention *Rosa punicea,* at the same time indicating an anomaly to which we will return later. Miller, in the first edition of his Dictionary, in 1731 (*The Gardener's Dictionary*), mentions under No 23 the Capucine Rose with Parkinson's synonymy under the name 'The Austrian Rose'; in the 8th edition, he repeats Cornuti's name, but in such a way as the reader would think he himself named it *Rosa punicea.* This last name would thus seem to have been adopted definitively—when, in 1770, the first of the Austrian botanists, Jacquin, made known a rose which had all the described characteristics and had been well known for more than a century. For him, it was *Rosa bicolor* (*Hortus vindobonensis,* I, p. 1, t. 1). The celebrated writer of floras maintained that he found no part of the synonymy to be adapted to this plant; that he was unaware of its place of origin, and that he considered it to be a new species. He adds that it was introduced to the gardens of Vienna from Holland, and that its elegance assured it of a place in gardens *'verum horti ornamentum'.* This is astonishing. Since 1640, all those mentioning this rose called it the Austrian Rose in 1770, the best flora-ist of Austria didn't know of it in his country, and said it came from Holland! We should wonder at this point what the specific standing of the Capucine Rose might be. Is it a single taxon? Is it simply a sport which occurred in the garden and was 'fixed'? For a long time, we have known a single yellow-flowered rose, *R. lutea* (*R. eglanteria* L. [our *R. foetida*]), which Daléchamps described and illustrated in 1587 in his *Historia generalis plantarum.* Lobel mentioned it in 1576 in talking about the yellow roses which were naturalized in France in his time (*Adversariorum volumen,* p. 446). It is this plant, originating in Asia Minor, Armenia, and Persia, which produced the Capucine Rose. Proof in support is not lacking: In 1720, Boerhaave mentions, as being grown at the Leyden garden, a Rose which would bear at the same time a branch of yellow flowers while all the others habitually bore Capucines. What was going on here was something which is always interesting to tell—a throwback from a horticultural form to the Type. Thory also noted that the two forms were likewise found on the same plant. Boerhaave's observation had

excited our strong interest, but it was only this year [1893] that we [author P. Hariot] were able to verify it. In a garden in Méry-sur-Seine (Aube) where *Rosa punicea* grew in abundance, we found, on two bushes of this last, some branches which bore only *Rosa lutea.* A person worthy of faith, Monsieur L. Hariot, to whom we showed this curious occurrence, stated to us that he also had seen it once a dozen years ago. We though that it would perhaps not be without interest to either the botanist nor to the grower to bring up this partial return to the original Type of a form long ago fixed, and which had acquired nearly all the characteristics of a single taxon. We have profited by the incident such that we feel we can hand back to its true promulgator, Jacques Cornuti, the name *Rosa punicea.*" [JR17/149–151]

Rosa foetida 'Persiana' Listed as 'Persian Yellow' (F).

Rosa lutea Listed as *Rosa foetida.*

Horticultural Varieties

À Fleurs Simples Couleur de Cire Listed as *Rosa foetida.*

Austrian Copper Listed as *Rosa foetida* 'Bicolor'.

Bicolor Listed as *Rosa foetida* 'Bicolor'.

Buisson d'Or
trans. "Golden Bush"
Barbier, 1928
From 'Mme. Édouard Herriot' (Pern) × 'Harison's Yellow' (F).

"Yellow, large, full, medium scent, tall." [Sn] "Type, 'Persian Yellow', but more vigorous and much larger. Bud large, ovoid; flower large, double, full, very lasting, extremely fragrant, canary-yellow, borne singly on medium-length stem. Foliage sufficient, large, rich green, wrinkled. Many thorns. Growth very vigorous, upright, bushy. Blooms in June. Hardy." [ARA28/237] "It grows to 3.5 feet [ca. 1.15 m], producing many flowers in early June. [The grower] thinks it is very beautiful and credits it with a faint fragrance. At Breeze Hill the plants, now three years old, produced big, fat buds along arching stems, opening to large, semi-double flowers of the 'Harison's Yellow' type, with an enormous mass of darker stamens. In flower it seems to be some improvement, but the plant is less vigorous and the stems are stockier and even more viciously thorny." [ARA31/194]

Capucine Listed as *Rosa foetida* 'Bicolor'.

Carnée Listed as 'Victoria' (F).

Comtesse Listed as *Rosa foetida* 'Bicolor'.

Cuivré Listed as *Rosa foetida* 'Bicolor'.

Double Blush Listed as 'Victoria' (F).

Double Yellow
syns. 'Jaune de William', 'Williams' Double Yellow'
J. Williams, ca. 1828

"Pale-yellow color." [FP] "Flower small, full; color, sulphur yellow." [S] "Medium-sized, double, cupped, bright yellow." [JR11/13] "Flowers bright yellow, of medium size, double; form, cupped. Habit, branching; growth, moderate. An abundant and early bloomer; requiring

Double Yellow *continued*

but little pruning. A good seed-bearer." [P] "A pretty double rose, raised from the Single Yellow Austrian a few years hence; this blooms more freely than the original species, and is a most desirable variety." [WRP] "Only a half double rose, of a very pale sulphur colour, about an inch and a half in diameter [ca. 4 cm]; a profuse bloomer, and of rather weak growth. It is said to have been grown from the Yellow Austrian [*Rosa foetida*], although I think it is more likely from a Scotch rose impregnated with that variety. It produces seed freely, and its capsule has more of the appearance of the Scotch than the Austrian Rose." [Bu] See also 'Jaune Double' (F).

Eglanteria Lutea Listed as *Rosa foetida*.

Eglanteria Punicea Listed as *Rosa foetida* 'Bicolor'.

[Globe Yellow]
Italy, pre-1846

"Bright lemon; form, globular." [P] "Flower large, full, globular, very well formed; color, bright golden yellow." [S] "Medium-sized, double, globular, bright citron yellow." [JR11/13] "A very pretty pale yellow rose, of humble growth; this variety was raised in Italy." [WRP]

Harisonii Listed as 'Harison's Yellow' (F).

[Harisonii No 1]
England, pre-1846

"Medium-sized, double, cupped, golden yellow." [JR11/13] "Numerous seedlings have been raised from ['Harison's Yellow'], but all that have come under my notice have proved very similar, or inferior to it. To one produced in England the name has been given of 'Harrisonii No 1' [*sic*]. This I have imported, and find the flower to be pale yellow, tinged with copper." [WRP]

[Harisonii No 2]
Breeder unknown, pre-1848

"Flowers buff, their centre reddish salmon; form, cupped." [P] "Medium-sized, double, cupped, yellowish white, salmony red center." [JR11/14]

Harison's Salmon
Stephen F. Hamblin, 1929
Seedling of 'Harison's Yellow' (F).

"Bud medium size, globular; flower medium size, semi-double, globular, lasting, moderately fragrant, pink and yellow in salmon color, borne singly on short stem. Foliage sufficient, small, rich green. Growth moderate (6 ft. [ca. 2 m]), bushy; profuse bloomer in May and June. Very hardy." [ARA30/219]

Harison's Yellow
syns. 'Harisonii', 'Hogg's Yellow'
Harison, ca. 1824
Conjecturally from *Rosa foetida* × *R. pimpinellifolia*.

"Flower soft gold and yellow, semi-double. Growth vigorous, summer flowering." [GeH] "Cupped." [JR11/12] "Golden yellow, medium size, semi-double; generally has nine leaflets, a freer bloomer than 'Persian Yellow'. This is believed to be a hybrid between the common Austrian and a Scotch rose." [EL] "The best hardy yellow rose, bright clear golden yellow, entirely hardy and fine for planting with hardy ornamental flowering shrubs; makes a grand display of bright golden yellow flowers early in Spring." [C&Js03] "Grows 3 to 4 feet high [ca. 1–1.3 m]." [C&Js07] "Do not prune it, except to take out dead canes." [C-Ps25] "As it is somewhat bare-legged, it is best planted among shrubs or perennials that will hide the base of the plant." [C-Ps29] "Plant it where you have plenty of room for it to spread." [C-Ps26] "I am vastly proud of my hedge of 'Harison's Yellow', and I wish you could see it. It extends for sixty feet [ca. 20 m] all along the driveway on a rather steep hill, then jumps across the lawn and takes possession of a little mound or bank about six feet high [ca. 2 m] which it has completely covered. The plants on top of the mound are about eight feet high [ca. 2.6 m], and their bases are hidden by the canes growing lower down. This mound is a miracle of soft yellow when they bloom, and the glory lasts for about two weeks. The whole collection or colony has sprung from one rather puny old plant which was established for Heaven knows how many years on the place when we bought it about fifteen years ago. Incidentally, there were fifty-six seed-pods on the 'Harison's Yellow' plants this year, the largest number I have ever known. The Rugosas, Multifloras, Sweetbriars, Spinosissimas and others were in full flower with the 'Harison's Yellow' this year, and that accounts for the heavy crop of seed." [ARA23/178]

"Plants of 'Harrison's Yellow' [*sic*] in dry situations occasionally seed with some freedom; but, although many hundreds of chance or self-fertilized seeds have been sown, I have never known one to germinate, and have never been able to secure seeds by pollinating its blooms from other roses, though as many as 600 trials have been made in a season." [ARA16/32] "One plant of our three seedlings of 'Harison's Yellow'—the entire outcome of years of seed-sowings—bloomed quite profusely the past season, the third from germination. The plant appears rather nearer *R. spinosissima* than *R. lutea*, one of the reputed parents of 'Harison's Yellow', and the blooms, though well finished and more double, are lighter in color than those of this most valuable variety. It, however, responds to cross-fertilization and perfects seeds with foreign pollen, which has never been the case in our trials with 'Harison's Yellow'." [ARA19/33]

"Sent out in 1830 by an American, Rev. George Harison. Nothing was given of its parentage, but supposedly it is the single yellow Austrian Brier crossed with some form of the Scotch rose . . . 'Harison's Yellow' is very vigorous and long-lived (fifty years or more in grass), suckers quite freely (so it may be divided), and is considerably free from leaf-troubles. The twig and short bristles are quite Scotch. It blooms freely and sets abundant seed . . . Seeds taken from isolated plants have germinated very well. The new plants are identical with other Scotch roses in leaf, growth, bristles, and suckering roots—there is nothing of Austrian Brier in this second generation. Except for flower color, they are Scotch roses. The flowers range from single to as double as 'Harison's Yellow', the yellows predominating from deep to pale, but with others white, pink, rose, and salmon, a very sturdy assortment of Scotch roses. One, identical with the parent, save in paler color, has been tagged 'Harison's Lemon', and resembles a theoretic double Hugonis. Seedlings of the third seed generation will bloom this year. Still there is no Austrian Brier in them." [ARA30/50–51] "This very beautiful yellow, and in fact the *only yellow* rose of this character that I have seen worth cultivating, was grown by a Mr. Harrison [*sic*], near New York, about twenty years ago, and is evidently a seedling from the Yellow Austrian; its growth, after being well established, is quite luxuriant, often making shoots six feet long [ca. 2 m] in one season. The wood is of a dark reddish brown colour, with strong straight thorns, the foliage small, of a dark rich green; the flowers open of a beautiful globular form, and appear like as many golden balls; when open they are about two inches in diameter [ca. 5 cm], and nearly double, blooming very early in the season, and in great profusion; it seeds rather sparingly, but will no doubt produce many fine varieties. It delights in a good deep loamy soil, although it may grow in any soil or exposure; seeds saved from it should be sown and protected with the greatest care, and at no distant period we may anticipate, from this very plant, yellow roses possessing all the requisites of colour and form that the amateur can desire. The pruning must be done very sparingly; if the plant gets crowded, thin out the branches; the overgrown and straggling shoots can be shortened to any required length." [Bu] "Raised from seed by the late Geo. Harrison [*sic*], Esq., of New-York, form whom I [William R. Prince] received the first plant he parted with, in exchange for a Camellia Aitoni, which I had just then imported at an expense of three guineas. It has proved not only brilliant and beautiful, but what was equally important, a most free and profuse bloomer; the flowers which are not quite full double are about two inches in diameter [ca. 5 cm] and globular before expansion, but a hot sun makes them expand and lose much of their beauty. It is a more robust grower than ['Double Yellow'], often forming shoots of five to six feet [to ca. 2 m] in a season; its flowers are also a little larger, and do not fade so soon. Numerous seedlings have been raised from this variety, but all that have come under my notice have proved very similar, or inferior to it." [WRP] "Absolutely indispensable for dooryard adornment throughout practically our whole country …It bears evidence of admixture between the Asiatic *Rosa lutea* and the Scotch rose, *R. spinosissima,* and is the only form of the bright yellow *Rosa lutea* thoroughly at home in our climate." [ARA16/28]

"Was considered a great acquisition, a few years since, but this is now entirely eclipsed by the 'Persian Yellow'." [BBF66] "A bush of 'Harison's Yellow', when fully grown, is a magnificent and heartsome sight in early spring, its blooms coming in such abundance as almost to cover the bush. It makes a beautiful specimen plant for a lawn." [C&Js21]

Hogg's Yellow Listed as 'Harison's Yellow' (F).

[Jaune d'Italie]
Italy, pre-1846

"Pale straw yellow." [P] "Straw colored flowers with a yellow center." [WRP] "Small, double, straw yellow." [JR11/14]

Jaune de William Listed as 'Double Yellow' (F).

[Jaune Double]
trans. "Double Yellow"
Breeder uncertain, pre-1802

"Large, very full, yellow." [R&M62] Rössig mentions, under his discussion of *Rosa foetida* (as *Rosa cerea*), "a rare variety with double flowers, of the same color, which shouldn't be confused with the sulphur-colored double yellow rose [*i.e., Rosa hemisphaerica*]." [Rsg] "I hear that a sub-variety [of *Rosa foetida*] with double flowers exists; I have never seen it; maybe someone grew it from seed." [BJ09] "Fanciers have long since desired a double Capucine; they have made great efforts to obtain it. Indeed, I am assured that it *has* been obtained; but that, in the press to propagate it by dividing the specimen in two, all was lost." [BJ24] "Though Monsieur Parmentier has cited a double *R. lutea* in his collection at Enghien, I have not yet seen anything of it." [BJ30] "I read in the February 1836 issue of *Horticulteur Belge* that Monsieur de Coster, the Duke of Aremberg's foreman at Louvain, successfully strove to double the Capucine or Poppy Rose, *Rosa bicolor* Jacq., Hort., Kew, a sort of yellow rose. This fact, which for several years had been falsely announced by some catalogs, would seem finally to be confirmed, not only by this article in *Horticulteur Belge,* but also by particular knowledge which I have of the existence of this double Rose at the homes of several fanciers. This is an interesting conquest for Horticulture—to get this Rose, which ought to eclipse the Type … Let us hope that this novelty will be quickly introduced into France through the zeal of our amateur horticulturalists." [An46/210] See also 'Double Yellow' (F).

Jaune Simple Listed as *Rosa foetida*.

Lawrence Johnston
Pernet-Ducher, 1923 (but see below)
From 'Mme. Eugène Verdier' (N) × 'Persian Yellow' (F).

"Deep yellow, medium size, lightly double, light scent, tall." [Sn] A rose with a rather tortuous path to recognition! As we read in detail in T4, the rose is a sibling of 'Le Rêve' (F), but, though raised in 1923 (or so writes Thomas; if indeed a sibling of 'Le Rêve', we have other suspicions; but see 'Le Rêve' below), was unappreciated by its raiser, who held it back from introduction. At length, the only specimen was purchased by Major Lawrence Johnston, who planted it at his garden at Hidcote Manor in England. Still unintroduced, some specimens were distributed under the name 'Hidcote Yellow'. It was at this stage that Graham S. Thomas became familiar with it, and subsequently exhibited it in 1948 with Major Johnston's approval under the name 'Lawrence Johnston'. Mr. Thomas finds it to be an improvement on 'Le Rêve'. We have alas been unable to pinpoint the actual date of introduction.

Le Rêve
trans. "The Dream"
Pernet-Ducher, 1923 (but see below)
From 'Souvenir de Mme. Eugène Verdier' (HP) × 'Persian Yellow' (F).

"Sun yellow." [Cw] "Yellow, medium size, single to lightly double, tall." [Sn] "Flower large, semi-double, pure, unfading sunflower-yellow, borne erect, in clusters. Foliage large, bright green. Very vigorous, semi-climbing; blooms from June to September. Very hardy." [ARA25/187] "One of the first to flower." [C-Ps31] "Wonderful in early summer, but soon sheds its foliage." [ARA31/181] "One of the best for a large bush." [NRS28/37] "This is a true Pernetiana, but grows with long, not too stiff, shoots, much the way of our true climbing roses. It blooms but once, the flowers coming in small corymbs, and they are of an intense, deep, sun-yellow. The plant is as hardy and healthy as a rose can be." [ARA26/166] "Plant strongly climbing, growing to 2–3 meters high [ca. 6–9 ft]. Absolutely winter hardy. Blooms solitary or up to five, the plant quite covered. Each blossom very large for the sort, half full, long-lasting bright sun yellow without any shading or fading." [Ck] "The bush is a semi-climber, with foliage of pleasing green, and wood red like [that of] *R. lutea.*" [ARA25/129] "Beyond doubt this is the finest clear, unfading yellow climbing rose which will grow in the northern states. The large, clear yellow buds and blooms are produced in bewildering profusion very early in the sea-

Le Rêve *continued*

son. Plant is moderately vigorous, reaching 12 to 15 feet [ca. 4–5 m]. Foliage is beautiful but very susceptible to disease, and the plant is usually bare from midsummer on. In spite of its disreputable appearance at that season, it is worth particular care because of its great beauty in springtime." [GAS] There is some question as to the parentage of 'Lawrence Johnston' and 'Le Rêve'. Said to be siblings, the pod-parent of one is reported as 'Mme. Eugène Verdier', the Noisette, and the pod-parent of the other is reported as 'Souvenir de Mme. Eugène Verdier', the Hybrid Perpetual.

"This Rose is a refined 'Star of Persia', producing abundantly its clear yellow, fragrant, semi-double flowers, but with better foliage and habit and it also blooms every year." [C-Ps29] "This Rose is a duplicate of 'Star of Persia' but it is more bushy and not so tall in growth." [C-Ps27] "Sweeter [than 'Star of Persia']." [C-Ps28] "'Le Rêve' and 'Star of Persia' seem so much alike that it is useless to grow both. 'Le Rêve' holds its flowers fully two weeks longer, and has a peculiar and pleasing fragrance. Neither is a vigorous climber, and although they make fair pillars, we believe they will eventually fall into the shrub class, with 'Harison's Yellow' and 'Persian Yellow'." [ARA27/136]

"Not in commerce [but extant, in 1906]." [LS] "[Pernet-Ducher] had produced 'Le Rêve' more than twenty years ago [*i.e.,* ca. 1905] and finally decided to send it out because of its great decorative value, its early blooming, abundant and of long duration, and its hardiness." [ARA25/129] See also 'Lawrence Johnston' (F) and 'Star of Persia' (F).

[Luteola]

syn. 'Serin'
Breeder unknown, pre-1821

"Rose with round seed-buds, smooth: peduncles slightly hispid: flowers single, of a pale yellow colour: leaves spreading: leaflets ovate, pointed, ribbed, and notched: stem and petioles very prickly. [Andrews'] drawing of this new species of Scotch Rose was taken last summer (1821) at the nursery of Mr. Knight, where it flowered early in July, and again in autumn; ripening the fruit of those that flowered first, whilst the autumnal flowers were blooming. It is said to be indigenous to Scotland, and to blossom there more freely than with us. At present it is of a very pale yellow colour, which careful cultivation might improve. It would then we more estimable, as yellow is a colour rarely to be found amongst the roses." [A] "Much branched *shrub* about 0.9 m tall [ca. 3 ft], similar to [*Rosa foetida*] . . . but smaller in all its parts and with the *stems* covered with a great number of prickles of different sizes. *Leaflets* 7–9(–11), rather dark green, small, subrotund, glabrous on both surfaces, serrulate, gland-edged; petioles glabrous, with small, yellowish prickles; stipules broadening above, gland-edged. *Flowers* 1–2 at the ends of the laterals, unpleasantly scented, but less fetid than those of [*Rosa foetida* 'Bicolor']; *receptacles* depressed globose, glabrous; pedicels long, glabrous; *sepals* entire or pinnatifid, downy within, densely covered with glands outside; *petals* 5, rather small, canary yellow, cordately notched. Dupont's 'Rose Tulipe' . . . is a derivative of this. They grow in France, England, Germany, Italy, and Spain." [T&R]

[Pallida]

Souchet, 1824
Seedling of *Rosa foetida* 'Bicolor'

"Blossoms a sulphur yellow; canes very prickly. Several persons confuse with this sort the double yellow rose which belongs to *sulphurea* [*i.e., Rosa hemisphaerica*], and not to *lutea* [*i.e., R. foetida*]." [No26] "This rose, grown in the great kitchen garden at Versailles, was raised, says Monsieur de Pronville, from seed of *lutea bicolor*. It differs from its mother in its very thorny canes, and its flowers which are a sulphur yellow." [S] "Sometime previous to 1824, Souchet raised, from seed of *R. lutea punicea,* a rose with very thorny canes and a pale yellow flower which he called *R. L. Var. Flore Pallida,* and which he grew then in the royal kitchen garden at the Trianon. Does this form still [1894] exist? We have no idea." [JR18/4]

Parkfeuer

trans. "Parkfire"
Lambert, 1906
Seedling of *Rosa foetida* 'Bicolor'

"Red, medium size, single, tall." [Sn] "Flower brilliant scarlet-red, medium size, semi-double, single; summer flowering. Growth vigorous." [GeH] "Another Rose of pillar-like habit of growth. Its flowers, red and yellow, were small and shapeless." [NRS25/113] "Blossom single, flame red. Foliage and wood reddish. Plant very strong-growing, quite beautiful; pendulous in habit, unrivalled bordering water." [Ck]

Persian Yellow   Plate 18

syn. *Rosa foetida* 'Persiana'
Willock, 1833

"Medium-sized, double, globular, golden yellow." [BJ58] "Large, full, globular, deep yellow." [JR11/13] "A handsome mass and a more brilliant color than 'Harison's [Yellow]', but without its spiritual charm." [ARA28/63] "Flowered finely this year [1844], and far eclipses all other yellow roses; it has a better habit than the Harrisonii [*sic;* 'Harison's Yellow'] and is equally as free a bloomer, and as double as the Cabbage Rose." [MH44/379] "The 'Persian Yellow' flowered in our collection last Summer and is the most superb of all the yellow roses. [Its rival] 'Chromatella' or 'Cloth of Gold' [the Noisette] is a fine rose, but not quite so yellow as was at first announced." [MH45/9] "Colour the most brilliant yellow that may be imagined, full, large (up to four inches in diameter [ca. 1 dm]), and free-flowering . . . Fat round buds[,] the early ones have a disinclination to open, and the first flowers are often divided or have green centres. When perfect[,] a most beautiful flower, and none of more intense yellow. Does best creeping up a south wall, flowers rather late." [B&V] "Very floriferous." [R&M62] "'Persian Yellow' cannot be recommended too highly; its moderately full flowers are a deep golden yellow color and the young leaves have the fragrance of the Sweet Briar. It blooms freely under ordinary treatment but requires care in pruning; the head should be well thinned and the shoots that are left for flowering should be allowed to remain long. Established plants should be pruned very little." [C&Js11] "Bright yellow, small, nearly full, well formed; small foliage, faintly scented like the Sweetbriar; seven leaflets; the wood is chocolate-brown in color, armed with numerous brown thorns; it is the finest of all hardy yellow roses. It must not be closely pruned; it is desirable to grow more than one plant, and by pruning one this year, in the usual way, and the other the next, annual crops of flowers may be had. Does not grow from cuttings." [EL] "It is one of those roses which are feeble on their own roots, but grow very vigorously either on the Dog Rose or on the Manetti[i] stock." [FP] "A prolific source of infection where Black Spot is concerned." [NRS28/36]

"A new yellow rose has been given to us from the land of flowers, Persia. This was introduced by the London Horticultural Society in 1838, and is now called the *Persian Yellow Rose*. In habit it is very like the Single Yellow Austrian Briar; it seems to grow readily budded on the Dog Rose, and plants so budded have made shoots three feet or more [ca. 1 m +] in length in one season. In color it is of a deeper yellow than ['Harison's Yellow'], quite double, cupped, and not so liable to become reflexed as that very pretty and brilliant rose. Like the Yellow Austrian Briar, it loves a pure air and rich soil, and will then grow and bloom most freely." [WRP] "It belongs to the Pimpinellifolia tribe and seems to be a sub-variety of *Rosa eglanteria punicea*. It makes an elegant, very bushy shrub, very thorny, in which the elegant foliage with small, very fresh green, foliage is enhanced by a multitude of little double yellow roses, producing a charming effect." [An46/210] "'Persian Yellow' is none other than a double variety of Miller's *Rosa lutea,* the *Rosa Eglanteria* of Linnaeus; it's a bush the vigor of which is acceptable when grafted on the Briar or on the Multiflora 'De la Grifferaie', but which never lasts long unless grown 'own root', which suits it the best. It doesn't need to be placed in a special site, because the blossoms, nearly always solitary on their stalks, come in multitudes all along the canes of the preceding year, and open well whatever the case … The blossom of this variety, growing sometimes to 10 cm [ca. 4 in] in size, is full, well formed, a beautiful shaded golden yellow, accentuated on occasion by a longitudinal carmine line in the middle of some ragged petals at the center of the blossom, which tends towards a cupped shape, an arrangement which allows the equally yellow stamens to show. As to hardiness, 'Persian Yellow' leaves nothing to be desired." [JR7/41] "It has been a dozen years [*making 1836 or 1837*] since this Capucine Rose with very full flowers was introduced in England. It was only in 1845 that it was let out into commerce, and only last year [1847] that it bloomed in France for the first time. We have had it painted at Monsieur Louis Chanet's, horticulturalist at Gentilly, known as an able and hard-working rosarian because of the beautiful rose 'Mme. Angélina [*extinct, forgotten Bourbon of 1844; syn., 'Mme. Angélique'*] which he bred three years ago. The rose 'Persian Yellow'—which it would be more logical to call 'Capucine Persian'—is a very full flower, 8–9 cm in size [to ca. 3½ in], beautiful golden yellow, sometimes sprinkled or striped with some veins of carmine which one might see at the center of the blossom. The wood of the bush is noticeable because of its intense red, which distinguishes it from the others; the thorns are red, like the wood, at the base, and green at the tip; the leaves are ample and denticulate; the ovary is smooth and enlarged at the tip. There is one sole thing for which this variety might be reproached: it doesn't rebloom. Culture: —This rose will only last long if it is grown own-root—that's for sure." [dH48/274] "Very vigorous; canes rather tapering, upright, developing flowering branchlets; bark smooth, brownish red, armed with numerous reddish prickles which are thin, straight, very sharp, and much enlarged at the base. Leaves smooth and glossy, beautiful green, paler beneath, giving a scent of Pippin apples, divided into 7 or usually 9 oval leaflets, slightly pointed, finely and regularly dentate; petiole straight, green, slightly reddish at the base. Flowers about 2.5 inches across [ca. 7 cm], fairly full, cupped, slightly hollow at the center, usually solitary, or in twos or threes; color, beautiful golden yellow; outer petals concave for the first 2–3 rows, those of the center smaller and ruffled, and a brighter yellow; peduncle slender and red-

dish. Calyx glabrous, nearly hemispherical. This rose is not remontant, but is to be recommended for its vigor, its hardiness, and for the beautiful color of its flowers, which unfortunately waft a disagreeable odor. Considering its bearing and foliage, it would seem to be descended from *R. foetida*. It was introduced from Persia to England in 1833 … by Mr. Henry Willock; and into France around 1842." [JF]

"The rose 'Persian Yellow' … was brought from Persia to England around 1838 by the traveler Willock; but it wasn't until about 1845 that you could see it in the French rose catalogs, and it was only in 1846 that France saw a blooming plant." [JR7/41] "This rose … was introduced from Persia into the gardens of the London Horticultural Society in 1838 by Sir H[enry] Willock, and, in France, by Portemer fils in February 1841 along with the HP's 'Prince Albert' and 'Rivers', which were not yet in French commerce (Mr. Rivers, English horticulturalist, had bought the rights to these two roses from their breeder, Mr. Laffay)." [JR11/14] "I also noted at Portemer's and at Verdier's the rose 'Persian Yellow', which came to us from England, whence it seems to have been imported from India." [An46/210] One also sees the attribution "Lemaire, 1837" for this cultivar, an attribution we have been unable to substantiate.

"On the fourth of July we were crossing middle Norway, about latitude 63° … At the end of the Sognefjord we came to a little village called Laerdal, and just outside our hotel window was the most magnificent bush of *Rosa lutea* (the Persian Yellow) I ever saw. It was some twelve feet high [ca. 4 m], and more than that in diameter. There were thousands of roses—more yellow roses than I ever saw before of this species." [ARA20/48]

See also 'Double Yellow' (F) and 'Jaune Double' (F), should you suppose that 'Persian Yellow' was the first double yellow Foetida.

Punicea Listed as *Rosa foetida* 'Bicolor'.

[Rose Tulipe]
trans. "Tulip Rose"
Dupont/Noisette, pre-1817
Descended, perhaps immediately, from 'Luteola' (F).

"Yellow with poppy bands." [BJ17] "In June, flowers yellow with poppy bands." [BJ24]

Rosier d'Autriche Listed as *Rosa foetida* 'Bicolor'.

Rosier-Ponceau Listed as *Rosa foetida* 'Bicolor'.

Rustica
Barbier, 1929
From 'Mme. Édouard Herriot' (Pern) × 'Harison's Yellow' (F).

"Yellow, light orange center, medium size, full, medium scent, tall." [Sn] "Bud medium size, globular, yellow, tinted red; flower medium size, semi-double, full, open, lasting, moderately fragrant, straw-yellow and gold, apricot at center, outside citron-yellow, borne several together on medium-length stem. Foliage abundant, medium size, rich green, glossy. Growth very vigorous, semi-climbing; profuse bloomer for four weeks in May and June. Very hardy." [ARA30/225]

Serin Listed as 'Luteola' (F).

Star of Persia
Pemberton, 1919
From *Rosa foetida* × 'Trier' (Lam).

"Bright yellow." [Ÿ] "Deep yellow, medium size, lightly double, tall."

Star of Persia *continued*

[Sn] "A marvelously vivid buttercup-yellow Rose … the color *does not fade* … You can use this Rose as a climber or grow it as a specimen bush." [C-Ps27] "Blooms latter part of May and beginning of June, and intermittently during the summer. A good pillar Rose." [ARA20/130] "Colour bright yellow with golden stamens. Flowers semi-single, about three inches across [ca. 7.5 cm], blooming at the end of May and early June. Summer flowering. Growth from eight to ten feet high [ca. 2.6–3.3 m]. A pillar Rose." [NRS19/167] "The golden yellow, semi-double flowers are about 3 inches across [ca. 7.5 cm], and with petals of remarkable substance and firmness. The plant is reported to be hardy and vigorous as a low climber, and seems to present a brilliant yellow analogy to 'Paul's Scarlet Climber'." [ARA25/196] "Strong-growing." [Ck] "Should not be planted in a conspicuous place because the foliage drops in midsummer." [C-Ps29] "Will not bloom and soon dies of stem-rust." [ARA31/181] "Black-spots; blooms only once; fine color; good growth … *Mass.*; although I have had my plant two full seasons and it has grown many 10-foot canes [ca. 3.3 m], making an enormous bush, I have not seen a bloom yet. Foliage beautiful in early summer, but by September 1 the canes are practically bare from black-spot … *R.I.*; … more a high bush than a climber … *N.Y.*" [ARA28/

191] "Moderately vigorous climber, generally classed as a hybrid of *Rosa foetida*. It bears large, single or semi-double, bright yellow flowers which do not fade white. The foliage is very bad, and it sometimes fails to bloom at all. Not a great deal unlike 'Le Rêve' but perhaps the flowers are a trifle smaller and a shade brighter. Very hardy." [GAS] "Enormous semi-single blooms, very freely produced, and not liable to much damage by rain, or sun. Colour bright yellow, with lovely golden stamens. Foliage and wood like [those of] 'Persian Yellow', but much larger. Free of mildew. Growth very vigorous, making a lovely pillar rose. Summer flowering only, but still very welcome." [NRS23/96] See also 'Le Rêve' (F).

[Victoria]

syns. 'Carnée', 'Double Blush'
Guérin, pre-1846

"Salmon blush color, with a buff centre, large, but not fully double." [WRP] "Small, double, cupped, light salmon pink, yellowish center." [JR11/13] "Flowers light rosy pink, their centre buff; form, cupped. Very sweet." [P]

Williams' Double Yellow Listed as 'Double Yellow' (F).

CHAPTER TWELVE

Pimpinellifolias

"Amongst the modern additions to the ornaments of our gardens [writing in 1820], the varieties of *Double Scotch Roses* stand deservedly very high in estimation; their beauty is undisputed, and as they come into flower full three weeks before the general collection of garden Roses [*a footnote adds:* The earliest varieties open before the end of May, and the succession of blossoms on the different plants is kept up till near the end of June], they thus protract the period of our enjoyment of this delightful genus. On the British collector's notice they have an additional claim, being almost exclusively the produce of our own country; for of the many kinds that I have observed there are only three which can by any possibility be supposed to have originated out of Great Britain. The Scotch Rose has been, and still is, sometimes called the Burnet Rose; it is the Rosa spinosissima of the English authors of authority who have written on the genus: they have united the Rosa pimpinellifolia and the Rosa spinosissima of Linnaeus, treating them as the same species, and not even separating them as varieties ... I do not mean to question the propriety of considering them as the same species, but they are, assuredly, so different from each other, that they ought to have been treated as varieties; and when all the plants usually called Scotch Roses are brought together, the Rosa pimpinellifolia above alluded to must be considered as the type of the species, for, if they have all been derived from one stock, I apprehend that was the original parent; for which reason if I were writing an account of the genus, or treating on the particular species, I should certainly adopt *pimpinellifolia* as the specific name." [JSp]

"The *Scotch Rose* is a race which is valuable due to its precocity. It is sometimes a full month ahead of other summer Roses. Alone, it makes the most charming dwarf bush one could see, covered with their little globular flowers in flesh, pink, poppy-red, or carmine-shaded—all these nuances being found in the different varieties. The bush blooms under the weakest of suns, and takes to pruning very well. Usually you prune it close to wintertime." [R-H63/126–127] "*Pimpinella Rose.* This species was so called by Linnaeus because its foliage resembles that of the plant which goes by that name. The Spinosissima is a variety of the Pimpinel-

lifolia, according to Lamarck, while Bosc has it that the Pimpinellifolia is a variety of the Spinosissima. Be that as it may, they are the same species, called the Scotch Rose by Poiret. The plant makes a stocky bush, not very high; the young stems are covered with stickers of various sizes, nearly straight, thin, close-set, and very sharp; they come off in the second or third year. The leaves are composed of nine to eleven leaflets which are rounded, obtuse, ashy green, simply dentate; the petioles have small hooked prickles; the blossoms, which are more or less large, are single or semi-double; their color is white or yellowish, sometimes washed with pink; its side branches grow as long as the main stem, and the blossoms grow singly at the tips of these canes; the fruits are round, compressed, brown or black, and glossy. The flowers of this species open at the same time as those of the *Genista*, which is to say while the other species are still in bud. Grafted on a short stem of the Briar, the Pimpinellifolia, with its short and stocky canes, makes a rounded head entirely covered with flowers, making an admirable effect. The scent of the blossoms is elegant. This rose, which has certain resemblances to the rose of the Alps, grows on certain mountains in France. Monsieur Noisette, however, received from England a variety which was said to have originated in Missouri. Between 1828 and 1830, they had at Lyon thirty or forty varieties of this species ... The Pimpinellifolia is very hardy, and demands no more effort than the Centifolia or the Gallica." [JDR54/31–32] "They are most useful for dwarf hedges of 2-ft. to 3-ft. [ca. 6 dm to 1 m] in height, the yellow form being the dwarfest, and will grow and flower well in the driest positions where few other Roses would thrive. To look well they are very dependent on fine weather happening at the time they come into flower." [NRS17/33] "Scotch roses may be grown as standards, and the yellow, and one or two of the more robust varieties, make good heads; but in general they form round and small dense heads, in ill accordance with good taste: when grown in beds or clumps, as dwarfs, they are beautiful, and in early seasons they will bloom nearly a fortnight before the other summer roses make their appearance, and this, of course, makes them desirable appendages to the flower garden." [WRP] "In early spring the colouring of the spinosissimas and 'Altaica' is a wonderfully vivid green, but later in the year they are perhaps apt to become a little rusty [-colored]." [NRS17/48] "The leaves of the little Scotch Roses take on a pleasant russet hue [*in Fall*]." [NRS20/112]

"A Rose with great liking for underground exploration ... It is very variable in size, some plants of this Species growing but two or three inches high [ca. 5–7.5 cm], and others as many feet ... I have played on two golf courses where this little Rose, whether from accident or design I know not, forms most effective bunkers, growing in the open less than a foot high [ca. 3 dm], and apparently all the better for the indiscriminate pruning it receives from the players; and very pleasant it is on an evening early in June, when the little Rose is fully out in bloom, to pass by the place where it is thickly planted, for it is delightfully fragrant, and perhaps I should add that one appreciates the perfume none the less if one has managed to avoid the [golfing] difficulties caused by its presence. The flowers are white with yellow stamens, though there is also a form with blush flowers, and the little branches are short, stiff, much divided, beset with very dense, unequal spines and prickles. The root growth is considerable in proportion to the size of the plant, and it seems quite happy if planted over with low growing greenery, such as *Hutchinsia alpina*. This is the way I am treating it, partly in the hope of keeping it dwarf, and partly because the green makes a good setting for the rather fleeting white flowers and the grey tinted leaves. The plant seems to like a sandy rather than a heavy soil, but cares little how dry the situation may be." [NRS10/122] "The little Scotch Roses ... making charming dwarf hedges, and need very little care beyond the removal of their suckers from time to time. In our own garden we have such a hedge planted on the low earth wall of a rock garden. It grows so densely that even when all the leaves have fallen it proves quite a stalwart little screen." [NRS24/29]

"No distinction is made here between Spinosissima and Pimpinellifolia. We do not mean by this observation that Botanists do not." [Cal] "Linnaeus calls this rose the Pimpinella-Leafed Rose [*pimpinellifolia*]; Haller, the Very Spiny Rose [*spinosissima*]; Poiret, the Scots Rose. But still this was not enough confusion! Monsieur Lamarck gives the Very Spiny Rose as a variety of the Pimpinella-Leafed Rose; and, *vice versa,* Monsieur Bosc regards the Pimpinella-Leafed Rose as a variety of the Very Spiny Rose. But Monsieur de Pronville, in the manner of several modern botanists, makes the Very Spiny Rose a distinct species." [CM] "*R. spinosissima,* the Burnet Rose, is a most charming little plant. It is a native of this country [*i.e.,* the United Kingdom], being particularly abundant near our Western coasts, Cornwall, Wales, Cumberland, and the West of Scotland, though by no means confined to these localities. It is particularly suitable for growing on the rockery where the poor soil keeps it dwarf, and it produces its comparatively large solitary flowers on stems only a few inches high. These flowers are cream colour, and look very well against the finely divided green foliage ... This Rose is often called *R. pimpinellifolia,* especially by continental writers. The names *spinosissima* and *pimpinellifolia* both go back to Linnaeus, and appear in the Second and Third Edition of his *Species Plantarum* (though only the former in the First Edition). Much learning has been devoted to the endeavour to ascertain what Roses Linnaeus meant by these two names, and it remains doubtful. Monsieur Déséglise suggests that *pimpinellifolia* should be confined to varieties with rose-coloured flowers. Professor Crépin thought that Linnaeus's *R. pimpinellifolia* represented our Burnet Rose, and that his *spinosissima* was our modern *R. cinnamomea*; while Major Wolley Dod, following Lindley, makes *R. spinosissima* a form with glandular or setose flower stalks (peduncles), *R. pimpinellifolia* being a similar Rose but with smooth flower stalks. If this be right, then the common Rose of Great Britain should be called *R. spinosissima* var. pimpinellifolia, for the form with smooth flowers stalks is decidedly the commoner of the two in this country. Botanists may find it useful to preserve these fine distinctions, but from the gardener's point of view it seems unnecessary to distinguish these two forms under different names, and we may perhaps conveniently refer to both forms under the name *R. spinosissima*. The chief characteristics of the group are that the sepals remain erect, crowning the fruit after flowering; the flowers are usually solitary, *i.e.,* produced singly, and not in bunches; the leaves have generally nine or more leaflets, and the prickles are straight, large and small ones being generally intermixed on the stems." [NRS17/32–33] "Its feeble stems are prodigiously thorny, and grow more than two feet high [ca. 6 dm], and by their number as much as by their semi-vertical direction, they make a pretty bush, noticeable first by the form of the leaves which cover them, which seem to be modeled on those of the Burnet [genus *Sanguisorba*]; then by the multitude of sessile flowers with which they are decked out, which sparkle in mid-Spring, and which you'd take for pretty pompoms; and finally by the spherical fruits which follow, which seem to be nothing so much as little knobs of ebony. This pretty shrub gives us three varieties: one has nearly white flowers, the next has flowers of a pale red, and the third unites these two tints in the manner called 'rayed' [*i.e.,* striped linearly, not transversely]." [Fr]

"The original Scotch Rose is a wild dwarf rose, common in Scotland and the north of England. As it bears seed in great abundance, as these seeds vegetate freely, and as the Scotch gardeners have taken pride in multiplying and improving this native growth of the soil, the number of varieties is nominally immense. Many of them, however, are scarcely to be distinguished the one from the other. The flowers are small, and exceedingly numerous. They bloom earlier than most roses, and show various shades of crimson, rose, white, and yellow, or rather straw-color; for the yellow Scotch Rose is apparently a hybrid. They are useful for covering banks and forming clumps where masses of bloom are required. Nothing can exceed their hardiness, and they increase abundantly by suckers." [FP] "It has been found growing in many of the Alpine districts of Europe, though it is generally known as the Scotch Rose, deriving its name from the fact of the first introduction of it in a double state having been by the Messrs. Browns [sic], nurserymen at Perth (Scotland). As a stimulant to rose growers, I will relate what I have heard from the lips of Mr. Robert Brown, who is now living near this city [Philadelphia], and is the very individual who planted the seeds and distributed thousands of this rose through the floricultural world. He says, that 'in or about the year 1793 he introduced to his nursery, from a hill in the neighborhood, seeds saved from this rose, which produced semi-double flowers, and by continuing a selection of seeds, and thus raising new plants every year, they in 1803 had eight good double varieties to dispose of; being white, yellow, shades of blush, red and marbled; from these the stock was increased, and hundreds of varieties obtained which have been diffused over all Europe.' Several of them are cultivated in this country [U.S.A.]. We may safely assert that this patriarch of horticulture was the first to grow roses from seed on a grand scale half a century ago. He still lives in the enjoyment of all his faculties, retaining at his advanced age much of his former originality of mind, and to him I am indebted for the communication of many practical facts, the result of his long and valuable experience." [Bu] "The first appearance of the Double Scotch Roses was in the nursery of Messrs. Dickson and Brown (now Dickson and Turnbull) of Perth, between twenty and thirty years since [writing in 1820]. I am indebted to Mr. Robert Brown, one of the partners of the firm at the above period, for the following account of their origin. In the year 1793, he and his brother transplanted some of the wild Scotch Roses from the Hill of Kinnoul, in the neighbourhood of Perth, into their nursery garden: one of these bore flowers slightly tinged with red, from which a plant was raised, whose flowers exhibited a monstrosity, appearing as if one or two flowers came from one bud, which was a little tinged with red: these produced seed, from whence some semi-double flowering plants were obtained; and by continuing a selection of seed, and thus raising new plants, they in 1802 and 1803, had eight good double varieties to dispose of; of these they subsequently increased the number, and from the stock in the Perth garden the nurseries both of Scotland and England were first supplied. In Scotland, Mr. Robert Austin, of Glasgow . . . (of the firm Austin and M'Aslan, nurserymen in Glasgow), about fifteen years since obtained the varieties from Perth, and has since cultivated them to a great extent, having now in his collection upwards of one hundred different new and undescribed sorts, some of which, perhaps, when compared with the best now cultivated, may not be deserving of notice; but many are of such beauty, and so decidedly distinct, that, when made public, they will greatly increase the catalogue of these ornamental plants. In England, Mr. William Malcolm, of Kensington, in the year 1805, purchased from the Perth collection six of their original sorts, and subse-

quently obtained the two others. They had been sold before that time to several noblemen and gentlemen, who were customers of Messrs. Dickson and Brown. Messrs. Lee and Kennedy, of Hammersmith, received the first of their stock from Mr. Drummond Burrell, now Lord Gwydir, who brought them from Perth, and their collection was afterwards encreased [sic] by purchases from the same quarter. The same kinds have since been also obtained by Messrs. Whitley, Brames, and Milne, of Fulham. But, though the above three collections are by far the most complete of any, yet more or less of all the varieties are to be found in the other nursery gardens near London. Mr. Lee has lately raised, in his ground at Bedfont, beyond Hounslow, a great variety of seedlings, possessing extraordinary beauty; they attained a size fit for observation only in the present year, but I was not so fortunate as to be able to visit them when in blossom; I have, however, seen specimens of their flowers; and from these I conceive that many of the plants will assimilate with kinds before known; though several are very different, and will become important additions to general collections." [JSp]

"They bear seed profusely; and raising new varieties from seed will be found a most interesting employment. To do this, all that is required is to sow the seed as soon as ripe, in October, in pots or beds of fine earth, covering it with nearly one inch [ca. 2.5 cm] of mould; the succeeding spring they will come up, and bloom in perfection the season following." [WRP] "The Double Scotch Roses are more especially the object of attention with ornamental gardeners. They are nearly all strictly referable to the True Scotch Rose, or Rosa pimpinellifolia above mentioned, for the variations from the type, in foliage, and mode of growth, are very trifling in most of them; the chief difference between them is in the colours, and the impletion of the flower. The older books on gardening make no mention of any varieties of Scotch Roses; even the last edition of Miller's *Dictionary* does not notice any double one. In the second edition of the *Hortus Kewensis,* though the list there given of the cultivated Roses is large, not more than six varieties of the Scotch Rose are mentioned, only one of which is double, and that even is not properly a Scotch Rose; so that they are, in fact, altogether new subjects to a writer." [JSp] "Many interesting and pretty varieties have been raised, but as none of them possess the properties of a florist's flower, they have been thought but little of; nevertheless, they are very pretty and sweet scented, and blooming so early in spring, before other roses, are desirable and well worthy of cultivation." [JC] "In some of the catalogues two or three hundred varieties are described, but many of them are so near alike, it would be difficult to see the difference." [BBF66] "Of the types which are somewhat forgotten and which have already had their day, I would like to bring one to your attention today— the Burnet-Leafed Rose (*Rosa pimpinellifolia*)—to recommend it as a sort with which one could probably breed roses which were both pretty and new. The doubting Thomases will probably exclaim to me, 'But, my dear Sir! You're going backwards! We have already sown these roses, our fathers before us—the Prévosts, Viberts, Calverts, Pelletiers, Noisettes, and all the others who released them into commerce by the dozen . . .' True, true; I know it well; I knew it already. And so, what does that prove? Your fathers sowed them, like some among you sow '[Général] Jacqueminot', 'Jules Margottin', 'Géant [des Batailles]', 'Victor Verdier', and other HP's. One time around and we stop!?! There's more to do. It's time to start over with other elements. Take as mother a freely remontant rose which seeds easily, and pollinate it with one of the yellow Pimpinellifolias, and maybe get some new varieties of interest. And, if not, don't despair—if at first you don't succeed, you know—try, try again; vary according to the needs of the mother, because, right now, the science of hybridization is still to a great degree a science of trial and error. The Burnet Rose is at least a subject which takes easily to crossing, even out in the wild. One sees crosses with *RR. alpina, tomentosa, canina, rubiginosa,* and several others. The collections of the past tell us that it is no less easy to hybridize with the other garden sorts. They had them with blossoms of pale yellow, white, flesh, pink, and red or purple; in short, they pretty much ran the whole gantlet. The catalogs of the *rosiéristes* are generally pretty poor in Burnets, and one will have his work cut out for him to try getting some of the curious sorts which were around prior to 1840." [JR25/166] "Five or six years ago [*making 1821 or 1820*], I [Vibert] grew from seed a semi-double Pimpinellifolia rose with blotched leaves—which proves that the variegation from birth can sometimes be comparable to that owing to sports. This specimen grew well, and had maintained its 'striped' foliage for two years without change; however, in the third year, some vigorous canes without any mottling suddenly shot up from the base. As they came up, I got rid of them. But the following year, I lost this specimen, after having done everything to force it to give me variegated canes. Nature was stronger—the plant surrendered to it. I had taken some grafts of the rose before losing it, and I still have one pot of it." [V2] "I [Vibert] have sown more than ten thousand seeds from my deep purple Pimpinellifolia, and have never been able to get a semi-double from it. A person can lose heart after six years of fruitless attempts." [V2] "I know of no attempt to mix with them the blood of the Hybrid Teas or Hybrid Perpetuals or of the Rugosa hybrids. In habit the Burnet Rose is splendid, its constitution perfect—surely it possesses possibilities." [ARA24/25]

Rosa pimpinellifolia

"Following other authors, we have united *Rosa pimpinellifolia* and *R. spinosissima*, which are only varieties of one species having in common simply dentate leaflets and unifloral peduncles." [T&R] "The True Scotch Rose in its perfectly natural state, is well known: growing abundantly on a dry soil, but more plentifully in the northern than the southern parts of the kingdom. Its general character is a compact, bushy shrub: low when in a wild state, but in gardens, though it begins to flower when very small, it grows to three and four feet [ca. 1–1.3 m], and even higher, extending widely at the base: some of the varieties are however more dwarf than others. The branches are very numerous, thickly covered with aculei of various sizes, some being larger, others smaller, and some like fine hairs or setae; the larger aculei of the root shoots are frequently recurved, and have a falcate or hooked appearance; the lower parts of the stronger ones are often very much dilated. The leaves, on the greater number of the branches, have, for the most part, three pairs of foliola; but on the surculi, or strong shoots which arise directly from the roots, they have usually five pairs in the first year. The petioles are almost always smooth, though, occasionally, they produce some scattered hairs; and a few aculei as well as small glands, are also sometimes found upon them. The foliola are small, elliptical or nearly round, with simple serratures, of a deep and opaque green above, paler beneath, and quite free from pubescence on both sides. The flowers come out singly, in great numbers, along the whole length of the branches, standing erect, and not nodding [*a footnote adds:* In some of the double varieties the weight occasioned by the increased number of petals causes the peduncle to bend, and consequently the flowers are pendulous]; the peduncles are smooth, though not uniformly so, in wild as well as cultivated specimens, some are covered with setae; even the same plant is liable to vary in this particular, and the variation is more considerable in some of the double flowering sorts. The germen [*a footnote adds:* For the sake of conciseness I shall call that part which afterwards becomes the fruit, the germen, as it used to be so denominated; in later times it has been a question whether it ought to be considered as the dilated receptacle of the flower or the tube of the calyx, and it us thus differently described by different writers] is generally globose, but in several double varieties it becomes flattened, swollen, and somewhat campanulate, owing to the enlargement arising from the impletion of the flower. The leafits [*sic*] of the calyx (now called sepals) are quite simple, that is, without small leaves or pinnae on their sides, but have generally a leavy [*sic*] termination, more or less elongated; when the flower opens they become reflex, and more so in the double than in the single varieties. The single flowers of the True Scotch Rose are cupped at first, but subsequently the petals become more expanded; the bud, before it opens, commonly shews a bright colour; the base or claw of the petals, whatever be the general colour of the flower, is usually white or greenish yellow. The scent, though very agreeable, is not so strong or fine as in many other Roses. The fruit is round, or nearly so, differing in size in the different varieties; it is dark coloured, becoming, when ripe, quite black, but in some plants it is of a deep reddish brown." [JSp] "Ovary and peduncle glabrous. Petioles rough. Leaves small, saw-toothed, obtuse, looking like those of the Burnet. Prickles sharp, rough, and numerous . . . The flowers, which bloom at the beginning of June, are small and rayed with red on the back of the petals at anthesis; otherwise, they are completely white with a little yellow at the nub; they open wide. The leaflets of the calyx [*i.e.,* sepals] have white bristles within, lack prickles, and have some bristles along the edges. The nearly globular ovary is quite smooth and light green, and becomes glossy black at maturity. The leaves, composed of seven to nine lobes which are glabrous on both sides, looking like Burnet leaves, are dark green above, paler beneath. The light green petioles have some isolated bristles and several hairs beneath. The stipules are lacy, with an erect tip. The young shoots are charged with reddish bristles and many prickles, while the black-green stem has few thorns." [Rsg] "*Shrub with suckering roots, forming a bush which is thick, much branched, normally not very tall, and much armed. Thorns numerous, nearly always unequal, ordinarily straight, inter-mixed with hairs. Canes always spindly, always red or brown when they are out in the open air and sunshine. Leaves composed of 5–13 leaflets, more usually 7, 9, or 11; small, rounded, oval or elliptical, rarely having double their width in their length; nearly always obtuse and lacking in pubescence, except in several hybrids. Peduncles nude or hispid, ordinarily solitary, and then lacking bracts, or in 2's, 3's, or more (depending on culture and pruning) with bracts at their base. Ovary very variable in form, hemispherical, digitate, and just about as long as wide, globular, oval, or ovoid-fusiform; glabrous and smooth, or hispid. Sepals ordinarily simple and glabrous, sometimes glandulose; accompanied, rarely, by some setiform appendages, per-sistent, reflexed during bloom, then erect in most varieties, but stay-ing outspread in several. Corolla small, compared with that of other species; ordinarily hypocrateriform* [a marginal note written by Pierre-Philémon Cochet in his copy of Prévost defines this for us: "In the form of an antique cup"], and longer than the sepals. Blooms in May and June, and sometimes as a happenstance in September. Fruit glabrous (hispid in several varieties), flattened, globular, oval or ovoid, brown-black (orange red in the Scots rose). About when the fruit matures, it can be noted in many varieties that the peduncle is thick, fleshy, and colored, like the pericarp. The Scots Rose and sev-eral related varieties are the largest of the sort; their shoots are up-right, thick, and very long; their 'armor' consists ordinarily of ac-uleiform hairs which are equal and very numerous." [Pf]

"The Burnet-Leafed Rose (*R. pimpinellifolia* L.) has a brother, the Very Spiny Rose (*R. spinosissima*), about which several very well-known authors find the distinctions between it and the other to be too minor to allow it the 'honor' of being elevated to the rank of a spe-cies. They have combined them. The stems of the Pimpinellifolias grow 30 cm–1 m high [to 3 ft], depending upon the variety and the terrain; they are reddish or brown, much branched, armed with an immense number of straight thorns which are unequal, quite close, slender, and sharp. The leaves are numerous, alternate, composed of 7–11 leaflets rather like those of the Burnet—quite small, oval-rounded, gay green, glabrous on both sides, a little paler and nicely veined beneath, toothed like a saw along the edge, opposite, pedicu-late, borne on a petiole which has very small prickles and very short stipules which are moderately enlarged, and denticulate at the edge. The blossoms are solitary, axillary, borne on simple peduncles usu-ally armed with short small stickers. The calyx is glabrous, with five narrow segments, entire or sometimes a little pinnatifid around the tip. The corolla is white, often touched yellow at the base; the oval petals are notched at their [outer] edge, making a heart; the ovaries are globular, smooth, and small. In [variety Pimpinellifolia, as dis-tinct from varieties Spinosissima (the Type) and Scotica], the stems are shorter, the leaves a little smaller and more rounded, the pedun-cles shorter and without stickers, the corollas a light pink color on a whitish ground. [Scotica] is smaller yet, barely rising up to a half-foot [ca. 1.5 dm]. Its leaves are very small, its peduncles short, thick, and glabrous; the sepals are entire; the corolla white or washed pink; the fruits rounded, deep purple, nearly black. It is known as the *Scotch*

Rose. These plants grow in Europe, in Germany, Switzerland, and France. [Variety Pimpinellifolia] can be found in our [French] south-erly *départements* on wild crags." [JR25/166]

"Rose, with smooth round seed-buds; peduncles and petioles of the leaf smooth; the leaflets are egg-shaped, notched, and smooth; flowers white; the stem and branches are very prickly; the prickles straight, and nearly white. Various are the opinions of cultivators with regard to what part of the world this Rose is in reality indige-nous. Its general appellation with us is 'Common Scotch Rose'; but Professor Afzelius, in his Observations on Swedish Roses, claims it as a native of Sweden, finding great fault with Linnaeus for the inaccu-racy of his description in confounding the *pimpinellifolia* with the *spinosissima*; an error, we have little doubt, originating merely from having two names for one individual plant: the one rather a taller plant, whose flowers and leaves are of a more luxuriant growth; the other and most material is one, said to be of recent importation from Holland, whose leaves are narrower, nor are the spines quite so nu-merous or perfectly straight as on the true *spinosissima*, but yet it is evidently the same plant. This slight variation of clime and culture, it is not at all improbable, might be the cause of the above confusion: we have so frequently seen it growing wild on the waste lands with-in ten miles of London, that, although it may be a native of Sweden, it nevertheless seems quite at home in Britain." [A] "Grows naturally in England, Fontainbleau, Dauphiné, and Burgundy, where it covers considerable space; indeed, it is used as furnace kindling . . . It is worth noting that this rose, which covers the mountains neighbor-ing Edinburgh, never grows in Scotland more than a few inches tall, while in Europe it attains two [ca. 6 dm] and indeed sometimes three feet [ca. 1 m]." [AC] "It can be found throughout Europe, and in cer-tain parts of France from the Mediterranean region to the sub-alpine sections . . . This rose, which enjoys the climate of *le Midi*, is easily propagated by suckers." [JF] "This rose is quite common in the moun-tains of Burgundy, where it nearly alone covers considerable space; it is used thereabouts to heat furnaces; it is a part of landscape gar-dens, but it isn't very effective there." [CM] "Grows in the sandy plains of the southern [French] provinces, having white flowers tipped with yellow, which have furnished many beautiful varieties." [Go]

"Here is a group . . . which takes its origin, according to certain au-thors, from the wild eglantine of the north of England and Scotland, and nearly all the varieties, to the number of more than 300, were raised from seed by Scots nurserymen. That's why the English call them Scotch Roses . . . Much as I have nothing more to add concern-ing what the English have written on the subject, perhaps I will how-ever be allowed to add something of my own, namely, that the [wild] plant also can be found in the Ardennes, Vosges, Dauphiné, Rouer-gue, Switzerland, and Italy, and that, in 1856, when traveling through *le Midi* of France, I found in several places, growing in a wild state, the Pimpinellifolia in company with the dwarf wild Eglantine, or *Rosa rubiginosa nana*. I found it principally near the ruins of the cas-tle Kalmont-d'Olst, and, farther, in the ruins of the convent of Bonne-val, *département* Aveyron (province Rouergue); and most certainly the specimens I saw in that area were not planted by the hand of Man, because the bushes covered an area of at least 8–10 meters [ca. 25–30 ft]; the trunks measures, at their base, from 25–30 cm in circumfer-ence [ca. 10–12 in], and the single blossoms were of three varieties or colors: blush white, deep pink, and carmine. The varieties com-

Rosa pimpinellifolia continued

posing this group were not of premier merit as flowers, the larger number being single, semi-double, or double, few with full flowers; but, in compensation, their colors were very well defined, varying from pure white to purple red, and from yellowish white to sulphur yellow. *Rosa spinosissima* was perfectly named by the botanists, in view of the infinite quantity of sharp, narrow stickers on the slender and often nodding branches; it is called more often by French rosarians the *Pimprenelle Rose* [*i.e.,* 'Burnet Rose'] because of its foliage, which has some similarity to that of the plant that shares its name. All these roses waft a very strong scent which is found in no other group of roses except for that of the Capucines [*i.e.,* Foetidas], in which the scent is yet stronger. As these roses do quite well on their own roots, separating the offshoot [from the mother plant], one can make borders of massed bushes or hedges demarcating various parts of the garden, where they produce, around the month of May, an infinite quantity of blossoms in all colors, if the varieties have been mixed. It doesn't take much to please this rose. It suffices, in Spring, to spade close by the specimens to stop the runners from spreading too far, as they are inclined to do. Grafted, these roses don't do very well on the ordinary Briar or Dog Rose; it is necessary to use the fragrant Eglantine or *R. rubiginosa,* which one knows easily by its thorns, which are more slender and paler than those of the Briar, and the leaves of which, on the young growths, have a very strong perfume, not unlike that of the rose with which we are concerned at present. It is certain that the first Burnets with double flowers were raised from seed by Mr. Brown, nurseryman of Perth (Scotland), and it is from there that part of the most beautiful varieties come. But these roses have never been popular, in France like elsewhere. I think that fanciers who would like to buy for themselves the several sorts mentioned below could perhaps find them in England or Scotland, where certain companies still grow them. There also exist some remontant varieties ['Estelle', 'Irène', 'Perpetual Scotch', 'Souvenir de Henry Clay', and 'Stanwell Perpetual'] which I cite from memory, and which it would also perhaps be possible to recover." [JR10/107–108]

Horticultural Varieties

À Tiges sans Épines Listed as 'Inermis' (Pim).

Aicha
Petersen/Verschuren, 1966
From 'Souvenir de Jacques Verschuren' (HT) × 'Guldtop' (unreleased yellow Pim).

"Deep yellow." [Ÿ] "Dark yellow, large, lightly double, very fragrant, tall." [Sn]

Alba Flore Multiplici Listed as 'Pompon Blanc' (Pim).

Albo Pleno Listed as 'Pompon Blanc' (Pim).

Altaica
syns. 'Grandiflora II', 'Northern Cherokee Rose', 'Pallasii'
Wild form, 1818

"Its flowers are nearly white with a tinge of sulphur, and three inches [ca. 7.5 cm] or more across when well grown and fully ex-

panded, and are succeeded by jet black berries." [NRS10/123] "The soft cream-white 'Altaica', belonging to the spinosissimas, is the easiest Rose imaginable. It makes a charming dwarf hedge if the new growths are kept well tied down, the older branches being cut right away from time to time." [NRS18/132] "Early summer flowering; dark brown hips." [NRS18/133] "At intervals through the summer a solitary flower will suddenly appear on the bush. The plant increases freely by means of suckers, and if these are removed and planted elsewhere they soon develop into separate bushes. It is, in fact, best to do this from time to time, getting rid of the old bushes after six or seven years. It forms a very pleasing subject for a dwarf hedge of 3-ft. or 4-ft. in height [ca. 1–1.3 m]. The berries are a fine purplish black, and though not so showy as those of the red-fruited Roses, look well when arranged with them in vases; it is generally necessary for this purpose to remove some of the foliage to get the best effect." [NRS17/35] "Hardly reaching to four feet [ca. 1.3 m], and spreading or 'stooling out' as it grows, the 'Altaica' form of the Scotch or Burnet rose (*R. spinosissima*), now sometimes known as *R. altaica,* is a very lovely shrub, from the earliest spring days when its abundant green leaves unfold until a real freeze removes them in late fall. Its great single white flowers almost hide the foliage for awhile. This 'Altaica' Rose is *par excellence* as a low shrub." [ARA22/47–48]

"It is a native of the Altai Mountains in Siberia, has been known to cultivation since 1818, and in 1895 was described as 'a rose almost lost to cultivation.' It has, unfortunately, also been known as *R. grandiflora,* a name also applied in European catalogues to a climbing form of the Polyantha rose ['*Polyantha Grandiflora*'], thus creating much confusion. In fact, my first effort to obtain this rose was suggested by reading a description of it under the name of *R. grandiflora.* I imported some plants, but received the climbing Polyantha, which went skating the first winter after planting and never returned. I had relied upon the reputed hardiness of the 'Altaica' form! The true *R. spinosissima altaica* is absolutely hardy without any winter protection, and seems free from the attacks of mildew or insects, though it is sometimes troubled with a scale that is easily controlled by spraying. It forms a bushy shrub about five feet tall [ca. 1.6 m] and in an open soil spreads freely, just as do other forms of the Scotch rose. In May and June it is smothered in large clusters of single, paper-white flowers, enhanced in their beauty by the numerous bright yellow stamens in their centers. One vigorous shoot will be crowned by a cluster of these pure white flowers large enough and handsome enough to creditably perform the function of a bridal bouquet at any wedding. I have often thought of this when its blooms were at the height of perfection, but it always happened that no swain of my acquaintance had popped the vital question at an opportune time, such as would bring the culmination of his ardent desire just when the blooms were at their best. Perhaps some loving couple will arrange with me to be married on the day of the maximum bloom of the Northern Cherokee roses; then I can happily provide the decorations . . . Enterprising nurserymen should resurrect this rose from the undeserved oblivion in which it rests and offer it to the general public. The beauty of its bloom ought to be enjoyed as well as its excellent quality as a lawn shrub." [ARA19/22–23]

Aristide
Scotland, date uncertain
"Pinkish." [Ÿ] *Cf.* 'Mlle. Aristide' (M).

Aux Cent Écus Listed as 'Belle Laure' (Pim).

Belle Estelle Listed as 'Estelle' (Pim).

[Belle Laure]
syns. 'Aux Cent Écus', 'Belle Laure No 1'; trans., "Beautiful Laura"
Dupont/Vibert, 1817

"Single, white, spotted with purple at the petals' nub." [No26] "Thorns, straight, curved, and unequal; flowers medium-sized, flesh-white, and speckled purple at the nubs of the petals." [J-A/561] "Pretty large; prickles mixed with bristles." [dP] "*Bush* low, wide-spreading. *Peduncle, ovary,* and *sepals* glabrous. *Flower* 15–20 *lignes* across [ca. 1.9–2.5 in], double (20–30 petals), marbled purple pink on a white ground." [Pf] "One of the most famous obtentions of Du Pont, who sold it for three hundred francs, whence came its occasional name of 'Pimprenelle aux Cent Écus'." [Gx]

Belle Laure No 1 Listed as 'Belle Laure' (Pim).

[Belle Laure No 2]
Descemet/Vibert, 1818

"Shrub tall and thorny …; peduncles hispid; calyx-tube glabrous; blossoms single, 16–24 *lignes* across [ca. 2–3 in], marbled white and purplish pink. Fruit oval-globular, brown." [S, after Pf] "Rather tufted *bush* about 0.6 m high [ca. 2 ft]; *canes* brown; *prickles* very numerous, dense, fine, unequal, almost straight. *Leaflets* 7–9(–11), obtuse ovate, simply dentate, quite entire at the base, glabrous all over; petioles glabrous; stipules acute. *Flowers* faintly scented, 1(–2) at the tips of the laterals; pedicels and *receptacles* glabrous or hispid; *sepals* entire, acute, or spatulate; *petals* 5, fairly large, attractively and irregularly variegated, grayish white, pale pink, or dark pink, yellow towards the base, cordately notched. *Hips* small, red at first, black at maturity. Vibert introduced this rose under the name 'Pimprenelle Belle Laure No 2'. Descemet had raised it as a seedling of a much smaller rose of Dupont's which died in 1819, surviving as only a single bush with Lemeunier. The blossom is finer and has a more vivid variegation. It blooms in May and seems hardier than its parent. It is rare in gardens, although available from Vibert." [T&R]

Belle Mathilde Listed as 'La Belle Mathilde' (Pim).

Bicolor
Breeder unknown, pre-1846

Possibly 'Bicolore Nana', for which see below. Otherwise, listed in 1846 without description. Also, a synonym for 'King of Scotland' (Pim), *q.v.*

Bicolore Nana
Smith, date uncertain

"Cream white, flecked with carmine, single, dwarf." [Jg] "Reddish white, medium size, single, average height." [Sn] See also 'Bicolor' (Pim).

Blanc à Fleurs Doubles Listed as 'Pompon Blanc' (Pim).

[Blanche Semi-Double]
syn. 'Semi-Double Blanche'; trans., "Semi-Double White"
Breeder unknown, pre-1819

In the absence of description in the literature, we will hazard a daring guess that this cultivar is white, and semi-double. "From the Pimpinellifolia rose 'Semi-Double Blanche', I [Vibert] obtained four

or five different forms of fruit—some were spindle-shaped and up to ten *lignes* long [ca. 1¼ in]; other, on the contrary, were very flat in form." [V1]

Carnea Double Listed as 'Double Carnée' (Pim).

Carnée Double Listed as 'Double Carnée' (Pim).

Cavallii Listed as 'Ravellae' (Pim).

Charpentier Listed as 'Estelle' (Pim).

Claus Groth
Tantau, 1951
From 'Queen Mary' (HT) × *Rosa pimpinellifolia.*

"Salmon orange yellow, large, full, very fragrant, tall." [Sn]

[De Marienbourg]
syns. 'Glauque à Feuille de Pimprenelle', 'Mariaeburgensis', 'Redouté', 'Redutea Glauca'; trans., "From Marienbourg"
H. Redouté, pre-1820

"Flowers single, whitish, streaked with red points at the tip." [Ty] "Blossoms single, medium-sized, white, marbled with pink." [AC] "*Shrub,* lofty. *Leaves,* glaucous. *Flowerstalks,* hispid. *Floral leaves,* glaucous, oval-lanceolated. *Tube of calyx,* usually smooth, oval, tightened at the throat. *Sepals,* simple, terminated by a leaf-like point; rather glandulous. *Flowers,* single, middle-sized. *Petals,* concave, white, marbled and spotted with pink at their interior summit." [Go] "*Peduncles,* hispid, often grouped 3–5" [Pf] "In habitat, scarcely 0.5 m high [ca. 1½ ft], but to 0.9–1.2 m high [ca. 3 ft] in cultivation. Stem *prickles* unequal, almost straight, falling in age to leave the *canes* rough, as with all this group. New shoots with uniform, somewhat reddish, dense, very sharp *prickles. Leaflets* 9 or 11, obtuse ovate, simply dentate but entire at the base; petiole with small, yellow, slightly curved prickles. *Flowers* 5 cm or more in diameter [ca. 2 in +], fragrant, solitary at the ends of the laterals; pedicel and *receptacles* glabrous; *sepals* simple, leanceolate; *petals* 5, white, yellowing towards the base, more or less notched; *stigmas* sessile. *Hip* black and nodding at maturity. This rose grows in the Alps and in the Ardennes near to the home country of the painter of this work [*Les Roses,* by Redouté and Thory], whose brother Henry Redouté, a member of the institute of Egypt and natural history painter, discovered it. It requires full sun and almost never blooms in the shade." [T&R] "Has the look of a *rubrifolia,* but it doesn't seem to me that it should constitute a species." [MonLdeP]

Didot
Scotland, date uncertain
"Blush white." [LS]

Dominie Sampson
Breeder unknown, pre-1848

"Flowers marbled blush." [P] Dominie Sampson, tutor in Sir Walter Scott's novel *Guy Mannering.*

Double Blanche
(syn. and trans., 'Double White'
Breeder unknown, pre-1818

"White, medium size, lightly double, tall." [Sn] "Much better known than all the others. There is a custom of grafting it on the Briar; the shears then give it a rounded form, and this rose covers itself in June with a multitude of small double blossoms, the white color of which

Double Blanche *continued*

contrasts nicely with the green of its leaves." [CM] See also 'Pompon Blanc' (Pim).

Double Blush Burnet

Breeder unknown, pre-1821

"Pink, medium size, full, tall." [Sn] Possibly the same as 'Double Carnée' (Pim), *q.v.*

Double Carnée

syns. 'Carnea Double', 'Carnée Double', 'Incarnata'; trans., "Double Flesh"

Prévost, pre-1826

"Small white flowers, very pretty and graceful." [J-A/561] "*Bush* thick, tall, much armed. *Peduncle* glabrous, sometimes hispid-glandulose. *Ovary* and *sepals* glabrous. *Flowers* medium-sized, flesh, hypocrateriform, double (15–25 petals)." [Pf]

Double Marbrée Listed as 'Maculata' (Pim).

Double Pink Edine

Scotland, date uncertain

"Pink." [Ÿ] See also 'Lady Edine' (Pim).

Double Purple

syns. 'Pourpre Double', 'Purpurea Plena', 'Violette Double'

Breeder unknown, pre-1820

"A very late as well as a bad flowering plant; but being distinct, and having been established in our gardens, it cannot be passed over. The peduncles are long, thickened, and smooth, the germen campanulate, and the sepals narrow, the whole tinged with a mahogany colour; the bud is much swollen, and of a palish hue; the flower, though not large, is thick, and full double; the petals grow upright, and are thus cupped, and do not expand freely; their inside is of a dark lake colour, more inclining to purple than any [other] variety I have described; the backs of the petals are much lighter than the inside, but not distinctly two-coloured, though sufficiently so to give a slight appearance of variation to the general effect of the flower. The styles in the centre are, in some cases, swollen into numerous elongated lumps. It does not, generally, produce fruits." [JSp] "*Peduncle, ovary,* and *sepals* glabrous. *Flower* hypocrateriform, fragrant, a beautiful light violet; 18–20 *lignes* across [ca. 2¼–2½ in], composed of 6–20 petals. *Fruit* black, globular or flattened, crowned by the *sepals,* which are more often wide-spreading than connivent." [Pf]

Double Red Listed as 'Rouge' (Pim).

Double White Listed as 'Double Blanche' (Pim).

Dr. Merkeley

Skinner, 1924

Fragrant double pink wild form of *Rosa pimpinellifolia* discovered in Siberia.

[Estelle]

syns. 'Belle Estelle', 'Charpentier'

Vibert, pre-1820

"Pink." [V4] "Pale pink, full, large." [LF] "Semi-double, a flesh white." [No26] "Flowers rose, small and double." [P] "Semi-double, with profuse, medium sized white blossoms lightly colored pink." [BJ24] "Small, double, pink." [R&M62] "Flower small, full; color pink, shaded

flesh white." [S] "Blossoms medium-sized, white lightly suffused pink; elegant form. Often, this plant blooms a second time in the Fall." [J-A/561] "Pink flowers; reblooms sometimes." [JDR54/32] "A small neat Scotch Perpetual, of a roseate hue." [WRP] "*Peduncle* hispid. *Ovary* glabrous, turbinate-digitate, or slightly gourd-shaped. *Sepals* glabrous, entire. *Flower* large, flesh-colored, in a cluster. This variety blooms a second time in August and September." [Pf] "'Estelle', that we doubtless owe to a pollination by a Quatre-Saisons [*i.e., Damask Perpetual*]." [V2] Synonymy with an obscure Pimpinellifolia 'Jenny' has been suggested. There is insufficient data at present to accept or reject this; should it at length prove valid, 'Jenny' would be the name with priority, and the attribution would be "Dupont, pre-1810."

Falkland

Ireland?, pre-1930

"Pale rose, changing to almost white. Double." [NRS30/218] "Light pink to white, medium size, lightly double, tall." [Sn]

Flore Albo Submultiplici Listed as 'Pompon Blanc' (Pim).

Frühlingsanfang

trans. "Spring's Onset"

Kordes, 1950

From 'Joanna Hill' (HT) × 'Altaica' (Pim).

"Light yellow, large, single, very fragrant, tall." [Sn]

Frühlingsduft

trans. "Spring's Scent"

Kordes, 1949

From 'Joanna Hill' (HT) × 'Altaica' (Pim).

"Dark yellow, large, full, very fragrant, tall." [Sn]

Frühlingsgold

trans. "Spring's Gold"

Kordes, 1937

From 'Joanna Hill' (HT) × 'Altaica' (Pim).

"Yellow." [Ÿ] "Yellow, large, single, very fragrant, tall." [Sn]

Frühlingsmorgen

trans. "Spring's Morn"

Kordes, 1942

From a seedling ('E. G. Hill' [HT] × 'Cathrine Kordes' [HT]) × 'Altaica' (Pim).

"Deep pink, large, single, tall." [Sn]

Frühlingsschnee

trans. "Spring's Snow"

Kordes, 1954

From 'Golden Glow' (HT) × 'Altaica' (Pim).

"White, large, full, light scent, tall." [Sn]

Frühlingsstunde

trans. "Spring's Hour"

Kordes, 1942

"Whitish pink, medium size, lightly double, light scent, tall." [Sn]

Frühlingstag

trans. "Spring's Day"

Kordes, 1949

From 'McGredy's Wonder' (HT) × 'Frühlingsgold' (Pim).

"Yellow and red, medium size, full, very fragrant, tall." [Sn]

Frühlingszauber
trans. "Spring's Magic"
Kordes, 1942
From a seedling ('E. G. Hill' [HT] × 'Cathrine Kordes' [HT]) × 'Altaica' (Pim).

"Red, pink center, large, single, medium scent, tall." [Sn]

Full White Listed as 'Pompon Blanc' (Pim).

Gil Blas
Breeder unknown, pre-1848

"Flowers light red." [P] Gil Blas, resourceful hero of the eponymous semipicaresque French novel by Lesage.

Glauque à Feuille de Pimprenelle Listed as 'De Marienbourg' (Pim).

Glory of Edzell
England, date uncertain

"Pink-yellow, striped salmon; medium sizes, single, tall." [Sn]

Grandiflora II Listed as 'Altaica' (Pim).

Hibernica
Templeton, 1802
Supposed to be from *Rosa canina × R. pimpinellifolia.*

"Tall bush, columnar, extraordinarily elegant, quite hardy. Blossom large, single, bright rose-red, in such abundance that the bush is best used free-standing." [Ck] "Shrub 3–4 feet tall [ca. 1–1.3 m], forming a thick bush with upright branches of a reddish brown with prickles which are equal, straight, and lacking bristles; leaves of about five leaflets, villose beneath, simply dentate; flowers solitary, ordinarily bractless; petals concave, emarginate; fruit a deep somber red." [No26] "The environs of Belfast produce an insignificant shrub, known as *Rosa Hibernica,* for the discovery [ca. 1795] of which Mr. [John] Templeton received a premium of fifty guineas from the Botanical Society of Dublin, as being a new indigenous plant; though since discovered to become the *Rosa spinosissima* in poor soils, and the *Rosa canina* in loamy land." [Go]

Incarnata Listed as 'Double Carnée' (Pim).

[Inermis]
syn. 'À Tiges sans Épines'; trans., "Unarmed"
Nestler/DeCandolle, pre-1824

"*Stems* 0.9 m high [ca. 1 ft], unarmed except in extreme youth when minute ephemeral prickles are to be seen. *Leaflets* 7, 9, or 11, rounded ovate, simply dentate, glabrous on both surfaces; petioles glabrous; stipules acute. *Flowers* solitary at the tips of the laterals; *receptacles* and pedicels glabrous; *sepals* glabrous, narrow, equal, entire; *petals* 5, fairly large, light to darker red; *stamens* short; *stigmas* amassed in a convex head. *Hips* as for other varieties of *R. pimpinellifolia.* Nestler found this wild in the Vosges and sent it to DeCandolle. It commonly turns up in sowings of seed of the *pimpinellifolia* with prickles, and vice-versa. It is sought out by fanciers and found in many gardens. It needs no special care, but requires full sun." [T&R]

[Irène]
Vibert, 1823

"White." [V4] "Blossoms double, large, flesh-colored." [AC] "White,

full." [BJ40] "Medium-sized, double, pure white." [JR10/108] "Thorns unequal." [S] "*Peduncle* long, hispid. *Ovary* glabrous, digitate, bulging at the base, slightly constricted beneath the tip, which is slightly widened. *Sepals* simple, glabrous or bestrewn with some glandular hairs. *Flower* large (24–30 *lignes* across [ca. 3–3³⁄₄ in]), slightly nodding, very multiplex (35–60 petals), flesh, becoming nearly white. *Fruit* globular or flattened, red or light brown. *Sepals* spreading widely." [Pf] Listed as being remontant.

Jaune Soufré Listed as 'Sulphurea' (Pim).

Jenny See 'Estelle' (Pim).

Karl Foerster
Kordes, 1931
From 'Altaica' (Pim) × 'Frau Karl Druschki' (HP).

"White, medium size, lightly double, light scent, tall." [Sn]

King of Scotland
syns. 'Bicolor', 'King of Scots', 'King of the Scotch', 'Large Double Two-Coloured', 'Roi d'Écosse'
R. Brown, 1803

"Red." [Cal] "Grayish." [LS] "Flowers rosy purple." [P] "Currant red." [Ÿ] "Blossom medium-sized, full; color, bright grenadine." [S] "Semi-double; the petals have a pale exterior; but, on their inside, instead of being mottled, are an uniform rich lake. The fruits are few, black, compressed, and open at the top." [JSp]

King of Scots Listed as 'King of Scotland' (Pim).

King of the Scotch Listed as 'King of Scotland' (Pim).

[La Belle Mathilde]
syn. 'Belle Mathilde'
Descemet, 1816

"Large and superb white blossoms washed pink." [J-A/561] "Blossoms semi-double, pale pink." [AC] "*Shrub* vigorous, forming a tall, thick bush. *Petiole* glandulose, sub-pubescent. *Leaflets* very close-set, silky or pubescent beneath, particularly along the mid-vein. Serration simple or double, very sharp. *Peduncle* glandulose, very hispid. *Bracts* oval-lanceolate. *Ovary* glabrous, oval-globular, with a constricted neck. *Sepals* glandulose and ciliate. *Flower* fragrant, hypocrateriform, 25–30 *lignes* across [ca. 3.13–3.75 in], double (25–45 petals), pale pink, becoming nearly white. *Fruit* brown, oval-globular. *Sepals* wide-spreading or connivent." [Pf] "Mentioned by Desportes as one of Descemet's obtentions." [Gx]

Lady Dunmore
England, pre-1906

"Delicate pink." [LS]

Lady Edine
Scotland, pre-1906

"Blush white." [LS]

Large Double Two-Coloured Listed as 'King of Scotland' (Pim).

Lemon
Scotland, date uncertain

"Yellowish white." [Ÿ]

Lutea Plate 19
Breeder unknown, pre-1838
    "The blossoms when first expanded are of a full golden yellow, al-
most as good as 'Maréchal Niel' or 'Persian Yellow'. I first saw this
beautiful plant in flower at Kew last spring and was greatly attracted
by its fine colour." [NRS10/124] Our Plate 19 is of an otherwise unspecified yellow Pimpinellifolia.

Lutea Plena Listed as 'Sulphurea' (Pim).

Maculata

syns. 'Double Marbrée', 'Marmorata', 'Marmoriata'; trans.,
    "Blotched"
Breeder unknown, pre-1770
    "Blush white." [Y] "Blossoms white, medium-sized, very beautiful,
and opening very well." [J-A/561] "Flower small, semi-full; color,
white marbled with pink." [S]

[Marbrée d'Enghien]

Parmentier/Van Houtte, 1850?
    "Medium-sized, double, cream yellow marbled with red." [R&M62]
"Thirty years of assiduous effort to put together a special collection
—a constant chase—active and often fortunate in new varieties, a
true fancier's passion seconded by the advantages of Fortune—this
is the rare confluence of circumstances explaining the exceptional
merit of the rose collection of the late Louis Parmentier, of Enghien .
. . Among these rarities set aside, which the death of their possessor,
followed by the dispersal of his plants, subsequently delivered to commerce, my lucky star saw to it that I received some excellent lots. One
of these, among the others, was designated under the name *Capucine
panachée* [*i.e.,* "striped 'Austrian Copper'"]—it was a rose I recognized at a glance as being a Pimpinellifolia, a prediction happily confirmed by the look of the blossoms, the result being that we have acquired a charming novelty in a grouping in which varying forms are
rare . . . Description. Bushy under-shrub, quite leafy, of elegant habit.
Canes thin, cylindrical, with a smooth epidermis, which is green and
reddish. Thorns numerous, unequal, narrow, straight, slightly thickened at the base, chestnut-rust in color. Leaves close-set, small, green
with bluish reflections when young, later a beautiful dark green
streaked brown, glabrous (with a smooth [growth] bud), glossy. Leaflets 7–9, small, oval-oblong, half backfolded above, pointed or more
or less obtuse at the tip, with simple or double serration which is sharp
and pretty open. Blossoms semi-double, solitary, tipping numerous
axillary branches. Peduncles short, thick, glabrous, and unarmed, as
is the calyx. Calyx tube globular, comparatively fat, with sepals which
are semi-lanceolate, cuspidate, tipped with a green tongue-let, the two
outer sepals having, on one side, some linear appendages. Petals (in 5
or 6 rows) forming a cup, cream in color, admirably marbled with
bright red. The culture of this new variety is exactly that of the [oth-
er] roses in the same section." [V-H50/151–152] Interesting information on Parmentier and "the dispersal of his plants" may be found in
the periodical *Rosa Belgica* nos. 63–64 (pp. 13–32, with a nice illustration of the Gallica 'Narcisse de Salvandy'), and 71–72 (pp. 42–47).

Mariaeburgensis Listed as 'De Marienbourg' (Pim).

Marmorata Listed as 'Maculata' (Pim).

Marmoriata Listed as 'Maculata' (Pim).

Mary Queen of Scots

Breeder unknown, date uncertain
    Gray-lilac and plum. See T4 for its supposititious history, voyag-
ing from France to Scotland to Ireland . . . Mary, queen of Scots; alias
Mary Stuart; lived 1542–1587.

Miss Frotter

Scotland, pre-1906
    "Fresh pink." [LS]

Mrs. Colville

Breeder unknown, date uncertain
    Crimson-purple, single. Graham S. Thomas believes it a hybrid
with *Rosa pendulina*. Colville, the influential British nursery run by
Colville father and son, ceased operation in 1834.

Nankin

Vibert, 1817
    "Flowers flesh-colored, perceptibly yellowish, single." [No26]
"Blush." [Cal] "Yellow, center pink." [Y] "Blossoms single, flesh yellow.
At Monsieur Vibert's, now it's semi-double." [BJ30] "Very large flowers, of a still-rare coloration." [J-A/561] "Single, medium-sized." [AC]
"*Thorns,* uneven, numerous, bristly." [Go] "*Peduncle* sub-pubescent,
nearly always bearing one or two ovoid-lanceolate *bracts* at its base,
though solitary. *Ovary* globular, glabrous. *Sepals* glandulose. *Corolla*
hypocrateriform, of 5 *petals* marbled pale yellow and pink, straw yellow on the back. *Fruit* globular or flattened, nearly black, crowned by
the connivent *sepals.* I have seen several people apportion this rose
to *Eglanteria Lutea* [*i.e., Rosa foetida*]; I am unable to adopt this classification because several characteristics oppose it, in particular the
absence of glands." [Pf] "This rose comes a little close to *Rosa lutea*
[*i.e., R. foetida*], but they can't be confused." [S] Nankin, alias (in English) nankeen, a brownish yellow cotton fabric, and, in particular
here, its color.

Neptune

Breeder unknown, pre-1848
    "Deep red." [Y] "Fine dark red." [P] "Blossom medium-sized, full;
color, deep crimson." [S] Neptune, alias Poseidon, implacable god of
the seven seas.

Northern Cherokee Rose Listed as 'Altaica' (Pim).

Pallasii Listed as 'Altaica' (Pim).

[Perpetual Scotch]

syn. 'Scotch Perpetual'
Scotland, 1819
    "Large, double, pale flesh pink." [JR10/108] "Blossom medium-
sized, full, flat, quite remontant; color, flesh." [S] "Flowers pale rosy
blush, large and double; form, expanded; growth, moderate." [P] "A
very pale blush rose, of twice the size of the ordinary Scotch varieties,
fragrant and pretty; the foliage and shoots are delicate, assimilating
to its Scotch parent." [WRP] Not to be confused with 'Stanwell Perpetual' (Pim).

Petite Écossaise

trans. "Wee Scots [Rose]"
Vibert, pre-1826
    "Double white." [BJ30] "Flesh." [LS] "White, double; peduncles the

same [*i.e.*, silky or prickly]." [No26] "Whitish pink, small, lightly full, average height." [Sn]

Pompon Blanc

syns. 'Alba Flore Multiplici', 'Albo Pleno', 'Blanc à Fleurs Doubles',
    'Flore Albo Submultiplici', 'Full White'; trans., "White Pompom"
Descemet, pre-1817

"*Thorns,* uneven, straight. *Peduncle, Sepals,* and *Tube of calyx,* smooth. *Flowers,* white, full, extremely large." [Go] "Branching *bush* about 75 cm high [ca. 30 in]; *prickles* very numerous, unequal, some straight, some recurved. *Leaflets* 5, 7, or 9, round or rounded ovate, deeply dentate, bright green above, paler and sometimes reddish beneath; petioles glabrous or more often with small yellowish hooked prickles; stipules fairly broad, denticulate. *Flowers* solitary at the ends of the laterals; pedicels broadening above and narrowing below, glandular hispid; *receptacles* subglobose, quite glabrous, in part flushed reddish brown; *sepals* entire, acute, glabrous outside, downy within; *petals* 8–10-seriate, white, some pointed, others cordately notched. *Hips* globose, bright red maturing to black. It is to Descemet that fanciers owe this rose with its remarkable elegance and beautiful blossoms. For long rare and expensive, today it is stocked under the name 'Pompon Blanc' by almost every nursery. It makes a fine display grafted rather low down on the Briar, on which it will grow vigorously and produce magnificent heads in the second year. For the fullest flowers to the maximum number, it needs a site facing east, and, especially, no pruning, except for dead wood. Additional blossoms in the Fall are not unknown." [T&R]

Pourpre Double   Listed as 'Double Purple' (Pim).

Purpurea Plena   Listed as 'Double Purple' (Pim).

Ravellae

syn. 'Cavallii'
Christ, date uncertain
    "Cream white." [Ÿ]

Redouté   Listed as 'De Marienbourg' (Pim).

Redutea Glauca   Listed as 'De Marienbourg' (Pim).

Rich Crimson

Descemet, 1820
    "Crimson." [Ÿ] We pass on this unlikely, but not impossible, attribution.

Roi d'Écosse   Listed as 'King of Scotland' (Pim).

Rouge

syns. 'Double Red', 'Rubra Plena'; trans., "Red"
Descemet, ca. 1808
    "This rare and beautiful variety makes a tufted *bush* about 0.5 m high [ca. 1½ ft]; *canes* divergent; *prickles* unequal, short, almost straight. *Leaflets* 5–7 (–9), round or elliptical, simply dentate; petiole glabrous, normally unarmed; stipules narrow, acute. *Flowers* delicate pink, faintly scented, solitary on the secondary branches; pedicels glabrous or hispid, often both types occurring from one root. Otherwise it differs from the common Burnet with single red blossoms only by the more or less double corolla of 6–7 series of *petals,* and the much lower habit. *Hips* the size of a small wild cherry, red at first,

blackening at maturity. Descemet, one of our most distinguished growers, obtained the seeds and distributed this rose, which is notable for its elegance and the profusion of blossoms in the Spring. His plant died in a hard Winter after three years, but was replaced from Brisset's garden in Paris in 1811. It is readily propagated by grafting, preferably as a cleft graft. It grows slowly and produces few suckers. It is still a rarity, although the double white-flowered variety is common." [T&R] "Rose with nearly round seed-buds, smooth. Peduncles hispid. Flowers semi-double, and flesh-coloured. Leaves spreading. Leaflets ovate, ribbed, and notched at the edges. Stem and petioles very prickly. This fine semi-double Rose is generally known by the appellation of the 'Double Red Scotch'. It is evidently a thorny Rose, and powerfully resembles the *spinosissima* in most particulars except the flowers, whose pale delicate character reminds us so much of the *Indica,* that, were a flower detached from the plant, and compared with that ever-blooming species in a confined mode of culture, the resemblance would be found considerable. how or by whom it was first cultivated, we have not been able to learn with any degree of certainty." [A] Interesting in that cultivar 'Rouge' is described as either "delicate pink" or "flesh-coloured," not red.

Rubra Plena   Listed as 'Rouge' (Pim).

Scotch Perpetual   Listed as 'Perpetual Scotch' (Pim).

Seager Wheeler

Wheeler/P. H. Wright, 1947
Seedling of 'Altaica' (Pim).
    Double, pink.

Semi-Double Blanche   Listed as 'Blanche Semi-Double' (Pim).

Souvenir de Henry Clay

Boll/Portemer, 1854
    "Light pink." [Mz55–56/38] "Medium-sized, very full, light lilac pink." [JR10/108] "Medium-sized, full, beautiful light pink, well-formed, freely remontant." [R&M62] "Vigorous growth, with a white flower; this variety blooms twice [a year]." [S] "Flower medium, full, very beautiful form, beautiful light pink. This rose was bred by Mr. Boll, of New York in the U.S. You can buy it at Monsieur Portemer's, grower at Gentilly (Seine)." [I'H55/34] Henry Clay, American politician, lived 1777–1852.

Stanwell Perpetual

Lee, pre-1836
    "Pale pink." [V4] "Pink, most beautiful." [BJ40] "Large, full, flesh pink." [BJ53] "Medium-sized, full, cupped, white with a light blush." [JR10/108] "Pale pink, full, flat, large, superb." [LF] "Large pink flowers, freely remontant." [JDR54/32] "Blooms from Spring up to Winter." [S] "Flowers rosy blush, their centre often pink, large, and double; form, cupped. Habit, branching; growth, moderate." [P] "Light pink, medium size, full, light scent, tall." [Sn] "Blush, medium size, double, delicately scented; foliage very small, nine to eleven leaflets; dark reddish-brown wood, numerous small spines. A hybrid which blooms in the autumn." [EL] "An accidental hybrid found in Mrs. Lee's garden at Stanwell." [Go] "In habit like the ['Perpetual Scotch'], but it blooms more constantly and more profusely; in short, it is a much better rose of the same family, and one of the prettiest and sweetest of autumnal roses." [WRP]

Stanwell Perpetual *continued*

"Very charming . . . The flowers are double but not full, of a pale blush colour, borne profusely in May and early summer, and flowering again, but to a somewhat less extent, in August and September and right into November. They have the charm of a delightful fragrance, and can be grown without trouble, for they require little pruning, and if the bed is tolerably made at the beginning, will continue to do well for many years without attention, beyond keeping the ground round them free from weeds. This is so charming a Rose that it might well be more extensively grown than is at present the case, and having regard to its many good qualities, it seems curious that it has not been employed for further hybridisation . . . I presume the Stanwell from which it takes its birth and name is the Middlesex village lying two or three miles northward of Staines in the direction of West Drayton. In habit and foliage the plant has considerable resemblance to the Scotch Roses; but in other respects, in flower and fragrance, one is reminded of the Damask Rose, and there can be little doubt that these two plants have played a part in its production." [NRS17/33–34] "This Rose is still blooming freely [in the Fall]; in fact one has not been without its lovely blooms since May. It is growing upon a lattice fence 7-ft. in height [ca. 2.3 m] and also running rampant among the neighbour's branches, a *Deutzia crenata*." [NRS20/70] "It is a free autumnal bloomer and deliciously fragrant; a beautiful and distinct rose." [JC]

Sulphurea

syns. 'Jaune Soufré', 'Lutea Plena'
Hardy, pre-1838

"Pale straw color." [WRP] "Full, large, semi-full, cupped." [LF] "*Shrub,* vigorous, of an elegant form. *Thorns,* very fine, uneven, rather crooked, axillary. *Leaves,* from nine to eleven leaflets. *Leaflets,* small, almost round, finely toothed; of a yellowish green. *Flowers,* rather large, semi-double; solitary, regular, sulphur-yellow. *Petals,* irregularly shaped." [Go]

Suzanne

Skinner, 1949
From 2nd generation *Rosa laxa* seedling × *R. pimpinellifolia.*

Fragrant wide-opening flesh-pink blossoms on a 4-ft or 1.3-m plant with chestnut-brown canes.

Townsend

Scotland, pre-1885

"Blossom small, full; color, carmine striped with crimson." [S, making his customary error of confusing Pimpinellifolias with Centifolia Pompons, an error-set assiduously copied by his disciples and successors] Also, see T4, in which we read of a "blush-pink fading to ivory" 'Townsend'.

Vierge

syn. 'Vierge de Cléry'; trans., "virgin"
Prévost, 1820
"White." [Cal] "White." [Ÿ]

Vierge de Cléry Listed as 'Vierge' (Pim).

Violette Double Listed as 'Double Purple' (Pim).

White Scotch

Breeder unknown, date uncertain
"Pure white, very pretty." [WRP]

Wilhelm III Listed as 'William III' (Pim).

William III

syn. 'Wilhelm III'
Breeder unknown, pre-1910

"Crimson purple." [Ÿ] "I must also mention . . . a tiny little Rose growing only a few inches high called 'William III'. It is, I believe, a hybrid of spinosissima, with double crimson flowers, and it should be of use for the Rock Garden." [NRS10/122] William III, the "William" of "William and Mary," king of England, lived 1650–1702; if 'Wilhelm III' is to be accepted, then, too optimistically and with awry prolepsis, Kaiser Wilhelm II's crown prince Friedrich Wilhelm Victor August Ernst, lived 1882–1951, who never actually became Wilhelm III.

William IV

England, pre-1838

"Pure white." [JR10/108] "Pink." [LS] "White, small, full, medium height." [Sn] "Pink." [Ÿ] "The largest white pure Scotch rose known; a luxuriant grower, and a good variety." [WRP] William IV of England, the "Sailor King", lived 1765–1837; as he reigned as William IV only from 1830–1837, and our first reference is from 1838, presumably this cultivar appeared between 1830 and 1838.

CHAPTER THIRTEEN

Rubiginosas

"The Eglantine [*Rosa rubiginosa*] has been the theme of poets and lovers for many centuries. It is to be found in some sort growing wild in may parts of both hemispheres. To the flower there is no special beauty attached, being a very simple looking single pink blossom. Although there may be great beauty in simplicity, yet to admirers of the rose, singleness is at once an objection. The odour emitted by the plant after a shower, or when fresh with the dews of evening and morning, is certainly very grateful, and even delicious. Wherever there is a hedge to be planted, it should have a few plants of the sweet brier interspersed; it bears clipping well, and even a hedge of itself would prove a garden ornament rarely equalled, being of a lively green, and its many associations will make it always pleasing. To keep it within bounds, it can be freely clipped or sheared twice a year, and should not be allowed to get over four feet high [ca. 1.3 m] ... Growers and sellers have taken the advantage either by hybridizing or natural appearance, and have introduced to our notice *Double Yellow Sweet Briers, Double White Sweet Briers, Double Red Sweet Briers, Celestial Sweet Briers, Double Striped Sweet Briers,* and what will come next cannot be divined. Some of these are certainly well worth attention, and others are about as much like a raspberry bush as a sweet brier." [Bu] "The Rusty Roses [*i.e.,* Rubiginosas] are hardly known by the fanciers of today, these shrubs never having been grown in France except as botanics. The several I have come across I found at the *Jardin des Plantes* in Paris; there still exist, I believe, after forty years, several varieties at Monsieur Laffay's, in Bellevue, near Paris, which grow pretty much in a wild state, among the brambles and chestnuts of his garden. To return, one finds them very frequently in England, usually in the countryside, around cottages, because no cottager with a garden can bear not to have one or several of these roses, not indeed because of the beauty of their blossoms, which nearly all are single, semi-double, or double [but not full]; but rather for the unique perfume of its leaves, possessed by no other group of roses. As to the Type with single flowers, one finds a few throughout Europe, principally in the south, growing wild in the hedges or at forest-edges, particularly in dry and stony soils. The several varieties I have known, and which are more or less hybridized, come to us from England, grown for the most part from seed by Mr. Martin of Rose Angle, near Dundee. The number of varieties in this group being very few, I will mention the names of them all; if fanciers want to have them, it still would be necessary for them to buy them in England from certain collectors. Nearly all the varieties mentioned below are very vigorous; one can use them as climbers to train on columns and covering arcades; one can also use them as very defensive hedges. In either case, they produce a certain effect by their great number of blossoms, and their beautiful shiny red fruit, and, above all, by the scent of their foliage. These roses have nothing to fear from the worst cold. The Type of *Rosa rubiginosa* is worthless as a stock for delicate varieties such as Chinas, Teas, Noisettes, Bourbons, and indeed HP's; only two do well: Centifolias and Centifolia Mosses." [JR10/153] "Its stems, armed with a very great number of hooked spines, grow 4 or 5 feet high [ca. 1.3–1.6 m], and are clothed in a very green bark. Its leaves are a very bright gay green, and, when you bruise them, they give out a light perfume which is rather like that of a well-ripened 'Pomme de Reinette'. The blossoms, while numerous, and slightly reddish, are less interesting than the leaves; later, however, they become a magnificent ornament because of the hips with which they are covered; they are long and colored a bright coral red which contrasts strikingly with the shade of the leaves, which only fall after the hips." [Fr]

Concerning the 'Pomme de Reinette' apple, just mentioned, we are advised by Theo C. J. Grootendorst, of Southmeadow Fruit Gardens, Baroda, Michigan, U.S.A., and of the Grootendorst family responsible for 'F. J. Grootendorst' (Rg), "During the Renaissance 1300–1400, the 'Reinette', the apple of the Queen, was the best of the then-known varieties. The apple had acid, refreshing, coarse flesh, and could be kept a long time. In the *'Cris de Paris'*, the singsong of the street vendors went as follows:

Pommes de Reinettes et Pommes d'api,
Calvi, calvi, calvi, rouge,
Pommes de Reinettes et Pommes d'api,
Calvi rouge et calvi gris ...

"The Reinettes were very popular; more than 200 new ones were found and named. This was usually done by adding an adjective that described color, form, or country—and a new variety was born."

"The blossoms of this rose are very pleasant to look at, but they drop their petals easily, and a person should gather them carefully when they begin to open." [AC] "Not very interesting in itself, very common in our hedges and uncultivated places where it really takes hold. It is very prickly, and has only single flowers that don't last very long; but it nevertheless is very important for rose fanciers, because it grows some vigorous shoots, tall and straight, that a person looks after and leaves to come to a certain size to subsequently serve as the stock for whatever rose he's interested in. To obtain these shoots, you need to go choose them in the Fall, then take them up and replant them in your garden, where you let them get well established before grafting them. One could sow seed in a bed, but this method takes too long." [BJ09] "LeJeune claims to have raised a typical *rubiginosa* from a seed of *R. centifolia*." [T&R]

"*Shrub* usually tall, forming a branched bush which is thick, diffuse, and much-armed. *Canes* upright or flexuose, sarmentose at the tip. *Thorns* strong, uneven, hooked (straight on the shoots). *Bristles* rare or lacking. *Petiole* glandulose and sometimes villose, armed with prickles beneath. *Stipules* glabrous, entire, with edges fringed with glands. *Leaflets* 5 to 7, ordinarily oval or rounded and obtuse, sometimes oval-lanceolate, acute, somber dark green and nearly always glabrous above, glandulose and ordinarily pubescent beneath. *Serration* double, glandulose. *Peduncles* branched into 3–5, or in corymbs, ordinarily glabrous beneath the bracts, and hispid-glandulose above; but sometimes hispid-glandulose over their whole length, or completely glabrous and unarmed. *Bracts* lanceolate, subulate, entire, glabrous, with glandulose edges. *Ovary* hispid-glandulose or glabrous, oval, ovoid or fusiform, with a long narrow neck. *Sepals* glandulose (sometimes glabrous), usually reflexed, terminating in a long foliaceous point; 3 are appendiculate or pinnatifid. *Disk* thick, convex. *Petals* notched. *Styles* 20–40, free, adherent or slightly protrusive. *Fruit* oval or ovoid-fusiform, cochineal red or bright red. The glands with which the various parts of this rose—especially the leaves—are abundantly provided, leave on the fingers a strong scent which, depending on the variety, is more or less agreeable." [Pf]

"Few, if any, of the Hybrids, have their leaves so highly scented as the native species, whose modest flowers delight us in summer, and whose bright scarlet hips enliven the hedges at the close of autumn. What school-boy, whose lot may have been cast amid its favourite haunts, is not familiar with the flavour of this latter?" [P]

"The *Illustrierte Garten-Zeitung* of Vienna (Austria) reports to us that the cross of the ordinary Eglantine ... with various equally single varieties gives varieties most remarkable in their abundant bloom and hardiness." [JR18/177] "The old English Sweet

Briar or Eglantine is highly valued for its pretty graceful flowers and the delicious fragrance of its leaves. These charming new varieties [*i.e.*, the Penzance hybrids] are a great improvement on the common kind, being hybrids between it and the finest old Garden Roses. The foliage of all is sweetly scented; the flowers are exceedingly beautiful, single and semi-double, and borne in great profusion. They are vigorous growers, throwing up shoots from the root, making strong graceful bushes, four to six feet high [ca. 1.3–2 m], and entirely hardy everywhere. Give plenty of room and do not prune unless to remove dead or unsightly branches." [C&Js98] "These Penzance Sweet Briars also need careful thinning and training if the base of the hedge is to be kept well covered." [NRS24/32] "They [*i.e.*, the Penzance hybrids] are wondrously free bloomers and vary in color from pale yellow and terra cotta to crimson; they are vigorous growers and perfectly hardy in any situation." [CA97] "These hybrids are crosses made by Lord Penzance between the common Sweetbriar and other Roses. The foliage is pungently perfumed and the flowers, produced in great abundance, are of the most beautiful tints. They should be cut back the first season after planting, after which they only require thinning to keep them in shape." [C-Ps26] "The Sweetbriar hybrids, with the exception of 'Lord-' and 'Lady Penzance', do not possess fragrant foliage in noticeable degree, though the blooms of several varieties are pleasantly perfumed." [ARA19/20] "The hedges of Lord Penzance's sweet briars, which in summer have been sheets of crimson, rose and pink, are lit up again in early autumn by their orange red hips, with which the old sweet briars are also ornamented. Unfortunately the thrushes and blackbirds are specially partial to these soft and attractive berries, and they soon rob the bushes of their fruits, picking out the seeds and strewing their skins untidily around." [NRS18/131] "It is a great mistake to plant these 'Penzance' or any other Sweet-Briars in Rose-beds; for they are very strong growers, thoroughly hardy, and should not be pruned *at all,* except to cut out dead wood. Their proper place is in a hedge or grown individually in bush form." [F-M] Aside from 'Lady Penzance' and 'Lord Penzance', the names of the Penzance hybrids are taken from characters in the novels of Sir Walter Scott.

"So delicious is the scent of the Sweet Briar that no rose garden, nor, in fact, any other garden of flowers, should be without a bush or two." [JC]

Rosa rubiginosa

"Shrub of 3–6 feet [ca. 1–2 m], much branched, thick, diffuse; shoots clothed with glands, and with thorns smaller than those on the branches; canes light green, flexible, slender, armed with numerous thorns which are hooked, sparse, and unequal; leaves somber green, fragrant, covered beneath with rust-colored glands, composed of 5–7 leaflets; stipules velvety beneath, dentate, dilate; petioles bearing some strong hooked prickles; leaflets rounded, pointed, slightly concave, doubly dentate, ordinarily smooth above, very pale, velvety, and rugose beneath; blossoms solitary or two or three together, pale, and cupped; bracts lanceolate, pointed, pale, concave, slightly tomentose, glandulose; peduncles hispid, with some feeble bristles, as is the calyx tube, which is oval; sepals reflexing, pinnate; petals somewhat cordiform; disk not much thickened, 30–40 ovaries; styles velvety, distinct; fruit nearly round, oblong, or obovate, orange red, hispid or glabrous, crowned by the sepals. This rose grows all over in abundance. It is found in the Caucasus, Russia, Germany, England, Sweden, and in France, [even] around Paris." [S] "In Europe, commencing to the north-west with Iceland . . . , we find the *Rosa rubiginosa*, with pale, solitary, cup-shaped flowers." [Go] "A European plant, growing in dry and chalky soils in some of the southern counties of England, and also abounding in various parts of France and other countries of Europe." [WRP] "Found in France, Italy, England, and Germany, where it grows spontaneously in hedges and rock-clefts. The stems grow ten to twelve feet long [ca. 3.3–4 m]; ovaries oblong and bestrewn with viscous glands; canes glabrous, armed with fawn-colored, straight, very sharp thorns; leaves composed of seven oval obtuse leaflets of an ashen green, glandulose along the edges and beneath; fairly glossy and dark green above; when it is warm, or they are bruised, they exhale a scent like that of the 'Reinette' apple; the flowers appear in June, July, and August in great number; they are reddish and lightly fragrant; fruits brown-red." [AC] "*Bristles* lacking. *Petiole* villose and glandulose. *Leaflets* rounded, obtuse or oval-acute, flat, glabrous above, pubescent and glandulose beneath. *Peduncles* trichome-bearing, glabrous beneath the bracts, hispid-glandulose above. *Sepals* glandulose. *Flower* small, single, flesh or pale pink. *Styles* 20–30, hardly protrusive, filiform, glabrous at the tip." [Pf] "Its leaves are . . . covered with a multitude of russet glands which make them a little sticky to the touch." [CM] "In some localities they lose their leaves early." [C-Ps25] "Stem and canes strong, having some big thorns, more numerous than on the Dog Rose [*Rosa canina*], very hooked, much compressed; leaves oval (rarely elliptical), having—particularly beneath—some glandular bristles which, bruised, waft a *pomme-de-reinette* fragrance; flowers a little smaller than those of the [Dog Rose], and of a marked carmine pink . . . Hip ovoid, a little smaller than that of [*Rosa canina*], a little more mossy, and as long-lasting. A variety can also be found having elliptical leaflets (*R. rubiginosa sepium*)." [JDR54/21] "The canes of the Fragrant Eglantine grow from five to six feet and more [ca. 1.6–2 m +]—they have been seen larger at Désert, near Versailles . . . The English have gotten some varieties of this Eglantine which ought to be sought out by fanciers. It is rarely found in gardens, though it is not without its attractions in giving us blossoms in several shades of red, some white-striped, some all white, some semi-doubles, some doubles; last of all, they are effective in the middle of lawns. The Sweetbriar does well in limy soils; it can also be found in some clayey soils; but in dry, arid regions, it grows hardly a foot tall [ca. 3 dm], and its leaves hardly exceed three or four *lignes* in size [ca. 1/2 in]. This rose varies infinitely; nevertheless, the scent of its leaves—a characteristic it has all to itself—always makes it easy to recognize . . . Sometimes this rose is used as a stock on which to graft other sorts; but the grafts have trouble taking." [CM]

"Height, about four feet [ca. 1.3 m], armed with a very great number of hooked thorns. Its leaves are small, fragrant, covered on the back and between their teeth with russet-colored bristles, which are slightly sticky. Its flowers are small and red, with cordiform petals. There's a larger variety, more hirsute, in which the hips bristle with soft points." [MaRu] "Its wood is very thorny; its only merit is the perfume which the wood, leaves, and flower waft, which can be smelled ten or twelve steps away—a distinct characteristic of this species. It can be used advantageously in shrubberies. Its blossom is small, and composed of five notched petals of a pretty pink color." [C-T] "Flowers worthless, but the foliage gives out after a rain, or when moistened by the morning dew, a delightful perfume, equaled by few rose blooms." [CA96] "There is nothing much sweeter than the early foliage of the native Sweet Briar (*R. rubiginosa*) some warm day in May." [NRS21/98] "Highly valued for the delightful fragrance of its young foliage as well as its pretty pink flowers. Entirely hardy and splendid for hedges." [C&Js21] "Bright pink flowers followed by varnished scarlet berries. "In planting for large hedges, they should be placed in a double row, staggered, with at least 5 feet [ca. 1.6 m] between the plants . . . In pruning, it is necessary to thin only the weak wood and keep the plants within bounds, remembering that these roses bloom mostly from old wood, and should not be cutback too severely." [Th2] "Foliage when moist has a delicious spicy fragrance." [C-Ps32] "A profusion of orange, then red, berries in late summer." [C-Ps27] "Very handsome in fruit, of bright red colour, egg-shaped, and crowned with persistent spreading sepals." [NRS17/63]

"It seems to me that it is often confused, in the synonymy, with *Rosa lutea* [*i.e., R. foetida*], and perhaps with *Rosa canina*, with which it indeed shares many characteristics. It differs from *Rosa canina*, which has thinner, glabrous leaflets lacking any scent; whitish or pink-tinted blossoms, and nearly glabrous peduncles and ovaries. It is distinguished from *R. lutea* by having red flowers, not at all foetid; by its leaflets which are ordinarily reddish and very glandulose; and by its recurving thorns. As to the rest, it might not be impossible that these three be varieties of the same [species], and that the only question is—which is the Type? I regard *this* as the true Eglantine, different further from *Rosa villosa*, which has leaves neither fragrant nor glandulose, but supple, soft, and nearly downy, and straight thorns . . . The fruits of the Eglantine have a sweet flavor, mixed with an agreeable acidity. The hairs which surround the seeds separate easily from them, attaching to the fingers when they touch, penetrating the skin, bringing on some very severe itching there . . . The blossoms of the Eglantine are purgative, but its syrup is astringent. The conserve prepared from the fruits is sweetly vinegarish, good for the gout, an excellent astringent, good in the digestive tract to moderate the heat of bile and sweetening the acidity of the urine." [Lam]

"Rose with ovate seed-buds: peduncles hispid: petioles and stem prickly: prickles red, and curved: leaflets sweet-scented, ovate, pilose and glandular beneath. This fragrant shrub is known amongst botanists by the specific title of rubiginosa: but we have adopted its old and softer title of Eglanteria; for, when the poet says, How sweet is the Eglantine breeze! the very name sounds dulcet to our ear. It is an old inhabitant of the gardens, and will always continue to be one of its sweetest ornaments." [A]

Horticultural Varieties

À Fleurs Doubles Listed as 'Petite Hessoise' (Rbg).

À Fleurs Semi-Doubles Listed as 'Petite Hessoise' (Rbg).

Amy Robsart
Penzance/Keynes, Williams & Co., 1894

"Poppy red." [JR26/182] "Deep pink." [JR18/177] "Deep red, delicate pink within." [Ck] "Lovely deep rose; buds and flowers most graceful sweet briar type; very sweet and an abundant bloomer." [C&Js98] "Deep pink, medium size, lightly double, medium scent, tall." [Sn] "Bright rose blooms of medium size. The foliage has the delightful Sweetbriar fragrance." [C&Js23] "Flower deep rose. Growth very vigorous." [GeH]

Anne of Geierstein
Penzance/Keynes, Williams & Co., 1894

"Deep carmine." [JR18/177] "Carmine with a white nub." [JR26/182] "Bright carmine-scarlet." [Ck] "Dark crimson, large handsome flowers." [C&Js98] "Very free in bloom." [C-Ps26] "Deep red, small, single, medium scent, tall." [Sn] "Flowers are dark, velvety crimson. Graceful branching habit. Foliage very fragrant." [C&Js23] "Deep crimson-rose, single. Growth very vigorous." [GeH] "Dark crimson flower, followed by an abundance of clustered branches of hips. Important foliage, a good grower with graceful branching habit." [B&V]

Aschermittwoch
trans. "Ash Wednesday"
Kordes, 1955

"Silver-gray white, large, full, tall." [Sn]

Brenda
Penzance, 1894
From *Rosa rubiginosa* var. *apricorum* × *R. foetida.*

"Maiden's blush or peach blossom, a very dainty shade contrasting finely with the bright golden anthers." [C&Js98] "Pale red." [JR18/177] "Peach-pink, single. Growth very vigorous." [GeH] "Foliage fragrant." [Th2]

Canary Bird
W. Paul, 1911
From *Rosa rubiginosa* var. *dimorphacantha* × *R. foetida.*

"Pure yellow." [Ÿ] "Golden yellow, then cream-colored." [Ck] "Yellow-orange, medium size, single, medium height." [Sn] "Canary-yellow, tinted with crimson, single, medium size; early flowering. Growth shrubby." [GeH]

Catherine Seyton
Penzance, 1895

"Delicate pink." [LS] "Soft rosy pink; medium size." [Th2] "Rosy pink with golden anthers, single. Growth very vigorous." [GeH] "Has a longer season of flowering than most of the Penzance Briars." [NRS30/217]

Clémentine
syn. 'Rose Jay'
Descemet, pre-1824

"Blossoms semi-double, medium-sized, striped pink and white." [AC] "Rosy blush, pretty and distinct." [WRP] "Flowers large, semi-double, plumed and striped with white." [No26] "Medium-sized, single, red-pink." [JR10/154] "Flamed and streaked." [GJB] *Leaflets* of a darker green, glossy, not villose, but slightly pubescent beneath. *Serration* divergent and creped. *Peduncles* more glabrous beneath the bracts, and less hispid above. *Ovary* larger, shorter, flattened or glob-

ular. *Sepals* more glandulose, less divided. *Flower* variegated. The *petals,* also 10–15 in number, are white in the center and intense dark pink or light red along the circumference. *Fruit* dark red, in a much flattened cone, very large all the way at the bottom, at least as wide as high." [Pf] "*Leaflets,* slightly pubescent underneath, with curled divergent toothing. *Tube of calyx,* depressed or globular. *Flowers,* variegated, semi-double; the petals white in the centre, and light red or pink at the circumference. *Fruit,* conical, depressed, deep red." [Go] 'Janet's Pride' (Rbg), below, is possibly a "rediscovery" of this.

Double Red   Listed as 'La Belle Distinguée' (Rbg).

Double Scarlet Sweet Briar   Listed as 'La Belle Distinguée' (Rbg).

Edith Bellenden
Penzance/Keynes, Williams & Co., 1895
From *Rosa rubiginosa* var. *consanguinea* × *R. foetida.*

"Delicate pink." [LS] "Pale pink." [Ÿ] "Pale rose." [Th2] "Light pink, small, single, tall." [Sn] "Pale rose, single, flowering in clusters. Growth very vigorous." [GeH] "[For] garden, pillar, hedge." [Cat12]

Flammentanz
trans. "Fire Dance"
Kordes, 1955

"Crimson red." [Ÿ] "Red, large, full, light scent, tall." [Sn]

Flora McIvor
Penzance/Keynes, Williams & Co., 1895

"Pure white with pink reflections." [JR18/177] "Violet pink with a white center." [JR26/182] "White, edged pink." [LS] "White, suffused rose; small; fragrant." [Th2] "Pure white delicately tinted with rose, very fine large flowers, highly scented." [C&Js98] "A pure white, blushed with rose, large flowers, graceful in growth and habit; useful for cutting. A desirable plant." [B&V] "Blush white, tinted rose, and single. Growth very vigorous." [GeH] "Violet pink, small, single, tall." [Sn]

Fritz Nobis
Kordes, 1940

"Yellowish pink, large, lightly double, very fragrant, tall." [Sn]

Goldbusch
Kordes, 1954

"Yellow, medium size, lightly double, tall." [Sn]

Greenmantle
Penzance, 1895
From *Rosa rubiginosa* var. *spineo-urceolata* × *R. foetida.*

"Lilac pink with a white nub." [JR26/182] "Pink, white center." [LS] "Rich pink, fine foliage. Growth vigorous." [GeH] "Rose-red, white center, medium size, single, tall." [Sn] "Especially good for hedges." [Th2]

Gruss an Koblenz
trans. "Greetings to Koblenz"
Kordes, 1963

"Light red, medium size, lightly double, tall." [Sn]

Hebe's Lip
syns. 'Margined Hip', 'Rubrotincta'
Lee, pre-1846
Of Damask × Rubiginosa heritage.

"Creamy white, with a pink border." [WRP] "Flowers creamy white, their margin pink, single; form, cupped." [P] "White, touched carmine." [LS] "The form . . . halfway between single and semi-double." [JR26/116] "Blush-white edged pink. Growth vigorous." [GeH] "White, edged red, medium size, lightly double, tall." [Sn] "White, with picotee edge of purple. —Vigorous. —Bush, hedge." [Cat12]

[Hessoise]

trans. "Hessian" [*i.e., having to do with Hesse, Germany*]
Schwarzkopf, pre-1811

"Light rose-red." [GJB] "I got it from the garden of the Natural History Museum in Paris. It is much thornier [*than Alba 'Regia Odorata' which possibly refers to what we list as the Alba 'Beauté Tendre'*], with strong, hooked prickles. Its foliage is beautiful. The blossoms aren't the least bit remarkable; it is . . . good where its foliage, flowers, and fruit can ornament the garden. Its fruits are large, numerous, and a beautiful red. There's also a variety ['Petite Hessoise'] of this rose which only differs by being smaller in its proportions." [C-T] "Its wood is very strong and tall, and well armed with strong hooked thorns. Its blossom is single, with five medium-sized petals of a sparkling deep pink, with some pretty stamens which make it show up gracefully in beds. Raised own-root, it serves as stock for grafts, which prosper on it. Only the semidouble [*? — "the semidouble" could refer to any of a number of Rubiginosa cultivars; perhaps most likely is 'Petite Hessoise'*] gives more sparkle, because of certain blue reflections which run across the petals due to the sun. All sorts take to it as a stock. Its buds and flowers are profuse on the same stem. Leaves medium-sized, marked with very pronounced veins. Opens June 1–9." [LeR]

Hessoise Anémone Listed as 'Zabeth' (Rbg).

[Iver Cottage]

Breeder unknown, pre-1846
"Pale rose." [WRP] "Flowers pale pink; form, cupped." [P] "Single, cupped, pale red." [JR10/154]

Janet's Pride

Whitwell/W. Paul, 1912
"White, shaded and tipped crimson. —Very vigorous. —Garden, bush, hedge." [Cat12] "White, striped orange, medium size, lightly double, tall." [Sn] "Grows naturally into a thick bush about seven feet high [ca. 2.3 m], and would be excellent where a tall hedge is required." [NRS24/32] "Mr. Whitwell, of Darlington, came to the front. He was ably assisted by his wife, Janet. A seedling Rose of the Penzance Briar type, which was discovered in their garden and shown to Mr. D'Ombrain when there for the Darlington Rose Show, was at once named 'Janet's Pride'." [NRS24/38] See also 'Clémentine' (Rbg).

Jeannie Deans

Penzance/Keynes, Williams & Co., 1895
"Sparkling crimson." [LS] "Rose-red, semi-double." [Ck] "Scarlet-crimson; semi-double, large." [Th2] "Red, medium size, lightly double, tall." [Sn] "Rosy crimson, early. Growth very vigorous." [GeH] "[For] garden, bush, hedge." [Cat12]

John Cant

B. R. Cant, 1895
"Deep pink, small, lightly double, light scent, tall." [Sn]

Joseph Rothmund

Kordes, 1940
"Yellowish pink, medium size, lightly double, very fragrant, tall." [Sn]

Julia Mannering

Penzance/Keynes, Williams & Co., 1895
"A very glowing pearl pink." [Ck] "Crimson and white." [JR26/182] "Pale pink." [NRS24/32] "Soft pearly pink." [Th2] "Delicate pink." [LS] "Pink-white, small, single, moderate scent, tall." [Sn] "Flower pearly pink, early. Growth vigorous." [GeH] "Pearly pink. —Very vigorous. —Garden, bush, hedge." [Cat12]

La Belle Distinguée

syns. 'Double Red', 'Double Scarlet Sweet Briar', 'La Petite Duchesse', 'Lee's Duchess', 'Scarlet'; trans., "The Beautiful Distinctive [One]"
Breeder unknown, pre-1844
"A pretty bright red, small, and compact rose, very distinct and good, but its leaves are entirely scentless." [WRP] "Flowers bright rosy crimson, small and very double; form, compact. Habit, erect; growth, moderate. Very pretty." [P] "Deliciously fragrant, very pretty and free-flowering; habit of growth moderate." [JC] "A strong stiff habit, with very large dark green foliage; flowers of a dark rosy red colour, quite large and perfectly double; its habit is quite dwarf and stiff." [Bu] "Rose-red, small, very full, light scent, medium height." [Sn] "Small, very double, sparkling crimson pink. One of the best of the group, but its foliage is nearly scentless." [JR10/154]

La Petite Duchesse Listed as 'La Belle Distinguée' (Rbg).

Lady Penzance

Penzance/Keynes, Williams & Co., 1894
From *Rosa rubiginosa* var. *dolorosa* × *R. foetida* 'Bicolor'.
"Fawn, changing to Austrian copper." [CA97] "Two-toned, outside pale yellow, inside salmon orange." [Ck] "Copper and yellow." [NRS30/203] "Fawn, yellow at the center, nuanced red." [JR18/177] "Copper-red, yellow center, medium size, single, moderate scent, tall." [Sn] "Soft copper; single. Medium growth only for this class." [Th2] "Flower coppery yellow, single, early. Growth vigorous, distinct." [GeH] "One of the prettiest of this class. It is a lovely soft coppery tint and the flowers come in great profusion. A vigorous grower. Makes fine specimens." [C-Ps26] "The most distinct Penzance briar." [Cat12]

Lee's Duchess Listed as 'La Belle Distinguée' (Rbg).

Lord Penzance

Penzance/Keynes, Williams & Co., 1894
From *Rosa rubiginosa* var. *baumgartneri* × either 'Harison's Yellow' (F) or *R. foetida* itself.
"Light fawn." [Ÿ] "Saffron red." [JR26/182] "Delicate salmon colored." [Ck] "Fawn, shaded salmon. Medium growth only for this class." [Th2] "Deep yellow, moderate size, single, moderate scent, tall." [Sn] "Fawn colour, with deeply serrated leaves, single, summer flowering. Growth vigorous." [GeH] "Soft shade of fawn, shaded off to a pretty emerald-green, yellow in the centre, occasionally toned with a delicate pink; very sweet, abundant bloomer and grows well." [B&V] "Single flowers, fawn and ecru color, tinted with lemon. Makes a

Lord Penzance *continued*
beautiful hedge where a 'wild' effect is wanted. Plant on the edge of a woods or among shrubbery." [C-Ps26]

[Lucy Ashton]
Penzance, 1894

"Snow-white, with fine rose-red border." [Ck] "Lovely white flowers with pink edges, very free bloomer, deliciously sweet." [C&Js98] "White with pink edges. Growth vigorous." [GeH]

Lucy Bertram
Penzance/Keynes, Williams & Co., 1895

"Violet purple." [JR26/182] "Deep cherry rose." [NRS30/217] "Bright purple-red, light, half full." [Ck] "Rich crimson, white centre. —Very vigorous." [Cat12] "Rose-red, white center, small, single, tall." [Sn]

Magnifica
Hesse, 1916

"Large blossom, good, half-full, shining carmine." [Ck] "Purple-red, medium size, full, light scent, tall." [Sn]

Maiden's Blush Listed as 'Manning's Blush' (Rbg).

Manning's Blush
syns. 'Maiden's Blush', 'Pubescens'
Manning, pre-1819

"Blush white." [Ÿ] "Double, pale pink." [JR10/154] "Double and pretty, with fragrant leaves like the original." [WRP] "Rose with nearly round seed-buds: peduncles hispid and glandular: flowers grow in racemes, flesh-coloured: leaflets oblong, pointed, and covered with soft hair: stem and petioles prickly. Amongst the Eglantine Roses, this we think is the only one (the *R. E. multiplex* [*i.e.,* 'Williams's Sweetbriar'] excepted) with downy foliage. [Andrews'] drawing was made at the Nursery of Mr. Lee in 1819, where it was then called the Maiden's Blush Sweet Briar. It blossoms towards the end of July, and during the months of August and September." [A] "These [mossy] Eglantine Roses are rather delicate plants, and difficult to preserve. The palest-coloured is known by the appellation of Manning's Sweetbriar, being first raised by a gardener of that name. It is also by some called the Mossy Sweetbriar." [A]

Margined Hip Listed as 'Hebe's Lip' (Rbg).

Max Haufe
Kordes, 1939

"Pink, medium size, lightly double, tall." [Sn]

Mechthilde von Neuerburg
M. Boden-Kurtscheid, 1920
From *Rosa rubiginosa* var. *consanguinea* × *R.* ×*damascena*.

"Blossom half-full, pure pink. Bush very tall-growing." [Ck] "Pink, medium size, lightly double, tall." [Sn] Neuerburg, alias Neuchatel, Swiss city.

Meg Merrilies
Penzance/Keynes, Williams & Co., 1894
From *Rosa rubiginosa* var. *camadrae* × *R. foetida*.

"Deep crimson." [NRS30/217] "Bright carmine." [JR18/177] "Rosy carmine, petals in two rows." [Ck] "Bright crimson, single, free flowering. Growth vigorous." [GeH] "Rose-red, small, single, medium scent, tall." [Sn] "Free flowering variety, bright crimson, great abundance of hips, with large foliage, and robust habit; it is about the best of any of this class." [B&V]

[Minna]
Penzance, 1895

"Lilac-y, with a white and yellow center." [JR26/182] "White, tinted pink." [LS] "Pure white, single, large, petals tinted pale blush. Growth bushy." [GeH]

Mossy Sweetbriar Listed as 'Manning's Blush' (Rbg).

Multiplex Listed as 'Williams's Sweetbriar' (Rbg).

Petite Hessoise
syns. 'À Fleurs Doubles', 'À Fleurs Semi-Doubles'; trans., "Small 'Hessoise'"
Redouté/Lahaye, ca. 1810

"Flowers small, semi-double, pink, numerous." [No26] "Blossoms less double, but more numerous." [BJ30] "A pretty French hybrid, with bright, rose colored flowers, and leaves not so fragrant as some others." [WRP] "Its wood is green, elongated, and strong, protrusive, fairly strong thorns; leaves light green, large, round, and pleasant; buds pointed; flowers well formed, fairly large; petals dainty but thick, not ragged, on which, around the white, it is washed the most beautiful delicate pink—delicate, but bright all the same . . . Is this the Museum's Double Briar? Whatever the case, this is a charming variety, and one of the best-formed ones in the group. Opens 9–10 June." [LeR] "0.9–1.2 m high [ca. 3 ft]; *stems* glabrous, branched; *prickles* sparse, recurved, some long, some short. *Leaflets* 5(–7), medium-sized, subrotund, almost glabrous above, covered beneath with sticky, glandular, rust-colored hairs giving an apple scent when rubbed; petioles villose, prickly; stipules fairly broad, glandular, as are all foliaceous parts. *Flowers* 1–4; pedicels and ovoid *receptacles* glandular hispid; *sepals* pinnatifid, glandular outside, whitish woolly within; *petals* 10–15(–20), notched, pale pink whitening towards the base. *Hips* orange-red, subglabrous at maturity, long persistent. This, the 'Petite Hessoise' of the trade, was introduced by Redouté, who raised it from seed 15 years ago and distributed it via nurseries throughout France and abroad. A derivative is known with much broader and more rounded leaves and subumbellate inflorescences." [T&R]

Pubescens Listed as 'Manning's Blush' (Rbg).

Refulgence
syn. 'Refulgens'
W. Paul, 1909

"Scarlet-crimson; a good dark hybrid Sweet Briar, almost single. Growth very vigorous." [GeH] "Deep red, medium size, single, light scent, tall." [Sn] "Half full, scarlet-vermilion. Strong-growing, floriferous bush." [Ck] "The best dark Hybrid Sweet-Briar. Hardy." [Cat12]

Refulgens Listed as 'Refulgence' (Rbg).

[Rose Angle]
Martin, pre-1838
Supposedly a Rubiginosa × Arvensis hybrid.

"Deep lilac rose." [WRP] "Semi-double, cupped, light lilac pink." [JR10/154] "Flowers bright lilac rose; form, cupped." [P] "Bright rosy red flowers, quite double, grows freely." [Bu] "Raised from seed by Mr. Martin, of Rose Angle, near Dundee: this produces large and very double flowers, of a bright rose color; its foliage is also very fragrant." [WRP]

Rose Bradwardine
Penzance/Keynes, Williams & Co., 1894

"Lustrous Centifolia-pink." [Ck] "Violet pink with a white nub." [JR26/182] "Bright pink." [JR18/177] "Clear rose, good shape and very profuse." [B&V] "Light violet pink, small, single, tall." [Sn] "Clear pink; semi-double. Foliage very fragrant. Very vigorous." [Th2] "Clear rose colour, large, single. Growth very vigorous." [GeH] "Beautiful rich pink; perfect shade, abundant bloomer; very handsome and fragrant." [C&Js98] "Rose-pink, single flowers with old-fashioned charm. Best as a pillar or on a fence." [C-Pf33]

Rose Jay   Listed as 'Clémentine' (Rbg).

Rosenwunder
Kordes, 1934

"Red." [Ÿ] "Rose-red, large, lightly double, light scent, tall." [Sn]

Rubrotincta   Listed as 'Hebe's Lip' (Rbg).

Scarlet   Listed as 'La Belle Distinguée' (Rbg).

[Williams's Sweetbriar]
syn. 'Multiplex'
Williams of Turnham Green, ca. 1800

"Of all the fragrant-leaved Roses, this is certainly the finest, and for which we are indebted to Mr. Williams, who discovered it in his nursery about 23 years ago, growing promiscuously in the same Sweetbriar-bush with the Eglanteria major; and although found vegetating at the same time, and under the same auspices, yet is its character altogether very different; this being as slow in growth as the other is quick. It is the only Eglantine Rose at present known with perfectly double flowers, and is with difficulty increased by layers, which are a long time in forming a root; and the seeds, which it very rarely ripens, remain in the ground a long time dormant." [A]

[Zabeth]
syns. 'Hessoise Anémone', 'Zabeth Bombifera'
Dupont, pre-1813

"Flowers medium-sized, semi-double, bright pink, numerous; leaves not as long." [No26] "Ovary ovoid, glabrous at the tip. Sepals long, foliaceous; 3 are pinnatifid. Flower medium-sized, multiplex, semi-globular, light pink." [Pf] "Bush 0.6–0.9 m high [ca. 2–3 ft]; stems glabrous, green; prickles long, recurved, almost absent from the blooming shoots. Leaflets oblong ovate, acute at both ends, glabrous above, underside and margins tomentose and with very numerous sessile viscous glands; petiole with small greenish prickles, similarly glandular; stipules acute, quite entire, gland-edged. Flowers lateral and terminal, subumbellate; receptacles globose, glabrous like the pedicels or sometimes puberulent; all lateral pedicels with small, ovate, acute, glandular bracteoles; peduncular bracts more or less leafy; sepals 3 pinnatifid and 2 simple, usually acute, some spatulate or leafy at the tip; corolla medium-sized; petals 2–3-seriate, pink, whitening towards the base, the innermost a little crumpled; styles villose, slightly more exserted than in other Rubiginosas. Hips globose, bright red, crowned by the persistent sepals . . . 'Zabeth' is strongly apple-scented [in the foliage], as is typical with the Rubiginosas . . . It was distributed in France by Dupont; but has been known for a long time, since, according to English tradition, it was dedicated to Queen Elizabeth." [T&R]

Zabeth Bombifera   Listed as 'Zabeth' (Rbg).

CHAPTER FOURTEEN

Caninas

"Bushy shrub which grows eight to ten feet [ca. 2.6–3.3 m] high—sometimes up to fifteen [ca. 5 m]. Canes glabrous, light green and glossy, armed with strong, hooked thorns; leaves composed of five to seven oval leaflets which are glabrous above and below, more or less glossy, sometimes evenly dentate, sometimes unequally so; flowers usually in twos or fours at the tips of the canes. This rose blooms in June and July; you'll find it in hedges, shrubberies, and along roadsides." [AC] "*Flower,* composed of five petals notched into a heart, adherent to the calyx, as are a great number of stamens. The calyx is one structure in a bell shape, nearly round at the base, cut at the tip into five sharp leaflets [*i.e.,* sepals], as long as the petals. *Fruit,* the base of the calyx becomes a fleshy fruit, colored, soft, oval, pinched at the tip, crowned by the dried sepals, in one single compartment enclosing several nearly round seeds, bristling with stiff hairs, sprinkled through a pulp which is coral-red in color. These fruits are called 'Chinorrodon' [*sic; attempting to signify "Dog Rose" in Greek*] or 'Gratte-cul'. *Leaves,* winged, tipped with an odd one; oval, dentate along the edge, surfaces nerved. The leaflets are pointed, and their petioles prickly. *Root,* woody, suckering, blackish. *Habit;* this shrub, so common in hedges, sometimes throws out canes six or seven feet long [ca. 2–2.3 m], if it's growing in good soil, particularly when a person makes the effort to get rid of the old canes . . . All the stems are covered with straight thorns. It has produced several varieties, one of which has leaves of a pretty dark red, another with white flowers, and a third with black leaves." [AbR] "Canes grayish, bearing—at least on the main stem—some pretty strong thorns which are compressed, fairly distant, and moderately hooked; the leaflets are oval, sharply dentate, stiff, flat, grayish green, usually smooth. At the moment of bloom, the buds are pointed, and pale pink at expansion; it can easily be distinguished from afar by its white petals which have a slight blush. The hip is elliptical, sealing-wax red, very long lasting, and thick-walled. There is also a bristly sort, which they call '*Rosier des Buissons*' (*R. canina dumetorum* of the botanists)." [JDR54/21] "Both species [*Rosa canina* and *R. rubiginosa*] have foliage very susceptible to fungous troubles in our climate, and have hitherto failed to give good results when used for breeding purposes." [ARA16/33–34]

"There are a great many varieties, which however are only for a botanical collection—except for the one with double flowers." [No26] "Already in 1889, I had in my garden two seedlings from *Rosa canina* which, kept where they were planted, grew to two meters [ca. 6 ft] high—and were absolutely thornless. For purposes of study and not commerce, I attended to my two wildlings so that they would set seed. In the two years that followed, I raised young specimens without any trace of thorns; the third year, some of them had thorns, but in small quantities; others had none. I re-selected among these last, and finally got seed-bearers which were completely thornless. The variety was definitely fixed [in this characteristic of thornlessness] such that I had a large bed in my garden replete with this sort of rose, down to the third generation. I thus can guarantee this variety of *Rosa canina* to be absolutely thornless . . . This variety is extremely vigorous and resists frost very well; since 1889, the mother plant has borne the worst cold. It resists cold much better than the thorny sorts, and I expect it won't be long before I have a great many of this delightful sort of *Rosa canina* [*signed,* R. Kokulinski, gardener at Tempelhof, near Berlin]." [JR26/36] "This rose takes in a multitude of varieties, as Monsieur Loiseleur-Deslongchamps well says; and so, with it, the leaves will be more glossy or less glossy—sometimes a gay green, sometimes nearly or indeed thoroughly glaucous; they will be edged with quite equal teeth, or on the contrary they will be unequal; the color of the flowers, generally light pink, varies similarly, as they can be a thoroughly pure white, or a yellowish white; they same blossoms have little or no scent, or they have one that is strong and agreeable; to end, then, the peduncles, the calyx tubes, the styles, etc., are more of the same—nothing could be more variable . . . The strong, straight stems of this rose are used for shield-grafts of most of the double varieties. The name 'Dog Rose' was given to this species, they say, because it passes for a specific against hydrophobia." [CM] "The hips of these roses have many uses in domestic economy. The Germans make a faintly acid and very piquant sauce from them, similar in color to tomato ketchup. The bedeguar or devil's pincushion occurs mainly on roses of this group—a soft, fuzzy gall caused by the Bedeguar Gall Fly. It does, however, occur—although rarely—on other species. Finally, we repeat, for those who do not already know it, the enigmatic verse referring to the five sepals of a Dog Rose:

> Five brothers we: two bearded, two beardless,
> And I with half a beard. [T&R]

Rosa canina

"*Shrub* tall. *Canes* diffuse. The largest [of them], as well as the shoots, project out, and are sarmentose at the tip, armed with strong *thorns* which are nearly even, thick, and long, numerous and nearly straight at their base, hooked and less close-set at their tip. On the weak canes, the prickles are sparse and much-hooked. The flowering *branchlets* are sometimes unarmed. *Bristles* lacking. *Petiole* armed beneath with hooked thorns, rarely bestrewn with the glands, which are always occasional [*i.e., never very numerous*]; normally villose, sometimes glabrous. *Stipules* entire, often narrow, glabrous, with glandulose edges, and sometimes pubescent. *Leaflets* 5–7, oval or lanceolate, acute; usually flat, stiff, glabrous and smooth above, villose or pubescent beneath in several varieties, glabrous in others. *Serration* sharp, usually simple, convergent, sometimes silky, rarely glandulose. *Peduncles* short, glabrous or bestrewn with glands, sometimes villose, solitary, in 3–5's, or in tight few-flowered corymbs. *Bracts* lanceolate, subulate, longer than the peduncles, glabrous, with glandular and often pubescent edges. *Ovary* glabrous, ovoid-fusiform or oblong, with a narrow throat. *Sepals* long, reflexed, glabrous; 3 are pinnatifid, with edges normally glandulose or pubescent. *Petals* notched. *Disk* thick, convex. *Styles* 20–30, glabrous or villose, free, not very salient. *Fruit* oval or ovoid, scarlet." [Pf]

"Ovary ovoid, glabrous. Peduncles short. Sepals hairy. Petioles spiny. Leaves oval-lanceolate, sawtoothed with sharp teeth. Stem spiny…The corolla is composed of five petals of a delicate pink, medium in size, cordiform, and slightly notched. The pistils are a yellow tending towards green, and the stamens are a brighter yellow. The blossoms, which come either solitary or two or three together, open at the beginning of June. The calyx segments are partially winged, lacy, slightly long, lanate, glandulose, and arching back under the nub of the petals. The ovoid ovary elongates in the upper portion, and forms a 'bottleneck'. The peduncles are glabrous and equipped with lanceolate bracts. The oval-lanceolate leaves, serrated with sharp teeth, deep grass green above with barely noticeable glossy touches, paler beneath, are borne on slender petioles, which have prickles on the underside, and very long stipules at the base. The stem and branches have prickles which are oval at the base, slightly backcurved, and often in twos or threes." [Rsg]

"This plant and the greater part of its varieties are encountered in the woods, brush, and hedges of the countries of northern Europe." [Lam] "In Egypt, too, grows the *Rosa canina*, or dog rose, so common throughout Europe." [Go] "Its roots were long considered a specific against bites from mad dogs, a remedy which, like many others, has been abandoned. It would seem that the blossoms can be substituted for those of the Eglantine [*i.e., Rubiginosa*], and that they have [the same properties]." [Lam]

Horticultural Varieties

Abbotswood
Hilling, 1954

"Pink, medium size, lightly double, tall." [Sn] Said to be a chance seedling; attractive hips; fragrant.

Andersonii
Breeder unknown, pre-1910

"Flower rose-pink, single summer-flowering. Growth vigorous." [GeH] "It will hold its own with many of the summer flowering Garden Roses. It is a fine rose-pink…and is sometimes good enough for exhibition among single Decorative Roses. It is not a very strong grower, but makes a nice little bush about three feet high [ca. 1 m] and of good shape, furnished in autumn with cheerful red berries." [NRS10/124] "Has blossoms of a specially attractive shade of bright pure pink, which are longer lived than most single Roses, and are followed by bright red berries. The berries appear to be unusually hard or bitter, for I always notice they are the last of the rose hips to fall victims to the onslaughts of the thrushes and blackbirds." [NRS28/28]

Crême
trans. "Cream"
Geschwind, 1895
From an unnamed seedling (parentage: Canina × Tea) × an unnamed seedling (parentage: Canina × Bourbon).

"Yellowish-pink, small, lightly double, very fragrant, tall." [Sn]

Freya
Geschwind, 1910

"Pink, medium size, single, tall." [Sn, connecting it with *Rosa corymbifera* var. *implexa*] "No scent, –3 m [less than ca. 9 ft]." [EU] Freya, Norse goddess of Love and compatible activities.

Griseldis
Geschwind, 1895
From an unnamed seedling (parentage: Canina × Tea) × an unnamed seedling (parentage: Canina × Bourbon).

"Pink, medium size, full, tall." [Sn] "No scent, −4 m [less than ca. 12 ft]." [EU]

Gruss an Rengsdorf
trans. "Greetings to Rengsdorf"
M. Boden-Kurtscheid, 1920

"Deep pink, medium size, single, tall." [Sn] "Park-rose, strong-growing, pink, single, floriferous, completely hardy." [Ck]

Kiese
Kiese, 1910

"Red." [Ÿ] "Light red, medium size, single to lightly double, tall." [Sn] Hermann Kiese, rose breeder located in Weiselbach, Germany.

[Rose à Bois Jaspé]
trans. "Rose with Mottled Wood"
Brassac, 1876

"[Brassac] has put into propagation in his nurseries a new rose which, they say, is very interesting in its colorless wood and the size of its blossoms. This new obtention will bear the name 'Rose à Bois

[Rose à Bois Jaspé] *continued*
Jaspé', we are assured. The bark of this rose allows a person to see some large bands or rays, during the Winter presenting a red tint in the yellow ray, all in all making for a curious mottling. The foliage of this rose is ample and a beautiful dark green; the very large flowers —full, perfect in form—are a bright carminy cherry red." [JR1/2/14] Possibly not introduced until 1877 or 1878.

Siwa
Geschwind, 1910
   "Pink, medium size, full, tall." [Sn] "No scent, −3 m [less than ca. 9 ft]." [EU]

Theresia
Alfons, 1925
   "Light pink, small, single, tall." [Sn]

Una
G. Paul, 1898
From 'Gloire de Dijon' (N) × *Rosa canina.*
   "Large, single and semi-double, pale buff flowers which fade nearly white." [GAS] "Yellowish white, large, single to lightly double, tall." [Sn] "Lovely creamy yellow buds. Good for hedges, banks, or wild garden; very vigorous." [P1] "The single flowers are a creamy white after opening, sulphur yellow as buds. This variety is good for making enclosures, beautifying hedges, etc." [JR24/162] "Pale buff. —Vigorous pillar. —Pillar, hedge. —Large, handsome semi-single blooms. —Distinct." [JP] "A beautiful, nearly single, pale creamy yellow flower of good size, lasting well on the plant, but summer flowering only. Does best as an isolated bush but can be grown as a dwarf pillar." [F-M] "Flower pale cream, semi-single, semi-climber; summer flowering. Growth vigorous." [GeH] "Small grower; quite shy bloomer; requires winter protection." [ARA18/121] "This makes a good pillar Rose if carefully pruned." [NRS18/133] "This new variety is shown in one of the latest numbers of *The Garden.* It is the result of a cross between a *Rosa indica* and *Rosa Canina* . . . A grand future can be predicted for it." [JR24/162]

Walküre
trans. "Valkyrie"
Geschwind/Lambert, 1909
From *Rosa canina* × a Tea.
   "Whitish pink, large, full, tall." [Sn] "No scent, −3 m [less than ca. 9 ft]." [EU] Valkyries, the battle maidens sent from Valhalla to look after and escort thence the dead but valiant warriors; the similarly characterized authors, too, we think.

Weidenia
Alfons, 1927
   "Light pink, medium size, single, tall." [Sn]

CHAPTER FIFTEEN

A Miscellany

We bring together in this chapter a number of distinct small groups of roses, some of them long honored in gardens—if not in today's gardens, then at least in those of the past. Perhaps their impact on rosedom will make itself felt in future breeding; perhaps they are destined always to be what they are today, fresh reminders that some of the precious groups which the Rose has to offer can be tiny in scope as well as large in beauty.

Turbinata

"The *Rosa turbinata* Ait., Kreisel, Tapestry Rose, also called Frankfurt Rose, . . . grows long upright canes, and is used for covering walls, etc. —but the flowers are not well formed; because of this, they are not much liked in cottage gardens." [JR8/61] "The roses which pertain to this sort are, in general, little made to attract fanciers of beautiful roses; but the most part of them will always be sought for adorning country gardens because of their vigor, the dimensions that they can attain, etc." [Pf] "Gardeners don't consider the Turbinata a fit subject for grafting, despite the strength of its growth." [BJ30]

"In the classification of Rosae Turbinatae given here, the group is mainly founded, so far as can be judged, on the turnip-shaped form of the receptacle as seen immediately before the opening of the flower—a constant and invariable character. The flowers of all roses of this Section rarely open well; mostly they open very badly." [T&R] "This sort is easily distinguished by the size and form of its ovaries, which are very thick and turbinate. Its stems grow to four to five feet high [ca. 1.3–1.6 m]; they branch into canes which are glabrous, cylindrical, greenish or ashen, armed with sparse and recurved thorns, clothed with leaves which are alternate, petiolate, winged, composed of seven to five oval leaflets which are opposite, nearly sessile, green above, whitish and pubescent beneath, fairly regularly dentate like a saw along the perimeter, borne by a pubescent petiole ordinarily lacking prickles, bearing at the base a large denticulate bract, pubescent beneath. The flowers are supported on solitary peduncles which are axillary, close-

set, bristling with little thorns and rough bristles, short, tuberculate. The corolla is a deep red, large, moderately fragrant; calyx slightly hispid; division [*i.e.,* sepals] subulate, entire, whitish within. Ovaries also hispid, especially at their base; thick, turbinate, enlarged nearly into a bell-shape; sometimes purplish in color. It is hinted that this plant originated in Germany. We hardly know it except for the double form, which sometimes doesn't open at all because of the overplus in the number of petals." [Lam] "*Shoots* bristling with strong thorns having large bases; they are uneven, hooked, and intermingled with bristles. The thorns are more hooked and less numerous at the tip of the shoot than at the base. On feeble canes, and branchlets, they are yet rarer, and indeed sometimes lacking, in which case the epidermis is glabrous and very smooth. [*Growth*] *Buds* protrusive, rounded. *Petiole* normally villose, glandulose, and armed. *Stipules* large, normally entire, with lanate and glandulose edges. *Leaflets* 5–7, oval or ovoid, villose beneath. *Peduncles* hispid-glandulose; branched, in corymbs. *Bracts* large, wide, orbicular or oval. *Ovary* large, turbinate, with a wide, unconstricted neck; glabrous at the tip. *Sepals* short, terminating in a point, usually glandulose; 3 bear several appendages." [Pf] "Illustrated by Miss Lawrance, Rössig, and Redouté, described by Guerrapain, cited in DuPont's catalog." [Gx]

Rosa campanulata   Listed as *Rosa ×turbinata*.

Rosa ×rapa   Listed as 'Turneps' (Turb).

Rosa ×turbinata

botanical syns. *R. campanulata*, *R. ×francofurtana*; horticultural syns.,'À Gros Cul','Francofurtana','Francofurtensis','Frankfort Rose','Rosier de Francfort'
Origin unknown, pre-1583
Possibly from *Rosa majalis* × *R. gallica*.

"Rose." [Cal] "Very large, blush." [WRP] "Flowers fairly double, but not always expanding well, of a beautiful color of pink, and with little scent, placed last of all upon a very fat ovary, succeeded by fat, short fruits which are in the shape of a top." [BJ09] "The very double flowers spring from an ovary in the form of a crest." [Go] "The Frankfurt Rose blooms . . . [at] the end of June. The wood is green and takes on a red tint on the sunny side; it is smooth, glossy, and has few

Rosa ×*turbinata continued*

thorns. The leaves are oval, terminating in a point, and very deeply toothed. The very large calyx is bestrewn with brown bristles. The bud, barely covered by the calyx membranes, which are large and thick, is also very large. The blossom is large, not very double, and cherry-color or light wine-lee; the petals are large and thick; it is very fragrant." [C-T] "A shrub of 4 to 6 feet [ca. 1.3–2 m], with the habit of *R. damascena*; the branches have equal straight prickles, but no setae; leaves villous beneath; flowers large, red, very double, the 'tube of the calyx turbinate'." [P] "It grows into a big, wide bush of 5–6 feet [ca. 1.6–2 m]; leaves with 5 leaflets which are oval, pointed, rough, green and glabrous above, glaucous beneath; all its other parts are villose and lanate; flowers a bright pink with little scent, and more than two inches in size [ca. 5 cm]; ovaries large and top-shaped, whence its name 'turbinata'. One variety has double flowers." [BJ17]

"This sort bears also the names Rosier à Gros-Cul and Rosier Turbiné. It passes for being very common in the environs of Frankfurt. Would that be its native land? Did it really come from Frankfurt as its name would indicate? It is supposed that this rose is indigenous to Europe and originates in the mountains of Germany. The ovaries of this rose are longer than they are wide, in the form of a top, whence comes the name *Turbiné*; its peduncles are bristly; its stems bear several scattered, hooked prickles; its leaves, ordinarily composed of five leaflets which are oval, acute, rough, dark above and glaucous beneath, have a common petiole which is villose, and which bears several prickles; its flowers, of a bright red, and more than two inches in size [ca. 5 cm], come in clusters at the cane tips, and have little scent. They appear in June, and have difficulty opening. This rose grows four to five feet high [ca. 1.3–1.6 m]. It is grown in gardens—not because people think much of it, because it looks better from a distance than close up—but it *is* very vigorous. It makes shrubberies in country gardens and beds, which indeed contrast with other sorts by the color of its leaves and flowers." [CM] "Its ovaries are as long as they are wide, and are in the shape of a top." [AC] "Ovary semi-globular, pear-shaped and partially hispid. Peduncles bristling with glandular hairs. Petioles with prickles beneath. Leaves ovoid, pointed, and strongly dentate. Stem armed with isolated prickles . ... The flowers of this rose—of a very deep pink inclining to purple and, here and there, sometimes, violet—are very double and very large, in a favorable exposure. Its petals are long, heart-shaped, and slightly folded in on themselves at the center; the pistils and filaments are sulphur-colored, and the anthers gold. They bloom around the end of June and beginning of July. The calyx segments are short, bulge slightly, have an exterior bestrewn with red glands, and are clothed with white hairs. The semi-globular ovary has, in its lower part, a sort of *bourlet*, giving it the look of a pear or a top; this is why this rose, better known as the Frankfurt Rose, is called 'the rose with a turbinate ovary.' The peduncles have rough and glandular hairs. The ovoid leaves, which are pointed and strongly dentate, are composed of five to seven lobes. They are light green above and a whitish green beneath, with well-pronounced veining. The stipules are large, notched, bulging, and glandulose. The young growths are a light green touched with pink, often reddish on the sunny side. There are a few prickles on the branches." [Rsg] "The young shootes of this Rose are couered with a pale purplish barke, set with a number of small prickes likes hairs, and the elder haue but very few thornes: the flower or rose it selfe hath a very great bud or button under it, more then in any other rose,

and is thicke and double as a red rose [*Gallica*], but so strongly swelling in the bud, that many of them break before they can be full blowen, and then they are of a pale red rose colour, that is, betweene a red and a damaske, with a very thicke broade and hard vmbone of short yellow threads or thrumes in the middle, the huske of the flower hauing long ends [*sepals*], which are called the beards of the rose, which in all other are iagged [*"jagged"*] in some of them, in this hath no iagge at all: the smell is neerest vnto a red Rose." [PaSo]

"*Shrub*, vigorous, forming a thick bush. *Suckers*, armed with strong, unequal, crooked thorns, mixed with bristles. *Leafstalks*, usually hairy, thorny, and glandulous. *Stipules*, large, cottonous on the edges; entire. *Leaflets*, five or seven; oval, hairy underneath. *Flowerstalk*, branching, hispid, glandulous. *Floral leaves*, large, wide, oval or orbicular. *Tube of calyx*, smooth at the summit, without tightening. *Sepals*, short, usually glandulous, terminated by a point; three of them bearing appendages. *Flowers*, double or full." [Go] "Bush 1.5–1.8 m tall [ca. 4.5–5.5 m]; current *shoots* glaucescent and almost glabrous; adult *canes* armed with a fair number of scattered, unequal *prickles*, some straight, others recurved, which are densely crowded on all old wood; flowering branches quite glabrous. Leaflets 5, ovate, subacute, green above, tomentose beneath; simply dentate; petioles villose; stipules slightly glandular. *Flowers* 1–3 at the branch tips, subcorymbose, with a soft, pleasant scent; pedicels glandular hispid in youth; bracts basal, ovate acuminate, quite entire, ciliate at the margins like the stipules; *receptacles* top-shaped, glabrous, sometimes dark red and armed at the base with small reflexed hairs tipped with brown glands; *sepals* shorter than the petals, tomentose within, glandular without, acuminate, entire or more often with broad-based linear appendages; *corolla* always double but never full, approaching the volume of *R. centifolia* but darker; *styles* very numerous, villose. A native of Northern Europe, this is grown in gardens under the names 'Top-Shaped Rose', 'Frankfort Rose', and so on. According to De Candolle, it is intermediate in habit between *R. villosa* and *R. centifolia*, although very different from either. The flowers often open imperfectly, as do all the roses with turbinate receptacles: *R. sulfurea* [*i.e., R. hemisphaerica*] and its cultivar 'Pompon Jaune', *R. alpina turbinata* [*R. pendulina* 'Turbinata'], *R. fraxinifolia* [probably referring to 'Turneps' (Turb)], *Rosa sanguisorbaefolia*, and so on." [T&R]

"Sometimes confused with the villose Rose [*i.e., Rosa villosa*], the Frankfort differs from it in the following characteristics: its canes are smooth, with few or no thorns; its leaves are only simply dentate; its calyxes are top-shaped; and its styles are eight or ten times more numerous than is the case with any other species." [AC] "*Shoots* much armed at the base. *Canes* glaucous, usually glabrous and unarmed. *Leaflets* close-set, veined, rough, grayish green above, very pale beneath. *Serration* simple, convergent. *Ovary* bristling at the base, glabrous and much widened at the tip. *Sepals* terminating in a glandular point. *Flower* medium-sized or large, nearly full, bluish purple-pink. This rose is considered the Type of the species." [Pf]

À Feuilles de Frêne   Listed as 'Turneps' (Turb).

À Gros Cul   Listed as *Rosa* ×*turbinata*.

Amélia   Listed as 'Belle Rosine' (Turb).

Ancelin
E. Noisette, 1829
From *Rosa* ×*turbinata* × ?

"Very large, full, deep pink." [V8] "Very large, deep rose, elegant." [WRP] "Blossoms double, large, in clusters, pale pink." [AC] "Hybrid from the Frankfurt Rose. Stem straight, very vigorous canes which are glaucous and slightly tinted on the sunny side; thorns pretty numerous, slightly enlarged at the base, terminating in a hooked tip. Leaves composed of five leaflets which are rounded, slightly dentate, whitish beneath, the young ones tinted pink. Flowers in a corymb of five to seven, well-borne on their peduncles, red, double, large, very beautiful. I grew it from seed in 1828." [SAP29/264–265]

[Anne de Boleyn]
syn. 'Anne de Boulen'
Girardon, 1829
Seedling of 'Grosse Mohnkopfs Rose' (Turb).

"Flowers large, of a pale pink, having a delicate green bud in the middle." [AC] "Blossoms solitary or paired, three inches [ca. 7.5 cm], delicate pink, central petals short and wavy surrounding a delicate green heart. From seed of the rose 'Pavot' [*i.e.,* 'Grosse Mohnkopfs Rose'], which didn't pass on to its child even one bit of its appearance." [R-H29] "Bush with numerous, straight, unequal thorns; petioles long; leaflets distant, finely dentate; buds pointed and long; flower solitary, slightly concave, having in the middle a delicate green bud formed by aborted ovaries; petals a delicate pink, those of the center short and slightly undulate, those around the edge large." [S] Anne de Boleyn, alias Anne Boleyn, lived 1507–1536; second wife of Henry VIII and mother of Queen Elizabeth I; decapitated; parallels between her fate and cutting rose blossoms should be neither drawn nor pondered.

Anne de Boulen   Listed as 'Anne de Boleyn' (Turb).

Belle Rosine
syns. 'Amélia', 'Cerise'
Descemet, pre-1820

"Cerise." [LS] "Bright red." [Cal] "Blossoms double, large, cerise pink." [AC] "*Shrub,* having very crooked branches." [Go] "*Thorns* much hooked. *Leaflets* very villose beneath. *Peduncles* nearly glabrous at their base, glandulose above the bracts, together in multifloral corymbs. *Ovary* glabrous at the tip. *Flower* medium-sized or large, quite double, bright cherry red." [Pf]

Cerise   Listed as 'Belle Rosine' (Turb).

Francofurtana   Listed as *Rosa ×turbinata.*

Francofurtensis   Listed as *Rosa ×turbinata.*

Frankfort Rose   Listed as *Rosa ×turbinata.*

Fraxinifolia   Listed as 'Turneps' (Turb); but see also below.

Grosse Mohnkopfs Rose
syns. 'Grandesse Royale', 'Papaverina Major', 'Pavot', 'Poppy Rose',
   'Tête de Pavot'; trans., "Big Poppy-Headed Rose"
Schwarzkopf, pre-1799
From *Rosa gallica* × ?

"Bright rose." [Cal] "Flowers very full, very regular, and a charming pink." [J-As/63] "Blossoms semi-double, large, bright red." [AC] "The full blossoms, light purple, are three inches across [ca. 7.5 cm]." [BJ30] "Blossom a light purple, more than two inches across [ca. 5

cm], the biggest of the sort." [No26] "Blossom a deep crimson. Calyx composed of narrow leaflets. Ovary globular. Leaves glandular, oval-acuminate . . . This flower of a full and deep crimson is beautiful; towards the base, the petals are so arranged as to give it the look of a poppy-head, whence its name. It takes its origin from the French Rose, *Rosa gallica*; it was raised in Weissenstein from Gallica seed. The sepals are large, fine, and not very villose; its ovary is globular; both are equipped with glands, as is the peduncle, which is thick and outwardly armed with very fine prickles, of which the canes have very few. The leaves are oval-acuminate, finely dentate, leaf-green above, very villose and dull green beneath." [Rsg] "*Bracts* at the base of the corymbs large and oval; those of the partial peduncles are lanceolate. *Ovary* turbinate-digitate, glabrous and glaucous. *Flower* large, double, red or purple, light and bright." [Pf]

Grandesse Royale   Listed as 'Grosse Mohnkopfs Rose' (Turb).

Impératrice Joséphine
Aiton, 1790

"Rose." [Cal] "Pink, veined." [Y] This cultivar name is much in the trade at present, though—as we see—very spottily documented in the past. Impératrice Joséphine, alias the Empress Joséphine, frequently mentioned in these pages, and deservedly so. Witness Vibert's thoughts on the matter: "The French were born to attempt to achieve all sorts of glory; direct their tastes, honor the goal, and soon you will see them carry out this new career [*i.e.,* the study of agriculture (including horticulture)] successfully, and occupy an honorable place in the empire of Flora. All the civilized peoples have accorded Agriculture special protection; but the example of the sovereign would go farther than regulations and ordinances. The Dutch have realized this important truth. Let us also note that the King and his children do not disdain taking part in their horticultural society, and of paying, like others, their tribute twice a year at public exhibitions. I am assured that the German emperor, often diverging from the usual attributes of the top rank, busies himself—alone—with efforts on behalf of greenhouse plants in particular. Here, then, are examples which are good to follow because they speak to the spirit of the people—which is obvious—people who hardly ever read ordinances. If anyone wants a yet more striking proof of the influence that can affect our tastes, our pleasures, and I could say our *morals*—those which, by the stature of their position, show the way to those who surround them—I would mention Joséphine Beauharnais, that virtuous woman, who, worthy because of her high qualities of at least the lofty level at which circumstances placed her, rendered such great services to ornamental horticulture. Who doesn't know that she brought together at Malmaison one of the richest collections of plants and shrubs; and that she took great pains, here and in other countries, to seek out whatever was rare. Roses were especially favored by her; she honored Monsieur Dupont with particular good will, and didn't think it beneath her to join him in their undertakings. The impetus that she gave to Horticulture was sooner felt where she lived; and it is really from that time that the importance of the discoveries in this genus dates, as well as the improvement of the methodology and the increase in the number of fanciers. Her virtues and good will would command love and respect; her example would enliven everyone around her—a friendly rivalry born in the hearts of those who weren't strangers to flower-growing. And when, at that same time, I would, with difficulty, pry some secrets from Nature,

Impératrice Joséphine *continued*

didn't the hope I had of such august protection guide my first tries? Didn't it keep my courage up? —because, at that time, the consideration of the Public had not yet compensated me for my work. Fanciers, mingle sometimes with your pleasures the memory of a woman on whom Virtue imposes silence from all cliques, and whose name was as dear to Flora as it was to Mankind. If, to know the whole worth of flowers and to grow them successfully, it is necessary to be pure of heart and hand, who better than she to figurehead such sweet rewards and bring among us a rebirth of taste for this interesting occupation? History, in carrying her name down to posterity, will make known her beauty and her good will. As far as we are concerned, let us enshrine this in our Annals, and some day the knowledge of fanciers will be able to place beside her name that of others yet more august!" [V2]

Papaverina Major Listed as 'Grosse Mohnkopfs Rose' (Turb).

Pavot Listed as 'Grosse Mohnkopfs Rose' (Turb).

Poppy Rose Listed as 'Grosse Mohnkopfs Rose' (Turb).

Rosier de Francfort Listed as *Rosa ×turbinata*.

Tête de Pavot Listed as 'Grosse Mohnkopfs Rose' (Turb).

Turgida Listed as 'Turneps' (Turb).

Turneps
botanical syn. *Rosa ×rapa*; horticultural syns., 'À Feuilles de Frêne',
    'Fraxinifolia', 'Turgida', 'Turnip Rose'; trans., "Turnip"
Breeder unknown, pre-1770

"Rose." [Cal] "This sort differs from [*Rosa ×turbinata*] by its glossy, entirely glabrous leaflets." [Ty] "Flowering *branches* unarmed; adult branches with a few *prickles*. *Leaflets* oblong ovate, glabrous, glossy as in *R. lucida* although of a darker green. *Flowers* slow to develop and most abort; *receptacles* turbinate; sepals very long, incised; *petals* 4–5-seriate. *Hips* globose." [T&R] "They [*the hips*] are found flat, round, oval, pear-shaped, and top-shaped." [Go] "The stems, and the leaves as well, are nearly entirely without thorns in this sort, which has similarities to *Rosa turbinata*. Its leaves are composed of seven oval leaflets, slightly elongated, slightly pointed, nearly glossy above, paler beneath, glabrous on both sides; stipules large, entire, with two divergent points; petioles and rachis often reddish; flowers nearly solitary; peduncles armed with little prickles which are glandulose; ovaries very large, globulose, quite bristly; calyx divisions slightly pinnatifid; corolla red. This plant grows in Scotland, and is cultivated in the *Jardin des Plantes* in Paris." [Lam/Poir] "Vigorous shrub without hairs, or with a small number of upright, pale, setiform prickles grading to rough bristles; canes very red, armed with sparse, unequal thorns, of which the largest are flattened and hooked, intermixed with crimson bristles; leaves remote, tinted red which intensifies in the Fall, composed of 3–9 leaflets, which are simply or doubly dentate, glabrous, undulate; stipules flat, naked, undulate, finely dentate, narrow or wide; petioles bearing few prickles which are short, straight, and glandular; blossoms double, numerous, light red, in corymbs of 2–3 or more." [S] "*Bush* diffuse. Blooming *canes* ordinarily nude, glabrous, and unarmed. Non-blooming *canes* nude and glabrous at the summit, covered at their base with unequal bristles, of which the strongest are aculeiform, intermixed with a small number of thorns. *Leaves* 7–9 leaflets. *Petiole* red; armed with prickles beneath, bestrewn above with some small glands. *Stipules* glabrous,

much widened at the summit, ciliate-glandulose along their edges. *Leaflets* ovoid-oblong, glabrous, smooth above, ordinarily tinted purple beneath (only in their youth). *Serration* undulate, ordinarily simple, sometimes double. *Peduncles* bearing trichomes, glabrous beneath the bracts, hispid-glandulose above; united into corymbs even with the surrounding foliage, rarely projecting further. *Bracts* oval-lanceolate, acuminate, glabrous, denticulate at the summit; undulate, in an arc, contorted at the tip. *Ovary* turbinate-hemispherical, laterally flattened, bristling with points in the central flower, hispid-glandulose with the lateral ones. *Sepals* hispid-glandulose, terminating in a linear-lanceolate leaflet which is glabrous; as long as the corolla; 3 are divided, nearly pinnatifid. The glands are fragrant. *Flower* medium-sized or large, multiplex, irregular, light pink; opens in June and June." [Pf] See also *Rosa virginiana*.

Turnip Rose Listed as 'Turneps' (Turb).

Villosa

Rosa pomifera Listed as *Rosa villosa*.

Rosa villosa
botanical syn. *R. pomifera*; horticultural syns., 'Rosier à Fruit', 'Rosier velu'

"The flowers sometimes white, sometimes crimson, blowing in pairs." [Go] "Pale lilac rose. Notable for its glorious foliage and apple-shaped hips." [NRS30/203] "An old-fashioned variety with glaucous foliage, single blush-colored flowers, and handsome ornamental scarlet fruits." [CA96] "Flower bright blush to pink, single, with large apple-like fruits, red and hairy. Growth vigorous." [GeH] "It could serve as a stock, but it would be necessary to attend to getting rid of the numerous growths [*i.e., suckers*] which would in short order starve the scions." [BJ24] "It got its name [*villosa*] from the quantity of bristles which cover the ovary and flower peduncles, more numerous than in any other species. Only the double flowered variety ['Duplex', *below*] is grown. Tournefort calls it *Rosa pomifera* because of its fruits, which are round and apple-shaped." [BJ09] "The seedlings of *villosa* have given me some fruits which were completely glabrous, and varied in form." [V1]

"The Fruit Rose, *Villosa Pomifera,* is still blooming towards the end of May. Its wood is big, strong, and vigorous, like that of the Briars. Its leaves are long, deeply dentate, and often doubly dentate, with five to seven leaflets on the same leafstalk. The thorns are numerous, wide at the base, green, tinted lightly with pink, straight, and very pointed. The bud is round, with one to six on the same petiole. The blossom is single, with five petals, of a beautiful cherry red. Its calyx is round, supplied, like its petiole, with feeble, flexuose thorns. This calyx changes into a fruit as large as the little *pommes d'api,* beautiful red, which stay on the bush up till frost. This hip can be eaten; it is from the countryside, where it is dried for winter-curing, like prunes." [C-T] "Flowers single, a beautiful red. Calyx winged and bristly. Ovary globular. Leaves lanate and lanceolate … This Rose, an agreeable red, has some yellowish green pistils and some pale yellow stamens. The calyx segments are hispid and glandulose. The globular ovary shows the same characteristics as the calyx. The peduncle is bestrewn further with hairs and glands. The leaves, being villose on both sides, are a dull green, lanceolate, and doubly dentate for the most part. The [main] stem and branches bear big shield-shaped thorns. The fruits are large, bristly, and apple-ish." [Rsg]

"This rose has much in common with *Rosa canina*; however, it seems sufficiently distinct not to be included as a variety of this latter species. Its fruits are more rounded, its peduncles and ovaries are charged with glandular hairs and very numerous fine prickles; its leaves are soft and tomentose or pubescent. Its stems rise to a height of three or four feet [ca. 1–1.3 m]; they are stiff, glabrous, branching into cylindrical canes, grayish, clothed with petiolate leaves which are alternate, stipulate, composed of five or seven leaflets of medium size, oval, soft, pleasant to the touch, green, and pubescent on their upper side, nearly tomentose, and whitish beneath, doubly dentate on their edges, supported by pubescent petioles charged with some short small prickles and some moderately enlarged stipules. The flowers are nearly solitary, lateral or terminal, borne on very bristly glandulose peduncles. The calyxes are pubescent, covered with small glands, divided into five oval portions, extended at their tip by a long linear strip, which is sometimes slightly pinnatifid. The corolla is ordinarily single, with five petals of a deep red, whitish around their base, with a yellowish touch at the nub; the globular or slightly oval ovaries bristle with glandulose hairs; the fruits are large and rounded; they often shed a part of their bristles. In variety [*mollissima*], the leaflets are much thicker and softer, as if drapery; the ovaries are very often lacking glandular bristles. This shrub grows in Europe in dry, stony terrain, and in the woods." [Lam] "This rose, originating in Europe, grows spontaneously in central England and in the mountainous districts of France. Monsieur Bosc collected some specimens of it nearly at the summit of Mt. St. Gothard. The main limbs of the Villose Rose ascend to eight to ten feet [ca. 2.6–3.3 m]; its branches and canes are armed with rather strong prickles which are nearly straight, and separated one from the next; its leaves are ordinarily composed of seven leaflets which are oval, lanate, slightly soft to the touch both on top and beneath, and quite often exhibiting a gland at the point of each tooth. Slightly bruised, these leaves waft a resinous scent which makes it easy to recognize; further, they are viscous, particularly in the Spring. The blossoms of the Villose Rose appear in June. They are numerous, bright red, pretty fragrant, two inches in size [ca. 5 cm], and disposed at the tip of the cane in a sort of corymb; the size varies depending on culture or climate. The peduncles of the Villose Rose bristle with rough hairs; its petals are notched into a heart; its corolla is pink, its styles not very salient, its stigmas clustered together; its large fruits—nearly round—are sometimes clothed with soft spines which enclose a flesh which is pleasant to the taste; it is eaten under the name Rose Apple. Some people use these fruits to make preserves which are served at table for dessert. It is indeed likely that a person could come up with *eau-de-vie* by fermenting them. The Villose Rose always looks good no matter what stage of growth it is in: In the Spring, because of its large whitish leaves; in Summer, because of its numerous flowers; in the Fall, by way of its fruits. It is widespread in landscape gardens, and for good reason—it grows anywhere. However, it should not be given too much shade. As the Villose Rose is one of the species which grows the strongest trunks, one might suppose it would be just the thing for the purposes of grafting other roses on; experience, however, has proved that this rarely works, no doubt because of the resinous quality of the sap." [CM] "*Stems* to more than 3.6 m tall [ca. 11 ft]; *prickles* sparse, almost straight, grayish. *Leaflets* 5 or 7, bidentate, soft to the touch,

woolly on both sides; petiole tomentose, often with small, very short prickles. *Flowers* faintly scented, 2–3 together at the tips of the canes; pedicels and *receptacles* glandular hispid; *sepals* a little pinnatifid, pubescent, glandular, with an elongated, often flattened, leaflike tip; *petals* 5, cordately notched, light red in cultivated plants, but sometimes off-white in the wild. *Rosa villosa* grows in Europe in hills, hedges, and thickets. It is somewhat altered by cultivation … It is easily distinguished by the numerous soft appressed grayish hairs covering the leaflets, and the very large bristly hips, giving it the name of Apple Rose. Two varieties which have been raised to specific rank by many authors are *R. mollissima* Willd., differing only by its glabrous receptacle, and *R. tomentosa* Smith, which has an ovoid receptacle and simply dentate leaflets. Desvaux has made *R. tomentosa* a variety of *R. canina*; and Rau makes a new variety *R. villosa minuta*, which differs only in the subovoid receptacle, more elongate leaflets, and hips smaller by half. In some locales, the hips are dried and eaten in Winter like prunes, or are made into a pleasant conserve. Trouble-free to grow, *R. villosa* prefers shade to full sun. Semi-double and double varieties are also grown." [T&R] "The largest shrub in the genus. *Trunk* very large. *Branches* and *canes* strong, grayish green, glaucous, armed with thorns which are few in number, sparse, strong, straight or slightly curved, sometimes stipulary. *Bristles* rare or lacking. *Leaves* gray, composed of 5 or 7 leaflets. *Petiole* glandulose, ordinarily villose, armed beneath with small hooked prickles. *Stipules* glaucous, entire, with glandulose edges. *Leaflets* elliptical or oblong, flat, villose on both sides. *Serration* double, glandulose. *Peduncles* short, hispid-glandulose, long, foliaceous; 3 bear several appendages. *Fruit* very large, oval, hispid, orange-red or purple, crowned with the connivent sepals. The glands are viscous and very fragrant on all parts of the bush; and the hairs with which the peduncles, ovaries—and at length the fruits—bristle are very long and rough. [*In the single form*] *stipules* short, glandulose beneath. *Peduncles* glabrous beneath the bracts. *Flower* small, single, pale pink." [Pf] "This species now takes in several varieties with double flowers." [BJ30]

Duplex
syns. 'Pommifère à Fleur Double', 'Velu à Fleur Double', 'Wolley Dod's Rose'; trans., "Double"
Breeder unknown, pre-1770

"Semi-double, medium-sized, light pink." [AC] "Pink, medium size, lightly double, light scent, tall." [Sn] "*Tube of calyx*, oval, glandulous. *Sepals* foliaceous. *Flowers*, semi-double, fragrant, middle-sized, of a vivid pink." [Go] "*Peduncles* hispid-glandulose, bestrewn with stickers. *Flower* medium-sized, light or pale pink; semi-double, multiplex, or double (6–15 petals)." [Pf]

Majalis

Rosa cinnamomea Listed as *Rosa majalis*.

Rosa majalis
botanical syn. *R. cinnamomea*; horticultural syns., 'Cannelle', 'Du St. Sacrément', 'May Rose', 'Rosier des Alpes', 'Spring Rose'

"The May Rose deserves a place of honor in our gardens; it has the quality of being more Spring-like [*printanière*] than others." [C'H] "Doesn't grow very tall, and … gives roses of a pale red before all the

Rosa majalis continued

others." [MaRu] "Epidermis purplish; leaves glabrous above, pubescent beneath; in *May,* small single bright red fragrant flowers." [J-A/575–576] "Fruit nude, globular, an orange red." [No26] "Known by the common name of May Rose because it blooms at that time, . . . also known by the name *Can[n]elle [Cin[n]amon]* because of the color of its wood and the scent of its blossom, and the name *Du Saint-Sacrement,* doubtless because the flowers come about the time of the *Fête-Dieu;* in Latin, it is called *Cinnamomea.* It's a sort of Centifolia. Its branches, green at first, become—when they enlarge—the color of cinnamon, [and are] armed with small, recurved thorns. Its leaves are long, profoundly dentate, and of five to seven leaflets on the same stalk. The calyx is small, smooth, nearly round, and pinched at the top. The flower buds are oval, very slightly covered with the calyx membranes, and two to three on the same petiole, which is smooth and without prickles. The blossoms are of medium size, and delicate pink, with a light cinnamon aroma. This rose makes very large bushes which are not unattractive. It has been my experience that, if one shears it soon after bloom, it will give, in the Fall, a great number of new blossoms which are nicer than those of the Spring." [C-T] "This abundant rose, which grows wild in almost all European countries, has received the name Cinnamon Rose because of the stem color, not because of the scent of the flowers. It is attractive and much besought because of its early bloom." [T&R] "From Sweden. Thorns sparse and nearly equal; stipules linear; leaflets flat, glaucous, and cottony beneath. It likes a slightly fresh terrain, growing poorly in a mediocre one. I have the variety 'Scandens' in Brie; its long, thin canes fall back in garlands and are covered with lateral flowers." [BJ30] "Finally, it is owed the name *de Saint-Sacrement* because of the office it serves during that solemn fête in adorning baskets and altars." [CM]

"*Bush* 1.2–1.5 m tall [ca. 3½–4½ ft], with many densely-crowded short almost straight *prickles* on their lower parts. *Leaflets* 7, ovate, simply dentate, glabrous above, slightly pubescent beneath, especially on the rachis. *Flowers* scented, several together at the tips of the canes, subcorymbose; *receptacles* subglobose, glabrous; pedicel also glabrous; *sepals* very long; *petals* 5, cordately notched, more or less red depending upon the shrub's exposure; *stigmas* gathered into a head. This Rose grows spontaneously in Southern Europe and blooms in May. The Cinnamon Roses have undergone many modifications as a result of cultivation, and some botanists have recognized these as species. However, the characteristics upon which they are founded are of little merit." [T&R]

Flore Pleno

Sweden/Holland, ca. 1500?

"Flowers double, red, clustered at the tips of the young branches, cinnamon-scented, an inch in diameter [ca. 2.5 cm]." [BJ17] "Double blossoms, which open better [*grafted*] on the Briar." [J-A/576] "From southern France. It grows 6 to 8 feet tall [ca. 2–2.6 m]; stem a brown red, glaucous, clothed with prickles only at the base; leaves ordinarily of 7 leaflets, dark green, glabrous." [BJ17] "Known around 1500. Form of the Cinnamon Rose, grown at first by the Dutch, who imported it from Sweden. Used for the Fête-Dieu because it blooms then. It is the *Rosa canella rubicunda* and *cinnamomea flore pleno* of the Sixteenth Century authors." [ExRé] "*Shrub* to 3 m or more [ca. 9 ft]; *stems* tawny red, pruinose, with paired *prickles* close to the leaf

stipules and also to the insertion of young branches which have at their bases other densely clustered, straight, unequal and recurved prickles. *Leaflets* simply dentate, acute at the base, almost always obtuse at the apex, bright green above, pubescent beneath; petiole villose. *Flowers* semi-double, pleasantly scented, 1(–3); *receptacles* subglobose; *sepals* entire, subspatulate; *petals* reddish, notched, in 3–4 series; *stigmas* in a globose head." [T&R] "This sub-variety is a favourite in all gardens." [Go]

"This rose comes from central Europe, growing naturally in the hills around Geneva's lake, in the Auvergne, and in the Alps . . . Its very vigorous stems grow to four to six feet [ca. 1.6–2 m]. It is too bad that it puts out so many runners! This inconveniency may be avoided by grafting it, by which it will form well-rounded globes. Its leaves are composed of seven oval-acute leaflets of a dark green above, and whitish beneath. Its blossoms, which are an inch and a half across [ca. 4 cm], are double. The central petals are short and not as dark as the outer ones, which are a light crimson. Its scent is that of the Carnation. It reblooms in the Fall if watered when it is hot. Opens May 5–15, depending on the weather." [LeR]

"*Bush* tall. *Canes* diffuse, spindly, purplish, glaucous, armed with stipulary thorns which are little curved if at all. *Shoots* covered to their base with bristles and setiform prickles. *Petiole* villose, glandulose, armed or unarmed. *Stipules* large, normally entire, edges glandulose and upturned. *Leaflets* 5 or 7, rarely 9, ovoid-lanceolate, flat, much-veined; glabrous, grayish green and somber above; villose, glaucous, and very pale gray beneath. *Dentation* simple, sharp, fine. *Peduncle* glabrous. *Bracts* large, lanate, concave, bluish gray, ordinarily red at the base and along the edge. *Ovary* globular, glabrous, often colored, as is the peduncle. *Sepals* simple, excepting those of the blossom at the center of each corymb, which altogether bear 4–5 small appendages, and all of which terminate in a lanceolate leaflet. *Flower* small, nearly full, lilac pink, fragrant. Opens in May." [Pf]

"Flowers moderately double, slightly flat. Ovary semi-ovoid. Leaves elliptical. Calyx segments without appendages. Prickles sharp, beak-shaped . . . The blossoms of the May Rose—of which we don't know the homeland—and which takes its name from when it blooms—are flat and of medium size; their petals, always smaller towards the center, are tightly muddled there; the flower is the sort that is a very dark red in that part; they usually come in twos or threes, have yellow filaments and anthers; short peduncles; glabrous short petioles, usually having obvious stipules. It blooms from the middle of May to the middle of June. The calyx segments, appendiculate at the tip, exceed the bud and indeed the fully-developed blossom. The slight, semi-globular, bright green ovary is sometimes a little reddish; the maturing fruit never changes. The leaves are composed of five to seven elliptical lobes of a grass-green, very dark above, pale green and bestrewn with bristles beneath; dentation is present from the tip along two-thirds of the length; they are borne on a common petiole of a light green charged with white bristles, bearing large bulging stipules, and armed at the base with two prickles which are light brown, sharp, aimed sideways, and slightly hooked. The brown-gray stem is bumpy and armed with thorns that are shield-shaped at the base, sharp, and hooked like a beak. The young shoots are a bright dark red. This rose likes a southern or western exposure, in protected places." [Rsg]

Rubrifolia and Glauca

The possible synonymy or separation of *Rosa rubrifolia* and *R. glauca* has been at times the subject of beguiling debate. We leave determination of this question to the lucubrations of each season's new crop of eager taxonomists and botanists, and include both here under the same heading, noting when the same author has different entries on each of them.

Rosa rubrifolia or *R. glauca*

"Flower bright pink with white eye, single, with small trusses, with reddish-grey wood and foliage; summer flowering. Growth vigorous." [GeH] "The red-tinted stems and leaves, as well as the pretty little blossoms of a deep crimson, form an agreeable variety to the verdure of the surrounding foliage." [Go] "Its blossoms are single, small, and pink; but the color of its leaves and canes is very pretty; it seems covered with a dust or 'bloom' like that covering the 'Reine-Claude' plum. It can be found in our [French] Alps." [BJ09] "Habit upright; pretty shrub, because of its canes and reddish leaves." [JR26/181] "Stems reddish, and armed with hooked thorns; forms wide bushes 5–6 feet high [ca. 1.6–2 m]; leaves of 7 oval, acute, glabrous leaflets, *reddish* in their youth, and *glaucous* when fully developed; flowers also reddish, more than an inch in size [ca. 2.5 cm], in a terminal corymb. There's a variety with semi-double flowers." [BJ17] "Bush with a stem which is red or deep purple, 8–10 feet in length [ca. 2.6–3.3 m], with thorns which are equal, small, short, sparse, curved; leaves reddish, very glaucous, rough, opaque, with oval-acute leaflets; flowers small, deep red; fruit oblong." [No26] "[Not good as a stock for grafting.]" [JDR54/31] "We have brought it into our landscape gardens because of its height, the moderate number of thorns, and particularly because of the color of its bark, leaves, and stipules …The fanciers find in it quite an object of curiosity; furthermore, it has the priceless advantage of neither demanding care nor being damaged by frost." [CM, of *Rosa glauca*]

"Not so universally grown as it deserves to be, and where foliage is admired, I know of no variety that will give more pleasure than this one. It is described in our 'Official Catalogue' as 'Soft Rose—stems and foliage very distinct in colour. Grown for the effect of foliage only. Summer-flowering; known also as "ferruginea".' The flowers are insignificant, but the glaucous green foliage is quite distinct, and the deep crimson hips are very pretty and freely borne in clusters. This latter characteristic enables me to advise its cultivation on its own roots from seed. Some, I believe, cannot get this Rose to grow freely, and I experienced the same difficulty until a chance seedling in my garden showed me that when growing on its own roots it proved more satisfactory than when budded. I have a row of plants at the present time, grown from seed, which quite commonly produce rods of 6-ft. [ca. 2 m] and 8-ft. [ca. 2.6 m], and even longer. To ensure plenty of laterals suitable for decorative use, these rods must be tied town horizontally and shortened, and the thin and old wood cut out. At the base of those laterals that make weak growth strong buds for next year will generally appear, and such laterals should be cut hard back." [NRS17/53] "*R. glauca* …, which was hybridized with two or three Pimpinellifolias, has not yet shown even slight differences among its own seedlings. I don't know a more intractable rose than this one; indeed,

at my place and elsewhere, I have seen a very great number of seedlings from this rose which do nothing but reproduce the Type." [V2]

"Comes from the mountains of Europe. Makes thick bushes growing five to six feet tall [ca. 1.6–2 m], the color of which contrasts singularly with the verdure of other shrubs; leaves comprised of seven oval acute leaflets, reddish at first, then glaucous when fully developed; flowers in a terminal corymb, single and a beautiful incarnate red; trunk upright and robust; bark brown-red and covered with small red spines; fruits oval at first, becoming perfectly round in maturity. Blooms in June. This rose has a semi-double flowered variety." [AC, of *Rosa glauca*] "Grows naturally in montane woodlands in Dauphiné, Provence, Savoy, the Cévennes, the Vosges, etc. Stem grows ten to fifteen feet high [ca. 3.3–5 m], branching most usually from the base into several branches; canes reddish, smooth, charged here and there with straight thorns which are fairly strong and very protrusive; leaves composed of five to seven oval leaflets which are simply dentate, acute, quite glabrous, and glaucous; flowers in clusters to the number of six to fifteen together at the tips of their canes, bearing a lanceolate bract at the base of their peduncles; calyx divisions narrow, entire, longer than the petals and charged with several glandular hairs; corollas composed of five petals which are cordate and light red; stamens numerous, shorter than the petals; stigmas villose, adherent on a convex disk; fruits globular, smooth, and glabrous. This rose blooms in May and June." [AC, of *Rosa rubrifolia*]

"Reddish, glaucous *bush* 2.4–3 m or more high [ca. 7–9 ft +]. Stem *prickles* stout, recurved. *Leaves* 5–7(–9), oblong-ovate, soft to the touch, serrate, glabrous, glaucous, wine-colored, particularly beneath; petiole with yellowish prickles; stipules entire. *Flower* red at first, greenish-white when fully developed, clustered at the branch tips; pedicels short, glabrous, with a lanceolate bract at the base; *receptacles* at first ovoid, subglobose at maturity; *sepals* entire, acute, glandular hairy, longer than the petals. This shrub grows naturally in the Dauphiné, the Vosges, and particularly in moist places in the mountains of the Auvergne, where we have seen bushes 3 m [ca. 9 ft] in height. It readily and promptly naturalizes from seed." [T&R]

Carmenetta
syn. 'Rubrosa'
Central Experimental Farm, 1923
From *Rosa rubrifolia* × *R. rugosa*.

"Pale pink." [Ÿ] "Pink, medium size, single, light scent, tall." [Sn] The consensus seems to be that the general effect is that of a more robust *Rosa rubrifolia*.

Flora Plena
trans. "Double Flower"
J. C. Schmidt, 1896

Light red flowers, which are small and double. No further information on this interesting cultivar!

Mechliniae
Breeder unknown, date uncertain

Mentioned by Testu as a form showing mauve touches in the foliage, giving a mauve look to the whole.

Pinnatifide
Introducer unknown, pre-1828

A wild form found in "Cévennes, Pyrenees [France]." [RG]

Rubrosa   Listed as 'Carmenetta' (Rubr).

[Semi-Double]
Noisette, pre-1817

"Bush with slender canes, three to four feet high [ca. 1–1.3 m]; thorns not very numerous, slender; flowers pink, semi-double. Very odd variety. From my [*i.e., Monsieur Noisette's*] sowings." [No26]

Sir Cedric Morris
Morris/Beales, 1979

From *Rosa rubrifolia* × *R. mulligani*.

Cross evidently taking after *Rosa mulligani* in blossom (white, single, small), inflorescence (clusters), and size of plant (9+ m or ca. 30 ft), and *R. rubrifolia* in leaf and cane coloration (red maturing to gray), as we read in Griffiths.

Macrantha

Rosa ×macrantha
"Pale flesh, tinged pink; vigorous; bush." [NRS18/135] "Flower flesh, summer flowering, single. Growth vigorous." [GeH] "Single large light pink flowers three and one-half inches across [ca. 9 cm] and usually in clusters of four. It was in full flower July 9. It is said to be a hybrid between *R. canina* and *R. gallica*." [ARA18/42] "Against a rough oak fence, this single Rose has literally run riot. It is a beautiful creation, full of foliage in the winter, and in summer a hundred flowers burst out—flowers as soft in colour as those of the hedgerow—with broad, silky petals that seem to glisten in the sunlight. A faint fragrance comes from them, but it is their size, colouring, and profusion that makes Macrantha one of the most acceptable of all garden Roses. Its growth is free, almost extravagant, but every year ... severe pruning is essential." [NRS12/181] "Well repays for its cultivation when consideration is taken of its orange-red berries." [NRS17/63]

Daisy Hill
T. Smith, 1906?

Said to be from *Rosa macrantha* × *R. chinensis*.

"Pink, medium size, single, light scent, tall." [Sn] "Flower rich crimson, beautifully shaped buds; very distinct. Growth vigorous." [GeH] "Of very vigorous growth, with full double flowers of a delicious shade of pale silvery blush, suffused with peach, and deliciously fragrant. Quite one of the finest of summer flowering garden roses, either as a bush or as a semi-climber. A seedling from Macrantha." [SDH] "Daisy Hill" was the name of T. Smith's nursery.

Düsterlohe
trans. "Gloomy Fire"
Kordes, after 1931

From 'Dance of Joy' (HT, Sauvageot, 1931) × 'Daisy Hill' (Macra).

"A prickly, sprawling rose, with neat, dark green leaves. The flowers are borne singly and in clusters all along the arching branches, semi-double ... bright, clear rose-pink." [T4]

Düsterlohe II
trans. "Gloomy Fire II"
Kordes, 1941

"Light red, large, single, tall." [Sn]

Elfenreigen
trans. "Elf-Dance"
M. Krause, 1939

"Pink, medium size, single, tall." [Sn]

Harry Maasz
Kordes, 1939

From 'Barcelona' (HT) × 'Daisy Hill' (Macra).

Crimson flowers, dark green foliage, climbing.

Professor Ibrahim
M. Krause, 1937

"Pink, yellow center, large, full, very fragrant, tall." [Sn]

Raubritter
Kordes, 1936

From 'Daisy Hill' (Macra) × 'Solarium' (W).

"Pink, medium size, full, light scent, tall." [Sn] "No other rose that I have met has such irresistible charm, with its low branches laden with ball-like blooms." [T4] Fritz de Sickingen, nicknamed "Raub Ritter"; fl. 1521.

Macrophylla

Rosa macrophylla
"So called from the size of its leaves, which are very long, composed, as a rule, of eleven leaflets of some size, which give the plant a handsome appearance; the flowers are a pale Rose colour with very long sepals and large bracts, and these are followed by curious urn-shaped berries which hang down, crowned by the persistent sepals. It makes a bush of 4-ft. [ca. 1.3 m] or 5-ft. [ca. 1.6 m] high, and 3-ft. [ca. 1 m] or 4-ft. [ca. 1.3 m] across." [NRS17/37] "For vigor few of the species can surpass *R. macrophylla*. It has foliage which is quite distinct from that of any other Rose, and it actually reminds one of an Acacia. The single, pink flowers are carried on very dark coloured stems. This species was one of the strongest I grew, and established plants about twelve feet [ca. 4 m] in height were always a pleasure in the height of the flowering season." [NRS28/37]

"Tall shrub; canes reddish brown, with no thorns; stipules concave, wide, sharp, in an arc, nude, and colored; petioles 8–9 inches [ca. 2.3 dm] long, with no prickles, very lanate, with some glands; leaves the largest in the genus, composed of 5–11 leaflets; leaflets lanceolate, flat, veined, with simple very sharp teeth, naked above, lanate and whitish beneath, throughout dark green nuanced purple; bracts lanceolate, large at the base, very long, nearly entire, ringed and colored with red, smooth except for the mid-vein which on both sides is velvety; peduncles velvety, bearing some colored, unequal bristles; calyx-tube oblong, smooth; sepals simple, narrow, triangular, very long, dentate and widened at the tip, bearing some colored points on the part just before the tip; blossoms single, pink, with obovate petals, shorter than the sepals, mucronate with a small red point." [S] "*Anthers*, large and oblong. *Disk*, very large, slightly raised at the orifice. *Ovaries*, very villose, to the number of 28. *Styles*, villose, projecting, distinct. *Fruit*, oval." [MaCo] "Flowers white, with obovate petals bearing one small point colored red; peduncles villose, with some bristles which are unequal and colored. No varieties." [No26]

"Lindley has placed this rose in the Cinnamomae tribe, in which it seems to be it does not belong. It comes close to the *alpina* of the same author, from which it differs by its fairly large bracts, and the form of its stipules, which are large, concave, arching, and nude, while in the other they are narrow and fringed at the edge, with glands. In any case, it forms a link in the chain from one to the other. This species is not yet grown in France—or, at least, I haven't seen it yet at any of the nurseries. It was collected in Gossan-Than by Dr. Wallich, and has only been grown in England since 1823." [MaCo]

Auguste Roussel
Barbier, 1913
From *Rosa macrophylla* × 'Papa Gontier' (T).

"Light salmon pink, large, lightly double, tall." [Sn] "Good growth and foliage; large blooms; nice color; requires winter protection." [ARA18/119] "A great big shrub twelve to fifteen feet high [ca. 4–5 m], with clusters of big, semi-double, pink flowers." [GAS] "Plant climbing, of great vigor. Leaves large, proof against disease. Blooms in clusters of 5–12 blossoms which are large, semi-double, and with contorted, wavy petals, giving the flower a look all its own. Color, a superb salmony flesh pink, fading to a fresh pink. Very well formed buds. This is a new addition to the series of climbing roses so appreciated for several years [*referring evidently to the series of Wichuraiana hybrids put out by Barbier*]." [JR37/167]

Château de Vaire
Sauvageot, 1934
"Deep red, medium size, full, tall." [Sn]

Coryana
Cambridge University Botanic Garden, 1926
From *Rosa macrophylla* × *R. roxburghii*.

As we read in Griffiths, flowers cerise-pink and single; summer-blooming only; growth upright and to 3 m high (ca. 9 ft).

Doncasterii
Breeder unknown, date uncertain
"Years ago I tried to breed on a *R. macrophylla* 'Doncasterii'—most unsuccessfully. It was a deep single pink which didn't repeat and carried comparatively few flowers. It gave me lovely long seed pods which point-blank refused to germinate. It was very hardy and healthy to about 8 feet [ca. 2.6 m] in the glasshouse…Very early in my career I met Gordon Rowley of Reading University—a very clever geneticist with an abiding interest in roses. I was very much a new boy in the rose breeding business and he pointed me in various directions, including the use of *R. macrophylla* for disease resistance." [McG]

Master Hugh
Mason, 1966
From seed collected in China.
"Pink, medium size, single, light scent, tall." [Sn]

Virginiana

Rosa virginiana
horticultural syns. 'Rosier-Corail sans Épines', 'Rosier d'Amérique à Feuilles de Grande Pimprenelle', 'Turneps Anglais'
"Shrub 6 feet high [ca. 2 m] with few or no suckers, prickles some-times hooked. Leaflets 7 to 9, dark green and shining above, thickish, .5 to 1.5 inches long [ca. 1.5–4 cm]. Flowers usually few or solitary, bright pink, about two inches across [ca. 5 cm]. Fruit .33 inch high [ca. 1 cm], depressed globular. Blooms June and July. Found from Newfoundland to New York and Pennsylvania; western states, from Ohio to Louisiana, Arkansas, and Alabama [*note residual pre-20th-century concept of 'western states'*]. Well adapted for borders of shrubberies; handsome in summer with its shining foliage and bright pink flowers, and ornamental in winter with its fruits." [ARA21/37] "Badly named because it ranges only from Newfoundland to Pennsylvania. Attains six feet [ca. 2 m] and has glossy foliage, while that of [*Rosa carolina*] is dull. Also, it has hooked prickles, while Carolina's are straight." [ARA17/13]

Plena
trans. "Double"
LeRouge, ca. 1819
"This is a real darling, this small, pretty maverick, which comes from the southern part of America. Thoroughly new, thoroughly charming is this rose! Its wood is pinkish, and nearly lacking in thorns, which are only found where the leaves attach to the cane. The leaves look like those of the Ash; … [*word indecipherable*] … and edged with pink, terminating in a point; its canes are slender and long—*very* long—and branching. Each one bears a corymb or umbel of pretty, very double, roses, three or four on each peduncle. They are quite raggedy, one petal arching back and another going straight. They stand up or nod limply and airily. Their color is the most beautiful cherry red. Twenty or thirty other buds form clusters around the ones opening. The buds are much overtopped by the calyx appendages. Truly, one would want to compare this rose, in bloom, to a gathering of flirtatious little girls—very fresh and very light—the rather irregular character would not seem able to bear close examination, but they always charm you with their vivacity. This bush, on a three or four year graft, can be covered with more than four hundred roses. It blooms again in the Fall, if you cut off all the old ones, and don't spare the water when it is dry. They bloom June 10–15." [LeR]

Rosier-Corail sans Épines Listed as *Rosa virginiana*.

Rosier d'Amérique à Feuilles de Grande Pimprenelle Listed as *Rosa virginiana*.

Turneps Anglais Listed as *Rosa virginiana*. See also 'Turneps' (Turb).

Nutkana

Rosa nutkana
"Deep rose, free flowering, bright red hips. Growth vigorous. Suited for wild garden." [GeH] "Stems stout, 5 feet high [ca. 1.6 m] with usually straight prickles and sometimes bristly. Leaflets 5 to 7, or sometimes 9 on some shoots, 1/2 to 2 inches long [ca. 1–5 cm]. Flowers usually solitary, pink, 2 to 2 1/2 inches across [ca. 5–6.5 cm]. Fruit globular without neck. June and July. From Alaska to Oregon and Utah. Has the largest flowers of the western [American] species." [ARA21/40]

Cantab

Hurst, 1927

From *Rosa nutkana* × 'Red Letter Day' (HT).

Single deep pink fragrant blossoms on a plant 3 × 3 m in size [ca. 9 × 9 ft].

Schoener's Nutkana

Schoener/Conard-Pyle, 1930

From *Rosa nutkana* × 'Paul Neyron' (HP).

"Bud medium size, long-pointed, deep rose-pink; flower large, single, open, lasting, fragrant, clear rose-pink, borne several together on short, strong stem. Foliage sufficient, medium size, leathery, rich green. Growth vigorous, upright, bushy, shrub or pillar; abundant bloomer in May and June. Very hardy." [ARA31/229]

Hulthemia

Hulthemia persica

botanical syns. *Rosa berberifolia, R. monophylla, R. persica, R. simplicifolia*; horticultural syns., 'À Feuilles d'Épine Vinette', 'À Feuilles Simples'

"In May, blossoms of a beautiful yellow with the petals' nubs obscurely touched crimson; ovary and peduncles prickly." [No26] "Leaves simple; flower yellow, single, with purple nubs, very pretty. This rose is still [1840] very rare in France, because it doesn't much take to the basic culture of other roses. It, however, has been shown to live a fairly long time grafted on the Pimpinellifolia. The only own-root specimens we know of have been at the garden of the Luxembourg [Palace, in Paris] since 1826." [BJ40] "This species is curious because of its leaf, which is entire instead of being composed of several leaflets like all other roses. A person can see it in the beautiful and unique collection of roses of Monsieur Dupont, fancier, in the rue St.-Jacques, former convent of Ste.-Marie." [BJ09] "Pubescent stem, armed with strong hooked thorns which are white, particularly in the young growths; leaves entire, pale green, oval, nearly sessile; flowers yellow with a purple touch at the base of the petals, oval, pedunculate, solitary, terminal; peduncles short and clothed with several prickles; ovaries globulose, covered with prickles." [BJ17] "Fruits globular, prickly, as are the peduncles. Thorns of the stem hooked and nearly geminate. Leaves simple, nearly sessile. Flowers pale yellow, with a reddish touch at the nub. From Persia. Rare and delicate. Monsieur Hardy grows a beautiful specimen…in the flower garden of the Luxembourg." [BJ30] "It is seldom met with in this country [England], and does not do well, being rather of a delicate nature." [GeH]

"Among the numerous species of this genus, none is more remarkable than this one because of its entire leaves, which are nearly sessile. Its canes are diffuse, pubescent, clothed with strong curved thorns shaped like fish-hooks pretty much in twos at the base of the petioles or where the young canes spring from. The leaves are alternate, barely petiolate, quite entire—rather like those of the *épine-vinette* in form and size—oval, green, slightly glaucous, dentate along the edge. The blossoms are solitary at the tip of the young canes, borne by short, simple, pubescent peduncles bestrewn with some prickles. All of the divisions of the calyx are entire, smooth, lanceolate, and acuminate. The corolla is composed of five oval petals, yellow in color, usually marked with a touch of bright red at their base; the fruits are globular, and armed with numerous prickles. This species grows in the northern parts of Persia, where it was discovered by Michaux." [Lam] "Shrub of 50–70 cm [ca. 20–28 in], glaucous in color; branches slender, with pubescence which is lacking on the secondary branchlets; thorns slender, hooked, nearly decurrent at the base, often paired at the base of the leafstalk or branch, sometimes compound; leaves sessile, oval, unarmed, downy, simply dentate at the tip; stipules lacking; flowers solitary, in a 'starry' [*i.e., pointed*] cup, deep yellow blotched obscurely with crimson at the nub, wafting a sweet scent, says Olivier; stamens not very numerous; styles velvety." [S] "At most 0.6 m high [ca. 2 ft]; *branches* spreading, pubescent, slender, with many small whitish somewhat recurved *prickles* most commonly in pairs. *Leaves* simple, very shortly petiolate, alternate, serrate, glaucous green. *Receptacles* bristly with numerous short straight prickles; *sepals* lanceolate, entire, simple, also bristly; *flowers* solitary at the branch tips; *corolla* of 5 canary-yellow *petals*, each with a basal purplish spot. This rose, distinguished from all others by the simple leaves, has been brought back from Persia, where it is very common, by Michaux père and Olivier. The latter sent it to Cels père, who flowered it for the first time in Paris. Up to the present, no one has successfully acclimatized it in France, almost all fanciers having lost their plants, and the few surviving seedlings being weak and languishing. Budding on *R. spinosissima* [*R. pimpinellifolia*] has given the greatest hope of success." [T&R]

Interestingly, Malo differentiates between 'À Feuilles Simples' and 'À Feuilles d'Épine-Vinette':

'À Feuilles Simples'. "We owe the possession of this rose to the celebrated Olivier, who brought it from Persia, where it grew exposed to the north. It is not yet very widespread in gardens (although it has bloomed in the greenhouses of Malmaison and the *Jardin des Plantes*) because it is difficult to propagate. In the orangery, it blooms in April and May. Grafts and shield-buds made up to now do indeed take, but they don't last. If we can believe Olivier, this lack of success comes from too much care being bestowed on it. The stem…is armed with white hooked prickles, particularly in the young growths. Its leaves are entire, oval, and pale green; its flowers are large, yellow, solitary, marked with a purple touch, blackish at the petal nub; its peduncles are short and clothed with thorns, as are its ovaries. Olivier gives an interesting description of this rose in the tale of his travels in Persia." [CM]

'À Feuilles d'Épine-Vinette'. "This rose is just a very small bush, the main stem of which—divided into numerous canes which spread out and are pubescent and charged with a multitude of small prickles which aren't much curved—doesn't grow more than two feet [ca. 6 cm]. Its leaves are entire, oval, oblong, constricted at the base, sawtoothed at their edges, and glaucous green; its flowers are solitary at the tips of the young canes; their calyx is globular and armed with prickles; the corolla is composed of five light yellow petals with a red touch at the nub. The stamens are red; and the stigmas form, at the center of the blossom, a small convex head. This rose grows in the north of Persia; and, there, it is so abundant that it is used to feed furnaces. It blooms in May and June. Monsieur Dupont has given to the *Jardin du Roi* the only specimen which he had." [CM]

Rosa berberifolia   Listed as *Hulthemia persica*.

Rosa monophylla   Listed as *Hulthemia persica*.

Rosa simplicifolia Listed as *Hulthemia persica*.

À Feuilles d'Épine-Vinette Listed as *Hulthemia persica*.

À Feuilles Simples Listed as *Hulthemia persica*.

Hardii Plate 20
syns. 'Hardyana', 'Hardyi'
Hardy/Cels, 1834
From *Rosa clinophylla* × *Hulthemia persica*.

"Flowers bright yellow, with a deep chocolate spot at the bottom of each petal, small and single; form, cupped. Habit, branching; growth, vigorous; shoots, slender." [P] "Habit dwarf, tender, and but short lived." [JC] "Hybrid variety of *Rosa Clymphylla* [*sic*] and *Rosa Berberifolia* (habit of Berberifolia); blossom medium-sized, single, with a purple nub; extremely delicate bush." [S] "Obtained in 1836 by Monsieur Hardy from a seeding of *Rosa clinophylla*—the seeds of which were presumably fecundated by a *Rosa berberifolia*—in recognition of which he gave it his name. This rose maintains the blossom of its father, and takes the leaves from its mother, with 5–7 leaflets." [BJ40]

"The original roses of the Luxembourg, as well as those of the royal nursery of Trianon, are not purchasable; but are given away to respectable applicants, or exchanged for other plants with eminent nurserymen, by whom they are propagated and dispersed. In this way the Rosa Hardii Berberifolia, obtained this year by the accidental impregnation of that remarkable plant the Rosa Simplicifolia, or Monophylla, by a Microphylla growing near it, has fallen into the hands of Cels, by whom it will be shortly placed in circulation." [Go] "This curious hybrid, like its Persian parent, has single yellow flowers with a dark eye (much like Cistus formosus), and evergreen foliage; it seems quite hardy, and forms the very prettiest little bush possible." [WRP] "Our variety, alas!, resembles too nearly the species: it is delicate, and has been pronounced by some unmanageable. It suffers greatly from mildew, damp, and cold. The best mode of treating it is to plant it in a peaty soil, in the sunniest and airiest spot in the garden, away from all trees and fences. Take it up every autumn, keeping it in a cold frame, where sheltered from rain and frost." [P]

"Small bush growing to about two feet [ca. 6 dm]; canes outspread, slender, flexible, reddish, dense, slightly hirsutulous, armed at the attachment of each leafstalk with two paired thorns and a third one beneath, forming a triangle, rarely disposed in a line, sometimes two thorns or four. Leaves composed of 5–7 leaflets, lanceolate, small, slender, with sharp dentations, pretty often irregular in form, rarely opposite; terminal leaflet generally bilobate or trilobate. Sometimes three leaflets come from the same point, rarely one only, which nevertheless seems trifoliate because of the bifoliate stipule. The rachis has, beneath, three or four sharp little hooked prickles. The color of the foliage is a dark green. Flowers numerous, single, larger than those of the *Berberidifolia,* with golden yellow petals having a nub with a purple spot larger than that of the parent. These blossoms, which open perfectly well, are sometimes in twos or threes, but usually are solitary. The peduncle is short and slightly hirsute, the calyx is spherical and bristling with fairly numerous straight little thorns. The numerous stamens are a beautiful yellow, slightly lighter than the yellow of the petals. This interesting rose, bred at the Luxembourg by our colleague Monsieur Hardy from *Clinophylla* and *Berberidifolia* is of easy culture. It will better *Berberidifolia* through its larger size, more profuse and perfect bloom, more graceful habit, and more elegant foliage. It is being propagated in our establishment [Cels'], where it is

found exclusively; in due course, we will be able to supply them at a price of 25 francs. Fanciers who would like to acquire a specimen are requested to send us an advance order." [An34/372–373]

Hardyana Listed as 'Hardii' (Hult).

Hardyi Listed as 'Hardii' (Hult).

Lovers of *Hulthemia* will wish to seek out the modern hybrids 'Euphrates', 'Tigris', and 'Nigel Hawthorne'.

Hugonis

Rosa hugonis

"The first Rose to bloom in the spring, coming into bloom from ten days to two weeks ahead of the early 'Harison's Yellow'. The color is intense canary-yellow, very bright and attractive, and the plant is noteworthy all the growing season by reason of its dainty foliage. The young shoots are rich crimson in color, lending an added beauty that is not seen in many varieties. Hugonis is hardy as an oak and suitable only for lawn specimens or planting among shrubbery, as it is an exceptionally vigorous grower." [C&Js17] "This Rose is a spectacular show in itself. Every branch of the previous year's growth becomes lined on all sides, to the very tip, with closely-set, wide-open, single flowers like dainty yellow hollyhocks, and the branches bend over with the weight of bloom . . . When through blooming you will still have a most beautiful bush, for the acacia-like foliage on arching branches makes a most decorative shrub which, as far as we are aware, is never touched by disease of any kind but is clean and healthy always." [C&Js19] "The long, arching sprays make rare and exquisite indoor decorations in early spring when other flowers are scarce. *On a dining-table they are charming*, the delicate yellow crepe-like blooms, harmonizing softly with the snowy linen and silver, making one think of a scene in fairyland. This unique species is fine for shrub planting and makes a symmetrical bush about 6 feet in height [ca. 2 m] and the same in diameter when fully matured. An added and unusual attraction is the beautiful reddish-maroon new growths springing from the roots to provide more canes for the next season's bloom . . . Think of the pleasure of looking forward daily from about the last week in April, when the buds begin to form, till the plant is a mass a fairy-like bloom the first week in May." [C&Js24] "A graceful shrub, growing rapidly to a form generally resembling that of the familiar Van Houtte spirea, and blooming gloriously for full two weeks before any other rose is awake to the spring. After blooming, its pale green foliage on its curious red-brown twigs continues until fall turns the leaves a soft purple. This rose is good in the border exactly twelve months in the year, for its twigs are beautiful against the winter's snow." [ARA22/47]

"This beautiful rose came to us from the Royal Gardens, Kew, where it was raised from seeds received from north-central China in 1899." [ARA16/39] "Introduced in 1899, seeds being sent to Kew in that year by Father Hugh Scallan from Western China." [NRS15/28]

"It is an upright-growing shrub 6 to 8 feet tall [ca. 2–2.6 m] and more in diameter, with slender and spreading branches. The fragrant flowers, each about 2½ inches across [ca. 6.5 cm], are produced all along the branches, and so freely that the branches become yard-long sprays of soft yellow. The leaves are small and of a pale green

Rosa hugonis continued

hue, but the foliage is ample, and as I write in mid-November is still on the shrub, and has assumed a dark purple tint." [ARA16/39] "It is a very charming plant, for it has a free and graceful habit, and bears a profusion of bright yellow flowers about two inches across [ca. 5 cm] in April and early May. These are single flowers terminating short axillary shoots, which spring from the branches of the previous year. Growing about eight feet high [ca. 2.6 m], it produces rather small leaves, which average about three inches in length [ca. 7.5 cm] and are made up of from five to eleven leaflets. Two forms appear to be in cultivation, one of rather denser habit and less free in flowering than the other." [NRS15/28] "The best new shrub in commerce. It seeds freely and the seeds come up the next spring. My bush is in a tulip bed, so the soil was not disturbed; and the bed had a good cover of leaves last fall. This spring, the seedlings were coming up in tufts, so I pricked them out. The best one grew 20 inches [ca. 5 dm] this season, and is a perfectly good Hugonis." [ARA24/178] "*Rosa hugonis* up to this time yields seedlings inferior in vigor and attractiveness to the species, both from chance and carefully controlled pollinations. The seeds, though abundantly produced, are low in germinative powers, scarcely one in a thousand coming up the first season after planting." [ARA17/42–43] "It seeds with great freedom and appears to hybridize readily with other wild and cultivated roses." [ARA16/36] "*R. hugonis* still proves refractory, the hybrids losing yellow coloring to a great extent, but showing improvement in form and substance of bloom." [ARA18/45]

Albert Maumené

Sauvageot, 1934

"Carrot-red." [Ÿ] "Copper-red, large, lightly double, medium scent, medium height." [Sn]

Cantabrigensis

Cambridge University Botanic Garden, ca. 1931

From *Rosa hugonis* × *R. sericea*.

"Fragrant single yellow flowers about 1.5 inches across [ca. 4 cm]; foliage dainty; shrub six feet or more in size [ca. 2 m]. A chance seedling." [T4]

Double Hugonis

Introducer unknown, pre-1932

"Growth-habit like *Rosa hugonis*. Stronger grower. Great numbers of double, yellow flowers." [C-Ps32]

Dr. E. M. Mills

Van Fleet/American Rose Society, 1926

From *Rosa hugonis* × 'Radiance' (HT); or *R. hugonis* × 'Altaica' (Pim); or *R. hugonis* × a Rugosa.

"Flower medium size, (2 to 2½ inches across [ca. 5–6 cm]), semi-double, globular, primrose with pink suffusion which becomes more pronounced in the later blooms." [ARA26/184] "Slightly fragrant." [C-Ps28] "A very pretty, early-blooming shrub growing to a height of 4 feet [ca. 1.3 m] ... Very hardy." [ARA29/124] "It seemed to delight in 31 degrees [F] below zero, making splendid growth and bloom." [ARA31/188] "It must be carefully pruned to produce a shapely bush." [ARA30/175] "Appears absolutely free from disease and insect trouble ... *N.Y.*; More or less a disappointment. Excellent growth, for bunching or hedging, but the flower, while attractive when it first comes out, soon becomes very light yellowish white and lasts only a short time

... *Syracuse, N.Y.*; ... Not of value in this locality. Color insignificant and form worse. Foliage falls very early and the long, bare stalks are most unattractive ... *Calif.*" [ARA28/155]

"A hybrid of *Rosa hugonis* ... showing traces of Rugosa blood. The color is light primrose, with pink suffusion that becomes more pronounced in the later blooms, which are medium in size, cupped form, and semi-double. Flowers come singly all along the stem, like 'Hugonis', are of good lasting quality, but impatient of wet weather. They are slightly fragrant. The foliage is abundant, dark green, small and wrinkled, like a Rugosa. Wood is reddish, fuzzy, and thorny. Will make a splendid lawn specimen as it grows to 5 feet [ca. 1.6 m]; bushy and very hardy." [C-Ps27] "An early-blooming, spreading shrub rose, 3 to 4 feet high [ca. 1–1.3 m], similar to the graceful Scotch roses in its habit and in its manner of spreading by underground rootstocks. Foliage is small and deep green, and the new growth is almost thornless, with sharp, straight thorns on the mature wood. Flowers are medium size, 2 to 2½ inches across, semi-double, peculiarly globular in shape, and profusely produced along and around the arching branches ... The effect is of wands of bloom somewhat like Hygonis. The parentage of this rose is in doubt, although Dr. Van Fleet regarded it as a cross between Hugonis and 'Altaica'. The foliage hints of Rugosa ancestry ... Vigorous and graceful in habit throughout the season, and the rose is valuable either as a lawn specimen or for use among shrubs." [ARA26/48]

Headleyensis

Warburg, 1920

From *Rosa hugonis* × 'Altaica' (Pim).

According to Griffiths, the flowers are single, creamy yellow, and fragrant, on a tall plant with ferny foliage. "Raised at Boidier, then the home of Sir Oscar Warburg, at Headley near Epsom, Surrey ... I consider this the most ornamental of all the hybrids of *R. hugonis* that I have seen so far." [T4]

Xanthina

Rosa xanthina

horticultural syn. 'Zantina'

"Single yellow." [CA07] "Canary yellow. Single." [CA10] "A strong-growing, broad-thorned, maroon-stemmed Rose of graceful habit coming from Turkestan and Afghanistan, and covered in early spring with sulphur yellow flowers of most distinct character." [C-Ps25] "Has given plants with double yellow blooms from collected seeds, but as yet does not fruit well here [*U.S.A.*]; more fertile forms may in time be imported." [ARA16/36] "This seems like a double variety of *Rosa hugonis*, with the flowers a more vivid, clear yellow. It blooms early in May and makes great masses of shining double yellow flowers that simply cover each bush. Makes an enchanting, early-blooming lawn specimen." [C-Ps29] "Grew well, but lost their foliage very early and did not bloom." [ARA24/90] "*R. xanthina* ... shows considerably more variation in its cross and self-pollinated seedlings [than does *Rosa hugonis*], the flower colors ranging from paper-white to a somewhat deeper yellow than has yet been developed in Hugonis. Many seedlings are free from the penetrating formic acid odor so objectionable about the young growth of the Type in moist weather." [ARA21/28]

"*R. xanthina* … has no setae … but thin straight spines. The flowers are deeper yellow than in *R. hispida*, and a well grown bush in full flower is a fine sight. The berries are blackish, but not so polished as in 'Altaica' [Pim]. It appears that double flowers of this species are cultivated in China, and that it was from a specimen of one of these that Lindley gave his short description of the species, the origin of which appears to be still somewhat obscure." [NRS17/35] "Not known to cultivation in our country [U.S.A.] until after Frank N. Meyer found it in the neighborhood of Peking. He collected 135 cuttings and sent them to the office of Foreign Seed and Plant Introduction on December 23, 1905. These cuttings reached this country in good condition, and plants were raised from some of them at the Washington greenhouses, and also at the Chico Plant Introduction Field Station, Chico, Calif. Mr. Meyer's description of this rose, which accompanied the cuttings, is as follows: 'A semi-double, yellow rose frequently met with in the gardens here. It is a very thrifty grower and able to withstand long drought; very well fit to serve as a background for smaller plants or to be used as a lining along a path. The straight young shoots, which grow 5 to 8 feet high [ca. 1.6–2.6 m], might, perhaps, furnish a fine stock for long-stemmed hybrid roses.' … Mr. Meyer also collected and sent to this country the single-flowered form of *R. xanthina*, which has been named *R. xanthina, forma normalis*, by Messrs. Rehder and Wilson in '*Plantae Wilsonianae*'. The seeds of this variety were first collected on August 23, 1907, at which time he wrote as follows: 'The beautiful single yellow rose, *Rosa xanthina*, growing in dry, rocky locations and mostly in sheltered places, produces masses of delicate yellow flowers in early summer. It is used by the Chinese as a grafting stock for the Tea varieties of roses. Might be utilized for the same purpose in the United States, and may also be utilized in hybridizing. Seed collected at Shushan, Shantung, China'. This single form of *R. xanthina* is very free in flower, and, blooming early in the season, makes a welcome addition to the roses available for mass effects, or for use as a shrub." [ARA19/39–40]

Zantina   Listed as *Rosa xanthina*.

Soulieana

Rosa soulieana

"Monsieur Maurice de Vilmorin introduced this Chinese species to cultivation rather more than twenty years ago [*making ca. 1894*]. It is a very strong growing plant of the *R. moschata* type, attaining more than 12-ft. [ca. 4 m] in height, with a dense habit, intensely spiny shoots, and rather glaucous leaves, which are 3-in. or 4-in. long [ca. 7.5 cm or 1 dm]. The creamy white flowers, each about 1½-in. in diameter [ca. 4 cm], are borne in large clusters in July, and are succeeded by orange coloured fruits." [NRS15/30] "The egg-shaped hips assume a rich colour in autumn, and may be described as orange-red in shade." [NRS17/64] "This species, one of the most vigorous of the Chinese wild Roses, was first introduced to Europe by Père Soulie from Western China in 1896. He sent seeds to Monsieur Maurice de Vilmorin, that gentleman sending young plants to Kew in 1899. The bushes are very strong in growth, young shoots 10 to 15 feet or more in length [ca. 3.3–5 m +] being common on healthy specimens in deeply cultivated ground. The stems are copiously armed with large

spines, giving it some considerable value as a subject for hedges and impenetrable barriers in public parks. The grey-green leaves are 3 to 4 inches long [ca. 7.5 cm to 1 dm], composed of five to nine leaflets. The white blossoms, with pale yellow centres, average 1½ inches across [ca. 4 cm], [and] are very freely produced in large, branching corymbs during July. The small, globular fruits are orange-red in colour, attractive in mid-winter in the garden, the sprays useful to cut during the Christmas season for large vases—but one must wear gloves." [NRS27/56]

"Robust shrub of the habit of *R. canina*, 2–3 m high [ca. 6–9 ft], with thorns either straight or curving on floriferous canes which are numerous and large, glabrous except for small glands on the short peduncle. Leaves a pale green, 5–9 leaflets (usually 7), 6–10 cm long (usually 6–8) [ca. 2¼–4 in, 'usually' ca. 2½–3⅛ in]; leaflets oval or oval-oblongate, growing to 3 cm [ca. 1⅛ in], with very short petioles, finely dentate like a saw; rachis prickly; stipules large, adnate, finely bordered with glands, sharp at the free portion. Blossoms ivory white, about 4 cm in size [ca. 1½ in], disposed in ample terminal corymbs, close-set and compound, or sometimes solitary on short branches; peduncles slender, clothed with very small glands; calyx not very glandulose, with lobes [*i.e.*, sepals] either entire or bearing some slightly acuminate dentations. Petals emarginate. Ovaries bristly, with persistent styles. Fruit ovoid or nearly globular, 1.5 cm across [ca. ½ in], cinnabar orange. *Rosa soulieana* is distinguished from *R. moschata* Miller by its smaller leaves, its oval petioles rounded at the two ends, its less glandulose pedicels, and its shortly acuminate sepals. It is one of the prettiest sorts of single-flowered Roses from the point of view of flowers and fruits. [*A footnote adds:* It was introduced by Monsieur Maurice de Vilmorin.] *Rosa brunonii* Lindl. …, often erroneously called *Brunonis*, is easily distinguished by its very bristly peduncles. Its leaves are more like those of *R. soulieana* than those of *R. moschata* with which it is sometimes grouped." [JR36/182]

"An extremely vigorous species of multiflora type, less hardy in wood but with far more resistant foliage and larger blooms, very plentifully produced. Some botanical specimens of *R. soulieana* show light yellow flowers, but those available in this country [U.S.A.] are of the white-flowered type. *R. soulieana* appears to be quite as readily hybridized as *R. wichuraiana* and may confidently be expected to produce varieties of interest. The only seedlings yet bloomed, with Cabbage or *Rosa centifolia* varieties as pollen parents, have delightful semi-double blooms, shell-pink and light crimson in color, fragrant and beautifully formed. The hybrid plants are rampant in growth, with very spiny stems, and preserve the resistant foliage of the species. The cross with *Rosa setigera*, as yet unbloomed, is especially vigorous." [ARA16/35] "A very vigorous, erect, climbing rose with remarkably fine grayish foliage bearing white flowers in unbelievable huge clusters. In the autumn the plant is a mass of orange berries from top to bottom, very showy and very beautiful. It accepts foreign pollen readily and several hybrids have been raised which are not without charm, but none of which so far seems to have any urgent excuse for being introduced to a world already crowded with mediocrity." [GAS]

Chevy Chase
N. J. Hansen, 1939
From *Rosa soulieana* × 'Éblouissant' (Pol).

"'Finest of the Ramblers,' it suggests an improved '[Turner's]

Chevy Chase *continued*

Crimson Rambler' with lovely, small, dark crimson, very double (60 to 70 petals) flowers, singly or in clusters of 10 to 20 on short stems. Profuse bloom comes May into June, and the color changes with age but not unpleasantly. The soft, smooth, small leaves are very different from those on 'Dorothy Perkins' [W]. It is practically mildew-proof." [W] "Deep red, small, full, medium scent, tall." [Sn]

Kew Rambler

Royal Botanic Gardens, Kew, 1912
From *Rosa soulieana* × 'Hiawatha' (W).

"Flower apple-blossom colour, single, in persistent clusters." [GeH] "A single-flowered hybrid . . . introduced in 1922. Flowers are pale pink with white centers. Useful in wild places." [GAS] "A vigorous rambling, not climbing, Rose with delicate pink-tinted blossoms with white centres." [NRS27/56] "Pink, medium size, single, tall." [Sn]

Wickwar

Steadman, date uncertain
From *Rosa soulieana*? × *R. brunonii*?

"It retains the vigour, grayish leaves and delicious fragrance of *R. soulieana,* but has clear pink single flowers and a more tractable climbing habit." [T4] Phillips and Rix note creamy flowers and grayish leaves similar to those of *R. brunonii.*

Uncertain

Coral Drops

T. Smith, pre-1927

"It forms a bush of very graceful habit, 6–7 feet high [ca. 2–2.3 m], with very pretty foliage and bunches of rose coloured flowers in June; these are followed by hanging sprays of bright coral-red fruit in Autumn, when it is a very striking object. A mysterious seedling which was found here in an old seed bed." [SDH]

Fraxinifolia

syns. 'À Feuilles de Frêne', 'À Feilles Luisantes', 'Laevis', 'Lucida Fraxinifolia'; trans., "Ash-Leafed"
Boulogne, pre-1811

"We have seen at Monsieur Dupont's place this very pretty sort of rose and its variety with double flowers." [BJ09] "Ash-Leafed Rose, Glossy-Leafed Rose, in Latin *Lucida fraxinifolia*. This one is still very effective, and generally popular because of the beautiful forms which it takes when grafted on the Briar, because of the brilliance of its foliage, and because of the immensity of the flowers it has. They are nearly as big as those of the Centifolia, and quite double; a specimen grafted three or four years previously, and which is vigorous, can give up to three or four hundred [blossoms]. After the first bloom, if you shear and prune it, it will bloom again later, when conditions suit, with blossoms even fresher and more pleasing than the early ones. The canes branch, and are nearly thornless—you only find prickles where the leaves are attached. These last are bright green, long, terminating in a point at both ends, to the number of seven to nine [leaflets] on the same petiole which, because of its brownish red color, redoubles the sparkle of the leaves. The buds are long, and

crowned with the calyx membranes [sepals] which are also long and elegantly cut. The calyx is round, large, compressed, and as shiny as the leaves. The blossoms are in umbels, to the number of three or four on the same petiole. The petals are a beautiful sparkly cherry red. There is a variety with single flowers which are the same color; it has numerous stamens of a beautiful bright yellow. Put together, these two colors produce a charming effect. This effect, though the blossoms are single, makes a place for it as an ornamental in shrubberies, as do its hips, which are quite rounded and of a bright red both beautiful and sparkling. They keep until hard frost, look like cherries, and are thus effective against the bright foliage of this shrub. Some fanciers have given me these sorts under the name *Pensilvanica à feuilles sauvages*; but there is already a species with that name that I had and lost, and which I have not been able to replace; this one is nicer because it blooms in several seasons, particularly the Fall." [C-T]

"From Scotland. Stems and petioles nearly unarmed; leaves of 7–9 leaflets like those of *Fraxinus excelsior* in the upper branches. In July, blossoms which are medium-sized, semi-double, pink, and terminal; ovary semi-globulose; sepals elongate and semi-pinnate; peduncles and calyxes covered with hispid, very short bristles." [BJ24]

"*Bush* thick, tall, unarmed except at the base of vigorous shoots, where there are rough, aculeiform bristles. *Stems* and *branches* purple brown, ordinarily cracked and grayish at the base. *Canes* smooth, glaucous, green and (usually) purple. *Leaves* glabrous, in 5's, more usually 7 or 9 leaflets. *Petiole* nude, unarmed, or armed beneath with little prickles. *Stipules* long, glabrous, glaucous beneath, dilated at the summit; denticulate along the edges, which are rolled under at the base only. *Leaflets* lanceolate, cramped at the base, smooth, but not glossy above, pale and veined beneath. *Serration* simple, sharp, ordinarily deep, wavy, divergent. *Peduncles* in 2's or 3's, or in few-flowered corymbs. *Bracts* large, glabrous and ordinarily glaucous, oval, entire or denticulate, bullate, wavy. *Ovary* globular, glabrous. *Sepals* simple, cramped, glandulose, terminating in a long point. *Styles* numerous, free, not protrusive. *Fruit* globular, orange red, crowned by the convergent sepals. Blooms in May and June. This sort produces a great quantity of runners. [For the common form] *shoots* bristling with bristles at their base. *Leaflets* dark green above, grayish beneath. *Serration* deep, seeming crinkled because of the waviness. *Peduncles* glabrous and glaucous, shorter than the surrounding foliage. *Bracts* glaucous, just as long as or longer than the peduncles. *Ovary* glaucous, sometimes slightly colored. *Flower* medium-sized, single, pale pink." [Pf]

"*Fraxinifolia* has been, for [various] authors, *virginiana, blanda, corymbosa,* and *alpina*. The only difference I can find from *cinnamomea* is the absence of prickles—and it is known that this characteristic is fugaceous." [MaCo] Not to be confused with Andrews' early blooming, white-flowered *Rosa fraxinellaefolia*. The attribution "Boulogne" probably indicates distribution via Dumont de Courset, who had a wide-ranging rose collection there.

Théano

Geschwind, 1894
From *R. californica*? × 'Turner's Crimson Rambler' (Mult).

"Pink." [LS] "Light pink, small, lightly double, tall." [Sn] "No scent, −2.5 m [less than ca. 7½ ft]" [EU] The stated parentage has been questioned.

CHAPTER SIXTEEN

Roxburghiis

"There is nothing in the whole family that we have been engaged upon, so distinctive in flower and character as this group. The plants of the true Microphylla Rose [*i.e., Rosa roxburghii*] are very beautiful; when in foliage, their small pinnated leaves are so unlike any other plant (except perhaps a Locust tree in miniature) that they are both interesting and agreeable. It has been known twenty years in Europe, having been brought from China ... The first of this rose, as we believe, was imported [to the United States] by us [the Buist firm] in 1830, and it is now extensively cultivated in every section of the country. Recent importations, denominated *Microphylla,* can barely be recognized as such; the popularity of the old variety has given circulation to many of the inferior *new* ones, which, after having been seen in bloom, are frequently thrown aside as useless. They are generally hardy, in dry soils giving a succession of flowers throughout the season. They are adapted for training against fences, or low outbuildings, or they may be formed into handsome bushes of any shape; but a hedge of them is the beau idéal of the flower garden, which all may enjoy in any latitude south of this [*i.e.,* Philadelphia]." [Bu]

"Its character is unique, with small neat dark green foliage. The flowers are large and very double, of a rose colour, produced at the extremity of the young shoots, in twos or threes, according to the strength of the plant; the calyx ...is thick and prickly; hence it is called the 'Burr Rose'." [Bu] "Has a remarkably well-dressed appearance, with its dainty leaves and widespread bloom, shading from tenderest pink to a full crimson centre, and its large round buds covered with stiff green bristles." [NRS21/99] "*Shrub,* low, compact, pale green. *Branches,* thin, smooth, flexible. *Thorns,* stipular, geminated, straight. *Stipules,* very narrow, enlarging at the summit. *Leafstalks,* rather thorny, very weak. *Leaves,* smooth, composite. *Leaflets,* from five to thirteen, very small, glossy, round, oval, lanceolated, pointed, finely toothed, without pubescence; thorny underneath on the mid-rib, which is very prominent. *Flowers,* solitary, very double, pale pink more vivid in the centre. *Bracteal leaves,* accompanying the flower, narrow, lanceolated, pointed, smooth, glandulous on the margin. *Tube of the ca-lyx,* round, covered, as well as the divisions, with straight close thorns, resembling those of a horse-chestnut. *Sepals,* dilated, pointed, cottonous on the margin, formed like those of the *Rosa bracteata.* This little shrub, a native of China, bears the cold of our winters without injury. Lindley places it in the tribe of *Rosa canina;* but, on the whole, it bears a closer affinity to the Macartney rose." [Go]

"The original imported plant bearing double flowers ['Pourpre Ancien'] was undoubtedly an improved garden variety. Mr. Rivers says he received seed from Italy of this rose, and finds that plants from it, to use a florist's term, sport amazingly, no two appearing alike." [WRP] "Beyond 'Pourpre Ancien', there are still several other very pretty hybrids of *Rosa Microphylla* due to the industrious and indefatigable breeders of Lyon. All these hybrids are climbers —which is to say that they can easily be trained into just about any shape a rose can take." [JR8/136–137] "A warm and dry border will suit these varieties admirably ...but to see these very curious roses bloom in perfection, bud them on short stems of the Dog rose, and treat them exactly as recommended for the Tea-scented Roses; they will then bloom freely, either in pots or in the flower-borders, and form delightful little plants, quite unique in their characters and appearance." [WRP]

Rosa microphylla Listed as *Rosa roxburghii*.

Rosa roxburghii
botanical syn. *R. microphylla*; horticultural syn., 'Chestnut Rose'

"The small-leaved *R. microphylla* [*an unfortunate typographical error has it as "R. macrophylla"*] is most distinct on account of its rose-pink flowers being succeeded by spiny apple-like fruits that are eaten as apples by the Japanese. It is most beautiful in berry, yellowish green in colour and very fragrant." [NRS17/63] "Canes armed with large, oblique thorns; spiny calyxes. To be used on rocks." [JR26/181] "This Rose is a native of the Himalaya Mountains, and also of China, and was introduced to England about twenty years hence [*making approximately 1828*]. It is a decided curiosity. The leaves are composed of numerous small leaflets, sometimes as many as fifteen ranging on the sides of the petiole; the branches are of a whitish

Rosa roxburghii continued

brown, the outer bark often peeling off in autumn: they are almost destitute of prickles, but the broad sepals of the calyx are densely covered with them, owing to which the flower-buds are as rough as a hedgehog. The Microphylla appears to delight in a warm sandy soil: it is rather tender, and requires a wall to ensure the production of its flowers in full beauty. It requires very little pruning. No varieties have yet been raised to surpass the original [*'the original' probably referring to 'Pourpre Ancien'*]." [P]

"A bush which, grafted on a tall stock and grown in a pot, is bushy and neat, but which, planted against a warm wall, can grow up to a height of 4 meters [ca. 12 ft]. It gets through the winters of Central Europe quite well under a covering of soil and dry leaves in the open ground, never however becoming climbing or scandent except when own-root and raised in the soil of a hot-house. Wood, foliage, thorns, and fruit are singular and thoroughly different from those of other sorts; because of this, this rose merits a warm recommendation though its blossoms don't have any good scent. The court gardener, Nietner, confuses this rose with [*Rosa bracteata*] into one sole variety, which doesn't seem justified at all." [JR8/61]

"In 1862, Dr. Maximowicz, and, nine years later, Dr. Savatier, found the Type of *Rosa microphylla* in a wild state near Lake Hakone in the central part of Japan, where, it would seem, it became a shrub growing sometimes up to 2.5 m [ca. 7½ ft]. It has numerous upright canes which are slightly geniculate; the sub-stipular paired thorns are straight or ascendant. The leaves are [of] 9–15 leaflets, which are more or less velvety beneath, small or medium-sized, and oval-elliptical in form, with small dentations. Flower-stem short; flowers solitary, with yellowish petals. (*Fl. Sulfureus. Rosa Chlorocarpa.* Maxim. botanical collection in St. Petersburg). The fruit bristles with small straight stickers, which are spiniform, giving it the look of a little chestnut. According to Dr. Savatier, this fruit, which is greenish, large, nearly round, and very pulpy, would seem edible, having a taste which he found not disagreeable. Among the specimens preserved at St. Petersburg and consulted by our honorable and most rare collaborator Monsieur Crépin, there is one which bears a ripe fruit which becomes reddish. Monsieur Crépin wonders if this coloration only appears late in the season, or if it is produced by desiccation. It would seem thus, as, up till now, no one yet has been able to fix which tint the fruit takes on at full maturity. The description given this rose by the translator of Lindley gives it leaflets without pubescence and a full, pale red blossom with a lacy bract, characters lacking in the plant discovered along the Japanese lake. But Lindley, like Roxburgh (manuscript: *Flora indica,* London) had seen only cultivated plants with double flowers, or the collected specimens above, which plants would indeed be modified in parts other than the corolla, be it by seed or sport, as often happens in genus *Rosa.* The *Microphylla* rose … is Chinese and Himalayan in origin, and was introduced into Europe at some time of which I have been unable to find the date. We nevertheless have information which relates that it was already in cultivation about 1825, and that it resisted the intense cold of 1829–1830—which we find difficult to believe, as to this last assertion, because we have seen it hurt by less." [JR8/136–137] "In 1825, [Vibert] introduced into France … the *Microphylla.*" [SHP29/149] "It bloomed for the first time in France in 1827." [MaCo]

Horticultural Varieties

Château de la Juvenie
Gravereaux, 1901
    "Delicate pink." [LS]

Chestnut Rose   Listed as *Rosa roxburghii* (Rox).

Domain de Chapuis
Gravereaux, 1901

"Violet red." [LS] "Monsieur Jules Gravereaux, a citizen of Paris, with a town house in the Avenue de Villars, and a charming country home in the village of l'Haÿ, is universally recognized as the leading French amateur rosarian. He is the permanent President of the French Rose Society, and Président d'Honneur of the Société Nationale d'Horticulture de France. Paris owes to him, in conjunction with Monsieur Forestier, the laying out of the extensive Rose garden at Bagatelle in the Bois de Boulogne. He also supplied all the botanical species and most of the large collection of modern Roses to be found there. Monsieur Gravereaux has written and edited several publications connected with the Rose … Monsieur and Madame Jules Gravereaux reside in a beautifully furnished house at l'Haÿ, a few miles out of Paris, and adjoining the house is the Rose garden … This garden contains the most complete collection of Roses in the world … The garden is open to the public on certain days in the year, and the owner is at all times delighted to show visitors round and take them through his Rose museum; it is best, however, to make an appointment. Such a visit is an education in itself, and all lovers of the Rose, when stopping in Paris, should go and see it. The village of l'Haÿ is about one mile from Bourg-la-Reine station, a twenty minutes' run from the Luxembourg terminus in Paris. A motor car from the centre of Paris will, in about half-an-hour, reach the 'Roseraie de l'Haÿ', the home of Monsieur Jules Gravereaux." [NRS14/20–21]

"At the Roseraie de l'Haÿ, near Paris, a maid took my card and soon returned with the head gardener, Monsieur David. As he spoke no English and my French was broken, we spent little time in useless conversation. However, the varieties were all distinctly labeled, and, fortunately, variety and species names do not change in French, so we had a basis of understanding … The gardens … are interesting and instructive because of their systematic arrangement.

"The Museum of Roses is unique: It is a low structure of pleasing architecture, located near the center of the garden. It is filled with beautiful paintings of roses, many of them done in the garden by noted artists. One of the most prominent paintings shows Monsieur Gravereaux among the flowers he loved so well. In the Museum are also many old and valuable prints of roses. One case is filled with specimens of insects destructive to the rose, and another shows the effect of injurious rose diseases. There is also a collection of rose perfumes." [ARA22/135]

"On June 17, I had the good fortune to be the guest of Monsieur Gravereaux at the Roseraie de l'Haÿ. This is assuredly the most wonderful rose-garden in the world, and one could here spend many weeks in profitable study. The gardens cover a long and rather irregular shaped piece of ground of about five acres. The beds and borders are of geometric design, and are divided each from the other by high trellises of climbing roses. Coming in from the entrance one enters first the great display garden where large beds, each containing only one or two varieties, make a brilliant exhibit of bloom …

"On the west side is the Garden-house and in the center of this building is the museum, with the walls decorated with paintings of roses and of the late Monsieur Gravereaux and his family in the garden. Here is also a showing of the use of roses in the arts: rare tapestries, china with rose designs, carved wood, bronze work, and old books. In ad adjoining room is the working library and office, with its card catalogue of the plants in the garden—for the collection contains upwards of 7,000 species and varieties. The view into the display garden from the Garden-house is charming. Great masses of color lie before one, broken by occasional standards, or by pillar roses or pieces of garden sculpture. In the center is a pool with a small fountain, and at the back and sides high trellises of climbers frame in the picture.

"From this display garden we walked under rose-arches into numerous smaller gardens, varying in size and shape. By the side of a long path is a collection of rose species from all parts of the world; along another, the roses mentioned in history or in literature. One small garden is devoted to roses valuable for perfume, and contains, among other things, a collection of Rugosa seedlings developed by Monsieur Gravereaux during his experiments with roses for commercial perfumes. Another garden contains Hybrid Perpetuals; another Hybrid Teas. One of the smallest enclosures is given over entirely to Polyanthas, and a special garden is devoted to trials of novelties. At the end of the series of gardens is an outdoor theater with raised seats of turf, where outdoor plays, pageants, classical dances, and musicales can be given.

"Everything is complete, and no obtainable rose is omitted from this wonderful garden, which serves not only as an object of beauty but as a living museum, showing the development of the rose during the centuries culminating in the wonderful hybrids of today. The gardens are kept immaculately clean from weeds or dead flowers." [ARA23/127–128]

[Hybride du Luxembourg]
trans. "Hybrid from the Luxembourg [Palace]"
Hardy, pre-1841
"Medium, full, deep pink." [V8] "Full, flat, medium-sized, beautiful." [LF] "Flowers deep pink, shaded with blush, large and full; form, cupped. Habit, branching; growth, moderate." [P] "Of rapid growth, and suitable for a pillar or wall, with flowers of a roseate hue." [WRP] "Calyx-tube short, glabrous, oval-pyriform; flowers full, small, regular, purple red, edges purple brown or deep violet." [S] "Appears to be a hybrid from some of the Noisettes, of whose character it greatly partakes; the flowers are in clusters of a dull purple, very double, and a little fragrant." [Bu]

[Imbricata]
Ducher, 1869
"Flowers large, full, cupped, delicate pink." [JR8/137] "Vigorous growth; flower large, full, cupped; color, very delicate pink." [S]

Ma Surprise
trans. "My Surprise"
Guillot fils, 1872
"Salmony white." [Ÿ] "Ravishing, and has flowers colored white

with a peachblossom pink center nuanced salmon." [JR7/154] "Flowers large, full, good form, peach pink in the center with a white edge. Sometimes the center is striped white and salmon." [JR8/137] "Flower white, rosy center, shaded salmon, large, full, hardy. Growth moderate." [GeH] "Very vigorous and climbing shrub; flower very large, full, very well formed, with a peach pink center nuanced salmon, Tea-scented." [S]

Pourpre Ancien Plate 21
syn. 'Purpurea Plena'; trans., "Old Purple"
Breeder unknown, ca. 1829
"Flower full, large, very full, purple sometimes striped with white." [BJ70] "Vigorous, dense-growing bushes of semi-climbing habit; nearly evergreen. Double red flowers. Very satisfactory for cemetery work." [C&Js12] "Small, glossy green foliage, nearly evergreen in habit, hardy and vigorous grower. Flowers red, semi-double, produced in great profusion; very pretty and sweet." [CA96] "In the gardens of Brie, the rose 'À Petites Feuilles', now known under the name 'Pourpre Ancien', sometimes has flowers of a red more vinous than that shown in the accompanying picture; pretty often they are striped instead of being shaded pale pink. It makes a small bush with nodding branches which really look quite nice." [JR8/136–137]

"This pretty rose bloomed for the first time last year [1829] at Monsieur Laffay's in Auteuil. It has several similarities to R. bracteata, but it differs from that not only in its leaflets, but also in its muricate calyx. This small shrub, coming from China, was brought to England by Mr. Wallich. It will soon make part of the great collections. Monsieur Rameau, fancier residing in Lille, grows under the name Microphylla a rose from England with slender canes covered with several thorns which are straight, axillary, and weak; petioles unarmed, leaflets 9–11, calyx muricate; sepals oval; flowers medium-sized or small, 2–3, more often solitary, double, an intense pink." [BJ30] See also 'Striata' (Rox).

[Premier Essai]
trans. "First Try"
Geschwind, 1866
From Rosa roxburghii × 'Reine de la Lombardie' (Ch).
"Flowers medium-sized, full, flesh white with a bright carminy center." [JR8/137] "Very vigorous; flowers medium-sized, full; outer petals well imbricated; color, flesh white, bright carmine red at the center, fading to very fresh pink." [RJC66/184] "The variety I raised, 'Premier Essai', is, up till now, not only the most beautiful in form and color, but also is the most vigorous, which lends it to the purposes of an espalier in the open ground." [JR8/61]

Purpurea Plena Listed as 'Pourpre Ancien' (Rox).

Rouge Striée Listed as 'Striata' (Rox).

Rubra Variegata Listed as 'Striata' (Rox).

Simplex
syn. 'Single'
Breeder unknown, pre-1841
"Violet red, large, single." [LF] "Flowers bright red, large and single; form, cupped." [P]

Single Listed as 'Simplex' (Rox).

[Striata]

syns.'Rouge Striée','Rubra Variegata'; trans.,"Striped"
England, pre-1817

"Flowers crimson, striped with white." [P] "A large red flower, the centre partially striped with white." [WRP] "Differs very little from [*Rosa roxburghii*]. The leaf is composed of seven leaflets; oval, finely and regularly toothed, of a pale green colour. The thorns are reddish in the young shoots." [Go] "Stems slender, climbing, with smooth bark armed with thorns which are equal, reddish on the young growths, sparse, often stipulary and paired, not much dilated at the base, some straight, others lightly curved; petioles prickly; leaves ordinarily composed of seven leaflets which are flat, oval, light green, finely and regularly dentate. We don't yet know the flower. It is grown in the orangery." [No28] "I saw this rose at the Cels place in 1828." [MaCo] Possibly synonymous with 'Pourpre Ancien' (Rox).

Triomphe de la Guillotière

trans. "Triumph of La Guillotière" ["La Guillotière" is a precinct of
    Lyon, France]

Guillot père, 1864

"Flowers fairly large, full, well-formed, light pink, very beautiful." [JR8/137] "Very vigorous growth; flower large, full; light pink, nuanced white." [S] "Very vigorous bush; blossoms large, full, light pink, opening very well." [I'H64/328]

[Triomphe de Macheteaux]

Breeder unknown, pre-1841

"Pink striped with white." [LF] "A new French variety of a pale rose color and shaded." [WRP] "Blush, edged with rose, of medium size, full; form, cupped." [P]

[Triomphe des Français]

trans. "Triumph of the French"
Lartay, 1854

"Vigorous bush; blossom large, full, flesh pink with a darker center." [JDR55/10]

CHAPTER SEVENTEEN

Bracteatas

"The single Macartney Rose [*Rosa bracteata*] was brought to Europe from China, in 1795, by Lord Macartney, on his return from his embassy to that country. It now forms the original of a pretty family; but as it has not produced seed freely, even in France, fine varieties, as yet, are not numerous; its strictly evergreen and shining foliage is a beautiful feature; and I hope ere long to see numerous varieties, with double flowers of the same brilliant hues as our other fine roses possess." [WRP] "The plants are evergreen; the foliage dark, and shining as if varnished; which feature, in contrast with the milk-white apricot-scented flowers, is striking and beautiful." [P] "These roses produce a beautiful effect trained against a wall; they are damaged by heavy frost." [BJ40]

"Small bush notable by way of the bracts which very nearly form a second calyx around its blossoms, and by the petals surmounted by a little point in their notch. Its stems are pubescent, charged with straight, solitary, sparse prickles; its leaves are alternate, petiolate; paired leaflets; composed of five or seven leaflets which are elliptical, nearly rounded, slightly coriaceous, glabrous on both sides, glossy on their upper face, crenelate along the edge, obtuse at their tip; petiole with some hooked prickles, as has also the rachis of the leaves; the stipules adhere at the base of the petiole, and are divided into two linear, pointed lobes. The flowers are terminal, solitary, very fragrant, borne on a very short peduncle. The calyx divides into five leaflets [*i.e.,* sepals], which are entire, oval, lanceolate, acuminate, pubescent, and silky; the corolla is a beautiful white, yellowish when dried; the petals are heart-shaped, mucronate within the notch; ovary oval, pyriform, covered with appressed soft bristles, enveloped at the base with six or eight bracts which are lanceolate, silky, pubescent, concave, cut, fringed on the upper edge, often terminating in an oval leaflet; anthers golden yellow, free; styles lateral, capillary, greenish; stigmas ciliate, widening into a cup, violet-purple." [Lam]

"I have found it to seed freely when pollinated with many varieties and other species. The few crosses that have bloomed include a lovely pink-flowered hybrid with *Rosa carolina,* with extremely long-pointed buds; and a fragrant, double-flowered, pure white variety of bushy form, the result of using pollen of the scentless 'Frau Karl Druschki'. *R. bracteata* promises well for the production of varieties suited to at least the South." [ARA16/32]

Rosa bracteata
horticultural syns. 'À Bractées', 'Macartney Rose'

"A southern favorite. Beautiful large single white flowers, with glistening golden stamens; an exquisite sort and very fragrant." [C&Js12] "From China and Formosa. Usually low-growing, with stout, hooked prickles. Flowers one or few, short-stalked, white, 2 to 2³/₄ inches across [ca. 5–7 cm]. Blooms June to October. Naturalized in Florida and Louisiana. Handsome half-evergreen climber. Not hardy north." [ARA21/38] "Canes sarmentose and strong, with hooked, opposite thorns and large solitary white blossoms." [JR26/181] "Leaves small, like the wood … persistent; its blossom is small and white, accompanied by bracts or floral leaves, a feature all its own … It is feeble on its own roots; it is charming grafted on a two-foot stock [ca. 6 dm], or on the China, or on the Multiflora, or indeed on the Musk, if it is destined for a pot. But out in the open, it should be grafted onto the Briar, because the others have sap constantly running, and this lattermost rests during the Winter. This rose can grow over ten feet tall [ca. 3.3 m] if well taken care of, and if it has the air which suits it. Its blossoms appear from June up till September." [LeR]

"An evergreen bush 1.5 to 4 m tall [ca. 4–12 ft] with glossy leaves and white blossoms which appear in Summer and Fall. Too tender for the open ground, better for adorning walls or lattices in a greenhouse; it can also be grown in a pot. In southern Europe and in England it is also grown out in the garden; one attempt at this didn't work in Karpfen, Hungary." [JR8/61] "Its wood is green, armed with paired thorns which are pink and wide at the base. The nearly round leaves, which number eight or nine on the same stalk, are a beautiful glossy green. Its blossoms are white and fragrant. You grow this rose in the orangery; however, on the Briar in my garden, it got through the Winter with neither shelter nor covering. It has a distinctive character all its own, that of having bracts or floral leaves. It is a very pretty species which merits the attentions of the fancier, be it as a greenhouse shrub or out in the open." [C-T] "Macartney Roses sometimes suffer when exposed to severe frost in the open borders of the flower garden: they will therefore require the same protection as recommended for the Noisette roses." [WRP] "Sensitive to strong frosts." [BJ30]

"*Canes* geniculate, lanate, sometimes glandulose; armed with paired, stipular, hooked or straight thorns, slightly villose or lanate,

Rosa bracteata continued

particularly in their youth; [*thorns*] fixed on the cane on a prolonged 'shield,' the length of which is pretty nearly that of the thorn. *Leaves* close-set. *Petiole* villose, armed beneath with thorns. *Stipules* small, nearly free, multipartite, with unequal divisions which are linear and often pinnatifid. Leaflets 5, 7, or 9, rough, thick, obovate or cuneiform, rounded at the tip; glabrous, smooth, and nearly glossy above; shallowly crenelate. *Flowers* solitary, nearly sessile, surrounded with 8 or 10 *bracts* which are oval, concave, imbricated, silky, and with pectinate edges. *Ovary* very villose, globular or slightly flattened. *Sepals* very villose, usually simple. The numerous whitish bristles with which the sepals and especially the ovary are covered have the softness and density of velvet. *Corolla* of 5 large, thick petals, beautiful white, notched at the tip. *Stamens* yellow, very numerous, unequal. *Styles* numerous, free, little protrusive or not at all, filiform, thickened at the summit. *Stigmas* villose. Blooms in August and September. [The common form has] much hooked thorns, with neither bristles nor glands." [Pf] "Fruits spherical, hirsute, an orange red." [No26]

"It is a shrub, the main stem of which divides into feeble, skinny canes, able to attain from six to twelve feet in length [ca. 2–4 m], and perhaps more stretching out over the ground or if supported by surrounding bushes. These canes are well covered with a short down, and are close-set, grayish, and charged here and there with one or two slightly curved prickles, most often at the base of each leaf. The ovaries of this rose are oval, silky, and accompanied by silky lanceolate bracts; its leaves are comprised of seven leaflets which are oval, very obtuse at the summit, glossy green above, paler beneath, glabrous on both sides except along the lower rachis, which is charged with bristles; the petioles are prickly and villose; its flowers, which appear in June and last until September, are solitary, yellowish-white, an inch and a half in size [ca. 4 cm], and fragrant; this scent seems to be rather like that of a well-ripened apricot. The corolla is a beautiful white, and is composed of five petals deeply notched into a heart; the stamens are very numerous, and the styles glabrous and very short, terminated by the stigmas which, being joined together, form a large convex head in the middle of the blossom. The Macartney Rose, or Bracted Rose, has difficulty bearing the frosts of the Paris environs; and so it is grown in the orangeries, where it holds its leaves all year and blooms in Spring. It is propagated by graft, shield-grafting, and budding. In the *Jardin des Plantes,* one can see a large specimen of this species. As much for the arrangement of its flowers as for the particular character of its foliage, the Macartney Rose merits a place not only in collections but also in ornamental gardens." [CM] "Rose with round seed-buds, shining, and silky, furnished at the base with silky toothed floral leaves. Flowers white. Leaves resembling box. Leaflets nearly egg-shaped, finely sawed, and shining. Peduncles and petioles very prickly. Stems very prickly and downy. Branches flexuose and spreading. This perfectly distinct species of Rose was introduced from China to this country by Lord Macartney, on his return from his embassy to that court. It is perfectly known under the title of Macartney Rose, and also by the name of *lucida.*" [A] "Brought to England by Sir George Staunton, secretary of Admiral Lord Macartney, British ambassador to China. It bloomed in France for the first time in 1798, at the Cels place at Petit-Montrouge, near Paris." [ExRé]

Rosa clinophylla

botanical syns. *R. clynophylla, R. involucrata;* horticultural syn., 'À Feuilles Penchées'

"Very large, flat." [LF] "Smooth, climbing *shrub* 0.9–1.2 m high [ca. 3–4 ft]; *stems* with a short, compact, whitish silky down and fine, straight, geminate *prickles,* scattered, but mainly at the base of the stipules. *Leaves* alternate, nodding; *leaflets* 9–11, elliptical, almost always doubly dentate, bright green, glossy above, tomentose beneath; petioles villose, glandular, sometimes with 2–3 small hooked prickles; stipules fringed, with elongated, pointed divisions. *Flowers* 1 (–3) at the cane tips on very short pedicels surrounded by alternate floral leaves and bracts like an involucre; pedicels, *receptacles,* and entire, subulate *sepals* downy like the stem and branches; *petals* 5, white, slightly yellow at the base; *styles* free, a little exserted; *stamens* almost as long as the sepals. *Rosa clinophylla* derives its name from the Greek *to droop* and *a leaf.* It is easily distinguished from all others by the posture of the leaves as well as by the involucre, which seems to enfold the blossom. It is grown in Boursault's garden … It blooms in July, and needs to spend the Winter in the conservatory, where it retains its leaves. Its native country is unknown." [T&R] "*Shrub,* bushy …; *leaves* oblong, elliptical, doubly dentate, glossy above, villose beneath; … *tube* of calyx rounded, villose, sometimes bearing floral leaves [bracts]; … *petals* white, slightly cordiform, yellowish at the base; *fruits* rounded." [MaCo] "Mr. N. Wallich, director of the Botanical Garden in Calcutta, sent me this rose this year [1820], and told me that it grows spontaneously in the Indies. This adept has kindly sent me several others which died en route." [Ty] "Imported to England by Whitley; described and illustrated by Redouté." [Gx] "Here is a species cited by all the authors from the text of Thory and the charming illustration of Redouté—a species which, I believe, exists nowadays only in Art. Thirty years from now, it will probably be the same with all these new species which people hurry to put into commerce, as if there could be any doubt that they could ever be something more than a flash-in-the-pan." [MaCo] Graham S. Thomas relays that it was (re-)introduced from India in 1917.

Rosa clynophylla   Listed as *Rosa clinophylla.*

Rosa involucrata   Listed as *Rosa clinophylla.*

ℋorticultural Varieties

À Bractées   Listed as *Rosa bracteata.*

À Feuilles Penchées   Listed as *Rosa clinophylla.*

À Petites Feuilles   Listed as 'Scabriusculus' (Brac).

Alba Odorata

Italy, pre-1835

From *Rosa bracteata* × *R. roxburghii.*

"Yellowish white." [Gp&f52] "Double, white." [BJ40] "Greenish white, full, flat, large." [LF] "Flowers white, with yellowish centre, large and full; form, cupped. Rarely opens well." [P] "Blooms fairly well." [S] "'Alba Odorata', from southern China, with very vigorous canes having quite large thorns; leaves with leaflets which are obovate, rounded, firm, persistent, and glossy; large white flower, full, light saffron at the center." [JR2/45] "From Italian seed we have 'Alba Odorata', a vigorous growing variety, partaking as much of the Macartney in its habit as of Rosa microphylla; in fact, it is a complete hybrid, and a very good evergreen rose, producing an abundance of pale sulphur, or rather cream-colored flowers: these are sweet-scented, but do not in general open frequently at the north." [WRP]

[Coccinea]
Breeder unknown, pre-1835
"Deep-red." [S-V] "Deep red." [BJ40]

Double White Listed as 'Plena' (Brac).

Dwarf Mermaid
Breeder unknown, date uncertain
Seedling of 'Mermaid' (Brac)?

Dwarf (ca. 3 × 3 ft or 1 × 1 m), fragrant version of 'Mermaid' (Brac). Possibly synonymous with 'Happenstance' (Brac), *q.v.* Not to be confused with 'Little Mermaid' (Brac; see last paragraph of this chapter).

Flore Pleno Listed as 'Plena' (Brac).

Happenstance
California, mid-1950s
Sport of 'Mermaid' (Brac).

"I'm a newcomer to 'Happenstance', having purchased it from Petaluma Rose Company sometime in early June. I kept it in a pot for several months, and only planted it sometime in August, so I'm not sure what its growth habit will be. So far, it stays low to the ground and spreads out, and is almost always full of somewhat small pale yellow single blooms (about 2–2.5 inches in diameter [ca. 5–6.5 cm]) with darker yellow stamens that are beautiful in their simplicity. The blooms only last about a day or two, but there are always plenty of them. I haven't grown 'Mermaid' . . . but as 'Happenstance' is a sport of it, apparently it shares its bloom habit with 'Mermaid'. From what I've seen of the two, Happenstance's foliage is much smaller than that of 'Mermaid'. A typical 5-leaflet leaf is about 1 inch [ca. 2.5 dm], dark shiny green, and there is lots of foliage, low to the ground . . . One more thing about 'Happenstance'. It has had no disease, so far at least, and I have had my share of mildew problems [with other roses] this fall." [jP] "Well, I'm growing something that was given to me as 'Happenstance', though I'm getting confused by the somewhat sparse and conflicting information I've found about this rose. I'm not sure what the actual differences are between 'Happenstance' and 'Little Mermaid' [*for 'Little Mermaid' and other more recent Bracteata hybrids, see the last paragraph in this chapter*]. But I will assume I have 'Happenstance' (with some reservations) . . . The plant I have is almost 3 years old and still doesn't reach my knee. It has sprawled quite daintily to a little shrub about 3 feet in diameter [ca. 1 m]. The main canes are interrupted every couple of inches with laterals which always seem to have buds or blooms on them. The flowers are identical to 'Mermaid', just smaller. The plant itself also strongly reminds me of the climber. The laterals are very red in color and the canes also have a reddish-brown wood. The leaflets are generally five to seven and the petioles have sharp, evenly spaced spines along their length. The leaflets are *very* 'Mermaid'-ish, showing an almost yellowish-green color in their early youth, which be-

comes a shiny bright green with age. There is a hint of red in the margins. They are quite lanceolate. But the real zinger is the thorns. They are very sharp, strongly recurved, and red. They are also arranged mostly (but not entirely) just below the stipules in pairs or sets of three. The paired thorns are so similar to those of 'Mermaid' (just much smaller) that I am led to think that it is, indeed, a sport. I've found this to be a very easy rose to grow and very satisfying. It is quite beautiful, makes a great ground cover rose, spent its last summer in my yard with no water, stays very clean and attractive, and is blooming at this moment [*12:28 p.m., November 23, 1996*]. I like it." [aF]

"In the mid-1950s at an estate on the San Francisco Peninsula, a 'Mermaid' was burned down to the ground. From the roots, 5 sports grew. These were given by the estate owner to a friend . . . He, in turn, gave them to [the owner of an "old rose" nursery in California]. She destroyed four and kept one, 'Happenstance'. Tom [Liggett] says he has heard a number of stories, but he feels the above is the most credible. The rose is usually a low grower to 12 to 18 inches [ca. 3–4.5 dm]; however, Tom has seen an 8 × 8 foot plant [ca. 2.6 × 2.6 m] trained as a climber . . . Tom's plant is about 5 feet wide [ca. 1.6 m] and about 20 inches tall [ca. 5 dm] and rambles near the ground. As others have said, it has small, disease resistant, medium green [description later revised to "dark green"], shiny foliage and miniature 'Mermaid'-like blooms. It is a very pleasant looking plant . . . I forgot to mention that Tom's source for the information passed on was [the estate owner's friend] . . . Looking at the 'Happenstance' and 'Little Mermaid' in the San Jose Heritage Rose Garden (they're next to each other), Tom has a hard time believing that they are really different cultivars." [tLmH]

Macartney Rose Listed as *Rosa bracteata*.

Maria Léonida
Lemoyne/Burdin, 1829
From *Rosa bracteata* × "an ordinary China-Tea" (but see below).

"Yellowish white." [V9] "White nuanced straw yellow." [Ÿ] "Flesh white, full, flat, large, superb." [LF] "Beautiful white flower in the form of a bird's nest." [I'H60/239] "Semi-double, creamy white flowers tinged with rose in the center." [GAS] "Flowers white, centre rosy, and sometimes creamy, large and full; form, cupped." [P] "White, centre blush, flowers large and double; a very distinct rose, and very pretty." [JC] "Flower large, nearly full, cupped, white with some yellow." [JR2/45] "An established favorite; its fine bell-shaped flowers of the purest white sometimes slightly tinged with pink towards their centre, and its bright red anthers peeping from among its central petals, give to it an elegant and pleasing character." [WRP] "Flower white, centre blush, glossy foliage. Growth vigorous, tender." [GeH] "Double, remontant." [BJ40] "Blooms up till frost." [V4] "Has much of the *Macartney Rose* habit; the foliage nearly round, quite dark green and shining, with a tinge of red on the young wood; the flowers are sweet scented, of a creamy-white colour, with a delicate blush centre." [Bu] "*Boughs,* reddish, zig-zag, with fine red thorns. *Leaves,* small, elliptic, dentated, glossy, and tough. *Flowers,* expanding flesh-coloured, becoming white after expansion; double, numerous, lateral." [Go] "A fine border rose, for, by pegging down its shoots as they are produced in summer, a few plants soon cover a bed, or clump, with a dense mass of foliage and flowers, ornamenting the flower-garden from three to four months in summer and autumn: it also forms a very fine standard." [WRP] "A variety raised in Nantes under the name 'Maria Leoni-

Maria Léonida *continued*

da' also does very well [as a hedge]; it defends itself—it would be a case of 'kicking against the pricks'!" [JR33/186]

"The result of successive crosses, first between the Bracteate Rose and the Musk Rose, then between the result and a Tea Rose." [ExRé] "Hybrid of the ordinary Tea rose [*presumably 'Hume's Blush Tea-Scented China'*] and *R. bracteata,* made by Monsieur Lemoyne at Nantes. The bush has points of resemblance to both its mother and father; its blossom is very double, flesh, and wafts a very pronounced tea scent. This cross, between two so different species, is a quite extraordinary development." [R-H29/113] "Monsieur Burdin, at Chabéry . . . has seen his homage [*to Flora*] rewarded by a rose which he presents under the name 'Maria Leonida', which, to its charming blossoms adds the merit of reblooming." [R-H29/358–359]

"We read in the periodical *Lyon-Horticole* the following note on the origin of the rose 'Maria Léonida': 'Several times, I have called this rose a hybrid of the bracteate rose pollinated with a Tea Rose. This supposed parentage now seems certain. Monsieur Gordé, of the *Société Nantaise des Amis de l'Horticulture* [*sic*], put out the following little note on this rose: "During a visit several of our colleagues made a few weeks ago to the garden of Mme. Béchat, they noticed a well-foliaged rose plant with white blossoms. This rose, they were told, is the rose 'Maria Léonida'. It was bred in Nantes. Perhaps this is the place in which to recall its origin. Our research has alas not been able to supply us with the name of the breeder, but a beautiful specimen of this new rose was shown at the Nantes Horticultural Exhibition September 30, 1832; its obtention was signalized in a speech given the same day by Monsieur Ursin, president of the *Société Nantaise des Amis d'Horticulture.* Here is the pertinent passage: 'It is to the miscegenation which gives rise to hybrids (he said), to this enchanted gift which allows Man to participate in the power of the Creator, that we owe all these new races of roses, pelargoniums, carnations, and fruits of all sorts which have come these last few years to inexpressibly charm our eyes, noses, and tongues. Art, in this, prevails over Nature, and often concentrates in one sole individual the heavy perfections that the Creator never took the trouble to unite. In illustration of this, I will cite only the recent success gained by one of our honorable colleagues. Up till now, some remontant roses have flattered our vision by the continuity of their blossoms—but they were either scentless in Summer, or leafless in Winter. The hand of an ingenious fancier arranged the union of two interesting sorts: the *Tea Rose* and the *Macartney Rose.* Nature smiled on this enterprise, and, with this Hymen working under the most favorable circumstances, the rose 'Maria Léonida' was born, a rose in which the persistence of the leaves, the sweetness of the perfume, and the purity and longevity of the flowers unite all the blessings which, otherwise, are scattered.'"" Now that we know the origins of 'Maria Léonida', it would be nice if the *Société Nantaise d'Horticulture* would do the necessary research to find out the breeder. Doubtless, some old horticulturalists remember the name of this breeder or fancier who gave Horticulture this pretty variety." [JR27/1–2] "To Monsieur Pierre Cochet, Publisher and Editor of the *Journal des Roses.* Sir, the January 1903 *Journal des Roses* reproduced a note from Monsieur Gordé, of the *Société Nantaise des Amis de l'Horticulture,* on the rose 'Maria Léonida'. After that item, you express a wish to know the breeder of this variety. I am pleased, Sir, to be able to make known to you this

name, and, what is more, to give you information both very precise and authentic on the obtention of this rose that some Nantais fanciers—among others, one of our lady patrons, Mme. Béchat, florist, Haute-Grande-Rue, Nantes—still grows for the beauty of its blossoms. The rose Mme. Béchat has, and which is the subject of Monsieur Gordé's communication, is always very vigorous; it is never pruned, and so is tree-like. Monsieur Lemoyne, one of the founders of the *Société Nantaise d'Horticulture,* sowed, in 1826, some seeds which he had collected from an ordinary China-Tea which was close to, among others, an *R. bracteata,* about four feet distant [ca. 1.3 m]. From this crop came an individual which bloomed for the first time in 1829. Monsieur Hectot (born near Falaise January 29, 1759, died at Nantes in 1843), a Nantais botanist, creator of the *Jardin des Plantes* in Nantes, and Vice-President and first juror of the *Société Nationale d'Horticulture,* made the following description at the time: 'From the neck of the roots come several stems which grow to about four feet high [ca. 1.3 m]; they are glabrous and reddish, and bear branches which arise from the axils of the first leaves. Each of these branches is tipped with one or several flowers, and each flower is borne on its own inch-and-a-half long stem [ca. 4 cm]. This peduncle is clothed with mossy prickles. The ovary which follows is rounded and covered with a whitish 'bloom'; the blossom surmounting all is regular in form, and an inch and a half across [ca. 4 cm]. The petals are faintly flesh-colored, and take on a yellowish tinge closer to the nub, which has a slightly pink tinge. They decrease in size from the edge to the middle, where arise a pretty good number of purple styles—but no stamens can be seen. This blossom, which wafts a very pronounced tea scent, goes nicely with the glossy green foliage which completely covers it in all seasons. Seen without its flowers, this pretty bush resembles—at first sight—*Rosa bracteata*; it is, however, less thorny; it is also smaller and less robust in all parts. The wood, the leaves, and especially the canes are, just like the thorns, a pretty dark red. The leaves, pinnate with the odd one, are composed of five or seven leaflets, and are persistent. But there is a major difference between this variety we are describing and *Rosa bracteata*—the longer peduncle, and the absence of sub-calicinate bracts. It seems to us (adds Monsieur Hectot) that here we have sufficient distinct characteristics that, confident that they will remain constant in propagation, allow it to be admitted to our catalog of native roses [under the name] 'Rosa Maria Léonida', a name given to the hybrid by the person introducing it to Nantais horticulture. The *Société* votes its thanks to that honorable member.' Monsieur Lemoyne was a fancier [*"amateur," as opposed to being a member of the nursery trade*], without a doubt; he was one of the founders of our Society; he was a jury member and very active at various meetings . . . The wood of the rose which is the subject of Monsieur Gordé's note is much as Monsieur Hectot describes. As to the blossom, the [present] season doesn't allow comparisons. Mme. Béchat tells me it is completely white; one of our oldest members, Monsieur Péan, who saw this rose at the home of one of his friends thirty years ago [ca. 1874], and who always kept it, also tells me that it is a beautiful matte white, with neither a tinge of pink nor one of yellow. It thus seems that the color has varied a little since the description was made in 1829, a point at which it no doubt was not firmly fixed. The rose 'Maria Léonida', continues Mme. Béchat, is no longer known here [Nantes], or at least is never asked for under that name—but it is one of those that never sits for long in my nursery; my customers show a marked enthusiasm for this rose whenever I put one out for sale. Such, Mr. Editor, is the information which I count myself lucky to be able to give you on this Nantais-bred rose, hoping that you have found here the information which will satisfy the curiosity of your readers. Please, accept, Sir, my kind regards. [signed] P. FROLIARD, General Secretary." [JR27/21–23] As we understand from the above information "both very precise and authentic," the modern assertion sometimes made that 'Maria Léonida' is a hybrid between *Rosa bracteata* and *R. laevigata* is incorrect. Thus do we see the importance of checking information contemporary with the release of any cultivar in question!

Mermaid

W. Paul, 1918

From *Rosa bracteata* × "a full yellow Tea."

"Immense, single blooms of sulphur-yellow, 4 inches across [ca. 1 dm]. A constant everbloomer." [C-Ps33] "Flower sulphury yellow, the deep amber stamens standing out prominently and throwing a rich shade of yellow over the whole of the blossom, of great size, single, produced continuously from early summer till late in autumn. Growth climbing; the foliage is most effective, the leaves being very large and massive, of a deep shining green, and the young shoots tinged with red." [GeH] "Foliage deep bronzy green." [ARA19/103] "A most remarkable hybrid of *R. bracteata,* with abundant, leathery, smooth-edged, dark green foliage and broad, flat, single flowers of pale sulphury yellow deepening to gold in the center. Blooms continuously from midsummer until frost and makes vigorous growth up to 18 to 20 feet [ca. 6–6.6 m]. It is hardy as far north as Long Island and southern New England along the coast, but is probably best adapted to the southern states, although worth protecting wherever it can be made to grow." [GAS] "It is hardy with protection, but should it freeze to the ground, will bloom the following spring on its new growth; it blooms sparsely all summer, and retains its wonderful glossy foliage." [ARA25/103] "It is now 10 feet high [ca. 3.3 m] on a north wall, and its shiny dark green leaves last all winter. The two plants I left in the mountains survived all this winter's ice and snow, and that would seem to test their hardiness." [ARA25/133] "Very fine, and well adapted to this [*Mississippi*] climate." [ARA26/118] "Now nearly 12 feet high [ca. 4 m], and keeps a beautiful green foliage summer and winter, free from mildew." [ARA26/169] "Free of mildew and other diseases. The wood is very thorny … At times shy in flowering … If wanted for house decoration [*i.e., cutting*], it should be cut in the bud form, and placed in water two days before wanted. If cut when the blooms are expanded the petals quickly curl up." [NRS23/93] "The best light-colored single, and far ahead of [the] Cherokee [*i.e., Rosa laevigata*]. Better used as ground-cover than as climber; fine growth and lovely foliage; large blooms continuously produced." [ARA28/97] "It blooms all the time (in California)." [CaRoll/8/2]

"A hybrid of *R. bracteata* of semi-climbing habit of growth, with large glossy deep green foliage and long shoots prettily tinted with red. The buds are carried in clusters of about a dozen, and the flowers which are single of an enormous size—from four to six inches [ca. 1–1.5 dm] across—but in spite of the number of buds the blooms only appear one at a time. The colour is a beautiful pale sulphur-yellow, with dainty golden anthers, perhaps best described as a glorified

'Jersey Beauty' [*W*]. Perpetual flowering, though towards the autumn the blooms do not attain the enormous size the early ones do. It is very suitable for growing on low trellis and walls, but its ideal purpose will be in forming a large specimen bush … Will be placed in commerce in May, 1918." [NRS18/164] "Takes time to start but makes a fine pillar …*Mass.*; … wonderful as climber, or if center is supported for two to three years, as a high bush with drooping branches. Bloom exquisite, scattered from June to November. Fine foliage … *Md.*; … In bloom every day …too fleeting for cut-flowers …*Stockton, Calif.*" [ARA28/173]

"I [Courtney Page], too, had my doubts, but they were entirely dispelled one fine morning in September, when visiting Messrs. Wm. Paul and Son's Nurseries at Waltham Cross, accompanied by Mr. Samuel McGredy, of Portadown. Mr. Arthur Paul very kindly conducted us round the extensive nursery … Unexpectedly, we came upon a large breadth of cutbacks of 'Mermaid', and what a sight it was! The sun had only recently broken through the autumn mist, and the beautiful shining foliage was still wet with dew. There were blooms by the thousand, enormous ones, too, many being five or six inches across [ca. to 4.5 dm]. We stood admiring them for some considerable time, when suddenly Mr. McGredy turned to Mr. Paul and said, 'I have seen the sight of my life, it's simply magnificent. I would not have missed it on any account.'" [NRS20/45] "Mr. A. Paul very kindly gave me a few notes of the history of this handsome addition to the single flowered Roses. This variety was obtained from a species that has hitherto been seldom hybridized, flowers of *R. bracteata* …having been fertilized with the pollen of a double yellow Tea Rose. He told me that about a dozen seedlings were obtained, most of which produced single pale yellow flowers which varied in size and regularity of petals, although two or three of the progeny gave double blossoms [*see 'Sea Foam' (Brac)*]. The former were tested side by side and 'Mermaid' was selected as being the finest, both for its colour and the unusual size of its flowers and also for the beauty of its foliage, the bright glossy green of its large leaves and the ruddy tinge of the young shoots contrasting beautifully with the pale waxen sulphur-yellow tint of the petals, the effect of the latter being heightened by large clusters of amber coloured stamens. It also differs from *Rosa bracteata* in its longer season of flowering, its more vigorous growth and its hardiness, plants standing quite unprotected in the open ground at Waltham Cross having withstood 28 and 29 degrees of frost last winter … It throws up strong shoots from the base 6 to 8 feet long [ca. 2–2.6 m] in a season, whilst as an ornamental shrub it will be unique, and to my mind the best way to grow it, producing its huge star-like blossoms (often measuring four to five inches in diameter [ca. 1–1.25 dm]) continuously from early in July until stopped by frost in the autumn." [NRS20/45–46] "Everyone who has grown it admires it immensely." [ARA31/186]

[Nerrière]

Vibert, pre-1847

"8 cm [ca. 3 in], full, yellowish white." [VPt48/app] "Flower large, full, wide-spreading; color, cream with a darker center." [S] "Flowers yellowish white, their centre of a deeper tint than their margin, large and full; form, cupped." [P]

Pink Mermaid

California, 1960?

According to Griffiths, 'Pink Mermaid' has single, light pink

Pink Mermaid *continued*
blossoms about 9 cm or 3¹/₂ in across, with growth characteristic of the Bracteata group. Others have strong doubts of its Bracteata ancestry . . .

[Plena]
syns. 'Double White', 'Flore Pleno', 'Very Double Macartney'; trans., "Double"
Breeder unknown, pre-1835
    "*Shrub,* branching. *Thorns,* large, crooked. *Leaflets,* tough, glossy, full. *Flowers,* of a pinkish white." [Go] "The first double variety raised from seed. The growth is vigorous and the foliage beautiful; in this latitude [*that of New York*] the flowers are very apt to drop off before expansion, but at the south, we believe such is not the case." [WRP]

[Rosea]
trans. "Pink"
Breeder unknown, pre-1840
    "Violet-y pink." [BJ40]

[Rubra Duplex]
trans. "Double Red"
Breeder unknown, pre-1836
    "Deep pink." [V4] "Double red." [BJ40]

[Scabriusculus]
syn. 'À Petites Feuilles'; trans., "Little Bristly One"
Noisette, pre-1822
    The blossoms were presumably white and single. "*Branches,* thin, bristly, with small, straight thorns, intermingled with red or brown bristles, usually glandulous." [Go] "Much smaller [than *Rosa bracteata* proper]; canes silky; thorns smaller and nearly straight." [No26] "This variety differs from the Type by the following characteristics: *Canes,* more slender. *Thorns,* needle-like, straight or nearly straight, intermixed with numerous red or brown bristles, which are ordinarily glandulose. *Leaves* a little smaller." [Pf] "This one's better known in collections [than *Rosa bracteata* itself]." [MonLdeP]

[Scarlet Maria Leonida]
Rivers, pre-1846
    "Flowers bright red; form, cupped." [P] "Large, full, wide-spreading [blossom]; color, bright crimson." [S] "A new variety originated by Mr. Rivers, with bright red flowers." [WRP]

[Sea Foam]
W. Paul, 1919
From *Rosa bracteata* × "a full yellow Tea."
    "White, shaded slightly with cream." [ARA21/148] "A handsome variety with small double milk-white flowers, very striking." [NRS20/46] "Flowers double, milk-white. Foliage glossy dark green. Blooms continuously from June to October. Quite hardy." [ARA20/130] Sister seedling of 'Mermaid' (Brac).

Very Double Macartney Listed as 'Plena' (Brac).

[Victoire Modeste]
trans. "Modest Victory" (but see below)
Guérin, pre-1835
    "Yellowish pink, large." [S-V] "Blossom full, yellowish pink." [BJ40] "Pale rose, very large and full; rarely opens well." [P] The name of this cultivar is Guérin's little joke; his first name was "Modeste."

The most recent Bracteata hybrids are beyond the scope of these lucubrations; we, however, list—without description—for the worthy interest of Bracteata enthusiasts those the names of which have come across our escritoire:

Little Mermaid Wimer/Moore; root sport of 'Mermaid'

Muriel Moore; from *Rosa bracteata* × 'Guinée' [HT Climber]

Pearl Drift Le Grice; from 'Mermaid' × 'New Dawn' [Climber]

Pink Powderpuff Moore; from 'Lulu' [HT] × 'Muriel' [Brac]

Star Magic Moore; "2nd generation cross from *Rosa bracteata.*"

CHAPTER EIGHTEEN

Rugosas

"The Rugosa Roses, also known as the Ramanas or Japanese Roses, form a very interesting group, but perhaps have scarcely attained the popularity that their merits deserve. Yet for certain purposes they are well worth the attention of rosarians." [NRS15/31–35] "The ever-growing number of roses of this race proves to us that rose fanciers appreciate—as do we—the many good points that these plants have: hardy in the worst cold, and so decorative in their flowers, foliage, and fruit. We have disquired elsewhere on the use to which these bushes can be put to adorn parks and gardens." [JR19/179] "These Roses are gaining in popularity every day, and rightly so, for flower, foliage, and seed pods are most attractive . . . They make good bushes, and can be used in the Rose garden to form a hedge, or they can be planted in groups. Very hardy, they require little attention either by way of pruning or feeding, but like all Roses, they respond to good treatment and attention. I have seen these Roses planted in open glades in woods with other berried shrubs, for their fruit in autumn is much loved by pheasants, and it helps to keep the birds from straying." [GeH] "The ruddy fruits, produced in abundance, give cheerful colour when the leaves put in their autumn tint." [NRS17/62] "They are wonderfully hardy, growing and flowering freely in most exposed situations, even close to the sea. They are attractive alike in their strong, handsome foliage, their delightfully fragrant flowers, and, most of them also, in their large, brightly coloured fruits. They vary considerably in habit of growth, some forming neat bushes about 3-ft. high [ca. 1 m] and 2-ft. or more across [ca. 6 dm +], while others if allowed will form huge shrubs 12-ft. to 15-ft. in stature [ca. 4–5 m], and there are sorts of intermediate sizes, the majority naturally growing into well shaped bushes 5-ft. or 6-ft. in height [ca. 1.6–2 m]. There are two of them, Rugosa 'Repens Alba' and Rugosa 'Repens Rosea', of a climbing or creeping habit of growth, which, if given sufficient room, grow into great masses 4-ft. to 6-ft. high [ca. 1.3–2 m] and 20-ft. or more through [ca. 6.6 m]; thus it will be seen they afford plenty of choice when the purpose for which they are wanted has been decided upon. In the whole Rose family there are none which as a group make more easily managed or better hedges, and it is for this purpose, or for growing as free bushes, either in isolated positions or in an open shrubbery, that they are more peculiarly adapted. The perfume of the flowers is very sweet throughout the whole group, and in those, such as 'Rose à Parfum de l'Haÿ', to which the damask scent is added, we get flowers which are perhaps the most fragrant of all Roses. In addition to these advantages the Rugosas are as a group comparatively free from disease, and they are perpetual, that is to say they flower a second time in autumn, and some will be found in flower practically the summer through." [NRS15/31–35] "The Rugosas, which make fine bushes of fragrant flowers from May all through the summer, are not specially good later in the year, but they should always be grown in a garden where autumn effects are desired on account, first, of their beautiful berries which in August and September are quite a feature, and secondly for their foliage. In a fine autumn like that of 1919, some of these Rugosas put on the most glowing tints of amber, rose and gold which light up the garden right through October and the early part of November." [NRS20/111–112] "For autumn effects in the Rose garden many of the rugosas are unsurpassed, their large, thick leaves turning from dark green to the most brilliant golden and yellow tints." [NRS17/49] "Rugosa Roses and their hybrids seem just suited for our North American climate as they are so tough and hardy. They make dense, sturdy, compact bushes, 6 to 9 feet high [ca. 2–3 m], according to variety. Their dark, rich leathery foliage is oddly wrinkled, shiny and remarkably free from insect pests. Some bloom all summer, others but once, but are followed in the autumn with a profusion of beautiful, orange-red or crimson fruits . . . The plants are hardy as oaks, and do well in the most trying places—seashore, mountains, or anywhere. On account of the shapeliness of their growth, these Roses are especially valuable for use as lawn specimens. Being well branched and very symmetrical, they make splendid hedges, having in their favor hardiness and freedom from insects and disease. The thorny nature of the plants helps to make a hedge almost impenetrable." [C&Js21] "The Japanese Rugosa Hybrids are as hardy here [in Stavanger, Norway] as anywhere." [ARA20/47] "For the sea-shore, for very cold or very dry areas, for untoward growing conditions anywhere, try the Rugosas as your climbers." [W] "The Rugosas are specially useful at the sea-side, for they will stand the salt laden winds better than any other class of Roses." [NRS24/31] "On the other hand they have certain, and rather decided, limitations. They do not in any way take the place of our ordinary garden Roses, such as the H.T.'s and Tea Roses, as occupants of our beds and Rose borders. Their petals are frequently apt to be somewhat floppy, and the flowers do not really last well when cut and placed in water, consequently they are seldom seen at our shows, and only a few of them are of much value for the decoration of the house. While the single flowered kinds are often very beautiful, the double forms that have been obtained hitherto are for the most part of rather poor quality in the matter of form. There are a few exceptions. 'Conrad Ferdinand Meyer' and its white sport 'Nova Zembla' are usually well shaped, frequently also 'Daniel Leseuer', 'Mme. Georges Bruant', 'Mme. Lucien Villeminot', and Messrs. Paul & Sons most recent addition to this group, 'Dolly Varden'. But taking the double members of the Rugosas all round, beauty of form is not their strong point." [NRS15/31–35]

"To those who make a specialty of garden design, I particular-ly recommend the four following varieties: 'Belle Poitevine', 'Blanc Double de Coubert', 'Calocarpa', and 'Souvenir de Chris-tophe Cochet'. These four varieties are from the *Rosa rugosa* clan; they are semidouble, and they all are equally valuable. Their foli-age keeps, until far into the Fall, a dark green color which has the prettiest effect in the middle of other roses, the leaves of which have lost their bright coloration. Up until late in the year, the plant keeps blooming as well with beautiful flowers. The hips, which are the size of a nut, are the most sparkling red, giving the bush a magnificent appearance. One of the grand things these four vari-eties have in common is their hardiness, needing no protection whatsoever during the worst Winter. This is the group of plants most recommendable for adorning a park." [JR23/41] "The major-ity are essentially outdoor plants, and perhaps in considering their place in the garden we ought to think of them rather as flowering shrubs than in the light we usually regard our garden Roses. This applies also to our pruning of them, and in this respect they are decidedly accommodating, for they will do very well with practi-cally no pruning at all, merely having the old wood removed every three or four years when the bush begins to become too dense, or if preferred, and the position they occupy seems to require it, they may be pruned either moderately or even rather hard each spring. It is usual to do what pruning is required during February, and it is certainly convenient to get their pruning finished before the bulk of our garden Roses require attention, but it may really be taken in hand in any spell of open weather during autumn or winter, for they are so hardy that there is little fear of the Rugosas suffering from frost by reason of the pruning being carried out too early." [NRS15/31–35]

"The history of the Rugosas bears some resemblance to that of the hybrids of *R. multiflora*, in the sense that something like a hundred years elapsed after the discovery of the species before their development as garden plants was at all seriously taken in hand. *R. rugosa* 'Rubra' and also the white form *R. rugosa* 'Alba' are generally attributed to the Swedish botanist and traveller Carl Pehr Thunberg, under the year 1784, in which he published his *Flora Japonica*. It seems, however, possible that this Rose was in-troduced even earlier than this, under the name *R. kamtchatika*. The early history of these Roses rests in some obscurity, but is not without interest and deserves a short notice. In the year VIII of the Republic (1800), Ventenat, the gardener of the Empress Joséphine, published his *Description of the Plants Cultivated in the Garden of J. M. Cels,* wherein he described *R. kamtchatika* and gave a fine plate of it drawn by Redouté. Later in 1817 and 1824, Thory and Redouté gave another picture of the same plant, and it had also been figured by Andrews in 1805. Now, looking at these pictures, though there are certain differences between the portraits of Re-douté, which Thory attributed to the effect of some eighteen years' cultivation, there can be little doubt that we have a plant of *R. rugosa* and nothing else, and in his *Prodromus* (1820), Thory expressly calls *R. rugosa* a synonym of Ventenat's *R. kamtchatika* and also of the *R. ferox* of Andrews. Lindley, in his *Monograph* (1820), sets out first the *R. ferox* of Andrews, confusing it with Marschall von Bieberstein's plant of the same name, which comes from the Caucasus, not from Japan, and is a member of the Sweet-briar group; next, *R. rugosa,* which he had not seen and knew only from Thunberg's description, and which, as he says, contains little to distinguish it from *R. ferox* and *R. kamtchatika,* and he gives a Japanese drawing of this Rose. And thirdly he gives *R. kamtchati-ka* itself, distinguishing it chiefly by its growth and the supposed possession of falcate thorns under the sepals.

"Now, there can be little doubt that Andrews' *R. ferox* is simply *R. rugosa*; Andrews himself says Willdenow's description of *R. ru-gosa* is meant for his *ferox,* as it accords with his figure. He adds that it seems by nature formed to be admired at a distance from the numerous large thorns with which the stem is surrounded. But what was Lindley's *R. kamtchatika*? Prof. Crépin investigated the question and came to the conclusion that it and *R. rugosa* were only two forms of the same specific Type, a conclusion in which, after going through the evidence available (which it would take too long to set out here), I have also arrived, with the proviso that *kamtchatika* may be a hybrid form. The interest of the enquiry lies in this: that Lindley tells us that *R. kamtchatika* had usually been considered of somewhat recent introduction to the gardens of Europe; but that it was certain that the period of its arrival might be fixed at somewhat beyond the middle of the seventeenth century. Sir James Smith possessed a specimen of it gathered in the Botanic Garden in Chelsea in 1791, but to Monsieur Ventenat must be given the credit of having first made it known. Moreover, in the *Botanical Register,* vol. 5, where figures are given of both *R.*

kamtchatika and *rugosa,* it is stated that *kamtchatika* was brought out by Cels in 1802 and *rugosa* by Lee and Kennedy in 1796. These dates may be accepted as the dates of their issue to the public. But although these Roses were introduced so long ago, the greater part of the eighteenth [*i.e.,* 19th] century was to elapse before they obtained a footing in our gardens." [NRS15/31–35]

As we read in *The Growth of Gardens* (by R. Gorer, 1978, London: Faber & Faber), the botanical collector Maximowicz—keeper of the herbarium of the Imperial Botanic Garden in St. Petersburg, Russia—sent to St. Petersburg, in 1861, from Japan, 250 sets of plant material; and, in 1864, he returned to St. Petersburg laden with chests of herbarium specimens, 300 different sorts of seeds, and approximately 400 living plants. Among his co-workers at the Imperial Botanic Garden were Prof. Eduard Regel (director) and Jakob Kesselring, who, in the 1870s, introduced two Rugosa roses deriving almost certainly from Maximowicz's Japanese material (see 'Regeliana' and 'Kaiserin des Nordens').

"In 1873, MM. Jamain and Forney state that they are too new to pronounce a definite judgement upon. *The Garden,* for May, 1876, contains a reference to the white form, *rugosa* 'Alba', and in 1880 a note from Lord Brownlow's gardener in *The Gardener's Chronicle* shows that he was then growing the rugosas. Otherwise we hear little of them. About this time, the hybridizers seem to have turned their attention to the group, for 'Mme. Georges Bruant', one of the first of the modern hybrids, appeared in 1887, and in 1889 Dr. Müller, working, I believe, in conjunction with Monsieur Jules Gravereaux, brought out 'Thusnelda'. Thenceforward, these raisers, together with Messrs. Paul & Son, Cochet-Cochet, and others, produced a great many varieties." [NRS15/35]

"Found during the third and final voyage of Capt. Cook. Collected by Sir Joseph Banks, then named by Thunberg in 1784. The hardiest and most remontant of all. Despite having been introduced so long ago, relatively, it was only recently that it began to play a part in breeding, whence came the modern hybrids." [Gx] "One small garden [at the Roseraie de l'Haÿ in 1923] is devoted to roses valuable for perfume, and contains, among other things, a collection of Rugosa seedlings developed by Monsieur Gravereaux during his experiments with roses for commercial perfumes." [ARA23/128] "As Georges Bruant puts his white Rugosa hybrid 'Mme. G. Bruant' on the market, some breeders are quickly setting their sights on the long-neglected *Rosa rugosa* Thunb. The unusual appearance and fine habit of this interesting and beautiful rose promise an extraordinary future. The complete hardiness, the fine growth—especially suitable for standards—the excellent enameled glossy and resistant foliage, the capability of recurrent bloom and of easily setting hips are attractive to the breeders." [URZ5/1/19] "Rugosa varieties and hybrids bid fair to become the most reliable and highly prized bush roses for the northern and Prairie States, and, when the choicer forms are known, to be valued far down toward the frostless regions. Rugosa hybrids, as a

rule, carry their vigor, beauty of foliage, frost- and disease-resistance well into the third and fourth dilution with Tea and Remontant blood, while gaining greatly in beauty of bloom and coloring; but the faults of excessive spininess and weak flower-stems also persist; and the rugosa type may be regarded as especially adapted for the garden and not likely to produce varieties having value for cutting and exhibition." [ARA16/30–31]

"Rose experts may have a low opinion of the quality of blooms of some of the hardiest hybrid Rugosas, but on the cold, wind-swept prairies, their cheery, fragrant flowers mean more to lonely hearts, hungry for beautiful things, than the most exquisite productions to people in more favored climes." [ARA29/122]

Rosa rugosa   Plate 22

horticultural syns. 'À Feuilles Ridées', 'Rosier Hérisson', 'Runzliche Rose'

"Not very tall bush, in which the canes are cylindrical, lightly tomentose, charged with numerous close-set prickles which are straight and whitish in color; some are very strong, others smaller. The leaves are alternate, [leaflets] in sets with an odd one, usually nine leaflets which are oval, obtuse, tipped with a distinct point, saw-toothed along the edges, rough on both sides, green above, tomentose and veined beneath, an inch long [ca. 2.5 cm], borne on a pubescent petiole armed with prickles which are sparse, straight, and whitish. The flowers have a calyx which is pubescent on the outside and tomentose on the inside of the sepals. The fruits are glabrous and globular. This plant grows in Japan. Its rough and mucronate leaves and extremely numerous prickles distinguish it from other species . . . (description from Thunberg)." [Lam] "It's not yet [1824] cultivated either in England or in France." [MonLdeP] "*Shrub* vigorous, making a thick and large bush. *Canes* stout, divergent, villose, covered with numerous prickles which are long, straight, and covered with down; ordinarily, the strongest have stipules. *Petiole* stout, long, cylindrical, very downy, as are the long, straight, and unequal prickles with which it is armed beneath. *Stipules* large, much widened at the tip; glabrous above, villose beneath, denticulate and wavy along the edges, which are often reflexed. *Leaflets* 7 or 9, elliptical, obtuse or pointed, hooked, reticulately veined; glabrous and dark green above, pale and villose beneath. *Serration* ordinarily simple. *Peduncle* villose, arching, short. *Bracts* orbicular or oval-acuminate, glabrous above, villose below, denticulate, slightly glandulose and strongly undulate along the edge. *Ovary* globular, glabrous, and glaucous. *Sepals* lacy, long, villose, simple at the base, terminating in a leaflet which is ordinarily lanceolate, incised, or pinnatifid. *Flower* large, single, light violet purple. Opens in April and May. *Fruit* large, poppy red, globular, sometimes gibbose, crowned by the adherent sepals. *Ovules* 20–40." [Pf] "Stems slender, downy, armed with straight and nearly equal thorns; no stipules; petioles emarginate; leaflets rugose, simply dentate, obtuse, and mucronate, with close-set veins; no bracts; peduncles covered with short thorns which are thick at the base, upright, and verticillate; calyx oblong or globular, smooth; sepals entire, very thin, reflexing, two of them having a foliaceous dentate tip. This variety [the typical form], native to Japan, has, I believe, never left there." [S] "Bushy plant, in the wild, from 1–1.5 m tall

Rosa rugosa continued

[ca. 3–4½ ft], with flexuous canes which are bristly and spiny, and leaves resembling those of the Briar; they are composed of 5–9 leaflets which are rugose, somewhat puffy, nearly sessile, elliptical or oval, elliptically pointed, dark green above, tomentose, white, and with raised veins beneath; the blossoms, which exhale a very fine perfume, are solitary and pedunculate; the color of this rose is dark purple in the Japanese variety; the blossom is single, and, in color, white or a more or less intense pink." [S] "Height 6 feet [ca. 2 m]. A trifle exotic in appearance because of its rough, dark green, shiny foliage. Stems are thickly covered with gray prickles. Flowers large, single, in some seedlings an ugly shade of rose, followed by large orange or red haws. The hybrids of this rose are better in flower and foliage and look less exotic." [ARA16/17] "Has the best foliage of any rose in cultivation—thick, shiny, wrinkled—and almost the biggest fruits, often an inch in diameter [ca. 2.5 cm]." [ARA17/13] "Was in the Cels nurseries; Bosc called it 'Rosier Hérisson'; the Nouveau Duhamel, 'Rosier à feuilles ridées'; it's the 'Runzliche Rose' of the Germans." [Gx]

"*Rosa rugosa* is a robust shrub, much branched; 1–1.5 m in height [ca. 3–4½ ft]; twigs, branches, and canes covered with numerous unequal thorns, the larger of which are rigid, upright, and frequently flattened at the base, the smaller ones being bristles which are occasionally glandular. The leaves are comprised of 7, or less often five or 9, leaflets; these are oval-oblong or oval, obtuse or pointed, entire or, more rarely, doubly dentate, but always stiff and made rugose by the deep channels of the network of veins; the lower side is paler, and is clothed with a variable pubescence. The flowers are solitary or in bunches of 2–3, sometimes in a cluster at the tip of vigorous canes; the peduncle and calyx are glabrous, or, on the same specimen, clothed with glandular hairs; the lobes of the calyx, shorter than the corolla, are entire or bearing some occasional lacinations to the base, longly acuminate, and often slightly dilated at the tip. The flowers are large (about 8 cm across [ca. 3 in]), most often a beautiful red, more rarely white, and sometimes semi-double (in the variety 'Kaiserin des Nordens'). The hip which succeeds them is large, globular, flattened, crowned by the upright sepals, and red. The synonymy of this Rose is no less knotty than that of the most litigious of the other species of this difficult genus; also, we believe we should let pass in silence the opinions of Ventenat, Thory, Lindley, Trattinick, Seringe, and their way of putting this species together and of limiting species and closely-related forms. However, we should not forget that it is *Rosa rugosa* Thunb., as the typical form, which was figured and described in the January 1871 number of *Illustration Horticole*, by MM. André (ed.) and Linden, under the name *Rosa Regeliana*, and again by Mr. Lange, in 1874, in the seed catalog of the Copenhagen botanical garden under the name *R. andreae*. As to its place in the classification of genus *Rosa*, Lindley created for *Rosa ferox, rugosa*, and *Kamtschatica*, all of which belong incontestably to the same group, a special section, that of the *Feroces*; but it seems more natural to put them into the *Cinnamomae* group beside *Rosa alpina* L., *blanda* Ait., *Woodsii* Lindl., *cinnamomae* L., *amblyotis* Mey., etc. This plant, so unusual in its upright stature, the abundance of its thorns, the stiffness and tint of its foliage, the size and bright color of its blossoms, as well as the intense color of its fruits, grows spontaneously in Japan, Manchuria, Kamchatka, and in the Amur region and the island of Sacchalin. It was introduced to France at the beginning of this [19th] century in the garden of Cels; in 1838, it was grown in the

Jardin des Plantes in Paris under the name *R. Kamschatika* Vent. after a specimen found by the renowned rosarian Crépin in the herbarium of Kunth. Today, it has gone out into the gardens of fanciers, and one can see some beautiful specimens among others in the beautiful dendrological collection of Monsieur Lavallée in Segrez [the 'Arboretum Segrezianum']. *Rosa rugosa* is in no way a delicate sort, as one might suppose at least, from its place of origin. It need not dread our Winters, even the worst of them. Its propagation is the same as for other species of roses, and we add that one has a chance of obtaining new varieties from seed." [JR6/89–90]

Rosa rugosa 'Alba' Plate 24
Thunberg, 1784

"Single pure white flowers of 5 petals and highly scented, followed by pretty berries." [C&Js07] "Bud is delicately tinted with pink." [C-Ps25] "Flowers white, large and single, followed by larger and brighter coloured fruit than [that of *R. rugosa* itself], though less abundant." [P1] "White; single, large, borne singly or in clusters. Good as a hedge. Red fruits in fall." [Th2] "This is the Type variety with white blossoms, coming from Japan and described by Thunberg, producing quantities of large red hips, giving the bush a very decorative effect around the end of September. The very thick foliage is a beautiful dark green; it's a plant much to be recommended." [JR30/124] "This has large single white flowers followed by round fruits. The plant is moderate in growth, forming a bush from 4-ft. to 6-ft. high [ca. 1.3–2 m]. It is a very lovely flower and a great favorite with me; the petals are a pure white and contrast well with the yellow anthers." [NRS15/36] "Vigorous in growth. Plant where it can grow without pruning." [C-Ps28]

Rosa rugosa 'Rubra' Plate 23
Thunberg, 1784 (described); Lee & Kennedy, 1796 (introduced)

"Deep rose tinged violet, single, fragrant." [CA96] "Blossom single, red." [S] "Flowers a beautiful bright rosy crimson and single, succeeded by large berries of rich, rosy red. Exceedingly ornamental." [C&Js07] "Rich ruby crimson, shaded violet, large, single, and fragrant . . . Growth very vigorous." [GeH] "Fine for massing or hedges; absolutely hardy. Vigorous, very spiny, with rough, wrinkled foliage. Flowers are large, five-petaled, and very fragrant, varying from bright pink to deep carmine, with big golden centers. It blooms very early, and continues all summer, leaving behind a wealth of enormous seed-hips like little apples." [C-Ps25] "This is Thunberg's Type. It has single reddish violet flowers of a rather ugly shade of colour, followed by bright fruits of good size. It appears to be synonymous with 'Regeliana', at least for garden purposes." [NRS15/43] See also 'Regeliana' (Rg).

Rosa ×kamtchatika
Ventenat, 1798

Possibly a natural hybrid between *Rosa davurica* and *R. rugosa*.

"Upright, to 2 m tall [ca. 6 ft]. Bush resembling Rosa rugosa. Blossom velvety purple-carmine, very beautiful." [Ck] "Only differs [from *Rosa rugosa*] by way of its smaller stickers and less villose leaves." [BJ24] "*Bush* low and diffuse. *Canes* arching, brown gray, covered with down, bristles, and prickles, of which the largest are also covered with down, and are slightly curved, and coming in 2's or 3's beneath the stipules. *Petiole* villose, armed. *Stipules* large, entire or denticulate, villose, undulate, with upturned edges. *Leaflets* 7, 9, or 11, ovoid or elliptical, rough-veined, grayish-green; glabrous above, pale and pubescent beneath. *Serration* simple. *Peduncle* ordinarily villose, with neither bristles nor glands. *Bracts* large. *Ovary* globular, glabrous, and glaucous. *Sepals* entire, terminating in a long point; ordinarily glabrous, persistent, convergent after the petals fall. *Flower* medium-sized, single, light violet. Opens in May. *Fruit* pendant, globular, red." [Pf] "Stems three to four feet in length [ca. 1–1.3 m], with pale brown branches from which often the bristles and thorns fall in age; thorns stipulary, large, hooked, placed two or three together, the middle ones shorter; leaves gray, opaque; stipules fringed and glandulose along the edges; petioles thornless; leaflets blunt, simply and profoundly dentate, teeth horny at the tip. Blossoms dark red; peduncles purple, velvety at the base; calyx globular, smooth; sepals feebly glandulose, slightly enlarged at the tip, longer than the petals; petals heart-shaped, mucronate; 160–170 stamens; disk elevated, visible; 50 ovaries. This rose grows spontaneously in Kamchatka." [S]

"This Rose … has Kamchatka for its homeland, that peninsula of eastern Siberia situated between the Behring Sea and that of Okhotsk, according to Mouillefert only a variety of *Rosa rugosa* Thunb., a very distinct species which is very hardy and which is found in Manchuria, Korea, Sakalin Island, Japan, the Kuril Islands, and—last but not least—in Kamchatka." [JR18/165] "This rose, to which the name Kamchatka Rose is given in memory of the unfortunate La Peyrouse, to whose companions we owe this rose, comes from Japan; it has been grown for a score of years in several gardens in the environs of Paris. Its main stems are villose, and grow to about two feet high [ca. 6 dm]; its thorns, numerous and nearly conical; its leaves, an inch long [ca. 2.5 cm], composed of nine leaflets which are oval, ashy green above, whitish beneath; its flowers, which appear in May and June, are fragrant, deep pink, and of medium size. This rose, should it become common, would make hedges providing good defense. The Kamchatka Rose is not—truth to tell—the one we call the Hedgehog Rose; since it only differs in its smaller thorns and less villose leaves, all the careful public gardens give it the name 'Kamtchatka'." [CM] "This bush grows naturally in Kamtzchatka [*sic*]; it has been under cultivation for several years in the garden of Monsieur Cels, where it spends the Winter out in the open, and blooms around the end of the Spring." [Lam] "This one was sent to me [*de Pronville*] from England by Mr. Sabine [*Secretary of the London Horticultural Society*]." [MonLdeP]

"*Bush* 0.6–0.9 m high [ca. 2–3 ft] at most; *stems* and *branches* downy and hispid; *prickles* numerous, straight, unequal, acute, whitish, the shortest often glandular. *Leaflets* 7–9 (–11), dark green above, paler beneath; soft to the touch, obtuse or more often acute ovate, with unequal glandular teeth; petioles downy, prickly; stipules elongate, ciliate, with purplish glands. *Flowers* 1 (–2), terminal, large, fragrant, red tinged violet, on short, reddish, glabrous pedicels; *receptacles* globose and glabrous; *sepals* entire, subulate, more or less as long as the petals, pubescent outside, tomentose within. *Hip* rounded, glabrous, reddish-brown, crowned by the long-persistent calyx. This native of Kamchatka blooms in June in France, and often repeats in the Fall. It makes a fine effect when grafted on the Briar, but blooms sparingly unless pruned. No double-flowered variety is known yet. Comparison with Cels' Fig. 67 of the same species reveals that in less than 18 years it has undergone changes in length and density of form of the leaflets." [T&R]

"The plant drawn by Redouté in *Les Roses* under this name is simply *rugosa*, while that drawn by the same artist and described by Ventenat in the *Jardin de Cels* is different, having fewer and more hooked thorns. *R. kamtchatika* is shown in a coloured plate in the *Botanical Register*, vol. 5, p. 419, with one falcate thorn under each stipule and densely covered with setae but no other thorns; otherwise, it is like *R. rugosa*, with the typical dull rose coloured flower. It is also illustrated in the *Botanical Magazine*, vol. 59, where more thorns are shown. These plates follow Lindley's description, who I fancy had seen only dried specimens. I have for some years grown a plant of this rose which corresponds fairly well with that in the *Botanical Magazine*, but is quite unlike that in the *Botanical Register*. It has reddish stems and all the appearance of a hybrid rugosa. There is a thorn larger than the average under each stipule, which is sometimes falcate, but nearly as often straight." [NRS15/40] There is, or was, also a single white form of *Rosa ×kamtchatika* called 'Alba Simplex', notably made use of in breeding in the 1890s by Monsieur Cochet-Cochet (for instance, see 'Souvenir de Christophe Cochet' [Rg]).

Horticultural Varieties

À Feuilles Ridées Listed as *Rosa rugosa*.

Adiantifolia
trans. "Leaves Like Those of the Maidenhair Fern"
Cochet-Cochet, 1907

"Pink." [Ÿ] "Very unique. I saw it last May in the gardens of Monsieur Gravereaux at the Roseraie de l'Haÿ, but cannot find it anywhere alluded to in any of my books." [NRS28/208] Probably another member of the experimental series of which Cochet-Cochet's 'Heterophylla' (from *Rosa rugosa × R. foetida*) also comprises a member; see 'Heterophylla' (Rg).

Agnes
Saunders/Central Experimental Farm, 1923
From *Rosa rugosa ×* 'Persian Yellow' (F).

"Straw yellow." [Ÿ] "Coppery yellow buds; flowers become pale amber-gold upon opening; sweetly fragrant. Freely produced. Six feet [ca. 2 m]." [Way45] "A worthy yellow Rugosa. Buttercup-yellow buds, passing to clear yellow and opening to full, large blooms of fawn color and fruity fragrance. Does not bleach much and is very lasting, rain or shine. The flowers come all along the branches early in June. This is the only reliably yellow Rugosa. Awarded the Dr. W. Van Fleet Gold Medal by the American Rose Society, 1926." [C-Ps27] "Bud medium size, ovoid; flower medium size, double, full, fairly lasting; pale amber; strong fragrance. Vigorous, bushy grower, reaching 6 feet [ca. 2 m]; profuse bloomer in June. Hardy." [ARA24/174] "Yellow, medium size, very full, very fragrant, tall." [Sn] "It is a tall grower to 7 feet [ca. 2.3 m]." [W] "Makes large bushes or may be trained as pillars." [C-Ps31]

"This hybrid rose is a cross between *Rosa rugosa* as the seed parent and 'Persian Yellow' as the pollen parent. The cross was made by the late Dr. William Saunders, at the Central Experimental Farm, Ottawa, Canada, about the year 1900. It bloomed first in 1902, and has been under test at Ottawa ever since, during all of which time, so far as the writer is aware (and he has seen it every year) it has never been noticeably injured by winter. The habit of the plant and the texture

Agnes *continued*

and color of the leaves somewhat resemble [those of] *R. rugosa*. The flowers, double, and pale amber in color, are borne singly and in great profusion. The originator described it as 'pale yellow, the outer petals with a delicate creamy salmon hue.' The form of the bud is good, but that of the flower only fair. It is fragrant, and blooms early, but only once in the season. Because of its extreme earliness, great hardiness, and the distinct and attractive color of the flower, this variety should prove a great addition to the roses of the Rugosa group. Although introduced by the Experimental Farm, Ottawa, only in 1923, it will be noted from the statement above that the rose has been given a thorough test there." [ARA24/80–81] "This straw-colored Rugosa hybrid is absolutely hardy here. A semi-shrub, 4 feet high [ca. 1.3 m]. Foliage very scant and plant not attractive. Entirely free from blackspot and mildew after four years' careful trial. Flowers early. Blooms good, medium size, choice in the bud, but flat when open. Stems short . . . *Simcoe, Ont.*; . . . A straw-colored 'Hermosa' [B] or sometimes an enlarged 'Gardenia' [HT or W]. Ovoid bud; small, cupped bloom, lasts poorly; slight fragrance. Growth moderate, straggling . . . *St. Louis, Mo.*; No merit here . . . *Beverly Hills, Calif.*" [ARA28/141]

"A real acquisition. True, it blooms only once, but against a background of a vigorous plant clothed with very distinctive, grayish, much pitted and wrinkled, disease-free foliage, its fine buds of coppery yellow, opening to well-formed, sweet-scented flowers of pale amber, are wonderfully attractive. It is a cross of Rugosa × 'Persian Yellow', and appears to be sterile. Of dependable hardiness, it should be pruned very little." [ARA29/124] "A wonder when in full bloom." [ARA31/180]

Agnes Emily Carman

syn. 'Agnes Emily Corman'
Carman, ca. 1895
Possibly from *Rosa rugosa* × 'Harison's Yellow' (F).

"Dark crimson." [ARA16/32] "It is semi-double, and flowers in clusters; a beautiful crimson shade like 'Général Jacqueminot' [HP]; a free and continuous bloomer." [C&Js07] "[The blossoms] come in clusters, making a perfect bouquet in themselves." [C&Js21] "Has not bloomed as freely in California as some of the other Hybrid Rugosas." [Th2] "*Gardening* tells us about a new Rugosa hybrid bred in Chicago. The blossom of this rose, called 'Agnes Emily Corman' [*sic*], is semi-double and bright red, exactly like 'Général Jacqueminot'. The bud is very beautiful, long, losing something of its sparkle before opening completely. The foliage and growth are the same as Rugosa. The bush is very hardy and easily withstands a pretty harsh winter." [JR20/2] "Justly compared with 'Général Jacqueminot', for color, fragrance, and florescence, but lacks in number of petals, in spite of which it is a worthy subject for any garden that tolerates varieties with but one blooming period." [ARA25/206] "Makes a vigorous bush 5 feet or more in height [ca. 1.6 m +], with fine foliage, quite large and fairly rugose. With me it bears a splendid crop of fairly double flowers of the richest Jacqueminot crimson shade in June, and scatteringly thereafter. In a great many districts this is reported to bloom only once. It is very hardy." [ARA29/122] "The most brilliant red Hybrid Rugosa . . . Flowers are large, cupped and delightfully fragrant. Recurrent in bloom. It is vigorous and bushy but shows little of the Rugosa influence in the foliage." [C-Ps27]

Agnes Emily Corman   Listed as 'Agnes Emily Carman' (Rg).

Alba   Listed as *Rosa rugosa* 'Alba'.

Alice Aldrich

Lovett/Conard & Jones, 1899
From *Rosa rugosa* × 'Colonel de Sansal' (HP) (or possibly 'Caroline de Sansal' [HP]).

"Wonderful carmine pink; very floriferous." [Ck] "Exceedingly sweet and beautiful." [C&Js07] "Deep pink, medium size, full, medium fragrance, tall." [Sn] "A remarkably fine bush rose for garden planting; lovely buds, and large double flowers, rich rosy pink; blooms the whole season and is perfectly hardy." [C&Js06] "Gives beautiful, medium-sized pink flowers, and is an intermittent summer bloomer with unusually handsome foliage. It is especially desirable as an ornamental shrub." [ARA25/206] Possibly bred by Van Fleet.

Amdo

Hansen, 1927
From 'Tetonkaha' (Rg) × 'La Mélusine' (Rg).

"A heavy bloomer through July and into August. The pink flowers appear 7 to 10 in a cluster and have about 16 petals and 8 petaloids." [ARA27/226] "Violet pink, medium size, lightly double, very fragrant, tall." [Sn]

Amélie Gravereaux

Gravereaux, 1900
From a seedling (resulting from a cross of *Rosa gallica* with 'Eugène Fürst' [HP]) × *R. rugosa*.

"Flower large, full, dark red." [JR30/186] "Carmine purple, shaded red, large, full. Growth vigorous." [GeH] "Deep purple red, medium size, full, very fragrant, tall." [Sn] "Especially desirable in extremely cold climates, making a strong shrub with fine foliage, and producing medium-sized, purplish red flowers; exceptionally fragrant. It is recurrent." [ARA29/124] "Shrub of good vigor with strong canes; leaflets of medium size, finely bullate. Flowers large, nearly full, superbly colored deep purple red, showing nicely the influence of the pollen of 'Eugène Fürst'. It is, again [*i.e.*, like 'Mme. Lucien Villeminot'], an absolutely new coloration among the *Rugosas*." [JR27/165] "This is a wonderful everblooming Rugosa hybrid that sends up long shoots, pillar fashion, to 10 feet high [ca. 3.3 m], that bear a continuous succession of immense bouquets of large, full blooms, brilliant scarlet-crimson in color and of true old-rose perfume. It may be trained as a climber, pillar, or shrub Rose. The foliage is more refined than [that of] the type, and it amply clothes the plant. It is immune from diseases and, in a measure, from insects. Hardy in coldest climates." [C-Ps30] "This is a strong grower of upright habit, making a bush 6-ft. to 8-ft. high [ca. 2–2.6 m] if unpruned, with large flowers rather more than semi-double of a deep purple-red colour, one of the best of its particular type." [NRS15/36]

America

Harvard University Gardens/G. Paul, 1893

"Bright crimson." [Ÿ] "Deep pink, large, lightly double, tall." [Sn] "Brilliant crimson. —Blossoms large, single; fruit long, red; very vigorous." [Cx] "The flowers are large and open and of a crimson lake colour. The shape is that sometimes called the American shape, which differs slightly from the true Japanese. It has large ovate fruit covered with long spines. Mr. G. L. Paul tells me that this Rose was sent to his firm in the year 1892 by Prof. Sargent, of the Hartford [*sic*] Botanic Gardens, U.S.A. It has proved with me to be one of the earliest to flower." [NRS15/36] "Tribe of *Rosa Rugosa,* introduced from the United States; neither the description nor an illustration appearing in the catalog." [JR17/178]

Arnoldiana
Dawson, 1914
From *Rosa rugosa* × 'Général Jacqueminot' (HP).

Crimson-purple, semi-double. "The hybrids of [*Rosa rugosa*] are better in flower and foliage and look less exotic, particularly 'Mme. Georges Bruant' and 'Arnoldiana'." [ARA16/17] We read in Griffiths that 'Arnoldiana' is upright and tall. The name commemorates the Arnold Arboretum of Harvard University at Jamaica Plain, Massachusetts.

Atropurpurea
G. Paul, 1899
From *Rosa rugosa* × *R.* ×*damascena.*

"Blackish crimson, passing to maroon-crimson." [ARA17/29] "Large, semi-double, bright carmine with chestnut brown." [Ck] "Dark red, medium size, single, tall." [Sn] "Flower deep blackish crimson; single. Growth vigorous." [GeH] "This has deep blackish crimson buds opening to maroon flowers, changing to purple as they fade. It is a most beautiful variety; perhaps the greatest advance yet attained in the singles. The berries which follow the flowers are rounded and slightly flattened. The plant is of moderate growth, from 3-ft. to 5-ft. high [ca. 1–1.6 m], and tolerably bushy." [NRS15/36] "The richest colour among the rugosas." [Cat12]

Belle Poitevine
trans. "Poitiers Beauty"
Bruant, 1894
Seedling of 'Regeliana' (Rg).

"Clear rose, large and double, sweetly scented." [GeH] "Pure pink." [Ÿ] "Pink, large, lightly double, very fragrant, tall." [Sn] "One of the finest hybrids. With its ideal habit of growth, rugose foliage, and very large, loosely formed flowers of rose to magenta-pink, borne in profusion all season, it is a wonderful decorative rose. It sets seed-hips and is entirely hardy." [ARA29/123] "Has long buds and semi-double rose-coloured flowers. It is a strong grower of upright habit, and will make a bush 6-ft. to 8-ft. high [ca. 2–2.6 m]." [NRS15/36] "Enormous bush, leaves nearly dark green, very large pink blossom, strongly scented." [Ck] "Very vigorous bush, magnificent foliage, dark green, with nine leaflets; canes numerous, large, and strong, tipped with immense clusters of very large, elegant blossoms of a beautiful pink, which are double without being very full, so consequently they open easily. These flowers come from the beginning of Spring up to frost without interruption. The buds are very long, and accompanied by foliaceous sepals; the blossoms, widely open when expansion is complete, waft an exquisite and penetrating perfume which resembles that of the Centifolia and the Carnation; it is perhaps the most agreeably scented of all roses. The mother of this hybrid, *Rosa Rugosa Regeliana,* described by Monsieur Édouard André in 1871 and 1872 in *Illustration Horticole,* gave it one of its best qualities, that of blooming in large bouquets; it is not unusual to count up to 20–25 blossoms together at the tip of a cane. It is enough to simply cut a stem to have a perfect bouquet which perfumes the air, being formed of roses from the elegant bud surrounded by sepals to the widely-expanded rose." [JR18/148]

[Bergers Erfolg]
trans. "Berger's Success"
V. Berger/Pfitzer, 1924
From a seedling (of *Rosa rugosa*) × 'Richmond' (HT); Jg advances the very unlikely ancestry 'King Georg[e] V' (HT) × 'Mrs. Aaron Ward' (HT).

"Flower large (3–4 inches across [ca. 7.5 cm to 1 dm]), single, very lasting, bright fire-red with golden yellow stamens, borne, several together, sometimes to clusters of 30. Foliage dark green, abundant, continuous bloomer from May to October. Hardy." [ARA25/190]

Bienvêtu Listed as 'Monsieur Gustave Bienvêtu' (Rg).

Bienyetu Listed as 'Monsieur Gustave Bienvêtu' (Rg).

Blanc Double de Coubert Plate 26
trans. "Double White from [the town of] Coubert"
Cochet-Cochet, 1892
From *Rosa rugosa* 'Alba' × *R.* ×*kamtchatika* (but see below).

"Sparkling white Rugosa, blossom nearly full, eglantine scent." [JR19/36] "Paper-white." [ARA17/29] "Most beautiful and valuable white Rugosa. Pure white, quite full, very large blossom of a dazzling white, constantly blooming." [Ck] "White, large, full, medium scent, tall." [Sn] "A most desirable hybrid. It is very strong-growing, with typical Rugosa foliage, and produces large, snowy white, fairly double flowers all season; the perfume is exceptionally fine. The half-blown buds are very pretty. Very hardy; sets many large scarlet fruits." [ARA29/122] "One of the earliest Roses to bloom…Maximum height 4 to 5 feet [ca. 1.3–1.6 m]." [Way45] "Pure white, very large, nearly full, fragrant. Growth very vigorous." [GeH] "A magnificent, double, pure white, and very fragrant Hybrid Rugosa which blooms throughout summer and fall. As it grows to about 4 feet [ca. 1.3 m], it easily makes a low and very lovely white-flowering hedge of real distinction. When thoroughly established it sends up many strong canes at some distance from the plant, which if removed and headed back can be developed into really successful everblooming tree Roses which are perfectly hardy." [C-Ps30] "This has pure white semi-double flowers, which it produces freely and constantly, so that in the autumn flowers and fruit may be seen on the plant at the same time. The fruits are large and a good scarlet colour. The flowers are noticeable for their fragrance even among a fragrant family. It is a fairly strong grower, forming a bush from 5-ft. to 7-ft. high [ca. 1.6–2.3 m] of a good shape. This is the best double white and quite one of the best of the group." [NRS15/37]

"This rose came from a natural pollination [*i.e., open pollination*] of the rose called 'rugosa alba' from which it takes all its characteristics except the flower, which is double, nearly full, purest white, 10–12 cm across [ca. 4 in], and giving off an elegant eglantine scent. The bloom occurs in clusters of 5-6-7-8-10 flowers, opening in twos or threes. The variety 'Blanc Double de Coubert' is one of the most remontant, and blooms up till frost." [JR16/165] "The [Natural History] Museum received this wonderful development from its breeder, Monsieur Cochet-Cochet of Coubert (Seine-et-Marne) the 25th of February, 1893—which is to say just as it was being released

Blanc Double de Coubert *continued*

to commerce. Since that date, 'Blanc Double de Coubert' has reveled in our collections, being a shrub of the first order. Here's a description taken from life: Vigorous bush with strong, erect, velvety canes of a more or less pronounced gray color, bearing numerous thorns of varying sizes but always straight and not hooked like those of most other roses. Leaves large, compound, much stipulated at the base, and usually bearing 4–5 pairs of opposite leaflets with the odd one. Rachis large, rounded, velvety, having beneath some rigid prickles like those of the cane. Leaflets obovate, the lower ones larger than those near the tip, sessile, thick, intense bright green above, and bullate because of the 'channels' at the veins; quite hirsute and whitish green beneath; regularly dentate along the edge. Flowers in a terminal cluster in which the number [of blossoms] varies most frequently with us from 5–10 or 15 blooms apiece … Buds pointed, extremely elegant, much resembling those of the Tea rose 'Niphetos'. Flowers large, double, but not full, very pure white [*a note adds:* 'special instruments' have found a tiny quantity of azure blue in the petals, rendering the white whiter than that of other roses, the white of which is sullied with yellow or red], freely remontant, with an uncommonly elegant perfume. Petals ruffled. Fruits no less decorative than the leaves and blossoms, globular, large for the group, beautiful cochineal red, surmounted by long sepals rarely … [This cultivar] is particularly recommendable as a single specimen on the lawn at the corner of allées where it always looks most decorative owing to its stature, its beautiful ample glossy foliage, and its abundant bloom which comes from Spring to the Autumn frosts. This variety propagates easily by budding, be it on Briar seedlings or on 'De la Grifferaie' [Mult]." [JR18/165] "The best white Rugosa." [C-Ps27] There is an oft-repeated claim, dating back at least to 1915, that 'Blanc Double de Coubert' derives from *Rosa rugosa* × 'Mlle. de Sombreuil' (Cl. T); see under 'Mme. Georges Bruant' (Rg). Cx, of which the breeder of 'Blanc Double de Coubert' Cochet-Cochet was an editor, gives only Rugosa 'Alba' as this cultivar's parent.

Calocarpa   Plate 24
trans. "Beautiful Fruit"
Bruant, 1894
From *Rosa rugosa* 'Rubra' × 'Parsons' Pink China' (Ch).

"Clear rose, single; good foliage. Growth vigorous." [GeH] "Obtained by crossing the Type *R. rugosa* with a pink China. It's a slightly less vigorous plant and more slender than its kin; it covers itself with a multitude of single blossoms of a beautiful pink—nearly pure—which at length are replaced by elongated fruits, yellowish in color, and good looking." [JR30/124–125] "Blossom single, carmine pink, 12 cm wide [ca. 4³⁄₄ in], in great abundance. As it is with the bloom, so is it later with its large scarlet-red fruit decorating it. Multiplies from the roots. One of the most beautiful fruit-shrubs." [Ck] "The fruits are not so large as in [*Rosa rugosa*], but they are produced in such abundance as to recommend it to a place in every garden. In shape they are globose, and colour being a rich scarlet." [NRS17/62] "The flowers are single and rosy pink in colour. The fruits are produced abundantly and are a bright scarlet and shiny. They are not quite so large as in some varieties, and are pendulous. This plant is a strong grower, reaching from 6-ft. to 8-ft. [ca. 2–2.6 m] if unpruned; it appears to be one of the most commonly grown." [NRS15/37]

"This hybrid was found in a crop which the firm's book referred

to the cross *Rosa Rugosa* × Pink China. It is particularly as a tree-rose that it makes a splash, usually after the second year, when it makes an enormous spherical head, borne on the Briar, which enlarges very quickly. These big leafy spheres are entirely covered, from Spring, with medium-sized single blossoms with an elegant perfume. They are the most beautiful pure pink, ornamented with numerous yellow stamens at the center, on which hordes of bees will gather, meanwhile fertilizing the blossom, taking away to the hive a scent of honey. To these innumerable flowers, no less abundant hips succeed in big clusters in which you could count 40–60 fruits—perhaps thousands on plants several years old. These fruits redden towards the end of Summer and keep in good shape up to Winter because they stay hard a long time, unlike *Rosa Rugosa,* in the Type of which the hips soften very quickly. It can be stated that *Rosa Calocarpa* is the most beautiful shrub grown for fruits … and has, what is more, a ravishing bloom. The purplish canes are smaller than those of *Rugosa,* but they are very stiff; the leaves are also different somewhat, the leaflets being smaller, very elegant, and keeping green a long time, only a strong frost making them fall. Seeds replicate the plant pretty well, though in slightly differing forms; one can soon plant charming hedges with the seedlings from this pretty hybrid rose, as defensive as those of the Thorn, covered with fragrant flowers and scarlet fruit." [JR18/148] "We found in another magazine, the *Wiener Illustrierten Garten-Zeitung*'s 5th volume, this year, on page 203, the following: 'Reporting about a new hybrid of *R. rugosa* achieved by the breeder Bruant crossing it with the common Bengal Rose [*i.e., 'Parsons' Pink China'*], written by Éd[ouard] André for *Revue Horticole* … This cross produced two seedlings which differ quite a bit; one shows half-double flowers with the color of the common Monthly Rose [*again, 'Parsons' Pink China'*], so it seemed evident that only a few people would be interested in it; and the other one, which E. André named *R. rugosa* 'Calocarpa'. The single blossoms are smaller than those of *R. rugosa,* are well-proportioned, and clear pink in color. They cover the whole bush from Spring until late Summer, and are replaced by handsome red hips which last until the end of December. The second year after propagation, the shrub's thorny twigs already show flowers very freely, and, contrary to its ancestor, they are clothed with smaller, more exquisite, almost evergreen foliage. A special feature of this novelty is the bushy growth, if grown as a standard.' … Apart from the fact that ['Calocarpa'] will not be very successful and will—to boot—disappear without a trace, as much better roses have, we are against naming a hybrid with botanical terms." [URZ5/1/20–21] Seems to have first bloomed for Bruant about 1890.

Carmen
Lambert, 1906
From *Rosa rugosa* × 'Princesse de Béarn' (HP).

"Vinous red." [Ÿ] "Single, light crimson flowers very continuously … It is very hardy." [ARA29/124] "Deep red, medium size, single, medium scent, tall." [Sn] "Grows very tall, strongly upright. Foliage dark green, large. Blossom single, very large, bright black-red. Reblooms unfailingly." [Ck] "This has bright crimson flowers with golden anthers, which are very fragrant. The blossoms are single and very freely and continuously produced, but it forms no bright coloured fruit. Sometimes there are a few green ones. It is of good habit and moderate growth, the bush being about 4-ft. or 5-ft. high [ca. 1.3–1.6 m]. It looks very well in the garden when in flower, for it is perhaps the best colour among the crimsons." [NRS15/37] Carmen, in Bizet's 1875 opera, the gypsy cigarette-girl with boyfriends whose lives went up in smoke; from Prosper Mérimée's story.

Chédane-Guinoisseau
syn. 'Monsieur Chédane'
Chédane-Guinoisseau, 1895

"Has deep rose coloured double flowers, followed by berries in autumn; it is fragrant and continuous." [NRS15/37] "Light pink, very large, full, tall." [Sn] "Flower crimson, borne in panicles, continuously produced in summer and autumn. Double flowered. Autumn blooms further enhanced by bright coral hips succeeding the earlier flowers. Growth vigorous." [GeH] "Very vigorous bush, foliage very green, glossy, nine leaflets; flower very large, very full, the beautiful satiny pink called 'old rose' (a new coloration), in a cluster, very floriferous. Of premier merit, to be recommended for pot culture and for forcing. Blooms till frost." [JR19/130]

Cibles
Kaufmann, 1894
From *Rosa rugosa* 'Rubra' × 'Perle de Lyon' (T).

"Carmine on a yellow ground." [Ÿ] "Carmine, white centre." [NRS15/45] "Red, medium size, single, medium scent, tall." [Sn] "Medium large, single flowers of carmine red with a yellow base, darker and a little velvety in the Fall, with a little scent. The buds are well-shaped, elongate, pointed, and short-stemmed. The large, strong, and dark green foliage, glossy and slightly wrinkled above, light green and not wrinkled beneath, consists of 7 lanceolate leaflets that are colored maroon when young. The growth is enormous. Fed well, it grows up to tree-size; the thick branches are densely covered with long, sharp, various-sized prickles. It blooms profusely in clusters throughout the Summer. Especially recommended as a single specimen growing on the lawn." [URZ7/2/6–8] "Blooming almost continuously during the Summer; only at the end of August are some thin twigs affected with mildew. Surely this rose would flourish more if cut back after the first crop … Though the growth is not adequate for growing as a standard, it is better as a naturally-growing shrub, especially because the buds are comparable to those of any known exhibition variety." [URZ8/2/4–5]

Comte d'Epremesnil
Nabonnand, 1881

"Lilac red." [Ÿ] "Violet pink, large, lightly double, very fragrant, tall." [Sn] "Has double flowers of a deep reddish violet, not one of the most attractive. It is a strong grower and will reach 7-ft. [ca. 2.3 m] or more if unpruned." [NRS15/37] "Violet-y lilac. —Flowers large, half-full, very fragrant; very large orange red fruits; has some flowers, ripe fruits, and green fruits all at the same time; vigorous; very remontant." [Cx] "Very vigorous bush, flower large, semi-full, very fragrant, violet-y lilac. This variety is a seedling of the single Japan Rose, of which it keeps the make-up. I [Nabonnand] have had this variety for two years; it came from seeds from the Universal Exposition of 1878 [in Paris]; only one seed of five sprouted." [JR5/148]

Conrad Ferdinand Meyer   Plate 37
Müller/Froebel, 1899
From a seedling (resulting from a cross of 'Gloire de Dijon' [N] and 'Duc de Rohan' [HP]) × 'Germanica' (Rg).

"Clear silvery rose, especially good in bud-form." [ARA17/29] "This remontant rose develops superb roses in which the tender pink coloration somewhat resembles that of 'La France' [B or HT]." [JR25/116–117] "Splendid, large, elegantly formed buds and flowers, 3½ to 4 inches across [ca. 9 cm to 1 dm] and perfectly double—color, rich peachy yellow, delicately tinged with silver rose; very fragrant, entirely hardy and valuable in every way." [C&Js07] "Light pink, large, full, medium scent, tall." [Sn] "Color is clear silvery rose; very attractive; intensely fragrant; hardy and a very vigorous grower. Makes a grand hedge with masses of Roses in June and occasional blooms until frost." [C&Js21] "It generally gives us the first well shaped double Rose in the garden towards the end of May. Everyone should grow it." [NRS15/38] "Does not bloom until the second year after planting. The foliage differs from [that of] the Type in being less corrugated and tinted with bronze." [C-Ps31] "Very fragrant, silvery pink flowers of large size, equal to [those of] Hybrid Teas in form. It blooms heavily in June and occasionally thereafter. The bush is extremely vigorous—give it plenty of room, at least 3 feet on every side [ca. 1 m]; or against a building or over an archway, its 6, 8, or 10 feet of growth may easily be trained [to ca. 3.3 m] … The plant, while not so hardy, is sufficiently rugged for almost all situations." [C-Ps25] "If there is a wet fall and it grows late, it frequently winterkills badly after several seasons of successful culture. The main thing is to restrict feeding it heavily after midsummer, so the wood has a chance to ripen properly. In the drier sections of the mid-West it appears to withstand more cold successfully." [ARA29/123] "In America, they very frequently talk about this beautiful Rugosa hybrid which has a superb flowering; *The American Florist* says that this rose is especially pretty when the wood of the previous year is not pruned; this is in a garden planted in groups of various specimens, producing a grand effect, not only because of its many blossoms, but also because of its beautiful foliage. Our colleague adds that it was Dr. Müller who had gotten a cross of 'Gloire de Dijon' [N] and 'Duc de Rohan' [HP]. Upon this specimen, he dusted the pollen which he had taken from the Rugosa 'Germanica', whence came 'Conrad Ferdinand Meyer', which is thus of mixed parentage. It can't be doubted that it is these crossings and recrossings which have given us our best varieties, such we believe being the case with 'Gruss an Teplitz' [B]. It is particularly in Western America that the rose in question pleases the most; they don't prune it, only curbing the strong growths, [making] new side-stems grow from the trunk, and giving an abundant bloom." [JR32/166]

"This variety offers the eye not only a flower of extraordinary beauty, but also a shrub truly perfect in form; it is remontant, resists frost quite well, and is not bothered by insects or fungus. It is evident that this rose is due great success. Dr. Müller, who has already endowed the world with several varieties of great value, raised this new seedling in 1893. As for the rest, here is what the breeder has written to us about this rose: This variety came from the cross of a seedling arising from a cross of 'Gloire de Dijon' and 'Duc de Rohan', this seedling being the mother, with the Rugosa 'Germanica' as the father. 'Germanica' is a chance seedling or indeed a sport of a seedling of 'Kaiserin des Nordens' [Rg] of 1887. As to the other details about it: It was the firm of Otto Froebel of Zurich which released this variety to commerce, giving it at that time the name of a celebrated breeder who had been dead for several years, Herr Conrad Ferdinand Meyer of Zurich. It is due to our particular request [*that of the editor of the*

Conrad Ferdinand Meyer *continued*

Rosen-Zeitung, *an article from which is being quoted in the* Journal des Roses] that this present article appears; though this rose has been out for two years and has been heard of, it is true, it is not as well known as it should be. During its first year [of release], some gardeners and fanciers grew this variety, and it is thereby that its value became known…Here is the description of this variety, as given in 1899: The plant is strong and grows well, bearing well the Winter's cold; the wood is very thorny; it is remontant and looks very much like a true Rugosa. The leaf is large, thick, and each one grows to 18 cm long [ca. 7 in]; the form of the leaf[let] is rounded, but very elegant. The blossom, which is large, grows to 10–12 centimeters across [ca. 4–4³/₄ in], is full, well-formed, silvery pink, and highly scented. The buds, which are very beautiful, resembling those of 'La France', except more erect, and then, when the rose opens, [a blossom of] 'Baronne [Adolphe de] Rothschild' with thicker petals. This variety is certainly one of the most beautiful of the Rugosas seen up till now; it is certainly one of the fullest, best formed, longest lasting, and most fragrant. That is why it is called upon to play a very great role in adorning the garden as well as in the uses of cut-flowers. Last year, we had in our garden a two-year-old plant that had, all at the same time, up to forty blossoms. These flowers seem to be made to be part of the prettiest vase of flowers you could imagine. The blooms fruit easily, and we hope to make some sowings which will give us a new variety. 'Conrad Ferdinand Meyer' is the perfect rose for a cottage gardener as well as for the mere fancier who can give his roses enough room. It's also an excellent variety for septentrional areas." [JR26/67–68]

"It has a very vigorous growth of stiff, upright, and only slightly branching habit. It throws up strong stems 8-ft. high [ca. 2.6 m], densely armed with very numerous prickles of two kinds, the one kind large, sharp, and straight, or sloping downwards and persistent, the other much smaller and weaker, straight, and falling off with the leaves in autumn. The stems are decidedly brittle, and if not looked after in the autumn will be found badly broken and lacerated by their own thorns when pruning time comes round again. The foliage is large, dark green, slightly glossy on the upper surface, and abundant, but standing well out from the upright stems it gives the plant rather the appearance of a flowering shrub than a garden Rose. It is a little liable to mildew, but not badly so, as a rule, though once or twice I have suffered from a bad attack. This is certainly a weakness, for the rugosas as a race are free from this trouble. It has two distinct flowering periods, the first in the beginning of June, the second the end of July and early August…This is not so profuse as the early flowering, nor so definite, and the plant continues to give occasional flowers into the late autumn…Miss Langton tells me of a plant that has failed for two years to flower at all. The blossoms are very large, full and shapely, and are carried singly, or in two's and three's; they are deliciously fragrant with a real Rose scent. The colour is satiny pink, with silvery pink edges. Though a beautiful soft colour it does not harmonise well with many of the modern highly-coloured Roses. It looks well in a vase indoors when first picked, but has no lasting power in water, the stems soon going limp, and the flowers drooping before they die. In this respect, it is a true rugosa … The Rose does not, as do the true rugosas, make a mass of red fruits in autumn … The strong points of 'Conrad Ferdinand Meyer' are its robust habit and hardiness, its earliness, the beauty and fragrance of its blossoms and—Mr. Molyneux

adds—its thorns. Its weakness is its short flowering period and the length of time during the season in which it has but few flowers on the plant." [NRS11/34–36]

Crispata Plate 24
Kiese/J. C. Schmidt, 1902
"A light carmine coloration, with single flowers, but beautiful in effect." [JR30/124]

[Daniel Lesueur]
Gravereaux/Cochet-Cochet, 1908
From a seedling (arising from a cross of 'Pierre Notting' [HP] and 'Safrano' [T]) × *Rosa rugosa*.
"Buds salmon-pink to coppery pink; open blooms light yellow, large, double, fair form; fruit in fall. Vigorous, but a poor grower, and should be trained to pillar or fence." [Th2] "Vigorous bush. Canes green, armed with sparse, remote, nearly straight thorns intermixed with some stickers. Leaves generally 5-foliage. Leaflets medium-sized, elliptical, lanceolate, a beautiful green, resembling in form and color the foliage of the Tea, not that of the Rugosa at all. Bud long, nankeen yellow, nuanced dawn-pink. Flower large, cupped, pale nankeen yellow, nub of the petals canary yellow." [JR32/168] Th2 gives the attribution and date as: Müller, 1909. Daniel Lesueur, *nom de plume* of Jeanne Lapauze, French novelist, lived 1860–1921.

Delicata
Cooling & Sons, 1898
"Flower soft rose; large double. Very free. Continuous." [GeH] "This variety is thoroughly distinct from the other Rugosas. It is an excellent plant for garden ornament. The double, delicate pink, large blossoms come in bouquets. The very hardy bush is extremely floriferous." [JR22/70] "This has soft, rose-pink flowers, freely produced. The petals are large and a pleasing colour when fresh. It is one of the best. It is a fairly strong grower and makes a big bush if left alone." [NRS15/38] "Pink, large, lightly double, tall." [Sn] "Vigorous." [Cat12]

[Dolly Varden]
G. Paul, 1914
"Light apricot-pink, with rosy flesh centre; cupped." [GeH] "Light apricot-pink with a yellow base; blooms well but is not of as large growth as [such cultivars as 'Blanc Double de Coubert' and 'Conrad Ferdinand Meyer']." [ARA17/29] "Buds show deep yellow, opening light salmon-peach; semi-double; of good shape when half open. Fairly vigorous. Continuous bloomer near Philadelphia. Needs thinning in spring. Evidently with HT or T [or Pern] blood." [Th2] "The flower is semi-double, of a soft peach pink colour, with orange pink buds, the petals are rather longer, and the buds more pointed than in the case with most of the Rugosas, and the flower is often prettily shaped. Its growth is of quite manageable dimensions, and it will form a neat bush when grown, from 3-ft. to 4-ft. high [ca. 1–1.3 m]." [NRS15/38–39]

Dr. Eckener
V. Berger/Teschendorff
From 'Golden Emblem' (HT) × *Rosa rugosa* cultivar.
"Pinkish yellow flowers; typical Rugosa plant; useful for parks and gardens." [ARA31/205] "Orange yellow, coppery pink center, large, lightly double, medium scent, tall." [Sn] "The flowers are delightfully perfumed and they have the simplicity and charm of a native wild

Rose . . . [It] blooms intermittently all season." [C-Ps32] "Large, fragrant, semi-double flowers of coppery rose and golden yellow; very fragrant. Really a Hybrid Tea flower on a Rugosa plant. Remontant. Five to six feet [ca. 1.6–2 m]." [Way45] "Bud large, ovoid, deep yellow; flower large, semi-double, cupped, lasting, fragrant, golden yellow when fully open, coppery rose color in the center on yellow ground (does not burn). Foliage sufficient, large. Growth very vigorous; abundant, intermittent bloomer all season. Very hardy." [ARA31/244] "Spinel pink. We observed this Rose most particularly in our trial-grounds last season because it is said to bloom yellow in its native Germany, but here the color is pink with a golden yellow base. The sweetly perfumed blooms open in a wide cup, almost 4 inches across [ca. 1 dm], and the spinel pink color is enchanting. The plant grows 4 feet high [ca. 1.3 m] and the foliage is large, leathery, and noticeably healthy. A truly fine acquisition that may bloom yellow in some localities or when the plant becomes acclimated." [C-Ps31] "A new, deep golden yellow Rugosa hybrid. It blooms very early and the plant is the same type as 'Conrad Ferdinand Meyer' [Rg]. We believe it will make a fine rose for hedges and park use." [ARA31/180] "An improvement on the hardy park roses. Flower large, yellow, tinted with orange. Growth very vigorous, healthy." [ARA30/225] "Especially handsome." [W] See also its sport, 'Golden King' (Rg).

F. J. Grootendorst

de Goey/Grootendorst, 1918
From *Rosa rugosa* 'Rubra' × 'Mme. Norbert Levavasseur' (Pol).

"Bright red, double, and fringed. A cross between Rugosa and Polyantha, produced in clusters from June until frost." [GeH] "A hundred times more satisfactory to use than its awkward Holland name is to say! It is a continuous bloomer of flowers that look like red carnations, but, as with all the continuous blooming roses, there is no great burst of bloom at one time." [ARA22/48–49] "Red, small, full, medium scent, tall." [Sn] "Bud small, ovoid; flower small, open, double, borne in clusters on average-length stems; very lasting; slight fragrance. Color bright red; edges of petals serrated like a carnation. Foliage sufficient, small, leathery, wrinkled, dark green; disease resistant. Vigorous grower of bushy habit, bearing a profusion of blooms from June to October. Very hardy." [ARA20/135] "Bright red flowers of small size, fringed and double, produced freely and continuously in large bunches, through spring, summer, and fall. It will, if allowed, in three years, reach a height of 5 feet or more [ca. 1.6 m +], with foliage almost equal to the original Rugosa. Though it can easily be kept lower, it makes a splendid shrub or specimen bush, or the finest type of everblooming hedge." [C-Ps25] "It will retain its qualities better if pruned each year, leaving only the wood formed the previous season." [C-Ps27] "Of vigorous, spreading habit, its thorny branches grow to a height f 6 feet or more [ca. 2 m +], with wonderful, large, disease-free foliage. It would be very ornamental even if it never bloomed, but covered as it is all season with its large clusters of small, bright red, double flowers with petals notched like carnations, it is a gem. The flowers are very durable, but scentless and sterile." [ARA29/124] "Its fine habit and good foliage afford a handsome background for its perpetual unfading red blossoms. It, and its pink sport already reported ['Pink F. J. Grootendorst'], reveal new possibilities for good hedge roses that may be evolved from the many colored ramblers and Polyanthas." [ARA25/206] "I [*unidentified 'Holland nurseryman'*] was among the jury that gave the first award to this rose. It was in the

nursery of a very small fellow, and I remember that we gave it the highest award because we thought of the great possibilities of this rose in a rough climate. Some people have blamed us for it, but I am still proud of my share in it." [ARA24/186] "Of much merit." [Th2]

Fimbriata Plate 25

syn. 'Phoebe's Frilled Pink'
Morlet, 1891
From *Rosa rugosa* × 'Mme. Alfred Carrière' (N).

"Delicate blush, edged like a Chinese Primula, semi-double. Growth vigorous." [GeH] "Light pink, medium size, lightly double, medium scent, tall." [Sn] "This is a very pretty variety. The flowers are white tinted and edged blush, and are remarkable in having the margins of the petals fringed or serrated, rather like a pink. The flowers are single. The growth is moderate, and it forms a bush about 4-ft. high [ca. 1.3 m]." [NRS15/39] "Vigorous bush, very floriferous, making a shrub 2–3 meters high and nearly the same across [ca. 6–9 ft], canes with mostly glabrous bark, sometimes bearing minuscule bristles; leaves divided into 5 rarely 7 sessile oval leaflets, terminal leaflet attenuate, rounded at the two ends, glabrous, a beautiful gay green, glossy above, glaucous green beneath; obviously and regularly, but shallowly, dentate; flowers numerous, usually in a slightly nodding cluster, sometimes making a bouquet of 15–25 blossoms; buds flesh pink; hip elongate, enveloped by sepals which are connate to the base, soon and completely reflexed after the flower opens; flower semi-double, fairly large, very well formed, very elegant before completely open; petals unequal, obovate, upright at first, fimbriated at the tip, fading to a very lightly fleshed pink; stamens numerous with subspherical anthers, unequal white filaments, styles irregular; peduncles glabrous, upright or slightly nodding, hip supspherical, often broader than long, very glabrous, glaucescent green, fruits abundant, smaller than those of [typical] Rugosa." [JR15/105] "Many a time have we spoken of *Rosa rugosa* and the ornamental effect which places it among our best shrubs. Each year, the number of varieties in this category grows, and this sort of rose certainly holds some pleasant surprises in store for us. Among the varieties already known, there is one which is particularly striking in its very odd way of blooming; it is *Rosa rugosa* 'Fimbriata', raised by Monsieur Morlet, horticulturist of Avon (Seine-et-Marne), and released by him to commerce in 1891 . . . [It] is the result of a cross between *R. rugosa* and 'Mme. Alfred Carrière'. It is a very vigorous bush, making a plant to two meters in height [ca. 6 ft] and about as wide. It is very floriferous, giving 15–20 blossoms [in a cluster], semi-full, pretty big, well formed, pale pink fading to light flesh white, with petals toothed like a saw, an anomaly which, to our knowledge, exists only in this rose and in the *R. Ciliato petala* that Besser reports having collected in Lithuania, and which is treated pretty lengthily in the 5th fascicle of Crépin's *Primatiae monographiae rosarum*. This variety blooms from June to October . . . We much recommend this Rugosa, which is very distinct from the others in its group." [JR20/136]

Frau Dagmar Hastrup Listed as 'Fru Dagmar Hartopp' (Rg).

Fru Dagmar Hartopp

syn. 'Frau Dagmar Hastrup'
Hastrup, 1914
Seedling of *R. rugosa*.

"Light pink, medium size, single, medium to tall." [Sn] Though we

Fru Dagmar Hartopp *continued*

have seen statements—and very self-assured ones, too—about the "Hastrup" version of the name being the correct one, no data or references have been offered to back these statements up; meantime, in the earliest reference we have found (Jg, which derives from data brought together in Germany in the 1920s and early 1930s), "Hartopp" is what is listed, without any mention of "Hastrup" as the name of the cultivar. The surname "Hartopp" does exist.

Fürstin von Pless

trans. "Princess von Pless"
Lambert, 1911
From 'Mme. Caroline Testout' (HT) × 'Conrad Ferdinand Meyer' (Rg).

"White with lemon centre, very large, full, sweetly scented. Vigorous." [GeH] "Full, medium scent, tall." [Sn] "Bush very vigorous, upright, with strongly-thorned canes; foliage rough; buds large, strong, solitary or perhaps in threes on long and vigorous shoots; opening without difficulty; flower large or very large, of very beautiful form, white with a yellow center tinted light pink; fragrant, perfume persists … Absolutely hardy. The Rugosa characteristics are evident." [JR36/41]

George Will

Skinner, 1939
From a seedling (resulting from a cross of *Rosa rugosa* and *R. acicularis*) × an unknown rose.

"Deep pink, medium size, full, medium scent, tall." [Sn]

Georges Cain

syn. 'Monsieur Georges Cain'
Gravereaux/Cochet-Cochet, 1908
From 'Pierre Notting' (HP) × *Rosa rugosa*.

"Amaranth, nuanced purple." [Ÿ] "Dark red, large, full, tall." [Sn] "The darkest Rugosa, and the tallest as well. Leaves and blossoms colossal, the latter being semi-double. Amaranth with purple and black." [Ck] "Very dark, fairly double flowers, freely produced on a bush with very large, rugose foliage. Extremely hardy." [ARA29/124] "Very vigorous bush. Canes upright, purplish, armed with thorns which are strong, nearly straight, sparse, apparently equal. Leaves 7-foliate; leaflets elliptical, bright green above, bullate as with the greater part of the Rugosa hybrids. Long bud. Flower large, double, amaranth nuanced purple." [JR32/166] Dr. Müller, of 'Conrad Ferdinand Meyer' fame, may have had a hand in the breeding of this.

Germanica

syn. 'Germanica A'
Müller, 1890
Seedling of or sport of a seedling of 'Kaiserin des Nordens' (Rg).

"Deep violet." [Ÿ] "Deep violet red, medium size, full, very fragrant, tall" [Sn] "This variety has single Rose coloured flowers. It is of moderate growth, making a bush 3-ft. or 4-ft. in height [ca. 1–1.3 m]. The chief interest of this plant, for the possession of which I am indebted to the kindness of Monsieur Jules Gravereaux, lies in its having been the parent of 'Conrad Ferdinand Meyer' [Rg] and some other members of the group. Dr. Müller seems to have brought out another Rose of the same name in 1900, which I have not seen." [NRS15/39] See also 'Germanica B' (Rg).

Germanica A   Listed as 'Germanica' (Rg).

Germanica B

Müller, 1900
"Red violet." [Ÿ]

Golden King

Beckwith, 1935
Sport of 'Dr. Eckener' (Rg).

"Light yellow, large, lightly double, very fragrant, tall." [Sn]

Goldener Traum

trans. "Golden Dream"
J. C. Schmidt/Türke, 1932
From 'Türke's Rugosa-Sämling' (Rg) × 'Constance' (Pern).

As we read in Griffiths, large, fragrant deep yellow flowers with pinkish red streaks on the buds on a healthy and vigorous plant.

Grootendorst Supreme

Grootendorst, 1936
Sport of 'F. J. Grootendorst' (Rg).

"Deep red, small, full, light scent, tall." [Sn] "An improved variety having large, fringed, cherry-red flowers borne on a fine, large, well-foliaged bush. Excellent as a hedge." [Way45]

Hansa

Schaunt & Van Tol, 1905
"Reddish purple; double. Very vigorous." [Th2] "Purple red, large, full, tall." [Sn] "Freely produces double reddish violet flowers on a very vigorous plant of exceptional hardiness; sets fruits." [ARA29/123] Ÿ gives the attribution "Joda Exp. Stat. Schaum, 1905." Not to be confused with 'Hansen' (Rg), *i.e.*, 'Prof. N. E. Hansen' (Rg).

Hansen   Listed as 'Prof. N. E. Hansen' (Rg).

Heterophylla

trans. "Differing Leaves"
Cochet-Cochet, 1899
From *Rosa rugosa* × *R. foetida*.

"Rather snowy white or cream coloured flowers, carried in small trusses, single or nearly so. It is a somewhat dwarf grower, my plant, which I have had for some years, never having attained more than 2-ft. in height [ca. 6 dm], and only possesses two shoots. I have never seen any berries on the plant, which appears to be quite sterile." [NRS15/46] "A small yellow rose of the cluster type and the forerunner of the Polyantha-Rugosa form, now [*1925*] typified in 'F. J. Grootendorst' [Rg]." [ARA25/59] "I don't sell this hybrid as a Decorative. In the final analysis, its semi-double white blossoms, three centimeters across [ca. 1¼ in], in false-corymbs of 5–10, bear little of interest to rose fanciers. But I strongly recommend this rose to botanists as being, like *R. berberifolia* (Pallas) and *Watsoniana* (Crépin), one of the most bizarre forms of genus *Rosa*. In Spring, the various leaves which come first are normal. But soon the bush covers itself with a multitude of leaves composed of three pairs of leaflets, 4–5 centimeters long [ca. 2 in] by 3–4 millimeters wide [ca. ⅛ in]. This very singular leaflet-form, added to a similarity in growth, gives 'Heterophylla' a general air more or less of 'Watsoniana' [Mult]." [JR23/170]

Hildenbrandseck

syn. 'Hildenbranseck'
Lambert, 1909
From 'Atropurpurea' (Rg) × 'Frau Karl Druschki' (HP).

"Bright carmine." [Ÿ] "Red, medium size, lightly double, tall." [Sn] "This plant makes a very pleasing bush or a bushy pillar up to 8-ft. high [ca. 2.6 m]. Its flowers are a silvery rose and produced quite continuously the summer through. It makes no red berries." [NRS15/39] "Makes a very vigorous shrub 6 feet or more in height [ca. 2 m +], clothed with waxy, rather small leaves having little trace of the Rugosa blood, but very healthy. It bears its semi-double, light carmine flowers in clusters, very continuously. Appears to be quite hardy, and though generally reported sterile, mine seeds sparingly." [ARA29/124]

Hildenbranseck Listed as 'Hildenbrandseck' (Rg).

Himalayensis Listed as 'Kaiserin des Nordens' (Rg).

Jelina
Kaufmann, 1894
From *Rosa rugosa* 'Rubra' × 'Perle de Lyon' (T).

"Dark velvety carmine." [Ÿ] "Large, scented, short-stemmed, double but irregular blossoms colored carmine red, blooming profusely, and recurrent. The huge leaf consists of 7 leaflets, and measures up to 20 cm [ca. 8 in] from bottom to top. The leaflets are elliptical, dark green, very stiff, and extremely resistant, enameled glossy and sulcate above, not glossy beneath. The plant is strong-growing, and has a fine bushy habit; the strong branches are densely covered with variously sized prickles. Because the flowers are irregular in form, this variety is more remarkable as a deciduous shrub. The unique foliage is recommended for festoons." [URZ7/2/6–8] "Its dense, glossy, and healthy foliage has proved extraordinary again. This rose with its fine bushy growth and dark green, unusual foliage would ornament any pleasure ground." [URZ8/2/4–5]

Jindřich Hanus Böhm
Böhm, 1937
"Red, large, full, very fragrant, tall." [Sn]

Kaiserin des Nordens
syns. 'Himalayensis', 'Regeliana Flore Pleno', 'Regeliana Rubra', 'Rouge Pleine', 'Rubra Flore Pleno', 'Rubra Plena', 'Zuccariniana'; trans., "Empress of the Northerners"
Regel, 1879
"Blossom purple violet." [S] "Crimson, large and double; growth moderate." [P1] *Cf.* 'Taïcoun' (Rg), which is possibly (or probably) synonymous.

Kitana
Hansen, 1927
From 'Tetonkaha' (Rg) × 'Rose Apples' (Rg).
"Violet pink, large, lightly full, very fragrant, medium to tall." [Sn] "A vigorous, hardy, semi-double pink rose, blooming very freely in June and into July. Flowers 3 inches in diameter [ca. 7.5 cm], intensely fragrant; about 36 petals and 25 petaloids. Red fruit sets freely. Flowers are somewhat globular with little pollen; deep lavender pink." [ARA27/227]

Koza
Hansen, 1927
From a seedling (resulting from a cross of 'Siberian Form' [Rg] and 'La France' [B or HT]) × 'La Mélusine' (Rg).
"Deep pink, medium size, lightly double, tall." [Sn] "Vigorous plant,

over 7 feet in height [ca. 2.3 m +]; a profuse bloomer through July and into August. Flowers semi-double; deep pink." [ARA27/227]

La Mélusine
Späth, 1906
"Carmine crimson." [NRS15/45] "Violet red." [Ÿ] "Rose-red, large, full, very fragrant, tall." [Sn] "Blossom large, full, quite abundant, deep carmine red. Bloom continuous in large clusters, very effective." [Ck] "Very similar [in color to 'Hansa' (Rg)], with a wonderful perfume, and is free-blooming." [ARA29/123] "Has been one of the outstanding Rugosa hybrids. The color is something of a purplish crimson, like 'Hansa'; the fragrance is powerful, and it blooms until frost. This variety seems to have been neglected by American propagators. 'La Mélusine' was imported from Europe some twenty years ago, and has proved hardy. It is one of my favorites, owing to its intense fragrance." [ARA28/71]

Lady Curzon
Turner, 1901
From *Rosa macrantha* × *R. rugosa* 'Rubra'; frequently called a Damask, for reasons as yet undetermined.
"Large single pink, with golden anthers; very effective massed in the wild garden and orchard hedgerow." [NRS30/216] "Delicate pale pink, single. A good hybrid damask; early summer flowering. Growth vigorous." [GeH] "Very large pale pink single flowers … it is one of the most fiercely armed of all roses, and if one of its wide-flung branches catches in one's clothing it is no pleasant task to get free with bare hands." [NRS20/30, where called a Hybrid Rugosa] "The only climber in the Damask family. Very interesting sort, almost high-climbing, with heavy, beautiful foliage. Blossoms large, single, centifolia pink —the plant is covered with pink stars." [Ck] "The beautiful 'Lady Curzon' is a modern addition [to the Damask race], and has all the ancient fragrance in its pale single pink flowers. The habit is strong and almost a climber, and it is thus very well placed in a shrubbery or against a low wall." [ARA30/33] "Very good. Can be grown as a pillar Rose." [NRS30/203]

Le Cid
Vigneron, 1908
From 'Conrad Ferdinand Meyer' (Rg) × 'Belle Poitevine' (Rg).
"Vermilion pink." [Ÿ] "Dazzling crimson, large. Growth vigorous." [GeH] "I have found this Rose somewhat disappointing. It is described as a bright crimson, but the flowers borne by my plant have been a dull reddish rose, semi-double. It has not developed proper berries." [NRS15/46] "Vigorous and bushy shrub, foliage very dark glossy green; flower very large, full, very beautifully colored vermilion pink, superb. The blossom, one of the largest in this group, is borne on a very strong stem, and is usually solitary." [JR32/134] Le Cid, alias El Cid, alias Roderigo (or Ruy) Diaz de Bivar, alias El Campeador, Spanish national hero, lived ca. 1040–1099.

Lilli Dieck
Dieck, 1899
From *Rosa rugosa* × *R. gallica*.
"Red." [Ÿ]

Magnifica
Van Fleet/Conard & Jones, 1907
"Deep red, large, full, tall." [Sn] "A free and constant bloomer, with

Magnifica *continued*

lovely, brilliant carmine buds, which develop into purplish flowers." [ARA25/206] "Wide, firm leaves. Blossom bright deep blood red; ever-blooming." [Ck] "Intense, pungent fragrance which is so strong it scents the air around. A specimen plant, 5 years old, has bloomed unceasingly from late May until November. This plant was on a N.E. corner and shaded from the hot afternoon sun." [C&Js13] "New 1907. Introduced and for sale only by the Conard and Jones Co. —A magnificent rose; a splendid acquisition in this valuable class; stock limited. Its foliage and habit of growth are quite as fine as [those of] 'New Century' [Rg] and 'Sir Thomas Lipton' [Rg] . . . and its flowers, we think, surpass anything in this line yet introduced. The color is brilliant carmine, which in the buds have a depth and richness beyond description. This shades to a rosier hue, as the flowers open full. Size is often 4 to 5 inches across [ca. 1–1.25 dm]. Deliciously fragrant and will thrive where others fail." [C&Js07]

Margheritae
Vilmorin, date uncertain

We have been unable to obtain any information on this cultivar, and record it to spur on others to research.

Mercedes
P. Guillot, 1900

"Very hardy and vigorous shrub; blossom large, full, well formed, very fragrant, delicate carnation pink on a white ground, outer petals white, new coloration for this series, very beautiful variety." [JR24/146]

Mikado
Morlet, 1888

"Bright red." [Ÿ] "Deep red, large, full, tall." [Sn] Mikado, title of the Emperor of Japan; more familiarly, and probably more to the point in this case, *The Mikado*, outstanding comic opera by William S. Gilbert and Arthur Sullivan that premiered March 14, 1885, to great popular and critical success.

Minisa
Hansen, 1927
From 'Siberian Form' (Rg) × 'Prince Camille de Rohan' (HP).

"Deep red, medium size, lightly double, very fragrant, medium to tall." [Sn] "Not very double, having only about 17 petals and petaloids. Deep crimson with rich fragrance. A free bloomer." [ARA27/227]

Mme. Alvarez del Campo
Gravereaux, 1903
From 'Gloire de Dijon' (N) × *Rosa rugosa*.

"Lightly salmoned flesh pink." [Ÿ] "Has large buds and flowers, rosy flesh tinted salmon. Of the many varieties of *rugosa* I have tried as pillar Roses this is one of the few I have retained in this form." [NRS15/46] "Very vigorous bush, with superb bright foliage seemingly proof against the fungal diseases which often affect hybrids—especially the *Rugosa* ones. Canes strong, with straight thorns, relatively few in number, interspersed with setaceous thorns and stipulate glands. Bud very large, perfectly formed. Flower very large, very fragrant, a superb light pink with some salmon, somewhat resembling [that of] 'Pink Rover' [Cl HT]. Absolutely unique coloration among the *Rugosas* and their hybrids." [JR27/165]

Mme. Ancelot
Gravereaux & Müller/Cochet-Cochet, 1905
Two slightly differing parentages have been published: (1) from a seedling (resulting from a cross of 'Reine des Île-Bourbons' [B] and 'Maréchal Niel' [N]) × a seedling (resulting from a cross of 'Perle des Jardins' [T] and 'Germanica' [Rg]); (2) from a seedling (resulting from the cross of another seedling [which itself resulted from a cross of 'Reine des Île-Bourbons' (B) and 'Perle des Jardins' (T)] and 'Maréchal Niel' [N]) × 'Germanica' (Rg).

"Delicate pink." [Ÿ] "Whitish pink, large, full, medium scent, tall." [Sn] "Glossy leaves; Tea-blood evident in the blossom, very large, quite full, fresh pink with silver reflection; blooms up until frost." [Ck] "This has large double flowers, flesh pink with lighter reflexes. It is a very big grower, and in good soil attained some 10-ft. or 12-ft. in height [ca. 3.3–4 m]. Not finding the flowers very attractive I moved it to a shrubbery border, where it has proved more manageable." [NRS15/40] "At Coubert (S[eine]-et-M[arne]), Monsieur Cochet-Cochet is selling this Fall a new sort of Kamchatka Rose (Rugosa) coming from a crop from the Roseraie de l'Haÿ. Here is the description: . . . Very vigorous bush with strong canes of a gray green, reddish around the tip and sometimes on the sunny side. Bark completely covered with very small straight thorns, which are unequal, setiform, glandular-stipitate, and mixed with a few strong somewhat hooked thorns. Foliage ample, of a beautiful bright green, the edge of the young leaflets reddish because of the Tea in its heritage. Blossoms very large, quite double, perfectly formed; color, very fresh flesh pink with silvery reflections. Flowers come singly or in few-flowered clusters, lasting until the autumnal frosts. This new Rugosa hybrid—very remontant—is certainly one of the best obtentions from the Roseraie de l'Haÿ." [JR29/152]

Mme. Ballu
Gravereaux/Cochet-Cochet, 1904
From 'Général Jacqueminot' (HP) × a seedling (which resulted from a cross between 'Souvenir de la Malmaison' [B] and *Rosa rugosa*).

"Soft rose pink, a pretty colour but poor shape. It is a strong grower reaching 6-ft. to 8-ft. in height [ca. 2–2.6 m]." [NRS15/40] "Deep violet pink, medium size, lightly double, tall." [Sn] "Very vigorous bush, with bloom continuing up until the Autumn frosts. Canes extrusive, with green or reddish bark bestrewn with large, nearly straight, reddish thorns. Foliage a beautiful green, having little in common with that of the Rugosa. Flower medium-sized, beautiful delicate pink, sometimes with silvery reflections." [JR28/156]

Mme. Charles Frédéric Worth
Widow Schwartz, 1889

"Carmine red." [Ÿ] "Semi-double; rosy carmine." [ARA17/29] "This has double carmine coloured flowers carried in large bunches. It is a vigorous grower and makes a good bush some 5-ft. or 6-ft. high." [NRS15/40] "Very vigorous bush forming a shrub; big-wooded, less thorny than the Type; foliage very abundant, a magnificent somber green, with rugose leaflets, glossy as if varnished. Flowers large, full, in clusters, well formed, beautiful carmine red, very fragrant." [JR13/163]

Mme. G. Bruant   Listed as 'Mme. Georges Bruant' (Rg)

Mme. Georges Bruant

Bruant, 1887

From *Rosa rugosa* 'Alba' × 'Mlle. de Sombreuil' (T).

"Large, loosely double flowers of pure white and richly fragrant. A very decorative Rose." [C&Js24] "The very large, loosely double flowers are lacking in petals, and are of the finest shade of delicate, pearly white, with as rich a fragrance as I have ever found in any rose." [ARA25/206] "Blossom large, nearly full, dazzling white, bud long, reblooms excellently up until frost. Top-of-the-line variety." [Ck] "A moderate grower, with very healthy, rugose foliage and bunches of loosely formed, fragrant flowers of the purest waxy white, very continuously produced. The flowers are delicate in texture, because of the Tea blood, and yet the plant is quite hardy." [ARA29/122] "Flower paper-white, large, semi-double, produced in corymbs. Growth very vigorous, very floriferous." [GeH] "This is a double white variety, nearly full, and often comes a fair shape. It comes into flower a little later than 'Blanc Double de Coubert', and though of better form is not so showy in the garden, nor is it quite so pure a white. It is said to have the same parentage as this Rose . . . but while 'Blanc Double de Coubert' is nearer to the typical *R. rugosa,* 'Mme. Georges Bruant' partakes more of the Hybrid Teas (see *Jo. R.H.S.,* vol. 29, p. 42). Both varieties have much the same vigour of growth, 5-ft. to 7-ft. [ca. 1.6–2.3 m]." [NRS15/41] "[It] was still not in bloom [at Cheshunt], but easy it was indeed to pick out in the middle of all the others, its wood covered with thorns and its foliage being nearly the same as that of Rugosa itself." [JR12/106]

"Monsieur Bruant, Poitiers horticulturist, sent us some blossoms of a rose arising from his sowings which he will have for sale this Fall under the name 'Mme. G. Bruant'. The stem he sent us arrived in pretty good condition despite the long trip; it seems very interesting. This product of a cross between Rosa Rugosa and the Tea '[Mlle. de] Sombreuil' is certainly a point of departure from the series of Japanese hybrids. The clustered flowers are numerous, double, and a beautiful white. This rose will be good for growing in the North, having the great hardiness of Rosa Rugosa, the principal characteristics of which it preserves." [JR11/162] "This new variety, which distinguishes itself at first sight from all others known, came from a cross of *Rosa Rugosa* (a Japanese species with single flowers) and the Tea '[Mlle. de] Sombreuil'; it is a starting point for a new class of hybrids deserving of all attention. The bush is extraordinarily vigorous, always growing and always covered with flowers up to when the frost would destroy them; it is the first rose to open, and the last to bud. The blossoms, in umbels of 6–12, are large, wide open, semi-full, and a sparkling white; they waft a delicious perfume which is very sweet and penetrating. The foliage resembles that of the Rugosa, but it nevertheless is modified by the influence of the pollen parent; it is always a beautiful green on the adult canes, while the young growths are purple. The Briar stock on which they graft this variety speeds growth right along; one gets, in pruning long—which is the way to go because of its vigor—bushes in the second year of a size rarely seen. The [growth] buds 'take' easily, and grafted or own-root plants force easily in the cold house for Winter bloom. The buds, elongated in the way of 'Niphetos' [T], will be much besought by florists. It is known that *Rosa Rugosa* resists the worst cold; this new variety can thus be grown in the North, where other roses usually freeze." [JR11/166–167]

Mme. Henri Gravereaux

Gravereaux/Cochet-Cochet, 1904

From 'Marie Zahn' (HT) × 'Conrad Ferdinand Meyer' (Rg).

"Salmony pink." [JR31/177] "A rather large double cream coloured flower with a pink centre. A strong grower." [NRS15/41] "Vigorous plant with heavy gray wood bearing some small upright thorns which are awl-shaped and sparse; the [growth] buds, borne on floriferous canes, are very large, very protrusive, and reddish. Leaflets a beautiful green, not bullate like those of the Rugosa. Blooms come singly usually. Bud round. Flowers cupped, very large, very full, very well formed. Outer petals nearly white, or slightly yellowish; those of the center, with some salmon. The form and superb shading of this flower—absolutely unique in the Rugosas—make it a top-notch variety." [JR28/156]

Mme. Julien Potin

Gravereaux/Cochet-Cochet, 1912

From 'Germanica' (Rg) × 'Gloire de Dijon' (N).

"Double flowers of a pretty carnation pink colour, but appears inclined to suffer somewhat from mildew." [NRS15/41] "Very vigorous bush. Canes green, armed with strong thorns which are slightly hooked, sometimes purplish, sparse, and intermixed with small cylindrical stickers and glandular bristles. Leaves 5–7-foliage. Leaflets elliptical or elliptical-lanceolate, ample, a beautiful bright delicate green on the upper side, paler and more sullied on the lower side. Dentation deep, sharp, often doubled. Stipules adnate to barely divergent auricles fringed with glands. Bloom rarely unifloral, most often in few-flowered clusters, with 2–7 blossoms, with bracts. Pedicel, receptacle, and sepals covered with shortly pedicelate glands. Buds round. Flowers very large—up to 12 cm [ca. 4³/₄ in] across—cupped, the center often quartered; double without being full, a pretty flesh pink which is very tender and very fresh. Freely remontant, this superb novelty is certainly one of the prettiest roses created by Monsieur Gravereaux." [JR36/168–169]

Mme. Lucien Villeminot

syn. 'Mme. Lucien Willeminot'

Gravereaux and Müller, 1903

From 'Conrad Ferdinand Meyer' (Rg) × 'Belle Poitevine' (Rg).

"Pinkish cream." [Ÿ] "A paler and softer pink [than has 'Conrad Ferdinand Meyer']." [NRS11/36] "Mr. George M. Taylor . . . states that on the authority of the raiser, Dr. Müller, it is a cross between 'Conrad Ferdinand Meyer' and 'Belle Poitevine' . . . The form of the flower and appearance of growth of the two [*i.e.,* of 'Conrad Ferdinand Meyer' and 'Mme. Lucien Villeminot'] is quite distinct and 'Mme. Lucien Villeminot' seems to have a greater number of and more definite though perhaps less prolonged periods of flowering." [NRS12/157] "This has double flowers nearly full and often a fair shape, of a soft salmon rose colour . . . In habit of growth it much resembles 'Conrad Ferdinand Meyer', but the flowers are not quite so full, softer in colour, and I think slightly more continuously produced. It is rather a favorite with me." [NRS15/41] "Foliage less ample, less brilliant, and shed more quickly in the Fall than is the case with ['Mme. Alvarez del Campo' (Rg)]. Leaflets often lightly purpled beneath and along the veins. Flowers large, nearly full, globular, and well-formed. The fairly vigorous bush is not without similarities to 'Conrad Ferdinand Meyer', from which it issued and from which it is neatly differentiated by its lighter pink blossoms." [JR27/165]

Mme. Lucien Willeminot Listed as 'Mme. Lucien Villeminot' (Rg).

Mme. Ph. Plantamour Listed as 'Mme. Philippe Plantamour' (Rg).

Mme. Philémon Plantamour Listed as 'Mme. Philippe Plantamour' (Rg).

Mme. Philippe Plantamour
syns. 'Mme. Ph. Plantamour', 'Mme. Philémon Plantamour', 'Mme. Plantamour'
Breeder/introducer unknown, ca. 1900
   "Flame red." [Ÿ] "Red, large, lightly double, tall." [Sn] "Leaves and blossoms like those of the HP's; healthy, strong, one of the most beautiful colors among the Rugosas. Velvety scarlet-purple." [Ck]

Mme. Plantamour Listed as 'Mme. Philippe Plantamour' (Rg).

Mme. Tiret
Gravereaux & Müller/Cochet-Cochet, 1901
From a seedling (resulting from a cross of 'Pierre Notting' [HP] and 'Cardinal Patrizzi' [HP]) × 'Germanica' (Rg).
   "Color, bright red, with a silvery pink exterior." [JR35/15] "Carmine centre and pale pink outside to the petals. It is a big grower with nice brownish wood." [NRS15/42] "Light red, large, lightly double, tall." [Sn] "Branches reddish, with small straight thorns. Blooms singly usually, large, cupped, nearly full, vivid red, back of petals blush." [Ck] "Vigorous shrub. Canes always purplish, armed with some straight, strong thorns—the only process on the bark. Leaves 7-foliate. Leaflets pretty large, light green, with very slight dentation. Bloomstalk few-flowered or uni-flowered. Blossom large, cupped, nearly full, beautiful bright red within, petal reverses much paler, with silvery reflections. Beautiful novelty." [JR31/136]

Moje Hammarberg
Hammarberg, 1931
   "Reddish violet, large, full, very fragrant, tall." [Sn]

Monsieur Bienvêtu Listed as 'Monsieur Gustave Bienvêtu' (Rg).

Monsieur Chédane Listed as 'Chédane-Guinoisseau' (Rg).

Monsieur Georges Cain Listed as 'Georges Cain' (Rg).

Monsieur Gustave Bienvêtu
syns. 'Bienvêtu', 'Bienyetu', 'Monsieur Bienvêtu'
Gravereaux/Cochet-Cochet, 1906
From a seedling (resulting from a cross of 'Pierre Notting' [HP] and 'Safrano' [T]) × 'Conrad Ferdinand Meyer' (Rg).
   "Bright salmony pink." [Ÿ] "This variety is double, but not full, the colour pink with a touch of salmon when fresh, but the form in the flower is poor. Left to itself the plant makes a bush of a nice rounded shape about 4-ft. high [ca. 1.3 m] and 7-ft. or so across [ca. 2.3 m +], the growth being spreading rather than upright. The foliage is good." [NRS15/36–37] "Very vigorous bush. Canes upright, ash gray, bearing relatively few thorns, which are straight or slightly hooked. Foliage ample, of a beautiful green with, sometimes, some leaflets that are slightly purplish beneath. Blooms come singly. Peduncle strong. Flower very large, perfect in form. Superbly colored bright salmony

pink, with darker reflections in which can be found fainter nuances of the ancestors of this superb hybrid." [JR30/168]

Monsieur Hélye
Morlet, 1900
   "Madder carmine." [Ÿ] "Pink, yellow center, medium size, lightly double, tall." [Sn] "Our much esteemed comrade Denis Hélye was born on the Rue de la Clef in Paris on June 7, 1827. He signed on with the *Jardin des Plantes* at the age of ten after the death of his father, having thus become the only means of support for his aged and infirm mother, receiving as an apprentice there only sixty centîmes a day, a sum indeed too small to meet his needs. This, however, did not defeat him. After work, he went to his night job as a stevedore. His taste for gardens and horticulture grew as he grew; the layouts he designed showed much intelligence, and his merit was noted by both fanciers and his superiors. At length, he was named Chief Horticulturalist at the Natural History Museum at the age of 20. Whenever offered more lucrative positions elsewhere, he would refuse them in order to retain his old post, which he indeed kept until his death last March 29 [1884] at the age of 57." [JR8/67]

Monsieur Morlet
Morlet, 1900
   "Deep carmine." [Ÿ] Morlet, nurseryman of Avon, near Fontainebleau, France; active 1854–1900.

Mrs. Anthony Waterer
Waterer/G. Paul, 1896
From *Rosa rugosa* × 'Général Jacqueminot' (HP).
   "Semi-double; deep crimson." [ARA17/29] "Purple red, large, full, tall." [Sn] "Very bright, semi-double crimson flowers, fragrant and free. Remontant." [Way45] "This has deep crimson carmine semi-double flowers, which are quite remarkable for their fragrance, which at times will scent the air around the plant. It is a moderate grower of slightly spreading habit, making a wide bush 3-ft. or 4-ft. high [ca. 1–1.3 m] …One of the best of this group, but I do not remember seeing any berries on the plant." [NRS15/42] "This variety, which has the vigor and beauty of *Rosa Rugosa* as well as its growth and handsome foliage, will be excellent for hybridizing other varieties. It was originated in the Knap Hill nurseries by a cross of *R. rugosa* × 'Général Jacqueminot', and dedicated to Mrs. Anthony Waterer. Its sweet and penetrating perfume as well as its abundant bloom place it among the best varieties of this section. The semi-double flowers attain 3–4 inches across [ca. 7.5 cm to 1 dm], and we have counted up to 80 on the same branch. The leaves, usually composed of 5 leaflets, look quite a bit like those of *R. rugosa*, but they aren't so nerved or lustrous. The canes have strong recurved thorns, and the manner of growth is much more graceful than that of its mother." [JR20/97]

[Nemo]
trans. "No One"
Conard-Pyle, 1928
   "The Mystery Rose 'that nobody knows'. A Rugosa. Large full blooms of brilliant scarlet-crimson with true old-rose perfume. Grows 10 feet or more [ca. 3.3 m +] and produces a succession of bloom all summer. Hardy everywhere. Splendid for tall pillars." [C-Ps28] Fanciers of Nemos will recall the mysterious captain of Jules Verne's *Twenty Thousand Leagues Under the Sea*.

New Century

syn. 'The New Century'
Van Fleet/Conard & Jones, 1901
From 'Clotilde Soupert' (Pol) × *Rosa rugosa* 'Alba'.

"Carmine bordered cream." [LS] "Purple." [CA05] "Carmine rose, semi-double." [NRS15/45] "Light pink, red center, large, full, medium scent, tall." [Sn] "Flowers large, pale pink, with deeper shaded canter; very double and fragrant. Blooms intermittently all summer; growth vigorous and hardy." [C-Ps25] "Large, fully double, fragrant flowers of clear flesh-pink, with a light red center and creamy edges. It is very free-blooming, with foliage like [that of] 'Sir Thomas Lipton' [Rg]; is scarcely as vigorous, but hardy." [ARA29/123]

"This magnificent Rose was originated by the noted American Hybridizer Dr. W. Van Fleet of the *Rural New Yorker,* who first called our attention to it; and after two years careful trial on our own grounds, we were so fully convinced of its great value that we purchased the entire stock, and now offer it for the first time. It is most appropriately named 'New Century' as it represents a new and distinct race of Hardy Continuous-Blooming Roses, entirely different from the old Ever-Blooming varieties. 'New Century' is a stout upright grower, making a strong compact bush of bold erect habit, and well furnished with bright glossy green foliage. It is entirely hardy in all localities where the temperature does not fall below 30° below zero, and it is believed it will stand 40° to 50° below with slight protection. It should be planted in good rich ground and well fertilized with stable manure, as a rose of this vigorous character requires good feeding for best results. It is also well to cut back the plants strongly every Spring, and again, to some extent, after the first bloom is over, which treatment will encourage new growth and fresh bloom. 'New Century' flowers are extra large, fully three to four inches across [ca. 7.5 cm to 1 dm], perfectly full and double, and borne in magnificent clusters: the color is bright rich carmine rose, with deep red center, and the petals are widely bordered with fine creamy white ... It is very sweet and has the delightful fragrance of the Wild Rose or Sweet Briar. Although the 'New Century' is one of the hardiest of all roses, and therefore particularly recommended for the coldest sections of the Great Northwest and Canada, it is equally satisfactory for planting in all parts of the U.S., and we recommend it as the hardiest and most distinct Continuous-Blooming Bush Rose for garden planting yet produced. 'New Century' is particularly valuable for planting with hardy shrubbery in lawns, parks and cemeteries, where its splendid flowers and delightful fragrance will be a constant delight during the whole season. The term 'iron-clad ever-blooming rose' describes it exactly, as, besides its extreme hardiness, it seems absolutely impervious to the attacks of insects, rust and blight which are so fatal to other roses." [C&Js01]

Newry Pink Listed as 'Repens Rosea' (Rg).

Nova Zembla

B. Ruys/H.-W. Mees, 1906
Sport of 'Conrad Ferdinand Meyer' (Rg)

"Very fine. The flowers are large and double. Pure white, with a pleasing flush of pink." [C&Js12] "Often a good white, but at times apt to come somewhat of a dirty colour." [NRS11/36] "Like most white sports, the colour of the flower is apt to vary somewhat. I have thought that in recent years they have been a better white than they used to be when my plant was young." [NRS15/42] "Light pink, large, full, medium scent, tall." [Sn] "Pure white, centre rosy white, large, full, fragrant. Growth vigorous, hardy." [GeH] "Scarcely as vigorous [as 'Conrad Ferdinand Meyer'], with flowers of white, tinted blush. It is considerably hardier and with me a freer bloomer." [ARA29/124] "Very vigorous bush; flower very large, very full." [JR33/186] "A magnificent Rose, perfectly formed. Resembles the 'Conrad F[erdinand] Meyer' in appearance and freedom of bloom." [C&Js21] "This new rose is a white sport of the Rugosa rose 'Conrad Ferdinand Meyer'. It is as hardy, and blooms as early, as its progenitor. The roses are beautiful and fragrant. It's an excellent development." [JR30/153] Nova Zembla, alias Novaya Zemlya, Russian island separating Barents Sea from the Kara Sea; residents there are probably quite familiar with the color white.

Parnassina Listed as 'Parnassine' (Rg).

[Parnassine]

syn. 'Parnassina'
E. Noisette, 1825

"There is a beautiful variety [of Rosa rugosa] with double flowers; it can be found at Monsieur Ét[ienne] Noisette's, nurseryman at LaQueue; it bloomed for the first time in 1825. They're calling it R. Parnassine." [BJ30] "Blossoms the same [*i.e.,* light violet], double." [BJ40] "Bush with erect canes armed with straight, unequal thorns; leaves lanate beneath, composed of seven leaflets which are elongate, partially overlapping, and with reddish veins; flowers grouped three to five on each stalk, full, fairly well formed; petals a deep pink." [S] Parnassine, of or relating to the home of the Muses, Mt. Parnassus, where we authors frequently gather for light snacks of nectar and ambrosia during breaks in our work.

Paulii Listed as 'Repens Alba' (Rg).

Paulii Rosea Listed as 'Repens Rosea' (Rg).

Pink Grootendorst

Grootendorst, 1923
Sport of 'F. J. Grootendorst' (Rg).

"Light pink." [Ÿ] "Double flowers of a clear pink. Everblooming Baby Rugosa type blooms." [Way45] "The shining, shell-pink, fringed flowers are borne on a continuous flowering bush, and resemble the 'F. J. Grootendorst' ... in form and habit. This Rose is also fine to use for low hedges." [C-Ps28] "Pink, small, full, tall." [Sn] "Bud medium size; flower double, clear pink, very lasting; very vigorous, upright, bushy; profuse bloomer. Very hardy." [ARA24/174] Further research *may* at length indicate the correct name of this cultivar to be 'Pink F. J. Grootendorst'; but do not jump the gun.

Potager du Dauphin

trans. "Kitchen-Garden of the Crown Prince"
Gravereaux, 1899
"Pink." [Ÿ]

Prof. N. E. Hansen

syn. 'Hansen'
Budd, 1892
Deep red.

Proteiformis

Breeder unknown, 1894

From *Rosa rugosa* 'Alba' × ?

Rose with variable foliage and clusters of semi-double white blossoms. *Cf.* 'Heterophylla' (Rg) and 'Rosier Tenuifolia' (Rg).

Regeliana

Regel, 1871

"Violet purple." [Ÿ] "Single red; varies. Fruits in fall." [Th2] "*Rosa Rugosa Regeliana*, described by Monsieur Édouard André in 1871 and 1872 in *Illustration Horticole*, gives [its daughter, 'Belle Poitevine'] one of its own most beautiful qualities, blooming in large bouquets." [JR18/148] "Appears to be synonymous with rugosa 'Rubra', at least for garden purposes." [NRS15/43]

Regeliana Flore Pleno   Listed as 'Kaiserin des Nordens' (Rg).

Regeliana Rubra   Listed as 'Kaiserin des Nordens' (Rg).

Régina Badet

Gravereaux and Müller/Cochet-Cochet, 1908

From 'Général Jacqueminot' (HP) × a seedling (resulting from a cross of 'Empereur du Maroc' (HP) and *Rosa rugosa*).

"Violet-red, large, full, tall." [Sn] "Very vigorous bush. Canes with varying thorns, usually green, purple in the sun. Leaves 7-foliate, with very ample stipules. Leaflets elliptical lanceolate, delicate green, slightly purple along the edge in youth. Bud pointed. Flower large, quite double, flat, often quartered; magenta red, reverse of petals paler." [JR32/168]

Repens Alba

syn. 'Paulii'

G. Paul, 1903

From *Rosa rugosa* × *R. wichuraiana*. Also said, evidently in error, to be a cross between *Rosa rugosa* and *R. arvensis*.

"Pure white, free, continuous, weeping habit. Vigorous." [GeH] "Of extraordinary growth. It should only be planted where it can have a great deal of room, and if properly cared for will form a striking object when in bloom." [F-M] "This has white flowers and long, creeping, flexuous, but stout stems, which will in course of time form a huge, impenetrable bush, 4-ft to 6-ft. high [ca. 1.3–2 m] and of great width. It was obtained by crossing *rugosa* with *wichuraiana* (*The Garden*, 1910, p.979)." [NRS15/43] "Hybrid plants are not uncommonly sterile. For example, there is an attractive rose known as *Rosa rugosa* 'Repens Alba', apparently a hybrid of Rugosa with a climber. One plant of this at the local test-garden of the American Rose Society has resisted all efforts to make it set seed. No hips have ever been observed on it, and it has failed to set fruit when carefully hand-pollinated. Repeated crossings with twenty-five different varieties of roses have failed to give any seed." [ARA24/34]

Repens Rosea

syns. 'Paulii Rosea', 'Newry Pink'

T. Smith, ca. 1904

Sport from 'Repens Alba' (Rg).

"Large deep rose flowers." [NRS15/43] "Similar to ['Repens Alba'], but of more vigorous growth, and its flowers, which are much larger, resemble a large Clematis of a beautiful rose colour, shading to white in centre." [sDHca03] "Very large, single, rose-colored flowers. Very vigorous." [Th2] Dr. Charles Nelson reports (in *The Rose*, Summer, 1992) the renaming of this cultivar as 'Newry Pink'.

Rose à Parfum de l'Haÿ   Plate 28

trans. "Perfume Rose from L'Haÿ"

Gravereaux, 1903

From a seedling (resulting from the cross of a Damask and 'Général Jacqueminot' [HP]) × 'Germanica' (Rg).

"Carminy cerise red." [Ÿ] "Purple-cochineal-carmine, very large, fairly full, globular, fragrant. Growth vigorous, floriferous." [GeH] "Light red, white center, large, lightly double, very fragrant, tall." [Sn] "Large full double flowers of a dark carmine crimson, not usually well shaped, though one occasionally comes across a nice flower, but so fragrant that this Rose was selected by Mons. Jules Gravereaux, as the most highly scented of all Roses, for the purpose of making perfume." [NRS15/43] "Blooms plentifully in June and at intervals throughout the summer and autumn, the later flowers being especially abundant in August." [ARA19/18] "One of the best and most floriferous Rugosas. From late May through October, it bears quantities of very large, globular, double flowers colored dark crimson and shaded with carmine. As the name suggests, the blossoms are intensely fragrant. Growth is very vigorous and extremely hardy." [C-Ps30] "Has Damask blood, is hardy and a healthy grower, with rugose foliage, producing double, dark carmine-crimson blooms continuously if seed-hips are removed; extremely fragrant, but blues in heat." [ARA29/123] "Vigorous plant, flower large, full, beautifully colored cerise red, perfume exquisite and bloom abundant." [JR30/186] "This variety . . . due to its exquisite and very pronounced perfume, and its abundant bloom, is cited as the one to replace those once-blooming sorts which, up till now, have been used in the production of rose essence. The plant is vigorous, and easy to grow and propagate. Its foliage resembles that of its maternal grandparent *R. gallica* [*presumably Rosa ×damascena is meant*]. The quite double blossom is globular, slightly flat, and a beautiful carmine cerise red, with a white nub." [JR27/165] "Distinctly meritorious; produces an intense and exquisite perfume, because of which it is used to make the attar of roses." [C&Js19] "It is strange that one sees this beautiful variety so seldom, and strange, also, that so few writers recommend it." [NRS27/64]

"A curious rose variety, bred by Monsieur Gravereaux, the distinguished rosomane of L'Haÿ (Seine). It began with the pollination of a *Damask* rose by the old HP 'Général Jacqueminot'. This operation, which took place in 1894, gave a plant which was in turn pollinated by *Rosa Rugosa Germanica* [*sic*], giving a plant which bloomed in 1900, and which quickly became known as an excellent obtention, as much because of its profusion as by the exquisite scent it wafts. Monsieur Éd[ouard] André, the knowledgeable editor-in-chief of the *Revue Horticole,* having received some branches of this plant, gave the following description in his periodical: 'Upright shrub, bushy, vigorous. Old wood thorny, with straight gray thorns, unequal like those of *Rosa rugosa*; young canes green with thorns which are staggered, close-set, widely thickened, straight, and pink; leaves tri-jugate, rather thick, with large elongate stipules having sharp, divergent auricles; petiole pink at the base, tomentose, glandulose, and armed with back-hooked prickles; leaflets oval-acute, finely serrate, sessile, glabrous, glaucescent beneath; adult leaves dark green above, strongly nerved and reticulate, and slightly bullate (from *Rosa rugosa*); inflorescence a paucifloral or plurifloral corymb (as with 'Général Jacqueminot'), with bristly glandular reddish peduncles, 3–5 cm long [ca. 1¹/₂–2 in]; calyx glabrous or slightly hispid, longly turbinate where the ovary is; sepals reflexing at anthesis, triangular, entire, with a cetaceous [*sic: "cétacée" or "whalish"; we hope that "sétacée," i.e., "setaceous," was intended*] point, slightly hispid and green outwardly, velvety and pinkish within; flower quite double, flattened globular, obcordate petals, notched or mucronate, beautiful silvery carmine cherry red, lighter at the edge, white at the nub; central petals muddled; stamens with incurving white filaments; anthers deep yellow; styles very short, with salient stigmas of a pale yellow. Exquisitely elegant perfume, like a mix of the Damask and 'Général Jacqueminot'. I have seen 'Rose à Parfum de l'Haÿ', and can only congratulate its fortunate owner on the results of his breeding. No doubt this remontant variety will be grown some day in great quantity for distillation, due to its strong and delicious scent." [JR27/25–26]

Rose Apples
G. Paul, 1895

"Delicate carminy pink." [Ÿ] "Pale silvery rose. This variety is of vigorous growth." [P1] "Flower pale carmine-rose, semi-double, large petals, free. Growth vigorous. A fragrant form of *R. rugosa*." [GeH] "A plant of good habit, about 5-ft. [ca 1.6 m], with pale rose flowers and large berries freely produced. A capital hedge plant." [NRS15/43]

Roseraie de l'Haÿ Plate 24
Cochet-Cochet, 1902
Seedling of *Rosa rugosa* 'Rubra'.

"Violety pink." [Ÿ] "Dark red double flowers, freely produced. It is a strong grower." [NRS15/43] "Purple red, large, full, very fragrant, tall." [Sn] "Crimson-red, changing to rosy magenta, large, double. Growth very vigorous." [GeH] "Distinctly meritorious; produces an intense and exquisite perfume, because of which it is used to make the otto of Roses. Flowers bright red and very free-bloomer." [C&Js13] "From single red *Rosa rugosa*. The fruits are exactly pear-shaped, the reddish color and the form of the leaflets makes us think this new variety sprang from the pollen of another [non-rugosa] fertilizing the [incipient] seed. The blossoms, in the same form as those of 'Souvenir de Pierre Leperdrieux' [Rg], are darker in color. It blooms so early in Spring that, of the 1,000 species and varieties we grow, 'Roseraie de l'Haÿ' is the first to bloom. It is very remontant. This new variety bears the name of the splendid rosarium created at l'Haÿ [near Paris, France] by Monsieur Gravereaux." [JR26/2] "The variety 'Roseraie de l'Haÿ', which the artist [of the accompanying plate in the *Journal des Roses*] attributes to Monsieur Gravereaux, came from a sowing made by Monsieur Cochet-Cochet, *rosiériste* at Coubert, who had it for sale in the Fall of 1902. It is very floriferous, but, as with all the flowers in this series, has a light wine-lee tint. Doubtless, someone will manage to get rid of this tint in new varieties, because it takes away from much of the charm of the Rugosa roses." [JR30/124]

Rosier Hérisson Listed as *Rosa rugosa*.

Rosier Tenuifolia
trans. "Delicately Foliaged Rose-Plant"
Bénard, 1904
From *Rosa rugosa* 'Alba' × *R. pimpinellifolia*.

"White." [Ÿ] "Vigorous bush, very hardy, with white flowers; foliage finely lacinate and curled; has a characteristic of little branchlets

forming at each [growth] bud, giving it the look of a bush overspread with moss … No fancier should be without it." [JR28/155]

Rouge Pleine Listed as 'Kaiserin des Nordens' (Rg).

Rubra Listed as *Rosa rugosa* 'Rubra'.

Rubra Flore Pleno Listed as 'Kaiserin des Nordens' (Rg).

Rubra Plena Listed as 'Kaiserin des Nordens' (Rg).

(Rugosa × 'Duc d'Edinburgh')
Vilmorin, 1907
From *Rosa rugosa* × 'Duc d'Edinburgh' (HP).

We have found no further information on this rose, alas.

Runzliche Rose Listed as *Rosa rugosa*.

Ruskin
Van Fleet/American Rose Society, 1928
From 'Souvenir de Pierre Leperdrieux' (Rg) × 'Victor Hugo' (HP).

"Violet-purple-red, large, full, very fragrant, tall." [Sn] "Combines the bloom beauty of the Hybrid Perpetuals with magnificent, large, healthy Rugosa foliage. Its pure crimson color, rich fragrance, and fine form marks a real advance in the Rugosas, as so many of the reds have a tendency to blue." [ARA29/125] "A rather scanty bloomer, although the flowers were good, and *Boone* does not think it equal to other red Rugosas of nearly the same shade. At Breeze Hill it is shy, but attractive when it does bloom." [ARA31/199–200] "Buds like those of a Hybrid Perpetual, developing into large, double, deep crimson flowers of about 50 petals, with Rugosa-like fragrance and excellent lasting quality. It blooms abundantly in June, and moderately thereafter. The plant is a strong, erect Rugosa type, with rough foliage, inclined to stiffness in budded plants. It is a tall pillar and entirely hardy." [C-Ps30] "Bud large, ovoid; flower large, double, full (50 petals), cupped, lasting, very fragrant, deep crimson, borne singly or several together on medium-strong stem. Foliage sufficient, large, rich green, leathery, disease-resistant. Many thorns. Growth moderate, upright, bushy; abundant bloomer in June and September and October. Hardy." [ARA28/246] "*Hamblin* thinks it the best dark red Rugosa. An enormous plant, extremely hardy and robust. *Preston* says it blooms well in July and September. *Cross* finds it adaptable as a bush or pillar, with deliciously scented blooms of the color and form of Hybrid Perpetuals, and an important addition to the Rugosa class. *Isham* finds it a shy bloomer, but with lasting qualities, and thinks it a good Rugosa." [ARA30/193] *Not* named after John Ruskin (lived 1819–1900), English *littérateur* and critic, but rather after the town of Ruskin, Tennessee, where Van Fleet lived for a time.

S.A.R. Ferdinand Ier
trans. "H.R.H. Ferdinand 1st"
Gravereaux, 1901

"Pink." [Ÿ] "S.A.R." is "Son Altesse Royale," *i.e.*, "His Royal Highness." Ferdinand I, king of Bulgaria; lived 1861–1948; reigned 1908–1918.

S.M.I. Abdul-Hamid
trans. "His Imperial Majesty Abdul-Hamid"
Gravereaux, 1901

"Purple red." [Ÿ] "S.M.I." is "Sa Majesté Impériale." Abdul-Hamid II, sultan of Turkey; lived 1876–1909; reigned 1876–1909.

Sanguinaire

trans. "Blood-Like"

Gillot, 1933

From 'Bergers Erfolg' (Rg) × 'Captain Ronald Clark' (HT).

"Orangey blood red." [Ÿ] "Reddish orange, large, lightly double, light scent, tall." [Sn] By *Gillot,* not *Guillot.*

Sarah Van Fleet

Van Fleet/American Rose Society, 1926

From *Rosa rugosa* × 'My Maryland' (HT).

"Pink." [Ÿ] "Light rose-pink, semi-double, fragrant flowers come on a plant of erect and spreading habit. Blooms are best in the fall." [C-Ps28] "Light pink, medium size, lightly double, medium scent, tall." [Sn] "With us this has been a very fine shrub, with large, fragrant flowers of clear color, much more desirable than 'Belle Poitevine' which it resembles in many respects . . . Very good, deep rose-pink, darker than 'Conrad Ferdinand Meyer', and not so rampant." [ARA30/ 178] "A very strong grower, hardy, with medium Rugosa foliage, immune to disease, and produces semi-double, fragrant flowers of a wild-rose pink very continuously. It fades in heat, but is very fine in the fall." [ARA29/123] "Bud large, ovoid; flower large, semi-double, open, cupped, moderately to intensely fragrant, lasting, wild-rose-pink, fading lighter in strong sunlight, borne singly and several together. Foliage abundant, normal green, leathery Rugosa type, resistant to disease. Growth compact (maximum height about 6 feet [ca. 2 m]; flowers abundantly in June and continues through summer with a good crop again in autumn." [ARA26/186] "Makes a shapely bush, perfectly hardy, and produces quantities of fragrant, cupped blooms of Hermosa pink [v. 'Hermosa' (B)] with deeper pink inside. The buds are long and dainty and the flowers are fairly large, semi-double, and come in clusters; they have an enchanting old-rose fragrance. It should be given a space of 4 to 5 feet [ca. 1.3–1.6 m] to allow it to develop symmetrically." [C-Ps30] "The fine erect bush covered with glossy leaves reaches 6 to 8 feet [ca. 2–2.6 m]." [W] "Available . . . for general distribution in the spring of 1927 . . . named . . . in honor of the Doctor's wife . . . Habit of plant, erect and spreading; character of foliage, Rugosa type, medium green; vigorous; very hardy; flower, three to four rows of petals, opens flat, shows stamens; color, wild-rose pink; form, cupped; fragrance, moderate; bud, medium size; petalage, twenty to thirty; freedom of bloom and lasting quality, excellent. This rose is distinct from all the [other] Rugosa hybrids in color and continuity of flowering." [ARA26/47] "Vigorous grower; disease free . . . Ont.; the best thing about it is its light green foliage. Bloom rather ragged. Fears dampness but a good shrub. It does not sucker as much as the original Rugosa . . . Pa.; Bloomed a little last summer and is beginning to bloom this spring. Flowers not as perfect as we would like . . . N. Dak.; An occasional flower after the first burst. Has no quality either in individual bloom or decorative value here. Useless . . . Calif.; An improvement on 'Belle Poitevine' in clearness of color. Otherwise, just a sweet-scented double Rugosa." [ARA28/187] It must be left to seers and epistemologists as to whether 'Sarah Van Fleet' was actually introduced in 1926 or 1927; we give, above, the traditionally accepted date (meantime reminding Readers that "traditional acceptance" does not confer actuality).

Schneelicht

trans. "Snowlight"

Geschwind, 1896

From *Rosa rugosa* × *R. phoenicia.*

"Sparkling snow white." [Ÿ] "Flowers white." [P1] "Cream." [NRS15/ 45] "Flower snow-white, perfect form. Growth very vigorous." [GeH] "White, medium size, single, tall." [Sn] "No scent, recurrent, –2 m [less than ca. 6 ft]." [EU] "A climbing Rugosa with large, very white flowers, borne on a strong-growing plant that is best used as a fence-cover, as its tremendous, thorny growth is almost impenetrable." [ARA29/125] Others have given a date of 1894; Ÿ attributes it to Schmidt, 1895.

Schneezwerg

trans. "Snow Dwarf"

Lambert, 1911

From *Rosa rugosa* × *R. bracteata.*

"Snow white and yellow." [Ÿ] "The . . . flowers . . . look like Japanese Anemones and appear from June to October." [W] "White, medium size, lightly double, average height." [Sn] "This is a beautiful little semi-double flower of a very pure white, freely produced. I have not noticed any berries. It . . . grows about 3-ft. high [ca. 1 m]." [NRS28/27] "It is a rather dwarf, spiny plant, with splendid foliage, and combines the hardiness of Rugosa with the free-blooming habit of Bracteata. It seems dependably hardy here, producing a continuous display of clusters of semi-double, snow-white flowers, with golden stamens, all season. These are followed by quantities of small red fruits that are very attractive in the autumn." [ARA29/124] "Makes a good dwarf bush if kept well pruned." [NRS28/27] "Vigorous bush, foliage of medium size, glossy, Rugosa-like, healthy. Flowers of medium size (5 [cm; ca. 2 in], the size of a Mark), pure snow white, flat, semi-full. Center studded with a crown of stamens all crowded together; extraordinarily pretty, 3–10 on each branch. Bloom lasts until frost; hips small, bright red. Particularly appropriate as a rose for parks, rocky outcroppings, and hedges; also good as a specimen rose." [JR36/41]

Schwabenland

Berger/Pfitzer, 1928

From a Rugosa seedling × 'Elizabeth Cullen' (HT).

"Pink." [ARA29/193] "Violet pink, large, full, medium scent, average height." [Sn] "Bud large to very large, globular; flower large to very large, extremely double, full, open, very lasting, moderately fragrant, amaranth-pink, borne singly on long, strong stem. Foliage sufficient, large, rich green, leathery, disease-resistant. Growth very vigorous (2 ft. [ca. 6 dm]), upright; profuse, continuous bloomer from June to October. Very hardy." [ARA30/226] "A hardy, masculine rose." [ARA31/ 207] Schwabenland, alias Swabia, region in southwest Germany.

[Siberian Form]

Hansen, 1907

"Flowers large, single, dark crimson. Tall growing, hardy." [ARA27/227]

Signe Relander

D. Poulsen, 1928

From a Rugosa cultivar × 'Orléans-Rose' (Pol).

"Light red, small, lightly double, medium scent, medium growth." [Sn]

Single Pink

A. Smith, 1930

"Pink, medium size, single, medium height." [Sn]

Sir Thomas Lipton

Van Fleet/Conard & Jones, 1905

Rosa rugosa × 'Clotilde Soupert' (Pol).

"Double white flowers of large size, borne freely all summer and fall on a sturdy, ironclad bush of great size, which has the desirable foliage of the original Rugosa." [C-Ps25] "Unsatisfactory in size and color of blooms and has never shown any second blossoming period." [ARA25/206] "To my mind, the finest of all the whites when well grown. It requires rich soil and good care to display its full possibilities. Planted where it has ample room to develop, it makes a magnificent vase-shaped shrub of wonderful vigor. I have an old specimen, 9 feet high [ca. 3 m] and of corresponding spread, that is a dream of beauty when loaded with its myriad of large, snow-white, double, slightly fragrant flowers in June, and thereafter more or less till heavy frost. Some years it is as beautiful in the fall as in June … It seems to be absolutely sterile, as I have never seen nor heard of it ripening seed-hips." [ARA29/123] "Beautiful in foliage, early and constant in bloom, of most vigorous habit, ironclad constitution, producing a bush 5 or 6 feet high [ca. 1.6–2 m] and as great in diameter. The original bush on our grounds (10 years old) is over 20 feet in circumference [ca. 6.6 m] and is seldom, if ever, without bloom from the 3rd week in May until November." [C&Js07]

"We have had this splendid rose on trial for several years, and now take pleasure in recommending it as the finest pure white Hybrid Rugosa Rose yet produced. It is a strong vigorous grower, making a handsome bush, 4 to 5 feet high [ca. 1.3–1.6 m], well covered with bright glossy green leaves, which shine as if varnished. The flowers are 3 to 4 inches across [ca. 7.5 cm to 1 dm], perfectly double and pure snow white. They are very fragrant and borne on strong upright stems all through the growing season. It is one of the hardiest roses in existence, and therefore particularly valuable for planting in cold climates and exposed localities where other roses do not thrive. It does well everywhere and can be depended on to make a strong handsome bush and produce plenty of large double pure white roses for several months every season. It is especially recommended for yard, park, and cemetery planting, because of its handsome appearance, perfect hardiness and entire freedom from insects, rust and disease. It is undoubtedly the finest pure white hardy Hybrid Rugosa Rose yet produced, and is certain to be a standard variety for years to come." [C&Js05] Sir Thomas Johnstone Lipton, lived 1850–1931; English businessman and yachtsman familiar to many tea drinkers.

Souvenir de Christophe Cochet   Plate 27

trans. "In Memory of Christophe Cochet"

Cochet-Cochet, 1894

From *Rosa ×kamtchatika* 'Alba Simplex' × 'Comte d'Epremesnil' (Rg).

"Bright flesh pink." [Ÿ] "Pink flowers flushed carmine, semi-double, and a few large berries." [NRS15/44] "Blossom beautiful deep rose-red, about 12 cm in diameter [ca. 4³/₄ in]. Fruit large and bright red." [Ck] "Flowers pink, semi-double, fruit extra large." [P1] "A very pretty variety of the Kamchatka Rose, called 'Souvenir de Christophe Cochet', will be for sale next November 1 at Monsieur Cochet-Cochet's,

Coubert rosarian. Our readers already know this beautiful newcomer from the chromo which appeared in last September's number of the *Journal des Roses,* and which certainly gives a good idea of its great value. Having been able for several years to appreciate the Rose 'Souvenir de Christophe Cochet' in its breeder's nurseries, which are close by, we don't hesitate to state that it's a top-notch variety. It's an extremely vigorous bush giving an abundance of large blossoms which measure up to 13 cm across [ca. 5 in] and which sometimes come in clusters of 15 flowers. The habit of growth is the same as that of its parents, which are K[amtchatika] 'Alba Simplex' and K. 'Comte d'Epresmenil'. The coloration of the blossom is pink lightly washed carmine, with a slightly darker center with light violet reflections. The numerous and enormous red fruits which cover the plant during the Fall make it extremely decorative." [JR18/149] Christophe Cochet, father of Scipion Cochet and Pierre-Philémon Cochet (père); Christophe Cochet stocked his rose garden from Descemet's nursery prior to 1814; first of several generations of Cochets important to rose progress.

Souvenir de Philémon Cochet

trans. "In Memory of Philémon Cochet"

Cochet-Cochet, 1899

Seedling of 'Blanc Double de Coubert' (Rg).

"White, salmon-pink center, large, very full, medium to tall." [Sn] "Has nearly double flowers, white tinged salmon. It is a natural seedling from 'Blanc Double de Coubert, but I do not like it so well. It is not, however, quite so strong in growth." [NRS15/44] "White, double, extra large. Growth vigorous." [GeH] "A fine, very double, white hybrid, with the typical foliage and habit of the Rugosa. It blooms very freely and its fragrant flowers are followed by good seed-hips … Very hardy." [ARA29/123] "This beautiful variety, grown from seed by my father, and dedicated to his memory, came from 'Blanc Double de Coubert' open-pollinated—and it's a great improvement over that variety. The general characteristics of the two plants are the same—vigor, stature, foliage—but the blossoms of 'Souvenir de Philémon Cochet' are absolutely full. They grow to 10–12 cm across [ca. 4–4³/₄ in], are a beautiful white with some flesh in the center, and, in form and doubleness, look exactly like the well-known 'Souvenir de la Malmaison' [B]. This resemblance to that beautiful Bourbon makes this one of the most recommendable roses, much superior to 'Blanc Double de Coubert', whence it came. The variety 'Souvenir de Philémon Cochet' is freely remontant, and very vigorous." [JR23/169] Pierre-Philémon Cochet (fils), grandson of Christophe Cochet, son of Pierre-Philémon Cochet (père), father of Charles Cochet-Cochet, lived 1822–1898.

Souvenir de Pierre Leperdrieux

Cochet-Cochet, 1895

From *Rosa ×kamtchatika* 'Alba Simplex' × 'Comte d'Epresmenil' (Rg).

"Bright vinous red." [Ÿ] "Blossom large, 9–10 cm [ca. 3¹/₂–4 in], nicely semi-full; handsome, regular form; carmine purple." [Ck] "Light purple-red, large, full, medium scent, tall." [Sn] "Flowers semi-double, of a bright red colour. Fruit and foliage very attractive." [P1] "Flower bright wine-red, semi-double. Growth vigorous." [GeH] "A fine vigorous grower that bears double flowers in immense clusters; color, brilliant vinous red. Deliciously sweet scented and followed by bright red

Suvenir de Pierre Leperdrieux *continued*

berries that remain on a long time—very ornamental." [C&Js07] "Blooms all season." [C&Js21] "Very free-blooming." [ARA29/123] "A large open flower, scarcely semi-double, and deep purplish rose or violet, very fragrant, with an added sweetbriar perfume. The plant grows 3-ft. to 4-ft. [ca. 1–1.3 m]. The colour is very distinct and pleasing when quite fresh, otherwise it is not specially attractive, and the chief point of this Rose is its fragrance." [NRS15/44] "The new variety 'Souvenir de Pierre Leperdrieux' is dedicated to the memory of our maternal great-grandfather. It sprang from seeds of *Kamschatika Alba Simplex* (our usual pod-parent) × *Comte d'Epresmenil*. It's an improvement over its father. The bloom is extremely abundant; the blossoms, bright vinous red, double, eglantine scent, grouped in clusters of 8, 10, 15, 20, and indeed 30 roses on vigorous canes, come from the first nice days [in Spring] and continue with slight interruptions up to the heavy autumnal frosts. They grow to 10–12 cm across [ca. 4–4¾ in]. Its great vigor, superb foliage, and very abundant hips are themselves enough to make this rose popular as a decorative." [JR19/180]

Souvenir de Yeddo
trans. "In Memory of Yeddo"
Morlet, 1874
From *Rosa rugosa* × a Tea.

"Flower large, full, China pink." [S] "Light pink, large, full, tall." [Sn] "Mentioned by Monsieur Emile Köhne in his *Deutsche Dendrologie*, 1893 … full pink, said by Monsieur Köhne to come from *R. rugosa* × [*Rosa*] *damascena*, but Prof. Crépin found it difficult to admit the latter parent." [NRS15/44] "Rosa rugosa × Rosa indica [*i.e., R. chinensis*]." [URZ5/1/19] Yeddo, alias Yedo, alias Edo, alias Tokyo, memorable Japanese city.

Stella Polaris
trans. "Polar Star"
Jensen, 1890

"White, large, single, tall." [Sn] "Blossom large, pure white, single; hip long; quite constant. Plant resembles Rugosa 'Alba'." [Ck]

Stern von Prag
trans. "Prague Star"
V. Berger/Faist, 1924
From a seedling of *Rosa rugosa* × 'Edward Mawley' (HT).

"Deep red, large, full, medium scent, tall." [Sn] "Bud large, ovoid; flower large, very double, full, very lasting, strong fragrance, velvety dark blood-red, generally borne singly on long stem. Foliage sufficient, large, dark green. Very vigorous, upright bushy grower; abundant, intermittent bloomer. Very hardy." [ARA25/193] "A strong grower, bears large, fragrant, very double flowers of a velvety dark red; looks like a find and blooms at intervals." [ARA29/125] "Grows like 'Conrad Ferdinand Meyer' [Rg], very strong. Blossoms large, full, well-formed, velvety black-red. Floriferous." [Ck] "Rather a Hybrid Perpetual than a Rugosa Hybrid, except for the thorns. Its deep purplish crimson blooms come in clusters at the end of long stems and are very fragrant. If disbudded to one or two, the remaining ones will be of mammoth size. Blooms are abundant and intermittent. A very vigorous, upright, bushy grower." [C-Ps30]

[Taïcoun]
syn. 'Taïkoun'; trans., "Tycoon" or "Shogun"
Breeder unknown, pre-1872

"Under the name *Rosier japonais Taïcoun,* I have found a variety which was sold—a few years ago—under the name *Rosa rugosa* à fleurs pleines [*i.e.,* "Double-Flowered Rosa rugosa"], and which rather differs from the type with a single flower—at which an illustrious opportunistic botanist unhesitatingly made it a new species, which he described in a foreign miscellany." [l'H72/166–167] *Cf.* 'Kaiserin des Nordens' (Rg).

Taïkoun Listed as 'Taïcoun' (Rg).

Tetonkaha
Hansen, 1912
For parentage, see below.

"Deep pink, large, lightly double, very fragrant, tall." [Sn] "Seed parent, wild prairie rose from Lake Tetonkaha, about 18 miles northwest of Brookings, S. Dak.; pollen parent, a hybrid *Rosa rugosa* [*possibly* 'La Mélusine'?] … Flowers, fully 3 inches across [ca. 7.5 cm], 18 to 25 petals, deep rich pink, very fragrant. The bush is perfectly hardy far north into Manitoba and is a very free bloomer. This is now becoming widely popular. The bush is of vigorous growth, attaining a height of fully 6 feet and 6 feet across [ca. 2 m], with hundreds of flowers. A pleasing sight when in bloom. The attractive Rugosa (wrinkled) foliage is attractive also." [ARA27/227–228]

The New Century
Listed as 'New Century' (Rg).

Thusnelda
Müller, 1886
From *Rosa rugosa* 'Alba' × 'Gloire de Dijon' (N).

"Delicate pink." [Ÿ] "Flowers light salmon pink, very free and perpetual flowering … [T]his variety resembles the Hybrid Perpetual in size of blossom." [Pl] "Pink, medium size, lightly double, very fragrant, tall." [Sn] "Has pale salmon pink semi-double flowers produced early and late. It is a strong grower and will make a bush 4-ft. to 7-ft. high [ca. 1.3–2.3 m] … It is a charming Rose of its type, and well worth a place." [NRS15/44] "Delicate light-pink colored, large, full, fragrant, well-formed blossom. Blooms early and frequently. Most beautiful of all the Rugosas." [Ck]

Türke's Rugosa-Sämling
trans. "Türke's Rugosa Seedling"
Türke, 1923
From 'Conrad Ferdinand Meyer' (Rg) × 'Mrs. Aaron Ward' (HT).

"Peach-pink, yellow ground, large, semi-double, good form, long-lasting, delicacy 1 [on a scale of 10], scent 7 [on a scale of 10], Centifolia perfume, medium floriferousness, good rebloom, bud cup-shaped, deep yellow, long stem, numerous thorns, growth 7 [on a scale of 10], upright, 2 m [ca. 6 ft], stiff." [Jg] Verrier adds that it has dark leathery foliage.

Vanguard
G. A. Stevens, 1932
From a seedling (resulting from a cross of *Rosa wichuraiana* and *R. rugosa* 'Alba') × 'Eldorado' (Pern).

"Salmon orange." [Ÿ] "Orange-salmon-pink, medium size, full, tall." [Sn] "Orange-salmon and copper . . . Very vigorous, and will make a large shrub or pillar with 8- to 10-foot canes [ca. 2.6–3.3 m]. Its foliage is large, dark green, and very beautifully varnished. The large, fragrant flowers are very much like [those of] 'Miss Lolita Armour' [Pern] in both form and color . . . This extremely hardy Rose is strongly recommended for northern climates and is suitable for planting among shrubs or for tall lawn specimens. A beautiful, decorative plant, even when not in bloom." [C-Ps33] G. A. Stevens, our oft-cited climbing rose author, reference GAS.

Villa des Tybilles

Gravereaux, 1899
   "Red." [Ÿ]

Wasagaming

Skinner, 1939
From a seedling (resulting from a cross of *Rosa rugosa* and *R. acicularis*) × 'Gruss an Teplitz' (B).
   Double pink, reblooming.

White Grootendorst

Eddy, 1962
Sport of 'Pink Grootendorst' (Rg).
   "White, small, full, medium scent, medium height." [Sn]

Zuccariniana   Listed as 'Kaiserin des Nordens' (Rg).

CHAPTER NINETEEN

Laevigatas

"Another rose originating in China, long since naturalized in the south of the U.S., is partially hardy in Belgium; it is quite pretty; *R. sinica* Mun., or, better, *R. laevigata* Michx.; its yellow stamens contrast with the immaculate, virginal ground of the corolla; its beauty gives it the common name Camellia Rose." [JR26/116] "Of this splendid evergreen species, the original or single flowering variety has become widely disseminated throughout our more southern States, under the title of Cherokee, Nondescript, or Georgian Evergreen Rose ... So vigorous is the growth of this admirable climber that it ascends the loftiest trees of the forest to the height of 80 to 100 feet [ca. 27–34 m], and hedges of the most impervious description, clad with highly attractive glossy evergreen foliage, exist in some cases of more than a mile in extent. It appears to have been introduced at the same remote and unknown period, as the Melia Azederach, Prunus Caroliniensis!? [*the punctuation, sic*], Sapindus Saponaria, Catalpa Syringifolia!?, Stillingia Sebifera, and Sterculia Platanifolia ... [It] has flowers of cupped form, ... fragrant, and beautiful; the foliage usually trifoliate, but occasionally pinnate, is very glossy, and peculiarly luxuriant and attractive." [WRP]

"Countless attempts have been made to blend it with the choicer garden roses, but failure has been so constant that Cherokee rose-breeding has been pronounced impracticable. The writer [Dr. W. Van Fleet] has squandered whole seasons of work on the Cherokee, and has little to show for it except 'Silver Moon' and a bushy seedling producing apple-blossom-pink semi-double blooms, of exquisite fragrance but of little garden value. Scores of hybrid offspring of the choicest parentage have been grown from this species only to perish before flowering, often without divesting themselves of immature foliage. A hybrid, Cherokee × 'Maréchal Niel' [N], promised much at the outset, repeatedly sending up shoots 8 to 10 feet high [ca. 1.6–3.3 m], only to have the juvenile-looking foliage fall before full development, and the shoots wither away. This variety was grown in the greenhouse and outside, on its own roots, budded on both parents and on other stocks, in the West, and was also well established in a favorable location in California; but it perished after four years of trial without developing a bloom. The Cherokee Rose, like 'Harison's Yellow', is indeed a hard

nut for the rose-breeder to crack; yet it has developed varieties of value like 'Anemonen Rose', a lovely pink-flowered form, thought to have an infusion of Tea-rose blood; and efforts to blend it with other types should not be abandoned." [ARA16/33] "Eliminating mildew seems ... possible through a new strain of hybrid Laevigata roses. Heretofore it was claimed that *R. laevigata* ... does not make seed, and that other species and types would not take its pollen. Such is not the case, as hundreds of combinations were made with Laevigata as seed-bearer, using pollen from Hybrid Teas, Teas, Hybrid Perpetuals, and Pernetianas. Pollen of Laevigata used on Gigantea has proved that even the Gigantea foliage can be improved, making it much more rigid and glossy, a sure preventive of mildew." [ARA31/50]

Rosa alba chesuanensis foliorum marginibus et rachi medio spinosis Listed as *Rosa laevigata*.

Rosa amygdalifolia Listed as *Rosa laevigata*.

Rosa camellia Listed as *Rosa laevigata*.

Rosa camelliaeflora Listed as *Rosa laevigata*.

Rosa cherokeensis Listed as *Rosa laevigata*.

Rosa cucumerina Listed as *Rosa laevigata*.

Rosa hystrix Listed as *Rosa laevigata*.

Rosa laevigata Plate 29
botanical syns. *R. alba chesuanensis foliorum marginibus et rachi medio spinosis, R. amygdalifolia, R. camelliaeflora, R. cherokeensis, R. cucumerina, R. hystrix, R. nivea, R. sinica, R. ternata, R. trifoliata*; horticultural syns., 'Blanc de Neige', 'Nivea', 'Rosa Camellia', 'Rosier de la Chine', 'Rosier Lisse', 'Rosier Trifolié', 'Ternata'

"Pure white, very large, flower curious." [LF] "Single and a climber. Pure white flower with brilliant yellow centre, beautiful foliage, highly polished. Very free-flowering and effective. Wall or summer-house covered with this rose in flower is a subject for admiration and astonishment to those not familiar with this striking variety. Has a very beautiful bud. Here [on the Riviera] one of the commonest, growing and flowering in profusion, but in England is a shy bloomer." [B&V] "Wonderful in *le Midi* with its large sarmentose canes, glossy persistent leaves, and its large white blossoms with their circlet of golden

golden

stamens."[JR26/181] "A strong grower. Flowers semi-double, and firm like pure white wax and show well against the deep green leaves." [C&Js12] "Though long considered a native, the Cherokee Rose is now believed to have originally been imported from China or Formosa. It is widely naturalized in the South, extending on the banks of irrigating canals far into Texas. Where it is sufficiently hardy to bloom well it is highly prized for its large and beautiful white blooms and shining deep green foliage." [ARA16/33] "From China, Formosa, and Japan, naturalized in southern states. High climber; slender green prickly branches. Flowers solitary, white and rarely rose, 2½ to 3½ inches across [ca. 6.5–9 cm]; fragrant. Blooms in June. Not hardy north." [ARA21/38]

"Though this rose has been grown for a pretty large number of years in several Parisian gardens—particularly that of Monsieur Dupont, who has devoted himself successfully to the culture and study of this beautiful genus—it has not yet been possible to get it to bloom." [Lam, under *Rosa ternata*] "This rose is not common; in our [French] gardens, it forms a medium-sized bush with thorns which are hooked, opposite, and red like the bark; its leaves are persistent, medium-sized, lanceolate, glossy, and a dark green—it doesn't drop them at all in Winter. Its blossoms are single, white, and two inches across [ca. 5 cm]; but they are never seen in the neighborhood of Paris. Monsieur le Marquis du Dresnay has, in his herbarium, a specimen of this rose collected in the gardens of Caserta, near Naples; its fruit is fairly large, a little constricted at the base, and covered—like the peduncles—with a great number of thick, russet bristles which are not glandulose, but narrowing. The calycinate divisions are entire. Judging by the specimen of Monsieur Dresnay's, the ternate-leafed rose needs a substantial soil mixed with heath soil; it should also be protected against strong frosts while it is still young." [CM]

"*Rootstock,* suckering somewhat; *canes* suberect, loosely tufted, branched, unarmed, 0.6–3(–4.5) m tall [ca. 2–13½ ft]; branches numerous, glabrous; *thorns* few, sparse, grayish, compressed and dilated lengthwise at the base, thin, hooked. Leaflets 3(–5), lanceolate ovate, simply serrate, quite glabrous, glossy, bright green; stipules narrow, sublinear, serrate, slightly glandular; petioles with 1–4 short, almost straight prickles. *Flowers* lateral or rarely terminal, solitary, quite single, 7.5 cm in diameter [ca. 3 in], scentless; ovoid *receptacles* and upper part of pedicels glandular hispid; *sepals* lanceolate, linear, glabrous, quite entire; *petals* rounded, very widespread, snow white, sub-crenate; *stamens* about 100; *styles* slender, villose, coherent; stigmas in a compact hemispherical head. This rose is probably native to China and was introduced to Europe by Lord Macartney. (Thory considers it to be native to New Georgia in America, collected by Michaux, and the same as *R. laevigata* of the *Jardin Royale*.) It is hardy at Montpellier and blooms in late May, before *R. bracteata*. It can be grafted on the Dog Rose, but does better on its own roots, the suckers being a means of propagation. It appreciates a porous but moist soil, its foliage yellowing with too much or too little moisture. A double variant, if obtainable, would be one of the most beautiful roses by virtue of the brilliant whiteness of the flowers and the beauty of the foliage. Dumont de Courset seems to have confused this species with *R. bracteata*. *R. nivea* [*i.e.*, *Rosa laevigata*] differs by the 3(–5) leaflets, glabrous branches, pedicels, and rounded entire petals. Equated with *R. sinica* L. by some, it differs by its globose, glabrous receptacle and differently shaped sepals. *Rosa trifoliata* is inapplicable as a

name here as there are sometimes 4 or 5 leaflets." [DeCandolle in T&R] "All the parts of this plant are glabrous; its canes bear sparse thorns, ordinarily in twos, hard, hooked, single at the base of the petioles. The leaves are alternate, stipulate, composed of leaflets which are very smooth, oval, lanceolate, nearly without evident veins, three to five in number; accompanied by narrow bracts, divided at their tip into two subulate and mucronate points. The calyx is oval, bearing on its tube some long narrow spines, and divided at its mouth into five [*sepals*] which are lanceolate, acuminate, and entire at their edges. This plant was collected by Michaux in the new Georgia in America … (description from Michaux)." [Lam, under *R. levigata* (sic)] "From China. Medium-sized bush; spines short, recurved, and red like the bark; leaves persistent, glossy and dark green; flowers white; fruits fairly large, a bit constricted around the base and covered, like the peduncles, with a great number of reddish bristles; calycinate divisions entire." [BJ24]

"The story of the Cherokee Rose is generally little known, and the differing appellations given this plant can be confusing—and so, it is perhaps not completely useless to devote a few words to the subject. Aiton erred in stating that Philip Miller grew it in 1759. The name *Rosa sinica* seems to have previously been given to a variety of *R. indica*. The French botanist Michaux (*Flora boreali-americana*, I, p. 295, 1803) described this rose under the name *Rosa Laevigata* after some specimens collected by Pursh in Georgia; it grew, at that time, in shady woods, climbing up to the tops of the tallest trees. Twenty years later, Elliott ([A] *Sketch of [the] Botany [of] South[-] Carolina and Georgia*, I, 1821, p. 566) mentions it as having been cultivated in Georgian gardens, for about 40 years, under the name 'Cherokee Rose', certainly the first common name. Its origin, according to Elliott, was rather obscure. Leonard Plukenet was the first one who mentioned this plant (*Amaltheum botanicum*, 1705, p. 185), working with a dried specimen sent from China by James Cunningham which is still preserved in the British Museum—without flowers. Plukenet made it known under the name *Rosa alba chesuanensis foliorum marginibus et rachi medio spinosis*. It is thus fully evident that it is indeed China from which this dried specimen came. *Cunninghamia sinensis* commemorates the name of the discoverer and introducer. According to Elliott, it [the rose] was grown in Georgia in 1780 and in France in 1804, from a Chinese introduction. Poiret (*Encyclopédie Supplément*, v. I, p. 284) published it under the name *Rosa ternata*. Some years later, Bosc called it *Rosa trifoliata*. According to Poiret, it had already been in cultivation for some time, though without yet having bloomed. The *Hortus cantabrigiensis* of Don talks about it as *Rosa cherokeensis*, in 1811, but without giving a description or its history. Lindley, in *Monographia Rosarum* (1820), maintains *Rosa sinica* and *trifoliata*; he [also] created *Rosa hystrix*, fully knowing that these three roses were extremely close to each other. In 1837, he figured *Rosa laevigata* under the name *Rosa sinica* (*Bot. Reg.* t. 1922) after some specimens grown at Fulham by Witley and Osborn. At that date, Lindley acknowledged the identification of the three species cited above, and added other synonyms. In 1813, DeCandolle had described the same plant as *Rosa nivea*, and it is under this name that Redouté illustrated it (*Liliacées* [sic] II, p. 81). Meantime, Aiton (*Hortus Kewensis*, id. 2, III, p. 261) had confused *Rosa laevigata* with the *R. sinica* of Linnaeus, which by all the evidence, is nothing other than *Rosa indica* [*i.e.*, *R. chinensis*]. The description given by Aiton for his *Rosa sinica*, copied from that by Linnaeus, has led most

Rosa laevigata continued

rhodologues to say that his plant was not the same as *Rosa laevigata*. In 1818, a book of pictures of Chinese plants (*Icones pictae indo-asiaticae, plantarum excerptae e codicibus Dom, Cattley*) reproduced the figure of *Rosa laevigata* which was published again, in 1821, in another publication, the title of which was *Icones plantarum × sponte, China nascentum e bibliotheca. braamiana excerptae*. It is singular that two monographs on roses would create a new species from that figure. Trattinick, in 1823, made *Rosa cucumerina,* which he considered as a totally distinct plant constituting a special series. Seringe, in 1825, created *Rosa amygdalifolia* from the same reference. Another synonym, *Rosa triphylla,* had been given by Roxburgh in his *Flora indica* (1832), where it is said that this species of Rose was introduced into the garden of Calcutta from China before 1794. The synonyms *Rosa Camellia* and *Camelliaeflora* are horticultural [*i.e., not botanical*]. The first, according to Crépin, is the name under which *Rosa laevigata* was introduced from Japan by Siebold. The first blossoming took place in England in the Glasgow botanical garden [*in Scotland, not England*], according to Sir William Hooker, in 1828. The blooming plant came from Savannah [*Georgia, U.S.A.*], and bore the name 'Cherokee Rose'. Crépin, in 1889, in accord—in this—with Thory and Trattinick, made *Rosa laevigata* the Type of one group; he attributed 'Fortuniana' [Bks] to a cross between this rose and *R. banksia*. Regel gave the name *R. laevigata* var. *Braamiana* to a rose which would only seem to be *R. involucrata* Roxb. [*i.e., Rosa bracteata*], though this last had not been found in China in a wild state. And so, summarizing the above, the synonymy of the Cherokee Rose is as follows: *Rosa alba chesuanensis,* Plukenet, 1705; *R. laevigata,* Mich., 1803; *R. ternata,* Poiret, 1804; *R. sinica,* Aiton, 1811, non L.; *R. cherokeensis,* Don, 1811; *R. nivea,* D.C., 1813; *R. trifoliata,* Bosc, date uncertain; *R. hystrix,* Lind., 1820; *R. cucumerina,* Tratt., 1823; *R. amygdalifolia,* Seringe, 1825; *R. triphylla,* Roxb., 1832; *R. Camellia* and *R. camelliaeflora,* date uncertain." [JR28/41–42] "Formerly, some people also knew it under the name 'Rosier de la Chine' [*i.e., "Rose from China"*]." [Gx]

Rosa nivea   Listed as *Rosa laevigata*.

Rosa sinica   Listed as *Rosa laevigata*.

Rosa ternata   Listed as *Rosa laevigata*.

Rosa trifoliata   Listed as *Rosa laevigata*.

Horticultural Varieties

Anemone Rose   Listed as 'Anemonenrose' (Lv).

Anemonoides   Listed as 'Anemonenrose' (Lv).

Anemonenrose
syns. 'Anemone Rose', 'Anemonoides', 'Sinica Anemone'
J. C. Schmidt, 1896
From *Rosa laevigata* × a Tea Rose.

"Silvery carnation pink." [Ÿ] "Bright rosy pink; shell-shaped petals; very vigorous but rather tender." [NRS18/135] "Single, a silvery white, somewhat inclined to shade to rose; floriferous. In every respect this is a bad imitation of [*Rosa laevigata*], but it is more hardy, and valu-

able because it flowers freely in England. The blooms bear a strong resemblance to Anemone Japonica Elegans." [B&V] "Stronger than the parent Cherokee (and its saucer-shaped flowers, of a striking and rather cold pink, are more than beautiful among purple wisteria here)." [ARA19/87] "Large silvery pink, single. Growth vigorous, climber, likes a warm wall." [GeH] "The most beautiful of all single Roses, the rose-pink sinica Anemone, is one of the earliest to bloom, coming into flower in the 'merry month of May.' It appreciates the protection of a south wall, and is capable of covering a large space; in pruning, only the oldest wood should be taken out, and plenty of liberty should be permitted to long new branches." [NRS18/132] "Useful in the South." [GAS] See also 'Pink Cherokee' (Lv) and 'Anemonaeflora' (Bks).

Blanc de Neige   Listed as *Rosa laevigata*.

[Double Cherokee]
California Nursery Co., pre-1891

"This is a strong climber, and has double white flowers." [CA93] "[The blossom [?] is] halfway in size between Cherokees and Banksias, a Climber, with double flowers produced in one long, spring blooming period . . . rare and very attractive as a large bush." [CaRoll/4/3] Possibly synonymous with 'Fortuneana' (Bks), *q.v.*

[Mrs. A. Kingsmill]
G. Paul, 1911
Seedling of 'Anemonenrose' (Lv).

"Pale pink, soft rose reverse." [NRS15/149] "Flower pale shell-pink, very free. Growth vigorous." [GeH] "Dwarf, perpetual flowering." [NRS11/197] "This hybrid . . . is dwarf, remontant, and has large single blossoms; the color resembles that of its mother, but in reverse. The variety 'Anemonenrose' has pink on the upper side of the petals, while 'Mrs. A. Kingsmill' has it on the underside." [JR36/57]

"I do not suppose there is any living person who is better acquainted with the Rose than our old friend Mr. George Paul. He was born and cradled amongst Roses, and has practically devoted his life to them, and many indeed have been the new varieties that have come from that home of the Rose, Cheshunt. In his early days, when nurserymen were almost the only exhibitors at the shows, there were four men whose names were then, so to speak, household words—Rivers, Lane, Paul and Wood—of whom Mr. Paul is the sole survivor . . . He told me that after leaving his school in Germany, he spent nearly two years with his father's old friend, Mr. Charles Fisher, at Handsworth, near Sheffield, leaving to join his father at Cheshunt in the autumn of 1860. He first began exhibiting in the summer of 1862 . . . The lamented death of his father, Mr. George Paul, at the early age of 57, left him in charge of the large nursery with other cultures besides Roses, an undertaking which luckily proved possible from his training at Handsworth.

"Pot Roses had attained in the early [18]70's their greatest development, and at the large summer shows in the Botanic Gardens of the R.H.S., and at the Manchester Exhibition, specimens were shown by Mr. Charles Turner and himself which probably will never be repeated. Some six or eight plants filled a railway truck, and he well remembers a 'Charles Lawson' [HB] 'tied out for show' with 70 or 80 perfect blooms. Mr. Charles Turner was indeed an opponent well worth fighting, and their respective Rose foremen, Charles Gater, of Cheshunt, and his brother William, of Slough—'a pair of Gaters!' Dean Hole called them—were probably the best growers of pot Roses the world has seen . . .

"He knew personally all the raisers in England—Ward, Laxton, Mr. Ingram of Windsor, the Cants, Bennett, the Dicksons, McGredy, and of the French raisers, Lacharme, the two Guillots, Liabaud, Pernet of Lyon, Margottin, Charles and Eugène Verdier, and Lévêque of Paris. In the early days he always spent a week amongst the raisers at Lyon and Paris to see their new novelties of the year—happy, pleasant holidays. Talking of judging at the Lyon exhibition, he tells me he well remembers suggesting Captain Christy's name being attached to Lacharme's new Rose of the year. For many years he used to judge Roses at the Paris Triennial Shows and also the Grand International Exhibition, and he was one of the judges in the Rose Section at the great Ghent Shows.

"He tells me 'I think perhaps the greatest happiness of my life has been the friendship of nearly all the Rose-growers of England ... And of the long list of amateurs—the Rev. H. D'ombrain, Dean Hole, Mr. Baker of Exeter, Mr. Lindsell, and the Rev. J. Pemberton, all ex-champions; and, further back, Mr. Hedge of Colchester ..., Mr. Perry of Birmingham, who first originated the 'pegged down' system for Roses, and the Rev. Alan Cheales,' and, he added, 'I had almost omitted my old friend the Rev. Page-Roberts." [NRS20/25–28] "It will always be a source of satisfaction to have known George Paul. I spent a delightful day with him at Cheshunt, Herts., on September 5. He died suddenly about two weeks later. Although nearly eighty years old, he was, when I saw him, apparently hale and hearty, and he showed a keen interest in everything that pertained to the rose. He welcomed me with cordial hospitality. The American rosarian always associates the name of Paul & Sons with the introduction of the first Hybrid Tea rose, 'Cheshunt Hybrid' [Cl HT; see *The Old Rose Advisor*]. Mr. Paul retained to the last his keen desire to produce 'something better.' He was most enthusiastic over two varieties which seem to be particularly promising. These were: 'The Premier', a climbing hybrid of *Rosa lutescens,* and Paul's Perpetual-flowering Lemon Pillar [*i.e.,* 'Paul's Lemon Pillar' (Cl HT)] ...'" [ARA22/133]

Nivea Listed as *Rosa laevigata.*

Pink Cherokee
syn. 'Rosea'
California, 1887?
"A pink flowering form of the Single Cherokee rose. Possesses all the merits of the original." [CA10]

Ramona
syn. 'Red Cherokee'
Dietrich & Turner/California Nursery Co., 1913
Sport of 'Pink Cherokee' (Lv) or possibly 'Anemonenrose' (Lv).
"A dark rose-pink or light red form of the Cherokee, popular in the South." [GAS] "Flowers on young plants variable from pink to brilliant cherry carmine. The red color becomes more fixed as the plants attain age and strength." [CA14] "[In the southern United States] 'Ramona' will give scattering flowers through a long period." [ARA16/98] "In my garden, always the magnificent and profuse herald of the entire rose season, the scattered petals on the ground—deep pink on one side, whitish on the other—themselves giving as festive a look to the scene as the hundreds of blossoms adorning the plant above. The first hint of a warm spell will bring on the bloom in the late Winter or earliest Spring, bringing the balm of hope to the patient—and the impatient—rosarian. The thorns are cruel, as if knowing that they must guard a treasure." [BCD] "Carmine pink, large, single, tall."

[Sn] "This sensational and magnificent new climbing rose occurred as a sport from the well-known 'Pink Cherokee' ... It is a stronger and more rampant grower than its parent, and produces during the spring and early summer months, flowers in such profusion as to entirely cover the plant; in autumn there is a secondary crop of bloom. The flowers are much larger than either the pink or white forms, with brilliant golden-yellow stamens and broad petals of a glorious carmine-crimson color; an unusual shade, wonderfully striking and effective; the foliage is absolutely mildew proof, a rich glossy-green, so bright that it appears as though varnished. 'Ramona' will be of special value as a garden rose to the entire Pacific Coast. For planting on pergolas, pillars, perches, etc., it is a rose of unique and beautiful effect; in addition, it makes an elegant hedge plant if properly trained and pruned." [CA13] Ramona, Indian heroine of the 1884 of the same name about Old California, by Helen Hunt Jackson. There is an annual pageant in Hemet, California, based on the novel.

Red Cherokee Listed as 'Ramona' (Lv).

Rosea Listed as 'Pink Cherokee' (Lv).

Rosier de la Chine Listed as *Rosa laevigata.*

Rosier Lisse Listed as *Rosa laevigata.*

Rosier Trifolié Listed as *Rosa laevigata.*

Silver Moon
Van Fleet/Henderson, 1909
From *Rosa wichuraiana × R. laevigata.*
"Pale cream yellow to silvery white, large and semi-single. Growth very vigorous." [GeH] "The cupped blossoms measure up to 11 cm across [ca 4¹/₄ in], and are a beautiful silvery white color. They are single and very fragrant. The bush is vigorous and very floriferous." [JR33/135] "Splendid blooming qualities." [ARA18/21] "Primrose buds of pleasing shape ... disease-resistant." [C-Ps26] "Extra large; single; silver-white with golden yellow stamens; of remarkably strong growth; very distinct. Foliage lasts well." [ARA17/28] "Flowers are extra large and freely produced on long, strong stems; fine for cutting. Color is silvery white with a mass of golden yellow stamens in the center of the flower, which is a very attractive feature. Fragrance delicious. Foliage is a beautiful bronzy green and does not mildew." [C7Js12] "The grandest white climbing Rose. Flowers are very large, semi-double, and when open resemble a white clematis with a center of golden anthers. A most vigorous grower with large, dark green, shiny foliage. Quite different from all other climbing Roses." [C7Js23] "Enormously vigorous Wichuraiana, said to carry a strain of Cherokee. Large, almost single, pure white flowers borne in great abundance. One of the finest white-flowered ramblers, but too tender for severe climates." [GAS] "It grows prodigiously, and has perhaps the finest foliage of any, save 'American Pillar'. Its elongated buds and huge creamy-white single flowers are most attractive." [NRS18/149–150] "I measured this year's growth of new canes. One cane measured 2⁷/₈ inches in circumference at base [ca. 7.5 cm], and was 24 feet long [ca. 8 m]. Another one was 2.75 inches at base [ca. 7 cm] and 23 feet long [ca. 7.6 m]. The total growth of all laterals and canes this year, on this one rose, was 261 feet [ca. 80 m]!" [ARA23/185] "We always like 'Silver Moon' on account of its wealth of bloom, extreme hardiness, and clean foliage. It is indeed a wonderful rose." [ARA24/189]

Sinica Anemone Listed as 'Anemonenrose' (Lv).

CHAPTER TWENTY

Banksias

"Though for a long time we have had the very prettiest sorts of roses, we have however sought to add yet further to our delight in this group. We have searched for new roses among the Chinese and Japanese who have several species unknown to us. Of this number is the Banksia [cultivar 'Alba Plena'], which the English imported from China to England in 1807, and which Monsieur Cels and Monsieur Noisette have grown for 4 years [*writing in 1824*] in Paris, where we saw it in bloom at the latter's premises." [BJ24] "In 1825, [Vibert] introduced into France...the *Yellow Banksia.*" [SHP29/149] "Named by the botanist Robert Brown for Lady Banks." [GAS] "Dedicated to Lady Banks, wife of Sir Joseph Banks, well known English collector, who traveled with Captain Cook. William Kerr brought the first plants, from Chinese gardens, in 1807." [ExRé] "There are records of Banksian roses in England with trunks 2 feet 4 inches in circumference [ca. 7 dm], and a spread of 75 feet [ca. 25 m], bearing 50,000 to 60,000 flowers at one time. Throughout the southern states and on the Pacific Coast many magnificent Banksias are to be seen." [GAS] "Quite a feature and glory of the Riviera...They like to take possession of rows of trees or buildings forming a sort of coronet on the top, from which depend long shoots covered with innumerable flowers; in the case of the double yellow sort, one is reminded of the 'shower of gold' at a display of fireworks." [B&V]

"This rose differs widely in appearance from other roses, and the difficulty experienced by many in inducing it to grow and bloom freely points out the error of treating it as other roses. It is met with in the regular course of business, and the question that it is a rose being satisfactorily determined, it is pruned as a rose, the how, when, and where being never once thought of. Hence, the cause of the disappointment that so frequently ensues. Now, how pleasant it would be, if, with a little management, the many barren plants could be induced to change their character, and thus convert barrenness into a course of admiration and delight! To accomplish this end, do not prune the Banksian at set seasons, as with other roses. It is disposed to form strong shoots in the summertime. Watch for the appearance of these, and, so soon as they are about a foot long [ca. 3 dm], pinch off their tops. In conse-

quence of this check, they will form laterals, which become well ripened, and flower with certainty. It is necessary to cut their tops off early in Spring, and from this period the plants should be watched throughout the growing season. Where too many shoots arise from one spot, let some be broken out entirely when young, and let the others be stopped when they attain the length before mentioned. There was a plant which covered one side of a house in this neighborhood, but which was unfortunately destroyed by the severe frost during the Winter of 1837–8. It was subjected to the treatment mentioned above, and produced annually thousands of its beautiful blossoms." [MH47/413]

"This shrub puts out, from its base, some long, slender, and thornless branches which can go very high against a wall or fence, as long as one makes the effort to cut out, in March or April, the dead wood, and to secure the green branches. The leaves vary from three to seven leaflets, elongate-oval in shape, glossy on both sides, and finely dentate. At the base of the young growth, one can see two stipules which desiccate, disappear, and soon fall. The elegantly-scented blossoms, small and in panicles, look like those of the Parma violet, and are borne on small laterals from the long stems. A person can only find, in this species, two colors—yellow and white. They don't set hips in our climates, and indeed, when they do, it is difficult to obtain hybrids from seed because, the flowers being early, are gone by the time other species bloom. Recently, however, someone has bred a thorny variety—which we haven't been able to assess yet because, so far, we haven't seen it bloom [*presumably 'Fortuneana'*]. We are told that the Banksia was brought from China to England in 1807. It was dedicated to Lady Banks, spouse of the savant of that name who accompanied Captain Cook on his travels. It was introduced into France by Monsieur Boursault in 1817, who grew it in a temperate house where, in 1819, it bloomed on very high branches. Today, this rose is grown in the open, against a wall, needing a warm and protected site. If, before Winter, measures aren't taken to cover it with straw up to a certain height to preserve at least part of the stems intended to bear the laterals in the Spring, one runs the risk of seeing no bloom. The canes freeze to the ground, and the new growths which sprout from the trunk can't bloom the same year. This rose has much in common, in its growth, with the more hardy species *R. sempervirens* and *R. multiflora*." [JDR55/23–24]

"*Banksia with small white flowers and with small yellow flowers*. Everybody knows these two charming varieties. The first was brought from China to England in 1807 and planted in the garden of Mr. J[oseph] Banks, at Spring Grove … According to Monsieur Déséglise, the second (Damper, 1823) was being grown in gardens in 1824. Climbing bush with thornless green stems; leaves comprised of 3, 5, and sometimes 7 glossy oval lanceolate leaflets; setaceous, fugaceous stipules at base of leafstalk; flowers small (about 3 cm [ca. $^3/_4$ in], numerous, borne on glabrous peduncles, and in tight clusters at the cane-tips; central petals ragged; scent of violets or raspberries. These varieties are very vigorous, and likely to climb to a great height; they make very beautiful weepers, but they only really do well in warm locales; the Banksias you see in the gardens of Paris give you no idea of the beautiful growth of these shrubs … In the north [of France], as in the east, I believe that one would do well to grow the Banksia in the ground in a temperate house as the sole means of getting good growth; to the greatest degree possible, however, one should avoid growing it in a pot, as this gives only mediocre results. It should not be forgotten that the flowers come on the canes of the preceding year; therefore, for a good bloom, it should not be pruned … It has been asked whether this rose might be useful as a stock …? Yes, evidently, but only if grown in *le Midi*, because, as I put, this rose is pretty sensitive to cold … All the same, let me add that, if one can, without difficulty, graft several varieties on HP's, Teas, or Noisettes on a vigorous branch of the Banksia, it gives the bush a look all its own, and one gets a very pretty effect." [JR10/21] "A southern publication has recommended to fanciers grafting remontant roses on the yellow Banksia: 'Monsieur A. L. [*probably Alphonse Lavallée*] came up with the idea of grafting our remontant roses on the Banksia. This is how he covers walls with long garlands of roses. The Banksia grows quite tall—it has vigorous growth; remontant roses, grafted on the stems, grow six to seven meters [ca. 18–21 ft] over the course of the year. The Banksia rose blooms earlier than our remontant roses; the bloom of these grafts is three weeks earlier than those grafted on the Briar.' Perhaps this methodology is practicable in *le Midi*—but around here [Lyon] and in the North, where the cold rages harshly, both the [white] Banksia and its yellow variety can't be protected without much effort. We don't think, all in all, that these grafts would be easy to duplicate nor last very long on this species. Several sorts of Multifloras, the growth of which is as luxuriant as that of the Banksia, would seem to us to offer more certain success to fanciers. Nevertheless, we intend to try out the experiment recommended by the growers in *le Midi*." [JDR57/4]

"Especially valuable for use in barrancas or to cover large outbuildings, etc." [CaRoII/4/3] "They are among the most rapid-growing climbers and most useful for covering arbors, bare walls, old stumps, and other unsightly objects. They are thornless, will succeed under any ordinary circumstances, and require but little care." [CA96]

Rosa banksiae

"The Banksia Type is a shrub with climbing stems which are glabrous and smooth, and thornless. Its leaves, composed of three to five glossy, glabrous, smooth leaflets, are accompanied by two very lacy stipules, distinct from or only slightly adherent to the leafstalk; the small, fragrant flowers are disposed several to a corymb at the tips of the canes; the fruit is glabrous and globular. Today [1851], we know of four varieties of this rose: 1. the Type [*Rosa banksiae*], with single white flowers; 2. A variety with full white flowers ['Alba Plena'], introduced in 1807 by William Kerr … 3. Another, with full yellow flowers ['Lutea'], brought to the London Horticultural Society in 1823 by Mr. John Damper Parks … In these three varieties, the stems are thornless, and the flowers, to nearly 3 cm in size [to 1¼ in], are clustered several to a 'bouquet' at the tips of the canes. Finally, 4. The Thorny Banksia ['Fortuneana'], recently introduced to England by Mr. Fortune, imported to France through the efforts of Messrs. Thibault and Keteléer, [and growing in the greenhouses at Hippolyte Jamain's]." [l'H51/49–50] As we read in Phillips & Rix, this single white form was introduced to Europe by Robert Drummond in 1796.

Horticultural Varieties

À Fleurs Jaunes Listed as 'Lutescens Simplex' (Bks).

[Alba Grandiflora]
Breeder unknown, pre-1846

"A large single white flower." [WRP] "Very small, full flowers, delicately scented." [EL] Perhaps WRP refers to *Rosa laevigata*, while EL possibly refers to 'Alba Plena', 'Anemonaeflora', or 'Fortuneana'. *Quien sabe, señor?*

Alba Plena
syns. 'Blanc Ancien', 'Double White'; trans., "Double White"
Kerr/Banks, 1807

"Small, full, violet scent." [LF] "*Flowers*, extremely small, very double, white; expanding from March till May; highly scented with violets." [Go] "Flowers little more than half an inch in diameter [ca. 1.5 cm], which are of the purest white, with a delicate pink centre of a very delightful violet perfume, and are produced in a profusion of small clusters." [Bu] "A sweet perfume as though it had just returned on a visit from the Violet." [H] "The *Double White* was introduced to the European gardens in 1807, and shortly after to those of America. The flowers are very small, of a pleasant violet-like perfume, and are produced in wreaths on very long flexible shoots, the bark of which is green." [WRP] "This rose, which originated in China, was introduced, in England, in 1807, and bloomed for the first time in Paris in 1819. It is extremely vigorous, and may be found growing to the tops of the tallest trees in *le Midi*. Its branches, very slender and long, have no thorns; the bark is smooth and pale green; its leaves, of 3–5 ferny pointed leaflets, are glossy on both sides; the flowers, in clusters, are numerous, on branchlets, and borne on a stem of about two inches [ca. 5 cm]; they are small, [*single*], white, and have a distinct fragrance of violets. This rose is very tender … There also exists a yellow flowered variety which seems less affected by cold." [JF] "It can only be grown successfully in the open air in the favorable climate of Austria, France, and Italy; in the north of Germany, it needs the protection of a hothouse or conservatory, where it grows so quickly that in only a short time it covers laths and walls, and impresses by its mass of blossoms which are quite different from those of other roses, being rather like those of the double-flowered cherry. The shoots, thornless or with isolated thorns, and the bright foliage mainly composed of leaves with three leaflets, make this rose very interesting. You can find it already in the southern Tyrol clothing walls, annually growing trunks an inch thick [ca. 2.5 cm] and 4–5 meters long [ca. 12–15 ft], ornamented with many flowers. Farther south, in Rome, or Naples, you can find colossal specimens, and the effect produced by such a climbing or scandent rose when it forms allées or crowns the top of trees is one of enchantment." [JR8/60] "In the middle of France, sometimes grows to the top of the tallest poplars, and covers walls and roofs with its green foliage and its myriads of small milk-white flowers." [JF] "In Italy and the south of France it grows to perfection, climbing with an astonishing vigor, and covering every object within its reach. According to the French writer Deslongchamps, there was in 1842 a Banksia Rose at Toulon, of which the stem was, at its base, two feet and four inches in circumference [ca. 7 dm]; while the largest of the six branches measured a foot in girth [ca. 3 dm]. Its foliage covered a space of wall seventy-five feet wide [ca. 25 m], and about eighteen feet high [ca. 6 m]; and it sometimes produced shoots fifteen feet long [ca. 5 m] in a single year. It flowered in April and May; from fifty to sixty thousand of its double white blossoms opening at once, with an effect which the writer describes as magical." [FP]

"Rose with round seed-buds and long smooth peduncles: flowers numerous, in racemes mostly of three and four flowers, small, and of many folds, of a whitish colour, and sweet-scented: leaflets lance-shaped, long, and shining, with finely serrated edges: stem and petioles smooth and unarmed. This elegant training [*sic; 'trailing'?*] Rose is a native of China, and was first introduced to the Royal Gardens at Kew by Mr. W. Kerr in 1807. It is named in honour of Lady Banks, and figured in the Botanical Magazine, pl. 1954; and although it has been 14 years in cultivation with us, we have not heard of its flowering in any of the nurseries round London: or, if it has, not in the perfection it does when further removed from the smoky atmosphere of the metropolis. [Andrews'] drawing was made from a fine specimen sent us by Mr. Fairbairn from the superb collection of Prince Leopold at Claremont. The only rose to which it bears any resemblance is the Autumnal-flowering or Musk-scented: but altogether it is a very distinct species from any that we are at present acquainted with." [A] "Basally branched *shrub,* rambling and climbing to a great height when supported; *canes* long, whiplike, glabrous, green, unarmed. *Leaflets* (3–)5–7, elliptic ovate, glossy on both surfaces, finely and simply dentate with a glandular hair on each tooth; petiole glabrous above; beneath, having soft recumbent hairs extending to the ribs of the leaflets; stipules 2, free, setaceous, villose, acute, withering and fugaceous. *Flowers* small, with a sweet penetrating scent like that of violets, 10–20 in simple umbels on the laterals; pedicels 3–4 cm long [to ca. 1½ in]; bracts 2, one simple, the other of 3(–5) leaflets; *recep-*

tacles globose, glabrous like the pedicels; *sepals* short, entire, acute, glabrous without, whitish woolly within; *petals* 4–5-seriate, pure clear white, those at the center curled and crumpled, almost hiding the remaining stamens; *styles* short, free; *stigmas* a rather bright red … Boursault brought it to France in 1817 and grew it planted out in peaty soil in his magnificent temperate house, where it exceeded 13 m [ca. 40 ft] … *Rosa banksiae* is related to *R. sempervirens* 'Globosa' Thory and *R. sempervirens* 'Microphylla' D.C., but differs in its glabrous stems, pedicels, and receptacles; large umbels; free, filiform, caducous stipules; no bracteoles, and free styles. Pot plants raised by Cels and Noisettes have done badly and not bloomed. It would be desirable if this could be acclimatized outdoors where it would be suitable for covering arbors, permeating them with the delicious fragrance of its blossoms." [T&R]

"When this rose first made its appearance in the time of Sir Joseph Banks, it was hailed with the greatest rapture by every lover of the tribe, and it was instantly complimented with the name of his lady. It is the states south of [Pennsylvania] where is must be seen to be pronounced the most graceful, luxuriant, and beautiful of roses; there it is a perfect evergreen, covering the ends, fronts, and, in some instances, the entire dwellings of many of the inhabitants, who name it the *'Evergreen Multiflora'.* To us [further north], the beauty of the plant is nearly lost, being too tender for planting in the garden, and when grown in the greenhouse, its beauty and luxuriance almost disappear. This thornless rose is so perfectly double that it rarely produces seed." [Bu] "This White Banksia was planted thirty-five years ago, and though numerous dead branches have been taken out of it for the past several years, it is still in a very healthy condition. The pergola which supports it is 7 to 8 feet [ca. 2.3–2.6 m] from where the roots come out of the ground, and the columns cover a space of about 7 by 19 feet [ca. 2.3–6.3 m]. It has a gnarled and twisted trunk, in several branches. With the dead bark on, it looks like an old cedar tree or much like an old Scuppernong grape. Several branches are 3 to 4 inches in diameter [ca. 7.5 cm to 1 dm] … Considering the age of the bush, its immense size, its curious trunk, and the fact that it blooms abundantly every spring, with occasional blooms in the autumn, it seems to me to be quite a remarkable rose bush. It is of unusual beauty when in bloom and even when there are no flowers it is very beautiful with foliage very much like smilax." [ARA30/212]

Anemonaeflora
syn. 'Banksiaeflora'
Fortune, 1844

"White, centre cream, small and double, beautiful shining foliage." [JC] "Pink in the bud fading to nearly white … Pretty, but not in the first flight of Ramblers." [T4] "Flowers cream with yellowish centre, of medium size, very double; form, cupped. A distinct and good Pillar or Climbing Rose; the foliage of a fine light green; the flowers produced in handsome clusters. Requires very little pruning." [P] See also 'Anemonenrose' (Lv).

Banksiaeflora Listed as 'Anemonaeflora' (Bks).

Blanc Ancien Listed as 'Alba Plena' (Bks).

Double White Listed as 'Alba Plena' (Bks).

Double Yellow Listed as 'Lutea' (Bks).

Épineux de la Chine Listed as 'Fortuneana' (Bks).

Fortuneana
Fortune, 1840
syns. 'Épineux de la Chine', 'Fortunei', 'Fortuniana', 'La Chinoise'
Fortune, 1840

"Blush-white." [EL] "Very large, double flowers, chamois orange." [Mz52–53s/12] "White, large, and very sweet." [JC] "Canes thorny; medium-sized, very full, pure white." [BJ58] "A perfectly formed flower three inches or so in diameter [ca. 7.5 cm +], very pure, making a great show from tree tops." [B&V]

"Introduced from China in 1840 by the explorer Fortune. It is ... very vigorous. Its branches ... are armed with occasional short and hooked thorns ...; the bark is smooth and dark green; the leaves, the petiole of which is prickly, are divided into three or five leaflets which are close-set and pointed, beautiful dark green, and glossy on both sides; they are very abundant and may be called persistent, because they don't fall until after Winter. The flowers, larger and more double than those of the Banksia, are white, either solitary or in clusters of 3–5, borne on branchlets which grow from the previous year's canes." [JF] "The Thorny Banksia Rose ... is a climbing shrub with smooth, glabrous stems of a dark green, sometimes tinted with brown, clothed with some occasional elongated thorns (two or more per inter-node), which are very sharp, slightly back-hooked, enlarged at the base, dark brown, and five to six mm long [ca. ¼ in]. The flowering stems which grow from the axil of each leaf have, at their bases, some small, caducous brown scales; they bristle their whole length with large thick transparent hairs, and are prolonged in a long delicate-green flower-stalk, which is also bristly. The leaves are usually composed of three (rarely one or five) pointed oblong-lanceolate leaflets which are glabrous, glossy, smooth, dark green above, and lighter and more glossy beneath; the edges have some fine dentations which are tipped with a transparent point; the rachis of the lower face of the leaflet bristles with large thick hairs or rudimentary prickles. The lateral leaflets are nearly sessile; the terminal one—larger—is borne on a stalk about a centimeter long [ca. ⅜ in]. The common petiole is caniculate and is edged, above, with kinds of cilia; beneath, it is armed with several thick bristles, of which some are developed to the state of small arc-ed prickles. At the base of these petioles can be found two very lacy stipules, distinct from the petiole, edged with glandular bristles. The blossoms, solitary at the tips of the canes, are very full, slightly ruffled, to five cm in size [ca. 2 in], with a light pale reflection, giving a certain shimmer to its appearance. The calyx-tube (the ovary of the horticulturalists) is semiglobular, not constricted at the tip, light green, glabrous, or bearing some bristles, but only at the base; the sepals are much elongated, entire, or sometimes terminated by a foliaceous appendage, edged with cilia and with a fine cottony surface, glabrous on the outer face, cottony white within. The petals are obovate, and undulate or slightly ragged; at the center appear several stamens and the stigmas which form the entrance to the calygeal tube. This new variety is a happy development for Floriculture! It has the benefit of producing, very young, a great quantity of large blossoms; and it takes with great ease to forcing. We have seen, at Monsieur Jamain's, some specimens at least fifty cm high [ca. 20 in] on which you could count fifteen to twenty perfectly-developed flowers." [l'H51/50–51]

"Climbing shrub, hardy, evergreen, with large solitary blossoms in the axils of the leaves comprised of 3–5 leaflets. This is one of the plants introduced from China by the well-known collector Fortune now in the garden of the London horticultural society. Its wide-ranging slender canes bear here and there some hooked prickles. The leaflets are oval-lanceolate, finely dentate like a saw, slender, gay green, and glossy on both sides. The small and subulate stipules are caducous as is the case with the Banksia. The flowers, borne on short setiferous stalks, have a calyx with a nude hemispherical tube; sepals oval, entire; petals white, grouped irregularly in a not-very-tight mass about 8 cm across [ca. 3⅛ in]. That this is not a Banksia is shown by the solitary blossoms and thorny canes; no more is it a form of *Rosa sinica* [i.e., *R. laevigata*], as we see by its less robust habit and the absence of thorns on the calyx-tube. Is it not possible that it is a hybrid between these two species?" [V-H51–52/257]

"Monsieur A. Boisselot, Nantes horticulturalist, sends us the following letter: 'I am going to try—me, too—to add my humble stone to the edifice you are constructing in honor of the Queen of Flowers. The question has come up in the *Journal des Roses* as to what climbing variety is the one I love above all others. It is Fortune's Banksia. I want to mention the one with very large white blossoms. The plant is extremely vigorous, with very large wood, and is perhaps the hardiest of the Banksias, as it got through the terrible Winter of 1880. The flower is big, white, and so full that it nearly forms a compact bowl; the ruffled petals recurve, making the flower resemble a pompom. Nothing is as beautiful in the beginning of Spring as to see these garlands of hundreds of blossoms covering a great area.'" [JR8/1] "At the beginning of last year, I sent you a little note on Fortune's Banksia. I am back today to confirm to you the eulogy I delivered on this variety. This rose being of extreme vigor the whole year, the sorts grafted on it profit greatly thereby. Fortune's Banksia never defoliates to speak of; and, at the beginning of Spring, a month before other roses, it covers itself with a multitude of flowers. One can leave it to itself to cover tunnels and walls, then, on its enormous growths which branch high above the trunk, can graft on it such varieties as 'Gloire de Dijon' [N], 'Belle Lyonnaise' [N], and 'Maréchal Niel' [N]. And that's what I have done. A bud of 'Belle Lyonnaise', taken only last Spring, gave me, about November 15 (despite heavy frosts), a dozen beautiful roses, and still had, the 22nd of the same month, an equal quantity of half-open buds, plus twenty-five less advanced. I must admit that I had pinched the hungry branches of this bud several times during the year. It is necessary to take the effort to prune out the numerous and heavy 'gourmands' which surge from the stock [i.e., from the 'Fortuneana' stock on which the scion is grafted]. It seems to me that, if a person doesn't want climbing roses, he can graft on this variety all the other remontant roses. To do just that, I have planted several of Fortune's Banksias in the ground to grow big bushes." [JR9/1] "Is greatly admired." [FP]

Fortunei Listed as 'Fortuneana' (Bks).

Fortuniana Listed as 'Fortuneana' (Bks).

Hybride di Castello
Italy, 1920
From 'Lutescens' (Bks) × 'Lamarque' (N).

As we read in Griffiths, a vigorous-growing plant with large pure white double flowers.

Jaune Listed as 'Lutescens Simplex' (Bks).

Jaunâtre Pleine Listed as 'Lutea' (Bks).

La Chinoise Listed as 'Fortuneana' (Bks).

Lutea
syns. 'Double Yellow', 'Jaunâtre Pleine', 'Luteo-Plena'; trans., "Straw-
    Yellow"
Parks, 1823
    "Primrose yellow." [FP] "No scent." [LF] "Pale yellow, or straw-
coloured flowers, in size rather larger than the white, being perfectly
imbricated, and really gems of beauty, but without odour; if either
this or the white were to be seen apart from the plant, by the inexperi-
enced, they would never be taken for a rose." [Bu] *Flowers,* yellow, in
clusters, scentless. Imported from the botanical garden of Calcutta,
where it is cultivated under the name of Wong-moue-heong." [Go]
"The *Double Yellow* was not brought to Europe until 1827. It is an
unique and beautiful variety, with small pale buff scentless flowers."
[WRP] "Contrary to the statements in many books, and to the usual
opinion, I find it is not by any means scentless." [T4] "According to
Déséglise (*Catalogue raisonné des espèces du genre rosier, numéro
37*), it was growing in our [French] gardens in 1824." [JR10/21]

Lutea Simplex Listed as 'Lutescens Simplex' (Bks).

Luteo-Plena Listed as 'Lutea' (Bks).

Lutescens Simplex
syns. 'À Fleurs Jaunes', 'Jaune', 'Lutea Simplex'; trans., "Single
    Straw-Yellowish"
Introducer unknown, pre-1829
    Light yellow. "A single variety." [GAS] "No scent." [LF] "This charm-
ing variety grows in a most graceful way, sending up long shoots of
twenty feet and more [ca. 6.6 m +], like supple fishing rods." [???] "This
rare and interesting variety can be seen in bloom during May and
June at Monsieur Cels', as well as at the Horticultural Institute of Fromont." [R-H29/78] Testu tells of a later (re-)introduction by Sir Thomas
Hanbury at the great botanical garden La Mortola in Italy in 1870.

Purezza
Mansuimo, 1961
From 'Tom Thumb' (Miniature China) × 'Lutescens' (Bks).
    As we read in Griffiths, the blossoms are double, fragrant, white,
and 3 cm [ca. 1¼ in], in clusters; the plant is vigorous and may rebloom. "Quinto Mansuimo of San Remo, Italy, reported on his work
in the ARA of 1960 . . . I don't know if he introduced it: Sweet-scented and white, the climber blooms continuously December through
July. He called it a 'candid cascade'. Just the thing for a Californian
who wants a white Christmas . . . From this he raised a very fertile
pink mini, which he called the world's first everblooming Banksia
hybrid." [kK] It is by compelling speculation that I connect Mansuimo's rose, with its ancestry, with Griffiths' 'Purezza'.

[Rosea]
Breeder unknown, pre-1846
    "Flowers vivid rose, double; form, cupped." [P] "A hybrid, with
very bright roseate flowers, the whole plant partaking as much of the
character of the Boursault Rose as of the Banksian: in fact, it is a most
complete mule; and though it has lost a little too much caste in the
shape and size of its flowers—for they are a degree larger, and not
quite so double as those of the true Banksian—it will prove a very
pretty climber, and is also quite hardy." [WRP]

CHAPTER TWENTY-ONE

Musks

"The *Musk Cluster* rose is an old inhabitant of our gardens. Botanists consider it a distinct species, and have named it from the peculiar and agreeable odour it exhales in the evening, and in the cool autumnal months, which is the season that it flowers most abundantly, in large clusters, of a yellowish-white colour. There are single, semi-double, and fully double varieties of it; the latter is the variety generally cultivated. It is a native of India, from whence it was introduced." [Bu] "This plant grows in Barbary, particularly in the realm of Tunisia, in the hedges . . . The Tunisians grow this rose in quantity. They extract a very fragrant essential oil from the petals, known under the name 'essence of roses,' and of which the perfume is one of the most agreeable known. This essence is very expensive, due to the very small quantity furnished by these blossoms. It is very probable that we may assign to this species several varieties, which only differ in the size of the plants, and by their nearly double or semi-double flowers." [Lam]

"This species comes to us from Alexandria. The Type has single flowers of a dirty white; its wood is green, very vigorous, and armed with numerous hooked thorns. These days, it can take our Winters without covering; it is, however, only necessary to grow its double varieties, one of which has white flowers, another with red, and the other black [!]. It is true that these give fewer blossoms than the Type; but if a person takes the effort to give them a southern exposure, and to graft them on vigorous Briars, they can be forced to bloom." [LeR]

"Originating on the Barbary Coast, it grows six to eight feet tall [ca. 2–2.6 m]; stems armed with occasional hooked thorns; leaves composed of five to seven oval, very pointed leaflets more than an inch long [ca. 2.5 cm], glabrous on both sides, glossy and dark green above, glaucous and tomentose beneath; petioles very prickly; flowers medium-sized, numerous, white, wafting a very pleasant musk scent, disposed in elongate terminal panicles; they appear in June and last until the month of August. This rose has two main varieties: one with entirely double roses; the other, more widespread, with semi-double blossoms." [AC]

"The Type of the Musk Rose, introduced into cultivation around the year 1596, originated on the island of Madeira, where it grows abundantly. You can find it as well in North Africa and Persia. It is a very vigorous bush with big glossy green canes; the large thorns aren't very numerous; the leaves, composed of 9–11 leaflets, are shiny, dark green, and much serrated. The blossoms, in large clusters, are medium-sized, double, semi-double, or single; they vary from pure white to straw yellow and from nankeen yellow to pale red. These flowers have a very pronounced musk scent which, along with its late bloom, is its distinctive characteristic. This rose has the quality of being remontant. Like the Multifloras, this group is very susceptible to cold, and one is obliged to protect it from the frost during the Winter." [JR5/133] "They have . . . certain resemblances to *Rosa alba.*" [Lam] "Its stems are clothed with a greenish bark, smooth and bearing remote leaves composed of three pairs of oval-lanceolate leaflets ending in one odd one, serrated like its brothers along the edge, and colored a bright green. The blossoms grow in large clusters, forming umbels at the tips of the canes; they appear in August and continue without interruption until frost. Though they have neither the size nor the doubleness of the preceding [*Centifolias, the 'Tous-les-Mois' Damask Perpetuals, 'Common Moss'*]—they gain interest by their number, their continuity, their beautiful white color, and by the elegant aroma of Musk which they waft. Both varieties, the single and the double, are equally well-liked because they have the same sparkle, duration, and perfume; but both are delicate, tender to heavy frosts, from which it is necessary to protect them, especially in the north. Both are difficult to propagate, particularly when the sun—by being too feeble or allowing too much dampness—doesn't suit them. A light rich soil, slightly cool and moderately deep, is the one they like the best." [Fr]

"Its very thorny stems grow to 10 or 12 feet [ca. 3.3–4 m]; but they are so slender that they arch back here and there, producing an irregular and diffuse mass when one doesn't train it on anything; a support lets it make a bushy and graceful shrub." [Fr] "They do well to be trained to pillars, fences, or trellises. In the eastern states they must be well protected in the winter season, covering their roots with a quantity of dry leaves. They delight in dry situations and rich soil. There is great room for improvement in this group." [Bu] "The Musk Rose is today [1854] pretty much abandoned in France, going by the catalogs, in which it no longer finds a place. But it lives still under some *noms d'emprunt,* and in a new family to which it gave the light of day: The Musk Rose lives on in the Trianons and Portlands [*i.e.,* the Damask Perpetuals] ... It still lives in the Noisettes, which it, with the China, created." [JDR54/43]

Rosa brownii Listed as *Rosa brunonii.*

Rosa brunonii

botanical syn. *R. brownii*; horticultural syns., 'Moschata Nivea', 'Nepaul Rose', 'Snow Bush'

"Flower single white, a variety of R. Moschata; sweetly scented. Growth vigorous." [GeH] Testu tells us that *R. brunonii* is found in the Himalayas and from Afghanistan to Nepal, and that it was introduced in 1822. "*Shrub,* having the appearance of the Musk rose. *Branches,* vigorous; rather hairy when old, the young ones cottonous. *Thorns,* scattered, short, strong, and crooked. *Stipules,* linear, adherent, subulated, and spreading at the end; glandular underneath. *Leafstalks,* hairy, having a few small scythe-shaped thorns. *Leaflets,* five or seven; lanceolated, flat, simply serrated, hairy on both surfaces; of a dull green on the upper, pale and glandular on the under; serrature convergent. *Flowers,* in bunches; white, single. *Floral leaves,* straight, lanceolated, hairy; rolled inwards at the edge, glandular without. *Flower-stalks,* bristly, brownish, covered with glands. *Tube of calyx,* oblong, villous. *Sepals,* reflexed, longer than the petals; nearly simple. *Stamens,* and *Styles,* resembling those of the Musk rose. *Fruit,* small, oval, red-orange. This rose was sent from Nepaul by Dr. Wallich, and named after the celebrated botanist Dr. Robert Brown. It is now [*1838*] cultivated in the gardens of France and England, but requires matting in severe frosts." [Go] "'Moschata Nivea', or the 'Snow Bush', and one or two other roses from Nepaul, have the scent peculiar to this group; but as they bloom but once in the summer, and differ totally in some other respects from the true Rosa moschata, I have not included them." [WRP]

Rosa moschata

horticultural syns. 'Muscade d'Alexandrie', 'Muscat', 'Musk Rose'

"This beautiful plant gives white blossoms with an elegant musk scent." [JF] "In Africa, on the borders of the vast desert of Sahara, and more especially in the plains towards Tunis, is found the *Rosa moschata,* whose tufts of white roses give out a musky exhalation. This charming species is also to be found in Egypt, Morocco, Mogadore, and the Island of Madeira." [Go] "Inhabits the banks and shores of the Mediterranean in Africa, Spain, and le Roussilon." [JF] "It is said that this rose originated in Hindustan." [JDR54/42–43] "This is the Musk Rose that the people of Tunis grow with so much care, not only because of the perfume of its blossoms, but indeed because they profit by it—they extract from their petals an oil known under the name 'Essence of Rose', one of the most agreeable a person could use. This oil always fetches a good price due to the small quantity supplied by the Musk Roses. Further, this is the Musk Rose that the celebrated Olivier saw forming trees thirty feet tall [ca. 10 m] in the gardens of the king of Persia at Ispahan ... The growth of the Musk Rose is so strong that it is necessary to place it against a wall or against any other construction so that it be exposed to the mid-day sun. It is not yet at all acclimated to the environs of Paris; sometimes it loses its canes in the middle of our hard Winters; but, for all that, it's grown none the

less, because it always comes back from the roots, the growths ordinarily giving some flowers in the first year; and because they can be protected by covering the branches with straw and soil during frosts. Grafting onto the Briar makes it more robust; this is what is done with all roses still grown in the orangery." [CM] "The *White Musk Rose* should always be pruned in Fall or Spring to a half-foot off the ground [ca. 1.5 dm]. It is necessary to clothe them with lengths of manure during the Winter so they don't get frost-bitten; and in the Spring, you cultivate the soil a little when you remove the manure. And when the flowers begin to appear, if there are shoots which don't have any, it is necessary to cut them back within a foot and a half of their base [ca. 4.5 dm]; each bud will produce a shoot which will bloom well around Fall." [LaQ]

"The Muske Rose both single and double, rise up oftentimes to a very great height, that it ouergroweth any arbour in a Garden, or being set by a house side, to bee ten or twelue foote high [ca. 3.3–4 m], or more, but more especially the single kinde, with many greene farre spread branches, armed with a few sharpe great thornes, as the wilder sorts of Roses are, whereof these are accounted to be kindes, hauing small darke greene leaues on them, not much bigger then the leaues of Eglantine: the flowers come forth at the toppes of the branches, many together as it were in an unbell or tuft, which for the most part doe flower all at a time, or not long one after another, euery one standing on a pretty long stalke, and are of a pale whitish or creame colour, both the single and the double; the single being small flowers, consisting of fiue leaues, with many yellow threads in the middle ... both of them of a very sweete and pleasing smell, resembling Muske: some there be that haue auouched, that the chiefest s[c]ent of these Roses consisteth not in the leaues [*i.e.,* petals], but in the threads of the flowers." [PaSo]

"The stems of this rose climb to the height of two meters [ca. 6 ft]; they are armed with occasional large, hooked thorns. The leaves are composed of five to nine oblong, dentate, and pointed leaflets which are dark green and glossy above, and tomentose beneath. The flowers, arranged in a panicle, are numerous, not very fragrant, white, slightly yellowish in the middle, and single or semi-double; the calyx-tube is oblong, the sepals inflexed; the styles are united in a column as with the Sempervirenses." [JDR54/42–43] "Charming shrub 3–6 feet in height [ca. 1–2 m]; stems and canes upright; epidermis glabrous and beautiful green; thorns red, sparse, and wide-based; leaflets glossy above and whitish beneath; from August to November, clusters of numerous white very elegantly-scented flowers." [J-A/575]

"*Stems* 1.8–2.1 m high [ca. 5–6 ft], armed with strong, stout, hooked *prickles*; petioles with smaller prickles. *Leaflets* 5–9, oblong, acute, serrate, dark green, glossy, tomentose beneath. *Flowers* paniculate, faintly scented, white, on slender glandular-hairy pedicels; *receptacles* oblong ovoid, slightly hairy; *sepals* lanceolate, a little shorter than the petals, 2 entire, 3 pinnatifid; styles villose, exserted in a small column the height of the stamens. This rose originates in Barbary. It is tender and requires shelter in Winter. It blooms late, holds its foliage for a long time, and resents pruning." [T&R] "Rose, with many-flowered panicles, scented like musk; seed-bud egg-shaped; peduncles villose; petioles prickly; the leaflets are oblong, acuminated, and smooth; the spines of the branches are large, scattered, and straight. As a perfectly distinct species, [*Andrews'*] figure is well deserving of notice. Its flowers are numerous, of a soft creamy white, and which are supposed to emit an odour resembling the perfume called musk. A specific name thus derived, we should not hold in much estimation were the plant ever so deficient in descriptive character but as the reverse is obvious in the present instance, it is still the more objectionable. Were it, therefore, a name of recent introduction, we should certainly take the liberty of altering it; but, as it has been long known under the title of Musk Rose, however vague and imperfect the reference, we do not think ourselves authorized to change it. It is a native of the island of Madeira, and a very desirable rose, although by no means splendid; but[,] as one of the latter blowing[,] it is a considerable addition, as it illumines that part of autumn, when the major part of this luxuriant tribe have ceased to bloom." [A] "Illustrated by J. Bauhin, Miss Lawrance, Redouté." [Gx] *See also* the discerning discussion in T4 concerning *Rosa moschata* and its usurper *R. brunonii*, which latter evidently began to fill Moschata's shoes about the second quarter of the 19th century. Moschata is an autumnal bloomer, blooming after Brunonii's flowery summer.

Horticultural Varieties

À Fleurs Doubles Listed as 'Double White' (Mk).

Brunonii Himalayica Listed as 'Paul's Himalayan Musk Rambler' (Mk).

Brunonii Flore Pleno Listed as 'Paul's Himalayica Alba Magna' (Mk).

Coroneola Listed as 'Double White' (Mk).

[De Tous Mois]
syn. 'Perpétuelle de St.-Ouen'; trans., "All Year Long"
Breeder unknown, pre-1828
   "White." [RG] See also 'Spanish Musk Rose' (Mk). These two mysterious cultivars, or some unknown congener, could well have played a part in the origins of the Damask Perpetuals.

Double Blanche Listed as 'Double White' (Mk).

Double White
syns. 'À Fleurs Doubles', 'Coroneola', 'Double Blanche', 'Flora Plena', 'Multiplex', 'Plena'
Breeder/Introducer unknown, pre-1629
   "Flower white, double, summer flowering. Growth vigorous." [GeH] "The double bearing more double flowers, as if they were once or twice more double then the single, with yellow thrummes also in the middle." [PaSo] "Not very striking. Its flowers are medium-sized and double, but not full; their color is a dirty white. They don't have a lot of scent, but what they do have is fairly fine and musky. They are the last roses; one sees them from August up to October, and indeed later. This shrub, coming from Barbary, needs protection in the Winter." [BJ09] "Has double flowers and a different scent from that of other Roses, as the Arab writers mention with good reason. Ibn-el-Façel indicates that it smells of camphor. Its distribution in North Africa and the south of Europe came about no doubt after the Muslim invasion. It still exists in Tehran and Ispahan." [ExRé]
   "Grows less vigorously than ['Semi-Double']; the branches and shoots are closer together, and it gives fewer flowers, but these are as double as the Centifolia rose. They bloom earlier than does the semi-double. These two sorts can get through the Winter out in the open;

however, it is necessary to take the precaution of covering and mounding them up with some compost, or with some light earth. They can both be grafted onto the Briar, making nice heads, particularly the double one. It can be combined on the same stem with the China rose to good effect." [C-T] "The wood is strong, vigorous, and armed with numerous hooked thorns, a little shorter than the Type. Its blossom is a beautiful pure white, well formed, very double. Some small green leaves replace the central stamens. They are numerous on the same stalk, and as large as those of the Bordeaux [*i.e.*, 'Rosier des Dames' (CP)], all packed together into a bouquet of the greatest freshness. Its scent is lightly musky. It is necessary to graft it as high as the Multiflora because of the length of their canes. It is pruned in the Spring when the frosts are done. They open from July up till frost. This is a precious sort to grow." [LeR]

[Double White Damask Musk Rose]
Breeder unknown, pre-1629
   "[As opposed to *Rosa moschata* (the single) and 'Double White'] this other kinde of Muske Rose (which with some is called the white Damaske Muske, but more truely the double white Cinamon [*sic*] Rose) hath his stemme and branches also shorter then the former, but as greene: the leaues are somewhat larger, and of a whiter greene colour; the flowers are also somewhat larger then the former double kinde, but standing in vmbels after the same manner, or somewhat thicker, and of the same whitish colour, or a little whiter, and somewhat, although but a little, neare the smell of the other, but nothing so strong. This flowreth at the time of other Roses, or somewhat later, yet much before the former two sorts of Muske Roses, which flower not vntill the end of Summer, and in Autumne; both which things, that is, the time of the flowring, and the s[c]ent[,] being both different, shew plainly it cannot be of the tribe of Muske Roses." [PaSo] See also under 'Spanish Musk Rose' (Mk).

Eponine
Breeder unknown, pre-1835
   "White, very multifloral." [S-V] "Medium-size, double, cupped, pure white." [JR5/133] "A pure white, fragrant and very double variety, one of the prettiest of the group." [WRP]

Flora Plena Listed as 'Double White' (Mk).

Francis E. Lester
Lester Rose Gardens, 1946
Seedling of 'Kathleen' (HMk).
   "White, medium size, single, tall." [Sn] Hybrid Musk in ancestry, but principally a once-bloomer like the Musks proper; good fall display of orange hips. More a large bush than a tall climber. A much beloved cultivar on which we alas have a dearth of information.

Fraser's Pink Musk Listed as a Noisette in Appendix 1.

Himalayica Alba Magna Listed as 'Paul's Himalayica Alba Magna' (Mk).

Hispanica Moschata Simplex Listed as 'Spanish Musk Rose' (Mk).

La Mortola
Hanbury/Bunyard/G. S. Thomas/Sunningdale Nurseries, 1954
   "White." [Ý] "Yellowish white, small, single, medium scent, tall." [Sn] "A particularly fine form of *Rosa brunonii*, which was brought [to

La Mortola *continued*

the United Kingdom] by E. A. Bunyard from the famous garden [in Italy] whose name it bears; I …introduced it …under this name." [T4]

Mme. d'Arblay
syn. 'Wells' White Climber'
Wells, ca. 1835

"Flowers delicate flesh, changing to white, of medium size, double; form, cupped. Habit very robust and vigorous." [P] "A pure white rose of the most vigorous growth." [JC] "A very old Musk hybrid of vigorous growth, with very fragrant, flesh-tinted white flowers." [GAS] "Of rapid growth, attaining gigantic dimensions, surpassing almost any other climbing variety; the foliage large and abundant; the flowers creamy white, very double and pretty, and produced in large clusters. It is very hardy, and suitable for stocks to bud on. It will form a tree or pillar of the largest size." [WRP] "Has been highly extolled; in growth it is the giant of climbers, for strength and rapidity excelling any that I have seen; the foliage is also very strong, partaking, in that respect, of the Bourbon family. Its flowers are pure white, like [those of 'The Garland'], and produced in very large bunches. It is of a very hardy nature, and will withstand severe cold without being the least affected. For covering arches, arbours, or such erections, it has no equal: there is no doubt of its also being an excellent variety to propagate for stocks whereon to bud or graft the finer sorts of Bengal [*i.e.,* China], Tea, or Bourbon Roses, having to appearance of being liable to sucker from the root." [Bu] G. S. Thomas relays ([T4]) Roy Shepherd's data that 'Mme. d'Arblay' and 'The Garland' were raised from the same hip, "the result of a cross between *Rosa moschata* and *R. multiflora,* occurring at Tunbridge Wells, Kent." Let us keep in mind GAS's enlightened comment that the cross was between "the Musk Rose and some other species which was called Multiflora at that time" (*v.* 'The Garland', below); we should also consider that Wells' third rose introduction, his only other release, 'Wells' Pink', was a Noisette …At any rate, Mme. d'Arblay, perhaps better known as Fanny Burney; lived 1752–1840; novelist, daughter of music historian Charles Burney.

Moschata Himalayica   Listed as 'Paul's Himalayan Musk Rambler' (Mk).

Moschata Nivea   Listed as *Rosa brunonii.*

Multiplex   Listed as 'Double White' (Mk).

Muscade d'Alexandrie   Listed as *Rosa moschata.*

Muscat   Listed as *Rosa moschata.*

Musk Rose   Listed as *Rosa moschata.*

Narrow Water
Daisy Hill Nurseries, ca. 1883

"A pink counterpart of [*Rosa pissardii*]." [sDHca05] Graham S. Thomas speculates relation to 'Blush Noisette' (N).

Nepaul Rose   Listed as *Rosa brunonii.*

Paul's Himalayan Musk Rambler
syns. 'Brunonii Himalayica', 'Moschata Himalayica', 'Paul's Himalayica'
Rev. Prebendary Earle/G. Paul, 1899

"White, with yellow stamens. —Very vigorous climber." [Cat12]

"Evidently a selected form of the species *R. brunonii* or the wild Himalayan Musk Rose. It is a very vigorous climber closely related to *R. moschata,* with huge clusters of rather large single white flowers." [GAS] "Violet-pink, small, full, very tall." [Sn, presumably from a misidentified specimen]

Paul's Himalayica   Listed as 'Paul's Himalayan Musk Rambler' (Mk).

[Paul's Himalayica Alba Magna]
syns. 'Brunonii Flore Pleno', 'Himalayica Alba Magna'
G. Paul, 1899

"This is another interesting variation of *R. brunonii,* with white, semi-double flowers in great clusters like hybrid rhododendrons." [GAS]

[Paul's Himalayica Double Pink]
G. Paul, 1899

"Another variation of *R. brunonii,* with large clusters of semi-double, light pink flowers." [GAS]

[Paul's Tree Climber]
G. Paul, 1916

"Vigorous hybrid of *Rosa brunonii* or *R. himalayica,* with masses of small, double, blush-white flowers. Reported to be almost evergreen." [GAS]

Perpétuelle de St. Ouen   Listed as 'De Tous Mois' (Mk).

Plena   Listed as 'Double White' (Mk).

Princesse de Nassau
Laffay, pre-1829

"Cream, changing to pure white, flowers double and very highly scented." [JC] "Blossoms very double, medium-sized, fragrant, a pale sulphur yellow." [AC] "Fragrant, white-flowered Musk climber." [GAS] "A pure Musk Rose, of a yellowish-white colour, very double, though not so profuse as some others." [Bu] "A distinct and good variety, very fragrant, and blooming in large clusters; the flower-buds, before they open, are nearly yellow, changing to cream color as they expand." [WRP] "Flower yellowish straw cut very sweet [*sic*], double. Growth vigorous." [GeH] "*Canes* geniculate. *Leaves* close-set, with 7–9 leaflets. *Petiole* armed, villose, and glandulose. *Leaflets* oval-lanceolate, villose beneath, edged undulate. *Flower* medium-sized, very double and very fragrant, sulphur yellow before fully open, becoming white. *Styles* numerous, filiform, very salient, ordinarily in a fascicle through adhesion, and dividing by the effect of pressure exercised on the tip of the column. *Petals* 40–50, spatulate, rounded, with a point at the tip. Blooms in August and September." [Pf]

Rivers' Musk
Rivers, pre-1846

"Pink, shaded with buff." [CA93] "Very sweetly scented, double. Growth vigorous." [GeH] "Rose-red, small, full, very fragrant, tall." [Sn]

Semi-Double
Cels, pre-1811

"This variety of the Musk Rose differs but little, if at all, from the single, except in its semi-double flowers, which in that particular give to the plant a very distinct appearance; but in every other respect it is so closely allied, that it may justly be called the prototype of the former; more especially as upon the single plant double flowers have sometimes been found, but not frequent; and careful cultivation has now rendered it a circumstance of very rare occurrence. Its blossoms certainly form a richer appearance than the single: their fragrance is by some stronger, by others weaker; on the propriety of which we shall make no further comment, than merely to observe that we regard an appeal to the olfactory organs of all references the most imperfect. This plant, as well as [the single], is frequently on the upper part of the branches free from spines, but on the lower part of the stems they are extremely large and strong." [A]

"Differs from the single-flowered *moschata* . . . only by the fewer, weaker prickles, leaflets tomentose beneath, and *corolla* of 3–4 series of petals. If it is true, as botanists and travelers have told us, that this rose is native to Hindustan, the exquisitely musk-scented blooms are those used along with the Kashmir Rose [?] as the source of the precious essence called Attar by the Indians. This is found floating on the surface of distilled rose water, and is gathered up with cotton at the end of a stick while still warm. The story of its discovery is as curious as it is unique. Langlès in 1804 quotes from a valuable Mogul history: 'At a feast given by the Princess Nour-Dyhan for the Emperor Jehangir, a small canal in the gardens was filled with rose water. When the Emperor was strolling beside the canal with her, they noticed a kind of foam floating on the surface: the essence of roses concentrated into a mass by the action of the sun. By common consent, this oily substance was pronounced the most delicate perfume known in all India. Subsequently, Art has striven to imitate what was a product of Chance and Nature'." [T&R]

Snow Bush Listed as *Rosa brunonii.*

[Spanish Musk Rose]
syn. 'Hispanica Moschata Simplex'
Breeder/Introducer unknown, pre-1629

"This Spanish Rose riseth to the height of the Eglantine, and sometimes higher, with diuers great greene branches, the leaues whereof are larger and greener then of the former kindes: the flowers are single Roses, consisting of fiue whiter leaues then in any of the former Muske Roses, and much larger, hauing sometimes an eye of a blush in the white, of a very sweete smell, comming nearest vnto the last recited Muske Rose [*'Double White Damask Musk Rose', q.v. above*], as also for the time of the flowering." [PaSo] Considering the reduced height of this Musk Rose—short in comparison with *Rosa moschata* or 'Double White'—perhaps this is the Musk Rose La Quintinye had in mind when he made, circa 1695, the otherwise inexplicable comment about the Damask Perpetual 'Tous-les-Mois' being a "sort of Red Musk Rose" [LaQ]—this or perhaps 'Double White Damask Musk Rose' (*q.v.*). Could the 'Spanish Musk Rose' be ancestral to some or all of the Damask Perpetuals? *Quien sabe, señor?* See also 'De Tous Mois' (Mk).

Splendid Garland Listed as 'The Garland' (Mk).

The Garland
syns. 'Splendid Garland', 'Wood's Garland', 'Woods' Garland'
Wells, 1835

"A light fawn-color, changing to white, and blooms in large clusters of double flowers, which turn to pink before fading." [FP] "White and pale lilac." [JC] "Medium-sized, double, yellowish, white when opening." [JR5/133] "Produced in large trusses, of medium size, double; form, expanded." [P] "A pretty white, producing its flowers in clusters, containing frequently from seventy-five to one hundred, forming a conical corymb of about sixteen inches in diameter [ca. 4 dm], the whole plant appearing in the distance like a pagoda of snow interspersed with foliage of the brightest green; the growth is very rapid, making ten to twelve feet [ca. 3.5–4 m] in a season." [Bu] "Has fragrant creamy white flowers, changing to pink after expansion; these are in corymbose clusters, often 70 to 100 united, fragrant, of compact form, and beautiful. The growth is very vigorous and rapid, making in a good soil, ten to twelve feet a year [ca. 3.5–4 m]." [WRP] "Light yellowish pink, small, lightly double, medium scent, tall." [Sn] "An interesting old hybrid of the Musk Rose and some other species which was called Multiflora at that time. It bears long, loose sprays of semi-double, whitish flowers. Not very vigorous and valuable only as an antique." [GAS] "A fine old English Climbing Rose, highly valued for training over walls, fences, embankments, etc. Grows 15 to 20 feet in a season [ca. 5–6.6 m], bearing enormous clusters of pure white roses, medium sized, very full and sweet." [C&Js98] "A snowdrift of flowers in early summer, but unfortunately they are quickly over. I first saw this rose in Miss Jekyll's garden at Munstead, and it is a favorite there, and I have planted it against an oak fence. It is very riotous but one enjoys the glorious mass of flowers in early summer, flowers of starry form and pure white in colouring." [NRS12/182]

"This is sometimes called a Hybrid China, but Mr. Paul, in *The Rose Garden*, regarded it as a Hybrid between moschata and multiflora, and its stipules seem to indicate a connexion with the last named family. It is at all events a rampant grower, of branching habit. When allowed to grow as a bush unrestrained, young growths are pushed up above the flowering branches and then arching over, produce the flower laterals of the following year. The branches are covered with numerous sharp black spines which are very typical. The foliage is good and tolerably lasting but is all fallen by Christmas, and it is scarcely at all subject to mildew. It has only one flowering period and that of only moderate length. The first flower opened with me this year (1910) on the 28th June, and it was fully out about a week later, for the flowers come with a rush, while on the 28th July I noted it was practically over. The flowers are carried in large trusses of small blooms, at first buff and white, fading to white, the anthers blackening before the petals fall, and it has a slight honey fragrance, some of my friends call it musk . . . Planted in tolerable soil it will cover an arch more quickly than any [other] rose with which I am acquainted, and I have seen it looking beautiful as a tall weeping standard. Planted in a small clump, with the help of a tripod or a few poles, it makes a handsome tall bush, and if allowed to grow untrimmed at all will make a tangled bush about ten feet through [ca. 3.3 m], and where room can be spared this is perhaps the most effective way to treat it. It looks beautiful too if allowed to grow up into a tree, as 'Dundee Rambler' [Arv] will do, and then it flowers all down its drooping branches." [NRS11/55–56] Sometimes also called a Hybrid Sempervirens. See also 'Mme. d'Arblay' for its sibling and background.

Wells' White Climber Listed as 'Mme . . . d'Arblay' (Mk).

Wood's Garland Listed as 'The Garland' (Mk).

Woods' Garland Listed as 'The Garland' (Mk).

CHAPTER TWENTY-TWO

Arvensises

"This family of Roses are great ramblers, producing a long, slender, luxuriant growth; but, in a northern climate, they cannot be relied on as being perfectly hardy, unless laid down and covered over. They produce very pretty flowers, in clusters, mostly white." [BBF] "They form good weeping Roses on tall stems, and flower from June to July. They need no pruning or training, and do best if allowed to ramble at will, growing where other Roses would not exist and thriving in the poorest of soil." [GeH]

"Throughout most of Europe, and particularly in Scotland and northern England, *Rosa arvensis* trails in abundance over wastelands, climbing through hedges and thickets, often completely hiding the undergrowth from view. Its solitary flowers are small and fragrant. They are borne in great profusion in June and July. The plant is exceedingly hardy and vigorous, existing in rough, sterile soil where few others plants will grow. The earliest garden varieties of *R. arvensis* were raised by a man named Martin, of Dundee, Scotland, in the early years of the nineteenth century. All of them were white or pink. But about 1838, the famous English rosarian, Thomas Rivers, produced a dark red variety called 'Ayrshire Queen' . . . In 1854, Rivers wrote that there seemed to be no limit to the vigorous growth of the Ayrshire roses, and he described two plants of 'Bennett's Seedling' two years old, with stems 10 inches in circumference [ca. 2.5 dm]. He also recommended them for planting in rough ground, on banks, in parks, and in shrubberies, for the roses of Arvensis blood are hardy enough to withstand severe winter weather and need little or no attention after planting. They are essentially trailing and should not be pruned. The true strain of the Ayrshires bears the flowers singly and not in clusters; only the later and more complex hybrids bear flowers in bunches . . . *R. arvensis* and the old varieties, if they can be obtained true to name, may still offer the rose-breeder something of value in their rapid, vigorous growth, fragrance, and extreme hardiness." [GAS]

Rosa arvensis
syn. 'Field Rose'
"Bush growing to twelve to fifteen feet [ca. 4–5 m], with thin, slightly glaucous stems; thorns equal, sparse, in an arc or straight;

leaves remote, of 5–7 flat, oval, simply dentate leaflets which are very glaucous beneath; flowers white, yellowish at the base of the petals, not very fragrant, in clusters of 3–7; fruit round." [No26] "Sweet scent." [BJ24] "Violet stems, creeping, glabrous, well clothed with large hooked thorns, growing sometimes to 20 feet [ca. 6.6 m]. It's only good for covering rocks. I only mention it to call for its removal, and especially to warn people to be on guard against sellers of the Briar [*R. rubiginosa*] who mix it in among hedges." [BJ17]

"Very easy to pick out by its feeble canes sprawling on the ground or over nearby shrubs, green, and with few thorns; leaflets oval, shorter, and more obtuse [than those of *Rosa rubiginosa*], dry, of a very light green. Blossoms constantly white, slightly larger than those of the Dog Rose [*Rosa canina*], and always showing at the center styles united into a obviously salient column in the middle of the stamens. The hips are shortly ovoid, light red, and wrinkle up in the Winter." [JDR54/21] "Often, this species has nearly procumbent canes, much branched, three to four feet long [ca. 1–1.3 m]; its branches are stiff, hard, bluish or deep purple, glabrous, cylindrical, and armed with strong, hooked, very sharp, sparse thorns; clothed in alternate, stipulate leaves composed of seven or five oval leaflets of a dark green above, slightly paler and clearer beneath, glabrous, sometimes slightly rounded, crenelate along the edge, obtuse at both ends; borne on some glabrous petioles bearing some short prickles as well as—at their base—an enlarged bract, entire or finely dentate around the tip. The blossoms are perfectly white, borne on mid-sized peduncles, solitary, often gathered into a cyme, lightly hispid or nearly smooth, depending upon the age and the variety. The calyx is nearly glabrous, its divisions [*i.e.,* sepals] entire or slightly pinnatifid around their tip, green or purplish. The corolla is pretty large; the petals notched at their tip. The ovary is slightly globular, or elongate, and glabrous; the styles are pubescent, and the same length as the stamens. This plant grows nearly throughout Europe, in hedges, along roads, and in uncultivated places." [Lam] "This rose grows naturally in woods and fields, among rocks and brush; this is also why it has long been confused with the Hedge Rose [*Rosa rubiginosa*], though the growth is easy to distinguish. It is found promiscuously in Germany, Sweden, England, Denmark, and France. This rose sometimes grows into a bushy shrub capable of reaching six feet [ca. 2 m] and even more; and sometimes its thinner canes grow along the ground, or simply borrow their support from close-by shrubs; sometimes, finally, its branches grow up to twenty feet long [ca. 6.6 m]. Also, while little attention has been given to grafting good varieties, it could serve to form pergolas to great effect, to cover a *berceau,* or indeed to clothe the rearwards of a rocky outcrop in our landscape gardens. The Field Rose has smooth globular ovaries; its peduncles, glabrous; its petioles, armed with prickles; its leaves, an umbrageous green above, slightly whitish beneath; its blossoms, which you see in May and June, are white, disposed in clusters of twelve to fifteen; their scent is sweet … The only variety of the Field Rose one can allow is the double one; but that one's so little known that you don't even see it in the nurserymen's catalogs!" [CM] "Singled out and described [ca. 1260] by the celebrated monk Albertus Magnus, who was the first to note the distinct congruent pistils." [ExRé] "This is the 'White Dog Rose' of Miss Lawrance." [Gx]

Horticultural Varieties

Aennchen von Tharau
Geschwind, 1886
From an Alba × *Rosa arvensis.*
"White, medium size, full, tall." [Sn] "No scent, −3 m [less than ca. 9 ft]." [EU]

Alice Gray Listed as 'Scandens' (Arv).

Ayrshire Queen
syn. 'Queen'
Rivers, 1835
From 'Ayrshirea' (Arv) × 'Tuscany' (G).
"Flowers dark purplish crimson, large and semi-double; form, cupped." [P] "Medium-sized, double deep crimson purple." [JR5/16] "Originated … from the Blush Ayrshire [*i.e.,* 'Ayrshirea'], impregnated with the Tuscany Rose. But one seed germinated, and the plant has proved a complete hybrid. Its flowers are of the same shape, and not more double than those of the Blush Ayrshire, its female parent; but they have all the dark purplish crimson of the Tuscany Rose. It has lost a portion of the vigorous climbing habit of the Ayrshire, but yet makes an excellent pillar rose. Until we can get a dark Ayrshire Rose, double as a Ranunculus, this will be acceptable." [WRP]

Ayrshire Rose Listed as 'Ayrshirea' (Arv).

Ayrshirea
syns. 'Ayrshire Rose', 'Blanda', 'Capreolata', 'Tuguriorum'
Loudon?/Dalrymple, 1768
"The beauty and usefulness of the *Ayrshire Rose* are not sufficiently known. The rapidity with which it covers walls and fences, or the sides of unsightly buildings, with its thick mass of branches and foliage, and the brilliant effect of its numerous white flowers during the month of July, in situations where it is well exposed to the sun, and particularly when trained over the roofs of cottages or garden seats, are such valuable properties that no ornamental grounds should be without it." [JSa]
"It is believed that this came from a cross of *R. arvensis* with an unknown climbing rose. It was found in 1768 in a garden in Ayrshire, Scotland. It is a vigorous rose, and very hardy. Its small, pale, very numerous blossoms make quite a sight when the plant blooms … It should be sparingly pruned." [JF] "[*As compared to* Rosa arvensis]

this one is higher-growing, its leaves are longer, and its clusters more numerous; but it is not well known in the nurseries." [BJ30] "The quickest and longest growers of all Roses, blooming in clusters in the summer only. There is nothing to equal them for quickly and thickly covering a space, either for walls, pillars, arches, pergolas, or even as hedges by themselves. Trained a little at first to grow among the branches of a half-dead tree, they should then be left to themselves, and the highest shoots will hang down when no longer supported, and will be a mass of bloom for a short time in the following summer. They will cover an ordinary-sized summer-house, forming in time a deep thick mat all over the roof. Budded on Standard stocks 8 or 9 feet high [ca. 2.6–3 m] they make the most perfect weeping Roses, at last quite hiding the stems, and becoming huge bushes." [F-M2] "It would be hard to overpraise the Ayrshires for clothing pillars, pergolas, and old tree trunks in parks and gardens." [JR34/39] "Clambers over everything that comes in its way … of exceptional value on account of its hips which, although small, are none the less attractive, and are produced in such profusion that autumn is by no means the least showy period with this beautiful Rose." [NRS17/63]

"Very vigorous bush with long climbing canes having brownish green wood clothed with numerous much-recurved reddish thorns; leaves composed of 5–7 leaflets, sometimes 3, lanceolate, fairly finely dentate, a gay green; blossoms semi-double, clustered in a group of 7–12 in terminal panicles; color, light flesh white. This sort blooms but once a year." [S] "*Shrub,* having long, slender, thorny branches. *Flowers,* numerous; white, single, cup-shaped. Raised at Loudoun Castle, in Ayrshire, from seeds imported from North America; but supposed by Lindley to have been originally carried to America from Europe." [Go] "It is the opinion of some cultivators, that the varieties of the Ayrshire Rose have been originated from the Rosa arvensis, or creeping single White Rose of the woods and hedges of England. But this is contradicted by botanists, who assert that the original Ayrshire Rose was raised in Scotland from foreign seed. This may have been; but to judge from its habit, I feel no hesitation in asserting, that it is merely a hybrid seedling from the Rosa arvensis, having acquired much additional vigor, as hybrid roses almost invariably do, from some accidental impregnation. Perhaps no rose can be more luxuriant than this; for the Single Ayrshire, and that semi-double variety known as the double white, will often make shoots in one season, twenty to thirty feet in length [ca. 9 m]. Several of the prettiest varieties have been raised by Mr. Martin, of Rose Angle, Dundee." [WRP] "The Field Rose originated in Europe, where one sees it nearly everywhere growing in cultivated ground, hedges, and copses where it blooms profusely. It is an extremely vigorous bush with branches growing 4–5 meters long [ca. 12–15 ft] in a year; they are slender and flexible, dark green on one side and brownish red on the other. The thorns are large, hooked, and not very numerous; the somber green leaves are composed of 9–11 leaflets, which are small, pointed, and very dentate. The solitary blossoms are small, single, semi-double, or double, and vary from white to bright pink. The Field Rose can make wonderful 'baskets' [*i.e.,* rose-covered frameworks], which they quickly cover, pillars, and weepers, grafted on Briar stocks 4–6 feet high [ca. 1.3–2 m]; they also are good for covering rocks and such. I have seen hedges of these roses planted amongst other shrubs producing a very beautiful effect at bloom-time, and making a quite impenetrable barrier. Field Roses take the cold quite well." [JR5/15]

Ayrshirea *continued*

"In the cultivation and management of the Ayrshire Rose there is little difficulty; layers of its shoots root easily, and it strikes readily from cuttings. When placed in good soil it grows so rapidly, that by the second summer, the planter, if he wishes to cover a considerable space with its branches, will be gratified by the attainment of his object."[JSa]

"A History of the Ayrshire Rose has been published by Mr. Neill, the Secretary of the Caledonian Horticultural Society, in a paper in the *Edinburgh Philosophical Magazine* [*a footnote adds:* Volume ii. page 102]; and communications which I have received relative to the plant from Mr. Robert Austin, of Glasgow, and Mr. George Douglas, of Rodinghead, near Kilmarnock, have enabled me to add some few particulars to Mr. Neill's account. It is stated to have been raised (in what manner I shall hereafter observe upon) in the garden of John Earl of Loudon, at Loudon Castle, in Ayrshire, in the year 1768 or 1769. Mr. Douglas, who at that period had the charge of the estate and gardens at Loudon, has informed me that he gave a plant of the Rose to his friend Mr. Charles Dalrymple of Orangefield, near Ayr, from whose garden it was introduced into the nurseries in his neighbourhood, as well as at Glasgow; it was at first called the *Orangefield Rose,* but subsequently received the more general appellation by which it is now known. It has been considered by some as a native wild plant of Ayrshire, but I believe there is little doubt, that it was first observed in the gardens of that county, where possibly the original plants, or at least some of their earliest offspring, are still to be seen . . . From Scotland, it reached the nurseries round London, but was not noticed by any of our periodical works on plants till 1819, when Dr. Sims published an account of it in the *Botanical Magazine* [*a footnote adds:* Botanical Magazine, 2054]. His description was made from specimens of plants which cover a building, in the garden of the late Sir Joseph Banks, at Spring Grove; these came from the nursery of Mr. Ronalds at Brentford, and were planted in February 1811. In January 1820, Mr. Neill, in the paper I have above alluded to, gave, besides a general description of the Rose, a botanical character of it, drawn up by Mr. David Don, son of the late Mr. George Don, of Forfar. To the accounts both of Dr. Sims and of Mr. Neill, Mr. Lindley has referred in his *Rosarum Monographia* [*a footnote adds:* Pages 112 and 117], under the heads of Rosa arvensis and Rosa sempervirens. My opinions respecting the Ayrshire Rose do not entirely coincide with those given in either of the publications I have mentioned. Dr. Sims considered it as a variety of Rosa arvensis, but his figure is certainly not that of the plant he has described, and therefore is likely to lead to error. Mr. Don, supposing it to be a distinct species, hitherto undescribed, has named it Rosa capreolata: and Mr. Lindley refers what he calls the true Ayrshire Rose to Rosa sempervirens. I have some observations to make on all these points, but it will be expedient first to give a description of the Rose, and to detail the particulars in which it differs both from Rosa arvensis and Rosa sempervirens.

"The Ayrshire Rose has slender branches, which grow rapidly in one season to a very great extent (thirty feet and upwards [ca. 9 m +]), but they are so weak as absolutely to require support; the older branches are greenish brown, with a few small pale falcate aculei growing on them; the younger branches are green, with a tinge of purplish red, and armed with falcate red aculei; those branches which grow to any extent are so slender and flexible as to hang down almost perpendicularly from the last point to which they are nailed or tied.

The smaller side branches are very numerous, and are abundantly covered with leaves, so as to form a thick close mass; the plant rarely throws up strong surculi, or root shoots. The leaves are deciduous; the stipulae long and narrow, red in the centre, edged with glands, but otherwise smooth; the petioli have a few uncinate aculei and some small glands scattered over them; the foliola are either five or seven in number, the lower pair being much the smallest; they are flat and smooth, shining on both sides, but paler though without glaucousness underneath, ovate, pointed, and simply serrated; the edges, and particularly those of the vigorous leaves, being sometimes tinged with red. The flowers are produced abundantly from the beginning to near the end of July; they rarely grow singly, but are often in threes, and on strong shoots the cymes contain many flowers, from ten to twenty or more; the bractae are tinged with red, pointed, waved, edged with glands, and bent backwards; the peduncles are long, fine, and covered with glanduliferous setae; the germen (tube of the calyx) is elliptic, contracted at the top, and covered with setae, but not so much so as the peduncle; the sepals (leaves of the calyx) have a few fine pinnae, are covered with glands, have a point at the end extending beyond the bud before it expands; and when the flower opens, they are reflexed; the bud is cream-coloured, the petals are large, obcordate, expanding flat, and their edges are somewhat lapped over each other; the stamina are numerous, and bright yellow; the stigmata are united, porrect, and hairy. The scent of the flower is very pleasant. The fruit when ripe preserves nearly its original shape, is elongated, and not much increased in size.

"The characters of the common Rosa arvensis, which do not agree with the preceding, are these: the plant, wherever situated, is not inclined to grow to the same extent; the branches are stronger, thicker, and more able to support themselves; the younger shoots have more the appearance of surculi (which often arise from the root), they are glaucous, on the unexposed side of a more blueish [*sic*] green, and on the exposed side purple and deeper coloured; they bear fewer leaves, and the bush is consequently not so thick and close. The foliola are most frequently seven, and, under similar circumstances, smaller; they are usually broader in proportion to their length, somewhat folded, not flat, more rugose on both sides, an opaque green above, pale, glaucous, and without any appearance of shining beneath, with serratures less sharp, and the mid-rib occasionally hairy on the under side. The flowers appear at the end of June, and often grow singly; the peduncles are thicker and stronger; the germen is shorter and thicker, less contracted at the top, and usually smooth: the sepals are either without pinnae or with only very slight ones, they frequently have no terminating point, and when the flowers open, are not reflexed; the flower at its first opening is cupped, and not flatly expanded; the stigmata are quite smooth, not hairy. The fruit, when ripe, is considerably swollen, and generally nearly globose, but its shape varies in different plants.

"The differences between the Evergreen [*i.e.,* Sempervirens] and the Ayrshire Rose are also capable of being distinctly described. The Evergreen Rose is by no means a free grower, and though it extends, when trained against a wall, to some distance, it does not do so, rapidly; its shoots are equally slender, but not quite so weak, and they are rather more purple; it forms, however, with its branches and leaves, a very thick bush. The leaves are evergreen, and though similar in shape, are readily distinguished by being much more glossy and shining on both surfaces, which occasions them to appear altogether of a darker hue; they are also of a thicker substance, have finer serratures, and are more inclined to bend back. The flowers appear from the middle to the end of July, they are less numerous, and generally weaker, but accord in all other points …

"Mr. Neill states that the seeds from whence the Ayrshire Rose was obtained were part of a packet received from Canada or Nova Scotia, and it appears by his account, that several plants of it were produced together. Mr. Douglas further mentions, that a person, under the direction of Dr. Hope of Edinburgh, was sent to Canada to collect hardy plants and their seeds, for several noblemen and gentlemen in Scotland, who defrayed the expense of the collection by subscription, and that the Ayrshire Rose was raised, in 1768 or 1769, from seeds in the Earl of Loudon's share of the produce of this mission [*a footnote adds:* I have received from Mr. James Smith, nurseryman of Monkwood Grove, near Ayr, an account of the introduction of the Ayrshire Rose into that country, which differs from the history of its origin in the Earl of Loudon's garden, and, if correct, would entirely remove the difficulty which exists of its being supposed to have been raised from North American seeds. Mr. Smith's account is, that he perfectly remembers the Rose, since he was eleven years of age, which, at that time (in 1776) was growing in Mr. Dalrymple's garden at Orangefield, where it was planted by John Penn, a Yorkshireman, who was employed by the gentlemen of Ayrshire to keep their foxhounds; Penn was a man of some education, and much attached to gardening, in consequence of which Mr. Smith became acquainted with him, and received the account now given from himself; his statement was, that having been on a visit to his friends in Yorkshire, he brought the original plant from gentleman's garden in that country, to which it was supposed to have been introduced from Germany, and planted it at Orangefield, when, from its covering some buildings within view of the high road, it attracted notice, and so becoming an object of curiosity, plants of it were distributed till it became generally cultivated in the neighbourhood.].

"No rose having the slightest resemblance to the Ayrshire, or to which it can possibly be assimilated, has been brought to us, or described, from the American continent, and as we are tolerably well acquainted with the plants of the northern part of that country, it may, I think, be safely alleged, that the seeds could not have been those of an indigenous Rose of America …

"Having now, as I hope, cleared away the difficulties which have hitherto prevented this charming shrub from being accurately known, which is certainly of considerable importance to those who may wish to possess it, and no garden ought to be without it; a more difficult task remains to be performed, that of ascertaining what it really is. That it cannot be identified with the type of any described species is clear; it is equally certain that it has not yet been found growing naturally wild any where, so as to enable us to treat it as a species, or as one of those varieties of ascertained species which, from their not being traceable to a single original, but being abundant in the districts where they are found, I consider as a higher class of variation, or as sub-species of a well defined type. If … several plants of it were raised together, we have still to look for its parent, which would probably agree with it, if several of its seeds produced similar plants; but it does not seem certain that more than one plant was first produced, and it may consequently be considered as an accidental variety, referable either to R. arvensis, or R. sempervirens.

"The Rosa arvensis is a very rare plant in Scotland, and does not, as I am informed, grow wild in Ayrshire, therefore no seed of that species could have come by chance from a native plant, to give it being; nor is it very likely that Rosa sempervirens, which, even in the south of England, is a tender plant, would have freely ripened its seeds in the climate of Scotland, so as to have casually produced the young plant there. I therefore consider it more probable that the new Rose did actually originate in the garden at Loudon Castle, from some seed transmitted to, or collected for, the Earl of Loudon; and I think that the seed must have been that of Rosa sempervirens, which if is was really imported from America, must have been the produce of a garden plant, since the species is exotic in that country.

"The Ayrshire Rose certainly has more affinity to R. sempervirens than to R. arvensis, the inflorescence especially accords exactly, the chief differences being that the leaves of the Ayrshire Rose are deciduous, and that it flowers a little earlier in the season. Under Rosa sempervirens I therefore propose to place it, considering it to be a deciduous and free growing variety of that species; in order to preserve Mr. Don's name, it may be called Rosa sempervirens capreolata.

"If a comparison be made of the Ayrshire Rose with Rosa arvensis, in the state we usually find it, the differences between them are so numerous that there cannot be a doubt about the propriety of separating them. But there are varieties of Rosa arvensis in which some of these differences are often less apparent, or altogether assimilated. For an acquaintance with these varieties I am indebted to Mr. William Borrer, with whom I have had an opportunity of personally examining them in their native habitats in Sussex. Rosa arvensis in accidental varieties has sported very much, and has produced some particularly ornamental plants, but those I am now about to mention are not single productions; they are found growing wild in various places unconnected with each other. Of these the first variety has the fruit slightly covered with setae, but does not differ in any other character from the common Rosa arvensis. In the second, the leaves are elongated, and sharply pointed, and the fruit is also elongated. The third accords with the second, except that the fruit of it is slightly hispid. The fourth has many peculiarities, it is far less robust than the common sort, having weak shoots, which are consequently very pendant, and the joints do not grow straight but in a zig-zag manner; the foliola are smaller, less rugose, flatter, rather bending back, and shining on the upper surface; below they have the glaucousness of the type, though less of it, and are somewhat shining; the flowers grow mostly singly, sometimes in cymes, but very seldom in great numbers. The first and third of these varieties agree with the Ayrshire Rose in the hispid fruit; the second and third in their lengthened leaves and elongated fruits; but they have no other peculiar points of accordance. When I first heard of the fourth variety, I expected we had got the Ayrshire Rose in a wild state; its weak and pendant branches, and the shining quality of the foliola encouraged the opinion, but the flexuose habit of its shoots, their shortness of extent, and the difference in the leaves, though approximating, overthrew my hope. Notwithstanding all their coincidences we have still the period of flowering, the fineness of the peduncles, the character of the sepals, their habit of being reflexed when the flower opens, and, above all, the hairiness of the stigmata, to separate the Ayrshire Rose from Rosa arvensis and all its variations, and to unite it to Rosa sempervirens." [JSa]

Ayrshirea *continued*

"Ayrshire Roses are, some of them, perhaps, surpassed in beauty by the varieties of Rosa sempervirens; still they have distinct and desirable qualities: they bloom nearly a fortnight earlier than the roses of that division; they will grow where no other rose will exist; and to climb up the stems of timber trees in plantations near frequented walks, and to form undergrowth, they are admirably well adapted: they also make graceful and beautiful standards, for the ends of the branches descend and shade the stems, which in consequence, increase rapidly in bulk. It seems probable that Ayrshire Roses will grow to an enormous size as standards, and surpass in the beauty of their singular dome-shaped heads many other roses more prized for their beauty." [WRP]

[Beacon Belle]

R. & J. Farquhar, 1919

From 'Orléans-Rose' (Pol) × a seedling (of 'Katharina Zeimet' [Pol] × *Rosa arvensis*).

"Reputed to be an Ayrshire hybrid with Polyantha blood. Flowers small, very double, pale pink, fading white. Not unlike a cluster-flowered Wichuraiana in habit, but the foliage is thin and scrawny." [GAS]

Bennett's Seedling

Usually considered synonymous with 'Thoresbyana' (Arv); but see under that cultivar's entry, below.

Blanda Listed as 'Ayrshirea' (Arv).

Capreolata Listed as 'Ayrshirea' (Arv).

Dundee Rambler

Martin, pre-1838

"White edged with pale pink." [BJ77] "Double, white flowers." [GAS] "White, often edged with pink." [WRP] "White, bordered pale pink, very floriferous." [JR2/43] "Medium-sized, double, pure white." [JR5/15] "White tinged with pink, very vigorous." [JC] "Flowers in large clusters, white, edged with pink." [BBF] "Whitish pink, small, full, moderate height." [Sn] "Vigorous climber, with small white flowers tinged rose as they open fully." [CA96] "White, pink edges. Growth very vigorous. Summer-flowering." [GeH] "Flowers white, of medium size, double; form, compact. A plant of this is growing here completely underneath a large elm tree, where it thrives and flowers well every year." [P] "The most double, and one of the best in this division; it blooms in very large clusters, much after the Noisette fashion, and is truly a desirable rose." [WRP]

Düsterlohe

trans. "Gloomy Fire"

Kordes, 1931

"Rose-red, medium size, single, light scent, tall." [Sn] "A recent attempt to resuscitate the Arvensis or Ayrshire class. Flowers single, rose-red, nearly three inches across [ca. 7.5 cm]. Extremely hardy and very vigorous." [GAS] *Cf.* the Macranthas of the same name and origin. Synonym(s)?

Field Rose Listed as *Rosa arvensis*; can also refer to 'Ayrshirea' (Arv).

Macrophylla Scandens Listed as 'Scandens' (Arv).

Major Listed as 'Scandens' (Arv).

Mill Beauty Listed as 'Miller's Climber' (Arv).

Miller's Climber

syns. 'Mill Beauty', 'Mill's Beauty'

England?, pre-1838

"Light purple." [BJ58] "Bright pink." [Ÿ] "Large, double, bright red striped white." [JR5/15, of 'Mill's Beauty'] "Large, semi-double, deep pink." [JR5/15, of 'Miller's Climber']. "Light purple, like the common Bengal [*i.e., China—presumably referring to 'Parsons' Pink China'*]." [JR2/43] "This rose plant makes quite a splash when its blossom is fresh and particularly when it is grown as a contrast to other roses of a pale pink or white color; of good vigor, its canes are tendentially vertical; those bearing the blossoms present them in profuse corymbs; these roses are nearly large, semi-double, quite acceptable, and held perfectly upright on their stems; their color is a slightly carminy pink, but extremely sparkling, accompanied by very large, beautiful green foliage. In vigor, hold, and brightness of color, this sort is superior to 'Beauty of the Prairies' [Set], even though this latter produces fuller blossoms of a pretty form." [S] The classification of 'Miller's Climber' is somewhat in doubt; it has been called both an Arvensis × Sempervirens cross, and a Setigera hybrid. It may be Monsieur Noisette's 1827 'Rouge Pleine'.

Mill's Beauty Listed as 'Miller's Climber' (Arv).

Miss Jekyll

England, pre-1934

"Flower white, single. Vigorous climber." [GeH] "Light pink, medium size, full, tall." [Sn]

Mme. Viviand-Morel

Schwartz, 1882

From *Rosa arvensis* × 'Cheshunt Hybrid' (Cl HT).

"Rose-red, medium size, full, medium scent, tall." [Sn] "Very vigorous bush with climbing canes, from seed of a double-flowered Ayrshire crossed with 'Cheshunt Hybrid'; foliage reddish green passing to purple; flower medium-sized, full, well formed, in a cluster, carmine pink tinted cerise, reverse of the petals violet white; tea-scented. A new sort." [JR6/148] Viviand-Morel, quondam editor of *Lyon-Horticole*.

Myrrh-Scented Listed as 'Splendens' (Arv).

Queen Listed as 'Ayrshire Queen' (Arv).

Repens Listed as 'Splendens' (Arv).

Ruga

syn. 'Tea-Scented Ayrshire'

Italy, pre-1820

"Pale flesh." [BJ58] "Whitish pink, splendid in bud." [JR7/154] "Pale flesh, deliciously fragrant, double, free-blooming, and very beautiful." [JC] "Flowers flesh-colour, changing to creamy white, large and double; form, cupped; very sweet. A good seed-bearer." [P] "White, medium size, very full, tall." [Sn] "Flower pale flesh, free flowering. Growth very vigorous." [GeH] "Blossom medium-sized, not very full, pale flesh, very floriferous; usually employed budded high on the Briar to make a weeper." [S] "Evidently a hybrid between the Tea Rose [*if pre-1820, then presumably the Tea Rose parent would be 'Hume's Blush Tea-Scented China'*] and the celebrated Ayrshire Rose, but has not wood nor foliage sufficient for covering walls or arbours." [Bu]

"Raised in Italy, and is quite hardy, notwithstanding the proverbial delicacy of the one parent." [P] "Introduced from Italy. One of the best Ayrshires, with small, flesh-colored flowers tinged with pink. May be the same as 'Venusta Pendula'." [GAS] "A most beautiful and fragrant rose." [WRP]

Scandens
syns. 'Alice Gray', 'Macrophylla Scandens', 'Major'
Italy, pre-1804

"Large beautiful blush." [WRP] "Flowers creamy salmon blush." [P] "White." [Ÿ] "Medium-sized, semi-double, salmony cream white." [JR5/16] "A hybrid Sempervirens, having much of the Ayrshire habit, and making shoots of an immense length in one season. Its flowers are of a delicate buff when they first open, but they soon change to a pale flesh color." [WRP] "*Shrub*, with pendant leaves. *Leaflets*, oval-lanceolated; shallow toothing, curved underneath. *Flowers*, single, white; the styles as long as the stamens; united only by the interlacing of their pubescence." [Go] "Comes from Italy, growing in the woods around Florence. Its canes creep along the ground when there's nothing to hold them up; being fastened to a support, they grow to from twelve to fourteen feet [ca. 4–4.6 m], armed with short reddish thorns. The leaves are small, oval, acuminate, glossy-green, and persistent. The flowers are white, small, and musky, and keep blooming for several months. In English gardens, they only bloom at the beginning of Summer." [Lam]

Splendens
syns. 'Myrrh-Scented', 'Repens', 'Splendeur'
England, pre-1838

"White, bordered with red." [BJ58] "Matte white." [Ÿ] "More matte white [than 'Thoresbyana' (Arv)]." [JR34/39] "Creamy white, globose." [WRP] "White tinged with pink, not very double; small and pretty." [JC] "A new variety, with very large cupped flowers, of a creamy blush; this rose has also that peculiar 'Myrrh-scented' fragrance." [WRP] "Blossoms with a tea-scent." [JR7/154] "White with some flesh, resembling the blossom of 'Mrs. Bosanquet' [B] in its beauty." [JR2/44] "Flowers flesh colour, large, full. Growth very vigorous." [GeH] "Flowers pale flesh, buds crimson when young, presenting a pretty effect on the tree, large and double; form, globular. One of the best of Weeping Roses. A good seed-bearer." [P]

Splendeur Listed as 'Splendens' (Arv).

Tea-Scented Ayrshire Listed as 'Ruga' (Arv).

Thoresbyana Plate 30
syn. 'Bennett's Seedling'? (see below)
Bennett of Thoresby, 1840

"Pure white, large clusters." [WRP] "Flowers white, of medium size, double; form, expanded. A free bloomer." [P] "Vigorous plant; flowers in panicles, white, small, flat, full. Extremely floriferous." [S] "Pure white, blooms in immensely large clusters, double, beautiful grown either as a climbing or weeping rose." [JC] "White, small, semi-double, flat, produced in panicles. Growth very vigorous, climbing, free." [GeH] "A new variety, found growing amongst some briars by a gardener of the name of Bennet [*sic*], in Nottinghamshire. It is a very pretty double, pure white variety." [WRP] "This kind, raised by Bennett in 1840, is certainly one of the prettiest [of the Arvensis group] by way of its heavy bloom, the plant's vigor, and the longevity of its flowers, which are a beautiful pure white. We know of several specimens, among others an enormous plant which covers the whole front of a building, though poorly tended. Every year when it blooms, the effect produced is absolutely marvelous, all the more so because this variety blooms several days later than the other climbing roses in this category. It is to be recommended for clothing pergolas, pillars, verandas, etc." [JR31/188]

"'Thoresbyana', often confused with 'Bennett's Seedling', is however far from being a copy of the other, which is nothing more than a seedling of 'Polyantha' [Mult]. Both of these came indeed from the same breeder, the first in 1840, and the second much more recently. The one has pure white blossoms, the other gives blossoms having a little yellow in the middle, and the bloom of this one ['Bennett's Seedling'] is much earlier than that of 'Thoresbyana'. The only plant of this group which is nearly synonymous with the variety in question would be 'Splendens' ('Repens'), in which, however, the color is a more matte white." [JR34/39]

Tuguriorum Listed as 'Ayrshirea' (Arv).

Venusta Pendula
Kordes, 1928

"Pink-white, medium size, full, tall." [Sn] "This is an old climber, introducer and date unknown, probably an Ayrshire, with pinkish white flowers. See 'Ruga' [Arv]." [GAS]

[Ville de St.-Maur]
Denis, 1909

"Rampant rose with very flexile branches. Does admirably well as a weeper, indeed without any training. Very vigorous plant; flowers medium-sized, snow white, blooming in corymbs." [JR33/169]

Virginian Rambler
U.S.A., pre-1855

"Whitish pink, small, full, tall." [Sn] "In the way of 'Dundee Rambler', but the flowers are shaded with pink." [GeH] "Medium size, whitish pink, strong growing, early blooming." [Ck] "Very vigorous shrub; canes nearly thornless; one of the best roses to use as a weeper; blossom medium-sized, nearly full, delicate pink, nearly blush white." [S] *Cf.* 'Virginia Lass' (Set).

CHAPTER TWENTY-THREE

Sempervirenses

"A hundred years ago [ca. 1833] all really high-class climbing roses belonged to this group. The original of the family was *Rosa sempervirens,* a wild rose which rambles all over central Europe. It is very hardy, and, unlike the Ayrshire, with which it mingles to some extent, its flowers are borne in clusters of ten to fifty. The foliage is relatively small, very glossy, and entirely evergreen in the southern part of its range. The blooms are not fragrant, and most of its hybrids have scentless flowers so double that they resemble tiny camellias or double buttercups. Like the Ayrshires, the Evergreen roses are extremely vigorous and resent any attempt at pruning. All of the hybrid varieties vary somewhat in hardiness according to that of their other parent. Evidently, *R. sempervirens* transmits little of its own hardiness to its offspring. Its evergreen foliage offers a new quality to the hybridizer, especially for use in the South. There is no reliable information concerning its resistance to disease, but if the foliage holds on as the older authorities claimed it did, it could not be very susceptible. At any rate, there would be no harm in raising a few thousand seedlings from any available variety, or to import *R. sempervirens* itself and make a fresh start." [GAS] "This rose and its varieties, although very popular in France and England, lose much of the character implied by the name when cultivated in this [Philadelphian] part of the United States, where they become deciduous, losing their foliage on the approach of severe frost. But in the more favored southern climes, they retain it during the winter, and there grow and bloom in profuse wreaths or garlands, making them an object of great attraction in their season. They are in colour generally pale, making a decided contrast with the Boursault family. They grow rapidly, and are well adapted for arches, grottos, rockwork, pillars, or trellises. The foliage is of a peculiarly bright shining green." [Bu] "It is suited for the same purposes as the Ayrshire, from which it differs by producing its flowers in corymbs instead of singly, and by holding its beautiful dark green leaves till the depth of winter . . . As Pillar Roses some are very beautiful, rising quickly to the height of ten or twelve feet [ca. 3.3–4 m], their pretty ranunculus-shaped flowers drooping in graceful corymbs of from ten to fifty blooms each." [P] "All these varieties have climbing canes, and will do for cover-

ing *berceaux,* clothing walls, or forming garlands. The persistence of their foliage adds further to their merit. Indeed, in the greenhouse, they don't cast them until March." [BJ30]

"The Sempervirens Rose abounds throughout the middle of Europe, and is supposed to have been introduced in 1629." [P] "This rose comes from Provence, Languedoc, and, in general, southern Europe." [CM] "All varieties of *R. sempervirens* come from Italy, mainly the Florence area, where they bloom almost throughout the year. In the climate of Paris and northern France, however, own-root plants have difficulty blooming, especially if pruned." [T&R] "The original of this beautiful family is the Rosa sempervirens, the climbing Wild Rose of Italy, with small single white flowers, and foliage nearly evergreen." [WRP] "The petals are made into a supposed purgative medicine used by the people of Tuscany, although probably in minute doses." [T&R] "Its habit and main characteristics bring it fairly close to the Musk Rose; but it differs from that in its persistent leaves of a deeper brighter green, and by its bracts. The Evergreen Rose has elongate ovaries and bristly peduncles; its stems are armed with numerous hooked prickles; its leaves are composed of five oval leaflets terminating in a sharp point, glossy green both above and below, and remaining until new growth; its flowers are borne in umbels at the branch-tips; they are white, single, fairly large, appear in July, and waft a quite pleasant musk scent. This rose keeps its leaves all year (it's this property which brings about the name 'Evergreen'), and would be quite the thing for covering *berceaux* or summer-houses in our landscape gardens; but it is sensitive to frost. It is therefore best to put it in a warm exposure, and to cover it with straw during the Winter. Much as it is worth growing, this species nevertheless isn't much sought out, the Musk Rose with its stronger and more elegant scent being preferred. The Evergreen Rose grafts quite nicely on the Briar, but it doesn't last long there. You can see it own-root at the Trianon—it grows there. Used in that way, it would perhaps be a better substitute for the Field Rose [*Rosa arvensis*]. Monsieur Descemet has a double-flowered variety of the Evergreen Rose." [CM] "In 1825, Monsieur Vibert obtained from seed several effective double varieties . . . Monsieur Jacques, gardener-in-chief of my lord the Duc d'Orléans at Neuilly also enriched this group with several double varieties of great merit." [BJ30] "Monsieur Jacques, the chief gardener at the Château de Neuilly, has had the pleasure of originating most of the varieties now in cultivation." [WRP]

"The varieties of Rosa Sempervirens are of the easiest culture, as they seem to flourish in all soils and situations. In sheltered places and under trees they are nearly evergreen, retaining their leaves till spring. This makes them valuable for covering banks, trees, or walls … To make them grow vigorously, give them a supply of manure on the surface, annually in the autumn, to be carried to their roots by the rains of winter. In the autumn or winter pruning, their branches must be left at their full length, for, if shortened, they will make prodigious long shoots the following season, but produce no flowers; the shoots being very flexible, they can be laid in and twisted in any direction, but the use of the knife must be avoided as much as possible." [WRP] "In pruning they require much thinning, and the shoots left should be merely tipped." [P]

Rosa sempervirens
horticultural syn. 'Evergreen Rose'

"We cite this species of rose because it has the privilege of keeping its leaves all year, and because it trims out in a nice way the *treillage* it is trained against. Its blossoms, small but white and finely musky, contrast pleasantly with the beautiful glossy green of the leaves. It comes from Italy, and requires the orangery for the Winter." [BJ09] "Common in the Balearic Islands, grows spontaneously throughout the south of Europe and in Barbary. Its foliage, of a glossy green, is intermingled with a profusion of small, white, highly scented flowers." [Go] "Common in the Mediterranean area, in France, Italy, Africa, as well as (so it is said) in Asia on this side of the Ganges. It is extremely vigorous, and with support will climb to a considerable height. Its branches are smooth, and have thorns; its leaves, with 3–5 or 7 dentate leaflets, are slightly pointed, somber green, and don't tall until after Winter. Its little blossoms, white or whitish, are fragrant, and bloom in threes or fives on their branchlets. This rose does not require much pruning." [JF] "Flower small, white, and single; calyx entire. Ovary oval. Short peduncle. Small oval leaf with large teeth … This flower is small, single and white; the shoot which bears it soon nods earthwards, curving. Its calyx isn't very pinnate; its ovary is an abbreviated oval, and a rather light green; its peduncle is short and bristles with small fine white points. The shoots exposed to the sun are a dark red, and have some red thorns shaped like carding teeth, often with one set against two. The leaves are small, lacy, and oval-acuminate with large teeth; above, they are a dark green; below, slightly villose and a matte green. The petioles are armed at the base with hooked thorns. When it is not pruned, and left to grow naturally, the bush is green all Winter." [Rsg] "Rose with egg-shaped seed-buds: empalements and peduncles hispid: petioles prickly: stem armed with crooked red spines: flowers grow in scattered umbels, with lance-shaped, reflexed floral leaves: blossoms white. Native of Germany. As a training Rose, this species is particularly estimable from the rapidity of its growth. It also retains its leaves longer than most roses, but is certainly, strictly speaking, not an evergreen. It so

much resembles the *Rosa arvensis,* that at first sight they might easily be taken one for the other. It is a native of Germany, and was introduced about the year 1629." [A]

"One of the principal characteristics of this rose, which has besides much in common with *Rosa moschata,* is that it retains green leaves all year. Its canes grow to a height of four to five feet [ca. 1.3–1.6 m], dividing into diffuse branches, which are cylindrical, glabrous, overspread with green bark, and armed with very strong, whitish, hooked thorns. The leaves are alternate, petiolate, stipulate, ordinarily composed of five thick, glossy, very glabrous, oval, lanceolate, acuminate leaflets which are lightly dentate like a saw along their edges, persistent, and borne on glabrous petioles bearing some prickles and moderately enlarged stipules, which are denticulate along their edge. The flowers are terminal, clustered into a near-umbel, borne on peduncles which are hispid as are the calyxes. The bracts are linear, lanceolate, lacy, acuminate; they form a sort of common involucre at the base of the peduncles. The calycinate leaflets [*sepals*] are oval, oblong, bristled, entire, subulate at their tip, whitish at their edges. The corollas are white, very fragrant, musky, with five petals slightly notched into a heart; sometimes they become double under cultivation. The ovaries are oval or slightly globular, rough, and hispid. This plant grows wild in Spain, and in several parts of Germany and of France. I have run across it around Marseille, along the banks of the Uveaune. It is grown in boskets, where the persistent leaves provide a nice verdure all year. Its flowers appear around the beginning of Summer, and keep coming into the Fall." [Lam] "Glossy, persistent foliage with white blossoms, garlanding the hottest, serest boulders. Taken into cultivation, it has provided much-esteemed climbing varieties." [JF]

Horticultural Varieties

Adélaïde d'Orléans
Jacques, pre-1829

"Flesh." [V9] "White, full, globular, medium-sized, beautiful." [LF] "Rose, shaded, small and pretty." [JC] "Medium-sized, globular, yellowish white." [JR5/70] "Blossom small, full, plump, blooming in corymbs; color white, spotted." [S] "Flowers of a pale rosy blush, very double and perfectly formed, in large clusters, valuable for blooming later than any of what are termed June Roses." [Bu] "Flowers creamy white, of medium size, full; form, globular. Blooms in large handsome clusters. A superb Climbing or Weeping Rose." [P] "Light pink, small, full, tall." [Sn] "Dark shining green foliage, and beautiful shaded pale rose colored flowers." [WRP] "Graceful, slender-stemmed climber … It has handsome clusters of medium-sized, globular, creamy white flowers tipped red." [GAS]

"*Shrub,* vigorous. *Stems,* creeping, rather kneed. *Thorns,* not numerous, reddish, short, even, scattered, slightly curved. *Bark,* smooth, glossy. *Leaves,* composed of five leaflets. *Leaflets,* thick, oblong, rather acuminated; toothing sloped and irregular. *Flowers,* large, full, regular; pure white." [Go] "*Canes* flexuose. *Thorns* hooked, sparse. *Bristles* lacking. *Petiole* bestrewn with pedicellate glands, armed beneath with hooked prickles. *Stipules* narrow, short, with long points which are linear, subulate, and having glandulose fringed or pectinate edges.

Adélaïde d'Orléans *continued*

Leaflets thick, stiff, distant, ovoid, acuminate, glabrous. *Serration* simple, acute, not very deep. *Peduncles* hispid-glandulose, ordinarily simple and gathered in umbelliform corymbs. *Bracts* lanceolate, acuminate, fringed with glands. *Ovary* narrow, turbinate, oblong, villose under the bud, usually glabrous after full anthesis. *Sepals* glandulose, short, subulate; 3 bearing altogether 5 appendages. *Bud* globular, red. *Flower* medium-sized (20–30 *lignes* across [ca. 6.35 cm or 2¹/₂ in to 9.52 cm or 3³/₄ in]), nearly full (60–80 petals), flesh, sometimes light pink, becoming nearly white. *Petals* concave, the inner ones narrow and spatulate. *Styles* projecting, filiform, free. This interesting variety blooms in June." [Pfs]

"A pretty bush, which grows vigorously; stems rampant, slightly angled, armed with a very small number of thorns which are reddish, short, slightly widened at the base, slightly curved, scattered; bark smooth, glossy green; leaves with prickly petioles; stipules short, clothed with bristles; leaflets to the number of five, thick, oblong, terminating in a small point, glossy green above, light beneath, with subtle and irregular dentation. Flowers very numerous, small, sometimes medium-sized, very double, elegant, perfectly formed, in a cluster to the number of eight, ten, and often twelve, in terminal corymbs. Petals white, with an evident nuance of lilac at the edge, crisped throughout the blossom, rolled at the center, irregularly incised at the tip; calycinate divisions [*sepals*] with several small glands; tube of calyx glabrous; peduncle with several small bristles." [No35] We cannot verify the "1826" date often given as this cultivar's date of introduction; indeed, that Prévost fils mentions it in his *Supplément* rather than in his main catalog argues for a date of introduction of 1829 or perhaps 1828.

Anatole de Montesquieu
Van Houtte, pre-1852

"Small, full, white, in a cluster." [Gp&f52] "White, small, full, medium to tall." [Sn] "Plant not very vigorous; blossom small, nearly full; color, pure white." [S] Not to be confused with Jacques' pre-1835 violet-purple Noisette of the same name (which was "medium-sized, full, lilac pink." [JR5/70]).

Ayez   Listed as 'Spectabilis' (Semp).

[De la Chine à Feuilles Longues]
trans. "From China, With Long Leaves"
Italy, pre-1810

"Here is what Monsieur de Launay says in the *Almanach du bon Jardinier* of 1810: 'We recommend this sort of rose to Germany because it has the virtue of keeping its leaves all year, pleasantly clothing trellises on which appear its blossoms, which are small but white and with a musk scent, contrasting agreeably with the beautiful glossy green of its leaves. It comes from Italy, and needs the orangery in the Winter.' I nevertheless assume, despite Monsieur de Launay's words, that this rose will grow out in the open, especially on the Briar." [C-T]

Dona Maria
Vibert, 1828

"Medium-sized, double, pure white." [V8] "Pure white, full, small, flat, beautiful." [LF] "Medium-sized, full, cupped, pure white." [JR5/70] "Flowers nearly white." [Bu] "Pink white." [Ÿ] "Pure white, small and double." [JC] "Flower small, single, white with a little pink, in a cluster."

[JR2/43] "*Flowers,* full, small, very pretty; pure white." [Go] "Flowers pure white, of medium size, full; form, cupped, fine. A beautiful Rose, blooming in large handsome trusses; foliage, pale green; growth less vigorous than others." [P] "Purest white, with fine dark green foliage, and very double flowers; a good and distinct rose." [WRP] "In 1825, Monsieur Vibert obtained from seed some very effective double-flowered varieties [of Sempervirens]. We'll take note of the one with double, pure white blossoms, 'Dona Maria', the flesh-colored one, and the pink." [BJ30] Raised in 1825, released in 1828. Dona Maria, possibly Maria II, queen of Portugal 1826–1853, lived 1819–1853.

[Eugène d'Orléans]
Jacques, pre-1829

"Plant vigorous; stems thick, reddish, creeping, very glabrous, smooth, slightly glossy, bearing a few prickles which are red and nearly straight; leaves composed of five leaflets—rarely of seven—nearly sessile, oval, glabrous, glossy, and leathery, irregularly toothed like a saw; one to three flowers at the tip of the branchlets; double, small, only 18–24 *lignes* across [ca. 5.72 cm or 2¹/₄ in], well formed; petals a delicate pink; calyx tube glabrous; peduncle bearing small glandular bristles." [No35]

Evergreen Rose   Listed as *Rosa sempervirens*.

Félicité et Perpétue   Plate 31
Jacques, 1828

"Flesh." [V9] "Flower quite medium-sized, full, edged white, with some flesh." [JR2/43] "Medium-sized, full, slightly flesh-colored, plump." [V8] "Flesh white, full, flat, medium-sized, beautiful." [LF] "Creamy-white, small, full. Must be sparingly pruned." [EL] "Light pink, medium size, full, tall." [Sn] "Growth very vigorous; blossom medium-sized, full, plump, flesh white." [S] "Pure white, blooms in large clusters, shining sub-evergreen foliage; a beautiful climbing rose." [JC] "Flowers flesh-colour, changing to white, produced in graceful trusses, drooping with their own weight, of medium size, full; form, compact. A superb Pillar or Climbing Rose." [P] "It is a very perfect rose, beautifully cupped, of a creamy-white colour, and when well grown makes a magnificent pyramid." [Bu] "*Branches,* red and creeping. *Thorns,* scattered, rather crooked." [Go]

"In spite of its preposterous name, is one of the most beautiful of climbing roses; and trained as it sometimes is in European Gardens, drooping in graceful festoons from pillar to pillar on supporting wires, or mantling some unsightly dead trunk with its foliage of shining green and its countless clusters of creamy white flowers, it forms one of the most attractive objects imaginable. Thin out its shoots; but do not prune them, since, if they are much shortened, they will yield no flowers whatever. Give it a rich soil, with autumnal top-dressing of manure." [FP] "No plant can be more lovely than a large specimen of this rose, covered with its double Ranunculus-like cream-colored flowers. It will not bloom if pruned much; therefore its shoots must be tied in of their full length, and thinned out if too numerous, but not shortened." [WRP]

"Among the charming obtentions of our late friend Jacques, then gardener at Neuilly-sur-Seine for the prince who later became King Louis-Philippe, 'Félicité [et] Perpétue' is one of the most recommendable because of its hardiness and extreme vigor. Due to this characteristic of luxuriant growth, it can form widely-extending hedges within a few years. Further, a few specimens of this variety planted alongside a house will, after three years [ca. 1095 days] of being trained against its walls, individually attain 7 meters in height [ca. 21 ft], with a spread of about 1.5 meters [ca. 4½ ft]. But it is not only under the protection of a wall that this pretty Sempervirens shows such growth. Out in the open and trained into a pyramid, it will also grow to a prodigious size. Before the disastrous Winter of 1880, the Luxembourg Garden in Paris displayed to the astonished eyes of strollers some pyramids of this variety comprised of bushes, each of which was 6 meters high [ca. 18 ft], and 3 meters around the bushier part [ca. 9 ft], having, what is more, an incalculable number of blossoms produced with such incredible abundance that each pyramid was literally covered with bloom . . . The flowers of 'Félicité [et] Perpétue' are medium-sized or nearly small, very full, appearing imbricated, globe-shaped when fully open, white with a light flesh tint, in clusters either few- or many-flowered, according to the vigor of the cane bearing them. This Sempervirens variety, which is not remontant, is generally propagated by cuttings, which root easily, and it is as own-root specimens that they make these gigantic plants we have just mentioned." [JR8/57] "Sometimes called 'White Pet'. Valued chiefly as an antique, and as the almost solitary relict of the Sempervirens class [*in 1933*]. Flowers white, small, very double, and perfect, in large clusters. Foliage nearly evergreen. Plant very vigorous. Rare and hard to get true to name." [GAS] Félicité and Perpétue— which is to say, St. Felicity and St. Perpetua, martyrs at Carthage in A.D. 203; "perpetual felicity" is perhaps to be found elsewhere than this sublunar world, as would be "felicitous perpetuity."

Flore

R. Lévêque, ca. 1830

"Still a very beautiful variety with white blossoms having a bright pink center, raised by Monsieur Lévêque père." [JR7/154] "A bright rose." [FP] "Pink going to coppery." [JR32/172] "Violet-pink, medium size, full, medium scent, tall." [Sn] "Medium-sized, full, flesh-colored with a pink center." [JR5/70] "Blossom large, full; color, bright pink." [S] "Flower medium-sized, very full, fading to delicate flesh, very floriferous. This is the prettiest of the sort." [JR2/143] "Quite unknown, splendid old sort. Very high climbing, healthy. Blossom large for the sort, absolutely wonderful pink, like a small Centifolia. An especially delightful kind." [Ck] "Sometimes called 'Williams Evergreen' [*sic; q.v. as 'William's Evergreen'*]. The flowers are small, cup-shaped, bright pink, darker in the center. A variety called 'Flora' is mentioned without description, which may be the same thing." [GAS] "Seems to have been driven out of remembrance by the host of newer free growing kinds, but it is still one of the most charming. When one sees the bloom, tending to globular in form, fully packed with petals, inclining to droop on the stem and in colour like a mushroom at its pinkest, one recognizes it, or something near it, as one of the few Roses of old pictures and of the embroideries of our great grandmothers." [NRS22/36–37] Flore, alias Flora, our horticultural patroness-goddess, lobbying at Olympus for us to good effect.

Galande
The listing "'Galande' (Semp)," which one sometimes sees, presumably refers to the cultivar 'The Garland', which see in Chapter 21 on Musks.

[Léopoldine d'Orléans]

Jacques, pre-1829

"Blush white." [God] "Beautiful blush." [WRP] "White, tinged with rose." [FP] "Plant vigorous, with stems and canes creeping, bearing prickles which are reddish, straight for the most part, some slightly curved, widened at the base, others scattered, and the greatest number stipulary; bark smooth, glossy, light green; leaves divergent, with petioles which are prickly, usually composed of five leaflets which are oblong, pointed, bright green; serration fine, slanted, and not very deep. Flowers numerous, double, medium in size, well formed, in corymbs which sometimes nod; petals pale pink, sometimes flesh color, small and ragged in the center, outer ones larger; some cordiform, others irregularly notched; nubs yellowish; buds oblong; calyx glabrous; peduncle with a light covering of glands." [No35]

[Mélanie de Montjoie]

Jacques, pre-1829

"White." [V9] "Pure white, large, full, flat, beautiful." [LF] "Large, pure white, expanded." [WRP] "Vigorous bush; canes climbing high; thorns not very numerous, equal, straight, thin, a little widened at their base; bark smooth, tinted reddish; leaves distant, with petioles having only a few small bristles; leaflets five, small, lanceolate, glossy green; dentations small and slanted, neither very deep nor very regular. Flowers numerous, very double, medium-sized, flat, in a corymb; petals a beautiful white, light pink in the middle, small, folded and ragged at the center, larger and often mucronate at the edge; calyx-tube silky, as are the sepals and the peduncles, which are long." [No35]

Noisette Ayez
Listed as 'Spectabilis' (Semp).

Princesse Louise

Jacques, 1829

"Flowers double, small, pale pink." [BJ30] "Medium-sized, full, cup-formed, white." [BJ53] "Flesh." [V9] "Pure white, full, flat, medium-sized." [LF] "Blossom medium-sized, full, cupped, very light pink." [JR2/43] "Flowers creamy white, the back petals shaded with rose, large and double; form, cupped." [P] "A fine and vigorous growing variety, with flowers of a creamy blush, very double and prettily cupped." [WRP] "Light pink, medium size, very full, tall." [Sn] "*Shrub*, vigorous. *Stems*, long, slender, armed with numerous scattered thorns; strong and straight. *Leaflets*, green and smooth on both surfaces, rather acuminated, sharply and regularly toothed. *Flowers*, united in clusters of three to twenty; small, double; the petals expanding of a pale pink, becoming pure white: the external ones large; those of the centre notched, and rather curled." [Go] "Stems slender, terete, climbing-like, attaining six to eight feet in height [ca. 2–2.6 m]; young growths tinged violet; thorns fairly numerous, strong, scattered, non-stipulary, violet on the young wood, ashy gray on the old; leaves of seven leaflets which are oval, regularly dentate with sharp teeth, green and glabrous on the two surfaces; stipules entire, with two teeth which are long and setaceous. Flowers in corymbs terminating the small branches, three to twenty per cluster; pedicels about an inch long [ca. 2.5 cm], bearing—like the tube and the calyx divisions—some red and glandulose [bristles]; calyx tube oval-rounded; sepals sometimes with two appendages; bud rounded, pink before opening; corolla a very pale pink while opening, passing then to nearly pure white; outer petals larger, central petals crenelate, slightly crinkled; flowers double, small, from 18–20 *lignes* across [ca. 5.715–6.35 cm or 2–2½ in], opening around the end of June and the beginning of July." [No35]

Princesse Louise *continued*

Princesse Louise, alias Adélaïde Eugénie Louise, Princesse d'Orléans (lived 1777–1847); sister of King Louis-Philippe, instrumental in convincing him to accept the crown.

Princesse Marie Plate 32

Jacques, 1829

"Blossoms double, deep pink, flesh when fully open." [BJ30] "Delicate pink, full, flat, medium-sized." [LF] "Medium-sized, full, very light pink, cupped." [V8] "White, edged." [God] "Reddish-pink." [FP] "Medium-sized, full, salmony light pink." [JR5/71] "Flower medium-sized, cupped, white." [JR2/43] "Flowers clear pink, of medium size, full." [P] "Pink, medium-sized, full, tall." [Sn] "The true 'Princesse Marie' is a very neat and pretty bright rose colored variety, and entirely distinct." [WRP]

"*Shrub,* vigorous. *Stems,* long and slender, armed with thorns less numerous than the preceding. *Leaflets,* oval, pointed, with sharp toothing. *Flowers,* in clusters of from three to twelve, small, well formed, cup-shaped; petals at first of a deep red, becoming afterwards flesh-colour, sloped at the summit." [Go] "Stems similar to those of ['Princesse Louise']; thorns less numerous; leaves with five or seven leaflets which are oval, pointed, with sharp and setaceous teeth at the tip. Flowers in corymbs of three to twelve; pedicels an inch long [ca. 2.5 cm], violet, and nearly glabrous; calyx-tube oval-elongate; sepals short, entire; bud a beautiful red; corolla a deep pink at first, then flesh-colored, small, well-formed, cupped; petals notched at the tip; styles numerous, barely or not at all united at the base. This is the reddest of the double Sempervirenses." [No35]

"The variety 'Princesse Marie'…preserves the extreme vigor and hardiness of its ancestor, and produces flexuous canes which can attain up to 6–7 meters in length [ca. 18–21 ft] in the open, without any protection. It gives a multitude of blossoms which are medium-sized, full, well formed, very bright light pink when opening, then becoming paler, in clusters so numerous that the bush disappears under an avalanche of flowers; it is in the thousands, the total one can reach in counting the blooms of a four or five year old 'Princesse Marie' in good soil…The pretty change from the Sempervirens Type was raised in 1829 from a sowing of seeds of Sempervirens Major by our late friend Jacques, then gardener-in-chief of the prince's estate of Neuilly-sur-Seine; it was dedicated to Princesse Marie, daughter of my lord the Duc d'Orléans, who was [later] King [Louis-]Philippe I. As all these varieties of this sort are easily propagated by grafting, it doesn't matter what stock is usually used; and it propagates no less easily by budding, which 'takes' perfectly, made in the Fall under a *cloche* or indeed out in the open, as one does those of 'Manettii' [N] or 'De la Grifferaie' [Mult]." [JR10/9] Princesse Marie, lived 1813–1839, artiste and wife of Prince Frederick of Württemberg; not to be confused with Princesse Marie-Louise (1812–1850; see 'Reine des Belges' [Semp]).

[Reine des Belges] Plate 33

trans. "Queen of the Belgians"

Jacques, 1832

"Creamy white flowers." [GAS] "A lightly pinked white, the most beautiful coloration." [S] "In his brochure *Taille et culture du Rosier,* Monsieur Eugène Fornay [*sic; rather* "Forney"] classes 'Reine des Belges' among the Ayrshires with 'Splendens' and 'Miller's Climbing' [*sic*], and then adds 'These three varieties are English; they can be found at Monsieur Jamain's, in Bourg-la-Reine.' First of all, it is an error to place this variety among the Ayrshires, since it is a Sempervirens; what is more, it is a French rose. Around 1830, Jacques, King Louis-Philippe's gardener at Neuilly, was much occupied with roses in general, and the climbers in particular; he released to commerce several Sempervirenses to which he gave the names of the royal Princesses—and the Belgian queen was indeed the king's daughter. As for the rest, in *Die Rose,* by Nietner, on page 114, this rose is mentioned under no 4,206 with the tag *Jacques, 1832.* We subscribe completely to Monsieur Nietner's opinion. The rose 'Reine des Belges' is extremely vigorous, throwing out from the trunk strong canes which grow up to 4 meters long [ca. 12 ft]. It covers itself with clusters of elegant pure white buds which become roses medium in size, very double, well formed, beautiful white slightly tinted light pink in age. Its vigor, its evergreen foliage, and its abundant bloom in the Spring make it one of the best roses for pillars, walls, etc." [JR21/136] Marie-Louise, lived 1812–1850, *reine des belges, i.e.,* queen of the Belgians, having married King Leopold I of Belgium.

Rose Ayez Listed as 'Spectabilis' (Semp).

Scandens Listed as an Arvensis.

Spectabilis

syns. 'Ayez', 'Noisette Ayez', 'Rose Ayez', 'Spectabile'

Breeder unknown, pre-1833

"Vinous red." [BJ40] "Purple-lilac, full, flat, large." [LF] "Medium-sized, double, salmony pink." [JR5/71] "Flower medium-sized, full, opening wide; color pale pink; often starts blooming as late as the Fall." [S] "Remarkable rose; flower vinous red." [I'H60/239] "Flowers rosy pink, of medium size, double; produced occasionally in the autumn; form, cupped, pretty and distinct." [P] "A fine and distinct climbing rose, with bright rosy lilac flowers, and curiously incised petals; a most vigorous growing and desirable variety." [WRP]

Spectabile Listed as 'Spectabilis' (Semp).

[William's Evergreen]

William, 1850

"White, center rosy flesh." [CA96] "A strong growing climbing rose with very large foliage and producing immense clusters of white flowers; foliage retained all year." [CA97] Possibly, or reputedly, synonymous with 'Flore' (Semp).

CHAPTER TWENTY-FOUR

Boursaults

"This tribe takes its name from the late Monsieur Boursault, a distinguished French amateur horticulturist. They are the hardiest of the climbing roses—easily known by their long flexible shoots, of a reddish-purple colour, and withstanding with impunity the severest of our winters, flowering profusely early in the season; they may well be termed the harbingers of the rosary. They are well adapted for covering arbours or concealing outbuildings, walls, or any other disagreeable objects. They are also frequently cultivated for stocks, whereon to bud other roses of more rare character, which purpose they will answer very well, though a plant thus formed renders its durability uncertain, being very liable to *sucker* ... thereby taking away nourishment from the part of the plant which most requires it; of course, all suckers or shoots below the bud or graft must be displaced." [Bu] "They are exceedingly well adapted for pillar roses: they owe their origin to the Rosa Alpina, a single red rose, a native of the Alps, and also of the hills in the south of France." [WRP] "The Boursault Rose; *Rosa reclinata* Thory; described in 1810. Resulted from a cross between the Alp Rose and the China Rose. We find it planted at the château Soucelles, between 1790 and 1810, by Monsieur de Ménage and his son. Dedicated to the member of the Convention, Boursault, who became a Rose fancier. Given to Thory by another fancier, Monsieur Cugnot, in 1824." [Gx]

"The Boursault Roses are very distinct from all others. The shoots are long, flexible, very smooth, in some instances entirely free from thorns; the one side often of a pale green, the other of a reddish tinge: the eyes are formed further apart than common. The flowers are produced in large clusters . . . Boursault Roses should be well thinned out in pruning; but the shoots that are left for flowering should be shortened-in very little." [P] "They should have, wherever planted, plenty of space allotted for them; for after being one or two years established, they will make shoots ten to twelve feet long [ca. 3.5–4 m]. In pruning, the oldest wood should be cut out, merely to keep the branches from being too crowded: the flowers are produced from the wood of the preceding year. They will grow freely in any soil or situation." [Bu] "The growths of this rose are, it is true, long and flexible, the bushes of vigorous growth, but not of a habit sufficiently pendant to make perfect climbers without the help of the gardener. As, however, the most part of these roses are frequently used for clothing walls, particularly on the north side, where other scandent or climbing roses don't do well and don't develop their flowers perfectly, we make no objection to grouping them with the scandents or climbers, all the more so because the color of their blossoms, varying from somber red and pink shades, contrasts agreeably with the pale and primarily white flowers of the others ... During ordinary Winters, and planted against a north-facing wall, these roses are thoroughly hardy; in Germany in the north, the hybridized sorts occasionally suffer in heavy frosts—it is thus a good idea to cover the rose . . . with matted straw or pine branches." [JR8/58] "Experience proves the Alpine Roses to be excellent grafting stocks." [T&R] "The Blush and the Crimson have been recommended by many as stocks for budding and grafting the Tea-Scented Roses on. The Blush has been used here, but is not approved of: it is the worst of all stocks; and more disposed to canker than any other with which we are acquainted. The Crimson, which appears more suitable for the purpose, has not been tried extensively." [P]

"The varieties of this series are few. The vigorous canes reach 2–4 meters [ca. 6–12 ft]. The flowers are generally very large, semi-double, and crimson and red in color; all are very floriferous in our climate [that of Paris, France]." [JR2/42] "No Boursault is really very vigorous as climbers go. The bushes lose their foliage very early and the flowers are rough and badly shaped. The merits of the race are fragrance, extreme hardiness, and a very early flowering season. The species, *R. pendulina,* has been worked with very sparingly, and who knows whether a dash of Boursault might not improve the hardiness of some of our modern climbers?" [GAS]

Rosa alpina Listed as *Rosa pendulina.*

Rosa alpina 'Speciosa' Listed as 'Drummond's Thornless' (Bslt).

Rosa inermis Listed as *Rosa pendulina.*

Rosa pendulina

botanical syns. *R. alpina, R. inermis*; horticultural syns., 'Alp Rose', 'Alpine Rose'

"Bush 5–6 feet high [ca. 1.6–2 m]; branches and canes supple and slender; leaves glabrous, beautiful green above, whitish beneath; petioles, stipules, and peduncles lightly ciliate; flowers small, single, early, and very dark red." [J-A/567] "Its blossoms are pink, but semi-double, and borne in terminal clusters. Their scent is sweet and agreeable." [BJ09] "Doesn't grow more than twelve or eighteen inches [ca. 3–4.5 dm], . . . doesn't have any thorns; . . . the leaves are comprised of seven or nine leaflets; . . . the sepals don't have any appendages; . . . the flowers are solitary, or in twos, of a very bright red, and small." [MaRu] "Upright shrub, canes nearly unarmed, smooth, pink flowers. Appropriate to adorn alpine scenes." [JR26/181] "Shrub of 7–8 feet [ca. 2.3–2.6 m], making a lax, diffuse bush; canes long, nearly upright, slightly climbing, greenish-brown, sometimes glaucous and somewhat purplish on one side, thornless, or bearing some feeble thorns at the bases of the canes; stipules narrow at their base, wide at the summit, nude, entire, fringed with glands; petioles with pedicellate glands or bristles; 5–9 slender leaflets, oval or oblong-lanceolate, pointed at the two ends, doubly and largely dentate, nude or rarely pubescent beneath; midvein sometimes scabrous, with some short prickles; blossoms upright, single, red, solitary, with obcordate and concave petals. This rose is common in England, Germany, France, and nearly throughout temperate Europe." [S] "This rose, originating in the Alps, the Pyrenees, the Cévennes, the Vosges, and the mountains of the Auvergne, blooms perhaps in May, perhaps in June, perhaps in July, depending upon the altitude of the site it has taken to. Its stem grows to five to six feet [ca. 1.6–2 m]; its ovaries are oval, glabrous, sometimes hispid; its peduncles and its petioles often have pink prickles. Its canes are numerous, wide-spreading, smooth, glabrous, brown-green or reddish; its leaves, ordinarily composed of nine finely dentate leaflets which are now a slightly dark green, now quite glaucous. Its blossoms, nearly always solitary, medium-sized, lightly fragrant, are more than an inch in size [ca. 2.5 cm], and reddish. As to the fruit of the Alpine Rose, it becomes a beautiful dark red once it reaches full maturity. The Alpine Rose shows—during bloo—mfruits which are sometimes oval and sometimes semi-globulose, which ordinarily round out in ripening; it is grown in several gardens." [CM] "It seems to be grown more to contradict the proverb which says 'Every rose has its thorn' than for the beauty of its blossom." [AbR]

"A somewhat commonplace plant, though welcome for its earliness, and the flowers, which are blood red when first opened, rapidly take a somewhat faded appearance. It is well known for its smooth stems without prickles. There is, however, a more beautiful form of this Rose, sold under the name *R. alpina pendulina* . . . in which the fruits are pendulous and urn shaped. Both in flower, fruit and foliage this form seems to me more attractive than the type. The foliage is darker than that of the type, and sometimes faintly tinged with red, particularly about the stipules. The flowers are a fine bloom red." [NRS17/36–37] "Cultivated in England since the latter part of the seventeenth century . . . It is one of the few species perfectly at home in the rock garden, and is particularly striking when in fruit. The hips are narrowly pear-shaped, bright red, and surmounted by erect, persistent sepals, and being freely borne they afford a cherished colour effect, glorious, unique, and unusual." [NRS17/62] "Rose unarmed,

with oblong seed-buds, and hispid petioles and peduncles. Blossoms of a deep red purple. Leaves smooth. Leaflets ovate, sharp-pointed, and sawed at the edges. Stem and branches smooth. Fruit pendulous. This thornless Rose may be almost considered as the exception to an otherwise general rule. A specific so unequivocally good seldom occurs; and yet this Rose, in the Hortus Kewensis, bears the name of *pendulina*, from its pendulous fruit; a character common to several other species. But had we not found this Rose to be as well known under the name of *inermis*, as by the title of *pendulina*, we should not (although for the better) have thought ourselves so well justified in altering it; regarding names of no further value than as they give us the most immediate direction to any object we may be in search of. It is an early-blooming Rose with single flowers of the finest purple colour; and frequently blooms a second time in the autumn: but its flowers then are not so large as in the early part of the season." [A]

"*Stems* 0.9–1.2 m high [ca. 3–4 ft], diffuse, quite unarmed as in almost all alpine roses. *Leaflets* 7–9, ovate, obtuse, bright green above, paler beneath; biserrate; petioles a little rough to the touch, with moderately large finely-toothed stipules which widen towards the tip. *Flowers* 1 (–2), nodding, sometimes re-erecting; pedicels glandular hispid; *receptacles* oblong, sometimes rounded, distended, glabrous, recurved at anthesis; *sepals* entire, greenish or purplish externally, downy within and on the margins; *petals* 5, emarginate, rose violet; *stamens* numerous; styles very short but distinct. Found in mountainous places in Europe and, according to Aiton, indigenous to North America. Like all alpine roses, this is very variable. Hips may be much elongated or subglobose, constricted above like a calabash or not at all constricted, sometimes all on the same root. The always-nodding hip, glandular hispid peduncles and absence of prickles are the only characters for certain identification. It produces a fine show of its odd pendulous red hips in our gardens in the Fall, and is the first of all to bloom in Paris when favorably sited. It demands little attention, and all soils seem to suit it." [T&R] "*Shrub* tall, unarmed except at the base of the vigorous shoots, where ordinarily there are some bristles or sparse setiform prickles. *Canes* jutting out, upright or climbing, diffuse, ordinarily glaucous, purple or greenish brown on one side. *Leaves* composed of 7 or 9 leaflets, rarely 5. *Petiole* glandulose or glabrous, unarmed, or armed beneath with some small prickles. *Stipules* constricted at the base, dilated at the tip, entire, edged with glands. *Leaflets* oval or oblong-lanceolate, obtuse or sharp, glabrous (sometimes pubescent beneath). *Serration* sharp, normally glandulose, simple or double. *Peduncles* hispid-glandulose or glabrous, ordinarily solitary and without bracts, but often in 2's–5's, and coming with bracts due to the effects of culture and pruning. (Here, as with the greater number of sorts, the presence of bracts is a condition necessary for the coming-together of the peduncles; when the peduncle is solitary, normally there aren't any bracts). *Ovary* hispid-glandulose or glabrous, oval, bottle-shaped or fusiform; always bulbous at the base and constricted at the summit into a more or less elongated collar in the single varieties; often, in the multiplex varieties, gourd-shaped or slightly constricted at the neck, which is wide-spreading. *Sepals* hispid-glandulose or glabrous, simple or appendiculate, ordinarily erect and connivent after the petals fall. *Fruit* red, pendant. Blooms in May. [*For the single sort*] *Shrub* very tall, forming a lax and diffuse plant. *Canes* long, climbing, glaucous, a little purplish on one side. *Leaves* composed of 7 leaflets (rarely, 9), which are oval, obtuse, pale and pubescent beneath. *Serration* flat, bulbous at the base, constricted into a bottleneck at the tip, hispid, ordinarily purple. *Sepals* hispid-glandulose, terminating in a point, which is simple or bearing several linear appendages. *Flower* small, single, light pink." [Pf] "It comes from the Swiss mountains, and can further be found in those of the Dauphiné. It differs from [*Rosa canina*] in, 1. its oblong fruit and its petals shaped like a heart, nearly divided into two lobes; 2. by its calyxes, which are entire; 3. by its glabrous leaves; 4. especially by its thornless, smooth canes, reddish in color." [AbR] "Described in the Nouveau Duhamel, described and illustrated by Redouté." [Gx]

"All of the efforts of the florists have still not [*in 1793*] been enough to produce a double one." [AbR] "There's [*in 1798*] a single one and a double one." [MaRu] "Desvaux has made an extensive study of [*the various subspecies*] and is the main authority for their naming. All the varieties are in demand for decorating large parks, their bright red hips persisting into Winter; but in small gardens, their roots are too invasive. Connoisseurs refrain from pruning, merely trimming to preserve a good shape." [T&R] "Fruit oblong and drooping, peduncles bristly; [*there are, as of 1830*] 4 varieties [*which we list below, with some synonymy*], all worth collecting, hybrids of the Alpina fertilized by the China: [*1*] 'Calypso' [*by*] Noisette / 'Floride' [*as listed by*] Vibert . . . ; [*2*] 'Boursault' . . . ; [*3*] 'L'Héritier' / 'Reversa' . . . ; [*and 4*] there is another variety mentioned by Prévost [*to wit, 'Maheca' (Bslt)*]." [BJ30, in a cryptic sentence that we have liberally dealt with to clarify]

Rosa pendulina 'Laevis'
trans. "Smooth"
Thory, ca. 1820

Botanical variety. "*Shrub* 1.2–1.5 m high [ca. 4–5 ft]; *stems* elongate, reddish in maturity as with the Cinnamon Rose, quite unarmed. *Leaflets* 5–9, ovate, glabrous, almost always bidentate; petioles slightly hispid; stipules large, denticulate. *Flowers* 1–3, terminal and axillary; pedicels glabrous; *bracts* ovate, slightly dentate; *receptacles* globose; *sepals* entire, linear, spatulate above, lanate-margined; *petals* 5, emarginate, bright red, whitening towards the base; *stamens* very numerous; *styles* free. This native of the Alps and southern France is often confused with *R. cinnamomea* on account of the globose receptacle and stem color; but the latter has prickles adjacent to the stipules, as well as elongate always simply dentate leaflets. It blooms in cultivation through the greater part of the Summer, and suckers freely." [T&R]

Horticultural Varieties

À Boutons Penchés Listed as 'Boursault' (Bslt).

[À Boutons Renversés à Fleurs Simples]
syn. 'Reclinata Flore Simplici'
Cugnot, pre-1824

"Five . . . petals . . . Can reach a great height if supported; *branches* unarmed or occasionally with prickles on the lower part. *Leaflets* (3–) 7, glabrous, simply dentate, light green above, paler beneath; petioles glabrous, with small reddish prickles; stipules decurrent, acute, denticulate, flushed red in youth, later greenish. *Flowers* most-

ly clustered at the tips of the laterals, the buds facing downwards at first but becoming erect at anthesis; *receptacles* short, subglobose, glabrous like the pedicels and calyx; *sepals* subsimple, as long as the petals, spatulate; *petals* cordately notched, pale pink. *Hips* subglobose, red . . . Probably a hybrid between the China Rose and the Alpine Rose; it was sent to us by Cugnot and is rather rare." [T&R]

À Fleurs Doubles Listed as 'Inermis' (Bslt).

À Fleurs Panachées
syn. 'Variegata'; trans., "With Plumed Flowers"
Poilpré/Lemeunier, ca. 1815

"*Shrub* 0.9–1.2 m high [ca. 3–4 ft], differing from *R. alpina* [*i.e., Rosa pendulina*] only in the petals being attractively striped with bright red on a pink base. The rather small flowers appear in succession from early Spring to the end of August, especially when it is given a northerly exposure. Poilpré gave this sport of the Alpine Rose to Lemeunier seven or eight years ago." [T&R]

Alp Rose Listed as *Rosa pendulina*.

Alpine Rose Listed as *Rosa pendulina*.

Amadis
syn. 'Crimson'
Laffay, 1829

"Crimson and velvety purple, full, medium-sized." [LF, as a "Hybrid of China, Bourbon, Noisette, etc."] "Brilliant, purplish-crimson, changing to purplish-lilac, a very showy semi-double rose, and one of the best." [JC] "Thornless, full flower, large, well-formed, purplish crimson red changing to violet." [JR2/42] "It is of rather harsh crimson colour." [NRS21/101] "Flowers deep crimson purple, shaded more or less with vivid crimson, large and semi-double; form, cupped. Habit, erect; growth, vigorous; the young wood of a whitish green. A showy Rose; one of the best of the group." [P] "Of rapid growth, makes a most magnificent pyramid of rich purple crimson; the flowers are produced in clusters, are perfectly double, and of considerable duration." [Bu] "A very fine pillar rose; its clusters of large, deep purple and crimson flowers are inclined to be pendulous, consequently they have a fine effect when on a tall pillar." [WRP] "Flower deep purplish crimson. Growth free and rampant; does well under adverse conditions." [GeH] "It is a hardy shrub, equally able to take full sun or shade, nearly uncaring about the sort of soil or exposure. Nothing is better than this climbing Rose for covering trellises or training on posts along walkways. Very floriferous, from the first, hundreds of the most beautiful flowers on entirely thornless canes. It should be pruned very little if you want to see it bloom well." [R-H63/126] "The easiest [Boursault] to grow and the most free of bloom." [NRS21/101]

Belle de Bouseaux Listed as 'Boursalt' (Bslt).

Belle de Lille Listed as 'Calypso' (Bslt).

Belle Sultane Listed as 'Maheca' (Bslt).

Bengale Angevin Listed as 'Calypso' (Bslt).

Bengale Cypress Listed as 'Calypso' (Bslt).

Bengale Cypris Listed as 'Calypso' (Bslt).

Bengale Florida Listed as 'Calypso' (Bslt).

Bengale Hollandaise Listed as 'Maheca' (Bslt).

Bengale Violet Listed as 'Reversa' (Bslt).

Blush Boursault Listed as 'Calypso' (Bslt).

Boursault

syns. 'À Boutons Penchés', 'Belle de Bourseaux', 'Boursault Bengal',
    'Boursaultiana Plena', 'Declinata', 'Old Red Boursault', 'Pink',
    'Reclinata Flore Sub-Multiplici', 'Red'
Boursault/Vibert, pre-1820

"Pink." [V9] "Blossoms very double, medium-sized, bright pink."
[AC] "The oldest variety with flowers only semidouble; the colour is
pretty, and its profusion, at a distance, makes up for deficiency of petals." [Bu] "[The flowers] are semi-double, and indifferently formed."
[FP] "The flower is however of a large size, and brilliant color; it may be
deemed as superseded by the numerous climbers of a superior character." [WRP] "Flowers bright cherry when first opening, gradually becoming paler; large and semi-double; form, expanded. Habit, pendulous; growth, vigorous. A showy pillar or weeping Rose. *The original
Boursault Rose.*" [P] "Covered in Spring with a great number of blooms
which persist up to the Fall on favorably sited plants. No special care
is needed." [T&R] "Quite tall, espaliered, where it is very effective due to
its numerous, full, medium-sized, purple blossoms." [BJ30, as a hybrid "of the Alpina, fertilized by the China"] "This one's a new China.
Its wood is well armed. Its leaves are typical of the group—glossy, a
little larger; buds numerous, continuous until frost. Its blossom is a
pretty large, semi-double, bright pink. In the middle, some golden stamens remain. Its perfume is that of the 'Tous-Mois' [DP]. We owe it to
a sowing by Mlle. de Bourseaux [*sic*]. It suffers in the Winter." [LeR]

"*Shrub* very tall and diffuse. *Canes* very long, climbing, purple-
green, glaucous, unarmed except at the base of the most vigorous,
and some shoots, where is a sprinkling of straight prickles and rough
bristles. *Leaves* composed of 5 or 7 leaflets. *Petiole* ordinarily red, and
bestrewn with several glands and hairs, more often glabrous; armed
beneath with hooked thorns. *Stipules* entire, ciliate with glands. *Leaflets* glabrous, oval or ovoid, acute. *Serration* normally simple. *Peduncles* branching into multifloral corymbs, glabrous up to the last ram-
ification, which, from the upper bracts to the ovary, has a scattering
of small glands. Ordinarily, they are curving-ascending or upright.
Bracts large, oval-acuminate, glabrous, entire, with ciliate-glandulose edges, wavy, bullate, alone or more often in pairs at the base of
each branching of the peduncles. *Ovary* glabrous, glaucous, oval-
pyriform or globular, sometimes digitate. *Sepals* glabrous, glandulose, simple or altogether bearing 2–5 small linear appendages, each
one terminating in a small, glabrous leaflet which is lanceolate-lin-
ear, and shorter than the corolla. *Corolla* medium-sized, multiple
(12–20 petals), bright pink." [Pf]

"It is this variety which is the one most frequently found in gardens…It was raised by Monsieur Boursault around 1818 or 1820 from
seeds collected from the rose 'Boursaultiana Simplex', which itself is
a hybrid of the Alps Rose and a China. Vigorous shrub with long and
climbing canes, pretty nearly unarmed; leaves of 7–9 lanceolate and
simply dentate leaflets; petiole armed with small reddish thorns;
flowers pink, medium sized, grouped at the tips of the branches which
spring from the main canes; peduncle long; sepals shorter than the
corolla. This rose was named 'Rosa declinata à boutons renversés' by
Thory because, before the blossoms open, the buds curve earthwards

in a remarkable fashion—but they straighten up again before expansion. It is robust, and is able, I believe, to resist 18 or 20 degrees of cold.
I have never used it as a stock, but it can easily be so used. To obtain a
good bloom, one should grow it on a sunny wall, and at pruning time
only cut back those canes which would spoil the plant's form and symmetry. Monsieur Boursault was a distinguished fancier who loved
roses with a passion. His gardens on the rue Pigalle enjoyed a great
reputation, and were known as the most beautiful in Paris." [JR10/60]

Boursault Bengal Listed as 'Boursault' (Bslt).

Boursaultiana Plena Listed as 'Boursault' (Bslt).

Calypso

syns. 'Belle de Lille', 'Bengale Angevin', 'Bengale Cypress', 'Bengale
    Cypris', 'Bengale Florida', 'Blush Boursault', 'De Lesle', 'Florida
    Rose', 'Rose de la Floride', 'Rose de Lisle', 'White Boursault'
L. Noisette?, pre-1810

"Best of all is the blush Boursault, one of the loveliest and cleanest
coloured of all Roses; it has the outer petals of a tender white of singularly pure quality, deepening to a delicate pink in the middle."
[NRS21/101] "Flesh." [V9] "Blush flowers, large and double; a beautiful
climbing or weeping rose." [JC] "White, center deep pink, very large
and full." [LF] "Blossom medium-sized, full, flesh pink." [JR2/42] "One
of the earliest of the sub-class, producing large blush flowers, with a
deep rose center, and perfectly double." [BBF66] "The flowers are very
large, of a blush colour, with a deep pink centre, pendulous, and very
showy, but occasionally do not open well." [Bu] "Whitish pink, small
to medium size, lightly double, tall." [Sn] "Bush with thin, climbing
canes; flower very large, full, flesh around the circumference, red in
the middle." [S] "Very climbing, appropriate for covering *berceaux*.
Blossoms full, white, with a bright pink heart." [BJ30, as a hybrid "of
the Alpina, fertilized by the China"] "Larger and more full than most
others of the species. They are of a deep flesh-color, passing into a
lighter shade towards the edge. It can scarcely owe its qualities to the
Boursault race alone, but seems to be a hybrid of some of the Chinese
roses. When in perfection, it is much the best of the group, but requires a warmer and brighter aspect than the others. It is, however,
perfectly hardy." [FP] "From, globular. Habit, pendulous; growth, vigorous, the plant holding its leaves longer than others of the group. Exceedingly rich as a climbing Rose when planted in a good aspect,
which it requires to develop its flowers in full beauty." [P] "A beautiful
rose, and when trained up a pillar, its large and delicately-coloured
flowers have a fine effect…they are produced in great profusion, and
expand among the earliest roses. It is one of the most vigorous of all
the rose family, often throwing out shoots of ten to fifteen feet in
length [ca. 3.3–5 m], and ascending to the height of thirty to forty feet
[ca. 9–12 m], spreading laterally to an equal or greater extent." [WRP]

"This rose, which was grown at the Soucelle château in 1810, was
described by Prévost." [Gx] "*Shrub* large and very vigorous, unarmed
except at the base of the shoots and vigorous canes, where will be
found short, large-based thorns. *Canes* very long, purple red, climbing. *Leaves* to 5, 7, or 9 leaflets, which are oval and slightly glossy.
Peduncle glabrous. *Ovary* glabrous, irregularly oval or lageniform,
normally widened at the base, and slightly constricted beneath the
wide-spreading tip. *Flower* very large, full, usually nodding, white
along the edge, bright and brilliant flesh in the center." [Pf]

"This rose is a hybrid of the Alps rose, very probably fertilized by a China. It was grown from seed by Monsieur Louis Noisette. When? In this, I can't be exact, but I can say it was before 1824, when Desportes mentioned it in his monograph on genus Rosa under number 71 ... It should be grown against a wall. It is hardy, but was unable to withstand Paris' terrible Winter of 1879–1880 ... At the time this rose was found, people frequently gave roses the name of a personage of mythology; it is supposed that it bears the name of the daughter of Oceanus and Thetis, who, according to Homer, fell in love with Ulysses and kept this hero on her islet for nearly 7 years." [JR10/75]

Common Purple Boursault Listed as 'Reversa' (Bslt).

Crimson Listed as 'Amadis' (Bslt).

De la Chine Double sans Aiguillons Listed as 'Inermis' (Bslt).

De Lesle Listed as 'Calypso' (Bslt).

Declinata Listed as 'Boursault' (Bslt).

[Drummond's Thornless]
syn. *Rosa alpina* 'Speciosa'
Drummond, pre-1846

"Flowers rosy carmine when first opening, changing to pink; large and semi-double; form, cupped. Habit, pendulous; growth, vigorous." [P] "Blossoms large, semi-full, cupped; color, carmine pink, pale pink at the second bloom." [S] "Is now an old variety [*as of 1846*], but it produces such a profusion of bright red flowers, that it ought to be in every collection of climbing roses." [WRP] According to Dr. Charles Nelson (*v. The Rose*, Spring, 1992), James Drummond was a Scots-born curator of the Cork Botanical Garden in Ireland, appointed in 1809.

Dutch Bengal Listed as 'Maheca' (Bslt).

Élégance Listed as 'Elegans' (Bslt).

Elegans
syn. 'Élégance'
Breeder unknown, pre-1844

"Blossom medium-sized, semi-full, blooming in corymbs; color, bright carmine, spotted white." [S] "A most beautiful vivid-colored rose; its purple and crimson flowers are often striped with white: this has a long succession of bloom, as it is one of the earliest and latest of summer roses." [WRP] "Flowers rosy crimson, sometimes purplish; often streaked with white; produced in very large clusters; of medium size, semi-double; form, expanded. Habit, erect; growth, vigorous. A very showy pillar Rose. Continues a long time in flower, owing to the large trusses it produces, bearing buds in different stages of forwardness." [P] Possibly synonymous with 'Maheca' (Bslt).

Florida Rose Listed as 'Calypso' (Bslt).

Full Boursault Rose Listed as 'Plena' (Bslt). See also 'Inermis' (Bslt).

Full-Flowering Boursault Listed as 'Inermis' (Bslt). See also 'Plena' (Bslt).

Gracilis
syn. 'Shailer's Provence'
Shailer, 1796

"Small, full, bright pink." [R&M62] "Flower medium-sized, very fresh bright pink." [JR2/42] "Bright purplish rose with curious foli-

age." [FICaVI/227] "Violet-pink, small to medium size, full, medium fragrance, tall." [Sn] "Pale rosy pink, their circumference lilac blush, of medium size, full; form, compact. Habit, branching; growth, small. A curious hybrid." [P] "Of slender growth, with bright pink flowers, not fully double, but very profuse." [Bu] "A very old and delicate-growing rose, unlike most other varieties of this family in its habit, as it seems to be [a cross] between the Boursault and the Provence Rose." [WRP] "Flowers lively cherry, shaded with lilac blush, of medium size, full; form, cupped, perfect. Habit, branching; growth, vigorous. Prickles singularly large and long; foliage of a rich dark green, the variety evidently being a hybrid." [P] "Of the most vigorous growth in good soils, often making shoots ten to twelve feet long in one season [ca. 3.3–4 m]; unlike the other varieties of this division, its shoots are covered with thorns. Nothing can be more graceful than the luxuriant foliage of this plant; it has also finely-cupped flowers, of the most vivid rose-color, and must be reckoned a beautiful and desirable rose." [WRP] "Rose with nearly round seed-buds, and peduncles slightly hispid and slender: flowers of many petals, imbricated, equal, and flesh-coloured. Stem smooth and flexible: spines scattered. This delicate Rose was raised about the year 1796 by Mr. Shailer, nurseryman, of Little Chelsea. It is as yet so little known, that a dwarf variety of the Province [*sic*] is frequently sold for it; a mistake most probably owing to its being commonly called amongst cultivators Shailer's Province Rose: but it certainly bears most resemblance to the Rosa Indica [*i.e., R. chinensis*], and is, as far as we can understand, a hybrid production between the two species; and if so, it might come under the description of variety only. But, whilst nature produces such distinct and beautiful varieties, specific titles can only be regarded as a variation of terms. It makes a most graceful appearance, from the drooping of its branches and nodding of its flowers, whose close and numerous petals are too heavy for its weak and slender stem to support. It appears to be a Rose calculated to train against a trellis to great advantage. It is as hardy as most Roses, and is increased (but not easily) by layers. Flowers during the months of June and July." [A]

Hollandaise Listed as 'Maheca' (Bslt).

Inermis
syns. 'À Fleurs Doubles', 'De la Chine Double sans Aiguillons', 'Full-Flowering Boursault', 'Inermis Sinensis', 'Multiplex', 'Pleine', 'Plena', 'Sans Épines', 'Sans Épines à Fleur Rose Double', 'Turbinata'; trans., "Unarmed"
Breeder unknown, pre-1770

"Double flowers, pink, fragrant ... warm and wet years bring out a second bud in the center of the flowers, forming a smaller rose or indeed a branch if, just when it appears, a person straightens out the branch and cuts the other branches a little short. By this method, I have obtained some 6-inch [ca. 1.5 dm] branches topped by flowers." [BJ17] "To the Alpine Rose is assigned a variety with double flowers, to which certain fanciers—and I have no idea why—give the name *Rose de Chine des Jardiniers* [*"Gardeners' China Rose"*]. The growth of this variety couldn't be any stronger; it would be to no end to graft it on the Briar—it grows so vigorously that it is able to cover every bit of a *berceau*." [CM] "*Shrub* very vigorous, forming a tall, wide bush, sometimes a small tree; unarmed, except at the base of the shoots and the vigorous canes. *Canes* glaucous, violet-purple on one side. *Leaflets* 7–9, rarely 5, glabrous. *Peduncle* glabrous at the base, and hispid-glan-

Inermis *continued*

dulose above the bracts. *Bracts* oval, sharp, wavy, entire. *Ovary* oval-globulose, spiny at the base, constricted in the middle, glabrous and wide-spreading at the tip. 2–4 of the *sepals* are pinnatifid. *Flower* medium-sized, full, pale pink. Opens in May and June." [Pf] "At about the same time [as certain extinct cultivars such as 'Gris Cendré' and 'Aculeata Incarnata'] bloom the *Thornless Roses,* with single blossoms, and with double. The first [*i.e.,* the single], violet in color, isn't worth growing. The second, *Rosa inermis Sinensis,* merits the efforts of the fancier. The leaves are long, lightly edged in red, and deeply toothed, with five to nine leaflets on the same petiole. The branches or canes are vigorous, long, smooth, and green; the side exposed to the midday sun is lightly tinted pink. The calyx is nearly round, and is covered, as is the petiole, with brown bristles. The flower bud is pointed, and over-topped by the calyx leaflets [*i.e., sepals*], which are slender and loose. The blossom, which is an inch and a half across [ca. 4 cm], is of a fairly beautiful form, a very delicate pink, and is slightly fragrant. This Rose takes well to the Briar, on which it grows vigorously and forms a beautiful head." [C-T] "Distinct sort, well acclimated, in which the wood is vigorous, long, smooth, and greenish; the leaves are long, edged in red, and profoundly dentate; the calyx is nearly round, and covered over with bristles, as is the peduncle; the bud is pointed, and much surpassed by the extensions of the calyx, which are incised, making little feathers. Flower very double, two inches across [ca. 5 cm], beautiful form, very delicate pink, lightly fragrant. It grows robustly grafted onto the Briar, and does wonderfully. The pink comprising the color is more intense in the middle, and lighter along the edges. This beautiful rose leaves no doubt as to the place of its birth; its lack of tenderness in the rigor of our Winters makes me believe it came from the Alps, or perhaps from some cold part of China. It opens with the single *Alpina* at the beginning of May." [LeR]

"This rose, which is said to originate in China, begins to show up in rosariums. Its canes are thoroughly without prickles; but its leaves, composed of seven to nine leaflets—which are oval, dentate, glabrous on both sides—have several prickles on their petioles; its flowers are a delicate pink, more than two inches in size [ca. 5 cm], and borne at the cane-tips on peduncles bristling with thick, glandulose bristles. This rose blooms in May and June. According to Monsieur Bosc, its blossoms should be single; and, in Monsieur Deslongchamps' view, all we know up till now is the *double* variety. This sort of contradiction produces a confusion much dismaying to the fancier!" [CM]

"Very tufted *bush* 1.2–1.5 m tall [ca. 3–4 ft]; *branches* smooth, greenish, well armed. *Leaves* medium-sized; *leaflets* 7–9, elliptic, unequally dentate, green above, paler beneath, glabrous on both surfaces; petioles roughish to the touch from small prickles; stipules a little dentate, gland-edged, dilated, not replicate as in *R. hudsoniana* with which it might be confused. *Flowers* almost always solitary at the ends of the laterals, 5–6 cm in diameter [ca. 2–2¼ in]; pedicels elongate, glandular-hispid; *receptacles* turbinate, similarly hispid at the base only; *sepals* 3 pinnatifid, 2 simple, longer than the petals in an open blossom, ciliate, downy within; *petals* 7–8-seriate, delicate pink, faintly scented; *styles* free; *stigmas* distinct. A common rose in our gardens, this is one of the first to bloom. Dupont was persuaded that it came from the Far East and called it *Rosa chinensis,* but it hails from the Swiss Alps … It blooms at the beginning of May, and is undemanding, all soils suiting it. It should only be grown on its own

roots, since, if grafted, it is inferior and the later flowers abort." [T&R] *Cf.* 'Plena' (Bslt), the name of which 'Inermis' shares as a synonym. Not to be confused with 'Inermis Morletii' (Bslt).

Inermis Morletii
syn. 'Morletii'
Morlet père & fils, 1883

"Light pink." [GAS] "Violet-pink, medium size, lightly double, medium scent, tall." [Sn] "Flower purplish rose, large, flat, showy. Growth vigorous." [GeH] "Very vigorous sort, with a semi-double flower, delicate pink, of a magnificent coloration; stem very vigorous, entirely lacking thorns." [S] Not to be confused with 'Inermis' (Bslt).

Inermis Sinensis   Listed as 'Inermis' (Bslt).

L'Héritiana   Listed as 'Reversa' (Bslt).

L'Héritier   Listed as 'Reversa' (Bslt).

L'Héritier Pourpre   Listed as 'Maheca' (Bslt).

L'Orléanaise
Vigneron, 1899
From 'Mme. de Sancy de Parabère' (Bslt) × 'Calypso' (Bslt).

"Very light pink." [LS] "Pink, large, very full, tall." [Sn] "Like its mother and father, this beautiful variety has very beautiful glaucous green foliage, [and] is thornless. Very large blossom of a beautiful very light delicate pink. When completely open, the petals edges are nearly white while the center of the blossom has a beautiful light coloration. This variety will be a great acquisition for clothing tree-trunks, grills, verandahs, etc." [JR23/149]

Laevis   Listed as *Rosa pendulina* 'Laevis' (Bslt).

Luxembourg Rosa Rubella   Listed as 'Rubella' (Bslt).

Maheca
syns. 'Bengale Hollandaise', 'Dutch Bengal', 'Hollandaise', 'L'Héritier
  Pourpre', 'Maheca of Bengal', 'Purple Noisette', 'Purpurea',
  'Reversa Pourpre', 'Reversa Purpurina'
Noisette, ca. 1815

"Purple crimson flowers, little more than half double; it is the most common of the tribe and … is cultivated and sold from the flat boats on the Ohio and Mississippi rivers." [Bu] "Blossoms double, medium-sized, in corymbs of nuanced colors." [AC] "Blossom medium-sized, full; color, purple." [S] "Differs from ['Reversa'] essentially in the following characteristics: *Corymbs* much more multifloral. *Flowers* purple crimson, nuanced light violet while opening. They then go to light purple and purple pink, which makes varying shads in each corymb, in which the blossoms succeed one another from the beginning of June to mid-July. The crimson petals are velvety; those of the center have a white ray down the middle. *Ovary* oval-globular, consistently shorter than with ['Reversa']." [Pf] "A climbing Chinese hybrid, which grows vigorously and blooms early and profusely; the flowers singly have but little beauty, as they are only semi-double, but being of a fine violet purple hue, the mass presented on large spreading plants is quite attractive." [WRP] Not to be confused with the curiously similarly colored 'Mahéca' (G); perhaps the similarity in color gives us a clue as to the meaning of 'Maheca' or 'Mahéca' (etc.).

Maheca of Bengal   Listed as 'Maheca' (Bslt).

Mme. de Sancy de Parabère Plates 34 & 35

syn. 'Mme. Sancy de Parabère'

Bonnet/Jamin (possibly also with Jean-Laurent Jamain), 1874

"Blossoms medium-sized, full, a beautiful pink." [JR2/42] "Flower rose, medium size, double, fragrant. Growth very vigorous, climbing, early flowering." [GeH] "A thornless, vigorous Boursault, hardy in difficult climates, and one of the earliest to bloom. The large flowers are semi-double, bright rose-pink, fragrant. A wonderfully free-blooming and attractive rose for severe climates." [GAS] "Light pink, medium size, lightly double, medium fragrance, tall." [Sn] "Pretty vigorous, pink flowers, full, of medium size." [JR22/45] "Very early. Medium size, informal, double flowers, clear pink and most delightfully fragrant. Blooms generally come two to four on a stem long enough for cutting, and they last a long time. The wood is thornless. A Rose that is so hardy as to need no protection here [in Pennsylvania]." [C-Ps27]

"Nobody is certain of the date that this magnificent variety of *Rosa Alpina* was raised … Be that as it may, it is to Monsieur Ferdinand Jamin, the great arboricultor of Bourg-la-Reine, that we owe the good luck of having this pretty climbing rose in cultivation today. It was in 1873, in a garden belonging to Monsieur Bonnet, horticulturalist at Vanves (Seine) at that time, that Monsieur F. Jamin saw it for the first time; and, on the wish of Mme. Bonnet, he gave it the provisional name 'Mme. de Sancy de Parabère'. On May 28, 1874, Monsieur Jamin took some blossoms to the *Société Centrale d'Horticulture de France,* and the annals of that time report the following …: 'Presented by Monsieur Jamin, Ferd., nurseryman of Bourg-la-Reine: some flowers of a climbing rose, thornless, seemingly unpublished. This rose was given to Monsieur Jamin in 1873 by Monsieur Bonnet, horticulturalist of Vanves (Seine), who, having conferred with various cognoscenti on the matter, determined that none of them was familiar with it. Supposing therefore that it was indeed nameless, Monsieur Bonnet proposed to call it—at least, provisionally—'Mme. de Sancy de Parabère'. Monsieur Bachoux remarked that he believed *he* had seen it growing about 40 years previously at Monsieur de Boismilon's under the name 'Inermis'. For his part, Monsieur Truffaut also believed he knew it. Monsieur Jamin, F., didn't think the quality of being *inermis*—that is, thornless—made this rose's name *Inermis,* as Monsieur Bachoux was saying, because there were many other thornless climbing roses. In his own establishment, he had many such, not one of which resembled this one. The roses this variety produces are not that pretty considered singly, but they come in such great quantities that the bush becomes magnificent, through profusion. What is more, it is very vigorous.' The following year, Monsieur Bonnet *again* took some blossoms to the *Société Centrale d'Horticulture,* where it was judged by the Floriculture Committee as being very floriferous and very fragrant. Monsieur Jamin, F., from whom we garner these details, believes this not to have been a new variety when he sold it in 1874. 'It is,' he writes us, 'some very old rose, doubtless, which was set aside and lost sight of. I should add that one of our great rosarians of the capital whom I believed should be consulted, did not remember having seen it [before].' The original plant is still to be found in Bonnet's old garden, belonging now to Monsieur Gérand, also a horticulturalist, where it easily came through the harsh Winter of 1879–1880. The rose 'Mme. de Sancy de Parabère' is extremely vigorous, growing its unarmed canes 5–6 meters long in one year [ca. 15–20 ft]. It is quite a Spring-bloomer with

abundant flowers, which are large or very large, fragrant, semi-full, and a beautiful bright pink. We don't know how this rose could be recommended *too* highly to fanciers of this beautiful genus!" [JR9/125]

Mme. Sancy de Parabère Listed as 'Mme. de Sancy de Parabère' (Bslt).

Morletii Listed as 'Inermis Morletii' (Bslt).

Multiplex Listed as 'Inermis' (Bslt).

Old Red Boursault Listed as 'Boursault' (Bslt).

Paniculé Listed as 'Reversa' (Bslt).

Pink Listed as 'Boursault' (Bslt).

Pleine Synonym shared by 'Inermis' (Bslt) and 'Plena' (Bslt).

[Plena]

syns. 'Inermis', 'Full Boursault Rose', 'Pleine', 'Thornless'; all of these syns. are shared specifically or generally with other Boursaults, 'Inermis' in particular

Cartier?, pre-1829

"A pretty variety, with flowers of a bright red, and a fine and luxuriant grower." [WRP] "*Shrub,* very vigorous, having great analogy with the common Boursault, as to wood and foliage. *Flowers,* double, of a brilliant velvet crimson. *Petals,* sloped towards the summit; the base white." [Go] "*Canes* very long, climbing, purple, glabrous and glaucous, unarmed. Normally, the most vigorous are bestrewn at the base with some strong pretty straight thorns with large bases. *Leaves* to 7–9 leaflets. *Petiole* red, glandulose, armed with prickles beneath. *Stipules* glabrous, entire, ciliate with glands. *Leaflets* glabrous, lanceolate, acute. *Serration* simple, convergent. *Peduncles* long, branched, glabrous beneath the bracts, bestrewn above with glandular bristles. *Bracts* lanceolate, acuminate, undulate, glabrous, entire, ciliate with glands. *Ovary* glabrous, glaucous, turbinate, wide-spreading at the tip. *Sepals* scabrous, glandulose, shorter than the corolla, terminating in a simple, linear leaflet, or altogether bearing 2–5 subulate appendages. *Flower* medium-sized, bright pink, full or much doubled. Against a wall, this rose opens better than out in the open, and is very pretty then." [Pf]

Purple Noisette Listed as 'Maheca' (Bslt).

Purpurea Listed as 'Maheca' (Bslt).

Reclinata Flore Simplici Listed as 'À Boutons Renversés à Fleurs Simples' (Bslt).

Reclinata Flore Sub-Multiplici Listed as 'Boursault' (Bslt).

Reversa

syns. 'Bengale Violet', 'Common Purple Boursault', 'L'Héritiana', 'L'Héritier', 'Paniculé', 'Violet Bengal'; trans., "Backturned"

Vilmorin, ca. 1810

"Blossoms semi-double, medium-sized, violet purple." [AC] "Elongated canes. Blossoms medium-sized, purple. Petals striped within; corolla full, very regular." [BJ30] "Canes thin and climbing; flower medium-sized, double, globular, deep lilac." [S] "For distant effect, the Common Purple Boursault is not without its merits. The flowers are semi-double, but are produced in immense numbers; and, then, it is very hardy." [BBF66] "*Canes* glaucous, usually purple, very long,

Reversa *continued*

climbing, unarmed or bestrewn at their base with some rare and strong straight non-stipulary thorns. *Leaves* 5, 7, or 9 leaflets. *Petiole* glabrous, ordinarily armed beneath with several thorns. *Stipules* glabrous, entire or denticulate, ciliate with glands. *Leaflets* lanceolate, glabrous, glaucous beneath, entire at the base, simply dentate at the tip. *Serration* convergent. *Peduncles* in multifloral corymbs, glabrous beneath the bracts, bristling with glandular hairs above. *Bracts* ovoid-lanceolate, acuminate, glabrous, entire, edged with several glands. *Ovary* ovoid, glabrous, glaucous. *Sepals* glabrous or with scattered glandular hairs, simple or bearing all together 3–5 small subulate appendages, and terminating in a linear leaflet. *Flower* medium-sized, multiplex, purple or pale violet. Interior *petals* rayed white. This rose has much the look of the *Cinnamomae,* but its very long climbing canes and its non-stipulary thorns place it alongside the 'Boursault' rose, which it would be difficult to better class than with the Alpinas." [Pf] "Profusely blooming *shrub* capable of reaching great height when supported; adult *branches* glabrous; *prickles* sparse, fairly stout, recurved, absent on inflorescences. *Leaflets* 5 or 7, large, acute, rounded at the base, glabrous on both surfaces, uniformly serrate, glossy above; petioles glabrous; stipules broad, decurrent, denticulate, with a sessile reddish gland on each tooth. *Flowers* clustered at the tips of the laterals; pedicels glandular hispid; bracts acute ovate, a little glandular at the tip; *sepals* acute, downy within, glandular outside; petals 4–5-seriate, incurved over the stamens almost as in the Centifolia 'Anémone', or the Eglantine, pink tinged violet, whitening towards the base and for the most part traversed inside by a more or less regular whitish line; *stamens* numerous, unequal; *styles* short, distinct. *Hips* ovoid, red. This fine rose is obviously a hybrid of *R. alpina* and *R. indica* [*i.e., Rosa chinensis*], having been raised from seeds of the latter by Vilmorin about twelve years ago. The beauty of its blossoms combined with the elegant habit have made it fairly common in the collections of fanciers. We do not know if it comes true from seed. Up to the present, we have only seen it grafted on *R. rubrifolia,* which seems to suit it well. It is well suited for covering arbors and tunnels. We have named it after l'Héritier (1746–1800), to whom Redouté dedicates this modest monument in tribute to his patronage and tuition at the start of his career." [T&R] (This is a good example of the bad habit Redouté and Thory had of spontaneously re-naming, with-

out authority, a rose already in commerce long-since released, by others, under another name; such re-baptisms are, of course, invalid.)

"There is no doubt that the rose 'Reversa', which came from a China, was hybridized when the bloom of this same China received the pollen of the Alpina—which upset its make-up to the greatest degree; but the characteristic of its climbing canes could not have been acquired except from a variety which [*already*] had something of the sort." [V2]

Reversa Pourpre Listed as 'Maheca' (Bslt).

Reversa Purpurina Listed as 'Maheca' (Bslt).

Rose de la Floride Listed as 'Calypso' (Bslt).

Rose de Lisle Listed as 'Calypso' (Bslt).

Sans Épines Listed as 'Inermis' (Bslt).

Sans Épines à Fleur Rose Double Listed as 'Inermis' (Bslt).

Shailer's Provence Listed as 'Gracilis' (Bslt).

Speciosa Listed as 'Drummond's Thornless' (Bslt).

Thornless Listed as 'Plena' (Bslt), though the name could indeed apply to most of the Boursaults, particularly, of course, 'Inermis'.

Turbinata Listed as 'Inermis' (Bslt).

Violet Bengal Listed as 'Reversa' (Bslt).

Weissrote Mme. Sancy de Parabère
Grimm, date uncertain
Sport of 'Mme. de Sancy de Parabère' (Bslt).
    Pale blush, streaked with rose.

White Boursault Listed as 'Calypso' (Bslt).

Zigeunerblut
trans. 'Gypsy Blood'
Geschwind, 1889
From *Rosa pendulina* × a Bourbon rose.
    "Boursault of vigorous growth, with large, cup-shaped flowers of deep crimson, tinged with purple." [GAS] "No scent, −2 m [less than ca. 6 ft]." [EU] "Purple-red, large, full, tall." [Sn]

CHAPTER TWENTY-FIVE

Setigeras

"Much the most valuable of all the non-remontant climbers . . . Seeds of the common variety were sown about 1836, by Messrs. Samuel and John Feast of Baltimore [Maryland, U.S.A.]. The seedlings from this sowing were fertilized by surrounding flowers, from some of the best varieties of roses grown at the time, and from this lot came 'Baltimore Belle' and 'Queen of the Prairies', the two best-known sorts. The foliage is rough, large, 5 to 7 leaflets, generally of a dark green color; for rapidity of growth they equal or excel the Ayrshires, and surpass all climbers in hardiness." [EL] "Three years ago [*making 1839*], I received from Mr. Samuel Feast, of Baltimore, a small lot of roses. One of them was a seedling of our superb native *Rosa rubifolia* [*i.e., R. setigera*], the Detroit or Michigan rose. The terms in which Mr. Feast mentioned it were not such as to excite very high expectations; being, however, a variety of a species that I greatly admired, it was planted in a good situation, and its period of flowering looked forward to with some anxiety. The first year it did nothing—gave no indications of excellence. But by the second spring, it had become well established, and then it fully vindicated its parentage—it indeed proved to be a variety of surpassing beauty. It is distinguished, like its parent, for luxuriance of growth, and, like it, produces its flowers in large clusters. The flower is very double, and of an exquisite form, being perfectly symmetrical and deeply cupped, with petals of a camellia-like appearance. Its color is a fine pink, with slight variations of brilliancy in the flowers of the same cluster; and it possesses the property most unusual in a rose, of retaining its beauty unaffected by our scorching suns, for several days. I have bloomed some of the best varieties of the Ayrshire, and several other fine running roses; but though they are very beautiful, this seedling is superior to any of them. Mr. Feast calls it the 'Beauty of the Prairies' . . . Some years ago, I had the two original species, *R. rubifolia* and *R. sempervirens* var. *capreolata* (Ayrshire) [*i.e.,* 'Ayrshirea' (Arv)], growing side by side, and was strongly impressed with the relative inferiority of the latter. I then looked forward to the time when the former should be the parent of more superb varieties of climbing roses than any that had ever yet gladdened the eyes of the amateur; but little did I imagine that my anticipations were so soon to be realized." [MH42/134–135]

"The Prairie, or Bramble-leaved Rose, is a North-American species, introduced to England in 1830 . . . Mr. [*Joshua*] Pierce . . . advocates the use of the Prairie Rose for hedges or line fences; and remarks, that having sown a lot of seeds in a wild state, for the purpose of obtaining stocks, he was surprised to find among the offspring twelve fine varieties of double Roses. The varieties . . . appear hybrids, partaking largely of the character of R. multiflora; . . . these varieties are remarkable for the large trusses of flowers they produce. Whether their introduction will greatly enrich the Rosarium is, I think, doubtful. Certain it is, they have not supported in this country [England] the high character given them by our Transatlantic [American] brethren. The Group is however in its infancy, and it would be premature to condemn them." [P] "This native rose has been much improved by Mr. Feast and others, and now has many varieties, some of which are evidently hybrids. The single variety is in itself very attractive; blooming in clusters, which last a long time, and exhibit a pleasing diversity of shade, since the flowers grow paler as they grow old. For our own part, we prefer to parent to most of its more pretending offspring. All of this family are held in great scorn by transatlantic [English] cultivators. Perhaps the climate of England is unfavorable to them; perhaps national prejudice may color the judgment; or perhaps the fact that a less rigorous climate permits the successful cultivation of many fine climbing roses which cannot well be grown here may explain the slight esteem with which these coarse children of the prairies are regarded." [FP] "The sorts which comprise this tribe have ascendant canes growing 3–4 m high [ca. 9–12 ft], flowers of variable size and color, double or semi-double, pretty floriferous, blooming only once in the year." [JR2/42] "The flowers of all the varieties are produced in clusters." [BBF] "This class of Roses lacks one important quality, that is, fragrance." [BBF] "They are all tall, vigorous, and hardy in character, with plentiful foliage, and all were somewhat subject to blackspot infection." [ARA18/132]

"Bush upright, glabrous; prickles stipulary, otherwise sparse; leaves of three or—but rarely—five leaflets, which are oval, pointed, glabrous, sharply dentate; flowers red, numerous, sometimes solitary, with peduncles which are both long and covered with bristles; fruit globular, glabrous." [No26] "Only one of the numerous wild roses native to North America is a climber. This is the Prairie or Michigan rose, known botanically as *Rosa setigera*. It abounds in the meadows of midwestern states, making great clumps in fence-corners and wastelands. It is a coarse, rough, viciously thorny shrub with downward sweeping canes that take root when the tips touch the ground. The foliage resembles blackberry leaves—large, light green, rough, and composed of three leaflets. Because the botanical name of the blackberries is *Rubus*, this rose was once called *R. rubifolia*. *Rosa setigera* blooms late in July or in August, the latest of the once-blooming wild roses to come into flower. Its scentless pink flowers are about 2 inches across [ca. 5 cm] and appear in sparse clusters over several weeks. The species is pretty, but not unduly exciting. Its greatest merit is its extreme hardiness." [GAS] "*Rosa Rubifolia* Brown (*Rosa Setigera* Mx.). The Prairie or Michigan Rose, or indeed Blackberry-Leafed Rose… The wild form, with white flowers, bush to 1.5 m in height [ca. 4½ ft] at home in North America, is not known in our [French] gardens; we grow only the varieties with full flowers that are hybrids (produced by pollinating with other scandent or climbing roses, particularly the Multifloras). Thus it is that all the varieties of this group have their flowers in clusters while the pure Rosa Rubifolia has solitary blossoms, emphatically showing the hybrid nature of our horticultural varieties. The Prairie Roses are pretty tough and can stand, when completely uncovered, a chill of 20° Réaumur. In the north of Germany, one does well to cover them lightly, but it is good meantime to cut all the unripened growth back to their bases … The varieties 'Baltimore Belle', 'Beauty of the Prairies', and 'Queen of the Prairies' are known by me as the hardiest." [JR8/59–60] "Few persons, comparatively, are aware of the great beauty of the hybrid Michigan roses, or of the facility of their cultivation. They delight in an eastern exposure, on a light, rich, well-worked soil, with an abundance of the most nutritious diet. I cannot better recommend their culture than by giving you the results of an experiment of my own, with a single plant of the 'Queen of the Prairies'. Early in the spring of 1844, I purchased at auction a slight sprig of that variety, potted and in bloom. As, however, upon examination, it proved to be covered with red spiders, I then plunged the pot in an out-of-the-way corner of my garden as of no value. In May of that year, I cut it to the ground, washed it carefully, and transplanted the root to a warm border, where it has since remained. That season it made two shoots, some seven or eight feet high [ca. 2.3–2.6 m] and of great strength. During the winter these were laid down and slightly covered. Last spring, those two shoots, shortened to six feet [ca. 2 m], threw out, though their whole length, lateral branches, from twelve to fifteen inches long [ca. 3–3.75 dm]. At the end of each lateral there was a cluster of blossoms of great size and beauty, giving me, on the whole plant, over forty clusters. They com-

menced opening in June, were all very large and perfect, continued a long time, and were greatly admired. Early last spring, the plant threw up two strong, vigorous shoots, which have continued their growth, with the utmost luxuriance, to the present time. They now measure over twenty feet in height [ca. 6.6 m], and are of corresponding size and strength. After the blossoms had all matured, I layered the old shoots, and all new ones except the above two, carefully slitting the old wood on the under side, below each lateral, which I retained. These have thrown out an abundance of roots. I addition, therefore, to the original plant, with its two shoots of, to me, surprising growth and vigor, I have now some twenty-five smaller plants for distribution among my friends. This is the second year's product of a plant which had paid its way many times over in its Beauty and its highly ornamental character. *New Haven* [*Connecticut, U.S.A.*] *Nov., 1845.* We trust the experiment of our correspondent, Mr. Robinson, will induce every one to cultivate the Prairie roses; not only the Queen, but the others, of which there are now fifteen or twenty, and some which are fully equal, if not superior to the former. Every body who owns a foot of ground should plant at least one of the Prairie Roses, and more if they have room. —*ed.*" [MH45/448–449]

"No productions of the flower garden have attracted more attention within a few years than the new and beautiful varieties of Prairie roses, which now form the principal ornaments of every good collection during the month of July, after other roses have gone. Mr. Feast, who was the first to give a new feature to our native Prairie, deserves the thanks of every lover of this beautiful tribe for the origination of his superb seedlings. For years, we have been cultivating foreign roses, very few of which, in comparison with the Prairies, deserve a place in the garden. Some of the Boursaults are exceedingly showy and brilliant, but, with a few exceptions, they, like all other varieties of climbing roses, must give way to the Prairies." [MH47/353] "Mr. Feast, we are gratified to know, has received some reward for his beautiful productions. We trust that Mr. Pierce, whose seedlings are fully equal to any which have been raised, will, in due time, also receive that token of merit which is justly his due." [MH47/356]

"Though inferior, say some, to Noisettes, this section has the great advantage of both vigor and hardiness, while the Noisettes are usually more delicate. 'Baltimore Belle' is especially to be recommended because of its wonderful bloom. It is thus much to be regretted that this section … has not been made use of more by those who practice cross-breeding to create new varieties, as, by crossing them with reblooming sorts, we would hopefully obtain hardy climbing varieties with larger flowers, freely remontant, and with varying colors." [JR4/59]

"For some strange reason, these double Prairie Roses were apparently sterile, except 'Gem of the Prairies', and failure attended every attempt to hybridize them. Ellwanger, in 1880, wrote of his failures to obtain good seed and seedlings, and Dr. W. Van Fleet had no success with them … But although *R. setigera* was refractory in the hands of a plant-breeder of such skill and knowledge as Dr. Van Fleet, nevertheless it has yielded to the work of another renowned rose-breeder, Mr. M. H. Horvath, who made the first hybrids of *R. wichuraiana*. At the show of the Syracuse Rose Society, in June, 1931, and again at the exhibition of the Rose Society of Ontario, in Toronto, 1932, Mr. Horvath exhibited flowers of a dozen or more Setigera hybrids of which many seemed equal in color and quality of flowers to the best modern climbers of other races. He claimed that these roses had proved hardy at temperatures of 20 degrees below zero Fahrenheit. His hybrids are now in the process of propagation for dissemination and doubtless they will be widely distributed, especially in that part of the country where the present climbing varieties are badly damaged in winter." [GAS] "Not all crosses with setigera, however, are good. When the species was bred with Hybrid Teas, the result was a number of exceedingly bright-colored varieties with thin unattractive foliage." [ARA16/34] "To the breeder of Climbing Roses, setigera offers vigorous 12- to 15-foot growth [ca. 4–5 m], disease resistance, and obviously wide adaptability to soil and climate, but the latter within some limits. Plants show considerable winter injury in the most northern states. Setigera is, however, scentless, also difficult to bud, slow to root from cuttings, and seeds germinate very slowly, but that arching, lengthy habit and the midsummer blooms make it valuable, nonetheless." [W]

Rosa rubifolia Listed as *Rosa setigera*.

Rosa setigera
syn. *Rosa rubifolia*

"Has profuse clusters of bright, deep pink flowers, and produces an abundance of seeds." [WRP] "Flower deep pink with golden stamens, single, in small trusses, with rounded red fruits. Growth vigorous." [GeH] "Very climbing, growing several yards high; flower medium-sized, semi-double, deep pink." [JR2/42] "A vigorous North American plant which has tall and slender canes with long and thin prickles. Its somber green leaves are glossy, have pronounced veins, and are deeply toothed. Its flowers are petite, pale pink to pink, and in clusters of 3–6 on the branchlets." [JF] "Height 4 to 6 feet [ca. 1.3–2 m]. Large single flowers in clusters, opening one at a time. Gracefully arching branches. The foliage is good, and turns dark bronzy red in the fall. It can be planted with other roses or in masses by itself back of lower roses." [ARA16/17] "Shrub attaining 6 feet [ca. 2 m], with long, prickly, slender recurving or climbing branches. Leaflets 3 to 5, 1 to 3 inches long [ca. 2.5–7.5 dm]. Flowers in rather few-flowered corymbs, deep rose fading to whitish, about 2 inches across [ca. 5 cm]; almost scentless. Fruit globular, 1/3 inch across [ca. 1 cm]. Blooms in June and July. Occurs from Ontario and Wisconsin to Texas and Florida." [ARA21/37] "The 'Prairie Rose' of eastern America, growing to 6 feet in height [ca. 2 m]; foliage bluish green color; in June and July has clusters of pink flowers 2 inches across [ca. 5 cm]. Will climb to 10 feet [ca. 3.3 m]." [C-Ps25] "Our only [U.S.-native] climbing rose, and the only native rose that commonly has three leaflets." [ARA17/13] "The … canes become ruddy along exposed upper surfaces, some-

times maroon all around … The Prairie rose … commonly has but three leaflets towards its [branch] tips, five lower down, all about the same size … A peculiarity of the Prairie rose, distinguishing it from all other American species, is that its styles are welded together into a single column, although in all our other wild roses the several styles in each flower stand separately, like the bristles of a paint-brush. The Prairie rose is always graceful, and useful to the gardener in several ways … It varies widely, showing four extremes, though all alike have a longer season of bloom than most of the other wild roses. There is a slim sort with wiry stems, blooming in larger clusters than the others; a fleshy sort with plump stems and coarser leaves, both these having small pods; the third sort has great red-maroon pods like the best of canning cherries, and big stems that are ruddy also. These three are heavily armed and love full sun during as much as half the day, though they will thrive in partial shade so far as they go without attaining their full stature. All these thorny sorts are common along roadsides, triumphing over barrenness and drought or wet, and making an old rail-fence beautifully picturesque. The fourth sort is very rare, growing along creeks in the shade, with green stems of great length and almost or entirely thornless. This is a distinct variety; the other variations may perhaps be produced by soil-conditions and location. All are sturdy enough to withstands pests and diseases, though they are not free from such attacks, the second sort—through whose stipules the midrib is often a striking blood-red—commonly being infested with tiny pith-borers of the rose-sawfly which appear to do no damage." [ARA29/78–79]

"*Shrub* 0.9–1.2 m tall [ca. 3–4 ft]; *prickles* small, reddish, hooked, sparse, sometimes infrastipular. *Leaflets* 3–5, soft and seemingly puckered, unequally dentate, glabrous and light green above, paler and tomentose beneath; petioles glandular and prickly; stipules reddish, denticulate. *Flowers* clustered at the branch tips, the long pedicels and globose receptacles being glandular hispid; bracts long, sometimes leafy, gland edged; *sepals* short, with filiform pinnules, glandular without, slightly tomentose within; *petals* 5, soft pink fading to white, cordately notched, mucronate; *stamens* very numerous; styles coherent into a glabrous column like *R. arvensis*. Quite a new rose for France, to which a living root was sent by [Joseph] Sabine [*of the London Horticultural Society*], it is a member of De Candolle's *Synstilae*. Lindley makes Donn's *R. fenestrata* a variety of his *R. fenestralis*, which differs from *R. rubifolia* only by the completely glabrous leaflets and solitary blossoms." [T&R] "The stems divide into glabrous cylindrical branches bearing two stipulary thorns at the base of the leaves and some others, much more rare, sparsely along the branches, which are clothed with leaves which are alternate, petiolate, stipulate, composed of three to five leaflets which are glabrous and acuminate, in which the petioles as well as each leaflet's rachis bear several small prickles. The calyx is globular; it divides into five elongated divisions, the edges of which have long cilia, setaceous, numerous, arranged like the barbs of a feather. [There is] a rather remarkable variety: The branches and canes spread out much further; the thorns are dispersed [throughout] without any order; the leaflets are lightly pubescent, particularly along the rachis; and the calyx divisions have a much skimpier supply of cilia along their edges. These plants were observed by Michaux in lower Carolina (description from Michaux)." [Lam] "DuPont grew it; I have seen it in the collection of the Luxembourg." [Ty] "Its pale pink flowers are exquisite, its

Rosa setigera continued

grayish foliage is distinct, and it lends to any garden an air of stability, of naturalness." [ARA22/48]

Horticultural Varieties

Alpenfee
trans. "Fairy of the Alps"
Geschwind, ca. 1890
"Light pink, medium size, full, tall." [Sn] "No scent." [EU]

Anna Maria   Listed as 'Anne Maria' (Set).

[Anne Maria]
syns. 'Anna Maria', 'Michigan Anna Maria'
Pierce, ca. 1846
"Very double, pale blush, with a pink centre, and beautiful." [WRP] "Very double flowers of pink and rose." [FP] "Pale pink, their centre rose, of medium size, very double; form, cupped, distinct." [P] "Flesh pink, flowers quite full, few thorns." [JR4/59] "Pale carnation pink with very few thorns. The foliage of this rose has the quality of wafting a perfume which is very penetrating and very agreeable." [JR16/36] "Flowers, medium size, pale pink, with rose centre, cupped and very double: clusters, large, numbering twenty to thirty flowers, and rather compact: foliage, medium size, very pale green, undulated, slightly serrated, and rather smooth: spines, strong, pale green: habit, robust, vigorous and good. It is quite distinct from any of the others." [MH47/353–356]

Baltimore Belle
Feast, 1843
"A pale blush, fading to nearly white, produces a profusion of very compact and perfectly double flowers in clusters of six to twelve." [Bu] "The flowers are a pale, waxy blush, almost white, very double, in large clusters . . . perfectly hardy." [BBF] "Pale blush, variegated carmine rose and white, very double; flowers in beautiful clusters." [CA88] "White, shaded with flesh, small and very double." [P] "As large in diameter as the 'Queen of the Prairies' [Set]." [WRP] "Pale carnation pink, often entirely white, almost always grown as a pillar rose; remarkable." [JR16/36] "Flower white, suffused yellow, of medium size, full, produced in clusters. Growth very vigorous, climbing, hardy." [GeH] "Variegated red and white flowers in immense clusters, the whole plant appearing one great mass of bloom." [C&Js98] "Pink-white, small, very full, light scent, tall." [Sn] "Low growth; foliage fair; blooms not especially attractive." [ARA18/121] "We have now in flower a beautiful specimen of the 'Baltimore Belle' rose, which in our opinion more than rivals the Queen [*i.e.*, 'Queen of the Prairies']. It has only been planted two years, and has now upon it more than a hundred clusters of buds, each cluster containing from ten to forty buds and flowers. It is the most beautiful object we ever saw." [MH46/267–268]

"Flowers white with a flesh center, full, good form. This variety probably has Noisette blood, making it a little more delicate in very bad Winters. It nevertheless continues to be one of the most besought, being one of the most beautiful." [JR4/59] "This American

rose has small or medium-sized blossoms, very full, slightly nodding on their stalk, well formed, though the center be slightly ragged, white, slightly flesh when opening, with a scent like that of the Noisette. The plant is very bushy, with pretty large leaves, with a non-glossy surface, pale green throughout. This rose blooms very abundantly in small and medium-sized corymbs, in the way of 'Aimée Vibert' [N], with which it has yet other points of resemblance easy to see. Very pretty variety of a very distinct appearance." [S] "It is evidently a hybrid of some tender, ever-blooming variety, apparently one of the Noisettes; and derives, from its paternal parent, qualities of delicacy and beauty which are not conspicuous in the maternal stock. At the same time, it has lost some of the robust and hardy character of the unmixed Prairie. In a severe New-England winter, its younger shoots are often killed back. It shows a tendency to bloom in the autumn; and a trifle more of the Noisette blood infused into it would, no doubt, make it a true autumnal rose. Some florists use it for spring forcing in the greenhouse; for which the delicacy of its clustering white flowers, shaded with a soft, flesh-color, well fits it." [FP] "Vigorous bush with delicate green canes, armed with occasional hooked pink thorns; leaves of 3–5 strongly dentate leaflets which are much veined; petiole fringed with bristles borne under white prickles; adnate stipules edged with bristles; blossom 5–6 cm wide [ca. 1½–2 in], full, with ragged center, light flesh color, in a cluster; sometimes solitary; scentless . . . It is very floriferous, and capable of growing to a pretty great height. It works well as a weeper. Among the Blackberry-Leafed Roses [*i.e.*, Setigeras], it is the one which resists cold the best, managing 25–30° very well. Prune very long." [JR10/35]

"Mrs. Moses Lyman, of Longmeadow, Mass., a sister of the lamented Dr. W. Van Fleet, America's great worker with roses, answers the Editor's query as to favorite old-time roses when she writes, 'Brother and I used to play in a summer-house up in the West Branch valley of the Susquehanna River in good old Pennsylvania, not far from Williamsport. The summer-house was covered with 'Baltimore Belle'. I still love that fragrant pink climbing rose, and I love the farm where we lived.'" [ARA22/162] "Probably the prettiest of the Prairie Roses." [GAS]

Bijou des Prairies   Listed as 'Gem of the Prairies' (Set).

Corporal Johann Nagy
Geschwind, 1890
"Crimson and violet." [LS] "No scent, −3 m [less than ca. 9 ft]." [EU] "Violet red, medium size, full, tall." [Sn]

Erinnerung an Brod   Plate 36
syn. 'Souvenir de Brod'; trans., "In Remembrance of Brod"
Geschwind, 1886
From *Rosa setigera* × 'Génie de Châteaubriand' (HP).
"Prune violet with reflections." [Ÿ] "Heavy scented, −2.5 m [less than ca. 8½ ft]." [EU] "Violet-purple-red, medium size, very full, medium scent, tall." [Sn] "Flower nearly purplish- or violet-blue, most often with a dark red center, large, very full, flat; it is the only rose that approaches true blue, and surpasses 'Reine des Violettes' [HP] . . . Very vigorous, with pendant branches." [JR10/26] "Just as winter-hardy as the rest of the group; large, healthy foliage, large full flowers, deep rose-red at first, then colored purple-lilac. Of unusually splendid appearance." [Ck] "One of the prettiest 'Hungarian Climbers' . . . Though the canes don't grow as long as those of the Ayrshires, the

Multifloras, and the Sempervirenses, it is nevertheless true that pillars of perhaps eight feet in height [ca. 2.25 m] when planted with this variety produce a superb effect during the flowering season … It is a very vigorous bush covered with handsome dark green foliage, giving many fragrant blossoms in clusters, the flowers being mid-sized or large, flat, blue-maroon or violet, especially in somewhat moist soil; center, darker … The name recalls a town which is in the Austrian province of Carniole." [JR31/156] 'Erinnerung an Brod' may be construed as either a Setigera or as a Hybrid Perpetual.

Eurydice
Geschwind, 1887
"Carmine flesh." [LS] "Light pink nuanced carmine." [Ÿ] Eurydice, too circumspect wife of Orpheus.

Eva Corinna   Listed as 'Eva Corinne' (Set).

Eva Corinne
syns. 'Eva Corinna', 'Michigan Eva Corinna'
Pierce, ca. 1846
"Large, double, light flesh." [JR5/134] "Large, double, light red." [JR2/42] "It is a large flower, exceedingly double, light blush and beautiful." [WRP] "Vigorous growth; flower light pink nuanced deep red; large, full." [S] "Flowers, large, very delicate blush, with beautiful carmine centre, globular and very double; clusters, medium size, containing from ten to twenty flowers, rather compact; foliage, medium size, rugose; spines, purplish; habit, vigorous, and very erect. This is the most delicate of all the Prairies, and its clusters of blush flowers, with their deep centre, which are perfectly globular and quite fragrant, entitle it to a prominent place in every garden. It blooms quite late." [MH47/354]

Forstmeisters Heim
trans. "Forest-Ranger's Home"
Geschwind, 1886
"Crimson." [LS, Ÿ] "Carmine, mid-sized, double, no scent, −3 m [less than ca. 9 ft]." [EU] Mr. Unmuth records this as a hybrid between a Bourbon and *Rosa pendulina*.

Gem of the Prairies
syn. 'Bijou des Prairies'
Burgesse, 1860
From 'Queen of the Prairies' (Set) × 'Mme. Laffay' (HP).
"Light pinkish crimson shaded white." [JR4/59] "Almost double, lively rose-pink flowers tinted white." [GAS] "Rosy-red. Occasionally blotched with white; large, flat flowers, slightly fragrant." [EL] "Medium-sized, full, light crimson with blush, shaded white." [JR5/134] "Blossom bright pink, shaded white, medium sized, nearly full, fragrant. Very vigorous growth; [blooms] in clusters." [S] "Pink, medium size, full, medium scent, tall." [Sn] "Growth as above [with 'Baltimore Belle' and 'Queen of the Prairies'], but even stronger. Blossoms giant-sized and quite full as the most beautiful exhibition rose. Color, a brilliant rose-red." [Ck] Ellwanger advances a date of "1865."

Himmelsauge
trans. "Heaven's Eye"
Geschwind/J. C. Schmidt, 1895
From *Rosa setigera* × *R. rugosa* 'Plena'.
"Flower dark velvety purple-red, large, fragrant. Growth vigor-

ous, floriferous." [GeH] "Deep purple red, large, full, very fragrant, tall." [Sn] "Heavy scented, good hips, −3 m [less than ca. 9 ft]." [EU] "The same main characteristics as [the Setigeras] except in the color of the fading blossom, a splendid deep velvety red." [Ck]

[Jane]
Pierce, ca. 1846
"Flesh pink, double, very well formed." [JR4/59] "Very double, of a deep rosy lilac color, and beautiful appearance." [WRP] "Flowers, medium size, of a beautiful light, or lilac[,] rose, imbricated, and very double: clusters, large and rather compact, numbering twenty-five or thirty flowers: foliage, large, coarsely and sharply serrated: habit, very strong and vigorous." [MH47/353–356]

Janet's Pride
Whitwell/W. Paul, 1892
"White, striped orange, medium size, lightly double, tall." [Sn] "Flower white, shaded and tipped crimson, semi-single; early summer flowering. Growth very vigorous." [GeH]

Mary Washington
Washington, ca. 1790?
"This fine, hardy, ever-blooming rose always attracts a great deal of attention. It is a pure white, hardy, constant blooming rose of strong, upright growth; suitable for porches and verandas, where vigorous growth and constant bloom is desired. The flowers are medium size, quite full and double, and very fragrant. They are borne in large clusters all over the bush, which is an enormous bloomer, and bears a great abundance of flowers during the whole season." [C&Js98] "Growth small; bloom quite attractive; needs winter protection." [ARA18/121] "Semi-climbing habit." [C&Js05] "Said to have been raised by George Washington on his estate at Mount Vernon, from seed, and named by him in honor of his mother." [ARA18/179] "George Washington grew a Setigera seedling. Whether he deliberately crossed it we do not know, but if he did he was the first rose-breeder of America. If it was a natural cross then he was a keen observer, for the result, the 'Mary Washington' rose, is in commerce today." [ARA23/181] Noisette affinity has also been suggested for this rose. *Cf.* 'Nelly Custis' (Set).

Michigan Anna Maria   Listed as 'Anne Maria' (Set).

Michigan Eva Corinna   Listed as 'Eva Corinne' (Set).

Michigan Perpetual   Listed as 'Perpetual Michigan' (Set).

[Miss Gunnell]
Pierce, ca. 1846
"Pale pink, with a tinge of buff. It is one of the best." [FP] "Medium-sized, double, cupped, flesh, nuanced yellow." [JR5/134] "Flowers, medium size, of a delicate blush or buff, precisely of the shade of 'Lady Hume' Camellia [*known also as 'Lady Hume's Blush', syn., 'Incarnata', imported in 1806 by Hume (whom rosarians know from the Tea Rose 'Hume's Blush Tea-Scented China' [Hume/Colville, 1810])*], cupped, very regular, and double: clusters, large and spreading, numbering twenty-five to thirty flowers: foliage, large, undulated, and partially rugose: habit, vigorous and good. This is quite unique for the delicate tint of its flowers, which are produced in large clusters. It is one of the very best." [MH47/353–356]

Mr. Feast's No 1   Listed as 'Queen of the Prairies' (Set).

Mrs. F. F. Prentiss

Horvath, 1925

From a seeding (resulting from a cross of *Rosa setigera* × *R. wichuraiana*) × 'Lady Alice Stanley' (HT).

"Light pink, large, full, tall." [Sn] "One of the new Setigera hybrids remarkable for extreme hardiness. Has been exhibited frequently but probably not yet in commerce. It is a strong climber with attractive, smoothly imbricated flowers of clear, fresh pink." [GAS] "Pale pink, double, large-flowered climber of the general type of 'Dr. W. Van Fleet'. Extremely hardy, having withstood severe sub-zero temperatures without freezing even the tips." [ARA26/185]

[Mrs. Hovey]

Pierce, ca. 1846

"Large, full, very beautiful pure white." [JR5/134] "Blossoms flesh, passing to white. Looks like 'Baltimore Belle', but is hardier." [JR4/59] "A superb white . . . Mr. Pierce speaks very highly of 'Mrs. Hovey', as being a fine white, the 'largest, doublest, and best' of all his seedlings; it is of superb habit, with splendid deep green foliage." [MH47/353–356, the editor, *Mr.* Hovey, writing]

Multiflore Tricolore   Listed as 'Tricolore' (Mult).

[Nelly Custis]

Conard-Pyle, 1934

"White. The 'Wishing Rose of Washington.' Our stock is from Mt. Vernon, Va. Tradition says that if a young lady will prick her finger on a thorn of the 'Nelly Custis' Rose, and make a wish, her dream the following night will surely come true. A small shrub Rose with little, white, delightfully fragrant flowers in clusters." [C-Pf34] *Cf.* 'Mary Washington' (Set).

Ovid

Geschwind, 1890

"Flesh and bright pink." [LS] "Flesh and velvety pink." [Ÿ] "No scent, −3 m [less than ca. 9 ft]." [EU] "Pink, large, full, tall." [Sn] Ovid, alias Publius Ovidius Naso, delightfully urbane Roman poet who made a mysterious "mistake," for which he paid with unredeemed exile to the shores of the Black Sea; lived 43 B.C. to ca. A.D. 17.

[Pallida]

trans. "Pale"

Feast, 1843

"Very pale blush, nearly white, perfectly double; this rose appears to bloom finest when lying on the ground; in such a position it forms a solid mass of flowers and pale green foliage." [Bu] "A very fine full double flower, of incarnate hue changing to white; so nearly resembling the 'Superba' [Set] in color, and in the habit of the plant, that it cannot be distinguished, and although said to be of distinct parentage, may be deemed identical. It blooms perhaps a few days later than the 'Superba'." [WRP]

Perpetual   Listed as 'Perpetual Michigan' (Set).

[Perpetual Michigan]

syns. 'Michigan Perpetual', 'Perpetual', 'Perpetual Pink', 'Purpurea'

Feast, 1843

"Flowers rosy pink, changing to purple." [P] "Large, double, incarnadine pink changing to purple." [JR5/134] "4 cm [ca. 1½ in], full, lilac-y pink, globular, mucronate." [R&M62] "Produces flowers in great profusion, which continue in long succession [hence, "perpetual"]; rather small, but in large clusters, varying from light pink to purple." [BBF] "Usually called, very inappropriately, *Perpetual Pink,* has no claim to be called Perpetual, as it but rarely produces any flowers after the usual period of flowering, and I have concluded to correct its erroneous title at once; the flowers are remarkably fine, full double, of a purplish violet hue, and as large as the 'Queen of the Prairies' [Set]." [WRP]

Perpetual Pink   Listed as 'Perpetual Michigan' (Set).

[President]

Pierce, ca. 1846

"Flowers deep pink, small and very double; form, compact. Flowers later than others of the group." [P] "Small, very double, deep reddish pink." [JR5/133] "Flower very small, full; color, deep scarlet." [S] "Flowers, small, deep pink, compact, and very double; clusters, medium size, and rather loose, numbering fifteen to twenty flowers; foliage, medium size, rugose, and rather deeply serrated; prickles, purplish red; habit, vigorous and good. This is one of the latest flowering varieties." [MH47/355]

[President Coolidge]

Horvath, 1925

From a seeding (resulting from a cross of *Rosa setigera* × *R. wichuraiana*) × 'Château de Clos-Vougeot' (HT).

"Flower very double, glowing crimson, similar to 'Château de Clos-Vougeot', borne profusely on a strong climbing plant of extreme hardiness, withstanding below-zero temperatures without protection and without damage." [ARA26/185] "This vigorous Setigera bears double, bright crimson, fragrant flowers. It should be hardy anywhere roses are grown in North America." [GAS] John Calvin Coolidge, laconic president of the United States of America, 1923–1929; lived 1872–1933.

[Pride of Washington]

Pierce, ca. 1846

"Of a roseate hue changing to lilac, full double, and beautiful." [WRP] "Medium sized, double, cupped, pale pink." [JR5/134] "Deep pink, flowers small but quite distinct and very double." [JR4/59] "Flowers, medium size, pale rose, cupped and double, somewhat resembling 'Jane' [Set]: clusters, medium size, numbering ten to twenty flowers: foliage, medium size, slightly serrated, and nearly smooth: habit, vigorous and good." [MH47/353–356]

Purpurea   Listed as 'Perpetual Michigan' (Set).

Queen of the Prairies

syn. 'Mr. Feast's No 1'

Feast, 1843

"Clear, bright pink, sometimes with a white stripe; large, compact, and globular; very double and full; blooms in clusters; one of the finest." [CA88] "Flowers rosy red, striped with white, large and very double." [P] "Medium-sized, violet pink." [JR2/42] "Extra large, full flowers; rich rose; immense bloomer; perfectly hardy." [C&Js98] "Medium scent." [Sn] "Blooms but once a year." [S] "Foliage large, five leaflets, quite deeply serrated." [EL] "Ample, well-serrated foliage." [JR4/60] "Strong growth; good foliage; quite a bloomer." [ARA18/121]

"In America as in Europe, this variety is often grown as a pot rose." [JR16/36] "Certainly the best of the group, having very large rose-coloured flowers three inches in diameter [ca. 7.5 cm], frequently showing a stripe of white in the centre of each petal. They are produced in clusters, in which they always appear cup-shaped, and stand for several days without being affected by our scorching sun. Its foliage is very large, of a dark green, wood strong and of luxuriant growth; its blooming succeeds to that of the Garden or June Rose, and is the link connecting its congeners with that family." [Bu] "The growth of the plant is rapid, throwing up very strong shoots which often attain a length of ten to fifteen feet or more [ca. 3.3–5 m], in a season; the leaves are large, dark green, and luxuriant, and the whole plant presents an imposing appearance." [WRP] "A most superb variety … This is Mr. Feast's first seedling, and considered by some the best. The flowers are of a deep rose color, with a white stripe in the center of each petal. They have a peculiar, cap-shaped form. This variety is the most luxurious grower of any of the class, making a surprising growth in rich soil." [BBF] "Individually, its flowers are as void of beauty as a rose can be. Sometimes they are precisely like a small cabbage, —not the rose so called, but the vegetable, —and they are as deficient in fragrance as in elegance. Yet we regard this rose as a most valuable possession. It will cover a wall, pillar, a bank, or a dead trunk, with a profusion of bloom, gorgeous as a feature of the garden landscape, though unworthy to be gathered or critically examined. It is perfectly hardy, and of the easiest culture. Those who can make no other rose grow rarely fail with this." [FP] "Best of the old Prairie roses, valued for its extreme hardiness. The fairly large, double, rosy red flowers are shapeless and scentless, and although in mild climates it is outclassed in every respect, where the winters are severe it is a dependable and attractive climbing rose." [GAS]

"The committee were unanimous in the opinion, that some token of grateful remembrance is due to Mr. Feast, from the Massachusetts Horticultural Society, for the valuable varieties of roses he has produced by cross impregnation, particularly the 'Queen of the Prairies', which has given so general satisfaction to florists and others, and for which they feel under great obligations to this enterprising cultivator. Mr. Feast has given the type of a new class of roses, in his new variety, *Rosa rubifolia* var. Queen of the Prairies. It is of the most hardy character; enduring the most severe New England winter, without injury, even to its tender extremities; of most luxuriant growth, making, in good soils, 15 to 20 feet [ca. 5–6.6 m] of wood in a season. The flowers are very double; color, light crimson, inclining to rosy lilac; produced in large clusters, on lateral branches; in bloom the beginning of July, after common hardy roses are out of flower. This rose is without a rival, in our climate, for pillars, arbors, &c. Its only deficiency appears to be a want of fragrance. We trust, by the further efforts of Mr. Feast, we shall yet be in possession of a variety having this desirable quality." [MH46/155]

[Ranunculiflora]
Pierce, ca. 1846

"Small, full, pale flesh, very fragrant." [JR5/134] "A flower of small or medium size, very pretty, of a light blush hue, with a pink centre, and greatly admired." [WRP] "Flowers, small, pale blush, very much resembling 'Baltimore Belle': clusters, large, usually twenty or thirty

flowers; foliage, very rugose: spines, purplish: habit, vigorous and good. This variety is slightly fragrant, and flowers rather late." [MH47/353–356]

Russell's Cottage Listed as 'Russelliana' (Mult).

[Superba]
Feast, 1843

"Pale pink, varying to flesh." [JR4/60] "Of perfectly beautiful form, very double, of a pale blush or incarnate hue, varying to white; it is an admirable rose, and one of the best of the incarnate varieties." [WRP] See also 'Pallida' (Set).

[Tennessee Belle]
U.S.A., pre-1898

"A strong, vigorous climber; bright rosy pink; free bloomer; very fragrant." [C&Js98] "Not new but very good. A strong vigorous climber that blooms freely; bright rosy blush flowers, full and fragrant. Will stand all sorts of rough treatment, and is worthy of a place." [C&Js07]

[Triumphant]
Pierce, ca. 1846

"Deep rose." [FP] "Deep pink, double." [JR4/60] "Medium size, very double, bright deep pink." [JR5/134] "A magnificent variety, full double, of a deep roseate color, changing to pale violet, and greatly admired." [WRP] "Flowers, medium size, deep brilliant rose, imbricated, very double, and finely formed: clusters, large, and rather compact, numbering from twenty to thirty flowers: foliage, very large and handsome, undulated and bright green, deeply and sharply serrated: habit, very strong and robust. This variety is remarkable for its ample and beautiful foliage, as well as its deep and brilliant rosy flowers." [MH47/353–356]

Viragó
Geschwind, 1887

"Deep flesh." [LS] "Whitish pink, large, full, tall." [Sn] "Light carmine. —Flowers large, half-full, cupped, very vigorous." [Cx] "No scent, −3 m [less than ca. 9 ft]." [EU] "Large leaves with infinitely graceful, $^3/_4$-full, bright, large pink roses. Quite unknown." [Ck]

[Virginia Lass]
Pierce, ca. 1846

"Medium-sized, full, blush white." [JR5/134] "Medium-sized, nearly full, color very delicate pink shaded with white. This rose is often budded on high stems to form weepers." [S]

Yuhla
Hansen, 1927
From a "wild rose from Lake Oakwood (S. Dak.)" × 'Général Jacqueminot' (HP)

"Flowers semi-double, crimson; blooms through July and August. Leaves of Rugosa type. About 20 petals and 26 petaloids." [ARA27/228] "Light purple red, large, lightly double, light scent, tall." [Sn] What the particular "wild rose" was is problematical—the late bloom argues for *Rosa setigera*—but perhaps *R. macounii* also should be considered.

CHAPTER TWENTY-SIX

Wichuraianas

"It's about two years since these novelties were bred; and today [in 1898], they are known for their great usefulness not only as climbers, but also and especially for forcing and giving, in that locale [New Jersey, U.S.A.], blossoms for Easter." [JR22/130] "The outstanding characteristics of the Wichuraianas are—glossy foliage, strong, broad-based thorns on the stems, and rampant growth. Roses displaying these features may be safely classed as Wichuraianas. The trailing habit has been largely overcome, but these roses are never as stiff as Multifloras and lack the coarseness of that type. Large flowers appear frequently in second-generation crosses, sometimes in the first, and rank high in quality. Everblooming varieties are scarce, but several have recently appeared which promise intermittent bloom at least. In respect to hardiness, the early small-flowered types, except those with yellowish flowers, yield nothing to the earlier Multifloras, but in regions of severe winters the large-flowered varieties need some protection ... Certain puzzling differences in Wichuraiana types from different sources have led some careful observers to believe that *R. luciae*, a closely related form or species, may have been used by some hybridists who probably believed it was *R. wichuraiana*." [GAS] Recent taxonomic wisdom has merged *Rosa wichuraiana* and *Rosa luciae*—for at least the time being; for the purposes of our deliberations here, however, we retain the old separation.

"The wichuraiana Hybrids may now fairly claim to be the most important group of rambling Roses. The reason for this popularity is not difficult to explain when we look at the main characteristics of the family. They are possessed of an astonishingly exuberant vitality; they are hardy; they thrive in almost any soil or situation and under any sort of treatment; their growth, whilst extraordinarily rapid and rampant, is clean and graceful; their flexible stems lend themselves to be trained readily in any way desired. Their beautiful foliage shows, in the different varieties, almost every shade of bright glossy green; it covers the plants from the roots to the tips of the stems; in many of the varieties it is evergreen; in many it is mildew-proof, and in none is it exceedingly liable to this, nor in fact to any other pest. The flowers are produced in splendid profusion from all parts of the plant; and though in most of the varieties the chief burst of bloom lasts for only a month or six weeks, if we take the family as a whole, we get a very long season. For example, in my garden in the past season I was never without some wichuraiana blooms from May to December. The flowers themselves may be either single or double, large or small, produced singly or in magnificent clusters. Some are most beautiful in the bud, others when full blown. Many are delicately or sweetly perfumed. In one variety or another we have almost every shade from white to pink, from rose to crimson, from cream to orange, or beautiful combinations of these colours. In most cases the blooms withstand well the vagaries of the weather. So rapidly have the wichuraianas come to the front that, though hardly known ten years ago [*i.e.*, ca. 1903], I have counted as many as 80 varieties in the catalogue of one individual grower; and this would be barely half the members of this family now on the market. The trouble is that almost all of them are good; and with bewildering embarrassment of riches it is difficult for the uninitiated to select the best varieties for the purpose he may have in view." [NRS13/91–92]

"Now, the species from which these Ramblers are derived has certain marked peculiarities; and, as most of the Hybrids partake largely of these, it will be well first to note some of the features of the type. *Rosa wichuraiana* is a rampant grower, which, when well established, sends up every year from the base a number of long flexible stems, about as thick as an ordinary lead pencil. These stems show little tendency to grow upwards; they prefer to ramble over the surface of the ground or, where possible, to hang downwards. Unless the growing point has received some check or injury, these stems do not as a rule throw off any branches in their first season. But very early in the ensuing spring, sometimes even before the winter is over, they begin to send out from the old leaf nodes, at almost any point from the base to the tip, numbers of leafy lateral shoots. These laterals will develop into the flowering trusses of the following summer. Here and there one of these shoots, instead of producing flowers, will grow strongly into a long 'continuing lateral,' which will in every respect resemble the basal shoot from which it has sprung. One often sees also similar continuing laterals push out from the flowering truss itself, even before the blooming is over … Time for Pruning. The earliness with which the laterals start in their growth makes it imperative that whatever we have to do in the way of pruning or training should be done at a much earlier date than would be necessary with many other families. This work should be undertaken as soon as possible after the flowering season is over, and it should be finished long before the winter is ended. If it is left until the end of February or March the vigorous young shoots will be irretrievably damaged and the crop of blooms destroyed. What Shoots are to be preserved and what part of them? From the fact that all the best flowering trusses spring from the strongly grown stems of the previous year's growth, it is evident that these long sucker-like shoots, which have grown within the last few months, must be carefully preserved; and as the flowering trusses may spring from any part of their length there is no need to shorten them in any way in order to induce flowering. No older stems need be saved, unless it be that they are carrying fresh continuing laterals which may be required for furnishing the more distant parts of the plant with fine foliage and flowers. All other old wood, all spindly growths, such as last year's laterals, all weak, damaged or dead shoots, should be rigorously removed. The old wood will not produce either good foliage or good flowers, and if left it will only crowd the plant and hamper the growth of the valuable fresh stems. In some varieties, 'Gerbe Rose' for instance, there is often a great dearth of strong basal shoots. Such obstinacy may often be overcome be bending down one or more of the existing stems to the ground for a few weeks in the spring. This will cause the buds near the base, which would otherwise have remained dormant, to start into growth and to form the strong stems that we desire. A similar result may be arrived at by cutting back the stem to within a foot or two [ca. 3–6 dm] of the ground. All newly planted specimens should, before the spring, be cut down to within a foot or two of the ground. If this is not done, though one may get a few poor blooms from the long stems that are left, there is little chance of any strong basal shoots being formed for the next season, and the plant is not likely to develop well for the next two or three years. Whereas the pruned plant is likely to at once push out several strong shoots from the base." [NRS12/150–153] "Grown on their own roots they soon make fine trees which require but little pruning beyond the removal of dead and weakly wood. However, as the trees grow too thick, young rods should be tied in and the old removed. All this class benefit by liberal cultivation, but at the same time they will do well on poor soil." [GeH] "As good [in southern California] as elsewhere." [ARA21/59]

"In 1860, Dr. Wichura, a famous botanist, discovered in Japan this species, and introduced it into Europe about 1873. Crossed with Tea, Noisette, Polyantha, and other Roses, *R. wichuraiana* has given to us a group of Roses that to-day is one of the most popular in the Rose world." [GeH] "In 1893, while I [M. H. Horvath] was employed by the Newport Nursery Co., at Newport, R.I., I first saw *Rosa wichuraiana*. Struck by its beautiful, lustrous, shiny foliage,

I thought it was too bad that such wonderful growth and foliage should be topped by the meager little flowers it bore. I decided that it would make a good subject to experiment on, and proceeded to pollinate some of its flowers. I had only two varieties of roses handy from which to get pollen, so I took what there was. One was a small Polyantha with apple-blossom-pink flowers [*probably 'Mignonette'*]; the other was the old 'Agrippina' [*i.e.,* 'Cramoisi Supérieur', a China]. The pink one I cannot name, and I think it is not now found in commerce. The flowers were of an imbricated type, and possibly it might be traced by searching through some old catalogues of the period of 1880 to 1890. 'Manda's Triumph' and 'Universal Favorite' resulted form the pollination of the Polyantha and *R. wichuraiana*; and 'Pink Roamer' and 'South Orange Perfection' from the pollination of *R. wichuraiana* and 'Agrippina'. These roses were introduced by W. A. Manda, of South Orange, N.J., in 1898 and 1899. When the American Rose Society had its first flower show at the Eden Museum in New York City, I exhibited a number of my hybrids … There were four *R. wichuraiana* hybrids and two *R. rugosa* hybrids in the lot. During the same year (1900), in June, one of the Barbier brothers, well-known nurserymen of Orléans, France, visited my experimental grounds at Glenville, Ohio, which was my residence at that time, and in consequence, hybridizing soon got under way in France, resulting in the production of numerous hybrids. *R. wichuraiana* was also taken up about the same time by M. H. Walsh at Woods Hole, Mass., who produced a large number of excellent varieties. The American Rose Society at that period paid no particular attention to rose-research work, and in discouragement I dropped out of the membership." [ARA30/203–204] "These first hybrids all came from America. Then came a rush of very beautiful novelties from many countries." [NRS29/161]

"The firm Barbier & Co., of Orléans [France], in the person of one of its members, René Barbier—who himself is particularly given to hybridizing the ordinary Wichuraiana with the Teas and Noisettes—had the good fortune to be able, after long and patient research, to get some varieties, some of which seem destined to be very popular. His first obtentions … were appreciated by connoisseurs from their first appearance. I can't do better, as for the rest, than to repeat the words with which Messieurs Barbier announced their new genre, under the name *Wichuraiana Hybrid*[s]: 'The varieties of which we give the names and descriptions below constitute a new group. They are the product of the pollination of a Japanese species of rampant growth, *R. wichuraiana*, by different Teas, Noisettes, etc., etc. These roses maintain the extraordinary vigor of their mother, with its glossy foliage and its rampant growth, allowing them to be used to clothe slopes and rocky outcrops. The long flexible branches often grow three to four meters long [to ca. 12 ft], on young specimens, making them suitable for use as climbing roses to train around three trunks, adorn pergolas, and [make] hedges. Grafted on [tree rose or long or standard] stems, they make magnificent weepers covered completely with flowers. We particularly recommend those varieties which, in Spring, give a substantial quantity of buds with which to make bouquets'." [JR30/14] "René Barbier was, it seems, the first to hybridize roses at Orléans. He told me that for several years he had tried crossing various species with the Rugosa. Discouraged by the results, he noticed, one day, on a young plant of Wichuraiana received from America the preceding season, a small cluster of flowers. He pollenized these as an experiment. The result was gratifying, as, of ten seeds harvested, five grew and gave 'Albéric Barbier', 'Paul Transon', 'François Foucard', 'René Barbier', and 'Elisa Robichon', 1900. Differing from Mr. Walsh, the producer of 'Excelsa', who, in the United States, used Hybrid Perpetual on Wichuraiana, Monsieur Barbier pollenized this species with Tea, Hybrid Tea, and even Pernetiana." [ARA26/174–175]

"The first hybrids of *R. wichuraiana* were produced at Newport, Rhode Island, by M. H. Horvath, not later than 1896, and probably about 1893. Four were originated, two of which came from pollen of an old Polyantha, thus early beginning the confusion with *R. multiflora* ... A representative of the Barbier Nursery in France visited his garden a few years later and became interested in his hybrids. As a result, the French firm soon became actively engaged in breeding hybrids with *R. wichuraiana,* and many of our finest climbing roses come from that nursery. About the same time, the late M. H. Walsh, of Woods Hole, Massachusetts, took up the work, producing a long line of wholly delightful and beautiful climbing roses of a distinct type, such as 'Evangeline', 'Hiawatha', 'Milky Way'. The earliest Wichuraiana hybrids were trailers like the parent, particularly those raised from China and Polyantha blood; but when the pollen of Hybrid Perpetuals, Hybrid Teas, and Teas was used, more or less erect varieties came into existence. The Barbier firm specialized in producing plants with superior foliage and flowers of a creamy or yellowish hue, evidently from Tea rose ancestry, and consequently most of them were a little tender in the coldest parts of this country [U.S.A.]. Their most popular early varieties of that type were 'Albéric Barbier' and 'Aviateur Blériot'. From Walsh came innumerable hardy climbers which produced small, double and single flowers in giant clusters. They are generally believed to be hybrids between *R. wichuraiana* and Hybrid Perpetuals. Many of Walsh's roses never became popular; but they were all good, and one of them, 'Excelsa', superseded '[Turner's] Crimson Rambler' in many American gardens." [GAS] "Consider the Walsh climbing roses, many of them of the utmost value and importance. They were the result first of the fostering support of Mr. J. S. Fay, who was Mr. Walsh's early employer, and later of the single-minded devotion of this genius to the work he loved. They possibly paid expenses, and no more." [ARA23/21–22] "But the most famous of all the early Wichuraianas was 'Dorothy Perkins', introduced by the Jackson & Perkins Company in 1901 ... Until the year 1910, all hybrid Wichuraianas belonged to the cluster-flowering type. That year is notable in the history of roses for the introduction of the famous variety 'Dr. W. Van Fleet'. The outstanding merit of this rose was its lovely large flowers, comparable in size to those of Teas or Hybrid Teas. It was also relatively hardy and exceedingly vigorous ... It resulted from two hybridizations and was consequently two generations away from *R. wichuraiana* . . . Introduced the year before 'Dr. W. Van Fleet', although they did not cause as much sensation, were 'Climbing American Beauty', and 'Christine Wright', both raised by James A. Farrell in the Hoopes, Bro. & Thomas Company's nurseries near Philadelphia. These roses were also second-generation hybrids. Both of them were good roses and became very popular, but they were not followed by others of equal merit from that firm except 'Purity' in 1917." [GAS] "A very different type of climbing rose has been worked out at the old establishment of Hoopes, Bro. & Thomas Co., of West Chester, Pa., under the hands of James A. Farrell, assistant superintendent of one of the nurseries. Mr. Farrell was guided in his earlier years by that notable botanist and able nurseryman, Josiah Hoopes, of whom he writes as follows: 'Aside from his wonderful knowledge of conifers and other ornamental trees, Mr. Hoopes was a great lover of the rose, and under his instructions in the year 1898 I fertilized *Rosa wichuraiana* with pollen from several Tea and Hybrid Tea roses, resulting in the introduction of four distinct varieties. Three of these were named 'Edwin Lonsdale' [*extinct; whitish orange; from Hoopes, Bro. & Thomas, 1903; parentage: Rosa wichuraiana ×* 'Safrano' *(T)*], 'Prof. C. S. Sargent', and 'Robert Craig' [*extinct; yellow with a darker center; from Hoopes, Bro. & Thomas, 1903; parentage: Rosa wichuraiana ×* 'Beauté Inconstante' *(T)*]. The fourth was a large single pink variety [*unintroduced; parentage: Rosa wichuraiana ×* 'Marion Dingee' *(T)*], which I crossed with 'American Beauty' [HP], producing the rose named as disseminated as 'Climbing American Beauty'. This same pink seedling was again crossed with 'Mme. Caroline Testout' [HT] as pollen parent, and there resulted four fertile seeds from the cross, all of which germinated and grew. One, when it bloomed, produced a flower similar to 'La France' ["HT"] in color, but with so many petals that it did not properly open, wherefore it was discarded. Of the other three seedlings, one has been named 'Christine Wright', another 'Columbia' [*extinct; color unknown; Hoopes, Bro. & Thomas, 1903*], and the third 'Purity'." [ARA16/46] "During the past thirty years [*i.e.,* from ca. 1900 to ca. 1930] a flood of climbing roses of the Wichuraiana type has risen. Hundreds of varieties have come into commerce, many of them quite similar ... Very few new small-flowered cluster-type Wichuraianas are coming into commerce at present, and no more are needed except a thoroughly hardy one with fadeless yellow flowers —an unfulfilled desire of more than thirty years' standing." [GAS] "The testing of a [new seedling] rambler is a lengthy process, requiring at least four or five years. For example, 'Emily Gray' [W], in her first year, grew only about two feet [ca. 6 dm]. In her second year she gave me two blooms, but she sent up two long basal shoots. In the third and fourth years she showed great promise, and in the fifth year I was able to cut enough trusses, from the original seedling plant only, to show for the Gold Medal, and this was in spite of incessant rain during the week before the Show. With some Roses it is the other way about; they may show great promise in their second or third years and then year by year they deteriorate, till they at last find their way into the bonfire." [NRS29/162]

"My [M. H. Horvath's] interest was early given to the development of better hardy Climbing Roses. In 1892 I obtained the first hybrid with the Rosa Wichuraiana of Japan, thus beginning the modern strain of large-flowered hardy Climbing Roses. In 1897 I exhibited 14 new varieties at the first show held by the American Rose Society in the famous Eden Musée of New York City. These were seen and admired by many rosarians, with the result that many similar hybrids were made. The continuous inbreeding in the attempt to get larger size and brighter color into the Wichuraiana strain weakened it to the point where most of its varieties failed in winter hardiness." [Way45/93] "The possibilities inherent in *R. wichuraiana* in conjunction with other species and varieties of the Rose are immense, and I believe that we shall see a great development among the Ramblers." [NRS19/60] "[As of 1929] in the Wichuraiana ramblers the rush of good new varieties has greatly diminished, and the characteristics of the period [1912–1929] has been the endeavour to obtain a larger flowered type." [NRS29/70]

Though our endeavors mainly encompass the Wichuraianas of the pre-1930 era, we list with minimal data a few interesting later cultivars of interest; we in particular wish to give a nod of respect—short though it be—to some of the releases of Dr. Walter D. Brownell and Capt. George C. Thomas which are later in date.

Rosa wichuraiana Plate 37
syn. 'Zaunrose'

"Flower glistening white, single, in clusters, with golden stamens, trailing habit, and glossy leaves. Growth very vigorous." [GeH] "The flowers are produced in the greatest profusion, in clusters, on the end of every branch. They are pure white, one and one-half to two inches across [ca. 2.5–5 cm], with yellow stamens, and are very fragrant. Valuable as a covering for banks, rockeries, etc., and for use in cemeteries." [CA95] "Will creep all over the ground like an Ivy, or can be trained up to a post or trellis. Hardy as grass, and will grow in sun or shade, poor ground or rich—needs no protection, will take care of itself and bloom profusely every season without attention. Particularly suitable for Cemetery and Park planting, for which immense numbers are used every season. The flowers are single and very large, frequently five or six inches in circumference [ca. 1.25–1.5 dm; *note: 'circumference,' not 'diameter'*]; pure satiny white with bright golden center; they are borne in large clusters, covering the plant with a sheet of snowy blossoms during the early Summer months." [C&Js99] "Bloom two weeks in mid-June." [ARA18/131] "Trailing over the ground as growing shoots perhaps 10 to 12 feet long [ca. 3.3–4 m]. This, unhappily called the 'Memorial Rose,' has the flower and habit

of a sublimated dewberry. Its green spiny stems with shiny leaves sprawl over the ground and are happier so than when on a support. The flowers are pure white with a large circle of yellow stamens and are followed by interesting fruit. It will grow over banks, over rocks, hang down on stone walls, and persists even in the grass." [ARA16/17]

"In 1860 Dr. Wichura, a famous botanist, discovered in Japan this species, and introduced it into Europe about 1873." [GeH] "*Rosa wichuraiana* is a creeper with almost evergreen foliage. It is a native of Korea, and therefore hardy. Plants of it were introduced into America about the middle of the nineteenth century, and attracted considerable attention as a ground cover because of the shiny, leathery foliage and clusters of frilly, fragrant, white flowers. The type is still offered by some nurseries, sometimes under the name of the 'Memorial Rose'." [GAS] "I have already read many articles on this rose, and I have myself written several; its name is well known, and indeed it is much seen. For several years [prior to 1902], this rose has served as pod-parent in the creation of various new varieties. America gave us the first in 1898, and some 18 may now be counted, all of which are distinguished by the beauty of their foliage, the vigor of the plants, and the richness of their summer bloom. This single rose of such artistic form seems made for breeding. Its upright stems, at the end of which the blooms stand so proudly, take well to grafting; and it's quite unusual for it not to work. The hips ripen up to October if not indeed December." [JR26/68] "Monsieur Grignan says, with reason, that, at first, this species of rose was largely ignored in France. However, it was not the same in the U.S.; the horticuluralists in that country saw in this species an extreme vigor and hardiness, to which one could add an abundant late bloom, shadowing forth its use in crossing with other varieties, some very decorative roses at length being released to commerce under the name 'Wichuraiana Hybrids.'" [JR32/24]

Rosa wichuraiana 'Bracteata'
Rose on which we have found no information saving that it was used as a parent of 'Ernst Grandpierre' (W).

Rosa wichuraiana 'Poteriifolia'
A botanical variety reduced in size from that characteristic of the basic species.

Rosa wichuraiana 'Yakachinensis'
As Testu relates, the leaflets are in the form of a reversed spoon, with its white blossom being only a centimeter across (ca. $^1/_3$ in). Its annual shoots are 1.5–2 m in length (ca. $4^1/_2$–6 ft).

Horticultural Varieties

Achievement
T. J. English, 1925
Sport of 'Dorcas' (W).

"Small pink flowers and variegated foliage." [GAS] "Deep pink, small, full, tall." [Sn] "Like 'Dorcas', but with variegated foliage." [ARA25/183] "Flower deep rose-pink shaded coral. This Rose is a short pillar rose. When grown in pots under glass the foliage is most attractive." [GeH] "I do not think it will ever be of much value outdoors, but as a pot plant it is most delightful. I saw some hundreds of

Achievement *continued*

plants growing under glass last year, and thought then, 'Here is surely a fine plant for the greenhouse and conservatory.'" [NRS28/208]

[Adélaïde Moullé]
Barbier, 1901
From *Rosa wichuraiana* × 'Souvenir de Catherine Guillot' (Ch).

"Delicate pink." [JR26/11] "Clusters of small, purplish pink flowers with yellowish tints at the base of the petals. Extremely vigorous. Good of its kind, but watch out for wrong labels." [GAS] "Very bushy shrub, glabrous, with the habit of 'Ophirie' [N]. Canes slender, dark red, as are the petioles and pedicels; thorns numerous, straight, slender, very sharp, dark brown. Leaves with 4 pairs of leaflets which are oval, acutisculous [*i.e.*, slightly pointed], reflexed, smooth on both sides, darker green above, sharply toothed like a saw; stipules sharply serrulate; inflorescence in pauciflorous clusters; peduncles slender, unifloral; calyx-tube shortly turbinate; sepals oval-very acute, reflexing; corolla double, 4 cm across [ca. 1½ in], delicate lilac pink; petals obovate-oblong, not notched, with pale yellow nub. The rose 'Adélaïde Moullé' came from a sowing of *Rosa wichuraiana* pollinated by the variety 'Souvenir de Catherine Guillot'." [JR26/4] "The ride from Paris to Orléans was quite varied. Monsieur René Barbier met me at the hotel, and the afternoon was spent at Barbier & Co.'s nurseries. These comprise about 25 acres in Orléans and about 180 acres situated 10 miles from the city. In Orléans, mostly roses, herbaceous material, and shrubs are grown, and in the larger section are fruit, ornamental, and forest trees." [ARA22/137]

Aëlita
Shtanko, 1952

"White, medium size, full, medium scent, tall." [Sn]

[Alba Rubifolia]
syns. 'Alba Rubrafolia', 'Alba Rubrifolia'
Van Fleet/Conard & Jones, 1901
From *Rosa wichuraiana* × 'Coquette de Lyon' (T).

"White blossom, very ornamental sort." [JR32/172] "Has large double, pure white flowers and bright shining evergreen foliage, tinted with bronzy-red. May be used as a creeping, climbing or weeping rose." [C&Js07] "Bloom moderate two weeks in June also makes a good ground-cover." [ARA18/130] "Probably a trailer." [GAS] "Flowers white, sometimes tinted red, foliage tinted crimson. Growth very vigorous." [GeH] "The finest hardy Memorial Rose for Cemetery planting yet produced. Has no equal . . . As the flowers are pure white and much of the foliage and young growth bright red, it is appropriately named 'Alba Rubifolia'. When trained up to post or pillar, it soon makes a beautiful weeping rose, or if left alone will form a broad natural bush of great beauty. It is evergreen and retains its foliage all Winter, which adds greatly to its beauty. Its round thick leaves are so bright and glossy they shine as if varnished. The flowers are large and fragrant, perfectly full and double to the center, and borne in great profusion for weeks at a time. It is entirely hardy, needs no protection, always looks bright and cheerful, and is undoubtedly the finest memorial rose, for cemetery planting, yet introduced." [C&Js02] The name should evidently be pronounced "Alba *Ruby*-folia," the latter portion of which should not be confused with the Latin *rubifolia*, "bramble-leaved," which is a synonym of *Rosa setigera.*

Alba Rubrafolia   Listed as 'Alba Rubifolia' (W).

Alba Rubrifolia   Listed as 'Alba Rubifolia' (W).

Albéric Barbier
Barbier, 1900
From Rosa wichuraiana × 'Shirley Hibberd' (T).

"Cream white, yellow center." [Ÿ] "Blossoms semi-double or double, opening well, 6–8 cm in size [ca. 2⅓–3 in], beautiful cream white, canary yellow in the middle. Bud rounded, darker yellow. Very pretty variety." [JR30/15] "Bloom free through June." [ARA18/130] "The buds of 'Albéric Barbier' are almost always a pure and softer shade of amber yellow of a self colour and only in exceptional cases splashed and then very slightly." [NRS11/26] "A charming flower of deep yellow in bud, and when partially open turning to buff, and almost white when fully open; the truss is not very full, though the size and shape of the individual flower makes up for that . . . I can strongly recommend it for a shady place. The foliage is strong and of a very dark green, what in paint is called 'bronze green', and as nearly evergreen as any Rose I know of." [NRS16/93] "Amid glistening and glossy foliage there come charming pointed yellow buds, which open to creamy white blooms." [C-Ps25] "A fine climber of much distinction, exquisitely formed, lemon-yellow buds opening white. Foliage superb. Extremely thorny." [GAS] "A very strong grower; leaves dark green, bronzy red in the spring and glossy; flowers in clusters, semi-double or double, creamy white with canary-yellow center. Flowers early." [C&Js12] "Whitish yellow, small, full, light scent, tall." [Sn] "Rampant growth. The foliage is dense, of firm, dark, glossy green, almost evergreen, and not liable to mildew. The trusses are small and are produced in great profusion. The flowers are of good size and form and fully double. The buds are a rich golden yellow, and open to creamy white blooms. A number of stray blooms appear in the autumn. One of the best rambling Roses for any purpose." [NRS13/96]

Albertine
Barbier, 1921
From *Rosa wichuraiana* × 'Mrs. Arthur Robert Waddell' (Pern).

"Coppery chamois." [Ÿ] "Yellow-orange flowers; looks very promising." [ARA26/112] "Coppery salmon pink, large, full, medium scent, tall." [Sn] "Buds are salmon-orange, with gold in the base. The blooms come profusely in bunches." [C-Pf31] "Flower salmon. Growth moderate." [GeH] "A strong grower with fine foliage and a beautiful, distinct color—coppery pink with inside of petals tending to coppery chamois." [ARA29/51] "Its flowers are large for a rambler, and they are of a wonderful colour, coppery chamois, passing to a coppery rose. The foliage is glossy and of a dark colour, wood reddish." [NRS24/215] "Bronze-red canes." [C-Ps28] "Large-flowered Wichuraiana. Buds reddish; flowers semi-double, over three inches across [ca. 7.5 cm], coppery pink shaded with yellow when fresh, paling to silvery pink as they age. Very vigorous and appears to be reliably hardy." [GAS] "Best climber of recent years; attractive color . . . *Mass.*; Good grower; ordinary in other respects . . . *Stratford, Conn.*; Not very hardy . . . *Ontario*; . . . Discarded because of mildew . . . *Memphis, Tenn.*" [ARA28/141] "Bud large, ovoid, dark vermilion; flower large, double, open, cupped, very lasting; coppery chamois inside, outside bright coppery salmon-pink; borne in cluster on medium-long stem fragrant. Foliage abundant, rich green, disease-resistant. Bark and twigs reddish brown; many thorns. Very vigorous, climbing, trailing habit; profuse bloomer in May and June; hardy." [ARA22/148] "An exceedingly vigorous climber with large, shiny foliage. The buds are orange-vermilion and the blooms come in bunches of five to ten large, double flowers, often 4 inches across [ca. 1 dm]. The petals are large and are coppery chamois inside with the reverse bright salmon, turning to coppery pink. The color is similar to [that of] the Rose 'Mrs. A[rthur] R[obert] Waddell' which is one of its parents. It is slightly fragrant and blooms best on old wood, so it does not show perfection until planted two years." [C-Ps27]

Alex Giraud   Listed as 'Alexandre Girault' (W).

Alexandre Girault
syn. 'Alex Giraud'
Barbier, 1907
From *Rosa wichuraiana* × 'Papa Gontier' (T).

"Brilliant carmine." [Y̆] "Deep carmine, shaded with pale orange, large and free." [GeH] "Flowers medium size, in small clusters, rose-pink in bud, opening rich pink over a yellow base. Well liked abroad, but little known here [in the United States]." [GAS] "A striking variety at its best, but colour easily spoilt by rain or strong sunshine." [NRS29/166] "Flowers large, very double, petals bright carmine red tinted salmony yellow at the base. Superb coloration making a real splash. Very vigorous plant with glossy dark green foliage." [JR31/166] "Growth fair; color distinct." [ARA18/119] "A very rampant grower with fine flexible stems of pale bronzy green colour. The foliage is light, glossy green, and free from mildew. The flowers are produced in the greatest profusion in small trusses of medium-sized double blooms. The colour is deep carmine with orange at base of petals." [NRS13/98]

Alexandre Trémouillet
Barbier, 1903
From *Rosa wichuraiana* × 'Souvenir de Catherine Guillot' (Ch).

"Blush white." [Y̆] "Flowers white, tinted with rose and salmon centre, panicles of large double flowers; dark green foliage. Vigorous." [GeH] "Climbing shrub; leaves glossy, dark green; inflorescences in loose panicles; corolla full, pinkish white with some salmon." [JR27/164] "Very thorny plant, very bushy, with pink upright thorns. Leaves glossy dark green, with 2 or 3 pairs of oval, abruptly acuminate leaflets, heavily toothed like a saw, subsessile; petiole armed, glandulose. Inflorescence in loose panicle, leafy with large dentate foliaceous bracts; peduncles strong, green tinted pink; calyx turbinate, smooth, big, with triangular appendiculate-spatulate sepals, hirsute within; corolla full, blush white; petals cuneiform, oblong, not notched. This very beautiful plant comes from a *Rosa wichuraiana* crossed with 'Souvenir de Catherine Guillot' [Ch]." [JR26/4] Though announced and named in 1901, not actually *introduced to commerce* until 1903 (and introduction is what counts!).

Alida Lovett
Van Fleet/Lovett, 1917
From *Rosa wichuraiana* × 'Souvenir de Président Carnot' (HT).

"Pearly pink." [Y̆] "Flowers are cup-shaped, large, and quite double; color tender salmon-pink." [C-Ps28] "Color is bright shell-pink, with shadings of sulphur-yellow at base of petals. The flowers are similar in size and form to the 'Dr. W. Van Fleet' Rose." [C&Js23] "Big handsome flowers of clear, shining pink. Somewhat eclipsed by 'Christine Wright' and 'Mary Wallace', but different and probably better than either." [GAS] "More double than 'Christine Wright' and 'Mary Wallace', and darker than 'Dr. W. Van Fleet'." [CaRol/6/3] "Flower a very pleasing shade of flesh-pink of good size. Growth vigorous." [GeH] "Not quite so vigorous as many; foliage black-spots slightly; bloom free through three weeks of June, begins early." [ARA18/130] "Pink, large, full, tall." [Sn] "It is of vigorous climbing habit and proved hardiness, having been under observation since 1909. The habit of growth and form of the flower resemble [those of] 'Dr. W. Van Fleet', but the color is better." [ARA17/40] "Made the biggest hit of the season at the shows. It is a very beautiful pale pink rose, shading to yellow at the base of the petals, and has long, pointed buds and elegant foliage." [ARA22/44] "Both buds and flowers are large and of ideal form and the color a lively, bright shell-pink with shading of rich sulphur at the base of the petals. The plant is of strong growth, flowering for a long season. In habit it is like the popular 'Dr. W. Van Fleet' Rose, but larger and more beautiful." [ARA29/x] Originally bred in 1905; not released until 1917.

America
Walsh, 1915

"Delicate pink shading to white." [ARA16/21] "Single flowered, delicate pink." [C&Js18] "Obscure hybrid of Wichuraiana and Multiflora strains. Flowers light pink, single, small, in large clusters." [GAS] "Closely resembling 'American Pillar' [W]." [C&Js19] "Fairly good—resembles 'Evergreen Gem' [W] and 'American Pillar' [W], only smaller; occasionally blooms in fall." [ARA18/119] America, land of much promise.

"[M. H. Walsh] has been growing roses since he was eleven years old, and runs parallel to 'Gurney' Hill in his half-century relation to the queen of flowers. He says: 'Roses were my first love, and I still cherish them and am happy in growing and experimenting with them. I have now eleven acres of roses in cultivation and grow roses exclusively . . . I am experimenting at the present time by crossing certain species of roses, in which way new blood is imparted from the original variety.' Mr. Walsh has to his credit a portentous array of medals and certificates, not only from American associations but from societies abroad." [ARA16/45–46] "Before the 1922 *Annual* went to press, the death of Dr. W. Van Fleet occurred, and in the month after it appeared, Michael H. Walsh, of Woods Hole, Mass., on April 10, died. He was of ripe age, having passed his 74th birthday. Born not far from Chester, in England, and beginning his garden work when but eleven years old, he came to America in 1868, bringing with him to Boston as a young man a predisposition toward rose culture. After two gardening experiences in Belmont and in Brighton, Mr. Walsh settled within the same state, at Woods Hole, where he took charge of the extensive estate of Joseph S. Hay, and began his intensive work toward the production of better climbing roses. Meanwhile, Mr. Walsh grew these roses out of season wonderfully. Never will the Editor forget the exquisite beauty of a plant of the lovely white trailer, 'Mrs. M. H. Walsh' [W; Walsh, 1911; extinct], exhibited at one of the earlier New York flower shows. Its long, flexible, pure white twigs depended from a top-worked plant some six feet high [ca. 2 m], and it was a shower, a cascade, of chaste beauty. But the enduring, living, blooming, glowing monuments to Mr. Walsh's hybridizing genius are all over America and Europe, in the hardy climbing roses he produced. With 'Excelsa' [W] taking the place of '[Turner's] Crimson Rambler' [Mult]; with 'Hiawatha', 'Paradise', 'Evangeline', and 'Milky Way' [all W], the

America *continued*

'Walsh Quartette' of single loveliness from deep scarlet-crimson to pure white; with 'Lady Gay' [W] and 'Mrs. M. H. Walsh' in daintily double flowers; with all of this plus quality in vigor and hardiness, we have reason long to remember the quiet worker of Woods Hole who never sent out a rose he did not believe in." [ARA23/188]

American Beauty, Climbing
Hoopes, Bro. & Thomas, 1909
From a seedling (which was the result of a cross of *Rosa wichuraiana* and the Tea 'Marion Dingee') × 'American Beauty' (HP).

"Rich rosy crimson." [ARA17/126] "Carmine to rich imperial pink —blues in heat, fades quickly; fine buds; large, double flowers . . . Gives one large burst of bloom only. Vigorous, foliage usually lost early." [Th2] "Blossom red nuanced vermilion as in its mother, and similarly perfumed as well. Grows very strongly, and annually gives canes of 9 to 12 feet [ca. 3–4 m], durable as an oak; flower large; blooms richly and early, over four weeks, then less abundantly up to Fall. A good variety for pillars and columns." [JR38/88–89] "If left on the bush, the petals do not drop but assume an unattractive magenta tint. The foliage is of medium size, glossy, handsome, and remarkably free from pests." [C-Ps29] "Cerise flowers blue with age. Very large, cupped . . . Vigorous to 12 to 15 feet [ca. 4–5 m]. Best grown in semi-shade to slow up fading . . . Sweet and heady damask fragrance." [W]

"Color rosy crimson, almost identical with its pollen parent 'American Beauty' [HP], and with the same exquisite fragrance, a quality rarely found in climbing Roses of strong habit of growth. Will thrive and bloom in almost any situation where a climbing or pillar Rose is desired. Flowers 3 to 4 inches in diameter [ca. 7.5 cm to 1 dm], finely formed on long stems, are produced in great profusion and are splendid for cutting. When well established, this Rose makes tremendous growth, sending up several canes from the base of the plant during the growing season, each cane from 10 to 15 feet in length [ca. 3.3–5 m]. These new canes produce the bloom spikes that will appear the next season covered with masses of lovely, rosy crimson Roses, on long stems, suitable for cutting and dozens of Roses can be cut from a single plant without being missed." [C&Js24] "This Rose has just one fault—it will not drop its dead petals; but simply cut off the faded bloom and then again enjoy another and another distinctive show of breath-taking beauty." [C-Ps25] "Has the bad habit of 'holding its dead', as one annoyed woman put it, referring to the hanging on of its faded, browned petals, so that the otherwise decorative plant looked as if it had been showered with boiling water." [ARA25/197] "The foliage is of medium size, glossy, handsome, and remarkably free from pests." [C-Ps31] "The '[Climbing] American Beauty' reposed in luxury less than a foot [ca. 3 dm] above the body of a finally useful cat that had been run over on the highway." [ARA25/23] "Very useful and very glorious in spring." [ET] Possibly bred by James A. Farrell.

American Pillar
Van Fleet/Conard & Jones, 1906
From *Rosa wichuraiana* × a seedling (from a cross of *R. setigera* × a red HP).

"Large single flowers of rich, rosy pink approaching brilliant carmine, just a glint of white in the center, and stamens yellow. It began blooming here in early June and continued till far past the Fourth of July." [C&Js11] "Bright pink on a white ground." [Ÿ] "Light red, white center, medium size, single." [Sn] "Flower bright rose with light centre, large, single, fine trusses; bold glossy foliage. Growth vigorous, climber, summer flowering." [GeH] "Large clusters; dark pink with a white center and yellow stamens; very large, single. Similar to 'Evergreen Gem' [W]. Foliage lasts quite well." [ARA17/28] "Perhaps the most handsome foliage of any Rose. It is large, very glossy dark green shading to deep brownish purple." [NRS17/49] "Foliage black-spots some in midsummer; bloom profuse last three weeks of June." [ARA18/130] "Superb climber of astounding vigor, with lustrous foliage and enormous trusses of single flowers nearly two inches across [ca. 5 cm]. Each bloom is vivid rose-red, paling to white at the centre, illumined with a showy cluster of yellow stamens. Severe cold damages it somewhat if unprotected, in spite of its reputed Setigera strain, and the flowers are wishy-washy in hot seasons. Barring these defects, no climber is more beautiful or easier to grow." [GAS] "This Wichuraiana hybrid, which made its European debut at the [London] Temple Show in 1909 quickly found its niche, and promises to take a place alongside the most beautiful garden climbers. Its growth is very vigorous; the foliage, which persists very late, is large, glossy dark green, and strikingly elegant, amply clothing the canes. The blossoms, grouped in voluminous clusters, are single, large (at least 7 cm across [ca. 2¾ in]), and superbly colored; the base of the petals is white, and the remainder is scarlet red when it opens, passing then to pinkish crimson. These flowers, which come earlier than those of 'Dorothy Perkins' [W] and 'Hiawatha' [Mult], last a long time, a remarkable characteristic in a single rose." [JR35/133] "Though single, the blooms last for a week or more when cut." [C-Ps33] "American Pillar's fruits are both numerous and attractive." [CaRoI/5/2] "An early spring letter from Mrs. Moses Lyman, of Longmeadow, Mass., sister of the late Dr. W. Van Fleet, tells this interesting occurrence 'We had a very severe ice and snowstorm which sealed the ground and encased the trees and shrubs with a thick covering of ice, so the robins, song sparrows, bluebirds, and many others, including a pair of thrushes, were foodless. To our surprise and joy, they came to the front porch and ate the 'American Pillar' hips that had been so cheery all the winter as we looked through and beyond from our living-room windows. Fortunately, the vines were heavily laden, and, protected by the roof, the birds could eat all they needed until we could prepare other food for them.'" [ARA23/182] "'American Pillar' makes strong canes that grow upright several feet before bending over." [C&Js21] "Best as a pillar rose or for fences and walls. Hardy." [ARA21/93]

"Introduced (1906) and for sale only by the Conard and Jones Co., West Grove, Pa. Makes strong, heavy bushes, entirely hardy, and covered early in Spring with immense clusters of large single flowers, three to five inches across [ca. 7.5 cm to 1.25 dm], with hundreds of bright yellow stamens in the center, followed by pretty clusters of bright red fruit in Fall and Winter; has thick, dark green foliage, and is altogether one of the best and handsomest Pillar Roses for porch or veranda yet produced." [C&Js06] "If ever there was a rose constituted to stand the trying conditions of our American climate, we have it in this unique New Hardy Rose . . . Will thrive in poor soil as well as in rich, and insists on growing vigorously. It has stout, thick curving branches, rather thorny, but furnished with an abundance of glossy dark green leaves. Each stem has 9 leaflets instead of the usual 7 or 5, a kind of double supply, which gives the bush a very rich effect. It is one of the first to start growth in the early spring, and here [Pennsylvania] holds its leaves of lively green till far past Thanksgiving Day [late November], and never have we seen it troubled with insects. In early June it begins to bloom; large single flowers measuring 3 to 5 inches across [ca. 7.5 cm to 1.25 dm], and very durable. They are borne in immense clusters and make a remarkable sight. The color is a chaste shade of pink, while in the center of each flower is a large cluster of bright yellow stamens; these are followed in the Autumn with pretty clusters of brilliant red seed hips, which hang on through the winter to brighten the bushes and feed the birds. 'American Pillar' is truly an ornamental and satisfactory addition to any lawn." [C&Js07] "From the polish of its leaves and the leafy character of the stipule it must have a good deal of wichuraiana blood in its composition. The growth is very vigorous and the habit upright and strong, drooping after the stem has grown somewhat. It throws up strong polished green stems 10 feet or more in height [ca. 3.3 m +] if trained, armed with strong slightly hooked thorns, red when young, and carrying right to the ground the finest foliage of perhaps any climbing Rose we have. The colour and vigour of the foliage are alike remarkable, the leaves have nine leaflets and are carried thickly on the stem. In summer they are dark green in colour, and in autumn these darken still more, and the young thorns and leaf stalks turn quite a brilliant red, particularly at the base, producing an effect of claret colour in the green which makes the pillar conspicuous and distinct. The foliage seems practically free from mildew. There is only one flowering season and this is late. I did not get a flower out till the 12th July, 1910, and assuming this to be a late year it still makes it correspond with 'Hiawatha' [Mult] in season. The flowering period is of moderate duration. The flowers are single, large in size, and the colour is a bright rose-pink with a white centre. They are very showy in the garden, stand out well from the foliage and are carried in rather large trusses, but they are quite scentless ... Its strong points appear to be its fine growth, lateness, and showy flowers, and its really magnificent foliage, which clothes the stems down to the base, the pillars looking in autumn as though clothed with ivy rather than Rose foliage. Its special uses are as a tall pillar or rambling over a pergola, arch or screen." [NRS11/29–30]

"As far back as 1893, [Dr. W. Van Fleet] had been hybridizing among the Rugosas, and even before that, when in Ruskin, Tenn., he had made numerous crosses. It was from among a bunch of these hybridized seedlings that the Doctor had grown in Ruskin, that the bright eye of J. Horace McFarland caught sight of a blooming plant of the 'American Pillar', the introduction of which had been under discussion for some time. Mr. McFarland's enthusiasm decided the question." [ARA22/20–21] "In England the National Rose Society recently voted this their most popular Climbing Rose; in America that is usually the verdict as fast as 'American Pillar' becomes known. We are naturally proud to have introduced it." [C-Ps26] "The best single rambler. The flowers keep very well, either picked or on the bush. When in bloom it never fails to stop the crowd." [ARA18/90] "Has never been superseded." [NRS20/163]

Andenken an Breslau

trans. "In Remembrance of Breslau," "Souvenir de Breslau"
Kiese, 1913

"Bright cherry-carmine, large for its class, very full, produced in large clusters. Growth like [that of] 'Dorothy Perkins' [W]." [GeH] "Light red, medium size, full, tall." [Sn] "Growth quite good; foliage sparse; bloom of no special merit." [ARA18/121] "This introduction resembles, in form, 'Dorothy Perkins' [W], but the coloration is much more intense. The flowers are 5–6 cm across [ca. 2–2½ in], and stand together in big corymbs. The color is bright cerise carmine, to grand effect. The blossoms are quite full, the foliage shiny, the stem strong, and it is very freely climbing." [JR38/39]

[André Louis]

Tanne/Turbat, 1920

"Flower large, full, well-formed, flesh-pink, borne in clusters of 4 to 5. Vigorous." [ARA21/160] "Charming old-fashioned flowers of light flesh-color, with a blushing spot of pink in the center; fairly large, very double and sweet. Distinct in many respects." [GAS]

Anna Rübsamen

Weigand, 1902

"Clear salmon-pink. —Pillar, arch, pergola, creeping. Mid-season. Very free-flowering." [Cat12] "Light pink, medium size, full, light scent, tall." [Sn] "The blossom ... is of medium size, but quite full. The petals ray out and are very quilled, making this rose resemble vaguely one of those new [cactus] Dahlias. The color is a very sweet pink, the perfume of the strongest sort. The buds rather look like those of the Tea Roses and seem made to be painted. The partially open buds and the expanded blossoms are equally beautiful, a thing found but rarely in the climbing sorts, making them especially pretty to see in groups. Its growth is vigorous and its habit climbing. 'Anna Rübsamen' is a variety destined to be universally admired not only for its beautiful flowers, but also because of its branches with their very light green foliage and the ease with which it takes to different sorts of palisading, weepers, boskets, *berceaux,* etc." [JR26/164–165]

Apricot Glow

Brownell/Bobbink & Atkins, 1936
From a seedling (resulting from a cross of 'Emily Gray' [W] and 'Dr. W. Van Fleet' [W]) × 'Jacotte' (W).

"Orange-pink, medium size, full, very fragrant, tall." [Sn] "The very double, apricot-pink flowers open in large trusses on long stems in June. The leaves are glossy and the vigorous plants grow to 20 feet [ca. 6.6 m]. There is an appropriate fruity FRAGRANCE." [W]

Arcadia

Walsh, 1913

"Bright rosy scarlet, double, flowering in large clusters, late. Growth vigorous." [GeH] "Red, medium size, full, tall." [Sn] "One of the many good bright red cluster-flowering Wichuraianas swamped by the ballyhoo for 'Excelsa' [W]." [GAS] Arcadia, a Greek locale in the Peloponnesus famed in classical times for its rustic happiness and the innocent simplicity and kindness of its denizens.

Ardon

Turbat, 1925

"Bunches of fairly large, pink and white flowers. Long since lost in the shuffle." [GAS] "Flower large, very full, bright Neyron rose, veined and stained with white, very lasting, borne in pyramidal panicles of 30 to 40. Foliage disease-resistant. Almost thornless. Very vigorous and hardy." [ARA27/222] "Pink-white, large, full, tall." [Sn]

Auguste Gervaise

Barbier, 1916

From *Rosa wichuraiana* × 'Le Progrès' (HT).

"Coppery yellow and salmon-rose, changing to chamois and creamy white, double, very large for its class; bud coppery apricot yellow, tinted aurora pink. Growth very vigorous, climbing." [GeH] "Salmon pink, medium size, lightly double, medium scent, tall." [Sn] "It is half-double and very big for a Wichuraiana Hybrid, with very numerous flowers; climbing; vigorous. The bloom is yellow, turning slightly to a copper color, and then yellow and bright pink, and at last white." [ARA20/123–124] "The buds are coppery yellow, tinted aurora-apricot, opening to coppery yellow and rosy salmon, passing to creamy white. The enormous flowers measure from 4 to 5 inches across [ca. 1–1.25 dm], and are produced in great abundance in clusters of ten to twenty. A very strong grower, and very effective." [ARA19/100]

Aunt Harriet

Van Fleet/Farm Journal of Philadelphia/Conard & Jones, 1918

From 'Apolline' (B) × *Rosa wichuraiana*.

"Another bright-colored rambler, somewhat on the order of 'American Pillar', but semi-double; it is quite attractive." [ARA22/44] "Uninteresting red-flowered Wichuraiana." [GAS] "Deep red, large, full, light scent, tall." [Sn] "Originated by the famous rose-hybridizer Dr. W. Van Fleet. Introduced in 1918 by the *Farm Journal of Philadelphia*. Grown and distributed by The Conard & Jones Co.... One of the finest dazzling red climbers to date. For porches, arbors, and arches this Rose will prove immensely popular, as it is among the finest of recent introductions in this hardy climbing class ... The wonderfully brilliant coloring and free-flowering habit of 'Apolline' [B] is retained and also the dark shiny foliage and rugged hardiness of Wichuraiana. In full bloom it is amazingly fine with its masses of dazzling scarlet-crimson Roses loading every branch. The bright effect is intensified by the pure white centers and brilliant golden anthers which shine out when the flowers are fully open." [C&Jf18]

Avenir   Listed as 'L'Avenir' (W).

Aviateur Blériot

Fauque & fils/Vigneron, 1909

From *Rosa wichuraiana* × 'William Allen Richardson' (N).

"Saffron yellow blossom, center golden yellow, medium-sized, full. Very vigorous shrub, climbing, foliage glossy deep green, blooms in corymbs. The most yellow of this series. Absolutely distinct." [JR33/152] "The buds are a rich gold, later fading to cream. Open bloom is about 2½ inches across [ca. 6.5 cm] and very full; has delicious fragrance and polished foliage. This is one of the notable climbers." [C-Ps29] "When in bloom its buds and flowers are like miniature 'Mrs. Aaron Ward's [HT] borne in clusters, and these, when arranged in combination with forget-me-nots or blue cornflowers, are lovely." [ARA16/102] "The ... brilliant orange buds against a blue sky were something never to be forgotten." [ARA21/127] "Clean yellow buds opening to lighter colored flowers which eventually fade to almost white, all the time carrying a fine magnolia fragrance." [ARA24/185] "Rich apricot-yellow blooms in small clusters. The form is disorderly with the large number of little petals. A moderate climber and good ground-cover." [C-Ps31] "Orange yellow, medium size, full, tall." [Sn] "A most distinct climber, which produces over a long early

summer season charming saffron buds, opening into small, most attractive, double, apricot and lighter Roses of exquisite magnolia fragrance. It is not a high climber. Can also be used as a ground-cover." [C-Ps25] "Makes clusters of perfectly double, medium-sized, fragrant blooms, of rich, deep, saffron-yellow, deepening in the center to copper or golden yellow. Foliage is so shiny it seems glazed and is insect- and disease-proof." [C&Js21] "Fair to good growth; blooms attractive—best in bud-form; foliage lasts quite well." [ARA18/119] "Its merits do not seem to have been discovered and appreciated by the majority of lovers of the Ramblers." [NRS19/59] "Few of the older Wichuraianas have won a stronger hold on popularity. The buds are coppery orange, the flowers saffron and gold, fading white. Foliage remarkably handsome. Needs protection north." [GAS]

Babette

Walsh, 1908

"Clusters of little, double, dark pink or crimson flowers, with paler edges. Nice, old-time Wichuraiana." [GAS] "Red, medium size, full, tall." [Sn] "Nice growth; good color; fair foliage." [ARA18/119]

Beauté Orléanaise

trans. "Orléans Beauty"

Turbat, 1919

"Double, white, small-flowered Wichuraiana, sometimes tinged salmon-pink." [GAS] "Flower pure white suffused salmon-rose, changing to bright flesh pink, very double, produced in large trusses. Growth very vigorous, climbing." [GeH] "White, medium size, full, medium scent, tall." [Sn] "Seedling from unnamed variety. Bud medium-size, ovoid; flower medium-size, full, very double, borne in clusters of 20 to 25, on long stems; slight fragrance. Color pure white, slightly suffused rosy salmon, passing to fleshy rose. Foliage abundant, medium size, glossy green; disease resistant. A very strong grower of climbing upright habit, blooming profusely during June and July. Very hardy." [ARA20/130]

Bess Lovett

Van Fleet/Lovett, 1917

"Light red, long-stemmed clusters." [ARA29/97] "Beautiful pure pink." [Y] "A large, full, deep red, a clearer color than [that of] 'Dr. Huey' [W], and larger than [that of] 'Aunt Harriet' [W]. It is really the only red hybrid Wichuraiana of large size." [CaRol/6/3/] "Exquisitely fragrant, a thing rare in Climbing Roses. Flowers are lavishly produced and of good size, being similar in form to [those of] the 'Climbing American Beauty' [W], but very much brighter red in color and more fragrant by far." [ARA29/x] "Just a little brighter in color than 'Climbing American Beauty' ... The petals drop cleanly as they fade." [C-Ps25] "More steadfast in color than 'Climbing American Beauty'." [C-Ps29] "Large-flowered Wichuraiana. Bright crimson flowers, large, fragrant, and loosely cup-shaped. Excellent habit and blooming, but commonplace color and form." [GAS] "Resembles 'Climbing American Beauty' in shape of bloom and the large foliage is very attractive. Color is clear bright red and the well-formed flowers are freely produced. Beautiful in bud and bloom and one of the most fragrant of the hardy climbers." [C&Js23] "Light red, medium size, full, light scent, tall." [Sn] "The lovely blooms, on long stems, are well formed, fragrant, and fine for cutting ... Almost as vigorous in growth as 'American Pillar' [W]." [C-Ps28] "Foliage black-spots very slightly; bloom profuse three weeks of June, some in July." [ARA18/

130] "Flowers medium to large, clear bright red, full, of fine form, lasting well; very fragrant. Glossy foliage, like that of 'Silver Moon' [Lv]. A vigorous grower and free bloomer. Hardy." [ARA21/93] "Seemingly overlooked for many years, ['Bess Lovett'] provides an even brighter color [than does 'Climbing American Beauty'], an equally beautiful open flower, a good bud, and is free from the bad habit [of holding onto its dead petals] … It is highly commended as an admirable climber." [ARA25/197] "A large red … well liked." [ARA22/44]

Bloomfield Courage
Capt. Thomas/Bobbink & Atkins and Howard & Smith, 1925

"Artistic, single flowers thickly cover the plant like a cloud of dark crimson butterflies." [C-Pf31] "Deep red and white, small, single, tall." [Sn] "The tiny blossoms are only an inch [ca. 2.5 cm], or even less, in diameter, but the plant is so floriferous that it is literally covered in June with the velvety dark red blossoms with their white eyes." [CaRol/6/6] "A prodigious bloomer that occasionally produces a second crop. The color of the small, vivid crimson flowers is intensified by white centers and prominent anthers of glowing gold. Very showy when grown on posts or pillars." [C-Ps30] "A small dark red with white center; fine growth and foliage. A Wichuraiana which in southern California seacoast gives five months of bloom and scattering blooms till Christmas." [ARA28/96] "Very attractive. Bloom single, delicate, small, brilliant; charming for six weeks. Growth vigorous (10 to 20 feet [ca. 3.3–6.6 m]). Foliage disease-resistant." [ARA28/147] "Wichuraiana of astounding vigor, completely hidden in season by enormous, loose clusters of small, single, blackish crimson flowers with quilled petals, followed by a fine display of scarlet hips in autumn. Has developed an everblooming character in California, but is once-blooming only in the North and East." [GAS] "Another Eastern hardy variety that gives repeated bloom in the Southwest. Dark maroon, small-sized flower with light center; very prolific, giving not only a spring season of several months with fine display, but continued flowers throughout the year; very vigorous; remarkable foliage. Thornless; good as groundcover." [CaRoll/4/2] "Almost thornless, vigorous-growing plant. Beautiful for fences." [C-Ps34] "Literally covered with red fruits of good size which last almost all Winter. This is one of the finest of climbing roses." [CaRol/5/2] "Bloomfield" was the singularly fortuitous name of the Thomas estate in Pennsylvania.

Bloomfield Endurance   Listed as 'W. Freeland Kendrick' (W).

Bloomfield Favorite
Capt. Thomas, 1924
From 'Debutante' (W) × 'Moonlight' (HMk).

"Bud deep salmon; flower very double, 1¹/₂ inch across [ca. 4 cm], full, slight fragrance, pinkish cream. Foliage perfect. Vigorous climber; profuse bloomer from June to November (400 blooms in Pa.) on old and new wood. Very hardy." [ARA25/195] "Small, very double flowers of pinkish cream color, virtually a 'Climbing Cécile Brunner' in appearance, but hardier. Continuous bloom, in the manner of 'Bloomfield Fascination' [HMk]." [GAS]

Bonfire
Turbat, 1928
From 'Turner's Crimson Rambler' (Mult) × Rosa wichuraiana.

"Brilliant red, double, cluster-flowered Wichuraiana, superior to 'Excelsa' [W] in freedom from mildew and uniformity of color. It blooms several weeks earlier." [GAS] "Lowell finds it a very pretty climber, blooming late in June and the first half of July, much like 'Excelsa'. We agree except that with us it blooms about two weeks ahead of 'Excelsa'." [ARA31/201] "Dazzling scarlet, very early variety, flowering a fortnight before 'Excelsa'. Growth vigorous." [GeH] "Flower double, dazzling scarlet, borne in large, elongated clusters of 20 to 25 blooms. Foliage light green. Growth very vigorous, climbing; very early bloomer." [ARA29/223]

Bonnie Belle
Walsh, 1911

"Pink, single, with yellow stamens, handsome foliage. Growth vigorous." [GeH] "Pink, medium size, single, light scent, tall." [Sn] Not to be confused with 'Bonny Belle', Hobbies' extinct Polyantha of 1912.

Boston Rambler   Listed as 'Farquhar' (W).

Bouquet Rose
trans. "Pink Bouquet"
Theunis/Eindhoven, 1912
From 'Turner's Crimson Rambler' (Mult) × 'Ernst Grandpierre' (W).

"Rose pink; double. Said to be perpetual flowering." [NRS13/101] "Rose-pink to lilac-white, early, perpetual flowering. Growth vigorous." [GeH] "Fair growth; blooms well." [ARA18/119] "Pink, small, full, tall." [Sn] "Climbing rose blooming early and very abundantly, and having vigorous and healthy growth, looking in form and appearance in between '[Turner's] Crimson Rambler' [Mult] and 'Dorothy Perkins' [W]. The quite full blossoms, from 4–5 cm across [ca. 1¹/₂–2 in], appear in large corymbs early, in the month of May. The color of the buds and of the open flowers is, the first day, bright carnation pink on a yellow ground passing subsequently to lilac pink and lilac white, sometimes pure white, thus forming a beautiful contrast of colors in each corymb. This beautiful rose has the characteristic scent of the flower of the Linden." [JR36/184–185]

Bracteata   Listed as Rosa wichuraiana 'Bracteata'.

Breeze Hill
Van Fleet/American Rose Society, 1926
From Rosa wichuraiana × 'Beauté de Lyon' (Pern).

"Deep cream with tints of pink and salmon. Does not reach its full quality until the second or third year after planting." [GeH] "Pink." [Ÿ] "Light orange red, medium size, full, medium scent, tall." [Sn] "Remarkable for its huge, very double, pale salmon flowers, flushed lightly with orange and buff, fading almost white as they mature. The plant has enormous vigor, with small, hard foliage so unlike Wichuraiana hybrids that the influence of R. soulieana is suspected." [GAS] "Bud large, ovoid, slightly darker than flower; flower very large (3 inch diameter [ca. 7.5 cm]), double (50 to 60 petals), full, cupped, lasting, moderately fragrant, flesh tinted with apricot, center rose, paling with age, borne singly and in clusters up to 7 on medium-length stem; drop off cleanly. Foliage abundant, large, normal green, leathery, glossy, disease-resistant. Few thorns. Growth very vigorous, upright, bushy; profuse, continuous bloomer. Hardy." [ARA27/218] "A fragrant, hardy climbing Rose with extra-large, fully double blooms of pink with fawn suffusion and yellow base. The opening flower reminds one of 'Gloire de Dijon' [N], then the sun brings on the opalescence of 'Souvenir de la Malmaison' [B]; fine for cutting and extra good. Not at its best until the plants are well matured." [C-Ps29]

Breeze Hill *continued*

"'Breeze Hill' *must* have growth and age to show what it is." [ARA29/ 183] "Will do well in partial shade." [C-Pf31] "Subject to black-spot at times." [ARA30/180] "Probably the largest-flowered hardy climber in existence, it is characterized by its lovely 'sunrise and sunset' tints, and the enormous flower clusters produced on its heavy wood . . . The plants start rather slowly, but grow very rapidly when established." [ARA27/213] Breeze Hill, quondam headquarters of the American Rose Society.

Brownell Yellow Rambler

From a seedling (resulting from a cross of 'Emily Gray' [W] and 'Ghislaine de Féligonde' [Mult]) × 'Golden Glow' (W).

Brownell, 1942

Flowers yellow, double, coming singly and in clusters, main bloom in Spring.

Buttermere

Chaplin, 1932

"Large trusses of creamy yellow flowers flushed pink. May be important." [GAS] "Yellow, medium size, lightly double, medium scent, tall." [Sn]

Carissima

Walsh, 1904

"Delicate flesh colour, small, and quilled, in large bunches. Growth vigorous." [GeH] "Light pink, small, full, medium scent, tall." [Sn] "Rampant Wichuraiana with clusters of double, soft light pink flowers. Late blooming." [GAS] "A rampant grower with glossy foliage. Flowers a little earlier than 'Dorothy Perkins' [W], in large pyramidal trusses of beautiful small rosettes of delicate flesh tint. The petals are often quilled or twisted." [NRS13/98] "An exceedingly pretty refined flower of softest light pink. It is a free flowerer and a good rampant grower." [NRS16/99]

Carpet of Gold

Brownell, 1939

From a seedling (resulting from a cross of 'Emily Gray' [W] and 'Brownell Yellow Rambler' [W]) × 'Golden Glow' (W).

"Yellow, medium size, full, medium scent, tall." [Sn] "The double, yellow, 2- to 3-inch flowers [ca. 5–7.5 cm] first open in early June and continue through the month. The shiny, resistant foliage covers a handsome plant which is one of my great favorites. It grows along to 12 to 15 feet [ca. 4–5 m], and sometimes in four years to 20 feet [ca. 6.6 m] . . . FRAGRANT." [W]

Casimir Moullé

syn. 'Mme. Casimir Moullé'

Barbier, 1910

From *Rosa wichuraiana* × 'Mme. Norbert Levavasseur' (Pol).

"Deep pink, whitish reverse." [Ÿ] "The small, double, purplish pink flowers are borne very profusely." [GAS] "Bright purplish rosy colour, reverse of petals silvery pink. Growth very vigorous." [GeH] "Vigorous plant, bright green foliage. Inflorescences in panicles composed of 20–50 blossoms of medium size, flat in form, imbricated, very unusual, very double; color, purple pink, intense within and silvery pink on the back of the petals, making a contrast. Late-blooming, and as abundant as 'Lady Gay' [W] and 'Dorothy Perkins' [W]." [JR34/150]

Chaplin's Crimson Glow

Chaplin, 1930

"Deep crimson with white base. Free and continuous flowering. Excellent pillar and pergola Rose." [GeH] "Deep red, large, full, tall." [Sn] "Probably a Wichuraiana of the 'Paul's Scarlet Climber' type, with relatively large crimson flowers marked with white lines at the bases of the petals. I have seen it only once, as a forced pot-plant, scarcely distinguishable from 'Paul's Scarlet Climber'." [GAS]

Chaplin's Pink Climber

Chaplin, 1928

From 'Paul's Scarlet Climber' [W] × 'American Pillar' [W].

"Bright pink." [Ÿ] "Large, handsome clusters of rich, lively pink, each bloom with a small central cluster of golden anthers." [ARA29/ 199] "Wide, flat flowers of brilliant, pure pink. A vigorous plant and profuse bloomer." [C-Pf31] "Flower large, semi-double, flat, extremely lasting; clear, soft pink; golden stamens; borne in large clusters. Growth vigorous; free bloomer." [ARA29/220] "A most vigorous Wichuraiana of the 'American Pillar' [W] type, with semi-double flowers in huge clusters. The color is a peculiarly vivid pink shade, distinct and handsome." [GAS] "Its size and habit are similar to [those of] 'Paul's Scarlet Climber' [W], but the color is Neyron-pink [*v. 'Paul Neyron' (HP)*], and it has slight fragrance. It was said to be remontant." [ARA29/187] "Pink, large, lightly double, tall." [Sn] "*Nicolas* says it has a good, sparkling color when the plant is vigorous, but rather dull on weak plants. *Hatton* reports pink flowers of the 'Paul's Scarlet Climber' shape, beautiful when first open but fading badly, and must be cut off to keep the plant looking well." [ARA31/201] "The habit of growth is medium, the plants reaching a height of about 7 feet [ca. 2.3 m]. The blooms are fairly large, carried in clusters, with pretty golden stamens. The colour is a soft pink. The foliage reminds one of [that of] 'American Pillar', bright, shining green, free of mildew." [NRS29/98] "Strong, sturdy growth, with healthy light green foliage. It has borne no blooms the first year." [CaRol/6/6] "This striking novelty originated at Waltham Cross, England, in the same nursery in which 'Paul's Scarlet Climber' was raised [*Chaplin's was the successor firm to W. Paul's*]. It is . . . of strong, vigorous growth, perfectly hardy with large, glossy, dark green foliage, producing its large flowers, similar in size and form to [those of] 'Paul's Scarlet Climber', very profusely in strong trusses of from eight to twelve flowers each, but in color it is a rich, lively pink." [ARA30/v] "Best described as a double pink climber of great value for arches and pillars." [GeH]

Chatillon-Rambler

Nonin, 1913

From 'Dorothy Perkins' (W) × 'Turner's Crimson Rambler' (Mult).

"Light salmon pink, small, lightly double, light scent, tall." [Sn] "Rose tinted flesh, with large white centre, large, semi-double. Growth very vigorous; late flowering." [GeH] "Wichuraiana with pink flowers not unlike 'Dorothy Perkins' [W]." [GAS] "Will . . . largely displace 'Dorothy Perkins'. It is earlier blooming and far superior in colour and size of truss." [NRS18/149] "It deserves to be more largely grown than it is at present, and a trial will soon reveal its merits. It is a grand grower, and a very late flowerer. It has exceedingly attractive trusses of what I call rosy-flesh flowers, but I see the colour is described by the raiser as being 'muslin-rose', whatever tint that may be . . . The superiority over 'Dorothy Perkins' is undoubted." [NRS19/

57] "Plant of very great vigor, producing very long and sturdy canes from which issue enormous thyrses of pretty, semi-double blossoms of a beautiful nuance of muslin pink tinted flesh; the petals are large and solid and of very long duration. The bloom of this beautiful novelty has the advantage of being very late and prolonged. It is the last to bloom of the Wichuraiana hybrids." [JR38/55] "A beautiful Rose." [NRS15/146] Not to be confused with Nonin's 'Chatillon Rose', a Polyantha of 1923. Chatillon, or, more fully, Chatillon-sous-Bagneux, the location of Nonin's firm in France.

Christian Curle
Cocker, 1910
Sport of 'Dorothy Perkins' (W).

"Light pink, small, full, tall." [Sn] "This is a much prettier 'Dorothy Perkins', having all the characteristics of this last save the color, which is pale salmony pink." [JR33/53] "Sport of 'Dorothy Perkins', with which it is in every way identical save colour, which is a pale flesh-pink." [GeH] "Indistinguishable from 'Lady Godiva' [W]." [GAS]

Christine Wright
Hoopes, Bro. & Thomas, 1909
From a seedling (which was the result of crossing *Rosa wichuraiana* and 'Marion Dingee' [T]) × 'Mme. Caroline Testout' (HT).

"Lovely shade of pink; long-stemmed clusters." [ARA29/97] "Good form, with a perfect bud and good petalage; color is wild-rose-pink; blooms best in spring. A few scattering flowers in autumn. A very satisfactory climbing rose. Foliage lasts well." [ARA17/26] "[Flowers are] 3½ to 4 inches in diameter [to ca. 1 dm], double, borne singly and in clusters." [C&Js21] "Produces a great burst of large, double, wild-rose-pink flowers, borne individually and in clusters. By some considered the best pure pink among the early-flowering hardy climbers. After the great display in early June, casual blooms give a dash of color until late fall." [C-Ps28] "Light pink, large, lightly double, light scent, tall." [Sn] "Good growth and bloom; color and form most attractive." [ARA18/119] "Almost entirely immune from attack by insects or disease." [C-Ps26] "Foliage black-spots very slightly; bloom moderate half the time during June and July." [ARA18/130] "Foliage stiff as leather, insensible to black spot. Blossom of the bright pink shade of the Eglantine, from 6–7 cm across [ca. 2½ in], full, in clusters and solitary buds, very beautiful, lasting a full several days. Rich bloom in June, and sometimes also at season's end. Very hardy; good for pillars, walls, grills, and arbors." [JR38/88] "A strong climbing Rose with large, thick, leathery foliage which is proof against mildew. It has the same habit of growth as 'Climbing American Beauty' [W], and the large bright, clear pink flowers make it a good companion for that variety. The plant is a perfect mass of bloom in June and flowers occasionally during the summer." [C&Js12] "Quite faithful in throwing a few flowers every summer and fall; no other climber has done so for me." [ARA24/90] "A strong upright thorny grower … Blooms in small trusses of large double flowers of a bright carmine pink opening to clear pink. It makes a fine pillar Rose." [NRS13/95] "Suitable for fences. Hardy." [ARA21/93] "Oldest of the large-flowered, bright pink Wichuraianas. Still good, but languishes under the awe-inspiring shadow of 'Mary Wallace' [W]." [GAS] Possibly bred by James A. Farrell.

Cinderella
Walsh, 1909
"Deep pink, small, full, medium scent, tall." [Sn] "One of the innu-

merable variations on the theme of 'Dorothy Perkins' [W], somewhat darker and late-flowering." [GAS] "Fair grower and bloomer; flowers do not all come at once." [ARA18/119] "Flower deeper shade of pink than 'Lady Gay' [W], end of petals quilled; double late flowering. Growth vigorous." [GeH] Not to be confused with Page's similarly named Noisette of 1859. Cinderella, the hearth-warming heroine of the fairy tale who showed the way to modern femaledom by owing it all to wise choice of footwear.

City of York Listed as 'Direktor Benschop' (W).

Claude Raabe
Buatois, 1941
"Carmine flesh pink on a yellow ground." [Ÿ]

Clematis
Turbat, 1924
"Red, white center, small, single, tall." [Sn] "Bud small; flower small, single, very lasting, dark red with prominent white eye, borne in clusters of 40 to 50. Foliage rich green, very resistant to black-spot. Very vigorous grower, climbing habit." [ARA25/187] "Strongly reminiscent of 'Bloomfield Courage' [W], which is just as good, if not better." [GAS] *Clematis*, the genus in the *Ranunculaceae*.

Climbing American Beauty Listed as 'American Beauty, Climbing' (W).

Copper Glow
Brownell, 1940
From 'Golden Glow' (W) × 'Break o'Day' (HT).
"Coppery yellow, large, full, very fragrant, tall." [Sn]

Coquina
Walsh, 1911
"Orange-pink, white center, small, single, light scent, tall." [Sn] "Pale pink; small cup-shaped blooms in clusters; the flowers, which last a long time, do not come out till mid July." [NRS18/184] "That pretty little climber 'Coquina', which I have only had since the spring, began to flower in August, and has gone on doing so ever since." [NRS11/26] "Flower pale pink; growth vigorous." [GeH] "Growth and blooming quite good." [ARA18/120] "One of the innumerable pink, single, cluster-flowered Wichuraianas now on their way to oblivion." [GAS]

Coral Satin
Zambory/Jackson & Perkins, 1966
From 'New Dawn' (W) × 'Fashion' (Fl).
"Coral pink." [Ÿ] "Light orange, large, full, medium scent, tall." [Sn]

Coronation
Turner, 1912
"Red, lightly striped white." [Ÿ] "Fine trusses of semi-double rosettes, crimson streaked with white. Late flowering, but earlier than 'Dorothy Perkins' [W]." [NRS13/101] "Makes beautiful sprays of exquisite crimson-scarlet flowers, with a dainty flake of white on some of the petals, which are quilled, giving a soft and unique appearance to each cluster. This Rose has our highest recommendation as it is a new and desirable change in this class." [C&Js19] "The heads of bloom come in such masses that they almost hide the foliage." [C&Js23] "Red, small, full, tall." [Sn] "A strong grower and perfectly hardy, making beautiful sprays of cherry-red or crimson-scarlet flowers, with

Coronation *continued*

some of the petals daintily marked with white." [C-Ps29] "The plant is good either as a low pillar or trellis Rose, or with Wichuraiana for trailing." [C-Ps26]

Coupe d'Or

trans. "Cup of Gold"
Barbier, 1930
Seedling from 'Jacotte' (W).

"Yellow, medium size, full, medium scent, tall." [Sn] "The latest bid for first place as a really good, yellow-flowered Wichuraiana. Blooms two inches across [ca. 5 cm], not noticeably clustered, fragrant, bright yellow, becoming lighter as they age. Partially trailing habit; reputed to be hardy." [GAS] "Bud and flower medium size, double, full, open, cupped, lasting, fragrant, canary-yellow, slightly paler on opening, borne several together on medium-length stem. Foliage sufficient, medium size, rich green, leathery, glossy, disease-resistant. Growth vigorous, climbing or trailing; abundant bloomer four weeks in May and June. Very hardy." [ARA31/235]

Cramoisi Simple

trans. "Single Crimson"
Barbier, 1901
From 'Rubra' (W) × 'Turner's Crimson Rambler' (Mult).

"Crimson red." [Ÿ] "Deep red with a white nub." [JR26/181] "Extremely vigorous bush with upright gay green canes armed with paired thorns of a bright pink. Leaves ample, robust and prickly petiole, stipules large and lacinate, 3–4 pairs of subsessile, serrulate, concolored leaflets. Inflorescence an upright pyramidal panicle, leafy, oval bracts which are glandulose and ciliate-lacinate; branchlets upright; peduncle hispidulous, dark bright red; calyx longly turbinate, smooth, green and red; sepals wide-spreading, oval-cucculate, lobed-dentate, subulate, edges and interior lanate; corolla single or semi-double, outspread, 4 cm wide [ca. 1³/₄ in], petals widely obcordate, concave, edges undulate and blunted, deep violet crimson red with a white nub. This beautiful plant has foliage just like that of the rose '[Turner's] Crimson Rambler', one of its parents. It was the pollen-bearer, while *Rosa Wichuraiana Rubra* was the seed-bearer. Its habit—extremely decorative—is less rampant than that of *R. wichuraiana*." [JR26/5]

Crimson Shower

Norman, 1951
Seedling of 'Excelsa' (W).
"Deep red, small, lightly double, light scent, tall." [Sn]

Daybreak

Dawson/Eastern, 1909

Long extinct hybrid of Wichuraiana × a blush Tea; only mentioned here because 'Daybreak' is also Van Fleet's original name for the important 'Dr. W. Van Fleet' (W). Neither to be confused with Pemberton's 1918 Hybrid Musk of the same name. Daybreaks, Breaks o' Day, Dawns, and such were evidently much on people's minds during that era.

De Candolle

Robichon, 1912
From *Rosa wichuraiana* × 'Eugenie Lamesch' (Pol).
"Deep yellow to salmon-yellow, large trusses, free flowering.

Growth very vigorous." [GeH] "Coppery salmon, medium size, full, tall." [Sn] "Very vigorous climbing shrub with glossy foliage; flowers medium-sized, full, presented in bouquets of 30–40 ochre yellow buds; the open blossom changes to salmony copper yellow, varying with the temperature; superb coloration." [JR37/105] Not to be confused with the Moss of the same name.

Debutante   Plate 39

Walsh, 1901
From *Rosa wichuraiana* × 'Baronne Adolphe de Rothschild' (HP).

"Pretty, double, soft pink, cluster-flowered Wichuraiana submerged in the fame of 'Dorothy Perkins' [W]." [GAS] "Pretty soft shade of pink belonging to the late flowering section of the Wichuraianas. Makes a good weeping standard." [F-M] "A most perfect, small, pure pink rosette flower in large clusters. Rampant grower. One of the prettiest." [NRS16/97] "Soft light pink, rosettes in clusters, very double, scented. Growth very vigorous." [GeH] "Bloom free last three weeks of June." [ARA18/130] "Double flowers of uniform size and a beautiful soft pink color. Blooms during July, September and October in graceful clusters and throws out the delicate odor of the Sweetbriar. Entirely hardy and splendid for climbing and trailing." [C&Js06] "Rather straggly growth; free bloomer, occasional blooms in fall." [ARA18/120] "A very rampant flexible grower, producing a profusion of graceful trusses of soft pink rosettes. Flowers about 10 days earlier than 'Dorothy Perkins'." [NRS13/99]

Delight

Walsh, 1906

"Single carmine red, base of petals white, filled with clusters of yellow stamens; very free flowering, and elegant in habit." [NRS28/149] "Another of Walsh's innumerable Wichuraianas, with single, deep pink flowers, very bright and pretty, reminiscent of 'Hiawatha' [Mult]." [GAS] "Rose-carmine with white centre, single, in large trusses, free flowering, resembling a Sweet Briar. Very vigorous." [GeH] "Red, white center, medium size, single, light scent, tall." [Sn] "A delightful single flower of carmine with white centre, giving a very bright effect. A vigorous grower. Very good as a weeping Standard. Forms rootlets on growing stems." [NRS16/97] "Strong growth; good foliage; blooms almost same color as [those of] 'Hiawatha' and 'Eisenach' [W]." [ARA18/120] "Rampant, flexible growth. Dark glazed foliage." [NRS13/100]

Denyse Ducas

Buatois, 1953
"Golden yellow, carmine red exterior." [Ÿ]

Desiré Bergera

Barbier, 1909
From *Rosa wichuraiana* × 'Aurore' (Ch).

"Coppery rose." [ARA19/86] "Coppery dawn pink." [Ÿ] "Coppery yellow, double, in small trusses, freely produced. Very vigorous." [GeH] "Clusters of very double, coppery pink flowers varying to light pink. Distinct and charming." [GAS] "Pale salmon pink, flushed yellow in bud, fading to pale pink. When full flowered shows centre. Strong grower, with nice coppery brown young shoots. Not very distinctive with me." [NRS16/95] "Gorgeous, large-blossomed Wichuraiana. Glossy green foliage, strong growth, mid-sized well-formed blossoms, coppery pink, rose-red within. Tea-scented." [Ck] "A rampant grower with strong reddish green thorny shoots. Dark green glossy foliage, slightly liable to mildew. It flowers freely in small trusses of double flowers of coppery yellow colour." [NRS13/97] "Climbing bush, vigorous and floriferous; bouquets of 2–6 very double, medium-sized blossoms of a beautiful coppery saffron pink and coppery light red within. Novel coloration among the climbers." [JR33/167]

Diabolo
trans. "Devil"
Fauque & fils, 1908
From *Rosa wichuraiana* × 'Xavier Olibo' (HP).

"Velvety crimson." [Ÿ] "Purple red, white center, medium size, single to semi-double, tall." [Sn] "Clusters of fairly large, fiery red, semi-double flowers shaded blackish purple. Handsome but rarely seen." [GAS] "Flower dark glowing crimson, large, with golden stamens, semi-single, early flowering. Growth very vigorous." [GeH] "Not very floriferous, but the flowers are borne in fairly large open clusters … Grows and shows to advantage in partial shade." [NRS16/93] "Climbing shrub, foliage dark green, blossom single or semi-double, large, in a corymb, velvety blackish purple and very bright flame, lasting. The white base of the petals and the numerous stamens of the most beautiful yellow lighten the center, making a most happy color contrast. Pillar rose, distinct coloration." [JR32/134] "A very strong, upright vigorous grower, with rigid stems of light green colour closely covered with small crimson thorns. The foliage is large and dark green with a somewhat rugose surface which is lightly glossed. It suffers a little from mildew. The flowers are produced in small trusses on long stiff stems. The individual blooms are large, semi-single; the petals are a deep glowing crimson with dark shading, and form a magnificent contrast to the rich golden stamens. It is very distinct in every way." [NRS13/95]

Direktor Benschop
syn. 'City of York'
Tantau, 1939
From 'Professor Gnau' (HT) × 'Dorothy Perkins' (W).
"White, large, lightly double, medium scent, tall." [Sn]

Donau!
trans. "Danube!"
Praskač, 1913
From 'Erinnerung an Brod' (Set) × 'Rubra' (W).
"Reddish lilac tinted slaty blue." [Ÿ] "Violet red, small, full, very fragrant, tall." [Sn] "An interesting mixture of Multiflora and Wichuraiana strains, bearing clusters of fragrant purple-violet flowers which fade steely blue." [GAS] "For those who like 'Veilchenblau' [Mult], … 'Donau[!]' is good; it is of a richer purple, and very fine at the end of blooming, when it is like the 'Royal Purple' sweet pea. It is a strong grower." [ARA19/86] "One of the most fragrant climbing roses grown up till now. It is, in any case, a very interesting development because of its unique color of lilac. It is a superb climbing variety covered with flowers from one end to the other. It produces large false umbels containing up to 30 well-developed roses. Each blossom is about 5 cm across [ca. 2 in]. When opening, it is reddish lilac, which then becomes reddish blue lilac, finally becoming a bright slaty blue, keeping this tint until the petals fall. The color varies according to the exposure and the nature of the soil. The blossom is pretty full, and this alone makes it surpass 'Veilchenblau' [Mult]. 'Donau!' has, as

mentioned above, a delicious perfume resembling that of the Lily of the Valley. Due to its scent and to its beautiful blue color, it takes First Place among climbing roses. The plant has strong canes, rapid growth, few thorns, and large bright green leaflets. 'Donau!' is particularly good, by reason of its unique lilac color and Lily of the Valley perfume, for covering frameworks, walls, pergolas, etc. It is the most beautiful rose of this color." [JR38/73] The Danube river, beautifully blue, often in three-quarter time.

Dorcas
T. J. English, 1922
"Deep pink, small, full, tall." [Sn] "Flower full, perfectly shaped, very lasting; deep rose-pink at edges, shading to coral-pink, with palest yellow at base; large, well-formed clusters. Foliage practically evergreen. Vigorous; profuse bloomer." [ARA24/168] "Large clusters carried on strong and long laterals. Ample foliage and a strong grower. Nilson pink at the edge of petals, tinted coral red and pale yellow at the base." [NRS24/163] "Very vigorous and mildew-proof." [GeH] "Vigorous, profuse Wichuraiana of 'Dorothy Perkins' type." [GAS] Dorcas, alias Tabitha, Biblical eleemosynary clothes-maker who got a second chance.

Dorothy Dennison
Dennison/A. Dickson, 1909
Sport of 'Dorothy Perkins' (W).
"Pale pink." [Ÿ] "Light pink, small, full, tall." [Sn] "Lovely salmon-pink flowers, perfectly double. Makes large clusters." [C&Js21] "Indistinguishable from 'Lady Godiva' [W]." [GAS] "Shell-pink flowers, borne in clusters all over a husky plant." [C-Ps25] "Palest shell-pink, large trusses … Very vigorous." [GeH] "Foliage black-spots slightly; bloom profuse last half of June, free through July." [ARA18/130] "Biggest blossoms of the 'Dorothy [Perkins]' sort … glossy, light green leaves. One of the most beautiful climbing roses." [Ck]

Dorothy Perkins   Plate 39
Jackson & Perkins, 1901
From "a variety of *Rosa wichuraiana*" × 'Mme. Gabriel Luizet' (HP)
"Satiny carmine pink." [Ÿ] "Beautiful bright carminy pink." [JR32/172] "Beautiful shell pink in immense clusters, quite full and double." [C&Js03] "Flowers are perfectly double with petals crinkled." [C&Js06] "The classic, small-flowered clustered wichuraiana, of such great popularity that varieties of similar type and color have never had a chance. It is a rose of supreme grace and beauty, bearing huge clusters of very double, shell-pink flowers with quilled petals." [GAS] "Very vigorous plant, salmony pink, good variety." [JR31/177] "Rose-pink, small, double, very sweet, produced in large clusters. Growth very vigorous, climbing, late flowering; bright glossy green foliage." [GeH] "Foliage lost quite early." [ARA17/28] "Foliage black-spots slightly, especially in late summer; bloom very profuse last three weeks of June and early July." [ARA18/131] "Fine growth and blooming qualities." [ARA18/120] "Blooms just in time for June weddings." [C&Js07] "For best results, prune out old canes at the base when bloom is over." [C-Ps30] "Of rampant growth; with fine glossy foliage which is unfortunately more liable to mildew than most of the class. Flowers in the greatest profusion from about the second week in July. The trusses are of immense size. The individual bloom is a small double rosette of soft rose pink colour. In some seasons the flowering is prolonged till late in the autumn." [NRS13/99]

Dorothy Perkins *continued*

"This newcomer of American origin is from a cross between the rose 'Mme. Gabriel Luizet' [HP] and a variety of *Rosa wichuraiana*. It is a climbing rose which will have the same vigor as '[Turner's] Crimson Rambler' [Mult], thus making it good for covering walls, trellises, and pergolas. The plant—which is floriferous—throws numerous blossoms up to the Fall; they come in corymbs, are a delicate pink with a white center, and are nicely scented." [JR26/129] "This is a grand new hardy climber, has stood a temperature of 20° below zero without injury. Grows 10 to 15 feet [ca. 3.3–5 m] in a season, blooms in immense clusters like the '[Turner's] Crimson Rambler', but the blooms are more double and of a beautiful shell-pink color passing to clear deep rose, makes large pointed buds and is a very satisfactory rose for general planting." [C&Js05]

"'Dorothy Perkins' and her sports are all of a very vigorous and rambling growth and a branching, drooping and spreading habit—the basal shoots running along the ground if not tied up. The shoots continue growing until very late in autumn. The young stems are smooth, almost polished, of a light green tint which browns a little in the autumn, and they are armed with sharp slightly hooked thorns about an inch apart [ca. 2.5 cm]. They are well clothed with good glossy lightish green foliage, the leaves have usually seven leaflets, but there is often another pair to be seen, either rudimentary or more or less developed. The stipules at the base of the leaf have their edges divided into a number of hair-like teeth, reminding one of those of '[Turner's] Crimson Rambler', but are a good deal more leafy than in that variety. The foliage lasts long on the plant so as to be nearly evergreen, becoming slightly darker and redder in the late autumn, and it is decidedly subject to mildew for a Rose of its class. There is only one true flowering period, but occasional flowers may be found on the plants as late as December in a warm autumn. They begin to flower late…, coming in at a useful time just as the Ramblers are going over…They continue in profuse flower till the end of August. After this, for the remainder of the season, there will be found from time to time a few blossoms…The flowers are semi-double to full, often of quite a pretty shape, produced in large trusses, sometimes of 20 or 30 blossoms, in the greatest profusion. The colour of 'Dorothy Perkins' is clear rose pink…'Dorothy Perkins' and its sports may be used in the garden for any purposes for which a free growing rambling Rose is adapted, and their drooping lax stems may be trained into almost any desired position. The great number of basal shoots produced every year make the plants specially useful for pillars and arches, and they make fine heads as weeping standards. They are also suitable for pergolas, screens, tall hedges, or trellis work. The strong points of these Roses are their freedom of growth and hardiness, the decorative effect of their striking colour, and the wonderful mass of bloom out at the same time in late July and August. They will grow in any soil, but a start in rich soil will save one or perhaps two years in the time taken for them to produce an effect in the garden." [NRS11/37–40] "It is *the* typical Rambler (as '[Turner's] Crimson Rambler' is *not*), still popular and rightly so. Huge clusters of small, double, clear, rose-pink flowers appear in July. Few roses give a greater effect in bloom, making even the battle with mildew worthwhile." [W]

Double Pink Memorial Rose   Listed as 'Universal Favorite' (W).

Double White Memorial Rose   Listed as 'Manda's Triumph' (W).

Dr. Huey

syn. 'Dr. Robert Huey'
Capt. Thomas/Bobbink & Atkins, A. N. Pierson, 1920
From 'Ethel' (W) × 'Gruss an Teplitz' (B).

"Fine Wichuraiana with fairly large, beautifully ruffled flowers of fiery maroon-red. A most profuse bloomer and extremely vigorous. Probably the finest dark red variety for garden effect." [GAS] "Drab crimson-maroon." [C-Ps29] "Deep red, medium size, lightly double, light scent, tall." [Sn] "The large semi-double flowers are of deepest crimson shaded black, and the unique colouring contrasts beautifully with the golden anthers. The flowers never turn blue and are very freely produced in large clusters on a vigorous plant." [GeH] "The hot sun does burn the petals, so the fading flowers should be removed." [C-Ps28] "A free-flowering climber having large, lasting, semi-double, dark carmine flowers and good foliage. A free-growing, hardy variety." [ARA20/168] "It has been tested for four years, and is distinct as a large, semi-double, deep red climber of one period of bloom. It is hardy." [ARA20/37] "An absolutely unique Rose in every respect. The color is an intense dark crimson-scarlet, comparing only with the Hybrid Tea Rose, 'Château de Clos-Vougeot'. The flowers are large, semi-double, and so closely spaced on the plant in its June burst of bloom as almost to conceal the excellent foliage. These flowers do not 'blue' as they fade, and the plant is attractive for many weeks in consequence. It can be treated as a pillar, but its 10-foot canes [ca. 3.3 m] will climb anywhere. It is a production of America's most acute amateur hybridizer, Capt. George C. Thomas, Jr." [C-Ps25] "[Raised by] Capt. George C. Thomas [in] 1914; intro. by Bobbink & Atkins and A. N. Pierson [in] 1920 . . . Bud medium size; flower medium-size (about 2 inches in diameter [ca. 5 cm]), semi-double (15 petals) to single, borne in clusters of 3 or 4 on good stems; lasting. Color dark crimson-maroon of great brilliancy; stamens and anthers light yellow. Foliage medium green; young growth reddish brown. Blooms continuously for three weeks." [ARA20/133] "Mildews in damp conditions." [Th2] "'Dr. Huey', after three years of indecision and no bloom, grew like a beanstalk this summer." [ARA28/62]

"The name for it . . . was announced at the meeting of the American Rose Society held in the Bloomfield Gardens on June 4, 1919, when the rose created great enthusiasm among the many experts there." [ARA20/37] "My [Dr. Robert Huey's] earliest rose recollection is of an attempt to pluck a moss rose in my grandmother's garden and of getting my fingers pricked by the sharp thorns. Rescued by the nurse, the thorns were removed, and I was turned loose in the belief that a lesson had been taught. Nevertheless, I wanted that rose, and returned to the attack with a like result. Mother then appeared on the scene, took in the situation, cut the rose, removed the thorns, and made me happy with the flower. I have loved roses ever since. Living in the city as a young man, and spending four years in the army during the [American] Civil War [1861–1865], there was no opportunity for attempting a rose-garden, but after being established in [medical] practice upon my return, and feeling the need for outdoor relaxation, I purchased a home and two acres of ground in 1877, and began to try to grow roses. There was then little reliable information to be had, and the flowers that resulted compared most unfavorably with the illustrations in the catalogues, while the plants would die by the dozen. Persevering, I finally met with success, and knowing that many others were thirsting for knowledge I began writing and talking of my experiences and how my difficulties were overcome, thus doing a sort of rose missionary work. Captain Thomas was so pleased over his success with a bed of fifty roses which I had given him that he got the rose fever too; and he has surely done splendid work since, making me very proud of my pupil." [ARA22/158] "[Dr. Huey] first heard of budded roses through Messrs. Alex. Dickson & Sons, the great Irish rose-growers, and his trial of these was really the beginning of a new era in outdoor rose-growing in America [*how singularly coincidental and appropriate is the name of this cultivar, then, 'Dr. Huey' having become one of the main stocks for budding roses in America*]. In 1898 his friend Alexander Scott gave him three plants of 'Killarney' [HT], and these were the first plants of this rose planted outdoors in America. The original plants were still doing well in 1918, when war changes connected with the establishment of the Hog Island shipyard put the Doctor out of his rose-garden. Many new roses have had their first American trial in Dr. Huey's garden, where they would always have the best care and his enlightened and critical judgment." [ARA22/158] "Dr. Robert Huey, who passed from this life on March 12, 1928, at the age of 85, stood during all his long and useful life as a great rose amateur. To his single-minded zeal is due much of the enthusiasm and interest manifested by many individuals in rose-growing. It was his example and spirit which started Captain George C. Thomas, Jr., on his career of rose investigation, trial and origination." [ARA29/209]

Dr. Robert Huey Listed as 'Dr. Huey' (W).

Dr. W. Van Fleet
Van Fleet/Henderson, 1910
From a seedling (resulting from *Rosa wichuraiana* × 'Safrano' [T]) × 'Souvenir du Président Carnot' (HT).

"The horticultural firm of Messrs. Peter Henderson & Co. announce the entry into commerce of two new varieties of Wichuraiana hybrid roses which have won some silver medals in the rose exhibitions of New York. They are: 'Dr. W. Van Fleet' . . . Vigorous plant, robust, covered with beautiful green foliage. The cupped blossoms measure about ten cm across [ca. 4 in]; the wavy petals are flesh pink at the base, and more delicate pink at the edge. The full flowers, borne on rigid stems, are extremely fragrant. [*The other introduction was 'Silver Moon' [Lv].*]" [JR33/135]

"Delicate flesh pink." [Ÿ] "Flesh-pink on the outer surface, deepening to rosy flesh in the centre, large, full and double, scented. Growth vigorous, climbing, free." [GeH] "Flowers soft flesh, shading to delicate peach-pink, and borne on long stems. Foliage very good and lasts well. Very vigorous grower; blooms well in spring and thereafter scattering ones. Suitable for arches, pergolas, summer-houses, fences, etc. Hardy." [ARA21/93] "Named in honor of its originator, Dr. Walter Van Fleet, who has been in charge of the U.S. Government Station for Plant Introduction at Chico, California, and who sent us plants of this rose for trial four years before its introduction to the public. This remarkable hardy climbing rose has retained the splendid characteristics of both its parents—the beautiful Hybrid Tea 'Souvenir du Président Carnot' and the vigorous *Rosa wichuraiana*. The color is a remarkably delicate shade of flesh pink on the outer surface, deepening to rosy flesh in the center. The flowers are full and double and when open run 4 inches [ca. 1 dm] and over in diameter. The center is built high and the petals are beautifully undulated and cupped. A

fine rose for cutting, as the stems run from 12 to 18 inches [ca. 3–4.5 dm]. The foliage is immune from mildew and is a pleasing shade of bronze green; large and glossy and apparently disease proof. It is a most abundant bloomer and enthusiastically praised by all who see it." [C&Js11] "I approach this rose with awe and humility, although I never liked it very much. Its color is a wishy-washy pink, characterless and flat, but its influence has been stupendous. Its introduction broke the garden's thralldom to innumerable, fussy little cluster-flowered ramblers which bore us to distraction with their infantile prettiness and indistinguishable differences. Here was an heroic rose, of noble size and perfect form, borne on a rampant plant, first of the new race of climbers. Its value and importance to rose-growers in cold climates can hardly be estimated, although it needs shelter in winter." [GAS] "Growth very vigorous; bloom free last three weeks of June." [ARA18/130] "Good growth and foliage; beautiful flowers of good form; blooms well in spring, an occasional bloom thereafter." [ARA18/120] "If not cut off, the blooms will produce lovely red 'cherries' (seed-hips) in the late fall and winter. Must not be pruned severely." [C-Ps29] "The hips . . . are about the size of a cherry, and, as they ripen, turn gradually from green to yellow to a handsome red. With me they hold their color well into the new year. A well established plant produced for me in 1929 about 1000 hips from which I took 770 seeds. The 'Dr. W. Van Fleet' hips usually contain one or two seeds, but many of them, that seem from the outside to be perfectly developed, contain no seed at all." [CaRol/5/2] "One matured plant will cover the side of a one-car garage." [C-Ps34] "All summer long, no matter how hot or dry or wet, each leaf shines as if it had been waxed and polished daily, making such a comfortable green spot for light-strained eyes that I often wish that Dr. Van Fleet's ambition to have a bush of it in every yard might be fulfilled." [ARA29/85]

"In the early 90's the Doctor and his wife were attracted to the remarkable colony at Ruskin, Tenn., to which came such men as the Russian Prince, Kropotkin, and the famous journalist, Arthur Brisbane. It was here that the rose later named for the Doctor was originated. He had taken South, along with a host of other seedlings, a weakly little plant which itself was a typical Wichuraiana, resulting from a cross with the 'Safrano' rose, a well-known old fashioned Tea. Using this seedling as the female parent, he worked upon it pollen from the French Hybrid Tea 'Souvenir du Président Carnot'. But three or four heps matured, and these he took with him, when his medical service at Ruskin terminated, back to Little Silver, N.J., where he later sowed the few sound seeds they contained. Of these seeds but a few germinated and grew. This was in the fall of 1899, and in 1901 the seedlings bloomed. Among about 150 others in bloom at the same time, this particular rose showed at once its remarkable freshness of color and unusual bud character. Mrs. Van Fleet and the Doctor agreed to name it 'Daybreak'. Then Patrick O'Mara of the firm Peter Henderson & Co., visited the gardens, and he said when saw in bloom the few plants of 'Daybreak' that the Doctor had propagated, 'We've got to have that at once,' though he criticized its seeming lack of vigor. The Doctor accepted O'Mara's offer carrying the right to name the new rose and fully control its sale, and he was paid $75, although at the time he thought it should have been worth $250. As was his custom, Dr. Van Fleet retained a plant for himself—a very fortunate thing! The several precious plants of this 'Daybreak' were delivered in the fall to Mr. O'Mara, and the latter was told to start its prop-

Dr. W. Van Fleet *continued*

agation slowly in a cool-house, but this was not done. The gardeners of the firm put the plants in a hothouse and forced them into bloom. The blooms were flimsy and did not impress the other members of the Henderson firm. O'Mara said, 'It looked devilish good to me, but it doesn't hold up.' . . . 'The plants were taken out of the greenhouse and sent to Charles Henderson's place at Hackensack, and planted there in their tender condition. Bitter weather came along and killed every one of them, but I [Van Fleet] was not told . . . When the 1906 Henderson catalogue came out and 'Daybreak' was not in it, I wrote to O'Mara, and he then told me he had lost it all. I told him that wouldn't do, that I had stock, and that it was the finest thing I had. I told him the public was entitled to it, and that if he wouldn't put it out I would. He said, "Bring some up and who it to Charles Henderson." It was in good bloom then, and I brought up to New York an armful of it, and also an armful of the 'Silver Moon' with its long-stemmed flowers. O'Mara was delighted when he saw these, and said, "Business or no business, we'll go right in and see Mr. Henderson!" The latter gentleman said at once, "We have had no such novelties as these for years. They are revelations. We want both of them." They both liked the 'Dr. [W.] Van Fleet' best, because a pink rose is a better seller. Henderson said, "I'll pay the Doctor anything he asks for 'Daybreak' and this white rose." They sent their propagator right down and took the bud wood. I asked him $100 for it. Then the Roses disappeared from view for three or four years, or until 1910, when the Henderson catalogue featured both of them . . . Patrick O'Mara wrote that Charles Henderson was going to name the . . . rose after me. I objected, and asked him to continue to call it 'Daybreak', but O'Mara insisted, and thus it was finally named 'Dr. W. Van Fleet'." [ARA22/16–17] "Dr. Van Fleet called the rose 'Daybreak', a much better name than it now has, but it was renamed by the introducers in honor of the Doctor himself making a splendid memorial to his genius, for no better variety of the class has even been produced." [GAS]

"On January 18, 1922, Dr. Van Fleet wrote the Editor that by reason of the results of the disastrous Easter Monday freeze the preceding season, his notes [*on hybridization, for the* American Rose Annual] would be shortened, but would be in hand by February 1. The Doctor added that his health was impaired, and that he was going South, hoping for relief. Then came the shocking news of his sudden death at Miami, Fla., as the result of an imperatively necessary operation, on January 26, 1922 . . . Though . . . Dr. Van Fleet produced many effective roses now in commerce, his work was extended in other directions. Strawberries, gooseberries, corn, tomatoes, peppers, cannas, gladioli, geraniums, honeysuckles felt the touch of his magic hand in improvement. He was seeking to replaced our destroyed chestnuts, and at one recent interview he announced that he had produced chestnuts eight-five per cent blight-proof, and was on the way to complete success. In hurriedly getting together this all too incomplete tribute to Dr. Van Fleet, the Editor has come to realize the impression is breadth of culture and sweetness of spirit made on all who came to really know him. He shunned notoriety, and it was impossible to get him to make a public address. With a small group, however, at his home or in the field, he was the brilliant, genial, human scientist whose memory will long live, certainly as that of the greatest rose hybridist and, probably, the greatest plant-breeder America has yet known . . .

"From his sister, Mrs. Moses Lyman, of Longmeadow, Mass., herself a notable plant-lover, come the following details: Walter Van Fleet was born at Piermont on the Hudson, Rockland County, New York, June 18, 1857. The forebears of the Van Fleets in America came from Utrecht, Holland, in 1692, to New Amsterdam, the direct ancestor of our immediate family settling in the Mohawk Valley, from whence, in course of time, our parents removed to Williamsport, Pa., eventually settling on a farm at Watsontown, Pa. Walter attended school in Williamsport and then at Watsontown, and with his brother and two sisters grew up in a real home, in which were books and music, and in which all joined in the love of the open as well as of dogs and horses and birds. It was characteristic of Walter that when he was interested in anything he always wanted to probe deeper to find out all that could be known about it. An omnivorous reader, it was natural for him to develop the interest which later ruled his life. All too soon we were grown, and then Walter became interested in ornithology, devoting much time to this study, and in time going to South America where he made a collection of butterfly and bird specimens for Harvard. Coming home, he studied medicine and went into active practice, both at Watsontown and later at Renovo. Finding that it was absorbing him to the exclusion of opportunity for following his deepening desire to hybridize plants, he gave up his practice and actively undertook his real life-work. Walter was a social being. He formed real friendships as a boy, even though he was quiet and even shy. In the family circle he was the favorite, and his older brother Frederick and my sister Ida, with myself, always turned to him for advice, because he was just and dependable, as he continued to be during his useful life . . .

"Another associate of Dr. Van Fleet in his departmental work adds further interesting details. Mr. F. L. Mulford, a horticulturist in the Bureau of Plant Industry, knew him and his work well. He writes thus: The ideal rose for which he was striving, in his later work at least, was a garden form, that variety that would compare in healthfulness and disease resistance with the best of the rose species; that would be hardy under ordinary garden culture; and that would be a continuous bloomer . . . His personality was altogether lovable, and those who came in contact with him day after day appreciated his kindly consideration. He was steadfast of purpose, as is shown by the ruthless manner in which he rooted out inferior seedlings so soon as he believed them to be valueless. Modest and retiring in the extreme, he had an intolerance of hypocrisy and cant that was notable . . .

"With Robert Pyle, now President of the American Rose Society, and long the head of the firm of Conard & Jones Co., which has introduced to the public more of his roses than any other firm, Dr. Van Fleet had much contact. Mr. Pyle writes thus of him: It was Dr. Van Fleet who did some of the first hybridizing of cannas in this country. He was associated with Antoine Wintzer at West Grove in 1893, and indeed it was really Dr. Van Fleet who started Wintzer on his career of canna-hybridizing . . . Dr. Van Fleet was also interested in gladioli, and has to his credit 'Princeps' [*"Gladiolus cruentus, blood red and white, pollenized with a selected Childsii variety resulted in the magnificent scarlet hybrid 'Princeps', acknowledged the first of its color yet produced"* [ThGl; photo of 'Princeps', p. 81]] and some other notable strains. His deepest interest, however, was in roses. As far back as 1893 he had been hybridizing among the Rugosas, and even before that, when in Ruskin, Tenn., he had made numerous crosses . . . No monument that we can raise will begin to mark so appropriately the memory we cherish of Dr. Van Fleet as do the thousands upon thousands of Dr. Van Fleet roses that are and will be planted about the homes throughout this nation." [ARA22/13–21]

Dr. Zamenhof
Brada/Böhm, 1935
From *Rosa wichuraiana* × an unnamed seedling.

"Red, yellow center, medium size, lightly double, medium scent, tall." [Sn]

Easlea's Golden Rambler
syn. 'Golden Rambler'
Easlea/Totty, 1932

"Citron chrome yellow." [Ÿ] "It is reported to be an extraordinarily fine Wichuraiana, with very large, double, lemon-yellow flowers flamed with orange and coppery tones." [GAS] "Deep yellow, large, full, very fragrant, tall." [Sn]

Edgar Andreu
syn. 'Edgar Andrieu'
Barbier, 1912
From *Rosa wichuraiana* × 'Cramoisi Supérieur' (Ch).

"A very excellent wichuraiana having, perhaps, the largest individual flowers of any of the cluster kinds. The colour is a reddish crimson." [NRS18/149] "Dark crimson-red, in large trusses; late. Growth vigorous." [GeH] "Blood-red Wichuraiana of the old type, which is said to resist mildew!" [GAS] "Red, medium size, full, tall." [Sn] "Blossom bright blood-red, tinted magenta, passing to bright crimson, reverse of petals bright pink. Inner petals striped with white. Corymbs with 5–15 blossoms. Leaves glossy deep green. Plant vigorous and very floriferous, making quite a splash." [JR36/153] "The flowers … are very much larger than those of 'Excelsa' [W], and they are different in colour. They are a bright blood-red, or really a bright crimson, having the reverse of the petals tinged with bright rose. The blossoms are borne in trusses of from 7 to 15 flowers, and apart from their beauty, the foliage is also very resistant to mildew. I am very fond of 'Edgar Andreu'; there is something about it so reminiscent of the fine old 'Cramoisi Supérieur' [Ch]." [NRS19/58–59]

Edgar Andrieu   Listed as 'Edgar Andreu' (W).

Edmond Proust
Barbier, 1901
From *Rosa wichuraiana* × 'Souvenir de Catherine Guillot' (Ch).

"Light pink and carmine." [Ÿ] "An early attempt at a large-flowered Wichuraiana with double, light pink flowers with coppery stains." [GAS] "Coppery carmine-pink, in clusters, large. Growth vigorous." [GeH] "Light pink, red center, medium size, full, tall." [Sn] "Shrub bushy, well ramified, canes undulate, green tinted with red, with fine, hooked, red thorns. Leaves of 3 pairs of leaflets, subsessile, longly ovate, strongly toothed like a saw, glossy dark green; petiole strongly prickled. Inflorescence in paucifloral cluster; flowers erect; peduncle coming from a thicket of foliaceous bracts; calyx-tube globular; sepals largely ovate-tubular, hirsute within, reflexing; corolla double, globular, 3–4 cm across [ca. 1–1¹/₂ in], flesh pink; petals ovate cucullate, edges slightly grooved. Seedling of *Rosa wichuraiana* pollinated by the variety 'Souvenir de Catherine Guillot' [Ch]." [JR26/4]

Eisenach
Kiese, 1910

"Bright red, simple, produced in large clusters. Growth extra vigorous." [GeH] "Bright red double rosettes." [NRS13/101] "Red, yellow center, small, single, tall." [Sn] "Good growth; fair foliage; blooms resemble [those of] 'Hiawatha' [Mult] —a trifle smaller and showing more copper; comes into bloom earlier than most varieties, with all flowers coming at once." [ARA18/120]

Elegance
Brownell, 1937
From 'Glenn Dale' (W) × an unnamed seedling (which resulted from a cross of 'Mary Wallace' [W] and 'Miss Lolita Armour' [HT]).

"Yellowish white, large, full, medium scent, tall." [Sn] "Double, 6- to 7-inch [ca. 1.5–1.8 dm], deep- to pale-yellow blooms, white at edges in fading. Long, strong stems; large, dark, glossy, resistant foliage. Glorious in bud and most effective bloom. For those who like exhibition-type flowers with heavy petalage, this is it. (Too big for me.) Vigorous to 15 to 20 feet [ca. 5–6.8 m] when established. If you grow it on a fence, allow 40 feet [ca. 12 m], not a rose for cramping! Very hardy. For many this is the favorite yellow climber." [W]

Elisa Robichon
Barbier, 1901
From *Rosa luciae* × 'L'Idéal' (N).

"Lilac-tinted flesh-pink." [JR26/181] "Pretty color." [ARA18/120] "Huge clusters of large, salmon-tinted flowers paling to rosy buff." [GAS] "Rose shaded pale yellow, semi-double, summer flowering. Growth vigorous." [GeH] "Trusses; single; rose, shaded old-gold. Especially good for covering banks. Holds foliage well." [ARA17/28] "A poor-shaped flower, but very effective in colouring, being a warm pink shaded with suspicion of salmon and copper; the bud is salmon coloured, and the plant a rampant grower." [NRS16/93] "Habit of a *Noisette*. Very glabrous bush; canes very smooth; thorns rare, brown, narrow, hooked; wood green, tinted dark red; petioles green and dark red, bearing two rows of distant, subsessile, oval-acuminate leaflets which are toothed like a saw; stipules longly auricled, upright; blossoms in a lax corymb; peduncles stout, uni-floral, tinted dark red, as is the globular or subturbinate calyx-tube; sepals oval-subulate, smooth, reflexing; corolla semi-double, 4–5 centimeters across [ca. 2–2¹/₂ in]; petals obovate-obtuse, notched, light lilac pink, pale yellow nub. This rose is the product of a Rosa Wichuraiana pollinated by 'L'Idéal'. It is from the same crop as 'François Foucard', 'Auguste Barbier' [Barbier, 1900; white-centered violet flowers; extinct, alas], 'René André', and 'Paul Transon'." [JR26/3–4]

Elise   Listed as 'Elsie' (W).

Elisie   Listed as 'Elsie' (W).

Elsie
syns. 'Elise', 'Elisie'
W. Paul, 1910

"Flesh-pink Wichuraiana with good trusses of flowers larger than the average." [GAS] "Fresh-coloured pink with deeper centres, large for its class, of nice rosette shape; extra large trusses. Growth vigorous." [GeH] "Pink, medium size, full, tall." [Sn] "Colored delicate flesh pink, the center of the blossom being a little darker. The form is per-

Elsie *continued*

fect and the numerous clusters last a long time. This is certainly a good development in the climbers." [JR34/85]

Émile Fortépaule

Barbier, 1903

From *Rosa wichuraiana* × 'Souvenir de Catherine Guillot' (Ch).

"Clusters of double, straw-colored flowers which fade white. One of the old Wichuraiana series." [GAS] "Tea-rose scented." [Ck] "Light yellow, medium size, full, tall." [Sn] "Vigorous bush, climbing; long bright green leaves; corymbose inflorescence; corolla very double, globular, from 5 to 7 cm across [ca. 2–2³/₄ in], white washed sulphur yellow; petals oblong, cucculate." [JR27/164] "Vigorous shrub with upright, floriferous canes bearing straight, very hooked, red thorns. Leaves long, bright green, with pointed green ciliate-glandulose stipules, 3 pairs of subsessile, oval-oblong, acuminate leaflets which are regularly toothed like a saw. Inflorescence a leafy corymb, peduncles glabrous, green or tinted red; calyx turbinate, with oblong sepals which are acuminate, reflexed, and hirsute within; corolla very double, globular, 4–5 cm across [ca. 1³/₄–2 in], white washed sulphur yellow; petals oblong, cucculate, entire or subemarginate." [JR26/5]

Emily Gray

A. H. Williams/B. R. Cant, 1918

From 'Jersey Beauty' (W) × 'Comtesse du Caÿla' (Ch).

"Deep fawn." [Ÿ] "Deep yellow, salmon center, large, full, tall." [Sn] "A new yellow climbing Rose with glossy, undulated, holly-like foliage. The buds are long and flowers of golden yellow are large and semi-double. A valuable acquisition." [C&Js24] "A marvellous Wichuraiana with foliage like [that of] *Berberis vulgaris,* great substance and very glossy; flowers rich golden yellow and almost as large as [those of] 'Mme. Ravary' [HT]. The finest yellow Wichuraiana Rose yet introduced." [GeH] "The large flowers are borne in clusters of ten or more. It is a robust grower with decidedly individual foliage of a thick, wavy texture very much like Holly. The new growth and young leaves are deep crimson. The yellow color is very fine, although it is a little paler when the flowers are open, and the plant is fairly hardy." [C-Ps25] "Now we may linger with royalty again. This large-flowered Wichuraiana has exceedingly lovely, semi-double, golden buff or tawny yellow flowers of inexpressible beauty. The foliage is marvelously glossy and fine. Alas, the tenderness of yellow climbers to frost finds it a shining example, for it needs careful protection wherever the thermometer goes below 20° F. in winter." [GAS] "With me a very shy bloomer." [NRS24/163] "Becomes hardier and blooms better as the plant ages." [C-Ps28] "In exposed places, it needs some winter protection, in the northern states, until fully established." [C-Ps30] "Prune very sparingly and retain old wood as much as possible." [C-Ps27] "Extraordinarily beautiful foliage; growth rather slight, but healthy. I did not see any flowers, but my father told me it had one or two of very beautiful yellow which faded white after the first day." [ARA24/90] "This is a hardy, strong, vigorous climber, with large, dark, glossy, mildew proof foliage of a fine bronze tone, which is very marked in the younger growth. The blooms are of a medium size, semi-double and deliciously fragrant, and are carried on long-stemmed trusses of any number up to ten. The colour is a rich orange gold, which the blooms retain until well expanded … It may perhaps be described as a glorified 'Shower of Gold' [W]." [NRS17/127] "Definitely clear yel-

low, the mature flower becoming a pleasing ecru on the second day. Then this rose has foliage so beautiful and individual that one would want it even if it did not bloom. It has a thick, waxy texture, and the young leaves are a deep crimson … [*quoting A. H. Williams:*] "Emily Gray' was the result of crossing 'Jersey Beauty' with the pollen of 'Comtesse du Caÿla'." have quite a number of seedlings from that particular cross. Most of them were strong climbers, but quite a fair proportion of them were dwarf and perpetual flowering. The foliage of all of them was good, but none had quite the robustness and individuality of 'Emily Gray'. The colors ranged from deep golden yellow through all stages of yellow to creamy white; one was coppery salmon, but it was most disappointing in that the blooms were borne on short stems and the plant is not a vigorous climber, though it was very effective pegged down.'" [ARA23/105]

Ernst Grandpierre

Weigand, 1900

From *Rosa wichuraiana* 'Bracteata' × 'Perle des Jardins' (T).

"Bright yellow, blooming in large corymbs." [JR32/172] "Yellowish white, small, full, medium scent, tall." [Sn] "A conventional, pale yellow cluster-flowering Wichuraiana of no great value." [GAS] "Yellow, small, full, very sweet, produced in corymbs. Growths very vigorous, climbing." [GeH] "Weak growth; not distinct." [ARA18/122] "The bush can be made into a climber or a groundcover. This novelty reproduces itself very well by seed. The perfume is of such sweetness that it is truly impossible to define, and is at the same time as penetrating as that of *Rosa wichuraiana*. When 'Ernst Grandpierre' is in full bloom, it is noticeable from a great distance. [*A black-and-white photo shows*] a plant of 'Ernst Grandpierre' in the form of a weeper four meters high [ca. 12 ft]. The bloom-time lasts longer than that of other climbing roses because the buds, instead of opening all at once, bloom, rather, one after the other, the clusters covering themselves with a succession of flowers. I have grown a great many specimens of 'Ernst Grandpierre' for exhibition, and have never regretted it because, in the midst of the climbing roses I have brought to exhibitions, 'Ernst Grandpierre' always sparkles like a pearl next to '[Turner's] Crimson Rambler' [Mult]." [JR26/168–169] We have as yet been unable to find any further information on *Rosa wichuraiana* 'Bracteata', this cultivar's pod-parent.

Erwin Hüttmann

Krause, 1941

"Rose-red, medium size, full, very fragrant, tall." [Sn]

Étendard

trans. "Standard"

Robichon, 1956

From 'New Dawn' (W) × an unnamed seedling.

"Scarlet red." [Ÿ]

Ethel

C. Turner, 1912

Seedling of 'Dorothy Perkins' (W).

"Blooms profusely in large trusses of semi-double flesh-pink rosettes. Late." [NRS13/101] "Whitish pink, small, lightly double, tall." [Sn] "Clear flesh-pink … Growth vigorous." [GeH] "One of the best pink climbing roses …; it stays a long time in bloom, and the large bunches of soft pink, crinkled flowers are very pretty." [ARA30/165] "Pink seedling from 'Dorothy Perkins', immortal because it bore the seed which produced 'Dr. Huey' [W]." [GAS]

Evangeline
Walsh, 1906
From *Rosa wichuraiana* × 'Turner's Crimson Rambler' (Mult).

"White edged with crimson." [Ÿ] "Lavender-pink with white centre, single, in large trusses. Growth very vigorous. Very fragrant." [GeH] "Whitish pink, medium size, single, moderate scent, tall." [Sn] "Flowers in large, loose clusters and in great abundance. The individual bloom is much like our Dog-Rose, but glorified both in size and substance." [NRS29/164] "A single flower of a bright apple blossom colour, very strongly scented—very strong grower—late flowering." [F-M] "Bloom profuse last two and a half weeks of June." [ARA18/131] "White edged, and in sunny weather suffused with blush pink; very vigorous and exquisitely fragrant. In autumn has pretty bunches of tiny orange hips." [NRS18/134] "For delicacy of coloring this Rose surpasses all others in the climbing class . . . quantities of red berries which remain on the bush until the middle of winter." [C&Js24] "The lovely pale pink blossoms are flushed dark at the edges; the individual flower is of a fair size. The trusses are long and open. A fairy-like Rose, and in a half-shaded place gives a most beautiful effect. It is one of the most rampant growers, and lends itself for growth into and over trees." [NRS16/99] "Flexible growth." [NRS13/100] "Very vigorous and sinuous. Fine foliage, large trusses of large single flowers, blush white—edged with carmine, very fragrant." [NRS29/164] "Delightful fragrance which perfumes the air for quite a distance from the plant." [ARA29/50] "This variety is very distinct; single flower, two inches in diameter [ca. 5 cm], growth very vigorous, flowers borne in large clusters. Color, white with tips of petals pink; deliciously fragrant." [C&Js09] "A good representative of the small-flowered, single, pale pink, cluster-flowering Wichuraianas. Any of a dozen similar varieties might be substituted, but this one has won favor for its peculiar fragrance and enormous vigor." [GAS] "Foliage dark green, glossy." [Th2] "A darling, 2-inch [ca. 5 cm], single pink that looks like a wild rose . . . Most growers have let this charmer fall by the wayside, yet it is one of the choicest of the Walsh introductions." [W] Evangeline, eponymous heroine of Longfellow's 1847 poem on Acadian yearnings; in a half-shaded place, she, too, gave a most beautiful effect.

[Evergreen Gem]
Horvath/Manda & Pitcher, 1898
From *Rosa wichuraiana* × 'Mme. Hoste' (T).

"Pretty buff-yellow flowers two to three inches in diameter [ca. 5–7.5 cm], perfectly double with a rich sweet-briar fragrance." [C&Js02] "Buff-yellow to white, double, in trusses. Growth vigorous." [GeH] "Small clusters, medium size, full, very fragrant, good form, short to medium stem. Growth weak; hardy. Fine foliage but sparse. Buff yellow fading to white." [ARA23/161] "Good growth and blooming qualities; resembles 'American Pillar'." [ARA18/120] "The plant grows vigorously and gives an abundance of very pretty double blossoms." [JR22/130] "Vigorous, trailing Wichuraiana with small, double, white flowers tinged with yellow in the bud. Good ground-cover." [GAS]

Excelsa
syn. 'Red Dorothy Perkins'
Walsh, 1908
"Bright scarlet red." [Ÿ] "Purple pink, small, full, tall." [Sn] "A dis-

tinct variety in form, color and habit. The color is an intense crimson-maroon, with tips of the petals tinged scarlet. Flowers are large and double, produced thirty to forty on a stem, and almost every eye produces a cluster of bright blossoms." [C&Js12] "Best red bloomer of class . . . good growth." [ARA18/120] "The most brilliant of the Wichuraiana hybrids." [NRS28/148] "Flowers in trusses, double, brilliant scarlet-crimson. Glossy green, healthy foliage. Fine for fences, walls, arches, pergolas, etc. Hardy." [ARA21/93] "Very 'climbing' and floriferous, producing some bouquets of double flowers, bright cherry red passing to scarlet, with a white center." [JR34/102] "Thick glossy foliage; late flowering." [GeH] "Good foliage which lasts especially well." [ARA17/28] "A mildewless vast improvement on '[Turner's] Crimson Rambler' [Mult]." [NRS23/178] "Resembles 'Dorothy Perkins' in growth and habit, but does not seem so liable to mildew. The colour is a fine rich scarlet crimson." [NRS13/100] "An exceedingly vigorous Wichuraiana that was high-pressured into great popularity to replace '[Turner's] Crimson Rambler', which it was wholly unfit to do. Its flowers are rosy crimson instead of scarlet, and very uncertain in shade, for many clusters have a disreputable, faded look. The foliage is so extremely subject to mildew that it is a pest. 'Bonfire' [W] and 'Fernand Rabier' [W] are ever so much better." [GAS] "This Rose is so far superior to the old '[Turner's] Crimson Rambler' as to have wholly taken its place in all wise practice. Its very double flowers, produced in immense clusters on each stem, cover a strong and vigorous plant for a longer time than most Roses of its type, and the flowers fade agreeably rather than otherwise." [C-Ps25] "Seems to have supplanted '[Turner's] Crimson Rambler' in cottage gardens." [NRS20/92] "Remove old canes at base soon after blooming, or they may mildew." [C-Ps29] "Foliage black-spots from midsummer on; bloom profuse last of June and early in July." [ARA18/131] "A joy to behold." [NRS30/249] "Quite one of the best." [NRS16/97]

Farquhar
syns. 'Boston Rambler', 'The Farquhar Rose'
Dawson/Farquhar, 1903
From *Rosa wichuraiana* × 'Turner's Crimson Rambler' (Mult).

"Blossom medium-sized, bright pink fading to pale pink and white." [JR32/172] "Clusters of small pale pink flowers. Unimportant." [GAS] "Pink-salmon, medium size, full, light scent, tall." [Sn] "Flower large, clusters of soft pink flowers, very rapid grower." [GeH] "Somewhat like 'Dorothy Perkins' [W] in bloom but more like '[Turner's] Crimson Rambler' [Mult] in habit." [C&Js09] "Foliage black-spots slightly; bloom profuse last two and a half weeks of June." [ARA18/131] "Very fine glossy foliage, well retained. Very vigorous. Might be called an early-blooming 'Dorothy Perkins'." [Th2] "The anonymous Society which has now replaced the firm Van Waveren & Son, of Hillegom (Holland), announces that Messrs. Farquhar and Company of Boston (U.S.) have entrusted it with the European sales of the new rose 'Farquhar'. This variety is a hybrid between *Rosa wichuraiana* and '[Turner's] Crimson Rambler'. It has the same characteristics and hardiness as this last; the color is pink fading to white, making an excellent contrast with the sparkling red of '[Turner's] Crimson Rambler'." [JR27/3] "Originated at Boston, Mass., and is a true hardy climber or rambler. Grows 10 to 12 feet [ca. 3.3–4 m] in a season, is entirely hardy, has handsome foliage and bears immense clusters of large double bright pink flowers, delightfully fragrant and exceedingly beautiful." [C&Js05]

Ferdinand Roussel
Barbier, 1903
From *Rosa wichuraiana* × 'Luciole' (T).

"Flesh colour, tinted with vinous red, large." [GeH] "Rather large, flesh-pink flowers stained with crimson." [GAS] "Light purple-red, small, full, tall." [Sn] "Climbing shrub, leaves medium-sized; corolla very double, wide-spreading, from 6 to 9 cm across [ca. 2½–3½ in]; petals cuneiform, slightly toothed at the tip, intense wine red." [JR27/164] "Shrub very bushy, glabrous, very thorny, wood tinted red; thorns straight, long and narrow. Leaves medium-sized or small, with two rows of leaflets which are oval short, subsessile, and edged with large saw-like teeth; petiole very slender and armed with pink prickles; stipules petite, ciliate-glandular. Peduncles uni-floral, red, slender; calyx with tube which is subspherical, with long subulate sepals of green and red; corolla double, wide-spreading, 3–4 cm across [ca. 1–1½ in]; petals cuneiform, slightly dentate at the tip, intense vinous red." [JR26/4]

Fernand Krier
Walter, 1925
Sport of 'Excelsa' (W).

"A sport of 'Excelsa' with peach-pink flowers." [GAS] "Pink, sometimes red, medium size, full, tall." [Sn]

Fernand Rabier
Turbat, 1918
From 'Delight' (W) × an unnamed seedling.

"Deep scarlet-red flowers." [ARA20/123] "A needed addition to the Perkins group, being two shades deeper than 'Excelsa' [W] . . . The color of this Rose is deep crimson-scarlet, almost as dark as the 'Dr. Huey' Rose [W]." [C-Ps28] "Almost as dark as 'Dr. Huey', but stands sun better." [C-Ps30] "A gorgeous, glowing scarlet, cluster-flowered Wichuraiana better than 'Excelsa'." [GAS] "The flowers are of good size, double, perfectly formed, pure deep scarlet, and are produced in large, erect corymbs of forty to fifty. Very vigorous and floriferous." [ARA19/101] "Deep red, medium size, lightly double, light scent, tall." [Sn]

Fernand Tanne
Tanne/Turbat, 1920

"Rather large yellow buds and flowers creamy-white when open. Pretty, but only one of many like it." [GAS] "Large, full, double; deep yellow passing to cream-yellow; Tea fragrance. Vigorous." [ARA21/160] "Deep yellow, large, full, very fragrant, tall." [Sn]

Flora Mitten   Listed as 'Miss Flora Mitten' (W).

Fragezeichen
trans. "Question Mark"
Böttner, 1910
From 'Dorothy Perkins' (W) × 'Marie Baumann' (HP).

"The most beautiful pink climbing rose. Flower large, full, in large bloom clusters, deep pink with lighter shadings. Big blossom, gorgeous large glossy green leaves, absolutely healthy." [Ck] "Pink, large, lightly double, tall." [Sn]

Fraîcheur
trans. "Freshness"
Turbat, 1921

"Pale lilac rose. One of the prettiest of its colour." [NRS29/248]

"Yields wonderful pyramidal trusses of a most exquisite soft tender pink colour. As I have seen it it surpasses all the pale pink ramblers." [NRS24/216] "One of the very late-blooming Wichuraianas, with pyramidal clusters of pale pink flowers." [GAS] "Pink, small, full, tall." [Sn] "Very lasting, soft pink blooms in pyramidal cluster. Foliage glossy dark green. Very vigorous." [ARA22/148]

François Foucard
syn. 'François Fouchard'
Barbier, 1900
From *Rosa luciae* × 'L'Idéal' (N).

"Cream white." [JR26/181] "Semi-double blossom, beautiful yellow passing to cream white." [JR32/172] "The buds of 'François Foucard' are beautiful, pointed and of a bright golden yellow opening to blossoms of a uniform light yellow, fading quickly to creamy white. The flowers are rather like those of 'Gardenia' [*probably referring to the Wichuraiana; but there was also an HT by the same name*] but smaller, a trifle fuller, and paler in colour." [NRS11/27] "Lemon-yellow, semi-double flowers. Said to have a Noisette strain." [GAS] "An early flowering Wichuraiana, pale lemon yellow flowers, medium size, slightly more perpetual than most of this class. Makes a good weeping standard." [F-M] "Light yellow, medium size, lightly double, tall." [Sn] "Small grower; bloom attractive, somewhat shy." [ARA18/120] "Pale yellow-lemon, beautiful bud. Growth vigorous; almost perpetual." [GeH]

François Fouchard   Listed as 'François Foucard' (W).

François Guillot
Barbier, 1905
From *Rosa wichuraiana* × 'Mme. Laurette Messimy' (Ch).

"Milk white." [Ÿ] "Yellow, white and pink. Growth vigorous." [GeH] "One of the early attempts at a yellow Wichuraiana. Pretty much like 'Gardenia' [*probably referring to the Wichuraiana; but there was also an HT of the same name*], with faintly yellow buds and very double white flowers. Rampantly vigorous." [GAS] "Climbing plant, vigorous and extremely floriferous. Foliage dark green, glossy. Buds yellowish white; flowers superb, 8–10 cm across [ca. 3½–4 in], double, milk white, dark yellow anthers. Magnificent variety producing a grand effect." [JR30/23] "Yellowish white, medium size, full, light scent, tall." [Sn] "Small growth; blooms large and double." [ARA18/122] "A rampant grower and very floriferous, with creamy white flowers, which turn almost dead white, and are well shaped. This is quite one of the best, and has glossy deep green foliage." [NRS16/93] "A good double white climber, blooming freely, and entirely worth while." [ARA18/91]

François Juranville
Barbier, 1906
From *Rosa wichuraiana* × 'Mme. Laurette Messimy' (Ch).

"A most charming salmon pink colour." [NRS16/95] "Fresh pink." [Ÿ] "Deep fawn-pink, with apple fragrance. Growth very vigorous. Weeping standard." [GeH] "Described abroad as a vigorous Wichuraiana with large or very large semi-double flowers of ruddy pink, tinged with salmon, but all specimens seen here [U.S.A.] are pale flesh-colored, cluster-flowered Wichuraianas of no particular note." [GAS] "Blossoms very large, full, very prettily colored fresh pink. Foliage large, glossy dark green. Very vigorous plant." [JR30/167] "Growth and foliage good; flowers pretty, not abundant." [ARA18/120] "I should put 'François Juranville' almost at the head of the Wichuraiana list for lovely foliage, good-sized individual flowers of a strawberry-pink, and some fragrance; it is never 'sick' and grows anywhere." [ARA19/86] "One of the most graceful pink ramblers we have. It is a rampant grower with flexible bronzy green stems and few thorns. The foliage is a glossy medium green, bronzy green when young; not liable to mildew. The flowers are freely produced in small trusses. They are fairly large, loosely double and of a beautiful shade of rosy salmon pink." [NRS13/94] "It has extra vigorous growth and a rambling, drooping habit. The stems are smooth and green, bronzing on the sunny side in autumn, armed with a moderate number of sharp thorns usually about an inch apart [ca. 2.5 cm], which are red when young and but very slightly hooked. The foliage is magnificent, of a dark green, covering the plant well to the ground, the under surface is slightly glossy, and the upper so much as to give an appearance of having been highly polished. It is not subject to mildew. It has only one true flowering period, though no doubt occasionally a late flower may be found. The first flower opened with me on the 26th June, 1910, and it has a moderate duration of flowering, lasting about six weeks. It is thus one of the mid-season wichuraianas. The flowers are large for its class, rather loose and double, freely produced and carried in small clusters, the buds and very young flowers are a coppery rose, opening to salmon rose, the petals having a faint yellow base. It is very fragrant, the scent being of a fruity character, somewhat resembling [that of] apples. To some of my friends it recalls the scent of the wild briar ... It may be used as a pillar, arch or pergola, or as a weeping standard. The strong points of this Rose are its beautiful colour, its perfume, its freedom of growth and flower, and fine foliage." [NRS11/41–42]

François Poisson
Barbier, 1902
From *Rosa wichuraiana* × 'William Allen Richardson' (N).

"Pure white." [JR26/181] "Light yellow, large, full, tall." [Sn] "A rose of the 'Albéric Barbier' [W] type, with double white flowers tinged yellow. Look out for the Noisette strain in this *yellow* Wichuraiana." [GAS] "Growth and foliage fair; attractive color; blooms quite well." [ARA18/120] "Climbing bush, vigorous. Inflorescence in a corymb, upright. Corolla quite double, from 5 to 7 cm across [ca. 2–2³/₄ in], white with a yellow center; petals cuneiform, those of the interior imbricated and upright." [JR28/155] "Vigorous bush, glabrous, having the habit of a *Noisette* rose. Canes upright, twisted, green tinted red, armed with wide red thorns. Leaves glossy deep green, slender glandulose petiole; joints prickly, red; 3 pairs of subsessile leaflets bordered with pointed and serrate saw-like teeth; very sharp stipules. Inflorescences in leafy bouquets, corymbiform, upright; peduncles strongly glandular, red; calyx-tube subspherical, green; sepals oval, much subulate, green, reflexing; corolla quite double, 4–5 cm across [ca. 1¹/₂–2 in], pure white; petals cuneiform, not notched, interior petals narrow and muddled. This variety sprang from a crop of *R. wichuraiana* pollinated by the variety 'William Allen Richardson' [N]." [JR26/4]

Frau A. von Brauer
Lambert, 1912
From 'Farquhar' (W) × 'Schneewittchen' (Pol); or from 'Farquhar' (W) × a seedling (which resulted from crossing *Rosa wichuraiana* and 'Turner's Crimson Rambler' [Mult]).

"Clusters of small white flowers which turn pink with age." [GAS]

"Whitish pink, small, very full, medium scent, tall." [Sn] "Fair growth; blooms inferior to others of same type." [ARA18/122] "Canes 2.5–4 m [ca. 7¹/₂–12 ft]. The general characteristics are those of ['Freifrau von Marschall'], of which this is the sister. The color of the blossom is pure white, with some flesh when the petals are about to fall. The thyrses are longer than [those of 'Freifrau von Marschall'], and grow to 30–35 cm [ca. 1 ft to 1 ft 2 in]. The flowers keep several weeks without falling. Very fragrant, this novelty is the best of all the white Wichuraianas." [JR37/9]

Frau Albert Hochstrasser
Weigand, 1906

"Flower yellow, changing to white, very sweet. Growth vigorous." [GeH] "Late-flowering Wichuraiana of 'Albéric Barbier' type. Buds said to be golden yellow." [GAS] "Pink, small, full, very fragrant, tall." [Sn]

Frau Liesel Brauer
Thönges, 1938

"Pink, medium size, lightly double, light scent, tall." [Sn]

Frau Marie Weinbach
Weigand, 1906

"White-flowered Wichuraiana with small blooms in gigantic clusters." [GAS] "White, small, full, medium scent, tall." [Sn]

Fraulein Octavia Hesse
H. A. Hesse, 1910
From *Rosa wichuraiana* × 'Kaiserin Auguste Viktoria' (HT).

"A yellowish creamy white, and the blooms have moderate fragrance. Though it is a delicate looking flower, it seems to get through the winter here [New Bedford, Mass.]." [ARA22/44] "Good, full petalled, flat, round flower in small trusses. Pure white, but flushed with yellow at centre, which gives a solidity to the look of the flower. The best and most distinctive white." [NRS16/96] "Yellowish white, small, full, light scent, tall." [Sn] "*Recurrent* bloom along with a vigorous habit. The small, double, yellowish-white flowers have darker yellow centers, and they are fragrant." [W] "A rampant grower with flexible light green stems. The foliage is fine, glossy, light green and free from mildew. The flowers are freely produced in small trusses. They are large, double, of good form; they are creamy white." [NRS13/95] "Good growth and foliage; bloom attractive, not profuse." [ARA18/120] "A very good but little-known Wichuraiana, with clusters of very double white flowers, deep yellow in the center. A very distinct rose, but watch out for winter damage." [GAS]

Freifrau von Marschall
Lambert, 1912
From 'Farquhar' (W) × 'Schneewittchen' (Pol).

"Clusters of bright pink flowers. Reported to be almost thornless." [GAS] "Yellowish pink, small, full, tall." [Sn] "Very vigorous plant giving canes 2–3 m long [ca. 6–9 ft] with occasional but very strong stipulary thorns. Foliage ample, very bright green. Blossoms in thyrses which are long and pyramidal; flowers small, full, well formed, very delicate light pink, staying fresh a long time, even after cutting. It is, *par excellence,* a rose to decorate espaliers, pillars, and garlands, and to make weepers." [JR37/9]

Gardenia

Horvath/Manda & Pitcher, 1899
From *Rosa wichuraiana* × 'Perle des Jardins' (T).

"Flower medium-sized, blooming in large corymbs, yellowish white passing to Gardenia white." [JR22/172] "Pure white, yellow bud." [Ÿ] "The buds of 'Gardenia' are a bright amber yellow always more or less streaked with carmine." [NRS11/26] "The very long buds are a sparkling yellow before opening, the open flower becoming white. The form resembles that of the blossom of the Gardenia, hence the name." [JR22/130] "Buds bright yellow; open flowers, lovely cream color, three to four inches in diameter [ca. 7.5 cm to 1 dm], delightfully fragrant." [C&Js02] "Deep, rich golden yellow flowers, passing to creamy white. Blooms profusely and is hardy as an oak. Flowers large and fine for cutting." [C&Js21] "Exquisite in the bud, useful for all purposes except as a weeping standard as the growths are too stiff. Early flowering." [F-M] "Yellowish white, medium size, full, very fragrant, tall." [Sn] "Bright yellow to cream, early summer flowering. Growth very vigorous." [GeH] "Strong grower with large green foliage. Flowers produced singly on stems one-half to one foot long [ca. 1.5–3 dm]; when in bud hardly distinguishable from 'Perle [des Jardins]', bright yellow, and when open cream color, three to three and one-half inches in diameter [ca. 7.5–9 cm], incurving towards evening to perfect imitation of [the] Gardenia, or Cape Jasmine, hence its name. Flowers are delightfully fragrant, and produced freely." [CA01] "The flowers are large, pale yellow in the bud, almost white when open. It is a tremendous grower, with extremely handsome foliage, and is, perhaps, the finest climber of this type. In spite of its fame as a 'Hardy Maréchal Niel', it is not reliably hardy in severe climates. I was never able to keep more than a few inches of the top alive in eastern Ohio." [GAS] "Blooms better on old wood." [C-Pf31] "Foliage very good and lasts well. Do not confound with 'Gardenia' [HT] of Soupert & Notting, which is inferior." [ARA17/28] "Fine glossy foliage, persistent, plentiful. Growth very vigorous; hardy." [ARA23/162] "The foliage lasts a long time on the plants and is practically evergreen—it is free from mildew." [NRS11/25] "Foliage black-spots very slightly, mildews in later summer; bloom moderate most of June." [ARA18/131] "A beautiful Rose, but not growing very vigorously or flowering very profusely with me." [NRS16/96] "Of rampantly vigorous growth, with numerous long canes that will go anywhere, and which produce in early summer quantities of pleasing small yellow buds opening to creamy white. The foliage is very good and would justify this Rose even if it had only a few blooms." [C-Ps28] "Good foliage; fairly good growth; somewhat lacking in number of canes; color pretty—most attractive in bud." [ARA18/120] "Finely formed, rich yellow buds, opening into medium to large, double gardenia-like flowers of creamy white, borne singly or in clusters and lasting well; quite fragrant. Foliage excellent and plentiful, nearly evergreen. Very vigorous climber if trained, as it has a tendency to trail; rampant, bushy growth; medium to long stems; profuse bloomer. Best for walls, fences, and banks. Hardy." [ARA21/93]

Garisenda

Gaetano, Bonfiglioli & figlio, 1911
From *Rosa wichuraiana* × 'Souvenir de la Malmaison' (B).

"Medium-sized, delicate rose-pink flowers, much like those of the old 'Souvenir de la Malmaison', which was one of its parents." [GAS] "Light pink, medium size, very full, tall." [Sn] "Good growth and blooming qualities; large, attractive flowers." [ARA18/120] "This very interesting newcomer . . . carries on its mother's large growth and way of blooming in big clusters of 20–30 large blossoms; from 'Souvenir de la Malmaison' it takes its pretty color, its form, and to some degree its large flower. This very remarkable variety is very floriferous; and when its flesh pink blossoms are fully open, the effect is truly incomparable and imposing, superior to the most part of known Wichuraiana hybrids. The bloom takes place when other roses are nearly done and lasts for a fairly long time." [JR35/133]

Gaston Lesieur

Turbat, 1915

"Bright red Wichuraiana of 'Excelsa' type." [GAS] "A variety similar to 'Excelsa', with bright red double flowers produced in clusters. Growth very vigorous, climbing." [GeH] "Red, medium size, full, tall." [Sn]

Général Testard

syn. 'Général Tétard'
Pajotin-Chédane, 1918
Sport of 'American Pillar' (W).

"Red obverse, white center." [Ÿ] "Red, white center, small, lightly double, tall." [Sn]

Général Tétard   Listed as 'Général Testard' (W).

Gerbe Rose

trans. 'Pink Cluster'
Fauque-Laurent/Vigneron, 1904
From *Rosa wichuraiana* × 'Baronne Adolphe de Rothschild' (HP).

"Delicate pink." [Ÿ] "A charming Wichuraiana with the pleasant habit of blooming a little in autumn. The flowers are fairly large, clear light pink, and slightly fragrant." [GAS] "Pure pink; cupped; good foliage; fragrant." [GeH] "Tolerably well known as a fine, large-flowered '[Mme. Caroline] Testout' [HT] pink Rose, with grand almost evergreen foliage." [NRS18/151] "A large, pale pink, double flower growing one to a stem, throws a large crop at first, then makes a new growth and bloom again on the new wood, thus providing a long season of flowers." [ARA22/43] "Pink, large, full, medium scent, tall." [Sn] "Very vigorous climbing shrub, foliage glossy deep green. Flowers double, large, cupped, opening well. Very beautifully colored delicate pink, resembling 'Baronne Adolphe de Rothschild' [HP]. Distinct and very beautiful variety." [JR28/154] "Nearly thornless." [Cat12] "Delightfully smooth, thick rods and large persistent green leaves." [NRS17/49] "Often a great dearth of strong basal shoots. Such obstinacy may often be overcome by bending down one or more of the existing stems to the ground for a few weeks in the spring. This will cause the buds near the base, which would otherwise have remained dormant, to start into growth and to form the strong stems that we desire. A similar result may be arrived at by cutting back the stem to within a foot or two of the ground [ca. 3–6 dm]." [NRS12/151–152] "A rigid upright grower with almost thornless stems, not so rampant as most. The foliage is dense, with large leaflets of a bright deep glossy green; persistent and mildew proof. The flowers are produced in small trusses; they are large for their class, double, of good form; they are a beautiful rich pink colour. One of the most sweetly fragrant of Roses." [NRS13/95]

Glenn Dale

syn. 'V.F.3'
Van Fleet/American Rose Society, 1927

From *Rosa wichuraiana* × possibly 'Isabella Sprunt' (T).

"Very pretty yellowish white Wichuraiana of the 'Gardenia' [W] type, but not enough different to be wildly exciting." [GAS] "Light yellow, large, lightly double, light scent, tall." [Sn] "Disseminated in 1927 by the American Rose Society. It is a vigorous climber, with tawny yellow buds, gradually opening to large, semi-double, creamy flowers fading pure white." [C-Ps29] "Among the finest of the white climbers. Graceful ivory buds; large, very double (30 to 50 petals), snow-white flowers in great clusters on long, strong stems. Dark, leathery, resistant foliage. Grows to 10 feet [ca. 3.3 m], an excellent pillar rose, and very hardy." [W] "Is resistant to black-spot and mildew." [C-Ps31] "*Boone* reports that it is one of the finest climbers he has in Idaho … It is attractive at Breeze Hill, but so much like dozens of others that the impression it makes is very watery." [ARA31/191] "A perfectly hardy and vigorous but not rampant climber, with heavy, dark green, Hybrid-Tea-like foliage, which does not spot or mildew. The lemon-colored buds are long, beautiful, and uniform in shape, like a Hybrid Tea. They are borne singly or in clusters of up to twenty flowers on one lateral, which can be separately cut. The flowers, which are slightly fragrant, open to white, and are produced in one crop. As this rose is a true climber, without tendency to form a bush, it can be so treated to advantage; when trained on a pillar, the heavy laterals droop and the buds give the pillar an appearance like a shower of stars. This variety is commended as different from any other climbing rose, particularly in its exquisite buds; and while it gives, while open, the general appearance of 'Silver Moon' [Lv], it is not so unmanageable in its growth." [ARA27/213]

Golden Climber Listed as 'Mrs. Arthur Curtiss James' (W).

Golden Glow
Brownell, 1937
From 'Glenn Dale' (W) × seedling (resulting from a cross of 'Mary Wallace' [W] and an HT).

"Yellow, large, full, medium scent, tall." [Sn] "A beauty, with double 3½-to 5-inch [ca. 9 cm to 1.3 dm] high-centered, spectrum-yellow flowers in abundance in June and well into July. The foliage is dark, leathery, and glossy. Vigorous to 20 feet either up or trailing [ca. 6.6 m]. The fragrance is of tea." [W] Not to be confused with the Pernetiana of the same name.

Golden Orange Climber
Brownell, 1937
Sport of 'Mrs. Arthur Curtiss James' (W).

"Orange yellow, large, lightly double, tall." [Sn] "Has considerable orange and orange-red in the gold." [W]

Golden Rambler Listed as 'Easlea's Golden Rambler' (W).

Greta Fey
Strassheim, 1909
"Clusters of fragrant and attractive creamy pink flowers." [GAS] "Whitish pink, small, lightly double, tall." [Sn]

Grevinde Silvia Knuth
D. T. Poulsen, 1913
"White, yellow center, small, lightly double, tall." [Sn]

Gruss an Freundorf!
trans. "Greetings to Freundorf!"
Praskač, 1913
From 'Rubra' (W) × 'Turner's Crimson Rambler' (Mult).

"Splendid, semi-double, deep velvety crimson flowers, not quite as maroon as [those of] 'Dr. Huey' [W], and borne in clusters; does not burn in the hot sun." [C-Ps29] "Its large flowers are very dark red, with a distinct white eye at the base of the petals. It bloomed heavily, keeping on a long time." [ARA22/44] "Red, white center, medium size, lightly double, tall." [Sn] "The rose which I have grown under this name is a vigorous Multiflora bearing huge clusters of deep velvety maroon-red flowers … [I]t is described abroad as a creeper, which the rose I know is not; but true to name or not, it is a superb variety of its type." [GAS] "Magnificent and precious new introduction in this class of climbers. The blossoms appear in large, bright, not very dense bouquets; some grow 4–5 cm across [ca. 2 in]. They are semi-full, with white nubs—sometimes some petals are spattered with pure white—and the anthers are golden yellow. Bright crimson red at the beginning, they become deep blackish red when completely open (the color of 'Prince Camille de Rohan' [HP]) to grand effect. This climbing variety has a long bloom season. The stems are 30–40 cm long [ca. 12–14 in], and the cut flowers last a long time in water. Of great vigor, the growths attain 3–4 m in a year [ca. 9–12 ft]; they are strongly armed with thorns. The small foliage is bright dark green. This sort, of rapid, rampant growth, is good particularly to edge ponds, cover rocky outcroppings, and, as well, as a border in place of ivy. As a cemetery rose, and for arches, it produces an effect unseen till now. It is, without a doubt, the most precious climbing rose of its color. 'Gruss an Freundorf!' is in red what 'Dorothy Perkins' [W] is in pink—it's a magnificent sequel to this latter." [JR38/73]

Harlequin
F. Cant, 1935
Sport of 'Excelsa' (W).

"Pink and dark red, small, full, tall." [Sn] Not to be confused with the Gallicas of the same name. Harlequin, the restless inamorato of Columbine in the *Commedia del'Arte*, particularly featured at present in the ever-delightful pantomime at Tivoli Gardens in Copenhagen.

Heart of Gold
syn. 'W.M. 5'
Van Fleet/American Rose Society & U.S. Dept. of Agriculture, 1926
From a seedling (resulting from a cross of *Rosa wichuraiana* and *R. setigera*) × *R. moyesii*.

"Red, white center, medium size, single, tall." [Sn] "Bud medium size; flower medium size, single, open, lasting, crimson shading to white at center with yellow stamens, borne in clusters on medium-length stems. Foliage abundant, medium size, rich green, glossy. Vigorous (10 feet), trailing,; profuse bloomer for four weeks in May and June. Very hardy." [ARA25/193] "The name of this Rose does not refer to the general colour but only to the golden stamens. The Rose is a very deep crimson with a band of clear white separating the crimson from the gold. Foliage is good throughout the season and not liable to Mildew or Black Spot. Habit is good and plant is exceptionally healthy and hardy." [GeH] "A free-growing climber with dark foliage resistant to disease. Flowers single, 2 to 3 inches across [ca. 5–7.5 cm], in large panicles, dark purplish crimson with white center and a

Heart of Gold *continued*

mass of showy golden stamens. Little fragrance." [C-Ps26] "It is christened 'Heart of Gold' by reason of its abundant stamens, showing in the center of a large and beautiful 'blackish crimson' (as Dr. Van Fleet called it) single flower in which a band of clear white separates the crimson and the gold . . . The plant is vigorous and sightly as a bush or pillar rose, covered with bloom in June." [ARA24/18] "Of no importance except that it was introduced as a hybrid of *R. wichuraiana* × the remarkable *R. moyesi*[*i*], which is highly dubious. The single, dark red flowers are large, white in the center, with enormous clusters of yellow stamens. Pretty at times, but fades disgustingly in hot seasons." [GAS] "Does not seem to do very well in France." [ARA28/129]

"'Heart of Gold' first puts into rose circulation absolutely new blood through the rare red Chinese *Rosa Moyesi* [*sic*] . . . as its pollen parent. The resulting plant, with the vigor of its Wichuraiana parent, and carrying foliage of enduring character good-looking throughout the season, is strong in growth and can be treated as a bush or pillar rose, or as a low climber. The plant in the Editor's garden has been with little effort kept in the fan shape made necessary by its location, and in June it is a wonderful sight, covered as it is for many days with its strikingly distinct and handsome single flowers. These are produced day after day, and they fade as they age to an agreeable lighter shade, and fall cleanly, so that for several weeks the plant is an object of the utmost attractiveness. Allowed to scramble on itself, it forms a bush of much the same type as 'Mary Wallace'. It is believed to be quite as hardy and dependable as that utterly different rose. Its foliage has not shown liability to either mildew or black-spot. Dr. Van Fleet thought well of it, for in the 1919 Annual he wrote: 'The plant appears exceptionally healthy and hardy'." [ARA25/69–70] "The most striking [*of Van Fleet's Moyesii hybrids*] is W.S. No. 5, with an unnamed Wichuraiana-Setigera hybrid as seed parent. This, at four years from germination, forms a fine plant with arching shoots six to eight feet high [ca. 2–2.6 m], covered in June with blackish crimson single blooms nearly three inches across [ca. 7.5 cm]. Even the filaments of the stamens are colored, as in *R. Moyesii*, but the petals have a white base, making a striking contrast with the deep coloring of the other portions of the flower. The plant appears exceptionally healthy and hardy, and will be propagated for dissemination and trial." [ARA19/32]

Henri Barruet

Barbier, 1918

"The bud is deep yellow at first, passing, while expanding, to coppery and clear yellow, and finally to white tinted lilaceous rose when fully open. The large flowers are borne in clusters of eight to fifteen, and the varying shades are effective. Strong grower; profuse bloomer." [ARA19/101] "Deep yellow in the bud state and changing to coppery yellow and clear yellow when opening, with edged purple-rose petals, passing to white tinted with lilac-rose and veined carmine when fully open; of fair size, produced in large clusters. Growth vigorous, climbing." [GeH] "A strange Wichuraiana with double flowers much like [those of] 'André Louis' [W] in form and size, but curiously tinted with coppery tones, yellow, and purplish pink. Scarcely a prize beauty but very interesting and would be more important if its foliage were not so defective." [GAS]

Huguette Despiney   Listed as 'Mme. Huguette Despiney' (W).

Île de France

Nonin, 1922

From 'American Pillar' (W) × a seedling.

"Bright red, white center." [Ÿ] "Enormous trusses of crimson flowers with white centres. Very effective." [NRS24/216] "Splendid Wichuraiana with huge clusters of semi-double, vivid pink flowers of almost the same brilliant effect as 'American Pillar'. It remains in bloom a long time and fades very little." [GAS] "A light red 'American Pillar', possibly an improvement. If it holds its red in the off seasons when 'American Pillar' has such a perfectly awful mushroom color, it will be worth having." [ARA27/134] "A semi-double form of the great 'American Pillar' Rose, but somewhat more cerise in the coloring, which it holds better in hot weather. Blooms come in large clusters." [C-Ps31] "Better bloom [*than has 'American Pillar'*], though not in as large heads; growth not so unruly." [ARA28/161] "Red, white center, medium size, lightly double, light scent, tall." [Sn] "Bud small, ovoid; flower medium size, semi-double, open, very lasting; bright scarlet, white center; slight fragrance. Very vigorous, grows 15 to 20 feet high [ca. 5–6.6 m]; profuse and continuous bloomer for five weeks. Hardy." [ARA24/172] "It will thrive almost anywhere and is universally admired." [C-Ps29]

Jacotte

Barbier, 1920

From *Rosa wichuraiana* × 'Arthur R. Goodwin' (Pern).

"Coppery orange." [Ÿ] "Large flowers of reddish copper, heavily shaded with yellow and quite fragrant." [C-Ps28] "The colour is rich coppery salmon, with saffron yellow base. The buds are a delightful shade of orange and yellow, tinted orange red, semi-double. The foliage is rich green and glistening." [NRS24/216] "The holly-like foliage makes it ornamental, even when out of bloom." [C-Ps30] "Coppery yellow, medium size, lightly double, medium scent, tall." [Sn] "Bud large, ovoid, orange and yellow; flower large, semi-double, open, cupped, very lasting; deep coppery yellow, tinted coppery red; borne several together, on long, strong stem; fragrant. Foliage abundant, leathery, glossy, dark green, of medium size, disease-resistant. Bark green; many thorns. Very vigorous, climbing, trailing habit; blooms profusely in May and June; hardy." [ARA22/149] "An astonishingly lovely, large-flowered Wichuraiana with bright orange-yellow blooms as large as those of Hybrid Teas. Hardier than most yellow-tinted climbers, with foliage of extraordinary beauty. Worth protecting in exposed gardens." [GAS] "Rich glossy foliage, but as hardy as any Wichuraiana and deliciously fragrant . . . It produces its best blooms after you have it planted two years." [C-Ps27] "Has . . . the richest fragrance of any climber. The flowers are semi-double, reddish copper and yellow, the plant has enormous thorns and holly-like foliage, and it will make 15 or 20-foot canes [ca. 5–6.6 m]." [CaRol/6/3] "Kills back in winter here. —*Washington, D.C.*; . . . Had it only this season; flowers of extreme beauty but has not grown well. —*Harrisburg, Pa.*" [ARA26/116] "Branches very brittle, and hard to train as they break readily . . . *Washington, D.C.*; . . . Dies back . . . *Wash.*; Very vigorous, with very little bloom . . . *B.C.*; One short blooming season. Unsuitable for this district . . . *Calif.*; Very attractive in flower and foliage. Has been difficult to establish at Breeze Hill and has made only moderate growth. Flowers very brilliant but fleeting—like small editions of 'Independence Day' [Pern]. Probably best hardy climber of its color."

[ARA28/165] "Rapidly and deservedly approaching the top in popularity." [C-Ps30] "A startling new color in climbing Roses." [C-Ps25]

Jean Girin
G. Girin, 1910

"Bright pink." [Ÿ] "Pink, medium size, full, tall." [Sn] "A pink Wichuraiana of the 'Dorothy Perkins' [W] type. Sometimes blooms in the autumn." [GAS] "The flowers are similar in form and color to the pink 'Dorothy Perkins'. The chief merit of this Rose is that after giving a mass of bloom in June, like the other climbers, it blooms again . . . Cut off all the old June blooms to help the plant produce more flowers during the summer and fall." [C&Js24] "Bloom abundant last two and a half weeks of June, moderate but occasional in July and August." [ARA18/131] "Flower pink, double, in clusters. Growth very vigorous." [GeH] "Rampant, flexible growth. Blooms in fine trusses of double pink rosettes. Said to be perpetual." [NRS13/101] "Tall, rather straggly growth; . . . quite a good bloomer—on order of 'Dorothy Perkins'." [ARA18/120] "Absolutely hardy as a climber . . . In the fall has a second blooming period, when it gives approximately half the number of blooms produced in the spring. Foliage lasts quite well." [ARA17/28] "This pretty Rose kept if not the entirety then at least a part of the characters which distinguish the Wichura roses from the Polyanthas or Multifloras. Its leaflets always have the bright varnish which seems to cover those of the Type; they are also a shorter oval, and thicker in texture. What is more, they are very glabrous." [JR35/169] "Vigorous shrub, very climbing, blooming in big corymbs; foliage of a beautiful bright green; blossom a bright medium pink, perfect in form and quite double, opening easily; the base of the petals in blush white with the reverse light bright pink; stamens grouped together, making a yellow area in the middle of the flowers, which come over a long period of time and last a good while, fading to delicate pink at the time the petals fall. This variety makes a superb weeper, constantly in bloom . . . From a Wichuraiana seedling." [JR34/168]

Jean Guichard
Barbier, 1905
From *Rosa wichuraiana* × 'Souvenir de Catherine Guillot' (Ch).

"Blossom large, bright carminy salmon fading to carmine pink." [JR32/172] "Showy, cluster-flowered Wichuraiana with yellowish red buds and bright salmon flowers." [GAS] "Salmon-pink-red, medium size, full, tall." [Sn] "Coppery carmine to salmon-rose. Growth very vigorous; weeping standard." [GeH] "Fair growth; bloom very distinct." [ARA18/120] "Of rampant flexible growth, with stems of coppery bronze to dark green. Foliage is dark green and glossy, and not liable to mildew. Flowers very freely in small trusses. The buds are bronzy crimson and open to large, flat, very double blooms of coppery pink. They are very fragrant." [NRS13/97] "Climbing shrub, very vigorous, floriferous. Beautiful glossy foliage. Bud vermilion red mixed with yellow and bright red. Flower from 7 to 8 cm across [ca. 2³/₄–3 in], quite full, bright carmine salmon going to carmine pink, a new coloration in the climbing roses." [JR30/23]

Jean L'Hoste
M. Congy/Cochet-Cochet, 1926
From 'Alexandre Girault' (W) × 'Gerbe Rose' (W).

"Large-flowered Wichuraiana with bright pink flowers, tinted white at the base of the petals." [GAS] "Pink, white center, medium size, full, tall." [Sn] "Very vigorous climbing growth with clear green glossy foliage, very resistant to disease. Flowers large, double, rosy carmine, base of petals flesh-white, and are produced in corymbs of 50 to 100 blooms." [GeH]

Jeanne Richert
Walter, 1929
From 'Léontine Gervaise' (W) × seedling.

"Cluster-flowered Wichuraiana with cream-colored blooms tinged with reddish brown in the center." [GAS] "Yellowish white, medium size, full, tall." [Sn]

Jersey Beauty
Horvath/Manda & Pitcher, 1899
From *Rosa wichuraiana* × 'Perle des Jardins' (T).

"White, shaded with yellow." [Ÿ] "Blossom large, single, pale yellow, beautifully effective in bloom." [JR32/172] "Elegant single flowers three inches in diameter [ca. 7.5 cm], pale yellow, very fragrant and a tremendous bloomer." [C&Js02] "Light yellow, large, single, medium scent, tall." [Sn] "Chrome-yellow to cream, single, small trusses, early, evergreen. Growth vigorous." [GeH] "A single rose, with numerous stamens of the most sparkling yellow color. The magnificently green foliage produces as pretty an effect as you could hope for." [JR22/130] "A very rampant grower with fine, flexible stems. The foliage is dark glossy green and is quite evergreen. The blossoms are produced in the greatest profusion in medium trusses on long stems. The buds are golden yellow, and open to large cream coloured single blooms with fine golden stamens." [NRS13/96] "A valuable trailing Wichuraiana with remarkably handsome foliage and large, single flowers of creamy yellow. Superb thing for covering banks in climates where it does not winter-kill. Difficult to obtain true-to-name." [GAS] "*The Garden* announces that the rose 'Jersey Beauty' will be a great success in the garden. Of substantial growth, which is to say that it is very 'climbing', it can easily be used for training on walls, buildings, rustic bridges, and colonnades. Grafted onto high stems of the Briar [*i.e., tree rose or standard style*], it will make admirable weepers. Its very well-formed buds are a beautiful light cream yellow. This variety . . . was admired by visitors to the Temple Show [*in London; forerunner of the Chelsea Garden Show*], where it was exhibited." [JR24/113] "A beautiful Rose, but with me it has not grown so vigorously or flowered in profusion sufficiently to make the show it may in warmer localities." [NRS16/96]

"Perhaps the strongest and most rampant of the hybrid 'wichs'. It has very vigorous stems, of a very branching and droopy habit, which are armed with fairly regular, nearly straight and sharp thorns, and carry a dense mass of dark green, thick, glossy foliage, lasting so long on the plant as to be practically evergreen. The foliage is carried well down to the base of the plant, and it is quite free from mildew. It has practically only one flowering period, though an occasional flower may be found in the autumn until the frosts come. In my garden the first flower opened on the 14th June . . . and it continued to bloom until the end of July . . . The flowers are large and single, carried in small clusters and freely produced. The blossoms have a certain fragrance, but it is not very great. The buds I call a bright cinnamon yellow, and the flowers open to a pale creamy yellow, in which the cluster of bright yellow stamens in the centre are a distinct feature . . . The extreme vigour of this plant is remarkable. I have pulled mine about in

Jersey Beauty *continued*

a disgraceful manner without the least ill result, and it will do well in partial shade, though it may not flower quite so freely. It may be used for a tall pillar, arch, or pergola, and is specially good for a high screen or tall hedge. The strong points of this Rose are its grand single blossoms and magnificent foliage, and there is nothing weak connected with it. Down to the present [1911] it is the best single-flowered wichuraiana." [NRS11/43–44]

Jessica
Walsh, 1909

"Old-fashioned Wichuraiana with creamy white flowers tinted pink in the middle. Blooms in autumn." [GAS] "Yellowish white, pink center, small, full, tall." [Sn] "Flower creamy white, pink centre. Growth very vigorous." [GeH] "A fine comparison [*i.e.,* 'complement'] to ['Gerbe Rose' (W)] is 'Jessica', a Rose with 'Maiden's Blush' flowers and very fine foliage." [NRS18/151]

Jitřenka
Mikeš-Böhm, 1933

"Light pink, medium size, lightly double, tall." [Sn]

Johanna Ropcke   Listed as 'Johanna Röpke' (W).

Johanna Röpke
syn. 'Johanna Ropcke'
Tantau, 1931
From 'Dorothy Perkins' (W) × 'Ophelia' (HT).

"Attractive Wichuraiana with clusters of beautifully shaped little flowers of pale salmon-pink and cream." [GAS] "Salmon pink, medium size, lightly double, tall." [Sn]

Joseph Billard
Barbier, 1905
From *Rosa wichuraiana* × 'Mme. Eugène Résal' (Ch).

"Wichuraiana with clusters of single, bright red flowers tinted yellow in the centers." [GAS] "Red, yellow center, medium size, single, tall." [Sn] "Crimson, with rich yellow to cream centre, single, early. Growth vigorous." [GeH] "A great climber, but as an effective garden Rose it is, to my mind, a complete failure. With me it is not very floriferous and the flowers do not seem to bloom together . . . To the ordinary mortal who does not get out early the crimson is an unwholesome magenta." [NRS16/94] "Growth fairly good; blooms large, single; nice color." [ARA18/120] "Plant climbing, and vigorous. Foliage glossy somber green. Flowers single, 7–9 cm across [ca. 2¾–3½ in], to superb effect, sparkling bright carmine, petal nubs bright yellow." [JR30/23–24] "A vigorous grower with strong prostrate stems. The foliage is large and fine, and of a dark glossy green, not subject to mildew. The flowers are produced in profusion in small trusses of large single blooms with fine stamens. As they open the outer part of the petals is bright crimson, and the inner part is golden or orange yellow, which soon fades to cream. A very distinct variety, and one of the greatest beauty when first opening. To see it at its best one must be out in the garden in the early morning before breakfast." [NRS13/98]

Joseph Liger
Barbier, 1909
From *Rosa wichuraiana* × 'Irène Watts' (Ch).

"Clusters of medium-sized, canary-yellow flowers, edged light pink." [GAS] "Yellow, white center, medium size, full, tall." [Sn] "Canary-yellow to creamy white, edged clear pink, free. Growth very vigorous." [GeH] "Very floriferous variety with vigorous growth. Blooms in panicles of 20–30 blossoms which are delicately shaded canary yellow within, the tip of the petals cream white. Flowers large, from 7–10 cm across [ca. 3½–4 in]." [JR33/167]

Jules Levacher
Barbier, 1908
From *Rosa wichuraiana* × 'Mme. Laurette Messimy' (Ch).

"Rampant Wichuraiana, with clusters of reddish buds and silvery pink flowers." [GAS] "Pink, medium size, lightly double, tall." [Sn] "Pale silver-pink, small, double, freely produced. Growth very vigorous." [GeH] "Pale pink, yellow at base of petals. It is a rampant grower and free flowerer." [NRS16/95] "Vigorous variety with dark green foliage, extremely floriferous. Blooms in bouquets of 5 to 10 blossoms, semi-double, beautiful China pink with silvery reflections; carmine pink bud." [JR32/152] "A rampant grower with light green stems and few thorns. The foliage is very dense—of graceful form and of pale yellowish green colour; it is not liable to mildew. It flowers very profusely in small trusses of medium-sized well-formed double blooms. The colour is pale Chinese pink." [NRS13/94]

July Glory
Chaplin, 1932

"Strong Wichuraiana with compact, stiff trusses of fully double, bright cerise-pink flowers." [GAS] "Pink, small, full, tall." [Sn]

L'Avenir
syn. 'Avenir'; trans., "The Future"
Corboeuf-Marsault, 1910

"Flower of beautiful yellow-brown colour and good holding." [GeH] "Whitish pink, small, lightly double, medium scent, tall." [Sn]

La Fiamma
trans. "The Flame"
Walsh, 1909

"Handsome Wichuraiana with clusters of single, flame-colored flowers." [GAS] "Red, medium size, single, tall." [Sn] "Strong grower; good blooming qualities; color much like [that of] 'Eisenach' [W], blooming period a trifle longer." [ARA18/120]

La Mexique   Listed as 'Le Mexique' (W).

La Perie   Listed as 'La Perle' (W).

La Perle
syn. 'La Perie'
Fauque-Laurent/Vigneron, 1904
From *Rosa wichuraiana* × 'Mme. Hoste' (T).

"Cream white." [Ÿ] "Yellowish white, large, full, medium scent, tall." [Sn] "Trusses of large, well-formed creamy yellow flowers." [GAS] "Flower creamy white, full, double. Growth very vigorous." [GeH] "Rampant bush of very great vigor, foliage glossy dark green. Flowers quite double, large, opening well, coming in panicles. A beautiful cream white color, fragrant. Very beautiful variety in this line." [JR28/154] "A well-formed large flower of cream yellow, going almost white, borne in open small trusses. A rampant grower. Young growth of coppery brown colour. It does not seem to be so well known as it deserves to be." [NRS16/96]

Lady Duncan
Dawson/Eastern, 1900
From *Rosa wichuraiana* × *R. rugosa*.

"Trailing Wichuraiana with bright pink flowers shaded yellow in center. Foliage resembles Rugosa, said to be one of its parents." [GAS] "A ruggedly hardy hybrid ... produced in 1900 by Jackson Dawson of the Arnold Arboretum, one of the first Americans to appreciate the possibility of *R. rugosa* as a parent plant in hybridization. The similarity to the parents is well divided, the flower resembling the pink form of Rugosa and its foliage that of the Wichuraiana, while the habit of growth is a compromise between the upright form of one parent and the trailing habit of the other. 'Lady Duncan' is a profuse June bloomer, and always handsome in its glistening foliage, which remains in good condition the season through. The plant ... was sent to me by Mr. Dawson before it was named, and is now some 10 to 12 feet in diameter [ca. 3.3–4 m]. I tried to train it up, but it showed evidence of displeasure. I [William C. Egan] removed the 'harness,' and it soon showed signs of joy by increased growth and denser foliage. The name 'Lady Duncan' implies English origin, and this fact aroused my curiosity and started me on a hunt to discover the 'whys and wherefores.' I found that Mr. Dawson had at one time been in the employ of an American family whose daughter married the youngest son of a Scotch peer named Duncan. Dawson was treated very kindly by this family, and he had great affection for them. He named the rose after the daughter, who was never 'Lady Duncan,' however, as she died before her husband became a lord." [ARA24/82]

Lady Gay
Walsh, 1905
From *Rosa wichuraiana* × 'Bardou Job' (B).

"Blossom small, cherry pink fading to blush white." [JR32/172] "Very vigorous bush, hardy; flower small, fairly full; coloration, cerise pink passing to white." [JR30/25] "Injured by thrips." [ARA26/201] "Pink-white, small, full, tall." [Sn] "The introducers say 'this Rose is fair superior to '[Turner's] Crimson Rambler' [Mult] of which it is a seedling [*no it isn't*] and which it closely resembles in habit of bloom and vigor of growth. The flowers (in large loose clusters) are of a delicate cherry pink color, fading to soft tinted white. The effect of a plant in full bloom with the combination of soft white flowers, cherry pink buds and deep green of the foliage is indeed charming. It is perfectly hardy and unsurpassed for climbing work." [C&Js07] "Vigorous growth; same color as [that of] 'Dorothy Perkins' [W], not quite so profuse." [ARA18/120] "Foliage black-spots very slightly; bloom profuse last half of June, moderate into July." [ARA18/131] "The rose 'Lady Gay' is one of the most attractive in this group. Its origins are not precisely known; we know only that it was born in the U.S., that it was shown for the first time in Boston by Mr. Walsh, horticulturist of Wood's Hole, Massachusetts, in March 1904, and two months later in London, England, at the Temple Show [*predecessor of the Chelsea Flower Show*], where it received a certificate of merit. We also know that it is considered to be a 'sport' of 'Dorothy Perkins' [*no it isn't*] ... the blossoms of 'Lady Gay' are more double than those of 'Dorothy Perkins', and are a bright delicate pink color; both of them keep their foliage until late in the season. All in all, this variety is one of the best of the climbing roses." [JR32/24]

"Walsh regarded this lovely Wichuraiana as an improvement on 'Dorothy Perkins', which it resembles. It has been widely distributed, and much of the stock passing under the name of 'Dorothy Perkins' may really be 'Lady Gay'. I know of no way in which the two varieties can be separated today. Some growers maintain that they are distinctly different, while others claim that they are identical ... Certain specimens labeled 'Lady Gay' sometimes produce autumn flowers, which I have never seen on 'Dorothy Perkins'." [GAS] "Very similar in appearance to 'Dorothy Perkins' ... There are two marked differences between them. 'Lady Gay' has stems so very much more flexible that it is almost impossible to arrange the trusses in a vase unless it is to be looked at from below, for they will persist in hanging downwards. The other great difference is that 'Lady Gay' gives practically no autumnal blooms. The colour in 'Lady Gay' has, I think, a shade more lilac in the tone of the pink ... They seem equally liable to mildew. If I were choosing between the two varieties I should select 'Dorothy Perkins'." [NRS13/99] "I have a leaning in favour of 'Lady Gay' as against 'Dorothy Perkins', as I think the flower is brighter and more distinctive. It is as well that we do not all admire the same lady!" [NRS16/98]

Lady Godiva
G. Paul, 1908
Sport of 'Dorothy Perkins' (W).

"Pale flesh pink." [Ÿ] "Pink mauve." [JR35/133] "A very beautiful soft creamy pink or pale salmon." [NRS20/92] "Flower soft pale flesh pink. Growth like [that of] 'Dorothy Perkins'." [GeH] "Whitish pink, small, full, medium scent, tall." [Sn] "Good growth; not a bloomer." [ARA18/122] "Comes out a few days after 'Dorothy Perkins', and is perhaps the most delicate colour of all. It is a beautiful shell pink. Last year we noticed Messrs. Paul & Son had a plant with a number of flowers out quite late in the autumn—the latter half of October." [NRS11/38] "Extremely attractive variation of 'Dorothy Perkins', with clusters of small, very double, pale pink flowers of the most exquisite tint. It is one of the finest cluster-flowering ramblers, although it has never achieved popularity. 'Christian Curle' [W] and 'Dorothy Dennison' [W] are practically identical with it." [GAS]

Laxton's Monthly Rambler Listed as 'Monthly Rambler' (W).

Le Mexique
syn. 'La Mexique'
A. Schwartz, 1912
From 'Dorothy Perkins' (W) × 'Marie Pavic' (Pol).

"Silvery pink flowers of medium size; said to be really perpetual." [NRS13/101] "Moderately vigorous Wichuraiana, with clusters of rather large pale silvery pink flowers. Occasionally blooms in autumn." [GAS] "Light pink, medium size, lightly double, light scent, tall." [Sn] "Pale silvery pink, large, full, free flowering. Growth very vigorous." [GeH] "Vigorous, pretty varnished foliage; silvery pink bud; flower large for the genre, full, opens well, pretty form, in corymbs; very pale silvery pink fading to blush white; reverse of petals light pink; this variety blooms continually—it's freely remontant." [JR36/169]

[Le Poilu]
trans. "The Whiskery One"
Barbier, 1915
From 'Wichmoss' (W) × 'Moussue de Japon' (M).

"A vigorous grower, having the branches quite covered with numerous hairs or small thorns. Flowers are satiny rose-color, turning

[**Le Poilu**] *continued*

to lilac-rose with silvery reflex. It is quite hardy. They come in bouquets of 8 to 15 at a time." [C&Js21]

Léontine Gervais

Barbier, 1904

From *Rosa wichuraiana* × 'Souvenir de Catherine Guillot' (Ch).

"Copper pink." [Ÿ] "Salmon red, medium size, full, tall." [Sn] "Superb plant, nasturtium red mixed with carmine and salmon." [JR32/172] "Salmon-rose, tinted yellow, very fragrant, early. Vigorous climber." [GeH] "A most beautifully coloured Rose with shades of salmon, copper, yellow, and sometimes, under certain climatic conditions, the outside petals are almost white and the centre coppery red. The buds are generally of this latter colour. I should call this one of the best, but with me it does not grow so freely as many of the others … This year, in October, I got quite a number of second crop buds." [NRS16/96] "Large reddish orange fruits shaped like a tangerine." [CaRol/2] "Superb plant of great vigor, extremely floriferous. Corymbs of 3–10 blossoms. Corolla double, having the same coloration as 'Souvenir de Catherine Guillot', though a little lighter: nasturtium red mixed with carmine and salmon, bright yellow nub. Superb color, till now unknown among climbers." [JR28/156] "Very vigorous and hardy variety blooming in clusters of 3–10 blossoms of a beautiful coloration: nasturtium red mixed with a slightly salmony carmine. Novel coloration. Meritorious plant." [JR31/177] "The true variety is a Wichuraiana with loose clusters of large salmon-yellow flowers tinged with copper and pink. It has long been one of the most famous Wichuraiana climbers in Europe, but the plants seen in this country do not fit this description. Decidedly worth growing if the true variety can be obtained." [GAS] "A rampant, vigorous grower with thorny wood. The leaves are of beautiful dark glossy green, but they fall early and are slightly liable to mildew. The flowers are freely produced in small trusses of large, thinly double blooms. The buds are coppery red, and open to a beautiful rosy salmon yellow. Tea scented." [NRS13/97]

"Makes fine vigorous growth of very lax and drooping habit, branching freely, green in colour, turning a rich russet brown on the sunny side in autumn, and plentifully but irregularly armed with sharp thorns only slightly hooked, averaging about half-an-inch apart [ca. 1.25 cm]. The foliage is rather lighter in tint and much less dense than [that of] most wichuraianas, and falls sooner than is usual with Roses of this class, being in fact rather delicate and meagre; but it is glossy on the upper surface and free from mildew. It has only one flowering period. The first flower opened with me on the 28th June, 1910 … and it continues in flower for about six weeks … It gives an occasional flower in autumn. The blossoms are carried on rather short side stalks in small trusses, occasionally almost singly, and are small in size but nearly full. They are sweetly scented, the fragrance being of a fruity character. The colour is remarkable and difficult to describe. It has quite a resemblance to its parent '[Souvenir de] Catherine Guillot', and might also bring to mind a soft tinted 'Comtesse du Caÿla' [Ch]. The buds are a coppery red, and the flowers open to a beautiful salmon rose tinged with yellow. This is the nearest I can get to it, but I fear it will convey little to one who has not seen the flower. The plant does not cover itself with bloom as do most of the wichuraianas, and I should not quarrel with anyone who called it disappointing in the garden … for the flowers do not stand rain well.

They are, however, very decorative and striking when cut and brought indoors, and may be said to last well in water. In the garden it may be used for pillar, arch, or pergola. The charm of this Rose lies in its wonderful colour and sweet fragrance. Its weak points are its somewhat meagre foliage for a Rose of this class and want of distant effect in the garden as a climber, and I am not sure that it is very hardy." [NRS11/45–46]

Little Compton Creeper

Brownell, 1938

"Deep pink, small, single, vigorous." [Sn] "Single, deep wild-rose-pink flowers come in open clusters amidst glossy dark foliage. Canes reach 15 feet [ca. 5 m] and 'grow naturally 10 to 15 degrees above the horizontal' —a beautiful robust plant with masses of yellow-orange-red hips in autumn." [W] Little Compton, Rhode Island, U.S.A., was where Brownell was located.

Louis Sauvage

Turbat, 1914

"Clusters of very double dark red flowers." [GAS] "Purple red, small, full, tall." [Sn]

Loveliness

Chaplin, 1933

"Attractive, double, light rose-pink Wichuraiana." [GAS] "Light pink, white center, medium size, full, tall." [Sn]

Madeleine Lemaire

Nonin, 1923

From 'Mrs. F. W. Flight' (W) × unnamed seedling.

"Bright salmon pink." [Ÿ] "Another of the endless pink-flowered ramblers intermediate between the Multiflora and the Wichuraiana types." [GAS] "Deep pink, medium size, lightly double, light scent, tall." [Sn] "Bud large, ovoid; flower large, semi-double, open, very lasting, slight fragrance, Nilson pink striated crimson-carmine passing to lighter pink, borne in clusters on long stem. Foliage disease-resistant. Few thorns. Very vigorous, climbing, upright; profuse bloomer in June and July." [ARA25/187] "Bud medium size, long-pointed; flower medium size, semi-double, cupped, very lasting; bright salmon-pink; slight fragrance. Foliage disease-resistant. Very vigorous, upright climber (15 to 20 feet [ca. 5–6.6 m]; profuse and continuous bloomer. Hardy." [ARA24/172]

Magic Carpet

Brownell, 1941

From 'Coral Creeper' (W) × 'Stargold' (HT).

"Yellowish orange red, large, lightly double, tall." [Sn] "Large double flowers open in a wonderful medley of yellow and orange shades. The shiny, resistant foliage covers vigorous 15-foot plants [ca. 5 m] which are lovely with 'Carpet of Gold' [W]." [W]

Manda's Triumph

syn. 'Double White Memorial Rose'

Horvath/Manda & Pitcher, 1898

From *Rosa wichuraiana* × either an HP or a Polyantha (possibly 'Mignonette').

"White." [Ÿ] "White, medium size, full, tall." [Sn] "Bloom abundant two weeks in early June." [ARA18/131] "A lovely sight in June." [W] "Gives a second bloom in the Fall, but the flowers are smaller." [JR26/

69] "One of the first four Wichuraiana hybrids. It is a vigorous, trailing plant with clusters of double white flowers." [GAS] "Straggly growth; poor foliage; bloom not attractive." [ARA18/122] "This grand rose is of free growth, luxuriant foliage, and produces large clusters of double pure white flowers, beautifully imbricated, and well formed, two inches in diameter [ca. 5 cm] and sweetly scented." [CA97] "A new Hybrid Wichuraiana of remarkable beauty. The flowers are medium size, perfectly double to the center, pure white and very fragrant. The plant is an erect grower, has handsome dark-green foliage, is entirely hardy and bears its lovely flowers in large clusters; valuable for all purposes where fine hardy roses are wanted." [C&Js99] "A white Wichuraiana with very full flowers. White blossoms with very regular form. You can count up to 150 flowers per plant. The canes are up to 5 meters long [ca. 15 ft]. Took the silver medal at the Florist's Exhibition in New York. Honorable mention at the Horticultural Society of New York, as well as that of Massachusetts. Much recommended by the horticultural press." [JR21/68]

Marco

P. Guillot, 1904

From *Rosa wichuraiana* × 'Souvenir de Catherine Guillot' (Ch).

"Rather large white flowers stained coppery orange in the center." [GAS] "Blossom medium-sized, full, well-formed, white with a dark coppery center fading to saffron white." [JR32/172] "White, yellow center, medium size, full, tall." [Sn] "Yellowish copper, fading to white. —Vigorous. —Arch, pergola, creeping, weeping standard. —Early." [Cat12] "Very vigorous bush, hardy, rampant; glossy purple foliage; numerous inflorescences, in clusters; blossom medium-sized, quite full, deep carminy orange yellow, edges white shading to white tinted saffron. Superb." [JR28/154]

Marie Dietrich

Walter, 1928

From 'Léontine Gervais' (W) × 'Eugénie Lamesch' (Pol).

"Yellowish red, small, lightly double, tall." [Sn] "Vigorous Wichuraiana with small pinkish red flowers shading white." [GAS] "Type, 'Léontine Gervais' in bud. Flower yellowish red, passing to white. Foliage bright green, glossy, disease-resistant. Profuse." [ARA30/224]

Marie Gouchault

Turbat, 1927

"Red blue passing to salmon pink." [Ÿ] "Light red, medium size, full, tall." [Sn] "No particular value outdoors, occasionally used for forcing. Flowers of bright reddish pink, turning salmon with age." [GAS] "Flower as large as [that of] 'Dorothy Perkins' [W], very lasting, double, clear red passing to brilliant salmon-rose, borne in large clusters of 30 to 40. Foliage abundant, shining green, disease-resistant. Few thorns. Growth very vigorous; blooms three weeks earlier than 'Dorothy Perkins'." [ARA28/239] "Growth very vigorous and almost thornless, beautiful glossy green foliage, large elongated clusters of 30 to 40 double flowers. Fine lighted red passing to bright salmon-pink, producing great effect. Very early and profuse-blooming variety, flowering three weeks before 'Dorothy Perkins'." [GeH]

Mary Lovett

Van Fleet, 1915

From *Rosa wichuraiana* × 'Kaiserin Auguste Viktoria' (HT).

"An exact counterpart of ['Dr. W. Van Fleet' (W)], but this Rose is *pearly white*. We are led to believe that this is the finest hardy climbing white Rose in existence." [C&Js15] "Identical with ['Dr. W. Van Fleet'] except in color, which is pure, waxy white." [ARA21/93] "Pink-white, medium size, full, medium scent, tall." [Sn] "One of the best large-flowered Wichuraianas, with fairly large, beautifully formed, double white blooms borne profusely in midsummer and occasionally in the autumn." [GAS] "A large-flowering, full, white Climbing Rose. It blooms freely in early June, and again sparingly throughout the summer and fall." [C-Ps29] "Seems to lose its buds from freezing and it fails to show many of them." [ARA29/84] "Good growth and blooming qualities; attractive flowers—more double than [those of] 'Silver Moon' [Lv]." [ARA18/121] "A really good, pure white, hardy climbing Rose has long been needed, and this is precisely what we have in the 'Mary Lovett'. The flowers of purest white, full and splendidly formed, are held on long strong stems and are delightfully fragrant—an unusual property in a climbing rose. It is . . . a strong grower with abundant large, glossy, mildew-proof leafage and is exceedingly free flowering." [C&Jf17] "Loses foliage early." [ARA17/27] "Foliage not so plentiful as in most Wichuraianas, black-spots very slightly in midsummer; bloom abundant two weeks in early June." [ARA18/131] "Always attracts attention; it is our best large double white climber." [ARA22/44]

Mary Wallace

syn. 'W.C. 124'

Van Fleet/American Rose Society, 1923

From *Rosa wichuraiana* × a pink HT.

"The large flowers of this Wichuraiana are brilliant pink, suffused with gold. The plant is prolific and vigorous and hardier than most of this type. Its withered flowers disfigure the clusters too long, but it has achieved a wider popularity than 'Alida Lovett' which is a much better rose." [GAS] "Pink, large, lightly double, light scent, tall." [Sn] "A darker companion to 'Dr. W. Van Fleet', and possibly not quite such a strong grower, but has exquisite, double flowers on long stems that are good for cutting." [ARA29/52] "The color has more life in it than that of 'Dr. W. Van Fleet' [W], but the flowers wilt miserably under hot sun." [ARA28/62] "The dead flowers do hang on instead of falling off cleanly at all times though they are not so offensive as some. Attracts attention by its outstanding quality of color, which is impossible to describe." [ARA27/137] "Generally graces us with a few blooms in the autumn." [C-Ps31] "Bud large, long-pointed; flower very large, cupped, semi-double, lasting; deep rose-pink; borne, several together, on long stem; fragrant. Foliage abundant, rich, glossy green, disease-resistant. Vigorous, climbing (8 to 12 feet); profuse bloomer in June and September; hardy." [ARA22/157] "This charming pillar rose has well-formed semi-double flowers, bright clear rose-pink, with salmon base to the petals; exceeding four inches in diameter [ca. 1 dm]. Makes a fine plant 6 to 8 feet high [ca. 2–2.6 m]. Grand mildew-proof foliage; very free flowering and always in flower." [GeH] "Named by the Rose Society of Portland in honor of the daughter of the U.S. Secretary of Agriculture . . . [It has been] under observation here for fully four years and [we] heartily endorse the following official description: '. . . Hardy Pillar Rose type. Makes a fine, strong, self-supporting Rose 6 to 8 feet high [ca. 2–2.6 m], with large, glossy foliage, resistant at Bell [Maryland, U.S.A.] to all diseases. Blooms with great freedom in spring, and bears a considerable number of fine buds in summer and fall. Flowers well-formed, semi-double, bright, clear

Mary Wallace *continued*

rose-pink, with salmon base to the petals. Largest in size of any Wichuraiana hybrid, often exceeding 4 inches in diameter [ca. 1 dm].'" [C&Js24] "It is, curiously enough, either a climber or a shrub, according to its handling. As it grew under Dr. Van Fleet's critical eye, in the poor soil to which he designedly subjected his seedlings, it made a wonderful mound of glossy foliage, covered early with very large, semi-double, rose-pink flowers, and followed later with some fine buds in summer and fall." [ARA22/49] "It will climb, if you want it to, 10 feet or more [ca. 3.3 m +] each year; it will make a graceful specimen plant, or a wonderful hedge, or a conspicuous pillar. 'Mary Wallace' stands alone. Lovely long buds of a shade of warm pink peculiar to itself and very attractive; great open flowers will halt the passerby; rich green leafage that resists bugs and bothers." [C-Ps25] "This spring (1924) I secured a plant of 'Mary Wallace'. It gave quite a number of blossoms and grew three stems over 8 feet tall [ca. 2.6 m +] and a number of others less high. The flowers are beautiful. But the most remarkable thing is that there has not been one leaf affected by mildew or black-spot. Have we, at last[,] a rose free from these troubles? All honor to Dr. Van Fleet." [ARA25/203] "Intro[duced] by American Rose Society, 1923." [ARA24/194]

Matka Vlast
Böhm, 1934

"Pink, striped red and white, small, full, tall." [Sn]

Max Graf
Bowditch, 1919

"Bright pink, center yellow." [Ÿ] "Pink, medium size, single, vigorous." [Sn] "Early. Large, rosy pink, single flowers, like crimped silk. For trailing over and covering embankments is one of the best. Grows rapidly; beautiful foliage. Left to itself, it makes a mound, not over 18 inches high [ca. 4.5 dm]." [C-Ps29] "Clusters of large and lovely bright rosy pink single flowers, borne freely in June, seldom blooming afterward. Extremely hardy, grows vigorously, and is highly desirable for planting on embankments or trailing over rocks, mixing splendidly with the Wichuraianas. The foliage is unique, fairly disease-proof, and very beautiful." [C-Ps25] "Here is a rose that should be planted by the thousands. Usually it is once-blooming, though it blooms a little in September sometimes." [ARA29/125] "Completely reliable." [W]

"The trailing rose, 'Max Graf', which was discovered by the foreman, Mr. Graf, in the nursery at Pomfret Center, Conn., owned by Mr. James H. Bowditch. In the nursery were growing several species of roses, including *R. rugosa, R. setigera,* and *R. wichuraiana.* Mr. Bowditch writes that 'the most likely crosses are *R. wichuraiana* and *R. setigera,* or *R. wichuraiana* and *R. rugosa.*' My guess is that the honor belongs to the two latter. The foliage strongly resembles that of the Wichuraiana, at the same time having suggestions of the ruggedness of the Rugosa foliage, while the flower is a good pink, resembling the pink form of the true Rugosa…'Max Graf' is a profuse June bloomer, some belated flowers appearing during July. But if this rose had never a flower on it, it would take place as a most handsome groundcover, because of its foliage of a rich dark green, unblemished by mildew, black-spot, or kindred ailments. No leaf-eating insect has yet discovered my plants, and I certainly will not advertise their presence to the bugs! These qualities explain why 'Max Graf' is admira-

bly adapted for a ground-cover or for hanging over steep banks or stone walls. Further, and importantly, it is reliably hardy without winter protection, even here at Egandale [*Highland Park, Illinois, U.S.A., the home of the writer, William C. Egan*]. It may also be used as a climber, reaching a height of ten or more feet [ca. 3.3 m +], though, as stated, it is essentially a trailing rose. Mr. Bowditch writes that he has 'a large plant about ten feet high growing on a red cedar post with side branches, making a thick, handsome bush with long shoots, that might easily be put up another five or even ten feet, apparently.' In established plantings, young canes emanating from the base rise up some eighteen or twenty inches [ca. 4.5–5 dm] for light, and then, arching over, lie prostrate upon their brethren. The growth is rapid and vigorous. This rose does not produce seed, which means that its splendidly rich appearance is not disfigured with more or less disreputable seed-pods. Also, it has so fair, unfortunately, escaped the propagating nurseryman. Perhaps this note about it will wake up some one or more of them." [ARA20/56] "In the American Rose Annual for 1920 I published an article on the 'Max Graf' rose, illustrating only its leafage. I wrote favorably of it, and its four years' summer behavior since then has still more impressed me with it as a plant of importance. It is very much admired by visitors, not only when in bloom but at all times. The three plants, originally set about 4 feet apart [ca. 1.3 m], now occupy a space of 18 feet [ca. 6 m]. It would have covered much more, only that the head of the house, who, like the natural head of all households, has a feminine profile, said that *she* wanted *some* lawn on the place where she could dampen her feet on dewy mornings so I had to curb the ambition of 'Max Graf'!" [ARA24/81] "It is undoubtedly due to [William C. Egan] that the super-hardy 'Max Graf' was rescued from oblivion." [ARA30/199]

Maxime Corbon
Barbier, 1918
From *Rosa wichuraiana* × 'Léonie Lamesch' (Pol).

"Light orange yellow, medium size, full, medium scent, tall." [Sn] "Deep coppery red buds; flowers deep coppery yellow, washed red, passing to apricot-yellow and white tinted straw-color, borne in panicles of six to twenty. Strong grower." [ARA19/101] "Coppery deep yellow striped with red, passing to apricot-yellow, centre white tinted straw-yellow, fairly large; buds bright deep coppery red. Growth vigorous, climbing. A climbing form of 'Léonie Lamesch' [Pol]." [GeH]

May Queen
Van Fleet/Conard & Jones, 1898
From *Rosa wichuraiana* × 'Mrs. DeGraw' (HB).

"Beautiful lilac." [JR26/181] "Coral." [Ÿ] "Pink, large, full, tall." [Sn] "Splendid large double roses of clear, bright pink, and deliciously sweet-scented. Blooms tremendously. Literally bushels of flowers can be picked from a fully grown bush." [C&Js07] "Clear coral-pink, large flowers, strong grower, early." [GeH] "Fairly large, double coral-pink flowers. A second rose by the same name, originated by Dr. W. Van Fleet, was put out by Conard & Jones Co. in 1911. Its description is the same. Evidently they are hopelessly mixed [*GAS appears incorrect in his supposition that there was a "second rose by the same name"; its "description is the same" because it* is *the same*]." [GAS] "Good, healthy foliage." [C&Js21] "Foliage not quite so plentiful as with most; bloom moderate through June." [ARA18/131] "Lilac pink, semidouble, short-stemmed, 3-inch [ca. 7.5 cm] flowers in garland effect. This will do well in almost complete shade provided this is open, as on the north side of a house. Good glossy foliage. Plant grows to at least 30 feet [ca. 10 m] and tends to bloom all season. On West Coast *does* so after a great May profusion. Strong, sweet fragrance." [W] "This splendid new Climbing Rose is a true Hybrid obtained by crossing the beautiful Tea [*sic; Hybrid Bourbon, rather*] Rose 'Mrs. DeGraw' with the hardy running rose [*R.*] *wichuraiana*. It partakes of the nature of both parents, being a vigorous erect growing climber well furnished with handsome foliage, and bearing great numbers of lovely large roses, fully as beautiful as the finest Tea Roses. The blooms are three inches and more across [ca. 7.5 cm +], perfectly double, with raised centre, delightfully sweet scented, and borne in clusters of five to seven all over the bush. The color is clear coral pink, very bright and handsome. 'May Queen' is a strong erect growing climber, entirely hardy, an early and abundant bloomer, and particularly recommended for all situations where hardy, free blooming climbing Roses are wanted. It is undoubtedly the greatest advance made in hardy climbing roses for many years, and must speedily take its place at the head of the list of this valuable class." [C&Js98]

"One of the top climbing roses is—like everyone says—the old thornless variety, the ever-beautiful 'Mme. [de] Sancy de Parabère' ..., classed among the Alpina Roses [*i.e., Boursaults*]. Beside it can be placed 'May Queen', a Wichuraiana of very pretty effect. Well before the first blossoms of 'Turner's Crimson Rambler' [Mult], 'May Queen' is in all its glory, giving a profusion of large and beautiful flowers, its bloom ending just as 'Turner's' is only just getting underway. Though in commerce some ten years, it doesn't seem to have become widely distributed, as all the fanciers who see it in our gardens are taken by surprise by its many virtues. We don't doubt that, before long, it will become one of the most valued early blooming climbers. Despite my research in several catalogs given me, I have never found any particulars on this rose. With its big flowers, it is a nice change from the series of Multiflora hybrids, which generally have small flowers; this, however, equals them in the number of inflorescences. Its beautiful coral pink color can't be equaled by any [other] climber introduced up till now; and its beautiful foliage, which is long-lasting, is proof against all maladies, indeed mildew, which ravages most Multifloras. 'May Queen' is of rapid growth, with very long, flexible, curving stems which have a tendency to 'set' themselves, an excellent quality for a climbing rose. In gardens with crags and rocky outcroppings, it clings to rocks, allowing its long blooming canes to cascade back, producing a magnificent effect. It can also be used advantageously to ornament thickets, grilles, pillars, and pyramids, or to form graceful festoons. In short, there's nothing it can't do without great success. Grown as a weeping rose, it is no less admirable because of its handsome foliage than because of its bloom. The blossoms come in a cluster—sometimes 36 in an umbel; they are full, flat in form, and long-lasting; they start to appear at the end of May or beginning of June, depending on the temperature, and they last about four weeks, without seeming to have gone downhill ... 'May Queen' ... was released to commerce in 1899 [*no it wasn't*]; it is from a cross of *R. wichuraiana* with another unspecified kind. Thus, it is a Wichuraiana hybrid. The following year, [Conard & Jones] released another beautiful variety of the same sort— 'Ruby Queen' [W; *no, it was the same year*] ... Both are very hardy and of exceptional merit." [JR34/125–126]

Melita

Easlea, 1933

Sport of 'Thelma' (W).

"Light orange pink, medium size, very full, tall." [Sn]

Merveille de la Brie

trans. "Brie Wonder"

Breeder unknown, date uncertain

"Scarlet red." [Ÿ]

Mičurin

Böhm, 1936

"Light red, large, lightly double, tall." [Sn]

[Milano]

Ingegnoli, 1923

"The largest, most perfect scented bloom I have ever seen on a Wichuraiana climber. Some day it will push off 'Coralie' [W], 'Paul Noël' [W], 'François Juranville' [W], and the whole tribe of salmon-pink Wichuraianas. It takes time to get started; then it runs." [ARA28/174] Milano, alias Milan, Italian city.

[Milky Way]

Walsh, 1900

"Excellent ... with huge clusters of single, pure white flowers infrequently tinged with pink. It is extremely decorative in rustic situations and is one of the best of the type." [GAS] "This variety, of which news comes from America, is a Wichuraiana hybrid in which the blossom exceed in size all the [previously] existing varieties in this section. The newcomer in question—called 'Milky Way', which is to say *'Voie Lactée'*, was raised by Mr. Walsh. The generally single blossoms are pure white and grow up to 63 mm across [ca. 2½ in]." [JR34/117] "Resembles the Type in colour, but the flowers are much larger." [NRS13/100] "Bloom moderate, intermittent during last half of June and some of July." [ARA18/131] "The pure waxy white, single flowers, with yellow stamens, are borne in immense clusters. Excellent foliage, well retained. Vigorous." [Th2]

Minnehaha

Walsh, 1904

From *Rosa wichuraiana* × 'Paul Neyron' (HP).

"Unchanging deep pink." [Ÿ] "Deep salmon pink, small, very full, very fragrant, tall." [Sn] "A much-neglected Wichuraiana of 'Dorothy Perkins' [W] type with flowers a little larger and a little lighter pink. All these variations on 'Dorothy Perkins' are more or less different and provide interesting variety in tints and seasons. 'Minnehaha' is one of the best." [GAS] "One of the best pink Wichuraianas. Medium sized flowers borne on an exceptionally large truss. Makes a handsome weeping standard, and is useful for all purposes. Late flowering." [F-M] "Much like 'Dorothy Perkins', perhaps lighter in bud; vigorous growth; wonderful amount of bloom." [ARA18/121] "Comes out a little earlier [than does 'Dorothy Perkins'] and does not last quite so long, the clusters of blossom are looser, and less closely packed, hanging down more like a bunch of grapes, so giving a lighter and more diaphanous effect, particularly when one is looking up at them as they hang from an arch. The colour is not so uniform as [that of] 'Dorothy Perkins', and the flowers have tints of paler pink, the general effect being a lighter tone than that of 'Dorothy Perkins'." [NRS11/

Minnehaha *continued*

38] "Deep pink rosettes; large, loose trusses; similar to 'Dorothy Per-kins'; late flowering. Growth vigorous." [GeH] "Hardy shrub; flower large, very full, fragrant; deep unchanging pink." [JR33/186] "A charming double satiny pink-flowering Rambler of a most pleasing color. Flowers are borne in clusters; foliage glossy green." [C&Js12] "Slightly liable to mildew." [NRS29/165] "Foliage black-spots very slightly in midsummer; bloom very profuse during last two and a half weeks of June." [ARA18/131] "The growth ... is thicker and stiffer [than that of 'Dorothy Perkins'] and the foliage larger ... The bunch is pyramidal shaped and the flowers are slightly darker pink and smaller ... This is a particularly good Rose for an arch because, look-ing at the bunches from below, they present a very diaphanous effect against the sky." [NRS20/92] "As a flower I do not admire it, but un-doubtedly it makes one of the finest weeping Standards by reason of its growth and the size and pyramidal form of its trusses. The growth seems to start early and makes enough wood each year to replace pruned out flowered wood, which so many of the other varieties do not. The general effect is as good as any of this class. It seems inclined to sport, and I have a pale variety from a chance cutting." [NRS16/98] "Of a strong, rampant, much stiffer growth, and with foliage that is larger and darker green than [that of] 'Dorothy Perkins'. It flowers a few days later in fine, long, upstanding pyramidal trusses. The indi-vidual blooms are smaller than in 'Dorothy' and of a much deeper pink colour. It is often described as the best pink in this section." [NRS13/99] "A neglected variety that deserves much wider recogni-tion. Although it was introduced only four years later than 'Dorothy Perkins', it has never really attained much popularity simply because that variety has always been kept so much in the foreground. And yet, grow the two together, test them in flower, truss, hardiness, and ro-bustness of growth, and I think it will be found that 'Minnehaha' must be voted the finer. Its large truss, with its exquisitely placed flowers, is indeed a thing of beauty and gracefulness." [NRS19/56] "Has a winsome appeal." [W] Minnehaha—alias Laughing Water—Hiawatha's love in Longfellow's poem *The Song of Hiawatha*.

Miss Flora Mitten

syn. 'Flora Mitten', 'Miss Florence Mitten'
Lawrenson, 1913
For possible parentage, see below.

"This introduction is of the 'American Pillar' [W] sort, with large single blossoms of a delicate pink with beautiful yellow stamens." [JR38/89] "This is a very pretty Rose, but in the rain its creamy-white flowers become spotted in an odd way with flecks of pink." [NRS18/133] "Pink, medium size, single, tall." [Sn] "Clear pink. [For] pillar, arch, pergola. Large single flowers." [NRS15/148] "Reported to be a hybrid of *R. wichuraiana* and *R. canina*, with very large, single, soft pink flowers illumined with gold stamens. Attractive but not espe-cially important." [GAS] "Every garden should possess a plant of ['Miss Flora Mitten']. It is one of the finest single flowered shrubbery Climbers we have, its fine clusters of glorified Wild Rose blossoms being magnificent." [NRS18/148]

Miss Florence Mitten Listed as 'Miss Flora Mitten' (W).

Miss Hellyett Listed as 'Miss Helyett' (W).

Miss Helyett

syns. 'Miss Hellyett', 'Miss Heylyett'
Fauque & fils, 1908
From *Rosa wichuraiana* × 'Ernest Metz' (T).

"Salmon." [Ỹ] "Rose-red, medium size, full, light scent, tall." [Sn] "Large and full; rosy pink with salmon-pink centre, a decided acqui-sition; mid-season." [GeH] "The blooms are very fine, and its buds are of a pinkish shade with deeper rose suffusion." [NRS18/150] "Bloom large and double; color attractive and holds well; good growth; blooming qualities during the second year rather shy, but may im-prove, as rose has been recommended highly." [ARA18/121] "A very attractive rose, making long slim growth which can be trained in any form. Flowers usually a combination of pink, apricot, and salmon." [ARA18/91] "Slim, rapid growers like 'Miss Helyett', 'White Dorothy' [W], and the like." [ARA18/89] "A most attractive, large-flowered Wi-churaiana of extremely vigorous, half-trailing growth. One of the ear-liest roses to bloom, producing large, long-stemmed, double flowers of pale pink tinged with dark rose on the outer petals. It is a neglect-ed worthy climber, hardy and attractive." [GAS] "Very climbing shrub, foliage dark green, glossy. Blossom large, full, solitary, bright carmine pink along the petal edges and yellowish salmon pink in the middle. Very early bloom. To be recommended for ornamenting shrubberies and for cut flowers." [JR32/134] "The largest flowered variety I have. A lovely shade of pale pink with the outside of the outer petals much darker, which in the bud and half-opened state give a very beautiful effect. The flowers come singly and might be more numerous. It is a rampant climber and makes a mass of lateral growth, and rather too vigorous for a 'weeper'; but over an arch or pillar is most effective and would do finely for a fence." [NRS16/94] "For some unaccountable reason, one seldom sees it referred to in the Gardening Press. Can it be that people have overlooked this grand Rambler? It is a very vig-orous grower with dark, handsome foliage. Its large, full flowers of a bright shade of carmine pink with yellowish salmon-pink centres, are very attractive and pleasing, and it is a variety which blooms early and lasts a long time in beauty. This, to my taste, is one of the grand-est of Ramblers. When thoroughly established, it is without a rival." [NRS19/60]

Miss Heylyett Listed as 'Miss Helyett' (W).

Miss Liberty

Boerner/Stuart, 1956
From 'New Dawn' (W) × 'Climbing World's Fair' (Cl Fl).

"Pink, large, lightly double, tall." [Sn] Miss Liberty, generally found disporting herself in New York Harbor, meanwhile attaining a nice verdigris.

Mme. Alice Garnier

Fauque & fils/Gouchault & Turbat, 1906
From *Rosa wichuraiana* × 'Mme. Charles' (T).

"Clusters of small, bright pink flowers tinted yellow." [GAS] "Buff yellow. —Vigorous climber. —Pillar, arch, pergola, weeping stan-dard. —Free. Early. Flowers again in Autumn." [Cat12] "Flowered well for me this autumn with, so far as I can judge, a true second bloom ... Its colour is washy." [NRS11/26] "Rampant shrub, very vigorous, canes growing to two to three meters [ca. 6–9 ft]. Foliage glossy dark green, bloom very profuse and of long duration, in bouquets or corymbs;

flowers small, quite double, perfect in form, opening easily. The bright pink color on a yellowish ground, light pink at the edge, resembles [that of] the charming '[Mlle.] Cécile Brunner' [Pol]." [JR30/136]

Mme. Auguste Nonin

Nonin, 1912
From 'Dorothy Perkins' (W) × 'Blush Rambler' (Mult).

"Wichuraiana of 'Dorothy Perkins' type, with pale pink flowers tinged white." [GAS] "Light violet pink, white center, small, lightly double, light scent, tall." [Sn] "Double, light pink, center white, succeeds well as a parasol, in which shape it is as a splendid specimen in the gardens of [the] Luxembourg [Palace] in Paris [France]." [ARA26/175] "Good growth and foliage; fair amount of bloom." [ARA18/120] "Very vigorous shrub, rapidly forming pretty columns covered with bouquets of upright, nearly double flowers of a shade of light mauve pink with a large white center; bloom late and lasting." [JR36/152]

Mme. Casimir Moullé   Listed as 'Casimir Moullé' (W).

Mme. Charles Lejeune

F. Vandevelde, 1924
From 'Dr. W. Van Fleet' (W) × 'La Perle' (W).

"Clusters of rather large, soft pink flowers." [GAS] "Pink, medium size, full, tall." [Sn] "Flowers soft pink. Foliage rich glossy. Growth very vigorous, climbing; very floriferous." [ARA26/187] "Beautiful glossy leaves." [Ck]

Mme. Constans

Gravereaux, 1902
"Delicate pink." [Ÿ]

Mme. Huguette Despiney

syn. 'Huguette Despiney'
G. Girin, 1911
Sport of 'Marco' (W).

"Interesting and bizarre, small-flowered Wichuraiana with clusters of buff-yellow flowers, edged with red." [GAS] "Salmon orange-yellow passing to pale pink, full, sweetly scented, produced in trusses. Growth vigorous, climbing." [GeH] "Very vigorous shrub, freely climbing, blooming in few-flowered clusters of 3–5 blossoms, sometimes singly; salmon orange yellow passing to delicate pink." [JR36/89]

Monthly Rambler

syn. 'Laxton's Monthly Rambler'
Laxton, 1926
From *Rosa wichuraiana* × "old crimson monthly" (presumably either 'Slater's Crimson China' [Ch] or, more likely, 'Cramoisi Supérieur' [Ch]).

"Crimson red." [Ÿ] "Brilliant crimson trusses." [GeH] "Clusters of small, brilliant crimson flowers of moderate size. Has a tendency to bloom in the autumn." [GAS] "Flower large, semi-double (more petals than most sorts), fragrant, brilliant crimson-red that is very lasting, borne in large, pendant clusters. Growth vigorous; continuous bloomer throughout summer and on young wood in autumn." [ARA28/236]

Morning Dawn

Boerner/Jackson & Perkins, 1955
From seedling (of 'New Dawn' [W]) × 'R.M.S. Queen Mary' (HT).
"Salmon pink, large, full, medium scent, tall." [Sn]

Mrs. Arthur Curtiss James

syn. 'Golden Climber'
Brownell/Jackson & Perkins, 1933
From 'Mary Wallace' (W) × seedling.

"Golden yellow." [Ÿ] "Deep yellow, large, full, medium scent, tall." [Sn] "Very vigorous hardy climber, buds marked like [those of] 'Golden Emblem' [Pern], large fragrant bloom golden yellow on long stems for cutting." [GeH] "Of all yellow climbers in general commerce today, this is the only rival of 'Le Rêve' [F] and 'Star of Persia' [F] in fastness and purity of color. The blooms are large, semi-double, clear bright yellow which does not fade. Hardy in central New York." [GAS] "Early. Something we have longed for—a yellow Climbing Rose which will stand zero temperatures. Perfectly formed buds of rich gold marked with orange-scarlet, open to large, semi-double blooms the color of pure gold, and fade very little. The open flower shows a mass of pale yellow stamens which add to its beauty. It is delightfully fragrant. Coming singly on 15- to 18-inch stems [ca. 3.75–4.5 dm], 'Golden Climber' makes a perfect cut-flower which lasts well. It blooms over a long period in early summer and produces quite a number of flowers again in late summer and autumn. The plants are vigorous and have handsome foliage." [C-Pf33] "Absolutely tops with me." [W]

Mrs. Littleton Dewhurst

Pearson, 1912
Sport of 'Lady Gay' (W).

"White, small, lightly double, tall." [Sn] "Pure white, double, in large loose trusses. Growth very vigorous." [GeH] "Similar in many respects to 'White Dorothy' [W]." [NRS13/98]

Mühle Hermsdorf

E. Dechant, 1928
From *Rosa wichuraiana* × 'Gruss an Zabern' (Mult).

"Prolific Wichuraiana with large clusters of double, fragrant, white flowers." [GAS] "White, medium size, full, very fragrant, tall." [Sn] "Flower full, double, very fragrant, pure white. Foliage large. Growth vigorous; free bloomer. All blooms open at same time." [ARA30/226]

New Dawn

Somerset/Dreer, 1930
Sport of 'Dr. W. Van Fleet' (W).

"Light pink, medium size, full, medium scent, tall." [Sn] "Reddening pink." [Ÿ] "Bud medium size; flower medium size, double, lasting, slightly fragrant, blush-pink, borne singly and several together on long stem. Foliage sufficient, medium size, dark green, glossy. Growth vigorous, climbing (15 to 20 ft. [ca. 5–6.6 m]); free, continuous bloomer from June to November. Very hardy." [ARA30/219] "Pale pink. An everblooming sport of the world's favorite Climbing Rose … They are identical in flower, but 'New Dawn' doesn't stop blooming after a few weeks. It makes a fine display in early summer and then keeps right on producing blooms until frost finally stops it. Dainty, pale pink, fragrant Roses on long stems for cutting." [C-Ps33] "Reputed to be an everblooming form of 'Dr. W. Van Fleet', but so far has evinced little tendency to grow or bloom freely." [GAS]

[Nokomis]

Walsh, 1918
From *Rosa wichuraiana* × 'Comte Raimbaud' (HP).

"Excellent Wichuraiana with large clusters of dark pink flowers,

[Nokomis] *continued*

larger and darker than those of 'Dorothy Perkins' [W]." [GAS] "Double, rose-pink flowers, larger than those of 'Dorothy Perkins', come in variable clusters of 5 to 30. A wonderful vigorous climber (rare now). Very fragrant." [W] Nokomis, mother of Hiawatha in Longfellow's poem *The Song of Hiawatha.*

Normandie
Nonin, 1929

"Salmon pink, medium size, full, tall." [Sn] "Late-blooming Wichuraiana with clusters of pretty salmon-pink flowers." [GAS]

Papa Rouillard
Turbat, 1923

From 'Léontine Gervais' (W) × unnamed seedling.

"Brilliant carmine." [Ÿ] "Light red, medium size, full, tall." [Sn] "Reported to be an almost thornless Wichuraiana with bright red flowers in long, pendulous clusters." [GAS] "Bud medium size, globular; flower medium size, full, double, very lasting, bright carmine, borne in long clusters of 15 to 25 flowers on long stem. Foliage sufficient, medium size, rich green, glossy. Thornless. Very vigorous climber; abundant bloomer in June and July." [ARA25/188]

Paradise
Walsh, 1907

"Graceful pink clusters of single, ruffled flowers, white toward the base, and a large cluster of yellow stamens." [ARA29/56] "Pink, large, single, light scent, tall." [Sn] "White, edged with pink, small petals, single flowers in large clusters, twisted. Growth very vigorous, distinct." [GeH] "Late." [Cat12] "Growth fair; not a bloomer." [ARA18/122] "Free grower. Very pretty single flower of pale pink with white centre. Dr. Williams says: 'White tipped with pink.' The flowers are of good size, as also the trusses. Good as a weeper." [NRS16/97] "Extremely vigorous Wichuraiana with huge, diffuse clusters of single flowers, with notched white petals deeply tinged with rose. Fragrant and handsome." [GAS]

Paul Noël   Plate 40
Tanne, 1912

From *Rosa wichuraiana* × 'Monsieur Tillier' (T).

"Old rose, then pale pink." [Ÿ] "Yellowish pink, medium size, lightly double, tall." [Sn] "A rarely beautiful Wichuraiana [*i.e., we hope, 'Of rare beauty'*], of a deep, warm coral-pink." [ARA21/126] "Rather large, very double, camellia-shaped flowers of a deep old-rose shade, blended with salmon-yellow. Some plants have a tendency to bloom in the fall." [GAS] "Yellowish salmon-rose. Growth very vigorous." [GeH] "Here we have an unusually attractive climber in bud, in bloom, and in foliage. Nature has made the canes of dark reddish brown, beautiful to look at even when in spots they are bare from the lovely shiny bronzed foliage. Its delightful fragrance adds another mark of distinction to the charm of the Rose 'Paul Noel' [*sic*]. The buds are salmon-orange-pink, with a yellow base, and open to perfectly double blooms with a tufted center of salmon-pink which holds while the flower lasts. It is a most vigorous climber, very profuse in bloom, and it always gives a few, heartily welcomed blooms, late in the summer." [C-Ps27] "Absolutely a new break in colour in the Rambler section. It is, unfortunately, somewhat variable in colour, but at its best it rivals the deeper tints of 'Lyon-Rose' [Pern] when it assumes that

coppery tone which everyone seems to appreciate so greatly. The flowers of 'Paul Noël' are large—fully double the size of those of 'Dorothy Perkins' [W] —and are borne in trusses of from four to six. The colour is often very light, but even when it comes toned down a bit by adverse climatic conditions it is still very beautiful. I would describe the softer tone as a mixture of old rose and pale yellow. This variety is a robust grower with highly-polished foliage of dark, bronzy green." [NRS19/59–60]

"Very vigorous bush, floriferous, giving roses in groups of two or three; [they are] medium-sized, early, and [the bloom] lasts about two months; color, shrimp pink mixed with sulphur yellow. Variety of the highest merit." [JR35/6] "In our number of last January, we announced on page 6 of this same chronicle that Mr. Tanne, distinguished rose-lover, released to commerce his two beautiful Wichuraiana varieties 'Dr. Henri Neuprez' [Plate 40] and 'Paul Noël'. The happy breeder of these pretty obtentions lets us know that, not having enough specimens to provide to buyers, he will wait some time before releasing them to the public. We will give our readers ample warning." [JR35/39] "Very vigorous plant, floriferous; pretty glossy green foliage; has a tendency to rebloom; bears full roses in clusters of two to five; very early and long-lasting; color, shrimp pink mixed with sulphur yellow; a variety of pretty effect." [JR36/154] It is interesting to compare Tanne's description of JR35/6 with Tanne's description after another season of growth in JR36/154!

Paul Ploton
Barbier, 1910

From *Rosa wichuraiana* × 'Mme. Norbert Levavasseur' (Pol).

"Glowing carmine, double, rosette shaped. Growth vigorous." [GeH] "Deep pink, medium size, full, tall." [Sn] "A dark 'Minnehaha' [W], the rosettes rather larger and flatter. The tone of colour is rather dull, but the pyramidal sprays are large and make a good effect at the end of the laterals which stand out from the main growth. A good pillar Rose." [NRS16/97] "Plant climbing, vigorous. Foliage bright green. Blooms in bouquets of 10–12 double blossoms colored bright amaranth within, passing to crimson when open; petal exteriors lilac-y pink. Very effective coloration. Bloom late and very abundant." [JR34/150] "A vigorous, rampant grower, with fine dark green glossy foliage, which is practically evergreen and untouched by mildew. It blooms in trusses of small double rosettes of glowing carmine colour." [NRS13/100]

Paul Transon
Barbier, 1900

From *Rosa wichuraiana* × 'L'Idéal' (N).

"Bright flesh pink." [Ÿ] "Light salmon pink, large, full, medium scent, tall." [Sn] "Flower rose coloured, flowers large and double, scented with Tea Rose scent. Growth vigorous." [GeH] "Shows more traces of the Tea than most of the Wichuraianas. Salmon pink, a good creeper, sweet scented, and mid season flowering." [F-M] "This is an early flowerer . . . The flower is flat, but in the bud is very attractive. The colour of the open flower varies in its shading of coppery salmon pink. It is a very vigorous grower." [NRS16/95] "Moderately vigorous Wichuraiana with rather large flowers of light salmon-pink. A sparse bloomer but continuous for a long time." [GAS] "Apricot; of fine size for this class; double. Splendid bloomer. Very vigorous. Foliage well retained." [Th2] "Good in growth, foliage and blooming qualities." [ARA18/121]

Paul's Scarlet Climber
W. Paul, 1916

"Bright scarlet red." [Ÿ] "Red, medium size, full, tall." [Sn] "Medium-sized flowers of *vivid scarlet,* shaded with bright crimson. We consider this the brightest red, hardy climbing Rose in existence, surpassing in brilliance even the famous 'Gruss an Teplitz' [B]." [C&Js21] "Wonderful shade of scarlet flowers which last until all have opened and make a brilliant show for a long time. The color does not turn blue or darken and the foliage is good." [ARA29/56] "For brilliancy of color this Rose outclasses every other climbing variety in the red shades. The color is gleaming vivid scarlet which does not fade but remains bright until the flowers fall. The blooms are medium in size, semi-double, and perfect in bud form. They come in clusters of from three to fifteen or more." [C&Js22] "Vivid scarlet, shaded with crimson, flowering in great profusion, large clusters of medium size, semi-double flowers. Growth very vigorous." [GeH] "The greatest profusion of bloom comes on the new growth." [CaRolII/6/5] "Very vigorous grower, blooms from middle of June profusely, but sparingly later until end of October." [NRS28/70] "Gives recurrent bloom in California." [CaRolI/4/2] "The most vivid scarlet climbing Rose yet grown. Its flowers come in beautiful open cluster-heads, with from 5 to 15 blooms, on strong stems. A plant of 'Paul's Scarlet' in full bloom is as spectacular during the day as fireworks at night. It makes a splendid pillar as it is medium in growth." [C-Ps30] "Strong climbing habit with good foliage, and flowers in the greatest profusion with clusters of medium-sized semi-double blooms. The colour is a scarlet shaded with crimson, and is well retained, without burning or fading, till the petals fall. The plant makes a magnificent display in the garden for five or six weeks. For pergolas or tall pillars this Rose has a great future in store." [NRS16/142] "Nothing so pure and bright in color has ever before been known in a climbing Rose. It needs, and deserves, to stand by itself, away from hardy climbers that are merely red, and with which it will not mix. Pleasing buds, quickly opening into large, flat, informal flowers, grow plentifully on a hardy, strong but not rampant plant carrying light green leaves. Sometimes it grows slowly, and sometimes there is also a scanty fall bloom, in addition to the scarlet splash of bloom in the spring. The garden without 'Paul's Scarlet Climber' is deficient … Use it as a pillar or bush— but if you value your eyesight, keep its dazzling scarlet as far away as possible from carmine or magenta flowers." [C-Ps25]

"The brightest red of all the pillar Roses. Colour, vivid scarlet, shaded with crimson. Flowers of medium size, produced in sprays. The raiser is to be congratulated in presenting us with such a beautiful and useful pillar variety, but why did he name it a climber? As we have it it is as pillar Rose growing from seven to eight feet high [ca. 2.3–2.6 m]. Although strictly speaking it should be classed as summer flowering and is at its best in July, nevertheless it has a long season, giving bloom well into September." [NRS21/65–66] "A very strong Climbing Hybrid wichuraiana with stout and rapid growth. The semi-double blooms, which are of a bright scarlet colour, are borne in clusters, and make the plant the most striking feature in the Rose Garden. It is an exceptional variety, as it has better manners than any of the [other] Climbing Roses. Some are apt to become bare at the base, but not so with '[Paul's] Scarlet Climber', who takes good care to hide her lower limbs with her blooms. The foliage is dark green and remains on the plant over a long period. It is almost perpetual flowering and the blooms last a long time on the plant. Unfortunately it is not fragrant, but in spite of that it is the best red Rose we have for pillars, or big bushes, or planting against an east wall. It does not like a lot of pruning, and while it will bloom well from last year's growths it will bloom equally well from the lateral shoots. If these are pruned back in the Spring to three eyes and the long shoots of last year tipped, no other pruning, beyond cutting out any dead wood, is necessary." [NRS30/154] "Moderate vigor, bearing clusters of beautifully formed, fairly large, vivid scarlet flowers shaded with crimson. This rose has fallen heir to the mantle of '[Turner's] Crimson Rambler' [Mult], and may be seen along roadsides everywhere. At present it is the most popular red climbing rose." [GAS]

[Pearl Queen]
Van Fleet/Conard & Jones, 1901

"An elegant new Hardy Climber, large perfectly double flowers, clear Pearl White, finely tinted with deep rose; fragrant and a tremendous bloomer." [C&Js01] "Bloom free most of June." [ARA18/131] "Resembles the beautiful '[Souvenir de la] Malmaison' rose so closely that it might easily be mistaken for it. Large full regular flowers, perfectly double and delightfully fragrant. Colour, clear pearl white faintly tinged with pale rose, deepening at center to bright red. A strong hardy grower and tremendous bloomer." [C&Js02]

Perfection Orange   Listed as 'South Orange Perfection' (W).

Petit Louis
Nonin, 1912
From 'Dorothy Perkins' (W) × seedling.

"Salmony pink." [Ÿ] "Flower salmon-rose. Growth very vigorous." [GeH] "Early-flowering pink Wichuraiana of the 'Dorothy Perkins' type. Sometimes used for forcing under glass." [GAS] "Plant growing strongly, rapidly clothing a wide area, blooming in enormous bouquets; large very double flowers of a beautiful tint of salmony pink frosted silver; early to bloom, and long-lasting." [JR36/152] "Growth and foliage quite good; blooming fair." [ARA18/121] "Foliage blackspots slightly from midsummer; bloom free two weeks in late June." [ARA18/131] "It was raised by Monsieur Nonin, of Chatillon, a very eminent French horticulturist, whose name is more associated with and better known in regard to the chrysanthemum than it is with the Rose. Mr. Robert Fife, of Edinburgh, was so greatly impressed with the beauty of this fine Rambler when he saw it exhibited in London that he at once procured plants from France and introduced it into commerce in this country [United Kingdom]. I am astonished that it has been so long neglected by other nurserymen, for, apart altogether from its beauty and its undoubted superiority over 'Dorothy Perkins', it flowers at least fourteen days earlier than the older and better known variety. 'Petit Louis' bears elegantly formed flowers of a soft pink disposed in charming sprays. It is a good grower, and is much less addicted to mildew than 'Dorothy Perkins' —this affliction is rarely seen with us on 'Petit Louis'." [NRS19/56–57]

Petit René
Nonin, 1925

"Clusters of small, double, bright red flowers." [GAS] "Red, small, very full, very fragrant, tall." [Sn] "Type, 'Excelsa' [W]. Bud small, globular; flower small, very double, full, very lasting, very fragrant, brilliant red, borne in clusters on short stem; hang on. Foliage abundant,

Petit René *continued*

glossy. Growth very vigorous (6 to 16 feet [ca. 2–5.3 m]; profuse bloomer for four weeks in June and July." [ARA27/223]

Pink Pearl
Horvath/Manda & Pitcher, 1901
From *Rosa wichuraiana* × 'The Meteor' (HT).

"Salmony pink." [Ÿ] "Old-fashioned Wichuraiana, with clusters of crimson buds and pale pink, double, fragrant flowers." [GAS] "This variety, which was bred by W. A. Manda, is a hybrid which always wins the highest awards wherever shown in America. It is a cross of *R. wichuraiana* and '[The] Meteor'. The buds are salmon pink fading to pale pink bit by bit as it opens. As for the blossoms, they attain a size which surpasses that of any of the other Wichuraianas." [JR24/129]

Pink Roamer
Horvath/Manda & Pitcher, 1898
From *Rosa wichuraiana* × either (1) 'The Meteor' (HT) or (2) 'Cramoisi Supérieur' (Ch).

"Pink, white center, small, single, medium scent, tall." [Sn] "Purple with a white center." [JR26/181] "Flower semi-full or single, bright pink with a large white eye." [JR32/172] "The flowers are single, and from two to three inches in diameter [ca. 5–7.5 cm]; rich pink, with silver-white center, and orange-red stamens; exceedingly fragrant, and picturesque." [C&Js99] "Old flowers shed petals." [ARA23/170] "Semi-double bright rose-colored flowers, centers white. A trailer." [GAS] "Pink with silvery white centre, very showy, clusters. Growth vigorous." [GeH] "Flowers pretty large, bright pink with a considerable number of dark stamens, very vigorous. Honorable mention by the New York Horticultural Society." [JR21/68] "'Pink Roamer' is a very vigorous climbing shrub, producing very long growths which cover themselves with a great quantity of flowers. These last are single, and richly colored deep pink with a pure white center—excepting the yellow anthers." [JR24/114] "Single, in small clusters, small to medium size, good form, cinnamon-scent, short to medium stem. Poor foliage, with faint scent, plentiful early in season, very sparse to none by end of June, subject to rust and red spider. Growth very vigorous; hardy. Deep rose-pink." [ARA23/170] "Foliage barely sufficient from midsummer on, very little black-spot in midsummer; bloom free for two weeks in mid-June." [ARA18/131]

Poteriifolia Listed as *Rosa wichuraiana* 'Poteriifolia'.

Primevère
syn. 'Primrose'; trans., "Primrose"
Barbier/Dreer, 1929
From *Rosa wichuraiana* × 'Constance' (Pern).

"Bright primrose yellow." [Ÿ] "Yellow, large, full, light scent, tall." [Sn] "At last a good, yellow, hardy, double climber. The fully double blooms are $2^{1}/_{2}$ inches in diameter [ca. 6.5 cm], borne in clusters of two to five, rich primrose-yellow which does not fade, fragrant. [*The writer*] is greatly pleased with the flowers, the strong climbing plant, and the foliage." [ARA30/197] "Rather large, very double bright yellow flowers which fade pale lemon but not white as the older yellow climbers do. It takes its time about establishing itself in the North, but flourishes greatly in Virginia." [GAS] "Type, 'Albéric Barbier' [W] but much larger. Bud medium-sized, very double, full, very lasting, primrose-yellow holding its color until petals drop, borne several to-

gether on long stem. Foliage disease-resistant. Growth vigorous, climbing; abundant bloomer. Very hardy." [ARA29/219] "Bud medium size to large, egg-yolk yellow; flower large, double, full, open, lasting, slightly fragrant, bright primrose-yellow, passing to canary-yellow, borne several together on long stem. Foliage abundant, medium size, rich green, glossy, disease-resistant. Growth very vigorous, climbing, and trailing; abundant bloomer for four weeks in May and June. Very hardy." [ARA30/225] "Beautiful shiny foliage . . . a moderate grower, making a splendid pillar rose. The buds are rich yellow, the open flowers soft but rich primrose, which color is held until the petals drop. The flowers are about two and one-half inches in diameter [ca. 6.5 cm], very double, perfect in shape and deliciously fragrant; they come in clusters of four or five." [CaRol/6/3] "*Nicolas* claims it is the only yellow climber that does not fade to a nondescript muddy cream. *Foote* admires it, but complains of black-spot . . . The correct name of this rose in 'Primrose'. We understand that the French originators agreed with the American introducers that it should have that name; but, in spite of this, introduced it in Europe under the French translation 'Primevère'." [ARA31/205] "A strong climber with glossy foliage that it held well into the autumn." [ARA31/181]

Primrose Listed as 'Primevère' (W).

Professor C. S. Sargent
Hoopes, Bro., & Thomas, 1903
From *Rosa wichuraiana* × 'Souvenir d'Auguste Métral' (HT).

"Delicate buff, with center of deep golden yellow, $2^{1}/_{2}$ inches across [ca. 6.5 cm]." [C&Js06] "One of the largest-flowered yellow-tinted climbers, and keeps its color better than most of them. The blooms are very double, and keep well, cut or on the bush." [ARA22/44] "Quite fragrant." [C&Js21] "A pillar Rose, giving delicate buff, fragrant flowers of medium size, and of a distinctly dainty expression." [C-Ps25] "Yellow, medium size, full, tall." [Sn] "When well established in a good protected early place, will give the best-colored apricot flowers of any climber. They are very double, slow about opening, and will keep a week after they open." [ARA18/91] "Singly and in small clusters, good form, medium size, double, quite fragrant, short to medium stem. Fine foliage, sufficient. Growth strong; hardy. Fine for banks. Buff-yellow to golden center, but fading to a creamy buff when fully open." [ARA23/171] "This extremely vigorous, trailing Wichuraiana is difficult to make grow erect. It produces yellow buds and semi-double, pale fawn-colored flowers, and is relatively hardy for a yellow climber, after it has been once established." [GAS] "Not same as 'Sargent' [W]." [Th2] Professor C. S. Sargent, of the Arnold Arboretum, Massachusetts.

Purity
Hoopes, Bro., & Thomas, 1917
From a seedling (resulting from a cross of *Rosa wichuraiana* and 'Marion Dingee' [T]) × 'Mme. Caroline Testout' (HT).

"Flowers pure white and about 4 inches in diameter [ca. 1 dm], with cupped petals." [C&Js21] "Semi-double white; an improvement on the others, with longer stems and larger flowers." [ARA18/91] "White, medium size, full, light scent, tall." [Sn] "Pure white with flesh centre, pointed, globular; handsome foliage, fragrant. Growth very vigorous; weeping standard." [GeH] "Remarkably fine Wichuraiana of the large-flowered type. Big, cup-shaped, pure white flowers borne with remarkable freedom. Plant is excessively thorny and extremely vigorous, but ranks near the top among white climbers." [GAS] "A rampant grower, with dark green or bronzy stems covered with magnificent thorns. The foliage is very fine, a dark, glossy green, and very dense; it is almost evergreen, and mildew-proof. The flowers are produced in small trusses; they are large, semi-double, of good form, with snow-white petals." [NRS13/92–93] "Very hardy, excellent foliage, and a good grower." [C-Ps26] "Foliage black-spots in midsummer, very slightly in late summer, slightly mildews in midsummer; bloom sparse in June." [ARA18/131] "It was sent out in 1917 as a Hybrid wichuraiana, but really there seems to be very little of the wichuraiana about it. It is a very vigorous growing Rose with large paper white blooms. Delightfully fragrant. The foliage is bright green and remains on the plant well into the Winter. It is best grown as a pillar, or spread out fanshape. Unfortunately it is not perpetual flowering, but on two occasions my plant has bloomed the second time in November. It is a Rose for some reason or other rarely seen, but one I would not like to be without." [NRS30/228] "Of the summer flowering group I know nothing to equal 'Purity' . . . which is altogether a charming Rose." [NRS20/94] Purity, like Chastity and Generosity, a virtue generally more valued in others than in one's self.

Purpurtraum
trans. "Purple Dream"
Kayser & Seibert, 1923

"Deep purple red, medium size, lightly double, tall." [Sn] "The introducers describe it as darkest of all cluster-flowering Wichuraianas. Probably red or violet." [GAS] "Flower medium large, in clusters. Vigorous growth." [ARA26/186] "The darkest of the ramblers. Blossom mid-sized, in a cluster. Moderate grower." [Ck]

Rambler-Königin
trans. "Rambler-Queen"
Kohler & Rudel, 1907

"Pink, small, full, tall." [Sn] "Flower full, pink. Very floriferous and remontant." [JR35/15] "Almost unknown pink, small-flowered Wichuraiana." [GAS] "Pink, very free. Growth very vigorous." [GeH]

Refresher
A. Clark/Hazlewood, 1929

"White, small, single, tall." [Sn] "Vigorous Wichuraiana strongly resembling a white-flowered 'American Pillar' [W]." [GAS]

Regierungsrat Rottenberger
Praskač, 1926

"Deep red, medium size, full, tall." [Sn] "Under this awful name may lie hidden a beautiful rose but the world will never know it. Reported to be a Wichuraiana, with clusters of double, rose-red flowers." [GAS]

René André   Plate 38
Barbier, 1900
From *Rosa wichuraiana* × 'L'Idéal' (N).

"Red and saffron yellow." [JR26/181] "Orange- or shrimp-pink." [ARA19/86] "Blossom semi-double, bright saffron at the tip, orange yellow around the base, passing to white." [JR32/172] "Deep dawn pink." [Ÿ] "'René André's lovely warm pink blossoms glowed." [ARA21/127] "The flowers are fairly large, saffron-yellow in the bud, tinged with pink as they open. Not a great deal unlike 'Paul Transon' [W]." [GAS] "Among the three varieties presented [*by Barbier Frères as their first offering of their new Wichuraiana hybrids, the other two being*

'Albéric Barbier' *and* 'Paul Transon'], 'René André' is without a doubt the most beautiful. Flowers semi-double, 6–7 cm across [ca. 2½–2¾ in]. Bud, deep saffron red. Petals bright saffron at the tip, orange yellow around the base, going to white around the center, veined carmine, becoming paler when fully open." [JR30/14–15] "Yellowish pink, medium size, lightly double, very fragrant, tall." [Sn] "Dark saffron-yellow, shaded orange-red, early, fragrant. Growth vigorous." [GeH] "A vigorous grower with strong, thorny stems of bronzy green. Foliage, large dark green, lightly glossed. It is rather liable to mildew. Flowers in small trusses of loosely double blooms. The buds are coppery red, and open to bronzy pink." [NRS13/97]

Renée Danielle
P. Guillot, 1913

"Jonquil yellow." [Ÿ] "Yellow, medium size, full, tall." [Sn] "A yellow-flowered Wichuraiana of the old type, with clusters of small blooms which fade white as they age. Sometimes blooms in the autumn." [GAS] "Here [in Ciampino, Italy], a very fine Wichuraiana, of glossy, persistent foliage and lovely jonquil-yellow flowers." [ARA19/86] "Plant of very great vigor, with long rampant climbing hardy canes; very beautiful lustrous purple foliage—very ornamental; inflorescences corymbiferous, sometimes solitary; flower medium-sized, quite full, cupped; color varies from jonquil yellow or deep golden yellow to white when the petals fall; very beautiful variety for garlands, pergolas, porticos, weepers, rocks, etc. It has a tendency to rebloom over the course of the high season." [JR37/151]

Romeo
Easlea, 1919

"Deep red, double and of perfect form; resembling a miniature 'Liberty' [HT]." [GeH] "Deep red, small, full, tall." [Sn] "A grand addition to the fast-growing ramblers. The flowers are deep red, double, and of perfect elongated form, resembling a miniature Hybrid Tea. Excellent for florists' work." [NRS19/171] "It hasn't many flowers, being like 'Emily Gray' [W] and 'Paul's Scarlet Climber' [W] in that respect, but each is quite perfect, like a deep red miniature Tea rose, and it makes a most effective table decoration." [ARA25/133] "Flowers perfectly formed, double, deep red. Vigorous grower; blooms continuously during June and July." [ARA20/130] "A most interesting early Wichuraiana of rigid, erect growth, at times bearing beautifully shaped little crimson flowers on individual stems, clothing the plant from top to bottom in a mass of bloom. At other times it has no distinctive character and looks more or less like 'Excelsa' [W]." [GAS] How well 'Romeo' (W) goes with 'Juliet' (Pern/HP) perhaps sheds exciting new light on Shakespeare's play.

Royal Scarlet Hybrid
Chaplin, 1926

"Bright crimson red." [Ÿ] "Early. Crimson-scarlet. A counterpart of 'Paul's Scarlet Climber' [W] but crimson instead of scarlet in color. We think it more beautiful than 'Paul's Scarlet [Climber]', but as it blooms about two weeks earlier, both are needed." [C-Pf33] "Type, 'Paul's Scarlet Climber', with flowers of similar shape but smaller and deeper in color. Free flowering." [ARA28/237] "Deep red, medium size, lightly double, tall." [Sn] "A valuable addition to red climbers. After the style of 'Paul's Scarlet [Climber]', the flowers being similar in shape to the latter, only rather smaller, and a shade deeper in colour; free flowering; fine pillar Rose." [GeH] "Here is a gorgeous member of the

Royal Scarlet Hybrid *continued*

rose aristocracy. A rose much finer than 'Paul's Scarlet Climber', of a glowing ruddy crimson shade intermediate between that flaming variety and 'Dr. Huey' [W]. It is one of the most effective Wichuraianas now in commerce." [GAS]

[Rubra]

Barbier, 1901

From *Rosa wichuraiana* × 'Turner's Crimson Rambler' (Mult).

"Blossom single, red lightly tinted orange, white center, blooming in clusters of 20 to 50 flowers." [JR32/172] "Blooms in clusters of single flowers, bright scarlet petals tinted orange-red and with numerous orange-red stamens." [C&Js07] "Vigorous, branching shrub with climbing canes which are long, green, glabrous, and armed with short upright or slightly curved whitish-gray thorns. Leaves glabrous, bright green, with two or three pairs of small, oval, sessile, serrate-crenulate leaflets, paler beneath, terminal leaflet larger and longly pedicelate; stipules large, lacinate, pointed at the tip; petiole caniculate, glandulose, armed with occasional small and back-hooked thorns. Inflorescence in leafy multifloral panicles, terminally or laterally branched, accompanied by green bracteate leaflets which are upright, foliaceous, lobed, and cuspidate on the lower branches, oval-acuminate, serrated like a saw, keeled; pedicels reddish, bearing similarly-colored glands; ovary glabrous, turbinate, green; calyx with reflexing sepals after anthesis; sepals oval-acuminate, concave, hispidulose, ciliate with white bristles; corolla 4 centimeters or more across [ca. 1 1/2 in +], spreading widely; petals cuneiform-obtuse, much notched, beautiful bright carmine-red washed orange, white at the base; stamens in a distinct central ring, long golden yellow filaments, with orange anthers; styles green, upright, claviform. This beautiful shrub, sparkling in bloom, was raised by Messrs. the Barbier Bros., horticulturalists of Orléans, from a sowing of *R. wichuraiana* pollinated by '[Turner's] Crimson Rambler'. They are releasing it to commerce in 1901. This cross gave several plants with blossoms which were more or less red, and one sole plant with blossoms of a pale pink; they don't seem to want to bloom abundantly. Seeds collected from 'Rubra' without artificial pollination reproduce the variety nearly identically. Of 70 specimens, not one was a return to the Type of either parent, likewise the foliage, which remains as described above; only the blossoms of these varieties have tints which vary to a greater or lesser red—but not a single plant had white flowers. The bloom-time of these seedlings, including 'Rubra', is the same as that of '[Turner's] Crimson Rambler', and little sooner than the white-blossomed *R. wichuraiana* Type. I would describe it as around mid-June, with bloom lasting until month's end. Use of this beautiful newcomer will be especially to clothe trellises, tunnels, and all the favorable sites on which climbing roses are used for decoration. But it is especially on isolated crags on slopes that it provides a magnificent cover in Spring, with its purple mantle. We have already gotten wonderful results in this genre with '[Turner's] Crimson Rambler'; the series will be able to continue and vary indefinitely, to the great advantage of our country houses, at which it will add to the picturesque element. Already, with the *Rugosa* crosses; with the new obtentions of Messrs. Barbier I wrote about last year; with the development which we have Mr. Manda of the U.S. to thank for; and with the *Rubiginosa* hybrids, said to be from Lord Penzance;—all of these have enriched our undertakings and brought precious elements of springtime decoration into the garden." [JR25/21]

Ruby Queen

Van Fleet/Conard & Jones, 1898

From 'Cramoisi Supérieur' (Ch; Van Fleet knew it under its synonyms 'Agrippina' or 'Queen's Scarlet') × *Rosa wichuraiana*.

"Lilac-y pink." [Ÿ] "Blossom medium-sized, double, bright carmine, backs of petals whitish." [JR32/172] "Lilac pink with a white center." [JR26/182] "One of the oldest Wichuraianas. Rather large, double, ruby-red flowers with white centers. Valuable only as a curiosity." [GAS] "Without fragrance." [C-Ps26] "Deep violet pink, medium size, full, tall." [Sn] "Bright carmine with white eye, large, semi-double. Growth very vigorous." [GeH] "The flowers are brilliant carmine with a pure white center. The similarly very vigorous plant [*i.e., similar to* 'May Queen' (W)] is admirable. Both of these are very hardy and of exceptional merit." [JR34/126] "Bright rich ruby red, with clear white center; flowers quite double, three to three and one-half inches across [ca. 8–9 cm], opening out flat and perfect; color brilliant carmine, base of petals pure white; the color is rich and velvety and the purest shade found in Roses, lasting without a tinge of purple for days. Blooms with great freedom in clusters of five to seven. The plant is a strong vigorous climber, with handsome glossy foliage, and entirely hardy. Its rapid hardy growth, early and abundant bloom, and bright rich colors will make it a favorite with rose-loving people everywhere." [C&Js98] "A strong upright grower with stiff, thorny stems. The foliage is dense, of medium green lightly glossed, almost evergreen, and mildew proof. The flowers are produced in the greatest profusion, in fairly large trusses. The blooms are of medium size, loosely double. The petals are a glowing carmine with a white base; late in the season the white base extends far up the petal, giving a more pink tone to the general appearance; very beautiful in either stage." [NRS13/95] "Fair in growth and bloom." [ARA18/121] "A fine pillar Rose." [C&Js22] "Not so well known as it deserves. Early loose flowers—in small truss. Recommended as a weeping standard." [F-M] "One 'rose for the million' which everyone has seen is 'Ruby Queen'. We have one growing over the end of an old stone house, where, with ample opportunity for climbing, it is, in its season of bloom, a wonderful sight. Yet while Dr. Van Fleet thought well of this variety, it was his ambition to produce the same richness of color and riot of growth with a better flower." [ARA22/19]

Ruby Ring

A. Clark, 1926

"Attractive Wichuraiana with large clusters of single, white flowers deeply edged with glowing red." [GAS] "Deep red, medium size, single, tall." [Sn]

Sander's White

Sander & Sons, 1912

"White, small, full, medium scent, tall." [Sn] "The slightly fragrant flowers, with golden stamens, come in panicles and appear earlier than [those of] 'White Dorothy' [W]." [C-Ps30] "Does not send up vigorous annual shoots from the base quite so freely as the white sport from 'Dorothy Perkins' [W]." [NRS28/148] "By all accounts and reports this is the finest cluster-flowering white Wichuraiana climber, with individual blooms of perfect rosette form, highly perfumed and desirable in every way. Occasional blooms are produced in autumn." [GAS] "Bloomed twice . . . as it does every year." [ARA22/43] "This rose is the prettiest and most floriferous of all the white Wichuraiana crosses. It was chosen from the best of about four thousand seedlings. The rose 'Sander's White' makes long vigorous growths completely covered with beautiful glossy green foliage, thereby forming an admirable contrast with the large, thick thyrses of snow white blossoms produced by this newcomer. Grown on a wall, this rose covers it completely the first year and presents a uniform mass of a white which could not be more beautiful mixed with pretty foliage." [JR36/155] "Fair growth; mass of bloom all at once—attractive." [ARA18/121] "Rampant grower; flowers profusely in large trusses of double snow-white blooms. Very well spoken of." [NRS13/101] "The best white wichuraiana we have. My opinion has been much criticised, and it has been urged that the flowers of this variety have a tendency to turn brown in the centre. That has not been my experience of it, however." [NRS18/151] "The finest white Rambler at present in commerce. The astonishing thing to me is the neglect of this Rambler by the trade. It was sent out in 1912 by the Continental House of Sander and Sons, a firm whose name is more associated with orchids than it is with Roses. I think that we owe the fact of this Rambler having been put into commerce to the perspicacity of a well-known British horticultural journalist, who is thoroughly *au fait* with all matters relating to his profession, and who is a real judge of flowers. He happened to be in Messrs. Sander's office in Belgium one morning, and a box of seedling Roses had just come in from some correspondent—he thinks—in Germany. As the firm were not in the Rose trade they were not disposed to consider the seedlings that had been sent for their inspection, but their visitor was greatly struck with the sprays of the white Rambler, and strongly advised them to send it out. They knew he was an experienced horticulturist, and, valuing his opinion, they took his advice—hence 'Sander's White Rambler'. The flowers ... are very beautifully shaped—and they are very fragrant, exhaling the real, so-called, 'old-fashioned' Rose perfume. In this respect no other Rambler can rival it. The foliage is mildew-proof, and it is a strong growing variety." [NRS19/58]

Sargent
Dawson, 1912
From *Rosa wichuraiana* × a seedling (resulting from a cross of 'Turner's Crimson Rambler' [Mult] and 'Baronne Adolphe de Rothschild' [HP]).

"Light pink, medium size, lightly double, tall." [Sn] "A rugged climber of moderate growth, with coarse foliage and stems, showing indications of Multiflora as well as Wichuraiana parentage. The single flowers are borne in huge clusters and vary from clear flesh-pink to creamy white, like huge apple-blossoms, very beautiful and fragrant." [GAS] "Called one of the handsomest roses that has been raised in the United States." [ARA16/17]

Schneeball
trans. "Snowball"
Weigand, 1906

"Clusters of medium-sized, double, snow-white flowers." [GAS] "White, medium size, lightly double, medium scent, tall." [Sn] "Snow-white, of medium size, produced in clusters. Growth very vigorous." [GeH]

Seagull
Pritchard, 1907

"White, medium size, single, tall." [Sn] "Flower white, free, sweetly scented. Growth vigorous." [GeH] "Early-flowering Wichuraiana with very large clusters of single, pure white flowers. Either the same rose or another is reported as a hybrid of *Rosa Brunoni* [*sic*]." [GAS] "Absolutely winter hardy, climbs high and wide. Fine leaves. Large clusters of snow-white blossoms." [Ck]

Shalimar
Burrell, 1914
Sport of 'Minnehaha' (W)

"Immense pyramidal clusters of creamy yellow flowers 'picoteed' bright rose pink." [GAS] "Creamy blush lightly flaked rose with picotee edge, large trusses, free flowering. Growth vigorous." [GeH] "Yellowish pink, medium size, full, tall." [Sn] "Growth good; not a profuse bloomer; sometimes gives an occasional bloom in fall." [ARA18/121]

Shower of Gold
G. Paul, 1910
From 'Jersey Beauty' (W) × 'Instituteur Sirdey' (HT).

"Deep yellow, medium size, full, tall." [Sn] "Light cream to pale yellow; spring only. Foliage fair." [ARA17/26] "I had quite a nice second crop of flowers this year." [NRS16/99] "Golden yellow, double, of rosette shape. Growth very vigorous, climbing, numerous laterals are produced, clad with beautiful glossy foliage." [GeH] "Wichuraiana with a queer, misleading name. The buds are yellowish, opening to rather large, double, white flowers, tinged with cream-color in the center. A vigorous grower with lovely foliage but extremely tender to frost." [GAS] "Fair growth; blooms distinct; needs winter protection." [ARA18/121] "A very vigorous grower with deep golden yellow and orange flowers borne in fine trusses. It produces a mass of bloom and the Wichuraiana foliage is beautiful in form, in color, and in its high metallic lustre." [C&Js12]

"The habit of growth is vigorous, and numerous laterals are produced which are densely clad in a glossy and beautiful foliage, almost fern-like in its effect. The leaves on the upper side are of a vivid glossy green, the under side reddish brown shaded with a silvery sheen, and the reddish-brown colour runs through the stems. The flowers are double, rosette shaped, and of medium size for the class to which it belongs. It is almost the colour of 'William Allen Richardson' [N], but with not quite so much orange; but perhaps its chief characteristic is that the majority of blooms, instead of changing to white as they age, retain to a considerable extent their rich yellow colour, the general effect rendering the appearance of the whole plant in bloom most striking." [NRS10/161] "It makes vigorous stems of somewhat branching habit which turn brown on the sunny side in autumn. The thorns on the stem are few and irregularly placed but the backs of the leaf stalks usually have from four to six small ones. The foliage is particularly good, dark green glossy and closely packed on the stems, and is moreover almost evergreen, and quite free from mildew. The flowering period begins, Dr. Williams tells me, on the 15th of June, and lasts for about six weeks. It seldom flowers again. The flowers are small and double, but not full, carried in medium-sized trusses, the colour golden yellow, sometimes shaded cream. It holds its colour well and is slightly fragrant ... Its strong points are its foliage, for which alone it is almost worth growing, and its colour, which is unique in its class, and makes it a great and useful addition to the wichuraianas." [NRS11/52–53]

Snowflake
F. Cant, 1923

"Clusters of semi-double, pure white flowers resembling tiny snowballs." [GAS] "White, medium size, lightly double, very fragrant, tall." [Sn] "A vigorous-growing rose with elegant trusses of pure white, semi-double, round flowers with pretty golden stamens, making it most enchanting. One is reminded very much of the old double ten-weeks stock. It is really a pure white rambler. In commerce in 1923." [ARA22/145] "White shading to yellow at base. Like a fall of snow on the green stems and foliage scented, foliage fine and glossy, late. Growth very vigorous." [GeH] "Bud medium size, ovoid; flower medium size, open, double, very lasting; pure white; borne in cluster on long, strong stem; strong fragrance. Foliage abundant, medium size, glossy dark green, disease-resistant. Few thorns. Climbing habit; profuse, intermittent bloomer during July and August." [ARA23/150] "Blossoms snow-white, shaped like snowballs, in large clusters, long-lasting. Plant of strong growth, very 'climbing.' Leaves healthy and free of mildew." [Ck] "The individual flowers have the appearance of miniature snowballs about the size of a walnut. It is extremely free flowering; the trusses are large and delightfully graceful, carried on long stems, and the general effect of a well furnished plant gives the impression of myriads of enormous snowflakes resting upon a shining green background. Late flowering. Its habit is vigorous, it is mildew-proof, and must be seen to be fully appreciated." [NRS22/226]

Sodenia
Weigand, 1911

"Pure brilliant carmine, nearly scarlet, fairly full; produced in the same profusion and in larger trusses than in 'Dorothy Perkins' [W]." [GeH] "Popular Wichuraiana, with clustered rosy scarlet flowers, varying to deep pink." [GAS] "Double rosettes, carmine scarlet." [NRS13/101] "A lighter red [than that of 'Excelsa' (W)] and highly desirable for its colour." [NRS18/150] "Delicate pink; tall bush; finely-cut foliage; flowers again a little in autumn." [NRS18/135] "Rose red, medium size, full, tall." [Sn] "Plant very 'climbing', proof against maladies; foliage bright dark green. Blossoms pure bright carmine, red, nearly scarlet, quite full and long-lasting. Sometimes reblooms in the Fall, like 'Dorothy Perkins'." [JR36/89] "Pretty good in growth and bloom." [ARA18/121] We exclude Ÿ's "Deep yellow" as being, presumably, a slip.

Solarium
Turbat, 1925

"A fine, brilliant vermilion Wichuraiana of 'Hiawatha' [Mult] type." [GAS] "Early. Velvety vermilion-red." [C-Pf33] "Deep orange red, medium size, single, tall." [Sn] "Type, 'Hiawatha', but larger and better color. Flower very large, single, very lasting, velvety vermilion-red, stamens yellow, borne in clusters of 30. Foliage normal, rich glossy green. Growth very vigorous." [ARA27/223] "Good growth. Blooms first year not impressive . . . *Mass.*; Another 'American Pillar' [W] type . . . *Pa.*; Grew 4 feet [ca. 1.3 m] with good foliage and pretty blooms . . . *Ohio*; No special merit . . . *Calif.*; . . . Almost, but not quite, as red as 'Paul's Scarlet Climber' [W]." [ARA28/189] "*Foote* calls it a very brilliant red, brighter than anything except 'Paul's Scarlet Climber'. *Ontario* finds it improves with age. The past year it was remarkably fine at Breeze Hill, and we believe it has been overlooked." [ARA31/193]

Source d'Or
trans. "Spring of Gold"
Turbat, 1912

"Deep yellow, large, full, very fragrant, tall." [Sn] "Golden yellow, changing to flesh yellow as the flower expands, large for its class, full. Growth very vigorous, climbing." [GeH] "Has a large flower and keeps its color well, but the blooms are too soft to keep very long." [ARA22/44] "Flowers in clusters of about four. Buds open a warm buff yellow, and the open flower retains its yellow colour for some time, eventually fading to a creamy white with a shade of yellow at base of petals, giving the flower a decidedly yellow tinge, and the later buds in truss being of a warm buff yellow, the whole effect is very good. Splendid pillar Rose of strong growth. One of the best." [NRS16/97] "Good Wichuraiana pillar with buff-yellow buds and creamy white flowers. Hardy for a yellow rambler." [GAS] "Very vigorous variety, big-wooded, nearly erect in growth; foliage bright dark green. Blooms in thyrses of numerous full flowers, large for the genre, golden yellow fading to fresh yellow upon expansion; buds golden yellow." [JR36/183] "High-climbing, foliage bronzy green-brown." [Ck] "Foliage mildews somewhat in late summer; bloom sparse and intermittent through mid-June." [ARA18/131] "An early-blooming, hardy, yellow climber with golden yellow buds which fade to amber. Flowers are fragrant. The plant grows 6 to 8 feet high [ca. 2–2.6 m] and is suitable for pillars or fences but not for arches or arbors." [C-Ps26]

South Orange Perfection
syn. 'Perfection Orange'
Horvath/Manda & Pitcher, 1897
From *Rosa wichuraiana* × either 'Mme. Hoste' (T) or 'Cramoisi Supérieur' (Ch), the Tea much more likely than the China.

"Flesh white." [Ÿ] "Blooms freely in clusters. Color, rosy-blush, changing to white; the flowers are perfect rosettes in form, very pretty and entirely distinct from all others." [C&Js99] "Very beautiful full but small flowers—Polyantha-sized—delicate pink, very vigorous, very resistant." [JR21/68] "Grows freely close to the ground and produces multitudes of small, most perfectly formed double flowers, soft blush pink at the tips changing to white; lasts a long time in perfection." [CA97] "Foliage black-spots slightly in midsummer, more later; bloom moderate last two and a half weeks in June." [ARA18/131] "As for 'Perfection Orange', I haven't had more than one single hip. I sowed the seeds in a flower pot and three or four weeks later, they sprouted. From the beginning, I noticed differences in growth. I left the plants in the same pot until May before transplanting them. As I set to this little task, I noticed that the young plant already had buds. Soon from these buds came ravishing roses in which the colors varied from pure white to pinks from the lightest tone to the deepest. The seedling grew with great rapidity and bore numerous blossoms. The plant had everything to be desired in a climber, looking like *R. multiflora* with Polyantha characteristics. At present, one can admire the blossoms of 'Perfection Orange' in a garden of a house on the Frankfurt road in Frieberg, in the middle of a group of Teas. The others—the seedlings—are coming along well; more than 60 bloomed the following year, and are different [from 'South Orange Perfection'] in wood and foliage. Unfortunately, these roses can't take any cold." [JR26/69]

Souvenir Adolf Chawoik Listed as 'Souvenir d'Adolphe de Charvoik' (W).

Souvenir d'Adolphe de Charvoik

syn. 'Souvenir Adolf Chawoik'; trans., "In Memory of Adolphe de Charvoik"

Breeder unknown, 1911

"Clusters of semi-double, pink flowers. Probably a Wichuraiana." [GAS] "Light pink, small, full, tall." [Sn]

Souvenir d'Ernest Thébault

trans. "In Memory of Ernest Thébault"

Thébault-Lebreton, 1921

"Clusters of small, double, dark red flowers." [GAS] "Deep red, medium size, full, tall." [Sn]

Souvenir de J. Mermet

trans. "In Memory of J. Mermet"

Mermet, 1934

"Light red, large, full, tall." [Sn]

Souvenir de Paul Raudnitz

trans. "In Memory of Paul Raudnitz"

Cochet-Cochet, 1908

From *Rosa wichuraiana* × 'Turner's Crimson Rambler' [Mult].

"White flowers tinged with salmon." [GAS] "Whitish pink, small, very full, tall." [Sn] "Extremely vigorous bush with long climbing canes. Canes green, armed with gray thorns which are strong, slightly hooked, and sparse. Leaves 9-foliate. Stipules very strongly pectinate. Leaflets elliptical, the terminal one lanceolate, extremely bright green, and looking as if varnished. Inflorescence very multifloral (25 to 35 blossoms grouped in a false corymb). Flower small (3 to 4 cm across [ca. $1^1/_4$–$1^1/_2$ in]), very double, porcelain white with a touch of flesh, slightly shaded Hydrangea pink, reverse of petals silvery. The open blossoms stay beautiful a very long time on this rose. This pretty newcomer sometimes blooms a second time in the Fall." [JR32/168]

Srdce Europy

Böhm, 1937

"Deep pink, white center, small, single, tall." [Sn]

Sweet Heart Listed as 'Sweetheart' (W).

Sweetheart

syn. 'Sweet Heart'

Walsh, 1899?

From *Rosa wichuraiana* × 'Bridesmaid' (T).

"Flowers white with faint blush, double." [GeH] "Red and white." [Ÿ] "A pretty palish pink, smallish flower, well worth having, though not so distinctive as some." [NRS16/99] "Rose-pink buds open to very double, $2^1/_2$-inch [ca. 6.5 cm], white flowers that are richly fragrant." [W] "Very sweet-scented." [C&Js17] "Color, bright pink in the bud, which fades to soft white when open. Very double and average $2^1/_4$ inches across [ca. 6 cm], deliciously fragrant, perfectly hardy." [C&Js06] "Of similar growth and colouring [to 'Carissima' (W)]; very fragrant." [NRS13/99] "Small grower; shy bloomer." [ARA18/122] "Grows like '[Turner's] Crimson Rambler' [Mult]." [C&Js07] An introduction date of 1901 is also seen.

Symbol Miru

Böhm, 1937

"White, medium size, full, tall." [Sn]

Syringa

Browning, 1931

"Trusses of large, single, pure white flowers, said to resemble those of a philadelphus or Mock Orange." [GAS] "White, small, single, tall." [Sn] GAS gives the attribution as J. Bond, 1931.

The Beacon

W. Paul, 1922

"Flowers bright fiery red, with a white eye, as in 'American Pillar' [W]; single and semi-double, produced in large clusters; handsome foliage; a very distinct and effective novelty." [NRS23/257] "Its brilliant flowers fairly glow for weeks on end and look like a guiding light when planted at the entrance to a garden." [C-Ps30] "This and 'Solarium' [W] are much alike, 'The Beacon' probably better . . . We compared it with 'Paul's Scarlet Climber' [W] and found it a half dozen shades bluer. Wouldn't trade 'Hiawatha' [Mult] for it." [ARA28/192] "Red, white center, medium size, single to semi-double, tall." [Sn] "Blooms are the same type as the famous 'American Pillar' . . . but the color is vivid, fiery red. It is most attractive when grown in pillar form, blooming in showy masses all over and around the branches. Foliage is large and something of the Hybrid Perpetual type. This Red 'American Pillar' is a real novelty as there are too few reds in the climbing class." [C-Ps27] "Strong-growing Wichuraiana with Multiflora characteristics. It bears huge clusters of rather large, single, fiery red flowers with white centers. Very showy but not at all distinct." [GAS] "Very hardy. — *Washington, D.C.*; Flowers single, bright red . . . Had it only this season, but has made excellent growth. —*Harrisburg, Pa.*" [ARA26/122]

The Farquhar Rose Listed as 'Farquhar' (W).

Thelma

Easlea, 1927

From *Rosa wichuraiana* × 'Paul's Scarlet Climber' (W).

"Most attractive Wichuraiana with huge clusters of large, single or semi-double flowers of pale salmon- or flesh-pink. Distinct color, unfading and attractive." [GAS] "Due for recommendation. It keeps its coral-pink color for a long time without getting dirty tones." [ARA31/181] "Light orange pink, medium size, lightly double, light scent, tall." [Sn] "The individual flowers possess 3 rows of petals. They are fully 3 inches across [ca. 7.5 cm], produced in sprays, from 3 to 18 flowers. Colour, lovely soft Coral Pink." [NRS26/257] "*Foote* likes the color of the flowers much better the second year than the first, but is not willing to commit herself to its value until she has seen it bloom in profusion. *Smith* had attractive blooms in large clusters, and at Breeze Hill a three-year-old plant was exquisitely lovely, with large clusters of semi-double, soft flesh-pink flowers." [ARA31/200] "The colour of the blooms is a delicate coral pink, which turns to carmine as they fade. The blooms are very numerous, and carried in clusters, and are remarkable for their lasting qualities, often remaining on the plant for eight or ten days after they are fully expanded. It comes into bloom the beginning of July, and carries a fair number of blooms in the Autumn. The foliage is a dark green, quite mildew proof. The wood is thornless." [NRS28/185] "Slightly fragrant, delicate coral-pink, suffused with carmine-red as it develops . . . Almost thornless. Growth very vigorous; profuse bloomer." [ARA28/237] "This is a rampant growing Climber of the 'Tausendschön' [Mult] type. The colour is a soft blush

Thelma *continued*

pink. It is very persistent flowering, and retains its blooms for a very great length of time." [NRS26/208] "A nice pillar rose with attractive foliage, free from disease, with semi-double pink flowers in clusters … It bloomed … in large sprays of flowers about 2 inches across [ca. 5 cm], of almost the same shade as [that of] 'Mrs. Charles Bell' [HT]. We think it is going to be a very attractive climber." [ARA30/194]

"The colour lasts well and is not affected by rain or sun. Mr. Easlea points out that as the trusses age there comes a slight crimson suffusion over the petals. The general habit is that of a pillar, or climbing Rose, the shoots being rather stiffer than in most of the wichuraianas. The plant comes into flower about the middle of July, and the trusses remain for a long time on the plant, continuing more or less decorative through August, the individual trusses lasting two or three weeks. There is no perfume. The flowers are semi-double, rather larger than most of its class, but not quite so large as those of 'Dr. W. Van Fleet'. They are very decorative, and retain their colour and freshness well on the plant. The foliage is somewhat lighter in colour than that of many Roses, of a beautiful soft green and glossy. No trouble from disease has been noticed … Several of my friends recommend 'Thelma' for use as a tall hedge. I have not tried it in this form, but the character of its growth seems to suggest it would be very suitable for the purpose, and I can imagine that a wall of soft coral colouring of the trusses of this Rose against the green background of foliage might be found very pleasing." [NRS30/72–73]

Theodora Milch

Weigand, 1906

"Pink, small, very full, medium scent, tall." [Sn]

Tricolore

trans. "Three-Color"

Weigand, 1906

"Clusters of small, double flowers, variegated red, white, and pink." [GAS] "Light pink to red, medium size, full, tall." [Sn]

Troubadour

Walsh, 1910

"Pretty, bright crimson Wichuraiana with a lovely name. The names of most of Walsh's roses were attractive and expressive." [GAS] "Deep red, medium size, full, tall." [Sn] "Bloom of 'Troubadour' almost identical with [that of] 'Excelsa' [W]." [ARA17/28] "Fine growth and foliage; profuse bloomer; resembles 'Excelsa' in color." [ARA18/121] "Perhaps too near 'Excelsa' [in colour] to be largely recommended." [NRS18/150] "Crimson, double, with dark glossy foliage, very free growth. Very vigorous." [GeH]

Universal Favorite

syn. 'Double Pink Memorial Rose'

Horvath/Manda & Pitcher, 1899

From *Rosa wichuraiana* × either 'American Beauty' (HP), or (less likely) some Polyantha such as 'Mignonette'.

"Pink." [Ÿ] "Delicate lilac and pure white." [JR26/181] "Clear, bright pink; equally as beautiful as ['Manda's Triumph' (W)], and a charming companion for it." [C&Js99] "Wonderful plant, China pink, exquisite perfume, very vigorous. It's a cross of Wichuraiana and 'American Beauty'. Honorable Mention by the New York Horticultural Society." [JR21/68] "One of the four original Wichuraiana hybrids. A

trailer with clusters of small, double, pink flowers." [GAS] "Foliage black-spots very slightly in midsummer, very sparse in late summer; bloom free through the first three weeks of June." [ARA18/131] "The most vigorous variety of its class; the long branching shoots are covered with bright green foliage; the double flowers of a beautiful rose color, similar to the 'Bridesmaid' [T], are deliciously fragrant; a grand variety for any purpose." [CA97] As we have just seen, listed in the California Nursery Company catalog of 1897, though all-important actual commercial release of the cultivar seems not to have occurred until 1899; many sources strike an average and list 1898 for the cultivar's introduction.

V.F. 3 Listed as 'Glenn Dale' (W).

Valentin Beaulien Listed as 'Valentin Beaulieu' (W).

Valentin Beaulieu

Barbier, 1904

From *Rosa wichuraiana* × 'Souvenir de Catherine Guillot' (Ch).

"Violet-pink, medium size, full, tall." [Sn] "Climbing bush. Inflorescence a loose panicle. Corolla very double, from 5 to 7 cm across [ca. 2–2¾ in], bright pink with lilac." [JR28/156] "Strong pillar rose with drooping laterals and irregular pale pink flowers." [GAS] "The bud and edges of the young leaves and mid ribs are of a coppery brown, too, which gives the plant a distinctive character. So far, with me, it has not bloomed freely. The flower is not very well formed, of a light pink." [NRS16/98] "A very rampant grower of trailing growth, with flexible shoots of bronzy green colour. The foliage is fine dark green and mildew-proof. The young graceful shoots have a peculiar fern-like appearance. The flowers are borne in small trusses of flat, very double blooms of deep pink colour shaded with yellow." [NRS13/97–98] "Shrub with floriferous, quite divergent red-tinted green canes armed with fine, slightly curved, red thorns. Leaves with slender armed petiole, 2 pairs of oval-elongate, subsessile leaflets, toothed like a saw, stipules ciliate-glandulose. Inflorescence a loose, slender panicle, branchlets tinted red, with pedicels and bracts glandulose; calyx with ovoid tube; sepals reflexing, ovate-subulate; corolla very double, lilac pink; petals widely obcordate, 4–5 cm across [ca. 1½–2 in]. From a crop of *R. wichuraiana* pollinated by 'Souvenir de Catherine Guillot' [Ch]." [JR26/4–5]

Variegata

trans. 'Variegated'

Conard & Jones?, 1915?

"The foliage only of this Rose is variegated, flowers white." [C&Js15] "Foliage beautifully variegated green and white, occasionally tinted pink. A novelty." [C&Js20] "Foliage not nearly so plentiful as most kinds, healthy; bloom free last two and a half weeks of June. A good ground-cover." [ARA18/131] "Foliage variegated green and cream, and has the appearance of being sickly. Growth poor; hardy. Ignoring season of planting as not fair test, no bloom was obtained in three seasons." [ARA23/174]

Vicomtesse de Chabannes

Buatois, 1921

"Interesting Wichuraiana, with large, semi-double, purplish crimson flowers tinted white in the center." [GAS] "Purple red, white center, medium size, lightly double, tall." [Sn] "New, good-growing sort, blossom fairly large, purple-scarlet with white center." [Ck] "Flower large, semi-double; purplish crimson, center white, forming a distinct eye; borne in enormous cluster. Very vigorous, climbing habit." [ARA22/151]

Victory
F. R. M. Undritz/R. Undritz, 1918
From 'Dr. W. Van Fleet' (W) × 'Mme. Jules Grolez' (HT).

"Deep pink, large, full, medium scent, tall." [Sn] "Large, dark pink flowers, admirable only for its vigorous growth." [GAS] Victory, commemorating the victory obtained in World War I; this cultivar is preserved notably in a German rosarium ...

W.C. 124 Listed as 'Mary Wallace' (W).

W. Freeland Kendrick
syn. 'Bloomfield Endurance'
Capt. Thomas/Andorra Nurs., 1921
From 'Aviateur Blériot' (W) × 'Mme. Caroline Testout' (HT).

"Whitish pink, orange pink center, large, full, medium scent, medium growth." [Sn] "Everblooming Wichuraiana of dwarf pillar growth. Flowers double, fragrant, pale silvery pink, sometimes white." [GAS] "Semi-Climber. Originally thought better for the coast but of good value throughout the South ... Resists disease. Double flowers of good size, paper white with light peach or fawn center. Continuous; prolific." [ARA28/104] "Bud medium size, globular; flower medium size, double, globular, lasting, borne singly and several together on medium length stem; fragrant. Color white, with peach-blush center. Foliage abundant, medium size, leathery, glossy, dark green, disease-resistant. Vigorous upright grower; profuse bloomer (189 blooms) from May to October. Practically hardy; tips freeze." [ARA21/163] "Bud medium size, ovoid, flesh-white; flower large, slightly globular, very double, full, very lasting, fragrant, flesh deepening to peach in center, borne singly and several together on medium-length, strong stem. Foliage abundant, medium size, dark bronzy green, leathery, glossy, very disease-resistant. Very vigorous, semi-climber (5 feet in Pa.); profuse, continuous bloomer (189 blooms in Portland [Oregon]) from May to November. Very hardy." [ARA25/195] GAS gives an attribution of: Capt. Thomas/Bobbink & Atkins, 1920.

W.M. 5 Listed as 'Heart of Gold' (W).

Weisse New Dawn
trans. "White New Dawn"
Berger, 1959
"White, medium size, full, medium scent, tall." [Sn]

White Dorothy
B. R. Cant, 1908
Sport of 'Dorothy Perkins' (W).

"A pure white sport from the invaluable 'Dorothy Perkins', which it resembles in all save colour." [GeH] "It comes somewhat creamy sometimes, but is most effective for a weeping standard." [NRS16/98] "The middle of the flowers is apt to become blackish, I suppose through the darkening stamens." [NRS20/92] "A nearly pure white, but perhaps a little dark in the middle. It is probably the best white rambler, but often sports back to its parent in the oddest fashion. I have had a branch with one truss pure pink and all the other trusses white. Sometimes half the flower will be pink and the other half

white, again one or two petals only may be pink, or a few trusses may have a faint pinkish flush. These irregularities, however, are exceptional, and not sufficient to mar the general beauty of the plant in full flower." [NRS11/39] "White, medium size, full, tall." [Sn] "Bloom profuse last two and a half weeks of June, moderate during large portion of July." [ARA18/131] "Its habit is altogether satisfactory, and its growth abundant and easily amenable to training." [C-Ps28] "It is astonishing how people will still cling to White Dorothy Perkins [sic]. I am told there are some stocks in commerce that retain their purity, but I must confess I have never seen them, and I always find a more or less reversion to the Type—that is, to 'Dorothy Perkins'. Even if 'White Dorothy' came white without any variation, I would still contend that its day has passed. It has been completely superseded by 'Sander's White'." [NRS19/57–58] "Surpassed in beauty by 'Sander's White' Rambler and perhaps several other cluster-flowered ramblers, this white sport of 'Dorothy Perkins' has become widely distributed. It produces clusters of snow-white flowers and is a plant of extraordinary vigor." [GAS] "A most valuable addition to this class." [C&Js11]

Wichmoss
Barbier, 1911
From *Rosa wichuraiana* × 'Salet' (MR).

"Whitish pink, small, lightly double, light scent, tall." [Sn] "Deep rosy white, buds well mossed, a hybrid of Wichuraiana and a moss. Growth vigorous." [GeH] "The flower is semi-double, with upper side of the petals pink while the reverse is somewhat darker. It is quite fragrant and has the flower stalks and sepals mossed like 'Salet'. It blooms in clusters." [C&Js12] "Inferior Wichuraiana, interesting because its buds are mossy. One of the few successful attempts at introducing the Moss rose characteristics into a modern race. The pale blush-pink flowers fade white." [GAS] "Vigorous grower; small trusses of small semi-double flesh white blooms. Buds heavily mossed. Very interesting novelty." [NRS13/101] "Foliage black-spots badly and mildews a good deal from midsummer on, but almost no loss of foliage; bloom abundant, almost continuously, from early June until last of month." [ARA18/131] "Very vigorous plant, very unusual, with branches covered over with a multitude of small stickers, like with the Moss Roses; pretty foliage—bright dark green. Flower semi-double, fragrant, with pink petals tinted carmine pink on the reverse. The receptacle and sepals are mossy like with the variety 'Salet'. Blooms in corymbs of 6–15 blossoms. Completely new sort of climbing rose; it's a veritable Climbing Moss Rose." [JR36/10]

Wichuraiana Alba Listed as *Rosa wichuraiana*.

Wichuraiana Hybride I
Rouland, 1980
"Pink." [Ÿ]

William C. Egan
Dawson/Hoopes, Bro., & Thomas, 1900
From *Rosa wichuraiana* × 'Général Jacqueminot' (HP).

"Delicate pink." [Ÿ] "Light pink, medium size, very full, medium scent, tall." [Sn] "Trailing Wichuraiana with rather large, pale flesh-pink flowers. Good color. Almost forgotten but valuable." [GAS] "Blooms in large attractive trusses. Flowers large, full and a beautiful pink; always hardy and dependable." [C&Js06] "Foliage black-spots from midsummer on; bloom free through nearly all of June."

William C. Egan *continued*

[ARA18/131] "The Garden Club of Illinois is arranging for a testimonial dinner to Mr. W. C. Egan, of Egandale, Highland Park, Ills., on his eightieth birthday, which is to occur April 1, 1921. The Editor, who has experienced the pleasure of visiting Mr. Egan many times and of hearing from him many more times, refers members of the American Rose Society to his piquant and delightful articles and notes which we have from time to time printed in the *Annual*, as evidence of the great youngness of this great lover of plants and trees. Egandale is a wonder-place, made up of not many acres, but the acres very large, because they have been stretched by Mr. Egan's plant-placing genius so as to be altogether beautiful and effective and proper. The rose at Egandale is in a climate anything but genial to it, and yet it smiles on Mr. Egan because he loves it and takes care of it." [ARA21/171] "'The Sage of Egandale' was one of the titles by which his friends hailed the great gardener whose patience, skill, and friendship had made his home at Highland Park, Ill., truly a Mecca for plant-lovers. With correspondents everywhere who were honored to have their best in plant life accepted at Egandale, the collection there became notable. With his rare Irish humor, Mr. Egan would tell to visitors the history of each fine thing. Of course he loved roses, though he had to fight hard to protect them from lake storms. Naturally he paid attention to those that could endure, and it is undoubtedly due to him that the super-hardy 'Max Graf' [W] was rescued from oblivion. He was young to the end, though had he lived until April 1 next, his friends would have joined in celebrating with him his eighty-sixth birthday. Bubbling with whimsical humor, always kindly, a great horticulturist, a genial philosopher, William C. Egan ended on January 2, 1930, a long life which left the world a better place to live in." [ARA30/199]

Windermere
Chaplin, 1932

"Light rose red, medium size, lightly double, medium scent, tall." [Sn] Windermere, English lake.

Yakachinensis Listed as *Rosa wichuraiana* 'Yakachinensis'.

[Yellow Minnehaha]
F. Cant, pre-1933

"Reported to have white flowers with yellow centers." [GAS]

Yvonne
F. Cant, 1920

"'Lady Godiva' [W] type, with clusters of blush-pink flowers tinged with yellow. Attractive." [GAS] "Light pink, medium size, full, light scent, tall." [Sn] "Soft pink with deeper centre and yellow base, in large loose trusses, good foliage. Growth very vigorous." [GeH] "The flowerets come in large trusses of a soft shell pink colour with a yellow base. It is a pretty decorative variety, but so far I am not satisfied that its growth is quite vigorous enough." [NRS25/178] "I cannot get this Rose to grow with any vigour. I have had it for three years and if it does not do better next year its doom it sealed." [NRS24/163] "This is a very lovely shell-pink colored rose . . . A vigorous grower, with large, upright trusses of bloom, lasting well, it will soon find its way into every garden." [ARA21/152] "It has delightful glossy foliage, which is mildew-proof. Very neat pretty buds, perfection in shape, the flowers are carried in large loose trusses of blooms, which are thrown well away from the plant. Its wonderful lasting properties when cut combine to make it a very graceful Rose for all decorative purposes. Colour a charming soft shade of pink, with deeper pink centre and yellow base, produced freely from July to September, and sweetly scented. In every way an exquisite variety, exceedingly vigorous in habit of growth, most suitable for arches, pergolas and screens." [NRS21/199] "A vigorous growing rambling Rose. The large clusters of blooms are liable to get spotted with rain. Fragrant. Colour pale pink, very much lighter than [that of] 'Lady Godiva'. Foliage and wood a peculiar shade of dark olive green. Free of mildew. A very pretty climber, quite one of the best." [NRS23/97]

Zaunrose Listed as *Rosa wichuraiana*.

CHAPTER TWENTY-SEVEN

Multifloras

"To Japan and China we look for the habitats of the type of this Group. It was introduced to England in 1804. These are also Climbing Roses, producing their flowers in large corymbs, and consequently continuing a long time in bloom ... The foliage of this Group is particularly elegant, and the branches have but few spines." [P] "With a few exceptions I should be inclined to have no Multiflora climbers; the foliage of the others is so much finer and more decorative, and the Multifloras are so easily mildewed." [ARA21/127] "Grafted on short stems and grown in large pots, they bloom freely, and form pretty objects, as they produce their myriads of elegant flowers during a great part of the summer." [WRP] "All the varieties have more or less climbing canes, often attaining a height of 10 or 12 feet [ca. 3–4 m]; they are fairly sensitive to cold in our climate [that of Paris] ... But, grown in the midlands of France where the climate is much more favorable, these varieties become much more vigorous with more abundant bloom." [JR2/42] "In dry soils it is tolerably hardy, and south of [Philadelphia] perfectly so. The flowers are produced in such profusion that it has often received the cognomen of *wreath-rose.*" [Bu]

"*Rosa multiflora* gets its name from the abundance of bloom it produces. The panicle of 60–100 flowers, pectinate stipules and bracts, and sarmentose branches make it easily distinguishable from all others, especially *R. moschata* which is close, but further differs in its coherent styles and disposition of flowers." [T&R] "The stipule of the multiflora is very curious, taking the form of a number of little teeth almost reduced to hairs on either side of the stem, and this characteristic is very markedly reproduced in the Ramblers, being most striking in those like '[Turner's] Crimson Rambler' which partakes in a great degree of the multiflora habit." [NRS11/24] "All the varieties reproduce with the greatest ease from cuttings and layers, and *multiflora* can be successfully grafted on the wild Briar. If [growth] buds are inserted on a solitary stem 2.4–3 m high [ca. 7–9 ft], the effect will be picturesque, like that of a weeping willow. To avoid frost damage, pruning should be postponed until the end of April. Inflorescences scarcely ever bloom twice, so sterile shoots should be pruned less severely to encourage new growth and flowers." [T&R] "The Multifloras, those

attractive rampant kinds that have come to us from China, begin to be Europeanized. Already, several years since, I developed [writing in 1843] some varieties—less beautiful than the Type, it is true, but which, in the second generation, crossed with our European roses and others, have given me some stronger and hardier sub-varieties to the point at which several are thoroughly unrecognizable [as Multifloras]. I await the bloom of these last with impatience; I am counting on it for next Spring [1844]." [R-H44/479]

"The roses commonly called Multiflora Ramblers or Hybrids make a highly complex, badly misunderstood group ... One of the Chinese forms of the species is *R. multiflora cathayensis,* which, as it grows in America, makes a wiry although sturdy bush with clusters of single pink flowers. It is presumed ... that *R. multiflora cathayensis* is the prototype of a garden variety discovered in China, known as *R. multiflora platyphylla,* which was brought into Europe early in the [19th] century and introduced under the name of ... 'Seven Sisters Rose' ... No Multiflora variety attained distinction until about 1890 when '[Turner's] Crimson Rambler' was introduced into England from Japan." [GAS] "The year 1893 was notable in the rose-world for the introduction by Charles Turner of the Royal Nurseries, Slough, England, of the Crimson Rambler, the first of the modern race of the Multiflora hybrids. According to a statement in the *Gardener's Chronicle* (Series 3, Vol. XVI, p. 249), a plant of this rose was sent from Japan to Mr. Jenner, a well-known horticulturist, by Mr. R. Smith, Professor of Engineering at Tokio [sic]. Mr. Jenner named it the Engineer, and subsequently gave the rose to J. Gilbert, a nurseryman of Lincoln, who exhibited some cut blooms in London in July, 1890, and received an Award of Merit from the Royal Horticultural Society. Soon after this Gilbert sold his stock to Mr. Turner, who renamed it Crimson Rambler and put it into commerce in 1893." [ARA18/82] "No one knows definitely what the ancestry of '[Turner's] Crimson Rambler' is. It is more vigorous and coarser than *R. multiflora cathayensis* or *R. multiflora platyphylla,* although it may be descended from them. Its Chinese name is Shi Tz-mei, or Ten Sisters, but it was called 'The Engineer' when first exhibited in England. Later it was put into commerce as 'Turner's Crimson Rambler'. The name was soon clipped, and as 'Crimson Rambler' it captured the fancy of the world in the decade following 1890. Bushes were planted by the thousands everywhere, and no man's home was considered complete without a 'Crimson Rambler' and a *Spiraea VanHouttei*." [GAS] "As was to be expected, its popularity gave a great stimulus to the production of roses of this type, and new varieties appeared in rapid succession. Some of these earlier sorts . . . showed a tendency to shed their leaves rather easily and to be somewhat subject to fungous diseases, so that experienced rose-growers came to regard the class as a whole with less enthusiasm than at first. But with the introduction, one after another, of later varieties that have shown marked improvement in these respects, the value of these ramblers seems now firmly established." [ARA18/82]

"There is nothing tender or delicate about 'Crimson Rambler'. It is one of the hardiest roses, and it quickly swept before it most of the Prairie Roses [*i.e.,* Setigera Hybrids] which had hitherto been relied upon for climbing forms in this country. Closely following 'Crimson Rambler' came its seedlings and hybrids . . . Multiflora Ramblers have somewhat large, coarse foliage, not particularly attractive either in shape or texture. The canes are thick, brittle, and inclined to be stubby or blunt, which permits the plants to be grown in bush form 12 to 14 feet high [ca. 4–4.6 m], and that much or more in diameter. They have a slight tendency toward everblooming and occasional flowers may be produced on almost any Multiflora hybrid at any time. They also tend to produce thornless varieties, of which 'Tausendschön' is, perhaps, the best example. But the Multiflora race has so far refused to depart from its cluster-blooming habit. All its seedlings and hybrids persist in bearing relatively small flowers in huge bunches. These blooms have a papery, uninteresting texture, and scent is either lacking or faintly disagreeable. The Multiflora race also enjoys the dubious distinction of producing the only *blue* roses which have been widely distributed as such. 'Veilchenblau', a descendant of '[Turner's] Crimson Rambler', was the first to attract attention, and it has been followed by several other varieties of varying degrees of 'blueness', the best of which is probably 'Violette' . . . The blueness of these Multiflora races is very different from the purplish shade common to most red roses, and which is intensified by their fading into the defect known as 'blueing.' It appears as a sort of turbid blue overlaying a ground-color of purple-pink or dull magenta. Most of their muddiness has disappeared from the color of 'Violette', and its clear shade of violet-purple is not so bad." [GAS]

"These roses have but few adaptations. I have stated . . . their appropriateness for pillar roses, and for warm situations against walls, where they are very ornamental: they also bloom in the greatest perfection as standards, but they will then require additional protection in winter." [WRP] "With the possible exception of the 'Blush Rambler', whose remarkable vigor of growth seems better adapted to tall arches and pergolas, the most effective way to grow roses of this class is as free bushes. Walls, arches, and per-

golas may be left to the Wichuraianas, for which they are admirably suited, but it is the great merit of the Multiflora ramblers that their stiffer habit of growth is well adapted to this form, and with some support, by judicious staking, they are capable of making very large and symmetrical bushes. So grown, with space to develop freely, they possess a natural beauty of form and foliage that gives a really wonderful decorative effect quite apart from the beauty of the bloom, striking as that is.

"Though these ramblers are naturally vigorous, to secure, year after year, the freedom and strength of growth that so enhances their beauty, first of all a careful preparation of the soil before planting is essential, and afterward an equally careful cultivation. This does not mean that any elaborate methods are required; on the contrary, everything necessary for success is simple and within the reach of all. The beds should be made three feet square [ca. 1 m square] and at least two feet deep [ca. 6 dm]. After the soil has been thrown out, the bottom of the bed should be well loosened to the depth of the spading-fork and a generous amount of rich barn-compost thoroughly mixed with the soil. Then alternate layers of soil and manure should be filled in, forked well together, and lightly tramped down till within eight inches [ca. 2 dm] of the top, when the bed may be filled in with plain loam. A generous quantity of coarse crushed bone should be added as the bed is made up, and, when the plant is set, a handful of bone-meal should be mixed with the soil around the roots. During the spring and early summer, till about July 1, the bushes should be watered and cultivated at intervals, and established plants will benefit by occasional liberal applications of liquid manure. About July 1 a mulch of spent hops or some coarse litter may be spread over the beds to keep the ground moist during the hot weather, and late in the fall a quantity of leaves should be drawn up around the base of the plants and kept in place by a light covering of salt-marsh hay or other litter.

"The best time for pruning is immediately after the blooming season, as this gives the new shoots a better opportunity to develop. In pruning, as many as necessary of the oldest stalks should be removed. For staking, galvanized iron water-pipes, painted dark green, are as satisfactory as anything for the older and larger bushes, while cedar poles or hardwood stakes may be used for those recently set out." [ARA18/82–83]

"This rose, originating in Japan, has given us several sub-varieties, of which certain have been set up as species by authors." [MaCo] "Several of the varieties in the catalogue have been raised in Italy, where these pretty roses flourish and bear seed abundantly." [WRP]

Rosa multiflora Plates 41–43

"I have received a new species [*writing in 1811*] which should be precious, according to what I have been told and if one may judge from the price I paid for two specimens five or six inches [to ca. 1.5 dm] high! It's the *Multiflora*. I am told that this species gives a multitude of flowers which, united on the same petiole, make a ball like the Hydrangea or Snow-Ball Plant do. I am told that it comes from the Orangery, but nevertheless has hopes of being able to get along o.k. out in the open. *And* I am told that it will grow vigorously and cover frameworks. Its wood, though slender and delicate, is said to be climbing or very elongated; it is green, its young growths have a pink tint, and it is armed with thorns of the same color. Its leaves, to the number of five or seven on the same stalk, are oval, regularly dentate, and edged pink. This rose is being announced with every favorable word, and would seem to be a wonderful acquisition." [C-T]

"Introduced into England by T. Evans in 1804, and into France by Boursault in 1808." [JR11/40] "This species is distinguished by its small flowers in a panicle, borne on pubescent, thornless peduncles. It's a shrub in which the stems are upright, branching into cylindrical canes which are glabrous, upright, purplish, and which bear prickles which are sparse and recurved; clothed in leaves which are opposite, sometimes alternate, sessile, oval, saw-toothed along the edges, green and glabrous above, pale and pubescent beneath, petioles also pubescent; bearing sparse, recurved prickles which are quite small. The flowers are terminal, and disposed in a wide, branching panicle; the peduncles and stems are pubescent and thornless. The calyx is all covered with white, thick bristles, especially on the edges of the sepals. The corolla is white, and the size of that of the bramble; the fruits are oval, pubescent, and thornless. This plant is found in Japan, where it was observed by Thunberg (description from Thunberg)." [Lam] "This rose originated in Japan. It was sent to us [the French] by the English a few years ago [*writing in 1819*]. Its wood is climbing, very elongate, extremely vigorous, clothed with hooked thorns. Its leaves are numerous, opposite, oval, and long, nearly two inches [ca. 5 cm]. Its innumerable blossoms appear around June and last until the end of July. They are borne at the tips of the canes on stout peduncles, forming large corymbs. Ordinarily, 18 to 30 may be counted on each cane—indeed, sometimes more than a hundred. Its scent is weak but elegant. They [*the flowers*] are a little larger than those of the 'Pompon de Bourgogne' [G], and are of a color of pink mixed with white. It is very double. It is necessary to graft it on a tall Briar, and to protect it with straw during the Winter. It is said that, being grafted on the Damask or the Common China ['*Parsons' Pink China*'], it would give more bloom and resist the Winter better. As for the rest, this delicate rose requires the warmest possible exposure, as well as the effort not to prune it until after frosts [no longer occur], which [frosts] destroy the new shoots. To get some nice own-root specimens to put in pots, as with all the Musks, you need to graft them on Briars cut back to six inches of the ground [ca. 4.5 dm] to make it easy to bury the growth of the grafts, which will be very long the following Spring. They will have their own roots and can be lifted and potted. When its long canes are grafted high, they need to be supported by small stakes, or on an arbor or by trellises." [LeR]

"Canes long, climbing, clothed with hooked thorns; leaves numerous; leaflets opposite, sessile, villose, as is the common petiole, which is caniculate; flowers small, double, in clusters of 3–20, pretty pink color which however pales at the end of several days; scent agreeable, especially in the evening, styles abortive and converted into narrow foliaceous extentions. This delicate species needs a warm site, protected from much cold, especially in the first year or two. The length of the canes makes it necessary to curb them in." [BJ24] "Canes

slender and out-thrust; climbing; small soft leaves of a more or less somber green depending upon the vigor of the plant; stipules ciliate; [blooms] from June to August, very numerous single blossoms, in clusters, of an ashen pink." [J-A/574]

"It has very great vigor; its canes, long and flexible, are smooth, with some small thorns. Its leaves, with 5–7 leaflets, are close-set, soft, and rugose, delicate green, slightly glaucous; its blossoms … are in clusters at the end of branchlets which grow on the previous year's canes; they are small, generally pale in color, on a long and hirsute stem." [JF] "Very tall bush; canes flagelliform, flexible, smooth, armed with hooked thorns placed in pairs under the stipules; leaves composed of 5–7 leaflets; stipules enlarged at the base, pointed, adherent, much dentate, tomentose beneath; petioles very velvety; leaflets close-set, wrinkled, lanceolate, obtuse, crenelate, somber green, villose on both sides; flowers numerous, small, in clusters, double, pale pink; bracts linear, dentate, very caducous, tomentose like the peduncles; calyx-tube turbinate; sepals oval; 18–25 lanate styles, longer than the interior petals, grouped in a column; fruit not crowned by the sepals, turbinate, light red." [S] See also below under cultivar 'Rose' (Mult), as well as 'Grevillii' (Mult) and 'Platyphylla' (Mult).

"Height 15 feet [ca. 5 m]. Forms a roundish dense shrub when grown alone. It will climb on trees or other shrubs. It has clusters of small white flowers with yellow stamens, a delicious spicy fragrance, and small red or orange fruits. It is very spiny and makes an impenetrable thicket." [ARA16/16–17] "The great importance of *R. multiflora* to American rose-growing is its use as an understock upon which to bud or graft other varieties. The type most favored for this purpose is *R. multiflora japonica*. Millions of seedlings and cuttings of this rose are budded to Hybrid Teas and other choice varieties every year." [GAS]

Rosa multiflora var. cathayensis

"During the 1900 Veitchian Expedition, Mr. Wilson collected seeds of a pretty, single, pink Rose common in Western Hupeh and Western Szechuan, since named var. cathayensis. It is a vigorous growing bush, with corymbs of pink-tinted blossoms, rather larger than the single white flowers of the Japanese [type]." [NRS27/52] "In June of 1913 the wild prototype of the Crimson Rambler blossomed for the first time in this country in the Arnold Arboretum, where it was raised from seeds collected in north-central China by William Purdom in 1910. This wildling has been named *Rosa multiflora* var. *cathayensis*, and is a rose of rare beauty and of great potential value. The flowers are borne in large clusters, as in all Rambler roses, and are clear pink, each 2 to 2$\frac{1}{2}$ inches across [ca. 5–7 cm], single of course, with a mass of yellow stamens; the foliage is perfect, and the plant is a vigorous grower and is absolutely hardy." [ARA16/38]

Rosa multiflora var. platyphylla Listed as 'Platyphylla' (Mult).

Horticultural Varieties

[À Bois Brun]
trans. "With Brown Wood"
Vibert, 1849

"Blossoms full, 5 cm across [ca. 2 in], carminy pink; petals notched, often with a line in the middle; blooms in corymbs." [M-V49/233]

À Feuilles Larges Listed as 'Platyphylla' (Mult).

À Fleurs Carnées Listed as 'Carnea' (Mult).

À Fleurs Roses Listed as 'Rose' (Mult).

À Grandes Feuilles Listed as 'Platyphylla' (Mult).

Agnes und Bertha
syn. 'Kala Agneta'; trans., "Agnes and Bertha"
Alfons, 1926
 "Pink, small, single, tall." [Sn]

Améthyste
Nonin, 1911
Either a sport of 'Non Plus Ultra' (Mult), or from a cross of 'Non
 Plus Ultra' and *Rosa multiflora*.
 "Odd steel-blue with violet crimson, semi-double, very large cluster." [Ck] "Violet-red, small, lightly full, tall." [Sn] "This is a vigorous
shrub, blooming abundantly in strong clusters. The semi-double
flowers have an unusual steel-blue color, tinted purplish crimson."
[JR36/9] "One of the course, unmanageable Multifloras, tolerated for
its strange, little, semi-double, steel-blue flowers with a purplish pink
undertone." [GAS] "Strong grower; poor color; not lasting." [ARA18/
121] "Nearer 'blue' than 'Veilchenblau' [Mult] with great clusters of
small, very double blooms in marvelously rich purple tones in spring.
Shiny, disease-resistant foliage and long arching branches to 12 feet
[ca. 4 m]." [W] "Nonin's Nursery is an exceedingly interesting place to
visit, for there are to be seen many fine specimens of roses. Among
them are many weeping standards . . . top-worked at a height of 6 to
8 and 10 feet [ca. 2–3.3 m]." [ARA23/127]

Anci Böhm Listed as 'Anci Böhmova' (Mult).

Anci Böhmova
syn. 'Anci Böhm'
Böhm, 1929
Sport of 'Marietta Sylva Tarouca' (Mult).
 "Deep violet pink, large, full, tall." [Sn] "The small, ruffled, rosy red
flowers with lilac shades are borne in big clusters. Wiry habit and almost thornless." [GAS] "Sport of 'Marietta Sylva Tarouca', and like it in
form, fullness, and color[,] but brighter. Bud medium size, globular;
flower large, double, full, globular, lasting, lilac to rosy red, borne in
large cluster on strong, medium-length stem. Foliage sparse, small,
gray-green, bronzy, soft, fern-like (divided into 9 leaves), disease-resistant. Growth very vigorous (3 to 4 ft. [ca. 1–1.3 m]), bush, pillar,
and climber; abundant bloomer in June and July. Hardy." [ARA31/243]

Andreas Hofer
Kiese, 1911
Seedling of 'Tausenschön' (Mult).
 "Red, small, full, tall." [Sn] "Vigorous growth, somber green leaf;
the small flowers are bright blood red." [JR36/55] "Foliage very plen-
tiful through season; bloom free middle of June." [ARA18/129]

Andrée Vanderschrick
E. M. Buatois, 1935
 "White, small, full, light scent, tall." [Sn]

Apple Blossom
Burbank, 1932

"Apparently a Multiflora of the common type, with large clusters
of single, salmon-pink flowers." [GAS]

Aristide Briand
Penny, 1928
 "Mauve pink." [Ÿ] "Violet pink, medium size, lightly double, medi-
um scent, tall." [Sn] "A great name apparently wasted on a most un-
promising bluish pink Multiflora of the 'Veilchenblau' [Mult] type."
[GAS]

Asta von Parpart
Geschwind/Lambert, 1909
From a Multiflora × a Hybrid Perpetual.
 "Purple, medium size, full, tall." [Sn] "Good rebloom. Blooms in
clusters; purple-carmine." [Ck] "No scent, good autumn flowers, −3 m
[less than ca. 9 ft]." [EU]

Aurélian Igoult
Igoult, 1924
 "Another of the many attempts to achieve a blue rose. The violet-
tinted flowers have a reddish tone." [GAS] "Violet red, medium size,
full, tall." [Sn]

Bagatelle
Soupert & Notting, 1908
From 'Turner's Crimson Rambler' (Mult) × 'Mignonette' (Pol).
 "White, washed very delicate pink, new in this group. Very vigor-
ous shrub, freely climbing, hardy. The blossoms come in large bou-
quets on very long stems; they are of medium size and long duration."
[JR32/153] "White, slightly tinged with pale rose. Growth vigorous."
[GeH] "White, medium size, full, tall." [Sn] For *Bagatelle*, see under
'Caroubier' (Mult).

Baronesse von Ittersum Listed as 'Jkvr. D. Baroness von
 Ittersum' (Mult).

Baronin Anna von Lüttwitz
Walter, 1909
From 'Euphrosine' (Lam) × 'Rösel Dach' (Pol).
 "Pink, medium size, full, tall." [Sn]

Bijou de Lyon
trans. "Lyon Gem"
Schwartz, 1882
 "Very vigorous bush with climbing canes; leaves composed of
5–7 beautiful bright green leaflets; flowers small, full, in a cluster, as
double as those of 'Pâquerette' [Pol], but one size larger, with imbricated petals of purest white. A superb plant." [JR6/148–149]

Blanda Egreta
Alfons, 1926
 "Pink, small, single, tall." [Sn]

Bleu Magenta Listed as 'Bleu Violette' (Mult).

Bleu Violette
syn. 'Bleu Magenta'; trans., "Violet Blue"
Van Houtte, 1900
Seedling of 'Turner's Crimson Rambler' (Mult).
 "Deep purple red." [Ÿ] "Deep purple red, small, full, very fragrant,

tall." [Sn] "Just recently we heard tell that the Remontant Turner's Crimson Rambler has been found—which doesn't surprise us a bit! Now today, our astonishment is redoubled when we read a note from the Louis Van Houtte père firm ... in which it is said 'Latest Novelty: Climbing Rose 'Bleu Violette' (seedling of '[Turner's] Crimson Rambler').' Here is their description of the plant: 'The art of the rosarian, after many years of effort, has at last been able to produce this eighth Wonder [of the World]: the *Blue Rose*!! This new climbing rose surpasses all its forerunners by the purity and intensity of its coloration. The blossoms, in corymbs, are half-double and of medium size; when they open, partially lilac-red and lilac-pink, they change first to amethyst blue, then to steel blue; the general look is of violet. Of robust growth, with beautiful green foliage and few thorns, this rose is among the hardiest. Every Rose Fancier will want to acquire this variety, which will probably, by continued crossings, bring us at last to the true blue rose, as blue as the Bluet of the fields.' We will reserve comment on this until we see it bloom on our own grounds." [JR33/22]

Blumen-Dankert
Kiese, 1904

"Light pink, medium size, lightly double, tall." [Sn]

Blush Rambler
B. R. Cant, 1903

"Delicate pink, pale at the center." [Ÿ] "Light pink, small, lightly double, tall." [Sn] "Of the colour of appleblossom, sweet-scented, remaining a long while in bloom, and to be recommended as a companion to the well-known parent variety [*poss. 'Turner's Crimson Rambler' (Mult)?*]." [F-M] "Flower blush rose colour, in large clusters, sweetly scented, free. Growth vigorous." [GeH] "Fair growth; good bloomer." [ARA18/119] "'Blush Rambler', whose remarkable vigor of growth seems better adapted to tall arches and pergolas." [ARA18/82] "Small, double in small clusters or sprays, old flowers shed petals, magnolia fragrance, stems short to long. Good plentiful foliage which is favored by the tent caterpillar, but since new growth is made constantly, the plant always shows a fair amount of foliage. Growth extremely vigorous and slender. Should be good for covering stumps and for the wild-flower garden. Flesh-pink, opening to flesh-white with orange stamens." [ARA23/157] "A semi-double rose of pale pink color, with lighter center, flowering in heavy clusters ... From its color, its vigorous growth, and its time of blooming, it is a good companion rose to 'American Pillar' [W] and should be grown with it whenever possible." [ARA18/84] "Counterpart to 'Mrs. [F. W.] Flight [Mult]." [Ck] "Huge clusters of single, light pink flowers adorn this rampant Multiflora. It fades badly and has been superseded." [GAS] "This is perhaps the best of the Ramblers. Its parentage is not stated, but its consanguinity with '[Turner's] Crimson Rambler' and the climbing Multifloras is clear. It has extraordinarily vigorous growth of upright habit, throwing up great strong basal shoots 12 to 15 feet in height [ca. 4–5 m], arching over if left untrained. They are smooth and light green in colour, and remain green in autumn, and are armed with strong thorns, straight or only slightly hooked, placed at intervals of two or three inches [ca. 5–7.5 dm]. The stems are clothed well downwards with magnificent foliage, the leaves are large, strong, light green in summer darkening a little in autumn, slightly glossy on the upper surface with narrow stipules at the bas, little more than an extension of the stem, the edges of which will be found to be devel-

oped into numerous hairs like the typical stipule of '[Turner's] Crimson Rambler' and the multifloras. The foliage is nearly free from mildew. 'Blush Rambler' has only one flowering period but that lasts a long time for a Rambler. The first flowers opened with me on the 28th June, 1910, and the show of blossom was at its best about the middle of July. This lasted till the second week in August ... The flowers are rather small, nearly single, and carried in very large clusters in the greatest profusion, but possess little or no fragrance. The colour is blush rose with a lighter centre, very much resembling the tints and effect of apple blossom ... A point in favour of 'Blush Rambler' is its green, handsome, and healthy appearance when its time of flowering has passed. The special use for 'Blush Rambler' in the garden is for tall pillars, arches, or pergolas; it will also do well on a trellis or screen, and is on the whole easy to manage for any of these purposes, but though it makes a big head it is a little too upright and unmanageable for a good standard. It is said to grow well up trees, and it is beautiful and effective as a pot plant under glass. Its strong points are its handsome stems and foliage, profusion of flower and delicacy of colouring, its hardiness, and the fact that it will flourish in almost any soil. I think it has no weak point except that there is no autumnal blooming." [NRS11/30–31]

Bobbie James
Sunningdale, 1960

"An unnamed foundling which it was my [G. S. Thomas'] privilege to name in memory of one of the grand old men of gardening ... It is extremely vigorous, with large, long-pointed, fresh green, glossy foliage and large heads of creamy white flowers." [T4]

Bocca Negra
Dubreuil, 1910
Seedling of 'Turner's Crimson Rambler' (Mult).

"Purple red, medium size, single, tall." [Sn] "Extra vigorous plant, blooming in large corymbs of 15–20 blossoms, which are single, purple crimson in color, with a large white eye, and cupped. Wonderful plant for pillars and pergolas with its beautiful rich green foliage and its clusters of sparkling red flowers." [JR34/168]

Bonnie Prince
T. N. Cook/Portland Rose Society, 1924
From 'White Tausendschön' (Mult) × a Wichuraiana seedling; but see below.

"Whitish yellow, medium size, full, light scent, tall." [Sn] "Very beautiful snow white climber. Long graceful clusters of medium size flowers of open frilled form abundantly produced on strong arching canes up to 20 feet long [ca. 6.6 m]. Hardy. Early and lasts well." [GeH] "Bud small, long-pointed; flower medium size, cupped, double, fragrant, white with tinge of yellow in center, borne in clusters. Foliage abundant, medium size, glossy rich green. Very vigorous climber, profuse bloomer in June and occasionally thereafter. Very hardy. Deep red heps ½ inch in diameter [ca. 1 cm]." [ARA25/189] "An early-flowering Multiflora of the 'Tausendschön' type, with huge clusters of pure white, semi-double flowers. Not important." [GAS] "Exquisite when grown as a specimen on a strong post. Specially fine in dry sections, as too much rain spoils the blooms." [C-Ps29] "'Oh, vision fugitive!' A rain, and my 'Prince' has vanished, leaving only the debris of the picnic ... *Pa*.; ... Much like a white 'Tausendschön', but the flowers are

Bonnie Prince *continued*

smaller and very, very fleeting. They scorch badly in sun and heat. Useful only for its earliness at Breeze Hill." [ARA28/148] "A new and very beautiful snow-white climber, distributed for the first time in this year [1925]. It was originated by the late Thomas N. Cook, a devoted Massachusetts rosarian . . . It bears fine full blooms, of better substance and in larger trusses than 'Tausendschön', and is of similar habit except that it has some thorns." [C-Ps25] "Rich, glossy green foliage that does not mildew. Practically thornless. Almost evergreen in Portland, Ore. Has twice withstood zero temperatures there." [Th2] "Kills back in winter here. — *Washington, D.C.* Not especially promising first year after planting. —*Central Point, Ore.* Virtually an improved 'White Tausendschön'. Has some thorns. Very pretty, and has proved hardy. —*Harrisburg, Pa.*" [ARA26/113] "Mr. Cook, with rare fineness of spirit, gave his rose wholly to the Portland Rose Society, and that body has arranged for its propagation and distribution so that the rose will be available in the fall of 1924, and whatever increment arises will be for the beneficent uses of that Society." [ARA24/184] "Mr. Cook, born in 1851, and in active business for a lifetime as senior member of a Boston wholesale paper house, was not only a rose-lover in the ordinary sense, but a hybridist and an investigator. As the latter he amassed a library of some three hundred books and pamphlets on roses, which he believed to be the second best collection of its kind in the United States. Its nucleus rested in a notable English rose library, bought in 1916 from the heirs of Lord Carmichael. Mr. Cook was particularly fond of the hardy climbers, and his own hybridizing was done to improve the quality of these useful roses . . . In July, 1916, one of Mr. Cook's seedlings, the result of a cross between 'Tausendschön' and an unnamed white seedling, was given honorable mention at the exhibition of the Massachusetts Horticultural Society, and in 1917 it won the First Class Certificate . . . Those who had the privilege of personal contact with Mr. Cook knew of his broad culture and his delightful friendliness. He was, as good rosarians are apt to be, a good man to know. [*He died October 22, 1924, just as his rose was being put to commerce*]." [ARA25/201–202]

Bordeaux

Soupert & Notting, 1907

From 'Turner's Crimson Rambler' (Mult) × 'Mlle. Blanche Rebatel' (Pol).

"Entirely new wine-red coloration. Very vigorous bush, climbing freely, and thoroughly hardy. The blossoms come in enormous bouquets on long stems; they have the size and form of those of '[Turner's] Crimson Rambler', but appearing long before those of the type variety, and lasting longer. 'Bordeaux' is unequalled as a variety to train on fences or walls or on pyramids. Because of its distinct color, it stands out clearly from all those now grown, and further has the great merit of blooming easily and abundantly in the cool house." [JR31/136] "Red, small, lightly double, tall." [Sn]

Buttercup

W. Paul, 1909

"Yellow, small, single to semi-double, tall." [Sn] "Poor growth; bloom goes fast." [ARA18/121]

[Carnea]

syn. 'À Fleurs Carnées'

Evans/Colville, 1804

"*Branches* long and climbing, straight, glabrous, reddish; *prickles* often geminate and infrastipular or more or less scattered. *Leaflets* 5 or 7, rather small, ovate to elongated ovate, almost sessile, soft to the touch, simply dentate, green and glabrous above, paler and pubescent beneath; petioles villose with small hooked prickles; stipules pectinately pinnatifid. *Flowers* numerous, in dense broad panicles borne on the laterals, small, almost full, faintly scented; bracts incised on both margins like the stipules; peduncles and pedicels villose like the petioles; *receptacles* ovoid to subglobose, pubescent; *sepals* 3 pinnatifid, 2 simple, acute, shorter than the petals, pubescent; *petals* multiseriate, pale pink; styles free, villose, central ones fasciculate, outer ones divergent. This native of China was introduced to England by T. Evans around 1804, where it bloomed for the first time in Colville's nursery. Boursault brought it from London to Paris in 1808, where it bloomed in August 1812 in Dr. Cartier's garden. The long branches of *multiflora* lend themselves to many uses: draping arbors and bowers, entwined into garlands or pyramids, and by means of support on trellises for covering walls to a great height. Grafted plants succeed the best. In the open air, winter frosts destroy *multiflora* in the Parisian area, unless it is covered for protection." [T&R]

Carolina Budde

Leenders, 1913

From 'Turner's Crimson Rambler' (Mult) × 'Léonie Lamesch' (Pol).

"Red, medium size, full, tall." [Sn] "Magnificent climbing rose with large and full crimson red blossoms. Very vigorous and winter-hardy plant. The foliage is shiny. Excellent for frameworks, arches, and pyramids." [JR38/21]

Caroline Bank

Geschwind, ca. 1890

"Pink, medium size, full, tall." [Sn] "No scent, −3 m [less than ca. 9 ft]." [EU]

Caroubier

Nonin, 1912

From 'Hiawatha' (Mult) × *Rosa multiflora*.

"Light red, medium size, single, tall." [Sn] "Clusters of brilliant, single, crimson-scarlet flowers, a little earlier than [those of] the Wichuraiana [*sic*] 'Hiawatha', from which it was raised." [GAS] "Vigorous growth; flowers attractive, not all in bloom at once; resembles 'Eisenach' [W] in color; occasionally gives a little fall bloom." [ARA18/119] "I have had a French variety named 'Caroubier' flowering here this autumn, and as late an November could cut some trusses from it. In colour it is lighter than 'Hiawatha' and deeper than 'Leuchtstern' [Mult], but possesses more of the multiflora strain. This is a type of Rambler wanted, as it will bloom fairly well again in autumn." [NRS18/149]

"From a subscriber to the *Journal des Roses,* we receive the following note: 'I saw at Bagatelle a climber of the 'Hiawatha' sort called 'Caroubier', which attracted me with its small single blossoms of a sparkling color. I have searched but in vain for it in all the catalogs. Could you tell me about it, or insert this small note in your estimable publication? [*signed*] T.H.'." [JR35/134] "One of our subscribers was so good as to favor us with a question on the rose 'Caroubier' which he saw at Bagatelle . . . The breeder of this pretty climber . . . sends us the following note: . . . 'Vigorous bush, producing large bouquets of single, upright blossoms of a very bright color—crimson red brightened with scarlet. It blooms ten days before 'Hiawatha', and gives a second bloom. The duration of the bloom is thus quite prolonged. The petals do not fall.'" [JR36/9] "This variety was awarded the *Prix des Dames Patronesses* at the 1911 Bagatelle concourse." [JR37/88]

Cato
Gratama, 1903

"Pink-yellow, medium size, full, tall." [Sn] "This newcomer ... was found by the firm Gratama Bros. & Co., horticulturists at Hoogeveen (Holland), in 1899. Its first bloom took place in 1901 in the aforementioned establishment; and, after closely scrutinizing their obtention, the breeders decided to release it to commerce. Shown last June to the Committee on Flowers and Plants, the rose 'Cato' —which belongs to the series of Climbing Polyanthas—was much noted by visitors. Compared to the variety 'Euphrosine' [Lam], to which it could be said to have some resemblance, the members of the Committee discerned that the blossoms of the novelty were larger, fuller, and more finely colored. The buds are crimson red before anthesis, the color little by little becoming lighter until achieving a beautiful delicate pink when fully open. When the petals fall, the light yellow stamens become very noticeable and make a magnificent effect with the pink color of the blossoms. The diameter of these last comes to 5 cm [ca. 2 in], and they are in panicles of 20–25 buds borne on long stems. The shallowly dentate leaves are a beautiful glossy dark green; the rearward portion is garnished with small pointed thorns which are back-pointing; such thorns are also found on the shrub's wood, excepting on the flower-bearing branches. What is more, the blossoms have the advantage of lasting a long time cut." [JR28/27–28] Cato, Roman statesman, whether the elder (lived 234–149 B.C.) or the younger (95–46 B.C.), his great-grandson the Stoic, we know not.

Charlotte Mackensen
Vogel, 1938

"Deep red, medium size, full, tall." [Sn]

Charlotte von Rathlef
Vogel, 1935

"Pink, medium size, full, tall." [Sn]

Chatter
Schmidt, 1960

"Light red, medium size, lightly double, medium scent, tall." [Sn]

Coccinea
Legris, 1843

"Carminy pink." [Ÿ] "Colors varied, white, pink, scarlet, and ashen blue, superb." [LF] "Small flowers of a carmine roseate hue." [WRP] "Full pink." [JR2/42] "Flowers rosy carmine, changeable, small and full." [P] "Small, full, carmine pink." [JR5/71] "Blossoms numerous, some 8 cm across [ca. 3 in], very full and quite open, scarlet pink passing to lilac pink in age. Doesn't rebloom." [dH44/429] Possibly a re-release of 'Platyphylla' (Mult), which also see. Also ascribed to Van Houtte, who perhaps sold it through his catalog at some point.

Coccinée   Listed as 'Platyphylla' (Mult).

Coralie
W. Paul, 1919

From 'Hiawatha' (Mult) × 'Lyon-Rose' (Pern).

"Orange-salmon. Coral buds opening orange-salmon, aging soft

pink. Although rarely seen it is one of the most beautiful Climbers grown." [C-Pf33] "A climbing 'Lyon-Rose', coral-red changing to deep pink, large for its class, double, distinct rambling variety." [GeH] "Large, coral-pink flowers resembling . . . 'Mme. Édouard Herriot' [Pern]. A superb thing in full bloom. Foliage particularly handsome. The best hardy climbing rose of this color." [GAS] "Light orange red, medium size, full, tall." [Sn] "Foliage glossy green." [ARA20/217] "Beautiful climber; fine growth . . . *Mass.*; A delightful new color effect. Vigorous, and increasingly so as it becomes established . . . *Md.*; No climber I have seen yields more pleasing flowers, and it blooms longer than the average, although not so many flowers as some others. Attractive salmon-pink blooms on nice stems, much larger than most climbers. Plant normally robust and rather abnormally free from pests . . . *Idaho*; Reported as doing well, but of no outstanding merit . . . *Calif.*" [ARA28/151] "Fine in colour and form, although not specially effective, as the blossoms are hardly numerous enough, and the growth is somewhat stiff. The colour is of the lovely shade seen in the 'Lyon-Rose', a very welcome tint when there are so many pinks and reds." [NRS24/217]

Countess M. H. Chotek   Listed as 'Gräfin Marie Henriette Chotek' (Mult).

Crimson Grandiflora
Ghys, 1912

"Purple red, small, full, tall." [Sn]

Crimson Rambler   Listed as 'Turner's Crimson Rambler' (Mult).

Crimson Rambler Remontant   Listed as 'Flower of Fairfield' (Mult).

Daisy Brazileir
Turbat, 1918

"Flower fire-red and purple-red with prominent yellow stamens. Growth vigorous, erect climbing." [GeH] "Light red, small, single, light scent, tall." [Sn] "Single flowers of fire-red and purple-red, with yellow anthers; very showy. Completely covered in autumn and winter with orange-red berries which create a gorgeous effect. Wood and foliage deep green. Vigorous, erect grower." [ARA19/101]

Daniel Lacombe   Plate 47
Allard/Moreau-Robert, 1885

Either a seedling of 'Polyantha' (Mult); or from a cross of *Rosa multiflora* × 'Général Jacqueminot' (HP).

"Yellowish pink-white, medium size, full, tall." [Sn] "Reported to be a Multiflora with yellow flowers stained pink." [GAS] "Flower white, yellow centre; very free. Growth very vigorous." [GeH] "Extremely vigorous bush, giving canes 3–4 m long [ca. 9–12 ft]; blossom medium-sized, full, chamois yellow upon opening, washed pink and fading to purest white; clusters comprised of 60–80 flowers; wood smooth and thornless; from the old 'Polyantha' [Mult], called 'À Fleurs de Ronce', from which it takes its vigor and eager bloom." [JR9/149]

Dawson
syns. 'Dawsoniana', 'The Dawson Rose'
Dawson/Strong, 1888

From a selfing of a seedling which resulted from crossing 'Polyantha' (Mult) and 'Général Jacqueminot' (HP).

"Pale rose. —Vigorous climber. —Pillar, arch, pergola. —Early

Dawson *continued*

flowering." [Cat12] "Pink, small, full, tall." [Sn] "Flower pale rose, semi-double. Growth very vigorous." [GeH] "It grows to several meters wide, and covers itself with semi-double pink blossoms." [JR26/115] "Growth fair; no special merit." [ARA18/122] "Foliage plentiful, almost very plentiful, black-spots and mildews in midsummer, black-spots badly in late summer, with practically no loss of foliage; bloom profuse in late May and early June." [ARA18/129] "This is a new rose coming from the Arnold Arboretum (Massachusetts, U.S.). Having been bred by Mr. Jackson Dawson, one of the people in charge of that renowned establishment, he dedicated it to himself. This variety is the product of *Rosa multiflora* (R. polyantha) crossed with 'Général Jacqueminot'; it is singularly beautiful and thoroughly distinct from the others in this category of hybrids. It is like '[Turner's] Crimson Rambler' in the way it blooms, but in growth is much superior to this last. The plant grows in all directions, with strong branches arching back to the ground which are covered right now (the beginning of June) with a multitude of semi-double pale pink blossoms. The size and form are pretty much those of the Crimson Rambler, but the blackish green leaves have much serrated stipules. The six plants shown at Kew, in the rose collection, were quite an attraction." [JR20/97] "The first authentic hybrid of *R. multiflora* made in America. The blooms are bright pink, double, clustered, and come very early. Of historical interest only." [GAS] "This rose-pink variety still holds its place as one of the earliest-flowering Multifloras, and in addition is a very charming rose." [ARA18/84] "The veteran superintendent of the Arnold Arboretum, Jackson Dawson, is another of the half-century rose workers to whom honor is due. His hybridizing work began with the introduction of the 'Dawson' rose, in 1888, and in the list presented in this *Annual* it will be seen that he has produced climbers of exceptional quality, and one single rose, 'Arnold' [Rg], which, not yet by any means well known, is certain to be used for lawn specimens in increasing degree." [ARA16/46]

Dawsoniana   Listed as 'Dawson' (Mult).

De la Grifferaie
Grille/Vibert, 1844
From 'Platyphylla' (Mult) × a form of *Rosa gallica*.

"Carminy purple." [Ÿ] "Often striped." [R&M62] "Flower large, full, crimson purple." [JR2/42] "Medium-sized, full, carminy purple." [BJ53] "Large, full, deep pink fading to delicate pink." [JR5/71] "Large for the sort, full, carminy purple." [Gp&f52] "Very large for the species, full, carminy purple, very vigorous, obtained from 'Cocciné' [*i.e.*, 'Platyphylla' (Mult)]." [V8] "Purple red, large, full, medium scent, tall." [Sn] "Flowers deep rose in bud, changing to blush, large and full; form, compact. Extremely robust." [P] "Lilac-rose. This variety makes a valuable stock on which to bud strong-growing kinds." [EL] "Of vigorous growth, and produces the largest flowers of this class, purplish carmine, and full double." [WRP] "May also be grown as a bush with perfect success as far North as Boston. It gives a great abundance of blush and rose-colored flowers, forming a high mound of bloom." [FP] "Very vigorous growth; large, full flower, crimson purple; resistant to heavy frost." [S] "Canes of medium size bark somber green, bearing sharp reddish-brown thorns which are slightly hooked. Much used as stock on which to graft Teas." [S] "Very vigorous; canes of medium size ...; bark somber green, reddish where the sun strikes,

with reddish brown thorns, tapered, slightly hooked, and very sharp. Leaves somber green, rugose, composed of 5–7 oval, pointed, dentate leaflets; basal leaflets very small; leafstalk pretty strong, slightly nodding, armed with 5–6 little prickles. Blossoms about two inches across [ca. 5 cm], very full, plump, rarely solitary, when so on twigs, usually in clusters in a number depending upon the vigor of the branch; color, purplish pink changing to vinous lilac-pink; outer petals fairly large for the type, center petals muddled; peduncle short and slender. Calyx rounded. This rose is extremely vigorous and blooms abundantly." [JF] "It is important because of its wide distribution in the rural districts where it is known as the Seven Sisters Rose in the North particularly, although that name justly belongs to ['Platyphylla']. 'De la Grifferaie' was once widely used as an understock ..., which accounts for its abundance, since it suckered vigorously when the rose budded upon it died. The plant is coarse, with large, rough foliage and long, arching stems, in a superficial way not unlike the old Prairie Rose [*i.e.*, Setigera] hybrids. The double flowers are shapeless and scentless, of various shades of purplish pink, rose-pink, and white, some part one color and part another. Plant is extremely hardy and has value in northern gardens where more highly developed strains perish without careful protection." [GAS] "De la Grifferaie" refers to a château built by Napoléon III in the Canton de Baugé, Département de Maine-et-Loire, near the community of Echemiré, but perhaps more pertinently near the city in which Vibert's nursery was located at the time of the introduction of this cultivar, Angers (information kindly supplied by Colette Tremblay).

Décoration de Geschwind   Listed as 'Geschwinds Orden' (Mult).

Dr. Reymond
L. Mermet, 1907
Seedling of 'Turner's Crimson Rambler' (Mult).

"White, large, full, tall." [Sn] "Fairly large, double white flowers tinged with green." [GAS] "Very vigorous and very hardy shrub, blooming abundantly in pyramidal corymbs, very elegantly formed; blossom large, full, pure white on a slightly greenish ground." [JR31/166]

Écarlate   Listed as 'Platyphylla' (Mult). Not to be confused with the HT 'Écarlate'.

Eichsfeldia
Alfons, 1925
   "Yellowish white, small, single, tall." [Sn]

Elisabeth
Alfons, 1926
   "Pink, small, full, medium scent, tall." [Sn]

Emerickrose
Alfons, 1922
   "Light pink, white center, small, full, medium scent, tall." [Sn]

Émile Nerini
Nonin, 1913
From 'Turner's Crimson Rambler' (Mult) × 'Dorothy Perkins' (W).

"Bright red cluster-flowered Multiflora." [GAS] "Shining pink, large-blooming." [Ck] "Double, carmine-red, very early, valuable for that feature." [ARA26/175] "Light pink, medium size, lightly double, tall." [Sn] "Vigorous plant, forming naturally a pretty bush, very floriferous, producing an abundance of large, upright bouquets; the numerous solid flowers are a pretty ruby red tint, with a large white center; very bright coloration. Forced, they resemble—to my way of thinking—enormous bushes of 'Orléans-Rose' [Pol]." [JR38/55]

Erato
Tantau, 1939

"Pink, small, lightly double, tall." [Sn] Erato, the Muse of lyric poetry, unconcerned with this present work, alas.

Erlkönig
probable syn., 'Roi des Aunes', *q.v.*
Geschwind, 1886
Seedling of 'De la Grifferaie' (Mult).

"Crimson carmine." [Y] "Carmine purple, middle-sized, double, no scent, −3 m [less than ca. 9 ft]." [EU]

Erna
Vogel, 1929

"Light pink, small, full, tall." [Sn]

Ernst Dechant
Vogel, 1928

"White, yellow center, small, lightly double, tall." [Sn]

Ernst G. Dörell
Geschwind, 1887

"Carmine." [LS] "Carmine pink, middle-sized, double, no scent, −3 m [less than ca. 9 ft]." [EU]

Evodia
Alfons, 1925

"Whitish pink, small, full, medium scent, tall." [Sn]

Exquisite
Praskač, 1926

"Salmon pink, small, full, tall." [Sn]

Fatinitza
Geschwind, 1886
From *Rosa multiflora* × *R. arvensis,* in the third generation.

"White and pink." [LS] "Varying light pink—deep pink with white stripes, middle-sized, double, no scent, −3 m [less than ca. 9 ft]." [EU]

Flower of Fairfield
syns. 'Crimson Rambler Remontant', 'Immerblühender Crimson Rambler'
Schultheis/Ludorf, 1908
Sport of 'Turner's Crimson Rambler' (Mult).

"Red, medium size, lightly double, tall." [Sn] "Flower bright crimson, medium, double. Growth vigorous, climbing, autumn-flowering." [GeH] "A perpetual flowering sport of '[Turner's] Crimson Rambler' that should be an acquisition as perpetual flowering Ramblers are scarce." [F-M] "This rose enjoyed brief fame as an Everblooming Crimson Rambler. It is evidently a bright red counterpart of that variety but its everblooming character is defective." [GAS] "A sport from the notable '[Turner's] Crimson Rambler', which it resembles in every respect except that it continues to bloom all Summer. Its European growers claim that it produces a marvelous succession of brilliant crimson clusters from early Spring till late Autumn." [C&Js11] "I am inclined to fear that if some of the brightness has not been lost, at least the less pleasing stage of colouring in the flower is reached ear-

lier in the sport than we find to be the case with '[Turner's] Crimson Rambler'." [NRS11/58] "Foliage very plentiful through season, blackspots slightly, especially in midsummer, mildews badly in late summer; bloom abundant in June, moderate and continuous till late summer." [ARA18/130]

Francis
Barbier, 1907
From *Rosa wichuraiana* × 'Turner's Crimson Rambler' (Mult).

"Red, white center, small, single, tall." [Sn] "Flower bright red, single, in bouquets of fifty followed by a profusion of red hips. Growth similar to [that of] '[Turner's] Crimson Rambler'." [GeH] "Stout, upright, rampant growth. Foliage large dark green with roughish surface. Blooms in large masses of small single flowers; crimson with white centre." [NRS11/101] "Bright pink, and, if seen in early morning with the others in their freshness, a showy flower, but later on it seems to want brightness and vigour in its flowering. The growth is somewhat after the manner of '[Turner's] Crimson Rambler', as it sends up long straight rods. Hitherto I have pruned out all old growth, but while making these notes it occurs to me to try flowering it on the laterals, and it may then give a better effect." [NRS16/100] "The plant has quite the same foliage, growth, and manner of bloom as '[Turner's] Crimson Rambler', but the blossoms, in large clusters of 25–50 flowers, are single, and a beautiful bright red fading to pale pink, with a cluster of golden yellow stamens. The plant covers itself with bright red hips, making a superb effect in the Fall." [JR31/166] Data on the 'Francis' Wichuraiana evidently offered by Fauque & fils in 1909 are hard to come by; the descriptions of the 'Francis' that presently exists in commerce and in rosaria agree with the description of Barbier's 'Francis'.

Frau Georg von Simson
Walter, 1909
From 'Helene' (Mult) × 'Rösel Dach' (Pol).

"Light pink, medium size, full, tall." [Sn]

Frau Käte Schmid
Vogel, 1931

"Deep pink, large, lightly double, light scent, tall." [Sn]

Frau Lina Strassheim
Strassheim, 1906
Sport of 'Turner's Crimson Rambler' (Mult).

"Salmon pink, medium size, full, tall." [Sn] "Climbing plant, blossom medium-sized, in a cluster, bright chamois pink." [JR33/186] "Like 'Flame' [extinct Mult of 1912 from Turner], a sport or seedling of '[Turner's] Crimson Rambler' with clusters of vivid salmon-pink flowers." [GAS]

Futtaker Schlingrose
Geschwind/Chotek, ca. 1900

"Deep red, medium size, full, tall." [Sn] "Slightly scented, good hips, −3 m [less than ca. 9 ft]." [EU] "One of the most beautiful red climbing roses. Entirely unknown. Climbs up to 4 m high [ca. 12 ft], heavy-blooming, splendid kind. Leaves quite healthy, dark green. Blossom well-formed, velvety dark red." [Ck]

G. F. Veronica
Demitrovisi, date uncertain

"Light yellow, small, lightly double, medium scent, tall." [Sn]

[Garden's Glory]

syn. 'Pink Mme. Plantier'
Conard & Jones, 1905
From 'Dawson' (Mult) × 'Clotilde Soupert' (Pol).

"A grand new Pillar or Veranda Rose, offered now for the first time after being thoroughly tested by us . . . Large fully double flowers, clear rose pink, very fragrant, borne in beautiful clusters, strong, vigorous grower and profuse bloomer, entirely hardy; almost thornless. Resembles '[Mme.] Plantier' [HN] in habit of growth and abundance of bloom." [C&Js05]

Gardeniaeflora

Benary/J. C. Schmidt, 1901

"Snow white." [Ÿ] "An early-flowering Multiflora with clusters of rather large, semi-double, pure white flowers." [GAS] "White, small, lightly double, light scent, tall." [Sn]

Geisha

Geschwind/Lambert, 1913

"Red, center striped white, medium size, full, tall." [Sn] "Moderate growth, probably related to 'Gruss an Teplitz' [B]. Flowers glowing red with white streaks on center petals." [GAS] "Some scent; bush to 2.5 m [ca. 7½ ft]." [EU] "Fair growth; bloom fades quickly." [ARA18/122] "Rapid and vigorous growth; beautiful foliage; this variety is completely different from the race from which it issued. Large flower, from 8–10 cm across [ca. 3–4 in], cupped, pretty full, sparkling scarlet crimson, like 'Gruss an Teplitz'. Central petals rayed white. The blossoms cover the plant; in full bloom, it is a veritable miracle of color. Much to be recommended. Resists cold very well." [JR38/89]

Gela Tepelmann

Tepelmann, ca. 1950

"Red, medium size, full, tall." [Sn]

Geschwinds Nordlandrose

Geschwind, 1884

"Light pink, medium size, very full, tall." [Sn] "No scent, recurrent, −3 m [less than ca. 9 ft]." [EU]

Geschwinds Nordlandrose II

Geschwind, 1929

"Cherry red." [EU]

Geschwinds Orden   Plate 49

syn. 'Décoration de Geschwind'; trans., "Geschwind's Medal"
Geschwind, 1886
From *Rosa rugosa* × *R. multiflora* (or *R. multiflora* cultivar).

"Bright violet pink." [Ÿ] "Violet purple-pink, white edges, medium size, very full, medium scent, tall." [Sn] "Purple-pink flowers edged white. Practically unknown in this country [U.S.A.] and does not seem important." [GAS] "The rose illustrated in our picture . . . was bred by Mr. Geschwind of Karpfen (Hungary) and released to commerce in 1886. This variety, called 'Geschwinds Orden' or 'Décoration de Geschwind', classes as one of that series of roses called 'Hungarian Climbing Roses.' The breeder, in selling this rose, states that it is the product of a cross between *Rosa rugosa* and a Multiflora. The slightly rugose foliage bespeaks its Rugosa heritage; as to the Multiflora presence, it can't be doubted. This is certainly one of the prettiest flowers from this series. Though it doesn't have the vigor of an Ayr-

shire or Sempervirens, a person still can put together pretty colonnades with this Hungarian rose. The abundance of its blossoms, their long duration, and the hardiness of specimens against cold are the great advantages that they have over some varieties with long canes. The flowers are deep bright pink with a touch of violet and a nearly pure white edging; they are medium-sized, very full, and nearly flat. At bloom-time, the effect produced by this bush is extremely beautiful. Unfortunately, it is not remontant." [JR20/56]

Geschwinds Schönste

trans. "Geschwind's Most Beautiful"
Geschwind, ca. 1900

"Light red, medium size, full, tall." [Sn] "No scent, −3 m [less than ca. 9 ft]." [EU] For full information on the important and imaginative breeder Rudolf Geschwind, we refer the reader to the excellent article on him by William Grant and Erich Unmuth in the 1994 *American Rose Annual*. In short, he was born on August 23, 1829, in Hredle, Bohemia, and lived in the city of Teplitz until age 18. He studied in Prague, and, that completed, was appointed a Forester Royal, retaining that position until retirement at age 77. He wrote three books on roses and rose breeding, but came to the world's attention at the Paris World's Fair of 1886, exhibiting there some of his "Hungarian Climbing Roses." He continued his wide-ranging breeding until July 2, 1910, and died on July 10, 1910.

Ghislaine de Féligonde

Turbat, 1916
From crossing a yellow Multiflora (or, probably, Lambertiana) with a red Multiflora (and see below).

"Lemon-colored flowers in great clusters. Charming because of its many tints and shades of soft yellow." [ARA29/98] "Must become a favorite. Its clusters of blooms are aurora yellow and pink, small, but wonderfully beautiful, very perpetual." [NRS20/70] "Bud nasturtium yellow." [Ÿ] "Clusters of small apricot yellow buds, opening pale buff with coppery tints; continuous; well retained foliage; canes almost thornless." [CaRoII/3/3] "Yellowish white, medium size, full, tall." [Sn] "Coppery greyish gold, base of petals golden yellow, passing to delicate yellowish white tinted flesh; buds bright capucin-yellow, borne in clusters. Growth very vigorous, climbing." [GeH] "Strong grower, freely perpetual and floriferous; flowers in clusters of ten to twenty; bright yellow;; opening coppery aurora, with golden yellow aiglets, passing to yellowish white, tinted delicate flesh-color. Very effective." [ARA18/108] "Has a tendency to bloom a second time, once, indeed, blooming on the root shoots of the current year." [ARA24/185] "My new bush bloomed from mid-June until the freeze in September without interruption. It did not seem to be much of a climber, and was rather slender in growth and twiggy, but very healthy, and the flowers are pretty. The yellow color lasts about a day, but the opening buds contrive to keep a yellow effect to the flower clusters all the time. Very dainty, sweet, and altogether lovely." [ARA24/90] "Loveliest of all Multifloras, and one of the few justifications for the race. The plants are sometimes relatively thornless, of moderate growth, and bloom profusely in early summer with occasional clusters in mid-summer and fall. The small buds are strongly tinged with orange, and open into delightfully fragrant little blooms, bright buff at first, but fading almost white. It is a degree or two hardier than most yellow Multifloras." [GAS] "Monsieur E. Turbat, of Orléans, France, tells us he produced it from two unnamed seedlings of Multiflora." [ARA24/186] "Sunday I was entertained by Monsieur Turbat. The most of the day was spent in his nurseries, principally among the roses, although the large collection of herbaceous plants interested me. There are about a hundred acres under cultivation. Before [U.S.] Quarantine No. 37 went into effect, 500,000 roses were propagated annually, but only 150,000 are now grown. In the Dwarf Polyantha section were many interesting unnamed seedlings . . ." [ARA22/137] "Monsieur Turbat modestly says that he has not worked as much as his neighbor and friend [René Barbier], adding that the unforeseen has often disturbed his plans. His original intention was to create plants suited as much as possible to culture in pots for forcing, but he has produced mostly decorative varieties . . . When entering it at Bagatelle, Mr. [sic] Turbat had no confidence in 'Ghislaine de Féligonde' [Mult], and he was very agreeably surprised to see it awarded a Certificate of Merit." [ARA26/175]

Gilda
Geschwind, 1887

"Reddish violet, medium size, very full, tall." [Sn] "No scent, −3 m [less than ca. 9 ft]." [EU] Gilda, daughter of the hunchbacked jester Rigoletto in Verdi's opera, involved in extensive operations mostly demonstrating various aspects of the proposition that you always hurt the one you love. Studies seem to indicate that we aren't particularly beneficial to those we hate, either.

Goldfinch
G. Paul, 1908
Seedling of 'Helene' (Mult).

"Yellow fading to white." [Ÿ] "Deep yellow, small, lightly double, medium scent, tall." [Sn] "Buds golden yellow, opening flowers [color-word missing here; "yellow," presumably], changing to white, semi-double. Growth very vigorous, climbing." [GeH] "Pale orange, changing to white; semi-double; trusses. Reported stronger in the extreme North than the Hybrid Wichuraianas." [ARA17/28] "The hardiest yellow rambler, blooming early in a good-sized cluster. The flowers fade to white." [ARA18/90] "Among the yellow climbers the hardiest and earliest is 'Goldfinch', a small-flowered variety." [ARA22/44] "The small compact buds open deep yellow and fade in a single day to a pale lemon-white. A very free-growing, free-blooming variety, with good foliage and no thorns, an advantage that is appreciated by anyone who has to prune one of these large ramblers. The blossom has a distinct and charming fragrance that is as fleeting as its color, and in autumn the bright orange hips are very attractive." [ARA18/84] "Foliage very plentiful till late summer, then plentiful, black-spots slightly from midsummer on, mildews very slightly in late summer; bloom free first half of June." [ARA18/130] Goldfinch, various of appropriately colored finches; in this case, probably *Carduelis carduelis*.

Graf Zeppelin Plate 54
Böhm, 1910
Sport of 'Non Plus Ultra' (Mult).

"Bright coral-red variation of '[Turner's] Crimson Rambler' [Mult]. Not much good, for the color fades abominably." [GAS] "A fine climbing Rose, similar to 'Tausendschön' [Mult] . . . , but the color is vivid pink with a fiery reflex which is very effective." [C&Js12] "It does not seem necessary to carry detestation of [World War I] German methods so far as to include their roses . . . It is an early bloomer, and the color is pure bright rose." [ARA18/84–85] "Light orange red, medium size, lightly double, tall." [Sn] "Foliage very plentiful till late summer, then plentiful, black-spots and mildews very slightly; bloom profuse through most of June, sparse and moderate in July." [ARA18/130] "Herr E. Böhm, nurseryman, Obercassel, near Bonn (Germany), released a new rose to commerce of the Multiflora sort with long canes—that is, 'climbing.' 'Graf Zeppelin' is the name of this introduction, which has bright coral red blossoms, a glowing coloration producing a superb effect. The panicles are numerous, large, and long-lasting. Mr. Kiese, the well-known raiser of 'Otto von Bismarck' [HT], who tried out 'Graf Zeppelin', says that he has seen flowers on this rose very late in the Fall, and that the specimen bore, without harm, 25° C. of frost. In a word, this will be a climber of the first order." [JR34/1]

Gräfin Ada von Bredow
Walter, 1909
From 'Thalia' (Lam) × 'Rösel Dach' (Pol).

"Whitish pink, small, lightly double, tall." [Sn] "Vigorous Multiflora with large, white and rose-pink flowers in big clusters." [GAS] "The Saverne Rose Society was organized thirty years ago by Monsieur Louis Walter who has been the moving spirit ever since. He has succeeded in establishing a public Roseraie that is the most cherished possession of the city. Monsieur Walter is called by his fellow citizens, 'Rosen Walter,' and a petition has been made to change the name of Saverne into Saverne-les-Roses." [ARA29/185] In many places of the world, civic enthusiasm and pride do much to encourage worthy personal exertion.

Gräfin Marie Henriette Chotek
syn. 'Countess M. H. Chotek', 'Marie Henriette Grafin Chotek'
Lambert, 1911
From 'Farquhar' (W) × 'Richmond' (HT).

"Red, medium size, full, medium scent, tall." [Sn] "Inflorescence very large; well formed, quite full, bright red. Blooms in giant clusters—each branch fills a vase. Plant very 'climbing,' erect, foliage beautiful, entirely healthy." [Ck] "A splendid hardy climber. Grows upright and bushy, and makes shoots 8 to 10 feet long [ca. 2.6–3.3 m] in a season. Blooms are medium sized, well formed, very fragrant, bright crimson." [C&Js13] "Foliage very plentiful, sufficient in midsummer, very sparse in late summer, black-spots very badly; bloom free about first two weeks of June." [ARA18/129] "[The growth of] 'Paul's Scarlet Climber' distinctly resembles [that of] that splendid Pillar Rose 'Grafin Marie Henriette Chotek' —a Rose with bloom and bud not unlike [those of] 'Richmond', which was one of its parents. To those who prefer a Rose that will give them a good button-hole flower, I commend this variety most heartily." [NRS18/149] Not to be confused with Kiese's 1910 Multiflora 'Gräfin Chotek', which was apple-blossom pink.

[Graulhié]
Van Houtte, pre-1842

"Double white flowers of a very small size, and particularly delicate and pretty." [WRP] "Medium-sized, full, white." [BJ53] "Very small, full, white." [R&M62] "Blossom very small, full, opening wide; color white, exterior of petals pink." [S] "Pure white, outer petals tinged with rose, of medium size, full; form, cupped. Good." [P]

Grevillea Listed as 'Grevillii' (Mult).

Grevillii

syns. 'Grevillea', 'Roxburghiana'
Breeder/Introducer unknown, pre-1828

"White." [RG] "*Shrub* smaller [than 'Platyphylla', etc.] in all its parts. *Canes* very slender. *Thorns* feebler. *Stipules* small, entire, edges simply ciliate. *Leaflets* smaller, relatively narrower, less villose. *Ovary* more elongate. *Corolla* of 4–5 narrow white petals." [Pf] "Monsieur Laffay, a man of much experience in the culture of these roses—and in general with all the species from the East—thinks that this could well be the Type of the Multifloras." [MaCo] 'Grevillii' and 'Grevillea' are sometimes seen as (incorrect) synonyms of 'Platyphylla' (Mult).

Grossherzogin Eléonore von Essen

Strassheim, 1906
From a Multiflora × 'Turner's Crimson Rambler' (Mult).

"Deep red, medium size, full, tall." [Sn] "Very vigorous shrub; flower medium-sized, full, blood red." [JR31/22]

Gruss an Breinegg

trans. "Greetings to Breinegg"
Alfons, 1925

"Light reddish violet, small, single, tall." [Sn]

Gruss an Germershausen

trans. "Greetings to Germershausen"
Alfons, 1926

"Violet pink, white center, small, single, tall." [Sn]

Gruss an Hannover

trans. "Greetings to Hanover"
Lahmann, 1938

"Orange pink, medium size, full, tall." [Sn]

Hackeburg Listed as 'Hakeburg' (Mult).

Hakeburg

syn. 'Hackeburg'
Kiese/Hake, 1912

"Light violet, white center, medium size, full, tall." [Sn] "Delicate lilac color. Plant hardy, prickly. Blooms in beautiful clusters." [Ck] "A very good Multiflora with abundant clusters of lilac-colored flowers, edged with white. Plant almost thornless." [GAS] "Fair growth and bloom; foliage light, but attractive." [ARA18/120] "Very vigorous climbing shrub, hardy, nearly thornless, very floriferous, producing enormous thyrses. Blossom fresh lilac pink, delicate, with a white center, in the middle of which are the yellow stamens. This rose, raised by Herr Kiese, was shown at Britz-Berlin, where it was noticed by Herr Hake, to whom Herr Kiese offered it, and who has it for sale at his horticultural firm, Klein Machnower Baumschulen, in Berlin." [JR37/76]

Hans Schmid

Vogel, 1934

"Deep pink, medium size, full, tall." [Sn]

Havering Rambler

Pemberton, 1920
Seedling of 'Turner's Crimson Rambler' (Mult).

"Deep cyclamen pink. Its huge trusses of almond blossom blooms make a wonderful show as a pillar." [NRS29/248] "Pink, small, full, tall." [Sn] "Large sprays of pale pink flowers like double almond-blossoms." [Sn] "A summer-flowering rambler. Colour, almond blossom, distinct. Large clusters of rosette flowers, well distributed. Growth very vigorous." [NRS20/201] "Flower small, double, rosette-form, almond-blossom pink, very lasting, borne in large clusters on long stem. Very vigorous blooms profusely." [ARA21/159] Havering-atte-Bower, Pemberton's home.

Helene

Lambert, 1897
From a HT seedling × an unnamed seedling (which resulted from crossing 'Aglaia' [Lam] and 'Turner's Crimson Rambler' [Mult]).

"Very good old Multiflora of pale lilac-pink as we know it. Described abroad as pure violet-rose on yellowish-white base." [GAS] "Delicate pink." [Ÿ] "Pale flesh tinted violet. Growth very vigorous, distinct; a good weeping Rose." [GeH] "Violet pink, white center, medium size, full, tall." [Sn] "Hardy thornless climber, violet crimson, quite double and borne in splendid clusters." [C&Js03] "This is a lovely rose of pale flesh-color, tinted violet, with flat, semi-double flowers of medium size. It has a very free, gracious habit of growth and is thornless." [ARA18/85] "This rose is thoroughly distinct and worthy of praise; but not, as some have claimed, better than '[Turner's] Crimson Rambler'. Color is soft violet rose with anthers and pistils of pure yellow, which gives the flowers a pleasing appearance. They bloom with 20 to 50 together in a cluster, and in habit and growth are very much like '[Turner's] Crimson Rambler'." [C&Js07] "As for 'Aglaia' seedlings, some do wonderfully well, as for example 'Helene'." [JR26/69]

Hiawatha Plate 52

Walsh, 1904
From 'Turner's Crimson Rambler' (Mult) × 'Paul's Carmine Pillar' (HCh).

"Single crimson red, in strong very effective umbels." [JR31/134] "Small single flower of a rich crimson on a cream ground." [JR35/119] "Brilliant scarlet; bears large clusters of single flowers; bright and effective. One of the best in this section." [C&Js09] "Burnt to a pale pink." [ARA21/126] "This Rose holds its intense bright color for a long time and is very spectacular when in full bloom." [C&Js23] "Colour is often disappointing in wet weather." [NRS29/167] "Rich crimson with white eye, small, single, produced in large and long clusters. Growth very vigorous, climbing, late flowering; foliage deep glossy green." [GeH] "Very hardy rose, blooming in a corymb of 30–40 blossoms, which are small, single, and a beautiful crimson color." [JR33/134] "The *most brilliant red* of the cluster-flowered, late-blooming climbers. Color is deep scarlet with orange suffusion, turning to bright pink with white center. It is remarkable for the length of time it remains in bloom. The long, thin growths are especially amenable to any kind of training. Fine for a trellis." [C-Ps28] "Large, single, in medium-sized clusters, good form, long stems. Fine foliage, plentiful. Very vigorous growth; hardy. Deep crimson shading to pure white bases. Fine for covering trellises, arbors, and banks." [ARA23/163] "This variety makes very long annual growths, with large clusters of blossoms for fully half their length." [NRS28/149] "Growth tall, but straggly; good bloomer." [ARA18/122] "Has the defect, to my mind, of throwing out fresh growth just below the flower truss at the time of flowering, and the effect of the flower is much spoilt by being partially hidden." [NRS16/98–99] "Foliage black-spots some in midsummer, severely later; bloom profuse last two and a half weeks of June and free into July." [ARA18/131] "Loses foliage early." [ARA17/28] "Masses of brilliant red berries follow the blooms and remain on the bush nearly all winter." [C&Js24]

"The rose 'Hiawatha', much noticed and besought when [first] released to commerce, seemed a little set aside for 2 or 3 years; but its exceptional qualities brought it back into favor with gardeners who see and take note of the real worth of a rose. This variety is again much in demand today. The rose 'Hiawatha' makes a plant of extreme vigor, with long climbing canes which are supple, a beautiful green, very lightly purpled on the sunny side, and armed with upright, sparse, gray thorns, with no other production of bark. Leaves 7-foliate, more rarely 9-foliate. Rachis armed, on the lower side, with small hooked prickles, and bestrewn with pedicellate glands; sometimes there is a slight tomentum around the odd leaflet. Leaflets small, bright green, particularly on the upper side, as with the *R. wichuraiana* Type, oval-rounded; the odd one is elliptical or lanceolate-elliptical; serration simple, not very profound. Stipules adnate, simple, pectinate. Bloom very multifloral, in a pyramidal cyme with up to 50 blossoms, often fewer. Flowers small, single, bright crimson red with a white center; stamens numerous and golden yellow, graceful in effect. The bloom, though late, lasts quite a long time, the petals changing color and passing to vinous red without falling. Summing it all up, the rose 'Hiawatha' is one of the best climbers known, due to its vigor, its abundant bloom, and the bright color of its flowers. These qualities combine to make a truly very decorative plant." [JR36/45]

"Obtained as a seedling from '[Turner's] Crimson Rambler', and is one of the best of the numerous progeny of this Rose. It has very vigorous growth of a branching and drooping habit. The stems are a bright light green, they retain their colour and do not turn red or brown in autumn, and are armed with a fair number of nearly straight sharp prickles, red at first but soon turning a light brown, they easily reach a height of 10 to 12 feet [ca. 3.3–4 m] in the season. They are clothed with close set, rather small but dense foliage, which lasts long on the plant, the upper surface of the leaves being slightly glossy. The stipules at the base of the leaves are green, and the edges end in a slight hairiness indicating its descent from '[Turner's] Crimson Rambler]. Unlike its parent it is quite free from mildew. It has only one true flowering period, though now and then a flower may be seen in the late autumn; the blossoms opened with me on the 23rd July, 1910, and lasted well into September; it is thus one of the latest of the Ramblers. The flowers are single, borne profusely and in large trusses, quite scentless, in colour scarlet-crimson with a white eye. They stand bad weather well on the plant, and are very striking in the garden at a time when many of the summer Roses are gone … I well remember the first time I saw this Rose. We were making our way to a daffodil show at Huntingdon on a wintry April morning when we met, a little way from the town, a cart full of pots of 'Hiawatha' in full flower, and very bright and strange it looked in a momentary gleam of wintry sunshine … In the garden it is useful in many ways from the great ease with which it can be trained. If you make it into a pillar you can (and should) wind it round and round, not tie it straight upward —for similar reasons it readily becomes a good weeping standard. To get this, let it go as it likes the first year from the bud, and begin to train round bamboo or other hoops the second year. Cottagers have

a wonderful instinct for finding what will do well in their gardens, and they have already found the value of 'Hiawatha'. Riding through a Hertfordshire village a year ago I noticed several of the cottagers had one, and sometimes two weeping standards of 'Hiawatha' in full flower, making the whole village quite gay. On arch or pergola this Rose gives no trouble, and it may be used with effect creeping over a bank. It is readily increased either from cuttings or by budding on the briar; for pillars I rather prefer it from a cutting, as I fancy it is slightly less vigorous when so reared. The strong points of this Rose are its fine foliage, brilliant colour and profusion of bloom, its lateness, its adaptability to many garden purposes and long flowering period, and, not least, its hardiness. The only things against it are its want of perfume and lack of a second flowering." [NRS11/42–43] "It looks particularly well in the evening sunlight of summer." [NRS20/90] "Still as popular as when first introduced." [NRS28/149] Hiawatha, hero of Longfellow's poem *The Song of Hiawatha*.

Hiawatha Remontant
trans. "Reblooming Hiawatha"
Sauvageot, 1931
From 'Hiawatha' (Mult) × 'Mme. Norbert Levavasseur' (Pol).

"Scarlet. The most brilliant red of the single, cluster-flowering, late climbers." [C-Pf31] "Orange red, white center, small, single, tall." [Sn] "Supposed to be an everblooming form of 'Hiawatha'." [GAS] "Gives repeated bloom throughout the season." [ARA30/143]

Hildeputchen
Alfons, 1922
"Pink, small, lightly double, medium scent, tall." [Sn]

Hugo Maweroff
Soupert & Notting, 1910
From 'Turner's Crimson Rambler' (Mult) × 'Mrs. W. H. Cutbush' (Pol).

"Deep red, small, full, tall." [Sn] "Warm carmine, small, double, produced profusely in large trusses. Growth very vigorous." [GeH] "Warm carmine color. Small blossom of a rigorously regular form, blooming in very full bouquets which are held very upright. Freely climbing bush, floriferous. Deliciously effective on a wall, or solitary. This newcomer, unique among climbers, is in the first rank." [JR34/183]

Ida Klemm
Walter, 1907
Sport of 'Turner's Crimson Rambler' (Mult).

"White, medium size, lightly double, tall." [Sn] "Excellent Multiflora with snow-white flowers." [GAS] "Growth and bloom quite good." [ARA18/120] "Giant cluster of almost large, half-full blossoms of fantastic white with conspicuous golden stamens. Leaves large, glossy dark green, quite healthy; infinitely lavish bloom; quite winter-hardy, extraordinarily gorgeous kind; further, is the last white Multiflora to bloom." [Ck] Ida Klemm, congener of the Klemm of Hoyer & Klemm, "rose-growers of Dresden." [JR37/10]

Immerblühender Crimson Rambler Listed as 'Flower of Fairfield' (Mult).

Indra
Tantau, 1937
"Pink, medium size, lightly double, light scent, tall." [Sn]

Jkvr. D. Baroness von Ittersum
syn. 'Baronesse von Ittersum'
Leenders, 1910

"Described as a brilliant scarlet-crimson on an orange-red ground." [ARA18/84] "Light red, medium size, lightly double, light scent, tall." [Sn] "A plant of 'Baroness von Ittersum' [*sic*], expected to be of the brightest red in flower, showed this season [1919] only a rather pale pink." [ARA20/161] "Orange-scarlet flowers, shading to yellow at base of petals, of rather large individual size, but in a small cluster. The blooms keep ten days after they are opened, without fading or losing a petal." [ARA18/90] "Flower glowing crimson, semi-double. Growth vigorous." [GeH] "Typical Multiflora with almost single, bright crimson flowers in the usual clusters. Vigorous, floriferous, and one of the best of its class." [GAS] "A charming Single variety. The blooms are cochineal colour, the foliage and wood of this charming variety being most beautiful." [NRS18/151] "Wonderful growth and blooming qualities." [ARA18/120] "A fine climber with glossy foliage; very early and free bloomer. Flowers are large and color is brilliant scarlet-crimson." [C&Js12] "Foliage very plentiful throughout season, black-spots badly in midsummer, mildews slightly; bloom moderate through June." [ARA18/129]

Josephine Ritter
Geschwind, ca. 1900
"Pink, medium size, full, tall." [Sn] "Bush to 3 m [ca. 9 ft]." [EU]

June Moon
Nicolas, 1939
"Red, yellow exterior, large, full, tall." [Sn]

Kala Agneta   Listed as 'Agnes und Bertha' (Mult).

Karl Schneider
Vogel, 1934
"Salmon pink, medium size, lightly double, tall." [Sn]

Kathleen   Plate 53
W. Paul, 1907
From 'Turner's Crimson Rambler' (Mult) × 'Félicité et Perpétue' (Semp).

"Rose-red, white center, small, single, tall." [Sn] "It gives quantities of large umbels of single blossoms richly colored carmine pink with a center marked with white. It is, it would seem, very ornamental." [JR32/38] "A cross between the Multiflora and Sempervirens classes, with single, white-eyed, pale pink flowers in pyramidal trusses." [GAS] "Soft carmine rose with white eye, very free, lasts well." [GeH] "A splendid sort with its large clusters looking like the Cineraria." [JR31/73] "This pretty variety belongs to the group of non-remontant climbing multiflora roses. It was released to commerce in 1907 by Messrs. William Paul & Sons, the celebrated rosiéristes of Waltham Cross, London, England, who raised it from seed. The very vigorous plant gives considerable quantities of large umbels of single blossoms of a carmine red, absolutely marvelous in effect, and long lasting. This very ornamental plant was recognized by the English Royal Horticultural Society by a certificate of merit. 'Kathleen' is to be recommended for clothing pillars, ironwork, pergolas, etc. These magnificent climbing roses are unfortunately under-used in gardens, in which they nevertheless are the most beautiful ornament from June

until the end of July." [JR32/58] Not to be confused with the similarly named Hybrid Musk.

Kde Domov Muj
Böhm, 1935
"Whitish pink, medium size, lightly double, tall." [Sn]

Kleine Rosel
Vogel, 1929
"Violet-red, medium size, single, medium height." [Sn]

Laure Davoust   Plate 46
Laffay, 1834

"Pink and lilac blush, blooms in immensely large clusters; the most beautiful of all climbing roses." [JC] "Small, very full, white, lilac pink." [BJ53] "Light carmine." [Ÿ] "Small, full, incarnate pink fading to deep flesh." [JR5/72] "Delicate pink, large, full, flat, superb." [LF] "Very small, full, delicate pink." [V8] "Very small, full, pink." [Gp&f52] "Small, full, white, flesh or pinkish, panicles of 50 and indeed 100 blossoms." [R&M62] "Its small double flowers of bright pink and flesh-color, changing to white, are produced in large and graceful clusters, beautiful from the varieties of shade which they exhibit." [FP] "Flowers clear pink, changing to flesh, dying off white, small and full; form, cupped. The flowers are produced in large and elegant trusses, the three colours shewing on the truss at the same time." [P] "Is a hybrid, and a most elegant and delicate rose, having all the peculiar neatness of the double red and white varieties, with larger flowers and more beautiful foliage." [WRP] "Bush with very climbing canes, often growing to 5–6 m [ca. 15–18 ft]; bloom very abundant; its light carmine blossoms are small, grouped in a corymb, and so great in number that the bush is covered. This variety should be protected against heavy frosts, or it will die when the cold becomes a little intense." [S] "It is notoriously liable to be damaged by frost. It bears clusters of perfectly formed, bright carmine-pink flowers, varying to white and flesh-colour." [GAS] "Is the climax of perfection in this family; with all the aid of the imagination its beauty on a well grown plant cannot be pictured. The flowers are of various shades of colour, from white to a lovely deep pink, perfect in form, the clusters are immense, and produced from almost every eye of the strong wood of the preceding year; it is of very strong growth, making shoots of twenty feet [ca. 6.6 m] in one season with very luxuriant foliage." [Bu] "It forms a magnificent Weeping Rose, but requires a sheltered situation. There is a plant here on a six-foot stem [ca. 2 m], only two years old, and whose branches droop to the ground, the foliage being completely hidden by the myriads of flowers." [P] "Strolling in an old Hertfordshire garden last summer, I was arrested by a delightful scent coming from a rampant climber which was covering part of a pergola near by. The blossoms, of a soft blush pink colour, tinged with lilac, hung in big bunches from the roof of the pergola. They were very pretty, wonderfully round and double, like little fairy balls made of tiny Rose petals; but to me their chief charm lay in the delicious old-world perfume they shed so generously around them." [NRS11/133]

"Very vigorous; branches large, very long and climbing; bark smooth, green, with remote, yellowish, very sharp, short prickles. Leaves ample, somber green above, glaucous beneath, of 5 or usually 7 oval leaflets, with nerves jutting out, and dentate; petiole green, pubescent, with some occasional thorns beneath. Flowers about 1½ inches across [ca. 4 cm], very full, plump, blooming in clusters in which the number of blossoms varies with the vigor of the branch; a person might see 80 or 100 . . . ; color bright flesh; stem slender and nodding; outer petals concave, inner ones petite and muddled; bud rounded. Calyx globular; sepals very short, leaf-like." [JF]

Laure Soupert
Soupert & Notting, 1927
From 'Tausendschön' (Mult) × 'George Elger' (Pol).

"Yellowish white, small, full, very fragrant, tall." [Sn] "Climbing Polyantha with large clusters of white flowers throughout the season." [GAS] "Bud small, ovoid, rosy white, opens freely; flower small, double, full, very lasting, strong fragrance, yellowish white changing to pure white, borne in clusters of 80 to 100 on strong stem. Foliage abundant, small, deep glossy green, disease-resistant. No thorns. Growth vigorous, climbing or trailing; free, continuous bloomer." [ARA28/243]

Le Droit Humain
trans. "Human Right"
Vilin (veuve) & fils, 1906

"Rose-red, medium size, very full, tall." [Sn] "Climbing shrub, blossom medium-sized, very full, bright crimson." [JR33/186]

Leopold Ritter
Geschwind, ca. 1900

"Red, medium size, lightly double, tall." [Sn] "No scent, recurrent, −3 m [less than ca. 9 ft]." [EU]

Leuchtstern
trans. "Shining Star"
Kiese/J. C. Schmidt, 1899
From 'Daniel Lacombe' (Mult) × 'Turner's Crimson Rambler' (Mult).

"Bright pink with a large white eye." [Ÿ] "Pink, white center, small, single, tall." [Sn] "A climbing rose . . . Its charming clusters of flowers—single and pink with a white center—are in form rather like a Cineraria." [JR26/149] "Flower bright rose, with white eye, small, single, produced in corymbs. Growth vigorous, climbing, floriferous." [GeH] "A good pillar or bush Rose, free flowering, colour—bright rose, with a prominent white eye, single flowers in clusters." [F-M] "A worthless, pale pink Multiflora with single flowers in this country [U.S.A.]. Abroad, the flowers are described as bright red with white centers." [GAS] "The colouring of this rambling Rose has been warmly criticized, but whether the contrast of a somewhat crude rose with white is to the taste of everyone or not, few kinds are more striking in effect when they are in flower. I have this in several places, against a pergola post and an outer fence, and in both it gives effective colouring to the surroundings. The output of flowers is enormous, and this combined with the colouring creates one of the richest Rose pictures amongst the climbers." [NRS12/182] "Very decorative, rich and continuous bloom; a very fragrant, very floriferous hybrid climber." [JR35/120] "Small, bushy growth; all blooms at once, fading quickly." [ARA18/122] "Liable to disfiguration by mildew." [NRS11/31] "Foliage very plentiful, black-spots slightly; bloom abundant in early June." [ARA18/130]

Lien Budde
Leenders, 1913

"Red, large, full, medium to tall." [Sn]

Lisbeth von Kamecke
Kiese, 1910
From 'Veilchenblau' (Mult) × 'Katharina Zeimet' (Pol).

"Light violet, small, lightly double, tall." [Sn] "Pale violet-coloured flowers. Growth very vigorous." [GeH] "Reported to be a very attractive Multiflora, with lilac flowers, like pale violets." [GAS] "To me, far more attractive than the so-called blue Rambler, which I cannot bring myself to admire. Its colour is a lovely pale lilac, something like the tint of 'Marie Louise' violets, only not quite so deep." [NRS18/150] "This rose is very beautiful; the flowers are an Elder-flower color—very novel—it has good umbels, pretty foliage, and it blooms very nicely." [JR36/55]

Lyon Rambler
Dubreuil, 1908
Sport of 'Turner's Crimson Rambler' (Mult).

"Bright rose-colored form of '[Turner's] Crimson Rambler'." [GAS] "Rose-red, medium size, lightly double, tall." [Sn] "Bright cherry-red with white centres, double. Growth very vigorous." [GeH] "Growth not of best—low and bushy; fair in blooming." [ARA18/120] "Rose of extreme vigor with long climbing canes like those of '[Turner's] Crimson Rambler', from which it sprang. Beautiful somewhat bullate dark green foliage. Bloom abundant and long-lasting, in umbelliform thyrsoid corymbs, to the greatest effect. Blossoms numerous (25 to 40 in a corymb), close-set in hemispherical clusters, perfectly cupped; petals very bright pink with some carmine and a large silvery white nub. Notable for its coloration, which is novel in the '[Turner's] Crimson Rambler' group." [JR32/135]

Madeleine Seltzer
Walter, 1926
From 'Tausendschön' (Mult) × 'Mrs. Aaron Ward' (HT).

"Whitish yellow, medium size, full, medium scent, tall." [Sn] "Introduced as a Yellow Tausendschön, which would be exciting if it were really true." [GAS] "Same form as 'Tausendschön' but yellow passing to brighter yellow. Very few thorns. Growth vigorous; profuse bloomer." [ARA28/239]

Malva Rambler
Puyravaud, 1908
Seedling of 'Turner's Crimson Rambler' (Mult).

"Multiflora with mauve-pink flowers." [GAS] "Violet pink, medium size, lightly full, very fragrant, tall." [Sn] "Blossom pure mauve pink, same form as '[Turner's] Crimson Rambler', very vigorous bush, very climbing; bloom early, very fragrant, non-remontant." [JR32/135]

Mánja Böhmová
Böhm, 1925
Sport of 'Tausendschön' (Mult).

"Yellowish white, medium size, full, medium scent, tall." [Sn] "Vigorous, white-flowered Multiflora of 'Tausendschön' type." [GAS] "Bud medium size, ovoid; flower large, double, full, globular, very lasting, intensely fragrant, greenish white, borne in cluster on long, strong stem. Foliage large, light green, soft, mildews and black-spots. No thorns. Growth very vigorous, bushy, climbing; abundant bloomer all season. Freezes to 15 inches [ca. 3.75 dm]." [ARA31/244]

Maria Liesa
Alfons, 1925

"Pink, small, single, tall." [Sn]

Marie Henriette Grafin Chotek Listed as 'Gräfin Marie Henriette Chotek' (Mult).

Marietta Silva Taroucová
Zeman, 1925
From 'Colibri' (Pol) × ? 'Flower of Fairfield' (Mult).

"Red, medium size, full, tall." [Sn] "Multiflora of slender growth, resembling a Wichuraiana in some respects. It produces huge clusters of small, frilled, purplish pink flowers of a very vivid shade." [GAS] "Originated in the Dendrological Gardens of Graf Silva Tarouca at Pruhonice, 1925 . . . Large, lasting flowers of bright rose-color, borne in clusters. Foliage abundant, normal green, medium size, resistant to disease. Growth very vigorous, climbing; profuse bloomer; hardy." [ARA26/186]

Mary Hicks
Hicks, 1927
"Deep red, medium size, full, medium fragrance, tall." [Sn] "More or less everblooming Climbing Polyantha, with clusters of rather large, full flowers, not unlike [those of] 'Excelsa' [W]." [GAS] "Fine crimson, deeper than [those of] 'Excelsa'. Very vigorous, fine foliage." [GeH] "Flowers deeper, fuller, and larger than [those of] 'Excelsa'. Foliage fine. Growth very vigorous." [ARA29/221]

[Menoux]
Jobert, 1848
Seedling of 'Laure Davoust' (Mult).
"Medium-sized, full, deep pink." [JR2/42] "Blossom medium-sized, nearly full; color, pink, with a bluing edge." [S] "This rose came from a seed of the Multiflora 'Laure Davoust' sown in November 1844. Its first bloom took place in 1846—it wasn't very remarkable. The vigorous specimen had grown some long canes which produced nothing but a few isolated pink roses of little worth. At its second bloom, in May 1847, this rose gave numerous panicles composed of several flowers of a bright pink and larger than those of other Multifloras; they were grouped elegantly on long strong stems . . . This year, 1848, this Rose, on a wall, forms an immense palisade, and its vigorous canes have given a magnificent bloom from May 15–30. While its relatives often perish in the cold, this one has nothing to fear from the frost." [SRh48/72]

Merveille Listed as 'Tausendschön' (Mult).

Mme. Charles Yojerot
Lebreton, 1933
"Red, large, full, tall." [Sn]

Mme. François Royet
Royet, 1926
"Bright red." [Ÿ] "Another edition of '[Turner's] Crimson Rambler' [Mult], with clusters of bright red flowers." [GAS] "Red, large, full, tall." [Sn]

Mme. Jenny
Nonin, 1925
"Pink, small, full, medium scent, tall." [Sn] "An attractive Multiflora, with clusters of delicately fragrant, bright pink, semi-double flowers." [GAS]

Mosellied
trans. "Song of the Mosel [River]"
Lambert, 1932
"Purple-red, white center, medium size, single, medium scent, tall." [Sn]

Mrs. F. W. Flight
Flight/Cutbush, 1905
From 'Turner's Crimson Rambler' (Mult) × 'The Garland' (Mk).

"Carminy cerise, white center." [Ÿ] "With immense clusters of very decorative big pink flowers." [JR31/73] "Attractive Multiflora with huge clusters of clear, light pink, semi-double flowers." [GAS] "Blossom large, semi-double, carmine cerise, center white, very noticeable." [JR32/171] "Flower deep pink with blush centre, semi-double, in large trusses. Growth vigorous, early flowering." [GeH] "Climbing bush; flower large, semi-double, cherry color with a white center." [JR33/186] "Very strong growth, producing its flowers in large loose panicles suitable for arches and pergolas." [F-M] "Growth rather small; blooms of good color fading quickly." [ARA18/121] "Foliage very plentiful, black-spots and mildews from midsummer on, foliage holds well; bloom profuse during most of June." [ARA18/130] "A little coarse in character as a decorative flower, and looks best on the bush at a distance." [NRS20/90]

Multiflore Tricolore Listed as 'Tricolore' (Mult).

Neige d'Avril
trans. "April Snow"
Robichon, 1908
"White." [Ÿ] "Charming, early-flowering Multiflora, with large, pyramidal clusters of semi-double white flowers adorned by bright golden yellow stamens. One of the best of the type." [GAS] "Very climbing shrub, without a single thorn, with beautiful light green foliage; blossom large, full, white, in large, pyramidal, very long-lasting corymbs; very early bloom." [JR32/153] "Dependably healthy, thorny." [Ck]

Newport Fairy
R. Gardner, 1908
From *Rosa wichuraiana* × 'Turner's Crimson Rambler' (Mult).

"Large umbel of salmon-orange-pink color." [Ck] "Deep pink, white center, small, single, tall." [Sn] "Pink with white eye, single, free flowering. Growth very vigorous." [GeH] "Very vigorous; less coarse than the usual Multifloras. Flowers small, single, and deep rosy pink." [GAS] "Vigorous growth; good amount of bloom; not among first to flower in spring." [ARA18/121]

Non Plus Ultra
syn. 'Weigand's Crimson Rambler'; trans., "Can't Be Exceeded"
Weigand, 1902
From 'Turner's Crimson Rambler' (Mult) × 'Mlle. Blanche Rebatel' (Pol).

"Bright red." [Ÿ] "Deep red, small, lightly double, tall." [Sn] "Much like '[Turner's] Crimson Rambler' but darker and earlier." [GAS] "Flower a dark colored form of '[Turner's] Crimson Rambler'. Growth very vigorous." [GeH] "This rose has the same foliage and vigor as '[Turner's] Crimson Rambler', with a darker coloration." [JR31/177] "This new wort of '[Turner's] Crimson Rambler' is a cross with a somewhat feeble variety: Polyantha '[Mlle.] Blanche Rebatel' × '[Turner's] Crimson Rambler'; the mother predominates in this cross, as it differs little from '[Turner's] Crimson Rambler' in growth and foliage. The blossom is also durable, and it will perhaps be more floriferous ... The umbels in which the flower-clusters come are perhaps more strongly colored and larger than with '[Turner's] Crimson Rambler'; they begin to appear at about 75 centimeters [ca. 30 in] ... This new variety has yet another advantage—that of blooming no less than eight or ten days before the older variety. Also, the bloom-period lasts longer, making it much superior to ['Turner's Crimson Rambler']." [JR26/165–166]

Nymphe Egeria

Geschwind/Ketten, 1892

"Fresh pink." [Ÿ] "Pink, middle-sized, double, no scent, −3 m [less than ca. 9 ft]." [EU] Egeria, Roman cult nymph, so distraught at the death of her beloved Numa Pompilius that she wept herself into being a running spring; those who are dubious have perhaps never loved.

Nymphe Tepla

Geschwind, 1886

Seedling of 'De la Grifferaie' (Mult)

"Carmine." [Ÿ] "Pink-carmine, middle-sized, very double, no scent, −3 m [less than ca. 9 ft]." [EU]

Olivet

Vigneron, 1892

From 'De la Grifferaie' (Mult) × 'Mme. Baron-Veillard' (B).

"Light red, large, full, tall." [Sn] "Extremely vigorous shrub with large and firm canes, very beautiful dark green foliage, flower of premier size, full, flat, perfectly held, very light red in color, center slightly darker. A top-of-the-line plant which will be much in demand as a climber due to its vigor and the beauty of its flowers." [JR16/153] Olivet, suburb of Orléans, France, where Vigneron's nursery was located.

Oriflamme

W. Paul, 1914

"Deep pink, yellow center, medium size, full, light scent, tall." [Sn] "Flower vivid rose suffused with coppery gold, fountain-like sprays, glossy foliage. Growth very vigorous." [GeH] "Small; bloom pretty, but shy." [ARA18/122] "Not a very robust grower as compared, for example, with 'Lady Gay' [W] or 'Excelsa' [W], produces exquisitely scented flowers of cream and salmon, eventually fading to light straw-color." [ARA24/185]

Památník Komenského

Bojan, 1936

"Salmon pink, medium size, full, medium fragrance, tall." [Sn]

Papa Gouchault

Turbat, 1922

"Red Multiflora with Wichuraiana characteristics. It resembles 'Excelsa' [W] but does not fade so badly and blooms earlier." [GAS] "Flowers pure crimson-red, of medium size, double, and of nice form; lasts long without losing colour. Growth very vigorous, with abundant glistening green foliage." [GeH] "Flower of good form, medium size, double, lasting; pure crimson-red, with no violet tinge (when forced very bright cardinal-red); borne in cluster of 10 to 20. Foliage bright green. Very vigorous, climbing." [ARA23/152] "The new '[Turner's] Crimson Rambler' [Mult], with all its good qualities and none

of its faults, except some of its stiffness. Flowers in large panicles, pure crimson red, lasting a long time without fading. Abundant, glistening green foliage." [C-Ps28] "Does not mildew." [C-Ps29] "Hardy. —*Washington, D.C.*" [ARA26/119] Auguste Gouchault, a nurseryman of Orléans, France. His son, Jules Gouchault, was a quondam business partner of Turbat.

Paulette Bentall

Bentall, 1916

"Purple-red, small, full, tall." [Sn]

Pemberton's White Rambler

Pemberton, 1914

"A dead white with very double flowers." [NRS18/150] "White, small, full, tall." [Sn] "Excellent Multiflora with large clusters of small, double, pure white, rosette-like flowers." [GAS] "Large trusses of white flowers, rosette, carried on upright stems, remaining in flower a long time both on the plant and cut. Not liable to mildew." [NRS15/165] "Pure white in color, very vigorous, and the best white rambler. It is a late bloomer, and the foliage is mildew-proof. A large-flowered, early-blooming white rambler is very much needed at present." [ARA18/85]

Perle des Neiges

trans. "Pearl of the Snows"

Dubreuil, 1902

"Sparkling white." [Ÿ] "Clusters of double white flowers over a long season." [GAS] "Remontant, white, medium size, lightly double, tall." [Sn] "Flower snow-white, double, large corymbs, free flowering. Growth vigorous." [GeH] "Plant having the look of the celebrated Japanese Rose '[Turner's] Crimson Rambler'; same foliage and same climbing canes; its pectinate stipules indicate its origin; it came from the 'Polyantha' [Mult] type. This variety is extremely floriferous; it blooms, bearing up to the latter season, corymbs of 25–30 blossoms borne on long canes; its quite double blossom, in the form of an expanded cup, is of a sparkling whiteness, and opens easily." [JR35/147] "Called the White Crimson Rambler." [JR35/120]

Perle vom Wienerwald!

trans. "Pearl of the Vienna Woods!"

Praskač, 1913

From 'Helene' (Mult) × 'Turner's Crimson Rambler' (Mult).

"Rose-red, small, lightly double, tall." [Sn] "Showy Multiflora with enormous clusters of fairly large, semi-double, unfading bright flesh-pink flowers." [GAS] "This is one of the best climbing varieties in pink up till now. Each blossom is about 4 cm across [ca. 1½ in]; it is semi-full and cupped, carmine pink within, delicate carnation pink on the outside. The flowers are borne on stems from 30 to 40 cm in length [ca. 12–16 in], giving it an appreciable value for cut flowers. They come in immense clusters composed, often, of fifty to a stem. The duration of the bloom is one of the longest for a climbing rose; it comes around the middle of June. Some cut flowers in a vase, in water, keep their color and all their freshness for fifteen full days. It's an excellent rose for a vase—which one sole umbel fills! Its vigor and manner of growth are perfect; the plant is very floriferous, has few thorns, and bright dark foliage. It is a superb climbing rose, and precious for covering walls, frameworks, and espaliers, and for planting in woodland and groups of conifers. It is of great beauty and of a strength of color

Perle vom Wienerwald! *continued*

that produces a strong effect at a great distance. It is a garden rose, a decorative, a cut rose—of the first class. In a few years, it will be widely known and loved by all as a pot plant." [JR38/72–73]

Perle von Britz

trans. "Pearl from Britz"
Kiese/J. C. Schmidt, 1911
Seedling of 'Tausendschön' (Mult).

"White, small, lightly double, tall." [Sn] "The buds are delicate pink surrounded with white; the umbels are very large, and the growth very strong." [JR36/55] "Floriferous, abundantly covered with soft white bloom clusters with pink buds. Infinitely decorative, grows strongly, healthy." [Ck]

Peter Lambert

Vogel, 1936

"Deep pink, medium size, full, tall." [Sn] "Lambert, Peter, Trier [Germany,] 1860–1939. [Released one rose, a China, at age 19; later was affiliated with Reiter for a short time, during which the great early HT 'Kaiserin Auguste Viktoria' was released.] In 1896 began his own rose-breeding [releasing, among many roses, the extremely influential HP 'Frau Karl Druschki' as well as many significant shrub roses and HTs] ... From 1890 to 1910 was editor of the *Rosen-Zeitung*." [Kr]

Philadelphia Rambler

Van Fleet/Conard & Jones, 1903
From 'Turner's Crimson Rambler' (Mult) × 'Victor Hugo' (HP).

"Deep crimson, double, in large trusses. In the way of '[Turner's] Crimson Rambler', but flowers brighter in colour." [GeH] "Much like '[Turner's] Crimson Rambler', slightly larger, bright red flowers tinted lighter in the center." [GAS] "Red, medium size, full, tall." [Sn] "This is a better '[Turner's] Crimson Rambler', having far brighter and more intense color than that old favorite, and holding its dazzling flowers a long time. It is a Van Fleet hybrid, and was introduced by us in 1904." [C-Ps25] "Introduced by ourselves in 1903." [C&Js05] "Has handsome foliage; does not mildew, and is a most abundant bloomer." [C&Js04]

"The American horticultural journal *Meehan's Monthly* announces the obtention of a new climbing rose, the 'Philadelphia Rambler', an improved seedling of 'Turner's Crimson Rambler' from which it is distinguished by its doubler flowers, and, particularly, by its foliage which is *never* attacked by mildew or the worm, as happens so often with that wonderful Japanese Rose ['Turner's Crimson Rambler'] when it is planted in a place sheltered from rain and dew. It will be released to commerce this year [1902] by the Dingee & Conard Co., in West Grove, Pennsylvania, U.S. of A." [JR26/114] "The most magnificent hardy climbing rose in existence. Blooms two weeks earlier than the old '[Turner's] Crimson Rambler'. Splendid flowers, 2½ inches across [ca. 7 cm] and perfectly double. Borne in grand clusters completely covering the whole bush. Color pure deep rich crimson, far brighter, more intense than the old '[Turner's] Crimson Rambler', which has heretofore been the standard for brilliant color, does not fade, bleach, or wash out, but holds its bright dazzling color to the last. Undoubtedly the brightest and best of all." [C&Js04]

Phyllis Bide To be found in *The Old Rose Advisor* as a Climbing Polyantha.

Pink Mme. Plantier Listed as 'Garden's Glory' (Mult).

Platyphylla Plate 44

syn. 'À Feuilles Larges', 'À Grandes Feuilles', 'Coccinée', 'Écarlate', 'Platyphylla', 'Pourpre', 'Rose Foncé', 'Rouge', 'Rubra', 'Seven Sisters', 'Thoryi'
Greville, 1815

"Various colors, white, pink, scarlet, and ashy blue, superb." [LF] "Small, full, carmine pink." [V8] "Light lilac." [JR7/154] "Delicate pink." [Ÿ] "Flowers bright rose, shaded, changeable, often presenting three or four shades of colour on the same truss." [P] "Deep pink." [V9] "Blush, tinted and striped with various shades, small or medium size; a tender variety of no value." [EL] "A hardy, vigorous climber, and a tremendous bloomer. Flowers in large clusters, varies in color from white to crimson, quite fragrant, showy and handsome; an old time favorite." [C&Js05] "A melody of lilac-rose, soft pink, and almost-white flowers, with 'seven tints in the same cluster'. The individual blooms are larger than those of *R. multiflora* and appear in pyramidal clusters in June. The plant is somewhat tender; can grow to 30 feet [ca. 9 m], but 8 to 10 feet [ca. 2.6–3.3 m] is more usual." [W] "Was at one time greatly esteemed and admired for its variety of character ... It is a fine grower, producing its flowers in large clusters, not two of which are alike; opening of every shade, from pure white to deep purple. Indeed this rose has no compeer; it produces its flowers single, semi-double, and double, and in such variety of shade and colour, that there are rarely two alike. An east or northeast situation suits it best; otherwise the effect of its variety is greatly diminished by the direct rays of the sun. It requires a dry sheltered spot." [Bu] "Foliage very plentiful, black-spots very slightly from midsummer on; bloom abundant during most of June." [ARA18/130] "[In Chelston, Bermuda] the old-fashioned 'Seven Sisters' grows easily and blooms freely." [ARA19/90]

"*Canes* tall, as in *R. multiflora* 'Rosea' but more robust. *Leaflets* more rounded and 3–4 times larger than those of the [type] species. *Flowers* also much larger though perhaps less numerous, an attractive shade of purple. This magnificent, remarkable for its foliage and petal color, was introduced [into France] by Noisette for whom it bloomed in September 1819. He had found it in 1817 in a market garden near London, to which it had come as seed from Japan. So far, it has been grown only in a peaty soil in a temperate house; but there is every likelihood of its being acclimated outdoors." [T&R] "*Shrub*, vigorous. *Branches*, thicker than [those of 'Rose' [Mult], etc.]. *Stipules*, long and linearly divided; very slightly pubescent. *Leaflets*, larger, almost smooth on the upper surface; teeth not bristly, curled underneath. *Flowerstalk*, having brown glands. *Tube of calyx*, rather tightened under the throat. *Sepals*, two simple; two pinnatifid; one elliptic, or pinnatifid on one side. *Flowers*, small, double, or full; light pink or light purple." [Go] "This is supposed to be an old Chinese garden rose brought to Europe in the early 1800's. Rehder calls it *Rosa multiflora platyphylla*, which may be correct; but it does not explain the extreme tenderness of the variety to frost which is commented upon by the earliest writers ... The small, double flowers vary from purplish red to white, through many intervening shades. It seems to be related to 'De la Grifferaie' in some way." [GAS]

Polyantha Plate 45

Von Siebold, 1827

"Yellowish." [LS] "Vigorous shrub, forming an enormous compact, subspherical bush, capable of attaining several meters [ca. yards] in diameter, with lengthily arching canes which are more or less thorny;

non-remontant; canes flexuose, angled, with reddish epidermis; leaves compound, pinnate, with the odd one, 7–9 leaflets which are oval, villose, felty beneath, light green above, soft and pleasant to the touch, rachis strongly prickly. Inflorescence in an enormous panicle which can grow to fifty centimeters [ca. 20 in] and indeed more in length, resembling that of the common bramble; flower single, fragrant, pure white or somewhat sulphury, with cuneate petals; fruits very small, with very caducous calycinate divisions, a beautiful shining red at maturity." [S]

"There are few roses which give us as much to talk about as the sort known under the name of *Rosa polyantha* Sieb. & Zucc. The horticulturists and botanists have been filled with jealousy about it since its introduction into cultivation. It has successively borne the names *Rosa thyrsiflora* Leroy, *Rosa intermedia* Carr., *Rosa Wichurae* K. Koch until the day when it was perceived that Siebold had described it under the name of *Rosa polyantha*. Will it retain this lattermost name? They talk about putting it under *Rosa multiflora* Thunberg, a species introduced into England by T. Evans in 1804, and into France by Bousault in 1808. From the horticultural point of view in which we are placed, it matters little to know what the botanists will at length decide upon when they have the question better in hand. What is certain is that the actual progenitor of *Rosa polyantha* should not be confused with that of *Rosa multiflora*. When all is said and done, we know that the *Rosa polyantha* introduced from Japan produced a series of varieties remarkable for their small size, their abundant bloom, and their minuscule roses. Each year, some new gains come to further enrich an already abundant group. The Type, *Rosa polyantha,* is equally something to be talked about—from another point of view: it is an excellent stock on which to graft other roses…If one adds to these merits the fact that its seeds germinate the same year sown, it's yet another characteristic making it an excellent stock." [JR11/40]

"This species originated in Japan, whence it was introduced into France for the first time, as far as we know, around 1862. It was the *Fleuriste de Paris* which received the first slip, which still exists, and which, planted in the nursery of Longchamps, grew into a strong shrub which, each year, is covered with thousands of blossoms of a very beautiful white. Here are the characteristics of the Type: Shrub extremely bushy, very vigorous; non-blooming branches nearly climbing, growing to nearly two meters [ca. 6 ft] in the case of young plants on their own roots; strong thorns, enlarged at the base, slightly hooked; 5–7 leaflets, sometimes even nine pairs of oval-elliptical leaflets, which are soft, gentle to the touch, villose, and thoroughly but shallowly dentate rachis rust-colored, with short prickles similarly colored, enlarged at the base and sharply barbed on each side; blooming branches comparatively slender, with smaller leaflets which are more rounded and more obviously dentate than those of the sterile branches; inflorescence in long, pyramidal, subconical panicles, quite upright, much branched; buds very small, solitary, or most often clustered, on a shortly villose flower stalk blossoms lightly and pleasantly fragrant, the scent somewhat resembling that of Tea roses, pure white, or slightly sulphurous; 5 wedge-shaped petals, very large at the summit, which, in the middle, displays a large notch, giving it the appearance of the 5-armed Maltese Cross…; hips…very small, with deciduous sepals, beautiful glossy red, as if varnished, at maturity, with many long and narrow seeds. It blooms around the end of May, and is very ornamental. If perhaps this species originat-

ed in Japan, it is also, we are told, found in China…It is from this latter country that Monsieur A. Leroy's firm has received it with no other name than that of 'new rose.'

"It is evidently quite variable, and the small number of seedlings it has given us have sometimes differed from the Type so much that none of the characteristics are preserved. Along the same lines, Monsieur Jean Sisley tells us, in a letter written September 8, 1873, 'This single 'Polyantha'…produced, *without artificial pollination,* very distinct and notable varieties. Guillot fils has obtained double blossoms, yellow as those of the Banksia, and double reds, as well as one he calls remontant, and one with foliage like that of *R. microphylla;* but *none* of these varieties has that characteristic that distinguishes the Type —blooming in a panicle, which, to my way of thinking, makes it distinct from all other roses—as well as more meritorious.' June 30 of that same year, Monsieur Sisley wrote to us, "Polyantha' is very hardy …It seeds easily, producing many varieties, which however are not out yet—single pinks, double pinks, single and double yellows, and a very double white. This last is going to be released to commerce. [*A footnote adds:* This very double white-blossomed plant looks like a miniature Noisette; it seems to be the equivalent of the Pompon Chinas, and could be used, like them, in borders…It was to be seen at the last exhibition at the *Palais d'Industrie,* in the booth of Mssrs. Lévêque and Son…under the name 'Pâquerette', in allusion to the small size of all its parts, and the elegance of its flower.] …Ph. Rambaux has shown some seedlings which he calls Noisettes, because they have that look—but they are from 'Polyantha'.'

"We have had a chance to see and study the growth and bloom of Monsieur Rambaux's plants, and cannot hesitate to state that they have the appearance of Teas and Noisettes, and that their flowers have, in color, fragrance, and general character, the look of these two groups. All the plants are freely remontant, blooming until frost stops them. The hips are nearly all subspherical, smooth, and glossy, varying from 7 to 10 millimeters [ca. ¼–½ in], and in color varying from orange red to brownish violet; one exceptional variety has longly oval-acuminate sepals which are persistent, while all the others are deciduous. In a letter of October 25, 1875, on the same subject, Monsieur Sisley adds, 'I forgot to tell you that the seeds of my children of 'Polyantha' are three or four times larger than those of their mother.'" [R-H76]

Polyantha Grandiflora Plate 48
Bernaix, 1886

"Large panicles of pure white bramble-like flowers produced in great profusion in the blooming season; of climbing habit and robust growth; very useful to cover old fences, trees, buildings, etc.; very hardy." [CA97] "Single, hardy, growth vigorous." [GeH] "Said to be a hybrid of *R. multiflora* × some Noisette. It bears great clusters of single or semi-double, flat white flowers." [GAS] "It is a hybrid of *polyantha* and *muscosa* [*sic; surely 'moschata' is intended*], with warm white flowers as large as those of the Musk Rose and the clambering habit that is common to both parents." [NRS20/30] "Bush of uncommon vigor; foliage shiny; flowers large, single, white, disposed in corymbs. Excellent stock for grafting all varieties known of roses, to which it communicates its vigor and earliness. It fruits abundantly, 4 or 5 times more than the Type, and its fruits—larger—contain many more seeds than the wild plant. Sown in February–March, its seeds

Polyantha Grandiflora *continued*

sprout after one month; and the young plants, in good soil, can be grafted that same year. This stock also has the advantage of not putting out runners. A bed of roses grafted on this stock was awarded a Grand Silver Medal at the Lyon Horticultural Exhibition in September, 1886." [JR10/172]

"If you'll take a look at the picture . . . representing a new single variety that Monsieur Alex. Bernaix, rosarian of Villeurbane (Rhône) has named Rosa polyantha grandiflora, you will quickly be convinced of its superiority to the Type. In effect, it is larger and more vigorous in all parts. Its flowers are very numerous and its seeds very abundant. Over and above its ornamental qualities which will perhaps not be appreciated by fanciers of double flowers, it demands the attention of rosarians due to its fecundity and of hybridizers due to the ease with which it can be crossed with other races to produce new varieties . . . The *Rosa polyantha grandiflora* makes a shrub of wonderful growth, covered with beautiful glossy green foliage. Its flowers, arranged in clusters, are very numerous, single but large, and a beautiful white." [JR11/40]

Pourpre Listed as 'Platyphylla' (Mult).

Printemps Fleuri

trans. "Flowery Springtime"
Turbat, 1922

"Clusters of curious, bright purplish pink flowers, displaying a mass of yellow stamens in the center. More strange than beautiful." [GAS] "Light purple, medium size, lightly double, light scent, tall." [Sn] "Flower large, peony-shaped; brilliant purple, passing to carmine-rose; borne in cluster of 10 to 15. Foliage glossy dark green. Blooms very early." [ARA23/152]

Prinz Hirzeprinzchen

Geschwind/Lambert, 1911

"Purple-red, striped white, medium size, full, medium scent, tall." [Sn] "Bloom of long duration; flower small, semi-full, carmine purple, petals rayed white; blooms in clusters." [JR36/42] "Scented, −3 m [less than ca. 9 ft]." [EU]

Prinzessin Ludwig von Bayern

Bróg, 1911
Seedling of 'Turner's Crimson Rambler' (Mult)

"Light red, medium size, full, tall." [Sn]

Prior M. Oberthau

Alfons, 1923

"Rose red, white center, small, full, tall." [Sn]

Psyche

G. Paul, 1898
From 'Turner's Crimson Rambler' (Mult) × 'Golden Fairy' (Pol).

"Fine creamy yellow tinged with rose." [C&Js03] "Crimson pink." [Ÿ] "Pale carnation pink on a salmony ground." [JR32/171] "It looks a little like 'Turner's Crimson Rambler', but the double flowers are pinker." [JR22/161] "Flower pale rosy flesh pink, base of petals suffused with yellow. Growth very vigorous." [GeH] "Not such a rampant grower [as 'Turner's Crimson Rambler']. Colour, pale flesh; flowers produced in trusses, suitable for arches." [F-M] "Good large blossoms borne in pretty clusters." [C&Js09] "Good growth, foliage and bloom." [ARA18/121] "The polyantha hybrid 'Psyche' is a seedling bred by crossing 'Golden Fairy' . . . by Bennett, with 'Turner's Crimson Rambler'. The form and growth are much like those of 'Turner's Crimson Rambler', this latter being perhaps a little less vigorous. The bush would seem thoroughly hardy, nearly insensible to the cold, and it gives an abundant bloom in the Spring, but it is not freely remontant. The blossoms are in panicles of 15–25 roses measuring 2½ inches by 2½ inches across (an *inch*—English measurement—is about 0 m 2 cm); the buds are very pretty and well formed. The color is white tinted salmon pink, with yellow at the base of the petals." [JR22/116] Psyche, a pretty young thing with marital difficulties, saved at length by a "cruel monster" who continues to practice his archery on us today.

Purple East

G. Paul, 1901
From 'Turner's Crimson Rambler' (Mult) × 'Beauté Inconstante' (T).

"Deep carmine purple." [Ÿ] "Gave freely of its semi-double, rosy pink flowers with a purplish tint; it is very distinct." [ARA22/43] "A very beautiful Multiflora with huge clusters of rather large, semi-double, brilliant purple flowers. It is a strange and rather violent color, bound to attract attention. An outstanding characteristic is its earliness." [GAS] "About 1.5 m high [ca. 4½ ft], climbing habit; as the name tells us, a beautiful purple color, covered with semi-double blooms." [Ck] "Clear deep pink, with purple shading; large to very large; semi-double. Vigorous." [Th2]

Queen Alexandra

Veitch, 1901
From 'Turner's Crimson Rambler' (Mult) × *Rosa multiflora simplex*.

"Terra-cotta pink." [F-M] "Bright clear rose." [C&Js09] "Blossom medium-sized, double, pink with a white center." [JR32/171] "Huge clusters of semi-double, rosy crimson flowers." [GAS] "Pink, white center, small, single, light scent, tall." [Sn] "Rosy pink flowers, in clusters, semi-double. Growth very vigorous." [GeH] "The top gold medal was awarded to Messrs. Veitch & Sons of Chelsea, London, for their wonderful novelty in climbing roses, dedicated to the new queen of England and called 'Queen Alexandra'. It is a development from '[Turner's] Crimson Rambler', pollinated by *Rosa multiflora simplex*, and which grows enormous bouquets of flowers which are deep pink on the outside and white on the inside of these charming roses." [JR25/116] "A hardy, vigorous climber. Color, exquisite shade of deep rose; one of the most beautiful roses of its class and suitable for the choicest places." [C&Js06]

Rambling Rector

England, 1910

"Pink-white, small, lightly double, tall." [Sn] "Its flowers are creamy on opening . . . the flowers fade to white, borne in large heads with yellow stamens which quickly turn dark on maturity . . . delicious *R. multiflora* fragrance. It was included in the Daisy Hill Nursery catalogue for 1912. Small oval heps." [T4]

Ratgeber Rose

Verlag Praktischer Ratgeber, 1930

"Light red, medium size, full, light scent, tall." [Sn]

Roby

P. Guillot, 1912
From 'Léonie Lamesch' (Pol) × 'Leuchtstern' (Mult).

"Rose red, yellow center, medium size, single, tall." [Sn] "Carmine."

[Ÿ] "Flower soft rose on a lemon ground, buds carmine, medium size, single, produced in corymbs, free. Growth vigorous." [GeH] "A sturdy Multiflora with clusters of medium-sized, single flowers, changing from red to pink." [GAS] "Fair growth; shy bloomer." [ARA18/122] "Very vigorous shrub, hardy, inflorescence a corymb of 30–50 blossoms; buds ovoid, bright carmine, with the exterior carmine attenuating to delicate pink on a ground of orange yellow, resembling the coloration of 'Léonie Lamesch', from which, in a cross with 'Leuchtstern', it came; very ornamental." [JR36/152] "A very beautiful single wichuraiana; I saw it at the raiser's, Mons. Guillot's, before it was introduced, and thought then it would be a favorite with us here [in England]. The colour is bronzy red and pink." [NRS18/149]

Roi des Aunes

trans. "King of the Dwarves"; probably synonymous with 'Erlkönig' [Mult]
Geschwind, 1885

"Purple carmine." [Ÿ] "Reputed to have large, globular, bright red flowers." [GAS]

Rose

syn. 'À Fleurs Roses', 'Rosé', 'Rosea'; trans., "Pink"
Breeder unknown, pre-1821

"Delicate pink." [V9] "4–5 cm [ca. to 2 in], globular, bright pink with some violet, and striped with purple." [R&M62] "Small, full, flat, superb." [LF] This rose, in our gardens, is regarded as the Type of the species; it however differs from it in its oval, concave bracts with incised or dentate edges, and by its free styles. Flowers very small, full, a light or pale pink." [MaCo] "Differing from the type in having oval, concave, bracteal leaves, with toothed edges; the styles detached. *Flowers*, very small, full; of a light or pale pink." [Go] "This rose of our gardens is regarded as the Type of the species; it however differs in its oval bracts, which are concave, with incised or toothed edges, and in its free styles; blossom very small, full, light or pale pink." [S]

"*Stipules* villose beneath and along the edges, which are pectinate-pinnatifid, and glandless. *Leaflets* nerved-reticulated, with edges simply and not very deeply dentate or crenelate. *Peduncles* very villose, much branched, being several times dichotomous or trichotomous. *Bracts* oval, concave, edges incised or serrate. *Ovary* villose, short, oval-digitate, not constricted at the tip. *Buds* small, globular. *Sepals* oval or ovoid, acute, concave, reflexed, villose and glandulose; 3 bearing several divergent appendages. *Flowers* very small, full, light or pale pink. *Styles* free." [Pf]

"This rose, originating in Japan, and of which the celebrated Thunberg was the first to give us a description, grows 'climbing' canes clothed with hooked thorns. Its leaves are numerous, composed of five to seven leaflets, opposite, oval, and nearly two inches long [ca. 5 cm]. Its blossoms, which appear around June and last until the end of July are borne at the tip of the canes on wide-spreading peduncles forming a large corymb; ordinarily, one can count eighteen to thirty on each cane—sometimes more than a hundred. Their scent is feeble but suave, especially in the evening. They are a little larger than those of the double [Centifolia] pompons, and of a pretty pink which nonetheless pales at the end of several days. The English have known the Multiflora since 1804; it was at least six years until it was taken from England to France and grown in the environs of Paris. It is one of the most pleasant roses to look at because of the multitude of flowers which deck it out. The red-brown color of its ovaries, peduncles, and indeed its canes is very noticeable. It especially produces a very beautiful effect when grafted on a slightly tall Briar. Thunberg and the botanists who, following his lead, have spoken of the Multifloral Rose give it white blossoms. It is true that one notes, in its numerous bouquets, some white flowers among the pink; be that as it may, we describe it with pink blossoms—such a mix is insufficient to establish a variety. Quite recently indeed someone has successfully grafted the Multiflora on the Damask and the common China ['Parsons' Pink China'], assuring a person thereby of it giving more flowers and resisting better the rigors of Winter. To draw to an end: This rose, naturally delicate, demands a warm exposure; it should be protected from much cold, especially in the first and second years. Its canes, having as well the inconvenience of extending far and wide, need to be supported by close-by trees, or leaned upon something, be it a wall or be it a pergola. Last year [1820?], Monsieur Noisette brought the Type with single flowers from England." [CM]

Rosé Listed as 'Rose' (Mult).

Rose Foncé Listed as 'Platyphylla' (Mult).

Rose-Marie Viaud

syn. 'Rosemary Viaud'
Igoult, 1924
Seedling of 'Veilchenblau' (Mult).

"Pink lilac." [Ÿ] "Violet red, small, lightly double, tall." [Sn] "A Multiflora of the 'Veilchenblau' strain, said to be even better." [GAS] "Seedling from 'Veilchenblau', which it resembles in color except that the blue is more pronounced and flowers are doubler." [ARA26/183]

Rosea Listed as 'Rose' (Mult).

Rosemary Viaud Listed as 'Rose-Marie Viaud' (Mult).

Roserie

Witterstaetter, 1917
Sport of 'Tausendschön' (Mult).

"Pink, base of petal white." [Ÿ] "Large (3³/₄-inch [ca. 9.5 cm]), semi-double, deep-pink flowers with a white base. A real beauty with a grand spell of blooming in June." [W] "Rose red, white center, medium size, lightly double, medium scent, tall." [Sn] "Like its excellent parent, but much darker, and of a more solid color. Wood thornless." [Th2] "A very lovely Multiflora with ruffled, rose-pink flowers, larger than most of its class. It is a sport of 'Tausendschön', which it resembles, and it fades badly in hot weather." [GAS] "Just the same as the notable 'Tausendschön', from which it varies in its uniform bright pink, but like it in its thornless branches and a generally gracious and pleasant habit of vigorous growth." [C-Ps25]

Rouge Listed as 'Platyphylla' (Mult).

Roxburghiana Listed as 'Grevillii' (Mult).

Royal Cluster

Conard & Jones, 1899
From 'Hermosa' (B) × 'Dawson' (Mult).

"Slightly blushing white." [Ÿ] "Whitish pink, small, single, tall." [Sn] "Forgotten Multiflora, with clusters of double, white flowers, tinged pink." [GAS] "Undoubtedly the most magnificent Double White Hardy Climbing Rose yet introduced. Blooms in immense clusters. The

Royal Cluster *continued*

name 'Royal Cluster' was given it because of the great size and beauty of its enormous clusters. 119 flowers and buds have been counted in one cluster at one time . . . The flowers are full medium size, quite double, and beautifully formed. The color is white, sometimes faintly tinted with blush . . . The 'Royal Cluster' has a delicious, spicy fragrance, very pleasing and attractive. The 'Royal Cluster' is a hardy, vigorous climber and prodigious bloomer. The bush has few thorns, does not mildew, and is remarkably free from insects and disease. Continues a long time in bloom and the flowers are very double. Recommended as the best all-around pure white hardy climbing rose to date. It has no equal." [C&Js99]

Rubin Plate 51

trans. "Ruby"

J. C. Schmidt, 1901

From 'Daniel Lacombe' (Mult) × 'Fellemberg' (N).

"Deep crimson. —Vigorous climber." [Cat12] "Bright pink." [Ÿ] "Deep red, medium size, full, tall." [Sn] "'[Turner's] Crimson Rambler' type, with attractive, large, bright crimson flowers." [GAS] "Flower small, pretty full, sparkling ruby red; blooms in big corymbs; hardy." [JR32/171] "Claimed to be a better rose than '[Turner's] Crimson Rambler', is a stronger grower, has better foliage, and does not mildew. Flowers are borne in loose graceful clusters and are larger and more double than [those of] '[Turner's] Crimson Rambler', colour is a bright shining carmine." [C&Js05] "Foliage and growth good; blooms attractive and last well." [ARA18/121] "Foliage very plentiful, trace of black-spot from midsummer on; bloom free and continuous in June, some in July." [ARA18/130] "Flower bright ruby-red, large, semi-double, produced in large clusters. Growth very vigorous, climbing, hardy; wood and foliage also tinged with red. Distinct." [GeH]

Rubra Listed as 'Platyphylla' (Mult).

Rudelsburg

Kiese, 1919

"Rose red, medium size, full, tall." [Sn] "Large clusters of bright rosy red flowers." [GAS] "Blooms in clusters, bright carmine pink. Plant climbs very strongly, thorny, beautiful foliage." [Ck]

Russell's Cottage Rose Listed as 'Russelliana' (Mult).

Russelliana

syn. 'Russell's Cottage Rose', 'Scarlet Grevillia', 'Souvenir de la Bataille de Marengo'

Breeder unknown, pre-1844

"Rose, changing to lilac, flowers of medium size; a distinct and pretty rose." [JC] "Deep carmine red." [Ÿ] "Violet red, medium size, full, tall." [Sn] "Flowers rich dark lake, gradually changing to lilac, of medium size, very double; form, expanded. A good and distinct Pillar Rose." [P] "Blooms in large clusters of a rich, dark lake, changing to various shades of red and lilac, so that the cluster presents a curious diversity of hue. As it is extremely vigorous in growth, it would make an admirable pillar or climbing rose, were it but a little more hardy . . . As 'Russelliana' bears pruning better than most climbing roses, it may be grown as a bush; in which state it has flourished here for a number of years without protection." [FP] "This sort is a Rubifolia which has the look of a gigantic Provins; the vinous red or deep purple color of its innumerable medium-sized blossoms, their perfect form, their

good hold, make them noticeable at once as something out of the ordinary in their shade; the glandular hairs with which it is literally covered make it easy to distinguish from others of its group—everything together giving it a look all its own. As to hardiness, the Rubifolias take the worst frosts without suffering." [S] "I have pillars of it twenty feet high [ca. 6.6 m], forming, during the month of June, a very attractive object, having a profusion of flowers of the richest shades of crimson many of them being striped with white. From the base to the pinnacle it is one mass of glowing beauty. Perfectly hardy in our coldest latitudes, it has large rich green foliage, very distinctly and deeply nerved, the shoots are strong and erect, and will grow freely in any soil or situation. The old shoots only should be thinned out; the young wood ought never to be shortened unless locality demands it." [Bu]

Scarlet Grevillia Listed as 'Russelliana' (Mult).

Schloss Friedenstein

J. C. Schmidt, 1917

From 'Veilchenblau' (Mult) × 'Mme. Norbert Levavasseur' (Pol).

"Purple lilac." [Ck] "Generally considered the bluest and least objectionable of the descendants of 'Veilchenblau'. It bears clusters of medium, dark blue flowers tinged with violet." [GAS] "Reddish violet, small, full, medium scent, tall." [Sn] "Flower darkish blue with reddish violet centre, large and full, produced in large corymbs. Growth very vigorous, climbing, deep green foliage, free from Mildew. The best blue rose in existence." [GeH]

Seven Sisters Listed as 'Platyphylla' (Mult), but the name is casually used for many cluster-flowered roses.

Souvenir de l'Exposition de Bordeaux 1905

Puyravaud, 1905

From 'Turner's Crimson Rambler' (Mult) × 'Simon de St.-Jean' (HP).

"Red." [Ÿ] "Light red, medium size, full, tall." [Sn] "Blossom a fresh cerise red, large, full, globular, in a near-pyramid of more than 40 flowers, producing a wonderful effect. Shrub very vigorous, climbing, big-wooded; thorns close-set, straight, reddish, very protrusive; foliage bright green, disease-resistant. This plant makes gigantic pillars." [JR29/151–152] "Strong-growing but undistinguished imitation of '[Turner's] Crimson Rambler'." [GAS]

Souvenir de la Bataille de Marengo Listed as 'Russelliana' (Mult).

Steiler Rambler Listed as 'Steyl Rambler' (Mult).

Stella

trans. "Star"

Soupert & Notting, 1905

From 'Turner's Crimson Rambler' (Mult) × a unnamed seedling.

"Clusters of bright red flowers with white centers." [GAS] "Blossoms single, in clusters, carmine red on a very bright white ground." [JR32/171] "Flowers bright carmine with white centre, single. Growth very vigorous." [GeH] "White, small, single, very fragrant, tall." [Sn] "Shrub of very great vigor, very climbing and with beautiful bright green foliage; blooms in large corymbs; the blossom is small and single but of a marvelous coloration: Carmine red on a very bright white ground, with golden yellow pistils. The very sharp white background with the carmine red gives the flower the look of a bright star; seen from afar in full bloom, the plant seems enveloped in a twinkling constellation! This novel variety is very floriferous, and the bloom lasts a long time. As soon as the flowers fall, some little green fruits appear which soon turn to a beautiful yellowish red, thus forming a novel ornament for this beautiful variety—which is also very fragrant." [JR29/135]

Steyl Rambler
syn. 'Steiler Rambler'
Leenders, 1915

"Light red, medium size, full, tall." [Sn] "Flower brilliant geranium-red, produced in large clusters, which in shape and type very closely resembles 'Orléans-Rose' [Pol]. Growth vigorous, climbing." [GeH] "Good bloomer; fairly good grower; poor foliage; occasional bloom after spring." [ARA18/121]

Svatopluk Čech
Brada, 1936

"Orange yellow, medium size, full, tall." [Sn]

Sweat Lavender Listed as 'Sweet Lavender' (Mult).

Sweet Lavender
syn. 'Sweat Lavender'
G. Paul, 1912

"Light violet pink, small, single, tall." [Sn] "Single flowered, produced in large bunches, bright mauve with golden stamens, the foliage dense dark green; most striking." [NRS12/208] "Flower light lavender-pink, with golden stamens, single, large clusters[,] distinct, free. Growth very vigorous." [GeH] "Poor growth and foliage; blooms not distinct." [ARA18/122] "Contrary to Mr. Thomas, we find 'Sweet Lavender' very good, with plenty of bloom and a lovely lilac-pink-cream color." [ARA19/86] "Vigorous Multiflora, with mauve-tinted, single flowers." [GeH] "Very handsome and makes a lovely group at one end of a very rustic pergola with 'Veilchenblau' [Mult] (here [near Rome, Italy], the hot sun quickly turns it a true violet color)." [ARA21/126–127] "Completely disease-free, beautiful light green foliaged climbing Rose, extremely floriferous, single, large blossoms of the most beautiful delicate lilac pink with conspicuous golden stamens." [Ck] "Very vigorous, with very dense dark green foliage; the roses are small, single, and pale mauve or lavender mauve in large bouquets. This rose approaches pale blue more closely than any other we have; we have long thought a Cambridge Blue was much to be desired, and this newcomer represents considerable progress towards this goal. Planted among climbers or other, yellow, roses, this rose produces a wonderful effect." [JR37/57]

Taunusblümchen
Weigand, 1902
From 'Turner's Crimson Rambler' (Mult) × 'Mlle. Blanche Rebatel' (Pol).

"Violet pink, small, lightly double, tall." [Sn] "The blossom of this newcomer—to which the name of 'Taunusblümchen has been given—is small, not very full, and pink with a tinge of violet. It is, you could say, the sister of . . . 'Non Plus Ultra' [Mult; *same parentage, and introduced same year, as 'Taunusblümchen'*], having much in common with it in growth, foliage, and habit; also, it's as floriferous. 'Taunusblümchen' also looks like ['Non Plus Ultra'] in growth and bloom, but it has the advantage in possessing a perfume like that of the Centifolia." [JR26/166–167]

Tausendschön
syn. 'Merveille'; trans., "Thousand Beauties"
Kiese/J. C. Schmidt, 1906
From 'Daniel Lacombe' (Mult) × 'Weisser Herumstreicher' (Mult).

"Delicate pink passing to carminy pink, and has no thorns." [JR35/119] "In large corymbs, medium-sized, full, delicate carminy pink." [JR32/171] "Colour bright satiny pink, the flowers produced in clusters with a pendulous habit that stand well out from the foliage." [F-M] "A well-known, thornless Multiflora, with huge clusters of large, semi-double, ruffled flowers which vary through tints of white, pale pink, rose and creamy yellow. A very fine variety, prettier than 'Roserie' [Mult] or any of its descendants." [GAS] "Differs from every other rose because the enormous clusters of large, double flowers vary in color from pink to white, the buds on first opening being a light cherry-pink, changing, when fully open, to a delightful rosy carmine, and then fading to white. At blooming-time the mass of flowers nearly hides the foliage. Strong, vigorous grower, almost thornless." [ARA21/93] "A splendid rose, most suitable for growing on a pole or pillar, as it is not so luxuriant as some other multifloras. The flowers are large, of soft rose colouring, and are very freely produced. A plant in bloom is remarkably showy." [OM] "Imagine a luxuriant climbing rose literally covered with thousands of bright blossoms, borne in clusters and quite double. Colors of every imaginable shade, from white to deep pink. A hardy vigorous grower with few thorns and handsome foliage." [C&Js09] "Good grower and bloomer; fairly good foliage." [ARA18/121] "Its excellent foliage endures throughout the season." [C-Ps25] "Foliage lasts fairly well. Reported hardier in the North than the Hybrid Wichuraianas." [ARA17/28] "Foliage very plentiful, black-spots very slightly from mid-summer on, mildews considerably in midsummer bloom free first half of June." [ARA18/130]

"This Rose makes good shoots, 7-ft. and sometimes 8-ft. in height [ca. 2.3 m and sometimes ca. 2.6 m], upright, and somewhat branching; it is properly described as a semi-climber. It has nice, perfectly smooth stems, which redden on the sunny side in the autumn, and have practically no prickles; but a few slender hooked thorns and setae are to be found on the leaf stalk. Its relationship to '[Turner's] Crimson Rambler' [Mult] appears in the stipules at the base of the leaf stalk, which, like that variety, instead of being leaf-like, are split into a dozen or more hair-like teeth on either side. The leaves are not large, and fairly glossy on the upper surface, but the foliage generally is rather meagre and badly subject to mildew. There is only one flowering period; the first flower opened in my garden on the 18th June, 1910 . . . The plant is fully out by the end of June, and thence lasts in flower for rather less than a month. The flowers are borne on short lateral growths from the stems of the previous year, these laterals growing out at right angles to the stem in a manner that is very characteristic. The flowers are decidedly larger than those of most ramblers, resembling [those of] 'Tea Rambler' [Mult] in size, being two or three inches across [ca. 5–7.5 cm], and in shape reminding one of an Oleander, but they are somewhat lacking in form, and rather flat when expanded, semi-double, with very crinkled petals. They are very freely produced in fair sized trusses, which from the size of the flowers appear rather tightly packed. In a sense they stand rain well. That is, they continue to look well on the plant when not too closely examined, but wet rapidly spoils the colour for close inspection, rendering the flowers discolored and streaky. The colour is

Tausendschön *continued*

mottled rose and pink . . . and fades to a rather pale washed out magenta and there is a faint scarcely noticeable yellow tinge at the base of the petal. The blossoms are quite scentless. I think the colour of this Rose is only seen in perfection in hot weather or under glass. In the garden the Rose makes an ideal pillar of seven or eight feet in height [ca. 2.3–2.6 m], and it more readily adapts itself to this purpose than any [other] Rose I know. It is not sufficiently strong growing for arch or pergola, and I do not very much care for it as a standard, while its liability to mildew makes it unsuited for a wall. It will also stand a certain amount of shade . . . The characteristic features of 'Tausendschön' are its smooth, almost thornless wood, the short lateral flowering shoots growing at right angles to the stem, and its fine effect of profuse trusses of large flowers. Its weak points are its somewhat meagre foliage, liability to mildew, and want of form in the individual flowers." [NRS11/54]

"Always outstanding in any collection of roses. Large, double, cupped flowers, both rose-pink and white, in large clusters on strong stems. Very early flowering, with profuse May-into-June bloom. It could drop its petals more cleanly; 'Roserie', which is similar, does this better. Foliage is soft; the canes thornless, and only 8 to 10 feet [ca. 2.6–3.3 m] . . . Only slightly FRAGRANT." [W] "This ravishing newcomer in climbing roses . . . surpasses in growth, handsome foliage, and bloom all the multiflora climbers known till now . . . Its dainty flowers have ruffled petals, and look quite a bit like those of a blush-white Balsam; when quite open, they take on more of a carmine shade such that, in full bloom, the plant seems to be developing two different sorts of blossoms. These latter are spaced among the others, and come from June up to the end of July in elongated, drooping clusters, producing a most charming and decorative effect. 'Merveille' will be of a vigor and hardiness surpassing those of '[Turner's] Crimson Rambler'." [JR31/2/27] "A well-grown and well-flowered bush of this rose is a very beautiful sight." [ARA18/85] "Trained as a weeping tree, is an unforgettable sight in the spring." [ARA35/101] "The most beautiful climber I have ever seen." [ARA31/118]

Tea Rambler

G. Paul, 1903

From 'Turner's Crimson Rambler' (Mult) × "a climbing Tea." (cognoscenti will suspect the Noisette 'Gloire de Dijon')

"Coppery salmon pink." [Ÿ] "Beautiful . . . deep coppery pink in the bud, changing to soft pink in the older flowers." [F-M] "Coppery pink to soft salmon-pink. Growth very vigorous." [GeH] "Moderately vigorous Multiflora with clusters of fragrant, coppery pink and salmon flowers. Very attractive." [GAS] "Among the novelties of Fall, 1902, it was also announced that Messrs. Paul & Sons . . . announced one of their originations, The Tea Rambler, which made quite a stir . . . The bush is very vigorous, developing numerous large leaves, and bearing quantities of petite blossoms of 'La France' [B or HT] coloration." [JR26/161] "Very vigorous upright stems . . . The foliage is particularly good and persistent; the leaves are moderately dark green in colour, surrounded with a faint red edge, with a fine glossy surface, while the young undeveloped leaves at the end of the shoots are delicate and fern-like. It is particularly free from mildew . . . only one flowering period . . . large clusters . . . tea-scented. The individual blossoms are rather large for a rambling rose, a little fuller than semi-

double, and somewhat loosely put together. The colour of the buds is cherry-carmine, that of the open flowers coppery pink, fading to 'La France' pink . . . more form than most ramblers." [NRS11/54–55] "Growth not of best; profuse bloomer; most attractive." [ARA18/121] "The leaves are unusually handsome, and persist on the stems until midwinter." [OM] "Unsuitable for northern gardens." [NRS/14]

The Dawson Rose   Listed as 'Dawson' (Mult).

The Lion

G. Paul, 1900

From 'Turner's Crimson Rambler' (Mult) × 'Beauté Inconstante' (T).

"Flower bright crimson, single." [GeH] "Rose red, white center, medium size, single, tall." [Sn] "This newcomer is a climbing rose with single flowers, from a sowing of '[Turner's] Crimson Rambler' fertilized by 'Beauté Inconstante'. Its numerous and elegant blossoms of a carmine pink are white in the middle." [JR25/117] "Popular, large-flowered, single, bright red Multiflora not a great deal unlike '[Paul's] Carmine Pillar'." [GAS] "Single blossom, like [that of] '[Paul's] Carmine Pillar', glossy carmine, late blooming, strong-climbing, floriferous, erect." [Ck] "This rose, with me, is not so vigorous in growth as others of this class, but the large, flat, crimson flowers, measuring two and a half inches in diameter [ca. 6 cm], make it perhaps the most striking and brilliant of all the single ramblers." [ARA18/85]

The Wallflower

G. Paul, 1901

"Rose red, medium size, lightly double, tall." [Sn] "Crimson." [Ÿ] "Excellent Multiflora with huge clusters of semi-double, bright red flowers. Very striking and effective." [GAS] "Flower soft rosy crimson, freely produced on the full length of the shoots. Growth very vigorous." [GeH] "A very showy rose with large, semi-double, and rather flat flowers that are very lasting. The color is a bright rosy crimson, and altogether it is one of the most effective and decorative roses in this or any other class." [ARA18/122] "Fair growth; blooms of no special merit." [ARA18/122] "One of the most beautiful, brightest climbing roses." [Ck]

Thoryi   Listed as 'Platyphylla' (Mult).

[Tricolore]

syn. 'Multiflore Tricolore'

Robert & Moreau, 1862

"Silvery pink." [Ÿ] "Small, full, globular, lilac, striped white and purple." [JR5/72] "Medium-sized, edged pink, toothed and deckled white, less vigorous and less floriferous than ['De La Grifferaie' (Mult)]." [JR2/42] "Vigorous growth; blossom lilac pink; edge of the petals toothed and pointed white; medium-sized, full, globular." [S] "A vigorous Multiflora with lilac-pink flowers, having serrated petals dotted white." [GAS] "4–6 cm [ca. 2 in], full, globular, lilac-y pink, ends of the petals dentate and stippled, with a nice center of white, corymbs of 20–50 blossoms, climbing, just the thing for training against walls and covering frameworks; plant very effective." [R&M62]

Trompeter von Säckingen

Geschwind, ca. 1890

Seedling of 'Geschwinds Nordlandrose' (Mult).

"Purple red, medium size, full, medium scent, tall." [Sn] "Scented, −3 m [less than ca. 9 ft]." [EU]

Turner's Crimson Rambler Plate 50

Turner, 1893

"Bright crimson." [Ÿ] "Blossom medium-sized, full, bright crimson red, bloom abundant, in corymbs which are pyramidal, very graceful." [JR32/171] "The whole plant appears a sheet of bloom for weeks at a time." [C&Js98] "Flowers bright carmine, not very full, small, and united in a cluster. Very vigorous plant, pyramidal in form; blooms in umbels, very hardy it would seem, coming from Japan. It is, up till now, the best shrub rose." [JR20/58–59] "The wood and foliage, covered with short hairs, are very distinct, and the trusses of small crimson flowers which come, in perfection, in the shape of a bunch of grapes, produced quite a sensation from their unique character when the Rose was first exhibited. It is not an autumnal, but lasts in bloom a fair time. It does not do well against a wall, fairly as a bush with the shoots supported by bamboos, and decidedly well as a pillar Rose, though autumnals are certainly best for that purpose. With the same reservation it will be found to answer well as a hedge, and it makes a fine standard." [F-M2]

"Both foliage and wood of the current year are light green in colour, the bark of the young wood is smooth and shiny, while the leaf stalks are covered with short hairs, and this hairy effect is increased by the stipules at the base of the leaves which, instead of being green and leaf like, are formed into a number of rather coarse hairs generally about a dozen on each side, a peculiarity often transmitted more or less markedly to its numerous progeny. After flowering [it] tends to throw up vigorous straight shoots from the base of the plant which will attain a height of ten feet [ca. 3.3 m] or more, arching over at the top if left at liberty. From these in the following year short laterals grow out on which the flowers are borne. The routine of culture therefore is to remove in the late summer the shoots that have flowered, carefully preserving the young growths, in order to secure the bloom for the following year. The foliage is badly subject to mildew. There is only one flowering period. The first flowers opened in my garden on the 22nd June, 1910, and the plant was fairly well out about ten days later and fully out by the 10th July from whence it continued till the middle of August. While the flowering period lasts the plant is covered with a wonderful profusion of flowers, rather small individually, about an inch across [ca. 2.75 cm], semi-double, and carried in clusters. The flowers are quite scentless, crimson in colour, and rather wanting in form, but they are exceptionally long lasting both on the plant and when cut ... '[Turner's] Crimson Rambler' is quite hardy, and to this and to the variety of purposes for which it may be used in the garden, it is, no doubt, largely indebted for the high place it holds in popular opinion ... The colour does not blend well with that of other flowers, and when fading it is not pleasing. There is no second flowering, and the wood is at times liable to canker ... I have a plant of it on a screen 10-ft. to 12-ft. in height [ca. 3.3–4 m], between 'Aglaia' [Lam] a pale yellow Rambler usually past its best before '[Turner's] Crimson Rambler' reaches its full glory of flower, and on the other side 'Aimée Vibert' [N], which flowers at the same time and contrasts well with '[Turner's] Crimson Rambler' both in flowers and foliage ... [It] will grow in almost any soil, though it is economical of time to give it a good root run at the start, and this appears specially desirable, as I have found it decidedly impatient of root disturbances. Sometimes the removal of the soil for purposes of renovation on one side only will give it a severe check from which it will take some years to recover. Many situations will suit it, but I think the sun during at least part of the day is essential." [NRS11/56–60] "It's not unusual to be able to mention someone who has a specimen of 'Turner's Crimson Rambler' that gives several hundred flowers and buds; but it *is* rare to be able to talk about a specimen bearing 32,000 blossoms at a time. This, however, is very much the case, and out particular correspondent tells us this number was counted this summer by Mr. Turner on a plant belonging to Mr. Marshall. When Mr. Turner presented, for the first time, in June 1892, some inflorescences of this pretty rose at the Earl's Court exhibition, Mr. Marshall knew right away this was a plant with a future, and soon bought a specimen which he planted in good ground. It is this seven-year-old plant which produced the prodigious quantity of flowers mentioned above. The 16 branches on this phenomenal rose are 34 feet long [ca. 10.4 m], each with 50 clusters of 40 blossoms and buds." [JR22/145–146]

"A climbing Polyantha which was named after Charles Turner, its *obtainer*, or, to put it more accurately, its *importer* to Europe. It can be said that, of all the seedlings put out in this class in the last six years, this variety is one of the most astonishing. If a person makes the effort to choose good ground for it, it gives within the year growths from 3 to 4 meters long [ca. 9–12 ft]. It takes easily to all sorts of treatments—tree-roses, weepers, espaliers, trained on a framework, etc. It can be used to hide the ugliness of a wall, or to decorate a colonnade or make a tunnel, etc. It blooms on the previous year's wood, and gives thickets of 50–80 blossoms per branch. The blossoms are bright red and have all the Polyantha characteristics. The duration of this flower is most astonishing, as, from the day it opens to the moment it's all over, fifteen days to three weeks can pass—something you don't see in any other variety ... There's one thing that surprises me greatly on the subject of the Crimson Rambler: The sluggish way in which the horticultural press took to talking about this variety. This rose was known in Japan from 1840, and took 50 years to come to us." [JR23/40–41] "Rarely has a rose been embraced so quickly by the public as has this one. It found a place in nearly every garden. It's not an English rose; it was, I believe, brought from Japan." [JR22/106] "It comes from Japan, where it is grown in gardens under the name 'Soukura-Ibara', which is to say 'Cherry Rose.' A navy mechanic going through Japan, struck by the variety's wonderful floriferousness, introduced it into Europe and sold it to Charles Turner, rosarian of Slough (England), who propagated it and released it to commerce in 1894 [sic] under the name 'Crimson Rambler'." [JR23/154] "Imported from Japan by the mechanic of a steam boat, from whom Mr. Turner, horticulturist of Slough (England) bought it, this rose is a member of the series of Multifloras better known under the name 'Polyantha' [Mult]. According to information we have been able to obtain, 'Turner's Crimson Rambler' would be very common in Japan, especially around the port of Nagasaki, where it is used to make garden enclosures. It is also reported that, in the same country, there is another variety with paler blossoms. It is an excellent importation, but we don't believe the plant as climbing as was said when it first came out in the English exhibitions. It can be classified among the semi-climbers pretty neatly, at least, based on the one specimen shown at the Paris show. The bush is vigorous, very hardy—easily bearing up under two harsh Winters—very floriferous, clad in bright and pretty dark green foliage, which holds until severe cold. Its crimson color somewhat resembles that of '[Mlle.] Blanche Rebatel'

Turner's Crimson Rambler *continued*
(Bernaix' dwarf Polyantha), but its blossoms are larger, and the doubling is better. A Gold Medal as well as numerous First-Class Certificates have been accorded this rose in England. Its entry into commerce will take place next November 1." [JR17/136] "The year 1893 was notable in the rose-world for the introduction by Charles Turner of the Royal Nurseries, Slough, England, of the Crimson Rambler, the first of the modern race of the Multiflora hybrids. According to a statement in the *Gardeners's Chronicle* (Series 3, Vol. XVI, p. 249), a plant of this rose was sent from Japan to Mr. Jenner, a well-known horticulturist, by Mr. R. Smith, Professor of Engineering at Tokio [*sic*]. Mr. Jenner named it the 'Engineer', and subsequently gave the rose to J. Gilbert, a nurseryman of Lincoln, who exhibited some cut blooms in July, 1890, and received an Award of Merit from the Royal Horticultural Society. Soon after this, Gilbert sold his stock to Mr. Turner, who renamed it Crimson Rambler and put it into commerce in 1893. Perhaps there was never a garden rose that had such a sudden and widespread popularity, both in England and America." [ARA18/82] "[In 1893] came 'Turner's Crimson Rambler', and Mr. [E. G.] Hill risked $200 on this novelty, receiving the first shipment that came to the United States. It was in immediate demand here, and great was the perplexity of the propagators when it was found to be a very different proposition in propagating from the familiar Polyanthas!" [ARA16/48]

"This pretty variety is not as hardy as was thought at first. The *Rosen-Zeitung* tells us that, last Winter, though the cold was not great, this rose lost many canes, more than other climbers that didn't suffer at all [*a note adds:* In Brie, this variety had no problems with the harsh Winter of 1894–1895.]." [JR20/97–98] "[In Florida] the old '[Turner's] Crimson Rambler' fortunately seldom blooms, and is much subject to mildew." [ARA16/98] "Here [on the Riviera] it never seems quite happy, and does not display that strength, vigour and health characteristic of successful cultivation, hence, as is often the case, the plant becomes a rendezvous for all varieties of the insect world. Does not flower till first week in May and therefore comparatively useless." [B&V] "Planting such [climatically unsuited] roses is as absurd as trying 'Maréchal Niel' [N] in Maine or '[Turner's] Crimson Rambler' in California." [ARA22/30] "One rose I never will have in my garden, as it is a leper, a mildew-breeder—the old '[Turner's] Crimson Rambler'. I have had no mildew to speak of since I discarded it." [ARA22/43] "I wish to say a word of vindication for the most abused, yet most beautiful and never yet equaled '[Turner's] Crimson Rambler'. True, it is subject to red spider, rust, scale, and what not, but the plant is not to blame. Its misfortunes started when it was improperly re-named, for it is not a rambler, but the truest type of 'biennial' pillar. Then man tried to confine it against a wall, often of wood, reflecting tremendous heat on a plant native to the 'wide open spaces,' literally suffocating it. Once against a house, man tried to make it climb, which it never was intended to do, and then forgot the use of pruning shears, letting old wood accumulate year after year, until degeneracy overtook it. Though I know I will be much criticized, I proclaim that, properly trained as a pillar in the open, where it will receive air-circulation from all sides, and with blooming canes removed each year, '[Turner's] Crimson Rambler' is the most beautiful red cluster rose in existence, and no more subject to pests than any other pillar." [ARA28/33] "My '[Turner's] Crimson Ramblers' have never

mildewed, except in one awful moisture-laden summer when we decided that the sun had departed for the season . . . There are better blooms than those of '[Turner's] Crimson Rambler', but it is so hardy, constant, and reliable, and it has such a neat restrained growth that doesn't sprawl all over the neighborhood with long, thorn-studded wands which grasp at everything within reach, that I speak my word for it." [ARA28/91] "'Excelsa' [W] is much superior, and 'Philadelphia [Rambler]' [Mult] . . . is considered far better by many." [Th2] "Although displaced by 'Excelsa' in many gardens, this Multiflora is a superior rose. It has much better brilliant red flowers in larger and handsomer trusses. Best grown as a big shrub away from walls, otherwise it suffers from mildew and rust." [GAS]

(Turner's Crimson Rambler × Veilchenblau)
Parentage as above.
J. C. Schmidt, 1925
  "Violet red, medium size, lightly double, tall." [Sn]

Unique
F. Evans, 1928
  "Orange salmon, large, full, tall." [Sn] "Climbing Polyantha with clustered tawny orange-salmon flowers. Blooms in autumn." [GAS] "Very tall, lovely flowers." [ARA31/205]

Veilchenblau
trans. "Violet Blue"
J. C. Schmidt, 1909
From 'Turner's Crimson Rambler' (Mult) × 'Erinnerung an Brod' (Set).

  "Reddish lilac." [Ÿ] "Lilac-rose to bluish purple and steel-blue, small, in large clusters." [GeH] "Reddish violet, white center, small, lightly double, medium scent, tall." [Sn] "Lilac changing to amethyst and steel-blue; medium size; produced in large clusters. Lower foliage lost early." [ARA17/28] "Blooms in clusters, half-full, reddish, petals become steel-blue, very effective. Does very well when not in full sun. Plant extremely strong-growing, rather thorny, with beautiful glossy foliage." [Ck] "Small, semidouble, cupped, purple flowers fading to magenta. The huge clusters come on short stems in June. The plant is so strong it has been used as an understock but fading spoils this for a garden plant. It is now of historic interest only. ('Violette' [Mult] is better.) It is FRAGRANT." [W] "A new Rose from Holland that originated from '[Turner's] Crimson Rambler'. It bears semi-double flowers of medium size, in large bunches. The originators describe the color as 'reddish or rosy lilac when opening, changing to *amethyst or metallic blue*.' We have bloomed it inside and outside and find it as described and a very distinct novelty. Thoroughly hardy and a vigorous tall growing climber." [C&Js11] "Sent out by the Germans, who call it 'the forerunner of a genuine cornflower-blue rose.' It is hardy, very vigorous and blooms profusely." [CA11] "Vigorous growth; good blooming qualities; odd in color; lower foliage lost early." [ARA18/121] "I get the brunt of every winter storm. On the windmill at the north side of the house, the most exposed position, a blue rose ('Veilchenblau') has grown unprotected for twelve or fifteen years, making robust growth, and is loaded with flowers each summer. I do not admire this rose, but the foliage is fine and free from insects, and for three years, now, the color seems to be changing to rose, so that I hope for rather attractive flowers another year." [ARA26/201] "A robust, hardy climbing Rose, with long-shaped leaves and heavy in growth. The flowers come in large clusters and are violet-blue in color. The color is decidedly odd, and visitors here are about equally divided in their opinion of it. Some think the color is too bizarre, others are highly delighted with the novelty as no other Rose has as yet approached this color. Quite a few red Roses 'blue' as the flowers age, but this one 'blues' to start with. As an oddity it is all right." [C-Ps26] "Ancestor of a long line of similar purplish pink Multifloras. It resembles '[Turner's] Crimson Rambler' strongly in habit, and produces large clusters of purplish pink buds which open to semi-double violet-toned flowers of a distinctly blue shade. The yellow stamens mar the effect by giving the plant a peculiar muddy color at a distance. Some people find it attractive, others despise it, but, nevertheless, it is interesting and, I believe, an important rose." [GAS]

Violetta Listed as 'Violette' (Mult).

Violette
syn. 'Violetta'
Turbat, 1921

"Pure violet." [Ÿ] "Violet red, medium size, full, light scent, tall." [Sn] "Is, for those who can admire the bluish tints a really great advance. The colour is a pure deep violet, making a striking effect among ramblers, and certainly more pleasing than 'Veilchenblau' [Mult]." [NRS24/216] "Finest of all the descendants of 'Veilchenblau' which I have seen. It is a Multiflora with large clusters of semi-double, ruffled, pure violet flowers, only occasionally tinged with magenta. It is most unusual and striking and I consider it a beautiful rose." [GAS] "An improvement on 'Veilchenblau' in habit of growth. Flower pure deep violet, in large cluster." [ARA22/151] "Practically alone among climbers for this violet color. The buds open maroon in large clusters of 1-inch [ca. 2.5 cm], ruffly, semidouble blossoms. The plant is not at all inclined to mildew. Outstanding in the garden, especially with a clear yellow . . . which [will] pick up the golden emphasis of Violette's stamens; or to separate pink Ramblers on a long fence, as 'Dorothy Perkins' [W] or 'Minnehaha' [W]. Because of color alone, this should be more widely planted. It reminds me of the wild purple aster." [W]

Vlatava
Böhm, 1936
"Violet red, medium size, full, tall." [Sn]

Waltham Bride
W. Paul, 1905

"White, medium size, full, tall." [Sn] "Early-flowering Multiflora, with clusters of snow-white, double flowers." [GAS] "This remarkable obtention is a climbing hybrid from the Multifloras, in which the bloom is both profuse and very early. Its charming blossoms, which have the advantage of being deliciously perfumed, are a snow white, and always open, when established, fifteen days before any of the other climbers in this group." [JR29/53] "Flower snow-white, double, large, clusters, early. Growth very vigorous." [GeH]

Wartburg
Kiese, 1910
Seedling of 'Tausendschön' (Mult).

"Magenta pink." [Ÿ] "Carmine rose. Twisted petals." [NRS13/172] "Rose red, small, full, tall." [Sn] "Multiflora of the 'Tausendschön' type, with clusters of double flowers in several shades of pink." [GAS] "Pro-

duces large clusters of flowers, well filled and carmine rose in color. The whole plant has a most effective appearance." [C&Js14] "Foliage very plentiful till late summer, then plentiful, black-spots slightly; bloom profuse most of June." [ARA18/130]

Watsoniana
New York, ca. 1870

"White or pink." [Ÿ] "Flower pinky white, tiny and single, in small clusters, with bamboo-like leaves and trailing stems. Growth vigorous. Found in an American garden in 1878." [GeH] "This variety is an importation from Japan, and is excellent in a park due to its beautiful foliage, but its flower is worthless." [JR23/42] "A curiosity due to its very lacy 3-leaflet leaves." [JR26/182] "Has been called 'the ostrich-feathered Rose' because of its peculiar cut foliage, utterly unlike that of any other Rose, making it a highly ornamental shrub which in late June presents great bunches of tiny white or pink flowers. It will need some protection north of Pittsburgh." [C-Ps25] "Rather quaint, and I have seen it effectively employed for table work." [NRS28/208]

Wedding Bells
Walsh, 1905
Seedling of 'Turner's Crimson Rambler' (Mult).

"Clusters of dark rose-pink flowers." [GAS] "Pink, white center, medium size, lightly double, tall." [Sn] "Flower rose-pink, free. Growth vigorous." [GeH] "Foliage not quite so plentiful as with most, black-spots somewhat; bloom abundant for two weeks in mid-June." [ARA18/131] "Good in growth, foliage, and blooming." [ARA18/121]

Weigand's Crimson Rambler Listed as 'Non Plus Ultra' (Mult).

[Weisser Herumstreicher]
trans. "White Rambler"
J. C. Schmidt, 1899
From 'Daniel Lacombe' (Mult) × 'Pâquerette' (Pol).

"Flower pure white, large for its class, full, produced in clusters. Growth very vigorous, climbing, free." [GeH] Evidently first bloomed in 1895.

White Flight Listed as 'White Mrs. Flight' (Mult).

White Mrs. Flight
syn. 'White Flight'
Rockford, 1916
Sport of 'Mrs. F. W. Flight' (Mult).

"Pure white." [GAS] "White, medium size, full, tall." [Sn] The same sport possibly also occurred for Koster in 1923.

White Tausendschön
Roehrs, 1918
Sport of 'Tausendschön' (Mult).

"Like 'Tausendschön' with pure white or pink-flaked, white flowers." [W] "Apt to have a few light pink markings." [ARA18/85]

Wodan
Geschwind, 1890
From 'Gloire des Rosomanes' (B) × ? *Rosa multiflora*.

"Crimson." [Ÿ] "Carmine-red, large, double, no scent, −2 m [less than ca. 6 ft]." [EU] Wodan, Wotan, Odin . . . by whatever name, formidable northern god of battle, treaties, and oaths. In the lattermost alone, he has played a large part in these proceedings.

CHAPTER TWENTY-EIGHT

Lambertianas

"Besides these summer-flowering multifloras, a new race has recently been introduced, the distinguishing feature of which is that the plants bloom again in autumn." [NRS12/157] "The group of roses known as Lambertianas was originated by Peter Lambert of Trier, Germany, who is famous as the originator of the great white rose 'Frau Karl Druschki' [HP]. Although they were introduced as everblooming hardy climbers, the varieties he sent out have proved to be Multifloras of commonplace appearance, rather less vigorous and less hardy than roses like 'Tausendschön' [Mult] and '[Turner's] Crimson Rambler' [Mult], but predisposed to bloom more or less continuously. These roses grow 6 to 7 feet high [ca. 2–2.3 m] and as much in diameter. Properly trained and pruned, they produce an enormous mass of bloom in June, followed by an occasional cluster throughout the summer, with a fairly good secondary burst of flowers in late autumn. They do not differ greatly in effect from the Hybrid Musks known as Pemberton roses, and have some affinities with them. On the whole, the Lambertianas and other roses of the Multiflora type are much better grown as large shrubs than as climbers. For that purpose they need plenty of room and thorough thinning of the old wood each summer after the first bloom has faded. No doubt, the Lambertianas are promising subjects for further breeding-work." [GAS] "The foliage is good and persists until frost. In spring, these bushes are masses of white, with some yellow or pink shading, and they tend toward recurrent blooming ... These aftermaths do not equal the June outburst, but the bushes are seldom without bloom." [ARA27/117] "Even the first year these bloom late on the tips of the season's basal shoots and consequently do not make such rampant growths as the summer flowering varieties; and it is advisable, once they have attained the desired height, not to shorten growth too much in pruning as they take longer to build up again." [NRS12/157] "We can't overdo calling our readers' attention to these climbing Polyanthas [*referring to the first Lambertianas 'Aglaia', 'Euphrosine', and 'Thalia'*]. For pillar roses, *berceaux,* walls, etc., you can't do better than these to produce the best results!" [JR20/2]

Adrian Reverchon

Lambert, 1909

"Pink, medium size, single, tall." [Sn] "Bright pink with white blaze, single, in large clusters. Everblooming." [Ck] "White edged Rose, blooms in clusters; makes a good bush or pillar; flowers again in autumn." [NRS18/133]

Aglaia

syn. 'Yellow Rambler'

Schmitt/Lambert, 1895

From *Rosa multiflora* × 'Rêve d'Or' (N).

"Blossom small, light canary yellow." [JR32/171] "Yellow, small, full, medium scent, tall." [Sn] "Canary-yellow, small, semi-double, of beautiful shell-shaped form, tea-perfumed, produced in large trusses. Growth vigorous, climbing." [GeH] "A new hardy climbing rose of the '[Turner's] Crimson Rambler' [Mult] type; flowers of medium size and double form produced in large clusters over the entire vine; color a fine shade of yellow, darker than 'Coquette de Lyon' [T]." [CA97] "This variety is entirely new, and undoubtedly the finest hardy yellow climbing rose yet introduced. It is a strong vigorous climber, resembling the '[Turner's] Crimson Rambler' in growth and foliage; blooms in immense clusters, often as many as 120 to 150 flowers in a bunch, and continues in bloom a long time; color, dark rich coppery yellow, sometimes creamy yellow; quite fragrant; entirely hardy, and a new and striking climber that few people have seen." [C&Js98] "Bush extremely vigorous, its branches attaining 3 and 4 m in length [ca. 9–12 ft] in one year; they have a small number of short thorns, and are adorned with pretty bright green foliage. The well-held, large blossoms come in small clusters like those of 'Turner's Crimson Rambler'. You can count up to 150 flowers on each plant. The color is greenish yellow, darker than that of 'Coquette de Lyon', and the middle of the blossom has some bluish reflections. The perfume is sweet, delicate, and very penetrating. You could call this the Yellow Rambler." [JR20/1] "This is the Yellow Rambler of the nursery 'plate-book' salesman. Thousands of people have been deluded into purchasing it for a yellow climbing rose. Instead, it has clusters of pretty white flowers, faintly tinged with sulphur-yellow in the bud." [GAS] "Foliage very plentiful, holds well; bloom moderate last of May till middle of June." [ARA18/21] "Only flowers freely on well-established plants." [Cat12]

"A climbing rose released to commerce by P. Lambert. At the exhibition at which I had an opportunity to see a two-year-old specimen, it excited much curiosity. It is pale yellow, while the Crimson Rambler is red, the only other differences being that ['Aglaia'] is less vigorous than ['Turner's Crimson Rambler'], and that ['Aglaia'] doesn't bloom in big clusters. Cultivated, however, as a tree rose, as we saw at the exhibition, it's very effective. Interplanting 'Aglaia' with 'Turner's' would make a most fetching combination, because ['Aglaia'] blooms less than three weeks before the other. 'Aglaia' looks a lot like 'Malton' [HCh], considering both flower and bush—and the length of bloom, about 15 days, is also much the same. The only big difference is that 'Aglaia' opens yellow to pale to white, while 'Malton' comes fiery red. I [C. P. Strassheim] have crossed the two in my rosarium, and am impatiently awaiting the results. 'Aglaia' is covered all autumn with hips, giving the plant the gayest appearance, not the case with 'Malton'." [JR23/43] "As for 'Aglaia' seedlings, some do wonderfully well, as for example 'Helene' [Mult]. The blossoms of all these seedlings are quite full. Right now (November 24 [1901]), 'Aglaia' is still covered with flowers. One of the seedlings of 'Aglaia' stays bushy, while the others are rampant." [JR26/69] Aglaia, one of the three Graces, representing Brilliance.

Arndt
Lambert, 1913
From 'Helene' (Mult) × 'Gustave Grünerwald' (HT).

"Salmony pink." [Y] "Light pink, medium size, full, tall." [Sn] "One of the best Lambertianas. Large, loose clusters of reddish yellow buds and pretty salmon-pink flowers. Fairly constant bloomer." [GAS] "Small growth; winterkilled." [ARA18/121] "Very vigorous semi-climbing plant with rough foliage; flowers erect in strong thyrses, light silvery pink. The bud is yellowish red, becoming salmony pink while opening; the semi-full blossom is fairly large. Extra-floriferous bush, and quite remontant." [JR38/56]

Ausonius
Lambert, 1932
From an unnamed seedling (resulting from a cross of 'Chamisso' [Lam] and 'Léonie Lamesch' [Pol]) × an unnamed seedling (resulting from a cross of 'Geheimrat Dr. Mitteweg' [Lam] and 'Tip-Top' [Pol]).

"Yellowish pink, medium size, lightly double, medium scent, tall." [Sn]

Birdie Blye
Van Fleet/Conard & Jones, 1906
From 'Helene' (Mult) × 'Bon Silène' (T).

"Very vigorous bush, floriferous; medium-sized blossom, quite full, shining carmine pink." [JR30/22] "Sometimes it is magenta-blooming." [ARA29/103] "A fine thing, blooming as late as the old blush China, with fine, bold clusters of a deep pink shade. As vigorous as the old 'Fellemberg' [N], it deserves a place in every garden." [NRS19/76] "Poor growth." [ARA18/121] "Introduced and for sale by only The Conard & Jones Company, West Grove, Pa. This splendid rose originated in 1900 and is the result of a cross between 'Helene', a fine hardy climbing rose of the '[Turner's] Crimson Rambler' type, and the popular Tea Rose 'Bon Silène'. It forms a fine, handsome bush 3 to 4 feet high [ca. 1–1.3 m] with glossy foliage and blooms constantly from early June till freezing weather, producing at the end of every shoot, clusters of bright, satiny rose blossoms, quite double, intensely fragrant, and over 3 inches in diameter [ca. 7.5 cm]. The buds

are long and pointed and in color a bright carmine until they open. It is exceedingly hardy and may be planted almost anywhere in the temperate zone (does well in the south also). By special permission we have named this splendid Rose in honor of Mlle. Birdice Blye, she whom the great Rubenstein declared to be 'the coming great American pianist' and who along with her fame has won the love and admiration of thousands of musical folk throughout the country and Europe. We have adopted her more popular name of 'Birdie Blye' and deem ourselves most fortunate in being able to offer a rose that is also destined, we believe, to take a foremost place in the hearts and homes of the American people. (Plant it in rich soil and full sunlight.)" [C&Js06] "This Rose has brought us more unsolicited testimonials than almost any other variety. It blooms continuously from June till frost and is one of Dr. W. Van Fleet's greatest productions, which we introduced. A perfectly hardy Rose with cup-shaped, faintly scented, bright satiny pink blossoms, which are only medium in size, but a well matured bush is always in bloom. Growth is about 4 feet [ca. 1.3 m], so do not use this in a Rose-bed. It makes a fine specimen bush or pillar Rose." [C-Ps25] "Makes a Pillar or climber in the South." [C-Ps29]

Blanche Frowein
Leenders, 1915

"Coppery yellow, medium size, full, very fragrant, tall." [Sn] "Copper suffused with golden yellow, passing to delicate yellow, of medium size, full and very fragrant. Growth vigorous, climbing free, and perpetual." [GeH] "Small growth; foliage not of best; blooms not distinct." [ARA18/121]

Buisman's Triumph
Buisman, 1952
"Pink, large, lightly double, tall." [Sn]

Chamiso   Listed as 'Chamisso' (Lam).

Chamisso
syn. 'Chamiso'
Lambert, 1922
From 'Geheimrat Dr. Mitteweg' (Lam) × 'Tip-Top' (Pol).

"Light pink and yellowish white, medium size, lightly double, medium scent, medium height." [Sn] "2–5 m high [ca. 6–15 ft]. Leaves brownish green, young shoots dark red. Blossom large, nearly full, light flesh pink on a yellow ground in large clusters, fragrant. Buds round, yellow-red." [Ck] "A big shrub of the Lambertiana race, with huge clusters of bright rosy pink flowers tinted yellow. Fall bloom scanty." [GAS] "Type, 'Trier'. Bud small, globular, yellowish red; flower medium; semi-double, lasting; flesh-pink, center yellowish white; borne in cluster on long stem; moderate fragrance. Foliage bronze-green. Few thorns. Vigorous, trailing; profuse and continuous bloomer; hardy." [ARA23/154] "Semi-climber; good for hedge . . . R.I.; The most charming of the Lambertianas, and truly 'perpetual' blooming . . . Pa." [ARA28/150]

Electra
Veitch, 1900
From Rosa multiflora × 'William Allen Richardson' (N).

"Golden yellow when opening, then cream yellow, mid-sized, semi-double, very strong climber, very beautiful." [Ck] "Yellow, dou-

Electra *continued*

ble, small, freely produced and more perpetual than 'Aglaia' [Lam]. Growth very vigorous." [GeH] "Clusters of moderately large bright yellow buds turning white as they open. Very beautiful." [GAS] "Yellowish white, medium size, lightly double, light scent, tall." [Sn] "Trusses of pale yellow rosettes paling to creamy white. Takes a few years to establish, and then very prolific and beautiful for its short season." [NRS29/167] "Foliage very plentiful, very little black-spot; bloom moderate through middle of June." [ARA18/129] "Very vigorous shrub, panicles with 40–60 blossoms, golden yellow in bud, paler when open." [JR32/171] "Comes highly recommended by the English growers who claim it is a strong rapid grower and free bloomer, bearing large double yellow roses in great abundance, it promises to be a valuable variety and is worthy of careful trial." [C&Js05] "Withstood 34 degrees of frost." [NRS14/167] Electra, daughter of Agamemnon and Clytemnestra.

Euphrosine

syn. 'Pink Rambler'
Schmitt/Lambert, 1895
From *Rosa multiflora* 'Sarmentosa' × 'Mignonette' (Pol).

"Pink, small, lightly double, medium scent, tall." [Sn] "Bright pink, when opened the yellow anthers are very effective. Growth very vigorous. Free flowering." [GeH] "The old 'Pink Rambler' of peripatetic nursery salesmen. A true Multiflora of the '[Turner's] Crimson Rambler' type, with small, double, bright pink flowers in clusters. Of no importance now [in 1933]." [GAS] "This rose comes from that pretty little 'Mignonette', which it much resembles in form and foliage. The blossom is pure pink, and the semi-open buds light carmine. The very numerous very deep yellow stamens enhance the sparkle of the flower." [JR20/1] "Belongs to the same class as ['Aglaia' and 'Thalia'], but is entirely different, and if possible more beautiful. A free rampant bloomer climbing many feet in a single season, and covered for weeks at a time with immense clusters of medium size, well filled fragrant flowers; bright glossy pink; very rich and handsome; remarkably striking and attractive. It is entirely hardy; produces an abundance of rich green foliage, and is very desirable for all positions where climbing roses are wanted." [C&Js98] Euphrosine, alias Euphrosyne, one of the three Graces, representing Joy.

Excellenz Kuntze

Lambert, 1909
From 'Aglaia' (Lam) × 'Souvenir de Catherine Guillot' (Ch).

"Light yellow, small, full, medium scent, tall." [Sn] "1–5 m high [ca. 3–15 ft], sulphur yellow, then pink-yellow. Blooms in clusters, everblooming." [Ck] "Reblooming climber." [JR33/183] "Poor growth and foliage." [ARA18/122]

Excellenz von Schubert

Lambert, 1909
From 'Mme. Norbert Levavasseur' (Pol) × 'Frau Karl Druschki' (HP).

"Cluster-flowered Multiflora of Lambertiana type, with dark pink flowers." [GAS] "Reblooming climber." [JR33/183] "Shrubby, well foliated. Blossoms of the size and form of [those of] 'Gloire des Polyantha' [Pol], late-blooming, deep carmine pink, quite full, from 5–20 in dense bunches at the end of every shoot. Very satisfying, rich bloom up till frost. Good as an espalier and breeding rose." [Ck]

Frau A. Weidling

Vogel, 1930
"White, small, lightly double, tall." [Sn]

Frau Eva Schubert

syn. 'Gregor Mendel'
Tepelmann, 1937
"Pink, small, lightly double, tall." [Sn]

Frau Helene Videnz

Lambert, 1904
From an unnamed seedling (which resulted from a cross of 'Euphrosine' [Lam] and 'Princesse Alice de Monaco' [T]) × 'Louis-Philippe' (Ch).

"Salmon pink, medium size, full, tall." [Sn] "Vigorous shrub, blooms in large panicles, pure light salmon pink, small, globular, and full." [JR30/24]

Frau Professor Grischko

Vogel, 1947
"Red, medium size, lightly double, tall." [Sn]

Frau Sophie Meyerholz

Vogel, 1942
"Pink, medium size, full, tall." [Sn]

Gartendirektor Otto Linne

Lambert, 1934
"Deep pink, yellow center, medium size, full, medium to tall." [Sn]

Gartenstadt Liegnitz

Lambert, 1911
From 'Frau Helene Videnz' (Lam) × 'Dr. Andry' (HP).

"Another 'blue rose,' with purple-red flowers turning slatey violet." [GAS] "Purple red, medium size, lightly double, tall." [Sn] "As a specimen or breeding rose, splendidly colored; winter hardy. Blooms in clusters at the tip [of the canes]; medium-sized, purple-red, becoming slate-red." [Ck]

Geheimrat Dr. Mitteweg

Lambert, 1909
From 'Mme. Norbert Levavasseur' (Pol) × 'Trier' (Lam).

"Rose-red, yellow center, large, full, medium scent, tall." [Sn] "Bush stout, bushy, upright; thorns strong but few. Leaves extra large, dark green. Blooms in large, loosely-built clusters, full, polyantha-like, wide, rose-red with yellow-white center. Gorgeous bouquet rose. Otherwise, for use in the foreground, breeding, and as a specimen. Keeps blooming until frost." [Ck] "Reblooming climber." [JR33/183–184]

Gneisenau

Lambert, 1924
From an unnamed seedling (which resulted from crossing 'Schneelicht' [Rg] with 'Killarney' [HT]) × 'Veilchenblau' (Mult).

"White, yellow center, medium size, full, very fragrant, tall." [Sn] "Rather large, semi-double snow-white flowers in clusters. Excellent Multiflora for hedges." [GAS] "Bud long-pointed, flower large (3 inches across [ca. 7.5 cm]), lasting, very fragrant, snow-white with ocher-yellow stamens, borne in clusters on long stem. Vigorous (5 to 6$\frac{1}{4}$ feet [ca. 1.6–2 m])." [ARA25/190]

Grandmaster
Kordes, 1952
"Light yellow-orange, large, single, light scent, medium height." [Sn]

Gregor Mendel Listed as 'Frau Eva Schubert' (Lam).

Gruss an Heidelberg
trans. "Greetings to Heidelberg"
Kordes, 1959
"Light red, large, full, tall." [Sn]

Gruss an Zabern
Lambert, 1903
From 'Euphrosine' (Lam) × 'Mme. Ocker Ferencz' (T).
"White." [Ÿ] "White, medium size, full, very fragrant, tall." [Sn] "Flower white, in clusters, large trusses. Growth vigorous, not perpetual." [GeH] "A very free-flowering semi-climbing pillar Rose, blooms in large trusses of sweet scented pure white flowers, summer flowering only." [F-M] "Another of the endless Multifloras with white flowers." [GAS]

[Hauff]
Lambert, 1911
From 'Aimée Vibert' (N) × 'Turner's Crimson Rambler' (Mult).
"One of the strongest Lambertianas, with clusters of purplish flowers on and off all summer." [GAS] "Seedling of '[Turner's] Crimson Rambler', but does not mildew. Very vigorous; almost thornless. Color intermediate between [those of] '[Turner's] Crimson Rambler' and 'Veilchenblau' [Mult]—a violet purple-red." [ARA18/91] "Strong growth, leaves wide, blossom mid-sized, full, violet; hardy, somewhat remontant." [Ck]

Heideröslein
Lambert, 1932
From 'Chamisso' (Lam) × 'Amalie de Greiff' (HT).
"Yellowish salmon pink, medium size, single, medium scent, tall." [Sn]

Heine
Lambert, 1912
From 'Trier' (Lam) × 'Frau Karl Druschki' (HP).
"Its large trusses of white flowers are distinguished by dark reddish stamens." [GAS] "White, small, full, tall." [Sn] Heinrich Heine, German *littérateur*, lived 1797–1856.

Heinrich Conrad Söth
Lambert, 1919
From 'Geheimrat Dr. Mitteweg' (Lam) × *Rosa foetida*.
"Another Lambertiana with rosy red flowers, white in the center. Good autumn bloomer." [GAS] "Pink, white center, small, single, medium scent, tall." [Sn] "Bud small; flower small, single, borne in pyramidal clusters; fragrant. Color light rosy red, with white eye—resembles 'Leuchtstern' [Mult], but redder. Foliage large, glossy dark green. A very vigorous grower of upright, bushy habit, and a continuous bloomer all season. Very hardy." [ARA20/136] "Bush strongly erect, 1.5–2 m [ca. 3¹/₂–6 ft], hardy. Leaves glossy. Very floriferous, blooming at the cane-tips in large, pyramidal clusters. Each blossom is single, bright, deep rose-red with a white eye. The bloom lasts, splendid ornamental and park rose." [Ck]

Hoffmann von Fallersleben
Lambert, 1917
"Yellowish salmon red, small, full, tall." [Sn] "Clusters of reddish salmon flowers on a Lambertiana of drooping habit." [GAS] "Strong-climbing plant, pendant, particularly rich bloom, 5–20 blossoms [per cluster], long stem, full, salmon red, becoming yellow and ochre-yellow, ending deep salmon." [Ck]

Kommerzienrat W. Rautenstrauch
Lambert, 1909
From 'Léonie Lamesch' (Pol) × *Rosa foetida* 'Bicolor'.
"Attractive Lambertiana, with clusters of salmon-pink flowers tinged with yellow." [GAS] "Salmon pink, yellow center, medium size, lightly double, tall." [Sn] "Small growth; not distinct." [ARA18/122] "Reblooming climber." [JR33/183–184]

Lausitz
Berger, 1959
"Pink, medium size, lightly double, light scent, tall." [Sn]

Lavender Lassie
Kordes, 1960
From 'Hamburg' (HMk) × 'Mme. Norbert Levavasseur' (Pol).
"Violet pink, medium size, full, very fragrant, tall." [Sn]

Lessing
Lambert, 1914
From 'Trier' (Lam) × 'Entente Cordiale' (HT).
"Bushy Lambertiana with clusters of small, double, dark pink flowers, striped white." [GAS] "Rose red, small, full, medium scent, tall." [Sn] "Strong-growing and climbing, thorny. Leaves large, light green. Blooms in large clusters, nearly full, small, reddish pink with white mid-line, citron-yellow in the center. Bud red-yellow, fragrant." [Ck] Gotthold Ephraim Lessing, German dramatist, lived 1729–1781.

Lichterloh
trans. "Ablaze"
Tantau, 1955
"Red, medium size, lightly double, light scent, tall." [Sn]

Lyric
DeRuiter, 1951
"Deep pink, medium size, full, light scent, tall." [Sn]

Max Singer
syn. 'Rosiériste Max Singer'
Lacharme, 1885
From 'Polyantha Alba Plena Sarmentosa' (Mult) × 'Général Jacqueminot' (HP).
"It is said to have medium-sized, ruby-red, cup-shaped flowers." [GAS] "Deep red, medium size, full, tall." [Sn] "Large, healthy leaves, quite beautiful, large, rose-red blossoms. Strong rebloomer." [Ck] "The second variety announced by Mons. Lacharme belongs to the series of polyantha hybrids and was dedicated to Monsieur Max Singer, great rose fancier of Tournai (Belgium), and author of the *Guide Général du Rosiériste* . . . Very vigorous bush; blossoms the size of those of the rose 'Hermosa' [B], full, bright red, passing to a lighter pink; effective plant." [JR9/166] Max Singer, preeminently important author of not only the above but, most importantly, the 1885 *Dictionnaire des Roses*, a wonderful, pioneering work preserving many what

Max Singer *continued*

would have otherwise have been unobtainable descriptions of mid-century rose cultivars, which we have frequently used in these present lucubrations, cited as S. His work is one of the main links in the great chain of rose nomenclatural and informational history, which is essentially Prévost to Singer to Simon to Jäger, each author subsuming his predecessor, with predecessor's errors intact, and then adding newer information up to date of publication of his own work. *The Old Rose Adventurer* and *The Old Rose Advisor,* full of respect for this chain and the work it represents, nevertheless have done what none of these workers did, gone back to original sources to verify and correct where necessary. Those who have preceded us in this work labored mightily and well!—and we feel not only inspired by their examples but also fortunate to have been able to build on their foundation. We wish our own successors as much good fortune—and more ease—in their endeavors!

Mosel
Lambert, 1920
From 'Mme. Norbert Levavasseur' (Pol) × 'Trier' (Lam).
    "Another strange violet form of *R. multiflora.* Occasionally flowers in autumn." [GAS] "Reddish violet, medium size, full, light scent, tall." [Sn] "Very strong growing shrub, up to 4 meters high [ca. 13 ft]; bloom very profuse; color like that of 'Schloss Friedenstein' [Mult], deep slaty violet; blossom medium-sized, full, in large clusters medium-early to late." [Ck] "Bud red; flower medium size, full, double, very lasting, violet, with reddish violet center; borne on strong stem; slightly fragrant. Foliage abundant, large, leathery, dark bronzy green, disease-resistant. Very vigorous; climbing habit; blooms profusely in June and July; sometimes again in September. Hardy." [ARA21/164] The Mosel, German river.

Mozart
Lambert, 1937
From 'Robin Hood' (HMk) × 'Rote Pharisäer' (HT).
    "Pink, white center, small, single, medium scent, tall." [Sn] Wolfgang Amadeus Mozart, musical genius showing abundantly all the scatter-shot ramifications of genius—not all of them as common minds would have them!; lived 1756–1791; those whom the gods love die young.

Neisse
Berger, 1959
    "Pink, medium size, full, tall." [Sn]

Oriole
Lambert, 1912
Seedling of 'Aglaia' (Lam).
    "Light yellow, small, full, tall." [Sn] "Beautiful pale yellow Multiflora with deep golden buds. Much neglected in favor of 'Goldfinch' [Mult] but is probably a better rose, although neither is scarcely worth growing nowadays." [GAS] "Foliage very plentiful, trace of black-spot in midsummer; bloom free first two weeks of June." [ARA18/130]

P. Rosegger Listed as 'Peter Rosegger' (Lam).

Perpetual Thalia Listed as 'Thalia Remontant' (Lam).

Peter Rosegger
syn. 'P. Rosegger'
Lambert, 1914
From 'Geheimrat Dr. Mitteweg' (Lam) × 'Tip-Top' (Pol).
    "Light orange pink, medium size, full, tall." [Sn] "Blossom nearly large, rosette-formed, beautifully structured, 5–15 [in a cluster], floriferous, and good rebloom." [Ck]

[Philippine Lambert]
Lambert, 1903
From an unnamed seedling (resulting from a cross of 'Euphrosine' [Lam] and 'Safrano' [T]) × 'Dr. Grill' (T).
    "Bright salmon and peach." [LS] "Light pink, in clusters." [CA05] "Flower silvery flesh with deeper centre. Growth vigorous and dwarf." [GeH]

Pink Rambler Listed as 'Euphrosine' (Lam).

Probuzeni
Böhm, 1935
    "Light pink, medium size, very full, medium scent, medium to tall." [Sn]

Prodaná Nevěsta
Brada, 1934
    "White, small, full, tall." [Sn]

Rosiériste Max Singer Listed as 'Max Singer' (Lam).

Rudolf von Bennigsen
Lambert, 1932
    "Pink, edged whitish yellow, large, full, tall." [Sn]

Saarbrücken
Kordes, 1959
    "Red, medium size, lightly double, tall." [Sn]

Thalia
syn. 'White Rambler'
Schmitt/Lambert, 1895
From 'Polyantha Alba Plena Sarmentosa' (Mult) × 'Pâquerette' (Pol).
    "A very pure white, giving beautiful panicles of blossoms borne on long stiff stems." [JR22/161] "Blossom full, small, pure white." [JR32/171] "White, small, full, medium scent, tall." [Sn] "Pure white, small, semi-double, fragrant, produced in clusters, very vigorous, climbing; very hardy." [GeH] "Blooms in large snowy clusters, very handsome and attractive, and entirely hardy." [C&Js98] "This is the 'White Rambler' of traveling nurserymen's plate-books. It is a strong-growing Multiflora, with huge clusters of semi-double, white flowers with a peculiar and not altogether odor." [GAS] "Foliage very plentiful, black-spots very slightly; bloom free early part of June." [ARA18/131] "From 'Ma Pâquerette' [*sic*], this Polyantha is exactly the same as ['Aglaia' (Lam) and 'Euphrosine' (Lam)] in growth and the way it blooms. Only the color is different—beautiful immaculate white—and the cluster is usually larger." [JR20/1–2] Thalia, one of the three Graces, representing Bloom.

Thalia Remontant
syn. 'Perpetual Thalia'
Lambert, 1903
From a seedling of 'Thalia' (Lam) × 'Mme. Laurette Messimy' (Ch).

"White, small, full, tall." [Sn] "Flower pure white, semi-double, in large clusters. Growth very vigorous." [GeH] "Probably one of the earliest of the Lambertiana race, with clusters of fairly double, white flowers, borne more or less intermittently all summer." [GAS] "This charming white-flowered climbing rose ['Thalia'], which belongs to the ravishing *Three Graces* group [*i.e.*, 'Aglaia', 'Euphrosine', and 'Thalia'], has—up till now—only produced one profuse bloom-period, in July-August. Crossing a seedling of 'Thalia' with the remarkable China '[Mme.] Laurette Messimy', Herr Peter Lambert of Trier obtained a freely remontant variety, which we have admired at his breeding-grounds, still in full bloom in the middle of September." [JR26/114]

Thermidor
Corboeuf-Marsault, 1909
From 'Turner's Crimson Rambler' (Mult) × 'Perle des Jardins' (T).

"Yellow, medium size, full, medium scent, tall." [Sn] Thermidor, eleventh month of the calendar of revolutionary France, July 19 through August 17.

Thiergarten Listed as 'Tiergarten' (Lam).

Tiergarten
syn. 'Thiergarten'
Lambert, 1904
From 'Euphrosine' (Lam) × 'Safrano' (T).

"Deep yellow." [Ÿ] "Multiflora with long-stemmed clusters of ochre-yellow flowers, paling to white." [GAS] "Shrub very vigorous and hardy. Blossom small, full, deep ochre yellow. Good plant for colonnades and weeping roses." [JR30/24] Tiergarten, the zoological garden.

Trier
Lambert, 1904
From 'Aglaia' (Lam) × 'Mrs. R. G. Sharman-Crawford' (HP).

"Cream white, salmony pink bud." [JR35/120] "Yellowish white, small, full, medium scent, tall." [Sn] "Flower creamy white, edged with fawn, semi-single. Growth vigorous." [GeH] "Flower medium-sized, in large corymbs, creamy white, remontant." [JR32/171] "Shrubby Lam-

bertiana with clusters of semi-double, pinkish white flowers tinged with yellow, borne more or less freely all season." [GAS] "A strong-growing climber of the Rambler type, producing immense trusses of pale rose-colored flowers, changing to white. It is ever blooming, flowering more or less all summer and fall; a decided improvement over white Rambler [*i.e.*, 'Thalia' (Lam)]." [C&Js07] "Fair growth; free bloomer—occasionally blooming a little in fall." [ARA18/121] "Foliage not quite so plentiful as many, black-spots slightly; bloom abundant in June, moderate till last of August, continuous." [ARA18/130] "Has been in flower all the season, but does not grow very high." [NRS14/162] "A very great acquisition to the pillar Roses—its small but beautifully shaped flowers are fully produced on long panicles—not a vigorous grower for a climber, but a Rose that should be in every garden." [F-M] Trier, or Trèves, German city, headquarters of Lambert.

Ufhoven
Berger, 1964
"Salmon pink, medium size, full, tall." [Sn]

Von Liliencron
Lambert, 1916
From 'Geheimrat Dr. Mitteweg' (Lam) × 'Mrs. Aaron Ward' (HT).

"Strong shrubby Lambertiana with clusters of yellowish red buds and light pink flowers throughout the season." [GAS] "Dark glossy leaves; small double flowers, light yellowish rose, deeper reverse. Seldom flowers much after the summer crop." [T4]

White Rambler Listed as 'Thalia' (Lam).

Wilhelm Marx
Vogel, 1939
"Red, medium size, full, tall." [Sn]

Yellow Rambler Listed as 'Aglaia' (Lam).

Zitronenfalter
trans. 'Lemon Butterfly'
Tantau, 1956
"Yellow, large, full, light scent, tall." [Sn]

CHAPTER TWENTY-NINE

Hybrid Musks

"Within the present century the Musk rose was used again to produce a new race of garden roses different from the Noisettes. The Reverend J. H. Pemberton, in England, originated a group of varieties which he called Hybrid Musks. They are large bushes, in bloom more or less continuously, bearing flowers of varying size and doubleness, mostly white, pale pink, and pale yellow, in gigantic clusters. The strong, basal shoots of most of Pemberton's roses have a way of bursting into great panicles of bloom about 4 to 5 feet [ca. 1.3–1.6 m] from the ground, especially in autumn." [GAS] "The Musk strain was perpetuated in the everblooming climbers produced by Captain George C. Thomas, Jr., who used some of Pemberton's roses as parents in his early hybridizing work. His roses, or his earlier varieties at least, are continuous-blooming shrubs which are reasonably hardy. The flowers are mostly single, and although he introduced them as hardy everblooming climbers, they never really climb much or bloom freely after the early summer display. When Captain Thomas moved to California he advanced his breeding-work more rapidly, and at the time of his death many hundreds of promising seedlings were being grown which will take some years to study and select ... Most of them show little Musk character and bear superficial resemblance to Climbing Hybrid Teas or Climbing Bengals." [GAS] "None of these Musk hybrids are much more than big shrubs." [GAS]

"Prune ... by the little-and-often system, removing the ends of the flowering stems all through the growing season. Occasionally cut off an old cane at the base in spring. Then you will reap a lovely, flowery reward." [W]

Andenken an Alma de l'Aigle
trans. "In Remembrance of Alma de l'Aigle"
Kordes, 1948
"Pink, medium size, full, light scent, tall." [Sn]

Aurora
Pemberton, 1923
From 'Danaë' (HMk) × 'Miriam' (HT).
"Golden canary. Growth vigorous." [GeH] "Flower 2 to 3½ inches in diameter [ca. 5–9 cm]; golden yellow, passing to pale creamy white[,] small clusters; moderately fragrant." [ARA24/168] "Light yel-

low, small, lightly double, medium scent, tall." [Sn] "Colour golden canary. Flowers medium size, semi-single, produced in corymbs, large sprays. Bush habit, tall, perpetual, late blooming. Not liable to mildew, fragrant." [NRS25/250] "Another new variety of the 'Nur Mahál' [HMk] type, of a deep yellow primrose colour. Very free flowering. The plant exhibited was vigorous and free of mildew. A good bedding Rose." [NRS24/214] Aurora, alias Eos, personification of the dawn.

Autumn Delight
Bentall, 1933
"Yellowish white, small, single, tall." [Sn] "A good display in summer from side-shoots, and magnificent heads of blossom in autumn." [T4]

Ballerina
Bentall, 1937
"Pink-white, small, single, tall." [Sn] Phillips & Rix report it as a *Rosa multiflora* seedling.

Belinda
Bentall, 1936
"Pink, medium size, lightly double, medium fragrance, tall." [Sn]

Bishop Darlington
Capt. Thomas/Dreer and Howard & Smith, 1926
From 'Aviateur Blériot' (W) × 'Moonlight' (HMk).
"Cream to flesh-pink with yellow glow; reverse light pink." [C-Pf34] "Bud medium size, ovoid, orange-red; flower large, semi-double, open, cupped, lasting, moderate fruity fragrance, cream to flesh-pink, with yellow glow through center, reverse light pink with broad light canary-yellow bas, borne singly and several together on medium to long stem; [the blossoms] hang on [after fading]. Foliage abundant, medium size, light bronzy green, soft, disease-resistant. Growth vigorous (8 feet [ca. 2.6 m]), climbing; profuse, continuous bloomer (200 [blossoms] in Pa. from May to November). Hardy in Pa." [ARA27/219] "Continuously in flower." [ARA31/189] "[For] cool zones. Good grower; very fine foliage; continuous bloomer; deep orange bud, opening semi-double up to 18 petals; color fades. Should do well in Pacific Northwest." [ARA28/99] "The Musk strain is evident in this ever-blooming climber, reminiscent of the Noisettes, although much hardier. One of its ancestors was 'Aviateur Blériot', which brought in a Wichuraiana strain. The flowers are large, almost single, with a somewhat unkempt appearance, when fully open. The buds are coppery yellow, fading lighter as they expand." [GAS] *Hamblin and Hatton* report that it suffers badly in winter in New England but pro-

duces new growth 4 to 5 feet tall [ca. 1.3–1.6 m] which blooms well in June, August, and September, with a few flowers all summer … *Cross* finds it very desirable for trellis or pillar and likes its splendid, long-pointed, orange buds, even if the semi-double flowers pass quickly. Thinks it might be better in shade. *Middleton* considers it one of Thomas' best introductions, with attractive blooms which ought to have more petals. It grows about 8 feet high [ca. 2.6 m] and is not troubled with disease." [ARA30/180] "A semi-climbing or pillar rose, hardly strong enough in habit to rank high; but it has a strongly individual semi-double bloom of a lovely soft fawn color shaded with salmon." [CaRol/6/6]

Bloomfield Comet
Capt. Thomas/Bobbink & Atkins, 1929
From 'Duchess of Wellington' (HT) × 'Danaë' (HMk).

"Large growth; very fine thick foliage, well retained. A single whose color is between that of 'Irish Fireflame' [HT] and 'Irish Elegance' [HT]; of large size and good substance; holds its color in sunlight. Continuous through long season. Quite hardy." [ARA28/99] "The Noisette class might be stretched to receive this combination of Musk and Hybrid Tea. Plant makes thick, lush stems of moderate length, and produces a sparse succession of reddish buds which expand to single coppery yellow flowers stained with red." [GAS] "Bud medium size, long-pointed, reddish orange; flower large to very large, single, open, very lasting, slight fragrance, orange suffused salmon with yellow base, borne, singly and several together, on medium to long, strong stem. Foliage sparse, medium to large, light bronzy green, soft, mildew-resistant. Few thorns. Vigorous climber (6 feet in Pa. [ca. 2 m]; 12 feet in Calif. [ca. 4 m]); free, intermittent bloomer. Tips freeze." [ARA25/194] Bloomfield, name of the Thomas estate in Pennsylvania.

[Bloomfield Completeness]
Capt. Thomas, 1931

"One of the last varieties originated by Capt. Thomas who believed it one of his best roses. Flowers double, fragrant, deep orange-yellow, and continuously produced." [GAS]

Bloomfield Culmination
Capt. Thomas/Bobbink & Atkins, 1925
From 'Sheilagh Wilson' (HT) × 'Danaë' (HMk).

"Bud medium size, long-pointed; flower large to very large, single, open, lasting, slight fragrance, deep rose-pink with white center, borne singly and several together, on medium-length, normal stem. Foliage sufficient, medium size, rich green, leathery, disease-resistant. Vigorous climber (7 feet [ca. 2.3 m] in Pa.), upright; abundant, continuous bloomer from May to November. Tips freeze." [ARA25/194] "Of moderate vigor and improved hardiness. Flowers are rose-pink, single, and about four inches across [ca. 1 dm]. Not especially valuable." [GAS]

Bloomfield Dainty
Capt. Thomas/Bobbink & Atkins, 1925
From 'Danaë' (HMk) × 'Mme. Édouard Herriot' (Pern).

"Orange buds, opening single, clear yellow blooms that fade to a pleasing cream. Foliage subject to black-spot. Made 4-foot [ca. 1.3 m] canes first season. Flowers are beautiful, but too few and fleeting … *R.I.*; … a canary-yellow everblooming climber with distinct, varnished, deep olive-green foliage, impervious to mildew … *Calif.*; The

best Bloomfield rose to my notion. Grows luxuriantly, with fine glossy foliage and lovely single yellow flowers that are very attractive. Rightly named … *Calif.*" [ARA28/147] "Good growth; may be used as climber or hedge; foliage impervious to mildew; lost at end of long season. A distinct single rose, deep canary, of medium size, which blooms through long season." [ARA28/99] "Bud medium size, long-pointed, deepest orange; flower large, single, open, lasting, slight fragrance, deep canary-yellow, borne singly and several together. Foliage sufficient, medium size, rich green, leathery, glossy, black-spots, mildew-resistant, many thorns. Vigorous, upright (5 feet [ca. 1.6 m] in Pa.); free, intermittent bloomer from May to November. Tips freeze." [ARA25/194] "Combination of Pernetiana and Musk, its clustered flowers claim Noisette kinship. Buds rich yellow; the single flowers are lighter. Blooms freely in early summer and scatteringly thereafter. Prettiest of Thomas' single-flowered climbers. Especially useful as a shrub." [GAS] "Very dark green, healthy foliage and medium climbing growth. Perhaps best near coast." [CaRoll/4/2] "Spurts of bloom occur all summer. The plant grows 6 to 8 feet [ca. 2–2.6 m] and makes an excellent ground cover or ornament for a low fence. Slightly FRAGRANT." [W]

Bloomfield Dawn
Capt. Thomas/Armstrong, 1931
From "a climbing rose" × 'Bloomfield Progress' (HMk).

"Flowers large and double, varying from light to dark pink. Reported to be everblooming, but suspected of tenderness in the North." [GAS] "Bud long, slender, rose-pink; flower large, semi-double, fragrant (Damask), soft light pink, yellow base, reverse deep pink, borne on long, strong stem. Foliage disease-resistant. Growth vigorous; profuse, continuous bloomer." [ARA31/226] "A good-sized, light silver-pink; decorative; exquisite perfume; continuity and retained foliage. Very vigorous." [CaRoll/4/2] "On a long fence at the bottom of the rose-garden grows a thick mat of glossy rose leaves which are almost hidden at the peak of the spring season with a multitude of good-sized single pink blossoms strongly suggesting in color the exquisite 'Dainty Bess' [HT]. This is 'Bloomfield Dawn', a charming thing, much handsomer in every way than the pink Cherokee." [ARA33/109]

Bloomfield Discovery
Capt. Thomas, 1925
From 'Danaë' (HMk) × an unnamed seedling (which resulted from crossing 'Frau Karl Druschki' [HP] and 'Mme. Caroline Testout' [HT]).

"Single, light pink flowers of the same type as 'Bloomfield Culmination' [HMk]." [GAS]

Bloomfield Fascination
Capt. Thomas/Bobbink & Atkins, 1925
From 'Danaë' (HMk) × 'Mme. Laurette Messimy' (Ch).

"Type, 'Danaë'. Bud small, ovoid; flower small, double, full, very lasting, slight fragrance, light canary-yellow, borne, singly and several together, on medium-length, strong stem. Foliage very abundant, medium to small, rich bronzy green, soft, very disease-resistant. Few thorns. Very vigorous climber (5 feet [ca. 1.6 m]; 12 feet [ca. 4 m] in Calif.); abundant, continuous bloomer from May to November. Tips freeze." [ARA25/195] "Canes 8 feet high [ca. 2.6 m]. Bloomed continuously until October 21. Small yellow flowers which fade soon but drop off clean. Foliage fair … *Ore.*" [ARA28/148] "A bushy plant much

Bloomfield Fascination *continued*

like Pemberton's Musks, with clusters of relatively small, buff-yellow flowers which fade nearly white. One of the best of this group." [GAS]

Bloomfield Favorite

Capt. Thomas, 1924

From 'Debutante' (W) × 'Moonlight' (HMk).

"Bud deep salmon; flower very double, 1¹/₂ inch across [ca. 3.5 cm], full, slight fragrance, pinkish cream. Foliage perfect. Vigorous climber; profuse bloomer from June to November (400 blooms in Pa.) on old and new wood. Very hardy." [ARA25/195] "Small, very double flowers of pinkish cream color, virtually a Climbing Cecile Brunner in appearance, but hardier. Continuous bloom." [GAS]

Bloomfield Perfection

Thomas/Bobbink & Atkins, 1927

From 'Danaë' (HMk) × 'Bloomfield Abundance' (Pol).

"Rather large, very double, creamy white flowers tinged pink in the center. Of Musk descent, but resembles a Wichuraiana of the 'André Louis' type, though it blooms oftener." [GAS] "Bud medium size, ovoid, orange and pink; flower medium size, very double, full, very lasting, slight fragrance (like honeysuckle), cream-yellow with lilac suffusion, borne, singly, several together, and in clusters, on short, weak stem. Foliage abundant, medium size, dark bronzy green, leathery, glossy, very disease-resistant. Vigorous, upright climber (8 feet [ca. 2.6 m] in one season in Calif.), bushy, strong; profuse, continuous bloomer. Tips freeze." [ARA25/195] "A strong-growing climber with perfect foliage, immune to disease and well retained. Gives constant bloom during the entire season. Flowers soft cream, with yellow or orange marking and a pink suffusion, extremely double, of medium size, and good lasting qualities, open well, strong honey perfume. Bred for an everblooming climber in the East, this rose is valuable in the South for its all-season decorative qualities." [ARA28/99]

"Superior in growth to both its parents. Its blooming, continuity, and profusion were equal to [those of] 'Bloomfield Abundance', but on a much larger plant. As a matter of fact, it gave more bloom than either parent. The flower was larger than [that of] 'Danaë' or 'Bloomfield Abundance', and probably came from 'Dorothy Page-Roberts' [HT, parent of 'Bloomfield Abundance']. Form and color were much better, and the fragrance, which was most distinct, exceeded its father and mother in intensity. The foliage, larger than that of either parent, was retained as well as that of 'Danaë', and had the glossy beauty of the leaves of 'Bloomfield Abundance'. In this particular experiment there was a great advance in all these properties, and 'Bloomfield Perfection' was almost a perfect achievement of our endeavor. Continued advance was halted a long time because 'Bloomfield Perfection' had one serious handicap. It did not set pods naturally, and it was most difficult to set them artificially. Such seed as we obtained did not germinate readily, and the seedlings were weak. At last, after some years of endeavor, a cross was made with 'Mme. Butterfly' [HT] as the pollen parent, and the 'Bloomfield Perfection' pod ripened healthy seeds. A few germinated, and the best of them was a seedling with the growth, foliage, type of flower, and fragrance of 'Bloomfield Perfection', but with some of Mme. Butterfly's spiral bud, which gave the new bloom a better shape than that of 'Bloomfield Perfection', while the color was slightly darker. Best of all, this new seedling set its own pods naturally." [ARA31/34–35]

Bonn

Kordes, 1950

"Orange red, large, full, medium scent, tall." [Sn] Bonn, quondam capital of West Germany.

Buff Beauty

Bentall, 1939

Seedling of 'William Allen Richardson' (N).

"Deep orange yellow, medium size, full, medium scent, tall." [Sn] "It has an excellent habit, with arching branches gradually building up." [T4]

Callisto

Pemberton, 1920

Seedling of 'William Allen Richardson' (N).

"Yellow, small, full, tall." [Sn] "Golden-yellow rosettes, in clusters; foliage dark green. Growth moderate, branching, free flowering." [GeH] "Flower of rosette form, golden yellow, very lasting, borne in clusters along the stem. Foliage abundant, leathery, dark green. Vigorous; bushy; blooms abundantly and continuously all season; fine in autumn. Hardy." [ARA21/158] "A yellow perpetual flowering cluster Rose. Flowering throughout the season to the middle of October. Good in autumn, of bush habit, growing about three feet high [ca. 1 m]." [NRS17/147] "A rampant, decorative climber, with small, double, light lemon- or straw-yellow flowers in clusters; very profuse and continuous bloomer. No cutting value. Foliage fairly well retained." [ARA28/101] Callisto, companion of Artemis, vowing to remain a virgin; Zeus had other ideas.

Cascadia

Capt. Thomas, 1925

"Small single blush to white flowers; blooms in large heads; foliage immune and retained; continuous during spring, summer and fall." [CaRoll/4/3] "A very good cluster-flowering white climber on the Pacific Coast. Probably a genuine Noisette hybrid, descended from the old 'Mme. d'Arblay', a forgotten Musk and Multiflora hybrid." [GAS]

Ceres

Pemberton, 1914

"Pink-yellow, small, lightly double, medium scent, medium height." [Sn] "Flowers semi-double, blush with yellow shading, produced in corymbs. Perpetual, good in autumn." [NRS15/165] "A good shrub with clusters of blush-white flowers tinged with yellow." [GAS] "A cluster Rose of perpetual flowering character. Good in autumn. Recommended for growth in bush form." [NRS14/156] "Growth vigorous." [GeH] "Fair growth; scattered blooms throughout season; better results if given winter protection." [ARA18/119] Ceres, alias Demeter, goddess of agriculture.

Chami

syn. 'Charmi'

Pemberton, 1929

"Deep pink, medium size, lightly double, very fragrant, medium height." [Sn] "A perpetual flowering Cluster Rose, colour bright rose pink, yellow stamens, semi-single, produced in corymbs, large sprays, bush habit, bedding, very strong Musk perfume, good in Autumn." [NRS29/312] "Reported to be a good autumnal rose of the Musk type. Flowers bright rose-pink." [GAS]

Charmi Listed as 'Chami' (HMk).

Clytemnestra
Pemberton, 1915
From 'Trier' (Lam) × 'Liberty' (HT).

"Yellowish salmon, small, full, light scent, tall." [Sn] "Perpetual flowering cluster, copper buds opening to salmon chamois, dark leathery foliage. Not liable to mildew." [NRS15/165] "Described as a perpetual flowering semi-climber. The flowers have slightly twisted petals that somewhat spoilt its effectiveness some thought, others liked the quaintness of the blooms. The flowers are small and would appear to have some polyantha blood." [NRS15/156] "A distinct Musk hybrid with clusters of coppery red and salmon-yellow flowers varying to pink and white as they open. Striking shrub-rose, and a fair autumn bloomer." [GAS] "Good foliage; strong growth; blooms small, attractive color, in clusters. Adaptable as a pillar rose." [ARA18/118] "Growth vigorous." [GeH] "A very pretty Rose, and is more vigorous than 'Danaë' [HMk], or 'Moonlight' [HMk], both of which with me make big bushes." [NRS18/148] "A low, wiry bush which finds a suitable place beside a stone terrace wall, over which it climbs and sprawls. The foliage is attractive, disease-resistant, and still perfect in November. The delicate variegated flowers come in clusters, and, while not profuse, are worth while the season long, developing in the latter part of the year, much after the habit of 'Ghislaine de Féligonde' [Mult], at the ends of new shoots. It is a cheerful, friendly little rose." [ARA27/118] Clytemnestra, cheerful, friendly little wife of Agamemnon, sister of Helen of Troy and Castor and Pollux; at length killed by her son Orestes for being rather a bad lot.

Cornelia
Pemberton, 1925

"Fresh pink, illumined with yellow." [Ÿ] "Light pink, orange center, small, lightly double, medium fragrance, tall." [Sn] "Flower nearly double, about 3 inches across [ca. 7.5 cm], pale pink deepening in center, borne profusely in flattish sprays." [ARA25/183] "Typical [Hybrid] Musk, with clusters of large, pale pink flowers flushed yellow." [GAS] "A perpetual flowering cluster Rose. Colour strawberry, flushed yellow. Flowers in clusters, rosette. Shrub habit, good for massing. Foliage handsome, leathery, dark green. Wood claret colour. Good in autumn. Fragrant musk perfume." [NRS25/250] "Small fawn-apricot flowers, terra-cotta in the bud. This is really everblooming from summer into autumn, when the plant is at its best, and the flowers are superb. Foliage is bronze and glossy, and the vigorous growth reaches 6 to 8 feet [ca. 2–2.6 m]. How excellent is this one to espalier against a high fence or train over a pillar, and it is well adapted to rather shady locations." [W]

Danaë
Pemberton, 1913
From 'Trier' (Lam) × 'Gloire de Chedane-Guinoisseau' (HP).

"Yellowish white, medium size, full, tall." [Sn] "Soft yellow, semi-double, in clusters, perpetual flowering. Growth very vigorous." [GeH] "Yellow blossoms coming in clusters, continually reblooming from June to October. The growth is vigorous, the canes branch, and the plant grows to 3 to 4 feet high [ca. 1–1.3 m], and is in top form in September." [JR37/120] "A perpetual flowering yellow cluster Rose. Habit, bushy and branching. Growth, active and vigorous, throwing up throughout the entire Rose season strong shoots from the base, about

four feet long [ca. 1.3 m], each shoot bearing cluster sprays of yellow flowers. Foliage, dark green, waxy. Flowering continuously from June to late in Autumn. Very good in September." [NRS14/187] "Grows into a nice shaped bush some 4-ft. high [ca. 1.3 m], and produces clusters of soft yellow semi-double flowers, which are useful for decorative purposes. It may be treated as a shrubbery Rose in an open situation." [NRS21/47] "Probably the best of the bushy Musk hybrids. It makes a fair climber, bearing clusters of light yellow flowers on and off throughout the whole season." [GAS] "Growth not especially tall but bushy; blooms in clusters, scattered throughout season, on wood of previous year; requires winter protection." [ARA18/120] "Has long been a favorite of mine because of its hardiness, perpetual-flowering habit, and clear, yellow color." [ARA22/134] Danaë, mother of Perseus by Zeus.

Daphne
Pemberton, 1912

"Rose pink. Vigorous." [NRS13/167] "Deep pink, small, lightly double, very fragrant, tall." [Sn] "A pink-colored shrub rose, blooming from June to November. Best in the Fall." [Ck] "Flower pink, clusters, perpetual flowering. Growth vigorous." [GeH] "Blush-pink [Hybrid] Musk which blooms well in autumn. Moderate growth." [GAS] "Carnation pink remontant variety. The blossoms come in bunches and open from June to October; but the roses have their best form in October. Dwarf and branching bush growing at least two to three feet high [ca. 6 dm to 1 m], just the thing for bedding." [JR37/120] Daphne, beloved by Apollo, much to her distress, finding relief in forestry.

Daybreak
Pemberton, 1918
From 'Trier' (Lam) × 'Liberty' (HT).

"Light yellow, small, lightly double, light scent, tall." [Sn] "Semi-single, golden yellow flowers, borne several on a stem. Foliage handsome dark green. Vigorous, bushy grower; perpetual bloomer." [ARA19/103] "Everblooming shrubby [Hybrid] Musk with clusters of single golden yellow flowers. Pemberton called it a Noisette." [GAS] "Forms a vigorous, low bush with profuse yellow buds opening to dainty white flowers, but the petals of fading blooms turn brown, curl up tightly, and soon spoil the appearance of the bush unless they are removed daily. This condemns it for a garden of many roses." [ARA27/118]

Eva
Kordes, 1933
From 'Robin Hood' (HMk) × 'J. C. Thornton' (HT).

"Carminy red, white center." [Ÿ] "Has a white center and looks more carmine than crimson." [W] "Light red, white center, medium size, full, medium scent, tall." [Sn]

Felicia
Pemberton, 1928
From 'Trier' (Lam) × 'Ophelia' (HT).

"Buds pink, fading to blush and partly white when opening to the semi-double blooms which are borne in large branching panicles, and have a pleasing musk perfume." [ARA28/233] "Very pretty cluster-flowering musk, with relatively large, light rose-pink, ruffled flowers, borne well into the autumn." [GAS] "Light pink, white center, medium size, lightly double, very fragrant, tall." [Sn] "China pink, shaded yellow, produced in large clusters, perpetual flowering, good in autumn, very

Felicia *continued*

fragrant. Growth vigorous." [GeH] "Another of the late Mr. Pemberton's Seedlings, and to me one of his best. The blooms, which are semi-double, are borne in clusters. The colour is white, overlaid with pale pink. The habit of growth is vigorous and bushy. Strong Musk scent. The foliage is a reddy green colour. Not liable to Mildew." [NRS28/151]

Fortuna
Pemberton, 1927
From 'Lady Pirrie' (HT) × 'Nur-Mahál' (HMk).

"A bushy Musk with very large, semi-double flowers of apple-blossom-pink, almost scarlet in bud. Good autumn bloomer, and very fragrant." [GAS] "Bud much splashed with red; flower large (3 to 4 inches in diameter [ca. 7.5 cm to 1 dm]), semi-double (12 to 15 petals), fruity fragrance, rose-pink, netted with fine veins and fading to rosy pink like apple-blossoms (center filled with golden anthers), borne freely in large sprays. Dwarf, bushy habit." [ARA28/233] "Flower large (4^1/$_2$ in. diam. [ca. 1.2 dm]), semi-single, moderately fragrant, soft China pink, borne in clusters. Growth dwarf; continuous bloomer. Good in autumn." [ARA30/221] "A large semi-double Rose for its type, produced in clusters. The colour is pale pink, flushed white. Musk scented. The habit appears to be fairly vigorous, and it should make a very pretty specimen bush." [NRS28/255] Fortuna, goddess of Chance, to whom authors in particular owe special devotions.

Francesca
Pemberton, 1922
From 'Danaë' (HMk) × 'Sunburst' (Pern).

"Copper orange, medium size, single, light scent, tall." [Sn] "Colour apricot. Flowers medium size, semi-single, produced in corymbs, large sprays. Bush habit, tall, spreading." [NRS22/224] "Very beautiful Musk, with large, golden apricot flowers in loose sprays. A big bush, but a sparse bloomer late in the season." [GAS] "Type, 'Pax' [HMk]. Bud small, long-pointed; flower medium-size, open, single, lasting; apricot; borne in long spray on long stem; slight fragrance. Foliage abundant, large, leathery, disease-resistant. Few thorns. Very vigorous, upright; abundant and continuous bloomer from June to September; hardy." [ARA23/148]

Galatea
Pemberton, 1914

"Queer, bushy Musk with clusters of small, double gray, or pinkish stone-colored flowers." [GAS] "Perpetual flowering cluster. Flowers stone colour, rosette, large trusses on long stems. Not liable to mildew. Very good in autumn." [NRS15/165] Galatea, quondam block of stone, beloved of Pygmalion, who found new interest in Art for Art's Sake.

Havering
Bentall, 1937

"Borne in small clusters, the flowers are of soft pink, large and semi-double. Sturdy upright growth. About 3 feet [ca. 1 m]." [T4] Havering-atte-Bower, home of Pemberton, who was probably responsible for the breeding of the Hybrid Musk seedlings released by Bentall after Pemberton's death.

Inspektor Blohm
Kordes, 1942

"White, medium size, very full, very fragrant, tall." [Sn]

Kathleen
Pemberton, 1922
From 'Daphne' (HMk) × 'Perle des Jardins' (T).

"Clusters of pink buds opening to single, white flowers." [GAS] "A perpetual free-flowering cluster Rose. Colour pink-blush, after the shade of *R. canina*. Large trusses of small single flowers, well distributed. Strong shrub habit, free flowering. Good in autumn." [NRS22/224] "Type, 'Moonlight' [HMk]. Bud small; flower small, open, single, very lasting; blush-pink; borne in clusters on long stem; slight fragrance. Foliage abundant, large, leathery, dark green, disease-resistant. Few thorns. Very vigorous (6 feet high [ca. 2 m]); profuse and continuous bloomer from May to November; hardy." [ARA23/148] "Healthy and hardy in sun or shade, will grow up to 15 feet [ca 5 m], bringing delicious scent to you at second-story windows, or will stop lower down and be shrubby. In constant bloom, it looks like a bough of apple blossoms, the small, single, white flowers, pink in the bud, appearing in long-stemmed clusters. Really FRAGRANT." [W] Not to be confused with W. Paul's 1907 Multiflora of the same name.

Maid Marian   Listed as 'Maid Marion' (HMk).

Maid Marion
syn. 'Maid Marian'
Pemberton/Bentall, 1930

"White, medium size, lightly double, tall." [Sn] "Flower light carmine-rose, reverse of petals silvery satin, large. Growth vigorous." [GeH] "A Hybrid Musk, somewhat like a vigorous Polyantha, with large trusses of white flowers turning pink with age." [GAS] "Bud and flower medium size, white, opening blush, borne in large cluster. Foliage sufficient, glossy. Growth very vigorous (3 to 4 ft. [ca. 1–1.3 m]); profuse, continuous bloomer all season." [ARA31/233] Maid Marion, of much interest to Robin Hood.

Moonlight
Pemberton, 1913
From 'Trier' (Lam) × 'Sulphurea' (T).

"White-colored Rose tinted cream white, enhanced by the sparkle of its gold-colored stamens, blooming in clusters from June to October. The foliage is bronzy green. The growth is vigorous." [JR37/120] "White, medium size, lightly double, medium fragrance, medium to tall." [Sn] "White flushed with lemon-yellow, with golden stamens, semi-single, in clusters, sweetly scented. Growth vigorous." [GeH] "A vigorous Musk, producing clusters of rather large, single, white flowers sparingly throughout the season." [GAS] "Good June blooms and a number of blooms thereafter; but the foliage mildews, color here, pure white; single." [ARA16/22] "A perpetual-flowering semi-climber, produces its lemon-white flowers in clusters. The golden stamens help to make a very pretty effect, and as it flowers again in the autumn it should be very useful. It is semi-single and mildew-proof." [NRS13/154] "Bushy growth, not especially tall; blooms in clusters, scattered throughout the season, on new wood; requires winter protection." [ARA18/121] "In growing 'Moonlight' as a hedge we must be careful to cut out the inferior old wood and lay in the long rods of new wood each spring." [NRS24/31]

"A delightful garden Rose of very free flowering character described as a Hybrid Tea, but some seemed to think it would have been more correctly sent out as a hybrid multiflora. It is a Rose flowering in clusters after the style of 'Trier', but paler in colour, with no pink in the buds." [NRS14/158] "Useful and reliable." [NRS20/94] "A perpetual flowering cluster Rose. Flowers, white flushed lemon, with prominent golden stamens. Sweetly scented. Habit, bushy and branching. Growth, active and vigorous, growing about four feet high [ca. 1–3 m]. Wood and foliage, dark claret red, in charming contrast to the moonlight colour of the flowers. Blooming continuously in large sprays from June to late in Autumn. The sprays when cut keeping fresh for several days." [NRS (specific ref. lost)] "Seems to me the best of Mr. Pemberton's introductions down to the present. The plant grows into a good bush or may be formed into a hedge; it has dark glossy foliage and throughout the season continually pushes up long flowering sprays, carrying very beautiful lemon white flowers, with a centre of orange stamens. The spikes are most effective if picked and the flowers allowed to open indoors, which they will continue to do for nearly a fortnight. 'Moonlight' is quite an excellent garden plant." [NRS21/48]

Moschata × Polyantha

Bernaix, 1886

"White, small, single, medium height." [Sn] Probably Bernaix's Multiflora 'Polyantha Grandiflora' of 1886. The date "1866" seen for this is a typographical or scribal error.

Nur-Mahál

trans. "The Fairy of the Palace" or "The Light of Palaces"
Pemberton, 1923
From 'Château de Clos-Vougeot' (HT) × an unnamed seedling.

"A crimson, everblooming pillar Rose. Semi-double, mildly scented blooms in clusters from May to November. This Rose has proved to be one of the most profuse and continuous bloomer among hardy pillar Roses." [C-Ps32] "Colour cramoisie; flowers medium, semi-single, produced in corymbs, large sprays; bush habit; flowers continuously; musk perfume." [NRS23/262] "Flowers continuously from June to November, every shoot carrying a truss of semi-single bright crimson flowers, carried erect, the blooms being Musk scented." [NRS25/91] "Ordinary color. Do not care for it . . . *Mass.*; The most conspicuous, pictorial, and all-round worthy of Pemberton's Musks; hardy as an oak. Hardly ever without great bouquets of cerise-pink blooms. This and 'Prosperity' [HMk] (pure white) are much better dooryard roses than anybody else has produced . . . *Pa.*; Continuous bloomer, and good for color-note as a shrub . . . *Calif.*" [ARA28/181] "A bright crimson semi-single Rose of vigorous habit, reminding one very much of *R. moyesii*. The blooms are very freely produced in clusters, on fairly stiff stems. Not liable to damage by rain. Musk scented. The habit of the plant exhibited was free and branching, the foliage not showing any trace of mildew. It will make a good bedding Rose, and apparently well able to hold its own in a wet season." [NRS23/39] "When first introduced this rose was an ordinary dwarf Musk, with rather large, ruffled flowers of a curious reddish purple. Recently it has developed a strong climbing habit, possibly a sport propagated inadvertently but not introduced as such. At any rate, while it is classed as a bedding rose in Europe, in this country it is a climber. It has a strange attraction in its rather violent color." [GAS] "A rather dwarf bush rose, which perhaps will eventually fit into the 'Gruss an Teplitz' [B] and 'Birdie Blye' [Lam] group. The flowers are produced almost continuously, in clusters, and they are similar to [those of] 'Tausendschön' [Mult] in form, though not as double, and

of a bright crimson purple. Very attractive, and we like it as a shrub." [ARA27/141]

"To meet the repeated enquiries as to the origin of this name for a Rose these brief remarks are offered. The Rose, 'Nur Mahál, on its first appearance in public under a number was named by a lady of long residence in India after an eminent lady in Indian history who lived in the 17th Century, Nurjahan the Beautiful, subsequently known as Nur Mahál, the Light of Palaces, or, as we should say in English, 'The Glory of the Home' . . . Nur Mahál from childhood was a lover of Roses. It was an Crown Princess of Persia, when in her Rose garden, that she first met her future husband, Jehangir . . . Jehangir, however, did not prove to be an ideal ruler, so Nur Mahál took in hand the reins of Government as the power behind the throne . . . As in Persia so in India, Nur Mahál had an extensive Rose garden, and doubtless sought and found both consolation of mind and invigoration of spirit, as many lovers of the Rose have since found, in her beautiful Rose garden. Her later name was given her by her devoted husband, who called her Nur Mahál, the Light of Palaces." [NRS25/188]

Nymphenburg

Kordes, 1954

"Orange salmon pink, large, lightly double, medium scent, tall." [Sn]

Pax

trans. "Peace"
Pemberton, 1918
From 'Trier' (Lam) × 'Sunburst' (Pern).

"White, large, lightly double, medium scent, moderate height." [Sn] "Buds tinged with fawn." [NRS21/196] "Pure white with golden anthers, semi-single, in large clusters, free flowering. Growth vigorous." [GeH] "Rather distinct carnation perfume, like *R. moschata*." [NRS21/106] "Shrubby Musk with rather large, almost single, pure white flowers. Free flowering in autumn." [GAS] "Semi-single flowers, 3 to 4 inches in diameter [ca. 7.5 cm to 1 dm]; white with golden anthers; buds tinted lemon; real musk fragrance. Foliage dark green, young shoots claret. Blooms produced in corymbs, on long stems." [ARA19/103] "Has creamy white flowers resembling [those of] 'Moonlight' [HMk], but slightly fuller and larger. The foliage is not quite so attractive, nor does it grow so strongly as that variety, which I prefer of the two, but it makes quite a good garden plant." [NRS21/57] "Grew well and bloomed well, but flowers are nearly single and of no especial attractiveness; scent was in no way remarkable. The bush is so susceptible to black-spot that I do not believe it is worth growing." [ARA24/84] "Quite a success. It is a large, flat, white rose of few petals, borne almost continuously until frost. The bush is tall, to 6 feet, and straggling, its longest shoots being of climbing habit. Planted beside a 'Climbing Gruss an Teplitz' [Cl B], their long branches mingle on an arch 9 feet high [ca. 3 m], making a pleasing combination." [ARA27/118] "'A new Hybrid Musk of the first order, very strongly perfumed —real musk—foliage dark green, the young shoots claret colour. The blooms are semi-single, three or four inches in diameter [ca. 7.5 cm to 1 dm]. Produced in corymbs, and carried on long stems, sometimes as many as thirty being on the one stem. The colour pure white, tinted lemon in the bud, with prominent golden anthers' . . . Continuous flowering, blooming more freely in the late autumn than midsummer. It is a pity it is not a vigorous climber, but as a big bush it

Pax *continued*

will be most effective." [NRS18/166–167] "The fine arching branches make this a most decorative trellis or fence rose." [W] Pax, alias Peace, commemorating the World War I armistice.

Pearl

Turner, 1915

"Pale pink." [Ÿ] "Whitish pink, small, single, tall." [Sn]

Penelope

Pemberton, 1924

From 'Ophelia' (HT) × an unnamed seedling.

"Shell-pink shaded saffron, borne in clusters; musk fragrance. Foliage dark green. Shrubby habit; perpetual flowering. Good in autumn." [ARA25/185] "Light violet pink, medium size, lightly double, very fragrant, tall." [Sn] "Small, ovoid buds and shell-pink flowers borne, several together, on short stems, semi-double, open form, very good lasting quality, and strong musk perfume. Leathery, resistant foliage; very vigorous growth; profuse and continuous bloom. A fine grower and very free." [ARA26/119] "A perpetual flowering cluster rose. Colour shell-pink shaded salmon. Flowers carried in corymbs. Shrub habit. Handsome dark green foliage. Wood claret colour. Good in autumn. Fragrant, musk perfume." [GeH] "Grows to about 8 feet [ca. 1.6 m]. A free-blooming Rose best treated as a pillar or spread against a fence. The pink and saffron flowers come in clusters of from 3 to 30. It makes a great show in autumn." [C-Ps34] "Glows from June to October and gets more and more beautiful as the season advances." [W] Penelope, Odysseus' patient and wily wife.

Pink Prosperity

Bentall, 1931

"Vigorous, pink-flowering form of the Musk rose 'Prosperity' [HMk]." [GAS] "Pink, medium size, full, medium fragrance, tall." [Sn] "An erect plant like a very large Polyantha." [T4]

Prosperity

Pemberton, 1919

From 'Marie-Jeanne' (Pol) × 'Perle des Jardins' (T).

"White, tinted pink in bud, rosette form, large clusters, perpetual flowering. Growth vigorous." [GeH] "White, medium size, full, medium scent, tall." [Sn] "Bushy Musk with extra-large clusters of white, rosette-like flowers, tinged with pale pink, intermittently throughout the entire season." [GAS] "It is seldom without bloom." [C-Ps32] "A perpetual flowering cluster Rose. Colour white, tinted pink in bud. Form rosette, flowers produced in extra large trusses, carried erect. Foliage dark green, waxy, not liable to mildew. Growth from three to four feet high [ca. 1–1.3 m], bushy. Cut sprays last over a week in water. Free flowering, bloom well into November." [NRS19/167] "Grows 4 to 5 feet high [ca. 1.3–1.6 m]. A joy to us all summer for it is as hardy as an oak, and the pink-tinted white flowers keep coming in fragrant clusters all the growing season." [C-Ps28] "Great clusters of small, fully-double, pink-tinted, white flowers, opening from rosetted buds, on strong stems from June to frost. Makes neat bushy pillar growth to 8 feet [ca. 1.6 m], also fine to spread out on a fence. If you want an *everblooming* white, look no further: this is a beauty. (Worthwhile, though is some seasons it will mildew somewhat.) FRAGRANT." [W] As we see, the end of World War I did indeed bring us both Peace (or at least 'Pax') and 'Prosperity'.

Queen Alexandra

syn. 'Queen Alexandra II'

Pemberton, 1915

"Pale yellow, flushed with pink, perpetual flowering, large and single, in clusters. Growth vigorous." [GeH] "Pink, white center, small, single, light scent, tall." [Sn] "Large single flowers, produced in corymbs, smooth petals, pale yellow flushed and edged with salmon pink, prominent golden stamens." [NRS15/165] "An upright grower (attaining about four or five feet [ca. 1.3–1.6 m]) and a persistent bloomer, sending up strong growths from the base, each carrying five to ten blooms. The flowers are large and *single* with smooth petals and prominent golden stamens. The colour of the petals is pale yellow flushed and edged with salmon." [NRS16/144] "Excellent for pillars, and is a perpetual flowerer. The blooms are perfectly single, reminding one of a glorified Dog-Rose; the colour is pale citron-yellow flushed with pink when young, and fading with age to white." [NRS18/139] "Trained on an iron fence, has proved so hardy that it has never been frosted even when on three occasions the thermometer has registered two or three degrees below zero Fahrenheit." [NRS14/167]

Queen Alexandra II   Listed as 'Queen Alexandra' (HMk).

Queen of the Musks

G. Paul, 1912

"Flesh white." [Ÿ] "Creamy white, with red buds. Dwarf." [NRS13/172] "Whitish pink, small, full, very fragrant, tall." [Sn] "Large bunches of creamy white flowers with pink centres, the buds rosy pink; very effective." [NRS12/208] "A continuous-blooming Musk, probably not unlike the type developed by Pemberton. The rosy white, fragrant flowers are relatively small and come in large clusters." [GAS] "Creamy white to pearl-pink, with red buds. Growth vigorous." [GeH] "Very floriferous sort of polyantha giving a profusion of pyramidal clusters of small white blossoms and pink buds. Extraordinarily floriferous bedding rose—and, what is more, it's perpetually in bloom." [JR37/57] "It is delightfully free-flowering, producing its flowers in large clusters in great profusion, sweet scented, dwarf habit of growth, and should make a beautiful bedding Rose. The colour is a pretty flesh with a pale yellow centre—one of these Roses that are always in flower, the true perpetuals." [NRS13/159]

Robin Hood

Pemberton, 1927

From an unnamed seedling × 'Edith Cavell' (Pol).

"Light red, small, single, medium to tall." [Sn] "Pink, nuanced carmine." [Ÿ] "Flower bright cherry-red, borne in large clusters. Growth vigorous (4 to 5 feet [ca. 1.3–1.6 m]); very free and continuous bloomer." [ARA28/237] "Polyantha type…Shrub habit, good for massing." [NRS27/265] Robin Hood, legendary agent of capital redistribution in Sherwood Forest.

Rosaleen

Bentall, 1933

Rarely mentioned Hybrid Musk that, as Griffiths reports, has clusters of double crimson blossoms on a large, healthy plant.

Rostock

Kordes, 1937

"Light pink, large, full, light scent, tall." [Sn]

Sammy

Pemberton, 1921

From an unnamed seedling (of 'Trier' [Lam]) × 'Gruss an Teplitz' (B).

"Red, small, lightly double, light scent, moderate height." [Sn] "Flower carmine, perpetual flowering, clusters, semi-single, produced in corymbs. Growth shrub[by], shoots from base 4 and 5 feet high [ca. 1.3–1.6 m]." [GeH] "Shrubby Musk producing clusters of almost single, bright rosy-red flowers throughout the season." [GAS] "Bud small; flower semi-single, very lasting; carmine; borne in erect cluster; fragrance slight. Foliage abundant, medium size, glossy, bronze-green. Very vigorous, bushy; profuse bloomer all season; hardy." [ARA22/153] "A perpetual flowering cluster Rose. Colour carmine. Flowers semi-single, produced in corymbs. Trusses carried erect. Foliage and wood bronze green. Almost thornless. A shrub Rose, throwing up from the base shoots four and five feet high [ca. 1.3–1.6 m]. A good autumnal, flowering well into November." [NRS21/197] "One of the best of the Hybrid Musks. In bloom from June to Christmas." [NRS29/248]

Sangerhausen

Kordes, 1938

"Luminous red." [Y] "Light red, medium size, lightly double, light scent, tall." [Sn] Sangerhausen, the great German rosarium.

Sea Spray

Pemberton, 1923

"Pink-white, small, lightly double, tall." [Sn] "Moderately vigorous Musk with clusters of dainty white and flesh-pink flowers." [GAS] "Stone-white flushed pink, distinct; large clusters of rosette flowers; foliage leathery dark green; Mildew-proof, growth very vigorous; a summer flowering Rambler." [GeH]

Skyrocket Listed as 'Wilhelm' (HMk).

Thisbe

Pemberton, 1918

From 'Marie-Jeanne' (Pol) × 'Perle des Jardins' (T).

"Chamois-yellow rosettes in clusters. Growth vigorous." [GeH] "Yellow, medium size, full, very fragrant, tall." [Sn] "Large trusses on long upright shoots. A vigorous, bushy grower; perpetual flowering." [ARA19/103] "I have tried 'Thisbe' but did not find much merit in it." [ARA27/118] "Erect growth and light green leaves … This is near to the Lambertiana group but on account of its fragrance should never be forgotten." [T4] Thisbe and Pyramus, unfortunate Babylonian lovers.

Vanity

Pemberton, 1920

From 'Château de Clos-Vougeot' (HT) × an unnamed seedling.

"Pink, medium size, lightly double, medium scent, tall." [Sn] "Rose pink, large, semi-single, free, in large clusters. Growth vigorous." [GeH] "Large, shrubby Musk, with loose sprays of single, rose-pink flowers throughout the season." [GAS] "A very pretty semi-double rose, carried on very long stems in enormous loose clusters—certainly the largest cluster rose we have. The color is a bright rose, shaded carmine at the edge of the petals, which, combined with the golden stamens, makes the blooms most elegant. The habit of growth is very vigorous. Recently I saw 'Vanity' in the raiser's garden. The large bushes, with their dark olive-green foliage, free from mildew, were very fine. Its perpetual flowering qualities, and its sweet scent, will make 'Vanity' a favorite as a specimen shrub." [ARA21/153] "Foliage and wood blue green, shaded red, fairly free of mildew. Growth very vigorous, both as a maiden and cutback. The huge trusses of bloom are carried on long stems anything up to 7 feet high [ca. 2.3 m]. A very interesting and useful shrubbery Rose." [NRS23/96] "A perpetual free-flowering cluster Rose. Colour rose pink. Flowers large, semi-single, produced in corymbs, well distributed. Trusses extra large, of distinct character. A bush Rose, throwing shoots from the base, four to seven feet high [ca. 1.3–2.3 m], all carrying sprays of flowers. Blooming well into October. Fragrant musk perfume." [NRS20/201] "A most remarkable plant." [T4] Vanity, perhaps the most delusive of the seven deadly sins.

Wilhelm

syn. 'Skyrocket'

Kordes, 1934

From 'Robin Hood' (HMk) × 'J. C. Thornton' (HT).

"Bright blood red." [Y] "Deep red, medium size, lightly double, medium fragrance, tall." [Sn] "Large trusses of as many as 75 semidouble, 2-inch [ca. 5 cm], rich-crimson flowers, black-red in the bud. Outstanding in any garden, does not fade. Abundant and continuous flowering. Glossy, dark, blue-green leaves. Grows to 7 feet [ca. 2.3 m] and is an eye-catcher. Excellent for pillar or trellis. The first time I saw it I walked the length of a long garden in the pouring rain to identify it … Sweet honey FRAGRANCE." [W] "A real everblooming Shrub Rose producing enormous flower clusters throughout the entire season. Makes a magnificent display with its large clusters composed of medium-sized brilliant red blooms. Of sturdy, upright habit which makes it most desirable planted either by itself or in combination with various kinds of shrubs. A forerunner of a distinct new race." [Way45]

Will Scarlet

G. S. Thomas/Hilling, 1950

Sport of 'Wilhelm' (HMk).

"Red, medium size, lightly double, medium fragrance, medium to tall." [Sn] "A sport which occurred on a plant of 'Wilhelm' under my care in 1947 and was introduced in 1950. It is identical to its parent in all respects except colour and scent." [T4] Will Scarlet, one of Robin Hood's coadjutors in the administration of financial redistribution.

Wind Chimes

Lester, ca. 1946

"Clusters of small, single, deep-pink flowers in the shade, lighter in full sun, followed by round orange fruits 'like little doorknobs.' In constant bloom, this is choice, with all the vigor, pest- and disease-resistance, and wonderful musky sweetness of its family … FRAGRANT." [W] "Colorful hips all winter." [W]

[Winter Cheer]

Pemberton, 1914

"Perpetual flowering cluster, semi-single crimson flowers, large upright spreading trusses. Flowering very late in autumn." [NRS15/165] "Fair growth; scattering blooms throughout season; better results if protected." [ARA18/121] "Does well everywhere … A valuable red decorative with plenty of hardiness and good foliage; no cut-flower value." [ARA28/95]

CHAPTER THIRTY

Old Hybrid Tea and Pernetiana Climbers

"The Climbing Hybrid Teas are sports, as a [*general*] rule, from dwarf Hybrid Tea varieties. They grow with varying degrees of vigor, and require the same care. The hardiness of this class varies considerably, reflecting their parentage to a large extent, and many of them will thrive on a sheltered wall much farther north than climbers of pure Tea ancestry ... Included in this class are climbing sports of the roses known as Pernetianas, distinguished by shades of yellow-orange and coppery pink foreign to the true Teas and Hybrid Teas. Some Climbing Hybrid Teas of the Pernetiana strain are much better varieties than their dwarf prototypes ... In spite of the fact that the yellow hue of Pernetiana roses is derived from the hardy *R. foetida,* the mutual antagonism of hardiness and yellowness persists in all their climbing sports, so that one may almost safely say that the yellower they are the tenderer they are. This is doubly true of those which derive part of their golden color from the old yellow Tea roses. While Climbing Hybrid Teas bare less hardy than the large-flowered Wichuraianas, and are much more subject to insect pests and diseases, their popularity is increasing in gardens farther north than might be expected. The flowers are so exquisitely beautiful and are borne in such profusion in early summer that the slight labor necessary to protect them in winter is amply rewarded ... A fault of this class is that some of the so-called climbing sports have a imperfect climbing habit and are only a little more vigorous than the original bush types. Such varieties are adapted to pillar use and for making bold displays of massed plants. Sometimes this weakness is only a failure of the individual plant and not of the variety. It has been discovered that plants propagated from short, blooming spurs of climbing sports occasionally revert to the bush type, and that buds from vigorous climbing canes must be used to insure the propagation of the climbing habit ... If a favorite Climbing Hybrid Tea does not grow properly, try a new plant. This second may reverse an unfavorable opinion." [GAS]

"There is no possible comparison between the performance of Climbing Hybrid Tea roses here [in southern California] and in the East. In my experiments with them there [in the East] we found very few which were good bloomers. They gave a mild spring burst of color and only an occasional scattering of flowers thereafter ... In California, these roses are remarkably good and have a very long blooming period. Their first display is very much like the spring bloom of Wichuraianas in the quantity of flowers." [ARA28/94]

"In planting climbers the bed should be prepared in exactly the same way as for an ordinary bed, excepting that it should be much smaller, but the roots of the climbers will naturally take up more space underground than the roots of the dwarf bushes, and climbers should have a bed of some extent. This is particularly necessary for the Hybrid Tea Climbers ... For each plant the bed should be about two feet wide [ca. 6 dm] and not less than four feet [ca. 1.3 m] in length. In planting climbers, especially the Hybrid Teas, it is hardly necessary to say that they will not do well on the north side of any arbor or wall. Roses must have the sun in order to flourish and, besides, many climbers on a north wall would be winter killed to a very great degree" [Th]

"It is not generally realized what beauty can be created with the climbing rose. The rapid, flexible growth, their generally excellent foliage and their superb display of blooms make them applicable to an almost unlimited variety of uses. They may be trained to cover walls; as hedges; as a ground cover on sloping banks; for shrubbery purposes; and in many other decorative ways. There are infinite different and fanciful ways of training the climbers on numerous styles of arches, fences and trellises to delight the imagination of even the most unimaginative.

"In planning the size of the trellis or arch, some thought must be given to the location of it and its harmonious relation to the buildings. A very satisfactory arch to span a garden walk three feet wide [ca. 1 m] can be made from three-quarter-inch pipe [ca. 2 cm]. Two pieces twenty-five feet long [ca. 8.3 m] are required. These are bent to form the arch and five bars of one-half inch pipe [ca. 1.2 cm] are used to join them. These bars may be any length according to the width of arch desired. Eighteen inches [ca. 4.5 dm] is suggested for making an arch of very pleasing proportions. The base of the arch is imbedded one and one-half feet deep [ca. 4.5 dm] in concrete. A wire of any desired mesh can be used to place across the top and sides. When completed the height will be about nine feet [ca. 3 m]. A pleasing arch for a screen can be made by having a single pipe bent in the arch shape, and set in concrete. Wire, such as commonly used for tennis courts[,] may be used to draw across the surface. This is very attractive. However if one does not wish to spend the time and extra cost of using such material, a coarser mesh wire could be used to very good advantage. The length of pipe needed will vary according to the size of screen desired. Five feet [ca. 1.6 m] is a good height for a fence used mainly for display purpose, for when the roses bloom they are within the line of vision, and within the reach of the average person. For a fence of this kind[,] two-and-one-half inch pipe [ca. 6 cm] seven feet long [ca. 2.3 m] should be used for the end posts and braces. These are imbedded two feet [ca. 6 dm] in concrete. For the line posts one and one-quarter inch pipe [ca. 3 cm] six feet long [ca. 2 m] will be needed. These need to be imbedded only one feet [ca. 3 dm] as the strain of the wire is mainly on the end posts. Smooth twisted wire about number ten gauge is stretched along these posts.

"In choosing a climbing rose some thought must be given to the characteristics of the plant in connection with the place in which it is to be used. That is, if one desires a plant for a small trellis from about eight to ten feet high [ca. 2.6–3.3 m], a Pillar Rose, for example[,] would be more satisfactory than a climber such as 'Belle of Portugal' [*i.e.*, 'Belle Portugaise', for which see p. 205 of *The Old Rose Advisor*] which is a rampant grower and would keep one endlessly cutting it back. When the rose is first planted, if in a dormant condition, cut down to about twelve inches [ca. 3 dm] from the ground. As the eyes break from these dormant canes choose those which show promise of strong growth, and which are most suitable, that is, pointing towards the desired direction, and rub or cut off all others. As the new canes are thrown up they should be trained in the way they are to follow. If for instance the canes are to run along a fence with four wires, and the bush is planted at the post, eight good canes should be trained, one on each wire running in both directions. The laterals which break from these canes on the second year will tend to grow upwards as the upper side will get the most sun. These laterals and sublaterals provide the flower and foliage to cover the space. An attractive way of training the canes on a narrow arch or trellis is to zig-zag from one side to the other. This criss-cross effect enables the laterals to break and shoot upwards, thus supplying density of foliage and greater profusion of blooms on the lower part of the support. This method requires constant attention to train and tie the canes in place when they reach the proper size for bending. The material we find most suitable for typing is raffia. One advantage in its use is that while it will hold the stem securely in place it rots in time and breaks away, thus preventing it from binding or cutting into the canes as most strings will do. In tying the canes we find a very convenient way is to tie the raffia first, in a slip knot, to the part of the trellis or fence where we wish to train the shoot. Then bring the raffia around the shoot and tie in a square knot.

"Pruning should be done when the plant is in its most dormant state, in Southern California, usually in the early part of January. The most convenient method we find is to cut the plant loose from the fence or trellis, so as to make it easy to handle. The best of the new canes of the current year should be saved for bloom in following years. The poorest of the old canes should be cut out to give room for this new growth. One should know, of course, before pruning, whether the plant put forth its best blooms on its first, second or third years' wood. Captain Thomas' 'Bloomfield Perfection' [HMk], for example, starts putting forth its blooms on the first year's growth. Therefore it is well to leave plenty of the new wood, though a good supply of second and third year's canes should also be left. When pruning a climber which puts forth its best blooms on the second or third year, one would naturally have to leave more of the older canes, for it one were to cut off all the second and third year's growth, the plant would never bloom. The density of foliage desired will determine to some extent the amount of canes to leave. Enough foliage should be left at all times to provide sufficient shade so the canes will not become sunburned. Too much sun will stop the flow of sap and seriously interfere with the growth of the plant. In pruning cut about one-eighth of an inch [ca. 3 mm] above the eye. The cut should slope in an angle slightly higher on the side on which the eye is located. The knife or shears should be sharp enough to insure a good clean cut, otherwise there may be danger of splitting or bruising the end, thus damaging the plant. All large cuts should be covered with a good pruning wax to stop the flow of sap. This practice will also help overcome die-back so often afflicting the popular Austrian Briar (Pernetiana). In this case cut at least one inch below the dead stem [ca. 2.5 cm] and apply the wax. When pruning is completed the remaining canes should be tied firmly back just where they are wanted.

"There are types of climbers which will, when given the proper care in pruning and training, produce blooms of excellent cutting value. Some of Captain Thomas' latest introductions are splendid for this purpose." [CaRoll/1/2–3]

"I think in a small garden one or two Climbing Roses will probably give more satisfaction than a number of Dwarf Roses, for they will get more air and sun. A Rose plant costs far, far less than its potential value, and therefore is worth some expenditure of work and material. In planting a Climbing Rose, just think how you may be creating a picture and a memory that will remain in someone's mind for life." [NRS28/67]

We should add a few notes to address some of the peculiarities with which this group presents us. It has become fairly customary in rose books to list climbing sports alphabetically under the name of the rose from which they sported, with the "Climbing" portion of the cultivar's name added after a comma—for instance, the cultivar correctly called 'Climbing Monsieur Paul Lédé' will be listed below as 'Monsieur Paul Lédé, Climbing'. All foreign equivalents of "Climbing," such as "Rankende" and "Grimpant," will appear as "Climbing." Entries on the climbing sports of Hybrid Teas introduced before 1900 (such as 'Climbing Captain Christy') will be found in *The Old Rose Advisor*. Occasionally, a cultivar will have sported another climbing sport at a separate location; and, theoretically, these different climbing sports could differ in other details such as vigor or floriferousness. When we know of a sport which has re-occurred thus, we list the attribution of the earliest sport in the usual way, with the attribution and date of the *subsequent* sport on the same line as (using 'Climbing H. Vessey Machin' as our example): "(also: Howard & Smith, 1922)". It is not impossible that in any of these cases the later sport predominates in commerce; to attempt to distinguish such different sportings would provide the dedicated but projectless researcher with a challenging way of improving his weary hours.

Allan Chandler

syn. 'Allen Chandler'
Chandler/G. Prince, 1924
From 'Hugh Dickson' (HP) × unnamed cultivar

"Cherry-red, single flower. Very lasting and slightly fragrant." [C-Ps31] "Blooms of vivid scarlet, of the same size as [those of] 'K. of K.' [HT]. It is very free-flowering the whole season, and I can highly commend this as a pillar rose." [ARA27/209] "Red, large, lightly double, light scent, tall." [Sn] "Strong growing, frequent bloom. Blooms in threes and fours, semi-double, bright scarlet." [Ck] "Flower vivid scarlet and of fine size. Growth vigorous." [GeH] "Effective Hybrid Tea of pillar habit, with large, semi-double, fragrant flowers of brilliant scarlet-crimson." [GAS] "The large blooms are ... not liable to damage by rain." [NRS24/113] "Crimson. A wonderful show during its first blooming period in June, and produces some fine blooms later. Leathery, glossy, disease-resistant foliage." [C-Ps34] "Bud medium-size, long-pointed, very dark red; flower large, single and semi-single, very lasting; brilliant crimson; long stem; slight fragrance. Foliage abundant, disease-resistant. Profuse and continuous bloomer. Hardy." [ARA24/168] "A strong-growing, semi-single rose of great merit. The large, delightfully fragrant, blooms are a vivid scarlet color, and are carried in clusters of three or four. The growth is very vigorous, and the plants I have seen were entirely free of mildew. A fine perpetual-flowering pillar rose, and one of the greatest acquisitions of recent years." [ARA24/164–165]

"What a lovely sight 'Allan Chandler' is, with his vivid scarlet single blooms produced both early and late. It is suitable for growing as a big bush, or pillar. I have a bed of 'Penelope' [HMk] overtopped by specimens of 'Allan Chandler', and the effect is very pleasing." [NRS29/192] "This is a fine plant and a real acquisition to the garden. The colour is a bright scarlet crimson; some call it scarlet, but that colour to me suggests the red geranium, or sealing wax, or the soldier's uniform, and it has nothing of this sort; and however it should be qualified, the Rose is certainly some shade of crimson. The colour lasts well, for a Rose of this colouring wonderfully well; it does not 'go blue', and will stand rain and sun. The habit of the plant is very vigorous, but not that of a climber. It will send up fine shoots of 5 or 6 feet in length [ca. 1.6–2 m]. It is admirable for pegging down in a large bed, or for a low wall, and might possibly make a big bush; but I have not yet seen it grown into a large shrub in the way 'Gruss an Teplitz' [B] can be grown, or 'Mrs. Wemyss Quin' [HT]. It begins to flower early, about the middle of June, or even a few days before this ... I hardly think we can call it continuous; one can usually find a flower or two on the plants, but by no means always. It flowers in autumn very well. The flower is single, or nearly so, and has fine large and stout petals, which are moderately fragrant. On the plant the flowers last well; several are borne in the head or bunch, and succeed one another; hence it forms a conspicuous object in the garden. It is highly decorative, and noticeable a long way from the plant; but the effect is of a number of single flowers. One never gets a display such as 'Paul's Scarlet Climber' [W] can give; the individual flowers, however, are more imposing than those of that Rose. I class it in my own mind rather with Roses of the type of 'François Crousse' [Cl T], or 'Sarah Bernhardt' [Cl HT]. Its growths are not long enough, I should suppose, for it to make a good arch Rose ... However it may best be applied there is no doubt that it makes a fine effect of colour. Its foliage is good and gives no trouble to keep free from disease, and I think few will regret introducing it into their garden." [NRS30/65–66]

Allen Chandler   Listed as 'Allan Chandler' (HT Cl).

Angelus, Climbing

Dixie, 1933
Sport of 'Angelus' (HT).

"White, large, full, medium scent, tall." [Sn]

Apotheker George Höfer, Climbing

M. Vogel, 1941
Sport of 'Apotheker Georg Höfer' (HT).

"Red, very large, full, very fragrant, tall." [Sn]

Ards Pillar

A. Dickson, 1902

"Velvety crimson." [Ÿ] "Good, full crimson flowers." [F-M4] "Hybrid Tea with large, velvety crimson, semi-double flowers." [GAS] "Of cupped form." [GeH] "Red, large, full, tall." [Sn] "Velvety crimson, semi-climbing." [JR32/139] "Flowers large, full, cupped, rich velvety crimson; vigorous growth; a fine pillar rose." [W/Hn] The Ards Peninsula, Ireland, where the A. Dickson nurseries were located.

Black Boy

A. Clark, 1919
From 'Étoile de France' (HT) × 'Bardou Job' (B).

"The blackest scarlet I have ever seen in a rose, and its great flowers will attract any observer." [CaRol/6/6] "Dark red satin petals shaded with black velvet." [ARA32/120] "Enormous blooms of scarlet overlaid with blackish shades, and very fragrant, lost but a few inches of its 12-foot canes [ca. 4 m] last Winter." [CaRol/6/6] "Reminiscent of 'Bardou Job' [B], but even darker in color, semi-double." [Ck] "Deep red, very large, full, medium scent, tall." [Sn] "Crimson, shaded with dark maroon. Vigorous climber, good foliage." [Au] "Semi-double." [Th2] "Deep crimson, shaded with blackish maroon, overlaying scarlet ... good mildew-proof foliage and fine climbing habit ... opens quickly, retains its rich color." [TS] "Without a peer ... in formation of flower, richness of color, and freedom of bloom." [PP28] "Excellent growth the first season, giving a few superb, dark red flowers, which blackened agreeably instead of fading." [ARA27/129] "Lustrous, mildew-free leaves." [ARA23/119] "Highly resistant to mildew and an intermittent bloomer until midsummer but sparingly thereafter." [ARA35/171] "15 ft tall [ca. 5 m] in a season." [ARA31/186] "Dark crimson blooms of medium size. A vigorous climber which comes into bloom early. It makes a fine splash of color." [ARA30/153] "In Australia this variety has achieved a wonderful popularity. In colour it is a deep velvety crimson, shaded blackish maroon, the reverse sides of the petals being somewhat lighter, just the colour we used to get in some of the old H.P.'s. It possesses a distinct but not overpowering fragrance. The bud is well shaped, and in this stage it makes a good buttonhole Rose. The blooms however open quickly, but even then they retain their good colour, which is blacker than any other Rose I know; a very vigorous and good climbing variety, quickly covering a large space of wall or fence." [NRS26/141] Not to be confused with the Moss of the same name.

Bloomfield Dawn Listed as a Climbing HT.

Bloomfield Improvement Listed as 'Ednah Thomas' (Cl HT).

Capitaine Soupa, Climbing
Vogel, 1938
Sport of 'Capitaine Soupa' (HT).
  "Rose-red, large, full, tall." [Sn]

Captain Thomas
Capt. Thomas/Armstrong Nurseries, 1938
From 'Bloomfield Completeness' (HMk) × 'Attraction' (HT).
  "Single yellow, fragrant." [W] "Being in Los Angeles about the first of April, I started for Beverly Hills, armed with a letter of introduction from our Editor, to look up Capt. George C. Thomas. After considerable climbing, I finally reached the top of his particular hill. His home is situated upon a crest from which the ground slopes two ways, on the one side rather abruptly . . . Leading to the top of the hill, are Captain Thomas' display roses, made up of the better-known varieties and some of his own productions. This part of the garden was well matured, and at the time I saw it, simply wonderful . . . Captain Thomas has constructed a cactus rock-garden, wherein he has a most complete and interesting assortment of those curious plants of California and the desert region. Distributed throughout the garden were specimen rose plants found in Arizona and his own state. Many of these have histories going back thirty or more years. Some of them looked like quince trees, with main stems 3 inches through [ca. 7.5 cm] . . . I must mention one Hybrid Tea as being the most beautiful flower I have ever seen. It was a 'Padre' [HT], and it was beyond description. Anyone who could see it would be almost ready to bow down and worship the California climate! Captain Thomas was a gracious host, and is a wonderful inspiration to the amateur. He is a hard-working, aggressive man in the prime of life, and we are going to hear more of him. His whole enthusiasm is with the amateur grower and against the kind of commercial men who advertise all roses as hardy in every location and each as the best in the world . . . The Captain has many plans for the future beautification of the estate, and lucky is he who will see it when his preparations are consummated." [ARA26/144–145] "SUDDEN DEATH OF CAPTAIN GEORGE C. THOMAS, JR. News of this sad event, which occurred Tuesday, February 28, 1932, in Beverly Hills, Calif., arrives as the last forms of the Annual are on press. A fitting appreciation of this great rosarian and generous friend will appear." [ARA32/210] "Funeral services for George C. Thomas, Jr., noted author and clubman, who died from a heart attack last Tuesday at the family residence . . . will be conducted at 11 a.m. tomorrow at All Saints' Church, Camden Drive and Santa Monica Boulevard . . . Later the body will be sent by Bresee Brothers to Philadelphia, to be laid beside the remains of the late Mr. and Mrs. George Clifford Thomas, the parents of Mr. Thomas. Mr. Thomas was born in Philadelphia. He became interested in social upbuilding, his father having been a noted churchman, philanthropist and banker. He was especially interested in horticulture and botany and when, eleven years ago, he came with his family to Beverly Hills, he continued his horticultural experiments which already have made him one of the foremost rosarians of America. In addition to his well-known works on rose culture, Mr. Thomas also was known for his books on golf and fishing. He was a prominent member of the California Club, the Los Angeles Country Club and the Tuna Club. An authority on golf and golf courses, Mr. Thomas was architect of many of the country's finest courses, including the Los Angeles municipal courses, the north course at Los Angeles Country Club and courses at Bel-Air, Ojai and other places. Mr. Thomas was a captain in the American Expeditionary Forces and commanded the first American bombing squadron to see active service in France. Deeply interested in the religious and social life of his community, Mr. Thomas was a leader in the building and furnishing of All Saints' Church, the organ in that church having been brought from the old Thomas home at Philadelphia. Besides his widow, Mr. Thomas leaves his son, George Thomas III, and his daughter, Mrs. Paul Gardner." [LATimes 2/25/32: Pt 2, p. 7]
  "Captain George C. Thomas, Jr. October 3, 1873–February 23, 1932. Tributes to a Great American Rosarian. It was the late Dr. Robert Huey, a sincere and famous rose amateur, of Philadelphia, who, by precept and example, interested George C. Thomas, Jr., in the rose about the year 1900, and later connected him with the American Rose Society. This was many years before his enthusiasm for aviation began, which later took him to France with the A.E.F., in which he became a Captain. When Captain Thomas became interested in anything, his interest was direct and dynamic. He read, studied, planted, tested, wrote. The appearance of his *Practical Book of Outdoor Rose-Growing,* dedicated to Dr. Huey in 1914, a superb book which ran into five editions by 1920, gave America its first comprehensive and serious book on rose-growing since the original publication in 1882 of *The Rose* by H. B. Ellwanger. For a whole generation, American rose-readers had had to be satisfied with numerous English publications, many of them unadapted to American conditions, although excellent in themselves, until Captain Thomas produced his monumental work . . . About 1912, Captain Thomas began to breed roses, and with a very definite ideal. He wanted to produce a satisfactory hardy everblooming climber, and he wanted better garden roses. No thought of profit for himself clouded his endeavor; on the contrary, almost at once, he provided that any gains from the sale of his roses should be turned over to the American Rose Society, the research fund of which profited materially from his wise generosity . . . Mr. John A. Armstrong of Ontario, Calif., knew Captain Thomas well, and assisted him materially in the difficult business of launching some of his new roses into world commerce. It is a pleasure to quote Mr. Armstrong's words, because they throw light on the careful and meticulous way in which the Captain conducted his negotiations with the nurserymen who propagated his varieties. That the Captain was always scrupulously fair was acknowledged by everyone, but there is no doubt that his rigid insistence upon points which

Captain Thomas *continued*

he considered important made him difficult to deal with at times: 'Because of our mutual interest in roses, I enjoyed many hours with Captain Thomas in his Beverly Hills rose-garden, observing his many seedlings and talking about roses. It was always a pleasure and an education for me because Captain Thomas knew roses thoroughly. He was very thorough in his hybridizing work and had definite purposes in mind, such as hardiness and adaptability to all climatic conditions, characteristics which are sometimes overlooked by hybridizers who adopt more spectacular methods. In all of Captain Thomas' business arrangements in connection with roses he was always very fair, and extremely punctilious in carrying out his part of the agreement. At the same time he insisted on the other parties to the arrangements being fair to him. Anyone who came in contact with Captain Thomas was always impressed by the enormous energy that he put into anything that he did, and he put and endless amount of thought and energy into roses ...'" [ARA33/107–110] "As I walked through the beauties of this place [Thomas' estate] and sat in a chair commanding a view of the gardens and the mountains in the background, an unforgettable impression was made upon my mind, and I could not help but think that here with my Creator I could be wholly, solely myself." [ARA26/145]

Chastity
F. Cant, 1924

"White, sometimes faint yellow shading base of petals; bright orange anthers, moderate size, perfectly formed, high pointed centre. Beautiful scent. Very early flowering." [GeH] "The elegant buds, of a clear primrose white, appealed to me." [NRS24/216] "Snowy white, semi-double, and star shaped. Very lovely and one of the very few really good white climbers." [GAS] "Larger than 'Purity' [W]." [ARA28/150] "White, yellow center, medium size, full, medium scent, tall." [Sn] "Flower pure white, well-formed, mid-sized, long-lasting. Plant strongly climbing, early blooming, in clusters of 5–10. Recommended newcomer." [Ck] "This is a pillar rose, somewhat after the type of 'Mme. Alfred Carrière' [N]. The scented blooms, which are about 3 inches in diameter [ca. 7.5 cm], are somewhat thin and open quite flat. They are produced in clusters of five or six and are not liable to damage by rain. The foliage and wood are a light green; quite free from mildew. A good acquisition." [ARA23/146] "A magnificent white pillar rose, but its great fault is a disposition toward mildew." [ARA27/209] "Yellowish white. This is a useful addition to the Pillar Roses. Clusters of well-formed medium size double blooms are produced early in the Summer. The only two faults seem to be that the blooms are inclined to mildew, and its flowering season is not as long as most." [NRS28/50] "The predominating colour of this magnificent Seedling is white . . . , with sometimes a faint yellow shading at the base of the petals in dull weather to which the bright orange anthers of the expanded flower lend a tone of the most picturesque harmony. The flowers are of moderate size, substantially and perfectly formed, with an unusually high pointed helix centre, and are carried erect in elegant trusses of from five to ten blooms. When disbudded, the individual flowers are not infrequently quite up to the standard required of exhibition Roses . . . Its habit of growth is vigorous . . . It has a most beautiful scent, and is the earliest of all white Roses to bloom." [NRS24/238] "Bud medium size, long-pointed; flower medium size, double, high center, very lasting, fragrant pure white shad-

ing to lemon at base, borne several together on medium-length stem. Foliage sufficient, medium size, light green, glossy. Few thorns. Vigorous grower, climbing, dwarf habit, blooms freely from May to July. Very hardy." [ARA25/183] Chastity, curious in being a virtue generally desired in anyone but one's self.

Château de Clos-Vougeot, Climbing
Morse, 1920
Sport of 'Château de Clos-Vougeot' (HT).

"Superb, everblooming, blackish red rose, turning darker with age . . . Fine growth (8 feet [ca. 2.6 m]) . . . holds foliage better than dwarf." [PP28] "Bloom full, roundish in form, most beautiful when fully developed, then long-lasting, deep red, quite our darkest rose. Leaves beautiful and healthy." [Ck] "Bud very large; flower very large, full, open form, very double, borne singly and together on long stems; very lasting; strong fragrance . . . Foliage abundant, medium size, leathery, rich green; disease resistant. Very vigorous and free blooming, producing its blooms from June to September. Very hardy." [ARA20/126] "Though a shy bloomer, is well worth growing." [ARA18/79] "Foliage is lost early." [Th2] "Growth usually poor . . . distinct. Valuable." [Capt28] "A light coloured wall covered with this almost black climber will be a glorious picture. It makes vigorous growths, and very few plants revert back, although if pruned hard the first year they refuse to produce climbing growths." [NRS22/159]

Christine, Climbing
Willink, 1936
Sport of 'Christine' (Pern).

"Deep yellow, small, lightly double, light scent, tall." [Sn]

Climbing Cracker   Listed as 'Cracker' (Cl HT).

Colcestria
B. R. Cant, 1916

"Satin pink." [Cw] "Flower satin rose in the centre, shading off to silver-pink in the outer petals, which are beautifully reflexed, large and full, possessing a most delightful perfume. Growth strong, climbing, with good stout foliage of a light green shade, and retained well in winter." [GeH] "Pink, large, full, very fragrant, tall." [Sn] "Strong Pillar in habit of growth . . . Very free in flowering when established." [NRS/17] "Hardly free enough." [NRS21/34] "A strangely neglected rose." [T4]

Columbia, Climbing
Totty, 1920 (also: E. G. Hill, 1920; Vestal, 1923; and Lens, 1929)
Sport of 'Columbia' (HT).

"Pink changing to brighter pink." [Ÿ] "Rose-red, very large, very full, very fragrant, tall." [Sn] "Bud very large, long-pointed; flower very large, double, full, very lasting; same color as [that of] 'Columbia'; moderate fragrance. Foliage disease-resistant. Very vigorous climber; profuse bloomer from April to November." [ARA24/174] "A poor bloomer. —*Oklahoma City, Okla.*" [ARA26/113] "Best in cool dampness. One of the best of the pink Hybrid Tea climbers, with the fault of discoloration in heat, but fine growth and foliage, long stems and lovely perfume; not a prolific bloomer, yet always furnishes fine blooms for cutting." [Capt28] "As large as the original. Plant very strong climbing, healthy, hardy." [Ck] "A well-defined climbing sport." [ARA31/240] "We had, last year [*1920, at E. G. Hill's*], a sport of 'Columbia' that ran up eight to ten feet [ca. 2.8–3.3 m]." [ARA22/132]

Comte F. de Chavagnac
Ch. Siret-Pernet, 1929
From 'Antoine Rivoire' (HT) × 'Zéphirine Drouhin' (B).

"Orange pink, medium size, full, tall." [Sn] "Flower peach-blossom-pink with rosy carmine center, borne on long, strong them. Foliage beautiful clear green. Thornless. Growth very vigorous, climbing." [ARA31/235] "Healthy foliage, light green, growth 6 [on a scale of 10]." [Jg]

Comtesse Vandal, Climbing
Jackson & Perkins, 1936
Sport of 'Comtesse Vandal' (Pern).

"Bright crimson, interior chamois." [Ÿ] "Salmon pink, very large, full, medium scent, tall." [Sn]

Condesa de Sástago, Climbing
Vestal, 1936
Sport of 'Condesa de Sastago' (Pern).

"Oriental red and yellow." [Ÿ] "Red and yellow, large, full, medium scent, tall." [Sn]

Countess of Stradbroke
A. Clark, 1928
Seedling of 'Walter C. Clark' (HT).

"Fine dark red color that holds well on the plant without bluing and is scented." [ARA30/146] "Unquestionably the most richly colored and most perfectly shaped Hybrid Tea. The blooms have magnificent form and depth of color, opening slowly from great blackish crimson buds to fully double velvety red flowers of rich and satisfying fragrance. A sparse but steady bloomer over a long period." [GAS] "Deep red, large, full, medium scent, tall." [Sn] "Pillar. Crimson." [C-Pf34] "A very rich red ... with wonderful fragrance and strong climbing growth." [ARA27/155]

Cracker
syn. 'Climbing Cracker'
A. Clark, 1927
Of *Rosa gigantea* heritage.

"Red with white, large, single, very fragrant, tall." [Sn] "A vigorous pillar Rose, also good as a bush. The flowers are single, about three inches across [ca. 7.5 cm], of a striking red shade with a distinct white zone, and handsome golden stamens help to make a very attractive variety. The flowers possess a faint sweetbriar fragrance; the foliage is abundant and mildew proof." [NRS26/142]

Crimson Conquest
Chaplin, 1931
Sport of 'Red-Letter Day' (HT).

"Red, medium size, single, medium scent, tall." [Sn] "A vigorous climbing sport ... bearing huge sprays of semi-double, scarlet flowers." [GAS]

Cupid
B. R. Cant, 1915
"Buff-pink single." [NRS29/192] "Blush-colour." [OM] "The flowers are produced in clusters, and are of a flesh-pink colour on pale primrose yellow." [NRS18/139] "Light orange-pink, large, single, tall." [Sn] "A Hybrid Tea with large, glowing flesh-colored blooms. A pillar rose of good habit." [GAS] "Flower pale peach flesh, large, single, in clusters.

Growth very vigorous; light green foliage, very large; summer." [GeH] "A pillar rose of strong growth ... of good habit and abundant foliage. The flowers are single, four to five inches across [ca. 1–1.25 dm], sometimes larger, and the colour in the half-developed stage is a glowing flesh, with a touch of peach, softening to delicate flesh and opal when fully expanded. In the Autumn it produces pretty rose-coloured seed pods." [NRS15/177] "A fine pillar Rose of good habit with fine foliage, freely producing clusters of large *single* blooms, which are four to five inches in diameter [ca. 1–1.25 dm], with very fine stamens. The colour is soft glowing flesh, softening to more delicate shades as the flowers expand." [NRS16/143] "A large-petalled single flowered Rose of pale blush colour—a lovely thing when well shown. Like most singles it seems best picked and opened indoors. I confess I have not quite discovered the best way to grow this plant. I tried it first as a climber, then as a pillar Rose, but though a strong grower its shoots are not long enough for either purpose, and I must now try it as a bush." [NRS21/52–53] "Undoubted 'Lyon[-Rose]' [Pern] blood in it." [NRS21/130] Cupid, troublesome young marksman with bow and arrow.

Dame Edith Helen, Climbing
Howard & Smith, 1930
Sport of 'Dame Edith Helen' (HT).

"Dark pink, very large, very full, very fragrant, tall." [Sn] "10-foot canes [ca. 3.3 m]." [ARA31/227] "While the other varieties go on blooming and one keeps wondering if they *are* going to climb, she has started with one single cane which is now nine feet tall [ca. 3 m]. There can be no doubt about her intentions." [CaRoIII/6/4]

Daydream
A. Clark, 1925
"Dainty shades of sunrise pink." [CaRoI/6/6] "Early. Blush-pink. An exquisite Climber from Australia, with 3-inch [ca. 7.5 cm], semi-double flowers of blush-pink, shading to a white center—a beautiful flower which lasts well. Moderate growth; makes a splendid pillar." [C-Pf33] "Good foliage and vigor, with semi-double flowers resembling large water-lilies of blush-pink shading. Quite distinct. Lasts well when cut. Makes large bush or pillar." [ARA26/188] "Probably a Hybrid Perpetual. Flowers large, ruffled, semi-double, light blush-pink at the edges, blending to pale yellow and white at the center. A profuse bloomer over a long season, and one of the finest modern climbers. Hardy for its class." [GAS]

Dr. J. H. Nicolas
Nicolas/Jackson & Perkins, 1940
"Deep pink, large, full, medium scent, tall." [Sn] "'Age cannot wither, nor custom stale' this superb rose-pink climber of dependable recurrent bloom. Very double, 5- to 6-inch [ca. 1.25–1.5 dm] flowers in clusters of 3 or 4, of old-fashioned Hybrid Perpetual form—sumptuous! This rose is a fine producer, even first-year plants do well if you cut blossoms with stems only to first true leaf. Dark leathery foliage and vigorous, but rather slow, pillar growth to 8 feet [ca. 2.6 m], nice for a front-door trellis. Very FRAGRANT. Tops with me!" [W]

[Ednah Thomas]
syn. 'Bloomfield Improvement'
Capt. Thomas/Howard & Smith, 1931
From a seedling × 'Bloomfield Progress' (HT).

"Large, double, rich salmon-rose, exhibition-quality blooms, sev-

[EdnahThomas] *continued*

eral in a cluster on long, strong stems. Recurrent bloom. Reaches 12 feet [ca. 4 m], and, if killed to ground, will grow up again vigorously. Hardiness depends on rootstock. 'Texas Wax' probably better than multiflora for this one. Semihardy in Philadelphia area. Marvelous FRAGRANCE." [W] "Flower large, double, fragrant, crimson-scarlet with considerable orange in its color, borne on strong stem. Foliage holds well. Growth vigorous, climbing; continuous bloomer." [ARA31/227] Ednah Thomas, Mrs. Paul Gardner, proud daughter of Capt. Thomas who favored us with the pleasure of her charming conversation one morning.

Effective

Hobbies, 1913

From an unnamed seedling (which was itself a seedling of 'General MacArthur' [HT]) × 'Paul's Carmine Pillar' (Mult).

"Brilliant scarlet red." [Ÿ] "Red, large, full, very fragrant, tall." [Sn] "This is a worthy companion to 'Pink Pearl' [W] with which it shares the wonderful trait of continuous bloom. We hope to have found [in this] the best autumnal climber …From 'General MacArthur' it takes its very pretty color, and from '[Paul's] Carmine Pillar' it obtained early bloom and climbing growth. The long buds are very fetching." [JR37/26]

Elvira Aramayo, Climbing

Ingegnoli, 1933

Sport of 'Elvira Aramayo' (Pern).

"Copper-orange red, medium size, lightly double, medium scent, tall." [Sn]

England's Glory

syn. 'Gloire d'Angleterre'

Wood/W. Paul, 1902

From a seedling (of 'Gloire de Dijon' [N]) × 'Mrs. W. J. Grant' (HT).

"Flesh-pink Hybrid Tea with rosy center." [GAS] "Towards the perimeter, they are a coppery yellow which is darker than that of 'Gloire de Dijon', with a delicate satiny pink color within; the roses are furthermore deliciously scented." [JR26/150] "Whitish pink, large, full, tall." [Sn] "Glossy foliage. Blossom well formed, beautiful pure pink." [Ck] "Flowers large, full, and well formed. The petals, larger than those of 'Gloire de Dijon', are, in the outer rows, flesh, and satiny pink in the center of the blossom. The growth is hardy and the plant erect. The breeder of this new variety was for a long time manager of the rose-nurseries at Henry Bennett's." [JR26/86]

Étoile de Hollande, Climbing

Leenders, 1931

Sport of 'Étoile de Hollande' (HT).

"Crimson red." [Ÿ] "Red, large, full, very fragrant, tall." [Sn] "During the spring blooming period the flowers completely cover the plant, with some recurrence on old wood." [ARA36/178] "Bright red, double …very large, cupped …Color is quite sun-resistant. Recurrent …soft foliage …to 8 feet [ca. 2.6 m] …Beautiful buds …Marvelous old-rose fragrance." [W] "One of the finest red climbers …Large blooms all season." [ARA37/213]

Florence Haswell Veitch

W. Paul, 1911

From 'Mme. Emile Metz' (extinct HT, Soupert & Notting, 1893, blush;

parentage: 'Mme. de Loeben-Sels' [HT] × 'La Tulipe' [T]) × 'Victor Hugo' (HP).

"One of the best rich crimsons." [NRS20/69] "Deep red, medium size, very full, medium scent, tall." [Sn] "Rich blackish crimson colour. It is not a fast grower, but with a little patience one is rewarded with a fine plant that yields its blossoms until quite late in the year." [NRS22/162] "Very free. Fragrant." [Cat12] "Blossom bright scarlet, shaded black, large, moderately full, perfect form, stiff petals. Bush very vigorous, nearly climbing. Wonderful scent, continuous bloom; excellent as a large bush, or for clothing walls of medium height." [JR35/101] "Many of the qualities of 'Sarah Bernhardt' [Cl HT], but it is a far better shaped flower, and seems to me most promising." [NRS14/63–64]

Frau Ida Münch

Beschnidt/Münch & Haufe, 1919

From 'Frau Karl Druschki' (HP) × 'Billard et Barré' (N).

"Light yellow, large, full, medium scent, tall." [Sn] "Buds long-pointed; flower perfectly formed, with high center, very lasting, light golden yellow, deeper in center, borne on long stems. Vigorous; bushy." [ARA21/163]

Gartendirektor Julius Schütze

Kiese, 1920

From 'Mme. Jules Gravereaux' (HT) × 'Pharisaër' (HT).

"Violet pink, large, full, medium scent, tall." [Sn] "Flower pale rosy pink and peach blossom, large, of fine form, carried on long and rigid stalks. Growth vigorous." [GeH]

General MacArthur, Climbing

H. Dickson, 1923

Sport of 'General MacArthur' (HT).

"Deep velvety crimson." [Ÿ] "Rose red, large, lightly double, very fragrant, tall." [Sn] "Orange-crimson; perfume; not a fine cut flower, but nevertheless worthwhile; nearly continuous." [CaRoll/4/2] "Quite longly climbing. Blossom bright blood red. Strongly scented." [Ck] "Seems to come a better colour in stiff red soil." [NRS28/66] "About 5 feet high [ca. 1.6 m] the first year." [ARA25/183] "Suitable for all purposes where Climbing Roses are required; will climb more quickly if shoots are tied in. Period of blooming is from middle of June until late Autumn." [NRS28/71] "Best near coast. Wonderful as a decorative rose; continuous bloomer, and fine in every way, though fails somewhat in cutting value." [Capt28] "The best tender climber of its color." [PP28]

General-Superior Arnold Janssen, Climbing

Böhm, 1931

Sport of 'General-Superior Arnold Janssen' (HT).

"Deep rose-red, large, full, moderate scent, tall." [Sn]

Gloire d'Angleterre   Listed as 'England's Glory' (Cl HT).

Gloire de Hollande, Climbing

trans. "Climbing Glory of Holland"

Breeder unknown, date uncertain

Sport of 'Gloire de Hollande' (HT).

"Deep red, large, full, medium scent, tall." [Sn]

Gruss an Aachen, Climbing

trans. "Climbing Greetings to Aachen"

Vogel/Kordes, 1937

Sport of 'Gruss an Aachen' (HT).

"Ivory-white…enriched with apricot pink…rich fragrance and full-petalled shape." [T4] "Pink-white, large, full, light scent, tall." [Sn] "Very vigorous." [ARA38/239]

[Gwen Nash]

A. Clark, 1920

"'Gwen Nash', which I think the loveliest rose that blooms, has four to five inch [ca. 1–1.25 dm], semi-double blossoms opening almost flat, of beautiful shell pink shading to white in the center. This gives a few blooms from June until frost, and retains enough wood to start out strong each Spring." [CaRoI/6/6] "Well worth a place where showy climbers are wanted, but it is a bit inclined to mildew." [NRS25/196] "This makes a large, healthy and vigorous bush. It is also a good climbing Rose and well worth growing. This is again a large, semi-double flower of a very lovely shade of cyclamen pink, with a white eye and striking stamens." [NRS26/142] "Not a rampant grower, but its bloom is one of the loveliest things that grows." [CaRoI/6/6] "An extraordinarily beautiful bush of small pillar rose, classed as a Hybrid Tea but Hybrid Perpetual in blooming habit. The large, saucer-shaped flowers are nearly single, pure white and gold in the center, flushed with deep pink at the edges, in picotee fashion. Tricky but very lovely." [GAS]

H. Vessey Machin, Climbing

H. Dickson, 1919 (also: Howard & Smith, 1922)
Sport of 'H. Vessey Machin' (HT).

"Bright crimson." [ARA19/v] "Deep red, very large, full, medium scent, tall." [Sn] "Bud large; flower large, full, double. Color deep scarlet, shaded crimson. Vigorous grower; profuse bloomer." [ARA20/126] "A full, double Rose of bright, true red, with blooms that last longer than [those of] most of the Hybrid Teas. Makes a fine specimen bush. It averages 4 to 5 feet in height [ca. 1.3–1.6 m]." [C-Ps29] "I know of no other climbing Hybrid Tea that will give such a succession of really large, crimson roses all through the spring and summer. Its color is intensely bright and its form is so good that it will compare favorably with any exhibition show rose. With me it starts blooming about the second week in June and continues until the end of August, with scattering bloom in September. However, I find it needs time to get established, and will not throw up shoots of 10 feet or more [ca. 3.3 m +] until three or four years after being planted." [ARA29/108] "A vigorous climbing sport of this well-known Rose. A climbing novelty of the greatest value, as, unlike many climbing sports, its flowers are produced in great profusion, and the plant is strong, clean, and fixed." [GeH] "This gentleman is not happy when on the ground. What a show he makes of himself when on high!" [ARA29/111]

Hadley, Climbing

Heizmann, 1927
Sport of 'Hadley' (HT).

"Red." [Ÿ] "Too thin for great heat. The best red climber for cutting, and certainly the best dark red; fine grower and better foliage than dwarf, with long stems and fine perfume…a splendid bloomer, and better all around than 'Climbing Château de Clos-Vougeot' [Cl HT], which varies in growth and loses foliage." [Capt28] "I wish that someone would suggest a red climbing rose that would take the place of our splendid old 'Hadley'. It blooms in the spring with long stems and there is always a rose to be had, if it is given half a chance; but oh, the mildew!" [CaRoIII/6/6] "A fine climbing form of 'Hadley'." [ARA30/225]

Hermann Robinow, Climbing

syn. 'Climbing Robinow'
Lambert, 1934
Sport of 'Hermann Robinow' (Pern).

"Salmon pink, center orange, large, full, medium scent, tall." [Sn] "Pillar. Creamy white flowers tinted pink, resembling [those of] 'Ophelia' [HT]. Growth about 6 feet [ca. 2 m]." [C-Pf34]

Hoosier Beauty, Climbing

Western, 1918 (also: W. R. Gray, 1925)
Sport of 'Hoosier Beauty' (HT).

"An attractive glowing crimson. Makes beautiful fragrant flowers." [C&Js22] "Deep red, large, full, very fragrant, tall." [Sn] "Not profuse, but attractive." [Th2] "Canes 14 to 15 feet in length [to ca. 5 m], throwing up stems 18 to 24 inches long [ca. 4.5–6 dm] by the score, surmounted with the rich, velvety crimson blooms…a delight not to be forgotten. One bloom will perfume a room with a fragrance that is all its own. I could not be without 'Climbing Hoosier Beauty'." [ARA29/109] "Fine here. —*Saratoga, Calif.*" [ARA26/113]

Independence Day, Climbing

W. & J. Brown/E. Murrell, 1930
Sport of 'Independence Day' (Pern).

"Red, orange yellow center, medium size, very full, very fragrant, tall." [Sn] "Golden yellow." [Ÿ]

Irène Bonnet

C. Nabonnand, 1920

"Briar pink." [Ÿ] "Full, sweet-scented, bright pink flowers." [GAS] "Salmon pink, medium size, full, medium height, tall." [Sn] "Outside of petals rosy pink, inside salmon pale lilac-rose, full, sweetly scented. Growth exceedingly vigorous, climbing." [GeH]

Irish Fireflame, Climbing

A. Dickson, 1916
Sport of 'Irish Fireflame' (HT).

Bronze-colored; see color descriptions of the bush form. "A grand introduction…not a tall climber, but bushy, and must be left to grow quite freely." [ARA18/47] "Growth uncertain so far; foliage good; apparently varies, and unless of large growth would prefer the dependable dwarf pruned for decoration." [Capt28] "Subject to mildew, but of non-fading colors…therefore attractive in the [California] interior." [CaRoII/4/2]

Jonkheer J. L. Mock, Climbing

Timmermans, 1923
Sport of 'Jonkheer J. L. Mock' (HT).

"Exterior light red, interior cerise." [Ÿ] "Carmine-pink, white within, hardy." [Ck] "Whitish pink, large, full, very fragrant, tall." [Sn] "Good stems, continuity and cutting value, but on account of slow opening and mildew must be restricted to use in the interior…not attractive during damp periods of the year." [CaRoII/4/2] "Best for interior with some altitude giving dry heat. A fine grower with good stem and fragrance, but balls easily in damp and mildews." [Capt28]

Julien Potin, Climbing

Bostick, 1935
Sport of 'Julien Potin' (Pern).

Yellow, with a blush. No further information! For data, extrapolate from descriptions of the bush form in Chapter 32 on Pernetianas.

Kitty Kininmonth

syns. 'Kitty Kinnonmonth', 'Kitty Kininmouth', etc.
A. Clark, 1922
Of *Rosa gigantea* heritage.

"Immense flowers of a deep, bright crimson." [CaRol/6/6] "Deep pink, lightly double, medium scent, tall." [Sn] "A semi-double; very large; brilliant salmon-pink; decorative; fine growth and with retained foliage." [CaRoll/4/2] "Bud large, globular; flower very large, semi-double, cupped, very lasting; pink—almost fadeless—with many golden stamens; slight fragrance. Very vigorous climber; moderate bloomer in spring." [ARA24/176] "[For] everywhere. A wonderful decorative rose with a specially clear, brisk color; flower very large; growth fine; foliage fair and will hold." [Capt28] "To 12 feet [ca. 4 m]. Dark wrinkled foliage, few thorns. Heavy June bloom … sparingly repeated. Slight fragrance." [W] "Early. Glowing pink. Flowers are extra large, semi-double, cupped form. Color deep, glowing pink, almost fadeless." [C-Ps34] "Good substance and growth. The colour is hard to describe, as it is unlike any other pink Rose that we have." [NRS25/196] "Very nearly the same vivid pink as the old favorite 'Zéphirine Drouhin' [B]." [ARA31/186] "It is my idea of a perfect rose; the heavy waxy petals of brilliant pink form a shapely flower that lasts for three days in our [Georgian] hot southern sunshine." [ARA32/120] "It does especially well in southern California, with mildew-proof foliage and very large, semi-double, rose-pink flowers … to 15 feet or more [ca. 4.5 m +]." [ARA31/186] "A vigorous climber, producing large semi-double blooms of a most striking carmine-rose color. Though distinctive to a degree in this country [Australia], this variety should improve considerably in a cooler climate." [ARA27/153]

Kitty Kinnonmonth Listed as 'Kitty Kininmonth' (Cl HT).

Kitty Kininmouth Listed as 'Kitty Kininmonth' (Cl HT).

Lady Forteviot, Climbing

Howard Rose Co., 1935
Sport of 'Lady Forteviot' (HT).

"Golden-yellow to apricot, wonderfully FRAGRANT." [W]

Lady Sylvia, Climbing

W. Stevens/Low, 1933
Sport of 'Lady Sylvia' (HT).

"Deep pink, large, full, medium scent, tall." [Sn] "Its 'Ophelia' [HT] -like flowers are of a little darker color and of the finest quality, produced throughout the entire season." [ARA36/178]

Lady Waterlow

P. & C. Nabonnand, 1902
From 'La France de 89' (Cl HT) × 'Mme. Marie Lavalley' (N).

"Salmon-rose, golden centres." [P1] "Very beautiful semi-double … clear salmon-pink petals edged with crimson; and when gathered in bunches its effect is most striking." [K1] "Light salmon pink, saffron nub; flower large, semi-double; very vigorous." [Cx] "Should become more popular not only for its intrinsic beauty, but it flowers freely in late autumn … There is an alluring charm in the large half-double flowers with petals of softest pink and white." [NRS/12] "Salmon flesh, margined rosy pink. A charming semi-climber, blooming from early Summer to late Autumn, and satisfactory in every way. Takes a little time to establish, and should be trained in palmate fashion." [NRS28/51] "Lovely light green foliage, which is not only distinct

…but…immune from disease [excepting blackspot] …carries twice, and often three times in the year quantities of most lovely pale salmon pink flowers, nearly single, with large petals held well up above the foliage. The bright cherry-coloured buds are very pleasing." [NRS/13] "Bud well formed; very large and handsome foliage; plant very vigorous, very floriferous." [JR26/149] "The hardihood of the growth is superlative, the foliage wonderful. I have had leaves 5 inches long by 4 wide [ca. 1.25 × 1 dm] … It is exempt from disease, both mildew and rust; it is one of the first to leaf out, and one of the last to shed in the fall; it climbs quite as high as 'Mme. Alfred Carrière' [N], while remaining clothed to the ground … The best climber I know." [JR36/106] "Extremely climbing, with strong, thorny wood … Three-year-olds have attained 18 feet in height [ca. 5.25 m] …Pruned specimens make very pretty shrubs." [JR36/123] "Vigorous; best suited for pillar or hedge; blooms early and at intervals until autumn." [NRS28/71] "A very charming rose." [OM]

Laurent Carle, Climbing

Rosen, 1923 (also: L. Mermet, 1924)
Sport of 'Laurent Carle' (HT).

"Deep carmine, then blood-red." [Ck] "Bright carminy red." [Y̆] "Brilliant crimson-carmine." [ARA26/183] "Red, large, full, very fragrant, tall." [Sn] "Not always a big grower." [CaRoll/4/2] "Best in dry heat. Not as good as others in growth, but with more resistant foliage, and a lasting rose with perfume. A great advance over the dwarf, but balls in dampness. Better than 'Climbing Étoile de France' and much finer than 'Climbing H. V[essey] Machin'." [ARA28/95] "'Climbing Laurent Carle', an Australian Rose, is a splendid doer and one that will be in great demand when it is better known." [NRS25/195]

Liberty, Climbing

H. B. May, 1908
Sport of 'Liberty' (HT).

"Dark red." [Y̆] "Velvety crimson; good bloomer." [Th2]

Los Angeles, Climbing

Howard & Smith, 1925
Sport of 'Los Angeles' (Pern).

"Light orange pink, yellow center, very large, full, very fragrant, tall." [Sn] "Magnificent flowers of coral-pink, salmon, and gold, exactly like those of the dwarf. Plant free-flowering early in season, but sparse afterward. Fairly hardy and moderately vigorous." [GAS] "Flowers larger than in parent, of more intense color. Very vigorous grower; continuous bloomer throughout season." [ARA27/219] "The best grower of all climbing Hybrid Teas I tried. Made two canes from its first spring planting, 20 feet [ca. 3.6 m] or more long, and several smaller ones … It has had a few blooms through the summer and some nearly out now … *Texas*; Fair growth (6 to 7 feet [ca. 2–2.3 m]; more flowers than dwarf, of equal quality. Does better second year. I like it … *Calif.*" [ARA28/50] "Best in cool districts. Fair growth only; good cutting value; slight perfume; loses foliage in long season but very beautiful." [ARA28/97] "This seems to be a fixed Sport, and is a colour much wanted amongst these Roses. Does not appear to be subject to Black Spot, which is so prevalent in this Rose when grown as a dwarf." [NRS28/50] "An exceedingly handsome rose and generally a satisfactory plant, whereas the dwarf 'Los Angeles' does not thrive except in a limited district in southern California." [GAS] Los Angeles, alias El Pueblo de Nuestra Señora la Reina de Los Angeles de Porciuncula, vivid Californian city with all the esprit of youth, all the awkwardness of promise, and all the vigor of hybridity.

Louis Barbier
syn. 'Louise Barbier'
Barbier, 1909
From 'Mme. Bérard' (N) × *Rosa foetida* 'Bicolor'.

"Copper red, striped yellow, medium size, lightly double, tall." [Sn] "The blooms, which are borne in clusters, are yellow and old Rose, semi-double. It is very useful for pillars, where the brown wood is very noticeable." [NRS13/162] "This is one of the earliest blooming Roses, and it is really lovely as an artistic Rose, the mixture of colours being so remarkable. Flowers semi-double, growth almost climbing. The result of a number of crosses in which 'Mme. Bérard' was employed, and this is very evident by its smooth reddish wood." [NRS21/131] "Plant very vigorous, climbing, giving growths from 1–3 m long [ca. 3–9 ft], entirely covered with flowers. Blooms very early, beginning in May. Flower semi-double, in clusters of 2 to 6, petals bright coppery red, sometimes striped yellow, fading to coppery pink and bright purple when opening; exterior coppery yellow, darker at the base. Novel coloration, sparkling, as brilliant as that of *R. foetida* 'Bicolor'. Foliage thick, glossy, dark green. Though also blooming during the course of Summer, this variety can't be considered absolutely remontant ... The plant keeps the great vigor of 'Mme. Bérard', while taking the tints of 'Bicolor' with its superb coloration, making a marvelous effect at a distance." [JR33/167–168] "The other day a Rose ('Louis Barbier') was handed to me to name which had distinctly the odour of violets." [NRS23/76]

Louise Barbier   Listed as 'Louis Barbier' (Cl Pern).

Louise Catherine Breslau, Climbing
Kordes, 1917
Sport of 'Louise Catherine Breslau' (Pern).

"Shrimp red." [Ÿ] "Copper orange red, large, very full, medium scent, tall." [Sn] "Very large, flat, double, orange-yellow and scarlet flowers, exactly like [those of] the dwarf form from which it sported." [GAS] "Flower of larger size [than that of bush form], same colour as the normal type, produced in great profusion. Growth very vigorous." [GeH] "Bud ovoid; flower very large, full, very double, open, very lasting; orange, yellow, and scarlet, reverse of petals red; borne several together on long, strong stem; slightly fragrant. Foliage abundant, large, leathery, glossy, bronzy green, practically black-spot resistant. Very vigorous; blooms profusely at intervals from June to October. Practically hardy; tips freeze." [ARA21/164] "Best in cool climate. Good growth and wonderful spring bloom, but lacks continuity, although it gives occasional flowers through season; very striking and has some fine blooms for cutting; foliage lost in long growing season." [ARA28/99]

Lyon-Rose, Climbing
Ketten, 1924
Sport of 'Lyon-Rose' (Pern).

"Copper pink, illumined by yellow-gold." [Ck] "Shrimp red, coral center." [Ÿ] "Has satisfied us; it grows very tall." [ARA28/133] "A climbing, very vigorous form of the well-known 'Lyon-Rose'." [ARA24/173]

Mady
Gemen & Bourg, 1925
"Light yellow, large, full, tall." [Sn]

Mamie, Climbing
Vogel, 1938
Sport of 'Mamie' (HT).
"Rose red, large, full, medium scent, tall." [Sn]

Marguerite Carels
C. Nabonnand, 1922
From 'Frau Karl Druschki' (HP) × 'General MacArthur' (HT).

"Pink, large, full, tall." [Sn] "Massive, fully double, eighty-petalled blooms of rich pink. Blooms profusely. The most voluptuous bloom of any climbing Rose we know." [C-Ps30] "Carmine. Produces immense blooms in overwhelming quantities surpassing any other climbing Rose we know. The long, ovoid buds are carmine, which becomes rich pink in the flower. It is best used as a pillar strongly supported to bear the weight of the extraordinary crop of blooms. Cut the blooms off when past their best." [C-Ps31] "Bud long-ovoid, Paul Neyron-carmine; flower large, full, globular; Paul Neyron-pink, center shaded deeper; borne on long, strong stem. Foliage dark green. Thorns few. Vigorous, climbing; profuse bloomer." [ARA23/151]

Mevrouw G. A. van Rossem, Climbing
Gaujard, 1937
Sport of 'Mevrouw G. A. van Rossem' (Pern).
"Dark orange yellow on a golden yellow ground." [Ÿ] "Orange yellow, large, full, very fragrant, tall." [Sn]

Miss Marion Manifold
Adamson/Brundrett, 1913
"Rich, glowing crimson. Vigorous climber; one of the very best." [Au] "Red, large, full, medium scent, tall." [Sn] "An exceedingly handsome Hybrid Perpetual or Bourbon, producing a super-abundance of very large, very full, and beautifully shaped glowing scarlet-crimson flowers over a period of many weeks." [GAS] "New plants are slow to establish their climbing habit. *Burgess* reports growth of only 5 feet [ca. 1.3 m] the first season. On the other hand, *Isham*, in California, calls it a good grower but a rather shy bloomer. After several years hesitancy, it made remarkable growth at Breeze Hill and supplied us with an abundance of lovely, velvety, crimson-scarlet flowers." [ARA31/186] "A vigorous climbing rose with full, large, well-formed flowers of rich, velvety crimson, and a free and continuous bloomer, opening well in all weathers. It has a slight Bourbon scent. In this country [Australia] it sends out strong, vigorous canes each year up to, and sometimes exceeding, nine feet [ca. 3 m], and when covered with bloom is a glorious sight. One of our growers recently counted 150 blooms on his bush, and experts here consider it the finest climbing rose in the world." [ARA28/112] GAS gives a date of 1911, which is perhaps date of first bloom rather than date of introduction.

Mme. Butterfly, Climbing
Smith, 1926
Sport of 'Mme. Butterfly' (HT).
"Bright pink [and] apricot yellow." [Ÿ] "Yellowish pink, large, full, very fragrant, tall." [Sn] "Flowers the same as [those of] the bush variety and salmon to cream color, with yellow base." [C-Ps30] "[As compared with the bush form] flower longer, outer petals cleaner, more fragrant, and altogether superior ... vigorous ... to 7 feet [ca. 2.3 m]." [ARA26/181]

Mme. Édouard Herriot, Climbing

Ketten, 1921

Sport of 'Mme. Édouard Herriot' (Pern).

"Coral red." [Ÿ] "Copper yellow red, large, lightly double, medium scent, tall." [Sn] "Brilliant orange coral-red to salmon-flame; fifteen petals; a marvelous decorative; recurrent; loses foliage; weak stems." [CaRoll/4/2] "Gorgeous coral and orange flowers in abandoned profusion early in the season, with a few afterward. A fine thing, but plants may vary in vigor, seldom any two achieving quite the same habit. If it were fixed, and bloomed just a little more, it would command more respect." [GAS] "Bloomed continuously until freezing weather." [ARA25/103] "Vigorous; profuse bloomer." [ARA22/157] "It flowers in profusion and the plant is strong, clean and fixed." [NRS23/258] "At times rather liable to revert to the dwarf form." [NRS24/217] "For cool seacoast climates. Blooms well but fades quickly; stems weak; loses foliage; distinct but disappointing." [ARA28/99] "Very fine here. —*Oakland, Calif.* Has grown 4½ to 5 feet high [ca. 1.45–1.6 m]. Not many flowers but the color was more intense than [that of blossoms of] the bush variety. —*San Francisco, Calif.*" [ARA26/113] "Does not make much lateral growth so far." [NRS25/173] "Some shoots very strong, others somewhat weak, free and branching, blooming quite freely early and late." [NRS28/71] "Very good; little black-spot …*Mass.*; …Really a pillar, with better blooms and foliage than 'Mme. Édouard Herriot'…*Pa.*; … The most beautiful pillar rose in my garden. Very vigorous; constant bloomer; satisfactory in every particular. Has a tendency to shoot upward; have checked this by spreading out the shoots in fan shape … *Calif.*; Half the plants climb here and give very fine bloom for garden decoration. Far superior to the dwarf. Loses foliage early, especially on heavy canes, and blooms in bursts. Fades like parent … *Calif.*; Fair growth (6 to 7 feet [ca. 2–2.3 m]. Many more flowers than dwarf. Very much to my liking … *Calif.*" [ARA28/151] "I an heartily recommend it to those who have the required space. It appears to be as hardy as an oak, produces canes 8 feet in length [ca. 2.6 m] which bend gracefully, and, with no pruning, produce hundreds of delightful blooms from mid-June to mid-July and a few scattered blooms until October. Like most others of its type, it requires two years to become established, but it is well worth waiting for. But such thorns!" [ARA29/61] "Not a true Climber, but it is an improvement on the older Dwarf type, and is much in demand." [NRS25/195]

Mme. Grégoire Staechelin

syn. 'Spanish Beauty'

Dot, 1927

From 'Frau Karl Druschki' (HP) × 'Château de Clos-Vougeot' (HT).

"Iridescent pearl-pink inside with splashes of ruby-carmine on the outside." [C-Ps33] "Light pink, very large, lightly double, medium scent, tall." [Sn] "The buds are brushed with deep maroon, which remains until the petals drop. The open blooms are flushed flesh-pink; they come on long rigid stems and are delightfully fragrant." [C-Ps32] "It is a very strong grower, with pink flowers and curly petals, much like 'Zéphirine Drouhin' [B] in form, but larger and very fragrant." [ARA28/124] "A little shy of bloom at first." [ARA30/184] "Outstanding among climbing roses for the great size and delicate beauty of its pale pink flowers, richly splashed with crimson in the bud and on the reverse of the outer petals. While classes as a Hybrid Perpetual, it is evidently so closely related to the old-time Bourbons that it could be easily assigned to that section. The plants grow very vigorously. Its flowers are produced on long stems and are followed by very large decorative hips." [GAS] "If the flowers are not cut off, you will get, in the fall, an abundant crop of large, orange-colored seed-pods, looking like little Seckel pears." [C-Ps29] "Fruits … hang on until December." [CaRol/5/2] "It is a magnificent acquisition, most beautiful, with ample foliage which seemed, possibly, sensitive to mildew, a sad inheritance, perhaps, from 'Frau Karl Druschki'. The bud and half-opened flower are perfect in form and color; the pink suffusion, shading from the base of the petals up, is exquisite. The bloom is not recurrent, but is of long duration and lasted at Bagatelle from the end of April to the early days of June." [ARA27/211] "It is richly perfumed and when full blown has a pleasant citronelle fragrance. Grows 12 feet [ca. 4 m] or more in a season, and has large, disease-resistant foliage. The main stem of the plant shoots upright and the long bloom-spurs stand out 18 inches [ca. 4.5 dm] or more at right angles, with exquisite, full, fragrant blooms at the tips. The blooms come early in June and last over a long period, as the come in succession and each bloom is long-lasting." [C-Ps28] "When the sepals of the long-pointed buds begin to divide, the first color is a deep maroon which will leave an indelible imprint to the last, but as the bud develops into the rare and graceful urn shape, that maroon stripe begins to 'run' into a graduated carmine, paling some as the bloom expands into a large, semi-double cup, each flower radiating a delightful fragrance of its own. It blooms but once a year, but as the buds come three to five on the stem, opening one after the other, the season is unusually long. Were they disbudded (side buds removed), the terminal ones would grow into mammoth blooms. The plant is extremely vigorous, growing easily 12 feet [ca. 4 m] or more, each year climbing higher. The foliage is beautiful olive color, ample and leathery. Its hardiness has been proved by six consecutive winters at West Grove [Pennsylvania]. Being a true climber, 'Mme. Grégoire Staechelin' can be used for wire fences (the long branches trained along the lateral wires), pergolas, tall pylons; as pillars when twined around a stout post, lamp-post, or telephone-pole. On the side of a house it will eventually reach over the roof. The most useful and effective perfectly hardy climbing Rose." [C-Ps30]

"There is no bush Rose grown to which we can compare this queen of Climbers. Two years ago, we sent Mr. J. H. Nicolas [*son of the gentleman commemorated in the Hybrid Perpetual 'Secrétaire J. Nicolas' (Schwartz, 1883)*] of our Research Department into Spain. Near Barcelona he discovered this wonderful Rose and immediately recognized its superior qualities." [C-Ps28] "Feliu de Llobregat is near the great city of Barcelona, about 5 miles [ca. 12.5 km] from the Mediterranean Sea. We enjoy a very good climate: it seldom freezes in winter, the heat is not excessive in summer, and fog is almost unknown. The place where I practice hybridizing is very well aërated and dry. I [Pedro Dot] do the hybridizing in the open air, and also sow the seed without the least precaution. I begin hybridizing in May, continuing and up to late July. Gathering the seeds in September and October, I plant them in November, and by January they begin to germinate. On April 18 of this year, I had the pleasure of seeing the first bloom of last season's hybrids … The method I am following in hybridization is first to picture to myself the rose I would like to produce. However, almost every time I have obtained the contrary, though often the results were better than the expectation, and agreeably surprising. Only once I actually got what I had desired." [ARA26/50–52] "From 'Frau Karl Druschki' × 'Château de Clos-Vougeot' I obtained a climbing seedling, extremely rampant in growth, producing great quantities of flowers that are very fragrant, of delicate rose-pink, and elegant in form, but not remontant." [ARA26/51] "At Bagatelle, I [J. H. Nicolas] met my old friend J. C. N. Forestier [*after whom the 1919 Pernetiana by Pernet-Ducher, 'Jean C. N. Forestier' was named (q.v.)*], retired superintendent of the parks of Paris … [*who said*] 'I named that rose for Mme. Staechelin'." [ARA31/166] "No unfavorable reports have been received." [ARA31/192] "An outstanding climber among once-bloomers." [W]

Mme. Segond-Weber, Climbing
Reymond, 1929
Sport of 'Mme. Segond-Weber' (HT).
"Salmon pink, very large, full, medium scent, tall." [Sn] "A climbing sport of vigorous growth and very free-flowering character." [ARA30/223] "[For] everywhere. A new introduction which gives very large blooms with fine stems for cutting. Seems most promising; strongly recommended." [Capt28]

Monsieur Paul Lédé, Climbing
syn. 'Paul Lédé, Climbing'
Low, 1913
Sport of 'Monsieur Paul Lédé' (HT).
"Carmine pink and dawn yellow." [JR38/109] "Dark yellow, large, full, very fragrant, tall." [Sn] "Yellow and apricot. Graceful in vigor and color, 'Climbing Paul Lédé' is a precious enrichment in yellow climbers." [JR38/72] "Another first-rate variety. It is as vigorous as 'Climbing Mme. Abel Chatenay', and we all know the lovely carmine and yellow flowers it produces." [NRS22/159] "Very constant and one of the most satisfactory of the Sports, especially as we have no other Sport in the same shade of colour." [NRS28/50] "Strong-climbing sport of '[Monsieur] Paul Lédé'. Blossoms intense saffron yellow." [Ck] "[For] everywhere. Not pure yellow, but otherwise very fine, with splendid growth, good foliage, and cutting value. A prolific and constant bloomer." [Capt28]

[Moonshine]
Breeder unknown, pre-1920
"Valuable only because of its glossy, blue-green foliage of rampant growth. Flowers are single, white." [GAS] "I would like to mention one [climber] I grow for one purpose only, viz., to give me an unlimited quantity of fine foliage of a glossy blue-green colour and wonderful lasting property when cut. I refer to a variety called 'Moonshine' (not 'Moonlight', a rampant climber rarely to be found in any catalogue. It is absolutely not worth growing for its blooms, which, although large and single of a lovely white with fine yellow stamens, are produced so sparsely as to be almost useless. If, however, you want to 'back' your buttonhole with a leaf, attractive looking, and free from mildew, and rarely attacked by insects, that will remain fresh for two or three days in a holder, this, I have found, [is] the one *par excellence*." [NRS22/174]

Morgenrot
syn. 'Morgenroth'; trans., "Dawn"
Lambert, 1903
"Bright carmine." [LS] "Dark carmine red." [Ÿ] "Light crimson, white edge; pillar or bush; flowers again in the autumn." [NRS18/135] "Pale scarlet, white eye. —Very vigorous. —Garden, bush, pillar,

pergola. —A perpetual-flowering single rose." [Cat12/44] "Park-shrub, large, single, burning poppy-red. Blooms till frost." [Ck] "Bright crimson, with white centre, large, very free, perpetual blooming. Growth vigorous." [GeH] "Showing only small growth so far; to be tested further." [ARA18/121] "It throws up well from the base, and should receive careful and rather thorough thinning, and fairly hard pruning … During the later part of the season it is seldom without flowers, but never again is so fully covered as at its first flowering … The autumn flowers are not so bright as the summer ones, but they are bright and useful even in autumn. If allowed to become too rampant the autumnal flowering is apt to supper. It keeps its foliage well and I have few complaints of mildew, but one or two of black spot. Being single, the flowers open readily, even late in the year." [NRS14/74] "The coming of 'Morgenroth' raised the hope that we had a perpetual flowering Rose to take its [that of 'Paul's Carmine Pillar'] place, but it is to be feared, though perpetual, brilliant and beautiful, it is hardly free enough to give the mass of colour we want." [NRS11/49]

Morgenroth Listed as 'Morgenrot' (Cl HT).

Mrs. Aaron Ward, Climbing
A. Dickson, 1922
Sport of 'Mrs. Aaron Ward' (HT).
"Indian yellow, nuanced salmon." [Ÿ] "Yellow, very large, full, medium scent, tall." [Sn] "Very strong-growing sport of 'Mrs. Aaron Ward'. Blossom the same, deep yellow overlaid ivory white." [Ck] "Has all the characteristics of the parent, but is a climber." [ARA23/148] "Grew 7 to 8 feet [ca. 2.3–2.6 m] first year. Very floriferous. Blooms same as dwarf. Holds foliage well. Very satisfactory." [ARA28/151]

Mrs. C. V. Haworth, Climbing
F. Cant, 1932
Sport of 'Mrs. C. V. Haworth' (HT).
"Dark orange pink, large, lightly double, very fragrant, tall." [Sn]

Mrs. Henry Morse, Climbing
Chaplin, 1929
Sport of 'Mrs. Henry Morse' (HT).
"Golden pink, very large, full, medium scent, tall." [Sn]

Mrs. Henry Winnett, Climbing
P. Bernaix, 1930
Sport of 'Mrs. Henry Winnett' (HT).
"Red, large, full, medium scent, tall." [Sn]

Mrs. Herbert Stevens, Climbing
Pernet-Ducher, 1922
Sport of 'Mrs. Herbert Stevens' (HT).
"Snow white." [Ÿ] "White, large, full, medium scent, tall." [Sn] "Semi-double and delightfully fragrant … A rampant grower." [GAS] "[For] everywhere. Fine grower; good foliage; a rose for cutting and far ahead of 'Niphetos' [T] and 'Devoniensis' [T]. Blooms through a long season. Prefer this to 'Climbing Frau Karl Druschki' [Cl HP]." [Capt28] "Has grown enormously under glass, but has so far given very little bloom." [NRS24/217] "Strong-climbing … heavy bloom, winter hardy." [Ck] "Strong grower, many shoots, very branching; but these bloom well, both early in the summer and late autumn." [NRS28/71] "This is undoubtedly a fine rose, and, if it should prove hardy, it will quickly win many friends." [NRS25/137]

Mrs. Pierre S. Dupont, Climbing
Hillock, 1933
Sport of 'Mrs. Pierre S. DuPont' (HT).

"Yellow on an ochre ground." [Y̌] "Deep yellow, large, full, medium scent, tall." [Sn]

Mrs. Sam McGredy, Climbing
Buisman, 1937
Sport of 'Mrs. Sam McGredy' (HT).

"Copper orange red, large, full, medium scent, tall." [Sn]

Nora Cuningham
A. Clark, 1920
Seedling of 'Gustav Grünerwald' (HT).

"Early. Rose-pink. An Australian everbloomer which is very beautiful. Large, semi-double, cupped blooms of rose-pink with light center; fragrant. Strong, climbing growth." [C-Pf33] "It is really brilliant, with such large and vivid pink flowers." [ARA31/177] "Whitish pink, large, lightly double, medium scent, medium growth." [Sn] "A most beautiful Hybrid Perpetual or Bourbon. The large, semi-double flowers of an exquisite shade of clear light rose-pink are produced over a long period, and frequently again in autumn. The plant is less vigorous than it might be, and the foliage is very thin and delicate." [GAS]

Ophelia, Climbing
A. Dickson, 1920
Sport of 'Ophelia' (HT).

"Light salmon, shaded pink." [Y̌] "Attractive for cut flower blooms near the coast where it does not open too quickly; lovely form and distinct perfume; good stem; nearly continuous." [CaRoll/4/3] "Very strong climbing sport of 'Ophelia'. Blossom very large, delicate flesh white shaded pink-yellow." [Ck] "Very reliable. In great heat, this rose opens flat. If possible, should be given partial shade in Southern Zones." [Th2] "Blooms early and late. The branches should be well spread out." [NRS28/70] "Very few plants revert. Inclined to be too vigorous in growth, and consequently must be very carefully pruned to obtain an adequate amount of blooms." [NRS28/50] "Will become exceedingly popular . . . superior flowers to the dwarf variety." [NRS22/159]

Paul Lédé, Climbing Listed as 'Monsieur Paul Lédé, Climbing' (Cl HT).

Paul's Lemon Pillar
G. Paul, 1915
From 'Frau Karl Druschki' (HP) × 'Maréchal Niel' (N).

"Probably this is the most beautiful white of any class." [GAS] "A lovely Rose. It makes a fine pillar 8 or 9-ft. high [ca. 2.6–3 m], bearing freely its lemon white flowers in early summer, every one of perfect shape. It has one fault, and that a serious one, that there is no autumn flowering." [NRS21/54] "Wonderful blooms—large and of fine form; fair growth; rather shy bloomer." [ARA18/120] "This is a strong branching pillar Rose with large, fine leathery foliage. The flowers are large, double, and of perfect form, and are carried on long erect shoots. The colour is pale lemon yellow in bud, opening to creamy sulphur white. The flowers are slightly fragrant." [NRS16/142] "Best in Pacific Northwest. Balls in dampness; mildews." [Capt28] "Three years of patience have rewarded me beyond words, not counting the

first year of planting. It has brought me the Sweepstakes honors that I have tried for years to win at our local rose shows. Sentiment do you call it? Not if you had seen this bush in all its glory, with hundreds of blooms, many of which were between 4 and 5 inches in length [ca. 1–1.25 dm], and stems 44 inches long [ca. 1.2 m]. This is actual measurement. Rain does not affect it. You can guess its delicious fragrance when I tell you one of its parents is 'Maréchal Niel'." [ARA29/111]

Président Vignet, Climbing
Vogel, 1942
Sport of 'Président Vignet' (HT).

"Deep red, large, full, light scent, tall." [Sn]

Professor Dr. Hans Molisch
Mühle, 1923

"Pink, large, full, tall." [Sn]

Queen of Hearts
A. Clark, 1919
From 'Gustav Grünerwald' (HT) × 'Rosy Morn' (HP).

"Orange pink, large, semi-double, very fragrant, tall." [Sn] "Always in bloom, and carries large blooms with fragrance. Very fine." [NRS29/248] "An easy-growing tall climber of Hybrid Tea appearance, although its everblooming qualities are slight in this country [U.S.A.]. Flowers are large, semi-double, bright reddish pink, sometimes tending towards crimson." [GAS] "Of the almost single varieties, in colour reminding me of 'Lady Inchiquin' [HT]. The individual petals are large and well-formed, and the flower is delightfully scented. I have never seen any trace of mildew on the bold, massive foliage of this variety, which should be grown either as a Climber or large bush." [NRS26/141–142]

Radiance, Climbing
Griffing, 1927
Sport of 'Radiance' (HT).

"Salmon pink and copper yellow, large, full, very fragrant, tall." [Sn] "Like parent in all respects except that it is of vigorous, climbing growth." [ARA30/218] "Report was made to the Editor by Norman A. Reasoner of Oneco, Fla., that there existed at Macclenny, in that state, a vigorous and free-blooming sport of 'Radiance', the one best-loved rose in all the world. Inquiry was at once instituted, with the result of bringing information from W. D. Griffing of Macclenny, as follows: 'The 'Climbing Radiance' is a sport fixed in one of our 'Radiance' nursery blocks during the summer of 1923. The original plant was set out in front of the residence of one of our foremen and has made a wonderful growth, with canes ranging from 10 to 15 feet [ca. 3.3–5 m] or more. The flowers are identical with [those of] 'Radiance', are freely produced, and the plant is making the most healthy and vigorous growth.'" [ARA26/211]

Red Radiance, Climbing
Pacific, 1927
Sport of 'Red Radiance' (HT).

"Bud very large, long-pointed; flower very large, full, double, very lasting, moderately fragrant, red, borne on a long stem; drop off cleanly. Foliage abundant, large, dark green, glossy, disease-resistant. Growth very vigorous, climbing, profuse, continuous bloomer from May to November. Hardy." [ARA27/219]

Réveil Dijonnais

trans. "Dijonnais Revival"
E. M. Buatois, 1931
From 'Eugène Fürst' (HP) × 'Constance' (Pern).

"Cerise madder lake." [Ÿ] "Orange red, orange center, large, lightly double, medium scent, tall." [Sn] "Clusters of large semidouble carmine-streaked yellow flowers, profuse in spring and remontant." [W] "Of Hybrid Perpetual and Pernetiana ancestry, probably reverting to the Bourbon strain. It bears medium-sized, golden yellow buds, striped with reddish pink, which open to semi-double, cup-shaped flowers of deep golden yellow suffused with pink. Very decorative and one of the most promising new climbers." [GAS]

Richmond, Climbing

A. Dickson, 1912
Sport of 'Richmond' (HT).

"Bright red." [Ÿ] "Red, medium size, full, medium scent, tall." [Sn] "Pure red scarlet ... of fair form only and blooming less freely in the autumn and summer." [Th] "A grand colour, rather stiff perhaps in growth ... The flowers seem to have more substance than the dwarf form." [NRS22/160] "Lighter red; is a very prolific rose with fair cutting value; best near coast; recurrent." [CaRoll/4/2] "Many basal shoots attained a length of from 6-ft. to 10-ft. [ca. 2–3.3 m]. These I carefully trained in, merely 'tipping' the ends ... The result was largely a thicket of flowerless laterals and only about a half-dozen blooms." [NRS22/173] "Best near coast. The best of the lighter reds, and a very prolific bloomer. Has fair cutting value; superior to 'Liberty' [HT; *presumably meaning 'Climbing Liberty'*]." [Capt28] "Very vigorous ... the best addition to the climbers for many years." [JR36/92] "Fairly good growth; sparse foliage; bloom not profuse." [ARA18/122] "Very strong-climbing and quite winter hardy." [Ck] "One of the best." [NRS28/67]

Robinow, Climbing Listed as 'Hermann Robinow, Climbing' (Cl Pern).

Rose Marie, Climbing

Pacific, 1927
Sport of 'Rose Marie' (HT).

"Light pink, very large, full, medium scent, tall." [Sn] "Does not last in heat. A fine rose, the climber better than the dwarf; foliage good, except in great dampness; cutting value and lovely perfume." [ARA28/98] "Bud very large, long-pointed; flower very large and double, full, very lasting, strong fragrance, deep pink (deeper than parent), borne on long (3-foot [ca. 1 m]) stem; drop off cleanly. Foliage abundant, large, dark green, glossy, disease-resistant. Growth very vigorous, climbing; profuse, continuous bloomer from May to November. Hardy." [ARA27/220] Not to be confused with 'Climbing Rosemary' (Cl HT).

[Rosella]

Dot/Conard-Pyle, 1931
From a seedling (of 'Mme. Édouard Herriot' [Pern]) × 'Roger Lambelin' (HP).

"Single blooms of unusually brilliant velvety carmine, touched with gold at the base. Moderate grower, but desirable for its color. Blooms intermittently till fall." [C-Ps31] "Bud long-pointed; flower medium size (2¾ inches across [ca. 7 cm]), single, slightly fragrant, brilliant velvety carmine, yellow base, strong orange undertone,

borne in cluster, opening consecutively. Foliage large (Pernetiana), glossy. Growth vigorous (8 ft. [ca. 2.6 m] or more), upright; blooms profusely in June." [ARA31/245] "An exciting pillar rose of erect, vigorous growth." [GAS]

Rosemary, Climbing

Dingee & Conard, 1920
Sport of 'Rosemary' (HT).

"Light pink, very large, full, tall." [Sn] Not to be confused with 'Climbing Rose Marie' (Cl HT).

Sarah Bernhardt

Dubreuil, 1906

"Rosy scarlet flowers shaded velvety red, semi-double and fragrant." [GAS] "Deep red, large, semi-double, moderate scent, tall." [Sn] "Non-remontant." [JR33/185] "Blossom very large, single, red, starry; quite healthy, large, light green foliage, grows about 1–1½ m high [ca. 3–4½ ft]." [Ck] "Growth very hardy, very vigorous and floriferous, with upright semi-climbing canes. Blossom full, very large, with large fleshy petals, bright scarlet crimson red nuanced velvety purple. The blossom is very fragrant with a scent of violets, and does not burn in the sun." [JR30/150] "Has a fine crimson colour and good perfume, and gets up to the top of an 8-ft. [ca. 2.6 m] bamboo without difficulty. The flowers are perhaps a little thin and sometimes apt to be rather ragged, but it is a Rose that has been rather overlooked, and seems to me quite useful for our purpose [*of making Pillars*]." [NRS14/63] Sarah Bernhardt, 1844–1923; French actress.

Scorcher

A. Clark/Hackett & Co., 1922
From 'Mme. Abel Chatenay' (HT) × an unnamed seedling.

"Red, large, lightly double, light scent, tall." [Sn] "Four-inch [ca. 1 dm], semi-double, ruffled flowers of crimson-scarlet. The September bloom of 'Scorcher' in our test-garden was very striking last fall. It is fragrant, too." [C-Ps34] "Early. Scarlet. One of the most brilliant introductions from Australia. Large, semi-double, very lasting blooms of vivid scarlet-crimson cover the plant in early June, and it blooms again, but not so freely, in the fall." [C-Pf33] "Bud large, ovoid; flower large, semi-double, open, lasting; carmine-crimson; slight fragrance. Foliage disease-resistant. Vigorous climber; free and continuous bloomer." [ARA24/176] "Stunning Australian variety of most vigorous growth, with very large, ruffled, semi-double flowers of blazing rosy-scarlet, a different 'Paul's Scarlet Climber' and even brighter. It is evidently a throw-back to the Bourbon type, as its parent was a Hybrid Tea. Occasional blooms are produced in midsummer and autumn. One of the finest modern climbers." [GAS]

Shot Silk, Climbing

Knight, 1931 (also: Low, 1935)
Sport of 'Shot Silk' (Pern).

"An aristocrat among blends. Large, high-centered, semidouble, pale-cerise blooms with a golden glow and an orange center; blooms in clusters all summer long, opening, and holding, exquisite form; excellent for trellis or pillar or arch. Strong stems and large, dark, glossy leaves. Vigorous to 10 feet [ca. 3.3 m]. One of the hardiest ... (much better than 'Cl. Talisman' of similar coloring). Very FRAGRANT." [W]

Souvenir d'Émile Zola

trans. "In Memory of Émile Zola"
Begault-Pigné, 1907
Seedling of 'La France de 89' (Cl HT).

"Delicate silvery pink." [Ÿ] "Bright pink in bud, delicate silvery pink upon opening, very large, full, very fragrant, distinctive perfume; vigor and stature of 'La France de 89'." [JR31/166] Émile Zola, French novelist, lived 1840–1902.

Souvenir de Claudius Denoyel

trans. "In Memory of Claudius Denoyel"
Chambard, 1920
From 'Château de Clos-Vougeot' (HT) × 'Commandeur Jules Gravereaux' (HP).

"Crimson red." [Ÿ] "A magnificent, perfectly formed flower of glistening crimson with shadings of vermilion. It will grow 7 to 8 feet high [ca. 2.3–2.6 m] and is the most desirable *Pillar Rose* we know. The fall blooms are exceptionally fine." [C-Ps28] "Does not blue or pale, it is of a vigorous habit and is very sweet scented." [CaRoll/1/8] "Good in all districts. A peculiar color, verging on dark brown; very large grower with particularly fine foliage. Opens a trifle flat, but with clothed center and good stems and perfume. A continuous but not prolific bloomer." [Capt28] "One of the best red climbers. It has the happy faculty of blooming all the way up the stalk. It is very fragrant and is of good color." [CaRol/5/7]

Souvenir de Claudius Pernet, Climbing

trans. "In Memory of Claudius Pernet, Climbing"
Western Rose Co., 1925 (also: Gaujard, 1932)
Sport of 'Souvenir de Claudius Pernet' (Pern).

"Pure sun yellow." [Ÿ] "Sunflower yellow. The old favorite yellow Rose in climbing form." [C-Ps33] "Deep yellow, large, full, medium scent, tall." [Sn] "Immense blooms." [C-Ps34] "Better than the dwarf; fair grower; foliage lost; some blooms very fine." [ARA28/99] "Better as a Climber than a Dwarf, giving more perfect flowers of large size; double; fine form, and usually without the black centers sometimes found in the Dwarf. A marvelous golden-yellow; not prolific, but of exhibition value. Produces in winter, but foliage lost early." [CaRoll/4/2]

Souvenir de Georges Pernet, Climbing

trans. "In Memory of Georges Pernet, Climbing"
Pernet-Ducher, 1927
Sport of 'Souvenir de Georges Pernet' (Pern).

"Red exterior, carmine petals." [Ÿ] "Orange pink, large, full, very fragrant, tall." [Sn] "Very vigorous; profuse bloomer." [ARA28/238] "*Foote* reports that it ought to make a fine pillar. Like the dwarf in all respects except the growth, which is very vigorous and apparently a free bloomer." [ARA31/194]

Spanish Beauty   Listed as 'Mme. Grégoire Staechelin' (Cl HT).

Sunday Best

A. Clark, 1924
From 'Frau Karl Druschki' (HP) × an unnamed seedling.

"Bright crimson ... Has a quality I have not seen in any other rose among the hundred and more climbers at Breeze Hill." [CaRol/6/6] "Its gorgeous, single red flowers have conspicuous white centers and are borne very freely early in the season. Autumn blooms scarce." [GAS] "Pillar. Early. Brilliant red with a large white eye." [C-Pf33] "Long,

pointed bud; 3-inch [ca. 7.5 cm], semi-double, ruffled flowers, vivid crimson to carmine with a white eye, richer coloring in partial shade. Starts to bloom early and goes right on even past a first light frost. Wrinkled foliage, not too attractive ... It appears to me ... it should branch more, great long canes springing from base are garlanded the entire length with bloom. Grows 8 to 10 feet [ca. 2.6–3 m]." [W]

Talisman, Climbing

Western, 1930 (also: Dixie, 1932)
Sport of 'Talisman' (Pern).

"Scarlet red and golden yellow." [Ÿ] "Copper yellow, medium size, lightly double, very fragrant, tall." [Sn] "Multicolored. Free bloomer when plant is matured." [C-Ps34]

The Queen Alexandra Rose, Climbing

Lindecke/Kordes, 1929
Sport of 'The Queen Alexandra Rose' (Pern).

"Light red, orange center, large, full, medium scent, tall." [Sn] "Hybrid Tea of the Pernetiana strain, with semi-double, scarlet and yellow flowers like those of the dwarf, borne intermittently all through the season." [GAS]

Vicomtesse Pierre de Fou

Sauvageot, 1923
From 'L'Idéal' (N) × 'Monsieur Joseph Hill' (HT).

"Deep magenta pink." [Ÿ] "Rose red, large, full, very fragrant, tall." [Sn] "Deep orange with rose and vermilion splashes; rather small, well-formed flower; double and very lasting; of remarkable decorative value; continuous and with healthy well-held foliage. Good on coast or interior." [CaRoll/4/2] "Bud medium size; flower medium size, deep pink to magenta-red, with a tip of yellow. Foliage large, dark green. Very hardy." [ARA24/173] "A striking Hybrid Tea of perpetual flowering habit, with large, double, deep salmon-pink flowers marked with red and yellow, and occasionally tinged with magenta. Foliage and buds very handsome." [GAS] "Very vigorous, beautiful foliage, pink colour." [NRS23/174] "The finest climber in the garden. An immense grower, it produces a constant succession of large double blooms of a wonderfully brilliant shrimp pink with gold shadings. By disbudding, excellent flowers for cutting may be secured. It made twenty-foot canes [ca. 6.6 m] the second year from budding, and has handsome, glossy, disease-resistant foliage." [CaRol/6/6]

Wenzel Geschwind, Climbing

Vogel, 1940
Sport of 'Wenzel Geschwind' (HT).

"Deep purple, large, full, medium scent, tall." [Sn]

Wilhelm Kordes, Climbing

Wood & Ingram, 1927
Sport of 'Wilhelm Kordes' (Pern).

"Salmon and copper yellow, large, full, medium scent, tall." [Sn] "Strong climbing." [ARA28/232] "A fine addition to the pillars." [ARA31/194]

Willowmere, Climbing

L. Mermet, 1924
Sport of 'Willowmere' (Pern).

"Bright salmon pink on a golden ground." [Ck] "Flower shrimp-red, shaded yellow at center." [ARA26/183] "Light orange pink and yellow, large, full, tall." [Sn]

Pl. IV.

Plate 1. 1, 'Manteau d'Évêque' and, 2, 'Panaché' (which latter is probably 'Rosa Mundi'), Gallicas

Plate 2. 'Oeillet Parfait', a Gallica

Plate 3. 'Tricolore de Flandre' (syn., 'Tricolore de Flandres'), a Gallica

Plate 4. 'Gros Provins Panaché', a Gallica

Plate 5. 'Félicité Hardy' (syn., 'Mme. Hardy'), a Damask

PL. 1

Plate 6. 1, 'Des Peintres', 3, 'Unique Panachée', and, 4, 'Unique' (syn., 'Unique Blanche'), Centifolias;
with, 2, 'Princesse Royale' (syn., 'Royale'), a Moss, and, 5, 'Multiplex' (syn., 'Jaune'), a Hemisphaerica

Plate 7. 'Dométile Bécar' (syn., 'Dométil Beckart'), a Centifolia

Plate 8. 'Cristata' (syn., 'Rosier Cent-Feuilles à Calice Crêté'), a Moss

Plate 9. 'Cristata', a Moss

Plate 10. 'Laneii', a Moss

Plate 11. 2, 'Impératrice Eugénie', a Mossy Remontant, and, 1, double California poppy, *Eschscholzia californica* cultivar

Plate 12. 'Eugénie Guinoisseau', a Mossy Remontant

Plate 13. 'Deuil de Paul Fontaine', a Mossy Remontant

Plate 14. 'Blanche Moreau', a Mossy Remontant

Plate 15. 1, 'Great Maiden's Blush' (syn., 'Cuisse de Nymphe'), an Alba; with, 2, 'Félicité Hardy' (syn., 'Mme. Hardy'), a Damask

Plate 16. *Rosa foetida* (syn., *R. lutea*), a Foetida

Plate 17. *Rosa foetida* 'Bicolor' (syn., 'Capucine Bicolor'), a Foetida

Plate 18. 'Persian Yellow', a Foetida

Plate 19. A yellow Pimpinellifolia, possibly 'Lutea'; with "new Bourbon hybrid"

Plate 20. 'Hardii', a Hulthemia

Plate 21. 'Pourpre Ancien', a Roxburghii

Plate 22. *Rosa rugosa*, a Rugosa

Plate 23. *Rosa rugosa* 'Rubra', a Rugosa

Plate 24. *Rosa rugosa* 'Alba', 'Calocarpa', 'Crispata', and 'Roseraie de l'Haÿ', Rugosas (original plate damaged)

Plate 25. 'Fimbriata', a Rugosa

Plate 26. 'Blanc Double de Coubert', a Rugosa

Plate 27. 'Souvenir de Christophe Cochet', a Rugosa

Plate 28. 'Rose à Parfum de l'Haÿ', a Rugosa

Plate 29. *Rosa laevigata,* a Laevigata

Plate 30. 'Thoresbyana', an Arvensis

Plate 31. 'Félicité et Perpétue', a Sempervirens

Plate 32. 'Princesse Marie', a Sempervirens

Plate 33. 'Reine des Belges', a Sempervirens

Plate 34. 'Mme. de Sancy de Parabère' (syn., Mme. Sancy de Parabère), a Boursault

Plate 35. 'Mme. de Sancy de Parabère' (syn., Mme. Sancy de Parabère'), a Boursault, as a weeper

Plate 36. 'Erinnerung an Brod', a Setigera

Plate 37. *Rosa wichuraiana,* left, a Wichuraiana; with 'Conrad Ferdinand Meyer', a Rugosa

Plate 38. 'René André', a Wichuraiana

Journal des Roses (Grisy-Suisnes) (S. & M.) France Juin 1908.

L.Schmidt-
Michel.

Dorothy Perkins,
(Wich.)
Jackson & Perkins 1902

Debutante (Wich.)
Walsh. 1901

Plate 39. 'Debutante' and 'Dorothy Perkins', Wichuraianas

Imp. De Tollenaere, Brux.

Plate 40. 1, 'Paul Noël' and, 2, 'Dr. Henri Neuprez' (Tanne, 1912), Wichuraianas, the latter extinct

Plate 41. A form of *Rosa multiflora*, a Multiflora

Plate 42. A form of *Rosa multiflora*, a Multiflora

Plate 43. A form of *Rosa multiflora*, a Multiflora

Plate 44. 'Platyphylla', a Multiflora

Plate 45. 'Polyantha', a Multiflora

Plate 46. 'Laure Davoust', a Multiflora

Plate 47. 'Daniel Lacombe', a Multiflora

Plate 48. 'Polyantha Grandiflora', a Multiflora

Plate 49. 'Geschwinds Orden' (syn., 'Décoration de Geschwind'), a Multiflora

Plate 50. 'Turner's Crimson Rambler', a Multiflora

Plate 51. 'Rubin', a Multiflora

Plate 52. 'Hiawatha', a Multiflora

Plate 53. 'Kathleen', a Multiflora

Plate 54. 'Graf Zeppelin', a Multiflora

Journal des Roses (Grisy-Suisnes) (S. & M.) France Juillet 1908.

Fr. Harms (Hybr. de thé) (Wefter 1901)
fyn. (Erz. Deegen) (H. de T.)

UNIV. OF
CALIFORNIA

Plate 55. 'Franz Deegen' (syn., 'Friedrich Harms'), a Hybrid Tea

Plate 56. 'Frau Peter Lambert', a Hybrid Tea

Plate 57. 'Étoile de France', a Hybrid Tea

L. Schmidt-Michel.

Mrs. Theodore Roosevelt.
(H. T.) L. G. Hill. 1902.

KUNST-ANSTALT E. GÜNTHER, GERA, REUSS.

Plate 58. 'Mrs. Theodore Roosevelt', a Hybrid Tea

Plate 59. 'Laurent Carle', a Hybrid Tea

Plate 60. 'Frau Oberhofgärtner Singer', a Hybrid Tea

Plate 61. 'My Maryland', a Hybrid Tea

Plate 62. 'Rhea Reid', a Hybrid Tea

Plate 63. 'Veluwezoom', a Hybrid Tea

Pöhls.

Chromolith. De Tollenaere Brux.

Plate 64. 'Kaiser Wilhelm II', a Hybrid Tea

Plate 65. 'Natalie Böttner', a Hybrid Tea

Plate 66. 'Stadtrat Glaser', a Hybrid Tea

Plate 67. 'Edward Mawley', a Hybrid Tea

Plate 68. 'Ophelia', a Hybrid Tea

Plate 69. 'Dr. G. Krüger', a Hybrid Tea

Plate 70. 'Lucien Chauré', a Hybrid Tea

Plate 71. 'Soleil d'Or', a Pernetiana

JOURNAL DES ROSES (SUISNES par GRISY-SUISNES (S.&M.) FRANCE. AÔUT 1907.

LYON-ROSE (ROSA PERNETIANA)

Plate 72. 'Lyon-Rose', a Pernetiana

Plate 73. 'Entente Cordiale', a Pernetiana

Plate 74. 'Arthur R. Goodwin', a Pernetiana

Plate 75. 'Rayon d'Or', a Pernetiana

SUNBURST
(Hybride de thé)

Plate 76. 'Sunburst', a Pernetiana

LOUISE-CATHERINE BRESLAU
(Pernetiana)

Plate 77. 'Louise Catherine Breslau', a Pernetiana

Plate 78. 'Mme. Édouard Herriot', a Pernetiana

Plate 79. 'Sonnenlicht', a Pernetiana

Plate 80. 'Willowmere', a Pernetiana

Plate 81. 'Leuchtfeuer', a Bourbon

Plate 82. 'Duc de Constantine', a Hybrid Perpetual

Thé Sombreuil.

Plate 83. 'Mlle. de Sombreuil' (syn., 'Sombreuil'), a Climbing Tea

CHAPTER THIRTY-ONE

Hybrid Teas, 1900–1920

In *The Old Rose Advisor,* our Chapter 10 on Hybrid Teas concentrated on the earliest members of that group, surveying the introductions and progress made particularly through the end of the 19th century. We now consider the next stage of the Hybrid Teas, a period in which they rose to preeminence over their predecessors in vogue, the Hybrid Perpetual and the Tea. During this period, the breeders worked successfully towards eliminating the early shortcomings of the group: plants that were delicate and gawky, blossoms that could not stand up to the weather and that nodded on their stems. The preferred appearance of rose blossoms was changing from that of the heavy, full, rounded flower, typified by Hybrid Perpetuals, to that of a lighter, less double, starry flower, heavily influenced by the Teas. Indeed, cultivars with single flowers now began to appear with increasing frequency and popularity. The range of color and the combinations of colors in one blossom were augmented, spurred on to some degree by the introduction of the Pernetianas with their hot, bright colors. For a time, particularly from 1900 to about 1920, the Hybrid Teas and Pernetianas continued side-by-side as separate groupings—and it is that period we examine in this volume.

Our lucubrations have been dominated up until this period by the French breeders. The French were indisputably the masters of the rose breeding world from 1815 until 1900!—and wielded their power with the wise benevolence, pride, and exacting taste that have always characterized French culture. Now, however, the Irish, the English, the Germans, and the Americans were coming on strong, each with their own ideals of what a rose should be. The cruel destruction arising from World War I hastened this change; and by the end of that war, and the beginning of the 1920s, it was clear that a new era had begun. Our next and final chapter, on Pernetianas, will glance—with blinking eyes—into what was a new epoch in rose history, the dawning of the present era of modern roses; but, with that bridge built towards what followed the age of Old Roses, we lay down our commission, and bid our successors Godspeed!

Abbé André Reitter
Welter, 1901
    "Delicate flesh." [LS] "Light pink, large, full, light fragrance, medium height." [Sn]

Adam Rackles
Rommel, 1905
Sport of 'Mme. Caroline Testout' (HT).
    "Pink on a ground of white." [LS] "Light pink, very large, full, light fragrance, moderately tall." [Sn]

Albast
Van Rossem, 1928
From 'Morgenglans' (HT) × 'Mrs. Wemyss Quin' (HT).
    "Light salmon orange, large, full, light scent, tall." [Sn] "Type, 'Mme. Leon Pain'. Bud medium size, ovoid; flower large, double, open, lasting, slightly fragrant, salmon-pink, borne several together on medium-length stem. Foliage sufficient, medium size, bronzy green, glossy, disease-resistant. Growth vigorous, upright; abundant bloomer from June to October. Very hardy." [ARA29/227]

Alexander Elmslie Listed as 'Alexander Emslie' (HT).

Alexander Emslie
syn. 'Alexander Elmslie'
A. Dickson, 1918
    "Quite a good Rose with flowers of a deep ruby colour. It is fairly free blooming, is useful as a decorative variety, and occasionally throws a bloom large enough for exhibition purposes." [NRS24/138] "Dark red, large, full, medium scent, medium height." [Sn] "Dwarf in habit and fairly free. The blooms are full and globular." [NRS24/152] "A crimson flower of fair but not first rate form; it is fragrant and the plant grows tolerably well." [NRS21/57] "Deep, globular bloom of pure solid ruby on deep, delicate, velvety crimson, with base slightly white; attar-of-rose perfume. Free grower, branching; very floriferous." [ARA19/102]

Alice Grahame
A. Dickson, 1903
    "White, large, very full, medium scent, medium height." [Sn] "Large, very full, sweet." [GeH] "Flowers very large, ivory white, tinted with salmon, produced freely and continuously; vigorous growth."

Alice Grahame *continued*

[W/Hn] "Vigorous growth, bushy, large leaves, large flower, full; color, ivory touched with salmon." [JR30/186] "Ivory-white, tinted salmon. In this variety we have an absolutely distinct and magnificent rose of the highest excellence. It is a strong, vigorous grower, of free and erect branching character, with very large and massive dark-green foliage. The growths are very smooth, with the appearance of being highly varnished. Every shoot is crowned with a bud, which develops into a flower of large size, enormous substance, and perfect form. This variety frequently varies both in form and colour … marvellously free and continuous blooming rose." [ADk03] "A new Rose, with stiff sturdy growth and good foliage. It is wanting in colour, and I have not been successful with it at present." [F-M4]

[Alice Kaempff]
Felberg-Leclerc, 1920
From 'General MacArthur' (HT) × 'Radiance' (HT).

"Bud medium size, long-pointed, pink, with light violet tint; flower large, full, globular, lasting; silvery rose-pink, center coppery yellow; strong fragrance. Foliage sufficient, medium size, glossy, rich green. Vigorous, bushy; free and continuous bloomer." [ARA22/154]

Alice Lindsell
A. Dickson, 1902

"Creamy white with a pink center." [JR27/40] "Blush, large, full, medium height." [Sn] "Very large and full, fine form, with high pointed centre." [GeH] "Flowers very large, of fine form, creamy white with a pink centre; vigorous growth." [W/Hn] "It is of fair growth and habit, and the blooms are unique in shape, being truly globular with yet a decided point in the centre. Unfortunately the colour is not very distinct, but the young flowers have colour in them, which fades, however, in the older flowers to nearly white." [F-M] Alice Lindsell, presumably wife or daughter of E. B. Lindsell, who himself "was in his time the most successful exhibitor the Society has ever known," and "was President" of the British National Rose Society "for the years 1907 to 1908." [NRS27/232]

Alsterufer
syn. 'Zwerg Teplitz'
Lambert, 1909
Seedling of 'Gruss an Teplitz' (B).

"Dark red, medium size, full, very fragrant, medium height." [Sn] "Rather low, moderately spreading; growth moderate, rather hardy; foliage barely sufficient; bloom free, continuous." [ARA18/124]

Amalie de Greiff
syn. 'Amalie de Grieff'
Lambert, 1912
From 'Herrin von Lieser' (HT, Lambert, 1905, cream yellow, extinct) × 'Mme. Mélanie Soupert' (HT).

"Salmon-red, large, full, medium scent, medium height." [Sn] "Large, well-formed, double flowers with long, shapely buds. Color, delicate satiny rose, with shadings of yellow in center which produces a tint of salmon." [C&Js24] "Vigorous. Flower very large, of very beautiful form, quite full; exterior petals readily reflexing. Long bud on a long and firm stem, often singly, sometimes in threes. The blossom is brick-color, with a salmon red center on an orange yellow ground, often resembling 'Lyon-Rose' [Pern]. Very remontant. Useful

both for cutting and the garden; very fragrant and long-lasting." [JR37/8–9] "Only fair; lacks distinctiveness." [ARA18/115]

Amalie de Grieff Listed as 'Amalie de Greiff' (HT).

Amateur André Fourcaud
Puyravaud, 1903
Seedling of 'Mme. Caroline Testout' (HT).

"Light pink, reverse darker." [Ÿ] "Flower handsome pink, reverse of petals very bright pink, very large, high-centered, bud very long, semi-double, fragrant, borne on a firm stem, very well branched, very floriferous, very beautiful." [JR27/149]

Ami Quinard
trans. "Friend Quinard"
Mallerin, 1927

"Maroon." [C-Ps31] "Deep red, medium size, lightly full, medium scent, medium growth." [Sn] "This velvety black beauty has long-pointed buds, flowers open, cup-shaped, semi-double, lasting, and fragrant, borne singly and sometimes in candelabras on long stems. Growth is vigorous and upright. 'Ami' is a tireless worker, producing flowers continuously, and her most enchanting blooms are shown if planted where shaded early from the hot afternoon sun." [C-Pf31] "Here is a dream come true; dream of a black-lustred red rose with a grace of petalage quite beyond this portrait of the bud just bursting. The blooms are semi-double, but they come profusely on a vigorous branching bush, giving a candelabra effect. The color, instead of fading, gets darker as the flower ages until it is almost black. Foliage is unusually disease-resistant. This Rose has been thoroughly tested in our test-garden and fields and we recommend it highly. It was first offered in the fall of 1930. An exclusive Star Novelty." [C-Ps31]

Andenken an Moritz von Fröhlich
trans. "In Memory of Moritz von Fröhlich"
Hinner, 1905
From 'Mme. Caroline Testout' (HT) × *possibly* 'Princesse de Béarn' (HP).

"Velvety dark red." [Ÿ] "Dark red, large, full, light scent, tall." [Sn]

[Angelus]
Lemon, 1920
From 'Columbia' (HT) × 'Ophelia' (HT).

"White with creamy centre. Growth vigorous." [GeH] "Flower large, full (40 to 45 petals), form similar to [that of] 'Premier' [HT] but higher center, lasting; white, cream tint at center; fragrant. Foliage dark green, disease-resistant. Vigorous; upright; free bloomer. Hardiness not tested. Similar to 'Kaiserin Auguste Viktoria' [HT], but more double; blooms in winter, and keeps longer." [ARA21/172] "I had poor success with this rose. New growth was very small; the flowers were too solid and turned yellowish before opening and never did open properly. It is a gummy sort of bloom and not attractive anyway." [ARA24/89] "Very seldom opened a bloom—mostly the weather destroyed them. The color is not bad and the perfume very strong, but in the open ground it is useless." [ARA25/137]

Apotheker Georg Höfer
trans. "Pharmacist Georg Höfer"
Welter, 1902
From either a seedling (which resulted from a cross between 'Mme.

Caroline Testout' [HT] and 'Mme. Lambard' [T]) × 'William Francis Bennett' (HT); or 'Mme. Caroline Testout' (HT) × a seedling (which resulted from a cross between 'Mme. Lambard' [T] and 'William Francis Bennett' [HT]).

"Described in all the catalogs as light purple red, in reality the color is a beautiful delicate pink; the flower is very large and very beautiful." [JR30/15] "Sweet-scented. Growth very vigorous." [GeH] "Going by the wood, at first sight it seems to be a hybrid from 'Mme. Caroline Testout', having the latter's vigorous growth, though being perhaps a little less thorny. It also has its mother's remontant qualities. The bud is long, and remains half open longer than does that of '[Mme.] Caroline Testout'; as for the flower itself, it is perhaps larger and fuller. The fiery red color is akin to that of 'Ulrich Brunner fils' [HP], except during great heat when the blossoms fade a little." [JR26/118] "Approximating to the H.P.s in foliage and habit, of very strong growth, with long buds, this Rose, which has large full flowers of a bright red colour, should be useful, with moderate pruning, in a cool season." [F-M4]

Arabella
Schilling/Tantau, 1917

"Deep pink, large, full, very fragrant, medium height." [Sn] "Form and growth resemble those of '[Mme.] Caroline Testout', only with considerably darker color. Fragrant." [Ck]

Argentine Cramon Listed as 'Mlle. Argentine Cramon' (HT).

Argyll
Dobbie, 1920
From 'Mme. Caroline Testout' (HT) × 'Marquise de Sinéty' (HT).

"A creamy yellow of large size. Purely a Rose for the keen exhibitor." [NRS24/148] "Buds and flowers large, pure white. Seems to be perpetual." [ARA20/126] "Large, full, moderate height." [Sn] "Described as an improved 'Mrs. David McKee' [HT], possessing a deeper cream tone. Growth robust." [GeH]

Augustus Hartmann
B. R. Cant, 1914

"Brilliant geranium-red, flushed with orange, sometimes bright cerise; flowers of large size and beautifully formed. The color is very striking." [C&Js15] "An unusual shade of red—the brightest in the garden—more scarlet than 'Richmond' [HT]; does not hold its color." [ARA18/133] "Carmine red, flushed orange. Exhibition, garden." [NRS15/146] "Light red, large, full, medium scent, tall." [Sn] "Large size and beautifully formed, nearly all blooms coming perfect and being carried erect on stout stems. Growth strong and sturdy, with deep green leathery foliage which does not readily mildew." [GeH] "Rather the shape of 'Ulrich Brunner [fils]' [HP]. The catalog description of 'bright metallic red' does not strike me as satisfactory. I think rosy carmine, flushed scarlet is the nearest I can get to it. When fresh it is very attractive. The plant is a strong grower, but is either delicate or resents being moved . . . When once established it grows well and flowers freely, but it is not a first class garden plant, because, though the flowers are bright and noticeable, those produced in late summer are apt to be of poor colour." [NRS21/50] "Best in cooler seasons, as hot weather causes it to lose shape and color badly. Growth rather weak, and foliage is lost early. Admirable for its color and fragrance." [C-Ps25] "It is a good grower, and carries its flowers on strong stems, and one

would hazard that it might have 'Captain Hayward' [HP] blood in its veins. The raisers state it is not subject to mildew." [NRS15/155] "This rose was of only fair growth in Central Zone, and was discarded there. Is a favorite in England . . . Can only be recommended for Pacific North-West, as it becomes flat in heat and loses foliage. Hardy in Central Zone, but of weak growth and sometimes winter-kills close to the ground." [Th2] "The chief merit of this Rose is its remarkable colouring, geranium red flushed orange. Flowers large, full and carried upright. It is especially good in autumn, but not sufficiently free flowering for general garden purposes." [NRS21/61–62]

Australia Felix
trans. "Felicitous Australia"
A. Clark, 1919
From 'Jersey Beauty' (W) × 'La France' (B or HT).

"Soft pink, outer petals deep reddish pink. Vigorous, free flowering, good foliage." [Au] "Pink, medium size, moderately full, moderate fragrance, moderate [growth]." [Sn] "Deliciously fragrant and everblooming." [ARA24/119] "Bud well-formed, deep reddish pink; flower open form, cupped; very lasting; 'La France' fragrance . . . Foliage abundant, glossy green. Vigorous, bushy grower, blooming continuously from June to October. Hardy. Rain does not affect flowers." [ARA20/136]

Australie
Kerslake, 1907
"Dark pink, large, full, tall." [Sn]

Aviateur Michel Mahieu
trans. "[Airplane] Pilot Michel Mahieu"
Soupert & Notting, 1912
From 'Mme. Mélanie Soupert' (HT) × 'Lady Ashtown' (HT).

"Coral red with a bright center. Flower large, perfect form, held upright above the ample and rich foliage. Petals thick. Splendid rose for bedding . . . Blooms without interruption until the first frosts. Very fragrant. Of the greatest value for all purposes." [JR37/10] "Pink, large, full, very fragrant, moderate height." [Sn] "Growth vigorous, upright, very floriferous." [GeH]

Avoca
A. Dickson, 1907

"Crimson scarlet, buds very long and pointed, flowers large and sweetly perfumed, foliage large and very dark green." [C&Js09] "One of the most beautiful of the old Remontants, blooming repeatedly when cut. Long-stemmed, very large, beautiful, well formed, splendid deep red." [Ck] "Deep scarlet crimson.—Very vigorous.—Exhibition, garden. —Very fragrant." [Cat12/16] "Very vigorous and has shapely flowers, which could do with a few more petals, as it does not last well when cut." [NRS23/201] "A beautiful shaped flower, of medium size, only useful for the late shows, as it is produced on the ends of long shoots which take time to grow. Colour crimson scarlet . . . Not very free flowering. Fragrant." [F-M] "The beautiful 'Avoca' may be grown as a pillar Rose, and is more free flowering in this way than when pruned hard, or it may be pegged down." [NRS21/114] "Very vigorous, semi-climbing." [JR35/14] "Very hardy. Crimson-scarlet; large, very long buds; perfumed. Does not bloom well in Central Zone; recommended for the Pacific North-West by Mr. Currey." [Th2]

Baron Palm

Lambert, 1913

From 'Étoile de France' (HT) × 'Mme. Ravary' (HT).

"Bush about two feet high [ca. 6 dm], bushy; foliage dark green; flowers large, cupped, full, pure velvety red with deep yellowish red and vermilion reflections; long-lasting, neither blues nor scorches. Good for bedding and cutting." [JR38/56] "Tall growth; pretty color; fragrant; blooming qualities fairly good." [ARA18/110]

Benedictus XV

Leenders, 1917

From 'Jonkheer J. L. Mock' (HT) × 'Marquise de Sinéty' (HT).

"White, center toned salmon. Shrubby." [Ck] "White, shaded soft salmon towards the centre, large, full, of perfect form, fragrant; buds long and pointed. Growth vigorous, very free flowering." [GeH] "Bud very large, long-pointed; flower very large, full, double, borne singly on long stems; lasting; strong fragrance. Color rosy white. Foliage sparse, large, glossy green. Very vigorous, upright grower, producing an abundance of bloom." [ARA20/134]

Bertha Kiese   Listed as 'Frau Berthe Kiese' (HT).

Bertha von Süffner   Listed as 'Bertha von Suttner' (HT).

Bertha von Suttner

syn. 'Bertha von Süffner'
Verschuren, 1918

"Light yellow with coppery pink, medium size, full, moderate height." [Sn] "Flower and colour like [those of] 'Mme. Abel Chatenay' [HT]; handsome foliage." [GeH] Bertha von Suttner, Austrian pacifist, lived 1843–1914.

Bessie Brown

A. Dickson, 1900

"A noble rose of extra fine quality and bears large full flowers of extraordinary depth and fullness and is deliciously sweet, color pure white, clouded and flushed with flesh pink." [C&Js07] "Lovely peachy pink, delicately shaded with rose and fawn." [C&Js02] "Creamy white; immense flowers of perfect shape and great substance; free blooming and vigorous. The flowers are impatient of wet, and they also droop." [P1] "Fine form, full, large to extra large, fine fragrance, medium long stems. Good foliage, sufficient. Growth strong, hardy. Soft ivory-white, very lightly blushed in cool weather." [ARA23/156] "Lovely new Rose, extra large, full and double and delightfully perfumed; healthy vigorous grower. Constant, profuse bloomer." [C&Js02] "Tall, almost climbing, vigorous, hardy; foliage plentiful, blackspots slightly in midsummer; bloom moderate, continuous, slight break in midsummer." [ARA18/124] "One of the best." [GeH]

"For exhibition, it is quite one of the best . . . The growth and foliage are strong, stout, and stiff; the blooms come exceedingly well, being rarely divided, and if there is any malformation it is usually of a slight nature. They are very large, sweet-scented, of perfect pointed semi-globular shape, and the fine petals open just as they should do, neither too stiffly nor too easily. The colour is a good true creamy white unstained; but it does not display the beauty of the flowers well upon the plant, for the stalk, though stout, is pliable, and the heavy blooms hang their heads . . . I have not found it affected by mildew; and though rain will harm it as it will all white Roses, its pendant position protects the centre. It is not so good in autumn, and I fear it will be rather an exhibitor's Rose." [F-M2]

Betty

A. Dickson, 1905

"A superb newcomer with marvelous coloration . . . its coppery salmon color is difficult to describe." [JR29/153] "Such glorious, long, coppery pink buds, and her stems and leaves are so glossy and rich! The flower is very large and rather single. 'Betty' never mildews or blackspots and is a great favorite." [ARA29/54] "In a cool season this Rose is indispensable, but from the small number of its petals it is quite useless to attempt to show it in a hot one. The petals are very large, few Roses have longer petals, but tied, and cut young, it is a beautiful flower useful for its colour, a coppery-yellow, tinted rose." [F-M] "Coppery rose—overspread with golden yellow. This is Dickson's description. With us, particularly in the late spring and summer, the rose verges more from cream to orange-salmon. In the autumn it more nearly approaches Dickson's description . . . Large growth, good foliage; very hardy, long stem, but not always erect; long, pointed bud; a poor keeper; opens quickly and with no great petallage; its blooming qualities, wonderful in spring and autumn, good in summer, secure it a place in the first list. Plant 18 inches [ca. 4.5 dm] center to center. Prune to 5 eyes." [Th] "Opens well in wet; rather thin." [NRS14/159] "Very long petals. Fragrant." [Cat12/17] "Fine form . . . deliciously perfumed. Growth very vigorous, continuous flowering." [GeH] "Its blooms are extremely large, fairly full, and of a glorious form. Its growth is extremely vigorous, erect and of very free branching habit, flowers all season and is deliciously perfumed." [C&Js07] "Strong upright growth; beautiful color; good bloomer, attractive bud." [ARA18/110] "Low, rather upright growth, moderately vigorous, hardy; foliage sufficient, blackspots slightly in midsummer; bloom moderate, continuous, slight break in midsummer." [ARA18/124] "A dependable Rose with beautiful, coppery buds of exquisite form, and large and very attractive pale pink flowers with a golden sheen; golden yellow center. The color fades quickly in hot weather, and then the flowers are apt to hang their heads. The bush is lusty, but its distinctive foliage sometimes blackspots. A hardy and satisfactory Rose, very fine early in the season, and even better in the fall, when the stems are stronger and the color does not fade." [C-Ps25] "We are so impressed with the value of this Rose that we commend it for mass planting." [C&Js21]

[Bianca]

W. Paul, 1913

"Creamy white, tinted peach or sometimes carmine. Moderate size, buds short pointed, double. Fragrance fait. Growth and production very good. Stems long and flowers mainly come singly." [CA17] "Color, cream white tinted peach; buds long, pointed, peachblossom pink; very decorative, blooming abundantly and continuously; vigorous growth." [JR37/88] Bianca, Baptista's *other* daughter in Shakespeare's *The Taming of the Shrew*.

[Bloomfield Progress]

Capt. Thomas/Bobbink & Atkins, 1920

From 'Mary, Countess of Ilchester' (HT) × 'General MacArthur' (HT).

"A strong-growing, bushy plant with very lasting, double (over 50 petals), red flowers having strong fragrance. This rose is similar to 'General MacArthur', but differs in habit, size, and form of flower, being superior in that it holds the center better and is larger in hot weather." [ARA20/168]

Blush o'Dawn   Listed as 'Flush o'Dawn' (HT).

British Queen

McGredy, 1912

"Pure white, unexpanded buds sometimes flushed peach. Open flowers without any trace of yellow. Beautifully formed, with pointed center and reflexed outer petals." [CA17] "The most beautiful white rose existing, surpassing, in perfection of form, all other white roses … The floriferousness is notable; it blooms from June to Winter. The blossom type is between [that of] 'Maman Cochet' [T] and 'Frau Karl Druschki' [HP] with a Tea rose form. The petals are large, and well arranged; we often note in the bud a light pink tint which disappears when the flowers opens and is transformed into immaculate white." [JR36/171] "Pure white in colour, tea-scented and of very refined shape—pointed centre with the outer petals beautifully reflexed. It is a vigorous grower, producing a number of branches almost horizontally all the way up the leading shoots, each of which carry two or three buds. It is very free and continuous flowering (my plants had some flowers on them at Christmas). The blooms all come of excellent shape and with good culture of large size, and there is a great deal of Tea blood in its veins … The raiser is to be congratulated … on the result of his endeavour to obtain a free flowering white Rose with perfume." [NRS13/157–158] "Large, full, of exquisite form, opening freely in all weathers, sweetly fragrant. Growth vigorous, branching, free flowering." [GeH] "The plant produces too much twiggy growth, and the flower stem usually bends over so much that the flower often rests face downwards on the ground." [NRS21/45] "Very dwarf spreading growth. Very little disbudding." [Th] "Low-growing, compact, apparently hardy; foliage almost sufficient, black-spots slightly in midsummer; bloom moderate, continuous." [ARA18/124] "The flowers are models of perfection." [C&Js13]

Bürgermeister Christen

Bergmann, 1911

From 'Mme. Caroline Testout' (HT) × 'Fisher-Holmes' (HP).

"Flower large, full, bright deep pink, fragrant. Pointed bud. Bush vigorous and floriferous." [JR36/88] "Fair; not so good as others of same type." [ARA18/115]

[C. W. Cowan]

syn. 'Improved Marquise Litta de Breteuil'

A. Dickson, 1912

"Carmine cerise about like 'Reine Marie-Henriette' [Cl HT]. Buds short pointed, opening rather flat. Flowers double, quite fragrant. Not of strong growth, but very free bloomer. Stems long and slender, carrying flowers erect." [CA17] "Deliciously perfumed." [GeH] "Warm cerise red; the blossoms are large, quite full, and imbricated, continuously produced in great profusion; the petals are thick, sweet, and round; the growth is vigorous and branching. It is considered by the cognoscenti as being much superior to 'Marquise Litta de Breteuil' in all ways. Its growth is more vigorous, its petals are as long, and the blossoms are larger. Equally good for exhibition and for garden; delicious Tea scent." [JR36/91]

Capitaine Georges Dessirier

Pernet-Ducher, 1919

Seedling of 'Château de Clos-Vougeot' (HT).

"Velvety deep red, strong growth, very good cutting-, forcing-, and bedding-rose." [Ck] "Bud large, globular; flower large, full, double, globular, borne singly on long, strong stem; very lasting; strong fragrance. Color dark velvety red, shaded with crimson and fiery red. Foliage abundant, large, glossy, dark green. Very vigorous grower of bushy habit and an abundant and continuous bloomer. Hardy." [ARA20/130] "Sweetly scented. Growth vigorous, of spreading habit, dark green foliage." [GeH] "Brought out as an improvement on 'Château de Clos-Vougeot', and, in respect of habit of growth, it undoubtedly is. In other respects, I prefer the latter. It, however, makes a nice dark crimson buttonhole Rose. Not over vigorous." [NRS24/153]

Capitaine Soupa

Laperrière, 1902

From 'Mme. Caroline Testout' (HT) × 'Victor Verdier' (HP).

"Growth vigorous, with heavy, erect wood; thorns strong and not very numerous; foliage light and dark green. Blossom a beautiful bright pink color, very large and quite double, borne on a long, strong, and upright stem; opens very well, not bothered by dampness or great heat." [JR26/162]

[Cardinal]

J. Cook, 1904

From 'Liberty' (HT) × a red seedling.

"Deep rich crimson; very fine. Makes large, finely formed flowers; double and full." [C&Js15] "A splendid new Hybrid Tea Rose, strong grower and free bloomer. Makes large finely formed flowers, very double and full, deep dark red center elegantly tinted with golden yellow. A true monthly rose with rich tea fragrance. Very beautiful and a constant bloomer." [C&Js/06]

Charles de Lapisse   Listed as 'Monsieur Charles de Lapisse' (HT).

[Charles J. Graham]

A. Dickson, 1906

"Thoroughly remarkable HT; its enormous flowers …are a superb orange crimson." [JR29/153] "Large, full, sparkling crimson orange." [JR22/190] "Very bright crimson. —Vigorous. —Exhibition, garden. —A cool season rose of fine colour. Fragrant." [Cat12/19] "Rather small with me, and not very perpetual." [NRS14/159] "A cool summer Rose only, but at its best there are few Roses brighter in colour. The flowers are excellent in shape, fragrant, but the number of petals is small. A good grower, apt to make one tall shoot, that must not be stopped as it will only shoot away again from the first eye." [F-M] "Dazzling." [CA10]

Charles K. Douglas

H. Dickson, 1919

"Intense flaming scarlet." [ARA19/v] "Flowers of a striking crimson-scarlet that does not fade. A vigorous grower with an abundance of disease-resistant foliage." [C-Ps26] "A mighty good red, too. For cutting it is perhaps a little better than 'Étoile de Hollande' [HT]." [ARA29/46] "Fairly large, semi-double flowers of striking scarlet, with crimson suffusion, that fades some, but not unpleasantly. It blooms continuously and in the evening the flowers fold up in graceful fashion." [C-Ps27] "One of the cheeriest red bedding kinds and is seldom without bloom until after hard frost." [C-Ps28] "Its blooms are not of the approved exhibition type … although lacking scent, they make up that deficiency by the brilliance of their intense scarlet color. The plant is perfectly hardy here [Toronto, Canada], a vigorous grower and a willing worker." [ARA29/59] "Although its petals are on the loose side they are long and of good texture. Blooms fairly full and shapely.

Charles K. Douglas *continued*

Growth free and vigorous and foliage handsome, but not altogether free from mildew." [NRS24/153] "Mildew-proof." [GeH] "Bud large, long-pointed; flower large, full, double; sweet fragrance. Color intense flaming scarlet, flushed bright velvety crimson. Foliage dark green; disease resistant. Vigorous, upright grower; produces an abundance of blooms from June to October." [ARA20/126]

Château de Clos-Vougeot
Pernet-Ducher, 1908

"Velvety maroon red nuanced and shaded dark maroon." [Riv] "Velvety maroon, shaded with fiery red. It is as dark as the famous 'black' rose, 'Prince Camille de Rohan' [HP] . . . but richer in color." [C&Js21] "Velvety scarlet, shaded with fiery red, changing to dark velvety crimson as the flowers expand; handsome foliage." [C&Js10] "Keeps its brilliant coloration despite the temperature." [JR32/85] "Delicious perfume." [JR32/124] "Perfume strong in the spring and fall, fair in summer; twenty-two blooms throughout the season on Multiflora; growth above the average. A rose worthy of cultivation for its unique and beautiful color." [ARA17/24] "Velvety scarlet to dark velvety crimson; low spreading growth. Darkest hybrid tea. Use Japanese Multiflora [*as budding stock*]. Disbud." [Th] "Growth above average; wonderful color; good fragrance; fair bloomer." [ARA18/110] "Good vigor, branching; foliage somber green; thorns occasional and slightly protrusive; flower large, globular, full, richly colored crimson scarlet nuanced fiery red passing to blackish velvety purple." [JR32/25] "Low, moderately spreading, not vigorous, apparently hardy; foliage almost sufficient, healthy; bloom moderate three-fourths of time, distributed well through season." [ARA18/124] "Straggly grower, weak in Central East, but hardy. Velvety scarlet to dark velvety crimson, with some shading almost black; fragrant. Loses foliage early. Stems strong, but necks often weak. A collector's rose." [Th2] "A difficult Rose to manage—it spreads out its branches in a curious and rather ineffective manner." [NRS21/111] "The sprawling bush should be trimmed so the branches grow upright, and then the stems will be long." [ARA29/55] "The plants are rather low and spreading in habit of growth, so should be planted on the outside edge of your bed of Hybrid Teas." [C&Js24] "I have overcome the bad effect of its awkward habit of growth by planting in a bed at the top of a low 'dry' containing wall. In this position the flowers appear to lean forward and look you in the face as you enter, as though extending a greeting of sweet perfume and beauty." [NRS20/161]

"Has a depth of velvety crimson unapproached by any other rose and, though a shy bloomer, is well worth growing." [ARA18/79] "It is a lovable, but often an exasperating Rose . . . Growth is uncertain and eccentric. It blooms well and seldom 'blues'; stems are usually strong but low and horizontal. The bush is quite hardy, but is apt to lose its foliage early." [C-Ps25] "A remarkable Rose." [C&Js15]

Chrissie MacKellar
syn. 'Chrissie McKellar'
A. Dickson, 1913

"Crimson-carmine on rich, deep ochrey-madder, becoming orange-pink as the semi-double blooms develop." [C&Js15] "Delicate luminous orange pink. Reverse, bright orange; very floriferous. Good size." [Ck] "Carmine crimson, passing to orange pink. Garden." [NRS15/147] "Very fragrant . . . must be classed as a semi-double. The colour

is brilliant carmine super-imposed on deep brownish red, and changing to orange pink as the blooms develop." [NRS18/139] "Orange pink, veined carmine. Coloring entirely unique and difficult to describe. Very free flowering and richly scented. Semi-double." [CA17] "Yellow-madder in bud, fading to orange-pink. Growth strong and bushy; foliage very good; a decorative only. Gives over sixty blooms in Central Zone." [Th2] "A sumptuous and magnificent rose, in which the pointed buds are intense crimson carmine veined madder and deep ochre, becoming more orange when the semi-double flowers open; the reverse of the petals is intense orange mixed with the above-mentioned colors . . . vigorous and branching growth . . . great abundance . . . intense green foliage . . . strongly and pleasantly scented." [JR37/105] "Perfume mild . . . growth splendid—high, strong and bushy, with many canes. Easily established and well adapted for decorative purposes." [ARA17/25] "Primrose Tea perfumed, buds long and pointed. Growth vigorous, branching; very free." [GeH] "A variety that requires slight pruning. When left almost unpruned it is seen at its best. Very free flowering. The colour is orange pink; flowers semi-single, beautiful in bud." [NRS21/62] "Splendid growth and foliage; color attractive; excellent bloomer, especially decorative." [ARA18/110] "Makes a pretty bed, if only by reason of its beautiful foliage, which is light brown when young, and its extremely free flowering habit. The flowers are thin, scarcely semi-double, of a light orange buff, with a faint tinge of pink. They look pretty when fresh, but go over too quickly. The plant grows well, and has a very branching habit, and, in spite of its rather strict limitations, is worth growing." [NRS21/47]

Chrissie McKellar   Listed as 'Chrissie MacKellar' (HT).

Circe
W. Paul, 1916

"Flesh-white shaded with carmine, base of petals deep yellow, large, and full, with handsome elongated buds." [GeH] "Whitish-pink, large, full, medium height." [Sn] "Good color and growth; large, attractive blooms." [ARA18/118] Circe, beguiling enchantress of Homer's *The Odyssey*.

Clarice Goodacre
A. Dickson, 1918

"Pure white, yellowish tinted center. Odor good. Weak stem. Bush very strong." [ARA26/94] "Ivory-white to lightest chrome; long spiral bud; medium size; good lasting qualities; claimed to have tangerine perfume. Small growth; fine stem; good foliage. An exhibition rose. Particularly adapted to Pacific North-West and Pacific South-West Zones." [Th2] "Of vigorous growth with pretty foliage. The blooms, which are somewhat thin, are finely pointed. Colour chrome on ivory white—very distinct. It will make a fine decorative and bedding variety." [NRS18/168] "Will give bloom for the exhibition box, as well as being a suitable bedding rose." [ARA18/47] "Its perfectly spiral globular-formed bloomed are three-quarter zoned biscuit-chrome on ivory-white stiff petals; long pointed buds carried on erect rigid flower stalks. Vigorous and erect wood festooned with ideal H.T. foliage." [GeH] "Somewhat scantily clad—*à la mode*—and with a stem not overstrong, this variety produces blooms which in their half-opened state cause one instinctively to remove his hat! She demands plenty of rich food if she is to appear at her best." [ARA29/59–60] "Growth, form, and color good. Tested by Dr. Huey as a seedling for some time and considered by him a valuable variety. Promising." [ARA18/118]

Clément Pacaud
Chambard, 1916

"Red, large, full, moderate height." [Sn] "Growth vigorous; flower very large, brilliant carmine; continuous bloomer." [ARA18/108]

Cleveland II   Listed as 'Mrs. Dunlop-Best' (HT).

Colonel Leclerc
Pernet-Ducher, 1909
From 'Mme. Caroline Testout' (HT) × 'Horace Vernet' (HP).

"A curious shade of cherry red, flushed with carmine. It is a Rose with a wonderful fragrance." [NRS27/63] "[Blossoms] produced singly. Growth vigorous, free flowering." [GeH] "Growth very vigorous with erect canes; leaves somber green; solitary bud; flower large, globular, pretty full; color, cerise red nuanced carmine lake . . . Like 'Mme. Caroline Testout', from which it takes certain characteristics, this variety is very floriferous; it will be an excellent garden rose which will add much to the category of continuous-blooming red roses." [JR33/23]

Columbia
E. G. Hill, 1917
From 'Ophelia' (HT) × 'Mrs. George Shawyer' (HT).

"Hydrangea pink." [Cw] "Clear rose-pink; almost thornless." [ARA22/xiv] "Sometimes lighter pink. A great prize-winner. It blooms freely and produces perfect blooms all season." [C&Js24] "True pink, of the shade of 'Mrs. George Shawyer', deepening as it opens to glowing pink, produced on long stiff stems; fragrant. It is a free grower, with beautiful foliage." [GeH] "Light pink, with full petalage; opens somewhat flat in heat; deliciously fragrant. Good but not strong grower . . . Of exceptional value in cool conditions; must be given careful protection. Good in early and late seasons in southern California. Scorches in heat." [Th2] "A lovely and very fragrant rose, usually at its best in the fall. It will keep a long time when cut and is a good hot-weather rose." [ARA29/54] "The blooms open slowly to large and shapely flowers of imbricated form, which are carried upright on stiff stems. It is quite free . . . Has some fragrance." [NRS24/153] "Perfume is its best point, although its keeping quality and form make it valuable as a cut-flower . . . The color does not spot in partial shade. It blooms freely." [ARA31/99] "The color of the bud is rose-pink, and it opens into a very large, full flower which deepens and brightens in color as the bloom expands. The plant grows freely, and the young growth is quickly produced. The stems are long and stiff, and the ample bronzy green foliage is itself of great beauty. It will thus be noted that this rose gives great promise as a forcing variety." [ARA17/35] "A very large free flowering Rose of good shape. The blooms are freely produced and not liable to much damage by rain. Very sweetly scented. Colour bright rose pink, becoming paler as the blooms age. Foliage and wood dark green, somewhat similar to that of 'Ophelia' . . . Fairly free of mildew. Growth vigorous and upright." [NRS23/90] "Beautiful foliage and fine, healthy growth." [ARA18/96]

"Its large and firm buds open very slowly to wide, impressive flowers whose color deepens as it expands to a rich rose-pink, slightly tinged with yellow at the base of the petals. The stems are long and very strong, making it ideal for cutting because of its heavy sub-stance and fine lasting quality. It is delightfully fragrant. This Rose is particularly good in the cooler seasons, when the color is richer, and it produces flower after flower with great freedom. It does not bloom so well in hot weather, when the buds may be short and puckery, and the flowers not so good. The plant grows fairly well, but is chiefly made up of flower-stems. Reasonably hardy, but careful protection in the colder regions will be found advisable. It has few thorns, and the foliage is healthy." [C&Js25] "The new rose, 'Columbia', which was introduced last year, met with instant and splendid appreciation on the part of the public. That the rose warrants it, goes without saying, but it is seldom that a rose will in one season establish itself as did 'Columbia'." [ARA19/109] "'Columbia' comes as near to perfection for the amateur as can possibly be expected from any rose." [C-Ps26] Columbia, poetical name for the United States of America in particular or for the Americas generally.

Commandant Letourneux
Bahaud/Ketten, 1903
Sport of 'Joséphine Marot' (HT).

"Bright, soft pink." [Y] "Pink, very large, very full, very fragrant, medium height." [Sn]

Comte de Torres   Listed as a Climbing HT.

Comte F. de Chavagnac   Listed as a Climbing HT.

Comte G. de Rochemur
A. Schwartz, 1911
From 'Xavier Olibo' (HP) × 'Gruss an Teplitz' (B).

"Fiery scarlet tinted satiny vermilion, with bright center and rosy white edged petals; perfume above the average; sixty-seven blooms throughout the season; growth average. An especially desirable rose on account of its blooming qualities." [ARA17/24] "A soft crimson Rose that seems to have become popular in America." [NRS21/44] "Good form, double, medium size, fragrance, and stem. Fine foliage, sufficient. Growth poor; hardy. Scarlet-red shaded vermilion, lighter edges." [ARA23/159] "Growth moderate." [GeH] "Very vigorous, holds its foliage very well; long bud, well held, fiery carmine red; flower large, full, very beautiful form, sparkling scarlet red nuanced satiny vermilion, center flame, petal edges tinted and nuanced whitish pink. Very beautiful coloration, very floriferous, very fragrant . . . doesn't blue." [JR35/166–167]

Comtesse Beatrix de Buisseret
Though sometimes seen listed under this name, and as from "Soupert & Notting, 1900," this is actually 'Béatrix, Comtesse de Buisseret' from Soupert & Notting in 1899, and will be found in *The Old Rose Advisor* under that name.

Comtesse de Cassagne
M. Guillot, 1919
"Rich coppery pink, shaded clear rose, occasionally quite yellow; large, lovely bud; holds center well. Growth and foliage good. Doing well in southern California, but lighter in color." [Th2] "Lovely buds and large, full flowers, slightly pink inside and ivory-white outside. The blooms are borne on strong stems and have a pronounced Hybrid Tea fragrance. It seems to be a vigorous grower and continuous bloomer." [ARA21/147] "Vigorous, very wide full petals, outside petals ivory yellow, inside slightly pinkish, very fine bud, rigid stem with

Comtesse de Cassagne *continued*

H.T. perfume, upright growth and continuous bloomer." [NRS21/105] "Bud elongated . . . glossy green foliage." [GeH] "Bud very large, long-pointed; flower very large, globular, very double, borne, several together, on long stems; very lasting; strong fragrance. Color coppery rose, shaded with bright rose—varies, sometimes being entirely yellow. Foliage abundant, large, light green; disease resistant. Very vigorous grower of bushy habit and bears a profusion of blooms all season." [ARA20/131] "Vigorous, with abundant dark glossy foliage. Bud and bloom large, very double, ivory-yellow, very lasting. Fair bloomer. No disease. Very lovely." [ARA28/151]

Comtesse Icy Hardegg

Soupert & Notting, 1907
From 'Mrs. W. J. Grant' (HT) × 'Liberty' (HT).

"Shining pure carmine, always constant . . . The blossoms are large and fuller than those of ['Mrs. W. J. Grant'], with larger petals of better consistency; the perfect bud is longer than that of its mother." [JR31/137] "Red, large, full, medium height." [Sn] "Glowing carmine, very large, full, elongated bud. Growth vigorous, very floriferous." [GeH] "Deep vivid carmine. —Garden, bedding. —Vigorous. —Fragrant." [Cat12/21] "A beautiful bright carmine color. Bud is very long and pointed; flowers very large, full, perfect form. A superb Rose and a decided acquisition." [C&Js11]

Contrast

Howard & Smith, 1937
"Deep pink, white exterior, large, full, medium scent, medium to tall." [Sn]

Cornelis Timmermans

Timmermans, 1919
From 'Pharisäer' (HT) × 'Le Progrès' (HT).

"Soft pink with yellow, very large, full, sweetly scented. Growth vigorous, bushy, free flowering." [GeH] "Clear pink, yellow edge; large; fragrant; forty petals; best in the half-open flower; discolors somewhat. Good foliage. Vigorous; free blooming. Has done well for Howard & Smith, Los Angeles, Calif." [Th2] "Type, foliage like [that of] 'Le Progrès'; blooms like [those of] 'Pharisäer', but more double. Flower very large, full, double, very lasting; clear pink, with deep yellow edge; fragrant. Vigorous; free bloomer." [ARA21/164]

Countess of Derby

A. Dickson, 1905
"Flesh-peach. —Vigorous. —Garden, bedding. —Very free flowering. Good in autumn." [Cat12/21] "Salmon center, shading off to delicate peach. Pointed buds. Very fragrant." [CA14] "Form identical with [that of] the elegant 'Catherine Mermet' [T] but infinitely superior in growth and quantity of bloom produced. Blooms are large and symmetrical with pointed centers; color, salmon in center with outer petals rose, growth vigorous and erect, branching freely; deliciously tea perfumed." [C&Js07] "A newcomer of the 'Catherine Mermet' sort, but much more vigorous and deliciously perfumed." [JR29/153] "Fair growth and foliage; some autumn bloom." [Th] "Fair growth; not a profuse bloomer." [ARA18/115] "Free flowering." [GeH] "A good garden Rose, opening well in all seasons." [NRS14/159] "Distinctly a cool season Rose, and perhaps one of those Roses that are best described as garden Roses first and exhibition Roses afterwards—meaning by that, that only occasionally will one get a flower large enough for exhibition. A good grower, very free flowering, so it must be rigorously thinned out, shoots and buds too, if exhibition flowers are desired. A good shape with a fine wing petal; not so subject to mildew as some of the 'Irish' Roses." [F-M]

Countess of Warwick

Easlea, 1919
"A lovely rose which merited a high award at the hands of the judges, but apparently did not appeal to them. The color is rich yellow, edged with pink. It should make a good exhibition rose, as the flowers are large, regular in form, and carried erect, not drooping." [ARA20/120] "This rose reminds one somewhat of 'Mrs. Foley-Hobbs' [T], though the blooms are not quite so large, but they are, nevertheless, very attractive; tea-scented. The color, a bright creamy yellow, is of particular charm by reason of the pale pink edges of the petals." [ARA20/117] "A charming Rose of exhibition form. Colour lemon yellow, edged pink. Growth dwarf." [NRS19/171] "Vigorous upright grower." [ARA20/126] "Grows well, and has lemon and pink flowers, which are often pretty." [NRS21/58] "Foliage dark olive green, wood red." [NRS23/90] "Vigorous upright habit of growth, and quite free from mildew. Tea scented. A valuable bedding Rose and good enough at times for exhibition." [NRS20/149]

Crimson Crown

A. Dickson, 1905
"Red, middle yellowish-white, medium size, not very full, dwarf." [Sn] "Growth vigorous, floriferous, produced in clusters of 6–9 blossoms; flower pretty large, full, bright deep crimson, nub lemon white." [JR30/26] "Extremely floriferous and robust, of the 'Étoile de France' [HT] sort, with an identical coloration." [JR29/153]

Crimson Emblem

McGredy, 1916
"Brilliant scarlet, constant bloom. Excellent bedding rose." [Ck] "The most beautiful of all glowing crimson Roses in existence, extraordinarily [*free(?)*-]growing and free blooming, with almost smooth wood and mildew-proof foliage. It is the most beautiful brilliant, dazzling crimson scarlet Rose in existence, and is a very superb variety. The flowers are perfect in shape and form, with fine long stems for cutting . . . delightfully sweet-scented." [NRS16/167]

Cynthia Forde

syns. 'Miss Cynthia Forde', 'Mrs. Cynthia Forde'
H. Dickson, 1909
"Rose-pink; tall, bushy." [ARA17/32] "A very beautiful shade of brilliant rose pink, unlike any other Rose I know. Habit. Excellent in every way, free and branching, with the foliage well displayed . . . Its free-flowering character, good shaped and beautiful coloured flowers, will render it of the greatest value as a bedding Hybrid Tea." [NRS10/147] "The largest and best of all clear pink Roses. The growth is remarkable." [ARA22/xiv] "A medium-sized bloom of pure silvery pink. The ovoid-pointed buds open well into perfectly formed flowers in sunshine or in cloudy weather. Its petals unroll gracefully and evenly into a well-formed, imbricated, deliciously fragrant bloom. The bush is vigorous, grows erect, very floriferous, and the foliage is healthy.

A most dependable Rose." [C-Ps27] "A lovely reminder of the days of 'prunes and prisms,' with every petal carefully arranged in its large and very perfect flowers. Sweetly scented blooms, very durable, and bright rose-pink, with sharply outlined edges. Bush is erect, with many vigorous canes. A dependable, steady and deliberate Rose— not a 'thriller' in any sense." [C-Ps25] "Growth, foliage, and color very good; blooming fair. Use Multiflora [*budding stock*]." [ARA18/113] "Almost tall, compact, hardy; foliage plentiful, black-spots slightly; bloom free, almost continuous." [ARA18/127] "The nearest approach to 'perpetual motion' in Roses." [C-Ps28]

Dame Edith Helen
A. Dickson, 1926
From 'Mrs. John Laing' (HP) × a Pernetiana?

"A very large and double flower of vivid, pure pink, on heavy and very rigid stem; foliage persistent; plant very vigorous." [ARA28/128] "Flower very large, conical center, exhibition form, pink, slightly more salmon and even-toned than 'Mme. Caroline Testout' [HT], borne on good stems." [ARA26/181] "Full as the old Cabbage Rose, on strong single stems. Excellent as cut-flower." [ARA28/153] "The raiser said, 'the bloom is so big and perfect that you cannot expect many.' The blooms are *very long lasting* when cut." [C-Ps30] "Very sweetly scented" [ARA28/133] "Beautiful, but not vigorous . . . shy after the first blooming . . . plants grow little, and seem to get smaller every year . . . leaves fall off early . . . very beautiful, fragrant blooms . . . Throughout the South, it seems to do well." [ARA30/175] "Unfortunately, it is not a free bloomer, save in the Far West, but each bloom is so impressive that it is worth the price of the bush. It has enough Pernetiana blood to have inherited the mean trait of losing its foliage and resting in summer." [C-Ps29] "Bloom very large, full, and double, cupped, very lasting, strong old rose fragrance, pure glowing pink, borne singly on long, strong stem. Foliage medium size, sufficient, rich green, leathery, disease-resistant. Growth vigorous, upright, bushy, profuse, continuous." [ARA28/232–233] "It is one new variety that, in California, at least, has lived up to the advertising given it. It has everything—color, size, fragrance, vigor, long stems, and good foliage—and is a most satisfactory garden rose." [ARA29/148] "A large, finely shaped, clear pink bloom, with plenty of substance, freely produced on long, stiff stems; sweetly scented. Vigorous; foliage free of mildew; good for garden purposes." [ARA26/178] "An utter flop as a decorative garden rose." [K] "Did wonderfully the first year but has done nothing since." [ARA31/97] "Opens up a new era in British Rose history, being a departure from the semi-double and single varieties that have lately exceeded the saturation point. The pendulum has swung to the other extreme, and we now have a great, full Rose of the type associated with romance and knighthood. The large bud, on an erect, well-clothed stem, slowly opens, exhaling that old Rose perfume, now so rare. The color from the early bud till the end of the bloom is a solid 'Paul Neyron' [HP] pink. Never known to ball." [C-Ps28] "Vigorous grower. Good foliage, free from disease. A beautiful shade of dark pink, well shaped, and very fragrant . . . *Calif.*; . . . Does not open properly . . . *Calif.*" [ARA28/153] "This is one of the best Roses of recent years. The blooms are large, well formed, with a high pointed centre. The color is a rich glowing pink, inclined to pale as the blooms expand. Deliciously scented. The habit of growth is vigorous and branching, and the foliage is dark green, leathery." [NRS27/57]

Dean Hole
A. Dickson, 1904
Sport of 'Mme. Caroline Testout' (HT).

"Intense salmon pink." [CA10] "Light carmine, shaded salmon, very large, full, and fine form, high pointed center, free and good; a grand rose." [HDk04] "Silvery carmine tinted salmon; flower very large, full, high-centered; very floriferous, very vigorous." [Cx] "Often not a clear color. In autumn, usually muddy." [Th] "Nice shape; substance varies; above average size and cuts well; fragrant." [Th2] "Plenty of buds, some of which failed to open on account of the wet. It requires shading to get the best out of this Rose." [NRS14/159] "The variety 'Dean Hole' is one of the best of today's roses, and indeed one of the best roses of any time. The growth is very vigorous, branching, and very floriferous. The bud is long and pointed, and of pretty shape; the flower is very large, very full, with a high center. The color is superb and very fresh, and is silvery carmine with salmon-tinted reflections." [JR37/30] "Pretty form; petals thick and strong." [JR31/177] "Occasionally comes split . . . impatient of too much wet . . . very free-flowering." [F-M] "Blooms of excellent form, long and pointed, though the colour is rather unattractive—silvery rose and salmon." [OM] "Subject, but not badly, to mildew . . . Good grower." [F-M] "Fair growth; color not of best; mildews." [ARA18/115] "Low, weak grower; foliage sufficient; bloom sparse, well scattered through season." [ARA18/124] "Superseded by 'Mrs. Henry Morse' [HT]." [C-Ps29]

"It was a singular coincidence that the last letter the Dean wrote on Roses had as its subject matter this Rose that had been named after him. He saw a flower of it, but never saw the plant growing." [F-M] S. Reynolds Hole—Dean Hole—one of the far-famed clerical rosarians of Britain whose prose on the Queen of Flowers testifies to his deep love of that monarch.

Decorator
Hobbies, 1913

"Reddish yellow, large, semi-full, medium height." [Sn] "Produces its flowers in clusters; the buds are bright carmine striped yellow. When the blossom is completely open, the colors pale. Growth very vigorous." [JR38/55]

Defiance
E. G. Hill, 1907
From 'Lady Battersea' (HT) × 'Gruss an Teplitz' (B).

"A huge, rich red Rose of great substance and fragrance; one of the largest and finest lately introduced." [C&Js15] "Red, large, full, medium scent, tall." [Sn] "Small growth; not distinct." [ARA18/115] "Moderate height; foliage sufficient, free from disease; bloom moderate, about half the time." [ARA18/124] There is confusion with a Hybrid Tea 'Defiance' attributed to Kress, 1914.

Dernburg
Krüger, 1915
From 'Mme. Caroline Testout' (HT) × 'Souvenir d'Aimée Terrel des Chênes (T).

"Blossom large, full, pink with coral red and yellow. Cutting- and bedding-rose, indescribably floriferous." [Ck] "Light orange-pink, large, full, medium height." [Sn]

Desdemona

G. Paul, 1911

"Opaque pale rose pink. Vigorous. Bedding, garden. Fragrant." [NRS13/167] "Large bold, autumnal-blooming flower; very fragrant." [NRS11/197] "Fair growth; color and form not good." [ARA18/115] "The bush is vigorous and bushy; beautiful ample foliage. Flower globular, double, large, full; color, an opaque light pink, very attractive and rare. Always in bloom, very fragrant. A good autumnal for fanciers." [JR36/57] Desdemona, the willowy wife of Othello in Shakespeare's tragedy.

Die Mutter von Rosa

Verschuren, 1906

"Pink, medium size, full, medium scent, medium height." [Sn] "Vigorous bush; flower large, very fresh pink." [JR31/22]

Die Spree

Nauke, 1906

"Whitish-pink, large, full, medium scent, medium height." [Sn] "Vigorous, flower large, full, fragrant, opens well; color, flesh pink, satiny whitish pink within." [JR31/22] The Spree, German river passing through Berlin.

Donald MacDonald

A. Dickson, 1916

"Chiefly notable for its colour, which is bright and attractive, a shade of rosy pink—the catalogues call it orange carmine. The plant is of dwarf branching habit, and the flowers are nicely shaped." [NRS21/62] "Blooms are full with shell-like petals which glow with exquisite intensely orange-carmine color and the buds develop naturally into miniature exhibition blooms, 3 1/2 to 4 inches across [ca. 9–10 cm], inexpressibly charming." [C&Js17] "Medium sized flowers, semi-double, produced in sprays, compact habit, good for massing." [NRS21/62] "Tea-perfumed. Growth perfect. A good bedder and a very attractive decorative variety." [GeH] "Of vigorous growth, with dark green foliage. The blooms are exquisitely formed, abundantly produced on strong stiff stems, and very sweetly scented. The colour, which is most attractive, is glowing carmine, suffused orange. It is a valuable addition to the bedding Hybrid Teas." [NRS17/128]

Dora Hansen

Jacobs, 1907

From 'Mme. Caroline Testout' (HT) × 'Mme. Jules Grolez' (HT).

"Salmon-pink, large, full, medium height." [Sn] "A fine Rose of good form, with long, shapely buds of pure, delicate salmon-pink. The edges of the petals are slightly curled." [C&Js24]

Dorothy Page-Roberts

A. Dickson, 1906

"A lovely shade of coppery pink, suffused with apricot yellow, especially at the base of petals, which are very large, massive and of great substance." [CA10] "Large, globular blooms of coppery pink, suffused apricot-yellow—a color difficult to describe but most attractive." [C&Js24] "Flower large, full, coppery carnation pink tinted apricot yellow." [JR35/14] "Coppery pink; odor good; opens almost single. Bush strong." [ARA26/94] "Semi-double; coppery pink, suffused with yellow; free-blooming; growth very vigorous, hardy, with splendid foliage." [ARA18/133] "Disbud." [Th] "Glowing pink buds of large size, opening to a coppery pink bloom with yellow shadings. The stems are

long and strong and the plant grows very tall. The color fades quickly, and the foliage is somewhat subject to disease. It is a moderate bloomer and not very fragrant. Notable for its beautiful color." [C-Ps25] "Very large, fairly full, elongated bud opening well. Growth vigorous." [GeH] "Fine form, short to medium stem, large, full, fragrant. Good foliage, sufficient. Growth strong, hardy." [ARA23/160] "A tall upright grower of excellent constitution. The flower has good substance of petal and stands rain better than most, but it is only semi-double and may be thought too thin, while ... there is too long a gap between its flowering periods." [NRS23/56] "Growth tall and upright; attractive dark leathery foliage; flower semi-double, nice color; does not last well; fair bloomer." [ARA18/110] "Tall, rather spreading, vigorous; foliage sufficient to plentiful, black-spots and mildews slightly; bloom moderate, almost continuous." [ARA18/124] "Despite its small size, it is a rose of exquisite coloration: light pink with yellow shadings, destined to surpass 'Mme. Léon Pain' [HT] in popularity." [JR31/73]

Double White Killarney

syn. 'Killarney Double White'

Budlong, 1913

Sport of 'White Killarney' (HT).

"The only good, first-class white rose that we have available today, commercially." [ARA21/138] "Beautiful in the bud in early spring, but ... not a good summer boarder." [ET] "'Double White [Killarney]' will not produce so many blooms per square foot as the single 'White [Killarney]'." [ARA16/115]

Dr. A. Hermans

Verschuren, 1907

Seedling of 'Rosa Verschuren' (HT).

"Yellowish pink, large, very full, medium height." [Sn]

Dr. G. Krüger   Plate 69

Ulbrich/Kiese, 1913

From a seedling (resulting from a cross of 'Mme. Victor Verdier' [HP] and a seedling of 'Mme. Caroline Testout' [HT]) × 'Mme. Falcot' (T).

"Wonderful for bedding, forcing, and cutting. Flower large, quite full, keeping as a big bud for a long time; color, carmine and crimson red. Stem upright and strong. Leaves large, dark green, healthy; buds long. Penetrating perfume. This newcomer is certainly the most beautiful crimson red rose to enter commerce in ten years." [JR38/40] "Not a strong grower; no special merit." [ARA18/115]

Dr. Helfferich

Lambert, 1919

From 'Gustav Grünerwald' (HT) × 'Mrs. Aaron Ward' (HT).

"Bud very large, ovoid, rose-orange; flower very large, full, cupped, double and semi-double, borne singly and several together on long, strong stems; lasting; strong fragrance. Color rose, center yellowish orange, edges silvery. Foliage sufficient, medium size, glossy green; disease resistant. Vigorous grower of upright habit, reaching a height of 2 feet [ca. 6 dm], and bearing an abundance of blooms intermittently. Hardy." [ARA20/136]

Dr. Joseph Drew

C. Page/Easlea, 1918

From 'Mme. Mélanie Soupert' (HT) × 'Comtesse Icy Hardegg' (HT).

"A fine growing Rose. The flowers are produced freely and are pale yellow, overlaid with pink towards the edges." [NRS21/57] "Resembles 'Mme. Mélanie Soupert', but superior in growth, with fine large flowers of salmon-yellow, richly suffused with pink, the latter color predominating as the bloom ages; very sweetly scented. Vigorous grower; free bloomer." [ARA19/102] "A vigorous-growing variety of free-branching habit. The blooms, which are carried on long, stiff stems, are of fine shape. The colour is a handsome tinted pale rose, with copper at the base of its large shell-shaped petals. Foliage dark green . . . to me it is one of the sweetest-scented Roses we have had for some time. When disbudded it makes a fine exhibition Rose, while as a bedding variety, it is especially good in the autumn . . . free from mildew." [NRS19/136]

Dr. Nicolas Welter
Soupert & Notting, 1912
From 'Mme. Mélanie Soupert' (HT) × 'Mme. Segond-Weber' (HT).

"Salmon pink, very delicate and pure, center more intense. Flower very large, pretty full, held upright. Bud long and pointed. Very floriferous up to fall. Magnificent exhibition rose. Excellent for all other uses as well. Very fragrant. Has all the good qualities of its parents." [JR37/10]

Dr. O'Donel Browne
A. Dickson, 1908

"Carminy pink." [Ÿ] "Carmine rose, large, full. Vigorous." [GeH] "Carmine rose; flowers very large, full and well formed; petals large, shell shaped and of fine texture; foliage large and of good color. A valuable rose for any purpose." [C&Js10] "It is early days to say very much of this variety, but what little has been seen of it has been satisfactory. In general habit and appearance it more nearly approaches the Hybrid Perpetual class than the Hybrid Tea class. It produces a large flower of good shape that opens well with a nice smooth petal, and should prove very useful to the exhibitor. Colour carmine rose, very strongly perfumed. A good grower." [F-M] "[For] exhibition, garden, standard, town." [Cat12/23]

Dr. Troendlin   Listed as 'Oberbürgermeister Dr. Troendlin' (HT).

Duchess of Sutherland
A. Dickson, 1912

"The color is certainly novel, being a delicate, warm rose-pink with lemon shading on the white base." [C&Js14] "Possessing a Sweet-Briar perfume." [GeH] "Bright rose pink. Buds very long pointed, on strong stems. Very double. Petals veined. Strong grower." [CA17] "Delicate rose-pink. Vigorous. Bedding." [NRS13/168] "Upright grower; delicate warm rose pink with salmon shading; olive green foliage. Very little disbudding." [Th] "Good growth, foliage, color, and form; fair in bloom." [ARA18/110] "The blossoms are produced abundantly, and are borne upright at the tip of the stems. They are large, full, and elongated in form; the petals are usually large, strong, and velvety, making a blossom which is a veritable nest of delight; elegant scent; a truly novel color, delicate warm red nuanced lemon yellow at the base of the petals; the canes are upright and vigorous. The foliage is olive green. A very pretty rose." [JR36/91]

Duchess of Wellington
syn. 'Orange Killarney'
A. Dickson, 1909

"Beautiful saffron yellow touched carmine, a coloration certain-

ly little enough known in Roses." [JR35/183] "Deep saffron yellow, outside petals orange. —Vigorous. —Garden. —A striking colour. Fragrant." [Cat12/23] "Intense saffron-yellow, stained with rich crimson; delicious apricot perfume." [ARA22/xiv] "Intense saffron-yellow, stained with rich crimson, which, as the flower develops, becomes deep, coppery, saffron-yellow. The blooms are fairly full; petals large and of great substance. Free-flowering and delightfully fragrant. We consider this about the best yellow Hybrid Tea." [C&Js22] "Disbud." [Th] "Alas, rain is fatal to her complexion, and her appearance in wet weather debars her from the leading position she would otherwise hold in the front rank of our yellow beauties." [NRS20/102] "Demands protection from the rain." [ARA29/111] "It may be damaged by excessive rains, but when this happens another crop of buds follows in quick order." [C-Ps30] "Very beautiful in cool weather, but comes single and white in heat." [ARA19/47] "The open flower is deficient in petals. The flowers are richly tea-scented, and freely produced, but often hang their heads." [C-Ps27] "Slight spicy perfume; forty-seven blooms throughout the season; growth next to the largest." [ARA17/24] "Moderate, bushy." [ARA17/32] "The bush is a lusty grower, spreading wide, and is unusually free from pests. It is often very hard to establish, but when it is really at home, it is entirely hardy and can be depended upon. The less it is pruned the better, particularly the lower, horizontal growths. 'Duchess of Wellington' is not perfect, but it is by far the finest, thoroughly tested yellow Rose, and will be indispensable for many years." [C-Ps25]

"Saffron-yellow, opens lighter, fades quickly but owing to substance of petal does not wilt; attractive bud, often stained crimson; open flowers loose, not fully double. Stems long and strong, neck very often weak. Growth very fine. Foliage good but lost sometimes in long seasons. Gives close to fifty blooms in Central Zone. Scored high in American Rose Society's votes. A rose which is not noted in English lists and will be displaced by new introductions. Good for cutting early and late in East where hardiness is valuable. Is a great favorite in Pacific North-West, being used there as a cut-flower on account of the improvement in neck and substance in that climate." [Th2] "Best described as vigorously robust, with growth sometimes as thick as one's little finger, the fine foliage contrasting well with the flowers. Free-flowering. I have known this Rose as the orange Killarney for many years, and it is undoubtedly of good constitution, and while it will, I doubt not, occasionally give us a flower good enough for exhibition, its proper place and use is as a bedding Rose. It makes a fine standard." [NRS10/146] "Medium to large growth, very hardy; fine foliage, fairly long erect stem; long, pointed bud, medium to large flower, but not of great petallage; only fair keeper but a wonderful bloomer from frost to frost; the best yellow rose beyond all question. Plant 18 inches [ca. 4.5 dm] center to center. Prune to 5 eyes." [Th] "If we could have but one yellow rose we would choose the Duchess for her abundance of bloom, her spicy perfume, and her strong, disease-resisting constitution. The Duchess likes central Kentucky." [ARA31/99]

Duchesse de la Mothe-Houdancourt
Mille-Toussaint, 1906
From 'Mme. Abel Chatenay' (HT) × 'Maman Cochet' (T).

"Rose-red, large, full, medium scent, medium height." [Sn] "Growth very vigorous, flower large, full, very fragrant, carmine pink shaded vermilion pink nuanced straw yellow and coppery red." [JR31/22]

Duisburg
Hinner, 1908

"Deep pink, large, full, medium scent, medium height." [Sn] "Fair; not so good as other reds of same type." [ARA18/115]

Earl of Gosford
McGredy, 1912

"Dark crimson, heavily shaded. Growth vigorous. Very fragrant. One of the deepest colored in this section." [CA17] "Deep scarlet. Strong growth; floriferous; fragrant." [Ck] "Color deep incarnadine shaded like 'Victor Hugo' [HP]; wonderfully vigorous, it is particularly adapted to harsh climates. Due to these qualities, it has a great future in store." [JR36/171] "A fine strong grower, a Rose particularly well adapted for growing in adverse climates; owing to its fine free habit is bound to be a very popular Rose." [NRS12/209]

[Earl of Warwick]
W. Paul, 1904

"Soft salmon pink, shaded in center with vermilion. Large and full." [CA14] "Fragrant, opening well . . . free flowering." [GeH] "The flower is a rich salmon pink color, shaded vermilion at the center; large and full, wonderful in form, and quite distinct from all other roses known. This variety is splendid and will be much appreciated as an exhibition flower—which takes nothing away from its use as a decorative. The plant is very vigorous." [JR28/80]

Écarlate
trans. "Scarlet"
Boytard/Gouchault & Turbat, 1906
Seedling or sport of 'Camoëns' (HT).

"Brilliant scarlet." [Th] "Medium-sized blooms of *an intensely brilliant scarlet*. This Rose produces more bloom in a season than any other in this class. Flowers are semi-double and have lovely bright golden anthers in the center." [C&Js21] "Semi-double; red. A fine late summer- and fall-blooming rose. At Ithaca [New York] it is surpassed by other reds early in the season." [ARA18/133] "A superb and distinct novelty with color an extremely brilliant scarlet. It is a robust grower with medium sized, full blooms, which are produced freely. A splendid rose, higher in color than 'Liberty' [HT] or 'Richmond' [HT]." [C&Js11] "Great bloomers, but do not stand hot weather very well." [ARA19/46] "Light scarlet; short in bud, opens flat; medium size; does not last; no fragrance. Low, bushy growth; weak stem. Very good foliage . . . Gives over one hundred blooms in Central Zone, but of no cutting value; fine as decorative or bedding sort or for a hedge." [Th2] "One hundred and eight blooms throughout the season on Multiflora, ninety-three blooms on Briar, fifty-nine blooms on plants on their own roots; growth strong and bushy, but not exceptionally tall. A splendid decorative rose." [AA17/24] "Dwarf growth, blooming continually and very abundantly in clusters of 5–6 blossoms, bud long, light sparkling purple, flower the same color, cupped, semi-double, medium size. From 'Camoëns', from which it takes its erect bearing; but 'Écarlate' is much more vigorous, and the leaves hang on a long time." [JR30/136] "Strong, bushy growth; splendid foliage, wonderful amount of bloom. Decorative rose, doing best on Multiflora [understock]." [ARA18/110] "A strong-growing, free-blooming Rose. A brilliant scarlet of the first magnitude, and one of the hardiest of the Hybrid Tea class. The blooms are loose-petaled, medium in size, and slightly fragrant. Their beauty lies in their great showiness.

Flowers cover the bush throughout the season. It grows about 3½ feet high [ca. 1.2 m] and is fine when used as a hedge or low screen." [C-Ps27] "A charming little Rose, always in bloom, and very bright, but the wood has too many thorns." [NRS29/249] "So much like 'K. of K.' [HT] that few people want both." [C-Ps26]

"The foliage is rather small, fairly dense, but not very bright; it is dark green in colour. The habit of the plant is very branching, each plant making quite a little thicket, from which the flower stems are thrown up erect and level. It is practically always in flower . . . and it is covered with flowers till very late in the year; perhaps it is one of the last in bloom in the garden. The flowers are only semi-double, light scarlet with a dash of crimson; they are carried in loose branching panicles, and are very showy and effective in the distance. The individual flowers have no beauty of shape, very little substance, and the colour soon goes; consequently they are very fleeting, but they are so quickly replaced by others that the general effect of the bed is good throughout the season . . . The flowers have a certain fragrance, but it is not very pronounced . . . The upright flower stalks of 'Écarlate' carry the flowers well above the foliage at a nearly uniform height . . . The plants seem practically free from mildew and other diseases. 'Écarlate' has a good constitution, and is very hardy, and makes an excellent bedding Rose. I think it must have some China blood in it, for it always reminds me of an upright growing China Rose, but, unlike this race, it had terribly numerous and strong prickles . . . As a bright and cheerful Rose, that demands little trouble or attention, it may be confidently recommended to those who are not seeking well-shaped flowers." [NRS12/81]

Edel
McGredy, 1919
From 'Frau Karl Druschki' (HP) × 'Niphetos' (T).

"Ivory white." [Ÿ] "White, on an ivory ground, then fading to pure white. Blossom enormous in size, flawless in form, with a long stem. A truly noble rose." [Ck] "Makes a magnificent bloom, full to the center, and unusually long lasting, the center still unfurling, dahlia style, while the concealed outer petals begin to wither . . . The best white Rose for warm and dry situations." [C-Ps29] "White, ovary flush at base; not as fine as 'Mrs. Charles Lamplough'; balls somewhat easily. Strong grower. Recommended for the west coast of Florida by Miss Creighton, and by Bobbink & Atkins for Central Zone." [Th2] "The large, globular buds contain nearly 100 petals and are liable to ball in damp weather, but in warm, dry weather they open to magnificent exhibition blooms. Sweetly fragrant. An irresistible Rose when it is happy." [C-Pf34] "A fine, promising exhibitor's rose . . . It is, perhaps, rather too heavy for an ordinary bedding variety, but has the good qualification of fragrance." [ARA20/122] "An enormous flower, perfectly formed, with high pointed centre—sweetly scented. The colour is a very pale cream. A good vigorous grower, it is an ideal Exhibition Rose." [NRS18/165] "Bud very large; flower very large, double, well-built, stately, opens well in all weathers; sweet fragrance. Color white, with the faintest ivory shading toward base, passing to pure white. Foliage bold and distinct. Very vigorous grower; free bloomer." [ARA20/127] "Excellent early in season, with long stems and shapely bud; not so good late." [ARA25/121] "Have had some fine upstanding blooms of this variety, and it is quite a good grower." [NRS24/154] "A fine grower, with uniform habit." [GeH] "A strong-growing Rose, producing very double ivory-white flowers of notable quality. Appears to be a vigorous grower, and quite healthy, although the flowers sometimes nod and fail to open in wet weather. Otherwise very promising." [C-Ps25]

Edgar Blanchard   Listed as 'Monsieur Edg. Blanchard' (HT).

Edgar M. Burnett
McGredy, 1914

"Flesh, tinted rose. Exhibition, bedding." [NRS15/148] "Very large full flowers, of fine shape and form, with large flesh petals tinted rose. A great improvement on 'La France' [B or HT] and may be regarded as an advance on the type of 'Lady Alice Stanley' [HT]; undoubtedly the sweetest scented Rose in existence." [NRS14/207] "A glorified 'La France', though it is a much better colour; does not blue. The blooms are a good shape, though perhaps not produced so generously as 'La France'. It is a good grower and a first class variety for any purpose." [NRS23/201–202] "A very large flower of fairly good form, but of those indefinite flesh tints which are seldom attractive … I have found the plant to grow fairly well." [NRS21/51] "Poor growth; small blooms; no distinguishing characteristics." [ARA18/115] "The gigantic size of the blooms was apparent. It is one of our largest Roses with a very great number of petals of a blush pink colour, with a deep edge of colour to each petal; deliciously fragrant. It is almost too large for a garden Rose, but it is so free flowering that it will no doubt find a place in many gardens. A good grower, and almost mildew proof." [NRS14/157]

Edith Cavell
Chaplin, 1918

"A large white rose, probably most useful for exhibition purposes. Good growth, but poor foliage, and the blooms looks as if they would split." [ARA20/120] "Of vigorous habit. The finely-shaped blooms are carried singly on long, upright stems. The colour, rather a cold lemony white, did not appeal to some experts." [NRS19/136] "Bud long-pointed; flower double, high center, well shaped, borne singly on long, strong stem. Color pale lemon-white. Vigorous, upright grower." [ARA20/127] Edith Cavell, heroic nurse in World War I; not to be confused with the Polyantha of 1917 'Miss Edith Cavell'.

[Edith Part]
McGredy, 1913

"Carmine with chamois, washed pink. Petals two-toned. Very beautiful." [CA17] "A coloration unknown till now. The tint is rich red, with deep salmon reflections, and yellow. The buds are darker red and yellow. The coloration is so pleasant and brilliant that there's no rose that can be compared to it … It is, in color, a mixture of 'Beauté Inconstante' [T] and 'Lady Pirrie' [HT] … admirable hold, grows well, very floriferous, of the greatest value for exhibition and decoration; very agreeably perfumed." [JR37/89] "Flower rich red, suffused with deep salmon and coppery yellow with a deeper shading in the bud stage of carmine and yellow, sweetly perfumed. Growth vigorous, free, branching." [GeH]

Edmée et Roger
Ketten, 1902
From 'Safrano' (T) × 'Mme. Caroline Testout' (HT).

"Flesh white, center salmon flesh pink, darker ground, large or very large, long bud, opens well, stem long and firm. Vigorous and floriferous … Dedicated to Dr. Dumas of Faverny and his wife." [JR26/163] "Large, full, fragrant. Growth erect, vigorous." [GeH]

Edmonde Deshayes
Bernaix, 1901

"Cream, center incarnadine." [Ÿ] "Creamy white with flesh-coloured centres, fine double flowers with evenly imbricated petals; growth moderate." [P1] "Creamy white, centre shaded white, large, full, and fine form; free and very good." [HDk] "Extra floriferous, moderate growth, flowers borne upright, quite double with numerous regularly imbricated petals … silky-looking, uniformly creamy white, nuanced blush at the center … abundant flowering." [JR25/147]

Edward Mawley   Plate 67
McGredy, 1911

"Said to be the finest of all dark velvety crimson Hybrid Tea Roses." [C&Js12] "Large, shell-shaped petals, their fine deep crimson colour, and its pronounced fragrance. The flower is large, and the form fairly good, but not first class, flowers with rounded or potato centres being too often produced. The colour, though good, is apt to blue somewhat in hot weather." [NRS21/41] "The foliage is not carried up the stem as well as one might desire." [ARA29/60] "Deep crimson, with darker shadings—varies; blues in extreme heat; good form, fairly full, remarkably fragrant; good stem. Foliage very fine and well retained. Growth medium. [For] South-east near coast, Pacific North-West, Pacific South-West." [Th2] "Truly superb, perfectly-formed blooms; the colour is a deep rich velvety crimson. The velvety bloom upon its huge petals is a revelation in colouring; the form of the blooms [is] faultless and perfect; very large and quite full with petals beautifully arranged, and of wonderful depth and substance … The growth is handsome, uniform, and perfect, holding every bloom rigidly upright, with the most delicious and sweetest perfume of any Rose grown … it never burns or goes off colour in the hottest weather … the warmer and hotter the sun, the more beautiful in both colour, shape, and form its flowers develop." [NRS11/78–79] "Shy bloomer." [Th] "Brilliant color; fragrant; good growth and form; fair blooming qualities. Use Multiflora [understock]." [ARA18/110] "Growth perfect, free flowering." [GeH] "A strong-growing, free-blooming variety, producing large, full flowers, of great depth and substance. Color is rich, velvety crimson and the blooms are delightfully fragrant." [C&Js21] "At the ripe age of seventy-four years there died at his home in Rosebank, Berkhamstead, England, on September 14, 1916, a man whose love and work for roses had given him a high place in the esteem of rose-growers the world over. Edward Mawley was made President of the National Rose Society of England in 1915, after having served it as Secretary for thirty-seven years. He was thus officially related to this greatest of all rose organizations for all but its first two years. To Mr. Mawley's zeal and ability may properly be ascribed the wonderful progress of the National Rose Society. He was greatly beloved by his associates." [ARA17/116]

Élégante
Pernet-Ducher, 1918

"Rich yellow bud, opening pale yellow and holding color well. Long, firm bud; full flower of fair odor. Medium petalage and substance … total of 10 [blossoms in the year]." [ARA27/147] "Long-pointed buds of deep chrome-yellow, on strong stems opening slowly [to] very large, fragrant, cupped blooms of deep yellow, fading to creamy [*several words lost due to damage to page*]." [C-Ps27] "The ideal yellow bedder of Tea habit. Spreading in growth, with a resistant foliage, it bears continuously long-pointed golden buds, gradually

Élégante *continued*

changing, when open, to a pleasing cream." [C-Ps29] "Always of good shape; bud long pointed on long stems; lasts well and color a very good yellow. Splendid foliage and strong growth. No disease." [ARA29/107] "Blossom very large, very well formed, gold-yellow. Plant very strong-growing; further, floriferous up until the Fall. Healthy leaves. To be recommended." [Ck] "Long sulphur-yellow bud, opening to a large, full flower of creamy yellow. Foliage bright green. A strong grower, with divergent branches; very floriferous." [ARA19/100] "Just that [*i.e., elegant*]! A very lovely flower. Low, spreading growth. Good in spring and fall. —*Harrisburg, Pa.* I like this yellow rose. It is a little pale in color but it has a beautifully pointed bud which opens slowly and well. Its shape is good, and the foliage is excellent. My bush has grown somewhat leggy but not spindly, and stems are quite vigorous. No mildew. —*Seattle, Wash.*" [ARA26/113]

[Elisabeth Barnes]
A. Dickson, 1907

"Satiny salmon rose with fawn center suffused with yellow. Outside of petals deep rosy red, shaded with copper and yellow. A charming rose, possessed of delightful fragrance." [CA10] "Growth vigorous." [GeH]

Elisabeth Didden
Leenders, 1918
From 'Mme. Caroline Testout' (HT) × 'General MacArthur' (HT).

"Red, large, semi-full, medium scent, medium height." [Sn] "Flower large, full; glowing carmine-red and scarlet; fragrant. Vigorous; free bloomer." [ARA21/165] "Blossom sufficiently full, with excellent form and poise; bright coral-red. Strong growth, erect, healthy foliage. Excellent garden- and cutting-rose." [Ck]

Elizabeth
B. R. Cant, 1911
Seedling of 'Frau Karl Druschki' (HP).

"Deep carnation pink at the center, lighter towards the petal edges; blossoms large and well-filled, with pointed petals. This variety is very pretty and quite decorative." [JR36/55–56] "Rose pink. —Vigorous. —Exhibition, garden. —Fragrant." [Cat12/65] "A pink flower of no very great distinction. The substance of petal and form of flower are both fair, and the plant grows sufficiently well . . . It is fragrant." [NRS21/42] "Fair growers with some autumn bloom." [Th]

[Elizabeth Cullen]
A. Dickson, 1919

"Scarlet crimson. Moderately vigorous." [NRS23/list] "It has proved with us a dwarf grower and not so free as we could have wished." [NRS24/141] "A vigorous growing Rose, of free branching habit. Blooms large, semi-double, produced in great profusion. Not liable to damage by rain. Fragrant. Colour a deep crimson, which it retains well. Foliage and wood reddy green. Fairly free of mildew. Said to be an improvement on 'K. of K.' [HT], but personally I prefer the older variety. An excellent bedding Rose, but one that requires a cool season." [NRS23/91] Unlikely parent of 'Schwabenland' (Rg).

Enchanter
J. Cook, 1903
From 'Mme. Caroline Testout' (HT) × 'Mlle. Alice Furon' (HT).

"Light pink, large, full, medium height." [Sn] Not to be confused with the "fawn with white center" 'Enchantress' (T). "Bearing a most

important relation to the production of Hybrid Tea roses is John Cook, of Baltimore. Mr. Cook is a veteran in working with the rose. His first successful hybrid, 'Souvenir of Wootton', was sent out in 1888, and but few years have passed without having a real achievement to record for Mr. Cook. To have is succession come forth from one grower 'My Maryland', 'Radiance', 'Panama', and 'Francis Scott Key' [all HT] is certainly an evidence of the extremely high standard set by Mr. Cook, as well as of his discrimination in selecting his winners. In a recent letter he says, referring to the roses that have actually gone into commerce under his name: 'Hundreds of other seedlings were raised, with fine flowers, but were lacking in stem and growth, and were never sent out.'" [ARA16/44] "The originator of the world's best loved rose, 'Radiance', closed well-nigh a century of beneficent life on October 9, 1929 . . . One of the Editor's 'Golden Memories' is of a day spent in the home of this rose veteran after his ninetieth birthday, when his keen rose judgment, his forward-looking mind, his citizenship and his culture were all in evidence. 'Radiance', the world-rose, was only one of Mr. Cook's contributions. Beginning in 1888 with the first American Hybrid Tea, 'Souvenir of Wootton', he sent out some 25 varieties . . . His standards were so high that he 'junked' hundreds of seedlings which were equal to or better than the average European introductions. John Cook was a father whose sons and daughters gave him great joy and do him vast credit. He was a lively citizen, an interested horticulturist, a warm friend, a great rosarian." [ARA30/198]

Enver Pascha
Kiese, 1916
From 'Frau Peter Lambert' (HT) × 'Baronne Henriette de Loew' (T).

"Flower fleshy white, outside of petals soft pink, very full, opening well in all weathers. Growth erect." [GeH] "Whitish pink, large, very full, medium height." [Sn]

Ernest Laurent
Viaud-Bruant, 1914
"Whitish pink, large, full, medium scent, tall." [Sn]

Ernst Hempel
Mietzsch, 1907
Seedling of 'Mme. Caroline Testout' (HT).
"Light pink, large, full, medium height." [Sn]

Ethel Dickson
H. Dickson, 1917

"Growth fair; blooms attractive in color and form." [ARA18/118] "Strong, upright, vigorous, branching growth, producing its large, full, and beautifully formed flowers in endless profusion. Flowers large and very full with high pointed centre, the flower resembles [that of] 'Mme. Abel Chatenay' [HT] in type, but in bloom, habit and inflorescence may be clearly stated to be a great advance on that well known rose. As a bedder it is superb, its growth being vigorous and very upright. Colour, deep salmon rose with silvery flesh reflexes." [NRS17/162]

Étincelante
trans. "Sparkling"
Chambard, 1913
From 'Gruss an Teplitz' (B) × 'Étoile de France' (HT).

"Very vigorous, bushy, tall; foliage bronzy green, purplish, compact, very healthy. Pretty bud, long, bright velvety crimson with purple. Flower large, double, well formed, opening easily, beautiful and bright intense red shaded purple; abundantly floriferous and fragrant." [JR37/167] "Sweetly scented." [GeH] "Growth good to very good; color and form pleasing; blooming qualities above the average. Use 'special bed' for best results." [ARA18/110]

Étoile de Bologne Listed as 'Stella di Bologna' (HT).

Étoile de France Plate 57
trans. "Star of France"
Pernet-Ducher, 1904
From 'Mme. Abel Chatenay' (HT) × 'Fisher-Holmes' (HP).

"Rich red, shaded velvety crimson." [CA10] "Sweetly scented." [GeH] "A sparkling red Rose of happy disposition, whose cheerful flowers ride high on graceful stems . . . unfavorable weather sometimes prevents the buds from opening . . . Foliage is good and fairly resistant to disease." [C-Ps25] "Velvety crimson, fair form; balls in Central Zone, but opens well in South-East Zone. Good grower and a fair cutting rose." [Th2] "Very little disbudding [needed]." [Th] "Growth and color quite good; foliage fair; form frequently balls." [ARA18/115] "This is undoubtedly the most magnificent new Rose introduced for many years; it is a strong healthy grower, quite hardy and a quick and abundant bloomer, makes beautiful large pointed buds and extra large fully double flowers, 3½ to 4½ inches across [ca. 9.5–12 cm]. Color, very bright dark rich crimson, exceedingly handsome and sure to take first place among the finest roses in cultivation. Its hardiness, vigorous growth and freedom of bloom make it particularly valuable for planting in the open ground, while the large size, exquisite color, and the delicious fragrance of its buds and flowers make it especially desirable as a cut flower and forcing Rose." [C&Js06] "Low-growing, weak; foliage sufficient, black-spots slightly; bloom sparse, intermittent." [ARA18/125]

"According to that important voice, the Horticultural Press, the new rose 'Étoile de France' will be classed alongside such varieties as 'K[aiserin] A[uguste] Viktoria [HT], 'Hon[ourable] Edith Gifford' [HT], 'Mme. Ravary' [HT], and 'Killarney' [HT]. This marvelous newcomer will be very floriferous and remontant; the roses are as bright and red as those of 'Fisher-Holmes', as deliciously perfumed as those of 'La France' [B or HT], and of a form resembling that of 'Victor Hugo' [HP]." [JR27/161] "We have heard tell time and time again about this sensational rose, have had the good fortune to receive specimens of its rare beauty—and we cannot hesitate to declare that this novelty is not only of the first order, but that it also will take first place in the roseries for the sale of cut flowers. 'Étoile de France' makes a bush of great vigor and robust constitution, not very branching, occasional thorns, beautiful bronzy foliage, pretty long bud nearly always solitary on each stem, which is long and strong. The very large flower, with regular petals, is magnificent in form—an elongated cup, quite full, always opening easily; superbly colored velvety grenadine red, bright cerise at center. Other than its color and its elegant perfume, one of the great things about this flower is that it lasts a long time." [JR28/40]

Étoile de Hollande
trans. "Star of Holland"
Verschuren, 1919
Two parentages have been put forward: (1) from 'General MacArthur' (HT) × 'Hadley' (HT) or (2) seedling of 'Château de Clos-Vougeot' (HT).

"Large semi-double, very fine scarlet red blooms." [NRS21/107] "Very dark red full blooms of good form and with a most delicious perfume, quite as strong as [that of] any of the Hybrid Perpetuals. It is evidently a good autumnal." [NRS24/139] "Large; rich deep red, gleaming with color." [ARA2/96] "Large, semi-double flowers of a very beautiful scarlet-red." [ARA21/148] "A truly magnificent rose that I do not hesitate to recommend. The blooms are rather full, with broad, heavy petals of dark velvety crimson which never fades or 'blues.' It opens well in the worst weather." [ARA23/141] "Lovely bud with strong Rose fragrance, borne on long stems. Flower of good size but rather scant petalage, though the texture of the petals is firm. Color is deep velvety crimson, without shading. It does not blue, but lightens with age. Vigorous, branching habit and healthy foliage. A new red Rose of first magnitude." [C-Ps27] "The buds are fine, but the glory of this flower is in the half-open bloom which comes as near perfection as any red Rose we have. The color is deep velvety crimson, without shading; petals are large and firm, making an unusually fine semi-double flower, which is deliciously fragrant, and freely produced from June until hard frost. A beautiful Rose for cutting. Has leathery, disease-resistant foliage and is a vigorous grower; stands some shade." [C-Ps29] "Medium-sized, ovoid buds and medium to small, cupped, deep bright red, double flowers of good lasting quality and strong fragrance, borne singly or several together on long, strong stems. Soft, disease-resistant foliage. Moderate, upright growth." [ARA27/132] "Will thrive in almost all soils and situations." [C-Ps33] "The bush is generally of a branching habit, but in its second growth it throws up one or sometimes more strong stems—a vigorous plant. The foliage is good, and of a dark green which contrasts well with the flowers . . . wonderful and curious musk-damask perfume . . . The substance of the petals is good, and the flowers stand wet well. In sun they do not 'blue' much, as is the fault with so many red Roses, but become duller in colour." [NRS29/102] "The finest red everblooming Rose in existence, barring none. The petals look like soft crimson velvety, restful to the eye and at peace with any other color. Lovely long buds with true Rose fragrance are borne on long stems. Flowers are of good size, with not many petals, but of firm texture which holds them up in the form of a chalice . . . Vigorous when once established and resistant to black-spot." [C-Ps28] "The rose of roses to me; a great, big, loose fellow of velvety crimson." [ARA29/48] "A prize. Fragrant, productive, inspiring, marvelous! If I could afford it, I'd plant a hundred of this variety. The effect would be dazzling. One never tires of it." [ARA29/46]

Eugène Boullet
Pernet-Ducher, 1910
From 'Liberty' (HT) × 'Étoile de France' (HT).

"Crimson red, shaded carmine. Practically no disbudding." [Th] "Crimson washed carmine." [Ÿ] "Deep carmine . . . very floriferous." [JR35/183] "A very free bloomer and has proved itself valuable as a bedder for the garden. Color is deep crimson to carmine, and the large flowers are so freely produced that they make a sheet of gorgeous color." [C&Js12] "Fair; good growth and color; fair blooming qualities; inferior to others of same type." [ARA18/115] "Strong growth with canes not often branching; beautiful bronze green foliage, and usually solitary buds; flower large, full, globular; color, crimson red shaded carmine lake . . . continuous bloom . . . excellent for bedding." [JR34/40] GeH's "China-rose shaded orange-yellow" is an error for 'Mme. Eugénie Boullet' (HT).

Eva de Grossouvre
P. Guillot, 1908
Seedling of 'Mrs. W. J. Grant' (HT).

"Salmon-pink, large, full, medium height." [Sn] "Vigorous, flower very large, full, globular, large petals varying from light salmon touched with carmine to beautiful delicate salmon pink." [JR32/134]

Evelyn
A. N. Pierson/W. Paul, 1918
Sport of 'Ophelia' (HT).

"Large, full, imbricated flowers of salmon-white, shaded and edged with rose, yellow at base." [ARA19/102] "Almost full, large, fine form, quite fragrant, long stem. Fine foliage, plentiful. Growth medium, strong; hardy. Almost the duplicate of 'Ophelia', except in number of petals, being more double, and is not as good as the latter in blooming qualities." [ARA23/161] "Growth vigorous, upright. Distinct." [GeH]

Excellenz M. Schmidt-Metzler
Lambert, 1911
From 'Frau Karl Druschki' (HP) × 'Franz Deegen' (HT).

"White. Garden." [NRS15/148] "White, large, full, lightly scented, tall." [Sn] "Small growth; poor bloomer." [ARA18/115] "White, large, full, sweet-scented. Growth vigorous." [GeH]

Farbenkönigin
syn. 'Reine des Couleurs'; trans., "Queen of Colors"
Hinner, 1902
From 'Grand-Duc Adolphe de Luxembourg' (HT) × 'La France' (B or HT).

"Bright carmine overlaid with silvery gloss. Color deep at base, light toward tips. Petals two-toned. Large and full. Free blooming. Very handsome." [CA17] "Imperial pink. Practically no disbudding." [Th] "Salmon rose, with pink reflex. —Vigorous. —Garden, bedding." [Cat12/25] "Bright red, changing to imperial pink, medium, full, very sweet. Growth vigorous, erect, free flowering." [GeH] "Growth tall; few canes; color and form quite good; not a bloomer." [ARA18/115] "Moderately tall, compact, hardy; foliage sufficient, healthy; bloom free, continuous." [ARA18/125] "Floriferous and very remontant; the bush develops large blossoms of a bright crimson red, tinted on the outside with silvery pink; its branches are of moderate vigor and usually bear two or three blossoms which are deliciously perfumed. As is the case with many varieties, this rose suffers under great heat, and is effective only in the Springtime, as well as from September until the late frosts of the Fall." [JR27/145–146]

Fliegerheld Öhring
trans. "Aviator-Hero Öhring"
Kiese, 1919

"Red-orange, medium size, full, medium height." [Sn]

Florence Edith Coulthwaite
A. Dickson, 1908

"Deep cream, stippled with bright rose on the inside of the petals and reflected on the back, thus creating an indescribable delicate orange and peach glow. Flowers large, full, imbricated; foliage deep green and highly varnished; delicately perfumed." [C&Js10] "Yellowish-white, medium size, full, medium scent, moderate height." [Sn]

"Very small [growth], compact, weak grower, tender; foliage sufficient, healthy; bloom sparse, occasional." [ARA18/125]

Florence Pemberton
A. Dickson, 1903

"Creamy white, edged blush. —Vigorous. —Exhibition, garden, standard. —Free flowering." [Cat12/26] "Flowers very large, full, fine form, creamy white flushed with pink, shading to peach at the edges . . . Resembles 'Alice Lindsell' [HT]." W/Hn] "Creamy white, suffused pink, large, full, perfect form, high pointed centre. Growth vigorous, floriferous." [GeH] "Cream-white, suffused pink—holds color quite well; of fair form, medium size and petalage. Foliage seldom diseased. Very vigorous growth; stems, however, not always strong, except in Pacific North-West. Recommended . . . as an exhibition variety. Gives over three dozen blooms in Central Zone; many more in Pacific North-West." [Th2] "Large, creamy white flowers with shadings of delicate lilac-pink—one of the most beautifully formed flowers, and carried well on rigid stems. The plant grows vigorously, but is not a prolific bloomer, and the foliage is apt to be lost early. A Rose for connoisseurs. Keeps splendidly when cut." [C-Ps25] "The blooms have wonderful lasting qualities, remaining fresh and lovely after being in water for five days." [C-Ps27] "Creamy-white with 'suspicion' of pink, the edges of the petals occasionally flushed peach, making a most effective combination, and contrasting well with the beautiful dark-green foliage. A superb variety . . . It is a strong and vigorous grower, of free branching habit, flowering continuously, and in the greatest profusion throughout the entire season. The blooms, which are carried on firm and erect stems, are of phenomenal size, very full, perfect in form, with very high pointed centre. The petals are massive, very smooth and of unusual depth." [ADk03] "This is a good all round Rose, an excellent grower and one that in an ordinary season may be relied on to produce large flowers of good quality. Its petals are slightly tissuey in texture and are somewhat impatient of wet—but it is one of those Roses that have improved very much since introduced and is quite first rate in every way." [F-M] "Excellent growth; color and form attractive, not of the best; fairly good bloomer. Use Multiflora [understock]." [ARA18/110] "Superseded by 'Miss Wilmott' [HT]." [C-Ps29]

Flush o'Dawn
syn. 'Blush o'Dawn'
Walsh, 1902
From 'Margaret Dickson' (HP) × 'Mlle. de Sombreuil' (Cl T).

"Carnation pink." [Ÿ] "Pinkish white, large, full, medium scent, moderate height." [Sn] "Creamy white, sometimes shaded pink, large, full. Growth vigorous, free." [GeH]

Fragrant Bouquet
Howard & Smith, 1922

"A flesh-pink, shaded gold, but slightly fragrant with good petalage." [ARA25/101] "Pink, yellow center, large, full, very fragrant, medium height." [Sn] "Would be fine if it could be brought to grow upright instead of creeping on the ground. The flowers are lovely and the perfume is delicious." [ARA25/137] "Cross of unnamed varieties. Bud long-pointed; flower full, double, cupped, very lasting; shell-pink, base of petals yellow; strong fragrance. Foliage leathery. Medium height, bushy habit; very free blooming." [ARA22/190] "It has all the good qualities they claim for it." [NRS25/194]

Frances Gaunt

A. Dickson, 1918

"Pure, deep, fawny apricot, toning to silvery flesh. Its lovely shell-shaped petals form a beautiful, globular, cup-shaped bloom on rigid flower-stalk. Strong Persian-rose fragrance. Foliage glossy. Vigorous grower; branching; very floriferous." [ARA19/102] "A vigorous growing Rose, with deep green foliage. The blooms are large and globular, with shell-shaped petals, which are carried on strong upright stems. The colour is a creamy buff. Should prove useful for bedding purposes." [NRS18/167] "A rather short vigorous upright bush, with fairly large semi-double salmony-yellow blooms." [NRS21/105] "Quite a good Rose and a vigorous grower." [NRS24/155] "Superseded by 'Mrs. A[rthur] R[obert] Waddell' [HT]." [C-Ps29]

[Francis Scott Key]

J. Cook, 1913

From 'Radiance' (HT) × a red seedling.

"Abundant bloom of exquisitely formed, rich crimson-red flowers." [C&Js15] "An immense flower of bright crimson, which changes to bluish crimson as the flower ages. Not until the plants have warmed up is the flower really good, but then it is a wonder for size and solidity. The innumerable petals with curled edges give the appearance of a great ball of scarlet-crimson, long lasting, never fully opening. Does not age gracefully, and the flowers should be removed when they turn to a dull magenta. During cold, rainy weather, the outside petals may stick and prevent the flowers opening. A glorious Rose for dry climates; especially fine in late summer." [C-Ps29] "A jolly, big Rose, chockfull of broad curled petals, with great round buds on tall strong stems—a Rose to love and cherish in these days of so many loose-petaled semi-double varieties. Its bright crimson color sometimes 'blues', and its buds fail to open well in hot weather." [C-Ps25] "A magnificent flower, of heavy petals; grew well into a large bush and bloomed very freely. I like it." [ARA24/90] "A strong-growing, sturdy Rose of American origin, which has proved valuable for garden planting. Color is a deep, even red, and the flowers are large, very double, well formed, and of unusual substance." [C&Js18] "Delightfully fragrant. A superior garden variety, named in honor of the writer of 'The Star Spangled Banner.'" [C&Js24]

Franz Deegan Listed as 'Franz Deegen' (HT).

Franz Deegen Plate 55

syns. 'Franz Deegan', 'Friedrich Harms'

Hinner, 1901

Seedling of 'Kaiserin Auguste Viktoria' (HT).

"Cream yellow." [CA06] "Golden yellow at the center, delicate yellow around the edges. Form of 'Kaiserin Auguste Viktoria'." [JR30/15] "Large, full, very fragrant, opening well. Growth vigorous." [GeH] "Growth very vigorous; flower very large, full, well formed; color, delicate yellow, deep golden yellow towards the center. Very beautiful variety, notable for its profusion, the form of its flowers, and the richness of its coloration—yet the variety is not very well-known! It is, however, much to be recommended for cutting and bedding; it gives great stems, and buds which are nearly always solitary." [JR30/17] "Golden yellow center, outer petals soft yellow, often white; odor slight. Bush medium. 19 blooms; 17 the second season." [ARA26/94] "Very small [growth], weak; foliage sufficient to sparse, especially in late summer; bloom sparse, occasional, best late in season." [ARA18/

125] "A strong vigorous grower, throwing up fine blooming shoots very freely; the foliage is dark green and so tough and glossy, it is not troubled with rust or mildew; the buds are clear yellow, shading to lovely golden orange at the center." [C&Js05]

Frau A. Lautz Listed as 'Frau Anna Lautz' (HT).

Frau Anna Lautz

Kiese, 1912

"Blossom full, graceful, carmine red; the buds are long; the plant bears its blossoms upright at the tip of the cane; one of the most beautiful roses of this color." [JR36/55] "Red, large, semi-full, medium scent, medium height." [Sn] "Low growth; shy bloomer." [ARA18/115]

Frau Berthe Kiese

syn. 'Bertha Kiese'

Jacobs/Kiese, 1913

From 'Kaiserin Auguste Viktoria' (HT) × 'Undine' (HT).

"Pure golden yellow." [ARA16/21] "Yellow, medium size, semi-double, light scent, medium height." [Sn] "Light yellow; moderate, bushy." [ARA17/32] "Golden yellow, long orange-carmine buds, large, full, well formed. Growth vigorous." [GeH]

Frau Bürgermeister Kirschstein

Jacobs, 1906

From 'Luciole' (T) × 'Mrs. W. J. Grant' (HT).

"Growth vigorous, erect, long bud, opens well, medium-sized flower, full, bright bronzy red tinted carmine lake." [JR31/22] "Semi-full, very fragrant, medium height." [Sn]

Frau Emma Sasse

Plog/Hinner, 1908

From 'Mrs. W. J. Grant' (HT) × 'Paul Neyron' (HP).

"Light pink, large, full, medium scent, tall." [Sn]

Frau J. Reiter

Welter, 1904

From 'Mlle. Augustine Guinoisseau' (HT) × a seedling (resulting from a cross of 'Viscountess Folkestone' [HT] and 'Kaiserin Auguste Viktoria' [HT]).

"Pure white, or slightly coppery." [Ÿ] "Flower very large, very full, cupped, very delicate flesh pink, or pure white." [JR31/178]

Frau Karl Smid Listed as 'Mme. Gustave Metz' (HT).

Frau Lilla Rautenstrauch

Lambert, 1902

From 'Mme. Caroline Testout' (HT) × 'Goldquelle' (T).

"Creamy white, apricot-orange in centre. —Vigorous. —Exhibition, garden, standard. —Very free flowering. Pendant blooms. Fragrant." [Cat12/27] "Silvery white, tinted rose; flower large, very full with high pointed center and perfect form." [C&Js09] "Rosy flesh, coppery orange buds. Growth moderate." [GeH] "Vigorous; pendant blooms." [Au] "This new Rose (whose name I hope I have spelled correctly) seems well worth a trial, as I have had a few fine, well-shaped flowers of it, of varied and pleasing tints of colour. The different shades seemed to differ a good deal, according to the strength of the bloom and the atmospheric influences." [F-M4] "Good large blooms without disbudding, and worth growing if drooping flowers are not objected to." [NRS14/160]

Frau Oberhofgärtner Singer Plate 60

Lambert, 1908

From 'Jules Margottin' (HP) × 'Eugène Boullet' (HT).

"Pink, large, very full, medium scent, medium height." [Sn]

[Frau Peter Lambert] Plate 56

Walter, 1902

From an unnamed seedling (arising from a cross of 'Kaiserin Auguste Viktoria' [HT] and 'Lady Caroline Testout' [HT]) × 'Mme. Abel Chatenay' (HT).

"Flower deep pink, shaded salmon, large and full, fragrant, opening well. Growth very vigorous, upright, free. Exhibition." [GeH] "The rose 'Frau Peter Lambert', which belongs to the Hybrid Tea group, is expected to render the same service to flower gardeners who already grow 'Kaiserin Auguste Viktoria' for cut-flowers, which [latter] has today become one of the most popular varieties." [JR26/114]

Frau Philipp Siesmayer

Lambert, 1908

From 'Mme. Caroline Testout' (HT) × 'Erzherzogin Marie Dorothea' (T).

"Yellowish pink." [Ÿ] "Yellow, suffused with pink. Growth vigorous." [GeH]

Frau Therese Lang

Welter, 1910

From 'Mme. Caroline Testout' (HT) × 'Johanna Sebus' (Cl HT).

"Red, large, very full, very fragrant, tall." [Sn]

Freiburg II

Krüger, 1917

From 'Dr. G. Krüger' (HT) × 'Frau Karl Druschki' (HP).

"Flower large, double, well-shaped, long-lasting, inside silver-rose, outside bright apricot-pink. Vigorous, healthy, and floriferous." [ARA26/186] "Medium-sized, long-pointed buds and globular flowers of peach-blossom pink with deeper shading, double, moderately fragrant, and of good lasting quality; borne singly on medium stems. Vigorous, upright growth and continuous bloom. Very free flowering and constant." [ARA26/114] "Very excellent rose. Blossom large, with completely high-centered, beautiful form, quite full, long-lasting, ready rebloomer. Inside of petals, white-pink; outside, pleasing Persian pink, quite wonderfully beautiful, matchless color. Growth erect, strong; blossoms come long-stemmed; foliage healthy and beautiful ... The most beautiful, most valuable rose from this breeder." [Ck]

Freifrau Ida von Schubert

Lambert, 1911

From 'Oskar Cordel' (HP) × 'Frau Peter Lambert' (HT).

"Dark crimson red." [Th] "Deep crimson, long pointed blood-red buds, petals broad. Growth erect." [GeH] "Color clear; growth and foliage above average; satisfactory bloomer. Form not of best." [ARA18/110] "Good growth, hardy; fine foliage, good stem; medium size, fair form, lasts well; color 'warm crimson-red,' delicious perfume; thirty blooms in 1915." [ARA16/19] "Bush upright, vigorous, woody, with large brown thorns; foliage dark bronze green, healthy; bud long, pointed, deep blood red; flower large, ³⁄₄ full, somber crimson red in the shape of a chalice; petals large, elliptical, upright, separated, long-footed; fragrance strong and very pleasant. Dedicated to her Excellency, the Baroness of Schubert." [JR36/41]

Friedrich Albert Krupp

syn. 'Friedrich Alfred Krupp'

Welter, 1903

"Yellowish salmon pink, large, very full, medium scent, medium height." [Sn] Possibly a Tea.

Friedrich Alfred Krupp Listed as 'Friedrich Albert Krupp' (HT).

Friedrich Harms Listed as 'Franz Deegen' (HT).

Friedricharah Listed as 'Friedrichsruh' (HT).

Friedrichsruh

syn. 'Friedricharah'

Türke, 1907

From 'Princesse de Béarn' (HP) × 'Francis Dubreuil' (T).

"Deep blood-crimson, very free and sweet. Growth vigorous." [GeH] "In color it is almost as deep as 'Château de Clos-Vougeot' [HT], but the plant is much more upright and hence more satisfactory." [C-Ps27] "Deep red; dwarf, bushy." [ARA17/31] "Deep red, large, very full, very fragrant, medium height." [Sn] "A profuse blooming, deliciously sweet-scented, almost black-red Rose with flowers that darken as they grow older, making one of the darkest red Roses known. It has short petals but is full to the center." [C-Ps26] "Cushion-shaped when fully opened ... A record variety for the amount of blooms produced in a season." [C-Ps28] "Large, full, good form, very fragrant, medium-long stems. Foliage good, sufficient. Growth low, strong, bushy; hardy. Dark maroon-red with blackish purple shadings." [ARA23/161]

Fürst Niclot Listed as 'Kaiser Wilhelm II' (HT).

Generaal Snijders

syn. 'General Snyders'

Leenders, 1917

From 'Mme. Mélanie Soupert' (HT) × 'George C. Waud' (HT).

"Bright carmine-red, shaded coral red, large and full, of fine form. Growth vigorous, of great freedom in blooming." [GeH]

General MacArthur

E. G. Hill, 1905

Possibly descended from 'Gruss an Teplitz' (B).

"Vivid scarlet, almost vermilion. Dazzling, with the effect of scarlet geraniums." [Dr] "Flower large, full, flat, fragrant." [JR30/25] "Bright crimson; perfume good ... of all-round worth." [ARA17/24] "Tending to blue; fragrance strong and enduring; buds attractive ... about 35 flowers in a season." [ARA21/90] "Lacks substance." [ARA25/105] "Blend of Musk and Damask [perfumes]." [NRS/17] "Perfectly magnificent in flower." [Fa] "The floral display comes in bursts with flowerless intervals." [NRS23/55] "A grand new everblooming rose; both buds and flowers are extra large, and bright glowing crimson scarlet; a vigorous grower, every shoot producing a flower of most intense brilliant color." [C&Js07] "One of the very best of the Hybrid Teas. It is of strong growth, and bears bright red flowers, which, if somewhat thin, are very freely produced. A splendid rose for the garden." [OM] "Always good, but too pinkish a red ... fragrance, form, fine foliage ... free-flowering." [RATS] "Color tends to blue ... small [blossoms] in hot weather . . . almost immune from mildew; slightly susceptible to [black] spot." [Th] "Fine in spring and fall, but comes small and burns quickly in hot weather." [ARA19/46] "In hot weather it is likely to open flat quickly with few petals and not much color." [C-Ps27] "Scarlet-crimson; tall, bushy." [ARA17/31] "Low, spreading, compact, weak; foliage plentiful, healthy; bloom moderate, intermittent." [ARA18/125] "Very vigorous, floriferous and remontant ... develops solitary blossoms on stems up to eighteen inches long [ca. 4.5 dm]! The flowers are a dark crimson of a very brilliant shade, and are deliciously fragrant." [JR28/30] "Medium to large growth, very hardy; fine leathery foliage, good stems; fairly long bud, opening into medium-sized bloom of fair substance; a very fine keeper and good bloomer from frost to frost. Not as large as '[Dr.] Huey' [HT] or '[Laurent] Carle' [HT]. Plant 18 inches [4.5 dm] center to center. Prune to 5 eyes." [Th] "[Does] only passably well [in Houston, Texas, in comparison to 'Red Radiance' (HT)]." [ET] "Wonderful rose in Pacific North-West and Pacific South-West, where it gives fine growth and blooms profusely during a long season. In England the most popular red rose for general cultivation." [Th2] "Growth above average." [ARA18/110] "Very vigorous." [M] "Revels in a moist, fairly heavy soil. It has a splendid habit of growth—upright and strong, its foliage is much handsomer than that of 'Richmond' [HT], but the flowers are never of so fine a form as those of 'Richmond' at its best, nor is the colour quite so pure ... has a delicious fragrance." [NRS21/112] "It was a failure on my light soil till I took it down to the wettest and heaviest part of my garden, where it received a half shade ... [Its] foliage ... is noteworthy. It has a blackish tinge in the green, joined with a bluish black shade, which pervades the whole plant ... The carriage of the flowers is excellent ... the open flowers rather soon lose their shape ... Very free flowering and continuous and not to suffer from mildew." [NRS/13]

"For years this Rose has been one of the foremost of the red Hybrid Teas for bedding. It is a most continuous bloomer, keeping up an array of brilliant glowing crimson-scarlet flowers from early in June until frost comes. It is deliciously scented and the blooms come on long stems, suitable for cutting. A favorite wherever grown, as it produces perfect blooms and does well, even during the hot months of summer. A highly satisfactory red Rose for amateurs." [C&Js24] "Notable for its fragrance. Summer disbudding will increase the beauty and number of the autumn blooms. Plant of average vigor, with foliage almost immune to disease." [C-Ps29] "It blooms persistently and is especially fine in autumn. Foliage is almost immune to disease; plant quite hardy, but not especially vigorous." [C-Ps25] "The plant makes a strong, well-balanced bush of vigorous habit with strong foliage, slightly glossy, which is not subject to fungoid disease. During its flowering periods the crimson blooms are produced in quantity, and there may be three and sometimes four flowering periods during the season, but between these periods the bed is usually flowerless ... The fragrance is strong, and of the true old Rose character ... The flowers are rather thin, with short centre petals, so that they open to a flat and confused centre, wanting in form. There is also an element of blue in the flower, which is rapidly developed by hot sunshine (Mr. Glassford says they remind him of red cabbage in vinegar, which is scarcely an exaggeration), so that in a warm Summer the August flowering is disappointing. The flowers, however, are not much affected by rain." [NRS29/107] "Do you know that the first rose I [E. G. Hill] got [i.e., bred] that gave me any encouragement was 'General MacArthur'?" [ARA22/131]

General Snyders Listed as 'Generaal Snijders' (HT).

General-Superior Arnold Janssen
Leenders, 1912
From 'Farbenkönigin' (HT) × 'General MacArthur' (HT).

"Bright crimson. With us dark pink." [Th] "Fiery red." [Ÿ] "Particularly intense deep carmine ... Large, full, and very fragrant flowers. The perfectly formed buds are very distinctive. The plant is vigorous, compact, and continuous." [JR36/74] "Bright crimson—in Central Zone is dark pink, nearly a solid color; form lasting; perfumed. Foliage seldom has disease. Not an exhibition rose. Thirty-four blooms in Central Zone." [Th2] "Carmine; tall, spare." [ARA17/32] "The flowers come on strong stems, suitable for cutting. The buds are long, finely formed, and the color of the open flowers is very effective." [C&Js24] "Glowing deep carmine, finely formed bud on perfect stems. Growth vigorous, compact, and continually blooming." [GeH] "Very ready re-bloomer." [Ck] "Keeps a steady pace but never rushes into a profusion of blooms." [C-Ps29] "Excellent in color and lasting qualities; nice growth; fairly good bloomer." [ARA18/110] "Almost tall, rather spreading, hardy; foliage plentiful, little black-spot; bloom free in summer, intermittent during season." [ARA18/125] "A fine, upstanding Rose of glowing carmine, darker than pink but not quite crimson. The well-formed buds open slowly into big sweet-scented flowers which hold their color well. The bush is vigorous, quite hardy, and little subject to disease. Its most serious fault is its long name." [C-Ps25] "Another excellent own-root rose in 'General-Superior Arnold Janssen'. I have found it a close competitor of 'Radiance' [HT] in the matter of growth and bloom. Its unusual color makes it a striking addition to any garden." [ARA20/156]

General Th. Peschkoff
Ketten, 1909
From 'Mme. Ravary' (HT) × 'Étoile de France' (HT).

"Salmon red, fading to 'Hermosa' [B] pink, nub Indian yellow, interior of petals blush white; bud long and solitary, opening well. Shrub vigorous, floriferous." [JR33/152–153] "Light pink, very large, full, medium scent, tall." [Sn] "Salmon-pink, passing to pale lilac-rose, base of petals Indian yellow, inside rosy white, large, fairly full. Growth vigorous, free." [GeH]

Generalin Isenbart
Lambert, 1915
From 'Triumph' (HT) × 'E. Veyrat Hermanos' (N).

"Coppery pink, yellow in the middle, large, full, medium scent, medium height." [Sn] "Reverse of petals yellowish white, bordered with rose, inside of petals coppery rose, large and full. Growth erect; thornless." [GeH]

Generaloberst von Kluck
Lambert, 1917
From 'Frau Geheimrat Dr. Staub' (HT, Lambert, 1908, red; parentage: 'Mrs. W. J. Grant' [HT] × 'Duke of Edinburgh' [HP]) × 'Germanica' (Rg).

"Red, large, full, very fragrant, medium height." [Sn] Could be called a Rugosa hybrid—but hasn't been.

George C. Waud
A. Dickson, 1909

"Orange vermilion. Disbud. Marked by Dr. Huey, who considers it one of the best red roses." [Th] "Scarlet-orange; moderate, bushy."

George C. Waud *continued*

[ARA17/31] "Rose, suffused orange ... This promising Rose is such a good grower and so distinct in colour that it is pretty certain shortly to take a more prominent place." [NRS11/80] "Unique color—a light red with a touch of orange and vermilion. The blooms are double and have high-pointed centers." [ARA29/55] "The flowers are large and full, of perfect form and very sweet scented. The color is a very distinct glowing vermilion suffused with orange-red. A splendid Rose for amateurs to grow for exhibition." [C&Js23] "Highly tea perfumed." [C&Js10] "Perfume quite marked; twenty-six blooms throughout the season on Multiflora [understock]; growth average. Useful as a cut-flower variety." [ARA17/24] "Cochineal-carmine, tinted vermilion and orange, large, very full, high centered, generally single [*i.e.*, solitary] on long stiff stems, very sweet. Growth robust, erect, free flowering." [GeH] "Good in early part of season, but not very perpetual." [NRS14/160] "A shade of color heretofore unknown among roses." [CA10] "The color seldom 'blues'. Its fragrance is pleasant and spicy. The stems are long and strong. It is good early in the season and is particularly fine in autumn; the summer bloom is scant, off-color, and would better be disbudded." [C-Ps27] "Foliage [is] large ... The plant is unusually hardy and one of the very few really good reds." [C-Ps29] "Moderate height, rather compact, not vigorous; foliage sufficient, black-spots slightly; bloom moderate, intermittent." [ARA18/125] "It is good early in the season and is particularly fine in autumn; the summer bloom is scant and off-color. Subject to black-spot, but is a good grower and quite hardy." [C-Ps25] "A promising new Rose, remarkable for its colour described by the raisers as glowing orange vermilion—it is a good grower, is sweetly scented and has been well exhibited." [F-M]

Germaine Chénault
P. Guillot, 1910
From 'Killarney' (HT) × 'Rosomane Gravereaux' (HT).
    "Bush vigorous with erect canes; long buds; blossoms very large, full, globular, fragrant, salmon white, deeper at the center, sometimes brightened with carmine." [JR34/167] "Fair growth only; poor foliage." [ARA18/116] "Growth vigorous." [GeH]

Gertrude
A. Dickson, 1903
Sport of 'Countess of Caledon' (HT).
    "Flesh pink." [Ÿ] "A blush sport from the well-known 'Countess of Caledon', which it resembles in all save colour." [HDk] "A very beautiful blush sport from 'Countess of Caledon', which is resembles in every particular excepting colour, and possessing all the good qualities of this grand rose. It is perfectly distinct, and is a most valuable addition to this now important class [*i.e.*, Hybrid Teas] either for exhibition, garden decoration, or for forcing purposes. It is a constant bloomer, opening its flowers freely until cut off by frost." [ADk03]

Gladys Harkness
A. Dickson, 1901
    "Deep salmon pink, silvery pink reflections; cupped." [JR30/16] "Bright pink, not unlike '[Mme.] Caroline Testout' [HT], good foliage. Vigorous, scented." [P1] "Very large, good constitution and fragrant. A fine Rose." [P1] "Inclining to the H.P. side of the class, this variety is sturdy and hardy in growth and foliage, and the pink blooms, though not of the most refined shape, are large, with fine petals, sweet-scented, and good in the autumn." [F-M] "Vigorous. —Exhibi-

tion, standard. —Good in autumn. Fragrant." [Cat12/28] "A splendid new Hybrid Tea, growth very erect and vigorous; large and beautifully formed buds and flowers, resembling the famous 'American Beauty' [HP] in size and fullness; color, bright rich salmon pink; very fragrant and first-class in every way." [C&Js02]

Gladys Holland
McGredy, 1917
    "Cream-salmon-pink with orange yellow. Blossom very large, quite full; nevertheless opening well." [Ck] "Buff- to orange-yellow. Twenty-fifth in English Annual for exhibition in 1923. Poor grower in Central Zone and discarded there for general cultivation. Exhibition only." [Th2] "A grand Rose, rich buff in colour, with lighter shadings, good shape and size, very free. The blooms come very much at the same time." [NRS23/203] "Continuous flowering." [GeH] "Magnificent form and size. Colour buff, shaded orange yellow, outside of petals soft rose and pearly peach ... perfect uniform habit of growth ... Delicately sweet scented." [NRS17/172] "A Rose of vigorous upright growth, with glossy and practically mildew-proof foliage. The blooms, which are of perfect form and freely produced, are carried on strong upright stems. The colour is a creamy white on the outer petals, centre buff yellow and apricot. It is a very fine exhibition Rose, and will also prove valuable for bedding and garden purposes." [NRS17/127]

Gloire de Hollande
trans. "Dutch Glory"
Verschuren, 1918
From 'General MacArthur' (HT) × 'Hadley' (HT).
    "Dark red colour, in the way of 'Château de Clos-Vougeot' [HT], not turning blue, large and very full." [GeH] "It has the most glowing blood-red flowers that one can imagine, but it is apt to 'blue' at times." [ARA23/141] "Deep red, large, full, medium scent, medium height." [Sn] "Blossom very large, with flawless form, fragrant, quite full and long-lasting, always opening. Color red, shaded blackish. Growth strong, quite upright, well-branched. A completely outstanding sort which is insufficiently known." [Ck]

[Goldelse]
Hinner, 1902
Seedling of 'Kaiserin Auguste Viktoria' (HT).
    "Deep yellow." [LS] "Golden yellow, medium size, bud large, moderately full." [Jg]

Golden Ophelia
B. R. Cant, 1918
From 'Ophelia' (HT) × 'Mrs. Aaron Ward' (HT).
    "Golden yellow in the centre, paling slightly at the outer petals, of fair size, very compact, opening in perfect symmetrical form." [GeH] "Deep yellow upon opening, it quickly fades lighter, but the center remains definitely yellow. A well-formed Rose, descended from 'Ophelia' and with many of its good qualities." [C-Ps25] "Shorter bud than 'Ophelia', but holding center better; smaller and less pointed; slight fragrance; petals have less substance than [those of] its parent, but lasts." [Th2] "A seedling from 'Ophelia', possessing many of its characteristics. Flower of fair size, very compact, opening in perfect symmetrical form, golden yellow in center, and paling to almost white at outer petals." [ARA19/102] "Odor slight; fine shape, rather small but exquisite; lasts well when cut. Bush slim but strong." [ARA26/94] "Very

pretty orange-yellow flowers, the outer petals of a lighter shade. The blooms are carried singly on long upright stems, and in shape remind one of 'Innocent[e] Pirola' [T], as it has that peculiarity about it what Foster-Melliar aptly describes as 'the whorl of a shell.' Foliage dark olive green, a good grower, and free from mildew. Should make a good bedding and pot Rose." [NRS19/134] "Popular [in Houston, Texas]." [ET] "Nice grower, with very fine and retained foliage; stems not so stout as [those of] 'Ophelia'. Does well in Pacific South-West and very well in winter in Southern zones. Much to be preferred to most yellows for general garden cultivation and ordinary cut-flowers." [Th2]

Grace Molyneux
A. Dickson, 1909

"Apricot at the center, cream around the edges." [Ÿ] "A fascinating rose of rare beauty and faultless form. The color is apricot, tinted flesh in center; but when fully developed the outer petals are creamy white on the inside with a pink sheen on the reverse." [CA10] "Blooms large, fine form and freely produced; petals large and of good texture; delicately tea perfumed." [C&Js10] "Carmine apricot with lighter flesh center. Very little disbudding." [Th] "Creamy apricot. —Vigorous. — Garden, bush, standard. —Fragrant." [Cat12/29] "Somewhat of the 'Pharisaër' [HT] sort." [JR31/73] "A constant bloomer, with good foliage, and grows very tall. It is nearly white, with a shade of apricot and light flesh-color; has Tea rose perfume." [ARA29/55] "Particularly attractive in growth, color and form; blooming qualities fairly good; foliage tends to mildew. Excellent cutting rose in spring." [ARA18/111] "Tall, compact, hardy, vigorous; foliage sufficient, mildews somewhat; bloom free, continuous." [ARA18/125] "A vigorous growing Hybrid Tea of good habit and constitution, the flowers are produced freely on long stalks—are sweetly scented and of refined shape—with high culture and severe disbudding will produce exhibition flowers . . . it is as a bedding and garden Rose that it can be most strongly recommended." [F-M]

Graf Fritz Schwerin
Lambert, 1916
From 'General MacArthur' (HT) × 'Goldelse' (HT).

"Rose-red, large, single, light scent, tall." [Sn]

Graf Fritz von Hochberg
Lambert, 1904
From 'Mme. Caroline Testout' (HT) × 'Goldquelle' (T; Lambert, 1899, reddish gold; parentage: 'Kaiserin Auguste Viktoria' [HT] × 'Mme. Eugène Verdier' [N]).

"Yellowish salmon pink, large, full, medium scent." [Sn] "Blossom large, pretty full, of beautiful form; color, very delicate flesh pink, center darker." [JR31/178]

Graf Silva Tarouca
Lambert, 1915
From 'Étoile de France' (HT) × 'Lady Mary Fitzwilliam' (HT).

"Red, large, full, tall." [Sn]

Grange Colombe
P. Guillot, 1911
Two parentages have been published: (1) 'Pharisaër' (HT) × an unnamed seedling; (2) 'Mme. Caroline Testout' (HT) × 'Lady Ashtown' (HT).

"Cream-white with salmon yellow and fawn center. Very little dis-

budding." [Th] "A beautifully formed flower of soft ivory-white, with fawn-colored center. As the flower expands it becomes slowly white." [C-Ps26] "Cream. Garden." [NRS15/148] "Ivory, with fawn-yellow, salmon center; almost white in heat; buds flushed pink; odor slight. Bush very strong and compact. 22 blooms; 32 the second season." [ARA26/94] "Of all-round worth. Color clear, attractive; form almost perfect in bud; strong grower; splendid bloomer." [ARA18/111] "Creamy white; tall, bushy." [ARA17/32] "Vigorous with erect canes, which are stiffly upright; ample foliage of a purplish light green; long bud; blossom large, full, cupped; petals large, regular, imbricated; color, cream white, tawny salmon yellow towards the center, fading to white when open, fragrant." [JR35/156] "Very hardy. Outer petals cream, center usually yellow-buff, with, sometimes, a tinge of shrimp-pink; bud long, but opens loose; good size, but does not last well; slight fragrance. Nice bushy growth; stem often strong and of fair length. Little affected by disease. Gives over fifty blooms in Central Zone, and does well there early and late, but needs a cool climate. Must be cut early in bud if at all. Does well in Pacific North-West." [Th2] "Growth sturdy and erect, with good number of canes. A good all-round rose." [ARA17/22] "A fine light rose we seldom hear about, but a new budded plant of it far surpassed anything [else] of its color." [ARA25/205] "Superseded by 'Lady Craig' [HT outside our era]." [C-Ps29]

Grossherzog Friedrich von Baden
Lambert, 1908
From 'Mme. Caroline Testout' (HT) × 'Meta' (T).

"Carmine rose pink. With us light pink. Disbud." [Th] "A valuable rose, notable for its color, fragrance, blooming and lasting qualities; growth good; form of open flower pleasing." [ARA18/111] "Medium height, rather compact, hardy; foliage plentiful, black-spots slightly; bloom moderate, almost continuous." [ARA18/125] "Perfume fair; fifty blooms throughout the season; growth very good. A splendid all-round rose." [ARA17/23]

Grossherzog Wilhelm Ernst von Sachsen
Welter, 1915
From 'Mme. Mélanie Soupert' (HT) × 'Lyon-Rose' (Pern).

"Rose-red, large, full, very fragrant, medium height." [Sn] "Bright scarlet with carmine-rose, large, fairly full, fragrant, long bud opening well. Growth vigorous, erect, flowering till late in autumn." [GeH]

Grossherzogin Alexandra
Jacobs, 1904
From 'Merveille de Lyon' (HP) × 'Kaiserin Auguste Viktoria' (HT).

"Yellowish-white, large, full, very fragrant, medium height." [Sn]

Gruss an Aachen
trans. "Greetings to Aachen"
Geduldig/Hinner, 1909
From 'Frau Karl Druschki' (HP) × 'Franz Deegen' (HT).

"Pale salmon shading to white, fragrant. Growth dwarf." [GeH] "Buds gold and red." [ARA29/97] "Valuable as a pot-rose. Flowers are yellowish pink, shaded red. Very free-flowering." [C&Js14] "Lighter in color in summer, but in fall the colors are superb." [C-Ps29] "Color fades quickly in hot weather, becoming almost white; perfume mild; growth fair." [ARA17/22] "Its only fault is that the fragrance is faint." [C-Ps28] "An unusual and distinctive Rose that we recommend high-

Gruss an Aachen *continued*

ly to anyone desiring a hardy, free-flowering variety of sturdy growth, with flowers as large as Tea Roses, fully double to the center. Remarkable for its beautifully colored flowers which show in shades of carmine, yellow, tinted and white on the same bush and at the same time. It deserves a place in the Hybrid Teas. Extremely hardy anywhere, and makes an ideal compact Memorial Rose. It actually improves with age, the open flowers being more beautiful than the buds." [C-Ps27] "Of good vigor; the branches are strong, rigid, fairly erect. Continuous-flowering . . . The bud is long and of attractive form; color, orange red strongly tinted yellow. The color of the rose is quite difficult to describe . . . truly very beautiful. One gathers that the blossom will attain perhaps six inches [ca. 1.5 dm] across—but I have never seen it that large." [ARA36/124] "Tall, vigorous; foliage very plentiful till late summer, then plentiful, black-spots . . . mildews . . . bloom moderate, continuous, size and quality compensate for lack of quantity." [ARA18/128] Aachen, or Aix-la-Chapelle, was Charlemagne's capital city. Those partial to 'Gruss an Aachen' may wish to know of its extant sports, which—oddly—are evasive in commerce for such a well-known and beloved parent!: 'Climbing Gruss an Aachen', 'Gruss an Aachen Superior', 'Jean Muraour', 'Minna', 'Rosa Gruss an Aachen'.

Gruss an Aachen Superior

Leenders, 1942
Presumably a "superior" sport of 'Gruss an Aachen' (HT).
   "Blush white, large, full, moderate height." [Sn]

Gruss an Sangerhausen

trans. "Greetings to Sangerhausen"
Müller/Soupert & Notting, 1904
From 'Pierre Notting' (HP) × 'Safrano' (T).
   "Brilliant scarlet, center crimson; flowers very large and full; of great beauty; most floriferous." [C&Js09] "Fragrant. Growth vigorous, very floriferous." [GeH] "Over seven years, we have watched this beautiful variety in our nurseries and we are able to recommend it as one of the most beautiful scarlet red hybrid tea roses. Growth of good vigor; beautiful dark green foliage; the wood, reddish. Flower large, full, of beautiful form; color, scarlet red, the center a very pronounced grenadine red. The buds are very long and well formed." [JR28/153]

Gruss an Zweibrücken

trans. "Greetings to Zweibrücken"
Lambert, 1915
From 'Charles Gater' (HP) × 'Mme. Caroline Testout' (HT).
   "Red, large, full, medium scent, tall." [Sn]

Gruss vom Westerwald

trans. "Greetings from the Westerwald"
Kettenbeil, 1914
From 'Mme. Caroline Testout' (HT) × 'Mme. Ravary' (HT).
   "Orange-pink, medium size, full, medium scent, dwarf." [Sn]

Gustav Grünerwald

Lambert, 1903
Two parentages have been published: (1) 'Safrano' (T) × 'Mme. Caroline Testout' (HT); (2) 'Bicolor' (F) × 'Grossherzogin Viktoria Melitta von Hessen' (HT; Lambert, 1897; cream; parentage, 'Safrano' [T] × 'Mme. Caroline Testout' [HT]).

"Bright carmine with yellowish center, outer petals of lighter shade; flowers cup-shaped, large and full." [C&Js15] "Carmine pink with a radiant center of yellow; blossom large, full, fragrant; floriferous; very vigorous." [Cx] "Flowers . . . cupped, with a high centre . . . buds yellowish red, long and pointed." [W/Hn] "A beautiful flower . . . of a very distinctive shade of bright carmine pink with pale orange shading at the base of the petal which lights up the flower well. It has a delicious perfume, being one of the best of the pink Roses in this respect. The flowers are not badly affected by either sun or rain, but in hot weather, especially in mid season, they are apt to get loose and lose their shape . . . The autumnal blooming is generally good and free." [NRS/12] "Free vigorous growth of an upright yet branching habit, and good though rather sparse dark green bold leathery foliage but little liable to mildew. It flowers fairly continuously and freely from early July till late autumn. The flowers are carried erect singly and on good stems, though full flowers will droop at times. The petals are strong and of good substance, bright carmine pink in colour, rather paler in hot weather . . . sweetly fragrant." [NRS/10] "Good autumnal." [JP] "A good early variety . . . must be disbudded freely." [F-M] "Not the most floriferous, despite being very vigorous." [JR32/33] "Pretty vigorous, floriferous, having buds which are elongate, pointed, and good for vases. The blossoms are large, cupped, of a pretty and fresh pink, the inwards of the petals being saffron yellow. Were it not for this last color, it would very much resemble the charming 'Mme. Caroline Testout', with which it shares many other characteristics, notably form, wood, and thorns." [JR29/92] "Moderate height, compact, vigorous, hardy; foliage plentiful, black-spots slightly; bloom almost free, continuous." [ARA18/125] "Everyone should grow this variety if only for the sake of the bright rose-pink colour of the flowers. There are many pink roses, but this is distinct from them all. It grows well and flowers freely." [OM] "Good . . . not one of the best." [ARA18/111] "An excellent Rose, opens well, seems to revel in the wet weather, sweetly scented. One of the best varieties for the North." [NRS14/160] "Grünerwald (Gustave [*sic*]), chief gardener to the Imperial Court at Gatchina." [FeR]

Gustav Sobry

Welter, 1902
From 'Kaiserin Auguste Viktoria' (HT) × 'Comte Chandon' (T).
   "Golden yellow and red." [Ÿ] "Reddish gold shading to clear yellow, large full long buds, sweet scented; free blooming." [P1] "Growth small and weak." [ARA18/116]

H. D. M. Barton

H. Dickson, 1917
   "Good [red] color and fair growth for new plants." [ARA18/118] "Strong, vigorous, upright, and freely branching growth, handsome dark green leathery foliage, wood and spines reddish, flowers moderately large and very full, with long pointed and beautifully formed buds, produced with extraordinary freedom right throughout the season. Colour, deep rich velvety crimson which does not blue with age. A Garden Bedding Rose of the type of 'General MacArthur', but far surpassing that grand bedder in the richness of its colour and the more freely branching and dwarfer habit of growth." [NRS17/162]

H. E. Richardson

H. Dickson, 1913
   "Deep, rich crimson of the 'Victor Hugo' [HP] shade, a Rose of

most pleasing build and dazzling brilliance." [C&Js14] "Deep rich crimson, large, beautifully formed, with high pointed centre, carried on strong and upright stems. Growth vigorous, upright; very free." [GeH] "Of beautiful shape, but on the small side for exhibition. It is very sweet scented, of fine colour, a good scarlet-crimson; growth, vigorous and erect; an excellent garden variety…; could be described as a small 'Horace Vernet' [HP], but is much freer than that variety." [NRS13/155] "Fragrant." [NRS13/168] "Vigorous, with very forthright and open growth. The blossoms, full and of very beautiful form, are large and bright crimson." [ARA18/116] "Tall growth, not bushy; not a bloomer." [ARA18/116]

H. F. Eilers
Lambert, 1913
From 'Gustav Grünerwald' (HT) × 'Luise Lilia' (HT).

"Carmine and reddish terra-cotta, outside of petals clearer, very large and full; buds very long and pointed, borne singly on long stems. Growth vigorous, upright, free flowering, with dark green foliage." [GeH] "Vigorous, floriferous bush. Blossom very large, long and strong stem, pretty full, high-centered; outer petals carmine, those of the center slaty velvety red. Good for forcing and cutting." [JR38/56] "Growth slightly above average; color distinct, not of best; form and blooming qualities fair." [ARA18/111] "Medium in height and compactness, reasonably vigorous, hardy; foliage sufficient, black-spots slightly; bloom moderate, intermittent first of season, continuous later." [ARA18/125]

H. P. Pinkerton
H. Dickson, 1918

"Long buds; large, full flowers of brilliant scarlet, heavily flamed velvety crimson. Very free-flowering. Mildew-proof." [ARA19/102] "Of strong, vigorous branching habit, with dark green foliage which is mildew proof. The blooms, which are very large, with high pointed centre, are freely produced and carried on erect stiff stems, and are very sweetly perfumed. The colour is a very brilliant scarlet, heavily flushed with velvety crimson. This will make a grand exhibition and garden Rose; and is undoubtedly the finest Rose of its colour yet produced." [NRS17/130]

H. V. Machin   Listed as 'H. Vessey Machin' (HT).

H. Vessey Machin
A. Dickson, 1914

"Intense, black-grained scarlet-crimson, of gigantic size, full, of perfect form with high pointed centre, carried on rigid flower stalks; faintly Tea perfumed. Growth sturdy and erect." [GeH] "Large and full, black-scarlet-vermilion. Gives solitary blossoms with long, erect stems. Splendid rose, quite fragrant. Cutting and forcing rose. Floriferous." [Ck] "Apt to 'blue' because the blooms last much longer than [those of] most H.T.'s." [C-Ps28] "A Hybrid Tea of great size and substance of petal; colour, rich crimson, flushed scarlet; as shown, a wonderful flower of highest exhibition standard; growth, robust rather than vigorous, holding its flowers erect; a great advance on the crimson Hybrid Teas." [NRS13/155] "One of the finest crimson Roses we have seen. The shade is a tint described as scarlet crimson; it is bright and attractive, and the flower is finely formed and fragrant. The plant, however, is a wretched grower." [NRS21/51] "Strong-growing plants with good foliage." [C&Js24] "Growth, foliage, and form good;

flowers large, beautiful color. Should rank with the Hybrid Perpetuals, there being little bloom after spring." [ARA18/111] "Good in the spring, but better still in the fall." [C-Ps29] "Medium in height and compactness, reasonably hardy; foliage sufficient, black-spots very slightly; bloom sparse, occasional." [ARA18/125] "This Rose makes a hearty splash of bright, true red, with brave flowers firmly set on sturdy stems. The large buds are very dark, and remain in the lovely half-open state for several days; they also sometimes ball. The open Rose is fully double, but quite loose in the center and much brighter than the bud, and is not very fragrant. The color is apt to 'blue.' It is not a continuous bloomer, the flowers coming in crops, two or three times a season. This Rose is very close to the Hybrid Perpetuals, which it resembles in vigor, but does not grow so tall. It is very hardy, but somewhat subject to black-spot. A Rose with certain failings, but too beautiful to miss; especially effective in masses." [C-Ps25] "The Council announce with great regret the death in August last [1919] of one of the Society's Vice-Presidents, Mr. H. V. Machin. Although not so well known to present-day Rosarians, a few years ago he was a most successful Amateur exhibitor at the Society's Provincial Shows. His loss will be keenly felt, the more so as he had endeared himself to so many friends." [NRS20/15]

Hadley
Montgomery/Pierson, 1914
From an unnamed seedling (parentage: 'Liberty' [HT] × 'Richmond' [HT]) × 'General MacArthur' (HT).

"Deep velvety crimson, retaining its brilliancy at all seasons of the year; double flowers and buds are well formed, and deliciously fragrant." [C&Js15] "Deep reddish purple, of good shape. Growth very free." [GeH] "Blossom very large, very well formed, erect, poised on a very long stem, particularly full, opens well, very long-lasting, dark blood red with blacker tints. Excellent color, constant bloom until frost. Commendable dark rose." [Ck] "Flowers are large, well-formed, and intensely fragrant. The long shapely buds make this Rose particularly pleasing before the flowers open, and the blooms are produced continuously and freely throughout the season. Color is a rich crimson, varying to deep velvety crimson, and most attractive." [C&Js24] "A rich crimson-red flower with velvety texture, lovely form, and perfume. Moderate in growth and bloom. Splendid color which blues very little. Flowers small in summer; superb in fall." [ARA26/110] "Velvety crimson to darkest black-purple—blues in extreme heat more than 'Hoosier Beauty' [HT]; double and attractive in form; fine fragrance. Foliage good. Stem usually long and strong. Weak grower in Central zone; satisfactory in cool, moist climates of Pacific North-West and Pacific South-West. Reported by Miss Creighton, of western Florida, as continuous." [Th2] "In the summer-time and all the time, 'Hadley' yields wonderfully fine blooms for cutting." [ARA29/106] "Not a robust grower but every bud comes perfect, and while not a good bedding Rose, it is very lasting when cut." [C-Ps28] "If you will cut the buds early, you will find little reason to object to its bad habit of losing its fine color when it fades. Fairly hardy, a moderate grower, but not a liberal bloomer, except as a greenhouse Rose. Best in the cooler sections of the country." [C-Ps25] "Free and constant flowerer." [Au] "The pre-disposition to blind wood…is the weak spot in 'Hadley'." [ARA16/116] "Produces so few flowers that it is hardly worth growing [in the florist trade]." [ARA22/140] "With its wonderful color and quality, is considered ideal by the buyer [of cut flowers], but not by

Hadley *continued*

the grower." [ARA23/108] "Has been almost entirely discarded [by commercial growers of cut flowers]." [ARA26/158]

"'Hadley' certainly is not [easy to grow]." [ARA25/170] "The plant grows well, but is of a rather straggling habit, and the carriage of the flowers is not good." [NRS21/51] "Of our dark red roses 'Hadley' is the favorite." [ARA21/142] "Superior to the reds I previously had." [ARA25/98] "Color distinct; growth and blooming fair; foliage quite good; best in the spring." [ARA18/111] "A grand rose." [ARA25/144] "In 1916 there was a flower show at Philadelphia ... Basing my opinion on the opinion of those with whom I talked after the show, it seems that 'Hadley' is 'some rose.' Those who saw this finest of the crimson roses at Philadelphia have something to remember ... Growers have decided that 'Hadley' is worth all the extra care which a good variety needs. It has come into its own. 'Montgomery's mistake' was the nickname tacked onto 'Hadley' by those who thought they knew more about roses than the originator of 'Hadley'." [ARA17/110] "Alexander W. Montgomery, Jr., of Hadley, Mass." [ARA16/44]

Hedwig Reicher

Hinner/Vogel-Hartweg, 1913

"Blossoms large, yellowish white." [JR38/90] "Large, full, white, yellow within. Cutting and forcing rose." [Ck] "Yellowish white, large, very full, medium scent, tall." [Sn]

Helvetia

trans. "Switzerland"

Heizmann, 1912

From 'Mme. Caroline Testout' (HT) × 'Farbenkökigin' (HT).

"Deep pink, large, full, moderate fragrance, moderate height." [Sn] "Small growth; not a bloomer." [ARA18/116] "At first named 'Alpengluhn' by its breeder, who changed its name due to the difficulty of translating 'Alpengluhn' into French ["Feu Alpin"] and English ["Alp-Glow"]." [JR36/42]

Henriette

A. Dickson, 1916

"Coppery orange red, large, full, medium height." [Sn] "Wonderful and distinct color; growth small." [ARA18/118] Probably a Pernetiana. Not to be confused with the coral-red 'Henrietta' HT of 1917 from Merryweather!

Herfsttooi

Van Rossem, 1919

From 'General MacArthur' (HT) × 'Leuchtfeuer' (extinct red B of 1909 from Kiese/Türke; parentage: 'Gruss an Teplitz' [B] × 'Cramoisi Supérieur' [Ch]).

"Flower brilliant purplish red. Vigorous, bushy grower; free bloomer." [ARA21/165] "Purplish red, medium size, full, light scent, medium height." [Sn]

Hermann Kiese

Geduldig, 1905

"Reddish yellow with pink, large, semi-full, very fragrant, medium height." [Sn] "Growth vigorous, with erect branches; flower large, nearly full, very fragrant; color, bright reddish yellow tinted pink; bud solitary, long, and borne on a long, strong stem." [JR30/26]

Herzogin Marie-Antoinette von Mecklembourg

Jacobs, 1910

From 'Frau Lilla Rautenstrauch' (HT) × 'Sunset' (T).

"Pure orange and golden yellow, large, full, sweetly scented, long bud opening well. Growth very vigorous, branching, floriferous." [GeH] "Deep orange. Garden." [NRS13/168] "Rather low bushy growth; color and form attractive; good bloomer. Use Multiflora [understock]." [ARA18/111] "Robust." [Au] "The shrub is vigorous and bushy, to 70–80 cm [ca. 2–3 ft], the long canes bearing large leaves of a handsome green shaded with red. The wood, which lasts well in winter, becomes very strong. The buds are long and bloom at all times; they are a superb orange yellow shaded salmon and striped carmine. Whether closed or open, they flower is always perfectly formed; color, beautiful orange yellow turning old gold; has a delicious perfume. It surpasses all Tea Roses because of its abundance, blooming as it does from July to the end of Fall." [JR35/37] "A very beautiful little flower of a fine orange colour, and nicely formed. It is so poor a grower that it cannot be generally recommended; its constitution, however, seems sound enough, and to those who will give themselves the trouble of growing it for the sake of its pretty little button-hole flowers I would say: Do not put it in a prominent place, and leave it alone; do not prune it at all, merely thin out old and extra thin twigs. Being of dwarf and branching habit it will stand this treatment without getting leggy." [NRS21/39]

Herzogin Viktoria Adelheid von Coburg-Gotha

Welter, 1905

From a seedling (which resulted from crossing 'Mme. Jules Grolez' [HT] and 'Kaiserin Auguste Viktoria' [HT]) × 'Capt. Hayward' (HP).

"Red, large, full, medium scent, medium height." [Sn]

Herzogin von Calabrien

Lambert, 1914

From 'Frau Karl Druschki' (HP) × a seedling (which resulted from crossing 'Hofgärtendirektor Graebener' [HT] and 'Herrin von Lieser' [HT]).

"Yellowish white, large, full, medium scent, moderate height." [Sn] "Creamy white, with clear sulphur-yellow centre, large, semi-double, sweetly scented; buds long and pointed. Growth vigorous, upright; free flowering." [GeH]

[Hilda Richardson]

A. Dickson, 1913

"Milk white, flushed rosy lilac at tips. Entirely different from the ordinary run of roses. Flowers are small to medium, semi-double, opening to saucer shape, with golden yellow stamens very conspicuous. Not at all adapted for cutting, but possessed of a refined, dainty elegance that with its freedom of bloom, unique coloring and delightfully rich fragrance may make it very popular as a garden rose." [CA17] "Its tint is delicate, its perfume delicious, and its bloom extremely abundant; its color ... is lilac pink stamped ... milk white. The center of the rose, which is globular and cupped, is carnation pink, dark but very delicate. The perfume is delicious: it combines the sweet geranium scent with the heady perfume of the primrose tea. The growth is vigorous and ideal; this rose is embellished with green foliage bordered yellow." [JR37/105]

His Majesty

McGredy, 1909

"Vermilion. Buds large and long. Fragrance like the H.P. class." [CA17] "Carmine-crimson. —Vigorous. —Exhibition, standard. — Subject to mildew."[Cat12/66] "Red, large, full, very fragrant, tall." [Sn] "Dark crimson shaded deep vermilion-crimson towards the edges, full, of great size, high pointed centre, sweetly perfumed. Growth vigorous, semi-climbing." [GeH] "Large growth without being 'climbing'; the quite erect blossoms are large, of good substance . . . beautiful deep crimson shaded blackish vermilion. One might call it the 'Red Frau Karl Druschki' due to its resemblance to that variety in form and growth . . . wafts the most elegant fragrance." [JR33/10]

Honourable Ina Bingham

A. Dickson, 1905

"Clear pink veined deep pink." [Ÿ] "Purest pink." [CA10] "Silver pink. Fair amount of disbudding." [Th] "Enormous blossoms of the most delicate pink."[JR29/153] "Silver-pink; semi-double; classed as a Hybrid Tea, but with Hybrid Perpetual characteristics." [ARA17/29] "Pure pink, large petals, semi-double, great substance and depth. Growth vigorous, good foliage. A fine rose." [GeH] "Robust, flower large, double, rigid stem, pure pink veined deep pink. Dedicated to a daughter of Lord Clanmorris." [JR30/26]

Hoosier Beauty

Dorner, 1915

From 'Richmond' (HT) × 'Château de Clos-Vougeot' (HT).

"Crimson; moderate, spare." [ARA17/32] "A promising red rose. Flowers of beautiful form, large; color good and lasting; very fragrant." [ARA18/133] "A large, full flower with well-shaped buds; color is glowing crimson; sweetly scented. Splendid for cutting."[C&Js15]"A small but glorious flower, full and well-formed, carried on stiff erect stems, with a tendency to flatness when fully expanded. The colour is a deep velvety crimson, which is quite unique, and the flower is very sweetly scented. It is a fine Rose for cut flower work and forcing, and should prove valuable for bedding." [NRS16/141] "Color brilliant and beautiful; growth and bloom not of the best." [ARA18/111] "Velvety crimson, with darker shadings; very nice form; fine fragrance. Stem long and fairly strong. Of only fair growth in Central Zone; much larger plants in Pacific North-West, and Pacific South-West. Continuous bloomer through season. Some mildew; no black-spot; holds foliage well. Blues less in great heat than 'Hadley' [HT], as noted in this country, and confirmed by letter from Poulsen Bros., of New Zealand."[Th2] "The blooms on my own-root 'Hoosier Beauty' plants surpass, both in quality and quantity, those on the grafted ones, and the growth is more vigorous." [ARA20/156] "A good grower, making long stems, suitable for cutting. We recommend this Rose highly to anyone growing Roses for show purposes as the flowers are firm and hold up well when cut." [C&Js24] "Low, compact; foliage plentiful, healthy; being transplanted fall, 1916, did not begin blooming till late, but bloomed continuously after beginning." [ARA18/125] "An American Rose of nice shape and fine crimson colour with good perfume . . . The growth proved rather long, untidy and spindly . . . a batch of plants have this year been free-flowering and pleasing." [NRS21/53] "Rather floppy in habit, but its dark crimson flowers, flushed with scarlet, are as fragrant as they are lovely." [NRS21/113] "I do not like the spindly way the bush grows, the leaf-buds are too far apart, and often the color of the

blooms is bad." [ARA29/109] "Some growers have already stated that 'Hoosier Beauty' is too weedy in growth, but they may prove entirely too hasty in their judgment . . . not prolific in growth or foliage . . . does not show the predisposition to blind wood which is the weak spot in 'Hadley'. The color, while a little dark, is more than offset by the wonderful fragrance." [ARA16/116] "Glowing crimson with darker shading, large, full, of good form, carried on erect stiff stems. Growth free; floriferous." [GeH] "Big, torch-like blooms of dusky red, opening from glowing slender buds; quite double, with wide-spreading butterfly petals surrounding an exquisite center. Among the better Roses for cutting, enduring a long while, retaining its color well, and keeping its full and fine perfume until the petals fall. Even in the garden it does not 'blue' so badly as many red Roses. Not a prolific bloomer, but may be depended upon to furnish a fair number of fine flowers. The plant is ordinarily a moderate grower, but often throws up vigorous branching canes bearing six or seven flowers on long, graceful stems like a giant candelabrum. It will sometimes hang its head. A rose of American origin whose rare beauty is unsurpassed in its color." [C-Ps25] "'Étoile de Hollande' [HT] is preferable." [C-Ps29] "The most beautiful red rose I have ever seen." [ARA23/64]

Hortulanus Albert Fiet

Leenders, 1919

From 'Mme. Mélanie Soupert' (HT) × 'Monsieur Paul Lédé' (HT).

"Salmony colour, back of petals yellow, which give their colour to the fairly large bud of elegant shape. When open, light salmony pink, scented, free bloomer."[NRS21/105] "Large, full, pure gold-yellow. The solitary blossoms are poised on long stems. Strong growth; healthy, glossy foliage. First-rate cutting and garden rose." [Ck] "Salmon rose shaded lilac-rose; buds long, apricot-yellow with coppery orange and lilac edges. Growth medium, very floriferous." [GeH] "Beautifully formed buds and flowers."[ARA21/147] "Bud very large, long-pointed; flower large, full, double, borne singly on average-length stems; lasting; strong fragrance. Color, apricot. Foliage sufficient, of medium size, glossy, green. A vigorous grower of bushy habit, bearing an abundance of blooms." [ARA20/135] Not to be confused with Verschuren's HT of 1919, 'Hortulanus Fiet'.

Improved Marquise Litta de Breteuil Listed as 'C. W. Cowan' (HT).

Intensity

Dingee & Conard, 1908

From 'Gruss an Teplitz' (B) × 'General MacArthur' (HT).

"Deep red, large, full, medium scent, medium height." [Sn] "A cross between 'Gruss an Teplitz' and 'General MacArthur', retaining all the admirable qualities of the latter with much of the darker beauty of the former. Color, a very dark crimson scarlet, approaching crimson maroon in the older flower." [C&Js08]

Irish Beauty

A. Dickson, 1900

"Single, pure white with yellow stamens. Large and free flowering. Deliciously fragrant." [CA14] "Pure white with golden stamens, single, large, fragrant. Vigorous." [GeH] "Moderately vigorous." [Cat12]

Irish Brightness

A. Dickson, 1904

"Crimson with pink base, single." [GeH] "Velvety crimson shading

Irish Brightness *continued*

pink at base of petals." [Th] "Light orange red, medium size, single, moderate height." [Sn] "Vivid crimson ... Very vigorous; single flowered." [Au]

Irish Elegance

A. Dickson, 1905

Supposedly either (1) from "a Hybrid Tea" × *Rosa eglanteria* or (2) from *R. ×hibernica* × "a Hybrid Tea."

"Single flowers of a bronze and orange color, from which the roses turn completely to a shade of apricot at maturity." [JR29/153] "A variegated rose with a lot of pink in the combination; it is beautiful but nothing to get excited about." [ARA34/81] "A very beautiful rose." [K2] "The long-pointed buds of deep bronze orange colour afford a warm contrast to the paler opened single flower of various shades of apricot." [NRS18/138] "Shades of terra cotta and pink; perpetual and free-flowering; makes a good bush or bedding Rose." [NRS18/134] "A delightful fragrance of cloves." [ARA24/95] "A wonderfully free bloomer." [ARA20/149] "Fades in heat ... opens quickly. Very good foliage. Very fine growth in Pacific North-West." [Th2] "The foliage is specially beautiful and harmonises well with the flowers, particularly in autumn, when it turns a ruddy green. The early foliage is also most beautiful, of a rich red tint. The habit is good and branching ... free flowering and fairly continuous ... The colour of the single flower is unique, the buds are a fine orange scarlet, and the petals of the open flower coppery fawn with a pink shade running through it. It has a sweet but not very strong fragrance, and good lasting flowers for a single Rose ... Its charm lies not merely in the flowers, lovely as they are, but in their delightful harmony with the foliage and in the good and healthy habit of the plants ... Decidedly liable to mildew." [NRS/12] "Has reached a height of fully 8-ft. [ca. 2.6 m] against the east wall of my house." [NRS20/70] "We have here the most charming of all the large-flowered, single, Hybrid Tea roses. The beautiful long-shaped buds are particularly attractive, being a bronzy orange-scarlet, which assumes apricot hues as the flower opens. The blooms often measure 5 inches across [ca. 1.25 dm] and are produced continuously from early June till frost. 2-yr. size, (budded), 50 cts., by express." [C&Js13]

Irish Fireflame

A. Dickson, 1913

Same supposed parentage(s) as 'Irish Elegance' (HT).

"Deep terra cotta opening to yellow; handsome dark foliage." [NRS18/134] "Orange yellow and red." [OM] "Deep maddery orange, splashed with crimson, single. Vigorous." [GeH] "Fiery crimson at the case, shading to orange-salmon ... in the bud state they are very attractive." [ARA16/117] "Deep madder-orange ... blossoms all season." [ARA25/121] "A reddish bronze yellow ... brilliant and very pleasing in the sunshine. A feature is the contrast in the varying shades of colour in the bud, half open and fully expanded flower; it is very striking and, combined with the deep bronze-green foliage, the whole makes a very fine decorative garden plant." [NRS/13] "Old gold, flushed with pure crimson when fully developed. Buds are very long and slender, beautifully spiral and richly colored a deep orange red, with golden base. The open flowers are quite large, often five inches broad [ca. 1.25 dm]. A further color effect is obtained from the extremely long, wiry, violet-colored stems. Foliage is glossy green. Delightfully

tea-scented. Remembering the prompt recognition secured by 'Irish Elegance', it is easy to prophecy a great future for this variety, which surpasses it in every respect." [CA17] "Not quite so strong as 'Irish Elegance'." [NRS21/47] "Perfumed. Foliage good. Stem weak; growth good in Southern zones; does well in shade in Pacific South-West, but flower and stem wilt in heat." [Th2] "Resembles 'Irish Elegance' in habit of growth. The colour of the shapely buds is a fiery orange splashed with scarlet, while the fully-developed large flowers are of golden apricot. The rich array of bright yellow anthers is an additional charm, and the pleasant perfume renders it a variety which will for a long time be regarded as being worthy of a place in every garden." [NRS18/138] "Dependable." [Capt28]

Irish Glory

A. Dickson, 1900

"A silvery-pink hue." [NRS18/137] "Rosy crimson, single, back of petals flamed with crimson, fragrant. Vigorous." [GeH] "Light pink, large, single, moderate scent, tall." [Sn] "Silvery pink. —Moderately vigorous. —Garden, bedding." [Cat12/32] "Rosy crimson; perpetual; good for bedding." [NRS18/134]

Irish Modesty

A. Dickson, 1900

"Charming coral-pink blooms." [NRS18/137] "Light orange pink, large, single, tall." [Sn] "Coral-pink with ecru base, single. Growth vigorous." [GeH]

[Irish Pride]

A. Dickson, 1904

"Single red, coppery center." [CA07] "Flower ecru and old rose. Growth vigorous, dwarf." [GeH]

Irish Simplicity   Listed as 'Simplicity' (HT).

[Irish Star]

A. Dickson, 1904

"Single red." [CA07] "Rosy red. Single." [CA10]

Isobel

McGredy, 1916

Same supposed parentage(s) as 'Irish Elegance' (HT).

"Single carmine flowers, base of petals shaded gold." [NRS18/140] "Light pink, large, single, light scent, medium height." [Sn] "Flame, copper, and gold ... my favorite among the singles of these blended shades." [ARA24/95] "Flowers of large size, single; scarlet-orange with clear yellow center and fading to a clear pink. A delightful rose in early summer *and a continuous bloomer*." [C-Ps25] "Huge petals of carmine pink, shaded orange; it is not too prolific, but of a remarkable distinctiveness." [CaRoll/3/3] "A most floriferous, single-flowered, decorative Rose. Color is rich crimson, flushed orange-scarlet, with faint copper shading and pure yellow center." [C&Js24] "Although single, the enormous petals, with their mingled shades of carmine, red, and orange, make a plant of 'Isobel', in bloom, a beautiful sight, and the manner in which the petals fold up after sundown is also delightful." [ARA29/48] "Delightfully sweet scented." [NRS16/166] "A large flower on a large bush ... light rose-pink, with apricot shadings." [ARA34/80–81] "A *single* Rose of remarkable beauty. The flowers are large, measuring 4$\frac{1}{2}$ inches across [ca. 1.15 dm]. The colour is a rich carmine shaded with copper, with a pure yellow zone in centre. The petals are of fine substance and the flower is fragrant. It will make a valuable decorative variety." [NRS16/145] "Of remarkable color. Fair growth." [ARA18/118] "Carmine flushed orange-scarlet, single flowered. Growth vigorous." [GeH] "Growth rather small, not bushy. Wonderful decorative rose where well grown." [Th2] "Free flowering, and tall in growth." [NRS21/63] "Rather scanty foliage." [NRS22/81] "The only single Rose we know that has enough 'pep' to do well almost anywhere. Light pink with salmon-orange tinge; of large size, folding up toward evening. Long lasting and a wonderful bud for boutonnière." [C-Ps29] "Makes a most charming shrub." [NRS28/37] "Said to be good." [ARA18/47] "Huge, warm, pink, five petaled, fragrant flowers ... an enchanting rose by any standards." [DP]

Jacques Hackenberg
Leenders, 1919
From 'Jonkheer J. L. Mock' (HT) × 'Marquise de Sinety' (HT).

"Silvery and lilac-rose with carmine, changing to flesh-pink with lilac shadings, large, of fine form, fragrant. Growth vigorous, branching; free flowering." [GeH] "Violet pink, large, full, medium scent, tall." [Sn] "Bud very large, long-pointed; flower very large, full, double, borne singly; lasting; strong fragrance. Color pale reddish lilac. Foliage abundant, large, glossy green. A vigorous, upright grower and abundant bloomer." [ARA20/135]

Jacque Poscher Listed as 'Jacques Porcher' (HT).

Jacques Porcher
syn. 'Jacque Poscher'
P. Guillot, 1914

"White shaded with carmine." [Ÿ] "Passing from white, shaded carmine on saffron center, to clear yellow with a darker center; perfume mild; sixty-nine blooms throughout the season; growth very good. A fine all-round rose, particularly desirable for garden decoration." [ARA17/22] "Flesh-pink, turning faint yellowish with carmine suffusion; buds and flowers small and crisp; odor delicious. Bush very strong. 31 blooms." [ARA26/94] "Cream-flesh to peach center, occasionally suffused light yellow; fair bud; open flower flat in heat but center full; medium to small; lasts well even with thin substance; little fragrance. Growth very tall and bushy; stem short yet fairly strong. Foliage very free from mildew and [black] spot and holds well. This variety is only fair for cutting, and the color is too light for great popularity. Gives well over sixty blooms in Central Zone, and many more in California where its size is greater. Has more virtues and less faults than many kinds. Discolors and balls in damp winds." [Th2] "Good strong growth; light yellow in color." [Th] "Large, full. Growth vigorous; very free." [GeH] "Bushy, moderately tall, compact, vigorous, hardy; foliage very plentiful, black-spots slightly; bloom moderate, intermittent." [ARA18/125] "An excellent rose. Splendid in color, foliage, blooming qualities, and growth." [ARA18/111]

Jacques Vincent
Soupert & Notting, 1908
From 'Mme. J. W. Budde' (HT) × 'Souvenir de Catherine Guillot' (Ch).

"Red with yellowish shade." [Th] "A deep coral pink ... an old favorite that of its kind has not yet been superseded. Here again we find very strong upright shoots carrying masses of bloom, and two feet apart [ca. 6 dm] is about the spacing needed." [NRS22/74] "Coloration very delicate, distinct, new, and striking: light yellowish coral red, like the shade of 'Lyon-Rose' [Pern], but more distinct; center saffron. The shape of the large blossom is uniquely elegant. 'Jacques Vincent' is a fascinating novelty which elbows out all other roses." [JR32/153]

Janet
A. Dickson, 1917

"Golden ochre on very delicate pearly champagne-biscuit fawn, with large imbricated globular-cupped formation, carried on long rigid flower-stalks; sweetly perfumed. Growth erect, leathery waxy foliage; exceptionally floriferous." [GeH] "Fawn-yellow in color and a large, fragrant, full bloom that closely resembles the glorious old 'Gloire de Dijon' [N]. A splendid grower with long, rigid flower-stalks. It is simply superb in the autumn." [C-Ps26] "Very large, good form, long-lasting, full, goldish ochre yellow. Plant strong-growing; rewarding bloomer, with good foliage; valuable rose." [Ck] "A sweet-smelling yellow Rose, and very floriferous." [NRS18/155] "Pretty; fair in growth; lacking in blooming." [ARA18/116] "The plants grew wonderfully and bloomed abundantly, having healthy and disease-resistant foliage. The blooms were of good form, size and color, and several of them in bouquets with a like proportion of 'Radiance' blooms, were the delight of all who saw them." [ARA23/177] "A Rose of moderate growth, with good dark foliage. The blooms, which are pointed with thick shell-like petals, are freely produced, carried on long stems well above the foliage, and sweetly scented. The colour of the outer petals is fawn, the centre chrome. This will make a fine bedding Rose, and may perhaps be described as a dwarf 'Gloire de Dijon', but the blooms do not open flat like that old variety." [NRS17/128] "Fragrant, attractive blooms in color and form. Good growth and foliage. A rose to make an amateur proud ... This is a variety which has never attained great popularity, although it is a favorite at Breeze Hill for growth, blooming quality, and its superb buds. It is roughly in the 'Lady Pirrie' [HT] and 'Mrs. A[rthur] R[obert] Waddell' [Pern] class, and while in no way superior to either it is worth growing with them. It is way ahead of many later Dickson roses." [ARA27/134] "But not up to the mark during hot weather." [C-Ps27]

Jean Muraour
Vogel, 1935
Sport of 'Gruss an Aachen' (HT).
"White, large, full, medium height." [Sn]

Jean Noté Listed as 'Jean Notté' (HT).

Jean Notté
Pernet-Ducher, 1908

"Citron, nuanced cream." [Ÿ] "Orange yellow, large, full, medium height." [Sn] "Chrome yellow, changing to creamy yellow, large and full, globular. Growth vigorous, floriferous." [GeH] "A small grower and not a profuse bloomer, even in 'special bed'." [ARA18/116] "Very vigorous bush with erect canes; beautiful reddish green foliage; flower very large, globular, quite full; color, yellow of a medium shade fading to cream yellow. Very floriferous." [JR32/25]

John Cook
Krüger, 1917
From 'La France' (B or HT) × ?

"Whitish pink, large, full, medium scent, tall." [Sn] "A seedling from 'La France', very similar in colour and habit." [GeH] "Large, full, fresh silvery pink, darker on the outside. Like the old, valuable, 'La France'.

John Cook *continued*
Healthy wood and foliage; grows happily, very floriferous, fragrant. Good cutting rose." [Ck] John Cook, American rose breeder.

[John Cuff]
A. Dickson, 1909
"Deep carmine pink with a most attractive and distinct yellow zone at the base of each petal; standing by itself on account of its novel and striking color." [CA10] "Large, full, well-shaped. Growth vigorous." [GeH]

John Ruskin
A. Dickson, 1903
"Sparkling flesh pink." [Ÿ] "Bright rosy carmine, the blooms are very large, perfectly formed; vigorous." [P1] "Deep pink, very large, full, medium scent, medium height." [Sn] "Free [blooming]. Growth vigorous." [GeH] John Ruskin, English art critic and *littérateur*, lived 1819–1900.

Jonkheer J. L. Mock
Leenders, 1909
From a seedling (resulting from crossing 'Mme. Caroline Testout' [HT] and 'Mme. Abel Chatenay' [HT]) × 'Farbenkönigin' (HT).
"A novelty of distinct merit. Color is carmine, changing to imperial pink. The blooms, which are produced with the greatest freedom, are carried on stiff and erect stems, and are of large size, perfect formation, and highly perfumed. Growth is vigorous and free." [C&Js11] "Mixture of ochre and light red." [Ÿ] "Large to extra large, full, fine form, tea fragrance, medium to long stem. Foliage good, sufficient. Growth vigorous, hardy. Inside of petals silvery pink, outside bright cherry-rose—very thick and leathery." [ARA23/164] "Carmine changing to Imperial pink ... foliage somewhat liable to mildew. Practically no disbudding." [Th] "Fine long bud." [GeH] "Distinct; notable for color, size, stem, and lasting qualities; tall growth, lacking in bushiness; fairly good bloomer." [ARA18/111] "Deep rose; tall, bushy." [ARA17/31] "Carmine and flesh pink. Has the wonderful two-toned petal effect shared by but two or three others. The inside of each petal is a soft, pearly blush, while the outside is bright carmine rose. As the flower opens, the outer portion shows the former shade and the high center the latter. Each petal just as it starts to curve away from the center will show both tones in a way that is truly charming. Flowers are large, beautifully formed, very fragrant and borne on splendid, strong, stiff stems. Will rank among the best." [CA17] "A tulip-shaped Rose of large size that never opens flat. Petals show light silvery pink against a background of brilliant deep carmine. Buds will not always open properly in wet weather, and extreme heat brings on a magenta tint. Quite hardy and almost thornless. Like most of the large-flowered full Roses it is not a profuse bloomer, but people who have it recommend it to their friends." [C-Ps29] "In growth resembles 'Mme. Caroline Testout' to some degree. Its blossoms are borne on upright and rigid stems, and are held well above the foliage; they are large, full, very fragrant, pink and light red with dawn-pink reflections, resembling 'Farbenkönigin' [HT] a little. The long bud opens well, and the form of the blossom much resembles that of 'La France'." [JR33/102] "Perfume fair in spring and fall, mild in summer; thirty-one blooms throughout the season on Multiflora [understock]; ... A majestic cut-flower." [ARA17/23] "Grafted specimens, while no more vigorous than own-root plants, are slightly more liberal in flowers." [ARA20/156] "Very handsome in the garden, and the perfect bloom lasts a long time, either on the bush or in water. I like to leave it on the bush, as it looks almost artificial in the house. It balls in wet weather." [ARA29/54] "Its color blues and the buds ball." [ARA23/64] "Very large growth and very hardy; only fair foliage, extremely long stems; long bud and large bloom of great substance; not a prolific but, considering the length of stems, a fine bloomer from frost to frost and a long keeper. Absolutely necessary to secure in two-year-old plants; yearlings do not appear to transplant with any success. Plant 20 inches [ca. 5 dm] center to center. Prune to 5 eyes." [Th]
"Carmine, with deep shadings, silvery pink inside; very large, with many petals of great substance, perfumed. Tall growth and very long, strong stem. Foliage mildews and is lost early. Very fine in heat but balls in dampness. A variety with bad faults and splendid virtues." [Th2] "An imposing Rose, of magnificent size, with petals of exceedingly heavy substance, delicately reflexed, showing light, creamy pink against a background of brilliant deep carmine. At its best in hottest weather, because its great petalage requires heat to develop and open properly. The color fades slightly, and its delicate perfume is quite fleeting. The flower-stems are notably erect and stiff. It grows tall, but is not bushy. The foliage is subject to black-spot and is likely to be lost early unless protected against it. The plant is quite hardy, but not a profuse bloomer. In spite of its faults, deserves a place in every garden." [C-Ps25] "Dedicated to Monsieur J. L. Mock, president of the Société des Rosiéristes de Hollande." [JR33/102]

Jonkheer Mr. G. Ruys de Beerenbrouck Listed as 'Jonkheer Ruis de Beerenbrouck' (HT).

Jonkheer Ruis de Beerenbrouck
syn. 'Jonkheer Mr. G. Ruys de Beerenbrouck'
Timmermans, 1919
From 'Mme. Mélanie Soupert' (HT) × 'Monsieur Joseph Hill' (HT).
"Flower large; full; orange-yellow, with light yellow flush." [ARA22/156] "Flower large, well-formed, full, double; light yellow over bright yellow. Vigorous; free bloomer." [ARA21/165] "Pure orange-yellow, changing to clear yellow, large and full. Growth vigorous." [GeH] "Medium height." [Sn]

Joseph Hill Listed as 'Monsieur Joseph Hill' (HT).

Jubiläumsrose
trans. "Jubilee Rose"
J. C. Schmidt, 1910
"Yellowish white, orange center, large, semi-full, medium height." [Sn]

Juwel
trans. "Jewel"
Hinner, 1910
"Lemon-white, large. Growth vigorous." [GeH] "White. Exhibition." [NRS15/148] "Yellowish white, large, full, medium scent, moderate height." [Sn] "This newcomer is of vigorous growth, putting forth long, rigid branches surmounted with enormous, full blossoms somewhat resembling those of 'K[aiserin] A[uguste] Viktoria [HT] and 'Frau Karl Druschki' [HP]." [JR34/105] "Much more full than 'Frau Karl Druschki'." [JR34/182]

K. of K.

syn. and trans. 'Kitchener of Khartoum'

A. Dickson, 1917

"Bright crimson . . . half-double, with large petals. Seems to be extremely floriferous." [ARA20/123] "Each petal resembling a piece of fine scarlet velvet." [ARA29/49] "Beautiful but somewhat weak-necked." [ARA26/21] "Never known to 'blue.' The large, single flowers come in masses almost continuously all summer . . . The foliage is rather small and scanty . . . Unsurpassed in the fall." [C-Ps29] "A Rose of vigorous free-branching habit, with dark green foliage. The blooms, which are freely produced and sweetly scented, are carried on fairly stiff stems. The colour is a brilliant scarlet crimson, which does not burn. It will prove an ideal bedding and decorative Rose, and is a great advance on 'Red-Letter Day' [HT]." [NRS17/128] "Similar to 'Red-Letter Day', but slightly larger." [ARA18/47] "An improvement on 'Red-Letter Day' . . . It is just the same bright crimson, but instead of being single . . . it is half-double, with large petals. Seems to be extremely floriferous." [ARA20/123] "A rather branching and free-growing bush; the flowering stems being pushed up nearly erect. It is not quite so strong as 'Red-Letter Day'. The foliage is good . . . it may sometimes get mildew, black-spot and rust . . . The flowers are a grand colour, nearly scarlet, carried in a good open truss, and come into bloom successively. They are produced with fair continuity . . . It has very high decorative value; in this respect it has few, if any, equals among the red Roses . . . The petal is large and of good substance . . . the buds are long, pointed and well shaped. It stands sun well for a red Rose, showing very little tendency to turn blue until the flower is quite faded, and it is not materially harmed by rain." [NRS29/115] "This brilliant Rose was named for the late Lord Kitchener of England. The color is a striking, intense brilliant scarlet, with a velvety sheen, making it stand out like a beauty-spot in a garden. The flowers are large, almost single, and slightly fragrant. You can rely on this Rose for almost continuous bloom all summer. Unusually hardy; very vigorous; fine when massed." [C-Ps27] "Quite took our fancy." [ARA18/47] Horatio Herbert, 1st Earl Kitchener of Khartoum and of Broome; British military man; lived 1850–1916.

[Kaiserin Goldifolia]

Conard & Jones, 1909

Presumably a sport of 'Kaiserin Auguste Viktoria' (HT).

"The flower of this variety is identical with [that of] 'Kaiserin Auguste Viktoria' but the distinction between the two Roses is the bright, golden yellow foliage of 'Kaiserin Goldifolia'. It is a decided novelty, beautifully attractive in leaf and flower." [C&Js09]

Kaiser Wilhelm II   Plate 64

syn. 'Fürst Niclot'

Jacobs/Welter, 1909

From a seedling (of 'Kaiserin Auguste Viktoria' [HT]) × 'Louis Van Houtte' (HP).

"Its bloom was good despite . . . continuous rain. 'Kaiser Wilhelm II' is the product of 'K[aiserin] A[uguste] Viktoria' × 'Louis van Houtte'. The shrub, moderately vigorous, with erect branches clad with beautiful dark green foliage, is proof against all disease . . . Each branch produces one or many blossoms (usually one) on a stiff stem. The buds are conical, long, open very easily, even when humid. The flower is large and full, fiery red and bloom red with poppy red re-

flections. The plant is very remontant and is able to give satisfaction as a cutting variety; further, it has the pleasant scent of the Centifolia." [JR35/27–28] "Weak growers in Middle Atlantic States." [Th]

Käthe von Saalfeld

Elbel, 1914

Sport of 'Grace Darling' (HT; Bennett, 1884).

"Orange yellow, large, very full, moderate scent, medium height." [Sn]

Killarney Brilliant

A. Dickson, 1914

Sport of 'Killarney' (HT; A. Dickson, 1899; pale pink).

"Large to very large, double, good to fine form, very fragrant, medium to long stem. Fine foliage, sufficient. Growth strong; hardy. Clear rosy crimson." [ARA23/164] "Fair, having the faults of parent, but not so good growers or bloomers." [ARA18/111]

Killarney Double White   Listed as 'Double White Killarney' (HT).

Killarney Queen

Budlong/Pierson, 1912

Sport of 'Killarney' (HT).

"Charming color, a deep brilliant pink . . . reliable blooming, and upright growth." [ARA29/51] "Bright pink . . . vigorous . . . 30 to 40 blooms per season." [ARA21/91] "The best of the Killarneys for outdoor planting. Flowers larger, color deeper and more lasting than [those of] . . . 'Killarney'; growth more vigorous." [ARA18/133] "Extremely heavy foliage . . . lesser production in bloom." [ARA18/99] "Tall, compact, free-growing, hardy; foliage sufficient, black-spots; bloom free, almost continuous." [ARA18/125] "For decoration or hedges in Interior South districts with dry conditions." [Th2] "Susceptible to mildew." [C-Ps28] "Considered the best of all the 'Killarney' sports because of its somewhat fuller flowers. It is a sprightly pink, and brightest in hot weather. The bud has the same lovely form as all the Killarneys, but slightly fuller, and is sweetly perfumed. The young growth and foliage is beautiful bronzy green. It is a vigorous grower, suitable for low hedges where the temperature does not drop to zero; but for general purposes it is quite hardy. It is a dependable bloomer and a very popular Rose in dry climates, where it mildews less." [C-Ps25]

Kitchener of Khartoum   Listed as 'K. of K.' (HT).

König Laurin

trans. "King Laurin"

Türke, 1910

From 'Mme. Caroline Testout' (HT) × 'White Maman Cochet' (T).

"Whitish pink, large, full, medium scent, tall." [Sn]

Königin Carola von Sachsen

syn. 'Reine Carola de Saxe'; trans., "Queen Carola of Saxony"

Türke/Mietzsch, 1903

From 'Mme. Caroline Testout' (HT) × 'Viscountess Folkestone' (HT).

"Satiny rose; reverse of petals silvery white. Disbud." [Th] "Satiny rose, extra large, full, produced singly. Growth robust, very free." [GeH] "Extra-large flowers that are perfect in bud and when fully expanded. Color is beautiful satiny rose with reverse of petals silvery rose." [C&Js23] "A distinctly better shape [than has 'Mme. Caroline Testout'], having a well-developed point. Its great fault is that sooner or later the blooms reveal a split." [F-M] "If a Rose should be called the 'Peony

Königin Carola von Sachsen *continued*

Rose,' this would be the one, as it looks like a peony in size and form when open. Buds are long and massive, bright, satiny, La-France-pink, with a silvery sheen on the reverse of the petals, which are uncommonly long-lasting. A steady but not profuse bloomer. Strong grower, with heavy, healthy foliage. A glorified 'Mme. Caroline Testout'." [C-Ps29] "Color and form good; lacking in growth and blooming qualities." [ARA18/116] "It flowers well in the fall and throughout the rest of the season." [C-Ps30] "Tall, compact, free-growing, hardy; foliage plentiful, black-spots; bloom free, almost continuous." [ARA18/125] "Large, perfectly formed buds. Open flower very large, double, and quite shapely. Bright rose with a satin sheen, reverse of petals lighter. Blooms singly on stiff stems of good length. Growth strong; fairly resistant to pests. A persistent, but not profuse[,] bloomer." [C-Ps25] "This seedling dates from 1896. It was bred by R. Türke, and propagated by the establishment of C.-W. Mietzsch, of Niedersedlitz, near Dresden, in Saxony…This plant is not slow to develop its well-formed blossoms of beautiful silvery pink…The growth is vigorous, hardy, and doesn't produce as many thorns or prickles as 'Mme. Caroline Testout'. The blossom is very big, of perfect form, and opens well; the imbricated petals are a wonderful deep pink at the center, and light silvery pink at the edge…the blossoms ordinarily develop on the very vigorous canes." [JR27/101] "We have looked at the dear old Queen a good many times when hunting for varieties to discard to make room for novelties, but she is too perfect in form and silvery beauty to lose. The big satiny silver-pink flowers are freely produced on vigorous plants. Continuously satisfactory." [C-Pf34] Not to be confused with Gamon's 1902 HT of the same color, named 'Reine Carola de Saxe'.

Königin Maria Theresia

trans. "Queen Maria Theresia"

Lambert, 1916

From 'Frau Karl Druschki' (HP) × 'Luise Lilia' (HT).

"Red, very large, very full, very fragrant, medium height." [Sn] "Long bud opening well." [GeH] "Strong growth; good foliage; prolific bloomer. Flowers bright carmine-red of great size and cutting value, although loose; distinct perfume. Strongly recommended." [ARA28/102] "Shrub, erect, heavy-wooded, growing very tall. Leaves very large, wide, dark green. Bud wonderfully beautiful, very long, bright lacquer red. Blossom extraordinarily large, wide, arching petals, form of '[Frau Karl] Druschki' [HP], full, fresh sparkle, uniquely bright carmine-rose-red. Doesn't blue, strong and pleasant scent; on single, erect, long stems. First-rate decorative rose, beautiful Fall-bloomer." [Ck]

Königin Viktoria von Schweden

trans. "Queen Victoria of Sweden"

Ries, 1919

From 'Mme. Segond-Weber' (HT) × 'Mrs. Joseph Hill' (HT).

"Light saffron yellow, going to pale salmon pink; come singly, good fulness and form." [Ck] "Light blush-yellow, much of the 'Ophelia' [HT] color, but distinctly superior in lasting qualities and larger bloom. Foliage and growth first class in every particular. Good cutting value." [ARA28/102] "Flower double, well-formed, borne singly. Color light saffron-yellow, passing to pale salmon-pink. Foliage glossy. Vigorous, upright grower." [ARA20/136] "Large, very full, with high centre, border of petals recurved; of fine growth, few thorns and deep glossy green foliage. Mildew-proof; very floriferous." [GeH]

Koningin Emma

trans. "Queen Emma"

Verschuren, 1903

From 'Kaiserin Auguste Viktoria' (HT) × a unnamed seedling.

"Fleshy white, with rosy centre, very large, full. Growth robust, floriferous." [GeH] "Foliage like that of 'K[aiserin] A[uguste] Viktoria', but very long and of very beautiful form. The blossom is very large, very full, and white with a little pink, the petals being very thick. A very beautiful variety!" [JR27/163]

Kootenay

syn. 'Mary Greer'

A. Dickson, 1917

"Primrose yellow." [Cw] "Yellowish white with pink, large, full, medium scent, medium height." [Sn] "Almost white, faint blush, tinged yellow; large; odor slight to good. Bush tall and strong." [ARA26/94] "Large size, globular form and good substance, produced in great profusion. Growth erect and vigorous." [GeH] "Of vigorous growth and branching habit; the blooms are freely produced on long rigid stalks. They are large and full and of perfect form, of primrose yellow colour, and strongly perfumed. The Rose is described as an improved 'Kaiserin Auguste Viktoria'." [NRS16/141] "Obtained some triumphs in America." [NRS21/57]

Kronprinzessin Cecilie

Kiese/J. C. Schmidt, 1907

From 'Mme. Caroline Testout' (HT) × 'Mrs. W. J. Grant' (HT).

"Light pink, large, very full, medium height." [Sn]

Kynast

Krüger, 1916

Seedling of 'Dr. G. Krüger' (HT).

"Deep red, large, full, very fragrant, medium height." [Sn]

La Detroit

Hopp & Lemke/Breitmeyer, 1904

From 'Mme. Caroline Testout' (HT) × 'Bridesmaid' (T).

"Shell pink." [CA05] "Flowers large, very full, and deliciously tea-scented. Color clear flesh-pink, shading to deep rose. Petals shell-shaped. Blooms freely until frost." [C&Js24] "A fair rose but inferior to the newer pinks." [Th] "A magnificent new Hybrid Tea Rose of largest size and splendid form; clear flesh pink, shading to deep rose, full and sweet." [C&Js06] "This variety was developed by a gardener from Grand Rapids, Mr. George Hopp…This rose will prove of great merit to flower-growers due to its abundance, remarkable coloration, and vigor. Its flowers are of perfect form, magnificently colored bright pink in the outer portion, with a more delicate pink tint towards the center. They are solitary, and borne on a stem both very long and abundantly clothed with large leaves; they are of moderate size and waft a delicious tea scent." [JR28/29] Not "*détroit*" —trans., geographical "straits"; that would be "*le* détroit"; rather, a femininization of the city of Detroit, Michigan, which city named from "geographical 'straits'."

La France Victorieuse

trans. "Victorious France"

Gravereaux/M. Guillot, 1919

"Silvery pink." [Ÿ] "Very wide full bloom, light pink, with deeper centre, very wide petals, rigid stem." [NRS21/105] "Shown by the

Roseraie de l'Haÿ, is a very large, full flower of tender pink, with darker center. The petals are very large and the stems strong." [ARA21/147] "A very beautiful Hybrid Tea rose with large petals of firm substance. The color approximates the light silvery salmon of my father's rose, 'Mme. Léon Pain' [HT], but the edges of the petals are bright carmine. The flower is very large, and borne upon long and stiff stems. The plant is of vigorous growth, of erect, branching habit." [ARA19/101–102] "Bud very large, long-pointed; flower very large, cupped, very double, borne singly on long stem; very lasting; fragrant. Color silvery carmine-pink, tinted with yellow on inside. Foliage sufficient, dark green, large; disease-resistant. Very vigorous, upright grower; bears an abundance of blooms intermittently during the season." [ARA20/131] "A lovely Hybrid Tea." [ARA20/124] France, *victorieuse* in World War I.

La Tosca

Widow Schwartz, 1900

From 'Joséphine Marot' (HT; Bonnaire, 1894; white) × 'Luciole' (T).

"Soft pink tinted with rosy white and yellow, large and full; very free flowering." [P1] "Pale reddish lilac. Very free blooming and most vigorous." [NRS29/250] "Delicate pink shaded blush." [Ÿ] "Silvery pink with deeper center. This rose does particularly well on the Pacific Coast. Very little disbudding." [Th] "Blooms fairly double, large, soft pink, shading to rose. Fine foliage. Strong, vigorous grower. Gives about 45 blooms per season. Hardy." [ARA21/92] "A charming new rose of strong vigorous growth and bearing large handsome buds and flowers all the season; color, a lovely shade of tender rose passing to flesh pink, but almost white, very sweet and beautiful." [C&J06] "One of the best light pinks. The cup-shaped buds and large, loose flowers are most attractive used alone or with pink roses of other shades." [ARA29/54] "Splendid for garden decoration. Noteworthy in growth, blooming, and hardiness; color good; bud fair in shape, but opens loose." [ARA18/112] "Medium to medium-large, double, good to fine form, very fragrant, medium to long stems. Fine foliage, sufficient, slight [black] spot. Growth very vigorous, tall, bushy; hardy." [ARA23/165] "Extremely hardy. Bright silvery pink, with darker center; bud short; flower loose; medium size; wilts in heat; slight fragrance. Remarkably fine growth and nice stem. Foliage very free from disease. Owing to lack of substance and petalage, this rose is mainly valuable in the extreme North on account of its great hardiness and growth, and its improvement under cool conditions. Over fifty blooms in Central Zone." [Th2] "Fifty-seven blooms throughout the season; growth exceptionally strong and vigorous. One of the best roses for garden decoration." [ARA17/23] "Tall, compact, vigorous, hardy; foliage plentiful, black-spots slightly; bloom abundant, continuous." [ARA18/125] "Growth vigorous, of good stature, the canes tinted purple and topped by a solitary blossom, which is large, well-formed, borne on a long stem, beautiful delicate pink nuanced blush white, nubs yellowish. Good for cutting." [JR24/163]

"It has fine foliage of a distinct colour, and free vigorous growth, with long, erect, nearly thornless stems of a light green colour; the habit of the plant is fairly symmetrical and the bush shapely. It flowers freely and nearly continuously from June till November … It is a Rose that seems to improve in freedom of flowering as the season advances, the second or summer bloom being often better than the early bloom, and the autumnal flowering best of all. The flowers are fairly well shaped and sometimes very good, but they are very loose, and

not full enough for exhibition. In hot weather they are rather quickly over. The colour of the buds, which are fairly large, is a soft pink, and the flowers are a pale blush flushed rosy white in the centre. Mr. Prior has noticed a yellow shade in the colouring and perhaps it is this that just prevents any appearance of real pink in them, and which leads Mr. Frank Cant to recall a salmon flesh tint. The flowers are fragrant with the perfume generally described as sweet, rather than that of the tea Rose. The plants are not very liable to mildew … Though a strong grower, it does not get out of hand … Its autumnal clusters of pale flowers looks very well on the plants, but its colour is then less pronounced than at its summer flowering … If very slightly pruned it is capable of growing into a very large bush, and seems to do fairly well with that treatment." [NRS12/98–99]

La Vendômoise

trans. "The [Female] One from Vendôme"

Moullière/Ketten, 1906

From 'Mrs. W. J. Grant' (HT) × 'Marie d'Orléans' (T).

"Rose-red, large, full, medium scent, tall." [Sn] "Flower China pink —very intense—lighter around the edges, very large, quite full, cupped, fragrant, very long bud, opens well. Growth vigorous, everblooming, hardy." [JR30/135]

Lady Alice Stanley

McGredy, 1909

"Deep coral-rose on outside … inside pale flesh; perfume mild to fair … growth fair." [ARA17/23] "Silvery pink; moderate [height], spare [growth]." [ARA17/32] "Full … coral-rose and pink. Good foliage. Medium grower. Averages 34 blooms per season." [ARA21/92] "Silvery pink, with rose reverse. Growth vigorous." [GeH] "Flesh-pink. The large, long-pointed buds open to cup-shaped flowers with a slight backward roll to the lip of each petal. Color is exquisite flesh-pink, lightened with rich coral on the reverse of the petals and a suspicion of salmon in the center of the bloom. Moderately fragrant." [C-Ps32] "The arrangement of petals, gently curved back just a trifle, even in the center, so gracefully overlapping and supporting one another, like the studied folds of a lovely frock, all so uniform, so well-proportioned, so regular, so strongly placed on its stem, and the whole so well guarded by its outer rows of petals—this it is which gives us the essence of ladyhood, the two tones of softer and deeper rose, together with a bountiful fragrance, that give its lovableness." [ARA30/36] "Good form." [OM] "Open flower very attractive … very little affected by mildew, but susceptible to [black] spot … growth, fair." [Th] "Exceptionally free-flowering. The blooms coming on good stiff stems make it ideal for cutting." [ARA22/xiv] "A magnificent Rose. Blooms are very large, very full and of great substance. The color on outside of petals is deep coral-rose; inside, pale flesh, slightly flushed deeper flesh. It is a stout, vigorous grower with free-branching habit and beautiful foliage; every shoot is crowned with a flower bud; deliciously fragrant." [C&Js12] "Very free flowering, useful for massing and at its best in September." [NRS21/63] "Gives its greatest number of flowers in July, with a second burst in September, although its total is only barely over thirty. The foliage is lost early by black-spot, but is almost proof against mildew." [Th2] "Extremely disease-resistant." [C-Ps31] "Growth is vigorous and the flowers large and of good shape and distinct colour." [F-M] "Low-growing, but healthy, with broad, distinctive, bronze-green foliage." [C-Ps29] "Height and compactness

Lady Alice Stanley *continued*

medium, vigorous, hardy; foliage plentiful, black-spots slightly; bloom free, almost continuous." [ARA18/125] "A most dependable Rose to use in solid beds, as it blooms freely and each flower is perfect. It opens well in all weathers." [C-Ps27] "A noble Rose of largest size and finest shape. Exquisite flesh-pink, shaded with rich coral in the center and on the reverse of petals. Flowers are borne on strong, erect stems—fine for cutting. Strong growing, healthy, with broad, distinctive foliage seldom attacked by insects." [C-Ps25] "[Very satisfactory in Brazil.]" [PS] "A gem that everyone admires." [Way45]

Lady Ashtown

A. Dickson, 1904
Seedling of 'Mrs. W. J. Grant' (HT).

"A light salmon pink. Disbud." [Th] "Flower very large, full, well-held; color, pale pink, shaded yellow, with silvery reflections." [JR31/178] "Pale rose, shading to yellow at the base of petals; reflex of petals silvery pink; flowers large, full, and pointed; and of erect branching character." [C&Js07] "Flowers large, globular, well formed; pale carmine-pink. Good foliage. Medium grower. Averages 40 blooms per season. Hardy." [ARA21/92] "Medium large, fine form, double, faint fragrance, medium stem. Fine foliage, sufficient. Growth medium strong; hardy. Light rose with silvery reflex, bases light yellow." [ARA23/165] "Light salmon-pink, variable; fine form; fair lasting qualities; trace of fragrance. Fair growth. Gives over thirty blooms in Central Zone. Does well in Washington, D.C.... when established on own root, with about an equal number of blooms, but comes smaller and lighter in heat, besides opening quickly in extreme heat, with weak neck; sometimes dies back. Always popular in England, and is listed there as pure deep pink. It needs coolness for perfection, and is of exhibition value in the Pacific Northwest Zone. Its extreme hardiness for an HT is proved by its northern record as well as by the almost entire lack of winter-killing of any of its wood in the Central Zone. Subject to mildew. Recommended for New York state." [Th2] "Brilliant shining pink with a golden underglow, unsurpassed in Rose colors. Flower moderately large, with a fine, high-pointed center, borne singly on erect stems. Blooms abundantly over a long season, but flowers are apt to lose shape in hot weather. Bush grows lustily, but is not always resistant to disease. Very hardy, and indispensable where winters are severe." [C-Ps25] "Distinct and attractive in color and form; good growth and foliage; blooming qualities fairly good. Also doing well on Multiflora [understock]." [ARA18/111] "Bushy, medium height, compact, hardy; foliage plentiful, black-spots slightly; bloom free, continuous." [ARA18/126]

"Growth vigorous, but not tall, habit branching and foliage strong, good and somewhat glossy. Opinion varies as to its liability to mildew. My own experience is that it is rather subject to this trouble... A few say 'very subject,' but I think it is not as bad as that, while many of my friends have found it 'fairly free from mildew.' It flowers very freely and continuously over a period from the end of June to late autumn. The flowers are carried fairly erect on slender stems, and although full flowers droop at times the habit is not generally drooping. The petals are large and of good substance, and the colour deep clear pink. The flowers come a beautiful shape, nicely pointed, and stand well. They last fairly well in water, though apt to lose colour, as they will also do in hot sun. They become rather spotted by rain, but do not ball or refuse to open. This is one of the very best gar-

den Roses; for bedding it is quite first class, its habit and profusion of bloom making it specially valuable for this purpose. It is also good for decorative purposes, particularly when young flowers are used, and for exhibition its place is 10th in Mr. Mawley's Analysis. It is unfortunately scarcely at all fragrant. It is not very particular as to soil or situation, and may be confidently recommended for almost all general purposes as one of the best Roses of recent introduction." [NRS10/31] "This is one of the most satisfactory Roses that have been introduced of recent years. It was unfortunate in missing the award of the N.R.S. Gold Medal, as few Roses have deserved it better. It has steadily increased in popular favour and is now to be found in every exhibitor's collection. It is easy to grow, generally comes of excellent shape, will stand high culture without getting coarse, and has few if any faults. It is subject to mildew, moderately vigorous, and very free flowering, and a good autumnal. It is high up in Mr. Mawley's analysis, and would be placed by most Rosarians in the best dozen H.Ps or H.T.s." [F-M] "While good at all times, it is especially glorious in midsummer and fall when the flowers are at their best. For those who are looking for an 'easy-to-grow' variety, this is it." [C-Ps31] "This is truly the pink Rose for everyone, everywhere." [C-Ps28]

[Lady Clanmorris]

A. Dickson, 1900

"Deep peach." [CA07] "Cream, salmon center, edges pink." [LS] "A grand new ever-blooming rose, perfectly distinct and different from all others; flowers very large and graceful, petals large and of excellent substance, color rich creamy-white with pale rose centre, edge of petals beautifully bordered with deep rose; altogether a rose of unusual excellence." [C&Js02]

[Lady Coventry]

Smith of Downley, 1913 (?)

"*Le Matin* tells us in its number of July 15 about an English horticulturalist who has finally discovered the *Blue Rose*. Mr. Smith, of Downley (Bucks.), devoted himself for many years to crossing some race of the Rose, and has concluded by obtaining this marvelous result. The English journals declare the shade wonderful; this variety bears the name '*Lady Coventry*'. We give this news *gratis prodéo*; for more, those who don't want to believe it should go there and see it for themselves." [JR34/117] "Growth not good; no special merit." [ARA18/116]

Lady Dunleathe

A. Dickson, 1913

"Pale yellow with deep golden center. Not among the big, bold, striking roses, but nevertheless one of the very best in our collection. It is surpassingly graceful and dainty at every stage. The buds are remarkably long pointed and slender, with noticeably elongated, narrow sepals. Open flowers are cupped and, as the bloom expands, the color greatly deepens. Stems are very long and slender, but strong enough to carry the flowers. Free blooming and delightfully fragrant." [CA17] "Petals long and pointed, ivory cream white, with egg-yellow tints, making the rose look much... like 'Betty' [HT]; the blossoms are strong, upright at the tip of their stems; the wood is dark brown, and the foliage is coppery, veined crimson . . . Continuous bloom. Truly a superb and charming variety." [JR37/106] "Beautiful color and form, especially in bud; growth average; foliage good; blooming qualities fairly good." [ARA18/111] "Good growth; hardy;

good foliage; fair stem; medium size; blooms well; beautiful in bud form; lasts well; . . . delicately perfumed." [Th] "Growth vigorous, free, continuous blooming." [GeH]

[Lady Faire]
Low, 1908
Sport of 'Mrs. W. J. Grant' (HT).

"Light carmine rose, shaded salmon." [CA10] "Flower salmon edged with flesh-pink." [GeH]

Lady Forteviot
B. R. Cant, 1928

"Very fine and free in early summer, with great promise in the early blooms, which were golden yellow and apricot with large petals, and fragrant." [ARA30/190] "This is a conical, high pointed Rose, even after the outer petals have spread widely. The colour is a brilliant orange on the inner face, with a bright canary yellow base, the back of the petals being paler and inclined to apricot. The leaves are large and glossy, and free of Mildew. The Rose was much admired." [NRS28/75] "Splendid growth, its shiny foliage free from disease . . . very wide, fluffy, beautiful flowers . . . fair fragrance . . . the flowers are over much too quickly and appear much too seldom." [ARA34/194] "To me, supersedes the old 'Angèle Pernet' [Pern], its perfume clinching the argument." [CaRoIII/5/3]

Lady Margaret Boscawen
A. Dickson, 1911

"Soft shell pink. Practically no disbudding." [Th] "Shell pink on fawn. —Vigorous. —Free. Garden, bedding. Fragrant." [Cat12/67] "A very good and beautiful variety in which the canes are erect, and strong, and the abundance very great. Foliage ample, thick, cypress green; the abundant blossoms are large, full, delicate pink on a fawn ground, with a strong Tea scent." [JR36/73]

[Lady Mary Ward]
McGredy, 1913

"'Rich orange, shaded deeper apricot orange, with a decided metallic veneering' (McGredy). His description was borne out in our tests and in addition we found the petals strongly veined carmine. Another perfectly unique color combination . . . Buds are long pointed; flowers of medium size, with pointed center and reflex outer petals, fairly double and apple-scented. Bears freely. Except for a weak stem, it is splendid in every way." [CA17] "Sweetly perfumed. Growth vigorous; free flowering." [GeH] "Extremely floriferous, and perfectly regular in growth . . . Nicely perfumed, attractive, and very effective." [JR37/90] "A wonderful color. Not a vigorous grower, but a fair bloomer; hardy." [C-Ps25]

Lady Moyra Beauclerc
A. Dickson, 1901

"Bright madder-rose with silvery reflexes, very large, full, massive, perfectly formed. Growth vigorous." [GeH] "Flesh color." [CA07] "Weak grower in Middle Atlantic States." [Th] "Growth and blooming not sufficient to warrant its inclusion among the better roses." [ARA18/116] "Being very vigorous and shooting out a quantity of branches which are, in the main, extremely floriferous, it is expected to quickly take a place of honor among the great favorites. The color may be said to be unique—very bright madder pink with silvery reflections, a color distinct both in its shade of pink and in its most attractive

combination of tones. The blossoms are large, indeed massive, and well formed, the center slightly drawn out into a point. The petals are somewhat oval like in 'La France' [B or HT]. The blossoms are supported on stems which are well clothed with leaves, which the flower stems easily clear. For forcing or pot-culture, this rose is absolutely ideal, being equally good for bedding or exhibition." [JR25/99–100] "A very fine variety, which for some reason never gained the Gold Medal, though it certainly deserved it. It is of long vigorous growth, showing a good deal of the Tea habit, but the shoots are slender and pliable and the heavy flowers will need support. They are very large, well shaped and beautifully tinted, but the freshness of the colour does not last in hot weather. This is a reliable Rose for exhibition, but variable in colour. Some exhibitors, notably Mr. E. B. Lindsell, think very highly of it." [F-M]

Lady Pirrie
H. Dickson, 1910

"Salmon-pink shaded with red and copper. Inside of petals apricot and fawn. A lovely Rose." [C&Js23] "Deep, coppery, reddish salmon, inside the petals apricot-yellow, flushed fawn and copper." [C&Js14] "Deep coppery reddish salmon; inside of petals apricot yellow—varies. Lighter with us. Very little disbudding." [Th] "Blooms come in great bouquets of deep, coppery reddish salmon, mixed with apricot yellow. Better disbud during July and August and enjoy the amazing tinted blooms in the autumn. Exquisite indoors when cut early in the morning." [C-Ps28] "Large, well-formed blooms, pointed and high in the center. Fragrant and fine for cutting." [C&Js24] "The flowers are very thin and open too quickly in hot weather, which usually detracts from the value of its second flowering in August." [NRS23/57] "Fair for decorative purposes; only good for cutting in cool weather." [ARA17/25] "The distinct colouring of this Rose at once attracts attention. I will attempt to do justice to it by calling it deep coppery reddish salmon on the outside of the petals, with a lighter shade of apricot flushed fawn on the inside, a delightful combination of colour that is unique. Habit. As the Rose is a decorative Rose this is of importance. It is of true 'bedding' habit, vigorous, free branching, and free flowering, good foliage and hardy. Altogether a promising variety." [NRS10/143] "Very hardy. Deep coppery salmon to apricot-yellow; bud attractive; flower loose and flat; color and form do not last; slight fragrance. Of fine strong growth, but subject to mildew." [Th2] "The colour is a delicate coppery pink, the bud long, pointed and well formed, but the number of petals is small, and the Rose opens rather rapidly, particularly in hot weather. The substance of the petals, however, is good, and they will stand a fair amount of rain . . . Has a good branching habit, with good foliage, slightly subject to mildew, but not badly so." [NRS21/35] "Very vigorous." [ARA29/54] "A tall, husky grower." [C-Ps28] "When it does well, this Rose makes a strong, branching bush . . . The foliage is a good brownish green, generally free from disease . . . it should not be pruned too hard, as the wood ripens well." [NRS29/108–109] "What fine growth, lovely foliage and finely coloured wood! She is never out of bloom, in fact I think she is most beautiful in autumn, the very tints of the petals appearing to be in harmony with the season." [NRS20/102] "In the garden this Rose has no equal . . . As a plant it does not reach its prime until it is two or three years old and allowed to develop into a large bush. In pruning it should be treated like '[Mme.] Caroline Testout' [HT] and 'Florence Pemberton' [HT], the old wood not shortened less than two or three

Lady Pirrie *continued*

feet from the ground [ca. 6 dm to 1 m]. It is free flowering and especially good in autumn." [NRS21/63] "A delightful combination of colour." [Cat12/67] "'Betty' [HT] ... will do as well." [C-Ps29]

[Lady Rossmore]

Campbell Hall/H. Dickson, 1907

"Reddish crimson with claret shading; medium size, fairly full. A
valuable addition to the darker colored Hybrid Teas." [C&Js10]

Lady Sylvia

Stevens, 1926
Sport of 'Ophelia' (HT).

Flesh-pink, fragrant, well-shaped sport of 'Ophelia'.

Lady Ursula

A. Dickson, 1909

"Blush flesh." [Ÿ] "A delightful shade of flesh pink. Flowers, produced on every shoot, are very large, full, and of perfect form, with
high center, from which the petals of great substance gracefully reflex." [CA10] "Petals large, smooth and circular; delicately tea perfumed." [C&Js10] "Its only serious fault is a tendency of the buds to
ball in unfavorable weather, otherwise a perfect garden Rose." [C-Ps29]
"Fine form, full, large, fragrant, long stems. Fine foliage, sufficient.
Vigorous upright growth; hardy." [ARA23/165] "Extremely hardy.
Flesh-pink, not always clear, fair form, though rather small; lasts
well; slight tea perfume. Fine, large, upright growth. Gives over sixty
blooms in Central Zone." [Th2] "A handsome rose of fine fragrance;
blooms of fine substance, smooth flesh-pink. Foliage sufficient. Averages 45 to 99 blooms per season. Thrives best in soil inclined to
dryness. Hardy." [ARA21/92] "A very dependable, almost flawless
Rose, distinguished by extremely vigorous growth. Practically immune to disease. Blooms continuously into freezing weather. Flowers of medium size, light flesh-pink, with shell-like petals reflexing
from a delicately shaped bud. Lasts well when cut. Charming, and an
easy Rose to grow." [C-Ps25] "Foliage is small but healthy." [C-Ps28]
"Tall, upright, vigorous, hardy; foliage very plentiful, rather subject
to black-spot; bloom profuse early in season, abundant later, continuous." [ARA18/126] "Remarkable for its vigor of growth and exceedingly free-blooming habit." [C&Js23] "Makes a splendid bush, 3 to 4
feet in height [ca. 1–1.3 m], and has blooms for cutting throughout
the entire growing season." [C-Ps30] "Grows 6 feet high [ca. 2 m] and
blooms faithfully all summer. In hot weather the blooms lose their
color and sometimes ball, but the buds are always good, and as we
cut our roses in the early morning, we enjoy the many buds in the
house during midsummer and find that no Hybrid Tea rose gives
more flowers and good healthy foliage in the spring and fall." [ARA31/
99] "Best pink decorative rose. Excellent in growth and blooming
qualities; good form and color. Use Multiflora [understock]."
[ARA18/111] "Exhibition, garden. A good all-round Rose." [Cat12/35]

Lady Wenlock

Bernaix, 1904

"Flowers large, pretty full, beautifully colored golden China pink
with a nankeen base." [JR31/102] "Flower large, of beautiful form,
thick; color, golden China pink passing to incarnadine." [JR31/178]
"Carmine-rose shaded china rose, base of petals Indian yellow, large,
full. Growth vigorous, free." [GeH] "Growth of moderate vigor, clad

with ample dark green foliage. Bud, elongate-ovoid, perfectly
formed, upright on a fairly long and firm stem, usually solitary; col-
or, golden China pink with a nankeen base, fading, when open, to a
very fresh blush with apricot reflections. This variety is extremely
noticeable due to the freshness of its nuances and the beauty of its
flowers." [JR28/155]

Laure Wattinne

Soupert & Notting, 1901
From 'Marie Baumann' (HP) × 'Mme. Caroline Testout' (HT).

"Pink, large, full, medium scent, moderate height." [Sn] "Growth
vigorous; handsome foliage; flower large and full, of beautiful form
and irreproachable bearing; bud long on a strong stem. Color, bright
pink, the center brighter and more intense. Very floriferous and fragrant." [JR25/162]

Laurent Carle   Plate 59

Pernet-Ducher, 1907

"Carmine-crimson flowers of great size and substance." [ARA22/
xiv] "Brilliant, velvety carmine. Flowers large, of perfect form, and intensely fragrant. One of the finest Roses grown as it produces its
splendid flowers throughout the season and the blooms come nearly
as good in hot, dry weather as under more favorable conditions."
[C&Js24] "Good keeping qualities, and it is a generous bloomer. One
can always tell 'Laurent Carle' by the little white streak on the inside
of one of the petals." [ARA29/55] "Beautiful cut-flower because of its
clear color, good shape, and lasting qualities; fair growth; fairly good
bloomer." [ARA18/112] "Fair amount of disbudding." [Th] "Brilliant
carmine; perfume fair to strong; thirty-one blooms throughout the
season on Multiflora [understock]; growth fair. Excellent for cutting."
[ARA17/24] "The massive glowing carmine blooms of this fine Rose
are probably the largest of all red Hybrid Teas. The buds are solid, very
dark, and open slowly to big, bold blooms of finest form, with broad,
deep petals of great substance. Its high-built, pointed center can only
be equaled by those Hybrid Perpetuals whose flowers were carefully
bred for exhibition. The wide-open flower is unusually pleasing in
shape, and holds its color. Fragrance is strong and well retained until
the petals fall. It is a dependable bloomer if protected against black-
spot, and even in the hottest weather will produce fine blooms, but not
in any great quantity at one time. It grows vigorously, but quite low
and branching, so that although the flowers are unsurpassed for cutting, the stems are not always long." [C-Ps25] "Does not enjoy summer
heat." [C-Ps29] "Fine foliage. Good grower. About 40 blooms per season. Hardy." [ARA21/92] "Of great vigor, with erect branches; beautiful
dark green foliage; long bud, usually solitary, borne on a long stem;
flower very large, of good form; moderately double; always opens easily; color, brilliant crimson carmine." [JR31/22–23] "Tall, compact,
growth moderate, hardy; foliage plentiful, healthy; bloom free, almost
continuous." [ARA18/126] "Growth vigorous; flowers very large, of
perfect form; buds long; color brilliant velvety carmine. A valuable
rose for exhibition or decorative purposes." [C&Js08] "Medium
growth, very hardy; fairly long, erect stem, good foliage, long, pointed
bud; medium to large flower of good substance and beauty. Blooms
well in the spring, fairly well in the summer, and quite well in the autumn. Plant 18 inches center to center [ca. 4.5 dm]. Prune to 4 eyes."
[Th] "Quite hardy. Deep crimson-rose; very attractive form, but petalage is very full and substance in only fair, so that under damp condi-

tions this rose does not open well; fine fragrance. Wood sometimes liable to die back. Foliage takes mildew and black-spot slightly. Growth rather small in Central Zone, where it gives an average of thirty-one blooms. Does well in South-East and Pacific South-West. In American Rose Annual vote in 1921 for southern states it scored more points than any other red HT." [Th2] "Good in all ways." [NRS14/160]

[Le Progrès]

trans. "Progress"
Pernet-Ducher, 1903

"Very vigorous bush with bushy canes, beautiful foliage, pretty ovoid golden yellow bud; very large cupped flower, full, opening easily; color, nankeen yellow, lighter when fully open. Superb, abundantly-blooming variety, one of the prettiest yellow roses." [JR27/130–131]

[Leslie Holland]

H. Dickson, 1911

"Flower deep scarlet-crimson, shaded velvety crimson, sweetly scented. Growth vigorous." [GeH] "This magnificent hybrid tea is by far the greatest leap forward in rose progress in recent years. It produces blossoms in profusion from June to October, bearing them upright at the tip of the canes. The blossom resists opening even on the hottest days, and without fading. It is of a deep crimson scarlet color, and has a very sweet scent." [JR36/56] Parent of 'Elvira Aramayo' (Pern).

Lia

Ketten, 1909

From 'Farbenkönigin' (HT) × 'Mme. Ravary' (HT).

"Clear rosy scarlet, reverse of petals crimson-pink, passing to rosy scarlet, base of petals Indian yellow, medium to large size, full. Growth vigorous, branching, very free." [GeH] "Purple red, yellow at the center, medium size, full, medium height." [Sn]

Liberty

A. Dickson, 1900

From 'Mrs. W. J. Grant' (HT) × 'Charles J. Graham' (HT).

"Undoubtedly the finest crimson rose of modern times. Color pure crimson scarlet; a steady and constant bloomer; flowers of large size, beautiful elongated form. A remarkable keeper when cut, preserving its brilliancy of color without change; very fragrant." [CA01] "Fairly mediocre by the end of September. Its color has a lilac tint." [JR28/10–11] "A good buttonhole rose. —Fragrant." [Cat12/37] "Rich velvety crimson, fine stiff petals . . . Growth fairly vigorous." [P1] "Deep bright crimson scarlet, one of the richest colored roses we have, beautiful buds and large double flowers, very fragrant and a constant bloomer, fine for house culture and cut flowers." [C&Js03] "Very floriferous, producing deliciously perfumed blossoms like those of 'American Beauty' [HP]; they are perhaps paler in summer, but in autumn their tint is much the same deep crimson as that of 'Gruss an Teplitz' [B]." [JR24/21] "One of the finest early-flowering roses; in color a warm rich crimson scarlet; surpassing its rival, the well-known '[The] Meteor' [HT], in abundance of bloom, size, and color." [CA02] "It seems to be a fairly good grower, with well-formed flowers not large enough for exhibition, but of a colour—bright crimson—which is much wanted in this section." [F-M2] "The ne plus ultra of red roses . . . very floriferous, remontant, and irreproachably held; the growth is vigorous, stocky, and clad in handsome, glossy foliage." [JR25/20] Liberty, referring in particular to Irish political aspirations.

Lieutenant Chauré

Pernet-Ducher, 1910

From 'Liberty' (HT) × 'Étoile de France' (HT).

"Carmine pink touched grenadine . . . ravishing. The blossom is large and full, with large petals." [JR36/183] "Among the largest [blossoms] of all red Hybrid Teas. The buds are solid, very dark, and open slowly to big, bold blooms of the finest form, with broad, deep petals of great substance. Its high-built, pointed center can only be equaled by [those of] Hybrid Perpetuals. The wide-open flower is unusually pleasing in shape, and holds its color. Fragrance is strong and well retained until the petals fall. It is a dependable bloomer, and even in the hottest weather will produce fine blooms, but not in any great quantity at one time." [C-Ps28] "A nice clear red, a little on the small side, but usually a good shape. Sweetly scented, it grows well, and although it is subject to mildew I would not care to be without it." [NRS23/201] "Twenty-three blooms throughout the season on yearling plants; growth fair. Promises to be a good all-round rose." [ARA17/24] "A crimson flower with a fine perfume, and is only of moderately satisfactory form, while the colour is scarcely 'fast' enough and does not last well . . . It grows fairly well and is popular with many." [NRS21/38] "Velvety crimson-red; fair form; petalage slightly thin, with good substance; fair fragrance. A good rose of nice growth and blooming qualities." [Th2] "Notable for its color and perfume. Growth and form fair; blooming qualities fairly good." [ARA18/112] "Velvety crimson, form globular, free flowering and fragrant. Holds its colour well. A good bedding Rose." [NRS21/63] "Crimson-red, shaded with garnet, large, fairly full, possessing petals of great depth and cupped form, fine long bud. Growth vigorous, upright, branching." [GeH] "Crimson; tall, bushy." [ARA17/31] "Medium to low-growing, compact, hardy; foliage very plentiful, black-spots somewhat, mildews slightly; bloom free, almost continuous." [ARA18/126] "Very vigorous with erect branches, large leaves which are dark green; long bud, velvety crimson red; flower large, pretty full, large petals, cupped; color, crimson red nuanced grenadine . . . an excellent garden rose for areas with moderate temperatures." [JR34/40] "A very good red rose." [ARA18/133]

Lilli von Posern

Kiese, 1910

From 'Mme. Caroline Testout' (HT) × 'Oberbürgermeister Dr. Troendlin' (HT).

"Pink, large, full, medium height." [Sn]

Lina Schmidt-Michel

Lambert, 1905

From 'Mme. Abel Chatenay' (HT) × 'Kleiner Alfred' (Pol).

"Soft bright pink. —Very vigorous. —Garden, pillar. —Semi-double." [Cat12/37] "A novelty dedicated to the artist whose watercolors . . . have appeared these last several years in the Journal des Roses. It is a vigorous rose . . . it grows to six to ten feet [ca. 2–3.3 m] in height, and blooms profusely in season. Its blossoms are semi-double, bright pink nuanced carmine, staying fresh and open a long time." [JR29/179] "While I myself regard this Rose as in some respects the most satisfactory Rose for a Pillar of any H.T. in my collection, I find this opinion by no means shared by my correspondents; several do not grow it at all, and the remainder are about equally divided for and against it . . . Those who approve it find it free from mildew and easy to grow. For this Rose a Pillar from 6 to 8 or 9 feet may

Lina Schmidt-Michel *continued*

be used [ca. 2–2.6–3 m]. In my own experience its great value lies in the readiness to make side shoots, which will clothe the Pillar well, and without requiring very constant attention. The flowers are freely produced in big showy clusters rather like those of 'Mme. Abel Chatenay' would be if it were to come nearly single, the petals being bicolor having a dark pink or brick red pink outside, and soft silvery pink on the inside; being only semi-double they open readily. The autumn flowering growths are long, pendant, and very graceful. In the annual pruning the rods of the year should be left full length except where they are cut to different heights to clothe the tree, the lateral growths being spurred in and old wood removed from time to time." [NRS14/72–73] Note the Floribunda-formula breeding.

Lohengrin
Kiese/J. C. Schmidt, 1903
From 'Mme. Caroline Testout' (HT) × 'Mrs. W. J. Grant' (HT).

"Silvery pink, pointed flowers. Growth moderate." [GeH] "Light pink, large, full, medium height." [Sn] "Purely an exhibitor's Rose of very fine shape, but fleeting colour, a medium grower, the flowers nearly always come good, but it is not recommended to the small grower." [F-M] Lohengrin, son of Parsifal, and knight of the Holy Grail.

Louis Baldwin   Listed as 'Louise Baldwin' (HT).

Louise Baldwin
syn. 'Louis Baldwin'
McGredy, 1919

"A graceful flower, extraordinarily long and pointed . . . Colour—rich orange, with soft apricot shading over the entire petal . . . Quite hardy, a good grower and very free blooming . . . Very sweet scented." [NRS19/163] "Bud long-pointed; flower full, high center; strong, sweet fragrance. Color rich orange, with soft apricot shading over the entire petal. Vigorous grower; abundant bloomer." [ARA20/128] "Of vigorous growth, with deep bronze-green foliage. The blooms, which are of a medium size and good shape, are very freely produced, and carried on long wiry stems. The colour is a very fine orange-apricot, which is quite unique in tint. It will prove a very fine bedding Rose." [NRS17/132]

Louise Criner
Chambard, 1919
Seedling of 'Louise Cretté' (HP).

"One of the best of the white Roses, and far too little known. Beautiful flowers of a splendid shape. A worthy descendant of the immaculate 'Louise Cretté', but far more shapely." [NRS24/145] "Medium-sized bud and bloom of white, with a cream center; only fair. Consider it overrated." [ARA27/136] "Blossom pure white, good fulness, good growth, continuous bloom. Cutting rose." [Ck] "Pure white. Bush slow-starting, low. 22 blooms." [ARA26/94] "Show-white; no fragrance. Growth slow starting; low bush but healthy. Disbudded, produced 23 blooms. Flowers droop and grow so low that they become mud-splashed in wet weather. —*Milton, Mass.* I think that this is the best-shaped white rose we have. It is very large and of excellent shape and never seems to show a center. Bud very long and shapely on a very strong stem and will last on the bush for days, or, when cut, in water. It will stand quite a lot of rain, never seeming to ball, but it is certainly inclined to mildew. —*Seattle, Wash.*" [ARA26/117]

Louise Lilia   Listed as 'Luise Lilia' (HT).

Louise Pernot
Robichon, 1903

"Delicate silvery pink." [Ÿ] "Whitish pink, middle salmon, large, full, medium height." [Sn] "Vigorous, with handsome light green foliage, flower large, full, well-formed; color, delicate silvery pink tinted salmon around the nub. Very handsome bud." [JR27/147]

Lucien Chauré   Plate 70
Soupert & Notting, 1913
From 'Mme. Abel Chatenay' (HT) × 'Pié X' (HP).

"Flesh pink illuminated with light cream pink, center glowing. Flower very large and regular, produced in profusion up till November. Excellent for cutting, forcing, and bedding. Top of the line variety, having all the good qualities of 'Mme. Abel Chatenay'." [JR37/183] "Attractive in color and form; foliage and growth quite good; a satisfactory bloomer in 'special bed'; in regular bed fair results may be expected." [ARA18/112] "Medium to tall, compact, hardy; foliage very plentiful, healthy; bloom moderate, almost continuous." [ARA18/126]

Lucien de Lemos
Lambert, 1905
From 'Princesse Alice de Monaco' (T) × 'Mme. Caroline Testout' (HT).

"Carnation pink." [Ÿ] "Light pink, large, full, medium scent, medium height." [Sn] "Flower large, full, globular, exterior petals very large, very warm carnation pink, center whitish pink; abundant bloom; well perfumed." [JR31/103] "Growth very vigorous; flower . . . erect, fragrant." [JR30/25]

Ludwig Möller
Kiese, 1915
From 'Frau Karl Druschki' (HP) × a seedling (of 'Maréchal Niel' [N]).

"Deep yellow, changing to pure white, of good form. Growth vigorous." [GeH] "Deep yellow, large, very full, tall." [Sn] "Has not yet shown particularly good results." [ARA18/112]

Luise Lilia
syn. 'Louise Lilia'
Lambert, 1912
From 'General MacArthur' (HT) × 'Frau Peter Lambert' (HT).

"Crimson. Garden." [NRS15/149] "Deep red, large, full, very fragrant, medium height." [Sn] "Deep blood-red, almost black; good shape, very fragrant, free blooming. Growth vigorous." [GeH] "Low-growing, stocky, hardy; foliage very plentiful, black-spots somewhat; bloom moderate, almost continuous." [ARA18/126] "Weak growth; winterkills." [ARA18/116]

Lulu
Easlea, 1919

"Orange-salmon and pink." [ARA25/102] "An abundant and continuous bloomer." [GeH] "This is said to hold the record for the longest bud yet produced." [ARA20/120] "Bud very long-pointed; flower orange, salmon, and pink. Vigorous grower of bushy habit . . . abundance of bloom all season." [ARA20/128] "A tall, eight petaled, very slender orange bud which was eye-catching . . . a charmer." [DP] "Pretty buds; opens too quick; too thin; fades quickly. Foliage crinkly; no [black] spot." [ARA26/117] "Foliage mildews. Growth good." [Th2]

"Growth very dense and vigorous." [NRS19/171] "Abundant foliage." [NRS24/157] "Has a most unusual, long, tapering bud ... Mr. Neal always wants me to place one of these in my refrigerator before breakfast for him to wear. In this way it will keep without opening up all day, even in hot weather. We love our 'Lulu'!" [ARA29/53]

Lydia Grimm
Geduldig, 1907
From a seeding (resulting from crossing 'Général Jacqueminot' [HP] with 'Mme. Caroline Testout' [HT]) × 'Kaiserin Auguste Viktoria' (HT).

"Yellowish white, large, full, medium scent, medium height." [Sn]

Madeleine Faivre
Buatois, 1902

"White, nubs yellow." [Ÿ] "Pinkish white, large, very full, medium height." [Sn] "Very vigorous, branches upright without being 'climbing.' Flower enormous, very double, opens very well. Color, flesh white, nubs yellow." [JR26/178]

Madeleine Gaillard
Bernaix, 1908

"Fresh pink." [Ÿ] "Vigorous, well held, quite special blooming qualities, flower large, beautifully formed, cupped, thick concave petals, beautiful pure white slightly nuanced pale cream. Beautiful and floriferous." [JR32/135]

[Magnafrano]
Van Fleet/Conard & Jones, 1900
From 'Magna Charta' (HP) × 'Safrano' (T).

"The outburst of blooms in June is gorgeous, and after that there is a frequent recurrence throughout the season. The flowers are large, of a brilliant cerise-red, coming several on each stem, every one opening perfectly; but if the side buds are pinched off while still small, the remaining bloom will be of gigantic size. The plant is very vigorous and can be trained as pillars, making a gorgeous sight. Large, handsome, disease-resistant foliage." [C-Pf29] "Low-growing, compact, reasonably hardy; foliage plentiful, healthy; bloom moderate, intermittent." [ARA18/26] "It combines the hardiness and vigor of the 'Magna Charta' with the free-blooming habit and delightful fragrance of the Tea Roses. The flowers are extra large, frequently four to five inches across [ca. 1–1.25 dm]; very regular, full and double, and deliciously sweet. The color is deep, bright, shining rose, very rich and handsome. The bush is a strong, upright grower, and a constant and most abundant bloomer." [C&Js02] Not mentioned in the Conard & Jones catalog until 1902, though there listed as "C.&J. Co., 1900."

Mama Looymans
syn. 'Mama Luymans'
Leenders, 1910
From 'Gruss an Teplitz' (B) × 'Hortensia' (T).

"Light orange red, medium size, light scent, moderate height." [Sn]

Mama Luymans   Listed as 'Mama Looymans' (HT).

Maman Lyly
trans. "Mama Lyly"
Soupert & Notting, 1911
From 'Mme. Mélanie Soupert' (HT) × 'Mrs. Peter Blair' (extinct HT; A. Dickson, 1906; yellow; parentage unk.).

"Whitish pink, large, semi-full, medium height." [Sn] "Flower of irreproachable form, and very large, resembling 'Souvenir de la Malmaison [B]. Color, very delicate flesh pink ...Surpasses all other light pink varieties." [JR35/168] "Delicate rosy flesh, large, well formed. Growth vigorous and very free." [GeH]

Mamie
syn. 'Mrs. Conway Jones'
A. Dickson, 1902

"Rosy carmine, with yellow base. Beautiful shape; growth vigorous." [P1] "A well-formed flower of good pointed shape, but rather undecided in colour." [F-M2] "Vigorous, well-spaced branches, very floriferous. It blooms early and continuously. The blossoms are fragrant, beautifully colored carmine pink with a splotch of yellow very evident at the base of the petals, which are large, smooth, and very sturdy. The blossom lasts a long time." [JR25/100] "Of strong healthy growth with good foliage. The buds are large and open slowly into very full flowers having fine petals and globular shape with high centre. A fine Rose for exhibition, and most reliable, as it is the best variety to 'stand' — i.e. keep its shape and colour—in a cut state I know, outside the pure Tea class. It is the only Rose, other than pure Tea, of which I have successfully shown the same bloom at two exhibitions." [F-M]

Manuel P. Azevedo
Soupert & Notting, 1910
From 'Étoile de France' (HT) × 'Ulrich Brunner fils' (HP).

"Color, fresh cerise red; upright; vigorous growth. Flower very large, perfect, full, firm petals. Beautiful long bud. This newcomer takes from 'Ulrich Brunner fils' its perfect form and vigor, and from 'Étoile de France' its abundant bloom. Its color is intermediate between those of its parents. The blossom opens easily no matter what, and can be found in both early and late beds. It has a long, rigid stem ...Long-lasting in water. A rare and unvarying color, and new among HT's. Very fragrant." [JR34/183] "Dedicated to an Argentine fancier. Its majestic deportment, the perfection of its form, and the richness of its color make it without equal." [JR35/183]

[Marcella]
W. Paul, 1913

"Salmon flesh. Buds stiff. Large, well formed and handsome. Growth strong and erect. Free and continuous bloomer. Good for cutting." [CA17] "Buds yellow, opening to a very large salmon-colored flower, quite full; at the tip of a long stem; bloom abundant and continuous; the very pretty rose is as good for cutting as it is for forcing." [JR37/89] "A splendid novelty; buds buff, the opening flower salmon-flesh, extra large, well filled and very handsome; of strong, erect growth, free and continuous in blooming." [C&Js16] Not to be confused with Liabaud's flesh-white HP of 1865.

Margaret Dickson Hamill
A. Dickson, 1915

"Straw, nuanced carmine." [Ÿ] "This is a beautiful Rose of a fine golden yellow." [NRS15/155] "An outstanding and magnificent Rose. Its delicate, solid, maize-straw-colored, deep, shell-like petals are edge-flushed with most delicate carmine on back of petals. Deliciously and powerfully fragrant." [C&Js16] "A fine bloom with yellow petals, reverse flushed carmine ... thoroughly perpetual flowering." [NRS18/154] "'Margaret Dickson Hamill' I should like better if she

Margaret Dickson Hamill *continued*

only had a longer petal. In other respects she is fine." [NRS20/162] "Fine in form and color but only a moderate bloomer." [ARA25/205] "Form, globular. Habit vigorous, branching and free flowering. It appears to be variable in colour, being described in some lists as lemon yellow, whereas with us the flowers are buff orange." [NRS21/64] "Large, globular; very fragrant. Growth vigorous, erect; free flowering; leathery green foliage, with deep crimson leaf stalks." [GeH] "The plant grows well, and the flowers are a straw yellow, destitute of form. Though I have grown in some years I have found little of interest in it as a garden plant." [NRS21/53] "Promises to be a beautiful bedding rose, blooming profusely even in October." [ARA18/47]

Margherita Croze
Ketten, 1913
From 'Étoile de France' (HT) × 'Earl of Warwick' (HT).

"Carmine purple fading to purplish pink when completely open, on a ground of Nilsson pink, large, full, fragrant; bud long, solitary, opens well; stem long and erect. Bush vigorous, very floriferous, ample foliage . . . Much to be recommended for bedding and cutting." [JR37/184] "Sweet-scented." [GeH] "Attractive color and form; growth good; blooming qualities fair." [ARA18/112]

Marguerite Guillot
P. Guillot, 1902
Seedling of 'Mme. Caroline Testout' (HT).

"Yellowish white, very large, full, medium scent, medium height." [Sn] "Growth vigorous, flower very large, full, globular, fragrant, cream white, fading to pure white. From 'Mme. Caroline Testout', from which it takes all its characteristics." [JR26/132]

Marianne Pfitzer
Jacobs, 1902
Seedling of 'Kaiserin Auguste Viktoria' (HT).

"Whitish pink, very large, full, medium height." [Sn] "Large, very full, flesh-coloured, with a deep pink and reddish sheen. Growth like that of 'K[aiserin] A[uguste] Viktoria', its parent." [Hn] "This newcomer is much the same in vigor, growth, and bloom as 'K[aisern] A[uguste] Viktoria', except that the color is just like that of 'Souvenir de la Malmaison' [B]." [JR26/49]

[Marichu Zayas]
Soupert & Notting, 1906
From an unnamed seedling × 'Mrs. W. J. Grant' (HT).

"Marvelous newcomer fitting into the top of the line, of inestimable value. Vigorous bush with beautiful dark green foliage. The blossom is large, full, finely and deliciously imbricated. —The long bud is held proudly on a straight, strong stem, and stands out to good effect against the foliage. Color very tender, very light crushed strawberry, nuanced a light bright pink. The bud of rare beauty destines 'Marichu Zayas' to a foremost place as a variety for hot-house cutting as well as in the open air; being extraordinarily floriferous, its place in beds is obvious. —Each branch bears an irreproachable flower or bud all year, without regard to the season, right up to the start of Winter. Has a distinct scent." [JR30/152]

Marie Henry
Buatois, 1900
From 'Irène Watts' (Ch) × 'Beauté Lyonnaise' (HT; Pernet-Ducher,

1895; white; parentage: 'Baronne Adolphe de Rothschild' [HP] × ?).

"Yellowish white, large, full, medium scent, tall." [Sn] "Blossom large, quite full, bud well formed, borne on a long, strong stem; white lightly tinted canary yellow within; petals firm. Growth vigorous, semi-climbing." [JR24/163]

Marie Isakoff
Dubreuil, 1901
Seedling of 'Mme. Caroline Testout' (HT).

"Orange yellow, large, full, medium scent, tall." [Sn] "Growth vigorous, very floriferous, canes upright, bearing solitary cupped blossoms which are large, full, and apricot yellow fading to pale canary at full expansion; the variety has the wood and foliage of 'Mme. Caroline Testout', from which it differs only in its charming color." [JR25/162]

Marie-Louise Mathian
Fugier, 1911

"Yellowish white, large, full, very fragrant, medium height." [Sn] "Growth very vigorous, with branching canes. Flower very large, very full, and well held. Color, cream white, with a salmon tint at the center when fully open. Bud long and well formed; flower has a delicate scent. Continuous bloom until frost." [JR36/23]

Marie Schmitt
Schmitt-Eltv., 1910
Sport of 'Mme. Caroline Testout' (HT).
"Light pink, large, full, tall." [Sn]

[Mark Twain]
E. G. Hill, 1902

"Rosy red." [CA10] "Satiny pink." [LS] "Fine pointed buds and large open flowers; deep rose-madder lightened with pink; very beautiful." [C&Js07] "Delicate pink tinted with deeper carnation pink. —Blossoms large, full; floriferous; vigorous; bushy." [Cx] Mark Twain, *nom de plume* of Samuel L. Clemens, thoroughly American *littérateur* and close observer of human nature, lived 1835–1910.

Marquis de Bouillé
A. Schwartz, 1904

"Light red tinted pale pink." [Ÿ] "Vigorous, foliage glaucous green; flower very large, very full, large petals." [JR28/154]

Marquise de Ganay
P. Guillot, 1909
From 'Liberty' (HT) × 'La France' (B or HT).

"Bright silvery pink. Vigorous. Exhibition, garden. Fragrant." [NRS11/100] "Light pink, very large, full, medium scent, medium height." [Sn] "Tea perfumed . . . free flowering." [GeH] "Very large, long-pointed buds, borne singly on long stems. Open flowers are a lovely silvery pink color. A vigorous growing, disease-resistant plant with dark green, leathery foliage. Moderately fragrant and lasting when cut." [C-Ps26] "Continuous blooms all season, until frost. A sturdy, erect grower producing large, bright, silvery pink flowers of fine form. Good for bedding." [C&Js24] "Growth very vigorous, with erect canes, ample dark green foliage; bud very large, borne on a long, fairly strong stem; flower enormous, cupped, full, large petals, well filled, beautiful silvery pink, nicely scented. The biggest of the HT's. From 'Liberty' × 'La France', it takes from 'Liberty' its rigid stems and the form of its flower (though with much greater fulness), and, from 'La

France', its extreme abundance and certain growth characteristics." [JR33/167]

[Marquise de Sinety]
Pernet-Ducher, 1906

"Yellow flushed orange. Buds are very deep golden yellow; pointed. Open flower cupped, with high center. Petals large and crisp. Fragrance rich. Stems very strong, but often curiously curved. Foliage very dark and handsome. Ranks very high." [CA17] "Flower ochre-yellow tinted bright rosy scarlet, changing paler with age, large, full, cupped, buds carmine-ochre. Growth moderate, floriferous." [GeH] "Growth vigorous; large reddish bronze green leaves; bud carmine ochre; flower very large, full, cupped; superbly colored Roman ochre nuanced Carthamine pink." [JR30/38] "Superseded by 'Élégante' [HT]." [C-Ps29]

Martha Drew
McGredy, 1919

"Creamy white with rose-coloured centre, sweetly scented, large, well formed. Growth vigorous." [GeH] "Yellowish white, pink in the middle, very large, full, medium scent, medium height." [Sn] "A fine, large-petaled rose of vigorous habit. The large blooms, which are carried erect on long, stiff stems, are of a fine pointed shape; sweetly scented. The color—flesh-tinted rose—somewhat reminds one of [that of] 'Mrs. Theodore Roosevelt' [HT]." [ARA20/116] "An improvement on 'Mrs. Theodore Roosevelt', which it resembles, though the blooms are larger and not inclined to flatness. It should make a good garden and exhibition rose." [ARA20/122]

Mary, Countess of Ilchester
A. Dickson, 1910

"Warm crimson carmine. Disbud." [Th] "A rose of great distinction and charm with vigorous and erect growth, and most attractive deep green foliage. Color is beautiful crimson carmine. It possesses unusually free and continuous blooming qualities; the flowers are of great size with massive petals, which are very smooth and circular. Sweetly perfumed. A rose of much merit." [C&Js11] "Dropped because it fades to magenta." [C-Ps29] "Extra large, warm crimson-carmine flowers, with large, smooth, circular petals; fine perfume. Sufficient foliage. Strong grower. Gives from 41 to 77 blooms per season. Hardy." [ARA21/92] "Fine cut-flower variety. Excellent in form, color, lasting qualities, foliage, and stem; growth good; shy bloomer." [ARA18/113] "Petals of immense size. Growth vigorous, erect, very free." [GeH] "Large, variable form, very double, fragrant, long stem. Foliage sufficient, subject to rust. Fair growth; hardy." [ARA23/166] "Moderate height, bushy, hardy; foliage plentiful, black-spots somewhat; bloom abundant, continuous." [ARA18/126]

Mary Greer Listed as 'Kootenay' (HT).

Max Herdoffer Listed 'Max Hesdörffer' (HT).

Max Hesdörffer
syn. 'Max Herdoffer'
Jacobs, 1902
Seedling of 'Kaiserin Auguste Viktoria' (HT).

"Deep rose." [JR32/140] "Pink, large, full, medium scent, medium height." [Sn] "This splendid new Hybrid Tea Rose is a strong vigorous grower; color, deep rose, bordered with silvery rose; flowers large, full and perfectly formed." [C&Js07]

May Miller
E. G. Hill, 1910
From an unnamed seedling × 'Paul Neyron' (HP).

"Glowing pink, large, full, medium height." [Sn] "Back of petals copper and bright pink, the upper surface being peach and apricot, the bud is long and pointed. Growth vigorous, free flowering." [GeH] "Fine form, large, double, long stem. Good foliage, sufficient. Growth strong; hardy. Coppery rose, blended peach-pink and apricot." [ARA23/166] "A strong growing, free flowering H.T. with large, dark foliage. The bud is long and pointed and opens into a flower of unusual beauty. The back of the petal is copper and bright pink, the upper surface peach and apricot shades." [C&Js13] "Medium high and compact, moderately hardy; foliage sufficient, black-spots somewhat; bloom moderate, intermittent." [ARA18/126]

Melody
Scott/A. Dickson, 1911

"Deep saffron-yellow, with primrose border. —Vigorous. —Garden, bedding, pot. Free-flowering. Fragrant." [Cat12/68] "Saffron yellow with primrose edges. Flower medium to large; very double and delightfully fragrant. Foliage dark violet green. Stems splendid. Very free bloomer. Unusually fine in every way." [CA17] "Of good size, well formed, perfumed. Growth vigorous, very free." [GeH] "Fair growth; lacking in distinctiveness." [ARA18/117] "Has garnered particular attention from all fanciers who have seen it these last two seasons by reason of its magnificent and abundant bloom, its pleasing color, and its brilliant dark green foliage. The very fragrant blooms, borne on strong stems, are intense saffron yellow bordered spring yellow, a very harmonious mix of colors. Of great merit for decoration and for forcing." [JR36/73]

Mevrouw A. del Court van Krimpen
Leenders, 1917
Seedling of 'Prince de Bulgarie' (HT).

"Pinkish white, large, full, medium scent, medium height." [Sn] "Bud very large, long-pointed; flower very large, full, borne, several together, on long stems; lasting; strong fragrance. Color rosy white and orange. Foliage abundant, large, glossy light green. A vigorous grower of bushy habit and a profuse bloomer." [ARA20/135]

Mevrouw Boreel van Hogelander
Leenders, 1918
From 'Mme. Léon Pain' (HT) × 'Mme. Antoine Mari' (T).

"Flesh coloured, shaded carmine and pink, medium size; full. Growth vigorous." [GeH] "Bud medium size, globular; flower medium size, globular, borne, several together, on average-length stems; very lasting; strong fragrance. Color rosy white and carmine. Foliage abundant, medium size, leathery, dark green. A vigorous grower of bushy habit and a profuse bloomer." [ARA20/135]

[Mevrouw C. van Marwyk Kooy]
Leenders, 1921
From 'Mme. Caroline Testout' (HT) × 'Mrs. Aaron Ward' (HT).

"Flower white, centre Indian yellow, sometimes coppery orange, large, full, fragrant. Growth vigorous; very floriferous." [GeH]

Mevrouw Dora van Tets
Leenders, 1912
From 'Farbenkönigin' (HT) × 'General MacArthur' (HT).

Mevrouw Dora van Tets *continued*

"Deep crimson with a velvety shading; flowers produced on elegant stems; free and continuous bloomer." [C&Js15] "Blossom medium sized, not very full, wafting an elegant, strong scent; color, brilliant deep crimson scarlet nuanced velvety, unchanging, the open flowers do not 'blue'; the best deep red among the HT's. The quite pretty buds are borne elegantly on their stems. Growth vigorous, compact, constant blooming." [JR37/10] "Collector's rose ... shy bloomer." [ARA16/20] "Hardy; fair growth; fair form; most distinct shade of 'deep velvety crimson'." [Th] "Brilliant and attractive color; foliage good; growth and form below average; fair bloomer." [ARA18/113] "Medium high, stocky, hardy; foliage plentiful, black-spots somewhat; bloom moderate, intermittent in warmer months." [ARA18/127] "A moderately good grower and produces nicely formed dark crimson flowers of medium size, which are very fragrant. It is not a tall Rose, though the growths are upright, and it makes an excellent bedding Rose, flowering freely and continuously, the chief merits being the good form of the flowers, their colour and fragrance." [NRS21/47] "Crimson. Garden, pot." [NRS15/149]

Mevrouw Smits Gompertz

Leenders, 1917

From 'Lady Wenlock' (HT; Bernaix, 1904; gold/pink; parentage unk.) × an unnamed seedling (resulting from a cross of 'Mme. J. W. Budde' [HT; Soupert & Notting, 1907; carmine] and 'Souvenir de Catherine Guillot' [Ch]).

"Yellowish salmon, shaded coppery orange and lilac-rose, medium size, full. Growth moderate, branching; very free flowering." [GeH] "Yellowish salmon orange, medium size, full, very fragrant, moderate height." [Sn] "Bud medium size, long-pointed; flower medium size, full, borne, several together, on medium-long stems; very lasting; strong fragrance. Color coppery orange and lilac. Foliage abundant, medium size, glossy dark green. A vigorous, bushy grower and a profuse bloomer." [ARA20/135]

Milady

Towill/Pierson, 1913

From 'J. B. Clark' (HP) × 'Richmond' (HT).

"Crimson scarlet. Flowers large, full, well formed on strong stems." [CA17] "Bright crimson, 'Richmond' type. Garden, pot." [NRS15/149] "In color resembling 'Richmond', and like 'Général Jacqueminot' [HP] in form and fragrance. Flower is large and double and opens perfectly." [C&Js14] "Large, pointed buds on strong stems, producing full, double, fragrant blooms of rich crimson-scarlet." [C&Js24] "Large, full, fine form, slight fragrance, short stem. Fine foliage and plentiful. Poor growth; not hardy. Clear rosy red." [ARA23/166] "Stiff erect stems. Growth vigorous." [GeH] "Low-growing, bushy, hardy; foliage sufficient, black-spots somewhat; bloom moderate, more in cool weather, less in hot months, almost continuous." [ARA18/127] "Being tested on Multiflora stock and showing up fairly well in growth, foliage, and blooming qualities." [ARA18/113] "The bush is vigorous and the foliage magnificent; the flower is large, quite double, and always opens easily, no matter what the time of year. The color is the same as that of 'Richmond', though the color of the buds is richer. The form of the flower much resembles that of 'Général Jacqueminot'; its excellent color, its vigor, its abundance and continuous bloom all make it particularly to be recommended for forcing."

[JR37/58] "It is not an ideal red rose, but, at the same time, it 'fills the bill' for very many." [ARA23/108] "Go west to see it right—there 'Milady' leads the list of red and crimson roses." [ARA21/131]

Mildred Grant

A. Dickson, 1901

From 'Niphetos' (T) × 'Mme. Mélanie Willermoz' (T).

"Flesh pink." [CA10] "Ivory white, tinted peach. —Robust. —Exhibition. —A fine exhibition variety." [Cat12/44] "Silvery white, flushed delicate pink." [CA17] "Blush white, large, full, medium height." [Sn] "The blossoms ... grow up to 12–15 cm across [ca. 4¾–6 in]; they are usually solitary and are borne by the vigorous branches, as with 'Captain Christy' [HT]. The roses are a silvery white tinted crimson pink towards the center, and deliciously perfumed. The bush is very floriferous, but, by reason of its upright stature, it does not do for making a tree rose. *Per contra*, it is at its best cultivated as a 'dwarf'. This variety is dedicated to a charming Miss, the daughter of one of the principal English rosarians." [JR27/20] "It appears to be the largest Rose of good pointed shape yet issued, almost dwarfing the blooms beside it of ordinary Show size, very fine indeed in form, petal and substance, but unfortunately undecided and whitish in colour." [F-M2] "The blossoms are quite large, have a high center, and keep a long time. The petals, which are very long, are very well formed, and, what is more, are enormous. The bush is vigorous, with the branches well placed and separate, each crowned with a flower, which is borne on an absolutely upright and very strong stem. The wood and foliage are very attractive, the latter being light green." [JR25/100] "Small growth; attractive blooms." [ARA18/113] "Very hardy. Silvery white in color, with shell-pink edges; lovely form; very large in size; lasts well. Bushy but short growth; nice stem. Foliage mildews. Good exhibition rose ... Has HP characteristics. Adapted to the Pacific North-West." [Th2]

"This is, no doubt, at its best one of the finest of all Show Roses, no well-shaped bloom of the true pointed refined form equalling it in size or in length and stoutness of petal. The habit is robust, the wood short and stout, and the leaf petioles very long. Each shoot produces a flower, and strong plants will bloom well again in the autumn. These great flowers take some time to develop, and it is probably best not to hurry them with liquid manure, as they are apt to come divided, and a full-sized bloom is not often perfect right through to the inside of the centre point. In perfection the faint pink tint on the cream-white veined petals is lovely, but very often the flowers are nearly white. It has improved in constitution of recent years, and though at one time could only be grown successfully as a maiden now many exhibitors find it equally good on cutbacks." [F-M] This cultivar, though always classed as a Hybrid Tea, has thoroughgoing and impeccable Tea parentage.

Minna

Kordes, 1930

Sport of 'Gruss an Aachen' (HT).

"A reddish pink sport of 'Gruss an Aachen'. It is not quite so full, but otherwise no different from the parent." [ARA31/181] "Pink, medium size, very full, light scent, dwarf." [Sn] "Bud medium size, ovoid, deeper in color than the flower; flower large, double, full, high-centered, very lasting, slightly fragrant, fine rosy pink, borne in cluster on medium-length, strong stem. Foliage sufficient, medium size, rich green, leathery, disease-resistant. Growth moderate, bushy, dwarf; profuse, intermittent bloomer all season. Tips freeze." [ARA31/242–243]

Miriam

Pemberton, 1919

"Flower capucine, of globular form, carried erect. Bed." [GeH] "Color capucine, distinct. Form globular, flowers carried erect. Foliage waxy, not liable to mildew. Growth compact, suitable for bedding and specimen blooms. Free flowering from early summer until late in autumn." [NRS19/ad]

Miss C. E. van Rossem

syn. 'Miss C. W. van Rossem'

Verschuren, 1919

From 'Leuchtfeuer' (B) × 'Red-Letter Day' (HT).

"Flower well-formed, velvety red; fragrant. Vigorous; bushy." [ARA21/165] "An intense and unvarying crimson. The blooms are of good shape but not too full. They are small, as is also the plant, and the scent reported by some growers is not apparent in my experience." [ARA29/62] "Has but little fragrance." [C-Ps29] "Sweetly scented. Growth vigorous and branching." [GeH] "A very dark Hybrid China, about the color of 'Cramoisi Supérieur' [Ch], but with full blooms, pointed buds, and is a better grower." [ARA24/107] "One of the first and one of the last to bloom, and there is scarcely a day in between when a healthy plant will not have some flowers. While small, the blooms are of nice shape, and the dark red color wears well." [ARA29/49] "The open bloom is rather small and of irregular form." [C-Ps28] "The flowers are deep glowing crimson, rather small, but well shaped, especially in the bud. They are freely and continuously produced . . . The growth is on the dwarf side." [NRS24/141] "The bush is compact and the foliage small but plentiful." [C-Ps30] "Extremely hardy, and one of the most beautifully colored reds." [C-Ps29]

"This makes a good branching little bush, from which rather tall and upright flowering stems are pushed up. The foliage is good, but not specially remarkable, and free from disease. The bright, velvety crimson flowers appear about mid-June, and are freely produced throughout the whole season. At times it is almost too free, as it is difficult to keep them properly disbudded. The flowers are highly decorative . . . The stems, however, are thin, and sometimes not strong enough to hold the flowers well . . . It has some fragrance, but it is not usually great, and varies much with the weather. The crimson flowers stand both sun and rain well." [NRS29/119] "Brilliant, glowing pure crimson which darkens with age but does not blue. The habit of growth is low and spreading, which makes this Rose ideal for bedding as it is continuously in bloom. The half-opened buds are just right for boutonnières. Really a splendid, satisfactory Rose with disease-resistant foliage." [C-Ps27]

Miss C. W. van Rossem Listed as 'Miss C. E. van Rossem' (HT).

Miss Cynthia Forde Listed as 'Cynthia Forde' (HT).

[Miss Kate Moulton]

J. Monson/Minneapolis Floral Co., 1906

From 'Mme. Caroline Testout' (HT) × an unnamed seedling (which resulted from crossing 'La France' [B or HT] and 'Mrs. W. J. Grant' [HT]).

"Pink tinted silvery flesh." [CA17] "A rose of entrancing beauty.

The flower is superb; large, full and perfectly formed. The color is beautiful silvery pink." [CA10] "Flower rosy pink shaded rosy salmon, large, full, long bud, opening well, carried on long stems. Growth vigorous, free." [GeH] "Vigorous bush, free from disease, very floriferous, flower large, full, borne solitary on long stem; color, carnation pink. Very good for forcing." [JR31/22]

Miss Willmott

McGredy, 1916

"A profuse bloomer, with perfectly formed flowers of soft sulphur-cream, faintly flushed with pink at the edges of the petals." [C&Js24] "Chaste as a lily; the faint flush of pink in the heart of the half-opened bloom enhances, rather than detracts from, her beauty." [ARA29/48] "Big buds, opening to large, cupped, white flowers, lightly tinted with pink, borne on long stems; deliciously fragrant." [C-Ps30] "Pale lemon with a tint of rose on edges of petals, large, exquisitely formed, sweet-scented. Growth free and branching." [GeH] "Fine and beautiful large flowers of pale sulphur-white, lightly tinted with pink. It is a remarkably free-blooming variety, especially in the fall, and should be widely tested." [C-Ps25] "Not a free-blooming variety, but every bloom is a perfect exhibition, prize-winning beauty." [C-Ps28] "A Rose of vigorous branching growth with dark glossy foliage. The blooms are of perfect form, with great depth of petal, very freely produced, and sweetly scented. The colour is a soft creamy yellow, with just the slightest flush of pink at the extreme tips of the petals. It is a fine exhibition and garden Rose, and I am inclined to think that it will rank as one of the raisers' best efforts." [NRS17/128]

Mlle. Argentine Cramon

syn. 'Argentine Cramon'

Chambard, 1915

"White, very large, full, medium height." [Sn] "A very double white Rose carried on rigid stems." [NRS18/155] "Fair growth; color clear and attractive." [ARA18/118] "Outside of petals white, tinted carnation rose at points of petals, interior of petals carnation-rose, very large, double and cupped. Growth very vigorous, strong and branching, beautiful purple green foliage, wood spineless." [GeH]

Mlle. Danielle Dumur

Laroulandie, 1909

Sport of 'Mme. Caroline Testout' (HT).

"Light pink, large, full, medium scent, medium height." [Sn] "Vigorous growth, sport of the beautiful 'Mme. Caroline Testout', from which it takes its good characteristic of floriferousness; very pretty coloration, delicate pink fading to silvery pink." [JR33/153]

Mlle. de Neux

Berland/Chauvry, 1901

Seedling of 'Mme. Caroline Testout' (HT).

"Pink, medium size, full, medium height." [Sn]

Mme. Alfred Digeon

Puyravaud, 1911

"Yellow, medium size, semi-full, tall." [Sn] "Flower lemon yellow tinted chamois, petal tips sometimes touched carmine, medium to large, full, very pretty bud for buttonholes, light scent, growth very branching, thornless, makes a beautiful bush, everblooming (dedicated to a devoted partisan of the Queen of Flowers)." [JR35/156]

Mme. Alfred Sabatier

Bernaix, 1904

"Bright peachblossom red." [Ÿ] "Sturdy, handsome, dark green foliage, plant of good vigor. Bud of pretty form, blossom fairly large, with thick wavy petals, gracefully intermingled at the center and delicately pleated towards the outside, bright satiny peach red, fading when open." [JR28/155]

Mme. Bardou Job

Dubreuil, 1913

Seedling of 'Prince de Bulgarie' (HT).

"Soft yellow center, almost white at edges; shaped like camellia, waxy and lovely; odor delicious. Bush strong and bushy. 26 blooms; 30 the second season." [ARA26/95] "It balls considerably and is generally out of date." [ARA27/138] "Very floriferous and quite remontant bush furnished with handsome bright green foliage. Buds held upright elegantly on the long, strong stems, often solitary; chrome yellow, lemon canary. Blossoms large, full, cupped, with satiny petals, opening very gracefully. Quite distinct from other Hybrid Teas." [JR37/184] "Another beautiful Rose with 'Ophelia' type of bud and flower. The buds are saffron color and come, sometimes singly and sometimes several together, on medium stems. The flowers are chrome-yellow and citron, with outside petals creamy white[,] and moderately fragrant. Is of upright bushy habit and glossy foliage. It does not bloom much during the hot summer months but it makes up for this with better blooms both spring and fall. Makes exquisite bouquets." [C-Ps27] "Growth vigorous." [GeH] "Average growth; very good color; especially attractive in bud-form; fair in blooming." [ARA18/112] Not to be confused with the red Bourbon 'Bardou Job'.

Mme. Butterfly

E. G. Hill, 1918

Sport of 'Ophelia' (HT).

"A glorified 'Ophelia'. Color is a harmony of pink, apricot, and gold. The flowers are larger than [those of] 'Ophelia' and more freely produced." [C&Js22] "Rather more salmon to apricot [than the blossoms of 'Ophelia'." [RP] "Similar to 'Ophelia' in all characteristics, except that the color is greatly intensified." [ARA19/159] "Soft flesh, shaded rose; beautiful spiral bud; attractive open flower of good size; lasts quite well; very fragrant. Stem very good. Foliage good ... Should be planted in partial shade in hot climates. In California coast areas does not discolor as quickly as its parent, and must be given the preference." [Th2] "A hot weather rose." [ARA24/95] "A little nonchalant in hot weather, but pepping up in the autumn when it gives some of its best blooms." [C-Ps29] "Very free-flowering." [ARA29/48] "Many admirers [in Houston, Texas]." [ET] "One of the few indispensable Roses ... The plant makes a good bush, the flowering shoots are long and upright, and the flowers carried erect when disbudded ... The foliage is deep green, hard and good, and not much affected by fungus. It is not carried high up the stem, which is an advantage for cutting, as the plant is not injured thereby ... The early flowers are frequently defective ... altogether a delightful Rose ... It has, however, two rather serious defects; one is that, if frost or cold weather occurs when the buds are forming, the flowers are often malformed, and the other is the serious liability of all its family to attack by stem fungus. In this respect, however, I think it does not suffer so much as 'Ophelia' and other

members of that family." [NRS29/105] "Delicately modeled flowers of tender pink and gold, and is one of the sweetest and most pleasing Roses. Its lovely spiral buds slowly unfold into a big, full-petaled flower of charming shape and dreamy color, very highly scented, and lasting unusually long. The stems are fine and very strong, making it one of the best Roses for cutting. It is better for a little shade in the garden, as the hot sun is likely to bleach it somewhat. The bush is quite vigorous, growing tall, but not bushy; and the flowers sometimes come in big branching sprays unless disbudded. A deliberate and steady bloomer, quite hardy, and fairly healthy." [C-Ps25] Mme. Butterfly, melodic sufferer in Puccini's opera of the same name.

Mme. C. Chambard

Chambard, 1911

From 'Frau Karl Druschki' (HP) × either 'Prince de Bulgarie' (HT) or possibly 'Lady Ashtown' (HT).

"Rosy flesh shaded salmon and saffron, base of petals deep yellow, very large, opening well, sweet-scented. Growth vigorous, erect, free." [GeH] "Fair growth; shy bloomer." [ARA18/116] "Growth very vigorous with erect canes, beautiful healthy light green foliage; bud long, solitary; borne on a long, stiff stem, silvery flesh pink with some salmon; flowers very large, opening easily, flesh pink, salmon nuanced dawn-pink, nubs deep yellow, fragrant and floriferous; excellent addition to the cut-rose roster ... It takes from 'Frau Karl Druschki' its great vigor as well as the beauty of its foliage, and from 'Prince de Bulgarie' its abundance." [JR35/156]

Mme. Caristie Martel

Pernet-Ducher, 1916

"Pure sulphur." [Ÿ] "A magnificent and very large straw-coloured Rose." [ARA18/154] "I would like to have 'Maréchal Niel' [N] blooms on a 'Mme. Caroline Testout' [HT] plant, and as free-flowering. ('Mme. Caristie Martel' approaches it slightly, but the rose must be good in all weathers.)" [ARA20/93] "Growth very vigorous, branching; flower very large (5 to 6 inches diameter [ca. 1.25–1.5 dm]), globular, large petals, pure sulphur-yellow, deeper in center. Its enormous size and pure yellow color, without any blending, make it quite a distinct novelty." [ARA18/108]

Mme. Charles de Lapisse

Laroulandie, 1910?

Sport of 'Mme. Caroline Testout' (HT).

"Pinkish pearly white." [Ÿ] In most probability, this is a synonym of 'Monsieur Charles de Lapisse' (HT), q.v.

Mme. Dailleux

Buatois, 1900

From 'Victor Verdier' (HP) × 'Dr. Grill' (T).

"Salmony pink, pink around the edges." [Ÿ] "Flower salmon pink, outer petals somewhat imbricated, center brighter pink on a coppery yellow ground, large, full; center petals muddled and, for the most part, folded inwards at a sharp angle for nearly their full length; very fragrant; conical bud opens well. Growth very vigorous." [JR24/163]

Mme. Desirée Bruneau

Moublot, 1907

"Pink." [Ÿ]

Mme. Edmond Rostand

Pernet-Ducher, 1912

From an unnamed rose × 'Prince de Bulgarie' (HT).

"Light pink." [Ÿ] "Pale flesh, shaded with salmon and reddish orange yellow in the center. A new rose which promises extremely well. Practically no disbudding." [Th] "Fine long buds opening well. Growth vigorous, free flowering." [GeH] "A vigorous grower with deep green, bronzed foliage. It produces fine long buds, opening to very large flowers . . . The color is somewhat variable but always charming." [C&Js13] "Color, form, and lasting qualities very good; growth above average; bloom fair. An improved 'Prince de Bulgarie', having less bloom." [ARA18/112] "Very vigorous, bushy; thorns numerous and not very protrusive; foliage dark green; bud long; flower very large, pretty full, globular, with large petals towards the outside; color, light pink nuanced salmon and reddish orange yellow at the center. This variety is not unlike the popular 'Prince de Bulgarie', but differs in its longer shoots and in its warmer, sharper color; an excellent garden and exhibition rose." [JR36/42]

Mme. Émile Lafond   Listed as 'Mme. Emilie Lafon' (HT).

Mme. Emilie Lafon

syn. 'Mme. Émile Lafond'

Moranville, 1905

Seedling of 'La France de 89' (Cl HT).

"Cerise red." [Ÿ] "Light red, large, full, medium height." [Sn]

Mme. Gustave Metz

syn. 'Frau Karl Smid'

Lamesch, 1905

From an unnamed seedling (of 'Mme. Caroline Testout' [HT]) × 'Viscountess Folkestone' (HT).

"Whitish pink, large, full, medium height." [Sn] "Vigorous, large and bright handsome foliage. Flower very large, large petals, magnificent form, quite full, nearly always solitary . . . Color creamy white, going to pink. The bloom is very abundant, and lasts until autumn." [JR29/22] "A vigorously growing Rose, producing large, very double blooms of soft, light pink, shading to creamy white in the center; the perfume slight. Recommended for cutting and for bedding—a good summer bloomer. Somewhat susceptible to mildew; quite hardy." [C-Ps25]

Mme. Henry Fontaine

P. Guillot, 1914

Seedling of 'Pharisäer' (HT).

"Yellowish pink, large, full, moderate scent, medium height." [Sn] "Growth quite tall; bloom lacks distinctiveness." [ARA18/116]

Mme. J.-P. Soupert

Soupert & Notting, 1900

From 'Mme. Caroline Testout' (HT) × 'Mlle. Alice Furon' (HT).

"Yellowish white, centre suffused clear rose, large, full, fragrant. Growth vigorous, free." [GeH] "Very vigorous, handsome foliage; bud magnificently formed; blossom very large, full; petals large and thick, well-held; color, white with a yellow glow. The forms of the buds and flowers resemble those of 'Mme. Caroline Testout' (HT). Very floriferous and fragrant." [JR24/149]

Mme. Jean Favre

Godard, 1900

From 'La France de 89' (Cl HT) × 'Xavier Olibo' (HP).

"White, pink reverse." [Ÿ] "Compact, foliage light green, bud long, deep carmine, flower large, well formed; when fully open, light carmine with bluish reflections." [JR25/6]

Mme. Jules Bouché

Croibier, 1910

"White. Garden, pot." [NRS15/149] "An almost perfect rose; it is not pure or 'paper' white, and is sometimes more than a little flushed, but its beautiful, fragrant, well-shaped flowers come singly at the end of long stems and it is a joy to the eye." [ARA25/132] "White, sometimes shaded primrose; odor good. Bush very strong and bushy. 30 blooms." [ARA26/95] "Practically no disbudding." [Th] "White, with centre shaded pink, pointed globular, flowers carried erect on tall stems, very active [*sic*] in habit, and flowers freely throughout the season. Especially good in September. Wood and foliage claret colour. A useful variety, far too little known." [NRS21/64] "Best light-colored rose; useful both for cutting and decorative purposes; growth and blooming qualities splendid; color clear, beautiful." [ARA18/112] "Substance somewhat thin; medium to small; lasts but may discolor slightly; slight perfume. Growth bushy and very fine; stem long but small and wilts in heat. Mildews in bad conditions. Holds foliage tenaciously in long seasons. This variety gives more flowers than any other cutting white HT, supplying over seventy in Central Zone . . . Is a fine rose and succeeds except in excessive damp or extreme heat. Does better in Central Zone than 'Frau Karl Druschki' [HP]." [Th2] "Relied on by many experienced gardeners to supply the bulk of their white Roses when 'Frau Karl Druschki' is out of flower." [C-Ps29] "A useful garden Rose, bearing its nicely formed cream coloured flowers on long upright stems . . . The foliage is good and the flower carried well . . . but in wet weather it is readily stained . . . We find it here a strong growing, free flowering plant." [NRS21/40] "Too readily spoiled by rain for our [English] climate." [NRS23/57] "Perfume mild; seventy-one blooms throughout the season; growth exceptionally fine; tall and plenty of canes. Excellent both for cutting and garden." [ARA17/22] "Vigorous, branches slender and strong, bud very long, flower large, full, well formed, petals of great substance, folding back at expansion. Color, salmon-white, center nuanced virginal pink, stem very strong. Good for all purposes." [JR34/169] "White—center shaded primrose or lightest blush—varies . . . Of medium to large growth, very hardy; good to very good foliage, long erect stem; long bud which develops into a medium-sized flower of wonderful substance and great lasting qualities. A splendid bloomer in spring, good in summer and remarkably good in fall. The best new rose since 'Duchess of Wellington' [HT] and by all means the best white to blush rose. Plant 18 inches center to center [ca. 4.5 dm]. Prune to 5 eyes." [Th] "Very disease-resistant. Its purple new growth is beautiful." [ARA29/67] "Growth vigorous, free flowering." [GeH] "Not very free blooming . . . The buds are long-pointed . . . Taller in growth than 'Kaiserin Auguste Viktoria' [HT]." [C-Ps28] "Noted for free blooming and fine growth, this Rose is part of the backbone of every Rose-garden. The flowers are very double, and are white, strongly tinged with pink in the center. The plant is hardy and very healthy. One of the best." [C-Ps25] "The most exquisitely perfect rose I have ever seen." [ARA28/116]

Mme. Léon Pain
P. Guillot, 1904
From 'Mme. Caroline Testout' (HT) × 'Souvenir de Catherine Guillot' (Ch).

"Flesh, center vermilion." [LS] "Silvery flesh-pink, center light orange-yellow." [Riv] "Silvery pink, sometimes shaded salmon. Buds pointed; flowers large and cupped. Blooms freely." [CA17] "Buds are carmine, and the open flower is light silvery pink with salmon tints, carmine on the outer petals. In cool weather it is suffused with an orange tint. Fragrant, well-formed, even the open state, and freely produced." [C-Ps25] "Very little disbudding." [Th] "Sweet [scent]." [GeH] "Perfume quite distinct; forty-one blooms throughout the season; growth above the average. Good for all purposes." [ARA17/23] "Flowers are large and full, with buds of salmon-pink, shaded to salmon-orange in delightful combination. A fine grower and does particularly well in the fall." [C&Js24] "A steady worker with strong stems of medium length. Thoroughly dependable, but not much as a plant." [ARA29/88] "Foliage and habit leave nothing to be desired." [C-Ps28] "Almost tall, inclined to be upright, hardy; foliage plentiful, black-spots slightly; bloom abundant, continuous." [ARA18/126] "Vigorous, robust, numerous somewhat branching canes, occasional thorns, handsome purplish foliage; flower very large, quite full, very well formed, fragrant, silvery flesh white, center brightened by orange yellow, petal reverse salmon tinted vermilion and chamois yellow; very beautiful." [JR28/154] "Silver flesh to Pearl salmon pink center … Of medium to large growth, very hardy; foliage perfect leathery green to reddish tea; long, erect stem; medium to large bud, opening into a bloom of substance, full, double, and of good lasting qualities; blooms very well in spring, summer, and autumn. This is the best of the lightest salmon pinks and a fine, reliable, all-round rose. 'Mme. Segond[-]Weber' is a more brilliant salmon than 'Mme. Léon Pain' and of more perfect form, but not as reliable a bloomer in the summer and autumn. Plant 18 inches center to center [ca. 4.5 dm]. Prune to 5 eyes." [Th]

"Lovely foliage, reddish when young, afterwards leathery, glossy, dark green and handsome, with red tinted stems. The habit of the plant is dwarf and branching, but the flower stems are carried high above the plant, stiff and erect. The bush is symmetrical and shapely. This Rose is very free flowering and almost always in flower, but rather late in starting … The flowers are a lovely shape carried upright and erect, they are fairly full, but hardly full enough for exhibition. The colour is not easy to describe, it contains tints of pale yellow, orange, pink and fawn, but the general effect of the Rose is a flesh coloured flower with salmon and orange in the centre. The buds are long and blunt, almost orange red, opening from the top in a very typical manner to large shell-like petals, of excellent substance. It is sometimes referred to as an improved 'Viscountess Folkestone'. It is not so full that that Rose … The flowers are fragrant and it scarcely ever suffers from mildew. The plants seem to grow very uniformly in a bed and the flowers are very level both in quality and height. 'Mme. Léon Pain' makes a grand bedding Rose. I would myself put it amongst the best four or five of the Hybrid Teas for this purpose … The blossoms harmonize very well with the lovely foliage, and a bed in full flower has a very delicate effect … The special merits of this Rose are its beautiful flowers and foliage, and the good contrast they afford, the fine shape and colour of the flowers, and their continuity; the

good habit and constitution of the plant, and freedom from disease. I know of no weak points, but some of my friends think the flowers a little too thin. It will, however, stand heat well, and bears the rain better than most, so I have little to complain of." [NRS12/88] "So free flowering and such a good grower that I have come to regard it as one of the most reliable varieties for decorative work. Its chief drawback being that the centre is not quite high enough so that the form is a little heavy and capable of improvement." [NRS20/93] "A good rose. Color most attractive; satisfactory in form, growth, and blooming qualities." [ARA18/112]

Mme. Léon Simon
Lambert, 1909
From 'Marie van Houtte' (T) × 'Mme. Caroline Testout' (HT).

"Deep pink on a light yellow ground. —Blossom large, full; floriferous; vigorous." [Cx] "Deep pink, yellow center, large, full, medium height." [Sn]

Mme. Léopold Dupuy
Robichon, 1911
From 'La France de 89' (Cl HT) × 'Mme. Ernst Calvat' (B).

"Pink, large, full, very fragrant, tall." [Sn] "Vigorous, producing very large flowers, which are full, very fragrant, and carmine China pink nuanced purple." [JR36/89]

Mme. Marcel Delanney
syn. 'Mme. Marcel Delauney'
Leenders, 1915

Color is pale pink or soft rose, shaded to Hydrangea-pink. Flowers are large, fragrant and freely produced." [C&Js24] "Clear, soft silvery rose, suffused with pale lilac; form opens cupped; very large size; lasting; lovely perfume. Bushy growth and strong stem. Resistant foliage. Has HP characteristics. A shy bloomer, but very good cutting rose. Good in Central and Pacific North-West Zones." [Th2] "Wonderful cut-flower, having beautiful color and fine long stems; fair bloomer; good foliage." [ARA18/112] "Large, full, and fragrant, perfect form. Growth vigorous and free. Distinct." [GeH] "Good growth, good foliage and stem; fine perfume. Not a profuse bloomer but a remarkable rose for cut blooms and with a possibility of being an all-round variety." [ARA17/30]

Mme. Marie Croibier
Croibier, 1901
Seedling of 'Mme. Caroline Testout' (HT).

"Deep pink, large, full, medium height." [Sn] "Growth very vigorous, foliage dark maroon green, thorns upright and numerous; flower full, very large; color, deep China pink; long bud, strong stem, very floriferous. This superb rose came from 'Mme. Caroline Testout', from which it takes its vigor and all its main characteristics of growth and bloom; its bud is longer, making the flower more graceful; its deep color never blues, and keeps until the petals fall." [JR25/147]

Mme. Marcel Delauney   Listed as 'Mme. Marcel Delanney' (HT).

Mme. Maurice de Luze
Pernet-Ducher, 1907
From 'Mme. Abel Chatenay' (HT) × 'Eugène Fürst' (HP).

"Deep rose-pink, carmine center, reverse of petals paler in color; perfume exceptionally strong and enduring; forty-five blooms throughout the season on Multiflora [understock]; growth very good. Useful for cutting or decorative purposes." [ARA17/23] "Large, full. Blossoms carnation pink with bright ground of carmine; very floriferous." [Ck] "Cupped form, sweet-scented, carried on long and stiff stems. Growth vigorous and free flowering." [GeH] "One of the best, always in bloom, and the flowers are a good size when disbudded." [NRS14/160] "Of good vigor, with upright canes, cheerful green foliage, superb buds borne on long and strong stems; flower very large, with large petals, in the form of a full cup. Color, Nilsson pink, center cochineal carmine, reverse of petals lighter." [JR31/103] "Blues in heat; attractive in form but not perfect; fine fragrance . . . Has never been largely planted, but deserves better support. Nice garden rose with tendency to mildew, and not an exhibition variety." [Th2] "Highly fragrant . . . The plant grows well and carries a well formed flower, often up to exhibition standard." [NRS23/56] "A fine large flower with large petals, a vigorous grower." [F-M] "Moderately high and compact, hardy; foliage plentiful, healthy; bloom moderate, almost continuous." [ARA18/126] "Growth vigorous, erect and branching." [C&Js08]

Mme. Maurice Fenaille
Boutigny, 1903
"Delicate pink." [Ÿ] "Whitish pink, large, full, tall." [Sn]

Mme. Méha Sabatier
Pernet-Ducher, 1916
From an unnamed seedling × 'Château de Clos-Vougeot' (HT).

"Deep crimson." [Ÿ] "Red, large, full, medium height." [Sn] "A very floriferous rose constantly in bloom, of a fine deep red colour. Its fault is the want of firmness of its stalk." [NRS19/121] "Growth very vigorous, spreading, branching; velvety crimson bud; flowers large, full, globular, bright crimson. Excellent bedding rose." [ARA18/108]

Mme. Mélanie Soupert
Pernet-Ducher, 1905
"Light cream to salmon yellow, with light carmine shades. Practically no disbudding." [Th] "Lovely cupped flower of good form, orange and yellow, strong stalk, free flowering; dark glossy foliage and good bedder." [GeH] "Large double flowers; fine salmon-yellow, suffused with carmine; freely borne on strong branching plants; quite hardy." [C&Js13] "Fairly hardy. Melon-yellow, suffused carmine to deep cream—holds color in heat by reason of its great substance; beautiful bud, opens loose; slight fragrance. Stems long and strong, but a poor grower. Foliage almost immune to mildew, but lost early. Twenty-five blooms in Central Zone. Of exhibition value in Pacific North-West." [Th2] "One of the most beautiful roses in cultivation. Especially good in color, size, substance, and stem . . . Blooming qualities only fair. Until grown on Multiflora [understock], was considered merely a collector's rose. On this stock better results are had than when grown in a 'special bed'." [ARA18/112] "The flowers are not all glorious . . . The numerous blossoms of the second or summer flowering are often wanting in character altogether . . . There is perhaps, also, rather too great a distance between the leaves, a defect partly made up by their large size; and the plant is not a very long-lived one." [NRS13/59–60] "Growth very vigorous, with erect canes, beautiful bronzy green foliage; blossoms with large petals, and themselves very large, globular, semi-full, superbly colored aurora on a ground of carmine yellow." [JR29/7] "Lovely buds. Bush tall and slim.

8 blooms." [ARA26/95] "Low-growing, weak; foliage sufficient, blackspots; few blooms each month." [ARA18/126] "Growth tall, but not bushy or uniform. One of the most beautiful roses grown; very large and with great substance." [ARA17/25]

"This beautiful Rose has a fine vigorous growth of upright habit, but like all the yellow Roses is somewhat tender. The foliage is large, stout and glossy, and free from mildew. It flowers well from the end of June to the end of September. The blossoms are carried on fine, long, stiff stems; perhaps they are a little thin, but the petals are most beautiful, shell-like, large and shapely. The colour is pale fawn and gold with a delicate shading of peach, and is most beautiful, attractive and unique among Roses. At its best I know no Rose of its type with an equal charm. The delicate colouring is very difficult to describe in words. I have as many different descriptions as I have correspondents, and probably that which I have given will please none of them. Though not devoid of fragrance, its scent is not very great, but sweet as far as it goes. It is most useful for decorative purposes and often gives good exhibition blooms . . . It is a fine Rose in the garden; in my opinion far best as a standard . . . When picked young, for a thin Rose, it lasts grandly in water for a time (but Mr. Molyneux says only two days), and it will stand a certain amount of wet. 'Mme. Mélanie' is one of the most distinct and beautiful of the newer Roses . . . As a dwarf it requires care and judgement in disbudding, specially after the July flowering is over. Leave it alone and, save for the early flowers which come singly, you may see little worth cutting and little colour, but it is worth time and worth trouble, all of which, when you get its perfect blossoms and charming colouring, will make you like it the more." [NRS10/34] "A very beautiful garden Rose that with high culture and much disbudding will yield good exhibition blooms, especially in a cool season. Its colour will make us want to exhibit it as often as possible as we are badly off for yellows. The petals are large but few in number, cut young it will keep its shape in the same way that 'Killarney' [HT] does, but too much heat and it collapses. Some very fine flowers have been exhibited this past season . . . It has been largely used by hybridists, but it is too soon to write about the results though we hear of great things." [F-M]

Mme. P. Euler
syn. 'Mme. Paul Euler', 'Mme. Pierre Euler', 'Prima Donna'
P. Guillot, 1907
From 'Antoine Rivoire' (HT) × 'Killarney' (HT).

"Vermilion silvery pink; large, very full, fragrant and possessing great lasting properties." [C&Js11] "Carmine rose.—Vigorous.—Garden, standard.—Fragrant." [Cat12/41] "Vigorous, blossom very large, supported on a long strong stem, very full, long duration, very beautifully colored silvery vermilion pink, fragrant." [JR31/139] "Moderately tall, quite compact, reasonably hardy; foliage plentiful and healthy; bloom abundant in July, other times almost continuous." [ARA18/126]

Mme. Paul Euler Listed as 'Mme. P. Euler' (HT).

[Mme. Philippe Rivoire]
Pernet-Ducher, 1905
"Plant of great vigor, with stocky canes and handsome bronzy green foliage; flower very large, full, globular; color, apricot yellow, center nankeen yellow, reverse of petals carminy." [JR29/151]

Mme. Pierre Euler Listed as 'Mme. P. Euler' (HT).

Mme. Raymond Poincaré

Gravereaux/Kieffer, 1919

From 'Antoine Rivoire' (HT) × ? 'Ophelia' (HT).

"Yellow with pink nuances." [Ÿ] "Flower bright nasturtium-yellow at center, salmon at edges. Vigorous; free bloomer." [ARA21/161] "Light salmon pink, yellow center, large, full, light scent, medium height." [Sn] "Flowers are bright Persian yellow in center with outer petals of salmon-pink and lighter yellow. The long buds open to full, cupped blooms of large size and are freely produced on rigid stems." [C-Ps25]

Mme. René André

Breeder unknown, 1906

"Whitish pink, large, full, light scent, medium height." [Sn] Cf. the Wichuraiana 'René André'.

Mme. René Collette

Gamon, 1909

From 'Mlle. Anna Charron' (T) × 'Kaiserin Auguste Viktoria' (HT).

"Yellowish red, red edges, large, full, very fragrant, medium height." [Sn]

Mme. René Oberthür

Vigneron, 1907

Seedling of 'Mme. Caroline Testout' (HT).

"Vigorous bush, with beautiful large dark green leaves. The blossom, large, full, has the form of that of 'Mme. Caroline Testout', from which it sprang. The color is a beautiful porcelain white, with the interior occasionally showing a very light salmon. This variety possesses all the merits of its mother." [JR31/138]

Mme. Segond-Weber

Soupert & Notting, 1907

From 'Antoine Rivoire' (HT) × 'Souvenir de Victor Hugo' (T).

"Rosy salmon. Very little disbudding." [Th] "Fine stiff petals, opening well. Growth vigorous, free flowering." [GeH] "A more brilliant salmon that [that of] 'Mme. Léon Pain' and of more perfect form, but not as reliable a bloomer in the summer and autumn." [Th] "Forty-nine blooms throughout the season on Multiflora [understock]; growth fair. Beautiful for cut-flowers." [ARA17/23] "Pure salmon pink, very delicate, new among HT's, bright center. The enormous blossom, with its large and strong petals, lasts a very long time; it is cupped, quite regular, and faultless in form. It is the largest of its class. With its magnificent ovoid, pointed buds borne on rigid stems, it has an upright and proud bearing. The vigorous and bushy shrub is clad in exuberant foliage. 'Mme. Segond-Weber' blooms without interruption from Spring to November." [JR31/136–137] "Rosy salmon, with cream-flesh edges; very fine form; lasting; slight fragrance. Foliage slightly affected by mildew and black-spot; holds fairly well. Fair growth; stem long and strong. Gives close to fifty blooms in Central Zone, and is a splendid cutting variety. On the California coast is much larger than in the East, but not so fine in substance, nor is the bud so spiral in form. Gives more perfect blooms than almost any other HT in Central Zone, and should be more widely planted ... has been overlooked for less worthy sorts." [Th2] "Fine form, double, very large, fragrant, long stem. Fine foliage, sufficient. Growth poor; fairly hardy." [ARA23/167] "Low, bushy." [ARA17/31] "The plant has a neat, compact habit of growth." [C-Ps28] "Height and compactness medium; foliage plentiful, healthy; bloom moderate, almost continuous."

[ARA18/126] "In warm sections, this Rose has no superior, with its long buds and fully double, fragrant flowers. Grow this Rose and you will love it as one of the 'old-fashioned' double Roses that have survived the onslaught of the semi-singles ... This Rose is a liberal bloomer, on strong stems, with good foliage." [C-Ps27]

Mme. Théodore Delacourt

Pernet-Ducher, 1913

"Long rosy scarlet bud ... few and small thorns." [GeH] "Poor growth and blooming qualities." [ARA18/42] "Growth very vigorous, with branching canes; foliage bronzy reddish green; thorns unequal and protrusive; bud long, grenadine red; flower large, pretty full, globular; color, reddish salmon nuanced light yellow. Excellent garden rose, generously abundant, and a recherché color." [JR37/42]

Mme. Viger

syn. 'Mme. Vigier'

Jupeau, 1900

From 'Heinrich Schultheis' (HP) × 'G. Nabonnand' (T).

"Soft rose, suffused carmine ... Growth vigorous." [GeH] "Light pink, very large, full, medium scent, medium height." [Sn] "Vigorous, upright branches, wood glaucous green, thorns rare, handsome foliage, very long and graceful buds, well held; borne on a long, strong stem; goes well with the foliage, nearly always solitary; flower very large, imbricated form, opens well; the most beautiful delicate pink, edges and reverse silvery pink touched carmine; nearly white in Fall ... Extra floriferous, always blooming." [JR24/146]

Mme. Vigier Listed as 'Mme. Viger' (HT).

Molly Bligh

A. Dickson, 1917

"Deep maddery pink, heavily zoned orange-madder at the base of the petals, large, ideal shape, musk-rose perfume. Growth vigorous, branching; very floriferous." [GeH] "Orange pink, large, full, light scent, medium height." [Sn] "Another really good pink of a deeper shade. She does very well here in this exposed garden ... It is a fine Rose, and the yellow at the base is most attractive." [NRS23/202]

Monsieur Charles de Lapisse

Laroulandie, 1909

Sport of 'Mme. Caroline Testout' (HT).

"Pale rose pink, of very vigorous growth, with well-shaped, full blooms." [NRS29/249] "Vigorous, well-branched growth; pretty buds, virginal pink when opening; blossom very large, full, pearly white, sometimes blush white fading to cream white, very pretty coloration for cutting or bedding." [JR33/153] "The value of this variety lies in its autumn flowering qualities. It is best described as a blush '[Mme.] Caroline Testout', resembling it in both habit and form of flower. The wood and foliage are claret colour, forming a beautiful setting to the pale blush bloom. This variety is good in September, and will be found in flower quite late in November. It is unaffected by wet. With us it is one of the best." [NRS21/62]

Monsieur Edg. Blanchard

syn. 'Edgar Blanchard'

Duron/Puyravaud, 1911

From 'Frau Karl Druschki' (HP) × ?

"Fresh blush white, center petals fringed; large, full, solitary, held on a stiff stem, bud spherical, growth very vigorous." [JR35/156] "Pinkish white, large, full, tall." [Sn] "Very floriferous." [JR36/43]

Monsieur Fraissenon

Gamon, 1911
Seedling of 'Lady Ashtown' (HT).

"Deep pink, large, full, medium scent, tall." [Sn] "Vigorous, long bud, flower large, full, deep frosty pink." [JR35/167]

Monsieur Joseph Hill

Pernet-Ducher, 1903
Seedling of 'Mme. Eugénie Boullet' (HT).

"Pink, shaded salmon; outside of petals coppery pink. Blooms very large, full and of perfect form. A superb variety." [CA11] "Soft salmony yellow; large, well-shaped, with many petals; odor delicious. Bush strong. 19 blooms." [ARA26/94] "Pink, salmon shaded; outside of petals pink copper. Practically no disbudding." [Th] "Flower salmon-pink shaded with yellow and ochre, outside of petals coppery pink, large, full, fine in bud and open flower, highly perfumed. Growth vigorous, free flowering." [GeH] "Growth very vigorous, with bushy canes; superb long bud, ovoid; flower very large, full, of the best in form; color, salmon pink shaded yellow; exterior of petals tinted coppery pink." [JR27/131] "A beautiful rose. Most attractive in color and form; growth and hardiness cannot be depended upon. Gives best results in 'special bed,' Multiflora [stock] ranking next." [ARA18/111] "Light salmon-pink, with orange to copper shadings; beautiful form; lasts well; slight perfume. Growth irregular; stem usually good. Foliage seldom mildews, but is lost in long seasons. Best in Pacific Northwest as an exhibition rose; shy in Central Zone and not hardy for Northern Zone; varies greatly. Some growers recommend a light soil." [Th2] "Another garden Rose that will give us an exhibition flower occasionally, especially at the end of the one long strong shoot that it is the custom of this variety so frequently to make. The flower requires careful shading to secure the orange-yellow tint in its petals which are of good size but rather more twisted than usual. It is moderately vigorous in growth, has very fine foliage of a deep bronze colour, leathery in texture, and is altogether a desirable variety. Not recommended for standards as it 'takes' very badly." [F-M] "I have found it hardier and even better as a standard than as a dwarf." [NRS13/57] "Bushy, low-growing, moderately compact, reasonably hardy; foliage sufficient, black-spots slightly; bloom moderate to free, continuous, except little while in midsummer." [ARA18/125]

"This Rose has vigorous but not tall growth of a somewhat spreading or branching habit. Like many Hybrid Teas it is somewhat apt to make one strong shoot with a pyramidal panicle of flowers, but does not behave worse in this respect than many others. The foliage is of a glossy olive green tinged with bronze, which seldom suffers from mildew. Its flowers, which are produced very freely and continuously from the end of June to late Autumn, are borne on stems of medium length, moderately erect, the full flowers drooping somewhat, and last well in water (four to five days). The petals are large, deep, stiff, and of fair substance. The colour is very variable and somewhat affected by weather. It is described in the Catalogue as coppery yellow, shaded salmon pink, and I have seen Roses almost as deep as this, but far the greater number of Roses of this variety gathered from the garden will be found much lighter in tint than this description conveys to my mind. The centre is deeper than the edges, and though

difficult to describe, it is a beautiful colour. It does well in bright weather, perhaps better if it be dull, and will stand a fair amount of rain. An excellent Rose this for bedding and decoration, whether in the garden or cut, and it often gives blooms good enough for exhibition. It also makes a fine standard and is somewhat fragrant with a Tea scent. A Rose to be safely recommended to anyone, for it is not particular as to soil or situation, but if choice is open select a sandy loam." [NRS10/28]

[Monsieur Paul Lédé]

Pernet-Ducher, 1902

"Apricot, shaded rose. —Moderately vigorous. —Garden, pot. —Fragrant." [Cat12/49] "Very sweet, elongated bud. Growth vigorous, very free flowering." [GeH] "Very vigorous, bushy; beautiful dark green foliage; blossom very large, full, superbly colored carmine pink nuanced and shaded yellow; very fragrant; continuous flowering." [JR26/131]

Morgenglans

trans. "Morning Glow"
Van Rossem, 1916

"Salmon, medium size, semi-full, light scent, medium height." [Sn] "Salmon-flesh, semi-double; bud coppery orange, opening well. Growth vigorous; free flowering." [GeH]

Morgentau

trans. "Morning Dew"
Hinner, 1908

"White, very large, full, medium scent, medium height." [Sn]

Mrs. Aaron Ward

Pernet-Ducher, 1907

"India yellow, occasionally washed with salmon rose. Some disbudding." [Th] "Whitish center to yellow-salmon-fawn, more buff in autumn; odor slight. Bush small. 7 blooms." [ARA26/95] "Yellow, tinted salmon rose. Very pale in spring, but highly colored in fall. Flowers handsomely formed and carried on strong stems." [CA17] "Large, full, elongated, opening well." [GeH] "An old Rose which is always in demand. Buff buds open to fully double flowers of yellow and pink. The plants are dwarf and are very free with their lovely blooms." [C-Pf34] "Fine form, large, double, quite fragrant, medium to medium-long stem. Fine foliage, sufficient. Growth poor; hardy. Nankeen-yellow and orange, changing when open to salmon-pink." [ARA23/167] "The blooms retain their beauty longer if partially shaded." [C-Ps29] "One of the most popular yellows. Blooms small, distinct in color but inclined to fade; foliage and form good; growth bushy; fair bloomer." [ARA18/113] "Bleaches badly; good form, but trifle short; slight fragrance. Compact, upright growth; good stems. Foliage very good . . . good in Central Zone, where it gives forty blooms . . . subject to black-spot . . . Is variable in color in some locations." [Th2] "This is a delightful Rose, with its frilly petals and varying but always exquisite color. In cool seasons, and on first opening, it is rich, golden fawn, but in bright sunlight it quickly fades to soft pink and white. Flowers are not large, but gracefully formed, fully double, and quite fragrant. The bush grows low, branches vigorously, and bears clean, pointed foliage which is almost immune to pests." [C-Ps25] "Flowers are full double and as attractive when full blown as in the bud state. The young foliage is a rich bronzy green. This Rose will probably produce more

Mrs. Aaron Ward *continued*

blooms for you than any other yellow H.T." [C&Js23] "Attractive irregularity of its form. I like the low, neat habit of the bush, the pointed, holly-like leaves, and the generous, successive crops of small blossoms." [ARA29/69] "Moderate vigor; blossom very large, very full." [JR35/14] "Growth very vigorous, with slightly branching canes, beautiful bronzy green foliage, long bud admirably held on a stiff stem, form resembles that of 'Catherine Mermet' [T], flower very large, in the form of a long cup, full; color, Indian yellow, sometimes nuanced salmon pink ... Its flowers, long-lasting, will make it much esteemed as an exhibition rose; it will also be excellent for cutting." [J31/23] "Moderately high, compact, and hardy; foliage plentiful, healthy; bloom free, continuous." [ARA18/127] "A good bloomer with dark green, waxy leaves. The open flower is not always of good form and quickly loses its color, but as the rich yellow, pointed buds with the attractive green leaves fit so well into a bouquet of pink, yellow, or tinted roses, we seldom allow a bud to reach the full-blown stage." [ARA31/98] "Exceptionally free-flowering; a favorite with the ladies." [ARA22/xiv] "I notice that men love to go from the garden wearing a 'Mrs. Aaron Ward'." [ARA29/52] "A very attractive and popular little rose; good for all purposes." [ARA17/25]

Mrs. Amy Hammond

McGredy, 1911

"Cream, shaded amber and apricot, large and full. Vigorous." [GeH] "A blend of ivory, amber and apricot. Practically no disbudding." [Th] "The flower is of perfect shape, petals long and pointed." [C&Js14] "A fair all-round Rose. The colour is cream, flushed pale pink, which is often deeper early in the year or under glass. The flower is of fair form and size, and the plant grows sufficiently well." [NRS21/43] "Flesh, shading to white; lovely shape. Bush strong and tall, somewhat leggy. 37 blooms." [ARA26/95] "It is an extraordinary, deep, long, very pointed flower, probably the most perfect shaped and most graceful in form of any Rose grown ... the marvellous freedom with which it grows and blooms throughout the entire season, and until quite late in the Autumn, will make it known as 'Everybody's Rose.' It opens freely in all weathers, is not affected by rain to any extent, and in hot weather retains its exquisite shape and graceful reflexed form better than any other variety we know of ... The colour is most pronounced, and develops during the best part of the flowering season to bright Apricot, especially towards the base of the flower. Many blooms develop all over this delightful Apricot shading ... delicious fragrance." [NRS11/177] "A good rose in all except blooming, which is fair." [ARA18/113] "A charming variety, but not robust." [NRS23/203]

Mrs. Andrew Carnegie

Cocker, 1913

From 'Frau Karl Druschki' (HP) × 'Niphetos' (T).

"White, occasionally beautifully lemon tinted, very large, well formed, and every flower perfectly shaped, with high centre. Growth robust; very free." [GeH] "A creamy white flower. The petals are thin, and under the conditions of 1917 the buds failed to open properly. Plant a weak grower, resembling in no way its parent, 'Frau Karl Druschki'. 'White Maman Cochet' [T] is superior to it." [ARA18/133] "A magnificent Rose of the colour of 'White Maman Cochet', but apparently of larger size with more substance and depth of petal. It is sweetly scented. The growth of the plant exhibited was very vigorous, as one might

expect from its parentage." [NRS13/151] "White, faintly tinged yellow, sometimes darker; beautiful form, large size; needs dryness and heat to open well; lasting. Foliage good. Growth fair in Central Zone, greater under more equable conditions. This rose has been reported as doing especially well in Lewiston, Idaho, where the elevation is less than 1,000 feet [ca. 300 m]. Needs a dry climate without cold extremes." [Th2] "Fairly good in growth and bloom. Does especially well in midsummer." [ARA18/113] "A sensational newcomer, the most beautiful of white roses, a Druschki with delicious perfume ... The blossoms are large, pretty, elegant, formed with absolute perfection, and high-centered. This rose is in all ways superior to Druschki. It looks like 'White Maman Cochet', but is larger. Sometimes some of the flowers have a light salmon tint. This wonderful contrast may be admired for a long time, as the open flowers last and last. The vigor of the bush is even greater than that of Druschki. This is a magnificent decorative, and marvelous for forcing; it adapts particularly well to American culture, the canes growing to 3–4 feet in length [ca. 1–1.3 m]." [JR37/76]

Mrs. Archie Gray

H. Dickson, 1914

"Deep creamy yellow, opening to clear, light canary-yellow; fine habit, and opens freely in all weathers, as the petals are firm and of good substance; flowers large and exquisitely formed." [C&Js16] "This is an exhibition Rose of such beauty that it will be a garden Rose too. A cream self of magnificent shape and all the points of an exhibition variety with a delightful fragrance coupled with a free flowering habit." [NRS14/155] "Small plants; winterkilled." [ARA18/117] "Growth upright, strong, vigorous, with beautiful brilliant foliage; blossoms large and exquisitely formed, produced in great profusion; buds long and pointed, cream yellow, opening light canary yellow; the blossoms open freely under all circumstances, the petals being strong and of good substance." [JR38/25]

Mrs. Bertram J. Walker

H. Dickson, 1915

"Very distinct, clear, bright cerise-pink, a shade of color quite novel and unlike that of any other known Rose. The color is even and dense throughout the flower and does not fade with age. A fine garden Rose of splendid bedding properties and a good exhibition Rose." [C&Js16] "I was much taken with this Rose—fragrant, and a fine bright colour —that one might describe as a deep cerise. Apparently a good grower and a good all-round variety." [NRS15/155] "Nicely formed cerise pink flowers. The plant is a fair grower, but rather stumpy in habit, and in this respect disappointing." [NRS21/54] "Strong, vigorous, upright branching growth attaining a uniform height of about two feet [ca. 6 dm], foliage abundant and very healthy. Flowers large, very full and of perfectly symmetrical form, freely and abundantly produced right throughout the season." [NRS15/170] "Fair growth only; large, very attractive blooms; foliage lost early; not a continuous bloomer. Retained for its beautiful spring blooms." [ARA18/113]

Mrs. C. V. Haworth

A. Dickson, 1919

"A really good many-colored rose (golden yellow with apricot-red was this summer's coloring of this changeable rose)." [ARA24/107] "Large, full, apricot-colored with chrome yellow and reddish shading." [Ck] "Flower of cinnamony apricot color as it expands, developing into a delicate biscuit-buff with very delicate cerise-rose sheen on the reflex of the large upstanding shell-shaped petals, which are deeply veined saffron-primrose, fairly full; highly perfumed Persian primrose and produced in great profusion on rigid flower stalks. Growth vigorous, erect, branching." [GeH]

Mrs. C. W. Dunbar-Buller

A. Dickson, 1919

"Bud very large, globular; flower very large, full, borne on long, strong stems; strong fragrance. Color rosy white, veined warm, clear rosy deep carmine, with lemon base, colorings which betoken a pure and lasting shade—rose-madder—throughout the bloom's existence; reflex of petal solid rosy cerise, edges silvery white when fully open. Foliage abundant, large, leathery, dark green. A vigorous, upright, bushy grower and continuous bloomer from June to October. Very hardy." [ARA20/128] "Poor growth; shy bloomer the first season." [ARA26/119] "Large, imbricated form, strongly perfumed…Distinct." [GeH]

Mrs. Charles Curtis Harrison   Listed as 'Mrs. Charles Custis Harrison' (HT).

Mrs. Charles Custis Harrison

syn. 'Mrs. Charles Curtis Harrison'
A. Dickson, 1910

"Carmine crimson. Garden." [NRS15/150] "Deep crimson pink on front of petals; deep crimson carmine on reverse side. Practically no disbudding." [Th] "Deep carmine-pink with shaded crimson reflex, large and free. Growth vigorous." [GeH] "This rose, of rare beauty, makes a vigorous bush with erect canes which produce a great quantity of flowers on stiff stems; the blossoms are large, full, globular, and with smooth petals, deep red on the obverse, more carminy on the reverse … very delicate perfume." [JR34/103] "Above average in color and fragrance; good grower; fairly good bloomer." [ARA18/113]

Mrs. Charles E. Russell

syn. 'Pink American Beauty'
Montgomery, 1913
From: "'Mme. Abel Chatenay' [HT], 'Marquise Litta [de Bretueil]' [HT], 'Mme. Caroline Testout' [HT], 'General MacArthur' [HT] and three seedlings resulting from these crosses are all combined to produce 'Mrs. Charles [E.] Russell'." [ARA16/125]

"Deep crimson carmine. Has the true old Rose perfume." [NRS29/251] "Bright rose-pink, deeper toward the center. The bud is fully as large as [that of] 'American Beauty' [HP], but more pointed." [C&Js15] "Rosy carmine. Exhibition, pot." [NRS15/150] "Rosy carmine with scarlet center. Color brilliant and pleasing. Flowers beautifully formed and last splendidly when cut. Stems extremely strong, with flowers always borne singly." [CA17] "Rosy carmine, with rosy scarlet centre, large, full, fine form. Growth vigorous, free branching." [GeH] "Large, full flowers of rosy carmine, on very strong stems, and quite fragrant. The flower does not keep well in the garden, but it has long been noted as one of the finest cut Roses when grown by the florist. A fair grower, resistant to disease, hardy, but not very free-blooming." [C-Ps25] "Alexander W. Montgomery, Jr., of Hadley, Mass., is responsible for three good roses now in commerce, of which two, 'Mrs. Charles [E.] Russell' and 'Hadley' [both HT], are very much in the rose eye of the cut-flower growers and the public today. There is much to hope for from Mr. Montgomery." [ARA16/44]

Mrs. Charles Hunter

W. Paul, 1912

"Cerise, nearly red. Stems strong. Very free bloomer." [CA17] "Rose-pink; tall, bushy." [ARA17/32] "Blossom pinkish crimson fading to pink when fully open. Flower very big, with large petals, wonderful for forcing and for the open ground. Vigorous." [JR36/103] "Rosy crimson, changing to rose colour as it expands, very bold, with large handsome petals, produced on strong upright stalks. Growth vigorous, free flowering." [GeH] "Fair in most characteristics; not distinct." [ARA18/117]

Mrs. Charles J. Bell

Mrs. C. J. Bell/Pierson, 1917
Sport of 'Red Radiance' (HT).

"*A true even shell-pink* with a heavy salmon suffusion, giving it the true opalescence of a pearl." [C-Ps30] "This is truly a superb sport of the famous 'Radiance' [HT], equal to that variety in most respects and superior to it in color, which is a fine light pink of a most distinct shade." [C-Ps25] "Of an unusual color … Very fine." [ARA24/90] "A lovely shade of soft or shell-pink … beautiful in bud or open flower. Fine foliage. Growth of the best. Continually in flower. Averages 45 blooms per season. Prune to 6 eyes. Hardy." [ARA21/91] "Superior in growth to 'Radiance', being equally vigorous but more robust in habit." [ARA17/140] "In some soils the color is a decided light salmon … The blooms are well formed, with petals of a heavy texture, so the cut-flowers keep a long time. The bush grows as tall as [that of] 'Radiance', the foliage is healthy, large, and disease-resistant and the flowers come continuously from June until hard frost." [C-Ps31] "Magnificent grower and bloomer, with flowers all season." [ARA29/52]

Mrs. Conway Jones   Listed as 'Mamie' (HT).

Mrs. Cynthia Forde   Listed as 'Cynthia Forde' (HT). See also 'Mrs. Forde' (HT).

[Mrs. David Jardine]

A. Dickson/Wm. Craig, 1908

"Beautiful pink color; blooms profusely." [JR32/38] "Has that powerful perfume which made 'La France' [B or HT] so popular." [C&Js09] "Very large, full, of imbricated form, highly perfumed. Growth vigorous, erect, floriferous." [GeH] "A glorious and most charming rose, possessing vigorous and erect growth, together with marvelously free flowering habit. The blooms, which are produced on every shoot, are of very large and perfect form; beautiful in its several stages of development. The color is a delightful shade of bright rosy pink, shading in outer petals to salmon pink." [CA11]

Mrs. David McKee

A. Dickson, 1904

"Cream-yellow; flowers large; excellent for exhibition." [C&Js12] "Sulphur white. A weakly grower, but produces blooms of perfect shape." [NRS29/251] "Very good big flowers, and opens well in all weathers." [NRS14/161] "Creamy yellow. —Vigorous. —Exhibition, garden. —A good garden rose." [Cat12/45] "Amber-white, changing to sulphury white, large, full, opening well, fragrant. Growth vigorous, free flowering." [GeH] "A Rose that has improved since it was introduced. It will give good shaped flowers in fair quantity and is to be preferred to the 'Duchess of Portland' [HT], a Rose of similar colour and better shape but of poor constitution. Its colour, pale creamy-yellow, makes it useful to the exhibitor and it was awarded the Gold Medal of the N.R.S." [F-M]

Mrs. Dunlop-Best

syn. 'Cleveland II'
Hicks, 1916

"Coppery yellow and reddish copper; splendidly formed blossom." [Ck] "The well-shaped, reddish apricot blooms appeal to me, and the shiny red-bronze foliage on slender, ruddy canes, makes a really beautiful plant." [ARA29/48] "Reddish apricot, base of petals coppery yellow; sweetly scented. Growth strong and branching; very free and decorative; free from Mildew." [GeH] "Not full enough for interior districts but remarkably fine for seacoast on account of its foliage and lack of balling. Has splendid cutting value, especially in the fall ... An old rose which is commencing to come into its own, and is far superior to many later introductions. Hardy." [ARA28/103] "Reddish apricot to coppery yellow at base; nice buds, though short; attractive open flower of fair size; holds color but is small in heat; slight fragrance. Long, strong stems as a rule; fair growth. Foliage attractive Tea color when young, and seldom mildews, besides holding well. Thirty-five flowers in Central Zone." [Th2] "Very promising variety; most distinct and attractive in color of flower; good in growth for new plants." [ARA18/119]

Mrs. E. Alford

Lowe & Shawyer, 1912

"Silvery pink, large, full and free. Vigorous." [GeH] "Whitish pink, large, full, medium height." [Sn] "This is a fine upstanding erect-growing Hybrid Tea ... The flower is pointed in shape, which is very full and quite up to exhibition standard. Colour, flesh pink in centre." [NRS13/154]

Mrs. E. G. Hill

Soupert & Notting, 1905
From 'Mme. Caroline Testout' (HT) × 'Liberty' (HT).

"Light rose, reverse of petals deep amaranth pink. One of the best of the bi-colour pinks." [NRS29/251] "Pointed, full buds. Growth vigorous." [GeH] "Has good foliage with large leaflets of a clean green, perhaps rather on the dark side, but not specially distinctive. The habit is vigorous and the flower stalks erect. The flowers come rather early ... and are produced continuously without a break in the whole season, and during the greater part of it in considerable quantity. This Rose is of the bicolor type, a most beautiful combination of colour, the petals being pale silvery pink on the inside, and the reverse coral rose. Occasionally they are a beautiful shape, and nearly always attractive, but sometimes perhaps a little thin and open. The petals are of good substance, shell-like, and a large size. The half open flowers are always attractive, and the flowers retain their colour well in warm or in wet weather. They are carried erect and well above the foliage ... It gives no trouble on account of mildew or any other disease. The flowers are fragrant, but not markedly so. As a bedding Rose it is quite first class. In fact, in my opinion, it has scarcely a rival among the H.T.'s for this purpose ... My principal bed is in half shade, but last year I planted another group in full sun, and they seem to be doing equally satisfactorily ... Mr. G. L. Paul has noticed that the colour of 'Mrs. E. G. Hill' does not harmonise well with all other Roses. It is well, therefore, to avoid associating in its near neighbourhood Roses of pronounced salmon or orange tints. The strong points of 'Mrs. E. G. Hill' are its lovely and distinct colour and erect carriage of the flowers, the quantity of flowers produced, and their continuity, the good habit of the plant, and its freedom from disease. I know of no bad points; some of my friends speak of it as too thin, but this is not always a defect in a bedding Rose, enabling it to open well in bad weather." [NRS12/88–90] "Growth of very great vigor; beautiful dark green foliage; bud long and pointed; flower extremely large, full, opening easily, borne on a very long stem; well held; petals coral red outside, alabaster white within. Good for cutting and bedding. Floriferous and fragrant ... dedicated to the wife of the well-known American rosarian Mr. Hill, who picked it out from a great number of seedlings." [JR29/136]

Mrs. E. Townsend

syn. 'Mrs. E. Townshend'
P. Guillot, 1910
From 'Mme. Laurette Messimy' (Ch) × 'Mme. Léon Pain' (HT).

"Apricot yellow." [Ÿ] "Soft rosy fawn, orange carmine on the reverse side. Practically no disbudding." [Th] "Yellowish pink, large, full, medium scent, medium height." [Sn] "Soft chamois-rose, reverse of petals orange-carmine, passing to rosy flesh towards the edge, large, full, globular. Growth vigorous, very free." [GeH] "Fine bloomer, of good color, form and growth; discarded on account of susceptibility to mildew." [ARA18/117]

Mrs. E. Townshend   Listed as 'Mrs. E. Townsend' (HT).

Mrs. Edward Powell

Bernaix, 1910

"Color is velvety crimson. The flowers are large, full, and freely produced on strong, vigorous canes." [C&Js24] "Bright scarlet crimson. Form cupped globular, but a little too hollow in the centre to be quite satisfactory. Nevertheless its brilliancy in colouring, together with its good autumnal flowering habit, combine to make it a desirable Rose for bedding purposes." [NRS21/64] "Scarlet, shaded purplish crimson. Garden, bedding. Deep purple-tinted foliage. Fragrant." [NRS13/170] "Brilliant color; growth and blooming fair; best in spring." [ARA18/113] "Perhaps one of the best bedding Roses we have among the crimson H.T.'s. It has lovely foliage, often suffused with a faint purple tinge; the flower stems are long and erect, and the flowers are carried well. They are of a scarlet crimson colour of fair form, but not first class in this respect, freely and continuously produced ... A good grower, and is easy to keep free from disease. Altogether it is a first class garden Rose. It has a certain perfume, but not that of the damask Rose." [NRS21/40] "An excellent garden Rose with lovely foliage and keeps its colour well ... The shade of crimson is bright and attractive and its only fault is that the shape of the flower, which, though not altogether bad, leaves something to be desired." [NRS20/93] "Brighter flowers, more continuously produced than those of 'General MacArthur' [HT]. Its foliage is dark, glossy, and abundant, its habit of growth is almost perfect for a bedding Rose, and it has a decided though rather curious scent. The shape of its flowers appears to be the only weak point of this Rose." [NRS21/112] "Large, full, of exquisite shape. Growth vigorous, very floriferous." [GeH] "Vigorous growth, of moderate length with ample glossy foliage. The upright bud is beautiful in form—long ovoid—and beautiful in color as well: scarlet lake going to purple grenadine. The large blossom is of exquisite form with thick petals which are firm, very large, imbricated but separate, uniformly velvety crimson red in color. Extremely floriferous, notable for its brilliant coloration and its rare perfection of form." [JR34/151]

Mrs. Forde

A. Dickson, 1913

"Carmine rose. Garden." [NRS15/150] "Deep carmine-rose on delicate rose-pink with yellow base, large, full, and perfect. Growth vigorous." [GeH] "Fairly vigorous." [Au] "Delightfully perfumed." [C&Js14] "Good growth, very hardy; fair foliage, good stem; medium to large size, blooms well, good form, lasts well, fragrant." [ARA16/20] "A good sprinkling of Tea blood in its veins ... It should have a useful career as an exhibition Rose, and its dainty and distinct colouring will appeal to many who will want it in their gardens. Of fine form and shape, colour dainty rose-pink, with that yellow base to the petal that betrays its Tea blood. Altogether a fine variety, a good erect grower with a strong fruity perfume." [NRS14/146–147] "The flowers, large, numerous, and always opening well, are borne upright on very rigid stems; they have a unique form: the center juts out, and the petals fall back gracefully around it. The perfectly formed blossom is of a splendid color ... delicate carmine red nuanced pink; it has a chrome yellow zone at the base of each petal. The branches are particularly strong and robust; the plant is much branched; the foliage is lime green; each branch is crowned with a bud; ... very strong, delicious Tea scent." [JR36/91–92]

Mrs. Franklin Dennison

McGredy, 1915

"Flesh, edged deep rose. Bush very strong. 21 blooms." [ARA26/95] "A large white flower of fair form and substance ... chiefly useful for exhibition." [NRS21/54] "A vigorously growing pearly white Rose of excellent form, lightly tinted with pink and cream. Very floriferous and hardy, but foliage could be better." [C-Ps25] "Vigor ... superb, full, high-centered blooms. The color is rather undecided and it varies with the season." [ARA29/62] "The blooms are a model of perfection, as large as [those of] 'Mildred Grant' [HT]. The colour is most difficult to describe—porcelain white, veiled primrose yellow deepening to ochre at the base ... The flower of enormous size, beautifully pointed, and of great substance ... quite full and a model exhibition bloom. It is as good a grower as 'Frau Karl Druschki' [HP], yet it flowers so freely it must be classes as a really good garden Rose, but as an exhibition Rose it stands unique among Hybrid Teas ... delightfully sweet perfumed." [NRS15/174] "Beautiful flower; tall growth; fair foliage and blooming qualities; most attractive cutting rose." [ARA18/113] "A very dependable Rose for cut-flowers." [C-Ps29] "Medium height, fairly compact, hardy; foliage sufficient, black-spots; bloom free, continuous." [ARA18/127] "Likely to prove a useful Rose for exhibition as well as garden purposes." [NRS14/156]

Mrs. Fred Searl

A. Dickson, 1917

"Fawny shell-pink, the reflex of petals warm silvery carmine-rose, deeper at edges, inside of petals richest fawn, large size, globular form, produced in profusion; Tea perfumed." [GeH] "Of a paler shade, and in a dry season very beautiful. She does much better with me tan 'Dean Hole' [HT]. They are very much alike in shape and in colour, and both rather thin in texture of petal." [NRS23/203] "Light pink, very large, full, medium scent, medium height." [Sn]

Mrs. Fred Staker Listed as 'Mrs. Fred Straker' (HT).

Mrs. Fred Strader Listed as 'Mrs. Fred Straker' (HT).

Mrs. Fred Straker

syn. 'Mrs. Fred Staker', 'Mrs. Fred Strader'

A. Dickson, 1910

"Salmon-pink, yellow base. Vigorous. Garden." [NRS11/100] "Orange crimson in the bud, developing as the bloom expands to silver fawn on front of the petals; delicate orange pink on back. Practically no disbudding." [Th] "A pretty little Rose in the early part of the season, the flowers were nicely formed and coloured salmon pink with a yellow base to the petal; the later flowers, however, usually proved of little value ... I regard it as one of the Roses of the past." [NRS21/36] "Spiral form, free. Growth free." [GeH] "Excellent color and form; growth good; hardiness varies; fair bloomer; small flowers best in spring." [ARA18/113] "The plant is of excellent growth, bearing vigorous, upright canes covered with flowers throughout the season. They are well formed, held upright, and colored orange at first, then becoming silvery gray at the petal edges and orange pink at the center. The buds are long, elegant, and spiraled, which allows the various colors to mix together. Endowed with a delicious perfume, this rose is perfection." [JR34/103–104]

Mrs. George Marriott

McGredy, 1918

"Deep cream and pearl, suffused rose and vermilion. Won Gold Medal of National Rose Society of England." [Th2] "Very large flowers, perfectly formed." [ARA19/103] "What a joy it is when you have finally raised a splendid flower of perfect form." [ARA29/112] "Deep cream and pearl, pencilled and suffused rose and vermilion ... splendid habit of growth and freedom of flowering." [NRS18/206] "Although free flowering, the growth on cut-backs is rather stumpy. The full large blooms seem to lose their freshness, and the rose and vermilion suffusion almost disappears, leaving the fully developed flower an insipid creamy white, with just a suspicion of the overlying colours." [NRS24/159] "A distinct and charming Rose of vigorous growth. The blooms are very large, high centre, of perfect shape and sweetly scented. The colour is a deep cream, suffused rose vermilion —quite unique. An ideal exhibition and garden Rose, and one that has come to stay." [NRS18/163]

Mrs. George Preston

A. Dickson, 1910

"Whitish pink, very large, full, medium scent, medium height." [Sn] "Very beautiful vigorous rose, very floriferous, giving large blossoms which are full and globular, with large and smooth petals; color, beautiful silvery pink. Sometimes, in the Fall, one might find a light tint of orange. Having a very penetrating perfume and being long-lasting, this variety will be a good addition to the exhibition sorts." [JR34/104] "Tall growth; distinct color; fair bloomer." [ARA18/113]

Mrs. George Shawyer

Lowe & Shawyer, 1911

"Brilliant rose pink, almost solid color. Large, full and well formed. Especially good for forcing." [CA17] "Pale rose. —Garden." [Cat12/69] "The color is a lovely bright shade of pink and the flowers are freely produced on straight, upright stems which shows them off to good advantage on the bush and makes them valuable for cutting." [C&Js12] "Perfume mild; thirty-one blooms throughout the season on two-year-old plants; growth well above the average. Very good for cutting." [ARA17/23] "Carried on stiff stems, long bud opening well."

Mrs. George Shawyer *continued*

[GeH] "A pink flower with a long pointed bud, and is very beautiful when grown under glass; in the open the colour is not so brilliant. The plant grows well, but is somewhat subject to black spot." [NRS21/43] "The color is a beautiful shade of pink, and very popular. In many sections, however, it is disposed to mildew, and on that account is not so extensively grown as its merits would otherwise entitle it to be." [ARA16/114] "Hardiness fair. Clear rose at its best, but often muddy; fine form. Foliage mildews very badly. Fair growth and stem. On account of its lasting qualities and freedom from mildew under dry heat, it is a good rose for Interior South." [Th2] "Gives beautiful long buds which keep well. It grows very tall, up to 7 feet [ca. 2.3 m], and does well for about ten years." [ARA30/151] "Rose-pink blooms of large size and excellent shape, both as bud and open flower. Has fine stems and is good for cutting; fairly fragrant in the early stages. Very susceptible to mildew in moist regions, but a good Rose for the drier sections, and at its best in hot weather. A good grower and bloomer; quite hardy." [C-Ps25] "Good to fine form, medium to large size, double, tea fragrance, medium to long stem. Foliage good, sufficient on own root and sparse on budded. Growth strong; medium hardy. Clear brilliant rose." [ARA23/168] "Satisfactory rose, particularly in color, lasting qualities, and stem; form good; growth above average; fair bloomer. Use Multiflora [understock]." [ARA18/113]

Mrs. Henry Morse

McGredy, 1919

From 'Mme. Abel Chatenay' (HT) × 'Lady Pirrie' (HT).

"Brilliant pink shaded vermilion red." [Riv] "Rose shot scarlet." [NRS21/58] "A sweetly scanted, large-flowered Rose with pointed buds. Color is striking because the light pink of the inner petals is in lovely contrast to the deep pink of the outer petals." [C-Ps26] "Bud very large, long pointed; flower very large, high center, double; fragrant. Color flesh-cream ground, with a sheen of bright rose, deeply impregnated and washed vermilion, with clear vermilion veining on petals. Very vigorous grower, bearing an abundance of bloom." [ARA20/129] "A rose that attracts the eye at a glance … The bud is long and opens freely. A good all-round rose, and every bloom comes good in form." [ARA20/121] "It can be grown to a huge size without becoming coarse." [ARA29/109] "Good substance in the petals, and the buds take quite a long time to develop. A constant bloomer and a good grower of free erect habit." [NRS23/202] "One of the most popular of all pink Roses. The buds are perfect in form, long, artistically formed, of a rich carmine-pink, and open to a high-pointed, two-toned, pink flower of great beauty. The outside of the petals is a clean, lustrous 'pink,' while the inside is pinkish flesh with a lovely sheen; there is an underlying yellow glow which brings out the fine shades. It has 30 petals and a fine Tea fragrance. A garden Rose which produces cut-flowers of highest quality. Moderate growth." [C-Pf34] "Bright rose, darker shadings; beautiful spiral bud, holding high center when open; good size; lasting; very free; thirty petals; fragrant. Tall but somewhat spindly growth, with good stem. Foliage mildews … would seem to mildew in moist heat rather than damp coolness, but would do better still in dry climates. A rose well worth test, particularly adapted to Central Zone conditions with altitude." [Th2] "It has a most artistically formed bud, followed by a long-lasting bloom of great size, pleasingly perfumed. A healthy and hardy bush, with

small but sturdy foliage, it sends up bloom after bloom of high quality on long stems for cutting." [C-Ps29]

"Of very vigorous habit and the blooms are long and shapely, of a lovely bright pink, shaded salmon, deeper at the base, with a distinct tea scent. An ideal rose for bedding and pot-work. May best be described as a glorified 'Mme. Abel Chatenay.'" [ARA20/116] "Invariably a prey to black-spot, but producing so freely blooms of such exquisite charm as to render it a favorite." [ARA29/62] "Until this Rose is well established, the foliage is liable to mildew late in the season. A superb Rose for cutting." [C-Ps27] "This Rose makes a good compact bush, and branches freely. The plant is rather dwarf, and it is only a strong one that will reach 2 feet [ca. 6 dm]. The foliage is fairly profuse, but in most localities it is sadly liable to mildew, and to some extent to black spot … The foliage also suffers somewhat from red rust … The flowers are beautiful in form, full, with a pointed centre; they are silvery rose on the outside of the petal, and rose pink on the inside … it is not, in my opinion, a continuous flowerer. In this respect some of my friends do not agree … The flowers last fairly well, the guard petals being strong and good, though the centre ones are at times weak … They are sweetly scented. The colour lasts fairly well in dull, cloudy weather, but is soon affected by sun, and I have at times seen this Rose of an appalling colour … Those who grow it must be prepared to give it some care to obtain it in perfection." [NRS29/106–107] "But can you tell me anything more entrancing to look upon than that delightful rose, 'Mrs. Henry Morse'?" [ARA29/46] "We have never raised or sent out a Rose with a feeling of greater pride than we do in offering this wonderful novelty to the Rose-loving world." [NRS19/163]

Mrs. Henry Winnett

Dunlop, 1917

From 'Mrs. Charles E. Russell' (HT) × 'Mrs. George Shawyer' (HT).

"A large, dark crimson, beautifully formed rose, with a high-pointed center, and grows with strong, heavy stems that are a delight to cut. The blooms last well, either cut or on the bush, keep their bright color, stand rain well, and have a delightful fragrance." [ARA29/108] "Deep scarlet crimson, which does not blue. Strong growth, and very good for cutting. Very sweet perfume." [NRS29/253] "Has a good-sized and well-formed bloom and is free from disease, though the color sometimes lacks a little luster." [ARA24/107] "Its foliage is characteristic of 'Mrs. [George] Shawyer', and the observer reports it as a 'big, strong, rank-growing rose, in color almost as dark as 'Hadley' [HT].' He adds, 'Though Mr. Dunlop has registered the rose as "brighter than 'Richmond' [HT]," it is not only brighter but darker than that variety. The color undoubtedly comes from its grandparents, and through 'Mrs. Charles [E.] Russell' from the fine 'General MacArthur' [HT] strain. Dunlop's rose has the fragrance of 'Hadley', though not quite so pronounced. It gives every indication of being a first-class forcing rose, and judging from the parentage and growth characteristics it should make a good garden rose." [ARA17/39]

Mrs. Herbert Stevens

McGredy, 1910

Supposedly from 'Frau Karl Druschki' (HP) × 'Niphetos' (T), but see below …

"Nearly pure white, with a fawn and peach base to the petal. Habit, free and vigorous for a Tea, of excellent bedding type. The flowers are remarkable for their 'pointed' character, with good length of petal and excellent shape." [NRS/10] "Beautiful buds of rather thin petalage, and balls slightly, although frequently of exhibition value." [Th2] "Grows strongly, has perfectly formed flowers, white tinged with a faint pink." [OM] "Growth and color good; foliage inclined to mildew; fairly good bloomer." [ARA18/113] "The best bloomer in whites in my garden." [ARA24/96] "Tall, compact, hardy; foliage very plentiful, black-spots and mildews somewhat; bloom free, continuous." [ARA18/127] "Very branching growth . . . To myself and some of my friends the foliage appears rather small and scanty, but others have referred to it as good dark foliage. It is always in flower throughout the season, and the blossoms are a nearly pure white (some notice a fawn and peach shading which I have not observed), and are a very beautiful shape, usually rather thin, and particularly elegant . . . One of the most beautiful decorative Roses we have had for a long time . . . rather bad in respect to mildew." [NRS/13] "I prefer this to any other white, for its shapely buds, its delicately toned color, and its healthy foliage. Not a rampant grower, but a very constant bloomer." [ARA29/52] "Growth vigorous, free-growing, very floriferous." [GeH] "I asked him [McGredy] if it was not from 'Niphetos'. He said, No! but it had some of that blood in it, but only indirectly. It was the result of no less than 6 different crossings with his own seedlings." [NRS22/26] "Produces an exquisite flower." [C&Js14]

Mrs. Hugh Dickson

H. Dickson, 1915

"Cream, suffused orange-buff; large, full, many petals; odor delicious. Bush strong. 19 blooms; 19 the second season." [ARA26/95] "The petals are large and of excellent substance and the flower of superb build, with high-pointed center and beautiful outline; deep cream with heavy suffusion of orange and apricot." [C&Js15] "A delightful Rose of exquisite form and fragrance, a Hybrid Tea of large size and good petal, cream, with a suffusion of orange and apricot. Judging from the plant exhibited the habit of the plant is excellent, branching, and not too vigorous." [NRS14/151] "Of superb build, with high-pointed centre, delightful perfume. Growth vigorous; very free flowering." [GeH] "Retained on account of its attractive color and foliage. Growth and blooming qualities not good; variable in hardiness." [ARA18/113] "Of strong, free-branching habit, with dark olive-green foliage . . . fairly stiff stems . . . a fine bedding Rose, and also valuable for exhibition." [NRS17/129] "A grand Rose for any purpose, a typical Hybrid Tea of a most delightful perfume, carrying its large handsome flowers in great freedom." [NRS15/170]

Mrs. Isabel Milner

W. Paul, 1907

From 'Princess of Wales' (HP) × 'Robert Duncan' (HP).

"Yellowish white, large, full, medium scent, medium height." [Sn] "Flower large, full; color, ivory white tinted pink. Vigorous growth." [JR35/14] "Ivory-white, suffused with pink, and delicately margined with mauve, extra large, good form. Growth vigorous." [GeH]

Mrs. John Forster   Listed as 'Mrs. John Foster' (HT).

Mrs. John Foster

syn. 'Mrs. John Forster'

Hicks, 1915

"Rich vermilion, sweetly scented. Growth vigorous." [GeH] "Deep red, large, full, medium scent, medium height." [Sn] "Growth rather tall; inclined to be shy bloomer." [ARA18/119]

Mrs. Joseph H. Welch

McGredy, 1911

"Brilliant rose pink. Very little disbudding. Not good in very hot weather." [Th] "Flower very large, delicate scent, irreproachable form, bright pink, very distinct." [JR36/74] "The colour of this wonderful Rose is a rich, brilliant Rose-Pink . . . It is undoubtedly the largest Rose in cultivation, and the most perfect type of the modern exhibition flower the Rose-world has yet seen . . . The growth is vigorous and upright, with the perpetual blooming habit of the true Hybrid Tea. Its rich, brilliant colour, perfect shape, and gigantic size and finish will compel attention in every Rose garden . . . Delicately sweet scented." [NRS11/176D] "A strong and vigorous grower, and has attained a high place as an exhibition Rose. The flower is rose pink and distinct in form from all other Roses; the petals, though few in number, are very large, and the centre ones fold inwards and retain their position unexpectedly well." [NRS21/43] "Very hardy. Brilliant rose-pink; very large, semi-double blooms. Splendid growth and foliage. Its greatest fault in Central Zone is short and weak stem and the fact that it wilts quickly. In Pacific North-West is very much better in these characteristics, and gives many more blooms. Decorative." [Th2] "Tall growth, good foliage, and large blooms; shy bloomer; not of best color. Retained for remarkably large and attractive spring flowers." [ARA18/113]

Mrs. MacKellar

A. Dickson, 1918

"Deep Naples yellow. An old Rose of good growth, its full blooms being always well shaped." [NRS29/253] "Beautiful clear color; bud almost perfect in form, not so good in open flower; fair growth; shy bloomer." [ARA18/113] "During the whole season gives a great number of canary-yellow blooms." [NRS18/154] "Centre deep citron or delicate pure canary, becoming pearly primrose-white as the blooms expand, large, with high-pointed centre, produced on rigid flower-stalks; fragrant. Growth vigorous, stiff and erect, floriferous." [GeH]

Mrs. Maud Dawson

A. Dickson, 1915

"Orange red, large, full, very fragrant, medium height." [Sn] "Brilliant orange-carmine or cerise; Tea Rose perfume, floriferous. Growth free." [GeH]

Mrs. Mona Hunting

H. Dickson, 1914

"Buff-yellow. Vigorous. Garden." [NRS13/171] "Pale buff. Blooms are always a good shape, and very free." [NRS29/253] "Chamois opening to pure fawn; very lovely, showing coppery in bud; odor slight. Bush medium; nearly winter-killed. 17 blooms." [ARA26/95] "A garden decorative Rose of great charm and beauty, growth free and branching, producing its flowers in the greatest profusion. Flowers medium sized and very full, bud long and pointed, colour deep chamois yellow, opening to pure fawn." [NRS16/177] "Growth and foliage poor." [ARA18/117] "A Hybrid Tea and a decorative Rose of much merit. Very free flowering, good branching habit of growth, flowers not very full but with a good outer petal. Delightful bright yellow in colour, of the shade called chamois, I believe. Sweet scented. Will be in request as a good bedder." [NRS13/153]

Mrs. Moorfield Storey

Waban, 1915

From 'General MacArthur' (HT) × 'Monsieur Joseph Hill' (HT)

"Light violet pink, large, full, medium height." [Sn] "Delicate pale pink, large, borne on stiff, erect stems. Growth strong, vigorous and upright." [GeH] "Weak growth; winterkills." [ARA18/117]

[Mrs. Muir MacKean]

McGredy, 1912

"Ruddy cerise. Buds large and very long pointed. Stems long and strong." [CA17] "Flower bright carmine-crimson, of perfect shape and form, fragrant. Growth vigorous, perpetual flowering." [GeH] "Unique; bright carmine without reflections; the flower is large, strong, very well formed, perfect in form of the modern sort. The bush is very floriferous." [JR36/171]

Mrs. Oakley Fisher

B. R. Cant, 1921

"A single tinted salmon-copper." [ARA23/125] "A uniform egg-yellow. It seems to be a good keeper, and the blooms appear in masses." [ARA23/140] "A very large, single-flowering rose, somewhat after the style of 'Irish Fireflame' ... dark red stems ... of good form, not apt to crinkle with age ... pale golden buff, with deeper-colored stamens." [ARA22/145] "Deep orange yellow, large, single, medium, moderate height." [Sn] "A very decorative single Rose of an attractive apricot orange colour. It is fairly vigorous, but does not bloom too freely." [NRS25/176] "Orange-apricot; single, very distinct; quite continuous; moderate growth." [CaRoll/3/3]

Mrs. R. D. McClure

H. Dickson, 1913

"Clear pink." [NRS21/49] "Large, full flowers of fine form, with large, shell[-shaped] petals, very firm and smooth, slightly reflexed at the edges; color brilliant, glistening salmon-pink." [C&Js14] "Bright salmon pink, full, globular. Flowers carried erect on short, stout stems. Free flowering, good in autumn, desirable for specimen blooms." [NRS21/64] "Strong, erect footstalks." [GeH] "Vigorous bush; open branching; flower very large, of exquisite form, and quite full. The bright salmon pink color inevitably keeps until the blossom is fully open." [JR37/58] "Fair in growth and blooming; color attractive." [ARA18/113] "Very pure colour, a soft rose salmon ... It is a fine pointed Rose of excellent shape and habit, which can be described as free branching, scented and useful for all purposes." [NRS13/155–156]

[Mrs. Sam Ross]

H. Dickson, 1912

"Pale straw-color to light chamois-yellow, with a distinct flush of buff on the reverse of petals." [C&Js14] "Flesh, suffused salmon and underlaid with buff. Color hard to describe, but delicate, unique and very pleasing. Flowers cupped, with outer petals slightly reflexed. Best in fall." [CA17] "Very large, full, very sweetly scanted. Growth strong, vigorous, and upright; very free." [GeH] "Strong, good growth; foliage dark green. The flower is beautiful, large, and quite double; the petals are delicate and wonderfully turned under at the edge. This newcomer is notable due to a coloration very difficult to describe. The petals are chamois and fawn yellow. Deliciously perfumed, the blossoms are borne upright at the tips of long stems which hold them above the foliage; they last a long time; very floriferous, it is, to our way of thinking, one of the best novelties." [JR36/170]

Mrs. Stewart Clark

H. Dickson, 1907

From 'Rubens' (T) × 'Tom Wood' (HP).

"Bright cerise pink ... a very vigorous grower, and fragrant withal." [NRS12/142] "Bright cerise-pink to brilliant rose, scented, free and perpetual, glossy green foliage. Growth vigorous and branching." [GeH] "A very promising variety of large size and fine shape. Its colour is a little against it, approaching the magenta shade that is objectionable to some. A very vigorous grower, almost too much so, it is deliciously fragrant and was awarded the N.R.S. Gold Medal." [F-M] "Plenty of wood and nothing else; does not want the knife." [NRS14/161] "It's a vigorous bush, robustly bearing blossoms of a color which is fairly difficult to describe, varying from pale cerise to very dark pink with a white tint at the base of the petals." [JR31/38] "Growth very good; flowers attractive; Hybrid Perpetual in blooming characteristics. Retained for its wonderful amount of spring bloom." [ARA18/113]

Mrs. T. Hillas

Pernet-Ducher, 1913

"Fine, pure chrome-yellow, without any suffusion; large, full flowers of elongated cu-shape." [C&Js15] "Deep cream, clear yellow center, almost white at times; large, perfect shape; odor good. Bush strong. 13 blooms; 18 the second season." [ARA26/95] "Buds golden yellow, long and pointed ... branching habit." [GeH] "Color attractive; pretty bud-form, poor open flower; growth good to fair; inclined to be shy bloomer." [ARA18/113] "Fair growth; hardy; fair foliage; good stem; medium size; fair bloomer; beautiful form; lasts well." [Th] "Very vigorous, with long and erect canes; foliage bronze green; thorns pretty numerous and salient; beautiful long bud, medium yellow; flower large, full, form of a long cup, beautifully colored pure chrome yellow ... Excellent garden rose; this new variety, of robust constitution, will be much appreciated for the elegance of its pretty blossoms." [JR37/42]

Mrs. Theodore Roosevelt   Plate 58

E. G. Hill, 1904

From 'La France' (B or HT) × ?

"Cream white with a pink center." [JR32/140] "Flesh pink; outer petals creamy white." [CA17] "Light pink." [CA07] "Flower silvery rose white, reverse of petals peach coloured, large, full, of imbricated form, sweet-scented. Growth vigorous, upright, very floriferous." [GeH] "Flesh, tinted pink. —Vigorous. —Exhibition, garden. —Erect growth. Flowers uniformly good." [Cat12/47] "Growth and blooming not of best." [ARA18/117] "This is undoubtedly one of the best exhibition Roses we have received from America. It has no bad manners and its customs are excellent. Its flowers almost always come clean and of good shape, and imbricated rather than pointed. Lasts well when cut, and in fact hasn't a bad feature. It has gained many Silver Medals for best blooms, and as it is easy to grow is strongly recommended to the small exhibitor. Makes a fair standard but does better, if anything, on dwarfs." [F-M] "Low-growing, small, not very hardy; foliage sufficient, black-spots; bloom moderate early and late, decreasing in hot weather, none in hottest." [ARA18/127] "Excellent mid-season variety; flowers large and full; does well." [NRS14/161]

Mrs. Wakefield Christie-Miller

McGredy, 1909

"Soft pearly blush, shaded salmon; outside of petal clear vermilion rose; loosely built with petals of good size." [Th] "Silvery pink shaded salmon; exterior light vermilion pink; flower very large, full, peony-shaped; very floriferous; very vigorous." [Cx] "Rosy carmine; outer petals soft pearly blush. Buds and flowers extremely large, borne perfectly erect on grand stems. Petals two-toned. Fine in every way." [CA17] "Inside of petals peachy blush, outside rose shaded vermilion. Flowers, large globular, irregular in outline, carried erect on short stiff stems. Striking colour, fragrant, and as an autumn bedding Rose it is unsurpassed. Most suitable for massing." [NRS21/64] "Blush, shaded salmon. The flowers open out like [those of] a big tree Paeony, and are most decorative. They are produced on erect, strong growths." [OM] "The deeper colour being on the outside of the petal and the lighter shade inside, respectively clear vermilion rose and soft blush shaded salmon—a very striking combination. Habit, very vigorous, branching and with good foliage. Flowers of an enormous size, as large as any of the Hybrid Teas, quite full, and retaining their colour well in the hottest sun. A remarkable decorative Rose." [NRS/10] "28 to 57 blooms per season." [ARA21/92] "Growth, fairly good; lacks in blooming; color and form not of best." [ARA18/117] "Tall, bushy, vigorous, hardy; foliage very plentiful, black-spots very much, bloom abundant, continuous." [ARA18/127] "Does especially well here [Denver, Colorado], especially in hot weather." [ARA24/95] "It will survive severe winters and seems to revel in summer heat. Its low habit makes it an ideal bedder ... The sweetly perfumed bloom on a stocky stem is large, with a heavy tuft of petals that look as if thrown in, thus giving an artistic touch. In color it is bright rosy pink, holding well. The plant is well clothed with ample and healthy foliage." [C-Ps29] "The large foliage is very ornamental and disease-resistant." [C-Ps27] "A laughing, tousle-headed pink Rose, so sturdy and dependable that it is a necessity in every garden. It is a stocky, stubby grower, with blunt canes bearing large bunches of big, fluffy flowers, bright rose and pearly pink. One of the very best for bedding, an exceptionally liberal bloomer, and very hardy. Its decidedly informal shape is its only handicap, but even that is pleasing. A Rose which grows in esteem more and more each year—a good friend and a jolly one." [C-Ps25]

[Mrs. Wallace H. Rowe]
McGredy, 1912

"Bright 'sweet pea mauve.' Flowers of good size and very well formed. Growth vigorous." [CA17] "Superb flower of remarkable coloration otherwise unknown among roses: bright mauve. The flower is superb in all ways, and is one of the most marvelous newcomers. Grows very well, and is very floriferous." [JR36/171] "Large, full, of good form. Growth perfect, free flowering. Distinct." [GeH]

Mrs. Walter Easlea
A. Dickson, 1910

"Glowing crimson-carmine, deepening to intense crimson-orange, back of petals satiny crimson, large, full, fragrant. Growth robust, vigorous and erect." [GeH] "Medium sized flowers of fair form, coloured carmine crimson; the flowers are good early and late, but in hot weather, and through August, there is too much rose in the crimson to be pleasing. The plant is a very fair grower, and I have picked a vase of it in a mild January, which illustrates its persistence in flowering." [NRS21/36] "Here we have a variety which is completely charming in both form and color. The growth is vigorous, with upright canes covered with beautiful dark green foliage. The flower is large,

full, solitary, and colored bright carmine, becoming orange when fully open, the backs of the petals being satiny crimson." [JR34/104] "Fairly good in growth and bloom when grown in 'special bed'." [ARA18/117] "Requires time to become established, then a good all-around rose." [Th]

Mrs. Wemyss Quin
A. Dickson, 1914
From 'Harry Kirk' (T) × ?

"Intense lemon-chrome, which is washed with a delicate, but solid, maddery orange, giving it a rare depth of color—virtually a golden orange, which, when open, becomes deep canary-yellow." [C&Js15] "The colour is a fine bright yellow, the leaves dark and glossy, and the growth excellent." [NRS20/93] "Lemon-chrome; moderate, spare." [ARA17/32] "Beautiful color; foliage wonderful in spring, lost early; only fair; shy bloomer." [ARA18/114] "The colour of the flowers varies from a canary yellow to a clear lemon chrome and sometimes approaches a golden yellow. The colour gets paler as the flowers open and is less good in autumn. Although I have seen the flowers grown large enough to take a place in an exhibition box, as a rule the flowers are only of medium and sometimes of small size. In form they leave somewhat to be desired, because, like nearly all Roses of this group, they are of the primitive type in which the petals get shorter towards the centre of the flower. The carriage of the flowers is good and they do not hang their heads. The foliage is a deep glossy green, practically unaffected by mildew, and though it is capable of invasion by black spot I have, down to the present, succeeded without much trouble in keeping my plants free from this disease. The glossy foliage is a feature of the variety, and a great addition to its value for bedding. The habit of the plant is good and fairly shapely ... The stems are armed with large thorns, reddish and somewhat translucent when young, the growth is more or less upright so that the plants may be placed fairly close together." [NRS22/49]

"It makes a strong, very branching bush, and, if planted where it can be allowed to develop, will make a plant 7- or 8-ft. high [ca. 2.3–2.6 m] and 4- or 5-ft. wide [ca. 1.3–1.6 m]. The foliage is dark green and glossy, not troubled with mildew, and very little affected by black spot, and it does not suffer from die back ... The flowers are very thin, rather small, and of poor form ... but they are decorative both in the bud and when further advanced ... They open rather too quickly, and are apt to fade to a paler tint in hot weather, and are somewhat liable to become spotted by rain." [NRS29/112] "Another good bedding rose, a fine grower, hardy, floriferous, and clean, is 'Mrs. Wemyss Quin', the best garden yellow of all I have tried, including 'Rayon d'Or' [Pern] and 'Constance' [Pern]." [ARA20/47] "The best yellow Rose since 'Mme. Ravary' [HT], and is useful both in the garden and for cutting. The foliage is a dark glossy green; the plant is a really good grower and flowers freely and continuously, giving no trouble; the flowers are of medium size and of tolerably good form, but do not retain it long; they are of a canary yellow colour throughout the summer and early autumn, but in late autumn, like so many yellow Roses, that colour seems to get washed out." [NRS21/49] "The leading yellow Rose in existence, and, with the exception of 'Lady Pirrie' [HT], the best hybrid tea of the last ten years ... Colour, chrome yellow. Very free flowering and excellent in autumn ... seen at its best on established plants two or three years old. It should be allowed to develop into a bush, having the old wood about two to three feet high [ca. 6 dm to 1 m]." [NRS21/64–65]

[My Maryland] Plate 61

Cook, 1908

From 'Madonna' (HT) × 'Enchanter' (HT).

"Flower bright salmon-pink with paler edges, free, fragrant. Vigorous." [GeH] "A grand pink variety that has come to the front with great strides. A splendid bloomer and superb rose." [CA10] "A very popular Rose on account of its beautiful form, color and free-flowering habit. Color is a lovely salmon-pink shade which lightens up beautifully as the flowers expand." [C&Js12] "Growth robust and very free flowering; flowers medium size, full; color bright salmon pink with paler edges; delightfully fragrant. Promises to be one of the most popular varieties in this country." [C&Js10] "Raised by Mr. John Cook of Baltimore, who has given us many now prominent Roses. His own admiration for this beautiful one is well shown by the name he gave it. But we honor still more his loyalty to his native State, for when offered a large sum of money by someone who wished the honor of giving this Rose another name, Mr. Cook refused the coin and held the name 'My Maryland'." [C&Js11]

Natalie Böttner Plate 65

Böttner, 1909

From 'Frau Karl Druschki' (HP) × 'Goldelse' (HT).

"Soft flesh to creamy yellow. Practically no disbudding." [Th] "Cream yellow, the superb blossom is held upright on its stem with a proud air, and is as large as [that of] 'K[aiserin] A[uguste] Viktoria' [HT]." [JR35/183] "This Rose is pure white and said to even excel '[Frau Karl] Druschki'. The shape of the flower is similar to [that of] 'Kaiserin Auguste Viktoria' and the blooms are borne on long, strong stems. Very choice." [C&Js12] "Soft flesh, becoming white with yellow base; odor slight. Bush medium. 18 blooms." [ARA26/95] "Large, full, perfectly formed. Growth vigorous, free." [GeH] "Pleasing in color and form, later tending to ball somewhat in wet weather; growth and bloom good." [ARA18/114] "Fair perfume; forty blooms throughout the season; growth well above the average. A good cut-flower." [ARA17/25] "Low-growing, slight, hardy; foliage sufficient, healthy; bloom moderate, intermittent." [ARA18/127]

Nederland

trans. "Netherlands"

Verschuren, 1919

From 'General-Superior Arnold Janssen' (HT) × 'George C. Waud' (HT).

"Deep red, very large, very full, tall." [Sn] "Flower large, full, double, beautiful red color. Vigorous." [ARA21/165] "Deep red. Moderate. Garden, bedding. Fragrant." [NRS23/insert] "Fine form, borne on strong flower stalks. Growth vigorous." [GeH] "Large, full, brilliant red. Blossom of good form. Growth strong and erect with healthy foliage. Valuable cutting and bedding rose." [Ck]

Nellie Parker

H. Dickson, 1916

"Pale creamy white, with deeper centre, frequently flushed with blush at the tips of the petals, large, very full, of beautiful form, freely and abundantly produced. Growth strong, vigorous, upright branching, large handsome foliage." [GeH] "Very full, perfect form, salmony centre; the bud comes out with a strong yellowish tint. This light tint gives a great delicacy to the colour of the bloom." [NRS19/121] "Attractive in color; somewhat lacking in growth and blooming." [ARA18/

114] "This is a very fine Rose, of vigorous upright growth, with dark olive-green foliage, which is mildew proof. The blooms, which are very large and of perfect shape, are freely produced on strong upright stems, and sweetly scented. The colour is a pale creamy flesh, with yellow at base, slightly tinted with pale pink on the tips of the petals. This is a beautiful variety, and in addition to its being a very fine exhibition Rose, it is also valuable for garden purposes." [NRS17/125]

Nelly Verschuren

Verschuren, 1918

"Light yellow, large, full, very fragrant, medium height." [Sn] "Clear yellow colouring; handsome foliage." [GeH]

Nerissa

W. Paul, 1912

"Creamy-yellow." [NRS13/171] "Pink, flushed carmine; buds cream, flushed salmon. Coloring resembles [that of] 'Antoine Rivoire' [HT]. Buds sharply short-pointed; open flowers have high center with reflexed outer petals." [CA17] "Creamy yellow, shaded with white, center tinted peach; very large, full, free and good." [C&Js16] "Cream, tinted white, darker in the center. Blossom very large, quite full, very graceful in form. Splendid for exhibition and magnificent for the garden. Vigorous." [JR36/103] "Creamy white flowers, full, and of fine form, lightly shaded with yellow and pale pink. A little-known Rose of excellent habit which deserves further trial." [C-Ps25] "Creamy white, tinted peach; large buds not opening well and blighted; black spot. 22 blooms." [ARA26/95] "Lightly scented, dwarf." [Sn] "A very fine, very large, full flower of good shape and firm petaled. Color is cream-white with peach-tinted center. Among the best in the light shades." [C&Js23] Nerissa, Portia's waiting-maid in Shakespeare's *The Merchant of Venice* (II:9) who reminds us of the thought-provoking advice that

> The ancient saying is no heresy, —
> Hanging and wiving goes by destiny.

Noblesse

McGredy, 1917

"Colour, apricot primrose-yellow, the outer portion of the petals being flushed deep pearl pink, tinged rose . . . Extra free flowering, carrying its blooms upright . . . Delicately sweet scented." [NRS17/173] "Light maize yellow petals, edged light rose. Not a strong grower." [NRS29/254] "A nicely formed primrose flower, with a touch of pink in the centre—a moderate grower." [NRS21/57] "Growth vigorous, very free flowering." [GeH] "A Rose of fine habit and great freedom. The blooms at times are large enough for exhibition, but specially good for decorative work. The colour is a combination of apricot and primrose, flushed with flesh-pink." [NRS16/145]

Nordlicht

trans. "Northern Light"

Kiese, 1910

From 'Mme. Caroline Testout' (HT) × 'Luciole' (T).

"Yellow, red center, large, semi-full, medium height." [Sn]

Oberbürgermeister Dr. Troendlin

Kaiser, 1904

Sport of 'Mme. Caroline Testout' (HT).

"Very delicate flesh pink." [Ÿ] "Light pink, large, very full, medium height." [Sn]

Ökonomierat Echtermeyer

Lambert, 1913

From 'Rose Benary' (HT) × ?

"Upright canes, vigorous. Flowers upright, in 3's on a long stem with large and strong petals, full, very large, deep carmine pink, shaded lighter, regular, fragrant, long-lasting; bud pointed. Very floriferous." [JR38/56] "Lacking in growth and blooming." [ARA18/117] "Regular form, fragrant, pointed buds. Growth vigorous, erect branching; very free." [GeH]

Ophelia   Plate 68

W. Paul, 1912

Seedling of 'Antoine Rivoire' (HT).

"Salmon flesh, shaded rose, with chamois center. Buds and flowers beautifully formed and color enhanced by rich veining on the petals. Stems long, carrying flowers erect. Could hardly be praised too highly." [CA17] "Salmon color, with pink reflections, perfect form, well-held—upright at the end of a long stem. Excellent for forcing and the garden." [JR36/103] "Salmon-flesh shaded rose . . . with a flush of pale apricot whilst in the opening stage . . . honey scent." [RP] "Fragrance quite marked for light-colored rose." [ARA18/114] "Fragrance, fair, very delicate; shape, very good in bud and open flower." [Th] "Chaste, maidenly, sweetly formed, and richly scented, its pearly blooms swaying on graceful stems, 'Ophelia' has been worshipped for many years by all lovers of good Roses . . . The plant grows tall, not bushy, and often throws up stout, branching canes bearing many flowers in long-stemmed bouquets . . . In hot weather, [the blossoms] are apt to be creamy white, while in cool autumn nights they develop rich tints of pink and shades of gold." [C-Ps27] "One unfurling bud on the desk fills one with awe and happiness. It is one of the most dependable bloomers and seldom has blackspot. In the early morning these creamy, pink-toned flowers with their high, deeper pink centers are lovely." [ARA31/99] "Brighter in autumn." [ARA26/95] "30 blooms a season." [ARA21/92] "Moderate, bushy." [ARA17/32] "Growth good; fine foliage; stem good; perfect form, lasts well; color beautiful." [ARA16/20] "Rather badly subject to stem fungus." [NRS29/115] "Foliage mildews slightly and may be lost by black-spot . . . In extreme heat, 'Ophelia' blasts in the bud." [Th2] "Blooms perfectly in our cool [Norwegian] summers." [ARA20/47] "Many admirers [in Houston, Texas]." [ET] "I cannot but feel that 'Antoine Rivoire' must have been very close to the place in the nursery from which that pod [containing the seed originating 'Ophelia'] was gathered." [ARA31/146] "Very few Ophelias are now grown in America, and most of the plants sold under that name really are 'Mme. Butterfly' from which bloom only an expert can tell 'Ophelia', but which is a better plant." [C-Ps30] "Charles H. Totty and I [E. G. Hill] went over there to see Mr. Paul, and I said to him, 'How many have you got of that?' 'Well,' he said, 'I have sold a good many of it.' I asked, 'How many can you let me have?' He said, 'Well, I am not going to let you have all I have. I have to keep some for my own trade.' I said, 'How many? Let's get down to business.' He said, 'About 300.' I was the happiest fellow in the world when I got those 300 over; but somebody put Mr. Eisele on it, and the Dreers had it in their catalogues, so I had to put 'Ophelia' on the market a year too soon. However, I have no cause to complain, because 'Ophelia' has been the mother of nearly all the good roses I have raised." [ARA22/131] "A favorite with everyone who grows it." [C&Js18] Ophelia, Hamlet's quondam girlfriend in Shakespeare's play. It is not true that Ophelia's remark "O, what a noble mind is here o'erthrown" (*Hamlet* III:1) was prompted by her perusal of early editions of *The Old Rose Adventurer* and *The Old Rose Advisor*.

Orange Killarney   Listed as 'Duchess of Wellington' (HT).

Othello

G. Paul, 1911

From ? × 'Gustav Grünerwald' (HT).

"Dark maroon red; most distinct; fragrant." [NRS11/197] "Dark crimson. Growth very vigorous." [GeH] "Deep red, large, full, light scent, medium height." [Sn] "Deep maroon. —Vigorous. —Garden." [Cat12/70] "Grows vigorously. Raised from the well-known 'Gustav Grünerwald', from which it takes its fragrance. Color, deep maroon red, like that of 'Charles Darwin' [HP]; the blossom is large and of beautiful form." [JR36/57] Othello, the Moor of Venice, Shakespeare's tragic figure whose "blood begins my safer guides to rule." [*Othello* II:3]

Otto von Bismarck

Kiese/J. C. Schmidt, 1908

From 'Mme. Caroline Testout' (HT) × 'La France' (B or HT).

"Pink, large, full, medium scent, medium height." [Sn] "Growth vigorous; of free branching habit, flowering freely and continuously; color somewhat like [that of] 'La France'; grand for massing; won over 'Frau Karl Druschki' [HP] in a contest for a prize of 3000 marks." [C&Js10] Prince Otto Eduard Leopold von Bismarck-Schönhausen, German Chancellor, lived 1815–1898.

P. L. Baudet

Lourens, 1915

From 'Veluwezoom' (HT) × 'Le Progrès' (HT).

Light pink, large, lightly double, light scent, medium height." [Sn] "Makes very large bushes, with lots of salmonpink blooms on very long stems." [ARA30/151]

[Papa Reiter]

Hinner/Ketten, 1900

Seedling of 'Mme. Caroline Testout' (HT).

"Cream tinted pink." [LS]

Paul Meunier

syn. 'Paul Monnier'

Buatois, 1902

"Straw yellow, strongly tinted salmon. —Flower very large, full, fragrant; floriferous; very vigorous." [Cx] "Strong stem, held on heavy wood, upright and strong . . . hardy and floriferous." [JR29/184] "Very vigorous with heavy, upright wood, handsome bronzy green foliage. Flower large, full, elongated bud." [JR26/178]

Paul Monnier   Listed as 'Paul Meunier' (HT).

[Perle von Godesburg]

Schneider, 1902

Sport of 'Kaiserin Auguste Viktoria' (HT).

"White tinted creamy yellow." [CA10] "A sport from and very much like 'Kaiserin Auguste Viktoria', only with more yellow in centre." [GeH] "Golden yellow, passing to light yellow. —Blossom large, full, fragrant; floriferous, vigorous." [Cx]

Pharisäer

trans. "Pharisee"

Hinner, 1901

Seedling of 'Mrs. W. J. Grant' (HT).

"Silvery pink, faintly suffused salmon. Petals unusually large and reflexed. Heavy fall bloomer." [CA17] "Pinkish yellow." [LS] "Large, full, whitish-pink with salmon-pink; fairly long-stalked, free-flowering." [Hn] "Buds long on stiff stems, of splendid texture, flower very large, rose colour shading to silver, with centre of salmon; very free." [P1] "The most perfect Rose in the garden; the blooms open in any weather; a good size, and when disbudded are very large." [NRS/14] "Very little disbudding." [Th] "A truly grand Rose; always in bloom; long pointed buds of delicious fragrance. Flesh-white flowers." [ARA22/xiv] "Opens somewhat loose but holds its center . . . Only fair foliage, but holds in long seasons. Fine, tall, fairly bushy growth . . . continuous bloomer." [Th2] "Large, silvery pink blooms with rosy tints in the center. It is not a very double Rose, but the bud is lovely, and the flower holds its shape well when fully open. The color seldom fades, and the light perfume is rather fleeting. The stems are long, slender, and not always sufficiently strong. A tall, rather bushy grower with slightly thin leaves, somewhat subject to black-spot, although often surprisingly resistant. A continuous, liberal bloomer, especially in the cooler parts of the country and in cool seasons. Hot weather causes it to open too quickly. The plant is very hardy. A deserving Rose, whose lack of fullness is its chief defect but one easily forgiven because of its other fine qualities." [C-Ps25] "Perfume mild . . . growth well above the average." [ARA17/22] "Low-growing, compact, hardy; foliage sufficient, black-spots somewhat; blooms free, continuous." [ARA18/127] "The flowers are carried erect and well above the foliage, and are sweet scented. Its strong points are the beautiful shape of its flowers and elongated buds, its good constitution and its autumnal blooming and erect habit. Its weak ones are not many, but it is too tall for an ideal bedder, and the substance of petal is rather thin." [NRS/12] "Vigorous and rather tall (4-ft. [ca. 1.3 m]) with a branching but erect habit. The young foliage is a beautiful red, getting greener with age, and it is not subject to mildew . . . It flowers very freely and continuously from the end of June till October . . . the flower, though nicely pointed, is not very full. The colour is somewhat difficult to describe. 'Rosy white, shaded pale salmon' . . . the centre is somewhat deeper . . . The buds are long and specially beautiful . . . It is a very beautiful garden Rose . . . though a fair-sized (often large) Rose, it never looks heavy . . . It has moderate fragrance. This is not perhaps everybody's Rose, but it is one of my chief favorites . . . The shade of colouring of the flowers is very delicate and they harmonise well with the foliage." [NRS/10] "A very pretty variety; its outstanding features are the vigor of its canes and the abundance of its bloom." [JR32/33]

[Pie X]

Hildebrand/Soupert & Notting, 1905

From 'Kaiserin Auguste Viktoria' (HT) × 'Mrs. W. J. Grant' (HT).

"Plant vigorous and bushy; bud very graceful and of magnificent form; flower large, very full, cupped; color, cream white passing to delicate pink, petals imbricated, edged very tender bright pink, center darker. Color extremely tender and full of grace. Floriferous, fragrant, good for forcing and cut flowers." [JR29/136]

Pierre Wattinne

Soupert & Notting, 1901

From 'Papa Gontier' (T) × an unnamed seedling.

"Deep pink, large, full, medium scent, medium height." [Sn] "Vigorous, handsome foliage; long bud; flower large, full, of a beautiful form; color, glossy cherry pink nuanced salmon yellow. Floriferous and fragrant." [JR25/162]

Pink American Beauty Listed as 'Mrs. Charles E. Russell' (HT).

Pink Gruss an Aachen Listed as 'Rosa Gruss an Aachen' (HT).

Pink Radiance Listed as 'Radiance' (HT).

Portia

W. Paul, 1910

"Flesh, shaded yellow in centre." [Cat12/70] "Deep reddish old rose. Though this variety varies in colour, it is always pleasing, and is especially good for massing." [NRS29/254] "The flowers are large, full, beautifully colored pink to the base of the petals, yellow at the center. Much to be recommended for pot-culture and exhibition." [JR34/85] "Light pink, middle yellow, large, full, medium height." [Sn] "Pale rose, base of petals and centre of flower shaded with yellow, large, full. Growth robust." [GeH] "Fair growth only; not a bloomer." [ARA18/117] Portia, the "rich heiress" of Shakespeare's *The Merchant of Venice* (IV:1) who points out that

> The quality of mercy is not strain'd;
> It droppeth as the gentle rain from heaven
> Upon the place beneath: it is twice bless'd;
> It blesseth him that gives and him that takes[.]

Keen rosarians might ponder replacing the word "mercy" with the word "fertilizer" in their copies of the play.

Premier

E. G. Hill, 1918

From an unnamed seedling (of 'Ophelia' [HT]) × 'Mrs. Charles E. Russell' (HT).

"Rose-red, large, full, medium scent, medium height." [Sn] "Rich dark pink—blues badly in heat; full; good form; blooms usually borne singly; fragrant." [Th2] "Pure rose-pink in summer, deep rose-pink in cooler weather, borne on stiff, thornless stems; deliciously fragrant. Growth free, like 'Ophelia', with good foliage." [GeH] "Very good, and given to producing large, high-centered flowers on long, stiff stems." [ARA25/132] "A magnificent novelty with splendid, double, large, fragrant flowers of rich, deep rose-color. It is practically thornless and is destined to become very popular." [C&Js20] "When 'Premier' is allowed to properly mature on the plant it is a wonderful rose. Its one fault is its liability to bruise in shipment . . . 'Premier' cut tight will never open." [ARA25/169] "A rich, dark pink, American-born Rose with fine, long buds and big, deep-petaled blooms. It is one of the most popular of cut-flowers, when grown by the florist, and always arouses enthusiasm when seen at its best in the garden. It is sweetly scented, of fine form, with splendid stems, but of quite varying performance outdoors. The color 'blues' badly in heat, and it seems to do best in the more northerly sections, where it is reported to be of fine growth and free-flowering. It has very few thorns, is reasonably hardy, and has fine foliage which needs protection from black-spot." [C-Ps25] "Large, fine form, double, fine fragrance, medium to medium-long stem. Foliage good, sufficient. Growth medium strong; hardy. Deep rose-pink." [ARA23/170] "Poor outdoors, but fine in the hothouse." [ARA23/139] "The best dark pink, and very widely grown." [ARA21/131] "The King of Pink Roses." [ARA19/v]

Président Vignet
Pernet-Ducher, 1911

"Brilliant red." [NRS13/26] "Vermilion red. Moderate. Garden." [NRS13/171] "Blossom large, quite full, bright red, fragrant, erect, with long stems. Valuable kind." [Ck] "Red, medium size, full, light scent, medium height." [Sn] "Growth vigorous, free branching." [GeH] "Bush of great vigor with usually unbranched canes; thorns not very protrusive; foliage gay green; blossom large, globular, full, usually solitary on a long stem; beautifully colored bright carmine red nuanced brilliant poppy-red. Excellent garden rose, robust, abundant bloom." [JR36/24]

Prima Donna Listed as 'Mme. P. Euler (HT).

Prince de Bulgarie
trans. "Prince of Bulgaria"
Pernet-Ducher, 1901

"Silvery flesh, shaded rosy salmon." [CA17] "Deep rosy flesh, shaded with salmon. Very little disbudding." [Th] "Pale tinted rose, shaded apricot. —Vigorous. —Garden, standard, bedding. —Variable in colour. Fragrant." [Cat12/51] "Large, full, elongated flowers, produced on long, strong stems, making this a splendid cut-flower. Color is silvery flesh, shaded deeper in center and tinted saffron-yellow." [C&Js24] "Occasional yellow tints; good form. Good growth and foliage. Fair for cutting. Only valuable in the North." [Th2] "Very vigorous; leaves large, bright green; bud long, very graceful; flower very large, quite full, in the form of an elongated cup; outer petals large; coloration superb, difficult to describe; silvery flesh pink, very delicately nuanced or shaded salmon and dawn-pink...form resembles that of 'Souvenir de Président Carnot' [HT]. Like it, 'Bulgarie' holds its blossoms on a strong and quite erect stem." [JR25/131] "Closely resembles 'Antoine Rivoire' [HT], than which it is much more free flowering. Long-petaled buds of pearly pink, flushed with salmon and yellow, on straight, wiry stems. An excellent Rose of variable color, being decidedly light pink early in the season, almost white in hot weather, and heavily shaded with golden yellow in the fall. It is sweetly fragrant, and good when cut; best in the cooler parts of the country, where the color is more intense and enduring. Grows tall and blooms well all summer." [C-Ps25] "There is a curious little fold of petals in the center to give it individuality, and the copperish colored new shoots are somewhat more pronounced in color in this rose than in its later relatives." [ARA29/69] "The special feature of 'Prince de Bulgarie' lies in the beauty of its young foliage, which is comparable to that of 'Gruss an Teplitz' [B]." [NRS22/61] "Medium height, bushy, hardy; foliage plentiful, black-spots somewhat; bloom moderate, almost continuous." [ARA18/127] "Badly attacked by black spot." [NRS12/91] "A very vigorous grower with large bright green foliage, flowers extra large and full, exquisite rosy flesh. Color very beautiful and sweet and a constant and abundant bloomer." [C&Js03]

"Growth vigorous and sturdy, but not tall[,] habit, bushy and spreading. Foliage good, rather glossy, reddish bronze when young,

and not subject to mildew. The flowers are produced from the end of June to the end of September, in my garden very freely at short intervals, but it is not a Rose from which one can expect to pick a flower every day in the summer. The flowers are carried fairly well on good, but not very stiff stems, and though not full enough for exhibition come a tolerable shape with petals of good substance. The colour varies considerably, sometimes, particularly in wet weather and autumn, they are a pale salmon flesh, and then much resemble a small 'Mme. Wagram [Comtesse de Turenne]' [HT], but the foliage is not so shiny. The typical flower, however, is a pale salmon yellow, and has a distinct orange shade, which is decidedly attractive, but to obtain this warm weather seems necessary. I have no doubt that it is a warm weather Rose, and I do not think it stands rain well, and the colour seems to get washed out at times in a bad year. The flowers last well in water (three days), and are particularly valuable for vases and decorative purposes generally. It makes a good garden Rose, and a fair bedding Rose, and should be more often grown for this purpose than one sees it. It is fragrant, and though not remarkably so the scent, such as there is, is sweet and pleasing. A bed of this Rose makes a good companion to one of '[Monsieur] Joseph Hill.'" [NRS10/39]

Prince Englebert Ch. d'Arenberg
Soupert & Notting, 1909
From 'Étoile de France' (HT) × 'Richmond' (HT).

"Color, shining scarlet shaded purple, noble and distinct. Flowers very large, irreproachably regular with strong petals. Buds elegant, held fairly upright. Good vigor. Fragrant." [JR33/183] "Large, full, sweet. Growth vigorous, very free." [GeH] "Not one of the best reds in growth and blooming qualities, but attractive as a cut-flower, and so retained." [ARA18/114]

Princesse Vera Orbelioni
A. Schwartz, 1908
From 'Kaiserin Auguste Viktoria' (HT) × 'Sénateur Saint-Romme' (HT).

"Whitish salmon pink, large, full, medium height." [Sn] "Cream white, nuanced carmine pink. —Blossom large, full, very floriferous; very vigorous." [Cx] "Vigorous, flower large, full, well formed, opens well, pretty bud, salmony creamy white nuanced salmon pink. Very floriferous." [JR32/136]

Prinses Juliana
Leenders, 1918
From 'General MacArthur' (HT) × 'Marie Van Houtte' (T).
"Deep red, medium size, full, very fragrant, medium height." [Sn]

Prinzessin Hildegard von Bayern
Lambert, 1914
From 'Frau Karl Druschki' (HP) × 'Franz Deegan' (HT).
"Yellowish white, very large, very full, medium scent, tall." [Sn] "Clear yellow, sometimes pure sulphur-yellow in the centre, changing to cream-yellow, large and full, of good substance, produced on stiff stems; perfumed. Growth vigorous, upright and free branching." [GeH]

Prinzessin Marie
Lindemann, 1907
From 'Mme. Caroline Testout' (HT) × 'Mme. Mélanie Willermoz' (T).
"Light pink, large, full, medium height." [Sn]

Queen Mary

A. Dickson, 1913

"Bright canary yellow—crayoned carmine. Fair amount of disbudding."[Th] "Creamy ground, brilliantly penciled and flushed cerise, with an underlying shade of yellow. Combination of colors is wonderful and almost impossible to describe. Buds are long and pointed, with an unusual spiral form and recurved tips. Open flowers are semi-double, loose and spreading, medium sized, fragrant and freely borne." [CA17] "The colors are zoned deep, bright canary-yellow on plenteous, shell-shaped petals, which are crayoned with pure deep carmine, the crayoning giving a gloriously warm coloring as the yellow and carmine do not commingle. Tea perfumed." [C&Js14] "Carmine-rose-yellow, rose predominating; odor sweet; opens full out; short stems; does not hold up head well. Low and bushy. 34 blooms." [ARA26/96] "Very dark canary yellow. The petals are shell-shaped, and bordered deep carmine; the flower is globular. The very fetching perfume is that of the primrose; the leaves are bronzy apple green." [JR37/106] "It is absolutely distinct among Roses—in its wonderful combination of beautiful shades of pink and yellow—the yellow is bright and clear, the pink soft and blush like in appearance. Excellent habit of growth and very free and perpetual flowering . . . I saw no traces of mildew on the plants. The flowers are medium-sized, but of exquisite shape, with quite a good point and a good number of petals for its size." [NRS13/154] "Remarkable color; fair in growth, form, bloom; hardiness varies." [ARA18/118] "A collector's rose. Weak growth; beautiful color . . . very fragrant; eight blooms in 1915." [ARA16/21] "I am now prepared to . . . express the bold opinion that it is the most beautiful of all Roses . . . It is purely a garden Rose, of dwarf rather than vigorous habit, free flowering and fragrant. Its lovely blending of colours is quite unique amongst Roses, a very bright shade of canary yellow, suffused with bright pink, the latter colour being laid on in a quite distinct fashion . . . It will be very popular for table decoration, as it looks particularly well under electric light." [NRS14/148]

Radiance

syn. 'Pink Radiance'

J. Cook/Henderson, 1908

From 'Enchanter' (HT) × 'Cardinal' (HT).

"Soft carmine pink. Flowers large, elongated cup-shaped; very double and sweetly scented." [CA17] "Carmine, shaded salmon and coppery red. Garden." [NRS15/151] "Brilliant rosy-carmine displaying beautiful opaline pink tints in the open flower." [C&Js11] "Carmine-rose; tall, bushy." [ARA17/31] "Light silver flesh to salmon pink . . . tends to blue slightly . . . shape, only fair . . . growth very strong . . . splendid constitution . . . the best pink rose in cultivation today [1920]." [Th] "Globular-shaped flower of even pink . . . Succeeds everywhere; always in bloom." [ARA22/xiv] "Blooms medium to large . . . Lasts well . . . slightly subject to mildew and [black] spot . . . average of 51 blooms per season." [ARA21/91] "A hot weather rose." [ARA24/95] "We can depend on it for blossoms at all times. While the form is not always good, nevertheless it is never so poor that it doesn't add to a bouquet . . . strong, disease-resisting plant." [ARA31/99] "Fine strong growth and apparently good constitution . . . The colour is a deep pink, possibly tinged red, not a clear pink, and the form of the flower is not specially good." [NRS21/44–45] "The form is fine; flower large and full with cupped petals. Splendid healthy foliage." [C&Js12]

"Foliage very abundant, blackspots slightly; bloom free, continuous all season." [ARA18/127] "A beauty both novel and remarkable. Its foliage is luxuriant; the plant, bushy, with voluptuous foliage, freely bearing buds emerging above the plant, everblooming . . . The blossoms have large rounded petals and long stems, are upright, and are of a brilliant carmine-lake, resembling a pretty 'Mme. Abel Chatenay' [HT]; the coppery shadings and gradations of red and yellow contrast strongly. These remarkable characteristics are accompanied by a sweet fragrance and extended bloom . . . beautiful and productive in Fall, and, up till now, healthy." [JR34/76] "Foliage little affected by disease and holds in long growing seasons. Remarkably strong growth and good stem—sometimes weak neck . . . especially fine in warm conditions. Severe damp and cold wind discolors outer petals . . . Considered by J. H. McFarland, Editor of *American Rose Annual*, to be, with its sports ('Red Radiance' and 'Mrs. Charles Bell'), the best American-raised garden HT." [Th2] "Too much cannot be said of 'Radiance' as an own-root subject. In my garden I have found this splendid variety more than satisfactory. No matter what weather conditions prevail, 'Radiance' may be depended upon to produce a goodly number of blooms from early summer to late fall." [ARA20/156]

"The best and most popular pink Rose in America . . . The fragrant flowers are large, globular but not compact, brilliant rose-pink, with lighter tints on the inner surface of the petals. The shapely, big buds are borne on long stems and open slowly. Wet weather sometimes interferes with the opening of the flowers. The plant grows tall and bushy, throwing up bud after bud with the utmost freedom. The foliage is disease-resistant, and the plant is one of the hardiest." [C-Ps25] "Valuable because of its all-round worth and wonderful constitution. Particularly notable for fragrance, strong growth, and very good blooming qualities." [ARA18/114] "It was with a dry chuckle that he [Cook] recorded for us the fact that he sold the entire stock of 500 plants to Peter Henderson for $500—probably the highest price ever paid for an outdoor rose, though that was not what Mr. Henderson bought it for, but rather for its greenhouse value." [ARA26/32]

[Radiance Sport]

Originator unknown, pre-1919

Sport of 'Radiance' (HT).

"Milky white, with delicate blush center. It is semi-double and very beautiful, especially in the half-open bud, but has not shown the amount of bloom of its parent." [ARA19/47]

Red Admiral

W. Paul, 1913

"Cerise red. Garden, bedding." [NRS15/151] "Color, bright cerise red; produces great quantities of very large blossoms. This variety grows very vigorously." [JR37/89] "[Flowers] large and handsome, produced in masses. Growth vigorous." [GeH] "Medium size, semi-double, good form, slight fragrance, medium stem. Foliage sufficient, slight [black] spot. Growth very low, bushy; hardy." [ARA23/171] "Good color and growth; fair bloomer; form not of best, not so satisfactory as other reds of same type." [ARA18/118]

[Red Chatenay]

Breeder unknown, pre-1910

"Red." [CA10] *Cf.* the extinct 'Crimson Chatenay' (Merryweather, 1915): "Very similar to the favourite variety 'Mme. Abel Chatenay'

[HT], from which it is a seedling; the colour is a beautiful bright crimson, fragrant." [GeH]

Red Cross

A. Dickson, 1916

"Orange-crimson-scarlet, Tea Rose perfume. Growth vigorous, erect, floriferous; vigorous bronzed branching wood, with waxy leathery foliage." [GeH] "Appears to be a more double 'Red-Letter Day' [HT]." [ARA18/133] "Notable for its very bright flowers of a light scarlet crimson, which stand sun better than most crimsons. They are, however, rather thin and not of perfect form. The plant is a fairly good but not a big grower." [NRS21/55]

Red-Letter Day

A. Dickson, 1914

"Scarlet crimson, semi-single, with rich golden stamens, retaining its colour throughout. Active of habit, continuous in flowering, and good in autumn. In the mass a glorious piece of colour." [NRS21/66] "A fiery crimson which does not fade or burn. It is very free-flowering and its season continuous." [NRS18/139] "An exceedingly beautiful, semi-double Rose, of infinite grace and charm. Its velvety, brilliant, glowing scarlet-crimson buds and fully opened, cactus-like flowers never fade." [C&Js15] "Semi-double, scarlet-crimson flowers which hold their color. Plant of upright habit, and the most vigorous grower of all the single class thus far tried. A really valuable rose." [ARA18/133] "A very fine decorative garden Rose this. The rows of it at Newtownards could be picked out half a mile away, so free flowering and bright its colouring ... not much more than semi-double; ... free branching habit ... notwithstanding its glorious crimson colouring, fragrance is not so pronounced as one would have wished." [NRS14/149–150] "Very free, cheerful and continuous but has no fragrance." [NRS23/55] "Semi-double, fine form, medium to large size, slightly fragrant, medium to medium-long stems. Fine foliage, sufficient. Growth strong; hardy. Brilliant scarlet with slight crimson tone." [ARA23/171] "Glowing scarlet-crimson—very brilliant and intense color; bud long and pointed; open flower, loose, few petals, good size and color; no fragrance. Foliage seldom has mildew, but is susceptible to black-spot. Upright growth; stems thin but fairly strong. A splendid bedding rose, but with little or no cutting value ... Very continuous bloomer—forty blooms in Central Zone ... ('K. of K.' [HT] is much the same in color, has some fragrance, and is possibly a better grower ...)." [Th2] "The flowers are carried on rather thin stalks, but being light the stalks are sufficient to support them. A long stem is thrown up, carrying a terminal flower, secondary flowering shoots of fair length afterwards appearing down the stem. Several of these long shoots are usually produced, giving the plant a good bushy habit which is quite satisfactory for bedding purposes ... It has very little, if any, fragrance ..." [NRS22/56] "Velvety, brilliant, glowing scarlet-crimson, opening to medium-sized curiously cactus-shaped flowers, which do not fade or burn in the sun, as the reflex of the petals is satiny crimson scarlet colourings devoid of blue or magenta, semi-double. Growth erect and free-branching; free and continuous flowering throughout the season." [GeH] "Moderately tall, bushy, hardy; foliage plentiful, black-spots slightly; bloom almost free, continuous." [ARA18/127] "The plant grows well and is of branching though upright habit, but requires careful watching to prevent the occurrence of black spot ... fairly tall habit." [NRS21/50]

Red Radiance

Gude Bros., 1916

Sport of 'Radiance' (HT).

"Brilliant cerise-red." [C-Ps28] "Clear cerise-red which does not fade. Makes a large, double bloom." [C&Js21] "Does not bloom quite so freely as 'Radiance'." [C-Ps34] "Beautiful color and is little affected by hot weather." [ARA19/46] "Lighter in heat." [Th2] "Dark, rich red ... quite fragrant; fine form; lasting about five days ... Growth vigorous ... average 45 blooms." [ARA21/91] "Red; tall, bushy." [ARA17/32] "Moderate height, compact, hardy; foliage very abundant, black-spots very slightly; bloom free, continuous." [ARA18/127] "Plant an entire bed of this vigorous, healthy rose, and you can depend upon having abundant, deliciously fragrant and handsome blooms for cutting from June until frost." [C&Js24] "Large to very large, fragrant, double, of fine cupped form, medium to long stems. Fine foliage, sufficient. Growth very strong; hardy. Clear dark cerise-red." [ARA23/171–172] "Its big, bouncing blooms of cerise-red endear this Rose to all lovers of the Queen of Flowers ... It is a spendthrift bloomer, and the buds are particularly fine in the half-open state, although the globular center has been known to ball. The flowers are quite good for cutting, but also endure well in the garden and hold their color. The fragrance is sweet, and fairly strong. Growth is exceptionally fine, equaling, if not better than, the famous 'Radiance' of which our 'Red Radiance' is the better one of two sports. It is dependably hardy, and while not entirely immune, the foliage is resistant to disease." [C-Ps25] "A dark, rich red, darker than Pierson's [rival 'Red Radiance'; *see below*] ... Large to extra-large flowers; quite fragrant; fine form; lasting about five days. Foliage fine, sufficient. Growth vigorous, bushy; medium to long stems, stronger than [those of] 'Radiance'. Free-blooming, average 45 blooms when pruned to 6 eyes. Hardy." [ARA21/91] "No other can take the place of this rose in the garden. The sturdiness of its growth, the splendid, heavy, green foliage, and its freedom of bloom must give it first place, and the blossoms themselves are handsome ... while I generally prefer a high-pointed center, these large, tulip-like blossoms, in their setting of dark green, command unfailing admiration." [ARA29/70]

[Red Radiance]

Pierson, 1916

Sport of 'Radiance' (HT).

"Clear rich red." [ARA21/91] "Differs from [Gude's 'Red Radiance'] only in color, a lighter shade of cerise-red." [ARA23/172] "Though not as deep and clear in color as Gude's, [Pierson's 'Red Radiance'] seems, in my garden, to be just a little freer in bloom." [ARA26/58]

Red Star

Verschuren, 1918

"Brilliant crimson-red. A Rose that is enthusiastically praised in Europe." [C-Ps26] "A very brilliant scarlet-red, vigorous grower." [NRS18/154] "Blossom giant-sized, semi-double, most beautiful fully open, quite flame-red. Plant unusually floriferous." [Ck] "Red, large, semi-full, medium scent, medium height." [Sn] "The very long buds are most attractive and the open, semi-double flower is vivid but not flashy. The blooms do not flatten out like most few-petaled Roses. A free bloomer which holds its color well." [C-Ps27] "The blooms flatten out like most few-petaled Roses. Plant grows tall and the foliage is good." [C-Ps28] "Fire red, medium; foliage like [that of] 'Général

Red Star *continued*

Jacqueminot' [HP]." [GeH] "To those who love the silkiness and brilliancy of the oriental poppy, this Rose should have a particular appeal." [C-Ps29]

Reine Carola de Saxe

trans. "Queen Carola of Saxony"

Gamon, 1902

"Flesh-pink, large, full, sweet-scented, elongated bud. Growth vigorous, continuous flowering." [GeH] "Vigorous, flower large, full, very well formed, flower solitary, beautiful delicate silvery pink on a deep salmony pink ground, fragrant . . . Dedicated to the memory of the great care exercised by Her Majesty on behalf of an ill, restless gentleman of Lyon at the town of Strehlen in Saxony, 1870–1871 [*during, it should be noted, the Franco-Prussian War; the "ill, restless gentleman of Lyon" is undoubtedly Gamon himself*]." [JR26/147] Not to be confused with, or indeed to be confused with, 'Königin Carola von Sachsen' (HT).

Reine des Couleurs   Listed as 'Farbenkönigin' (HT).

Reine Marguerite d'Italie

trans. "Queen Marguerite of Italy"

Soupert & Notting, 1904

From 'Baron Nathaniel de Rothschild' (HP) × 'Mme. la Princesse de Bessaraba de Brancovan' (T).

"Bright carmine red, center vermilion. A vigorous grower. Flowers large, full, and good form. Very floriferous." [C&Js11] "Deep carmine, medium, full, sweet. Growth vigorous, branching, very floriferous." [GeH] "One of the most reliable of roses, has a large, double, red flower of good shape and fragrance. Healthy and blooms all the time." [ARA29/49] "Vigorous, handsome dark green foliage; the bud is magnificently formed, and held proudly above the foliage. Blossom very large, very full, of great beauty, and of excellent poise. Color, shining carmine red, the center brightened with vermilion red . . . literally covered with blossoms and buds throughout the season. Centifolia fragrance." [JR28/153]

Reine Mère d'Italie

trans. "Queen Mother of Italy"

Bernaix, 1910

"A very new yellow." [JR35/183] "Deep yellow. Vigorous. Garden." [NRS13/172] "Medium-sized, distinct, apricot-ochre-yellow blooms, sometimes showing pink markings. Foliage well retained. Recommended." [ARA28/104] "Small in growth; poor in color." [ARA18/118] "The bush is vigorous and semi-upright, richly clad in strong, shiny foliage. The bud, of beautiful ovoid form, is borne on a rigid, upright stem, extremely beautiful while opening—a seductive apricot ochre yellow. The blossom of nice size and moderate fulness opens well; color, also apricot ochre yellow, washed Nilson pink at the center, somewhat resembling the shade of 'Soleil d'Or' [Pern] . . . Very floriferous." [JR34/151] What with its "shiny" foliage and blossom-coloration, this could well be a Pernetiana.

Renée Wilmart-Urban

Pernet-Ducher, 1907

"Salmon-flesh; edges of petals carmine. Disbud." [Th] "Flowers large and full." [C&Js10] "Vigorous. —Garden, bedding. —A beautiful rose." [Cat12/52] "Growth very vigorous, beautiful light green foliage, long bud, flower large, full, graceful in form; color salmon incarnadine, petal edges bordered and nuanced bright carmine . . . Excellent garden rose." [JR31/23]

[Rhea Reid]   Plate 62

E. G. Hill, 1908

From 'American Beauty' (HP) × a red seedling.

"Rich, dark, velvety red; full, double flowers of good form, and as fragrant as 'La France' [B or HT]. A rose of great excellence." [CA10] "It is a rich red, very double, fine form and a constant bloomer." [C&Js09] "Splendid form; rich cherry-crimson." [C&Js15] "Flower deep crimson, with full centre, an improved 'Lady Battersea' [HT]. Growth vigorous and free." [GeH] "Coloration varying with the temperature from cerise pink in Summer to 'Richmond' [HT] red when forced in Winter; flowers large, full, very abundant, opening perfectly well in Winter, as large and full as those of 'Mme. Ferdinand Jamin' [HP, but doubtless meaning 'American Beauty']. Easy to grow, and upright in stature." [JR33/54]

[Richmond]

E. G. Hill, 1905

From 'Lady Battersea' (HT) × 'Liberty' (HT).

"Bright crimson." [CA07] "Scarlet, lightly shaded crimson." [CA17] "Pure red scarlet. At times varies greatly. Fragrant." [Th] "Bright light crimson. —Vigorous . . . Fragrant. Very free flowering." [Cat12/53] "Scarlet crimson; flower large, full, fragrant; blooms continuously; very vigorous." [Cx] "Very small in heat and its form is flat; fragrant." [Th2] "Too single (many better reds)." [ARA25/105] "Continuous bloom . . . gorgeous in the spring and fall, although they fade and blue in the sun, and the midsummer blooms are not very attractive." [ARA29/70] "'Richmond' is still the most popular rose for Christmas; the color is just right, being wonderfully brilliant . . . Richmond's chief handicap is that it opens too quickly in the summer." [ARA16/116] "The plants require a lot of disbudding to get the flowers at their best, the August blooming is not altogether satisfactory, as the colour is apt to 'blue' somewhat in hot sun, and the growth and foliage, though fair, are not so good as with 'Mrs. [Edward] Powell' [HT]. The fragrance is good but not equal to that of 'Hugh Dickson' [HP]." [NRS23/54] "Brilliant color; fairly good growth; blooming qualities good on Multiflora [understock]; not dependable; varies greatly; seldom grown well." [ARA18/118] "Pure scarlet-red, large, fairly full, generally carried single on long and stiff stems, sweetly perfumed. Growth vigorous, free." [GeH] "The roses are generally solitary and . . . develop of long, firm, and erect stems. The foliage . . . is a dark green . . . the color of this variety, which is delicately perfumed, is a bright scarlet crimson." [JR28/182] "Another florist's rose, like 'Mme. Abel Chatenay' [HT]." [JR37/171] "Moderately high, compact, and hardy; foliage abundant, black-spots some; bloom moderate, continuous spring and fall, almost continuous in midsummer." [ARA18/127] "Delightful . . . more continuously produced with me than those of any other Rose in my garden . . . a most grateful and refreshing perfume." [NRS/12] "This Rose makes but moderate growth with stems rather twiggy and thin, in habit rather a poor bush, not very hardy. The foliage is nice when young and only of fair substance, but clean and little affected by mildew. The flowers are carried splendidly erect and well above the foliage in a way that is quite remarkable considering their thin stems. The flowers are produced most freely . . . the bud and half opened flowers are very beautiful, and the summer flowers come an almost perfect shape . . . bright crimson without any trace of purple . . . It flowers so much that it seems almost to flower itself to death, and the plants are apt to dwindle away . . . I was inclined to think it a weakly edition of 'Liberty'." [NRS/10] "Has the drawback that it wants continual disbudding if the later flowers are to be of any individual beauty. In June it will produce many really lovely flowers, and it is constantly in bloom. It seems to prefer a light soil." [NRS21/111–112] "E. G. Hill, of Richmond, Indiana." [ARA16/47]

Ricordo di Geo Chavez

trans. "In Memory of Geo Chavez"
Gaetano, Bonfiglioli & figlio, 1911
From 'Kaiserin Auguste Viktoria' (HT) × 'La France de 89' (Cl HT).
    "Rose-red, large, full, tall." [Sn]

Ricordo di Giosue Carducci

syn. 'Souvenir de Giosue Carducci'; trans., "In Memory of Giosue Carducci"
Gaetano, Bonfiglioli & figlio, 1909
From 'Anna Olivier' (T) × 'La France de '89' (Cl HT).
    "Whitish pink, very large, very full, medium height." [Sn] "Blossom enormous, very double, opens well; exterior petals very large, reflexed, blush white nuanced 'La France' pink, bordered light bright pink; interior petals small, peachblossom pink, reverse of petals satiny and darker in color; musk scent particularly strong in Fall. Bud large, round, often solitary, on an erect stem 50–80 cm long [ca. 20–32 in]. Very vigorous and very floriferous." [JR33/182]

Rosa Gruss an Aachen

syn. and trans. 'Pink Gruss an Aachen'
Spek, 1930
Sport of 'Gruss an Aachen' (HT).
    "Yellowish pink, large, full, moderate height." [Sn]

Rosalind Orr English

E. G. Hill, 1905
From 'Mme. Abel Chatenay' (HT) × 'Papa Gontier' (T).
    "Bright scarlet pink." [CA10] "Salmon pink, large, full, medium height." [Sn] "Growth vigorous . . . ; flower large, very full, well held, and long-lasting; color, cherry pink." [JR30/26]

Rose Benary

Lambert, 1908
From 'Ferdinand Batel' (HT) × 'Liberty' (HT).
    "Pink, yellow center, large, full, medium scent, medium to tall." [Sn]

Rose d'Espérance

trans. "Rose of Hope"
Verschuren, 1918
    "Dark red to deep black colour, after the style of 'Château de Clos-Vougeot', of medium size." [GeH] "Deep red, small, full, dwarf." [Sn]

Rose Marie

Dorner, 1918
From 'Hoosier Beauty' (HT) × 'Sunburst' (Pern).
    "Clear rose-pink, long shapely buds, good form. Growth free." [GeH] "Well-formed buds; lovely, fragrant flowers of gleaming pink." [ARA29/96] "Most lovely, with such a perfect shape and clean color,

and very free-flowering." [ARA25/132] "A very free spring bloomer and fair bloomer all season. Strikingly fine in bud, and fragrant." [ARA29/88] "Mildly fragrant." [C-Ps29] "Good, but in hot weather it could have a few more petals. The color keeps well, and the bud is pointed and large." [ARA24/108] "Bright rose-pink, nearly solid color; fine shape; often quite large; fragrant. Foliage almost free of mildew. Growth and stem both good. Thirty-one flowers in Spokane . . . Strongly recommended for southern California, and for Washington State . . . , and for New Mexico . . . No mildew in 1923, no black-spot, and does not lose its foliage early." [Th2] "Light rose pink . . . strong perfume. A good grower, that is suitable alike for Exhibition and decorative purposes." [NRS29/254] "Beautiful form, especially in the bud. A lovely, clear pink which varies in shade according to the weather but is always pleasing. It resists black-spot and winters well." [ARA31/98] "A big, splendid American Rose in all phases; the buds are long, smooth, and delicately curved; the open flowers exquisitely pointed and clear rose-pink, unmixed with other shades. Both buds and blooms are fine for cutting, being borne on long stems which are not always erect, and sometimes a trifle weak. The plant grows vigorously, is of branching habit, not very thorny, and is both hardy and healthy. It blooms with remarkable freedom and opens its flowers well." [C-Ps25] "Not very vigorous." [C-Ps28] "Good, but the growth is not all that could be desired." [ARA26/209] "Bud large, globular; flower very large, cupped, double, borne singly on long stem; fragrant. Color clear rose-pink. Foliage abundant, glossy dark green, large; disease resistant. Vigorous grower of upright habit; produces a profusion of bloom during July and August." [ARA20/134] "The foliage is good; the plant of medium height and spreading. Makes a good bedder." [C-Ps30] "Considered the best bedding Rose in this color." [C&Js22]

[Rose Queen]

E. G. Hill, 1911
    "Color is much the same shade of pink as [that of] 'Mme. Caroline Testout' [HT], with yellow at base of petals. Buds very beautifully formed and intensely colored; borne on long stems. Particularly fine for cutting." [CA13] "Vigorous plant with erect canes; floriferous. Bud long and pointed, borne on a long stem. Blossom opens well, intense pink, nubs of petals yellowish." [JR36/89] The Rose Queen, monarch of the Tournament of Roses that takes place New Year's Day in beautiful Pasadena, California.

Rosemary

E. G. Hill, 1907
    "Light pink, very large, very full, medium height." [Sn] "Deep carmine, reverse of petals permeated old gold, medium size, abundant and continuous, delightful bush or pillar Rose with sweet scent. Growth vigorous." [GeH]

Rosita Mauri

Ketten, 1913
From 'Mme. Abel Chatenay' (HT) × 'Étoile de France' (HT).
    "Pink." [Ÿ] "Pure brilliant Nilsson pink, large, full, fragrant; long bud, opening well; stem long, firm, and erect. Growth vigorous, floriferous." [JR37/184] "Pure deep rose-pink, large, full, sweetly scented, elongated bud, produced singly on long and stiff stems. Growth vigorous, erect, free flowering." [GeH] "Fairly good bloomer; tall grower; color and form good, not of best. Useful decorative." [ARA18/114]

Rostelfe Listed as 'Rotelfe' (HT).

[Rotelfe]
syn. 'Rostelfe'; trans., "Red Elf"
Tantau, 1922
Sport of 'Château de Clos-Vougeot' (HT).

"Blackish red, mid-sized, healthy growth. Cutting and forcing rose. Quite out of the ordinary; floriferous." [Ck] "Has very dark blackish semi-double blooms very freely produced; it is a good garden rose." [ARA24/109] "Bud medium size, ovoid; flower medium size, full, double, globular, lasting; scarlet, overlaid and mottled maroon, like 'Château de Clos-Vougeot'; borne, several together, on long stem. Foliage dark bronzy green. Vigorous, upright; free, intermittent bloomer. An upright-growing 'Château de Clos-Vougeot'." [ARA23/154] "Of moderate, branching growth; foliage quite small; stems stiff; blooms small to medium . . . *Maine*; The rose is much like 'Château de Clos-Vougeot' but a little brighter. Upright grower, and flowers constantly in clusters on strong stems. I like it. Bore 26 blooms . . . *R.I.*; Profuse bloom in June, but practically a 'dud' afterward. Not as beautiful as 'Château', and hardly worth bothering with." [ARA28/186]

Rübezahl
Krüger, 1917
From 'Julius Fabianics de Misefa' (T) × 'Mrs. W. J. Grant' (HT).
"Red, large, full, light scent, tall." [Sn]

Ruhm der Gartenwelt
trans. "Glory of the Garden-World"
Jacobs/Lambert, 1904
From 'American Beauty' (HP) × 'Francis Dubreuil' (T).
"Brilliant fiery red." [Ÿ] "Very vigorous, blooms profusely, giving globular blossom, a non-bluing blood red." [JR28/166]

Sachsengruss
trans. "Saxon Greeting"
Neubert/Hoyer & Klemm, 1912
From 'Frau Karl Druschki' (HP) × 'Mme. Jules Gravereaux' (Cl HT).
"Pink." [Ÿ] "Delicate flesh on a white ground. Center blush with China pink reflections. Form and placement of the blossoms just like those of 'Frau Karl Druschki' [HP]." [JR37/10] "Do you know the rose 'Sachsengruss'? Here [Brazil] it is huge, with thick texture, semi-double, and just the color of a baby's skin, or a pink geode. It seems to bloom only on the tips of canes or branches, and has no side buds, so that we must wait for new, long canes to get flowers." [ARA29/199] "Large, full. Growth similar to [that of] 'Frau Karl Druschki'." [GeH] "Blossom giant-sized, sufficiently full, lasting, on long stem, tender flesh-pink colored on a lighter ground. Plant big, strong-growing . . . with beautiful leaves. Splendid rose." [Ck]

Seabird
H. Dickson, 1913
"Clear primrose yellow, paling with age to creamy yellow, medium, of fine form and good substance, produced on long upright stems. Growth vigorous and free branching; flowering freely and continuously." [GeH] "Low-growing, slender, moderately hardy; foliage plentiful, black-spots somewhat in midsummer; bloom moderate, intermittent." [ARA18/127] "Growth vigorous, with strong, slender canes;

extremely floriferous. Blossom medium-sized or large, of elegant form, light primrose yellow. This new variety is a splendid garden rose." [JR37/58]

[Sénateur Saint-Romme]
A. Schwartz, 1904
"Salmon on a pink ground." [LS] "Vigorous bush; foliage icy green, tinted purple; blossom large, full, well formed, opening well, well held, solitary; color, coppery salmony China pink, nuances carminy saffron, on a golden yellow ground; bud, light red. Floriferous. Beautiful variety." [JR28/154]

[Sensation]
J. H. Hill, 1922
From 'Hoosier Beauty' (HT) × 'Premier' (HT).
"Type, 'Hoosier Beauty'. Bud very large, long-pointed; flower very large (5 inches across [ca. 1.25 dm]), open, double (36 petals), very lasting; borne singly on long, strong stems; moderate fragrance. Scarlet-crimson, with maroon markings (like 'Château de Clos-Vougeot' [HT]). Foliage dark green. Free branching; profuse bloomer." [ARA23/175] "Mildews so badly that it makes a record for that and beats poor 'Killarney' [HT]." [ARA26/121]

September Morn
Dietrich & Turner, 1915
Sport of 'Mme. P. Euler' (HT).
"The bloom: Color, silvery pink; bloom size, 4–5 in [ca. 1–1.25 dm]; bloom style, high-centered, many-petaled, like a more rounded 'Mlle. de Sombreuil'; petals, 100–150 (just counted a swollen bud to confirm); fragrance, intense sweet damask with citrus overtones; remontancy, profuse, near-continuous bloom, still at it in December in northern California. The plant: Form, spreading, up to 6 ft tall [ca. 2 m] and 4 ft wide [ca. 1.3 m]; foliage, dull gray-green, 5-leaflet leaves, reddish green canes, reasonably full form; small, straight prickles of various sizes, rounded leaflets. Standard: Makes a very effective 4 ft standard [ca. 1.3 m]. Environment and culture: Enjoys hot weather. Plant in hot spot in the garden. Needs budding to a vigorous rootstock. Does poorly on its own roots. Dislikes heavy pruning. Susceptible to some disease. December example after rain has some mildew and a bit of rust. Other information: Four bushes and one standard are in the San Jose Heritage Rose Garden. Tom Liggett found it years ago in Willow Glen, California, when pruning roses for a lady who said she had bought it at Woolworth's before 1920 for a nickel (5¢)! He took cuttings and has kept it since. Its only reversion [to 'Mme. P. Euler'] was destroyed. Named after the painting of a nude girl standing at water's edge which became famous when in 1910 it was placed in a New York department store window raising the ire of the then-puritanical. The rose did not receive the attention it should have at the time because the blooms had too much of an old rose look. Today, it is a Hybrid Tea that surpasses the best of the English Roses with its beauty and fragrance. Tom Liggett reports that Miriam Wilkins said of it, 'These are the most beautiful roses I've ever seen.' As Alice Flores reports, Mel Hulse's comment was 'Why would you hybridize another pink HT after seeing this one?'." [tLmH] "Low-growing, inclined to be compact, moderately hardy; foliage plentiful, healthy; bloom moderate through midsummer, almost continuous, spring and fall occasionally." [ARA18/127]

[Silver Wedding]

Albert F. Amling Co., 1921

Sport of 'Ophelia' (HT).

"Exactly like 'Ophelia', except that foliage is cream-colored, with red tinge on young growth." [ARA22/190]

Simplicity

syn. 'Irish Simplicity'

H. Dickson, 1909

"Pure white, large . . . Single." [Th] "The buds are cup-shaped in form and the large flowers, occasionally having two rows of petals, are produced in quantity. The yellow anthers lend their charm, and when seen in the distance the flowers resemble a mass of pigmy white water lilies." [NRS18/138] "The best white single Hybrid Tea. Flowers large, with a mass of golden stamens." [ARA18/137] "Very big and effective." [ARA25/132] "Pure white, scented, immense size, showing gold and yellow anthers, single, free flowering. Growth vigorous, branching." [GeH] "Moderate height, bushy, almost hardy; foliage plentiful, subject to midsummer drop, black-spots slightly; bloom free, almost continuous." [ARA18/127] "Very vigorous." [Cat12/55]

Souvenir d'Anne-Marie

trans. "In Memory of Anne-Marie"

Ketten, 1902

From 'Safrano' (T) × 'Mme. Caroline Testout' (HT).

"Yellowish salmon-pink, large, full, medium to tall." [Sn] "[Bud] opening well." [GeH] "Flower salmon, yellowish flesh, creamy white around the edge, large, full, fragrant, long bud, stem long and erect. Growth vigorous, very floriferous . . . Dedicated to the memory of Mlle. Gicquel des Touches, of Pouprière." [JR26/163]

Souvenir d'E. Guillard

trans. "In Memory of E. Guillard"

Chambard, 1912

From 'Beauté Inconstante' (T) × 'Le Progrès' (HT).

"Saffron, shaded coppery carmine; large, full; sweetly scented; very floriferous." [C&Js16] "Saffron, shaded carmine. Garden. Fragrant." [NRS15/152] "[Blossoms] carried erect on long and stiff flower stalks. Growth vigorous, branching, very floriferous." [GeH] "Very vigorous, with upright canes which branch a little; beautiful deep purplish red foliage; big-wooded with few thorns. Pretty bud borne on a long stiff stem, deep coppery orange yellow. Blossom large, full, dawn yellow shaded coppery carmine; very floriferous and fragrant." [JR36/169] "Moderate, bushy." [ARA17/32]

Souvenir de Giosue Carducci Listed as 'Ricordo di Giosue Carducci' (HT).

Souvenir de Gustave Prat

trans. "In Memory of Gustave Prat"; possibly the full name is
   'Souvenir de Gustave Prat de Stadhal Glaser'

Pernet-Ducher, 1910

"One of the prettiest newcomers among the yellow roses. The tint is a very light sulphur yellow shaded darker yellow and delicately touched pink. The center of the blossom is nearly white." [JR35/183] "Clear, light sulphur-yellow; large, full flowers of fine form, freely and abundantly produced." [C&Js16] "Sulphur-yellow, paling at edges; lovely shape but small. Bush weak. 2 blooms." [ARA26/96] "A very charming flower. The colour is pale sulphur yellow, with a deeper cen-

tre, and the plant grows well and has a nicely pointed form, though this does not last very long . . . Not especially effective as a bedding plant." [NRS21/37] "Vigorous growth with branching canes, gay green leaves; buds ovoid, light sulphur yellow; flower very large, pretty full, globular, sulphur white or light sulphur yellow without tincture of any other color . . . Excellent garden rose, very floriferous." [JR34/40] "Fair to good growth; hardy; good foliage; good stem; medium size; blooms best in the spring; very good form; lasts well; does best on Multiflora." [Th] "Moderate, bushy." [ARA17/31] "Low-growing, compact; foliage plentiful, healthy; bloom free, continuous." [ARA18/127] "Vigorous, erect. Garden, bedding. Very promising." [NRS11/101]

[Souvenir de Maria de Zayas]

trans. "In Memory of Maria de Zayas"

Soupert & Notting, 1905

From an unnamed seedling × 'Papa Gontier' (T).

"Bush very vigorous and bushy; bud long and pointed on a long, erect peduncle; flower very large, full, beautiful form; color, carmine red veined deep red. This variety continues the series of dark red hybrid teas begun several years ago by the Soupert & Notting firm. Excellent variety for forcing and the open ground; floriferous and fragrant." [JR29/136] Not to be confused with 'Souvenir de Maria Zozaya' (HT), nor with 'Marichu Zayas' (HT).

[Souvenir de Maria Zozaya]

trans. "In Memory of Maria Zozaya"

Soupert & Notting, 1903

From 'Souvenir de Wootton' (HT) × 'Mrs. W. J. Grant' (HT).

"Coral, silvery center." [LS] "Vigorous growth, beautiful foliage, long bud of a graceful and exquisite form, magnificent coral red in color, opening as easily in great heat as in heavy rains; the open blossom is of extraordinary size, full, perfectly held on a very long, stiff stalk; camellia form, petals large and thick, coral red on the exterior, silvery pink within, the center more intense. This is one of the largest flowers among the Hybrid Teas, an excellent variety for frameworks and for cutting, and a beautiful exhibition rose—it has a great future ahead of it because it has all the good characteristics: Profusion, beauty, scent, a beautiful shape, and perfect hold." [JR27/148] Not to be confused with 'Souvenir de Maria de Zayas' (HT).

Souvenir de Mme. F. Zurich

trans. "In Memory of Mme. F. Zurich"

Puyravaud, 1910

From 'Laure Wattine' (HT) × 'Mme. Bérard' (N).

"Light salmon, large, full, medium height." [Sn] "Flower salmon, nuanced silvery, large, pretty double, imbricated, buds spherical, solitary at the ends of the canes which are very rigid and adorned with ample and beautiful dark green foliage; young canes carmine red; growth 'climbing', hardy, floriferous . . . dedicated to the memory of a Swiss lady." [JR34/150–151]

Souvenir de Monsieur Frédéric Vercellone

trans. "In Memory of Monsieur Frédéric Vercellone"

A. Schwartz, 1906

From 'Antoine Rivoire' (HT) × 'André Schwartz' (T).

"Vigorous, blossom large, full, very well formed, good poise, opens well, fragrant; carmine pink, lightly coppery, nuanced blush white tinted bright carmine." [JR30/136]

Souvenir du Capitaine Fernand Japy

trans. "In Memory of Captain Fernand Japy"
Sauvageot, 1923

"Purple pink, large, full, moderate height." [Sn] "Flower enormous, cupped, fuschine-pink, shaded purple, reverse silvery. Very hardy." [ARA24/173]

Souvenir du Président Daurel

trans. "In Memory of President Daurel"
Chauvry, 1905
Sport of 'Mme. Caroline Testout' (HT).

"Deep pink, large, full, medium height." [Sn] "Sport of 'Mme. Caroline Testout', of darker color, a beautiful metallic pink. All other characteristics are the same as those of its mother." [JR30/23]

[St. Helena]

B. R. Cant, 1912

"Blossom white with a red spot at the center; the base of the petals is yellow, and, in certain cases, the yellow extends over the center. The large flower is perfectly formed, with long petals, and is upright at the tip of the stem." [JR36/169] "Flower cream with a pink blush in centre, yellow at the base of petals and in some instances coming yellow well up the centre of the bloom, large, full, perfectly formed, with long shell-shaped petals, carried erect. Growth vigorous." [GeH]

Stadtrat F. Kähler

Geduldig, 1905

"Light red, large, full, dwarf." [Sn] "Growth vigorous, hardy, and floriferous; blossom very large, very full, round, exterior petals reflexed; bud solitary and pointed; color, light fiery red." [JR30/26]

Stadtrat Glaser   Plate 66

Kiese, 1910
From 'Pharisäer' (HT) × a yellow seedling.

"Light yellow, large, very full, medium height." [Sn] "Clear sulphur-yellow edged soft red, large, full, long bud, opening well on long and stiff stems. Growth vigorous, free flowering." [GeH]

Stella di Bologna

syn. 'Étoile de Bologne'; trans. "Star of Bologna"
Gaetano, Bonfiglioli & figlio, 1909
Seedling of 'L'Innocence' (HT).

"Violet pink, large, full, medium scent, medium height." [Sn] "Flower very large, pretty double, petals large, violet pink, lighter at the base, nuanced and bordered fuchsia; scent penetrating and delicious. Bud long, solitary, opening well; stem very long (sometimes 80 cm [ca. 32 in]), and stiff. Growth vigorous with erect canes, very floriferous." [JR33/182]

Sunny South

A. Clark, 1918
From 'Gustav Grünerwald' (HT) × 'Betty Berkeley' (T).

"Pink flushed carmine, yellow base. Vigorous, free flowering, good foliage." [Au] "A semi-double flower, and in my opinion very beautiful." [NRS27/142] "Slightly fragrant." [C-Ps33] "It is the freshest, cleanest pink Rose we have ever seen and the flowers come in stems from 2 to 3 feet long [ca. 6 dm to 1 m]. Entirely distinct." [C-Ps34] "The flowers are a lovely shade of pink flushed with carmine on a yellow base and are carried erect on good long stiff stems." [GeH] "A richly colored pink decorative rose of great vigor of growth, length of stem, and continuous bloom." [ARA24/119] "The color is pink, flushed with carmine on a yellow base—a most distinct and charming combination. It possesses a strong constitution and good habit, growing naturally five to six feet high [ca. 1.6–2 m], sometimes very much taller, and flowering practically throughout the year." [ARA28/112] "A beauty, with pale pink buds showing a 'spot' of dark rose when they begin to open. In full bloom the flower is a lovely soft rose-pink, tea-scented. The plant is about 4 feet tall [ca. 1.3 m], with flowers produced singly on thornless canes 2 to 3 feet long [ca. 6 dm to 1 m]." [ARA31/187] "A very robust grower with blooms of a good color." [ARA30/151] "An Australian introduction of highest value for decorative purposes and as a cut-flower. Very bushy up to 10 feet [ca. 3.3 m]. Flowers continuously and freely; soft pink with yellow shadings. Foliage remarkably resistant to disease. Almost in a class by itself for hedge or massing." [Capt28] "Foliage handsome. Strong constitution; good habit. A continuous bloomer from June to October." [ARA20/136]

T. F. Crozier

H. Dickson, 1918

"Deep canary buds, full, firm; lemon-white blooms; odor spicy. Strong stem. Bush strong. 15 blooms; 16 the second season." [ARA26/96] "A vigorous-growing rose with full flowers on long, strong stems. The bud is yellow and the flowers white when fully open; not very large." [ARA21/148] "Flowers large, full and globular, with high-pointed canter, deep canary-yellow. Strong, vigorous, branching growth." [ARA19/103] "A Rose of great beauty. Fine, vigorous branching habit, with deep olive green foliage, free from mildew. The flowers are large and full with high centre—apparently freely produced. The colour is a beautiful clear canary yellow. A fine Rose for garden purposes, and occasionally large enough for Exhibition." [NRS18/166]

[Taft Rose]

Breeder unknown, pre-1911
From 'Kaiserin Auguste Viktoria' (HT) × 'Mme. Cusin' (T).

"Salmon-pink, shaded with chrome-yellow." [C&Js12] "Novelties of such high order as this variety appear but few times in a life-time. We find it one of the most profusely blooming, brightest colored, sweetest scented pink roses we have ever grown. One of the really good new bedding roses of recent years with stem enough for satisfactory cutting." [C&Js11]

The Dandy

G. Paul, 1905
Seedling of 'Bardou Job' (B).

"Fiery maroon crimson." [Ÿ] "Flower small, sparkling blackish crimson." [JR30/25] "Glowing crimson. —Vigorous. —A buttonhole rose. Fragrant." [Cat12/57]

Toreador

W. Paul, 1919

"Rose-red, medium size, semi-full, medium height." [Sn] "Bud crimson; flower semi-double, rosy red, outside of petals golden yellow. Vigorous grower; abundant bloomer." [ARA20/130] "Growth upright; very free blooming. Distinct." [GeH]

Totote Gélos

Pernet-Ducher, 1915

"White or Nearly White [*as a garden rose* "*With Flowers Approach-*

ing Exhibition Standard"]." [NRS24/184, 186] "Pinkish-white, large, full, medium height." [Sn] "Flesh-white shaded with chrome-yellow in the autumn, large, full, and globular, with long and pointed buds." [GeH] "Growth and blooming below average; lacks distinctiveness." [ARA18/118]

Troja

Mikeš/Böhm, 1927

Sport of 'Mrs. Herbert Stevens' (HT).

"Bud long-pointed, cream-yellow; flower full, lasting, fragrant (sweet), creamy white, borne on long, strong stem. Foliage disease-resistant. Growth vigorous, bushy, upright; free bloomer. Reported to be unusually hardy." [ARA31/244]

Ulster Standard

H. Dickson, 1917

"A single Rose of great merit, free branching growth and dark green wood and foliage. The shoots, which grow to a uniform height of about 2 feet [ca. 6 dm], branching into large, loose, evenly disposed corymbs of intense deep crimson, open to large smooth flowers with prominent yellow anthers, making an ideal bedding single Rose in a much needed colour. The blooms, which are about 3 inches in diameter [ca. 7.5 cm], are of bright crimson, which does not fade as the flower ages." [NRS17/162] "A single Rose of great value, the colour standing throughout the age of the flowers." [NRS18/140]

Veluwezoom   Plate 63

Pallandt/Lourens, 1908

From 'Mme. Caroline Testout' (HT) × 'Soleil d'Or' (Pern).

"Brilliant carmine passing to deep rose, large, full, opening well. Growth vigorous, very free." [GeH] "Color is brilliant, dark carmine rose in the centre with golden yellow reflex. A strong grower which makes long pointed buds and large double flowers. Useful for cut flowers and also for bedding on account of its free flowering habit." [C&Js11] "Bush of great vigor, with upright canes, small round leaves, and strong thorns. Long bud borne on long, strong stem; flower very large, full, pointed, opening well, bright coloration—deep carmine pink with a glowing center touched golden yellow." [JR32/168]

[Verna MacKay]

A. Dickson, 1912

"Fawn, suffused sulphur. Buds very beautifully formed. Fragrance unusually rich." [CA17] "Delicate ivory sulphur-buff, changing to brilliant lemon as the flower expands, medium-sized, of exquisite spiral formation, carried on erect stems, distinctly potpourri perfumed. Growth vigorous, erect, free branching." [GeH] "Delicate ivory white changing to bright lemon yellow when the flower opens; the form . . . is a sort of spiral . . . The blossoms are borne upright at the tips of the stems and are produced in marvelous profusion the whole season. The growth is vigorous, the bush well branched, each branch tipped by a flower. Perfect decorative; it has a distinctive potpourri scent." [JR36/91]

Vinoca

Amaury-Fonseca, 1906

"Satiny pink." [Ÿ]

W. C. Clark   Listed as 'Walter C. Clark' (HT).

W. C. Gaunt

A. Dickson, 1917

"Brilliant (velvet) vermilion, tipped scarlet, reverse of petals crimson-maroon, of medium size, pointed and perfectly formed, carried erect; Tea-rose perfumed. Growth vigorous, branching, with handsome large oval beech-green foliage." [GeH] "Wanting in perfume." [NRS22/112] "A Rose of moderately vigorous growth, with fine olive-green foliage. The blooms, which are a perfect shape, pointed, and have handsome guard petals, are of delicious Tea-Rose perfume. The colour is a rich bright vermilion, shaded crimson maroon. It is a charming Rose, and its not too vigorous habit will make it a fine bedding variety." [NRS17/125]

W. E. Lippiatt

A. Dickson, 1907

"Brilliant velvety crimson shaded maroon; the flowers are large, full; symmetrically formed center. Very sweet." [C&Js10] "Velvet-crimson. —Vigorous. —Exhibition, garden, standard. —A good dark H.T. Very fragrant." [Cat12/59] "Probably the best dark HT in cultivation—the colour is deep crimson shaded maroon. Rather late flowering, but particularly good in autumn . . . a good grower, free from mildew, fragrant, and the flowers are of good size and shape." [F-M] "Tall, bushy, hardy; foliage very plentiful, black-spots somewhat; bloom moderate and intermittent first half of season." [ARA18/128] W. E. Lippiatt, rosarian; introduced, among other cultivars, the China 'Primrose Queen'.

Walküre

trans. "Valkyrie"

Ebeling, 1919

From 'Frau Karl Druschki' (HP) × 'Mme. Jenny Gillemot (HT; Pernet-Ducher, 1905; yellow; parentage: 'Lady Mary Fitzwilliam' [HT] × 'Honourable Edith Gifford' [T]).

"Yellowish white, large, full, medium height." [Sn] "Bud long-pointed; flower double, with high center, borne singly. Color cream-white, ochre-yellow toward the center. Vigorous grower. Hardy." [ARA20/136]

Walter C. Clark

syn. 'W. C. Clark'

W. Paul, 1917

"Deep red, large, full, very fragrant, tall." [Sn] "Deep maroon-crimson shaded black, large, moderately full, very fragrant. Growth very vigorous, with handsome dark green foliage, the young shoots being beautifully tinted with red." [GeH] "Has considerable fragrance." [NRS22/112] "A good dark Rose with the blooms carried on long arching stems. Well formed and fairly full, and fragrant. Not over free and somewhat subject to mildew." [NRS24/160]

Weddigen

syn. 'Weddingen'

Lambert, 1916

From 'General MacArthur' (HT) × 'Goldelse' (HT).

"Salmon pink, large, full, very fragrant, tall." [Sn] "Fresh silvery salmon-rose, passing to salmon-carmine towards the centre, large, full, fragrant. Growth bushy, erect, hardy; free, continuous flowering." [GeH]

Weddingen Listed as 'Weddigen' (HT).

Weisse Gruss an Aachen
trans. "White Gruss an Aachen"
Vogel, 1944
Presumably a sport of 'Gruss an Aachen' (HT).

"White, large, very full, medium scent, medium height." [Sn]

Wenzel Geschwind
Geschwind, 1902
From 'Princesse de Sagan' (Ch) × 'Comte de Bobrinsky' (HP).

"Deep purplish red, medium-large to large, full, medium scent, dwarf." [Sn]

Westfield Star
Morse, 1920
Sport of 'Ophelia' (HT).

"The white replica of the famous 'Ophelia', with all Ophelia's good qualities. Petals have good substance and the flowers, lemon-yellow in the bud, open cream and then turn to pure glistening white till the end." [C-Ps27] "When fully open, the petals quill and form like a star." [C-Ps28] "Faintly but sweetly perfumed." [C-Ps29] "Fine form, fragrant, and a good keeper, the finest blooms coming in the fall." [C-Ps34] "Dwarf; stems short; disease-resistant; very little bloom. Buds good shape but blooms open flat, lemon-yellow which soon fades creamy white . . . [*Ontario*]; Yellowish buds, opening to nearly perfect glistening white blooms of delightful fragrance, the same lovely shape as [those of] 'Ophelia'. Foliage large, free from disease; blooms singly on strong stems . . . the best white rose we have [*Rhode Island*]." [ARA28/194–195] "I prefer this to the American '[Lady] Sylvia' [HT], as it is slightly more double and will stand heat better, being in all respects a real 'Ophelia' but for the color—the bud being sulphur-yellow and the open bloom 'Kaiserin [Auguste Viktoria' white." [ARA24/107–108]

White Killarney
Waban/F. R. Pierson, 1909
Sport of 'Killarney' (HT).

"Snowy white blooms with enormous petals. The opening buds are beautiful, but the flower is lacking in petals. Practically identical with the other forms of 'Killarney' except in color, and has their faults and virtues. It is one of the really reliable white Roses for bedding and cutting." [C-Ps25] "Ofttimes with a light pearl or lemon tint in the center." [C-Ps29] "Large, good to fine form, semi-double, quite fragrant, short to long stem. I prefer this to the double form, being freer in bloom. Fine foliage, sufficient. Growth medium strong; hardy. Pure white." [ARA23/174] "Flowers more double than those of 'Killarney' and pure waxy white. Foliage sufficient to plentiful, subject, however, to mildew. Growth medium. Averages 42 blooms per season. Hardy." [ARA21/91] "Not as good a bloomer as 'Killarney' and with the same foliage. Disbud." [Th] "A disappointing sport of 'Killarney'. Nice color and growth; not so good a bloomer as parent, and has same faulty foliage." [ARA18/114] "In my opinion, there can be no doubt that this rose is more vigorous than its mother; the blossoms are larger and have more petals; the consistent quality of the flowers is also notable. In a vase, they seem superior to [those of] 'Killarney', the blossoms of which sometimes leave much to be desired. The coloration of 'White Killarney' much resembles that of 'K[aiserin] A[uguste] Viktoria'; the bud is tinted green, but goes to creamy white or ivory as the flower opens. The form is identical to that of 'Killarney', though with larger petals . . . Another white sport of 'Killarney' exists in America, but, not having seen it, I can't outline its merits." [JR33/40–41] "Tall, compact, hardy; foliage plentiful, black-spots somewhat; bloom free, almost continuous." [ARA18/128] "I have one 'White Killarney' which makes fine growth and has perfect foliage, is always in bloom, and is probably way above its class." [ARA19/46] "A better white than the well known '[The] Bride' rose [T]." [C&Js09]

William Notting
Soupert & Notting, 1904
From 'Mme. Abel Chatenay' (HT) × 'Antoine Rivoire' (HT).

"Bright rosy cerise with center deeper. Very sweet." [C&Js21] "Large, full, fine form, fragrant, long stem. Sufficient, healthy foliage. Growth average; hardy." [ARA23/174] "Growth vigorous, beautiful dark green foliage; bud long, of beautiful and imposing appearance on a long and firm stem; blossom extraordinarily large, quite full, of magnificent form, and irreproachably well held; the reverse of the petals, coral red; within, salmon, the center glowing in the way of 'Mme. Abel Chatenay', but of a color more pronounced and brighter, the blossom much larger and the plant more vigorous . . . It is, what is more, extremely floriferous and very fragrant." [JR28/41]

Young America
E. G. Hill, 1902
From 'Duke of Edinburgh' (HP) × 'The Meteor' (HT).

"Deep red, medium size, full, medium scent, medium height." [Sn] "The rose tourist abroad who announces himself to one of the rose-masters of Great Britain, France, or Germany as an American will always be considered in relation to his acquaintance with the best-known American rosarian—E. G. Hill, of Richmond, Ind. He it is who has, in his long half-century of clean and fine work with the queen of flowers, most definitely impressed himself and his productions upon the acute growers abroad.

"Born in England in 1847, his plant-loving father brought the boy to Geneva, N.Y., in 1851, where, after the brief schooldays of those times were over, he was employed by the then notable nursery firm of T. C. Maxwell & Bro., who were leaders in outdoor-grown roses. Naturally 'Gurney' Hill became familiar with all the best sorts then in commerce. In 1865 his father came to Richmond, Ind., and in 1881 he and his son began a general florist's catalogue business, from which developed the extensive business of today . . .

"An insistent demand always creates a supply, and it was about this time [ca. 1893], full twenty-five years ago, that 'Gurney' Hill fostered the introduction of the earlier Hybrid Tea roses, so much desired for cut-flower needs as well as for outdoor bloom, by buying and testing all the many foreign productions. It was thankless and expensive work; but it had one merit—it turned the mind of this able rosarian to the production of better varieties. Only those who have watched the work of such men realize the care, the expense, and the time required to conduct rose-breeding with success. As Miss Hill—the interested sister of 'Gurney' Hill—has well said, it is 'a still more expensive undertaking than testing European novelties, for these were at least up with the average rose, while the seedlings require not less than three years' trial. The first test merely sorts out the singles and the defective roses, after which comes the 'watchful waiting' required to separate those good enough for rigid trial in the best part of a forcing-house.'

"Mr. Hill's standards were high, and it was not until 1904 that two roses resulted which he believed were superior. These were 'General MacArthur' and 'Mrs. Theodore Roosevelt' [both HT], both yet very much 'on the map.' The famous 'Richmond' [HT] was sent out in 1905 as the best amongst an unprecedentedly large production of red seedlings. It was seeded from 'Lady Battersea' [HT], and had 'Liberty' [HT] blood in its petals. An international honor came in the Paris gold medal for 'Rhea Reid' [HT] in 1908, as tested in the Bagatelle Gardens . . .

"Nearly threescore and ten, Mr. Hill's rose ability is keener than ever, and his vision clearer. Writes Miss Hill: 'No rose is as yet perfect as measured by the arbitrary demands of the forcer, and for this reason the rose-breeder's work is not done . . .'

"Now notice what Mr. Hill, this veteran of a half-century's efforts, failures, successes, has for the immediate future: 'Sixty seedlings, selected from something like 5,000, are now being grafted to furnish a test for the coming season. Visiting florists have been surprised and delighted with the novel combinations of color, the size and the freedom of growth, of many of them.'" [ARA16/47–49]

"The Editor demands of me some reminiscences covering the time since the Hybrid Tea rose began. He must have been thinking of my life-long habit of visiting with the great European rose-hybridizers . . . My thought does go back to my first introduction to those rosarians of Lyons.

"Unluckily, it was not my good fortune to meet in person that prince of the great contemporary rosarians, François Lacharme, but I well remember his statement in correspondence with me that 'Safrano', a Tea rose of that period which we all grew considerably, was responsible for the break in the old type of Hybrid Perpetuals, becoming the parent for the distinct type of roses represented by the since-abandoned 'Victor Verdier' [HP] and 'Countess of Oxford' ['Comtesse d'Oxford' (HP)], and later for that wonderful variety, 'Mme. Ferdinand Jamain' [i.e., 'Mme. Ferdinand Jamin' (HP)], originated around 1885 by Lédéchaux, and coming to America before 1886 to be introduced here as 'American Beauty' [HP; 'Mme. Ferdinand Jamin' and 'American Beauty' were long thought to be synonymous, but differences between them have been noted, and the originator of 'American Beauty' was 'very positive' about his origination of that cultivar] . . . This new type of Hybrid Perpetual showed a very distinctive departure in growth, with its smooth stems, few thorns, and a soft, pleasing color of the foliage, which is a distinct character of the class . . .

"My first flying visit to Lyons [i.e., 'flying' as in 'hurried,' not as in 'aeronautical'] was in quest of information relative to the raising of new rose varieties. At that time Jean Sisley, a prominent French amateur rosarian, who also dealt comfortably with the English language, acted as intermediary in most of the correspondence between the English and French rosarians. I found at that early date that, with few exceptions, the raisers of new roses largely depended on natural cross-fertilization for the hybrids between the Teas and the Hybrid Perpetuals which gave rise to the Hybrid Teas. They did not, indeed, at all recognize that they were creating a new class, for the earlier varieties . . . were sent out as Hybrid Perpetual roses. Not one of those acute rosarians recognized that a new class had been created which was shortly to dominate the rose-world.

"Shortly after this, Henry Bennett, of Shepperton, England, came to the forefront with his additions to the Hybrid Tea section . . . long since forgotten for better sorts, though they were great advances at the time. Mr. Bennett's untimely death was a serious mishap to the progress he was making in the introduction of crosses between the Hybrid Perpetuals and the various members of the *Rosa indica* family. It seems hardly thirty years since Alexander Dickson gave us 'Killarney', followed in two years by 'Liberty', both being distinct advances in themselves, and as the parents of numerous Hybrid Tea roses which have proved amenable to winter forcing.

"Here in my recollections enters the later Pernet-Ducher, who, in 1896, gave us 'Antoine Ducher' [HT], yet a splendid garden rose and the progenitor of many good outside and inside roses. Indeed, we must give this great Frenchman a prominent position, if not the first place among the world's rosarians . . .

"It was about 1905 that I had the good fortune to originate 'General MacArthur' [HT] and 'Richmond' [HT], which undoubtedly started the line of great red roses we now have. I think that 'General MacArthur' had 'Gruss an Teplitz' [B] as a parent on one side, but I am not at all positive about it. In the early days I was so anxious to produce varieties of value from the crosses I made that I confess I did not keep records as I should have done. I tried pollen from many varieties on both seedlings, and named varieties, but I did not put any special stress on their lineage . . .

"I can do no more than give a slight glimpse into the rich past of two generations in this brief story. I have seen the rose in the greenhouse assume a vastly important position, and I only hope that someone more gifted than I am will take up the work and give the world the even better roses it deserves. No one who has ever visited me will deny my statement that I enjoy working with roses, and that, indeed, they have kept me alive in more than one sense for a long lifetime." [ARA31/144–146]

Zwerg Teplitz Listed as 'Alsterufer' (HT).

CHAPTER THIRTY-TWO

Pernetianas

"A new class of Rose, originating with that eminent raiser, Monsieur Pernet-Ducher, of Lyons. They have rapidly gained popularity on account of their unique colouring. There are really two sections of these beautiful and novel Roses, one having very strong, erect growth, with glistening foliage, and bearing a strong resemblance to the Persian Briar ['Persian Yellow' (F)]; the other similar in every way to the Hybrid Teas, but inclined to follow the Briar in the appearance of growth and foliage. They require to be kept well nourished, and should be carefully but lightly pruned." [Au] "The characteristic of the Pernet group has been the great improvement and variety of colouring in the flower; but this was accompanied by a loss as compared with the Hybrid Tea of the quality of form, at least in the earlier members of the group, and the absence of the pronounced fragrance so much valued in the Rose. It may possibly be that the coalescence of the two groups . . . is resulting from an attempt to get into the Pernet group with its magnificence of colour the beauty of form which many of the Hybrid Teas have already achieved, and the fragrance which is so much desired." [NRS29/67]

"Pernetianas are at [their] best in regions of a long vegetative season, like southern France, the birthplace of the race, and this season is divided in two distinct growing periods—an early spring, and a long spring-like autumn, intervened by a hot summer, because there is enough growing weather when they awake from the summer rest enforced by natural defoliation to come again to a useful life. This new growth may mature before winter, if winter there is. The obvious foreign conclusion is that Pernetianas are out of place where the season is short, with late spring and early winter, and in place in a climate with a long growing season." [ARA29/196] "Pernetianas, as a rule, do not do well in this [Brazilian] climate." [ARA28/116] "The use of Pernetianas in humid climates was discouraged." [ARA29/181] "Only those who truly love to work with roses as well as gather them should try to grow Pernetianas in Kentucky." [ARA31/98] "Frankly, I do not believe any Pernetiana roses are worth a 'hoorah' in the South." [ARA26/116] "I find that the Pernetianas, taken as a whole (there are a few exceptions), are quite unsuitable to Australian conditions. They are subject to black-spot and die-back, and are at their best for a very short period, while their time of usefulness is by no means lengthy. The best results are to be obtained by growing a bed of one variety. Prune them very lightly, removing only the dead and sickly wood, feed and water them well, and as soon as they begin to go off, throw them out and replant with growing stock." [ARA30/152] "We must get away from Roses of the 'Rayon d'Or' [Pern] type. The reason for this is because that sort is typical of a variety that dies back quickly, is liable to Black Spot, and has a poor constitution. Its descendants inherit its undesirable characters, and seedlings bred from it would require to be selected very cautiously." [NRS25/112] "The Pernetiana Roses have a bad character for black spot, and some trace this back to 'Persian Yellow'. I cannot deny this impeachment, although black spot is not confined to this particular tribe . . . There is one feature . . . that requires special consideration, and that is their pruning. I am strongly of opinion many kinds would be far more successfully grown, if not pruned at all, or at any rate pruned very moderately. I have seen huge plants of 'Lyon-Rose' that had never known the painful operation of pruning, and I am told 'Rayon d'Or' in some soils, and in sheltered gardens, make wonderful plants on this let-alone plan. I have tried it myself with 'Golden Emblem' [Pern], and the result was really marvellous, huge basal growths springing up from the non-pruned plants." [NRS21/128–129]

"I have been told Monsieur Pernet-Ducher has a remarkably coloured seedling, from which he obtains many of his crosses, and possibly this accounts for so large a number of this tribe originating with him." [NRS21/131] "Iron caused the intensified orange colors [in rose blossoms at Villeurbanne, suburb of Lyon, France]." [ARA31/171] "It is evident that most of our yellow Roses of to-day owe their colour to the influence of 'Soleil d'Or' [Pern] through its parent 'Persian Yellow'. Some of the grand old Tea Roses were yellow; but, I think, their influence—whilst notable in some Hybrid Teas—is almost negligible, and it is to the yellow species [*Rosa foetida*] that we owe the golden tones found in some of our Roses to-day." [NRS25/113] "The recent infusion of Austrian briar 'blood' has deepened the yellows and supplied us also with wonderful orange, salmon and terra-cotta shades . . . True pinks—in fact, 'rose' pinks, or cold pinks—are at present out of favour among Rose growers. Warmth and fire is what is appreciated in pink Roses. Coldness, then, as regards pinkness, may be considered a fault, and this is about the only one attributed to that fine H.P. 'Mrs. John Laing'. We may be a little too captivated by the recent brilliant breaks in colour, and inclined to under-rate the real pinks. May we not become in time rather eye-wearied by the 'heat' and glare of some of the recent introductions and return to the appreciation of the milder and softer colours [*and, bringing us full circle, perhaps we see here the beginnings of the reawakening of interest in "old" roses!*]? The colder pink, along with the blushes, whites and pale yellows, would seem to be the Roses to suggest coolness in the heat of summer. On a sweltering day in July, a scheme of indoor floral decoration composed, say, of 'Mrs. John Laing' and the Snow Queen ['Frau Karl Druschki'], both possessing pure green foliage, would be more restful than one of 'Mme. Édouard Herriot' [Pern] and 'Rayon d'Or'; whereas, in the cool of the autumn, a suggestion of warmth is wanted in our decorative schemes and colouring, to harmonise with the changing foliage around us, and we naturally turn to the Pernetiana roses." [NRS22/140–141]

"What we see in the Rose is certain colours of the spectrum, of the rainbow, that range from indigo, through blue, green, yellow and orange into red. To eliminate the indigo and blue, which have little luminosity, would leave us only the series from greenish-yellow, through yellow and orange, into the red, to deal with, and give us the maximum of hue, luminosity and purity. Consideration of this point narrowed the problem and pointed along the line to its solution. That was, to breed Roses which would not reflect the blue, which would, in fact, make a selective absorption of colour. We must remember we have to deal with light and not pigment, and there is no other course. I [Dr. Arthur Robert Waddell, of Cambridge] happened to have in my possession at this time certain colour screens for experimental purposes in another subject. Among them was one which had been wrongly dyed and which thus, from the intensity of its blue, cut off yellow light. When I looked at a yellow or orange flower through this—a dandelion, for instance—it appeared vermilion, while owing to a red dye present in the screen a red flower flashed up brilliantly, the explanation of the latter condition being that, with the absorption of yellow, the source of so much white light was cut off at the same time. Here was the answer required: Employ yellow to reverse the process and cut off blue. To be more explicit: To infuse such a powerful yellow strain into our Roses that the rough, diffracting surfaces of their petals would be so changed as not to reflect blue but to absorb it entirely. They would retain their capacity for reflecting the red-yellow end of the spectrum only, and nothing beyond. At the same time, in losing blue we would get rid of a great factor in the production of white light, which is, after all, only a

diluent and darkener, and leave us, instead, bright, glowing, pure colours in the above yellows, oranges and reds.

"Just at this time, 1900, Monsieur Pernet-Ducher introduced 'Soleil d'Or', the very thing that was wanted. Evidently he had got on a right line. But I cannot say how many of our British raisers grasped the real significance of this momentous arrival. Realising what Monsieur Pernet-Ducher was doing, about 1902 I wrote to him, setting out all that the elimination of blue implied, pointing out how imperative it was to strengthen his yellow strain, at the same time sending him a duplicate of the colour screen I have referred to. He replied promptly with all his native courtesy indicating how I had given him a clearer outlook on his own line of advance. The next step was in 1906–7. I received from him a mysterious packet of twelve Roses, labelled 'Canari'; I was to put them safely by themselves and watch. Lest the secret should leak out I had every flower bud pinched off the moment it appeared. One only I allowed to bloom, so that I might see it for myself before removing it also. In the morning it was opening and by afternoon it had spread its petals. 'Rayon d'Or' was born, and a revolution in modern Rose growing was accomplished . . . Of course, 'Rayon d'Or' is not perfect; it may have its defects. But its fragrant, shining foliage is a feature, and its lustrous yellow blooms mark the emancipation of the Hybrid Tea from the thraldom of the Blue." [NRS24/219–220]

"Since 1883, Monsieur Pernet-Ducher had sought to raise crosses between 'Persian Yellow' . . . and other[,] remontant[,] roses. [*For the beginning of Pernet-Ducher's search for better yellow roses, see under 'Comte Henri Rignon' (HT) in* The Old Rose Advisor.] This knowing *rosiériste* was haunted by the superb yellow color of the Persian, which he strongly wished to have in a remontant. The enterprise seemed bold, because Mother Nature doesn't always deign to cooperate, particularly where hybridization is concerned, and often gives just the opposite of what was intended! In a word, Pernet-Ducher stuck to his idea, and over and over again hybridized Hybrid Perpetuals with the pollen of 'Persian Yellow'. After many vicissitudes, he noted that the rose 'Antoine Ducher' took more easily than others to crossing with *Rosa lutea*. In 1888, he pricked out the seedlings obtained by these hybridizations, which, planted in the nursery, bloomed one after the other. The plants were certainly quite unusual—very interesting from the botanical point of view in their variations, but nothing showed commercial value. Only one of them was noted in 1891 and 1892 when it bloomed; it gave semi-double blossoms which were bright pink with whitish petal bases making a star, petal reverses bright yellow, and having the foetid scent of *Rosa lutea*. It ['Rhodophile Gravereaux' (Pern)] would have been gotten rid of, or at least forgotten right away, if a certain small incident hadn't happened. In a friendly dispute which Pernet-Ducher was having with the simpatico editor of *Lyon-Horticole*, Monsieur Viviand-Morel, the latter challenged his friend to come up with some descendants of

Rosa lutea, which another horticulturist of Lyon, the late Alegatière, had never been able to make seed. The following season, which is to say May 1893, at the bloom-time of the notorious semi-double pink-flowered rose mentioned above, the dispute was decided in favor of Viviand-Morel. But in looking for stems to send to his friend, Pernet-Ducher noticed that [the 'plant' consisted of] two specimens growing next to each other, the one being the pink semi-double rose, the other quite small specimen showing for the first time quite full blossoms of a beautiful yellow color—'Soleil d'Or' was found. Pernet thus found doubled his means of convincing Viviand-Morel of the possibility of growing varieties of *Rosa lutea* from seed—not only in making *R. lutea* seed, but by means of using its pollen to fertilize other species or varieties … Following the precedent of Noisette, who gave his name to a much appreciated group of roses, Monsieur Pernet-Ducher gave, with reason, the designation *Pernet Rose, Rosa Pernetiana,* to this new series in the genus Rosa, to perpetuate the knowledge of its origin." [JR24/87–89 *passim*]

Evidently without knowing of the simultaneous efforts of Pernet-Ducher, "I [Lord Penzance] collected a quantity of the pollen of these Roses [*viz.,* *Rosa foetida,* 'Persian Yellow', and 'Harison's Yellow' (F)] and operated on the blooms of several Hybrid Perpetuals, notably 'Général Jacqueminot' and 'Jean Cherpin' [this operation taking place sometime prior to 1896]. I obtained abundance of hips, and in due time plenty of seed, and again in due time, some hundreds of plants. But excepting perhaps in two or three cases no sign is visible in their wood, foliage, or growth of the Yellow Briar; no doubt the greater part of them have not yet flowered, but I confess my hope of success with them is pretty well extinct. One plant, indeed, about three or four years ago, did give unmistakeable signs of the Briar parentage, the foliage was almost identical with that of ['Harison's Yellow'], and when the flower showed itself it presented a pretty mixture of crimson and yellow. But it was very shapeless, and out of a dozen blooms there would perhaps be only one that in shape could be said to give any pleasure to the eye. Moreover, it proved itself to be very difficult to propagate by either bud or graft; it is even difficult to keep it alive, one branch after another dying down more quickly than they are reproduced. The plant seems, if I may use such an expression[,] to resent the attempt to unite such incongruous parents, and to make continual protest against its having been called into existence." [NRS25/110–111, quoting from the *Rosarian's Year Book* for 1896]

"This relatively recent sort was bred in 1900 by the well-known horticulturist and rose breeder Monsieur Joseph Pernet-Ducher of Lyon. The Pernet rose came from crossing 'Persian Yellow' (sulphur yellow) with the HP 'Antoine Ducher'. The first variety obtained was 'Soleil d'Or'; 'Lyon-Rose', 'Rayon d'Or', etc., saw the light of day later. To these new hybrids, the creator gave the name Pernetiana Roses (Roses of Pernet), as Noisette did for his obtentions. The appearance of this new race showed the way for new crosses, and now, there is already a whole category of different varieties which, quite distinct and differing much among themselves, all belong to the same class. The coloration varies from sun yellow up to apricot yellow and coppery orange, and isn't equaled in any other sort of rose. Before the appearance of the Pernetiana, there weren't any freely remontant [yellow] roses, except among the Tea roses and Hybrid Teas, and even then the yellow shade wasn't very pure. It had much of a chamois tint to it. Thus it was that the Pernetianas came as a true surprise to fanciers. They inherited the pure yellow color from 'Persian Yellow'. The first variety, 'Soleil d'Or', still wasn't pure yellow. Later, by crossing '[Mme.] Mélanie Soupert' [HT] with 'Soleil d'Or', 'Rayon d'Or' came along in 1910 with its relatively pure shade of yellow. The Pernetiana roses distinguish themselves from all the other sorts of roses grown by their large thorns and glossy green leaves, which are characteristics of *Rosa lutea* [i.e., R. foetida] … The greater part of the early varieties give a lot of dead wood and die young … As for the more recent ones, they have a vigor, a greater strength, and can be compared to the other Hybrid Teas." [Cw] "After 1910, progress was very rapid." [NRS25/115] "The introduction of new Hybrid Perpetuals has practically ceased, and the place of this type has been assumed first by the Hybrid Tea group, and secondly the Pernet Roses, and these two later groups are still being propagated and improved; they are, in fact, showing a tendency to coalesce." [NRS29/66] "The new varieties are now so very mixed that their classification becomes more and more difficult." [ARA21/152]

"Rosarians in the future will have a wealth of colour undreamed of before that happy match between 'Persian Yellow' [F] and 'Antoine Ducher' [HP], and will all agree that they have lived 'happily ever after.'" [NRS13/166]

Adolf Kärger
syn. 'Adolphe Kärzer'
Kordes, 1918
From 'Cissie Easlea' (Pern) × 'Sunburst' (Pern).

"Yellow, very large, full, medium scent, medium height." [Sn] "Cadmium yellow. Vigorous. Garden, bedding." [NRS23/list] "Chrome yellow without shading, large and full, produced on long, stiff stems; long bud. Growth vigorous, deep green foliage; free and late flowering." [GeH] "Unusually floriferous, even blooming spontaneously and quite profusely in October with its long-stemmed blossoms. The bud is long, sometimes nearly 8–10 cm long [to ca. 1 dm], quite full, of excellent form, pure deep yellow without any secondary tone … The leaf is large, deep green, and completely disease-free. The plant is upright and strong-growing; long stems." [Ck] "Bud long-pointed; flower very large, double, open, high center, clear golden yellow, fading lighter in the full sun; lasting, borne singly on long stem; slightly fragrant. Foliage abundant, large, glossy, rich green. Very vigorous; bushy; profuse and continuous bloomer." [ARA21/163] "Said to be an improvement upon ['Sunburst']. It is decidedly nothing of the kind." [NRS22/184]

[Adolf Koschel]
syn. 'Adolphe Koschel'
Kordes, 1918
From 'Harry Kirk' (T) × 'Louise Catherine Breslau' (Pern).

"Light orange yellow, nuanced red." [Cw] "Large, deep ochre-yellow blossom with blood-red shading; continuous bloom." [Ck] "Flower intense orange-yellow with reddish shadings, large, very full, produced on long and stiff stems, tea scent. Growth vigorous, erect, branching; perpetual flowering." [GeH] "A pretty Rose and is one of a most attractive character. It has done very well and it is always notable for its perfectly formed flowers of good substance, and they are full, but not too full. The colour is a deep orange yellow heavily flushed with red. It is quite distinct from anything we have, and there is a decided opening for it. The growth and habit are good, and it flowers very freely all through the season." [NRS22/184] "Type, 'Karry Kirk' as a plant. Bud long-pointed, orange-yellow; flower large, very double, open, high center, orange-yellow, very lasting, borne singly on long, strong stem; strong Tea fragrance. Foliage sufficient, medium size, leathery, bronzy green, sometimes black-spots. Vigorous; bushy; blooms abundantly and continuously all season. Practically hardy, but tips freeze." [ARA21/163]

Adolphe Kärzer Listed as 'Adolf Kärger' (Pern).

Adolphe Koschel Listed as 'Adolf Koschel' (Pern).

Ambassador
Premier Rose Gardens, 1930
"Bronzed salmon." [Ÿ] "Bronze salmon, very large, full, medium scent, medium height." [Sn]

Amélie de Bethune
Pernet-Ducher, 1924
"Coral red." [Cw] "Coral red, medium size, lightly double, light scent, dwarf." [Sn] "Mid-sized blossom, full, coral pink. Plant strong, growth quite upright, very floriferous." [Ck] "Very good bloom in autumn." [ARA26/112] "Type, 'Mme. Édouard Herriot' [Pern]. Bud medium size, ovoid; flower medium size, semi-double, open, fairly lasting; coral-red, shaded yellow at base; slight fragrance. Moderate grower, upright, 2½ feet high [ca. 7.5 dm]; free and continuous bloomer. Freezes to 10 inches [ca. 2.5 dm]." [ARA24/171]

Angel Guiméra
Dot, 1925
From 'Frau Karl Druschki' (HP) × 'Souvenir de Claudius Pernet' (Pern).

"Sulphur-yellow, a very strong grower, and in type of plant like 'Souvenir de Claudius Pernet'. The blooms are very full but open well." [ARA27/205] "Tested two years. The best white in captivity. Prolific bloomer. Double, fragrant blooms, straw-yellow in the center, turning to pure, gleaming white. Good foliage. Vigorous. As hardy as its mother, '[Frau Karl] Druschki'." [ARA28/142] "A very vigorous variety, with large, thick foliage. The very fragrant bloom is white, with clear yellow in the center; the plant is extremely floriferous, and one may say that it is a true intermediate type between 'Frau Karl Druschki' and 'Souvenir de Claudius Pernet'." [ARA26/50–51] "Bud medium, long-pointed; flower medium size, double, full, moderately fragrant, amber-yellow, borne, singly or several together, on long stem. Foliage abundant, normal, soft, large. Growth very vigorous, upright, bushy

(one-year plants, 2 feet [ca. 6 dm]); profuse, continuous bloomer." [ARA26/188]

Angèle Pernet
Pernet-Ducher, 1924
"Reddish orange." [Ÿ] "Reddish orange nuanced golden yellow." [Cw] "Very beautiful in a rich yet soft amber-orange; it seems very promising." [ARA26/170] "Orange-yellow, shaded rosy apricot. Compact bud, opening with many petals of good substance. Slight odor." [ARA27/147] "A striking color—copper-red and cadmium-yellow with capucine bicolor brownish shades. The plant seems to be a strong grower, and the blooms come freely, only the shape is a little flat." [ARA26/167] "Exceedingly brilliant color, reputed to be most floriferous and healthy. Orange-red edged chrome-yellow, and outside petals golden yellow. Bushy, upright in growth, and has very few thorns." [C-Ps25] "A really enchanting color—there is no other Rose just like it. The lovely cupped blooms of brownish orange red, are edged with chrome-yellow, with golden yellow outside petals. In the autumn the flowers last longer, and have better coloring; very brilliant and attractive, especially in the morning. Makes bushy, upright growth and blooms freely." [C-Ps29] "Globular, of fairly good form, both in the bud and when fully expanded, dark apricot, with a rosy sheen, very attractive, sweetly scented. Vigorous, branching, with very beautiful bright, glossy green foliage, quite free of mildew and black-spot." [ARA26/178] "Fades quickly in the sun . . . Bushy, upright in growth." [C-Ps27] "There are not many of the enchanting, orange blooms but each one is a gem laden with perfume." [C-Pf34] "The flower is semi-single, thus adding to its charm . . . Handsome, holly-like foliage." [C-Ps30] "Not a full Rose but a free bloomer and exceedingly brilliant in color when the bloom opens. It is glorious early in the morning." [C-Ps26] "In cool weather it can be of marvelous color, but for hot seasons it is a little thin, and will bleach. I did not notice black-spot on the plants, and it would be a valuable addition to our sorts if this should prove right. It is a good grower, and covered well by luxuriant, glossy leaves; grows a little sideways." [ARA27/204] "Type, 'Souvenir de Claudius Pernet' [Pern]. Bud medium size, pointed; flower medium size, semi-double, cupped; tango color; moderate fragrance. Moderate grower, upright, open habit, 2½ feet high [ca. 7.5 dm]; free and continuous bloomer. Freezes to 10 inches [ca. 2.5 dm]." [ARA24/172] "Tolerably continuous, but with a few blank periods." [NRS29/113] "I have, in the Santa Clara valley [in California], a nursery-row of 'Angèle Pernet' budded [on 'Odorata'] just a year ago. The plants are 3 to 4 feet high [ca. 1–1.3 m], with beautiful, shiny, abundant foliage, free of mildew and black-spot, although surrounded by rows of mildewed roses and with black-spot not far away." [ARA31/221]

"Another widely heralded introduction which so far has only the merit of being an odd color, but this fades quickly, and the rose opens up in very poor form, and has a very worn-out appearance. —*Beverly Hills, Calif.* Looks good for California. —*Oakland, Calif.* 'Angèle Pernet' is superb. —*San Francisco, Calif.* Has come to stay, and seems to be one of Pernet-Ducher's masterpieces. It is an outstanding individual among a class of roses that seem to be perfectly at home here. The color is new and distinct, and the growth is typical and that is good with every rose of the Pernet type here. —*Caldwell, Idaho* . . . Medium-sized, ovoid buds; medium-sized, open flowers, borne singly on medium stems; semi-double and slightly fragrant, coppery cream color. Plant grew 14 inches [ca. 3.5 dm]; of open habit; foliage

Angel Guiméra *continued*

normal and black-spots. Six blooms the first season. —*South Bend, Ind.* Small growth, thin petalage, but most attractive color *which keeps well*. Very interesting and expect more from it another year. —*Harrisburg, Pa.*" [ARA26/112] "Medium-sized buds and full flowers of red-orange and chrome-yellow; the most beautiful copper-colored rose …*Old Lyme, Conn.*; Large ovoid buds; flowers of open form, good lasting quality, and slight fragrance, borne singly or several together on long, strong stems. Color is like an Early Crawford peach, edged with fawn, the back of the petals yellow. Is semi-double, of the 'Killarney' [HT] type. Foliage is glossy and resistant to disease. Open habit (3 feet [ca. 1 m]); bore 54 blooms and was uninjured last winter … *Caldwell, Idaho*; … Fair lasting quality … *Woods Hole, Mass.*; … Foliage …lost early in the fall. A striking color, but flower rarely of good shape. Some early fall blooms were perfect …*Seattle, Wash.*" [ARA27/127–128] "Moderate grower; rather slow to establish itself. A steady bloomer throughout season. Foliage good … *Milton, Mass.*; … Dies back … *Tenn.*; … Fine plant with glossy, bronze foliage, resistant to disease. Flowers deep orange, semi-double, globular. One of the most beautiful copper-colored roses … *Santa Barbara, Calif.*; Has not bloomed at all this fall …*Redlands, Calif.*; Wonderful color throughout the year, and very attractive. Loses foliage easily and not so vigorous as I would like. Have twelve bushes and want at least a dozen more …*California.*" [ARA28/143] "Improves on acquaintance." [ARA27/207] "Angèle is a sister of the late Claudius and Georges Pernet." [C-Ps30]

Angels Mateu
Dot, 1934

"Coppery-carminy." [Ÿ] "Yellowish pink, very large, full, medium scent, tall." [Sn] "Flowers of orange-rose, with an iridescent sheen which is very lovely. It is fully double, having 50 to 75 petals, but always opens well. Delightful blackberry fragrance." [C-Pf34] "One [private rosarium] which I [Pedro Dot] had the honor of visiting lately is that of a great amateur rose-grower, Monsieur Miguel Mateu, in the park of his ancient and beautiful historic chateau of Perelada, near the French border. This rosary was designed by Monsieur Mateu, and comprises all the novelties, foreign and national. Monsieur Mateu is very particular about the nomenclature of the plants, and he has a porcelain label for each one, with the name of the rose, the raiser, and the date." [ARA28/134]

Annette Gravereaux
Leenders, 1929
From 'Mevrouw C. van Marwyk Kooy' (HT) × 'Golden Emblem' (Pern).

"Light orange yellow, very large, full, light scent, medium height." [Sn] "Bud very large, ovoid; flower very large, double, lasting, moderately fragrant, lemon-yellow, shaded orange-cadmium, borne singly on long, strong stem. Foliage sufficient, medium size, dark green, disease-resistant. Growth vigorous, upright; abundant bloomer." [ARA30/228]

Antonio Relleri de Peluffo Listed as 'Antonio Rolleri de Peluffo' (Pern).

Antonio Rolleri de Peluffo
syn. 'Antonio Relleri de Peluffo'
Soupert & Notting, 1926

From 'General MacArthur' (HT) × 'Mme. Édouard Herriot' (Pern).

"Brilliant red with deeper shading in centre carried on strong stems. Growth vigorous." [GeH] "Red, very large, full, medium scent, dwarf." [Sn] "Type, 'General MacArthur'. Bud large, ovoid; flower very large and double, full, lasting, very fragrant, brilliant red, darker at center, borne singly on long, strong stem; drop off cleanly. Foliage normal, large, normal green, leathery. Many thorns. Vigorous, bushy, dwarf; abundant, continuous bloomer. Very hardy." [ARA27/225]

Apotheker Franz Hahne
trans. "Pharmacist Franz Hahne"
Müller, 1920

"Salmon pink, large, full, medium scent, tall." [Sn] "Salmon, rose, base of petals orange-yellow, large, full; hues of distinct red-orange colouring. Growth vigorous, similar to 'Gloire de Dijon' [N]." [GeH] "Flowers large, full, salmon-rose on orange-yellow ground. Very free bloomer." [ARA21/163]

[Ariel]
Bees, 1921
From 'Mme. Édouard Herriot' (Pern) × 'Natalie Böttner' (HT).

"Orange yellow, large, full, medium scent, moderate height." [Sn] "A rose of the 'Independence Day' [Pern] type, with somewhat similar coloring, but the blooms are much larger and better shaped, and are sweetly scented. The habit of growth is upright and vigorous." [ARA21/153] "Bud apricot-flame-orange, opening soft orange-buff; buds fine shape, but open rather loosely and deficient in petals; odor spicy; foliage good. Bush small but healthy; many thorns." [ARA26/98] "Blossoms orange-yellow in the middle and tinted scarlet red on the outside of the petal; medium to large in size, good form, very fragrant, slightly full, often several to a stem. Growth strong, bushy. Plant unusually floriferous." [Ck] Ariel, airy spirit of Shakespeare's comedy *The Tempest*; these days, more frequently seen on the roofs of houses with televisions.

Arthur R. Goodwin Plate 74
Pernet-Ducher, 1909
Either from (1) an unnamed seedling × 'Soleil d'Or' (Pern) or (2) a sport of 'Soleil d'Or' (Pern).

"Coppery orange-red, passing to salmon pink as the flowers expand; flowers medium to large and full." [C&Js14] "Apricot, flushed salmon. Petals numerous and narrow. Very free bloomer." [CA17] "Coppery orange with a trace of orange red over the whole petal; really charming, it blooms freely, has fierce red thorns, a spreading habit of growth, and is deliciously scented. In fact, it is one of the best of its class, blooming all through the season, and its shape is peculiarly Pernetiana." [NRS13/162] "Has a beautiful bud, opening to a nearly flat flower. The lovely orange colour is most attractive. The habit of growth is fair but not very strong, and though the plants may go on for some years they may in any bad weather suffer a good deal." [NRS20/89] "Coppery orange buds, opening into double flowers of bright salmon-pink, which fades in hot weather. Growth low, very branching and thorny. Foliage needs protection against black-spot. Fairly hardy." [C-Ps25] "Coppery orange colour, very beautiful in the bud, opening to a flat centred flower faintly flushed with pink. The plant is not a very strong grower, but makes good stems, a couple of feet long, armed with numerous strong thorns, and carrying good shiny foliage. The flower is not large, but on account of its brilliant colouring it makes a very useful decorative variety." [NRS21/35] "Attractive color; good form; growth, foliage, and bloom fair only; kills back to ground." [ARA18/110] "Rather low, spreading; foliage sufficient, free from disease; bloom moderate and continuous." [ARA18/124] "It is a fine sturdy grower and good solid wood that stands winter well. The general tone of colour is pinkish orange. Flowers rather flat, but lovely buds and very floriferous. A fine bedder. Growths covered with formidable prickles. We have here a sweetly fragrant variety, a rather uncommon feature of this tribe." [NRS21/131] "Very vigorous plant with bushy habit; foliage reddish green; flower medium-sized or large, full, imbricated form; magnificently colored reddish coppery orange passing to salmon pink when the petals fall. Continuous bloom . . . A superb variety of novel coloration, very floriferous and hardy. This will be an excellent garden rose, which will enrich this new group [Pernetianas] very nicely." [JR33/23]

Autumn

Coddington, 1930

From 'Sensation' (HT) × 'Souvenir de Claudius Pernet' (Pern).

"Stained and splashed with red, orange, and various shades of pink—a regular rainbow." [C-Pf34] "Sparkling crimson red." [Ÿ] "Crimson-scarlet and yellow. Growth moderate." [GeH] "Orange red, medium size, full, moderate height." [Sn] "The most gorgeous combination of crimson-scarlet and yellow which we have ever seen. The firm, compact buds are medium size, bright golden yellow, stained crimson without, and deepening to luscious orange in the center. They open to double, splendidly shaped flowers of glorious crimson and gold, with stiff petals that endure much handling without injury . . . These Roses will be disseminated in 1930." [ARA29/xix] "'Autumn' has a good name and because of its strong colors is going to be popular, although the shape of the flowers is nothing to boast about and it has the bad habit of holding the dead flowers on the bush. Its rich reds and yellows are too startling to be passed by, however." [CaRoll/10/3] "The darkest flower among the 'fancy' Roses. The short buds are deep burnt-orange, opening to medium-sized, very double, fragrant flowers of the same burnt-orange, stained with red and orange at the edges and base of the inner petals. It fades somewhat lighter with age but is always striking. It resembles 'Talisman' [Pern] in form of flower, but is much more richly colored." [C-Ps33] "Bud medium size, ovoid, burnt orange; flower medium size, double, cupped, lasting, moderately fragrant, burnt orange, streaked with red, borne singly on medium-length stem. Foliage abundant, medium size, leathery, glossy, disease-resistant. Growth moderate, upright; free, continuous bloomer." [ARA29/218] "Healthy growth." [C-Pf32] "*Hatton's* report is characteristic—'probably the darkest of the "fancy" roses, burnt-orange streaked with red, slightly fragrant and a shy bloomer. The early blooms were blotchy but the autumn blooms were superb. I am anxious to see it on good plants.' *Goodwin* says it is exactly the color the introducer and the catalogues say it is. He had only one gorgeous bloom in September and felt amply repaid for the three months' wait he had for it. *Hampton* finds it a remarkably good plant, and *Covell* enjoyed the few small, brilliant orange and yellow flowers from a very little plant." [ARA31/201]

Autumn Tints

B. R. Cant, 1914

"Copper red and yellow, medium size, full, medium height." [Sn]

"Colour, coppery-red shaded with orange and salmon, medium-size flowers produced in great profusion throughout the Summer and Autumn; the growth is strong and branching and the foliage a rich bronzy green, not liable to mildew. An exceedingly attractive bedding and decorative variety of similar colouring to [that of] 'Mme. Édouard Herriot' [Pern]." [NRS15/177] "Rather on the small side." [NRS21/135] "Growth and blooming qualities not sufficient to warrant its being retained." [ARA18/115]

Barbara

W. Paul, 1923

"Flower very bright red, with yellow base and reverse of petals pale yellow." [ARA24/168] "Orange red, very large, lightly full, medium height." [Sn] "Of excellent shape and substance and one of the brightest orange-reds in the garden; but it bloomed so little that we fear it will never amount to much." [ARA27/128] "Needs heat without dampness. Very brilliant orange shades; continuous bloomer; may be trained as pillar or climber; foliage mildews. Valuable for distinct color; little perfume or cutting value." [ARA28/95] "Doubtless a Pernetiana, it forms a larger bush, much in the way of the old 'Général Jacqueminot' [HP], but blooms all summer. The strong shoots are each crowned by a bud, and soon break, to bring a second lot of blooms on shorter stems. The color reminds me of [that of] 'The Queen Alexandra Rose' [Pern]." [ARA26/166] "For massing." [GeH]

Barbara Richards

A. Dickson, 1930

"Yellow, very large, full, medium scent, medium height." [Sn] "Inner face: bright maize-yellow with buff reverse; the bud and young flower are washed and flushed warm rose, blooms of exhibition size and sweetly scented." [GeH] "Bud very large, ovoid, maize-yellow, washed rose; flower very large, extremely double, full, high-centered, unusually lasting, intensely fragrant (sweet), maize-yellow with buff reverse flushed warm rose, borne singly on long, strong stem. Foliage sufficient, large, rich green, leathery, disease-resistant. Growth vigorous, bushy; abundant, continuous bloomer all season. Very hardy." [ARA31/230]

[Beauté de Lyon]

trans. "Beauty from Lyon"

Pernet-Ducher, 1910

From 'Soleil d'Or' (Pern) × an unnamed seedling.

"Very charming. The huge red thorns, with brilliant green fragrant foliage, show up the handsome flowers, which are coral red and yellow, or pale terra-cotta blended with yellow. It has bloomed all through the past season and is very vigorous in growth." [NRS13/163] "Bush of great vigor, with strong and upright canes; gay green foliage; flower large, full, globular, always opening well; superbly colored coral, slightly nuanced yellow . . . Absolutely hardy, this new rose is distinguished from 'Soleil d'Or' by its stronger canes, more ample foliage, and blossoms which, though less full, have larger petals; while remontant, it can't be called floriferous. The unique coloration of 'Beauté de Lyon' will ensure it a place in the most modest collection." [JR34/40] "Unique, and I would not be without it. The plant is first to bloom in June and is through when '[Mme. Édouard] Herriot' [Pern] and some of the early ones begin. I do not cut this rose back unless some cane looks unhealthy, but I simply cut off the ends of the canes. It stands about 4 feet high [ca. 1.3 m], with large, strong stems

[Beauté de Lyon] *continued*

covered with huge thorns. These stems are staked to the ground in winter. There were seventy-five large, perfect blooms at one time on one bush this year. The color is deep copper-yellow and the flower is semi-double and very fragrant." [ARA29/53–54] "The foliage is of a greyish hue, most distinct. Practically only a summer-bloomer." [NRS21/131] "Fine but it flowers only once." [ARA27/206] "Distinct in colour." [Cat12] "A pillar Rose of a very fine colour. In this variety Pernet-Ducher was getting near to what he ultimately gave us in 'Mme. Édouard Herriot'. 'Beauté de Lyon' has still its admirers." [NRS25/114] See also under 'Rayon d'Or' (Pern).

Belle Cuivrée

trans. "The Beautiful Coppery One"
Pernet-Ducher, 1924

"Orange red, medium size, full, medium height." [Sn] "Almost a ringer for 'Angèle Pernet' [Pern] at first glance. A little more red in the color and of a cup-like shape. It bloomed so little that there was small opportunity to observe it." [ARA27/128] "No bloom is carried upright." [ARA27/204] "Type, 'Mme. Édouard Herriot' [Pern]. Flower medium size, nearly full, coral-red, shaded coppery yellow. Foliage dark green. Vigorous grower, branching habit. It is a hybrid of two un-named seedlings." [ARA26/182] "Buds crimson, flushed orange; blooms medium size, bright coppery orange, with slight fragrance. Different and decorative, but not vigorous. Wintered badly and had 60 per cent black-spot. Gave 11 blooms ... *Ontario*; A little bloom of grand color, but quick to go. Weak ... *Calif*." [ARA28/144]

Bénédicte Seguin

Pernet-Ducher, 1918

"Apricot." [C-Ps29] "A beautiful yellow, and fragrant, but such a shy bloomer." [ARA30/164] "Copper orange, large, full, medium scent, moderate height." [Sn] "Brownish terra cotta, shaded coppery orange, large, full, and globular, buds reddish apricot shaded carmine. Growth very vigorous, erect, branching; foliage bronzed reddish green. Distinct." [GeH] "Bud reddish apricot, shaded carmine; flowers large, full, globular, Roman ocher, shaded coppery orange. Foliage reddish, bronzy green. Strong, erect grower." [ARA19/100] "A superb new orange-yellow rose ... A very vigorous plant with bronzy green foliage and an abundance of flowers." [ARA20/124] "The blooms are carried on long straight stems and the buds are most attractive, being reddish-apricot, shaded with carmine. It is, however, too thin and short in the petals. It is also not free enough to my mind, so I cannot recommend it to the small amateur." [NRS24/152] "Large petals, very fine in bud ...; its colour is golden-yellow, with fine dark foliage, and very long firm stem. It is more of an H.T. than a Pernetiana; it has besides the delicate and penetrating perfume of the Hybrid Tea, a quality worthy of note in a yellow Rose, especially one so highly coloured as this one." [NRS21/104–105] "One of the finest roses for exhibition that I had in my garden last year." [ARA26/112]

Betty Uprichard

A. Dickson, 1922

"Color striking—outside copper, inside silvery salmon." [ARA29/96] "Carmine pink." [Ÿ] "Soft pink flushed orange, with deeper centre, full and pointed, fragrant." [GeH] "Salmon pink, large, lightly double, very fragrant, tall." [Sn] Carmine-colored buds; open flowers salmon, suffused with orange on the inside, with coppery carmine reverse, of

medium size and not full." [C-Ps26] "The somewhat scanty number of fine long petals stand erect and hold fast their colors on both sides under any weather, at no time showing fatigue. Not very scented outdoors, but the perfume develops indoors when used as cut-flowers. A worthy Rose of unusual color." [C-Ps28] "The colour is always good in rain or sunshine." [NRS24/150] "Difficult to describe. One writer has it: 'The outer face of the petals is orange-scarlet, inner face soft pink, shaded with apricot towards the base.' I have it as a mixture of salmon and orange. The blooms are small and rather thin, but they are most attractive, having a distinct verbena scent. The plants shown were vigorous and free from mildew." [ARA21/153] "Medium-sized, long-pointed buds and large, semi-double flowers of beautiful deep pink and flesh. Grew vigorously in early summer; not so good later." [ARA27/128] "Bud medium size, long-pointed; flower large, full, open, semi-double to double, high centered; delicate salmon-pink, reverse glowing carmine with coppery sheen and suffusion of orange; borne singly and several together, on long, strong stem; strong fragrance. Foliage abundant, large, leathery, glossy, light bronze-green. Few thorns. Vigorous, bushy, profuse and continuous bloomer from June to October; hardy." [ARA23/148] "Our customers' enthusiasm over this Rose increases every year. A vigorous grower, it emulates 'Radiance' [HT] in performance. It is one of the best of the two-tone type ... The plant is healthy and vigorous." [C-Ps29] "It is a rampant grower, bearing, on very long shoots, fine colored blooms that show on the outside a deep coral-carmine whilst the inner face of the petals is a delightful soft orange-pink. This rose has perhaps but one fault—its weak neck; sometimes the large blooms bow their heads. In spite of this, it is a grand rose." [ARA25/135] "Vigorous upright growth, but sometimes it develops the '[Mme. Abel] Chatenay' [HT] habit of throwing up one strong shoot and the rest nowhere." [NRS24/171] "Vigorous, reaching about 2½ feet [ca. 7.5 dm]. Blooms freely. Stems long and strong. Foliage not over-plentiful, slightly susceptible to mildew and black-spot." [ARA28/145] "A strong grower and an abundant bloomer. In color it is a coral-rose of most striking shade which combines beautifully with 'Los Angeles' [Pern] or 'Souvenir de Georges Pernet' [Pern]. Like 'Padre' [Pern], it causes much favorable comment from all who visit our garden. It is best in the fall when the blooms are deeper color and fuller. As our autumn in central Kentucky is long, we find the roses that do exceptionally well at that time are those to be well considered when planning the garden." [ARA31/99] "Fine to go with 'Padre'." [ARA26/170] "Deserves to be planted in numbers, near 'Padre' and 'Elvira Aramayo' [Pern]." [ARA28/136]

"Looks like a splendid grower; liked it very much. —*Rutherford, N.J.* Vigorous growth; profuse bloom; heat-resisting quality; brilliant color. One of the most promising. —*Editor's Observation*. A very pretty rose but also one of those semi-double flowers of which we are now getting so many. Its colors are glorious and its shape more pretty than good. Will make an excellent bedding rose where color is desired as it has lots of bloom and its color is so striking. Mildewed with me but not badly. —*Seattle, Wash.* Every bloom perfect. —*Birmingham, England*." [ARA26/113] "A ravishing flower, rather single, but of a perfect form and of coloring most happily shaded." [ARA25/128] "Should prove a good acquisition, for it has really a quite unique and novel coloring—a deep salmon-pink, with a lighter surface on the petals. The bud is pointed, and the large flower opens well; it is one of the best of the newer roses." [ARA24/108] "Worth trying." [NRS24/152]

California
Howard & Smith, 1916

"Deep orange yellow, large, full, medium scent, moderate height." [Sn] Not to be confused with the 1940 HT of much the same color. California, the Golden State, both geologically and in spirit.

Cambrai
syn. 'Cambraia'
Smith, 1920
Sport of 'Mme. Édouard Herriot' (Pern).

"Light orange, medium size, full, moderate height." [Sn] "Rich deep apricot, semi-double, free. A sport of 'Mme. Édouard Herriot', with all its characteristics. [GeH] Cambrai, alias Cambray, city in northern France.

Cambraia Listed as 'Cambrai' (Pern).

Cardinal Mercier
Lens, 1930

"Salmony pink, orange reverse." [Ÿ] "Orange salmon pink, very large, full, moderate height." [Sn]

Cécile Ratinckx
Vandevelde, 1924

"Copper yellow, large, full, moderate height." [Sn] "Coppery yellow. Foliage glistening green. Growth vigorous; very floriferous." [ARA26/186]

Ceres
Spek, 1922
From 'Sunburst' (Pern) × 'Mme. Edmond Rostand' (HT).

"Deep orange, large, full, medium height." [Sn] "Flower deep orange, salmon in center. Very vigorous; continuous bloomer." [ARA24/173] Not to be confused with the similarly named Hybrid Musk. Ceres, goddess of Agriculture, whence "cereal."

[Christine]
McGredy, 1918

"Superb citron-yellow." [Cw] "Clear yellow, occasional red splash on bud; odor fair. Bush strong." [ARA26/94] "Flower deepest and clearest golden yellow, perfectly shaped, with petals of good substance; sweetly scented. Growth vigorous; deep glossy green mildew-proof foliage." [GeH]

Cissie Easlea
Pernet-Ducher, 1913
From 'Mme. Mélanie Soupert' (HT) × 'Rayon d'Or' (Pern).

"Its colouring is a dream. A very clear saffron yellow, with carmine center, large, a full globular bloom of special charm." [NRS13/164] "Yellow, red center, very large, full, moderate height." [Sn] "Form, roundish; full, lasting, saffron yellow with orange; leaves healthy, glossy." [Ck] "In the matter of foliage, however, 'Cissie Easlea'—a good clear yellow—has the finest of all." [ARA25/132] "Perhaps the most beautiful foliage of any Rose grown. It is really remarkable in size, colour and brightness. The flowers are large, of a saffron yellow shade, passing to Naples yellow." [NRS21/134] "Green bronzed foliage, oval-shaped bud of pale buff tint, shaded with bright carmine; flower large, full and globular, coloring clear saffron-yellow with carmine passing to Naples-yellow when expanding." [C&Js14] "Few thorns."

[GeH] "Very vigorous bush with upright canes; foliage bronzy green; thorns fairly numerous and protrusive; bud ovoid, reddish nankeen shaded bright carmine; blossom very large, full, globular, colored light saffron yellow with a carminy center, fading to Naples yellow when the petals fall. Excellent garden and exhibition rose." [JR37/42]

Collette Clément
Mallerin, 1931

"Coppery rose. Not entirely single but almost so. A Rose for brightening garden-beds as it is so free in bloom and vigorous in growth." [C-Pf34] "Red-orange, medium size, lightly double, light scent, moderate height." [Sn] "Flower semi-double, nasturtium-red. Foliage disease-resistant. Growth very vigorous." [ARA31/235] "Use it along the shrub-border where color is wanted and cut-flowers are not expected." [C-Ps34]

Comtesse Vandal
syn. and trans. 'Countess Vandal'
Leenders, 1932
From an unnamed seedling (which resulted from a cross of 'Ophelia' [HT] and 'Mrs. Aaron Ward' [HT]) × 'Souvenir de Claudius Pernet' (Pern).

"Brilliant chamois." [Ÿ] "Salmon pink, very large, full, medium to tall." [Sn] "An upright-growing, vigorous Rose with rich-colored, attractive, disease-resistant foliage. The perfumed, perfectly formed blooms, which come from long, tapering buds, are a blending of copper, salmon, and gold in color, and they are produced almost continuously on long, erect, rigid stems. This delightful, decorative, cutting rose was the sensation at the 1931 foreign Rose shows where it won many medals and trophies." [C-Ps33] "Bud double, high-centered, very lasting, fragrant, brilliant pink lightened with salmon, yellow at base, borne singly on long stem. Foliage abundant, large, leathery, dark green, disease-resistant. Growth vigorous (2 to 2½ feet [ca. 6–7.5 dm]), upright, bushy; profuse, continuous bloomer. Very hardy in Holland." [ARA31/239]

Condesa de Sástago
Dot, 1932

"Red interior, golden yellow exterior." [Ÿ] "Red and yellow, large, lightly double, medium scent, tall." [Sn] "Open, spicy blooms." [Way45] "Copper and yellow. This Spanish novelty is the first double Rose to carry the vivid colors of the brilliant species Rose, 'Austrian Copper' [F]. There is a lot of Hybrid Perpetual blood in it, as well as species and Hybrid Tea, so that the plant is unusually strong and upright in growth, with foliage well up on the flower-stem. The blooms are fully double, reddish copper on the inside of the petals and deep yellow on the outside, a combination which attracts immediate attention. Unlike many high-colored Roses, this one is fragrant, having an alluring spicy scent." [C-Ps33]

[Constance]
Pernet-Ducher, 1915
Seedling of 'Rayon d'Or' (Pern).

"Golden yellow; moderate, spare." [ARA17/32] "With intense golden yellow flowers of medium size, of fair, globular form, 'Constance' was a step in advance toward the perfect yellow Rose. Its color is somewhat fleeting. It is much better in the southern part of the country." [C-Ps25] "It has not enough substance and opens too quickly, also

[Constance] *continued*

fades to some extent." [ARA25/99] "[The color] will hold if the plant were partially shaded." [C-Ps29] "Wonderful color; growth and foliage only fair; hard to establish—liable to winterkill." [ARA18/110] "Buds deep orange, splashed vermilion, opening to handsome, clear rich yellow; flowers of good size, with good stems; odor fair. Foliage good. Bush medium strong with good growth in spite of bad start. 12 blooms." [ARA26/98] "A very vigorous grower, of spreading, branching habit; glossy green foliage; long, orange-yellow bud, streaked with crimson; large, full-globular flower of beautiful cadmium-yellow coloring, passing to golden yellow." [C&Js15] "Large to extra large, fine form, double, slight scent, medium to long stem. Glossy foliage, sufficient. Growth poor; hardy. Deep yellow changing to buff-yellow." [ARA23/159] "Sometimes a martyr to 'black-spot'." [NRS20/161] "Not unlike 'Rayon d'Or', but a superior Rose." [C&Js24] "Far superior in growth to 'Rayon d'Or'." [NRS21/135]

Countess Vandal   Listed as 'Comtesse Vandal' (Pern).

Daily Mail Rose   Listed as 'Mme. Édouard Herriot' (Pern).

Dannenberg
Kiese, 1916
From 'Gruss an Teplitz' (B) × 'Lyon-Rose' (Pern).

"Coral with blood-red; bud cherry pink, with touches of yellow-pink; large; quite full." [Jg] "Rose-red, large, full, medium scent, medium height." [Sn]

Dazla
B. R. Cant, 1930

"Brilliant orange-scarlet, with yellow base; buds long and pointed. Flowers semi-double, large waved petals." [GeH] "Orange red, yellow center, large, lightly double, medium height." [Sn] "Bud long-pointed; flower large (nearly 6 in. across [ca. 1.5 dm]), semi-double, with waved petals, brilliant orange-scarlet with golden yellow base and reverse. Foliage dark green. Growth very vigorous. Extremely hardy." [ARA31/213] "Of the same brilliantly colored, few petaled type as 'I Zingari' [Pern] and 'Gwyneth Jones' [Pern], but just how well it will compete with these two remains to be seen. It has possibilities." [CaRoll/10/4] "[The Queen] stopped a few moments to admire a great vase of the new rose 'Dazla', which really was dazzling." [ARA31/168]

[Deutschland]
trans. "Germany"
Kiese, 1910
From 'Frau Karl Druschki' (HP) × 'Soleil d'Or' (Pern).

"Cream, opening to golden yellow." [Cat12] "This was a big yellow Rose . . . I could never get it to grow. It gave some nice flowers, but it was a martyr to Black Spot." [NRS25/114] "Golden yellow, with faint rosy yellow fusion in the centre of the bloom. It grows somewhat like '[Frau Karl] Druschki', showing this parentage in the wood." [NRS13/162] One also sees an attribution of "Zuchtunger, 1911," of unknown validity.

Dilly's Wiederkehr
trans. "Dilly's Return"
Schwartzbach, 1925

"Pink, large, full, medium height." [Sn]

Director Rubió
Dot, 1927
From 'O. Junyent' (Pern) × 'Jean C. N. Forestier' (Pern).

"Cerise-red, large, and fragrant, with healthy foliage . . . a splendid variety." [ARA29/186] "A very vigorous plant and large blooms of a very beautiful red." [ARA27/212] "The color is unique and the laminated [*sic; 'fimbriated,' perhaps?*] petals of the fully opened flower bring to mind the ruffled feathers of a swan." [C-Ps31] "Red, large, lightly double, light scent, medium height." [Sn] "Bud large, long-pointed; flower very large, semi-double, lasting, moderately fragrant, magenta-red, borne singly on stiff stem. Foliage abundant, large, disease-resistant. Growth very vigorous, bushy; abundant bloomer from May to November." [ARA29/229] "One of the most striking Roses we have ever grown, and produces the largest Rose-blooms we have ever seen—one great flower measured $7^{1}/_{2}$ inches in diameter [ca. 1.9 dm]. The color is cochineal-pink . . . but that does not describe the brilliance and beauty of the flower at all stages, from the mammoth, long-pointed bud to the loose, ruffled, open flower, and it doesn't fade. The plant is hardly of average height, but is extra-sturdy, like a low-growing Hybrid Perpetual, and the flowers are held rigidly erect on stout stems." [C-Pf34] "*Nicolas* calls it his pet, a 'he' rose, hardy as an oak, and simply handsome. In growth it reminds us of 'H. V[essey] Machin' [HT], 'Mrs. Wakefield Christie-Miller' [HT], and 'Mme. Albert Barbier' [HP] —stiff, stubby and erect, each stem topped by flaring, flat, brilliant pink flowers of enormous size. It is exceedingly handsome, but there are long periods without flowers." [ARA30/195] "It is all that its friends claim for it when it blooms, but it blooms too seldom at Breeze Hill, and the plants do not grow." [ARA31/202] "Very vigorous." [C-Pf31]

"Director Rubió, in charge of Barcelona (Spain) public parks and Royal Gardens, is a critical judge of Roses, and to have permitted his name to be given a Rose is in itself a guarantee of quality. Twin of the now popular 'Mari Dot' [extinct], grandchild of 'Frau Karl Druschki' [HP] and 'Mme. Édouard Herriot' [Pern] with 'J[ean] C. N Forestier' [Pern] as a father, 'Director Rubió' is a blue-blooded grandee! Of medium height and compact form, it makes an ideal bedder. It outshone every other brilliant pink Rose in our Rose-fields last summer. The bud, borne on [an] erect pedicel, is cerise-scarlet, opening to a very large and fairly double bloom, sweetly scented, of a solid cochineal-pink, holding its color long, rain or shine; then it pales some and dies gracefully. The petals are uneven in shape, some notched. The span from the first color of the bud to the drop of the petals is unusually long. We have had 'Director Rubió' under observation for five years and we highly recommend it as the most vivid, yet refined, bedding or cut-flower variety." [C-Ps30] "The Pedralbes rose-garden is laid out in a superbly beautiful spot and is not open to the general public. The roses are cultivated, under the patronage of the King, by the park department of the city of Barcelona, whose accomplished superintendent, Señor Nicolas M. Rubió, a former pupil of Monsieur J. C. N. Forestier, of France, is the architect who recently redesigned with great skill the whole ancient enclosure of the Palace of Pedralbes." [ARA30/144]

Dr. Augustin Wibbelt
Leenders, 1928
Sport of 'Los Angeles' (Pern).

"Deep yellow, large, lightly double, light scent, medium height." [Sn] "Bud medium size, long-pointed; flower large, semi-double, open, moderately fragrant, golden yellow shaded orange-cadmium, medium-length stem. Foliage abundant, medium size, light green. Growth bushy; profuse bloomer." [ARA29/227]

Dr. Edward Deacon
Morse, 1926
From 'Mme. Édouard Herriot' (Pern) × 'Gladys Holland' (HT).

"The margin of the petals being pale shrimp-pink, gradually emerging into a deep salmon-orange towards the base of the petals giving the flower a wonderful appearance, each petal being artistically reflexed. The habit of the plant is upright and free. Bold, glossy, leathery foliage, and is practically disease-proof." [GeH] "Bud very large, globular; flower very large and double, full, globular, very lasting, moderately fragrant, deep salmon-orange, fading to shrimp-pink, borne several together on medium-length stems; drop off cleanly. Foliage abundant, large, rich, glossy green, leathery, disease-resistant. Few thorns. Growth vigorous, upright, bushy; free, continuous bloomer in June, July, September, and October. Hardy." [ARA27/215] "*Lowell* thinks it is pretty and has a very vigorous plant growing about 3 feet high [ca. 1 m]. For *Ontario* it wintered well and yielded many fragrant blooms, much better in 1930 than in 1929." [ARA31/190] "Will supersede 'Mme. Édouard Herriot'." [ARA29/210] "Good." [ARA27/207]

Dr. Müller
Müller, 1905

"Salmon pink to red, medium size, lightly double, tall." [Sn]

Duquesa de Peñaranda
syn. 'Duquesa del Peñaranda'
Dot, 1931
From 'Souvenir de Claudius Pernet' (Pern) × 'Rosella' (Cl HP).

"Orange passing to salmon." [Ÿ] "Orange red, very large, full, medium scent, tall." [Sn] "This glorious Rose produces two distinct types of flowers. During the summer the pointed buds are a blend of apricot-orange and dark pink, opening to splendid blooms of coppery apricot. In the autumn great brownish buds open slowly to finely formed flowers of a luscious cinnamon-peach color, truly enchanting to visitors to our gardens who delight in the new art shades. It is sweetly perfumed and one of the loveliest Roses for cutting." [Way45] "Bud very large, long-pointed; flower very large, double, cupped, extremely lasting, fragrant, orange, borne several together on long stem. Foliage abundant, large, rich green, glossy, disease-resistant. Growth very vigorous, upright; free, continuous bloomer all season." [ARA31/244]

Duquesa del Peñaranda   Listed as 'Duquesa de Peñaranda' (Pern).

E. P. H. Kingma
Verschuren, 1919
From 'Mme. Édouard Herriot' (Pern) × 'Duchess of Wellington' (HT).

"Flower full, double, apricot-color and orange-yellow." [ARA21/165] "Orange yellow, medium size, full, moderate height." [Sn] "Deep apricot orange; habit of 'Mme. Édouard Herriot'." [NRS21/141] "Very fine in the half-opened bud, which is a rich, glowing orange shaded apricot. Flowers are semi-double and come almost continuously." [C-Ps28] "Described abroad as apricot-yellow, of fine substance, and the type of 'Mme. Édouard Herriot'. Flower more double than that vari-

ety, with better stem. Foliage and growth reputed to be excellent. An interesting and probably a valuable novelty." [C-Ps25] "Similar to 'Independence Day' [Pern]." [C-Ps29]

[Eldorado]
Howard & Smith, 1923
From an unnamed seedling × 'Mme. Édouard Herriot' (Pern).

"Lovely, double, yellow rose, tinged with red." [ARA29/96] "Bud and flower very large, very double, full, lasting; copper, suffused orange and salmon; borne singly on strong stem; moderate fragrance. Vigorous, bushy; free bloomer." [ARA24/174] "No good here; has a weak neck, and no form … *Grand Junction, Colo.*; Large globular buds and very double flowers of full form, pure yellow with no red streaks, slight fragrance, of very good lasting quality, borne singly on long, strong stems. Abundant, glossy foliage, resistant to disease. Vigorous growth (2 feet [ca. 6 dm]); 45 blooms in the season; uninjured in the winter … *Caldwell, Idaho* … Notched petals, edged pink, and do not fade, of good lasting quality, moderate fragrance, borne singly on short, normal stems. Glossy foliage which black-spots slightly. Upright growth (1½ feet [ca. 5 dm] / Although in a bed of 'Souvenir de Claudius Pernet' [Pern] which were badly black-spotted, it was almost free from the disease … *Meshanticut Park, R.I.*; A favorite with us. The heavy flowers droop in wet and heat, but it has so much more substance and form than 'Souvenir de Claudius Pernet' that we like it better." [ARA27/130–131] Eldorado, alias El Dorado, the Land of Gold, a land of legend frequently associated with the great State of California, where the breeders were located.

Elvira Aramayo
Looymans, 1922
From 'Feu Joseph Looymans' (Pern) × an unnamed seedling (which resulted from a cross of 'Leslie Holland' [HT] and 'Rayon d'Or' [Pern]).

"Indian red best describes its queer flower. The petals curl lengthwise, cactus-like, as they mature." [ARA29/67] "Orange red, medium size, lightly double, medium scent, medium height." [Sn] "The petals are small but long, and the open flower shows a fancy form, much in the way of an aster or chrysanthemum." [ARA26/166] "A beautiful rose of a unique colour, namely Indian red; growth fairly strong, straight and bushy; very free flowering; fine as a decorative and bedding variety." [GeH] "Brilliant unfading color; flower thin but most attractive irregular form. —*Harrisburg, Pa.*" [ARA26/114] "Buds long and pointed; flower of the cactus type with quilled petals. Free-blooming, and a fairly vigorous grower." [C-Ps25] "Has much of the color of 'Mme. Édouard Herriot' [Pern], if it is not still more intense. The open flower, with its many small petals curled and twisted in all directions, shows a new type of rose beauty … This rose is very free and healthy, and I think it will soon be found in most gardens, because it is fuller and a little more intense in its coloring than 'Mme. Édouard Herriot'." [ARA25/136] Growth straight and bushy." [NRS23/258] "It is a seedling of 'Independence Day' from which it has inherited the good qualities and faults a Pernetiana is heir to. The bush is vigorous when once established and a prolific bloomer. Gorgeous in masses." [C-Ps27] "Continually black-spotted." [C-Ps29] "Poor grower; black-spots. Wonderful color; attractive … *Mass.*; Long-pointed buds, opening to medium-sized cactus-like vermilion blooms; fragrance slight. Medium growth. No mildew but bad black-spot. A very striking rose of unusual color. Bore 44 blooms … *R.I.*; … Habit not over-

Elvira Aramayo *continued*

strong…*Conn.*;…'Elvira Aramayo' is the rose best beloved by black-spot. Has never been very popular, and 'Cuba' [Pern; Pernet-Ducher, 1926; like 'Padre' (Pern); extinct] will push it off its perch … *Pa.*" [ARA28/157] "Large, long-pointed buds and flowers of the 'La France' [B or HT] type, with fair lasting quality and slight fragrance, borne on long, strong stems. It is red all the time. Foliage abundant, normal green, and medium size, mildews. Compact, upright-growing (1½ feet [ca. 4.5 dm]); 31 flowers in the season … *Caldwell, Idaho*; Unlike any other rose I know. It has a slight resemblance to a carnation. The orange-scarlet buds are of medium size and long-pointed; flower small, semi-double, the base deep orange, shading into orange-scarlet, very brilliant, paling to cerise-rose as it develops, of open form, good lasting quality, slight fragrance, borne several together on short, normal stems. Abundant, glossy foliage, resistant to disease. Upright, symmetrical growth (2 to 2½ feet [ca. 6–7.5 dm]; 72 flowers in the season; uninjured by winter. Murderous thorns! Color so dazzling it kills other rose effects. Excellent for a decorative vase … *Toronto, Ontario.*" [ARA27/131]

Émile Charles

Bernaix, 1922

Sport of 'Mme. Édouard Herriot' (Pern).

"Light orange red, medium size, full, medium height." [Sn] "Metallic yellow; fair style." [ARA28/157] "Bud fiery red, shaded golden yellow; flower coral-red, edges eglantine pink, shaded crushed strawberry, flame color at base. Vigorous; continuous bloomer." [ARA23/150] "Beautifully colored buds and open flowers of yellow in novel shades, and with ample foliage and good growth." [ARA25/127]

Emma Wright

McGredy, 1918

"Wonderful orange-flame color; odor slight and spicy. Buds fine shape, open too quickly, and almost single. 27 blooms; 19 the second season." [ARA26/94] "Pure orange without shading. An attractive bedding variety of good habit … noted by Hazlewood, of New South Wales, as single. Of decorative value in cool climates; foliage reported good." [Th2] "For a boutonnière, the last word is 'Emma Wright', producing, with amazing freedom, long buds of exquisite shape and startling brilliant orange color." [ARA29/60] "Free-flowering." [ARA19/102] "A good doer and free bloomer, semi-double, of fine salmon-red." [ARA24/107] "Orange yellow, large, lightly double, light scent, medium height." [Sn] "Blooms freely produced on upright stems. Thin but not liable to damage by rain. Colour pure orange, shaded pink, edge of petals paler. Foliage and wood bright reddy [*sic*] green, free of mildew. Growth fairly vigorous and branching, both as a maiden and cutback. A fine bedding and decorative Rose." [NRS23/91] "A very fine decorative Rose. When I first saw this Rose I thought it too much like the H.T. 'Old Gold', but it is really a great improvement on that well-known variety. The blooms are of a pure orange colour, which it retains until the petals fall; … sweetly scented. The foliage is bright and glossy, and quite free from mildew." [NRS18/165] "The foliage is dark, good and glossy, and is not much affected by mildew or black spot." [NRS29/104]

Entente Cordiale   Plate 73

P. Guillot, 1908

From 'Mme. Caroline Testout' (HT) × 'Soleil d'Or' (Pern).

"Coppery-yellow, edged rose. Vigorous." [NRS11/99] "A loose flower of quaint colouring, colours cherry red and yellow. An interesting Rose, but hardly worth growing to-day." [NRS21/131] "Blooms in clusters of six or eight large, loosely built, cherry red and yellow blooms. When well dined and disbudded the blooms are full and very handsome, the colour standing out well." [NRS13/161] "Red, yellow center, large, lightly double, medium scent, medium height." [Sn] "Very vigorous plant, bushy, canes rather out-thrust, thorns numerous, fine, thickened at the base; foliage pretty ample, light green; inflorescences few-flowered; peduncles flexuose; buds long; sepals filiform, very elongated; flowers large, double, cupped, nasturtium red on a large golden yellow ground; stamens the same color; petal reverse golden salmon at the base shading to a lighter salmony carmine at the tip. Very elegant and floriferous variety." [JR32/134] "Quite distinct from the rose of the same name raised by Pernet-Ducher, which is creamy-white." [Cat12]

Étoile de Feu

trans. 'Fire-Star'

Pernet-Ducher, 1921

"Flaming orange flowers, with glow of pink." [ARA29/96] "Pink to salmon red, large, full, medium height." [Sn] "Salmon-pink and coral-red, shaded with flame colour, large, full, globular; fine foliage. Growth vigorous." [GeH] "Upstanding center petals … 'Fiery Star', as the name implies, it throws out glowing flame tints which make it really unique." [C-Ps29] "Superb orange-rose and holds its color. Brighter and better in blooming, growth and foliage than 'Louise Catherine Breslau' [Pern]." [ARA26/114] "Is a little freer than 'Louise Catherine Breslau', and slightly more constant, but the color is much the same." [ARA24/108] "Quite similar to 'Louise C[atherine] Breslau', but holds its foliage better." [C-Ps26] "The flower, and manner of growth, are much like the old 'Louise Catherine Breslau', but the foliage is prettier and the flower has more 'fire.' The blooms are also more freely produced, immense in size and cup-shaped, opening flat, but the center is filled with short petals. In addition to its attractiveness, the foliage of this rose is very little troubled by disease." [CaRoll/4/1] "A cupped bloom of reddish orange, quite similar to 'Beauté de Lyon' [Pern], but on a low-growing branching bush. Apparently a free bloomer and reasonably healthy." [C-Ps25] "Seems rather weak." [ARA25/120] "An abundant bloomer throughout the season." [C-Ps33] "Flower large, full, globular, salmon-pink and coral-red, shaded with flame tint. Foliage glossy bronze-green. Very vigorous, bushy, branching habit; very hardy." [ARA22/148] "Too tender for this [Connecticut] climate." [ARA27/131] "The globular buds of glowing flame tints gradually open to blooms of coral-pink and reddish salmon, which are full, cactus-form, and very large. A vigorous grower, branching in habit, with beautiful, shiny, dark green foliage, more resistant to disease than [that of] most other Pernetianas." [C-Ps27] "Long, pointed buds; full, double gorgeous orange-flame flowers, fading coral-pink; exquisite fragrance; very good keeper; 50 petals. Bore 19 blooms. Medium, branching growth. Beautiful holly-like foliage. A great favorite and one of the best new roses … *Buffalo, N.Y.*; Very good. Color varies but mostly flame at first opening, passing to salmon-yellow … Beautiful, leathery green leaves. No disease … *Washington, D.C.*; … It does not keep well when cut, and gives fewer blooms than 'Independence Day' [Pern] … *Wis.*; Moderate growth; rather free bloomer. Flowers resemble a full double water-lily … *Minn.*" [ARA28/157] "The plants, when young, are of spreading habit, but become more upright and branching when they are established." [C-Ps31] "The foliage is glossy and the plant is branching, and blooms well until late fall—a rose I would not be without." [ARA25/101]

Feu Joseph Looymans

trans. "The Late Joseph Looymans"
Looymans, 1921
From 'Sunburst' (Pern) × 'Rayon d'Or' (Pern).

"Apricot yellow." [Cw] "Indian yellow." [Ÿ] "Yellow-orange bud, opening deep yellow-orange, veined apricot. Large, perfect buds, opening well to medium-full flowers of good substance. Last well when cut. Slight odor. Very lovely." [ARA27/147] "Vigorous. Yellow, with vivid apricot. Buds long and pointed, well-formed blooms." [GeH] "Yellow, light orange center, large, full, medium height." [Sn] "A brilliant and effective yellow with vivid apricot centre; buds well formed, long and pointed; flowers large, fairly full; growth strong, straight and bushy; strongly recommended for garden and exhibition purposes. A Rose of undoubted merit." [NRS23/208] "A very large but not too full golden yellow rose, that sometimes has a bronze shading. A rampant grower, and well covered with luxuriant foliage. The blooms are borne on long shoots, and give fine material for decorative purposes." [ARA25/136] "Bud very large, long-pointed; flower very large, cupped, very double, lasting; Indian yellow; borne on long, weak stem. Foliage abundant, leathery, dark green, disease-resistant. Vigorous; blooms abundantly and continuously; hardy." [ARA22/155] "Good as a 'maiden'; not so good as 'cut-back'." [ARA28/157] "Would be worth growing for its foliage alone." [ARA29/60] "Plant extremely strong-growing and erect, with beautiful, healthy foliage and long stems. The blossom opens well, sufficiently full, reddish yellow. A stand-out in the newcomers." [Ck] "The last production of Joseph Looymans, and dedicated to him by his sons." [ARA28/158]

Flammenrose

trans. "Flame-Rose"
Türke/Kiese, 1920
From either 'Mrs. E. G. Hill' (HT) or 'Mrs. Joseph Hill' (HT) × 'Mme. Édouard Herriot' (Pern).

"Coppery red." [Cw] "Rosy red, buds striped orange and yellow, large and full; well-shaped on strong upright stems." [GeH] "Light orange yellow, medium size, lightly double, light scent, medium height." [Sn] "Flower more orange-yellow and more intense than [that of] 'Mme. Édouard Herriot' [Pern], borne, singly and several together, on long, strong stem. Foliage leathery, disease-resistant." [ARA22/154]

Florence L. Izzard

syn. 'Florence M. Izzard'
McGredy, 1923

"A good deep cadmium-yellow, but the bloom is sometimes crippled and, as a rule, is too small." [ARA26/166] "Copper yellow, medium size, lightly double, very fragrant, moderate height." [Sn] "The colour is a pure deep buttercup yellow, blooms long and beautifully pointed, of fine substance, perfect form and delightfully scented. Foliage mildew-proof and glossy, with few spines, with an ideal habit of growth." [NRS23/260] "Gorgeous color and queer, lopsided shape. Plant grows sideways, and not very vigorously." [ARA27/132] "A delightful rose, of a glorious golden yellow color; quite one of the best of that shade the raiser has given us ... We now have in this rose the

full pointed center that has long been the aim of rose-growers. The blooms are of medium size, with a distinct trace of tea scent. The plants exhibited did not show such strong growth as one would have liked to have seen, but it was evident that that was only a passing fault, doubtless caused by over-propagation." [ARA22/146] "A very beautiful rose. Color rich yellow, which it retains well. The blooms are fairly large and of good form, but liable to be, perhaps, a little rough when fully expanded; deliciously scented—in fact, the judges were of unanimous opinion that the perfume was identical to that grand old variety 'Maréchal Niel' [N]. Not liable to damage by rain. It is, undoubtedly, at its best in the half-open stage, when the petals recurve in a very delicate way. The foliage is a bright holly-green, shaded red; wood and spines bright red. The plant shown was of vigorous habit and free from mildew. A magnificent rose. In this rose the Pernetiana blood is almost entirely eliminated, and it is practically a pure Hybrid Tea." [ARA23/144] "For exhibition, bedding, garden and cut-flower purposes." [GeH] "'Mrs. E[rskine] P[embroke] Thom' [Pern] is better." [C-Ps29] "Good as maiden only; dies the second year. Same report from Europe. I have done my best to grow it for four years, and am still trying ... Pa.; ... Beautiful, but too thin to consider as a standard variety ... Calif." [ARA28/159]

Florence M. Izzard   Listed as 'Florence L. Izzard' (Pern).

Frau Felberg-Leclerc

Felberg-Leclerc, 1921
Sport of 'Louise Catherine Breslau' (Pern).

"Yellow, medium size, full, light scent, medium height." [Sn] "Bud medium size, globular; flower medium size, full, double, cupped, lasting; pure golden yellow; borne singly on good stem; slight fragrance. Foliage sufficient, leathery, bronze-green. Growth moderate, dwarf, branches divergent; profuse and continuous bloomer all season; tips freeze." [ARA22/154]

Geisha

Van Rossem, 1920
Sport of 'Mme. Édouard Herriot' (Pern).

"Golden yellow orange." [Cw] "Very fine Rose, perpetual flowering, colour pink apricot." [NRS23/173] "Orange-apricot-yellow-buff, all blended and fading to rosy buff. Long, well-shaped buds, opening rather too quickly to a flower lacking in petals. Odor fair. Bush strong." [ARA27/147] "Deep orange, striped red, large, full, light scent, medium height." [Sn] "Pure deep orange-yellow, gradually changing to golden yellow when opening; the buds are long, pointed, streaked with garnet. Growth vigorous, of branching habit, and green bronzed foliage; perpetual flowering." [GeH] "Bud medium size, long-pointed, orange, marked coral-red; flower large, open, double, lasting; golden yellow; borne, several together, on good stem; slight fragrance. Foliage sufficient, medium size, glossy dark green; disease-resistant. Many thorns. Vigorous, upright, bushy; blooms profusely all season; hardy." [ARA22/155–156] "Same as '[Miss] May Marriott' [Pern], with habit of 'Mme. Édouard Herriot'. —*Hamilton, Ont.* Bright color but hardly worth bothering with. —*Harrisburg, Pa.*" [ARA26/114]

Georges Clemenceau

Lévêque, 1919
Sport of 'Mme. Édouard Herriot' (Pern).

"Carmine red, nuanced yellow." [Cw] "Bright orange, shaded car-

Georges Clemenceau *continued*

mine, splendid and very effective." [NRS21/140] "Orange red, large, very full, medium height." [Sn] "Flower large, well-formed, very full; bright orange, shaded with umber and carmine. Very vigorous; profuse bloomer." [ARA21/160] "Bright orange tinted and shaded with carmine, large, well formed; elongated bud of fine form. Growth very vigorous; handsome glossy green foliage." [GeH] Georges Clemenceau, French politician, lived 1841–1929.

[Golden Emblem]
McGredy, 1916

"Golden citron yellow." [Cw] "Rich yellow blooms." [ARA20/122] "A real, dependable yellow." [ARA25/205] "Golden-yellow, splashed crimson on outer petals; full, strong stems; mildly scented; fine foliage. Recurrent." [CaRoll/3/2] "The peerless yellow rose. This summer, in the mountains, I had two plants of it which during three months were never a week without bloom." [ARA25/131–132] "Golden Emblem's buds are a delight, but I do not much care for the expanded bloom. It has more substance than 'Christine' [Pern], but the flowers are fewer and the color disappears almost as quickly. The foliage is glossy and apparently resistant to disease." [ARA25/204] "A remarkable Rose, somewhat resembling 'Rayon d'Or' [Pern] in colour, but perhaps a shade deeper in its golden yellow. The flowers are fuller and of better form, with petals of greater substance, and are sweetly fragrant. It is said to be a fine grower, flowering in greatest profusion. The foliage is a fine deep glossy green, and not liable to mildew." [NRS16/146] "A great improvement on 'Rayon d'Or', the colour being richer and deeper, with larger and more perfect blooms. It is so perpetual flowering that as a bedding and garden Rose it is without a rival. At its best it surpasses 'Maréchal Niel' [N] in shape and formation, and with its wonderful colouring will be a telling Exhibition flower. The habit of growth is ideal: free and branching, with a splendid constitution, holding every bloom rigidly upright. It has glossy, holly-like green foliage of wonderful substance and beauty. Mildew proof and delightfully sweet scented." [NRS17/172] "A fine garden Rose of deep yellow, sometimes orange yellow colour, which is retained better than the colour of any other yellows. It seems the best of the 'Rayon d'Or' class, having the dark glossy foliage of that Rose, and it is hardier—at least, it has not died back in winter so far. Its drawbacks are that the flowers are rather too cupped and not high enough in the centre to be of really good form, and there are not quite enough of them." [NRS21/54–55] "His star rose for the season was 'Golden Emblem', which bore over twenty buds and blossoms on Armistice Day." [ARA26/199]

Goldenes Mainz
Kröger, 1927

"Orange yellow, large, lightly double, medium scent, moderate height." [Sn]

Gooiland Beauty
Van Rossem, 1924
From 'Sunburst' (Pern) × 'Golden Emblem' (Pern).

"Delicate orange yellow." [Cw] "Yellowish orange, large, lightly double, light scent, medium height." [Sn] "A very strong grower, with a golden orange color. The flower is nice, but semi-double." [ARA27/208] "Vigorous. Clear golden orange. The blooms keep their colour very long and shade off to a creamy yellow. Semi-double, prominent yellow stamens. Very free flowering." [GeH] "Bud medium size; flower very large, semi-double, open, lasting, slight fragrance, clear golden orange, borne, several together, on medium-length stem. Foliage abundant, large, dark green, leathery, disease-resistant. Very vigorous, bushy grower; abundant, continuous bloomer from May to November. Very hardy." [ARA25/191]

Gooiland Glory
Van Rossem, 1925
From 'General MacArthur' (HT) × 'Mme. Édouard Herriot' (Pern).

"Light red, medium size, lightly double, light scent, medium height." [Sn] "Cherry-red and coral-red shades. Resembles 'Padre' [Pern], but is deeper. Large semi-double flowers. Scented. Strong upright stems. A good garden rose." [GeH] "Type, 'Padre'. Bud medium size, long-pointed, coral; flower moderately large, open, semi-double, very lasting, slightly fragrant, orange-red, borne, several together, on normal stem. Foliage abundant, glossy, dark green, large. Growth vigorous, upright, bushy; blooms abundantly and continuously." [ARA26/187]

Gorgeous
H. Dickson, 1915

"Deep orange-yellow, veined reddish copper; shape loose, good petalage, large; lasts well. Growth, stem, and foliage good ... Recommended especially for Pacific North-West Zone. Opens too quickly in heat." [Th2] "'Gorgeous', like 'Ophelia' [HT], could hardly, perhaps, be classed as a pink, since the developed flower is a golden salmon flushed with rose." [ARA16/114] "Orange-yellow, suffused rose; odor delicious. Full rounded bud, open flower compact and handsome. Bush weak. 11 blooms." [ARA26/94] "Blossom very large, roundish form, long-lasting, nicely full, deep orange yellow with a salmon tone, veined copper." [Ck] "A very fine flower, and the first exhibition variety to give us the new colours, the result of the Pernet-Ducher cross ... Here you have a variety that could hold its own with the best. The name is quite justified—flesh, orange, apricot and copper are its colours. Fragrant and a good grower." [NRS14/150] "Beautiful and distinct color; growth is fair; blooming qualities not especially good." [ARA18/111] "Sometimes the blooms come faulty—inclined to split —but it is worth growing if only for the perfect flower it produces now and again." [NRS23/204] "Large, full and exquisitely formed; produced in endless profusion; deep orange, flushed copper-yellow and heavily veined with reddish copper." [C&Js15] "Large, fine form, double, fine fragrance, medium stem. Fine foliage, sufficient. Low weak growth; medium hardy." [ARA23/162] "The plant is healthy but not a tall grower." [C-Ps29] "Low, moderately compact, hardy; foliage very abundant, mildews slightly; bloom moderate, intermittent." [ARA18/125] "Strong, vigorous, free branching growth, handsome dark olive green foliage. Flowers large, full and exquisitely formed, produced in endless profusion on stiff erect stems. Colour, deep orange yellow, flushed copper yellow and heavily veined with reddish copper." [NRS15/170] "Well named for its fine orange flowers with a flush of pink. Their form is only fairly good ... The plant is a fairly good grower, and a bed of it in early summer looks well. Down to the present [1921] it has not been so satisfactory in its later flowering, much of the colour being lacking, but I hope it may improve in this respect." [NRS21/54] "A prolific fall bloomer." [C-Ps27] "Gorgeous indeed is this well-named Rose, for so it is in size, form, and color, which is soft orange, flushed with copper, coral-red, and shrimp-pink. The flowers are very large, fragrant and double, and particularly 'gorgeous' in the autumn. Partial shade helps retain the lovely colors. When the blooms are developing, the buds are deep coppery yellow, heavily veined and flushed with salmon-rose. The strong, smooth stems are well provided with olive-green, disease-resistant foliage. While the plant is healthy, it is not a tall grower." [C-Ps30] "A promising variety. Appears to be an intensified 'Mme. Mélanie Soupert' [HT]." [ARA18/133]

Gottfried Keller
Müller, 1894
From an unnamed seedling (which resulted from a cross of 'Mme. Bérard' [N] and 'Persian Yellow' [F]) × an unnamed seedling (which resulted from a cross of an unnamed seedling [itself resulting from a cross of 'Pierre Notting' (HP) and 'Mme. Bérard'] and 'Persian Yellow').

"Bicolored blossom, varying from orange yellow to coppery pink, flower single, medium sized." [JR33/134] "Orange yellow, medium size, lightly double, medium scent, moderate height." [Sn] "Deep yellow, suffused terra cotta pink. —Moderately vigorous. —Garden. —Charming in colour and perpetual flowering. Nearly single-flowered." [Cat12] "Deep apricot colour flushed with red ... [The flowers] were very shapeless and the growth was tall. This was the character of growth of all the early Pernet[iana] Roses." [NRS25/113] Possibly not commercially introduced until 1904.

Gruss an Coburg
syn. 'I. Gruss an Coburg'; trans. "Greetings to Coburg"
Felberg-Leclerc, 1927
From 'Alice Kaempff' (HT) × 'Souvenir de Claudius Pernet' (Pern).

"Bud brilliant coppery pink, opening to a large, full flower, of changing effect, inside of petals yellow, fawn and brown, base of petals golden yellow, outside of petals brownish red overshaded with coppery golden yellow and reddish and violet. A unique colouring. Very fragrant." [GeH] "Yellow." [Ÿ] "Copper yellow, large, full, very fragrant, medium height." [Sn] "A brilliant coppery pink. Its one fault seems to be that the bloom is a little too flat." [ARA30/152] "A large flower in the color of 'Louise Catherine Breslau' [Pern], and seems to be a first-rate, well-scented garden rose." [ARA29/201] "Good for moist climates; in dry seasons the blooms will be too small. It is a bicolor—inside deep yellow, outside of petals salmon-red, and a very strong grower." [ARA30/162] "Bud brilliant coppery orange-red; flower large, double, full, very fragrant, yellowish brown to golden yellow at base, outside brownish red with coppery golden yellow, reddish and violet sheen. Foliage bronzy green, disease-resistant. Growth vigorous, upright; continuous bloomer from June to November." [ARA28/242] "Growth is vigorous, with upright, branching habit; flowers of good form, on long stems. Colour, apricot-yellow, light yellow at base. A garden and bedding Rose of high merit." [NRS30/262]

Gwyneth Jones
McGredy, 1925
"Red and orange, medium size, lightly double, light scent, moderate height." [Sn] "Flower of unique coloring—rich carmine-orange without shading, semi-double to moderately full, with faint lemon perfume. Growth very bushy, strong, and free; flowers continually throughout the season. An ideal Rose for bedding." [C-Ps30] "The petals are large and of good texture, and the flowers semi-double to moderately full, the average number of petals of each bloom being from fifteen to seventeen." [NRS25/237] "A remarkable color, but untidy."

[ARA27/208] "Bud medium size, long-pointed; flower medium size, semi-double, open, very lasting, slight fragrance, brilliant carmine-orange, borne, singly and several together, on medium-length stem. Foliage abundant, medium size, light green, leathery, mildews and black-spots. Vigorous, bushy; profuse and continuous bloomer. Very hardy." [ARA25/184] "This is a most attractive rose. The blooms, which are very large with loose petals, are freely produced on long stems, and the color is a brilliant, rich vermilion that stands out among all other colors in the garden; moderately scented. It has bright green foliage, free of mildew and black-spot; vigorous. I have had it in my garden two years, and it has attracted more attention than any other." [ARA26/178] "The blooms retain their fascinating colour until they drop ... Foliage is dark green and Mildew-proof and the stems are strong with few thorns ... An ideal Rose for bedding, decoration and the garden." [GeH] "Does not appear to be over-robust in growth, but will probably improve." [ARA27/133] "Too thin, but fine color ... Conn.; Single, copper-orange blooms with orange base; slight fragrance. Fades badly, and not outstanding. Black-spots 20 per cent. Bore 13 blooms ... Ont.; ... Good foliage ... Calif.; A gorgeous, red-hot copper bowl of a flower, but of weak growth and a shy bloomer. A stunner, and well worth the trouble to get good flowers occasionally." [ARA28/161]

Hermann Robinow
Lambert, 1918
From 'Frau Karl Druschki' (HP) × 'Lyon-Rose' (Pern).

"Orange salmon pink, large, full, medium scent, medium height." [Sn] "Salmon-orange, shaded with salmon-rose and deep yellow, large and full, sweetly scented; buds long, carried erect on long stiff stems. Growth dwarf, vigorous." [GeH]

Hortulanus Budde
Verschuren, 1919
From 'General MacArthur' (HT) × 'Mme. Édouard Herriot' (Pern).

"Dark velvet, shaded yellow. Vigorous. Garden, bedding." [NRS23/insert] "Flower large, full, double, luminous fiery carmine-red, showing yellow center when expanded; very lasting. Profuse bloomer." [ARA21/165] "If you took 'Mme. Édouard Herriot' and made it bloom more freely, then gave it a glowing fiery red color, you would come near having a rose like 'Hortulanus Budde'." [ARA23/141] "It has, unfortunately, Herriot's fault of drooping flowers, but not quite so pronounced. A good grower and free bloomer." [NRS24/145] "Medium size, produced in great profusion throughout the season." [GeH] "The flowers are wonderfully bright in colour and are set off by clear dark green foliage; they are very freely produced and are sweet scented." [NRS24/139] "Blossom fairly full, fiery orange red on an orange-yellow ground, with a novel brilliance. Growth bushy. Plant unusually floriferous." [Ck]

I. Gruss an Coburg   Listed as 'Gruss an Coburg' (Pern).

I Zingari
syn. 'I Zingary'
Pemberton, 1925
"A brilliant gypsy red." [CaRoIII/8/1] "Orange red, medium size, lightly double, moderate height." [Sn] "Blooms coppery rose, bright yellow center; single, 3 inches in diameter [ca. 7.5 cm]; no fragrance. Black-spots 10 per cent. Bore 8 blooms ... Ont.; A splendid decorative

I Zingari *continued*

which is beginning to be quite vigorous."[ARA28/164] "Loses its shape very quickly and is rather a ragged bloom when open." [ARA27/134] "Type, 'Mme. Édouard Herriot' [Pern]. Flower semi-single, orange-scarlet, continuously produced in corymbs. Foliage dark green; stems claret. Especially vivid color, resembling the colors of the I Zingari Cricket Club, for which it was named." [ARA26/181] "Perpetual and free flowering. Sweetly scented. Fine habit." [GeH] "It makes more or less shrubby growth and blooms sparingly." [ARA31/188] "I saw this Rose growing in the Raiser's garden during the Summer, and was greatly impressed with its striking colour … Mr. Pemberton said its colour reminded him of the old I Zingari C.C. colours—orange scarlet, to which I must add shaded gold. The blooms are semi-double, and very freely produced on strong upright stems. The foliage is very dark green, the wood light claret colour, and the plants were sturdy and well grown. A very interesting decorative Rose, well worth a trial." [NRS25/107] Not a nurseryman's rose, but one which many ladies may like because of its art shades." [ARA28/138]

I Zingary Listed as 'I Zingari' (Pern).

Independence Day

Bees, 1919

From 'Mme. Édouard Herriot' (Pern) × 'Souvenir de Gustave Prat' (HT).

"Gold, stained flame, overlaid with orange and apricot." [ARA25/102] "Sun yellow on an orange apricot ground." [Cw] "A beautiful yellow with no touch of lemon." [ARA27/206] "Not really yellow and lacks fragrance but it is a wonder." [ARA26/98] "Large flowers, shrimp pink, free flowering." [NRS23/174] "Yellowish red, orange yellow center, medium size, very full, very fragrant, moderate height." [Sn] "The buds are long, freely produced, and the flowers are deliciously fragrant. Color is rich orange-apricot, suffused with sunflower-yellow. A sensationally attractive Rose." [C-Ps26] "While the blooms are semi-double, the petals are large, making a fine flower. A sensationally attractive Rose when it can be shaded in the afternoon. At its best in the morning, for boutonnières as the fresh blooms open." [C-Ps28] "Flame, gold, and apricot; exquisite in bud; opens too quickly and fades soon; odor slight, if any. Bush very strong. 39 blooms; 36 the second season." [ARA26/94] "Free blooming and lovely in the bud stage, but its beauties are too fleeting." [NRS24/160] "The blooms are of a good shape and are carried erect on strong stems. The color, a bright flame, is very attractive. The foliage is a bright, shiny dark green, and there was no trace of mildew or black spot to be detected in the unusually large, massed exhibit … It is a good grower and will be excellent for garden and bedding purposes." [ARA20/116] "A typical bedding Rose where quantity dominates the quality of individual blooms, thus affording always a splash of color in the garden. The semi-double flowers, generally in clusters on small, stubby stems, are apricot, suffused with golden yellow, and are somewhat fragrant. Like most yellow Roses the sun will fade the color, wherefore it is at its best in the early morning. Would prefer a location where sun does not touch it until afternoon … Color especially fine in the fall." [C-Ps29] "Bud medium size, long-pointed; flower medium-size, globular, double, high center, borne, several together, on long, strong stem; very lasting; strong fragrance. Color sunflower-gold, stained with flame-color, overlaying orange-apricot, all of which tints are fused together in the

mature bloom. Foliage abundant, medium size, leathery, glossy, dark green; disease-resistant. A vigorous, upright grower, reaching a height of 2 to 2½ feet [ca. 6–7.5 dm]; free and continuous bloomer from June to October." [ARA20/128] "Flame colour on petals of sunflower-gold, overlaying orange-apricot, all of which tints are fused together in the mature bloom, the centre of which glows with warmth and intensity; sweetly scented. Growth vigorous and free; of wonderful flowering capacity, every shoot bears a large number of fine blooms and buds; foliage glossy, dark green; Mildew-proof." [GeH] "Freedom from pests, wonderful color and foliage." [ARA29/111] "Very vigorous growth and beautiful foliage." [ARA20/120] "Leathery leaves; blossoms freely." [ARA25/121] "It ranks next to 'Gruss an Teplitz' [B] in quantity of bloom." [ARA29/66] "A vigorous-growing Rose, with dark glossy foliage. The blooms, carried on erect stems, are of a bright apricot colour, sweetly scented. A very pretty bedding and decorative Rose." [NRS19/136] "This Rose marks a new era in the Herriot type, the blooms being erect and the centre petals taking a more pointed shape. It is a good grower and will be excellent for garden and bedding purposes." [NRS20/153]

"I can see little difference between this Rose and 'Miss May Marriot' [Pern]. If anything I think the latter is the best … Perhaps it carries its flowers more upright than [does] 'Miss May Marriot', but after what I have seen at the shows frankly I am disappointed with this Rose." [NRS21/139] "Good yellow. Not so profuse as 'Lady Hillingdon' [T] but blooms more freely than 'Mme. Édouard Herriot' [Pern]. —*San Francisco, Calif.* Apricot-yellow. A beautiful rose but not immune to mildew. 'E. P. H. Kingma' [Pern] is advertised as a better rose, but in one year we cannot agree. —*Saratoga, Calif.* Fine; continuous bloomer. —*Ailene, Kansas.* Flame-color, showing suffusion of gold and buff-apricot. Growth very strong; wintered without being killed back at all. Fragrance, very slight if any. Disbudded, produced 39 blooms. Exquisite in bud; opens too soon, with insufficient petals; fades quickly in hot weather. —*Milton, Mass.* … Put out thirty plants last spring; got a wealth of bloom in the spring, most of them being short-stemmed and useless for cutting, but the hot summer and defoliation which happens to most Pernetiana roses was very disastrous. I did not lose any plants, but they were now about half the size they were in the spring, and I expect next year will see their finish. Frankly, I do not believe any Pernetiana roses are worth a 'hoorah' in the South. In fact, I have not yet discovered any Hybrid Tea rose in any of the shades of yellow which is worth growing outdoors here. —*Vicksburg, Miss.* … Growth strong; blooms finely; somewhat inclined to sprawl. —*East Mauch Chunk, Pa.*" [ARA26/116] "Blooms of medium size, with high pointed centre, freely produced, not liable to damage by rain. Sweetly scented. Colour variable, sunflower gold, shaded red. Foliage shiny bright green, free of mildew. Growth vigorous and branching. Very good as a cutback. The blooms are somewhat thin, and the colour, which pales in the summer, is particularly bright in the autumn. A good Rose." [NRS23/92]

Jean C. N. Forestier

Pernet-Ducher, 1919

From an unnamed cultivar × 'Mme. Édouard Herriot' (Pern).

"Carminy lake, nuanced red." [Ÿ] "A large-flowered, deep pink variety." [ARA22/136] "Orange red, large, full, medium scent, tall." [Sn] "Beautiful rose. Blossom large, full, durable, even more beautiful when [fully] open, lacquer-carmine with flame red and yellow nuances. Plant strong, hardy, bushy, erect, uncommonly floriferous, with beautiful, healthy foliage. Of the '[Mme. Édouard] Herriot' tribe, but completely different from that." [Ck] "Bud large, ovoid, Lincoln red; flower very large, full, double, borne singly on long, strong stems; very lasting; fragrant. Color carmine-lake, slightly tinted with Chinese orange and yellow. Foliage abundant, large, glossy bronze-green; disease-resistant. A very vigorous, upright grower bearing a profusion of blooms from June till October." [ARA20/131] "A fine grower, but the flowers seem to be of bad form." [NRS21/139] "Blooms very large, full and globular, liable to damage by rain. Sweetly scented. Colour crimson lake, tinted with yellow. Foliage bronzy green, with reddish wood. Growth vigorous and branching, both as a maiden and cutback. Fairly free of mildew. Free flowering, and a good bedding variety." [NRS23/92] "The park of Montjuich, at Barcelona, Spain, the most beautiful public park in the world (I am told, and I believe it), designed by J. C. N. Forestier." [ARA26/29] "The name of Forestier is intimately connected with Bagatelle, because it was he who organized that contest in 1907 . . . Monsieur Forestier was the foremost garden designer of the modern school, and to him is due the innovation of using herbaceous plants in public planting . . . Besides being a great garden designer and engineer he was a keen plantsman, and, above all, a connoisseur of roses whose infallible judgment was sought alike by friends and foes. He was keen in detecting talent, helping and protecting young hybridizers who without his advice and encouragement might have remained in obscurity." [ARA31/155] See also under 'Mme. Grégoire Staechelin' (Cl HT).

Jeanne Escoffier   Listed as 'Jeanne Excoffier' (Pern).

Jeanne Excoffier
syn. 'Jeanne Escoffier'
Buatois, 1921
From 'Mme. Philippe Rivoire' (HT) × 'Mme. Édouard Herriot' (Pern).

"Salmon pink, large, full, moderate height." [Sn] "Bud large, long-pointed; flower large, full; daybreak-pink, inside of petals buff-colored. Vigorous, branching." [ARA22/149]

Johannisfeuer
trans. "St. John's Fire"
Türke, 1910
From an unnamed seedling (resulting from a cross of 'Princesse de Béarn' [HP] and 'Deutschland' [Pern]) × *Rosa foetida* 'Bicolor'.

"Red, yellow center, large, full, very fragrant, tall." [Sn] "The colour is brilliant red, each petal merging into yellow at the base. It is semi-climbing, and the full-cupped blooms are very sweetly scented." [NRS13/162]

Joseph Baud
Gillot, 1920
From 'Rayon d'Or' (Pern) × an unnamed seedling (but see below).

"Orange yellow, very large, full, medium scent, moderate height." [Sn] "From seedling from 'Rayon d'Or'. —Orange red and carmine red, changing to golden yellow, very large and full. Vigorous." [NRS21/140] "Golden and orange-yellow, very large, full, and sweetly perfumed; elongated bud of orange-yellow and carmine. Growth vigorous, branching; free flowering." [GeH] "Bud large, long-pointed, orange-yellow, streaked carmine-red; flower very large, full, double,

lasting, golden yellow and orange-yellow, borne singly on long, strong stem; very fragrant. Foliage light green. Vigorous, abundant bloomer." [ARA21/160] Note that the breeder is "Gillot," which is not a mistake for "Guillot."

Jubiläumsrose
trans. "Jubilee Rose"
J. C. Schmidt, 1929

"Pink, large, full, medium height." [Sn] Not to be confused with Schmidt's creamy HT of the same name from 1910.

Julien Potin
Pernet-Ducher, 1927
From 'Souvenir de Claudius Pernet' (Pern) × an unnamed seedling.

"Primrose yellow." [Ÿ] "Golden perfection. The long buds show color for several days, and after opening last a long time, fading but little; also, it is sweetly fragrant, a rare quality in a yellow rose." [ARA29/48] "Yellow, large, full, medium scent, moderate height." [Sn] "Almost a duplicate of 'Ville de Paris' [Pern], but it is from ten to fourteen days later coming into bloom. Flowers are buttercup-yellow, with outside edges of petals lighter." [C-Ps30] "A clear yellow, said to be a free bloomer and a good grower, with good foliage." [ARA28/124] "In long-pointed form and rich coloring this is the aristocrat of pure yellow Roses. Of medium to large size, the pointed, clear yellow buds open to splendid golden yellow blooms which hold their color well. The finest yellow for exhibition. The fragrant flowers are quite freely produced on upright plants." [C-Ps34] "It keeps a long time when cut." [C-Pf34] "Rich golden yellow that grows deeper and more intense as the flowers mature. The buds are long and shapely and develop into large full flowers of beautiful form. Delightfully sweet scented. Growth upright, with ample glossy bronzy green foliage and very floriferous." [GeH] "Bud long-pointed, chrome citron-yellow; flower large, double, full, cupped, high centered, pure primrose-yellow, borne on long, strong stem. Foliage bright green, disease-resistant. Few thorns. Growth very vigorous, upright; profuse bloomer." [ARA28/238] "Long, sturdy pedicels and a moderately vigorous bush." [C-Ps31] "It is a beautiful plant, full of vigor, giving large, double, yellow flowers on long, strong stems. The only fault is that it whitens somewhat along the edges, the general defect of yellow roses." [ARA28/126] "Fewer thorns [than has 'Souvenir de Claudius Pernet' (Pern)]." [ARA28/201] "Not so vigorous as 'Souvenir de Claudius Pernet' but is far superior in other ways, and in bud and open bloom is similar, without the disfiguring center. The color is more golden and holds well in the hottest sun without scorching." [ARA29/72] "Evidently not a rose for humid climates. Growers experienced with it say it does not bloom enough in the garden." [ARA29/189] "Liked the hot summer. This rose is good, but has some faults that must be reckoned with in its culture. It produces some of the 'bullheads,' so well known from 'Souvenir de Claudius Pernet', and these must be quickly disbudded, so that the new break may bring a better bloom. Also, the old blooms must be taken off early, otherwise the plant gets too hard and takes a long time to break again. A good bloom of it is a sensation, but the yellow is not so hard or deep as that of 'Souvenir de Claudius Pernet'. The growth is strong but a little thin, and the plant easily becomes top-heavy." [ARA30/162] "Considering that at Breeze Hill we were unable to distinguish 'Julien Potin' from 'Ville de Paris', we are inclined to believe that 'Ville de Paris' has been sent out by some nurseries as 'Julien Potin', and in

Julien Potin *continued*

such cases more or less favorable reports have resulted. Where the true variety has been sent out, opinion is almost unanimously against it." [ARA31/197] "This is an exceedingly pretty rose. The bright yellow, fragrant blooms, which are carried on long stems, are well formed, with high-pointed centers. Under glass, they open cupped, but outdoors a little ragged. The habit of growth is vigorous. Foliage dark olive-green, with younger growths red, and inclined to mildew at times. On maiden plants the blooms are inclined to pale, but on cutbacks it keeps its color well. A first-rate bedding variety." [ARA30/156] "Dedicated to Monsieur Julien Potin, one of our great orchid amateurs and rose-lovers ... It is a real beauty with pointed buds on erect stems, and flowers of a magnificent yellow, warmer than either 'Souvenir de Claudius Pernet' or 'Ville de Paris', from which it is very different in form." [ARA27/211]

Juliet

Easlea/W. Paul, 1910

From 'Captain Hayward' (HP) × 'Soleil d'Or' (Pern).

"Color quite particularly striking. Exterior, gold-yellow; interior, blood red; attractive, effective color-contrast. Very floriferous plant." [Ck] "Orange red, center yellowish pink, large, full, very fragrant, moderate height." [Sn] "Outside of petals old gold; interior rich rosy red changing to deep rose. Very remarkable color. Fragrant ... Foliage, poor." [Th] "Vermilion-red, reverse of petals old gold. Very vigorous." [NRS/11] "Really a most incongruous mixture of colours, but at the same time nearly everyone admits that it is fascinating and very beautiful." [NRS/12] "The color of the flower is somewhat variable. When it is warm and humid, weather often found in England during the Summer, the predominating color is a crimson-rose ... the petal exterior taking on a golden color, richly and noticeably contrasting with the red shades. When cold and dry, the crimson shades are replaced by a bright pink lit by scarlet, with the exteriors still yellow, though perhaps a little more brilliant. This rose blooms during the Summer and Fall ... Of remarkable vigor, this is a good variety to choose for making shrubberies in the garden." [JR34/140–141] "Early bloom only." [M-P] "A very pretty novelty which blooms as well in Fall as it does in Summer ... The very large flowers have an exquisite scent." [JR34/85] "A lovely variety, and as fragrant as beautiful." [OM] "Blend of Damask and Fruit-scented [perfumes]." [NRS/17] "Does not ball ... does not do well in extremely hot climates ... Prune very lightly." [Th2] "Seemingly a strong grower, it had also the following points to its credit—a highly perfumed flower, undamaged by rain and borne on a stiff stalk, and further, a point not often mentioned, fragrant foliage like that of the Sweet Briar. Its defects are evident in its lack of form, the flowers often coming double-centred, and in a certain unreliability as to colour. The blooms, especially in dry, sunny weather, are apt to lack the gold, its chief attraction, and in a vase this colour is not long sustained. In fact, 'Juliet' often wears a 'washy' look ... Great susceptibility to that bane of the rose-grower, black spot." [NRS23/211–212] From Shakespeare's *Romeo and Juliet* (II:2), Juliet, who knows true love well in reminding us that

> My bounty is as boundless as the sea,
> My love as deep; the more I give to thee
> The more I have, for both are infinite.

Konrad Thönges

Thönges, 1929

"Deep yellow and salmon, large, lightly double, moderate height." [Sn]

[La Giralda]

Dot, 1926

From 'Frau Karl Druschki' (HP) × 'Mme. Édouard Herriot' (Pern).

"Pink; fragrance 7 [on a scale of 10]; growth 7 [on a scale of 10]." [Jg] La Giralda, name of an old, tall tower of the Cathedral in Seville, Spain (data kindly supplied by Mel Hulse).

La Mie au Roy

trans. [from rather antique French], "The King's Beloved"

Bernaix, 1927

From 'Duchess of Wellington' (HT) × 'Pax Labor' (Pern).

"Coppery salmon yellow, large, full, medium scent, moderate height." [Sn] "Flower extra large, full, globular, beautiful apricot colour, base of petals saffron-yellow, the extremities of the petals dark carmine passing to creamy yellow." [GeH] "A very warm orange bud." [ARA31/178] "An interesting, large saffron-yellow, with fine foliage, and it did well." [ARA30/189] "'Bullheaded', hardly opening indoors." [ARA30/162] "A very vigorous Pernetiana it is, with persistent foliage, ovoid bud and flower yellow, salmon, and copper." [ARA28/127] "Bud very large, coppery salmon, striped salmon-rose; flower very large, double, full, globular, apricot, base saffron-yellow, edges shaded carmine, passing to cream-yellow, borne on long, strong stem; foliage large, leathery, disease-resistant. Growth vigorous, upright, branching." [ARA28/239]

La Somme

Barbier, 1919

From 'Mme. Caroline Testout' (HT) × 'Rayon d'Or' (Pern).

"Coral red, coppery reflections." [Ÿ] "Orange red and deep copper. As large as '[Mme.] Caroline Testout'. Vigorous." [NRS21/140] "Deep coral red with coppery reflexes, changing to bright salmon, of '[Mme.] Caroline Testout' form. Growth vigorous and floriferous, with deep glossy green foliage." [GeH] "Bud large, ovoid, orange-red, with coppery red markings; flower large, semi-double, open, cupped, lasting; deep coral-red, with coppery reflex turning light salmon; borne, several together, on strong, medium long stem; fragrant. Foliage sufficient, medium size, leathery, glossy dark green, disease-resistant. Bark green and reddish brown; few thorns. Vigorous, bushy; blooms freely and continuously from June to October; hardy." [ARA22/149] La Somme, the French river, but also recalling the World War I battle of La Somme.

Lady Elphinstone

Dobbie, 1921

Sport of 'Mme. Édouard Herriot' (Pern).

"Brilliant apricot, flushed with Japanese yellow, fine habit and free flowering. Growth vigorous." [GeH] "Many flowers; colour straw yellow, lightly tinted pink." [NRS23/174] "Yellow, very large, lightly double, dwarf." [Sn] "[As compared to 'Emma Wright' (Pern)], 'Lady Elphinstone', a rich apricot orange, holds its colour better and it is less affected by insolation in this respect. It is, too, a much freer bloomer. So far as I am concerned, and I hope I am totally unbiased, I think this Rose is superior to 'Independence Day' [Pern] and vastly so to '[Miss] May Marriott' [Pern], 'Midas' [extinct Pern], 'Geisha' [Pern] and a host of other sports or descendants from 'Mme. Édouard Herriot'." [NRS24/144] "Bud long-pointed; flower very large, open, semidouble, very lasting; Indian yellow, passing to clear rose; borne singly on strong stem. Foliage abundant, large, glossy dark green, disease-resistant. Moderate grower, bushy; profuse bloomer, from June to October; hardy." [ARA22/152]

Lady Inchiquin

A. Dickson, 1921

"A mixture of pink, orange, and cerise, and a very beautiful mixture it is." [NRS24/171] "Orangy cherry red." [Cw] "Rose pink, suffused orange. [Growth] moderate." [NRS23/list] "A quite unique color—cherry-red with intense orange tint; the bud is large and opens to good blooms. I had better color in the open bloom when grown under glass than when grown outdoors." [ARA24/109] "Orange red, large, very full, medium scent, moderate height." [Sn] "'Lady Inchiquin' also delighted on account of its marvelous coral-red color. It is a good grower and always brings well-formed large blooms. The neck could be a little stronger. It is undoubtedly a new color in Roses." [ARA25/135] "Undoubtedly a Rose of grand colour. Insolation does not appear to affect its brilliancy as it does other similarly tinted sorts. Its constitution is not of the most robust, unfortunately." [NRS24/150] "The perfectly formed blooms were carried on fairly stiff stems. Its colourings will make it an ideal bedder, but the plants exhibited were not quite as vigorous as one would have wished." [NRS21/169] "Vigorous. Orange-cerise. Large, full, and perfect in shape. Free flowering. A rose of marvellous beauty. Valuable for all purposes." [GeH] "Large well-formed blooms that are toned a lovely coral-red … it may be subject to most of the leaf-diseases known to fall on the Pernetianas." [ARA26/166] "The color is quite new, the flower full and of fair size … I have not seen any mildew on it." [ARA27/206] "This Rose is usually of moderate growth and vigour, with very thorny stems. It is evident that it varies greatly with the soil and position in which it is growing … The right conditions appear to be a clayey loam, neither too light nor too heavy. The foliage is only fairly good; it is rather glossy and lightish green, somewhat liable to mildew, and not immune from black spot … The flower stalk is not often strong enough to keep the flower upright … It does not make a satisfactory standard." [NRS29/116] "Best on Brier stock; very thorny; no color like it—have had it four or five summers; growth moderate to vigorous; fall bloomer … Mass.; … Too tender for this climate. In all other respects, fine … Conn.; Rather dwarf. Foliage ample and free from disease. Blooms rather scarce but delightful color—cerise with orange shades—very brilliant, scentless, of good shape and substance, although not very large … Ont.; … Rather seriously affected with blackspot about midsummer … Ont.; … Bad, scant, and small foliage. Bloom good, but similar to [that of] 'Director Rubió' [Pern], which has good healthy foliage … Pa." [ARA28/168] "This much-abused rose is one of my strong favorites, and I cannot understand why it is not more popular. It is a beautiful pink, of a wonderful shape, and full enough to please anybody. And, thank goodness, it is a Hybrid Tea, though one can't help wondering if it didn't get its color from the Pernetianas." [ARA29/109] "If only it gave more blooms and was a better doer it would be in the front rank." [NRS25/179]

Les Rosati

Gravereaux/Kieffer, 1906

From either (1) 'Persian Yellow' (F) × an unnamed seedling (resulting from a cross of an HP with a Tea) or (2) Rosa foetida 'Bicolor' × an unnamed seedling (resulting from a cross of an HP with a Tea); see also below.

"Bright carmine." [Ÿ] "A curiously formed deep crimson with yellow backed petals." [NRS13/161] "Light red, yellow center, medium size, full, medium scent, tall." [Sn] "Flowers cochineal carmine, reverse of petals rosy white, base of petals sulphur yellow. Medium size, full, imbricated. Growth vigorous, erect and hardy." [NRS21/130] "Floriferous." [GeH] "A seedling from 'Persian Yellow' crossed with a seedling from a Hybrid Perpetual and a Hybrid Tea. This had flat, carmine rose-coloured flowers and a strong habit of growth." [NRS25/114] "Vigorous bush; blossom medium-sized, with creased and imbricated petals, bright carmine with cherry red reflections, bright yellow nub. Hardy and quite distinct variety." [JR33/186] NRS25/114 has Müller as the breeder.

Lilly Jung

syn. 'Lily Jung'

Leenders, 1925

"Deep yellow and red, large, full, very fragrant, moderate height." [Sn] "Scented, deep golden yellow flowers on strong, rigid stems; it is a nice garden rose." [ARA28/133] "From unnamed varieties, ['Lilly Jung'] has a very vigorous plant, pointed bud, and large, full flower of a beautiful golden yellow." [ARA27/210] "Fragrant. Very vigorous. Free. [For] cutting and the garden." [GeH] "It grew satisfactorily, but failed to bloom. Ontario had sturdy plants and fragrant yellow blooms." [ARA30/177] "Bud large, ovoid; flower double, large, intensely fragrant, very lasting, deep golden yellow, borne several together on long stem. Foliage normal, bronzy, leathery, medium size. Growth very vigorous, upright." [ARA26/187]

Lily Jung   Listed as 'Lilly Jung' (Pern).

Lord Lambourne

McGredy, 1922

"Deep buttercup-yellow, flushed carmine. A magnificent rose, opening well in all weather. Good grower and very attractive. A good bed of this Rose is a sight not to be forgotten. Fragrant." [GeH] "Flower enormous, perfectly formed, very lasting; golden buff, base of petals old burnished gold, shaded strawberry pink. Blooms from July to November." [ARA23/149] "Yellow, large, full, very fragrant, moderate height." [Sn] "Flowers too floppy and not lasting." [ARA27/136] "Mr. Easlea, I think, has hit the nail on the head when he said it was the grandest individual bloom ever produced. It is a super '[Mme.] Mélanie Soupert' [HT], with enormous stiff petals, 5 inches long [ca. 1.25 dm], perfectly formed. The colour is a golden buff with base of petals old burnished gold, shaded strawberry pink, almost too wonderful in colour to be a real live bloom. Its lasting qualities are extraordinary, the bloom remaining perfect for over a week. An exhibition Rose of the first magnitude, and has been named after that well-known horticulturist, Lord Lambourne." [NRS22/191] "Has been a disappointment from the beginning." [ARA30/171] "This is the rose we have been waiting for so long, but, as exhibited, was a little disappointing, which was entirely owing to the season. The color is golden yellow, with a

Lord Lambourne *continued*

deeper golden base, and, at times, the edges of the petals are shaded with carmine. At first, the blooms are of good shape, but afterward become somewhat of a loose habit, and while the petals are a bit soft, they will stand a fair amount of wet. The wood is light green, with few thorns, and the foliage is a very rich green. The blooms are a little inclined to be top-heavy when fully expanded, but they are lasting, and with a strong Pernetiana scent." [ARA25/178] "The colour is a deep absolutely unfading buttercup yellow, each and every individual petal being heavily margined all round carmine scarlet ... The foliage is bright glossy green and mildew proof. Stems are long and stout with very few thorns. The habit of growth is very free, strong and upright ... The flowers have a strong fruity scent." [NRS25/236] "Bud very large, long-pointed; flower very large, double, high center, very lasting, fragrant, deep buttercup-yellow heavily edged carmine-scarlet, borne, singly and several together, on long stem. Foliage abundant, large, light green, leathery, glossy, mildews and black-spots. Few thorns. Very vigorous, upright, bushy; profuse continuous bloomer from May to October. Very hardy." [ARA25/184] "An oversized 'Sunstar' [Pern], perhaps deeper yellow. Impatient of hot sun; lovely long bud in the morning. A typical 'two-hour' rose for shaded, fairly humid locations and sheltered from the wind. Worthy in the right location if seen in the early morning ... *Pa.*; ... a decorative rose worth growing; free blooming, with good constitution ... *B.C.*; ... 'Norman Lambert' [Pern] is better than either this or 'Sunstar'." [ARA28/171] "Perhaps best described as a glorified 'Sunstar'. In my own garden it has been very fine, especially in the Autumn." [NRS25/116]

Los Angeles

Howard & Smith, 1916

From 'Mme. Segond-Weber' (HT) × 'Lyon-Rose' (Pern).

"Pinkish flame tinted coral red." [Ÿ] "Bright pink with coral red, nuanced golden yellow." [Cw] "Wonderful rosy-orange/salmon-gold colored; good scent; most recommendable for cutting and forcing." [Ck] "Salmon red, yellow center, large, lightly double, very fragrant, medium height." [Sn] "Light, silvery, salmon-pink, with golden suffusion; double; fair stem; mild perfume; exquisite form; loses foliage early. Continuous." [CaRoll/3/2] "A luminous flame pink, toned with coral and shaded with translucent gold at the base of the petals, fragrance equals in intensity [that of] 'Maréchal Niel' [N]. The buds are long and pointed, and expand into a flower of mammoth proportions. Growth very vigorous, producing a continuous succession of long-stemmed flowers." [GeH] "The perfume is entrancing though not strong." [C-Ps31] "Some have said that 'Los Angeles' has only a slight fragrance, and others that it is one of the most fragrant. I rather think, myself, that the temperature and humidity have a good deal to do with the fragrance of the rose." [ARA24/181] "Flame-pink, shaded to yellow, toned with salmon, much on the order of the 'Lyon-Rose'. Gives promise of being a good bedding variety with some value for cutting. Reported to be a strong grower and a good bloomer." [ARA17/30] "A new Rose from the 'Land of Sunshine and Flowers' [*i.e.*, California] ... surpassingly brilliant in color, beautiful in form, and exceedingly free in bloom. The color is entirely new in roses—flame-pink toned with coral and shaded with translucent gold at base of the petals. The flowers are produced in almost unbroken succession from early summer to late fall. The plant is a vigorous grower, with many strong

canes, each one crowned with superb blooms." [ARA17/xx] "Coral with yellow suffusion. Bush slow to start; medium strong. 9 blooms." [ARA26/94] "The blooms come true to shape, are held well erect, and as beautiful when past their prime as in the bud state. It is really a continuous bloomer, and still makes efforts to bloom yet again in spite of frosts." [NRS22/74] "Well-formed flowers, alike attractive in bud and bloom, and showing shades of salmon-pink, apricot and orange almost impossible to describe. Plant vigorous where it is happy, and with good foliage, needing easily given protection from blackspot. It is a somewhat temperamental Rose of varying performance ... and is, perhaps, the most popular Rose of American origin—next to 'Radiance' [HT]. 'Los Angeles' has made perhaps the biggest sensation of any Rose since the introduction of the Pernetiana race." [C-Ps26] "Hard to establish. Only one out of six has made sturdy growth but it is now one of our dependable bloomers. It always attracts attention either as a cut-flower or in the garden." [ARA31/98] "No other Rose can be as lovely—and also as mean—as this much-lauded variety. It will do well here and positively refuse to grow there. Yet it is worth growing even if you get but one good bloom in a season! It is certain in but one thing—its foliage will likely drop in midsummer, no matter what you do. When it blooms, the color is a glowing salmon-pink, washed with gold at the base ... There's no question about it; one good bloom of 'Los Angeles' is worth more than a bouquet of many other Roses." [C-Ps29] "This is quite a good Rose, but the rapidity with which it has sprung into popular favour is somewhat remarkable. It flowers freely and its continuity is good. The colour is that of a pale 'Lyon-Rose' ... Salmon rose shaded apricot, is nearer the mark provided rather subdued shades of these colours are understood. The form of the flower is good and the flower double. It has a fair number of petals, but not so many as to prevent it opening well. They will stand some rain and are of fair substance ... The flowers are carried well and upright on good stalks. The secondary blossoms are at times apt to nod somewhat ... The foliage is sufficient but not remarkable, and during the year I have grown it I have found no disease. The habit of the plant is quite satisfactory for a bedding Rose; because, like many H.T.'s, it is apt to throw a strong shoot carrying a terminal flower followed by secondary flower shoots lower down the stem ... Its constitution appears excellent ... It has some fragrance." [NRS22/54–55] "An excellently erect habit." [NRS22/107]

"[In southern California] 'Los Angeles' ... is a glory." [ARA21/58] "Without a doubt, the most satisfactory rose in all sections of California is 'Los Angeles'." [ARA29/145] "In spite of high praise elsewhere, ['Los Angeles'] has been a total failure with me, as it refuses obstinately to grow, sheds its leaves three times a year, and is very shy in blooming, although I will admit that what flowers I got were perfect, gorgeous in color and perfume, but small. 'Willowmere' [Pern] is so much superior in every way except color that there is no comparison." [ARA22/161] "Truly a magnificent Rose in vigor of growth, color, form, fragrance, and, in fact, in everything required of a first-class Rose." [C&Js17] "I tried this rose again because of its immense reputation. I had a very healthy looking and lusty plant to start with last spring, but there is scarcely a living cane on it this fall. It bloomed well, the flowers were fine, but it died back from leaf to leaf, new growth as well as old, like a pear tree with the blight." [ARA24/89] "Shoots occasionally die back in the winter." [NRS24/161] "The faults of this Rose are a certain tendency to black-spot; the tendency of the full flower to hang its head, though some will carry themselves well; and the over-rapid opening of the flower … Some of the plants are not very long-lived, though I still have in my garden the batch I got when it first came out. On the other hand, it is a lovely colour and a beautiful flower, and with me has grown strong and vigorously, making a successful garden plant." [NRS29/110]

"The plant is so strong and shapely, it blooms so freely, its blooms lasts so well cut or on the tree, its petal is of such substance, its colour so warm and attractive, that it stands easily our first bedder to-day. Its habit of yielding a panicle of blossom on a stem, each blossom a good bloom, makes it especially desirable as a bedder." [NRS22/67] "An entire bed of this wonderful Rose is not too much to have, for it is one of the finest and most notable varieties ever produced." [C&Js23] "Delighted everybody as a mass and as a single flower [*i.e.*, lone specimen] (our field of 8,000 plants never was without blooms)." [ARA24/107] "I shall never forget the sight of a bed of this Rose in Balboa Park, the old exhibition grounds at San Diego. The plants were five years old, sixty-six in the bed … The plants in this bed were over seven feet high [ca. 2.3 m] … All the nice things that are said of this Rose are not overdone. I think it is one of the grandest Roses raised, good in every respect." [NRS23/133]

"It was early in 1916 that mail contact with Mr. Fred H. Howard, of Los Angeles, California, brought to the Editor's garden certain plants labeled 'Seedling 101'. Admiring the vigor, both of the plant and of the stock on which it was budded, these roses were early put into the ground. They started with unreasonable promptness, grew with unusual vigor, and bloomed both earlier and stronger than it was right to expect newly transplanted material to do. The flowers were most attractive and different. Though the coloring is similar to [that of] several of the Pernetiana roses, it is deeper, and the vigor and foliage of 'Los Angeles' commend it as utterly different." [ARA17/38] "Since the first plant of 'Los Angeles' flowered with me, I have seen no other rose to compare with it in several ways: First, in color: The glow of this rose, the suffusion of pink and yellow, producing an effect of illumination—in this respect 'Los Angeles' is incomparable . . . This miracle of color persists with remarkable purity till the petals fall. Second, in form: The charming proportions of this rose set it apart. The flat, full-petaled roundness of its cup when fully expanded gives it a decorative quality not often seen in roses. There is distinction in the flower from the day its pointed bud is formed to the moment of its first loosening petal. Third, in foliage and habit of growth: The rich green of the leaves of 'Los Angeles' make a fine setting for the brilliant flowers. The rose is held well up at the top of straight, stiff stems, and the dark foliage is almost of an ivy-green—a very satisfactory color. The keeping quality of 'Los Angeles', when cut, is another valuable characteristic. Brought in from the garden when color first shows in the bud, it develops fast in water and holds its perfect beauty much longer than almost any other of its comrades. Its fragrance is delicious. In short, it is a rose to marvel at and to revel in … Lavender candytuft is a most lovely companion flower for this rose when cut—or the lavender statices." [ARA20/157] "The best garden rose." [ARA29/109] "Once having seen the luminosity of 'Los Angeles', we needs must believe there is something 'Beyond the sunset's radiant glow'." [ARA29/102] The dynamic Los Angeles, California—exciting, sprawling city built of diversity and dreams.

Louise Catherine Breslau Plate 77
Pernet-Ducher, 1912
From an unknown rose × an unnamed seedling (of 'Soleil d'Or' [Pern]).

"Coppery orange red." [Cw] "Shrimp red nuanced orange." [Ÿ] "Light orange red, very large, full, medium scent, moderate height." [Sn] "Superb coloring of shrimp-pink, shaded with reddish coppery orange, and chrome-yellow on the reverse of petals." [C&Js14] "Flowers . . . when full blown present many novel shades from pink to apricot." [C&Js24] "Terra cotta shade; good-sized double, but loose; striking color; plant's habit one of best; a dependable kind; fine foliage." [CaRoll/3/3] "Large, full, globular, bud coral-red, shaded with chrome-yellow. Growth vigorous, branching, free flowering; distinct." [GeH] "An exceedingly handsome, bold bloom, reddish fawn and coppery orange, in which fawn predominates. A good shaped bloom from an unnamed seedling crossed with a seedling from 'Soleil d'Or'. The foliage is thick and leathery and quite mildew proof." [NRS13/164] "The form of this rose suggests a water-lily, fully open. The color is a glowing yellowish salmon, and not the least of its beauties is its dark green, burnished foliage. It has grave faults—I have no rose in my garden more susceptible to black-spot, and it is not a free bloomer." [ARA29/69] "Astonishing in color. Salmon-red buds, opening to large flowers of orange-pink, glowing with yellow and copper. Double, but not of the finest form when fully open. Color fades in strong sunlight, but is retained well when cut. Stem is stiff, but not long. Growth bushy and vigorous; foliage glossy. Repays extra care and is effective in beds." [C-Ps25] "Pernetiana of wonderful color; foliage particularly glossy and attractive, but, like the majority of roses of the type, is lost early; fair in growth; shy in blooming." [ARA18/112] "Chiefly remarkable for its colour, which is a coppery salmon pink, often with a buff shading. The flowers have no great pretension to beauty of form, but the plant is a good grower—dwarf but branching." [NRS21/44] "Good growth, hardy; beautiful foliage, lost early, fair stem; medium size, fair form, fair lasting qualities; color distinct … thirty-three blooms in 1915." [ARA16/19] "Bush of great vigor and robust constitution, with branching canes; thorns close-set and not very protrusive; beautiful glossy bronze-green foliage; buds large, ovoid, coral red tinted chrome yellow; flowers very large, quite full, globular, with large outer petals; superbly colored shrimp red nuanced reddish coppery orange and chrome yellow on the reverse of the petals. Abundantly floriferous and of a coloration all its own, this magnificent variety will certainly have the same success as that enjoyed by its predecessor 'Lyon-Rose', which it surpasses in hardiness." [JR36/42] "It possesses remarkable thick leathery foliage of a glistening nature. Quite a fine bedder, and well worth growing until something better comes along." [NRS21/133]

Louise Joly
Buatois, 1922
From 'Mme. Édouard Herriot' (Pern) × an unnamed seedling.

"Yellowish salmon, large, full, light scent, moderate height." [Sn] "Bud large, long-pointed, coral-red, shaded shrimp-pink; flower large, double, cupped, lasting; lake, tinted salmon and yellow; borne singly, on medium strong stem; moderate fragrance. Foliage glossy green, disease-resistant. Few thorns. Vigorous, upright, bushy; profuse and continuous bloomer; hardy." [ARA23/151]

Lyon-Rose Plate 72
Pernet-Ducher, 1907

From 'Mme. Mélanie Soupert' (HT) × an unnamed seedling (descended from crosses between 'Soleil d'Or' [Pern] and unnamed Hybrid Teas; see under the sibling of 'Lyon-Rose', 'Rayon d'Or' [Pern]).

"Monsieur Pernet-Ducher has let us in on his magnificent new rose 'Lyon-Rose', to be released to commerce next Fall. This variety . . . will make a splash, it is said." [J31/23] "The greatest and most beautiful rose of the century." [CA11]

"Monsieur Pernet-Ducher will have for sale this Fall, after October 15, his new and pretty rose of the Pernetiana series: LYON ROSE [sic]. It's a very vigorous bush with slightly branching canes, straight thorns which are sparse and unequal; ample foliage composed of 5–7 reddish somber green leaflets; blossoms usually solitary, sometimes two or three buds on each stem. Buds large and rounded, coral red strongly tinted medium chrome yellow at the base; flower very large with large petals, full, globular; color, lobster red along the edge (petal tips), center of the blossom coral red or salmon red, nuanced chrome yellow, producing a fortuitous color contrast. Very fragrant. 'Lyon-Rose' comes from 'Mme. Mélanie Soupert' (HT) pollinated by an unreleased variety which itself came directly from 'Soleil d'Or'. Though by its origin, this pretty newcomer falls into the Pernetiana category, it has all the qualities of the Hybrid Teas, especially in its abundant bloom. It is certainly a plant of high worth." [JR31/71] "These colors [in the JR31/71 quote] were determined with the assistance of the *'Répertoire des couleurs'* published by the French Chrysanthemist Society." [JR31/138] "Orange red, salmon center, large, full, very fragrant, moderate height." [Sn] "Flowers very large and of good shape when the second bud is retained. Excellent grower on briar stock, but no good otherwise." [NRS14/160] "Very vigorous bush; flower very large, full, globular . . . This superb variety, because of the richness of its coloration, is of incomparable beauty, and constitutes one of the joyful beauties of the Queen of Flowers." [JR35/15] "'Lyon-Rose' produces blossoms of a large size, sufficiently double to be called full, but in which the large petals aren't so compacted as to interfere with the blossom's opening . . . While the beauty of its flowers gains the admiration of all visitors, its ravishing and delicious coloration comes as a real surprise." [JR31/138] "Wonderful color; growth good; stem usually weak; fair bloomer only; needs 'special bed'." [ARA18/112] "I was assured not only by Monsieur Bernaix but by its famous creator, Monsieur Pernet himself—it is never out of flower, and remarkably vigorous in constitution." [NRS10/113] "This is a most welcome addition to our gardens if only by reason of its unique colour. On that account and its other good qualities it can be pardoned the unfortunate habit it has of dropping its lower leaves prematurely at the end of the summer." [NRS11/80] "The fruity fragrance of the foliage, resembling pineapple, the fierce red prickles, and the reddish wood, traceable in 'Persian Yellow' [F]." [NRS13/161]

"Distinct." [GeH] "We feel that we can safely recommend it as one of the best of the new roses." [C&Js08] "Finally, 'Lyon-Rose', that magnificent variety bred by Pernet-Ducher, the able rose-sower of Lyon, will be made available to the public. Every fancier will be able to buy and admire it at its next bloom. Having seen this novelty at several exhibitions, and indeed at its breeder's, we don't hesitate to declare it a rose of the first merit . . . Our heartiest congratulations to Monsieur Pernet-Ducher." [JR31/123–124]

Mabel Lynas
McGredy, 1926

"Deep red, yellow center, large, full, very fragrant, medium size." [Sn] "Bud very large, long-pointed; flower large to very large, double, full, strong fragrance, deep brilliant crimson-scarlet, borne singly and several together. Foliage abundant, medium to large, rich green, leathery, glossy. Few thorns. Vigorous to very vigorous, upright, bushy." [ARA25/185] "Bud large, ovoid; flower very large, extremely double, high-centered, very lasting, wonderful fragrance, dark crimson with a yellow base, borne singly or several together on long stem. Foliage abundant, medium size, light green, leathery, glossy, very disease-resistant. Growth very vigorous, upright; profuse, continuous bloomer from June to November. Hardy." [ARA28/235] "Somewhat on the border line of the Pernetiana. The colour is a rich velvety crimson with a slight shade of maroon. The blooms are large and double, and carried well on long stiff stems above the foliage. The plant shown was vigorous, and free of mildew. A good garden Rose with a delicious perfume." [NRS25/124] "Only valuable as a curious example of an ugly crimson rose on Pernetiana foliage . . . *Armstrong* calls it very poor, no growth, and unattractive." [ARA30/190] "A very good grower, varies in color but is sometimes good." [ARA29/201] "Though a Pernetiana, it favours the H.T. in habit and freedom of flower, and the H.P. as regards hardiness. Unlike some Pernetianas, it is so exceedingly hardy that it never dies back, no matter how severe the weather, and the growth though typical Pernetiana is unusual in its freedom, bushiness and strength. The colour of the flowers is dark crimson with a yellow base, and the only dark crimson we know with typical Pernetiana growth. Another outstanding feature is that the flowers have probably the strongest and sweetest scent of any Rose in cultivation, and this is the first of the Pernetiana type with outstanding fragrance. The flowers are very large, full, and of fine form, and petals of stout, heavy texture. The foliage is of medium size, bright glossy green, as though it had been varnished, and mildew proof. The stems are the same colour as the foliage, and thinly covered with crimson thorns. The habit of growth is very free, vigorous and upright, and altogether new in crimson Roses. A very free and perpetual flowering garden and bedding variety." [NRS27/263]

Madette
P. Guillot, 1922

"Coppery orange pink, medium size, full, moderate height." [Sn] "Bud medium size, long-pointed, dark nasturtium-red; flower medium size; coppery orange-pink; borne in cluster. Foliage bronzy green. Vigorous; continuous bloomer from May to October; hardy." [ARA23/151]

Mary Pickford
Howard & Smith, 1923

From an unnamed seedling × 'Souvenir de Claudius Pernet' (Pern).

"Pale yellow buds, opening clear yellow with the center of the flower deep yellow. Slightly deficient in petalage and substance. Very dainty and lovely in half-open state. No odor." [ARA27/147] "Orange yellow, large, full, medium scent, moderate height." [Sn] "Deep orange-yellow, shading lighter during hot dry weather, of moderate size and of delicious Tea perfume. In habit of growth it is strong and vigorous." [GeH] "A new Rose from California. It is a seedling of 'Souvenir de Claudius Pernet', with some resemblance to the parent plant. It has a ravishing bud, deeper yellow than [that of] Claudius, with carmine markings on reverse of the petals, reminiscent of 'Golden Emblem' [Pern]. Petals unroll and recurve gracefully. The sweet-scented flower is medium in size and the color fades in bright, hot weather." [C-Ps27] "Good in hot weather . . . *Mass.*; . . . Good new growth and kept its foliage. The flowers look like [those of] 'Souv[enir] de Claudius Pernet', but are orange in the bud. I like it . . . *Westwood, Mass.*; . . . Disease-resistant . . . *Ind.*; 'Mary Pickford' is close to '[Souvenir de Claudius] Pernet' in foliage and bloom, but center of flower is not nearly so unsightly, and in the spring the blooms are much better . . . *Idaho.*" [ARA28/173] "Medium-sized, ovoid buds and semi-double flowers of pale yellow with deeper center, of open form, fair lasting quality, and without fragrance, borne singly. Healthy foliage. Moderate growth and sparse bloom—4 in the season." [ARA27/137] "A very cheerful bloomer with only medium-sized flowers, but lots of them, and a good clear orange-yellow." [ARA29/52] "Bud large, long-pointed, orange-yellow; flower large, double, full, very lasting; light orange-yellow; borne singly on long stem; very fragrant. Very vigorous, bushy; profuse bloomer." [ARA24/175] "Does not produce enough flowers, but still is a favorite. The buds open up beautifully, and while the deep yellow at the center fades to almost white on the outside petals at time, I rather like that color combination. And you can always count on having a strong, tall bush and stout stems." [ARA29/146] "'Mrs. E[rskine] P[embroke] Thom' [Pern] is better." [C-Ps29] Mary Pickford, beloved American film actress prominent in the silent era.

Mevrouw G. A. van Rossem

syn. 'Mrs. G. A. van Rossem'
van Rossem, 1926
From 'Gorgeous' (Pern) × 'Souvenir de Georges Pernet' (Pern) [or possibly 'Souvenir de Claudius Pernet' (Pern)].

"Deep orange yellow." [Ÿ] "It is dark orange-apricot, a combination of colors new to the rose." [ARA28/132] "A showy variety of rich golden yellow color, flushed and lined with peach-pink on the outer petals." [ARA29/200] "The background is brownish yellow but the general color effect is orange, due to the very prominent orange veins." [CaRoll/3/8] "The bud is of deep burnt-orange, gradually opening to tangerine, heavily veined with maroon, with a golden yellow reverse and base. Gradually the many pigments fuse into an old-rose tint which remains pleasant to see till the petals drop." [C-Ps29] "A deep sun-yellow overlaid and shaded by scarlet. Its faults are that the bloom does not hold color and opens very rapidly." [ARA29/201] "Orange yellow, large, full, medium scent, medium height." [Sn] "Red-orange . . . A spectacular Rose which shows best in the half-open bud stage when it is of the deepest red-orange, almost brownish, with deeply impressed maroon veins. Toward the end the color tones to old-rose. It is delicately perfumed. The bush is vigorous and produces freely." [C-Pf31] "Undoubtedly one of the best roses of the year and is very beautiful in form and of new coloring—golden yellow with veins and reflex of reddish apricot. The plant is vigorous, very floriferous, and has persistent foliage." [ARA28/127] "A truly spectacular Rose . . . The bloom opens rather quickly and shows a gracefully disarranged center as if a handful of small petals had been added . . . Delicate perfume. The plant is vigorous, with red wood and deep green, holly-like foliage. It is prolific and blooms well in summer. A bedding rose with a great future." [C-Ps30] "Bud ovoid, opens freely in dull and moist weathers. Flower large, double, full, very fragrant,

heavily flamed and shaded orange and apricot on a dark golden yellow ground, reverse of petals often dark bronze and nearly brown when first open; borne on long, strong stem. Foliage very large, dark bronzy green, leathery, disease-resistant. Average number of large red thorns. Growth vigorous, upright; abundant bloomer." [ARA28/241] "*Ontario* rather hopefully calls it interesting, but neither vigorous nor free enough, and we are inclined to agree that that report is about correct. Its curious, incurved flowers, filled with a tuft of small petals, like a topknot on a bantam hen, certainly make no claim to excellence of form. Its color, when good, is universally admired, but so often it is wishy-washy and ordinary dirty pink." [ARA31/198] "In some respects, it comes near 'Wilhelm Kordes' [Pern] in color, but the bud is not pointed. Growth is very strong and it is a free bloomer. The foliage is a beautiful polished light green and is seemingly quite free from fungous pests." [ARA28/130] "The true color of 'Soleil d'Or' [Pern] in a finished garden rose! Foliage and habit good." [ARA28/177] "Bizarre and highly colored, and one of the better roses in its class, although a little lacking in vigor." [ARA30/191]

Miss May Marriott

Robinson, 1918
Sport of 'Mme. Édouard Herriot' (Pern).

"Rich apricot to orange-red. Growth vigorous." [GeH] "Orange yellow, large, lightly full, medium scent, moderate height." [Sn] "A fine orange gold sport of 'Mme. Édouard Herriot'. There have appeared three or four sports of a similar character . . . but I think this is the best." [NRS21/137] "This is a rich glowing apricot-coloured sport from 'Mme. Édouard Herriot'. The foliage and habit of growth are identical with [those of] that well-known variety. Quite distinct, it will prove a very valuable companion to its parent." [NRS18/165] "Good foliage." [GeH]

Mme. Édouard Herriot Plate 78

syn. 'Daily Mail Rose'
Pernet-Ducher, 1913
From 'Mme. Caroline Testout' (HT) × a Pernetiana.

"Deep coral red, nuanced scarlet red." [Cw] "Crushed strawberry, but in fact almost any colour from salmon pink to brick red." [NRS20/88] "It starts a brick-red, finishing a washy faded rose." [NRS22/69] "Terra-cotta; tall, spare." [ARA17/31] "Yellow, red center, very large, full, medium scent, tall." [Sn] "Not always a vigorous grower but its coral-red and orange buds, developing into moderate-sized flowers of orange-red and salmon, are beautiful." [ARA29/52] "Superb coral-red shaded with yellow, and bright rosy scarlet, passing to prawn-red, of medium size, semi-double; bud coral-red shaded with yellow on the base. Growth vigorous, of spreading branching habit with many long thorns and green-bronzed foliage; perpetual flowering." [GeH] "Twenty-five blooms in 1915." [ARA16/20] "The earliest to bloom in its class." [C-Ps27] "Most of its blooms after the early spring are too thin. At its best it can hardly be equaled." [ARA23/65] "A Rose of such unusual and pleasing color that it is a favorite wherever grown . . . A free-blooming Rose, producing fine flowers all summer and until frost." [C&Js24] "Does not stand rain specially well." [NRS29/121] "Not a good Rose for cutting." [C-Ps32] "Placed in a bowl with yellow, apricot, and salmon roses, the Madame attracts attention." [ARA29/53] "Strikes a spot in my color-consciousness that no other rose touches." [ARA29/102] "This vivid Rose, before any other, gets and grips the

Mme. Édouard Herriot *continued*

gaze of visitors as they enter our Rose-Garden. The large buds glow like dusky fire, and the newly opened blooms like red-hot copper which soon changes to a pleasing orange pink. Its fairly large, semi-double flowers are well formed in the early stage, but open too quickly in hot weather; the stems are often weak. The bush blooms freely, in several successive crops, and is a tall, bushy grower, with many thorns, and dark foliage requiring protection against black-spot. It is very hardy, and is the best of the tested varieties in this color. Winner of . . . [the] $5,000 [*sic*] prize offered by the *Daily Mail* newspaper of London. Will produce many more of its marvelously colored flowers if it is only lightly pruned." [C-Ps25] "[Pernet-Ducher] sent me [E. G. Hill] 'Mme. Édouard Herriot', the rose that the *Daily Mail* people offered a $500 [*sic*] prize for at the great International Show. He thought it would bring far more money than 'Sunburst' [Pern]. It would not bloom in the winter." [ARA22/131] "A glorious color, but a poor bush." [ARA23/84] "The plant is not only free flowering but constantly putting up fresh growths, so that a bed of it has some flowers in bloom throughout the season." [NRS21/48] "A particularly good bedding Rose and quite hardy, almost always in flower through the season. In form it is only fair, and the carriage of the flowers, which are produced in succession at the top of the stalk, leaves much to be desired. Its attraction lies in its colour, which is very striking but harmonises with few other Roses except white ones." [NRS20/89]

"The colour is terra-cotta with various shades of pink and orange, passing to a strawberry rose tint. In hot weather this colour rather quickly becomes unattractive. The form of the bud and opening flower is good, but is rapidly lost as the blossom expands. A strong upright stem carries at its extremity 3 or 4 flowers on short foot stalks which open successively. They are only semi-double. It is a defect of the plant that the flowers are apt to hang their heads, the foot stalks not being strong enough to support them, and this is particularly marked in the secondary flowers. The foliage is a fine glossy green colour and free from mildew, which, however, occasionally attacks the stems; it is liable to invasion by black spot, but with a little trouble this can usually be kept in check. The stems are copiously armed with large thorns, which are reddish and partially translucent when young. The habit of the plant is excellent, a good plant producing several upright stems, which carry the flowers well above the foliage, and make a neat bush. The constitution of the plant has proved unexpectedly good, and it seems quite free from the 'die back' which has affected so many of the varieties of this group. To me it possesses no fragrance, but some detect a fruity perfume." [NRS22/58–59]

"This is the most sensational Rose introduced for many years." [C&Js14] "Best of the Pernetianas so far [1918]. Attractive and distinct color; perfectly hardy; foliage beautiful in spring, but lost early; fairly good bloomer." [ARA18/110] "As soon as a variety of similar colouring that carries its blooms erect is introduced, this Rose will decline in popularity." [NRS21/65] "Mayor [of Lyon] Édouard Herriot, himself a rose-lover." [ARA30/158]

Mme. Eugène Picard
Gillot, 1929
Sport of 'Ariel' (Pern).

"Deep yellow, medium size, lightly double, medium scent, moderate height." [Sn] "Bud medium size, oval, carmine-red; flower medium size, semi-double, high-centered, lasting, moderately fragrant,

yellow, borne several together on medium-length, strong stem. Foliage abundant, medium size, dark green, leathery. Growth vigorous, bushy; abundant, continuous bloomer." [ARA30/224]

Mme. Georges Landard
Walter, 1925
From 'Mme. Abel Chatenay' (HT) × 'Lyon-Rose' (Pern).

"Rose-red, large, full, medium scent, moderate height." [Sn] "Color and form similar to [those of] 'Mme. Abel Chatenay', but the foliage is shining like [that of] 'Louise Catherine Breslau' [Pern]. Blooms borne singly on long stems. Very free flowering." [ARA26/183]

Mme. Henri Quenille   Listed as 'Mme. Henri Queuille' (Pern).

Mme. Henri Queuille
syn. 'Mme. Henri Quenille'
Pernet-Ducher/Gaujard, 1928

"Light orange red, large, full, very fragrant, moderate height." [Sn] "The colour is in the way of 'Los Angeles' [Pern], with a copper shading towards the base of the petals; a fine Rose for all florists and the garden." [GeH] "*San Diego* reports that it does well, rather spreading, bloom moderate, color admired, and seems promising. *Isham* calls the color lovely, flowers well-shaped, foliage good. *Hatton* thinks the flower very attractive if cut and opened in the house; it fades too much in the garden. It does not bloom freely with him." [ARA30/196] "*Foote* found it very satisfactory the second year, and of excellent growth. *McMurry* reports interesting color. *Nicolas* calls it a tall, vigorous 'Étoile de Feu' [Pern] with fewer petals. *Huntingdon* reports total failure. We liked the flowers at Breeze Hill but gagged at the name and its tendency to fade quickly to a rather uninteresting pink." [ARA31/204] "Bud long-pointed; flower very lasting, deliciously fragrant, very bright shrimp-pink, deeper at center, shaded coppery and gold on reverse. Foliage bronzy green, disease-resistant. Few thorns. Growth very vigorous, branches long and flexible." [ARA29/224]

Mme. Ruau
Gravereaux/Kieffer & fils, 1909
From 'Pharisäer' (HT) × 'Les Rosati' (Pern).

"Orange pink, yellow center, large, full, medium height." [Sn] "More like the Hybrid Teas . . . large globular blooms, a fusion of yellow and old Rose—very attractive. It is free blooming, perpetual and sweetly scented." [NRS13/162] "A Rose after the style of 'Lyon[-Rose]' [Pern], but not so full or shapely. It makes a pretty shrub." [NRS21/132] "This is a very vigorous plant, bushy, with erect canes; fairly abundant, unequal, not very protrusive, thorns; leaves composed of 5–7 oblong, gay green leaflets; bud long; blossom large, quite full, in the form of an elongated cup; color, carminy shrimp pink; petal edges and reverse are neatly shaded with yellow; this tone is warmer and more accentuated at the base of the petals; blooms continuously all summer." [JR33/168] "I was very fond of this pretty Rose with its charming flowers of deep old rose flushed with orange. It was hopeless, however, owing to its awful addiction to mildew." [NRS25/114] "Free flowering. Distinct." [GeH]

Morgenster
syn. 'Morgenstern'; trans. "Morning Star"
Nyvelt, 1916
Sport of 'Mme. Édouard Herriot' (Pern).

"Coppery orange, large, lightly double, medium height." [Sn]

Morgenstern Listed as 'Morgenster' (Pern).

Mrs. Ambrose Ricardo Listed as 'Mrs. Ambrose Riccardo' (Pern).

Mrs. Ambrose Riccardo
syn. 'Mrs. Ambrose Ricardo'
McGredy, 1914

"Straw yellow, nuanced coppery." [Cw] "Deep honey yellow overlaid brighter yellow, of great size and substance. Among yellow Roses this is the largest of all yet raised ... A really magnificent Rose, delightfully sweet perfume." [NRS14/207] "Deep yellow, large, full, very fragrant, moderate height." [Sn] "The blooms, when open, are cup-shaped and very large, with center petals standing up." [C-Ps29] "Beautiful at all stages, changing from creamy yellow to delicate pink. The form is always good, and in the spring and fall the blossoms are very large. However, it is subject to black-spot and winter-kills easily. It is not an abundant bloomer, but, like some few people, has such rare charm that we feel we have gained much by knowing it." [ARA31/98] "Amongst yellow Roses, this [is] the largest of all yet raised; free-flowering; delightfully sweet perfume." [C&Js16] "An exhibition variety of great size and substance—I won't say an improved, but an enlarged form of 'Mrs. Amy Hammond' [HT]. I heard someone say it was too much like 'Mme. Jules Gravereaux' [Cl HT], but I failed to see any resemblance ... Colour, flesh and cream; very fragrant, as all this raiser's Roses are. A good grower, and likely to be very useful." [NRS14/152–153] "One large bloom of this will attract more attention in a room than a whole bowl of beautiful mixed varieties." [ARA29/53] "The large, chalice-shaped blossoms are of an indescribable creaminess, and the center honey-golden, each succeeding row of petals growing paler and changing ultimately to a faint pink. Its fragrance is good but not strong. The bush is subject to black-spot and needs care to prevent it from dying out. While the number of blossoms is not great, their quality is supreme." [ARA29/68] "A magnificent, large-flowered Rose, strong-growing and very free in bloom. The flowers are quite double, of good form, and exquisitely colored a tender flesh-pink overlaid with honey-yellow. Very sweetly scented and attractive in every way. A Rose we can highly recommend. Order at least ten of this choice variety so that you can have flowers for cutting all season." [C&Js23] "Growth and form above average; color distinct; blooming qualities fairly good." [ARA18/113] "Popular among bedding Roses for its great size and lovely color. Flowers are light orange-yellow, paling later to soft pink. They are unusually large, full, but not too full, and of good, globular form. Sometimes they open too quickly. Blooms come in big sprays on a lusty branching plant. The foliage is handsome, but needs protection against black-spot." [C-Ps25] "A beautiful flower of honey yellow colour in early summer, but the plant is so susceptible to black spot that it defoliates early, and the flowers seldom appear late." [NRS21/52] "Small, upright; foliage sufficient, healthy; bloom moderate, intermittent." [ARA18/127] "It is a haughty Rose aristocrat in appearance and requires just a little more care than ordinary to get from it the best blooms." [C-Ps26] "Quite first rate in every respect." [NRS21/134]

Mrs. Arthur Robert Waddell
Pernet-Ducher, 1908

"Orange pink or reddish salmon. Outer petals flesh. Of medium size and semidouble. Very free bloomer." [CA17] "Exquisite and delicate combination of colors; buds gold and copper, developing into flowers of pink and apricot shades. It is a very consistent bloomer." [ARA29/52] "Rosy scarlet bud, opening reddish salmon; reverse of petals rosy scarlet, semi-double. Fair amount of disbudding." [Th] "Bleaches slightly." [ARA26/202] "Semi-double, soft rosy-salmon flowers, suffused with a golden sheen. Good foliage. Medium height; poor grower and bloomer when budded. Gives from 31 to 62 blooms per season. Hardy." [ARA21/92] "Deep apricot, paling to orange-salmon; rose-pink predominating in late autumn; beautiful bud opening too loose. Weak stem; odor slight but fresh. Medium bushy. 25 blooms." [ARA26/95] "Reddish salmon, reverse rosy scarlet, fading to cream when open; attractive bud; semi-double flower of medium size; does not last. Foliage fair. Poor stem and weak neck; spreading and bushy growth ... Needs cool climate for perfection ... shows Foetida blood." [Th2] "A copper-headed tomboy among Roses. Remarkable for its vigorous, branching growth and its long reddish buff buds of finest shape. The open flowers are coppery gold, but quickly fade to pink. They are almost single, and so freely produced, especially in autumn, that the bush is nearly always a spot of rollicking color." [C-Ps25] "Mild perfume; fifty-seven blooms throughout the season on Multiflora [understock]; growth above the average. An excellent decorative rose." [ARA17/25] "Growth very vigorous, robust constitution, bushy; beautiful bronze green foliage; bud grenadine red; flower large, semi-full; bicolored, reddish salmon, grenadine red on the reverse of the petals." [JR32/25–26] "Vigorous; growth similar to [that of] Tea Roses; flowers semi-double, fine buds." [Au] "Tall, bushy, vigorous, hardy; foliage very plentiful, black-spots and mildews somewhat; bloom free and continuous." [ARA18/127] "Medium spreading growth, fine foliage; very hardy, fair stem; pretty bud, but opens somewhat single; in summer not a good keeper. Undoubtedly the best of its color, and a wonderful bloomer in spring, moderate in summer and very good in autumn. Plant 18 inches [ca. 4.5 dm] center to center. Prune to 4 eyes." [Th] "A useful decorative rose, doing best on Multiflora [understock]. Notable for its growth, blooming qualities, and distinct color." [ARA18/113] "A lovely, decorative, free-blooming Rose that apparently thrives in any climate. It is unusually free flowering." [C-Ps27] "Makes enormous bushes [in New South Wales, Australia] and covers itself with bloom. It also hangs its head but nevertheless is good; does well for twenty-five years." [ARA30/152] "A wonderful grower; the color is most attractive, and while somewhat loose as to shape, its many fine qualities entitle it to very high rank as a garden rose." [ARA23/63] For Dr. Robert Arthur Waddell, see this chapter's head-note.

Mrs. Bullen
Pernet-Ducher, 1916

"Cochineal-carmine, shaded with yellow, passing to carmine-lake, large, moderately full. Growth vigorous, branching; continuous flowering." [GeH] "From unnamed varieties. —A Rose of artistic beauty, yielding cochineal carmine flowers in large clusters of semi-double character. A fine bedder, and will be valued for those who admire this *négligé* type of Rose." [NRS21/137] "Red, large, very full, moderate height." [Sn]

Mrs. C. E. Pearson Listed as 'Mrs. Charles E. Pearson' (Pern).

[Mrs. Charles E. Pearson]
McGredy, 1913

"'Orange, flushed red, apricot, fawn and yellow' (McGredy). Col-

[Mrs. Charles E. Pearson] *continued*

oring may be said to be intermediate between 'Lyon[-Rose]' [Pern] and 'Mme. Édouard Herriot' [Pern]. Buds are pointed; open flowers reflexed-globular to nearly flat, double and faintly fragrant. Growth moderate or rather short. Stems short, but strong, carrying flowers finely. Blooms freely and has a very high coloring." [CA17] "Plants are literally covered with flowers up to the autumnal frosts; blossoms large; canes vigorous, always holding the rose well above the foliage; in fragrance, deliciously sweet … very sweet." [JR37/89] "[Flowers] of medium size … Growth vigorous, free branching." [GeH] "One of the very beautiful roses that will not grow … The colour is a lovely salmon rose with a tinge of yellow, and the flower is of beautiful form. The pity is the beauty is so frail." [NRS21/48] "Splendid bedding variety." [C&Js15] "A dwarf stumpy grower, and a very beautiful front row plant. Splendid for edging a Rose bed. The blooms much resemble [those of] 'Lyon-Rose', but smaller. Although dwarf, it is by no means weakly, and I can recommend it." [NRS21/134] "Very distinct color; good form; poor growth; shy bloomer. Retained merely for its attractive color." [ARA18/113]

Mrs. Erskine Pembroke Thom
Howard & Smith, 1926
From 'Grange Colombe' (HT) × 'Souvenir de Claudius Pernet' (Pern).

"Pure lemon yellow; double; long shapely buds; mildly scented; good growth; prolific." [CaRoll/3/2] "Light yellow, large, full, medium scent, medium height." [Sn] "Double flowers of clear, deep, canary-yellow without a trace of shading, borne singly on long stems. Moderately fragrant. The plant is upright, branching, with attractive foliage resistant to disease." [GeH] "Long buds of good pointed shape, developing into perfectly formed, high-centered, fully double flowers of clear, deep canary-yellow without a trace of shading, long lasting and moderately fragrant, borne singly on long stems. The plant is upright, branching with attractive foliage resistant to disease, and is very free flowering." [ARA26/185] "Medium-sized, semi-double, long buds of perfect form, which open to a flower of clear, deep lemon-yellow. Makes a strong, upright-growing plant with quantities of flowers in June and in the fall. the foliage is notably free from disease and is dark, bronzy green. It is different from 'Souvenir de Claudius Pernet', being wholly free from the black center which frequently spoils that variety in cool weather." [C-Ps30] "Probably the best yellow Pernetiana we have today. It has an ovoid, pointed bud of deep ochre-yellow, sometimes splashed with carmine, opening to semi-double sunflower-yellow, medium-size blooms on short but firm stems, and has some perfume. The plant is robust, though not tall-growing, and the wood reddish brown with few thorns. Unusually good foliage for the class. A heavy spring bloomer and also in the fall, with some activity between the two seasons." [C-Ps29] "Very free in bloom, owing to the tendency of the lower eyes to 'break' while the terminal bud is still forming." [ARA28/177] "I believe I have not seen a more symmetrical plant, and the foliage is almost proof against black-spot, which is our greatest rose enemy. The blooms are a true yellow and are produced freely, their only fault being lack of petals. [The variety] holds her color in hot weather better than most yellow roses." [ARA29/92] "*Hatton* finds it a good fall bloomer, but shy in midsummer. *Lines* objects to the divided center of the open bloom which he calls as unforgivable fault. *Rice* says it lacks petals. *Nicolas* calls it a useful mediocrity with unsteady foliage." [ARA30/178] "Grows and blooms well in hot weather. Free; good color; no black-spot … *Mass.*; … The only fault I found was that blooms were weak and thin during July and August … *Ohio*; … Superfine growth and foliage, and habit all that is to be desired. Color is similar to [that of] 'Souv[enir] de Claudius Pernet', though deeper and more lasting. Does not come bull-headed nor have the ugly black centers '[Souvenir de Claudius] Pernet' has at times. I congratulate Fred Howard on this signal achievement. It is the best yellow rose in my garden … *Calif.*" [ARA28/177] "A true yellow utility garden Rose. Should be planted in masses to be appreciated, as its main feature is to give the yellow color to the garden." [C-Ps29]

Mrs. Frederick W. Vanderbilt
McGredy, 1912

"Deep orange, large, full, medium scent, moderate height." [Sn] "Coppery rose; moderate; bushy." [ARA17/32] "'Deep orange red, shaded bronze apricot red' (McGredy). Here it runs more toward a salmon ground, with carmine, yellow and flesh mixed in. Buds are moderately pointed and open flowers very double, of medium size and slightly fragrant. Growth moderate and spreading. Stems short but strong." [CA17] "More or less Pernet [*i.e.*, Pernetiana], with the character of an H.T., old gold, salmon, and yellow, and very free flowering." [NRS13/165] "Wonderful color; good form, which is retained; growth only fair; shy bloomer." [ARA18/113] "Large, perfect in shape and form; very fragrant … very free flowering." [GeH] "Very fine, with large blooms, much resembling 'Lyon[-Rose]' [Pern] at times. Its one fault is a sprawling type of growth, which suggests various methods of growing other than the ordinary bush form. As a standard it would be grand." [NRS21/134] "Perfect flowers of good substance. Good show and decorative quality." [C&Js15] "A decorative garden Rose of great beauty, to my mind the best of all those Roses that own to a cross with the Pernet-Ducher blood … A good grower; unique colouring, copper apricot and orange on a flesh ground—nearly mildew proof —and fragrant." [NRS14/155] "Quite distinct from any other Rose in cultivation, a marvellously attractive variety … The flower is absolutely perfect in shape and form with petals of wonderful depth and substance, blooming freely throughout the entire season, and suitable alike for exhibition purposes, garden culture or decorative work. It is a fine, strong, free grower, quite the best among the deep shaded Roses of this type, and regarded, by the Rev. Joseph Pemberton, as the finest and most useful decorative Rose of the year." [NRS13/215]

Mrs. G. A. van Rossem   Listed as 'Mevrouw G. A. van Rossem' (Pern).

Mrs. Pierre S. Dupont
Mallerin, 1929
From an unnamed seedling (arising from a cross between 'Ophelia' [HT] and 'Rayon d'Or' [Pern]) × an unnamed seedling (arising from a cross between another unnamed seedling [which resulted from a cross between 'Ophelia' and 'Constance' (Pern)] and 'Souvenir de Claudius Pernet' [Pern]).

"The 'perpetual motion' golden yellow, perfumed Rose, seldom without buds or blooms, and of the petalage and form of 'Mme. Butterfly' [HT] at its best." [ARA30/vii] "Bud medium size, long-pointed, reddish gold; flower medium size, semi-double, cupped, very lasting, moderately fragrant, deep golden yellow, becoming slightly lighter with age, borne singly or several together on stem of average length. Foliage abundant, rich green, disease-resistant. Growth vigorous (2 ft. [ca. 6 dm]), compact; profuse, continuous bloomer." [ARA30/224] "*Spillers* had no growth and no bloom." [ARA31/207] "*Pyle* calls it an irrepressibly constant bloomer with lovely buds for cutting all through the season. He thinks it the most beautiful of the new yellow roses. *Nicolas* states 'a dandelion-yellow rose that stays yellow, the most constant bloomer I know; extremely resistant to black-spot'." [ARA30/197]

Mrs. Ramon de Escofet
Easlea, 1919

"Red, very large, full, tall." [Sn] "Flower of intense flame-crimson colour, in the way of 'George C. Waud' [HT], but larger. Growth vigorous; very perpetual." [GeH] "A very large show bloom of intense flame crimson colouring. Will probably eclipse 'George C. Waud', and its growth is very vigorous." [NRS19/171] "A strong grower with large full blooms carried on long stems. Quite free . . . Mildews on the spines." [NRS24/161] "Its failing is a weak flower stalk and liable to mildew on its thorns." [NRS21/140] "Blooms large, good shape and freely produced on long stiff stems. A little impatient of wet. Colour a fiery crimson. Foliage dark green, fairly free from mildew and black spot. Growth vigorous, both as a maiden and cutback. Perpetual flowering. A good garden Rose." [NRS23/94]

Mrs. Redford
McGredy, 1919

"Soft apricot, with yellow suffusion. Good petalage and substance. Odor slight." [ARA27/147] "Orange yellow, medium size, very full, very fragrant, dwarf." [Sn] "A Rose with a future. The flowers are borne erect, and are of an intense apricot orange and of fine shape, if a little thin." [NRS21/139] "Flower full, of perfect shape; petals gracefully reflexed; opens freely in all weathers; sweet fragrance. Color bright apricot-orange. Foliage leathery, glossy; disease-resistant. Vigorous, upright grower; abundant bloomer." [ARA20/129] "By far the most striking variety in this lovely and pleasing tone of colour. A splendid upright grower with extraordinary beautiful holly-like, mildew-proof foliage. The blooms are solidly built, every petal gracefully reflexed and as perfect in shape and form as 'A[lfred] K. Williams' [HP]. Very free blooming and sweetly scented, opening its flowers freely in all weathers." [NRS19/163] "Long-pointed buds and medium-sized, full, double, soft apricot flowers, with a yellow sheen, of good lasting quality and slight fragrance, borne singly on medium-length stems. Foliage normal and glossy. Growth poor; 5 flowers in the season." [ARA27/141] "A fine bedding Rose of vigorous growth, with deep glossy green foliage—apparently mildew proof. The blooms are small, of faultless shape. The colour is one of those difficult to describe—a brilliant orange, suffused copper and apricot. Quite unique." [NRS18/167] "Very promising.—*Simcoe, Ont.* Plant so poor that it passed away without blooming. —*Harrisburg, Pa.*" [ARA26/119] "If heavily fed and well cared for, this Rose produces abundant blooms of bright orange and apricot, not very double but fragrant and lasting. A strong grower with shiny foliage. Fine for bedding." [C-Ps27]

Mrs. Robert Mitchell
Jersey Nurseries, 1926
From 'St. Helena' (HT) × 'Mrs. Redford' (Pern).

"Salmon pink, very large, full, moderate height." [Sn] "Flower very large, distinct salmon-rose, overlaid with coppery pink and distinctly lighted up with golden gleams, borne well above the foliage. Foli-

age rich green, glossy, mildew-resistant. Growth vigorous, compact." [ARA28/236] "Fine habit." [GeH]

Mrs. S. Paton
McGredy, 1928

"Orange red, medium size, very full, medium scent, moderate height." [Sn] "Brilliant orange, scarlet carmine, without any variation, running to an orange base. The orange scarlet sheen is very pronounced and makes the flower positively glow. The flowers are full, moderately large and of fine form, with petals of heavy texture. The habit of growth is of ideal bedding type, very free flowering, vigorous, branching and bushy, and the flowers are carried upright on long, stiff dark stems having few thorns. The foliage is a delightful dark reddish bronzy green, showing the colour of the flowers to great advantage, and has the appearance of being just newly varnished. It is quite mildewproof, and the blooms are extremely pretty. A very fine hardy Bedding Rose, flowering continuously from early Summer to late Autumn, and unaffected by the worst weather." [NRS28/301] "Very lovely, good, but not a profuse bloomer, foliage good, medium tall, and branching." [ARA30/197] "A fine rose for the amateur, is much the same shade as 'Charles P. Kilham' [HT], but darker and keeps its color for a long time. The plant grows well and has splendid, luxuriant foliage that has been healthy here. Its bud is of ideal form and the flower is large and full." [ARA30/161]

Mrs. Sam McGredy
McGredy, 1929

"Copper orange red, large, full, medium scent, moderate height." [Sn] "Reddish copper outside and coppery orange inside makes it very distinct. Slight fragrance, a moderate bloomer, and a strong, healthy plant." [ARA31/207] "A fine, well-shaped rose of a somewhat difficult color to describe—orange-red, shaded apricot, reverse of petals red. The blooms are large, of good shape, produced on long stems, and moderately fragrant. It is a rather vigorous grower with dark red foliage. A good bedding variety." [ARA30/156] "This is a very pretty and attractive Rose. The blooms are a good shape, and carried erect. The colour is a combination of shades of scarlet, copper, orange and red that produce a dazzling effect. Sweetly scented. The foliage is a dark bronzy red. The habit of the plant is vigorous and upright." [NRS29/123] "The colour is quite distinct . . . a wonderful dual combination of vivid shades. A beautiful scarlet coppery orange is heavily flushed with Lincoln red on the outside of the petals, and these colours together give a rich and almost dazzling effect. They are particularly brilliant in sunshine, which seems to illumine the flower . . . The flowers are of large size and beautiful form, and they possess the proper fulness to make them useful for all purposes. They are very freely produced and delicately perfumed. The foliage is a handsome dark reddish bronzy-green and mildew-proof, the stems are very long and strong—not thorny—and the blooms erect. The plant has a vigorous and exceptionally free habit." [NRS29/308] "Bud large, long-pointed; flower large, double, high-centered, very lasting, moderately fragrant, scarlet-coppery-orange, heavily flushed with Lincoln red on the outside of the petals, borne singly, several together, and in clusters on long stem. Foliage abundant, medium size, glossy bronze-green, disease-resistant. Growth vigorous, upright; profuse, continuous bloomer. Very hardy." [ARA30/222] "A truly grand rose when it comes anything like perfect . . . I find the bush a little thin, al-

Mrs Sam McGredy *continued*
though it seems to be healthy, and that means much for one of the new fancy-colored roses. It is a deep, glowing, uniform orange and copper-red. The bud is ideally formed but the bloom none too full." [ARA31/179] "I think a bud of Mrs. Sam is just about as handsome a thing as we have in this coloring, but I would not complain if the bush would grow a little stronger." [CaRoll/10/4]

Mrs. Talbot O'Farrell
McGredy, 1926

"Yellow, splashed cerise, veined orange, moderate size, fragrant." [GeH] "Red, medium size, full, medium scent, moderate height." [Sn] "Gorgeous color, but no more." [ARA28/131] "A highly colored little bud, but you have to look quickly or it's gone." [ARA29/147] "Type,'Killarney' [HT]. Bud small to medium, long-pointed; flower small to medium, double, high center, very lasting, fragrant, old-gold heavily stippled with rose on the upper surface, borne, singly and several together, on long stem. Foliage sufficient, small, dark bronzy green, leathery, glossy. Few thorns. Vigorous or moderate grower, upright, bushy habit; profuse, continuous bloomer from June to October." [ARA25/185] "A rose of unusual coloring, difficult to describe; small blooms; upright and fairly vigorous ... *Wash.*; Lovely, but shy. A collector's rose ... *Calif.*" [ARA28/180]

Mrs. W. E. Nickerson
McGredy, 1927

"Chrome-yellow at center passing to rich warm rosy salmon; reverse rich orange-cadmium at base, passing to salmon." [ARA27/226] "Yellowish salmon pink, very large, full, medium scent, moderate height." [Sn] "Rosy salmon shaded yellow. The flowers are large, full, and of perfect shape. A valuable bedding and exhibition variety." [GeH] "Too thin; also, I do not like these mixed-up colors." [ARA30/161] "Wonderful growth; good color; very free; semi-double, but keeps well when cut. No black-spot ... *Mass.*; Fragrance and open flower fair; growth, foliage, stem, size, form, petalage, bud and color good; general effect very good ... *N.Y.*; ... Holds form better than many roses with more petals. In color of foliage, bloom, and vigor, well to the front as a garden and cut rose ... *Wash.*; Very vigorous, and one of the best-shaped blooms; beautiful two-toned salmon and orange color. At times stems are a little weak for so large a flower ... *Wash.*" [ARA28/180] "The stems are weak-necked at times, and the blooms magnificent in early summer and autumn. The mid-summer flowers are likely to be thin, few-petaled, and of muddy color ... *Middleton* praises its perfect form, but admits a little mildew. *Ontario* is non-committal, but reports 23 per cent black-spot." [ARA30/184] "All correspondents condemn its weak neck. *Foote* finds it a steady bloomer, tall grower, and a good bedder ... *Ontario* thought it rather spasmodic ... *McMurry* has good plants on own roots ... The most comprehensive report comes from *Huntingdon* who calls it 'a rose with very pronounced virtues and faults, bud and half-open flower superb, good size, rich color; open flower a worthless, hollow bowl with a harsh, unattractive color.' She found the plant healthy, amazingly free in the first season, but less and less liberal in two succeeding years." [ARA31/199] "Bud large, long-pointed; flower very large, double, high centered, very lasting, moderately fragrant, deep chrome-yellow on the lower half veining out and passing to a warm rich rosy salmon, reverse heavily veined with *rose d'or* [?] and shaded orange-cadmium,

borne singly and several together on long stem. Foliage abundant, large, dark green, leathery, disease-resistant. Average number thorns. Growth very vigorous, upright; profuse, continuous bloomer from June to November. Hardy." [ARA28/236]

Nona
Easlea, 1924
From 'Mme. Édouard Herriot' (Pern) × 'Constance' (Pern).

"Long tapering buds of flame and orange colour, open flowers flame to pink. Buds carried erect. The colours are a blending of [those of] 'Betty Uprichard' [Pern] and 'Mme. Édouard Herriot' [Pern]." [GeH] "Red and pink, medium size, lightly double, medium scent, moderate height." [Sn] "Bud medium size, long-pointed; flower medium-size, semi-double, open, very lasting, fragrant, flame and pink (like 'Mme. Édouard Herriot', but deeper vermilion tint), borne erect, several together, on medium-length stem. Foliage sufficient, medium size, rich green, leathery. Vigorous, upright; profuse bloomer." [ARA25/185]

Norman Lambert
McGredy, 1926

"Salmon orange, yellow center, large, full, medium scent, moderate height." [Sn] "Copper-orange. Large, well-formed buds and unique, multi-colored, semi-double blooms, predominantly copper-orange. Splendid bedding variety." [C-Ps31] "Very fine. Buds deep orange and gold, opens to rich orange." [ARA31/178] "In this rose the Pernet blood is almost entirely displaced by the Hybrid Tea, and the color is a golden yellow, shaded terra-cotta—a very charming combination. The blooms are of good shape, with high-pointed centers, and delightfully fragrant. The plant was vigorous and free. It will be a popular decorative variety." [ARA25/178] "Perhaps the best of the numerous modern art shades for cutting, as the blooms are carried on long, stiff stems." [NRS29/146] "Gorgeous color, but no more." [ARA28/131] "The brilliant coloring of this variety is its great attraction—deep chrome yellow, margined and splashed with orange-scarlet. It is not a strong grower, but is quite liberal with its flowers." [ARA29/52] "It is a strong grower, and [fades very quickly]." [ARA28/133] "Lovely, thumb-thick canes over 2 feet long [ca. 6 dm]." [ARA29/113] "Subject to black-spot ... *Mass.*; Fragrance, stem, size, form, petalage, bud, open flower, fair; growth, foliage, color, good; general effect very good ... *N.Y.*; Not over-strong; stems average; slight black-spot but no mildew; blooms freely, with attractive color, poor shape, little substance, bronzy orange, fading somewhat with age, insufficient petalage, and petals too short slight scent noticeable at times ... *Ont.*; ... Orange-yellow and burnt-orange blooms on long, strong stems; vigorous growth, and foliage resists disease ... *Va.*; ... Does not last ... *Texas*; ... Has no special merit ... *Calif.*" [ARA28/181] "Bud large, long-pointed; flower large, double, high-centered, very lasting, slightly fragrant, deep salmon-orange, suffused bronze and yellow, fading to yellow at the base, reverse deep buttercup-yellow, borne on long, strong stem; drop off cleanly. Foliage abundant, large, normal green, leathery, glossy, disease-resistant. Few thorns. Growth very vigorous, upright, bushy profuse, continuous bloomer. Hardy." [ARA27/218]

[O. Junyent]
not "O'Junyent"
Dot, 1924
From 'Frau Karl Druschki' (HP) × 'Mme. Édouard Herriot' (Pern).

"Has grown less than a foot high [ca. 3 dm], and not very bushy.

The flowers are attractive orange-pink, beautifully and regularly ruffled." [ARA27/141] "Type, 'Antoine Rivoire' [HT]. Bud large, ovoid; flower large, semi-double, open, lasting, coral-red on yellow base, borne, several together, on short, strong stem. Foliage abundant, large, dark green, glossy, disease-resistant. Many thorns. Very vigorous, bushy, dwarf habit (grows 2½ feet high [ca. 7.5 dm]); profuse, continuous bloomer from May to November. Very hardy." [ARA25/192]

Old Gold

McGredy, 1913

"Vivid reddish orange with rich coppery red and coppery apricot shadings, of medium size, moderately full, carried rigidly upright; sweetly scented." [GeH] "Reddish orange yellow, medium size, lightly double, medium scent, tall." [Sn] "Orange red, very beautiful in the bud." [OM] "Reddish orange, semi-double. —Moderately vigorous." [JP] "Strong growth…a deep coppery old gold." [NRS/13] "Best in the bud. While it is orange at first, the color fades to light buff as the flower opens." [ARA34/81] "The fault of 'Old Gold' is the very fleeting period during which the buds retain their beautiful form." [NRS20/87] "The most glorious color that has ever been seen in any Rose the tint is a vivid reddish orange with rich coppery red and coppery apricot shadings. A gem for cut-flower work and all kinds of decorations." [C&Js14] "Great beauty of colour, which the raisers call reddish rouge, with rich coppery red and apricot shadings … a very beautiful and striking decorative plant … spreading and not too tall. It has very dark coppery foliage, which appeared quite mildew proof … very free-flowering. It is sweetly scented and lasts well when cut." [NRS13/215] "Does not last; especially fragrant…Foliage good." [Th2] "Messrs. S. McGredy & Son…have struck yet another line. They have been busy infusing the colour of the Pernet roses into Hybrid Teas with great success, having combined 'Rayon d'Or' [Pern] colour with a specially free habit of growth. The sheets of colour are perfectly dazzling. The best, 'Old Gold', has annexed the dark coppery green foliage and strong growth. It is quite mildew proof, showing the long-pointed blooms to perfection. A deep coppery old gold." [NRS13/165] "Without a doubt the most beautiful decorative existing, its color never having been equaled by another rose the color is orange-red tinted apricot-red. It is a gem for vases, as the roses last a very long time in the best condition. The foliage is a somber coppery green, making a delicious contrast. The blossom is pleasantly perfumed; this variety is continuously in bloom and grows vigorously; the roses are always borne singly at the ends of the long stems." [JR37/89] "Medium to large, fine form, single, slightly fragrant, long stems. Fine foliage, sufficient. Growth strong, bushy, slender; hardy." [ARA23/169]

Padre

B. R. Cant, 1920

"Large, coppery scarlet blooms, slightly flushed with deep yellow at the base of the petals." [C-Ps29] "A suffusion of copper that gives it a unique, brilliant tonality." [C-Ps31] "Dazzling color and keeping qualities." [ARA29/111] "Copper red, yellow center, medium size, lightly double, medium scent, moderate height." [Sn] "Coppery scarlet, similar to 'Mme. Édouard Herriot' [Pern]. An attractive rose, but had some black-spot." [ARA25/121] "Fine long petals of coppery scarlet colouring, flushed with yellow at the base; produced on long shoots. Growth strong and upright; free flowering." [GeH] "A 'Mme. Édouard Herriot' of improved form and even more brilliant color—intense orange-

red. A tall-growing Rose, and a very free bloomer; foliage quite healthy. Cut when in bud." [C-Ps25] "The handsome semi-single flowers are borne in clusters on long, candelabra-like stems, and the unusually charming color attracts attention anywhere. Fine in the spring and fall, but in summer the blooms open too quickly. Should be planted back of low-growing varieties." [C-Ps27] "Growth appeared to be very similar to that of 'Lady Pirrie' [HT], and the color of bloom also; though, if anything, it seemed slightly darker." [ARA20/120] "This rose appeared to me to be more of a Pernetiana than a Hybrid Tea, but the new varieties are now so very mixed that their classification becomes more and more difficult. It is a good-shaped cerise-cherry colored rose, fragrant, and apparently a good grower." [ARA21/152] "Blooms of medium size, with loose petals. Liable to damage by rain. Moderately scented. Colour orange scarlet, with gold at base of petals, fading with age. Foliage dark green. Fairly free of mildew. Growth as a maiden vigorous, but inclined to weaken as a cutback. The blooms have a tendency to hang their heads, and are shyly produced, with me practically only flowering twice during the year. Liable to lose its leaves in the early autumn." [NRS23/95] "The foliage is small and scanty." [C-Ps28] "Foliage subject to mildew." [NRS24/161] "Growth upright (3 feet [ca. 1.m]); 60 flowers throughout the season…*Caldwell, Idaho*; …Fades considerably the second or third day. The plants are tall, with sparse foliage…It is one of the freest blooming of its type, and a most excellent decorative rose." [ARA27/141] "Very graceful." [ARA29/55]

Pardinas Bonet

Dot, 1929

From 'La Giralda' (Pern) × 'Souvenir de Claudius Pernet' (Pern).

"Pink and orange. A low-growing Rose with large, semi-double, cupped blooms of pinkish orange; peculiar fragrance." [C-Ps33] "Deep yellow, large, full, very fragrant, dwarf." [Sn] "Yellow and red. Great oval buds open to intensely fragrant, cup-shaped flowers with broad outer petals of carmine-red. The center is glowing yellow and composed of narrow, incurved petals striped with pale carmine. This Rose has few thorns, is moderate in growth, but blooms all season." [C-Ps31] "Bud large, oval; flower large, double, globular, lasting, intensely fragrant, deep yellow, outside red, borne singly on a long stem. Foliage sufficient, medium size, shiny, disease-resistant. Few thorns. Growth moderate, dwarf; abundant, continuous bloomer from May to December." [ARA29/229] "An excellent plant, very vigorous, very healthy and very floriferous. Its double flowers are of a pretty color where the yellow and red blend harmoniously." [ARA28/127] "A descendant of '[Frau Karl] Druschki' [HP], '[Mme. Édouard] Herriot' [Pern], and '[Souvenir de Claudius] Pernet', interesting parents. The water-lily-like flowers are different." [C-Ps34]

[Pax Labor]

Chambard, 1918

Sport of 'Beauté de Lyon' (Pern).

"Golden yellow, nuanced coppery red." [Cw] "A large, full rose, clear yellow centre." [NRS19/120] "A Rose to be noted. It is a fine big flower on a very sturdy growth, as stiff as [that of] 'Louise Catherine Breslau' [Pern]. Colour pale yellow, edged carmine." [NRS21/138] "Very large bud of orange-gold, bordered with carmine; flowers very large, full, pale golden yellow, slightly shaded coppery carmine when opening, passing to sulphur-yellow when fully open. Foliage deep bronzy green. Hardy and vigorous." [ARA19/100] "Vigorous. Exhibition." [NRS23/list]

Président Bouché

Pernet-Ducher, 1916

From an unnamed seedling × 'Lyon-Rose' (Pern).

"Shrimp red with coral red, nuanced yellow." [Cw] "Yellowish orange red, medium size, full, moderate height." [Sn] "Gorgeous bright copper red gold, luminous color, very large, quite full. Growth strong; good stem." [Ck] "A splendid upright grower, with lovely shapely blooms. Perhaps wanting a little in fulness, but still a variety of much merit. The colour is coral red, shaded prawn carmine." [NRS21/136] "Coral-red, shaded with prawn-carmine-red, medium sized. Growth vigorous, branching, continuous flowering." [GeH] "It is finer than 'Mme. Édouard Herriot' [Pern]." [NRS22/65]

President Wilson

Easlea, 1918

"Orange pink, large, full, moderate height." [Sn] "Flower butter yellow. Growth vigorous." [GeH] "A most delightful shade of shrimp pink, reminding one of 'Willowmere' [Pern], but of a clearer and more refined hue. The flowers are very large, of exhibition quality, and they are freely produced upon vigorous erect growths." [NRS18/202] "Very large flowers of a clear pink, but for the past five years it balls at intervals each season, and is subject to mildew and black-spot." [ARA25/102] "The blooms are very large and of bright pink with a luminous glow. They resemble [those of] 'Willowmere' but have less salmon in the color. Grows vigorously and blooms liberally on robust, thorny stems." [C-Ps29] "More nearly a warm shrimp-pink than the usual Pernetiana, ['President Wilson'] was large, double, freely produced, and exceedingly handsome; in fact, it stood out in comparison with other roses as different, notable, and desirable. It ought to have a great future." [ARA24/185] Thomas Woodrow Wilson, 28th president of the United States of America, a pacifist who presided over the American role in World War I, lived 1856–1924.

Princesse de Béarn-Deutschland

Status unclear; either a garbled reference to 'Deutschland' (Pern) itself, *q.v.,* or (perhaps more likely) an unreleased hybrid between the indicated HP and 'Deutschland' by Kiese, used as a parent of 'Johannisfeuer' (Pern).

Professor Schmeil

Kröger, 1925

"Orange yellow, striped light red, large, lightly double, moderate height." [Sn]

[Rayon d'Or] Plate 75

trans. "Beam of Gold"

Pernet-Ducher, 1910

From 'Mme. Mélanie Soupert' (HT) × an unnamed seedling (descended from crosses between 'Soleil d'Or' [Pern] and unnamed Hybrid Teas; see below).

"A sheet of purest brightest yellow close before me. Here was the exact colour of 'Persian Yellow' [F], seen in a great Hybrid Tea Rose, a yellow holding its own even in the burning rays of the August sun. 'Marvel of marvels! What have you here, Monsieur?' I cried [to Monsieur Pernet-Ducher, continuing:] '*Voici la rose jaune que nous attendons depuis vingt ans* [Here is the yellow rose that we have waited for for twenty years].' '*C'est vrai* [Quite so],' was the proud, quiet answer [from Pernet-Ducher]. 'Rayon d'Or' is without doubt the best yellow Rose which exists!" [NRS10/115] "A magnificent golden yellow Rose with large, glossy foliage which appears immune to the attacks of mildew. It is a strong, vigorous grower with large globular flowers, cadmium-yellow in color as the buds begin to expand, toning to golden yellow as they develop. A gorgeous Rose and one we highly recommend." [C&Js18] "Very much the same as 'Constance' [Pern]. Wonderful color; growth and bloom fair. Has tendency to [winter] kill back to ground level." [ARA18/114] "Marred by the crimson streaks on its outer petals. I grant the buds are very lovely, but for colour schemes in planting it is a defect. The wood is very pithy, and it suffers badly in winter. In some parts it does marvellously well, and I am told it loves a peaty soil." [NRS21/132] "Must rely on its colour for its form is poor in all stages; the foliage is brilliant and glossy and the growth usually good, but it has a most abominable habit of dying back in winter." [NRS20/89] "A lovely rose, is a very shy bloomer, and the bush is irregular in shape." [ARA23/84] "It bloomed excellently in June, but the real flowers came in September, several of them over 5 inches across [ca. 1.25 dm], of a golden shade that leaves no room for improvement. The plant was healthy and green without mildew or black-spot. It was located to catch only the forenoon sun, since I had an idea that our hot sunlight was too violent a change from European conditions." [ARA24/186] "At its first blooming-time, I had one flower 6 inches in diameter [ca. 1.5 dm] and others almost as large. At the present writing (July, 1924), it is bearing its third crop of flowers on an extra-strong shoot that has a dozen buds and blooms. The bush is perfectly healthy, no disease of any sort." [ARA26/205] "A warm sandy soil suits it best. It is a good plan to lift and replant it yearly or every two years." [NRS21/66]

"This variety so impatiently awaited by rose fanciers will be released to commerce this Fall, and, due to the large number of specimens he has, the distinguished breeder, Monsieur Pernet-Ducher, *rosiériste* of Vénissieux-lès-Lyon (Rhône), will be able to supply them at a price which is relatively moderate for a sort so worthy of interest. We have indeed been able to size up this plant for several years; in 1907, at Lyon, where we were of a Jury consisting also of our colleagues Messrs. Alex. Dickson, of Newtownards (Ireland) G. Paul, of Cheshunt (England); and Turbat, of Orléans. We were struck at once by the form of the blossom and by its marvelous coloration of coppery orange rayed bright carmine. Also, the highest honors were awarded to this precious newcomer. 'Rayon d'Or' takes its origin from 'Soleil d'Or'. Having gained this latter, Monsieur Pernet-Ducher —an indefatigable seeker—made crosses with various Hybrid Teas, and, in 1898, obtained from an unreleased Hybrid Tea always kept for his work, several varieties among which was 'Beauté de Lyon' [Pern], released to commerce this Spring, as well as—important fact!—a series of roses with continuous bloom, like the H.T.'s themselves. Some attempts at crosses were tried with these plants, taking their pollen to fertilize some Hybrid Teas, and the experimenter noted that one of the products of this crossing gave some magnificent roses, which specimen he kept as a pod-parent, and which, crossed with 'Mme. Mélanie Soupert', gave birth to 'Lyon-Rose' and 'Rayon d'Or'. With his 'Persian Yellow' hybridizing, and with their reblooming hybrids, Monsieur Pernet-Ducher always hopes to progress from generation to generation in raising very yellow rebloomers, and, by mixing pollen, some Hybrid Teas with the maximum floribundity . . . 'Rayon d'Or' makes a vigorous shrub with bushy canes; beautiful bronzy-green foliage, glossy as if varnished; bud ovoid, coppery orange rayed deep carmine; flower large, of beautiful globular form, full, superbly colored cadmium yellow at anthesis and solar yellow when fully open ... To this description, the breeder adds, *'Rayon d'Or' is, without argument, the most yellow rose with continuous bloom now grown; its superb yellow color keeps as long as the blossom itself; in the opinion of all rose growers who have looked it over at my breeding-grounds, be they amateur or professional, it is an incomparable yellow rose.* To all the qualities listed above, we should like to add here that 'Rayon d'Or' blooms abundantly, the flowers always opening very well. During harsh Winters, though the plant be pretty hardy, it would be a good idea to give it some light protection." [JR34/125]

We have unexpectedly been left a glimpse of the "unnamed seedling" which was a parent of 'Rayon d'Or' and 'Lyon-Rose' (one might note in passing that the description of this seedling comes exceedingly close to the description of the co-founder of the Pernetiana race, 'Rhodophile Gravereaux'): "[On a visit to the premises of Pernet-Ducher] that which I treasured most highly was a somewhat loose-petalled flower of yellow-orange and flame-pink. I espied it growing out of the open roof of a little forcing house, and its colour was so vivid and so unusual that I asked what it could possibly be, as I was certain it was a rose I had never seen before. Monsieur Pernet [-Ducher], with his usual courteous kindness, promptly gathered me a blossom, adding, in answer to my eager enquiries, that he did not sell it—'it was not sufficiently *rustique* [hardy].' And then came the exciting announcement that this Rose was the pollen parent of both 'Soleil d'Or' [Pern] and 'Lyon[-]Rose' [Pern]." [NRS10/116] This about being the pollen parent of 'Soleil d'Or' is surely a misremembrance for 'Rayon d'Or' [Pern]; the pollen parent of 'Soleil d'Or' was, of course, 'Persian Yellow' (F), and the pod-parent 'Antoine Ducher' (HP).

Recuerdo de Angel Peluffo
trans. "In Memory of Angel Peluffo"
Soupert & Notting, 1927
From 'Mme. Édouard Herriot' (Pern) × 'Duchess of Wellington' (HT).

"Red, large, full, medium scent, moderate height." [Sn] "Bud large, ovoid; flower large, double, full, very lasting, moderately fragrant, cardinal-red, center garnet-red, borne singly on long, strong stem. Foliage abundant, large, rich green, disease-resistant. Average number of thorns. Growth vigorous, bushy; profuse continuous bloomer from May to November." [ARA28/243]

Reims
trans. "Rheims"
Barbier, 1924

"Yellowish orange red, large, full, medium height." [Sn] "Bud long-pointed; flower very large, flesh-pink, shaded apricot and coppery orange; petals sometimes imbricated." [ARA25/188] "Too pale to make much of an impression here; the bloom is large but bleaches to white as it expands." [ARA27/205] "Very lovely, but the imported plant was extremely weak." [ARA26/120] "Blossom large, full, flesh-colored on a yellowish ground, shaded flame at the center. Plant strong, hardy, healthy." [Ck] "In spite of its too erect branches and somewhat bare appearance, ['Reims'] is interesting because of its magnificent flowers of perfect form, resembling a large camellia, and with firm round petals sometimes imbricated, and in shades of yellow." [ARA25/128] "Long bud of nice form opening to a fine full flower. Back of petals flesh-pink.

Inside bright nankin yellow, apricot orange and copper-pink. A very beautiful colouring. Vigorous and very free-flowering. A grand bedding variety." [GeH] Reims, alias Rheims, the French cathedral city.

Reinhard Bädecker
Kordes, 1918
From 'Frau Karl Druschki' (HP) × 'Rayon d'Or' (Pern).

"Deep yellow." [Cw] "Deep yellow, striped red around the edges, very large, very full, medium scent, moderate height." [Sn] "Flower resembling [that of] 'Rayon d'Or' in colour, intense yellow with saturnine red shadings on reverse of petals, very large and full. Growth like [that of] 'Frau Karl Druschki', vigorous and upright; foliage large, deep glossy green and free from Mildew." [GeH] "Bud globular, golden yellow, with scarlet stripes; flower very large, extremely double, full, open, very lasting; clear golden yellow, unfading borne singly on strong stem of average length; slightly fragrant. Foliage abundant, large, leathery, glossy dark green. Very vigorous; upright; blooms profusely at intervals from June to October. Practically hardy; tips freeze." [ARA21/164] "As a yellow Rose it is not wanted." [NRS22/183]

Reverend David R. Williamson Listed as 'Reverend
Williamson' (Pern).

Reverend David Williamson Listed as 'Reverend Williamson'
(Pern).

Reverend F. Page-Roberts
B. R. Cant, 1921

"Yellow, shaded red." [Ÿ] "Orange yellow, large, very full, very fragrant, moderate height." [Sn] "Soft buff with reverse of deep salmon; coppery red bud; good stem fine form; light fragrance; good growth. Recurrent." [CaRoll/3/2] "A two-toned yellow and apricot, opening deeper yellow; blooms full and large, with a decided fruity scent." [ARA25/101] "Too apricot for my taste." [ARA30/164] "At its best in hot weather, and rain is apt to destroy the petals." [NRS29/118] "A gloriously yellow Rose of fine form. The buds are deeply stained with tawny orange, but the open flower is deep yellow and unfading. Its fine and vigorously branching growth and free blooming habit mark this as a yellow Rose which has probably come to stay. Very fragrant." [C-Ps25] "A pure honey-yellow rose of good build ad substance, [this rose] is a fine garden acquisition, but its habit of bearing its blooms sideways instead of upright may bring it into disrepute. It is obviously fungous-proof and a vigorous grower." [ARA23/140] "One of the most beautiful and satisfactory of the new two-tone Roses. The long-shaped buds are Indian yellow, splashed with carmine, a charming color, covering the reverse of the petals when the blooms open; the inside of the petals is rich yellow, almost like 'Maréchal Niel' [N]. In form it is good, the inner petals standing upright as long as the flower lasts; not easily damaged by rain. The bush is spreading in growth, with abundant, dark green foliage, not entirely disease-resistant. The new foliage is as ornamental as polished bronze. Blooms come freely from June until frost, borne singly on long stems, delightful for cut-flowers. A noteworthy feature of this Rose is its piquant fruit-like fragrance." [C-Ps27] "Long and shapely buds of Indian yellow are washed with deep carmine which 'runs' as the bud unfurls but never disappears. In the half-open stage, the flower is nearly perfect in form. The interior of the bloom has that peculiar and rare 'Maréchal Niel' tint, and the open flower is a cup that never flattens, from which comes a

Reverend F. Page-Roberts *continued*

sweet and spicy fragrance. The stems are long enough for cutting. Foliage dark olive-green, rather scant, and not over-persistent. The plant is low-growing and branching, a quality that brings it to the front as a mass bedder." [C-Ps29] "Rich golden yellow, with buff shading and apricot suffusion. Very double and of good substance. Stems slightly weak. Odor delicious. Bush slow to take hold and rather dwarf." [ARA27/147] "A fine rose of a vigorous habit, with good shaped blooms, which are carried erect on long, stiff stems and are very sweetly scented. The colour is an orange-yellow, becoming lighter at the edges of the petals." [ARA21/151] "Disbudding is desirable during the summer, but not necessary in the autumn. The growth is vigorous and branching. The foliage is reddish when young and dark green when mature." [NRS24/166] "Good bronzy foliage. Growth strong and branching." [GeH] "It is not so easy to get established as many other Roses, and when first planted it should be cut back in the spring to about 2 inches [ca. 5 cm]." [C-Ps30]

"Have had very good success with it, and it is our favorite rose. — *Grand Junction, Colo.*; . . . The plant seems normally healthy, but it is not mildew-proof here. —*Caldwell, Idaho*; . . . Disappointing during the hot weather, but superb in fall. One of the most distinct and exquisitely beautiful of all roses; definitely superior, and a real rose advance. —*Harrisburg, Pa.*" [ARA26/120] "Fair; good shade of yellow with bright yellow center; small flowers; wilts in sun . . . *Washington, D.C.*; . . . No mildew or black-spot so far. Not prolific, but very fine; growth moderate. The best of its color I have seen . . . *Mo.*; Has done well in this rainy and cool summer . . . *Mo.*; . . . Color orange-apricot with flame-red on outer petals . . . *Calif.*; Everybody likes it, but its growth has been uniformly disappointing." [ARA28/184] "It possesses all the characteristics that a good Rose should have—strong upright growth, good foliage, not addicted to mildew, sweet fruity scent, and exceedingly perpetual flowering; indeed, late in the autumn it was the most consistent and best rose we had in the Nursery, carrying its colour to the end. The blooms are large, full and well formed, of a beautiful rich 'Maréchal Niel' [N] yellow colour, occasionally veined with buff markings in the bud and young stages. The blooms last well." [NRS21/206] "Blooms very large, of a good shape, with high pointed centre, flattening somewhat when fully expanded. Not liable to damage by rain. Colour bright golden yellow. Sweetly scented. Foliage shiny green, free of mildew. Growth vigorous as a maiden, and fairly so as a cutback. Good alike for exhibition and bedding. Magnificent under glass." [NRS23/95] "It sports very freely and does not seem a properly fixed variety." [NRS25/194] "Will prove a fine garden rose." [ARA24/107]

Reverend Williamson

syn. 'Reverend David R. Williamson', 'Reverend David Williamson'
Pernet-Ducher, 1921

"Colour coral red, tinted orange." [NRS23/175] "Coral red nuanced carmine red." [Cw] "Light orange red, large, very full, moderate height." [Sn] "Good; a fine pointed rose with a glorious coloring resembling that of 'Mme. Édouard Herriot'." [ARA24/108] "It produces its flowers freely, and is good for cutting, while the growth is fairly vigorous. The blooms are globular in shape." [NRS25/176] "Blossom large, comes singly, coral red shaded carmine red, full, lasting, very beautiful even though quite open. Striking coloration. Plant very strong . . . with healthy foliage." [Ck] "Bud long-pointed, deep coral-red; flower large,

full, globular; coral-red shaded carmine-lake. Foliage reddish bronze-green. Very vigorous, spreading, branching habit." [ARA22/150]

Rhodophile Gravereaux

Pernet-Ducher, ca. 1900
From 'Antoine Ducher' (HP) × 'Persian Yellow' (F).

"Rose red, yellow center, large, lightly double, tall." [Sn] "A single climbing Rose, of a pleasing shade of pale carmine pink, with yellow centre." [NRS13/162] "Semi-double flowers, bright pink, with petal bases whitish, making a star; reverse of petals light yellow, and having the foetid scent of *Rosa lutea* [*R. foetida*]." [JR24/87–88] "'Rhodophile Gravereaux', with a flower that's single or pretty nearly so . . . [The thorns] are *dark brown*, some strong and hooked, the feebler ones straight and pretty much like bristles." [JR30/123] For particulars on the history of cultivar 'Rhodophile Gravereaux', see our entry on 'Soleil d'Or', its more-famous co-founder of the Pernetiana race. Commandeur Jules Gravereaux, rhodophile, rhodologue, and rosomane, amateur breeder, and founder of the Roseraie de l'Haÿ.

Rising Sun

Hicks, 1924

"Copper yellow, large, full, medium height." [Sn] "Rich copper shaded old-gold at base. Vigorous." [ARA25/185] "Would be better called 'Sunset', as the blooms will be lying on the ground as soon as they try to open their petals." [ARA27/205]

Schleswig-Holstein

Engelbrecht, 1921
Sport of 'Mme. Édouard Herriot' (Pern).

"Reddish yellow, large, lightly double, medium height." [Sn] "Bud medium size, ovoid; flower medium size, cupped, semi-double, lasting; deep, clear yellow with reddish sheen, turning to lighter yellow; borne, singly or several together, on good stem; fragrant. Foliage sufficient, glossy, rich green, disease-resistant. Vigorous; profuse and continuous bloomer." [ARA22/155] Schleswig-Holstein, northern province of Germany bordering—and formerly partially in—Denmark.

Schmetterling

Müller, 1905

"Yellow and red, medium size, lightly double, medium scent, tall." [Sn]

Secretaris Zwart

Van Rossem, 1920
From 'General MacArthur' (HT) × 'Lyon-Rose' (Pern).

"Flower bright rose, shaded salmon, large. Growth vigorous; free and late flowering." [GeH] "Light pink, large, full, medium height." [Sn] "Flower large, very attractive, bright rose, reverse of petals silvery rose. Foliage glossy; disease-resistant. Vigorous; very free blooming." [ARA22/157]

Shot Silk

A. Dickson, 1924

"The delicate color—cherry-cerise, overshot with salmon—is most attractive, especially late in the season. It gives a plentiful crop of flowers." [ARA29/52] "Salmon orange red, yellow center, medium size, full, medium scent, moderate height." [Sn] "Blossom cherry red with salmon-orange wash, full. Good bloomer in any weather, strong-scented. Strong-growing plant." [Ck] "The fragrant blooms of this fairly vigorous rose are produced on short, stiff stems, are rather round and loosely made, and of a very attractive color." [ARA24/165] "[The color] is extraordinarily variable in different flowers, often of the same plant, and in different stages of their growth, the older flowers becoming pink, and not infrequently, especially in cold weather, fading to a pale yellow. The brilliant colouring is in the young flowers, and to secure this they must be picked when just opening. It comes into flower from the third week until towards the end of June, and thence onwards the bed is continuously in flower till stopped by frost." [NRS29/103] "Sometimes brings wonderful blooms of a solid cherry-pink, with golden shadings. The plant grows only moderately. Blooms are carried well up. A fine garden rose." [ARA27/205] "A very beautiful rose which well deserves its name for its coloring and its entrancing appearance in the bud or when half open. It fades too quickly and discolors at the end." [ARA27/211] "The defect of the flower is its want of form when open, the centre petals being too short, and even in the bud the form is somewhat too rounded." [NRS29/104] "Distinctive in color and fragrant, but not full enough." [ARA30/172] "Has an altogether delightful odour." [NRS29/72] "Beautiful foliage . . . large, shining, dark green. The plant is tall and with its glossy foliage is very attractive. The fragrant flowers are described as 'orange-rose, overshot with golden yellow and flushed soft rose'." [CaRoll/4/1] "Bud medium size, ovoid; flower medium size, double, full, high-centered, lasting; cherry-cerise, shot with golden yellow very fragrant. Foliage disease-resistant. Vigorous, upright, bushy; profuse and continuous bloomer. Hardy." [ARA24/171] "Free branching growth with glossy green foliage not liable to Mildew. A variety of great merit." [GeH] "Fine bloom and growth in early summer; some black-spot not so good in fall . . . *Mass.* Thin, but fine color; none too free . . . *Conn.*; . . . Fears hot sun and black-spot. In cool weather the buds are entrancing . . . *Pa.*; . . . Nice foliage, but small growth ad flower. Not as good as 'Gorgeous' [Pern], which it resembles . . . *Ga.*; . . . Compact bush; healthy and free blooming. The elusive color is splendid in late summer and fall. Average, 42 blooms. Like it . . . *Calif.*" [ARA28/187–188] "'Shot Silk' may, perhaps, be considered the crown of the group [*to wit, the group of roses developed between 1912 and 1929 having the 'pinker shades'*], its fault being the fleeting character of both colour and the flower itself." [NRS29/70] "Color and fragrance alone compel me to grow it." [ARA29/113]

Soleil d'Angers

trans. "Sun of Angers"
Détriché, 1909
Sport of 'Soleil d'Or' (Pern).

"Flower deep yellow and vermilion scarlet, free. Growth vigorous." [GeH] "Deep yellowish pink, medium size, very full, tall." [Sn] "Not unlike 'Juliet' [Pern] in colour, but a confused shape, yellow and vermilion with fragrant foliage." [NRS13/162] "Flower large, globular, full, vermilion red, pretty, petal bases ochre yellow, with vermilion red, a lasting and rich coloration. Altogether, it might be called a red-flowered 'Soleil d'Or'. The wood and thorns are very dark brownish red, and the leaves are also of a green much darker than the Type variety." [JR33/167] "Really not worth growing." [NRS21/132]

Soleil d'Or Plate 71

trans. "Sun of Gold"
Pernet-Ducher, 1900
From 'Antoine Ducher' (HP) × 'Persian Yellow' (F).

"Praised by some and cursed by others, the rose 'Soleil d'Or' shows that, with Roses like with people, you can't please everybody and his uncle. 'This variety is changeable,' says one fancier, and the next one adds, 'Yes, and it doesn't grow here.' A third opines that, in an equable climate, it's a wonderful variety. 'Bad form!', 'Unique color!', 'Quartered!', 'Yellow and carmine!', 'Variable in color!', 'Grows poorly!', 'Grows well!', 'Reblooms?', 'Doesn't rebloom!'. Yes, we know all that: Praised by some, cursed by others, the rose 'Soleil d'Or' nevertheless calmly goes about its business. I have always sung the praises of this rose. Were it to have every fault in the world, I would still extoll it, first of all because it is a new type, the creation of which many hybridizers attempted in vain—and its color is unique. What is more, I have always thought that it would be the point of departure for new creations which would relieve us a little from the monotony of the old nuances." [JR30/122]

"Bright yellow and gold." [Ÿ] "Yellowish orange red, large, full, tall." [Sn] "The flowers are large and globular, perfectly full and double. The color is a mixture of reddish gold, orange-yellow, nasturtium-red and rosy pink, a combination difficult to describe. Has spicy orange fragrance." [C&Js13] "Fragrance of pineapple." [NRS13/160] "An agreeable scent much like that of the Centifolia." [JR24/88] "Flower golden yellow shaded with orange and crimson, the orange often predominating, large, full, very sweet. Growth very vigorous, flowering both in summer and autumn. Distinct." [GeH] "One of the grandest new roses ever introduced, a strong robust grower and entirely hardy; extra large perfectly double flowers, reddish gold shaded nasturtium red, very beautiful and distinct." [C&Js06] "In announcing its release to commerce for November 1, 1900, Monsieur Pernet-Ducher supplies the following description: 'Very vigorous bush, 60–80 centimeters high [ca. 2–3 ft]; canes upright, pretty thick; wood brown foliage close-set on the stem, beautiful gay green bud conical, beautiful yellow; flower very large, 7–10 centimeters wide [ca. 3–4 in], very full, globular, central petals reflexing inwardly superbly colored orange golden yellow to reddish golden yellow nuanced nasturtium pink; very fragrant. The coloration is so resistant to the sun that it doesn't pale a bit; in cool temperatures, the color is lighter and comes quite close to that of 'Persian Yellow'." [JR24/89] "We cut only unhealthy wood and clip the tips of the long canes. In this way, a blossoming branch will come from every eye." [ARA29/54] "I want to say a word for the much-abused 'Soleil d'Or'. With me the foliage has been perfect, and although it has but one real blooming season . . . the flowers it does produce are so lovely and so deliciously fragrant that it is worthy of trial in every garden." [ARA27/149] "Why slave for a puny reluctant 'Souv[enir] de Claudius Pernet' [Pern] when 'Soleil d'Or' will give you bowls of gorgeous-colored roses as vivid and as delightfully tangible—chunky, almost—as a Cézanne landscape, with an old-fashioned beauty that Cézanne has not? What if they are short-stemmed—they smell like roses! What if they bloom but once—one tawny lion cub is worth a lot of weaklings, and one needs some time free for sweet peas and the rest of the garden." [ARA28/63]

"Changeable, the rose 'Soleil d'Or'! I have had in my garden for four years a specimen grafted on the Briar which remained languishing and sickly. It grew little, it bloomed poorly, and validated the opinion of those who had nothing good to say about this variety. But see the outcome of these [first] impressions: Having grafted two dormant eyes of this malingerer on a vigorous stem of the Briar, today I

Soleil d'Or *continued*

have a superb 'Soleil d'Or' with ten canes, some of them tipped with one blossom, others with two, some indeed with three—superb flowers, well held, with leaves intact. It's this magnificent specimen of mine that is the source of my description. Its foliage is its own shade of green, something like a somewhat glaucescent cobalt green. It is of medium size, with elliptical leaflets having simple teeth, and glabrous; its pale green thorns are long, thin, hooked, and barely flattened. Those of its brother, 'Rhodophile Gravereaux' [Pern] are *dark brown,* some of them strong and hooked, the weakest ones straight, and nearly like a bristle. Before anthesis, the bud is ovoid, and the receptacle is glabrous, smooth, light green, and longly turbinate. The sepals are also glabrous, but depending on their position and strength, they bear either hairs both short and glandular or appendages which are glandulose and more or less foliaceous. The open blossom is pretty flat, in quarters ('quartered,' say the English), the petals often folding back on the center, but nicely arranged along the edge. Its coloration is unique in rosedom, though of a changeable appearance. The outer face of the petals is golden yellow, the interior saffron yellow—intense at the nub—passing to orange red and shaded pink around the upper part. The varying nuances presented by its petals give a multi-colored effect to the rose 'Soleil d'Or'. From one angle, it seems yellow, from another, orange pink. Indeed, sometimes a quarter or half of the blossom is one shade, and the rest another. It can be said that 'Soleil d'Or' has a pleasant scent. This is a remarkable characteristic which alone suffices to demonstrate its hybrid origin. It takes this trait from its mother, the variety 'Antoine Ducher', a fragrant HP in which you can recognize this particular characteristic from the Centifolias, in which group it is fairly pronounced. It doesn't come from its father 'Persian Yellow', which is pretty much scentless, though belonging to a group in which the flowers exhale the disagreeable odor of coriander. The hybrid character of 'Soleil d'Or' manifests itself in its coloration, in the sterility of its flowers, and in the intermediate characteristics of its bush. It seems to do much better in temperate climes than in *le Midi.* At the altitude of 500–800 m [to ca. 2400 ft], it is absolutely remarkable, like its paternal ancestors." [JR30/122–123]

"Several foreign horticultural journals have recently discussed the question of the floriferousness of this new and superb rose, particularly concerning whether or not it can be considered as a *freely remontant* variety. It will be necessary to grow it another couple of years, watching it closely to see if it lives up to the descriptions with which this magnificent variety was announced. Meanwhile, we have noticed now and then that rose varieties which are very remontant in certain areas of France are not so in Germany or England; the climate of these latter two countries influences the bloom of roses there to a greater or lesser degree—more the roses which do better generally in a sunny land than those which subsist under more or less damp periods during a part of the growing season. According to one of the correspondents of the *Rosen-Zeitung* of Trier, the rose 'Soleil d'Or' would bloom generally better in Germany, and also produce a few midsummer blooms. We have observed the same thing in Brie, in the important nurseries of our editor-in-chief of the *Journal des Roses* [Cochet], where this variety opened its blossoms, despite great heat and dryness, up to last September. In the mountains, at Châlet à Gobet, in the Vaudois Jurat (Switzerland), at 800 meters in altitude

[ca. 2400 ft], the specimen we planted in our alpine rosery still produced its last bud at the end of September then it bore very well a lowering of the temperature to −29° C. Right now (May, 1902), it is already covered with foliage and buds, which are well advanced over [those of] other rose varieties I have planted at the same altitude, excepting only those of the *Rugosa* section. Another specimen that I planted at Vevey (Switzerland), at the edge of *Lac Léman,* in a warm situation, very well protected from north winds, grew its last blooms in November, 1901, and the first of Spring 1902 opened at the beginning of May; but, curiously, after those of the Banksia, 'Maréchal Niel' [N], 'Reine Marie Henriette' [Cl HT] etc., and Camellias, grown out in the open in the same garden in that area which enjoys a privileged climate. All of these observations concerning the new rose 'Soleil d'Or' occurred naturally in plants in the 1900–1901 Winter that Monsieur Pernet-Ducher of Lyon, the happy breeder, had graciously given to me to study in diverse areas—their hardiness, as well as their habit of growth." [JR26/67]

"Hybridizers had tried to pollinate that remarkable double yellow Persian rose—the English call it 'Persian Yellow'—but nothing came of it. Knowing very well that often sterility in roses is due to the viscous conformation of the pistil and ovaries, but that the stamens—that is, the male organ—can at the same time be in good shape, Monsieur Pernet-Ducher had the idea of taking a separate route from that of his predecessors by performing the inverse operation. Out of this operation were born 'Soleil d'Or', with a double flower, and 'Rhodophile Gravereaux' [Pern], with a blossom which is single or pretty nearly so, both of them celebrated as the first representatives of a new group." [JR30/122–123] "This newcomer, from Monsieur Pernet-Ducher, the able and very well-known Lyonnais breeder, was drawn especially for our readers so that we could give them a true idea of the blossom. It comprises a thoroughly unique hybrid in genus *Rosa*—not one of those everyday roses that a person sees alas much too often in commerce, but indeed a fortuitous cross owing to the perseverance of an indefatigable researcher to whom we are already in debt for a long list of beautiful and good varieties. Here is the story of that famous flower that today we call 'Soleil d'Or'—a name bestowed on it by its breeder.

"Since 1883, Monsieur Pernet-Ducher had sought to raise crosses between 'Persian Yellow' (*Rosa lutea* [*i.e., R. foetida*]) and other[,] remontant[,] roses. This knowing *rosiériste* was haunted by the superb yellow color of the Persian, which he strongly wished to have in a remontant. The enterprise seemed bold!—because Mother Nature doesn't always deign to cooperate, particularly where hybridization is concerned, and often gives just the opposite of what was intended. In a word, Pernet-Ducher stuck to his idea, and over and over again hybridized Hybrid Perpetuals with the pollen of 'Persian Yellow'. After many vicissitudes, he noted that the rose 'Antoine Ducher' took more easily than others to crossing with *Rosa lutea.* In 1888, he pricked out the seedlings obtained by these hybridizations, which, planted in the nursery, bloomed one after the other. The plants were certainly quite unusual—very interesting from the botanical point of view in their variations, but nothing showed commercial value. Only one of them ['Rhodophile Gravereaux' (Pern)] was noted in 1891 and 1892 when it bloomed; it gave semi-double flowers which were bright pink with whitish petal bases making a star, petal reverses light yellow, and having the foetid scent of *Rosa lutea.* It would have been gotten rid of, or at least forgotten right away, if a certain small incident hadn't happened.

"In a friendly dispute which Pernet-Ducher was having with the sympatico editor of *Lyon-Horticole,* Monsieur Viviand-Morel, the latter challenged his friend to come up with some descendants of *Rosa lutea,* which another horticulturist of Lyon, the late Alegatière, had never been able to make seed. The following season—to be precise, May, 1893—at the bloom-time of the notorious semi-double pink-flowered rose mentioned above, the dispute was decided in favor of Viviand-Morel. But in looking for stems to send to his friend, Pernet-Ducher noticed that [the 'plant' consisted of] two specimens growing next to each other, the one as ever the pink semi-double rose, the other quite small specimen showing for the first time quite full blossoms of a beautiful yellow color—'Soleil d'Or' was found! Pernet thus found doubled his means of convincing Viviand-Morel of the possibility of growing varieties of *Rosa lutea* from seed—not only in making *R. lutea* seed, but also by means of using its pollen to fertilize other species or varieties; the course taken, while diametrically opposite, came nevertheless to the same end.

"'Soleil d'Or' was immediately grafted on several specimens, and was carefully scrutinized; in 1896, it gave a repeat bloom, and its floriferous remontant canes were carefully picked out and planted, producing some reblooming plants. A fact worth noting is that the first plants, grafted in 1893, which were at first only occasionally remontant, became freely remontant afterwards simply due to the nature of the variety, which took several years to manifest its characteristics. 'Soleil d'Or', bred in 1888, kept father Persian Yellow's floral coloration, though slightly changed the reddish-barked wood, like the Lutea Type, though bigger and more erect; the foliage, though having a certain resemblance to that of *R. lutea,* is more ample and a darker green; when it is bruised, it gives out its own scent, resembling the fragrance of Apples. As to the scent of the blossom, everyone knows that 'Persian Yellow' produces roses which are foetid and offensive by nature; 'Soleil d'Or', on the other hand, wafts an agreeable perfume much like that of the Centifolia. This variety has also inherited the hardiness of the Persian and can withstand very low temperatures without suffering. If this variety keeps a certain number of its father's characteristics, such is also no less the case with its mother, 'Antoine Ducher', which it resembles in pretty nearly only three things: the shape of its pericarp, the perfume of its flowers, and its precious characteristic of re-blooming. As to the habit of the bush, it's intermediate between the two parents.

"'Soleil d'Or' will be for sale by its breeder this Fall [of 1900] at a price sufficiently moderate that all the trade will be able to buy it the stock available is adequate to meet demand . . .

"Following Noisette's precedent, who gave his name to a much-appreciated group of roses, Monsieur Pernet-Ducher gave, with reason, the designation *Pernet Rose, Rosa Pernetiana,* to this new series in the genus *Rosa,* to perpetuate the memory of its origin. Though 'Soleil d'Or' is not yet in commerce, we [*the reporter, Pierre Cochet*] have been called upon to examine it under various conditions—particularly by a letter which its fortunate breeder was so kind as to send us—and we do not hesitate to sing its praises, certain that the future will validate our appreciation. As for anything more, the following awards bestowed on this new variety are sufficiently eloquent to preclude further paeans: [*briefly put, numerous awards presented 1898–*

1900 at exhibitions or by horticultural societies in Lyon, Tours, Dijon, Paris, Vienna, Budapest, Dresden, etc.] . . . 'Soleil d'Or' is a worthy successor to the beautiful roses that Monsieur Pernet-Ducher has bred these last years . . . We give Monsieur Pernet-Ducher all our congratulations! Due to his perseverance, the future holds yet further happy surprises for us." [JR24/87–89]

Solliden
Leenders, 1924
From an unnamed seedling (resulting from a cross of 'Mme. Mélanie Soupert' [HT] and 'George C. Waud' [HT]) × 'Mme. Édouard Herriot' (Pern).

"Red, large, lightly double, light scent, dwarf." [Sn] "Bud large, long-pointed; flower large, semi-double, open, lasting, slight fragrance, carmine-lake with reverse shaded ochre, borne several together. Foliage sufficient, dark green. Many thorns. Vigorous, bushy habit; abundant, continuous bloomer." [ARA25/192]

Sonnenlicht Plate 79
trans. 'Sunlight'
Krüger/Kiese, 1913
From 'Lady Mary Fitzwilliam' (HT) × 'Harison's Yellow' (F).

According to Testu, this is a once-blooming rose, blooming at the beginning of Summer, the flowers being semi-double, pure canary yellow, and fragrant, on a vigorous bush. "Canes, red-brown." [Jg]

Souvenir d'Angèle Opdebeeck
Verschuren, 1926
"The flowers are very fine golden yellow in the bud, changing to butter-yellow as the blooms develop." [GeH] "Bud long-pointed, perfectly formed, orange-yellow, streaked carmine-red; flower large, full, double, moderately fragrant, canary-yellow." [ARA27/223] "Yellow, large, full, medium scent, moderate height." [Sn]

Souvenir de Charles Laemmel
trans. "In Memory of Charles Laemmel"
Gillot, 1920
From 'Frau Karl Druschki' (HP) × 'Soleil d'Or' (Pern).

"Yellow, striped orange, large, full, very fragrant, moderate height." [Sn] "A large and full golden yellow flower, slightly shaded rose pink. Vigorous and very floriferous." [NRS21/140] "Flower golden and orange yellow, slightly shaded with rose, large, full, and fragrant; ovoid bud of clear yellow colour on stiff stem. Growth very vigorous, erect, exceedingly free flowering; foliage deep glossy green." [GeH] "Bud very large, ovoid, clear yellow; flower very large, full, double, borne on long, strong stem; golden yellow, streaked orange and shaded pink; very fragrant. Foliage round, rich green. Very vigorous; upright; free and continuous bloomer." [ARA21/162]

Souvenir de Claudius Pernet
trans. "In Memory of Claudius Pernet"
Pernet-Ducher, 1920
From 'Constance' (Pern) × an unnamed variety.

"Pure sun yellow." [Ÿ] "Deep yellow, large, full, medium scent, moderate height." [Sn] "Flowers of the most striking sunflower-yellow, with the recurving outer petals becoming cream with sharp demarcations very large and full, beautifully formed, with elongated thick petals . . . Left on the plant, blooms deteriorate more rapidly and are marred by rain or heavy dew, while the sun 'eats it up.' Does not give

Souvenir de Claudius Pernet *continued*

its best blooms until the weather has become permanently warm. If disbudded to one bloom per stem and 'fed,' it will give exhibition blooms of great beauty." [C-Ps31] "A Rose of unusual beauty of form and coloring and in great demand on account of its bright, sunflower-yellow flowers which retain their color better than any other yellow Rose, both in bud and open bloom. The buds are very fine, long-shaped, full, and firm, and they come on strong, upright stems, with brilliant green foliage." [C&Js24] "A new, clear yellow Rose which has made a tremendous sensation because of its practically unfading color and excellent habit of growth. The outer petals sometimes bleach a little, but the flower is sun-flower yellow until it drops. Bloom is of large size, and in its early stages almost perfectly formed. (Cut early to avoid unsightly center.) Foliage is extraordinarily dark, glossy, and fairly resistant to disease. Growth vigorous and very thorny." [C-Ps25] "Flower sunflower-yellow colour, deeper in the centre, without any other blending, very large and full, beautifully formed with elongated deep petals. A vigorous grower, of erect branching habit; brilliant green foliage; few thorns." [GeH] "Very liable to damage by rain. Sweetly scented. Colour deep orange yellow in centre, outside petals lighter. Foliage dark shiny olive green, hard and holly like, quite free of mildew and black spot. Growth both as a maiden and cutback vigorous. Blooms very freely in the late autumn. This is a variety that requires a warm season for the blooms to open well. Very beautiful under glass." [NRS23/95–96] "The foliage is holly-like and olive-green. This Rose performs best in hot, dry, bright weather. Flowers often appear in clusters." [C-Ps27] "We have discovered that by taking out the center bud of the cluster on 'Souvenir de Claudius Pernet', the other buds develop into better flowers and retain the color under normal circumstances." [ARA24/183] "Sunflower-yellow throughout; odor slight if any. Did not open well until I tried removing terminal bud, then got some perfect flowers through August but a certain percentage of buds will not open in spite of anything. Bush strong. 17 blooms; 22 the second season." [ARA26/96] "Bud large, long-pointed; flower very large, full, double, borne singly on long, strong stem; very lasting fragrant. Color pure sunflower-yellow, deeper in center. Foliage abundant, glossy green, large; disease-resistant. Very vigorous, upright grower, producing an abundance of blooms from May to October. Hardy." [ARA20/132] "Bright yellow; long stem; leathery foliage; wintered well. A very fine rose, and the best yellow." [ARA25/121]

"Has done well [in Oklahoma], and it holds its yellow color." [ARA25/203] "Practically worthless outdoors in the South. The first blooms are greenish white and there are only a few good yellow ones late in the summer." [ARA29/93] "Scotland, with its sunless skies, is by no means its spiritual home." [NRS24/148] "It is not a good sort for every location, but neither is it deserving of utter rejection . . . Our 7,000 plants have taught us a lesson, for they only open their wonderful blooms in dry, warm weather. A wet season, such as we had last year, will cause all the buds to rot on the plant." [ARA23/141] "Balls badly in wet weather and will, therefore, I am afraid, never be popular. Flowers best from side shoots." [NRS24/161] "A rather small, grafted or budded plant from a pot. Probably it had been grown all winter and consequently it was inclined to rest all summer. It had a flower or two of a rather cold and sickly yellow and of absolutely no form. The color did not fade, however, nor was it afflicted with blackspot or mildew, and it did not die back." [ARA24/89] "It came into its

own only when it was worked on Odorata stock." [ARA26/157] "The rose is a good grower; it provides a well-formed flower of a good and clear color, and keeps well—all qualities that are essential. It is certainly proving its worth as a commercial rose." [ARA24/160] "While lacking somewhat in vigor [it] gives beautiful yellow blooms of ideal shape and fullness. The color remains longer than in ['Christine' (Pern), 'Mabel Morse' (extinct Pern), or 'Golden Emblem' (Pern)], and I consider this rose to be the most satisfying yellow of the four . . . The blooms are not as plentiful as I would like . . . None of the four varieties possesses fragrance to any degree." [ARA25/204] "It is a 'Rayon d'Or' [Pern] with an elongated bud, long stems, and a large, full flower." [ARA20/124] "Particularly, in bud, half open or wide open . . . a superb rose, holding its clear yellow color perfectly. It carries plenty of thorns but this apparently makes little difference [in its use as a cut flower]." [ARA25/173] "It is one of the most wonderful roses I have ever beheld. It is not only of good size, but the coloring is simply superb—a clear, shining, golden yellow. It has health, vigor, and all the characteristics that are necessary for an excellent garden rose." [ARA22/130] "Certainly Monsieur Pernet's masterpiece. It is a strong grower and has been described as brilliant sunflower-yellow, which is not far wrong. Surely this is the finest of the entire Pernetiana type." [ARA21/155] "The name was given by Monsieur Pernet-Ducher to perpetuate the memory of his eldest son, who gloriously fell on the battlefield." [NRS21/104]

Souvenir de Georges Pernet

trans. "In Memory of Georges Pernet"
Pernet-Ducher, 1921
From an unnamed variety × 'Mme. Édouard Herriot' (Pern).

"Cochineal carmine red." [Cw] "Orient red." [Ÿ] "Deep salmon-pink, lovely form, and lasting bloom." [ARA29/45] "Red, large, full, moderate height." [Sn] "It is a very good pink, much the shade of 'Columbia' [HT] or 'Premier' [HT], and altogether, a promising rose." [ARA23/107] "Large, coral-red blooms with good pointed buds, which sometimes rot easily; the too-large blooms hang on account of the rather weak neck." [ARA24/108] "Pink, slightly tinted with yellow, with a firm stem and fine foliage, a healthy and vigorous bush, producing wide and large blooms, whose 'turbinated' bud is very nicely shaped." [NRS21/106] "Deep rose-red; very large; fine foliage; winters well. One of my favorites." [ARA25/121] "Flowers pink, slightly shaded yellow, on strong stems. A vigorous grower with beautiful disease-resistant foliage. It produces an abundance of beautifully formed buds and large, full flowers." [ARA21/148] "Large, ovoid bud of oriental-red, shaded yellow; flowers large and full; bush quite branching; flowers seem too heavy for the stems; branches so weak that buds sometimes lie on the ground." [ARA25/102] "Flowers large, of globular form, and the bush is vigorous and free in growth. Color, orient-red shading to cochineal-carmine at the end of the petals, the whole being overspread with a golden sheen." [C&Js24] "Last year this rose did not win our good opinion so much, but this summer it proved a rare gem, as so rain could spoil the multitude of beautiful blooms that decked the plants. The color is a glorious deep coral-red, and is not given to much alteration by changing temperatures and sunshine." [ARA25/136] "Provides brick-red buds which open into fragrant, deep pink blooms of enormous size. Like '[Souvenir de] Claudius Pernet' [Pern], it is hard to establish, but it pays if you have patience to wait." [ARA29/55] "Beautiful all the way from bud to open flower. It is immense without being coarse, and is very generous." [ARA29/48] "Its large blossoms of salmon, rose, and gold made one of the most beautiful spots in our garden last summer ... To produce its most perfect tones, it must have partial shade, and it needs much spraying to prevent black-spot, but is worth it. Only those who truly love to work with roses as well as gather them should try to grow Pernetianas in Kentucky." [ARA31/98]

"Practically every Rose has its duplicates or 'just as good' substitutes, but 'Souvenir de Georges Pernet' has never yet been matched and stands alone in his splendid isolation—long-pointed buds of rich oriental-red, tipped with deep carmine, on a pedestal of buttercup-yellow. As the petals unfurl slowly, these tints blend into a shimmering cochineal old-rose. In form it is nearer perfection than any [other] Rose we know. The flower is of very large size and unusually long lasting, rain or shine, and the plant it vigorous, branching and rather sprawly. Foliage a deep green with a purplish edge, large and of average persistence." [C-Ps28] "Bud very large, ovoid; flower very large, full, globular; oriental red, shaded with yellow, ends of petals cochineal-carmine; borne on long, strong stem. Foliage dark bronzy green. Very vigorous, upright, bushy, branching; extremely hardy." [ARA22/150] "Astonishingly large, this new bright-colored beauty is worth a place in every garden. The big, fat buds are borne on strong, short stems and disclose fiery copper hues as they open slowly to an enormous, globular flower of many petals, brilliant orange-pink, sweetly perfumed, and very lasting. The bush is a stubby grower, branching, and very thorny. The foliage is hard and shining, apparently more resistant to black-spot than most varieties of this type of Roses." [C-Ps25] "It has dark, shiny disease resistant foliage and in this respect it is a great advance over other Pernetiana Roses." [C-Ps26] "In memory of his youngest son whom he lost during the World War ... not a profuse bloomer, but a prize-winner at all shows." [C-Ps31] "Not yet matched for form and color." [C-Pf31] "For size and shape of flowers and for constant blooming, I know no bright, dark pink that equals it." [ARA29/52] "The best of the so-called orient-red coloured Roses." [NRS24/149]

Souvenir de Gustave Schickelé

trans. "In Memory of Gustave Schickelé"

Ketten, 1927

From 'Mme. Édouard Herriot' (Pern) × 'Duchess of Wellington' (HT).

"Deep orange yellow, large, very full, moderate height." [Sn] "Flower of very remarkable colouring, outside of petals bright rosy scarlet, shaded with apricot, inside of petals chrome-yellow, blooms large, fairly full, buds long and pointed. Growth vigorous, erect and floriferous." [GeH] "Bud long-pointed, opens well in all weathers; bloom large, double, full, deep chrome-yellow, reverse bright rosy scarlet, shaded with apricot. Foliage abundant, glossy Quaker green, disease-resistant. Growth very vigorous, upright, bushy, free-branching; continuous bloomer from June to November. Hardy." [ARA28/243]

Souvenir de Jean Soupert

trans. "In Memory of Jean Soupert"

Soupert & Notting, 1929

From 'Ophelia' (HT) × 'Feu Joseph Looymans' (Pern).

"Yellow, large, lightly double, very fragrant, moderate height." [Sn] "Bud very large, long-pointed; flower very large, semi-double, cupped, lasting, intensely fragrant, golden yellow, borne singly on long stem. Foliage abundant, large, bronze-green, leathery. Growth vigorous, upright; profuse bloomer from May to November." [ARA30/229]

Souvenir du Reverend Père Planque

trans. "In Memory of Reverend Père Planque"

Bel, 1932

"Orange yellow, large, full, moderate height." [Sn]

[Sunburst] Plate 76

Pernet-Ducher/E. G. Hill, 1911

"Cadmium yellow." [JR37/80] "A magnificent yellow, shaded orange copper; long buds on long stems; flowers very large; unusually vigorous and healthy. Has scored highest honors wherever exhibited. The only yellow." [CA13] "Lovely even if it does sometimes come almost white." [NRS20/161] "That colour is deep yellow, much to be desired, cadmium deepening to orange is the shade . . . It is a slightly larger bud than [that of] 'Mme. Ravary' [HT], and distinctly better shaped, but not very full. It is a good grower, but not very vigorous." [NRS13/158]" Medium large, fine form, double, tea fragrance, long stem. Foliage fine, sufficient. Growth strong, hardy. Deep yellow to orange-yellow." [ARA23/173] "Superb cadmium-yellow, with orange-yellow centre, large, fairly full, cupped form, the buds generally borne singly on long, stout stems. Growth very vigorous, upright, and free flowering." [GeH] "Thirteen blooms in 1915." [ARA16/20] "Not always reliable but an excellent bloomer when thoroughly established. Growth low and somewhat spreading. Very few thorns and foliage good." [C-Ps25] "Beautiful shade at best, but color varies greatly; growth fair; blooming shy; hardiness not dependable." [ARA18/118] "A vigorous and healthy Rose, with long, pointed buds and splendid flowers, which are produced on strong, upright stems. The color is an intense orange-copper and golden yellow, extremely brilliant in effect. A splendid variety which does well both for forcing in the greenhouse and for garden planting." [C&Js14] "Low-growing, compact, winterkills a good deal; foliage sufficient, black-spots slightly; bloom moderate, almost continuous." [ARA18/128] "Has proved a most disappointing Rose. I well remember the pleasure I felt in the first exhibit of it I saw. The centre of the flowers was a bright glowing orange, paling slightly at the edges of the petals. I came back to it again and again, and thought the flower was most appropriately named. Later I procured some plants, and when I found it a fine and strong grower my hopes were high till the flowers appeared. With a few exceptions they proved to be of a dull cream colour, which steadily deteriorated as we came to autumn. Then we were told that we should get the colour by taking out the terminal bud and allowing the side shoots to develop. But this proved of no avail. Only occasionally, in a spell of very hot weather, did we find a flower with any approach to the colour we desired, and it seems clear this country [England] is too cold for it." [NRS21/41] "Now [in 1925] grown very little [as a florist's rose]." [ARA25/173]

"When I was at Lyons, with Monsieur Pernet[-Ducher], and he was showing me his roses and dilating upon them, I caught sight of a couple of yellow roses that were sticking up, and kept looking at them. Pernet said to me, 'What are you looking at?'. I said, 'I am looking at that yellow rose. Let's go over there, and then we can come back here.' But he said, 'Come right along; we will get there.' We got over there after a while, and I was captivated by that rose. I said to Monsieur Pernet, 'I would like to buy that rose.' 'Well,' he said, 'what will you give?'. I looked them over, and I said, 'I will risk $500 on that.' 'Well,' he said, 'I will not take that much money for it; I would not feel right to take $500 for that rose. When we go in to dinner I will make

[Sunburst] *continued*

you a price.' So when we got to the dinner, and the old gentleman said, 'Mr. [E. G.] Hill, if you will give me 1500 francs ($292.50) for that Rose that would be about right.' I said, 'That is not enough.' He said, 'Yes, I do not want more.' I replied, 'I want you to reserve the European rights. I will exploit it in America, and the information will get back to England, and I am sure you will sell a good lot of them.' It worked that way, and Monsieur Pernet got more money out of 'Sunburst' over there than I got out of it in the sale over here." [ARA22/130–131]

[Sunstar]

A. Dickson, 1921

"Salmon red, shaded yellow." [NRS23/list] "Flower salmon-red with deep crimson base, the flowering growth erect, branching." [GeH] "Too thin and fleeting." [NRS24/162] "A bedding and decorative variety of vigorous growth. The predominant colour is a salmon-red, and base of the petals is a deep crimson. A distinct and beautiful variety, which will not, however, be placed in commerce until after the war." [NRS18/164] "Bud long-pointed; flower medium size, orange, edged and veined vermilion; honey fragrance. Vigorous; bushy; very free bloomer." [ARA21/160] "Buds orange, yellow, crimson, vermilion, and all the rest; half-open flowers beautiful with opalescent tints, but the open flowers after a few hours recall three-day-old Climbing American Beauties; strong grower; blooms singly on short stems; very little disease . . . R.I.; I like this rose about which there is such a difference of opinion, but realize its faults. Each season the blooms are larger, but almost single. Since the wide-open flower has such a sickly lemon tint outside, I nearly always cut the buds and let them open in the house, thus saving the pure orange and crimson tints. It is one of my favorites . . . *Ont.*" [ARA28/192]

Talisman

Montgomery/A. N. Pierson, 1929

From 'Ophelia' (HT) × 'Souvenir de Claudius Pernet' (Pern).

"A mixture of orange, yellow, and rose-red in irregular proportions." [C-Pf31] "Scarlet red, golden yellow." [Ÿ] "Golden yellow with crimson shading." [GeH] "Orange and scarlet." [CaRoll/3/2] "A wonderful red and yellow Rose of American origin just being sent out." [C-Ps29] "Copper yellow, medium size, full, medium scent, moderate height." [Sn] "It would be much the better for a few petals more and a little more constant color." [ARA31/179] "Very showy scarlet and gold blooms, so far a little on the small side grows and blooms well." [ARA30/153] "Exquisite buds on long, straight stems . . . It is deservedly popular because of its unusual coloring and freedom of bloom." [C-Ps31] "The fragrant flowers are much more highly colored in autumn." [C-Ps33] "During hot weather the blooms are apt to be off color and of poor form, but simply pinch them off and your fall crop will be that much better." [C-Ps34] "A most attractive and distinct rose of what is usually called the 'novelty' type . . . The rose averages twenty-five petals, opens pleasingly, and lasts well. The foliage is full and good, and the unusually long calyx-lobes are very decorative." [ARA28/208] "A florist's Rose that has proved very good outdoors. Our experience with it has been a mixture of orange, yellow, and cream in irregular proportions, varying from plant to plant, with handsome foliage. The flowers are fairly full, fragrant, cup-shaped, with the petals standing upright, the center ones crinkled. In spite of the current adverse criticism you should try this Rose and see how near you can

approach in form and color the greenhouse-grown blooms shown on 'Talisman' color plates." [C-Ps30] "'Talisman' will be a fine rose, not only on account of the color, but also for its tremendous growth, in which it here [Germany] ranks with 'Radiance' [HT]." [ARA30/161] "Bud medium size, long-pointed; flower medium size, double, high-centered, very lasting, extremely fragrant, golden yellow and copper, borne singly on long stem. Foliage abundant, large, rich green, leathery, mildews. Average number of thorns. Growth very vigorous, upright; free bloomer." [ARA28/246] "Tall, upright plants with light green foliage healthier than most Pernetianas." [C-Pf34] "The reports are as various as the colors and forms which the flowers assume. Except in very favored regions, 'Talisman' is likely to produce a great many short-petaled, rather nondescript flowers in hot weather, frequently assuming the ugly black-ball center of 'Souv[enir] de Claudius Pernet' [Pern]. Even where this fault is most evident, it disappears in cool weather, and large, deep-petaled, marvelously colored blooms result. The plants thrive everywhere and have fine foliage which is somewhat subject to mildew in certain sections." [ARA31/200]

"There are so many reports on 'Talisman' and they vary so widely that it seems best to quote from all of them. *Elliot* found moderate growth and no disease. *Foote* was disappointed in the early bloom, but had plenty of lovely flowers in the autumn, though not to be compared with those grown under glass. *Clement* reports all the faults of 'Souvenir de Claudius Pernet', with more poor buds than good ones. Sometimes very beautiful. *Hatton* finds the flowers splendid if cut in the bud and opened indoors; outdoors they vary and fade so badly in the sun that it is a disappointment after seeing them inside. It is very fragrant and free-flowering. *Mitchell* thinks it will be satisfactory outside but the flowers are a gamble, some satisfactory and some with small, imperfect petals. B. & A. check it very good. *Nicolas* cannily reserves his judgment, but thinks it is a cool-weather variety if the loudly trumpeted colors are to be expected. *Cross* notes a bewildering range in excellency of bloom and variable color, some flowers matching the famous illustration. The plants are not strong, but he thinks that due to over-propagation. *Fay* says it does not like the heat. *Kirk* found excellent growth, healthy foliage, with blooms in form and color like the well-known picture. *Davis* was delighted with its color and found the plant disease-resistant. He thinks it will be popular, but reports only moderate growth. *Dunning* says it is a wonderful combination of colors, beautiful in bud when half-open, but semi-double and flat after the first day, with stamens dark brown; and inclined to be deformed late in the season. He prefers 'Angèle Pernet' [Pern]. *Rice* praises the color. *Webster* thinks it is a flop outdoors, but possibly due to over-propagation. He does not regard it favorably. *Connors* states that it has proved to be all that is claimed for it. He is more than pleased with it, although it does fade in July and August. It has been resistant to disease. *O'Roark* calls it a red and yellow prize package. He had flowers exactly like those shown in the illustration in the 1928 *Annual*, and 'What more can one ask?' quoth he. *McGalliard* recommends it. *Schirmer* was a little disappointed. *Furniss* likes it and reports wonderful foliage and flowers of unusual color. *Isham* had wonderful color in bud and bloom, and thinks it promises well. *Armstrong* will grow it for color, size, and fragrance, but wishes that many of the blooms were not malformed and that it would not mildew so badly. It blooms better than any other rose *Hampton* has, and she thinks it is simply perfect. At Breeze Hill, the plants made moderate growth, bloomed perpetually, and had good foliage. The flowers were occasionally a very fine color, fully equal to the illustration in the 1928 *Annual*, but much of the time they were pale and disfigured by a black center inherited from 'Souvenir de Claudius Pernet'. Superb in autumn." [ARA30/193–194]

[The Queen Alexandra Rose]
McGredy, 1918

"This Rose is arrayed like a gypsy queen. The complex old-gold of the bud is revealed as the petals unfurl, gradually showing the most brilliant vermilion-scarlet at the top, with pure gold settling at the base of the petals as if by gravity, both being reabsorbed again into a minimum-red as the flower ages. A Rose of absolutely unique coloration." [C-Ps29] "The large petals unfurl slowly until we have a good-sized Rose, fairly double and cup-formed … The bush is sprawly in habit, which puts it in the bedding class, and the foliage not too persistent." [C-Ps30]

United States
Verschuren, 1918

"Yellowish salmon pink, large, lightly double, moderate height." [Sn] "Flower deep lemon-yellow. Growth like [that of] 'Arthur R. Goodwin' [Pern]." [GeH]

Ville de Malines
trans. "City of Malines"
Lens, 1929

"Reddish yellow, large, full, medium height." [Sn] "Bud long-pointed; flower yellow shaded cherry-red, inside of petals orange with a tint of tango, passing to pink with golden yellow shadings. Growth vigorous, bushy profuse, continuous bloomer. Reported unusually hardy." [ARA31/238]

[Ville de Paris]
trans. "City of Paris"
Pernet-Ducher, 1925

"Sun yellow." [Cw] "Comes on a long stem of purple-brown colour, and its fine foliage is free of disease. Its yellow colour does not fade, and it opens in all weathers." [NRS29/146] "Type, 'Souvenir de Claudius Pernet' [Pern], but considered better in form and blooming qualities. A glorious yellow rose said to surpass any other seen." [ARA26/183] "With us a poor grower and a worse bloomer. Flowers cold, hard yellow of the 'Souv[enir] de Claudius Pernet' shade and of the same balloon shape as [that of] 'Radiance' [HT]." [ARA28/194] "The flowers are too round and globular, but the color is fine, they open well, and the long, wiry stems are clothed with the finest of shiny, leathery Pernetiana foliage." [ARA29/146] "A consistent disappointment … New plants and the old have steadily deteriorated for several years." [ARA30/179] "Is a fine grower. I thought at first this rose was too thin, but many will like it." [ARA28/138] "In the 1925 Bagatelle contest, this Rose was declared the most important yellow garden Rose, and deemed worthy of the name 'Ville de Paris' for which honor a large cash premium had been posted several years previously—to be awarded when a Rose good enough for it could be produced. Every French hybridizer competed for that greatest honor—and purse. After winning it, Monsieur Pernet declared this to be the crowning of his long career, and retired from business. (He died Nov. 23, 1928.) Its buds are long and flowers fairly large, not very full, but their charm

lies in their fragrance, and the gleaming buttercup-yellow color. The bush is tall, with rich holly-green foliage on wiry stems. While superior as a garden Rose, it is good also for cutting." [C-Ps29] "Of all dandelion-yellow Roses of Austrian Briar (Pernetiana) ancestry, this is about the tallest grower, its long, wiry stems gently waving in the breeze like spears of wheat … The bud is generally of the pointed form, with broad base and the open bloom is of medium petalage, fairly large and fragrant, with a center that does not turn black. It is a steady doer throughout the season. Stands rain and extreme heat better than most other yellow Roses, and the foliage is notably resistant to diseases." [C-Ps30]

Von Scharnhorst
Lambert, 1921
From 'Frau Karl Druschki' (HP) × 'Gottfried Keller' (Pern).

"Light yellow, medium size, lightly double, light scent, tall." [Sn] "Bud medium size, ovoid, yellow flower; medium size, open, semi-double, lasting; sulphur-yellow, turning to yellowish white with age; borne, several together, on short stem; slight fragrance. Foliage abundant, medium size, glossy, soft, light green, disease-resistant. Very vigorous, upright; blooms profusely in May and June and again in August and September; hardy." [ARA22/155]

Wildenfels Gelb
trans. "Wild Crag Yellow"
Dechant, 1929

"Yellow, medium size, single, tall." [Sn]

Wildenfels Rosa
trans. "Wild Crag Pink"
Dechant, 1928

"Pink, medium size, single, light scent, tall." [Sn]

Wilhelm Kordes
Kordes, 1922
From 'Gorgeous' (Pern) × 'Adolf Koschel' (Pern).

"Nasturtium red nuanced golden yellow." [Cw] "Coppery salmon yellow, large, full, medium scent, moderate height." [Sn] "When well grown, produces gorgeous blooms of salmon, gold, copper, and red. Worth a trial." [C-Ps32] "Surely the wonder of the year. The bloom has much of the perfect form of 'Mme. Abel Chatenay' [HT], and the bud is high and well-formed, always opening to perfect blooms. The first flowers are very large, but the medium-sized ones that follow have the better color. The ground-color is a solid golden yellow on the outer face of the petals and at the bottom of the flowers, but when the sunlight touches it, it takes on a color that ranges from the brownish red of *Rosa lutea* [*i.e.*, *R. foetida*] to the crimson of 'Hugh Dickson' [HP]." [ARA23/141] "Requires a special description for each bloom each hour of each day throughout the season. Cannot be averaged in a short space, but some blooms will be 'plus,' others 'minus.' Buds ovoid, opening to double flowers of nasturtium-red to salmon on gold base; fragrant—particularly good in the autumn. Young foliage deep bronze." [C-Ps29] "Golden yellow at base, it graduates to capucine-red, with deep carmine veins. Bud beautifully formed. The plant is not very vigorous, but has handsome purplish red foliage, turning to deep green. Not very hardy north of Philadelphia." [C-Ps30] "Capucine-red on a golden yellow ground, gradually toning to golden yellow striped with red when expanding. Fairly full, of good form and

Wilhelm Kordes *continued*

carried on stiff stems. Tall and upright; opens well and lasts. Foliage fair and free from disease." [GeH] "Multi-colored, combining red and salmon; varies; double; long bud; mild fragrance. Exquisite but difficult to establish." [CaRoll/3/2] "Has different colors than any other rose, old or new. It has the red, salmon, and golden shades all blended into one flower with prominent veining. It might be called an autumn-hued rose. The flowers are large and have great substance; the buds hold well in the center as the petals unfold. I also like the beautiful bronze foliage of its new growths, and with me it is a very sturdy, satisfactory grower." [ARA29/66] "Bud large, long-pointed; flower large, double, full, high-centered, very lasting; golden yellow, with coppery yellow at edges and on petals exposed to the sun; borne singly on long, strong stems; strong fragrance, like ripe apples. Foliage sufficient, medium size, leathery, glossy, disease-resistant. Vigorous, upright, bushy; abundant and continuous bloomer." [ARA22/155] "Best as a maiden." [NRS26/list] "A marvelous flower. Growth weak and plant hard to establish … *Calif.*; … To our mind it has everything a rose should have except size, blooming quality, fragrance, and decent growth. Color is splendid." [ARA28/196] "If you want a real thrill in rose-growing, try a couple of these." [ARA29/105]

Willowmere Plate 80
Pernet-Ducher, 1913
From an unnamed seedling × 'Lyon-Rose' (Pern).

"Rich shrimp-pink, shaded yellow in the center, and toning to carmine-pink toward the edges of petals. Long, carmined coral-red buds, carried on long, stout flower stems; very large flower, full and of elongated cup shape. An excellent feature of this rose is its splendid substance. Habit of growth promises to be everything that can be desired." [C&Js14] "Orange pink, yellow center, medium size, full, moderate height." [Sn] "In our Rose garden it stands out prominently among the best of the pink colored varieties." [C-Ps30] "The colour is remarkable. It is an improved 'Lyon-Rose' which does not fade. It is very vigorous and hardy; the blooms are long and pointed, carried on erect stems, and are very attractive with their fierce red thorns." [NRS13/164] "Most attractive and distinct in color and form; strong growth; foliage fair; inclined to be rather shy bloomer." [ARA18/114] "Fine growth, hardy; fair foliage, good stem; medium size, beautiful form, lasts well … twelve blooms in 1915." [ARA16/21] "Tall, spare." [ARA17/31] "Low-growing, moderately compact; foliage plentiful, blackspots somewhat; bloom moderate, almost continuous." [ARA18/128] "While not as good a bloomer as it might be, ['Willowmere'] is a good grower, very hardy, and of the most lovely shade of pink." [ARA23/65] "A strong growing plant, with flowers which are often beautiful. At their best they are a peach pink, often full enough for exhibition, and well formed. It is as a garden plant that it should be principally considered, and its defect in this respect is that the flowers are rather readily injured by rain, and a proportion are not so well formed as they should be, while the plant is subject to stem mildew." [NRS21/49] "A good-natured, handsome Rose of largest size and splendid form, showing clear pink, glowing with yellow, like sunshine in its heart. A steady, repeating blooming, with husky, thorny canes and excellent foliage which is much less subject to disease than others of its class. Prune but little. It never sulks." [C-Ps25]

"Bush of great vigor with erect canes; foliage light green; thorns

numerous and not very protrusive; bud elongate in form, borne on a long and strong peduncle, carminy coral red; flower very large, full, in form an elongated cup, richly colored shrimp red nuanced yellow at the center, petal edges carmine pink. Continuous bloom. This superb newcomer, much noted at the London Exhibition of 1912, approaches 'Lyon-Rose' in color; but it is one up on 'Lyon-Rose' in producing flowers which are more graceful and lighter in effect; the bush is absolutely hardy. It is one of the prettiest of the Pernetiana race." [JR37/42] "In many ways this Rose resembles 'Los Angeles' [Pern] but it is more free in bloom and very much stronger in growth. A favorite of the great rosarian, the late Admiral Aaron Ward." [C-Ps27] "Named by Pernet for the estate of his friend, Admiral Ward … The large flowers are salmon-pink flushed with gold. The plants are bushy and free blooming but the foliage needs careful protection." [C-Ps34] "Has been one of the best-loved garden Roses for years." [C-Ps33]

"On June 28, I arrived in Lyons and at once set out to visit Monsieur Pernet-Ducher. I found that to do so was by no means easy, as to go to Venissieux is a long ride in one of the roughest trams I was ever on. Although the tram went slowly, it seemed every minute that it would jump the track, and I cannot imagine that riding on a camel would be any worse. Arriving at the little public square of Venissieux, I asked for Monsieur Pernet-Ducher, finding, as is so often the case with a famous person in his own town, that he was apparently totally unknown! After enquiry in five or six little shops, I finally found an old butcher who knew the way. He directed me to take the first turn to the right and then the second turn to the left, following which, after several miles of hard walking in the hot sun on a very dusty road, I found the house of Monsieur Pernet-Ducher. It opens directly on the street, and behind it is a little nursery. What view there is over the high walls around it shows the nursery to be entirely surrounded by factories, so that it is far from an attractive place.

"Monsieur Pernet-Ducher apologized profusely for his roses 'on account of the poor weather,' which seemed entirely unwarranted, as the plants looked good to me, being quite healthy and literally covered with bloom. The center of attraction was, of course, 'Souvenir de Claudius Pernet', and near the large block of this variety was 'Souvenir de Georges Pernet', another great rose. There was also a collection of the older Pernetiana varieties, and, yet more interesting, thousands of seedlings which are being tested, but about which Monsieur Pernet-Ducher was very disdainful, saying there was very little among them of any value. I was interested to see also thousands of little twisted papers on the rose stems, covering flowers which had been crossed by hand this season, and from which we have every right to expect many fine new varieties to come.

"I had never seen hybridization on such a large scale, and the procedure interested me greatly. I was also much impressed by the care with which Monsieur Pernet-Ducher tested and judged his new garden roses. His standard is high, and other people might name and send out hundreds of varieties each year from seedlings he has produced. He insists, quite truthfully, that his care in the past has given him a high reputation, which he must keep up, and he is therefore most careful to select only the very best of his seedlings for naming." [ARA23/129–130]

"The Pernet-Ducher firm is certainly the oldest rose establishment still fully in business. It is more than a century since Claude

Ducher set up at Lyon in the Madeleine quarter of the city, and in 1845 he was already inviting Lyon's fanciers to come visit his roseries. Despite vicissitudes, the firm of Pernet-Ducher never ceased to work for the improvement of Roses. Pernet-Ducher had the misfortune to lose his two sons to the War, and in 1924 called upon Monsieur Jean Gaujard to aid him in his work. During long months, master and student worked together, and in Summer 1925 Pernet-Ducher sold his firm and seedlings to Monsieur Gaujard to allow him to continue his work. Monsieur Jean Gaujard continued the work of his predecessor with success." [LADR210/26]

"Pernet-Ducher was born at Lyon in November of 1859. He died in November, 1928, at the age of 69, surrounded by the acknowledgements of the whole horticultural world, having sought neither publicity nor honors. His father Jean Pernet—known under the name 'Pernet père' among breeders—was born on the route de Vaulx, Villeurbanne, near Lyon, in 1832, and died in February, 1896, at the age of 64. He was still fully active when death surprised him. Always occupied with roses, he was one of the first hybridizers who sought out novelties. A *rosiériste* both of repute and counsel, from 1865 he was located at 64 route de Vaulx.

"His son Joseph Pernet (who would become Pernet-Ducher) showed from his youth an interest in the Rose. In 1878, he began to pursue his apprenticeship at other firms; then one day he got the idea of working with hybridizers, and came to the gate of the Widow Ducher, located at the corner of Chemin des Quatre-Maisons and Avenue des Deux-Ponts (today Avenue Berthelot). The firm of Widow Ducher had always been located near the Cemetery of La Guillotière; today, where the nursery had been is a large bus garage.

"Young Joseph Pernet worked conscientiously at hybridizing roses. On the far side of Widow Ducher's nursery lived a carnation-grower known at the time, Alégatière [*he was also a rose breeder*], and he is the one who gave young Pernet the idea of putting caps on the hybridized rose-blossoms to keep insects from getting to them and disturbing the cross.

"The Ducher firm was one of the oldest rose-houses. Its founder, [Jean-]Claude Ducher, born at Lyon in 1820, was the first [Ducher] to interest himself exclusively in new roses, and his fame mounted on May 16, 1845, when an exhibition of unreleased seedlings was took place at the Palace of Arts. This was, without a doubt, the first exhibition ever in the world totally devoted to new roses …

"Mme. Widow Ducher had a daughter, Marie, who married Joseph Pernet in 1882; the two houses were thus united in taking the name Pernet-Ducher … Continuing the work of Claude Ducher and of his own father, Pernet-Ducher very quickly created some very beautiful varieties. Two of the best known would be 'Mme. Caroline Testout' (1890) and 'Mme. Abel Chatenay' (1894) …

"The masterwork of his life of research was without a doubt the creation of a new race of roses, the Pernetianas … Pernet-Ducher had noted that the roses grown around 1880–1885 didn't have sparkling coloring, the yellows coming from the Teas not being a pure yellow. One day in June 1885, walking in the Parc de la Tête-d'Or [in Lyon], still quite a young park, he was struck by the luxuriant bloom of a 'Persian Yellow' [F] and a *Rosa foetida* 'Bicolor'. This was a wake-up call, an enlightenment which excited his imagination; and soon he had plotted out his way: 'to bring large, reblooming flowers the yellow and coppery tints of these two varietis'. But the difficulties were great, because 'Persian Yellow' and 'Bicolor' had small, non-remontant flowers …

"Nevertheless, he put his shoulder to the task, and only thirteen years later, in 1898, he convoked the rosarians at his new nursery at 114 route d'Heyrieux, at Lyon-Monplaisir, to admire a sensational rose, 'Soleil d'Or' …

"At the beginning of the war in 1914, Pernet-Ducher had the great misfortune to lose over the course of a few days his two sons Claudius and Georges. Claudius fell October 24, 1914, brought down by the Germans during the night at 2 in the morning, only 32 years old. No sooner had Pernet-Ducher gotten this terrible news than he found out, a few days later, about the death of his second son, Georges, struck down at the age of 28 at Fontenelle …

"Pernet-Ducher had the reputation of a taciturn, eccentric man, especially at the end of his life after he lost his two sons. Undermined by illness, he had some sad years. But he had always detested interviews, reporters, and publicity—and quite often, when journalists would pay him a visit, he would slam the door in their faces! …

"He always dressed extremely simply, hating pomp, and received the highest personages while he was in the course of his work. Everyone knew to stand in awe of the omnipresent blue apron, with his straw hat on in nearly all seasons as he walked through his nurseries, back bent, hands behind his back, eyes bright behind his glasses. Often, he would stay for whole hours among his roses, observing them, and thinking out the crosses he wanted to make.

"Despite his difficult manner, he had the esteem of his colleagues, and some fanciers had indeed for him a true veneration. He always imbued the value of a rose with his opinion of the person it came from; and, in his judgments, it was impossible for him to be impartial. Not putting himself to the trouble of beating around the bush, he would state succinctly his point of view, in which he would always strive to say the most precise thing to make the most beautiful rose come out on top. His whole life was research, and the rest of the world had little interest to him. This great simplicity certainly contributed yet more to his greatness …

"Jean Gaujard, who was at that time [1925] 21 years old, came to help him with his hybridization; and several months later, Pernet-Ducher sold him his firm. He was sick, sad, and weary, and in November of 1928, he breathed his last …

"Pernet-Ducher was, for all his life, simply a researcher, and never a man of money. His great artlessness was that of many scholars who never leave their laboratory—he never left his roses. An intelligent observer, a dogged worker, he created beautiful roses for professional and fancier alike. He paid no attention to either of them!—and this is what we should be thankful for. For 50 years, his fame was universal, living like an artist, working like a scientist. It is perhaps only today [after his death] that we can appreciate all the more the importance of his work. He stamped his indelible mark on the world of Horticulture." [LADR258/8–13]

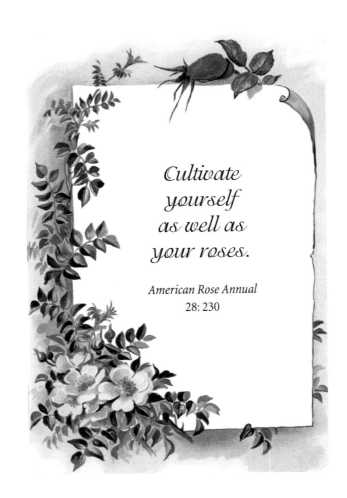

*Cultivate
yourself
as well as
your roses.*

American Rose Annual
28: 230

Additions and Corrections

"When I find out about any errors, I am eager to correct them; it is a duty, which I fulfill." [JPV]

Another few years of research have brought to light a few more facts, as well as a few more "extant or important" cultivars in the groups surveyed in *The Old Rose Advisor,* dealing with the repeat-blooming old roses. It is, of course, not always completely certain that the cultivars listed, seemingly as extant, in current catalogs, or in current books, are correctly identified. We nevertheless are optimistic about the information published by others, and include the following as addenda, including as well some new bits of information on a few cultivars otherwise already treated in our previous book. The order followed will be the order of the book itself; additions and corrections made should also be reflected in the index and appropriate appendices:

Dust Jacket. The rose illustrated on the front of the dust jacket of *The Old Rose Advisor* is the Hybrid Tea 'Mrs. W. J. Grant'; that on the back is the Hybrid Perpetual 'Gustave Piganeau'.

CHAPTER TWO: Damask Perpetuals

[Amanda Patenotte]
syn. 'Amande Patenotte'
Vibert, 1845

"Pale rose color, very double, protuberant fine globose form, large, splendid." [WRP] "7 cm [ca. 2³/₄ in], full, deep pink, globular, very fragrant." [VPt47/127] "Blossom medium-sized, full, plump, of a bright purple pink. Elegant foliage." [An46-47/209] "Dark rose, large and full; form, globular. Habit, erect; growth, moderate." [P] "Canes hardly thorny at all; foliage medium, of a light green; flower nestling within the foliage (peduncle about a centimeter long [ca. ³/₈ in]), ovary smooth, glabrous; calycinate divisions medium-sized; corolla a very bright cerise red." [dH47/253] "(By some ranked as a Hybrid Perpetual, and perhaps justly so)…one of the very finest of this class; it is a most admirable flower…it is new, and in great request even in France at 15 to 20 francs each plant. I last year paid 22 francs, and was deemed favored." [WRP]

Belle Fabert
We can add to the information supplied in *The Old Rose Advisor* that the introducer is Fabert.

Blanche-Vibert
To the biography of Jean-Pierre Vibert can be added two new facts: (1) that as a sergeant in the elite corps that became *les Voltigeurs* (see frontispiece) in Napoléon's First Army of the Republic, Vibert was seriously wounded in the siege of Naples [V2]; (2) that sometime in the mid to late 1820s, Vibert offered to donate for study purposes a large collection of rose cultivars to the Paris *Jardin des Plantes,* which donation was refused, the stated reason being that the *Jardin* was only interested in species roses, not cultivars [MaCo].

Buffon
syns. 'Joséphine', 'Rose Buffon'
Breeder unknown, pre-1821

"Pale rose." [Cal] "Having large plump [*pommées*] blossoms, like the Centifolia; very double, flesh." [BJ30] "*Flowers,* middle-sized, very full, pale pink." [Go] Comte Georges Louis Leclerc de Buffon, influential French naturalist and theorist, lived 1707–1788.

Capitaine Rénard
syns. 'Capitaine Raynard', 'Rose du Roi Strié', 'Striped Crimson Perpetual'
Breeder unknown, pre-1843

"A very fickle flower, is usually pale flesh color, striped with crimson, but some flowers lose the stripe entirely." [WRP] "Blossom large, very full; color, white." [S]

Casimir Delavigne
Vibert, 1848

"Blossom large, full, nuanced lilac." [S] "Flowers full, from 8–9 cm across [ca. 3¹/₄ in], violet-red and crimson; globular form." [M-V49/233]

Céline Bourdier
Robert, 1852

"6–7 cm [ca. 2¹/₂ in], full, bright red." [R&M62] "Vigorous bush; canes upright, very thorny; flower medium-sized, full; petals folded, giving it the form of a rose-window; color, red shaded with lilac." [S]

Césonie
Vibert, pre-1836

"Flowers dark rose, large and full; form, compact." [P]

Christophe Colombe
Robert, 1854

"Blossom from 11 to 15 centimeters [ca. 4¹/₄–5⁷/₈ in], very full, flat,

Christophe Colombe *continued*
amaranth purple, darker at the center." [I'H55/51] "From 11–13 cm [ca. 4^1/$_4$–5 in], full, flat, amaranth." [R&M62] "Blossom very large, full, flat; color, grenadine, with a deep ruby center." [S] Christophe Colombe, alias Christopher Columbus, alias Cristoforo Colombo, discovered a New World, or at least a world new to southern Europeans, lived 1451–1506.

Desdémona
Vibert, 1841
   "Medium-sized, double, carmine-red." [V8] "Of a carmine red hue, delightfully fragrant, but sometimes fails to bloom well in autumn." [WRP] "For its delicate colour, and exquisite fragrance, is worthy of culture, though its tendency to autumnal blooming merely, is discouraging." [Bu] Desdemona, Othello's wife in Shakespeare's tragedy.

[Duchesse de Montmorency]
R. Lévêque, 1844
   "Flower, double, large, globular, and of a fine bright satiny rose color." [MH45/28] "Blossom large, very full, cupped; color, delicate pink, shaded lilac; much to be recommended for its late bloom." [S]

[Ebène]
trans. "Ebony"
Boyau, 1844
   "Medium-sized, full, changeable violet purple." [BJ53] "Medium-sized, double, violety purple, the darkest of the sort." [V8] "Weak-growing plant; blossom medium-sized, full; color, violet purple." [S]

[Henriette]
syn. 'Bifera Italica'
Italy, pre-1811
   "Wood strong and vigorous, not very many thorns. Leaves very beautiful, deeply cut, gay green. Calyx big, elongate, glabrous, tip constricted. Bud pointed, beautiful shape, overtopped by its sepals, seven or eight on the same stem. The blossom is large, not very double, but well formed, a beautiful delicate pink, very fragrant, blooming from June 10 to 15. A single stem, with its leaves and half-open buds, makes a nice bouquet." [C-T] "This variety of the Damask Rose came to us from Italy; wood strong, vigorous, clothed with few thorns; its leaves are a light gay green; calyx fat, elongate, and glabrous. Buds pointed and well covered by the extension of the calyx, seven or eight on the same peduncle; flower large, and not very double, well formed, of a delicate color of pink, very fragrant. One lone branch, accompanied by its leaves, buds, and blossoms, can make a perfect bouquet of the nicest appearance. Opens from the 10th to the 19th [of June]." [LeR] There is probable synonymy between 'Henriette', 'Henriette Boulogne', and 'Quatre Saisons d'Italie', with which lattermost 'Henriette' already shares its synonym 'Bifera Italica'.

Henriette Boulogne
Breeder unknown, pre-1839
   "Pink, large, full, cupped." [LF] "A good rose, but rather an inconstant autumnal bloomer." [WRP] Probably synonymous with 'Henriette' and 'Quatre Saisons d'Italie', *qqv.* If we accept this synonymy, the "Boulogne" part of the name of this cultivar is possibly owing to the arrival of this cultivar from Italy via the much-respected rosarium of the botanist Dumont de Courset, located in Boulogne, France.

[Indigo]
syn. 'Perpétuelle Indigo'
Laffay, pre-1845
   "Bluish violet, velvety, quite novel in tint." [MH45/Aug.Ad.3] "Blossom large, full, flat; color, deep grenadine." [S] "Medium-sized, double, slaty deep violet, flat." [R&M62] "Flowers medium size, very double, flat, and of a very dark purple. This is one of the Portland or old perpetuals." [MH45/28]

[Jeanne Hachette]
Vibert, pre-1844
   "Flowers lilac rose, large and double; form, globular." [P]

Joasine Hanet
   It appears that the correct date for this cultivar by Vibert is 1846, not 1847. We can also add the following to the description in *The Old Rose Advisor*: "6 cm [ca. 2^1/$_3$ in], full, purple red, corymbiferous, in a rosette." [VPt47/126]

Jules Lesourd
Robert & Moreau, 1863
   "Light red." [Jg] "7–8 cm [ca. 3 in], full, globular, very bright red." [M-R65]

La Moderne
syns. 'À Fleur Double', 'Double', 'Gros Fruit'; trans., "The Modern [One]"
Breeder unknown, pre-1820
   "Blush." [Cal] "*Shrub*, with feeble thorns. *Flowers*, large, semi-double, of a pale purplish pink." [Go]

[La Volumineuse]
trans. "The Massy [One]"
Breeder unknown, pre-1835
   "Flesh pink." [S-V] "Rosy blush, worthless." [P] See also 'Volumineuse' (Ag).

Laurent Heister
   The firm releasing this variety was "Robert & Moreau," not "Moreau-Robert." We can also add the following to our description in *The Old Rose Advisor*: "Very remontant." [AnM-L59/36] "Vigorous bush, blossom from 7–9 cm across [ca. 2^3/$_4$–3^1/$_2$ in], full, light lilac pink, perfect form. In form, this plant resembles [that of] the Gallica 'Comte [Boula] de Nanteuil'." [AnM-L59/212]

Le Prince de Galles
Breeder unknown, pre-1826
   "Deep pink." [V3] "Deep pink." [BJ40] "Bush with purplish, unarmed canes; leaflets smooth, large, dark green, sharply dentate; calyx-tube narrow and extremely long; sepals terminating in a very long point; blossom large, full; light red, or deep bright pink." [S] Not to be confused with the ca. 1845 Hybrid Perpetual, which was cerise, lighter at the edges.

Lesueur
Robert, 1853
   "7–9 cm [ca. 2^3/$_4$–3^1/$_2$ in], full, violety red pink, cupped, in a rosette, in clusters." [R&M62] "Flowers large, full, violet red-pink, cupped, well-formed, in a rosette; in a corymb; wood and foliage dark green." [I'H54/12] "Very vigorous bush; flower large, full, formed of very muddled petals, and growing in corymbs; color, reddish violet." [S]

Marquise de Boccella

We can add the following to our description in *The Old Rose Advisor*: "Light pink; a stout and short grower; the petals are singularly reflexed." [MH51] "Very pale flesh; habit dwarf—more so than any of the preceding [*a group including, in part, 'Baronne Prévost' (HP), 'Duchesse de Sutherland' (HP), and 'La Reine' (HP)*], and very compact." [MH49]

Mathilde Jesse

Laffay, 1847

"Fiery red." [Jg] "Flame pink." [LS]

Portland Blanc

trans. "White Portland"
Vibert, 1836

"Very pure white." [V4] "Flower medium-sized, double, white, with some flesh before opening." [S] "Biferous, pure white, full, flat, large, superb." [LF] "Medium-sized, full, white, not always opening well." [V8] "Nearly white, a rose of large size, perfect in form, quite fragrant, and a good grower; it is yet scarce, but a few seasons will make it nearly as plentiful as any other variety." [Bu]

Portland Pourpre

Prévost, ca. 1830

"Deep bright crimson, semi-double." [WRP] "Semi-double, medium, deep purple." [V8] "Bush with weak thorns; flower large, semi-double, light purplish pink." [S]

Préval

Préval, ca. 1821

"Delicate blush, large and full; form, expanded." [P] "Flowers very double, large, and of a pale pink." [AC] "A fine large flower, of a pale roseate hue, perfect compact form, and fragrant; a free bloomer." [WRP] "Raised, around 1821, by Monsieur Préval, at Eturqueray, between Bourg-Achard and Pont-Audemer, département of Eure. *Ovary*, obconical, glabrous and smooth at the summit, often rayed green on a pale ground. *Flower* large, full or very multiple, pale pink. This rose is freely biferous, and ordinarily gives more beautiful flowers at the second bloom. Grafted, it is rare that it keeps good growth after the first year." [Pf]

Quatre Saisons d'Italie

syns. 'Bifera Italica', 'D'Italie', 'D'Italie Rose', 'Damas d'Italie', 'Rosier de la Malmaison'; (see also below)
Florence/Dupont, pre-1812

"Delicate pink." [RG] "Vermilion, sometimes striped." [Ÿ] "Flowers medium-sized, fairly double, flesh, well-formed as well as plenteous." [J-A] "Bush with diffuse canes; leaflets oval-lanceolate, acute, with teeth which are pointed, villose, and non-glandulose; peduncles glandulose; tube of calyx obconical, glabrous at the tip; flowers medium-sized, semi-double, fragrant, a light pink or bright flesh in the middle, pale at the edges." [MaCo] "Open *bush* about 0.6 m high [ca. 2 ft]; *prickles* very numerous, small, short, unequal, almost straight. *Leaflets* 5 or 7, large, ovate, bright green, simply serrate, glabrous above, paler and slightly hairy beneath and on margins; petioles villose, with small, yellowish prickles; stipules fairly broad, acute, glandedged. *Flowers* in three at the cane-tips; bracts subtending the lateral pedicels elongate, acute; pedicels and *receptacles* glandular-hispid;

sepals overtop the bud, 3 pinnatifid, 2 simple; *petals* in 4–5 ranks, large, delicate pink, paler towards the base, cordately notched. *Hips* elongate-ovoid, red. This rose stands out among the Damasks by way of its large flowers, often over 7.5 cm across [ca. 3 in]—but only when on its own roots, as the size is noticeably smaller in grafted specimens. Dupont received it from Florence twenty years ago [ca. 1805?] and distributed it. It has little scent, but compensates for this by its grace and elegance. Although long known, it remains rare, but can be seen grafted in Catel's fine collection. On its own roots, it is tender and needs full sun." [T&R] Evidently re-introduced by Victor Verdier in 1865. There was also a white version. Alongside the above-listed synonyms, there are other very probable ones: Vibert lists, in 1820, a non-remontant Quatre Saisons 'Rose d'Italie', and W. Paul, in 1848, a deep rose 'Belle Italienne'. All of these should be compared with two Damask Perpetuals which we also list in this appendix, 'Henriette' and 'Henriette Boulogne'; it should be noted that 'Quatre Saisons d'Italie' at least shares its synonym 'Bifera Italica', if not indeed its very identity, with 'Henriette'. We replace the entry in *The Old Rose Advisor* with this augmented and completely revised one.

CHAPTER THREE: Chinas

Animating

syn. 'Bengale Animée'
England, pre-1817

We restore the original name, and correct the attribution, from the information presented in *The Old Rose Advisor*.

Beauty of Glenhurst

Morley/Nottle, 1985

The introducer of this cultivar, Trevor Nottle, tells us (in unpublished correspondence): "The rose 'Beauty of Glenhurst' was named by me and raised and grown by June & Brian Morley. I introduced it in the one year I was a rose wholesaler! It would have been 1985 so it would have been raised from seed June gathered in 1979 and grown in 1980. It is a very vigorous bush to about 3.5 meters (about 10 feet) and the same across. It flowers in huge corymbs and while the flowers are not large (about 5–7 cm [ca. 2–3 in]), they are so dense that the impact overall is that of a mass of pink color."

Belle Hébé

syn. 'Hébé'; trans., "Beautiful Hebe"
Laffay, pre-1836

"Blossoms double, medium-sized, bright pink around the edges, flesh in the middle." [MaCo]

Eugène de Beauharnais

We must correct our slip; Eugène de Beauharnais was of course Empress Joséphine's *son*; his name in the last line of the entry should also have had an *accent grave* over the second "e" (as above here), not an *accent aigue*.

Pompon de Paris

For information on the various Lawrencianas or Miniature Chinas, of which this is the most notorious, please see Appendix 2 in the present volume.

[Reine de la Lombardie]

trans. "Queen of Lombardy"
Breeder unknown, pre-1835

"Deep cerise." [S-V] "Large, very multiplex or full, red passing to purple." [Gp] "Blush, changing to rosy crimson, large and full; form, expanded." [P] "Medium-sized, double, purple." [R&M62] "Blossom large, full, flat; color, pale pink, passing to crimson." [S] "Of a brilliant and beautiful cherry color, of globular form and full double; the plant is of rapid growth, very hardy and blooms profusely." [WRP] A parent of Geschwind's Roxburghii 'Premier Essai'.

Unermüdliche

We add a little to the three words of description in *The Old Rose Advisor*: "Purple-red, center white, medium size, semi-double, dwarf." [Sn]

CHAPTER FOUR: Teas

Tea Roses. It is perhaps worth noting that we find a reference to "yellow roses" in section 74 ("Things That Lose by Being Painted") of the 11th century Japanese *The Pillow Book of Sei Shonagon*, probably a reference to Tea Roses.

Blanche Duranthon

This occasionally seen reference is most likely a reference to 'Mme. Lucien Duranthon' (T), *q.v.* below.

Charles Rovolli

Should be 'Charles Rovelli'. The Messers Rovelli, nurserymen of Pallanza, Italy.

[Duchesse de Bragance]

Dubreuil, 1886
Seedling of 'Coquette de Lyon' (T).

"Much-branched bush, with upright canes bestrewn with occasional thorns. Foliage dark green with red young shoots. Calyx reddish in youth, with foliaceous sepals exceeding the bud, which is oval. Blossom very full, and opening well, with a very firm stem; beautiful canary yellow, intense at the center, paler along the edges; outer petals gracefully recurve to the tip. Very meritorious for cut flowers." [JR10/149] Plate 148 in *The Old Rose Advisor*, mistakenly listed as referring to the Hybrid Perpetual 'Duchesse de Bragance', actually refers to this extinct Tea of the same name.

Fortune's Five-Colored Rose

syn. 'À Cinq Couleurs'
Fortune, 1843

"Yellowish-white, sometimes lined with bright pink." [BJ58] "Medium-sized, full, cream white, lined purple." [R&M62] "Bush vigorous; canes bright green; thorns dark green, flat at the base; flower large, full; color, cream-white striped with pink, touched with crimson and spotted with pink and with violet." [S] "You remember—don't you, Readers? —those charlatans who would sell so-called White-and-Red Roses, Blue Dahlias, Tri-Colored Camellias, etc.? The Roubaix Correctional Facility has sent some of these to prison, and do you know why? It is because they were poor devils, uneducated, ignorant of how to announce such things as these. Here, then, is how a very se-rious compilation expresses itself on the subject of the rose called 'Five-Colored': 'It seems to belong'—it says—'to the China Rose group; but it shows a very beautiful and unique aspect. Sometimes it is uni-colored, then white or red all at the same time on the same specimen, while often being striped with all these colors. Here, it will be as hardy as other Roses', etc. Did the poor devils who are serving out their time for their 'moment of error' (as they say when talking about prevaricating functionaries) promise anything more than that? No! —but it is necessary to put these things in quotation-marks; otherwise, one has recourse to the botheration of Police. Be that as it may, the bush which supposedly produces these roses is in Paris in the company of two Briars, or single Dog Roses." [dH44/328–329] Particularly considering the cream or yellow tinge in this rose, noted not only in the above descriptions but also in the blossoms on our own specimen, as well as characteristics of the leaves and hips, we believe this rose to pertain more to the Tea group than to the China—another Tea of the original, delicate sort.

Laurette

Robert, 1853

"Seven to eight cm. [ca. 3 in], full, salmony flesh, peduncles strong, bearing their blossoms well, wood not very thorny, vigorous." [M-L53/323] "Bush vigorous, climbing canes; flower large, full; color, salmony yellow." [S] "Insignificant." [JDR56/49] "Pretty good variety, though ordinary." [I'H56/246]

[Meta]

This cultivar, with an entry in *The Old Rose Advisor*, was named after Meta Weldon, Irish rosarian.

Mme. Lucien Duranthon

Bonnaire, 1898

"Bush of great vigor without being 'climbing,' with strong, rigid canes and peduncles; blossom solitary; bloom abundant and continual; blossom large, cupped, colored cream white around the edge, center coppery and salmony; very distinct variety." [JR22/147]

[Mme. Ocker Ferencz]

Bernaix, 1892

"Canary yellow washed carminy pink; blossom large, full, imbricated, vigorous." [Cx] "Beautiful bush of moderate size. Buds long, washed outside with violet pink. Flower of very beautiful form, with petals which are thick, satiny, glossy, and colored a very light pale canary yellow—nearly white—tinted chrome, fading towards the nub. Outer petals often washed along the edges with carminy pink." [JR16/164] A parent of 'Gruss an Zabern' (Lam).

Regulus

This cultivar, with an entry in *The Old Rose Advisor*, should be attributed to "Robert & Moreau," not to "Moreau-Robert."

Safrano

The garbled line on p. 57 of *The Old Rose Advisor*, 11 lines down in the left-hand column, should read, "low Tea, and was entered into commerce in the autumn without much hoopla; the . . ."

[Souvenir de Clairvaux]

The Old Rose Advisor's last quote on this cultivar should refer to the Hybrid Perpetual 'Mlle. Thérèse Levet', not to the Tea 'Souvenir de Thérèse Levet'.

CHAPTER FIVE: Bourbons

Amarante
trans. "Amaranth"
Page, 1859

"Crimson purple." [LS] "Blossom medium-sized, full, cup-shaped; color, bright cerise red." [S] "Carmine purple, with cherry red, medium size." [Jg]

Capitaine Sisolet
On the basis of FlCa41/31, the following changes to *The Old Rose Advisor* should be made: The name should be changed to 'Capitaine Sissolet', the date should be changed to pre-1841, the classification should be changed to Hybrid China, and the following description may be added: "Rich fulgent rose colour."

Delille
Breeder unknown, pre-1848

"Flesh." [LS] "Rosy lilac, large and very double; form, compact. Growth, moderate. Uncertain." [P]

Euphémie
Vibert, 1847

"Delicate rose, of medium size, full." [P] "7 cm [ca. 2¾ in], full, delicate pink, mucronate." [M-L47/362] "Flower full, large; petals very pointed, giving a particular form to this rose; color, delicate pink." [S]

Gruss an Teplitz
We supply a corrected—and complicated!—parentage, thanks to Erich Unmuth. An unnamed seeding (parentage: 'Sir Joseph Paxton' [HB] × 'Fellemberg' [N]) was crossed with 'Papa Gontier' (T); the resulting seedling was crossed with 'Gloire des Rosomanes' (B), thus producing 'Gruss an Teplitz'!

J. B. M. Camm
We add the following to the entry in *The Old Rose Advisor*: "I [exhibitor Arthur Soames] was specially complimented ... by the Rev. J. B. M. Camm in the *Journal of Horticulture*, to which, under the pseudonym of 'Wyld Savage,' he contributed articles so long as Rose Shows were in progress." [NRS28/114]

[Leuchtfeuer] Plate 81
trans. "Beacon-Fire"
Türke/Kiese, 1909
From 'Gruss an Teplitz' (B) × 'Cramoisi Supérieur' (Ch).

"Flower bright red, large, full, sweetly scented. Growth vigorous, free." [GeH]

Lorna Doone
W. Paul, 1894

"The blossoms of this variety are magenta carmine, shaded with scarlet; they are large, globular, well formed, and very abundant. The bush is very vigorous for the sort." [JR18/4] "The flowers have a sweet perfume; they bloom just as well out in the open in the Fall. This is a desirable addition to the roses which bloom late ... The buds are very large and of good substance." [JR18/67]

Louise Odier
We add to the entry in *The Old Rose Advisor* our speculation that this rose was named after the wife or daughter of James Odier, nurseryman of Bellevue, near Paris, who was active at the time 'Louise Odier' was introduced. Monsieur Odier was indeed also a rose breeder, having bred and introduced the early (1849) Hybrid Tea 'Gigantesque'. He may well thus have been the actual breeder of 'Louise Odier', Margottin later purchasing full propagation rights from him.

Philémon Cochet
The attribution listed in *The Old Rose Advisor* should be augmented to specify "S. Cochet."

Souvenir d'un Frère
trans. "In Memory of a Brother"
Oger, 1850

"Purple-red and carmine." [S] "Medium-sized, full, deep red nuanced with crimson." [BJ58] "6–7 cm [ca. 2½ in], nearly full, very dark red mixed with crimson." [R&M62] "Vigorous plant; blossoms medium-sized, nearly full, deep violet red sometimes having a white line down the middle of several petals." [l'H53/202]

Victoire Fontaine
Fontaine, 1882
Seedling of 'Catherine Guillot' (B).

"Vigorous plant; flower medium-sized or large, very full, well formed; color rich, a beautiful bright satiny purple pink ... very floriferous. Flower very beautiful, opening perfectly." [JR6/164]

CHAPTER SIX: Hybrid Bourbons, Hybrid Chinas, and Hybrid Noisettes

Arthur Young
Portemer, 1863
Hybrid China

"Blossom large, full, very dark, velvety purple." [S]

Belle de Crécy
Roeser/Hardy, 1829
Hybrid China

We correct, update, and augment our entry in *The Old Rose Advisor*; note the vice versa in attribution. "Deep violet." [V4] "Blackish purple, full, medium-sized." [LF] "Medium-sized, very full, deep purple." [BJ53] "Purple-red, medium size, very full, very fragrant, tall." [Sn] "Shrub with upright, slender stems; prickles fairly numerous, dark brown, slightly hooked; leaves a very dark green, composed of elongate leaflets with very pronounced, irregular dentations; blossoms arranged in corymbs, numerous, medium-sized, full; petals violet, velvety and shaded, rolled at the center, symmetrically arranged in the other parts, irregularly notched at the tip. Hybrid China." [SAP29/266] "Raised by Monsieur Roeser, a fancier in Crécy, and published by Monsieur Hardy." [BJ30]

[Belle de Vernier]
Breeder unknown, pre-1827
Hybrid China

"Flowers rosy crimson, marbled with dark purplish slate, more slaty towards their circumference, of medium size, full; form, cupped. Habit, erect; growth, moderate." [P] The cultivars 'Belle de Vernier', 'Belle Violette', and 'De Vergnies' are locked in a struggle con-

[Belle de Vernier] *continued*

cerning possible synonymy, it being quite a horse race which will turn out to be the name with priority should they all indeed be the same rose; we include entries for them all here until the situation is resolved.

[Belle Violette]

De Vergnies, pre-1830

Hybrid China

"Beautiful bright violet." [S] "Medium-sized, full, violet." [R&M62] "Dark bluish violet, large, superb." [WRP] "Flowers violet, of medium size, full. Raised at Angers. Introduced in 1845." [P] P is incorrect in his latter information, as BJ30 lists it (in 1830) as "'Belle Violette' de Verny," and tells us that it is a seedling from the (royal) flower nursery at Sèvres, where presumably De Vergnies worked; it is not listed in the 1824 *Bon Jardinier. Cf.* 'Belle de Vernier' and 'De Vergnies'.

Bijou des Amateurs

trans. "Fanciers' Gem"

Breeder unknown, pre-1835

Hybrid China

"Pinkish red." [Ÿ] "Dark cerise, large." [S-V] "Medium-sized, full, crimson." [V8] "Blossom very large, full, sparkling red, violet at the petals' edges." [S] "Flowers crimson spotted, their circumference inclining to violet, of medium size, full." [P] Usually construed a Gallica, but known as a Hybrid China in its heyday.

Capitaine Sissolet

See above, in the Bourbon section, under 'Capitaine Sisolet'.

Cardinal de Richelieu

Adding to our information in *The Old Rose Advisor,* we read in Verrier (original source not specified) that the Dutch breeder Van Sian bred it and provided Laffay with it, unnamed.

Catherine Ghislaine

Emiliana, 1885?

Hybrid China

"Blossom small, semi-full; color, white, marbled with violet." [S] Often called a Damask.

Céline

Laffay, 1835

Hybrid Bourbon

We add to our information in *The Old Rose Advisor*: "Deep pink." [Ÿ] "A deep shaded blush, splendid." [WRP]

Charles Lawson

We add words about this important Hybrid Bourbon cultivar to our entry in *The Old Rose Advisor*: "Discovered amongst some Roses from the Continent, and its origin is a mystery." [NRS28/35]

[Comtesse de Coutard]

E. Noisette, 1829

Hybrid China

"A pretty pink." [S] "Very vigorous shrub, canes not very numerous; many thorns of very unequal sizes, some long and recurved, others very slender; leaves composed of five to seven leaflets which are elongate, glabrous, lightly dentate, slack; blossoms pink, very double, large, in a bouquet of five to seven, borne short peduncles." [SAP29/

308] "Raised by my brother Ét[ienne] Noisette." [No35] *Cf.* the Centifolia, 'Duchesse de Coutard'.

[Comtesse Molé]

Laffay, ca. 1845

Hybrid Bourbon

"Pure flesh color, superb." [WRP] "Flowers large and double; color fine clear flesh; habit robust." [MH45/Aug.Ad.3] "Very vigorous growth; canes strong, bright green, clothed with thorns that are flattened at the base; leaves glossy dark green, regularly dentate; blossom large, full, cupped; color, very fresh pink shaded bright grenadine." [S]

[De Vergnies]

De Vergnies, 1824

Hybrid China

"*Ovary* oval, glandulose, with a constricted neck. *Blossom* medium-sized, full, semi-globular, blackish violet. *Petals* wavy along the edge." [Pf] *Cf.* 'Belle de Vernier' and 'Belle Violette'.

[Deuil du Maréchal Mortier]

syn. 'Maréchal Mortier'; trans., "Mourning for Marshal Mortier"

Breeder unknown, pre-1841

Hybrid China

"Velvety maroon purple. Superb." [LF] "Flower large, full, cup-shaped; color, velvety purple crimson; base of petals, pure white; towards the end of the season, the coloration alters to purple marbled with white." [S] "Flowers crimson purple, very velvety, the base of the petals white, giving to the center of the flower a whitish appearance, the flowers sometimes open of a light vivid crimson, afterwards becoming marbled with purple, large and double; form, cupped. Habit, branching; growth, vigorous; shoots, very spinous." [P] *Cf.* 'Dumortier' (G).

Duc de Sussex

Laffay, pre-1841

Hybrid China

"Pale pink, center velvety ruby, full, large, flat, superb." [LF] "Large, full, plump, shaded pink." [BJ53] "Blossom large, full, globular; color, cream, nuanced pink." [S] "Yellowish white and pink, large, full, tall." [Sn] Often construed a Damask.

Duchesse de Montebello

Laffay, pre-1826

Hybrid Noisette

We augment the date and data found in *The Old Rose Advisor,* including words from the breeder and his most famous fellow breeder: "Delicate pink, full, flat, medium-sized, beautiful." [LF] "Medium-sized, full, pink." [V8] The Duchess of Montebello, wife of the ennobled soldier Maréchal Lannes.

Ekta

Hansen, 1927

Hybrid China

From *Rosa gallica* 'Grandiflora' × 'American Beauty' (HP).

"Of tall, upright habit; very hardy and vigorous. Flowers, single, pink; blooming freely throughout June and a few days in July. Since the flowers are single, this plant may not be a hybrid. However, the flowers are pink while the flowers of the *R. gallica* parent are dark crimson. Also, it blooms earlier than *R. gallica*. This plant sprouts freely. May be useful for screens, hedges, or as an ornamental shrub." [ARA27/226–227] "White, medium size, single to semi-double, moderate scent, tall." [Sn]

[Gloriette]
Vibert, 1836
Hybrid Noisette
"Small, flesh, full, tender." [R&M62] "Delicate flesh colour, small and full." [P] "Bush not very vigorous; canes feeble, nearly without thorns; color, pink-white, with a bright pink center." [S] *Cf.* the Centifolia and the Gallica of the same name.

Jenny
syn. 'Jenny Duval'
Duval, pre-1846
Hybrid China
"Flowers rosy blush." [P] "In color rather a deep rose, with flowers beautifully cupped." [WRP] "Flower medium-sized, full; color, bright red." [S] See also our remarks under 'Louis-Philippe' (HCh), below.

La Saumonée
trans. "The Salmony [One]"
Margottin fils, 1877
Hybrid China
"Vigorous growth; blossom large, full, cupped; beautiful salmony pink. Sometimes reblooms in the Fall; climbing." [S] Most likely of Hybrid Perpetual parentage, but reverting to Hybrid China characteristics, like 'Paul's Carmine Pillar' (HCh), below.

Le Météore
trans. "The Meteor"
Thierry, pre-1846
Hybrid China
"Blossom very large, full; color, carmine, nuanced purple." [S] "Flowers bright red, large and semi-double. Habit, branching; growth, vigorous. A very showy Rose; good for a pillar." [P] "From the same origin [as 'Chénédolé' (HCh [*in* The Old Rose Advisor])]; in color bright rosy red, very striking, and when blooming in large clusters on the plant, always much admired." [WRP]

[Louis-Philippe]
Miellez, pre-1835
Hybrid Bourbon
"Purple." [V4] "Crimson, center pinkish." [BJ40] "One of the older varieties, light reddish crimson." [WRP] "Bright pink, very large." [S-V] "Flowers purplish rose, large and very double; form, cupped. Habit, branching; growth, vigorous." [P] King Louis-Philippe, the "Citizen-King", lived 1773–1850. Considering this 'Louis-Philippe' alongside the China 'Louis-Philippe' (Guérin, 1834), we have an illustration of how some cultivars have names that "grow." The China will often be listed as 'Louis-Philippe d'Angers', not because King Louis-Philippe had anything in particular to do with Angers, but rather because it was bred there by Guérin and people wanted to differentiate it from this present 'Louis-Philippe' sent out by Miellez. In much the same way would something like 'Jenny' (HCh) grow into 'Jenny Duval'.

Malton
We add to the entry in *The Old Rose Advisor* a quotation attesting to its early importance in the breeding of Hybrid Perpetuals: "I [Mauget] have sown a lot of 'Malton', which has given me some good rebloomers pretty much of the same shade—sanguine purple—and which I am going to propagate." [SHP45/309]

(Mme. Caroline Testout × *R. gallica splendens*)
Breeder unknown, date uncertain
Hybrid China
From 'Mme. Caroline Testout' (HT) × *Rosa gallica* 'Splendens'.
"Pink, large, full, tall." [Sn]

Paul's Carmine Pillar
syn. "The Clematis-Flowered Rose"
G. Paul, 1895
Hybrid China
Seedling of 'Gloire de Margottin' (HP).
"Blossom large, beautiful shining carmine red." [JR32/171] "Bright carmine pink, very floriferous, single." [JR35/120] "Beautiful large single flowers, soft pale pink; a vigorous grower and entirely hardy." [C&Js99] "Variously classed as a hybrid of *R. gallica*, as a Multiflora, or as a Hybrid Tea. In some ways, it resembles all three. It is moderately vigorous, fairly hardy, blooms only once a season. The large, brilliant crimson flowers are single, borne in clusters, and very effective on a pillar." [GAS]

Chapter Seven: Hybrid Perpetuals

Alba Carnea
Touvais, 1867
"Plant not very vigorous; branches draggle along the ground; very delicate foliage; color of the rose slightly blushing—nearly white; form of the blossom, plump; [blossom] pretty strong and nearly full." [S] Some are confused by the name of this cultivar, and class it as an Alba.

Alba Mutabilis
E. Verdier, 1865
"Blossom well formed, pretty strong, quite full; color, delicate pink clouded with [deeper] pink." [S] Has been listed as a Moss.

Angèle Fontaine
Fontaine, 1877
"Vigorous bush; flower medium-sized or large, full; bright and delicate pink, good form." [JR1/12/12]

Arthur de Sansal
Despite the quote in *The Old Rose Advisor* about this being "a seedling of Monsieur Pierre Cochet's" [JR10/20], it is possible that this cultivar should only be attributed to Scipion Cochet (his son), or to the Cochet Bros.; research continues.

[Baron Chaurand]
Liabaud, 1869
Possibly a seedling of 'Monsieur Bonçenne' (HP).
"Growth very vigorous; canes upright, with few nodes; thorns straight, very strong at the base, slightly flattened; foliage very beautiful; bushy, complementing the blossoms very well, which latter are large, full, cupped, and irreproachably shaped; color, velvety scarlet; very deep grenadine in the center." [S]

[Bicolore Incomparable]

Touvais, 1861

"Medium-sized, full, black center, top of the petals delicate pink." [M-R65] Has been listed as a Gallica.

[Comte de Nanteuil]

Quétier, 1852

"Large, full, bright pink." [R&M62] "Vigorous growth; blossom large, full, globular; color, bright pink, petal edges deep crimson." [S] "Pale flesh, a most beautifully formed, cup-shaped rose, distinct, and of good free habit of growth." [JC] Has been listed as a Gallica.

[Comte Raimbaud]

Rolland/E. Verdier, 1867

"Flowers large, full, deep carminy cerise." [I'H68/49] "Flower large, semi-full; color, deep cerise." [S] A parent of 'Nokomis' (W).

[Comtesse Duchatel]

Laffay, 1842

"Blossom large, very full, cupped; color, purple pink." [S] "Medium-sized or large, bright carminy pink, cupped." [R&M62] "Flower large, double and cupped; petals finely imbricated, of a bright rose color. This superb variety remains a much longer time expanded than the 'Mme. Laffay' [HP]." [MH45/28]

Dr. Jamain

The mysterious word "flag" just under the heading of the entry in *The Old Rose Advisor* may be deleted.

Duc de Constantine   Plate 82

Soupert & Notting/Schmitt, 1857

"Bright lilac-y pink. —flower very large, full, cupped, fairly vigorous." [Cx] "Very vigorous growth; blossom satiny pink, large, *puriforme* [?], full." [S] "Large, full, bright pink, center lighter, vigorous." [R&M62] Evidently has some Arvensis or Multiflora heritage.

Duchess of Fife

The parentage given in *The Old Rose Advisor* should be only "sport" and not "seedling."

Duchesse de Bragance

Reference in *The Old Rose Advisor* to Plate 148 should be deleted, as the illustration is of the Tea of the same name.

Duhamel-Dumonçeau

The Old Rose Advisor's attribution should specify "Hugues Vilin." Also, this cultivar could be a Bourbon rather than an HP.

Empress of India

Adding to *The Old Rose Advisor*'s description, "A strong grower and a very free autumnal." [Cr76]

François Arago

Parentage may be added to the entry in *The Old Rose Advisor*: Seedling of 'Géant des Batailles' (HP).

(Frau Karl Druschki × Cristata)

Jacobs, ca. 1938

From 'Frau Karl Druschki' (HP) × 'Cristata' (M).

"White, large, full, medium to tall." [Sn]

Gaspard Monge

Moreau-Robert, 1874

"Flower large, full, globular; color, crimson and lilac." [S] Not to be confused with the light pink and lilac Centifolia.

Général Duc d'Aumale

Expanding *The Old Rose Advisor*'s entry, "Large, full, finely shaped flowers; superb, growth vigorous." [Cr76]

John Hopper

We can correct the entry in *The Old Rose Advisor*—the correct illustration is Plate 101, not Plate 10.

L'Étincelante

Adding to *The Old Rose Advisor*'s entry, "The most dazzling scarlet imaginable, flowers very large and nearly full, an abundant bloomer, and very effective, growth vigorous." [Cr76]

Louise Peyronny

Let us be less certain about the parentage, and change the line in *The Old Rose Advisor* to read, "Supposedly a seedling of 'La Reine' (HP)."

Merveille de Lyon

Again, a parentage change. The line in *The Old Rose Advisor* may be altered to read, "'Baronne Adolphe de Rothschild' (HP) × 'Safrano' (T)."

Mlle. Berthe Lévêque

The Old Rose Advisor's attribution and date should be corrected to "Céchet père/Lévêque, 1865."

Mlle. Élise Chabrier

The attribution in *The Old Rose Advisor* should be augmented to state, "Gautreau/S. Cochet, 1867," as I am informed by Philippe Gautreau, the breeder's very kind grand-nephew (responsible for informing me of several of these new facts and corrections)!

Mme. A. Labbley

syn. 'Mme. A. Labbey'

Breeder unknown, pre-1885

"Pink or lilac-y." [LS] "Blossom medium-sized, full; color, pink, shaded lilac." [S]

Mme. Charles Montigny

Corboeuf-Marsault, 1900

From 'Prince Camille de Rohan' (HP) × 'Éclair' (HP).

"Red, large, full, tall." [Sn] "Vigorous bush, well-branched; flower large, full, very well formed; bud conical; color, blackish red, nuanced velvet and flame; very fragrant and very floriferous." [JR24/165]

Mme. Ferdinand Jamin

Let us augment *The Old Rose Advisor*'s description: "Deep carmine-rose, colour of old 'William Jesse' [HB], a large globular flower with deep broad petals, highly scented, a good rose." [Cr76]

Mme. Prosper Laugier

Reference to Plate 125 should be added to the entry in *The Old Rose Advisor*.

Mme. Scipion Cochet

The attribution and date listed in *The Old Rose Advisor* should be corrected to state "Desmazures/S. Cochet, 1872."

[Mrs. Cripps]

Laffay, pre-1845

"Flower large and double: petals undulated and numerous, of a fine rose, the centre of a brighter shade." [MH45/28] "Blossom large, full; color, delicate pink, with a deep pink center." [S] Mrs. Cripps, probably wife of Thomas Cripps, English nurseryman of the time located in Tunbridge Wells, Kent. Has been listed as a Gallica.

Paula Clegg

Parentage listed in *The Old Rose Advisor* should be, "From 'Kaiserin Auguste Viktoria' (HT) × *Rosa foetida* 'Bicolor'."

[Perpétuelle de Neuilly]

A further idea of the appearance of this, one of the first Hybrid Perpetuals, and otherwise with an entry in *The Old Rose Advisor,* may be gained by reviewing our entry in this present volume on the Mossy Remontant 'Impératrice Eugénie'. It is interesting that this very old HP evidently continued to be grown and known at least some 20 years after introduction!

[Ponctué]

trans. "Spotted"

Laffay, pre-1845

"Flower medium size, double, flat, of a bright rose color, spotted with lilac and pure white." [MH45/28]

Reine d'Espagne

trans. "Queen of Spain"

Fontaine, 1861

"Blossom medium-sized, full; color, flame red." [S] Has been listed as a Gallica.

Souvenir de Béranger

The entry in *The Old Rose Advisor* should be fine-tuned to specify the breeder as François-René Bruant.

Souvenir de Mme. Hennecourt

The synonym listed in *The Old Rose Advisor* turns out to be the valid name of this cultivar: 'Souvenir de Mme. Hennecart'; and the attribution should be "Carré/S. Cochet, 1869."

Souvenir de Pierre Sionville

trans. "In Memory of Pierre Sionville"

J.-P. Boutigny, 1906

"Bright red." [Ÿ] "Blossom large, very full, cupped, beautiful bright pink; very vigorous growth, covered with beautiful green foliage like the Centifolia, from which it arose. The bloom is continuous. Very meritorious variety." [JR30/153] Has been listed as a Hybrid Tea.

Souvenir du Président Porcher

The Old Rose Advisor's attribution to Granger should specify "T. Granger." See also our note below correcting Appendix 7.

Thyra Hammerich

The attribution in *The Old Rose Advisor* should specify Hugues Vilin as the breeder.

CHAPTER EIGHT: Noisettes and Climbers

Belle Portugaise

Parentage should be 'Souvenir de Mme. Léonie Viennot' (N) × *R. gigantea.*

Blairii No 1

The "two parentages" given in *The Old Rose Advisor* are simply two halves of the same parentage: 'Parks' Yellow Tea-Scented China' (T) × 'Tuscany' (G).

[Dr. Kane]

Pentland, 1856

Noisette

"Vigorous; flowers large, sulphur yellow, held in much esteem in the South [of theUnited States]." [JR4/60] Something "held in much esteem in the South" could well turn up as an "unknown" somewhere there.

Fraser's Pink Musk

syns. 'Blush', 'Carné', 'Flesh-Coloured', 'Frazerii'

Fraser, ca. 1810

Noisette

"Small, semi-double, cupped, pale red." [JR5/133] "Not a pure Musk Rose, but a hybrid of the Noisette class, which was raised at Charleston, S.C., about the same time as the Champney[s] and Noisette Roses, and was carried thence to England by Mr. John Fraser; it is of a blush color, and quite fragrant; its flowers are semi-double, in large clusters, but it has now been cast aside." [WRP] "Rose with oval seed-buds and many-flowered panicles: footstalks prickly: leaflets oblong, pointed, finely sawed, and smooth: stem climbing: spines of the branches scattered and straight. This Rose, we believe, was first raised from seed in America, sent to France, and from thence to England. It is evidently a variety of the old Autumnal Rose, beginning in the summer season to unfold its delicate pink blossoms with an abundant succession till the month of November. [Andrews'] figure is from a large plant trained against an old barn in the Hammersmith Nursery, in 1824." [A] "It is true we have the 'Pink Musk Cluster', 'Red Musk Cluster', 'Frazerii', and some others, but … they are worthless." [Bu]

Jacques Amyot

The situation with 'Jacques Amyot' is very confused. We have documentation, as listed, of the DP 'Jacques Amyot' (see p. 24 of *The Old Rose Advisor*); but there are also persistent reports of a Noisette 'Jacques Amyot', with attribution "Varangot, 1850." If the two are to be separated, the DP is red-purple, and the N is deep rose or lilac-pink.

Lady Clonbrock

Smith of Daisy Hill, 1903

Noisette

We add to data given in *The Old Rose Advisor*. "A vigorous-growing Noisette, which produces immense trusses of pale rose-coloured flowers in summer and late autumn." [sDH/03] "Found in an old Irish garden." [sDH/29] Thus, 'Lady Clonbrock' should be regarded as a temporary "study name" for an older, as yet unidentified, Noisette. Information kindly supplied by Dr. E. Charles Nelson, formerly of Dublin, Ireland.

Madeleine Lemoine
Franceschi-Fenzi, date uncertain
Noisette
From *Rosa moschata* × *R. gigantea*.

Griffiths relays that the blossoms are cream-white, slightly semi-double, large, and fragrant.

Mlle. de Sombreuil Plate 83
We are happy to be able to add to the description in *The Old Rose Advisor* a plate contemporary with the original release of this cultivar of so much beauty and interest. See our Plate 83. Also, the parentage of 'Mlle. de Sombreuil' is 'Gigantesque' (Hardy/Sylvain-Péan, 1835; T).

Mme. Pierre Cochet
We correct *The Old Rose Advisor*'s reference: Plate 199, not 198.

Mock's Rosa Druschki
trans. "Mock's Pink '[Frau Karl] Druschki'"
Mock, ca. 1935
Climbing Hybrid Perpetual
We alas have no information on this cultivar, but record the name to spur on others to research.

Summer Snow, Climbing
Couteau, Jackson & Perkins, 1936
Climbing Polyantha
Seedling of 'Tausendschön' (Mult).
We correct our slip in *The Old Rose Advisor* as to parentage.

CHAPTER NINE: Polyanthas

Dopey
Evidently there was or is a Polyantha cultivar synonymously named 'Dopey', contrary to our impression in *The Old Rose Advisor*. Mon dieu!

Evaline
Prosser, 1920
From 'Orléans-Rose' (Pol) × 'Rayon d'Or' (Pern).

"Light pink, edged bright pink, small, full, petals rolled; in clusters, fragrance 6 [on a scale of 10], constant, growth 6 [on a scale of 10], bushy." [Jg] "Produces an abundance of small light pink flowers with rolled petals." [ARA21/148]

[Golden Fairy]
Bennett, 1889
"Flower bright fawn-yellow with lighter edges. Growth moderate." [GeH] "This Polyantha which was bred by the late Bennett certainly couldn't be compared with 'Gloire des Polyantha' [Pol] as a decorative plant, but the form is so perfect and the blossoms so full that it deserves to be much more often grown than it is at present. It's quite an exaggeration to say that this rose is golden: The open flower is pure white with a light touch of a cream tone at the nub of the petals. Sometimes, however, you can find several blossoms lightly tinted pale apricot. The bushy plant is more vigorous than the major part of varieties of this category." [JR22/145]

La Proserpine
Ketten, 1897
From 'Georges Schwartz' (Pol) × 'Duchesse Marie Salviati' (T).

"Peach, yellow center." [Ÿ] "Peach-colored Multiflora tinted yellow." [GAS] "Blossom peach red, center tinted orange chrome yellow, edge fading to blush white, medium-sized, fairly full, fragrant, long stem. Vigorous, heavy continuous bloom. Valuable for cutting." [JR21/135] Proserpine, alias Persephone, unwilling co-regent of Hades who returns seasonally to visit us.

Le Loiret
Turbat, 1920
"Flowers very brilliant pink, passing to tender salmon-rose, borne in clusters of 10 to 15 on very long stems. Foliage disease-resistant. Vigorous; bushy." [ARA21/161] "Flower brilliant rose with fire-red shading, changing to soft salmon-rose. Growth vigorous, branching; foliage deep glossy green." [GeH] Loiret, *département* of France in which is situate Turbat's city of Orléans.

Marguerite Rose
trans. "Pink Marguerite [Daisy]"
Robichon, 1904
"Growth vigorous, compact, big-wooded, foliage light green, blossom full, well formed, imbricated at the edges, color 'Hermosa' [B] pink, larger than this last, blooms in well-held clusters." [JR28/155] Though we do not know the parentage of this cultivar, there are indications that this is an early example of Floribunda-formula breeding (*i.e.,* Polyantha × Hybrid Tea).

[Mme. Alégatière]
Alégatière, 1888
From 'Jules Margottin' (HP) × "a Polyantha."
"Bright rose." [CA96] "Bright pink. —Blossom large, fragrant; floriferous; vigorous." [Cx] "Bush everblooming, canes upright; numerous thorns, fawn-green; foliage small, of 3–5 leaflets; flower of medium size, beautiful bright pink, full, and keeps an admirable form for a long time." [JR12/165]

Perle Angevin
trans. "Pearl of Anjou"
Délépine, 1920
From 'Jeanne d'Arc' (Pol) × 'Mrs. W. H. Cutbush' (Pol).
"Blush pink, small, full, open, long-lasting, in clusters, floriferous, constant, few thorns, growth 5 [on a scale of 10], upright." [Jg] "Bud small; flower small, open, double, lasting, pale rose, borne in cluster on strong stem. Foliage sufficient, medium size, rich green, disease-resistant. Few thorns. Moderate grower, upright, bushy; blooms profusely from June to October." [ARA22/150]

Rödhätte
trans. "Red-Hat" [or "Little Red Riding-Hood"])
Poulsen, 1911
From 'Mme. Norbert Levavasseur' (Pol) × 'Liberty' (HT) or 'Richmond' (HT).
"Flower clear cherry-red, fairly large, semi-double. Growth vigorous and free-flowering." [GeH] "Cherry-red; semi-double, large, Continuous bloomer. Foliage mildews in damp conditions. Rather small growth." [Th2] And so the Floribunda division gets underway!

CHAPTER TEN: Hybrid Teas

Chloris
Geschwind/Ketten, 1890

"Scarlet, large, very double, 1 m [ca. 3 ft]." [EU] "Blossom light purple crimson, very large, full, very fragrant. Bush of medium vigor and very floriferous. One of the biggest Hybrid Tea roses. Chloris, spouse of Zephyrus." [JR14/146–147] Further gossip on Chloris may be found in the entry on the Alba of that name.

[Clara Barton]
Van Fleet/Conard & Jones, 1898
From 'Cl. Clotilde Soupert' (Cl Pol) × 'American Beauty' (HP).

"After years of careful study and hybridizing the most beautiful varieties, we at last succeeded in obtaining this *grand new constant-blooming rose,* which has attracted so much attention, and proved of such remarkable beauty and value that we requested permission of Miss Clara Barton, President of the world's Red Cross Society, to give it her name … The color is a rare and exquisite shade of delicate amber pink, entirely different from any other rose with which we are acquainted. The flowers are quite large, three to three and one-half inches in diameter [ca. 7.75–9 cm], and double to the center; they are delightfully fragrant, and each one is set in a lovely rosette of leaves, completely encircling the flower and making it a lovely bouquet in itself. It is a most constant and abundant bloomer, continuously loaded with flowers during the whole growing season, and if taken indoors before cold weather, will bloom all winter as well. We think the plant will prove hardy with usual protection as far north as New York, unless in very exposed situations … It is an exquisite Rose in every way." [C&Js98]

[Clara Watson]
We add the following to *The Old Rose Advisor*'s description: "Bright salmon, center tinted rosy peach, free, fine form and habit." [HuD/04]

Danmark
Augmenting *The Old Rose Advisor,* "Very like 'La France' [B or HT], but stouter in growth and stiffer in petal." [HuD/04]

Ferdinand Batel
Adding to *The Old Rose Advisor,* "Fair size." [HuD/04]

Ferdinand Jamin
Again, adding to *The Old Rose Advisor,* "Fine form, long pointed bud; good." [HuD/04] Not to be confused with the HP 'Mme. Ferdinand Jamin'.

Gertrude
Continuing to expand on *The Old Rose Advisor*: Of parent 'Countess of Caledon,': "Large, full, and well formed, very free and good." [HuD] Of 'Gertrude': "A blush sport of 'Countess of Caledon' which it resembles in all save color." [HuD/04]

Jules Girodit
Buatois, 1899

"Light orange pink, large, full, medium height." [Sn]

La Favorite
Widow Schwartz, 1899
From 'Mme. Caroline Testout' (HT) × 'Reine Emma des Pays-Bas' (T).

"Blush white washed cream. —Flower fairly large, full, cupped; floriferous; vigorous." [Cx] "Pink, large, full, medium height." [Sn]

Mme. Georges Bénard
Bénard/Corboeuf-Marsault, 1899
Seedling of 'Grace Darling' (HT).

"Pink, yellow center, large, full, medium height." [Sn]

Appendix 7: Cultivars by Breeder or Introducer

Aside from making the corrections and additions as indicated by the above entries, an injustice to *gens* Granger must be corrected. Of roses attributed to Granger in *The Old Rose Advisor*, only the last, 'Souvenir du Président Porcher', should be attributed to Théophile Granger; the rest are due to the much more significant Louis-Xavier Granger. Also, the breeder Dr. J. Campbell Hall should be located as in Rowantree House, Monaghan, Ireland. Finally, there is some dubiety whether the breeder's name should be spelled "Varangot" or "Varengot"; research continues …

APPENDIX TWO

Lawrencianas

"The first of these interesting Roses was introduced from China in 1810. The varieties form pretty objects cultivated in pots, rarely exceeding a foot in height [ca. 3 dm]. Thousands of them are sold in our markets every year, and beautiful they are when covered with their tiny blossoms. In dry soils the Fairy Roses may be planted in masses, also as edgings for the beds in the Rosarium: for the latter purpose the hardiest kinds should be chosen. They require the same treatment as [Teas]." [P]

"Habitat: Île Maurice; China? Introduced into England in 1810; to Paris by Monsieur L. Noisette." [RG] "*Bush* from two inches [ca. 5 cm] to two feet [ca. 6 dm] in height. *Canes* numerous, upright, very slender, armed with prickles which are red, and either straight or hooked; *petioles* glandulose and prickly; *leaves* composed of three to five *leaflets* which are very small, oval, lanceolate, acute, glabrous, stiff, smooth, and glossy above, glaucous and often purplish beneath, the odd leaflet larger, finely and simply dentate; *stipules* lacy, subulate, ciliate with glands; peduncles glabrous or glandulose; *calyx tube* oval or pyriform, often glabrous and glaucous; *sepals* simple and glandulose, or glabrous and appendiculate; *flowers* very small, nearly scentless, with acuminate petals; from twenty to sixty *styles* which are free and ordinarily projecting. These roses, originating from the Île-Bourbon, where they were developed by the horticulturalist's art— if not taken from China—and only differ from *semperflorens* [*i.e.,* Chinas of the 'Slater's Crimson China' race] by their small stature." [MaCo]

Lawrencianas are the direct predecessors of today's typical Miniature Roses, and constitute a subrace of China Roses. Of these early cultivars, it appears that every last one is extinct! We list a handful that remained in commerce for some length of time. The perhaps anticipated 'Pompon de Paris' does not appear, as this name had no currency among horticulturists or rosarians during the period in which Lawrencianas were current; see 'Pompon' (Law), below.

[Alba]
syn. 'Blanc'; trans. "White"
Mauget, 1827
"Flowers white, delicate." [P] "Very small, full, white." [V8] "Flowers small, full, white, often with flesh-color." [MaCo] "Blossom very small, notable because of its rich bloom and fine scent; color, virginal white." [S]

[Blush]
syns. 'Ancien', 'Fairy'
Breeder unknown, pre-1846
"Pale pink." [P] "Flower small, nearly full, pink." [JR4/21] Probably synonymous with 'Pompon' (Law).

[Caprice des Dames]
trans. "Whimsy of the Ladies"
Miellez, pre-1831
"Purple." [S-V] "Deep pink." [V9] "Vivid rose." [P] "Flower small, flat; color, bright pink." [S] "Canes from five to six inches high [ca. 1.3–1.5 dm]; leaflets oval lanceolate, glaucous beneath, with sharp dentations; blossoms the size of those of the ordinary Lawrenciana, but a purplish red." [MaCo]

[De Chartres]
syn. 'Nain'; trans., "From Chartres"
Laffay, pre-1829
"Pale pink." [V9] "Very small, full, pink." [V8] "Blossom very small, double or very double; pink." [JR4/21] "Bush from two to five inches in height [ca. 5 cm to 1.25 dm] . . . leaflets one to two *lignes* across, by four to six long [ca. 3.175–6.35 mm × 1.27–1.90 cm or ca. ¹⁄₈–¹⁄₄ in × ¹⁄₂–³⁄₄ in]." [MaCo] "Yet smaller and bushier than ['Simple' (Law)]. *Leaves* the same size. *Ovary* ovoid, pyriform, glabrous. *Sepals* glabrous, terminating in a leaflet which is oblong, incised, and serrated. *Corolla* pink, very doubled, 6–9 *lignes* across [ca. 1.90–2.86 cm or ca. ³⁄₄–1 in]. *Petals* oblong or cuneiform, pointed, often shorter than the sepals. *Styles* 20–25, red, filiform." [Pf]

[Dieudonné]
syn. 'Violet'
Mauget, 1827
"Crimson purple." [V9] "Pink." [P] "Very small, full, purple." [V8] Not to be confused with Paillard's pre-1828 Hybrid China of the same name and color.

[Double]
syn. 'Multiflore'
Vibert, pre-1819
"Pink." [V9] "Flowers rose." [P] "Nuanced pink, full, flat, very small." [LF] "Very small, full, deep pink." [V8] "Flower very small, very full, plump, pink." [JR4/21] "Bush larger than that of ['De Chartres'], and forming a looser shrub; leaflets two to five *lignes* across [ca. 6.35 mm

to 1.59 cm or ca. $^1/_4–^1/_2$ in], by six to twelve in length [ca. 1.90 cm to 3.81 cm or ca. $^3/_4–1^1/_2$ in], tinted purple beneath in their youth; calyx-tube glabrous, short, gibbose; sepals simple or foliaceous; flowers full, very small, a purplish pink; styles, thirty to fifty, red, filiform." [MaCo]

[Duc de Chartres]
Breeder unknown, pre-1831
"Flowers pink." [P] Probably synonymous with 'De Chartres' (Law).

[Jenny]
syn. 'Rubra'
Breeder unknown, pre-1836
"Fiery purple." [V4] "Bright crimson." [P]

[La Desirée]
trans. "The Desired [One]"
Breeder unknown, pre-1848
"Flower very small, full; pink." [JR4/21] "Medium-sized, full; color, white." [S]

[La Gloire des Laurencias]
trans. "Glory of the Laurencias" [sic]
Miellez, pre-1829
"Crimson." [S-V] "Bright purple." [V9] "Dark crimson." [P] "The darkest of all." [BJ30] "Pale pink." [BJ40] "Small, full, crimson." [JR4/21] "Light red, full, flat, very small." [LF] "Very small, double; color, bright pink." [S] "Very small, full, bright purple." [V8]

[La Laponne]
syn. 'Petite Laponne'; trans., "The [Female] Lapplander" [slightly misspelled]
Breeder unknown, pre-1829
"Cerise." [V9] "Pink." [BJ40] "Violet-y red." [S-V] "Flower very small, full, pink." [JR4/21] "Violet-y pink, full, flat, very small." [LF] Could 'La Laponne' be a mishearing of 'La Liliputienne'? —but Laffay lists them both.

[La Liliputienne]
syn. 'Belle Liliputienne'; trans., "The [Female] Native of Lilliput"
Miellez, pre-1829
"Deep pink." [V9] "Light violet." [S-V] "Deep pink." [BJ40] "Flower very small; deep pink." [JR4/21] "Very small, full, flat, nuanced." [LF] "Bush very small; flowers extremely petite, full, a very bright pink." [MaCo, attributing this cultivar to Laffay]

[La Mouche]
trans. "The Fly"
Miellez, pre-1830
"Cerise." [V9] "Pink." [BJ40] "Flower very small, full; light red." [JR4/

21] "Pale pink, full, flat, very small." [LF] "Very small, full, pink-red." [V8] "Very small, full, flat; color, blood red." [S] "One of the smallest." [BJ30] "Canes no more than three or four inches tall [ca. 7.5 cm to 1 dm]; flowers don't exceed three or four lignes in size [ca. 9.53 mm to 1.27 cm or ca. 0.39–0.5 in], full, flat, well-formed, a flesh pink." [MaCo]

[Nigra]
trans. "Black"
Breeder unknown, pre-1835
"Very dark purple." [S-V] "Very dark crimson." [P]

[Pompon]
syns. 'Bijou', 'Commun', 'Nain', 'Pompon Bijou', 'Pumila'
Colville, ca. 1806
"Pink." [RG] "Pale rose." [P] "Pale pink." [V9] "Flower small, nearly full, light pink." [JR4/21] "Flesh, medium-sized, full, flat, beautiful." [LF] "Bush one to two feet high [ca. 3–6 dm]; leaflets the same size as those of ['Double' (Law)], never tinted purple; calyx-tube oval, glabrous; blossoms semi-double, light pink, twelve to twenty lignes across [ca. 3.81–6.35 cm or ca. $1^1/_2–2^1/_2$ in; surely these measurements are misstated?]." [MaCo] If, as its synonym tells us, this was the "common" form, it is perhaps what became known as 'Pompon de Paris'. Meanwhile, modernity appears to question whether the introducer's name has or has not an "e" at the end ("Colvill"?).

[Pourpre Brun]
trans. "Purple Brown"
Breeder unknown, pre-1844
"Purplish crimson." [P] "Very small, full, brown purple." [V8]

[Retour du Printemps]
trans. "Spring's Return"
Breeder unknown, pre-1835
"Bright pink." [S-V] "Flowers bright rose." [P] "Flower medium-sized, semi-double; color, bright pink." [S]

[Simple]
syns. 'Simple', 'Single Lawrence'
Noisette, 1827
"Bush thick, extraordinarily small. Leaflets a little purpled beneath in their youth, 3 lignes in breadth and 4–8 in length [breadth ca. 9.53 mm or ca. 0.39 in, and length ca. 1.27–2.54 cm or ca. 0.5–1 in]. Ovary ovoid or fusiform, ordinarily glabrous. Flower very small, pink, from 5–8 oblong petals, which are pointed." [Pf] "Bush three to six inches high [ca. 7.5 cm to 1.5 dm], making a tight shrub; leaflets very small, a little purplish in youth; calyx-tube fusiform, glabrous; flowers very small, pink, having five to eight petals." [MaCo]

APPENDIX THREE

Differentiating Similarities

While the groupings of old roses are fairly well defined, the names that have been given often vary from author to author. It cannot be assumed that one author's *Provence* is another author's *Provence*; indeed, though it is common nowadays to hear that *a Provence Rose is a Centifolia Rose,* such was not the case at all when these roses were in their heyday, as we are about to see. Researchers will run across a grouping called *Belgica* in the older works; *Belgica* can refer to *Damask,* or to *part of Damask,* or to *Agathe.* One must, in researching, set aside the name an author gives to a grouping, and attend only to the characteristics he lists in order to clarify that author's intentions.

Frequently, authors would split up, or lump together, groupings; the reader will note below that what we have classed as *Gallica* was broken down by Prévost fils into *Provence, Provins,* and *Gallica.* This is not to be scoffed at; anyone who could set 'Globe White Hip', 'Tuscany', and 'Rosa Mundi' cheek to jowl would find differences between them as compelling as those between 'Cramoisi Supérieur' (Ch) and 'Safrano' (T). Until someone has the time and resources to complete Prévost's project, however, of separating out all these cultivars into these three groupings (with a fourth one of their hybrids), we retain the more inclusive, "lumping," structure of classification for these subgroupings.

On the other hand, various of the contemporary savants, intellectuals, and adepts would scatter our *Agathe* cultivars among the Gallicas, Damasks, Centifolias, and Turbinatas; it could be debated whether their attitude could be considered "lumping" or very extreme "splitting" —labels lose their meaning with concepts as well as with roses! At any rate, in this particular case, it seems clear to us that the Agathes show a consistent set of characteristics that, though some of these characteristics be shared with one other grouping, and other characteristics with yet another, still the consistency of the association of this set in each individual Agathe cultivar marks them as a distinct—and exceedingly interesting—group.

We have mentioned above how our Gallica group may be split. The *Damask* group is similarly amorphous, depending upon each individual author what form it is to take. Some authors, as we see Prévost doing below, will split it into Damask, Portland, and Belgica. Others will add, as just mentioned, some of the Agathes, and/or farm out some Damasks to the Gallicas, the Centifolias, and even in some cases to the Albas; when what is perhaps the best-known Damask, 'Belle Couronnée' ('Celsiana'), first came out, a very respected periodical, the annual *Bon Jardinier,* indeed referred it to the Alba section.

What the reader must get out of all of this is that these groupings are to a great degree mere intellectual artificialities. Nature, with its ever-abundant cornucopia, was not set up to fulfill our concepts; quite the opposite, it strains to beggar our concepts, playfully mocks them, and laughs flirtatiously at our presumption.

At any rate, as an example of one noble attempt to come to terms with a knotty problem, we first present how Prévost fils tried to put it all together:

"*Provins Roses.* Nowadays, three species, their varieties, and the very numerous hybrids which some from them are confused under this name. These species are:

The Provence Rose, *Rosa Provincialis*
The Provins Rose, *Rosa Provinalis*
and   The French Rose, *Rosa Gallica.*

"The first, with which few botanists concern themselves, shows up in several catalogs with a certain number of varieties which really hardly belong to it. The two others, better known, have been described more frequently—pretty nearly such that what we are calling the Provins Rose has been entered under the name Provence Rose.

"These three sorts of roses, quite distinct each in its Type and proper varieties, have so much aptitude for cross-fertilization that the numerous more or less hybrid varieties that they have produced have effaced these differences. Thus it is that our *embarrassment of riches* has made us unite them under one common name. However, it seems to me that it would be useful to keep these three divisions, be it only to have that many sections in which to place the *pure* varieties. A fourth division would receive all the more or less hybrid varieties which, by that very fact, could not be put into any of the three first divisions. The flower color, the thorns on the canes, or any other visible characteristic—any of these could serve as a basis for some subdivisions ever-useful for facilitating research. Such is the plan I have sketched out for myself, and which I have begun to carry out. However, lacking the time necessary to accomplish this long and close scrutiny, I have only been able to classify a small number of *Provence Roses,* and one part of their hybrids ... Nevertheless, I am not giving up on this idea; it is something for the future.

"At this point, I will lay out for you the comparative characteristics of these three sorts of roses, and cite as examples some varieties of each. These characteristics, compared to those of the Centifolia, Belgica, Portland, and Damask . . . , will serve to distinguish those species from these with which I am concerned at the moment" [the following listing adapted from Pf]:

Shrub:
Provence: Tall.
Provins: Tall.
Gallica: Not very tall.

Canes:
Provence: Straight, slender, vertical or spreading.
Provins: Straight, slender, vertical, arching depending upon their length.
Gallica: Less slender, not as long as the two preceding sorts, and not taking on as vertical a direction as the Provins Rose.

Epidermis:
Provence: Rarely purplish, usually greenish.
Provins: Nearly always very purple, at least on one side of the cane.
Gallica: Ordinarily greenish, sometimes slightly purplish on one side.

Growth Buds:
Provence: Protrusive, forming and developing rapidly.
Provins: Hardly protruding at all, forming late.
Gallica: Not very protrusive, forming slightly late.

Thorns:
Provence: Very feeble, composed of not very numerous bristles, the smallest of which are glandulose; intermingled on the strongest canes only with several remote prickles which are short, large-based, acicular, and straight or bent.
Provins: Very feeble, composed of numerous straight bristles which are very fine, of which the smallest are glandulose; intermingled at the base of only the largest canes with several very remote, very slender, setiform prickles, straight or slightly inclined but without curvature, only distinct from the bristles due to their larger size.
Gallica: Feeble; composed of bristles, part of which are glandulose, and of prickles which are slender and straight or inclined; more numerous than in the two preceding sorts, and stronger than those of the Provins.

Leaves:
Provence: 7 leaflets, sometimes only 5.
Provins: 5 or 7 leaflets.
Gallica: 5 or 7 leaflets.

Petiole:
Provence: Villose and glandulose, unarmed or armed with several small prickles.
Provins: Villose, very glandulose, usually long and slender, unarmed or armed with several small, slender, straight prickles.
Gallica: Villose and glandulose, ordinarily armed with hooked or falcate thorns.

Stipules:
Provence: Usually simple, with fringed-glandulose edges, villose beneath.
Provins: Sub-orbicular, oval or elliptical, obtuse or pointed, sub-pubescent beneath.
Gallica: Ordinarily simple, with ciliate-glandulose edges, villose beneath.

Leaflets:
Provence: Oval-elliptical or oblong, obtuse, pointed or acute, villose or silky beneath.
Provins: Sub-orbicular, oval or elliptical, obtuse or pointed, sub-pubescent beneath.
Gallica: Oval or elliptical, obtuse or acute, sub-pubescent beneath.

Serration:
Provence: Usually simple, sharp, bristly.
Provins: Simple or double, bristly and glandulose.
Gallica: Usually simple, pointed, hardly deep at all, slightly bristly, rarely glandulose.

Peduncles:
Provence: Long, straight, hispid-glandulose, usually together in multifloral corymbs.
Provins: Long, straight, vertical, hispid-glandulose, in 2s to 5s, or in few-flowered corymbs.
Gallica: Short, straight, hispid-glandulose, in 2s to 5s, or in few-flowered corymbs.

Ovary:
Provence: Oblong, inflated around the middle, constricted at the neck, twice as high as wide, glandulose or glabrous at the base, always glabrous at the tip.
Provins: Oval-globular, much constricted at the neck, glandulose across the whole surface.
Gallica: Oval, slightly constricted at the neck, ordinarily glandulose across the whole surface; sometimes glabrous, particularly at the tip.

Sepals:
Provence: Glandulose, long, terminating in an appendage or linear-lanceolate leaflet, usually denticulate or incised. 3 or more are edged with numerous long appendages which are long, linear-lanceolate, and very acute; the lower, larger ones are themselves divided or pinnatifid.
Provins: Glandulose, long, terminating in a lanceolate leaflet, ordinarily incised or denticulate. 3 or more are edged with numerous appendages which are lanceolate or spatulate; the lower, larger ones are often divided.
Gallica: Glandulose, short, concave, terminating in a short, subulate point. 2 bear several linear subulate appendages on both sides, and a third on one side only.

Corolla:
Provence: Medium-sized or large, most usually the color is flesh or pink.
Provins: Small or medium-sized, rarely large; the predominating color is usually red, purple, or brown. The petals are often velvety.
Gallica: Small, medium, or large, rarely flesh-colored, most usually pink, red, or purple.

Fruit:
Provence: Oval or oblong.
Provins: Globular.
Gallica: Globular or rounded.

Pure Varieties:

Provence: 'Globe White Hip', 'Grande Sultane', '[La] Porcelaine', etc.
Provins: 'Aigle Brun', 'Uniflore', 'La Comtesse', etc.
Gallica: 'Versicolor', 'Pourpre de Tyr', 'Grand Mogol', etc.

Now let us review Prévost's differentiation of Centifolia, "Belgica," Portlandica, and Damascena:

"The botanists and horticulturists who have written upon the genus *Rosa* have not been entirely in accord about *Rosa Centifolia, Belgica, Portlandica,* and *Damascena.* Few recognize *Portlandica* as a species, and nearly all of them for the most part confuse the varieties of *Centifolia, Belgica,* and *Damask.* Indeed, those who admit these four types as distinct species nearly always attribute the varieties of one to another, and vice-versa … It seems to me that a careful scrutiny of the Types, and especially of the fairly numerous varieties which pertain to each of them, would as a matter of course give rise to some more complete descriptions, which would facilitate positive knowledge of these sorts as well as to a more exact classification of their varieties …" [Pf, from whom the following is adapted]

Canes:

Centifolia: Divergent, forming a diffuse, not very tall bush, with a greater or lesser number of leaves, which drop off early and easily.

Belgica: Slender, diffuse, vigorous, geniculate or flexuose, much armed, making a thick, strong bush, continuously growing, keeping its leaves for a long time.

Portlandica: Upright, much armed in most varieties, nearly thornless in several others; making a thick, tall bush, ornamented with its foliage a long time in the varieties which bloom only once or twice a year; weaker and soon losing its leaves in the perpetual varieties.

Damascena: Upright or flexuose, vertical or diffuse, ordinarily much armed, not much in several varieties; depending upon the variety, the form and dimensions of the bush will vary a great deal they lose their leaves at the usual time.

Leaves:

Centifolia: Distant and not very numerous; very subject to rust.
Belgica: Abundant and at an ordinary distance, slightly subject to rust.
Portlandica: Same as *Belgica.*
Damascena: Same as *Belgica,* but very little subject to rust.

Petiole:

Centifolia: Always glandulose, rarely villose, ordinarily unarmed.
Belgica: Villose and glandulose, ordinarily armed beneath with hooked prickles.
Portlandica: Same.
Damascena: Same.
Serration of the Leaflets:
Centifolia: Often double, nearly always glandulose.
Belgica: Ordinarily simple and villose, rarely glandulose.
Portlandica: Same.
Damascena: Same. Sometimes glandulose.

Peduncles:

Centifolia: Long, bestrewn or covered with pediculate glands, solitary or together in 2s to 5s, or in few-flowered corymbs which project from the surrounding foliage.

Belgica: Very long, bearing trichomes, armed with thorns beneath and above the bracts, glandulose above, in elegant multifloral corymbs which are open, and projecting from the surrounding foliage.

Portlandica: Short, simple or trichome-bearing, hispid-glandulose, often bristling with prickles beneath the bracts, crowded with fastigiate corymbs which are shorter than the surrounding foliage.

Damascena: Hispid-glandulose, or simply glandulose. Normally in open, multifloral corymbs, which project from the surrounding foliage.

Ovary:

Centifolia: Glandulose, oval, oblong or fusiform, rarely turbinate, always longer than wide and more or less constricted at the neck.

Belgica: Glandulose, narrow, very long, fusiform, constricted at the neck; at the base, always distinct from the tip of the peduncle.

Portlandica: Glandulose or glabrous. Very long (often as long as and sometimes longer than the peduncle), narrow, obconical, fusiform or claviform, always narrowing at the base, and grading insensibly into the thick top of the peduncle.

Damascena: Glandulose or glabrous, rarely hispid, short, turbinate or obconical, always widened at the neck and without obvious narrowing.

Sepals:

Centifolia: Foliaceous, longer than the bud, shorter than the petals.
Belgica: Foliaceous, longer than the bud, shorter than the petals.
Portlandica: Very foliaceous, longer than the bud, equaling or surpassing the length of the petals.
Damascena: Foliaceous or non-foliaceous, surpassing or only equaling the height of the bud.

Bud:

Centifolia: Conical.
Belgica: Same.
Portlandica: Same.
Damascena: Never round as in many Gallicas, but normally shorter than with the 3 preceding sorts.

Corolla:

Centifolia: Very fragrant.
Belgica: Same.
Portlandica: Same.
Damascena: Generally less fragrant.

Petals:

Centifolia: Concave, regularly arranged.
Belgica: Less regularly arranged.
Portlandica: Same.
Damascena: Same.

[Some Examples from Pf**]**

Centifolia: 'Oeillet', 'Bullata', 'Des Peintres', 'Unique'.
Belgica: 'York & Lancaster', 'La Félicité'.
Portlandica: 'Palmyre', 'Rose du Roi', 'Préval', 'Bifera', 'Le Prince de Galles'
Damascena: 'Argentée', 'Damas Violacé', 'Duc de Chartres', 'Henri IV', 'Triomphe de Lille' [*Prévost also includes here some cultivars that we have as Gallicas: 'Claire d'Olban', 'Mme. de Tressan'*].

De Pronville (1822) adds something to our deliberations:

"32. *Rosa damascena* . . . [syn.] *Rosa bifera* . . . Var. b, Portlandica. Found in Syria . . . Variety b comes from England. We think that this indeed is the rose which is the true *damascena,* and we persist in separating it from the following rose [*Belgica*], as Bosc and de Courset have done.

"33. *Rosa belgica* . . . Found in Belgium, in France . . . Of smaller size, branches less charged with prickles, oval fruits and long, divergent peduncles—these characteristics are sufficient to distinguish this rose from the preceding [de Pronville's *Rosa damascena, i.e.,* 'Bifera']; further, it isn't biferous at all as *damascena* is.

"34. *Rosa centifolia* . . . Found in the forests of the eastern part of the Caucasus . . .

"35. *Rosa provincialis* . . . Found in central France . . .

"36. *Rosa parvifolia* . . . Found in the mountains around Dijon . . . [*This is our 'Pompon de Bourgogne' (CP)*].

"37. *Rosa gallica* . . . Found in the hedges near Montauban . . . , in the scrub near Würtzburg . . ." [dP]

Thus, we see that, for de Pronville, the common Damask would be 'Bifera' (which Prévost classed not as *damascena* but as *Portlandica*), the Belgica would be (as in Prévost) the nonreblooming plants that we today regard as the "true" Damasks, the original Type of the Centifolia is a wild plant, and *provincialis* is to be distinguished from *centifolia*.

Let us go back yet further. Rössig, in 1799, differentiates *Rosa centifolia* from *R. provincialis* ("this blossom is single, and has large, light or deep [*hoch*] red petals" [OB]), saying, "It is not so closed-up as the Centifolia is, but is flatter" [OB]. *Rosa Belgica* is, for Rössig, not the once-blooming Damask Rose as Prévost and de Pronville would have it, but rather the 'Blush Belgic' rose—which is to say, the original Agathe, with Rössig having a separate category for *Rosa damascena*.

In 1793, Monsieur l'Abbé Rozier has, among others, *Rosa gallica, R. centifolia, R. damascena* ("grows to a height of 8 to 10 feet [ca. 2.6–3.3 m], with a prickly stem covered with a greenish bark . . . the blossoms, of a pale and tender red, are barely double; their scent is very agreeable; the fruits are long and smooth" [AbR]), *R. belgica* ("Its stems grow to a height of three feet [ca. 1 m], and are prickly . . . the very double flowers are light flesh, and have very little scent. This bush produces them in great quantity" [AbR]; this is clearly, as with Rössig, the 'Blush Belgic' Agathe), and "the Rose of Provins, *Rosa provincialis* . . . It is easy to distinguish this rose from all the others by the color of its scanty petals—a beautiful sparkling red, golden yellow at the heart. The blossom is single and large; its scent is strong and agreeable near Provins more than anywhere else. The bush grows many stems from its roots" [AbR].

Then, what sense are we to derive from all of this? We can only repeat what we stated above: One must, in researching, set aside the name an author gives to a grouping, and attend only to the characteristics he lists in order to clarify that author's intentions.

Let's Visit Some Nurseries!

It will be refreshing and give some idea of the horticultural flavor of our era if we join several writers in surveying the scene, or indeed paying calls upon some personalities, nurseries, and gardens. Put on your hat and coat; our carriage and driver are waiting . . .

1824

"I believe that nobody occupied themselves with propagating species and varieties of roses until about fifty years ago; at least, we haven't seen any catalogs of double roses before that which Miller published on the plants grown at the royal garden at Chelsea (England); and, among the collections of fanciers at the time (1764), that of Mr. Telson near London is noted. The nurserymen of Haarlem in Holland had raised from seedlings of *R. gallica* and several other sorts a very great number of varieties, as can be noted in the catalog of the Van-Eden [*sic*] Bros. It can be assumed that Holland and England had the first collections of double roses, with those bizarre and often ridiculous names with which the Dutch gardeners often baptized them.

"Messrs. Richard père & fils established at the Trianon a beautiful collection of roses, while that of Monsieur Dupont made them known in Paris. Monsieur Dumont de Courset had not neglected to bring together the species and varieties of this charming shrub in his botanical garden situated near Boulogne. Day by day, one could see the beautiful assembly [in France] of roses growing, making admirable the garden of the Luxembourg [Palace, in Paris], augmented by the seedlings of Monsieur Charpentier, and followed-up with yet more zeal by Monsieur Hardy, head of that wonderful establishment. Over about twenty-five years, the taste for roses has been brought to such a point that, casting our attention beyond the capital [Paris] and its environs, there is not one province, nor indeed one canton in France where a person couldn't find a collection worthy of holding the attention of the fancier. It would be impossible to give notes on all of them; I will content myself with mentioning the main rose collections, royal and private gardens, and the nurseries where they can be bought.

"1. The royal *Jardin des Plantes* in Paris: Messrs. Thouin, directors. Several foreign species can be found there, grown large, such as *R. bracteata*.

"2. The royal *Jardin du Luxembourg*: Monsieur Hardy, chief gardener. It brings together the most complete collection I know of, be it of botanical species, be it of cultivated varieties.

"3. The flower garden of the King at Sèvres, park of St.-Cloud: Monsieur Lécoffé [*sic*; should be "Écoffay"], gardener-in-chief. The collection prospered for a long time under Monsieur Lelieur of Ville-sur-Arce; it has brought together several varieties of roses still little known.

"4. Offshoot of the [above] flower garden, at the *porte Jaune* of the park of St.-Cloud: Monsieur Putaux, gardener-in-chief. The immense collection of roses that can be seen there is, I believe, a duplicate of other nurseries; but I have seen there some pretty rare varieties.

"5. The nursery of the Trianon: gardener-in-chief, Monsieur Gondouin. When the demonstration garden of trees and shrubs is fully established, I have no doubt that it will become one of the most interesting for the fancier as well as for the botanist: the hopes that I have suspend the regret I feel about the destruction of the old demonstration garden, so well directed by Monsieur Bosc. [J-A/ 577 would add (in 1826): 6. "Fontainebleau, Monsieur S[o]uchet." See below for more from J-A]

"As for private collections, we note that of the château of Malmaison, that Dupont put together, and which had been one of the most considerable; it took in some species and varieties that Mr. Kennedy had sent from England.

"Monsieur le Duc d'Orléans, horticulture fancier, has had a beautiful series of roses planted in his gardens at Neuilly-sur-Seine. Monsieur Jacques is the gardener-in-chief there. [*We cannot resist noting that the copy of* MonL/deP *that we are consulting, and from which we extract these present paragraphs, was a gift from Monsieur Jacques, just mentioned, to Pierre-Philémon Cochet (bearing marginalia by the latter); certainly the pleased eyes of Monsieur Jacques himself rested for at least a moment on the very printed words from which we translate here!*]. One can see equally lush collections at the properties of Messrs. Thory at Clamart, Redouté at Fleury, Lelieur, Lixon, and Deschiens at Versailles, and Dubourg at Vaucresson. It would be easy to mention many others—but let us pass on to the nurseries.

"I have no doubt that, whether considering botany or pleasure-gardens, there is no collection comparable to that of Monsieur Noisette; he has brought together species newly-discovered as well as old; and though Monsieur Noisette hasn't yet published a catalog of his plant treasures, a person can find at his place, as at others, everything seductive that the art of Gardening offers fanciers.

"Monsieur Boursault possesses in his magnificent collection at the *rue Blanche* some very rare roses which he grew before the big nurseries did.

"That of Monsieur Godefroy of Ville d'Avray, formed with care and arranged methodically, is also one of the most complete that I know of. But the most considerable, as far as kinds of seedlings go, is, without contradiction, that of Monsieur Vibert at Chennevières-sur-Marne. The kernel of this immense amassment is the old collection of Descemet's, at St.-Denis, which then passed—and quite properly so—for the most notable in the environs of Paris [*marginalia by Pierre-Philémon Cochet adds:* It is from Monsieur Descemet's place that my grandfather, Christophe Cochet, got his collection before the [anti-Napoléon allied] invasion of 1814]. The varieties that Monsieur Vibert has obtained from seed make an even greater number; and, each year, at bloom-time, no gardener or fancier neglects a visit to Chennevières, where the only embarrassment that they experience is an embarrassment of riches.

"The environs of Paris aren't the only ones where you find rose nurseries; the ones of Rouen are much talked about, and among the ones there, the collection of Monsieur Calvert. In the *départements* of Haut- and of Bas-Rhin, Baumann Frères grow a great number there. [*A note adds:* We have a catalog of roses grown at Dôle in Franche-Comté by Monsieur Lerouge, businessman and organist of that city [*this "catalog" is an unpublished manuscript of very great interest that we have been able to consult in the writing of* The Old Rose Adventurer]. Messrs. Miellez, gardeners located at Esquermes, near Lille, have one of the most beautiful collections I have seen.] And a person has not yet seen everything on the subject of roses until he visits the gardens of Ghent and Brussels, as well as that of Enghien, where Monsieur Parmentier has brought together such a large collection of diverse plants that it can be compared to that of Monsieur de Courset near Boulogne.

"But the big nurserymen who can get French fanciers some rare plants—those who betake themselves to England to seek out imports from the Cape [of Good Hope] and from New Holland—can find them in the vast collections of Messrs. Kennedy and Lee, and above all in the new firm of Mr. Loddiges, will find there as well some roses from India and China which have never been seen in France, and will also find some singular varieties such as the Mossy Pompon, of which the price is still too high for wide distribution. The catalog of roses from that nursery comes—it is said—to twelve hundred varieties." [MonL/deP]

1826

"The gardens of the Luxembourg, at Paris; of St.-Cloud, at Sèvres; of Fontainebleau, Trianon, etc., offer to the view of the fancier each year everything that rose-culture can offer of the most remarkable and complete.

"Monsieur Noisette, one of our most recommendable merchants, presents in his vast nurseries and greenhouses (which he devotes to growing ornamentals, and to economical and botanical instruction) the most happy resources for organizing, undertaking, or completing collections of the most choice items in this beautiful genus, as well as in all others. This year, he has obtained some very beautiful plants; and received from America, from his brother, his correspon-

dent, some roses the flowers of which are awaited with impatience…

"Monsieur Vibert, grower at Chennevières-sur-Marne, near Paris, also brings to commerce some very precious progress in this category, which he particularly specializes in. This year, he has made yet more notable gains with his very numerous seedlings. Further, he is known for neglecting neither effort nor sacrifice to care for his beautiful collection; and his business relations are equally conducted with all the precision desirable.

"Many other merchants, such as Messrs. Vilmorin, Grand-Didier (quai de la Mégisserie, at Paris), etc., etc. [*the instances of "etc." are characteristic of the writer, Pirolle*], also have some very beautiful collections, and take the greatest interest in satisfying all the needs of commerce.

"Many fanciers have, in Paris, collections which are smaller, but by that very fact more choice by their owners having to choose the most dainty among the 1,000 and more varieties which can be counted these days, aside from (you understand) some 'resemblers' or 'pretty nearlies', of which just one can console a person about not having the other 9 or 10.

"One notes in particular among these growers Monsieur le docteur Cartier, faubourg Poissonière, no. 99: his rich collection, supported by his very numerous seedlings, is as incomparable in beauty as it is fortunate in his success in keeping his patients healthy and free from Illness, which spends its time admiring the beauty of his roses, inhaling their perfume, and receiving the succor of the most celebrated children of the god of Epidaurus [*the figures of speech, sic; Vibert, in a controversy with the writer, Pirolle, a few years later, noted that Pirolle "does everything but write plain French." The "children of the god of Epidaurus" would be physicians; the god of Epidaurus was, of course, Aesculapios*].

"Messrs. Catel, distinguished composer and member of the Institute, rue Bleu; and Vandaël, one of our most able painters, at the des Feuillantines cul-de-sac in the faubourg St.-Jacques, no. 14, also posseses some of the most choice collections which can serve as models to those who would limit their choices to the most beautiful.

"Monsieur Hardy, in charge of the flower garden of the Luxembourg, and Monsieur le docteur Cartier, have also both made this year some progress in coloration and rare form…" [J-A/586–587]

1827

"We … limit ourselves, this year, to talking about the Luxembourg, Sèvres, St.-Cloud, and the Grand and Petit Trianon, the roses kept there, with the greatest *éclat*, the lustre they lend to the growing in these places, and the reputation of the estimable growers who are in charge of them. The seedlings add much each year in several of these establishments to the treasures they have already; and in others, they promise the most interesting and gratifying results for next year in the particular characteristics they display.

"At Versailles I saw Monsieur Deschiens' collection of roses. It brings together some rare and very precious varieties. Alongside some which are grown by a number of fanciers one finds some Chinas and Hybrid Chinas of premier merit; among these latter can be distinguished, in particular, the one they call *obscurité-bengale* [*sic*], of which the density and the deep purple brown of the petals gives the blossoms—which are of the largest size and very well formed—a merit and transcendent sparkle; a Provins, under the name of *Grand César,* which still sparkles very much beside the flowers of the same group known as *Ninon, Duc de Guiche,* etc.; a double white *Musk,* very well formed, having the merit, like the Chinas, of blooming all year long. Certainly, it will replace for the better the Musk which only blooms in the Fall.

"I visited the same day, at the pools of Versailles, the beautiful collection of Monsieur Lelieur, former manager of the royal gardens of Sèvres and St.-Cloud. As I was waiting there, I noted in this precious collection the most beautiful plants possible, under his able direction, and which still today ornament the gardens of that palace. Over the last several years, plants of particular interest to fanciers have been added, plants owing to his own breeding. I noted especially some beautiful Albas, which he called *Belle de Ségur, Belle Catel;* a Portland which he called *Douce Mélie,* with a well-formed, beautiful sweet pink flower of the second size, and which blooms twice [a year] like *Perpétuelle Lelieur,* also called *Rose du Roi.* Finally at the place of this able amateur [*i.e., non-commercial*] grower, to whose efforts we owe some very beautiful plants, I admired a number of very precious new Chinas—as many of them his own as from Monsieur Laffay, grower at Auteuil. Monsieur Lelieur find himself at the head of the fanciers who begin to renew their collection, admitting only roses called perpetual and biferous ...

"Tuesday, last June 21, we got together with several rose fanciers at Monsieur Grandidier's place. At exactly six in the morning, we began our excursion to the fanciers' and growers' places, those who, in the area of Paris, are most particularly known to us for being worthy of the interest of connoisseurs for the culture, beauty, and choiceness of their roses. Mme. Widow Desfossés, nurserywoman, on the St.-Marceau pavement, at Orléans, came to Paris to look at the roses and set her collection alongside those of the individuals and names of this capital [Paris], and was the first at the rendezvous, the charm of which was thereby augmented by the prize of her gracious friendliness. Before 7 a.m., we had already gotten to Auteuil and the grounds of Monsieur Laffay. This able grower showed us his precious collection, as robust as it is rich in all the beautiful varieties already known, as well as those which he recently raised in his fields of seedlings.

"Among these last, we particularly noticed his rose *Corvisart,* Hybrid China of the second size, carved into ranunculus form, and colored white, flesh, and blended pink. The blossom was proliferous; but, this year, I noted that this sport was common on many plants on which I never saw it before; another unnamed hybrid, a perfect flower of the second size, colored cerise and shaded deep violet, with pink-violet edges; an Agathe named *Irène* with flowers of the fourth size; a rose *Cels,* new, but very full; a Provence called *Incomparable d'Auteuil* of the fourth size, with a raggedy center, the edges shell-shaped, light pink standing out clearly from the bright crimson of the center; another Provence of the same size, bright pink spotted white; a Centifolia *Globuleuse* in the style and color of *Ninon* or *Belle de Storrs*; another Centifolia of the fourth size, in which the pinkish-violet color is much tigered grayish wine-lee. Several of us went back to look again at the true *Centfeuilles d'Auteuil,* pink lightly misted with violet, gray edges, flowers charming and of the fourth size.

"At the start of the first area beyond Auteuil, to which Monsieur Laffay conducted us, leaving the gardens of Monsieur Ternaux, we saw right away a Hybrid China with flowers of the second size, cut in the most elegant fashion; the petals poised in cups along the edge and gracefully imbricated at the center were a purple lightened with the finest and lightest violet red. This plant, which everyone likes, received the first as well as last votes of admiration from the party, which had many to bestow on this beautiful field of roses. The following, also Hybrid Chinas of the same flower size, also arrested its particular attention: *Nubienne,* beautiful pink violet of charming form; *Renoncule Rose,* which, in its tints and forms brought to the mind's eye the superb blossoms of the Provins *Belle Esquermoise* reduced by a third; *Miaulis,* pretty much the same style, size, and color; another choice still unnamed, but numbered 264, uniting the richness of the bright form of *Ninon de Lenclos* with flames of pink and violet, to very good effect ...

"We observed with no less interest the China roses raised last year by Monsieur Laffay ... They were also of notable beauty. I should tell you, however, that *Bigottini* did not sustain its reputation this year; I had already seen it at Versailles and Paris a few days before, and found, as here, nearly all its petals rolled lengthwise, to not very graceful effect; but, to tell all, some fanciers liked it, and were waiting for it to be added to the number of [available] varieties with perpetual bloom. They also think, grown on the north side, and in the open air, it would bloom much better.

"Among the new Chinas, we have noted the plant called *Denon*; leaves a very dark green, pretty flowers of the first size, of a fairly bright crimson; *Reine de Golconde,* a new Tea rose of a beautiful white, fairly double, a little smaller than the other, but very floriferous; *Isabelle d'Orléans,* charming blossoms of a very pure white ... The new China *Duc de Grammont* ... presents its first flowers which are so full that they don't open without the greatest difficulty; but this fault is redeemed by the later blossoms, in particular those of the Fall, which, less full, are of great beauty.

"We had already taken note in the same area of a Damask called *Caroline Mitchels,* leaflets of large size, corollas the same and very full, color blush white, very nice form ... Monsieur Laffay dedicated, in this area, two of his most beautiful roses to two fanciers of the party visiting. You may guess that Mme. Widow Desfossés is one who received this tribute, and that her name, as was so appropriate, was given to one of the brightest new roses. We had all noted a rose on which the purple bark, the sparse thorns, fairly strong all their length, the Indian foliage [?], and the charming small cupped blossoms, anemone-like—it could not escape our notice. This plant was known by Monsieur Hardy as an exact duplicate of the one already known to fanciers under the two names *Zerbine* and *Desbrosses.*

"In a third area, we also found some very beautiful plants, notably a Damask with small flesh blossoms lightly tinted lilac in the center, with the most graceful form: it was under no. 178; another, with flowers of the second size, semi-full, colored lilac, with large edges in a whitish halo, to grand effect. This last is also known already to duplicate quite exactly a new flower already known under the name *Gourgaud.*

"Finishing off our visit, we invited Monsieur Laffay to be so good as to bring us together again so that we could continue our explorations, which he accepted with an openness of heart which we will remember warmly.

"The we descended upon the flower-garden of Sèvres, where

Monsieur Écoffay, gardener-in-chief, very kindly let us see the beautiful collection of that establishment. We admired there the proud sparkle, ever worthy of its old reputation, the beautiful conquests made in the seedlings of the preceding years, and the rich hopes of the coming year. After this interesting review, we also requested that able and fortunate grower who received us with so much courtesy to bring his kindness to an acme by attending us for the quiet hour which we proposed to spend at St.-Cloud, as much to refresh ourselves as to talk over our observations, to which his own observations could do nothing but add a value much to the taste of all fanciers, ourselves included. He was so good as to put aside his work to comply with our wishes . . .

We regretted yet more . . . that Messrs. Cartier, Sommesson, etc., held back by business, were not able to realize their intention of joining us in our rounds; but they will not refuse us the precious tribute of their knowledge to give our work all the merit it could have in the interest of fanciers as well as those of good faith in commerce.

"After this stop, we met in this park of St.-Cloud to see there the works at the Porte-Jaune, where Monsieur Putaud, gardener-in-chief, took us along an allée of several hundred *toises* [*a toise is a linear measure of 6 1/2 ft*], bordered left and right with a line of roses which, much resembling the beautiful collection at Sèvres which we had visited a little before, nevertheless had no less claim to be examined with an interest which was well justified. We saw at the same time, on the long walls which enclosed the park on each side, some espaliers of which the good hold, the vigor, and the cut all were to the honor of Monsieur Putaud's talents.

"From the nurseries at Porte-Jaune we went right along to Vaucresson and Monsieur Dubourg's place, who also received us with the greatest urbanity. At his place, we found one of the richest collection of any fancier. Many plants, though familiar to us, seemed not one whit the less new to us, notably the Provins with a very brown tint, as well as those called *Proserpine, Tête* or *Bouche de Nègre*. We noted in particular a Hybrid China which just received the name *Duchesse de Reggio,* which we had known from a few days earlier as coming from that same fancier who sent it to us under the name *Belle de Vernier*; one of us knew it also under the name *Etrennes de Gossart,* indeed coming from the same source. Be that as it may, it is a rose of the second size, richly sculpted with the rarest nuances of the colors crimson, violet, and very rare and pronounced lapis-lazuli blue. It is a gem to collect! It is only to be regretted that, at its entry into the world, it already bears three different names. It came from Douai. Monsieur Dubourg retains for it the synonymy already given. We found in the rose *Merveille de l'Univers* (hybrid prov. [*sic*]), with flowers of the fourth size, a style and a coloration yet more perfect than that of *Ninon de Lenclos*; in his *Délicat* (prov.), a superb rose of the second size, with a bright cerise and violet heart, very well formed and with large lilac-blue edges of the rarest: this plant comes very close to that we know under the name of *la Cosaque*; and, finally, a number of other very precious roses from our collections.

"We had already noted several beautiful plants among the seedlings; particularly a Provins, flowers very full, of the fourth size, centre angularly folded, color bright purple on a thick velvet, outer petals in a large saucer with lilac-gray edges. We have named this beautiful plant rose *Dubourg*. Another Provins hybrid with flowers in a ranunculus form, cerise heart passing to violet brown, outer petals

formed into a cup, bordered carmine, of the second size, named rose *Lucile* in memory of the lady who, with Monsieur Dubourg, did us the honor of a gracious reception . . . A third Provins with very full and charming flowers, velvety violet brown, ranunculus form, first to second size, has received the name rose *Grandidier,* because the beautiful blossoms of this plant resembled also the memory of one of our most estimable traveling companions. With the same intentions, we also named rose *Lincell* a quarter-Provins with flowers of the second size, cupped into an anemone at the heart, petals quite velvety, brown lamé bordered flame.

"The sun told us that, despite ourselves, it was time to take leave of our amiable hosts, and to quit the beautiful gardens of Vaucresson to be off to Versailles, where Monsieur Barrier showed us, at the Grand Trianon, a very superb collection of choice and precious roses. We also found there, as elsewhere, some plants with several names, which, despite their novelty, contributed also to the confusion about which fanciers so properly complain. In the seedlings from the China, Monsieur Barrier had his rose *Nini*, quite double, second size, beautiful form, tea-scent, a rose which required a long-sustained effort to propagate. He then conducted us towards Monsieur Gondouin's, chief grower at the Petit Trianon. Though, this day, he would only look at roses, we were distracted from our intentions without realizing it by the rich and varied horticulture so admirably run and planned by Monsieur Gondouin. Still young, he already shows himself worthy of the reputation of his respectable uncle Monsieur Gondouin, one of our premier growers. Finally, returning to roses, we were forced to pass rapidly by the plants of his collection to turn our attention to his seedlings lest the waning day decline to allow us. We noted there two beautiful Centifolias of the large fourth size, of which the Sparkle waged a victorious battle against the shade of Night; a Damask with blossoms of the third size in which the beautiful forms and the flesh white shed light making them admirable in the midst of the darkness which surrounded them. There we terminated our observations so that we wouldn't abuse the kindness of Messrs. Barrier and Gondouin, it being time to foster their ease by giving them our heart-felt appreciation combined with the thoughtfulness of leave-taking . . .

"The following days, I revisited [in Paris] the collections of the Luxembourg, and of Monsieur Cartier at the faubourg Poissonière. There, not only the specimens in the collection, but also the seedlings, offer the richest objects of admiration to fanciers of the genus. It is to these sources and to that at Auteuil, at Monsieur Laffay's, that we would owe, in a few days, a completely new collection.

"Our roses were visited by Monsieur de Jessaint, prefect of La Marne, after the creation of the prefectures. We want to mention this illustrious fancier because, like Cincinnatus, Malesherbes, etc., he furnishes to his contemporaries an example of sparkle and influence in which the private virtues of the Friend of Men and of Plants adds to public virtues and the sageness of a judge. Everybody knows, and History will tell it, that Monsieur de Jessaint has risen over all our political tempests, fortunately for him and his administrants because he unites eminently his great wisdom and equitable goodwill which captivates every heart and conciliates every spirit.

"In 1821, we saw Monsieur de Jessaint's pleasure gardens at Châlons. We had, at the time, admired the good stewardship and the beautiful plants. The choice in these latter still shows the best taste of all . . .

"I had the opportunity to accompany this fancier to the flower garden of the Luxembourg. He saw there, with admiration, the beautiful collection of roses. Leaving, he demonstrated some regret at not having been able to congratulate Monsieur Hardy on the beauty and the gratifying culture of the rich collection at that establishment. Monsieur Hardy was, at that moment, at his home, but the modest Monsieur de Jessaint would not permit anyone to announce him for fear of putting out this estimable and able grower. He contented himself merely with saying a few obliging things to him.

"We then went to visit the beautiful collection of Monsieur Noisette. We found there, beside the roses that we knew—and which, as far as that goes, were nonetheless brilliant—several new and quite precious plants. Monsieur de Jessaint much admired, in particular, the new rose *Unique Panachée,* coloration and size the same as old, but better formed, and lined rose carmine on its snowy white. This rose, though non-remontant, will long be sought out by fanciers. We much noted no. 963, a violet pink Quatre-Saisons [*i.e.,* Damask Perpetual], beautiful in form and of the third size: it was presented as a remontant rose. Several beautiful new roses among the Chinas also flattered the knowing eye of Monsieur de Jessaint, which were quickly marked for his own collection. Monsieur Noisette counted among his new roses a Pimpinellifolia *Belle Laure,* but with double flowers, and another Pimpinellifolia with double blossoms of a beautiful violet. If these two plants had been blooming, we would still be there admiring them.

"Monsieur de Jessaint also counted off the growers and rose fanciers of his *département*; he found, at Vitry, being grown by them a snow-white rose in particular, of the second size, well formed, and with a red border, called *Admirable Bordée Rouge.* He bought it, and already he has given it to some fanciers. With the intention of adding a number of new flowers to his collection, he brought back from Holland last year two hundred roses, the names of which were unknown in our catalogs; and, when they bloomed, he didn't find more than fifteen new sorts, of which only three were not to be found in Paris, at least not in the collections which he had time to visit. As he has had the generosity to let me pass judgment on the same next year, this will be a scrutinizing to which I will bring to bear all my efforts, in the interest of synonymy.

"During the following days, I visited, with several Flemish fanciers, the collection of Monsieur Grandidier, so rich in the beautiful plants of France, England, and Holland. We much admired in particular the Île Bourbon Chinas [*i.e.,* the Bourbons]; colored a pink of the most seductive freshness and vividness, third size, flowers very beautiful, numerous, and very fecund; a Hybrid China called no. 15 with bright cerise blossoms of the second size, very well formed, superb; a Provins under the name rose *Professeur* with flowers of the second size, very well formed, petals waffly and nuanced with two very pronounced tints of pink ...

"Monsieur Sommesson, in his garden of Batignoles, near the Clichy gate, also showed us that year a vast field covered with own-root roses chosen from the élite of all the collections. It is not possible to present to fanciers anything more sumptuous or more stunning than a bed so rich and brilliant. It was necessary to take a good deal of time to admire it all and take down the details, which all accrued to the good taste and choice of this great fancier.

"Mme. Olry, at St.-Leu, valley of Montmorency, also offered our eyes a collection to mention for the richness and good management of the plants. This woman, who grows, grafts, and sows with as much success as grace, has raised a pure China with beautiful white roses of the second size, which should take its place in any new collection.

"Monsieur Toussaint la Prairie, at Pierrefitte, near St.-Denis, showed us a collection which he proposes to complete this Fall, with some roses which he got in Flanders. What we have seen gives us very great hopes. We have in the main noted among his seedlings several Hybrid Chinas of great merit, notably a rose of the fourth size in which the coloration of flesh and icy lilac couple admirably with the beauty of a rich form.

"Messrs. Jacquin Bros. have, this Spring, taken their whole beautiful collection of roses from the countryside to Paris: it is great food for the curiosity of Parisian fanciers. We already know that it offers great resources to the friends of these plants. We know as well that these estimable merchants know very well, as do the most recommendable of their brothers in the trade, the sources from which each of them can surely draw new plants and more from commerce in any case in which they need them.

"To bring this article to an end ..., Messrs. Hardy and Grandidier, who went visiting the collections of Rouen this year, report that Monsieur Lecomte of that city has raised a rose a very great size with the most elegant form, and of a beautiful lilac color. This beautiful plant is also as much to be known for its very large and much-serrated foliage. Presumably, it is a re-bloomer. It was so notably beautiful and precious that Monsieur Savoureux, gardener-florist at Rouen, rue de Grammont, no. 32, faubourg St.-Sévère, has a contract for exclusive rights to it and to putting it into commerce. It is probable that this plant, for a year or two, will hold to a price less moderate than that of other roses. Monsieur Savoureux will be the one to ask about it." [J-As/112–128]

"I still think that all these details about outings, compliments, and comings and goings are at least superfluous. The suavity of the people he writes about is well known; and, if their politeness is less ceremonious than that of the author, it is at least a little more sincere. Perhaps I can't appreciate manners, but these pompous curlicues seem to me to be out of place." [JPV]

1829

"*Messieurs,* the Rose has always been the Queen of Flowers ... Vilmorin *père,* Dupont, and Descemet were the first French adepts who devoted their talents to the classification and description of the characteristics of the genus *Rosa* ... In 1810, the time when breeding of some interest began to take place, Monsieur Descemet was the grower who brought together the greatest number of varieties; but in 1814 and 1815, the peaceful retreat of this able gardener was turned upside-down to such a point that he was obliged to leave commerce. Our honorable colleague, Monsieur Vibert, bought his roses, and created from it the firm about which you have charged me to report.

"Monsieur Vibert, for about twenty years, has confined himself to the culture of the Rose. Then, around the year 1812, he obtained some good results from seed; in the Summer of 1815, following the enemy's invasion, the collection of Monsieur Descemet was due to be sold and dispersed by the third of August. In those fateful days, aside from the fears about transplanting the bushes at that time of year, no one was thinking about matters relating to the pleasurable side of Life! Only Monsieur Vibert, moved by his taste, listened to his zeal alone, braving the promptings of experience and the heat of the Dog Days, and had the heart to acquire and save, by sheer effort, that precious collection, which counted up to two hundred and fifty species or varieties, and which encompassed ten thousand seedlings, of which have were three or four years old. These young seedling roses, transplanted into the garden of Monsieur Vibert, nearly all bloomed the following years, and gave more than a hundred pretty varieties which later were of consequence in the culture of this plant.

"Monsieur Vibert resided, twenty months ago, at Chennevières-sur-Marne, where he had put six *arpens* of ground to the cultivation of roses. Persecuted without relief by the white worm, which over two years devoured more than fifty thousand plants of every sort—many stock-plants and several varieties—he was forced to move his firm to St.-Denis, where he has devoted his time to discovering new varieties of roses, which are studied by him in a very orderly way with the most scrupulous assiduity. These seedlings are divided into beds one next to the other from their birth, and the observations this grower makes are kept in a daily journal which lists the name and class of the rose, as well as the day and year when the crop was planted. To escape the problems which the underground runners of roses can give, particular beds are devoted to varieties of the same species, that species to be studied. Each variety, particularly of the Provins, is separated off by another less runnery sort of another species. Some labels, placed with precision, make it easy to tell what's what when they bloom. It is from these beds that come every year those charming new varieties which are the delight of our country's fanciers, and which enrich the collections of foreigners.

"I cannot tell you, Gentlemen, how many species or varieties Monsieur Vibert has, be it in seedlings or anything else. This distinguished gardener does not know himself; but it can be told that he doesn't release to commerce any Rose until after having observed each individual for two or three years. Rigorous in his principles, he'll only allow as [new] varieties those which present some observable difference [from those that already exist]. He takes every precaution possible to avoid mistakes; and for the few on which he has doubts, he puts it into a special bed for the purpose of observing it again at next bloom. If, after that, it shows some constancy in these same distinct, new characteristics, he propagates it with confidence, and it goes into commerce. If it changes, he rejects it.

"His collection is divided into twenty-six classes, of which each has a special bed, marked and numbered. The *Centifolias,* for instance, are divided into *Centifolias Proper, Mossy Centifolias,* and *Hybrid Centifolias.* Of these latter, there are ten of his breeding which are widely distributed in commerce. After the Centifolias, the *Alba* class is one of those which gives our horticulturist the widest divergence from Nature, and in which he takes special interest. In 1810, in Dupont's time, only four varieties of Alba were known. In 1815, Descemet had no more than a dozen. In 1829, Monsieur Vibert grows more than sixty varieties, of which about twenty-five come from his own breeding.

"The *Provins* class, despite the changes taking place all over [*referring to the onset of the new hybrids involving Chinas and the like*], has nevertheless doubled; but the Roses which have for some years

been the object of special efforts among horticulturists are the *Chinas,* which Monsieur Vibert has made special efforts with, and which have given him yet more remarkable results; he counts these days three hundred varieties, and hopes to add to the number every year.

"This horticulturist has, each year, introduced to France, or discovered, several of those Roses that, by the uniqueness of their characteristics or the perfection of their qualities, are beyond the caprice of Taste and the evanescence of Today. In 1817, among the Perpetuals which are so stingily supplied by Nature, he found *Palmyre,* which then had no rivals. In 1824, in obtaining from the Noisettes, *Isabelle d'Orléans,* and several others from *Semperflorens major,* he proved that the industriousness of Man can do much with Nature, and that knowledgeable work is rarely without reward.

"In 1825, he introduced into France the *Yellow Tea,* the *Yellow Banksia,* the *Microphylla,* and several other varieties of no less interest. Forcing Nature to bring us new pleasures, he then raised, that same year, three varieties of *double Sempervirens,* of which we yet had only the single Type. Since then, we have added more than eight varieties of this charming climbing species in the colors white, blush, and pink. In 1828, he put into commerce *Centifolia cristata,* the distinctive characteristic of which reveals the origin of the Moss Roses.

"Among the *Noisettes,* I noted one under the name *Aimée Vibert* which rivals *Isabelle d'Orléans* and *Princesse d'Orange*; it opens more easily, and its color white is purer. Good father of his family, and worthy admirer of the qualities of his daughter, Monsieur Vibert has dedicated this Rose to Mlle. Vibert, who combines the grace of her age to the virtues of her gender.

"But Monsieur Vibert is not only an excellent horticulturist; he is also an enlightened writer. Aside from his work on the white worm, which merited your praise, his *Essais sur les Roses,* accorded the greatest favor by all those who are engaged in rose culture, attest to the zeal and profound knowledge of this horticulturist. It is in this work that he predicted the success that would come from the creation of a horticultural society in France, and in which he announced, two years before its formation, the services which it would render to the country, if were came under the patronage of the King and the members of his august family ...

"The catalogs of this horticulturist began to appear in 1816, and have continued every year without interruption. Some day, they will be consulted rewardingly by those who want to understand the success which we have obtained in this interesting field. His catalogs show that, in a dozen years, Monsieur Vibert has enriched commerce with more than three hundred and thirty beautiful varieties coming from his seed. That which will appear in 1830 will be one of the most notable of the series. More than seventy-five beautiful [new] varieties will take their places there. Fanciers will be charmed to know half this number will be put into commerce this autumn.

"One notes, this year, a *Hybrid China with pure white flowers,* and several Provence roses or Damasks also white and full; the blossoms of one of these varieties contain 140 to 150 petals: we don't have anything like it of the sort and color, except 'Boule de Neige'.

"In the gardens of Monsieur Vibert, there is something particular about the way things grow. This horticulturist, used to forcing Nature to new productions, seems to possess also the secret of making it do his bidding to give him quick results. This Spring, I saw a bed of roses, sown in the open ground fifteen months ago, two-thirds of which were in bloom and already with several varieties worthy of attention. Their canes were at the time 3 feet long [ca. 1 m], and had many secondary branches. Such rapid growth with a rose from seed is completely new to French horticulture. Backed by a terrain rendered cooperative by his efforts, and served by abundant water, propagation, whenever the situation demands, goes forward with astonishing rapidity. Nobody knows better than Monsieur Vibert how to budget time and opportunity with nursery operations. Everything is long foreseen, sometimes indeed months in advance. Mastering the flow of the sap, he makes it go dormant, or halt, or speed up nearly at will. Thoroughgoing experience allows him to determine in a quite precise way the time necessary for such and such an operation, if accidents don't come along to foil the calculations of his forethought.

"Despite the many duties which claim every day of the nursery business, Monsieur Vibert has not neglected to make them agreeable to the eye. More than two thousand five hundred beautiful grafted or own-root specimens, placed tastefully in borders, represent nearly every one of the most beautiful species or varieties grown. These specimens are not meant for commerce; they serve to decorate the garden and are a means of demonstrating how each does when it blooms. An intelligent gardener, versed in this culture, is given the responsibility of imparting all the information one could desire to anyone who asks for it, without any obligation. Still unique in its genre as a nursery devoted to one plant, this firm has every right to not only the confidence but also the admiration of fanciers and others, and the many visits which make his nursery their goal show that people know its director gives value. Forced to pay considerable amounts to take care of his nursery, Monsieur Vibert only grows notable Roses, especially those which flatter the taste of fanciers, without however neglecting those destined to give seed, be it for the decoration of country gardens, be it for botanical study. Every year, he weeds out a certain number of common varieties, particularly among the Provinses, varieties which recede in value as their seedlings advance.

"Monsieur Vibert is one of those enlightened men who have contributed the most to extend the taste for gardening and for ornamental plants; his wide knowledge and his merited success have borne his reputation beyond our borders. In private life, a member of the Council, having a claim to a Medal of Encouragement, I propose to you, *Messieurs,* that this estimable grower be given a proof of our interest by ordaining the insertion of this report in our *Annales.*" [SHP29/145–152]

1836

"Messieurs, at our meeting of June 15 last, you named a Commission composed of the undersigned to visit the nurseries of our *confrère* Monsieur Vibert, at Longjumeau (Seine-et-Oise), and to give you a report on it. We herewith fulfill the second of these duties.

"It is primarily as a grower and seller of Roses that Monsieur Vibert is known in Horticulture, in plant commerce, and among the fanciers. At first a fancier himself, he soon became an expert at Rose culture, in how to develop new and more beautiful varieties, in the appreciation of their merits, and in the choice of the best procedures to maintain them …

"You well know, gentlemen, that Monsieur Vibert, in leaving Chennevières to avoid the white worms, had looked into the matter to find out if there was any problem with them at the grounds he chose at St.-Denis. The response being made that none had ever been seen there, he re-established there with confidence. In the event, he didn't see any during the first years; then there were a few, then a greater number, but never enough to cause a lot of concern. Were it demonstrated that it was Monsieur Vibert's Roses which brought the white worms to this ground, Science would respond that the cockchafer knows that the roots of roses are good nourishment for its larvae, and so this insect, which hadn't had the habit of laying its eggs in this district, did so when it found Roses there. We won't go on, gentlemen, about the nurseries of Monsieur Vibert at St.-Denis, because then it would make a report; we will only tell you that, after seven years there, Monsieur Vibert moved his firm to Longjumeau, in January 1835. It is for there that last June the Commission charged us with rendering a report, which charge we will have the honor of fulfilling.

"The garden of Monsieur Vibert is 3 *arpens* in extent; it forms a long rectangle arranged north-south, a little sloping on the north side, and ending on that side at the Yvette River, which flows east, never overflowing, never dwindling, rather like a lock placed there for the good of the community. The three other sides are bordered by espaliered walls. The most elevated portion of the ground is a heavy yellowish soil lying on a clayey bed which affects the absorption of the rainwater, and forces it to flow, in part, into a large reservoir that Monsieur Vibert has constructed to receive it; the lower part is a black earth, lighter, which previously part of the meadow across which the river flows. These two sorts of ground are both excellent for growing all kinds of plants. Last of all, all the ground is regularly planted and forms an ornamental garden at the same time as being a nursery.

"The Commission knowing that Monsieur Vibert only planted this as recently as January 1836, it marveled at the size, vigor, and neatness of all the plants that it contains in the face of the extreme dryness of 1835 and 1836. This wonderful growth is due to the good terrain which Monsieur Vibert knew how to choose, and to the efforts which he has put into his planting, and which he gives to all his nurseries.

"Though different catalogs bring the number of Roses to more than two thousand, Monsieur Vibert is too good a judge to take in all of them. His demonstration garden only contains about 1,200; these are the best of both the old and the new—those which good taste will always choose. As merchant and fancier, Monsieur Vibert takes upon himself to procure novelties which come from sources other than himself; but he allows them into his demonstration garden only after having verified their merit; and if they don't subsequently show marked quality, he rejects them and doesn't introduce them into his inventory, high though the price be that he paid for them. Transitory fashion exercises its powers among Roses just as it does elsewhere. A person longs for a Rose today that he would turn his nose up at tomorrow. The prudent businessman knows what's what in this regard, and is very wary of propagating a lot of something that will only have a short vogue. In this, Monsieur Vibert is a paragon of judgment, prudence, and good faith.

"You will recall, gentlemen, the warm and sparkling words of our General Secretary, Monsieur Soulange-Bodin, in which he set out before you the rapidity, dexterity, and success with which French gardeners propagate foreign plants in their firms. At that time, this astonishing rapidity, this wonderful success—they weren't known in

Rose propagation. Today, we march forward with no less success: the hot-house, the lath-house, the *cloche* all contribute to speeding up the propagation of Roses as they do that of Camellias, to satisfy the impatience of the fancier and the interest of the grower. If Monsieur Vibert receives a [growth] bud of a new and meritorious Rose in the Spring, by Fall he can supply 200 or 300 plants of it . . . [*The report goes on to discuss Monsieur Vibert's serious work and indeed Homeric efforts with fruit trees and grape (raisin) vines.*]

"Our Commission has the honor of proposing to the Council:

"First, that it address its congratulations to Monsieur Vibert, our colleague, on the perfection of his nurseries;

"Second, that Monsieur Vibert be requested to look well after his seedling Pears and Apples, sown in 1829, until the Society has a chance to examine and report on them;

"Third, that the present Report be conducted to the Editorial Committee.

"[Signed:] Jacques, Jacquin aîné, Quiclet, Berlèse, Boussière, and Poiteau *reporter.*" [SHP36/139–149]

1844

"The following day [in September, 1844] we visited the Gardens of the Luxembourg, so long famous for its collection of grapes. It is now under the superintendence of Monsieur Hardy, well known for his success in producing new varieties of roses from seed. The Gardens are several acres in extent, and are laid out in the geometrical style. In front of the palace there is a large piece of water, surrounded with terraces, terminating at their extremities by stone balustrades, decorated with two groups in marble, representing wreaths, and four small figures supporting vases, in which are planted pelargoniums and other flowers. The sloping banks which form the terraces, were planted with a profusion of flowers, particularly of German asters, and ornamented with statues. On the borders of the walks were also placed the large orange trees, which are kept in opaque roofed houses in winter. At the opposite end of this sheet of water, steps from the palace ascend to the broad central avenue, which terminates in an observatory. To the right and left are groves of trees, affording umbrageous retreats to the immense concourse of people who throng the gardens from daylight to dark.

"The nursery attached to the gardens is situated to the right of the palace, beyond the plantations of wood, and is six or eight acres in extent. It is laid out in four squares, with a slip or border on the outside. One of these squares was wholly devoted to fruit trees; one of them to roses; a third to the Alpine strawberry and the Dahlia; and the fourth to miscellaneous objects. The collection of grapes is cultivated around the several squares on espalier rail or trellises erected for that purpose. We called on Monsieur Hardy, previous to our visit to the garden, but he was absent . . .

"In the quarter devoted to roses, we saw many of the perpetuals and tender kinds in flower; they are mostly cultivated as standards, which appear to do finely in the climate of Paris, attaining to a large size. Monsieur Hardy, the director, has been a successful rose-grower as the many varieties in the catalogues, bearing the name of his family, attest; he has a great number of seedlings planted . . ." [MH45/245–246]

"Proceeding along the Boulevard de l'Hôpital, one of the broadest in the city [Paris], and passing out at the Barrière d'Italie, we found the garden of Monsieur [Victor] Verdier, celebrated for its fine collection of roses. The grounds are not extensive, containing two or three acres, and Monsieur Verdier devotes a particular attention to the rose, which occupied a greater portion of the premises. Two small greenhouses, built low, as a greater part of such structures are, around Paris, contained a variety of new plants.

"The roses are nearly all cultivated as standards or half-standards, and set out in rows two or three feet apart [ca. 6 dm to 1 m]. As a greater portion of them were Bourbons and hybrid perpetuals, which are now taking the place of other roses, from their perpetual blooming, the garden was almost as gay with flowers, as it is in June [*the visit took place in September*]. The first variety which we particularly noticed, was a large specimen of Tea 'Safrano', two feet or more high [ca. 6 dm +], in the open border, and covered with an abundance of its beautiful saffron-colored flowers; when in bud, they are darker and more beautiful than when fully expanded . . . Among the miscellaneous plants, we found a fine collection of phloxes, comprising nearly fifty varieties . . . Monsieur Verdier's collection of Paeonies, both shrubby and herbaceous, is extensive . . . Monsieur Modeste Guérin was one of the first to produce [peony] seedlings in any great quantity, but he has had great success in raising several very beautiful varieties. The new phloxes and other more rare herbaceous plants are all cultivated in small pots, and plunged in the ground under a north fence, wall, or hedge. This method allows their sale at all seasons of the year, and with the certainty of living . . .

"Monsieur Verdier is very successful in his management of the rose, and his plants were in most excellent order. He has formed a plantation of fifteen hundred varieties, selected from above twenty-five hundred cultivated by him since 1827. From such a plantation selections may be made when the plants are in flower. Monsieur has produced several fine varieties from seed, and has also introduced many others, raised by his uncle, Monsieur Jacques, gardener to the king, Neuilly. His whole collection gave us much gratification." [MH45/247–249]

"Meudon is about six miles [ca. 9.6 km] from Paris, on the route of the Versailles railroad, from the southern bank of the Seine. Mr. Laffay's garden has been recently established here, on an elevated and airy spot, with a deep, rich, heavy loam, in which roses thrive admirably, and form vigorous plants. The weather had been cool, with a heavy rain the day previous, and few roses were in bloom. Monsieur Laffay was not at home, and his aged father could tell us nothing in relation to the private marks and numbers which were attached to most of the varieties we saw in flower. The distance and the time occupied in accomplishing a visit, rendering it quite impossible for us to call again, we noted such as we saw interesting, not knowing whether some of them were new seedlings, or older kinds. The splendid 'La Reine' [HP], no one could mistake, who had read a description of it; and the very first bloom we saw assured us it could be no other flower: we were right in our conjecture. At least twenty different plants were in bloom, producing their immensely large, highly fragrant, and superbly cupped flowers, very freely . . .

"Monsieur Laffay has had great success in raising roses from seed; his experiments have been mostly confined to the hybrid perpetual, and he has produced several of much merit . . . He informed us, that he had more than six thousand seedlings then growing, many of which will bloom the present year, when more new and fine varieties may be expected. Monsieur Laffay cultivates mainly his own seedlings, and finds a large commerce in the disposal of the plants. Hundreds of the 'La Reine' have been sent to England during the last year.

"Besides the cultivation of roses, Monsieur Laffay gives considerable attention to fruit, particularly pears, and the growth of new and superior kinds; on the borders of the walks, dwarf trees were planted, trained in the pyramidal form, and some of them were in bearing. His principal object, however, is the cultivation of seedling roses." [MH45/249–250]

"*Sept. 17th.* —Fromont is about twenty miles [ca. 32 km] from Paris, and is easy of access by the Orléans and Corbeil Railroad, one of the stations being only a few rods from the entrance to the grounds. The whole extent of Monsieur Soulange-Bodin's place is upwards of sixty-four acres, beautifully situated on a gentle declivity, sloping to the Seine. It was first commenced upwards of thirty years ago, and was intended as a school, where every department of gardening could be thoroughly learnt. For a long time, this was carried into effect, and Monsieur Soulange-Bodin's place was well known as the *Institute of Horticulture at Fromont.* In connection with it a journal was published, called the *Annales Horticole de Fromont,* edited by the proprietor, and containing all the lectures delivered by the professors in the several departments of the establishment. Five volumes were completed, when its publication was stopped, and it forms one of the most valuable works to the amateur.

"Fromont is laid out in the English style, and the taste displayed is highly creditable to the proprietor. Monsieur Soulange-Bodin, to use the language of Mr. Loudon, is at one a 'skilful cultivator, a marchand grenatier (seedsman), a scholar, and an accomplished gentleman.' In his younger days he was attached to the army, and travelled all over Europe; he afterwards had the charge of the gardens of the Empress Josephine at Malmaison; and about 1814, retired to his present situation, and commenced the formation of the nursery and Institute, intending to combine science with picturesque beauty. Since its establishment the proprietor informed us he had laid out *two million francs,* in improvements upon the grounds.

"The entrance is through a long and winding avenue of evergreens and forest trees, disposed in picturesque groups, admitting of no view, until it opens upon a broad and beautiful lawn, sloping away from the Chateau, and backed by plantations of lofty trees. Formerly the nursery contained all kinds of trees, both hardy and tender, and a general collection of every thing wanted in such an establishment; but the care attendant upon so extensive a place was to much for the health of Monsieur Soulange-Bodin, now upwards of seventy years of age . . .

"The plants were now all laid out in the open air in various parts of the grounds, disposed in places made for the purpose, where they are sheltered from high winds and the rays of the sun. These places are formed of hedges of the beech, or arbor vitae running east and west, planted about seven feet apart [ca. 2.3 m], so that the sun does not shine upon the plants only at morning and night . . . The only place where we noticed hedges to any thing like the same extent as at Fromont, was in the nursery of Mr. Rivers, of Sawbridgeworth [in England] . . . who from his frequent visits to the Continent, had probably seen the good effects of the plan, and, throwing aside all prejudice, adopted it himself.

"The inspection of the propagating department afforded us great gratification. The principal part of the houses are in a walled enclosure of about half an acre, sloping to the south, and the back part of most of them was sunk in the earth, about two feet [ca. 6 dm], and an additional embankment was made by the earth which was thrown out to form the one in the rear, there being several of them one before the other. In this way they are protected from the cold with the exception of the roof, and being narrow, many of them have shutters. A single broad shelf, with a walk on the back, is all the interior fitting of several of the ranges, these being adapted for holding young stock, very few large plants being allowed to accumulate and occupy room.

"The houses devoted exclusively to propagation face the north, running in a transverse direction of the others, occupying the whole of the west wall, and are of similar construction, as regards size, but they are built with a central bed for holding bark or leaves, or some other heating material; the hot water pipes are in front, and a walk in the rear. No where did we ever see so much neatness and method in a propagating department; three rows of large bell glasses [*cloches*], fifteen inches broad and fifteen high [ca. 3.75 dm], were arranged lengthwise of the bed, each of them containing ten or twelve plants, which had been grafted in August, and which were now nearly ready for removal. All the brick and wood work was white-washed, the surface of the beds raked level, and the walks perfectly clean. Instead of being made a place of confusion, as it too often is, much to the injury of the plants, the propagating department was a perfect model of neatness. No nursery establishment that we visited presented so much system, and we only wish that our own cultivators might have the opportunity to inspect a place so worthy of imitation.

"Our time being limited, our walk through the grounds was rather hasty. A great number of fine trees and shrubs are planted out in groups, and on the borders of the walks, and a small spot of ground is entirely devoted to the magnolia, to which splendid group the proprietor has given much attention, and raised one fine variety, M. *Soulangeàna.* We saw upwards of twenty species and varieties, among them some very fine specimens. Half shady aspects are selected, and heath soil mixed with the loam, which is naturally too stiff for a majority of the kinds. In this way, all the American plants are grown to a large size, and in great beauty.

"We left no place with more regret than Fromont. The hearty welcome with which we were received, the kindness with which we were entertained, united with our respect for the skill and intelligence of the gentlemanly proprietor, made us only wish for another day to devote to an inspection of a place so full of interest." [MH45/283–286]

"The kitchen gardens at Versailles occupy twelve acres, and are mostly remarkable for the number of the pear trees, which are planted on the borders of all the walks, trained *en pyramid* [*sic*], and produce good crops. The pineapple is cultivated to a great extent, and there is one house devoted to the banana. The whole is well kept, and we can only again repeat our regret at being deprived on a full inspection of the whole grounds [by a sudden drenching rain]." [MH45/287]

1860

"The rose is the Queen of Flowers, *Messieurs.* It is sufficient, to show the interest which attaches to the review with which we have been charged, to remember this old saying—old as the world, no doubt! —one which, despite our progress in horticulture and the precious importations of our modern travelers, no one dares to challenge. We thus shouldn't be surprised at the important place which this plant occupies in the nurseries of a province which, like its neighbor, may be called the Garden of France . . .

"The culture of the Rose, gentlemen, occupies, in Angers, in the twenty firms which we have visited, an area of ten to twelve hectares . . . Commerce in the Briar has acquired a growing importance during these last years, and [what we have] threatens to be insufficient to the needs of horticulturists, unless a proper preference for own-root roses does not grow in equal proportion. Annually, the trade in roses now attains the level of 75 to 80 thousand *francs,* and we supply for sale about a hundred thousand grafted roses, and forty thousand own-root, without counting a great number of Chinas and others which are sold by the thousand for beds and borders. The greater part of these bushes go to America, England, Belgium, and Portugal; the rest are sold retail in France.

"It is for nearly half a century that we have been occupied with trying to perfect our old sorts of roses . . . During several years, we had within our walls [*Angers is a walled city*] one of the most able and persevering [rose] seed sowers, Monsieur Vibert, several years now retired to Montfort-l'Amaury (Seine-et-Oise). This distinguished horticulturist, to whom we further owe some of our most precious and magnificent [varieties of] table raisins, brought with his seedlings an intelligence, a spirit of order, and an admirable perseverance which were crowned year after year by the most marvelous results.

"The success of Vibert, Laffay, etc., quickly awakened the desires and emulation of other horticulturists; and, before long, the number of varieties grew prodigiously . . ." [AnM-L59/207–209]

1865

"The topographical situation of the city of Angers [France] is fairly well known, close to, and indeed nearly at, the junction of four navigable rivers, numerous routes, and from which begin three and soon four important railway tracks. The ways of the population derive from the situation in which they are placed: active, industrious, honest, given to agricultural and industrial work, they're right there contributing to the progress and development of the diverse branches of cultural endeavor. Horticulture, in particular, arboriculture, market gardening, nurseries—many firms for all of these are found here.

"There is one which, above all, by its importance, well deserves close study. The nurseries of Monsieur André Leroy have, these days, a reputation not only European but also extending to America. Founded more than a century ago, but modest in its beginnings, this establishment, today one of the glories of French Horticulture, was for a long time all that it could be in an age when the taste for gar-

dening and planting wasn't very far developed. In 1820, when Monsieur André Leroy took charge, it was no more than 4 hectares in size; now, it extends to about a hundred and sixty . . .

"This vast manufactory of trees and shrubs—as Monsieur Turgan calls it—makes itself known from afar to visitors, and its outskirts give advance warning of what one is going to see. Some long avenues of American walnut trees and Red Chestnuts lead one to a large circular plaza planted with evergreen Magnolias of a beautiful lustrous green. At the time of our visit, these trees were covered with large pure white blossoms.

"An elegant grille, which stands at the entrance to this plaza, gives entry to a country garden, where wild flowers from throughout the globe are represented by some specimens which a person could call *gigantic,* were they to be compared to what one has seen up till now in gardening. Among these trees . . . we can mention a *Sequoia gigantea* from California, about eight meters high [ca. 24 ft] by a meter and a half at the base [ca. 4 1/2 ft]; several Himalayan cedars, a little taller; an Atlas cedar . . . [etc., etc.]

"The nurseries of Monsieur André Leroy contain, as we have mentioned above, a total extent of about a hundred and sixty hectares, which are subdivided as follows: a hundred in fruit trees of all sorts, twenty-five in forest and ornamental trees, ten in saplings for nurseries, ten in shrubs both deciduous and evergreen, five in rhododendrons, three in large-flowered magnolias, three in roses, one in tall camellias in the open ground, etc.

"These vast works are divided further into various enclosures close-set one to the other, and connected by large and commodious lanes. This arrangement, made necessary by circumstances, has the advantage of presenting the most varied cultural conditions . . ." [*La Patrie,* 1865]

1866

"Monsieur Moreau-Robert has been asking, since June last, for the naming of a Committee charged with visiting his collection, and particularly to take note of the roses blooming . . .

"The old living quarters which were there previously were taken down to make room for some new construction, built higher at some distance, and in another direction. The location of the demolished house has become a verdant lawn of beds and specimen plants, which will continue to be embellished as time goes on, because the planting there is quite new.

"What strikes a person at first at Monsieur Moreau's is the considerable quantity of [grape] vines which cover the walls, making them entirely disappear under the curtain of the foliage; no space is empty or unoccupied . . .

"The rose seedlings of Monsieur Moreau are no less fortunate [than those of the grapevines]; the varieties obtained by him are, for the most part, of the greatest merit—as we can demonstrate by recalling that beautiful Mossy Remontant, of dark shades, shown at the meeting of last June and dedicated by Monsieur Moreau as a mark of filial affection to the memory of Monsieur Jean-Pierre Vibert, founder of this present firm.

"The Queen of Flowers extends widely its so rich and numerous varieties to all parts of the garden. One sees that Monsieur Moreau loves roses, and that he grows them with the care and attention of a passionate fancier. Despite the advance of the season, most of the blossoms were full of freshness and beauty. We were fortunate to be able to admire anew 'Empereur du Maroc' [HP], one of the first dark-shaded roses, grown from seed at Angers by Monsieur Guinoisseau. The own-root roses, arranged in beds by sort, were all coming along very well, and very considerable in number.

"We can't leave the main grounds without speaking of the Yuccas, which Monsieur Moreau grows with a particular tenderness and care; several varieties of this beautiful plant, some of which are very rare and of high price, are notable in several ways. All his specimens appear to be in the most robust health. It is the same with a pretty collection of Agaves, which are found arranged around the entrance of the garden and the house.

"From the main grounds, Monsieur Moreau took us to the plot which he owns at Maître-École. There can be found tree-roses, Briars destined to receive the graft in August …

"Several beds of budded roses attracted attention by their air of good health and their vigorous growth. The quantity of own-root roses, or those grafted high [*i.e.,* tree roses], is so considerable that you could compare them to a standing army!

"Monsieur Moreau's nurseries are very carefully looked to, well thought-out, and do him the greatest honor. The firm which he runs was founded, as you know, by Monsieur Jean-Pierre Vibert, who brought it to Angers after having seen several seasons of his rose plantations ravaged by the white worm. That distinguished horticulturist, who died last January, was unrivalled in France in rose culture. Monsieur Robert, his worthy successor, followed honorably in the footsteps of Monsieur Vibert, and passed on to Monsieur Moreau an establishment which could not be in better hands." [AnM-L66/115–118] The firm continued its work hybridizing and selling roses for another 30 years.

Breeding Conditions and Practices

"To produce beautiful roses having double flowers, it is necessary to sow among the prettiest those which, aside from the number of petals, still have enough stamens to produce pollen; lacking them, one sows semi-doubles, the seed of which gives some doubles, but fewer than the first way; a person will find many more semi-doubles and even more singles. If one sows singles, one can, with an infinite quantity of individuals, obtain several semi-doubles, which, sown later, give us some doubles; this is how Nature and Chance gave us the beautiful Centifolia roses before anyone occupied himself with rose breeding." [BJ24]

"Messrs. the Fanciers and Growers of Roses . . . sow some seeds of the Centifolia, and obtain some roses which have some analogy with the Damask, the Alba, etc.; they quickly decide that these roses are hybrids of the Centifolia and the Damask, or the Alba, etc.—a little too quickly! Others, however, are quicker still: they sow seeds gathered at random; then, when the specimens which result bloom, they study them, and class them arbitrarily among the hybrids of such and such species because they believe they see in them specific characteristics of these two species; or it can happen—and it does, pretty frequently!—that these supposed hybrids come from seed of neither sort of which they show characteristics . . . [Several pages intervening] . . . Here are some examples. Monsieur Noisette sowed some Chinas, and obtained some Pimpinellifolias; Monsieur Prévost sowed some seeds from the Noisette, and obtained the pure Type of the Musk. All sow with neither rhyme nor reason, and they obtain the Type with single flowers, the Type of their supposed species—but the Type obtained at Rouen differs from that obtained at Paris, and the types obtained at Paris differ from those obtained in London. To convince yourself of what I have just advanced, all you need to do is to compare the very well done descriptions by Lindley with better yet ones by Prévost fils. There are not more than four which accord to the point at which one cannot make of them different species established upon the specific characteristics adopted by these gentlemen. But then if you go on and compare them with the descriptions of Thory and of other authors, you will have the opportunity to create species by the hundreds or the thousands—if these descriptions have been made in differing localities." [MaCo]

"[By 1814], Monsieur Descemet put together a very great quantity of notes on the sowings he had made; the origin of a part of his roses is set down there. This precious work, which would have supplied us with some very valuable ideas about the tricks of Nature and which are the best varieties from which to sow seed, was destroyed as a result of the events of the war; the little bit which by chance was saved has made me [Vibert] regret strongly the loss of a set of observations which would have spared me much time and many trials." [V1]

"My [Mauget's] work, in the beginning [ca. 1825], had little to recommend it, having at that time as Types or seed-bearers only a few varieties from the Orient among the Chinas, Noisettes, Teas, and Bourbons, and only a few Portlands and Perpetual hybrids [i.e., Damask Perpetual]. I nevertheless desired to increase my efforts in breeding, particularly with perpetual roses. Trying to enrich the then-poor selection of Perpetuals, I drummed up, at the offices of all my brothers in the trade—as much in Belgium as in France—all those which seemed to me to have merit. I planted in my nursery all I was able to obtain, for the purposes of study. Heaven knows I was taken in by the blandishments of the shopkeepers! Finally, after several years, my plants gave me some seeds which I sowed with care. To be sure, I had taken as my motto two words which turned out to be quite necessary indeed: Patience and Perseverance . . . Now, the greater part of my seedlings come from mother seed-bearers which themselves were my developments. The people who wish to visit my breeding-grounds during the bloom-season to assure themselves of what I have written need go but 14 yards [ca. 14 m] from the Paris platform at the railway station in Orléans." [SHP45/308]

"I cannot help mentioning the jealousies which exist among some of the 'Cultivateurs de Rosiers' in France. I once visited the gardens of a noted grower, in company with a grower of less celebrity. I was surprised to see so little in these grounds, and to find the owner careless as to shewing what he possessed. Although exceedingly polite and talkative on other subjects, he was disinclined to speak on Roses. The mystery was cleared up by a letter received soon afterwards. In it were words to this effect: 'If you visit my establishment again, which I beg of you to do, pray do not bring any French Rose grower with you, for I cannot shew them my rarities and beauties.' This opened my eyes: I concluded I had not seen 'the lions'; and an after visit proved this to be the case." [P]

"Our colleague, Monsieur Oscar Leclerc, in telling you about a successful way to obtain double Ranunculi, has given me [Vibert] the opportunity to let you know about an analogous fact which particularly struck my attention, and which tends to confirm fully the report in the Gardener's Magazine on the subject of artificially-bred Ranunculi.

"About two years ago [ca. 1829], one of my German correspondents—a great Rose fancier—told me that one of his friends, who for a long time had been occupied with the artificial breeding of Carnations, had done the same with Roses, and that he had gotten such results that he believed he could do no better than to describe to me some of the roses obtained by this procedure. To be brief, among thirty varieties of Roses of which the detailed description was sent to me, the greater portion showed, in flowers and foliage, variations and characteristics so pronounced and at the same time so different from those ordinarily found in our seedlings that my first impression was that there had been a great deal of exaggeration in the report. I was told, among other things, of the existence of a China-Moss and of a Pimpinellifolia-Moss!

"I have grown roses for twenty years; I have made many sowings and seen much with my own two eyes—but I declare that I was unable to believe that a singularity which was only a sport, and found in but one sort of Centifolia, could be transferred to another sort, and particularly to a China. This is what I told to my correspondent in a very detailed letter on the subject. I requested new explanations, and, in particular, to indeed be able to correspond directly with his friend. Soon, new information came in confirmation of the first news, and I understood from that distinguished fancier that he could cross one species with another with equal ease, that he preferred double roses to others for pollination, that he could tell if the fertilization had taken place, and that if it had not, he would try again. I owe to the good will of this estimable person my knowledge of the principal means he employed; and so, with this under my belt, at the last bloom [of the season], I made several attempts of the sort myself. Owing, however, to the continual rains of the season, my first tries did not take. These facts are well known in the part of Germany where this person resides; his social position, which allows him to keep to his work, and the range and number of details which were supplied to me are the foundation of my complete belief in the existence of these new Roses . . .

"I am of the opinion, gentlemen, that artificial breeding can be employed with success with a great number of plants, and that in this case the hand of Man will be a great aid to Nature, bringing together species of the same family which, up till now, had refused to ally. Judging from the material which Monsieur Oscar Leclerc reported to you concerning Ranunculi, as well as the present information which I have had the honor of presenting to you, it would seem evident that the most double flowers of these two genera are the best for production of seed. As a consequence of this important discovery, it is easy to see what a vast field opens up to Thought and Industry. We are far from being able to tell where these detours from Nature might lead, and I think it would be useful if the Society were to study what has been written or tried on the subject. This would be how to set on their way some people whose taste or nature inclines them towards the goal of extending the frontiers of our knowledge. Monsieur Sageret and, I believe, some others among us were themselves formerly occupied with artificial breeding . . . Artificial breeding is certainly nothing new, but one can't deny, at least, that this area of Science is still obscure, and well merits clarification." [SHP31]

"One never knows what the fertilization of any two varieties will produce; or, more correctly, how many different varieties may result. One seed-pod containing four seeds may, and has to my knowledge,

produced four seedlings absolutely distinct in every conceivable respect. Many a time I have seen produced from the seeds sown from one hip, half a dozen seedlings absolutely distinct in color and form, some as single as the ordinary Dog Rose, and some so full in substance that it was impossible to get them to open, even under glass . . . The system we [at A. Dickson's] ultimately adopted was hybridization in the first instance between two varieties, then inbreeding from their offspring upon the following lines: We took a seedling of our own, which gave some evidence of possessing at least some of the qualities aimed at, and, in the first instance, this seedling was crossed with the male parent; secondly, the seedling crossed with the female parent; thirdly, the male parent crossed with the seedling; fourthly, the female parent crossed with the seedling. As soon as we were able to form an opinion on the results of this inter-breeding, we again made a selection of those most closely approaching our ideal, then again inbreeding, but with this difference, that we made use of only a limited number of parents, but in almost every instance making a double cross. For example, if we made a seedling with, say, 'Marie Van Houtte' [T] as the male parent, then during that season we reversed the cross, making 'Marie Van Houtte' the seed-bearing parent and the seedling the male parent." [ARA25/62, quoting from the American Rose Society Bulletin of 1908]

"Development [of seed] without fertilization (apogamy) [is] a phenomenon that is not uncommon in the rose, as shown by the work of Dingler of Germany and Almquist of Sweden." [ARA24/36]

"In 1816, I [Vibert] sowed the seed of 'Belle Herminie' [G] (single rose, Descemet), the only [spotted rose] we had in the Provins group at that time; and over twenty-five years, I have constantly sown the seeds of improvements of this rose. Today [in 1844], there are at my place more than four thousand seedlings of these sorts of [spotted and striped] roses." [V8]

"This year [1843], I [Laffay] have developed among my seedlings (which total 60 to 100 thousand) a spotted one which will have the benefit of being perpetual on all its canes; its blossom, well formed, is flat in form and a vinous pink, spotted with very large white points. And so, Monsieur, you see the strategy of my march—always to plant seeds of the latest arrivals (the newest varieties developed); I will end of not by concluding but by continuing with novelties which will allow us to week yet other [older] varieties out of our collections." [R-H44/479] "Monsieur Laffay . . . has been highly successful in the raising of seedlings, and besides several new ones which he brings out this year [1845] for the first time, he has an immense stock of young seedlings, to the number we think of 6000." [MH45/27]

"In the first place, the hips, to be ripe, should not be picked until they have turned, some orange, some scarlet, or crimson, some darker, and begin to wrinkle; but should not be left on the plant to dry up. Then the seed should be planted at once, as I think, and many authorities agree with me, that many people make the mistake of keeping the seed out of the ground too long. If allowed to get very dry, the shell hardens and the germination will be much slower." [ARA25/63] "One gathers seed from roses when they are quite ripe. One then sows them in a pot, or, most favorably, in a bed near an east-facing wall. The seeds are covered in Winter. A person could indeed sow with the same success in Spring, but it would be necessary to soak the seeds in water mixed with a fifth part of eau-de-vie for 12–24 hours before planting. It is not at all necessary to plant the seeds more than 5–6 lignes deep [ca. $^1/_2$–$^3/_4$ in or ca. 1.5–1.9 cm]. Nearly all of them sprout in the Spring, some of them the following year. The young plants are grown with the same care recommended for all other seedlings. The seeds of the rose called the China Rose, though sown in the Spring, nevertheless bloom the same year in June-July; and the others the year following, according to how well they are taken care of. One would do well to sow thinly so that the plants don't etiolate when left in place to bloom." [BJ24]

"The seeds are principally grown in frames and beds under lathe shade, and in the open air, retaining natural conditions so far as possible, but the results of certain of the more difficult crosses were planted in pots under glass. The tardy germination of many kinds of rose seeds is very trying. A small proportion of the seeds taken from the hips of Multiflora, Tea, and Wichuraiana varieties may promptly germinate when grown under favorable conditions, but rarely all. Many will be delayed until the following season, and others may not sprout until they have been in the soil several years. Seeds of the great majority of rose species, native and exotic, and their hybrids, consistently refuse to grow until the second year after planting, and individual seeds have been known to 'hang fire' for as long as seven years, growing with full energy when they did start. We find it advisable to keep all sowings of rare hybridized seed in view for at least five years . . . Seedlings require from one to four years of growth to show their full characteristics, though everblooming varieties often attempt to bloom within a few weeks after coming up." [ARA18/44] "The location [for raising the seedlings] was chosen because of its favorable soil and aspect, and the neighborhood of predatory rabbits, moles and field-mice had to be accepted. Against these animals it is necessary to protect by underground wire-screening as well as by overhead frames, and every new stem must have its collar to defy to teeth of the cottontails! 'They prefer and always choose the rare things,' plaintively remarked the Doctor." [ARA19/126] "I got a fairly good crop of seed from hybridized plants and a few good heps from seedlings which I have raised. I discarded about two hundred seedlings in October as worthless, and kept, possibly, a half dozen. I think that is too many." [ARA24/90]

"A new rose may make a hit in California, and succeed to a certain extent in New Jersey. It is at once sold throughout the land, perhaps on a stock which thrives only under certain conditions. Who can tell what it will do in northern New York?" [ARA22/30] "There is one difficulty which the producer of new varieties must overcome in order to get his roses before the public. Like the writer who must interest the publisher in his story, so the man with the new rose must interest the nurseryman. The nurseryman must see a profit before he will undertake the work of propagating and selling a new variety. As a rule, he also wants to be the only original introducer of the rose in question. Under this arrangement, he can work up a large stock and bring it before the public in his own good time, without competition, and at his own price. Sometimes a man who overcomes all the minor difficulties necessary to hybridize and grow a rose which he considers needed, not to speak of major troubles relating to the same, has almost the hardest part of the operation before him in getting his product marketed, for[,] although, after years of patient effort, with the attendant expense, he secures what he started out to evolve, his new rose may never be widely grown if it does not hit the fancy of a nurseryman. Yet, it is only fair to the nursery firms to say that they must protect themselves, and see a possible profit in the same way as any other business man before they take up new varieties tendered them by amateurs, no matter how enthusiastic the latter may be. In a way, the public is most to blame, because the public buys what it considers is best for it, and very often it is not capable of judging. If the public clamors for '[Turner's] Crimson Rambler' [Mult], the grower must produce and deliver this rose in order to do business, even if he knows it is inferior to some other variety. If he grows a better rose, he may not sell it." [ARA20/39]

A Royal Rose Garden

Now that, in previous appendices, we have visited various nurseries, and learned some aspects of breeding and the nursery trade, it is time that we take a close look at the final product, the rose garden. Of great interest is the manuscript inventory of roses for the royal rose labyrinth in Stockholm's *Linnés Park,* a list compiled by Gustaf Johan Billberg, in 1836. (Historical details on Billberg and the park may be found in *Rosenbladet* [the publication of the Swedish Rose Society] No. 2, 1996, in the article "Rosenlabyrinten i Humlegården" by Maria Flinck; another version of this present appendix, in Swedish, has been published in *Rosenbladet,* No. 4, 1997, and No. 1, 1998.)

The list is a labyrinth in itself! Many cultivars are listed, with a few of them well known, many somewhat obscure, many completely obscure, and one or two seemingly otherwise unknown. The complete understanding of such a document is desirable from many points of view. First of all, on the primary level, it tells us what was in commerce or at least available to those in a certain location with the means to purchase such material. Second, it reveals or verifies the existence of a particular cultivar by a particular date; there are indeed a few items here that push back the known date for the listed cultivar by several years! Third, it provides us with an interesting snapshot of the taste of the buyer or designer at one point in his or her life; we begin to understand the goals of the person in charge to a greater or lesser degree of clarity in accordance with the skill with which the person manifested his or her intentions through the choices made. Fourth, simply through "scribal variation"—mistakes!—we are provided with more synonymy, some of which may provide a link that will allow us to make a connection with a yet more wayward synonym, a link that perhaps will in some cases finally bring about the return of a "prodigal son" to the "home" of its more valid, and perhaps previously unsuspected, synonym. Finally, it gives us an opportunity to indulge ourselves with the delights of rose history!

Without further preface, then, let us proceed to the list itself and the information relating to its cultivars. Quite a number of them are extinct, and do not otherwise appear in this book. I retain the numbering of Billberg's list, but supply—in place of his version of the name and his other few-worded remarks, usually including a vague indication of the color—the valid name of the cultivar, then adding the name of the breeder and/or introducer, if known (in some cases nothing is known; in a few cases, only the city or country from which the variety came is known), as well as either the date of introduction of the particular cultivar or the earliest date of written record for the

cultivar, ending with an indication of the group to which the cultivar belongs. Abbreviations are as follows: A minus sign before a date means that the cultivar was introduced *by* that date; in other words " –1828" means "1828 or before." "Br. unk." means "Breeder and/or introducer unknown."

1–375.	Not roses.
376.	*Rosa rubiginosa*
377.	*Rosa canadensis* (*R. americana*)
379–381.	These are botanical color forms of the variable *Rosa rubiginosa.*
382.	'Inodora' (Br. unk., –1826) Rbg
383.	*Rosa setigera*
384–386.	These are botanical forms of the variable *Rosa canina.*
387.	*Rosa setigera,* again.
388.	The list's *crassifolia* is a bit of a mystery; due to the literal meaning of the name, confirmed by the common Swedish name listed (tjockblads), it is likely that this is the well-known and still-extant Centifolia 'Bullata' (Dupont, –1809).
389.	If we accept our theory about no. 388, then variety ß of *crassifolia* would most likely be the white sport of 'Bullata', called 'Bullata Alba'. If this is the case, then Billberg's list would be the first record we have so far of this cultivar, otherwise only known as –1845, with introducer unknown. I know of no other subvarieties or variations of 'Bullata'.
390.	*columnifera.* Again, an unfamiliar name, otherwise unrecorded as far as I am aware. Again going by the literal meaning of the name, this could be the Centifolia cultivar 'Childling' (Br. unk., –1759), perhaps better known under its later synonyms 'Mère Gigogne' or 'Prolifera', in which a column of successively smaller buds arises from the heart of preceding blossoms.
391.	'Belle Laure' (Dupont/Vibert, 1817) Pim
xxx.	'Zerbine' (Vibert, 1822) Pim
392.	'Blanche Double' (Prévost, –1826) Pim
393.	'Carnée' (Vibert, 1820) Pim
394.	Not "Des brossy" but rather 'Desbrosses' (Angers, –1828) Pim
395.	'Hardy' (Girardon, –1835) Pim

396. 'Pourpre' (Descemet, –1820) Pim

397. *carlina.* This rose is a complete mystery. Its proximity on the list to *Rosa carolina* is perhaps implicative; possibly the person who wrote the label or tag for the plant, from which Billberg was reading, loyally had the current king Carl or Karl on his mind (Karl XIV Johan), and simply left out the "o" of "carolina"!

398. *fenestralis* is a botanical variety of *Rosa setigera.*

399, 400. *Rosa carolina* and a botanical variety of same.

401. 'Common Centifolia' (Br. unk., –1596) C

402. 'Cristata' (Kitzer/Vibert-Portemer-Roblin, 1827) M

403. 'D'Anjou' (Br. unk., –1829) C

404. 'Des Peintres' (Br. unk., –1806) C

405. 'Oeillet' (Poilpré, 1789) C

406. 'Unique Rouge' (Br. unk., –1824) C

407. 'Unique' (Richmond, 1777) C

408. *Rosa lucida*

409. 'Common Moss' (Br. unk., –1720) M

410. 'À Feuille de Sauge' (Shailer, 1820) M

411. 'White Moss' (Shailer, 1788) M

412. 'Vilmorin' (Vilmorin, ca. 1805) M

413. 'Panachée' (Shailer, 1818) M

414. 'Zoe' (Forest, 1829) M

415. Billberg's list has the word "Briard" (*i.e.,* "pertaining to Brie"), which one sees in rose literature here and there; it is undoubtedly an understandable French misunderstanding of the English word "Briar," which is the common name of *Rosa rubiginosa.*

416. 'Clémentine' (Descemet, –1824) Rbg

417. 'Descemet' (Br. unk., –1836) Rbg. This is the only record of a Rubiginosa cultivar with this name; the breeder Descemet did, however, release several Rubiginosas, as did his prolific colleague and successor Vibert, for either of whom it would have been natural to have named a release 'Descemet'.

418. 'Hessoise' (Schwarzkopf, –1811) Rbg

419. 'Hessoise Pourpre Double' (Descemet, –1820) Rbg

420. 'Zabeth' (Dupont, –1813) Rbg

421. 'Poniatowsky' (Cartier, 1821) Rbg

422. *Rosa gallica*

423. 'Adèle Heu' (Vibert, 1816) G

424. 'Adonis' (Descemet, –1814) G

425. 'Aimable Rose' (Vibert, 1819) G

426. 'Aimable Hortense' (Vibert, 1819) G

427. 'Aimable Pourpre' (Holland, pre-1811) G

428. 'Belle Hélène' (Descemet, –1818) G

429. 'Ariane' (Vibert, 1818) G

430. 'Arethuse' (Vibert, 1819) G

431. 'Aglaé de Marsilly' (Vibert, 1822) G

432. 'Aimée Roman' (Prévost, –1826) G

433. 'Adéline' (Vibert, –1826) G

434. 'Arsinoé' (Vibert, 1816) G

435. 'Beauté Parfaite

436. 'Beauté Incomparable' (Miellez, –1828) G

437. 'Beauté Merveilleuse' (Br. unk., –1831) G

438. 'Beauté du Jour' (Miellez, 1822) G

439. 'Beauté Pourpre' (Br. unk., –1831) G

440. 'Barbanègre' (Vibert, 1820) G

441. 'Belle Abosine' (Br. unk., –1836) G. This is one of those names that cries out as being wrong—what is an "Abosine"? No doubt some day someone will run across the correct, slightly different, name, and we will all say, "Oh, of *course*! Why didn't *we* think of that?"

442. 'Belle Adélaïde' (Miellez, –1828) G

443. 'Belle Gabrielle' (Miellez, –1828) G

444. 'Belle Cramoisie' (Descemet, –1820) G

445. 'Belle Africaine' (Prévost, –1824) G. Attributed to Vibert by Desportes.

446. 'Belle Esquermoise' (Miellez, –1821) G

447. 'Belle de Desbrosses' (Br. unk., –1831) G. Probably from Desbrosses, as the name tells us, whom we meet again (see no. 394).

448. 'Busard Triomphant' (Br. unk., –1811) G

449. 'Boïldieu' (Prévost, 1828) G

450. 'Cadisché' (Vibert, 1830) G

451. 'Casimier Périer' (Lecomte, –1828) G

452. 'Champion' (Vibert, 1831) G

453. 'Charles Auguste' (Paillard, 1824) G

454. 'La Circassienne' (Vibert, 1821) G

455. 'Cire d'Espagne' (Miellez, –1830) G

456. 'Claire d'Olban' (Vibert, 1825) G

457. 'Clémentine'. There were two Gallicas at this date by this name, choose either the –1811 one with breeder unknown, or Vibert's 1818 release.

458. 'Clorinde' (Miellez, –1828) G

459. 'Comte Foy [de Rouen]' (Lecomte, –1827) G. The name is probably only 'Comte Foy', but as there were other roses 'Comte Foy' around at the time, it has always been called 'Comte Foy *de Rouen*'.

460. 'Comte Lacépède' (Vibert, –1836) G

461. 'Cora' (Lecomte, –1828) G

462. 'Cornélie' (Garilland, ca. 1825) G

463. 'Délices de Flore' (Br. unk., –1829) G; there was also a Centifolia 'Délices de Flandre' (Miellez, –1828).

464. 'Duc de Bordeaux' (Vibert, 1820) G

465. 'Duc de Guiche' (Br. unk., –1810) G

466. 'Duc d'Orléans'. There were two Gallicas by this name in this era, one Écoffay, 1819, the other Vibert, 1831.

467. 'Empereur' (Br. unk., –1810) G. It is interesting to note political realities in horticulture. Often the roses which were named after, or which alluded to, Napoléon, were not acknowledged by their breeder or namer in the post-Napoleonic era.

468. 'L'Enchanteresse' (François, 1826) G

469. 'Enfant de France' (Holland, –1802) G. There was also an Agathe by this name, with attribution Brussels, –1824.

470. 'Eucharis' (Descemet/Vibert, –1820) G

471. 'Ex Albo Violacea' (Noisette, –1829) G

472. 'Fanny Bias' (Vibert, 1819) G. Vibert, as something of a *parvenu,* had a number of enemies who were troublesome particularly in the 1820s; these enemies attempted to make it appear as if Vibert were attempting to pass off, in this case, an older variety of Descemet's as 'Fanny Bias'; Vibert stated the case cleanly by responding that he found 'Fanny Bias' among his seedlings—not, perhaps, specifying whether it was among his *own* seed-

lings, or among the ones to which he bought full proprietary rights from Descemet, but, still, Vibert was accurate; it was *his* seedling, and not a re-release of an older cultivar. Vibert was very exact and just; in his early catalogs, varieties coming from Descemet are clearly marked with a "D"; as Vibert wrote in one response to an attack, "Even the most junior gardener at the Luxembourg [Palace garden] would have to be a booby not to understand [what roses in my catalog] came from Monsieur Descemet" [V2]

473. 'Fontenelle' (Trébucien, –1829) G
474. 'Gloire des Jardins' (Descemet, –1815) G
475. 'Gloire des Pourpres' (Vibert, –1826) G
476. 'Grain d'Or' (Brussels, –1826) G
477. 'Grande Beauté' (Vibert, 1830) G
478. 'Grand Mogol' (Holland, –1828) G
479. 'Grand Papa' (Brussels, –1828) Hybrid G × C
480. 'Hervy' (Hardy, –1820) G
481. 'Heureuse Surprise' (Br. unk., –1835) Hybrid China
482. 'Illustre Gris-de-Lin' (Miellez, –1828) G
483. Blank. Perhaps the plant in this position in the rosarium was dead!
484. 'Incomparable de Lille' (Miellez, –1821) G
485. 'L'Infant' (Vibert, 1829) G
486. 'Soleil Brillant' (Holland, –1811) G
487. 'Iris' (Br. unk., 1820) G
488. 'Jeanne Seymour' (Vibert, 1829) G
489. 'Labbey de Pompières' (Prévost, 1827) G
490. 'Laborde' (Vibert, 1823) G
491. 'La Moskawa' (Delaâge, 1824) G. Delaâge was one of Napoléon's generals (as, of course, had been the King of Sweden, Karl XIV Johan, the quondam Général Bernadotte) and served for instance at Austerlitz; at length he retired to rose breeding at Angers, France, often giving his roses names relating to his war experiences.
492. 'La Rochefoucault' (Coquerel, 1825) G
493. 'Latone' (Vibert/Laffay, 1829) G. A rare instance of Vibert selling proprietary rights to his own rose to another breeder.
494. 'Léa' (Vétillart, ca. 1825) G
495. 'Loisiel' (Prévost, 1826) G
496. 'Louis XVIII' is a synonym of 'À Fleurs Gigantesques' (Sèvres, 1813) G. Écoffay, responsible for the well-known 'Rose du Roi' (DP), is usually responsible for roses emanating from Sèvres during this era.
497. 'Mme. Sommesson' (Br. unk., –1831) G
498. 'Manteau Pourpre' (Br. unk., –1811) G
499. 'Marguerite de Valois' (Vibert, 1829) G
500. 'Marie-Antoinette' (Vibert, 1829) G. It should be noted that the teenage Vibert was in Paris during the French Revolution.
501. 'Marie Stuart' (Dubourg, 1820) G. Desportes dates this 1826.
502. 'Monthyon' (Vibert, 1828) G
503. 'Néala' (Vibert, 1822) G
504. 'Ninon de Lenclos' (Vibert, 1817) G
505. 'La Noble Fleur' (Descemet, –1820) G
506. 'Noble Pourpre' (Vibert, 1828) G
507. Blank
508. 'Ombrée d'Hollande' (Holland?, –1826) G

509. 'Ombre Parfaite' (Vibert, 1823) G
510. 'Orphise' (Vibert, –1826) G
511. 'Othello' (Trébucien, –1829) G
512. 'Ourika' (Hardy/Vibert, 1825) G
513. 'Passe-Velours' (Descemet, –1820) G
514. 'Pierre Corneille' (Trébucien, –1829) G
515. 'Pierret' (Vibert, 1819) G
516. 'Bourbon' (Br. unk., –1811) G
517. 'Pourpre Triomphant' (Vibert, –1829) G
518. 'Pourpre Royale' (Br. unk., –1828) G
519. 'Pourpre Obscur' (Godefroy/Vibert, 1820) G
520. 'Pourpre sans Épine' (Godefroy, 1818) G
521. 'Reine des Amateurs' (Hébert, –1829) G
522. 'Reine des Roses' (Vibert, –1820) G
523. 'Renoncule' (Cartier/Dupont, –1810) G
524. 'Rien Ne Me Surpasse' (Miellez, –1826) G
525. 'Roi des Pourpres' (Descemet, –1817) G
526. 'Roi de Rome' is a synonym of the troublesome 'Enfant de France' (Holland, –1802) G (see no. 469). You see, the "child of France" was Napoléon's little boy, who was made "king of Rome."
527. 'Roi d'Angleterre' could be either Margat, –1829, or Vibert, –1831; in either case, G
528. 'Rosalba' (Vibert, 1829) G
529. 'Fénélon' (Vibert, –1836) G. The nonalphabetic placement of this cultivar in the garden, and its mangled name in Billberg's list, testify to a number of vicissitudes both scribally and perhaps horticulturally; perhaps it was sent in haste to replace a dead plant—we may note that it is at the very center of the garden. 'Fénélon' was the newest of the new when it appeared in the Labyrinth; Billberg's list is the earliest mention of it yet found.
530. 'Pourpre Charmant' (Holland, –1811) G
531. 'Rouge Brillante' (Vibert, –1821) G
532. 'Sidonie' (Vibert, 1829) G
533. 'Stratonice' (Br. unk., –1828) G
534. 'Superbe Violette' (Vibert, 1825) G
535. 'Talma' (Prévost, –1826) G
536. 'Télémaque' (Vibert, 1830) G
537. 'Théagène' (Vibert, 1820) G
538. 'Tricolore' (Vibert, –1821) or (Lahaye, 1827) G
539. 'Le Triomphe de Beauté' (Holland, –1826) G
540. 'Triomphe d'Europe' (Holland, –1828) G
541. 'Triomphe de Flore' (Descemet, –1821) G
542. 'Vandaëls' (Vibert, 1820) G
543. 'Vanneau' (Vibert, 1830) G
544. 'Véturie' (Vibert, –1828) G
545. 'Violette san Pareille' (Holland, –1821) or (Vibert, 1822) G
546. 'Virginie' (Descemet, –1820) G. The novel *Paul et Virginie* was popular at the time.
547. 'Wellington' (Br. unk., –1826) G
548. 'Ypsilanti' (Vibert, 1821) G
549. 'Zuléma' (Vibert, 1828) G
550. 'Adrienne Lecouvreur' (Vibert, 1830) G
551. 'Belle Herminie' (Coquerel, 1819) G
552. 'Belle Cramoisie' ("M"/Vibert, 1829) G; or (Descemet, –1820) G. There were two. "M" may well be Mauget, of Orléans.
553. 'Belle de Marly' (Br. unk., –1836) G

554. 'Belle Double' (Br. unk., –1836) G

555. 'Belle de Fontenay' (Boutigny, –1828) G

556. 'Camaieux' (Vibert, 1830) G

557. 'Charlotte de Lacharme' (Vibert, 1822) G

558. 'Duc d'Orléans' (Vibert, 1831) G

559. 'Emilie la Jolie' (Rouen, 1826) G. Desportes dates 1825, perhaps referring to the first bloom of the cultivar, rather than its commercial introduction.

560. 'Pourpre Strié de Blanc' (Br. unk., –1831) G

561. 'Admirable Panaché' (François, 1827) G

562. 'Pourpre Charmant Strié' (Hardy, 1824) G

563. 'Uniflore Marbrée' (Vibert, 1830) G

564. *Hulthemia persica*

565. The list's Lawrenciana refers to one of the series of miniature Chinas (which lie behind the present-day Miniature Roses); it is unlikely that this very delicate plant lasted very long in the winters of Stockholm.

566. *Rosa ×kamtchatika*

567. 'Parnassina' (Noisette, 1825) Rg

568. *Rosa bracteata*

569. 'Maria Léonida' (Lemoyne/Burdin, 1829) Brac

570. *Rosa roxburghii*

571. 'Turneps' (Br. unk., –1770) Cin

572. 'Luisante à Grande Fleur' (Hardy, 1818) Vir

573. 'Hudsoniana' refers to either *Rosa blanda* or *R. palustris.*

574. 'Lucida' is synonymous with *Rosa virginiana.*

575. 'Boursault' (Boursault/Vibert, –1820) Bslt

576. 'Calypso' (Noisette, –1810) Bslt

577. 'Inermis' (Br. unk., –1775) Bslt

578. 'Reversa' (Vilmorin, ca. 1810) Bslt

579. 'Multiplex' (Br. unk., –1629) Hem

580. 'Pompon Minor' (Br. unk., –1806) Hem

581. *Rosa foetida*

582. *Rosa foetida* 'Bicolor'

583. *Rosa carolina* 'Parviflora'

584. *Rosa carolina* 'Parviflora' forma 'Humilis'

585. *Rosa majalis*

586. *Rosa majalis* 'Flore Pleno'

587. 'York and Lancaster' (Br. unk., –1551) D

588. 'Belle Couronnée' (Cels, –1817) D

589. 'Portland Rose' (Br. unk., –1775) DP

590. 'Jeune Henry' (Descemet, –1815) DP

591. 'Le Prince de Galles' (Br. unk., –1826) DP

592. 'Triomphe de Rouen' (Lecomte, 1826) D or DP

593. 'Varrata' (Br. unk., –1826) DP

594. 'Félicité Hardy' (Hardy, ca. 1831) D. Billberg's listing as 'Félicité Hardy' is the latest record I have run across of use of the correct name of what came to be known as 'Mme. Hardy'.

595. 'Admirable' (The Netherlands, –1787) Ag

596. 'Belle d'Auteuil' (Prévost?, –1826) D

597. 'Venusta' (Descemet, –1814) DP

598. 'Monstrueuse' (Br. unk., –1821) Ag

599. 'Pourpre' (Descemet, –1820) D

600. 'Du Luxembourg' (Hardy, –1826) D

601. 'Tomenteux à Fleurs Panachées' (Girardon, –1829) DP

602. 'Dame Blanche' (Miellez, –1828) D or A

603. 'Delphine Gay' (Vibert, 1823) D

604. 'Henri IV' (Trébucien, –1829) D

605. 'Jeanne Hachette' (Coquerel, –1829) D

606. 'La Constance' (Vibert, –1831) DP

607. 'La Gracieuse' (Holland, –1818) D

608. 'Leda' (D). This problematical cultivar beguiles us all not only with its beauty but also with its history. If we are dealing with what we construe 'Leda' to be today—a white flower, with red markings—the earliest listing found for a white 'Leda' (and Billberg indeed lists it as "white") is, as one gathers, in England in 1831. Mention is made of a *pink* Damask 'Leda', however, in 1827. And so, attribution: if pink, (Br. unk., –1827); if white, (England, –1831).

609. 'Léontine Faye' (Vibert, 1831) D

610. 'Roi des Pays-Bas' (Brussels, –1826) D

611. 'Lodoïska Marin' (Prévost, –1822) DP. It is possible, however, that Prévost obtained this from one Marin of the city of Angers, France; as with everything in old roses, research continues.

612. 'Louis XVI' (Miellez, –1828) D

613. 'Oeillet Blanc' (Miellez, –1826) D

614. 'Lavallette' (Vibert, 1823) D

615. 'Admirable' (Holland, –1787) Ag. No. 595, again.

616. 'Adonis' (Stegerhoek, –1828) Ag. There were three cultivars named 'Adonis' in the era with which we are concerned; one red Gallica, our no. 424; one pink Gallica (Vibert, –1829); and one Agathe, our present entry. Stegerhoek's name has been forgotten for about 170 years; it is time to restore to him what is his.

617. 'Amande' (Br. unk., –1826) G. The Agathes have much in common with Damasks, Damask Perpetuals, Gallicas, and Centifolias; an Agathe may be found in any of these categories, depending upon how a particular writer construes each of these groupings. It is clear that the designer of our Labyrinth regarded nos. 615 through 634 as a special group of some kind, "Provincialis," whatever may be intended by that (clearly not Province Roses or Centifolias, which are nos. 401–407), though indeed we list some as Agathes, and most as Gallicas.

618. 'Amphitrite' (Vibert, –1829) G

619. 'Augustine Bertin' (Vibert, 1818) G

620. 'Beauté Suprenante' (Descemet/Vibert, –1820) G

621. 'Belle Auguste' (Descemet/Vibert, 1817) G

622. 'Boule de Neige' (Vibert, 1826) G

623. 'Belle Hélène' (Descemet, –1818) G. Repeating no. 428.

624. 'Couronnée Double' (Br. unk., –1836) G

625. 'Duchesse d'Angoulême' (Miellez, 1818?) G

626. 'Duchesse de Berry' (Vibert, 1818) G

627. 'Élisa Descemet' (Descemet, –1820) G

628. 'Élisa LeMesle' (Vibert, 1832) G

629. 'Grande Merveilleuse' (Vibert, –1826) G

630. 'Grande Souveraine' (Vibert, 1825) G

631. 'Grand Sultan' (Descemet, –1820) G

632. 'Mademoiselle' (Vibert, 1820) G

633. 'Ornement de Parade' (Holland, –1811) G

634. 'Psyché' (Vibert, 1818) G

635. 'Grande Pivoine de Lille' (Godefroy, 1820) Turb

636. 'Belle Rosine' (Descemet, –1820) Turb

637. 'Aimable Éléonore' (Coquerel, –1828) Turb

638. *Rosa villosa*
639. 'Isménie' (Vibert, 1823) Pom
640. 'Adda' (Vibert, 1825) A
641. 'Antoinette' (Descemet, –1826) A
642. 'Belle de Ségur' (Lelieur/Vibert, –1826) A
643. 'Lesser Maiden's Blush' (Kew, 1797) A
644. 'Plena' (Br. unk., –1770) A
645. 'Bouquet Parfait' (Vibert, 1826) A
646. 'Camille Bouland' (Prévost, –1826) A
647. 'Cécile Loisiel' (Loisiel, 1825) A
648. 'Céleste Blanche' (Vibert, –1820) A
649. 'Chloris' (Descemet, –1820) A
650. 'Fanny-Sommesson' (Vibert, –1826) A. Again, a rose that may have been originally bred by Sommesson, with proprietary rights subsequently sold to Vibert.
651. 'Gabrielle d'Estrées' (Vibert, 1819) A
652. 'Jeanne d'Arc' (Vibert, 1818) A
653. 'Joséphine' ("E"/Vibert, –1826) A. "E" may well be Écoffay, of Sèvres.
654. 'Joséphine Beauharnais' (Vibert, 1823) A
655. 'La Seduisante' (Miellez, –1826) A
656. 'La Surprise' (Poilpré, 1823) A
657. 'Petite Cuisse de Nymphe' (Br. unk., –1811) A. 'Lesser Maiden's Blush' again (see no. 643).
658. 'Pompon Bazard' (Bazard/Vibert, 1818) A
659. 'Pompon Carné' (Br. unk., –1826) A. The seeming "D" in the MS for nos. 659 and 660 is evidently a "P" standing for "Pompon" Albas.
660. 'Caméllia' (St.-Cloud/Prévost, –1824) A
661. 'Catel' (Vibert, –1826) A
662. 'Chaptal' (Vibert, 1823) A
663. 'Chaussée' (Vibert, 1823) A
664. 'Gracilis' (Noisette, –1824) A
665. 'Great Maiden's Blush' (Br. unk., –1754) A
666. 'Sophie de Bavière' (Rouen, 1826) A
667. 'York Rouge' (Miellez, –1826) A
668. 'Evratina' (Bosc, 1809) A
669. 'Pompon de Bourgogne' (Br. unk., –1629) G
670. The list's 'Carnea' could be any of a number of things. Placed as it is between 'Pompon de Bourgogne' and (low-growing) forms of *Rosa pimpinellifolia*, let us choose a famous cultivar that otherwise would have escaped the Labyrinth: 'Carné', a synonym of 'Blush Belgic' (Br. unk., –1754), the original Agathe.
671–676. Unspecified forms of *Rosa pimpinellifolia*.

Thus, then, with Billberg's list. The reader must be left to draw his or her own conclusions from it, according to the nature of the research being done; but perhaps one or two observations would be appropriate.

Cultivars that would have seemed "old" at the time—those antedating about 1815—are few and are mainly very famous roses of indisputable interest and beauty, most of which are indeed still with us today: 'Common Centifolia', 'White Moss', 'Duc de Guiche', Hemisphaerica 'Multiplex', 'York and Lancaster', the three venerable Albas 'Plena', 'Great Maiden's Blush', and 'Lesser Maiden's Blush', and 'Pompon de Bourgogne' to name most of them. The only "very old" favorite which comes to mind as being conspicuous by its absence is 'De Meaux' (Seguier, 1637) CP. Otherwise, the cultivars in the Labyrinth are a festival of roses from primarily the 1820s, but also the 1810s and the early 1830s, quite as one would expect—the notion was probably to supply mainly "new but proven roses," much as would be the direction given by a city council to someone planning a civic rose garden today.

The great preponderance of Vibertian varieties will at once strike the reader; less evident, but also present, is a strong tendency towards French versions of names (for instance, the original list has 'La Royale' instead of 'Great Maiden's Blush'). From Vibert's earliest offerings ('Adèle Heu' of 1816, for instance) to those released within a few years of the appearance of Billberg's list ('Télémaque' of 1830, 'Duc d'Orléans' of 1831, 'Élisa LeMesle' of 1832, and of course 'Fénélon' of ca. 1836, as some examples), the list comprises a very rich survey of Vibert's *oeuvre*, so rich indeed that it is likely that the main supplier of roses to the rosarium was Vibert's nursery itself, which we know to have had commercial dealings throughout Europe. However, a few cultivars on the list could not have come from Vibert; intriguingly, for instance, Vibert never offered 'Belle Couronnée' (alias 'Celsiana'), possibly because of a lasting personal animus against the Cels firm, which was very much a part of the court clique with which Vibert was in disfavor.

But let us draw towards an end with some intriguing speculation. One fact from Vibert's life is very interesting to consider in relation to this rose garden. At some point in the mid to late 1820s, Vibert offered to donate to the Paris *Jardin des Plantes* his collection of rose cultivars, as he felt it would assist them in their research on the genus. This gift was refused, the given reason being that the *Jardin* was primarily interested in studying pure species, the clandestine reason being perhaps the machinations of the court clique against Vibert. Could it be that this offer, or some part of it, is what was finally realized in Stockholm? Perhaps Vibert's wish to promote serious botanical study of rose cultivars, scorned in his own land, at last found consummation in the welcoming land of Linnaeus' student.

Cultivars by Year

Noting the chronological ebb and flow of the various groups, either absolutely or relatively to each other, is essential to a full understanding of rose history. The following lists are also intended to assist those designing "period gardens" so that they can find easily and plant what was grown by a specific year (though, of course, these listings include many extinct cultivars). Additionally, the changing styles of naming roses are well worth a moment or two of reflection. We arrange the groupings in the order in which they appear in this volume. These are, of course, not *all* cultivars, but rather only those with entries in *The Old Rose Adventurer*.

Gallicas

Wild Species
Rosa gallica
Circa 1200
'Officinalis'
Pre-1581
'Rosa Mundi'
Pre-1629
'Holoserica'
'Holoserica Duplex'
'Holoserica Multiplex'
'Pompon de Bourgogne'
Early 18th Century
'Macrantha Rubicunda'
Pre-1754
'Marmorea'
Pre-1770
'Purpurine de France'
1773
'Perle de Weissenstein'
Pre-1787
'Admirable'
Pre-1790
'L'Évêque'
Pre-1791
'Cramoisie'
'Regina Dicta'
Pre-1799
'Pluton'
Pre-1806
'Belle sans Flatterie'
'Rosier d'Amour'

1809
'Grand Napoléon'
Pre-1810
'Achille'
'Beauté Tendre'
'De Van Eeden'
'Duc de Guiche'
'Empereur'
'Estelle'
'Grosse Cerise'
'La Maculée'
'Noire Couronnée'
'Renoncule'
'Superbe en Brun'
Pre-1811
'Aigle Brun'
'Aimable Poupre'
'Aimable Rouge'
'Alector Cramoisi'
'Bacchante'
'Beauté Insurmontable'
'Beauté Renommée'
'Belle Aimable'
'Belle Brun'
'Belle Parade'
'Bouquet Charmante'
'Bourbon'
'Busard Triomphant'
'Cérisette la Jolie'
'Couronnée'
'Cramoisie Éblouissante'
'Cramoisie Triomphante'
'Feu Amoureux'

'Gallica Alba'
'Gallica Alba Flore Plena'
'Grande Brique'
'Grande et Belle'
'Junon'
'Grande Violette Claire'
'La Pucelle'
'Mahaeca'
'Manteau Pourpre'
'Minerve'
'Nouveau Intelligible'
'Nouveau Monde'
'Nouveau Rouge'
'Ombre Panachée'
'Ombre Superbe'
'Ornement de Parade'
'Pallas'
'Panachée Superbe'
'Perle de l'Orient'
'Pourpre Charmant'
'Rouge Formidable'
'Rouge Superbe Actif'
'Sans Pareille Pourpre'
'Sans Pareille Rose'
'Subnigra'
'Velours Pourpre'
1811
'Roxelane'
Pre-1813
'Beauté Touchante'
'Belle Flore'
'Belle Galathée'
'Belle Pourpre'

'Carmin Brillant'
'Cocarde Pâle'
'Great Royal'
'Incomparable'
'Joséphina'
'Nouvelle Gagnée'
'Ornement de la Nature'
'Passe-Princesse'
'Pourpre Ardoisée'
Pre-1814
'Adèle'
'Adonis'
Pre-1815
'Gloire des Jardins'
'Holoserica Regalis'
'Jeannette'
'Jeune Henry'
1816
'Adèle Heu'
'Aline'
'Temple d'Apollon'
Pre-1817
'Pintade'
'Roi des Pourpres'
Pre-1818
'À Grand Cramoisi'
'Aimable Amie'
'Belle Hélène'
'Grand Monarche'
'Nouvelle Pivoine'
1818
'Aigle Noir'
'Ariane'

Gallicas

1818 *continued*
'Bérénice'
'Duchesse d'Angoulême'
'Duchesse de Berry'
'Grand Cramoisi de Vibert'
'Phoebus'
Pre-1819
'Belle Mignonne'
'Couronne de Salomon'
'Hector'
'La Provence'
'Le Grand Sultan'
'Lustre d'Église'
'Manteau d'Évêque'
1819
'Baraguay'
'Belle Herminie'
'Capricorn'
'Daphné'
'Fanny Bias'
'Fanny Parissot'
Pre-1820
'Beauté Surprenante'
'Belle Olympe'
'Clio'
'Belle Biblis'
'Cynthie'
'Grand Sultan'
'Eucharis'
'Eudoxie'
'Illustre'
'Isabelle'
'L'Obscurité'
'La Tendresse'
'Manteau Royal'
'Passe-Velours'
'Sanguineo-Purpurea Simplex'
'Tuscany'
1820
'Duc de Bordeaux'
'Manette'
'Marie Stuart'
Pre-1821
'Arlequin'
'Ponctué'
'Pourpre Marbrée'
'Tricolore'
'Triomphe de Flore'
1821
'Henri Quatre'
'Ypsilanti'
1822
'Charlotte de Lacharme'
'Mme. de Tressan'
'Néala'

1823
'Aglaé Adanson'
'Assemblage des Beautés'
'Dupuytren'
'Les Trois Mages'
'Ombrée Parfaite'
Pre-1824
'Fleurs de Pelletier'
1824
'Grand Palais de Laeken'
'Louis-Philippe'
Pre-1825
'Reine de Perse'
Circa 1825
'Léa'
'Pelletier'
1825
'Claire d'Olban'
'Virginie'
Pre-1826
'Abailard'
'Bellotte'
'Globe White Hip'
'Le Pérou'
'Orphise'
'Princesse Éléonore'
'Revenante'
'Zoé'
1826
'Fornarina'
'L'Enchanteresse'
Pre-1827
'Comte Foy de Rouen'
1827
'Général Foy'
'Pompon de Bourgogne à Fleur
    Blanche'
'Tricolore'
Pre-1828
'À Fleurs de Rose Tremière de
    la Chine'
'Beau Narcisse'
'Belle Virginie'
'Cora'
'Galatée'
'Horatius Coclès'
'Juliette'
'Princesse de Portugal'
'Pucelle de Lille'
1828
'Anacréon'
'Moïse'
'Président de Sèze'
Pre-1829
'Adonis'

'Belle Hélène'
'Belle Villageoise'
'Bérénice'
'Feu de Vesta'
'Grand Corneille'
'Octavie'
'Reine des Amateurs'
1829
'Marie-Antoinette'
'Marjolin'
Pre-1830
'Montézuma'
Circa 1830
'Fulgens'
'Helvetius'
1830
'Camayeux'
1831
'Du Maître d'École'
'Duc d'Orléans'
1832
'Agénor'
1833
'Alfieri'
'Ingénue'
'Renoncule Ponctuée'
Pre-1834?
'Ledonneau-Leblanc'
1834
'Alcine'
'Comte Boula de Nanteuil'
'Cramoisi Picoté'
'Héloïse'
'Hortense de Beauharnais'
'Julie d'Étanges'
'Malesherbes'
'Nestor'
Pre-1835
'Belle de Yèbles'
Circa 1835
'Edmond Duval'
'Oeillet Double'
1835
'Antonine d'Ormois'
'Fanny Elssler'
'Gonzalve'
'Lycoris'
'Nouvelle Transparente'
Pre-1836
'Adèle Prévost'
'Duc d'Arenberg'
'Gloire de France'
'Gracilis'
'La Nationale'
'Orpheline de Juillet'

'Rouge Admirable Strié'
1836
'D'Aguesseau'
'Juanita'
'Lucile Duplessis'
'Séguier'
Pre-1837
'Duc de Fitzjames'
'Royal Marbré'
1837
'Duchesse de Buccleuch'
'Sanchette'
Pre-1838
'Superb Tuscan'
1838
'Catinat'
'Ohl'
1839
'Belle Villageoise'
Pre-1840
'Catinat'
Circa 1840
'De Schelfhont'
'Joséphine Parmentier'
'Prince Frédéric'
'Princesse de Nassau'
1840
'Emilie Verachter'
Pre-1841
'Desiré Parmentier'
'Mazeppa'
'Paquita'
1841
'Columelle'
'Fornarina'
'Néron'
'Oeillet Parfait'
Pre-1842
'Adèle Courtoise'
'Amélie de Mansfield'
'Bellard'
'Château de Namur'
'Crignon de Montigny'
'Double Brique'
'Elise Rovella'
'Ferdinand de Buck'
'Général Donadieu'
'Henri Foucquier'
'Hippolyte'
1842
'Cosimo Ridolfi'
'Dona Sol'
'Jeanne Hachette'
'Madelon Friquet'
'Rosemary'

Pre-1843
'Captain Williams'
'Dumortier'
'Gazelle'
'Gil Blas'
'Kean'
'Petite Orléanaise'
1843
'Agar'
'Giselle'
'Narcisse de Salvandy'
'Phénice'
Pre-1844
'La Ville de Londres'
1844
'Mécène'
Circa 1845
'Van Huyssum'
1845
'Abaillard'
'Alcime'
'Aramis'
'Esther'
'Oeillet Flamand'
'Perle des Panachées'
Pre-1846
'Bossuet'
'Don de Guérin'
'Louis Van Tyll'
'Marie Tudor'
1846
'Ambrose Paré'
'Napoléon'
'Tricolore de Flandre'
'Turenne'
Pre-1847
'Belle Doria'
'Van Artevelde'
'Victor Parmentier'
1847
'Mercédès'
'Triomphe de Sterckmanns'
Pre-1848
'Nanette'
1849
'L'Ingénue'
Circa 1850
'Pepita'
Pre-1852
'Gros Provins Panachée'
1852
'Montalembert'
1853
'Georges Vibert'
'La Neige'

1855
'César Beccaria'
1856
'Tour Malakoff'
1857
'Pompon'
1872
'Belle des Jardins'
1876
'Ville de Toulouse'
1878
'König von Sachsen'
1880?
'Valence Dubois'
Pre-1885
'Alexandre Laquement'
'Beauté de la Malmaison'
'Chapelain d'Arenberg'
'Charles de Mills'
'Charles Lemayeux'
'Charles Lemoine'
'François Foucquier'
'Général Moreau'
'Gloriette'
'Mme. Ville'
'Nouveau Vulcain'
1898
'Marcel Bourgoin'
1900
'Conditorum'
'Oleifolia'
Pre-1906
'Gazella'
'Provins Ancien'
'Rosier des Parfumeurs'
1906
'Alika'
Pre-1929
'La Plus Belle des Ponctuées'
1952
'Scharlachglut'
Date Uncertain
'Complicata'
'Haddington'
'Les Saisons d'Italie'

Damasks

Wild
Rosa ×damascena
Ancient
'Sancta'
Pre-1551
'York and Lancaster'

1689?
'Kazanlyk'
Pre-1789
'Red Damask'
1801?
'Parure des Vierges'
Pre-1806
'Blush Damask'
Pre-1810
'La Félicité'
Pre-1811
'Argentée'
'Don Pedro'
'Virginale'
Pre-1813
'L'Amitié'
Pre-1817
'Belle Couronnée'
Pre-1818
'Fausse Unique'
1818
'Pénélope'
1819
'Silvia'
Circa 1820
'Panachée'
1820
'Damas Violacé'
'Duc de Chartres'
1823
'Lavalette'
Pre-1824
'Belle Auguste'
1825
'Boutigny'
'Rosemonde'
Pre-1826
'Belle d'Auteuil'
'Périclès'
'Roi des Pays-Bas'
'Rose de Puteau'
'Triomphe de Lille'
1826
'Triomphe de Rouen'
Pre-1827
'Pink Leda'
1827
'Déesse Flore'
Pre-1828
Rosa ×damascena 'Subalba'
Pre-1829
'Bélisaire'
'Henri IV'
Pre-1830
'Dame Blanche'
'Monstrueux'

1830
'Mme. Zoutmann'
Pre-1831
'Leda'
Pre-1832
'Ispahan'
1832
'Félicité Hardy'
Pre-1836
'Coralie'
1836
'La Ville de Bruxelles'
Pre-1838
'Babet'
1840?
'Rosier de Damas'
Pre-1841
'Duc de Cambridge'
1841
'Sémiramis'
1842
'La Négresse'
'Véturie'
1843
'Olympe'
Pre-1844
'Bella Donna'
'Pope'
1845
'Ismène'
'Noémie'
Pre-1846
'Angèle'
Pre-1848
'Eudoxie'
'Mme. Lambert'
'Mme. Stolz'
'Phoebus'
'Rose Verreux'
Pre-1850
'Louis Cazas'
1854?
'Léon Lecomte'
1856
'Botzaris'
Pre-1885
'Marguerite de Flandre'
'Mme. Carré'
1901
'Lady White'
'Turner's Crimson Damask'
1931
'Professeur Émile Perrot'
1939
'Oratam'

Damasks *continued*
1947
'Omar Khayyám'
1949
'Gloire de Guilan'
1950
'St. Nicholas'
Date Uncertain
'Rose à Parfum de Bulgarie'
'Rose à Parfum de Grasse'
'Rose d'Hivers'

Agathes

Pre-1754
'Blush Belgic'
Pre-1790
'Majestueuse'
'Soleil Brillante'
Pre-1791
'Rouge Belgic'
Circa 1802
'Enfant de France' (Holland)
Pre-1804
'Prolifère'
Pre-1810
'Henriette'
Pre-1811
'Beauté Superbe Agathée'
'Feunon Rouge'
'Francfort Agathé'
'Royale'
'Victorine la Couronnée'
1811?
'Marie-Louise'
1816
'Héloïse'
1818
'Sapho'
Pre-1819
'Bouquet Rose de Vénus'
Pre-1820
'Belle Hébé'
'Petite Renoncule Violette'
'Sommesson'
1820
'Fatime'
Pre-1824
'Enfant de France' (Brussels)
Pre-1826
'De la Malmaison'
Pre-1828
'Volumineuse'
Circa 1845
'Belle Isis'

Centifolias

Pre-1596
'Common Centifolia'
Pre-1616
'Grande Centfeuille de
    Hollande'
Pre-1629
'Rubra'
Pre-1695
'Hollandica'
Pre-1759
'Childling'
Pre-1775
'Alba'
'Variegata'
1777
'Unique'
1789
'Oeillet'
Circa 1800
'Vilmorin'
Pre-1802
'À Feuilles de Céleri'
Pre-1804
'À Feuilles Crénelées'
'À Fleurs Simples'
Pre-1806
'Des Peintres'
Pre-1808
'Foliacée'
1809
'Bullata'
Pre-1810
'La Louise'
'Le Rire Niais'
'Unique Rose'
Pre-1811
'À Feuille de Chêne'
'À Feuilles de Chanvre'
'Aglaia'
'Capricornus'
'Euphrosine l'Élégante'
'Thalie la Gentille'
1818
'Héloïse'
Pre-1819
'My Lady Kensington'
1819
'Minette'
Pre-1820
'Descemet'
'Gros Chou d'Hollande'
'Théone'
'Unique Admirable'

Pre-1821
'Yorkshire Provence'
1821
'Duc d'Angoulême'
'Unique Panachée'
Pre-1824
'Unique Rouge'
1824
'Reine des Centfeuilles'
Pre-1826
'Grand Bercam'
1829
'Goliath'
1830
'Adéline'
1832
'Wellington'
1835
'Blanchefleur'
Pre-1836
'Laure'
1837
'Anaïs Ségales'
1839
'Alain Blanchard'
Pre-1844
'Hypacia'
1845
'Adrienne de Cardoville'
'Eulalie LeBrun'
'Hulda'
'Justine Ramet'
Pre-1846
'Mme. L'Abbey'
Pre-1848
'Jacquinot'
1848
'Comtesse de Ségur'
Pre-1853
'Dométile Bécar'
Pre-1854
'Duc de Brabant'
1854
'Gaspard Monge'
'Gloriette'
1855
'Juanita'
1856
'Charles-Quint'
1857
'La Noblesse'
'Mme. d'Hébray'
'Tour de Malakoff'
Pre-1862
'Marguerite de Flandre'

Pre-1885
'Duchesse de Coutard'
'Grande Renoncule Violette'
'Regina'
'Robert le Diable'
1888
'Vierge de Cléry'
Pre-1906
'Leea Rubra'
1934
'Ballady'
'Stratosféra'
1938
'Röte Centifolie'
1958
'Black Boy'
'Blue Boy'
Date Uncertain
'À Fleurs Doubles Violettes'
'Ciudad de Oviedo'
'Eugénie Chamusseau'
'Fantin-Latour'
'Reine de Saxe'

Centifolia Pompons and Pompon Mosses

1637
'De Meaux'
Pre-1791
'Rosier des Dames'
1805
'Spong's'
1807
'À Fleurs Presque Simples'
Circa 1810
'Comtesse de Chamoïs'
Pre-1811
'Nouveau Petit Serment'
'Pompon Blanc'
Pre-1813
'Mossy De Meaux'
Pre-1817
'Pompon de Kingston'
Pre-1819
'Pompon Varin'
Pre-1820
'Calypso Petite'
'Petite Junon de Hollande'
Pre-1824
'White De Meaux'
1880
'Little Gem'
Date Uncertain
'Decora'

Mosses

Pre-1720
'Common Moss'
Pre-1777
'Rubra'
1788
'White Moss Rose'
Circa 1805
'Vilmorin'
1807
'Single'
1817
'White Bath'
1818
'Panachée'
1824
'De La Flèche'
Pre-1826
'Prolifère'
Pre-1826
'Semi-Double'
Pre-1827
'Crimson'
1827
'Cristata'
Pre-1829
'Gracilis'
1829
'Zoé'
Pre-1834
'Ferrugineux du Luxembourg'
Pre-1838
'Blush'
'Miniature Moss'
'Rivers' Single Crimson'
1839
'Angélique Quétier'
1840
'Asepala'
'Mauget'
1841
'Malvina'
Pre-1843
'Célina'
1843
'Alice Leroi'
'Catherine de Wurtemburg'
'Comtesse de Murinais'
'Précoce'
Pre-1844
'Panachée Pleine'
'Panaget'
1844
'Anémone'
'Unique de Provence'

1845
'Etna'
'Général Clerc'
'Indiana'
'Jenny Lind'
'Nuits d'Young'
'Princesse Adélaïde'
Pre-1846
'Delphinie'
'Joséphine'
'Lansezeur'
1846
'Laneii'
'Ponctuée'
'Princesse Royale'
1847
'Parmentier'
1848
'Jean Bodin'
'L'Obscurité'
'La Diaphane'
'Pourpre du Luxembourg'
'Soeur Marthe'
1849
'Aristobule'
'Bérangère'
'Pélisson'
'Routrou'
'Zaïre'
1850
'Barillet'
'Mme. Rose Chéri'
1851
'À Long Pédoncle'
'Adèle Pavié'
'D'Arcet'
'Duchesse d'Abrantès'
'Mme. Clémence Beauregard'
'Mme. De la Roche-Lambert'
'Mme. Soupert'
'Princesse Amélie'
1852
'Gloire des Mousseux'
'Ismène'
'Lafontaine'
'Marie de Blois'
1853
'Jeanne de Montfort'
'Maréchal Davoust'
'Princess Alice'
'Robert Fortune'
1854
'Capitaine John Ingram'
'Comtesse Doria'
'François de Salignac'

'Frédéric Soullier'
'Julie de Mersan'
'Lucie Duplessis'
'Princesse de Vaudémont'
1855
'Duchesse d'Istrie'
'William Lobb'
1856
'Duchesse de Verneuil'
'Général Kléber'
1857
'De Candolle'
'Ducis'
'La Caille'
'Ninette'
'Reine-Blanche'
1858
'Ménage'
'Mlle. Aristide'
'William Grow'
1859
'Emmeline'
'John Grow'
Circa 1860
'Coralie'
'Reine des Moussues'
1860
'Dr. Marjolin'
'Lane'
'Louise Verger'
1861
'Alcime'
'James Mitchell'
Pre-1862
'Pourpre Violet'
1862
'Blanche Simon'
1863
'Henri Martin'
Pre-1866
'Félicité Bohain'
1866
'Princesse Bacciochi'
Pre-1870
'Purpurea Rubra'
1872
'Eugène Verdier'
1876
'Violacée'
1877
'Louis Gimard'
Pre-1885
'Emilie'
Pre-1888
'Elisabeth Rowe'

1888
'Oeillet Panaché'
1890
'Capitaine Basroger'
'Crimson Globe'
1892
'Zenobia'
1900
'Cumberland Belle'
1905
'La Neige'
'Marie-Victoria Benoît'
Pre-1906
'Moussue du Japon'
1906
'Anni Welter'
1911
'Goethe'
1932
'Golden Moss'
'Olavus'
'Waltraud Nielsen'
'Yellow Moss'
1941
'Robert Léopold'
1956
'Parkjuwel'
'Parkzauber'
Date Uncertain
'Don Pedro'
'Le Lobèrde'

Mossy Remontants

1835
'Quatre Saisons Blanc
 Mousseux'
1844
'Perpétuelle Mauget'
1847
'Général Drouot'
'Mme. de Villars'
1849
'Hermann Kegel'
'Pompon Perpétuel'
1852
'Delille'
1853
'Céline Briant'
'Marie de Bourgogne'
'Oscar Leclerc'
'René d'Anjou'
1854
'Baron de Wassenaër'
'Mme. Édouard Ory'
'Salet'

Mossy Remontants
continued
1855
'Alfred de Dalmas'
'Bicolor'
'Circé'
'Gloire d'Orient'
'Impératrice Eugénie'
1856
'Mlle. Alice Leroy'
'Raphael'
1857
'Ma Ponctuée'
'Mme. de Staël'
'Validé'
1859
'Césonie'
1860
'Eugène de Savoie'
1861
'Fornarina'
'Hortense Vernet'
'John Fraser'
'John Cranston'
1863
'Clémence Robert'
'Mme. Legrand'
'Sophie de Marsilly'
1864
'Eugénie Guinoisseau'
'James Veitch'
'Mme. Platz'
1865
'Marie Leczinska'
'Mélanie Waldor'
1867
'Mme. Charles Salleron'
'Souvenir de Pierre Vibert'
1868
'Maupertuis'
1869
'Mme. William Paul'
1872
'Mme. Moreau'
1873
'Deuil de Paul Fontaine'
'Mme. Landeau'
1874
'Soupert et Notting'
1880
'Blanche Moreau'
1881
'Mousseline'

1890
'Mlle. Marie-Louise
    Bourgeoise'
1898
'Mme. Louis Lévêque'
1904
'Venus'
1933
'Gabriel Noyelle'

Albas

Wild Species
Rosa ×alba
Pre-1754
'Great Maiden's Blush'
'Semi-Plena'
Pre-1770
'Plena'
1797
'Lesser Maiden's Blush'
Pre-1799
'Belle Aurore'
1802
'Belle Thérèse'
1807
'Cymbaefolia'
1809
'Evratina'
Pre-1810
'Céleste'
'Elisa'
Pre-1813
'Beauté Tendre'
Pre-1815
'Semonville'
Pre-1817
'À Feuilles de Pêcher'
1817
'Fanny Rousseau'
'Petite Lisette'
Pre-1818
'Duc d'York'
1818
'Armide'
'Jeanne d'Arc'
1819
'Gabrielle d'Estrées'
Pre-1820
'Chloris'
1820
'Placidie'
1822
'Caroline d'Angleterre'

1823
'Amélia'
'Claudine'
'Joséphine Beauharnais'
'La Surprise'
'Semonville à Fleurs Doubles'
Pre-1826
'Belle de Ségur'
'Camille Bouland'
'Fanny-Sommesson'
1826
'Königin von Dannemark'
1828
'Monique'
Pre-1829
'Maxima Multiplex'
Circa 1830
'Alice'
Pre-1830
'Henriette Campan'
'Princesse de Lamballé'
1831
'Candide'
Pre-1833
'La Remarquable'
Pre-1836
'Félicité'
Pre-1838
'Monica'
Pre-1842
'Astrée'
1843
'Alba Bifera'
Pre-1844
'Étoile de la Malmaison'
'Ferox'
'Marie de Bourgogne'
'Zénobie'
1844
'Mme. Audot'
Pre-1846
'Blanche de Belgique'
'Blush Hip'
'Mme. Legras de St.
    Germain'
'Superbe'
'Vénus'
1847
'Esmeralda'
'Lucrèce'
'Ménage'
Pre-1848
'Fanny'
1876
'Pompon Blanc Parfait'

Pre-1885
'Vaucresson'
1911
'Arva Leany'
Date Uncertain
'Belle Amour'

Hemisphaericas

Wild Species
Rosa hemisphaerica
Pre-1629
'Multiplex'
Pre-1806
'Pompon Jaune'

Foetidas

Wild Species
Rosa foetida
1596
Rosa foetida 'Bicolor'
Pre-1802
'Jaune Double'
Pre-1817
'Rose Tulipe'
Pre-1821
'Luteola'
Circa 1824
'Harison's Yellow'
1824
'Pallida'
Circa 1828
'Double Yellow'
1833
'Persian Yellow'
Pre-1846
'Globe Yellow'
'Harisonii No 1'
'Jaune d'Italie'
'Victoria'
Pre-1848
'Harisonii No 2'
1906
'Parkfeuer'
1919
'Star of Persia'
1923
'Lawrence Johnston'
'Le Rêve'
1928
'Buisson d'Or'
1929
'Harison's Salmon'
'Rustica'

Pimpinellifolias

Wild Species
Rosa pimpinellifolia
Pre-1770
'Maculata'
1802
'Hibernica'
1803
'King of Scots'
Circa 1808
'Rouge'
1816
'La Belle Mathilde'
Pre-1817
'Pompon Blanc'
1817
'Belle Laure'
'Nankin'
Pre-1818
'Double Blanche'
1818
'Altaica'
'Belle Laure No 2'
Pre-1819
'Blanche Semi-Double'
1819
'Perpetual Scotch'
Pre-1820
'De Marienbourg'
'Double Purple'
'Estelle'
1820
'Rich Crimson'
'Vierge'
1821
'Double Blush Burnet'
1823
'Irène'
Pre-1824
'Inermis'
Pre-1826
'Double Carnée'
'Petite Écossaise'
Pre-1836
'Stanwell Perpetual'
Pre-1838
'Lutea'
'Sulphurea'
'William IV'
Pre-1846
'Bicolor'
Pre-1848
'Dominie Sampson'
'Gil Blas'
'Neptune'

1850?
'Marbrée d'Enghien'
1854
'Souvenir de Henry Clay'
Pre-1885
'Townsend'
Pre-1906
'Lady Dunmore'
'Lady Edine'
'Miss Frotter'
'White Scotch'
Pre-1910
'William III'
1924
'Dr. Merkeley'
1931
'Karl Foerster'
1937
'Frühlingsgold'
1942
'Frühlingsmorgen'
'Frühlingsstunde'
'Frühlingszauber'
1947
'Seager Wheeler'
1949
'Frühlingsduft'
'Frühlingstag'
'Suzanne'
1950
'Frühlingsanfang'
1951
'Claus Groth'
1954
'Frühlingsschnee'
1966
'Aicha'
Date Uncertain
'Aristide'
'Bicolore Nana'
'Didot'
'Double Pink Edine'
'Falkland'
'Glory of Edzell'
'Lemon'
'Mary Queen of Scots'
'Mrs. Colville'
'Ravellae'

Rubiginosas

Wild Species
Rosa rubiginosa
Circa 1800
'Williams's Sweetbriar'

Circa 1810
'Petite Hessoise'
Pre-1811
'Hessoise'
Pre-1813
'Zabeth'
Pre-1819
'Manning's Blush'
Pre-1824
'Clémentine'
Pre-1838
'Rose Angle'
Pre-1844
'La Belle Distinguée'
Pre-1846
'Hebe's Lip'
'Iver Cottage'
1892
'Janet's Pride'
1894
'Amy Robsart'
'Anne of Geierstein'
'Brenda'
'Lady Penzance'
'Lord Penzance'
'Lucy Ashton'
'Meg Merrilies'
'Rose Bradwardine'
1895
'Catherine Seyton'
'Edith Bellenden'
'Flora McIvor'
'Greenmantle'
'Jeannie Deans'
'John Cant'
'Julia Mannering'
'Lucy Bertram'
1909
'Refulgence'
1911
'Canary Bird'
1916
'Magnifica'
1920
'Mechthilde von Neuerburg'
1934
'Rosenwunder'
1939
'Max Haufe'
1940
'Fritz Nobis'
'Joseph Rothmund'
1954
'Goldbusch'

1955
'Aschermittwoch'
'Flammentanz'
1963
'Gruss an Koblenz'

Caninas

Wild Species
Rosa canina
1876
'Rose à Bois Jaspé'
1895
'Crême'
'Griseldis'
1898
'Una'
1909
'Walküre'
Pre-1910
'Andersonii'
1910
'Freya'
'Kiese'
'Siwa'
1920
'Gruss an Rengsdorf'
1925
'Theresia'
1927
'Weidenia'
1954
'Abbotswood'

A Miscellany

Due to the diverse nature of this section, we indicate for each cultivar its affiliation.

Wild Species
Hulthemia persica (Hult)
Rosa hugonis (Hug)
Rosa macrantha (Macra)
Rosa macrophylla (Macro)
Rosa majalis (Maj)
Rosa nutkana (Nut)
Rosa rubrifolia (Rubr)
Rosa soulieana (Soul)
Rosa villosa (Vil)
Rosa virginiana (Vir)
Rosa xanthina (Xan)

Circa 1500?
'Flore Pleno' (Maj)
Pre-1583
'Francofurtana' (Turb)

A Miscellany *continued*
Pre-1770
'Duplex' (Vil)
'Turneps' (Turb)
1790
'Impératrice Joséphine' (Turb)
Pre-1799
'Pavot' (Turb)
Pre-1811
'Fraxinifolia' (unk.)
Pre-1817
'Semi-Double' (Rubr)
Circa 1819
'Plena' (Vir)
Pre-1820
'Belle Rosine' (Turb)
Pre-1828
'Pinnatifide' (Rubr)
1829
'Ancelin' (Turb)
'Anne de Boleyn' (Turb)
1836
'Hardii' (Hult)
1894
'Théano' (unk.)
1896
'Flora Plena' (Rubr)
1906?
'Daisy Hill' (Macra)
1912
'Kew Rambler' (Soul)
1913
'Auguste Roussel' (Macro)
1920
'Headleyensis' (Hug)
1923
'Carmenetta' (Rubr)
1926
'Coryana' (Macro)
'Dr. E. M. Mills' (Hug)
Pre-1927
'Coral Drops' (unk.)
1927
'Cantab' (Nut)
1930
'Schoener's Nutkana' (Nut)
Circa 1931
'Cantabrigensis' (Hug)
After 1931
'Düsterlohe' (Macra)
Pre-1932
'Double Hugonis' (Hug)
1934
'Albert Maumené' (Hug)
'Château de Vaire' (Macro)

1936
'Raubritter' (Macra)
1937
'Professor Ibrahim' (Macra)
1939
'Chevy Chase' (Soul)
'Elfenreigen' (Macra)
'Harry Maasz' (Macro)
1941
'Düsterlohe II' (Macra)
1966
'Master Hugh' (Macro)
1979
'Sir Cedric Morris' (Rubr)
Date Uncertain
'Doncasterii' (Macro)
'Harvest Song' (Vir)
'Mechliniae' (Rubr)
'Wickwar' (Soul)

Roxburghiis

Wild Species
Rosa roxburghii
Pre-1817
'Striata'
Circa 1829
'Pourpre Ancien'
Pre-1841
'Hybride du Luxembourg'
'Simplex'
'Triomphe de Macheteaux'
1854
'Triomphe des Français'
1864
'Triomphe de la Guillotière'
1866
'Premier Essai'
1869
'Imbricata'
1872
'Ma Surprise'
1901
'Château de la Juvenie'
'Domaine de Chapuis'

Bracteatas

Wild Species
Rosa bracteata
Rosa clinophylla
Pre-1822
'Scabriusculus'
1829
'Maria Léonida'

Pre-1835
'Alba Odorata'
'Coccinea'
'Plena'
'Victoire Modeste'
Pre-1836
'Rubra Duplex'
Pre-1840
'Rosea'
Pre-1846
'Scarlet Maria Leonida'
Pre-1847
'Nerrière'
1918
'Mermaid'
1919
'Sea Foam'
Mid-1950s
'Happenstance'
1960?
'Pink Mermaid'
Date Uncertain
'Dwarf Mermaid'

Rugosas

Wild Species
Rosa ×kamtchatika
Rosa rugosa
Rosa rugosa 'Alba'
Rosa rugosa 'Rubra'
1825
'Parnassine'
Pre-1872
'Taïcoun'
1874
'Souvenir de Yeddo'
1879
'Kaiserin des Nordens'
1881
'Comte d'Epremesnil'
1886
'Thusnelda'
1887
'Mme. Georges Bruant'
1888
'Mikado'
1889
'Mme. Charles Frédéric Worth'
1890
'Germanica'
'Stella Polaris'
1891
'Fimbriata'

1892
'Blanc Double de Coubert'
'Prof. N. E. Hansen'
1893
'America'
1894
'Belle Poitevine'
'Calocarpa'
'Cibles'
'Jelina'
'Proteiformis'
'Souvenir de Christophe Cochet'
Circa 1895
'Agnes Emily Carman'
1895
'Chédane-Guinoisseau'
'Rose Apples'
'Souvenir de Pierre Leperdrieux'
1896
'Mrs. Anthony Waterer'
'Schneelicht'
1898
'Delicata'
1899
'Alice Aldrich'
'Atropurpurea'
'Conrad Ferdinand Meyer'
'Heterophylla'
'Lilli Dieck'
'Potager du Dauphin'
'Souvenir de Philémon Cochet'
'Villa des Tybilles'
Circa 1900
'Mme. Philippe Plantamour'
1900
'Amélie Gravereaux'
'Germanica B'
'Mercedes'
'Monsieur Hélye'
'Monsieur Morlet'
1901
'Lady Curzon'
'Mme. Tiret'
'New Century'
'S.A.R. Ferdinand Ier'
'S.M.I. Abdul-Hamid'
1902
'Crispata'
'Roseraie de l'Haÿ'
1903
'Mme. Alvarez del Campo'
'Mme. Lucien Villeminot'

'Repens Alba'
'Rose à Parfum de l'Haÿ'
Circa 1904
'Repens Rosea'
1904
'Mme. Ballu'
'Mme. Henri Gravereaux'
'Rosier Tenuifolia'
1905
'Hansa'
'Mme. Ancelot'
'Sir Thomas Lipton'
1906
'Carmen'
'La Mélusine'
'Monsieur Gustave Bienvêtu'
'Nova Zembla'
1907
'Adiantifolia'
'Magnifica'
'Rugosa × Duc d'Edinburgh'
'Siberian Form'
1908
'Daniel Lesueur'
'Georges Cain'
'Le Cid'
'Régina Badet'
1909
'Hildenbrandseck'
1911
'Fürstin von Pless'
'Schneezwerg'
1912
'Mme. Julien Potin'
'Tetonkaha'
1914
'Arnoldiana'
'Dolly Varden'
'Fru Dagmar Hartopp'
1918
'F. J. Grootendorst'
1923
'Agnes'
'Pink Grootendorst'
'Türke's Rugosa-Sämling'
1924
'Bergers Erfolg'
'Stern von Prag'
1926
'Sarah Van Fleet'
1927
'Amdo'
'Kitana'
'Koza'
'Minisa'

1928
'Nemo'
'Ruskin'
'Schwabenland'
'Signe Relander'
1930
'Dr. Eckener'
'Single Pink'
1931
'Moje Hammarberg'
1932
'Goldener Traum'
'Vanguard'
1933
'Sanguinaire'
1935
'Golden King'
1936
'Grootendorst Supreme'
1937
'Jindřich Hanus Böhm'
1939
'George Will'
'Wasagaming'
1962
'White Grootendorst'
Date Uncertain
'Margheritae'

Laevigatas

Wild Species
Rosa laevigata
1887?
'Pink Cherokee'
Pre-1891
'Double Cherokee'
1896
'Anemonenrose'
1909
'Silver Moon'
1911
'Mrs. A. Kingsmill'
1913
'Ramona'

Banksias

Wild Species
Rosa banksiae
1807
'Alba Plena'
1823?
'Lutea'

Pre-1829
'Lutescens'
1840
'Fortuneana'
1844
'Anemonaeflora'
Pre-1846
'Alba Grandiflora'
'Rosea'
1920
'Hybride di Castello'
1961
'Purezza'

Musks

Wild Species
Rosa brunonii
Rosa moschata
Pre-1629
'Double White Damask Musk Rose'
'Spanish Musk Rose'
Pre-1640
'Double White'
Pre-1821
'Semi-Double'
Pre-1828
'De Tous Mois'
Pre-1829
'Princesse de Nassau'
Pre-1835
'Eponine'
Circa 1835
'Mme. d'Arblay'
1835
'The Garland'
Pre-1846
'Rivers' Musk'
Circa 1883
'Narrow Water'
1899
'Paul's Himalayan Musk Rambler'
'Paul's Himalayica Alba Magna'
'Paul's Himalayica Double Pink'
1916
'Paul's Tree Climber'
1946
'Francis E. Lester'
1954
'La Mortola'

Arvensises

Wild Species
Rosa arvensis
1768
'Ayrshirea'
Pre-1804
'Scandens'
Pre-1820
'Ruga'
1835
'Ayrshire Queen'
Pre-1838
'Dundee Rambler'
'Miller's Climber'
'Splendens'
1840
'Thoresbyana'
Pre-1846
'Alice Gray'
Pre-1855
'Virginian Rambler'
1882
'Mme. Viviand-Morel'
Pre-1885
'Capreolata'
1886
'Aennchen von Tharau'
1909
'Ville de St.-Maur'
1919
'Beacon Belle'
1928
'Venusta Pendula'
1931
'Düsterlohe'
Pre-1934
'Miss Jekyll'

Sempervirenses

Wild Species
Rosa sempervirens
Pre-1810
'De la Chine à Feuilles Longues'
1828
'Dona Maria'
'Félicité et Perpétue'
Pre-1829
'Adélaïde d'Orléans'
'Eugène d'Orléans'
'Léopoldine d'Orléans'
'Mélanie de Montjoie'

Sempervirenses *continued*
1829
'Princesse Louise'
'Princesse Marie'
Circa 1830
'Flore'
1832
'Reine des Belges'
Pre-1833
'Spectabilis'
1850
'William's Evergreen'
Pre-1852
'Anatole de Montesquieu'

Boursaults

Wild Species
Rosa pendulina
Rosa pendulina 'Laevis'
Pre-1770
'Inermis'
1796
'Gracilis'
Pre-1810
'Calypso'
Circa 1810
'Reversa'
Circa 1815
'À Fleurs Panachées'
'Maheca'
Pre-1820
'Boursault'
Pre-1824
'À Boutons Renversés à Fleurs
    Simples'
Pre-1829
'Plena'
1829
'Amadis'
Pre-1844
'Elegans'
Pre-1846
'Drummond's Thornless'
1874
'Mme. de Sancy de Parabère'
1883
'Inermis Morletii'
1889
'Zigeunerblut'
1899
'L'Orléanaise'
Date Uncertain
'Weissrote Mme. Sancy de
    Parabère'

Setigeras

Wild Species
Rosa setigera
Circa 1790?
'Mary Washington'
1843
'Baltimore Belle'
'Pallida'
'Perpetual Pink'
'Queen of the Prairies'
'Superba'
Circa 1846
'Anne Maria'
'Eva Corinne'
'Jane'
'Miss Gunnell'
'Mrs. Hovey'
'President'
'Pride of Washington'
'Ranunculiflora'
'Triumphant'
'Virginia Lass'
1860
'Gem of the Prairies'
1886
'Erinnerung an Brod'
'Forstmeisters Heim'
1887
'Eurydice'
'Viragó'
Circa 1890
'Alpenfee'
1890
'Corporal Johann Nagy'
'Ovid'
1895
'Himmelsauge'
Pre-1898
'Tennessee Belle'
1925
'Mrs. F. F. Prentiss'
'President Coolidge'
1927
'Yuhla'
1934
'Nelly Custis'

Wichuraianas

Wild Species
Rosa wichuraiana
Rosa wichuraiana 'Bracteata'
Rosa wichuraiana 'Poteriifolia'
1897
'South Orange Perfection'

1898
'Evergreen Gem'
'Manda's Triumph'
'May Queen'
'Pink Roamer'
'Ruby Queen'
1899
'Gardenia'
'Jersey Beauty'
'Sweetheart'
'Universal Favorite'
1900
'Albéric Barbier'
'Ernst Grandpierre'
'François Foucard'
'Lady Duncan'
'Milky Way'
'Paul Transon'
'René André'
'William C. Egan'
1901
'Adélaïde Moullé'
'Alba Rubifolia'
'Cramoisi Simple'
'Debutante'
'Dorothy Perkins'
'Edmond Proust'
'Elisa Robichon'
'Pearl Queen'
'Pink Pearl'
'Rubra'
1902
'Anna Rübsamen'
'François Poisson'
'Mme. Constans'
1903
'Alexandre Trémouillet'
'Émile Fortépaule'
'Farquhar'
'Ferdinand Roussel'
'Professor C. S. Sargent'
1904
'Carissima'
'Gerbe Rose'
'La Perle'
'Léontine Gervais'
'Marco'
'Minnehaha'
'Valentin Beaulieu'
1905
'François Guillot'
'Jean Guichard'
'Joseph Billard'
'Lady Gay'
1906
'American Pillar'

'Delight'
'Evangeline'
'François Juranville'
'Frau Albert Hochstrasser'
'Frau Marie Weinbach'
'Mme. Alice Garnier'
'Schneeball'
'Theodora Milch'
'Tricolore'
1907
'Alexandre Girault'
'Paradise'
'Rambler-Königin'
'Seagull'
1908
'Babette'
'Diabolo'
'Excelsa'
'Jules Levacher'
'Lady Godiva'
'Miss Helyett'
'Souvenir de Paul Raudnitz'
'White Dorothy'
1909
'American Beauty, Climbing'
'Aviateur Blériot'
'Christine Wright'
'Cinderella'
'Désiré Bergera'
'Dorothy Dennison'
'Greta Fey'
'Jessica'
'Joseph Liger'
'La Fiamma'
1910
'Casimir Moullé'
'Christian Curle'
'Dr. W. Van Fleet'
'Eisenach'
'Elsie'
'Fragezeichen'
'Fraulein Octavia Hesse'
'Jean Girin'
'L'Avenir'
'Paul Ploton'
'Shower of Gold'
'Troubadour'
1911
'Bonnie Belle'
'Coquina'
'Garisenda'
'Mme. Huguette Despiney'
'Sodenia'
'Souvenir d'Adolphe de
    Charvoik'
'Wichmoss'

1912
'Bouquet Rose'
'Coronation'
'De Candolle'
'Edgar Andreu'
'Ethel'
'Frau A. von Brauer'
'Freifrau von Marschall'
'Le Mexique'
'Mme. Auguste Nonin'
'Mrs. Littleton Dewhurst'
'Paul Noël'
'Petit Louis'
'Sander's White Rambler'
'Sargent'
'Source d'Or'
1913
'Andenken an Breslau'
'Arcadia'
'Chatillon-Rambler'
'Donau!'
'Grevinde Silvia Knuth'
'Gruss an Freundorf!'
'Miss Flora Mitten'
'Renée Danielle'
1914
'Louis Sauvage'
'Shalimar'
1915
'America'
'Gaston Lesieur'
'Le Poilu'
'Mary Lovett'
'Variegata'
1916
'Auguste Gervaise'
'Paul's Scarlet Climber'
1917
'Alida Lovett'
'Bess Lovett'
'Purity'
1918
'Aunt Harriet'
'Emily Gray'
'Fernand Rabier'
'Général Testard'
'Henri Barruet'
'Maxime Corbon'
'Nokomis'
'Victory'
1919
'Beauté Orléanaise'
'Max Graf'
'Romeo'
1920
'André Louis'

'Dr. Huey'
'Fernand Tanne'
'Jacotte'
'Yvonne'
1921
'Albertine'
'Fraîcheur'
'Souvenir d'Ernest Thébault'
'Vicomtesse de Chabannes'
'W. Freeland Kendrick'
1922
'Dorcas'
'Île de France'
'The Beacon'
1923
'Madeleine Lemaire'
'Mary Wallace'
'Milano'
'Papa Rouillard'
'Purpurtraum'
'Snowflake'
1924
'Bloomfield Favorite'
'Clematis'
'Mme. Charles Lejeune'
1925
'Achievement'
'Ardon'
'Bloomfield Courage'
'Fernande Krier'
'Petit René'
'Solarium'
1926
'Breeze Hill'
'Heart of Gold'
'Jean L'Hoste'
'Monthly Rambler'
'Regierungsrat Rottenberger'
'Royal Scarlet Hybrid'
'Ruby Ring'
1927
'Glenn Dale'
'Marie Gouchault'
'Thelma'
1928
'Bonfire'
'Chaplin's Pink Climber'
'Marie Dietrich'
'Mühle Hermsdorf'
1929
'Jeanne Richert'
'Normandie'
'Primevère'
'Refresher'
1930
'Chaplin's Crimson Glow'

'Coupe d'Or'
'New Dawn'
1931
'Johanna Röpke'
'Syringa'
1932
'Buttermere'
'Easlea's Golden Rambler'
'July Glory'
'Windermere'
Pre-1933
'Yellow Minnehaha'
1933
'Jitřenka'
'Loveliness'
'Melita'
'Mrs. Arthur Curtiss James'
1934
'Matka Vlast'
'Souvenir de J. Mermet'
1935
'Dr. Zamenhof'
'Harlequin'
1936
'Apricot Glow'
'Mičurin'
1937
'Elegance'
'Golden Glow'
'Golden Orange Climber'
'Srdce Europy'
'Symbol Miru'
1938
'Frau Liesel Brauer'
'Little Compton Creeper'
1939
'Carpet of Gold'
'Direktor Benschop'
1940
'Copper Glow'
1941
'Claude Rabbe'
'Erwin Hüttmann'
'Magic Carpet'
1942
'Brownell Yellow Rambler'
1951
'Crimson Shower'
1952
'Aëlita'
1953
'Denyse Ducas'
1955
'Morning Dawn'
1956
'Étendard'

'Miss Liberty'
1959
'Weisse New Dawn'
1966
'Coral Satin'
1980
'Wichuraiana Hybride I'
Date Uncertain
'Merveille de la Brie'

Multifloras

Wild Species
Rosa multiflora
Rosa multiflora var. *cathayensis*
1804
'Carnea'
1815
'Platyphylla'
Pre-1821
'Rose'
1827
'Polyantha'
Pre-1828
'Grevillii'
1834
'Laure Davoust'
Pre-1842
'Graulhié'
1843
'Coccinea'
Pre-1844
'Russelliana'
1844
'De La Grifferaie'
1848
'Menoux'
1849
'À Bois Brun'
1862
'Tricolore'
Circa 1870
'Watsoniana'
1882
'Bijou de Lyon'
1884
'Geschwinds Nordlandrose'
1885
'Daniel Lacombe'
'Roi des Aunes'
1886
'Erlkönig'
'Fatinitza'
'Geschwinds Orden'
'Nymphe Tepla'
'Polyantha Grandiflora'

Multifloras *continued*
1887
'Ernst G. Dörell'
'Gilda'
1888
'Dawson'
Circa 1890
'Caroline Bank'
'Trompeter Von Säckingen'
1890
'Wodan'
1892
'Nymphe Egeria'
'Olivet'
1893
'Turner's Crimson Rambler'
1897
'Helene'
1898
'Psyche'
1899
'Leuchtstern'
'Royal Cluster'
'Weisser Herumstreicher'
Circa 1900
'Futtaker Schlingrose'
'Geschwinds Schönste'
'Josephine Ritter'
'Leopold Ritter'
1900
'Bleu Violette'
'The Lion'
1901
'Gardeniaeflora'
'Purple East'
'Queen Alexandra'
'Rubin'
'The Wallflower'
1902
'Non Plus Ultra'
'Perle des Neiges'
'Taunusblümchen'
1903
'Blush Rambler'
'Cato'
'Philadelphia Rambler'
'Tea Rambler'
1904
'Blumen-Dankert'
'Hiawatha'
1905
'Garden's Glory'
'Mrs. F. W. Flight'
'Souvenir de l'Exposition de
      Bordeaux 1905'
'Stella'

'Waltham Bride'
'Wedding Bells'
1906
'Frau Lina Strassheim'
'Grossherzogin Eléonore von
      Essen'
'Le Droit Humain'
'Tausendschön'
1907
'Bordeaux'
'Dr. Reymond'
'Francis'
'Ida Klemm'
'Kathleen'
1908
'Bagatelle'
'Flower of Fairfield'
'Goldfinch'
'Lyon Rambler'
'Malva Rambler'
'Neige d'Avril'
'Newport Fairy'
1909
'Asta von Parpart'
'Baronin Anna von Lüttwitz'
'Buttercup'
'Frau Georg von Simson'
'Gräfin Ada von Bredow'
'Veilchenblau'
1910
'Bocca Negra'
'Graf Zeppelin'
'Hugo Maweroff'
'Jkvr. D. Baronesse von
      Ittersum'
'Lisbeth von Kamecke'
'Rambling Rector'
'Wartburg'
1911
'Améthyste'
'Andreas Hofer'
'Gräfin Marie Henriette
      Chotek'
'Perle von Britz'
'Prinz Hirzeprinzchen'
'Prinzessin Ludwig von
      Bayern'
1912
'Caroubier'
'Crimson Grandiflora'
'Hakeburg'
'Roby'
'Sweet Lavender'
1913
'Carolina Budde'
'Emile Nerini'

'Geisha'
'Lien Budde'
'Perle vom Wienerwald!'
1914
'Oriflamme'
'Pemberton's White Rambler'
1915
'Steyl Rambler'
1916
'Ghislaine de Féligonde'
'Paulette Bentall'
'White Mrs. Flight'
1917
'Roserie'
'Schloss Friedenstein'
1918
'Daisy Brazileir'
'White Tausendschön'
1919
'Coralie'
'Rudelsburg'
1920
'Havering Rambler'
1921
'Violette'
1922
'Emerickrose'
'Hildeputchen'
'Papa Gouchault'
'Printemps Fleuri'
1923
'Prior M. Oberthau'
1924
'Aurélian Igoult'
'Bonnie Prince'
'Rose-Marie Viaud'
1925
'Eichsfeldia'
'Evodia'
'Gruss an Breinegg'
'Mánja Böhmová'
'Maria Liesa'
'Marietta Silva Taroucová'
'Mme. Jenny'
'Turner's Crimson Rambler ×
      Veilchenblau'
1926
'Agnes und Bertha'
'Blanda Egreta'
'Elisabeth'
'Exquisite'
'Gruss an Germershausen'
'Madeleine Seltzer'
'Mme. François Royet'
1927
'Laure Soupert'

'Mary Hicks'
1928
'Aristide Briand'
'Ernst Dechant'
'Unique'
1929
'Anci Böhmova'
'Erna'
'Geschwinds Nordlandrose II'
'Kleine Rosel'
1930
'Ratgeber Rose'
1931
'Frau Käte Schmid'
'Hiawatha Remontant'
1932
'Apple Blossom'
'Mosellied'
1933
'Mme. Charles Yojerot'
1934
'Hans Schmid'
'Karl Schneider'
1935
'Andrée Vanderschrick'
'Charlotte von Rathlef'
'Kde Domov Muj'
1936
'Památnik Komenského'
'Peter Lambert'
'Svatopluk Čech'
'Vlatava'
1937
'Indra'
1938
'Charlotte Mackensen'
'Gruss an Hannover'
1939
'Erato'
'June Morn'
Circa 1950
'Gela Tepelmann'
1960
'Bobbie James'
'Chatter'
Date Uncertain
'G. F. Veronica'

Lambertianas

1885
'Max Singer'
1895
'Aglaia'
'Euphrosine'
'Thalia'

1900
'Electra'
1903
'Gruss an Zabern'
'Philippine Lambert'
'Thalia Remontant'
1904
'Frau Helene Videnz'
'Tiergarten'
'Trier'
1906
'Birdie Blye'
1909
'Adrian Reverchon'
'Excellenz Kuntze'
'Excellenz von Schubert'
'Geheimrat Dr. Mitteweg'
'Kommerzienrat W.
    Rautenstrauch'
'Thermidor'
1911
'Gartenstadt Liegnitz'
'Hauff'
1912
'Heine'
'Oriole'
1913
'Arndt'
1914
'Lessing'
'Peter Rosegger'
1915
'Blanche Frowein'
1916
'Von Liliencron'
1917
'Hoffmann von Fallersleben'
1919
'Heinrich Conrad Söth'
1920
'Mosel'
1922
'Chamisso'
1924
'Gneisenau'
1930
'Frau A. Weidling'
1932
'Ausonius'
'Heideröslein'
'Rudolf von Bennigsen'
1934
'Gartendirektor Otto Linne'
'Prodaná Nevěsta
1935
'Probuzeni'

1937
'Frau Eva Schubert'
'Mozart'
1939
'Wilhelm Marx'
1942
'Frau Sophie Meyerholz'
1947
'Frau Professor Grischko'
1951
'Lyric'
1952
'Buisman's Triumph'
'Grandmaster'
1955
'Lichterloh'
1956
'Zitronenfalter'
1959
'Gruss an Heidelberg'
'Lausitz'
'Neisse'
'Saarbrücken'
1960
'Lavender Lassie'
'Ufhoven'

Hybrid Musks

1886
'Moschata × Polyantha'
1912
'Daphne'
'Queen of the Musks'
1913
'Danaë'
'Moonlight'
1914
'Ceres'
'Galatea'
'Winter Cheer'
1915
'Clytemnestra'
'Pearl'
'Queen Alexandra'
1918
'Daybreak'
'Pax'
'Thisbe'
1919
'Prosperity'
1920
'Callisto'
'Vanity'
1921
'Sammy'

1922
'Francesca'
'Kathleen'
1923
'Aurora'
'Nur-Mahál'
'Sea Spray'
1924
'Penelope'
1925
'Bloomfield Culmination'
'Bloomfield Dainty'
'Bloomfield Discovery'
'Bloomfield Fascination'
'Cascadia'
'Cornelia'
1926
'Bishop Darlington'
1927
'Bloomfield Perfection'
'Fortuna'
'Robin Hood'
1928
'Felicia'
1929
'Bloomfield Comet'
'Chami'
1930
'Maid Marion'
1931
'Bloomfield Completeness'
'Bloomfield Dawn'
'Pink Prosperity'
1933
'Autumn Delight'
'Eva'
'Rosaleen'
1934
'Wilhelm'
1936
'Belinda'
1938
'Ballerina'
'Havering'
'Rostock'
'Sangerhausen'
1939
'Buff Beauty'
1942
'Inspektor Blohm'
Circa 1946
'Wind Chimes'
1948
'Andenken an Alma de l'Aigle'
1950
'Bonn'

'Will Scarlet'
'Nymphenburg'

Old Hybrid Tea and Pernetiana Climbers

1902
'Ards Pillar'
'England's Glory'
'Lady Waterlow'
1903
'Morgenrot'
1906
'Sarah Bernhardt'
1907
'Souvenir d'Émile Zola'
1908
'Liberty, Climbing'
1909
'Louis Barbier'
1911
'Florence Haswell Veitch'
1912
'Richmond, Climbing'
1913
'Effective'
'Miss Marion Manifold'
'Monsieur Paul Lédé,
    Climbing'
1915
'Cupid'
'Paul's Lemon Pillar'
1916
'Colcestria'
1917
'Irish Fireflame, Climbing'
'Louise Catherine Breslau,
    Climbing'
1918
'Hoosier Beauty, Climbing'
1919
'Black Boy'
'Frau Ida Münch'
'H. Vessey Machin, Climbing'
Pre-1920
'Moonshine'
1920
'Château de Clos-Vougeot,
    Climbing'
'Gartendirektor Julius Schütze'
'Gwen Nash'
'Irène Bonnet'
'Nora Cuningham'
'Ophelia, Climbing'
'Rosemary, Climbing'
'Souvenir de Claudius Denoyel'

Old Hybrid Tea and Pernetiana Climbers
continued

1921
'Mme. Édouard Herriot, Climbing'

1922
'Kitty Kininmonth'
'Marguerite Carels'
'Mrs. Aaron Ward, Climbing'
'Mrs. Herbert Stevens, Climbing'
'Scorcher'

1923
'General MacArthur, Climbing'
'Jonkheer J. L. Mock, Climbing'
'Laurent Carle, Climbing'
'Professor Dr. Hans Molisch'
'Vicomtesse Pierre de Fou'

1924
'Allan Chandler'
'Chastity'
'Lyon-Rose, Climbing'
'Sunday Best'
'Willowmere, Climbing'

1925
'Daydream'
'Los Angeles, Climbing'
'Mady'
'Souvenir de Claudius Pernet, Climbing'

1926
'Mme. Butterfly, Climbing'
'Queen of Hearts'

1927
'Cracker'
'Hadley, Climbing'
'Mme. Grégoire Staechelin'
'Radiance, Climbing'
'Red Radiance, Climbing'
'Rose Marie, Climbing'
'Souvenir de Georges Pernet, Climbing'
'Wilhelm Kordes, Climbing'

1928
'Countess of Stradbroke'

1929
'Columbia, Climbing'
'Comte F. de Chavagnac'
'Mme. Segond-Weber, Climbing'
'Mrs. Henry Morse, Climbing'
'The Queen Alexandra Rose, Climbing'

1930
'Dame Edith Helen, Climbing'
'Independence Day, Climbing'

'Mrs. Henry Winnett, Climbing'
'Talisman, Climbing'

1931
'Crimson Conquest'
'Ednah Thomas'
'Étoile de Hollande, Climbing'
'Général-Superior Arnold Janssen, Climbing'
'Réveil Dijonnais'
'Rosella'
'Shot Silk, Climbing'

1932
'Mrs. C. V. Haworth, Climbing'

1933
'Angelus, Climbing'
'Elvira Aramayo, Climbing'
'Lady Sylvia, Climbing'
'Mrs. Pierre S. Du Pont, Climbing'

1934
'Hermann Robinow, Climbing'

1935
'Julien Potin, Climbing'
'Lady Forteviot, Climbing'

1936
'Christine, Climbing'
'Comtesse Vandal, Climbing'
'Condesa de Sástago, Climbing'

1937
'Gruss an Aachen, Climbing'
'Mevrouw G. A. van Rossem, Climbing'
'Mrs. Sam McGredy, Climbing'

1938
'Capitaine Soupa, Climbing'
'Captain Thomas'
'Mamie, Climbing'

1940
'Dr. J. H. Nicolas'
'Wenzel Geschwind, Climbing'

1941
'Apotheker Georg Höfer, Climbing'

1942
'Président Vignet, Climbing'

Date Uncertain
'Gloire de Hollande, Climbing'

Hybrid Teas, 1900–1920

1900
'Bessie Brown'
'Irish Beauty'
'Irish Glory'

'Irish Modesty'
'La Tosca'
'Lady Clanmorris'
'Liberty'
'Magnafrano'
'Marie Henry'
'Mme. Dailleux'
'Mme. J.-P. Soupert'
'Mme. Jean Favre'
'Mme. Viger'
'Papa Reiter'

1901
'Abbé André Reitter'
'Edmond Deshayes'
'Franz Deegen'
'Gladys Harkness'
'Lady Moyra Beauclerc'
'Laure Wattinne'
'Marie Isakoff'
'Mildred Grant'
'Mlle. de Neux'
'Mme. Marie Croibier'
'Pierre Wattinne'
'Pharisäer'
'Prince de Bulgarie'

1902
'Alice Lindsell'
'Apotheker Georg Höfer'
'Capitaine Soupa'
'Edmée et Roger'
'Farbenkönigin'
'Flush o'Dawn'
'Frau Lilla Rautenstrauch'
'Frau Peter Lambert'
'Goldelse'
'Gustav Sobry'
'Madeleine Faivre'
'Mamie'
'Marguerite Guillot'
'Marianne Pfitzer'
'Mark Twain'
'Max Hesdörffer'
'Monsieur Paul Lédé'
'Paul Meunier'
'Perle von Godesburg'
'Reine Carola de Saxe'
'Souvenir d'Anne-Marie'
'Wenzel Geschwind'
'Young America'

1903
'Alice Grahame'
'Amateur André Fourcaud'
'Commandant Letourneux'
'Enchanter'
'Florence Pemberton'
'Friedrich Albert Krupp'

'Gertrude'
'Gustav Grünerwald'
'John Ruskin'
'Königin Carola von Sachsen'
'Koningin Emma'
'Le Progrès'
'Lohengrin'
'Louise Pernot'
'Mme. Maurice Fenaille'
'Monsieur Joseph Hill'
'Souvenir de Maria Zozaya'

1904
'Cardinal'
'Dean Hole'
'Earl of Warwick'
'Étoile de France'
'Frau J. Reiter'
'General MacArthur'
'Graf Fritz von Hochberg'
'Grossherzogin Alexandra'
'Gruss an Sangerhausen'
'Irish Brightness'
'Irish Pride'
'Irish Star'
'La Detroit'
'Lady Ashtown'
'Lady Wenlock'
'Marquis de Bouillé'
'Mme. Alfred Sabatier'
'Mme. Léon Pain'
'Mrs. David McKee'
'Mrs. Theodore Roosevelt'
'Oberbürgermeister Dr. Troendlin'
'Reine Marguerite d'Italie'
'Ruhm der Gartenwelt'
'Sénateur Saint-Romme'
'William Notting'

1905
'Adam Rackles'
'Andenken an Moritz von Fröhlich'
'Betty'
'Countess of Derby'
'Crimson Crown'
'Hermann Kiese'
'Herzogin Viktoria Adelheid von Coburg-Gotha'
'Honourable Ina Bingham'
'Irish Elegance'
'Lina Schmidt-Michel'
'Lucien de Lemos'
'Mme. Mélanie Soupert'
'Mrs. E. G. Hill'
'Mme. Emilie Lafon'
'Mme. Gustave Metz'

'Mme. Philippe Rivoire'
'Pie X'
'Richmond'
'Rosalind Orr English'
'Souvenir de Maria de Zayas'
'Souvenir du Président Daurel'
'Stadtrat F. Kähler'
'The Dandy'
1906
'Charles J. Graham'
'Die Mutter von Rosa'
'Die Spree'
'Dorothy Page-Roberts'
'Duchesse de la Mothe-
    Houdancourt'
'Écarlate'
'Frau Bürgermeister
    Kirschstein'
'La Vendômoise'
'Marichu Zayas'
'Marquise de Sinety'
'Miss Kate Moulton'
'Mme. René André'
'Souvenir de Monsieur
    Frédéric Vercellone'
'Vinoca'
1907
'Australie'
'Avoca'
'Comtesse Icy Hardegg'
'Defiance'
'Dora Hansen'
'Dr. A. Hermans'
'Elisabeth Barnes'
'Ernst Hempel'
'Friedrichsruh'
'Kronprinzessin Cecilie'
'Lady Rossmore'
'Laurent Carle'
'Lydia Grimm'
'Mme. Desirée Bruneau'
'Mme. Maurice de Luze'
'Mme. P. Euler'
'Mme. René Oberthür'
'Mme. Segond-Weber'
'Mrs. Aaron Ward'
'Mrs. Isabel Milner'
'Mrs. Stewart Clark'
'Prinzessin Marie'
'Renée Wilmart-Urban'
'Rosemary'
'W. E. Lippiatt'
1908
'Dr. O'Donel Browne'
'Duisburg'
'Eva de Grossouvre'

'Florence Edith Coulthwaite'
'Frau Emma Sasse'
'Frau Oberhofgärtner Singer'
'Frau Philipp Siesmayer'
'Grossherzog Friedrich von
    Baden'
'Intensity'
'Jacques Vincent'
'Jean Notté'
'Lady Faire'
'Madeleine Gaillard'
'Morgentau'
'Mrs. David Jardine'
'My Maryland'
'Otto von Bismarck'
'Princesse Vera Orbelioni'
'Radiance'
'Rose Benary'
'Rhea Reid'
'Veluwezoom'
1909
'Alsterufer'
'Colonel Leclerc'
'Cynthia Forde'
'Duchess of Wellington'
'General Th. Peschkoff'
'George C. Waud'
'Grace Molyneux'
'Gruss an Aachen'
'His Majesty'
'John Cuff'
'Jonkheer J. L. Mock'
'Kaiser Wilhelm II'
'Kaiserin Goldifolia'
'Lady Alice Stanley'
'Lady Ursula'
'Lia'
'Marquise de Ganay'
'Mlle. Danielle Dumur'
'Mme. Léon Simon'
'Mme. René Collette'
'Monsieur Charles de Lapisse'
'Mrs. Wakefield Christie-Miller'
'Natalie Böttner'
'Prince Englebert Ch.
    d'Arenberg'
'Ricordo di Giosue Carducci'
'Simplicity'
'Stella di Bologna'
'White Killarney'
Pre-1910
'Red Chatenay'
1910
'Eugène Boullet'
'Frau Therese Lang'
'Germaine Chénault'

'Herzogin Marie-Antoinette
    von Mecklembourg'
'Jubiläumsrose'
'Juwel'
'König Laurin'
'Lady Pirrie'
'Lieutenant Chauré'
'Lilli von Posern'
'Mama Looymans'
'Manuel P. Azevedo'
'Marie Schmitt'
'Mary, Countess of Ilchester'
'May Miller'
'Mme. Charles de Lapisse'
'Mme. Jules Bouché'
'Mrs. Charles Custis Harrison'
'Mrs. E. Townsend'
'Mrs. Edward Powell'
'Mrs. Fred Straker'
'Mrs. Herbert Stevens'
'Mrs. Walter Easlea'
'Mrs. George Preston'
'Nordlicht'
'Portia'
'Reine Mère d'Italie'
'Souvenir de Gustave Prat'
'Souvenir de Mme. F. Zurich'
'Stadtrat Glaser'
Pre-1911
'Taft Rose'
1911
'Bürgermeister Christen'
'Comte G. de Rochemur'
'Desdemona'
'Edward Mawley'
'Elizabeth'
'Excellenz M. Schmidt-
    Metzler'
'Freifrau Ida von Schubert'
'Grange Colombe'
'Lady Margaret Boscawen'
'Leslie Holland'
'Maman Lyly'
'Marie-Louise Mathian'
'Melody'
'Mme. Alfred Digeon'
'Mme. C. Chambard'
'Mme. Léopold Dupuy'
'Monsieur Edg. Blanchard'
'Monsieur Fraissenon'
'Mrs. Amy Hammond'
'Mrs. George Shawyer'
'Mrs. Joseph H. Welch'
'Othello'
'Président Vignet'
'Ricordo di Geo Chavez'

'Rose Queen'
1912
'Amalie de Greiff'
'Aviateur Michel Mahieu'
'British Queen'
'C. W. Cowan'
'Dr. Nicolas Welter'
'Duchess of Sutherland'
'Earl of Gosford'
'Frau Anna Lautz'
'General-Superior Arnold
    Janssen'
'Helvetia'
'Killarney Queen'
'Luise Lilia'
'Mevrouw Dora van Tets'
'Mme. Edmond Rostand'
'Mrs. Charles Hunter'
'Mrs. E. Alford'
'Mrs. Muir MacKean'
'Mrs. Sam Ross'
'Mrs. Wallace H. Rowe'
'Nerissa'
'Ophelia'
'Sachsengruss'
'Souvenir d'E. Guillard'
'St. Helena'
'Verna Mackay'
1913
'Baron Palm'
'Bianca'
'Chrissie MacKellar'
'Decorator'
'Double White Killarney'
'Dr. G. Krüger'
'Edith Part'
'Étincelante'
'Francis Scott Key'
'Frau Berthe Kiese'
'H. E. Richardson'
'H. F. Eilers'
'Hedwig Reicher'
'Hilda Richardson'
'Irish Fireflame'
'Lady Coventry'
'Lady Dunleathe'
'Lady Mary Ward'
'Lucien Chauré'
'Marcella'
'Margherita Croze'
'Milady'
'Mme. Bardou Job'
'Mme. Théodore Delacourt'
'Mrs. Andrew Carnegie'
'Mrs. Charles E. Russell'
'Mrs. Forde'

Hybrid Teas, 1900–1920
1913 *continued*
'Mrs. R. D. McClure'
'Mrs. T. Hillas'
'Ökonomierat Echtermeyer'
'Queen Mary'
'Red Admiral'
'Rosita Mauri'
'Seabird'
1914
'Augustus Hartmann'
'Edgar M. Burnett'
'Ernest Laurent'
'Gruss vom Westerwald'
'H. Vessey Machin'
'Hadley'
'Herzogin von Calabrien'
'Jacques Porcher'
'Käthe von Saalfeld'
'Killarney Brilliant'
'Mrs. Archie Gray'
'Mrs. Mona Hunting'
'Mrs. Wemyss Quin'
'Prinzessin Hildegard von
    Bayern'
'Red-Letter Day'
1915
'Dernburg'
'Generalin Isenbart'
'Graf Silva Tarouca'
'Grossherzog Wilhelm Ernst
    von Sachsen'
'Gruss an Zweibrücken'
'Hoosier Beauty'
'Ludwig Möller'
'Margaret Dickson Hamill'
'Mlle. Argentine Cramon'
'Mme. Marcel Delauney'
'Mrs. Bertram J. Walker'
'Mrs. Franklin Dennison'
'Mrs. Hugh Dickson'
'Mrs. John Foster'
'Mrs. Maud Dawson'
'Mrs. Moorfield Storey'
'P. L. Baudet'
'September Morn'
'Totote Gélos'
1916
'Circe'
'Clément Pacaud'
'Crimson Emblem'
'Donald MacDonald'
'Enver Pascha'
'Graf Fritz Schwerin'
'Henriette'

'Isobel'
'Königin Maria Theresia'
'Kynast'
'Miss Wilmott'
'Mme. Caristie Martel'
'Mme. Méha Sabatier'
'Morgenglans'
'Mrs. Dunlop-Best'
'Nellie Parker'
'Red Cross'
'Red Radiance' (Gude)
'Red Radiance' (Pierson)
'Weddigen'
1917
'Arabella'
'Benedictus XV'
'Columbia'
'Ethel Dickson'
'Freiburg II'
'Generaal Snijders'
'Generaloberst von Kluck'
'Gladys Holland'
'H. D. M. Barton'
'Janet'
'John Cook'
'K. of K.'
'Kootenay'
'Mevrouw A Del Court van
    Krimpen'
'Mevrouw Smits Gompertz'
'Molly Bligh'
'Mrs. Charles J. Bell'
'Mrs. Fred Searl'
'Mrs. Henry Winnett'
'Noblesse'
'Rübezahl'
'Ulster Standard'
'W. C. Gaunt'
'Walter C. Clark'
1918
'Alexander Emslie'
'Bertha von Suttner'
'Clarice Goodacre'
'Dr. Joseph Drew'
'Edith Cavell'
'Élégante'
'Elisabeth Didden'
'Evelyn'
'Frances Gaunt'
'Gloire de Hollande'
'Golden Ophelia'
'H. P. Pinkerton'
'Mevrouw Boreel van
    Hogelander'
'Mme. Butterfly'

'Mrs. George Marriot'
'Mrs. MacKellar'
'Nelly Verschuren'
'Premier'
'Prinses Juliana'
'Red Star'
'Rose d'Espérance'
'Rose Marie'
'Sunny South'
'T. F. Crozier'
Pre-1919
'Radiance Sport'
1919
'Australia Felix'
'Capitaine Georges Dessirier'
'Charles K. Douglas'
'Château de Clos-Vougeot'
'Comtesse de Cassagne'
'Cornelis Timmermans'
'Countess of Warwick'
'Dr. Helfferich'
'Edel'
'Elizabeth Cullen'
'Étoile de Hollande'
'Fliegerheld Öhring'
'Herfsttooi'
'Hortulanus Albert Fiet'
'Jacques Hackenberg'
'Jonkheer Ruis de
    Beerenbrouck'
'Königin Viktoria von
    Schweden'
'La France Victorieuse'
'Louise Baldwin'
'Louise Criner'
'Lulu'
'Martha Drew'
'Miriam'
'Miss C. E. van Rossem'
'Mme. Henry Fontaine'
'Mme. Raymond Poincaré'
'Mrs. C. V. Haworth'
'Mrs. C. W. Dunbar-Buller'
'Mrs. Henry Morse'
'Nederland'
'Toreador'
'Walküre'
1920
'Alice Kaempff'
'Angelus'
'Argyll'
'Bloomfield Progress'
'Westfield Star'
1921
'Mevrouw C. van Marwyk Kooy'

'Mrs. Oakley Fisher'
'Silver Wedding'
1922
'Fragrant Bouquet'
'Rotelfe'
'Sensation'
1923
'Souvenir de Capitaine
    Fernand Japy'
1926
'Dame Edith Helen'
'Lady Sylvia'
1927
'Ami Quinard'
'Troja'
1928
'Albast'
'Lady Forteviot'
1930
'Minna'
'Rosa Gruss an Aachen'
1935
'Jean Muraour'
1937
'Contrast'
1942
'Gruss an Aachen Superior'
1944
'Weisse Gruss an Aachen'

Pernetianas

1894
'Gottfried Keller'
1900
'Rhodophile Gravereaux'
'Soleil d'Or'
1905
'Dr. Müller'
'Schmetterling'
1906
'Les Rosati'
1907
'Lyon-Rose'
1908
'Entente Cordiale'
'Mrs. Arthur Robert Waddell'
1909
'Arthur R. Goodwin'
'Mme. Ruau'
'Soleil d'Angers'
1910
'Beauté de Lyon'
'Deutschland'
'Johannisfeuer'

'Juliet'
'Rayon d'Or'
1911
'Sunburst'
1912
'Louise Catherine Breslau'
'Mrs. Frederick W. Vanderbilt'
1913
'Cissie Easlea'
'Mme. Édouard Herriot'
'Mrs. Charles E. Pearson'
'Old Gold'
'Sonnenlicht'
'Willowmere'
1914
'Autumn Tints'
'Mrs. Ambrose Riccardo'
1915
'Constance'
'Gorgeous'
1916
'California'
'Dannenberg'
'Golden Emblem'
'Los Angeles'
'Morgenster'
'Mrs. Bullen'
'Président Bouché'
1918
'Adolf Kärger'
'Adolf Koschel'
'Bénédicte Seguin'
'Christine'
'Emma Wright'
'Hermann Robinow'
'Miss May Marriot'
'Pax Labor'
'President Wilson'
'The Queen Alexandra Rose'
'United States'
'Reinhard Bädecker'

1919
'E. P. H. Kingma'
'Georges Clemenceau'
'Hortulanus Budde'
'Independence Day'
'Jean C. N. Forestier'
'La Somme'
'Mrs. Ramon de Escofet'
'Mrs. Redford'
1920
'Apotheker Franz Hahne'
'Cambrai'
'Flammenrose'
'Geisha'
'Joseph Baud'
'Padre'
'Secretaris Zwart'
'Souvenir de Charles Laemmel'
'Souvenir de Claudius Pernet'
1921
'Ariel'
'Étoile de Feu'
'Feu Joseph Looymans'
'Frau Felberg-Leclerc'
'Jeanne Excoffier'
'Lady Elphinstone'
'Lady Inchiquin'
'Reverend F. Page-Roberts'
'Reverend Williamson'
'Schleswig-Holstein'
'Souvenir de Georges Pernet'
'Sunstar'
'Von Scharnhorst'
1922
'Betty Uprichard'
'Ceres'
'Elvira Aramayo'
'Émile Charles'
'Lord Lambourne'
'Louise Joly'
'Madette'

'Wilhelm Kordes'
1923
'Barbara'
'Eldorado'
'Florence L. Izzard'
'Mary Pickford'
1924
'Amélie de Bethune'
'Angèle Pernet'
'Belle Cuivrée'
'Cécile Ratinckx'
'Gooiland Beauty'
'Nona'
'O. Junyent'
'Reims'
'Rising Sun'
'Shot Silk'
'Solliden'
1925
'Angel Guiméra'
'Dilly's Wiederkehr'
'Gooiland Glory'
'Gwyneth Jones'
'I Zingari'
'Lilly Jung'
'Mme. Georges Landard'
'Professor Schmeil'
'Ville de Paris'
1926
'Antonio Rolleri de Peluffo'
'Dr. Edward Deacon'
'La Giralda'
'Mabel Lynas'
'Mevrouw G. A. van Rossem'
'Mrs. Erskine Pembroke Thom'
'Mrs. Robert Mitchell'
'Mrs. Talbot O'Farrell'
'Norman Lambert'
'Souvenir d'Angèle Opdebeeck'
1927
'Director Rubió'

'Goldenes Mainz'
'Gruss an Coburg'
'Julien Potin'
'La Mie au Roy'
'Mrs. W. E. Nickerson'
'Recuerdo de Angel Peluffo'
'Souvenir de Gustave
    Schickelé'
1928
'Dr. Augustin Wibbelt'
'Mme. Henri Queuille'
'Mrs. S. Paton'
'Wildenfels Rosa'
1929
'Annette Gravereaux'
'Jubiläumsrose'
'Konrad Thönges'
'Mme. Eugène Picard'
'Mrs. Pierre S. du Pont'
'Mrs. Sam McGredy'
'Pardinas Bonet'
'Souvenir de Jean Soupert'
'Talisman'
'Ville de Malines'
'Wildenfels Gelb'
1930
'Ambassador'
'Autumn'
'Barbara Richards'
'Cardinal Mercier'
'Dazla'
1931
'Collette Clément'
'Duquesa de Peñaranda'
1932
'Comtesse Vandal'
'Condesa de Sástago'
'Souvenir du Reverend Père
    Planque'
1934
'Angels Mateu'

Cultivars by Breeder or Introducer

It is interesting to follow the careers of breeders by seeing how the course of their offerings developed! Close study of the listings, particularly for those breeders who undertook their crossings in a "scientific" manner, will provide many insights. We do not list here breeders or introducers with only one introduction represented in *The Old Rose Adventurer*, unless that breeder or introducer is part of a family group, or had a cultivar with a listing also in *The Old Rose Advisor*. Family groups (as *Lévêque*) with the same last name are listed with the elder generation preceding the younger; family groups with differing last names (as *Jacques* [uncle] and *Verdier* [nephew]) are listed separately under the last name. Arrangement under each heading is chronological, then alphabetical within each year. As always, the date is intended to be that of *commercial introduction*, as is the stan-

dard practice, not that of *raising*. In a number of cases, the breeder's company continued to release new offerings under his name after his decease. This listing does not include *all* of the cultivars released by any of these breeders or introducers, but rather only those cultivars having entries in this volume. Comparison of the list for a particular breeder in *The Old Rose Adventurer* with that for the same breeder in *The Old Rose Advisor* will of course give a fuller idea of the interests and career goals of the breeder; the way in which the breeder's "profile" changes from volume to volume can be instructive (for an extreme example, compare the lists for *Lévêque* in each volume). We include the appropriate *addenda* (but not *corrigenda*) from Appendix 1, as well as the appropriate cultivars from Appendix 2.

Alfons
Germany?
1922 'Emerickrose' (Mult)
1922 'Hildeputchen' (Mult)
1923 'Prior M. Oberthau' (Mult)
1925 'Eichsfeldia' (Mult)
1925 'Evodia' (Mult)
1925 'Gruss an Breinegg' (Mult)
1925 'Maria Liesa' (Mult)
1925 'Theresia' (Mult)
1926 'Agnes und Bertha' (Mult)
1926 'Blanda Egreta' (Mult)
1926 'Elisabeth' (Mult)
1926 'Gruss an Germershausen' (Mult)
1927 'Weidenia' (Can)

Barbier Frères & Compagnie
Orléans, France
1900 'Albéric Barbier' (W)
1900 'François Foucard' (W)
1900 'Paul Transon' (W)
1900 'René André' (W)
1901 'Adélaïde Moullé' (W)
1901 'Cramoisi Simple' (W)
1901 'Edmond Proust' (W)
1901 'Elisa Robichon' (W)

1901 'Rubra' (W)
1902 'François Poisson' (W)
1903 'Alexandre Trémouillet' (W)
1903 'Émile Fortépaule' (W)
1903 'Ferdinand Roussel' (W)
1904 'Léontine Gervais' (W)
1904 'Valentin Beaulieu' (W)
1905 'François Guillot' (W)
1905 'Jean Guichard' (W)
1905 'Joseph Billard' (W)
1906 'François Juranville' (W)
1907 'Alexandre Girault' (W)
1907 'Francis' (Mult)
1908 'Jules Levacher' (W)
1909 'Désiré Bergera' (W)
1909 'Joseph Liger' (W)
1909 'Louis Barbier' (Cl Pern)
1910 'Casimir Moullé' (W)
1910 'Paul Ploton' (W)
1911 'Wichmoss' (W)
1912 'Edgar Andreu' (W)
1913 'Auguste Roussel' (Macro)
1915 'Le Poilu' (W)
1916 'Auguste Gervaise' (W)
1918 'Henri Barruet' (W)
1918 'Maxime Corbon' (W)

1919 'La Somme' (Pern)
1920 'Jacotte' (W)
1921 'Albertine' (W)
1924 'Reims' (Pern)
1928 'Buisson d'Or' (F)
1929 'Primevère' (W)
1929 'Rustica' (F)
1930 'Coupe d'Or' (W)

Baron-Veillard, Auguste Alexandre
Orléans, France
1888 'Vierge de Cléry' (C)

Bee's Ltd.
Chester, England
1919 'Independence Day' (Pern)
1921 'Ariel' (Pern)

Beluze, Jean
Lyon, France
1847 'Mme. de Villars' (MR)
1855 'Gloire d'Orient' (MR)

Bénard, Georges
Orléans, France
1899 'Mme. Georges Bénard' (HT)
1904 'Rosier Tenuifolia' (Rg)

Bennett, Henry
Manor Farm Nursery
Shepperton, Stapleford, England
1889 'Golden Fairy' (Pol)

Bentall, J. A.
Havering, Essex, England
1916 'Paulette Bentall' (Mult)
1931 'Pink Prosperity' (HMk)
1933 'Autumn Delight' (HMk)
1933 'Rosaleen' (HMk)
1936 'Belinda' (HMk)
1937 'Ballerina' (HMk)
1937 'Havering' (HMk)
1939 'Buff Beauty' (HMk)

Berger, Vincenz
Bad-Harzburg, Germany
1924 'Bergers Erfolg' (Rg)
1924 'Stern von Prag' (Rg)
1928 'Schwabenland' (Rg)
1930 'Dr. Eckener' (Rg)

Berger, W.
Germany?
1959 'Lausitz' (Lam)
1959 'Neisse' (Lam)
1959 'Weisse New Dawn' (W)
1964 'Ufhoven' (Lam)

Berland
Bordeaux?, France
1901 'Mlle. de Neux' (HT)

Bernaix, Alexandre
Villeurbanne-Lyon, France
1886 'Moschata × Polyantha' (HMk)
1886 'Polyantha Grandiflora' (Mult)
1892 'Mme. Ocker Ferencz' (T)

Bernaix fils (Pierre)
Villeurbanne-Lyon, France
1901 'Edmond Deshayes' (HT)
1904 'Lady Wenlock' (HT)
1904 'Mme. Alfred Sabatier' (HT)
1908 'Madeleine Gaillard' (HT)
1910 'Mrs. Edward Powell' (HT)
1910 'Reine Mère d'Italie' (HT)
1922 'Émile Charles' (Pern)
1927 'La Mie au Roy' (Pern)
1930 'Climbing Mrs. Henry Winnett'
   (Cl HT)

Boden, M.
Germany?
1920 'Gruss an Rengsdorf' (Can)
1920 'Mechthilde von Neuerburg' (Rbg)

Boerner, E. S.
U.S.A.
1955 'Morning Dawn' (W)
1956 'Miss Liberty' (W)

Böhm, Jan
Blatná-Cechy, Czechoslovakia
1910 'Graf Zeppelin' (Mult)
1925 'Mánja Böhmová' (Mult)
1929 'Anci Böhmova' (Mult)
1931 'Climbing General-Superior Arnold
   Janssen' (Cl. HT)
1934 'Matka Vlast' (Mult)
1934 'Stratosféra' (C)
1935 'Kde Domov Muj' (Mult)
1935 'Probuzeni' (Lam)
1936 'Mičurin' (Mult)
1936 'Vlatava' (Mult)
1937 'Jindřich Hanus Böhm' (Rg)
1937 'Srdce Europy' (W)
1937 'Symbol Miru' (W)

Boll, Daniel
New York City, New York, U.S.A.
1854 'Souvenir de Henry Clay' (Pim)

Bonnaire, Joseph
Lyon, France
1898 'Mme. Lucien Duranthon' (T)

Bonnet
Vanves, France
1874 'Mme. de Sancy de Parabère' (Bslt)

Böttner
Germany?
1909 'Natalie Böttner' (HT)
1910 'Fragezeichen' (W)

Boutigny, Jules-Philibert
Rouen, France
1903 'Mme. Maurice Fenaille' (HT)
1906 'Souvenir de Pierre Sionville' (HP)

Boyau, Joseph
Angers, France
1844 'Ebène' (DP)

Boytard, A.
Orléans, France
1906 'Écarlate' (HT)

Brada, Dr. Gustav
Czechoslovakia
1934 'Prodaná Nevěsta' (Lam)
1935 'Dr. Zamenhof' (W)
1936 'Svatopluk Čech' (Mult)

Brassac, François
Toulouse, France
1876 'Rose à Bois Jaspé' (Can)
1876 'Ville de Toulouse' (G)

Brownell, Walter D. & Josephine
Little Compton, Rhode Island, U.S.A.
1933 'Mrs. Arthur Curtiss James' (W)
1936 'Apricot Glow' (W)
1937 'Elegance' (W)
1937 'Golden Glow' (W)
1937 'Golden Orange Climber' (W)
1938 'Little Compton Creeper' (W)
1939 'Carpet of Gold' (W)
1940 'Copper Glow' (W)
1941 'Magic Carpet' (W)
1942 'Brownell Yellow Rambler' (W)

Bruant, François-René
Poitiers, France
1887 'Mme. Georges Bruant' (Rg)
1894 'Belle Poitevine' (Rg)
1894 'Calocarpa' (Rg)

Buatois, Emmanuel
Dijon, France
1899 'Jules Girodit' (HT)
1900 'Marie Henry' (HT)
1900 'Mme. Dailleux' (HT)
1902 'Madeleine Faivre' (HT)
1902 'Paul Meunier' (HT)
1921 'Jeanne Excoffier' (Pern)
1921 'Vicomtesse de Chabannes' (W)
1922 'Louise Joly' (Pern)
1931 'Réveil Dijonnais' (Cl HT)
1933 'Gabriel Noyelle' (MR)
1935 'Andrée Vanderschrick' (Mult)
1941 'Claude Rabbe' (W)
1941 'Robert Léopold' (M)
1953 'Denyse Ducas' (W)

Budlong & Son Company
Auburn, Rhode Island, U.S.A.
1912 'Killarney Queen' (HT)
1913 'Double White Killarney' (HT)

Buisman & Son
Heerde, The Netherlands
1937 'Climbing Mrs. Sam McGredy' (Cl HT)
1952 'Buisman's Triumph' (Lam)

Burbank, Luther
Santa Rosa, California, U.S.A.
1932 'Apple Blossom' (Mult)

California Nursery Company
Niles, California, U.S.A.
pre-1891 'Double Cherokee' (Lv)

Calvert & Company
Rouen, France, *and* **London, England**
1821 'Henri Quatre' (G)
1822 'Caroline d'Angleterre' (A)
1832 'Wellington' (C)

Cambridge University Botanic Garden
Cambridge, England
1926 'Coryana' (Macro)
ca. 1931 'Cantabrigensis' (Hug)

Cant, Benjamin R.
Colchester, England
1895 'John Cant' (Rbg)
1903 'Blush Rambler' (Mult)
1908 'White Dorothy' (W)
1911 'Elizabeth' (HT)
1912 'St. Helena' (HT)
1914 'Augustus Hartmann' (HT)
1914 'Autumn Tints' (Pern)
1915 'Cupid' (Cl HT)
1916 'Colcestria' (Cl HT)
1918 'Golden Ophelia' (HT)
1920 'Padre' (Pern)
1921 'Mrs. Oakley Fisher' (HT)
1921 'Reverend F. Page-Roberts' (Pern)
1928 'Lady Forteviot' (HT)
1930 'Dazla' (Pern)

Cant, Frank
Colchester, England
1920 'Yvonne' (W)
1923 'Snowflake' (W)
1924 'Chastity' (Cl HT)
1932 'Climbing Mrs. C. V. Haworth'
pre-1933 'Yellow Minnehaha' (W)
1935 'Harlequin' (W)

Cartier, Dr.
Paris, France
pre-1810 'Renoncule' (G)
1823 'Dupuytren' (G)
pre-1829 'Plena' (Bslt)

Cels Frères
Montrouge, Paris, France
pre-1810 'Unique Rose' (C)
pre-1817 'Belle Couronnée' (D)
pre-1821 'Semi-Double' (Mk)

Chambard, C.
Lyon, France
1911 'Mme. C. Chambard' (HT)
1912 'Souvenir d'E. Guillard' (HT)
1913 'Étincelante' (HT)
1915 'Mlle. Argentine Cramon' (HT)
1916 'Clément Pacaud' (HT)
1918 'Pax Labor' (Pern)
1919 'Louise Criner' (HT)
1920 'Souvenir de Claudius Denoyel' (Cl HT)

Chaplin Bros.
Waltham Cross, England
1918 'Edith Cavell' (HT)
1926 'Royal Scarlet Hybrid' (W)

1928 'Chaplin's Pink Climber' (W)
1929 'Climbing Mrs. Henry Morse' (Cl HT)
1930 'Chaplin's Crimson Glow' (W)
1931 'Crimson Conquest' (Cl HT)
1932 'Buttermere' (W)
1932 'July Glory' (W)
1932 'Windermere' (W)
1933 'Loveliness' (W)

Charpentier
Sablé, France
1807 'À Fleurs Presque Simples' (CP)
pre-1810 'Elisa' (A)
pre-1815 'Semonville' (A)

Chauvry, J.-B.
Bordeaux, France
1905 'Souvenir du Président Daurel' (HT)

Chédane-Guinoisseau
Angers, France
1895 'Chédane-Guinoisseau' (Rg)

Clark, Alister
Bulla, Australia
1918 'Sunny South' (HT)
1919 'Australia Felix' (HT)
1919 'Black Boy' (Cl HT)
1920 'Gwen Nash' (Cl HT)
1920 'Nora Cuningham' (Cl HT)
1922 'Kitty Kininmonth' (Cl HT)
1922 'Scorcher' (Cl HT)
1924 'Sunday Best' (Cl HT)
1925 'Daydream' (Cl HT)
1926 'Queen of Hearts' (Cl HT)
1926 'Ruby Ring' (W)
1927 'Cracker' (Cl HT)
1928 'Countess of Stradbroke' (Cl HT)
1929 'Refresher' (W)

Cochet, Pierre (fils)
Grisy-Suisnes, France
pre-1906 'Provins Ancien' (G)
pre-1906 'Rosier des Parfumeurs' (G)

Cochet-Cochet, Charles
Coubert, France
1892 'Blanc Double de Coubert' (Rg)
1894 'Souvenir de Christophe Cochet' (Rg)
1895 'Souvenir de Pierre Leperdrieux' (Rg)
1899 'Heterophylla' (Rg)
1899 'Souvenir de Philémon Cochet' (Rg)
1902 'Roseraie de l'Haÿ' (Rg)
1907 'Adiantifolia' (Rg)
1908 'Souvenir de Paul Raudnitz' (W)

Cocker, James (& Sons)
Aberdeen, Scotland
1910 'Christian Curle' (W)
1913 'Mrs. Andrew Carnegie' (HT)

Conard & Jones Company
West Grove, Pennsylvania, U.S.A.
1899 'Royal Cluster' (Mult)
1905 'Garden's Glory' (Mult)
1909 'Kaiserin Goldifolia' (HT)
1915? 'Variegata' (W)

Conard-Pyle Company
West Grove, Pennsylvania, U.S.A.
1928 'Nemo' (Rg)
1934 'Nelly Custis' (Set)

Cook, John (& Son)
Baltimore, Maryland, U.S.A.
1903 'Enchanter' (HT)
1904 'Cardinal' (HT)
1908 'My Maryland' (HT)
1908 'Radiance' (HT)
1913 'Francis Scott Key' (HT)

Cooling & Son
Bath, England
1898 'Delicata' (Rg)

Coquereau
Maître-École, Angers, France
1831 'Du Maître d'École' (G)

Coquerel
Le Hâvre, France
1819 'Belle Herminie' (G)
pre-1829 'Feu de Vesta' (G)
pre-1829 'Octavie' (G)
pre-1830 'Montézuma' (G)

Corboeuf-Marsault
Orléans, France
1890 'Mlle. Marie-Louise Bourgeoise' (MR)
1898 'Marcel Bourgoin' (G)
1900 'Mme. Charles Montigny' (HP)
1909 'Thermidor' (Lam)
1910 'L'Avenir' (W)

Croibier & fils
Vénissieux, Lyon, France
1901 'Mme. Marie Croibier' (HT)
1910 'Mme. Jules Bouché' (HT)

Dawson, Jackson
Arnold Arboretum, Jamaica Plain,
**   Massachusetts, U.S.A.**
1888 'Dawson' (Mult)
1900 'Lady Duncan' (W)
1900 'William C. Egan' (W)
1903 'Farquhar' (W)
1909 'Daybreak' (W)
1912 'Sargent' (W)
1914 'Arnoldiana' (Rg)

De Ruiter, G.
Hazerswoude, The Netherlands
1951 'Lyric' (Lam)

De Vergnies
Douai, France
1824 'De Vergnies' (HCh)
pre-1830 'Belle Violette' (HCh)

Dechant, Ernst
Hohenstein-Ernstthal, Germany
1928 'Mühle Hermsdorf' (W)
1928 'Wildenfels Rosa' (Pern)
1929 'Wildenfels Gelb' (Pern)

Descemet, Jacques-Louis
St.-Denis, France
ca. 1808 'Rouge' (Pim)
ca. 1810 'Comtesse de Chamoïs' (CP)
pre-1811 'Aglaia' (C)
pre-1811 'Euphrosine l'Élégante' (C)
pre-1811 'Thalie la Gentille' (C)
pre-1811 'Virginale' (D)
pre-1814 'Adèle' (G)
pre-1814 'Adonis' (G)
pre-1815 'Gloire des Jardins' (G)
pre-1815 'Jeannette' (G)
pre-1815 'Jeune Henry' (G)
1816 'Héloïse' (Ag)
1816 'La Belle Mathilde' (Pim)
pre-1817 'Pompon Blanc' (Pim)
pre-1817 'Roi des Pourpres' (G)
pre-1818 'Belle Hélène' (G)
1818 'Belle Laure No 2' (Pim)
pre-1819 'Belle Flore' (G)
pre-1820 'Beauté Surprenante' (G)
pre-1820 'Belle Biblis' (G)
pre-1820 'Belle Galathée' (G)
pre-1820 'Belle Olympe' (G)
pre-1820 'Belle Rosine' (Turb)
pre-1820 'Calypso Petite' (CP)
pre-1820 'Chloris' (A)
pre-1820 'Clio' (G)
pre-1820 'Cynthie' (G)
pre-1820 'Descemet' (C)
pre-1820 'Eucharis' (G)
pre-1820 'Eudoxie' (G)
pre-1820 'Grand Sultan' (G)
pre-1820 'Illustre' (G)
pre-1820 'Isabelle' (G)
pre-1820 'Manteau Royale' (G)
pre-1820 'Passe-Velours' (G)
pre-1820 'Unique Admirable' (C)
1820 'Fatime' (Ag)
1820 'Rich Crimson' (Pim)
pre-1821 'Triomphe de Flore' (G)
pre-1824 'Clémentine' (Rbg)

Desprez, Jean
Yèbles, France
ca. 1830 'Belle de Yèbles' (G)
ca. 1830 'Helvetius' (G)

Dickson, Alexander
Newtownards, Ireland
1900 'Bessie Brown' (HT)
1900 'Irish Beauty' (HT)
1900 'Irish Glory' (HT)
1900 'Irish Modesty' (HT)
1900 'Lady Clanmorris' (HT)
1900 'Liberty' (HT)
1901 'Gladys Harkness' (HT)
1901 'Lady Moyra Beauclerc' (HT)
1901 'Mildred Grant' (HT)
1902 'Alice Lindsell' (HT)
1902 'Ards Pillar' (Cl HT)
1903 'Mamie' (HT)
1903 'Alice Grahame' (HT)
1903 'Florence Pemberton' (HT)
1903 'Gertrude' (HT)
1903 'John Ruskin' (HT)
1904 'Dean Hole' (HT)
1904 'Irish Brightness' (HT)
1904 'Irish Pride' (HT)
1904 'Irish Star' (HT)
1904 'Lady Ashtown' (HT)
1904 'Mrs. David McKee' (HT)
1905 'Betty' (HT)
1905 'Countess of Derby' (HT)
1905 'Crimson Crown' (HT)
1905 'Honourable Ina Bingham' (HT)
1905 'Irish Elegance' (HT)
1906 'Charles J. Graham' (HT)
1906 'Dorothy Page-Roberts' (HT)
1907 'Avoca' (HT)
1907 'Elisabeth Barnes' (HT)
1907 'W. E. Lippiatt' (HT)
1908 'Dr. O'Donel Browne' (HT)
1908 'Florence Edith Coulthwaite' (HT)
1908 'Mrs. David Jardine' (HT)
1909 'Duchess of Wellington' (HT)
1909 'George C. Waud' (HT)
1909 'Grace Molyneux' (HT)
1909 'John Cuff' (HT)
1909 'Lady Ursula' (HT)
1910 'Mary, Countess of Ilchester' (HT)
1910 'Mrs. Charles Custis Harrison' (HT)
1910 'Mrs. Fred Straker' (HT)
1910 'Mrs. Walter Easlea' (HT)
1910 'Mrs. George Preston' (HT)
1911 'Lady Margaret Boscawen' (HT)
1912 'C. W. Cowan' (HT)
1912 'Climbing Richmond' (Cl HT)
1912 'Duchess of Sutherland' (HT)

1912 'Verna Mackay' (HT)
1913 'Chrissie MacKellar' (HT)
1913 'Hilda Richardson' (HT)
1913 'Irish Fireflame' (HT)
1913 'Lady Dunleathe' (HT)
1913 'Mrs. Forde' (HT)
1913 'Queen Mary' (HT)
1914 'H. Vessey Machin' (HT)
1914 'Killarney Brilliant' (HT)
1914 'Mrs. Wemyss Quin' (HT)
1914 'Red-Letter Day' (HT)
1915 'Margaret Dickson Hamill' (HT)
1915 'Mrs. Maud Dawson' (HT)
1916 'Climbing Irish Fireflame' (Cl HT)
1916 'Donald MacDonald' (HT)
1916 'Henriette' (HT)
1916 'Red Cross' (HT)
1917 'Janet' (HT)
1917 'K. of K.' (HT)
1917 'Kootenay' (HT)
1917 'Molly Bligh' (HT)
1917 'Mrs. Fred Searl' (HT)
1917 'W. C. Gaunt' (HT)
1918 'Alexander Emslie' (HT)
1918 'Clarice Goodacre' (HT)
1918 'Frances Gaunt' (HT)
1918 'Mrs. MacKellar' (HT)
1919 'Elizabeth Cullen' (HT)
1919 'Mrs. C. V. Haworth' (HT)
1919 'Mrs. C. W. Dunbar-Buller' (HT)
1920 'Climbing Ophelia' (Cl HT)
1921 'Lady Inchiquin' (Pern)
1921 'Sunstar' (Pern)
1922 'Betty Uprichard' (Pern)
1922 'Climbing Mrs. Aaron Ward' (Cl HT)
1924 'Shot Silk' (Pern)
1926 'Dame Edith Helen' (HT)
1930 'Barbara Richards' (Pern)

Dickson, Hugh
Belfast, Ireland
1907 'Mrs. Stewart Clark' (HT)
1909 'Cynthia Forde' (HT)
1909 'Simplicity' (HT)
1910 'Lady Pirrie' (HT)
1911 'Leslie Holland' (HT)
1912 'Mrs. Sam Ross' (HT)
1913 'H. E. Richardson' (HT)
1913 'Mrs. R. D. McClure' (HT)
1913 'Seabird' (HT)
1914 'Mrs. Archie Gray' (HT)
1914 'Mrs. Mona Hunting' (HT)
1915 'Gorgeous' (Pern)
1915 'Mrs. Bertram J. Walker' (HT)
1915 'Mrs. Hugh Dickson' (HT)
1916 'Nellie Parker' (HT)

Dickson, Hugh *continued*
1917 'Ethel Dickson' (HT)
1917 'H. D. M. Barton' (HT)
1917 'Ulster Standard' (HT)
1918 'H. P. Pinkerton' (HT)
1918 'T. F. Crozier' (HT)
1919 'Charles K. Douglas' (HT)
1919 'Climbing H. Vessey Machin' (Cl HT)
1923 'Climbing General MacArthur' (Cl HT)

Dieck, Dr. Georg
Göschen, Germany
1899 'Lilli Dieck' (Rg)
1900 'Conditorum' (G)
1900 'Oleifolia' (G)

Dietrich & Turner
Montebello, California, U.S.A.
1913 'Ramona' (Lv)
1915 'September Morn' (HT)

Dingee & Conard Company
West Grove, Pennsylvania, U.S.A.
1908 'Intensity' (HT)
1920 'Climbing Rosemary' (Cl HT)

Dobbie & Company, Ltd.
Edinburgh, Scotland
1920 'Argyll' (HT)
1921 'Lady Elphinstone' (Pern)

Dorner & Sons Company
Lafayette, Indiana, U.S.A.
1915 'Hoosier Beauty' (HT)
1918 'Rose Marie' (HT)

Dot, Pedro
Barcelona, Spain
1924 'O. Junyent' (Pern)
1925 'Angel Guimérá' (Pern)
1926 'La Giralda' (Pern)
1927 'Director Rubió' (Pern)
1927 'Mme. Grégoire Staechelin' (Cl HT)
1929 'Pardinas Bonet' (Pern)
1931 'Duquesa de Peñaranda' (Pern)
1931 'Rosella' (Cl Pern)
1932 'Condesa de Sástago' (Pern)
1932 'Golden Moss' (M)
1934 'Angels Mateu' (Pern)

Dubourg
Vaucresson, France
pre-1811 'La Pucelle' (G)
1820 'Marie Stuart' (G)
pre-1828 'Galatée' (G)

Dubreuil, Francis
Lyon, France
1886 'Duchesse de Bragance' (T)
1901 'Marie Isakoff' (HT)

1902 'Perle des Neiges' (Mult)
1906 'Sarah Bernhardt' (Cl HT)
1908 'Lyon Rambler' (Mult)
1910 'Bocca Negra' (Mult)
1913 'Mme. Bardou Job' (HT)

Ducher, Jean-Claude
Lyon, France
1869 'Imbricata' (Rox)

Dupont, André
Paris, France
pre-1802 'À Feuilles de Céleri' (C)
pre-1804 'À Feuilles Crénelées' (C)
pre-1804 'À Fleurs Simples' (C)
pre-1804 'Prolifère' (Ag)
1809 'Bullata'
pre-1810 'Beauté Tendre' (G)
pre-1810 'Céleste' (A)
pre-1810 'Henriette' (Ag)
pre-1810 'La Félicité' (D)
pre-1810 'La Louise' (C)
pre-1810 'La Maculée' (G)
pre-1810 'Le Rire Niais' (C)
pre-1810 'Noire Couronnée' (G)
pre-1810 'Superbe en Brun' (G)
pre-1811 'Alector Cramoisi' (G)
pre-1811 'Junon' (G)
pre-1813 'Belle sans Flatterie' (G)
pre-1813 'Zabeth' (Rbg)
pre-1817 'Rose Tulipe' (F)
1817 'Belle Laure' (Pim)
pre-1820 'La Tendresse' (G)

Duval, Charles
Montmorency, France
pre-1846 'Jenny' (HCh)

Easlea, Walter
Leigh-on-Sea, Manchester, England
1910 'Juliet' (Pern)
1918 'President Wilson' (Pern)
1919 'Countess of Warwick' (HT)
1919 'Lulu' (HT)
1919 'Mrs. Ramon de Escofet' (Pern)
1919 'Romeo' (W)
1924 'Nona' (Pern)
1927 'Thelma' (W)
1932 'Easlea's Golden Rambler' (W)
1933 'Melita' (W)

Écoffay
Sèvres, France
1820 'Manette' (G)

English, T. J.
Barnwood, Gloucester, England
1922 'Dorcas' (W)
1925 'Achievement' (W)

Fauque-Laurent
Orléans, France
1904 'Gerbe Rose' (W)
1904 'La Perle' (W)

Fauque & fils
Orléans, France
1906 'Mme. Alice Garnier' (W)
1908 'Diabolo' (W)
1908 'Miss Helyett' (W)
1909 'Aviateur Blériot' (W)

Feast, Samuel J. & John
Baltimore, Maryland, U.S.A.
1843 'Baltimore Belle' (Set)
1843 'Pallida' (Set)
1843 'Perpetual Michigan' (Set)
1843 'Queen of the Prairies' (Set)
1843 'Superba' (Set)

Felberg-Leclerc, Walter
Trier, Germany
1920 'Alice Kaempff' (HT)
1921 'Frau Felberg-Leclerc' (Pern)
1027 'Gruss an Coburg' (Pern)

Fontaine, François
Clamart, France
pre-1852 'Gros Provins Panachée' (G)
1861 'Reine d'Espagne' (HP)
1863 'Mme. Legrand' (MR)
1867 'Mme. Charles Salleron' (MR)
1873 'Deuil de Paul Fontaine' (MR)
1877 'Angèle Fontaine' (HP)
1880? 'Valence Dubois' (G)
1882 'Victoire Fontaine' (B)

Fortune, Robert
London, England
1840 'Fortuneana' (Bks)
1843 'Fortune's Five-Colored Rose' (T)
1844 'Anemonaeflora' (Lv)

Foulard, Oscar
Le Mans, France
1840 'Asepala' (M)
1841 'Oeillet Parfait' (G)
1849 'Aristobule' (M)

Franceschi-Fenzi, Dr.
Santa Barbara, California, U.S.A.
date unk. 'Madeleine Lemoine' (Cl T)

Gaetano, Bonfiglioli & figlio
Bologna, Italy
1909 'Ricordo di Giosue Carducci' (HT)
1909 'Stella di Bologna' (HT)
1911 'Garisenda' (W)
1911 'Ricordo di Geo Chavez' (HT)

Gamon, André
Lyon, France
1902 'Reine Carola de Saxe' (HT)
1909 'Mme. René Collette' (HT)
1911 'Monsieur Fraissenon' (HT)

Geduldig, Philipp
Aachen, Germany
1905 'Hermann Kiese' (HT)
1905 'Stadtrat F. Kähler' (HT)
1907 'Lydia Grimm' (HT)
1909 'Gruss an Aachen' (HT)

Geschwind, Rudolf
Karpona, Hungary
1866 'Premier Essai' (Rox)
1884 'Geschwinds Nordlandrose' (Mult)
1885 'Roi des Aunes' (Mult)
1886 'Aennchen von Tharau' (Arv)
1886 'Erinnerung an Brod' (Set)
1886 'Erlkönig' (Mult)
1886 'Fatinitza' (Mult)
1886 'Forstmeisters Heim' (Set)
1886 'Geschwinds Orden' (Mult)
1886 'Nymphe Tepla' (Mult)
1887 'Ernst G. Dörell' (Mult)
1887 'Eurydice' (Set)
1887 'Gilda' (Mult)
1887 'Viragó' (Set)
1889 'Zigeunerblut' (Bslt)
1890 'Chloris' (HT)
1890 'Corporal Johann Nagy' (Set)
1890 'Ovid' (Set)
1890 'Wodan' (Mult)
ca. 1890 'Alpenfee' (Set)
ca. 1890 'Caroline Bank' (Mult)
ca. 1890 'Trompeter von Säckingen' (Mult)
1892 'Nymphe Egeria' (Mult)
1894 'Théano' (unk. affiliation)
1895 'Crême' (Can)
1895 'Griseldis' (Can)
1895 'Himmelsauge' (Set)
1896 'Schneelicht' (Rg)
ca. 1900 'Futtaker Schlingrose' (Mult)
ca. 1900 'Geschwinds Schönste' (Mult)
ca. 1900 'Josephine Ritter' (Mult)
ca. 1900 'Leopold Ritter' (Mult)
1902 'Wenzel Geschwind' (HT)
1909 'Asta von Parpart' (Mult)
1909 'Walküre' (Can)
1910 'Freya' (Can)
1910 'Siwa' (Can)
1911 'Arva Leany' (A)
1911 'Prinz Hirzeprinzchen' (Mult)
1913 'Geisha' (Mult)
1929 'Geschwinds Nordlandrose II' (Mult)

Gillot, Francis
Trepillot-Besançon, France
1920 'Joseph Baud' (Pern)
1920 'Souvenir de Charles Laemmel' (Pern)
1929 'Mme. Eugène Picard' (Pern)
1933 'Sanguinaire' (Rg)

Girardon, Victor
Bar-sur-Aube, France
1829 'Anne de Boleyn' (Turb)
1829 'Goliath' (C)

Girin, Guillaume
St.-Romaine-de-Popey, France
1910 'Jean Girin' (W)
1911 'Mme. Huguette Despiney' (W)

Godard, Antoine
Lyon, France
1900 'Mme. Jean Favre' (HT)

Godefroy
Ville d'Avray, France
pre-1811 'Aimable Rouge' (G)
pre-1811 'Royale' (Ag)
1818 'Aigle Noir' (G)
ca. 1820 'Panachée' (D)
1820 'Damas Violacé' (D)
1820 'Duc de Chartres' (D)

Granger, Louis-Xavier
Grisy-Suisnes, France
1861 'John Fraser' (MR)

Gratama Bros. & Company
Hoogeveen, The Netherlands
1903 'Cato' (Mult)

Gravereaux, Commandeur Jules
L'Haÿ-les-Roses, France
1899 'Potager du Dauphin' (Rg)
1899 'Villa des Tybilles' (Rg)
1900 'Amélie Gravereaux' (Rg)
1901 'Château de la Juvenie' (Rox)
1901 'Domaine de Chapuis' (Rox)
1901 'Mme. Tiret' (Rg)
1901 'S.A.R. Ferdinand Ier' (Rg)
1901 'S.M.I. Abdul-Hamid' (Rg)
1902 'Mme. Constans' (W)
1903 'Mme. Alvarez del Campo' (Rg)
1903 'Mme. Lucien Villeminot' (Rg)
1903 'Rose à Parfum de l'Haÿ' (Rg)
1904 'Mme. Ballu' (Rg)
1904 'Mme. Henri Gravereaux' (Rg)
1905 'Mme. Ancelot' (Rg)
1906 'Les Rosati' (Pern)
1906 'Monsieur Gustave Bienvêtu' (Rg)
1908 'Daniel Lesueur' (Rg)
1908 'Georges Cain' (Rg)

1908 'Régina Badet' (Rg)
1909 'Mme. Ruau' (Pern)
1912 'Mme. Julien Potin' (Rg)
1919 'La France Victorieuse' (HT)
1919 'Mme. Raymond Poincaré' (HT)

Grootendorst, F. J.
Boskoop, The Netherlands
1923 'Pink Grootendorst' (Rg)
1936 'Grootendorst Supreme' (Rg)

Guérin, Modeste
Angers, France
pre-1835 'Victoire Modeste' (Brac)
pre-1846 'Victoria' (F)

Guillot père (Laurent)
Lyon, France
1855 'Impératrice Eugénie' (MR)
1864 'Triomphe de la Guillotière' (Rox)

Guillot père & Clément
Lyon, France
1857 'Ma Ponctuée' (MR)

Guillot fils (Jean-Baptiste)
Lyon, France
1872 'Belle des Jardins' (G)
1872 'Ma Surprise' (Rox)

Guillot, Pierre
Lyon, France
1900 'Mercedes' (Rg)
1902 'Marguerite Guillot' (HT)
1904 'Marco' (W)
1904 'Mme. Léon Pain' (HT)
1907 'Mme. P. Euler' (HT)
1908 'Entente Cordiale' (Pern)
1908 'Eva de Grossouvre' (HT)
1909 'Marquise de Ganay' (HT)
1910 'Germaine Chénault' (HT)
1910 'Mrs. E. Townsend' (HT)
1911 'Grange Colombe' (HT)
1912 'Roby' (Mult)
1913 1912 'Renée Danielle' (W)
1914 'Jacques Porcher' (HT)
1914 'Mme. Henry Fontaine' (HT)
1922 'Madette' (Pern)

Guillot, Marc
St.-Priest, France
1919 'Comtesse de Cassagne' (HT)

Guinoisseau-Flon
Angers, France
1864 'Eugénie Guinoisseau' (MR)

Hall, Dr. J. Campbell
Rowantree House, Monaghan, Ireland
1907 'Lady Rossmore' (HT)

Hansen, Professor N. E.
Brookings, South Dakota, U.S.A.
1906 'Alika' (G)
1907 'Siberian Form' (Rg)
1912 'Tetonkaha' (Rg)
1927 'Amdo' (Rg)
1927 'Ekta' (HCh)
1927 'Kitana' (Rg)
1927 'Koza' (Rg)
1927 'Minisa' (Rg)
1927 'Yuhla' (Set?)

Hardy, Alexandre
Luxembourg Palace Gardens, Paris,
    France
1819 'Baraguay' (G)
1823 'Semonville à Fleurs Doubles' (A)
1824? 'Louis-Philippe' (G)
1829 'Marjolin' (G)
1832 'Félicité Hardy' (D)
pre-1834 'Ferrugineux du Luxembourg'
    (M)
pre-1836 'Gloire de France' (G)
1836 'Hardii' (Hult)
pre-1838 'Sulphurea' (Pim)
1838? 'Ohl' (G)
pre-1841 'Hybride du Luxembourg' (Rox)
pre-1843 'Célina' (M)
pre-1844 'Hypacia' (C)
1846 'Napoléon' (G)
1848 'Pourpre du Luxembourg' (M)

Hébert, Mme.
Rouen, France
1828 'Président de Sèze' (G)
1829 'Reine des Amateurs' (G)

Heizmann, E.
Vevey, Switzerland
1912 'Helvetia' (HT)
1927 'Climbing Hadley' (Cl HT)

Hesse, H. A.
Baumschulen, Weener, Ems, Germany
1910 'Fraulein Octavia Hesse' (W)
1916 'Magnifica' (Rbg)

Hicks, Elisha J.
Hurst, Twyford, Berkshire, England
1915 'Mrs. John Foster' (HT)
1916 'Mrs. Dunlop-Best' (HT)
1924 'Rising Sun' (Pern)
1927 'Mary Hicks' (Mult)

Hill, E. Gurney
Richmond, Indiana, U.S.A.
1902 'Mark Twain' (HT)
1902 'Young America' (HT)
1904 'General MacArthur' (HT)
1904 'Mrs. Theodore Roosevelt' (HT)
1905 'Richmond' (HT)
1905 'Rosalind Orr English' (HT)
1907 'Defiance' (HT)
1907 'Rosemary' (HT)
1908 'Rhea Reid' (HT)
1910 'May Miller' (HT)
1911 'Rose Queen' (HT)
1917 'Columbia' (HT)
1918 'Mme. Butterfly' (HT)
1918 'Premier' (HT)

Hill, Joseph H.
Richmond, Indiana, U.S.A.
1922 'Sensation' (HT)

Hilling & Company Ltd.
Woking, Surrey, England
1949 'Gloire de Guilan' (D)
1950 'Will Scarlet' (HMk)
1954 'Abbotswood' (Can)

Hinner, Wilhelm
Trier, Germany
1900 'Papa Reiter' (HT)
1901 'Franz Deegen' (HT)
1901 'Pharisäer' (HT)
1902 'Farbenkönigin' (HT)
1902 'Goldelse' (HT)
1905 'Andenken an Moritz von Frölich'
    (HT)
1908 'Duisburg' (HT)
1908 'Morgentau' (HT)
1910 'Juwel' (HT)
1913 'Hedwig Reicher' (HT)

Hobbies, Ltd.
Dereham, England
1913 'Decorator' (HT)
1913 'Effective' (Cl HT)

Hoopes, Bro. & Thomas Company
West Chester, Pennsylvania, U.S.A.
1903 'Professor C. S. Sargent' (W)
1909 'Climbing American Beauty' (W)
1909 'Christine Wright' (W)
1917 'Purity' (W)

Horvath, M. H.
Newport, Rhode Island, U.S.A.; *later,*
    Mentor, Ohio, U.S.A.
1897 'South Orange Perfection' (W)
1898 'Evergreen Gem' (W)
1898 'Manda's Triumph' (W)
1898 'Pink Roamer' (W)
1899 'Gardenia' (W)
1899 'Jersey Beauty' (W)
1899 'Universal Favorite' (W)
1901 'Pink Pearl' (W)
1925 'Mrs. F. F. Prentiss' (Set)
1925 'President Coolidge' (Set)

Howard & Smith Company
Montebello, California
1916 'California' (Pern)
1916 'Los Angeles' (Pern)
1922 'Fragrant Bouquet' (HT)
1923 'Eldorado' (Pern)
1923 'Mary Pickford' (Pern)
1925 'Climbing Los Angeles' (Cl Pern)
1926 'Mrs. Erskine Pembroke Thom' (Pern)
1930 'Climbing Dame Edith Helen' (Cl HT)
1937 'Contrast' (HT)

Howard Rose Company
Hemet, California, U.S.A.
1935 'Climbing Lady Forteviot' (Cl. HT)

Igoult, M.
Poitiers?, France
1924 'Aurélian Igoult' (Mult)
1924 'Rose-Marie Viaud' (Mult)

Ingegnoli Bros.
Milano, Italy
1923 'Milano' (W)
1933 'Climbing Elvira Aramayo' (Cl Pern)

Jackson & Perkins Company
Medford, Oregon, U.S.A.
1901 'Dorothy Perkins' (W)
1936 'Climbing Comtesse Vandal' (Cl Pern)

Jacobs, O.
Weitendorf, Mecklenburg, Germany
1902 'Marianne Pfitzer' (HT)
1902 'Max Hesdörffer' (HT)
1904 'Grossherzogin Alexandra' (HT)
1904 'Ruhm der Gartenwelt' (HT)
1906 'Frau Bürgermeister Kirschstein' (HT)
1907 'Dora Hansen' (HT)
1909 'Kaiser Wilhelm II' (HT)
1910 'Herzogin Marie-Antoinette von
    Mecklembourg' (HT)
1913 'Frau Berthe Kiese' (HT)
ca. 1938 '(Frau Karl Druschki × Cristata)'
    (HP)

Jacques, Antoine A.
Neuilly, France
1828 'Félicité et Perpétue' (Semp)
pre-1829 'Adélaïde d'Orléans' (Semp)
pre-1829 'Eugène d'Orléans' (Semp)
pre-1829 'Léopoldine d'Orléans' (Semp)
pre-1829 'Mélanie de Montjoie' (Semp)
1829 'Princesse Louise' (Semp)

1829 'Princesse Marie' (Semp)
1832 'Reine des Belges' (Semp)

Kaufmann, Dr. Ernst
Szabolas, Hungary, *now* **Timisoara, Romania**
1894 'Cibles' (Rg)
1894 'Jelina' (Rg)

Ketten Bros.
Luxembourg
1897 'La Proserpine' (Pol)
1902 'Edmée et Roger' (HT)
1902 'Souvenir d'Anne-Marie' (HT)
1909 'General Th. Peschkoff' (HT)
1909 'Lia' (HT)
1913 'Margherita Croze' (HT)
1913 'Rosita Mauri' (HT)
1921 'Climbing Mme. Édouard Herriot' (Cl Pern)
1924 'Climbing Lyon-Rose' (Cl Pern)
1927 'Souvenir de Gustave Schickelé' (Pern)

Kew, Royal Botanic Gardens
Kew, Richmond, Surrey, England
1797 'Lesser Maiden's Blush' (A)
1912 'Kew Rambler' (Soul)

Kiese, Hermann
Wieselbach-Erfurt, Germany
1899 'Leuchtstern' (Mult)
1902 'Crispata' (Rg)
1903 'Lohengrin' (HT)
1904 'Blumen-Dankert' (Mult)
1906 'Tausendschön' (Mult)
1907 'Kronprinzessin Cecilie' (HT)
1908 'Otto von Bismarck' (HT)
1910 'Deutschland' (Pern)
1910 'Eisenach' (W)
1910 'Kiese' (Can)
1910 'Lilli von Posern' (HT)
1910 'Lisbeth von Kamecke' (Mult)
1910 'Nordlicht' (HT)
1910 'Stadtrat Glaser' (HT)
1910 'Wartburg' (Mult)
1911 'Andreas Hofer' (Mult)
1911 'Perle von Britz' (Mult)
1912 'Frau Anna Lautz' (HT)
1912 'Hakeburg' (Mult)
1913 'Andenken an Breslau' (W)
1915 'Ludwig Möller' (HT)
1916 'Dannenberg' (Pern)
1916 'Enver Pascha' (HT)
1919 'Fliegerheld Öhring' (HT)
1919 'Rudelsburg' (Mult)
1920 'Gartendirektor Julius Schütze' (Cl HT)

Kordes, Wilhelm
Sparrieshoop, Holstein, Germany
1917 'Climbing Louise Catherine Breslau' (Cl Pern)
1918 'Adolf Kärger' (Pern)
1918 'Adolf Koschel' (Pern)
1918 'Reinhard Bädecker' (Pern)
1922 'Wilhelm Kordes' (Pern)
1928 'Venusta Pendula' (Arv)
1930 'Minna' (HT)
1931 'Düsterlohe' (Arv)
1931 'Karl Foerster' (Pim)
Post-1931 'Düsterlohe' (Macra)
1933 'Eva' (HMk)
1934 'Rosenwunder' (Rbg)
1934 'Wilhelm' (HMk)
1936 'Raubritter' (Macra)
1937 'Climbing Gruss an Aachen' (Cl HT)
1937 'Frühlingsgold' (Pim)
1937 'Rostock' (HMk)
1938 'Sangerhausen' (HMk)
1939 'Harry Maasz' (Macra)
1939 'Max Haufe' (Rbg)
1940 'Fritz Nobis' (Rbg)
1940 'Joseph Rothmund' (Rbg)
1941 'Düsterlohe II' (Macra)
1942 'Frühlingsmorgen' (Pim)
1942 'Frühlingsstunde' (Pim)
1942 'Frühlingszauber' (Pim)
1942 'Inspektor Blohm' (HMk)
1948 'Andenken an Alma de l'Aigle' (HMk)
1949 'Frühlingsduft' (Pim)
1949 'Frühlingstag' (Pim)
1950 'Bonn' (HMk)
1950 'Frühlingsanfang' (Pim)
1952 'Grandmaster' (Lam)
1952 'Scharlachglut' (G)
1954 'Frühlingsschnee' (Pim)
1954 'Goldbusch' (Rbg)
1954 'Nymphenburg' (HMk)
1955 'Aschermittwoch' (Rbg)
1955 'Flammentanz' (Rbg)
1956 'Parkjuwel' (M)
1956 'Parkzauber' (M)
1958 'Black Boy' (C)
1958 'Blue Boy' (C)
1959 'Gruss an Heidelberg' (Lam)
1959 'Saarbrücken' (Lam)
1960 'Lavender Lassie' (Lam)
1963 'Gruss an Koblenz' (Rbg)

Krause, Max
Hasloh, Holstein, Germany
1937 'Professor Ibrahim' (Macra)
1938 'Röte Centifolie' (C)
1939 'Elfenreigen' (Macra)
1941 'Erwin Hüttmann' (Mult)

Kröger
Germany?
1925 'Professor Schmeil' (Pern)
1927 'Goldenes Mainz' (Pern)

Krüger, Dr. G.
Freiburg, Baden, Germany
1913 'Sonnenlicht' (Pern)
1915 'Dernburg' (HT)
1916 'Kynast' (HT)
1917 'John Cook' (HT)
1917 'Freiburg II' (HT)
1917 'Rübezahl' (HT)

Lacharme, François
Lyon, France
1848 'L'Obscurité' (M)
1854 'Salet' (MR)
1855 'Bicolor' (MR)
1885 'Max Singer' (Lam)

Laffay, Jean
Auteuil, *then* **Bellevue-Meudon, France**
pre-1826 'Duchesse de Montebello' (HN)
pre-1829 'De Chartres' (Law)
pre-1829 'Princesse de Nassau' (Mk)
1829 'Amadis' (Bslt)
1834 'Laure Davoust' (Mult)
1835 'Céline' (HB)
1835 'Quatre Saisons Blanc Mousseux' (MR)
pre-1836 'Belle Hébé' (Ch)
pre-1841 'Duc de Cambridge' (D)
pre-1841 'Duc de Sussex' (HCh)
1841 'Néron' (G)
1842 'Comtesse Duchatel' (HP)
pre-1843 'Kean' (G)
pre-1844 'Pope' (D)
pre-1845 'Indigo' (DP)
pre-1845 'Mrs. Cripps' (HP)
pre-1845 'Ponctué' (HP)
1845 'Général Clerc' (M)
1845 'Jenny Lind' (M)
1845 'Nuits d'Young' (M)
1845 'Princesse Adélaïde' (M)
1845 'Comtesse Molé' (HB) ca.
1846 'Laneii' (M)
1846 'Ponctuée' (M)
1847 'Mathilde Jesse' (DP)
1848 'La Diaphane' (M)
1850 'Mme. Rose Chéri' (M)
1851 'Mme. Clémence Beauregard' (M)
1852 'Gloire des Mousseux' (M)
1854 'Capitaine John Ingram' (M)
1854 'Frédéric Soullier' (M)
1855 'Alfred de Dalmas' (MR)
1855 'William Lobb' (M)
1858 'Mlle. Aristide' (M)
1858 'William Grow' (M)

Laffay, Jean *continued*
1859 'John Grow' (M)
1863 'Henri Martin' (M)

Lambert, Peter
Trier, Germany
1897 'Helene' (Mult)
1902 'Frau Lilla Rautenstrauch' (HT)
1903 'Gruss an Zabern' (Lam)
1903 'Gustav Grünerwald' (HT)
1903 'Morgenrot' (Cl HT)
1903 'Philippine Lambert' (Lam)
1903 'Thalia Remontant' (Lam)
1904 'Frau Helene Videnz' (Lam)
1904 'Graf Fritz von Hochberg' (HT)
1904 'Tiergarten' (Lam)
1904 'Trier' (Lam)
1905 'Lina Schmidt-Michel'
1905 'Lucien de Lemos' (HT)
1906 'Carmen' (Rg)
1906 'Parkfeuer' (F)
1908 'Frau Oberhofgärtner Singer' (HT)
1908 'Frau Philipp Siesmayer' (HT)
1908 'Grossherzog Friedrich von Baden' (HT)
1908 'Rose Benary' (HT)
1909 'Adrian Reverchon' (Lam)
1909 'Alsterufer' (HT)
1909 'Excellenz Kuntze' (Lam)
1909 'Excellenz von Schubert' (Lam)
1909 'Geheimrat Dr. Mitteweg' (Lam)
1909 'Hildenbrandseck' (Rg)
1909 'Kommerzienrat W. Rautenstrauch' (Lam)
1909 'Mme. Léon Simon' (HT)
1911 'Excellenz M. Schmidt-Metzler' (HT)
1911 'Freifrau Ida von Schubert' (HT)
1911 'Fürstin von Pless' (Rg)
1911 'Gartenstadt Liegnitz' (Lam)
1911 'Gräfin Marie Henriette Chotek' (Mult)
1911 'Goethe' (Cl M)
1911 'Hauff' (Lam)
1911 'Schneezwerg' (Rg)
1912 'Amalie de Greiff' (HT)
1912 'Frau A. von Brauer' (W)
1912 'Freifrau von Marschall' (W)
1912 'Heine' (Lam)
1912 'Luise Lilia' (HT)
1912 'Oriole' (Lam)
1913 'Arndt' (Lam)
1913 'Baron Palm' (HT)
1913 'H. F. Eilers' (HT)
1913 'Ökonomierat Echtermeyer' (HT)
1914 'Herzogin von Calabrien' (HT)
1914 'Lessing' (Lam)
1914 'Peter Rosegger' (Lam)

1914 'Prinzessin Hildegard von Bayern' (HT)
1915 'Blanche Frowein' (Lam)
1915 'Generalin Isenbart' (HT)
1915 'Graf Silva Tarouca' (HT)
1915 'Gruss an Zweibrücken' (HT)
1916 'Graf Fritz Schwerin' (HT)
1916 'Königin Maria Theresia' (HT)
1916 'Von Liliencron' (Lam)
1916 'Weddigen' (HT)
1917 'Generaloberst von Kluck' (HT)
1917 'Hoffmann von Fallersleben' (Lam)
1918 'Hermann Robinow' (Pern)
1919 'Dr. Helfferich' (HT)
1919 'Heinrich Conrad Söth' (Lam)
1920 'Mosel' (Lam)
1921 'Von Scharnhorst' (Pern)
1922 'Chamisso' (Lam)
1924 'Gneisenau' (Lam)
1932 'Ausonius' (Lam)
1932 'Heideröslein' (Lam)
1932 'Mosellied' (Mult)
1932 'Rudolf von Bennigsen' (Lam)
1934 'Gartendirektor Otto Linne' (Lam)
1934 'Climbing Hermann Robinow' (Cl Pern)
1937 'Mozart' (Lam)

Laperrière, Joseph
Champagne-au-Mont-d'Or, France
1902 'Capitaine Soupa' (HT)

Laroulandie, F.
Bordeaux, France
1909 'Mlle. Danielle Dumur' (HT)
1909 'Monsieur Charles de Lapisse' (HT)
1910? 'Mme. Charles de Lapisse' (HT)

Lartay, Clémence?
Bordeaux, France
1854 'Triomphe des Français' (Rox)

Laxton Bros.
Bedford, England
1926 'Monthly Rambler' (W)

Lecomte
Rouen, France
1826 'Triomphe de Rouen' (D)
pre-1827 'Comte Foy de Rouen' (G)
pre-1828 'Cora' (G)

Lee, James
Hammersmith, London, England
pre-1826 'Globe White Hip' (G)
pre-1827 'Crimson' (M)
pre-1836 'Stanwell Perpetual' (Pim)
pre-1846 'Hebe's Lip' (Rbg)

Leenders Bros.
Tegelen, The Netherlands
1909 'Jonkheer J. L. Mock' (HT)
1910 'Jkvr. D. Baroness von Ittersum' (Mult)
1910 'Mama Looymans' (HT)
1912 'General-Superior Arnold Janssen' (HT)
1912 'Mevrouw Dora van Tets' (HT)
1913 'Carolina Budde' (Mult)
1913 'Lien Budde' (Mult)
1915 'Mme. Marcel Delauney' (HT)
1915 'Steyl Rambler' (Mult)
1917 'Benedictus XV' (HT)
1917 'Generaal Snijders' (HT)
1917 'Mevrouw A. Del Court van Krimpen' (HT)
1917 'Mevrouw Smits Gompertz' (HT)
1918 'Elisabeth Didden' (HT)
1918 'Mevrouw Boreel van Hogelander' (HT)
1918 'Prinses Juliana' (HT)
1919 'Hortulanus Albert Fiet' (HT)
1919 'Jacques Hackenberg' (HT)
1921 'Mevrouw C. van Marwyk Kooy' (HT)
1924 'Solliden' (Pern)
1925 'Lilly Jung' (Pern)
1928 'Dr. Augustin Wibbelt' (Pern)
1929 'Annette Gravereaux' (Pern)
1931 'Climbing Étoile de Hollande' (Cl HT)
1932 'Comtesse Vandal' (Pern)
1942 'Gruss an Aachen Superior' (HT)

Lens, Louis
Wavre-Notre-Dame, Belgium
1929 'Ville de Malines' (Pern)
1930 'Cardinal Mercier' (Pern)

LeRouge
Dôle, France
ca. 1819 'Plena' (Vir)
pre-1820 'Belle Hébé' (Ag)

Lester Rose Gardens
Watsonville, California, U.S.A.
ca. 1946 'Francis E. Lester' (Mk)
ca. 1946 'Wind Chimes' (HMk)

Lévêque, René
Paris, France
ca. 1830 'Flore' (Semp)
1844 'Duchesse de Montmorency' (DP)

Lévêque, Louis
Ivry-sur-Seine, France
1898 'Mme. Louis Lévêque' (MR)

Lévêque, P.
Ivry-sur-Seine, France
1919 'Georges Clemenceau' (Pern)

Liabaud, Jean
Lyon, France
1869 'Baron Chaurand' (HP)

Looymans, P. J.
Oudenbosch, The Netherlands
1921 'Feu Joseph Looymans' (Pern)
1922 'Elvira Aramayo' (Pern)

Low, Stuart
Bush Hill Park, Enfield, Middlesex,
England
1908 'Lady Faire' (HT)
1913 'Climbing Monsieur Paul Lédé'
  (Cl HT)

Lowe & Shawyer
Uxbridge, England
1911 'Mrs. George Shawyer' (HT)
1912 'Mrs. E. Alford' (HT)

Mallerin, Charles
Isère, France
1927 'Ami Quinard' (HT)
1929 'Mrs. Pierre du Pont' (Pern)
1931 'Collette Clément' (Pern)

Marest
Paris, France
1830 'Mme. Zoutmann' (D)

Margottin fils (Jules)
Pierrefitte, France
1877 'La Saumonée' (HCh)

Martin
Rose Angle, Scotland
pre-1838 'Rose Angle' (Rbg)
pre-1838 'Dundee Rambler' (Arv)

Mauget
Orléans, France
1827 'Alba' (Law)
1827 'Dieudonné' (Law)
1827 'Pompon de Bourgogne à Fleurs
  Blanches' (G)
1844 'Anémone' (M)
1844 'Perpétuelle Mauget' (MR)

May, H. B.
Summit, New Jersey, U.S.A.
1908 'Climbing Liberty' (Cl HT)

McGredy, Samuel
Portadown, Ireland
1909 'His Majesty' (HT)
1909 'Lady Alice Stanley' (HT)
1909 'Mrs. Wakefield Christie-Miller' (HT)
1910 'Mrs. Herbert Stevens' (HT)
1911 'Edward Mawley' (HT)
1911 'Mrs. Amy Hammond' (HT)

1911 'Mrs. Joseph H. Welch' (HT)
1912 'British Queen' (HT)
1912 'Earl of Gosford' (HT)
1912 'Mrs. Frederick W. Vanderbilt' (Pern)
1912 'Mrs. Muir MacKean' (HT)
1912 'Mrs. Wallace H. Rowe' (HT)
1913 'Edith Part' (HT)
1913 'Lady Mary Ward' (HT)
1913 'Mrs. Charles E. Pearson' (Pern)
1913 'Old Gold' (Pern)
1914 'Edgar M. Burnett' (HT)
1914 'Mrs. Ambrose Riccardo' (Pern)
1915 'Mrs. Franklin Dennison' (HT)
1916 'Crimson Emblem' (HT)
1916 'Golden Emblem' (Pern)
1916 'Isobel' (Pern)
1916 'Miss Wilmott' (HT)
1917 'Gladys Holland' (HT)
1917 'Noblesse' (HT)
1918 'Christine' (Pern)
1918 'Emma Wright' (Pern)
1918 'Mrs. George Marriot' (HT)
1918 'The Queen Alexandra Rose' (Pern)
1919 'Edel' (HT)
1919 'Louise Baldwin' (HT)
1919 'Martha Drew' (HT)
1919 'Mrs. Henry Morse' (HT)
1919 'Mrs. Redford' (Pern)
1922 'Lord Lambourne' (Pern)
1923 'Florence L. Izzard' (Pern)
1925 'Gwyneth Jones' (Pern)
1926 'Mabel Lynas' (Pern)
1926 'Mrs. Talbot O'Farrell' (Pern)
1926 'Norman Lambert' (Pern)
1927 'Mrs. W. E. Nickerson' (Pern)
1928 'Mrs. S. Paton' (Pern)
1929 'Mrs. Sam McGredy' (Pern)

Mermet, Louis
Lyon, France
1907 'Dr. Reymond' (Mult)
1924 'Climbing Willowmere' (Cl Pern)
1934 'Souvenir de J. Mermet' (W)

Miellez, Auguste
Esquermes-lès-Lille, France
pre-1811 'Minerve' (G)
pre-1811 'Pallas' (G)
pre-1813 'Beauté Touchante' (G)
pre-1813 'Nouvelle Gagnée' (G)
pre-1818 'Duc d'York' (A)
1818? 'Duchesse d'Angoulême' (G)
1819 'Capricorn' (G)
pre-1826 'Princesse Éléonore' (G)
pre-1826 'Revenante' (G)
pre-1826 'Zoé' (G)
pre-1828 'Beau Narcisse' (G)

pre-1828 'Horatius Coclès' (G)
pre-1828 'Juliette' (G)
pre-1828 'Pucelle de Lille' (G)
pre-1829 'La Gloire des Laurencias' (Law)
pre-1829 'La Liliputienne' (Law)
pre-1830 'Dame Blanche' (D)
pre-1830 'La Mouche' (Law)
pre-1830 'Princesse de Lamballé' (A)
pre-1831 'Caprice des Dames' (Law)
pre-1835 'Louis-Philippe' (HB)
1835 'Nouvelle Transparente' (G)
ca. 1840 'Princesse de Nassau' (G)
ca.1860 'Coralie' (M)

Mietzsch, L. W.
Dresden, Germany
1907 'Ernst Hempel' (HT)

Mikeš
Troja, Czechoslovakia
1927 'Troja' (HT)
1933 'Jitřenka' (Mult)

Mille-Toussaint fils
Lyon, France
1906 'Duchesse de la Mothe-Houdancourt'
  (HT)

Montgomery, Alexander W.
Hadley, Massachusetts, U.S.A.
1913 'Mrs. Charles E. Russell' (HT)
1914 'Hadley' (HT)
1929 'Talisman' (Pern)

Moranville
France
1905 'La Neige' (M)
1905 'Mme. Emilie Lafon' (HT)

Moreau, Félix
Fontenay-aux-Roses, France
ca. 1850 'Pepita' (G)
pre-1885 'Général Moreau' (G)

Moreau-Robert
Angers, France
1862 'Blanche Simon' (M)
1864 'Mme. Platz' (MR)
1865 'Marie Leczinska' (MR)
1865 'Mélanie Waldor' (MR)
1866 'Princesse Bacciochi' (M)
1867 'Souvenir de Pierre Vibert' (MR)
1868 'Maupertuis' (MR)
1869 'Mme. William Paul' (MR)
1872 'Mme. Moreau' (MR)
1873 'Mme. Landeau' (MR)
1874 'Gaspard Monge' (HP)
1880 'Blanche Moreau' (MR)
1881 'Mousseline' (MR)
1890 'Capitaine Basroger' (M)

Morlet fils
Avon, France
1874 'Souvenir de Yeddo' (Rg)
1883 'Inermis Morletii' (Bslt)
1888 'Mikado' (Rg)
1891 'Fimbriata' (Rg)
1900 'Monsieur Hélye' (Rg)
1900 'Monsieur Morlet' (Rg)

Morse, Henry
Norwich, England
1920 'Climbing Château de Clos-Vougeot'
    (Cl HT)
1920 'Westfield Star' (HT)
1926 'Dr. Edward Deacon' (Pern)

Müller, Dr. Fr.
Weingarten, Bavaria, Germany
1886 'Thusnelda' (Rg)
1890 'Germanica' (Rg)
1894 'Gottfried Keller' (Pern)
1899 'Conrad Ferdinand Meyer' (Rg)
1900 'Germanica B' (Rg)
1904 'Gruss an Sangerhausen' (HT)
1905 'Dr. Müller' (Pern)
1905 'Schmetterling' (Pern)
1920 'Apotheker Franz Hahne' (Pern)

Nabonnand, Gilbert
Golfe-Juan, France
1881 'Comte d'Epremesnil' (Rg)

Nabonnand, Paul & Clément
Golfe-Juan, France
1902 'Lady Waterlow' (Cl HT)

Nabonnand, Clément
Esterel Parc par Mandelieu, France
1920 'Irène Bonnet' (Cl HT)
1922 'Marguerite Carels' (Cl HT)

Nicolas, J. H.
Newark, New Jersey, U.S.A.
1939 'June Moon' (Mult)
1940 'Dr. J. H. Nicolas' (Cl HT)

Nielsen
Denmark?
1932 'Olavus' (M)
1932 'Waltraud Nielsen' (M)

Noisette, Louis Claude
La-Queue-en-Brie, France
ca. 1815 'Maheca' (Bslt)
pre-1817 'Semi-Double' (Rubr)
pre-1820 'Théone' (C)
pre-1822 'Scabriusculus' (Brac)
1827 'Simple' (Law)

Noisette, Étienne
La-Queue-en-Brie, France
1825 'Parnassine' (Rg)
1829 'Ancelin' (Turb)
1829 'Comtesse de Coutard' (HCh)

Nonin, Auguste
Chatillon-sous-Bagneux, France
1911 'Améthyste' (Mult)
1912 'Caroubier' (Mult)
1912 'Mme. Auguste Nonin' (W)
1912 'Petit Louis' (W)
1913 'Chatillon-Rambler' (W)
1913 'Émile Nerini' (Mult)
1922 'Île de France' (W)
1923 'Madeleine Lemaire' (W)
1925 'Mme. Jenny' (Mult)
1925 'Petit René' (W)
1929 'Normandie' (W)

Oger, Pierre
Caen, France
1850 'Souvenir d'un Frère' (B)

Pacific Rose Company
Los Angeles, California, U.S.A.
1927 'Climbing Red Radiance' (Cl HT)
1927 'Climbing Rose Marie' (Cl HT)

Page, C. G.
Washington, D.C., U.S.A.
1859 'Amarante' (B)

Pajotin-Chédane
Angers, France
1918 'Général Testard' (W)

Parks, John Damper
London, England
1823? 'Lutea' (Bks)

Parmentier, Louis-Joseph-Ghislain
Enghien, Belgium
1828 'Moïse' (G)
ca. 1830 'Alice' (A)
ca. 1835 'Edmond Duval' (G)
pre-1836 'Félicité' (A)
1840 'Emilie Verachter' (G)
ca. 1840 'De Schelfhont' (G)
ca. 1840 'Joséphine Parmentier' (G)
ca. 1840 'Prince Frédéric' (G)
pre-1843 'Dumortier' (G)
1843 'Narcisse de Salvandy' (G)
ca. 1845 'Belle Isis' (Ag)
ca. 1845 'Van Huyssum' (G)
pre-1847 'Belle Doria' (G)
pre-1847 'Van Artevelde' (G)
pre-1847 'Victor Parmentier' (G)
1850? 'Marbrée d'Enghien' (Pim)

Pastoret
France
1857 'La Noblesse' (C)
1857 'Tour de Malakoff' (C)

Paul, Adam
Cheshunt, Hertfordshire, England
1853 'Princess Alice' (M)

Paul, George
Cheshunt, Hertfordshire, England
1895 'Paul's Carmine Pillar' (HCh)
1895 'Rose Apples' (Rg)
1898 'Psyche' (Mult)
1898 'Una' (Can)
1899 'Atropurpurea' (Rg)
1899 'Paul's Himalayica Alba Magna' (Mk)
1899 'Paul's Himalayica Double Pink' (Mk)
1900 'The Lion' (Mult)
1901 'Purple East' (Mult)
1901 'The Wallflower' (Mult)
1903 'Repens Alba' (Rg)
1903 'Tea Rambler' (Mult)
1905 'The Dandy' (HT)
1908 'Goldfinch' (Mult)
1908 'Lady Godiva' (W)
1910 'Shower of Gold' (W)
1911 'Desdemona' (HT)
1911 'Mrs. A. Kingsmill' (Lv)
1911 'Othello' (HT)
1912 'Sweet Lavender' (Mult)
1912 'Queen of the Musks' (HMk)
1914 'Dolly Varden' (Rg)
1915 'Paul's Lemon Pillar' (Cl HT)
1916 'Paul's Tree Climber' (Mk)

Paul, William
Waltham Cross, England
1880 'Little Gem' (M)
1890 'Crimson Globe' (M)
1892 'Zenobia' (M)
1894 'Lorna Doone' (B)
1904 'Earl of Warwick' (HT)
1905 'Waltham Bride' (Mult)
1907 'Kathleen' (Mult)
1907 'Mrs. Isabel Milner' (HT)
1909 'Buttercup' (Mult)
1909 'Refulgence' (Rbg)
1910 'Elsie' (W)
1910 'Portia' (HT)
1911 'Canary Bird' (Rbg)
1911 'Florence Haswell Veitch' (Cl HT)
1912 'Mrs. Charles Hunter' (HT)
1912 'Nerissa' (HT)
1912 'Ophelia' (HT)
1913 'Bianca' (HT)
1913 'Marcella' (HT)

1913 'Red Admiral' (HT)
1914 'Oriflamme' (Mult)
1916 'Circe' (HT)
1916 'Paul's Scarlet Climber' (W)
1917 'Walter C. Clark' (HT)
1918 'Mermaid' (Brac)
1919 'Coralie' (Mult)
1919 'Sea Foam' (Brac)
1919 'Toreador' (HT)
1922 'The Beacon' (W)
1923 'Barbara' (Pern)

Pelletier, Amédé
Mesnil-le-Montant, France
pre-1817 'À Feuilles de Pêcher' (A)
pre-1820 'Sommesson' (Ag)
pre-1824 'Fleurs de Pelletier' (G)
ca. 1825 'Pelletier' (G)
pre-1826 'De la Malmaison' (Ag)
1827 'Général Foy' (G)
pre-1828 'À Fleurs de Rose Tremière de Chine' (G)
pre-1828 'Princesse de Portugal' (G)

Pemberton, Joseph Hardwick
Havering-atte-Bower, Essex, England
1912 'Daphne' (HMk)
1913 'Danaë' (HMk)
1913 'Moonlight' (HMk)
1914 'Ceres' (HMk)
1914 'Galatea' (HMk)
1914 'Pemberton's White Rambler' (Mult)
1914 'Winter Cheer' (HMk)
1915 'Clytemnestra' (HMk)
1915 'Queen Alexandra' (HMk)
1918 'Daybreak' (HMk)
1918 'Pax' (HMk)
1918 'Thisbe' (HMk)
1919 'Miriam' (HT)
1919 'Prosperity' (HMk)
1919 'Star of Persia' (F)
1920 'Callisto' (HMk)
1920 'Havering Rambler' (Mult)
1920 'Vanity' (HMk)
1921 'Sammy' (HMk)
1922 'Francesca' (HMk)
1922 'Kathleen' (HMk)
1923 'Aurora' (HMk)
1923 'Nur-Mahál' (HMk)
1923 'Sea Spray' (HMk)
1924 'Penelope' (HMk)
1925 'Cornelia' (HMk)
1925 'I Zingari' (Pern)
1927 'Fortuna' (HMk)
1927 'Robin Hood' (HMk)
1928 'Felicia' (HMk)

1929 'Chami' (HMk)
1930 'Maid Marion' (HMk)

Penzance (Lord). James Plaisted Wilde, 1st Baron Penzance
Eashing Park, England
1894 'Amy Robsart' (Rbg)
1894 'Anne of Geierstein' (Rbg)
1894 'Brenda' (Rbg)
1894 'Lady Penzance' (Rbg)
1894 'Lord Penzance' (Rbg)
1894 'Lucy Ashton' (Rbg)
1894 'Meg Merrilies' (Rbg)
1894 'Rose Bradwardine' (Rbg)
1895 'Catherine Seyton' (Rbg)
1895 'Edith Bellenden' (Rbg)
1895 'Flora McIvor' (Rbg)
1895 'Greenmantle' (Rbg)
1895 'Jeannie Deans' (Rbg)
1895 'Julia Mannering' (Rbg)
1895 'Lucy Bertram' (Rbg)
1895 'Minna' (Rbg)

Pernet père (Jean)
Lyon, France
1874 'Soupert & Notting' (MR)
1877 'Louis Gimard' (M)

Pernet-Ducher, Joseph (Pernet fils)
Lyon, France
1900 'Rhodophile Gravereaux' (Pern)
1900 'Soleil d'Or' (Pern)
1901 'Prince de Bulgarie' (HT)
1902 'Monsieur Paul Lédé' (HT)
1903 'Le Progrès' (HT)
1903 'Monsieur Joseph Hill' (HT)
1904 'Étoile de France' (HT)
1905 'Mme. Mélanie Soupert' (HT)
1905 'Mme. Philippe Rivoire' (HT)
1906 'Marquise de Sinety' (HT)
1907 'Laurent Carle' (HT)
1907 'Lyon-Rose' (Pern)
1907 'Mme. Maurice de Luze' (HT)
1907 'Mrs. Aaron Ward' (HT)
1907 'Renée Wilmart-Urban' (HT)
1908 'Château de Clos-Vougeot' (HT)
1908 'Jean Notté' (HT)
1908 'Mrs. Arthur Robert Waddell' (Pern)
1909 'Arthur R. Goodwin' (Pern)
1909 'Colonel Leclerc' (HT)
1910 'Beauté de Lyon' (Pern)
1910 'Eugène Boullet' (HT)
1910 'Lieutenant Chauré' (HT)
1910 'Rayon d'Or' (Pern)
1910 'Souvenir de Gustave Prat' (HT)
1911 'Président Vignet' (HT)
1911 'Sunburst' (Pern)

1912 'Louise Catherine Breslau' (Pern)
1912 'Mme. Edmond Rostand' (HT)
1913 'Cissie Easlea' (Pern)
1913 'Mme. Édouard Herriot' (Pern)
1913 'Mme. Théodore Delacourt' (HT)
1913 'Mrs. T. Hillas' (HT)
1913 'Willowmere' (Pern)
1915 'Constance' (Pern)
1915 'Totote Gélos' (HT)
1916 'Mme. Caristie Martel' (HT)
1916 'Mme. Méha Sabatier' (HT)
1916 'Mrs. Bullen' (Pern)
1916 'Président Bouché' (Pern)
1918 'Bénédicte Seguin' (Pern)
1918 'Élégante' (HT)
1919 'Capitaine Georges Dessirier' (HT)
1919 'Jean C. N. Forestier' (Pern)
1920 'Souvenir de Claudius Pernet' (Pern)
1921 'Étoile de Feu' (Pern)
1921 'Reverend Williamson' (Pern)
1922 'Souvenir de Georges Pernet' (Pern)
1922 'Climbing Mrs. Herbert Stevens' (Cl HT)
1923 'Lawrence Johnston' (F)
1923 'Le Rêve' (F)
1924 'Amélie de Bethune' (Pern)
1924 'Angèle Pernet' (Pern)
1924 'Belle Cuivrée' (Pern)
1925 'Ville de Paris' (Pern)
1927 'Julien Potin' (Pern)
1927 'Climbing Souvenir de Georges Pernet' (Cl Pern)
1928 'Mme. Henri Queuille' (Pern)

Perrot
France?
1931 'Professeur Émile Perrot' (D)
1934? 'Ballady' (C)

Pierce, Joshua
Washington, D.C., U.S.A.
ca. 1840 'Anne Maria' (Set)
ca. 1846 'Eva Corinne' (Set)
ca. 1846 'Jane' (Set)
ca. 1846 'Miss Gunnell' (Set)
ca. 1846 'Mrs. Hovey' (Set)
ca. 1846 'President' (Set)
ca. 1846 'Pride of Washington' (Set)
ca. 1846 'Ranunculiflora' (Set)
ca. 1846 'Triumphant' (Set)
ca. 1846 'Virginia Lass' (Set)

Pierson, A. N.
Cromwell, Connecticut, U.S.A.
1916 'Red Radiance' (HT)
1918 'Evelyn' (HT)

Poilpré
Le Mans, France
1789 'Oeillet' (C)
ca. 1815 'À Fleurs Panachées' (Bslt)
1823 'La Surprise' (A)

Portemer père
Gentilly, France
1846 'Princesse Royale' (M)
1849 'Hermann Kegel' (MR)
1854 'Comtesse Doria' (M)
1855 'Duchesse d'Istrie' (M)
1856 'Duchesse de Verneuil' (M)
1857 'De Candolle' (M)
1863 'Arthur Young' (HCh)

Poulsen, D. T.
Kvistgaard, Denmark
1911 'Rödhätte' (Pol)
1913 'Grevinde Silvia Knuth' (W)
1928 'Signe Relander' (Rg)

Pradel, Henri (père) & Giraud (fils)
Montauban, France
1857 'Mme. d'Hébray' (C)

Praskač, Franz
Freundorf-Tulin, Austria
1913 'Donau!' (W)
1913 'Gruss an Freundorf!' (W)
1913 'Perle vom Wienerwald!' (Mult)
1926 'Exquisite' (Mult)
1926 'Regierungsrat Rottenberger' (W)

Prévost fils
Rouen, France
pre-1813 'Passe-Princesse' (G)
1820 'Placidie' (A)
1820 'Vierge' (Pim)
pre-1826 'Camille Bouland' (A)
pre-1826 'Double Carnée' (Pim)
pre-1826 'Belle d'Auteuil' (D)
pre-1826 'Grand Bercam' (C)
1828 'Monique' (A)
pre-1829 'Gracilis' (M)
pre-1829 'Maxima Multiplex' (A)
ca. 1830 'Portland Pourpre' (DP)
ca. 1835 'Oeillet Double' (G)
1840 'Mauget' (M)

Puyravaud, Jouannem
Ste.-Foy-la-Grande, France
1903 'Amateur André Fourcaud' (HT)
1905 'Marie-Victoria Benoît' (M)
1905 'Souvenir de l'Exposition de
    Bordeaux 1905' (Mult)
1908 'Malva Rambler' (Mult)
1910 'Souvenir de Mme. F. Zurich' (HT)
1911 'Mme. Alfred Digeon' (HT)

Quétier, Pierre-Victor
Meaux, France
1839 'Angélique Quétier' (M)
pre-1842 'Château de Namur' (G)
1852 'Comte de Nanteuil' (HP)

**Regel (Prof. Eduard) & Kesselring
    (Jakob)**
**Imperial Botanic Garden,
    St. Petersburg, Russia**
1871 'Regeliana' (Rg)
1879 'Kaiserin des Nordens' (Rg)

Rivers, Thomas
Sawbridgeworth, England
1835 'Ayrshire Queen' (Arv)
pre-1838 'Miniature Moss' (M)
pre-1838 'Rivers' Single Crimson' (M)
pre-1846 'Rivers' Musk' (Mk)
pre-1846 'Scarlet Maria Leonida' (Brac)

Robert
Angers, France
1844 'Unique de Provence' (M)
1845 'Abaillard' (G)
1847 'Parmentier' (M)
1851 'À Long Pédoncle' (M)
1851 'D'Arcet' (M)
1851 'Duchesse d'Abrantès' (M)
1851 'Mme. De la Roche-Lambert' (M)
1851 'Mme. Soupert' (M)
1851 'Princesse Amélie' (M)
1852 'Céline Bourdier' (DP)
1852 'Delille' (MR)
1852 'Ismène' (M)
1852 'Lafontaine' (M)
1852 'Marie de Blois' (M)
1852 'Montalembert' (G)
1853 'Céline Briant' (MR)
1853 'Georges Vibert' (G)
1853 'Jeanne de Montfort' (M)
1853 'La Neige' (G)
1853 'Laurette' (T)
1853 'Lesueur' (DP)
1853 'Maréchal Davoust' (M)
1853 'Marie de Bourgogne' (MR)
1853 'Oscar Leclerc' (MR)
1853 'René d'Anjou' (MR)
1853 'Robert Fortune' (M)
1854 'Christophe Colombe' (DP)
1854 'François de Salignac' (M)
1854 'Gaspard Monge' (C)
1854 'Gloriette' (C)
1854 'Lucie Duplessis' (M)
1854 'Mme. Édouard Ory' (MR)
1854 'Princesse de Vaudémont' (M)
1855 'César Beccaria' (G)

1855 'Circé' (MR)
1855 'Juanita' (C)
1856 'Botzaris' (D)
1856 'Charles-Quint' (C)
1856 'Général Kléber' (M)
1856 'Raphael' (MR)
1856 'Tour Malakoff' (G)

Robert & Moreau
Angers, France
1857 'Ducis' (M)
1857 'La Caille' (M)
1857 'Mme. de Staël' (MR)
1857 'Ninette' (M)
1857 'Pompon' (G)
1857 'Reine-Blanche' (M)
1857 'Validé' (MR)
1858 'Ménage' (M)
1859 'Césonie' (MR)
1859 'Emmeline' (M)
1859 'Laurent Heister' (DP)
1860 'Dr. Marjolin' (M)
1860 'Eugène de Savoie' (MR)
1860 'Lane' (M)
1860 'Louise Verger' (M)
ca. 1860 'Reine des Moussues' (M)
1861 'Alcime' (M)
1861 'Fornarina' (MR)
1861 'Hortense Vernet' (MR)
1862 'Tricolore' (Mult)
1863 'Clémence Robert' (MR)
1863 'Jules Lesourd' (DP)
1863 'Sophie de Marsilly' (MR)

Robichon, Altin
Orléans, France
1903 'Louise Pernot' (HT)
1904 'Marguerite Rose' (Pol)
1908 'Neige d'Avril' (Mult)
1911 'Mme. Léopold Dupuy' (HT)
1912 'De Candolle' (W)

Roeser
Crécy-en-Brie, France
1834 'Comte Boula de Nanteuil' (G)

Ruschpler
Germany?
1878 'König von Sachsen' (G)

Sauvageot, J.
Doubs, France
1923 'Souvenir du Capitaine Fernand Japy'
    (HT)
1923 'Vicomtesse Pierre de Fou' (Cl HT)
1931 'Hiawatha Remontant' (Mult)
1934 'Albert Maumené' (Hug)
1934 'Château de Vaire' (Macro)

Schoener, George M. A.
Santa Clara, California, U.S.A.
1930 'Schoener's Nutkana' (Nut)

Schmidt, J. C.
Erfurt, Germany
1896 'Anemonenrose' (Lv)
1896 'Flora Plena' (Rubr)
1899 'Weisser Herumstreicher' (Mult)
1901 'Rubin' (Mult)
1909 'Veilchenblau' (Mult)
1910 'Jubiläumsrose' (HT)
1917 'Schloss Friedenstein' (Mult)
1925 '(Turner's Crimson Rambler ×
    Veilchenblau)'
1929 'Jubiläumsrose' (Pern)
1932 'Goldener Traum' (Rg)

Schmitt
Bischweiler, Germany
1895 'Aglaia' (Lam)
1895 'Euphrosine' (Lam)
1895 'Thalia' (Lam)
1910 'Marie Schmitt' (HT)

Schwartz, Joseph
Lyon, France
1882 'Bijou de Lyon' (Mult)
1882 'Mme. Viviand-Morel' (Arv)

Schwartz, Widow
Lyon, France
1889 'Mme. Charles Frédéric Worth' (Rg)
1899 'La Favorite' (HT)
1900 'La Tosca' (HT)

Schwartz, André
Lyon, France
1904 'Marquis de Bouillé' (HT)
1904 'Sénateur Saint-Romme' (HT)
1906 'Souvenir de Monsieur Frédéric
    Vercellone' (HT)
1908 'Princesse Vera Orbelioni' (HT)
1911 'Comte G. de Rochemur' (HT)
1912 'Le Mexique' (W)

Schwarzkopf, Daniel August
Weissenstein & Napoleonshohe,
    Germany
1773 'Perle de Weissenstein' (G)
pre-1799 'Grosse Mohnkopfsrose' (Turb)
pre-1811 'Hessoise' (Rbg)
pre-1811 'Perle de l'Orient' (G)
pre-1815 'Holoserica Regalis' (G)

Shailer, Henry
Battersea, Chelsea, & Kensington,
    England
1788 'White Moss Rose' (M)

1796 'Gracilis' (Bslt)
1818 'Panachée' (M)

Skinner, Dr. F. L.
Dropmore, Manitoba, Canada
1924 'Dr. Merkeley' (Pim)
1939 'George Will' (Rg)
1939 'Wasagaming' (Rg)
1949 'Suzanne' (Pim)

Smith, T.
Daisy Hill Nursery, Newry, Ireland
ca. 1883 'Narrow Water' (Mk)
ca. 1904 'Repens Rosea' (Rg)
1906? 'Daisy Hill' (Macra)
pre-1927 'Coral Drops' (unk. affiliation)

Sommesson
Porte de Clichy, Paris, France
1822 'Mme. de Tressan' (G)
pre-1826 'Abailard' (G)

Souchet, Charles
Bagnolet, France
1824 'Pallida' (F)

Soupert (Jean) & Notting (Pierre)
Luxembourg
1857 'Duc de Constantine' (HP)
1876 'Violacée' (M)
1900 'Mme. J.-P. Soupert' (HT)
1901 'Laure Wattinne' (HT)
1901 'Pierre Wattinne' (HT)
1903 'Souvenir de Maria Zozaya' (HT)
1904 'Reine Marguerite d'Italie' (HT)
1904 'William Notting' (HT)
1905 'Mrs. E. G. Hill' (HT)
1905 'Souvenir de Maria de Zayas' (HT)
1905 'Stella' (Mult)
1906 'Marichu Zayas' (HT)
1907 'Bordeaux' (Mult)
1907 'Comtesse Icy Hardegg' (HT)
1907 'Mme. Segond-Weber' (HT)
1908 'Bagatelle' (Mult)
1908 'Jacques Vincent' (HT)
1909 'Prince Englebert Ch. d'Arenberg'
    (HT)
1910 'Hugo Maweroff' (Mult)
1910 'Manuel P. Azevedo' (HT)
1911 'Maman Lyly' (HT)
1912 'Aviateur Michel Mahieu' (HT)
1912 'Dr. Nicolas Welter' (HT)
1913 'Lucien Chauré' (HT)
1926 'Antonio Rolleri de Peluffo' (Pern)
1927 'Laure Soupert' (Mult)
1927 'Recuerdo de Angel Peluffo' (Pern)
1929 'Souvenir de Jean Soupert' (Pern)

Spek, Jan
Boskoop, The Netherlands
1922 'Ceres' (Pern)
1930 'Rosa Gruss an Aachen' (HT)

Stegerhoek, Cornelius
Nordwyck, The Netherlands
pre-1813 'L'Amitié' (D)
pre-1821 'Tricolore' (G)
pre-1828 'Adonis' (Ag)

Stevens, Walter
Hoddesdon, Hertfordshire, England
1926 'Lady Sylvia' (HT)
1933 'Climbing Lady Sylvia' (Cl HT)

Strassheim, C. P.
Sachsenhausen, Frankfurt-am-Main,
    Germany
1906 'Frau Lina Strassheim' (Mult)
1906 'Grossherzogin Eléonore von Essen'
    (Mult)
1909 'Greta Fey' (W)

Tanne, Remi
Rouen, France
1912 'Paul Noël' (W)
1920 'André Louis' (W)
1920 'Fernand Tanne' (W)

Tantau, Mathias
Ütersen, Germany
1922 'Rotelfe' (HT)
1931 'Johanna Röpke' (W)
1937 'Indra' (Mult)
1939 'Direktor Benschop' (W)
1939 'Erato' (Mult)
1951 'Claus Groth' (Pim)
1955 'Lichterloh' (Lam)
1956 'Zitronenfalter' (Lam)

Tepelmann
Germany?
1937 'Frau Eva Schubert' (Lam)
ca. 1950 'Gela Tepelmann' (Mult)

Thierry
Calvados, France
pre-1846 'Le Météore' (HCh)

Thomas, Desiré
St.-Denis, France
1854 'Julie de Mersan' (M)

Thomas, Capt. George C.
Beverly Hills, California, U.S.A.
1920 'Bloomfield Progress' (HT)
1920 'Dr. Huey' (W)
1921 'W. Freeland Kendrick' (W)
1924 'Bloomfield Favorite' (W)

Thomas, Capt. George C. *continued*
1925 'Bloomfield Courage' (W)
1925 'Bloomfield Culmination' (HMk)
1925 'Bloomfield Dainty' (HMk)
1925 'Bloomfield Discovery' (HMk)
1925 'Bloomfield Fascination' (HMk)
1925 'Cascadia' (HMk)
1926 'Bishop Darlington' (HMk)
1927 'Bloomfield Perfection' (HMk)
1929 'Bloomfield Comet' (HMk)
1931 'Bloomfield Completeness' (HMk)
1931 'Bloomfield Dawn' (HMk)
1931 'Ednah Thomas' (Cl HT)
1938 'Captain Thomas' (Cl HT)

Thönges
Germany
1929 'Konrad Thönges' (Pern)
1938 'Frau Liesel Brauer' (Mult)

Timmermans, Joseph
Herten, Roermond, The Netherlands
1919 'Cornelis Timmermans' (HT)
1919 'Jonkheer Ruis de Beerenbrouck' (HT)
1923 'Climbing Jonkheer J. L. Mock' (Cl HT)

Touvais, Jean
Petit-Montrouge, France
1861 'Bicolore Incomparable' (HP)
1867 Alba Carnea' (HP)

Trébucien
Rouen, France
pre-1829 'Grand Corneille' (G)
pre-1829 'Henri IV' (D)

Trouillard, Victor
Angers, France
1856 'Mlle. Alice Leroy' (MR)

Turbat (Eugène) & Compagnie
Orléans, France
1912 'Source d'Or' (W)
1914 'Louis Sauvage' (W)
1915 'Gaston Lesieur' (W)
1916 'Ghislaine de Féligonde' (Mult)
1918 'Daisy Brazileir' (Mult)
1918 'Fernand Rabier' (W)
1919 'Beauté Orléanaise' (W)
1920 'Le Loiret' (Pol)
1921 'Fraîcheur' (W)
1921 'Violette' (Mult)
1922 'Papa Gouchault' (Mult)
1922 'Printemps Fleuri' (Mult)
1923 'Papa Rouillard' (W)
1924 'Clematis' (W)
1925 'Ardon' (W)

1925 'Solarium' (W)
1927 'Marie Gouchault' (W)
1928 'Bonfire' (W)

Türke, Robert
Meissen, Germany
1903 'Königin Carola von Sachsen' (HT)
1907 'Friedrichsruh' (HT)
1909 'Leuchtfeuer' (B)
1910 'Johannisfeuer' (Pern)
1910 'König Laurin' (HT)
1920 'Flammenrose' (Pern)
1923 'Türke's Rugosa-Sämling' (Rg)

Turner, Charles
Slough, Berkshire, England
1893 'Turner's Crimson Rambler' (Mult)
1901 'Lady Curzon' (Rg)
1901 'Lady White' (D)
1901 'Turner's Crimson Damask' (D)
1912 'Coronation' (W)
1912 'Ethel' (W)
1915 'Pearl' (HMk)

Van Eeden Bros.
Haarlem, The Netherlands
1810 'De Van Eeden' (G)
pre-1820 'L'Obscurité' (G)

Van Fleet, Dr. Walter
Glenn Dale, Maryland, U.S.A.
1898 'Clara Barton' (HT)
1898 'May Queen' (W)
1898 'Ruby Queen' (W)
1900 'Magnafrano' (HT)
1901 'Alba Rubifolia' (W)
1901 'New Century' (Rg)
1901 'Pearl Queen' (W)
1903 'Philadelphia Rambler' (Mult)
1905 'Sir Thomas Lipton' (Rg)
1906 'American Pillar' (W)
1906 'Birdie Blye' (Lam)
1907 'Magnifica' (Rg)
1909 'Silver Moon' (Lv)
1910 'Dr. W. Van Fleet' (W)
1915 'Mary Lovett' (W)
1917 'Alida Lovett' (W)
1917 'Bess Lovett' (W)
1918 'Aunt Harriet' (W)
1923 'Mary Wallace' (W)
1926 'Breeze Hill' (W)
1926 'Dr. E. M. Mills' (Hug)
1926 'Heart of Gold' (W)
1926 'Sarah Van Fleet' (Rg)
1927 'Glenn Dale' (W)
1928 'Ruskin' (Rg)

Van Houtte, Louis
Ghent, Belgium
pre-1842 'Graulhié' (Mult)
1846 'Tricolore de Flandre' (G)
pre-1852 'Anatole de Montesquieu' (Semp)
1900 'Bleu Violette' (Mult)

Van Rossem, G. A.
Naarden, The Netherlands
1916 'Morgenglans' (HT)
1919 'Herfsttooi' (HT)
1920 'Geisha' (Pern)
1920 'Secretaris Zwart' (Pern)
1924 'Gooiland Beauty' (Pern)
1925 'Gooiland Glory' (Pern)
1926 'Mevrouw G. A. Van Rossem' (Pern)
1928 'Albast' (HT)

Vandevelde, F.
Belgium?
1924 'Cécile Ratinckx' (Pern)
1924 'Mme. Charles Lejeune' (W)

Veitch (James) & Son
Chelsea, England
1900 'Electra' (Lam)
1901 'Queen Alexandra' (Mult)

Verdier, Victor
Paris, France
1844 'Mme. Audot' (A)
1845 'Adrienne de Cardoville' (C)
1847 'Esmeralda' (A)
1848 'Comtesse de Ségur' (C)
1850 'Barillet' (M)

Verdier, Victor & Charles
Paris, France
1854 'Baron de Wassenaër' (MR)

Verdier, Eugène
Paris, France
1861 'James Mitchell' (M)
1861 'John Cranston' (MR)
1864 'James Veitch' (MR)
1865 'Alba Mutabilis' (HP)
1872 'Eugène Verdier' (M)
1876 'Pompon Blanc Parfait' (A)

Verdier, Charles
Paris, France
1888 'Oeillet Panaché' (M)

Verschuren (H. A.) & Sons
Haps, The Netherlands
1903 'Koningin Emma' (HT)
1906 'Die Mutter von Rosa' (HT)
1907 'Dr. A. Hermans' (HT)
1918 'Bertha von Suttner' (HT)

1918 'Gloire de Hollande' (HT)
1918 'Nelly Verschuren' (HT)
1918 'Red Star' (HT)
1918 'Rose d'Espérance' (HT)
1918 'United States' (Pern)
1919 'E. P. H. Kingma' (Pern)
1919 'Étoile de Hollande' (HT)
1919 'Hortulanus Budde' (Pern)
1919 'Miss C. E. Van Rossem' (HT)
1919 'Nederland' (HT)
1926 'Souvenir d'Angèle Opdebeeck' (Pern)

Vestal (Joseph W.) & Son
Little Rock, Arkansas, U.S.A.
1923 'Climbing Columbia' (Cl HT)
1936 'Climbing Condesa de Sastago'
   (Cl Pern)

Vétillart
Le Mans, France
ca. 1825 'Léa' (G)
1826 'Fornarina' (G)

Viaud-Bruant
Poitiers, France
1914 'Ernest Laurent' (HT)

Vibert, Jean-Pierre
Chennevières-sur-Marne, St.-Denis,
   Longjumeau, *and* **Angers, France**
1816 'Adèle Heu' (G)
1816 'Aline' (G)
1817 'Fanny Rousseau' (A)
1817 'Nankin' (Pim)
1817 'Petite Lisette' (A)
1818 'Ariane' (G)
1818 'Armide' (A)
1818 'Bérénice' (G)
1818 'Duchesse de Berry' (G)
1818? 'Grand Cramoisi de Vibert' (G)
1818 'Jeanne d'Arc' (A)
1818 'Pénélope' (D)
1818 'Sapho' (Ag)
pre-1819 'Double' (Law)
1819 'Daphné' (G)
1819 'Fanny Bias' (G)
1819 'Gabrielle d'Estrées' (A)
1819 'Minette' (C)
1819 'Silvia' (D)
pre-1820 'Estelle' (Pim)
pre-1820 'Gros Chou d'Hollande' (C)
pre-1820 'Petite Renoncule Violette' (Ag)
1820 'Duc de Bordeaux' (G)
pre-1821 'Arlequin' (G)
pre-1821 'Ponctué' (G)
1821 'Ypsilanti' (G)
1822 'Charlotte De Lacharme' (G)

1822 'Néala' (G)
1823 'Aglaé Adanson' (G)
1823 'Amélia' (A)
1823 'Claudine' (A)
1823 'Irène' (Pim)
1823 'Joséphine Beauharnais' (A)
1823 'Lavalette' (D)
1823 'Ombrée Parfaite' (G)
pre-1824 'Belle Auguste' (D)
1825 'Claire d'Olban' (G)
1825 'Virginie' (G)
pre-1826 'Bellotte' (G)
pre-1826 'Fanny-Sommesson' (A)
pre-1826 'Orphise' (G)
pre-1826 'Péricles' (D)
pre-1826 'Petite Écossaise' (Pim)
pre-1826 'Semi-Double' (M)
pre-1826 'Triomphe de Lille' (D)
1827 'Déesse Flore' (D)
1828 'Anacréon' (G)
1828 'Dona Maria' (Semp)
pre-1829 'Belle Hélène' (G)
1829 'Marie-Antoinette' (G)
1830 'Adéline' (C)
ca. 1830 'Fulgens' (G)
1831 'Candide' (A)
1831 'Duc d'Orléans' (G)
1832 'Agénor' (G)
1833 'Alfieri' (G)
1833 'Ingénue' (G)
1833 'Renoncule Ponctuée' (G)
1834 'Alcine' (G)
1834 'Cramoisi Picoté' (G)
1834 'Héloïse' (G)
1834 'Hortense de Beauharnais' (G)
1834 'Julie d'Étanges' (G)
1834 'Malesherbes' (G)
1834 'Nestor' (G)
1835 'Antonine d'Ormois' (G)
1835 'Blanchefleur' (C)
1835 'Fanny Elssler' (G)
1835 'Gonzalve' (G)
1835 'Lycoris' (G)
pre-1836 'Césonie' (DP)
pre-1836 'Gracilis' (G)
pre-1836 'Rouge Admirable Strié' (G)
1836 'D'Aguesseau' (G)
1836 'Gloriette' (HN)
1836 'Juanita' (G)
1836 'La Ville de Bruxelles' (D)
1836 'Lucile Duplessis' (G)
1836 'Portland Blanc' (DP)
1836? 'Séguier' (G)
1837 'Anaïs Ségales' (C)
1837 'Duchesse de Buccleuch' (G)

1837 'Sanchette' (G)
1838 'Catinat' (G)
1839 'Alain Blanchard' (C)
1839 'Belle Villageoise' (G)
1839 'Omphale' (G)
1841 'Columelle' (G)
1841 'Desdémona' (DP)
1841 'Fornarina' (G)
1841 'Malvina' (M)
1841 'Sémiramis' (D)
1842 'Cosimo Ridolfi' (G)
1842 'Dona Sol' (G)
1842 'Jeanne Hachette' (G)
1842 'La Négresse' (D)
1842 'Madelon Friquet' (G)
1842 'Rosemary' (G)
1842 'Véturie' (D)
1843 'Agar' (G)
1843 'Alice Leroi' (M)
1843 'Catherine de Wurtemburg' (M)
1843 'Comtesse de Murinais' (M)
1843 'Giselle' (G)
1843 'Olympe' (D)
1843 'Phénice' (G)
1843 'Précoce' (M)
pre-1844 'Jeanne Hachette' (DP)
pre-1844 'La Ville de Londres' (G)
pre-1844 'Marie de Bourgogne' (A)
pre-1844 'Zénobie' (A)
1844 'Mécène' (G)
1845 'Alcime' (G)
1845 'Amanda Patenotte' (DP)
1845 'Aramis' (G)
1845 'Esther' (G)
1845 'Etna' (M)
1845 'Eulalie LeBrun' (C)
1845 'Hulda' (C)
1845 'Indiana' (M)
1845 'Ismène' (D)
1845 'Justine Ramet' (C)
1845 'Noémie' (D)
1845 'Oeillet Flamand' (G)
1845 'Perle des Panachées' (G)
1846 'Ambrose Paré' (G)
1846 'Turenne' (G)
pre-1847 'Nerrière' (Brac)
1847 'Euphémie' (B)
1847 'Général Drouot' (MR)
1847 'Lucrèce' (A)
1847 'Ménage' (A)
1847 'Mercédès' (G)
1847 'Triomphe de Sterckmanns' (G)
1848 'Casimir Delavigne' (DP)
1848 'Jean Bodin' (M)
1848 'Soeur Marthe' (M)

Vibert, Jean-Pierre *continued*
1849 'À Bois Brun' (Mult)
1849 'Bérangère' (M)
1849 'L'Ingénue' (G)
1849 'Pélisson' (M)
1849 'Pompon Perpétuel' (MR)
1849 'Routrou' (M)
1849 'Zaïre' (M)
1851 'Adèle Pavié' (M)

Vigneron, Jacques
Olivet, France
1892 'Olivet' (Mult)
1899 'L'Orléanaise' (Bslt)
1907 'Mme. Renée Oberthür' (HT)
1908 'Le Cid' (Rg)

Vilin (veuve) & fils
Grisy-Suisnes, France
1906 'Le Droit-Humain' (Mult)

Vilmorin
Paris, France
ca. 1800 'Unique Carnée' (C)
ca. 1805 'Vilmorin' (M)
ca. 1810 'Reversa' (Bslt)
1907 '(Rugosa × Duc d'Edinburgh)' (Rg)
date unk. 'Margheritae' (Rg)

Vogel, Max
Sangerhausen, Germany
1928 'Ernst Dechant' (Mult)
1929 'Erna' (Mult)
1929 'Kleine Rosel' (Mult)
1930 'Frau A. Weidling' (Lam)
1931 'Frau Käte Schmid' (Mult)
1934 'Hans Schmid' (Mult)
1934 'Karl Schneider' (Mult)
1935 'Charlotte von Rathlef' (Mult)
1935 'Jean Muraour' (HT)
1936 'Peter Lambert' (Mult)
1938 'Climbing Capitaine Soupa' (Cl HT)
1938 'Charlotte Mackensen' (Mult)
1938 'Climbing Mamie' (Cl HT)
1939 'Wilhelm Marx' (Lam)
1940 'Climbing Wenzel Geschwind' (Cl HT)

1941 'Climbing Apotheker Georg Höfer'
   (Cl HT)
1942 'Frau Sophie Meyerholz' (Lam)
1942 'Climbing Président Vignet' (Cl HT)
1944 'Weisse Gruss an Aachen' (HT)
1947 'Frau Professor Grischko' (Lam)

Waban Rose Conservatories
Natick & Boston, Massachusetts, U.S.A.
1909 'White Killarney' (HT)
1915 'Mrs. Moorfield Storey' (HT)

Walsh, Michael H.
Wood's Hole, Massachusetts, U.S.A.
1899? 'Sweetheart' (W)
1900 'Milky Way' (W)
1901 'Debutante' (W)
1902 'Flush o'Dawn' (HT)
1904 'Carissima' (W)
1904 'Minnehaha' (W)
1904 'Hiawatha' (Mult)
1905 'Lady Gay' (W)
1905 'Wedding Bells' (Mult)
1906 'Delight' (W)
1906 'Evangeline' (W)
1907 'Paradise' (W)
1908 'Babette' (W)
1908 'Excelsa' (W)
1909 'Cinderella' (W)
1909 'Jessica' (W)
1909 'La Fiamma' (W)
1910 'Troubadour' (W)
1911 'Bonnie Belle' (W)
1911 'Coquina' (W)
1913 'Arcadia' (W)
1915 'America' (W)
1918 'Nokomis' (W)

Walter, Louis
Saverne, France
1902 'Frau Peter Lambert' (HT)
1907 'Ida Klemm' (Mult)
1909 'Baronin Anna von Lüttwitz' (Mult)
1909 'Frau Georg von Simson' (Mult)
1909 'Gräfin Ada von Bredow' (Mult)

1925 'Fernande Krier' (W)
1925 'Mme. Georges Landard' (Pern)
1926 'Madeleine Seltzer' (Mult)
1928 'Marie Dietrich' (W)
1929 'Jeanne Richert' (W)
1932 'Yellow Moss' (M)

Weigand, Christoph
Bad Sonen a Taunus, Germany
1900 'Ernst Grandpierre' (W)
1902 'Anna Rübsamen' (W)
1902 'Non Plus Ultra' (Mult)
1902 'Taunusblümchen' (Mult)
1906 'Frau Albert Hochstrasser' (W)
1906 'Frau Marie Weinbach' (W)
1906 'Schneeball' (W)
1906 'Theodora Milch' (W)
1906 'Tricolore' (W)
1911 'Sodenia' (W)

Wells, William
Redleaf, Kent, England
1835 'The Garland' (Mk)
ca. 1835 'Mme. d'Arblay' (Mk)

Welter, Nicola
Trier, Germany
1901 'Abbé André Reitter' (HT)
1902 'Apotheker Georg Höfer' (HT)
1902 'Gustav Sobry' (HT)
1903 'Friedrich Albert Krupp' (HT)
1904 'Frau J. Reiter' (HT)
1904 'Venus' (MR)
1905 'Herzogin Viktoria Adelheid von
   Coburg-Gotha' (HT)
1906 'Anni Welter' (M)
1910 'Frau Therese Lang' (HT)
1915 'Grossherzog Wilhelm Ernst von
   Sachsen' (HT)

Western Rose Company
San Fernando, California, U.S.A.
1918 'Climbing Hoosier Beauty' (Cl HT)
1925 'Climbing Souvenir de Claudius
   Pernet' (Cl Pern)
1930 'Climbing Talisman' (Cl Pern)

Cultivars by Color

Roses are variable!—in color, particularly. In the following, we try to strike an average where there has been a range of opinion; where dubieties remain, we try to go by what seems to be the general effect of the blossom in the garden as opposed to what one obtains from a close-up examination. These proud flowers will never consent to be regimented; planting all the roses listed as "white to near-white" will not result in a homogeneous sheet of paper-white during the blooming season! And many "yellows" will, for instance, show a lot of pink in warm weather. There are few absolutes in the world of Roses . . .

We arrange the cultivars by color, then in the order in which they appear in *The Old Rose Adventurer*. The delightful but anomalous cultivars from Chapter 15, A Miscellany, are listed together, but with indications as to their specific group (as, "Rubr" for the Rubrifolias). As always, pure ("wild") species are given pride of place. The cultivars that have their entries only in Appendix 1 or Appendix 2 are not included here.

White to Near-White

Gallicas
'De Schelfhont'
'Gallica Alba Flore Plena'
'Globe White Hip'
'Gracilis'
'L'Ingénue'
'La Neige'
'Ledonneau-Leblanc'
'Pompon de Bourgogne à Fleurs Blanches'

Damasks
'Botzaris'
'Dame Blanche'
'Fausse Unique'
'Félicité Hardy'
'Parure des Vierges'
'Rose d'Hivers'

Agathes
—None—

Centifolias
'Alba'
'Unique'
'Vierge de Cléry'

Centifolia Pompons and Pompon Mosses
'Pompon Blanc'
'White De Meaux'

Mosses
'Blanche Simon'
'Comtesse de Murinais'
'Emilie'
'Emmeline'
'La Neige'
'Reine-Blanche'
'Unique de Provence'
'White Bath'
'White Moss Rose'

Mossy Remontants
'Blanche Moreau'
'Mlle. Marie-Louise Bourgeoise'
'Quatre Saisons Blanc Mousseux'

Albas
Rosa ×alba
'À Feuilles de Pêcher'
'Blanche de Belgique'
'Claudine'
'Cymbaefolia'
'Ferox'
'La Remarquable'
'La Surprise'
'Maxima Multiplex'
'Mme. Legras de St. Germain'
'Plena'
'Princesse de Lamballé'
'Semi-Plena'

'Superbe'
'Vénus'

Hemisphaericas
—None—

Foetidas
—None—

Pimpinellifolias
'Altaica'
'Blanche Semi-Double'
'Double Blanche'
'Frühlingsschnee'
'Karl Foerster'
'Pompon Blanc'
'Vierge'
'White Scotch'
'William IV'

Rubiginosas
'Minna'

Caninas
Rosa canina

A Miscellany
Rosa soulieana
'Sir Cedric Morris' (Rubr)

Roxburghiis
—None—

Bracteatas
Rosa bracteata

Rosa clinophylla
'Alba Odorata'
'Plena'
'Scabriusculus'
'Sea Foam'

Rugosas
Rosa rugosa 'Alba'
'Blanc Double de Coubert'
'Fürstin von Pless'
'Heterophylla'
'Mme. Georges Bruant'
'Nova Zembla'
'Proteiformis'
'Repens Alba'
'Rosier Tenuifolia'
'Schneelicht'
'Schneezwerg'
'Sir Thomas Lipton'
'Stella Polaris'
'White Grootendorst'

Laevigatas
Rosa laevigata
'Double Cherokee'
'Silver Moon'

Banksias
Rosa banksiae
'Alba Grandiflora'
'Alba Plena'
'Fortuneana'

White to Near-White
continued
'Hybride di Castello'
'Purezza'

Musks
Rosa brunonii
Rosa moschata
'De Tous Mois'
'Double White'
'Double White Damask Musk
    Rose'
'Eponine'
'Francis E. Lester'
'La Mortola'
'Mme. d'Arblay'
'Paul's Himalayan Musk
    Rambler'
'Paul's Himalayica Alba Magna'
'Semi-Double'
'Spanish Musk Rose'

Arvensises
Rosa arvensis
'Aennchen von Tharau'
'Ayrshirea'
'Dundee Rambler'
'Thoresbyana'
'Ville de St.-Maur'

Sempervirenses
Rosa sempervirens
'Anatole de Montesquieu'
'De la Chine à Feuilles Longues'
'Dona Maria'

Boursaults
—None—

Setigeras
'Mary Washington'
'Mrs. Hovey'
'Nelly Custis'

Wichuraianas
Rosa wichuraiana
Rosa wichuraiana 'Bracteata'
Rosa wichuraiana 'Poteriifolia'
'Aëlita'
'Alba Rubifolia'
'Direktor Benschop'
'Evergreen Gem'
'Frau Marie Weinbach'
'Glenn Dale'
'Grevinde Silvia Knuth'
'Manda's Triumph'
'Mary Lovett'
'Milky Way'

'Mrs. Littleton Dewhurst'
'Mühle Hermsdorf'
'Purity'
'Refresher'
'Sander's White'
'Schneeball'
'Seagull'
'Snowflake'
'Symbol Miru'
'Syringa'
'Variegata'
'Weisse New Dawn'
'White Dorothy'

Multifloras
'Andrée Vanderschrick'
'Bijou de Lyon'
'Bobbie James'
'Bonnie Prince'
'Dr. Reymond'
'Ernst Dechant'
'Gardeniaeflora'
'Graulhié'
'Ida Klemm'
'Mánja Böhmová'
'Neige d'Avril'
'Pemberton's White Rambler'
'Perle des Neiges'
'Polyantha'
'Polyantha Grandiflora'
'Waltham Bride'
'Weisser Herumstreicher'
'White Flight'
'White Tausendschön'

Lambertianas
'Frau A. Weidling'
'Gneisenau'
'Gruss an Zabern'
'Heine'
'Prodaná Nevěsta'
'Thalia'
'Thalia Remontant'

Hybrid Musks
'Cascadia'
'Inspektor Blohm'
'Moschata × Polyantha'
'Pax'
'Prosperity'

Old Hybrid Tea and
Pernetiana Climbers
'Angelus, Climbing'
'Chastity'
'Moonshine'
'Mrs. Herbert Stevens,
    Climbing'

Hybrid Teas, 1900–1920
'Angelus'
'British Queen'
'Double White Killarney'
'Edel'
'Edith Cavell'
'Excellenz M. Schmidt-Metzler'
'Irish Beauty'
'Jean Muraour'
'Kaiserin Goldifolia'
'Louise Criner'
'Madeleine Gaillard'
'Marguerite Guillot'
'Mlle. Argentine Cramon'
'Morgentau'
'Mrs. Andrew Carnegie'
'Mrs. Herbert Stevens'
'Simplicity'
'Weisse Gruss an Aachen'
'White Killarney'

Pernetianas
—None—

Flesh and Blush

Gallicas
'Adèle Prévost'
'Adonis'
'Aline'
'Antonine d'Ormois'
'Belle Galathée'
'Belle Hélène'
'Clio'
'Duchesse d'Angoulême'
'Elise Rovella'
'Fanny Bias'
'Galatée'
'Gallica Alba'
'Héloïse'
'Mme. de Tressan'

Damasks
'Babet'
'Bélisaire'
'Belle Auguste'
'Blush Damask'
'Coralie'
'Duc de Chartres'
'Ismène'
'Marguerite de Flandre'
'Mme. Carré'
'Mme. Zoutmann'
'Sancta'
'Virginale'

Agathes
'Belle Isis'

'Blush Belgic'
'Bouquet Rose de Vénus'
'Enfant de France' (Brussels)
'Marie-Louise'

Centifolias
'Blanchefleur'
'Comtesse de Ségur'
'Gloriette'
'Héloïse'
'Unique Carnée'

Centifolia Pompons and
Pompon Mosses
'Petite Junon de Hollande'

Mosses
'Adèle Pavié'
'Blush'
'Coralie'
'Duchesse d'Abrantès'
'Duchesse de Verneuil'
'Ismène'
'Lane'
'Lucie Duplessis'
'Vilmorin'

Mossy Remontants
'Alfred de Dalmas'
'Mme. de Staël'
'Mme. Louis Lévêque'
'Mousseline'
'Raphael'

Albas
'Alba Bifera'
'Alice'
'Armide'
'Beauté Tendre'
'Belle de Ségur'
'Belle Thérèse'
'Blush Hip'
'Caroline d'Angleterre'
'Céleste'
'Chloris'
'Duc d'York'
'Elisa'
'Esmeralda'
'Étoile de la Malmaison'
'Evratina'
'Fanny Rousseau'
'Fanny-Sommesson'
'Félicité'
'Gabrielle d'Estrées'
'Great Maiden's Blush'
'Jeanne d'Arc'
'Joséphine Beauharnais'
'Lesser Maiden's Blush'
'Ménage'

'Mme. Audot'
'Petite Lisette'
'Pompon Blanc Parfait'
'Vaucresson'

Hemisphaericas
—None—

Foetidas
—None—

Pimpinellifolias
'Bicolore Nana'
'Didot'
'Double Blush Burnet'
'Double Carnée'
'Estelle'
'Falkland'
'Frühlingsstunde'
'Inermis'
'Irène'
'La Belle Mathilde'
'Lady Edine'
'Perpetual Scotch'
'Petite Écossaise'
'Stanwell Perpetual'

Rubiginosas
Rosa rubiginosa
'Manning's Blush'
'Petite Hessoise'
'Williams's Sweetbriar'

Caninas
'Walküre'

A Miscellany
'Kew Rambler' (Soul)

Roxburghiis
'Triomphe des Français'

Bracteatas
'Maria Léonida'

Rugosas
'Conrad Ferdinand Meyer'
'Fimbriata'
'Mercedes'
'Mme. Ancelot'
'Mme. Julien Potin'
'Souvenir de Philémon Cochet'

Laevigatas
—None—

Banksias
—None—

Musks
'Paul's Tree Climber'

Arvensises
'Beacon Belle'
'Miss Jekyll'
'Ruga'
'Scandens'
'Splendens'
'Venusta Pendula'
'Virginian Rambler'

Sempervirenses
'Adélaïde d'Orléans'
'Félicité et Perpétue'
'Léopoldine d'Orléans'
'Mélanie de Montjoie'
'Reine des Belges'
'William's Evergreen'

Boursaults
'Calypso'

Setigeras
'Baltimore Belle'
'Eva Corinne'
'Miss Gunnell'
'Pallida'
'Ranunculiflora'
'Superba'
'Viragó'
'Virginia Lass'

Wichuraianas
'Alexandre Trémouillet'
'André Louis'
'Beauté Orléanaise'
'Carissima'
'Dr. W. Van Fleet'
'Elsie'
'Frau A. von Brauer'
'Greta Fey'
'New Dawn'
'Sargent'
'South Orange Perfection'
'Souvenir de Paul Raudnitz'
'Sweetheart'
'W. Freeland Kendrick'
'Wichmoss'
'William C. Egan'

Multifloras
Rosa multiflora
Rosa multiflora var. *cathayensis*
'Bagatelle'
'Blush Rambler'
'Carnea'
'Evodia'
'Kde Domov Muj'
'Perle von Britz'
'Rambling Rector'

'Royal Cluster'
'Watsoniana'

Lambertianas
'Philippine Lambert'

Hybrid Musks
'Ceres'
'Kathleen'
'Maid Marion'
'Queen of the Musks'
'Sea Spray'

Old Hybrid Tea and Pernetiana Climbers
'Cupid'
'Daydream'
'Gruss an Aachen, Climbing'
'Hermann Robinow, Climbing'
'Ophelia, Climbing'

Hybrid Teas, 1900–1920
'Abbé André Reitter'
'Alice Grahame'
'Alice Lindsell'
'Benedictus XV'
'Circe'
'Die Spree'
'Edgar M. Burnett'
'Edmée et Roger'
'Edmond Deshayes'
'Enver Pascha'
'Ernest Laurent'
'Evelyn'
'Flush o'Dawn'
'Frau J. Reiter'
'Germaine Chénault'
'Gertrude'
'Graf Fritz von Hochberg'
'Gruss an Aachen'
'Gruss an Aachen Superior'
'König Laurin'
'Koningin Emma'
'Lucien Chauré'
'Madeleine Faivre'
'Maman Lyly'
'Marianne Pfitzer'
'Martha Drew'
'Mevrouw A. Del Court van Krimpen'
'Mevrouw Boreel van Hogelander'
'Mildred Grant'
'Mme. Charles de Lapisse'
'Mme. Gustave Metz'
'Mme. Léon Pain'
'Mme. Maurice Fenaille'
'Mme. René André'

'Mme. René Oberthür'
'Monsieur Charles de Lapisse'
'Monsieur Edg. Blanchard'
'Mrs. E. Alford'
'Mrs. Franklin Dennison'
'Mrs. George Preston'
'Nellie Parker'
'Ophelia'
'Pharisäer'
'Radiance Sport'
'Renée Wilmart-Urban'
'Silver Wedding'
'St. Helena'
'Totote Gélos'

Pernetianas
—None—

Shades of Pink

Gallicas
'Abailard'
'Adèle'
'Adèle Courtoise'
'Bellard'
'Belle Biblis'
'Belle Mignonne'
'Belle Sultane'
'Bérénice' (Vibert)
'Bérénice' (Racine)
'Bouquet Charmante'
'Chapelain d'Arenberg'
'Complicata'
'Comte Foy de Rouen'
'Cynthie'
'Daphné'
'Desiré Parmentier'
'Duchesse de Berry'
'Dumortier'
'Edmond Duval'
'Estelle'
'Fulgens'
'Grand Palais de Laeken'
'Grand Sultan'
'Grande Brique'
'Henri Foucquier'
'Incomparable'
'Julie d'Étanges'
'Junon'
'König von Sachsen'
'L'Enchanteresse'
'Les Trois Mages'
'Mazeppa'
'Nouvelle Gagnée'
'Octavie'
'Ornement de Parade'
'Pelletier'

Shades of Pink
Gallicas continued
'Pepita'
'Petite Orléanaise'
'Provins Ancien'
'Reine de Perse'
'Revenante'
'Rosier des Parfumeurs'
'Triomphe de Flore'
'Valence Dubois'

Damasks
'Argentée'
'Don Pedro'
'Gloire de Guilan'
'Henri IV'
'Ispahan'
'Kazanlyk'
'Louis Cazas'
'Monstrueux'
'Pink Leda'
'Professeur Émile Perrot'
'Roi des Pays-Bas'
'Rose à Parfum de Grasse'
'Rose de Puteau'
'Rose de Damas'
'St. Nicholas'
'Triomphe de Rouen'

Agathes
'Beauté Superbe Agathée'
'De la Malmaison'
'Majestueuse'
'Prolifère'
'Volumineuse'

Centifolias
'À Feuille de Chêne'
'À Feuilles Crénelées'
'À Feuilles de Céleri'
'À Feuilles de Chanvre'
'À Fleurs Simples'
'Ballady'
'Bullata'
'Common Centifolia'
'Des Peintres'
'Descemet'
'Duchesse de Coutard'
'Fantin-Latour'
'Foliacée'
'Gaspard Monge'
'Goliath'
'Grand Bercam'
'Grande Renoncule Violette'
'Gros Chou d'Hollande'
'Hollandica'
'La Louise'

'La Noblesse'
'Le Rire Niais'
'Leea Rubra'
'Minette'
'My Lady Kensington'
'Oeillet'
'Regina'
'Reine de Saxe'
'Reine des Centfeuilles'
'Thalie la Gentille'
'Théone'
'Unique Rose'

Centifolia Pompons and Pompon Mosses
'À Fleurs Presque Simples'
'Comtesse de Chamoïs'
'De Meaux'
'Decora'
'Mossy De Meaux'
'Pompon de Kingston'
'Pompon Varin'
'Rosier des Dames'
'Spong's'

Mosses
'À Long Pédoncle'
'Alice Leroi'
'Bérangère'
'Catherine de Wurtemburg'
'Common Moss'
'Cristata'
'Cumberland Belle'
'De Candolle'
'Delphinie'
'Don Pedro'
'Ducis'
'Elizabeth Rowe'
'Félicité Bohain'
'Général Kléber'
'Gloire des Mousseux'
'Jean Bodin'
'Jenny Lind'
'La Caille'
'La Diaphane'
'Lafontaine'
'Le Lobèrde'
'Louise Verger'
'Marie-Victoria Benoît'
'Mauget'
'Mme. Rose Chéri'
'Parmentier'
'Pompon'
'Princesse Amélie'
'Princesse Bacciochi'
'Princesse de Vaudémont'
'Princesse Royale'

'Prolifère'
'Reine des Moussues'
'Semi-Double'
'Single'
'Soeur Marthe'
'Zenobia'
'Zoé'

Mossy Remontants
'Céline Briant'
'Clémence Robert'
'Impératrice Eugénie'
'Mlle. Alice Leroy'
'Mme. Platz'
'Salet'

Albas
'Amélia'
'Astrée'
'Belle Amour'
'Camille Bouland'
'Fanny'
'Königin von Dannemark'
'Lucrèce'
'Monica'
'Monique'
'Placidie'
'Zénobie'

Hemisphaericas
—None—

Foetidas
'Victoria'

Pimpinellifolias
'Aristide'
'Double Pink Edine'
'Dr. Merkeley'
'Lady Dunmore'
'Miss Frotter'
'Seager Wheeler'
'Souvenir de Henry Clay'
'Suzanne'

Rubiginosas
'Brenda'
'Edith Bellenden'
'Iver Cottage'
'Julia Mannering'
'Max Haufe'
'Mechtilde von Neuerburg'
'Zabeth'

Caninas
'Abbotswood'
'Freya'
'Griseldis'
'Siwa'

'Theresia'
'Weidenia'

A Miscellany
Rosa macrantha
Rosa macrophylla
Rosa nutkana
Rosa rubrifolia
Rosa virginiana
'Anne de Boleyn' (Turb)
'Auguste Roussel' (Macro)
'Carmenetta' (Rubr)
'Elfenreigen' (Macra)
'Master High' (Macro)
'Mechliniae' (Rubr)
'Pinnatifide' (Rubr)
'Plena' (Vir)
'Professor Ibrahim' (Macra)
'Raubritter' (Macra)
'Semi-Double' (Rubr)
'Théano' (unk.)
'Wickwar' (Soul)

Roxburghiis
'Château de la Juvenie'
'Imbricata'
'Triomphe de la Guillotière'

Bracteatas
'Pink Mermaid'
'Victoire Modeste'

Rugosas
'Adiantifolia'
'Amdo'
'Belle Poitevine'
'Calocarpa'
'Delicata'
'Fru Dagmar Hartopp'
'Hildenbrandseck'
'Lady Curzon'
'Mme. Alvarez del Campo'
'Mme. Ballu'
'Mme. Lucien Villeminot'
'Monsieur Gustave Bienvêtu'
'Pink Grootendorst'
'Potager du Dauphin'
'S.A.R. Ferdinand Ier'
'Sarah Van Fleet'
'Schwabenland'
'Single Pink'
'Souvenir de Christophe
   Cochet'
'Souvenir de Yeddo'
'Tetonkaha'
'Thusnelda'
'Türke's Rugosa-Sämling'
'Wasagaming'

Laevigatas

'Anemonenrose'
'Mrs. A. Kingsmill'
'Pink Cherokee'

Banksias

—None—

Musks

'Narrow Water'
'Paul's Himalayica Double Pink'

Sempervirenses

'Eugène d'Orléans'
'Flore'
'Princesse Louise'
'Princesse Marie'

Boursaults

Rosa pendulina
'À Boutons Renversés à Fleurs
    Simples'
'Gracilis'
'Inermis'
'Inermis Morletii'
'L'Orléanaise'
'Mme. de Sancy de Parabère'
'Plena'

Setigeras

Rosa setigera
'Alpenfee'
'Anne Maria'
'Eurydice'
'Jane'
'Mrs. F. F. Prentiss'
'Ovid'
'Pride of Washington'
'Tennessee Belle'

Wichuraianas

'Adélaïde Moullé'
'Alida Lovett'
'America'
'Anna Rübsamen'
'Ardon'
'Bloomfield Favorite'
'Bonnie Belle'
'Chaplin's Pink Climber'
'Chatillon-Rambler'
'Christian Curle'
'Christine Wright'
'Coquina'
'Debutante'
'Dorothy Dennison'
'Edmond Proust'
'Elisa Robichon'
'Ethel'
'Evangeline'
'Farquhar'

'Fernande Krier'
'Fragezeichen'
'Fraîcheur'
'François Juranville'
'Frau Liesel Brauer'
'Freifrau von Marschall'
'Garisenda'
'Gerbe Rose'
'Île de France'
'Jean Girin'
'Jean L'Hoste'
'Jitřenka'
'Johanna Röpke'
'Jules Levacher'
'Lady Duncan'
'Lady Gay'
'Lady Godiva'
'Le Mexique'
'Loveliness'
'Madeleine Lemaire'
'Mary Wallace'
'Milano'
'Miss Flora Mitten'
'Miss Helyett'
'Miss Liberty'
'Mme. Auguste Nonin'
'Mme. Charles Lejeune'
'Mme. Constans'
'Morning Dawn'
'Normandie'
'Petit Louis'
'Pink Pearl'
'Rambler-Königin'
'Sodenia'
'Souvenir d'Adolphe de
    Charvoik'
'Thelma'
'Theodora Milch'
'Universal Favorite'
'Valentin Beaulieu'
'Wichuraiana Hybride I'
'Yvonne'

Multifloras

'Agnes und Bertha'
'Apple Blossom'
'Baronin Anna von Lüttwitz'
'Blanda Egreta'
'Blumen-Dankert'
'Caroline Bank'
'Cato'
'Charlotte von Rathlef'
'Dawson'
'Elisabeth'
'Emerickrose'
'Émile Nerini'
'Erato'

'Erna'
'Exquisite'
'Fatinitza'
'Frau Georg von Simson'
'Frau Lina Strassheim'
'Geschwinds Nordlandrose'
'Geschwinds Nordlandrose II'
'Hakeburg'
'Havering Rambler'
'Helene'
'Hildeputchen'
'Indra'
'Josephine Ritter'
'Karl Schneider'
'Leuchtstern'
'Maria Liesa'
'Mme. Jenny'
'Mrs. F. W. Flight'
'Newport Fairy'
'Nymphe Egeria'
'Památník Komenského'
'Platyphylla'
'Rose'
'Roserie'
'Taunusblümchen'

Lambertianas

'Arndt'
'Birdie Blye'
'Buisman's Triumph'
'Euphrosine'
'Frau Eva Schubert'
'Frau Helene Videnz'
'Frau Sophie Meyerholz'
'Kommerzienrat W.
    Rautenstrauch'
'Lausitz'
'Mozart'
'Neisse'
'Probuzeni'
'Ufhoven'
'Von Liliencron'

Hybrid Musks

'Andenken an Alma de l'Aigle'
'Ballerina'
'Belinda'
'Bloomfield Dawn'
'Bloomfield Discovery'
'Daphne'
'Felicia'
'Fortuna'
'Havering'
'Pearl'
'Penelope'
'Pink Prosperity'
'Rostock'

Old Hybrid Tea and Pernetiana Climbers

'Colcestria'
'Columbia, Climbing'
'Comte F. de Chavagnac'
'England's Glory'
'Gartendirektor Julius
    Schütze'
'Gwen Nash'
'Kitty Kininmonth'
'Lady Sylvia, Climbing'
'Lady Waterlow'
'Mme. Butterfly, Climbing'
'Mme. Grégoire Staechelin'
'Mme. Segond-Weber,
    Climbing'
'Nora Cuningham'
'Professor Dr. Hans Molisch'
'Radiance, Climbing'
'Rosemary, Climbing'
'Souvenir d'Émile Zola'

Hybrid Teas, 1900–1920

'Adam Rackles'
'Alice Kaempff'
'Amateur André Fourcaud'
'Arabella'
'Capitaine Soupa'
'Commandant Letourneux'
'Dame Edith Helen'
'Desdemona'
'Die Mutter von Rosa'
'Dora Hansen'
'Elizabeth'
'Enchanter'
'Ernst Hempel'
'Fragrant Bouquet'
'Frau Emma Sasse'
'Frau Oberhofgärtner Singer'
'Freiburg II'
'Grossherzog Friedrich von
    Baden'
'Hilda Richardson'
'Honourable Ina Bingham'
'Isobel'
'Jacques Hackenberg'
'John Cook'
'John Ruskin'
'Kronprinzessin Cecilie'
'La Detroit'
'La France Victorieuse'
'La Tosca'
'Lady Alice Stanley'
'Lady Ashtown'
'Lady Faire'
'Lady Margaret Boscawen'
'Lady Sylvia'

Shades of Pink
Hybrid Teas, 1900–1920
continued
'Lady Ursula'
'Lady Wenlock'
'Laure Wattinne'
'Lilli von Posern'
'Lina Schmidt-Michel'
'Lohengrin'
'Louise Pernot'
'Lucien de Lemos'
'Marichu Zayas'
'Marie Schmitt'
'Marquise de Ganay'
'May Miller'
'Minna'
'Miss Kate Moulton'
'Mlle. Danielle Dumur'
'Mlle. de Neux'
'Mme. Butterfly'
'Mme. Dailleux'
'Mme. Desirée Bruneau'
'Mme. Edmond Rostand'
'Mme. Marcel Delauney'
'Mme. P. Euler'
'Mme. Segond-Weber'
'Mme. Viger'
'Mrs. Charles J. Bell'
'Mrs. David Jardine'
'Mrs. Forde'
'Mrs. Fred Searl'
'Mrs. Henry Morse'
'Mrs. Joseph H. Welsh'
'Mrs. Moorfield Storey'
'Mrs. R. D. McClure'
'Mrs. Wakefield Christie-Miller'
'My Maryland'
'Oberbürgermeister Dr.
    Troendlin'
'Otto von Bismarck'
'P. L. Baudet'
'Pierre Wattinne'
'Portia'
'Prince de Bulgarie'
'Prinzessin Marie'
'Radiance'
'Reine Carola de Saxe'
'Ricordo di Giosue Carducci'
'Rosalind Orr English'
'Rose Benary'
'Rose Queen'
'Rosemary'
'Rosita Mauri'
'Sachsengruss'
'September Morn'
'Souvenir du Président Daurel'

'Stella di Bologna'
'Taft Rose'
'Vinoca'
'Weddigen'
Pernetianas
'Dilly's Wiederkehr'
'Jubiläumsrose'
'La Giralda'
'Wildenfels Rosa'

Deep Pink to Rose and Rose-Red

Gallicas
'À Fleurs de Rose Tremière de
    la Chine'
'Adèle Heu'
'Adonis'
'Aimable Amie'
'Aimable Rouge'
'Alaine'
'Amélie de Mansfield'
'Beauté Tendre'
'Bellotte'
'Capricorn'
'Cérisette la Jolie'
'Claire d'Olban'
'Couronne de Salomon'
'Crignon de Montigny'
'Don de Guérin'
'Duchesse de Buccleuch'
'Emilie Verachter'
'Empereur'
'Eucharis'
'Eudoxie'
'Fanny Parissot'
'Ferdinand de Buck'
'Gazella'
'Gazelle'
'Général Moreau'
'Gil Blas'
'Gloire des Jardins'
'Grand Monarche'
'Grande et Belle'
'Great Royal'
'Henri Quatre'
'Horatius Coclès'
'Jeune Henry'
'Joséphine Parmentier'
'La Pucelle'
'La Tendresse'
'La Ville de Londres'
'Léa'
'Louis-Philippe'
'Lustre d'Église'
'Lycoris'

'Marie Stuart'
'Minerve'
'Moïse'
'Nanette'
'Napoléon'
'Nouvelle Transparente'
'Oleifolia'
'Omphale'
'Phoebus'
'Princesse de Nassau'
'Princesse de Portugal'
'Pucelle de Lille'
'Roxelane'
'Sanchette'
'Triomphe de Sterckmanns'
'Turenne'
'Van Artevelde'
'Ville de Toulouse'
'Virginie'
'Ypsilanti'

Damasks
Rosa ×damascena
'Eudoxie'
'Général Foy'
'La Ville de Bruxelles'
'Léon Lecomte'
'Noémie'
'Omar Khayyám'
'Pénélope'
'Rose à Parfum de Bulgarie'
'Silvia'
'Véturie'

Agathes
'Belle Hébé'
'Enfant de France' (Holland)
'Rouge Belgique'
'Soleil Brillant'

Centifolias
'Adéline'
'Adrienne de Cardoville'
'Anaïs Ségales'
'Belle Junon'
'Childling'
'Ciudad de Oviedo'
'Duc d'Angoulême'
'Duc de Brabant'
'Eugénie Chamusseau'
'Euphrosine l'Élégante'
'Grande Centfeuille de Hol-
    lande'
'Justine Ramet'
'Laure'
'Mme. L'Abbey'
'Wellington'
'Yorkshire Provence'

*Centifolia Pompons and
Pompon Mosses*
'Calypso Petite'

Mosses
'Angélique Quétier'
'Anni Welter'
'De La Flèche'
'Duchesse d'Istrie'
'Gracilis'
'Indiana'
'Joséphine'
'Louis Gimard'
'Malvina'
'Marie de Blois'
'Ménage'
'Miniature Moss'
'Mme. Clémence Beauregard'
'Précoce'
'Princess Alice'
'Princesse Adélaïde'
'Rubra'
'Waltraud Nielsen'
'Zaïre'

Mossy Remontants
'Baron de Wassenaër'
'Césonie'
'Delille'
'Marie de Bourgogne'
'Mme. Édouard Ory'
'Mme. Legrand'
'Mme. William Paul'
'Perpétuelle Mauget'
'Soupert et Notting'
'Validé'

Albas
'Henriette Campan'

Hemisphaericas
—None—

Foetidas
—None—

Pimpinellifolias
'Frühlingsmorgen'
'Hibernica'

Rubiginosas
'Amy Robsart'
'Catherine Seyton'
'Clémentine'
'Greenmantle'
'Hessoise'
'Jeannie Deans'
'John Cant'
'La Belle Distinguée'
'Rose Angle'

'Rose Bradwardine'
'Rosenwunder'

Caninas
'Andersonii'
'Gruss an Rengsdorf'

A Miscellany
Rosa majalis
'Ancelin' (Turb)
'Cantab' (Nut)
'Coral Drops' (unk.)
'Coryana' (Macro)
'Daisy Hill' (Macra)
'Doncasterii' (Macro)
'Duplex' (Pom)
'Düsterlohe' (Macra)
'Flore Pleno' (Maj)
'Francofurtana' (Turb)
'Harvest Song' (Vir)
'Impératrice Joséphine' (Turb)
'Schoener's Nutkana' (Nut)

Roxburghiis
Rosa roxburghii

Bracteatas
'Rubra Duplex'

Rugosas
'Alice Aldrich'
'Chédane-Guinoisseau'
'George Will'
'Kitana'
'Koza'
'Repens Rosea'
'Rose Apples'

Laevigatas
'Ramona'

Banksias
'Rosea'

Musks
'Rivers' Musk'

Arvensises
'Capreolata'
'Düsterlohe'
'Miller's Climber'
'Mme. Viviand-Morel'

Sempervirenses
'Spectabilis'

Boursaults
'Boursault'
'Drummond's Thornless'

Setigeras
'Gem of the Prairies'

'Perpetual Michigan'
'President'
'Queen of the Prairies'
'Triumphant'

Wichuraianas
'Achievement'
'American Beauty, Climbing'
'American Pillar'
'Andenken an Breslau'
'Babette'
'Casimir Moullé'
'Cinderella'
'Claude Rabbe'
'Delight'
'Dorothy Perkins'
'Erwin Hüttmann'
'July Glory'
'Le Poilu'
'Little Compton Creeper'
'Max Graf'
'May Queen'
'Minnehaha'
'Nokomis'
'Paul Transon'
'Pink Roamer'
'Regierungsrat Rottenberger'
'Srdce Europy'
'Victory'
'Windermere'

Multifloras
'À Bois Brun'
'Anci Böhmova'
'Ernst G. Dörell'
'Frau Käte Schmid'
'Garden's Glory'
'Gruss an Germershausen'
'Hans Schmid'
'Le Droit Humain'
'Malva Rambler'
'Marietta Silva Taroucová'
'Menoux'
'Nymphe Tepla'
'Oriflamme'
'Perle vom Wienerwald!'
'Peter Lambert'
'Prior M. Oberthau'
'Queen Alexandra'
'Rudelsburg'
'The Wallflower'
'Wartburg'
'Wedding Bells'

Lambertianas
'Excellenz von Schubert'
'Gartendirektor Otto Linne'
'Geheimrat Dr. Mitteweg'

'Heinrich Conrad Söth'
'Lyric'
'Max Singer'

Hybrid Musks
'Bloomfield Culmination'
'Chami'
'Cornelia'
'Vanity'
'Wind Chimes'

Old Hybrid Tea and Pernetiana Climbers
'Capitaine Soupa, Climbing'
'Dame Edith Helen, Climbing'
'Dr. J. H. Nicolas'
'Ednah Thomas'
'General MacArthur, Climbing'
'Général-Superior Arnold Janssen, Climbing'
'Irène Bonnet'
'Jonkheer J. L. Mock, Climbing'
'Mamie, Climbing'
'Queen of Hearts'
'Rose Marie, Climbing'

Hybrid Teas, 1900–1920
'Apotheker Georg Höfer'
'Australia Felix'
'Australie'
'Aviateur Michel Mahieu'
'Bürgermeister Christen'
'Columbia'
'Cynthia Forde'
'Dean Hole'
'Dr. O'Donel Browne'
'Duchess of Sutherland'
'Duisburg'
'Ethel Dickson'
'Farbenkönigin'
'Frau Peter Lambert'
'General MacArthur'
'Gladys Harkness'
'Graf Fritz Schwerin'
'Grossherzog Wilhelm Ernst von Sachsen'
'Gustav Grünerwald'
'Helvetia'
'Irish Glory'
'Irish Pride'
'John Cuff'
'Jonkheer J. L. Mock'
'Killarney Brilliant'
'Killarney Queen'
'Königin Carola von Sachsen'
'La Vendômoise'
'Lady Moyra Beauclerc'
'Magnafrano'

'Mamie'
'Margherita Croze'
'Mark Twain'
'Max Hesdörffer'
'Mme. Léon Simon'
'Mme. Léopold Dupuy'
'Mme. Marie Croibier'
'Mme. Maurice de Luze'
'Monsieur Fraissenon'
'Mrs. Bertram J. Walker'
'Mrs. C. W. Dunbar-Buller'
'Mrs. Charles Custis Harrison'
'Mrs. Charles E. Russell'
'Mrs. Charles Hunter'
'Mrs. George Shawyer'
'Mrs. Stewart Clark'
'Ökonomierat Echtermeyer'
'Premier'
'Ricordo di Geo. Chavez'
'Rose Marie'
'Souvenir de Monsieur Frédéric Vercellone'
'Souvenir du Capitaine Fernand Japy'
'Sunny South'
'Toreador'
'Veluwezoom'
'William Notting'

Pernetianas
'Dannenberg'
'Dr. Müller'
'Mme. Georges Landard'
'Rhodophile Gravereaux'
'Secretaris Zwart'

Shades of Red

Gallicas
'Admirable'
'Alika'
'Beauté Touchante'
'Belle Flore'
'Belle Olympe'
'Bossuet'
'Captain Williams'
'Carmin Brillant'
'Conditorum'
'Cramoisie Éblouissante'
'D'Aguesseau'
'Feu de Vesta'
'Fleurs de Pelletier'
'Foucheaux'
'François Foucquier'
'Général Donadieu'
'Gonzalve'
'Grand Corneille'

Shades of Red

Gallicas continued

'Grand Cramoisi de Vibert'
'Grosse Cerise'
'Hippolyte'
'Jeannette'
'Juliette'
'Louis Van Tyll'
'Macrantha Rubicunda'
'Malesherbes'
'Manteau Royal'
'Mme. Ville'
'Nestor'
'Nouveau Rouge'
'Nouvelle Pivoine'
'Officinalis'
'Pompon de Bourgogne'
'Prince Frédéric'
'Princesse Éléonore'
'Purpurine de France'
'Rouge Formidable'
'Rouge Superbe Actif'
'Scharlachglut'
'Van Huyssum'
'Victor Parmentier'

Damasks

'Angèle'
'Mme. Lambert'
'Red Damask'
'Rose Verreux'
'Turner's Crimson Damask'

Agathes

'Feunon Rouge'
'Henriette'
'Royale'

Centifolias

'Capricornus'
'Röte Centifolie'
'Rubra'
'Unique Admirable'
'Unique Rouge'

Centifolia Pompons and Pompon Mosses

'Little Gem'

Mosses

'Anémone'
'Comtesse Doria'
'Crimson'
'D'Arcet'
'Dr. Marjolin'
'Eugène Verdier'
'Ferrugineux du Luxembourg'
'Goethe'

'Henri Martin'
'Laneii'
'Maréchal Davoust'
'Mme. Soupert'
'Moussue du Japon'
'Ninette'
'Parkjuwel'
'Pélisson'
'Rivers' Single Crimson Moss'

Mossy Remontants

'Eugène de Savoie'
'Eugénie Guinoisseau'
'Fornarina'
'John Fraser'
'Marie Leczinska'
'Maupertuis'
'Mme. Charles Salleron'
'Mme. Landeau'
'René d'Anjou'
'Venus'

Albas

—None—

Hemisphaericas

—None—

Foetidas

—None—

Pimpinellifolias

'Frühlingszauber'
'Gil Blas'
'King of Scots'
'Rich Crimson'
'Rouge'
'William III'

Rubiginosas

'Flammentanz'
'Gruss an Koblenz'
'Lucy Bertram'
'Meg Merrilies'
'Refulgence'

Caninas

'Kiese'
'Rose à Bois Jaspé'

A Miscellany

Rosa villosa (Vil)
'Belle Rosine' (Turb)
'Düsterlohe II' (Macra)
'Flore Plena' (Rubr)
'Fraxinifolia' (unk.)
'Grosse Mohnkopfs Rose' (Turb)
'Harry Maasz' (Macra)
'Turneps' (Turb)

Roxburghiis

—None—

Bracteatas

'Scarlet Maria Leonida'

Rugosas

'Agnes Emily Carman'
'America'
'Bergers Erfolg'
'Carmen'
'Cibles'
'Crispata'
'F. J. Grootendorst'
'Jindřich Hanus Böhm'
'Le Cid'
'Lilli Dieck'
'Magnifica'
'Mme. Charles Frédéric Worth'
'Mme. Philippe Plantamour'
'Mme. Tiret'
'Monsieur Hélye'
'Nemo'
'Rose à Parfum de l'Haÿ'
'Roseraie de l'Haÿ'
'Signe Relander'
'Taïcoun'
'Villa des Tybilles'

Laevigatas

—None—

Banksias

—None—

Musks

—None—

Arvensises

—None—

Sempervirenses

—None—

Boursaults

Rosa pendulina 'Laevis'

Setigeras

'Forstmeisters Heim'
'President Coolidge'
'Yuhla'

Wichuraianas

'Alexandre Girault'
'Arcadia'
'Aunt Harriet'
'Bess Lovett'
'Bonfire'
'Chaplin's Crimson Glow'
'Dr. Zamenhof'
'Eisenach'

'Excelsa'
'Ferdinand Roussel'
'Fernand Rabier'
'Gaston Lesieur'
'Général Testard'
'Joseph Billard'
'La Fiamma'
'Mičurin'
'Monthly Rambler'
'Papa Rouillard'
'Paul Ploton'
'Paul's Scarlet Climber'
'Petit René'
'Royal Scarlet Hybrid'
'Rubra'
'Ruby Queen'
'Solarium'
'Souvenir de J. Mermet'
'The Beacon'
'Troubadour'

Multifloras

'Andreas Hofer'
'Bordeaux'
'Carolina Budde'
'Caroubier'
'Chatter'
'Daisy Brazileir'
'Erlkönig'
'Flower of Fairfield'
'Francis'
'Futtaker Schlingrose'
'Geisha'
'Gela Tepelmann'
'Geschwinds Schönste'
'Gräfin Marie Henriette Chotek'
'Grossherzogin Eléonore von Essen'
'Hiawatha'
'Hiawatha Recurrent'
'Hugo Maweroff'
'Jkvr. D. Baroness von Ittersum'
'Kathleen'
'Kleine Rosel'
'Leopold Ritter'
'Lien Budde'
'Lyon Rambler'
'Mary Hicks'
'Mme. Charles Yojerot'
'Mme. François Royet'
'Olivet'
'Papa Gouchault'
'Philadelphia Rambler'
'Prinzessin Ludwig von Bayern'
'Ratgeber Rose'

'Roi des Aunes'
'Rubin'
'Souvenir de l'Exposition
    Bordeaux 1905'
'Steyl Rambler'
'The Lion'
'Turner's Crimson Rambler'
'Wodan'

Lambertianas
'Frau Professor Grischko'
'Gruss an Heidelberg'
'Lichterloh'
'Saarbrücken'
'Wilhelm Marx'

Hybrid Musks
'Eva'
'Robin Hood'
'Rosaleen'
'Sammy'
'Sangerhausen'
'Wilhelm'
'Will Scarlet'
'Winter Cheer'

Old Hybrid Tea and Pernetiana Climbers
'Allan Chandler'
'Apotheker Georg Höfer,
    Climbing'
'Ards Pillar'
'Cracker'
'Crimson Conquest'
'Effective'
'Florence Haswell Veitch'
'H. Vessey Machin, Climbing'
'Laurent Carle, Climbing'
'Marguerite Carels'
'Morgenrot'
'Mrs. Henry Winnett, Climbing'
'Président Vignet, Climbing'
'Red Radiance, Climbing'
'Richmond, Climbing'
'Sarah Bernhardt'
'Scorcher'
'Sunday Best'

Hybrid Teas, 1900–1920
'Alexander Emslie'
'Augustus Hartmann'
'Avoca'
'Baron Palm'
'Bloomfield Progress'
'C. W. Cowan'
'Cardinal'
'Charles J. Graham'
'Charles K. Douglas'

'Clément Pacaud'
'Colonel Leclerc'
'Comte G. de Rochemur'
'Comtesse Icy Hardegg'
'Crimson Crown'
'Crimson Emblem'
'Defiance'
'Donald MacDonald'
'Dr. G. Krüger'
'Earl of Gosford'
'Écarlate'
'Edward Mawley'
'Elizabeth Cullen'
'Étoile de France'
'Eugène Boullet'
'Francis Scott Key'
'Frau Anna Lautz'
'Frau Therese Lang'
'Freifrau Ida von Schubert'
'Generaal Snijders'
'General-Superior Arnold
    Janssen'
'Generaloberst von Kluck'
'Graf Silva Tarouca'
'Gruss an Sangerhausen'
'Gruss an Zweibrücken'
'H. D. M. Barton'
'H. E. Richardson'
'H. F. Eilers'
'H. P. Pinkerton'
'H. Vessey Machin'
'Herzogin Viktoria Adelheid
    von Coburg-Gotha'
'Irish Brightness'
'Irish Star'
'K. of K.'
'Kaiser Wilhelm II'
'Königin Maria Theresia'
'Lady Rossmore'
'Laurent Carle'
'Leslie Holland'
'Lia'
'Liberty'
'Lieutenant Chauré'
'Manuel P. Azevedo'
'Marquis de Bouillé'
'Mary, Countess of Ilchester'
'Mevrouw Dora van Tets'
'Milady'
'Miss C. E. van Rossem'
'Mme. Alfred Sabatier'
'Mme. Emilie Lafon'
'Mme. Jean Favre'
'Mme. Méha Sabatier'
'Mrs. Edward Powell'
'Mrs. Henry Winnett'

'Mrs. John Foster'
'Mrs. Muir MacKean'
'Mrs. Walter Easlea'
'Nederland'
'Président Vignet'
'Prince Englebert Ch.
    d'Arenberg'
'Red Admiral'
'Red Chatenay'
'Red Cross'
'Red-Letter Day'
'Red Radiance' (Gude)
'Red Radiance' (Pierson)
'Red Star'
'Reine Marguerite d'Italie'
'Richmond'
'Rose d'Espérance'
'Rübezahl'
'Ruhm der Gartenwelt'
'Sensation'
'Souvenir de Maria de Zayas'
'Souvenir de Maria Zozaya'
'Stadtrat F. Kähler'
'Ulster Standard'
'W. C. Gaunt'
'W. E. Lippiatt'

Pernetianas
'Les Rosati'
'Mabel Lynas'
'Mrs. Bullen'
'Recuerdo de Angel Peluffo'
'Solliden'

Deep Red, Maroon, Purple, and Deep Violet

Gallicas
Rosa gallica
'À Grand Cramoisi'
'Achille'
'Agénor'
'Aigle Brun'
'Aigle Noir'
'Aimable Pourpre'
'Alcime'
'Alector Cramoisi'
'Alfieri'
'Ambrose Paré'
'Ariane'
'Assemblage des Beautés'
'Bacchante'
'Beau Narcisse'
'Beauté Renommée'
'Belle Brun'

'Belle Hélène'
'Belle Pourpre'
'Château de Namur'
'Columelle'
'Comte Boula de Nanteuil'
'Cora'
'Cramoisie'
'De Van Eeden'
'Double Brique'
'Feu Amoureux'
'Fornarina' (Vétillart)
'Grand Napoléon'
'Haddington'
'Hector'
'Holoserica'
'Holoserica Duplex'
'Holoserica Multiplex'
'Holoserica Regalis'
'Isabelle'
'Kean'
'L'Obscurité'
'La Provence'
'Le Grand Sultan'
'Le Pérou'
'Mahaeca'
'Manteau Pourpre'
'Marcel Bourgoin'
'Marjolin'
'Nouveau Intelligible'
'Nouveau Monde'
'Nouveau Vulcain'
'Ombre Panachée'
'Ombre Superbe'
'Ombrée Parfaite'
'Orpheline de Juillet'
'Pallas'
'Passe-Velours'
'Perle de l'Orient'
'Perle de Weissenstein'
'Pluton'
'Pourpre Charmant'
'Roi des Pourpres'
'Sanguineo-Purpurea Simplex'
'Sans Pareille Pourpre'
'Subnigra'
'Superb Tuscan'
'Superbe en Brun'
'Temple d'Apollon'
'Tuscany'
'Velours Pourpre'

Damasks
'Duc de Cambridge'
'La Négresse'
'Olympe'
'Périclès'
'Pope'

Deep Red, Maroon, Purple, and Deep Violet
continued

Agathes
'Petite Renoncule Violette'

Centifolias
'À Fleurs Doubles Violettes'
'Black Boy'
'Hulda'
'Robert le Diable'
'Stratosféra'
'Tour de Malakoff'

Centifolia Pompons and Pompon Mosses
'Nouveau Petit Serment'

Mosses
'Alcime'
'Barillet'
'Capitaine Basroger'
'Capitaine John Ingram'
'Célina'
'Crimson Globe'
'Etna'
'François de Salignac'
'Frédéric Soullier'
'Général Clerc'
'John Grow'
'L'Obscurité'
'Lansezeur'
'Mlle. Aristide'
'Mme. De la Roche-Lambert'
'Nuits d'Young'
'Parkzauber'
'Pourpre du Luxembourg'
'Pourpre Violet'
'Purpurea Rubra'
'William Grow'
'William Lobb'

Mossy Remontants
'Deuil de Paul Fontaine'
'Général Drouot'
'James Veitch'
'John Cranston'
'Souvenir de Pierre Vibert'

Albas
—None—

Hemisphaericas
—None—

Foetidas
—None—

Pimpinellifolias
'Mrs. Colville'
'Neptune'

Rubiginosas
'Anne of Geierstein'
'Magnifica'

Caninas
—None—

A Miscellany
'Château de Vaire' (Macro)
'Chevy Chase' (Soul)

Roxburghiis
'Domaine de Chapuis'
'Hybride du Luxembourg'
'Pourpre Ancien'
'Simplex'

Bracteatas
'Coccinea'

Rugosas
Rosa ×kamtchatika
Rosa rugosa 'Rubra'
'Amélie Gravereaux'
'Arnoldiana'
'Atropurpurea'
'Georges Cain'
'Germanica'
'Germanica B'
'Grootendorst Supreme'
'Hansa'
'Jelina'
'Kaiserin des Nordens'
'La Mélusine'
'Mikado'
'Minisa'
'Moje Hammarberg'
'Monsieur Morlet'
'Mrs. Anthony Waterer'
'Prof. N. E. Hansen'
'Régina Badet'
'Ruskin'
'S.M.I. Abdul-Hamid'
'Siberian Form'
'Souvenir de Pierre Leperdrieux'
'Stern von Prag'

Laevigatas
—None—

Banksias
—None—

Musks
—None—

Arvensises
'Ayrshire Queen'

Sempervirenses
—None—

Boursaults
'Amadis'
'Maheca'
'Zigeunerblut'

Setigeras
'Corporal Johann Nagy'
'Erinnerung an Brod'
'Himmelsauge'

Wichuraianas
'Bloomfield Courage'
'Clematis'
'Cramoisi Simple'
'Crimson Shower'
'Diabolo'
'Dr. Huey'
'Edgar Andreu'
'Gruss an Freundorf!'
'Heart of Gold'
'Louis Sauvage'
'Purpurtraum'
'Romeo'
'Souvenir d'Ernest Thébault'
'Vicomtesse de Chabannes'

Multifloras
'Asta von Parpart'
'Bocca Negra'
'Charlotte Mackensen'
'Crimson Grandiflora'
'Gilda'
'Mosellied'
'Non Plus Ultra'
'Paulette Bentall'
'Printemps Fleuri'
'Purple East'
'Trompeter von Säckingen'

Lambertianas
'Hauff'

Hybrid Musks
'Nur-Mahál'

Old Hybrid Tea and Pernetiana Climbers
'Black Boy'
'Château de Clos-Vougeot, Climbing'
'Countess of Stradbroke'
'Étoile de Hollande, Climbing'
'Gloire de Hollande, Climbing'
'Hadley, Climbing'
'Hoosier Beauty, Climbing'
'Liberty, Climbing'
'Miss Marion Manifold'

'Rosella'
'Souvenir de Claudius Denoyel'

Hybrid Teas, 1900–1920
'Alsterufer'
'Ami Quinard'
'Andenken an Moritz von Fröhlich'
'Capitaine Georges Dessirier'
'Château de Clos-Vougeot'
'Chrissie MacKellar'
'Étincelante'
'Étoile de Hollande'
'Friedrichsruh'
'Gloire de Hollande'
'Hadley'
'Herfsttooi'
'His Majesty'
'Hoosier Beauty'
'Intensity'
'Kynast'
'Louise Lilia'
'Othello'
'Prinses Juliana'
'Rhea Reid'
'Rotelfe'
'The Dandy'
'Walter C. Clark'
'Young America'

Pernetianas
—None—

Light Purple, Light Violet, Lilac, Slate, Gray, Ashen, and "Blue"

Gallicas
'Baraguay'
'Belle Doria'
'Belle Parade'
'Belle sans Flatterie'
'Belle Virginie'
'Busard Triomphant'
'Charles de Mills'
'Charles Lemayeux'
'Charles Lemoine'
'Couronnée'
'Du Maître d'École'
'Duc d'Arenberg'
'Duc de Bordeaux'
'Duc de Fitzjames'
'Duc de Guiche'
'Grande Violette Claire'
'Les Saisons d'Italie'
'Manette'
'Marie-Antoinette'

'Marie Tudor'
'Montézuma'
'Oeillet Double'
'Ornement de la Nature'
'Orphise'
'Paquita'
'Passe-Princesse'
'Pourpre Ardoisée'
'Président de Sèze'
'Reine des Amateurs'
'Tour Malakoff'

Damasks
'Bella Donna'
'Belle d'Auteuil'
'Lavalette'

Agathes
'Sommesson'

Centifolias
'Blue Boy'
'Marguerite de Flandre'

Centifolia Pompons and Pompon Mosses
—None—

Mosses
'James Mitchell'
'Robert Fortune'
'Routrou'
'Violacée'

Mossy Remontants
'Mélanie Waldor'

Albas
—None—

Hemisphaericas
—None—

Foetidas
—None—

Pimpinellifolias
'Double Purple'
'Mary Queen of Scots'

Rubiginosas
'Aschermittwoch'

Caninas
—None—

A Miscellany
—None—

Roxburghiis
—None—

Bracteatas
'Rosea'

Rugosas
Rosa rugosa
'Comte d'Epremesnil'
'Parnassine'

Laevigatas
—None—

Banksias
—None—

Musks
—None—

Arvensises
—None—

Sempervirenses
—None—

Boursaults
—None—

Setigeras
—None—

Wichuraianas
'Donau!'
'Marie Gouchault'

Multifloras
'Améthyste'
'Aristide Briand'
'Aurélian Igoult'
'Bleu Violette'
'Coccinea'
'De La Grifferaie'
'Geschwinds Orden'
'Gruss an Breinegg'
'Lisbeth von Kamecke'
'Rose-Marie Viaud'
'Schloss Friedenstein'
'Sweet Lavender'
'Turner's Crimson Rambler ×
    Veilchenblau'
'Veilchenblau'
'Violette'
'Vlatava'

Lambertianas
'Gartenstadt Liegnitz'
'Lavender Lassie'
'Mosel'

Hybrid Musks
'Galatea'

Old Hybrid Tea and Pernetiana Climbers
'Wenzel Geschwind, Climbing'

Hybrid Teas, 1900–1920
'Lady Coventry'

'Mrs. Wallace H. Rowe'
'Wenzel Geschwind'

Pernetianas
—None—

Cream to Sulphur, Light Yellow, and Pale Buff

Gallicas
'Ingénue'

Damasks
'Mme. Stolz'

Agathes
—None—

Centifolias
—None—

Centifolia Pompons and Pompon Mosses
—None—

Mosses
'Yellow Moss'

Mossy Remontants
—None—

Albas
'Arva Leany'

Hemisphaericas
Rosa hemisphaerica
'Multiplex'
'Pompon Jaune'

Foetidas
'Double Yellow'
'Globe Yellow'
'Harisonii No 1'
'Harisonii No 2'
'Jaune d'Italie'
'Luteola'
'Pallida'

Pimpinellifolias
'Frühlingsanfang'
'Lemon'
'Lutea'
'Ravellae'
'Sulphurea'

Rubiginosas
'Goldbusch'

Caninas
'Crême'
'Una'

A Miscellany
Rosa hugonis
'Cantabrigensis' (Hug)
'Double Hugonis' (Hug)
'Dr. E. M. Mills' (Hug)
'Headleyensis' (Hug)

Roxburghiis
—None—

Bracteatas
'Dwarf Mermaid'
'Happenstance'
'Mermaid'
'Nerrière'

Rugosas
'Agnes'
'Daniel Lesueur'
'Golden King'

Laevigatas
—None—

Banksias
'Anemonaeflora'
'Lutea'
'Lutescens Simplex'

Musks
'Princesse de Nassau'
'The Garland'

Arvensises
—None—

Sempervirenses
—None—

Boursaults
—None—

Setigeras
—None—

Wichuraianas
'Albéric Barbier'
'Aviateur Blériot'
'Buttermere'
'Coupe d'Or'
'Elegance'
'Émile Fortépaule'
'Emily Gray'
'Ernst Grandpierre'
'Fernande Tanne'
'François Foucard'
'François Guillot'
'François Poisson'
'Frau Albert Hochstrasser'
'Fraulein Octavia Hesse'
'Gardenia'
'Golden Glow'

**Cream to Sulphur,
Light Yellow, and Pale Buff**
Wichuraianas
continued
'Jeanne Richert'
'Jersey Beauty'
'Joseph Liger'
'L'Avenir'
'La Perle'
'Mrs. Arthur Curtiss James'
'Primevère'
'Professor C. S. Sargent'
'Renée Danielle'
'Shalimar'
'Shower of Gold'
'Source d'Or'
'Yellow Minnehaha'

Multifloras
'Buttercup'
'Daniel Lacombe'
'Eichsfeldia'
'G. F. Veronica'
'Ghislaine de Féligonde'
'Goldfinch'
'Laure Soupert'
'Madeleine Seltzer'
'Psyche'

Lambertianas
'Aglaia'
'Electra'
'Excellenz Kuntze'
'Grandmaster'
'Oriole'
'Thermidor'
'Tiergarten'
'Trier'
'Zitronenfalter'

Hybrid Musks
'Aurora'
'Autumn Delight'
'Bishop Darlington'
'Bloomfield Dainty'
'Bloomfield Fascination'
'Callisto'
'Danaë'
'Daybreak'
'Moonlight'
'Thisbe'

*Old Hybrid Tea and
Pernetiana Climbers*
'Captain Thomas'
'Frau Ida Münch'
'Mady'
'Paul's Lemon Pillar'

Hybrid Teas, 1900–1920
'Albast'
'Argyll'
'Bertha von Suttner'
'Bessie Brown'
'Bianca'
'Clarice Goodacre'
'Countess of Derby'
'Élégante'
'Florence Edith Coulthwaite'
'Florence Pemberton'
'Frances Gaunt'
'Franz Deegen'
'Frau Lilla Rautenstrauch'
'Gladys Holland'
'Grace Molyneux'
'Grange Colombe'
'Grossherzogin Alexandra'
'Hedwig Reicher'
'Herzogin von Calabrien'
'Irish Modesty'
'Janet'
'Jean Notté'
'Jubiläumsrose'
'Juwel'
'Königin Viktoria von
    Schweden'
'Kootenay'
'Lady Dunleathe'
'Le Progrès'
'Lydia Grimm'
'Marcella'
'Marie Henry'
'Marie-Louise Mathian'
'Melody'
'Mevrouw C. van Marwyk
    Kooy'
'Miss Wilmott'
'Mme. Alfred Digeon'
'Mme. Bardou Job'
'Mme. C. Chambard'
'Mme. Caristie Martel'
'Mme. J.-P. Soupert'
'Mme. Jules Bouché'
'Mme. Mélanie Soupert'
'Mme. Philippe Rivoire'
'Mrs. Amy Hammond'
'Mrs. Archie Gray'
'Mrs. C. V. Haworth'
'Mrs. David McKee'
'Mrs. E. Townsend'
'Mrs. George Marriot'
'Mrs. Hugh Dickson'
'Mrs. Mona Hunting'
'Mrs. Sam Ross'
'Mrs. T. Hillas'

'Mrs. Theodore Roosevelt'
'Mrs. Wemyss Quin'
'Natalie Böttner'
'Nelly Verschuren'
'Nerissa'
'Noblesse'
'Papa Reiter'
'Paul Meunier'
'Perle von Godesburg'
'Pie X'
'Princesse Vera Orbelioni'
'Prinzessin Hildegard von
    Bayern'
'Reine Mère d'Italie'
'Seabird'
'Souvenir de Gustave Prat'
'Souvenir de Mme. F. Zurich'
'T. F. Crozier'
'Troja'
'Verna Mackay'
'Walküre'
'Westfield Star'

Pernetianas
'Angel Guiméra'
'Ariel'
'Cissie Easlea'
'Von Scharnhorst'
'Wildenfels Gelb'

Deep Yellow to Deeper Buff, Fawn, Bronze, Apricot, Copper, Coral, Coral-Pink, Salmon, Orange, Nasturtium, Coppery Red, Orange-Red, and Scarlet

Gallicas
'Gloriette'

Damasks
'Oratam'
'Sémiramis'

Agathes
—None—

Centifolias
—None—

*Centifolia Pompons and
Pompon Mosses*
—None—

Mosses
'Golden Moss'

'Olavus'
'Robert Léopold'

Mossy Remontants
'Gabrielle Noyelle'

Albas
'Semonville'
'Semonville à Fleurs Doubles'

Hemisphaericas
—None—

Foetidas
Rosa foetida
'Buisson d'Or'
'Harison's Salmon'
'Harison's Yellow'
'Jaune Double'
'Lawrence Johnston'
'Le Rêve'
'Parkfeuer'
'Persian Yellow'
'Star of Persia'

Pimpinellifolias
'Aicha'
'Claus Groth'
'Frühlingsduft'
'Frühlingsgold'

Rubiginosas
'Canary Bird'
'Fritz Nobis'
'Joseph Rothmund'
'Lady Penzance'
'Lord Penzance'

Caninas
—None—

A Miscellany
Hulthemia persica
Rosa xanthina
'Albert Maumené' (Hug)
'Hardii' (Hult)

Roxburghiis
—None—

Bracteatas
—None—

Rugosas
'Dolly Varden'
'Dr. Eckener'
'Goldener Traum'
'Sanguinaire'
'Vanguard'

Laevigatas
—None—

Banksias
—None—

Musks
—None—

Arvensises
—None—

Sempervirenses
—None—

Boursaults
—None—

Setigeras
—None—

Wichuraianas
'Albertine'
'Apricot Glow'
'Auguste Gervaise'
'Breeze Hill'
'Brownell Yellow Rambler'
'Carpet of Gold'
'Copper Glow'
'Coral Satin'
'De Candolle'
'Denyse Ducas'
'Désiré Bergera'
'Dorcas'
'Easlea's Golden Rambler'
'Étendard'
'Golden Orange Climber'
'Henri Barruet'
'Jacotte'
'Jean Guichard'
'Léontine Gervais'
'Magic Carpet'
'Marco'
'Marie Dietrich'
'Maxime Corbon'
'Melita'
'Merveille de la Brie'
'Mme. Huguette Despiney'
'Paul Noël'
'René André'

Multifloras
'Coralie'
'Graf Zeppelin'
'Gruss an Hannover'
'Svatopluk Čech'
'Tea Rambler'
'Unique'

Lambertianas
'Ausonius'
'Blanche Frowein'

'Heideröslein'
'Hoffmann von Fallersleben'
'Peter Rosegger'

Hybrid Musks
'Bloomfield Comet'
'Bloomfield Completeness'
'Bonn'
'Buff Beauty'
'Clytemnestra'
'Francesca'
'Nymphenburg'

Old Hybrid Tea and Pernetiana Climbers
'Christine, Climbing'
'Elvira Aramayo, Climbing'
'Irish Fireflame, Climbing'
'Julien Potin, Climbing'
'Lady Forteviot, Climbing'
'Los Angeles, Climbing'
'Louis Barbier'
'Louise Catherine Breslau, Climbing'
'Lyon-Rose, Climbing'
'Mevrouw G. A. van Rossem, Climbing'
'Mme. Édouard Herriot, Climbing'
'Mrs. Aaron Ward, Climbing'
'Mrs. C. V. Haworth, Climbing'
'Mrs. Henry Morse, Climbing'
'Mrs. Pierre S. Du Pont, Climbing'
'Mrs. Sam McGredy, Climbing'
'Réveil Dijonnais'
'Shot Silk, Climbing'
'Souvenir de Claudius Pernet, Climbing'
'Souvenir de Georges Pernet, Climbing'
'The Queen Alexandra Rose, Climbing'
'Wilhelm Kordes, Climbing'
'Willowmere, Climbing'

Hybrid Teas, 1900–1920
'Amalie de Greiff'
'Betty'
'Comtesse de Cassagne'
'Decorator'
'Dernburg'
'Dorothy Page-Roberts'
'Dr. A. Hermans'
'Dr. Helfferich'
'Dr. Joseph Drew'
'Dr. Nicolas Welter'

'Duchess of Wellington'
'Duchesse de la Mothe-Houdancourt'
'Earl of Warwick'
'Elisabeth Barnes'
'Elisabeth Didden'
'Eva de Grossouvre'
'Fliegerheld Öhring'
'Frau Berthe Kiese'
'Frau Bürgermeister Kirschstein'
'Friedrich Albert Krupp'
'Generalin Isenbart'
'George C. Waud'
'Goldelse'
'Golden Ophelia'
'Gruss vom Westerwald'
'Gustav Sobry'
'Henriette'
'Herzogin Marie-Antoinette von Mecklembourg'
'Hortulanus Albert Fiet'
'Irish Elegance'
'Irish Fireflame'
'Jacques Vincent'
'Jonkheer Ruis de Beerenbrouck'
'Käthe von Saalfeld'
'Lady Forteviot'
'Lady Mary Ward'
'Lady Pirrie'
'Louise Baldwin'
'Ludwig Möller'
'Lulu'
'Mama Looymans'
'Margaret Dickson Hamill'
'Marie Isakoff'
'Mevrouw Smits Gompertz'
'Miriam'
'Mme. Henry Fontaine'
'Mme. Raymond Poincaré'
'Mme. René Collette'
'Mme. Théodore Delacourt'
'Molly Bligh'
'Monsieur Joseph Hill'
'Morgenglans'
'Mrs. Aaron Ward'
'Mrs. Dunlop-Best'
'Mrs. Fred Straker'
'Mrs. MacKellar'
'Maud Dawson'
'Mrs. Oakley Fisher'
'Rosa Gruss an Aachen'
'Sénateur Saint-Romme'
'Souvenir d'Anne-Marie'
'Souvenir d'E. Guillard'

Pernetianas
'Adolf Kärger'
'Adolf Koschel'
'Ambassador'
'Amélie de Bethune'
'Angèle Pernet'
'Angels Mateu'
'Annette Gravereaux'
'Antonio Rolleri de Peluffo'
'Apotheker Franz Hahne'
'Arthur R. Goodwin'
'Autumn'
'Autumn Tints'
'Barbara'
'Barbara Richards'
'Beauté de Lyon'
'Belle Cuivrée'
'Bénédicte Seguin'
'Betty Uprichard'
'California'
'Cambrai'
'Cardinal Mercier'
'Cécile Ratinckx'
'Ceres'
'Christine'
'Collette Clément'
'Constance'
'Dazla'
'Deutschland'
'Director Rubió'
'Dr. Augustin Wibbelt'
'Dr. Edward Deacon'
'Duquesa de Peñaranda'
'E. P. H. Kingma'
'Eldorado'
'Elvira Aramayo'
'Émile Charles'
'Emma Wright'
'Entente Cordiale'
'Étoile de Feu'
'Feu Joseph Looymans'
'Flammenrose'
'Florence L. Izzard'
'Frau Felberg-Leclerc'
'Geisha'
'Georges Clemenceau'
'Golden Emblem'
'Goldenes Mainz'
'Gooiland Beauty'
'Gooiland Glory'
'Gorgeous'
'Gottfried Keller'
'Gwyneth Jones'
'Hermann Robinow'
'Hortulanus Budde'
'I Zingari'

Deep Yellow to Deeper Buff, Fawn, Bronze, Apricot, Copper, Coral, Coral-Pink, Salmon, Orange, Nasturtium, Coppery Red, Orange-Red, and Scarlet

Pernetianas continued
'Independence Day'
'Jean C. N. Forestier'
'Jeanne Excoffier'
'Johannisfeuer'
'Joseph Baud'
'Julien Potin'
'Konrad Thönges'
'La Mie au Roy'
'La Somme'
'Lady Elphinstone'
'Lady Inchiquin'
'Lilly Jung'
'Lord Lambourne'
'Los Angeles'
'Louise Catherine Breslau'
'Louise Joly'
'Lyon-Rose'
'Madette'
'Mary Pickford'
'Mevrouw G. A. van Rossem'
'Miss May Marriot'
'Mme. Édouard Herriot'
'Mme. Eugène Picard'
'Mme. Henri Queuille'
'Mme. Ruau'
'Morgenster'
'Mrs. Ambrose Riccardo'
'Mrs. Erskine Pembroke Thom'
'Mrs. Frederick W. Vanderbilt'
'Mrs. Pierre S. Du Pont'
'Mrs. Ramon de Escofet'
'Mrs. Redford'
'Mrs. Robert Mitchell'
'Mrs. S. Paton'
'Mrs. W. E. Nickerson'
'Nona'
'O. Junyent'
'Old Gold'
'Padre'
'Pax Labor'
'Président Bouché'
'President Wilson'
'Rayon d'Or'
'Reverend Williamson'
'Rising Sun'
'Schleswig-Holstein'
'Shot Silk'
'Soleil d'Or'

'Sonnenlicht'
'Souvenir d'Angèle Opdebeeck'
'Souvenir de Charles Laemmel'
'Souvenir de Claudius Pernet'
'Souvenir de Georges Pernet'
'Souvenir de Jean Soupert'
'Souvenir du Reverend Père
    Planque'
'Sunburst'
'Sunstar'
'The Queen Alexandra Rose'
'United States'
'Ville de Paris'
'Willowmere'

Mixed Coloration

Gallicas
'Beauté Surprenante'
'Belle de Yèbles'
'Dupuytren'
'Général Foy'
'Gloire de France'
'Helvetius'
'Illustre'
'Narcisse de Salvandy'
'Néala'
'Ohl'
'Panachée Superbe'
'Regina Dicta'
'Renoncule'
'Rosier d'Amour'
'Sans Pareille Rose'
'Zoé'

Damasks
'À Pétale Teinté de Rose'
'Belle Couronnée'
'Damask Violacé'
'Déesse Flore'
'Lady White'
'Leda'
'Phoebus'
'Triomphe de Lille'

Agathes
'Francfort Agathé'
'Héloise'
'Sapho'

Centifolias
'Aglaia'
'Charles-Quint'

Centifolia Pompons and Pompon Mosses
—None—

Mosses
'Asepala'
'Jeanne de Montfort'

Mossy Remontants
'Hortense Vernet'

Albas
'Belle Aurore'
'Candide'

Hemisphaericas
—None—

Foetidas
Rosa foetida 'Bicolor'
'Rustica'

Pimpinellifolias
'Frühlingstag'
'Nankin'

Rubiginosas
'Flora McIvor'
'Hebe's Lip'
'Janet's Pride'
'Lucy Ashton'

Caninas
—None—

A Miscellany
—None—

Roxburghiis
'Ma Surprise'
'Premier Essai'

Bracteatas
—None—

Rugosas
'Mme. Henri Gravereaux'
'New Century'

Laevigatas
—None—

Banksias
—None—

Musks
—None—

Arvensises
'Alice Gray'

Sempervirenses
—None—

Boursaults
—None—

Setigeras
—None—

Wichuraianas
'Bouquet Rose'
'Harlequin'
'Jessica'
'Mme. Alice Garnier'
'Paradise'
'Pearl Queen'
'Ruby Ring'

Multifloras
'Gräfin Ada von Bredow'
'Grevillii'
'June Morn'
'Laure Davoust'
'Roby'
'Russelliana'
'Stella'
'Tausendschön'

Lambertianas
'Adrian Reverchon'
'Chamisso'
'Rudolf von Bennigsen'

Hybrid Musks
'Bloomfield Perfection'
'Queen Alexandra'

Old Hybrid Tea and Pernetiana Climbers
'Comtesse Vandal, Climbing'
'Condesa de Sástago, Climbing'
'Independence Day, Climbing'
'Monsieur Paul Lédé,
    Climbing'
'Talisman, Climbing'
'Vicomtesse Pierre de Fou'

Hybrid Teas, 1900–1920
'Contrast'
'Cornelis Timmermans'
'Countess of Warwick'
'Edith Part'
'Frau Philipp Siesmayer'
'General Th. Peschkoff'
'Hermann Kiese'
'Jacques Porcher'
'Lady Clanmorris'
'Marquise de Sinety'
'Monsieur Paul Lédé'
'Mrs. E. G. Hill'
'Mrs. Isabel Milner'
'Nordlicht'
'Queen Mary'
'Stadtrat Glaser'

Pernetianas
'Comtesse Vandal'

'Condesa de Sástago'
'Gruss an Coburg'
'Juliet'
'Mrs. Arthur Robert Waddell'
'Mrs. Charles E. Pearson'
'Mrs. Sam McGredy'
'Mrs. Talbot O'Farrell'
'Norman Lambert'
'Reims'
'Reinhard Bädecker'
'Reverend F. Page-Roberts'
'Schmetterling'
'Soleil d'Angers'
'Souvenir de Gustave
    Schickelé'
'Talisman'
'Ville de Malines'
'Wilhelm Kordes'

Striped or Mottled

Gallicas
'Abaillard'
'Agar'
'Aglaé Adanson'
'Alexandre Laquement'
'Anacréon'
'Aramis'
'Arlequin'
'Beauté de la Malmaison'
'Beauté Insurmontable'
'Belle Aimable'
'Belle des Jardins'
'Belle Herminie'
'Belle Villageoise'
'Bourbon'
'Camayeux'
'Catinat'
'César Beccaria'
'Charlotte de Lacharme'
'Cocarde Pâle'
'Cosimo Ridolfi'
'Cramoisi Picoté'
'Cramoisie Triomphante'
'Dona Sol'
'Duc d'Orléans'
'Esther'
'Fanny Elssler'
'Fornarina' (Vibert)
'Georges Vibert'
'Giselle'
'Gros Provins Panaché'
'Hortense de Beauharnais'
'Jeanne Hachette'
'Joséphina'

'Juanita'
'L'Évêque'
'La Maculée'
'La Nationale'
'La Plus Belle des Ponctuées'
'Lucile Duplessis'
'Madelon Friquet'
'Manteau d'Évêque'
'Marmorea'
'Mécène'
'Mercédès'
'Montalembert'
'Néron'
'Noire Couronnée'
'Oeillet Flamand'
'Oeillet Parfait'
'Perle des Panachées'
'Phénice'
'Pintade'
'Pompon'
'Ponctué'
'Pourpre Marbrée'
'Renoncule Ponctuée'
'Rosa Mundi'
'Rosemary'
'Rouge Admirable Strié'
'Royal Marbré'
'Séguier'
'Tricolore' (Vibert)
'Tricolore' (Lahaye)
'Tricolore de Flandre'

Damasks
'L'Amitié'
'La Félicité'
'Panachée'
'Rosemonde'
'York and Lancaster'

Agathes
'Fatime'
'Victorine la Couronnée'

Centifolias
'Alain Blanchard'
'Dométile Bécar'
'Eulalie LeBrun'
'Hypacia'
'Jacquinot'
'Juanita'
'Mme. d'Hébray'
'Unique Panachée'
'Variegata'

Centifolia Pompons and Pompon Mosses
—None—

Mosses
'Aristobule'
'Julie de Mersan'
'Oeillet Panachée'
'Panachée'
'Panachée Pleine'
'Panaget'
'Ponctuée'

Mossy Remontants
'Bicolor'
'Circé'
'Gloire d'Orient'
'Hermann Kegel'
'Ma Ponctuée'
'Mme. de Villars'
'Mme. Moreau'
'Oscar Leclerc'
'Pompon Perpétuel'
'Sophie de Marsilly'

Albas
'Marie de Bourgogne'

Hemisphaericas
—None—

Foetidas
'Rose Tulipe'

Pimpinellifolias
'Belle Laure'
'Belle Laure No 2'
'Bicolor'
'De Marienbourg'
'Dominie Sampson'
'Glory of Edzell'
'Maculata'
'Marbrée d'Enghien'
'Townsend'

Rubiginosas
—None—

Caninas
—None—

A Miscellany
—None—

Roxburghiis
'Striata'
'Triomphe de Macheteaux'

Bracteatas
—None—

Rugosas
—None—

Laevigatas
—None—

Banksias
—None—

Musks
—None—

Arvensises
—None—

Sempervirenses
—None—

Boursaults
'À Fleurs Panachées'
'Elegans'
'Reversa'
'Weissrote Mme. Sancy de
    Parabère'

Setigeras
—None—

Wichuraianas
'Coronation'
'Matka Vlast'
'Tricolore'

Multifloras
'Prinz Hirzeprinzchen'
'Tricolore'

Lambertianas
'Lessing'

Hybrid Musks
—None—

Old Hybrid Tea and Pernetiana Climbers
—None—

Hybrid Teas, 1900–1920
—None—

Pernetianas
'Pardinas Bonet'
'Professor Schmeil'

Leaves or Stems Striped or Mottled, or of Coloration Unusual for the Group

'Rosemary' (G), 'Oscar Leclerc' (MR), 'Rose à Bois Jaspé' (Can), 'Variegata' (W), and 'Kaiserin Goldifolia' and 'Silver Wedding' (both HT)

APPENDIX TEN

Loose Ends

Final words, or nearly. We read somewhere of "that kind senescence" that comes at the end of any endeavor; we leave to the Reader to decide the degree to which this enters into a final appendix of loose ends.

Descriptions

"On looking over a good collection of Roses a keen observer, even if he be unlearned in their culture, cannot fail to be struck with the difference observable in what is called the 'habit' of each sort, for there is almost endless variety in wood, leaves, thorns, strength, and manner of growth, apart from the blooms themselves. He would also probably notice a good many of what he would call 'red' Roses, very much alike to his untrained eyes in general appearance, and he might wonder how they could be all distinguished apart. But as a good shepherd can tell every member of a large flock of sheep by a diligent study of their faces, and an English apple, or even apple-tree without its leaves, can be correctly named by some clever pomologists, so a fairly representative bloom of any Rose can be distinguished by a thoroughly expert Rosarian.

"Descriptions of the different varieties are to be found in the catalogues issued by nurserymen, and many of these are now fairly full and accurate. The colour, naturally enough, occupies the principal part of the descriptions; but the different shades . . . are very difficult to express to ordinary readers in language that they will clearly understand, for some are extremely variable in their tints, and others come much fuller in colour when grown strongly.

"It is not every one who is, without studying the matter, well conversant with the different tints expressed in the terms frequently used. Among these may be found—ivory, cream, lemon, chrome, straw, canary sulphur, nankeen, saffron, apricot, fawn, buff, salmon, copper, bronze, blush, flesh, peach, rose, cerise, coral, cherry, currant, madder, vermilion, scarlet, lake, carmine, lilac, plum, violet, magenta, claret, maroon, and amaranth. It requires not only a good eye for colour, but also a certain amount of training, for an ordinary man to distinguish accurately between these shades; perhaps the description 'a soft shade of écru, passing to a lovely golden yellow' might leave him not much wiser than he was before. I confess that some of them beat me, and that even the first two on the list, ivory and cream, as seen in Roses, would present very slight distinctions to my eyes . . .

"My endeavour will be to supplement these descriptions with other matters that the purchaser and chooser would like to know as an addition to and commentary upon published catalogues. For instance, the novice student of these seductive pamphlets will only require a little knowledge of human nature to enable him to take a fair discount off the description given by the raiser himself of any one sort: and he will find it advantageous to be acquainted with some slight vagaries in catalogue-English which custom has sanctioned. In this language 'medium-sized' means 'small,' and 'pretty' generally implies the same. In growth, 'moderate' means 'weakly,' 'free' describes a plant which is rather weakly but branching, and 'vigorous' stands for ordinary growth. 'A good pot Rose' might very likely mean that it would not stand any bad weather out of doors, a 'nearly full' one mean[s that it] shows an eye, and we should probably be doing no injustice in supposing that a Rose which is 'good when caught right' is bad as a rule." [F-M]

Terminology

"When *I* use a word," Humpty Dumpty said in rather a scornful tone, "it means just what I choose it to mean—neither more nor less.

"'The question is,' said Alice, 'whether you *can* make words mean so many different things.'

"'The question is,' said Humpty Dumpty, 'which is to be master—that's all.'" [TTL-G]

It is interesting to note the different terms used for floral variegation by the French, who are, as always, much more sensitive and exact in their descriptions than English speakers tend to be. We provide a short glossary of such words, with their implications, and encourage their use by those aiming at exactitude:

Aspergé: Sprinkled.
Bicolor: Having distinct, well-separated, large zones of either one or another of two colors, in the manner of 'York and Lancaster' (D).
Jaspé: Marbled, mottled, or streaked in the manner of the mineral jasper.
Ligné: Lined with striations of a tendentially regular shape.
Liséré: Edged; synonymous with English "picotee."
Marbré: Veined with two or more colors, looking like marble.
Moiré: Watered, referring to the artistic process of putting one color on another by use of the sponge, one color fading into another insensibly, with some areas distinct in one or the other color. This appearance is particularly common in many Tea Roses.

Mouchété: Flecked.

Nuagé: Clouded.

Nuancé: Nuanced.

Oeillé: Eyed; the contrasting color inhabits the center of the blossom in a definite zone.

Panaché: Plumed or flamed with two or more colors irregularly accompanying each other. In this book, we usually translate this as "plumed," as (1) this is the literal meaning and (2) the appearance of the variegation is usually rather closer to a feathery pattern than to one of flames.

Piqueté: Spotted or marked with small irregular colorations; not to be confused with the English "picotee," which is the French *liséré*.

Pointillé: Dotted with small points.

Rayé: Striped radially; *i.e.*, arranged lengthwise from the heart of the blossom towards the perimeter.

Rubané: Banded or ribboned; like "striped," but with wider zones of contrast.

Sablé: Discolored with some regularity, like heraldic sable.

Sillonné: Streaked, as if furrowed or grooved.

Soufflé: Puffed; like *nuagé*.

Strié: Striped or striated with two or more distinct colors in a more or less irregular but generally linear shape.

Taché: Blotched.

Tigré: Striped or banded irregularly, like the stripes on a tiger, rather like *zebré*.

Vergeté: Streaked, as if brushed.

Zebré: Striped or banded irregularly, like the stripes on a zebra, rather like *tigré*, the striations more bold and less irregular than those of *strié* or *panaché*.

Names

"The Dutch and the Flemings, who grew the first [roses], sent them to us with names which were emphatic and often ridiculous. Soon flower-growers called to their aid Mythology (then used by Entomologists), history both ancient and modern; sovereigns, ministers, magistrates, men of war, illustrious men of all nations, celebrated women—all gave their names to so many varieties of roses. Now that the number of varieties increases each year by hundreds, nurserymen and fanciers go the route of dedicating their newcomers to kin and friends. All these names put together in a fairly limited space make a rather curious assemblage. Young men who join the gardener in looking through a collection of roses find a remembrance of the schoolwork of their childhood at each name; fully considered, a collection of roses is a new course in History! All the celebrated people and the men of the age grow there peacefully, often mixed together. In the same glance, one admires the Prince de Condé and Lafayette, the King of Rome and the Duc de Bordeaux, Sister Joseph and Fanny Bias, Joan of Arc and the Comtesse de Genlis. There is, there, a fusion, an amalgam which brings no consequences; and the fancier, bewildered by having to choose between flowers so fresh, so brilliant, chooses them all—to the great satisfaction of the nurseryman." [BJ30]

"Vibert said that it was the privilege of beautiful roses to have several names. Guillemeau stated that it wasn't unusual to find one variety bearing up to ten names. Prévost received 'Rouge Formidable'

under fourteen different titles. It is easy to explain this abundance of names at the beginning of the Nineteenth Century. For the most part, Roses came from Holland, most frequently without either name or name of breeder. Each grower or fancier who received them baptized them to his taste … This right of baptism practiced on unnamed roses was an excusable practice; it is worse to de-baptize them. Redouté and Thory themselves unfortunately dreamed up a few; not only did they give Latin appellations to some varieties in their work which bore [also] their usual French names, but they indeed were also so bold as to [re]name some roses which they did not originate. Thus it is that, with 'Rouge Formidable', they write 'We believe that we ought to suppress the bizarre name which this Rose already bears in the trade, and to substitute for it that of André Du Pont.' Then they go on to call horticulture's 'Belle Aurore' 'Belle Aurore Poniatowska' instead, to honor the daughter of the great Polish nobleman. And then they dedicate *Rosa hudsoniana* to the well-known English navigator, even though it was already known under another name. Let us be indulgent. The names from this era are generally charming, and it is tempting to dedicate a rose to a friend or a beloved! But it is easy to see the confusion into which rose history is thrown by this overplus of synonyms, making the ordering of the chaos a delicate affair, with synonymy frequently impossible to establish." [Gx]

"These days [1873], rosarians have a trying habit of giving their introductions names too long or too difficult to pronounce; such must be admitted after reviewing the catalogs: 'Souvenir du Voyage de Sa Majesté la Reine d'Angleterre', 'Mme. la Comtesse Lucie de Barante de Monthozon', 'Monsieur le Baron de Heckeren de Wassenaer', [*not to forget* 'Société d'Agriculture de la Marne', 'Souvenir de la Princesse Alexandra Swiatopolk Czetwertinski', 'Société d'Horticulture de Melun et Fontainebleau', 'Les Fiançailles de la Princesse Stéphanie et de l'Archiduc Rodolphe'] etc. Such names are also the ones most often mangled, and it is rarely wisely that it is left to the whim of the gardener's ear, which will transform such a name as 'Marquis de Dreux-Brézé' into 'Marquée de Deux Baisers' [*i.e.*, "Marked with Two Kisses," etc.]." [JF]

Passions

"Stealing Rose Trees. —Two young Devonshire men were charged the other day with stealing Rose trees from a villa garden at Paignton [England]. One of them was acquitted; but concerning the other it was said the Bench had taken some time to consider their decision in the case. They had no difficulty at all in convicting the defendant of having stolen the Rose trees; the only doubt in the minds of the magistrates was whether they should send him to prison or not; but they were willing to take a more lenient view of the case. They should inflict a penalty of £10, or two months' imprisonment, with hard labour. —Prisoner said he should appeal against the decision. The fine, however, was paid." [R3/216]

"It is the Editor's thought that devotion to the rose not only promotes long life but creates in the men and women who recognize roses as God's best floral gift to mankind a sweetness of spirit and an enjoyment of life well worth emulation." [ARA26/33]

"There is nothing in which deduction is so necessary as in religion," said [Sherlock Holmes], leaning with his back against the shutters. "It can be built up as an exact science by the reasoner. Our highest assurance of the goodness of Providence seems to me to rest in the flowers. All other things, our powers, our desires, our food, are all really necessary for our existence in the first instance. But this rose is an extra. Its smell and its colour are an embellishment of life, not a condition of it. It is only goodness which gives extras, and so I say again that we have much to hope from the flowers." [ACD]

"I [E. G. Hill] like to work with flowers and plants, and study them. Really few people know, and a great many of the florists do not understand, that the sexual relation exists in plants just the same as in the animal kingdom. When we keep that thing in mind, and remember it is God's plan and purpose to benefit the world, to make things more beautiful, we can work with Him. I despise the man who says he creates anything. I tell you, God alone creates the flowers and beautiful things in life; but we can be co-workers with Him in the fertilization, in the production of new plants and new flowers. In the sixteenth chapter of *Proverbs* we read, 'Jehovah hath made everything for its own end.' And how true that is; the man that dares to believe that he creates anything without the Divine assistance is a man on unsafe ground and he is not right in his thought and mind. In Westminster Abbey, last year, I noticed two tablets not more than ten feet apart [ca. 3.3 m]. One was to Charles Darwin, the revelator of God's laws concerning plants and animals in the material world; the other was to John Wesley, the interpreter of the spiritual life as revealed by God through Jesus Christ. I thought how broad a platform that is and how sincerely the thought should be that the same God, the same Jehovah who made man and created him after his own image, also made the plants and the fishes, the fowls, the birds and the animals.

"To be a successful hybridist, or to attain success in fertilization, we have to have idealism, we must have a vision of the thing we want to aim at. Young men must get this thoroughly ground into their minds and into their thoughts. *Dreams! Dreams!* some may say. If it were not for the dreamers, there would not be much accomplished in this world. Have a vision of the things you want to do, and then have the purpose of mind, the stability to stick at it and work it out and you will get results." [ARA22/129]

Method

As, following the publication of *The Old Rose Advisor,* we noted some interest expressed in print in the history and manner in which these works were compiled and written, we will draw aside the authorial curtain for a moment.

In 1982, our increasing interest in Old Roses frequently met with points of frustration due to (1) the unsatisfactory state of information supplied by many works on the subject; (2) the fact that most catalogs listed their cultivars in an alphabetical mêlée of sorts, rather than one listing for Teas, one for Chinas, etc., making it difficult to compare members of the same classification with each other; and (3) the concentration of most works then coming out on artistic photography rather than on information (as remains the case today). To enable us to conduct our own studies more efficiently, we had "a vision of the things we wanted to do," and began (1) to put together a collection of index cards on "extant or important" cultivars, each one bearing handwritten excerpts from this work or that on the pertinent cultivar, and

(2) to compile a complete list of all Old Rose cultivars, important or unimportant, extant or extinct, developed up through 1920, with breeder, date, and synonymy, to aid in our understanding the development of each group, the contribution of each breeder, and the significance of genealogies, the listing first arranged alphabetically by cultivar name, and then arranged chronologically by name of breeder. This methodology proved useful, and no changes were made in it between work on *The Old Rose Advisor* and that on *The Old Rose Adventurer.*

To clear up paradoxical elements, we widened our researches continually until a reasonable breadth of material had been encompassed. At a certain point, we realized that this material could perhaps be of service to others as well, and so commenced to prepare the easier groups for trial publication. This eventuated in the previous volume, *The Old Rose Advisor,* dealing mainly with repeat bloomers. These were "easier" because most of the groups began more recently, and were, for the most part, fairly well documented, particularly as compared to their relatives, the mist-shrouded once-blooming old European roses.

The treatment given having met with approbation upon the publication of that first book, we continued our work—with a little more zest—on the groups and cultivars inhering to *The Old Rose Adventurer.* As the reader will have noted, our system in the previous volume of having each group divided into separate alphabetical listings for cultivars expected to be in commerce and those noncommercial and less important was the one major change between the two books. Though valid in the mid-1980s, when conceptualization of the first took place, the idea became invalid due to the fact that obscure, formerly noncommercial, cultivars were now entering the marketplace with increasing frequency—a fact to be hailed not only because wonderful rare roses were becoming available to more rosarians, but also because it would simplify our chapters both for reader and writer!

At length, the time came to call a halt to increasingly far-flung and decreasingly useful efforts at research, and to publish our results. As with the first book, we examined our index cards one by one, judging the ensemble of remarks, comparing the descriptions and opinions with each other carefully, piecing them together so that a reader would be able to understand each cultivar or group in as many facets as possible. This operation once completed, the index cards were reordered into as many permutations and transformations of order as the appendices seemed to require. It was with a sad smile that we read in a few reviews that what we had done would not have been possible before the age of computers! In truth, as you see, our process has been the same as that of compilers for the last couple of millennia, the computer only coming into it as something of a glorified typewriter, or enchanted scribe, if you will. Any future efforts on our part will possibly benefit from the increasing sophistication of the computer; but, in this case, we wished to finish as we began, in the traditional way.

It has been an exciting journey!—but a long one. "To be sure, I had taken as my motto two words which turned out to be quite necessary indeed: Patience and Perseverance." [SHP35/308]

"The moments were numbered; the strife was finished; the vision was closed. In the twinkling of an eye, our flying horses had carried us to the termination of the umbrageous aisle; at right angles we wheeled into our former direction; the turn of the road carried the scene out of my eyes in an instant, and swept it into my dreams forever." [DeQ]

Bibliography

Key to Citations

These should not be confused with other abbreviations, which are listed prior to Chapter 1.

A: *Roses, or A Monograph . . . ,* by Henry Andrews, 1805 and 1828.
AbR: *Cours Complet d'Agriculture . . . ,* by Abbé Rozier, 1793.
AC: *La Rose,* by A. de Chesnel, 1838.
ACD: Short story *The Naval Treaty,* by Arthur Conan Doyle.
ADE: Departmental Archives of Essonne at Corbeil, France.
ADk: *Catalogue,* by Alexander Dickson, year as indicated.
ADVDM: Departmental Archives of Val-de-Marne at Creteil, France.
ADY: Departmental Archives of Yvelines at Versailles, France.
aF: Information kindly supplied via the Internet by Alice Flores.
AHB: *The Tree Rose,* by A[rthur] H[enry] B[osanquet], 1845.
An: *Annales de Flore et de Pomone,* 1832–1848.
AnM-L: *Annales du Comice Horticole de Maine-et-Loire,* 1859.
ARA16 (*et seq.*): *American Rose Annual,* 1916–1940. Quoted by kind permission of the American Rose Society.
Au: *The Australasian Rose Book,* by R. G. Elliott, ca. 1925.
BBF: *The Flower-Garden, or Breck's Book of Flowers,* by Joseph Breck, 1851.
BBF66: *New Book of Flowers,* by Joseph Breck, 1866.
BCD: Interpolated commentary by Brent C. Dickerson.
BJ: *Le Bon Jardinier,* 1865 edition.
BJ06: *Le Bon Jardinier,* 1806 edition.
BJ09: *Le Bon Jardinier,* 1809 edition.
BJ09s: *Supplément à . . . Bon Jardinier,* 1809.
BJ17: *Le Bon Jardinier,* 1817 edition.
BJ24: *Le Bon Jardinier,* 1824 edition.
BJ30: *Le Bon Jardinier,* 1830 edition.
BJ40: *Le Bon Jardinier,* 1840 edition.
BJ53: *Le Bon Jardinier,* 1853 edition.
BJ58: *Le Bon Jardinier,* 1858 edition.
BJ63: *Le Bon Jardinier,* 1863 edition.
BJ70: *Le Bon Jardinier,* 1870 edition.
BJ77: *Le Bon Jardinier,* 1877 edition.
Bk: *Roses and How to Grow Them,* by Edwin Beckett, 1918.
Br: *A Year in a Lancashire Garden,* by Henry Bright, 1879.
BSA: *The Garden Book of California,* by Belle Sumner Angier, 1906.

Bu: *The Rose Manual,* by Robert Buist, 1844.
B&V: *List of Roses Now in Cultivation at Chateau Eléonore, Cannes . . . ,* by Henry Charles Brougham, 3rd Baron Brougham & Vaux, 1898.
C: *Beauties of the Rose,* by Henry Curtis, 1850–1853. Facsimile reprint, 1980, by Sweetbriar Press; additional material by Leonie Bell.
CA88 (*et seq.*): *Descriptive Catalogue,* California Nursery Company, 1888 *et sequitur.*
Cal: *Catalogue* of Calvert & Company, 1820.
Capt27: Article "Tea Roses for Southern Climates," by Capt. George C. Thomas, in ARA27.
Capt28: Article "Climbing Roses for Southern Climates," by Capt. George C. Thomas, in ARA28.
CaRoI (*et seq.*): *The California Rosarian,* published by the California Rose Society 1930–1932.
Cat12: *Official Catalogue of Roses,* by the [British] National Rose Society, 1912 edition.
CBë: *Biographical Notice of Ellis and Acton Bell,* by Charlotte Brontë, 1850.
CC: *Catalogue* for the Wasamequia Nurseries, New Bedford, MA, by Henry H. Crapo, 1848. In ARA26.
CdF: *La Culture des Fleurs,* anonymous, 1712.
C'H: *Dictionnaire Universel des Plantes . . . ,* by Pierre-Joseph Buc'hoz, 1770.
C&Jf: *Fall Catalog,* The Conard & Jones Co., 1897–1924, edition as specified. Quoted by kind permission of The Conard-Pyle Co.
C&Js: *Spring Catalog,* The Conard & Jones Co., 1897–1924, edition as specified. Quoted by kind permission of The Conard-Pyle Co.
Ck: *Catalogue, Marie Henriette Chotek Rosenschulen,* by Marie Henriette Chotek, 1926.
CM: *Histoire des Roses,* by Charles Malo, 1821.
C-Pf: *Fall Catalog,* The Conard-Pyle Co., 1925–1934, edition as specified. Quoted by kind permission of the Conard-Pyle Co.
C-Ps: *Spring Catalog,* The Conard-Pyle Co., 1925–1934, edition as specified. Quoted by kind permission of The Conard-Pyle Co.
Cr: *Catalogue* of Cranston's Nurseries, various years as noted.
C-T: *Almanach des Roses,* by Claude-Thomas Guerrapain, 1811.
Cw: *La Rose Historique,* by Edm. Van Cauwenberghe, 1927.
Cx: *Les Plus Belles Roses au Debut de IIème Siècle,* by the Société Nationale d'Horticulture de France, 1912.
Cy: *The French Revolution. A History,* by Thomas Carlyle, 1837.

Cy2: *Oliver Cromwell's Letters and Speeches,* 3rd edition, by Thomas Carlyle, 1849.

Cy3: *The History of Friedrich II of Prussia, Called Frederick the Great,* by Thomas Carlyle, 1865.

D: *A General History and Collection of Voyages and Travels,* by Robert Kerr, 1824.

DeQ: From "The Vision of Sudden Death", from *The English Mail-Coach,* by Thomas De Quincy, 1849.

dH: *Journal d'Horticulture Pratique et de Jardinage,* 1844–1847, edited by Martin-Victor Paquet.

DO: *Roses for Amateurs,* by Rev. H. Honywood D'Ombrain, 1908.

dP: *Sommaire d'une Monographie du Genre Rosier . . . ,* by M. de Pronville, 1822.

DP: Article "My Favorites . . . ," by D. Bruce Phillips, in *Pacific Horti-culture,* vol. 43, no. 3, 1982. Quoted by kind permission of *Pacific Horticulture.*

Dr: *Everblooming Roses,* by Georgia Torrey Drennan, 1912.

DuC: *The Flowers and Gardens of Madeira,* by Florence DuCane, 1909.

E: *Gardens of England,* by E. T. Cook, 1911.

ECS: City Archives of Soisy-sous-Etioles, France.

Ed: *The Amateur's Rosarium,* by R. Wodrow Thomson, 1862.

EER: Article "A Short History of the Tea Rose," by E. E. Robinson, in *The Rose,* vol. 17, no. 3, 1969.

EER2: Article "The Early Hybrid Perpetuals," by E. E. Robinson, in *The Rose,* vol. 13, no. 3, 1965.

EJW: *California Garden-Flowers,* by E. J. Wickson, 1915.

EL: *The Rose,* by Henry B. Ellwanger, 1882.

ElC: Article "Old Roses and New Roses," by Henry B. Ellwanger, in *Century Magazine,* vol. 4, 1883.

ET: Article "Help Wanted in Texas?" by Edward Teas, from ARA28.

EU: Unpublished material compiled and very kindly shared by Mr. Erich Unmuth of Vienna, Austria.

ExRé: *Guide pour servir à la visite de notre Exposition Rétrospective de la Rose,* by Roseraie de l'Haÿ, 1910.

F: *Les Roses,* by Louis Fumierre, 1910.

Fa: *In a Yorkshire Garden,* by Reginald Farrer, 1909.

FeR: *La France en Russie,* by Eugène Delaire, 1900.

Fl: *The Florist,* vol. 1, 1848.

FlCa: *Floricultural Cabinet,* date as specified.

F-M: *The Book of the Rose,* 4th edition, by Andrew Foster-Melliar, 1910.

F-M2: *The Book of the Rose,* 2nd edition, by Andrew Foster-Melliar, 1902.

F-M3: *The Book of the Rose,* 1st edition, by Andrew Foster-Melliar, 1894.

F-M4: *The Book of the Rose,* 3rd edition, by Andrew Foster-Melliar, 1905.

FP: *The Book of Roses,* by Francis Parkman, 1871.

Fr: *Dictionnaire du Jardinier Français,* by Monsieur Fillassier, 1791.

FRB: *Tea Roses,* by F. R. Burnside, 1893.

GAS: *Climbing Roses,* by G. A. Stevens, 1933. Quoted by kind per-mission of the copyright holder, The McFarland Co.

G&B: *Roses,* by Gemen & Bourg, ca. 1908.

GeH: *The Rose Encyclopaedia,* by Geoffrey W. Henslowe, 1934.

Gf: *Catalogue,* J.-B. Guillot fils, 1856.

GG: *In a Gloucestershire Garden,* by Henry N. Ellacombe, 1896.

GJB: *Vägledning genom Linnés park 1836,* manuscript by G. J. Billberg, 1836.

Gl: *The Culture of Flowers and Plants,* by George Glenny, 1861.

Go: *The Rose Fancier's Manual,* by Mrs. Gore, 1838.

God: *Catalogue des Rosiers,* by Godefroy, 1831.

Gp: *Catalogue,* by J.-B. Guillot, 1844–1845.

Gp&f: *Catalogue,* J.-B. Guillot père & fils, 1852.

Gx: *"La Malmaison" Les Roses de l'Impératrice Joséphine,* by Jules Gravereaux, 1912.

H: *A Book About Roses,* by S. Reynolds Hole, 1906.

Hd: *The Amateur's Rose Book,* by Shirley Hibberd, 1874.

HDk: *Catalog,* year as indicated, by Hugh Dickson.

Hj: Unpublished correspondence with Thomasville Nurseries, Inc. Quoted by kind permission of Thomasville Nurseries, Inc.

HmC: *My Roses and How I Grew Them,* by Helen (Crofton) Milman, 1899.

Hn: *The Amateur Gardener's Rose Book,* by Julius Hoffmann, English translation by John Weathers, 1905.

HoBoIV: *The Horticultural Review and Botanical Magazine,* 1854.

HRH: *A Gardener's Year,* by H. Rider Haggard, 1905.

HstI (*et seq.*): *The Horticulturist,* 1846–1875.

Ht: *Le Livre d'Or des Roses,* by Paul Hariot, 1904.

HUM: *An Essay Concerning Human Understanding,* by John Locke, 1690.

Hÿ: *Les Roses Cultivées à l'Haÿ en 1902,* by Roseraie de l'Haÿ, 1902.

J: *Roses for English Gardens,* by Gertrude Jekyll, 1902.

J-A: *Le Jardinier-Amateur,* edited by Eugène Pirolle, 1826.

J-As: *Premier Supplément, Le Jardinier-Amateur,* edited by Eugène Pirolle, 1827.

JC: *Cultural Directions for the Rose,* 6th edition, by John Cranston, 1877.

JDR54 (*et seq.*): *Journal des Roses* 1854–1859, edited by Jean Cherpin.

JF: *Les Roses,* by Hippolyte Jamain & Eugène Forney, 1873.

Jg: *Rosenlexikon,* by Auguste Jäger, 1970.

jP: Information kindly supplied via the Internet by Judy Pineda.

JP: *Roses: Their History, Development, and Cultivation,* by Rev. Joseph H. Pemberton, 1920.

JPV: *Réponse à . . . Pirolle,* by Jean-Pierre Vibert, 1827.

JR1 (*et seq.*): *Journal des Roses,* 1877–1914, edited by Cochet & Bernardin.

JSa: Article "On the Ayrshire Rose" by Joseph Sabine, in *Transactions of the London Horticultural Society,* 1822.

JSp: Article "Double Scotch Roses" by Joseph Sabine, in *Transactions of the London Horticultural Society,* 1822.

K: *The Rose Manual,* by J. H. Nicolas, 1938. Quoted by kind permis-sion of the publishers, Doubleday & Co., Inc.

K1: *Eversley Gardens and Others,* by Rose G. Kingley, 1907.

K2: *Roses and Rose-Growing,* by Rose G. Kingley, 1908.

kK: Information kindly supplied by e-mail by Karl King.

Kr: *The Complete Book of Roses,* by Gerd Krüssmann, 1981. Quoted by kind permission of the publisher, Timber Press.

L: *Gardening in California,* 3rd revised edition, by William S. Lyon, 1904.

LADR: *Les Amis des Roses,* issues 1946–1962.

Lam: *Encyclopédie Méthodique . . .* , section on roses by Lamarck, 1804.

Lam/Poir: *Encyclopédie Méthodique. Botanique. Supplément,* by J. L. M. Poiret, 1816.

LaQ: *Instruction Pour les Jardins Fruitiers et Potagiers . . . ,* by Jean de la Quintinye, 1695.

Lc: *Les Rosiers,* by Jean Lachaume, revised by Georges Bellair, ca. 1921.

L-D: *La Rose . . . ,* by Jean Louis Augustin Loiseleur-Deslongchamps, 1844.

LeB: *Traité des Jardins . . . ,* by Abbé Le Berriays, 1789.

LeR: *Histoire Généalogique des Rosiers,* by Antoine LeRouge, un-published manuscript dated 1819, with additional material from 1820.

LF: *Prix Courant des Espèces et Variétés de Roses,* by Jean Laffay, 1841.

LF1: Death Certificate of Jean Laffay, town records of the Munici-pality of Cannes, France, 1878.

l'H: *L'Horticuleur Français,* 1851–1872.

LR: *La Rose,* by J. Bel, 1892.

LS: *Nomenclature de Tous les Noms de Roses,* 2nd edition, by Léon Simon, 1906.

Lu: *Luther Burbank. His Methods and Discoveries,* vol. 9, by Luther Burbank, 1914.

M: *Gardening in California,* by Sidney B. Mitchell, 1923. Quoted by kind permission of the publishers, Doubleday & Co., Inc.

MaCo: *Manuel Complet de l'Amateur des Roses,* by Boitard, 1836.

MaRu: *La Nouvelle Maison Rustique . . . ,* by J.-F. Bastien, 1798.

McG: Unpublished e-mail to the author kindly supplied by Sam McGredy IV, OBN.

MCN: *Minutier Central des Notaires* at the French National Archives in Paris, France.

MH: *The Magazine of Horticulture,* edited by C. M. Hovey, Boston & New York, various years as indicated.

M'I: *The Book of the Garden,* by Charles M'Intosh, 1855.

M-L: *Travaux du Comice Horticole de Maine-et-Loire.*

MLS: Article "Roses in Kansas City," by Minnie Long Sloan, in ARA28.

MonL/deP: *Monographie du Genre Rosier,* translation of Lindley by de Pronville, with an added appendix, 1824.

M-P: *The Culture of Perennials,* by Dorothy M-P. Cloud, 1925. Quoted by kind permission of the publishers, Dodd, Mead & Co., Inc.

M-R: *Catalogue,* by Moreau-Robert, year as indicated.

MR8: *Modern Roses 8,* published by The McFarland Company, 1980. Quoted by kind permission of The American Rose Society and The McFarland Company.

M-V: *L'Instructeur Jardinier,* 1848–1851, edited by Martin-Victor Paquet.

Mz: *Catalogue* of Miellez of Esquermes, various years as indicated.

N: *Die Rose,* by Thomas Nietner, 1880.

No: *Manuel Complet du Jardinier,* by Louis Noisette, 1825.

No26: *Manuel Complet du Jardinier,* by Louis Noisette, 1826 edition.

No28: *Manuel Complet du Jardinier, Supplément No I,* by Louis Noisette, 1828.

No35: *Manuel Complet du Jardinier, Supplément No II,* by Louis Noisette, 1835.

NRS10 (*et seq.*): *Rose Annual,* 1910–1930, by the [British] National Rose Society. Quoted by kind permission of the Royal National Rose Society.

OB: *Oekonomisch-Botanische Beschreibung,* by Rössig, 1799.

OM: *The Rose Book,* by H. H. Thomas, 1916.

P: *The Rose Garden,* 1st edition, by William Paul, 1848.

P1: *The Rose Garden,* 10th edition, by William Paul, 1903.

P2: *Contributions to Horticultural Literature, 1843–1892,* by William Paul, 1892.

PaSo: *Paradisi in Sole: Paradisus Terrrestris,* by John Parkinson, 1629.

Pd: *Le Bilan d'un Siècle,* by Alfred Picard, tome 3, 1906.

Pf: *Catalogue Descriptif . . . du Genre Rosa,* by Prévost fils, 1829.

Pfs: *Supplément au Catalogue des Roses . . . ,* by Prévost fils, 1830.

pH: *Henderson's Handbook of Plants and General Horticulture,* "New Edition" (*i.e.,* 2nd), by Peter Henderson, 1889.

PlB: *Choix des Plus Belles Roses,* by Martin-Victor Paquet *et al.,* 1845–1854.

PP28: Article "Proof of the Pudding" in ARA28.

Pq: *Le Jardinier Pratique,* by Jacquin & Rousselon, 1852.

PS: Article "Roses in Brazil," by Mrs. Paul C. Schilling, in ARA28.

R1 (*et seq.*): *The Garden,* vols. 1–7, "founded and conducted by William Robinson," 1872–1875.

R8: *The Rose-Amateur's Guide,* 8th edition, by Thomas Rivers, 1863.

RATS: Article "Roses Across the Sea" in ARA28.

RG: *Rosetum Gallicum,* by Desportes, 1828.

R-H29 (*et seq.*): *Revue Horticole,* issues 1829–1877. Quoted by kind permission of the publishers.

R-HC: *Revue Horticole,* centenary number, 1929. Quoted by kind permission of the publishers.

Riv: *Roses et Rosiers,* by Rivoire père & fils, with Marcel Ebel, 1933.

RJC60 (*et seq.*): *Revue des Jardins et des Champs,* 1860–1871, edited by Jean Cherpin.

R&M: *Catalogue,* by Robert & Moreau, year as indicated.

Ro: *The English Flower-Garden,* 8th edition, by William Robinson, 1903.

RP: Article "Roses—The Ophelia Strain and Kindred Spirits," by Reginald Parker, in *The Rose,* vol. 13, no. 3, 1965.

RR: Article "Check List of Red Tea Roses," by R. Robinson, in *The Rose,* vol. 13, no. 1, 1964.

Rsg: *Die Rosen / Les Roses.* Rössig's *Die Rosen,* translated into French by de Lahitte, 1802–1820.

RZ: *Rosen-Zeitung,* vol. 1, 1886.

S: *Dictionnaire des Roses,* by Max Singer, 1885.

SAP: *Journal de la Société d'Agronomie Pratique.* 1829.

SBP: *Parsons on the Rose,* by Samuel B. Parsons, 1888.

sDH03 (*et seq.*): *Newry Roses* catalogs, by T. Smith of Daisy Hill Nursery, 1903–1929.

SHj: Article "Old Roses for the South," 1949, and address "Tea Roses for Florida," 1951, by Samuel J. Hjort. Quoted by kind permission of Sarah L. Hjort of Thomasville Nurseries, Inc.

SHP: *Annales de la Société d'Horticulture de Paris.*

Sn: *Rosenverzeichnis,* 3rd edition, Rosarium Sangerhausen, 1976.

SNH: *Journal de la Société Nationale d'Horticulture.*

SRh: *Société d'Horticulture Pratique du Rhône,* year as specified.

S-V: *Catalogue des Plantes . . . ,* by J. Sisley-Vandael, 1835–1836.

S-Vs: *Supplément . . . ,* by J. Sisley-Vandael, 1839.

Sx: *The American Rose Culturist,* by C. M. Saxton, 1860.

T1: *The Old Shrub Roses,* by Graham S. Thomas, 1956. Quoted by kind permission of the author and of the publishers J. M. Dent & Sons, Ltd.

T1H: Writings of Dr. Hurst in *The Old Shrub Roses* by Graham S. Thomas.

T2: *Climbing Roses Old and New,* by Graham S. Thomas, 1983. Quoted by kind permission of the author and of the publishers J. M. Dent & Sons, Ltd.

T3: *Shrub Roses of Today,* by Graham S. Thomas, 1980. Quoted by kind permission of the author and of the publishers J. M. Dent & Sons, Ltd.

T4: *The Graham Stuart Thomas Rose Book,* by Graham Stuart Thomas, 1994. Quoted by kind permission of the publishers, Sagapress & Timber Press.

Th: *The Practical Book of Outdoor Rose Growing,* by Capt. George C. Thomas, 1920. Quoted by very kind permission of the Thomas family.

Th2: *Roses for All American Climates,* by Capt. George C. Thomas, 1924. Quoted by very kind permission of the Thomas family.

ThGl: *The Gladiolus,* by Matthew Crawford, 1911.

tLmH: Oral history kindly supplied by Tom Liggett kindly relayed via the Internet by Mel Hulse.

T&R: *Les Roses,* by Claude-Antoine Thory and Pierre-Joseph Redouté, 1817–1824.

TS: Article "Roses of Australia," by T. A. Stewart, in ARA28.

TTL-G: *Through the Looking-Glass,* by Lewis Carroll.

TW: *Cultivated Roses,* by T. W. Sanders, 1899.

Ty: *Prodrome de la Monographie . . . du Genre Rosier . . . ,* by Claude-Antoine Thory, 1820.

UB28: Article "Unfinished Business" in ARA28.

URZ: *Ungarische Rosenzeitung,* edited by Ernst Kaufmann, date as indicated. Basic translation kindly supplied by Mr. Erich Unmuth.

V1: *Observations sur la Nomenclature et le Classement des Roses,* by Jean-Pierre Vibert, 1820.

V2: *Essai sur les Roses,* by Jean-Pierre Vibert, 1824–1830.

V3: *Catalogue,* by Jean-Pierre Vibert, 1826.

V4: *Catalogue,* by Jean-Pierre Vibert, 1836.

V5: Page from town records of Montfort l'Amaury containing *l'Acte de décès* concerning the death of Jean-Pierre Vibert, 1866.

V6: *Le Mouvement Horticole,* 1866.

V7: Minutes of the February 8, 1866, meeting of the *conseil d'administration de la Société Nationale d'Horticulture.*

V8: *Catalogue,* by Jean-Pierre Vibert, 1844.

V9: *Catalogue,* by Jean-Pierre Vibert, 1831.

VD: Article "Roses on the Mexican Coast," by V. E. Dillon, in ARA28.

V-H: *Flore des Serres et des Jardins de l'Europe,* by Louis Van Houtte, 1845–1880.

VPt: *Almanach Horticole,* 1844–1848, edited by Martin-Victor Paquet.

W: *Climbing Roses,* by Helen Van Pelt Wilson, 1955. Quoted by kind permission of Helen Van Pelt Wilson.

War: *Warren's Descriptive Catalogue,* by J. L. L. F. Warren, 1844.

Way45: *Catalog,* by Wayside Gardens, 1945.

WD: *Roses and Their Culture,* 3rd edition, by W. D. Prior, 1892.

W/Hn: Interpolations by translator John Weathers in *The Amateur Gardener's Rose Book,* by Julius Hoffmann, 1905.

WHoI (*et seq.*): *The Western Horticultural Review,* 1850–1853.

Wr: *Roses and Rose Gardens,* by Walter P. Wright, 1911.

WRP: *Manual of Roses,* by William R. Prince, 1846.

Ÿ: *Inventaire de la Collection,* by Roseraie de l'Haÿ, 1984. Quoted by kind permission of the *Service des Espaces Verts du Conseil Général du Val de Marne,* France.

Works Consulted

Almanach Horticole. 1844–1848. Edited by Martin-Victor Paquet. Paris: Cousin.

American Rose Annual. 1916–1940. American Rose Society.

Les Amis des Roses. 1946–1961. Société Français des Rosiéristes.

Anderson, Frank J. 1979. *An Illustrated Treasury of Redouté Roses.* New York: Abbeville Press.

Andrews, H. C. 1805 & 1828. *Roses or A Monograph of the Genus Rosa.* Knightsbridge: Andrews.

Annales de Flore et de Pomone. 1832–1848. Paris: Rousselon.

Annales du Comice Horticole de Maine-et-Loire. 1859. Angers.

Angier, Belle Sumner. 1906. *The Garden Book of California.* San Francisco: P. Elder & Co.

Anonymous. 1712. *La Culture des Fleurs.* Lyon: Besson.

Anonymous. 1764. *L'École du Jardinier Fleuriste.* Paris: Panckoucke.

Barron, Leonard. 1905. *Roses and How to Grow Them.* New York: Doubleday.

Bastien, J.-F. 1798. *La Nouvelle Maison Rustique . . .* Paris.

Beales, Peter. 1979. *Edwardian Roses.* Norwich: Jarrold.

Beales, Peter. 1979. *Late Victorian Roses.* Norwich: Jarrold.

Beales, Peter. 1985. *Classic Roses.* London: Collins Harvill.

Bean, W. J. 1970– . *Trees and Shrubs Hardy in the British Isles,* 8th edition. London: Murray.

Beckett, Edwin. 1918. *Roses and How to Grow Them.* London: C. A. Pearson.

Bel, J. 1892. *La Rose.* Paris: Baillière.

Billberg, Gustaf Johan. 1836. *Vägledning genom Linnés Park.* Manuscript unpublished until 1996, until it appeared with an article "Rosenlabyrinten i Humlegården" by Maria Flinck in *Rosenbladet* 2: 18–21. Stockholm.

Boitard, Pierre. 1836. *Manuel Complet de l'Amateur de Roses, leur Monographie, leur Histoire et leur Culture.* Paris: Roret.

Le Bon Jardinier, Almanach pour l'Année 1806. 1806. Paris: Onfroy.

Le Bon Jardinier, Supplément . . . to the 1806 edition. Paris: Onfroy.

Le Bon Jardinier . . . 1809. Paris: Onfroy.

Le Bon Jardinier . . . 1817. Paris: Audot.

Le Bon Jardinier . . . 1824. Paris: Audot.

Le Bon Jardinier . . . 1830. Paris: Audot.

Le Bon Jardinier . . . 1840. (Title page missing).

Le Bon Jardinier . . . 1853. Paris: Dusacq.

Le Bon Jardinier . . . 1858. Paris: Maison Rustique.

Le Bon Jardinier . . . 1863. Paris: Maison Rustique.

Le Bon Jardinier . . . 1865. Paris: Maison Rustique.

Le Bon Jardinier . . . 1869. Paris: Maison Rustique.

Le Bon Jardinier . . . 1870. Paris: Maison Rustique.

Le Bon Jardinier . . . 1877. Paris: Maison Rustique.

Bosanquet, Arthur Henry (as "A.H.B."). 1845. *The Tree Rose.* London: Gardener's Chronicle.

Breck, Joseph. 1851. *The Flower Garden; or, Breck's Book of Flowers.* Boston: Jewett.

Breck, Joseph. 1866. *New Book of Flowers.* New York: Orange Judd.

Breon, Nicolas. 1825. *Catalogue des Plantes Cultivées aux Jardins Botanique et de Naturalisation de l'Île Bourbon.* St.-Denis, Île-Bourbon: Impr. du Gouv.

Bright, Henry. 1879. *A Year in a Lancashire Garden.* London: Macmillan.

Brontë, Charlotte. 1850. *Biographical Notice of Ellis and Acton Bell.* Republished in Penguin Classics edition of Anne Brontë's *Agnes Gray,* 1988.

Brougham, Henry Charles, 3rd Baron Brougham & Vaux. 1898. *List of Roses Now in Cultivation at Château Éléonore, Cannes* . . . London: Bumpus.

Brown, Thomas A. 1998. *19th Century Horticulturists and Plant Raisers.* Petaluma: Thomas A. Brown.

Buc'hoz, Pierre-Joseph. 1770. *Dictionnaire Universel des Plantes* . . . Paris: Lacombe.

Buist, Robert. 1844. *The Rose Manual.* Philadelphia: Buist.

Bunyard, Edward A. 1936. *Old Garden Roses.* London: Country Life.

Burbank, Luther. 1914. *Luther Burbank. His Methods and Discoveries.* New York & London: Luther Burbank Press.

Burnside, F. R. 1893. *Tea Roses.* Hereford: Jakeman & Carver.

California Nursery Company. 1888 *et sequitur. Catalogue.* Niles, CA: California Nursery Company.

The California Rosarian. 1930–1932. Point Loma, CA: California Rose Society.

Calvert & Company. 1821. *Catalogue of Roses.* Calvert: Rouen.

Cannes, France. Town records.

Carlyle, Thomas. 1837. *The French Revolution. A History.* Reprint (no date). New York: Modern Library.

Carlyle, Thomas. 1849. *Oliver Cromwell's Letters and Speeches,* 3rd edition. Chicago: Belford, Clark & Co.

Carlyle, Thomas. 1858–1865. *The History of Friedrich II of Prussia, Called Frederick the Great.* Republication (no date). New York: Merrill & Baker.

Carroll, Lewis (pseudonym for Charles Lutwidge Dodgson). Republished 1950. *Through the Looking-Glass.* New York: Arcadia.

Cauwenberghe, Edm. Van. 1927. *La Rose Historique* . . . Brussels: Féd. des Soc. Hort.

Chotek, Marie Henriette. 1926. *Catalogue, Marie Henriette Chotek Rosenschulen.* Trnava: Chotek.

Cloud, Dorothy M.-P. 1925. *The Culture of Perennials.* New York: Dodd, Mead & Company.

Comice Horticole de Maine-et-Loire. Various dates, 1830s–1850s. *Travaux du Comice Horticole de Maine-et-Loire.*

The Conard & Jones Company. 1897–1924. *Catalog.* West Grove, PA.: Conard & Jones.

The Conard-Pyle Company. 1925–1934. *Catalog.* West Grove, PA.: Conard-Pyle.

Cook, E. T. 1911. *Gardens of England.* London: Black.

Cours Complet d'Agriculture. 1793. Abbé Rozier, ed. Paris.

Cranston, John. 1877. *Cultural Directions for the Rose,* 6th edition. Liverpool: Blake & Mackenzie.

Cranston and Mayo's. Various dates. *A Descriptive Catalogue* . . . King's Acre: Cranston and Mayo's.

Crapo, Henry H. 1848. *Catalogue for the Wasamequia Nurseries, New Bedford, Mass.* Reprint ARA26.

Crawford, Matthew. 1911. *The Gladiolus.* Appendix by Dr. Walter Van Fleet. Chicago & New York: Vaughan's.

Curtis, Henry. 1850–1853. *Beauties of the Rose.* Bristol: Lavars.

de Chesnel, A. 1838. *La Rose,* 2nd edition. Paris: Soc. Repr. des Bons Livres.

de Pronville, Aug. 1818. *Nomenclature Raisonnée . . . du Genre Rosier.* Paris: Huzard.

de Pronville, Aug. 1822. *Sommaire d'une Monographie du Genre Rosier.* Paris: Huzard.

de Pronville, Aug. 1824. Appendix to *Monographie du Genre Rosier, Traduite de l'Anglais de M. J. Lindley.* Paris: Audot.

De Quincey, Thomas. 1849. "The Vision of Sudden Death" from *The English Mail-Coach.* Reprint. New York: Holt, Rinehart & Winston.

Descemet, Jean. 1741. *Catalogue des Plantes du Jardin de M[essieu]rs les Apoticaires de Paris.* Paris: no imprint.

Desportes, Narcisse Henri François. 1828. *Rosetum Gallicum* . . . Le Mans: Pesche & Paris: Huzard.

Dickerson, Brent C. 1982–1983. "Education of a Gardener." *Pacific Horticulture* 43(4): 8–10.

Dickerson, Brent C. 1989. "The Portland Rose." *The Garden, Journal of the Royal Horticultural Society* (January): 9–14.

Dickerson, Brent C. 1990. "Notes Towards an Understanding of 19th Century Rose-Breeding. *The Yellow Rose* (March): 2–6.

Dickerson, Brent C. 1992. *The Old Rose Advisor.* Portland, OR: Timber Press.

Dickerson, Brent C. 1997. *Handbook of Old Roses.* In manuscript.

Dickerson, Brent C. 1997–1998. "Åter till Rosenlabyrinten." *Rosenbladet* 1997(4), 1998(1). Stockholm.

Dickson, Alexander. Various dates. *Catalogue,* Royal Irish Nurseries. Newtownards: Dickson.

Dickson, Hugh. Various dates. *Catalogue,* Royal Nurseries. Belfast: Dickson.

Dobson, Beverly. 1985. *Combined Rose List 1985.* Irvington, NY: Dobson.

Dobson, Beverly. 1987. *Combined Rose List 1987.* Irvington, NY: Dobson.

D'Ombrain, Rev. H. Honywood. 1908. *Roses for Amateurs.* London: L. Upcott Gill.

Doyle, Arthur Conan. Short story "The Naval Treaty."

Drennan, Georgia Torrey. 1912. *Everblooming Roses.* New York: Duffield.

DuCane, Florence. 1909. *The Flowers and Gardens of Madeira.* London: Black.

Ellacombe, Henry N. 1896. *In a Gloucestershire Garden.* London: Arnold.

Elliott, R. G. No date (ca. 1925). *The Australasian Rose Book.* Melbourne: Whitcombe & Tombs.

Ellwanger, Henry B. 1883. "Old and New Roses." *Century Magazine* 26: 350–358.

Ellwanger, Henry B. 1896. *The Rose.* New York: Dodd, Mead & Company.

Encyclopédie Méthodique. 1804. Botanical contributions by Lamarck. Paris.

Encyclopédie Méthodique. Botanique . . . Supplément. 1816. Continuation by J. L. M. Poiret. Paris.

Farrer, Reginald. 1909. *In a Yorkshire Garden.* London: Arnold.

Festing, Sally. 1986. "The Second Duchess of Portland and Her Rose." *Garden History* 14: 194–200.

Fillassier, Monsieur. 1791. *Dictionnaire du Jardinier Français.* Paris: Desoer.

Fillery, J. W. 1960. *Old Fashioned Roses in New Zealand.* Ilfracombe: Stockwell.

The Floricultural Cabinet 4: 224–231; 1838. London.

The Floricultural Cabinet 9: 30–31; 1841. London.

The Florist & Horticultural Journal. 1852. Philadelphia.

The Florist & Pomologist. 1848. London.

Foster-Melliar, Andrew. 1894. *The Book of the Rose,* 1st edition. London: Macmillan.

Foster-Melliar, Andrew. 1902. *The Book of the Rose,* 2nd edition. London: Macmillan.

Foster-Melliar, Andrew. 1905. *The Book of the Rose,* 3rd edition. London: Macmillan.

Fumierre, Louis. 1910. *Les Roses.* Rouen: Cagniard.

The Garden. 1872–1875. London.

The Garden. 1987. London.

Gautreau, Philippe. Unpublished correspondence with the present author.

Gemen & Bourg. No date (ca. 1908). *Roses.* Luxembourg: Buck.

Glenny, George. 1861. *The Culture of Flowers and Plants.* London: Houlston.

Godefroy. 1831. *Catalogue des Rosiers cultivées Chez M. Godefroy . . .* Paris: Huzard & Audot.

Gore, Mrs. Catherine Grace Francis. 1838. *The Rose Fancier's Manual.* London: Colburn.

Gravereaux, Jules. 1912. *"La Malmaison" Les Roses de l'Impératrice Joséphine.* Paris: Ed. d'Art.

Griffiths, Trevor. 1984. *The Book of Old Roses.* London: Michael Joseph.

Griffiths, Trevor. 1987. *The Book of Classic Old Roses.* London: Michael Joseph.

Griffiths, Trevor. 1990. *A Celebration of Old Roses.* London: Michael Joseph.

Grimm, Hedi, & Wernt Grimm. Unpublished correspondence with the present author.

Guerrapain, Claude-Thomas. 1811. *Almanach des Roses.* Troyes: Gobelet.

Guillot, Jean-Baptiste (père). 1844. *Catalogue . . .* Lyon: Guillot.

Guillot, Jean-Baptiste (père et fils). 1852. *Catalogue . . .* Lyon: Guillot.

Guillot, Jean-Baptiste (fils). 1856. *Catalogue . . .* Lyon: Guillot.

Haggard, H. Rider. 1905. *A Gardener's Year.* London: Longmans Green.

Harkness, Jack. 1978. *Roses.* London: Dent.

Hariot, Paul. 1904. *Le Livre d'Or des Roses.* Paris: Laveur.

Henderson, Peter. 1889. *Henderson's Handbook of Plants and General Horticulture.* New York: Henderson.

Henslow, T. Geoffrey W. 1934. *The Rose Encyclopaedia.* London: Pearson.

Hibberd, Shirley. 1874. *The Amateur's Rose Book.* London: Groomsbridge.

Hoffmann, Julius. 1905. *The Anateur's Rose Book.* John Weathers, trans. London: Longmans Green.

Hole, S. Reynolds. 1906. *A Book About Roses.* London: E. Arnold.

L'Horticulteur Français. 1851–1872. Paris: Hérincq.

The Horticultural Review and Botanical Magazine. 1854. Cincinnati.

The Horticulturist. 1846–1875. Edited by A. J. Downing *et alia.* New York.

How to Grow Roses. 1980. Editors of Sunset Books. Menlo Park: Lane.

L'Instructeur Jardinier. 1848–1851. Paris: Paquet.

Jacquin, P.-J., & H. Rousselon. 1852. *Le Jardinier Pratique.* Paris: Lefèvre & Guérin.

Jäger, August. 1970. *Rosenlexikon.* Leipzig: Zentralantiquariat.

Jamain, Hippolyte, & Eugène Forney. 1873. *Les Roses.* Paris: Rothschild.

Le Jardinier-Amateur. 1826. Eugène Pirolle, ed. Paris: Renard.

Le Jardinier-Amateur, Premier Supplément. 1826–1827. Eugène Pirolle, ed. Paris: Renard.

Le Jardinier Prévoyant, Almanach pour . . . MDCCLXXII. 1772. Paris: Didot.

Jekyll, Gertrude. 1902. *Roses for English Gardens.* London: Country Life.

Journal de la Société d'Agronomie Pratique. 1829. Paris.

Journal de la Société d'Horticulture Pratique du Rhône. Issues 1859–1863. Lyon.

Journal de la Société Nationale d'Horticulture. 1863, 1865, 1869. Paris: Société Nationale d'Horticulture.

Journal des Roses. 1854–1859. J. Cherpin, ed. Lyon: Cherpin.

Journal des Roses. 1877–1914. Cochet & Bernardin, eds. Melun: Cochet.

Journal d'Horticulture Pratique et de Jardinage. 1844–1847. Paris: Cousin.

Joyaux, François. 1998. *La Rose de France.* Paris: Imprimerie Nationale.

Keays, Ethelyn Emery. 1936. *Old Roses.* New York: Macmillan.

Kerr, Robert. 1824. *A General History and Collection of Voyages and Travels.* Edinburgh: Blackwood.

Kingsley, Rose G. 1907. *Eversley Gardens and Others.* London: Allen.

Kingsley, Rose G. 1908. *Roses and Rose-Growing.* New York: Macmillan.

Krüssmann, Gerd. 1981. *The Complete Book of Roses.* Portland, OR: Timber Press.

Lachaume, Jean. No date (ca. 1921). *Les Rosiers.* Revised by Georges Bellair. Paris: Maison Rustique.

Laffay, Jean. 1841. *Prix Courant des Espèces et Variétés de Roses . . .* Bellevue-Meudon: Laffay.

La Quintinye, Jean de. 1693. *The Complete Gard'ner.* John Evelyn, trans. London: Gillyflower.

La Quintinye, Jean de. 1695. *Instructions pour les Jardins Fruitiers et Potagers . . .* Geneva: Ritter.

Le Berriays. 1789. *Traité des Jardins, ou Le Nouveau De La Quintinye,* 3rd edition. Paris.

Lemonnier, Daniel. Unpublished correspondence with the present author.

Leproux, Dominique. 1986. "Les Roses Anciennes, un marché en expansion." *Revue-Horticole*, pp. 40–41.

LeRouge, Antoine. 1819–1820. *Histoire Généalogique des Rosiers en deux volumes contenans 560 Espèces et variétés / Dediée à mon Amie*. Unpublished manuscript, partially based on Guerrapain. From the Cochet collection.

Locke, John. 1690 *et sequitur. An Essay Concerning Human Understanding*. Collated edition of 1894 by Alexander Campbell Fraser; facsimile reprint by Dover Books, 1959. Originally published London: Basset.

Loiseleur-Deslongchamps, Jean Louis Augustin. 1844. *La Rose . . .* Paris: Audot.

Louette, Ivan. Unpublished correspondence with the present author.

Lyon, William S. 1904. *Gardening in California*. 3rd revised edition. Los Angeles: G. Rice.

McFarland, J. Horace. 1928. *Roses and How to Grow Them*. Garden City: Doubleday.

M'Intosh, Charles. 1855. *The Book of the Garden*. Edinburgh: Blackwood.

The Magazine of Horticulture. Examined were issues from 1840 through 1852. Boston & New York: Hovey & Company.

Malo, Charles. 1821. *Histoire des Roses*. Paris: Janet.

Massiot, Georges. Unpublished correspondence with the present author.

Miellez. 1853. *Plantes de Serres et de Pleine Terre / Prix-Courant*. Lille: Miellez.

Miellez. 1853. *Supplément*. Lille: Miellez.

Miellez. 1854. *Plantes de Serres et de Pleine Terre / Prix-Courant*. Lille: Miellez.

Miellez. 1856. *Plantes de Serres et de Pleine Terre / Prix-Courant*. Lille: Miellez.

Milman, Helen (Crofton). 1899. *My Roses and How I Grew Them*. London: Lane.

Mitchell, Sydney B. 1923. *Gardening in California*. New York: Doubleday.

Modern Roses 8. 1980. Harrisburg, PA: McFarland Company.

Montaigne, Michel Eyquem de. 1962. *Oeuvres Complètes*. Stanford, CA: Stanford University Press.

Montfort l'Amaury, France. Town records.

Moreau-Robert. 1865. *Catalogue Générale*. Angers: Moreau-Robert.

Le Mouvement Horticole. 1866.

National [British] Rose Society. 1912. *Official Catalogue of Roses*. Croyden: National Rose Society.

Nelson, E. Charles. Unpublished correspondence with the present author.

Nicolas, J. H. 1938. *The Rose Manual*. New York: Doubleday.

Nietner, Thomas. 1880. *Die Rose*. Berlin: Hempel & Parey.

Noisette, Louis. 1825. *Manuel Complet du Jardinier*. Paris: Rousselon.

Noisette, Louis. 1826. *Manuel Complet du Jardinier . . . tome quatrième*. Paris: Rousselon.

Noisette, Louis. 1828. *Manuel Complet du Jardinier . . . Supplément No 1*. Paris: Rousselon.

Noisette, Louis. 1829. *Manuel Complet du Jardinier . . . Brussels edition*. Brussels: Wahlen & Tarlier.

Noisette, Louis. 1835. *Manuel Complet du Jardinier . . .* Paris: Rousselon.

Nottle, Trevor. 1983. *Growing Old-Fashioned Roses*. Australia: Kangaroo Press.

Nottle, Trevor. Unpublished correspondence with the present author.

Paquet, Martin-Victor (*inter alia*). 1845–1854. *Choix des Plus Belles Roses*. M.-V. Paquet, ed. Paris: Dusacq.

Parker, Reginald. 1965. "Roses, the Ophelia Strain and Kindred Spirits," *The Rose* 13: 173–180.

Parkinson, John. 1629. *Paradisi in Sole Paradisus Terrestris*; facsimile reprint (1976) by Dover Books. Originally published London.

Parkman, Francis. 1871. *The Book of Roses*. Boston: Tilton.

Parsons, Samuel B. 1888. *Parsons on the Rose*. New York: Orange Judd.

Paul, William. 1848. *The Rose Garden*, 1st edition. London: Sherwood, Gilbert & Piper.

Paul, William. 1892. *Contributions to Horticultural Literature, 1843–1892*. Waltham Cross: Paul.

Paul, William. 1903. *The Rose Garden*, 10th edition. London: Simpkin.

Pemberton, Rev. Joseph J. 1920. *Roses: Their History, Development, and Cultivation*. London: Longmans Green.

Phillips, Roger, & Martyn Rix. 1988. *Roses*. New York: Random House.

Phillips, Roger, & Martyn Rix. 1993. *The Quest for the Rose*. New York: Random House.

Picard, Alfred. 1906. *Le Bilan d'un Siècle*. Paris: Impr. Nationale.

Prévost fils. 1829. *Catalogue Descriptif, Méthodique et Raisonné, des Espèces, Variétés et Sous-Variétés du Genre Rosier, Cultivées chez Prévost fils . . .* Rouen: Prévost.

Prévost fils. 1830. *Supplément au Catalogue des Roses . . .* Rouen: Prévost.

Prince, William R. 1846. *Prince's Manual of Roses*. New York: Clark & Austin.

Prior, W. D. 1892. *Roses and Their Culture*. 3rd edition. London: Routledge.

Redouté, Pierre-Joseph. 1828. *Les Roses*, 3rd edition. Text by Claude-Antoine Thory. Paris: Dufart.

Redouté, Pierre-Joseph. 1833. *Choix des Plus Belles Fleurs*. Paris: Roret.

Redouté, Pierre-Joseph. 1978. *P. J. Redouté Roses*. Locality unknown: Miller Graphics.

Redouté, Pierre-Joseph. 1990 (reprint). *Redouté's Roses*. Secaucus, NJ: Wellfleet.

Revue des Jardins et des Champs. 1860–1862. Paris: Cherpin.

Revue-Horticole. 1829–1877. Paris: Librarie Agricole.

Revue-Horticole. 1929. Special centenary number. Paris: Maison Rustique.

Rivers, Thomas. 1863. *The Rose-Amateur's Guide*, 8th edition. London: Longmans Green.

Rivoire père & fils, & Marcel Ebel. 1933. *Roses et Rosiers*. Paris: Baillière.

Robert & Moreau. 1862. *Extrait du Catalogue des Rosiers, Vignes, et Diverses Plantes . . .* Angers: Robert & Moreau.

Robinson, William. 1903. *The English Flower-Garden*, 8th edition. London: Murray.

Rockwell [F. F.] and Grayson [Esther C.]. 1966. *The Rockwells' Complete Book of Roses.* New York: Doubleday.

Rosarium Sangerhausen. 1976. *Rosenverzeichnis,* 3rd edition. Sangerhausen: Rosarium Sangerhausen.

Rosarium Sangerhausen. No date (ca. 1980). *Der Welt Bedeutendster Rosengarten.* Sangerhausen: Rosarium Sangerhausen.

Rose Annual. 1910–1930. Croyden: National Rose Society.

Rosen-Zeitung. 1886. Frankfurt: Fey.

Roseraie de l'Haÿ. 1902. *Les Roses Cultivées à l'Haÿ en 1902.* Grisy-Suisnes: Cochet.

Roseraie de l'Haÿ. 1910. *Guide pour servir à la visite de notre Exposition Rétrospective de la Rose.* Paris: Exp. Int. d'Hort. de Paris.

Roseraie de l'Haÿ. 1984. *Inventaire de la Collection.* L'Haÿ: Cons. Gén. du Val-de-Marne.

Rössig, D. 1799. *Oekonomisch-Botanische Beschreibung...der Rosen.* Leipzig.

Rössig, D. 1802–1820. *Die Rosen / Les Roses.* German / French edition, French translation by M. de Lahitte. Leipzig.

Sabine, Joseph. 1822. Article "Double Scotch Roses" in *Transactions of the London Horticultural Society* 4: 281–305. London.

Sabine, Joseph. 1822. Article "On the Ayrshire Rose" in *Transactions of the London Horticultural Society* 4: 456–467. London.

Sanders, Thomas William. 1899. *Cultivated Roses.* London: Collingridge.

Simon, Léon. 1906. *Nomenclature de Tous les Noms de Roses,* 2nd edition. Paris: Libr. Hort.

Singer, Max. 1885. *Dictionnaire des Roses.* Tournai: Singer.

Sisley-Vandael, J. 1835–1836. *Catalogue de Plantes...* Paris: Sisley-Vandael.

Sisley-Vandael, J. 1839. *Supplément...* Paris: Sisley-Vandael.

Smith, Thomas. Various dates. Catalogs for *Newry Roses.* Ireland.

Société Nationale d'Horticulture de France. 1912. *Les Plus Belles Roses au Debut du XXème Siècle.* Paris: Société Nationale d'Horticulture.

Soulange-Bodin. 1835. *Coup-d'Oeil Historique sur les Progrès de l'Horticulture Française depuis 1789.* Paris: Soc. Roy. d'Hort.

The Southern Horticulturalist. 1869. Tangipahoa, LA.

Stevens, G. A. 1933. *Climbing Roses.* New York: Macmillan.

Testu, Charlotte. 1984. *Les Roses Anciennes.* Paris: Flammarion.

Thomas, Capt. George C. 1920. *The Practical Book of Outdoor Rose Growing.* Philadelphia: J. B. Lippincott & Co.

Thomas, Capt. George C. 1924. *Roses for All American Climates.* New York: Macmillan.

Thomas, Graham S. 1956. *The Old Shrub Roses.* London: Dent.

Thomas, Graham S. 1980. *Shrub Roses of Today.* London: Dent.

Thomas, Graham S. 1983. *Climbing Roses Old and New.* London: Dent.

Thomas, Graham S. 1994. *The Graham Stuart Thomas Rose Book.* Portland, OR: Sagapress & Timber Press.

Thomas, Harry H. 1916. *The Rose Book.* London: Cassell.

Thomson, R. Wodrow. 1862. *The Amateur's Rosarium.* Edinburgh: Paton & Ritchie.

Thomson, Richard. 1959. *Old Roses for Modern Gardens.* Princeton: Van Nostrand.

Thory, Claude Antoine. 1820. *Prodrome de la Monographie des Espèces et Variétés Connues du Genre Rosier...* Paris: Dufart.

Ungarische Rosenzeitung, edited by Ernst Kaufmann. Selections with basic translation kindly supplied by Mr. Erich Unmuth.

Unmuth, Erich. Unpublished correspondence with the present author.

Van Houtte, Louis. 1845–1880. *Flore des Serres et des Jardins de l'Europe.* Ghent: Van Houtte.

Van Mons, J. B. 1835. *Arbres Fruitiers...* Louvain.

Verrier, Suzanne. 1991. *Rosa Rugosa.* Deer Park, WI: Capability's.

Verrier, Suzanne. 1995. *Rosa Gallica.* Deer Park, WI: Capability's.

Vibert, Jean-Pierre. 1820. *Observations sur la Nomenclature et le Classement des Roses.* Paris: Huzard.

Vibert, Jean-Pierre. 1824–1830. *Essai sur les Roses.* Paris: Huzard.

Vibert, Jean-Pierre. 1826. *Catalogue.* Paris: Huzard.

Vibert, Jean-Pierre. 1827. *Réponse de M. Vibert...aux Assertions de M. Pirolle...* Paris: Huzard.

Vibert, Jean-Pierre. 1831. *Catalogue.* Paris: Huzard.

Vibert, Jean-Pierre. 1836. *Catalogue.* Paris: Huzard.

Vibert, Jean-Pierre. 1844. *Catalogue.* Angers: Vibert.

Warren, J. L. L. F. 1844. *Annual Descriptive Catalogue of Fruit and Ornamental Trees, Grape-Vines, Shrubs and Herbaceous Plants, Roses, Dahlias, Green-House Plants, etc., etc.* Boston: Warren.

Wayside Gardens. 1945. *Catalog.*

The Western Horticultural Review. 1850–1853. Cincinnati.

Weston, Richard. 1770. *The Universal Botanist and Nurseryman...* London: Bell.

Weston, Richard. 1775. *The English Flora...* London: Weston.

Wickson, E. J. 1915. *California Garden-Flowers.* San Francisco: Pacific Rural.

Wilson, Helen Van Pelt. 1955. *Climbing Roses.* New York: Barrows.

Wright, Walter P. 1911. *Roses and Rose Gardens.* London: Headley.

Young, Norman. 1971. *The Complete Rosarian.* New York: St. Martin's.

The present author would be remiss were he not to cite three books, the high standards and adroit execution of which have always inspired him with a wonderful vision of Possibility:

Jacobsen, Hermann. 1960. *A Handbook of Succulent Plants,* English edition. Poole: Blandford.

Reynolds, Gilbert Westacott. 1966. *The Aloes of Tropical Africa and Madagascar.* Cape Town: Trustees, Aloes Book Fund.

Reynolds, Gilbert Westacott. 1974. *The Aloes of South Africa,* 3rd edition. Cape Town & Rotterdam: Balkema.

Index

Items that are not cultivar names—names of breeders or such special subjects—are listed in **boldface**. Where there could be confusion between two cultivars of the same name, we indicate whatever is necessary to distinguish the differing roses. Readers looking under an invalid synonym for a rose will be referred to the valid synonym. It is, we know, painful to forgo an old familiar name for a less familiar other that happens to have priority; but when one bows to Truth over Personal Preference, one has made great progress. We had intended to index these roses by a matrix of average number of serrations per leaf of each cultivar as figured against stable characteristics of the rugosities on the peduncle; the demands of time intervening, however, we present this listing in alphabetical form, hoping that the Reader will not be disappointed.

Some Numbers

In *The Old Rose Adventurer,*

of *Gallicas,* there are entries for 349
of *Damasks,* 74
of *Agathes,* 24
of *Centifolias,* 80
of *Centifolia Pompons* and *Mossy Pompons,* 15
of *Mosses,* 131
of *Mossy Remontants,* 52
of *Albas,* 61
of *Hemisphaericas,* 3
of *Foetidas,* 22
of *Pimpinellifolias,* 63
of *Rubiginosas,* 41
of *Caninas,* 14
of *Hugonises,* 6
of *Hulthemias,* 2
of *Macranthas,* 8
of *Macrophyllas,* 6

of *Nutkanas,* 3
of *Villosas,* 2
of *Rubrifolias,* 7
of *Soulieanas,* 4
of *Majalises,* 2
of *Turbinatas,* 7
of *Virginianas,* 3
of *Xanthinas,* 1
of *Unknown Position,* 3
of *Roxburghiis,* 13
of *Bracteatas,* 17
of *Rugosas,* 113
of *Laevigatas,* 7
of *Banksias,* 10
of *Musks,* 19
of *Arvensises,* 18
of *Sempervirenses,* 15
of *Boursaults,* 19
of *Setigeras,* 31
of *Wichuraianas,* 237
of *Multifloras,* 180
of *Lambertianas,* 55
of *Hybrid Musks,* 57

of *Old Hybrid Tea* and *Pernetiana Climbers,* 100
of *Hybrid Teas, 1900–1920,* 478
of *Pernetianas,* 154

Making a *total* of 2,506 in *The Old Rose Adventurer.*

In the previous book, *The Old Rose Advisor,* there were

of *Damask Perpetuals,* 42; to which *The Old Rose Adventurer* adds another 23; for a combined total of 65
of *Chinas,* 75; added, 2; combined total, 77
of *Teas,* 424; added, 5; combined total, 429
of *Bourbons,* 143; added, 7; combined total, 150
of *Hybrid Bourbons, Hybrid Chinas,* and *Hybrid Noisettes,* 55; added, 20; combined total, 75

of *Hybrid Perpetuals,* 831; added, 17; combined total, 848
of *Noisettes* and *Climbers,* 307; added, 6; combined total, 313
of *Polyanthas,* 213; added, 8; combined total, 221
of the earliest *Hybrid Teas,* 242; added, 5; combined total, 247

Making a *total* of 2,332 in *The Old Rose Advisor.*

Total additions to *The Old Rose Advisor* in *The Old Rose Adventurer,* 93

Total for groups primarily in *The Old Rose Advisor,* 2,425

Total for new groups in *The Old Rose Adventurer,* 2,506

Grand total for both books of all cultivars covered, **4,931**

Adieu, good readers; bad also, adieu.

Thomas Carlyle
*The History of Friedrich II of Prussia,
Called Frederick the Great*